The Longman Anthology
of Women's Literature

The Longman Anthology of Women's Literature

Mary K. DeShazer

Editor

Wake Forest University

Longman

New York San Francisco Boston
London Toronto Sydney Tokyo Singapore Madrid
Mexico City Munich Paris Cape Town Hong Kong Montreal

Editor-in-Chief: *Joseph Terry*
Acquisitions Editor: *Erika Berg*
Marketing Manager: *Melanie Goulet*
Supplements Editor: *Donna Campion*
Media Supplements Editor: *Nancy Garcia*
Senior Production Manager: *Eric Jorgensen*
Project Coordination, Text Design and Electronic Page Makeup: *WestWords, Inc.*
Cover Designer: *Wendy Stolberg*
Cover Design Manager: *Nancy Danahy*
Cover Image: *"Sinnende," 1917, by Gabrielle Münter © 2001 Artists Rights Society (ARS), New York/VG Bild-Kunst, Bonn*
Photo Researcher: *PhotoSearch, Inc.*
Manufacturing Buyer: *Al Dorsey*
Printer and Binder: *Quebecor World-Taunton*
Cover Printer: *Phoenix Color Corp.*

For permission to use copyrighted material, grateful acknowledgment is made to the copyright holders on pages 1451-1459, which are hereby made part of this copyright page.

Library of Congress Cataloging-in-Publication Data

The Longman anthology of women's literature / Mary K. DeShazer, [editor].
    p. cm.
    Includes bibliographical references and index.
    ISBN 0-321-01006-X
    1. English literature — Women authors. 2. Commonwealth literature (English) — Women authors. 3. American literature — Women authors. 4. Women — Literary collections. I. DeShazer, Mary K.

PR1110.W6 L66 2000
820.8'09287—dc21

00-063216

Please visit our website at http://www.ablongman.com/deshazer.

ISBN 0-321-01006-X

34567890–QWT–05

In memory of my mother, Marian Montgomery DeShazer,
and
for my father, Henry Gaines DeShazer

CONTENTS

Alternate Table of Contents—
A Historical Chronology of Writers   *xxi*

Alternate Table of Contents—
Thematic Approaches to Women's Literature   *xxxv*

Preface   *xlv*

Section I

Engendering Language, Silence, and Voice

INTRODUCTION   1

ANNOTATED BIBLIOGRAPHY   11

VIRGINIA WOOLF (1882–1941)   14
  A Room of One's Own   16

BELL HOOKS (1955–)   72
  Talking Back   73

LEOBA OF ENGLAND AND GERMANY (700?–779)   76
  Letter to Lord Boniface   77

MATILDA, QUEEN OF ENGLAND (1080–1118)   78
  Letter to Archbishop Anselm   79
  Letter to Pope Pascal   80

ANNE LOCK (FL. 1556–1590)   81
  from A Meditation of a Penitent Sinner, upon the 51 Psalm   82

ISABELLA WHITNEY (FL. 1567–1573?)   85
  The Author . . . Maketh Her Will and Testament   85
  from The Manner of Her Will   86

MARGARET CAVENDISH, DUCHESS OF NEWCASTLE
(1623?–1673)   89
  The Poetess's Hasty Resolution   90
  The Poetess's Petition   90

An Excuse for So Much Writ upon My Verses   91
Nature's Cook   91
from To All Writing Ladies   92

ANNE KILLIGREW (1660–1685)   93
Upon the Saying that My Verses Were Made by Another   94
On a Picture Painted by Herself   95

ANNE FINCH, COUNTESS OF WINCHILSEA (1661–1720)   96
The Introduction   97
A Nocturnal Reverie   98
Ardelia to Melancholy   100
Friendship Between Ephelia and Ardelia   101
The Answer   101

FRANCES (FANNY) BURNEY (1752–1840)   102
from The Diary of Frances Burney   103

MARIA EDGEWORTH (1768–1849)   105
from Letters for Literary Ladies   106

JANE AUSTEN (1775–1817)   112
Northanger Abbey   114

MARY SHELLEY (1797–1851)   232
Introduction to *Frankenstein*   233

CHARLOTTE BRONTË (1816–1855)   236
Letter from Robert Southey   238
Letter to Robert Southey   239
Letter to George Henry Lewes   240

EMILY BRONTË (1818–1848)   241
[Alone I Sat; the Summer Day]   242
To Imagination   243
The Night Wind   243
R. Alcona to J. Brenzaida   244
[No Coward Soul is Mine]   245
Stanzas   246

GEORGE ELIOT (1819–1880)   247
Silly Novels by Lady Novelists   248

CHARLOTTE PERKINS GILMAN (1860–1935)   263
The Yellow Wallpaper   264

EDITH WHARTON (1862-1937)   274
   A Journey   275

GERTRUDE STEIN (1874-1946)   282
   from Patriarchal Poetry   284

ZORA NEALE HURSTON (1891-1960)   288
   from Dust Tracks on a Road   289

STEVIE SMITH (1902-1971)   292
   My Muse   292
   A Dream of Comparison   293
   Thoughts about the Person from Porlock   293

MAY SARTON (1912-1995)   295
   Journey Toward Poetry   296
   The Muse as Medusa   296
   Of the Muse   297

HISAYE YAMAMOTO (1921-)   298
   Seventeen Syllables   299

MAXINE HONG KINGSTON (1940-)   307
   No Name Woman   308

GLORIA ANZALDÚA (1942-)   315
   Speaking in Tongues: A Letter to Third World Women Writers   316

ALICE WALKER (1944-)   323
   In Search of Our Mothers' Gardens   324

MEDBH MCGUCKIAN (1950-)   331
   To My Grandmother   332
   From the Dressing Room   332
   Turning the Moon into a Verb   333

CAROL ANN DUFFY (1955-)   333
   Standing Female Nude   334
   Litany   335
   Mrs. Aesop   335

GCINA MHLOPHE (1959-)   336
   The Toilet   337
   Sometimes When It Rains   341
   The Dancer   343
   Say No   344

INTERTEXTUALITIES   **345**
   TOPICS FOR DISCUSSION, JOURNALS, AND ESSAYS   345
   GROUP WRITING AND PERFORMANCE EXERCISE   346
   BARBARA CHRISTIAN (1943–)   346
      The Highs and Lows of Black Feminist Criticism   347
   ELAINE SHOWALTER (1941–)   352
      Feminist Criticism in the Wilderness   353

Section II

Writing Bodies/Bodies Writing

INTRODUCTION   375

ANNOTATED BIBLIOGRAPHY   388

HÉLÈNE CIXOUS (1937–)   390
   The Laugh of the Medusa   391

NANCY MAIRS (1943–)   405
   Reading Houses, Writing Lives: The French Connection   406

ANONYMOUS   416
   The Wife's Lament (8th century?)   417

ANONYMOUS   418
   Wulf and Eadwacer (8th century?)   419

MARGERY KEMPE (1373?–1438?)   419
   from The Book of Margery Kempe   420

MARGERY BREWS PASTON (1457?–1495)   425
   Letters to her Valentine/fiance   425
   Letter to her husband, John Paston   427

ELIZABETH I (1533–1603)   427
   On Monsieur's Departure   428
   When I was Fair and Young   429

MARY WROTH (1587?–1653?)   429
   from Pamphilia to Amphilanthus   430

APHRA BEHN (1640–1689)   433
   The Lucky Chance, or an Alderman's Bargain   434

JANE BARKER (1652–1727)   492
   A Virgin Life   493

DELARIVIER MANLEY (1663–1724)   494
   from The New Atalantis   495

ELIZA HAYWOOD (1693?–1756)   498
   from The Female Spectator   499

HARRIET JACOBS (1813?–1897)   506
   from Incidents in the Life of a Slave Girl, Written by Herself   507

CHRISTINA ROSSETTI (1830–1894)   512
   Monna Innominata   513

DJUNA BARNES (1892–1982)   519
   from Ladies Almanack   520
   To the Dogs   523

EDNA ST. VINCENT MILLAY (1892–1950)   529
   from Fatal Interview   530

ANNE SEXTON (1928–1974)   531
   The Abortion   532
   In Celebration of My Uterus   533
   For My Lover, Returning to His Wife   534

AUDRE LORDE (1934–1992)   535
   Uses of the Erotic: The Erotic as Power   536
   Love Poem   540
   Chain   541
   Restoration: A Memorial—9/18/91   542

BHARATI MUKHERJEE (1938–)   544
   A Wife's Story   545

TONI CADE BAMBARA (1939–1996)   553
   My Man Bovanne   554

SHARON OLDS (1942–)   558
   That Year   559
   The Language of the Brag   559
   The Girl   560
   Sex Without Love   561

SLAVENKA DRAKULIĆ (1949-)   562

Make-up and Other Crucial Questions   563

JOY HARJO (1951-)   568

Fire   569
Deer Ghost   569
City of Fire   570
Heartshed   571

DIONNE BRAND (1953-)   572

Madame Alaird's Breasts   573

SANDRA CISNEROS (1955-)   576

I the Woman   576
Love Poem #1   578

JACKIE KAY (1961-)   578

Close Shave   579
Other Lovers   580

INTERTEXTUALITIES   582

TOPICS FOR DISCUSSION, JOURNALS, AND ESSAYS   582
GROUP WRITING AND PERFORMANCE EXERCISE   583
CATHERINE GALLAGHER (1945-)   584
Who Was That Masked Woman? The Prostitute and the Playwright
in the Comedies of Aphra Behn   585
SHARI BENSTOCK (1944-)   597
The Lesbian Other   598

Section III

Rethinking the Maternal

INTRODUCTION   605

ANNOTATED BIBLIOGRAPHY   617

SUSAN RUBIN SULEIMAN (1939-)   620

Writing and Motherhood   621

PATRICIA HILL COLLINS (1948-)   638

Shifting the Center: Race, Class, and Feminist Theorizing About
Motherhood   638

JULIAN OF NORWICH (1343-1416)   654

from Showings   655

JULIANA BERNERS (CA. 1486)   658
   from The Book of Hunting   659

DOROTHY LEIGH (?–1616)   660
   from The Mother's Blessing   661

ELIZABETH CLINTON, THE COUNTESS OF LINCOLN
(1574?–?)   664
   from The Countess of Lincoln's Nursery   665

ANNE BRADSTREET (1612–1672)   668
   The Author to Her Book   669
   Before the Birth of One of Her Children   670
   In Reference to her Children, 23 June, 1656   670

LADY MARY WORTLEY MONTAGU (1689–1762)   672
   To Lady Bute   673

MARY BARBER (1690–1757)   676
   Written for My Son, and Spoken by Him at His First Putting
      on Breeches   676
   The Conclusion of a Letter to the Rev. Mr. C—   678

CHARLOTTE SMITH (1749–1806)   679
   The Glow-Worm   680
   Verses Intended to Have Been Prefixed to the Novel of Emmeline, but
      then Suppressed   681

MARY TIGHE (1772–1810)   682
   Sonnet Addressed to My Mother   682

LYDIA SIGOURNEY (1791–1865)   683
   Death of an Infant   684
   The Last Word of the Dying   684
   Dream of the Dead   686

FELICIA HEMANS (1793–1835)   687
   Casabianca   688
   The Hebrew Mother   689

GRACE AGUILAR (1816–1847)   690
   from The Exodus—Laws for the Mothers of Israel   692

KATE CHOPIN (1851–1904)   695
   The Awakening   696

TILLIE OLSEN (1913–)   778
Tell Me a Riddle   779

JUDITH WRIGHT (1915–)   803
Stillborn   804
Letter   805

GWENDOLYN BROOKS (1917–)   806
the mother   808
A Bronzeville Mother Loiters in Mississippi. Meanwhile, A Mississippi
    Mother Burns Bacon   808
The Last Quatrain of the Ballad of Emmett Till   812

SYLVIA PLATH (1932–1963)   812
The Disquieting Muses   814
Medusa   815
Nick and the Candlestick   816
Childless Woman   817
Edge   817

LUCILLE CLIFTON (1936–)   818
june 20   819
daughters   819
sarah's promise   819
naomi watches as ruth sleeps   820

BESSIE HEAD (1937–1986)   820
The Village Saint   822

MARGARET ATWOOD (1939–)   826
Giving Birth   827

ROSELLEN BROWN (1939–)   836
Good Housekeeping   837

BETH BRANT (1941–)   838
A Long Story   839

AMA ATA AIDOO (1942–)   844
A Gift from Somewhere   845

MINNIE BRUCE PRATT (1944–)   851
Poem for My Sons   852

KERI HULME (1947–)   853
One Whale, Singing   854

RITA DOVE (1952–)   860

Demeter Mourning   861
Demeter, Waiting   862
Mother Love   862

CHERRÍE MORAGA (1952–)   863

La Güera   863
For the Color of My Mother   869

KATE DANIELS (1953–)   870

Genesis I:28   871
Love Pig   872
In My Office at Bennington   872
After Reading Reznikoff   873
Prayer for My Children   874

INTERTEXTUALITIES   875

TOPICS FOR DISCUSSION, JOURNALS, AND ESSAYS   875
CREATIVE WRITING EXERCISE   876
ORAL HISTORY PROJECT   876
MARGIT STANGE (1949–)   876
    Personal Property: Exchange Value and the Female Self in
    The Awakening   877
PAULA GUNN ALLEN (1939–)   888
    Who Is Your Mother? Red Roots of White Feminism   889

Section IV
Identity and Difference

INTRODUCTION   899

ANNOTATED BIBLIOGRAPHY   911

MICHELLE CLIFF (1946–)   916

If I Could Write This in Fire, I Would Write This in Fire   917

TRINH T. MINH-HA (1952–)   928

Not You/Like You: Postcolonial Women and the Interlocking Questions of Identity
    and Difference   929

MARY SIDNEY HERBERT (1561–1621)   933

The Doleful Lay of Clorinda   934

AEMILIA LANYER (1569–1645)   936

from Salve Deus Rex Judaeorum   937

KATHERINE PHILIPS (1632–1664)   939

 To the Excellent Mrs. A.O. upon her Receiving the name of Lucasia,
  and Adoption into our Society   940
 Friendship's Mysteries, to my Dearest Lucasia   941
 On Rosania's Apostasy, and Lucasia's Friendship   942
 Lucasia, Rosania, and Orinda, Parting at a Fountain   942

MARY ROWLANDSON (1636?–1710)   943

 from The Sovereignty and Goodness of God, Together with the
  Faithfulness of His Promises Displayed, Being a Narrative of the
  Captivity and Restoration of Mrs. Mary Rowlandson   944

HANNAH MORE (1745–1833)   947

 from The Black Slave Trade   948

PHILLIS WHEATLEY (1753?–1784)   949

 On Being Brought from Africa to America   950
 To S.M., A Young African Painter, On Seeing His Works   950
 To the Right Honorable William, Earl of DARTMOUTH, His Majesty's Principal
  Secretary of State for North America, & c.   951

DOROTHY WORDSWORTH (1771–1855)   952

 from The Grasmere Journal   953

MARGARET FULLER (1810–1850)   955

 from Woman in the Nineteenth Century   957

EMILY DICKINSON (1830–1886)   966

 Poem 258 (There's a certain Slant of light,)   968
 Poem 280 (I felt a Funeral, in my Brain,)   968
 Poem 303 (The Soul selects her own Society—)   969
 Poem 341 (After great pain, a formal feeling comes—)   969
 Poem 365 (Dare you see a Soul *at the White Heat*?)   969
 Poem 508 (I'm ceded—I've stopped being Theirs—)   970
 Poem 512 (The Soul has Bandaged moments—)   970
 Poem 709 (Publication—is the Auction)   971
 Poem 754 (My Life had Stood—a Loaded Gun—)   971
 Poem 1072 (Title divine—is mine!)   972

ALICE DUNBAR-NELSON (1875–1935)   972

 I Sit and Sew   973
 The Proletariat Speaks   974

ZITKALA-SÄ (GERTRUDE SIMMONS BONNIN) (1876–1938)   975

 The Tree-Bound   976

SUSAN GLASPELL (1882–1948)   980

 Trifles   981

MARIANNE MOORE (1887–1972)   990

The Fish   991
The Paper Nautilus   992
The Mind Is an Enchanting Thing   993
In Distrust of Merits   994
Like a Bulwark   996

KATHERINE MANSFIELD (1888–1923)   996

The Doll's House   997

EUDORA WELTY (1909–)   1002

Why I Live at the P.O.   1003

DORIS LESSING (1919–)   1010

An Old Woman and Her Cat   1012

OODGEROO OF THE TRIBE NOONUCCAL (1920–1993)   1021

We Are Going   1022

ANITA DESAI (1937–)   1022

Surface Textures   1023

PAULA GUNN ALLEN (1939–)   1026

Molly Brant, Iroquois Matron, Speaks   1027
Taku Skansken   1030

ANGELA CARTER (1940–1992)   1031

Wolf Alice   1032

BUCHI EMECHETA (1944–)   1038

A Cold Welcome   1038

JAMAICA KINCAID (1949–)   1043

Xuela   1044

INGRID DE KOK (1951–)   1058

Our Sharpeville   1059
Small Passing   1060
Transfer   1061

INTERTEXTUALITIES   1062

TOPICS FOR DISCUSSION, JOURNALS, AND ESSAYS   1063
CREATIVE WRITING EXERCISE   1063
JUNE JORDAN (1936–)   1064
    The Difficult Miracle of Black Poetry in America or Something Like a
    Sonnet for Phillis Wheatley   1065

JOANNE FEIT DIEHL (1947–)   1073
Selfish Desires: Dickinson's Poetic Ego and the Rites of Subjectivity   1073

Section V

Resistance and Transformation

INTRODUCTION   1079

ANNOTATED BIBLIOGRAPHY   1091

ADRIENNE RICH (1929–)   1094
Notes toward a Politics of Location   1095
Diving into the Wreck   1106
from Inscriptions   1108
  One: Comrade   1108
  Two: Movement   1109
  Three: Origins   1110
  Four: History   1111

ELLEN KUZWAYO (1914–)   1112
Nkosi Sikelel'i Afrika (God Bless Africa)   1113

RACHEL SPEGHT (1597?–1630?)   1116
from A Muzzle for Melastomus   1117

MARY ASTELL (1666–1731)   1124
from A Serious Proposal to the Ladies   1125

SARAH FYGE (1670–1723)   1129
The Liberty   1130

MARY WOLLSTONECRAFT (1759–1797)   1131
from A Vindication of the Rights of Woman   1133

MARY HAYS (1760–1843)   1140
from Appeal to the Men of Great Britain in Behalf of Women   1141

SOJOURNER TRUTH (1797?–1883)   1145
Ain't I a Woman?   1146
Keeping the Thing Going While Things Are Stirring   1146

HARRIET MARTINEAU (1802–1876)   1147
from Society in America   1148
  Citizenship of People of Color   1148
  Political Nonexistence of Women   1150

ELIZABETH BARRETT BROWNING (1806-1861)   1152
The Runaway Slave at Pilgrim's Point   1153
A Curse for a Nation   1160

FRANCES ELLEN WATKINS HARPER (1825-1911)   1163
The Slave Mother   1164
Free Labor   1165
An Appeal to My Country Women   1166
Learning to Read   1167

REBECCA HARDING DAVIS (1831-1910)   1168
Life in the Iron-Mills   1169

ANZIA YEZIERSKA (1881?-1970)   1192
Soap and Water   1193

H.D. (HILDA DOOLITTLE) (1886-1961)   1197
Eurydice   1198
Oread   1201
from The Walls Do Not Fall (I-IV)   1202

MURIEL RUKEYSER (1913-1980)   1205
Bubble of Air   1206
from Letter to the Front (VII)   1207
Käthe Kollwitz   1207
Despisals   1211

NADINE GORDIMER (1923-)   1212
Amnesty   1213

JANET FRAME (1924-)   1218
The Chosen Image   1219

MAYA ANGELOU (1928-)   1221
Still I Rise   1223

TONI MORRISON (1931-)   1224
Recitatif   1225

CARYL CHURCHILL (1938-)   1237
Vinegar Tom   1238

IRENA KLEPFISZ (1941-)   1268
from Bashert   1269
death camp   1271
Etlekhe verter oyf mame-loshn/A few words in the mother
    tongue   1272

EAVAN BOLAND (1944–)   1273
   Inscriptions   1274
   Writing in a Time of Violence   1275

ZOË WICOMB (1948–)   1277
   Bowl Like Hole   1278

CAROLYN FORCHÉ (1950–)   1282
   The Colonel   1283
   Message   1284
   Ourselves or Nothing   1285
   The Garden Shukkei-en   1288
   The Testimony of Light   1289

LOUISE ERDRICH (1954–)   1289
   Fleur   1290

INTERTEXTUALITIES   1298
   TOPICS FOR DISCUSSION, JOURNALS, AND ESSAYS   1299
   GROUP RESEARCH ASSIGNMENT   1299
   ANN PARRY (1949?–)   1300
      Sexual Exploitation and Freedom: Religion, Race, and
      Gender in Elizabeth Barrett Browning's "The Runaway Slave at
      Pilgrim's Point"   1300
   NELL IRVIN PAINTER (1942–)   1309
      "Ar'n't I a Woman?"   1309

Historical Appendices   1319

   Old English and Middle English Literature—449-1485   1319
   Renaissance and Early Seventeenth-Century Literature—
      1485-1660   1334
   Late Seventeenth and Eighteenth-Century Literature—
      1660-1800   1352
   Nineteenth-Century Literature—1800-1900   1369
   Modernist Literature—1900-1945   1385
   Contemporary Literature—1945-2000   1401

Selected Bibliographies   1419

Credits   1449

Index   1458

A HISTORICAL CHRONOLOGY OF WRITERS

I. Old English and Middle English Literature

LEOBA OF ENGLAND AND GERMANY (700?-779)   76
  Letter to Lord Boniface   77

ANONYMOUS   416
  The Wife's Lament (8th century?)   417

ANONYMOUS   418
  Wulf and Eadwacer (8th century?)   419

MATILDA, QUEEN OF ENGLAND (1080-1118)   78
  Letter to Archbishop Anselm   79
  Letter to Pope Pascal   80

JULIAN OF NORWICH (1343-1416)   654
  from Showings   655

MARGERY KEMPE (1373?-1438?)   419
  from The Book of Margery Kempe   420

MARGERY BREWS PASTON (1457?-1495)   425
  Letters to her Valentine/fiance   425
  Letter to John Paston   427

JULIANA BERNERS (CA. 1486)   658
  from The Book of Hunting   659

II. Renaissance and Early Seventeenth-Century Literature

ELIZABETH I (1533-1603)   427
  On Monsieur's Departure   428
  When I was Fair and Young   429

ANNE LOCK (FL. 1556-1590)   81
  from A Meditation of a Penitent Sinner, upon the 51 Psalm   82

MARY SIDNEY HERBERT (1561–1621)   933
    The Doleful Lay of Clorinda   934

ISABELLA WHITNEY (FL. 1567–1573?)   85
    The Author . . . Maketh Her Will and Testament   85
    from The Manner of Her Will   86

AEMILIA LANYER (1569–1645)   936
    from Salve Deus Rex Judaeorum   937

DOROTHY LEIGH (?–1616)   660
    from The Mother's Blessing   661

ELIZABETH CLINTON, THE COUNTESS OF LINCOLN (1574?–?)   664
    from The Countess of Lincoln's Nursery   665

MARY WROTH (1587?–1653?)   429
    from Pamphilia to Amphilanthus   430

RACHEL SPEGHT (1597?–1630?)   1116
    from A Muzzle for Melastomus   1117

ANNE BRADSTREET (1612–1672)   668
    The Author to Her Book   669
    Before the Birth of One of Her Children   670
    In Reference to her Children, 23 June, 1656   670

MARGARET CAVENDISH, DUCHESS OF
NEWCASTLE (1623?–1673)   89
    The Poetess's Hasty Resolution   90
    The Poetess's Petition   90
    An Excuse for So Much Writ upon My Verses   91
    Nature's Cook   91
    from To All Writing Ladies   92

III. Late Seventeenth and Eighteenth-Century Literature

KATHERINE PHILIPS (1632–1664)   939
    To the Excellent Mrs. A.O. upon her Receiving the Name of Lucasia,
        and Adoption into our Society   940
    Friendship's Mysteries, to my Dearest Lucasia   941
    On Rosania's Apostasy, and Lucasia's Friendship   942
    Lucasia, Rosania, and Orinda, Parting at a Fountain   942

MARY ROWLANDSON (1636?–1710)   943
    from The Sovereignty and Goodness of God, Together with the Faithfulness
        of His Promises Displayed, Being a Narrative of the Captivity and
        Restoration of Mrs. Mary Rowlandson   944

APHRA BEHN (1640-1689)   433
    The Lucky Chance, or an Alderman's Bargain   434

JANE BARKER (1652-1727)   492
    A Virgin Life   493

ANNE KILLIGREW (1660-1685)   93
    Upon the Saying that My Verses Were Made by Another   94
    On a Picture Painted by Herself   95

ANNE FINCH, COUNTESS OF WINCHILSEA (1661-1720)   96
    The Introduction   97
    A Nocturnal Reverie   98
    Ardelia to Melancholy   100
    Friendship Between Ephelia and Ardelia   101
    The Answer   101

DELARIVIER MANLEY (1663-1724)   494
    from The New Atalantis   495

MARY ASTELL (1666-1731)   1124
    from A Serious Proposal to the Ladies   1125

SARAH FYGE (1670-1723)   1129
    The Liberty   1130

LADY MARY WORTLEY MONTAGU (1689-1762)   672
    To Lady Bute   673

MARY BARBER (1690-1757)   676
    Written for My Son, and Spoken by Him at His First Putting on Breeches   676
    The Conclusion of a Letter to the Rev. Mr. C—   678

ELIZA HAYWOOD (1693?-1756)   498
    from The Female Spectator   499

HANNAH MORE (1745-1833)   947
    from The Black Slave Trade   948

CHARLOTTE SMITH (1749-1806)   679
    The Glow-Worm   680
    Verses intended to have been Prefixed to the Novel of Emmeline, but then
        Suppressed   681

FRANCES (FANNY) BURNEY (1752-1840)   102
    from The Diary of Frances Burney   103

PHILLIS WHEATLEY (1753?–1784)   949
    On Being Brought from Africa to America   950
    To S.M., A Young African Painter, On Seeing His Works   950
    To the Right Honorable William, Earl of DARTMOUTH, His Majesty's Principal
        Secretary of State for North America, & c.   951

MARY WOLLSTONECRAFT (1759–1797)   1131
    from A Vindication of the Rights of Woman   1133

MARY HAYS (1760–1843)   1140
    from Appeal to the Men of Great Britain in Behalf of Women   1141

IV. Nineteenth-Century Literature

MARIA EDGEWORTH (1767–1849)   105
    from Letters for Literary Ladies   106

DOROTHY WORDSWORTH (1771–1855)   952
    from The Grasmere Journal   953

MARY TIGHE (1772–1810)   682
    Sonnet Addressed to My Mother   682

JANE AUSTEN (1775–1817)   112
    Northanger Abbey   114

LYDIA SIGOURNEY (1791–1865)   683
    Death of an Infant   684
    The Last Word of the Dying   684
    Dream of the Dead   686

FELICIA HEMANS (1793–1835)   687
    Casabianca   688
    The Hebrew Mother   689

MARY SHELLEY (1797–1851)   232
    Introduction to Frankenstein   233

SOJOURNER TRUTH (1797?–1883)   1145
    Ain't I a Woman?   1146
    Keeping the Thing Going While Things Are Stirring   1146

HARRIET MARTINEAU (1802–1876)   1147
    from Society in America   1148
        Citizenship of People of Color   1148
        Political Nonexistence of Women   1150

ELIZABETH BARRETT BROWNING (1806–1861)   1152

    The Runaway Slave at Pilgrim's Point   1153
    A Curse for a Nation   1160

MARGARET FULLER (1810–1850)   955

    from Woman in the Nineteenth Century   957

HARRIET JACOBS (1813?–1897)   506

    from Incidents in the Life of a Slave Girl, Written by Herself   507

GRACE AGUILAR (1816–1847)   690

    from The Exodus—Laws for the Mothers of Israel   692

CHARLOTTE BRONTË (1816–1855)   236

    Letter from Robert Southey   238
    Letter to Robert Southey   239
    Letter to George Henry Lewes   240

EMILY BRONTË (1818–1848)   241

    [Alone I Sat; the Summer Day]   242
    To Imagination   243
    The Night Wind   243
    R. Alcona to J. Brenzaida   244
    [No Coward Soul is Mine]   245
    Stanzas   246

GEORGE ELIOT (1819–1880)   247

    Silly Novels by Lady Novelists   248

FRANCES ELLEN WATKINS HARPER (1825–1911)   1163

    The Slave Mother   1164
    Free Labor   1165
    An Appeal to My Country Women   1166
    Learning to Read   1167

EMILY DICKINSON (1830–1886)   966

    Poem 258 (There's a certain Slant of light,)   968
    Poem 280 (I felt a Funeral, in my Brain,)   968
    Poem 303 (The Soul selects her own Society—)   969
    Poem 341 (After great pain, a formal feeling comes—)   969
    Poem 365 (Dare you see a Soul *at the White Heat?*)   969
    Poem 508 (I'm ceded—I've stopped being Theirs—)   970
    Poem 512 (The Soul has Bandaged moments—)   970
    Poem 709 (Publication—is the Auction)   971
    Poem 754 (My Life had Stood—a Loaded Gun—)   971
    Poem 1072 (Title divine—is mine!)   972

CHRISTINA ROSSETTI (1830-1894)   512
  Monna Innominata 513

REBECCA HARDING DAVIS (1831-1910)   1168
  Life in the Iron-Mills 1169

KATE CHOPIN (1851-1904)   695
  The Awakening 696

CHARLOTTE PERKINS GILMAN (1860-1935)   263
  The Yellow Wallpaper 264

V. Modernist Literature

EDITH WHARTON (1862-1937)   274
  A Journey 275

GERTRUDE STEIN (1874-1946)   282
  from Patriarchal Poetry 284

ALICE DUNBAR-NELSON (1875-1935)   972
  I Sit and Sew 973
  The Proletariat Speaks 974

ZITKALA-SÄ (GERTRUDE SIMMONS BONNIN) (1876-1938)   975
  The Tree-Bound 976

ANZIA YEZIERSKA (1881?-1970)   1192
  Soap and Water 1193

SUSAN GLASPELL (1882-1948)   980
  Trifles 981

VIRGINIA WOOLF (1882-1941)   14
  A Room of One's Own 16

H.D. (HILDA DOOLITTLE) (1886-1961)   1197
  Eurydice 1198
  Oread 1201
  from The Walls Do Not Fall (I-IV) 1202

MARIANNE MOORE (1887-1972)   990
  The Fish 991
  The Paper Nautilus 992
  The Mind Is An Enchanting Thing 993
  In Distrust of Merits 994
  Like a Bulwark 996

KATHERINE MANSFIELD (1888-1923)   996
  The Doll's House   997

ZORA NEALE HURSTON (1891-1960)   288
  from Dust Tracks on a Road   289

DJUNA BARNES (1892-1982)   519
  from Ladies Almanack   520
  To the Dogs   523

EDNA ST. VINCENT MILLAY (1892-1950)   529
  from Fatal Interview   530

STEVIE SMITH (1902-1971)   292
  My Muse   292
  A Dream of Comparison   293
  Thoughts About the Person from Porlock   293

VI. Contemporary Literature

EUDORA WELTY (1909-)   1002
  Why I Live at the P.O.   1003

MAY SARTON (1912-1995)   295
  Journey Toward Poetry   296
  The Muse as Medusa   296
  Of the Muse   297

TILLIE OLSEN (1913-)   778
  Tell Me a Riddle   779

MURIEL RUKEYSER (1913-1980)   1205
  Bubble of Air   1206
  from Letter to the Front (VII)   1207
  Käthe Kollwitz   1207
  Despisals   1211

ELLEN KUZWAYO (1914-)   1112
  Nkosi Sikelel'i Afrika (God Bless Africa)   1113

JUDITH WRIGHT (1915-)   803
  Stillborn   804
  Letter   805

GWENDOLYN BROOKS (1917-)   806
the mother   808
A Bronzeville Mother Loiters in Mississippi. Meanwhile, A Mississippi Mother
    Burns Bacon.   808
The Last Quatrain of the Ballad of Emmett Till   812

DORIS LESSING (1919-)   1010
An Old Woman and Her Cat   1012

OODGEROO OF THE TRIBE NOONUCCAL (1920-1993)   1021
We Are Going   1022

HISAYE YAMAMOTO (1921-)   298
Seventeen Syllables   299

NADINE GORDIMER (1923-)   1212
Amnesty   1213

JANET FRAME (1924-)   1218
The Chosen Image   1219

MAYA ANGELOU (1928-)   1221
Still I Rise   1223

ANNE SEXTON (1928-1974)   531
The Abortion   532
In Celebration of My Uterus   533
For My Lover, Returning to His Wife   534

ADRIENNE RICH (1929-)   1094
Notes toward a Politics of Location   1095
Diving into the Wreck   1106
from Inscriptions   1108
    One: Comrade   1108
    Two: Movement   1109
    Three: Origins   1110
    Four: History   1111

TONI MORRISON (1931-)   1224
Recitatif   1225

SYLVIA PLATH (1932-1963)   812
The Disquieting Muses   814
Medusa   815
Nick and the Candlestick   816
Childless Woman   817
Edge   817

AUDRE LORDE (1934–1992)   535

Uses of the Erotic: The Erotic as Power   536
Love Poem   540
Chain   541
Restoration: A Memorial—9/18/91   542

LUCILLE CLIFTON (1936–)   818

june 20   819
daughters   819
sarah's promise   819
naomi watches as ruth sleeps   820

JUNE JORDAN (1936–)   1064

The Difficult Miracle of Black Poetry in America or Something Like A Sonnet
   for Phillis Wheatley   1065

HÉLÈNE CIXOUS (1937–)   390

The Laugh of the Medusa   391

ANITA DESAI (1937–)   1022

Surface Textures   1023

BESSIE HEAD (1937–1986)   820

The Village Saint   822

CARYL CHURCHILL (1938–)   1237

Vinegar Tom   1238

BHARATI MUKHERJEE (1938–)   544

A Wife's Story   545

PAULA GUNN ALLEN (1939–)   1026

Molly Brant, Iroquois Matron, Speaks   1027
Taku Skansken   1030
Who Is Your Mother? Red Roots of White Feminism   889

MARGARET ATWOOD (1939–)   826

Giving Birth   827

TONI CADE BAMBARA (1939–1996)   553

My Man Bovanne   554

ROSELLEN BROWN (1939–)   836

Good Housekeeping   837

SUSAN RUBIN SULEIMAN (1939–)   620

Writing and Motherhood   621

ANGELA CARTER (1940–1992)   1031
    Wolf Alice   1032

MAXINE HONG KINGSTON (1940–)   307
    No Name Woman   308

BETH BRANT (1941–)   838
    A Long Story   839

IRENA KLEPFISZ (1941–)   1268
    from Bashert   1269
    death camp   1271
    Etlekhe verter oyf mame-loshn/A few words in the mother tongue   1272

ELAINE SHOWALTER (1941–)   352
    Feminist Criticism in the Wilderness   353

AMA ATA AIDOO (1942–)   844
    A Gift from Somewhere   845

GLORIA ANZALDÚA (1942–)   315
    Speaking in Tongues: A Letter to Third World Women Writers   316

SHARON OLDS (1942–)   558
    That Year   559
    The Language of the Brag   559
    The Girl   560
    Sex Without Love   561

NELL IRVIN PAINTER (1942–)   1309
    "Ar'n't I a Woman?"   1309

BARBARA CHRISTIAN (1943–)   346
    The Highs and Lows of Black Feminist Criticism   347

NANCY MAIRS (1943–)   405
    Reading Houses, Writing Lives: The French Connection   406

SHARI BENSTOCK (1944–)   597
    The Lesbian Other   598

EAVAN BOLAND (1944–)   1273
    Inscriptions   1274
    Writing in a Time of Violence   1275

BUCHI EMECHETA (1944–)   1038
    A Cold Welcome   1038

MINNIE BRUCE PRATT (1944-)   851
  Poem for My Sons   852

ALICE WALKER (1944-)   323
  In Search of Our Mothers' Gardens   324

CATHERINE GALLAGHER (1945-)   584
  Who Was That Masked Woman? The Prostitute and the Playwright
    in the Comedies of Aphra Behn   585

MICHELLE CLIFF (1946-)   916
  If I Could Write This in Fire, I Would Write This in Fire   917

JOANNE FEIT DIEHL (1947-)   1073
  Selfish Desires: Dickinson's Poetic Ego and the Rites of Subjectivity   1073

KERI HULME (1947-)   853
  One Whale, Singing   854

PATRICIA HILL COLLINS (1948-)   638
  Shifting the Center: Race, Class, and Feminist Theorizing About
    Motherhood   638

ZOË WICOMB (1948-)   1277
  Bowl Like Hole   1278

SLAVENKA DRAKULIĆ (1949-)   562
  Make-up and Other Crucial Questions   563

JAMAICA KINCAID (1949-)   1043
  Xuela   1044

ANN PARRY (1949?-)   1300
  Sexual Exploitation and Freedom: Religion, Race, and Gender in Elizabeth
    Barrett Browning's "The Runaway Slave at Pilgrim's Point"   1300

MARGIT STANGE (1949-)   876
  Personal Property: Exchange Value and the Female Self in
    The Awakening   877

CAROLYN FORCHÉ (1950-)   1282
  The Colonel   1283
  Message   1284
  Ourselves or Nothing   1285
  The Garden Shukkei-en   1288
  The Testimony of Light   1289

MEDBH MCGUCKIAN (1950–)   331
    To My Grandmother   332
    From the Dressing Room   332
    Turning the Moon into a Verb   333

INGRID DE KOK (1951–)   1058
    Our Sharpeville   1059
    Small Passing   1060
    Transfer   1061

JOY HARJO (1951–)   568
    Fire   569
    Deer Ghost   569
    City of Fire   570
    Heartshed   571

RITA DOVE (1952–)   860
    Demeter Mourning   861
    Demeter, Waiting   862
    Mother Love   862

CHERRÍE MORAGA (1952–)   863
    La Güera   863
    For the Color of My Mother   869

TRINH T. MINH-HA (1952–)   928
    Not You/Like You: Postcolonial Women and the Interlocking Questions
        of Identity and Difference   929

DIONNE BRAND (1953–)   572
    Madame Alaird's Breasts   573

KATE DANIELS (1953–)   870
    Genesis I:28   871
    Love Pig   872
    In My Office at Bennington   872
    After Reading Reznikoff   873
    Prayer for My Children   874

LOUISE ERDRICH (1954–)   1289
    Fleur   1290

SANDRA CISNEROS (1955–)   576
    I the Woman   576
    Love Poem #1   578

CAROL ANN DUFFY (1955–)   333

Standing Female Nude   334
Litany   335
Mrs. Aesop   335

BELL HOOKS (1955–)   72

Talking Back   73

GCINA MHLOPHE (1959–)   336

The Toilet   337
Sometimes When It Rains   341
The Dancer   343
Say No   344

JACKIE KAY (1961–)   578

Close Shave   579
Other Lovers   580

THEMATIC APPROACHES TO WOMEN'S LITERATURE

Women and the Sacred

LEOBA OF ENGLAND AND GERMANY (700?-779)   76
Letter to Lord Boniface   77

MATILDA, QUEEN OF ENGLAND (1080-1118)   78
Letter to Archbishop Anselm   79
Letter to Pope Pascal   80

JULIAN OF NORWICH (1343-1416)   654
from Showings   655

MARGERY KEMPE (1373?-1438?)   419
from The Book of Margery Kempe   420

ANNE LOCK (FL. 1556-1590)   81
from A Meditation of a Penitent Sinner, upon the 51 Psalm   82

AEMILIA LANYER (1569-1645)   936
from Salve Deus Rex Judaeorum   937

DOROTHY LEIGH (?-1616)   660
from The Mother's Blessing   661

ELIZABETH CLINTON, THE COUNTESS OF LINCOLN (1574-?)   664
from The Countess of Lincoln's Nursery   665

ANNE BRADSTREET (1612-1672)   668
Before the Birth of One of Her Children   670

MARY ROWLANDSON (1636?-1710)   943
from The Sovereignty and Goodness of God, Together with the Faithfulness
of His Promises Displayed, Being a Narrative of the Captivity and
Restoration of Mrs. Mary Rowlandson   944

PHILLIS WHEATLEY (1753?-1784)   949
On Being Brought from Africa to America   950
To the Right Honorable William, Earl of DARTMOUTH, His Majesty's Principal
Secretary of State for North America, & c.   951

FELICIA HEMANS (1792–1835)   687
    The Hebrew Mother   689

GRACE AGUILAR (1816–1847)   690
    from The Exodus—Laws for the Mothers of Israel   692

H.D. (HILDA DOOLITTLE) (1886–1961)   1197
    Eurydice   1198

TILLIE OLSEN (1913–)   778
    Tell Me a Riddle   779

MURIEL RUKEYSER (1913–1980)   1205
    Bubble of Air   1206
    from Letter to the Front (VII)   1207

OODGEROO OF THE TRIBE NOONUCCAL (1920–1993)   1021
    We Are Going   1022

AUDRE LORDE (1934–1992)   535
    Uses of the Erotic: The Erotic as Power   536

LUCILLE CLIFTON (1936–)   818
    sarah's promise   819
    naomi watches as ruth sleeps   820

PAULA GUNN ALLEN (1939–)   1026
    Taku Skanksen   1030
    Who Is Your Mother? Red Roots of White Feminism   889

IRENA KLEPFISZ (1941–)   1268
    from Bashert   1269
    death camp   1271

AMA ATA AIDOO (1942–)   844
    A Gift from Somewhere   845

ALICE WALKER (1944–)   323
    In Search of Our Mothers' Gardens   324

CAROLYN FORCHÉ (1950–)   1282
    Message   1284
    Ourselves or Nothing   1285
    The Garden Shukkei-en   1288

JOY HARJO (1951-)   568

Fire   569
Deer Ghost   569

KATE DANIELS (1953-)   870

Genesis I:28   871
After Reading Reznikoff   873
Prayer for My Children   874

Coming of Age

DOROTHY LEIGH (?-1616)   660

from The Mother's Blessing   661

FRANCES (FANNY) BURNEY (1752-1840)   102

from The Diary of Frances Burney   103

PHILLIS WHEATLEY (1753?-1784)   949

On Being Brought from Africa to America   950

JANE AUSTEN (1775-1817)   112

Northanger Abbey   114

HARRIET JACOBS (1813?-1897)   506

from Incidents in the Life of a Slave Girl, Written by Herself   507

ANZIA YEZIERSKA (1881?-1970)   1192

Soap and Water   1193

KATHERINE MANSFIELD (1888-1923)   996

The Doll's House   997

EUDORA WELTY (1909-)   1002

Why I Live at the P.O.   1003

HISAYE YAMAMOTO (1921-)   298

Seventeen Syllables   299

TONI MORRISON (1931-)   1224

Recitatif   1225

SYLVIA PLATH (1932-)

The Disquieting Muses   814

AUDRE LORDE (1934-1992)

Chain   541

JUNE JORDAN (1936-)   1064
    The Difficult Miracle of Black Poetry in America or Something Like a Sonnet
        for Phillis Wheatley   1065

ANGELA CARTER (1940-1992)   1031
    Wolf Alice   1032

SHARON OLDS (1942-)   558
    That Year   559
    The Girl   560

MICHELLE CLIFF (1946-)   916
    If I Could Write This in Fire, I Would Write This in Fire   917

ZOË WICOMB (1948-)   1277
    Bowl Like Hole   1278

JAMAICA KINCAID (1949-)   1043
    Xuela   1044

INGRID DE KOK (1951-)   1058
    Our Sharpeville   1059

CHERRÍE MORAGA (1952-)   863
    La Güera   863

DIONNE BRAND (1953-)   572
    Madame Alaird's Breasts   573

CAROL ANN DUFFY (1955-)   333
    Litany   335

BELL HOOKS (1955-)   72
    Talking Back   73

GCINA MHLOPHE (1959-)   336
    The Toilet   337

Women and Aging

ELIZABETH I (1533-1603)   427
    When I was Fair and Young   429

ISABELLA WHITNEY (FL. 1567-1573?)   85
    The Author . . . Maketh Her Will and Testament   85
        In The Manner of Her Will   86

LYDIA SIGOURNEY (1791–1865) 683
  The Last Word of the Dying 684
  Dream of the Dead 685

SOJOURNER TRUTH (1797?–1883) 1145
  Ain't I a Woman? 1146
  Keeping the Thing Going While Things Are Stirring 1146

FRANCES ELLEN WATKINS HARPER (1825–1911) 1163
  Learning to Read 1167

CHRISTINA ROSSETTI (1830–1894) 512
  Monna Innominata 513

EDITH WHARTON (1862–1937) 274
  A Journey 275

EDNA ST. VINCENT MILLAY (1892–1950) 529
  from Fatal Interview 530

MAY SARTON (1912–1995) 295
  Of the Muse 297

TILLIE OLSEN (1913–) 778
  Tell Me a Riddle 779

MURIEL RUKEYSER (1913–1980) 1205
  Käthe Kollwitz 1207

DORIS LESSING (1919–) 1010
  An Old Woman and Her Cat 1012

OODGEROO OF THE TRIBE NOONUCCAL (1920–1993) 1021
  We Are Going 1022

AUDRE LORDE (1934–1992) 535
  Restoration: A Memorial—9/18/91 542

LUCILLE CLIFTON (1936–) 818
  daughters 819
  sarah's promise 819
  naomi watches as ruth sleeps 820

BESSIE HEAD (1937–1986) 820
  The Village Saint 822

PAULA GUNN ALLEN (1939-)   1026
   Molly Brant, Iroquois Matron, Speaks   1027
   Who Is Your Mother? Red Roots of White Feminism   889

TONI CADE BAMBARA (1939-1996)   553
   My Man Bovanne   554

NANCY MAIRS (1943-)   405
   Reading Houses, Writing Lives: The French Connection   406

ALICE WALKER (1944-)   323
   In Search of Our Mothers' Gardens   324

MEDBH MCGUCKIAN (1950-)   331
   To My Grandmother   332

RITA DOVE (1952-)   860
   Demeter Mourning   861
   Demeter, Waiting   862
   Mother Love   862

CHERRÍE MORAGA (1952-)   863
   For the Color of My Mother   869

Gender and Postcolonialism

ELLEN KUZWAYO (1914-)   1112
   Nkosi Sikelel'i Africa (God Bless Africa)   1113

OODGEROO OF THE TRIBE NOONUCCAL (1920-1993)   1021
   We Are Going   1022

NADINE GORDIMER (1923-)   1212
   Amnesty   1213

ADRIENNE RICH (1929-)   1094
   Notes toward a Politics of Location   1095

ANITA DESAI (1937-)   1022
   Surface Textures   1023

BESSIE HEAD (1937-1986)   820
   The Village Saint   822

BHARATI MUKHERJEE (1938-)   544
   A Wife's Story   545

BETH BRANT (1941-) 838
A Long Story 839

AMA ATA AIDOO (1942-) 844
A Gift from Somewhere 845

GLORIA ANZALDÚA (1942-) 315
Speaking in Tongues: A Letter to Third World Women Writers 316

EAVAN BOLAND (1944-) 1273
Inscriptions 1274
Writing in a Time of Violence 1275

BUCHI EMECHETA (1944-) 1038
A Cold Welcome 1038

MICHELLE CLIFF (1946-) 916
If I Could Write This in Fire, I Would Write This in Fire 917

KERI HULME (1947-) 853
One Whale, Singing 854

ZOË WICOMB (1948-) 1277
Bowl Like Hole 1278

JAMAICA KINCAID (1949-) 1043
Xuela 1044

INGRID DE KOK (1951-) 1058
Our Sharpeville 1059
Small Passing 1060
Transfer 1061

TRINH T. MINH-HA (1952-) 928
Not You/Like You: Postcolonial Women and the Interlocking Questions
of Identity and Difference 929

DIONNE BRAND (1953-) 572
Madame Alaird's Breasts 573

GCINA MHLOPHE (1959-) 336
The Toilet 337
Sometimes When It Rains 341
The Dancer 343
Say No 344

U.S. Ethnic Literatures

PHILLIS WHEATLEY (1753?–1784)   949
    On Being Brought from Africa to America   950
    To S.M., a Young African Painter, on Seeing His Work   950
    The Right Honorable William, Earl of DARTMOUTH, His Majesty's Principal
        Secretary of State for North America, & c.   951

SOJOURNER TRUTH (1797?–1883)   1145
    Ain't I a Woman?   1146
    Keeping the Thing Going While Things Are Stirring   1146

HARRIET JACOBS (1813?–1897)   506
    from Incidents in the Life of a Slave Girl, Written by Herself   507

GRACE AGUILAR (1816–1847)   690
    from The Exodus—Laws for the Mothers of Israel   692

FRANCES ELLEN WATKINS HARPER (1825–1911)   1163
    The Slave Mother   1164
    Free Labor   1165
    An Appeal to My Country Women   1166
    Learning to Read   1167

ALICE DUNBAR-NELSON (1875–1935)   972
    I Sit and Sew   973
    The Proletariat Speaks   974

ZITKALA-SÄ (GERTRUDE SIMMONS BONNIN) (1876–1938)   975
    The Tree-Bound   976

ANZIA YEZIERSKA (1881?–1970)   1192
    Soap and Water   1193

ZORA NEALE HURSTON (1891–1960)   288
    from Dust Tracks on a Road   289

TILLIE OLSEN (1913–)   778
    Tell Me a Riddle   779

MURIEL RUKEYSER (1913–1980)   1205
    Bubble of Air   1206
    from Letter to the Front (VII)   1207
    Käthe Kollwitz   1207
    Despisals   1211

GWENDOLYN BROOKS (1917–)   806

the mother   808
A Bronzeville Mother Loiters in Mississippi. Meanwhile, A Mississippi
   Mother Burns Bacon   808
The Last Quatrain of the Ballad of Emmett Till   812

HISAYE YAMAMOTO (1921–)   298

Seventeen Syllables   299

MAYA ANGELOU (1928–)   1221

Still I Rise   1223

TONI MORRISON (1931–)   1224

Recitatif   1225

AUDRE LORDE (1934–1992)   535

Uses of the Erotic: The Erotic as Power   536
Love Poem   540
Chain   541
Restoration: A Memorial—9/18/91   542

LUCILLE CLIFTON (1936–)   818

june 20   819
daughters   819
sarah's promise   819
naomi watches as ruth sleeps   820

JUNE JORDAN (1936–)   1064

The Difficult Miracle of Black Poetry in America or Something Like a
   Sonnet for Phillis Wheatley   1065

PAULA GUNN ALLEN (1939–)   1026

Molly Brant, Iroquois Matron, Speaks   1027
Taku Skansken   1030
Who is Your Mother? Red Roots of White Feminism   889

TONI CADE BAMBARA (1939–1996)   553

My Man Bovanne   554

MAXINE HONG KINGSTON (1940–)   307

No Name Woman   308

IRENA KLEPFISZ (1941–)   1268

from Bashert   1269
death camp   1271
Etlekhe verter oyf mame-loshn/ A few words in the mother tongue   1272

GLORIA ANZALDÚA (1942-)   315

Speaking in Tongues: A Letter to Third World Women Writers   316

NELL IRVIN PAINTER (1942-)   1309

"Ar'n't I a Woman?"   1309

BARBARA CHRISTIAN (1943-)   346

The Highs and Lows of Black Feminist Criticism   347

ALICE WALKER (1944-)   323

In Search of Our Mothers' Gardens   324

PATRICIA HILL COLLINS (1948-)   638

Shifting the Center: Race, Class, and Feminist Theorizing About
        Motherhood   638

JOY HARJO (1951-)   568

Fire   569
Deer Ghost   569
City of Fire   570
Heartshed   571

RITA DOVE (1952-)   860

Demeter Mourning   861
Demeter, Waiting   862
Mother Love   862

CHERRÍE MORAGA (1952-)   863

La Güera   863
For the Color of My Mother   869

LOUISE ERDRICH (1954-)   1289

Fleur   1290

SANDRA CISNEROS (1955-)   576

I the Woman   576
Love Poem #1   578

BELL HOOKS (1955-)   72

Talking Back   73

PREFACE

The Longman Anthology of Women's Literature is an innovative text for the twenty-first century: multicultural, thematic, theoretical, and historical. Designed for courses in women's literature and women's studies, this comprehensive book offers challenging literary works by more than 140 women writing in English from fifteen countries, women from the eighth century to the present. Biographical headnotes discuss the life and work of each writer, allowing readers to consider a particular woman's accomplishments in historical perspective, and thirty-five author photographs present a compelling visual representation of these outstanding women. Selections are glossed as needed so that newcomers to a particular era's language or milieu can appreciate each writer's allusions and context. As with all good literature, these selections both reflect and transcend the time period in which they were written.

Organized thematically, the anthology emphasizes five important topics for women writers: engendering language, silence, and voice; writing the body; rethinking the maternal; identity and difference; and resistance and transformation. In addition, the text incorporates recent insights in feminist and postmodern theory, African-American and ethnic studies, and postcolonial and cultural studies into its framework and content. In the words of South African fiction writer Zoë Wicomb, readers of this anthology can "hear the variety of discourses."

As editor, I have envisioned The Longman Anthology of Women's Literature as a major contribution to the lively debates engendered by the rise of women's studies in academia. During the 1980s and 1990s a series of "culture wars" pitted advocates of aesthetic considerations as central to what makes a work of literature "great" against those who privileged political and social concerns. My own belief is that both canonical and non-canonical works of women's literature make for exciting reading, and that both aesthetic and cultural questions are necessary to pose if one is to read with discernment and pleasure.

DEPTH AND BREADTH OF SELECTIONS

When asked to imagine an ideal anthology of women's literature, many readers envision a collection of dynamic works by women across historical time periods, an approach that is multicultural and global, and a diverse array of literary genres—in short, a source of new knowledge. The Longman Anthology of Women's Literature offers a site where such knowledge can be constructed. The writers represented here hail from Antigua, Australia, Canada, Croatia, England, Ghana, India, Ireland, Jamaica, New Zealand, Nigeria, Scotland, South Africa, and Trinidad as well as the United States. The U.S. writers embrace African-American, Native-American, Latina, Chinese-American, Japanese-American, Vietnamese-American, Jewish-American, and European-American identities. Represented are the voices of eighth-century anonymous lyricists, medieval nuns and mystics, early modern poets and polemicists, Restoration and eighteenth-century wits, Victorian sages, modernist experimenters, and contemporary feminists. Even more than male writers, these women express themselves in a variety of genres: in poems, novels, plays, short stories, and autobiographies to be sure, but also in diaries, letters, speeches, polemical tracts, essays in "life writing," and conduct manuals.

Included are a number of full-length essays and works of fiction often considered "classic" texts of women's literature: Virginia Woolf's landmark feminist treatise *A Room of One's Own* (1929); Jane Austen's mock-gothic novel *Northanger Abbey* (1817); George Eliot's wry review of nineteenth-century popular literature, "Silly Novels by Lady Novelists" (1856); Rebecca Harding Davis's tale of class struggle in industrial America, *Life in the Iron-Mills* (1861); Kate Chopin's novella about desire and autonomy, *The Awakening* (1899); Tillie Olsen's novella of a Jewish woman's dying memories, *Tell Me A Riddle* (1960); and Audre Lorde's meditative essay on women's sexuality, "Uses of the Erotic: The Erotic as Power" (1980). A number of long poems appear, among them Mary Sidney Herbert's "The Doleful Lay of Clorinda" (1595), Elizabeth Barrett Browning's "The Runaway Slave at Pilgrim's Point" (1850), Christina Rossetti's *Monna Innominata* (1881), Gwendolyn Brooks's "A Bronzeville Mother Loiters in Mississippi. Meanwhile, A Mississippi Mother Burns Bacon" (1960), and Muriel Rukeyser's "Käthe Kollwitz" (1968). Four plays—Aphra Behn's *The Lucky Chance* (1686), Susan Glaspell's *Trifles* (1916), Djuna Barnes's *To the Dogs* (1923), and Caryl Churchill's *Vinegar Tom* (1976)—reflect the historical, thematic, and stylistic range of explorations by women in this important genre.

Among the many distinguished writers of short fiction are Antigua's Jamaica Kincaid, Canada's Margaret Atwood, India's Anita Desai, Native America's Louise Erdrich, New Zealand's Keri Hulme, Nigeria's Buchi Emecheta, and South Africa's Nadine Gordimer. Letter writers and diarists range from the eighth-century Leoba of England and Germany to the fifteenth-century iconoclast Margery Kempe, from the beloved Victorian novelist Charlotte Brontë to the insouciant African-American autobiographer Zora Neale Hurston. Included also are feminist polemics from Rachel Speght, Mary Wollstonecraft, Margaret Fuller, and Alice Walker, to name only a few. An early modern treatise on breast-feeding by Elizabeth Clinton, suffragist speeches by Sojourner Truth, a captivity narrative by Mary Rowlandson, and a legendary Indian tale by Zitkala-Sä further exemplify the variety of literary discourses recorded here—a feast for readers of both genders and all nationalities, races, classes, and ages.

THEMATIC ORGANIZATION

The U.S. poet Adrienne Rich has claimed that women's literature represents "a whole new psychic geography to be explored." The possibilities of this terrain are evident in the five thematic categories around which this anthology is organized. The literary and feminist topics that these categories raise are among the most intellectually stimulating and fiercely debated in today's universities. These conceptual themes are designed to elicit active reading and informed, impassioned discussion.

The first section of the anthology, "Engendering Language, Silence, and Voice," addresses the issue of what it means for a woman to be so bold as to write in a man's literary world. How does she find her own voice—that tentative, inspired speaking subject—when she takes up the pen or sits before the computer? As a landmark work of feminist criticism, Woolf's *A Room of One's Own* explores the difficulties, psychological and material, that women writers have had to confront; it also foregrounds the power of women who express anger or lyricism or androgyny. Included in this section are several of the "mothers" whose writing Woolf "thinks back through" in her treatise—Margaret Cavendish, Anne Finch, Jane Austen, Charlotte and Emily Brontë—as well as modern writers who address silence and voice, writers such as Edith Wharton, Gertrude Stein, and Maxine Hong Kingston.

The second section, "Writing Bodies/Bodies Writing," departs from the French feminist theorist Hélène Cixous. "Write your self," she admonishes in "The Laugh of the Medusa." "Your body must be heard. Only then will the immense resources of the unconscious spring forth." How have women through the ages written (about) their bodies, claiming or responding ambivalently to their cycles, illnesses, strengths, desires? Answers to this question emerge from the anonymous "The Wife's Lament," an Old English elegy attributed to a woman; Margery Kempe's writing on celibacy and godly coupling in the fifteenth century; a play by the lusty Aphra Behn from the seventeenth century; and the nineteenth-century slave narrative of Harriet Jacobs. This section concludes with the erotic musings of modern women, among them Anne Sexton, Toni Cade Bambara, Sandra Cisneros, and Joy Harjo; it reveals a range of responses to embodiment, from denial to *jouissance,* or sexual pleasure.

Section three, "Rethinking the Maternal," explores the concepts of motherhood and maternity and raises the question, "in what diverse ways have the experience of mothering and the mother-daughter or mother-son bond been represented in literature by women?" Included are Julian of Norwich's fourteenth-century treatise on God as Mother, Puritan poet Anne Bradstreet's meditations on and for her children, poems on mothers by Sylvia Plath and Cherríe Moraga, Kate Chopin's *The Awakening,* and stories by Canadian Indian writer Beth Brant, Ghanaian writer Ama Ata Aidoo, and South African writer Bessie Head. What pregnancy, lactation, maternity, and daughterhood have meant to writing women of different classes, races, nationalities, sexualities, and time periods is a central topic here.

Section four, "Identity and Difference," explores how women writers depict the self-other relationship in its enactment of friendship, love, and power relations; it further considers issues of identity politics and women's writing. Selections range from Katherine Philips's seventeenth-century Orinda and Lucasia poems to Phillis Wheatley's problematic presentation of subjectivity under slavery, from Emily Dickinson's creative manifesto, "Dare you see a Soul *at the White Heat?*" to Jamaica Kincaid's story of selfhood and postcolonialism, "Xuela." This part of the anthology explores women's varied depictions of identity, subjectivity, commonality, and difference. In turn, it encourages readers, in the words of Trinh T. Minh-ha, to "unsettle every definition of otherness" that they encounter.

The final section, "Resistance and Transformation," moves women's literature overtly into the political sphere by way of cultural and feminist studies. Resistance writing, as the critic Barbara Harlow explains, "actively engages in the historical process of struggle against cultural oppression." Contrary to the easy assumption that political writing by women is a recent phenomenon, women for centuries have challenged the status quo in verse, fiction, and prose. Included here are selections from Mary Hays's "Appeal to the Men of Great Britain in Behalf of Women"; Elizabeth Barrett Browning's "A Curse for a Nation"; poems of resistance by Frances Ellen Watkins Harper,

Adrienne Rich, Irena Klepfisz, Eavan Boland, and Maya Angelou; a story about a complex interracial friendship, Toni Morrison's "Recitatif"; and Carolyn Forché's poems documenting the war in El Salvador during the 1980s. These and other selections reveal that today as throughout history, women's rights are human rights.

Although these thematic categories are especially crucial for understanding women's literature in English, other significant approaches are reflected in the anthology's alternate tables of contents. Included is a chronological listing of writers as well as five additional thematic tables of contents: Women and the Sacred, Coming of Age, Women and Aging, Gender and Postcolonialism, and U.S. Ethnic Literatures.

SECTIONAL INTRODUCTIONS AND BIBLIOGRAPHIES

Each of the book's five sections begins with an introduction that explores key critical concepts. The introduction overviews the works of literature included there and places each writer in her thematic and theoretical context. An annotated bibliography follows each section, listing and describing all works cited as well as scholarly works for further reading on each topic. Both the sectional introductions and the bibliographies foreground useful critical and theoretical material from feminist, postmodern, cultural studies, and Afrocentric perspectives. They also provide insight into feminist research methodology. In addition, the anthology includes selected bibliographies for each author at the end of the book. An instructor's manual is available to adopters of this edition; it contains further discussion of how to use this material.

ENGAGING FEMINIST THEORY

During the past three decades feminist theory has transformed the academy across disciplines and especially in literary studies, as scholars have recovered the works of forgotten or neglected women and studied the role of gender on literary production and productivity. This anthology reflects the current emphasis in the field of women's literature on interweaving texts and critical contexts. More specifically, it features essays by ten important feminist thinkers, thus revealing the various historical and theoretical lenses that can be grouped under the rubric of "feminisms." Each of the anthology's five sections begins with two of these essays.

Virginia Woolf's *A Room of One's Own* theorizes the economic obstacles, loss of creative identity, and self-doubt—as well as the imaginative power and personal triumphs—of women writers throughout history. This pivotal text considers, too, the literary possibilities of a "woman's sentence" and the aesthetic ideal of "incandescence." In "Talking Back," bell hooks claims that for black women, the challenge is to "change the nature and direction of our speech," to "talk back" against sexism and racism regardless of their source. Hélène Cixous's "The Laugh of the Medusa" identifies writing as an act that allows women to "realize the decensored relation of woman to her sexuality, to her womanly being, giving her access to her native strength." Nancy Mairs's "Reading Houses, Writing Lives: The French Connection" combines theory, autobiography, and praxis to consider how French feminist theory has posited ways of reconceptualizing women's bodies in the 1990s; it also documents Mairs's own struggle with multiple sclerosis. In "Writing and Motherhood," Susan Rubin Suleiman overviews psychoanalytic perspectives on motherhood and explores maternity in women's literature "as mothers see it." "Shifting the Center: Race, Class, and Feminist Theorizing about Motherhood," by Patricia Hill Collins, challenges feminists to consider race and class issues when examining the complex terrain of "motherwork" and creativity.

Michelle Cliff's "If I Could Write This in Fire, I Would Write This in Fire" invites readers to examine the connection between the politics of identity and issues of race, class, sexual orientation, and postcolonialism. Trinh T. Minh-ha, in "Not You/Like You: Postcolonial Women and the Interlocking Questions of Identity and Difference," claims that raising the question of identity "reopens the discussion on the self-other relationship in its enactment of power relations." She further suggests that no "I" is ever unitary or monolithic, but is instead connected and contingent. In "Notes toward a Politics of Location" Adrienne Rich interrogates her own position as a white, North American, lesbian poet undergoing "a struggle to keep moving, a struggle for accountability." And Ellen Kuzwayo's "Nkosi Sikelel'i Afrika" documents the struggle against apartheid and explores women's changing roles in South Africa.

Taken together, these ten essays comprise an exciting "crash course" in contemporary feminist thought and provide readers with valuable historical knowledge, theoretical vocabulary, and conceptual tools for examining women's literature through the ages.

USING INTERTEXTUALITIES

As a vehicle for examining diverse texts in dialogue across times, styles, and genres, this anthology offers a section entitled "Intertextualities" at the end of each thematic unit. Connecting texts and contexts, "Intertextualities" foregrounds five authors from each of the anthology's thematic sections and provides students with stimulating questions for class discussion and journal writing. To help students better understand and link texts by the featured writers, "Intertextualities" includes ten valuable essays of feminist literary or historical criticism. The distinguished critics whose essays appear here are Barbara Christian, Elaine Showalter, Catherine Gallagher, Shari Benstock, Margit Stange, Paula Gunn Allen, June Jordan, Joanne Feit Diehl, Ann Parry, and Nell Irvin Painter. The purpose of "Intertextualities" is to invite readers to think critically about scholarly discourse and textual intersections.

READING HISTORICALLY

For readers who emphasize a historical approach to the study of literature by women, this anthology features appendices that cover six literary periods: Old and Middle English literature, Renaissance and early seventeenth-century literature, late seventeenth and eighteenth-century literature, nineteenth-century literature, modernist literature, and contemporary literature. Each accessible, comprehensive essay puts women's writing in its historical context by discussing together men's and women's literature of the period. These historical appendices invite readers to consider the gendered nature of literary history and periodicity.

To read historically, one must have a broad range of texts from each period from which to choose. This anthology compares favorably to its predecessors in providing such breadth and scope. Indeed, it offers eight writers from the Anglo-Saxon and medieval periods, eleven from the Renaissance and early seventeenth century, eighteen from the late-seventeenth and eighteenth centuries, twenty-two from the nineteenth century, fourteen modernists, and over seventy contemporary writers.

The Longman Anthology of Women's Literature is, therefore, a historically rich, multicultural, and multigeneric book that diverse audiences can enjoy. I trust that after a semester—or longer!—of perusing this anthology, readers will proclaim with Virginia Woolf, "literature is open to everybody. . . . there is no gate, no lock, no bolt that you can set upon the freedom of my mind."

A WORD ON THE EDITORIAL PROCEDURES

In pre-eighteenth century texts I have modernized the spelling except in those instances in which it seemed appropriate to leave archaic forms. In selections that include footnotes by both the author and myself as editor, I have placed the author's footnotes in brackets. Dates at the end of each work reflect the year of composition, if known, and the year of publication.

ACKNOWLEDGMENTS

I am indebted to many people who offered intellectual support during the course of this project. The anthology would still be in process were it not for the skillful work and dedication of my research assistant and dear friend Kim Kessaris, to whom I am very grateful. Carla Cummins also provided valuable research assistance. I deeply appreciate the consultants who contributed their expertise to the anthology's historical appendices: Anita Helle (Nineteenth Century and Modernism), Kathleen Hickok (Nineteenth Century and Contemporary Literature), Claudia Thomas Kairoff and Cynthia Caywood (Late-Seventeenth and Eighteenth Centuries), Olga Valbuena and Elizabeth Hageman (Renaissance and Early Seventeenth-Century Literature), and Gillian Overing and Denise Baker (Old and Middle English Literature). Any errors are, of course, my own. Many present and former colleagues in the English Department at Wake Forest University generously shared with me their knowledge of women's literature, especially Elizabeth Phillips, Dolly McPherson, Andrew Ettin, Nancy Cotton, Anne Boyle, Jane Mead, Lisa Sternlieb, Gale Sigal, Kate Daniels, and Andrea Atkin.

I am grateful to the English Department, the Women's Studies Program, and the Graduate School at Wake Forest for financial and practical support; and to Isabel Zuber and Jill Carraway of the WFU Library for their help in locating crucial books. In addition, I thank my students in Women Writers in Society, Mothers and Daughters, and Global Women's Literature for allowing me to share new ideas and texts with them.

My friends and family have seen me through this project with humor and grace. For love and friendship over many years I thank Anita Helle, Gillian Overing, Susan Carlson, Lynda Hart, Catherine Keller, Sandra and Alan Bryant, Sarah Lu Bradley, E. J. Essic, Inzer Byers, Patti Patridge, Elizabeth Phillips, Eva Rodtwitt, Sally Barbour, Ulrike Wiethaus, Linda Nielsen, Nancy Winbigler, Cathy Simard, Martha Kierstead, Monza Naff, Sharon Ellison, Marilyn Farwell, Cynthia Caywood, Tyrone Williams, and Valerie Leeper. I am also grateful to Kevin and Robyn Dettmar, Beth Daniell, Susan Hilligoss, and Barbara Heifferon for their interest in my work. My family in

Kentucky and Indiana have been supportive, and I appreciate them all: my father, Henry DeShazer; my brother and sister-in-law, Sam and Vickie DeShazer; my nephews, Ryan and Will DeShazer; and my sisters and brothers-in-law, Kathy DeShazer and Ron Flora and Bettye and Richard Grogan.

My greatest debt is to my husband, Martin Jacobi, and my stepsons, Evan and Andy, for their love and patience during those long summers I spent at the computer. I also appreciate the affection and support of Sasha Jacobi, Bob and Nan Jacobi, and John Jacobi and Mary McVeigh.

My editors at Longman have been wonderful allies, and I am particularly grateful to Lisa Moore, Meg Botteon, Laura McKenna, and Joseph Terry for their wisdom. I also appreciate the advice of Rich Wohl, Mark Getlein, Ruth Halikman, Robert Ravas, Allison Ellis, Kathy Smeilis, and Patrick Burt.

In addition, the following professors reviewed this book in manuscript and offered valuable insights: Elaine Lawless, University of Missouri; Kathleen Hickok, Iowa State University; Kristina Groover, Appalachian State University; Bonnie Zimmerman, San Diego State University; Sandra Clark, Anderson University; Lillian Robinson, East Carolina State University; Yvonne Gaudelius, The Pennsylvania State University; Jan VanStavern, Dominican College of San Rafael; Cynthia Caywood, University of San Diego; Heather G. Hathaway, Marquette University; Susan Radner, William Paterson University; Elizabeth Renfro, California State University, Chico; Mary Terchek, University of Maryland at College Park; Laura L. Runge, University of South Florida, St. Petersburg; Rose Norman, University of Alabama, Huntsville; and Ophelia Jane Allen, New Mexico State University.

SECTION I

Engendering Language, Silence, and Voice
❖━━❖━❖━❖━━❖

> Literature is open to everybody. I refuse to allow you, Beadle though you
> are, to turn me off the grass. Lock up your libraries if you like; but there is
> no gate, no lock, no bolt that you can set upon the freedom of my mind.
>
> *Virginia Woolf, A Room of One's Own*

> Certainly for black women, our struggle has not been to emerge from
> silence into speech but to change the nature and direction of our speech,
> to make a speech that compels listeners, one that is heard.
>
> *bell hooks, "Talking Back"*

The concept of engendering language, silence, and voice offers insight to readers who
approach this anthology eager to explore women's ideas and experiences but who
also seek inspiration from women who have successfully made the enormous leap
from anonymity to literary recognition. A multifaceted word, to *engender* means not
only to produce or originate but also to consider the gendered implications of a term
or a concept. The original meaning of *engendering* is both "begetting" and "procreat-
ing"; to beget has conventionally described men's roles in creative process, while to
procreate has described women's. The first section in this anthology focuses on the
generative activities of literary women from the Middle Ages to the present, women
who have both begotten and procreated memorable texts.

To examine women's literature from a feminist perspective is to assume that the
distinction between "masculine" and "feminine" is important to the generation of all
writing. The term *feminist* evokes a long and distinguished history of women and
enlightened men who have raised consciousness about the oppression of women
across cultures and who have argued for gender equality in the social, political, economic, and domestic spheres. In literary theory and criticism, feminist practice
includes a variety of approaches that consider the ways in which gender is a cultural
construction rather than a biological given, examine the parameters of male and
female experience, and analyze the representations of women and men in specific
texts. In addition, feminist theory has interrogated how readers bring their society's
assumptions about gender difference to a text. Although one need not be a feminist
to enjoy writing by women, the field of women's literature has been greatly enhanced
by the insights of feminism.

The wellsprings of this inquiry into women's writing are two important essays of
feminist theory: VIRGINIA WOOLF's *A Room of One's Own* (1929), a key work of modern feminist literary criticism; and "Talking Back" (1989) by BELL HOOKS, a reflection
on race, gender, and voice by a contemporary American intellectual. Like many

1

other scholars, Woolf and hooks assume that literature, language, gender, and class interact in a variety of ways, and that understanding such interactions is crucial to any revision of literary history. To this equation hooks adds the category of race, using it to reflect upon the situation of African-American women writing today. Both Woolf and hooks foreground the cultural and historical repression of women writers struggling for what Woolf calls the "freedom to think of things in themselves" (*LAWL* 34).

As critical as it may be to examine such repression, it is enriching and powerful to inquire in a related vein: why, then, *have* women written? According to their journals and essays, they write to express deep feelings, send messages to others, create alternate worlds, make order of chaos, seek transcendence, celebrate themselves. In her journal the novelist KATHERINE MANSFIELD documents the intense desire with which many women approach writing: "*Work*. Shall I be able to express one day my love of work—my desire to be a better writer—my longing to take greater pains. . . . Oh, to be a *writer*, a real writer given up to it and it alone" (112, 151). For feminist theorist TRINH T. MINH-HA, writing well has traditionally meant using literary conventions skillfully to express reality, but she sees this meaning as reductive: "Yet I-the-writer do not *express* (a) reality more than (a) reality *impresses* itself on me. Expresses me." In Trinh's view, a writer writes "to possess and depossess herself of the power of writing" (18).

Literary studies have traditionally been dominated by the myth of the author's sovereignty, by the notion of a work as original and the (male) writer's perspective as objective and universal. Feminist literary theory has challenged this dominant myth, as have other contemporary critical approaches such as deconstruction, which seeks to dismantle established systems of thought regarding authorial and textual production. For women, writing may involve expression of the self *and* the loss of self; a fluidity often emerges that allows the "speaking subject" to represent in language both her individuality and her relations with others, including her readers. As Trinh notes, women writers have often been "concerned not with inserting a 'me' into language, but with creating an opening where the 'me' disappears while 'I' endlessly come and go, as the nature of language requires" (35). Such fluidity allows writing women to move organically from language to silence and back again. To reveal themselves as individual and collective "gendered voices" constitutes an act that Myriam Díaz-Diocaretz has termed "reterritorialization," a metaphoric seizure of verbal and linguistic space. Such reclamations occur when women's writing challenges notions of women as passive receivers of discourse, claiming their strong voices *and* their textual methods as forms of resistance (91).

Nancy K. Miller concurs with Díaz-Diocaretz that a deconstructionist view of literature—an approach that "erases" the author and privileges the text—does not necessarily work well for analyzing women's writing. "Because women have not had the same historical relation of identity to origin, institution, production that men have had, they have not, I think, (collectively) felt burdened by *too much* Self, Ego, Cogito, etc.," Miller asserts. Certainly many women have been excluded throughout history from structures of authority, including the literary authority long granted to upper-class white men. Therefore, women writers' "relation to integrity and textuality, desire and authority, displays structurally important differences from that universal position." Women need to claim their voices as female subjects, Miller concludes, so that their authorial perspectives can offer "a different staging of the drama of the writing subject"—a representation in which women's experience and witness can be viewed as authoritative, valuable, perhaps even "universal" (6–7).

Many of the women in "Engendering Language, Silence, and Voice" write about the process of writing itself: its pleasures and complications, their ambivalence toward its power, the tensions it produces between what contemporary poet ADRIENNE RICH calls "the energy of creation" and "the energy of relation," the intricacies of technical and stylistic experimentation, the transgressive potential of language (43). As Woolf suggests, literary women are both inheritors and originators. Woolf herself struggled to claim her right to write. Anticipating negative reviews of *A Room of One's Own*, she worried in her diary that she would be "attacked for a feminist and hinted at for a sapphist," or lesbian, by male colleagues and reviewers; yet she wrote the book "with ardour & conviction" (262). Other women, too, have often hesitated to write, and with good reason. As Woolf notes, women have typically been misrepresented in or absent from texts authored by men. Throughout literary history male writers have disparaged women's writing, identified creativity as a male prerogative, and claimed that women who practice literary arts are not "real women." A 1650 letter from Thomas Parker to his sister attacks her for publishing: "Your printing of a book beyond the custom of your sex doth rankly smell" (Gilbert and Gubar 74). ANNE FINCH, Countess of Winchilsea, was widely satirized by eighteenth-century English men of letters as a "bluestocking" who scribbled. In 1837 the English poet laureate, Robert Southey, wrote to CHARLOTTE BRONTË that "literature cannot be the business of a woman's life: and it ought not to be" (*LAWL* 239). Guy Butler, a South African literary critic, claimed in 1959 that poetry was "an educated man's affair" (qtd. in Lockett v). Most graphically, contemporary novelist Norman Mailer has asserted that "the one thing a writer has to have is balls" (qtd. in Olsen 29–31).

Assaulted by such misrepresentations, some women have feared and doubted their written work. Anne Finch describes the source and nature of this anxiety in the introductory poem to her only published volume:

> Alas! A woman that attempts the pen,
> Such an intruder on the rights of men,
> Such a presumptuous creature is esteemed,
> The fault can by no virtue be redeemed. (*LAWL* 97)

EMILY BRONTË, one of the nineteenth century's finest lyric poets, has the speaker in "Alone I sat; the summer day" express doubts about her literary merits:

> I asked myself, "O Why has heaven
> Denied the precious gift to me,
> The glorious gift to many given
> To speak their thoughts in poetry?" (*LAWL* 242)

In the twentieth century the confessional poet SYLVIA PLATH expresses doubts about the power of her creativity: "What I fear most, I think, is the death of the imagination" (110). In *Silences*, novelist TILLIE OLSEN explores the reasons that more women writers than men have historically been or felt silenced; she asserts that the circumstances of creation have differed radically for women, and that these circumstances have been punitive. Women who have written despite the demands to care for young children, husbands or lovers, and elderly relatives, and despite economic and psychic deprivation, she concludes, are "survivors, 'only's.' One out of twelve" (39).

Yet many women have resisted public derision and their own self-doubt to claim a writer's identity. In her poem "Upon the Saying That My Verses Were Made by Another," the eighteenth-century poet ANNE KILLIGREW chastises her culture for denigrating her work and expresses her determination to persevere:

> The Envious Age, only to Me alone,
> Will not allow, what I do write, my Own;
> But let them Rage, and 'gainst a Maid Conspire,
> So Deathless numbers from my Tuneful Lyre
> Do ever flow. (*LAWL* 95)

One hundred years later FRANCES BURNEY gleefully celebrates in her diary the publication of her novel *Evelina*: "This year was ushered in by a grand and most important event, for at the latter end of January the literary world was favoured with the first publication of the ingenious, learned, and most profound Fanny Burney!" (*LAWL* 103). Although both Killigrew's and Burney's writing fell into relative obscurity shortly after their deaths, feminist scholars of the past thirty years have unearthed their work and that of many silenced or forgotten counterparts. It is therefore possible, in Woolf's words, to "think back through our mothers if we are women" to a greater extent than ever before (*LAWL* 53). Adrienne Rich has applauded feminist scholars for "challenging the sacredness of the gentlemanly canon, sharing the rediscovery of buried works by women, asking women's questions, bringing literary history and criticism back to life in both senses" (33). At the dawn of a millennium, readers have available an astounding number of new and recovered books that offer vital knowledge by and about women. Yet most would agree with Rich that there remains, for women, "a whole new psychic geography to be explored" (35). This geography maps a complex terrain that reveals literature as more than the representation of a language system or the expressive and social use of style. It maps the ways that literature functions as a social institution, defining what voices can be heard and what value those voices can be given.

Because the engendering of language requires time, acumen, and perseverance, many women who lack these resources feel guilty about writing instead of fulfilling countless other demands. They may also feel selfish, and with some justification: "Writing in such a context is always practiced at the cost of other women's labor" (Trinh 7). Doubts, frustration, and despair can thus result for women who do write. Attempting to publish adds another layer of anxiety for many, since it includes painful scrutiny that women may eschew, fearing ridicule, invasion of privacy, and rejection. For nineteenth-century American poet EMILY DICKINSON, publication is "the Auction / Of the Mind of Man—"; yet for Plath, publication is essential: "I justified my writing by saying it would be published, give me life" (*LAWL* 971; Plath 110). Olsen comments on the difficulties women have experienced in getting their writing published; in the 1970s works by women comprised about 8 percent of the material in literary anthologies, regardless of the genres, nationalities, or time periods covered (Olsen 241). The questions that Trinh raises for herself may well loom for other women: "Why write? For whom? What necessity? What writing?" (Trinh 9).

Some women have objected to being identified as "women writers." The American poet Louise Bogan refused to edit an anthology of "female songbirds" in 1935;

her peer, the poet Elizabeth Bishop, rejected anthologies composed solely of women on the grounds that they were ghettoizing. Bishop as well as British poets Kathleen Raine and Laura Riding Jackson left codicils in their wills forbidding the publication of their work in women's anthologies. The novelist Cynthia Ozick puts it this way: "The term 'woman writer' . . . has no meaning, not intellectually, not morally, not historically. A writer is a writer" (qtd. in Olsen 251). However, if one agrees with the French philosopher Simone de Beauvoir that one is not born but is made a woman, any limiting notion of what constitutes "womanhood" can be avoided. Many women see themselves as "women writers," fully conscious of the limitations and possibilities that social roles and gendered self-definitions have brought them. Others claim to write androgynously, as "man-womanly" or "woman-manly," in Woolf's terms (*LAWL* 64). Still others consider themselves writers pure and simple, rejecting any gender-specific designation at all.

Despite some women's reservations about the label "woman writer," most feminist critics dispute Ozick's suggestion that writing transcends gender identity and takes place outside of the social order. Instead, they have asserted the need for scholars and students to investigate what it has meant historically to write as a woman, as well as the need to examine women's writing separately from that of men. In the late 1970s ELAINE SHOWALTER coined the term "gynocriticism" to describe this type of study, as distinct from an approach that foregrounds images of women in literature by men. Gynocritics study the history, themes, structures, and genres of literature written by women, as well as issues of female creativity and the literary strategies of particular writers and works. In her 1980 essay "Feminist Criticism in the Wilderness," Showalter explains the logic of gynocriticism:

> To see women's writing as our primary subject forces us to make the leap to a new conceptual vantage point and to redefine the nature of the theoretical problem before us. It is no longer the ideological dilemma of reconciling revisionary pluralisms but the essential question of difference. How can we constitute women as a distinct literary group? What is *the difference* of women's writing? (*LAWL* 357)

A gynocritical approach lends itself well to a study of the literature by women included in Section I of this anthology. These writers help us as readers to consider silence and speech as forces that compel women to ask of themselves: why write?

BREAKING (OR EMBRACING) SILENCE

> When the claims of creation cannot be primary, the results are atrophy, unfinished work; minor effort and accomplishment; silences.
>
> *Tillie Olsen, Silences*

> As thoughts like clouds traverse my human eyes,
> Silence opens the world that I explore:
> Mozartian gaiety, the lightest presence,
> At last I welcome back my wandering soul
> Into these regions of strange transcendence,
> And find myself again, alive and whole.
> *May Sarton, "A Divorce of Lovers," Collected Poems*

In *Silences* Olsen distinguishes between what she calls natural silence—the gestation time needed for creativity to flourish—and the "unnatural thwarting of what struggles to come into being but cannot" (6). In the excerpts above Olsen presents silence as oppressive, while MAY SARTON shows it as enlightening. Hence the conundrum of silence must be examined to enhance our awareness of what it means to engender language and voice.

Many creative women have embraced natural silence as a source of strength and inspiration, a means of hearing the rich chords of daily sounds that busy lives obscure. Virginia Woolf, for example, recognizes the power of silence as well as that of language. In writing her novel *The Waves*, she was torn between presenting two central characters, a man and a woman, sitting at a table talking or remaining silent. Her own writing process reflects this dilemma, and many excerpts from her diary reveal that her more fecund choice is silence: "As for my next book, I am going to hold myself from writing till I have it impending in me; grown heavy in my mind like a ripe pear, pendant, gravid, asking to be cut or it will fall" (*Diary* 3: 209). Like Sarton, Woolf realizes the value of silence to the creative enterprise.

Unnatural silence, as Olsen suggests, is quite a different matter. The literary critic Ihab Hassan, in *The Literature of Silence,* offers a trajectory of modern works (almost entirely by men) that traces the contours of a tradition in which an oppressive silence is paramount to meaning. This tradition ranges from Samuel Beckett's tendency to obliterate language at one extreme and, at the other, Henry Miller's postorgiastic silence, having worn out language at the behest of graphic sexual description. To many women, however, imposed silence seems a state from which it is crucial to break free. Rich argues that systemic silencing of women's work is one reason that so many women have believed themselves to be writing in isolation, with no viable tradition behind them:

> The entire history of women's struggle for self-determination has been muffled in silence over and over. One serious obstacle encountered by any feminist writer is that each feminist work has tended to be received as if it emerged from nowhere; as if each one of us had lived, thought, worked, without any historical past or contextual present. This is one of the ways in which women's work and thinking has been made to seem sporadic, errant, orphaned of any tradition of its own. (11)

Although she claims that contemporary black women have not been silenced so much as they have been taught "the right speech of womanhood," bell hooks nonetheless believes that her mother's language was restricted. What hooks feared most as a young writer, she explains, was not punishment for her transgressive speech but enforced silence, a suppression of words. The imposition of silence, she concludes, is a "terrorism that breaks spirits, that makes creativity impossible" (*LAWL* 75).

Breaking silence can be cannily strategic, as it is for MAXINE HONG KINGSTON'S Chinese-American protagonist in "No Name Woman" (*LAWL* 308), who analyzes her family's code of silence even as she reveals hidden secrets about her suicidal aunt. It can be a defiant and self-affirming act, as it is for ALICE WALKER: "In search of my mother's garden, I found my own" (*LAWL* 331). Embracing silence, too, can be an aesthetic choice, as it is for Sarton's speaker upon meeting "The Muse as Medusa": "Your silence is my ocean, / And even now it teems with life" (*LAWL* 297). As these examples reveal, silence functions in more complex ways than merely as an absence in a representational system. Finally, silence and language cannot be separated, for stillness leads to thought, which in turn gives rise ineluctably to words.

COMING TO LANGUAGE

I'll walk where my own nature would be leading:
It vexes me to choose another guide.

Emily Brontë, "Stanzas"

I *lack imagination* you say
No. I lack language.
The language to clarify
my resistance to the literate.

Cherríe Moraga, This Bridge Called My Back

What is "language"? Feminist theory can help us forge a working definition and thereby scrutinize this concept so crucial to women writers. For French feminist thinkers, claims theorist Toril Moi, language is "a heterogeneous signifying process located in and between speaking subjects"; it produces multiple meanings in our private reflections, our dialogues with others, and the texts we read (154). For postmodern scholars and readers, language is not a monolithic structure; it is dynamic rather than static, and it is productive, not merely reflective, of diverse realities. Language both erupts and disrupts. It is also the most visible and audible sign of our humanity, the means by which we express ourselves and connect with others. As TONI MORRISON claims in her Nobel Prize lecture, "word-work" is generative; language alone "protects us from the scariness of things with no names. Language alone is meditation" (22, 28). Language can thus be angry or tender, accusing or conciliatory, diminishing or empowering to ourselves and those with whom we communicate.

In "'When We Dead Awaken': Writing as Re-Vision," Adrienne Rich explores "the visible effects on women's lives of seeing, hearing our wordless or negated experience affirmed and pursued further in language." Although language has the power to trap as well as to liberate, women have often used it to "see and name—and therefore live—afresh," for "writing is re-naming" (34–35, 43). But finding language and images for this new consciousness can be difficult and dangerous, Rich acknowledges, and using language to turn things into their opposites is risky business. As the French feminist HÉLÈNE CIXOUS explains, "every woman has known the torture of beginning to speak aloud, heart beating as if to break, occasionally falling into loss of language, ground and language slipping out from under her, because for woman speaking—even just opening her mouth—in public is something rash, a transgression" (92). Not only gender but race, class, and sexual orientation can serve as barriers to emergent speech. GLORIA ANZALDÚA claims, for instance, that lesbians of color are invisible in white- and straight-dominated society, and thus their speech is inaudible. As Anzaldúa notes, certain social locations forbid intellectual work: "How dare I even consider becoming a writer as I stooped over the tomato fields bending, bending under the hot sun, hands broadened and calloused, not fit to hold the quill, numbed into an animal stupor by the heat. . . . Does not our class, our culture as well as the white man tell us writing is not for women such as us?" (*LAWL* 317-18). Literature, that is, must be recognized as an institutional product, and one to which not all emergent writers are granted equal access. Cynthia Ozick alleges, in this vein, that when she writes in English, as a Jew, she is conscious of writing in Christendom—outside of the dominant hegemony. As humans, perhaps none of us are ever totally comfortable with words, which come to us relatively late in our interaction with the world; certainly this linguistic "dis-ease," along with institutional biases that prohibit certain forms of speech, can cause ambivalence and despair. But dis-ease can also fuel the imagination, as Anzaldúa has realized: "Living in a state of psychic unrest, in a Borderland, is what makes poets write and artists create" (73).

To make literature with language brings with it an ethical responsibility of which many women are particularly aware, given their social positioning on the margins of the dominant discourse. The writer serves a social as well as a linguistic function, conveying political as well as other forms of knowledge. Thus women writers sometimes find conflicting goals between writing as what Trinh has called a "free agent" and writing as "the people's messenger" (15). Whether these two stances can be united, whether women as a historically oppressed group—despite their differences of race, class, etc.—have written autonomously or connectedly, remains contested ground among feminist scholars and women writers themselves. Most would agree, however, with African-American poet AUDRE LORDE when she claims that "for those of us who write, it is necessary to scrutinize not only the truth of which we speak, but the truth of that language by which we speak it" (43). Only then can silence be transformed into powerful language and action.

FINDING VOICES(S)

If we wish to increase the supply of rare and remarkable women like the Brontës, we should give the Joneses and the Smiths rooms of their own and five hundred a year. One cannot grow fine flowers in a thin soil.

Virginia Woolf, Women and Writing

Then I noticed that the door had been painted, and that a new window pane had replaced the old broken one. I smiled to myself as I reached the door. Before long I was sitting on that toilet seat, writing a poem.

Many more mornings saw me sitting there writing.

Gcina Mhlophe, "The Toilet"

For writers, having one's voice emerge out of silence—whether repressive or fertile—can seem a miraculous feat indeed. When composing The Waves, Woolf wrestled repeatedly with the thorny issue of finding voice: "I have not yet mastered the speaking voice," she admits in her diary of 1931, "and I propose to go on pegging it down, arduously, then re-write, reading much of it aloud, like poetry." When this elaborate process works, the results amaze the author, who describes writing the last words of her novel "with some moments of such intensity and intoxication that I seemed only to stumble after my own voice, or almost, after some sort of speaker (as when I was mad). I was almost afraid, remembering the voices that used to fly ahead. . . . How physical the sense of triumph and relief is!" (Diary 4). As Woolf's

description suggests, such triumphs are most likely to occur when writers have sufficient time to meditate and revise, luxuries not available historically to many female
"Joneses and Smiths," who often must settle for a smile to themselves when they find
time and space to write, as GCINA MHLOPHE'S South African protagonist does. For
Woolf, finding voice is "the greatest rapture known to me"; for Mhlophe it is a source
of rare relief.

A well-known advocate of "cultural feminism," Woolf stressed the disparities
between women and men rather than their commonalities. Indeed, she believed that
women's creative power "differs greatly from the creative power of men," not because
of some innate, biological distinction but because of historical circumstances and literary biases that for centuries robbed the world of women's voices (LAWL 59).
Women writers today, she asserts, speaking in A Room of One's Own of her fictive
Mary Carmichael, have the opportunity to "light a torch in that vast chamber where
nobody has yet been" by writing about women from their own perspectives—by
catching "those unrecorded gestures, those unsaid or half-said words" that form when
women are alone, no longer (mis)interpreted by the male gaze (LAWL 57). But such
chambers have been illuminated, as Woolf herself notes, by numerous women from
the Middle Ages onward, women who inserted their own voices into the dominant
literary discourse, forever changing its boundaries. One of the earliest women to publish a book of poems in English, ISABELLA WHITNEY, claims her writing voice fiercely:

> Now stand aside and give me leave
> to write my latest Will;
> And see that none you do deceive,
> of that I leave them till. (LAWL 86)

MARGARET CAVENDISH, that seventeenth-century puzzle whom Woolf describes mis-
leadingly as "harebrained, fantastical Margaret of Newcastle," exudes confidence in
her own emerging voice and is reined in only slightly by the ill opinions of her male
readers:

> Reading my Verses, I liked them so well,
> Self-love did make my judgment to rebel:
> Thinking them so good, I thought more to write;
> Considering not How others would them like. (LAWL 90)

Nineteenth-century women writers sometimes adopted pseudonyms to disguise their
voices, for, as Charlotte Brontë noted, "no author should be without the advantage
of being able to walk invisible." Currer, Ellis, and Acton Bell; GEORGE ELIOT;
France's George Sand—all hid at first their sex but heeded the call to write. "Imagination is a strong, restless faculty which claims to be heard and exercised," Brontë
asserted in a letter to George Henry Lewes, the literary scholar with whom George
Eliot lived out of wedlock, thus losing her reputation but not her creativity. "Are we
not quite deaf to her cry and insensate to her struggles?" (LAWL 241). Personified as
female, the imagination for Brontë emerges as a poignant sister whose desires must be
honored. Even when a woman's fancy runs amok—as is the case with Catherine
Morland in JANE AUSTEN's Gothic parody, Northanger Abbey—a vivid imagination
emerges as essential to the "good nature" and "good humour" of anyone "born to be
an heroine" (LAWL 114).

Modern women, too, record their sense of accomplishment and joy at finding imaginative voice. The experimental novelist and poet GERTRUDE STEIN had no hesitancy in proclaiming herself a genius: "Einstein was the creative philosophic mind of the century and I have been the creative literary mind of the century" (qtd. in Gilbert and Gubar 1275). Similarly, ZORA NEALE HURSTON, who in the early twentieth century coped not only with sexist but also with racist discrimination, describes herself in "How It Feels to Be Colored Me" as "the cosmic Zora . . . the eternal feminine with its strand of beads" (*I Love Myself* 155). Women also record their frustrations and fears. Speaking in turn-of-the-century America as an outsider by virtue of class and national origin, ANZIA YEZIERSKA laments that the immigrant experience, when recorded, falls on deaf ears: "As one of the dumb, voiceless ones I speak. One of the millions of immigrants beating, beating out their hearts at your gates for a breath of understanding" (92). Attempting to keep silent, Maxine Hong Kingston, the daughter of Chinese immigrants, speaks only because she is plagued by an avenging relative: "My aunt haunts me—her ghost drawn to me because now, after fifty years of neglect, I alone devote pages of paper to her" (*LAWL* 315). Gloria Anzaldúa summarizes well the combination of pride and risk that has characterized the voices of many literate women throughout history: "Writing is the most daring thing I have ever done and the most dangerous" (*LAWL* 321).

One distinctive strategy that allows many women writers to find their own voices is their invocation of a female muse, an actual or imagined source of creative inspiration to whom they pay homage. This is not to say that some women do not envision their muse as male: witness Dickinson's "Loaded Gun," who depends on an owner yet is more powerful than any master; or the Irish poet MEDBH MCGUCKIAN'S comic dressing-room intruder: "I can take anything now, even his being / Away, for it always seems to me his / Writing is for me" (*LAWL* 332). But relying on a male inspirer—one who enchants but may also overpower—raises for many the complex issue of authority: will a patriarchal muse inspire or control, aid or appropriate their writing? Many women, therefore, re-imagine the muse as female: as goddesses, mythic women, figures from history or their own lives—extensions of their creative selves. Woolf "thinks back through our mothers," giving praise to literary predecessors who enable her and other women to find voice. Alice Walker similarly honors her foremothers, from anonymous black quilters in Alabama to famous jazz and blues singers, for handing down to their daughters a strong creative legacy. "They were women then / My mama's generation / . . . How they knew what we / *Must* know / Without knowing a page / Of it / Themselves" (*LAWL* 330-31). Even when the muse refuses her presence she is invariably female, as in British poet STEVIE SMITH'S wry limerick: "My Muse sits forlorn / She wishes she had not been born / She sits in the cold / No word she says is ever told" (*LAWL* 292). More often, however, the female muse sustains the woman writer because the bond between author and muse is one of reciprocity; creator and inspirer are envisioned as one. In identifying female muses, therefore, women writers sing themselves. Anzaldúa's exhortation to third world women writers makes explicit the interwoven nature of the poet-muse relationship: "Find the muse within you. The voice that lies buried under you, dig it up. Do not fake it, try to sell it for a handclap or your name in print" (*LAWL* 323).

Taken together, the writers in this section of the anthology exhibit remarkable stylistic and generic range. Represented here are women's letters, diaries, poems, reviews, essays, autobiographies, autoethnographies, and fiction. Within a genre, for instance fiction, we find an array of thematic, formal, and aesthetic strategies. Kingston's "No Name Woman" is fictively autobiographical; Mhlophe's "The Toilet" is autobiographically fictive. CHARLOTTE PERKINS GILMAN'S "The Yellow Wallpaper" chronicles a silenced woman's struggle to write, while EDITH WHARTON'S "A Journey" portrays a woman's self-protective use of silence. The poetry included here ranges from Whitney's mock assertion of women's legal autonomy to Smith's mock lament at the absence of her muse, from Cavendish's apology for her writing's insurrection to Killigrew's defense of women's right to voice. Brontë and Finch compose lyrical meditations on the natural world; Stein and Duffy write free-verse satires; Sarton and McGuckian perfect the elegy as a form for lamenting the loss of a beloved woman. Women write letters to their male spiritual advisors, to popes and kings and men in power, to women in their families, to other "writing ladies." Their autobiographies claim their creative identity exuberantly—Hurston asserts, "once I found the use of my feet, they took to wandering"—and reveal excruciating pains taken to conceal that identity: Burney foresees "a thousand dangers of discovery"—"I never could believe they did not suspect me" (*LAWL* 291, 105). These writers from the eighth century to the present have overcome psychic and institutional obstacles to explore the multifaceted dimensions of their creativity. With Virginia Woolf, it is the privilege of contemporary readers to honor and enjoy them.

> What genius, what integrity it must have required in face of all that criticism, in the midst of that purely patriarchal society, to hold fast to the thing as they saw it without shrinking. (*LAWL* 52)

[handwritten annotation: Tribute to women writers]

⊰ Works Cited—Section I ⊱

Note: In the introductory essay, all citations of works included in this anthology are indicated by *LAWL*, followed by the page number.

Anzaldúa, Gloria. *Borderlands/La Frontera: The New Mestiza.* San Francisco: Spinsters/aunt lute, 1987. This collection of poems and essays discusses Latina women's efforts to break silence and the psychological, social, and material difficulties of being a lesbian *mestiza* writing on the borderlands between cultures.

Cixous, Hélène, and Catherine Clément. *The Newly Born Woman.* Trans. Betsy Wing. Minneapolis: University of Minnesota Press, 1986. This work of French feminist theory considers the way women have been pathologized as either hysterics or sorceresses and explores the multifaceted power of female sexual pleasure, or *jouissance*, as women "come to writing."

de Beauvoir, Simone. *The Second Sex.* Trans. H. M. Parshley. Harmondsworth, Eng: Penguin, 1972. This classic feminist text analyzes ways in which women have been constructed as Other in patriarchal society.

Díaz-Diocaretz, Myriam. "'I will be a scandal in your boat': Women Poets and the Tradition." *Knives and Angels: Women Writers in Latin America.* Ed. Susan Bassnett. London: Zed Books, 1990. This essay considers the obstacles faced by Latin American women poets undertaking acts of "deterritorialization" as they write scripts that challenge patriarchal aesthetic assumptions.

Gilbert, Sandra M., and Susan Gubar, eds. *The Norton Anthology of Literature by Women.* 2nd ed. New York: Norton, 1996. This highly respected anthology of women's literature includes selections by more than 170 writers in English from the Middle Ages to the present, as well as valuable historical introductions to each period and lengthy biographies for each author.

Hassan, Ihab. *The Literature of Silence: Henry Miller and Samuel Beckett*. New York: Knopf, 1967. Although this critical work deals with male writers, its theoretical insights on the problems and possibilities of silence as a literary motif are applicable to some modernist women's literature.

Hurston, Zora Neale. *I Love Myself When I Am Laughing . . . A Zora Neale Hurston Reader*. Ed. Alice Walker. Old Westbury, NY: Feminist Press, 1979. This selection of Hurston's work includes excerpts from *Dust Tracks on a Road* and other autobiographical works, including "How It Feels to Be Colored Me," as well as Hurston's fiction and critical essays by Walker and Mary Helen Washington.

Lockett, Cecily, ed. *Breaking the Silence: A Century of South African Women's Poetry*. Johannesburg: Ad. Donker Publisher, 1990. This anthology contains a useful introduction to South African women's literature and offers poems by Mhlophe, de Kok, and others included in this anthology.

Lorde, Audre. *Sister Outsider: Essays and Speeches*. Trumansburg, NY: Crossing Press, 1984. This collection by a prominent "black lesbian feminist warrior poet" contains such essays as "Poetry Is Not a Luxury" and "The Transformation of Silence into Language and Action."

Mansfield, Katherine. *Journal of Katherine Mansfield*. Ed. J. Middleton Murry. New York: Knopf, 1933. In her journal of 1914–1922 Mansfield records her struggle to write despite ill health, along with the pleasure she receives from creative work. The journal also includes vignettes and early drafts of stories.

Miller, Nancy K. "Changing the Subject." *Coming to Terms: Feminism, Theory, Politics*. Ed. Elizabeth Weed. New York: Routledge, 1989. In this essay Miller considers how feminist writers can claim the value of a "female authorial project" given that postmodern tenets can undermine an author's authority and agency.

Moi, Toril. *Sexual/Textual Politics: Feminist Literary Theory*. New York: Methuen, 1985. Moi offers a cogent analysis and critique of gynocriticism and evaluates the differences between Anglo-American and French feminist theory.

Moraga, Cherríe, and Gloria Anzaldúa, eds. *This Bridge Called My Back: Writings by Radical Women of Color*. 1981. Rpt. Latham, NY: Kitchen Table Women of Color Press, 1983. This collection of essays and poems by Native American, African American, Latina, and Asian American feminist writers is an excellent introduction to issues and images of language, silence, and voice in their work.

Morrison, Toni. *The Nobel Lecture in Literature, 1993*. New York: Knopf, 1994. This lecture discusses the value of "word-work" in freeing the imaginative spirit and the writer's voice.

Olsen, Tillie. *Silences*. New York: Delacorte, 1978. This pivotal study on the ways in which women writers have been silenced provides important background to more recent debates about coming to voice; it also contains many excerpts from men and women writers' journals about combating silence.

Plath, Sylvia. *The Journals of Sylvia Plath*. Eds. Ted Hughes and Frances McCullough. New York: Ballantine, 1982. These journals record with urgent energy this writer's self-doubt as well as her triumphant sense of genius. They date from her college years (1950–55) to her suicide in 1963.

Rich, Adrienne. *On Lies, Secrets, and Silence: Selected Prose, 1966–1978*. New York: Norton, 1979. Many essays in this collection address issues of breaking silence and finding voice, but see especially Rich's autobiographical essay "'When We Dead Awaken': Writing as Re-Vision" for valuable theorizing of these issues.

Sarton, May. *Collected Poems 1931–1973*. New York: Norton, 1974. This book offers selections from eleven volumes of Sarton's poetry and includes many poems that address the themes of silence, voice, and the female muse.

Trinh T. Minh-ha. *Woman, Native, Other: Writing Postcoloniality and Feminism*. Bloomington: Indiana UP, 1989. This series of theoretical essays includes a powerful section entitled "Commitment from the Mirror-Writing Box" in which Trinh examines the triple bind of women writers of color, their "silence in time," "vertically imposed language," and ways of "writing woman."

Woolf, Virginia. *The Diary of Virginia Woolf*. Ed. Anne Olivier Bell. 5 vols. New York: Harcourt, 1977–81. This excellent edition of Woolf's diaries includes accounts of her creative struggles and reflections on her writing.

———. *Women and Writing*. Ed. Michele Barrett. New York: Harcourt, 1979. Barrett has collected here many of Woolf's best essays and reviews on women's writing, and she offers as well a cogent overview of Woolf's feminist work and the conflict in *A Room of One's Own* between aesthetic and material concerns.

Yezierska, Anzia. "America and I." *America and I: Short Stories by American Jewish Women Writers*. Ed. Joyce Antler. Boston: Beacon, 1990. This story offers Yezierska's viewpoint on what it means to be a Jewish immigrant in early twentieth-century America.

⊰⊱ Suggestions for Further Reading ⊱⊰

Bowlby, Rachel. *Virginia Woolf: Feminist Destinations*. Oxford: Blackwell, 1988. This study of Woolf's narrative strategies and feminist vision includes a strong chapter on the importance of *A Room of One's Own* as a work of feminist theory.

DeShazer, Mary K. *Inspiring Women: Reimagining the Muse*. New York: Pergamon, 1986. This study examines how women poets through the ages have invoked female muses, women from history, mythology, and their own lives. See especially the introductory chapter and the essay on Sarton's solitary muse.

Ettin, Andrew Vogel. *Speaking Silences: Stillness and Voice in Modern Thought and Jewish Tradition*. Charlottesville: U of Virginia P, 1994. This book offers an intellectual and a spiritual meditation on how silence has functioned in numerous texts written out of Jewish traditions.

Gates, Henry Louis, Jr., ed. *Reading Black, Reading Feminist: A Critical Anthology*. New York: Meridian, 1990. This collection of essays examines how black women writers have engendered language and voice in the face of racism and offers black feminist critical perspectives on such writers as Hurston and Walker. The book includes Barbara Christian's essay "The Highs and the Lows of Black Feminist Criticism."

Gilbert, Sandra M., and Susan Gubar. *The Madwoman in the Attic: The Woman Writer and the Nineteenth-Century Literary Imagination*. New Haven: Yale UP, 1979. This landmark study of nineteenth-century women's literature examines the "anxiety of authorship" felt by women such as Eliot and the Brontës who presumed to write in a culture that demanded their silence.

hooks, bell. *Talking Back: Thinking Feminist, Thinking Black*. Boston: South End, 1989. In this collection of essays, hooks explores how black women come to voice as writers and theorists in a society often hostile to their work.

Jones, Suzanne W., ed. *Writing the Woman Artist: Essays on Poetics, Politics, and Portraiture*. Philadelphia: U of Pennsylvania P, 1991. This collection of feminist critical essays contains useful approaches to issues of silence and voice in such writers as Eliot, Woolf, and

Anzaldúa. The essays also examine the representation of women artist figures in women's texts.

Madison, D. Soyini, ed. *The Woman That I Am: The Literature and Culture of Contemporary Women of Color.* New York: St. Martin's, 1994. This anthology introduces writings by Native American, African American, Latina American, and Asian American women. It includes poetry, short stories, plays, cultural narratives, and critical perspectives.

Showalter, Elaine, ed. *The New Feminist Criticism: Essays on Women, Literature, and Theory.* New York: Pantheon, 1985. One of America's foremost proponents of gynocriticism, Showalter has collected important feminist essays by such critics as Sandra Gilbert, Annette Kolodny, Lillian S. Robinson, Barbara Smith, Susan Gubar, and Nancy K. Miller; many deal with language and voice. The collection includes Showalter's "Feminist Criticism in the Wilderness."

Stimpson, Catharine R. "Woolf's Room, Our Project: The Building of Feminist Criticism." *The Future of Literary Theory.* Ed. Ralph Cohen. New York: Routledge, 1989. This essay examines *A Room of One's Own* as a pivotal work of feminist literary criticism and defines what feminist criticism needs to be for the 1990s and beyond.

—◆—

Virginia Woolf
1882–1941

she / Joyce born + died in same year

An innovative modernist writer of fiction, VIRGINIA WOOLF also wrote impassioned polemics on behalf of women's rights and pacifism. Although her early novels—*The Voyage Out* (1915) and *Night and Day* (1919)—were written in traditional form, the stream-of-consciousness style that would characterize her finest work was developing even then. This fluid, impressionistic technique, which presented lyrical accounts of "moments of being" experienced by a broad range of exquisitely drawn characters, appears in her major novels: *Jacob's Room* (1922), *Mrs. Dalloway* (1925), *To the Lighthouse* (1927), and *The Waves* (1931). *The Years* (1937) and *Between the Acts* (1941) returned to the formal realism of her earlier fiction but with a new approach to time and structure. In her novels Woolf explores the complexities of claiming an artistic identity, the vicissitudes of personal relationships, and such philosophical issues as the passing of time, the bearing of loss, and the power of memory to sustain the human spirit.

Woolf's most memorable feminist essays are *A Room of One's Own* (1929), an important work of feminist literary criticism and a witty indictment of patriarchal restrictions on women's creative agency; and *Three Guineas* (1938), an epistolary defense of women's education as well as a scathing response to the encroachment of fascism on Europe in the late 1930s. Her feminist views abound in the historical fantasy, *Orlando* (1928), which playfully investigates the possibilities of androgynous vision, a concept developed theoretically in *A Room of One's Own.* Woolf wrote numerous essays and reviews focusing on women's writing, a number of which are collected in the two-volume *The Common Reader* (1925, 1932) and in *Contemporary Writers* (1965, published posthumously). Among the subjects of her essays are many of her female literacy predecessors—MARGARET CAVENDISH, APHRA BEHN, ELIZA HAYWOOD, MARY WOLLSTONECRAFT, JANE AUSTEN, the BRONTËS, GEORGE ELIOT, ELIZABETH BARRETT BROWNING, and CHRISTINA ROSSETTI—as well as such contemporaries as KATHERINE MANSFIELD, Dorothy Richardson, and Olive Schreiner. In these essays Woolf offers incisive analyses of the psychic and material difficulties that women writers have historically faced.

Sir

Born in 1882, Woolf was the third child of Leslie Stephen, a renowned late Victorian critic and biographer, and his second wife, Julia Jackson Duckworth, who brought to the marriage three children of her own. She grew up in London in a large household open to many prominent writers, artists, and scholars of the era. In 1895 her mother died, a trauma that Woolf would explore indirectly in *To the Lighthouse* through the emotionally charged relationship of Lily Briscoe and Mrs. Ramsay. When her father passed away in 1904, Virginia left the family home at 22 Hyde Park Gate and moved with her two brothers, Thoby and Adrian, and her sister, Vanessa, to 46 Gordon Square in the Bloomsbury district of London. Here she became associated, through her brothers, with the artistic circle that came to be called the "Bloomsbury Group," which included the writer Lytton Strachey, the economist John Maynard Keynes, art critics Roger Fry and Clive Bell, the novelist E.M. Forster, the historian and scholar Leonard Woolf and, later, the dancer Lydia Lopokova (Keynes's wife) and the artist Dora Carrington (Strachey's life companion). In 1912 Virginia married Leonard Woolf, in whom she apparently found a compatible and supportive mate. Biographers suggest that the relationship might have been platonic; the couple had no children. Patrons as well as practitioners of the arts, the Woolfs in 1917 founded the Hogarth Press, which published work by such prominent figures as Sigmund Freud, T. S. Eliot, and Katherine Mansfield; several volumes of memoirs by working-class women; Leonard's historical treatises, Virginia's novels, and books by other "Bloomsberries."

Women's issues and friendships with women played a significant role in Woolf's life and literary career. She worked for suffrage from 1910 to 1911, taught classes for working women off and on during much of her adult life, and gave lectures to academic women—two of which resulted in *A Room of One's Own*. She also supported the unbanning of Radclyffe Hall's lesbian novel, *The Well of Loneliness* (1928). Woolf had a relationship in the late 1920s with Vita Sackville-West, an heiress and author whose intellectual vitality and open lesbianism intrigued her. Both *Orlando* and *A Room of One's Own* were written, at least in part, for Vita. Woolf's sister, Vanessa Bell, a prominent artist, was a friend and ally throughout her life, and in the 1930s she established a close friendship with the composer ETHEL SMYTH.

From 1895 until her death Woolf suffered from severe depression. Scholars have speculated variously as to its causes: the pain of losing her mother at a vulnerable age, the trauma caused by her half-brother George Duckworth's incestuous advances toward her in her teens, the ambivalence she experienced at the death of her iron-willed father, the stresses incumbent upon a "woman who attempts the pen" (the eighteenth-century poet ANNE FINCH'S phrase), her response to the horrors of war. Whatever the causes, Woolf experienced massive mood swings and psychic terrors that led to several mental breakdowns. Her illness worsened in early 1940, and in 1941 she committed suicide by drowning herself in the River Ouse near the Woolfs's home in Sussex.

The essay by Woolf included here, *A Room of One's Own*, raises several issues important to an understanding of women's literary achievements. What do women need in order to create? Historically, what barriers have prevented women from reaching their creative potentials? What might women's writing become in the future? To enhance her reader's journey across the landscape of women's artistic struggle, Woolf invents the marvelous character of Judith Shakespeare, gifted sister to William, whose story dramatizes the plight of women during the Renaissance. Yet she cannily undermines her own assertion that women have not written meaningful literature by recounting, in Chapter 4, an extensive female literary tradition, from Cavendish through the Brontës. For Woolf, "we think back through our mothers if we are women. It is useless to go to the great men writers for help, however much one may go to them for pleasure."

Virginia Woolf remains a pivotal figure to any conception of women's literary history. As a prodigious stream-of-consciousness novelist comparable in scope and originality to James Joyce, she offers powerful examples of modernist experimentation and brilliant, meditative prose. As a feminist essayist she chronicles the difficulties and rewards of breaking silence about women's writing lives. Finally, she traces with exuberance the contours, however vexed, of a distinctive female literary tradition in English—a tradition to which she is a major contributor.

⊰ A Room of One's Own ⊱

ONE

But, you may say, we asked you to speak about women and fiction—what has that got to do with a room of one's own? I will try to explain. When you asked me to speak about women and fiction I sat down on the banks of a river and began to wonder what the words meant. They might mean simply a few remarks about Fanny Burney; a few more about Jane Austen; a tribute to the Brontës and a sketch of Haworth Parsonage under snow; some witticisms if possible about Miss Mitford; a respectful allusion to George Eliot; a reference to Mrs. Gaskell and one would have done.[1] But at second sight the words seemed not so simple. The title women and fiction might mean, and you may have meant it to mean, women and what they are like; or it might mean women and the fiction that they write; or it might mean women and the fiction that is written about them; or it might mean that somehow all three are inextricably mixed together and you want me to consider them in that light. But when I began to consider the subject in this last way, which seemed the most interesting, I soon saw that it had one fatal drawback. I should never be able to come to a conclusion. I should never be able to fulfill what is, I understand, the first duty of a lecturer—to hand you after an hour's discourse a nugget of pure truth to wrap up between the pages of your notebooks and keep on the mantelpiece for ever. All I could do was to offer you an opinion upon one minor point—a woman must have money and a room of her own if she is to write fiction; and that, as you will see, leaves the great problem of the true nature of woman and the true nature of fiction unsolved. I have shirked the duty of coming to a conclusion upon these two questions—women and fiction remain, so far as I am concerned, unsolved problems. But in order to make some amends I am going to do what I can to show you how I arrived at this opinion about the room and the money. I am going to develop in your presence as fully and freely as I can the train of thought which led me to think this. Perhaps if I lay bare the ideas, the prejudices, that lie behind this statement you will find that they have some bearing upon women and some upon fiction. At any rate, when a subject is highly controversial—and any question about sex is that—one cannot hope to tell the truth. One can only show how one came to hold whatever opinion one does hold. One can only give one's audience the chance of drawing their own conclusions as they observe the limitations, the prejudices, the idiosyncrasies of the speaker. Fiction here is likely to contain more truth than fact. Therefore I propose, making use of all the liberties and licenses of a novelist, to tell you the story of the two days that preceded my coming here—how, bowed down by the weight of the subject which you have laid upon my shoulders, I pondered it, and made it work in and out of my daily life. I need not say that what I am about to describe has no existence; Oxbridge is an invention; so is Fernham; "I" is only a convenient term for somebody who has no real being. Lies will flow from my lips, but there may perhaps be some truth mixed up with them; it is for you to seek out this truth and to decide whether any part of it is worth keeping. If not, you will of course throw the whole of it into the wastepaper basket and forget all about it.

1. Frances Burney, Jane Austen, Charlotte Brontë, Emily Brontë, George Eliot, and Elizabeth Gaskell (1810–65) were highly regarded nineteenth-century British novelists. Mary Russell Mitford (1787–1855) was a prominent nineteenth-century poet and essayist who wrote about English rural life.

Here then was I (call me Mary Beton, Mary Seton, Mary Carmichael or by any name you please—it is not a matter of any importance) sitting on the banks of a river a week or two ago in fine October weather, lost in thought. That collar I have spoken of, women and fiction, the need of coming to some conclusion on a subject that raises all sorts of prejudices and passions, bowed my head to the ground. To the right and left bushes of some sort, golden and crimson, glowed with the colour, even it seemed burnt with the heat, of fire. On the further bank the willows wept in perpetual lamentation, their hair about their shoulders. The river reflected whatever it chose of sky and bridge and burning tree, and when the undergraduate had oared his boat through the reflections they closed again, completely, as if he had never been. There one might have sat the clock round lost in thought. Thought—to call it by a prouder name than it deserved—had let its line down into the stream. It swayed, minute after minute, hither and thither among the reflections and the weeds, letting the water lift it and sink it, until—you know the little tug—the sudden conglomeration of an idea at the end of one's line: and then the cautious hauling of it in, and the careful laying of it out? Alas, laid on the grass how small, how insignificant this thought of mine looked; the sort of fish that a good fisherman puts back into the water so that it may grow fatter and be one day worth cooking and eating. I will not trouble you with that thought now, though if you look carefully you may find it for yourselves in the course of what I am going to say.

But however small it was, it had, nevertheless, the mysterious property of its kind—put back into the mind, it became at once very exciting, and important; and as it darted and sank, and flashed hither and thither, set up such a wash and tumult of ideas that it was impossible to sit still. It was thus that I found myself walking with extreme rapidity across a grass plot. Instantly a man's figure rose to intercept me. Nor did I at first understand that the gesticulations of a curious-looking object, in a cutaway coat and evening shirt, were aimed at me. His face expressed horror and indignation. Instinct rather than reason came to my help; he was a Beadle; I was a woman. This was the turf; there was the path. Only the Fellows and Scholars are allowed here; the gravel is the place for me. Such thoughts were the work of a moment. As I regained the path the arms of the Beadle sank, his face assumed its usual repose, and though turf is better walking than gravel, no very great harm was done. The only charge I could bring against the Fellows and Scholars of whatever the college might happen to be was that in protection of their turf, which has been rolled for 300 years in succession, they had sent my little fish into hiding.

What idea it had been that had sent me so audaciously trespassing I could not now remember. The spirit of peace descended like a cloud from heaven, for if the spirit of peace dwells anywhere, it is in the courts and quadrangles of Oxbridge on a fine October morning. Strolling through those colleges past those ancient halls the roughness of the present seemed smoothed away; the body seemed contained in a miraculous glass cabinet through which no sound could penetrate, and the mind, freed from any contact with facts (unless one trespassed on the turf again), was at liberty to settle down upon whatever meditation was in harmony with the moment. As chance would have it, some stray memory of some old essay about revisiting Oxbridge in the long vacation brought Charles Lamb to mind—Saint Charles, said Thackeray, putting a letter of Lamb's to his forehead. Indeed, among all the dead (I give you my thoughts as they came to me), Lamb is one of the most congenial; one to whom one would have liked to say, Tell me then how you wrote your essays? For his essays are superior even to Max Beerbohm's, I thought, with all their perfection, because of that wild flash of imagination, that lightning crack of genius in the middle of them which leaves them flawed and imperfect, but starred with poetry. Lamb then came to Oxbridge perhaps a hundred years ago. Certainly he wrote an essay—the name escapes me—about the manuscript of one of Milton's poems which he saw here. It was *Lycidas* perhaps, and Lamb wrote how it shocked him to think it possible that any word in *Lycidas* could have been different from what it is. To think of Milton changing the words in that poem seemed to him a sort of sacrilege.[2] This led me to remember what I could of *Lycidas* and to amuse myself with guessing which word it could have been that Milton had altered, and why. It then occurred to me that the very manuscript itself which Lamb had looked at was only a few hundred yards away, so that one could follow Lamb's footsteps across the quadrangle to that famous library where the treasure is kept. Moreover, I recollected, as I put this plan into execution, it is in this famous library that the manuscript of Thackeray's *Esmond* is also preserved.[3] The critics often say that *Esmond* is Thackeray's most perfect novel. But the affectation of the style, with its imitation of the eighteenth century, hampers one, so far as I remember; unless indeed the eighteenth-century style was natural to Thackeray—a fact that one might prove by looking at the manuscript and seeing whether the alterations were for the benefit of the style or of the sense. But then one would have to decide what is style and what is meaning, a question which—but here I was actually at the door which leads into the library itself. I must have opened it, for instantly there issued, like a guardian angel barring the way with a flutter of black gown instead of white wings, a deprecating, silvery, kindly gentleman, who regretted in a low voice as he waved me back that ladies are only admitted to the library if accompanied by a Fellow of the College or furnished with a letter of introduction.

That a famous library has been cursed by a woman is a matter of complete indifference to a famous library. Venerable and calm, with all its treasures safe locked within its breast, it sleeps complacently and will, so far as I am concerned, so sleep for ever. Never will I wake those echoes, never will I ask for that hospitality again, I vowed as I descended the steps in anger. Still an hour remained before luncheon, and what was one to do? Stroll on the meadows? sit by the river? Certainly it was a lovely autumn morning; the leaves were fluttering red to the ground; there was no great hardship in doing either. But the sound of music reached my ear. Some service or celebration was going forward. The organ complained magnificently as I passed the chapel door. Even the sorrow of Christianity sounded in that serene air more like the recollection of sorrow than sorrow itself; even the groanings of the ancient organ seemed lapped in peace. I had no wish to enter had I the right, and this time the verger might have stopped me, demanding perhaps my baptismal certificate, or a letter of introduction from the Dean. But the outside of these magnificent buildings is often as beautiful as the inside. Moreover, it was amusing enough to watch the congregation assembling, coming in and going out again, busying themselves at the door of the chapel like bees at the mouth of a hive. Many were in cap and gown; some had tufts of fur on their shoulders; others were wheeled in bath-chairs; others, though not past middle age, seemed creased and crushed into shapes so singular that one was

2. Charles Lamb (1775–1834), was an English essayist and poet admired by William Makepeace Thackeray (1811–63), English novelist and critic. Woolf alludes here to Lamb's famous essay "Oxford in the Vacation." Max Beerbohm (1872–1956) was an essayist and a caricaturist known as "the Incomparable Max." John Milton (1608–74), best

known as the author of the epic poem *Paradise Lost* (1667), also wrote the pastoral elegy *Lycidas* (1638) on the death of his friend from Cambridge, Edward King.
3. *The History of Henry Esmond* (1852), a novel, tells the life story of the son of the third Viscount Castlewood and the political intrigue in which he is engaged.

reminded of those giant crabs and crayfish who heave with difficulty across the sand of an aquarium. As I leant against the wall the University indeed seemed a sanctuary in which are preserved rare types which would soon be obsolete if left to fight for existence on the pavement of the Strand. Old stories of old deans and old dons came back to mind, but before I had summoned up courage to whistle—it used to be said that at the sound of a whistle old Professor _____ instantly broke into a gallop—the venerable congregation had gone inside. The outside of the chapel remained. As you know, its high domes and pinnacles can be seen, like a sailing-ship always voyaging never arriving, lit up at night and visible for miles, far away across the hills. Once, presumably, this quadrangle with its smooth lawns, its massive buildings, and the chapel itself was marsh too, where the grasses waved and the swine rootled. Teams of horses and oxen, I thought, must have hauled the stone in wagons from far countries, and then with infinite labour the grey blocks in whose shade I was now standing were poised in order one on top of another, and then the painters brought their glass for the windows, and the masons were busy for centuries up on that roof with putty and cement, spade and trowel. Every Saturday somebody must have poured gold and silver out of a leathern purse into their ancient fists, for they had their beer and skittles presumably of an evening. An unending stream of gold and silver, I thought, must have flowed into this court perpetually to keep the stones coming and the masons working; to level, to ditch, to dig and to drain. But it was then the age of faith, and money was poured liberally to set these stones on a deep foundation, and when the stones were raised, still more money was poured in from the coffers of kings and queens and great nobles to ensure that hymns should be sung here and scholars taught. Lands were granted; tithes were paid. And when the age of faith was over and the age of reason had come, still the same flow of gold and silver went on; fellowships were founded; lectureships endowed; only the gold and silver flowed now, not from the coffers of the king, but from the chests of merchants and manufacturers, from the purses of men who had made, say, a fortune from industry, and returned, in their wills, a bounteous share of it to endow more chairs, more lectureships, more fellow-ships in the university where they had learnt their craft. Hence the libraries and labo-ratories; the observatories; the splendid equipment of costly and delicate instruments which now stands on glass shelves, where centuries ago the grasses waved and the swine rootled. Certainly, as I strolled round the court, the foundation of gold and sil-ver seemed deep enough; the pavement laid solidly over the wild grasses. Men with trays on their heads went busily from staircase to staircase. Gaudy blossoms flowered in window-boxes. The strains of the gramophone blared out from the rooms within. It was impossible not to reflect—the reflection whatever it may have been was cut short. The clock struck. It was time to find one's way to luncheon.

It is a curious fact that novelists have a way of making us believe that luncheon parties are invariably memorable for something very witty that was said, or for some-thing very wise that was done. But they seldom spare a word for what was eaten. It is part of the novelist's convention not to mention soup and salmon and ducklings, as if soup and salmon and ducklings were of no importance whatsoever, as if nobody ever smoked a cigar or drank a glass of wine. Here, however, I shall take the liberty to defy that convention and to tell you that the lunch on this occasion began with soles, sunk in a deep dish, over which the college cook had spread a counterpane of the whitest cream, save that it was branded here and there with brown spots like the spots on the flanks of a doe. After that came the partridges, but if this suggests a cou-ple of bald, brown birds on a plate you are mistaken. The partridges, many and vari-ous, came with all their retinue of sauces and salads, the sharp and the sweet, each in its order; their potatoes, thin as coins but not so hard; their sprouts, foliated as rose-buds but more succulent. And no sooner had the roast and it retinue been done with than the silent serving-man, the Beadle himself perhaps in a milder manifestation, set before us, wreathed in napkins, a confection which rose all sugar from the waves. To call it pudding and so relate it to rice and tapioca would be an insult. Meanwhile the wineglasses had flushed yellow and flushed crimson; had been emptied, had been filled. And thus by degrees was lit, halfway down the spine, which is the seat of the soul, not that hard little electric light which we call brilliance, as it pops in and out upon our lips, but the more profound, subtle and subterranean glow, which is the rich yellow flame of rational intercourse. No need to hurry. No need to sparkle. No need to be anybody but oneself. We are all going to heaven and Vandyck is of the company—in other words, how good life seemed, how sweet its rewards, how trivial this grudge or that grievance, how admirable friendship and the society of one's kind, as, lighting a good cigarette, one sunk among the cushions in the window-seat.

If by good luck there had been an ash-tray handy, if one had not knocked the ash out of the window in default, if things had been a little different from what they were, one would not have seen, presumably, a cat without a tail. The sight of that abrupt and truncated animal padding softly across the quadrangle changed by some fluke of the subconscious intelligence the emotional light for me. It was as if some one had let fall a shade. Perhaps the excellent hock was relinquishing its hold. Certainly, as I watched the Manx cat pause in the middle of the lawn as if it too questioned the universe, some-thing seemed lacking, something seemed different. But what was lacking, what was dif-ferent, I asked myself, listening to the talk. And to answer that question I had to think myself out of the room, back into the past, before the war indeed, and to set before my eyes the model of another luncheon party held in rooms not very far distant from these; but different. Everything was different. Meanwhile the talk went on among the guests, who were many and young, some of this sex, some of that; it went on swimmingly, it went on agreeably, freely, amusingly. And as it went on I set it against the background of that other talk, and as I matched the two together I had no doubt that one was the descendant, the legitimate heir of the other. Nothing was changed; nothing was differ-ent save only—here I listened with all my ears not entirely to what was being said, but to the murmur or current behind it. Yes, that was it—the change was there. Before the war at a luncheon party like this people would have said precisely the same things but they would have sounded different, because in those days they were accompanied by a sort of humming noise, not articulate, but musical, exciting, which changed the value of the words themselves. Could one set that humming noise to words? Perhaps with the help of the poets one could. A book lay beside me and, opening it, I turned casually enough to Tennyson. And here I found Tennyson was singing:

> There has fallen a splendid tear
>   From the passion-flower at the gate.
> She is coming, my dove, my dear;
>   She is coming, my life, my fate;
> The red rose cries, "She is near, she is near";
>   And the white rose weeps, "She is late";
> The larkspur listens, "I hear, I hear";
>   And the lily whispers, "I wait."[4]

4. Alfred, Lord Tennyson (1809–92) was a popular British poet who was appointed poet laureate in 1850. His poem *The Princess* (1847), from which Woolf quotes, glorified the institution of marriage.

Was that what men hummed at luncheon parties before the war? And the women?

> My heart is like a singing bird
> Whose nest is in a watered shoot;
> My heart is like an apple tree
> Whose boughs are bent with thick-set fruit;
> My heart is like a rainbow shell
> That paddles in a halcyon sea;
> My heart is gladder than all these
> Because my love is come to me.[5]

Was that what women hummed at luncheon parties before the war?

There was something so ludicrous in thinking of people humming such things even under their breath at luncheon parties before the war that I burst out laughing, and had to explain my laughter by pointing at the Manx cat, who did look a little absurd, poor beast, without a tail, in the middle of the lawn. Was he really born so, or had he lost his tail in an accident? The tailless cat, though some are said to exist in the Isle of Man, is rarer than one thinks. It is a queer animal, quaint rather than beautiful. It is strange what a difference a tail makes—you know the sort of things one says as a luncheon party breaks up and people are finding their coats and hats.

This one, thanks to the hospitality of the host, had lasted far into the afternoon. The beautiful October day was fading and the leaves were falling from the trees in the avenue as I walked through it. Gate after gate seemed to close with gentle finality behind me. Innumerable beadles were fitting innumerable keys into well-oiled locks; the treasure-house was being made secure for another night. After the avenue one comes out upon a road—I forget its name—which leads you, if you take the right turning, along to Fernham. But there was plenty of time. Dinner was not till half-past seven. One could almost do without dinner after such a luncheon. It is strange how a scrap of poetry works in the mind and makes the legs move in time to it along the road. Those words—

> There has fallen a splendid tear
> From the passion-flower at the gate.
> She is coming, my dove, my dear—

sang in my blood as I stepped quickly along towards Headingley. And then, switching off into the other measure, I sang, where the waters are churned up by the weir:

> My heart is like a singing bird
> Whose nest is in a watered shoot;
> My heart is like an apple tree . . .

What poets, I cried aloud, as one does in the dusk, what poets they were!

In a sort of jealousy, I suppose, for our own age, silly and absurd though these comparisons are, I went on to wonder if honestly one could name two living poets now as great as Tennyson and Christina Rossetti were then. Obviously it is impossible, I thought, looking into those foaming waters, to compare them. The very reason why the poetry excites one to such abandonment, such rapture, is that it celebrates

---

5. This quotation is the first stanza of "A Birthday" (1861) by Christina Rossetti, one of Victorian England's foremost women poets.

some feeling that one used to have (at luncheon parties before the war perhaps), so that one responds easily, familiarly, without troubling to check the feeling, or to compare it with any that one has now. But the living poets express a feeling that is actually being made and torn out of us at the moment. One does not recognize it in the first place; often for some reason one fears it; one watches it with keenness and compares it jealously and suspiciously with the old feeling that one knew. Hence the difficulty of modern poetry; and it is because of this difficulty that one cannot remember more than two consecutive lines of any good modern poet. For this reason—that my memory failed me—the argument flagged for want of material. But why, I continued, moving on towards Headingley, have we stopped humming under our breath at luncheon parties? Why has Alfred ceased to sing

> She is coming, my dove, my dear?

Why has Christina ceased to respond

> My heart is gladder than all these
> Because my love is come to me?

Shall we lay the blame on the war? When the guns fired in August 1914, did the faces of men and women show so plain in each other's eyes that romance was killed? Certainly it was a shock (to women in particular with their illusions about education, and so on) to see the faces of our rulers in the light of the shell-fire. So ugly they looked—German, English, French—so stupid. But lay the blame where one will, on whom one will, the illusion which inspired Tennyson and Christina Rossetti to sing so passionately about the coming of their loves is far rarer now than then. One has only to read, to look, to listen, to remember. But why say "blame"? Why, if it was an illusion, not praise the catastrophe, whatever it was, that destroyed illusion and put truth in its place? For truth . . . those dots mark the spot where, in search of truth, I missed the turning up to Fernham. Yes indeed, which was truth and which was illusion, I asked myself. What was the truth about these houses, for example, dim and festive now with their red windows in the dusk, but raw and red and squalid, with their sweets and their boot-laces, at nine o'clock in the morning? And the willows and the river and the gardens that run down to the river, vague now with the mist stealing over them, but gold and red in the sunlight—which was the truth, which was the illusion about them? I spare you the twists and turns of my cogitations, for no conclusion was found on the road to Headingley, and I ask you to suppose that I soon found out my mistake about the turning and retraced my steps to Fernham.

As I have said already that is was an October day, I dare not forfeit your respect and imperil the fair name of fiction by changing the season and describing lilacs hanging over garden walls, crocuses, tulips and other flowers of spring. Fiction must stick to facts, and the truer the facts the better the fiction—so we are told. Therefore it was still autumn and the leaves were still yellow and falling, if anything, a little faster than before, because it was now evening (seven twenty-three to be precise) and a breeze (from the southwest to be exact) had risen. But for all that there was something odd at work:

> My heart is like a singing bird
>   Whose nest is in a watered shoot;
> My heart is like an apple tree
>   Whose boughs are bent with thick-set fruit—

perhaps the words of Christina Rossetti were partly responsible for the folly of the fancy—it was nothing of course but a fancy—that the lilac was shaking its flowers over the garden walls, and the brimstone butterflies were scudding hither and thither, and the dust of the pollen was in the air. A wind blew, from what quarter I know not, but it lifted the half-grown leaves so that there was a flash of silver grey in the air. It was the time between the lights when colours undergo their intensification and purples and golds burn in window-panes like the beat of an excitable heart; when for some reason the beauty of the world revealed and yet soon to perish (here I pushed into the garden, for, unwisely, the door was left open and no beadles seemed about), the beauty of the world which is soon to perish, has two edges, one of laughter, one of anguish, cutting the heart asunder. The gardens of Fernham lay before me in the spring twilight, wild and open, and in the long grass, sprinkled and carelessly flung, were daffodils and bluebells, not orderly perhaps at the best of times, and now wind-blown and waving as they tugged at their roots. The windows of the building, curved like ships' windows among generous waves of red brick, changed from lemon to silver under the flight of the quick spring clouds. Somebody was in a hammock, somebody, but in this light they were phantoms only, half guessed, half seen, raced across the grass—would no one stop her?—and then on the terrace, as if popping out to breathe the air, to glance at the garden, came a bent figure, formidable yet humble, with her great forehead and her shabby dress—could it be the famous scholar, could it be J ____ H____ herself?[6] All was dim, yet intense too, as if the scarf which the dusk had flung over the garden were torn asunder by star or sword—the flash of some terrible reality leaping, as its way is, out of the heart of the spring. For youth——

Here was my soup. Dinner was being served in the great dining-hall. Far from being spring it was in fact an evening in October. Everybody was assembled in the big dining-room. Dinner was ready. Here was the soup. It was a plain gravy soup. There was nothing to stir the fancy in that. One could have seen through the transparent liquid any pattern that there might have been on the plate itself. But there was no pattern. The plate was plain. Next came beef with its attendant greens and potatoes—a homely trinity, suggesting the rumps of cattle in a muddy market, and sprouts curled and yellowed at the edge, and bargaining and cheapening, and women with string bags on Monday morning. There was no reason to complain of human nature's daily food, seeing that the supply was sufficient and coal-miners doubtless were sitting down to less. Prunes and custard followed. And if any one complains that prunes, even when mitigated by custard, are an uncharitable vegetable (fruit they are not), stringy as a miser's heart and exuding a fluid such as might run in misers' veins who have denied themselves wine and warmth for eighty years and yet not given to the poor, he should reflect that there are people whose charity embraces even the prune. Biscuits and cheese came next, and here the water-jug was liberally passed round, for it is the nature of biscuits to be dry, and these were biscuits to the core. That was all. The meal was over. Everybody scraped their chairs back; the swing-doors swung violently to and fro; soon the hall was emptied of every sign of food and made ready no doubt for breakfast next morning. Down corridors and up staircases the youth of England went banging and singing. And was it for a guest, a stranger (for I had no more right here in Fernham than in Trinity or Somerville or Girton or Newnham or Christchurch), to say, "The dinner was not good," or to say (we were now, Mary Seton and I, in her sitting-room), "Could we not have dined up here alone?" for if I had said anything of the kind I should have been prying and searching into the secret economies of a house which to the stranger wears so fine a front of gaiety and courage. No, one could say nothing of the sort. Indeed, conversation for a moment

6. Jane Harrison (1850–1928) was a British classical scholar and social anthropologist who lectured at Newnham Hall, Cambridge, from 1898 to 1922.

flagged. The human frame being what it is, heart, body and brain all mixed together, and not contained in separate compartments as they will be no doubt in another million years, a good dinner is of great importance to good talk. One cannot think well, love well, sleep well, if one has not dined well. The lamp in the spine does not light on beef and prunes. We are all *probably* going to heaven, and Vandyck is, we *hope,* to meet us round the next corner—that is the dubious and qualifying state of mind that beef and prunes at the end of the day's work breed between them. Happily my friend, who taught science, had a cupboard where there was a squat bottle and little glasses—(but there should have been sole and partridge to begin with)—so that we were able to draw up to the fire and repair some of the damages of the day's living. In a minute or so we were slipping freely in and out among all those objects of curiosity and interest which form in the mind in the absence of a particular person, and are naturally to be discussed on coming together again—how somebody has married, another has not; one thinks this, another that; one has improved out of all knowledge, the other most amazingly gone to the bad—with all those speculations upon human nature and the character of the amazing world we live in which spring naturally from such beginnings. While these things were being said, however, I became shamefacedly aware of a current setting in of its own accord and carrying everything forward to an end of its own. One might be talking of Spain or Portugal, of book or racehorse, but the real interest of whatever was said was none of those things, but a scene of masons on a high roof some five centuries ago. Kings and nobles brought treasure in huge sacks and poured it under the earth. This scene was for ever coming alive in my mind and placing itself by another of lean cows and a muddy market and withered greens and the stringy hearts of old men—these two pictures, disjointed and disconnected and nonsensical as they were, were for ever coming together and combating each other and had me entirely at their mercy. The best course, unless the whole talk was to be distorted, was to expose what was in my mind to the air, when with good luck it would fade and crumble like the head of the dead king when they opened the coffin at Windsor. Briefly, then, I told Miss Seton about the masons who had been all those years on the roof of the chapel, and about the kings and queens and nobles bearing sacks of gold and silver on their shoulders, which they shovelled into the earth; and then how the great financial magnates of our own time came and laid cheques and bonds, I suppose, where the others had laid ingots and rough lumps of gold. All that lies beneath the colleges down there, I said; but this college, where we are now sitting, what lies beneath its gallant red brick and the wild unkempt grasses of the garden? What force is behind the plain china off which we dined, and (here it popped out of my mouth before I could stop it) the beef, the custard and the prunes?

Well, said Mary Seton, about the year 1860—Oh, but you know the story, she said, bored, I suppose, by the recital. And she told me—rooms were hired. Committees met. Envelopes were addressed. Circulars were drawn up. Meetings were held; letters were read out; so-and-so has promised so much; on the contrary, Mr. ___ won't give a penny. The *Saturday Review* has been very rude. How can we raise a fund to pay for offices? Shall we hold a bazaar? Can't we find a pretty girl to sit in the front row? Let us look up what John Stuart Mill said on the subject.[7] Can any one persuade the editor of the ___ to print a letter? Can we get Lady ___ to sign it? Lady ___ is out of town. That was the way it was done, presumably, sixty years ago, and it was a prodigious effort, and a great deal of time was spent on it. And it was only after a long struggle and with the utmost difficulty that they got thirty

7. John Stuart Mill (1806–73) wrote *The Subjection of Women* (1869), a tract in favor of liberating women from slavery into the status of individuals.

thousand pounds together.[8] So obviously we cannot have wine and partridges and servants carrying tin dishes on their heads, she said. We cannot have sofas and separate rooms. "The amenities," she said, quoting from some book or other, "will have to wait."[9]

At the thought of all those women working year after year and finding it hard to get two thousand pounds together, and as much as they could do to get thirty thousand pounds, we burst out in scorn at the reprehensible poverty of our sex. What had our mothers been doing then that they had no wealth to leave us? Powdering their noses? Looking in at shop windows? Flaunting in the sun at Monte Carlo? There were some photographs on the mantelpiece. Mary's mother—if that was her picture—may have been a wastrel in her spare time (she had thirteen children by a minister of the church), but if so her gay and dissipated life had left too few traces of its pleasures on her face. She was a homely body; an old lady in a plaid shawl which was fastened by a large cameo; and she sat in a basket-chair, encouraging a spaniel to look at the camera, with the amused, yet strained expression of one who is sure that the dog will move directly the bulb is pressed. Now if she had gone into business; had become a manufacturer of artificial silk or a magnate on the Stock Exchange; if she had left two or three hundred thousand pounds to Fernham, we could have been sitting at our ease tonight and the subject of our talk might have been archaeology, botany, anthropology, physics, the nature of the atom, mathematics, astronomy, relativity, geography. If only Mrs. Seton and her mother and her mother before her had learnt the great art of making money and had left their money, like their fathers and their grandfathers before them, to found fellowships and lectureships and prizes and scholarships appropriated to the use of their own sex, we might have dined very tolerably up here alone off a bird and a bottle of wine; we might have looked forward without undue confidence to a pleasant and honourable lifetime spent in the shelter of one of the liberally endowed professions. We might have been exploring or writing; mooning about the venerable places of the earth; sitting contemplative on the steps of the Parthenon, or going at ten to an office and coming home comfortably at half-past four to write a little poetry. Only, if Mrs. Seton and her like had gone into business at the age of fifteen, there would have been—that was the snag in the argument—no Mary. What, I asked, did Mary think of that? There between the curtains was the October night, calm and lovely, with a star or two caught in the yellowing trees. Was she ready to resign her share of it and her memories (for they had been a happy family, though a large one) of games and quarrels up in Scotland, which she is never tired of praising for the fineness of its air and the quality of its cakes, in order that Fernham might have been endowed with fifty thousand pounds or so by a stroke of the pen? For, to endow a college would necessitate the suppression of families altogether. Making a fortune and bearing thirteen children—no human being could stand it. Consider the facts, we said. First there are nine months before the baby is born. Then the baby is born. Then there are three or four months spent in feeding the baby. After the baby is fed there are certainly five years spent in playing with the baby. You cannot, it seems, let children run about the streets. People who have seen them running wild in Russia say that the sight is not a pleasant one. People say, too, that human nature takes its shape in the years between

8. ["We are told that we ought to ask for £30,000 at least . . . . It is not a large sum, considering that there is to be but one college of this sort for Great Britain, Ireland and the Colonies, and considering how easy it is to raise immense sums for boys' schools. But considering how few people really wish women to be educated, it is a good deal."—LADY STEPHEN, *Life of Miss Emily Davies*.]

9. [Every penny which could be scraped together was set aside for building, and the amenities had to be postponed.—R. STRACHEY, *The Cause*.]

one and five. If Mrs. Seton, I said, had been making money, what sort of memories would you have had of games and quarrels? What would you have known of Scotland, and its fine air and cakes and all the rest of it? But it is useless to ask these questions, because you would never have come into existence at all. Moreover, it is equally useless to ask what might have happened if Mrs. Seton and her mother and her mother before her had amassed great wealth and laid it under the foundations of college and library, because, in the first place, to earn money was impossible for them, and in the second, had it been possible, the law denied them the right to possess what money they earned. It is only for the last forty-eight years that Mrs. Seton has had a penny of her own. For all the centuries before that it would have been her husband's property— a thought which, perhaps, may have had its share in keeping Mrs. Seton and her mothers off the Stock Exchange. Every penny I earn, they may have said, will be taken from me and disposed of according to my husband's wisdom—perhaps to found a scholarship or to endow a fellowship in Balliol or Kings, so that to earn money, even if I could earn money, is not a matter that interests me very greatly. I had better leave it to my husband.

At any rate, whether or not the blame rested on the old lady who was looking at the spaniel, there could be no doubt that for some reason or other our mothers had mismanaged their affairs very gravely. Not a penny could be spared for "amenities"; for partridges and wine, beadles and turf, books and cigars, libraries and leisure. To raise bare walls out of the bare earth was the utmost they could do.

So we talked standing at the window and looking, as so many thousands look every night, down on the domes and towers of the famous city beneath us. It was very beautiful, very mysterious in the autumn moonlight. The old stone looked very white and venerable. One thought of all the books that were assembled down there; of the picture of old prelates and worthies hanging in the panelled rooms; of the painted windows that would be throwing strange globes and crescents on the pavement; of the tablets and memorials and inscriptions; of the fountains and the grass; of the quiet rooms looking across the quiet quadrangles. And (pardon me the thought) I thought, too, of the admirable smoke and drink and the deep armchairs and the pleasant carpets: of the urbanity, the geniality, the dignity which are the offspring of luxury and privacy and space. Certainly our mothers had not provided us with anything comparable to all this—our mothers who found it difficult to scrape together thirty thousand pounds, our mothers who bore thirteen children to ministers of religion at St. Andrews.

So I went back to my inn, and as I walked through the dark streets I pondered this and that, as one does at the end of the day's work. I pondered why it was that Mrs. Seton had no money to leave us; and what effect poverty has on the mind; and what effect wealth has on the mind; and I thought of the queer old gentlemen I had seen that morning with tufts of fur upon their shoulders; and I remembered how if one whistled one of them ran; and I thought of the organ booming in the chapel and of the shut doors of the library; and I thought how unpleasant it is to be locked out; and I thought how it is worse perhaps to be locked in; and, thinking, of the safety and prosperity of the one sex and of the poverty and insecurity of the other and of the effect of tradition and of the lack of tradition upon the mind of a writer, I thought at last that it was time to roll up the crumpled skin of the day, and its arguments and its impressions and its anger and its laughter, and cast it into the hedge. A thousand stars were flashing across the blue wastes of the sky. One seemed alone with an inscrutable society. All human beings were laid asleep—prone, horizontal, dumb.

Nobody seemed stirring in the streets of Oxbridge. Even the door of the hotel sprang open at the touch of an invisible hand—not a boots was sitting up to light me to bed, it was so late.

TWO

The scene, if I may ask you to follow me, was now changed. The leaves were still falling, but in London now, not Oxbridge; and I must ask you to imagine a room, like many thousands, with a window looking across people's hats and vans and motor-cars to other windows, and on the table inside a room a blank sheet of paper on which was written in large letters WOMEN AND FICTION, but no more. The inevitable sequel to lunching and dining at Oxbridge seemed, unfortunately, to be a visit to the British Museum. One must strain off what was personal and accidental in all these impressions and so reach the pure fluid, the essential oil of truth. For that visit to Oxbridge and the luncheon and the dinner had started a swarm of questions. Why did men drink wine and women water? Why was one sex so prosperous and the other so poor? What effect has poverty on fiction? What conditions are necessary for the creation of works of art?—a thousand questions at once suggested themselves. But one needed answers, not questions; and an answer was only to be had by consulting the learned and the unprejudiced, who have removed themselves above the strife of tongue and the confusion of body and issued the result of their reasoning and research in books which are to be found in the British Museum. If truth is not to be found on the shelves of the British Museum, where, I asked myself, picking up a notebook and a pencil, is truth?

Thus provided, thus confident and enquiring, I set out in the pursuit of truth. The day, though not actually wet, was dismal, and the streets in the neighborhood of the Museum were full of open coal-holes, down which sacks were showering; four-wheeled cabs were drawing up and depositing on the pavement corded boxes containing, presumably, the entire wardrobe of some Swiss or Italian family seeking fortune or refuge or some other desirable commodity which is to be found in the boarding-houses of Bloomsbury in the winter. The usual hoarse-voiced men paraded the streets with plants on barrows. Some shouted; others sang. London was like a workshop. London was like a machine. We were all being shot backwards and forwards on this plain foundation to make some pattern. The British Museum was another department of the factory. The swing-doors swung open; and there one stood under the vast dome, as if one were a thought in the huge bald forehead which is so splendidly encircled by a band of famous names. One went to the counter; one took a slip of paper; one opened a volume of the catalogue, and . . . . . the five dots here indicate five separate minutes of stupefaction, wonder and bewilderment. Have you any notion how many books are written about women in the course of one year? Have you any notion how many are written by men? Are you aware that you are, perhaps, the most discussed animal in the universe? Here had I come with a notebook and a pencil proposing to spend a morning reading, supposing that at the end of the morning I should have transferred the truth to my notebook. But I should need to be a herd of elephants, I thought, and a wilderness of spiders, desperately referring to the animals that are reputed longest lived and most multitudinously eyed, to cope with all this. I should need claws of steel and beak of brass even to penetrate the husk. How shall I ever find the grains of truth embedded in all this mass of paper, I asked myself, and in despair began running my eye up and down the long lists of titles. Even the names of the books gave me food for thought. Sex and its nature might well attract doctors and biologists; but what was surprising and difficult of explanation was the fact that sex—woman, that is to say—also attracts agreeable essayists, light-fingered novelists, young men who have taken the M.A. degree; men who have taken no degree; men who have no apparent qualification save that they are not women. Some of these books were, on the face of it, frivolous and facetious; but many, on the other hand, were serious and prophetic, moral and hortatory. Merely to read the titles suggested innumerable schoolmasters, innumerable clergymen mounting their platforms and pulpits and holding forth with a loquacity which far exceeded the hour usually allotted to such discourse on this one subject. It was a most strange phenomenon; and apparently—here I consulted the letter M—one confined to male sex. Women do not write books about men—a fact that I could not help welcoming with relief, for if I had first to read all that men have written about women, then all that women have written about men, the aloe that flowers once in a hundred years would flower twice before I could set pen to paper. So, making a perfectly arbitrary choice of a dozen volumes or so, I sent my slips of paper to lie in the wire tray, and waited in my stall, among the other seekers for the essential oil of truth.

What could be the reason, then, of this curious disparity, I wondered, drawing cartwheels on the slips of paper provided by the British taxpayer for other purposes. Why are women, judging from this catalogue, so much more interesting to men than men are to women? A very curious fact it seemed, and my mind wandered to picture the lives of men who spend their time in writing books about women; whether they were old or young, married or unmarried, red-nosed or hump-backed—anyhow, it was flattering, vaguely, to feel oneself the object of such attention, provided that it was not entirely bestowed by the crippled and the infirm—so I pondered until all such frivolous thoughts were ended by an avalanche of books sliding down on to the desk in front of me. Now the trouble began. The student who has been trained in research at Oxbridge has no doubt some method of shepherding his question past all distractions till it runs into its answer as a sheep runs into its pen. The student by my side, for instance, who was copying assiduously from a scientific manual was, I felt sure, extracting pure nuggets of the essential ore every ten minutes or so. His little grunts of satisfaction indicated so much. But if, unfortunately, one has had no training in a university, the question far from being shepherded to its pen flies like a frightened flock hither and thither, helter-skelter, pursued by a whole pack of hounds. Professors, schoolmasters, sociologists, clergymen, novelists, essayists, journalists, men who had no qualification save that they were not women, chased my simple and single question—Why are women poor?—until it became fifty questions; until the fifty questions leapt frantically into mid-stream and were carried away. Every page in my notebook was scribbled over with notes. To show the state of mind I was in, I will read you a few of them, explaining that the page was headed quite simply, WOMEN AND POVERTY, in block letters; but what followed was something like this:

> Condition in Middle Ages of,
> Habits in the Fiji Islands of,
> Worshipped as goddesses by,
> Weaker in moral sense than,
> Idealism of,
> Greater conscientiousness of,
> South Sea Islanders, age of puberty among,

Attractiveness of,
Offered as sacrifice to,
Small size of brain of,
Profounder sub-consciousness of,
Less hair on the body of,
Mental, moral and physical inferiority of,
Love of children of,
Greater length of life of,
Weaker muscles of,
Strength of affections of,
Vanity of,
Higher education of,
Shakespeare's opinion of,
Lord Birkenhead's opinion of,
Dean Inge's opinion of,
La Bruyère's opinion of,
Dr. Johnson's opinion of,
Mr. Oscar Browning's opinion of, . . .

Here I drew breath and added, indeed, in the margin, Why does Samuel Butler say, "Wise men never say what they think of women"? Wise men never say anything else apparently. But, I continued, leaning back in my chair and looking at the vast dome in which I was a single but by now somewhat harassed thought, what is so unfortunate is that wise men never think the same thing about women. Here is Pope:

Most women have no character at all.

And here is La Bruyère:

Les femmes sont extrêmes; elles sont meilleures ou pires que les hommes—

a direct contradiction by keen observers who were contemporary. Are they capable or incapable? Napoleon thought them incapable. Dr. Johnson thought the opposite.[10] Have they souls or have they not souls?[11] Some savages say they have none. Others, on the contrary, maintain that women are half divine and worship them on that account.[12] Some sages hold that they are shallower in the brain; others that they are deeper in the consciousness. Goethe honored them; Mussolini despises them.[13] Wherever one looked men thought about women and thought differently. It was impossible to make head or tail of it all, I decided, glancing with envy at the reader next door who was making the neatest abstracts, headed often with an A or a B or a C, while my own notebook rioted with the wildest scribble of contradictory jottings.

10. ["'Men know that women are an overmatch for them, and therefore they choose the weakest or the most ignorant. If they did not think so, they never could be afraid of women knowing as much as themselves,' . . . In justice to the sex, I think it but candid to acknowledge that, in a subsequent conversation, he told me that he was serious in what he said."—BOSWELL, The Journal of a Tour to the Hebrides.]

11. Samuel Butler (1835–1902) was a British novelist and satirist. Alexander Pope (1688–1741) was the eighteenth century's most famous poet and wit. Jean de La Bruyère (1645–96) was a French moralist; his quotation reads, "Women are extreme; they are either better or worse than

men." Dr. Samuel Johnson (1709–84) was a famous eighteenth-century editor and man of letters; James Boswell (1740–95) was his friend and biographer. Napoleon Bonaparte (1769–1821) was a French military commander who crowned himself emperor in 1804.

12. ["The ancient Germans believed that there was something holy in women, and accordingly consulted them as oracles."—FRAZER, The Golden Bough.]

13. Johann Wolfgang van Goethe (1749–1832) was a German poet and novelist who was celebrated as the foremost writer of his time; his masterpiece was Faust (1808–32). Benito Mussolini (1883–1945) was an Italian dictator and the leading proponent of fascism.

It was distressing, it was bewildering, it was humiliating. Truth had run through my fingers. Every drop had escaped.

I could not possibly go home, I reflected, and add as a serious contribution to the study of women and fiction that women have less hair on their bodies than men, or that the age of puberty among the South Sea Islanders is nine—or is it ninety?—even the handwriting had become in its distraction indecipherable. It was disgraceful to have nothing more weighty or respectable to show after a whole morning's work. And if I could not grasp the truth about W. (as for brevity's sake I had come to call her) in the past, why bother about W. in the future? It seemed pure waste of time to consult all those gentlemen who specialize in woman and her effect on whatever it may be—politics, children, wages, morality—numerous and learned as they are. One might as well leave their books unopened.

But while I pondered I had unconsciously, in my listlessness, in my desperation, been drawing a picture where I should, like my neighbor, have been writing a conclusion. I had been drawing a face, a figure. It was the face and the figure of Professor von X engaged in writing his monumental work entitled *The Mental, Moral, and Physical Inferiority of the Female Sex*. He was not in my picture a man attractive to women. He was heavily built; he had a great jowl; to balance that he had very small eyes; he was very red in the face. His expression suggested that he was laboring under some emotion that made him jab his pen on the paper as if he were killing some noxious insect as he wrote, but even when he had killed it that did not satisfy him; he must go on killing it; and even so, some cause for anger and irritation remained. Could it be his wife, I asked, looking at my picture. Was she in love with a cavalry officer? Was the cavalry officer slim and elegant and dressed in astrachan? Had he been laughed at, to adopt the Freudian theory, in his cradle by a pretty girl? For even in his cradle the professor, I thought, could not have been an attractive child. Whatever the reason, the professor was made to look very angry and very ugly in my sketch, as he wrote his great book upon the mental, moral and physical inferiority of women. Drawing pictures was an idle way of finishing an unprofitable morning's work. Yet it is in our idleness, in our dreams, that the submerged truth sometimes comes to the top. A very elementary exercise in psychology, not to be dignified by the name of psychoanalysis, showed me, on looking at my notebook, that the sketch of the angry professor had been made in anger. Anger had snatched my pencil while I dreamt. But what was anger doing there? Interest, confusion, amusement, boredom—all these emotions I could trace and name as they succeeded each other throughout the morning. Had anger, the black snake, been lurking among them? Yes, said the sketch, anger had. It referred me unmistakably to the one book, to the one phrase, which had roused the demon; it was the professor's statement about the mental, moral and physical inferiority of women. My heart had leapt. My cheeks had burnt. I had flushed with anger. There was nothing specially remarkable, however foolish, in that. One does not like to be told that one is naturally the inferior of a little man—I looked at the student next to me—who breathes hard, wears a ready-made tie, and has not shaved this fortnight. One has certain foolish vanities. It is only human nature, I reflected, and began drawing cart-wheels and circles over the angry professor's face till he looked like a burning bush or a flaming comet—anyhow, an apparition without human semblance or significance. The professor was nothing now but a faggot burning on the top of Hampstead Heath. Soon my own anger was explained and done with; but curiosity remained. How explain the anger of the professors? Why were they angry? For when it came to analyzing the impression left by these books there was always an element of heat. This heat took many forms; it showed itself in satire, in sentiment, in curiosity, in reprobation. But there was another element which was often present and could not immediately be identified. Anger, I called it. But it was anger that had gone underground and mixed itself with all kinds of other emotions. To judge from its odd effects, it was anger disguised and complex, not anger simple and open.

Whatever the reason, all these books, I thought, surveying the pile on the desk, are worthless for my purposes. They were worthless scientifically, that is to say, though humanly they were full of instruction, interest, boredom, and very queer facts about the habits of the Fiji Islanders. They had been written in the red light of emotion and not in the white light of truth. Therefore they must be returned to the central desk and restored each to his own cell in the enormous honeycomb. All that I had retrieved from that morning's work had been the one fact of anger. The professors—I lumped them together thus—were angry. But why, I asked myself, having returned the books, why, I repeated, standing under the colonnade among the pigeons and the prehistoric canoes, why are they angry? And, asking myself this question, I strolled off to find a place for luncheon. What is the real nature of what I call for the moment their anger? I asked. Here was a puzzle that would last all the time that it takes to be served with food in a small restaurant somewhere near the British Museum. Some previous luncher had left the lunch edition of the evening paper on a chair, and, waiting to be served, I began idly reading the headlines. A ribbon of very large letters ran across the page. Somebody had made a big score in South Africa. Lesser ribbons announced that Sir Austen Chamberlain was at Geneva.[14] A meat axe with human hair on it had been found in a cellar. Mr. Justice—commented in the Divorce Courts upon the Shamelessness of Women. Sprinkled about the paper were other pieces of news. A film actress had been lowered from a peak in California and hung suspended in mid-air. The weather was going to be foggy. The most transient visitor to this planet, I thought, who picked up this paper could not fail to be aware, even from this scattered testimony, that England is under the rule of a patriarchy. Nobody in their senses could fail to detect the dominance of the professor. His was the power and the money and the influence. He was the proprietor of the paper and its editor and sub-editor. He was the Foreign Secretary and the Judge. He was the cricketer; he owned the racehorses and the yachts. He was the director of the company that pays two hundred per cent to its shareholders. He left millions to charities and colleges that were ruled by himself. He suspended the film actress in mid-air. He will decide if the hair on the meat axe is human; he it is who will acquit or convict the murderer, and hang him, or let him go free. With the exception of the fog he seemed to control everything. Yet he was angry. I knew that he was angry by this token. When I read what he wrote about women I thought, not of what he was saying, but of himself. When an arguer argues dispassionately he thinks only of the argument; and the reader cannot help thinking of the argument too. If he had written dispassionately about women, had used indisputable proofs to establish his argument and had shown no trace of wishing that the result should be one thing rather than another, one would not have been angry either. One would have accepted the fact, as one accepts the fact that a pea is green or a canary yellow. So be it, I should have said. But I had been angry because he was angry. Yet it seemed absurd, I thought, turning over the evening paper, that a man with all this power should be angry. Or is anger, I wondered, somehow, the familiar, the attendant sprite

14. Sir Austen Chamberlain (1863–1937) was a British politician who served as Foreign Secretary from 1924 to 1929.

on power? Rich people, for example, are often angry because they suspect that the poor want to seize their wealth. The professors, or patriarchs, as it might be more accurate to call them, might be angry for that reason partly, but partly for one that lies a little less obviously on the surface. Possibly they were not "angry" at all; often, indeed, they were admiring, devoted, exemplary in the relations of private life. Possibly when the professor insisted a little too emphatically upon the inferiority of women, he was concerned not with their inferiority, but with his own superiority. That was what he was protecting rather hot-headedly and with too much emphasis, because it was a jewel to him of the rarest price. Life for both sexes—and I looked at them, shouldering their way along the pavement—is arduous, difficult, a perpetual struggle. It calls for gigantic courage and strength. More than anything, perhaps, creatures of illusion as we are, it calls for confidence in oneself. Without self-confidence we are as babes in the cradle. And how can we generate this imponderable quality, which is yet so invaluable, most quickly? By thinking that other people are inferior to oneself. By feeling that one has some innate superiority—it may be wealth, or rank, a straight nose, or the portrait of a grandfather by Romney—for there is no end to the pathetic devices of the human imagination—over other people.[15] Hence the enormous importance to a patriarch who has to conquer, who has to rule, of feeling that great numbers of people, half the human race indeed, are by nature inferior to himself. It must indeed be one of the chief sources of his power. But let me turn the light of this observation on to real life, I thought. Does it help to explain some of those psychological puzzles that one notes in the margin of daily life? Does it explain my astonishment the other day when Z, most humane, most modest of men, taking up some book by Rebecca West and reading a passage in it, exclaimed, "The arrant feminist! She says that men are snobs!"[16] The exclamation, to me so surprising— for why was Miss West an arrant feminist for making a possibly true if uncomplimentary statement about the other sex?—was not merely the cry of wounded vanity; it was a protest against some infringement of his power to believe in himself. Women have served all these centuries as looking-glasses possessing the magic and delicious power of reflecting the figure of man at twice its natural size. Without that power probably the earth would still be swamp and jungle. The glories of all our wars would be unknown. We should still be scratching the outlines of deer on the remains of mutton bones and bartering flints for sheepskins or whatever simple ornament took our unsophisticated taste. Supermen and Fingers of Destiny would never have existed. The Czar and the Kaiser would never have worn their crowns or lost them. Whatever may be their use in civilized societies, mirrors are essential to all violent and heroic action. That is why Napoleon and Mussolini both insist so emphatically upon the inferiority of women, for if they were not inferior, they would cease to enlarge. That serves to explain in part the necessity that women so often are to men. And it serves to explain how restless they are under her criticism; how impossible it is for her to say to them this book is bad, this picture is feeble, or whatever it may be, without giving far more pain and rousing far more anger than a man would do who gave the same criticism. For if she begins to tell the truth, the figure in the looking-glass shrinks; his fitness for life is diminished. How is he to go on giving judgment, civilizing natives, making laws, writing books, dressing up and speechifying at banquets, unless he can see himself at breakfast and at dinner at least twice the size he really is? So I reflected, crumbling my bread and stirring my coffee and

15. George Romney (1734–1802) was an English portrait painter whose patrons were aristocrats.
16. Rebecca West (1892–1983) was a novelist and jour-
nalist of Scottish-Irish descent and a chronicler of the women's suffrage movement.

now and again looking at the people in the street. The looking-glass vision is of supreme importance because it charges the vitality; it stimulates the nervous system. Take it away and man may die, like the drug fiend deprived of his cocaine. Under the spell of that illusion, I thought, looking out of the window, half the people on the pavement are striding to work. They put on their hats and coats in the morning under its agreeable rays. They start the day confident, braced, believing themselves desired at Miss Smith's tea party; they say to themselves as they go into the room, I am the superior of half the people here, and it is thus that they speak with that self-confidence, that self-assurance, which have had such profound consequences in public life and lead to such curious notes in the margin of the private mind.

But these contributions to the dangerous and fascinating subject of the psychology of the other sex—it is one, I hope, that you will investigate when you have five hundred a year of your own—were interrupted by the necessity of paying the bill. It came to five shillings and ninepence. I gave the waiter a ten-shilling note and he went to bring me change. There was another ten-shilling note in my purse; I noticed it, because it is a fact that still takes my breath away—the power of my purse to breed ten-shilling notes automatically. I open it and there they are. Society gives me chicken and coffee, bed and lodging, in return for a certain number of pieces of paper which were left me by an aunt, for no other reason than that I share her name.

My aunt, Mary Beton, I must tell you, died by a fall from her horse when she was riding out to take the air in Bombay. The news of my legacy reached me one night about the same time that the act was passed that gave votes to women. A solicitor's letter fell into the postbox and when I opened it I found that she had left me five hundred pounds a year forever. Of the two—the vote and the money—the money, I own, seemed infinitely the more important. Before that I had made my living by cadging odd jobs from newspapers, by reporting a donkey show here or a wedding there; I had earned a few pounds by addressing envelopes, reading to old ladies, making artificial flowers, teaching the alphabet to small children in a kindergarten. Such were the chief occupations that were open to women before 1918. I need not, I am afraid, describe in any detail the hardness of the work, for you know perhaps women who have done it; nor the difficulty of living on the money when it was earned, for you may have tried. But what still remains with me as a worse infliction than either was the poison of fear and bitterness which those days bred in me. To begin with, always to be doing work that one did not wish to do, and to do it like a slave, flattering and fawning, not always necessarily perhaps, but it seemed necessary and the stakes were too great to run risks; and then the thought of that one gift which it was death to hide—a small one but dear to the possessor—perishing and with it myself, my soul—all this became like a rust eating away the bloom of the spring, destroying the tree at its heart. However, as I say, my aunt died; and whenever I change a ten-shilling note a little of that rust and corrosion is rubbed off; fear and bitterness go. Indeed, I thought, slipping the silver into my purse, it is remarkable, remembering the bitterness of those days, what a change of temper a fixed income will bring about. No force in the world can take from me my five hundred pounds. Food, house and clothing are mine for ever. Therefore not merely do effort and labor cease, but also hatred and bitterness. I need not hate any man; he cannot hurt me. I need not flatter any man; he has nothing to give me. So imperceptibly I found myself adopting a new attitude towards the other half of the human race. It was absurd to blame any class or any sex, as a whole. Great bodies of people are never responsible for what they do. They are driven by instincts which are not within their control. They too, the patriarchs, the professors, had endless difficulties, terrible drawbacks to contend with. Their education had been in some ways as faulty as my own. It had bred in them defects as great. True, they had money and power, but only at the cost of harboring in their breasts an eagle, a vulture, forever tearing the liver out and plucking at the lungs—the instinct for possession, the rage for acquisition which drives them to desire other people's fields and goods perpetually; to make frontiers and flags; battle-ships and poison gas; to offer up their own lives and their children's lives. Walk through the Admiralty Arch (I had reached that monument), or any other avenue given up to trophies and cannon, and reflect upon the kind of glory celebrated there. Or watch in the spring sunshine the stockbroker and the great barrister going indoors to make money and more money and more money when it is a fact that five hundred pounds a year will keep one alive in the sunshine. These are unpleasant instincts to harbor, I reflected. They are bred of the conditions of life; of the lack of civilization, I thought, looking at the statue of the Duke of Cambridge, and in particular at the feathers in his cocked hat, with a fixity that they have scarcely ever received before. And, as I realized these drawbacks, by degrees fear and bitterness modified them-selves into pity and toleration; and then in a year or two, pity and toleration went, and the greatest release of all came, which is freedom to think of things in them-selves. That building, for example, do I like it or not? Is that picture beautiful or not? Is that in my opinion a good book or a bad? Indeed my aunt's legacy unveiled the sky to me, and substituted for the large and imposing figure of a gentleman, which Mil-ton recommended for my perpetual adoration, a view of the open sky.

So thinking, so speculating, I found my way back to my house by the river. Lamps were being lit and an indescribable change had come over London since the morning hour. It was as if the great machine after laboring all day had made with our help a few yards of something very exciting and beautiful—a fiery fabric flashing with red eyes, a tawny monster roaring with hot breath. Even the wind seemed flung like a flag as it lashed the houses and rattled the hoardings.

In my little street, however, domesticity prevailed. The house painter was descending his ladder; the nursemaid was wheeling the perambulator carefully in and out back to nursery tea; the coal-heaver was folding his empty sacks on top of each other; the woman who keeps the green-grocer's shop was adding up the day's takings with her hands in red mittens. But so engrossed was I with the problem you have laid upon my shoulders that I could not see even these usual sights without referring them to one center. I thought how much harder it is now than it must have been even a century ago to say which of these employments is the higher, the more necessary. Is it better to be a coal-heaver or a nursemaid; is the charwoman who has brought up eight children of less value to the world than the barrister who has made a hundred thousand pounds? It is useless to ask such questions; for nobody can answer them. Not only do the comparative values of charwomen and lawyers rise and fall from decade to decade, but we have no rods with which to measure them even as they are at the moment. I had been foolish to ask my professor to furnish me with "indis-putable proofs" of this or that in his argument about women. Even if one could state the value of any one gift at the moment, those values will change; in a century's time very possibly they will have changed completely. Moreover, in a hundred years, I thought, reaching my own doorstep, women will have ceased to be the protected sex. Logically they will take part in all the activities and exertions that were once denied them. The nursemaid will heave coal. The shop-woman will drive an engine. All assumptions founded on the facts observed when women were the protected sex will have disappeared—as, for example (here a squad of soldiers marched down the street), that women and clergymen and gardeners live longer than other people. Remove that protection, expose them to the same exertions and activities, make them soldiers and sailors and engine-drivers and dock laborers, and will not women die off so much younger, so much quicker, than men that one will say, "I saw a woman today," as one used to say, "I saw an aeroplane"? Anything may happen when womanhood has ceased to be a protected occupation, I thought, opening the door. But what bearing has all this upon the subject of my paper, Women and Fiction? I asked, going indoors.

THREE

It was disappointing not to have brought back in the evening some important statement, some authentic fact. Women are poorer than men because—this or that. Perhaps now it would be better to give up seeking for the truth, and receiving on one's head an avalanche of opinion hot as lava, discolored as dish-water. It would be better to draw the curtains; to shut out distractions; to light the lamp; to narrow the enquiry and to ask the historian, who records not opinions but facts, to describe under what conditions women lived, not throughout the ages, but in England, say in the time of Elizabeth.[17]

For it is a perennial puzzle why no woman wrote a word of that extraordinary literature when every other man, it seemed, was capable of song or sonnet. What were the conditions in which women lived, I asked myself; for fiction, imaginative work that is, is not dropped like a pebble upon the ground, as science may be; fiction is like a spider's web, attached ever so lightly perhaps, but still attached to life at all four corners. Often the attachment is scarcely perceptible; Shakespeare's plays, for instance, seem to hang there complete by themselves. But when the web is pulled askew, hooked up at the edge, torn in the middle, one remembers that these webs are not spun in mid-air by incorporeal creatures, but are the work of suffering human beings, and are attached to grossly material things, like health and money and the houses we live in.

I went, therefore, to the shelf where the histories stand and took down one of the latest, Professor Trevelyan's *History of England*.[18] Once more I looked up Women, found "position of," and turned to the pages indicated. "Wife-beating," I read, "was a recognized right of man, and was practiced without shame by high as well as low. . . . Similarly," the historian goes on, "the daughter who refused to marry the gentleman of her parents' choice was liable to be locked up, beaten and flung about the room, without any shock being inflicted on public opinion. Marriage was not an affair of personal affection, but of family avarice, particularly in the 'chivalrous' upper classes. . . . Betrothal often took place while one or both of the parties was in the cradle, and marriage when they were scarcely out of the nurses' charge." That was about 1470, soon after Chaucer's time.[19] The next reference to the position of women is some two hundred years later, in the time of the Stuarts. "It was still the exception for women of the upper and middle class to choose their own husbands, and when the husband had been assigned, he was lord and master, so far at least as law and custom could make him. Yet even so," Professor Trevelyan

17. Elizabeth I was queen of England from 1558 to 1603.
18. Sir George Macaulay Trevelyan (1876–1962) was a historian and a professor at Cambridge; his *History of*

England appeared in 1926.
19. Geoffrey Chaucer (c. 1340–1400) wrote *The Canterbury Tales* in the 1380s.

concludes, "neither Shakespeare's women nor those of authentic seventeenth-century memoirs, like the Verneys and the Hutchinsons, seem wanting in personality and character." Certainly, if we consider it, Cleopatra must have had a way with her; Lady Macbeth, one would suppose, had a will of her own; Rosalind, one might conclude, was an attractive girl.[20] Professor Trevelyan is speaking no more than the truth when he remarks that Shakespeare's women do not seem wanting in personality and character. Not being a historian, one might go even further and say that women have burnt like beacons in all the works of all the poets from the beginning of time—Clytemnestra, Antigone, Cleopatra, Lady Macbeth, Phèdre, Cressida, Rosalind, Desdemona, the Duchess of Malfi, among the dramatists; then among the prose writers: Millamant, Clarissa, Becky Sharp, Anna Karenina, Emma Bovary, Madame de Guermantes—the names flock to mind, nor do they recall women "lacking in personality and character."[21] Indeed, if woman had no existence save in the fiction written by men, one would imagine her a person of the utmost importance; very various; heroic and mean; splendid and sordid; infinitely beautiful and hideous in the extreme; as great as a man; some think even greater.[22] But this is woman in fiction. In fact, as Professor Trevelyan points out, she was locked up, beaten and flung about the room.

A very queer, composite being thus emerges. Imaginatively she is of the highest importance; practically she is completely insignificant. She pervades poetry from cover to cover; she is all but absent from history. She dominates the lives of kings and conquerors in fiction; in fact she was the slave of any boy whose parents forced a ring upon her finger. Some of the most inspired words, some of the most profound thoughts in literature fall from her lips; in real life she could hardly read, could scarcely spell, and was the property of her husband.

It was certainly an odd monster that one made up by reading the historians first and the poets afterwards—a worm winged like an eagle; the spirit of life and beauty in a kitchen chopping up suet. But these monsters, however amusing to the imagination, have no existence in fact. What one must do to bring her to life was to think poetically and prosaically at one and the same moment, thus keeping in touch with fact—that she is Mrs. Martin, aged thirty-six, dressed in blue, wearing a black hat and brown shoes; but not losing sight of fiction either—that she is a vessel in which all sorts of spirits and forces are coursing and flashing perpetually. The moment, however, that one tries this method with the Elizabethan woman, one branch of illumination fails; one is held up by the scarcity of facts. One knows nothing detailed, nothing perfectly true and substantial about her. History scarcely mentions her. And

20. Female protagonists in Shakespeare's *Antony and Cleopatra, Macbeth,* and *As You Like It.*

21. Characters in Aeschylus's *Agamemnon;* Sophocles' *Antigone;* Shakespeare's *Antony and Cleopatra* and *Macbeth;* Racine's *Phèdre;* Shakespeare's *Troilus and Cressida, As You Like It,* and *Othello;* Webster's *The Duchess of Malfi;* Congreve's *The Way of the World;* Richardson's *Clarissa;* Thackeray's *Vanity Fair;* Tolstoy's *Anna Karenina;* Flaubert's *Madame Bovary;* and Proust's *Remembrance of Things Past.*

22. ["It remains a strange and almost inexplicable fact that in Athena's city, where women were kept in almost Oriental suppression as odalisques or drudges, the stage should yet have produced figures like Clytemnestra and Cassandra, Atossa and Antigone, Phèdre and Medea, and all the other heroines who dominate play after play of the 'misogynist' Euripides. But the paradox of this world where in real life a respectable woman could hardly show her face alone in the street, and yet on the stage woman equals or surpasses man, has never been satisfactorily explained. In modern tragedy the same predominance exists. At all events, a very cursory survey of Shakespeare's work (similarly with Webster, though not with Marlowe or Jonson) suffices to reveal how this dominance, this initiative of women, persists from Rosalind to Lady Macbeth. So too in Racine; six of his tragedies bear their heroines' names; and what male characters of his shall we set against Hermione and Andromaque, Bérénice and Roxane, Phèdre and Athalie? So again with Ibsen; what men shall we match with Solveig and Nora, Hedda and Hilda Wangel and Rebecca West?"—F. L. LUCAS, *Tragedy,* pp. 114–15.]

I turned to Professor Trevelyan again to see what history meant to him. I found by looking at his chapter headings that it meant—

"The Manor Court and the Methods of Open-field Agriculture . . . The Cistercians and Sheep-farming . . . The Crusades . . . The University . . . The House of Commons . . . The Hundreds Years' War . . . The Wars of the Roses . . . The Renaissance Scholars . . . The Dissolution of the Monasteries . . . Agrarian and Religious Strife . . . The Origin of English Sea-power . . . The Armanda . . ." and so on. Occasionally an individual woman is mentioned, an Elizabeth, or a Mary; a queen or a great lady. But by no possible means could middle-class women with nothing but brains and character at their command have taken part in any one of the great movements which, brought together, constitute the historian's view of the past. Nor shall we find her in any collection of anecdotes. Aubrey hardly mentions her. She never writes her own life and scarcely keeps a diary; there are only a handful of her letters in existence. She left no plays or poems by which we can judge her. What one wants, I thought—and why does not some brilliant student at Newnham or Girton supply it?—is a mass of information; at what age did she marry; how many children had she as a rule; what was her house like; had she a room to herself; did she do the cooking; would she be likely to have a servant? All these facts lie somewhere, presumably, in parish registers and account books; the life of the average Elizabethan woman must be scattered about somewhere, could one collect it and make a book of it. It would be ambitious beyond my daring, I thought, looking about the shelves for books that were not there, to suggest to the students of those famous colleges that they should re-write history, though I own that it often seems a little queer as it is, unreal, lop-sided; but why should they not add a supplement to history? calling it, of course, by some inconspicuous name so that women might figure there without impropriety? For one often catches a glimpse of them in the lives of the great, whisking away into the background, concealing, I sometimes think, a wink, a laugh, perhaps a tear. And, after all, we have lives enough of Jane Austen; it scarcely seems necessary to consider again the influence of the tragedies of Joanna Baillie upon the poetry of Edgar Allan Poe;[23] as for myself, I should not mind if the homes and haunts of Mary Russell Mitford were closed to the public for a century at least. But what I find deplorable, I continued, looking about the bookshelves again, is that nothing is known about women before the eighteenth century. I have no model in my mind to turn about this way and that. Here am I asking why women did not write poetry in the Elizabethan age, and I am not sure how they were educated; whether they were taught to write; whether they had sitting-rooms to themselves; how many women had children before they were twenty-one; what, in short, they did from eight in the morning till eight at night. They had no money evidently; according to Professor Trevelyan they were married whether they liked it or not before they were out of the nursery, at fifteen or sixteen very likely. It would have been extremely odd, even upon this showing, had one of them suddenly written the plays of Shakespeare, I concluded, and I thought of that old gentleman, who is dead now, but was a bishop, I think, who declared that it was impossible for any woman, past, present, or to come, to have the genius of Shakespeare. He wrote to the papers about it. He also told a lady who applied to him for information that cats do not as a matter of fact go to heaven, though they have, he added, souls of a sort. How much

---

23. Joanna Baillie (1762–1851) was a popular Scottish dramatist and poet; Edgar Allan Poe (1809–1849) was an American poet and writer of horror and detective fiction.

thinking those old gentlemen used to save one! How the borders of ignorance shrank back at their approach! Cats do not go to heaven. Women cannot write the plays of Shakespeare.

Be that as it may, I could not help thinking, as I looked at the works of Shakespeare on the shelf, that the bishop was right at least in this; it would have been impossible, completely and entirely, for any woman to have written the plays of Shakespeare in the age of Shakespeare. Let me imagine, since facts are so hard to come by, what would have happened had Shakespeare had a wonderfully gifted sister, called Judith, let us say. Shakespeare himself went, very probably—his mother was an heiress—to the grammar school, where he may have learnt Latin—Ovid, Virgil and Horace—and the elements of grammar and logic.[24] He was, it is well known, a wild boy who poached rabbits, perhaps shot a deer, and had, rather sooner than he should have done, to marry a woman in the neighborhood, who bore him a child rather quicker than was right. That escapade sent him to seek his fortune in London. He had, it seemed, a taste for the theater; he began by holding horses at the stage door. Very soon he got work in the theater, became a successful actor, and lived at the hub of the universe, meeting everybody, knowing everybody, practicing his art on the boards, exercising his wits in the streets, and even getting access to the palace of the queen. Meanwhile his extraordinarily gifted sister, let us suppose, remained at home. She was as adventurous, as imaginative, as agog to see the world as he was. But she was not sent to school. She had no chance of learning grammar and logic, let alone of reading Horace and Virgil. She picked up a book now and then, one of her brother's perhaps, and read a few pages. But then her parents came in and told her to mend the stockings or mind the stew and not moon about with books and papers. They would have spoken sharply but kindly, for they were substantial people who knew the conditions of life for a woman and loved their daughter—indeed, more likely than not she was the apple of her father's eye. Perhaps she scribbled some pages up in an apple loft on the sly, but was careful to hide them or set fire to them. Soon, however, before she was out of her teens, she was to be betrothed to the son of a neighboring wool-stapler. She cried out that marriage was hateful to her, and for that she was severely beaten by her father. Then he ceased to scold her. He begged her instead not to hurt him, not to shame him in the matter of her marriage. He would give her a chain of beads or a fine petticoat, he said; and there were tears in his eyes. How could she disobey him? How could she break his heart? The force of her own gift alone drove her to it. She made up a small parcel of her belongings, let herself down by a rope one summer's night and took the road to London. She was not seventeen. The birds that sang in the hedge were not more musical than she was. She had the quickest fancy, a gift like her brother's, for the tune of words. Like him, she had a taste for the theater. She stood at the stage door; she wanted to act, she said. Men laughed in her face. The manager—a fat, loose-lipped man—guffawed. He bellowed something about poodles dancing and women acting—no woman, he said, could possibly be an actress. He hinted—you can imagine what. She could get no training in her craft. Could she even seek her dinner in a tavern or roam the streets at midnight? Yet her genius was for fiction and lusted to feed abundantly upon the lives of men and women and the study of their ways. At last—for she was very young, oddly like Shakespeare the poet in her face, with the same grey eyes and rounded brows—at last Nick Greene the

---

24. Ovid, Virgil, and Horace were the Latin poets of the Augustan period (27 BCE–14 CE) whose works were taught in English primary school.

actor-manager took pity on her; she found herself with child by that gentleman and so—who shall measure the heat and violence of the poet's heart when caught and tangled in a woman's body?—killed herself one winter's night and lies buried at some crossroads where the omnibuses now stop outside the Elephant and Castle.

That, more or less, is how the story would run, I think, if a woman in Shakespeare's day had had Shakespeare's genius. But for my part, I agree with the deceased bishop, if such he was—it is unthinkable that any woman in Shakespeare's day should have had Shakespeare's genius. For genius like Shakespeare's is not born among laboring, uneducated, servile people. It was not born in England among the Saxons and the Britons. It is not born today among the working classes. How, then, could it have been born among women whose work began, according to Professor Trevelyan, almost before they were out of the nursery, who were forced to it by their parents and held to it by all the power of law and custom? Yet genius of a sort must have existed among women as it must have existed among the working classes. Now and again an Emily Brontë or a Robert Burns blazes out and proves its presence.[25] But certainly it never got itself on to paper. When, however, one reads of a witch being ducked, of a woman possessed by devils, of a wise woman selling herbs, or even of a very remarkable man who had a mother, then I think we are on the track of a lost novelist, a suppressed poet, of some mute and inglorious Jane Austen, some Emily Brontë who dashed her brains out on the moor or mopped and mowed about the highways crazed with the torture that her gift had put her to. Indeed, I would venture to guess that Anon, who wrote so many poems without signing them, was often a woman. It was a woman Edward Fitzgerald, I think, suggested who made the ballads and the folk-songs, crooning them to her children, beguiling her spinning with them, or the length of the winter's night.[26]

This may be true or it may be false—who can say?—but what is true in it, so it seemed to me, reviewing the story of Shakespeare's sister as I had made it, is that any woman born with a great gift in the sixteenth century would certainly have gone crazed, shot herself, or ended her days in some lonely cottage outside the village, half witch, half wizard, feared and mocked at. For it needs little skill in psychology to be sure that a highly gifted girl who had tried to use her gift for poetry would have been so thwarted and hindered by other people, so tortured and pulled asunder by her own contrary instincts, that she must have lost her health and sanity to a certainty. No girl could have walked to London and stood at a stage door and forced her way into the presence of actor-managers without doing herself a violence and suffering an anguish which may have been irrational—for chastity may be a fetish invented by certain societies for unknown reasons—but were none the less inevitable. Chastity had then, it has even now, a religious importance in a woman's life, and has so wrapped itself round with nerves and instincts that to cut it free and bring it to the light of day demands courage of the rarest. To have lived a free life in London in the sixteenth century would have meant for a woman who was poet and playwright a nervous stress and dilemma which might well have killed her. Had she survived, whatever she had written would have been twisted and deformed, issuing from a strained and morbid imagination. And undoubtedly, I thought, looking at the shelf where there are no plays by women, her work would have gone unsigned. That refuge

---

25. Emily Brontë was an English poet and the author of the novel *Wuthering Heights* (1847); Robert Burns (1759–96) was a Scottish poet who wrote in dialect.

26. Edward Fitzgerald (1809–83) as an English poet and translator.

she would have sought certainly. It was the relic of the sense of chastity that dictated anonymity to women even so late as the nineteenth century. Currer Bell, George Eliot, George Sand, all the victims of inner strife as their writings prove, sought ineffectively to veil themselves by using the name of a man.[27] Thus they did homage to the convention, which if not implanted by the other sex was liberally encouraged by them (the chief glory of a woman is not to be talked of, said Pericles, himself a much-talked-of man), that publicity in women is detestable.[28] Anonymity runs in their blood. The desire to be veiled still possesses them. They are not even now as concerned about the health of their fame as men are, and, speaking generally, will pass a tombstone or a signpost without feeling an irresistible desire to cut their names on it, as Alf, Bert or Chas. must do in obedience to their instinct, which murmurs if it sees a fine woman go by, or even a dog, Ce chien est à moi. And, of course, it may not be a dog, I thought, remembering Parliament Square, the Sièges Allée and other avenues; it may be a piece of land or a man with curly black hair. It is one of the great advantages of being a woman that one can pass even a very fine negress without wishing to make an Englishwoman of her.

That woman, then, who was born with a gift of poetry in the sixteenth century, was an unhappy woman, a woman at strife against herself. All the conditions of her life, all her own instincts, were hostile to the state of mind which is needed to set free whatever is in the brain. But what is the state of mind that is most propitious to the act of creation, I asked. Can one come by any notion of the state that furthers and makes possible that strange activity? Here I opened the volume containing the Tragedies of Shakespeare. What was Shakespeare's state of mind, for instance, when he wrote Lear and Antony and Cleopatra? It was certainly the state of mind most favorable to poetry that there has ever existed. But Shakespeare himself said nothing about it. We only know casually and by chance that he "never blotted a line." Nothing indeed was ever said by the artist himself about his state of mind until the eighteenth century perhaps. Rousseau perhaps began it. At any rate, by the nineteenth century self-consciousness had developed so far that it was the habit for men of letters to describe their minds in confessions and autobiographies. Their lives also were written, and their letters were printed after their deaths. Thus, though we do not know what Shakespeare went through when he wrote Lear, we do know what Carlyle went through when he wrote the French Revolution; what Flaubert went through when he wrote Madame Bovary; what Keats was going through when he tried to write poetry against the coming of death and the indifference of the world.[29]

And one gathers from this enormous modern literature of confession and self-analysis that to write a work of genius is almost always a feat of prodigious difficulty. Everything is against the likelihood that it will come from the writer's mind whole and entire. Generally material circumstances are against it. Dogs will bark; people will interrupt; money must be made; health will break down. Further, accentuating all these difficulties and making them harder to bear is the world's notorious indifference. It does not ask people to write poems and novels and histories; it does not need them. It does not care whether Flaubert finds the right word or whether Carlyle scrupulously

27. The pen names of Charlotte Brontë, Mary Ann Evans, and Aurore Dupin.
28. Pericles (495–29 BCE) was an Athenian orator and statesman.
29. Jean-Jacques Rousseau (1712–78) was a French philosopher and the author of Confessions (1781); Thomas Carlyle (1795–1881) was a British writer and historian; Gustave Flaubert (1821–80) was a French novelist; John Keats (1795–1821) was a British Romantic poet.

verifies this or that fact. Naturally, it will not pay for what it does not want. And so the writer, Keats, Flaubert, Carlyle, suffers, especially in the creative years of youth, every form of distraction and discouragement. A curse, a cry of agony, rises from those books of analysis and confession. "Mighty poets in their misery dead"—that is the burden of their song. If anything comes through in spite of all this, it is a miracle, and probably no book is born entire and uncrippled as it was conceived.

But for women, I thought, looking at the empty shelves, these difficulties were infinitely more formidable. In the first place, to have a room of her own, let alone a quiet room or a sound-proof room, was out of the question, unless her parents were exceptionally rich or very noble, even up to the beginning of the nineteenth century. Since her pin money, which depended on the good will of her father, was only enough to keep her clothed, she was debarred from such alleviations as came even to Keats or Tennyson or Carlyle, all poor men, from a walking tour, a little journey to France, from the separate lodging which, even if it were miserable enough, sheltered them from the claims and tyrannies of their families. Such material difficulties were formidable; but much worse were the immaterial. The indifference of the world which Keats and Flaubert and other men of genius have found so hard to bear was in her case not indifference but hostility. The world did not say to her as it said to them, Write if you choose; it makes no difference to me. The world said with a guffaw, Write? What's the good of your writing? Here the psychologists of Newnham and Girton might come to our help, I thought, looking again at the blank spaces on the shelves. For surely it is time that the effect of discouragement upon the mind of the artist should be measured, as I have seen a dairy company measure the effect of ordinary milk and Grade A milk upon the body of the rat. They set two rats in cages side by side, and of the two one was furtive, timid and small, and the other was glossy, bold and big. Now what food do we feed women as artists upon? I asked, remembering, I suppose, that dinner of prunes and custard. To answer the question I had only to open the evening paper and to read that Lord Birkenhead is of opinion—but really I am not going to trouble to copy out Lord Birkenhead's opinion upon the writing of women. What Dean Inge says I will leave in peace. The Harley Street specialist may be allowed to rouse the echoes of Harley Street with his vociferations without raising a hair on my head. I will quote, however, Mr. Oscar Browning, because Mr. Oscar Browning was a great figure in Cambridge at one time, and used to examine the students at Girton and Newnham.[30] Mr. Oscar Browning was wont to declare "that the impression left on his mind, after looking over any set of examination papers, was that, irrespective of the marks he might give, the best woman was intellectually the inferior of the worst man." After saying that Mr. Browning went back to his rooms—and it is this sequel that endears him and makes him a human figure of some bulk and majesty—he went back to his rooms and found a stable-boy lying on the sofa—"a mere skeleton, his cheeks were cavernous and sallow, his teeth were black, and he did not appear to have the full use of his limbs. . . . 'That's Arthur' [said Mr. Browning]. 'He's a dear boy really and most high-minded.'" The two pictures always seem to me to complete each other. And happily in this age of biography the two pictures often do complete each other, so that we are able to interpret the opinions of great men not only by what they say, but by what they do.

---

30. Oscar Browning, or O.B. as he was known, was a writer, a permanent Fellow of Kings College, Cambridge, and a homosexual whom Woolf considered misogynist; see Jane Marcus, *Virginia Woolf and the Languages of Patriarchy* (Indiana UP, 1987), ch. 8 163–213.

But though this is possible now, such opinions coming from the lips of important people must have been formidable enough even fifty years ago. Let us suppose that a father from the highest motives did not wish his daughter to leave home and become writer, painter or scholar. "See what Mr. Oscar Browning says," he would say; and there was not only Mr. Oscar Browning; there was the *Saturday Review*; there was Mr. Greg—the "essentials of a woman's being," said Mr. Greg emphatically, "are that *they are supported by, and they minister to, men*"—there was an enormous body of masculine opinion to the effect that nothing could be expected of women intellectually. Even if her father did not read out loud these opinions, any girl could read them for herself; and the reading, even in the nineteenth century, must have lowered her vitality, and told profoundly upon her work. There would always have been that assertion—you cannot do this, you are incapable of doing that—to protest against, to overcome. Probably for a novelist this germ is no longer of much effect; for there have been women novelists of merit. But for painters it must still have some sting in it; and for musicians, I imagine, is even now active and poisonous in the extreme. The woman composer stands where the actress stood in the time of Shakespeare. Nick Greene, I thought, remembering the story I had made about Shakespeare's sister, said that a woman acting put him in mind of a dog dancing. Johnson repeated the phrase two hundred years later of women preaching. And here, I said, opening a book about music, we have the very words used again in this year of grace, 1928, of women who try to write music. "Of Mlle. Germaine Tailleferre one can only repeat Dr. Johnson's dictum concerning a woman preacher, transposed into terms of music. 'Sir, a woman's composing is like a dog's walking on his hind legs. It is not done well, but you are surprised to find it done at all.'"[31] So accurately does history repeat itself.

Thus, I concluded, shutting Mr. Oscar Browning's life and pushing away the rest, it is fairly evident that even in the nineteenth century a woman was not encouraged to be an artist. On the contrary, she was snubbed, slapped, lectured and exhorted. Her mind must have been strained and her vitality lowered by the need of opposing this, of disproving that. For here again we come within range of that very interesting and obscure masculine complex which has had so much influence upon the woman's movement; that deep-seated desire, not so much that *she* shall be inferior as that *he* shall be superior, which plants him wherever one looks, not only in front of the arts, but barring the way to politics too, even when the risk to himself seems infinitesimal and the suppliant humble and devoted. Even Lady Bessborough, I remembered, with all her passion for politics, must humbly bow herself and write to Lord Granville Leveson-Gower: ". . . notwithstanding all my violence in politics and talking so much on that subject, I perfectly agree with you that no woman has any business to meddle with that or any other serious business, farther than giving her opinion (if she is ask'd)."[32] And so she goes on to spend her enthusiasm where it meets with no obstacle whatsoever upon that immensely important subject, Lord Granville's maiden speech in the House of Commons. The spectacle is certainly a strange one, I thought. The history of men's opposition to women's emancipation is more interesting perhaps than the story of that emancipation itself. An amusing book might be made of it if some young student at Girton or Newnham would collect examples and deduce a theory—but she would need thick gloves on her hands, and bars to protect her of solid gold.

31. [*A Survey of Contemporary Music*, Cecil Gray, p. 246.]
32. Lord Granville Leveson-Gower (1758–1833) was an English politician and philanthropist.

But what is amusing now, I recollected, shutting Lady Bessborough, had to be taken in desperate earnest once. Opinions that one now pastes in a book labelled cock-a-doodle-dum and keeps for reading to select audiences on summer nights once drew tears, I can assure you. Among your grandmothers and great-grandmothers there were many that wept their eyes out. Florence Nightingale shrieked aloud in her agony.[33] Moreover, it is all very well for you, who have got yourselves to college and enjoy sitting-rooms—or is it only bed-sitting-rooms?—of your own to say that genius should disregard such opinions; that genius should be above caring what is said of it. Unfortunately, it is precisely the men or women of genius who mind most what is said of them. Remember Keats. Remember the words he had cut on his tombstone. Think of Tennyson; think—but I need hardly multiply instances of the undeniable, if very unfortunate, fact that it is the nature of the artist to mind excessively what is said about him. Literature is strewn with the wreckage of men who have minded beyond reason the opinions of others.

And this susceptibility of theirs is doubly unfortunate, I thought, returning again to my original enquiry into what state of mind is most propitious for creative work, because the mind of an artist, in order to achieve the prodigious effort of freeing whole and entire the work that is in him, must be incandescent, like Shakespeare's mind, I conjectured, looking at the book which lay open at *Antony and Cleopatra*. There must be no obstacle in it, no foreign matter unconsumed.

For though we say that we know nothing about Shakespeare's state of mind, even as we say that, we are saying something about Shakespeare's state of mind. The reason perhaps why we know so little of Shakespeare—compared with Donne or Ben Jonson or Milton—is that his grudges and spites and antipathies are hidden from us.[34] We are not held up by some "revelation" which reminds us of the writer. All desire to protest, to preach, to proclaim an injury, to pay off a score, to make the world the witness of some hardship or grievance was fired out of him and consumed. Therefore his poetry flows from him free and unimpeded. If ever a human being got his work expressed completely, it was Shakespeare. If ever a mind was incandescent, unimpeded, I thought, turning again to the bookcase, it was Shakespeare's mind.

Four

That one would find any woman in that state of mind in the sixteenth century was obviously impossible. One has only to think of the Elizabethan tombstones with all those children kneeling with clasped hands; and their early deaths; and to see their houses with their dark, cramped rooms, to realize that no woman could have written poetry then. What one would expect to find would be that rather later perhaps some great lady would take advantage of her comparative freedom and comfort to publish something with her name to it and risk being thought a monster. Men, of course, are not snobs, I continued, carefully eschewing "the arrant feminism" of Miss Rebecca West; but they appreciate with sympathy for the most part the efforts of a countess to write verse. One would expect to find a lady of title meeting with far greater encouragement than an unknown Miss Austen or a Miss Brontë at that time would have

---

33. [See *Cassandra*, by Florence Nightingale, printed in *The Cause*, by R. Strachey.] Florence Nightingale (1820–1910) was a famous nurse and hospital administrator who founded a training school for midwives; she wrote a feminist tract, *Cassandra*, between 1852 and 1859, but it remained unpublished until 1928.

34. John Donne (1572–1631) was a poet and prose writer and the dean of St. Paul's Cathedral; Ben Jonson (1572–1637) was a dramatist and Shakespeare's most distinguished rival.

met with. But one would also expect to find that her mind was disturbed by alien emotions like fear and hatred and that her poems showed traces of that disturbance. Here is Lady Winchilsea, for example, I thought, taking down her poems.[35] She was born in the year 1661; she was noble both by birth and by marriage; she was childless; she wrote poetry, and one has only to open her poetry to find her bursting out in indignation against the position of women:

> How are we fallen! fallen by mistaken rules,
> And Education's more than Nature's fools;
> Debarred from all improvements of the mind,
> And to be dull, expected and designed;
> And if some one would soar above the rest,
> With warmer fancy, and ambition pressed,
> So strong the opposing faction still appears,
> The hopes to thrive can ne'er outweigh the fears.

Clearly her mind has by no means "consumed all impediments and become incandescent." On the contrary, it is harassed and distracted with hates and grievances. The human race is split up for her into two parties. Men are the "opposing faction"; men are hated and feared, because they have the power to bar her way to what she wants to do—which is to write.

> Alas! a woman that attempts the pen,
> Such a presumptuous creature is esteemed,
> The fault can by no virtue be redeemed.
> They tell us we mistake our sex and way;
> Good breeding, fashion, dancing, dressing, play,
> Are the accomplishments we should desire;
> To write, or read, or think, or to enquire,
> Would cloud our beauty, and exhaust our time,
> And interrupt the conquests of our prime,
> Whilst the dull manage of a servile house
> Is held by some our utmost art and use.

Indeed she has to encourage herself to write by supposing that what she writes will never be published; to soothe herself with the sad chant:

> To some few friends, and to thy sorrows sing,
> For groves of laurel thou wert never meant;
> Be dark enough thy shades, and be thou there content.

Yet it is clear that could she have freed her mind from hate and fear and not heaped it with bitterness and resentment, the fire was hot within her. Now and again words issue of pure poetry:

> Nor will in fading silks compose,
> Faintly the inimitable rose.

—they are rightly praised by Mr. Murry,[36] and Pope, it is thought, remembered and appropriated those others:

35. Anne Finch, Countess of Winchilsea was an eighteenth-century poet and a friend of Alexander Pope.
36. John Middleton Murry (1889–1957) was a literary critic who edited The Athenaeum (1919–21) and The Adelphi, which he founded in 1923.

> Now the jonquille o'ercomes the feeble brain;
> We faint beneath the aromatic pain.

It was a thousand pities that the woman who could write like that, whose mind was turned to nature and reflection, should have been forced to anger and bitterness. But how could she have helped herself? I asked, imagining the sneers and the laughter, the adulation of the toadies, the scepticism of the professional poet. She must have shut herself up in a room in the country to write, and been torn asunder by bitterness and scruples perhaps, though her husband was of the kindest, and their married life perfection. She "must have" I say, because when one comes to seek out the facts about Lady Winchilsea, one finds, as usual, that almost nothing is known about her. She suffered terribly from melancholy, which we can explain at least to some extent when we find her telling us how in the grip of it she would imagine:

> My lines decried, and my employment thought,
> An useless folly or presumptuous fault:

The employment, which was thus censured, was, as far as one can see, the harmless one of rambling about the fields and dreaming:

> My hand delights to trace unusual things,
> And deviates from the known and common way,
> Nor will in fading silks compose,
> Faintly the inimitable rose.

Naturally, if that was her habit and that was her delight, she could only expect to be laughed at; and, accordingly, Pope or Gay is said to have satirized her "as a blue-stocking with an itch for scribbling."[37] Also it is thought that she offended Gay by laughing at him. She said that his *Trivia* showed that "he was more proper to walk before a chair than to ride in one." But this is all "dubious gossip" and, says Mr. Murry, "uninteresting." But there I do not agree with him, for I should have liked to have had more even of dubious gossip so that I might have found out or made up some image of this melancholy lady, who loved wandering in the fields and thinking about unusual things and scorned, so rashly, so unwisely, "the dull manage of a servile house." But she became diffuse, Mr. Murry says. Her gift is all grown about with weeds and bound with briars. It had no chance of showing itself for the fine distinguished gift it was. And so, putting her back on the shelf, I turned to the other great lady, the Duchess whom Lamb loved, hare-brained, fantastical Margaret of Newcastle, her elder, but her contemporary.[38] They were very different, but alike in this that both were noble and both childless, and both were married to the best of husbands. In both burnt the same passion for poetry and both are disfigured and deformed by the same causes. Open the Duchess and one finds the same outburst of rage, "Women live like Bats or Owls, labor like Beasts, and die like Worms. . . ." Margaret too might have been a poet; in our day all that activity would have turned a wheel of some sort. As it was, what could bind, tame or civilize for human use that wild, generous, untutored intelligence? It poured itself out, higgledy-piggledy, in torments of rhyme and prose, poetry, and philosophy which stand congealed in quartos and folios that nobody ever reads. She should have had a microscope put in her hand. She should have been taught to look

---

37. John Gay (1685–1732) was an English poet and dramatist, his poem *Trivia, or, The Art of Walking the Streets of London*, appeared in 1716.

38. Margaret Cavendish, Duchess of Newcastle was a poet, playwright, and author of *Female Orations* (1662).

at the stars and reason scientifically. Her wits were turned with solitude and freedom. No one checked her. No one taught her. The professors fawned on her. At Court they jeered at her. Sir Egerton Brydges complained of her coarseness—"as flowing from a female of high rank brought up in the Courts."[39] She shut herself up at Welbeck alone.

What a vision of loneliness and riot the thought of Margaret Cavendish brings to mind! as if some giant cucumber had spread itself over all the roses and carnations in the garden and choked them to death. What a waste that the woman who wrote "the best bred women are those whose minds are civilest" should have frittered her time away scribbling nonsense and plunging ever deeper into obscurity and folly till the people crowded round her coach when she issued out. Evidently the crazy Duchess became a bogey to frighten clever girls with. Here, I remembered, putting away the Duchess and opening Dorothy Osborne's letters, is Dorothy writing to Temple about the Duchess's new book.[40] "Sure the poor woman is a little distracted, she could never be so ridiculous else as to venture at writing book's and in verse too, if I should not sleep this fortnight I should not come to that."

And so, since no woman of sense and modesty could write books, Dorothy, who was sensitive and melancholy, the very opposite of the Duchess in temper, wrote nothing. Letters did not count. A woman might write letters while she was sitting by her father's sick-bed. She could write them by the fire whilst the men talked without disturbing them. The strange thing is, I thought, turning over the pages of Dorothy's letters, what a gift that untaught and solitary girl had for the framing of a sentence, for the fashioning of a scene. Listen to her running on:

> After dinner we sit and talk till Mr. B. comes in question and then I am gone. The heat of the day is spent in reading or working and about six or seven a Clock, I walk out into a Common that lies hard by the house where a great many young wenches keep Sheep and Cows and sit in the shades singing of Ballads; I go to them and compare their voices and Beauties to some Ancient Shepherdesses that I have read of and find a vast difference there, but trust me I think these are as innocent as those could be. I talk to them, and find they want nothing to make them the happiest People in the world, but the knowledge that they are so. Most commonly when we are in the midst of our discourse one looks about her and spies her Cows going into the Corn and then away they all run, as if they had wings at their heels. I that am not so nimble stay behind, and when I see them driving home their Cattle I think tis time for me to retire too. When I have supped I go into the Garden and so to the side of a small River that runs by it where I sit down and wish you with me. . . .

One could have sworn that she had the makings of a writer in her. But "if I should not sleep this fortnight I should not come to that"—one can measure the opposition that was in the air to a woman writing when one finds that even a woman with a great turn for writing has brought herself to believe that to write a book was to be ridiculous, even to show oneself distracted. And so we come, I continued, replacing the single short volume of Dorothy Osborne's letters upon the shelf, to Mrs. Behn.[41]

And with Mrs. Behn we turn a very important corner on the road. We leave behind, shut up in their parks among their folios, those solitary great ladies who wrote without audience or criticism, for their own delight alone. We come to town and rub shoulders with ordinary people in the streets. Mrs. Behn was a middle-class woman with all the plebeian virtues of humor, vitality and courage; a woman forced

39. Sir Egerton Brydges (1762–1837) was an English writer and editor of seventeenth-century texts.
40. Dorothy Osborne (1627–95) was an English letter

writer known for her acerbic wit.
41. Aphra Behn was an English poet, playwright, and wit of the Restoration period.

by the death of her husband and some unfortunate adventures of her own to make her living by her wits. She had to work on equal terms with men. She made, by working very hard, enough to live on. The importance of that fact outweighs anything that she actually wrote, even the splendid, "A Thousand Martyrs I have made," or "Love in Fantastic Triumph sat," for here begins the freedom of the mind, or rather the possibility that in the course of time the mind will be free to write what it likes. For now that Aphra Behn had done it, girls could go to their parents and say, You need not give me an allowance; I can make money by my pen. Of course the answer for many years to come was, Yes, by living the life of Aphra Behn! Death would be better! and the door was slammed faster than ever. That profoundly interesting subject, the value that men set upon women's chastity and its effect upon their education, here suggests itself for discussion, and might provide an interesting book if any student at Girton or Newnham cared to go into the matter. Lady Dudley, sitting in diamonds among the midges of a Scottish moor, might serve for frontispiece. Lord Dudley, *The Times* said when Lady Dudley died the other day, "a man of cultivated taste and many accomplishments, was benevolent and bountiful, but whimsically despotic. He insisted upon his wife's wearing full dress, even at the remotest shooting-lodge in the Highlands; he loaded her with gorgeous jewels," and so on, "he gave her everything—always excepting any measure of responsibility." Then Lord Dudley had a stroke and she nursed him and ruled his estates with supreme competence for ever after. That whimsical despotism was in the nineteenth century too.

But to return. Aphra Behn proved that money could be made by writing at the sacrifice, perhaps, of certain agreeable qualities; and so by degrees writing became not merely a sign of folly and a distracted mind, but was of practical importance. A husband might die, or some disaster overtake the family. Hundreds of women began as the eighteenth century drew on to add to their pin money, or to come to the rescue of their families by making translations or writing the innumerable bad novels which have ceased to be recorded even in textbooks, but are to be picked up in the fourpenny boxes in the Charing Cross Road. The extreme activity of mind which showed itself in the later eighteenth century among women—the talking, and the meeting, the writing of essays on Shakespeare, the translating of the classics—was founded on the solid fact that women could make money by writing. Money dignifies what is frivolous if unpaid for. It might still be well to sneer at "blue-stockings with an itch for scribbling," but it could not be denied that they could put money in their purses. Thus, towards the end of the eighteenth century a change came about which, if I were rewriting history, I should describe more fully and think of greater importance than the Crusades or the Wars of the Roses. The middle-class woman began to write. For if *Pride and Prejudice* matters, and *Middlemarch* and *Villette* and *Wuthering Heights* matter, then it matters far more than I can prove in an hour's discourse that women generally, and not merely the lonely aristocrat shut up in her country house among her folios and her flatterers, took to writing.[42] Without those forerunners, Jane Austen and the Brontës and George Eliot could no more have written than Shakespeare could have written without Marlowe,[43] or Marlowe without Chaucer, or Chaucer without those forgotten poets who paved the ways and tamed the natural savagery of the tongue. For masterpieces are not single and solitary births; they are the outcome

42. Novels by Jane Austen, George Eliot, Charlotte Brontë, and Emily Brontë, respectively.

43. Christopher Marlowe (1564–93) was the most innovative Renaissance dramatist other than Shakespeare.

of many years of thinking in common, of thinking by the body of the people, so that the experience of the mass is behind the single voice. Jane Austen should have laid a wreath upon the grave of Fanny Burney, and George Eliot done homage to the robust shade of Eliza Carter—the valiant old woman who tied a bell to her bedstead in order that she might wake early and learn Greek.[44] All women together ought to let flowers fall upon the tomb of Aphra Behn which is, most scandalously but rather appropriately, in Westminster Abbey, for it was she who earned them the right to speak their minds. It is she—shady and amorous as she was—who makes it not quite fantastic for me to say to you tonight: Earn five hundred a year by your wits.

Here, then, one had reached the early nineteenth century. And here, for the first time, I found several shelves given up entirely to the works of women. But why, I could not help asking, as I ran my eyes over them, were they, with very few exceptions, all novels? The original impulse was to poetry. The "supreme head of song" was a poetess. Both in France and England the women poets precede the women novelists. Moreover, I thought, looking at the four famous names, what had George Eliot in common with Emily Brontë? Did not Charlotte Brontë fail entirely to understand Jane Austen? Save for the possibly relevant fact that not one of them had a child, four more incongruous characters could not have met together in a room—so much so that it is tempting to invent a meeting and a dialogue between them. Yet by some strange force they were all compelled, when they wrote, to write novels. Had it something to do with being born of the middle class, I asked; and with the fact, which Miss Emily Davies a little later was so strikingly to demonstrate, that the middle-class family in the early nineteenth century was possessed only of a single sitting-room between them?[45] If a woman wrote, she would have to write in the common sitting-room. And, as Miss Nightingale was so vehemently to complain,—"women never have an half hour . . . that they can call their own"—she was always interrupted. Still it would be easier to write prose and fiction there than to write poetry or a play. Less concentration is required. Jane Austen wrote like that to the end of her days. "How she was able to effect all this," her nephew writes in his Memoir, "is surprising, for she had no separate study to repair to, and most of the work must have been done in the general sitting-room, subject to all kinds of casual interruptions. She was careful that her occupation should not be suspected by servants or visitors or any persons beyond her own family party."[46] Jane Austen hid her manuscripts or covered them with a piece of blotting-paper. Then, again, all the literary training that a woman had in the early nineteenth century was training in the observation of character, in the analysis of emotion. Her sensibility had been educated for centuries by the influences of the common sitting-room. People's feelings were impressed on her; personal relations were always before her eyes. Therefore, when the middle-class woman took to writing, she naturally wrote novels, even though, as seems evident enough, two of the four famous women here named were not by nature novelists. Emily Brontë should have written poetic plays; the overflow of George Eliot's capacious mind should have spread itself when the creative impulse was spent upon history or biography. They wrote novels, however; one may even go further, I said, taking *Pride and*

44. Elizabeth Carter (1717–1806) was an English poet, linguist, letter writer, and translator.
45. Emily Davies (1830–1921) was a British suffragist.

46. [*Memoir of Jane Austen*, by her nephew, James Edward Austen-Leigh.]

Prejudice from the shelf, and say that they wrote good novels. Without boasting or giving pain to the opposite sex, one may say that *Pride and Prejudice* is a good book. At any rate, one would not have been ashamed to have been caught in the act of writing *Pride and Prejudice*. Yet Jane Austen was glad that a hinge creaked, so that she might hide her manuscript before any one came in. To Jane Austen there was something discreditable in writing *Pride and Prejudice*. And, I wondered, would *Pride and Prejudice* have been a better novel if Jane Austen had not thought it necessary to hide her manuscript from visitors? I read a page or two to see; but I could not find any signs that her circumstances had harmed her work in the slightest. That, perhaps, was the chief miracle about it. Here was a woman about the year 1800 writing without hate, without bitterness, without fear, without protest, without preaching. That was how Shakespeare wrote, I thought, looking at *Antony and Cleopatra*; and when people compare Shakespeare and Jane Austen, they may mean that the minds of both had consumed all impediments; and for that reason we do not know Jane Austen and we do not know Shakespeare, and for that reason Jane Austen pervades every word that she wrote, and so does Shakespeare. If Jane Austen suffered in any way from her circumstances it was in the narrowness of life that was imposed upon her. It was impossible for a woman to go about alone. She never traveled; she never drove through London in an omnibus or had luncheon in a shop by herself. But perhaps it was the nature of Jane Austen not to want what she had not. Her gift and her circumstances matched each other completely. But I doubt whether that was true of Charlotte Brontë, I said, opening *Jane Eyre* and laying it beside *Pride and Prejudice*.

I opened it at chapter twelve and my eye was caught by the phrase, "Anybody may blame me who likes." What were they blaming Charlotte Brontë for, I wondered? And I read how Jane Eyre used to go up on to the roof when Mrs. Fairfax was making jellies and looked over the fields at the distant view. And then she longed—and it was for this that they blamed her—that

> "then I longed for a power of vision which might overpass that limit; which might reach the busy world, towns, regions full of life I had heard of but never seen: that then I desired more of practical experience than I possessed; more of intercourse with my kind, of acquaintance with variety of character than was here within my reach. I valued what was good in Mrs. Fairfax, and what was good in Adèle; but I believed in the existence of other and more vivid kinds of goodness, and what I believed in I wished to behold.
>
> "Who blames me? Many, no doubt, and I shall be called discontented. I could not help it: the restlessness was in my nature; it agitated me to pain sometimes. . . .
>
> "It is vain to say human beings ought to be satisfied with tranquillity: they must have action; and they will make it if they cannot find it. Millions are condemned to a stiller doom than mine, and millions are in silent revolt against their lot. Nobody knows how many rebellions ferment in the masses of life which people earth. Women are supposed to be very calm generally: but women feel just as men feel; they need exercise for their faculties and a field for their efforts as much as their brothers do; they suffer from too rigid a restraint, too absolute a stagnation, precisely as men would suffer; and it is narrow-minded in their privileged fellow-creatures to say that they ought to confine themselves to making puddings and knitting stockings, to playing on the piano and embroidering bags. It is thoughtless to condemn them, or laugh at them, if they seek to do more or learn more than custom has pronounced necessary for their sex.
>
> "When thus alone I not unfrequently heard Grace Poole's laugh. . . ."

That is an awkward break, I thought. It is upsetting to come upon Grace Poole all of a sudden. The continuity is disturbed. One might say, I continued, laying the book down beside *Pride and Prejudice*, that the woman who wrote those pages had more genius in her than Jane Austen; but if one reads them over and marks that jerk in them, that indignation, one sees that she will never get her genius expressed whole and entire. Her books will be deformed and twisted. She will write in a rage where she should write calmly. She will write foolishly where she should write wisely. She will write of herself where she should write of her characters. She is at war with her lot. How could she help but die young, cramped and thwarted?

One could not but play for a moment with the thought of what might have happened if Charlotte Brontë had possessed say three hundred a year—but the foolish woman sold the copyright of her novels outright for fifteen hundred pounds; somehow possessed more knowledge of the busy world, and towns and regions full of life; more practical experience, and intercourse with her kind and acquaintance with a variety of character. In those words she puts her finger exactly not only upon her own defects as a novelist but upon those of her sex at that time. She knew, no one better, how enormously her genius would have profited if it had not spent itself in solitary visions over distant fields; if experience and intercourse and travel had been granted her. But they were not granted; they were withheld; and we must accept the fact that all those good novels, *Villette, Emma, Wuthering Heights, Middlemarch,* were written by women without more experience of life than could enter the house of a respectable clergyman; written too in the common sitting-room of that respectable house and by women so poor that they could not afford to buy more than a few quires of paper at a time upon which to write *Wuthering Heights* or *Jane Eyre*. One of them, it is true, George Eliot, escaped after much tribulation, but only to a secluded villa in St. John's Wood. And there she settled down in the shadow of the world's disapproval. "I wish it to be understood," she wrote, "that I should never invite any one to come and see me who did not ask for the invitation"; for was she not living in sin with a married man and might not the sight of her damage the chastity of Mrs. Smith or whoever it might be that chanced to call? One must submit to the social convention, and be "cut off from what is called the world." At the same time, on the other side of Europe, there was a young man living freely with this gipsy or with that great lady; going to the wars; picking up unhindered and uncensored all that varied experience of human life which served him so splendidly later when he came to write his books. Had Tolstoi lived at the Priory in seclusion with a married lady "cut off from what is called the world," however edifying the moral lesson, he could scarcely, I thought, have written *War and Peace*.[47]

But one could perhaps go a little deeper into the question of novel-writing and the effect of sex upon the novelist. If one shuts one's eyes and thinks of the novel as a whole, it would seem to be a creation owning a certain looking-glass likeness to life, though of course with simplifications and distortions innumerable. At any rate, it is a structure leaving a shape on the mind's eye, built now in squares, now pagoda shaped, now throwing out wings and arcades, now solidly compact and domed like the Cathedral of Saint Sofia at Constantinople. This shape, I thought, thinking back over certain famous novels, starts in one the kind of emotion that is appropriate to it. But that emotion at once blends itself with others, for the "shape" is not

47. Leo Tolstoy (1828–1910), a Russian novelist, wrote *War and Peace* (1865–69) and *Anna Karenina* (1875–77).

made by the relation of stone to stone, but by the relation of human being to human being. Thus a novel starts in us all sorts of antagonistic and opposed emotions. Life conflicts with something that is not life. Hence the difficulty of coming to any agreement about novels, and the immense sway that our private prejudices have upon us. On the one hand, we feel You—John the hero—must live, or I shall be in the depths of despair. On the other, we feel, Alas, John, you must die, because the shape of the book requires it. Life conflicts with something that is not life. Then since life it is in part, we judge it as life. James is the sort of man I most detest, one says. Or, This is a farrago of absurdity. I could never feel anything of the sort myself. The whole structure, it is obvious, thinking back on any famous novel, is one of infinite complexity, because it is thus made up of so many different judgments, of so many different kinds of emotion. The wonder is that any book so composed holds together for more than a year or two, or can possibly mean to the English reader what it means for the Russian or the Chinese. But they do hold together occasionally very remarkably. And what holds them together in these rare instances of survival (I was thinking of *War and Peace*) is something that one calls integrity, though it has nothing to do with paying one's bills or behaving honorably in an emergency. What one means by integrity, in the case of the novelist, is the conviction that he gives one that this is the truth. Yes, one feels, I should never have thought that this could be so; I have never known people behaving like that. But you have convinced me that so it is, so it happens. One holds every phrase, every scene to the light as one reads—for Nature seems, very oddly, to have provided us with an inner light by which to judge of the novelist's integrity or disintegrity. Or perhaps it is rather that Nature, in her most irrational mood, has traced in invisible ink on the walls of the mind a premonition which these great artists confirm; a sketch which only needs to be held to the fire of genius to become visible. When one so exposes it and sees it come to life one exclaims in rapture, But this is what I have always felt and known and desired! And one boils over with excitement, and, shutting the book even with a kind of reverence as if it were something very precious, a stand-by to return to as long as one lives, one puts it back on the shelf, I said, taking *War and Peace* and putting it back in its place. If, on the other hand, these poor sentences that one takes and tests rouse first a quick and eager response with their bright coloring and their dashing gestures but there they stop: something seems to check them in their development: or if they bring to light only a faint scribble in that corner and blot over there, and nothing appears whole and entire, then one heaves a sigh of disappointment and says, Another failure. This novel has come to grief somewhere.

And for the most part, of course, novels do come to grief somewhere. The imagination falters under the enormous strain. The insight is confused; it can no longer distinguish between the true and the false; it has no longer the strength to go on with the vast labor that calls at every moment for the use of so many different faculties. But how would all this be affected by the sex of the novelist, I wondered, looking at *Jane Eyre* and the others. Would the fact of her sex in any way interfere with the integrity of a woman novelist—that integrity which I take to be the backbone of the writer? Now, in the passages I have quoted from *Jane Eyre*, it is clear that anger was tampering with the integrity of Charlotte Brontë the novelist. She left her story, to which her entire devotion was due, to attend to some personal grievance. She remembered that she had been starved of her proper due of experience—she had been made to stagnate in a parsonage mending stockings when she wanted to wander free over the world. Her imagination swerved from indignation and we feel it swerve. But there were many more influences than anger tugging at her imagination and deflecting it from its path. Ignorance, for instance. The portrait of Rochester is drawn in the dark. We feel the influence of fear in it; just as we constantly feel an acidity which is the result of oppression, a buried suffering smouldering beneath her passion, a rancour which contracts those books, splendid as they are, with a spasm of pain.

And since a novel has this correspondence to real life, its values are to some extent those of real life. But it is obvious that the values of women differ very often from the values which have been made by the other sex; naturally, this is so. Yet it is the masculine values that prevail. Speaking crudely, football and sport are "important"; the worship of fashion, the buying of clothes "trivial." And these values are inevitably transferred from life to fiction. This is an important book, the critic assumes, because it deals with war. This is an insignificant book because it deals with the feelings of women in a drawing-room. A scene in a battlefield is more important than a scene in a shop—everywhere and much more subtly the difference of value persists. The whole structure, therefore, of the early nineteenth-century novel was raised, if one was a woman, by a mind which was slightly pulled from the straight, and made to alter its clear vision in deference to external authority. One has only to skim these old forgotten novels and listen to the tone of voice in which they are written to divine that the writer was meeting criticism; she was saying this by way of aggression, or that by way of conciliation. She was admitting that she was "only a woman," or protesting that she was "as good as a man." She met that criticism as her temperament dictated, with docility and diffidence, or with anger and emphasis. It does not matter which it was; she was thinking of something other than the thing itself. Down comes her book upon our heads. There was a flaw in the center of it. And I thought of all the women's novels that lie scattered, like small pock-marked apples in an orchard, about the secondhand book shops of London. It was the flaw in the center that had rotted them. She had altered her values in deference to the opinion of others.

But how impossible it must have been for them not to budge either to the right or to the left. What genius, what integrity it must have required in face of all that criticism, in the midst of that purely patriarchal society, to hold fast to the thing as they saw it without shrinking. Only Jane Austen did it and Emily Brontë. It is another feather, perhaps the finest, in their caps. They wrote as women write, not as men write. Of all the thousand women who wrote novels then, they alone entirely ignored the perpetual admonitions of the eternal pedagogue—write this, think that. They alone were deaf to that persistent voice, now grumbling, now patronizing, now domineering, now grieved, now shocked, now angry, now avuncular, that voice which cannot let women alone, but must be at them, like some too conscientious governess, adjuring them, like Sir Egerton Brydges, to be refined; dragging even into the criticism of poetry criticism of sex;[48] admonishing them, if they would be good and win, as I suppose, some shiny prize, to keep within certain limits which the gentleman in question thinks suitable: ". . . female novelists should only aspire to excellence by courageously acknowledging the limitations of their

48. ["[She] has a metaphysical purpose, and that is a dangerous obsession, especially with a woman, for women rarely possess men's healthy love of rhetoric. It is a strange lack in the sex which is in other things more primitive and more materialistic."—*New Criterion*, June 1928.]

sex."[49] That puts the matter in a nutshell, and when I tell you, rather to your surprise, that this sentence was written not in August 1828 but in August 1928, you will agree, I think, that however delightful it is to us now, it represents a vast body of opinion—I am not going to stir those old pools, I take only what chance has floated to my feet— that was far more vigorous and far more vocal a century ago. It would have needed a very stalwart young woman in 1828 to disregard all those snubs and chidings and promises of prizes. One must have been something of a firebrand to say to oneself, Oh, but they can't buy literature too. Literature is open to everybody. I refuse to allow you, Beadle though you are, to turn me off the grass. Lock up your libraries if you like; but there is no gate, no lock, no bolt that you can set upon the freedom of my mind.

But whatever effect discouragement and criticism had upon their writing—and I believe that they had a very great effect—that was unimportant compared with the other difficulty which faced them (I was still considering those early nineteenth-century novelists) when they came to set their thoughts on paper—that is that they had no tradition behind them, or one so short and partial that it was of little help. For we think back through our mothers if we are women. It is useless to go to the great men writers for help, however much one may go to them for pleasure. Lamb, Browne, Thackeray, Newman, Sterne, Dickens, De Quincey—whoever it may be— never helped a woman yet, though she may have learnt a few tricks of them and adapted them to her use.[50] The weight, the pace, the stride of man's mind are too unlike her own for her to lift anything substantial from him successfully. The ape is too distant to be sedulous. Perhaps the first thing she would find, setting pen to paper, was that there was no common sentence ready for her use. All the great novelists like Thackeray and Dickens and Balzac have written a natural prose,[51] swift but not slovenly, expressive but not precious, taking their own tint without ceasing to be common property. They have based it on the sentence that was current at the time. The sentence that was current at the beginning of the nineteenth century ran something like this perhaps: "The grandeur of their works was an argument with them, not to stop short, but to proceed. They could have no higher excitement or satisfaction than in the exercise of their art and endless generations of truth and beauty. Success prompts to exertion; and habit facilitates success." This is a man's sentence; behind it one can see Johnson, Gibbon and the rest.[52] It was a sentence that was unsuited for a woman's use. Charlotte Brontë, with all her splendid gift for prose, stumbled and fell with that clumsy weapon in her hands. George Eliot committed atrocities with it that beggar description. Jane Austen looked at it and laughed at it and devised a perfectly natural, shapely sentence proper for her own use and never departed from it. Thus, with less genius for writing than Charlotte Brontë, she got infinitely more said. Indeed, since freedom and fullness of expression are of the essence of the art, such a lack of tradition, such a scarcity and inadequacy of tools, must have told enormously upon the writing of women. Moreover, a book is

49. ["If, like the reporter, you believe that female novelists should only aspire to excellence by courageously acknowledging the limitations of their sex (Jane Austen [has] demonstrated how gracefully this gesture can be accomplished). . . ."—*Life and Letters*, August 1928.]

50. Sir Thomas Browne (1605–82) was a physician and the author of *Religio Medici* (1642); John Henry Cardinal Newman (1801–90) was a Catholic theologian and a distinguished writer of prose; Laurence Sterne (1713–68)

was the author of *Tristram Shandy*; Charles Dickens (1812–70) was a prominent Victorian novelist; and Thomas De Quincey (1785–1859) was a British scholar and essayist.

51. Honoré de Balzac (1799–1850) was a French novelist and social critic.

52. Samuel Johnson (1709–84), eighteenth-century British editor and man of letters; Edward Gibbon (1737–94), a prominent British historian.

not made of sentences laid end to end, but of sentences built, if an image helps, into arcades or domes. And this shape too had been made by men out of their own needs for their own uses. There is no reason to think that the form of the epic or of the poetic play suits a woman any more than the sentence suits her. But all the older forms of literature were hardened and set by the time she became a writer. The novel alone was young enough to be soft in her hands—another reason, perhaps, why she wrote novels. Yet who shall say that even now "the novel" (I give it inverted commas to mark my sense of the words' inadequacy), who shall say that even this most pliable of all forms is rightly shaped for her use? No doubt we shall find her knocking that into shape for herself when she has the free use of her limbs; and providing some new vehicle, not necessarily in verse, for the poetry in her. For it is the poetry that is still denied outlet. And I went on to ponder how a woman nowadays would write a poetic tragedy in five acts—would she use verse—would she not use prose rather?

But these are difficult questions which lie in the twilight of the future. I must leave them, if only because they stimulate me to wander from my subject into trackless forests where I shall be lost and, very likely, devoured by wild beasts. I do not want, and I am sure that you do not want me, to broach that very dismal subject, the future of fiction, so that I will only pause here one moment to draw your attention to the great part which must be played in that future so far as women are concerned by physical conditions. The book has somehow to be adapted to the body, and at a venture one would say that women's books should be shorter, more concentrated, than those of men, and framed so that they do not need long hours of steady and uninterrupted work. For interruptions there will always be. Again, the nerves that feed the brain would seem to differ in men and women, and if you are going to make them work their best and hardest, you must find out what treatment suits them—whether these hours of lectures, for instance, which the monks devised, presumably, hundreds of years ago, suit them—what alternations of work and rest they need, interpreting rest not as doing nothing but as doing something but something that is different; and what should that difference be? All this should be discussed and discovered; all this is part of the question of women and fiction. And yet, I continued, approaching the bookcase again, where shall I find that elaborate study of the psychology of women by a woman? If through their incapacity to play football women are not going to be allowed to practice medicine—

Happily my thoughts were now given another turn.

FIVE

I had come at last, in the course of this rambling, to the shelves which hold books by the living; by women and by men; for there are almost as many books written by women now as by men. Or if that is not yet quite true, if the male is still the voluble sex, it is certainly true that women no longer write novels solely. There are Jane Harrison's books on Greek archaeology; Vernon Lee's books on aesthetics; Gertrude Bell's books on Persia.[53] There are books on all sorts of subjects which a generation ago no woman could have touched. There are poems and plays and criticism; there are histories and biographies; books of travel and books of scholarship and research;

---

53. Vernon Lee (1856–1935) was the pseudonym of Violet Paget, a French woman who wrote essays and novels in English; Gertrude Bell (1868–1926) was an archeologist and a travel writer.

there are even a few philosophies and books about science and economics. And though novels predominate, novels themselves may very well have changed from association with books of a different feather. The natural simplicity, the epic age of women's writing, may have gone. Reading and criticism may have given her a wider range, a greater subtlety. The impulse towards autobiography may be spent. She may be beginning to use writing as an art, not as a method of self-expression. Among these new novels one might find an answer to several such questions.

I took down one of them at random. It stood at the very end of the shelf, was called *Life's Adventure*, or some such title, by Mary Carmichael, and was published in this very month of October. It seems to be her first book, I said to myself, but one must read it as if it were the last volume in a fairly long series, continuing all those other books that I have been glancing at—Lady Winchilsea's poems and Aphra Behn's plays and the novels of the four great novelists. For books continue each other, in spite of our habit of judging them separately. And I must also consider her—this unknown woman—as the descendant of all those other women whose circumstances I have been glancing at and see what she inherits of their characteristics and restrictions. So, with a sigh, because novels so often provide an anodyne and not an antidote, glide one into torpid slumbers instead of rousing one with a burning brand, I settled down with a notebook and a pencil to make what I could of Mary Carmichael's first novel, *Life's Adventure*.

To begin with, I ran my eye up and down the page. I am going to get the hang of her sentences first, I said, before I load my memory with blue eyes and brown and the relationship that there may be between Chloe and Roger. There will be time for that when I have decided whether she has a pen in her hand or a pickaxe. So I tried a sentence or two on my tongue. Soon it was obvious that something was not quite in order. The smooth gliding of sentence after sentence was interrupted. Something tore, something scratched; a single word here and there flashed its torch in my eyes. She was "unhanding" herself as they say in the old plays. She is like a person striking a match that will not light, I thought. Buy why, I asked her as if she were present, are Jane Austen's sentences not of the right shape for you? Must they all be scrapped because Emma and Mr. Woodhouse are dead? Alas, I sighed, that it should be so. For while Jane Austen breaks from melody to melody as Mozart from song to song, to read this writing was like being out at sea in an open boat. Up one went, down one sank. This terseness, this short-windedness, might mean that she was afraid of something; afraid of being called "sentimental" perhaps; or she remembers that women's writing has been called flowery and so provides a superfluity of thorns; but until I have read a scene with some care, I cannot be sure whether she is being herself or some one else. At any rate, she does not lower one's vitality, I thought, reading more carefully. But she is heaping up too many facts. She will not be able to use half of them in a book of this size. (It was about half the length of *Jane Eyre*.) However, by some means or other she succeeded in getting us all—Roger, Chloe, Olivia, Tony and Mr. Bigham—in a canoe up the river. Wait a moment, I said, leaning back in my chair, I must consider the whole thing more carefully before I go any further.

I am almost sure, I said to myself, that Mary Carmichael is playing a trick on us. For I feel as one feels on a switchback railway when the car, instead of sinking, as one has been led to expect, swerves up again. Mary is tampering with the expected sequence. First she broke the sentence; now she has broken the sequence. Very well, she has every right to do both these things if she does them not for the sake of breaking, but for the sake of creating. Which of the two it is I cannot be sure until she has faced herself with a situation. I will give her every liberty, I said, to choose what that situation shall be; she shall make it of tin cans and old kettles if she likes; but she must convince me that she believes it to be a situation; and then when she has made it she must face it. She must jump. And, determined to do my duty by her as reader if she would do her duty by me as writer, I turned the page and read . . . I am sorry to break off so abruptly. Are there no men present? Do you promise me that behind that red curtain over there the figure of Sir Chartres Biron is not concealed?[54] We are all women, you assure me? Then I may tell you that the very next words I read were these—"Chloe liked Olivia . . ." Do not start. Do not blush. Let us admit in the privacy of our own society that these things sometimes happen. Sometimes women do like women.

"Chloe liked Olivia," I read. And then it struck me how immense a change was there. Chloe liked Olivia perhaps for the first time in literature. Cleopatra did not like Octavia. And how completely *Antony and Cleopatra* would have been altered had she done so! As it is, I thought, letting my mind, I am afraid, wander a little from *Life's Adventure*, the whole thing is simplified, conventionalized, if one dared say it, absurdly. Cleopatra's only feeling about Octavia is one of jealousy. Is she taller than I am? How does she do her hair? The play, perhaps, required no more. But how interesting it would have been if the relationship between the two woman had been more complicated. All these relationships between women, I thought, rapidly recalling the splendid gallery of fictitious women, are too simple. So much has been left out, unattempted. And I tried to remember any case in the course of my reading where two women are represented as friends. There is an attempt at it in *Diana of the Crossways*.[55] They are confidantes, of course, in Racine and the Greek tragedies. They are now and then mothers and daughters. But almost without exception they are shown in their relation to men. It was strange to think that all the great women of fiction were, until Jane Austen's day, not only seen by the other sex, but seen only in relation to the other sex. And how small a part of a woman's life is that; and how little can a man know even of that when he observes it through the black or rosy spectacles which sex puts upon his nose. Hence, perhaps, the peculiar nature of woman in fiction; the astonishing extremes of her beauty and horror; her alternations between heavenly goodness and hellish depravity—for so a lover would see her as his love rose or sank, was prosperous or unhappy. This is not so true of the nineteenth-century novelists, of course. Woman becomes much more various and complicated there. Indeed it was the desire to write about women perhaps that led men by degrees to abandon the poetic drama which, with its violence, could make so little use of them, and to devise the novel as a more fitting receptacle. Even so it remains obvious, even in the writing of Proust, that a man is terribly hampered and partial in his knowledge of women, as a woman in her knowledge of men.

Also, I continued, looking down at the page again, it is becoming evident that women, like men, have other interests besides the perennial interests of domesticity. "Chloe liked Olivia. They shared a laboratory together. . . ." I read on and discovered that these two young women were engaged in mincing liver, which is, it seems, a cure for pernicious anemia: although one of them was married and had—I think I am right in

54. According to Jane Marcus, Sir Chartres Biron was the presiding magistrate at the trial for obscenity of lesbian novelist Radclyffe Hall (1880–1943) in 1928; at issue was her novel *The Well of Loneliness* (1928). See ch. 8 in *Virginia Woolf and the Languages of Patriarchy*.

55. *Diana of the Crossways* (1885) was a novel by George Meredith; its central character is accused of adultery and divorce proceedings ensue.

stating—two small children. Now all that, of course, has had to be left out, and thus the splendid portrait of the fictitious woman is much too simple and much too monotonous. Suppose, for instance, that men were only represented in literature as the lovers of women, and were never the friends of men, soldiers, thinkers, dreamers; how few parts in the plays of Shakespeare could be allotted to them; how literature would suffer! We might perhaps have most of Othello; and a good deal of Antony; but no Caesar, no Brutus, no Hamlet, no Lear, no Jaques[56]—literature would be incredibly impoverished, as indeed literature is impoverished beyond our counting by the doors that have been shut upon women. Married against their will, kept in one room, and to one occupation, how could a dramatist give a full or interesting or truthful account of them? Love was the only possible interpreter. The poet was forced to be passionate or bitter, unless indeed he chose to "hate women," which meant more often than not that he was unattractive to them.

Now if Chloe likes Olivia and they share a laboratory, which of itself will make their friendship more varied and lasting because it will be less personal; if Mary Carmichael knows how to write, and I was beginning to enjoy some quality in her style; if she has a room to herself, of which I am not quite sure; if she has five hundred a year of her own—but that remains to be proved—then I think that something of great importance has happened.

For if Chloe likes Olivia and Mary Carmichael knows how to express it she will light a torch in that vast chamber where nobody has yet been. It is all half lights and profound shadows like those serpentine caves where one goes with a candle peering up and down, not knowing where one is stepping. And I began to read the book again, and read how Chloe watched Olivia put a jar on a shelf and say how it was time to go home to her children. That is a sight that has never been seen since the world began, I exclaimed. And I watched too, very curiously. For I wanted to see how Mary Carmichael set to work to catch those unrecorded gestures, those unsaid or half-said words, which form themselves, no more palpably than the shadows of moths on the ceiling, when women are alone, unlit by the capricious and colored light of the other sex. She will need to hold her breath, I said, reading on, if she is to do it; for women are so suspicious of any interest that has not some obvious motive behind it, so terribly accustomed to concealment and suppression, that they are off at the flicker of an eye turned observingly in their direction. The only way for you to do it, I thought, addressing Mary Carmichael as if she were there, would be to talk of something else, looking steadily out of the window, and thus note, not with a pencil in a notebook, but in the shortest of shorthand, in words that are hardly syllabled yet, what happens when Olivia—this organism that has been under the shadow of the rock these million years—feels the light fall on it, and sees coming her way a piece of strange food—knowledge, adventure, art. And she reaches out for it, I thought, again raising my eyes from the page, and has to devise some entirely new combination of her resources, so highly developed for other purposes, so as to absorb the new into the old without disturbing the infinitely intricate and elaborate balance of the whole.

But, alas, I had done what I had determined not to do; I had slipped unthinkingly into praise of my own sex. "Highly developed"—"infinitely intricate"—such are undeniable terms of praise, and to praise one's own sex is always suspect, often silly; moreover, in this case, how could one justify it? One could not go to the map and say Columbus discovered America and Columbus was a woman; or take an apple and

---

56. These are characters in the plays of Shakespeare.

remark, Newton discovered the laws of gravitation and Newton was a woman; or look into the sky and say aeroplanes are flying overhead and aeroplanes were invented by women. There is no mark on the wall to measure the precise height of women. There are no yard measures, neatly divided into the fractions of an inch, that one can lay against the qualities of a good mother or the devotion of a daughter, or the fidelity of a sister, or the capacity of a housekeeper. Few women even now have been graded at the universities; the great trials of the professions, army and navy, trade, politics and diplomacy have hardly tested them. They remain even at this moment almost unclassified. But if I want to know all that a human being can tell me about Sir Hawley Butts, for instance, I have only to open Burke or Debrett[57] and I shall find that he took such and such a degree; owns a hall; has an heir; was Secretary to a Board; represented Great Britain in Canada; and has received a certain number of degrees, offices, medals, and other distinctions by which his merits are stamped upon him indelibly. Only Providence can know more about Sir Hawley Butts than that.

When, therefore, I say "highly developed," "infinitely intricate," of women, I am unable to verify my words either in Whitaker, Debrett or the University Calendar. In this predicament what can I do? And I looked at the bookcase again. There were the biographies: Johnson and Goethe and Carlyle and Sterne and Cowper and Shelley and Voltaire and Browning and many others.[58] And I began thinking of all those great men who have for one reason or another admired, sought out, lived with, confided in, made love to, written of, trusted in, and shown what can only be described as some need of and dependence upon certain persons of the opposite sex. That all these relationships were absolutely Platonic I would not affirm, and Sir William Joynson Hicks would probably deny. But we should wrong these illustrious men very greatly if we insisted that they got nothing from these alliances but comfort, flattery and the pleasures of the body. What they got, it is obvious, was something that their own sex was unable to supply; and it would not be rash, perhaps, to define it further, without quoting the doubtless rhapsodical words of the poets, as some stimulus, some renewal of creative power which is in the gift only of the opposite sex to bestow. He would open the door of drawing-room or nursery, I thought, and find her among her children perhaps, or with a piece of embroidery on her knee—at any rate, the center of some different order and system of life, and the contrast between this world and his own, which might be the law courts or the House of Commons, would at once refresh and invigorate; and there would follow, even in the simplest talk, such a natural difference of opinion that the dried ideas in him would be fertilized anew; and the sight of her creating in a different medium from his own would so quicken his creative power that insensibly his sterile mind would begin to plot again, and he would find the phrase or the scene which was lacking when he put on his hat to visit her. Every Johnson has his Thrale, and holds fast to her for some such reasons as these, and when the Thrale marries her Italian music master Johnson goes half mad with rage and disgust, not merely that he will miss his pleasant evenings at Streatham, but that the light of his life will be "as if gone out."[59]

And without being Dr. Johnson or Goethe or Carlyle or Voltaire, one may feel, though very differently from these great men, the nature of this intricacy and the power

57. Burke and Debrett give listings of the lineage and titles of the English nobility.
58. William Cowper (1731–1800) was a popular British poet who struggled with madness. Percy Bysshe Shelley (1792–1822) was a British Romantic poet; the French writer Voltaire (1694–1778) wrote about English liberalism; Robert Browning (1812–1889) was a British poet known for his use of dramatic monologues.
59. Hester Thrale (1741–1821) was a British writer and close friend of Dr. Samuel Johnson.

of this highly developed creative faculty among women. One goes into the room—but the resources of the English language would be much put to the stretch, and whole flights of words would need to wing their way illegitimately into existence before a woman could say what happens when she goes into a room. The rooms differ so completely; they are calm or thunderous; open on to the sea, or, on the contrary, give on to a prison yard; are hung with washing; or alive with opals and silks; are hard as horsehair or soft as feathers—one has only to go into any room in any street for the whole of that extremely complex force of femininity to fly in one's face. How should it be otherwise? For women have sat indoors all these millions of years, so that by this time the very walls are permeated by their creative force, which has, indeed, so overcharged the capacity of bricks and mortar that it must needs harness itself to pens and brushes and business and politics. But this creative power differs greatly from the creative power of men. And one must conclude that it would be a thousand pities if it were hindered or wasted, for it was won by centuries of the most drastic discipline, and there is nothing to take its place. It would be a thousand pities if women wrote like men, or lived like men, or looked like men, for if two sexes are quite inadequate, considering the vastness and variety of the world, how should we manage with one only? Ought not education to bring out and fortify the differences rather than the similarities? For we have too much likeness as it is, and if an explorer should come back and bring word of other sexes looking through the branches of other trees at other skies, nothing would be of greater service to humanity; and we should have the immense pleasure into the bargain of watching Professor X rush for his measuring-rods to prove himself "superior."

Mary Carmichael, I thought, still hovering at a little distance above the page, will have her work cut out for her merely as an observer. I am afraid indeed that she will be tempted to become, what I think the less interesting branch of the species—the naturalist-novelist, and not the contemplative. There are so many new facts for her to observe. She will not need to limit herself any longer to the respectable houses of the upper middle classes. She will go without kindness or condescension, but in the spirit of fellowship into those small, scented rooms where sit the courtesan, the harlot and the lady with the pug dog. There they still sit in the rough and ready-made clothes that the male writer has had perforce to clap upon their shoulders. But Mary Carmichael will have out her scissors and fit them close to every hollow and angle. It will be a curious sight, when it comes, to see these women as they are, but we must wait a little, for Mary Carmichael will still be encumbered with that self-consciousness in the presence of "sin" which is the legacy of our sexual barbarity. She will still wear the shoddy old fetters of class on her feet.

However, the majority of women are neither harlots nor courtesans; nor do they sit clasping pug dogs to dusty velvet all through the summer afternoon. But what do they do then? and there came to my mind's eye one of those long streets somewhere south of the river whose infinite rows are innumerably populated. With the eye of the imagination I saw a very ancient lady crossing the street on the arm of a middle-aged woman, her daughter, perhaps, both so respectably booted and furred that their dressing in the afternoon must be a ritual, and the clothes themselves put away in cupboards with camphor, year after year, throughout the summer months. They cross the road when the lamps are being lit (for the dusk is their favorite hour), as they must have done year after year. The elder is close on eighty; but if one asked her what her life has meant to her, she would say that she remembered the streets lit for the battle of Balaclava, or had heard the guns fire in Hyde Park for the birth of King Edward the Seventh. And if one asked her, longing to pin down the moment with date and season, but what were you doing on the fifth of April 1868, or the second of November 1875, she would look vague and say that she could remember nothing. For all the dinners are cooked; the plates and cups washed; the children set to school and gone out into the world. Nothing remains of it all. All has vanished. No biography or history has a word to say about it. And the novels, without meaning to, inevitably lie.

All these infinitely obscure lives remain to be recorded, I said, addressing Mary Carmichael as if she were present; and went on in thought through the streets of London feeling in imagination the pressure of dumbness, the accumulation of unrecorded life, whether from the women at the street corners with their arms akimbo, and the rings embedded in their fat swollen fingers, talking with a gesticulation like the swing of Shakespeare's words; or from the violet-sellers and match-sellers and old crones stationed under the doorways; or from drifting girls whose faces, like waves in sun and cloud, signal the coming of men and women and the flickering lights of shop windows. All that you will have to explore, I said to Mary Carmichael, holding your torch firm in your hand. Above all, you must illumine your own soul with its profundities and its shallows, and its vanities and its generosities, and say what your beauty means to you or your plainness and what is your relation to the everchanging and turning world of gloves and shoes and stuffs swaying up and down among the faint scents that come through chemists' bottles down arcades of dress material over a floor of pseudo-marble. For in imagination I had gone into a shop; it was laid with black and white paving; it was hung, astonishingly beautifully, with colored ribbons. Mary Carmichael might well have a look at that in passing, I thought, for it is a sight that would lend itself to the pen as fittingly as any snowy peak or rocky gorge in the Andes. And there is the girl behind the counter too—I would as soon have her true history as the hundred and fiftieth life of Napoleon or seventieth study of Keats and his use of Miltonic inversion which old Professor Z and his like are now inditing. And then I went on very warily, on the very tips of my toes (so cowardly am I, so afraid of the lash that was once almost laid on my own shoulders), to murmur that she should also learn to laugh, without bitterness, at the vanities—say rather at the peculiarities, for it is a less offensive word—of the other sex. For there is a spot the size of a shilling at the back of the head which one can never see for oneself. It is one of the good offices that sex can discharge for sex—to describe that spot the size of a shilling at the back of the head. Think how much woman have profited by the comments of Juvenal; by the criticism of Strindberg.[60] Think with what humanity and brilliancy men, from the earliest ages, have pointed out to women that dark place at the back of the head! And if Mary were very brave and very honest, she would go behind the other sex and tell us what she found there. A true picture of man as a whole can never be painted until a woman has described that spot the size of a shilling. Mr. Woodhouse and Mr. Casaubon are spots of that size and nature.[61] Not of course that any one in their senses would counsel her to hold up to scorn and ridicule of set purpose—literature shows the futility of what is written in that spirit. Be truthful, one would say, and the result is bound to be amazingly interesting. Comedy is bound to be enriched. New facts are bound to be discovered.

However, it was high time to lower my eyes to the page again. It would be better, instead of speculating what Mary Carmichael might write and should write, to see

---

60. Juvenal was a Roman satirist during the Augustan era (27 BCE–14CE). August Strindberg (1849–1912) was a Swedish playwright and novelist.

61. Mr. Woodhouse and Mr. Casaubon are characters in Jane Austen's *Emma* (1816) and George Eliot's *Middlemarch* (1871–72).

what in fact Mary Carmichael did write. So I began to read again. I remembered that I had certain grievances against her. She had broken up Jane Austen's sentence, and thus given me no chance of pluming myself upon my impeccable taste, my fastidious ear. For it was useless to say, "Yes, yes, this is very nice; but Jane Austen wrote much better than you do," when I had to admit that there was no point of likeness between them. Then she had gone further and broken the sequence—the expected order. Perhaps she had done this unconsciously, merely giving things their natural order, as a woman would, if she wrote like a woman. But the effect was somehow baffling; one could not see a wave heaping itself, a crisis coming round the next corner. Therefore I could not plume myself either upon the depths of my feelings and my profound knowledge of the human heart. For whenever I was about to feel the usual things in the usual places, about love, about death, the annoying creature twitched me away, as if the important point were just a little further on. And thus she made it impossible for me to roll out my sonorous phrases about "elemental feelings," the "common stuff of humanity," "depths of the human heart," and all those other phrases which support us in our belief that, however clever we may be on top, we are very serious, very profound and very humane underneath. She made me feel, on the contrary, that instead of being serious and profound and humane, one might be—and the thought was far less seductive—merely lazy minded and conventional into the bargain.

But I read on, and noted certain other facts. She was no "genius"—that was evident. She had nothing like the love of Nature, the fiery imagination, the wild poetry, the brilliant wit, the brooding wisdom of her great predecessors, Lady Winchilsea, Charlotte Brontë, Emily Brontë, Jane Austen, and George Eliot; she could not write with the melody and the dignity of Dorothy Osborne—indeed she was no more than a clever girl whose books will no doubt be pulped by the publishers in ten years' time. But, nevertheless, she had certain advantages which women of far greater gift lacked even half a century ago. Men were no longer to her "the opposing faction"; she need not waste her time railing against them; she need not climb on to the roof and ruin her peace of mind longing for travel, experience and a knowledge of the world and character that were denied her. Fear and hatred were almost gone, or traces of them showed only in a slight exaggeration of the joy of freedom, a tendency to the caustic and satirical, rather than to the romantic, in her treatment of the other sex. Then there could be no doubt that as a novelist she enjoyed some natural advantages of a high order. She had a sensibility that was very wide, eager and free. It responded to an almost imperceptible touch on it. It feasted like a plant newly stood in the air on every sight and sound that came its way. It ranged, too, very subtly and curiously, among almost unknown or unrecorded things; it lighted on small things and showed that perhaps they were not small after all. It brought buried things to light and made one wonder what need there had been to bury them. Awkward though she was and without the unconscious bearing of long descent which makes the least turn of the pen of a Thackeray or a Lamb delightful to the ear, she had—I began to think— mastered the first great lesson; she wrote as a woman, but as a woman who has forgotten that she is a woman, so that her pages were full of that curious sexual quality which comes only when sex is unconscious of itself.

All this was to the good. But no abundance of sensation or fineness of perception would avail unless she could build up out of the fleeting and the personal the lasting edifice which remains unthrown. I had said that I would wait until she faced herself with "a situation." And I meant by that until she proved by summoning, beckoning and getting together that she was not a skimmer of surfaces merely, but had looked beneath into the depths. Now is the time, she would say to herself at a certain moment, when without doing anything violent I can show the meaning of all this. And she would begin—how unmistakable that quickening is!—beckoning and summoning, and there would rise up in memory, half forgotten, perhaps quite trivial things in other chapters dropped by the way. And she would make their presence felt while some one sewed or smoked a pipe as naturally as possible, and one would feel, as she went on writing, as if one had gone to the top of the world and seen it laid out, very majestically, beneath.

At any rate, she was making the attempt. And as I watched her lengthening out for the test, I saw, but hoped that she did not see, the bishops and the deans, the doctors and the professors, the patriarchs and the pedagogues all at her shouting warning and advice. You can't do this and you shan't do that! Fellows and scholars only allowed on the grass! Ladies not admitted without a letter of introduction! Aspiring and graceful female novelists this way! So they kept at her like the crowd at a fence on the race-course, and it was her trial to take her fence without looking to right or left. If you stop to curse you are lost, I said to her; equally, if you stop to laugh. Hesistate or fumble and you are done for. Think only of the jump, I implored her, as if I had put the whole of my money on her back; and she went over it like a bird. But there was a fence beyond that and a fence beyond that. Whether she had the staying power I was doubtful, for the clapping and the crying were fraying to the nerves. But she did her best. Considering that Mary Carmichael was no genius, but an unknown girl writing her first novel in a bed-sitting-room, without enough of those desirable things, time, money and idleness, she did not do so badly, I thought.

Give her another hundred years, I concluded, reading the last chapter—people's noses and bare shoulders showed naked against a starry sky, for some one had twitched the curtain in the drawing-room—give her a room of her own and five hundred a year, let her speak her mind and leave out half that she now puts in, and she will write a better book one of these days. She will be a poet, I said, putting *Life's Adventure*, by Mary Carmichael, at the end of the shelf, in another hundred years' time.

Six

Next day the light of the October morning was falling in dusty shafts through the uncurtained windows, and the hum of traffic rose from the street. London then was winding itself up again; the factory was astir; the machines were beginning. It was tempting, after all this reading, to look out of the window and see what London was doing on the morning of the twenty-sixth of October 1928. And what was London doing? Nobody, it seemed, was reading *Antony and Cleopatra*. London was wholly indifferent, it appeared, to Shakespeare's plays. Nobody cared a straw—and I do not blame them—for the future of fiction, the death of poetry or the development by the average woman of a prose style completely expressive of her mind. If opinions upon any of these matters had been chalked on the pavement, nobody would have stooped to read them. The nonchalance of the hurrying feet would have rubbed them out in half an hour. Here came an errand-boy; here a woman with a dog on a lead. The fascination of the London street is that no two people are ever alike; each seems bound on some private affair of his own. There were the businesslike, with their little bags; there were the drifters rattling sticks upon area railings; there were affable characters to whom the streets serve for clubroom, hailing men in carts and giving information without being asked for it. Also there were funerals to which men, thus suddenly reminded of the passing of their own bodies, lifted their hats. And then a very distinguished gentleman came slowly down a doorstep and paused to avoid collision with a bustling lady who had, by some means or other, acquired a splendid fur coat and a bunch of Parma violets. They all seemed separate, self-absorbed, on business of their own.

At this moment, as so often happens in London, there was a complete lull and *Androgyny* suspension of traffic. Nothing came down the street; nobody passed. A single leaf detached itself from the plane tree at the end of the street, and in that pause and suspension fell. Somehow it was like a signal falling, a signal pointing to a force in things which one had overlooked. It seemed to point to a river, which flowed past, invisibly, round the corner, down the street, and took people and eddied them along, as the stream at Oxbridge had taken the undergraduate in his boat and the dead leaves. Now it was bringing from one side of the street to the other diagonally a girl in patent leather boots, and then a young man in a maroon overcoat; it was also bringing a taxi-cab; and it brought all three together at a point directly beneath my window; where the taxi stopped; and the girl and the young man stopped; and they got into the taxi; and then the cab glided off as if it were swept on by the current elsewhere.

The sight was ordinary enough; what was strange was the rhythmical order with which my imagination had invested it; and the fact that the ordinary sight of two people getting into a cab had the power to communicate something of their own seeming satisfaction. The sight of two people coming down the street and meeting at the corner seems to ease the mind of some strain, I thought, watching the taxi turn and make off. Perhaps to think, as I had been thinking these two days, of one sex as distinct from the other is an effort. It interferes with the unity of the mind. Now that effort had ceased and that unity had been restored by seeing two people come together and get into a taxi-cab. The mind is certainly a very mysterious organ, I reflected, drawing my head in from the window, about which nothing whatever is known, though we depend upon it so completely. Why do I feel that there are severances and oppositions in the mind, as there are strains from obvious causes on the body? What does one mean by "the unity of the mind," I pondered, for clearly the mind has so great a power of concentrating at any point at any moment that it seems to have no single state of being. It can seperate itself from the people in the street, for example, and think of itself as apart from them, at an upper window looking down on them. Or it can think with other people spontaneously, as, for instance, in a crowd waiting to hear some piece of news read out. It can think back through its fathers or through its mothers, as I have said that a woman writing thinks back through her mothers. Again if one is a woman one is often surprised by a sudden splitting off of consciousness, say in walking down Whitehall, when from being the natural inheritor of that civilization, she becomes, on the contrary, outside of it, alien and critical. Clearly the mind is always altering its focus, and bringing the world into different perspectives. But some of these states of mind seem, even if adopted spontaneously, to be less comfortable than others. In order to keep oneself continuing in them one is unconsciously holding something back, and gradually the repression becomes an effort. But there may be some state of mind in which one could continue without effort because nothing is required to be held back. And this perhaps, I thought, coming in from the window, is one of them. For certainly when I saw the couple get into the taxicab the mind felt as if, after being divided, it had come together again in a natural fusion. The obvious reason would be that it is natural for the sexes to co-operate. One has a profound, if irrational, instinct in favor of the theory that the union of man and woman makes for the greatest satisfaction, the most complete happiness. But the sight of two people getting into the taxi and the satisfaction it gave me made me also ask whether there are two sexes in the mind corresponding to the two sexes in the body, and whether they also require to be united in order to get compete satisfaction and happiness. And I went on amateurishly to sketch a plan of the soul so that in each of us two powers preside, one male, one female; and in the man's brain, the man predominates over the woman, and in the woman's brain, the woman predominates over the man. The normal and comfortable state of being is that when the two live in harmony together, spiritually co-operating. If one is a man, still the woman part of the brain must have effect; and a woman also must have intercourse with the man in her. Coleridge perhaps meant this when he said that a great mind is androgynous.[62] It is when the fusion takes place that the mind is fully fertilized and uses all its faculties. Perhaps a mind that is purely masculine cannot create, any more than a mind that is purely feminine, I thought. But it would be well to test what one meant by man-womanly, and conversely by woman-manly, by pausing and looking at a book or two.

Coleridge certainly did not mean, when he said that a great mind is androgynous, that it is a mind that has any special sympathy with women; a mind that takes up their cause or devotes itself to their interpretation. Perhaps the androgynous mind is less apt to make these distinctions than the single-sexed mind. He meant, perhaps, that the androgynous mind is resonant and porous; that it transmits emotion without impediment; that it is naturally creative, incandescent and undivided. In fact one goes back to Shakespeare's mind as the type of the androgynous, of the man-womanly mind, though it would be impossible to say what Shakespeare thought of women. And if it be true that it is one of the tokens of the fully developed mind that it does not think specially or separately of sex, how much harder it is to attain that condition now than ever before. Here I came to the books by living writers, and there paused and wondered if this fact were not at the root of something that had long puzzled me. No age can ever have been as stridently sex-conscious as our own; those innumerable books by men about women in the British Museum are a proof of it. The Suffrage campaign was no doubt to blame. It must have roused in men an extraordinary desire for self-assertion; it must have made them lay an emphasis upon their own sex and its characteristics which they would not have troubled to think about had they not been challenged. And when one is challenged, even by a few women in black bonnets, one retaliates, if one has never been challenged before, rather excessively. That perhaps accounts for some of the characteristics that I remember to have found here, I thought, taking down a new novel by Mr. A, who is in the prime of life and very well thought of, apparently, by the reviewers. I opened it. Indeed, it was delightful to read a man's writing again. It was so direct, so straightforward after the writing of women. It indicated such freedom of mind, such liberty of person, such confidence in himself. One had a sense of physical well-being in the presence of this well-nourished, well-educated, free mind, which had never been thwarted or opposed, but had had full liberty from birth to stretch itself in whatever way it liked. All this was admirable. But after reading a chapter or two a shadow seemed to lie across the page. It was a straight dark bar, a shadow shaped something like the letter "I." One began dodging this way and that to catch a glimpse of the landscape behind it. Whether that was indeed a tree or a woman walking I was not quite sure. Back one was always hailed to the letter "I." One began to be tired of "I." Not but what this "I" was a most respectable "I"; honest and logical; as hard as a nut, and polished for centuries by good teaching and good feeding. I respect and admire that "I" from the bottom of my heart. But—here I turned a page or two, looking for something or other—the worst of it is that in the shadow of the letter "I" all is shapeless as mist. Is that a tree? No, it is a woman. But . . . she has not a bone in her body, I thought, watching Phoebe, for that was her name, coming across the beach. Then Alan got up and the shadow of Alan at once obliterated Phoebe. For Alan had views and Phoebe was quenched in the flood of his views. And then Alan, I thought, has passions; and here I turned page after page very fast, feeling that the crisis was approaching, and so it was. It took place on the beach under the sun. It was done very openly. It was done very vigorously. Nothing could have been more indecent. But . . . I had said "but" too often. One cannot go on saying "but." One must finish the sentence somehow, I rebuked myself. Shall I finish it, "But—I am bored!" But why was I bored? Partly because of the dominance of the letter "I" and the aridity, which, like the giant beech tree, it casts within its shade. Nothing will grow there. And partly for some more obscure reason. There seemed to be some obstacle, some impediment of Mr. A's mind which blocked the fountain of creative energy and shored it within narrow limits. And remembering the lunch party at Oxbridge, and the cigarette ash and the Manx cat and Tennyson and Christina Rossetti all in a bunch, it seemed possible that the impediment lay there. As he no longer hums under his breath, "There has fallen a splendid tear from the passion-flower at the gate," when Phoebe crosses the beach, and she no longer replies, "My heart is like a singing bird whose nest is in a watered shoot," when Alan approaches what can he do? Being honest as the day and logical as the sun, there is only one thing he can do. And that he does, to do him justice, over and over (I said, turning the pages) and over again. And that, I added, aware of the awful nature of the confession, seems somehow dull. Shakespeare's indecency uproots a thousand other things in one's mind, and is far from being dull. But Shakespeare does it for pleasure; Mr. A, as the nurses say, does it on purpose. He does it in protest. He is protesting against the equality of the other sex by asserting his own superiority. He is therefore impeded and inhibited and self-conscious as Shakespeare might have been if he too had known Miss Clough and Miss Davies.[63] Doubtless Elizabethan literature would have been very different from what it is if the woman's movement had begun in the sixteenth century and not in the nineteenth.

What, then, it amounts to, if this theory of the two sides of the mind holds good, is that virility has now become self-conscious—men, that is to say, are now writing only with the male side of their brains. It is a mistake for a woman to read them, for she will inevitably look for something that she will not find. It is the power of suggestion that one most misses, I thought, taking Mr. B the critic in my hand and reading, very carefully and very dutifully, his remarks upon the art of poetry. Very able they were, acute and full of learning; but the trouble was, that his feelings no longer communicated; his mind seemed separated into different chambers; not a sound carried from one to the other. Thus, when one takes a sentence of Mr. B into the mind it falls plump to the ground—dead; but when one takes a sentence of Coleridge into the mind, it explodes and gives birth to all kinds of other ideas, and that is the only sort of writing of which one can say that it has the secret of perpetual life.

But whatever the reason may be, it is a fact that one must deplore. For it means—here I had come to rows of books by Mr. Galsworthy and Mr. Kipling—that

---

63. Anne Clough (1820–92) and Emily Davies (1830–1921) were British suffragists and advocates of women's higher education.

some of the finest works of our greatest living writers fall upon deaf ears. Do what she will a woman cannot find in them that fountain of perpetual life which the critics assure her is there. It is not only that they celebrate male virtues, enforce male values and describe the world of men; it is that the emotion with which these books are permeated is to a woman incomprehensible. It is coming, it is gathering, it is about to burst on one's head, one begins saying long before the end. That picture will fall on old Jolyon's head; he will die of the shock; the old clerk will speak over him two or three obituary words; and all the swans on the Thames will simultaneously burst out singing. But one will rush away before that happens and hide in the gooseberry bushes, for the emotion which is so deep, so subtle, so symbolical to a man moves a woman to wonder. So with Mr. Kipling's officers who turn their backs; and his Sowers who sow the Seed; and his Men who are alone with their Work; and the Flag—one blushes at all these capital letters as if one had been caught eavesdropping at some purely masculine orgy. The fact is that neither Mr. Galsworthy nor Mr. Kipling has a spark of the woman in him.[64] Thus all their qualities seem to a woman, if one may generalize, crude and immature. They lack suggestive power. And when a book lacks suggestive power, however hard it hits the surface of the mind it cannot penetrate within.

And in that restless mood in which one takes books out and puts them back again without looking at them I began to envisage an age to come of pure, of self-assertive virility, such as the letters of professors (take Sir Walter Raleigh's letters, for instance) seem to forebode, and the rulers of Italy have already brought into being.[65] For one can hardly fail to be impressed in Rome by the sense of unmitigated masculinity; and whatever the value of unmitigated masculinity upon the state, one may question the effect of it upon the art of poetry. At any rate, according to the newspapers, there is a certain anxiety about fiction in Italy. There has been a meeting of academicians whose object it is "to develop the Italian novel." "Men famous by birth, or in finance, industry or the Fascist corporations" came together the other day and discussed the matter, and a telegram was sent to the Duce expressing the hope "that the Fascist era would soon give birth to a poet worthy of it." We may all join in that pious hope, but it is doubtful whether poetry can come out of an incubator. Poetry ought to have a mother as well as a father. The Fascist poem, one may fear, will be a horrid little abortion such as one sees in a glass jar in the museum of some county town. Such monsters never live long, it is said; one has never seen a prodigy of that sort cropping grass in a field. Two heads on one body do not make for length of life.

However, the blame for all this, if one is anxious to lay blame, rests no more upon one sex than upon the other. All seducers and reformers are responsible, Lady Bessborough when she lied to Lord Granville; Miss Davies when she told the truth to Mr. Greg. All who have brought about a state of sex-consciousness are to blame, and it is they who drive me, when I want to stretch my faculties on a book, to seek it in that happy age, before Miss Davies and Miss Clough were born, when the writer used both sides of his mind equally. One must turn back to Shakespeare then, for Shakespeare was androgynous; and so was Keats and Sterne and Cowper and Lamb and Coleridge. Shelley perhaps was sexless. Milton and Ben Jonson had a dash too much of the male in them. So had Wordsworth and Tolsoi.[66] In our time Proust

---

64. John Galsworthy (1867–1933) and Rudyard Kipling (1865–1936) were prominent British novelists; Galsworthy won the Nobel Prize for Literature in 1932.

65. Sir Walter Raleigh (1554–1618) was a Renaissance courtier, poet, and historian. Woolf refers negatively here to Mussolini's Italy.

66. William Wordsworth (1770–1850) was a British Romantic poet.

was wholly androgynous, if not perhaps a little too much of a woman. But that failing
is too rare for one to complain of it, since without some mixture of the kind the intellect seems to predominate and the other faculties of the mind harden and become
barren. However, I consoled myself with the reflection that this is perhaps a passing
phase; much of what I have said in obedience to my promise to give you the course of
my thoughts will seem out of date; much of what flames in my eyes will seem dubious
to you who have not yet come of age.

Even so, the very first sentence that I would write here, I said, crossing over to
the writing-table and taking up the page headed Women and Fiction, is that it is
fatal for any one who writes to think of their sex. It is fatal to be a man or woman
pure and simple; one must be woman-manly or man-womanly. It is fatal for a woman
to lay the least stress on any grievance; to plead even with justice any cause; in any
way to speak consciously as a woman. And fatal is no figure of speech; for anything
written with that conscious bias is doomed to death. It ceases to be fertilized. Brilliant and effective, powerful and masterly, as it may appear for a day or two, it must
wither at nightfall; it cannot grow in the minds of others. Some collaboration has to
take place in the mind between the woman and the man before the act of creation
can be accomplished. Some marriage of opposites has to be consummated. The whole
of the mind must lie wide open if we are to get the sense that the writer is communicating his experience with perfect fullness. There must be freedom and there must be
peace. Not a wheel must grate, not a light glimmer. The curtains must be close
drawn. The writer, I thought, once his experience is over, must lie back and let his
mind celebrate its nuptials in darkness. He must not look or question what is being
done. Rather, he must pluck the petals from a rose or watch the swans float calmly
down the river. And I saw again the current which took the boat and the undergraduate and the dead leaves; and the taxi took the man and the woman, I thought, seeing them come together across the street, and the current swept them away, I
thought, hearing far off the roar of London's traffic, into that tremendous stream.

[handwritten margin notes: Man & Woman working together, androgyny at its best. Paradox]

Here, then, Mary Beton ceases to speak. She has told you how she reached the
conclusion—the prosaic conclusion—that it is necessary to have five hundred a year
and a room with a lock on the door if you are to write fiction or poetry. She has tried
to lay bare the thoughts and impressions that led her to think this. She has asked you
to follow her flying into the arms of a Beadle, lunching here, dining there, drawing
pictures in the British Museum, taking books from the shelf, looking out of the window. While she has been doing all these things, you no doubt have been observing
her failings and foibles and deciding what effect they have had on her opinions. You
have been contradicting her and making whatever additions and deductions seem
good to you. That is all as it should be, for in a question like this truth is only to be
had by laying together many varieties of error. And I will end now in my own person
by anticipating two criticisms, so obvious that you can hardly fail to make them.

No opinion has been expressed, you may say, upon the comparative merits of the
sexes even as writers. That was done purposely, because, even if the time had come for
such a valuation—and it is far more important at the moment to know how much money women had and how many rooms than to theorize about their capacities—even if the
time had come I do not believe that gifts, whether of mind or character, can be weighted
like sugar and butter, not even in Cambridge, where they are so adept at putting people into classes and fixing caps on their heads and letters after their names. I do not
believe that even the Table of Precedency which you will find in Whitaker's *Almanac*
represents a final order of values, or that there is any sound reason to suppose that a

Commander of the Bath will ultimately walk in to dinner behind a Master of Lunacy. All this pitting of sex against sex, of quality against quality; all this claiming of superiority and imputing of inferiority, belong to the private-school stage of human existence where there are "sides," and it is necessary for one side to beat another side, and of the utmost importance to walk up to a platform and receive from the hands of the Headmaster himself a highly ornamental pot. As people mature they cease to believe in sides or in Headmasters or in highly ornamental pots. At any rate, where books are concerned, it is notoriously difficult to fix labels of merit in such a way that they do not come off. Are not reviews of current literature a perpetual illustration of the difficulty of judgment? "This great book," "this worthless book," the same book is called by both names. Praise and blame alike mean nothing. No, delightful as the pastime of measuring may be, it is the most futile of all occupations, and to submit to the decrees of the measurers the most servile of attitudes. So long as you write what you wish to write, that is all that matters; and whether it matters for ages or only for hours, nobody can say. But to sacrifice a hair of the head of your vision, a shade of its color, in deference to some Headmaster with a silver pot in his hand or to some professor with a measuring-rod up his sleeve, is the most abject treachery, and the sacrifice of wealth and chastity which used to be said to be the greatest of human disasters, a mere flea-bite in comparison.

Next I think that you may object that in all this I have made too much of the importance of material things. Even allowing a generous margin for symbolism, that five hundred a year stands for the power to contemplate, that a lock on the door means the power to think for oneself, still you may say that the mind should rise above such things; and that great poets have often been poor men. Let me then quote to you the words of your own Professor of Literature, who knows better than I do what goes to the making of a poet. Sir Arthur Quiller-Couch writes:[67]

> What are the great poetical names of the last hundred years or so? Coleridge, Wordsworth, Byron, Shelley, Landor, Keats, Tennyson, Browning, Arnold, Morris, Rossetti, Swinburne— we may stop there.[68] Of these, all but Keats, Browning, Rossetti were University men; and of these three, Keats, who died young, cut off in his prime, was the only one not fairly well to do. It may seem a brutal thing to say, and it is a sad thing to say: but, as a matter of hard fact, the theory that poetical genius bloweth where it listeth, and equally in poor and rich, holds little truth. As a matter of hard fact, nine out of those twelve were University men: which means that somehow or other they procured the means to get the best education England can give. As a matter of hard fact, of the remaining three you know that Browning was well to do, and I challenge you that, if he had not been well to do, he would no more have attained to write *Saul* or *The Ring and the Book* than Ruskin would have attained to writing *Modern Painters* if his father had not dealt prosperously in business. Rossetti had a small private income; and, moreover, he painted. There remains but Keats; whom Atropos slew young, as she slew John Clare in a mad-house, and James Thomson by the laudanum he took to drug disappointment.[69] These are dreadful facts, but let us face them. It is—however dishonoring to us as a nation—certain that, by

---

67. [*The Art of Writing*, by Sir Arthur Quiller-Couch.]
68. Sir Arthur Quiller-Couch (1863–1944), known by his pen name, "Q," was an English critic, novelist, and poet; George Gordon, Lord Byron (1788–1824) was a British Romantic poet; Walter Savage Landor (1775–1864) was a minor British poet associated with the Romantics; Matthew Arnold (1822–88) was an eminent Victorian poet and essayist; William Morris (1834–96) was a socialist, artist, and writer; both he and Dante Gabriel Rossetti (1828–82) were associated with the Pre-Raphaelites; Algernon Charles Swinburne (1837–1909) was a bohemian poet.

69. Robert Browning's dramatic monologue *Saul* is widely considered a lesser work than *The Ring and the Book* (1868–69), his longest poem; John Ruskin (1819–1900) was a leading art and social critic of Victorian England and the author of *Modern Painters* (1843); John Clare (1793–1864) was a working-class British poet who became mentally ill and was institutionalized in 1837; James Thomson (1834–82) was a British poet and essayist who suffered from melancholia.

some fault in our commonwealth, the poor poet has not in these days, nor has had for two hundred years, a dog's chance. Believe me—and I have spent a great part of ten years in watching some three hundred and twenty elementary schools—we may prate of democracy, but actually, a poor child in England has little more hope than had the son of an Athenian slave to be emancipated into that intellectual freedom of which great writings are born.

Nobody could put the point more plainly. "The poor poet has not in these days, nor has had for two hundred years, a dog's chance . . . a poor child in England has little more hope than had the son of an Athenian slave to be emancipated into that intellectual freedom of which great writings are born." That is it. Intellectual freedom depends upon material things. Poetry depends upon intellectual freedom. And women have always been poor, not for two hundred years merely, but from the beginning of time. Women have had less intellectual freedom than the sons of Athenian slaves. Women, then, have not had a dog's chance of writing poetry. That is why I have laid so much stress on money and a room of one's own. However, thanks to the toils of those obscure women in the past, of whom I wish we knew more, thanks, curiously enough, to two wars, the Crimean which let Florence Nightingale out of her drawing-room, and the European War which opened the doors to the average woman some sixty years later, these evils are in the way to be bettered. Otherwise you would not be here tonight, and your chance of earning five hundred pounds a year, precarious as I am afraid that it still is, would be minute in the extreme.

Still, you may object, why do you attach so much importance to this writing of books by women when, according to you, it requires so much effort, leads perhaps to the murder of one's aunts, will make one almost certainly late for luncheon, and may bring one into very grave disputes with certain very good fellows? My motives, let me admit, are partly selfish. Like most uneducated Englishwomen, I like reading—I like reading books in the bulk. Lately my diet has become a trifle monotonous; history is too much about wars; biography too much about great men; poetry has shown, I think, a tendency to sterility, and fiction—but I have sufficiently exposed my disabilities as a critic of modern fiction and will say no more about it. Therefore I would ask you to write all kinds of books, hesitating at no subject however trivial or however vast. By hook or by crook, I hope that you will possess yourselves of money enough to travel and to idle, to contemplate the future or the past of the world, to dream over books and loiter at street corners and let the line of thought dip deep into the stream. For I am by no means confining you to fiction. If you would please me—and there are thousands like me—you would write books of travel and adventure, and research and scholarship, and history and biography, and criticism and philosophy and science. By so doing you will certainly profit the art of fiction. For books have a way of influencing each other. Fiction will be much the better for standing cheek by jowl with poetry and philosophy. Moreover, if you consider any great figure of the past, like Sappho, like the Lady Murasaki, like Emily Brontë, you will find that she is an inheritor as well as an originator, and has come into existence because women have come to have the habit of writing naturally; so that even as a prelude to poetry such activity on your part would be invaluable.[70]

But when I look back through these notes and criticize my own train of thought as I made them, I find that my motives were not altogether selfish. There runs through

---

70. Sappho was a Greek poet from Lesbos who lived during the 7th and 6th centuries BCE; Lady Shikibu Murasaki (978?–1026?) was a Japanese courtier and author of the *Tale of Genji*, which is widely viewed as the first novel in world literature.

these comments and discursions the conviction—or is it the instinct?—that good books are desirable and that good writers, even if they show every variety of human depravity, are still good human beings. Thus when I ask you to write more books I am urging you to do what will be for your good and for the good of the world at large. How to justify this instinct or belief I do not know, for philosophic words, if one has not been educated at a university, are apt to play one false. What is meant by "reality"? It would seem to be something very erratic, very undependable—now to be found in a dusty road, now in a scrap of newspaper in the street, now in a daffodil in the sun. It lights up a group in a room and stamps some casual saying. It overwhelms one walking home beneath the stars and makes the silent world more real than the world of speech—and then there it is again in an omnibus in the uproar of Piccadilly. Some-times, too, it seems to dwell in shapes too far away for us to discern what their nature is. But whatever it touches, it fixes and makes permanent. That is what remains over when the skin of the day has been cast into the hedge; that is what is left of past time and of our loves and hates. Now the writer, as I think, has the chance to live more than other people in the presence of this reality. It is his business to find it and collect it and communicate it to the rest of us. So at least I infer from reading *Lear* or *Emma* or *La Recherche du Temps Perdu*. For the reading of these books seems to perform a curi-ous couching operation on the senses; one sees more intensely afterwards; the world seems bared of its covering and given an intenser life. Those are the enviable people who live at enmity with unreality; and those are the pitiable who are knocked on the head by the thing done without knowing or caring. So that when I ask you to earn money and have a room of your own, I am asking you to live in the presence of reality, an invigorating life, it would appear, whether one can impart it or not.

Here I would stop, but the pressure of convention decrees that every speech must end with a peroration. And a peroration addressed to women should have something, you will agree, particularly exalting and ennobling about it. I should implore you to remember your responsibilities, to be higher, more spiritual; I should remind you how much depends upon you, and what an influence you can exert upon the future. But those exhortations can safely, I think, be left to the other sex, who will put them, and indeed have put them, with far greater eloquence than I can compass. When I rum-mage in my own mind I find no noble sentiments about being companions and equals and influencing the world to higher ends. I find myself saying briefly and prosaically that it is much more important to be oneself than anything else. Do not dream of influencing other people, I would say, if I knew how to make it sound exalted. Think of things in themselves.

And again I am reminded by dipping into newspapers and novels and biographies that when a woman speaks to women she should have something very unpleasant up her sleeve. Women are hard on women. Women dislike women. Women—but are you not sick to death of the word? I can assure you that I am. Let us agree, then, that a paper read by a woman to women should end with something particularly disagreeable.

But how does it go? What can I think of? The truth is, I often like women. I like their unconventionality. I like their subtlety. I like their anonymity. I like—but I must not run on this way. That cupboard there,—you say it holds clean table-napkins only; but what if Sir Archibald Bodkin were concealed among them?[71] Let me then adopt a sterner tone. Have I, in the preceding words, conveyed to you sufficiently the

---

71. According to Jane Marcus, Sir Archibald Bodkin was Director of Public Prosecutions at the trial for obscenity of les-bian novelist Radclyffe Hall in 1928. See ch. 8 in *Virginia Woolf and the Languages of Patriarchy*.

warnings and reprobation of mankind? I have told you the very low opinion in which you were held by Mr. Oscar Browning. I have indicated what Napoleon once thought of you and what Mussolini thinks now. Then, in case any of you aspire to fiction, I have copied out for your benefit the advice of the critic about courageously acknowledging the limitations of your sex. I have referred to Professor X and given prominence to his statement that women are intellectually, morally and physically inferior to men. I have handed on all that has come my way without going in search of it, and here is a final warning—from Mr. John Langdon Davies.[72] Mr. John Langdon Davies warns women "that when children cease to be altogether desirable, women cease to be altogether necessary." I hope you will make a note of it.

How can I further encourage you to go about the business of life? Young women, I would say, and please attend, for the peroration is beginning, you are, in my opinion, disgracefully ignorant. You have never made a discovery of any sort of importance. You have never shaken an empire or led an army into battle. The plays of Shakespeare are not by you, and you have never introduced a barbarous race to the blessings of civilization. What is your excuse? It is all very well for you to say, pointing to the streets and squares and forests of the globe swarming with black and white and coffee-colored inhabitants, all busily engaged in traffic and enterprise and love-making, we have had other work on our hands. Without our doing, those seas would be unsailed and those fertile lands a desert. We have borne and bred and washed and taught, perhaps to the age of six or seven years, the one thousand six hundred and twenty-three million human beings who are, according to statistics, at present in existence, and that, allowing that some had help, takes time.

There is truth in what you say—I will not deny it. But at the same time may I remind you that there have been at least two colleges for women in existence in England since the year 1866; that after the year 1880 a married woman was allowed by law to possess her own property; and that in 1919—which is a whole nine years ago—she was given a vote? May I also remind you that the most of the professions have been open to you for close on ten years now? When you reflect upon these immense privileges and the length of time during which they have been enjoyed, and the fact that there must be at this moment some two thousand women capable of earning over five hundred a year in one way or another, you will agree that the excuse of lack of opportunity, training, encouragement, leisure and money no longer holds good. Moreover, the economists are telling us that Mrs. Seton has had too many children. You must, of course, go on bearing children, but, so they say, in twos and threes, not in tens and twelves.

Thus, with some time on your hands and with some book learning in your brains—you have had enough of the other kind, and are sent to college partly, I suspect, to be uneducated—surely you should embark upon another stage of your very long, very laborious and highly obscure career. A thousand pens are ready to suggest what you should do and what effect you will have. My own suggestion is a little fantastic, I admit; I prefer, therefore, to put it in the form of fiction.

I told you in the course of this paper that Shakespeare had a sister; but do not look for her in Sir Sidney Lee's life of the poet.[73] She died young—alas, she never wrote a word. She lies buried where the omnibuses now stop, opposite the Elephant

72. [*A Short Story of Women,* by John Langdon Davies.]
73. Sir Sidney Lee (1859–1926) was a biographer of Shakespeare.

and Castle. Now my belief is that this poet who never wrote a word and was buried at the crossroads still lives. She lives in you and in me, and in many other women who are not here tonight, for they are washing up the dishes and putting the children to bed. But she lives; for great poets do not die; they are continuing presences; they need only the opportunity to walk among us in the flesh. This opportunity, as I think, it is now coming within your power to give her. For my belief is that if we live another century or so—I am talking of the common life which is the real life and not of the little separate lives which we live as individuals—and have five hundred a year each of us and rooms of our own; if we have the habit of freedom and the courage to write exactly what we think; if we escape a little from the common sitting-room and see human beings not always in their relation to each other but in relation to reality; and the sky, too, and the trees or whatever it may be in themselves; if we look past Milton's bogey, for no human being should shut out the view; if we face the fact, for it is a fact, that there is no arm to cling to, but that we go alone and that our relation is to the world of reality and not only to the world of men and women, then the opportunity will come and the dead poet who was Shakespeare's sister will put on the body which she has so often laid down. Drawing her life from the lives of the unknown who were her forerunners, as her brother did before her, she will be born. As for her coming without that preparation, without that effort on our part, without that determination that when she is born again she shall find it possible to live and write her poetry, that we cannot expect, for that would be impossible. But I maintain that she would come if we worked for her, and that so to work, even in poverty and obscurity, is worth while.   *1929*

W. Woolf's conclusion

<hr />

bell hooks
1955–

A socialist-feminist scholar, theorist, and essayist, bell hooks is one of the foremost public intellectuals of our time. Her first book, *Ain't I A Woman: Black Women and Feminism* (1981), begun when she was nineteen, offers a searing analysis of racial and sexual politics, racist practices within feminism, and the need for black women and their male allies to build a strong women's movement. She expands this argument in *Feminist Theory: From Margin to Center* (1984), claiming that if feminism is to be a successful mass movement, it must include the voices of marginalized women. Hooks is the author of many other books on feminist struggle and the representations of black women in popular culture, including *Talking Back: Thinking Feminist, Thinking Black* (1989), *Yearning: Race, Gender, and Cultural Politics* (1990), *Breaking Bread* (with Cornel West, 1991), *Black Looks* (1992), *Outlaw Culture: Resisting Representations* (1994), and *Killing Rage: Ending Racism* (1995). Her essays treat a broad range of contemporary issues, such as date rape, censorship, misogyny in rap music, and sexist and racist violence in film. Known also for her writing about pedagogy, hooks asserts in *Teaching to Transgress: Education as the Practice of Freedom* (1994) that only a radical teaching style will produce the kinds of new knowledge that will lead students toward revolutionary change for the twenty-first century.

Born Gloria Watkins, hooks grew up in the segregated South in a family and community that loved her but could not always understand her need to speak and write. She has written

extensively and movingly about her struggles as an outspoken child often punished for insubordination. Her decision to adopt a pseudonym while writing an early volume of poetry was an
important strategy that freed her voice. Bell Hooks was the name of her great-grandmother, a
woman known for speaking her mind and a figure who represented for her granddaughter
courage and strength; the choice to refuse capitalization was a means of distinguishing her
voice from her grandmother's. Hooks studied at Stanford University, where she wrote a Ph.D.
dissertation on the novels of Toni Morrison. A teacher as well as a writer, she has taught at
Oberlin College and Yale University and is currently Distinguished Professor of English at
City College in New York. Much of her life story can be found in *A Woman's Mourning Song*
(1993), a collection of poems; *Sisters of the Yam* (1993), a study of "black women and self
recovery"; *Bone Black: Memories of Girlhood* (1996), a coming-of-age memoir; and *Wounds of
Passion: A Writing Life* (1997), an exploration of the links between sexuality and writing.

In all of her work, hooks addresses the urgent need for discursive and political resistance
to sexism, racism, and cultural imperialism. The essay included here, "Talking Back," reveals
the complexities that many women of color experience in engendering language, silence, and
voice. She calls upon black women to "talk back"—speak the truth, reject self-censorship—to
family members and friendship networks, racist feminists, white supremacists. Black women
traditionally have not been silenced, hooks asserts, revising Virginia Woolf's and Tillie
Olsen's arguments across racial differences; instead, they have been taught a self-denying kind
of domestic discourse, "the right speech of womanhood." It is time to "change the nature and
direction of our speech," she proclaims, without dishonoring the women whose speech she
both learned and unlearned—for "it was in this world of woman talk . . . that I made speech
my birthright."

⊰ Talking Back ⊱

In the world of the southern black community I grew up in, "back talk" and "talking
back" meant speaking as an equal to an authority figure. It meant daring to disagree
and sometimes it just meant having an opinion. In the "old school," children were
meant to be seen and not heard. My great-grandparents, grandparents, and parents
were all from the old school. To make yourself heard if you were a child was to invite
punishment, the back-hand lick, the slap across the face that would catch you
unaware, or the feel of switches stinging your arms and legs.

To speak then when one was not spoken to was a courageous act—an act of risk
and daring. And yet it was hard not to speak in warm rooms where heated discussions
began at the crack of dawn, women's voices filling the air, giving orders, making
threats, fussing. Black men may have excelled in the art of poetic preaching in the
male-dominated church, but in the church of the home, where the everyday rules of
how to live and how to act were established, it was black women who preached.
There, black women spoke in a language so rich, so poetic, that it felt to me like
being shut off from life, smothered to death if one were not allowed to participate.

It was in that world of woman talk (the men were often silent, often absent) that
was born in me the craving to speak, to have a voice, and not just any voice but one
that could be identified as belonging to me. To make my voice, I had to speak, to hear
myself talk—and talk I did—darting in and out of grown folks' conversations and dialogues, answering questions that were not directed at me, endlessly asking questions,
making speeches. Needless to say, the punishments for these acts of speech seemed
endless. They were intended to silence me—the child—and more particularly the girl

child. Had I been a boy, they might have encouraged me to speak believing that I might someday be called to preach. There was no "calling" for talking girls, no legit-imized rewarded speech. The punishments I received for "talking back" were intended to suppress all possibility that I would create my own speech. That speech was to be suppressed so that the "right speech of womanhood" would emerge.

Within feminist circles, silence is often seen as the sexist "right speech of womanhood"—the sign of woman's submission to patriarchal authority. This emphasis on woman's silence may be an accurate remembering of what has taken place in the households of women from WASP backgrounds in the United States, but in black communities (and diverse ethnic communities), women have not been silent. Their voices can be heard. Certainly for black women, our struggle has not been to emerge from silence into speech but to change the nature and direction of our speech, to make a speech that compels listeners, one that is heard.

Our speech, "the right speech of womanhood," was often the soliloquy, the talk-ing into thin air, the talking to ears that do not hear you—the talk that is simply not listened to. Unlike the black male preacher whose speech was to be heard, who was to be listened to, whose words were to be remembered, the voices of black women—giving orders, making threats, fussing—could be tuned out, could become a kind of background music, audible but not acknowledged as significant speech. Dialogue—the sharing of speech and recognition—took place not between mother and child or mother and male authority figure but among black women. I can remember watching fascinated as our mother talked with her mother, sisters, and women friends. The intimacy and intensity of their speech—the satisfaction they received from talking to one another, the pleasure, the joy. It was in this world of woman speech, loud talk, angry words, women with tongues quick and sharp, tender sweet tongues, touching our world with their words, that I made speech my birthright—and the right to voice, to authorship, a privilege I would not be denied. It was in that world and because of it that I came to dream of writing, to write.

Writing was a way to capture speech, to hold onto it, keep it close. And so I wrote down bits and pieces of conversations, confessing in cheap diaries that soon fell apart from too much handling, expressing the intensity of my sorrow, the anguish of speech—for I was always saying the wrong thing, asking the wrong questions. I could not confine my speech to the necessary corners and concerns of life. I hid these writings under my bed, in pillow stuffings, among faded underwear. When my sisters found and read them, they ridiculed and mocked me—poking fun. I felt violated, ashamed, as if the secret parts of my self had been exposed, brought into the open, and hung like newly clean laundry, out in the air for everyone to see. The fear of exposure, the fear that one's deepest emotions and innermost thoughts will be dis-missed as mere nonsense, felt by so many young girls keeping diaries, holding and hiding speech, seems to me now one of the barriers that women have always needed and still need to destroy so that we are no longer pushed into secrecy or silence.

Despite my feelings of violation, of exposure, I continued to speak and write, choosing my hiding places well, learning to destroy work when no safe place could be found. I was never taught absolute silence, I was taught that it was important to speak but to talk a talk that was in itself a silence. Taught to speak and yet beware of the betrayal of too much heard speech, I experienced intense confusion and deep anxiety in my efforts to speak and write. Reciting poems at Sunday afternoon church service might be rewarded. Writing a poem (when one's time could be "better" spent sweep-ing, ironing, learning to cook) was luxurious activity, indulged in at the expense of

others. Questioning authority, raising issues that were not deemed appropriate subjects brought pain, punishments—like telling mama I wanted to die before her
because I could not live without her—that was crazy talk, crazy speech, the kind that
would lead you to end up in a mental institution. "Little girl," I would be told, "if you
don't stop all this crazy talk and crazy acting you are going to end up right out there
at Western State."

Madness, not just physical abuse, was the punishment for too much talk if you
were female. Yet even as this fear of madness haunted me, hanging over my writing
like a monstrous shadow, I could not stop the words, making thought, writing speech.
For this terrible madness which I feared, which I was sure was the destiny of daring
women born to intense speech (after all, the authorities emphasized this point daily),
was not as threatening as imposed silence, as suppressed speech.

Safety and sanity were to be sacrificed if I was to experience defiant speech.
Though I risked them both, deep-seated fears and anxieties characterized my childhood days. I would speak but I would not ride a bike, play hardball, or hold the gray
kitten. Writing about the ways we are traumatized in our growing-up years, psychoanalyst Alice Miller makes the point in *For Your Own Good* that it is not clear why
childhood wounds become for some folk an opportunity to grow, to move forward
rather than backward in the process of self-realization. Certainly, when I reflect on
the trials of my growing-up years, the many punishments, I can see now that in resistance I learned to be vigilant in the nourishment of my spirit, to be tough, to courageously protect that spirit from forces that would break it.

While punishing me, my parents often spoke about the necessity of breaking my
spirit. Now when I ponder the silences, the voices that are not heard, the voices of
those wounded and/or oppressed individuals who do not speak or write, I contemplate the acts of persecution, torture—the terrorism that breaks spirits, that makes
creativity impossible. I write these words to bear witness to the primacy of resistance
struggle in any situation of domination (even within family life); to the strength and
power that emerges from sustained resistance and the profound conviction that these
forces can be healing, can protect us from dehumanization and despair.

These early trials, wherein I learned to stand my ground, to keep my spirit intact,
came vividly to mind after I published *Ain't I A Woman* and the book was sharply
and harshly criticized. While I had expected a climate of critical dialogue, I was not
expecting a critical avalanche that had the power in its intensity to crush the spirit,
to push one into silence. Since that time, I have heard stories about black women,
about women of color, who write and publish (even when the work is quite successful) having nervous breakdowns, being made mad because they cannot bear the
harsh responses of family, friends, and unknown critics, or becoming silent, unpro-
ductive. Surely, the absence of a humane critical response has tremendous impact on
the writer from any oppressed, colonized group who endeavors to speak. For us, true
speaking is not solely an expression of creative power: it is an act of resistance, a
political gesture that challenges politics of domination that would render us nameless
and voiceless. As such, it is a courageous act—as such, it represents a threat. To those
who wield oppressive power, that which is threatening must necessarily be wiped out,
annihilated, silenced.

Recently, efforts by black women writers to call attention to our work serve to
highlight both our presence and absence. Whenever I peruse women's bookstores, I
am struck not by the rapidly growing body of feminist writing by black women, but by
the paucity of available published material. Those of us who write and are published

remain few in number. The context of silence is varied and multi-dimensional. Most obvious are the ways racism, sexism, and class exploitation act to suppress and silence. Less obvious are the inner struggles, the efforts made to gain the necessary confidence to write, to re-write, to fully develop craft and skill—and the extent to which such efforts fail.

Although I have wanted writing to be my life-work since childhood, it has been difficult for me to claim "writer" as part of that which identifies and shapes my everyday reality. Even after publishing books, I would often speak of wanting to be a writer as though these works did not exist. And though I would be told, "you are a writer," I was not yet ready to fully affirm this truth. Part of myself was still held captive by domineering forces of history, of familial life that had charted a map of silence, of right speech. I had not completely let go of the fear of saying the wrong thing, of being punished. Somewhere in the deep recesses of my mind, I believed I could avoid both responsibility and punishment if I did not declare myself a writer.

One of the many reasons I chose to write using the pseudonym bell hooks, a family name (mother to Sarah Oldham, grandmother to Rosa Bell Oldham, great-grandmother to me), was to construct a writer-identity that would challenge and subdue all impulses leading me away from speech into silence. I was a young girl buying bubble gum at the corner store when I first really heard the full name bell hooks. I had just "talked back" to a grown person. Even now I can recall the surprised look, the mocking tones that informed me I must be kin to bell hooks—a sharp-tongued woman, a woman who spoke her mind, a woman who was not afraid to talk back. I claimed this legacy of defiance, of will, of courage, affirming my link to female ancestors who were bold and daring in their speech. Unlike my bold and daring mother and grandmother, who were not supportive of talking back, even though they were assertive and powerful in their speech, bell hooks as I discovered, claimed, and invented her was my ally, my support.

That initial act of talking back outside the home was empowering. It was the first of many acts of defiant speech that would make it possible for me to emerge as an independent thinker and writer. In retrospect, "talking back" became for me a rite of initiation, testing my courage, strengthening my commitment, preparing me for the days ahead—the days when writing, rejection notices, periods of silence, publication, ongoing development seem impossible but necessary.

Moving from silence into speech is for the oppressed, the colonized, the exploited, and those who stand and struggle side by side a gesture of defiance that heals, that makes new life and new growth possible. It is that act of speech, of "talking back," that is no mere gesture of empty words, that is the expression of our movement from object to subject—the liberated voice.   1989

Leoba of England and Germany
700?–779

A scholar, poet, and nun, Leoba served as abbess of Bischofsheim in Franconia in the diocese of Mainz for most of her life. Her *Vita* was written in 836 by Rudolf, a monk of Fulda, who emphasizes her love of scholarship and explains that she went to Bischofsheim at the request of Boniface, a famous missionary saint and martyr. During this period scores of English women lived in monasteries, many of them in what are now Germany and Holland, and devoted their lives to God and his works.

Leoba, whose given name was Thrutgeba, was born in Wessex around 700. The daughter of an older aristocratic couple, Dynne and Aebbe, she earned the nickname Leoba, which means beloved, from her parents. She entered the novitiate as a young girl under the supervision of the abbess Tetta of Winbourne, who released Leoba when Boniface asked her to come to supervise thirty nuns at his monastery in Franconia. Rudolf, who knew her as an elderly nun then living at his monastery in Hesse, undertook the task of recording her life; he presents Leoba as an avid student of the Old and New Testaments, the works of the church fathers, and council decrees. Saintly in her manner and vision, Leoba became friends with the first wife of Charlemagne, Lady Hildegard, and was loved by her sister-nuns, Agatha, Thecla, Nana, and Eolaba, whom Rudolf interviewed while writing the biography. According to that document, Leoba once cured a woman with severe hemorrhoids by feeding her milk with the nun's own spoon; on another occasion she exacted a confession of infanticide from a physically handicapped woman. Among the other oddities that he records is a dream Leoba had of an endless purple thread that twined from her mouth, only to be gathered up in her hands. Rudolf's biography takes pains to show that the love between Leoba and Boniface was mutual and deep. Shortly before his death, Boniface begged her to continue her work at the abbey and gave her the hood of his cloak, the insignia of a monk's calling, thus naming her implicitly as his successor. He also asked that after Leoba's death her bones be interred in his tomb next to his own remains, a request that the monks who buried her did not honor, apparently out of fear of disturbing Boniface's grave. Leoba was instead buried on the north side of a nearby altar.

Letter writing plays a major part in the Anglo-Saxon literary tradition, and the types of letters that are extant range from practical epistles to offerings of advice, friendship, love, and condolence. Boniface, by all accounts a dedicated and busy man, was assisted in his mission by a variety of women and men in different locations in what is now Europe, most of whom wrote frequent letters in Latin. Surviving from this correspondence to Boniface are letters from five holy women, one of whom in Leoba. A recurring theme in these women's documents is their love of books. According to Rudolf, Leoba exhibited a particular affinity for poetry and enjoyed memorizing ecclesiastical law in verse form. Although she probably wrote much poetry, the quatrain at the end of the letter that is reprinted here is her only surviving verse, a prayer for Boniface's safety. Leoba's letter also pays tribute to her teacher, the prioress Eadburga, affirming the opportunities for sharing knowledge between women that medieval monasteries offered their nuns and abbesses.

⊰ Letter to Lord Boniface ⊱

To the most reverend lord Boniface, noble in worth, dearly beloved in Christ and close to me in kinship, Leobgytha—the lowest servant of those who bear the gentle yoke of Christ—sends her greeting for his continuing health.[1]

I beg you in your kindness to keep in memory the long friendship that you shared with Dynne, my father, in our west country. Eight years have run their course since he has departed from the light of day, and so I plead with you not to refuse to offer

---

1. St. Boniface (c. 675–754), an English Benedictine missionary, was called the Apostle of Germany.

your prayers to God for his soul. No less do I ask you also to remember my mother Aebbe, who, as you are well aware, is related to you by ties of blood. She is still alive and much burdened by illness. I am the only daughter of both my parents. Undeserving as I am, I should be very privileged if I might welcome you as my brother, for no man of our family gives me so much trustworthiness and hope as I find in you.

I am sending you a very small gift, not because it is worthy of your favor, but so that you will remember me only a little and not hand me over to the blankness of oblivion just because you are far away, and so we shall be closely entwined with the cords of true affection forever.

Dearest brother, I beg you even more earnestly that with the leathern shield of your prayers you will protect me against the poison darts of my secret enemy. And another favor I ask you, and that is to deign to correct the countrified diction of this letter of mine and that you won't fail in your generosity to send me a model I can follow in just a few words of your own, for I am filled with breathless longing to hear from you.

These little verses written below I struggled to compose according to the rules of poetic versification. It isn't because I'm bold enough to think I have any talent but because I'm eager to practice my meager rudiments of graceful composition, and I hope to have your help. I learned the art from my schoolmistress Eadburga, who continues to persevere ceaselessly in her holy reading of Scripture.

Farewell, live longer, be happier, and pray for me!

> May the all-powerful Judge, who alone created all,
> Who pours forth light in the realm of the father
> Where it steadfastly gleams so Christ's glory may reign,
> Keep you unharmed forever in his eternal law.

732

Matilda, Queen of England
1080–1118

Matilda, or "Maud the good Queen," as she was known after her marriage to Henry I of England on November 11, 1100, was a beneficent and effective ruler, a woman of letters, and a generous patron of literature. She was named Edith at her birth in 1080 to Malcolm Canmore, the king of Scotland who regained his throne when the rebellious Macbeth was killed, and his Hungarian-born wife, Margaret. As an adolescent Edith lived at Wilton Monastery under the care of her aunt Christina, abbess of Romsey and Wilton. Although she received an excellent education in Latin there, Edith detested the monastery and her cloistered life; she later admitted tearing off the black hood she was forced to wear daily and trampling it on the ground "to vent my rage and hatred of it." Clearly Matilda was strong-willed and high-spirited even before her reign as queen.

On August 5, 1100, Henry I seized the English throne that by right belonged to his older brother, Robert Curthose, who was away on crusade. Henry thus had a political reason for wishing to marry the young Scottish princess Edith: an alliance with Scotland would help to protect him against the challenge to his reign posed by Norman barons who wished Henry's brother to assume the throne. From the perspective of Edith's family the marriage was also desirable, since it would strengthen their hereditary claim to the throne of England; Edith's uncle, Edgar Atheling, was descended from Alfred the Great and would have become king of England in 1066 had he not been forced to yield to William the Conquerer after the Battle of Hastings.

As queen, Matilda occasionally traveled with her husband to Normandy but more often represented him in his absence. She is believed to have convinced the king's brother not to contest Henry's ascension by appealing to his sympathies: she was in childbed and should not be disturbed by an invasion. During her reign she handed down official writs on behalf of royal physicians, witnessed charters at Exeter and Canterbury, and in 1117 founded the Hospital of St. Giles as a refuge for lepers, whose wounds she sometimes helped to treat. She bore two sons, one of whom died in infancy, the other at age seventeen in a shipwreck, and one daughter, who became the mother of Henry II and thereby ensured her family's right of succession. Toward the end of her life she generously endowed Wilton Monastery, which had been for centuries both a haven and an educational institution for aristocratic girls, because, according to one contemporary historian, she realized that women had fewer resources for learning than did men.

At Wilton Matilda had shown a talent for letters, and as queen she commissioned writings in French and Latin, ordering among other works the poetic version of the *Voyage of St. Brendan* and requesting that a biography of her mother, Margaret, be written by the scholar Turgot, later bishop of St. Andrews. *The Life of St. Margaret* became the book Matilda most highly prized and often read. What remains of her own writing are six letters to Anselm, Archbishop of Canterbury—as Queen she had become friends with this man of God—and one letter to Pope Pascal. Prior to the ascension of Henry, Anselm had become embroiled in a religious controversy that escalated during Henry's reign; Anselm was thus in and out of favor with the king, and in and out of exile. Matilda's letters repeatedly urge Anselm to return, and they promote a reconciliation between the archbishop and her husband, which did eventually take place. To Pope Pascal she writes in hopes that he will intervene in the dispute between Henry and Anselm and thus facilitate the speedy return from exile of the man she calls "our preacher, the most prudent comforter of the people, and their most devoted father." Matilda's letters bear witness to her considerable rhetorical skills, her political acumen, and her multiple roles as Queen of the English people.

⊰ Letter to Archbishop Anselm ⊱

To her lord and father, Anselm Archbishop of Canterbury, both revered and cherished, Matilda, devout handmaiden of his Holiness, sends her greetings in Christ:

As often as you have shared the citadel of holiness with me through the kindness of your letters, just so often have you brightened the clouded darkness of my spirit with the light of renewed joy. For even when you are absent, there is a certain revisiting with you, as it were, the repeated touching of your bits of writing, and the thoroughly joyful and frequent rereading of your letters, which have been committed to memory.

Now, my lord, what is more elegant in style, more bursting with significance than your letters? The seriousness of Fronto, of Cicero, of Fabius, the subtlety of Quintilian are not lacking in them. The wisdom of Paul wells up in them, the diligence of Jerome, the midnight labor of Gregory, the exegesis of Augustine—and what is even greater than these—the sweetness of evangelical eloquence that distils from your writing.[1] Because of this grace that pours from your lips, therefore, my heart and my body have exulted with deep affection in your love, and in carrying out your fatherly teaching.

Relying on the support of Your Holiness, therefore, I have entrusted the abbacy of Malmesbury to Eudolph, monk of Winton—formerly known to you, I believe, as the sexton. To you is entirely reserved anew whatever pertains to the investiture and the decree, of course, so that the mandate of the staff as well as of the pastoral care shall be bestowed through the process of your own judgment.

May the power of heavenly grace grant a worthy recompense to the favor of your goodwill, which has not grown cool toward me. Concerning the rest, may Christ safeguard your office, and may he who blesses you on earth gladden me with your swift return. Amen.   1105?

ᴈ Letter to Pope Pascal ᴇ

To the highest pontiff and universal father, Pope Pascal, Matilda, Queen of the English by the grace of God. May he so administer the authority of the apostolic high office on earth that he shall deserve to be enrolled— together with the hosts of the just—among the apostolic senate in the joys of perpetual peace.

I bring the greatest thanks and praises that I can to Your Sublime Holiness, O apostolic man, for those things that your fatherly kindness has deigned to bestow upon the king, my lord, and me, by way of religious instruction. These dispatches you have both entrusted to the living voices of legates and included with your own writings.

I do not desist and I will not desist from what is proper and what I am able to do with my whole heart, soul, and mind: I will frequent the threshold of the most holy Roman apostolic see, embrace the ground on which my holy Father and apostolic pope has walked, and while prostrating myself at their paternal knees, pray with fitting urgency. I will steadfastly remain until I feel I am being heard by you, either because of my submissive humility or rather because of the persistent importuning of my entreaties.

Let Your Excellency not be angered by this boldness of mine and because I dare to speak this way. And let the wisdom of the Roman clergy, the people, and the Senate not be astounded. For under your apostolic high office, Anselm, our Archbishop, was indeed once a protégé of the Holy Spirit. He *was*, I say, for us and for the people of the English—so blessed as we were then—our preacher, the most prudent comforter of the people, and their most devoted father.

What he took in abundance from his Lord's most opulent treasury—whose key-bearer we acknowledged him to be—he distributed among us even more lav-

---

1. Marcus Cornelius Fronto (c. 100–166 CE) was a Roman lawyer, orator, and grammarian; Marcus Tullius Cicero (106–143 CE) was a Roman orator, statesman, and philosopher; Quintus Fabius Vibulanus served as Roman consul from 485–479 BCE; Marcus Fabius Quintilian (c. 35–c. 100 CE) was a Roman rhetorician. St. Paul became a Christian on the road to Damascus and wrote the Pauline epistles to the New Testament; St. Jerome (c. 347–419) was a Church father who published a Latin version of the Bible known as the Vulgate; Pope Gregory I (c. 540–604) was pope from 590 until his death and the author of dialogues and homilies; St. Augustine (354–430) was an early Christian philosopher and Church father.

ishly. As his Lord's loyal minister and wise steward he seasoned each morsel he paid out to us with a generous serving of the condiment of wisdom, softened it with the sweetness of eloquence, and flavored it with the marvelous charm of his speech. And so it happened that the tender lambs did not lack the Lord's abundance of milk, nor did the sheep lack pasturage of the richest fertility, nor did the shepherds lack the most plentiful abundance of provisions. Now that all these things have ceased to be, however, there is nothing left but the shepherd who—hungry for food—weeps with many a groan, the sheep that hungers for its grazing, and the lamb that longs for its udder.

As long as the greatest shepherd, namely Anselm, is absent, not only is each one deprived of each of these things, but rather all of them are deprived of everything.

In such sorrowful weeping, in such shameful grief, in such disgrace to our realm, in the outrage arising from so great a loss, nothing remains to me—dazed and suffering as I am—but to fly for help to the blessed Peter's apostle and vicar, the apostolic man.

And so I appeal to your generosity, lord, lest we and the people of the English realm should, because of so great an eclipse, sink into an equally great decline. For what use are our life and our lineage, as long as we are descending into error?

Therefore, let your fatherhood think well of it, insofar as it touches us, to deign to open your paternal heart to us within the time period that my lord the king asks of your goodness. Allow us to rejoice in the return of our most beloved father, the Archbishop Anselm, and to preserve our dutiful subjection to the Holy Apostolic See. Certainly, I have been instructed by your most wholesome and beloved reminders. To the extent that my woman's strength is available to me and the help of good men is provided me, I will strive to the utmost, so that my humility discharges as far as possible what Your Highness advises. May Your Fatherhood blessedly thrive.   *1106?*

Anne Lock
fl. 1556–1590

An early modern poet, translator, and letter writer, Anne Lock published a sequence of religious sonnets, *A Meditation of a Penitent Sinner, upon the 51 Psalm,* in 1560. Using the English sonnet form devised by Henry Howard, Earl of Surrey, Lock crafted twenty-one aggregated poems, each of which paraphrases a verse of the fifty-first biblical Psalm. Preceding the sequence were five of her own introductory sonnets. Lock included the sonnets with her translation, *Sermons of John Calvin, upon the Song that Ezechias Made . . . Translated Out of French into English,* printed by John Day in London. Two copies of this work are extant, one housed at the British Library in London, the other at the Folger Shakespeare Library in Washington, D.C. Most Renaissance scholars agree that Lock's was the first sonnet sequence written in English, predating Philip Sidney's *Astrophel and Stella* by thirty-one years.

The daughter of Stephen Vaughan, Lock married twice after her first husband, Henry Lock, died in 1576; her second husband, Edward Dering, was a Protestant minister. Her son, Henry Lock (sometimes spelled Lok), became a minor Renaissance devotional poet whose *Ecclesiasticus . . . Sundry Sonnets of Christian Passions* was printed in 1597 by Richard Field. Influenced by her stepmother, Margery Brinklow, and by the Scottish reformer John Knox, whom she met in 1552, Lock became a zealous Protestant. As Patrick Collinson notes in *The Elizabethan Puritan Movement,* Lock went into exile in Geneva with her infant son and daughter in 1557 to avoid persecution during the reign of Queen Mary; she remained there until

1559. In Geneva she completed her translation of Calvin's sermons, which she dedicated to Katharine Bertie, Duchess of Suffolk, another devout Protestant and a likely patron. Thirteen letters, all written by Knox, remain of the correspondence that took place between Lock and Knox from 1556 to 1562. In 1590 Lock translated John Taffin's *Of the Markes of the Children of God,* a work composed to comfort Protestants experiencing religious persecution in the Netherlands; apparently she feared that English Protestants would soon suffer as well. In her preface to that work and her dedication to the Countess of Warwick, Lock describes herself as a religious writer "bound to do somewhat to the furtherance of the holy bidding" yet hampered by her sex in achieving "great things" or "strengthening the walls of Jerusalem."

Included here are seven sonnets from *A Meditation of a Penitent Sinner.* Lock's poetic persona is a development of the "I" of the Psalms, as the critic Michael Spiller notes, and her verse is simple but eloquent. Her sonnets present a vivid Calvinist view of original sin and the need for salvation by grace. Moreover, several sonnets, most notably "For lo, in sin, Lord, I begotten was," raise issues of carnal sin, gender, and redemption. In "With sweet hyssop besprinkle thou my sprite" Lock develops what the scholar Olga Valbuena calls "a productive tension between the eternal laws of God and the fickle tyrannical powers of humanity"; it reveals the poet's suffering as a Marian exile and her anticipation of a return to England, the "new Zion." Lock's final poems present a political call for the destruction of the "new Israel's foes"—the Catholics. Indeed, Catholics and Protestants were competing throughout the Reformation to show that their respective faiths closely resembled the original Hebrew religion. *A Meditation of a Penitent Sinner* thus reveals not only Lock's piety but also the political nature of her Protestant affiliation.

⇥ *from* A Meditation of a Penitent Sinner, upon the 51 Psalm ⇤

1

Have mer-cy upon me (O God) after thy great mercy	

Have mercy, God, for thy great mercy's sake,
O God: my God, unto my shame I say,
Being fled from thee, so as I dread to take
Thy name in wretched mouth, and fear to pray
5   Or ask the mercy that I have abused,
But, God of mercy, let me come to thee:
Not for justice, that justly am accused:
Which self word Justice so amazeth me,
That scarce I dare thy mercy sound again,
10   But mercy, Lord, yet suffer me to crave.
Mercy is thine: Let me not cry in vain,
Thy great mercy for my great fault to have.
Have mercy, God, pity my penitence
With greater mercy than my great offense.

For lo, I was shaped in wicked-ness, and in sin my mother con-ceived me.	

7

For lo, in sin, Lord, I begotten was,
With seed and shape my sin I took also,[1]

1. I.e., I assumed the burden of original sin from the moment of conception.

Sin is my nature and my kind alas,
In sin my mother me conceived: Lo
5 I am but sin, and sinful ought to die,
Die in his wrath that hath forbidden sin.
Such bloom and fruit lo sin doth multiply,
Such was my root, such is my wise within.
I plead not this as to excuse my blame,
10 On kin or parents my own guilt to lay:
But by disclosing of my sin, my shame,
And need of help, the plainer to display
Thy mighty mercy, if with plenteous grace
My plenteous sins it please thee to deface.

> *Sprinkle me, Lord, with hyssop and I shall be clean: wash me and I shall be whiter than snow.*

9

With sweet hyssop besprinkle thou my sprite:[2]
Not such hyssop, nor so besprinkle me,
As law unperfect shade of perfect light
Did use as an appointed sign to be
5 Foreshowing figure of thy grace behight,[3]
With death and bloodshed of thine only son,
The sweet hyssop, cleanse me defilèd wyght,[4]
Sprinkle my soul. And when thou so hast done,
Bedewed with drops of mercy and of grace,
10 I shall be clean as cleansed of my sin.
Ah wash me, Lord: for I am foul alas:
That only canst, Lord, wash me well within,
Wash me, O Lord: when I am washèd so,
I shall be whiter than the whitest snow.

> *Turn away thy face from my sins, and do away all my mis-deeds.*

11

Look on me, Lord: though trembling I beknow,
That sight of sin so sore offendeth thee,
That seeing sin, how it doth overflow
My whelmèd soul, thou canst not look on me,
5 But with disdain, with horror and despite.
Look on me, Lord: but look not on my sin.
Not that I hope to hide it from thy sight,
Which seest me all without and eke within,
But so remove it from thy wrathful eye,
10 And from the justice of thine angry face,
That thou impute it not. Look not how I
Am foul by sin: but make me by thy grace
Pure in thy mercy's sight, and Lord, I pray,
That hatest sin, wipe all my sins away.

2. Hyssop is a plant used by the ancient Hebrews in   3. *Behight* means to promise.
purification rites; sprite is archaic for spirit.   4. *Wyght* means being or person.

14

Restore to
me the com-
fort of thy
saving help,
& establish
me with thy
free spirit.

But render me my wonted joys again,
Which sin hath reft,[5] and planted in their place
Doubt of thy mercy ground of all my pain.
The taste, that thy love whilome[6] did embrace
5   My cheerful soul, the signs that did assure
My feeling ghost of favor in thy sight,
Are fled from me, and wretched I endure
Senseless of grace the absence of thy sprite.
Restore my joys, and make me feel again
10   The sweet return of grace that I have lost,
That I may hope I pray not all in vain.
With thy free sprite confirm my feeble ghost,
To hold my faith from ruin and decay
With fast alliance and assuréd stay.

20

Show fa-
vor, o lord
in thy good
will unto
Zion, that
its walls
of Jerusa-
lem may be
built.

Show mercy, Lord, not unto me alone:
But stretch thy favor and thy pleasèd will,
To spred thy bounty and thy grace upon
Zion, for Zion is thy holy hill;
5   That thy Jerusalem with mighty wall[7]
May be enclosed under thy defense,
And built so that it may never fall
By myning fraud[8] or mighty violence.
Defend thy church, Lord, and advance it so,
10   So in despite of tyranny to stand,
That trembling at thy power the world may know
It is upholden by thy mighty hand:
That Zion and Jerusalem may be
A safe abode for them that honor thee.

21

Thou shalt receive the pleasing sacrifice,
The brute shall of thy praised name resound
In thankful mouths, and then with gentle eyes
Thou shall behold upon thine altar lie
5   Many a yelden[9] host of humbled hart,
And round about then shall thy people cry:
We praise thee, God our God: thou only art
The God of might, of mercy, and of grace.
That I then, Lord, may also honor thee,
10   Relieve my sorrow, and my sins deface:
Be, Lord of mercy, merciful to me:
Restore my feeling of thy grace again:
Assure my soul, I crave it not in vain.

1560

5. Past tense of *reave*, which means "to burst."
6. At some past time.
7. Zion refers to England, the new Zion; Jerusalem is a
city holy to Christians.
8. Undermining fraud.
9. Past participle of *yield*.

+·+ ☷◈☲ +·+

Isabella Whitney
fl. 1567–1573?

Little biographical information exists about Isabella Whitney, the first Englishwoman to identify herself as a professional poet. Scholars have determined that she wrote two secular works between 1567 and 1573, using simple themes, restrained language, and classical allusions. It is speculated that she came from a middle-class family and was the sister of Geoffrey Whitney of Cheshire, the author of a 1586 emblem-book, a collection of poems to accompany pictures of everyday objects. Whitney's poetic persona appears self-reliant, confident, almost without cares; in short, according to the scholar Betty Travitsky, she was the sort of Elizabethan woman of letters that VIRGINIA WOOLF claims in A *Room of One's Own* did not exist.

Whitney's first publication was entitled "A Copy of a Letter Lately Written in Meeter by a Yonge Gentilwoman to Her Unconstant Lover" (1567?) and was joined upon its publication to two other poems on this same theme of betrayal. Her poetic sequence, A *Sweet Nosegay or Pleasant Posye: Contayning a Hundred and Ten Philosophicall Flowers,* was published in 1573. At the beginning Whitney tells the reader how she became self-educated: "subject unto sickness, that / abroad I could not goe / Had leasure good (though learning lackt) / some study to apply; / To reade such Bookes, whereby I thought / my selfe to edify." A *Sweet Nosegay* ends with the poet's mock will and testament, in which she leaves everything to her beloved city of London, "because I there was bred." Determined to achieve verisimilitude, Whitney dates her verse epistle "This xx, of October, / in ANNO DOMINI / A thousand: v hundred seventy three" and calls upon "standers by" and "my nearer kyn" to testify if necessary to the veracity of her document. Unfortunately, despite her vivid depiction of sixteenth-century London and the paucity of poems by early modern women available to readers today, a definitive collection of Whitney's entire body of work has not yet been published.

⊰ The Author . . . Maketh Her Will and Testament ⊱

```
        The time is come I must depart,
        From thee ah famous City:
        I never yet to rue my smart,¹
        did find that thou hadst pity.
5       Wherefore small cause there is, that I
        should grieve from thee to go:
        But many women foolishly,
        like me and other more²
        Do such a fixed fancy set,
10      on those which least deserve,
        That long it is ere wit³ we get,
        away from them to swerve.
        But time with pity oft will tell
        to those that will her try:
15      Whether it best be more to mell⁴
        or utterly defy.
```

1. To my regret.
2. Many others.
3. Intelligence.
4. Interfere.

And now hath time me put in mind,
of thy great cruelness:
That never once a help would find,
20   to ease me in distress.
Thou never yet, would credit give
to board me for a year:
Nor with Apparel me relieve
except thou paid were.[5]
25   No, no, thou never didst me good,
nor ever will I know:
Yet am I in no angry mood,
but will, or ere I go
In perfect love and charity,
30   my Testament here write:
And leave to thee such Treasury,
as I in it recite.
Now stand aside and give me leave
to write my latest Will.
35   And see that none you do deceive,
of that I leave them till.[6]

1573

⁍ *from* The Manner of Her Will ⁌

And What She Left to London and to All Those in It at Her Departing

I whole in body and in mind,
but very weak in Purse:
Do make, and write my Testament
for fear it will be worse.
5   And first I wholly do commend,
my Soul and Body eke:[7]
To God the Father and the Son,
so long as I can speak.
And after speech: my Soul to him,
10   And Body to the Grave:
Till time that all shall rise again,
their Judgement for to have.

.   .   .   .

And now let me dispose such things,
as I shall leave behind:
15   That those which shall receive the same,
may know my willing mind.
I first of all to London leave

---

5. Unless you were paid.   7. As well.
6. That I rob them of their legacy.

because I there was bred:
Brave buildings rare, of Churches store,
20   and Paul's to the head.[8]
Between the same: fair streets there be,
and people goodly store:
Because their keeping craveth cost,[9]
I yet will leave him more.
25   First for their food, I Butchers leave,
that every day shall kill:
By Thames you shall have Brewers store,
and Bakers at your will.
And such as orders do observe,
30   and eat fish thrice a week:
I leave two Streets, full fraught therewith
they need not far to seek.

. . . .

For Women shall you Taylors have,
by Bow, the chiefest dwell:[10]
35   In every Lane you some shall find,
can do indifferent well.
And for the men, few Streets or Lanes,
but Bodymakers[11] be:
And such as make the sweeping cloaks,
40   with Gardes[12] beneath the knee.

. . . .

Now when thy folk are fed and clad
with such as I have named:
For dainty mouths, and stomachs weak
some Junckets must be framed.[13]
45   Wherefore I Poticaries leave,
with Banquets in their Shop:[14]
Physicians also for the sick,
Diseases for to stop.

. . . .

If they that keep what I you leave,
50   ask Money: when they sell it:
At Mint there is such store, it is
impossible to tell it.[15]

. . . .

Now for the people in thee left,
I have done as I may:
55   And that the poor, when I am gone,
have cause for me to pray.
I will to prisons portions leave,
what though but very small:

---

8. A reference to St. Paul's Cathedral, London's greatest church.
9. Requires money.
10. A London street on which tailors had their shops.
11. Clothiers.

12. Stripes.
13. Confections must be made available.
14. Apothecaries, or drugstores, once sold "banquets" (sweets).
15. To count it.

Yet that they may remember me,
60   occasion be it shall:

    . . . .

Now London have I (for thy sake)
within thee, and without:
As comes into my memory,
dispersed round about
65   Such needful things, as they should have
here left now unto thee,
When I am gone, with conscience
let them dispersed be.
And though I nothing named have,
70   to bury me withall:
Consider that above the ground,
annoyance be I shall.[16]

    . . . .

Rejoice in God that I am gone,
out of this vale so vile.
75   And that of each thing, left such store,
as may your wants exile,
I make thee sole executor, because
I loved thee best.
And thee I put in trust, to give
80   the goods unto the rest.

    . . . .

And (though I am persuaded) that I
shall never more thee see:
Yet to the last, I shall not cease
to wish much good to thee.
85   This xx, of October,
in ANNO DOMINI[17]
A thousand: v hundred seventy three
as Almanacs describe,
Did write this Will with my own hand
90   and it to London gave:
In witness of the standers by,
whose names if you will have,
Paper, pen and Standish[18] were:
at that same present by:
95   With Time, who promised to reveal,
so fast as she could hie[19]
The same: least of my nearer kin,
for anything should vary:
So finally I make an end
100   no longer can I tarry.

                                          1573

---

16. I will be an annoyance.   18. Inkstand.
17. The year of our Lord.   19. Could go.

—·—✕◆✕—·—

Margaret Cavendish, Duchess of Newcastle
1623?–1673

Margaret Cavendish, a noblewoman turned writer, produced poems, plays, letters, autobiographical sketches, essays on science and philosophy, utopian fiction, and a biography of her husband. Her best known works include *Poems and Fancies: Written by the Right Honourable, the Lady Newcastle* (1653, reissued in 1664) and *Nature's Pictures Drawn by Fancies Pencil* (1656). *Poems and Fancies*, in which most of her verse is collected, was dedicated (in the custom of the times) to her childhood friend Elizabeth Chaplain, "Mistris Toppe"; its dedicatory poem reveals the psychic conflict Cavendish experienced in choosing to write and publish. *Nature's Pictures*, subtitled "A True Relating of My Birth, Breeding, and Life," presents the author's childhood, fostered by loving parents and close siblings, as happy and secure. Cavendish's plays were performed in London in the 1660s; Virginia Woolf described them as "swarming with a diffused, uneasy, contorted vitality."

Cavendish was born Margaret Lucas in Colchester around 1623, the youngest of eight children of Sir Thomas Lucas, Earl of Colchester, and Elizabeth Leighton. After the death of her father during her infancy, Margaret was raised by her mother in Essex and educated at home. When the English Civil War broke out, she served for two years as Maid of Honor to Queen Henrietta Maria, who fled to Oxford with King Charles I; Cavendish followed the Queen into exile in France in 1644. There she met her husband, the Marquis (later Duke) of Newcastle, a poet, philosopher, playwright, and horseman thirty years her senior; they lived in exile, dependent on the Queen's largesse, for the next fifteen years. The marriage, described by Cavendish as "honest and honourable," was childless and apparently compatible; her autobiography recounts frequent and lively exchanges between husband and wife about their writing. *Poems and Fancies*, written during a trip to England in 1651 and published two years later, was admired by Charles Lamb and Thomas Hobbes. Not all of her contemporaries shared their opinion, however; after reading Cavendish's biography of her husband, the diarist Samuel Pepys declared her "a mad, conceited ridiculous woman and he an ass to suffer [her] to write what she writes to him and of him."

Once the Duke and Duchess returned to England, she continued with her literary career despite receiving both public and familial censure for her eccentricity and presumption as a writing woman. Among her important later works are *Observations Upon Experimental Philosophy* (1668), which analyzes how art "produces hermaphroditical effects," and the utopian fantasy that accompanied it, *The Description of a New World, Called the Blazing World*. Cavendish died in London in 1673 and was buried in Westminster Abbey. Shortly after her death a volume of poems in tribute to her was published; contributors included Thomas Hobbes, Joseph Glanvill, Sir George Etherege, and Thomas Shadwell. Her work fell into obscurity thereafter, to be rescued in part by Virginia Woolf in a 1925 essay about the Duchess's life and work. "What a vision of loneliness and riot the thought of Margaret Cavendish brings to mind," she concludes. Many recent feminist critics, however, have viewed Cavendish more positively as a shrewd writer who deliberately represents herself as "a fantastic and singular woman."

Cavendish's large body of work is represented here by four poems and one prose piece, "To All Writing Ladies." Although Cavendish claimed not to revise her poems—she said there was "more pleasure in making them than in mending"—changes in the 1664 edition reveal extensive and meticulous editing. "To All Writing Ladies" astutely analyzes the effect of changing cultural landscapes on the status of women. In some historical periods leaders are more masculine than in others, she posits; only occasionally have women been perceived as heroic. A fresh and vivid writer, Cavendish exemplifies the determination characteristic of many creative women to persevere despite considerable adversity, to claim the right to write.

⇥ The Poetess's Hasty Resolution ⇤

Reading my Verses, I liked them so well,
Self-love *did make my* Judgement to rebel:

Thinking them so good, I thought more to write:
Considering not how others would them like.
5   *I wrote so fast. I thought, if I lived long,*

A Pyramid *of* Fame, *to build thereon.*
Reason *observing which way I was bent,*
Did stay my hand, and asked me what I meant;
Will you, said she, thus waste your time in vain,
10   On that which in the World small praise shall gain?
For shame leave off, said she, the Printer *spare,*
He'll lose by your ill Poetry, *I fear*
Besides the World hath already such a weight
Of useless Books, as it is over fraught.
15   Then pity take, do the World a good turn,
And all you write cast in the fire, and burn.
Angry I was, and Reason *strode away,*
When I did hear what she to me did say.
Then all in haste, I to the Press *it sent,*
20   *Fearing* Persuasion *might my* Book *prevent:*
But now 'tis done, with grief repent do I,
Hang down my head with shame, blush, sigh, and cry.
Take pity, *and my* drooping Spirits *raise,*
Wipe off my tears with Handkerchiefs *of* Praise.

1653

⇥ The Poetess's Petition ⇤

Like to a Fever's pulse *my heart* doth beat,
For fear my Book *some great repulse should meet.*
If it be naught, let her in silence lie,
Disturb her not, let her in quiet die;
5   Let not the Bells *of your* dispraise *ring loud,*
But wrap her up in silence as a Shroud:
Cause black oblivion *on her* Hearse *to hang,*
Instead of Tapers, *let dark night there stand;*
Instead of Flowers *to the grave her strow*
10   *Before her* Hearse, *sleepy, dull* Poppy *throw;*
Instead of Scutcheons,[1] *let my* Tears *be hung,*
Which grief and sorrow from my eyes out wrung:
Let those that bear her Corps, no Jesters be,
But sad, *and* sober, grave Mortality:
15   No Satyr Poets *to her* Funeral *come;*
No Altars *raised to write* Inscriptions *on:*

---

1. Eschutcheons, the part of a shield on which armorial bearings are displayed.

Let dust of all forgetfulness be cast
Upon her Corps, there let them lie and waste:
Nor let her rise again; unless some know,
20   *At Judgements, some good Merits she can show:*
Then she shall live in Heavens *of high praise:*
And for her glory, Garlands *of fresh Bays.*[2]

1653

◄ An Excuse for So Much Writ upon My Verses ►

Condemn me not for making such a coyle[3]
About my Book, *alas it is my Child.*
Just like a Bird, *when her* Young *are in Nest,*
Goes in, and out, and hops and takes no Rest;
5   *But when their* Young *are fledged, their heads out peep,*
Lord what a chirping does the Old *one keep.*
So I, for fear my Strengthless Child should fall
Against a door, or stool, aloud I call,
Bid have a care of such a dangerous place:
Thus write I much, to hinder all disgrace.

1653

◄ Nature's Cook ►

Death is the *Cook* of *Nature:* and we find
Meat dressed several ways to please her *Mind.*
Some *Meats* she roasts with *Fevers, burning hot,*
And some *she* boils with *Dropsies* in a *Pot.*
5   Some for *Jelly* consuming by degrees,
And some with *Ulcers,* Gravy out to squeeze.
Some *Flesh* as *Sage* she stuffs with *Gouts* and *Pains,*
Others for tender *Meat* hang up in *Chains.*
Some in the *Sea* she pickles up to keep,
10   Others, as *Brawn* is soused, those in *Winesteep.*
Some with the *Pox,* chops *Flesh,* and *Bones* so small,
Of which *She* makes a *French Fricasse* withall.
Some on *Gridirons* of *Calentures* is broiled[4]
And some is trodden on, and so quite spoiled.
15   But those are *baked,* when smothered they do die,
By *Hectic Fevers* some *Meat* She doth fry.
In *Sweat* sometimes *she* stews with *savoury smell,*
A *Hodge-Podge* of *Diseases* tasteth well.
Brains dressed with *Apoplexy* to *Nature's* wish,

2. Bay laurel, given as a prize for victory or excellence.
3. Such an issue.

4. Calentures are tropical fevers brought on by overexposure to heat.

20   Or swims with *Sauce* of *Megrimes*[5] in a *Dish*.
     And *Tongues* she dries with *Smoke* with *Stomachs* ill,
     Which as the second *Course* she sends up still.
     Then *Death* cuts *Throats*, for *Blood-puddings* to make,
     And puts them in the *Guts*, which *Colics* rack.
25   Some hunted are by *Death*, for *Deer* that's red,
     Or *Stall–fed Oxen*, knocked on the *Head*.
     Some for *Bacon* by *Death* are *Singed*, or *scaled*,
     Then powdered up with *Phlegm*, and *Rheum* that's salt.

1653

⊰ *from* To All Writing Ladies ⊱

It is to be observed, that there is a secret working by Nature, as to cast an influence upon the minds of men: like as in Contagions, when as the Air is corrupted, it produced several Diseases: so several distempers of the mind, by the imflammations of the spirits. And as in healthful Ages, bodies are purified, so wits are refined; yet it seems to me as if there were several invisible spirits that have several, but visible powers, to work in several Ages upon the minds of men. For in many Ages men will be affected and disaffected alike: as in some Ages so strongly and superstitiously devout, that they make many gods: and in another Age so atheistical, as they believe in no God at all, and live to those Principles. Some Ages again have such strong faiths, that they will not only die in their several Opinions, but they will Massacre, and cut one another's throats, because their opinions are different. In some Ages all men seek absolute power, and every man would be Emperour of the World; which makes Civil Wars: for their ambition makes them restless, and their restlessness makes them seek change. Then in another Age all live peaceable, and so obedient, that the very Governors rule with obedient power. In some Ages again, all run after Imitation, like a company of Apes, as to imitate such a Poet, to be of such a Philosopher's opinion. Some Ages mixed, as Moralists, Poets, Philosophers, and the like: and in some Ages again, all affect singularity; and they are thought the wisest that can have the most extravagant opinions. In some Ages Learning flourishes in Arts and Sciences; other Ages so dull, as they lose what former Ages had taught. And in some Ages it seems as if there were a Commonwealth of those governing spirits, where most rule at one time. Some Ages, as in Aristocracy, when some part did rule; and other Ages a pure Monarchy, when but one rules; and in some Ages, it seems as if all those spirits were at defiance, who should have most power, which makes them in confusion and War; so confused are some Ages, and it seems as if there were spirits of the Feminine Gender, as also the Masculine. There will be many Heroic Women in some Ages, in others very Prophetical: in some Ages very pious and devout: For our Sex is wonderfully addicted to the spirits. But this Age hath produced many effeminate Writers,[1] as well as Preachers, and many effeminate Rulers, as well as Actors. And if it be an Age when the effeminate spirits rule, as most visible they do in every Kingdom, let us take the advantage, and make the best of our time, for fear their reign should not last long; whether it be in the Amazonian Government, or in

---

5. Migraines—i.e., bad headaches.   1. Writers sympathetic to women, or perhaps androgynous.

the Politic Commonwealth, or in flourishing Monarchy, or in Schools of Divinity, or in Lectures of Philosophy, or in witty Poetry, or anything that may bring honor to our Sex: for they are poor, dejected spirits that are not ambitious of Fame. And though we be inferior to Men, let us show ourselves a degree above Beasts; and not eat, and drink, and sleep away our time as they do; and live only to the sense, not to the reason: and so turn into forgotten dust. But let us strive to build us Tombs while we live, of Noble, Honorable, and good Actions, at least harmless;

> *That though our Bodies die,*
> *Our Names may live to after memory.*

I *Wonder any should laugh, or think it ridiculous to hear of* Fairies, *and yet verily believe there are spirits: which spirits can have no description, because no dimension: And of* Witches, *which are said to change themselves into several forms, and then to return into their first form again ordinarily, which is altogether against nature: yet laugh at the report of* Fairies, *as impossible; which are only small bodies, not subject to our sense, although it be to our reason. For Nature can as well make small bodies as great, and thin bodies as well as thick. We may as well think there is no Air, because we do not see it; or to think there is no Air in an empty Barrel or the like, because when we put our hands and arms into the same, we do not feel it. And why should not they get through doors or walls, as well as Air doth, if their bodies were as thin? And if we can grant there may be a substance, although not subject to our sense, then we must grant that substance must have some form; And why not of man, as of any thing else? and why not rational souls live in a small body, as well as in a gross, and in a thin, as in a thick?*

Shall we say Dwarfs *have less souls, because less or thinner bodies? And if rational souls, why not saving souls? So there is no reason in Nature, but that there may not only be such things as* Fairies, *but these be as dear to God as we.*

1653

Anne Killigrew
1660–1685

Maid of honor to the Duchess of York, Anne Killigrew was a painter as well as a poet; her only volume of verse was published posthumously at her father's arrangement and had attached to it an engraving of a self-portrait by the author. Her father was Dr. Henry Killigrew, chaplain to the Duke of York and his first wife, Judith; her uncle Thomas Killigrew, a playwright, founded the Theatre Royal, which later became the Drury Lane. A victim of smallpox, Anne Killigrew died at age twenty-five at her family home in the cloisters of Westminster Abbey. Three months after her death, her father published a collection of her verse, prefaced with a poem by John Dryden, "To the Pious Memory of the Accomplished Young Lady, Mrs. Anne Killigrew, Excellent in the two Sister-Arts of Poesie and Painting." Dryden's ode praises the young poet's portraits of James II and Mary Modena, his second wife, as well as her pastoral landscapes and her modesty. Killigrew's interest in art is evident in "On a Picture Painted by Herself," which refers to a painting that represents the nymph Diana in two poses, hunting and bathing.

In addition to paying the requisite tributes to the various members of the royal family with which she was associated, Killigrew's poems suggest an absorption in her own creative process and identity. In a poem not included here, "To the Queen," the poet exhorts her Muse to "give me Prowess" to sing the worth of so great a queen as Mary Modena, who ascended to the throne four months before Killigrew's death. She appears to have been subtly asking the new Queen to appoint her as a court attendant, thus ensuring her economic security and prestige. The poem of most interest to many readers is "Upon the Saying that My Verses Were Made by Another." Although the title represents a commonplace theme of early women's writing, the need to defend their work against accusations of plagiarism, and is often an excuse for the poet to strike a modest pose, in this poem the speaker expresses what seems to be genuine anger at those who would denigrate her verse. Killigrew likens her fate to that of the Trojan princess Cassandra, destined "to speak the Truth, although believ'd too late."

⊰ Upon the Saying that My Verses Were Made by Another ⊱

    Next Heaven my Vows to thee (O Sacred *Muse!*)
    I offered up, nor didst thou them refuse.
       O Queen of Verse, said I, if thou'lt inspire,
    And warm my Soul with thy Poetic Fire,
5   No Love of Gold shall share with thee my Heart,
    Or yet Ambition in my Breast have Part,
    More Rich, more Noble I will ever hold
    The *Muse's* Laurel, than a Crown of Gold.
    An Undivided Sacrifice I'll lay
10   Upon thine Altar, Soul and Body pay;
    Thou shalt my Pleasure, my Employment be,
    My All I'll make a Holocaust[1] to thee.

       The Deity that ever does attend
    Prayers so sincere, to mine did condescend.
15   I write, and the Judicious praised my Pen:
    Could any doubt Insuing Glory then?
    What pleasing Raptures filled my Ravished Sense?
    How strong, how Sweet, Fame, was thy Influence?
    And thine, False Hope, that to my flattered sight
20   Didst Glories represent so Near, and Bright?
    By thee deceived, methought each Verdant Tree
    Apollós transformed *Daphne* seemed to be;[2]
    And every fresher Branch, and every Bough
    Appeared as Garlands to impale my Brow.
25   The Learned in Love say, Thus the Winged Boy[3]
    Does first approach, dressed up in welcome Joy;
    At first he to the Cheated Lovers' sight
    Nought represents, but Rapture and Delight,
    Alluring Hopes, Soft Fears, which stronger bind
30   Their Hearts, than when they more assurance find.

       Emboldened thus, to Fame I did commit
    (By some few hands) my most Unlucky Wit.
    But, ah, the sad effects that from it came!
    What ought t'have brought me Honor, brought me shame!

1. A burnt offering.
2. Apollo, Greek god of the sun and poetry, made sexual advances to the nymph Daphne, whom the gods turned into a laurel tree for her protection.
3. Cupid.

35 Like *Aesop's* Painted Jay[4] I seemed to all,
 Adorned in Plumes, I not my own could call:
 Rifled like her, each one my Feathers tore,
 And, as they thought, unto the Owner bore.
 My Laurels thus another's Brow adorned,
40 My Numbers they Admired, but Me they scorned:
 Another's Brow, that had so rich a store
 Of Sacred Wreaths, that circled it before;
 Where mine quite lost, (like a small stream that ran
 Into a Vast and Boundless Ocean)
45 Was swallow'd up, with what it joined and drowned,
 And that Abyss yet no Accession found.

  Orinda,[5] (*Albion's* and her Sex's Grace)
 Owed not her Glory to a Beauteous Face,
 It was her Radiant Soul that shone Within,
50 Which struck a Lustre through her Outward Skin;
 That did her Lips and Cheeks with Roses dye,
 Advanced her Height, and Sparkled in her Eye.
 Nor did her Sex at all obstruct her Fame,
 But higher 'mong the Stars it fixed her Name;
55 What she did write, not only all allowed,
 But every Laurel, to her Laurel, bowed!

  The Envious Age, only to Me alone,
 Will not allow, what I do write, my Own,
 But let 'em Rage, and 'gainst a Maid Conspire,
60 So Deathless Numbers from my Tuneful Lyre
 Do ever flow; so *Phoebus* I by thee
 Divinely Inspired and possessed may be;
 I willingly accept *Cassandra's* Fate,
 To speak the Truth, although believed too late.[6]

             1686

⊰ On a Picture Painted by Herself, ⊱

Representing Two Nymphs of DIANA*'s,*[7]
One in a Posture to Hunt, the Other Bathing

 We are *Diana's* Virgin-Train,
 Descended of no Mortal Strain;
 Our Bows and Arrows are our Goods,
 Our Palaces, the lofty Woods,
5 The Hills and Dales, at early Morn,
 Resound and Echo with our Horn;

4. This line alludes to Aesop's fable in which a bluejay is attacked by other birds when he dresses himself in peacock feathers.
5. The pen name of the poet Katherine Philips, whom Killigrew admired.

6. Apollo angrily condemned the Trojan princess Cassandra by giving her the skills of prophecy but having no one listen to her.
7. Roman goddess of the moon and the hunt, often portrayed as a virgin.

We chase the Hind and Fallow-Deer,
The Wolf and Boar both dread our Spear;
In Swiftness we out-strip the Wind,
10   An Eye and Thought we leave behind;
We *Fawns* and Shaggy *Satyrs* awe;
To *Sylvan Powers* we give the Law:
Whatever does provoke our Hate,
Our Javelins strike, as sure as *Fate;*
15   We Bathe in Springs, to cleanse the Soil,
Contracted by our eager Toil;
In which we shine like glittering Beams,
Or Crystal in the Crystal Streams;
Though *Venus*[8] we transcend in Form,
20   No wanton Flames our Bosoms warm!
If you ask where such Wights[9] do dwell,
In what Blessed Clime, that so excel?
The Poet's only that can tell.[10]

1686

⊷ ⧓ ⊶

Anne Finch, Countess of Winchilsea

1661–1720

Anne Finch is best known for her lyrical meditations on nature, which William Wordsworth praised in 1815, and for her poems defending women's right to write. Born to a prominent family, Anne Kingsmill was orphaned at the age of three and grew up close to only one relative, her half-sister Dorothy Ogle, the model for Teresa in several of Finch's poems. With ANNE KILLIGREW she served as one of six maids of honor to Mary of Modena, the second wife of the Duke of York, soon to be James II. When James was deposed, Anne and her husband, Hineage Finch, a government official whom she had met at court, fled London to live at a home of the Earl of Winchilsea in Kent. Apparently the couple's country life together was a happy one, as her poems from "Ardelia" (her pen name) to "Daphnis" reveal. Finch spent most of her time writing poetry, encouraged by her husband, who pursued his own scholarly interests.

During her years at court Finch had hidden her poetry, fearful of ridicule as what she termed a "Versifying Maid of Honour," but in Kent she shared her manuscripts with a coterie of friends, and her writing flourished. Although she lived some distance from London, Finch became known as a female wit to many leading male literary figures of the time and received both their admiration and their condescension. In 1709 Jonathan Swift noted that he found occasional amusement in "writing verses to Mrs. Finch" and praised her in "Apollo Outwitted" for writing poems but doing so in secret. Alexander Pope visited Finch shortly after her husband had inherited the Earl of Winchilsea's property and title and she had thus become the Countess of Winchilsea. After listening to a reading of her play, *Aristomenes*, Pope complained in a letter to a friend that he had "sat in great disorder with sickness at my head and stomach." Nonetheless, he and the countess apparently remained friendly for many years, exchanging witticisms over his negative portrayals of women in *The Rape of the Lock* and wrangling in a jocular but pointed style.

8. Roman goddess of love.
9. Human beings.

10. The poet is the only one who can tell.

Although Finch published a collection of her verse, *Miscellany Poems on Several Occasions*, in 1713, she left many other poems in an unpublished but carefully arranged manuscript upon her death. These poems demonstrate the variety of her concerns, from women's writing to friendship to melancholia. "The Introduction," written for the manuscript edition of her poems, defends her verse as legitimate and powerful, though "by a Woman writ." "The Answer," a response to Pope's "Impromptu," mocks her literary acquaintance for the misrepresentation of women in his work. In "Friendship Between Ephelia and Ardelia" she defends women's love for one another, while in "Ardelia to Melancholy" she acknowledges despondency. For an eighteenth-century woman of letters Finch led a remarkably sanguine life, freed by birth and social status from economic worries and supported in her writing by a loving partner and many friends. Yet while secure in many ways, she suffered from a depression caused in part, as the scholar Katharine Rogers suggests, by the stress of being a distinguished literary woman in an age known to "lump together all women writers, as if no distinctions among them could counterbalance the one anomaly they shared: being writers and being female." Her impressive body of poetry demonstrates that Finch ultimately enticed her muse to prevail, proving herself neither Nature's nor Education's fool.

⇥ The Introduction ⇤

Did I my lines intend for public view,
How many censures, would their faults pursue,
Some would, because such words they do affect,
Cry they're insipid, empty, uncorrect.
5 And many have attained, dull and untaught
The name of Wit, only by finding fault.
True judges might condemn their want of wit,
And all might say, they're by a Woman writ.
Alas! a woman that attempts the pen,
10 Such an intruder on the rights of men,
Such a presumptuous Creature is esteemed,
The fault can by no virtue be redeemed.
They tell us, we mistake our sex and way;
Good breeding, fashion, dancing, dressing, play
15 Are the accomplishments we should desire;
To write, or read, or think, or to enquire
Would cloud our beauty, and exhaust our time,
And interrupt the Conquests of our prime;
Whilst the dull manage of a servile house
20 Is held by some our outmost art, and use.
　　　Sure 'twas not ever thus, nor are we told
Fables, of Women that excelled of old;
To whom, by the diffusive hand of Heaven
Some share of wit and poetry was given.
25 On that glad day, on which the Ark returned,
The holy pledge, for which the Land had mourned,[1]
The joyful Tribes, attend it on the way,
The Levites do the sacred Charge convey,
Whilst various Instruments, before it play;

---

1. An allusion to the Ark of the Covenant, a chest believed to contain the tablets on which the ten commandments were written.

30   Here, holy Virgins in the Concert join,
      The louder notes to soften and refine,
      And with alternate verse, complete the Hymn Divine.
      Lo! the young Poet, after God's own heart,
      By Him inspired, and taught the Muses' Art,
35   Returned from Conquest, a bright Chorus meets,
      That sing his slain ten thousand in the streets.[2]
      In such loud numbers they his acts declare,
      Proclaim the wonders of his early war,
      That Saul upon the vast applause does frown,
40   And feels its mighty thunder shake the Crown.
      What, can the threatened Judgment now prolong?
      Half of the Kingdom is already gone;
      The fairest half, whose influence guides the rest,
      Have David's Empire, o'er their hearts confessed.
45   A Woman here, leads fainting Israel on,
      She fights, she wins, she triumphs with a song,
      Devout, Majestic, for the subject fit,
      And far above her arms exalts her wit,
      Then, to the peaceful, shady Palm withdraws,
50   And rules the rescued Nation with her Laws.[3]
      How are we fallen, fallen by mistaken rules?
      And Education's, more than Nature's fools,
      Debarred from all improvements of the mind,
      And to be dull, expected and designed;
55   And if some one would Soar above the rest,
      With warmer fancy and ambition pressed,
      So strong, th' opposing faction still appears,
      The hopes to thrive can ne'er outweigh the fears.
      Be cautioned then my Muse, and still retired;
60   Nor be despised, aiming to be admired;
      Conscious of wants, still with contracted wing,
      To some few friends and to thy sorrows sing;
      For groves of Laurel thou wert never meant;
      Be dark enough thy shades, and be thou there content.

                                                      1689?/1713

ᳵ A Nocturnal Reverie ᳶ

      In such a *Night*, when every louder Wind
      Is to its distant Cavern safe confined;
      And only gentle *Zephyr* fans his Wings,
      And lonely *Philomel*, still waking, sings;[4]

2. An allusion to the Old Testament David, a musician and warrior who killed the giant Goliath and conquered the Philistines, incurring the envy of the Israelite King Saul.
3. An allusion to Deborah, the judge who led Israel into battle and wrote a victory song (Judges 4 and 5).
4. Zephyr is the west wind; Philomel a Greek woman changed by the gods into a nightingale.

5   Or from some Tree, famed for the *Owl's* delight,
She, hollowing clear, directs the Wanderer right:
In such a *Night*, when passing Clouds give place,
Or thinly veil the Heavens' mysterious Face;
When in some River, overhung with Green,
10   The waving Moon and trembling Leaves are seen;
When freshened Grass now bears itself upright,
And makes cool Banks to pleasing Rest invite,
Whence springs the *Woodbind*, and the *Bramble*-Rose,
And where the sleepy *Cowslip* sheltered grows;
15   Whilst now a paler Hue the *Foxglove* takes,
Yet checkers still with Red the dusky brakes
When scattered *Glow-worms*, but in Twilight fine,
Show trivial Beauties watch their Hour to shine;
Whilst *Salisbury* stands the Test of every Light,[5]
20   In perfect Charms, and perfect Virtue bright:
When Odors, which declined repelling Day,
Through temperate Air uninterrupted stray;
When darkened Groves their softest Shadows wear,
And falling Waters we distinctly hear;
25   When through the Gloom more venerable shows
Some ancient Fabric,[6] awful in Repose,
While Sunburnt Hills their swarthy Looks conceal,
And swelling Haycocks thicken up the Vale:
When the loosed *Horse* now, as his Pasture leads,
30   Comes slowly grazing through the adjoining Meads,
Whose stealing Pace, and lengthened Shade we fear,
Till torn up Forage in his Teeth we hear:
When nibbling *Sheep* at large pursue their Food,
And unmolested Kine[7] rechew the Cud;
35   When *Curlews* cry beneath the Village-walls,
And to her straggling Brood the *Partridge* calls;
Their shortlived Jubilee the Creatures keep,
Which but endures, whilst Tyrant-*Man* does sleep;
When a sedate Content the Spirit feels,
40   And no fierce Light disturb, whilst it reveals;
But silent Musings urge the Mind to seek
Something, too high for Syllables to speak;
Till the free Soul to a composedness charmed,
Finding the Elements of Rage disarmed,
45   O'er all below a solemn Quiet grown,
Joys in th' inferior World, and thinks it like her Own:
In such a *Night* let Me abroad remain,
Till Morning breaks, and All's confused again;
Our Cares, our Toils, our Clamors are renewed,
50   Or Pleasures, seldom reached, again pursued.

1713

---

5. Salisbury alludes to Anne Tafton, Countess of Salis-   6. Building.
bury, a close friend.   7. Cattle.

⊰ Ardelia to Melancholy ⊱

At last, my old inveterate foe,
No opposition shalt thou know.
Since I by struggling can obtain
Nothing, but increase of pain,
5   I will at last no more do so,
Tho' I confess, I have applied
Sweet mirth and music, and have tried
A thousand other arts beside,
To drive thee from my darkened breast,
10   Thou who hast banished all my rest.
But though sometimes a short reprieve they gave,
Unable they, and far too weak, to save;
All arts to quell did but augment thy force,
As rivers checked break with a wilder course.

15   Friendship I to my heart have laid,
Friendship, th' applauded sovereign aid,
And thought that charm so strong would prove
As to compell thee to remove;
And to myself I boasting said,
20   Now I a conquerer sure shall be,
The end of all my conflicts see,
And noble triumph wait on me;
My dusky, sullen foe will sure
N'er this united charge endure.
25   But leaning on this reed, even whilst I spoke
It pierced my hand and into pieces broke.
Still, some new object or new interest came
And loosed the bonds, and quite dissolved the claim.

These failing, I invoked a Muse,
30   And Poetry would often use
To guard me from thy Tyrant power;
And to oppose thee every hour
New troops of fancies did I choose.
Alas! in vain, for all agree
35   To yield me Captive up to thee,
And heaven alone can set me free.
Thou, through my life, will with me go,
And make the passage sad and slow.
All that could ere thy ill got rule invade,
40   Their useless arms before thy feet have laid;
The Fort is thine, now ruined all within,
Whilst by decays without thy Conquest too is seen.

1713

ᚼ Friendship Between Ephelia and Ardelia ᚼ

EPH.   What Friendship is, Ardelia, show.
ARD.   'Tis to love, as I love You.
EPH.   This Account, so short (though kind)
       Suits not my inquiring Mind.
5   Therefore farther now repeat;
       What is Friendship when complete?
ARD.   'Tis to share all Joy and Grief;
       'Tis to lend all due Relief
       From the Tongue, the Heart, the Hand;
10   'Tis to mortgage House and Land;
       For a Friend be sold a Slave;
       'Tis to die upon a Grave,
       If a Friend therein do lie.
EPH.   This indeed, though carried high,
15   This, though more than e'er was done
       Underneath the rolling Sun,
       This has all been said before.
       Can Ardelia say no more?
ARD.   Words indeed no more can show:
20   But 'tis to love, as I love you.

1713

ᚼ The Answer ᚼ

[To Pope's Impromptu][8]

Disarmed with so genteel an air,
    The contest I give o'er;
Yet, Alexander, have a care,
    And shock the sex no more.
5   We rule the world our life's whole race,
    Men but assume that right;
First slaves to every tempting face,
    Then martyrs to our spite.
You of one Orpheus sure have read,
10   Who would like you have writ
Had he in London town been bred,
    And polish'd too his wit;
But he poor soul thought all was well,
    And great should be his fame,
15 When he had left his wife in hell,
    And birds and beasts could tame.

---

8. Alexander Pope wrote his short poem "Impromptu" to make peace with his friend Anne Finch, who had found Pope's mock epic *The Rape of the Lock* insulting to women writers, whom he called hysterical. The "Impromptu" claims that Finch outshines all other women poets; hence her response is conciliatory but admonitory as well.

Yet venturing then with scoffing rhymes
   The women to incense,
Resenting Heroines of those times
20   Soon punished his offense.[9]
And as the Hebrus rolled his scull,
   And harp besmeared with blood,
They clashing as the waves grew full,
   Still harmonized the flood.
25 But you our follies gently treat,
   And spin so fine the thread,
You need not fear his awkward fate,
   The lock won't cost the head.
Our admiration you command
30   For all that's gone before;
What next we look for at your hand
   Can only raise it more.
Yet sooth the Ladies I advise
   (As me too pride has wrought),
35 We're born to wit, but to be wise
   By admonitions taught.

1717

+—✠✦✠—+

Frances (Fanny) Burney
1752–1840

Frances Burney published novels, an autobiographical journal, a memoir of her father, and several plays, only one of which, *Edwy and Elgiva,* was ever performed. One of six children of a prominent musicologist, Dr. Charles Burney, and his wife, Esther, she lost her mother at the age of ten, just after the family had moved from King's Lynn to London, and never warmed to her stepmother, who objected to her writing on the grounds that it would impede her marital prospects. Burney wrote her first novel, *Evelina,* in secret and published it anonymously in 1778; its spectacular success brought her almost as much pleasure as did the ruses she contrived to hide her identity as its author. Her diary from that year reveals her delight in learning that even her friends had "not the smallest suspicion of the author, and that they had concluded it to be the work of a *man!*"

Her second novel, *Cecilia; or, Memoirs of an Heiress,* was published in 1782 just prior to Burney's acceptance of a post as Second Keeper of the Robes to Queen Charlotte, a prestigious position that provided her with the access to court that she chronicles so vividly in her journal. She hated the post because of its restrictiveness, however, and was not sorry when, several years later, a serious though short-lived illness enabled her release from it. In 1793, at the age of forty-one, she married a destitute Frenchman, Alexandre D'Arblay, and lived with him and their son in France for the next decade, bearing witness to the French Revolution and its bloody aftermath. She wrote her didactic novel *Camilla; or, Female Difficulties* (1796) and her

---

9. An allusion to Orpheus, the musician and poet from Greek myth who entered Hades in search of his abducted wife, Eurydice, and whose music was said to tame wild animals. Mythical women known as Furies later beheaded Orpheus and threw his head and lyre into the River Hebrus.

last novel, *The Wanderer* (1814), a protest against tyranny, to earn an income for her family. She also composed what might well be the first breast cancer narrative after being stricken with that disease in 1811, a series of letters to a beloved sister telling "the whole history" of the event. Upon her husband's death in 1818 she edited her father's memoirs, which appeared in 1832. Her own journal and letters, in seven volumes, were published in 1889 as *The Diary and Letters of Madame D'Arblay.*

The epistolary saga of a bashful girl in danger of being thwarted by her villainous grandmother, who threatens to ruin her socially, *Evelina* is an early novel of manners, both realistic and didactic in its perspective and voice. The novel's success helped Burney to become acquainted with the eighteenth century's most famous man of letters, Dr. Samuel Johnson, and his friend, the writer Hester Thrale. Burney was especially pleased with the latter's enthusiastic response to *Evelina*. *Cecilia* brought Burney less critical acclaim than did *Evelina* but is widely considered a more substantial novel; it defies the prevailing societal opinions about women's social and economic rights. This perhaps is why a later and more famous practitioner of the developing art form to which Burney contributed, JANE AUSTEN, took both the title of *Pride and Prejudice* and its central theme from *Cecilia*.

Burney became known as one of England's pioneer women novelists despite the fact that she lacked a formal education. Indeed, one of the most amusing moments in her early diary recalls a conversation she overheard between her beloved father and his good friend Samuel Crisp shortly after they had realized that Fanny was the author of a successful novel. "The variety of characters," exclaimed her father, "—the variety of scenes—and the language—why she has had very little education but what she has given herself—less than any of the others!" and Mr. Crisp responded, "Wonderful!—it's wonderful!" As the excerpts below reveal, Burney's diary of 1778 records her glee at her greatest accomplishment: becoming a published writer.

⇥ *from* The Diary of Frances Burney ⇤

March is almost over—and not a word have I bestowed upon my Journal!— n'importe,—I shall now whisk on to the present time, mentioning whatever occurs to me promiscuously.

This year was ushered in by a grand and most important event,—for at the latter end of January the literary world was favoured with the first publication of the ingenious, learned, and most profound Fanny Burney!—I doubt not but this memorable affair will, in future times, mark the period whence chronologers will date the zenith of the polite arts in this island! This admirable authoress has named her most elaborate performance "*Evelina, or a Young Lady's Entrance into the World.*" Perhaps this may seem a rather bold attempt and title for a female whose knowledge of the world is very confined, and whose inclinations, as well as situation, incline her to a private and domestic life. All I can urge is, that I have only presumed to trace the accidents and adventures to which a "young woman" is liable. I have not pretended to shew the world what it actually *is*, but what it *appears* to a girl of seventeen:—and so far as that, surely any girl who is *past* seventeen may safely do?

The motto of my excuse shall be taken from Pope's "Temple of Fame,"—

> In every Work, regard the Writer's end,
> None e'er can compass more than they intend. . . .
>
> March 26th

I have now to trace some curious anecdotes for about a fortnight past.

My cousin Richard has continued gaining strength and health with a daily rapidity of recovery, that has almost as much astonished as it has delighted us, and that is saying very much, for his truly amiable behaviour during his residence here, has so much encreased the regard I always had for him, that I have never in my life been more heartily rejoiced than upon his restoration to his friends.

On Friday se'night, my mother accompanied my father to Streatham, on a visit to Mrs. Thrale for four or five days.[1] We invited Edward to drink tea with us, and, upon the plan of a *frolic*, we determined upon going to Bell's circulating Library, at which my father subscribes for new books, in order to ask some questions about Evelina, however, when we got to the shop, I was ashamed to speak about it, and only enquired for some magazines, at the backs of which I saw it advertised. But Edward, the moment I walked off, asked the shop-man if he had . . . my little book, I am told, is now at all the circulating libraries.

I have an exceeding odd sensation, when I consider that it is now in the power of *any* and *every* body to read what I so carefully hoarded even from my best friends, till this last month or two,—and that a work which was so lately lodged, in all privacy in my bureau, may now be seen by every butcher and baker, cobler and tinker, throughout the three kingdoms, for the small tribute of three pence. . . .

[*Burney takes tea with friends, who read her book without knowing of her authorship.*]

I must own I suffered great difficulty in refraining from laughing upon several occasions,—and several times, when they praised what they read, I was upon the point of saying—"You are very good!—" and so forth, and I could scarce keep myself from making acknowledgements, and bowing my head involuntarily.

However, I got off *perfectly* safely.

MONDAY, Susan and I went to tea at Brompton. We met Miss Humphries coming to town. She told us she had just finished—"Evelina"—and gave us to understand that she could not get away till she had done it. We heard afterwards, from my aunt, the most flattering praises,—and Richard could talk of nothing else! His encomiums gave me double pleasure, from being wholly unexpected: for I had prepared myself to hear that he held it extremely cheap. And I was yet more satisfied, because I was sure they were sincere, as he convinced me that he had not the most distant idea of suspicion, by finding great fault with Evelina herself for her bashfulness with such a man as Lord Orville.[2]—"A man," continued he—"whose politeness is so extraordinary,—who is so elegant, so refined,—so—so—*unaccountably* polite,—for I can think of no other word.—I never read, never heard such language in my life!—and then, just as he is speaking to her, she is *so confused,*—that she always runs out of the room!"

[I *could* have answered him, that he ought to consider the original character of Evelina,—that she had been brought up in the strictest retirement, that she knew nothing of the world, and only acted from the impulses of Nature; and that her timidity always prevented her from daring to hope that Lord Orville was seriously attached to her. In short, I *could* have bid him read the Preface again, where she is called—"the offspring of Nature, and of Nature in her simplest attire"—but I *feared* appearing too well acquainted with the book, and I *rejoiced* that an *unprejudiced* reader should make no weightier objection.]

---

1. Hester Thrale (1741–1821), an English poet and diarist, was a close friend of England's premier man of let-   ters, Dr. Samuel Johnson.
2. The hero of *Evelina*.

Edward walked home with us; I railed at him violently for having bought the book, and charged him to consult with me before he again put it into any body's hands: but he told me he hoped that, as it had gone off so well, I should not regret it. Indeed he seems quite delighted at the approbation it has met with. He was extremely desirous that his brother should be made acquainted with the author, telling me that he wished to plead for him, but did not know how.

The next day, my father and mother returned to town. On Thursday morning, we went to a delightful Concert at Mr. Harris's. The sweet Rauzini was there, and sung four Duets with Miss Louisa Harris. He has now left the Opera, where he is succeeded by Roncaglia. I was extremely delighted at meeting with him again, and again hearing him sing. La Motte, Cervetto, . . . played several Quartettos divinely, and the morning afforded me the greatest entertainment.

There was nobody we knew but Lady Hales and Miss Coussmaker, who were as usual very civil.

Friday

Miss Humphries, Charlotte, Edward and I went to the Oratorio of Judas Maccabeus. Oratorios I don't love, so I shall say nothing of the performance. We were, also, a few nights since, at Giardini's Benefit, and heard a most charming Concert. . . .

Edward talked only of Evelina, and frequently. . . . It seems,—to my utter amazement, Miss Humphries has guessed the author to be *Anstey*, who wrote the Bath Guide!—How improbable—and how extraordinary a supposition. But they have both of them done it so much honour that, but for Richard's anger at Evelina's bashfulness, I never could believe they did not suspect me.   *1778/1889*

✦ ⇥⊰⊱⇤ ✦

Maria Edgeworth
1768–1849

An English novelist best known for *Castle Rackrent* (1800), a work that addresses the decline of the Anglo-Irish aristocracy and the problems of landlord-tenant relationships, Maria Edgeworth also wrote numerous essays on education as well as a feminist treatise, *Letters for Literary Ladies* (1795). Born in England to Anna Maria Ellers and Richard Lovell Edgeworth, she moved with her father after her mother's death in 1783 to Edgeworthstown, the family's Irish estate, where her father married the second of his four wives; there Edgeworth lived until her death. As the eldest of many children, she assumed both maternal and educational duties toward her younger siblings. An interest in education led her to collaborate with her father, a liberal man who espoused the utilitarian beliefs of Jeremy Bentham, on a series of educational essays and didactic stories. In 1798 they published an account of their educational theories, *Practical Education*.

With the publication of *Castle Rackrent*, widely viewed today as one of the first regional novels in English literature, Edgeworth began what would become a prolific career as a novelist. Although she traveled widely in Europe, many of her novels focus on the domestic space of the drawing room, most notably *Belinda* (1801) and *Ormond* (1817). *The Absentee* (1812) addresses themes similar to those of *Castle Rackrent* in criticizing those members of the Irish gentry who were absentee landlords. Other works include *Popular Tales* (1804), *The Modern Griselda* (1805), *Leonora* (1806), *Patronage* (1814), and *Helen* (1834). Edgeworth did relief work during the Irish potato famine of 1847, and late in her life she was awarded an honorary membership in the Irish Royal Academy.

Letters for Literary Ladies, her powerful defense of women's education, might well have been a response to Thomas Day, a friend of her father who opined, in a letter to Edgeworth, that "the extent of a woman's erudition should consist in her knowing simple letters, without their mischievous combinations." In these epistles exchanged between a conventional gentleman and a man of her father's persuasions, Edgeworth claims that women can and should be educated in politics, literature, and other fields; she also portrays men who are involved in child-raising. "Letter from a Gentleman to his Friend upon the Birth of a Daughter" takes as its speaker a man unconvinced of the merits of women's equality. In turn, his respondent cleverly shifts the terms of the argument, claiming that he is more concerned with women's happiness than with their rights. In *Letters for Literary Ladies* Edgeworth skillfully deploys her considerable rhetorical talents to claim dignity and equality for half of the human population.

⊰ *from* Letters for Literary Ladies ⊱

Letter From a Gentleman to His Friend upon the Birth of a Daughter

I congratulate you, my dear Sir, upon the birth of your daughter; and I wish that some of the Fairies of ancient times were at hand to endow the damsel with health, wealth, wit, and beauty—Wit?———I should make a long pause before I accepted of this gift for a daughter—you would make none.

As I know it to be your opinion, that it is in the power of education, more certainly than it was ever believed to be in the power of Fairies, to bestow all mental gifts; and as I have heard you say that education should begin as early as possible, I am in haste to offer you my sentiments, lest my advice should come too late.

Your general ideas of the habits and virtues essential to the perfection of the female character nearly agree with mine; but we differ materially as to the cultivation, which it is necessary or expedient to bestow upon the understandings of women: you are a champion for the rights of woman, and insist upon the equality of the sexes. But since the days of chivalry are past, and since modern gallantry permits men to speak, at least to one another, in less sublime language of the fair, I may confess to you that I see neither in experience or analogy much reason to believe that, in the human species alone, there are no marks of inferiority in the female;—curious and admirable exceptions there may be, but many such have not fallen within my observation. I cannot say that I have been much enraptured either on a first view or on a closer inspection with female prodigies. Prodigies are scarcely less offensive to my taste than monsters; humanity makes us refrain from expressing disgust at the awkward shame of the one, whilst the intemperate vanity of the other justly provokes ridicule and indignation. I have always observed in the understandings of women who have been too much cultivated, some disproportion between the different faculties of their minds. One power of the mind undoubtedly may be cultivated at the expence of the rest, as we see that one muscle or limb may acquire excessive strength and an unnatural size at the expence of the health of the whole body: I cannot think this desirable either for the individual or for society.—The unfortunate people in certain mountains in Switzerland are, some of them, proud of the excrescence by which they are deformed. I have seen women vain of exhibiting mental deformities, which to me appeared no less disgusting. In the course of my life it has never been my good fortune to meet with a female whose mind, in strength, just proportion, and activity, I could compare to that of a sensible man.—

Allowing, however, that women are equal to our sex in natural abilities, from their situation in society, from their domestic duties, their taste for dissipation, their love of romance, poetry, and all the lighter parts of literature, their time must be so fully occupied, that they could never have leisure, even supposing that they had inclination, for that severe application to which our sex submit.—Between persons of equal genius, and equal industry, time becomes the only measure of their acquirements———Now calculate the time, which is wasted by the fair sex, and tell me how much the start of us they ought to have in the beginning of the race, if they are to reach the goal before us?—It is not possible that women should ever be our equals in knowledge, unless you assert that they are far our superiors in natural capacity.——— Not only time but opportunity must be wanting to complete female studies—we mix with the world without restraint, we converse freely with all classes of people, with men of wit, of science, of learning, with the artist, the mechanic, the labourer; every scene of life is open to our view;—every assistance, that foreign or domestic ingenuity can invent, to encourage literary studies, is ours almost exclusively. From academies, colleges, public libraries, private associations of literary men, women are excluded, if not by law, at least by custom, which cannot easily be conquered.——— Whenever women appear, even when we seem to admit them as our equals in understanding, every thing assumes a different form; our politeness, delicacy, habits towards the sex forbid us to argue, or to converse with them as we do with one another—we see things as they are, but women must always see things through a veil, or cease to be women.—With these insuperable difficulties in their education and in their passage through life, it seems impossible that their minds should ever acquire that vigor and *efficiency*, which accurate knowledge and various experience of life and manners can bestow.

Much attention has lately been paid to the education of the female sex, and you will say, that we have been amply repaid for our care—That ladies have lately exhibited such brilliant proofs of genius as must dazzle and confound their critics. I do not ask for proofs of genius,—I ask for solid proofs of utility. In which of the useful arts, in which of the exact sciences have we been assisted by female sagacity or penetration?—I should be glad to see a list of discoveries, of inventions, of observations, evincing patient research, of truths established upon actual experiment, or deduced by just reasoning from previous principles—If these or any of these can be presented by a female champion for her sex, I shall be the first to clear the way for her to the Temple of Fame.

I must not speak of my contemporaries, else candor might oblige me to allow, that there are some few instances of great talents applied to useful purposes—But, except these, what have been the literary productions of women?—In poetry, plays and romances, in the art of imposing upon the understanding by means of the imagination, they have excelled—but to useful literature they have scarcely turned their thoughts—I have never heard of any female proficients in science—few have pretended to science till within these few years.—I know of none of their inventions, and few of their discoveries.

You will tell me, that in the most difficult and most extensive science of politics women have succeeded—you will cite the names of some illustrious queens—I am inclined to think, with the Duke of Burgundy, that "queens who reigned well were governed by men, and kings who reigned ill were governed by women."

The isolated examples of a few heroines cannot convince me that it is safe or expedient to trust the sex with power—their power over themselves has regularly been found to diminish, in proportion as their power over others has been increased.—I should not refer you to the scandalous chronicles of modern times, to volumes of private anecdotes, or to the abominable secret histories of courts, where female influences, and female depravity are synonymous terms, but I appeal to the open equitable page of history, to a body of evidence collected from the testimony of ages, for experiments tried upon the grandest scale of which nature admits, registered by various hands without the possibility of collusion and without a view to any particular system—from these you must be convinced, that similar consequences have uniformly resulted from the same causes in nations the most unlike, and at periods the most distant. Follow the history of female nature from the court of Augustus, to the court of Lewis the Fourteenth, and tell me whether you can hesitate to acknowledge, that the influence, the liberty, and the *power* of women have been constant concomitants of the moral and political decline of empires—I say the concomitants: where events are thus invariably connected I might be justified in saying, that they were *causes*—you would call them *effects*, but we need not dispute about the momentary precedence of evils, which are found to be inseparable companions—they may be alternately cause and effect,—the reality of the connection is established, it may be difficult to ascertain precisely its nature.[1]

You will assert, that the fatal consequences which have resulted from our trusting the sex with liberty and power, have been originally occasioned by the subjection and ignorance in which they had previously been held, and of our subsequent folly and imprudence in *throwing the reins of dominion into hands unprepared and uneducated to guide them.* I am at a loss to conceive any system of education that can properly prepare women for the exercise of power:—Cultivate their understandings, "cleanse the visual orb with Euphrasy and Rue,"[2] till they can with one comprehensive glance take in "one half at least of round eternity," still you have no security that their reason shall govern their conduct. The moral character seems, even amongst men of superior strength of mind, to have no certain dependence upon the reasoning faculty;—habit, prejudice, taste, example, and the different strength of various passions, form the moral character. We are impelled to action frequently contrary to the belief of our sober reason, and we pursue what we could, in the hour of deliberation, demonstrate to be inconsistent with *that greatest possible share of happiness,* which it is the object of every rational creature to secure. We frequently "think with one species of enthusiasm, and act with another:" and can we expect from women more consistency of conduct, if they are allowed the same liberty. No one can feel more strongly than you do the necessity and the value of female integrity; no one can more clearly perceive how much in society depends upon the honour of women, and how much it is the interest of every individual, as well as of every state, to guard their virtue, and to preserve inviolate the purity of their manners. Allow me, then, to warn you of the danger of talking in loud strains to the sex of the noble contempt of prejudice. You would look with horror at one who should go to sap the foundations of the building;

1. Augustus was the first Roman emperor; he reigned from 27 BCE to 14 CE. Louis XIV was king of France from 1643 to 1715.

2. An allusion to Book 11 of John Milton's *Paradise Lost* (1667).

beware then how you venture to tear away the ivy which clings to the walls, and braces the loose stones together. . . .

. . . Besides, it must take a length of time to alter associations and opinions, which, if not *just*, are at least *common* in our sex. You cannot expect even that conviction should operate immediately upon the public taste. You will, in a few years, have educated your daughter; and if the world be not educated exactly at the right time to judge of her perfections, to admire and love them, you will have wasted your labor, and you will have sacrificed your daughter's happiness: that happiness, analyze it as a man of the world or as a philosopher, must depend on friendship, love, the exercise of her virtues, the just performance of all the duties of life, and the self-approbation arising from the consciousness of good conduct.

I am, my dear friend,
Yours sincerely

ANSWER TO THE PRECEDING LETTER

If I were not naturally of a sanguine temper, your letter, my dear friend, would fill my mind with so many melancholy fears for the fate of literary women, that I should be tempted to educate my daughter in the secure "bliss of ignorance."

I am sensible that we have no right to try new experiments and fanciful theories at the expence of our fellow-creatures, especially on those who are helpless, and immediately under our protection. Who can estimate the anguish which a parent must feel from the ruin of his child, when joined to the idea that it may have been caused by imprudent education: but reason should never be blinded by sentiment, when it is her proper office to guide and enlighten. There is scarcely any family, I hope, which does not feel within itself the happy effects of the improvements in modern education; but we could never have felt these advantages, if we had resisted all attempts at alteration.

Do not, my dear Sir, call me *"a champion for the rights of women"*; I am more intent upon their happiness than ambitious to enter into a metaphysical discussion of their rights. Their happiness is so nearly connected with ours, that it seems to me absurd to manage any argument so as to set the two sexes at variance by vain contention for superiority. It is not our object to make an invidious division of rights and privileges, but to determine what is most for our general advantage.

I shall not, therefore, examine with much anxiety how far women are naturally inferior to us either in strength of mind or body. The strength of the one has no necessary connection with the other, I may observe; and intellectual ability has ever conquered mere bodily strength, from the times of Ajax and Ulysses to the present day.[3] In civilized society, that species of superiority which belongs to superior force, is reduced to little in the lowest classes, to less in the higher classes of life.

The invention of fire-arms renders address and presence of mind more than a match for force, or at least reduces to an affair of chance the pretensions of the feeble and the strong. The art of printing has extended the dominion of the mind, as much by facilitating the intercourse and combination of persons of literature, as by the rapid and universal circulation of knowledge. Both these inventions have tended to alter the relative situation of women in modern society.

---

3. Ajax was the greatest of Greek warriors after Achilles; when Achilles died, he carried his body from the field while the Greek leader, Ulysses, held back the Trojan warriors. Ajax and Ulysses also engaged in a wrestling match designed to pit strength against cunning.

I acknowledge that, with respect to the opportunities of acquiring knowledge, institution and manners are much in favor of our sex; but your argument concerning *time* appears to me to be inaccurate. Whilst the knowledge of the learned languages continues to form an indispensable part of a gentleman's education, many years of childhood and youth must be devoted to their attainment. During these studies, the general cultivation of the understanding is in some degree retarded. All the intellectual powers are cramped, except the memory, which is sufficiently exercised, but which is overloaded with words, and with words which are seldom understood. The genius of living and of dead languages differs so much, that the pains which are taken to write elegant Latin, frequently spoil the English style. Girls usually write much better than boys: they think and express their thoughts clearly at an age when young men can scarcely write an easy letter upon any common occasion. Women do not read the best authors of antiquity as school books; but they can have excellent translations of most of them, when they are capable of tasting their beauties. I know that it is supposed no one can judge of the classics by translations; and I am sensible that much of the merit of the originals may be lost; but I think the difference in pleasure is more than overbalanced to women, by the *time* they save, and by the labor and misapplication of abilities which is spared. If they do not acquire a classic taste, neither do they acquire classic prejudices: nor are they early disgusted with literature, by pedagogues, lexicons, grammars, and all the melancholy apparatus of learning. Fieldsports, travelling, gaming, lounging, and what is called pleasure in various shapes, usually fill the interval between quitting the college and settling for life: this period is not lost by the other sex. Women begin to taste the real pleasures of reading just at the age when young men, disgusted with their studies, begin to be ashamed amongst their companions of alluding to literature. When this period is past, business, the necessity of pursuing a profession, the ambition of shining in parliament, or of rising in public life, occupy a large portion of their lives. The understanding is but partially cultivated for these purposes; men of genius must contract their enquiries, and concentrate their powers; they must pursue *the expedient*, even when they distinguish that it is not *the right*, and they are degraded to "*literary artisans*". The other sex have no such constraint upon their understandings; neither the necessity of earning their bread, nor the ambition to shine in public life, hurry or prejudice their minds; in domestic life, "they have leisure to be wise." Women, who do not love dissipation, must have more time for the cultivation of their understandings, than men can have if you compute the whole of life.

You apprehend that knowledge must be hurtful to the sex, because it will be the means of their acquiring power. It seems to me impossible that women can acquire the species of direct power which you dread: the manners of society must totally change before women can mingle with men in the busy and public scenes of life. They must become Amazons before they can effect this change; they must cease to be women before they can desire it. The happiness of neither sex could be increased by this metamorphosis: the object cannot be worth the price. Power, supposing it to be a certain good to its possessor, is like all our other pleasures, capable of being appreciated; and if women are taught to estimate their pleasures, they will be governed in their choice by the real, not by the imaginary, value. They will be convinced, not by the voice of the moralist alone, but by their own observation and experience, that power is an evil in most cases; and to those who really wish to do good to their fellow-creatures, it is at best but a painful trust. If, my dear Sir, it be your object to monopolize power for our sex, you cannot possibly better secure it from the wishes of the other, than by enlightening their minds, and enlarging their view of human affairs. The common fault of ignorant and ill-educated women is a love for dominion: this they show in every petty struggle where they are permitted to act in private life. You are afraid that the same disposition should have a larger field for its display; and you believe this temper to be inherent in the sex. I doubt whether any temper be *natural*, as it is called: certainly this disposition need not be attributed to any innate cause; it is the consequence of their erroneous education. The belief that pleasure is necessarily connected with the mere exercise of free-will, is a false and pernicious association of ideas, arising from the tyranny of those who have had the management of their childhood, from their having frequently discovered that they have been more happy in chusing about trifles, when they have acted in opposition to the maxims of those who govern them, than when they have followed their advice. I shall endeavor to prevent this from happening in my daughter's early education, and shall thus, I hope, prevent her acquiring any unconquerable prejudice in favour of her own wishes, or any unreasonable desire to influence the opinions of others. People, who have reasons for their preferences and aversions, are never so zealous in the support of their own tastes, as those are who have no arguments either to convince themselves or others that they are in the right. *Power* over the minds of others will not, therefore, in domestic, any more than in public life, be an object of ambition to women of enlarged understandings.

You appeal to history to prove to me that great calamities have ensued whenever the female sex has been indulged with liberty, yet you acknowledge that we cannot be certain whether these evils have been the effects of our trusting them with liberty, or of our not having previously instructed them in the use of it: upon the decision of this rests your whole argument. Women have not erred from having knowledge, but from not having had experience: they may have grown vain and presumptuous when they have learned but little, they will be sobered into good sense when they shall have learned more.

But you fear that knowledge should injure the delicacy of female manners, that truth would not keep so firm a hold upon the mind as prejudice, and that the conviction of the understanding will never have a permanent, good effect upon the conduct. I agree with you in thinking, that the strength of mind, which makes people govern themselves by reason, is not always connected with abilities in their most cultivated state. I deplore the instances I have seen of this truth; but I do not despair: I am, on the contrary, excited to examine into the causes of this phenomenon in the human mind: nor, because I see some evil, would I sacrifice the good on a motive of bare suspicion. It is a contradiction to say, that to give the power of discerning what is good, is to give a disposition to prefer what is bad. All that you prove when you say that prejudice, passion, habit, often impel us to act in opposition to our reason, is, that there exist enemies to reason, which have not yet been subdued. Would you destroy her power because she has not been always victorious? rather think on the means by which you may extend her dominion, and secure to her in future the permanent advantages of victory.

Women, whose talents have been much cultivated, have usually had their attention distracted by subordinate pursuits, and they have not been taught that the grand object of life is to be happy; to be prudent and virtuous that they may be happy: their ambition has been directed to the acquisition of knowledge and learning, merely as other women have been excited to acquire accomplishments, for the purposes of ostentation, not with a view to the real advantage of the acquisition. But, from the abuse, you are not to argue against the use of knowledge. Place objects in a just view before the understanding, show their different proportions, and the mind will make a wise choice. "You think yourself happy because you are wise", said a philosopher; "I think myself wise because I am happy."

No woman can be happy in society who does not preserve the peculiar virtues of her sex. When this is demonstrated to the understanding, must not those virtues, and the means of preserving them, become objects of the first and most interesting importance to a sensible woman? I would not rest her security entirely upon this conviction, when I can increase it by all the previous habits of early education: these things are not, as you seem to think, incompatible. Whilst a child has not the use of reason, I would guide it by my reason, and give it such habits as my experience convinces me will tend to its happiness. As the child's understanding is enlarged, I can explain the meaning of my conduct, and habit will then be confirmed by reason: I lose no time, I expose myself to no danger by this system. On the contrary, those who depend merely on the force of habit and of prejudice alone, expose themselves to perpetual danger. If once their pupils begin to reflect upon their own hood-winked education, if once their faith is shaken in the dogmas which have been imposed upon them, they will probably believe that they have been deceived in every thing which they have been taught, and they will burst their former bonds with indignation: credulity is always rash in the moment of detection. . . .

. . . Women have not the privilege of choice as we have; but they have the power to determine. Women cannot precisely force the tastes of the person with whom they may be connected, yet their happiness will greatly depend upon their being able to conform their tastes to his. For this reason, I should rather, in female education, cultivate the general powers of the mind than any particular faculty. I do not desire to make my daughter a musician, a painter, or a poetess; I do not desire to make her a botanist, a mathematician, or a chemist; but I wish to give her the habit of industry and attention, the love of knowledge and the power of reasoning: these will enable her to attain excellence in any pursuit of science or of literature. Her tastes and her occupations will, I hope, be determined by her situation, and by the wishes of her friends: she will consider all accomplishments and all knowledge as subordinate to her first object, the contributing to their happiness and her own.

I am, my dear friend,
Yours sincerely
1795

Jane Austen
1775–1817

"Mrs. Hall of Sherborne was brought to bed yesterday of a dead child, some weeks before she expected, owing to a fright. I suppose she happened unawares to look at her husband." So wrote the witty Jane Austen in 1798 to her sister, Cassandra, with whom she loved to share the local news. A major English novelist of manners and morals, Austen was born into a prominent middle-class family in Steventon, Hampshire, in the south of

England; she was the seventh of eight children of a country parson and scholar, George Austen, and Cassandra Leigh Austen, whose uncle was an Oxford don. Educated primarily at home, Austen spent time reading and discussing books with her brothers and sister; she was especially fond of novels and wrote parodies of those she found excessively sentimental or gothic. She composed many works of juvenilia, including partial drafts of three of her later novels, but wrote considerably less between 1801 and 1806, when her father retired and the family moved to the bustling city of Bath. After George Austen's death she shared a cottage on her brother's estate at Chawton with her mother, her sister, and an unmarried female friend. At Chawton she wrote six novels during the last ten years of her life, initially publishing them anonymously, although the works' popular success led to an almost immediate discovery of their author's identity. Austen's male contemporaries hailed her writing: Sir Walter Scott praised her "elegance" and "precision," while Tennyson deemed her a "prose Shakespeare."

Austen's novels examine the complexities of gender and social class in early nineteenth-century England; among the subjects she critiqued were the vicissitudes of the marriage market, the restrictions on women's education, and the pretensions of certain members of the British aristocracy. Many of her novels feature an intelligent but economically vulnerable young woman, motherless or with a feckless father, who rejects an unsuitable man in favor of one more suitable as a husband. To this comic situation Austen adds irony and trenchant social commentary, satirizing pompous clergymen, arrogant aristocrats, silly girls, and frivolous balls. Her first novel, *Sense and Sensibility* (1811), portrays the dilemma of the Dashwood sisters, left in financial ruin when their father dies and his estate falls to their half-brother, whose wife convinces him to keep it for himself. Only through marriage to reliable men can the vivacious Marianne and the sensible Elinor secure their futures. *Pride and Prejudice* (1813) features Elizabeth Bennet and her four sisters, all of whom their flighty mother seeks to marry off. It falls to Elizabeth to reject the advances of the obnoxious Mr. Collins and to overcome her initial prejudice against a finer suitor, the wealthy Mr. Darcy. *Mansfield Park* (1814) focuses on the lack of economic options for single women; its protagonist, Fanny Price, abhors her dependence upon male relatives but finds "tranquillity and comfort" in the country, while her equally dependent companion, Mary Crawford, sees in rural life only "tediousness and vexation."

Many critics consider *Emma* (1816) Austen's finest novel, despite the author's belief that its protagonist was someone whom "no one but myself will much like." Lively and opinionated, Emma Woodhouse misinterprets social cues to her own detriment and that of others; ultimately she must overcome her youthful indiscretions. Another critically acclaimed work, *Persuasion*, was written in 1815 and published in 1817, when Austen described herself as "a very genteel, portable sort of invalid." This novel presents the ethical independence of Anne Elliott, an impoverished spinster who initially rejects her suitor, Captain Wentworth, as socially inferior but grows to believe in the integrity of her own feelings. Three of Austen's novels—*Sense and Sensibility*, *Emma*, and *Persuasion*—were made into popular Hollywood or BBC films during the 1990s.

Included here is *Northanger Abbey*, a satire of popular gothic literature and a *bildungsroman*, or novel of initiation. *Northanger Abbey* explores what feminist critics Sandra Gilbert and Susan Gubar, in *The Madwoman in the Attic*, have called "the necessity of female submission for female survival." Its protagonist, Catherine Morland, struggles to suppress her lively imagination and thereby meet the requirements of her suitor, Henry Tilney, the son of a wealthy, tyrannical general. Despite its parodic elements, the novel appropriates gothic conventions to a serious end, as Austen critiques officious patriarchs and allows her protagonist to question codes of propriety and patriarchal authority. Austen completed *Northanger Abbey* in 1808 but, according to her sister, she wrote it between 1798 and 1799; the novel was published posthumously in 1817.

⊰ Northanger Abbey ⊱

Volume I

ADVERTISEMENT,
BY THE AUTHORESS,
TO
NORTHANGER ABBEY.

This little work was finished in the year 1803, and intended for immediate publication. It was disposed of to a bookseller, it was even advertised, and why the business proceeded no farther, the author has never been able to learn. That any bookseller should think it worth while to purchase what he did not think it worth while to publish seems extraordinary. But with this, neither the author nor the public have any other concern than as some observation is necessary upon those parts of the work which thirteen years have made comparatively obsolete. The public are entreated to bear in mind that thirteen years have passed since it was finished, many more since it was begun, and that during that period, places, manners, books, and opinions have undergone considerable changes.

CHAPTER I

No one who had ever seen Catherine Morland in her infancy would have supposed her born to be an heroine. Her situation in life, the character of her father and mother, her own person and disposition, were all equally against her. Her father was a clergyman, without being neglected, or poor, and a very respectable man, though his name was Richard—and he had never been handsome. He had a considerable independence, besides two good livings—and he was not in the least addicted to locking up his daughters. Her mother was a woman of useful plain sense, with a good temper, and, what is more remarkable, with a good constitution. She had three sons before Catherine was born; and instead of dying in bringing the latter into the world, as any body might expect, she still lived on—lived to have six children more—to see them growing up around her, and to enjoy excellent health herself. A family of ten children will be always called a fine family, where there are heads and arms and legs enough for the number; but the Morlands had little other right to the word, for they were in general very plain, and Catherine, for many years of her life, as plain as any. She had a thin awkward figure, a sallow skin without colour, dark lank hair, and strong features; so much for her person; and not less unpropitious for heroism seemed her mind. She was fond of all boys' plays, and greatly preferred cricket not merely to dolls, but to the more heroic enjoyments of infancy, nursing a dormouse, feeding a canary-bird, or watering a rosebush. Indeed she had no taste for a garden; and if she gathered flowers at all, it was chiefly for the pleasure of mischief—at least so it was conjectured from her always preferring those which she was forbidden to take.—Such were her propensities—her abilities were quite as extraordinary. She never could learn or understand any thing before she was taught; and sometimes not even then, for she was often inattentive, and occasionally stupid. Her mother was three months in teaching her only to repeat the "Beggar's Petition;"[1] and after all, her next sister, Sally, could say it better than she did. Not that Catherine was always stupid, by no means; she learnt the fable of "The Hare and Many Friends," as quickly as any girl in England. Her mother wished her to learn music;

---

1. A poem by Thomas Moss published in *Poems on Several Occasions* (1769).

the work of women

and Catherine was sure she should like it, for she was very fond of tinkling the keys of the old forlorn spinnet; so, at eight years old she began. She learnt a year, and could not bear it; and Mrs. Morland, who did not insist on her daughters being accomplished in spite of incapacity or distaste, allowed her to leave off. The day which dismissed the music-master was one of the happiest of Catherine's life. Her taste for drawing was not superior; though whenever she could obtain the outside of a letter from her mother, or seize upon any other odd piece of paper, she did what she could in that way, by drawing houses and trees, hens and chickens, all very much like one another. Writing and accounts she was taught by her father; French by her mother: her proficiency in either was not remarkable, and she shirked her lessons in both whenever she could. What a strange, unaccountable character! For with all these symptoms of profligacy at ten years old, she had neither a bad heart nor a bad temper; was seldom stubborn, scarcely ever quarrelsome, and very kind to the little ones, with few interruptions of tyranny; she was moreover noisy and wild, hated confinement and cleanliness, and loved nothing so well in the world as rolling down the green slope at the back of the house.

Such was Catherine Morland at ten. At fifteen, appearances were mending; she began to curl her hair and long for balls; her complexion improved, her features were softened by plumpness and colour, her eyes gained more animation, and her figure more consequence. Her love of dirt gave way to an inclination for finery, and she grew clean as she grew smart; she had now the pleasure of sometimes hearing her father and mother remark on her personal improvement. "Catherine grows quite a good-looking girl—she is almost pretty to day," were words which caught her ears now and then; and how welcome were the sounds! To look *almost* pretty, is an acquisition of higher delight to a girl who has been looking plain the first fifteen years of her life, than a beauty from her cradle can ever receive.

Mrs. Morland was a very good woman, and wished to see her children every thing they ought to be; but her time was so much occupied in lying-in and teaching the little ones, that her elder daughters were inevitably left to shift for themselves; and it was not very wonderful that Catherine, who had by nature nothing heroic about her, should prefer cricket, base ball, riding on horseback, and running about the country at the age of fourteen, to books—or at least books of information—for, provided that nothing like useful knowledge could be gained from them, provided they were all story and no reflection, she had never any objection to books at all. But from fifteen to seventeen she was in training for a heroine; she read all such works as heroines must read to supply their memories with those quotations which are so serviceable and so soothing in the vicissitudes of their eventful lives.

From Pope, she learnt to censure those who

> bear about the mockery of woe.

From Gray, that

> Many a flower is born to blush unseen,
> And waste its fragrance on the desert air.

From Thompson, that

> ————It is a delightful task
> To teach the young idea how to shoot.[2]

Training to be a heroine

2. The first quotation comes from Alexander Pope's "Elegy to the Memory of an Unfortunate Lady" (1717); the second is a misquote of Thomas Gray's "Elegy Written in a Country Churchyard" (1751); the third is taken from James Thomson's "Spring" in *The Seasons* (1726).

And from Shakspeare she gained a great store of information—amongst the rest, that

> ————Trifles light as air,
> Are, to the jealous, confirmation strong,
> As proofs of Holy Writ.

That

> The poor beetle, which we tread upon,
> In corporal sufferance feels a pang as great
> As when a giant dies.

And that a young woman in love always looks

> ————like Patience on a monument
> Smiling at Grief.[3]

So far her improvement was sufficient—and in many other points she came on exceedingly well; for though she could not write sonnets, she brought herself to read them; and though there seemed no chance of her throwing a whole party into raptures by a prelude on the pianoforte, of her own composition, she could listen to other people's performance with very little fatigue. Her greatest deficiency was in the pencil—she had no notion of drawing—not enough even to attempt a sketch of her lover's profile, that she might be detected in the design. There she fell miserably short of the true heroic height. At present she did not know her own poverty, for she had no lover to portray. She had reached the age of seventeen, without having seen one amiable youth who could call forth her sensibility; without having inspired one real passion, and without having excited even any admiration but what was very moderate and very transient. This was strange indeed! But strange things may be generally accounted for if their cause be fairly searched out. There was not one lord in the neighbourhood; no—not even a baronet. There was not one family among their acquaintance who had reared and supported a boy accidentally found at their door—not one young man whose origin was unknown. Her father had no ward, and the squire of the parish no children.

But when a young lady is to be a heroine, the perverseness of forty surrounding families cannot prevent her. Something must and will happen to throw a hero in her way.

Mr. Allen, who owned the chief of the property about Fullerton, the village in Wiltshire where the Morlands lived, was ordered to Bath for the benefit of a gouty constitution; and his lady, a good-humoured woman, fond of Miss Morland, and probably aware that if adventures will not befall a young lady in her own village, she must seek them abroad, invited her to go with them. Mr. and Mrs. Morland were all compliance, and Catherine all happiness.

CHAPTER II

In addition to what has been already said of Catherine Morland's personal and mental endowments, when about to be launched into all the difficulties and dangers of a six weeks' residence in Bath, it may be stated, for the reader's more certain information, lest the following pages should otherwise fail of giving any idea of what her

---

3. *Othello* 3.3.; *Measure for Measure* 3.1.; and *Twelfth Night* 2.4.

description of Catherine at 17

character is meant to be; that her heart was affectionate, her disposition cheerful and open, without conceit or affectation of any kind—her manners just removed from the awkwardness and shyness of a girl; her person pleasing, and, when in good looks, pretty—and her mind about as ignorant and uninformed as the female mind at seventeen usually is.

When the hour of departure drew near, the maternal anxiety of Mrs. Morland will be naturally supposed to be most severe. A thousand alarming presentiments of evil to her beloved Catherine from this terrific separation must oppress her heart with sadness, and drown her in tears for the last day or two of their being together; and advice of the most important and applicable nature must of course flow from her wise lips in their parting conference in her closet. Cautions against the violence of such noblemen and baronets as delight in forcing young ladies away to some remote farm-house, must, at such a moment, relieve the fulness of her heart. Who would not think so? But Mrs. Morland knew so little of lords and baronets, that she entertained no notion of their general mischievousness, and was wholly unsuspicious of danger to her daughter from their machinations. Her cautions were confined to the following points. "I beg, Catherine, you will always wrap yourself up very warm about the throat, when you come from the Rooms at night; and I wish you would try to keep some account of the money you spend; I will give you this little book on purpose."

Sally, or rather Sarah, (for what young lady of common gentility will reach the age of sixteen without altering her name as far as she can?) must from situation be at this time the intimate friend and confidante of her sister. It is remarkable, however, that she neither insisted on Catherine's writing by every post, nor exacted her promise of transmitting the character of every new acquaintance, nor a detail of every interesting conversation that Bath might produce. Every thing indeed relative to this important journey was done, on the part of the Morlands, with a degree of moderation and composure, which seemed rather consistent with the common feelings of common life, than with the refined susceptibilities, the tender emotions which the first separation of a heroine from her family ought always to excite. Her father, instead of giving her an unlimited order on his banker, or even putting an hundred pounds bank-bill into her hands, gave her only ten guineas, and promised her more when she wanted it.

Under these unpromising auspices, the parting took place, and the journey began. It was performed with suitable quietness and uneventful safety. Neither robbers nor tempests befriended them, nor one lucky overturn to introduce them to the hero. Nothing more alarming occurred than a fear on Mrs. Allen's side, of having once left her clogs behind her at an inn, and that fortunately proved to be groundless.

They arrived at Bath. Catherine was all eager delight; her eyes were here, there, every where, as they approached its fine and striking environs, and afterwards drove through those streets which conducted them to the hotel. She was come to be happy, and she felt happy already.

They were soon settled in comfortable lodgings in Pulteney-street.

It is now expedient to give some description of Mrs. Allen, that the reader may be able to judge, in what manner her actions will hereafter tend to promote the general distress of the work, and how she will, probably, contribute to reduce poor Catherine to all the desperate wretchedness of which a last volume is capable—whether by her imprudence, vulgarity, or jealousy—whether by intercepting her letters, ruining her character, or turning her out of doors.

Mrs. Allen was one of that numerous class of females, whose society can raise no other emotion than surprise at there being any men in the world who could like them well enough to marry them. She had neither beauty, genius, accomplishment, nor manner. The air of a gentle-woman, a great deal of quiet, inactive good temper, and a trifling turn of mind, were all that could account for her being the choice of a sensible, intelligent man, like Mr. Allen. In one respect she was admirably fitted to introduce a young lady into public, being as fond of going every where and seeing every thing herself as any young lady could be. Dress was her passion. She had a most harmless delight in being fine; and our heroine's entrée into life could not take place till after three or four days had been spent in learning what was mostly worn, and her chaperon was provided with a dress of the newest fashion. Catherine too made some purchases herself, and when all these matters were arranged, the important evening came which was to usher her into the Upper Rooms. Her hair was cut and dressed by the best hand, her clothes put on with care, and both Mrs. Allen and her maid declared she looked quite as she should do. With such encouragement, Catherine hoped at least to pass uncensured through the crowd. As for admiration, it was always very welcome when it came, but she did not depend on it.

Mrs. Allen was so long in dressing, that they did not enter the ball-room till late. The season was full, the room crowded, and the two ladies squeezed in as well as they could. As for Mr. Allen, he repaired directly to the card-room, and left them to enjoy a mob by themselves. With more care for the safety of her new gown than for the comfort of her protegée, Mrs. Allen made her way through the throng of men by the door, as swiftly as the necessary caution would allow; Catherine, however, kept close at her side, and linked her arm too firmly within her friend's to be torn asunder by any common effort of a struggling assembly. But to her utter amazement she found that to proceed along the room was by no means the way to disengage themselves from the crowd; it seemed rather to increase as they went on, whereas she had imagined that when once fairly within the door, they should easily find seats and be able to watch the dances with perfect convenience. But this was far from being the case, and though by unwearied diligence they gained even the top of the room, their situation was just the same; they saw nothing of the dancers but the high feathers of some of the ladies. Still they moved on—something better was yet in view; and by a continued exertion of strength and ingenuity they found themselves at last in the passage behind the highest bench. Here there was something less of crowd than below; and hence Miss Morland had a comprehensive view of all the company beneath her, and of all the dangers of her late passage through them. It was a splendid sight, and she began, for the first time that evening, to feel herself at a ball: she longed to dance, but she had not an acquaintance in the room. Mrs. Allen did all that she could do in such a case by saying very placidly, every now and then, "I wish you could dance, my dear,—I wish you could get a partner." For some time her young friend felt obliged to her for these wishes; but they were repeated so often, and proved so totally ineffectual, that Catherine grew tired at last, and would thank her no more.

They were not long able, however, to enjoy the repose of the eminence they had so laboriously gained.—Every body was shortly in motion for tea, and they must squeeze out like the rest. Catherine began to feel something of disappointment—she was tired of being continually pressed against by people, the generality of whose faces possessed nothing to interest, and with all of whom she was so wholly unacquainted, that she could not relieve the irksomeness of imprisonment by the exchange of a syllable with any of her fellow captives; and when at last arrived in the tea-room, she felt yet more the awkwardness of having no party to join, no acquaintance to claim, no gentleman to assist them. They saw nothing of Mr. Allen; and after looking about them in vain for a more eligible situation, were obliged to sit down at the end of a table, at which a large party were already placed, without having any thing to do there, or any body to speak to, except each other.

Mrs. Allen congratulated herself, as soon as they were seated, on having preserved her gown from injury. "It would have been very shocking to have it torn," said she, "would not it? It is such a delicate muslin. For my part I have not seen any thing I like so well in the whole room, I assure you."

"How uncomfortable it is," whispered Catherine, "not to have a single acquaintance here!"

"Yes, my dear," replied Mrs. Allen, with perfect serenity, "it is very uncomfortable indeed."

"What shall we do? The gentlemen and ladies at this table look as if they wondered why we came here—we seem forcing ourselves into their party."

"Aye, so we do. That is very disagreeable. I wish we had a large acquaintance here."

"I wish we had *any*;—it would be somebody to go to."

"Very true, my dear; and if we knew anybody we would join them directly. The Skinners were here last year—I wish they were here now."

"Had not we better go away as it is? Here are no tea things for us, you see."

"No more there are, indeed. How very provoking! But I think we had better sit still, for one gets so tumbled in such a crowd! How is my head, my dear? Somebody gave me a push that has hurt it I am afraid."

"No, indeed, it looks very nice. But, dear Mrs. Allen, are you sure there is nobody you know in all this multitude of people? I think you *must* know somebody."

"I don't upon my word—I wish I did. I wish I had a large acquaintance here with all my heart, and then I should get you a partner. I should be so glad to have you dance. There goes a strange-looking woman! What an odd gown she has got on! How old fashioned it is! Look at the back."

After some time they received an offer of tea from one of their neighbours; it was thankfully accepted, and this introduced a light conversation with the gentleman who offered it, which was the only time that any body spoke to them during the evening, till they were discovered and joined by Mr. Allen when the dance was over.

"Well, Miss Morland," said he, directly, "I hope you have had an agreeable ball."

"Very agreeable indeed," she replied, vainly endeavouring to hide a great yawn.

"I wish she had been able to dance," said his wife, "I wish we could have got a partner for her. I have been saying how glad I should be if the Skinners were here this winter instead of last; or if the Parrys had come, as they talked of once, she might have danced with George Parry. I am so sorry she has not had a partner!"

"We shall do better another evening I hope," was Mr. Allen's consolation.

The company began to disperse when the dancing was over—enough to leave space for the remainder to walk about in some comfort; and now was the time for a heroine, who had not yet played a very distinguished part in the events of the evening, to be noticed and admired. Every five minutes, by removing some of the crowd, gave greater openings for her charms. She was now seen by many young men who had not been near her before. Not one, however, started with rapturous wonder on beholding her, no whisper of eager inquiry ran round the room, nor was she once called a divinity by any body. Yet Catherine was in very good looks, and had the company only seen her three years before, they would *now* have thought her exceedingly handsome.

She *was* looked at however, and with some admiration; for, in her own hearing, two gentlemen pronounced her to be a pretty girl. Such words had their due effect; she immediately thought the evening pleasanter than she had found it before—her humble vanity was contented—she felt more obliged to the two young men for this simple praise than a true quality heroine would have been for fifteen sonnets in cele-bration of her charms, and went to her chair in good humour with every body, and perfectly satisfied with her share of public attention.

CHAPTER III

Every morning now brought its regular duties; shops were to be visited; some new part of the town to be looked at; and the Pump-room to be attended, where they paraded up and down for an hour, looking at every body and speaking to no one. The wish of a numerous acquaintance in Bath was still uppermost with Mrs. Allen, and she repeated it after every fresh proof, which every morning brought, of her knowing nobody at all.

They made their appearance in the Lower Rooms; and here fortune was more favourable to our heroine. The master of the ceremonies introduced to her a very gentlemanlike young man as a partner;—his name was Tilney. He seemed to be about four or five and twenty, was rather tall, had a pleasing countenance, a very intelligent and lively eye, and, if not quite handsome, was very near it. His address was good, and Catherine felt herself in high luck. There was little leisure for speaking while they danced; but when they were seated at tea, she found him as agreeable as she had already given him credit for being. He talked with fluency and spirit—and there was an archness and pleasantry in his manner which interested, though it was hardly understood by her. After chatting some time on such matters as naturally arose from the objects around them, he suddenly addressed her with—"I have hither-to been very remiss, madam, in the proper attentions of a partner here; I have not yet asked you how long you have been in Bath; whether you were ever here before; whether you have been at the Upper Rooms, the theatre, and the concert; and how you like the place altogether. I have been very negligent—but are you now at leisure to satisfy me in these particulars? If you are I will begin directly."

"You need not give yourself that trouble, sir."

"No trouble I assure you, madam." Then forming his features into a set smile, and affectedly softening his voice, he added, with a simpering air, "Have you been long in Bath, madam?"

"About a week, sir," replied Catherine, trying not to laugh.

"Really!" with affected astonishment.

"Why should you be surprised, sir?"

"Why, indeed!" said he, in his natural tone, "but some emotion must appear to be raised by your reply, and surprize is more easily assumed, and not less reasonable than any other. Now let us go on. Were you never here before, madam?"

"Never, sir."

"Indeed! Have you yet honoured the Upper Rooms?"

"Yes, sir, I was there last Monday."

"Have you been to the theatre?"

"Yes, sir, I was at the play on Tuesday."

"To the concert?"

"Yes, sir, on Wednesday."

"And are you altogether pleased with Bath?"

"Yes—I like it very well."

"Now I must give one smirk, and then we may be rational again."

Catherine turned away her head, not knowing whether she might venture to laugh.

"I see what you think of me," said he gravely—"I shall make but a poor figure in your journal to-morrow."

"My journal!"

"Yes, I know exactly what you will say: Friday, went to the Lower Rooms; wore my sprigged muslin robe with blue trimmings—plain black shoes—appeared to much advantage; but was strangely harassed by a queer, half-witted man, who would make me dance with him, and distressed me by his nonsense."

"Indeed I shall say no such thing."

"Shall I tell you what you ought to say?"

"If you please."

"I danced with a very agreeable young man, introduced by Mr. King; had a great deal of conversation with him—seems a most extraordinary genius—hope I may know more of him. *That*, madam, is what I *wish* you to say."

"But, perhaps, I keep no journal."

"Perhaps you are not sitting in this room, and I am not sitting by you. These are points in which a doubt is equally possible. Not keep a journal! How are your absent cousins to understand the tenour of your life in Bath without one? How are the civilities and compliments of every day to be related as they ought to be, unless noted down every evening in a journal? How are your various dresses to be remembered, and the particular state of your complexion, and curl of your hair to be described in all their diversities, without having constant recourse to a journal?—My dear madam, I am not so ignorant of young ladies' ways as you wish to believe me; it is this delightful habit of journalizing which largely contributes to form the easy style of writing for which ladies are so generally celebrated. Every body allows that the talent of writing agreeable letters is peculiarly female. Nature may have done something, but I am sure it must be essentially assisted by the practice of keeping a journal."

"I have sometimes thought," said Catherine, doubtingly, "whether ladies do write so much better letters than gentlemen! That is—I should not think the superiority was always on our side."

"As far as I have had opportunity of judging, it appears to me that the usual style of letter-writing among women is faultless, except in three particulars."

"And what are they?"

"A general deficiency of subject, a total inattention to stops, and a very frequent ignorance of grammar."

"Upon my word! I need not have been afraid of disclaiming the compliment. You do not think too highly of us in that way."

"I should no more lay it down as a general rule that women write better letters than men, than that they sing better duets, or draw better landscapes. In every power, of which taste is the foundation, excellence is pretty fairly divided between the sexes."

They were interrupted by Mrs. Allen: "My dear Catherine," said she, "do take this pin out of my sleeve; I am afraid it has torn a hole already; I shall be quite sorry if it has, for this is a favourite gown, though it cost but nine shillings a yard."

"That is exactly what I should have guessed it, madam," said Mr. Tilney, looking at the muslin.

"Do you understand muslins, sir?"

"Particularly well; I always buy my own cravats, and am allowed to be an excellent judge; and my sister has often trusted me in the choice of a gown. I bought one for her the other day, and it was pronounced to be a prodigious bargain by every lady who saw it. I gave but five shillings a yard for it, and a true Indian muslin."

Mrs. Allen was quite struck by his genius. "Men commonly take so little notice of those things," said she: "I can never get Mr. Allen to know one of my gowns from another. You must be a great comfort to your sister, sir."

"I hope I am, madam."

"And pray, sir, what do you think of Miss Morland's gown?"

"It is very pretty, madam," said he, gravely examining it; "but I do not think it will wash well; I am afraid it will fray."

"How can you," said Catherine, laughing, "be so———" she had almost said, strange.

"I am quite of your opinion, sir," replied Mrs. Allen; "and so I told Miss Morland when she bought it."

"But then you know, madam, muslin always turns to some account or other; Miss Morland will get enough out of it for a handkerchief, or a cap, or a cloak.—Muslin can never be said to be wasted. I have heard my sister say so forty times, when she has been extravagant in buying more than she wanted, or careless in cutting it to pieces."

"Bath is a charming place, sir; there are so many good shops here. We are sadly off in the country; not but what we have very good shops in Salisbury, but it is so far to go; eight miles is a long way; Mr. Allen says it is nine, measured nine; but I am sure it cannot be more than eight; and it is such a fag—I come back tired to death. Now here one can step out of doors and get a thing in five minutes."

Mr. Tilney was polite enough to seem interested in what she said; and she kept him on the subject of muslins till the dancing recommenced. Catherine feared, as she listened to their discourse, that he indulged himself a little too much with the foibles of others. "What are you thinking of so earnestly?" said he, as they walked back to the ball-room; "not of your partner, I hope, for, by that shake of the head, your meditations are not satisfactory."

Catherine coloured, and said, "I was not thinking of any thing."

"That is artful and deep, to be sure; but I had rather be told at once that you will not tell me."

"Well then, I will not."

"Thank you; for now we shall soon be acquainted, as I am authorized to tease you on this subject whenever we meet, and nothing in the world advances intimacy so much."

They danced again; and, when the assembly closed, parted, on the lady's side at least, with a strong inclination for continuing the acquaintance. Whether she thought of him so much, while she drank her warm wine and water, and prepared herself for bed, as to dream of him when there, cannot be ascertained; but I hope it was no more than in a slight slumber, or a morning doze at most; for if it be true, as a celebrated writer has maintained, that no young lady can be justified in falling in love before the gentleman's love is declared,[4] it must be very improper that a young lady should dream of a gentleman before the gentleman is first known to have dreamt of her. How proper Mr. Tilney might be as a dreamer or a lover, had not yet perhaps

4. [Vide a letter from Mr. Richardson, No. 97, vol. ii. Rambler.]

entered Mr. Allen's head, but that he was not objectionable as a common acquaintance for his young charge he was on inquiry satisfied; for he had early in the evening taken pains to know who her partner was, and had been assured of Mr. Tilney's being a clergyman, and of a very respectable family in Gloucestershire.

Chapter IV

With more than usual eagerness did Catherine hasten to the Pump-room the next day, secure within herself of seeing Mr. Tilney there before the morning were over, and ready to meet him with a smile: but no smile was demanded—Mr. Tilney did not appear. Every creature in Bath, except himself, was to be seen in the room at different periods of the fashionable hours; crowds of people were every moment passing in and out, up the steps and down; people whom nobody cared about, and nobody wanted to see; and he only was absent. "What a delightful place Bath is," said Mrs. Allen, as they sat down near the great clock, after parading the room till they were tired; "and how pleasant it would be if we had any acquaintance here."

This sentiment had been uttered so often in vain, that Mrs. Allen had no particular reason to hope it would be followed with more advantage now; but we are told to "despair of nothing we would attain," as "unwearied diligence our point would gain;" and the unwearied diligence with which she had every day wished for the same thing was at length to have its just reward, for hardly had she been seated ten minutes before a lady of about her own age, who was sitting by her, and had been looking at her attentively for several minutes, addressed her with great complaisance in these words: "I think, madam, I cannot be mistaken; it is a long time since I had the pleasure of seeing you, but is not your name Allen?" This question answered, as it readily was, the stranger pronounced her's to be Thorpe; and Mrs. Allen immediately recognized the features of a former school-fellow and intimate, whom she had seen only once since their respective marriages, and that many years ago. Their joy on this meeting was very great, as well it might, since they had been contented to know nothing of each other for the last fifteen years. Compliments on good looks now passed; and, after observing how time had slipped away since they were last together, how little they had thought of meeting in Bath, and what a pleasure it was to see an old friend, they proceeded to make inquiries and give intelligence as to their families, sisters, and cousins, talking both together, far more ready to give than to receive information, and each hearing very little of what the other said. Mrs. Thorpe, however, had one great advantage as a talker, over Mrs. Allen, in a family of children; and when she expatiated on the talents of her sons, and the beauty of her daughters, when she related their different situations and views—that John was at Oxford, Edward at Merchant-Taylors', and William at sea—and all of them more beloved and respected in their different stations than any other three beings ever were, Mrs. Allen had no similar information to give, no similar triumphs to press on the unwilling and unbelieving ear of her friend, and was forced to sit and appear to listen to all these maternal effusions, consoling herself, however, with the discovery, which her keen eye soon made, that the lace on Mrs. Thorpe's pelisse was not half so handsome as that on her own.

"Here come my dear girls," cried Mrs. Thorpe, pointing at three smart looking females, who, arm in arm, were then moving towards her. "My dear Mrs. Allen, I long to introduce them; they will be so delighted to see you: the tallest is Isabella, my eldest; is not she a fine young woman? The others are very much admired too, but I believe Isabella is the handsomest."

The Miss Thorpes were introduced; and Miss Morland, who had been for a short time forgotten, was introduced likewise. The name seemed to strike them all; and, after speaking to her with great civility, the eldest young lady observed aloud to the rest, "How excessively like her brother Miss Morland is!"

"The very picture of him indeed!" cried the mother—and "I should have known her any where for his sister!" was repeated by them all, two or three times over. For a moment Catherine was surprised; but Mrs. Thorpe and her daughters had scarcely begun the history of their acquaintance with Mr. James Morland, before she remembered that her eldest brother had lately formed an intimacy with a young man of his own college, of the name of Thorpe; and that he had spent the last week of the Christmas vacation with his family, near London.

The whole being explained, many obliging things were said by the Miss Thorpes of their wish of being better acquainted with her; of being considered as already friends, through the friendship of their brothers, &c. which Catherine heard with pleasure, and answered with all the pretty expressions she could command; and, as the first proof of amity, she was soon invited to accept an arm of the eldest Miss Thorpe, and take a turn with her about the room. Catherine was delighted with this extension of her Bath acquaintance, and almost forgot Mr. Tilney while she talked to Miss Thorpe. Friendship is certainly the finest balm for the pangs of disappointed love.

Their conversation turned upon those subjects, of which the free discussion has generally much to do in perfecting a sudden intimacy between two young ladies; such as dress, balls, flirtations, and quizzes. Miss Thorpe, however, being four years older than Miss Morland, and at least four years better informed, had a very decided advantage in discussing such points; she could compare the balls of Bath with those of Tunbridge; its fashions with the fashions of London; could rectify the opinions of her new friend in many articles of tasteful attire; could discover a flirtation between any gentleman and lady who only smiled on each other; and point out a quiz through the thickness of a crowd. These powers received due admiration from Catherine, to whom they were entirely new; and the respect which they naturally inspired might have been too great for familiarity, had not the easy gaity of Miss Thorpe's manners, and her frequent expressions of delight on this acquaintance with her, softened down every feeling of awe, and left nothing but tender affection. Their increasing attachment was not to be satisfied with half a dozen turns in the Pump-room, but required, when they all quitted it together, that Miss Thorpe should accompany Miss Morland to the very door of Mr. Allen's house; and that they should there part with a most affectionate and lengthened shake of hands, after learning, to their mutual relief, that they should see each other across the theatre at night, and say their prayers in the same chapel the next morning. Catherine then ran directly up stairs, and watched Miss Thorpe's progress down the street from the drawing-room window; admired the graceful spirit of her walk, the fashionable air of her figure and dress, and felt grateful, as well she might, for the chance which had procured her such a friend.

Mrs. Thorpe was a widow, and not a very rich one; she was a good-humoured, well-meaning woman, and a very indulgent mother. Her eldest daughter had great personal beauty, and the younger ones, by pretending to be as handsome as their sister, imitating her air, and dressing in the same style, did very well.

This brief account of the family is intended to supersede the necessity of a long and minute detail from Mrs. Thorpe herself, of her past adventures and sufferings, which might otherwise be expected to occupy the three or four following chapters; in which the worthlessness of lords and attornies might be set forth, and conversations, which had passed twenty years before, be minutely repeated.

Chapter V

Catherine was not so much engaged at the theatre that evening, in returning the nods and smiles of Miss Thorpe, though they certainly claimed much of her leisure, as to forget to look with an inquiring eye for Mr. Tilney in every box which her eye could reach; but she looked in vain. Mr. Tilney was no fonder of the play than the Pump-room. She hoped to be more fortunate the next day; and when her wishes for fine weather were answered by seeing a beautiful morning, she hardly felt a doubt of it; for a fine Sunday in Bath empties every house of its inhabitants, and all the world appears on such an occasion to walk about and tell their acquaintance what a charming day it is.

As soon as divine service was over, the Thorpes and Allens eagerly joined each other; and after staying long enough in the Pump-room to discover that the crowd was insupportable, and that there was not a genteel face to be seen, which every body discovers every Sunday throughout the season, they hastened away to the Crescent, to breathe the fresh air of better company. Here Catherine and Isabella, arm in arm, again tasted the sweets of friendship in an unreserved conversation; they talked much, and with much enjoyment; but again was Catherine disappointed in her hope of re-seeing her partner. He was no where to be met with; every search for him was equally unsuccessful, in morning lounges or evening assemblies; neither at the upper nor lower rooms, at dressed or undressed balls, was he perceivable; nor among the walkers, the horsemen, or the curricle-drivers of the morning. His name was not in the Pump-room book, and curiosity could do no more. He must be gone from Bath. Yet he had not mentioned that his stay would be so short! This sort of mysteriousness, which is always so becoming in a hero, threw a fresh grace in Catherine's imagination around his person and manners, and increased her anxiety to know more of him. From the Thorpes she could learn nothing, for they had been only two days in Bath before they met with Mrs. Allen. It was a subject, however, in which she often indulged with her fair friend, from whom she received every possible encouragement to continue to think of him; and his impression on her fancy was not suffered therefore to weaken. Isabella was very sure that he must be a charming young man; and was equally sure that he must have been delighted with her dear Catherine, and would therefore shortly return. She liked him the better for being a clergyman, "for she must confess herself very partial to the profession;" and something like a sigh escaped her as she said it. Perhaps Catherine was wrong in not demanding the cause of that gentle emotion—but she was not experienced enough in the finesse of love, or the duties of friendship, to know when delicate raillery was properly called for, or when a confidence should be forced.

Mrs. Allen was now quite happy—quite satisfied with Bath. She had found some acquaintance, had been so lucky too as to find in them the family of a most worthy old friend; and, as the completion of good fortune, had found these friends by no means so expensively dressed as herself. Her daily expressions were no longer, "I wish we had some acquaintance in Bath!" They were changed into—"How glad I am we have met with Mrs. Thorpe!"—and she was as eager in promoting the intercourse of the two families, as her young charge and Isabella themselves could be; never satisfied with the day unless she spent the chief of it by the side of Mrs. Thorpe, in what they called conversation, but in which there was scarcely ever any exchange of opinion, and not often any resemblance of subject, for Mrs. Thorpe talked chiefly of her children, and Mrs. Allen of her gowns.

The progress of the friendship between Catherine and Isabella was quick as its beginning had been warm, and they passed so rapidly through every gradation of increasing tenderness, that there was shortly no fresh proof of it to be given to their friends or themselves. They called each other by their Christian name, were always arm in arm when they walked, pinned up each other's train for the dance, and were not to be divided in the set; and if a rainy morning deprived them of other enjoyments, they were still resolute in meeting in defiance of wet and dirt, and shut themselves up, to read novels together. Yes, novels; for I will not adopt that ungenerous and impolitic custom so common with novel writers, of degrading by their contemptuous censure the very performances, to the number of which they are themselves adding—joining with their greatest enemies in bestowing the harshest epithets on such works, and scarcely ever permitting them to be read by their own heroine, who, if she accidentally take up a novel, is sure to turn over its insipid pages with disgust. Alas! if the heroine of one novel be not patronized by the heroine of another, from whom can she expect protection and regard? I cannot approve of it. Let us leave it to the Reviewers to abuse such effusions of fancy at their leisure, and over every new novel to talk in threadbare strains of the trash with which the press now groans. Let us not desert one another; we are an injured body. Although our productions have afforded more extensive and unaffected pleasure than those of any other literary corporation in the world, no species of composition has been so much decried. From pride, ignorance, or fashion, our foes are almost as many as our readers. And while the abilities of the nine-hundredth abridger of the History of England, or of the man who collects and publishes in a volume some dozen lines of Milton, Pope, and Prior, with a paper from the Spectator, and a chapter from Sterne, are eulogized by a thousand pens,[5] there seems almost a general wish of decrying the capacity and undervaluing the labour of the novelist, and of slighting the performances which have only genius, wit, and taste to recommend them. "I am no novel reader—I seldom look into novels—Do not imagine that I often read novels—It is really very well for a novel." Such is the common cant. "And what are you reading, Miss ———?" "Oh! it is only a novel!" replies the young lady; while she lays down her book with affected indifference, or momentary shame. "It is only Cecilia, or Camilla, or Belinda;"[6] or, in short, only some work in which the greatest powers of the mind are displayed, in which the most thorough knowledge of human nature, the happiest delineation of its varieties, the liveliest effusions of wit and humour are conveyed to the world in the best chosen language. Now, had the same young lady been engaged with a volume of the Spectator, instead of such a work, how proudly would she have produced the book, and told its name; though the chances must be against her being occupied by any part of that voluminous publication, of which either the matter or manner would not disgust a young person of taste: the substance of its papers so often consisting in the statement of improbable circumstances, unnatural characters, and topics of conversation, which no longer concern any one living; and their language, too, frequently so coarse as to give no very favourable idea of the age that could endure it.

5. Allusions to the English poets John Milton (1608–74), Alexander Pope (1688–1744), and Matthew Prior (1664–1721). The Spectator was a newspaper edited by Joseph Addison (1672–1719) and Richard Steele (1672–1729). Laurence Sterne (1713–68) was a British novelist.

6. Allusions to Cecilia, or Memoirs of an Heiress (1782) and Camilla, or a Picture of Youth (1796) by the English novelist Frances Burney and Belinda (1801) by the Scottish novelist Maria Edgeworth.

CHAPTER VI

The following conversation, which took place between the two friends in the Pump-room one morning, after an acquaintance of eight or nine days, is given as a specimen of their very warm attachment, and of the delicacy, discretion, originality of thought, and literary taste which marked the reasonableness of that attachment.

They met by appointment; and as Isabella had arrived nearly five minutes before her friend, her first address naturally was—"My dearest creature, what can have made you so late? I have been waiting for you at least this age!"

"Have you, indeed! I am very sorry for it; but really I thought I was in very good time. It is but just one. I hope you have not been here long?"

"Oh! these ten ages at least. I am sure I have been here this half hour. But now, let us go and sit down at the other end of the room, and enjoy ourselves. I have an hundred things to say to you. In the first place, I was so afraid it would rain this morning, just as I wanted to set off; it looked very showery, and that would have thrown me into agonies! Do you know, I saw the prettiest hat you can imagine, in a shop window in Milsom-street just now—very like yours, only with coquelicot ribbons instead of green; I quite longed for it. But, my dearest Catherine, what have you been doing with yourself all this morning?—Have you gone on with *Udolpho*?"[7]

"Yes, I have been reading it ever since I woke; and I am got to the black veil."

"Are you, indeed? How delightful! Oh! I would not tell you what is behind the black veil for the world! Are not you wild to know?"

"Oh! yes, quite; what can it be? But do not tell me—I would not be told upon any account. I know it must be a skeleton, I am sure it is Laurentina's skeleton. Oh! I am delighted with the book! I should like to spend my whole life in reading it. I assure you, if it had not been to meet you, I would not have come away from it for all the world."

"Dear creature! how much I am obliged to you; and when you have finished *Udolpho*, we will read the Italian together; and I have made out a list of ten or twelve more of the same kind for you."

"Have you, indeed! How glad I am!—What are they all?"

"I will read you their names directly; here they are, in my pocket-book. *Castle of Wolfenbach, Clermont, Mysterious Warnings, Necromancer of the Black Forest, Midnight Bell, Orphan of the Rhine,* and *Horrid Mysteries.*[8] Those will last us some time."

"Yes, pretty well; but are they all horrid, are you sure they are all horrid?"

"Yes, quite sure; for a particular friend of mine, a Miss Andrews, a sweet girl, one of the sweetest creatures in the world, has read every one of them. I wish you knew Miss Andrews, you would be delighted with her. She is netting herself the sweetest cloak you can conceive. I think her as beautiful as an angel, and I am so vexed with the men for not admiring her!—I scold them all amazingly about it."

"Scold them! Do you scold them for not admiring her?"

"Yes, that I do. There is nothing I would not do for those who are really my friends. I have no notion of loving people by halves, it is not my nature. My attachments are always excessively strong. I told Capt. Hunt at one of our assemblies this

---

7. *The Mysteries of Udolpho, a Romance* (1794) by Ann Radcliffe (1764–1823), a Gothic novelist.
8. *The Castle of Wolfenbach* (1793) and *The Mysterious Warning* (1796) are Gothic novels by a Mrs. Parsons; *Clermont: A Tale* (1798) is by Regina Maria Roche; *The*

Necromancer; or the Tale of the Black Forest (1794) is by Peter Teuthold; *The Midnight Bell* (1798) is by Francis Lathom; *The Orphan of the Rhine, a Novel* (1798) is by Eleanor Sleath; and *Horrid Mysteries: A Story* (1796) is by Peter Will.

(handwritten margin note at top: "Men believe women cannot be friends: Isabella disagrees")

(handwritten margin note at left: "The men they prefer")

winter, that if he was to tease me all night, I would not dance with him, unless he would allow Miss Andrews to be as beautiful as an angel. The men think us incapable of real friendship you know, and I am determined to shew them the difference. Now, if I were to hear any body speak slightingly of you, I should fire up in a moment: but that is not at all likely, for *you* are just the kind of girl to be a great favourite with the men."

"Oh! dear," cried Catherine, colouring, "how can you say so?"

"I know you very well; you have so much animation, which is exactly what Miss Andrews wants, for I must confess there is something amazingly insipid about her. Oh! I must tell you, that just after we parted yesterday, I saw a young man looking at you so earnestly—I am sure he is in love with you." Catherine coloured, and disclaimed again. Isabella laughed. "It is very true, upon my honour, but I see how it is; you are indifferent to every body's admiration, except that of one gentleman, who shall be nameless. Nay, I cannot blame you—(speaking more seriously)—your feelings are easily understood. Where the heart is really attached, I know very well how little one can be pleased with the attention of any body else. Every thing is so insipid, so uninteresting, that does not relate to the beloved object! I can perfectly comprehend your feelings."

"But you should not persuade me that I think so very much about Mr. Tilney, for perhaps I may never see him again."

"Not see him again! My dearest creature, do not talk of it. I am sure you would be miserable if you thought so."

"No, indeed, I should not. I do not pretend to say that I was not very much pleased with him; but while I have *Udolpho* to read, I feel as if nobody could make me miserable. Oh! the dreadful black veil! My dear Isabella, I am sure there must be Laurentina's skeleton behind it."

"It is so odd to me, that you should never have read *Udolpho* before; but I suppose Mrs. Morland objects to novels."

"No, she does not. She very often reads *Sir Charles Grandison* herself;[9] but new books do not fall in our way."

"*Sir Charles Grandison*! That is an amazing horrid book, is it not? I remember Miss Andrews could not get through the first volume."

"It is not like *Udolpho* at all; but yet I think it is very entertaining."

"Do you indeed!—you surprize me; I thought it had not been readable. But, my dearest Catherine, have you settled what to wear on your head to-night? I am determined at all events to be dressed exactly like you. The men take notice of *that* sometimes you know."

"But it does not signify if they do;" said Catherine, very innocently.

"Signify! Oh, heavens! I make it a rule never to mind what they say. They are very often amazingly impertinent if you do not treat them with spirit, and make them keep their distance."

"Are they?—Well, I never observed *that*. They always behave very well to me."

"Oh! they give themselves such airs. They are the most conceited creatures in the world, and think themselves of so much importance!—By the bye, though I have thought of it a hundred times, I have always forgot to ask you what is your favourite complexion in a man. Do you like them best dark or fair?"

"I hardly know. I never much thought about it. Something between both, I think. Brown—not fair, and not very dark."

9. *Sir Charles Grandison* (1754) is a novel by Samuel Richardson (1689–1761).

"Very well, Catherine. That is exactly he. I have not forgot your description of Mr. Tilney; 'a brown skin, with dark eyes, and rather dark hair.' Well, my taste is different. I prefer light eyes, and as to complexion—do you know—I like a sallow better than any other. You must not betray me, if you should ever meet with one of your acquaintance answering that description."

"Betray you! What do you mean?"

"Nay, do not distress me. I believe I have said too much. Let us drop the subject."

Catherine, in some amazement, complied; and after remaining a few moments silent, was on the point of reverting to what interested her at that time rather more than any thing else in the world, Laurentina's skeleton; when her friend prevented her, by saying, "For Heaven's sake! let us move away from this end of the room. Do you know, there are two odious young men who have been staring at me this half hour. They really put me quite out of countenance. Let us go and look at the arrivals. They will hardly follow us there."

Away they walked to the book; and while Isabella examined the names, it was Catherine's employment to watch the proceedings of these alarming young men.

"They are not coming this way, are they? I hope they are not so impertinent as to follow us. Pray let me know if they are coming. I am determined I will not look up."

In a few moments Catherine, with unaffected pleasure, assured her that she need not be longer uneasy, as the gentlemen had just left the Pump-room.

"And which way are they gone?" said Isabella, turning hastily round. "One was a very good-looking young man."

"They went towards the churchyard."

"Well, I am amazingly glad I have got rid of them! And now, what say you to going to Edgar's Buildings with me, and looking at my new hat? You said you should like to see it."

Catherine readily agreed. "Only," she added, "perhaps we may overtake the two young men."

"Oh! never mind that. If we make haste, we shall pass by them presently, and I am dying to shew you my hat."

"But if we only wait a few minutes, there will be no danger of our seeing them at all."

"I shall not pay them any such compliment, I assure you. I have no notion of treating men with such respect. *That* is the way to spoil them."

Catherine had nothing to oppose against such reasoning; and therefore, to shew the independence of Miss Thorpe, and her resolution of humbling the sex, they set off immediately as fast as they could walk, in pursuit of the two young men.

Chapter VII

Half a minute conducted them through the Pump-yard to the archway, opposite Union-passage; but here they were stopped. Every body acquainted with Bath may remember the difficulties of crossing Cheap-street at this point; it is indeed a street of so impertinent a nature, so unfortunately connected with the great London and Oxford roads, and the principal inn of the city, that a day never passes in which parties of ladies, however important their business, whether in quest of pastry, millinery, or even (as in the present case) of young men, are not detained on one side or other by carriages, horsemen, or carts. This evil had been felt and lamented, at least three times a day, by Isabella since her residence in Bath; and she was now fated to feel and lament it once more, for at the very moment of coming opposite to Union-passage, and within view of the two gentlemen who were proceeding through the crowds, and threading the gutters of that interesting alley, they were prevented crossing by the approach of a gig, driven along on bad pavement by a most knowing-looking coachman with all the vehemence that could most fitly endanger the lives of himself, his companion, and his horse.

"Oh, these odious gigs!" said Isabella, looking up, "how I detest them." But this detestation, though so just, was of short duration, for she looked again and exclaimed, "Delightful! Mr. Morland and my brother!"

"Good heaven! 'tis James!" was uttered at the same moment by Catherine; and, on catching the young men's eyes, the horse was immediately checked with a violence which almost threw him on his haunches, and the servant having now scampered up, the gentlemen jumped out, and the equipage was delivered to his care.

Catherine, by whom this meeting was wholly unexpected, received her brother with the liveliest pleasure; and he, being of a very amiable disposition, and sincerely attached to her, gave every proof on his side of equal satisfaction, which he could have leisure to do, while the bright eyes of Miss Thorpe were incessantly challenging his notice; and to her his devoirs were speedily paid, with a mixture of joy and embarrassment which might have informed Catherine, had she been more expert in the developement of other people's feelings, and less simply engrossed by her own, that her brother thought her friend quite as pretty as she could do herself.

John Thorpe, who in the mean time had been giving orders about the horses, soon joined them, and from him she directly received the amends which were her due; for while he slightly and carelessly touched the hand of Isabella, on her he bestowed a whole scrape and half a short bow. He was a stout young man of middling height, who, with a plain face and ungraceful form, seemed fearful of being too handsome unless he wore the dress of a groom, and too much like a gentleman unless he were easy where he ought to be civil, and impudent where he might be allowed to be easy. He took out his watch: "How long do you think we have been running it from Tetbury, Miss Morland?"

"I do not know the distance." Her brother told her that it was twenty-three miles.

"*Three*-and-twenty!" cried Thorpe; "five-and-twenty if it is an inch." Morland remonstrated, pleaded the authority of road-books, innkeepers, and milestones; but his friend disregarded them all; he had a surer test of distance. "I know it must be five-and-twenty," said he, "by the time we have been doing it. It is now half after one; we drove out of the inn-yard at Tetbury as the town-clock struck eleven; and I defy any man in England to make my horse go less than ten miles an hour in harness; that makes it exactly twenty-five."

"You have lost an hour," said Morland; "it was only ten o'clock when we came from Tetbury."

"Ten o'clock! it was eleven, upon my soul! I counted every stroke. This brother of yours would persuade me out of my senses, Miss Morland; do but look at my horse; did you ever see an animal so made for speed in your life?" (The servant had just mounted the carriage and was driving off.) "Such true blood! Three hours and a half indeed coming only three-and-twenty miles! look at that creature, and suppose it possible if you can."

"He *does* look very hot to be sure."

"Hot! he had not turned a hair till we came to Walcot Church: but look at his forehand; look at his loins; only see how he moves; that horse *cannot* go less than ten

horses = symbol of Mr. Thorpe's arrogance

miles an hour: tie his legs and he will get on. What do you think of my gig, Miss Morland? a neat one, is not it? Well hung; town built; I have not had it a month. It was built for a Christchurch man, a friend of mine, a very good sort of fellow; he ran it a few weeks, till, I believe, it was convenient to have done with it. I happened just then to be looking out for some light thing of the kind, though I had pretty well determined on a curricle too; but I chanced to meet him on Magdalen Bridge, as he was driving into Oxford, last term: 'Ah! Thorpe,' said he, 'do you happen to want such a little thing as this? it is a capital one of the kind, but I am cursed tired of it.' 'Oh! d———,' said I, 'I am your man; what do you ask?' And how much do you think he did, Miss Morland?"

"I am sure I cannot guess at all."

"Curricle-hung you see; seat, trunk, sword-case, splashing-board, lamps, silver moulding, all you see complete; the iron-work as good as new, or better. He asked fifty guineas; I closed with him directly, threw down the money, and the carriage was mine."

"And I am sure," said Catherine, "I know so little of such things that I cannot judge whether it was cheap or dear."

"Neither one nor t'other; I might have got it for less I dare say; but I hate haggling, and poor Freeman wanted cash."

"That was very good-natured of you," said Catherine, quite pleased.

"Oh! d——— it, when one has the means of doing a kind thing by a friend, I hate to be pitiful."

An inquiry now took place into the intended movements of the young ladies; and, on finding whither they were going, it was decided that the gentlemen should accompany them to Edgar's Buildings, and pay their respects to Mrs. Thorpe. James and Isabella led the way; and so well satisfied was the latter with her lot, so contentedly was she endeavouring to ensure a pleasant walk to him who brought the double recommendation of being her brother's friend, and her friend's brother, so pure and uncoquettish were her feelings, that, though they overtook and passed the two offending young men in Milsom-street, she was so far from seeking to attract their notice, that she looked back at them only three times.

John Thorpe kept of course with Catherine, and, after a few minutes' silence, renewed the conversation about his gig—"You will find, however, Miss Morland, it would be reckoned a cheap thing by some people, for I might have sold it for ten guineas more the next day; Jackson, of Oriel, bid me sixty at once; Morland was with me at the time."

"Yes," said Morland, who overheard this; "but you forget that your horse was included."

"My horse! oh, d——— it! I would not sell my horse for a hundred. Are you fond of an open carriage, Miss Morland?"

"Yes, very; I have hardly ever an opportunity of being in one; but I am particularly fond of it."

"I am glad of it; I will drive you out in mine every day."

"Thank you," said Catherine, in some distress, from a doubt of the propriety of accepting such an offer.

"I will drive you up Lansdown Hill to-morrow."

"Thank you; but will not your horse want rest?"

"Rest! he has only come three-and-twenty miles today; all nonsense; nothing ruins horses so much as rest; nothing knocks them up so soon. No, no; I shall exercise mine at the average of four hours every day while I am here."

"Shall you indeed!" said Catherine very seriously, "that will be forty miles a day."

"Forty! aye fifty, for what I care. Well, I will drive you up Lansdown to-morrow; mind, I am engaged."

"How delightful that will be!" cried Isabella, turning round; "my dearest Catherine, I quite envy you; but I am afraid, brother, you will not have room for a third."

"A third indeed! no, no; I did not come to Bath to drive my sisters about; that would be a good joke, faith! Morland must take care of you."

This brought on a dialogue of civilities between the other two; but Catherine heard neither the particulars nor the result. Her companion's discourse now sunk from its hitherto animated pitch, to nothing more than a short decisive sentence of praise or condemnation on the face of every woman they met; and Catherine, after listening and agreeing as long as she could, with all the civility and deference of the youthful female mind, fearful of hazarding an opinion of its own in opposition to that of a self-assured man, especially where the beauty of her own sex is concerned, ventured at length to vary the subject by a question, which had been long uppermost in her thoughts; it was, "Have you ever read *Udolpho,* Mr. Thorpe?"

"*Udolpho!* Oh, Lord! not I; I never read novels; I have something else to do."

Catherine, humbled and ashamed, was going to apologize for her question, but he prevented her by saying, "Novels are all so full of nonsense and stuff; there has not been a tolerably decent one come out since *Tom Jones,* except *The Monk;*[10] I read that t'other day; but as for all the others, they are the stupidest things in creation."

"I think you must like *Udolpho,* if you were to read it; it is so very interesting."

"Not I, faith! No, if I read any, it shall be Mrs. Radcliffe's; her novels are amusing enough; they are worth reading; some fun and nature in *them.*"

"*Udolpho* was written by Mrs. Radcliffe," said Catherine, with some hesitation, from the fear of mortifying him.

"No sure; was it? Aye, I remember, so it was; I was thinking of that other stupid book, written by that woman they make such a fuss about, she who married the French emigrant."

"I suppose you mean *Camilla?*"

"Yes, that's the book; such unnatural stuff!—An old man playing at see-saw! I took up the first volume once, and looked it over, but I soon found it would not do; indeed I guessed what sort of stuff it must be before I saw it: as soon as I heard she had married an emigrant, I was sure I should never be able to get through it."

"I have never read it."

"You had no loss I assure you; it is the horridest nonsense you can imagine; there is nothing in the world in it but an old man's playing at see-saw and learning Latin; upon my soul there is not."

This critique, the justness of which was unfortunately lost on poor Catherine, brought them to the door of Mrs. Thorpe's lodgings, and the feelings of the discerning and unprejudiced reader of *Camilla* gave way to the feelings of the dutiful and affectionate son, as they met Mrs. Thorpe, who had descried them from above, in the passage. "Ah, mother! how do you do?" said he, giving her a hearty shake of the hand: "where did you get that quiz of a hat, it makes you look like an old witch? Here is Morland and I come to stay a few days with you, so you must look out for a couple of good beds some where near." And this address seemed to satisfy all the fondest

10. Henry Fielding (1707–54) published his novel *Tom Jones* in 1749; Matthew Gregory Lewis's *The Monk: A Romance* appeared in 1796.

wishes of the mother's heart, for she received him with the most delighted and exult-ing affection. On his two younger sisters he then bestowed an equal portion of his fra-ternal tenderness, for he asked each of them how they did, and observed that they both looked very ugly.

These manners did not please Catherine; but he was James's friend and Isabella's brother; and her judgment was further bought off by Isabella's assuring her, when they withdrew to see the new hat, that John thought her the most charming girl in the world, and by John's engaging her before they parted to dance with him that evening. Had she been older or vainer, such attacks might have done little; but, where youth and diffidence are united, it requires uncommon steadiness of reason to resist the attraction of being called the most charming girl in the world, and of being so very early engaged as a partner; and the consequence was, that, when the two Morlands, after sitting an hour with the Thorpes, set off to walk together to Mr. Allen's, and James, as the door was closed on them, said, "Well, Catherine, how do you like my friend Thorpe?" instead of answering, as she probably would have done, had there been no friendship and no flattery in the case, "I do not like him at all;" she directly replied, "I like him very much; he seems very agreeable."

"He is as good-natured a fellow as ever lived; a little of a rattle; but that will rec-ommend him to your sex I believe: and how do you like the rest of the family?"

"Very, very much indeed: Isabella particularly."

"I am very glad to hear you say so; she is just the kind of young woman I could wish to see you attached to; she has so much good sense, and is so thoroughly unaf-fected and amiable; I always wanted you to know her; and she seems very fond of you. She said the highest things in your praise that could possibly be; and the praise of such a girl as Miss Thorpe even you, Catherine," taking her hand with affection, "may be proud of."

"Indeed I am," she replied; "I love you exceedingly, and am delighted to find that you like her too. You hardly mentioned any thing of her, when you wrote to me after your visit there."

"Because I thought I should soon see you myself. I hope you will be a great deal together while you are in Bath. She is a most amiable girl; such a superior under-standing! How fond all the family are of her; she is evidently the general favourite; and how much she must be admired in such a place as this—is not she?"

"Yes, very much indeed, I fancy; Mr. Allen thinks her the prettiest girl in Bath."

"I dare say he does; and I do not know any man who is a better judge of beauty than Mr. Allen. I need not ask you whether you are happy here, my dear Catherine; with such a companion and friend as Isabella Thorpe, it would be impossible for you to be otherwise; and the Allens I am sure are very kind to you?"

"Yes, very kind; I never was so happy before; and now you are come it will be more delightful than ever; how good it is of you to come so far on purpose to see *me*."

James accepted this tribute of gratitude, and qualified his conscience for accept-ing it too, by saying with perfect sincerity, "Indeed, Catherine, I love you dearly."

Inquiries and communications concerning brothers and sisters, the situation of some, the growth of the rest, and other family matters, now passed between them, and continued, with only one small digression on James's part, in praise of Miss Thor-pe, till they reached Pulteney-street, where he was welcomed with great kindness by Mr. and Mrs. Allen, invited by the former to dine with them, and summoned by the latter to guess the price and weigh the merits of a new muff and tippet. A pre-engagement in Edgar's Buildings prevented his accepting the invitation of one friend, and obliged him to hurry away as soon as he had satisfied the demands of the other. The time of the two parties uniting in the Octagon Room being correctly adjusted, Catherine was then left to the luxury of a raised, restless, and frightened imagination over the pages of *Udolpho,* lost from all worldly concerns of dressing and dinner, incapable of soothing Mrs. Allen's fears on the delay of an expected dressmaker, and having only one minute in sixty to bestow even on the reflection of her own felicity, in being already engaged for the evening.

Chapter VIII

In spite of *Udolpho* and the dress-maker, however, the party from Pulteney-street reached the Upper-rooms in very good time. The Thorpes and James Morland were there only two minutes before them; and Isabella having gone through the usual ceremonial of meeting her friend with the most smiling and affectionate haste, of admiring the set of her gown, and envying the curl of her hair, they followed their chaperons, arm in arm, into the ballroom, whispering to each other whenever a thought occurred, and supplying the place of many ideas by a squeeze of the hand or a smile of affection.

The dancing began within a few minutes after they were seated; and James, who had been engaged quite as long as his sister, was very importunate with Isabella to stand up; but John was gone into the card-room to speak to a friend, and nothing, she declared, should induce her to join the set before her dear Catherine could join it too: "I assure you," said she, "I would not stand up without your dear sister for all the world; for if I did we should certainly be separated the whole evening." Catherine accepted this kindness with gratitude, and they continued as they were for three minutes longer, when Isabella, who had been talking to James on the other side of her, turned again to his sister and whispered, "My dear creature, I am afraid I must leave you, your brother is so amazingly impatient to begin; I know you will not mind my going away, and I dare say John will be back in a moment, and then you may easily find me out." Catherine, though a little disappointed, had too much good-nature to make any opposition, and the others rising up, Isabella had only time to press her friend's hand and say, "Good bye, my dear love," before they hurried off. The younger Miss Thorpes being also dancing, Catherine was left to the mercy of Mrs. Thorpe and Mrs. Allen, between whom she now remained. She could not help being vexed at the non-appearance of Mr. Thorpe, for she not only longed to be dancing, but was likewise aware that, as the real dignity of her situation could not be known, she was sharing with the scores of other young ladies still sitting down all the discredit of wanting a partner. To be disgraced in the eye of the world, to wear the appearance of infamy while her heart is all purity, her actions all innocence, and the misconduct of another the true source of her debasement, is one of those circumstances which peculiarly belong to the heroine's life, and her fortitude under it what particularly dignifies her character. Catherine had fortitude too; she suffered, but no murmur passed her lips.

From this state of humiliation, she was roused, at the end of ten minutes, to a pleasanter feeling, by seeing, not Mr. Thorpe, but Mr. Tilney, within three yards of the place where they sat; he seemed to be moving that way, but he did not see her, and therefore the smile and the blush, which his sudden reappearance raised in Catherine, passed away without sullying her heroic importance. He looked as handsome and as lively as ever, and was talking with interest to a fashionable and pleasing-looking young woman, who leant on his arm, and whom Catherine immediately guessed to be his sister; thus unthinkingly throwing away a fair opportunity of considering him lost to her for ever, by being married already. But guided only by what was simple and probable, it had never entered her head that Mr. Tilney could be married; he had not behaved, he had not talked, like the married men to whom she had been used; he had never mentioned a wife, and he had acknowledged a sister. From these circumstances sprang the instant conclusion of his sister's now being by his side; and therefore, instead of turning of a deathlike paleness, and falling in a fit on Mrs. Allen's bosom, Catherine sat erect, in the perfect use of her senses, and with cheeks only a little redder than usual.

Mr. Tilney and his companion, who continued, though slowly, to approach, were immediately preceded by a lady, an acquaintance of Mrs. Thorpe; and this lady stopping to speak to her, they, as belonging to her, stopped likewise, and Catherine, catching Mr. Tilney's eye, instantly received from him the smiling tribute of recognition. She returned it with pleasure, and then advancing still nearer, he spoke both to her and Mrs. Allen, by whom he was very civilly acknowledged. "I am very happy to see you again, sir, indeed; I was afraid you had left Bath." He thanked her for her fears, and said that he had quitted it for a week, on the very morning after his having had the pleasure of seeing her.

"Well, sir, and I dare say you are not sorry to be back again, for it is just the place for young people—and indeed for every body else too. I tell Mr. Allen, when he talks of being sick of it, that I am sure he should not complain, for it is so very agreeable a place, that it is much better to be here than at home at this dull time of year. I tell him he is quite in luck to be sent here for his health."

"And I hope, madam, that Mr. Allen will be obliged to like the place, from finding it of service to him."

"Thank you, sir. I have no doubt that he will. A neighbour of ours, Dr. Skinner, was here for his health last winter, and came away quite stout."

"That circumstance must give great encouragement."

"Yes, sir—and Dr. Skinner and his family were here three months; so I tell Mr. Allen he must not be in a hurry to get away."

Here they were interrupted by a request from Mrs. Thorpe to Mrs. Allen, that she would move a little to accommodate Mrs. Hughes and Miss Tilney with seats, as they had agreed to join their party. This was accordingly done, Mr. Tilney still continuing standing before them; and after a few minutes consideration, he asked Catherine to dance with him. This compliment, delightful as it was, produced severe mortification to the lady; and in giving her denial, she expressed her sorrow on the occasion so very much as if she really felt it, that had Thorpe, who joined her just afterwards, been half a minute earlier, he might have thought her sufferings rather too acute. The very easy manner in which he then told her that he had kept her waiting, did not by any means reconcile her more to her lot; nor did the particulars which he entered into while they were standing up, of the horses and dogs of the friend whom he had just left, and of a proposed exchange of terriers between them, interest her so much as to prevent her looking very often towards that part of the room where she had left Mr. Tilney. Of her dear Isabella, to whom she particularly longed to point out that gentleman, she could see nothing. They were in different sets. She was separated from all her party, and away from all her acquaintance; one mortification succeeded another, and from the whole she deduced this useful lesson, that to go previously engaged to a ball does not necessarily increase either the dignity or enjoyment of a young lady. From such a moralizing strain as this, she was suddenly roused by a touch on the shoulder, and turning round, perceived Mrs. Hughes directly behind her, attended by Miss Tilney and a gentleman. "I beg your pardon, Miss Morland," said she, "for this liberty, but I cannot any how get to Miss Thorpe, and Mrs. Thorpe said she was sure you would not have the least objection to letting in this young lady by you." Mrs. Hughes could not have applied to any creature in the room more happy to oblige her than Catherine. The young ladies were introduced to each other, Miss Tilney expressing a proper sense of such goodness, Miss Morland with the real delicacy of a generous mind making light of the obligation; and Mrs. Hughes, satisfied with having so respectably settled her young charge, returned to her party.

Miss Tilney had a good figure, a pretty face, and a very agreeable countenance; and her air, though it had not all the decided pretension, the resolute stilishness of Miss Thorpe's, had more real elegance. Her manners shewed good sense and good breeding; they were neither shy, nor affectedly open; and she seemed capable of being young, attractive, and at a ball, without wanting to fix the attention of every man near her, and without exaggerated feelings of extatic delight or inconceivable vexation on every little trifling occurrence. Catherine, interested at once by her appearance and her relationship to Mr. Tilney, was desirous of being acquainted with her, and readily talked therefore whenever she could think of any thing to say, and had courage and leisure for saying it. But the hindrance thrown in the way of a very speedy intimacy, by the frequent want of one or more of these requisites, prevented their doing more than going through the first rudiments of an acquaintance, by informing themselves how well the other liked Bath, how much she admired its buildings and surrounding country, whether she drew, or played or sang, and whether she was fond of riding on horseback.

The two dances were scarcely concluded before Catherine found her arm gently seized by her faithful Isabella, who in great spirits exclaimed—"At last I have got you. My dearest creature, I have been looking for you this hour. What could induce you to come into this set, when you knew I was in the other? I have been quite wretched without you."

"My dear Isabella, how was it possible for me to get at you? I could not even see where you were."

"So I told your brother all the time—but he would not believe me. Do go and see for her, Mr. Morland, said I—but all in vain—he would not stir an inch. Was not it so, Mr. Morland? But you men are all so immoderately lazy! I have been scolding him to such a degree, my dear Catherine, you would be quite amazed. You know I never stand upon ceremony with such people."

"Look at that young lady with the white beads round her head," whispered Catherine, detaching her friend from James—"It is Mr. Tilney's sister."

"Oh! heavens! You don't say so! Let me look at her this moment. What a delightful girl! I never saw any thing half so beautiful! But where is her all-conquering brother? Is he in the room? Point him out to me this instant, if he is. I die to see him. Mr. Morland, you are not to listen. We are not talking about you."

"But what is all this whispering about? What is going on?"

"There now, I knew how it would be. You men have such restless curiosity! Talk of the curiosity of women, indeed!—'tis nothing. But be satisfied, for you are not to know any thing at all of the matter."

"And is that likely to satisfy me, do you think?"

"Well, I declare I never knew any thing like you. What can it signify to you what we are talking of? Perhaps we are talking about you, therefore I would advise you not to listen, or you may happen to hear something not very agreeable."

In this common-place chatter, which lasted some time, the original subject seemed entirely forgotten; and though Catherine was very well pleased to have it dropped for a while, she could not avoid a little suspicion at the total suspension of all Isabella's impatient desire to see Mr. Tilney. When the orchestra struck up a fresh dance, James would have led his fair partner away, but she resisted. "I tell you, Mr. Morland," she cried, "I would not do such a thing for all the world. How can you be so teasing; only conceive, my dear Catherine, what your brother wants me to do. He wants me to dance with him again, though I tell him that it is a most improper thing, and entirely against the rules. It would make us the talk of the place, if we were not to change partners."

"Upon my honour," said James, "in these public assemblies, it is as often done as not."

"Nonsense, how can you say so? But when you men have a point to carry, you never stick at any thing. My sweet Catherine, do support me, persuade your brother how impossible it is. Tell him, that it would quite shock you to see me do such a thing; now would not it?"

"No, not at all; but if you think it wrong, you had much better change."

"There," cried Isabella, "you hear what your sister says, and yet you will not mind her. Well, remember that it is not my fault, if we set all the old ladies in Bath in a bustle. Come along, my dearest Catherine, for heaven's sake, and stand by me." And off they went, to regain their former place. John Thorpe, in the meanwhile, had walked away; and Catherine, ever willing to give Mr. Tilney an opportunity of repeating the agreeable request which had already flattered her once, made her way to Mrs. Allen and Mrs. Thorpe as fast as she could, in the hope of finding him still with them—a hope which, when it proved to be fruitless, she felt to have been highly unreasonable. "Well, my dear," said Mrs. Thorpe, impatient for praise of her son, "I hope you have had an agreeable partner."

"Very agreeable, madam."

"I am glad of it. John has charming spirits, has not he?"

"Did you meet Mr. Tilney, my dear?" said Mrs. Allen.

"No, where is he?"

"He was with us just now, and said he was so tired of lounging about, that he was resolved to go and dance; so I thought perhaps he would ask you, if he met with you."

"Where can he be?" said Catherine, looking round; but she had not looked round long before she saw him leading a young lady to the dance.

"Ah! he has got a partner, I wish he had asked you," said Mrs. Allen; and after a short silence, she added, "he is a very agreeable young man."

"Indeed he is, Mrs. Allen," said Mrs. Thorpe, smiling complacently; "I must say it, though I am his mother, that there is not a more agreeable young man in the world."

This inapplicable answer might have been too much for the comprehension of many; but it did not puzzle Mrs. Allen, for after only a moment's consideration, she said, in a whisper to Catherine, "I dare say she thought I was speaking of her son."

Catherine was disappointed and vexed. She seemed to have missed by so little the very object she had had in view; and this persuasion did not incline her to a very gracious reply, when John Thorpe came up to her soon afterwards, and said, "Well, Miss Morland, I suppose you and I are to stand up and jig it together again."

...ch obliged to you, our two dances are over; and, besides, I am ...a to dance any more."

...n let us walk about and quiz people. Come along with me, and ...ur greatest quizzers in the room; my two younger sisters and ...een laughing at them this half hour."

...excused herself; and at last he walked off to quiz his sisters by himself. The rest of the evening she found very dull; Mr. Tilney was drawn away from their party at tea, to attend that of his partner; Miss Tilney, though belonging to it, did not sit near her, and James and Isabella were so much engaged in conversing together, that the latter had no leisure to bestow more on her friend than one smile, one squeeze, and one "dearest Catherine."

CHAPTER IX

The progress of Catherine's unhappiness from the events of the evening, was as follows. It appeared first in a general dissatisfaction with every body about her, while she remained in the rooms, which speedily brought on considerable weariness and a violent desire to go home. This, on arriving in Pulteney-street, took the direction of extraordinary hunger, and when that was appeased, changed into an earnest longing to be in bed; such was the extreme point of her distress; for when there she immediately fell into a sound sleep which lasted nine hours, and from which she awoke perfectly revived, in excellent spirits, with fresh hopes and fresh schemes. The first wish of her heart was to improve her acquaintance with Miss Tilney, and almost her first resolution, to seek her for that purpose, in the Pump-room at noon. In the Pump-room, one so newly arrived in Bath must be met with, and that building she had already found so favourable for the discovery of female excellence, and the completion of female intimacy, so admirably adapted for secret discourses and unlimited confidence, that she was most reasonably encouraged to expect another friend from within its walls. Her plan for the morning thus settled, she sat quietly down to her book after breakfast, resolving to remain in the same place and the same employment till the clock struck one; and from habitude very little incommoded by the remarks and ejaculations of Mrs. Allen, whose vacancy of mind and incapacity for thinking were such, that as she never talked a great deal, so she could never be entirely silent; and, therefore, while she sat at her work, if she lost her needle or broke her thread, if she heard a carriage in the street, or saw a speck upon her gown, she must observe it aloud, whether there were any one at leisure to answer her or not. At about half past twelve, a remarkably loud rap drew her in haste to the window, and scarcely had she time to inform Catherine of there being two open carriages at the door, in the first only a servant, her brother driving Miss Thorpe in the second, before John Thorpe came running up stairs, calling out, "Well, Miss Morland, here I am. Have you been waiting long? We could not come before; the old devil of a coachmaker was such an eternity finding out a thing fit to be got into, and now it is ten thousand to one, but they break down before we are out of the street. How do you do, Mrs. Allen? a famous ball last night, was not it? Come, Miss Morland, be quick, for the others are in a confounded hurry to be off. They want to get their tumble over."

"What do you mean?" said Catherine, "where are you all going to?"

"Going to? why, you have not forgot our engagement! Did not we agree together to take a drive this morning? What a head you have! We are going up Claverton Down."

"Something was said about it, I remember," said Catherine, looking at Mrs. Allen for her opinion; "but really I did not expect you."

"Not expect me! that's a good one! And what a dust you would have made, if I had not come."

Catherine's silent appeal to her friend, meanwhile, was entirely thrown away, for Mrs. Allen, not being at all in the habit of conveying any expression herself by a look, was not aware of its being ever intended by any body else; and Catherine, whose desire of seeing Miss Tilney again at that moment bear a short delay in favour of a drive, and who thought there could be no impropriety in her going with Mr. Thorpe, as Isabella was going at the same time with James, was therefore obliged to speak plainer. "Well, ma'am, what do you say to it? Can you spare me for an hour or two? shall I go?"

"Do just as you please, my dear," replied Mrs. Allen, with the most placid indifference. Catherine took the advice, and ran off to get ready. In a very few minutes she reappeared, having scarcely allowed the two others time enough to get through a few short sentences in her praise, after Thorpe had procured Mrs. Allen's admiration of his gig; and then receiving her friend's parting good wishes, they both hurried down stairs. "My dearest creature," cried Isabella, to whom the duty of friendship immediately called her before she could get into the carriage, "you have been at least three hours getting ready. I was afraid you were ill. What a delightful ball we had last night. I have a thousand things to say to you; but make haste and get in, for I long to be off."

Catherine followed her orders and turned away, but not too soon to hear her friend exclaim aloud to James, "What a sweet girl she is! I quite doat on her."

"You will not be frightened, Miss Morland," said Thorpe, as he handed her in, "if my horse should dance about a little at first setting off. He will, most likely, give a plunge or two, and perhaps take the rest for a minute; but he will soon know his master. He is full of spirits, playful as can be, but there is no vice in him."

Catherine did not think the portrait a very inviting one, but it was too late to retreat, and she was too young to own herself frightened; so, resigning herself to her fate, and trusting to the animal's boasted knowledge of its owner, she sat peaceably down, and saw Thorpe sit down by her. Every thing being then arranged, the servant who stood at the horse's head was bid in an important voice "to let him go," and off they went in the quietest manner imaginable, without a plunge or a caper, or any thing like one. Catherine, delighted at so happy an escape, spoke her pleasure aloud with grateful surprize; and her companion immediately made the matter perfectly simple by assuring her that it was entirely owing to the peculiarly judicious manner in which he had then held the reins, and the singular discernment and dexterity with which he had directed his whip. Catherine, though she could not help wondering that with such perfect command of his horse, he should think it necessary to alarm her with a relation of its tricks, congratulated herself sincerely on being under the care of so excellent a coachman; and perceiving that the animal continued to go on in the same quiet manner, without shewing the smallest propensity towards any unpleasant vivacity, and (considering its inevitable pace was ten miles an hour) by no means alarmingly fast, gave herself up to all the enjoyment of air and exercise of the most invigorating kind, in a fine mild day of February, with the consciousness of safety. A silence of several minutes succeeded their first short dialogue; it was broken by Thorpe's saying very abruptly, "Old Allen is as rich as a Jew—is not he?" Catherine did not understand him—and he repeated his question, adding in explanation, "Old Allen, the man you are with."

"Oh! Mr. Allen, you mean. Yes, I believe, he is very rich."

"And no children at all?"

"No—not any."

"A famous thing for his next heirs. He is *your* godfather, is not he?"

"My godfather!—no."

"But you are always very much with them."

"Yes, very much."

"Aye, that is what I meant. He seems a good kind of old fellow enough, and has lived very well in his time, I dare say; he is not gouty for nothing. Does he drink his bottle a-day now?"

"His bottle a-day!—no. Why should you think of such a thing? He is a very temperate man, and you could not fancy him in liquor last night?"

"Lord help you! You women are always thinking of men's being in liquor. Why you do not suppose a man is overset by a bottle? I am sure of *this*—that if every body was to drink their bottle a-day, there would not be half the disorders in the world there are now. It would be a famous good thing for us all."

"I cannot believe it."

"Oh! lord, it would be the saving of thousands. There is not the hundredth part of the wine consumed in this kingdom, that there ought to be. Our foggy climate wants help."

"And yet I have heard that there is a great deal of wine drank in Oxford."

"Oxford! There is no drinking at Oxford now, I assure you. Nobody drinks there. You would hardly meet with a man who goes beyond his four pints at the utmost. Now, for instance, it was reckoned a remarkable thing at the last party in my rooms, that upon an average we cleared about five pints a head. It was looked upon as something out of the common way. *Mine* is famous good stuff to be sure. You would not often meet with any thing like it in Oxford—and that may account for it. But this will just give you a notion of the general rate of drinking there."

"Yes, it does give a notion," said Catherine, warmly, "and that is, that you all drink a great deal more wine than I thought you did. However, I am sure James does not drink so much."

This declaration brought on a loud and overpowering reply, of which no part was very distinct, except the frequent exclamations, amounting almost to oaths, which adorned it, and Catherine was left, when it ended, with rather a strengthened belief of there being a great deal of wine drank in Oxford, and the same happy conviction of her brother's comparative sobriety.

Thorpe's ideas then all reverted to the merits of his own equipage, and she was called on to admire the spirit and freedom with which his horse moved along, and the ease which his paces, as well as the excellence of the springs, gave the motion of the carriage. She followed him in all his admiration as well as she could. To go before, or beyond him was impossible. His knowledge and her ignorance of the subject, his rapidity of expression, and her diffidence of herself put that out of her power; she could strike out nothing new in commendation, but she readily echoed whatever he chose to assert, and it was finally settled between them without any difficulty, that his equipage was altogether the most complete of its kind in England, his carriage the neatest, his horse the best goer, and himself the best coachman. "You do not really think, Mr. Thorpe," said Catherine, venturing after some time to consider the matter as entirely decided, and to offer some little variation on the subject, "that James's gig will break down?"

"Break down! Oh! lord! Did you ever see such a little tittuppy thing in your life? There is not a sound piece of iron about it. The wheels have been fairly worn out these ten years at least—and as for the body! Upon my soul, you might shake it to pieces yourself with a touch. It is the most devilish little ricketty business I ever beheld! Thank God! we have got a better. I would not be bound to go two miles in it for fifty thousand pounds."

"Good heavens!" cried Catherine, quite frightened, "then pray let us turn back; they will certainly meet with an accident if we go on. Do let us turn back, Mr. Thorpe; stop and speak to my brother, and tell him how very unsafe it is."

"Unsafe! Oh, lord! what is there in that? they will only get a roll if it does break down; and there is plenty of dirt, it will be excellent falling. Oh, curse it! the carriage is safe enough, if a man knows how to drive it; a thing of that sort in good hands will last above twenty years after it is fairly worn out. Lord bless you! I would undertake for five pounds to drive it to York and back again, without losing a nail."

Catherine listened with astonishment; she knew not how to reconcile two such very different accounts of the same thing; for she had not been brought up to understand the propensities of a rattle, nor to know to how many idle assertions and impudent falsehoods the excess of vanity will lead. Her own family were plain matter-of-fact people, who seldom aimed at wit of any kind; her father, at the utmost, being contented with a pun, and her mother with a proverb; they were not in the habit therefore of telling lies to increase their importance, or of asserting at one moment what they would contradict the next. She reflected on the affair for some time in much perplexity, and was more than once on the point of requesting from Mr. Thorpe a clearer insight into his real opinion on the subject; but she checked herself, because it appeared to her that he did not excel in giving those clearer insights, in making those things plain which he had before made ambiguous; and, joining to this, the consideration, that he would not really suffer his sister and his friend to be exposed to a danger from which he might easily preserve them, she concluded at last, that he must know the carriage to be in fact perfectly safe, and therefore would alarm herself no longer. By him the whole matter seemed entirely forgotten; and all the rest of his conversation, or rather talk, began and ended with himself and his own concerns. He told her of horses which he had bought for a trifle and sold for incredible sums; of racing matches, in which his judgment had infallibly foretold the winner; of shooting parties, in which he had killed more birds (though without having one good shot) than all his companions together; and described to her some famous day's sport, with the foxhounds, in which his foresight and skill in directing the dogs had repaired the mistakes of the most experienced huntsman, and in which the boldness of his riding, though it had never endangered his own life for a moment, had been constantly leading others into difficulties, which he calmly concluded had broken the necks of many.

Little as Catherine was in the habit of judging for her self, and unfixed as were her general notions of what men ought to be, she could not entirely repress a doubt, while she bore with the effusions of his endless conceit, of his being altogether completely agreeable. It was a bold surmise, for he was Isabella's brother; and she had been assured by James, that his manners would recommend him to all her sex; but in spite of this, the extreme weariness of his company, which crept over her before they had been out an hour, and which continued unceasingly to increase till they stopped in Pulteney-street again, induced her, in some small degree, to resist such high authority, and to distrust his powers of giving universal pleasure.

When they arrived at Mrs. Allen's door, the astonishment of Isabella was hardly to be expressed, on finding that it was too late in the day for them to attend her friend into the house:—"Past three o'clock!" it was inconceivable, incredible, impossible! and she would neither believe her own watch, nor her brother's, nor the servant's; she would believe no assurance of it founded on reason or reality, till Morland produced his watch, and ascertained the fact; to have doubted a moment longer *then*, would have been equally inconceivable, incredible, and impossible; and she could only protest, over and over again, that no two hours and a half had ever gone off so swiftly before, as Catherine was called on to confirm; Catherine could not tell a falsehood even to please Isabella; but the latter was spared the misery of her friend's dissenting voice, by not waiting for her answer. Her own feelings entirely engrossed her; her wretchedness was most acute on finding herself obliged to go directly home. It was ages since she had had a moment's conversation with her dearest Catherine; and, though she had such thousands of things to say to her, it appeared as if they were never to be together again; so, with smiles of most exquisite misery, and the laughing eye of utter despondency, she bade her friend adieu and went on.

Catherine found Mrs. Allen just returned from all the busy idleness of the morning, and was immediately greeted with, "Well, my dear, here you are;" a truth which she had no greater inclination than power to dispute; "and I hope you have had a pleasant airing?"

"Yes, ma'am, I thank you; we could not have had a nicer day."

"So Mrs. Thorpe said; she was vastly pleased at your all going."

"You have seen Mrs. Thorpe then?"

"Yes, I went to the Pump-room as soon as you were gone, and there I met her, and we had a great deal of talk together. She says there was hardly any veal to be got at market this morning, it is so uncommonly scarce."

"Did you see any body else of our acquaintance?"

"Yes; we agreed to take a turn in the Crescent, and there we met Mrs. Hughes, and Mr. and Miss Tilney walking with her."

"Did you indeed? and did they speak to you?"

"Yes, we walked along the Crescent together for half an hour. They seem very agreeable people. Miss Tilney was in a very pretty spotted muslin, and I fancy, by what I can learn, that she always dresses very handsomely. Mrs. Hughes talked to me a great deal about the family."

"And what did she tell you of them?"

"Oh! a vast deal indeed; she hardly talked of any thing else."

"Did she tell you what part of Gloucestershire they come from?"

"Yes, she did; but I cannot recollect now. But they are very good kind of people, and very rich. Mrs. Tilney was a Miss Drummond, and she and Mrs. Hughes were school-fellows; and Miss Drummond had a very large fortune; and, when she married, her father gave her twenty thousand pounds, and five hundred to buy wedding-clothes. Mrs. Hughes saw all the clothes after they came from the warehouse."

"And are Mr. and Mrs. Tilney in Bath?"

"Yes, I fancy they are, but I am not quite certain. Upon recollection, however, I have a notion they are both dead; at least the mother is; yes, I am sure Mrs. Tilney is dead, because Mrs. Hughes told me there was a very beautiful set of pearls that Mr. Drummond gave his daughter on her wedding-day and that Miss Tilney has got now, for they were put by for her when her mother died."

"And is Mr. Tilney, my partner, the only son?"

"I cannot be quite positive about that, my dear; I have some idea he is; but, however, he is a very fine young man Mrs. Hughes says, and likely to do very well."

Catherine inquired no further; she had heard enough to feel that Mrs. Allen had no real intelligence to give, and that she was most particularly unfortunate herself in having missed such a meeting with both brother and sister. Could she have foreseen such a circumstance, nothing should have persuaded her to go out with the others; and, as it was, she could only lament her ill-luck, and think over what she had lost, till it was clear to her, that the drive had by no means been very pleasant and that John Thorpe himself was quite disagreeable.

CHAPTER X

The Allens, Thorpes, and Morlands, all met in the evening at the theatre; and, as Catherine and Isabella sat together, there was then an opportunity for the latter to utter some few of the many thousand things which had been collecting within her for communication, in the immeasurable length of time which had divided them.—"Oh, heavens! my beloved Catherine, have I got you at last?" was her address on Catherine's entering the box and sitting by her. "Now, Mr. Morland," for he was close to her on the other side, "I shall not speak another word to you all the rest of the evening; so I charge you not to expect it. My sweetest Catherine, how have you been this long age? but I need not ask you, for you look delightfully. You really have done your hair in a more heavenly style than ever: you mischievous creature, do you want to attract every body? I assure you, my brother is quite in love with you already; and as for Mr. Tilney—but *that* is a settled thing—even *your* modesty cannot doubt his attachment now; his coming back to Bath makes it too plain. Oh! what would not I give to see him! I really am quite wild with impatience. My mother says he is the most delightful young man in the world; she saw him this morning you know: you must introduce him to me. Is he in the house now?—Look about for heaven's sake! I assure you, I can hardly exist till I see him."

"No," said Catherine, "he is not here; I cannot see him any where."

"Oh, horrid! am I never to be acquainted with him? How do you like my gown? I think it does not look amiss; the sleeves were entirely my own thought. Do you know I get so immoderately sick of Bath; your brother and I were agreeing this morning that, though it is vastly well to be here for a few weeks, we would not live here for millions. We soon found out that our tastes were exactly alike in preferring the country to every other place; really, our opinions were so exactly the same, it was quite ridiculous! There was not a single point in which we differed; I would not have had you by for the world; you are such a sly thing, I am sure you would have made some droll remark or other about it."

"No, indeed I should not."

"Oh, yes you would indeed; I know you better than you know yourself. You would have told us that we seemed born for each other, or some nonsense of that kind, which would have distressed me beyond conception; my cheeks would have been as red as your roses; I would not have had you by for the world."

"Indeed you do me injustice; I would not have made so improper a remark upon any account; and besides, I am sure it would never have entered my head."

Isabella smiled incredulously, and talked the rest of the evening to James.

Catherine's resolution of endeavouring to meet Miss Tilney again continued in full force the next morning; and till the usual moment of going to the Pump-room, she felt some alarm from the dread of a second prevention. But nothing of that kind occurred, no visitors appeared to delay them, and they all three set off in good time for the Pump-room, where the ordinary course of events and conversation took place; Mr. Allen, after drinking his glass of water, joined some gentlemen to talk over the politics of the day and compare the accounts of their newspapers; and the ladies walked about together, noticing every new face, and almost every new bonnet in the room. The female part of the Thorpe family, attended by James Morland, appeared among the crowd in less than a quarter of an hour, and Catherine immediately took her usual place by the side of her friend. James, who was now in constant attendance, maintained a similar position, and separating themselves from the rest of their party, they walked in that manner for some time, till Catherine began to doubt the happiness of a situation which confining her entirely to her friend and brother, gave her very little share in the notice of either. They were always engaged in some sentimental discussion or lively dispute, but their sentiment was conveyed in such whispering voices, and their vivacity attended with so much laughter, that though Catherine's supporting opinion was not unfrequently called for by one or the other, she was never able to give any, from not having heard a word of the subject. At length however she was empowered to disengage herself from her friend, by the avowed necessity of speaking to Miss Tilney, whom she most joyfully saw just entering the room with Mrs. Hughes, and whom she instantly joined, with a firmer determination to be acquainted, than she might have had courage to command, had she not been urged by the disappointment of the day before. Miss Tilney met her with great civility, returned her advances with equal good will, and they continued talking together as long as both parties remained in the room; and though in all probability not an observation was made, nor an expression used by either which had not been made and used some thousands of times before, under that roof, in every Bath season, yet the merit of their being spoken with simplicity and truth, and without personal conceit, might be something uncommon.—

"How well your brother dances!" was an artless exclamation of Catherine's towards the close of their conversation, which at once surprized and amused her companion.

"Henry!" she replied with a smile. "Yes, he does dance very well."

"He must have thought it very odd to hear me say I was engaged the other evening, when he saw me sitting down. But I really had been engaged the whole day to Mr. Thorpe." Miss Tilney could only bow. "You cannot think," added Catherine after a moment's silence, "how surprized I was to see him again. I felt so sure of his being quite gone away."

"When Henry had the pleasure of seeing you before, he was in Bath but for a couple of days. He came only to engage lodgings for us."

"That never occurred to me; and of course, not seeing him any where, I thought he must be gone. Was not the young lady he danced with on Monday a Miss Smith?"

"Yes, an acquaintance of Mrs. Hughes."

"I dare say she was very glad to dance. Do you think her pretty?"

"Not very."

"He never comes to the Pump-room, I suppose?"

"Yes, sometimes; but he has rid out this morning with my father."

Mrs. Hughes now joined them, and asked Miss Tilney if she was ready to go. "I hope I shall have the pleasure of seeing you again soon," said Catherine. "Shall you be at the cotillion ball to-morrow?"

"Perhaps we——— yes, I think we certainly shall."

"I am glad of it, for we shall all be there." This civility was duly returned; and they parted—on Miss Tilney's side with some knowledge of her new acquaintance's feelings, and on Catherine's, without the smallest consciousness of having explained them.

She went home very happy. The morning had answered all her hopes, and the evening of the following day was now the object of expectation, the future good. What gown and what head-dress she should wear on the occasion became her chief concern. She cannot be justified in it. Dress is at all times a frivolous distinction, and excessive solicitude about it often destroys its own aim. Catherine knew all this very well; her great aunt had read her a lecture on the subject only the Christmas before; and yet she lay awake ten minutes on Wednesday night debating between her spotted and her tamboured muslin, and nothing but the shortness of the time prevented her buying a new one for the evening. This would have been an error in judgment, great though not uncommon, from which one of the other sex rather than her own, a brother rather than a great aunt might have warned her, for man only can be aware of the insensibility of man towards a new gown. It would be mortifying to the feelings of many ladies, could they be made to understand how little the heart of man is affected by what is costly or new in their attire; how little it is biassed by the texture of their muslin, and how unsusceptible of peculiar tenderness towards the spotted, the sprigged, the mull or the jackonet. Woman is fine for her own satisfaction alone. No man will admire her the more, no woman will like her the better for it. Neatness and fashion are enough for the former, and a something of shabbiness or impropriety will be most endearing to the latter. But not one of these grave reflections troubled the tranquillity of Catherine.

She entered the rooms on Thursday evening with feelings very different from what had attended her thither the Monday before. She had then been exulting in her engagement to Thorpe, and was now chiefly anxious to avoid his sight, lest he should engage her again; for though she could not, dared not expect that Mr. Tilney should ask her a third time to dance, her wishes, hopes and plans all centered in nothing less. Every young lady may feel for my heroine in this critical moment, for every young lady has at some time or other known the same agitation. All have been, or at least all have believed themselves to be, in danger from the pursuit of some one whom they wished to avoid; and all have been anxious for the attentions of some one whom they wished to please. As soon as they were joined by the Thorpes, Catherine's agony began; she fidgetted about if John Thorpe came towards her, hid herself as much as possible from his view, and when he spoke to her pretended not to fear him. The cotillions were over, the country-dancing beginning, and she saw nothing of the Tilneys. "Do not be frightened, my dear Catherine," whispered Isabella, "but I am really going to dance with your brother again. I declare positively it is quite shocking. I tell him he ought to be ashamed of himself, but you and John must keep us in countenance. Make haste, my dear creature, and come to us. John is just walked off, but he will be back in a moment."

Catherine had neither time nor inclination to answer. The others walked away, John Thorpe was still in view, and she gave herself up for lost. That she might not appear, however, to observe or expect him, she kept her eyes intently fixed on her fan; and a self-condemnation for her folly, in supposing that among such a crowd they should even meet with the Tilneys in any reasonable time, had just passed through her mind, when she suddenly found herself addressed and again solicited to dance, by Mr. Tilney himself. With what sparkling eyes and ready motion she granted his request, and with how pleasing a flutter of heart she went with him to the set, may be easily imagined. To escape, and, as she believed, so narrowly escape John Thorpe, and to be asked, so immediately on his joining her, asked by Mr. Tilney, as if he had sought her on purpose!—it did not appear to her that life could supply any greater felicity.

Scarcely had they worked themselves into the quiet possession of a place, how-ever, when her attention was claimed by John Thorpe, who stood behind her. "Hey-day, Miss Morland!" said he, "what is the meaning of this?—I thought you and I were to dance together."

"I wonder you should think so, for you never asked me." "That is a good one, by Jove!—I asked you as soon as I came into the room, and I was just going to ask you again, but when I turned round, you were gone!—this is a cursed shabby trick! I only came for the sake of dancing with *you,* and I firmly believe you were engaged to me ever since Monday. Yes; I remember, I asked you while you were waiting in the lobby for your cloak. And here have I been telling all my acquaintance that I was going to dance with the prettiest girl in the room; and when they see you standing up with somebody else, they will quiz me famously."

"Oh, no; they will never think of *me,* after such a description as that."

"By heavens, if they do not, I will kick them out of the room for blockheads. What chap have you there?" Catherine satisfied his curiosity. "Tilney," he repeated, "Hum—I do not know him. A good figure of a man; well put together. Does he want a horse? Here is a friend of mine, Sam Fletcher, has got one to sell that would suit any body. A famous clever animal for the road—only forty guineas. I had fifty minds to buy it myself, for it is one of my maxims always to buy a good horse when I meet with one; but it would not answer my purpose, it would not do for the field. I would give any money for a real good hunter. I have three now, the best that ever were back'd. I would not take eight hundred guineas for them. Fletcher and I mean to get a house in Leicester-shire, against the next season. It is so d———— uncomfortable, living at an inn."

This was the last sentence by which he could weary Catherine's attention, for he was just then born off by the resistless pressure of a long string of passing ladies. Her partner now drew near, and said, "That gentleman would have put me out of patience, had he staid with you half a minute longer. He has no business to withdraw the attention of my partner from me. We have entered into a contract of mutual agreeableness for the space of an evening, and all our agreeableness belongs solely to each other for that time. Nobody can fasten themselves on the notice of one, without injuring the rights of the other. I consider a country-dance as an emblem of marriage. Fidelity and complaisance are the principal duties of both; and those men who do not chuse to dance or marry themselves, have no business with the partners or wives of their neighbours."

"But they are such very different things!"

"—That you think they cannot be compared together."

"To be sure not. People that marry can never part, but must go and keep house together. People that dance, only stand opposite each other in a long room for half an hour."

"And such is your definition of matrimony and dancing. Taken in that light cer-tainly, their resemblance is not striking; but I think I could place them in such a view. You will allow, that in both, man has the advantage of choice, woman only the power of refusal; that in both, it is an engagement between man and woman, formed for the advantage of each; and that when once entered into, they belong exclusively

to each other till the moment of its dissolution; that it is their duty, each to endeavour to give the other no cause for wishing that he or she had bestowed themselves
elsewhere, and their best interest to keep their own imaginations from wandering
towards the perfections of their neighbours, or fancying that they should have been
better off with any one else. You will allow all this?"

"Yes, to be sure, as you state it, all this sounds very well; but still they are so very
different. I cannot look upon them at all in the same light, nor think the same duties
belong to them."

"In one respect, there certainly is a difference. In marriage, the man is supposed
to provide for the support of the woman; the woman to make the home agreeable to
the man; he is to purvey, and she is to smile. But in dancing, their duties are exactly
changed; the agreeableness, the compliance are expected from him, while she fur-
nishes the fan and the lavender water. *That*, I suppose, was the difference of duties
which struck you, as rendering the conditions incapable of comparison."

"No, indeed, I never thought of that."

"Then I am quite at a loss. One thing, however, I must observe. This disposition
on your side is rather alarming. You totally disallow any similarity in the obligations;
and may I not thence infer, that your notions of the duties of the dancing state are
not so strict as your partner might wish? Have I not reason to fear, that if the gentleman who spoke to you just now were to return, or if any other gentleman were to
address you, there would be nothing to restrain you from conversing with him as long
as you chose?"

"Mr. Thorpe is such a very particular friend of my brother's, that if he talks to
me, I must talk to him again; but there are hardly three young men in the room
besides him, that I have any acquaintance with."

"And is that to be my only security? alas, alas!"

"Nay, I am sure you cannot have a better; for if I do not know any body, it is
impossible for me to talk to them; and, besides, I do not *want to talk to any body*."

"Now you have given me a security worth having; and I shall proceed with
courage. Do you find Bath as agreeable as when I had the honour of making the
inquiry before?"

"Yes, quite—more so, indeed."

"More so!—Take care, or you will forget to be tired of it at the proper time.—
You ought to be tired at the end of six weeks."

"I do not think I should be tired, if I were to stay here six months."

"Bath, compared with London, has little variety, and so every body finds out
every year. 'For six weeks, I allow Bath is pleasant enough; but beyond *that*, it is the
most tiresome place in the world.' You would be told so by people of all descriptions,
who come regularly every winter, lengthen their six weeks into ten or twelve, and go
away at last because they can afford to stay no longer."

"Well, other people must judge for themselves, and those who go to London may
think nothing of Bath. But I, who live in a small retired village in the country, can
never find greater sameness in such a place as this, than in my own home; for here are
a variety of amusements, a variety of things to be seen and done all day long, which I
can know nothing of there."

"You are not fond of the country."

"Yes, I am. I have always lived there, and always been very happy. But certainly
there is much more sameness in a country life than in a Bath life. One day in the
country is exactly like another."

"But then you spend your time so much more rationally in the country."

"Do I?"

"Do you not?"

"I do not believe there is much difference."

"Here you are in pursuit only of amusement all day long."

"And so I am at home—only I do not find so much of it. I walk about here, and so I do there; but here I see a variety of people in every street, and there I can only go and call on Mrs. Allen."

Mr. Tilney was very much amused. "Only go and call on Mrs. Allen!" he repeated. "What a picture of intellectual poverty! However, when you sink into this abyss again, you will have more to say. You will be able to talk of Bath, and of all that you did here."

"Oh! yes. I shall never be in want of something to talk of again to Mrs. Allen, or any body else. I really believe I shall always be talking of Bath, when I am at home again—I *do* like it so very much. If I could but have papa and mamma, and the rest of them here, I suppose I should be too happy! James's coming (my eldest brother) is quite delightful—and especially as it turns out, that the very family we are just got so intimate with, are his intimate friends already. Oh! who can ever be tired of Bath?"

"Not those who bring such fresh feelings of every sort to it, as you do. But papas and mammas, and brothers and intimate friends are a good deal gone by, to most of the frequenters of Bath—and the honest relish of balls and plays, and every-day sights, is past with them."

Here their conversation closed; the demands of the dance becoming now too importunate for a divided attention.

Soon after their reaching the bottom of the set, Catherine perceived herself to be earnestly regarded by a gentleman who stood among the lookers-on, immediately behind her partner. He was a very handsome man, of a commanding aspect, past the bloom, but not past the vigour of life; and with his eye still directed towards her, she saw him presently address Mr. Tilney in a familiar whisper. Confused by his notice, and blushing from the fear of its being excited by something wrong in her appearance, she turned away her head. But while she did so, the gentleman retreated, and her partner coming nearer, said, "I see that you guess what I have just been asked. That gentleman knows your name, and you have a right to know his. It is General Tilney, my father."

Catherine's answer was only "Oh!"—but it was an "Oh!" expressing every thing needful; attention to his words, and perfect reliance on their truth. With real interest and strong admiration did her eye now follow the General, as he moved through the crowd, and "How handsome a family they are!" was her secret remark.

In chatting with Miss Tilney before the evening concluded, a new source of felicity arose to her. She had never taken a country walk since her arrival in Bath. Miss Tilney, to whom all the commonly-frequented environs were familiar, spoke of them in terms which made her all eagerness to know them too; and on her openly fearing that she might find nobody to go with her, it was proposed by the brother and sister that they should join in a walk, some morning or other. "I shall like it," she cried, "beyond any thing in the world; and do not let us put it off—let us go to-morrow." This was readily agreed to, with only a proviso of Miss Tilney's, that it did not rain, which Catherine was sure it would not. At twelve o'clock, they were to call for her in Pulteney-street—and "remember—twelve o'clock," was her parting speech to her new friend. Of her other, her older, her more established friend, Isabella, of whose fidelity and worth she had enjoyed a fortnight's experience, she scarcely saw any thing during the evening. Yet, though longing to make her acquainted with her happiness, she cheerfully submitted to the wish of Mr. Allen, which took them rather early away, and her spirits danced within her, as she danced in her chair all the way home.

CHAPTER XI

The morrow brought a very sober looking morning; the sun making only a few efforts to appear; and Catherine augured from it, every thing most favourable to her wishes. A bright morning so early in the year, she allowed would generally turn to rain, but a cloudy one foretold improvement as the day advanced. She applied to Mr. Allen for confirmation of her hopes, but Mr. Allen not having his own skies and barometer about him, declined giving any absolute promise of sunshine. She applied to Mrs. Allen, and Mrs. Allen's opinion was more positive. "She had no doubt in the world of its being a very fine day, if the clouds would only go off, and the sun keep out."

At about eleven o'clock however, a few specks of small rain upon the windows caught Catherine's watchful eye, and "Oh! dear, I do believe it will be wet," broke from her in a most desponding tone.

"I thought how it would be," said Mrs. Allen.

"No walk for me to-day," sighed Catherine;—"but perhaps it may come to nothing, or it may hold up before twelve."

"Perhaps it may, but then, my dear, it will be so dirty."

"Oh! that will not signify; I never mind dirt."

"No," replied her friend very placidly, "I know you never mind dirt."

After a short pause, "It comes on faster and faster!" said Catherine, as she stood watching at a window.

"So it does indeed. If it keeps raining, the streets will be very wet."

There are four umbrellas up already. How I hate the sight of an umbrella!"

"They are disagreeable things to carry. I would much rather take a chair at any time."

"It was such a nice looking morning! I felt so convinced it would be dry!"

"Any body would have thought so indeed. There will be very few people in the Pump-room, if it rains all the morning. I hope Mr. Allen will put on his great coat when he goes, but I dare say he will not, for he had rather do any thing in the world than walk out in a great coat; I wonder he should dislike it, it must be so comfortable."

The rain continued—fast, though not heavy. Catherine went every five minutes to the clock, threatening on each return that, if it still kept on raining another five minutes, she would give up the matter as hopeless. The clock struck twelve, and it still rained. "You will not be able to go, my dear."

"I do not quite despair yet. I shall not give it up till a quarter after twelve. This is just the time of day for it to clear up, and I do think it looks a little lighter. There, it is twenty minutes after twelve, and now I *shall* give it up entirely. Oh! that we had such weather here as they had at Udolpho, or at least in Tuscany and the South of France!—the night that poor St. Aubin died!—such beautiful weather!"

At half past twelve, when Catherine's anxious attention to the weather was over, and she could no longer claim any merit from its amendment, the sky began voluntarily to clear. A gleam of sunshine took her quite by surprise; she looked round; the clouds were parting, and she instantly returned to the window to watch over and encourage the happy appearance. Ten minutes more made it certain that a bright afternoon would succeed, and justified the opinion of Mrs. Allen, who had "always thought it would clear up." But whether Catherine might still expect her friends, whether there had not been too much rain for Miss Tilney to venture, must yet be a question.

It was too dirty for Mrs. Allen to accompany her husband to the Pump-room; he accordingly set off by himself, and Catherine had barely watched him down the street, when her notice was claimed by the approach of the same two open carriages, containing the same three people that had surprized her so much a few mornings back.

"Isabella, my brother, and Mr. Thorpe, I declare! They are coming for me perhaps—but I shall not go—I cannot go indeed, for you know Miss Tilney may still call." Mrs. Allen agreed to it. John Thorpe was soon with them, and his voice was with them yet sooner, for on the stairs he was calling out to Miss Morland to be quick. "Make haste! make haste!" as he threw open the door—"put on your hat this moment—there is no time to be lost—we are going to Bristol.—How d'ye do, Mrs. Allen?"

"To Bristol! Is not that a great way off? But, however, I cannot go with you to-day, because I am engaged; I expect some friends every moment." This was of course vehemently talked down as no reason at all; Mrs. Allen was called on to second him, and the two others walked in, to give their assistance. "My sweetest Catherine, is not this delightful? We shall have a most heavenly drive. You are to thank your brother and me for the scheme; it darted into our heads at breakfast-time, I verily believe at the same instant; and we should have been off two hours ago if it had not been for this detestable rain. But it does not signify, the nights are moonlight, and we shall do delightfully. Oh! I am in such extasies at the thoughts of a little country air and quiet!—so much better than going to the Lower Rooms. We shall drive directly to Clifton and dine there; and, as soon as dinner is over, if there is time for it, go on to Kingsweston."

"I doubt our being able to do so much," said Morland.

"You croaking fellow!" cried Thorpe, "we shall be able to do ten times more. Kingsweston! aye, and Blaize Castle too, and any thing else we can hear of; but here is your sister says she will not go."

"Blaize Castle!" cried Catherine; "what is that?"

"The finest place in England—worth going fifty miles at any time to see."

"What, is it really a castle, an old castle?"

"The oldest in the kingdom."

"But is it like what one reads of?"

"Exactly—the very same."

"But now really—are there towers and long galleries?"

"By dozens."

"Then I should like to see it; but I cannot———I cannot go."

"Not go!—my beloved creature, what do you mean?"

"I cannot go, because"———(looking down as she spoke, fearful of Isabella's smile) "I expect Miss Tilney and her brother to call on me to take a country walk. They promised to come at twelve, only it rained; but now, as it is so fine, I dare say they will be here soon."

"Not they indeed," cried Thorpe; "for, as we turned into Broad-street, I saw them—does he not drive a phaeton with bright chestnuts?"

"I do not know indeed."

"Yes, I know he does; I saw him. You are talking of the man you danced with last night, are not you?"

"Yes."

"Well, I saw him at that moment turn up the Lansdown Road,—driving a smart-looking girl."

"Did you indeed?"

"Did upon my soul; knew him again directly, and he seemed to have got some very pretty cattle too."

"It is very odd! but I suppose they thought it would be too dirty for a walk."

"And well they might, for I never saw so much dirt in my life. Walk! you could no more walk than you could fly! it has not been so dirty the whole winter; it is ancle-deep every where."

Isabella corroborated it: "My dearest Catherine, you cannot form an idea of the dirt; come, you must go; you cannot refuse going now."

"I should like to see the castle; but may we go all over it? may we go up every staircase, and into every suite of rooms?"

"Yes, yes, every hole and corner."

"But then,—if they should only be gone out for an hour till it is drier, and call by and bye?"

"Make yourself easy, there is no danger of that, for I heard Tilney hallooing to a man who was just passing by on horseback, that they were going as far as Wick Rocks."

"Then I will. Shall I go, Mrs. Allen?"

"Just as you please, my dear."

"Mrs. Allen, you must persuade her to go," was the general cry. Mrs. Allen was not inattentive to it:—"Well, my dear," said she, "suppose you go." And in two minutes they were off.

Catherine's feelings, as she got into the carriage, were in a very unsettled state; divided between regret for the loss of one great pleasure, and the hope of soon enjoying another, almost its equal in degree, however unlike in kind. She could not think the Tilneys had acted quite well by her, in so readily giving up their engagement, without sending her any message of excuse. It was now but an hour later than the time fixed on for the beginning of their walk; and, in spite of what she had heard of the prodigious accumulation of dirt in the course of that hour, she could not from her own observation help thinking, that they might have gone with very little inconvenience. To feel herself slighted by them was very painful. On the other hand, the delight of exploring an edifice like Udolpho, as her fancy represented Blaize Castle to be, was such a counterpoise of good, as might console her for almost any thing.

They passed briskly down Pulteney-street, and through Laura-place, without the exchange of many words. Thorpe talked to his horse, and she meditated, by turns, on broken promises and broken arches, phaetons and false hangings, Tilneys and trapdoors. As they entered Argyle-buildings, however, she was roused by this address from her companion, "Who is that girl who looked at you so hard as she went by?"

"Who?—where?"

"On the right-hand pavement—she must be almost out of sight now." Catherine looked round and saw Miss Tilney leaning on her brother's arm, walking slowly down the street. She saw them both looking back at her. "Stop, stop, Mr. Thorpe, she impatiently cried, it is Miss Tilney; it is indeed.—How could you tell me they were gone?—Stop, stop, I will get out this moment and go to them." But to what purpose did she speak? Thorpe only lashed his horse into a brisker trot; the Tilneys, who had soon ceased to look after her, were in a moment out of sight round the corner of Laura-place, and in another moment she was herself whisked into the Market-place. Still, however, and during the length of another street, she intreated him to stop. "Pray, pray stop, Mr. Thorpe. I cannot go on. I will not go on. I must go back to Miss Tilney." But Mr. Thorpe only laughed, smacked his whip, encouraged his horse, made odd noises, and drove on; and Catherine, angry and vexed as she was, having no power of getting away, was obliged to give up the point and submit. Her reproach-es, however, were not spared. "How could you deceive me so, Mr. Thorpe? How could you say, that you saw them driving up the Lansdown-road? I would not have had it happen so for the world. They must think it so strange; so rude of me! to go by them, too, without saying a word! You do not know how vexed I am.—I shall have no pleasure at Clifton, nor in any thing else. I had rather, ten thousand times rather get out now, and walk back to them. How could you say, you saw them driving out in a phaeton?"[11] Thorpe defended himself very stoutly, declared he had never seen two men so much alike in his life, and would hardly give up the point of its having been Tilney himself.

Their drive, even when this subject was over, was not likely to be very agreeable. Catherine's complaisance was no longer what it had been in their former airing. She listened reluctantly, and her replies were short. Blaize Castle remained her only com-fort; towards *that*, she still looked at intervals with pleasure; though rather than be disappointed of the promised walk, and especially rather than be thought ill of by the Tilneys, she would willingly have given up all the happiness which its walls could supply—the happiness of a progress through a long suite of lofty rooms, exhibiting the remains of magnificent furniture, though now for many years deserted—the hap-piness of being stopped in their way along narrow, winding vaults, by a low, grated door; or even of having their lamp, their only lamp, extinguished by a sudden gust of wind, and of being left in total darkness. In the meanwhile, they proceeded on their journey without any mischance; and were within view of the town of Keynsham, when a halloo from Morland, who was behind them, made his friend pull up, to know what was the matter. The others then came close enough for conversation, and Mor-land said, "We had better go back, Thorpe; it is too late to go on to-day; your sister thinks so as well as I. We have been exactly an hour coming from Pulteney-street, very little more than seven miles; and, I suppose, we have at least eight more to go. It will never do. We set out a great deal too late. We had much better put it off till another day, and turn round."

"It is all one to me," replied Thorpe rather angrily; and instantly turning his horse, they were on their way back to Bath.

"If your brother had not got such a d——— beast to drive," said he soon after-wards, "we might have done it very well. My horse would have trotted to Clifton within the hour, if left to himself, and I have almost broke my arm with pulling him in to that cursed broken-winded jade's pace. Morland is a fool for not keeping a horse and gig of his own."

"No, he is not," said Catherine warmly, "for I am sure he could not afford it."

"And why cannot he afford it?"

"Because he has not money enough."

11. A light, four-wheeled, horse-drawn vehicle.

Thorpe

"And whose fault is that?"

"Nobody's, that I know of." Thorpe then said something in the loud, incoherent way to which he had often recourse, about its being a d——— thing to be miserly; and that if people who rolled in money could not afford things, he did not know who could; which Catherine did not even endeavour to understand. Disappointed of what was to have been the consolation for her first disappointment, she was less and less disposed either to be agreeable herself, or to find her companion so; and they returned to Pulteney-street without her speaking twenty words.

As she entered the house, the footman told her, that a gentleman and lady had called and inquired for her a few minutes after her setting off; that, when he told them she was gone out with Mr. Thorpe, the lady had asked whether any message had been left for her; and on his saying no, had felt for a card but said she had none about her, and went away. Pondering over these heart-rending tidings, Catherine walked slowly up stairs. At the head of them she was met by Mr. Allen, who, on hearing the reason of their speedy return, said, "I am glad your brother had so much sense; I am glad you are come back. It was a strange, wild scheme."

They all spent the evening together at Thorpe's. Catherine was disturbed and out of spirits; but Isabella seemed to find a pool of commerce, in the fate of which she shared, by private partnership with Morland, a very good equivalent for the quiet and country air of an inn at Clifton. Her satisfaction, too, in not being at the Lower Rooms, was spoken more than once. "How I pity the poor creatures that are going there! How glad I am that I am not amongst them! I wonder whether it will be a full ball or not! They have not begun dancing yet. I would not be there for all the world. It is so delightful to have an evening now and then to oneself. I dare say it will not be a very good ball. I know the Mitchells will not be there. I am sure I pity every body that is. But I dare say, Mr. Morland, you long to be at it, do not you? I am sure you do. Well, pray do not let any body here be a restraint on you. I dare say we could do very well without you; but you men think yourselves of such consequence."

Isabella

Catherine could almost have accused Isabella of being wanting in tenderness towards herself and her sorrows; so very little did they appear to dwell on her mind, and so very inadequate was the comfort she offered. "Do not be so dull, my dearest creature," she whispered. "You will quite break my heart. It was amazingly shocking to be sure; but the Tilneys were entirely to blame. Why were not they more punctual? It was dirty, indeed, but what did that signify? I am sure John and I should not have minded it. I never mind going through any thing, where a friend is concerned; that is my disposition, and John is just the same; he has amazing strong feelings. Good heavens! what a delightful hand you have got! Kings, I vow! I never was so happy in my life! I would fifty times rather you should have them than myself."

And now I may dismiss my heroine to the sleepless couch, which is the true heroine's portion; to a pillow strewed with thorns and wet with tears. And lucky may she think herself, if she get another good night's rest in the course of the next three months.

Narrator

CHAPTER XII

"Mrs. Allen," said Catherine the next morning, "will there be any harm in my calling on Miss Tilney to-day? I shall not be easy till I have explained every thing."

"Go by all means, my dear; only put on a white gown; Miss Tilney always wears white."

Catherine cheerfully complied; and being properly equipped, was more impatient than ever to be at the Pump-room, that she might inform herself of General Tilney's lodgings, for though she believed they were in Milsom-street, she was not certain of the house, and Mrs. Allen's wavering convictions only made it more doubtful. To Milsom-street she was directed; and having made herself perfect in the number, hastened away with eager steps and a beating heart to pay her visit, explain her conduct, and be forgiven; tripping lightly through the church-yard, and resolutely turning away her eyes, that she might not be obliged to see her beloved Isabella and her dear family, who, she had reason to believe, were in a shop hard by. She reached the house without any impediment, looked at the number, knocked at the door, and inquired for Miss Tilney. The man believed Miss Tilney to be at home, but was not quite certain. Would she be pleased to send up her name? She gave her card. In a few minutes the servant returned, and with a look which did not quite confirm his words, said he had been mistaken, for that Miss Tilney was walked out. Catherine, with a blush of mortification, left the house. She felt almost persuaded that Miss Tilney *was* at home, and too much offended to admit her; and as she retired down the street, could not withhold one glance at the drawing-room windows, in expectation of seeing her there, but no one appeared at them. At the bottom of the street, however, she looked back again, and then, not at a window, but issuing from the door, she saw Miss Tilney herself. She was followed by a gentleman, whom Catherine believed to be her father, and they turned up towards Edgar's-buildings. Catherine, in deep mortification, proceeded on her way. She could almost be angry herself at such angry incivility; but she checked the resentful sensation; she remembered her own ignorance. She knew not how such an offence as her's might be classed by the laws of worldly politeness, to what a degree of unforgivingness it might with propriety lead, nor to what rigours of rudeness in return it might justly make her amenable.

Dejected and humbled, she had even some thoughts of not going with the others to the theatre that night; but it must be confessed that they were not of long continuance: for she soon recollected, in the first place, that she was without any excuse for staying at home; and, in the second, that it was a play she wanted very much to see. To the theatre accordingly they all went; no Tilneys appeared to plague or please her; she feared that, amongst the many perfections of the family, a fondness for plays was not to be ranked; but perhaps it was because they were habituated to the finer performances of the London stage, which she knew, on Isabella's authority, rendered every thing else of the kind "quite horrid." She was not deceived in her own expectation of pleasure; the comedy so well suspended her care, that no one, observing her during the first four acts, would have supposed she had any wretchedness about her. On the beginning of the fifth, however, the sudden view of Mr. Henry Tilney and his father, joining a party in the opposite box, recalled her to anxiety and distress. The stage could no longer excite genuine merriment—no longer keep her whole attention. Every other look upon an average was directed towards the opposite box; and, for the space of two entire scenes, did she thus watch Henry Tilney, without being once able to catch his eye. No longer could he be suspected of indifference for a play; his notice was never withdrawn from the stage during two whole scenes. At length, however, he did look towards her, and he bowed—but such a bow! no smile, no continued observance attended it; his eyes were immediately returned to their former direction. Catherine was restlessly miserable; she could almost have run round to the box in which he sat, and forced him to hear her explanation. Feelings rather natural than heroic possessed her; instead of considering her own dignity injured by this ready condemnation—instead of proud-ly resolving, in conscious innocence, to shew her resentment towards him who could harbour a doubt of it, to leave to him all the trouble of seeking an explana-tion, and to enlighten him on the past only by avoiding his sight, or flirting with somebody else, she took to herself all the shame of misconduct, or at least of its appearance, and was only eager for an opportunity of explaining its cause.

The play concluded—the curtain fell—Henry Tilney was no longer to be seen where he had hitherto sat, but his father remained, and perhaps he might be now coming round to their box. She was right; in a few minutes he appeared, and, making his way through the then thinning rows, spoke with like calm politeness to Mrs. Allen and her friend. Not with such calmness was he answered by the latter: "Oh! Mr. Tilney, I have been quite wild to speak to you, and make my apologies. You must have thought me so rude; but indeed it was not my own fault,—was it, Mrs. Allen? Did not they tell me that Mr. Tilney and his sister were gone out in a phaeton together? and then what could I do? But I had ten thousand times rather have been with you; now had not I, Mrs. Allen?"

"My dear, you tumble my gown," was Mrs. Allen's reply.

Her assurance, however, standing sole as it did, was not thrown away; it brought a more cordial, more natural smile into his countenance, and he replied in a tone which retained only a little affected reserve: "We were much obliged to you at any rate for wishing us a pleasant walk after our passing you in Argyle-street: you were so kind as to look back on purpose."

"But indeed I did not wish you a pleasant walk; I never thought of such a thing; but I begged Mr. Thorpe so earnestly to stop; I called out to him as soon as ever I saw you; now, Mrs. Allen, did not———Oh! you were not there; but indeed I did; and, if Mr. Thorpe would only have stopped, I would have jumped out and run after you."

Is there a Henry in the world who could be insensible to such a declaration? Henry Tilney at least was not. With a yet sweeter smile, he said every thing that need be said of his sister's concern, regret, and dependence on Catherine's honour. "Oh! do not say Miss Tilney was not angry," cried Catherine, "because I know she was; for she would not see me this morning when I called; I saw her walk out of the house the next minute after my leaving it; I was hurt, but I was not affronted. Perhaps you did not know I had been there."

"I was not within at the time; but I heard of it from Eleanor, and she has been wishing ever since to see you, to explain the reason of such incivility; but perhaps I can do it as well. It was nothing more than that my father———they were just preparing to walk out, and he being hurried for time, and not caring to have it put off, made a point of her being denied. That was all, I do assure you. She was very much vexed, and meant to make her apology as soon as possible."

Catherine's mind was greatly eased by this information, yet a something of solic-itude remained, from which sprang the following question, thoroughly artless in itself, though rather distressing to the gentleman: "But, Mr. Tilney, why were you less generous than your sister? If she felt such confidence in my good intentions, and could suppose it to be only a mistake, why should you be so ready to take offence?"

"Me! I take offence!"

"Nay, I am sure by your look, when you came into the box, you were angry."

"I angry! I could have no right."

"Well, nobody would have thought you had no right who saw your face." He replied by asking her to make room for him, and talking of the play.

He remained with them some time, and was only too agreeable for Catherine to be contented when he went away. Before they parted, however, it was agreed that the projected walk should be taken as soon as possible; and, setting aside the misery of his quitting their box, she was, upon the whole, left one of the happiest creatures in the world.

While talking to each other, she had observed with some surprise, that John Thorpe, who was never in the same part of the house for ten minutes together, was engaged in conversation with General Tilney; and she felt something more than surprize, when she thought she could perceive herself the object of their attention and discourse. What could they have to say of her? She feared General Tilney did not like her appearance: she found it was implied in his preventing her admittance to his daughter, rather than postpone his own walk a few minutes. "How came Mr. Thorpe to know your father?" was her anxious inquiry, as she pointed them out to her companion. He knew nothing about it; but his father, like every military man, had a very large acquaintance.

When the entertainment was over, Thorpe came to assist them in getting out. Catherine was the immediate object of his gallantry; and, while they waited in the lobby for a chair, he prevented the inquiry which had travelled from her heart almost to the tip of her tongue, by asking, in a consequential manner, whether she had seen him talking with General Tilney: "He is a fine old fellow, upon my soul! Stout, active—looks as young as his son. I have a great regard for him, I assure you: a gentleman-like, good sort of fellow as ever lived."

"But how came you to know him?"

"Know him!—There are few people much about town that I do not know. I have met him for ever at the Bedford; and I knew his face again to-day the moment he came into the billiard-room. One of the best players we have, by the bye; and we had a little touch together, though I was almost afraid of him at first: the odds were five to four against me; and, if I had not made one of the cleanest strokes that perhaps ever was made in this world———I took his ball exactly———but I could not make you understand it without a table; however I did beat him. A very fine fellow; as rich as a Jew. I should like to dine with him; I dare say he gives famous dinners. But what do you think we have been talking of? You. Yes, by heavens!—and the General thinks you the finest girl in Bath."

"Oh! nonsense! how can you say so?"

"And what do you think I said?" (lowering his voice) "Well done, General, said I, I am quite of your mind."

Here, Catherine, who was much less gratified by his admiration than by General Tilney's, was not sorry to be called away by Mr. Allen. Thorpe, however, would see her to her chair, and, till she entered it, continued the same kind of delicate flattery, in spite of her entreating him to have done.

That General Tilney, instead of disliking, should admire her, was very delightful; and she joyfully thought, that there was not one of the family whom she need now fear to meet. The evening had done more, much more, for her, than could have been expected.

Chapter XIII

Monday, Tuesday, Wednesday, Thursday, Friday and Saturday have now passed in review before the reader; the events of each day, its hopes and fears, mortifications and pleasures have been separately stated, and the pangs of Sunday only now remain to be described, and close the week. The Clifton scheme had been deferred, not relinquished, and on the afternoon's Crescent of this day, it was brought forward again. In a private consultation between Isabella and James, the former of whom had particularly set her heart upon going, and the latter no less anxiously placed his upon pleasing her, it was agreed that, provided the weather were fair, the party should take place on the following morning; and they were to set off very early, in order to be at home in good time. The affair thus determined, and Thorpe's approbation secured, Catherine only remained to be apprized of it. She had left them for a few minutes to speak to Miss Tilney. In that interval the plan was completed, and as soon as she came again, her agreement was demanded; but instead of the gay acquiescence expected by Isabella, Catherine looked grave, was very sorry, but could not go. The engagement which ought to have kept her from joining in the former attempt, would make it impossible for her to accompany them now. She had that moment settled with Miss Tilney to take their promised walk to-morrow; it was quite determined, and she would not, upon any account, retract. But that she *must* and *should* retract, was instantly the eager cry of both the Thorpes; they must go to Clifton to-morrow, they would not go without her, it would be nothing to put off a mere walk for one day longer, and they would not hear of a refusal. Catherine was distressed, but not subdued. "Do not urge me, Isabella. I am engaged to Miss Tilney. I cannot go." This availed nothing. The same arguments assailed her again; she must go, she should go, and they would not hear of a refusal. "It would be so easy to tell Miss Tilney that you had just been reminded of a prior engagement, and must only beg to put off the walk till Tuesday."

"No, it would not be easy. I could not do it. There has been no prior engagement." But Isabella became only more and more urgent; calling on her in the most affectionate manner; addressing her by the most endearing names. She was sure her dearest, sweetest Catherine would not seriously refuse such a trifling request to a friend who loved her so dearly. She knew her beloved Catherine to have so feeling a heart, so sweet a temper, to be so easily persuaded by those she loved. But all in vain; Catherine felt herself to be in the right, and though pained by such tender, such flattering supplication, could not allow it to influence her. Isabella then tried another method. She reproached her with having more affection for Miss Tilney, though she had known her so little a while, than for her best and oldest friends; with being grown cold and indifferent, in short, towards herself. "I cannot help being jealous, Catherine, when I see myself slighted for strangers, I, who love you so excessively! When once my affections are placed, it is not in the power of any thing to change them. But I believe my feelings are stronger than any body's; I am sure they are too strong for my own peace; and to see myself supplanted in your friendship by strangers, does cut me to the quick, I own. These Tilneys seem to swallow up every thing else."

Catherine thought this reproach equally strange and unkind. Was it the part of a friend thus to expose her feelings to the notice of others? Isabella appeared to her ungenerous and selfish, regardless of every thing but her own gratification. These painful ideas crossed her mind, though she said nothing. Isabella, in the meanwhile, had applied her handkerchief to her eyes; and Morland, miserable at such a sight, could not help saying, "Nay, Catherine. I think you cannot stand out any longer now. The sacrifice is not much; and to oblige such a friend—I shall think you quite unkind, if you still refuse."

This was the first time of her brother's openly siding against her, and anxious to avoid his displeasure, she proposed a compromise. If they would only put off their

resentment

scheme till Tuesday, which they might easily do, as it depended only on themselves, she could go with them, and every body might then be satisfied. But "No, no, no!" was the immediate answer; "that could not be, for Thorpe did not know that he might not go to town on Tuesday." Catherine was sorry, but could do no more; and a short silence ensued, which was broken by Isabella; who in a voice of cold resentment said, "Very well, then there is an end of the party. If Catherine does not go, I cannot. I cannot be the only woman. I would not, upon any account in the world, do so improper a thing."

"Catherine, you must go," said James.

"But why cannot Mr. Thorpe drive one of his other sisters? I dare say either of them would like to go."

"Thank ye," cried Thorpe, "but I did not come to Bath to drive my sisters about, and look like a fool. No, if you do not go, d———— me if I do. I only go for the sake of driving you."

"That is a compliment which gives me no pleasure." But her words were lost on Thorpe, who had turned abruptly away.

The three others still continued together, walking in a most uncomfortable manner to poor Catherine; some times not a word was said, sometimes she was again attacked with supplications or reproaches, and her arm was still linked within Isabella's, though their hearts were at war. At one moment she was softened, at another irritated; always distressed, but always steady.

"I did not think you had been so obstinate, Catherine," said James; "you were not used to be so hard to persuade; you once were the kindest, best-tempered of my sisters."

"I hope I am not less so now," she replied, very feelingly; "but indeed I cannot go. If I am wrong, I am doing what I believe to be right."

"I suspect," said Isabella, in a low voice, "there is no great struggle."

Catherine's heart swelled; she drew away her arm, and Isabella made no opposition. Thus passed a long ten minutes, till they were again joined by Thorpe, who coming to them with a gayer look, said, "Well, I have settled the matter, and now we may all go to-morrow with a safe conscience. I have been to Miss Tilney, and made your excuses."

"You have not!" cried Catherine.

Manipulation by Thorpe

"I have, upon my soul. Left her this moment. Told her you had sent me to say, that having just recollected a prior engagement of going to Clifton with us to-morrow, you could not have the pleasure of walking with her till Tuesday. She said very well, Tuesday was just as convenient to her; so there is an end of all our difficulties.—A pretty good thought of mine—hey?"

Isabella's countenance was once more all smiles and good-humour, and James too looked happy again.

"A most heavenly thought indeed! Now, my sweet Catherine, all our distresses are over; you are honourably acquitted, and we shall have a most delightful party."

Catherine rejects idea

"This will not do," said Catherine; "I cannot submit to this. I must run after Miss Tilney directly and set her right."

Isabella, however, caught hold of one hand; Thorpe of the other; and remonstrances poured in from all three. Even James was quite angry. When every thing was settled, when Miss Tilney herself said that Tuesday would suit her as well, it was quite ridiculous, quite absurd to make any further objection.

"I do not care. Mr. Thorpe had no business to invent any such message. If I had thought it right to put it off, I could have spoken to Miss Tilney myself. This is only

Peer Pressure!

doing it in a ruder way; and how do I know that Mr. Thorpe has———he may be mistaken again perhaps; he led me into one act of rudeness by his mistake on Friday. Let me go, Mr. Thorpe; Isabella, do not hold me."

Thorpe told her it would be in vain to go after the Tilneys; they were turning the corner into Brock-street, when he had overtaken them, and were at home by this time.

"Then I will go after them," said Catherine; "wherever they are I will go after them. It does not signify talking. If I could not be persuaded into doing what I thought wrong, I never will be tricked into it." And with these words she broke away *the trick* and hurried off. Thorpe would have darted after her, but Morland withheld him. "Let her go, let her go, if she will go."

"She is as obstinate as———" *Insult to Catherine.*

Thorpe never finished the simile, for it could hardly have been a proper one.

Away walked Catherine in great agitation, as fast as the crowd would permit her, fearful of being pursued, yet determined to persevere. As she walked, she reflected on what had passed. It was painful to her to disappoint and displease them, particularly to displease her brother; but she could not repent her resistance. Setting her own inclination apart, to have failed a second time in her engagement to Miss Tilney, to have retracted a promise voluntarily made only five minutes before, and on a false pretence too, must have been wrong. She had not been withstanding them on selfish principles alone, she had not consulted merely her own gratification; *that* might have been ensured in some degree by the excursion itself, by seeing Blaize Castle; no, she had attended to what was due to others, and to her own character in their opinion. Her conviction of being right however was not enough to restore her composure, till she had spoken to Miss Tilney she could not be at ease; and quickening her pace when she got clear of the Crescent, she almost ran over the remaining ground till she gained the top of Milsom-street. So rapid had been her movements, that in spite of the Tilneys' advantage in the outset, they were but just turning into their lodgings as she came within view of them; and the servant still remaining at the open door, she used only the ceremony of saying that she must speak with Miss Tilney that moment, and hurrying by him proceeded up stairs. Then, opening the first door before her, which happened to be the right, she immediately found herself in the drawing-room with General Tilney, his son and daughter. Her explanation, defective only in being—from her irritation of nerves and shortness of breath—no explanation at all, was instantly given. "I am come in a great hurry—It was all a mistake—I never promised to go—I told them from the first I could not go.—I ran away in a great hurry to explain it.—I did not care what you thought of me.—I would not stay for the servant."

The business however, though not perfectly elucidated by this speech, soon ceased to be a puzzle. Catherine found that John Thorpe *had* given the message; and Miss Tilney had no scruple in owning herself greatly surprized by it. But whether her brother had still exceeded her in resentment, Catherine, though she instinctively addressed herself as much to one as to the other in her vindication, had no means of knowing. Whatever might have been felt before her arrival, her eager declarations immediately made every look and sentence as friendly as she could desire.

The affair thus happily settled, she was introduced by Miss Tilney to her father, and received by him with such ready, such solicitous politeness as recalled Thorpe's information to her mind, and made her think with pleasure that he might be sometimes depended on. To such anxious attention was the general's civility carried, that not aware of her extraordinary swiftness in entering the house, he was quite angry with the servant whose neglect had reduced her to open the door of the apartment herself. "What did William mean by it? He should make a point of inquiring into the matter." And if Catherine had not most warmly asserted his innocence, it seemed likely that William would lose the favour of his master for ever, if not his place, by her rapidity.

Invited to dinner

After sitting with them a quarter of an hour, she rose to take leave, and was then most agreeably surprized by General Tilney's asking her if she would do his daughter the honour of dining and spending the rest of the day with her. Miss Tilney added her own wishes. Catherine was greatly obliged; but it was quite out of her power. Mr. and Mrs. Allen would expect her back every moment. The general declared he could say no more; the claims of Mr. and Mrs. Allen were not to be superseded; but on some other day he trusted, when longer notice could be given, they would not refuse to spare her to her friend. "Oh, no; Catherine was sure they would not have the least objection, and she should have great pleasure in coming." The general attended her himself to the street-door, saying every thing gallant as they went down stairs, admiring the elasticity of her walk, which corresponded exactly with the spirit of her dancing, and making her one of the most graceful bows she had ever beheld, when they parted.

Catherine, delighted by all that had passed, proceeded gaily to Pulteney-street; walking, as she concluded, with great elasticity, though she had never thought of it before. She reached home without seeing any thing more of the offended party; and now that she had been triumphant throughout, had carried her point and was secure of her walk, she began (as the flutter of her spirits subsided) to doubt whether she had been perfectly right. A sacrifice was always noble; and if she had given way to their entreaties, she should have been spared the distressing idea of a friend displeased, a brother angry, and a scheme of great happiness to both destroyed, perhaps through her means. To ease her mind, and ascertain by the opinion of an unprejudiced person what her own conduct had really been, she took occasion to mention before Mr. Allen the half-settled scheme of her brother and the Thorpes for the following day. Mr. Allen caught at it directly. "Well," said he, "and do you think of going too?"

"No; I had just engaged myself to walk with Miss Tilney before they told me of it; and therefore you know I could not go with them, could I?"

"No, certainly not; and I am glad you do not think of it. These schemes are not at all the thing. Young men and women driving about the country in open carriages! Now and then it is very well; but going to inns and public places together! It is not right; and I wonder Mrs. Thorpe should allow it. I am glad you do not think of going; I am sure Mrs. Morland would not be pleased. Mrs. Allen, are not you of my way of thinking? Do not you think these kind of projects objectionable?"

Mr Allen agrees with Catherine

"Yes, very much so indeed. Open carriages are nasty things. A clean gown is not five minutes wear in them. You are splashed getting in and getting out; and the wind takes your hair and your bonnet in every direction. I hate an open carriage myself."

"I know you do; but that is not the question. Do not you think it has an odd appearance, if young ladies are frequently driven about in them by young men, to whom they are not even related?"

"Yes, my dear, a very odd appearance indeed. I cannot bear to see it."

"Dear madam," cried Catherine, "then why did not you tell me so before? I am sure if I had known it to be improper, I would not have gone with Mr. Thorpe at all; but I always hoped you would tell me, if you thought I was doing wrong."

"And so I should, my dear, you may depend on it; for as I told Mrs. Morland at parting, I would always do the best for you in my power. But one must not be over particular. Young people *will* be young people, as your good mother says herself. You know I wanted you, when we first came, not to buy that sprigged muslin, but you would. Young people do not like to be always thwarted."

"But this was something of real consequence; and I do not think you would have found me hard to persuade."

"As far as it has gone hitherto, there is no harm done," said Mr. Allen; "and I would only advise you, my dear, not to go out with Mr. Thorpe any more."

"That is just what I was going to say," added his wife.

Catherine, relieved for herself, felt uneasy for Isabella; and after a moment's thought, asked Mr. Allen whether it would not be both proper and kind in her to write to Miss Thorpe, and explain the indecorum of which she must be as insensible as herself; for she considered that Isabella might otherwise perhaps be going to Clifton the next day, in spite of what had passed. Mr. Allen however discouraged her from doing any such thing. "You had better leave her alone, my dear, she is old enough to know what she is about; and if not, has a mother to advise her. Mrs. Thorpe is too indulgent beyond a doubt; but however you had better not interfere. She and your brother chuse to go, and you will be only getting ill-will."

Catherine submitted; and though sorry to think that Isabella should be doing wrong, felt greatly relieved by Mr. Allen's approbation of her own conduct, and truly rejoiced to be preserved by his advice from the danger of falling into such an error herself. Her escape from being one of the party to Clifton was now an escape indeed; for what would the Tilneys have thought of her, if she had broken her promise to them in order to do what was wrong in itself? if she had been guilty of one breach of propriety, only to enable her to be guilty of another?

Chapter XIV

The next morning was fair, and Catherine almost expected another attack from the assembled party. With Mr. Allen to support her, she felt no dread of the event: but she would gladly be spared a contest, where victory itself was painful; and was heartily rejoiced therefore at neither seeing nor hearing any thing of them. The Tilneys called for her at the appointed time; and no new difficulty arising, no sudden recollection, no unexpected summons, no impertinent intrusion to disconcert their measures, my heroine was most unnaturally able to fulfil her engagement, though it was made with the hero himself. They determined on walking round Beechen Cliff, that noble hill, whose beautiful verdure and hanging coppice render it so striking an object from almost every opening in Bath.

"I never look at it," said Catherine, as they walked along the side of the river, "without thinking of the south of France."

"You have been abroad then?" said Henry, a little surprised.

"Oh! no, I only mean what I have read about. It always puts me in mind of the country that Emily and her father travelled through, in the 'Mysteries of Udolpho.' But you never read novels, I dare say?"

"Why not?"

"Because they are not clever enough for you—gentlemen read better books."

"The person, be it gentleman or lady, who has not pleasure in a good novel, must be intolerably stupid. I have read all Mrs. Radcliffe's works, and most of them with great pleasure. The *Mysteries of Udolpho,* when I had once begun it, I could not lay down again;—I remember finishing it in two days—my hair standing on end the whole time."

"Yes," added Miss Tilney, "and I remember that you undertook to read it aloud to me, and that when I was called away for only five minutes to answer a note, instead of waiting for me, you took the volume into the Hermitage-walk, and I was obliged to stay till you had finished it."

"Thank you, Eleanor;—a most honourable testimony. You see, Miss Morland, the injustice of your suspicions. Here was I, in my eagerness to get on, refusing to wait only five minutes for my sister; breaking the promise I had made of reading it aloud, and keeping her in suspense at a most interesting part, by running away with the volume, which, you are to observe, was her own, particularly her own. I am proud when I reflect on it, and I think it must establish me in your good opinion."

"I am very glad to hear it indeed, and now I shall never be ashamed of liking Udolpho myself. But I really thought before, young men despised novels amazingly."

"It is amazingly; it may well suggest amazement if they do—for they read nearly as many as women. I myself have read hundreds and hundreds. Do not imagine that you can cope with me in a knowledge of Julias and Louisas. If we proceed to particulars, and engage in the never-ceasing inquiry of 'Have you read this?' and 'Have you read that?' I shall soon leave you as far behind me as—what shall I say?—I want an appropriate simile;—as far as your friend Emily herself left poor Valancourt when she went with her aunt into Italy. Consider how many years I have had the start of you. I had entered on my studies at Oxford, while you were a good little girl working your sampler at home!"

"Not very good I am afraid. But now really, do not you think Udolpho the nicest book in the world?"

"The nicest;—by which I suppose you mean the neatest. That must depend upon the binding."

"Henry," said Miss Tilney, "you are very impertinent. Miss Morland, he is treating you exactly as he does his sister. He is for ever finding fault with me, for some incorrectness of language, and now he is taking the same liberty with you. The word 'nicest,' as you used it, did not suit him; and you had better change it as soon as you can, or we shall be overpowered with Johnson and Blair all the rest of the way."[12]

"I am sure," cried Catherine, "I did not mean to say any thing wrong; but it is a nice book, and why should not I call it so?"

"Very true," said Henry, "and this is a very nice day, and we are taking a very nice walk, and you are two very nice young ladies. Oh! it is a very nice word indeed!—it does for every thing. Originally perhaps it was applied only to express neatness, propriety, delicacy, or refinement;—people were nice in their dress, in their sentiments, or their choice. But now every commendation on every subject is comprised in that one word."

"While, in fact," cried his sister, "it ought only to be applied to you, without any commendation at all. You are more nice than wise. Come, Miss Morland, let us leave him to meditate over our faults in the utmost propriety of diction, while we praise Udolpho in whatever terms we like best. It is a most interesting work. You are fond of that kind of reading?"

"To say the truth, I do not much like any other."

"Indeed!"

"That is, I can read poetry and plays, and things of that sort, and do not dislike travels. But history, real solemn history, I cannot be interested in. Can you?"

---

12. An allusion to Dr. Samuel Johnson (1709–84) and his Dictionary (1755); and to Hugh Blair (1718–1800) and his Lectures on Rhetoric and Belles Lettres (1789).

history — typical argument

Eleanor Tilney

modern idea

"Yes, I am fond of history."

"I wish I were too. I read it a little as a duty, but it tells me nothing that does not either vex or weary me. The quarrels of popes and kings, with wars or pestilences, in every page; the men all so good for nothing, and hardly any women at all—it is very tiresome: and yet I often think it odd that it should be so dull, for a great deal of it must be invention. The speeches that are put into the heroes' mouths, their thoughts and designs—the chief of all this must be invention, and invention is what delights me in other books."

"Historians, you think," said Miss Tilney, "are not happy in their flights of fancy. They display imagination without raising interest. I am fond of history—and am very well contented to take the false with the true. In the principal facts they have sources of intelligence in former histories and records, which may be as much depended on, I conclude, as any thing that does not actually pass under one's own observation; and as for the little embellishments you speak of, they are embellishments, and I like them as such. If a speech be well drawn up, I read it with pleasure, by whomsoever it may be made—and probably with much greater, if the production of Mr. Hume or Mr. Robertson, than if the genuine words of Caractacus, Agricola, or Alfred the Great."[13]

"You are fond of history!—and so are Mr. Allen and my father; and I have two brothers who do not dislike it. So many instances within my small circle of friends is remarkable! At this rate, I shall not pity the writers of history any longer. If people like to read their books, it is all very well, but to be at so much trouble in filling great volumes, which, as I used to think, nobody would willingly ever look into, to be labouring only for the torment of little boys and girls, always struck me as a hard fate; and though I know it is all very right and necessary, I have often wondered at the person's courage that could sit down on purpose to do it." *Change*

"That little boys and girls should be tormented," said Henry, "is what no one at all acquainted with human nature in a civilized state can deny; but in behalf of our most distinguished historians, I must observe, that they might well be offended at being supposed to have no higher aim; and that by their method and style, they are perfectly well qualified to torment readers of the most advanced reason and mature time of life. I use the verb 'to torment,' as I observed to be your own method, instead of 'to instruct,' supposing them to be now admitted as synonimous."

"You think me foolish to call instruction a torment, but if you had been as much used as myself to hear poor little children first learning their letters and then learning to spell, if you had ever seen how stupid they can be for a whole morning together, and how tired my poor mother is at the end of it, as I am in the habit of seeing almost every day of my life at home, you would allow that to *torment* and to *instruct* might sometimes be used as synonimous words."

"Very probably. But historians are not accountable for the difficulty of learning to read; and even you yourself, who do not altogether seem particularly friendly to very severe, very intense application, may perhaps be brought to acknowledge that it is very well worth while to be tormented for two or three years of one's life, for the sake of being able to read all the rest of it. Consider—if reading had not been taught, Mrs. Radcliffe would have written in vain—or perhaps might not have written at all."

13. David Hume (1711–76) was a Scottish philosopher and historian; William Robertson (1721–93) was a Scottish historian; Caractacus was a first-century Celtic king; Gnaeus Julius Agricola (40–93 CE) was a Roman general; Alfred the Great (849–899) was king of Wessex from 871 to 899.

Catherine assented—and a very warm panegyric from her on that lady's merits, closed the subject. The Tilneys were soon engaged in another on which she had nothing to say. They were viewing the country with the eyes of persons accustomed to drawing, and decided on its capability of being formed into pictures, with all the eagerness of real taste. Here Catherine was quite lost. She knew nothing of drawing—nothing of taste: and she listened to them with an attention which brought her little profit, for they talked in phrases which conveyed scarcely any idea to her. The little which she could understand however appeared to contradict the very few notions she had entertained on the matter before. It seemed as if a good view were no longer to be taken from the top of an high hill, and that a clear blue sky was no longer a proof of a fine day. She was heartily ashamed of her ignorance. A misplaced shame. Where people wish to attach, they should always be ignorant. To come with a well-informed mind, is to come with an inability of administering to the vanity of others, which a sensible person would always wish to avoid. A woman especially, if she have the misfortune of knowing any thing, should conceal it as well as she can.

The advantages of natural folly in a beautiful girl have been already set forth by the capital pen of a sister author;—and to her treatment of the subject I will only add in justice to men, that though to the larger and more trifling part of the sex, imbecility in females is a great enhancement of their personal charms, there is a portion of them too reasonable and too well informed themselves to desire any thing more in woman than ignorance. But Catherine did not know her own advantages—did not know that a good-looking girl, with an affectionate heart and a very ignorant mind, cannot fail of attracting a clever young man, unless circumstances are particularly untoward. In the present instance, she confessed and lamented her want of knowledge; declared that she would give any thing in the world to be able to draw; and a lecture on the picturesque immediately followed, in which his instructions were so clear that she soon began to see beauty in every thing admired by him, and her attention was so earnest, that he became perfectly satisfied of her having a great deal of natural taste. He talked of fore-grounds, distances, and second distances—side-screens and perspectives—lights and shades; and Catherine was so hopeful a scholar, that when they gained the top of Beechen Cliff, she voluntarily rejected the whole city of Bath, as unworthy to make part of a landscape. Delighted with her progress, and fearful of wearying her with too much wisdom at once, Henry suffered the subject to decline, and by an easy transition from a piece of rocky fragment and the withered oak which he had placed near its summit, to oaks in general, to forests, the inclosure of them, waste lands, crown lands and government, he shortly found himself arrived at politics; and from politics, it was an easy step to silence. The general pause which succeeded his short disquisition on the state of the nation, was put an end to by Catherine, who, in rather a solemn tone of voice, uttered these words, "I have heard that something very shocking indeed, will soon come out in London."

Miss Tilney, to whom this was chiefly addressed, was startled, and hastily replied, "Indeed!—and of what nature?"

"That I do not know, nor who is the author. I have only heard that it is to be more horrible than any thing we have met with yet."

"Good heaven!—Where could you hear of such a thing?"

"A particular friend of mine had an account of it in a letter from London yesterday. It is to be uncommonly dreadful. I shall expect murder and every thing of the kind."

"You speak with astonishing composure! But I hope your friend's accounts have been exaggerated;—and if such a design is known beforehand, proper measures will undoubtedly be taken by government to prevent its coming to effect."

"Government," said Henry, endeavouring not to smile, "neither desires nor dares to interfere in such matters. There must be murder; and government cares not how much."

The ladies stared. He laughed, and added, "Come, shall I make you understand each other, or leave you to puzzle out an explanation as you can? No—I will be noble. I will prove myself a man, no less by the generosity of my soul than the clearness of my head. I have no patience with such of my sex as disdain to let themselves sometimes down to the comprehension of yours. Perhaps the abilities of women are neither sound nor acute—neither vigorous nor keen. Perhaps they may want observation, discernment, judgment, fire, genius, and wit."

"Miss Morland, do not mind what he says; but have the goodness to satisfy me as to this dreadful riot."

"Riot! What riot?"

"My dear Eleanor, the riot is only in your own brain. The confusion there is scandalous. Miss Morland has been talking of nothing more dreadful than a new publication which is shortly to come out, in three duodecimo volumes, two hundred and seventy-six pages in each, with a frontispiece to the first, of two tombstones and a lantern—do you understand? And you, Miss Morland—my stupid sister has mistaken all your clearest expressions. You talked of expected horrors in London—and instead of instantly conceiving, as any rational creature would have done, that such words could relate only to a circulating library, she immediately pictured to herself a mob of three thousand men assembling in St. George's Fields; the Bank attacked, the Tower threatened, the streets of London flowing with blood, a detachment of the 12th Light Dragoons, (the hopes of the nation,) called up from Northampton to quell the insurgents, and the gallant Capt. Frederick Tilney, in the moment of charging at the head of his troop, knocked off his horse by a brickbat from an upper window. Forgive her stupidity. The fears of the sister have added to the weakness of the woman; but she is by no means a simpleton in general."

Catherine looked grave. "And now, Henry," said Miss Tilney, "that you have made us understand each other, you may as well make Miss Morland understand yourself—unless you mean to have her think you intolerably rude to your sister, and a great brute in your opinion of women in general. Miss Morland is not used to your odd ways."

"I shall be most happy to make her better acquainted with them."

"No doubt; but that is no explanation of the present."

"What am I to do?"

"You know what you ought to do. Clear your character handsomely before her. Tell her that you think very highly of the understanding of women."

"Miss Morland, I think very highly of the understanding of all the women in the world—especially of those—whoever they may be—with whom I happen to be in company."

"That is not enough. Be more serious."

"Miss Morland, no one can think more highly of the understanding of women than I do. In my opinion, nature has given them so much, that they never find it necessary to use more than half."

"We shall get nothing more serious from him now, Miss Morland. He is not in a sober mood. But I do assure you that he must be entirely misunderstood, if he can ever appear to say an unjust thing of any woman at all, or an unkind one of me."

It was no effort to Catherine to believe that Henry Tilney could never be wrong. His manner might sometimes surprize, but his meaning must always be just: and what she did not understand, she was almost as ready to admire, as what she did. The whole walk was delightful, and though it ended too soon, its conclusion was delightful too; her friends attended her into the house, and Miss Tilney, before they parted, addressing herself with respectful form, as much to Mrs. Allen as to Catherine, petitioned for the pleasure of her company to dinner on the day after the next. No difficulty was made on Mrs. Allen's side—and the only difficulty on Catherine's was in concealing the excess of her pleasure.

The morning had passed away so charmingly as to banish all her friendship and natural affection; for no thought of Isabella or James had crossed her during their walk. When the Tilneys were gone, she became amiable again, but she was amiable for some time to little effect; Mrs. Allen had no intelligence to give that could relieve her anxiety, she had heard nothing of any of them. Towards the end of the morning however, Catherine having occasion for some indispensable yard of ribbon which must be bought without a moment's delay, walked out into the town, and in Bond-street overtook the second Miss Thorpe, as she was loitering towards Edgar's Buildings between two of the sweetest girls in the world, who had been her dear friends all the morning. From her, she soon learned that the party to Clifton had taken place. "They set off at eight this morning," said Miss Anne, "and I am sure I do not envy them their drive. I think you and I are very well off to be out of the scrape. It must be the dullest thing in the world, for there is not a soul at Clifton at this time of year. Belle went with your brother, and John drove Maria."

Catherine spoke the pleasure she really felt on hearing this part of the arrangement.

"Oh! yes," rejoined the other, "Maria is gone. She was quite wild to go. She thought it would be something very fine. I cannot say I admire her taste; and for my part I was determined from the first not to go, if they pressed me ever so much."

Catherine, a little doubtful of this, could not help answering, "I wish you could have done too. It is a pity you could not all go."

"Thank you; but it is quite a matter of indifference to me. Indeed, I would not have gone on any account. I was saying so to Emily and Sophia when you over took us."

Catherine was still unconvinced; but glad that Anne should have the friendship of an Emily and a Sophia to console her, she bade her adieu without much uneasiness, and returned home, pleased that the party had not been prevented by her refusing to join it, and very heartily wishing that it might be too pleasant to allow either James or Isabella to resent her resistance any longer.

Chapter XV

Early the next day, a note from Isabella, speaking peace and tenderness in every line, and entreating the immediate presence of her friend on a matter of the utmost importance, hastened Catherine, in the happiest state of confidence and curiosity, to Edgar's Buildings. The two youngest Miss Thorpes were by themselves in the parlour; and, on Anne's quitting it to call her sister, Catherine took the opportunity of asking the other for some particulars of their yesterday's party. Maria desired no greater pleasure than to speak of it; and Catherine immediately learnt that it had been altogether the most delightful scheme in the world; that nobody could imagine how charming it had been, and that it had been more delightful than any body could conceive. Such was the information of the first five minutes; the second unfolded thus much in detail—that they had driven directly to the York Hotel, ate some soup, and bespoke an early dinner, walked down to the Pump-room, tasted the water, and laid out some shillings in purses and spars; thence adjourned to eat ice at a pastry-cook's, and hurrying back to the Hotel, swallowed their dinner in haste, to prevent being in the dark; and then had a delightful drive back, only the moon was not up, and it rained a little, and Mr. Morland's horse was so tired he could hardly get it along.

Catherine listened with heartfelt satisfaction. It appeared that Blaize Castle had never been thought of; and, as for all the rest, there was nothing to regret for half an instant. Maria's intelligence concluded with a tender effusion of pity for her sister Anne, whom she represented as insupportably cross, from being excluded the party.

"She will never forgive me, I am sure; but, you know, how could I help it? John would have me go, for he vowed he would not drive her, because she had such thick ancles. I dare say she will not be in good humour again this month; but I am determined I will not be cross; it is not a little matter that puts me out of temper."

Isabella now entered the room with so eager a step, and a look of such happy importance, as engaged all her friend's notice. Maria was without ceremony sent away, and Isabella, embracing Catherine, thus began: "Yes, my dear Catherine, it is so indeed; your penetration has not deceived you. Oh! that arch eye of yours! It sees through every thing."

Catherine replied only by a look of wondering ignorance.

"Nay, my beloved, sweetest friend," continued the other, "compose yourself. I am amazingly agitated, as you perceive. Let us sit down and talk in comfort. Well, and so you guessed it the moment you had my note? Sly creature! Oh! my dear Catherine, you alone who know my heart can judge of my present happiness. Your brother is the most charming of men. I only wish I were more worthy of him. But what will your excellent father and mother say? Oh! heavens! when I think of them I am so agitated!"

Catherine's understanding began to awake: an idea of the truth suddenly darted into her mind; and, with the natural blush of so new an emotion, she cried out, "Good heaven! my dear Isabella, what do you mean? Can you—can you really be in love with James?"

This bold surmise, however, she soon learnt comprehended but half the fact. The anxious affection, which she was accused of having continually watched in Isabella's every look and action, had, in the course of their yesterday's party, received the delightful confession of an equal love. Her heart and faith were alike engaged to James. Never had Catherine listened to any thing so full of interest, wonder, and joy. Her brother and her friend engaged! New to such circumstances, the importance of it appeared unspeakably great, and she contemplated it as one of those grand events, of which the ordinary course of life can hardly afford a return. The strength of her feelings she could not express; the nature of them, however, contented her friend. The happiness of having such a sister was their first effusion, and the fair ladies mingled in embraces and tears of joy.

Delighting, however, as Catherine sincerely did in the prospect of the connexion, it must be acknowledged that Isabella far surpassed her in tender anticipations. "You will be so infinitely dearer to me, my Catherine, than either Anne or Maria: I feel that I shall be so much more attached to my dear Morland's family than to my own."

This was a pitch of friendship beyond Catherine.

"You are so like your dear brother," continued Isabella, "that I quite doated on you the first moment I saw you. But so it always is with me; the first moment settles every thing. The very first day that Morland came to us last Christmas—the very first moment I beheld him—my heart was irrecoverably gone. I remember I wore my yellow gown, with my hair done up in braids; and when I came into the drawing-room, and John introduced him, I thought I never saw any body so handsome before."

Here Catherine secretly acknowledged the power of love; for, though exceedingly fond of her brother, and partial to all his endowments, she had never in her life thought him handsome.

"I remember too, Miss Andrews drank tea with us that evening, and wore her puce-coloured sarsenet; and she looked so heavenly, that I thought your brother must certainly fall in love with her; I could not sleep a wink all night for thinking of it. Oh! Catherine, the many sleepless nights I have had on your brother's account! I would not have you suffer half what I have done! I am grown wretchedly thin I know; but I will not pain you by describing my anxiety; you have seen enough of it. I feel that I have betrayed myself perpetually; so unguarded in speaking of my partiality for the church! But my secret I was always sure would be safe with *you*."

Catherine felt that nothing could have been safer; but ashamed of an ignorance little expected, she dared no longer contest the point, nor refuse to have been as full of arch penetration and affectionate sympathy as Isabella chose to consider her. Her brother she found was preparing to set off with all speed to Fullerton, to make known his situation and ask consent; and here was a source of some real agitation to the mind of Isabella. Catherine endeavoured to persuade her, as she was herself persuaded, that her father and mother would never oppose their son's wishes. "It is impossible," said she, "for parents to be more kind, or more desirous of their children's happiness; I have no doubt of their consenting immediately."

"Morland says exactly the same," replied Isabella; "and yet I dare not expect it; my fortune will be so small; they never can consent to it. Your brother, who might marry any body!"

Here Catherine again discerned the force of love.

"Indeed, Isabella, you are too humble. The difference of fortune can be nothing to signify."

"Oh! my sweet Catherine, in *your* generous heart I know it would signify nothing; but we must not expect such disinterestedness in many. As for myself, I am sure I only wish our situations were reversed. Had I the command of millions, were I mistress of the whole world, your brother would be my only choice."

This charming sentiment, recommended as much by sense as novelty, gave Catherine a most pleasing remembrance of all the heroines of her acquaintance; and she thought her friend never looked more lovely than in uttering the grand idea. "I am sure they will consent," was her frequent declaration; "I am sure they will be delighted with you."

"For my own part," said Isabella, "my wishes are so moderate, that the smallest income in nature would be enough for me. Where people are really attached, poverty itself is wealth: grandeur I detest: I would not settle in London for the universe. A cottage in some retired village would be extasy. There are some charming little villas about Richmond."

"Richmond!" cried Catherine.—"You must settle near Fullerton. You must be near us."

"I am sure I shall be miserable if we do not. If I can but be near *you*, I shall be satisfied. But this is idle talking! I will not allow myself to think of such things, till we have your father's answer. Morland says that by sending it to-night to Salisbury, we may have it to-morrow. To-morrow? I know I shall never have courage to open the letter. I know it will be the death of me."

A reverie succeeded this conviction—and when Isabella spoke again, it was to resolve on the quality of her wedding-gown.

Their conference was put an end to by the anxious young lover himself, who came to breathe his parting sigh before he set off for Wiltshire. Catherine wished to congratulate him, but knew not what to say, and her eloquence was only in her eyes. From them however the eight parts of speech shone out most expressively, and James could combine them with ease. Impatient for the realization of all that he hoped at home, his adieus were not long; and they would have been yet shorter, had he not been frequently detained by the urgent entreaties of his fair one that he would go. Twice was he called almost from the door by her eagerness to have him gone. "Indeed, Morland, I must drive you away. Consider how far you have to ride. I cannot bear to see you linger so. For Heaven's sake, waste no more time. There, go, go—I insist on it."

The two friends, with hearts now more united than ever, were inseparable for the day; and in schemes of sisterly happiness the hours flew along. Mrs. Thorpe and her son, who were acquainted with every thing, and who seemed only to want Mr. Morland's consent, to consider Isabella's engagement as the most fortunate circumstance imaginable for their family, were allowed to join their counsels, and add their quota of significant looks and mysterious expressions to fill up the measure of curiosity to be raised in the unprivileged younger sisters. To Catherine's simple feelings, this odd sort of reserve seemed neither kindly meant, nor consistently supported; and its unkindness she would hardly have forborn pointing out, had its inconsistency been less their friend; but Anne and Maria soon set her heart at ease by the sagacity of their "I know what;" and the evening was spent in a sort of war of wit, a display of family ingenuity; on one side in the mystery of an affected secret, on the other of undefined discovery, all equally acute.

Catherine was with her friend again the next day, endeavouring to support her spirits, and while away the many tedious hours before the delivery of the letters; a needful exertion, for as the time of reasonable expectation drew near, Isabella became more and more desponding, and before the letter arrived, had worked herself into a state of real distress. But when it did come, where could distress be found? "I have had no difficulty in gaining the consent of my kind parents, and am promised that every thing in their power shall be done to forward my happiness," were the first three lines, and in one moment all was joyful security. The brightest glow was instantly spread over Isabella's features, all care and anxiety seemed removed, her spirits became almost too high for controul, and she called herself without scruple the happiest of mortals.

Mrs. Thorpe, with tears of joy, embraced her daughter, her son, her visitor, and could have embraced half the inhabitants of Bath with satisfaction. Her heart was overflowing with tenderness. It was "dear John," and "dear Catherine" at every word;—"dear Anne and dear Maria" must immediately be made sharers in their felicity; and two "dears" at once before the name of Isabella were not more than that beloved child had now well earned. John himself was no skulker in joy. He not only bestowed on Mr. Morland the high commendation of being one of the finest fellows in the world, but swore off many sentences in his praise.

The letter, whence sprang all this felicity, was short, containing little more than this assurance of success; and every particular was deferred till James could write again. But for particulars Isabella could well afford to wait. The needful was comprised in Mr. Morland's promise; his honour was pledged to make every thing easy; and by what means their income was to be formed, whether landed property were to be resigned, or funded money made over, was a matter in which her disinterested spirit took no concern. She knew enough to feel secure of an honourable and speedy establishment, and her imagination took a rapid flight over its attendant felicities. She saw herself at the end of a few weeks, the gaze and admiration of every new acquaintance at Fullerton, the envy of every valued old friend in Putney, with a carriage at her command, a new name on her tickets, and a brilliant exhibition of hoop rings on her finger.

When the contents of the letter were ascertained, John Thorpe, who had only waited its arrival to begin his journey to London, prepared to set off. "Well, Miss Morland," said he, on finding her alone in the parlour, "I am come to bid you good bye." Catherine wished him a good journey. Without appearing to hear her, he walked to the window, fidgetted about, hummed a tune, and seemed wholly self-occupied.

"Shall not you be late at Devizes?" said Catherine. He made no answer; but after a minute's silence burst out with, "A famous good thing this marrying scheme, upon my soul! A clever fancy of Morland's and Belle's. What do you think of it, Miss Morland? I say it is no bad notion."

"I am sure I think it a very good one."

"Do you? That's honest, by heavens! I am glad you are no enemy to matrimony however. Did you ever hear the old song, 'Going to one wedding brings on another?' I say, you will come to Belle's wedding, I hope."

"Yes; I have promised your sister to be with her, if possible."

"And then you know"—twisting himself about and forcing a foolish laugh—"I say, then you know, we may try the truth of this same old song."

"May we? But I never sing. Well, I wish you a good journey. I dine with Miss Tilney to-day, and must now be going home."

"Nay, but there is no such confounded hurry. Who knows when we may be together again? Not but that I shall be down again by the end of a fortnight, and a devilish long fortnight it will appear to me."

"Then why do you stay away so long?" replied Catherine— finding that he waited for an answer.

"That is kind of you, however—kind and good-natured. I shall not forget it in a hurry. But you have more good-nature and all that, than any body living I believe. A monstrous deal of good-nature, and it is not only good-nature, but you have so much, so much of every thing; and then you have such—upon my soul I do not know any body like you."

"Oh! dear, there are a great many people like me, I dare say, only a great deal better. Good morning to you."

"But I say, Miss Morland, I shall come and pay my respects at Fullerton before it is long, if not disagreeable."

"Pray do. My father and mother will be very glad to see you."

"And I hope—I hope, Miss Morland, you will not be sorry to see me."

"Oh! dear, not at all. There are very few people I am sorry to see. Company is always cheerful."

"That is just my way of thinking. Give me but a little cheerful company, let me only have the company of the people I love, let me only be where I like and with

whom I like, and the devil take the rest, say I. And I am heartily glad
the same. But I have a notion, Miss Morland, you and I think pretty
most matters."

"Perhaps we may; but it is more than I ever thought of. And as 1
say the truth, there are not many that I know my own mind about."

"By Jove, no more do I. It is not my way to bother my brains with what does not
concern me. My notion of things is simple enough. Let me only have the girl I like,
say I, with a comfortable house over my head, and what care I for all the rest? Fortune *Thorpe*
is nothing. I am sure of a good income of my own; and if she had not a penny, why so *✓*
much the better." *does*

not

"Very true. I think like you there. If there is a good fortune on one side, there *want*
can be no occasion for any on the other. No matter which has it, so that there is
enough. I hate the idea of one great fortune looking out for another. And to marry for
money I think the wickedest thing in existence. Good day. We shall be very glad to
see you at Fullerton, whenever it is convenient." And away she went. It was not in
the power of all his gallantry to detain her longer. With such news to communicate,
and such a visit to prepare for, her departure was not to be delayed by any thing in his
nature to urge; and she hurried away, leaving him to the undivided consciousness of
his own happy address, and her explicit encouragement. *He thinks he has been successful.*

The agitation which she had herself experienced on first learning her brother's
engagement, made her expect to raise no inconsiderable emotion in Mr. and Mrs.
Allen, by the communication of the wonderful event. How great was her disappointment! The important affair, which many words of preparation ushered in, had been
foreseen by them both ever since her brother's arrival; and all that they felt on the
occasion was comprehended in a wish for the young people's happiness, with a
remark, on the gentleman's side, in favour of Isabella's beauty, and on the lady's, of
her great good luck. It was to Catherine the most surprizing insensibility. The disclosure however of the great secret of James's going to Fullerton the day before, did raise
some emotion in Mrs. Allen. She could not listen to that with perfect calmness; but *A secret*
repeatedly regretted the necessity of its concealment, wished she could have known
his intention, wished she could have seen him before he went, as she should certainly have troubled him with her best regards to his father and mother, and her kind
compliments to all the Skinners.

 END OF VOLUME I *15 chapters*

Volume II

CHAPTER 1

Catherine's expectations of pleasure from her visit in Milsom-street were so very
high, that disappointment was inevitable; and accordingly, though she was most
politely received by General Tilney, and kindly welcomed by his daughter, though
Henry was at home, and no one else of the party, she found, on her return, without
spending many hours in the examination of her feelings, that she had gone to her
appointment preparing for happiness which it had not afforded. Instead of finding
herself improved in acquaintance with Miss Tilney, from the intercourse of the day,
she seemed hardly so intimate with her as before; instead of seeing Henry Tilney to
greater advantage than ever, in the ease of a family party, he had never said so little,
nor been so little agreeable; and, in spite of their father's great civilities to her—in

spite of his thanks, invitations, and compliments—it had been a release to get away from him. It puzzled her to account for all this. It could not be General Tilney's fault. That he was perfectly agreeable and good-natured, and altogether a very charming man, did not admit of a doubt, for he was tall and handsome, and Henry's father. He could not be accountable for his children's want of spirits, or for her want of enjoyment in his company. The former she hoped at last might have been accidental, and the latter she could only attribute to her own stupidity. Isabella, on hearing the particulars of the visit, gave a different explanation: "It was all pride, pride, insufferable haughtiness and pride! She had long suspected the family to be very high, and this made it certain. Such insolence of behaviour as Miss Tilney's she had never heard of in her life! Not to do the honours of her house with common good-breeding! To behave to her guest with such superciliousness! Hardly even to speak to her!"

"But it was not so bad as that, Isabella; there was no superciliousness; she was very civil."

"Oh! don't defend her! And then the brother, he, who had appeared so detached to you! Good heavens! well, some people's feelings are incomprehensible. And so he hardly looked once at you the whole day?"

"I do not say so; but he did not seem in good spirits."

"How contemptible! Of all things in the world inconstancy is my aversion. Let me entreat you never to think of him again, my dear Catherine; indeed he is unworthy of you."

"Unworthy! I do not suppose he ever thinks of me."

"That is exactly what I say; he never thinks of you. Such fickleness! Oh! how different to your brother and to mine! I really believe John has the most constant heart."

"But as for General Tilney, I assure you it would be impossible for any body to behave to me with greater civility and attention; it seemed to be his only care to entertain and make me happy."

"Oh! I know no harm of him; I do not suspect him of pride. I believe he is a very gentleman-like man. John thinks very well of him, and John's judgment————"

"Well, I shall see how they behave to me this evening; we shall meet them at the rooms."

"And must I go?"

"Do not you intend it? I thought it was all settled."

"Nay, since you make such a point of it, I can refuse you nothing. But do not insist upon my being very agreeable, for my heart, you know, will be some forty miles off. And as for dancing, do not mention it I beg; that is quite out of the question. Charles Hodges will plague me to death I dare say; but I shall cut him very short. Ten to one but he guesses the reason, and that is exactly what I want to avoid, so I shall insist on his keeping his conjecture to himself."

Isabella's opinion of the Tilneys did not influence her friend; she was sure there had been no insolence in the manners either of brother or sister; and she did not credit there being any pride in their hearts. The evening rewarded her confidence; she was met by one with the same kindness, and by the other with the same attention as heretofore: Miss Tilney took pains to be near her, and Henry asked her to dance.

Having heard the day before in Milsom-street, that their elder brother, Captain Tilney, was expected almost every hour, she was at no loss for the name of a very fashionable-looking, handsome young man, whom she had never seen before, and who now evidently belonged to their party. She looked at him with great admiration, and even supposed it possible, that some people might think him handsomer than his brother, though, in her eyes, his air was more assuming, and his countenance less prepossessing. His taste and manners were beyond a doubt decidedly inferior; for, within her hearing, he not only protested against every thought of dancing himself, but even laughed openly at Henry for finding it possible. From the latter circumstance it may be presumed, that, whatever might be our heroine's opinion of him, his admiration of her was not of a very dangerous kind; not likely to produce animosities between the brothers, nor persecutions to the lady. He cannot be the instigator of the three villains in horsemen's great coats, by whom she will hereafter be forced into a travelling-chaise and four, which will drive off with incredible speed. Catherine, meanwhile, undisturbed by presentiments of such an evil, or of any evil at all, except that of having but a short set to dance down, enjoyed her usual happiness with Henry Tilney, listening with sparkling eyes to every thing he said; and, in finding him irresistible, becoming so herself.

At the end of the first dance, Captain Tilney came towards them again, and, much to Catherine's dissatisfaction, pulled his brother away. They retired whispering together; and, though her delicate sensibility did not take immediate alarm, and lay it down as fact, that Captain Tilney must have heard some malevolent misrepresentation of her, which he now hastened to communicate to his brother, in the hope of separating them for ever, she could not have her partner conveyed from her sight without very uneasy sensations. Her suspense was of full five minutes' duration; and she was beginning to think it a very long quarter of an hour, when they both returned, and an explanation was given, by Henry's requesting to know, if she thought her friend, Miss Thorpe, would have any objection to dancing, as his brother would be most happy to be introduced to her. Catherine, without hesitation, replied, that she was very sure Miss Thorpe did not mean to dance at all. The cruel reply was passed on to the other, and he immediately walked away.

"Your brother will not mind it I know," said she, "because I heard him say before, that he hated dancing; but it was very good-natured in him to think of it. I suppose he saw Isabella sitting down, and fancied she might wish for a partner; but he is quite mistaken, for she would not dance upon any account in the world."

Henry smiled, and said, "How very little trouble it can give you to understand the motive of other people's actions."

"Why? What do you mean?"

"With you, it is not, How is such a one likely to be influenced? What is the inducement most likely to act upon such a person's feelings, age, situation, and probable habits of life considered?—but, how should I be influenced, what would be my inducement in acting so and so?"

"I do not understand you."

"Then we are on very unequal terms, for I understand you perfectly well."

"Me?—yes; I cannot speak well enough to be unintelligible."

"Bravo!—an excellent satire on modern language."

"But pray tell me what you mean."

"Shall I indeed? Do you really desire it? But you are not aware of the consequences; it will involve you in a very cruel embarrassment, and certainly bring on a disagreement between us."

"No, no; it shall not do either; I am not afraid."

"Well then, I only meant that your attributing my brother's wish of dancing with Miss Thorpe to good-nature alone, convinced me of your being superior in good-nature yourself to all the rest of the world."

Catherine blushed and disclaimed, and the gentleman's predictions were verified. There was a something, however, in his words which repaid her for the pain of confusion; and that something occupied her mind so much, that she drew back for some time, forgetting to speak or to listen, and almost forgetting where she was; till, roused by the voice of Isabella, she looked up and saw her with Captain Tilney preparing to give them hands across.

Isabella shrugged her shoulders and smiled, the only explanation of this extraordinary change which could at that time be given; but as it was not quite enough for Catherine's comprehension, she spoke her astonishment in very plain terms to her partner.

"I cannot think how it could happen! Isabella was so determined not to dance."

"And did Isabella never change her mind before?"

"Oh! but, because———and your brother!—After what you told him from me, how could he think of going to ask her?"

"I cannot take surprize to myself on that head. You bid me be surprized on your friend's account, and therefore I am; but as for my brother, his conduct in the business, I must own, has been no more than I believed him perfectly equal to. The fairness of your friend was an open attraction; her firmness, you know, could only be understood by yourself."

"You are laughing; but, I assure you, Isabella is very firm in general."

"It is as much as should be said of any one. To be always firm must be to be often obstinate. When properly to relax is the trial of judgment; and, without reference to my brother, I really think Miss Thorpe has by no means chosen ill in fixing on the present hour."

The friends were not able to get together for any confidential discourse till all the dancing was over; but then, as they walked about the room arm in arm, Isabella thus explained herself: "I do not wonder at your surprize; and I am really fatigued to death. He is such a rattle! Amusing enough, if my mind had been disengaged; but I would have given the world to sit still."

"Then why did not you?"

"Oh! my dear! it would have looked so particular; and you know how I abhor doing that. I refused him as long as I possibly could, but he would take no denial. You have no idea how he pressed me. I begged him to excuse me, and get some other partner—but no, not he; after aspiring to my hand, there was nobody else in the room he could bear to think of; and it was not that he wanted merely to dance, he wanted to be with *me*. Oh! such nonsense! I told him he had taken a very unlikely way to prevail upon me; for, of all things in the world, I hated fine speeches and compliments; and so———and so then I found there would be no peace if I did not stand up. Besides, I thought Mrs. Hughes, who introduced him, might take it ill if I did not: and your dear brother, I am sure he would have been miserable if I had sat down the whole evening. I am so glad it is over! My spirits are quite jaded with listening to his nonsense: and then, being such a smart young fellow, I saw every eye was upon us."

"He is very handsome indeed."

"Handsome!—Yes, I suppose he may. I dare say people would admire him in general; but he is not at all in my style of beauty. I hate a florid complexion and dark eyes in a man. However, he is very well. Amazingly conceited, I am sure. I took him down several times you know in my way."

When the young ladies next met, they had a far more interesting subject to discuss. James Morland's second letter was then received, and the kind intentions of his father fully explained. A living, of which Mr. Morland was himself patron and incumbent, of about four hundred pounds yearly value, was to be resigned to his son as soon as he should be old enough to take it; no trifling deduction from the family income, no niggardly assignment to one of ten children. An estate of at least equal value, moreover, was assured as his future inheritance.

James expressed himself on the occasion with becoming gratitude; and the necessity of waiting between two and three years before they could marry, being, however unwelcome, no more than he had expected, was born by him without discontent. Catherine, whose expectations had been as unfixed as her ideas of her father's income, and whose judgment was now entirely led by her brother, felt equally well satisfied, and heartily congratulated Isabella on having every thing so pleasantly settled.

"It is very charming indeed," said Isabella, with a grave face. "Mr. Morland has behaved vastly handsome indeed," said the gentle Mrs. Thorpe, looking anxiously at her daughter. "I only wish I could do as much. One could not expect more from him you know. If he finds he *can* do more by and bye, I dare say he will, for I am sure he must be an excellent good hearted man. Four hundred is but a small income to begin on indeed, but your wishes, my dear Isabella, are so moderate, you do not consider how little you ever want, my dear."

"It is not on my own account I wish for more; but I cannot bear to be the means of injuring my dear Morland, making him sit down upon an income hardly enough to find one in the common necessaries of life. For myself, it is nothing; I never think of myself."

"I know you never do, my dear; and you will always find your reward in the affection it makes every body feel for you. There never was a young woman so beloved as you are by every body that knows you; and I dare say when Mr. Morland sees you, my dear child—but do not let us distress our dear Catherine by talking of such things. Mr. Morland has behaved so very handsome you know. I always heard he was a most excellent man; and you know, my dear, we are not to suppose but what, if you had had a suitable fortune, he would have come down with something more, for I am sure he must be a most liberal-minded man."

"Nobody can think better of Mr. Morland than I do, I am sure. But every body has their failing you know, and every body has a right to do what they like with their own money." Catherine was hurt by these insinuations. "I am very sure," said she, "that my father has promised to do as much as he can afford."

Isabella recollected herself. "As to that, my sweet Catherine, there cannot be a doubt, and you know me well enough to be sure that a much smaller income would satisfy me. It is not the want of more money that makes me just at present a little out of spirits; I hate money; and if our union could take place now upon only fifty pounds a year, I should not have a wish unsatisfied. Ah! my Catherine, you have found me out. There's the sting. The long, long, endless two years and half that are to pass before your brother can hold the living."

"Yes, yes, my darling Isabella," said Mrs. Thorpe, "we perfectly see into your heart. You have no disguise. We perfectly understand the present vexation; and every body must love you the better for such a noble honest affection."

Catherine's uncomfortable feelings began to lessen. She endeavoured to believe that the delay of the marriage was the only source of Isabella's regret; and when she saw her at their next interview as cheerful and amiable as ever, endeavoured to forget that she had for a minute thought otherwise. James soon followed his letter, and was received with the most gratifying kindness.

Chapter II

The Allens had now entered on the sixth week of their stay in Bath; and whether it should be the last, was for some time a question, to which Catherine listened with a beating heart. To have her acquaintance with the Tilneys end so soon, was an evil which nothing could counterbalance. Her whole happiness seemed at stake, while the affair was in suspense, and every thing secured when it was determined that the lodgings should be taken for another fortnight. What this additional fortnight was to produce to her beyond the pleasure of sometimes seeing Henry Tilney, made but a small part of Catherine's speculation. Once or twice indeed, since James's engagement had taught her what *could* be done, she had got so far as to indulge in a secret "perhaps," but in general the felicity of being with him for the present bounded her views: the present was now comprised in another three weeks, and her happiness being certain for that period, the rest of her life was at such a distance as to excite but little interest. In the course of the morning which saw this business arranged, she visited Miss Tilney, and poured forth her joyful feelings. It was doomed to be a day of trial. No sooner had she expressed her delight in Mr. Allen's lengthened stay, than Miss Tilney told her of her father's having just determined upon quitting Bath by the end of another week. Here was a blow! The past suspense of the morning had been ease and quiet to the present disappointment. Catherine's countenance fell, and in a voice of most sincere concern she echoed Miss Tilney's concluding words, "By the end of another week!"

"Yes, my father can seldom be prevailed on to give the waters what I think a fair trial. He has been disappointed of some friends' arrival whom he expected to meet here, and as he is now pretty well, is in a hurry to get home."

"I am very sorry for it," said Catherine dejectedly, "if I had known this before—"

"Perhaps," said Miss Tilney in an embarrassed manner, "you would be so good— it would make me very happy if—"

The entrance of her father put a stop to the civility, which Catherine was beginning to hope might introduce a desire of their corresponding. After addressing her with his usual politeness, he turned to his daughter and said, "Well, Eleanor, may I congratulate you on being successful in your application to your fair friend?"

"I was just beginning to make the request, sir, as you came in."

"Well, proceed by all means. I know how much your heart is in it. My daughter, Miss Morland," he continued, without leaving his daughter time to speak, "has been forming a very bold wish. We leave Bath, as she has perhaps told you, on Saturday se'nnight. A letter from my steward tells me that my presence is wanted at home; and being disappointed in my hope of seeing the Marquis of Longtown and General Courteney here, some of my very old friends, there is nothing to detain me longer in Bath. And could we carry our selfish point with you, we should leave it without a single regret. Can you, in short, be prevailed on to quit this scene of public triumph and oblige your friend Eleanor with your company in Gloucestershire? I am almost ashamed to make the request, though its presumption would certainly appear greater to every creature in Bath than yourself. Modesty such as your's—but not for the world would I pain it by open praise. If you can be induced to honour us with a visit, you will make us happy beyond expression. 'Tis true, we can offer you nothing like the gaieties of this lively place; we can tempt you neither by amusement nor splendour, for our mode of living, as you see, is plain and unpretending; yet no endeavours shall be wanting on our side to make Northanger Abbey not wholly disagreeable."

Northanger Abbey!—These were thrilling words, and wound up Catherine's feelings to the highest point of extasy. Her grateful and gratified heart could hardly restrain its expressions within the language of tolerable calmness. To receive so flattering an invitation! To have her company so warmly solicited! Every thing honourable and soothing, every present enjoyment, and every future hope was contained in it; and her acceptance, with only the saving clause of papa and mamma's approbation, was eagerly given.—"I will write home directly," said she, "and if they do not object, as I dare say they will not"—

General Tilney was not less sanguine, having already waited on her excellent friends in Pulteney-street, and obtained their sanction of his wishes. "Since they can consent to part with you," said he, "we may expect philosophy from all the world."

Miss Tilney was earnest, though gentle, in her secondary civilities, and the affair became in a few minutes as nearly settled, as this necessary reference to Fullerton would allow.

The circumstances of the morning had led Catherine's feelings through the varieties of suspense, security, and disappointment; but they were now safely lodged in perfect bliss; and with spirits elated to rapture, with Henry at her heart, and Northanger Abbey on her lips, she hurried home to write her letter. Mr. and Mrs. Morland, relying on the discretion of the friends to whom they had already entrusted their daughter, felt no doubt of the propriety of an acquaintance which had been formed under their eye, and sent therefore by return of post their ready consent to her visit in Gloucestershire. This indulgence, though not more than Catherine had hoped for, completed her conviction of being favoured beyond every other human creature, in friends and fortune, circumstance and chance. Every thing seemed to co-operate for her advantage. By the kindness of her first friends the Allens, she had been introduced into scenes, where pleasures of every kind had met her. Her feelings, her preferences had each known the happiness of a return. Wherever she felt attachment, she had been able to create it. The affection of Isabella was to be secured to her in a sister. The Tilneys, they, by whom above all, she desired to be favourably thought of, outstripped even her wishes in the flattering measures by which their intimacy was to be continued. She was to be their chosen visitor, she was to be for weeks under the same roof with the person whose society she mostly prized—and, in addition to all the rest, this roof was to be the roof of an abbey!—Her passion for ancient edifices was next in degree to her passion for Henry Tilney—and castles and abbies made usually the charm of those reveries which his image did not fill. To see and explore either the ramparts and keep of the one, or the cloisters of the other, had been for many weeks a darling wish, though to be more than the visitor of an hour, had seemed too nearly impossible for desire. And yet, this was to happen. With all the chances against her of house, hall, place, park, court, and cottage, Northanger turned up an abbey, and she was to be its inhabitant. Its long, damp passages, its narrow cells and ruined chapel, were to be within her daily reach, and she could not entirely subdue the hope of some traditional legends, some awful memorials of an injured and ill-fated nun.

It was wonderful that her friends should seem so little elated by the possession of such a home; that the consciousness of it should be so meekly born. The power of early habit only could account for it. A distinction to which they had been born gave no pride. Their superiority of abode was no more to them than their superiority of person.

Many were the inquiries she was eager to make of Miss Tilney; but so active were her thoughts, that when these inquiries were answered, she was hardly more assured than before, of Northanger Abbey having been a richly-endowed convent at the time of the Reformation, of its having fallen into the hands of an ancestor of the Tilneys on its dissolution, of a large portion of the ancient building still making a part of the present dwelling although the rest was decayed, or of its standing low in a valley, sheltered from the north and east by rising woods of oak.

Chapter III

With a mind thus full of happiness, Catherine was hardly aware that two or three days had passed away, without her seeing Isabella for more than a few minutes together. She began first to be sensible of this, and to sigh for her conversation, as she walked along the Pump-room one morning, by Mrs. Allen's side, without any thing to say or to hear; and scarcely had she felt a five minutes' longing of friendship, before the object of it appeared, and inviting her to a secret conference, led the way to a seat. "This is my favourite place," said she, as they sat down on a bench between the doors, which commanded a tolerable view of every body entering at either, "it is so out of the way."

Catherine, observing that Isabella's eyes were continually bent towards one door or the other, as in eager expectation, and remembering how often she had been falsely accused of being arch, thought the present a fine opportunity for being really so; and therefore gaily said, "Do not be uneasy, Isabella. James will soon be here."

"Psha! my dear creature," she replied, "do not think me such a simpleton as to be always wanting to confine him to my elbow. It would be hideous to be always together; we should be the jest of the place. And so you are going to Northanger!—I am amazingly glad of it. It is one of the finest old places in England, I understand. I shall depend upon a most particular description of it."

"You shall certainly have the best in my power to give. But who are you looking for? Are your sisters coming?"

"I am not looking for any body. One's eyes must be somewhere, and you know what a foolish trick I have of fixing mine, when my thoughts are an hundred miles off. I am amazingly absent; I believe I am the most absent creature in the world. Tilney says it is always the case with minds of a certain stamp."

"But I thought, Isabella, you had something in particular to tell me?"

"Oh! yes, and so I have. But here is a proof of what I was saying. My poor head! I had quite forgot it. Well, the thing is this, I have just had a letter from John; you can guess the contents."

"No, indeed, I cannot."

"My sweet love, do not be so abominably affected. What can he write about, but yourself? You know he is over head and ears in love with you."

"With _me_, dear Isabella!"

"Nay, my sweetest Catherine, this is being quite absurd! Modesty, and all that, is very well in its way, but really a little common honesty is sometimes quite as becoming. I have no idea of being so overstrained! It is fishing for compliments. His attentions were such as a child must have noticed. And it was but half an hour before he left Bath, that you gave him the most positive encouragement. He says so in this letter, says that he as good as made you an offer, and that you received his advances in the kindest way; and now he wants me to urge his suit, and say all manner of pretty things to you. So it is in vain to affect ignorance."

Catherine, with all the earnestness of truth, expressed her astonishment at such a charge, protesting her innocence of every thought of Mr. Thorpe's being in love with her, and the consequent impossibility of her having ever intended to encourage him. "As to any attentions on his side, I do declare, upon my honour, I never was sensible of them for a moment—except just his asking me to dance the first day of his coming. And as to making me an offer, or any thing like it, there must be some unaccountable mistake. I could not have misunderstood a thing of that kind, you know! And, as I ever wish to be believed, I solemnly protest that no syllable of such a nature ever passed between us. The last half hour before he went away! It must be all and completely a mistake—for I did not see him once that whole morning."

"But *that* you certainly did, for you spent the whole morning in Edgar's Buildings—it was the day your father's consent came—and I am pretty sure that you and John were alone in the parlour, some time before you left the house."

"Are you? Well, if you say it, it was so, I dare say—but for the life of me, I cannot recollect it. I *do* remember now being with you, and seeing him as well as the rest—but that we were ever alone for five minutes. However, it is not worth arguing about, for whatever might pass on his side, you must be convinced, by my having no recollection of it, that I never thought, nor expected, nor wished for any thing of the kind from him. I am excessively concerned that he should have any regard for me—but indeed it has been quite unintentional on my side, I never had the smallest idea of it. Pray undeceive him as soon as you can, and tell him I beg his pardon—that is—I do not know what I ought to say—but make him understand what I mean, in the properest way. I would not speak disrespectfully of a brother of your's, Isabella, I am sure; but you know very well that if I could think of one man more than another—*he* is not the person." Isabella was silent. "My dear friend, you must not be angry with me. I cannot suppose your brother cares so very much about me. And, you know, we shall still be sisters."

"Yes, yes," (with a blush) "there are more ways than one of our being sisters. But where am I wandering to? Well, my dear Catherine, the case seems to be, that you are determined against poor John—is not it so?"

"I certainly cannot return his affection, and as certainly never meant to encourage it."

"Since that is the case, I am sure I shall not tease you any further. John desired me to speak to you on the subject, and therefore I have. But I confess, as soon as I read his letter, I thought it a very foolish, imprudent business, and not likely to promote the good of either; for what were you to live upon, supposing you came together? You have both of you something to be sure, but it is not a trifle that will support a family now-a-days; and after all that romancers may say, there is no doing without money. I only wonder John could think of it; he could not have received my last."

"You *do* acquit me then of any thing wrong? You are convinced that I never meant to deceive your brother, never suspected him of liking me till this moment?"

"Oh! as to that," answered Isabella laughingly, "I do not pretend to determine what your thoughts and designs in time past may have been. All that is best known to yourself. A little harmless flirtation or so will occur, and one is often drawn on to give more encouragement than one wishes to stand by. But you may be assured that I am the last person in the world to judge you severely. All those things should be allowed for in youth and high spirits. What one means one day, you know, one may not mean the next. Circumstances change, opinions alter."

"But my opinion of your brother never did alter; it was always the same. You are describing what never happened."

"My dearest Catherine," continued the other without at all listening to her, "I would not for all the world be the means of hurrying you into an engagement before you knew what you were about. I do not think any thing would justify me in wishing you to sacrifice all your happiness merely to oblige my brother, because he is my brother, and who perhaps after all, you know, might be just as happy without you, for people seldom know what they would be at, young men especially, they are so amazingly changeable and inconstant. What I say is, why should a brother's happiness be dearer to me than a friend's? You know I carry my notions of friendship pretty high. But, above all things, my dear Catherine, do not be in a hurry. Take my word for it, that if you are in too great a hurry, you will certainly live to repent it. Tilney says, there is nothing people are so often deceived in, as the state of their own affections, and I believe he is very right. Ah! here he comes; never mind, he will not see us, I am sure."

Catherine, looking up, perceived Captain Tilney; and Isabella, earnestly fixing her eye on him as she spoke, soon caught his notice. He approached immediately, and took the seat to which her movements invited him. His first address made Catherine start. Though spoken low, she could distinguish, "What! always to be watched, in person or by proxy!"

"Psha, nonsense!" was Isabella's answer in the same half whisper. "Why do you put such things into my head? If I could believe it—my spirit, you know, is pretty independent."

"I wish your heart were independent. That would be enough for me."

"My heart, indeed! What can you have to do with hearts? You men have none of you any hearts."

"If we have not hearts, we have eyes; and they give us torment enough."

"Do they? I am sorry for it; I am sorry they find any thing so disagreeable in me. I will look another way. I hope this pleases you, (turning her back on him,) I hope your eyes are not tormented now."

"Never more so; for the edge of a blooming cheek is still in view—at once too much and too little."

Catherine heard all this, and quite out of countenance could listen no longer. Amazed that Isabella could endure it, and jealous for her brother, she rose up, and saying she should join Mrs. Allen, proposed their walking. But for this Isabella shewed no inclination. She was so amazingly tired, and it was so odious to parade about the Pump-room; and if she moved from her seat she should miss her sisters, she was expecting her sisters every moment; so that her dearest Catherine must excuse her, and must sit quietly down again. But Catherine could be stubborn too; and Mrs. Allen just then coming up to propose their returning home, she joined her and walked out of the Pump-room, leaving Isabella still sitting with Captain Tilney. With much uneasiness did she thus leave them. It seemed to her that Captain Tilney was falling in love with Isabella, and Isabella unconsciously encouraging him; unconsciously it must be, for Isabella's attachment to James was as certain and well acknowledged as her engagement. To doubt her truth or good intentions was impossible; and yet, during the whole of their conversation her manner had been odd. She wished Isabella had talked more like her usual self, and no so much about money; and had not looked so well pleased at the sight of Captain Tilney. How strange that she should not perceive his admiration! Catherine longed to give her a hint of it, to put her on her guard, and prevent all the pain which her too lively behaviour might otherwise create both for him and her brother.

The compliment of John Thorpe's affection did not make amends for this thoughtlessness in his sister. She was almost as far from believing as from wishing it to be sincere; for she had not forgotten that he could mistake, and his assertion of the offer and of her encouragement convinced her that his mistakes could sometimes be very egregious. In vanity therefore she gained but little, her chief profit was in wonder. That he should think it worth his while to fancy himself in love with her, was a matter of lively astonishment. Isabella talked of his attentions; *she* had never been sensible of any; but Isabella had said many things which she hoped had been spoken in haste, and would never be said again; and upon this she was glad to rest altogether for present ease and comfort.

CHAPTER IV

A few days passed away, and Catherine, though not allowing herself to suspect her friend, could not help watching her closely. The result of her observations was not agreeable. Isabella seemed an altered creature. When she saw her indeed surrounded only by their immediate friends in Edgar's Buildings or Pulteney-street, her change of manners was so trifling that, had it gone no farther, it might have passed unnoticed. A something of languid indifference, or of that boasted absence of mind which Catherine had never heard of before, would occasionally come across her; but had nothing worse appeared, *that* might only have spread a new grace and inspired a warmer interest. But when Catherine saw her in public, admitting Captain Tilney's attentions as readily as they were offered, and allowing him almost an equal share with James in her notice and smiles, the alteration became too positive to be past over. What could be meant by such unsteady conduct, what her friend could be at, was beyond her comprehension. Isabella could not be aware of the pain she was inflicting; but it was a degree of wilful thoughtlessness which Catherine could not but resent. James was the sufferer. She saw him grave and uneasy; and however careless of his present comfort the woman might be who had given him her heart, to *her* it was always an object. For poor Captain Tilney too she was greatly concerned. Though his looks did not please her, his name was a passport to her good will, and she thought with sincere compassion of his approaching disappointment; for, in spite of what she had believed herself to overhear in the Pump-room, his behaviour was so incompatible with a knowledge of Isabella's engagement, that she could not, upon reflection, imagine him aware of it. He might be jealous of her brother as a rival, but if more had seemed implied, the fault must have been in her misapprehension. She wished, by a gentle remonstrance, to remind Isabella of her situation, and make her aware of this double unkindness; but for remonstrance, either opportunity or comprehension was always against her. If able to suggest a hint, Isabella could never understand it. In this distress, the intended departure of the Tilney family became her chief consolation; their journey into Gloucestershire was to take place within a few days, and Captain Tilney's removal would at least restore peace to every heart but his own. But Captain Tilney had at present no intention of removing; he was not to be of the party to Northanger, he was to continue at Bath. When Catherine knew this, her resolution was directly made. She spoke to Henry Tilney on the subject, regretting his brother's evident partiality for Miss Thorpe, and entreating him to make known her prior engagement.

"My brother does know it," was Henry's answer.

"Does he?—then why does he stay here?"

He made no reply, and was beginning to talk of something else; but she eagerly continued, "Why do not you persuade him to go away? The longer he stays, the worse it will be for him at last. Pray advise him for his own sake, and for every body's sake, to leave Bath directly. Absence will in time make him comfortable again; but he can have no hope here, and it is only staying to be miserable." Henry smiled and said, "I am sure my brother would not wish to do that."

"Then you will persuade him to go away?"

"Persuasion is not at command; but pardon me, if I cannot even endeavour to persuade him. I have myself told him that Miss Thorpe is engaged. He knows what he is about, and must be his own master."

"No, he does not know what he is about," cried Catherine; "he does not know the pain he is giving my brother. Not that James has ever told me so, but I am sure he is very uncomfortable."

"And are you sure it is my brother's doing?"

"Yes, very sure."

"Is it my brother's attentions to Miss Thorpe, or Miss Thorpe's admission of them, that gives the pain?"

"Is not it the same thing?"

"I think Mr. Morland would acknowledge a difference. No man is offended by another man's admiration of the woman he loves; it is the woman only who can make it a torment."

Catherine blushed for her friend, and said, "Isabella is wrong. But I am sure she cannot mean to torment, for she is very much attached to my brother. She has been in love with him ever since they first met, and while my father's consent was uncertain, she fretted herself almost into a fever. You know she must be attached to him."

"I understand: she is in love with James, and flirts with Frederick."

"Oh! no, not flirts. A woman in love with one man cannot flirt with another."

"It is probable that she will neither love so well, nor flirt so well, as she might do either singly. The gentlemen must each give up a little."

After a short pause, Catherine resumed with "Then you do not believe Isabella so very much attached to my brother?"

"I can have no opinion on that subject."

"But what can your brother mean? If he knows her engagement, what can he mean by his behaviour?"

"You are a very close questioner."

"Am I?—I only ask what I want to be told."

"But do you only ask what I can be expected to tell?"

"Yes, I think so; for you must know your brother's heart."

"My brother's heart, as you term it, on the present occasion, I assure you I can only guess at."

"Well?"

"Well! Nay, if it is to be guess-work, let us all guess for ourselves. To be guided by second-hand conjecture is pitiful. The premises are before you. My brother is a lively, and perhaps sometimes a thoughtless young man; he has had about a week's acquaintance with your friend, and he has known her engagement almost as long as he has known her."

"Well," said Catherine, after some moments' consideration, "*you* may be able to guess at your brother's intentions from all this; but I am sure I cannot. But is not your father uncomfortable about it? Does not he want Captain Tilney to go away? Sure, if your father were to speak to him, he would go."

"My dear Miss Morland," said Henry, "in this amiable solicitude for your brother's comfort, may you not be a little mistaken? Are you not carried a little too far? Would he thank you, either on his own account or Miss Thorpe's, for supposing that her affection, or at least her good-behaviour, is only to be secured by her seeing nothing of Captain Tilney? Is he safe only in solitude? Or, is her heart constant to him only when unsolicited by any one else? He cannot think this—and you may be sure that he would not have you think it. I will not say, 'Do not be uneasy,' because I know that you are so, at this moment; but be as little uneasy as you can. You have no doubt of the mutual attachment of your brother and your friend; depend upon it therefore, that real jealousy never can exist between them; depend upon it that no disagreement between them can be of any duration. Their hearts are open to each other, as neither heart can be to you; they know exactly what is required and what can be borne; and you may be certain, that one will never tease the other beyond what is known to be pleasant."

Perceiving her still to look doubtful and grave, he added, "Though Frederick does not leave Bath with us, he will probably remain but a very short time, perhaps only a few days behind us. His leave of absence will soon expire, and he must return to his regiment.—And what will then be their acquaintance? The mess-room will drink Isabella Thorpe for a fortnight, and she will laugh with your brother over poor Tilney's passion for a month."

Catherine would contend no longer against comfort. She had resisted its approaches during the whole length of a speech, but it now carried her captive. Henry Tilney must know best. She blamed herself for the extent of her fears, and resolved never to think so seriously on the subject again.

Her resolution was supported by Isabella's behaviour in their parting interview. The Thorpes spent the last evening of Catherine's stay in Pulteney-street, and nothing passed between the lovers to excite her uneasiness, or make her quit them in apprehension. James was in excellent spirits, and Isabella most engagingly placid. Her tenderness for her friend seemed rather the first feeling of her heart; but that at such a moment was allowable; and once she gave her lover a flat contradiction, and once she drew back her hand; but Catherine remembered Henry's instructions, and placed it all to judicious affection. The embraces, tears, and promises of the parting fair ones may be fancied.

CHAPTER V

Mr. and Mrs. Allen were sorry to lose their young friend, whose good-humour and cheerfulness had made her a valuable companion, and in the promotion of whose enjoyment their own had been gently increased. Her happiness in going with Miss Tilney, however, prevented their wishing it otherwise; and, as they were to remain only one more week in Bath themselves, her quitting them now would not long be felt. Mr. Allen attended her to Milsom-street, where she was to breakfast, and saw her seated with the kindest welcome among her new friends; but so great was her agitation in finding herself as one of the family, and so fearful was she of not doing exactly what was right, and of not being able to preserve their good opinion, that, in the embarrassment of the first five minutes, she could almost have wished to return with him to Pulteney-street.

Miss Tilney's manners and Henry's smile soon did away some of her unpleasant feelings; but still she was far from being at ease; nor could the incessant attentions of the General himself entirely reassure her. Nay, perverse as it seemed, she doubted whether she might not have felt less, had she been less attended to. His anxiety for her comfort—his continual solicitations that she would eat, and his often-expressed fears of her seeing nothing to her taste—though never in her life before had she beheld half such variety on a breakfast-table—made it impossible for her to forget for a moment that she was a visitor. She felt utterly unworthy of such respect, and knew not how to reply to it. Her tranquillity was not improved by the General's impatience for the appearance of his eldest son, nor by the displeasure he expressed at his laziness when Captain Tilney at last came down. She was quite pained by the severity of his father's reproof, which seemed disproportionate to the offence; and much was her concern increased, when she found herself the principal cause of the lecture; and that his tardiness was chiefly resented from being disrespectful to her. This was placing her in a very uncomfortable situation, and she felt great compassion for Captain Tilney, without being able to hope for his good-will.

He listened to his father in silence, and attempted not any defence, which confirmed her in fearing, that the inquietude of his mind, on Isabella's account, might, by keeping him long sleepless, have been the real cause of his rising late. It was the first time of her being decidedly in his company, and she had hoped to be now able to form her opinion of him; but she scarcely heard his voice while his father remained in the room; and even afterwards, so much were his spirits affected, she could distinguish nothing but these words, in a whisper to Eleanor, "How glad I shall be when you are all off."

The bustle of going was not pleasant. The clock struck ten while the trunks were carrying down, and the General had fixed to be out of Milsom-street by that hour. His great coat, instead of being brought for him to put on directly, was spread out in the curricle in which he was to accompany his son. The middle seat of the chaise was not drawn out, though there were three people to go in it, and his daughter's maid had so crowded it with parcels, that Miss Morland would not have room to sit; and, so much was he influenced by this apprehension when he handed her in, that she had some difficulty in saving her own new writing-desk from being thrown out into the street. At last, however, the door was closed upon the three females, and they set off at the sober pace in which the handsome, highly-fed four horses of a gentleman usually perform a journey of thirty miles: such was the distance of Northanger from Bath, to be now divided into two equal stages. Catherine's spirits revived as they drove from the door; for with Miss Tilney she felt no restraint; and, with the interest of a road entirely new to her, of an abbey before, and a curricle behind, she caught the last view of Bath without any regret, and met with every mile-stone before she expected it. The tediousness of a two hours' bait at Petty-France, in which there was nothing to be done but to eat without being hungry, and loiter about without any thing to see, next followed—and her admiration of the style in which they travelled, of the fashionable chaise-and-four—postilions handsomely liveried, rising so regularly in their stirrups, and numerous out-riders properly mounted, sunk a little under this consequent incon-

venience. Had their party been perfectly agreeable, the delay would have been nothing; but General Tilney, though so charming a man, seemed always a check upon his
children's spirits, and scarcely any thing was said but by himself; the observation of
which, with his discontent at whatever the inn afforded, and his angry impatience at
the waiters, made Catherine grow every moment more in awe of him, and appeared to
lengthen the two hours into four.—At last, however, the order of release was given;
and much was Catherine then surprized by the General's proposal of her taking his
place in his son's curricle for the rest of the journey:—"the day was fine, and he was
anxious for her seeing as much of the country as possible."

The remembrance of Mr. Allen's opinion, respecting young men's open carriages, made her blush at the mention of such a plan, and her first thought was to
decline it; but her second was of greater deference for General Tilney's judgment; he
could not propose any thing improper for her; and, in the course of a few minutes, she
found herself with Henry in the curricle, as happy a being as ever existed. A very
short trial convinced her that a curricle was the prettiest equipage in the world; the
chaise-and-four wheeled off with some grandeur, to be sure, but it was a heavy and
troublesome business, and she could not easily forget its having stopped two hours at
Petty-France. Half the time would have been enough for the curricle, and so nimbly
were the light horses disposed to move, that, had not the General chosen to have his
own carriage lead the way, they could have passed it with ease in half a minute. But
the merit of the curricle did not all belong to the horses; Henry drove so well—so
quietly—without making any disturbance, without parading to her, or swearing at
them; so different from the only gentleman-coachman whom it was in her power to
compare him with! And then his hat sat so well, and the innumerable capes of his
great coat looked so becomingly important! To be driven by him, next to being dancing with him, was certainly the greatest happiness in the world. In addition to every
other delight, she had now that of listening to her own praise; of being thanked at
least, on his sister's account, for her kindness in thus becoming her visitor; of hearing
it ranked as real friendship, and described as creating real gratitude. His sister, he
said, was uncomfortably circumstanced—she had no female companion—and, in the
frequent absence of her father, was sometimes without any companion at all.

"But how can that be?" said Catherine, "are not you with her?"

"Northanger is not more than half my home; I have an establishment at my own
house in Woodston, which is nearly twenty miles from my father's, and some of my
time is necessarily spent there."

"How sorry you must be for that!"

"I am always sorry to leave Eleanor."

"Yes; but besides your affection for her, you must be so fond of the abbey!—After
being used to such a home as the abbey, an ordinary parsonage-house must be very
agreeable."

He smiled, and said, "You have formed a very favourable idea of the abbey."

"To be sure I have. Is not it a fine old place, just like what one reads about?"

"And are you prepared to encounter all the horrors that a building such as 'what
one reads about' may produce? Have you a stout heart? Nerves fit for sliding pannels
and tapestry?"

"Oh! yes—I do not think I should be easily frightened, because there would be so
many people in the house—and besides, it has never been uninhabited and left
deserted for years, and then the family come back to it unawares, without giving any
notice, as generally happens."

"No, certainly. We shall not have to explore our way into a hall dimly lighted by the expiring embers of a wood fire—nor be obliged to spread our beds on the floor of a room without windows, doors, or furniture. But you must be aware that when a young lady is (by whatever means) introduced into a dwelling of this kind, she is always lodged apart from the rest of the family. While they snugly repair to their own end of the house, she is formally conducted by Dorothy the ancient housekeeper up a different staircase, and along many gloomy passages, into an apartment never used since some cousin or kin died in it about twenty years before. Can you stand such a ceremony as this? Will not your mind misgive you, when you find yourself in this gloomy chamber—too lofty and extensive for you, with only the feeble rays of a single lamp to take in its size—its walls hung with tapestry exhibiting figures as large as life, and the bed, of dark green stuff or purple velvet, presenting even a funereal appearance. Will not your heart sink within you?"

"Oh! but this will not happen to me, I am sure."

"How fearfully will you examine the furniture of your apartment! And what will you discern? Not tables, toilettes, wardrobes, or drawers, but on one side perhaps the remains of a broken lute, on the other a ponderous chest which no efforts can open, and over the fire-place the portrait of some handsome warrior, whose features will so incomprehensibly strike you, that you will not be able to withdraw your eyes from it. Dorothy meanwhile, no less struck by your appearance, gazes on you in great agitation, and drops a few unintelligible hints. To raise your spirits, moreover, she gives you reason to suppose that the part of the abbey you inhabit is undoubtedly haunted, and informs you that you will not have a single domestic within call. With this parting cordial she curtseys off—you listen to the sound of her receding footsteps as long as the last echo can reach you—and when, with fainting spirits, you attempt to fasten your door, you discover, with increased alarm, that it has no lock."

"Oh! Mr. Tilney, how frightful! This is just like a book! But it cannot really happen to me. I am sure your housekeeper is not really Dorothy. Well, what then?"

"Nothing further to alarm perhaps may occur the first night. After surmounting your *unconquerable* horror of the bed, you will retire to rest, and get a few hours' unquiet slumber. But on the second, or at farthest the *third* night after your arrival, you will probably have a violent storm. Peals of thunder so loud as to seem to shake the edifice to its foundation will roll round the neighbouring mountains—and during the frightful gusts of wind which accompany it, you will probably think you discern (for your lamp is not extinguished) one part of the hanging more violently agitated than the rest. Unable of course to repress your curiosity in so favourable a moment for indulging it, you will instantly arise, and throwing your dressing-gown around you, proceed to examine this mystery. After a very short search, you will discover a division in the tapestry so artfully constructed as to defy the minutest inspection, and on opening it, a door will immediately appear—which door being only secured by massy bars and a padlock, you will, after a few efforts, succeed in opening—and, with your lamp in your hand, will pass through it into a small vaulted room."

"No, indeed; I should be too much frightened to do any such thing."

"What! not when Dorothy has given you to understand that there is a secret subterraneous communication between your apartment and the chapel of St. Anthony, scarcely two miles off—Could you shrink from so simple an adventure? No, no, you will proceed into this small vaulted room, and through this into several others, without perceiving any thing very remarkable in either. In one perhaps there may be a dagger, in another a few drops of blood, and in a third the remains of some instrument of torture; but there being nothing in all this out of the common way, and your lamp being nearly exhausted, you will return towards your own apartment. In repassing through the small vaulted room, however, your eyes will be attracted towards a large, old-fashioned cabinet of ebony and gold, which, though narrowly examining the furniture before, you had passed unnoticed. Impelled by an irresistible presentiment, you will eagerly advance to it, unlock its folding doors, and search into every drawer;—but for some time without discovering any thing of importance—perhaps nothing but a considerable hoard of diamonds. At last, however, by touching a secret spring, an inner compartment will open—a roll of paper appears: you seize it—it contains many sheets of manuscript—you hasten with the precious treasure into your own chamber, but scarcely have you been able to decipher 'Oh! thou—whomsoever thou mayst be, into whose hands these memoirs of the wretched Matilda may fall'—when your lamp suddenly expires in the socket, and leaves you in total darkness."

"Oh! no, no—do not say so. Well, go on."

But Henry was too much amused by the interest he had raised, to be able to carry it farther; he could no longer command solemnity either of subject or voice, and was obliged to entreat her to use her own fancy in the perusal of Matilda's woes. Catherine, recollecting herself, grew ashamed of her eagerness, and began earnestly to assure him that her attention had been fixed without the smallest apprehension of really meeting with what he related. "Miss Tilney, she was sure, would never put her into such a chamber as he had described! She was not at all afraid."

As they drew near the end of their journey, her impatience for a sight of the abbey—for some time suspended by his conversation on subjects very different—returned in full force, and every bend in the road was expected with solemn awe to afford a glimpse of its massy walls of grey stone, rising amidst a grove of ancient oaks, with the last beams of the sun playing in beautiful splendour on its high Gothic windows. But so low did the building stand, that she found herself passing through the great gates of the lodge into the very grounds of Northanger, without having discerned even an antique chimney.

She knew not that she had any right to be surprised, but there was a something in this mode of approach which she certainly had not expected. To pass between lodges of a modern appearance, to find herself with such ease in the very precincts of the abbey, and driven so rapidly along a smooth, level road of fine gravel, without obstacle, alarm or solemnity of any kind, struck her as odd and inconsistent. She was not long at leisure however for such considerations. A sudden scud of rain driving full in her face, made it impossible for her to observe any thing further, and fixed all her thoughts on the welfare of her new straw bonnet—and she was actually under the Abbey walls, was springing, with Henry's assistance, from the carriage, was beneath the shelter of the old porch, and had even passed on to the hall, where her friend and the General were waiting to welcome her, without feeling one aweful foreboding of future misery to herself, or one moment's suspicion of any past scenes of horror being acted within the solemn edifice. The breeze had not seemed to waft the sighs of the murdered to her; it had wafted nothing worse than a thick mizzling rain; and having given a good shake to her habit, she was ready to be shewn into the common drawing-room, and capable of considering where she was.

An abbey! Yes, it was delightful to be really in an abbey!—but she doubted, as she looked round the room, whether any thing within her observation, would have given her the consciousness. The furniture was in all the profusion and elegance of modern taste. The fire-place, where she had expected the ample width and ponderous carving of former times, was contracted to a Rumford, with slabs of plain though handsome marble, and ornaments over it of the prettiest English china. The windows, to which she looked with peculiar dependence, from having heard the General talk of his pre-serving them in their Gothic form with reverential care, were yet less what her fancy had portrayed. To be sure, the pointed arch was preserved—the form of them was Gothic—they might be even casements—but every pane was so large, so clear, so light! To an imagination which had hoped for the smallest divisions, and the heaviest stone-work, for painted glass, dirt and cobwebs, the difference was very distressing.

The General, perceiving how her eye was employed, began to talk of the small-ness of the room and simplicity of the furniture, where every thing being for daily use, pretended only to comfort, &c.; flattering himself however that there were some apartments in the Abbey not unworthy her notice—and was proceeding to mention the costly gilding of one in particular, when taking out his watch, he stopped short to pronounce it with surprize within twenty minutes of five! This seemed the word of separation, and Catherine found herself hurried away by Miss Tilney in such a man-ner as convinced her that the strictest punctuality to the family hours would be expected at Northanger.

Returning through the large and lofty hall, they ascended a broad staircase of shining oak, which, after many flights and many landing-places, brought them upon a long wide gallery. On one side it had a range of doors, and it was lighted on the oth-er by windows which Catherine had only time to discover looked into a quadrangle, before Miss Tilney led the way into a chamber, and scarcely staying to hope she would find it comfortable, left her with an anxious entreaty that she would make as little alteration as possible in her dress.

Chapter VI

A moment's glance was enough to satisfy Catherine that her apartment was very unlike the one which Henry had endeavoured to alarm her by the description of. It was by no means unreasonably large, and contained neither tapestry nor velvet. The walls were papered, the floor was carpeted; the windows were neither less perfect, nor more dim than those of the drawing-room below; the furniture, though not of the lat-est fashion, was handsome and comfortable, and the air of the room altogether far from uncheerful. Her heart instantaneously at ease on this point, she resolved to lose no time in particular examination of any thing, as she greatly dreaded disobliging the General by any delay. Her habit therefore was thrown off with all possible haste, and she was preparing to unpin the linen package, which the chaise-seat had conveyed for her immediate accommodation, when her eye suddenly fell on a large high chest, standing back in a deep recess on one side of the fireplace. The sight of it made her start; and, forgetting every thing else, she stood gazing on it in motionless wonder, while these thoughts crossed her:

"This is strange indeed! I did not expect such a sight as this! An immense heavy chest! What can it hold? Why should it be placed here? Pushed back too, as if meant to be out of sight! I will look into it—cost me what it may, I will look into it—and directly too—by day-light. If I stay till evening my candle may go out." She advanced and examined it closely: it was of cedar, curiously inlaid with some darker wood, and raised, about a foot from the ground, on a carved stand of the same. The lock was sil-ver, though tarnished from age; at each end were the imperfect remains of handles also of silver, broken perhaps prematurely by some strange violence; and, on the centre of the lid, was a mysterious cypher, in the same metal. Catherine bent over it intently, but without being able to distinguish any thing with certainty. She could not, in whatever direction she took it, believe the last letter to be a T; and yet that it should be any thing else in that house was a circumstance to raise no common degree of astonishment. If not originally their's, by what strange events could it have fallen into the Tilney family?

Her fearful curiosity was every moment growing greater; and seizing, with trembling hands, the hasp of the lock, she resolved at all hazards to satisfy herself at least as to its contents. With difficulty, for something seemed to resist her efforts, she raised the lid a few inches; but at that moment a sudden knocking at the door of the room made her, starting, quit her hold, and the lid closed with alarming violence. This ill-timed intruder was Miss Tilney's maid, sent by her mistress to be of use to Miss Morland; and though Catherine immediately dismissed her, it recalled her to the sense of what she ought to be doing, and forced her, in spite of her anxious desire to penetrate this mystery, to proceed in her dressing without further delay. Her progress was not quick, for her thoughts and her eyes were still bent on the object so well calculated to interest and alarm; and though she dared not waste a moment upon a second attempt, she could not remain many paces from the chest. At length, however, having slipped one arm into her gown, her toilette seemed so nearly finished, that the impatience of her curiosity might safely be indulged. One moment surely might be spared; and, so desperate should be the exertion of her strength, that, unless secured by supernatural means, the lid in one moment should be thrown back. With this spirit she sprang forward, and her confidence did not deceive her. Her resolute effort threw back the lid, and gave to her astonished eyes the view of a white cotton counterpane, properly folded, reposing at one end of the chest in undisputed possession!

She was gazing on it with the first blush of surprize, when Miss Tilney, anxious for her friend's being ready, entered the room, and to the rising shame of having harboured for some minutes an absurd expectation, was then added the shame of being caught in so idle a search. "That is a curious old chest, is not it?" said Miss Tilney, as Catherine hastily closed it and turned away to the glass. "It is impossible to say how many generations it has been here. How it came to be first put in this room I know not, but I have not had it moved, because I thought it might sometimes be of use in holding hats and bonnets. The worst of it is that its weight makes it difficult to open. In that corner, however, it is at least out of the way."

Catherine had no leisure for speech, being at once blushing, tying her gown, and forming wise resolutions with the most violent dispatch. Miss Tilney gently hinted her fear of being late; and in half a minute they ran down stairs together, in alarm not wholly unfounded, for General Tilney was pacing the drawing-room, his watch in his hand, and having, on the very instant of their entering, pulled the bell with violence, ordered "Dinner to be on table *directly!*"

Catherine trembled at the emphasis with which he spoke, and sat pale and breathless, in a most humble mood, concerned for his children, and detesting old chests; and the General recovering his politeness as he looked at her, spent the rest of his time in scolding his daughter, for so foolishly hurrying her fair friend, who was absolutely out of breath from haste, when there was not the least occasion for hurry in the world: but Catherine could not at all get over the double distress of having involved her friend in a lecture and been a great simpleton herself, till they were happily seated at the dinner-table, when the General's complacent smiles, and a good appetite of her own, restored her to peace. The dining-parlour was a noble room, suitable in its dimensions to a much larger drawing-room than the one in common use, and fitted up in a style of luxury and expense which was almost lost on the unpractised eye of Catherine, who saw little more than its spaciousness and the number of their attendants. Of the former, she spoke aloud her admiration; and the General, with a very gracious countenance, acknowledged that it was by no means an ill-sized room; and further confessed, that, though as careless on such subjects as most people, he did look upon a tolerably large eating-room as one of the necessaries of life; he supposed, however, "that she must have been used to much better sized apartments at Mr. Allen's?"

"No, indeed," was Catherine's honest assurance; "Mr. Allen's dining-parlour was not more than half as large:" and she had never seen so large a room as this in her life. The General's good-humour increased. Why, as he *had* such rooms, he thought it would be simple not to make use of them; but, upon his honour, he believed there might be more comfort in rooms of only half their size. Mr. Allen's house, he was sure, must be exactly of the true size for rational happiness.

The evening passed without any further disturbance, and, in the occasional absence of General Tilney, with much positive cheerfulness. It was only in his presence that Catherine felt the smallest fatigue from her journey; and even then, even in moments of languor or restraint, a sense of general happiness preponderated, and she could think of her friends in Bath without one wish of being with them.

The night was stormy; the wind had been rising at intervals the whole afternoon; and by the time the party broke up, it blew and rained violently. Catherine, as she crossed the hall, listened to the tempest with sensations of awe; and, when she heard it rage round a corner of the ancient building and close with sudden fury a distant door, felt for the first time that she was really in an Abbey. Yes, these were characteristic sounds; they brought to her recollection a countless variety of dreadful situations and horrid scenes, which such buildings had witnessed, and such storms ushered in; and most heartily did she rejoice in the happier circumstances attending her entrance within walls so solemn! *She* had nothing to dread from midnight assassins or drunken gallants. Henry had certainly been only in jest in what he had told her that morning. In a house so furnished, and so guarded, she could have nothing to explore or to suffer; and might go to her bedroom as securely as if it had been her own chamber at Fullerton. Thus wisely fortifying her mind, as she proceeded up stairs, she was enabled, especially on perceiving that Miss Tilney slept only two doors from her, to enter her room with a tolerably stout heart; and her spirits were immediately assisted by the cheerful blaze of a wood fire. "How much better is this," said she, as she walked to the fender—"how much better to find a fire ready lit, than to have to wait shivering in the cold till all the family are in bed, as so many poor girls have been obliged to do, and then to have a faithful old servant frightening one by coming in with a faggot! How glad I am that Northanger is what it is! If it had been like some other places, I do not know that, in such a night as this, I could have answered for my courage: but now, to be sure, there is nothing to alarm one."

She looked round the room. The window curtains seemed in motion. It could be nothing but the violence of the wind penetrating through the divisions of the shutters; and she stept boldly forward, carelessly humming a tune, to assure herself of its being so, peeped courageously behind each curtain, saw nothing on either low window seat to scare her, and on placing a hand against the shutter, felt the strongest conviction of the wind's force. A glance at the old chest, as she turned away from this examination, was not without its use; she scorned the causeless fears of an idle fancy, and began with a most happy indifference to prepare herself for bed. "She should take her time; she should not hurry herself; she did not care if she were the last person up in the house. But she would not make up her fire; *that* would seem cowardly, as if she wished for the protection of light after she were in bed." The fire therefore died away, and Catherine, having spent the best part of an hour in her arrangements, was beginning to think of stepping into bed, when, on giving a parting glance round the room, she was struck by the appearance of a high, old-fashioned black cabinet, which, though in a situation conspicuous enough, had never caught her notice before. Henry's words, his description of the ebony cabinet which was to escape her observation at first, immediately rushed across her; and though there could be nothing really in it, there was something whimsical, it was certainly a very remarkable coincidence! She took her candle and looked closely at the cabinet. It was not absolutely ebony and gold; but it was Japan, black and yellow Japan of the handsomest kind; and as she held her candle, the yellow had very much the effect of gold. The key was in the door, and she had a strange fancy to look into it; not however with the smallest expectation of finding any thing, but it was so very odd, after what Henry had said. In short, she could not sleep till she had examined it. So, placing the candle with great caution on a chair, she seized the key with a very tremulous hand and tried to turn it; but it resisted her utmost strength. Alarmed, but not discouraged, she tried it another way; a bolt flew, and she believed herself successful; but how strangely mysterious! The door was still immoveable. She paused a moment in breathless wonder. The wind roared down the chimney, the rain beat in torrents against the windows, and every thing seemed to speak the awfulness of her situation. To retire to bed, however, unsatisfied on such a point, would be vain, since sleep must be impossible with the consciousness of a cabinet so mysteriously closed in her immediate vicinity. Again therefore she applied herself to the key, and after moving it in every possible way for some instants with the determined celerity of hope's last effort, the door suddenly yielded to her hand: her heart leaped with exultation at such a victory, and having thrown open each holding door, the second being secured only by bolts of less wonderful construction than the lock, though in that her eye could not discern any thing unusual, a double range of small drawers appeared in view, with some larger drawers above and below them; and in the centre, a small door, closed also with a lock and key, secured in all probability a cavity of importance.

Catherine's heart beat quick, but her courage did not fail her. With a cheek flushed by hope, and an eye straining with curiosity, her fingers grasped the handle of a drawer and drew it forth. It was entirely empty. With less alarm and greater eagerness she seized a second, a third, a fourth; each was equally empty. Not one was left unsearched, and in not one was any thing found. Well read in the art of concealing a treasure, the possibility of false linings to the drawers did not escape her, and she felt round each with anxious acuteness in vain. The place in the middle alone remained now unexplored; and though she had "never from the first had the smallest idea of finding any thing in any part of the cabinet, and was not in the least disappointed at her ill success thus far, it would be foolish not to examine it thoroughly while she was about it." It was some time however before she could unfasten the door, the same difficulty occurring in the management of this inner lock as of the outer; but at length it did open; and not vain, as hitherto, was her search; her quick eyes directly fell on a roll of paper pushed back into the further part of the cavity, apparently for concealment, and her feelings at that moment were indescribable. Her heart fluttered, her knees trembled, and her cheeks grew pale. She seized, with an unsteady hand, the precious manuscript, for half a glance sufficed to ascertain written characters; and while she acknowledged with awful sensations this striking exemplification of what Henry had foretold, resolved instantly to peruse every line before she attempted to rest.

The dimness of the light her candle emitted made her turn to it with alarm; but there was no danger of its sudden extinction, it had yet some hours to burn; and that she might not have any greater difficulty in distinguishing the writing than what its ancient date might occasion, she hastily snuffed it. Alas! it was snuffed and extinguished in one. A lamp could not have expired with more awful effect. Catherine, for a few moments, was motionless with horror. It was done completely; not a remnant of light in the wick could give hope to the rekindling breath. Darkness impenetrable and immoveable filled the room. A violent gust of wind, rising with sudden fury, added fresh horror to the moment. Catherine trembled from head to foot. In the pause which succeeded, a sound like receding footsteps and the closing of a distant door struck on her affrighted ear. Human nature could support no more. A cold sweat stood on her forehead, the manuscript fell from her hand, and groping her way to the bed, she jumped hastily in, and sought some suspension of agony by creeping far underneath the clothes. To close her eyes in sleep that night, she felt must be entirely out of the question. With a curiosity so justly awakened, and feelings in every way so agitated, repose must be absolutely impossible. The storm too abroad so dreadful! She had not been used to feel alarm from wind, but now every blast seemed fraught with awful intelligence. The manuscript so wonderfully found, so wonderfully accomplishing the morning's prediction, how was it to be accounted for? What could it contain? To whom could it relate? By what means could it have been so long concealed? And how singularly strange that it should fall to her lot to discover it! Till she had made herself mistress of its contents, however, she could have neither repose nor comfort; and with the sun's first rays she was determined to peruse it. But many were the tedious hours which must yet intervene. She shuddered, tossed about in her bed, and envied every quiet sleeper. The storm still raged, and various were the noises, more terrific even than the wind, which struck at intervals on her startled ear. The very curtains of her bed seemed at one moment in motion, and at another the lock of her door was agitated, as if by the attempt of somebody to enter. Hollow murmurs seemed to creep along the gallery, and more than once her blood was chilled by the sound of distant moans. Hour after hour passed away, and the wearied Catherine had heard three proclaimed by all the clocks in the house, before the tempest subsided, or she unknowingly fell fast asleep.

Chapter VII

The housemaid's folding back her window-shutters at eight o'clock the next day, was the sound which first roused Catherine; and she opened her eyes, wondering that they could ever have been closed, on objects of cheerfulness; her fire was already burning, and a bright morning had succeeded the tempest of the night. Instantaneously with the consciousness of existence, returned her recollection of the manuscript; and springing from the bed in the very moment of the maid's going away, she eagerly collected every scattered sheet which had burst from the roll on its falling to the ground, and flew back to enjoy the luxury of their perusal on her pillow. She now plainly saw that she must not expect a manuscript of equal length with the generality of what she had shuddered over in books, for the roll, seeming to consist entirely of small disjointed sheets, was altogether but of trifling size, and much less than she had supposed it to be at first.

Her greedy eye glanced rapidly over a page. She started at its import. Could it be possible, or did not her senses play her false? An inventory of linen, in coarse and modern characters, seemed all that was before her! If the evidence of sight might be trusted, she held a washing-bill in her hand. She seized another sheet, and saw the same articles with little variation; a third, a fourth, and a fifth presented nothing new. Shirts, stockings, cravats and waistcoats faced her in each. Two others, penned by the same hand, marked an expenditure scarcely more interesting, in letters, hair-powder, shoe-string and breeches-ball. And the larger sheet, which had inclosed the rest, seemed by its first cramp line, "To poultice chesnut mare,"—a farrier's bill! Such was the collection of papers, (left perhaps, as she could then suppose, by the negligence of a servant in the place whence she had taken them,) which had filled her with expectation and alarm, and robbed her of half her night's rest! She felt humbled to the dust. Could not the adventure of the chest have taught her wisdom? A corner of it catching her eye as she lay, seemed to rise up in judgment against her. Nothing could now be clearer than the absurdity of her recent fancies. To suppose that a manuscript of many generations back could have remained undiscovered in a room such as that, so modern, so habitable!—or that she should be the first to possess the skill of unlocking a cabinet, the key of which was open to all!

How could she have so imposed on herself? Heaven forbid that Henry Tilney should ever know her folly! And it was in a great measure his own doing, for had not the cabinet appeared so exactly to agree with his description of her adventures, she should never have felt the smallest curiosity about it. This was the only comfort that occurred. Impatient to get rid of those hateful evidences of her folly, those detestable papers then scattered over the bed, she rose directly, and folding them up as nearly as possible in the same shape as before, returned them to the same spot within the cabinet, with a very hearty wish that no untoward accident might ever bring them forward again, to disgrace her even with herself.

Why the locks should have been so difficult to open however, was still something remarkable, for she could now manage them with perfect ease. In this there was surely something mysterious, and she indulged in the flattering suggestion for half a minute, till the possibility of the door's having been at first unlocked, and of being herself its fastener, darted into her head, and cost her another blush.

She got away as soon as she could from a room in which her conduct produced such unpleasant reflections, and found her way with all speed to the breakfast-parlour, as it had been pointed out to her by Miss Tilney the evening before. Henry was alone in it; and his immediate hope of her having been undisturbed by the tempest, with an arch reference to the character of the building they inhabited, was rather distressing. For the world would she not have her weakness suspected; and yet, unequal to an absolute falsehood, was constrained to acknowledge that the wind had kept her awake a little. "But we have a charming morning after it," she added, desiring to get rid of the subject; "and storms and sleeplessness are nothing when they are over. What beautiful hyacinths! I have just learnt to love a hyacinth."

"And how might you learn? By accident or argument?"

"Your sister taught me; I cannot tell how. Mrs. Allen used to take pains, year after year, to make me like them; but I never could, till I saw them the other day in Milsom-street; I am naturally indifferent about flowers."

"But now you love a hyacinth. So much the better. You have gained a new source of enjoyment, and it is well to have as many holds upon happiness as possible. Besides, a taste for flowers is always desirable in your sex, as a means of getting you out of doors, and tempting you to more frequent exercise than you would otherwise take. And though the love of a hyacinth may be rather domestic, who can tell, the sentiment once raised, but you may in time come to love a rose?"

"But I do not want any such pursuit to get me out of doors. The pleasure of walking and breathing fresh air is enough for me, and in fine weather I am out more than half my time. Mamma says, I am never within."

"At any rate, however, I am pleased that you have learnt to love a hyacinth. The mere habit of learning to love is the thing; and a teachableness of disposition in a young lady is a great blessing. Has my sister a pleasant mode of instruction?"

Catherine was saved the embarrassment of attempting an answer, by the entrance of the General, whose smiling compliments announced a happy state of mind, but whose gentle hint of sympathetic early rising did not advance her composure.

The elegance of the breakfast set forced itself on Catherine's notice when they were seated at table; and, luckily, it had been the General's choice. He was enchanted by her approbation of his taste, confessed it to be neat and simple, thought it right to encourage the manufacture of his country; and for his part, to his uncritical palate, the tea was as well flavoured from the clay of Staffordshire, as from that of Dresden or Sève. But this was quite an old set, purchased two years ago. The manufacture was much improved since that time; he had seen some beautiful specimens when last in town, and had he not been perfectly without vanity of that kind, might have been tempted to order a new set. He trusted, however, that an opportunity might ere long occur of selecting one—though not for himself. Catherine was probably the only one of the part who did not understand him.

Shortly after breakfast Henry left them for Woodston, where business required and would keep him two or three days. They all attended in the hall to see him mount his horse, and immediately on re-entering the breakfast room, Catherine walked to a window in the hope of catching another glimpse of his figure. "This is a somewhat heavy call upon your brother's fortitude," observed the General to Eleanor. "Woodston will make but a sombre appearance to-day."

"Is it a pretty place?" asked Catherine.

"What say you, Eleanor? Speak your opinion, for ladies can best tell the taste of ladies in regard to places as well as men. I think it would be acknowledged by the most impartial eye to have many recommendations. The house stands among fine meadows facing the southeast, with an excellent kitchen-garden in the same aspect; the walls surrounding which I built and stocked myself about ten years ago, for the benefit of my son. It is a family living, Miss Morland; and the property in the place being chiefly my own, you may believe I take care that it shall not be a bad one. Did Henry's income depend solely on this living, he would not be ill provided for. Perhaps it may seem odd, that with only two younger children, I should think any profession necessary for him; and certainly there are moments when we could all wish him disengaged from every tie of business. But though I may not exactly make converts of you young ladies, I am sure your father, Miss Morland, would agree with me in thinking it expedient to give every young man some employment. The money is nothing, it is not an object, but employment is the thing. Even Frederick, my eldest son, you see, who will perhaps inherit as considerable a landed property as any private man in the county, has his profession."

The imposing effect of this last argument was equal to his wishes. The silence of the lady proved it to be unanswerable.

Something had been said the evening before of her being shewn over the house, and he now offered himself as her conductor; and though Catherine had hoped to explore it accompanied only by his daughter, it was a proposal of too much happiness in itself, under any circumstances, not to be gladly accepted; for she had been already eighteen hours in the Abbey, and had seen only a few of its rooms. The netting-box, just leisurely drawn forth, was closed with joyful haste, and she was ready to attend him in a moment. "And when they had gone over the house, he promised himself moreover the pleasure of accompanying her into the shrubberies and garden." She curtsied her acquiescence. "But perhaps it might be more agreeable to her to make those her first object. The weather was at present favourable, and at this time of year the uncertainty was very great of its continuing so. Which would she prefer? He was equally at her service. Which did his daughter think would most accord with her fair friend's wishes? But he thought he could discern. Yes, he certainly read in Miss Morland's eyes a judicious desire of making use of the present smiling weather. But when did she judge amiss? The Abbey would be always safe and dry. He yielded implicitly, and would fetch his hat and attend them in a moment." He left the room, and Catherine, with a disappointed, anxious face, began to speak of her unwillingness that he should be taking them out of doors against his own inclination, under a mistaken idea of pleasing her; but she was stopt by Miss Tilney's saying, with a little confusion, "I believe it will be wisest to take the morning while it is so fine; and do not be uneasy on my father's account, he always walks out at this time of day."

Catherine did not exactly know how this was to be understood. Why was Miss Tilney embarrassed? Could there be any unwillingness on the General's side to shew her over the Abbey? The proposal was his own. And was not it odd that he should *always* take his walk so early? Neither her father nor Mr. Allen did so. It was certainly very provoking. She was all impatience to see the house, and had scarcely any curiosity about the grounds. If Henry had been with them indeed! but now she should not know what was picturesque when she saw it. Such were her thoughts, but she kept them to herself, and put on her bonnet in patient discontent.

She was struck however, beyond her expectation, by the grandeur of the Abbey, as she saw it for the first time from the lawn. The whole building enclosed a large court; and two sides of the quadrangle, rich in Gothic ornaments, stood forward for admiration. The remainder was shut off by knolls of old trees, or luxuriant plantations, and the steep woody hills rising behind to give it shelter, were beautiful even in the leafless month of March. Catherine had seen nothing to compare with it; and her feelings of delight were so strong, that without waiting for any better authority, she boldly burst forth in wonder and praise. The General listened with assenting gratitude; and it seemed as if his own estimation of Northanger had waited unfixed till that hour.

The kitchen-garden was to be next admired, and he led the way to it across a small portion of the park.

The number of acres contained in this garden was such as Catherine could not listen to without dismay, being more than double the extent of all Mr. Allen's, as well as her father's, including church-yard and orchard. The walls seemed countless in number, endless in length; a village of hot-houses seemed to arise among them, and a whole parish to be at work within the inclosure. The General was flattered by her looks of surprize, which told him almost as plainly, as he soon forced her to tell him in words, that she had never seen any gardens at all equal to them before; and he then modestly owned that, "without any ambition of that sort himself—without any solicitude about it, he did believe them to be unrivalled in the kingdom. If he had a hobby-horse, it was *that*. He loved a garden. Though careless enough in most matters of eating, he loved good fruit—or if he did not, his friends and children did. There were great vexations however attending such a garden as his. The utmost care could not always secure the most valuable fruits. The pinery had yielded only one hundred in the last year. Mr. Allen, he supposed, must feel these inconveniences as well as himself."

"No, not at all. Mr. Allen did not care about the garden, and never went into it."

With a triumphant smile of self-satisfaction, the General wished he could do the same, for he never entered his, without being vexed in some way or other, by its falling short of his plan.

"How were Mr. Allen's succession-houses worked?" describing the nature of his own as they entered them.

"Mr. Allen had only one small hot-house, which Mrs. Allen had the use of for her plants in winter, and there was a fire in it now and then."

"He is a happy man!" said the General, with a look of very happy contempt.

Having taken her into every division, and led her under every wall, till she was heartily weary of seeing and wondering, he suffered the girls at last to seize the advantage of an outer door, and then expressing his wish to examine the effect of some recent alterations about the tea-house, proposed it as no unpleasant extension of their walk, if Miss Morland were not tired. "But where are you going, Eleanor?—Why do you chuse that cold, damp path to it? Miss Morland will get wet. Our best way is across the park."

"This is so favourite a walk of mine," said Miss Tilney, "that I always think it the best and nearest way. But perhaps it may be damp."

It was a narrow winding path through a thick grove of old Scotch firs; and Catherine, struck by its gloomy aspect, and eager to enter it, could not, even by the General's disapprobation, be kept from stepping forward. He perceived her inclination, and having again urged the plea of health in vain, was too polite to make further opposition. He excused himself however from attending them: "The rays of the sun were not too cheerful for him, and he would meet them by another course." He turned away; and Catherine was shocked to find how much her spirits were relieved by the separation. The shock however being less real than the relief, offered it no injury; and she began to talk with easy gaiety of the delightful melancholy which such a grove inspired.

"I am particularly fond of this spot," said her companion, with a sigh. "It was my mother's favourite walk."

Catherine had never heard Mrs. Tilney mentioned in the family before, and the interest excited by this tender remembrance, shewed itself directly in her altered countenance, and in the attentive pause with which she waited for something more.

"I used to walk here so often with her!" added Eleanor; "though I never loved it then, as I have loved it since. At that time indeed I used to wonder at her choice. But her memory endears it now."

"And ought it not," reflected Catherine, "to endear it to her husband? Yet the General would not enter it." Miss Tilney continuing silent, she ventured to say, "Her death must have been a great affliction!"

"A great and increasing one," replied the other, in a low voice. "I was only thirteen when it happened; and though I felt my loss perhaps as strongly as one so young could feel it, I did not, I could not then know what a loss it was." She stopped for a moment, and then added, with great firmness, "I have no sister, you know—and though Henry—though my brothers are very affectionate, and Henry is a great deal here, which I am most thankful for, it is impossible for me not to be often solitary."

"To be sure you must miss him very much."

"A mother would have been always present. A mother would have been a constant friend; her influence would have been beyond all other."

"Was she a very charming woman? Was she handsome? Was there any picture of her in the Abbey? And why had she been so partial to that grove? Was it from dejection of spirits?"—were questions now eagerly poured forth; the first three received a ready affirmative, the two others were passed by; and Catherine's interest in the deceased Mrs. Tilney augmented with every question, whether answered or not. Of her unhappiness in marriage, she felt persuaded. The General certainly had been an unkind husband. He did not love her walk: could he therefore have loved her? And besides, handsome as he was, there was a something in the turn of his features which spoke his not having behaved well to her.

"Her picture, I suppose," blushing at the consummate art of her own question, "hangs in your father's room?"

"No; it was intended for the drawing-room; but my father was dissatisfied with the painting, and for some time it had no place. Soon after her death I obtained it for my own, and hung it in my bed-chamber—where I shall be happy to shew it you; it is very like." Here was another proof. A portrait—very like—of a departed wife, not valued by the husband! He must have been dreadfully cruel to her!

Catherine attempted no longer to hide from herself the nature of the feelings which, in spite of all his attentions, he had previously excited; and what had been terror and dislike before, was now absolute aversion. Yes, aversion! His cruelty to such a charming woman made him odious to her. She had often read of such characters; characters, which Mr. Allen had been used to call unnatural and overdrawn; but here was proof positive of the contrary.

She had just settled this point, when the end of the path brought them directly upon the General; and in spite of all her virtuous indignation, she found herself again obliged to walk with him, listen to him, and even to smile when he smiled. Being no longer able however to receive pleasure from the surrounding objects, she soon began to walk with lassitude; the General perceived it, and with a concern for her health, which seemed to reproach her for her opinion of him, was most urgent for returning with his daughter to the house. He would follow them in a quarter of an hour. Again they parted—but Eleanor was called back in half a minute to receive a strict charge against taking her friend round the Abbey till his return. This second instance of his anxiety to delay what she so much wished for, struck Catherine as very remarkable.

CHAPTER VIII

An hour passed away before the General came in, spent, on the part of his young guest, in no very favourable consideration of his character. "This lengthened absence, these solitary rambles, did not speak a mind at ease, or a conscience void of reproach." At length he appeared; and, whatever might have been the gloom of his meditations, he could still smile with *them*. Miss Tilney, understanding in part her friend's curiosity to see the house, soon revived the subject; and her father being, contrary to Catherine's expectations, unprovided with any pretence for further delay, beyond that of stopping five minutes to order refreshments to be in the room by their return, was at last ready to escort them.

They set forward; and, with a grandeur of air, a dignified step, which caught the eye, but could not shake the doubts of the well-read Catherine, he led the way across the hall, through the common drawing-room and one useless anti-chamber, into a room magnificent both in size and furniture—the real drawing-room, used only with company of consequence. It was very noble—very grand—very charming!—was all that Catherine had to say, for her indiscriminating eye scarcely discerned the colour of the satin; and all minuteness of praise, all praise that had much meaning, was supplied by the General: the costliness or elegance of any room's fitting-up could be nothing to her; she cared for no furniture of a more modern date than the fifteenth century. When the General had satisfied his own curiosity, in a close examination of every well-known ornament, they proceeded into the library, an apartment, in its way, of equal magnificence, exhibiting a collection of books, on which an humble man might have looked with pride. Catherine heard, admired, and wondered with more genuine feeling than before—gathered all that she could from this storehouse of knowledge, by running over the titles of half a shelf, and was ready to proceed. But suites of apartments did not spring up with her wishes. Large as was the building, she had already visited the greatest part; though, on being told that, with the addition of the kitchen, the six or seven rooms she had now seen surrounded three sides of the court, she could scarcely believe it, or overcome the suspicion of there being many chambers secreted. It was some relief, however, that they were to return to the rooms in common use, by passing through a few of less importance, looking into the court, which, with occasional passages, not wholly unintricate, connected the different sides; and she was further soothed in her progress, by being told, that she was treading what had once been a cloister, having traces of cells pointed out, and observing several doors, that were neither opened nor explained to her; by finding herself successively in a billiard-room, and in the General's private apartment, without comprehending their connexion, or being able to turn aright when she left them; and lastly, by passing through a dark little room, owning Henry's authority, and strewed with his litter of books, guns, and great coats.

From the dining-room of which, though already seen, and always to be seen at five o'clock, the General could not forgo the pleasure of pacing out the length, for the more certain information of Miss Morland, as to what she neither doubted nor cared for, they proceeded by quick communication to the kitchen—the ancient kitchen of the convent, rich in the massy walls and smoke of former days, and in the stoves and hot closets of the present. The General's improving hand had not loitered here: every modern invention to facilitate the labour of the cooks, had been adopted within this, their spacious theatre; and, when the genius of others had failed, his own had often produced the perfection wanted. His endowments of this spot alone might at any time have placed him high among the benefactors of the convent.

With the walls of the kitchen ended all the antiquity of the Abbey; the fourth side of the quadrangle having, on account of its decaying state, been removed by the General's father, and the present erected in its place. All that was venerable ceased here. The new building was not only new, but declared itself to be so; intended only for offices, and enclosed behind by stable-yards, no uniformity of architecture had been thought necessary. Catherine could have raved at the hand which had swept away what must have been beyond the value of all the rest, for the purposes of mere domestic economy; and would willingly have been spared the mortification of a walk through scenes so fallen, had the General allowed it; but if he had a vanity, it was in the arrangement of his offices; and as he was convinced, that, to a mind like Miss Morland's, a view of the accommodations and comforts, by which the labours of her inferiors were softened, must always be gratifying, he should make no apology for leading her on. They took a slight survey of all; and Catherine was impressed, beyond her expectation, by their multiplicity and their convenience. The purposes for which a few shapeless pantries and a comfortless scullery were deemed sufficient at Fullerton, were here carried on in appropriate divisions, commodious and roomy. The number of servants continually appearing, did not strike her less than the number of their offices. Wherever they went, some pattened girl stopped to curtsey, or some footman in dishabille sneaked off. Yet this was an Abbey! How inexpressibly different in these domestic arrangements from such as she had read about—from abbeys and castles, in which, though certainly larger than Northanger, all the dirty work of the house was to be done by two pair of female hands at the utmost. How they could get through it all, had often amazed Mrs. Allen; and, when Catherine saw what was necessary here, she began to be amazed herself.

They returned to the hall, that the chief stair-case might be ascended, and the beauty of its wood, and ornaments of rich carving might be pointed out: having gained the top, they turned in an opposite direction from the gallery in which her room lay, and shortly entered one on the same plan, but superior in length and breadth. She was here shewn successively into three large bed-chambers, with their dressing-rooms, most completely and handsomely fitted up; every thing that money and taste could do, to give comfort and elegance to apartments, had been bestowed on these; and, being furnished within the last five years, they were perfect in all that would be generally pleasing, and wanting in all that could give pleasure to Catherine. As they were surveying the last, the General, after slightly naming a few of the distinguished characters, by whom they had at times been honoured, turned with a smiling countenance to Catherine, and ventured to hope, that henceforward some of their earliest tenants might be "our friends from Fullerton." She felt the unexpected compliment, and deeply regretted the impossibility of thinking well of a man so kindly disposed towards herself, and so full of civility to all her family.

The gallery was terminated by folding doors, which Miss Tilney, advancing, had thrown open, and passed through, and seemed on the point of doing the same by the first door to the left, in another long reach of gallery, when the General, coming forwards, called her hastily, and, as Catherine thought, rather angrily back, demanding whither she were going? And what was there more to be seen? Had not Miss Morland already seen all that could be worth her notice? And did she not suppose her friend might be glad of some refreshment after so much exercise? Miss Tilney drew back directly, and the heavy doors were closed upon the mortified Catherine, who, having seen, in a momentary glance beyond them, a narrower passage, more numerous openings, and symptoms of a winding stair-case, believed herself at last within the reach of something worth her notice; and felt, as she unwillingly paced back the gallery, that she would rather be allowed to examine that end of the house, than see all the finery of all the rest. The General's evident desire of preventing such an examination was an additional stimulant. Something was certainly to be concealed; her fancy, though it had trespassed lately once or twice, could not mislead her here; and what that something was, a short sentence of Miss Tilney's, as they followed the General at some distance down stairs, seemed to point out: "I was going to take you into what was my mother's room—the room in which she died———" were all her words; but few as they were, they conveyed pages of intelligence to Catherine. It was no wonder that the General should shrink from the sight of such objects as that room must contain; a room in all probability never entered by him since the dreadful scene had passed, which released his suffering wife, and left him to the stings of conscience.

She ventured, when next alone with Eleanor, to express her wish of being permitted to see it, as well as all the rest of that side of the house; and Eleanor promised to attend her there, whenever they should have a convenient hour. Catherine understood her: the General must be watched from home, before that room could be entered. "It remains as it was, I suppose?" said she, in a tone of feeling.

"Yes, entirely."

"And how long ago may it be that your mother died?"

"She has been dead these nine years." And nine years, Catherine knew was a trifle of time, compared with what generally elapsed after the death of an injured wife, before her room was put to rights.

"You were with her, I suppose, to the last?"

"No," said Miss Tilney, sighing; "I was unfortunately from home. Her illness was sudden and short; and, before I arrived it was all over."

Catherine's blood ran cold with the horrid suggestions which naturally sprang from these words. Could it be possible? Could Henry's father?——And yet how many were the examples to justify even the blackest suspicions! And, when she saw him in the evening, while she worked with her friend, slowly pacing the drawing-room for an hour together in silent thoughtfulness, with downcast eyes and contracted brow, she felt secure from all possibility of wronging him. It was the air and attitude of a Montoni! What could more plainly speak the gloomy workings of a mind not wholly dead to every sense of humanity, in its fearful review of past scenes of guilt? Unhappy man! And the anxiousness of her spirits directed her eyes towards his figure so repeatedly, as to catch Miss Tilney's notice. "My father," she whispered, "often walks about the room in this way; it is nothing unusual."

"So much the worse!" thought Catherine; such ill-timed exercise was of a piece with the strange unseasonableness of his morning walks, and boded nothing good.

After an evening, the little variety and seeming length of which made her peculiarly sensible of Henry's importance among them, she was heartily glad to be dismissed; though it was a look from the General not designed for her observation which sent his daughter to the bell. When the butler would have lit his master's candle, however, he was forbidden. The latter was not going to retire. "I have many pamphlets to finish," said he to Catherine, "before I can close my eyes; and perhaps may be poring over the affairs of the nation for hours after you are asleep. Can either of us be more meetly employed? My eyes will be blinding for the good of others; and *yours* preparing by rest for future mischief."

But neither the business alleged, nor the magnificent compliment, could win Catherine from thinking, that some very different object must occasion so serious a delay of proper repose. To be kept up for hours, after the family were in bed, by stupid pamphlets, was not very likely. There must be some deeper cause: something was to be done which could be done only while the household slept; and the probability that Mrs. Tilney yet lived, shut up for causes unknown, and receiving from the pitiless hands of her husband a nightly supply of coarse food, was the conclusion which necessarily followed. Shocking as was the idea, it was at least better than a death unfairly hastened, as, in the natural course of things, she must ere long be released. The suddenness of her reputed illness; the absence of her daughter, and probably of her other children, at the time—all favoured the supposition of her imprisonment. Its origin—jealousy perhaps, or wanton cruelty—was yet to be unravelled.

In revolving these matters, while she undressed, it suddenly struck her as not unlikely, that she might that morning have passed near the very spot of this unfortunate woman's confinement—might have been within a few paces of the cell in which she languished out her days; for what part of the Abbey could be more fitted for the purpose than that which yet bore the traces of monastic division? In the high-arched passage, paved with stone, which already she had trodden with peculiar awe, she well remembered the doors of which the General had given no account. To what might not those doors lead? In support of the plausibility of this conjecture, it further occurred to her, that the forbidden gallery, in which lay the apartments of the unfortunate Mrs. Tilney, must be, as certainly as her memory could guide her, exactly over this suspected range of cells, and the stair-case by the side of those apartments of which she had caught a transient glimpse, communicating by some secret means with those cells, might well have favoured the barbarous proceedings of her husband. Down that stair-case she had perhaps been conveyed in a state of well-prepared insensibility!

Catherine sometimes started at the boldness of her own surmises, and sometimes hoped or feared that she had gone too far; but they were supported by such appearances as made their dismissal impossible.

The side of the quadrangle, in which she supposed the guilty scene to be acting, being, according to her belief, just opposite her own, it struck her that, if judiciously watched, some rays of light from the General's lamp might glimmer through the lower windows, as he passed to the prison of his wife; and, twice before she stepped into bed, she stole gently from her room to the corresponding window in the gallery, to see if it appeared; but all abroad was dark, and it must yet be too early. The various ascending noises convinced her that the servants must still be up. Till midnight, she supposed it would be in vain to watch; but then, when the clock had struck twelve, and all was quiet, she would, if not quite appalled by darkness, steal out and look once more. The clock struck twelve—and Catherine had been half an hour asleep.

CHAPTER IX

The next day afforded no opportunity for the proposed examination of the mysterious apartments. It was Sunday, and the whole time between morning and afternoon service was required by the General in exercise abroad or eating cold meat at home; and great as was Catherine's curiosity, her courage was not equal to a wish of exploring them after dinner, either by the fading light of the sky between six and seven o'clock, or by the yet more partial though stronger illumination of a treacherous lamp. The day was unmarked therefore by any thing to interest her imagination beyond the sight of a very elegant monument to the memory of Mrs. Tilney, which immediately fronted the family pew. By that her eye was instantly caught and long retained; and the perusal of the highly-strained epitaph, in which every virtue was ascribed to her by the inconsolable husband, who must have been in some way or other her destroyer, affected her even to tears.

That the General, having erected such a monument, should be able to face it, was not perhaps very strange, and yet that he could sit so boldly collected within its view, maintain so elevated an air, look so fearlessly around, nay, that he should even enter the church, seemed wonderful to Catherine. Not however that many instances of beings equally hardened in guilt might not be produced. She could remember dozens who had persevered in every possible vice, going on from crime to crime, murdering whomsoever they chose, without any feeling of humanity or remorse; till a violent death or a religious retirement closed their black career. The erection of the monument itself could not in the smallest degree affect her doubts of Mrs. Tilney's actual decease. Were she even to descend into the family vault where her ashes were supposed to slumber, were she to behold the coffin in which they were said to be enclosed—what could it avail in such a case? Catherine had read too much not to be perfectly aware of the ease with which a waxen figure might be introduced, and a supposititious funeral carried on.

The succeeding morning promised something better. The General's early walk, ill-timed as it was in every other view, was favourable here; and when she knew him to be out of the house, she directly proposed to Miss Tilney the accomplishment of her promise. Eleanor was ready to oblige her; and Catherine reminding her as they went of another promise, their first visit in consequence was to the portrait in her bed-chamber. It represented a very lovely woman, with a mild and pensive countenance, justifying, so far, the expectations of its new observer; but they were not in every respect answered, for Catherine had depended upon meeting with features, air, complexion that should be the very counterpart, the very image, if not of Henry's, of Eleanor's;—the only portraits of which she had been in the habit of thinking, bearing always an equal resemblance of mother and child. A face once taken was taken for generations. But here she was obliged to look and consider and study for a likeness. She contemplated it, however, in spite of this drawback, with much emotion; and, but for a yet stronger interest, would have left it unwillingly.

Her agitation as they entered the great gallery was too much for any endeavour at discourse; she could only look at her companion. Eleanor's countenance was dejected, yet sedate; and its composure spoke her enured to all the gloomy objects to which they were advancing. Again she passed through the folding-doors, again her hand was upon the important lock, and Catherine, hardly able to breathe, was turning to close the former with fearful caution, when the figure, the dreaded figure of the General himself at the further end of the gallery, stood before her! The name of "Eleanor" at the same moment, in his loudest tone, resounded through the building, giving to his daughter the first intimation of his presence, and to Catherine terror upon terror. An attempt at concealment had been her first instinctive movement on perceiving him, yet she could scarcely hope to have escaped his eye; and when her friend, who with an apologizing look darted hastily by her, had joined and disappeared with him, she ran for safety to her own room, and, locking herself in, believed that she should never have courage to go down again. She remained there at least an hour, in the greatest agitation, deeply commiserating the state of her poor friend, and expecting a summons herself from the angry General to attend him in his own apartment. No summons however arrived; and at last, on seeing a carriage drive up to the Abbey, she was emboldened to descend and meet him under the protection of visitors. The breakfast-room was gay with company; and she was named to them by the General, as the friend of his daughter, in a complimentary style, which so well concealed his resentful ire, as to make her feel secure at least of life for the present. And Eleanor, with a command of countenance which did honour to her concern for his character, taking an early occasion of saying to her, "My father only wanted me to answer a note," she began to hope that she had either been unseen by the General, or that from some consideration of policy she should be allowed to suppose herself so.

Upon this trust she dared still to remain in his presence, after the company left them, and nothing occurred to disturb it.

In the course of this morning's reflections, she came to a resolution of making her next attempt on the forbidden door alone. It would be much better in every respect that Eleanor should know nothing of the matter. To involve her in the danger of a second detection, to court her into an apartment which must wring her heart, could not be the office of a friend. The General's utmost anger could not be to herself what it might be to a daughter; and, besides, she thought the examination itself would be more satisfactory if made without any companion. It would be impossible to explain to Eleanor the suspicions, from which the other had, in all likelihood, been hitherto happily exempt; nor could she therefore, in *her* presence, search for those proofs of the General's cruelty, which however they might yet have escaped discovery, she felt confident of somewhere drawing forth, in the shape of some fragmented journal, continued to the last gasp. Of the way to the apartment she was now perfectly mistress; and as she wished to get it over before Henry's return, who was expected on the morrow, there was no time to be lost. The day was bright, her courage high; at four o'clock, the sun was now two hours above the horizon, and it would be only her retiring to dress half an hour earlier than usual.

It was done; and Catherine found herself alone in the gallery before the clocks had ceased to strike. It was no time for thought; she hurried on, slipped with the least possible noise through the folding doors, and without stopping to look or breathe, rushed forward to the one in question. The lock yielded to her hand, and, luckily, with no sullen sound that could alarm a human being. On tip-toe she entered; the room was before her; but it was some minutes before she could advance another step. She beheld what fixed her to the spot and agitated every feature. She saw a large, well-proportioned apartment, an handsome dimity bed, arranged as unoccupied with an housemaid's care, a bright Bath stove, mahogany wardrobes and neatly-painted chairs, on which the warm beams of a western sun gaily poured through two sash windows! Catherine had expected to have her feelings worked, and worked they were. Astonishment and doubt first seized them; and a shortly succeeding ray of common sense added some bitter emotions of shame. She could not be mistaken as to the room; but how grossly mistaken in every thing else! in Miss Tilney's meaning, in her own calculation! This apartment, to which she had given a date so ancient, a position so awful, proved to be one end of what the General's father had built. There were two other doors in the chamber, leading probably into dressing-closets; but she had no inclination to open either. Would the veil in which Mrs. Tilney had last walked, or the volume in which she had last read, remain to tell what nothing else was allowed to whisper? No: whatever might have been the General's crimes, he had certainly too much wit to let them sue for detection. She was sick of exploring, and desired but to be safe in her own room, with her own heart only privy to its folly; and she was on the point of retreating as softly as she had entered, when the sound of footsteps, she could hardly tell where, made her pause and tremble. To be found there, even by a servant, would be unpleasant; but by the General, (and he seemed always at hand when least wanted,) much worse! She listened—the sound had ceased; and resolving not to lose a moment, she passed through and closed the door. At that instant a door underneath was hastily opened; some one seemed with swift steps to ascend the stairs, by the head of which she had yet to pass before she could gain the gallery. She had no power to move. With a feeling of terror not very definable, she fixed her eyes on the staircase, and in a few moments it gave Henry to her view. "Mr. Tilney!" she exclaimed in a voice of more than common astonishment. He looked astonished too. "Good God!" she continued, not attending to his address, "how came you here? How came you up that staircase?"

"How came I up that staircase!" he replied, greatly surprised. "Because it is my nearest way from the stable-yard to my own chamber; and why should I not come up it?"

Catherine recollected herself, blushed deeply, and could say no more. He seemed to be looking in her countenance for that explanation which her lips did not afford. She moved on towards the gallery. "And may I not, in my turn," said he, as he pushed back the folding doors, "ask how *you* came here? This passage is at least as extraordinary a road from the breakfast-parlour to your apartment, as that staircase can be from the stables to mine."

"I have been," said Catherine, looking down, "to see your mother's room."

"My mother's room! Is there any thing extraordinary to be seen there?"

"No, nothing at all. I thought you did not mean to come back till to-morrow."

"I did not expect to be able to return sooner, when I went away; but three hours ago I had the pleasure of finding nothing to detain me. You look pale. I am afraid I alarmed you by running so fast up those stairs. Perhaps you did not know—you were not aware of their leading from the offices in common use?"

"No, I was not. You have had a very fine day for your ride."

"Very; and does Eleanor leave you to find your way into all the rooms in the house by yourself?"

"Oh! no; she shewed me over the greatest part on Saturday—and we were coming here to these rooms—but only—(dropping her voice)—your father was with us."

"And that prevented you;" said Henry, earnestly regarding her. "Have you looked into all the rooms in that passage?"

"No, I only wanted to see——Is not it very late? I must go and dress."

"It is only a quarter past four, (shewing his watch) and you are not now in Bath. No theatre, no rooms to prepare for. Half an hour at Northanger must be enough."

She could not contradict it, and therefore suffered herself to be detained, though her dread of further questions made her, for the first time in their acquaintance, wish to leave him. They walked slowly up the gallery. "Have you had any letter from Bath since I saw you?"

"No, and I am very much surprised. Isabella promised so faithfully to write directly."

"Promised so faithfully! A faithful promise! That puzzles me. I have heard of a faithful performance. But a faithful promise—the fidelity of promising! It is a power little worth knowing however, since it can deceive and pain you. My mother's room is very commodious, is it not? Large and cheerful-looking, and the dressing closets so well disposed! It always strikes me as the most comfortable apartment in the house, and I rather wonder that Eleanor should not take it for her own. She sent you to look at it, I suppose?"

"No."

"It has been your own doing entirely?" Catherine said nothing. After a short silence, during which he had closely observed her, he added, "As there is nothing in the room in itself to raise curiosity, this must have proceeded from a sentiment of respect for my mother's character, as described by Eleanor, which does honour to her memory. The world, I believe, never saw a better woman. But it is not often that virtue can boast an interest such as this. The domestic, unpretending merits of a person never known, do not often create that kind of fervent, venerating tenderness which would prompt a visit like yours. Eleanor, I suppose, has talked of her a great deal?"

"Yes, a great deal. That is—no, not much, but what she did say, was very interesting. Her dying so suddenly," (slowly, and with hesitation it was spoken,) "and you—none of you being at home—and your father, I thought—perhaps had not been very fond of her."

"And from these circumstances," he replied, (his quick eye fixed on her's,) "you infer perhaps the probability of some negligence—some—(involuntarily she shook her head)—or it may be—of something still less pardonable." She raised her eyes towards him more fully than she had ever done before. "My mother's illness," he continued, "the seizure which ended in her death was sudden. The malady itself, one from which she had often suffered, a bilious fever—its cause therefore constitutional. On the third day, in short as soon as she could be prevailed on, a physician attended her, a very respectable man, and one in whom she had always placed great confidence. Upon his opinion of her danger, two others were called in the next day, and remained in almost constant attendance for four-and-twenty hours. On the fifth day she died. During the progress of her disorder, Frederick and I (we were both at home) saw her repeatedly; and from our own observation can bear witness to her having received every possible attention which could spring from the affection of those about her, or which her situation in life could command. Poor Eleanor was absent, and at such a distance as to return only to see her mother in her coffin."

"But your father," said Catherine, "was he afflicted?"

"For a time, greatly so. You have erred in supposing him not attached to her. He loved her, I am persuaded, as well as it was possible for him to. We have not all, you know, the same tenderness of disposition—and I will not pretend to say that while she lived, she might not often have had much to bear, but though his temper injured her, his judgment never did. His value of her was sincere; and, if not permanently, he was truly afflicted by her death."

"I am very glad of it," said Catherine, "it would have been very shocking!"——

"If I understand you rightly, you had formed a surmise of such horror as I have hardly words to——Dear Miss Morland, consider the dreadful nature of the suspicions you have entertained. What have you been judging from? Remember the country and the age in which we live. Remember that we are English, that we are Christians. Consult your own understanding, your own sense of the probable, your own observation of what is passing around you. Does our education prepare us for such atrocities? Do our laws connive at them? Could they be perpetrated without being known, in a country like this, where social and literary intercourse is on such a footing; where every man is surrounded by a neighbourhood of voluntary spies, and where roads and newspapers lay every thing open? Dearest Miss Morland, what ideas have you been admitting?"

They had reached the end of the gallery; and with tears of shame she ran off to her own room.

Tilney
accuses

CHAPTER X

The visions of romance were over. Catherine was completely awakened. Henry's address, short as it had been, had more thoroughly opened her eyes to the extravagance of her late fancies than all their several disappointments had done. Most grievously was she humbled. Most bitterly did she cry. It was not only with herself that she was sunk—but with Henry. Her folly, which now seemed even criminal, was all exposed to him, and he must despise her for ever. The liberty which her imagination had dared to take with the character of his father, could he ever forgive it? The absurdity of her curiosity and her fears, could they ever be forgotten? She hated herself more than she could express. He had—she thought he had, once or twice before this fatal morning, shewn something like affection for her. But now—in short, she made herself as miserable as possible for about half an hour, went down when the clock struck five, with a broken heart, and could scarcely give an intelligible answer to Eleanor's inquiry, if she was well. The formidable Henry soon followed her into the room, and the only difference in his behaviour to her, was that he paid her rather more attention than usual. Catherine had never wanted comfort more, and he looked as if he was aware of it.

The evening wore away with no abatement of this soothing politeness; and her spirits were gradually raised to a modest tranquillity. She did not learn either to forget or defend the past; but she learned to hope that it would never transpire farther, and that it might not cost her Henry's entire regard. Her thoughts being still chiefly fixed on what she had with such causeless terror felt and done, nothing could shortly be clearer, than that it had been all a voluntary, self-created delusion, each trifling circumstance receiving importance from an imagination resolved on alarm, and every thing forced to bend to one purpose by a mind which, before she entered the Abbey, had been craving to be frightened. She remembered with what feelings she had prepared for a knowledge of Northanger. She saw that the infatuation had been created, the mischief settled long before her quitting Bath, and it seemed as if the whole might be traced to the influence of that sort of reading which she had there indulged.

Charming as were all Mrs. Radcliffe's works, and charming even as were the works of all her imitators, it was not in them perhaps that human nature, at least in the midland counties of England, was to be looked for. Of the Alps and Pyrenees, with their pine forests and their vices, they might give a faithful delineation; and Italy, Switzerland, and the South of France, might be as fruitful in horrors as they were there represented. Catherine dared not doubt beyond her own country, and even of that, if hard pressed, would have yielded the northern and western extremities. But in the central part of England there was surely some security for the existence even of a wife not beloved, in the laws of the land, and the manners of the age. Murder was not tolerated, servants were not slaves, and neither poison nor sleeping potions to be procured, like rhubarb, from every druggist. Among the Alps and Pyrenees, perhaps, there were no mixed characters. There, such as were not as spotless as an angel, might have the dispositions of a fiend. But in England it was not so; among the English, she believed, in their hearts and habits, there was a general though unequal mixture of good and bad. Upon this conviction, she would not be surprized if even in Henry and Eleanor Tilney, some slight imperfection might hereafter appear; and upon this conviction she need not fear to acknowledge some actual specks in the character of their father, who, though cleared from the grossly injurious suspicions which she must ever blush to have entertained, she did believe, upon serious consideration, to be not perfectly amiable.

Her mind made up on these several points, and her resolution formed, of always judging and acting in future with the greatest good sense, she had nothing to do but to forgive herself and be happier than ever; and the lenient hand of time did much for her by insensible gradations in the course of another day. Henry's astonishing generosity and nobleness of conduct, in never alluding in the slightest way to what had passed, was of the greatest assistance to her; and sooner than she could have supposed it possible in the beginning of her distress, her spirits became absolutely comfortable, and capable, as heretofore, of continual improvement by any thing he said. There were still some subjects indeed, under which she believed they must always tremble—the mention of a chest or a cabinet, for instance—and she did not love the sight of japan in any shape: but even *she* could allow, that an occasional memento of past folly, however painful, might not be without use.

The anxieties of common life began soon to succeed to the alarms of romance. Her desire of hearing from Isabella grew every day greater. She was quite impatient to know how the Bath world went on, and how the Rooms were attended; and especially was she anxious to be assured of Isabella's having matched some fine netting-cotton, on which she had left her intent; and of her continuing on the best terms with James. Her only dependence for information of any kind was on Isabella. James had protested against writing to her till his return to Oxford; and Mrs. Allen had given her no hopes of a letter till she had got back to Fullerton. But Isabella had promised and promised again; and when she promised a thing, she was so scrupulous in performing it! this made it so particularly strange!

For nine successive mornings, Catherine wondered over the repetition of a disappointment, which each morning became more severe: but, on the tenth, when she entered the breakfast-room, her first object was a letter, held out by Henry's willing hand. She thanked him as heartily as if he had written it himself. "'Tis only from James, however," as she looked at the direction. She opened it; it was from Oxford; and to this purpose:

> Dear Catherine,
>
> Though, God knows, with little inclination for writing, I think it my duty to tell you, that every thing is at an end between Miss Thorpe and me. I left her and Bath yesterday, never to see either again. I shall not enter into particulars, they would only pain you more. You will soon hear enough from another quarter to know where lies the blame; and I hope will acquit your brother of every thing but the folly of too easily thinking his affection returned. Thank God! I am undeceived in time! But it is a heavy blow! After my father's consent had been so kindly given—but no more of this. She has made me miserable for ever! Let me soon hear from you, dear Catherine; you are my only friend; *your* love I do build upon. I wish your visit at Northanger may be over before Captain Tilney makes his engagement known, or you will be uncomfortably circumstanced. Poor Thorpe is in town: I dread the sight of him; his honest heart would feel so much. I have written to him and my father. Her duplicity hurts me more than all; till the very last, if I reasoned with her, she declared herself as much attached to me as ever, and laughed at my fears. I am ashamed to think how long I bore with it; but if ever man had reason to believe himself loved, I was that man. I cannot understand even now what she would be at, for there could be no need of my being played off to make her secure of Tilney. We parted at last by mutual consent—happy for me had we never met! I can never expect to know such another woman! Dearest Catherine, beware how you give your heart.
>
> Believe me, &c.

Catherine had not read three lines before her sudden change of countenance, and short exclamations of sorrowing wonder, declared her to be receiving unpleasant news; and Henry, earnestly watching her through the whole letter, saw plainly that it ended no better than it began. He was prevented, however, from even looking his surprize by his father's entrance. They went to breakfast directly; but Catherine could hardly eat any thing. Tears filled her eyes, and even ran down her cheeks as she sat. The letter was one moment in her hand, then in her lap, and then in her pocket; and she looked as if she knew not what she did. The General, between his cocoa and his newspaper, had luckily no leisure for noticing her; but to the other two her distress was equally visible. As soon as she dared leave the table she hurried away to her own room; but the house-maids were busy in it, and she was obliged to come down again. She turned into the drawing-room for privacy, but Henry and Eleanor had likewise retreated thither, and were at that moment deep in consultation about her. She drew back, trying to beg their pardon, but was, with gentle violence, forced to return; and the others withdrew, after Eleanor had affectionately expressed a wish of being of use or comfort to her.

After half an hour's free indulgence of grief and reflection, Catherine felt equal to encountering her friends; but whether she should make her distress known to them was another consideration. Perhaps, if particularly questioned, she might just give an idea—just distantly hint at it—but not more. To expose a friend, such a friend as Isabella had been to her—and then their own brother so closely concerned in it! She believed she must wave the subject altogether. Henry and Eleanor were by themselves in the breakfast-room; and each, as she entered it, looked at her anxiously. Catherine took her place at the table, and, after a short silence, Eleanor said, "No bad news from Fullerton, I hope? Mr. and Mrs. Morland—your brothers and sisters—I hope they are none of them ill?"

"No, I thank you," (sighing as she spoke,) "they are all very well. My letter was from my brother at Oxford."

Nothing further was said for a few minutes; and then speaking through her tears, she added, "I do not think I shall ever wish for a letter again!"

"I am sorry," said Henry, closing the book he had just opened; "if I had suspected the letter of containing any thing unwelcome, I should have given it with very different feelings."

"It contained something worse than any body could suppose! Poor James is so unhappy! You will soon know why."

"To have so kind-hearted, so affectionate a sister," replied Henry, warmly, "must be a comfort to him under any distress."

"I have one favour to beg," said Catherine, shortly afterwards, in an agitated manner, "that, if your brother should be coming here, you will give me notice of it, that I may go away."

"Our brother! Frederick!"

"Yes; I am sure I should be very sorry to leave you so soon, but something has happened that would make it very dreadful for me to be in the same house with Captain Tilney."

Eleanor's work was suspended while she gazed with increasing astonishment; but Henry began to suspect the truth, and something, in which Miss Thorpe's name was included, passed his lips.

"How quick you are!" cried Catherine: "you have guessed it, I declare! And yet, when we talked about it in Bath, you little thought of its ending so. Isabella— no wonder *now* I have not heard from her—Isabella has deserted my brother, and is to marry your's! Could you have believed there had been such inconstancy and fickleness, and every thing that is bad in the world?"

"I hope, so far as concerns my brother, you are misinformed. I hope he has not had any material share in bringing on Mr. Morland's disappointment. His marrying

Miss Thorpe is not probable. I think you must be deceived so far. I am very sorry for Mr. Morland—sorry that any one you love should be unhappy; but my surprize would be greater at Frederick's marrying her, than at any other part of the story."

"It is very true, however; you shall read James's letter yourself.—Stay——there is one part——" recollecting with a blush the last line.

"Will you take the trouble of reading to us the passages which concern my brother?"

"No, read it yourself," cried Catherine, whose second thoughts were clearer. "I do not know what I was thinking of," (blushing again that she had blushed before,)—"James only means to give me good advice."

He gladly received the letter; and, having read it through, with close attention, returned it saying, "Well, if it is to be so, I can only say that I am sorry for it. Frederick will not be the first man who has chosen a wife with less sense than his family expected. I do not envy his situation, either as a lover or a son."

Miss Tilney, at Catherine's invitation, now read the letter likewise; and, having expressed also her concern and surprize, began to inquire into Miss Thorpe's connexions and fortune.

"Her mother is a very good sort of woman," was Catherine's answer.

"What was her father?"

"A lawyer, I believe. They live at Putney."

"Are they a wealthy family?"

"No, not very. I do not believe Isabella has any fortune at all: but that will not signify in your family. Your father is so very liberal! He told me the other day, that he only valued money as it allowed him to promote the happiness of his children." The brother and sister looked at each other. "But," said Eleanor, after a short pause, "would it be to promote his happiness, to enable him to marry such a girl?—She must be an unprincipled one, or she could not have used your brother so.—And how strange an infatuation on Frederick's side! A girl who, before his eyes, is violating an engagement voluntarily entered into with another man! Is not it inconceivable, Henry? Frederick too, who always wore his heart so proudly! who found no woman good enough to be loved!"

"That is the most unpromising circumstance, the strongest presumption against him. When I think of his past declarations, I give him up. Moreover, I have too good an opinion of Miss Thorpe's prudence, to suppose that she would part with one gentleman before the other was secured. It is all over with Frederick indeed! He is a deceased man—defunct in understanding. Prepare for your sister-in-law, Eleanor, and such a sister-in-law as you must delight in! Open, candid, artless, guileless, with affections strong but simple, forming no pretensions, and knowing no disguise."

"Such a sister-in-law, Henry, I should delight in," said Eleanor, with a smile.

"But perhaps," observed Catherine, "though she has behaved so ill by our family, she may behave better by your's. Now she has really got the man she likes, she may be constant."

"Indeed I am afraid she will," replied Henry; "I am afraid she will be very constant, unless a baronet should come in her way; that is Frederick's only chance. I will get the Bath paper, and look over the arrivals."

"You think it is all for ambition then? And, upon my word, there are some things that seem very like it. I cannot forget, that, when she first knew what my father would do for them, she seemed quite disappointed that it was not more. I never was so deceived in any one's character in my life before."

"Among all the great variety that you have known and studied."

"My own disappointment and loss in her is very great; but, as for poor James, I suppose he will hardly ever recover it."

"Your brother is certainly very much to be pitied at present; but we must not, in our concern for his sufferings, undervalue your's. You feel, I suppose, that, in losing Isabella, you lose half yourself: you feel a void in your heart which nothing else can occupy. Society is becoming irksome; and as for the amusements in which you were wont to share at Bath, the very idea of them without her is abhorrent. You would not, for instance, now go to a ball for the world. You feel that you have no longer any friend to whom you can speak with unreserve; on whose regard you can place dependence; or whose counsel, in any difficulty, you could rely on. You feel all this?"

"No," said Catherine, after a few moments' reflection, "I do not—ought I? To say the truth, though I am hurt and grieved, that I cannot still love her, that I am never to hear from her, perhaps never to see her again, I do not feel so very, very much afflicted as one would have thought."

"You feel, as you always do, what is most to the credit of human nature. Such feelings ought to be investigated, that they may know themselves."

Catherine, by some chance or other, found her spirits so very much relieved by this conversation, that she could not regret her being led on, though so unaccountably, to mention the circumstance which had produced it.

CHAPTER XI

From this time, the subject was frequently canvassed by the three young people; and Catherine found, with some surprize, that her two young friends were perfectly agreed in considering Isabella's want of consequence and fortune as likely to throw great difficulties in the way of her marrying their brother. Their persuasion that the General would, upon this ground alone, independent of the objection that might be raised against her character, oppose the connexion, turned her feelings moreover with some alarm towards herself. She was as insignificant, and perhaps as portionless as Isabella; and if the heir of the Tilney property had not grandeur and wealth enough in himself, at what point of interest were the demands of his younger brother to rest? The very painful reflections to which this thought led, could only be dispersed by a dependence on the effect of that particular partiality, which, as she was given to understand by his words as well as his actions, she had from the first been so fortunate as to excite in the General; and by a recollection of some most generous and disinterested sentiments on the subject of money, which she had more than once heard him utter, and which tempted her to think his disposition in such matters misunderstood by his children.

They were so fully convinced, however, that their brother would not have the courage to apply in person for his father's consent, and so repeatedly assured her that he had never in his life been less likely to come to Northanger than at the present time, that she suffered her mind to be at ease as to the necessity of any sudden removal of her own. But as it was not to be supposed that Captain Tilney, whenever he made his application, would give his father any just idea of Isabella's conduct, it occurred to her as highly expedient that Henry should lay the whole business before him as it really was, enabling the General by that means to form a cool and impartial opinion, and prepare his objections on a fairer ground than inequality of situations. She proposed it to him accordingly; but he did not catch at the measure so eagerly as she had expected. "No," said he, "my father's hands need not be strengthened, and Frederick's confession of folly need not be forestalled. He must tell his own story."

"But he will tell only half of it."

"A quarter would be enough."

A day or two passed away and brought no tidings of Captain Tilney. His brother and sister knew not what to think. Sometimes it appeared to them as if his silence would be the natural result of the suspected engagement, and at others that it was wholly incompatible with it. The General, meanwhile, though offended every morning by Frederick's remissness in writing, was free from any real anxiety about him; and had no more pressing solicitude than that of making Miss Morland's time at Northanger pass pleasantly. He often expressed his uneasiness on this head, feared the sameness of every day's society and employments would disgust her with the place, wished the Lady Frasers had been in the country, talked every now and then of having a large party to dinner, and once or twice began even to calculate the number of young dancing people in the neighbourhood. But then it was such a dead time of year, no wild-fowl, no game, and the Lady Frasers were not in the country. And it all ended, at last, in his telling Henry one morning, that when he next went to Woodston, they would take him by surprize there some day or other, and eat their mutton with him. Henry was greatly honoured and very happy, and Catherine was quite delighted with the scheme. "And when do you think, sir, I may look forward to this pleasure? I must be at Woodston on Monday to attend the parish meeting, and shall probably be obliged to stay two or three days."

"Well, well, we will take our chance some one of those days. There is no need to fix. You are not to put yourself at all out of your way. Whatever you may happen to have in the house will be enough. I think I can answer for the young ladies making allowance for a bachelor's table. Let me see; Monday will be a busy day with you, we will not come on Monday; and Tuesday will be a busy one with me. I expect my surveyor from Brockham with his report in the morning; and afterwards I cannot in decency fail attending the club. I really could not face my acquaintance if I staid away now; for, as I am known to be in the country, it would be taken exceedingly amiss; and it is a rule with me, Miss Morland, never to give offence to any of my neighbours, if a small sacrifice of time and attention can prevent it. They are a set of very worthy men. They have half a buck from Northanger twice a year; and I dine with them whenever I can. Tuesday, therefore, we may say is out of the question. But on Wednesday, I think, Henry, you may expect us; and we shall be with you early, that we may have time to look about us. Two hours and three quarters will carry us to Woodston, I suppose; we shall be in the carriage by ten; so, about a quarter before one on Wednesday, you may look for us."

A ball itself could not have been more welcome to Catherine than this little excursion, so strong was her desire to be acquainted with Woodston; and her heart was still bounding with joy, when Henry, about an hour afterwards, came booted and great coated into the room where she and Eleanor were sitting, and said, "I am come, young ladies, in a very moralizing strain, to observe that our pleasures in this world are always to be paid for, and that we often purchase them at a great disadvantage, giving ready-monied actual happiness for a draft on the future, that may not be honoured. Witness myself, at this present hour. Because I am to hope for the satisfaction of seeing you at Woodston on Wednesday, which bad weather, or twenty other causes may prevent, I must go away directly, two days before I intended it."

"Go away!" said Catherine, with a very long face; "and why?"

"Why! How can you ask the question? Because no time is to be lost in frightening my old housekeeper out of her wits, because I must go and prepare a dinner for you to be sure."

"Oh! not seriously!"

"Aye, and sadly too—for I had much rather stay."

"But how can you think of such a thing, after what the General said? when he so particularly desired you not to give yourself any trouble, because *any thing* would do."

Henry only smiled. "I am sure it is quite unnecessary upon your sister's account and mine. You must know it to be so; and the General made such a point of your providing nothing extraordinary: besides, if he had not said half so much as he did, he has always such an excellent dinner at home, that sitting down to a middling one for one day could not signify."

"I wish I could reason like you, for his sake and my own. Good bye. As to-morrow is Sunday, Eleanor, I shall not return."

He went; and, it being at any time a much simpler operation to Catherine to doubt her own judgment than Henry's, she was very soon obliged to give him credit for being right, however disagreeable to her his going. But the inexplicability of the General's conduct dwelt much on her thoughts. That he was very particular in his eating, she had, by her own unassisted observation, already discovered; but why he should say one thing so positively, and mean another all the while, was most unaccountable! How were people, at that rate, to be understood? Who but Henry could have been aware of what his father was at?

From Saturday to Wednesday, however, they were now to be without Henry. This was the sad finale of every reflection:—Captain Tilney's letter would certainly come in his absence; and Wednesday she was very sure would be wet. The past, present, and future, were all equally in gloom. Her brother so unhappy, and her loss in Isabella so great; and Eleanor's spirits always affected by Henry's absence! What was there to interest or amuse her? She was tired of the woods and the shrubberies—always so smooth and so dry; and the Abbey in itself was no more to her now than any other house. The painful remembrance of the folly it had helped to nourish and perfect, was the only emotion which could spring from a consideration of the building. What a revolution in her ideas! she, who had so longed to be in an abbey! Now, there was nothing so charming to her imagination as the unpretending comfort of a well-connected Parsonage, something like Fullerton, but better: Fullerton had its faults, but Woodston probably had none. If Wednesday should ever come!

It did come, and exactly when it might be reasonably looked for. It came—it was fine—and Catherine trod on air. By ten o'clock, the chaise-and-four conveyed the trio from the Abbey; and, after an agreeable drive of almost twenty miles, they entered Woodston, a large and populous village, in a situation not unpleasant. Catherine was ashamed to say how pretty she thought it, as the General seemed to think an apology necessary for the flatness of the country, and the size of the village; but in her heart she preferred it to any place she had ever been at, and looked with great admiration at every neat house above the rank of a cottage, and at all the little chandler's shops which they passed. At the further end of the village, and tolerably disengaged from the rest of it, stood the Parsonage, a new-built substantial stone house, with its semi-circular sweep and green gates; and, as they drove up to the door, Henry, with the friends of his solitude, a large Newfoundland puppy and two or three terriers, was ready to receive and make much of them.

Catherine's mind was too full, as she entered the house, for her either to observe or to say a great deal; and, till called on by the General for her opinion of it, she had very little idea of the room in which she was sitting. Upon looking round it then, she perceived in a moment that it was the most comfortable room in the world; but she was too guarded to say so, and the coldness of her praise disappointed him.

"We are not calling it a good house," said he. "We are not comparing it with Fullerton and Northanger—We are considering it as a mere Parsonage, small and confined, we allow, but decent perhaps, and habitable; and altogether not inferior to the generality; or, in other words, I believe there are few country parsonages in England half so good. It may admit of improvement, however. Far be it from me to say otherwise; and any thing in reason—a bow thrown out, perhaps—though, between ourselves, if there is one thing more than another my aversion, it is a patched-on bow."

Catherine did not hear enough of this speech to understand or be pained by it; and other subjects being studiously brought forward and supported by Henry, at the same time that a tray full of refreshments was introduced by his servant, the General was shortly restored to his complacency, and Catherine to all her usual ease of spirits.

The room in question was of a commodious, well-proportioned size, and handsomely fitted up as a dining parlour; and on their quitting it to walk round the grounds, she was shewn, first into a smaller apartment, belonging peculiarly to the master of the house, and made unusually tidy on the occasion; and afterwards into what was to be the drawing-room, with the appearance of which, though unfurnished, Catherine was delighted enough even to satisfy the General. It was a prettily-shaped room, the windows reaching to the ground, and the view from them pleasant, though only over green meadows; and she expressed her admiration at the moment with all the honest simplicity with which she felt it. "Oh! why do not you fit up this room, Mr. Tilney? What a pity not to have it fitted up! It is the prettiest room I ever saw; it is the prettiest room in the world!"

"I trust," said the General, with a most satisfied smile, "that it will very speedily be furnished: it waits only for a lady's taste!"

"Well, if it was my house, I should never sit any where else. Oh! what a sweet little cottage there is among the trees—apple trees too! It is the prettiest cottage!"

"You like it—you approve it as an object; it is enough. Henry, remember that Robinson is spoken to about it. The cottage remains."

Such a compliment recalled all Catherine's consciousness, and silenced her directly; and though pointedly applied to by the General for her choice of the prevailing colour of the paper and hangings, nothing like an opinion on the subject could be drawn from her. The influence of fresh objects and fresh air, however, was of great use in dissipating these embarrassing associations; and, having reached the ornamental part of the premises, consisting of a walk round two sides of a meadow, on which Henry's genius had begun to act about half a year ago, she was sufficiently recovered to think it prettier than any pleasure-ground she had ever been in before, though there was not a shrub in it higher than the green bench in the corner.

A saunter into other meadows, and through part of the village, with a visit to the stables to examine some improvements, and a charming game of play with a litter of puppies just able to roll about, brought them to four o'clock, when Catherine scarcely thought it could be three. At four they were to dine, and at six to set off on their return. Never had any day passed so quickly!

She could not but observe that the abundance of the dinner did not seem to create the smallest astonishment in the General; nay, that he was even looking at the side-table for cold meat which was not there. His son and daughter's observations were of a different kind. They had seldom seen him eat so heartily at any table but his own; and never before known him so little disconcerted by the melted butter's being oiled.

At six o'clock, the General having taken his coffee, the carriage again received them; and so gratifying had been the tenor of his conduct throughout the whole visit, so well assured was her mind on the subject of his expectations, that, could she have felt equally confident of the wishes of his son, Catherine would have quitted Woodston with little anxiety as to the How or the When she might return to it.

CHAPTER XII

The next morning brought the following very unexpected letter from Isabella:

Bath, April——

My dearest Catherine,

I received your two kind letters with the greatest delight, and have a thousand apologies to make for not answering them sooner. I really am quite ashamed of my idleness; but in this horrid place one can find time for nothing. I have had my pen in my hand to begin a letter to you almost every day since you left Bath, but have always been prevented by some silly trifler or other. Pray write to me soon, and direct to my own home. Thank God! we leave this vile place to-morrow. Since you went away, I have had no pleasure in it—the dust is beyond any thing; and every body one cares for is gone. I believe if I could see you I should not mind the rest, for you are dearer to me than any body can conceive. I am quite uneasy about your dear brother, not having heard from him since he went to Oxford; and am fearful of some misunderstanding. Your kind offices will set all right: he is the only man I ever did or could love, and I trust you will convince him of it. The spring fashions are partly down; and the hats the most frightful you can imagine. I hope you spend your time pleasantly, but am afraid you never think of me. I will not say all that I could of the family you are with, because I would not be ungenerous, or set you against those you esteem; but it is very difficult to know whom to trust, and young men never know their minds two days together. I rejoice to say, that the young man whom, of all others, I particularly abhor, has left Bath. You will know, from this description, I must mean Captain Tilney, who, as you may remember, was amazingly disposed to follow and tease me, before you went away. Afterwards he got worse, and became quite my shadow. Many girls might have been taken in, for never were such attentions; but I knew the fickle sex too well. He went away to his regiment two days ago, and I trust I shall never be plagued with him again. He is the greatest coxcomb I ever saw, and amazingly disagreeable. The last two days he was always by the side of Charlotte Davis: I pitied his taste, but took no notice of him. The last time we met was in Bath-street, and I turned directly into a shop that he might not speak to me; I would not even look at him. He went into the Pump-room afterwards; but I would not have followed him for all the world. Such a contrast between him and your brother!—pray send me some news of the latter—I am quite unhappy about him, he seemed so uncomfortable when he went away, with a cold, or something that affected his spirits. I would write to him myself, but have mislaid his direction; and, as I hinted above, am afraid he took something in my conduct amiss. Pray explain every thing to his satisfaction; or, if he still harbours any doubt, a line from himself to me, or a call at Putney when next in town, might set all to rights. I have not been to the Rooms this age, nor to the Play, except going in last night with the Hodges's, for a frolic, at half-price: they teased me into it; and I was determined they should not say I shut myself up because Tilney was gone. We happened to sit by the Mitchells, and they pretended to be quite surprized to see me out. I knew their spite: at one time they could not be civil to me, but now they are all friendship; but I am not such a fool as to be taken in by them. You know I have a pretty good spirit of my own. Anne Mitchell had tried to put on a turban like mine, as I wore it the week before at the Concert, but made wretched work of it—it happened to become my odd face I believe, at least Tilney told me so at the time, and said every eye was upon me; but he is the last man whose word I would take. I wear nothing but purple now: I know I look hideous in it, but no matter—it is your dear brother's favourite colour. Lose no time, my dearest, sweetest Catherine, in writing to him and to me,

Who ever am, &c.

Such a strain of shallow artifice could not impose even upon Catherine. Its inconsistencies, contradictions, and falsehood, struck her from the very first. She was ashamed of Isabella, and ashamed of having ever loved her. Her professions of attachment were now as disgusting as her excuses were empty, and her demands impudent. "Write to James on her behalf! No, James should never hear Isabella's name mentioned by her again."

On Henry's arrival from Woodston, she made known to him and Eleanor their brother's safety, congratulating them with sincerity on it, and reading aloud the most material passages of her letter with strong indignation. When she had finished it, "So much for Isabella," she cried, "and for all our intimacy! She must think me an idiot, or she could not have written so; but perhaps this has served to make her character better known to me than mine is to her. I see what she has been about. She is a vain coquette, and her tricks have not answered. I do not believe she had ever any regard either for James or for me, and I wish I had never known her."

"It will soon be as if you never had," said Henry.

"There is but one thing that I cannot understand. I see that she has had designs on Captain Tilney, which have not succeeded; but I do not understand what Captain Tilney has been about all this time. Why should he pay her such attentions as to make her quarrel with my brother, and then fly off himself?"

"I have very little to say for Frederick's motives, such as I believe them to have been. He has his vanities as well as Miss Thorpe, and the chief difference is, that, having a stronger head, they have not yet injured himself. If the *effect* of his behaviour does not justify him with you, we had better not seek after the cause."

"Then you do not suppose he ever really cared about her?"

"I am persuaded that he never did."

"And only made believe to do so for mischief's sake?"

Henry bowed his assent.

"Well, then, I must say that I do not like him at all. Though it has turned out so well for us, I do not like him at all. As it happens, there is no great harm done, because I do not think Isabella has any heart to lose. But, suppose he had made her very much in love with him?"

"But we must first suppose Isabella to have had a heart to lose, consequently to have been a very different creature; and, in that case, she would have met with very different treatment."

"It is very right that you should stand by your brother."

"And if you would stand by *your's*, you would not be much distressed by the disappointment of Miss Thorpe. But your mind is warped by an innate principle of general integrity, and therefore not accessible to the cool reasonings of family partiality, or a desire of revenge."

Catherine was complimented out of further bitterness. Frederick could not be unpardonably guilty, while Henry made himself so agreeable. She resolved on not answering Isabella's letter; and tried to think no more of it.

Chapter XIII

Soon after this, the General found himself obliged to go to London for a week; and he left Northanger earnestly regretting that any necessity should rob him even for an hour of Miss Morland's company, and anxiously recommending the study of her comfort and amusement to his children as their chief object in his absence. His departure gave Catherine the first experimental conviction that a loss may be sometimes a gain. The happiness with which their time now passed, every employment voluntary, every laugh indulged, every meal a scene of ease and good-humour, walking where they liked and when they liked, their hours, pleasures and fatigues at their own command, made her thoroughly sensible of the restraint which the General's presence had imposed, and most thankfully feel their present release from it. Such ease and such delights made her love the place and the people more and more every day; and had it not been for a dread of its soon becoming expedient to leave the one, and an apprehension of not being equally beloved by the other, she would at each moment of each day have been perfectly happy; but she was now in the fourth week of her visit; before the General came home, the fourth week would be turned, and perhaps it might seem an intrusion if she staid much longer. This was a painful consideration whenever it occurred; and eager to get rid of such a weight on her mind, she very soon resolved to speak to Eleanor about it at once, propose going away, and be guided in her conduct by the manner in which her proposal might be taken.

Aware that if she gave herself much time, she might feel it difficult to bring forward so unpleasant a subject, she took the first opportunity of being suddenly alone with Eleanor, and of Eleanor's being in the middle of a speech about something very different, to start forth her obligation of going away very soon. Eleanor looked and declared herself much concerned. She had "hoped for the pleasure of her company for a much longer time—had been misled (perhaps by her wishes) to suppose that a much longer visit had been promised—and could not but think that if Mr. and Mrs. Morland were aware of the pleasure it was to her to have her there, they would be too generous to hasten her return." Catherine explained: "Oh! as to *that*, papa and mamma were in no hurry at all. As long as she was happy, they would always be satisfied."

"Then why, might she ask, in such a hurry herself to leave them?"

"Oh! because she had been there so long."

"Nay, if you can use such a word, I can urge you no farther. If you think it long—"

"Oh! no, I do not indeed. For my own pleasure, I could stay with you as long again." And it was directly settled that, till she had, her leaving them was not even to be thought of. In having this cause of uneasiness so pleasantly removed, the force of the other was likewise weakened. The kindness, the earnestness of Eleanor's manner in pressing her to stay, and Henry's gratified look on being told that her stay was determined, were such sweet proofs of her importance with them, as left her only just so much solicitude as the human mind can never do comfortably without. She did—almost always—believe that Henry loved her, and quite always that his father and sister loved and even wished her to belong to them; and believing so far, her doubts and anxieties were merely sportive irritations.

Henry was not able to obey his father's injunction of remaining wholly at Northanger in attendance on the ladies, during his absence in London; the engagements of his curate at Woodston obliging him to leave them on Saturday for a couple of nights. His loss was not now what it had been while the General was at home; it lessened their gaiety, but did not ruin their comfort; and the two girls agreeing in occupation, and improving in intimacy, found themselves so well-sufficient for the time to themselves, that it was eleven o'clock, rather a late hour at the Abbey, before they quitted the supper-room on the day of Henry's departure. They had just reached the head of the stairs, when it seemed, as far as the thickness of the walls would allow them to judge, that a carriage was driving up to the door, and the next moment confirmed the idea by the loud noise of the house-bell. After the first perturbation of surprize had passed away, in a "Good Heaven! what can be the matter?" it was quickly decided by Eleanor to be her eldest brother, whose arrival was often as sudden, if not quite so unseasonable, and accordingly she hurried down to welcome him.

Catherine walked on to her chamber, making up her mind as well as she could, to a further acquaintance with Captain Tilney, and comforting herself under the unpleasant impression his conduct had given her, and the persuasion of his being by far too fine a gentleman to approve of her, that at least they should not meet under such circumstances as would make their meeting materially painful. She trusted he would never speak of Miss Thorpe; and indeed, as he must by this time be ashamed of the part he had acted, there could be no danger of it; and as long as all mention of Bath scenes were avoided, she thought she could behave to him very civilly. In such considerations time passed away, and it was certainly in his favour that Eleanor should be so glad to see him, and have so much to say, for half an hour was almost gone since his arrival, and Eleanor did not come up.

At that moment Catherine thought she heard her step in the gallery, and listened for its continuance; but all was silent. Scarcely, however, had she convicted her fancy of error, when the noise of something moving close to her door made her start; it seemed as if some one was touching the very doorway—and in another moment a slight motion of the lock proved that some hand must be on it. She trembled a little at the idea of any one's approaching so cautiously; but resolving not to be again overcome by trivial appearances of alarm, or misled by a raised imagination, she stepped quietly forward, and opened the door. Eleanor, and only Eleanor, stood there. Catherine's spirits however were tranquillized but for an instant, for Eleanor's cheeks were pale, and her manner greatly agitated. Though evidently intending to come in, it seemed an effort to enter the room, and a still greater to speak when there. Catherine, supposing some uneasiness on Captain Tilney's account, could only express her concern by silent attention; obliged her to be seated, rubbed her temples with lavender-water, and hung over her with affectionate solicitude. "My dear Catherine, you must not—you must not indeed—" were Eleanor's first connected words. "I am quite well. This kindness distracts me—I cannot bear it—I come to you on such an errand!"

"Errand!—to me!"

"How shall I tell you!—Oh! how shall I tell you!"

A new idea now darted into Catherine's mind, and turning as pale as her friend, she exclaimed, "'Tis a messenger from Woodston!"

"You are mistaken, indeed," returned Eleanor, looking at her most compassionately—"it is no one from Woodston. It is my father himself." Her voice faltered, and her eyes were turned to the ground as she mentioned his name. His unlooked-for return was enough in itself to make Catherine's heart sink, and for a few moments she hardly supposed there were any thing worse to be told. She said nothing; and Eleanor endeavouring to collect herself and speak with firmness, but with eyes still cast down, soon went on. "You are too good, I am sure, to think the worse of me for the part I am obliged to perform. I am indeed a most unwilling messenger. After what has so lately passed, so lately been settled between us—how joyfully, how thankfully on my side!—as to your continuing here as I hoped for many, many weeks longer, how can I tell you that your kindness is not to be accepted—and that the happiness your company has hitherto given us is to be repaid by——but I must not trust myself with words. My dear Catherine, we are to part. My father has recollected an engagement that takes our whole family away on Monday. We are going to Lord Longtown's, near Hereford, for a fortnight. Explanation and apology are equally impossible. I cannot attempt either."

"My dear Eleanor," cried Catherine, suppressing her feelings as well as she could, "do not be so distressed. A second engagement must give way to a first. I am very, very sorry we are to part—so soon, and so suddenly too; but I am not offended, indeed I am not. I can finish my visit here you know at any time; or I hope you will come to me. Can you, when you return from this lord's, come to Fullerton?"

"It will not be in my power, Catherine."

"Come when you can, then."

Eleanor made no answer; and Catherine's thoughts recurring to something more directly interesting, she added, thinking aloud, "Monday—so soon as Monday—and you *all* go. Well, I am certain of——I shall be able to take leave however. I need not go till just before you do, you know. Do not be distressed, Eleanor, I can go on Monday very well. My father and mother's having no notice of it is of very little consequence. The General will send a servant with me, I dare say, half the way—and then I shall soon be at Salisbury, and then I am only nine miles from home."

"Ah, Catherine! were it settled so, it would be somewhat less tolerable, though in such common attentions you would have received but half what you ought. But—how can I tell you?—To-morrow morning is fixed for your leaving us, and not even the hour is left to your choice; the very carriage is ordered, and will be here at seven o'clock, and no servant will be offered you."

Catherine sat down, breathless and speechless. "I could hardly believe my senses, when I heard it; and no displeasure, no resentment that you can feel at this moment, however justly great, can be more than I myself——but I must not talk of what I felt. Oh! that I could suggest any thing in extenuation! Good God! what will your father and mother say! After courting you from the protection of real friends to this—almost double distance from you home, to have you driven out of the house, without the considerations even of decent civility! Dear, dear Catherine, in being the bearer of such a message, I seem guilty myself of all its insult; yet, I trust you will acquit me, for you must have been long enough in this house to see that I am but a nominal mistress of it, that my real power is nothing."

"Have I offended the General?" said Catherine in a faltering voice.

"Alas! for my feelings as a daughter, all that I know, all that I answer for is, that you can have given him no just cause of offence. He certainly is greatly, very greatly discomposed; I have seldom seen him more so. His temper is not happy, and something has now occurred to ruffle it in an uncommon degree; some disappointment, some vexation, which just at this moment seems important; but which I can hardly suppose you to have any concern in, for how is it possible?"

It was with pain that Catherine could speak at all; and it was only for Eleanor's sake that she attempted it. "I am sure," said she, "I am very sorry if I have offended him. It was the last thing I would willingly have done. But do not be unhappy, Eleanor. An engagement you know must be kept. I am only sorry it was not recollected sooner, that I might have written home. But it is of very little consequence."

"I hope, I earnestly hope that to your real safety it will be of none; but to every thing else it is of the greatest consequence; to comfort, appearance, propriety, to your family, to the world. Were your friends, the Allens, still in Bath, you might go to them with comparative ease; a few hours would take you there; but a journey of seventy miles, to be taken post by you, at your age, alone, unattended!"

"Oh, the journey is nothing. Do not think about that. And if we are to part, a few hours sooner or later, you know, makes no difference. I can be ready by seven. Let me be called in time." Eleanor saw that she wished to be alone; and believing it better for each that they should avoid any further conversation, now left her with "I shall see you in the morning."

Catherine's swelling heart needed relief. In Eleanor's presence friendship and pride had equally restrained her tears, but no sooner was she gone than they burst forth in torrents. Turned from the house, and in such a way! Without any reason that could justify, any apology that could atone for the abruptness, the rudeness, nay, the insolence of it. Henry at a distance—not able even to bid him farewell. Every hope, every expectation from him suspended, at least, and who could say how long? Who could say when they might meet again? And all this by such a man as General Tilney, so polite, so well-bred, and heretofore so particularly fond of her! It was as incomprehensible as it was mortifying and grievous. From what it could arise, and where it would end, were considerations of equal perplexity and alarm. The manner in which it was done so grossly uncivil; hurrying her away without any reference to her own convenience, or allowing her even the appearance of choice as to the time or mode of her travelling; of two days, the earliest fixed on, and of that almost the earliest hour, as if resolved to have her gone before he was stirring in the morning, that he might not be obliged even to see her. What could all this mean but an intentional affront? By some means or other she must have had the misfortune to offend him. Eleanor had wished to spare her from so painful a notion, but Catherine could not believe it possible that any injury or any misfortune could provoke such ill-will against a person not connected, or, at least, not supposed to be connected with it.

Heavily past the night. Sleep, or repose that deserved the name of sleep, was out of the question. That room, in which her disturbed imagination had tormented her on her first arrival, was again the scene of agitated spirits and unquiet slumbers. Yet how different now the source of her inquietude from what it had been then—how mournfully superior in reality and substance! Her anxiety had foundation in fact, her fears in probability; and with a mind so occupied in the contemplation of actual and natural evil, the solitude of her situation, the darkness of her chamber, the antiquity of the building were felt and considered without the smallest emotion; and though the wind was high, and often produced strange and sudden noises throughout the house, she heard it all as she lay awake, hour after hour, without curiosity or terror.

Soon after six Eleanor entered her room, eager to show attention or give assistance where it was possible; but very little remained to be done. Catherine had not loitered; she was almost dressed, and her packing almost finished. The possibility of some conciliatory message from the General occurred to her as his daughter appeared. What so natural, as that anger should pass away and repentance succeed it? and she only wanted to know how far, after what had passed, an apology might properly be received by her. But the knowledge would have been useless here, it was not called for; neither clemency nor dignity was put to the trial—Eleanor brought no message. Very little passed between them on meeting; each found her greatest safety in silence, and few and trivial were the sentences exchanged while they remained up stairs, Catherine in busy agitation completing her dress, and Eleanor with more good-will than experience intent upon filling the trunk. When every thing was done they left the room, Catherine lingering only half a minute behind her friend to throw a parting glance on every well-known cherished object, and went down to the breakfast-parlour, where breakfast was prepared. She tried to eat, as well to save herself from the pain of being urged, as to make her friend comfortable; but she had no appetite, and could not swallow many mouthfuls. The contrast between this and her last breakfast in that room, gave her fresh misery, and strengthened her distaste for every thing before her. It was not four-and-twenty hours ago since they had met there to the same repast, but in circumstances how different! With what cheerful ease, what happy, though false security, had she then looked around her, enjoying every thing present, and fearing little in future, beyond Henry's going to Woodston for a day! Happy, happy breakfast! for Henry had been there, Henry had sat by her and helped her. These reflections were long indulged undisturbed by any address from her companion, who sat as deep in thought as herself; and the appearance of the carriage was the first thing to startle and recall them to the present moment. Catherine's colour rose at the sight of it; and the indignity with which she was treated striking at that instant on her mind with peculiar force, made her for a short time sensible only of resentment. Eleanor seemed now impelled into resolution and speech.

"You *must* write to me, Catherine," she cried, "you *must* let me hear from you as soon as possible. Till I know you to be safe at home, I shall not have an hour's comfort. For *one* letter, at all risks, all hazards, I must entreat. Let me have the satisfaction of knowing that you are safe at Fullerton, and have found your family well, and then, till I can ask for your correspondence as I ought to do, I will not expect more. Direct to me at Lord Longtown's, and, I must ask it, under cover to Alice."

"No, Eleanor, if you are not allowed to receive a letter from me, I am sure I had better not write. There can be no doubt of my getting home safe."

Eleanor only replied, "I cannot wonder at your feelings. I will not importune you. I will trust to your own kindness of heart when I am at a distance from you." But this, with the look of sorrow accompanying it, was enough to melt Catherine's pride in a moment, and she instantly said, "Oh, Eleanor, I *will* write to you indeed."

There was yet another point which Miss Tilney was anxious to settle, though somewhat embarrassed in speaking of. It had occurred to her, that after so long an absence from home, Catherine might not be provided with money enough for the expenses of her journey, and, upon suggesting it to her with most affectionate offers of accommodation, it proved to be exactly the case. Catherine had never thought on the subject till that moment; but, upon examining her purse, was convinced that but for this kindness of her friend, she might have been turned from the house without even the means of getting home; and the distress in which she must have been thereby involved filling the minds of both, scarcely another word was said by either during the time of their remaining together. Short, however, was that time. The carriage was soon announced to be ready; and Catherine, instantly rising, a long and affectionate embrace supplied the place of language in bidding each other adieu; and, as they entered the hall, unable to leave the house without some mention of one whose name had not yet been spoken by either, she paused a moment, and with quivering lips just made it intelligible that she left "her kind remembrance for her absent friend." But with this approach to his name ended all possibility of restraining her feelings; and, hiding her face as well as she could with her handkerchief, she darted across the hall, jumped into the chaise, and in a moment was driven from the door.

<h2 style="text-align:center">Chapter XIV</h2>

Catherine was too wretched to be fearful. The journey in itself had no terrors for her; and she began it without either dreading its length, or feeling its solitariness. Leaning back in one corner of the carriage, in a violent burst of tears, she was conveyed some miles beyond the walls of the Abbey before she raised her head; and the highest point of ground within the park was almost closed from her view before she was capable of turning her eyes towards it. Unfortunately, the road she now travelled was the same which only ten days ago she had so happily passed along in going to and from Woodston; and, for fourteen miles, every bitter feeling was rendered more severe by the review of objects on which she had first looked under impressions so different. Every mile, as it brought her nearer Woodston, added to her sufferings, and when within the distance of five, she passed the turning which led to it, and thought of Henry, so near, yet so unconscious, her grief and agitation were excessive.

The day which she had spent at that place had been one of the happiest of her life. It was there, it was on that day that the General had made use of such expressions with regard to Henry and herself, had so spoken and so looked as to give her the most positive conviction of his actually wishing their marriage. Yes, only ten days ago had he elated her by his pointed regard—had he even confused her by his too significant reference! And now—what had she done, or what had she omitted to do, to merit such a change?

The only offence against him of which she could accuse herself, had been such as was scarcely possible to reach his knowledge. Henry and her own heart only were privy to the shocking suspicions which she had so idly entertained; and equally safe did she believe her secret with each. Designedly, at least, Henry could not have betrayed her. If, indeed, by any strange mischance his father should have gained intelligence of what she had dared to think and look for, of her causeless fancies and injurious examinations, she could not wonder at any degree of his indignation. If aware of her having viewed him as a murderer, she could not wonder at his even turning her from this house. But a justification so full of torture to herself, she trusted would not be in his power.

Anxious as were all her conjectures on this point, it was not, however, the one on which she dwelt most. There was a thought yet nearer, a more prevailing, more impetuous concern. How Henry would think, and feel, and look, when he returned on the morrow to Northanger and heard of her being gone, was a question of force and interest to rise over every other, to be never ceasing, alternately irritating and soothing; it sometimes suggested the dread of his calm acquiescence, and at others was answered by the sweetest confidence in his regret and resentment. To the General, of course, he would not dare to speak; but to Eleanor—what might he not say to Eleanor about her?

In this unceasing recurrence of doubts and inquiries, on any one article of which her mind was incapable of more than momentary repose, the hours passed away, and her journey advanced much faster than she looked for. The pressing anxieties of thought, which prevented her from noticing any thing before her, when once beyond the neighbourhood of Woodston, saved her at the same time from watching her progress; and though no object on the road could engage a moment's attention, she found no stage of it tedious. From this, she was preserved too by another cause, by feeling no eagerness for her journey's conclusion; for to return in such a manner to Fullerton was almost to destroy the pleasure of a meeting with those she loved best, even after an absence such as her's—an eleven weeks absence. What had she to say that would not humble herself and pain her family; that would not increase her own grief by the confession of it, extend an useless resentment, and perhaps involve the innocent with the guilty in undistinguishing ill-will? She could never do justice to Henry and Eleanor's merit; she felt it too strongly for expression; and should a dislike be taken against them, should they be thought of unfavourably, on their father's account, it would cut her to the heart.

With these feelings, she rather dreaded than sought for the first view of that well-known spire which would announce her within twenty miles of home. Salisbury she had known to be her point on leaving Northanger; but after the first stage she had been indebted to the post-masters for the names of the places which were then to conduct her to it; so great had been her ignorance of her route. She met with nothing, however, to distress or frighten her. Her youth, civil manners and liberal pay, procured her all the attention that a traveller like herself could require; and stopping only to change horses, she travelled on for about eleven hours without accident or alarm, and between six and seven o'clock in the evening found herself entering Fullerton.

A heroine returning, at the close of her career, to her native village, in all the triumph of recovered reputation, and all the dignity of a countess, with a long train of noble relations in their several phaetons, and three waiting-maids in a travelling chaise-and-four, behind her, is an event on which the pen of the contriver may well delight to dwell; it gives credit to every conclusion, and the author must share in the glory she so liberally bestows. But my affair is widely different; I bring back my heroine to her home in solitude and disgrace; and no sweet elation of spirits can lead me into minuteness. A heroine in a hack post-chaise, is such a blow upon sentiment, as no attempt at grandeur or pathos can withstand. Swiftly therefore shall her post-boy drive through the village, amid the gaze of Sunday groups, and speedy shall be her descent from it.

But, whatever might be the distress of Catherine's mind, as she thus advanced towards the Parsonage, and whatever the humiliation of her biographer in relating it, she was preparing enjoyment of no every-day nature for those to whom she went; first, in the appearance of her carriage—and secondly, in herself. The chaise of a traveller being a rare sight in Fullerton, the whole family were immediately at the window; and to have it stop at the sweep-gate was a pleasure to brighten every eye and occupy every fancy—a pleasure quite unlooked for by all but the two youngest children, a boy and girl of six and four years old, who expected a brother or sister in every carriage. Happy the glance that first distinguished Catherine!—Happy the voice that proclaimed the discovery!—But whether such happiness were the lawful property of George or Harriet could never be exactly understood.

Her father, mother, Sarah, George, and Harriet, all assembled at the door, to welcome her with affectionate eagerness, was a sight to awaken the best feelings of Catherine's heart; and in the embrace of each, as she stepped from the carriage, she found herself soothed beyond any thing that she had believed possible. So surrounded, so caressed, she was even happy! In the joyfulness of family love every thing for a short time was subdued, and the pleasure of seeing her, leaving them at first little leisure for calm curiosity, they were all seated round the tea-table, which Mrs. Morland had hurried for the comfort of the poor traveller, whose pale and jaded looks soon caught her notice, before any inquiry so direct as to demand a positive answer was addressed to her.

Reluctantly, and with much hesitation, did she then begin what might perhaps, at the end of half an hour, be termed by the courtesy of her hearers, an explanation; but scarcely, within that time, could they at all discover the cause, or collect the particulars of her sudden return. They were far from being an irritable race; far from any quickness in catching, or bitterness in resenting affronts: but here, when the whole was unfolded, was an insult not to be overlooked, nor, for the first half hour, to be easily pardoned. Without suffering any romantic alarm, in the consideration of their daughter's long and lonely journey, Mr. and Mrs. Morland could not but feel that it might have been productive of much unpleasantness to her; that it was what they could never have voluntarily suffered; and that, in forcing her on such a measure, General Tilney had acted neither honourably nor feelingly—neither as a gentleman nor as a parent. Why he had done it, what could have provoked him to such a breach of hospitality, and so suddenly turned all his partial regard for their daughter into actual ill-will, was a matter which they were at least as far from divining as Catherine herself; but it did not oppress them by any means so long; and, after a due course of useless conjecture, that, "it was a strange business, and that he must be a very strange man," grew enough for all their indignation and wonder; though Sarah indeed still indulged in the sweets of incomprehensibility, exclaiming and conjecturing with youthful ardour. "My dear, you give yourself a great deal of needless trouble," said her mother at last; "depend upon it, it is something not at all worth understanding."

"I can allow for his wishing Catherine away, when he recollected this engagement," said Sarah, "but why not do it civilly?"

"I am sorry for the young people," returned Mrs. Morland; "they must have a sad time of it; but as for any thing else, it is no matter now; Catherine is safe at home, and our comfort does not depend upon General Tilney." Catherine sighed. "Well," continued her philosophic mother, "I am glad I did not know of your journey at the time; but now it is all over perhaps there is no great harm done. It is always good for young people to be put upon exerting themselves; and you know, my dear Catherine, you always were a sad little shatter-brained creature; but now you must have been forced to have your wits about you, with so much changing of chaises and so forth; and I hope it will appear that you have not left any thing behind you in any of the pockets."

Catherine hoped so too, and tried to feel an interest in her own amendment, but her spirits were quite worn down; and, to be silent and alone becoming soon her only wish, she readily agreed to her mother's next counsel of going early to bed. Her parents seeing nothing in her ill-looks and agitation but the natural consequence of mortified feelings, and of the unusual exertion and fatigue of such a journey, parted from her without any doubt of their being soon slept away; and though, when they all met the next morning, her recovery was not equal to their hopes, they were still perfectly unsuspicious of there being any deeper evil. They never once thought of her heart, which, for the parents of a young lady of seventeen, just returned from her first excursion from home, was odd enough!

As soon as breakfast was over, she sat down to fulfil her promise to Miss Tilney, whose trust in the effect of time and distance on her friend's disposition was already justified, for already did Catherine reproach herself with having parted from Eleanor coldly; with having never enough valued her merits or kindness; and never enough commiserated her for what she had been yesterday left to endure. The strength of these feelings, however, was far from assisting her pen; and never had it been harder for her to write than in addressing Eleanor Tilney. To compose a letter which might at once do justice to her sentiments and her situation, convey gratitude without servile regret, be guarded without coldness, and honest without resentment—a letter which Eleanor might not be pained by the perusal of—and, above all, which she might not blush herself, if Henry should chance to see, was an undertaking to frighten away all her powers of performance; and, after long thought and much perplexity, to be very brief was all that she could determine on with any confidence of safety. The money therefore which Eleanor had advanced was inclosed with little more than grateful thanks, and the thousand good wishes of a most affectionate heart.

"This has been a strange acquaintance," observed Mrs. Morland, as the letter was finished; "soon made and soon ended. I am sorry it happens so, for Mrs. Allen thought them very pretty kind of young people; and you were sadly out of luck too in your Isabella. Ah! poor James! Well, we must live and learn; and the next few friends you make I hope will be better worth keeping."

Catherine coloured as she warmly answered, "No friend can be better worth keeping than Eleanor."

"If so, my dear, I dare say you will meet again some time or other; do not be uneasy. It is ten to one but you are thrown together again in the course of a few years; and then what a pleasure it will be!"

Mrs. Morland was not happy in her attempt at consolation. The hope of meeting again in the course of a few years could only put into Catherine's head what might happen within that time to make a meeting dreadful to her. She could never forget Henry Tilney, or think of him with less tenderness than she did at that moment; but he might forget her; and in that case to meet!——Her eyes filled with tears as she pictured her acquaintance so renewed; and her mother, perceiving her comfortable suggestions to have had no good effect, proposed, as another expedient for restoring her spirits, that they should call on Mrs. Allen.

The two houses were only a quarter of a mile apart; and, as they walked, Mrs. Morland quickly dispatched all that she felt on the score of James's disappointment. "We are sorry for him," said she; "but otherwise there is no harm done in the match going off; for it could not be a desirable thing to have him engaged to a girl whom we had not the smallest acquaintance with, and who was so entirely without fortune; and now, after such behaviour, we cannot think at all well of her. Just at present it comes hard to poor James; but that will not last for ever; and I dare say he will be a discreeter man all his life, for the foolishness of his first choice."

This was just such a summary view of the affair as Catherine could listen to; another sentence might have endangered her complaisance, and made her reply less rational; for soon were all her thinking powers swallowed up in the reflection of her own change of feelings and spirits since last she had trodden that well-known road. It was not three months ago since, wild with joyful expectation, she had there run backwards and forwards some ten times a-day, with an heart light, gay, and independent; looking forward to pleasures untasted and unalloyed, and free from the apprehension of evil as from the knowledge of it. Three months ago had seen her all this; and now, how altered a being did she return!

She was received by the Allens with all the kindness which her unlooked-for appearance, acting on a steady affection, would naturally call forth; and great was their surprize, and warm their displeasure, on hearing how she had been treated, though Mrs. Morland's account of it was no inflated representation, no studied appeal to their passions. "Catherine took us quite by surprize yesterday evening," said she. "She travelled all the way post by herself, and knew nothing of coming till Saturday night; for General Tilney, from some odd fancy or other, all of a sudden grew tired of having her there, and almost turned her out of the house. Very unfriendly, certainly; and he must be a very odd man; but we are so glad to have her amongst us again! And it is a great comfort to find that she is not a poor helpless creature, but can shift very well for herself."

Mr. Allen expressed himself on the occasion with the reasonable resentment of a sensible friend; and Mrs. Allen thought his expressions quite good enough to be immediately made use of again by herself. His wonder, his conjectures, and his explanations, became in succession her's, with the addition of this single remark—"I really have not patience with the General"—to fill up every accidental pause. And, "I really have not patience with the General," was uttered twice after Mr. Allen left the room, without any relaxation of anger, or any material digression of thought. A more considerable degree of wandering attended the third repetition; and, after completing the fourth, she immediately added, "Only think, my dear, of my having got that frightful great rent in my best Mechlin so charmingly mended, before I left Bath, that one can hardly see where it was. I must shew it you some day or other. Bath is a nice place, Catherine, after all. I assure you I did not above half like coming away. Mrs. Thorpe's being there was such a comfort to us, was not it? You know you and I were quite forlorn at first."

"Yes, but *that* did not last long," said Catherine, her eyes brightening at the recollection of what had first given spirit to her existence there.

"Very true: we soon met with Mrs. Thorpe, and then we wanted for nothing. My dear, do not you think these silk gloves wear very well? I put them on new the first time of our going to the Lower Rooms, you know, and I have worn them a great deal since. Do you remember that evening?"

"Do I! Oh! perfectly."

"It was very agreeable, was not it? Mr. Tilney drank tea with us, and I always thought him a great addition, he is so very agreeable. I have a notion you danced with him, but am not quite sure. I remember I had my favourite gown on."

Catherine could not answer; and, after a short trial of other subjects, Mrs. Allen again returned to—"I really have not patience with the General! Such an agreeable, worthy man as he seemed to be! I do not suppose, Mrs. Morland, you ever saw a better-bred man in your life. His lodgings were taken the very day after he left them, Catherine. But no wonder; Milsom-street you know."

As they walked home again, Mrs. Morland endeavoured to impress on her daughter's mind the happiness of having such steady well-wishers as Mr. and Mrs. Allen, and the very little consideration which the neglect or unkindness of slight acquaintance like the Tilneys ought to have with her, while she could preserve the good opinion and affection of her earliest friends. There was a great deal of good sense in all this; but there are some situations of the human mind in which good sense has very little power; and Catherine's feelings contradicted almost every position her mother advanced. It was upon the behaviour of these very slight acquaintance that all her present happiness depended; and while Mrs. Morland was successfully confirming her own opinions by the justness of her own representations, Catherine was silently reflecting that *now* Henry must have arrived at Northanger; *now* he must have heard of her departure; and *now*, perhaps, they were all setting off for Hereford.

CHAPTER XV

Catherine's disposition was not naturally sedentary, nor had her habits been ever very industrious; but whatever might hitherto have been her defects of that sort, her mother could not but perceive them now to be greatly increased. She could neither sit still, nor employ herself for ten minutes together, walking round the garden and orchard again and again, as if nothing but motion was voluntary; and it seemed as if she could even walk about the house rather than remain fixed for any time in the parlour. Her loss of spirits was a yet greater alteration. In her rambling and her idleness she might only be a caricature of herself; but in her silence and sadness she was the very reverse of all that she had been before.

For two days Mrs. Morland allowed it to pass even without a hint; but when a third night's rest had neither restored her cheerfulness, improved her in useful activity, nor given her a greater inclination for needle-work, she could no longer refrain from the gentle reproof of, "My dear Catherine, I am afraid you are growing quite a fine lady. I do not know when poor Richard's cravats would be done, if he had no friend but you. Your head runs too much upon Bath; but there is a time for every thing—a time for balls and plays, and a time for work. You have had a long run of amusement, and now you must try to be useful."

Catherine took up her work directly, saying, in a dejected voice, that "her head did not run upon Bath——much."

"Then you are fretting about General Tilney, and that is very simple of you; for ten to one whether you ever see him again. You should never fret about trifles." After a short silence—"I hope, my Catherine, you are not getting out of humour with home because it is not so grand as Northanger. That would be turning your visit into an evil indeed. Wherever you are you should always be contented, but especially at home, because there you must spend the most of your time. I did not quite like, at breakfast, to hear you talk so much about the French-bread at Northanger."

"I am sure I do not care about the bread. It is all the same to me what I eat."

"There is a very clever Essay in one of the books up stairs upon much such a subject, about young girls that have been spoilt for home by great acquaintance—'The Mirror,' I think. I will look it out for you some day or other, because I am sure it will do you good."

Catherine said no more, and, with an endeavour to do right, applied to her work; but, after a few minutes, sunk again, without knowing it herself, into languor and listlessness, moving herself in her chair, from the irritation of weariness, much oftener than she moved her needle. Mrs. Morland watched the progress of this relapse; and seeing, in her daughter's absent and dissatisfied look, the full proof of that repining spirit to which she had now begun to attribute her want of cheerfulness, hastily left the room to fetch the book in question, anxious to lose no time in attacking so dreadful a malady. It was some time before she could find what she looked for; and other family matters occurring to detain her, a quarter of an hour had elapsed ere she returned down stairs with the volume from which so much was hoped. Her avocations above having shut out all noise but what she created herself, she knew not that a visitor had arrived within the last few minutes, till, on entering the room, the first object she beheld was a young man whom she had never seen before. With a look of much respect, he immediately rose, and being introduced to her by her conscious daughter as "Mr. Henry Tilney," with the embarrassment of real sensibility began to apologise for his appearance there, acknowledging that after what had passed he had little right to expect a welcome at Fullerton, and stating his impatience to be assured of Miss Morland's having reached her home in safety, as the cause of his intrusion. He did not address himself to an uncandid judge or a resentful heart. Far from comprehending him or his sister in their father's misconduct, Mrs. Morland had been always kindly disposed towards each, and instantly, pleased by his appearance, received him

Her mother

with the simple professions of unaffected benevolence; thanking him for such an attention to her daughter, assuring him that the friends of her children were always welcome there, and intreating him to say not another word of the past.

He was not ill inclined to obey this request, for, though his heart was greatly relieved by such unlooked-for mildness, it was not just at that moment in his power to say any thing to the purpose. Returning in silence to his seat, therefore, he remained for some minutes most civilly answering all Mrs. Morland's common remarks about the weather and roads. Catherine meanwhile,—the anxious, agitated, happy, feverish Catherine—said not a word; but her glowing cheek and brightened eye made her mother trust that this good-natured visit would at least set her heart at ease for a time, and gladly therefore did she lay aside the first volume of the *Mirror* for a future hour.[14]

Desirous of Mr. Morland's assistance, as well in giving encouragement, as in finding conversation for her guest, whose embarrassment on his father's account she earnestly pitied, Mrs. Morland had very early dispatched one of the children to summon him; but Mr. Morland was from home—and being thus without any support, at the end of a quarter of an hour she had nothing to say. After a couple of minutes unbroken silence, Henry, turning to Catherine for the first time since her mother's entrance, asked her, with sudden alacrity, if Mr. and Mrs. Allen were now at Fullerton? and on developing, from amidst all her perplexity of words in reply, the meaning, *Cath. shows* which one short syllable would have given, immediately expressed his intention of paying his respects to them, and, with a rising colour, asked her if she would have the goodness to shew him the way. "You may see the house from this window, sir," was information on Sarah's side, which produced only a bow of acknowledgment from the gentleman, and a silencing nod from her mother; for Mrs. Morland, thinking it probable, as a secondary consideration in his wish of waiting on their worthy neighbours, that he might have some explanation to give of his father's behaviour, which it must be more pleasant for him to communicate only to Catherine, would not on any account prevent her accompanying him. They began their walk, and Mrs. Morland was not entirely mistaken in his object in wishing it. Some explanation on his father's account he had to give; but his first purpose was to explain himself, and before they reached Mr. Allen's grounds he had done it so well, that Catherine did not think it could ever be repeated too often. She was assured of his affection; and that heart in return was solicited, which, perhaps, they pretty equally knew was already entirely his own; for, though Henry was now sincerely attached to her, though he felt and delighted in all the excellencies of her character and truly loved her society, I must confess that his affection originated in nothing better than gratitude, or, in other words, that a persuasion of her partiality for him had been the only cause of giving her a serious thought. It is a new circumstance in romance, I acknowledge, and dreadfully derogatory of an heroine's dignity; but if it be as new in common life, the credit of a wild imagination will at least be all my own.

A very short visit to Mrs. Allen, in which Henry talked at random, without sense or connection, and Catherine, wrapt in the contemplation of her own unutterable happiness, scarcely opened her lips, dismissed them to the extasies of another tête-à-tête; and before it was suffered to close, she was enabled to judge how far he was sanctioned by parental authority in his present application. On his return from Woodston, two days before, he had been met near the Abbey by his impatient father, hastily informed in angry terms of Miss Morland's departure, and ordered to think of her no more.

14. The *Mirror* was edited by the writer Henry Mackenzie from 1779 to 1780.

Henry + his father

Such was the permission upon which he had now offered her his hand. The affrighted Catherine, amidst all the terrors of expectation, as she listened to this account, could not but rejoice in the kind caution with which Henry had saved her from the necessity of a conscientious rejection, by engaging her faith before he mentioned the subject; and as he proceeded to give the particulars, and explain the motives of his father's conduct, her feelings soon hardened into even a triumphant delight. The General had had nothing to accuse her of, nothing to lay to her charge, but her being the involuntary, unconscious object of a deception which his pride could not pardon, and which a better pride would have been ashamed to own. She was guilty only of being less rich than he had supposed her to be. Under a mistaken persuasion of her possessions and claims, he had courted her acquaintance in Bath, solicited her company at Northanger, and designed her for his daughter in law. On discovering his error, to turn her from the house seemed the best, though to his feelings an inadequate proof of his resentment towards herself, and his contempt of her family.

John Thorpe had first misled him. The General, perceiving his son one night at the theatre to be paying considerable attention to Miss Morland, had accidentally inquired of Thorpe, if he knew more of her than her name. Thorpe, most happy to be on speaking terms with a man of General Tilney's importance, had been joyfully and proudly communicative; and being at that time not only in daily expectation of Morland's engaging Isabella, but likewise pretty well resolved upon marrying Catherine himself, his vanity induced him to represent the family as yet more wealthy than his vanity and avarice had made him believe them. With whomsoever he was, or was likely to be connected, his own consequence always required that theirs should be great, and as his intimacy with any acquaintance grew, so regularly grew their fortune. The expectations of his friend Morland, therefore, from the first over-rated, had ever since his introduction to Isabella, been gradually increasing; and by merely adding twice as much for the grandeur of the moment, by doubling what he chose to think the amount of Mr. Morland's preferment, trebling his private fortune, bestowing a rich aunt, and sinking half the children, he was able to represent the whole family to the General in a most respectable light. For Catherine, however, the peculiar object of the General's curiosity, and his own speculations, he had yet something more in reserve, and the ten or fifteen thousand pounds which her father could give her, would be a pretty addition to Mr. Allen's estate. Her intimacy there had made him seriously determine on her being handsomely legacied hereafter; and to speak of her therefore as the almost acknowledged future heiress of Fullerton naturally followed. Upon such intelligence the General had proceeded; for never had it occurred to him to doubt its authority. Thorpe's interest in the family, by his sister's approaching connection with one of its members, and his own views on another, (circumstances of which he boasted with almost equal openness,) seemed sufficient vouchers for his truth; and to these were added the absolute facts of the Allens being wealthy and childless, of Miss Morland's being under their care, and—as soon as his acquaintance allowed him to judge—of their treating her with parental kindness. His resolution was soon formed. Already had he discerned a liking towards Miss Morland in the countenance of his son; and thankful for Mr. Thorpe's communication, he almost instantly determined to spare no pains in weakening his boasted interest and ruining his dearest hopes. Catherine herself could not be more ignorant at the time of all this, than his own children. Henry and Eleanor, perceiving nothing in her situation likely to engage their father's particular respect, had seen with astonishment the suddenness, continuance and extent of his attention; and though latterly, from some hints which had accompanied an almost positive command to his son of doing every thing in his power to attach her, Henry was convinced of his father's believing it to be an advantageous connection, it was not till the late explanation at Northanger that they had the smallest idea of the false calculations which had hurried him on. That they were false, the General had learnt from the very person who had suggested them, from Thorpe himself, whom he had chanced to meet again in town, and who, under the influence of exactly opposite feelings, irritated by Catherine's refusal, and yet more by the failure of a very recent endeavour to accomplish a reconciliation between Morland and Isabella, convinced that they were separated for ever, and spurning a friendship which could be no longer serviceable, hastened to contradict all that he had said before to the advantage of the Morlands; confessed himself to have been totally mistaken in his opinion of their circumstances and character, misled by the rhodomontade[15] of his friend to believe his father a man of substance and credit, whereas the transactions of the two or three last weeks proved him to be neither; for after coming eagerly forward on the first overture of a marriage between the families, with the most liberal proposals, he had, on being brought to the point by the shrewdness of the relator, been constrained to acknowledge himself incapable of giving the young people even a decent support. They were, in fact, a necessitous family; numerous too almost beyond example; by no means respected in their own neighbourhood, as he had lately had particular opportunities of discovering; aiming at a style of life which their fortune could not warrant; seeking to better themselves by wealthy connexions; a forward, bragging, scheming race.

The terrified General pronounced the name of Allen with an inquiring look; and here too Thorpe had learnt his error. The Allens, he believed, had lived near them too long, and he knew the young man on whom the Fullerton estate must devolve. The General needed no more. Enraged with almost every body in the world but himself, he set out the next day for the Abbey, where his performances have been seen.

I leave it to my reader's sagacity to determine how much of all this it was possible for Henry to communicate at this time to Catherine, how much of it he could have learnt from his father, in what points his own conjectures might assist him, and what portion must yet remain to be told in a letter from James. I have united for their ease what they must divide for mine. Catherine, at any rate, heard enough to feel, that in suspecting General Tilney of either murdering or shutting up his wife, she had scarcely sinned against his character, or magnified his cruelty.

Henry, in having such things to relate of his father, was almost as pitiable as in their first avowal to himself. He blushed for the narrow-minded counsel which he was obliged to expose. The conversation between them at Northanger had been of the most unfriendly kind. Henry's indignation on hearing how Catherine had been treated, on comprehending his father's views, and being ordered to acquiesce in them, had been open and bold. The General, accustomed on every ordinary occasion to give the law in his family, prepared for no reluctance but of feeling, no opposing desire that should dare to clothe itself in words, could ill brook the opposition of his son, steady as the sanction of reason and the dictate of conscience could make it. But, in such a cause, his anger, though it must shock, could not intimidate Henry, who was sustained in his purpose by a conviction of its justice. He felt himself bound as much in honour as in affection to Miss Morland, and believing that heart to be his own which he had been directed to gain, no unworthy retraction of a tacit consent,

15. Boasting speech.

no reversing decree of unjustifiable anger, could shake his fidelity, or influence the resolutions it prompted.

He steadily refused to accompany his father into Herefordshire, an engagement formed almost at the moment, to promote the dismissal of Catherine, and as steadily declared his intention of offering her his hand. The General was furious in his anger, and they parted in dreadful disagreement. Henry, in an agitation of mind which many solitary hours were required to compose, had returned almost instantly to Woodston; and, on the afternoon of the following day, had begun his journey to Fullerton.

Chapter XVI

Mr. and Mrs. Morland's surprize on being applied to by Mr. Tilney, for their consent to his marrying their daughter, was, for a few minutes, considerable; it having never entered their heads to suspect an attachment on either side; but as nothing, after all, could be more natural than Catherine's being beloved, they soon learnt to consider it with only the happy agitation of gratified pride, and, as far as they alone were concerned, had not a single objection to start. His pleasing manners and good sense were self-evident recommendations; and having never heard evil of him, it was not their way to suppose any evil could be told. Good-will supplying the place of experience, his character needed no attestation. "Catherine would make a sad heedless young housekeeper to be sure," was her mother's foreboding remark; but quick was the consolation of there being nothing like practice.

There was but one obstacle, in short, to be mentioned; but till that one was removed, it must be impossible for them to sanction the engagement. Their tempers were mild, but their principles were steady, and while his parent so expressly forbade the connexion, they could not allow themselves to encourage it. That the General should come forward to solicit the alliance, or that he should even very heartily approve it, they were not refined enough to make any parading stipulation; but the decent appearance of consent must be yielded, and that once obtained—and their own hearts made them trust that it could not be very long denied—their willing approbation was instantly to follow. His consent was all that they wished for. They were no more inclined than entitled to demand his money. Of a very considerable fortune, his son was, by marriage settlements, eventually secure; his present income was an income of independence and comfort, and under every pecuniary view, it was a match beyond the claims of their daughter.

The young people could not be surprized at a decision like this. They felt and they deplored—but they could not resent it; and they parted, endeavouring to hope that such a change in the General, as each believed almost impossible, might speedily take place, to unite them again in the fullness of privileged affection. Henry returned to what was now his only home, to watch over his young plantations, and extend his improvements for her sake, to whose share in them he looked anxiously forward; and Catherine remained at Fullerton to cry. Whether the torments of absence were softened by a clandestine correspondence, let us not inquire. Mr. and Mrs. Morland never did—they had been too kind to exact any promise; and whenever Catherine received a letter, as, at that time, happened pretty often, they always looked another way.

The anxiety, which in this state of their attachment must be the portion of Henry and Catherine, and of all who loved either, as to its final event, can hardly extend, I fear, to the bosom of my readers, who will see in the tell-tale compression of the pages before them, that we are all hastening together to perfect felicity. The means by which their early marriage was effected can be the only doubt; what probable circumstance could work upon a temper like the General's? The circumstance which chiefly availed, was the marriage of his daughter with a man of fortune and consequence, which took place in the course of the summer—an accession of dignity that threw him into a fit of good-humour, from which he did not recover till after Eleanor had obtained his forgiveness of Henry, and his permission for him "to be a fool if he liked it!"

The marriage of Eleanor Tilney, her removal from all the evils of such a home as Northanger had been made by Henry's banishment, to the home of her choice and the man of her choice, is an event which I expect to give general satisfaction among all her acquaintance. My own joy on the occasion is very sincere. I know no one more entitled, by unpretending merit, or better prepared by habitual suffering, to receive and enjoy felicity. Her partiality for this gentleman was not of recent origin; and he had been long withheld only by inferiority of situation from addressing her. His unexpected accession to title and fortune had removed all his difficulties; and never had the General loved his daughter so well in all her hours of companionship, utility, and patient endurance, as when he first hailed her, "Your Ladyship!" Her husband was really deserving of her; independent of his peerage, his wealth, and his attachment, being to a precision the most charming young man in the world. Any further definition of his merits must be unnecessary; the most charming young man in the world is instantly before the imagination of us all. Concerning the one in question therefore I have only to add—(aware that the rules of composition forbid the introduction of a character not connected with my fable)—that this was the very gentleman whose negligent servant left behind him that collection of washing-bills, resulting from a long visit at Northanger, by which my heroine was involved in one of her most alarming adventures.

The influence of the Viscount and Viscountess in their brother's behalf was assisted by that right understanding of Mr. Morland's circumstances which, as soon as the General would allow himself to be informed, they were qualified to give. It taught him that he had been scarcely more misled by Thorpe's first boast of the family wealth, than by his subsequent malicious overthrow of it; that in no sense of the word were they necessitous or poor, and that Catherine would have three thousand pounds. This was so material an amendment of his late expectations, that it greatly contributed to smooth the descent of his pride; and by no means without its effect was the private intelligence, which he was at some pains to procure, that the Fullerton estate, being entirely at the disposal of its present proprietor, was consequently open to every greedy speculation.

On the strength of this, the General, soon after Eleanor's marriage, permitted his son to return to Northanger, and thence made him the bearer of his consent, very courteously worded in a page full of empty professions to Mr. Morland. The event which it authorized soon followed: Henry and Catherine were married, the bells rang and every body smiled; and, as this took place within a twelve-month from the first day of their meeting, it will not appear, after all the dreadful delays occasioned by the General's cruelty, that they were essentially hurt by it. To begin perfect happiness at the respective ages of twenty-six and eighteen, is to do pretty well; and professing myself moreover convinced, that the General's unjust interference, so far from being really injurious to their felicity, was perhaps rather conducive to it, by improving their knowledge of each other, and adding strength to their attachment, I leave it to be settled by whomsoever it may concern, whether the tendency of this work be altogether to recommend parental tyranny, or reward filial disobedience.

1798–99/1817

Mary Shelley
1797–1851

Mary Shelley was the daughter of the feminist writer MARY WOLL-
STONECRAFT, author of *A Vindication of the Rights of Women* (1792),
and the philosopher William Godwin, one of the most radical
thinkers of his age. Although neither Godwin nor Wollstonecraft
believed in marriage as an institution—he deemed it "the worst of
all laws" while she considered it "legal prostitution"—they did
marry shortly before Wollstonecraft gave birth to their daughter
and died of childbed fever. Young Mary and her half-sister, Fanny
Imlay (her mother's illegitimate daughter) were raised by Godwin
and his second wife, Mary Jane Clairmont, who by all accounts
treated her own two children more kindly than her stepchildren. Estranged from her step-
mother, Mary was sent to live with family friends in Scotland, where for several years she wandered the countryside happily, "indulging in waking dreams," as she would later claim. At
sixteen she returned to England and met the poet Percy Bysshe Shelley, unhappily married and
a frequent visitor to her father's house; he left his wife for Mary and the couple eloped first to
Switzerland and then to Italy, taking Mary's stepsister Claire Clairmont with them.

For a time the trio led an artistically rich life, interacting with close friends such as the
Romantic poets John Keats, Leigh Hunt, and George Gordon, Lord Byron, by whom Claire
Clairmont became pregnant. A number of misfortunes occurred, however, that dampened
their spirits. Between 1815 and 1818 Mary gave birth to three children, all of whom died in
infancy. In 1816, moreover, both Fanny Imlay and Shelley's wife, Harriet, the mother of his
two children, committed suicide; Shelley married Mary shortly thereafter but was denied custody of his children on the grounds that he was unfit. Although Mary Shelley at last gave birth
to a son who survived, Percy Florence, tragedy struck again in 1822, when Percy Shelley
drowned in a boating accident in Italy. For the next thirty years Mary Shelley raised her son,
edited her husband's poetry, and wrote novels, plays, stories, and essays of her own. She died at
fifty-three, nursed by her son and his wife.

Shelley's best known work, *Frankenstein* (1818), brought its author enduring fame and
encouraged her to write other tales of horror, published in this century as *Mary Shelley: Collected
Tales and Stories* (1976). Between 1835 and 1839 she published critical biographies of European
authors in the *Cabinet Cyclopedia*. Her other novels include *Valperga* (1823), *The Last Man*
(1826), *Perkin Warbeck* (1830), *Lodore* (1835), and *Falkner* (1837). The best of these, *The Last
Man*, explores the ambiguous status of an unhappy hero who outlives all of his contemporaries.
Having survived her mother, sister, husband, and three children, Shelley herself had experienced
something of her protagonist's lonely grief. "I am now on the eve of completing my five and
twentieth year," she wrote in her journal in 1822, "how drearily young for one so lost as I!. . . .
What I have suffered . . . will write years on my brow and intrench them in my heart."

As indicated in her retrospective account of writing *Frankenstein*, Shelley's novel emerged
as part of a contest Lord Byron proposed in which each member of the Shelley circle would
write a ghost story for the entertainment of the others. Initially intimidated by this exercise, the
nineteen-year-old Shelley struggled to imagine a tale that "would speak to the mysterious fears
in our nature and awaken thrilling horror" in its readers. At last she dreamed one night "so very
hideous an idea," that of the birth of a terrible "phantasm of a man" at the hands of a brilliant
but misguided creator. Encouraged by her husband to expand the story into a novel, Shelley
took care to insist that the final work was hers, not his. At the end of her introduction she
speaks with nostalgic pride of her brilliant creation: "And now, once again, I bid my hideous

progeny go forth and prosper. I have an affection for it, for it was the offspring of happy days, when death and grief were but words, which found no true echo in my heart."

⊰ Introduction to *Frankenstein* ⊱

The Publishers of the Standard Novels,[1] in selecting "Frankenstein" for one of their series, expressed a wish that I should furnish them with some account of the origin of the story. I am the more willing to comply, because I shall thus give a general answer to the question, so very frequently asked me—"How I, then a young girl, came to think of, and to dilate upon, so very hideous an idea?" It is true that I am very averse to bringing myself forward in print; but as my account will only appear as an appendage to a former production, and as it will be confined to such topics as have connection with my authorship alone, I can scarcely accuse myself of a personal intrusion.

It is not singular that, as the daughter of two persons of distinguished literary celebrity, I should very early in life have thought of writing. As a child I scribbled; and my favourite pastime, during the hours given me for recreation, was to "write stories." Still I had a dearer pleasure than this, which was the formation of castles in the air—the indulging in waking dreams—the following up trains of thought, which had for their subject the formation of a succession of imaginary incidents. My dreams were at once more fantastic and agreeable than my writings. In the latter I was a close imitator—rather doing as others had done, than putting down the suggestions of my own mind. What I wrote was intended at least for one other eye—my childhood's companion and friend;[2] but my dreams were all my own; I accounted for them to nobody; they were my refuge when annoyed—my dearest pleasure when free.

I lived principally in the country as a girl, and passed a considerable time in Scotland. I made occasional visits to the more picturesque parts; but my habitual residence was on the blank and dreary northern shores of the Tay, near Dundee. Blank and dreary on retrospection I call them; they were not so to me then. They were the eyry of freedom, and the pleasant region where unheeded I could commune with the creatures of my fancy. I wrote then—but in a most common-place style. It was beneath the trees of the grounds belonging to our house, or on the bleak sides of the woodless mountains near, that my true compositions, the airy flights of my imagination, were born and fostered. I did not make myself the heroine of my tales. Life appeared to me too commonplace an affair as regarded myself. I could not figure to myself that romantic woes or wonderful events would ever be my lot; but I was not confined to my own identity, and I could people the hours with creations far more interesting to me at that age, than my own sensations.

After this my life became busier, and reality stood in place of fiction. My husband, however, was from the first, very anxious that I should prove myself worthy of my parentage, and enroll myself on the page of fame. He was forever inciting me to obtain literary reputation, which even on my own part I cared for then, though since I have become infinitely indifferent to it. At this time he desired that I should write, not so much with the idea that I could produce anything worthy of notice, but that he might himself judge how far I possessed the promise of better things hereafter. Still I did nothing. Traveling, and the cares of a family, occupied my time; and study,

---

1. A reference to the series in which *Frankenstein* was to be published in its third edition.

2. Isabel Baxter, a friend during the author's childhood in Scotland.

in the way of reading, or improving my ideas in communication with his far more cultivated mind, was all of literary employment that engaged my attention.

In the summer of 1816, we visited Switzerland, and became the neighbours of Lord Byron.[3] At first we spent our pleasant hours on the lake, or wandering on its shores; and Lord Byron, who was writing the third canto of Childe Harold, was the only one among us who put his thoughts upon paper. These, as he brought them successively to us, clothed in all the light and harmony of poetry, seemed to stamp as divine the glories of heaven and earth, whose influences we partook with him.

But it proved a wet, ungenial summer, and incessant rain often confined us for days to the house. Some volumes of ghost stories, translated from the German into French, fell into our hands. There was the History of the Inconstant Lover, who, when he thought to clasp the bride to whom he had pledged his vows, found himself in the arms of the pale ghost of her whom he had deserted. There was the tale of the sinful founder of his race, whose miserable doom it was to bestow the kiss of death on all the younger sons of his fated house, just when they reached the age of promise. His gigantic, shadowy form, clothed like the ghost in Hamlet, in complete armour, but with the beaver up, was seen at midnight, by the moon's fitful beams, to advance slowly along the gloomy avenue. The shape was lost beneath the shadow of the castle walls; but soon a gate swung back, a step was heard, the door of the chamber opened, and he advanced to the couch of the blooming youths, cradled in healthy sleep. Eternal sorrow sat upon his face as he bent down and kissed the forehead of the boys, who from that hour withered like flowers snapt upon the stalk. I have not seen these stories since then; but their incidents are as fresh in my mind as if I had read them yesterday.

"We will each write a ghost story," said Lord Byron; and his proposition was acceded to. There were four of us. The noble author began a tale, a fragment of which he printed at the end of his poem of Mazeppa.[4] Shelley, more apt to embody ideas and sentiments in the radiance of brilliant imagery, and in the music of the most melodious verse that adorns our language, than to invent the machinery of a story, commenced one founded on the experiences of his early life. Poor Polidori[5] had some terrible idea about a skull-headed lady, who was so punished for peeping through a key-hole—what to see I forget—something very shocking and wrong of course; but when she was reduced to a worse condition than the renowned Tom of Coventry, he did not know what to do with her, and was obliged to dispatch her to the tomb of the Capulets, the only place for which she was fitted.[6] The illustrious poets also, annoyed by the platitude of prose, speedily relinquished their uncongenial task.

I busied myself *to think of a story*—a story to rival those which had excited us to this task. One which would speak to the mysterious fears of our nature, and awaken thrilling horror—one to make the reader dread to look round, to curdle the blood, and quicken the beatings of the heart. If I did not accomplish these things, my ghost story would be unworthy of its name. I thought and pondered—vainly. I felt that blank incapability of invention which is the greatest misery of authorship, when dull Nothing replies to our anxious invocations. *Have you thought of a story?* I was asked each morning, and each morning I was forced to reply with a mortifying negative.

3. George Gordon, Lord Byron (1788–1824), a poet and friend of the Shelleys; *Childe Harold's Pilgrimage* (1812–18) is a travelogue written in four cantos.
4. *Mazeppa* (1819) tells the life story of a Polish nobleman and adventurer.

5. Shelley refers to Percy Bysshe Shelley (1792–1822), the author's husband; Polidori to another member of their circle, an Italian writer.
6. The Capulets were Juliet's family in Shakespeare's *Romeo and Juliet.*

Everything must have a beginning, to speak in Sanchean phrase; and that beginning must be linked to something that went before. The Hindoos give the world an elephant to support it, but they make the elephant stand upon a tortoise. Invention, it must be humbly admitted, does not consist in creating out of void, but out of chaos; the materials must, in the first place, be afforded: it can give form to dark, shapeless substances, but cannot bring into being the substance itself. In all matters of discovery and invention, even of those that appertain to the imagination, we are continually reminded of the story of Columbus and his egg. Invention consists in the capacity of seizing on the capabilities of a subject, and in the power of moulding and fashioning ideas suggested to it.

Many and long were the conversations between Lord Byron and Shelley, to which I was a devout but nearly silent listener. During one of these, various philosophical doctrines were discussed, and among others the nature of the principle of life, and whether there was any probability of its ever being discovered and communicated. They talked of the experiments of Dr. Darwin,[7] (I speak not of what the Doctor really did, or said that he did, but, as more to my purpose, of what was then spoken of as having been done by him,) who preserved a piece of vermicelli in a glass case, till by some extraordinary means it began to move with voluntary motion. Not thus, after all, would life be given. Perhaps a corpse would be re-animated; galvanism had given token of such things: perhaps the component parts of a creature might be manufactured, brought together, and endued with vital warmth.

Night waned upon this talk, and even the witching hour had gone by, before we retired to rest. When I placed my head on my pillow, I did not sleep, nor could I be said to think. My imagination, unbidden, possessed and guided me, gifting the successive images that arose in my mind with a vividness far beyond the usual bounds of reverie. I saw—with shut eyes, but acute mental vision—I saw the pale student of unhallowed arts kneeling beside the thing he had put together. I saw the hideous phantasm of a man stretched out, and then, on the working of some powerful engine, show signs of life, and stir with an uneasy, half vital motion. Frightful must it be; for supremely frightful would be the effect of any human endeavour to mock the stupendous mechanism of the Creator of the world. His success would terrify the artist; he would rush away from his odious handiwork, horror-stricken. He would hope that, left to itself, the slight spark of life which he had communicated would fade; that this thing, which had received such imperfect animation, would subside into dead matter; and he might sleep in the belief that the silence of the grave would quench for ever the transient existence of the hideous corpse which he had looked upon as the cradle of life. He sleeps; but he is awakened; he opens his eyes; behold the horrid thing stands at his bedside, opening his curtains, and looking on him with yellow, watery, but speculative eyes.

I opened mine in terror. The idea so possessed my mind, that a thrill of fear ran through me, and I wished to exchange the ghastly image of my fancy for the realities around. I see them still; the very room, the dark *parquet,* the closed shutters, with the moonlight struggling through, and the sense I had that the glassy lake and white high Alps were beyond. I could not so easily get rid of my hideous phantom; still it haunted me. I must try to think of something else. I recurred to my ghost story—my tiresome unlucky ghost story! O! if I could only contrive one which would frighten my reader as I myself had been frightened that night!

7. Charles Darwin (1809–82), the English naturalist who developed the theory of evolution.

Swift as light and as cheering was the idea that broke in upon me. "I have found it! What terrified me will terrify others; and I need only describe the spectre which had haunted my midnight pillow." On the morrow I announced that I had *thought of a story*. I began that day with the words, *It was on a dreary night of November*, making only a transcript of the grim terrors of my waking dream.

At first I thought but of a few pages—of a short tale; but Shelley urged me to develope the idea at greater length. I certainly did not owe the suggestion of one incident, nor scarcely of one train of feeling, to my husband, and yet but for his incitement, it would never have taken the form in which it was presented to the world. From this declaration I must except the preface. As far as I can recollect, it was entirely written by him.

And now, once again, I bid my hideous progeny go forth and prosper. I have an affection for it, for it was the offspring of happy days, when death and grief were but words, which found no true echo in my heart. Its several pages speak of many a walk, many a drive, and many a conversation, when I was not alone; and my companion was one who, in this world, I shall never see more. But this is for myself; my readers have nothing to do with these associations.

I will add but one word as to the alterations I have made. They are principally those of style. I have changed no portion of the story, nor introduced any new ideas or circumstances. I have mended the language where it was so bald as to interfere with the interest of the narrative; and these changes occur almost exclusively in the beginning of the first volume. Throughout they are entirely confined to such parts as are mere adjuncts to the story, leaving the core and substance of it untouched.

1831

Charlotte Brontë
1816–1855 — 51 years old

Author of the much-loved *Jane Eyre* (1847), Charlotte Brontë was raised in the Yorkshire village of Haworth, where her father, Patrick Brontë, was a minister in the Church of England. She enjoyed the companionship of her siblings, Emily, Anne, and Branwell; their mother, Maria Branwell Brontë, had died in 1821 of stomach cancer, and the children's care had been assumed by their maternal aunt, Elizabeth Branwell. During this time of industrial growth, Yorkshire was a dangerous place, with polluted rivers, frequent outbreaks of cholera and typhoid, and an extremely high infant mortality rate. Traveling to the county's villages with her father and witnessing disease run rampant might well have contributed to Brontë's famous depiction of Lowood School in *Jane Eyre*; the experience of her two elder sisters, Maria and Elizabeth, at Cowan Bridge School, where they died of tuberculosis in 1825, certainly influenced her portrayal. After their sisters' deaths, the remaining Brontë children were educated at home, where they spent much time writing stories of imaginary kingdoms populated by powerful queens and brutal courtiers. According to Charlotte, the siblings were remarkably close, "their minds cast in the same mould, their ideas drawn from the same source."

In 1830, friends of the Brontë family, the Reverend Thomas Atkinson and his wife, offered to fund Charlotte Brontë's attendance at their new boarding school for girls, Roe Head.

15 years old

After a brief but difficult period of adjustment, she flourished at the school, reading Shakespeare and Milton and winning several academic prizes during her year there. She developed a friendship with her professor and mentor, Margaret Wooler, and met two young women who became lifelong friends, Ellen Nussey and Mary Taylor. Upon returning to Haworth, Brontë again took up writing with her siblings, leaving home only for brief periods during which she worked, unhappily, as a governess. In 1842, Brontë traveled with Emily to study at the Pensionnat Heger in Brussels, Belgium, where she developed an apparently unrequited attachment to her married tutor, Monsieur Heger. Eventually the household arrangement became strained and Brontë returned home, but the experience in Brussels provided her with material and characters for two later novels, *Villette* (1853) and *The Professor* (1857).

When she settled again at Haworth Parsonage, Brontë convinced her sisters to join her in submitting a volume of their poems for publication under the pseudonyms Currer, Ellis, and Acton Bell. Although their *Poems* were published in 1846 and received two positive reviews, sales of the volume were quite poor. Nonetheless determined to achieve literary success, Brontë urged each of her sisters to "set to work on a prose tale." Her own submission, *The Professor*, was rejected and remained unpublished during her lifetime, but Emily's *Wuthering Heights* and Anne's *Acton Grey* were accepted, provided that the authors would bear some of the publishing costs themselves. Undaunted by her own rejection, and indeed buoyed by her sisters' success, Brontë composed *Jane Eyre: An Autobiography* by Currer Bell, which was published in 1847 to widespread critical acclaim. Praised for its distinctive style and vision, the novel recounts in compelling first-person narrative the coming of age of a young governess whose ethical foundation is swayed by love but who ultimately is governed by the desire for dignity and liberty. Equally compelling is Brontë's presentation of the rugged iconoclast Rochester and his "madwoman in the attic," Bertha Mason Rochester, whom feminist critics Sandra M. Gilbert and Susan Gubar have posited as Jane's dark double.

When the public demanded more fiction by the mysterious Currer Bell, Brontë determined to write another novel but was slowed in this project by the painful and consecutive deaths of her alcoholic brother, Branwell, in September 1848, her beloved sister Emily in December of that year, and her younger sister, Anne, in May of 1849. Despite her shock and grief, Brontë was resolute in her desire to complete and publish *Shirley* (1849), a fictional account of the problems of mill owners and workers during the Luddite riots of 1812, riots that her father as a young man had witnessed in nearby Dewsbury. The novel provided Charlotte with some comfort, since she modeled her protagonist, Shirley Keeldar, after her sister Emily. By 1849 Brontë's identity as the author of *Jane Eyre* was known, and she traveled regularly to visit her publisher, George Smith, in London, where she on one occasion met the novelist she most admired, William Makepeace Thackeray, to whom she had dedicated the second edition of *Jane Eyre*. She became friends with the novelist Elizabeth Gaskell, who would later write her biography, and gained a circle of admiring readers in and around Haworth. One of these was her father's curate, Arthur Bell Nicholls, whom she married in 1854, the same year that her new novel, *Villette*, earned the same spectacular reception that *Jane Eyre* had received. Her life with Nicholls was brief, however, for in March 1855, ill from influenza and the complications of pregnancy, Charlotte Brontë died, survived by her new husband and her aged father.

While Brontë's major achievement certainly lies in her novels, her letters reveal much about her creative process and ambition. In 1838 she wrote boldly to England's poet laureate, Robert Southey, acknowledging her literary aspirations; his response both angered and energized her. She also corresponded about literary matters with the renowned man of letters George Henry Lewes, who urged her to avoid melodrama and choose sex-appropriate subject matter in her future novels. Certainly Brontë's letters demonstrate her remarkable determination to succeed as a writer on her own terms.

⊰ Letter from Robert Southey[1] ⊱

12 March 1837

Keswick

Madam,

You will probably ere this have given up all expectation of receiving an answer to your letter of Decr. 29. I was on the borders of Cornwall when that letter was written. It found me a fortnight afterwards in Hampshire. During my subsequent movements in different parts of the country, and a tarriance of 3 busy weeks in London, I had no leisure for replying to it. And now that I am once more at home and am clearing the arrears of business which had accumulated during a long absence, it has lain unanswered till the last of a numerous pile—not from disrespect or indifference to its contents, but in truth, because it is not an easy task to answer it, nor a pleasant one to cast a damp over the high spirits and the generous desires of youth.

What you are I can only infer from your letter, which appears to be written in sincerity, tho' I may suspect that you have used a fictitious signature.[2] Be that as it may, the letter and the verse bear the same stamp, and I can well understand that state of mind which they indicate. What I am, you might have well learnt by such of my publications as have come into your hands: but you live in a visionary world and seem to imagine that this is my case also, when you speak of my "stooping from a throne of light and glory." Had you happened to be acquainted with me, a little personal knowledge would have tempered your enthusiasm. You who so ardently desire "to be for ever known" as a poetess might have had your ardor in some degree abated, by seeing a poet in the decline of life, and witnessing the effect which age produces upon our hopes and aspirations. Yet I am neither a disappointed man, nor a discontented one, and you would never have heard from me any chilling sermonizings upon the text that all is vanity.

It is not my advice that you have asked as to the direction of your talents, but my opinion of them, and yet the opinion may be worth little, and the advice much. You evidently possess and in no inconsiderable degree what Wordsworth calls "the faculty of Verse." I am not depreciating it when I say that in these times it is not rare. Many volumes of poems are now published every year without attracting public attention, any one of which, if it had appeared half a century ago, would have obtained a high reputation for its author. Whoever therefore is ambitious of distinction in this way ought to be prepared for disappointment.

But it is not with a view to distinction that you should cultivate this talent, if you consult your own happiness. I who have made literature my profession, and devoted my life to it, and have never for a moment repented of the deliberate choice, think myself nevertheless bound in duty to caution every young man who applies as an aspirant to me for encouragement and advice, against taking so perilous a course. You will say that a woman has no need of such a caution, there can be no peril in it for her: and in a certain sense this is true. But there is a danger of which I would with all kindness and all earnestness warn you. The daydreams of which you habitually indulge are likely to induce a distempered state of mind, and in proportion as all the "ordinary uses of the world" seem to you "flat and unprofitable," you will be unfitted

---

1. England's poet laureate from 1813 to 1843, Robert Southey (1774–1843) was also a historian and a literary critic.

2. Brontë had, in fact, signed her own name.

for them, without becoming fitted for anything else. Literature cannot be the business of a woman's life: and it ought not to be. The more she is engaged in her proper duties, the less leisure will she have for it, even as an accomplishment and a recreation. To those duties you have not yet been called, and when you are you will be less eager for celebrity. You will then not seek in imagination for excitement, of which the vicissitudes of this life and the anxieties, from which you must not hope to be exempted be your station what it may, will bring with them but too much.

But do not suppose that I disparage the gift which you possess, nor that I would discourage you from exercising it. I only exhort you so to think of it and so to use it, as to render it conducive to your own permanent good. Write poetry for its own sake, not in a spirit of emulation, and not with a view to celebrity: the less you aim at *that*, the more likely you will be to deserve, and finally to obtain it. So written, it is wholesome both for the heart and soul. It may be made next to religion the surest means of soothing the mind and elevating it. You may embody in it your best thoughts and your wisest feelings, and in so doing discipline and strengthen them.

Farewell Madam! It is not because I have forgotten that I was once young myself that I write to you in this strain—but because I remember it. You will neither doubt my sincerity, nor my good will. And however ill what has been said may accord with your present views and temper, the longer you live the more reasonable it will appear to you. Though I may be but an ungracious adviser, you will allow me therefore to subscribe myself,

With the best wishes for your happiness, here and hereafter,
Your true friend
Robert Southey   *1837*

⊰ Letter to Robert Southey ⊱

16 March 1837

Roe Head

Sir,
I cannot rest until I have answered your letter, even though by addressing you a second time I should appear a little intrusive; but I must thank you for the kind and wise advice you have condescended to give me. I had not ventured to hope for such a reply, so considerate in its tone, so noble in its spirit. I must suppress what I feel, or you will think me foolishly enthusiastic.

At the first perusal of your letter I felt only shame and regret that I had ever ventured to trouble you with my crude rhapsody; I felt a painful heat rise to my face, when I thought of the quires of paper I had covered with what once gave me so much delight, but which now was only a source of confusion; but, after I had thought a little and read it again and again, the prospect seemed to clear. You do not forbid me to write; you do not say that what I write is utterly destitute of merit. You only warn me against the folly of neglecting real duties, for the sake of imaginative pleasures; of writing for the love of fame; for the selfish excitement of emulation. You kindly allow me to write poetry for its own sake, provided I leave undone nothing which I ought to do, in order to pursue that single absorbing exquisite gratification. I am afraid, Sir, you think me very foolish. I know the first letter I wrote to you was all senseless trash from beginning to end; but I am not altogether the idle dreaming being it would seem to denote. My Father is a clergyman of limited, though competent, income, and I am the eldest of his children. He expended quite as much in my education as he could afford in justice to the rest. I thought it therefore my duty, when I left school, to become a governess. In that capacity, I find enough to occupy my thoughts all day long, and my head and hands too, without having a moment's time for one dream of the imagination. In the evenings, I confess, I do think, but I never trouble anyone else with my thoughts. I carefully avoid any appearance of preoccupation, and eccentricity, which might lead those I live amongst to suspect the nature of my pursuits. Following my Father's advice—who from my childhood has counselled me just in the wise and friendly tone of your letter—I have endeavored not only attentively to observe all the duties a woman ought to fulfill, but to feel deeply interested in them. I don't always succeed, for sometimes when I'm teaching or sewing I would rather be reading or writing; but I try to deny myself, and my Father's approbation amply rewarded me for the privation. Once more allow me to thank you with sincere gratitude. I trust I shall never more feel ambitious to see my name in print: if the wish should rise, I'll look at Southey's letter, and suppress it. It is honor enough for me that I have written to him, and received an answer. That letter is consecrated; no one shall ever see it, but Papa and my brother and sisters. Again I thank you. This incident I suppose will be renewed no more; if I live to be an old woman I shall remember it thirty years hence as a bright dream. The signature which you suspected of being fictitious is my real name. Again, therefore, I must sign myself,

C. Brontë

P.S. Pray, Sir, excuse me for writing to you a second time; I could not help writing, partly to tell you how thankful I am for your kindness, and partly to let you know that your advice shall not be wasted, however sorrowfully and reluctantly it may be at first followed. C. B.   *1837*

⊰ Letter to George Henry Lewes[3] ⊱

6 November 1847

Haworth

Dear Sir,
    Your letter reached me yesterday; I beg to assure you that I appreciate fully the intention with which it was written, and thank you sincerely both for its cheering commendation and valuable advice.
    You warn me to beware of Melodrame and you exhort me to adhere to the real. When I first began to write, so impressed was I with the truth of the principles you advocate that I determined to take Nature and Truth as my sole guides and to follow in their very footprints; I restrained imagination, eschewed romance, repressed excitement: over-bright colouring too I avoided, and sought to produce something which should be soft, grave, and true.
    My work (a tale in I vol.) being completed, I offered it to a publisher. He said it was original, faithful to Nature, but he did not feel warranted in accepting it; such a

3. George Henry Lewes (1817–78) was a renowned English philospher and literary critic, he wrote for a number of journals, including *Frazer*.

work would not sell. I tried six publishers in succession; they all told me it was deficient in "startling incident" and "thrilling excitement," that it would never suit the circulating libraries, and as it was on those libraries the success of works of fiction mainly depended they could not undertake to publish what would be overlooked there—"Jane Eyre" was rather objected to at first [on] the same grounds—but finally found acceptance.

I mention this to you not with a view of pleading exemption from censure, but in order to direct your attention to the root of certain literary evils—if in your forthcoming article in "Frazer" you would bestow a few words of enlightenment on the public who support the circulating libraries, you might, with your powers, do some good.

You advise me too, not to stray far from the ground of experience as I become weak when I enter the region of fiction; and you say "real experience is perennially interesting and to all men. . . ."

I feel that this also is true, but, dear Sir, is not the real experience of each individual very limited? And if a writer dwells upon that solely or principally is he not in danger of repeating himself, and also of becoming an egotist?

Then too, Imagination is a strong, restless faculty which claims to be heard and exercised; are we to be quite deaf to her cry and insensate to her struggles? When she shews us bright pictures are we never to look at them and try to reproduce them? And when she is eloquent and speaks rapidly and urgently in our ear are we not to write to her dictation?

I shall anxiously search the next number of "Frazer" for your opinions on these points.

Believe me, dear Sir,
Yours gratefully
C Bell[4]   *1847*

Emily Brontë
1818–1848

Emily Jane Brontë, the author of *Wuthering Heights* (1847), was the most inscrutable of the famous Brontë siblings. Exactly how her distinctive artistic vision and complex understanding of the human psyche and its darker passions developed is shrouded in mystery. "My sister Emily loved the moors," CHARLOTTE BRONTË wrote after her younger sibling's death; "she found in the bleak solitude many and dear delights; and not the least and best loved—was liberty." Emily Brontë was raised by her maternal aunt, Elizabeth Branwell, and her father, Patrick Brontë, a curate, for whom Aunt Branwell kept house after Maria Brontë's death in 1821. With her younger sister, Anne, Emily composed stories and poems set in an imaginary kingdom called Gondal, whose amoral Queen, Augusta Geraldine Almeda, reigned with passion and brute force. Although she lived briefly at several boarding schools and studied for a year in Brussels with her sister Charlotte, Emily acquired most of her literary education at home. The sisters once attempted to establish their own school but were unable to attract any pupils.

Emily Brontë's poetry was arranged for publication by Charlotte, who found the poems by accident in 1845 and realized that "these were not common effusions, not at all like the poetry

---

4. Currer Bell was Charlotte Brontë's pen name.

women generally write." Although it was difficult to convince the reticent Emily to consider publication, she acquiesced when Charlotte and Anne agreed to include their own poems in the manuscript they sent forward, and in 1846 *Poems by Currer, Ellis, and Acton Bell* was published. When only two copies were sold, the sisters, undeterred, decided they would write novels. Under the leadership of Charlotte, Emily Brontë began composing *Wuthering Heights*, a brooding saga of the quasi-incestuous love of Catherine Earnshaw and her foster brother, Heathcliff. Brontë's characterization of the malevolent Heathcliff owes much to the poetry of Lord Byron, whom she read with guilty pleasure. Although *Wuthering Heights* garnered almost as much critical attention as *Jane Eyre*, it was more ambivalently received; reviewers found it baffling and immoral in its portrayal of fiendishness and vengeance. *Wuthering Heights* was to be Brontë's only novel, for in 1848 she died of consumption at Haworth, nursed by a grieving Charlotte. Her identity as the author of this controversial novel did not emerge until the appearance of its second edition in 1850. *Wuthering Heights* today is admired for its poetic language, imaginative power, and mystical vision.

The Complete Poems of Emily Jane Brontë, edited by C. W. Hatfield, appeared in 1941, solidifying her reputation as a distinguished poet. Charlotte Brontë described her sister's verses as having "a peculiar music—wild, melancholy, and elevating," a vivid and accurate assessment of their power. Although the authorship of "Stanzas" was for years disputed, Charlotte Brontë included it as one of Emily's poems when she edited, in 1850, a volume entitled *Selections from Poems by Ellis Bell*. Whereas the poem's assertion of independent creative identity has caused some scholars to argue that Charlotte wrote it, the romantic evocation of Emily's beloved moors suggests it is her voice.

⊰ [Alone I Sat; the Summer Day] ⊱

Alone I sat; the summer day
Had died in smiling light away;
I saw it die, I watched it fade
From misty hill and breezeless glade;

5   And thoughts in my soul were gushing,
And my heart bowed beneath their power;
And tears within my eyes were rushing
Because I could not speak the feeling,
The solemn joy around me stealing
10 In that divine, untroubled hour.

I asked myself, "O why has heaven
Denied the precious gift to me,
The glorious gift to many given
To speak their thoughts in poetry?

15 "Dreams have encircled me," I said,
"From careless childhood's sunny time;
Visions by ardent fancy fed
Since life in its morning prime."

But now, when I had hoped to sing,
20 My fingers strike a tuneless string;
And still the burden of the strain
Is "Strive no more; 'tis all in vain."

1837/1941

⊰ To Imagination ⊱

When weary with the long day's care,
And earthly change from pain to pain,
And lost, and ready to despair,
Thy kind voice calls me back again—
5   O my true friend, I am not lone
While thou canst speak with such a tone!

So hopeless is the world without,
The world within I doubly prize;
Thy world where guile and hate and doubt
10   And cold suspicion never rise;
Where thou and I and Liberty
Have undisputed sovereignty.

What matters it that all around
Danger and grief and darkness lie,
15   If but within our bosom's bound
We hold a bright unsullied sky,
Warm with ten thousand mingled rays
Of suns that know no winter days?

Reason indeed may oft complain
20   For Nature's sad reality,
And tell the suffering heart how vain
Its cherished dreams must always be;
And Truth may rudely trample down
The flowers of Fancy newly blown.

25   But thou art ever there to bring
The hovering visions back and breathe
New glories o'er the blighted spring
And call a lovelier life from death,
And whisper with a voice divine
30   Of real worlds as bright as thine.

I trust not to thy phantom bliss,
Yet still in evening's quiet hour
With never-failing thankfulness
I welcome thee, benignant power,
35   Sure solacer of human cares
And brighter hope when hope despairs.

1844/1846

⊰ The Night Wind ⊱

In summer's mellow midnight,
A cloudless moon shone through
Our open parlour window
And rosetrees wet with dew.

ilent musing,
wind waved my hair:
.ne Heaven was glorious,
..u sleeping Earth was fair.

I needed not its breathing
10 To bring such thoughts to me,
But still it whispered lowly,
"How dark the woods will be!

"The thick leaves in my murmur
Are rustling like a dream,
15 And all their myriad voices
Instinct with spirit seem."

I said, "Go, gentle singer,
Thy wooing voice is kind,
But do not think its music
20 Has power to reach my mind.

"Play with the scented flower,
The young tree's supple bough,
And leave my fellow feelings
In their own course to flow."

25 The wanderer would not leave me;
Its kiss grew warmer still—
"O come," it sighed so sweetly,
"I'll win thee 'gainst thy will.

"Have we not been from childhood friends?
30 Have I not loved thee long?
As long as thou hast loved the night
Whose silence wakes my song.

"And when thy heart is laid at rest
Beneath the church-yard stone
35 I shall have time enough to mourn
And thou to be alone."

1840/1850

⊰ R. Alcona to J. Brenzaida[1] ⊱

Cold in the earth, and the deep snow piled above thee!
Far, far removed, cold in the dreary grave!
Have I forgot, my Only Love, to love thee,
Severed at last by Time's all-wearing wave?

5 Now, when alone, do my thoughts no longer hover
Over the mountains on Angora's shore;
Resting their wings where heath and fern-leaves cover
That noble heart for ever, ever more?

1. Lovers in Brontë's imaginary Gondal, a kingdom she invented with her sister Anne.

Cold in the earth, and fifteen wild Decembers
10 From those brown hills have melted into spring—
Faithful indeed is the spirit that remembers
After such years of change and suffering!

Sweet Love of youth, forgive if I forget thee
While the World's tide is bearing me along:
15 Sterner desires and darker hopes beset me,
Hopes which obscure but cannot do thee wrong.

No other Sun has lightened up my heaven;
No other Star has ever shone for me:
All my life's bliss from thy dear life was given—
20 All my life's bliss is in the grave with thee.

But when the days of golden dreams had perished
And even Despair was powerless to destroy,
Then did I learn how existence could be cherished,
Strengthened and fed without the aid of joy;

25 Then did I check the tears of useless passion,
Weaned my young soul from yearning after thine;
Sternly denied its burning wish to hasten
Down to that tomb already more than mine!

And even yet, I dare not let it languish,
30 Dare not indulge in Memory's rapturous pain;
Once drinking deep that divinest anguish,
How could I seek the empty world again?

1845/1846

⊰ [No Coward Soul is Mine] ⊱

No coward soul is mine
No trembler in the world's storm-troubled sphere
I see Heaven's glories shine
And Faith shines equal arming me from Fear

5 O God within my breast
Almighty ever-present Diety
Life, that in me hast rest
As I Undying Life, have power in Thee

Vain are the thousand creeds
10 That move men's hearts, unutterably vain,
Worthless as withered weeds
Or idlest froth amid the boundless main

To waken doubt in one
Holding so fast by thy infinity
15 So surely anchored on
The steadfast rock of Immortality

With wide-embracing love
Thy spirit animates eternal years
Pervades and broods above,
20   Changes, sustains, dissolves, creates and rears

Though Earth and moon were gone
And suns and universes ceased to be
And thou wert left alone
Every Existence would exist in thee

25   There is not room for Death
Nor atom that his might could render void
Since thou art Being and Breath
And what thou art may never be destroyed.

1846/1850

Stanzas

Often rebuked, yet always back returning
    To those first feelings that were born with me,
And leaving busy chase of wealth and learning
    For idle dreams of things which cannot be:

5   Today, I will seek not the shadowy region;
    Its unsustaining vastness waxes drear;
And visions rising, legion after legion,
    Bring the unreal world too strangely near.

I'll walk, but not in old heroic traces,
10   And not in paths of high morality,
And not among the half-distinguished faces,
    The clouded forms of long-past history.

I'll walk where my own nature would be leading:
    It vexes me to choose another guide:
15   Where the gray flocks in ferny glens are feeding;
    Where the wild wind blows on the mountain side.

What have those lonely mountains worth revealing?
    More glory and more grief than I can tell:
The earth that wakes *one* human heart to feeling
20   Can centre both the world of Heaven and Hell.

1850

George Eliot
1819–1880

Considered by critics of her own day to be the greatest living British novelist, George Eliot located most of her novels in the English Midlands during the time of her own childhood, combining realism and compassion in her portraits of the ethical lives of ordinary villagers. Born Mary Ann Evans, Eliot was the daughter of Robert Evans, an estate manager in Warwickshire, and Christiana Pearson, his second wife. A precocious child, she read widely in philosophy and religion at an early age and went on to pursue her education rigorously, both in and out of school. In her youth Eliot converted to Evangelicism but eventually renounced it; nevertheless, many of  her novels portray Dissenters and clergymen with affection and sympathy. When her mother died, Eliot was forced at the age of sixteen to leave school; there followed a period of intermittent depression until she moved with her father in 1840 to Coventry, where she became associated with a circle of intellectuals and free thinkers. Her engagement with theological concerns led to her 1846 translation of D. F. Strauss's *Life of Jesus*, which was published without her name attached to it. Strauss was one of several German scholars whose use of modern research to question the historical accuracy of biblical stories influenced Eliot's own religious thinking.

She began her professional career in 1850 as an essayist and a translator for one of the nineteenth century's preeminent journals, *The Westminster Review*, for which she became assistant editor in 1851. Among the essays that she wrote for the review were several that dealt with women's writing, including "Margaret Fuller and Mary Wollstonecraft," in which she examines these feminists' perspectives on the "woman question." In 1854 her translation of Feuerbach's *Essence of Christianity* was published; Eliot was intrigued by his unorthodox belief that humans project onto religion their interest in their own species. She was encouraged to write fiction by George Henry Lewes, a distinguished literary critic whom she met through her work at *The Westminster Review*. Although Lewes was married and the father of three children, he was separated from his wife, and Eliot lived with him from 1854 until his death in 1878, a relationship that caused her to become a social outcast. The first sequence of *Scenes of Clerical Life*, "The Sad Fortunes of the Rev. Amos Barton," was published in 1857 in *Blackwood's Magazine*, followed by "Mr. Gilfil's Love Story" and "Janet's Repentance." But *Adam Bede* (1859) established Eliot as a major novelist. Like many of her novels, it depicts characters who must make agonizing moral decisions, as Eliot herself had to do in deciding to live with Lewes.

Middlemarch, published in installments in 1871 and 1872, is widely considered Eliot's finest novel; indeed VIRGINA WOOLF considered it "one of the few English novels written for grown-up people." In *The Rise of the Novel* (1957) Ian Watt describes it as a work following "in the Puritan tradition of the tragedy of feminine individualism," but contemporary feminist critics have viewed its heroine, Dorothea Brooke, as a strong, intelligent woman determined to survive on her own terms. In one of the novel's best-known passages, Eliot sets forth her philosophy of fiction. Rather than attempt universal scope, as such predecessors in the genre as Henry Fielding had set out to do, she determines to be a different sort of "belated historian": "I at least have so much to do in unravelling certain human lots, and seeing how they were woven and interwoven, that all the light I can command must be concentrated on this particular web, and not dispersed over that tempting range of relevancies called the universe."

Other novels by Eliot include *The Mill on the Floss* (1860), *Silas Marner* (1861), and *Felix Holt, The Radical* (1866). *Romola*, which Eliot conceived of during a visit to Florence in 1860, was published serially in the *Cornhill* in 1862 and 1863; her last novel, the critically acclaimed *Daniel Deronda*, was also published in installments between 1874 and 1876. Eliot published some poetry, including "Brother and Sister," a sonnet sequence celebrating her happy childhood with her brother, Isaac, from whom she was estranged during much of her adult life because of her relationship with Lewes. Among her best known short stories are "The Lifted Veil" (1859) and "Brother Jacob" (1864). After Lewes' death she married John Walter Cross, a younger man whom she had met in Rome some years earlier and who served as her financial adviser; he edited her letters and journals in three volumes in 1885. Her complete letters were not published until the twentieth century, when they were edited between 1955 and 1978 by Gordon Haight.

Eliot published "Silly Novels by Lady Novelists" in October 1856 in *The Westminster Review*. A delightfully satirical response to the melodramatic writing that she calls the "*mind-and-millinery* species" of nineteenth-century women's popular fiction, this review illustrates her keen intellect, barbed wit, and lack of sympathy for women who stereotype and thereby misrepresent the intellectual capacities of other women, real or imagined. This review shows the high aesthetic and ethical standards and seriousness of purpose to which Eliot holds the novel, still an evolving genre in her time, as well as the outrage she experiences when through their "lack of verisimilitude" women writers trivialize other women, and thus themselves.

⊱ Silly Novels by Lady Novelists ⊰

Silly novels by Lady Novelists are a genus with many species, determined by the particular quality of silliness that predominates in them—the frothy, the prosy, the pious, or the pedantic. But it is a mixture of all these—a composite order of feminine fatuity, that produces the largest class of such novels, which we shall distinguish as the *mind-and-millinery* species. The heroine is usually an heiress, probably a peeress in her own right, with perhaps a vicious baronet, an amiable duke, and an irresistible younger son of a marquis as lovers in the foreground, a clergyman and a poet sighing for her in the middle distance, and a crowd of undefined adorers dimly indicated beyond. Her eyes and her wit are both dazzling; her nose and her morals are alike free from any tendency to irregularity; she has a superb *contralto* and a superb intellect; she is perfectly well-dressed and perfectly religious; she dances like a sylph, and reads the Bible in the original tongues. Or it may be that the heroine is not an heiress—that rank and wealth are the only things in which she is deficient; but she infallibly gets into high society, she has the triumph of refusing many matches and securing the best, and she wears some family jewels or other as a sort of crown of righteousness at the end. Rakish men either bite their lips in impotent confusion at her repartees, or are touched to penitence by her reproofs, which, on appropriate occasions, rise to a lofty strain of rhetoric; indeed, there is a general propensity in her to make speeches, and to rhapsodize at some length when she retires to her bedroom. In her recorded conversations she is amazingly eloquent, and in her unrecorded conversations, amazingly witty. She is understood to have a depth of insight that looks through and through the shallow theories of philosophers, and her superior instincts are a sort of dial by which men have only to set their clocks and watches, and all will go well. The men play a very subordinate part by her side.

You are consoled now and then by a hint that they have affairs, which keeps you in mind that the working-day business of the world is somehow being carried on, but ostensibly the final cause of their existence is that they may accompany the heroine on her "starring" expedition through life. They see her at a ball, and are dazzled; at a flower-show, and they are fascinated; on a riding excursion, and they are witched by her noble horsemanship; at church, and they are awed by the sweet solemnity of her demeanour. She is the ideal woman in feelings, faculties, and flounces. For all this, she as often as not marries the wrong person to begin with, and she suffers terribly from the plots and intrigues of the vicious baronet; but even death has a soft place in his heart for such a paragon, and remedies all mistakes for her just at the right moment. The vicious baronet is sure to be killed in a duel, and the tedious husband dies in his bed, requesting his wife, as a particular favour to him, to marry the man she loves best, and having already dispatched a note to the lover informing him of the comfortable arrangement. Before matters arrive at this desirable issue our feelings are tried by seeing the noble, lovely, and gifted heroine pass through many *mauvais moments*, but we have the satisfaction of knowing that her sorrows are wept into embroidered pocket-handkerchiefs, that her fainting form reclines on the very best upholstery, and that whatever vicissitudes she may undergo, from being dashed out of her carriage to having her head shaved in a fever, she comes out of them all with a complexion more blooming and locks more redundant than ever.

We may remark, by the way, that we have been relieved from a serious scruple by discovering that silly novels by lady novelists rarely introduce us into any other than very lofty and fashionable society. We had imagined that destitute women turned novelists, as they turned governesses, because they had no other "lady-like" means of getting their bread. On this supposition, vacillating syntax and improbable incident had a certain pathos for us, like the extremely supererogatory pincushions and ill-devised nightcaps that are offered for sale by a blind man. We felt the commodity to be a nuisance, but we were glad to think that the money went to relieve the necessitous, and we pictured to ourselves lonely women struggling for a maintenance, or wives and daughters devoting themselves to the production of "copy" out of pure heroism—perhaps to pay their husband's debts, or to purchase luxuries for a sick father. Under these impressions we shrank from criticizing a lady's novel: her English might be faulty, but, we said to ourselves, her motives are irreproachable; her imagination may be uninventive, but her patience is untiring. Empty writing was excused by an empty stomach, and twaddle was consecrated by tears. But no! This theory of ours, like many other pretty theories, has had to give way before observation. Women's silly novels, we are now convinced, are written under totally different circumstances. The fair writers have evidently never talked to a tradesman except from a carriage window; they have no notion of the working classes except as "dependants"; they think five hundred pounds a year a miserable pittance; Belgravia and "baronial halls" are their primary truths; and they have no idea of feeling interest in any man who is not at least a great landed proprietor, if not a prime minister. It is clear that they write in elegant boudoirs, with violet-coloured ink and a ruby pen; that they must be entirely indifferent to publishers' accounts, and inexperienced in every form of poverty except poverty of brains. It is true that we are constantly struck with the want of verisimilitude in their representations of the high society in which they seem to live; but then they betray no closer acquaintance with any other form of life. If their peers and peeresses are improbable, their literary men, tradespeople, and cottagers are impossible; and their intellect seems to have the peculiar impartiality of reproducing both what they *have* seen and heard, and what they have *not* seen and heard, with equal unfaithfulness.

There are few women, we suppose, who have not seen something of children under five years of age, yet in "Compensation,"[1] a recent novel of the mind-and-millinery species, which calls itself a "story of real life," we have a child of four and half years old talking in this Ossianic[2] fashion—

"Oh, I am so happy, dear gran'mamma; I have seen, I have seen such a delightful person: he is like everything beautiful, like the smell of sweet flowers, and the view from Ben Lomond; or no, *better than that*—he is like what I think of and see when I am very, very happy; and he is really like mamma, too, when she sings; and his forehead is like *that distant sea*," she continued, pointing to the blue Mediterranean, "there seems no end—no end; or like the clusters of stars I like best to look at on a warm fine night . . . Don't look so . . . your forehead is like Loch Lomond, when the wind is blowing and the sun is gone in; I like the sunshine best when the lake is smooth . . . So now—I like it better than ever . . . it is more beautiful still from the dark cloud that has gone over it, *when the sun suddenly lights up all the colours of the forests and shining purple rocks, and it is all reflected in the waters below.*"

We are not surprised to learn that the mother of this infant phenomenon, who exhibits symptoms so alarmingly like those of adolescence repressed by gin, is herself a phoenix. We are assured, again and again, that she had a remarkably original mind, that she was a genius, and "conscious of her originality," and she was fortunate enough to have a lover who was also a genius, and a man of "most original mind."

This lover, we read, though "wonderfully similar" to her "in powers and capacity," was "infinitely superior to her in faith and development," and she saw in him the "'Agape'—so rare to find—of which she had read and admired the meaning of her Greek Testament; having, *from her great facility in learning languages*, read the Scriptures in their original *tongues*." Of course! Greek and Hebrew are mere play to a heroine; Sanskrit is no more than *a b c* to her; and she can talk with perfect correctness in any language except English. She is a polking polyglot, a Creuzer[3] in crinoline. Poor men! There are so few of you who know even Hebrew; you think it something to boast of if, like Bolingbroke,[4] you only "understand that sort of learning, and what is writ about it"; and you are perhaps adoring women who can think slightingly of you in all the Semitic languages successively. But, then, as we are almost invariably told, that a heroine has a "beautifully small head," and as her intellect has probably been early invigorated by an attention to costume and deportment, we may conclude that she can pick up the Oriental tongues, to say nothing of their dialects, with the same aerial facility that the butterfly sips nectar. Besides, there can be no difficulty in conceiving the depth of the heroine's erudition, when that of the authoress is so evident.

In "Laura Gay",[5] another novel of the same school, the heroine seems less at home in Greek and Hebrew, but she makes up for the deficiency by a quite playful familiarity with the Latin classics—with the "dear old Virgil," "the graceful Horace, the humane Cicero, and the pleasant Livy";[6] indeed, it is such a matter of course with her to quote Latin, that she does it at a picnic in a very mixed company of ladies and gentlemen, having, we are told, "no conception that the nobler sex were capable of

1. A novel written in 1856 by Lady Chatterton.
2. In the fashion of Ossian, a legendary Gaelic poet whose work was parodied in 1762 by the Scots writer James Macpherson as part of a literary hoax.
3. Friedrich Creuzer (1771–1858) was a German philologist.
4. Henry St. John, the first Viscount Bolingbroke

(1678–1751), an English writer and politician.
5. A novel of 1856 whose author was anonymous.
6. Virgil and Horace were Latin poets of the Augustan period (27 BCE–14 CE); Cicero (106–43 BCE) was a Roman orator; Livy(59 BCE–17 CE) was a Roman historian.

jealousy on this subject. And if, indeed," continues the biographer of Laura Gay, "the wisest and noblest portion of that sex were in the majority, no such sentiment would exist; but while Miss Wyndhams and Mr Redfords abound, great sacrifices must be made to their existence." Such sacrifices, we presume, as abstaining from Latin quotations, of extremely moderate interest and applicability, which the wise and noble minority of the other sex would be quite as willing to dispense with as the foolish and ignoble majority. It is as little the custom of well-bred men as of well-bred women to quote Latin in mixed parties; they can contain their familiarity with "the humane Cicero" without allowing it to boil over in ordinary conversation, and even references to "the pleasant Livy" are not absolutely irrepressible. But Ciceronian Latin is the mildest form of Miss Gay's conversational power. Being on the Palatine with a party of sightseers, she falls into the following vein of well-rounded remark:

> Truth can only be pure objectively, for even in the creeds where it predominates, being subjective, and parcelled out into portions, each of these necessarily receives a hue of idiosyncrasy, that is, a taint of superstition more or less strong; while in such creeds as the Roman Catholic, ignorance, interest, the bias of ancient idolatries, and the force of authority, have gradually accumulated on the pure truth, and transformed it, at last, into a mass of superstition for the majority of its votaries; and how few are there, alas! whose zeal, courage, and intellectual energy are equal to the analysis of this accumulation, and to the discovery of the pearl of great price which lies hidden beneath this heap of rubbish.

We have often met with women much more novel and profound in their observations than Laura Gay, but rarely with any so inopportunely long-winded. A clerical lord, who is half in love with her, is alarmed by the daring remarks just quoted, and begins to suspect that she is inclined to free-thinking. But he is mistaken; when in a moment of sorrow he delicately begs leave to "recall to her memory, a *depôt* of strength and consolation under affliction, which, until we are hard pressed by the trials of life, we are too apt to forget," we learn that she really has "recurrence to that sacred *depôt*," together with the tea-pot. There is a certain flavour of orthodoxy mixed with the parade of fortunes and fine carriages in "Laura Gay," but it is an orthodoxy mitigated by study of "the humane Cicero," and by an "intellectual disposition to analyze."

"Compensation" is much more heavily dosed with doctrine, but then it has a treble amount of snobbish worldliness and absurd incident to tickle the palate of pious frivolity. Linda, the heroine, is still more speculative and spiritual than Laura Gay, but she has been "presented," and has more, and far grander, lovers; very wicked and fascinating women are introduced—even a French *lionne*; and no expense is spared to get up as exciting a story as you will find in the most immoral novels. In fact, it is a wonderful *potpourri* of Almack's, Scotch second-sight, Mr Rogers's breakfasts,[7] Italian brigands, deathbed conversions, superior authoresses, Italian mistresses, and attempts at poisoning old ladies, the whole served up with a garnish of talk about "faith and development," and "most original minds." Even Miss Susan Barton, the superior authoress, whose pen moves in a "quick decided manner when she is composing," declines the finest opportunities of marriage; and though old enough to be Linda's mother (since we are told that she refused Linda's father), has her hand sought by a young earl, the heroine's rejected lover. Of course, genius and morality must be backed by eligible offers, or they would seem rather a dull affair; and piety,

---

7. Samuel Rogers (1763–1855) gave breakfasts for wealthy friends.

like other things, in order to be *comme il faut,* must be in "society," and have admittance to the best-circles.

"Rank and Beauty"[8] is a more frothy and less religious variety of the mind-and-millinery species. The heroine, we are told, "if she inherited her father's pride of birth and her mother's beauty of person, had in herself a tone of enthusiastic feeling that perhaps belongs to her age even in the lowly born, but which is refined into the high spirit of wild romance only in the far descended, who feel that it is their best inheritance." This enthusiastic young lady, by dint of reading the newspaper to her father, falls in love with the *prime minister,* who, through the medium of leading articles and "the *resumé* of the debates," shines upon her imagination as a bright particular star, which has no parallax for her, living in the country as simple Miss Wyndham. But she forthwith becomes Baroness Umfraville in her own right, astonishes the world with her beauty and accomplishments when she bursts upon it from her mansion in Spring Gardens, and, as you foresee, will presently come into contact with the unseen *objet aimé.* Perhaps the words "prime minister" suggest to you a wrinkled or obese sexagenarian; but pray dismiss the image. Lord Rupert Conway has been "called while still almost a youth to the first situation which a subject can hold in the *universe,*" and even leading articles and a *resumé* of the debates have not conjured up a dream that surpasses the fact.

> The door opened again, and Lord Rupert Conway entered. Evelyn gave one glance. It was enough; she was not disappointed. It seemed as if a picture on which she had long gazed was suddenly instinct with life, and had stepped from its frame before her. His tall figure, the distinguished simplicity of his air—it was a living Vandyke, a cavalier, one of his noble cavalier ancestors, or one to whom her fancy had always likened him, who long of yore had, with an Umfraville, fought the Paynim far beyond sea. Was this reality?

Very little like it, certainly.

By and by, it becomes evident that the ministerial heart is touched. Lady Umfraville is on a visit to the Queen at Windsor, and,—

> The last evening of her stay, when they returned from riding, Mr Wyndham took her and a large party to the top of the Keep, to see the view. She was leaning on the battlements, gazing from that "stately height" at the prospect beneath her, when Lord Rupert was by her side. "What an unrivalled view!" exclaimed she.
>
> "Yes, it would have been wrong to go without having been up here. You are pleased with your visit?"
>
> "Enchanted! A Queen to live and die under, to live and die for!"
>
> "Ha!" cried he, with sudden emotion, and with a *eureka* expression of countenance, as if he had *indeed found a heart in unison with his own.*

The "*eureka* expression of countenance," you see at once to be prophetic of marriage at the end of the third volume; but before that desirable consummation, there are very complicated misunderstandings, arising chiefly from the vindictive plotting of Sir Luttrell Wycherley, who is a genius, a poet, and in every way a most remarkable character indeed. He is not only a romantic poet, but a hardened rake and a cynical wit; yet his deep passion for Lady Umfraville has so impoverished his epigrammatic talent, that he cuts an extremely poor figure in conversation. When she rejects him, he rushes into the shrubbery, and rolls himself in the dirt; and on recovering, devotes

8. Another anonymous novel of 1856.

himself to the most diabolical and laborious schemes of vengeance, in the course of which he disguises himself as a quack physician, and enters into general practice, foreseeing that Evelyn will fall ill, and that he shall be called in to attend her. At last, when all his schemes are frustrated, he takes leave of her in a long letter, written, as you will perceive from the following passage, entirely in the style of an eminent literary man:

> Oh, lady, nursed in pomp and pleasure, will you ever cast one thought upon the miserable being who addresses you? Will you ever, as your gilded galley is floating down the unruffled stream of prosperity, will you ever, while lulled by the sweetest music—thine own praises—hear the far-off sigh from that world to which I am going?

On the whole, however, frothy as it is, we rather prefer "Rank and Beauty" to the two other novels we have mentioned. The dialogue is more natural and spirited; there is some frank ignorance, and no pedantry; and you are allowed to take the heroine's astounding intellect upon trust, without being called on to read her conversational refutations of skeptics and philosophers, or her rhetorical solutions of the mysteries of the universe.

Writers of the mind-and-millinery school are remarkably unanimous in their choice of diction. In their novels, there is usually a lady or gentleman who is more or less of a upas tree: the lover has a manly breast; minds are redolent of various things; hearts are hollow; events are utilized; friends are consigned to the tomb; infancy is an engaging period; the sun is a luminary that goes to his western couch, or gathers the rain-drops into his refulgent bosom; life is a melancholy boon; Albion and Scotia are conversational epithets. There is a striking resemblance, too, in the character of their moral comments, such, for instance, as that "It is a fact, no less true than melancholy, that all people, more or less, richer or poorer, are swayed by bad example"; that "Books, however trivial, contain some subjects from which useful information may be drawn"; that "Vice can too often borrow the language of virtue"; that "Merit and nobility of nature must exist, to be accepted, for clamour and pretension cannot impose upon those too well read in human nature to be easily deceived"; and that, "In order to forgive, we must have been injured." There is, doubtless, a class of readers to whom these remarks appear peculiarly pointed and pungent; for we often find them doubly and trebly scored with the pencil, and delicate hands giving in their determined adhesion to these hardy novelties by a distinct *très vrai*, emphasized by many notes of exclamation. The colloquial style of these novels is often marked by much ingenious inversion, and a careful avoidance of such cheap phraseology as can be heard every day. Angry young gentlemen exclaim—"'Tis ever thus, methinks"; and in the half hour before dinner a young lady informs her next neighbour that the first day she read Shakespeare she "stole away into the park, and beneath the shadow of the greenwood tree, devoured with rapture the inspired page of the great magician." But the most remarkable efforts of the mind-and-millinery writers lie in their philosophic reflections. The authoress of "Laura Gay," for example, having married her hero and heroine, improves the event by observing that "if those skeptics, whose eyes have so long gazed on matter that they can no longer see aught else in man, could once enter with heart and soul into such bliss as this, they would come to say that the soul of man and the polypus are not of common origin, or of the same texture." Lady novelists, it appears, can see something else besides matter; they are not limited to phenomena, but can relieve their eyesight by occasional glimpses of the *noumenon*, and are, therefore, naturally better able than any one else to confound skeptics, even of that remarkable, but to us unknown school, which maintains that the soul of man is of the same texture as the polypus.

#2 *type*

oracular species

The most pitiable of all silly novels by lady novelists are what we may call the oracular species—novels intended to expound the writer's religious, philosophical, or moral theories. There seems to be a notion abroad among women, rather akin to the superstition that the speech and actions of idiots are inspired, and that the human being most entirely exhausted of common sense is the fittest vehicle of revelation. To judge from their writings, there are certain ladies who think that an amazing ignorance, both of science and of life, is the best possible qualification for forming an opinion on the knottiest moral and speculative questions. Apparently, their recipe for solving all such difficulties is something like this: Take a woman's head, stuff it with a smattering of philosophy and literature chopped small, and with false notions of society baked hard, let it hang over a desk a few hours every day, and serve up hot in feeble English, when not required. You will rarely meet with a lady novelist of the oracular class who is diffident of her ability to decide on theological questions, who has any suspicion that she is not capable of discriminating with the nicest accuracy between the good and evil in all church parties, who does not see precisely how it is that men have gone wrong hitherto, and pity philosophers in general that they have not had the opportunity of consulting her. Great writers, who have modestly contented themselves with putting their experience into fiction, and have thought it quite a sufficient task to exhibit men and things as they are, she sighs over as deplorably deficient in the application of their powers. "They have solved no great questions"—and she is ready to remedy their omission by setting before you a complete theory of life and manual of divinity, in a love story, where ladies and gentlemen of good family go through genteel vicissitudes, to the utter confusion of Deists, Puseyites, and ultra-Protestants,[9] and to the perfect establishment of that particular view of Christianity which either condenses itself into a sentence of small caps, or explodes into a cluster of stars on the three hundred and thirtieth page. It is true, the ladies and gentlemen will probably seem to you remarkably little like any you have had the fortune or misfortune to meet with, for, as a general rule, the ability of a lady novelist to describe actual life and her fellow-men, is in inverse proportion to her confident eloquence about God and the other world, and the means by which she usually chooses to conduct you to true ideas of the invisible is a totally false picture of the visible.

As typical a novel of the oracular kind as we can hope to meet with, is "The Enigma: a Leaf from the Chronicles of the Wolchorley House."[10] The "enigma" which this novel is to solve, is certainly one that demands powers no less gigantic than those of a lady novelist, being neither more nor less than the existence of evil. The problem is stated, and the answer dimly foreshadowed on the very first page. The spirited young lady, with raven hair, says, "All life is an inextricable confusion"; and the meek young lady, with auburn hair, looks at the picture of the Madonna which she is copying, and *"There* seemed the solution of that mighty enigma." The style of this novel is quite as lofty as its purpose; indeed, some passages on which we have spent much patient study are quite beyond our reach, in spite of the illustrative aid of italics and small caps; and we must await further "development" in order to under-

9. Deists believed in a natural religion and denied that a Creator interfered with the laws of the universe. Puseyites were followers of the English theologian

Edward Pusey (1800–82).
10. Yet another anonymous novel of 1856.

stand them. Of Ernest, the model young clergyman, who sets every one right on all occasions, we read, that "he held not of marriage in the marketable kind, after a social desecration"; that, on one eventful night, "sleep had not visited his divided heart, where tumultuated, in varied type and combination, the aggregate feelings of grief and joy"; and that, "for the *marketable* human article he had no toleration, be it of what sort, or set for what value it might, whether for worship or class, his upright soul abhorred it, whose ultimatum, the self-deceiver, was to him THE *great spiritual lie*, 'living in a vain show, deceiving the being deceived'; since he did not suppose the phylactery and enlarged border on the garment to be *merely* a social trick." (The italics and small caps are the author's, and we hope they assist the reader's comprehension.) Of Sir Lionel, the model old gentleman, we are told that "the simple ideal of the middle age, apart from its anarchy and decadence, in him most truly seemed to live again, when the ties which knit men together were of heroic cast. The first-born colours of pristine faith and truth engraven on the common soul of man, and blent into the wide arch of brotherhood, where the primaeval law of *order* grew and multiplied, each perfect after his kind, and mutually interdependent." You see clearly, of course, how colours are first engraven on a soul, and then blent into a wide arch, on which arch of colours—apparently a rainbow—the law of order grew and multiplied, each—apparently the arch and the law—perfect after his kind? If, after this, you can possibly want any further aid towards knowing what Sir Lionel was, we can tell you, that in his soul "the scientific combinations of thought could educe no fuller harmonies of the good and the true, than lay in the primaeval pulses which floated as an atmosphere around it!" and that, when he was sealing a letter, "Lo! the responsive throb in that good man's bosom echoed back in simple truth the honest witness of a heart that condemned him not, as his eye, bedewed with love, rested, too, with something of ancestral pride, on the undimmed motto of the family—*Loiauté*."

The slightest matters have their vulgarity fumigated out of them by the same elevated style. Commonplace people would say that a copy of Shakespeare lay on a drawing-room table; but the authoress of "The Enigma," bent on edifying periphrasis, tells you that there lay on the table, "that fund of human thought and feeling, which teaches the heart through the little name, 'Shakespeare.'" A watchman sees a light burning in an upper window rather longer than usual, and thinks that people are foolish to sit up late when they have an opportunity of going to bed; but, lest this fact should seem too low and common, it is presented to us in the following striking and metaphysical manner: "He marvelled—as man *will* think for others in a necessarily separate personality, consequently (though disallowing it) in false mental premise— how differently *he* should act, how gladly *he* should prize the rest so lightly held of within." A footman—an ordinary Jeames, with large calves and aspirated vowels— answers the door-bell, and the opportunity is seized to tell you that he was a "type of the large class of pampered menials, who follow the curse of Cain—'vagabonds' on the face of the earth, and whose estimate of the human class varies in the graduated scale of money and expenditure . . . These, and such as these, O England, be the false lights of thy morbid civilization!" We have heard of various "false lights," from Dr Cumming to Robert Owen, from Dr Pusey to the Spirit-rappers, but we never before heard of the false light that emanates from plush and powder.

In the same way very ordinary events of civilized life are exalted into the most awful crises, and ladies in full skirts and *manches à la Chinoise*, conduct themselves not unlike the heroines of sanguinary melodramas. Mrs. Percy, a shallow woman of the world, wishes her son Horace to marry the auburn-haired Grace, she being an heiress; but he, after the manner of sons, falls in love with the raven-haired Kate, the heiress's portionless cousin; and, moreover, Grace herself shows every symptom of perfect indifference to Horace. In such cases, sons are often sulky or fiery, mothers are alternately maneuvering and waspish, and the portionless young lady often lies awake at night and cries a good deal. We are getting used to these things now, just as we are used to eclipses of the moon, which no longer set us howling and beating tin kettles. We never heard of a lady in a fashionable "front" behaving like Mrs Percy under these circumstances. Happening one day to see Horace talking to Grace at a window, without in the least knowing what they are talking about, or having the least reason to believe that Grace, who is mistress of the house and a person of dignity, would accept her son if he were to offer himself, she suddenly rushes up to them and clasps them both, saying "with a flushed countenance and in an excited manner"—"'This is indeed happiness; for, may I not call you so, Grace?—my Grace—my Horace's Grace!—my dear children!" Her son tells her she is mistaken, and that he is engaged to Kate, whereupon we have the following scene and tableau:

> Gathering herself up to an unprecedented height, (!) her eyes lightning forth the fire of her anger:
>
> "Wretched boy!" she said, hoarsely and scornfully, and clenching her hand. "Take then the doom of your own choice! Bow down your miserable head and let a mother's—"
>
> "Curse not!" spake a deep low voice from behind, and Mrs Percy started, scared, as though she had seen a heavenly visitant appear, to break upon her in the midst of her sin.
>
> Meantime, Horace had fallen on his knees at her feet, and hid his face in his hands.
>
> Who, then, is she—who! Truly his "guardian spirit" hath stepped between him and the fearful words, which, however unmerited, must have hung as a pall over his future existence—a spell which could not be unbound—which could not be unsaid.
>
> Of an earthly paleness, but calm with the still, iron-bound calmness of death—the only calm one there—Katherine stood; and her words smote on the ear in tones whose appallingly slow and separate intonation rung on the heart like the chill, isolated tolling of some fatal knell.
>
> "He would have plighted me his faith, but I did not accept it; you cannot, therefore—you *dare* not curse him. And here" she continued, raising her hand to heaven, whither her large dark eyes also rose with a chastened glow, which, for the first time, *suffering* had lighted in those passionate orbs, "here I promise, come weal, come woe, that Horace Wolchorley and I do never interchange vows without his mother's sanction—without his mother's blessing!"

Here, and throughout the story, we see that confusion of purpose which is so characteristic of silly novels written by women. It is a story of quite modern drawing-room society—a society in which polkas are played and Puseyism discussed; yet we have characters, and incidents, and traits of manner introduced, which are mere shreds from the most heterogeneous romances. We have a blind Irish harper "relic of the picturesque bards of yore," startling us at a Sunday-school festival of tea and cake in an English village; we have a crazy gypsy, in a scarlet cloak, singing snatches of romantic song, and revealing a secret on her death-bed which, with the testimony of a dwarfish miserly merchant, who salutes strangers with a curse and a devilish laugh, goes to prove that Ernest, the model young clergyman, is Kate's brother; and we have an ultra-virtuous Irish Barney, discovering that a document is forged, by comparing the date of the paper with the date of the alleged signature, although the same document has passed through a court of law, and occasioned a fatal decision. The "Hall" in which Sir Lionel lives is the venerable country-seat of an old family, and this, we suppose, sets the imagination of the authoress flying to donjons and battlements, where "lo! the warder blows his horn"; for, as the inhabitants are in their bedrooms on a night certainly within the recollection of Pleaceman X., and a breeze springs up, which we are at first told was faint, and then that it made the old cedars bow their branches to the greensward, she falls into this mediaeval vein of description (the italics are ours): "The banner *unfurled it* at the sound, and shook its guardian wing above, while the startled owl *flapped her* in the ivy; the firmament looking down through her argus eyes—

> Ministers of heaven's mute melodies.

And lo! two strokes tolled from out the warder tower, and 'Two o'clock' re-echoed its interpreter below."

Such stores as this of "The Enigma" remind us of the pictures clever children sometimes draw "out of their own head," where you will see a modern villa on the right, two knights in helmets fighting in the foreground, and a tiger grinning in a jungle on the left, the several objects being brought together because the artist thinks each pretty, and perhaps still more because he remembers seeing them in other pictures.

But we like the authoress much better on her mediaeval stilts than on her oracular ones, when she talks of the *Ich* and of "subjective" and "objective," and lays down the exact line of Christian verity, between "right-hand excesses and left-hand declensions." Persons who deviate from this line are introduced with a patronizing air of charity. Of a certain Miss Inshquine she informs us, with all the lucidity of italics and small caps, that "*function, not form, as the inevitable outer expression of the spirit in this tabernacled age*, weakly engrossed her." And *à propos* of Miss Mayjar, an evangelical lady who is a little too apt to talk of her visits to sick women and the state of their souls, we are told that the model clergyman is "not one to disallow, through the *super* crust, the undercurrent towards good in the *subject*, or the positive benefits, nevertheless, to the *object*." We imagine the double-refined accent and protrusion of chin which are feebly represented by the italics in this lady's sentences. We abstain from quoting any of her oracular doctrinal passages, because they refer to matters too serious for our pages just now.

The epithet "silly" may seem impertinent, applied to a novel which indicates so much reading and intellectual activity as "The Enigma"; but we use this epithet advisedly. If, as the world has long agreed, a very great amount of instruction will not make a wise man, still less will a very mediocre amount of instruction make a wise woman. And the most mischievous form of feminine silliness is the literary form, because it tends to confirm the popular prejudice against the more solid education of women. When men see girls wasting their time in consultations about bonnets and ball dresses, and in giggling or sentimental love-confidences, or middle-aged women mismanaging their children, and solacing themselves with acrid gossip, they can hardly help saying, "For Heaven's sake, let girls be better educated; let them have some better objects of thought—some more solid occupations." But after a few hours' conversation with an oracular literary women, or a few hours' reading of her books, they are likely enough to say, "After all, when a woman gets some knowledge, see what use she makes of it! Her knowledge remains acquisition, instead of passing into culture; instead of being subdued into modesty and simplicity by a larger acquaintance with thought and fact, she has a feverish consciousness of her attainments; she keeps a sort of mental pocket-mirror, and is continually looking in it at her own 'intellectuality'; she spoils the taste of one's muffin by questions of metaphysics; 'puts down' men at a dinner-table with her superior information; and seizes the opportunity of a *soirée* to catechize us on the vital question of the relation between mind and matter. And then, look at her writings! She mistakes vagueness for depth, bombast for eloquence, and affectation for originality; she struts on one page, rolls her eyes on another, grimaces in a third, and is hysterical in a fourth. She may have read many writings of great men, and a few writings of great women; but she is as unable to discern the difference between her own style and theirs as a Yorkshireman is to discern the difference between his own English and a Londoner's: rhodomontade is the native accent of her intellect. No—the average nature of women is too shallow and feeble a soil to bear much tillage; it is only fit for the very lightest crops."

It is true that the men who come to such a decision on such very superficial and imperfect observation may not be among the wisest in the world; but we have not now to contest their opinion—we are only pointing out how it is unconsciously encouraged by many women who have volunteered themselves as representatives of the feminine intellect. We do not believe that a man was ever strengthened in such an opinion by associating with a woman of true culture, whose mind had absorbed her knowledge instead of being absorbed by it. A really cultured woman, like a really cultured man, is all the simpler and the less obtrusive for her knowledge; it has made her see herself and her opinions in something like just proportions; she does not make it a pedestal from which she flatters herself that she commands a complete view of men and things, but makes it a point of observation from which to form a right estimate of herself. She neither spouts poetry nor quotes Cicero on slight provocation; not because she thinks that a sacrifice must be made to the prejudices of men, but because that mode of exhibiting her memory and Latinity does not present itself to her as edifying or graceful. She does not write books to confound philosophers, perhaps because she is able to write books and delight them. In conversation she is the least formidable of women, because she understands you, without wanting to make you aware that you *can't* understand her. She does not give you information, which is the raw material of culture—she gives you sympathy, which is its subtlest essence.

A more numerous class of silly novels than the oracular, (which are generally inspired by some form of High Church, or transcendental Christianity,) is what we may call the *white neck-cloth* species, which represent the tone of thought and feeling in the Evangelical party. This species is a kind of genteel tract on a large scale, intended as a sort of medicinal sweetmeat for Low Church young ladies; an Evangelical substitute for the fashionable novel, as the May Meetings[11] are a substitute for the Opera. Even Quaker children, one would think, can hardly have been denied the indulgence of a doll; but it must be a doll dressed in a drab gown and a coal-scuttle bonnet—not a worldly doll, in gauze and spangles. And there are no young ladies, we imagine—unless they belong to the Church of the United Brethren, in which people are married without any love-making—who can dispense with love stories. Thus, for Evangelical young ladies there are Evangelical love stories, in which the vicissitudes of the tender passion are sanctified by saving views of Regeneration and the Atonement. These novels differ from the oracular ones, as a Low Churchwoman often differs from a High Churchwoman: they are a little less supercilious, and a great deal more ignorant, a little less correct in their syntax, and a great deal more vulgar.

11. The Church of England held its Missionary Society meetings each year in May.

*Sh.
As You Like It*

The Orlando[12] of Evangelical literature is the young curate, looked at from the point of view of the middle class, where cambric bands are understood to have as thrilling an effect on the hearts of young ladies as epaulettes have in the classes above and below it. In the ordinary type of these novels, the hero is almost sure to be a young curate, frowned upon, perhaps, by worldly mammas, but carrying captive the hearts of their daughters, who can "never forget *that* sermon"; tender glances are seized from the pulpit stairs instead of the opera-box; *têta-à-têtes* are seasoned with quotations from Scripture, instead of quotations from the poets; and questions as to the state of the heroine's affections are mingled with anxieties as to the state of her soul. The young curate always has a background of well-dressed and wealthy, if not fashionable society—for Evangelical silliness is as snobbish as any other kind of silliness; and the Evangelical lady novelist, while she explains to you the type of the scapegoat on one page, is ambitious on another to represent the manners and conversation of aristocratic people. Her pictures of fashionable society are often curious studies considered as efforts of the Evangelical imagination; but in one particular the novels of the White Neck-cloth School are meritoriously realistic—their favourite hero, the Evangelical young curate, is always rather an insipid personage.

The most recent novel of this species that we happen to have before us, is "The Old Grey Church."[13] It is utterly tame and feeble; there is no one set of objects on which the writer seems to have a stronger grasp than on any other; and we should be entirely at a loss to conjecture among what phases of life her experience has been gained, but for certain vulgarisms of style which sufficiently indicate that she has had the advantage, though she has been unable to use it, of mingling chiefly with men and women whose manners and characters have not had all their bosses and angles rubbed down by refined conventionalism. It is less excusable in an Evangelical novelist, than in any other, gratuitously to seek her subjects among titles and carriages. The real drama of Evangelicalism—and it has abundance of fine drama for any one who has genius enough to discern and reproduce it—lies among the middle and lower classes; and are not Evangelical opinions understood to give an especial interest in the weak things of the earth, rather than in the mighty? Why then, cannot our Evangelical lady novelists show us the operation of their religious views among people (there really are many such in the world) who keep no carriage, "not so much as a brass-bound gig," who even manage to eat their dinner without a silver fork, and in whose mouths the authoress's questionable English would be strictly consistent? Why can we not have pictures of religious life among the industrial classes in England, as interesting as Mrs. Stowe's pictures of religious life among the negroes?[14] Instead of this, pious ladies nauseate us with novels which remind us of what we sometimes see in a worldly woman recently "converted"; she is as fond of a fine dinner table as before, but she invites clergymen instead of beaux; she thinks as much of her dress as before, but she adopts a more sober choice of colours and patterns; her conversation is as trivial as before, but the triviality is flavoured with Gospel instead of gossip. In "The Old Grey Church," we have the same sort of Evangelical travesty of the fashionable novel, and of course the vicious, intriguing baronet is not wanting. It is worthwhile to give a sample of the style of conversation attributed to this high-born rake—a style that in its profuse italics and palpable innuendoes, is worthy of Miss

*Praises
Stowe*

*dinner
party
changes*

12. The hero in Shakespeare's *As You Like It*.
13. A novel published in 1856 by Lady Scott.
14. Harriet Beecher Stowe (1811–96) was the American antislavery activist and author of *Uncle Tom's Cabin* (1852).

Squeers.[15] In an evening visit to the ruins of the Colosseum, Eustace, the young clergyman, has been withdrawing the heroine, Miss Lushington, from the rest of the party, for the sake of a *tête-à-tête*. The baronet is jealous, and vents his pique in this way:

> There they are, and Miss Lushington, no doubt, quite safe; for she is under the holy guidance of Pope Eustace the First, who has, of course, been delivering to her an edifying homily on the wickedness of the heathens of yore, who, as tradition tells us, in this very place let loose the wild *beasties* on poor Saint Paul!—Oh, no! by the bye, I believe I am wrong, and betraying my want of clergy, and that it was not at all Saint Paul, nor was it here. But no matter, it would equally serve as a text to preach from, and from which to diverge to the degenerate *heathen* Christians of the present day, and all their naughty practices, and so end with an exhortation to "come out from among them, and be separate"; and I am sure, Miss Lushington, you have most scrupulously conformed to that injunction this evening, for we have seen nothing of you since our arrival. But everyone seems agreed it has been a *charming party of pleasure*, and I am sure we all feel *much indebted* to Mr Grey for having *suggested* it; and as he seems so capital a cicerone, I hope he will think of something else equally agreeable to *all*.

This drivelling kind of dialogue, and equally drivelling narrative, which, like a bad drawing, represents nothing, and barely indicates what is meant to be represented, runs through the book; and we have no doubt is considered by the amiable authoress to constitute an improving novel, which Christian mothers will do well to put into the hands of their daughters. But everything is relative; we have met with American vegetarians whose normal diet was dry meal, and who, when their appetite wanted stimulating, tickled it with *wet* meal; and so, we can imagine that there are Evangelical circles in which "The Old Grey Church" is devoured as a powerful and interesting fiction.

But, perhaps, the least readable of silly women's novels, are the *modern-antique* species, which unfold to us the domestic life of Jannes and Jambres, the private love affairs of Sennacherib, or the mental struggles and ultimate conversion of Demetrius the silversmith.[16] From most silly novels we can at least extract a laugh; but those of the modern-antique school have a ponderous, a leaden kind of fatuity, under which we groan. What can be more demonstrative of the inability of literary women to measure their own powers, than their frequent assumption of a task which can only be justified by the rarest concurrence of acquirement with genius? The finest effort to reanimate the past is of course only approximative—is always more or less an infusion of the modern spirit into the ancient form—

> Was ihr den Geist der Zeiten heisst,
> Das ist im Grund der Herren eigner Geist,
> In dem die Zeiten sich bespiegeln.[17]

Admitting that genius which has familiarized itself with all the relics of an ancient period can sometimes, by the force of its sympathetic divination, restore the missing notes in the "music of humanity," and reconstruct the fragments into a whole which will really bring the remote past nearer to us, and interpret it to our duller apprehension, this form of imaginative power must always be among the very rarest, because it demands as much accurate and minute knowledge as creative vigour. Yet we find ladies constantly choosing to make their mental mediocrity more conspicuous,

---

15. A character in *Nicholas Nickleby* (1838–39) by Charles Dickens.
16. Biblical allusions: see 2 Timothy 3 and Acts 19.

17. This passage from Goethe's *Faust* reads as follows: "What some call the spirit of the age / is fundamentally the gentlemen's own spirit, / which mirrors the age."

Exotic
Orientalism
Said

by clothing it in a masquerade of ancient names; by putting their feeble sentimentality into the mouths of Roman vestals or Egyptian princesses, and attributing their rhetorical arguments to Jewish high-priests and Greek philosophers. A recent example of this heavy imbecility is "Adonijah, a Tale of the Jewish Dispersion,"[18] which forms part of a series, "uniting," we are told "taste, humour, and sound principles." *Adonijah*, we presume, exemplifies the tale of "sound principles"; the taste and humour are to be found in other members of the series. We are told on the cover, that the incidents of this tale are "fraught with unusual interest," and the preface winds up thus: "To those who feel interested in the dispersed of Israel and Judea, these pages may afford, perhaps, information on an important subject, as well as amusement." Since the "important subject" on which this book is to afford information is not specified, it may possibly lie in some esoteric meaning to which we have no key; but if it has relation to the dispersed of Israel and Judea at any period of their history, we believe a tolerably well-informed school-girl already knows much more of it than she will find in this "Tale of the Jewish Dispersion." "Adonijah" is simply the feeblest kind of love story, supposed to be instructive, we presume, because the hero is a Jewish captive, and the heroine a Roman vestal; because they and their friends are converted to Christianity after the shortest and easiest method approved by the "Society for Promoting the Conversion of the Jews"; and because, instead of being written in plain language, it is adorned with that peculiar style of grandiloquence which is held by some lady novelists to give an antique colouring; and which we recognize at once in such phrases as these: "the splendid regnal talents undoubtedly possessed by the Emperor Nero"—"the expiring scion of a lofty stem"—"the virtuous partner of his couch"—"ah, by Vesta!"—and "I tell thee, Roman." Among the quotations which serve at once for instruction and ornament on the cover of this volume, there is one from Miss Sinclair,[19] which informs us that "Works of imagination are *avowedly* read by men of science, wisdom, and piety"; from which we suppose the reader is to gather the cheering inference that Dr. Daubeny, Mr. Mill, or Mr. Maurice,[20] may openly indulge himself with the perusal of "Adonijah," without being obliged to secrete it among the sofa cushions, or read it by snatches under the dinner-table.

"Be not a baker if your head be made of butter," says a homely proverb, which, being interpreted, may mean, let no woman rush into print who is not prepared for the consequences. We are aware that our remarks are in a very different tone from that of the reviewers who, with a perennial recurrence of precisely similar emotions, only paralleled, we imagine, in the experience of monthly nurses, tell one lady novelist after another that they "hail" her productions "with delight": We are aware that the ladies at whom our criticism is pointed are accustomed to be told, in the choicest phraseology of puffery, that their pictures of life are brilliant, their characters well-drawn, their style fascinating, and their sentiments lofty. But if they are inclined to resent our plainness of speech, we ask them to reflect for a moment on the chary praise, and often captious blame, which their panegyrists give to writers whose works are on the way to become classics. No sooner does a woman show that she has genius or effective talent, than she receives the tribute of being moderately praised and severely criticized. By a peculiar thermometric adjustment, when a woman's talent is at zero, journalistic approbation is at the boiling pitch; when she attains mediocrity,

18. A novel by Jane Margaret Strickland, published in 1856.
19. The Scottish novelist Catherine Sinclair (1800–64), a moralist.

20. Charles G. Daubeny (1795–1867), British novelist; John Stuart Mill (1800–73), philosopher and essayist; Frederick D. Maurice (1805–72), a theologian at King's College, London.

it is already at no more than summer heat; and if ever she reaches excellence, critical enthusiasm drops to the freezing point. Harriet Martineau, Currer Bell, and Mrs. Gaskell have been treated as cavalierly as if they had been men.[21] And every critic who forms a high estimate of the share women may ultimately take in literature, will, on principle, abstain from any exceptional indulgence towards the productions of literary women. For it must be plain to everyone who looks impartially and extensively into feminine literature, that its greatest deficiencies are due hardly more to the want of intellectual power than to the want of those moral qualities that contribute to literary excellence—patient diligence, a sense of the responsibility involved in publication, and an appreciation of the sacredness of the writer's art. In the majority of women's books you see that kind of facility which springs from the absence of any high standard; that fertility in imbecile combination or feeble imitation which a little self-criticism would check and reduce to barrenness; just as with a total want of musical ear people will sing out of tune, while a degree more melodic sensibility would suffice to render them silent. The foolish vanity of wishing to appear in print, instead of being counterbalanced by any consciousness of the intellectual or moral derogation implied in futile authorship, seems to be encouraged by the extremely false impression that to write *at all* is a proof of superiority in a woman. On this ground, we believe that the average intellect of women is unfairly represented by the mass of feminine literature, and that while the few women who write well are very far above the ordinary intellectual level of their sex, the many women who write ill are very far below it. So that, after all, the severer critics are fulfilling a chivalrous duty in depriving the mere fact of feminine authorship of any false prestige which may give it a delusive attraction, and in recommending women of mediocre faculties—as at least a negative service they can render their sex—to abstain from writing.

The standing apology for women who become writers without any special qualification is, that society shuts them out from other spheres of occupation. Society is a very culpable entity, and has to answer for the manufacture of many unwholesome commodities, from bad pickles to bad poetry. But society, like "matter," and Her Majesty's Government, and other lofty abstractions, has its share of excessive blame as well as excessive praise. Where there is one woman who writes from necessity, we believe there are three women who write from vanity; and, besides, there is something so antiseptic in the mere healthy fact of working for one's bread, that the most trashy and rotten kind of feminine literature is not likely to have been produced under such circumstances. "In all labour there is profit"; but ladies' silly novels, we imagine, are less the result of labour than of busy idleness.

Happily, we are not dependent on argument to prove that Fiction is a department of literature in which women can, after their kind, fully equal men. A cluster of great names, both living and dead, rush to our memories in evidence that women can produce novels not only fine, but among the very finest; novels, too, that have a precious specialty, lying quite apart from masculine aptitudes and experience. No educational restrictions can shut women out from the materials of fiction, and there is no species of art which is so free from rigid requirements. Like crystalline masses, it may take any form, and yet be beautiful; we have only to pour in the right elements—genuine observation, humour, and passion. But it is precisely this absence of rigid requirement which constitutes the fatal seduction of novel-writing

[Margin handwritten note: Eliot's defense of fine woman writer]

21. Harriet Martineau (1802–76) was an essayist and woman of letters; Currer Bell was the pen name of novelist Charlotte Bronte; Elizabeth Gaskell (1810–65) was a popular Victorian novelist.

to incompetent women. Ladies are not wont to be very grossly deceived as to their power of playing on the piano; here certain positive difficulties of execution have to be conquered, and incompetence inevitably breaks down. Every art which has its absolute *technique* is, to a certain extent, guarded from the instrusions of mere left-handed imbecility. But in novel-writing there are no barriers for incapacity to stumble against, no external criteria to prevent a writer from mistaking foolish facility for mastery. And so we have again and again the old story of La Fontaine's ass, who puts his nose to the flute, and, finding that he elicits some sound, exclaims, "Moi aussi, je joue de la flute";—a fable which we commend, at parting, to the consideration of any feminine reader who is in danger of adding to the number of "silly novels by lady novelists."[22]   1856

Charlotte Perkins Gilman *married Stetson*
1860–1935

Famous today as the author of "The Yellow Wallpaper," the grim portrait of a young woman imprisoned by a postpartum "rest cure" that her physician prescribes, Charlotte Perkins Gilman was renowned in her own time for her studies of economic and social theory. Born Charlotte Anna Perkins in Hartford, Connecticut, she was raised by her mother, Mary A. Fitch, after her father, Frederick Beecher Perkins, a member of the distinguished New England Beecher family of intellectuals, abandoned his wife shortly after his daughter's birth. Gilman's childhood was unstable: her mother, her brother, and she lived in poverty and moved frequently. After studying briefly at the Rhode Island School of Design, Gilman began to earn a living as an art teacher and a designer of greeting cards. Her marriage to Charles Walter Stetson, a fellow artist, was unhappy; he complained shortly before their separation that she was "too affectionately expressive." When Charlotte Stetson became severely depressed after the *post partum* birth of her daughter, Katharine, she sought treatment at her husband's urging from the Philadelphia neurologist S. Weir Mitchell, whose field of specialization was women's "nervous disorders." A famous proponent of the rest cure about which Gilman writes in "The Yellow Wallpaper," Mitchell required of his patients extended periods of complete isolation and passivity that were anathema to the artistic Gilman, forbidden to paint or write; nor did she adapt well to Mitchell's philosophy of the physician as the patient's moral adviser. In 1888 she left both husband and doctor, seeking temporary haven at the California home of her closest friend, Grace Ellery Channing. After a short time Gilman and her daughter moved permanently to California, where she and her former husband, who by then, ironically, had married Channing, shared custody of Katharine. Together with her mother, Gilman ran a boardinghouse, and she increasingly turned her attention to political activism and writing.

"The Yellow Wallpaper" (1892), her first publication, sought revenge on Mitchell by exposing the ineffectiveness of his method of treatment in fiction that was thinly veiled autobiography. She reports happily in "Why I Wrote 'The Yellow Wallpaper,'" an essay published in 1913, that "the great specialist" had altered his treatment of women's neurasthenia upon reading her story. Shortly after publishing her first story, Gilman became active in the women's suffrage movement; with Helen Campbell, she edited *The Impress, A Journal of the Pacific Coast Women's Press Association,* in 1894, and soon she began to earn money as a public

22. Jean de LaFontaine (1621–95) was a French writer of charming fables as well as a poet. The passage in French reads, "And I, too, enjoy the flute."

lecturer. Although Gilman refused to call herself a feminist, claiming that she was merely trying to restore human fairness to a "masculinist" world, she became known as a radical woman not only because of her writings but also because, during her five years on the road lecturing, she sent her daughter to live with her father. Gilman believed that women's subordination began with men's expropriation of women's agricultural production, thus depriving women of equality in work and of economic independence; a balanced world required that women's autonomy be restored. Her 1898 treatise *Women and Economics* employed history, sociology, and philosophy to advance these theories, for as Gilman once said, "until we can see what we are, we cannot take steps to become what we should be."

In 1900 Gilman married George Houghton Gilman, her first cousin and friend, with whom she lived happily for thirty-four years until his death, continuing to write and lecture. That same year she published *Concerning Children*, a study arguing that children can best be cared for collectively, sometimes by their biological mother but not necessarily, for loving attention to children's socialization is the shared responsibility of all members of a community. Although she never directly challenged traditional marriage or the nuclear family, her theories implicitly offer a socialist and communal alternative. In *The Home: Its Work and Influence* (1903) and *Human Work* (1904) Gilman sets forth her ideas of state-provided child care for all and cooperative kitchens, among many innovations. Other works of feminist-socialist theory include *Man-Made World* (1911) and *His Religion and Hers* (1923), subtitled, "A Study of the Faith of Our Fathers and the Work of Our Mothers." Her autobiography, *The Living of Charlotte Perkins Gilman*, appeared in 1935, shortly before her death by suicide, an act that she considered rational because she was suffering from terminal cancer.

Between 1909 and 1916 Gilman edited *The Forerunner*, a monthly magazine in which much of her short fiction was published. Her stories and novels reflect both her socialist-humanist critique of past and present and her vision of a more equitable future. Men in Gilman's fiction are usually portrayed as conventional, but well intended and capable of conversion, as can be seen in her three utopian novels: *Moving the Mountain* (1911), *Herland* (1915), and *With Her in Ourland* (1916). The most widely read of these, *Herland*, depicts a peaceful, communal, futuristic society populated only by women, who reproduce parthenogenically. When three American men arrive, the introduction of hetrosexuality and sexual difference into the environment causes intriguing complications.

Although Gilman attained international recognition as an innovative social thinker, her brand of socialist feminism lost favor with the reading public after World War I, and by 1920 there were fewer requests for her books and lectures. Her writing was reclaimed during the 1970s by feminist scholars such as Elaine Hedges, who edited the Feminist Press's edition of "The Yellow Wallpaper" in 1973, and Ann J. Lane, who wrote Gilman's definitive biography. In the early twentieth century "The Yellow Wallpaper" was viewed by critics such as William Dean Howells as a chilling Gothic tale, but many feminists have read it as an allegory describing what can happen to oppressed women who lack the support to rise up, as Gilman did, to name the source of their oppression.

has the best of intentions

⇥ The Yellow Wallpaper ⇤

It is very seldom that mere ordinary people like John and I secure ancestral halls for the summer.

A colonial mansion, a hereditary estate, I would say a haunted house, and reach the height of romantic felicity—but that would be asking too much of fate!

Still I would proudly declare that there is something queer about it. Else why should it be let so cheaply? And why have stood so long untenanted?

emerging voice

Draws describe John

John laughs at me of course, but one expects that in marriage.
John is practical in the extreme.

He has no patience with faith, an intense horror of superstition, and he scoffs openly at any talk of things not to be felt and seen and put down in figures.

John is a physician, and *perhaps*—I wouldn't say it to a living soul of course, but this is dead paper, and a great relief to my mind—*perhaps* that is one reason I do not get well faster.

You see, he does not believe I am sick! And what can one do? If a physician of high standing, and one's own husband, assures friends and relatives that there is really nothing the matter with one but temporary nervous depression—a slight hysterical tendency—what is one to do? My brother is also a physician and also of high standing, and he says the same thing.

So I take phosphates or phosphites—whichever it is, and tonics, and journeys, and air, and exercise, and am absolutely forbidden to "work" until I am well again.

Personally, I disagree with their ideas.

Personally, I believe that congenial work with excitement and change would do me good.

But what is one to do?

I did write for a while in spite of them; but it *does* exhaust me a good deal—having to be so sly about it, or else meet heavy opposition.

I sometimes fancy that in my condition if I had less opposition and more society and stimulus—but John says the very worst thing I can do is to think about my condition, and I confess it always makes me feel badly.

So I will let it alone, and write about the house. — *Jung — the soul*

The most beautiful place!

It is quite alone, standing well back from the road, and quite three miles from the village. It makes me think of English places that you read about, for there are hedges, and walls, and gates that lock, and lots of separate little houses for the gardeners and people.

There is a *delicious* garden. I never saw such a garden, large and shady, full of box-bordered paths, and lined with long grape-covered arbors with seats under them.

There were greenhouses too, but they are all broken now.

There was some legal trouble, I believe, something about the heirs and co-heirs; anyhow, it has been empty for years and years.

That spoils my ghostliness, I am afraid, but I don't care—there *is* something strange about the house—I can feel it. I even said so to John one moonlit evening, but he said what I felt was a *draught*, and shut the window.

I get unreasonably angry with John sometimes. I'm sure I never used to be so sensitive. I think it is due to this nervous condition.

But John says if I feel so I shall neglect proper self-control; so I take pains to control myself—before him at least, and that makes me very tired.

woman express

I don't like our room a bit. I wanted one downstairs, that opened on the piazza and had roses all over the windows, and such pretty old-fashioned chintz hangings; but John wouldn't hear of it.

He said there was only one window and not room for two beds, and no near room for him if he took another.

He is very careful and loving, hardly lets me stir without special direction; I have a schedule prescription for each hour in the day, he takes every care, and I feel basely ungrateful not to value it more. He said we came here solely on my account, that I was to have perfect rest, and all the air I could get. "Your exercise depends on your strength my dear" said he, "and your food somewhat on your appetite; but air you can absorb all the time". So we took the nursery at the top of the house.

It is a big airy room, the whole floor nearly, with windows that look all ways, and air and sunlight galore. It was nursery first, and then playroom and gymnasium, I should judge, for the windows are barred for little children and there are rings and things in the walls. The paint and paper look as if a boy's school had used it. It is stripped off—the paper—in great patches, all around the head of my bed about as far as I can reach, and in a great place on the other side of the room, low down.

I never saw a worse paper in my life. One of those sprawling, flamboyant patterns, committing every artistic sin. It is *dull* enough to confuse the eye in following, pronounced enough to constantly irritate and provoke study, and when you follow the lame uncertain curves for a little distance they suddenly commit suicide—plunge off at outrageous angles, destroy themselves in unheard of contradictions.

The color is repellant, almost revolting; a smouldering unclean yellow, strangely faded by the slow-turning sun.

It is a dull yet lurid orange in some places, a sickly sulphur tint in others.

No wonder the children hated it! I should hate it myself if I had to live in this room long.

There comes John, and I must put this away—he hates to have me write a word.

We have been here two weeks, and I haven't felt like writing before since that first day.

I am sitting by the window now, up in this atrocious nursery, and there is nothing to hinder my writing as much as I please, save lack of strength.

John is away all day, and even some nights, when his cases are serious. I am glad my case is not serious.

But these nervous troubles are dreadfully depressing.

John doesn't know how much I really suffer. He knows there is no *reason* to suffer, and that satisfies him. Of course it is only nervous [sic]. It does weigh on me so not to do my duty in any way. I meant to be such a help to John, such a real rest and comfort, and here I am a comparative burden already! Nobody would believe what an effort it is just to do what little I am able. To dress and entertain and order things. It is fortunate Mary is so good with the baby. Such a dear baby!

And yet I can *not* be with him, it makes me so nervous.

I suppose John was never nervous in his life. He laughs at me so about this wallpaper! At first he meant to repaper the room, but afterwards he said that I was letting it get the better of me, and that nothing was worse for a nervous patient than to give way to such fancies. He said that after the wallpaper was changed it would be the heavy bedstead, and then the barred windows, and then the gate at the head of the stairs, and so on. "You know the place is doing you good" he said, "and really, dear, I don't care to renovate the house just for a three months rental."

"Then do let us go down stairs" I said, "there are such pretty rooms there!"

Then he took me in his arms and called me a blessed little goose, and said he would go down cellar if I wished, and have it white-washed into the bargain!

But he is right enough about the beds and windows and things. It is as airy and comfortable a room as anyone need wish, and of course I wouldn't be so silly as to make him uncomfortable just for a whim.

I'm really getting quite fond of the big room, all but that horrid paper.

Out of one window I can see the garden, those mysterious deep-shaded arbors, the riotous old-fashioned flowers and bushes, the gnarly trees. Out of another I get a lovely view of the bay and a little private wharf that belongs to the estate. There is a beautiful shaded lane that runs down there from the house. I always fancy I see people walking in these numerous paths and arbors, but John has cautioned me not to give way to fancy in the least. He says that with my imaginative power and habit of story making, a nervous weakness like mine is sure to lead to all manner of excited fancies, and that I ought to use my will and good sense to check the tendency. So I try.

I think sometimes that if I were only well enough to write a little it would relieve the pressure of ideas and rest me.

But I find I get pretty tired when I try. It is so discouraging not to have any advice and companionship about my work. When I get really well John says we will ask Cousin Henry and Julia down for a long visit: but he says he would as soon put fireworks in my pillowcase as to let me have those stimulating people about now. I wish I could get well faster. But I *mustn't* think about that.

This paper looks to me as if it *knew* what a vicious influence it had!

There is a recurrent spot where the pattern lolls like a broken neck, and two bulbous eyes stare at you upside down.

I get positively angry with the impertinence of it, and the everlastingness. Up and down and sideways they crawl, and those absurd unblinking eyes are everywhere. There is one place where two breadths didn't match; and the eyes go all up and down the line, one a little higher than the other. I never saw so much expression in an inanimate thing before, and we all know how much expression inanimate things have! I used to lie awake as a child, and get more entertainment and terror out of blank walls and plain furniture than most children could find in a toystore. I remember what a kindly wink the knobs of our big old bureau used to have; and there was one chair that always seemed like a strong friend.

I used to feel that if any of the other things looked too fierce I could always hop into that chair and be safe.

The furniture in this room is no worse than inharmonious, however, for we had to bring it all from down stairs. I suppose when this was used as a play room they had to take the nursery things out—and no wonder! for I never saw such ravages as the children have made here.

The wallpaper, as I said before, is torn off in spots, and it sticketh closer than a brother—they must have had perseverance as well as hatred. Then the floor is scratched and gouged and splintered, the plaster itself is dug out here and there, and this great heavy bed which is all we found in the room, looks as if it had been though the wars. But I don't mind it a bit—only the paper.

There comes John's sister—such a dear girl as she is, and so careful of me! I mustn't let her find me writing.

She is a perfect—an enthusiastic—housekeeper, and hopes for no better profession. I verily believe she thinks it is the writing which made me sick!

But I can write when she is out, and see her a long way off from these windows.

There is one that commands the road, a lovely shaded winding road; and one that just looks off over the country. A lovely country too, full of great elms and velvet meadows.

This wallpaper has a kind of subpattern in a different shade, a particularly irritating one, for you can only see it in certain lights, and not clearly then. But in the places where it isn't faded, and when the sun is just so, I can see a strange provoking

eyes as symbol

formless sort of figure, that seems to skulk about behind that silly and conspicuous front design.

humor

— There's sister on the stairs!

Well the Fourth of July is over! The people are all gone and I am tired out.

John thought it might do me good to see a little company, so we just had Mother and Nellie and the children down for a week.

Of course I didn't do a thing—Jennie sees to everything now. But it tired me all the same. John says if I don't pick up faster he shall send me to Weir Mitchell in the fall.[1]

But I don't want to go there at all, I had a friend who was in his hands once, and she says he is just like John and my brother only more so!

Besides it is such an undertaking to go so far. I don't feel as if it were worth while to turn my hand over for anything, and I'm getting dreadfully fretful and querulous. I cry at nothing and cry most of the time. Of course I don't when John is here, or anybody else, but when I am alone.

post partum

And I am alone a good deal just now. John is kept in town very often by serious cases, and Jennie is good and lets me alone when I want her to. So I walk a little in the garden or down that lovely lane, sit on the porch under the roses, and lie down up here a good deal.

I'm getting really fond of the room in spite of the wallpaper.

Perhaps *because* of the wallpaper! It dwells in my mind so! I lie here on this great immovable bed (—it's nailed down, I believe!) and follow that pattern about by the hour.

It is as good as gymnastics, I assure you. I start, we'll say, at the bottom, down in the corner over there where it hasn't been touched; and I determine, for the thousandth time, that I *will* follow that pointless pattern to some sort of a conclusion.

I know a little of the principles of design, and I know this thing was not arranged on any laws of radiation, or alternation, or repetition, or symmetry, or anything else that I ever heard of. It is repeated of course, by the breadth, but not otherwise.

Looked at in one way each breadth stands alone, the bloated curves and flourishes—a kind of debased Romanesque with *delirium tremens*—go waddling up and down in isolated columns of fatuity.

But on the other hand they connect diagonally, and the sprawling outlines run off in great slanting waves of optic horror like a lot of wallowing sea-weeds in full chase.

The whole thing goes horizontally, too, at least it seems so, and I exhaust myself in trying to distinguish the order of its going in that direction. They have used a horizontal breadth for a border, and that adds wonderfully to the confusion.

There is one end of the room where it is almost intact, and there, when the cross-lights fade and the low sun shines directly on it, I can almost fancy radiation after all; the interminable grotesques seem to form around a common center and rush off in headlong plunges of equal distraction.

It makes me tired to follow it. I will take a nap I guess.

I don't know why I should write this.
I don't want to.

---

1. S. Weir Mitchell (1829–1914) was a physician and a leading proponent of the "rest cure" for women's neurasthenia; at one time he treated Gilman.

I don't feel able.

And I know John would think it absurd. But I *must* say what I feel and think in some way—it is such a relief.

But the effort is getting to be greater than the relief.

Half the time now I am lazy, awfully lazy, and lie down ever so much. John says I mustn't lose my strength, and has me take codliver oil and lots of tonics and things, to say nothing of ale and wine and rare meat.

Dear John! He loves me very dearly, and hates to have me sick. I tried to have a real earnest reasonable talk with him the other day, and tell him how I wish he would let me go and make a visit to Cousin Henry and Julia.

But he said I wasn't able to go, nor able to stand it after I got there; and I did not make out a very good case for myself, for I was crying before I had finished.

It is getting to be a great effort for me to think straight—just this nervous weakness, I suppose.

And dear John gathered me up in his strong arms and just carried me up stairs and laid me on the bed, and sat by me, and read to me till it tired my head.

He said I was his darling, and his comfort, and all he had, and that I must take care of myself for his sake, and keep well.

He says no one but myself can help me out of it, that I must use my will and self-control and not let any silly fancies run away with me.

————There's *one* comfort, the baby is well and happy, and does not have to occupy this nursery with the horrid wall-paper. If I had not used it that blessed child would have!

What a fortunate escape!

Why, I wouldn't have a child of mine, an impressionable little thing, live in such a room for worlds.

I never thought of it before, but it is lucky that John kept me here after all.

I can stand it so much easier than a baby you see!

Of course I never mention it to them any more—I am too wise, but I keep watch of it all the same. There are things in that paper that nobody knows but me, or ever will. Behind that outside pattern the dim shapes get clearer every day. It is always the same shape, only very numerous. And it's like a woman stooping down, and creeping about behind that pattern. I don't like it a bit. I wonder—I begin to think—.

I wish John would take me from here!————

It is so hard to talk with John about my case, because he is so wise, and because he loves me so.

But I tried it last night.

It was moonlight. The moon shines in all round just as the sun does.

I hate to see it sometimes, it creeps so slowly, and always comes in by one window or another.

John was asleep and I hated to waken him, so I kept still and watched the moonlight on that undulating wallpaper till it made me creepy.

The faint figure behind seemed to shake the pattern, just as if she wanted to get out.

I got up softly and went to feel and see if the paper *did* move, and when I came back John was awake.

"What is it little girl?" he said. "Don't go walking about like that—you'll get cold."

I thought it was a good time to talk, so I told him that I really was not gaining here, and that I wished he would take me away.

"Why, darling", said he, "our lease will be up in three weeks, and I can't see how to leave before. The repairs are not done at home, and I can't possibly leave town just now. Of course if you were in any danger I could and would, but you really are better, dear, whether you can see it or not.

I am a doctor, dear, and I know. You are gaining flesh and color, your appetite is better, I feel really much easier about you."

"I don't weigh a bit more", said I, "nor as much; and my appetite may be better in the evening when you are here, but it is worse in the morning when you are away."

patronizing "Bless her little heart!" said he, with a big hug, "she shall be as sick as she pleases! But now let's improve the shining hours by going to sleep, and talk about it in the morning!"

"And you won't go away?" I asked gloomily.

"Why, how can I, dear? It is only three weeks more and then we will take a nice little trip of a few days while Jennie is getting the house ready. Really, dear, you are better!"

stern "Better in *body*, perhaps"—I began, and stopped short; for he sat up straight and looked at me with such a stern reproachful look that I could not say another word.

"My darling," said he, "I beg of you, for my sake and our child's sake, as well as for your own, that you will never for one instant let *that* idea enter your mind. There is nothing so dangerous, so fascinating, to a temperament like yours. It is a false and foolish fancy. Can you not trust me as a physician when I tell you so?"

So of course I said no more on that score, and he went to sleep before long.

He thought I was asleep first, but I wasn't. I lay there for hours trying to decide whether the front pattern and the back pattern really did move together or separately.

In a pattern like this, by daylight, there is a certain lack of sequence, a defiance of law that is a constant irritant to a normal mind.

The color is hideous enough, and unreliable enough, and infuriating enough, but the pattern is torturing.

You think you have mastered it, but just as you get well underway in following it, it turns a back somersault and there you are! It slaps you in the face, knocks you down and tramples on you. It is like a bad dream. The outside pattern is a florid arabesque, reminding one of a fungus. If you can imagine a toadstool in joints, an interminable string of toadstools, budding and sprouting in endless convolutions— why, that is something like it.

That is, *sometimes!*

There is one marked peculiarity about this paper, a thing nobody seems to notice but myself, and that is that it changes as the light changes.

When the sun shoots in through the east window—I always watch for that first long straight ray—it changes so quickly that I never can quite believe it. That is why I watch it always? By moonlight—the moon shines in all night when there is a moon—I wouldn't know it was the same paper.

Bars At night, in any kind of light, in twilight, candlelight, lamplight, and worst of all by moonlight—it becomes *bars!* The outside pattern, I mean. And the woman behind is as plain as can be.

Jail I didn't realize for a long time what the thing was that showed behind, the dim sub-pattern, but now I am quite sure it is a woman. — *behind the wall paper,*

By daylight she is subdued—quiet. I fancy it is the pattern that keeps her so still. It is so puzzling. It keeps me quiet by the hour. I lie down ever so much now. John says it is good for me, and to sleep all I can. Indeed he started the habit—by making me lie down for an hour after each meal. It is a very bad habit I am convinced, for you see I don't sleep!

And that cultivates deceit, for I don't tell *them* I'm awake—O no!

hanges
are
The fact is I am getting a little afraid of John. He seems very queer sometimes. And even Jennie has an inexplicable look.

It strikes me occasionally, just as scientific hypothesis—that perhaps it is the paper!

I have watched John when he didn't know I was looking—and come into the room suddenly on the most innocent excuses, and I've caught him several times *looking at the paper!* And Jennie, too.

I caught Jennie with her hand on it once.

She didn't know I was in the room, and when I asked her in a quiet, a very quiet voice, with the most restrained manner possible, what she was doing with the paper? she turned around as if she had been caught stealing and looked quite angry—asked me why I should frighten her so!

Then she said that the paper stained everything it touched, that she had found yellow smooches on all my clothes and John's, and she wished we would be more careful!

Did not that sound innocent? But I know she was studying that pattern, and I am determined that nobody shall find it out but myself!

Life is very much more exciting now than it used to be. You see I have something to expect, to look forward to, to watch. I really do eat better, and am much more quiet than I was. John is so pleased to see me improve.

He laughed a little the other day and said I seemed to be flourishing in spite of my wallpaper. I turned it off with a laugh. I had no intention of telling him it was *because* of the wallpaper!

He would make fun of me. He might even take me away. I don't want to leave now until I have found it out. There is a week more, and I think that will be enough.

I'm feeling ever so much better! I don't sleep much at night, for it is so interesting to watch developments, but I sleep a good deal in the daytime. In the daytime it is tiresome and perplexing. There are always new shoots on the fungus, and new shades of yellow all over it. I can not keep count of them, though I have tried conscientiously. It is the strangest yellow—that paper! A sickly penetrating suggestive yellow. It makes me think of all the yellow things I ever saw—not beautiful ones like buttercups, but old foul bad yellow things.

But there is another thing about that paper—the smell!   *The smell*

I noticed it the moment we came into the room, but with so much air and sun it was not bad. Now we have had a week of fog and rain, and whether the windows are open or not the smell is here. It creeps all over the house. I find it hovering in the dining room, skulking in the parlor, hiding in the hall, lying in wait for me on the stairs. It gets into my hair. Even when I go to ride, if I turn my head suddenly and surprise it there is that smell!

Such a peculiar odor too! I have spent hours in trying to analyze it, to find what it smelled like. It is not bad—at first, and very gentle, but quite the subtlest, most enduring odor I ever met.   *post partum*

In this damp weather it is awful. I wake up in the night and find it hanging over me. It used to disturb me at first. I thought seriously of burning the house to reach the smell. But now I am used to it. The only thing I can think of that it is like is the *color* of the paper! A yellow smell.

There is a very funny mark on this wall, low down, near the mop-board. A streak that runs all round the room.

It goes behind every piece of furniture except the bed; a long straight even smooch, as if it had been rubbed over and over.

I wonder how it was done, and who did it, and what they did it for!

Round and round and round—round and round and round—it makes me dizzy!

I really have discovered something at last. Through watching so much at night, when it changes so, I have finally found out.

The front pattern *does* move—and no wonder!

The woman behind shakes it! Sometimes I think there are a great many women behind, and sometimes only one and she crawls around fast. And her crawling shakes it all over.

Then in the very bright spots she keeps still, and in very shady spots she just takes hold of the bars and shakes them hard.

And she is all the time trying to climb through.

But nobody could climb through that pattern, it strangles so. I think that is why it has so many heads. They get through, and then the pattern strangles them off, and turns them upside down and makes their eyes white!

If those heads were covered or taken off it would not be half so bad.

I think that woman gets out in the day time! And I'll tell you why—privately— I've seen her! I can see her out of every one of my windows! It is the same woman, I know, for she is always creeping, and most women do not creep by daylight.

I see her in that long shaded lane, creeping up and down. I see her in those dark grape arbors, creeping all around the garden.

I see her on that long road under the trees, creeping along, and when a carriage comes she hides under the blackberry vines. I don't blame her a bit. It must be very unpleasant to be caught creeping by daylight! I always lock the door when I creep by daylight. I can't do it at night, for I know John would suspect something at once. And John is so queer now that I don't want to irritate him. I wish he would take another room!

Besides I don't want anybody to get that woman out at night but me.

I often wonder if I could see her out of all the windows at once. But turn as fast as I can I can only see out of one at a time.

And though I always see her she may be able to creep faster than I can turn!

I have watched her sometimes away off in the open country, creeping as fast as a cloud shadow in a high wind.

If only that top pattern could be gotten off from the under one! I mean to try tearing it, little by little.

I have found out another funny thing, but I shan't tell it this time! It does not do to trust people too much.

There are only two more days to get this paper off, and I believe John is beginning to notice.

I don't like the look in his eyes. And I heard him ask Jennie a lot of professional questions about me. She had a very good report to give.

She said I slept a good deal in the daytime. John knows I don't sleep very well at night, for all I'm so quiet. He asked me all sorts of questions, too, and pretended to be very loving and kind. As if I couldn't see through him!

Still I don't wonder he acts so, sleeping under this paper for three months.

It only interests me, but I feel sure John and Jennie are secretly affected by it.

Hurrah! This is the last day, but it is enough. John had to stay in town overnight, and won't be out till this evening.

Jennie wanted to sleep with me—the sly thing!—but I told her I should undoubtedly rest better for a night all alone.

That was clever, for really I wasn't alone a bit! As soon as it was moonlight and that poor thing began to crawl and shake the pattern, I got up and ran to help her.

I pulled and she shook, I shook and she pulled, and before morning we had peeled off yards of that paper.

A strip about as high as my head, and half around the room.

And then when the sun came and that awful pattern began to laugh at me I declared I would finish it today!

We go away tomorrow, and they are moving all my furniture down again to leave things as they were before.

Jennie looked at the wall in amazement, but I told her merrily that I did it out of pure spite at the vicious thing.

She laughed and said she wouldn't mind doing it herself, but I must not get tired. How she betrayed herself that time!

But I am here, and no person touches this paper but me—not *alive*!

She tried to get me out of the room—it was too patent! But I said it was so quiet and empty and clean now that I believed I would lie down again and sleep all I could; and not to wake me even for dinner—I would call when I woke!

So now she is gone, and the servants, and the things, and there is nothing left but that great bedstead, nailed down, with the canvas mattress we found on it.

We shall sleep down stairs tonight, and take the boat home tomorrow.

I quite enjoy the room now it is bare again.

How those children did tear about here! This bedstead is fairly gnawed!

But I must get to work.

I have locked the door and thrown the key down into the front path.

I don't want to go out, and I don't want to have anybody come in until John comes. I want to astonish him.

I've got a rope up here that even Jennie did not find. If that woman does get out, and tries to get away, I can tie her!

But I forgot I couldn't reach far without anything to stand on! The bed will not move. I tried to lift or push it till I was lame, and then I got so angry I bit off a little piece at one corner—but it hurt my teeth.

Then I peeled off all the paper I could reach standing on the floor. It sticks horribly. And the pattern just enjoys it. All those strangled heads and bulbous eyes and waddling fungus growths just shriek with derision!

I am getting angry enough to do something desperate. To jump out the window would be admirable exercise, but the bars are too strong even to try. Besides, I wouldn't do it of course! I know well enough that a step like that is improper and might be misconstrued.

I don't like to look out of the windows even—there are so many of those creeping women, and they creep so fast.

I wonder if they all came out of that wallpaper as I did? But I am securely fastened now by my well-hidden rope—you don't get me out in the road there.

I suppose I shall have to get back behind the pattern when it comes night, and that is hard!

It is so pleasant to be out in this great room and creep around as I please!

I don't want to go outside. I won't, even if Jennie asks me to. For outside, you have to creep on the ground, and everything is green instead of yellow.

But here I can creep smoothly on the floor, and my shoulder just fits in that long smooch around the wall, so I cannot lose my way.

Why there's John at the door!

It is no use, young man, you can't open it!

How he does call and pound?

Now he's crying for an ax!

It would be a shame to break that beautiful strong door!

"John dear!" sad I in the gentlest voice—"The key is down by the front steps, under a plantain leaf ."

That silenced him for a few moments.

Then he said—very quietly indeed—"Open the door, my darling!"

"I can't," said I, "The key is down by the front steps under a plantain leaf."

And then I said it again, several times, very gently and slowly.

I said it so often that he had to go and see, and he got it of course, and came in.

He stopped short, by the door. "What is the matter!" he cried. "For God's sake what are you doing!"

I kept on creeping just the same, but I looked at him over my shoulder.

"I've got out at last," said I, "in spite of you and Jane! And I've pulled off most of the paper, so you can't put me back!"

Now why should that man have fainted?

But he did, and right across my path by the wall, so that I had to creep over him!

1892

Edith Wharton
1862–1937

Author of the Pulitzer Prize–winning novel *The Age of Innocence* (1920), Edith Wharton is known for her fictional portraits of the tragic lives and moral quandries of aristocratic Americans, depicting what she called their "blind dread of innovation" and "instinctive shrinking from responsibility." Born Edith Newbold Jones in New York City, she grew up in one of those wealthy, conservative families about which she would later write. She was educated by tutors while her family traveled in Europe. In 1855 she married Edward Wharton, a member of a patrician family in Boston, with whom she lived unhappily for twenty-eight years; the couple moved to France in 1910 and divorced in 1913. Two early stories, "Souls Belated" (1899) and "The Other Two" (1904), take divorce as their subject, exploring the ways in which traditional gender roles and conventional social mores affect well-to-do women in bad marriages, taught to view divorce as scandalous. Wharton published her first collection of stories, *The Greater Inclination*, in 1899. It was *The House of Mirth* (1905), however, that won her acclaim and introduced her to a distinguished group of artists and intellectuals in Europe and America, including Henry James, whose fiction she admired and emulated. James once praised her work because "the masculine conclusion" in it outweighed "the feminine observation." Other members of her circle were the novelist Sinclair Lewis, who dedicated his grim novel *Babbitt* to her, and the French surrealist and dramatist Jean Cocteau, whom she met during the years that she resided in France. Despite her lifelong struggle with a nervous disorder similar to the neurasthenia about which CHARLOTTE PERKINS GILMAN wrote, Wharton managed to produce more than fifty volumes of fiction and nonfiction. In 1934 she became one of the first women honored by the American Academy of Arts and Letters.

The House of Mirth contains the subject matter Wharton would address in much of her subsequent fiction: the conflicts between aristocratic New Yorkers and the newly rich, and the ethical dilemmas of naïve or self-deluding characters caught up in these class-related tensions. Like James, she often chose as her narrator a sensitive observer who both judges the society he or she witnesses and becomes its victim. *The Custom of the Country* (1913), for years one of Wharton's least-known works, is considered by many critics today her most successful; in it she chronicles the machinations of Undine Spragg, an ambitious American woman who casts off four husbands and several lovers at home and abroad to rise to success. In *The Age of Innocence* Ellen Olenska, an American woman living in France, acquires a somewhat scandalous reputation and is rejected by the New York elite, with their rigid notions of propriety. Other works examine the difficult lives of the rural poor. In *Ethan Frome* (1911), a study of the damaging effects of patriarchal family structures, an unhappily married New England farmer takes a young lover; after the guilt-ridden pair unsuccessfully attempt suicide, Frome must assume the burden of care for both his lover and his wife. The highly acclaimed *Summer* (1917) depicts the narrow provincialism of a small American town. In these and other novels Wharton criticized America's consumer capitalism during the "Gilded Age" and its restrictive sexual mores.

The fiercely satiric writing that characterized Wharton's early novels gave way in the 1920s to more gentle criticism or, as some would say, nostalgia. Most critics agree that her novels subsequent to 1920 do not measure up to their predecessors, although her short stories remain consistently fine. In 1925 Wharton published a study of the art of the novel, and in 1934 she published a memoir of her early life, *A Backward Glance*, in which she extols traditional domestic duties as appropriate work for women, criticizes women's pursuits for equal education and suffrage, and reveals her ambivalence toward a female literary tradition. Although she admired JANE AUSTEN and GEORGE ELIOT, for example, she dismissed CHARLOTTE BRONTË'S writing as trivial, was "exasperated by the laxities" of Louisa May Alcott, and responded with hostility to the novels of VIRGINIA WOOLF. Given these ambivalent attitudes toward women writers, it seems ironic that in many of her novels and in such stories as "A Journey," Wharton insightfully critiques traditional constructions of femininity and explores with compassion the difficulty some women have in finding their voice.

⊰ A Journey ⊱

As she lay in her berth, staring at the shadows overhead, the rush of the wheels was in her brain, driving her deeper and deeper into circles of wakeful lucidity. The sleeping-car had sunk into its night-silence. Through the wet window-pane she watched the sudden lights, the long stretches of hurrying blackness. Now and then she turned her head and looked through the opening in the hangings at her husband's curtains across the aisle. . . .

She wondered restlessly if he wanted anything and if she could hear him if he called. His voice had grown very weak within the last months and it irritated him when she did not hear. This irritability, this increasing childish petulance seemed to give expression to their imperceptible estrangement. Like two faces looking at one another through a sheet of glass they were close together, almost touching, but they could not hear or feel each other: the conductivity between them was broken. She, at least, had this sense of separation, and she fancied sometimes that she saw it reflected in the look with which he supplemented his failing words. Doubtless the fault was hers. She was too impenetrably healthy to be touched by the irrelevancies of disease. Her self-reproachful tenderness was tinged with the sense of his irrationality: she had a vague feeling that there was a purpose in his helpless tyrannies. The suddenness of the change had found her so unprepared. A year ago their pulses had beat to one robust measure; both had the same prodigal confidence in an exhaustless future. Now their energies no longer kept step: hers still bounded ahead of life, preëmpting unclaimed regions of hope and activity, while his lagged behind, vainly struggling to overtake her.

When they married, she had such arrears of living to make up: her days had been as bare as the white-washed school-room where she forced innutritious facts upon reluctant children. His coming had broken in on the slumber of circumstance, widening the present till it became the encloser of remotest chances. But imperceptibly the horizon narrowed. Life had a grudge against her: she was never to be allowed to spread her wings.

At first the doctors had said that six weeks of mild air would set him right; but when he came back this assurance was explained as having of course included a winter in a dry climate. They gave up their pretty house, storing the wedding presents and new furniture, and went to Colorado. She had hated it there from the first. Nobody knew her or cared about her; there was no one to wonder at the good match she had made, or to envy her the new dresses and the visiting-cards which were still a surprise to her. And he kept growing worse. She felt herself beset with difficulties too evasive to be fought by so direct a temperament. She still loved him, of course; but he was gradually, undefinably ceasing to be himself. The man she had married had been strong, active, gently masterful: the male whose pleasure it is to clear a way through the material obstructions of life; but now it was she who was the protector, he who must be shielded from importunities and given his drops or his beef-juice though the skies were falling. The routine of the sick-room bewildered her; this punctual administering of medicine seemed as idle as some uncomprehended religious mummery.

There were moments, indeed, when warm gushes of pity swept away her instinctive resentment of his condition, when she still found his old self in his eyes as they groped for each other through the dense medium of his weakness. But these moments had grown rare. Sometimes he frightened her: his sunken expressionless face seemed that of a stranger; his voice was weak and hoarse; his thin-lipped smile a mere muscular contraction. Her hand avoided his damp soft skin, which had lost the familiar roughness of health: she caught herself furtively watching him as she might have watched a strange animal. It frightened her to feel that this was the man she loved; there were hours when to tell him what she suffered seemed the one escape from her fears. But in general she judged herself more leniently, reflecting that she had perhaps been too long alone with him, and that she would feel differently when they were at home again, surrounded by her robust and buoyant family. How she had rejoiced when the doctors at last gave their consent to his going home! She knew, of course, what the decision meant; they both knew. It meant that he was to die; but they dressed the truth in hopeful euphuisms, and at times, in the joy of preparation, she really forgot the purpose of their journey, and slipped into an eager allusion to next year's plans.

At last the day of leaving came. She had a dreadful fear that they would never get away; that somehow at the last moment he would fail her; that the doctors held one of the accustomed treacheries in reserve; but nothing happened. They drove to the station, he was installed in a seat with a rug over his knees and a cushion at his back, and she hung out the window waving unregretful farewells to the acquaintances she had really never liked till then.

The first twenty-four hours had passed off well. He revived a little and it amused him to look out of the window and to observe the humours of the car. The second day he began to grow weary and to chafe under the dispassionate stare of the freckled child with the lump of chewing-gum. She had to explain to the child's mother that her husband was too ill to be disturbed: a statement received by the lady with a resentment visibly supported by the maternal sentiment of the whole car. . . .

That night he slept badly and the next morning his temperature frightened her: she was sure he was growing worse. The day passed slowly, punctuated by the small irritations of travel. Watching his tired face, she traced in its contractions every rattle and jolt of the train, till her own body vibrated with sympathetic fatigue. She felt the others observing him too, and hovered restlessly between him and the lines of interrogative eyes. The freckled child hung about him like a fly; offers of candy and picture-books failed to dislodge her: she twisted one leg around the other and watched him imperturbably. The porter, as he passed, lingered with vague proffers of help, probably inspired by philanthropic passengers swelling with the sense that "something ought to be done;" and one nervous man in a skull-cap was audibly concerned as to the possible effect on his wife's health.

The hours dragged on in a dreary inoccupation. Towards dusk she sat down beside him and he laid his hand on hers. The touch startled her. He seemed to be calling her from far off. She looked at him helplessly and his smile went through her like a physical pang.

"Are you very tired?" she asked.

"No, not very."

"We'll be there soon now."

"Yes, very soon."

"This time to-morrow—"

He nodded and they sat silent. When she had put him to bed and crawled into her own berth she tried to cheer herself with the thought that in less than twenty-four hours they would be in New York. Her people would all be at the station to meet her—she pictured their round unanxious faces pressing through the crowd. She only hoped they would not tell him too loudly that he was looking splendidly and would be all right in no time: the subtler sympathies developed by long contact with suffering were making her aware of a certain coarseness of texture in the family sensibilities.

Suddenly she thought she heard him call. She parted the curtains and listened. No, it was only a man snoring at the other end of the car. His snores had a greasy sound, as though they passed through tallow. She lay down and tried to sleep . . . Had she not heard him move? She started up trembling . . . The silence frightened her more than any sound. He might not be able to make her hear—he might be calling her now . . . What made her think of such things? It was merely the familiar tendency of an over-tired mind to fasten itself on the most intolerable chance within the range of its forebodings . . . Putting her head out, she listened; but she could not distinguish his breathing from that of the other pairs of lungs about her. She longed to get up and look at him, but she knew the impulse was a mere vent for her restlessness, and the fear of disturbing him restrained her. . . . The regular movement of his curtain reassured her, she knew not why; she remembered that he had wished her a cheerful good-night; and the sheer inability to endure her fears a moment longer made her put them from her with an effort of her whole sound tired body. She turned on her side and slept.

She sat up stiffly, staring out at the dawn. The train was rushing through a region of bare hillocks huddled against a lifeless sky. It looked like the first day of creation. The air of the car was close, and she pushed up her window to let in the keen wind. Then she looked at her watch: it was seven o'clock, and soon the people about her would be stirring. She slipped into her clothes, smoothed her dishevelled hair and crept to the dressing-room. When she had washed her face and adjusted her dress she felt more hopeful. It was always a struggle for her not to be cheerful in the morning. Her cheeks burned deliciously under the coarse towel and the wet hair about her temples broke into strong upward tendrils. Every inch of her was full of life and elasticity. And in ten hours they would be at home!

She stepped to her husband's berth: it was time for him to take his early glass of milk. The window-shade was down, and in the dusk of the curtained enclosure she could just see that he lay sideways, with his face away from her. She leaned over him and drew up the shade. As she did so she touched one of his hands. It felt cold. . . .

She bent closer, laying her hand on his arm and calling him by name. He did not move. She spoke again more loudly; she grasped his shoulder and gently shook it. He lay motionless. She caught hold of his hand again: it slipped from her limply, like a dead thing. A dead thing? . . . Her breath caught. She must see his face. She leaned forward, and hurriedly, shrinkingly, with a sickening reluctance of the flesh, laid her hands on his shoulders and turned him over. His head fell back; his face looked small and smooth; he gazed at her with steady eyes.

She remained motionless for a long time, holding him thus; and they looked at each other. Suddenly she shrank back: the longing to scream, to call out, to fly from him, had almost overpowered her. But a strong hand arrested her. Good God! If it were known that he was dead they would be put off the train at the next station—

In a terrifying flash of remembrance there arose before her a scene she had once witnessed in travelling, when a husband and wife, whose child had died in the train, had been thrust out at some chance station. She saw them standing on the platform with the child's body between them; she had never forgotten the dazed look with which they followed the receding train. And this was what would happen to her. Within the next hour she might find herself on the platform of some strange station, alone with her husband's body. . . . Anything but that! It was too horrible—She quivered like a creature at bay.

As she cowered there, she felt the train moving more slowly. It was coming then—they were approaching a station! She saw again the husband and wife standing on the lonely platform; and with a violent gesture she drew down the shade to hide her husband's face.

Feeling dizzy, she sank down on the edge of the berth, keeping away from his outstretched body, and pulling the curtains close, so that he and she were shut into a kind of sepulchral twilight. She tried to think. At all costs she must conceal the fact that he was dead. But how? Her mind refused to act: she could not plan, combine. She could think of no way but to sit there, clutching the curtains, all day long . . .

She heard the porter making up her bed; people were beginning to move about the car; the dressing-room door was being opened and shut. She tried to rouse herself. At length with a supreme effort she rose to her feet, stepping into the aisle of the car and drawing the curtains tight behind her. She noticed that they still parted slightly with the motion of the car, and finding a pin in her dress she fastened them together. Now she was safe. She looked round and saw the porter. She fancied he was watching her.

"Ain't he awake yet?" he enquired.

"No," she faltered.

"I got his milk all ready when he wants it. You know you told me to have it for him by seven."

She nodded silently and crept into her seat.

At half-past eight the train reached Buffalo. By this time the other passengers were dressed and the berths had been folded back for the day. The porter, moving to and fro under his burden of sheets and pillows, glanced at her as he passed. At length he said: "Ain't he going to get up? You know we're ordered to make up the berths as early as we can."

She turned cold with fear. They were just entering the station.

"Oh, not yet," she stammered. "Not till he's had his milk. Won't you get it, please?"

"All right. Soon as we start again."

When the train moved on he reappeared with the milk. She took it from him and sat vaguely looking at it: her brain moved slowly from one idea to another, as though they were stepping-stones set far apart across a whirling flood. At length she became aware that the porter still hovered expectantly.

"Will I give it to him?" he suggested.

"Oh no," she cried rising, "He—he's asleep yet, I think—"

She waited till the porter had passed on; then she unpinned the curtains and slipped behind them. In the semi-obscurity her husband's face stared up at her like a marble mask with agate eyes. The eyes were dreadful. She put out her hand and drew down the lids. Then she remembered the glass of milk in her other hand: what was she to do with it? She thought of raising the window and throwing it out; but to do so she would have to lean across his body and bring her face close to his. She decided to drink the milk.

She returned to her seat with the empty glass and after a while the porter came back to get it.

"When'll I fold up his bed?" he asked.

"Oh, not now—not yet; he's ill— he's very ill. Can't you let him stay as he is? The doctor wants him to lie down as much as possible."

He scratched his head. "Well, if he's *really* sick—"

He took the empty glass and walked away, explaining to the passengers that the party behind the curtains was too sick to get up just yet.

She found herself the center of sympathetic eyes. A motherly woman with an intimate smile sat down beside her.

"I'm really sorry to hear your husband's sick. I've had a remarkable amount of sickness in my family and maybe I could assist you. Can I take a look at him."

"Oh, no—no, please! He mustn't be disturbed."

The lady accepted the rebuff indulgently.

"Well, it's just as you say, of course, but you don't look to me as if you'd had much experience in sickness and I'd have been glad to assist you. What do you generally do when your husband's taken this way?"

"I—I let him sleep."

"Too much sleep ain't any too healthful either. Don't you give him any medicine?"

"Y—yes."

"Don't you wake him to take it?"

"Yes."

"When does he take the next dose?"

"Not for—two hours—"

The lady look disappointed. "Well, if I was you I'd try giving it oftener. That's what I do with my folks."

After that many faces seemed to press upon her. The passengers were on their way to the dining-car, and she was conscious that as they passed down the aisle they glanced curiously at the closed curtains. One lantern-jawed man with prominent eyes stood still and tried to shoot his projecting glance through the division between the folds. The freckled child, returning from breakfast, waylaid the passers with a buttery clutch, saying in a loud whisper, "He's sick;" and once the conductor came by, asking for tickets. She shrank into her corner and looked out the window at the flying trees and houses, meaningless hieroglyphs of an endlessly unrolled papyrus.

Now and then the train stopped, and the newcomers on entering the car stared in turn at the closed curtains. More and more people seemed to pass—their faces began to blend fantastically with the images surging in her brain . . .

Later in the day a fat man detached himself from the mist of faces. He had a creased stomach and soft pale lips. As he pressed himself into the seat facing her she noticed that he was dressed in black broadcloth, with a soiled white tie.

"Husband's pretty bad this morning, is he?"

"Yes."

"Dear, dear! Now that's terribly distressing, ain't it?" An apostolic smile revealed his gold-filled teeth. "Of course you know there's no such thing as sickness. Ain't that a lovely thought? Death itself is but a deloosion of our grosser senses. On'y lay yourself open to the influx of the sperrit, submit yourself passively to the action of the divine force, and disease and dissolution will cease to exist for you. If you could indooce your husband to read this little pamphlet—"

The faces about her again grew indistinct. She had a vague recollection of hearing the motherly lady and the parent of the freckled child ardently disputing the relative advantages of trying several medicines at once, or of taking each in turn; the motherly lady maintaining that the competitive system saved time; the other objecting that you couldn't tell which remedy had effected the cure; their voices went on and on, like bellbuoys droning through a fog . . . The porter came up now and then with questions that she did not understand, but that somehow she must have answered since he went away again and again without repeating them; every two hours the motherly lady reminded her that her husband ought to have his drops; people left the car and others replaced them. . . .

Her head was spinning and she tried to steady herself by clutching at her thoughts as they swept by, but they slipped away from her like bushes on the side of a sheer precipice down which she seemed to be falling. Suddenly her mind grew clear again and she found herself vividly picturing what would happen when the train reached New York. She shuddered as it occurred to her that he would be quite cold and that some one might perceive he had been dead since morning.

She thought hurriedly: "If they see I'm not surprised they will suspect something. They will ask questions, and if I tell them the truth they won't believe me—no one would believe me! It will be terrible"—and she kept repeating to herself: "I must pretend I don't know. I must pretend I don't know. When they open the curtains I must go up to him quite naturally—and then I must scream." . . . She had an idea that the scream would be very hard to do.

Gradually new thoughts crowded upon her, vivid and urgent: she tried to separate and restrain them, but they beset her clamorously, like her school-children at the end of a hot day, when she was too tired to silence them. Her head grew confused, and she felt a sick fear of forgetting her part, of betraying herself by some unguarded word or look.

"I must pretend I don't know," she went on murmuring. The words had lost their significance, but she repeated them mechanically, as though they had been a magic formula, until suddenly she heard herself saying: "I can't remember, I can't remember!"

Her voice sounded very loud, and she looked about her in terror; but no one seemed to notice that she had spoken.

As she glanced down the car her eye caught the curtains of her husband's berth, and she began to examine the monotonous arabesques woven through their heavy folds. The pattern was intricate and difficult to trace; she gazed fixedly at the curtains and as she did so the thick stuff grew transparent and through it she saw her husband's face—his dead face. She struggled to avert her look, but her eyes refused to move and her head seemed to be held in a vice. At last, with an effort that left her weak and shaking, she turned away; but it was no use; close in front of her, small and smooth, was her husband's face. It seemed to be suspended in the air between her and the false braids of the woman who sat in front of her. With an uncontrollable gesture she stretched out her hand to push the face away, and suddenly she felt the touch of his smooth skin. She repressed a cry and half started from her seat. The woman with the false braids looked around, and feeling that she must justify her movement in some way she rose and lifted her traveling-bag from the opposite seat. She unlocked the bag and looked into it; but the first object her hand met was a small flask of her husband's, thrust there at the last moment, in the haste of departure. She locked the bag and closed her eyes . . . his face was there again, hanging between her eyeballs and lids like a waxen mask against a red curtain. . . .

She roused herself with a shiver. Had she fainted or slept? Hours seemed to have elapsed; but it was still broad day, and the people about her were sitting in the same attitudes as before.

A sudden sense of hunger made her aware that she had eaten nothing since morning. The thought of food filled her with disgust, but she dreaded a return of faintness, and remembering that she had some biscuits in her bag she took one out and ate it. The dry crumbs choked her, and she hastily swallowed a little brandy from her husband's flask. The burning sensation in her throat acted as a counter-irritant, momentarily relieving the dull ache of her nerves. Then she felt a gently-stealing warmth, as though a soft air fanned her, and the swarming fears relaxed their clutch, receding through the stillness that enclosed her, a stillness soothing as the spacious quietude of a summer day. She slept.

Through her sleep she felt he impetuous rush of the train. It seemed to be life itself that was sweeping her on with headlong inexorable force—sweeping her into darkness and terror, and the awe of unknown days. Now all at once everything was still—not a sound, not a pulsation. . . . She was dead in her turn, and lay beside him with smooth upstaring face. How quiet it was!—and yet she heard feet coming, the feet of the men who were to carry them away. . . . She could feel too—she felt a sudden prolonged vibration, a series of hard shocks, and then another plunge into darkness: the darkness of death this time—a black whirlwind on which they were both spinning like leaves, in wild uncoiling spirals, with millions and millions of the dead . . .

She sprang up in terror. Her sleep must have lasted a long time, for the winter day had paled and the lights had been lit. The car was in confusion, and as she regained her self-possession she saw that the passengers were gathering up their wraps and bags. The woman with the false braids had brought from the dressing-room a sickly ivy-plant in a bottle, and the Christian Scientist was reversing his cuffs. The porter passed down the aisle with impartial brush. An impersonal figure with a gold-banded cap asked for her husband's ticket. A voice shouted "Baig-gage express!" and she heard the clicking of metal as passengers handed over their checks.

Presently her window was blocked by an expanse of sooty wall, and the train passed into the Harlem tunnel. The journey was over; in a few minutes she would see her family pushing their joyous way through the throng at the station. Her heart dilated. The worst terror was past. . . .

"We'd better get him up now, hadn't we?" asked the porter, touching her arm.

He had her husband's hat in his hand and was meditatively revolving it under his brush.

She looked at the hat and tried to speak; but suddenly the car grew dark. She flung up her arms, struggling to catch at something, and fell face downward, striking her head against the dead man's berth.   *1914*

━━┥◆┝━━

Gertrude Stein
1874–1946

One of the most important of modernism's literary experimenters, Gertrude Stein commented often on the philosophy that guided her innovations. "Write as you are to be writing," she claimed in *Lectures in America* (1935). "If you write the way it has already been written . . . then you are serving mammon, because you are living by something some one has already been earning or has earned." The youngest of five children, Stein was born in Allegheny, Pennsylvania, to well-to-do parents of German Jewish descent. The family lived in Europe during Stein's infancy and moved to California when she was five. When her parents died during Stein's adolescence, she became especially close to her brother Leo, whom she accompanied to Boston in 1892. Her brother enrolled at Harvard University, while Stein studied at Radcliffe College.

After graduation, both brother and sister enrolled at Johns Hopkins, he to pursue graduate work in biology and she to attend medical school, which she failed in her second year—deliberately, according to most biographers; Stein wished to travel to Europe with Leo, who had developed an interest in modern art. By the time she and her brother moved to Paris in 1902, Stein had begun to write fiction whose linguistic innovations resembled bold brushstrokes on a canvas; thus she flourished in an environment in which she met many prominent and innovative painters, including Georges Braque, Henri Matisse, and Pablo Picasso, who became an influential friend and artistic confidant. As the Steins began to collect Cubist and other experimental paintings, Gertrude became increasingly convinced that art should represent a visual experience unmediated by cultural points of reference. Paradoxically, she began as well to see the order of words as directly tied to social orders of gender, race, sexuality, and economics.

When Leo Stein moved to Austria in 1909, Gertrude was joined by another American expatriate, Alice B. Toklas, who became her lover, assistant, and life companion. At their Parisian flat the two women hosted frequent literary salons at which French writers and artists and American intellectuals gathered. Here Stein served as a mentor to American writers such as Ernest Hemingway and F. Scott Fitzgerald ("you are all," she claimed, "a lost generation"), experimented in a range of writing techniques from stream of consciousness fiction to lesbian erotica—sometimes both in the same work, and sat for portraits by Picasso and other artists in her circle. In the 1920s Stein and Toklas left Paris for a cottage in the south of France, where Stein spent more time writing, Toklas gardened, and both cooked and entertained numerous visitors, including American soldiers during World War II. Stein returned only once to the United States, to give a successful lecture tour in 1934, but she always considered herself an American and an admirer of technological progress.

Several of Stein's early literary works owe much to the philosophy of one of her most distinguished teachers at Harvard, William James, who viewed human consciousness as an ongoing present, unique to each individual. *Three Lives* (1909), for example, attempts to represent the passing of time as filtered through the psychic lens of three ordinary women. The ways in which a person's experience of life can shift from second to second provides the subject for *The Making of Americans* (written in 1908, published in 1925). Known for her humorous and sometimes absurd repetition of words and sounds, Stein often ironizes the erotic, as in her novel *Tender Buttons* (1914) and her poem "Lifting Belly" (1915–17). In these works language both encodes and decodes a lesbian sexuality which is multifaceted, incoherent, improvisational. In *The Autobiography of Alice B. Toklas* (1933) Stein subverts generic conventions by playfully assuming the voice of Toklas in order to (mis)represent the life of Stein herself. Although some critics have argued that Toklas actually wrote this work, most scholars continue to attribute it to Stein; still, her collaboration with Toklas certainly influenced its composition. *Ida, A Novel* (1941) portrays a character who, like Stein when she met Toklas, was "tired of being just one." In addition to these works, Stein wrote rhetorical theory, most notably *Composition as Explanation* (1926), and several operas and plays. *Four Saints in Three Acts* (1934) was set to music by the American composer Virgil Thompson, as was *The Mother of Us All*, which was produced as an opera in 1947; this opera featured as one of its main characters the nineteenth-century suffragist Susan B. Anthony. Thompson once called Stein, ironically, "a Founding Father of her century" because she "dominated language."

In *Patriarchal Poetry* (1927), a work that defies generic categorization, Stein slyly refutes the premises of orderly, hierarchical, masculinist poetics. As feminist critics Sandra M. Gilbert and Susan Gubar have argued in *No Man's Land* (1988), *Patriarchal Poetry* is written in "Steinese," which has been variously described as similar to chanting, automatic writing, Cubist painting, and atonal music. Although it is difficult to know whether Stein's strategy is one of deliberate obfuscation or clever subversion (or both), this work clearly signals her dissatisfaction with conventional gender binaries and with modernist dicta regarding what poetry is or ought to be.

⇥ *from* Patriarchal Poetry ⇤

Their origin and their history patriarchal poetry their origin and their history patriarchal poetry their origin and their history.

Patriarchal Poetry.

Their origin and their history.

Patriarchal Poetry their origin and their history their history patriarchal poetry their origin patriarchal poetry their history their origin patriarchal poetry their history patriarchal poetry their origin patriarchal poetry their history their origin.

That is one case.

Able sweet and in a seat.

Patriarchal poetry their origin their history their origin. Patriarchal poetry their history their origin.

Two make it do three make it five four make it more five make it arrive and sundries.

Letters and leaves tables and plainly restive and recover and bide away, away to say regularly.

Never to mention patriarchal poetry altogether.

Two two two occasionally two two as you say two two two not in their explanation two two must you be very well apprised that it had had such an effect that only one out of a great many and there were a great many believe in three relatively and moreover were you aware of the fact that interchangeable and interchangeable was it while they were if not avoided. She knew that is to say she had really informed herself. Patriarchal poetry makes no mistake.

Never to have followed farther there and knitting, is knitting knitting if it is only what is described as called that they should not come to say and how do you do every new year Saturday. Every new year Saturday is likely to bring pleasure is likely to give pleasure is likely to bring pleasure every new year Saturday is likely to bring pleasure.

Day which is what is which is what is day which is what is day which is which is what is which is what is day.

I double you, of course you do. You double me, very likely to be. You double I double I double you double. I double you double me I double you you double me.

When this you see remarkably.

Patriarchal poetry needs rectification and there about it.

Come to a distance and it still bears their name.

Prosperity and theirs prosperity left to it.

To be told to be harsh to be told to be harsh to be to them.

One.

To be told to be harsh to be told to be harsh to them.

None.

To be told to be harsh to be told to be harsh to them.

When.

To be told to be harsh to be told to be harsh to them.

Then.

What is the result.

The result is that they know the difference between instead and instead and made and made and said and said.

The result is that they might be as very well two and as soon three and to be sure, four and which is why they might not be.

Elegant replaced by delicate and tender, delicate and tender replaced by one from there instead of five from there, there is not there this is what has happened evidently.

Why while while why while why why identity identity why while while why. Why while while while while identity.

Patriarchal Poetry is the same as Patriotic poetry is the same as patriarchal poetry is the same as Patriotic poetry is the same as patriarchal poetry is the same.

Patriarchal poetry is the same.

If in in crossing there is a if in crossing if in in crossing nearly there is a distance if in crossing there is a distance between measurement and exact if in in crossing if in in crossing there is a measurement between and in in exact she says I must be careful and I will.

If in in crossing there is an opportunity not only but also and in in looking in looking in regarding if in in looking if in in regarding if in in regarding there is an opportunity if in in looking there is an opportunity if in in regarding there is an opportunity to verify verify sometimes as more sometimes as more sometimes as more.

Fish eggs commonly fish eggs. Architects commonly fortunately indicatively architects indicatively architects. Elaborated at a time with it with it at a time with it at a time attentively today.

Does she know how to ask her brother is there any difference between turning it again again and again and again or turning it again and again. In resembling two brothers.

That makes patriarchal poetry apart.

Intermediate or patriarchal poetry.

If at once sixty-five have come one by one if at once sixty five have come one by one if at once sixty-five have come one by one. This took two and two have been added to by Jenny. Never to name Jenny. Have been added to by two. Never have named Helen Jenny never have named Agnes Helen never have named Helen Jenny. There is no difference between having been born in Brittany and having been born in Algeria.

These words containing as they do neither reproaches nor satisfaction may be finally very nearly rearranged and why, because they mean to be partly left alone. Patriarchal poetry and kindly, it would be very kind in him in him of him of him to be as much obliged as that. Patriotic poetry. It would be as plainly an advantage if not only but altogether repeatedly it should be left not only to them but for them but for them. Explain to them by for them. Explain shall it be explain will it be explain can it be explain as it is to be explain letting it be had as if he had had more than wishes. More than wishes.

Patriarchal poetry more than wishes.

Assigned to Patriarchal Poetry.

Assigned to patriarchal poetry too sue sue sue sue shall sue sell and magnificent can as coming let the same shall shall shall shall let it share is share is share shall shall shall shall shell shell shall share is share shell can shell be shell be shell moving in in in inner moving move inner in in inner in meant meant might might may collect collected recollected to refuse what it is is it.

Having started at once at once.

Put it with it with it and it and it come to ten.

Put it with it with it and it and it for it for it made to be extra.

With it put it put it prepare it prepare it add it add it or it or it would it would it and make it all at once.

Put it with it with it and it and it in it in it add it add it at it at it with it with it put it put it to this to understand.

Put it with it with it add it add it at it at it or it or it to be placed intend.

Put it with it with it in it in it at it at it add it add it or it or it letting it be while it is left as it might could do their danger.

Could it with it with it put it put it place it place it stand it stand it two doors or two doors two tables or two tables two let two let two let two to be sure.

Put it with it with it and it and it in it in it add it add it or it or it to it to be added to it.

There is no doubt about it.

Actually.

To be sure.

Left to the rest if to be sure that to be sent come to be had in to be known or to be liked and to be to be to be to be to be mine.

It always can be one two three it can be always can can always be one two three. It can always be one two three.

It is very trying to have him have it have it have him. have it as she said the last was very very much and very much to distance to distance them.

Every time there is a wish wish it. Every time there is a wish wish it. Every time there is a wish wish it.

Every time there is a wish wish it.

Dedicated to all the way through. Dedicated to all the way through.

Dedicated too all the way through. Dedicated too all the way through.

Apples and fishes day-light and wishes apples and fishes day-light and wishes day-light at seven.

All the way through dedicated to you.

Day-light and wishes apples and fishes, dedicated to you all the way through day-light and fishes apples and wishes dedicated to all the way through dedicated to you dedicated to you all the way through day-light and fishes apples and fishes day-light and wishes apples and fishes dedicated to you all the way through day-light and fishes apples and wishes apples and fishes day-light and wishes dedicated to dedicated through all the way through dedicated to.

Not at once Tuesday.

They might be finally their name name same came came came came or share sharer article entreat coming in letting this be there letting this be there.

Patriarchal poetry come too.

When with patriarchal poetry when with patriarchal poetry come too.

There must be more french in France there must be more French in France patriarchal poetry come too.

Patriarchal poetry come too there must be more french in France patriarchal come too there must be more french in France.

Patriarchal Poetry come to.

There must be more french in France.

Helen greatly relieves Alice patriarchal poetry come too there must be patriarchal poetry come too.

In a way second first in a way first second in a way in a way first second in a way.

Rearrangement is nearly rearrangement. Finally nearly rearrangement is finally nearly rearrangement nearly not now finally nearly nearly finally rearrangement nearly rearrangement and not now how nearly finally rearrangement. If two tables are near together finally nearly not now.

Finally nearly not now.

Able able nearly nearly nearly nearly able able finally nearly able nearly not now finally finally nearly able.

They make it be very well three or nearly three at a time.

Splendid confidence in the one addressed and equal distrust of the one who has done everything that is necessary. Finally nearly able not now able finally nearly not now.

Rearrangement is a rearrangement a rearrangement is widely known a rearrangement is widely known. A rearrangement is widely known. As a rearrangement is widely known.

As a rearrangement is widely known.

So can a rearrangement which is widely known be a rearrangement which is widely known which is widely known.

Let her be to be to be to be let her be to be to be let her to be let her to be let her be to be when is it that they are shy.

Very well to try.

Let her be that is to be let her be that is to be let her be let her try.

Let her be let her be let her be to be to be shy let her be to be let her be to be let her try.

Let her try.

Let her be let her be let her be let her be to be to be let her be let her try.

To be shy.

Let her be.

Let her try.

Let her be let her let her let her be let her be let her be let her be shy let her be let her be let her try.

Let her try.

Let her be.

Let her be shy.

Let her be.

Let her be let her be let her let her try.

Let her try to be let her try to be let her be shy let her try to be let her try to be let her be let her be let her try.

Let her be shy.

Let her try.

Let her try.

Let her be

Let her let her be shy.

Let her try.

Let her be.

Let her let her be shy.

Let her be let her let her be shy

Let her let her let her let her try.

Let her try.

Let her try.
Let her try.
Let her be.
Let her be let her
Let her try.   *1927*

⊷ ⊷ ≍⟡≍ ⊷ ⊷

Zora Neale Hurston
1891–1960

Recognized today as one of the finest American writers of the twentieth century, Zora Neale Hurston spent the last twenty years of her
life as an impoverished domestic worker in Florida. She was rediscovered after her death by ALICE WALKER, who in 1973 went "looking for Zora" as a role model and source of creative inspiration, and
by the scholar Robert Hemenway, who published her definitive
biography in 1977. Hurston was born in Eatonville, Florida, an all-
black town whose environment she describes vividly in her essay
"How It Feels to Be Colored Me" (1928). Although her childhood
was difficult—her father, John Hurston, a Baptist preacher, did not
support his wife and eight children, and her mother, Lucy, died
when Hurston was eleven—she grew up sheltered from racism and

nurtured by a proud black community in which she developed the self-esteem and humor that
served her well in later years. After a childhood of being cared for by various relatives, she supported herself as a teen, working for a time as a maid in a traveling theater company. In 1919
she won a scholarship to Howard University, at that time the nation's leading black college.
There she studied with a renowned African-American teacher and patron of the arts, Alain
Locke, editor of an influential anthology entitled *The New Negro* (1925).

    In the early 1920s Hurston took Harlem by storm, turning her extraordinary storytelling
abilities into impromptu performance art and joining the group of writers responsible for initiating the cultural movement that became known as the Harlem Renaissance. During this time
Hurston entered graduate school in anthropology at Barnard College, where she was the only
black student; she studied with renowned anthropologist Franz Boas and earned her tuition by
working as a private secretary to a liberal white novelist, Fannie Hurst. When she graduated in
1927, Hurston won a grant to return to Eatonville to study her community's oral traditions;
thereafter, she divided her time between gathering oral histories as a folklorist and writing fiction. She experienced both the positive and the negative aspects of a white patronage system
when she was given money to continue her research as an oral historian by Mrs. R. Osgood
Mason, a wealthy supporter of the arts who ordered Hurston to seek her permission before publishing any of her own work and expected her to perform on demand as a representative of the
"primitive" to Mason's white friends. Hurston's writing was controversial among the leading
male figures of the Harlem Renaissance; at one time she was quite close to Langston Hughes,
but the two had a falling out over differences in their political and literary philosophies. Refusing to become aligned with any particular black political agenda, Hurston rejected both the
notion that black literature should take as its goal the positive representation of black culture
to white audiences and the idea of "uplifting" the race through inspirational portrayals of black
life. Instead, she created realistic black characters, good and bad, and did not hesitate to tackle
in her fiction such subjects as domestic violence and a wife's revenge, the theme of her story

"Sweat." Some writers felt that her use of black dialect was demeaning, but Hurston prided herself on treating with dignity those whose idioms and speech patterns she captured in her writing.

Hurston's body of work, from fiction to autobiography to ethnography, has contributed significantly to the African-American literary canon. Although her story "Drenched in Light" appeared in *Opportunity*, a black magazine published in New York, in the early 1920s, most of her writing was published in the 1930s after the Harlem Renaissance had ended, a fact that negatively affected its critical reception. *Jonah's Gourd Vine* (1934) takes as its central character a man with wanderlust who is modeled after Hurston's father. *Mules and Men* (1935) presents the folktales and lore that she gathered during her research in Eatonville; this work was her best seller, earning just under $1,000 in all. In her finest novel, *Their Eyes Were Watching God* (1937), Hurston employs a variety of sophisticated and indigenous narrative strategies, such as a choral swell of voices from the front porch or the country store to comment on the protagonists and their tensions, and a "call and response" technique similar to that used by many African-American preachers to revitalize their congregations. *Seraph on the Suwanee* (1948), her last novel, features white protagonists and critiques white Southern culture. As the foremost American literary practitioner of orature, Hurston offers vivid dialogue that captures the rhythms and cadences of black dialects and idioms.

Hurston had two brief marriages, one in 1927 to Herbert Sheen, whom she had met at Howard University, and another in the late 1930s to Albert Price, a much younger man. During the 1930s she earned her living teaching at Bethune-Cookman College and working with the Federal Theater Project in New York. Her play *Singing Steel* (1934) offered a challenge to "the current mammy-song-Jolson conception of the Southern Negro" and was well reviewed. In 1936 and 1937 she received Guggenheim fellowships to travel and do research in the Caribbean, some of which she includes in her ethnographic studies and novels. During the 1940s and 1950s her views against integration became unpopular with many other black intellectuals, and in 1954 she wrote a letter to a Florida newspaper criticizing the Supreme Court's decision in *Brown v. Board of Education of Topeka, Kansas* to support desegregation on the grounds that it implicitly denigrated all-black institutions.

Dust Tracks on a Road (1942), a chapter of which is included here, appeared only after Hurston's publishers insisted on editing out statements critical of whites. Organized thematically rather than strictly chronological in form, *Dust Tracks* contains chapters with titles such as "Religion," "Research," "Race Pride," and "Seeing the World As It Is." Having left Eatonville after her mother's death to journey into an unwelcoming world, Hurston became aware and protective of her own singularity: "I had a feeling of difference from my fellow men, and I did not want it to be found out." Although most readers desire revelations of a private self in autobiography, in *Dust Tracks* Hurston offers instead what the literary critic Francoise Lionnet calls "a 'figural anthropology' of the self," thus inventing a unique "braiding" of generic and cultural forms.

⊰ *from* Dust Tracks on a Road ⊱

I Get Born

This is all hear-say. Maybe some of the details of my birth as told me might be a little inaccurate, but it is pretty well established that I really did get born.

The saying goes like this. My mother's time had come and my father was not there. Being a carpenter, successful enough to have other helpers on some jobs, he was away often on building business, as well as preaching. It seems that my father was away from home for months this time. I have never been told why. But I did hear that he threatened to cut his throat when he got the news. It seems that one daughter was all that he figured he could stand. My sister, Sarah, was his favorite child, but that one girl was enough. Plenty more sons, but no more girl babies to wear out shoes and bring in nothing. I don't think he ever got over the trick he felt that I played on him by getting born a girl, and while he was off from home at that. A little of my sugar used to sweeten his coffee right now. That is a Negro way of saying his patience was short with me. Let me change a few words with him—and I am of the word-changing kind—and he was ready to change ends. Still and all, I looked more like him than any child in the house. Of course, by the time I got born, it was too late to make any suggestions, so the old man had to put up with me. He was nice about it in a way. He didn't tie me in a sack and drop me in the lake, as he probably felt like doing.

People were digging sweet potatoes, and then it was hog-killing time. Not at our house, but it was going on in general over the country like, being January and a bit cool. Most people were either butchering for themselves, or off helping other folks do their butchering, which was almost just as good. It is a gay time. A big pot of hasslits cooking with plenty of seasoning, lean slabs of fresh-killed pork frying for the helpers to refresh themselves after the work is done. Over and above being neighborly and giving aid, there is the food, the drinks and the fun of getting together.

So there was no grown folks close around when Mama's water broke. She sent one of the smaller children to fetch Aunt Judy, the mid-wife, but she was gone to Woodbridge, a mile and a half away, to eat at a hog-killing. The child was told to go over there and tell Aunt Judy to come. But nature, being indifferent to human arrangements, was impatient. My mother had to make it alone. She was too weak after I rushed out to do anything for herself, so she just was lying there, sick in the body, and worried in mind, wondering what would become of her, as well as me. She was so weak, she couldn't even reach down to where I was. She had one consolation. She knew I wasn't dead, because I was crying strong.

Help came from where she never would have thought to look for it. A white man of many acres and things, who knew the family well, had butchered the day before. Knowing that Papa was not at home, and that consequently there would be no fresh meat in our house, he decided to drive the five miles and bring a half of a shoat, sweet potatoes, and other garden stuff along. He was there a few minutes after I was born. Seeing the front door standing open, he came on in, and hollered, "Hello, there! Call your dogs!" That is the regular way to call in the country because nearly everybody who has anything to watch has biting dogs.

Nobody answered, but he claimed later that he heard me spreading my lungs all over Orange County, so he shoved the door open and bolted on into the house.

He followed the noise and then he saw how things were, and, being the kind of a man he was, he took out his Barlow Knife and cut the navel cord, then he did the best he could about other things. When the mid-wife, locally known as a granny, arrived about an hour later, there was a fire in the stove and plenty of hot water on. I had been sponged off in some sort of a way, and Mama was holding me in her arms.

As soon as the old woman got there, the white man unloaded what he had brought, and drove off cussing about some blankety-blank people never being where you could put your hands on them when they were needed.

He got no thanks from Aunt Judy. She grumbled for years about it. She complained that the cord had not been cut just right, and the belly-band had not been put on tight enough. She was mighty scared I was going to have a weak back, and that I would have trouble holding my water until I reached puberty. I did.

The next day or so a Mrs. Neale, a friend of Mama's, came in and reminded her that she had promised to let her name the baby in case it was a girl. She had picked up a name somewhere which she thought was very pretty. Perhaps she had read it somewhere, or somebody back in those woods was smoking Turkish cigarettes. So I became Zora Neale Hurston.

There is nothing to make you like other human beings so much as doing things for them. Therefore, the man who grannied me was back next day to see how I was coming along. Maybe it was pride in his own handiwork, and his resourcefulness in a pinch, that made him want to see it through. He remarked that I was a God-damned fine baby, fat and plenty of lung-power. As time went on, he came infrequently, but somehow kept a pinch of interest in my welfare. It seemed that I was spying noble, growing like a gourd vine, and yelling bass like a gator. He was the kind of a man that had no use for puny things, so I was all to the good with him. He thought my mother was justified in keeping me.

But nine months rolled around, and I just would not get on with the walking business. I was strong, crawling well, but showed no inclination to use my feet. I might remark in passing, that I still don't like to walk. Then I was over a year old, but still I would not walk. They made allowances for my weight, but yet, that was no real reason for my not trying.

They tell me that an old sow-hog taught me how to walk. That is, she didn't instruct me in detail, but she convinced me that I really ought to try.

It was like this. My mother was going to have collard greens for dinner, so she took the dishpan and went down to the spring to wash the greens. She left me sitting on the floor, and gave me a hunk of cornbread to keep me quiet. Everything was going along all right, until the sow with her litter of pigs in convoy came abreast of the door. She must have smelled the cornbread I was messing with and scattering crumbs about the floor. So, she came right on in, and began to nuzzle around.

My mother heard my screams and came running. Her heart must have stood still when she saw the sow in there, because hogs have been known to eat human flesh.

But I was not taking this thing sitting down. I had been placed by a chair, and when my mother got inside the door, I had pulled myself up by that chair and was getting around it right smart.

As for the sow, poor misunderstood lady, she had no interest in me except my bread. I lost that in scrambling to my feet and she was eating it. She had much less intention of eating Mama's baby, than Mama had of eating hers.

With no more suggestions from the sow or anybody else, it seems that I just took to walking and kept the thing a-going. The strangest thing about it was that once I found the use of my feet, they took to wandering. I always wanted to go. I would wander off in the woods all alone, following some inside urge to go places. This alarmed my mother a great deal. She used to say that she believed a woman who was an enemy of hers had sprinkled "travel dust" around the doorstep the day I was born. That was the only explanation she could find. I don't know why it never occurred to her to connect my tendency with my father, who didn't have a thing on his mind but this town and the next one. That should have given her a sort of hint. Some children are just bound to take after their fathers in spite of women's prayers.

1942

‹ ›

Stevie Smith
1902–1971

The English poet and novelist Stevie Smith was born in Hull, Yorkshire, and raised in North London, first by her mother and later by a beloved aunt. Although her given name was Florence Margaret, she was nicknamed "Stevie" at an early age when a friend jokingly likened her riding abilities to those of a jockey named Steve Donoghue. Smith lived most of her adult life in London with her aunt, whom she memorialized in her fiction as "the noble aunt" and "the Lion of Hull." For thirty years Smith worked as a secretary for a publishing house, Newnes and Pearson, and did frequent broadcasts for the British Broadcasting Company. Her writing has been praised for its originality and wit, and she received the Cholmondely Award (1966) and the Queen's Gold Medal for Poetry (1969).

Smith's poetry appears simpler than it is. Her first volume of poetry, *A Good Time Was Had By All* (1937), reveals Smith's attraction to colloquialisms and their inherently ironic capacities, as well as her reliance on internal rhyme and assonance. *Not Waving But Drowning* (1957) uses humor to mask a persistent pessimism, while *The Frog Prince and Other Poems* (1966) employs fairy-tale themes to explore sexual anxiety and social anarchy. Many of her books of poetry are accompanied by the author's whimsical line drawings. Other collections by this prolific poet include *Tender Only to One* (1938), *Mother, What Is Man?* (1942), *Harold's Leap* (1950), *Some Are More Human than Others* (1958), and *Scorpion and Other Poems* (1971). Smith's collected poems were published in 1975, and *Me Again: Uncollected Writings of Stevie Smith* appeared in 1981. In addition to her poetic works, Smith received modest recognition as a novelist. *Novel on Yellow Paper* (1936), her first publication, defies generic categorization because it includes long passages of poetry in an otherwise prose text. Smith's novels can be viewed as extensions of her poetry in that their dominant narrative voices are lyrical and meditative. Other novels include *Over the Frontier* (1938) and *The Holiday* (1949), the most melancholy of her fictional works.

Charmingly subversive, the poems included here reveal Smith's playful dismantling of literary and religious canons. "My Muse Sits Forlorn" both acknowledges and undermines centuries of poetic invocations of an absent muse. "A Dream of Comparison" presents a philosophical dialogue between Eve and Mary that reveals Smith's ambivalence toward orthodox Christianity. In "Thoughts about the Person from Porlock" the poet again explores the vicissitudes of the writing process. Taken together, these poems reveal the technical and verbal virtuosity that led the poet MURIEL RUKEYSER to describe Stevie Smith as "our acrobat of simplicity."

⊰ My Muse ⊱

My Muse sits forlorn
She wishes she had not been born
She sits in the cold
No word she says is ever told.

Why does my Muse only speak when she is unhappy?
She does not, I only listen when I am unhappy
When I am happy I live and despise writing
For my Muse this cannot but be dispiriting.

1962

⊰ A Dream of Comparison ⊱

After reading Book Ten of 'Paradise Lost'[1]

Two ladies walked on the soft green grass
On the bank of a river by the sea
And one was Mary and the other Eve
And they talked philosophically.

5   "Oh to be Nothing," said Eve, "oh for a
Cessation of consciousness
With no more impressions beating in
Of various experiences."

"How can Something envisage Nothing?" said Mary,
10   "Where's your philosophy gone?"
"Storm back through the gates of Birth," cried Eve,
"Where were you before you were born?"

Mary laughed: "I love Life,
I would fight to the death for it,
15   That's a feeling you say? I will find
A reason for it."

They walked by the estuary,
Eve and the Virgin Mary,
And they talked until nightfall,
20   But the difference between them was radical.

1957

⊰ Thoughts About the Person from Porlock ⊱

Coleridge received the Person from Porlock
And ever after called him a curse,
Then why did he hurry to let him in?
He could have hid in the house.

5   It was not right of Coleridge in fact it was wrong
(But often we all do wrong)
As the truth is I think he was already stuck
With Kubla Khan.[2]

He was weeping and wailing: I am finished, finished,
10   I shall never write another word of it,
When along comes the Person from Porlock
And takes the blame for it.

1. The epic poem by John Milton (1608–74).
2. Samuel Taylor Coleridge (1772–1834), the British Romantic poet, wrote his poetic dream vision *Kubla Khan* in 1797 during an illness he experienced while staying in a farmhouse near the village of Porlock. A person from the village called to conduct business and robbed the poet of the end of his vision.

It was not right, it was wrong,
But often we all do wrong.

*

15   May we inquire the name of the Person from Porlock?
Why, Porson, didn't you know?
He lived at the bottom of Porlock Hill
So had a long way to go,

He wasn't much in the social sense
20   Though his grandmother was a Warlock,
One of the Rutlandshire ones I fancy
And nothing to do with Porlock,

And he lived at the bottom of the hill as I said
And had a cat named Flo,
25   And had a cat named Flo.

I long for the Person from Porlock
To bring my thoughts to an end,
I am becoming impatient to see him
I think of him as a friend,

30   Often I look out of the window
Often I run to the gate
I think, He will come this evening,
I think it is rather late.

I am hungry to be interrupted
35   For ever and ever amen
O Person from Porlock come quickly
And bring my thoughts to an end.

*

I felicitate the people who have a Person from Porlock
To break up everything and throw it away
40   Because then there will be nothing to keep them
And they need not stay.

*

Why do they grumble so much?
He comes like a benison
They should be glad he has not forgotten them
45   They might have had to go on.

*

These thoughts are depressing I know. They are depressing,
I wish I was more cheerful, it is more pleasant,
Also it is a duty, we should smile as well as submitting
To the purpose of One Above who is experimenting
50   With various mixtures of human character which goes best,
All is interesting for him it is exciting, but not for us.
There I go again. Smile, smile, and get some work to do
Then you will be practically unconscious without positively
        having to go.

1962

—+ ☰◊☰ +—

May Sarton
1912–1995

"We have to make myths of our lives," May Sarton says in *Plant Dreaming Deep*. "It is the only way to live them without despair." Of the many modern American women poets who are mythmakers, Sarton speaks most urgently and often about what it means to be a woman and a writer and about the female muse as a primary source of poetic inspiration. Sarton's source of inspiration represents a lesbian variation on the standard muse of heterosexual male poets, their female lover. But for her the muse is also a demonic shadow, a crucial Medusa-self against whom the poet struggles and yet through whom she ultimately transforms her wildness into vital creative energy.

Sarton is the author of fifteen volumes of poetry, twenty novels, twelve autobiographical works, and several children's books. She was born in Belgium to distinguished parents, George Sarton, a renowned historian of science, and Mabel Elwes Sarton, a painter, an embroider of fabrics, and a furniture designer. May was raised in Cambridge, Massachusetts, after her parents moved to the United States in 1916. Her education at Shady Hill School in Cambridge influenced her artistic development, as did an internship with Eva LaGallienne's Civic Repertory Theatre in New York, an experience that led Sarton to attempt, unsuccessfully, to establish a theatrical troupe of her own. In her autobiography *I Knew A Phoenix* (1959) she chronicles her life as a young writer enamored of Elizabeth Bowen and VIRGINIA WOOLF, two British writers whom she met during her visits to England. The pleasure and drawbacks of solitude and the writer's life are documented in her most famous journals, *Journal of a Solitude* (1973) and *The House by the Sea* (1977). The vicissitudes of old age never quelled her indomitable spirit, as is evident in her journals from the 1980s and 1990s: *At Seventy, After the Stroke, Endgame,* and *Encore: A Journal of the Eightieth Year.*

Sarton's novels address such themes as women's friendships, marriage, lesbian love, and aging. *A Small Room* (1961) explores life at an insular women's college and the student-teacher relationship. *As We Are Now* (1973) offers a sympathetic portrayal of the sorrows and frailties of residents in a nursing home, a scathing indictment of the way the elderly are often treated, and the experience of one rebellious woman determined to outwit the system. *Kinds of Love* (1970) depicts marriage and friendship as different but equally intense types of relationships, while *The Education of Harriet Hatfield* (1989) presents the complexities of love between women. Sarton indirectly came out as a lesbian in 1965 with the publication of *Mrs. Stevens Hears the Mermaids Singing,* several years before the Stonewall Rebellion (1969) and the advent of gay liberation; she claimed that publishing the novel cost her several teaching jobs. In her later years, however, she was vocal about her lesbian and feminist identities.

Although her journals and novels brought her a wide audience, Sarton considered her primary art form to be poetry. Her first volume, *Encounter in April,* appeared in 1937, her last, *The Silence Now,* in 1988. Her *Collected Poems 1930–1973* contains thirty-five years worth of poems; its major themes are the natural and animal worlds, the role of art in a changing society, the endurance of passionate love, and the joy as well as the loneliness to be found in silence and solitude. In *Journal of a Solitude* she asserts that while a novel represents a dialogue with others, poetry focuses on the inner world. "Why is it," she wonders, "that poetry always seems to me so much more of a true work of the soul than prose? . . . Perhaps it is that prose is earned and poetry given." One elects to be a novelist but is "chosen" to be a poet. The poems included here reveal the centrality of the muse, Sarton's primal source of creative inspiration. In "Journey Toward Poetry" stillness, not motion, "changes light to shadow," giving birth to creation. "The Muse as Medusa," in contrast, describes the poet's encounter with a mythical fury who can only be met one on one, "straight in the cold eye, cold." "Of the Muse" offers a powerful and moving assessment of Sarton's poetic philosophy as it developed over more than fifty years. Through the female muse, "all things are made new."

⊰ Journey Toward Poetry ⊱

First that beautiful mad exploration
Through a multiple legend of landscape
When all roads open and then close again
Behind a car that rushes toward escape,
5   The mind shot out across foreign borders
To visionary and abrupt disorders.
The hills unwind and wind up on a spool;
Rivers leap out of their beds and run;
The pink geranium standing on the wall
10   Rests there a second, still, and then breaks open
To show far off the huge blood-red cathedral
Looming like magic against a bright blue sky;
And marble graveyards fall into the sea.

After the mad beautiful racing is done,
15   To be still, to be silent, to stand by a window
Where time not motion changes light to shadow,
Is to be present at the birth of creation.
Now from the falling chaos of sensation
A single image possesses the whole soul:
20   The field of wheat, the telegraph pole.
From them the composed imagination reaches
Up and down to find its own frontier.
All landscapes crystallize and focus here—
And in the distance stand five copper beeches.

                                            1953

⊰ The Muse as Medusa ⊱

I saw you once, Medusa; we were alone.
I looked you straight in the cold eye, cold.
I was not punished, was not turned to stone—
How to believe the legends I am told?

5   I came as naked as any little fish,
Prepared to be hooked, gutted, caught;
But I saw you, Medusa, made my wish,
And when I left you I was clothed in thought . . .

Being allowed, perhaps, to swim my way
10   Through the great deep and on the rising tide,
Flashing wild streams, as free and rich as they,
Though you had power marshaled on your side.

The fish escaped to many a magic reef;
The fish explored many a dangerous sea—
15   The fish, Medusa, did not come to grief,
But swims still in a fluid mystery.

Forget the image: your silence is my ocean,
And even now it teems with life. You chose
To abdicate by total lack of motion,
20   But did it work, for nothing really froze?

It is all fluid still, that world of feeling
Where thoughts, those fishes, silent, feed and rove;
And, fluid, it is also full of healing,
For love is healing, even rootless love.

25   I turn your face around! It is my face.
That frozen rage is what I must explore—
Oh secret, self-enclosed, and ravaged place!
This is the gift I thank Medusa for.

                                         1971

⇥ Of the Muse ⇤

There is no poetry in lies,
But in crude honesty
There is hope for poetry.
For a long time now
5   I have been deprived of it
Because of pride,
Would not allow myself
The impossible.
Today, I have learned
10   That to become
A great, cracked,
Wide-open door
Into nowhere
Is wisdom.

15   When I was young,
I misunderstood
The Muse.
Now I am older and wiser,
I can be glad of her
20   As one is glad of the light.
We do not thank the light,
But rejoice in what we see
Because of it.
What I see today
25   Is the snow falling:
All things are made new.

                                         1980

↦— ⋈◊⋈ —↤

Hisaye Yamamoto

1921–

One of the first Japanese American writers to achieve critical attention after World War II, Hisaye Yamamoto is best known today for her short stories of life among *issei* (Japanese immigrants) and *nisei* (second generation Japanese Americans). She was born in Redondo Beach, California, to Japanese parents who emigrated from Kumamoto a decade prior to the passage of the Asian Exclusion Act of 1924, by which the U.S. government outlawed further Japanese immigration. As a teenager Yamamoto began to write poems and stories, using the pseudonym Napoleon because, as she later recounted, the name served as "an apology for my little madness"; she contributed regularly to the English section of a Japanese-language newspaper, *Kashu Mainichi*. Yamamoto attended Compton Junior College, where she majored in Latin, French, German, and Spanish; she also studied Japanese intensively for twelve years.

As a young woman during World War II, Yamamoto, with her father and brothers, was interned in a detention camp in Poston, Arizona, which housed thousands of Japanese Americans during a time of unfounded governmental suspicion of these citizens' loyalty. There she edited the camp newspaper, the *Poston Chronicle*, and published a serialized mystery, "Death Rides the Rails to Poston." From 1945 to 1948 she served as a columnist for the *Los Angeles Tribune*, a predominately black newspaper published weekly. After publishing her first story, Yamamoto left journalism to write full-time, aided by an inheritance from her brother Johnny, who had been killed during the war fighting with the American army in Italy. In 1948 she adopted a five-year-old boy, Paul, and in 1953 she volunteered on a Catholic Worker farm on Staten Island that was devoted to the pacifist principles of Dorothy Day. There she met and married Anthony DeSoto in 1955 and went on to give birth to four children after the couple returned to Los Angeles, where she has lived ever since. Although Yamamoto had several opportunities to pursue the formal study of writing, she never did so. When offered a Stanford University Writing Fellowship in the early 1950s, she turned it down "regretfully" in the belief that "I didn't contain enough information to be a writer."

Yamamoto's first story, "The High-Heeled Shoes," appeared in *Partisan Review* in 1948; it was followed by "Seventeen Syllables" in 1949. Two stories, "The Brown House" (1951) and "Epithalamium" (1960) were listed as "Distinctive Short Stories" during their year of publication; "Yoneko's Earthquake" was included in *Best Short Stories of 1952*. Several of Yamamoto's stories and essays address the experience of the internment camps, including "The Legend of Miss Sasagawara" (1950), which is set in Poston, and "I Still Carry It Around," a study of literature written about the internment. After 1961 Yamamoto published sporadically and began listing her occupation as "housewife." A collection of her stories did not appear until 1985, when *Seventeen Syllables: Five Stories of Japanese American Life* was published in Japan. Fifteen of her stories were collected in *Seventeen Syllables and Other Stories*, published in America by Kitchen Table Press in 1988. A screenplay by Emiko Omori, *Hot Summer Winds*, took its subject from "Seventeen Syllables" and "Yoneko's Earthquake"; this film appeared on PBS's *American Playhouse* in 1991. Yamamoto has received several awards for her writing, most notably a John Hays Whitney Foundation Opportunity Fellowship in 1950 and the American Book Award for Lifetime Achievement from the Before Columbus Foundation in 1986.

Most of Yamamoto's stories address issues of dislocation and relocation as Japanese tradition and American experience intersect. She has acknowledged that "Seventeen Syllables," reprinted here, tells her mother's story, even though its specific events were fabricated; her mother, who died in 1939, had regularly published *senryu*, a traditional type of Japanese poetry, during Yamamoto's childhood and adolescence. The story also explores the silences that can develop between *issei* parents and *nisei* children. Although Rosie Hayashi studies Japanese and courteously reads her mother's haiku, she fully understands neither the language nor the art; Tome Hayashi thus must share her enthusiasm for Japanese poetry with people outside her family and keep the secret of her past to herself. In the words of the scholar King-Kok Cheung, editor of a volume of critical essays entitled *Seventeen Syllables* (1994), Yamamoto "uses muted plot, symbolic scene, and understatement to evoke feelings that lie beneath the surface of language, compelling her readers to grapple with what is left unsaid."

⊰ Seventeen Syllables ⊱

The first Rosie knew that her mother had taken to writing poems was one evening when she finished one and read it aloud for her daughter's approval. It was about cats, and Rosie pretended to understand it thoroughly and appreciate it no end, partly because she hesitated to disillusion her mother about the quantity and quality of Japanese she had learned in all the years now that she had been going to Japanese school every Saturday (and Wednesday, too, in the summer). Even so, her mother must have been skeptical about the depth of Rosie's understanding, because she explained afterwards about the kind of poem she was trying to write.

See, Rosie, she said, it was a *haiku*, a poem in which she must pack all her meaning into seventeen syllables only, which were divided into three lines of five, seven, and five syllables. In the one she had just read, she had tried to capture the charm of a kitten, as well as comment on the superstition that owning a cat of three colors meant good luck.

"Yes, yes, I understand. How utterly lovely," Rosie said, and her mother, either satisfied or seeing through the deception and resigned, went back to composing.

The truth was that Rosie was lazy; English lay ready on the tongue but Japanese had to be searched for and examined, and even then put forth tentatively (probably to meet with laughter). It was so much easier to say yes, yes, even when one meant no, no. Besides, this was what was in her mind to say: I was looking through one of your magazines from Japan last night, Mother, and towards the back I found some *haiku* in English that delighted me. There was one that made me giggle off and on until I fell asleep—

> It is morning, and lo!
> I lie awake, comme il faut,
> sighing for some dough.

Now, how to reach her mother, how to communicate the melancholy song? Rosie knew formal Japanese by fits and starts, her mother had even less English, no French. It was much more possible to say yes, yes.

It developed that her mother was writing the *haiku* for a daily newspaper, the *Mainichi Shimbun*, that was published in San Francisco. Los Angeles, to be sure, was closer to the farming community in which the Hayashi family lived and several Japanese vernaculars were printed there, but Rosie's parents said they preferred the tone of the northern paper. Once a week, the *Mainichi* would have a section devoted to *haiku*, and her mother became an extravagant contributor, taking for herself the blossoming pen name, Ume Hanazono.

So Rosie and her father lived for awhile with two women, her mother and Ume Hanazono. Her mother (Tome Hayashi by name) kept house, cooked, washed, and, along with her husband and the Carrascos, the Mexican family hired for the harvest, did her ample share of picking tomatoes out in the sweltering fields and boxing them in tidy strata in the cool packing shed. Ume Hanazono, who came to life after the dinner dishes were done, was an earnest, muttering stranger who often neglected speaking when spoken to and stayed busy at the parlor table as late as midnight scribbling with pencil on scratch paper or carefully copying characters on good paper with her fat, pale green Parker.

The new interest had some repercussions on the household routine. Before, Rosie had been accustomed to her parents and herself taking their hot baths early and going to bed almost immediately afterwards, unless her parents challenged each other to a game of flower cards or unless company dropped in. Now if her father wanted to play cards, he had to resort to solitaire (at which he always cheated fearlessly), and if a group of friends came over, it was bound to contain someone who was also writing *haiku*, and the small assemblage would be split in two, her father entertaining the nonliterary members and her mother comparing ecstatic notes with the visiting poet.

If they went out, it was more of the same thing. But Ume Hanazono's life span, even for a poet's, was very brief—perhaps three months at most.

One night they went over to see the Hayano family in the neighboring town to the west, an adventure both painful and attractive to Rosie. It was attractive because there were four Hayano girls, all lovely and each one named after a season of the year (Haru, Natsu, Aki, Fuyu), painful because something had been wrong with Mrs. Hayano ever since the birth of her first child. Rosie would sometimes watch Mrs. Hayano, reputed to have been the belle of her native village, making her way about a room, stooped, slowly shuffling, violently trembling (*always* trembling), and she would be reminded that this woman, in this same condition, had carried and given issue to three babies. She would look wonderingly at Mr. Hayano, handsome, tall, and strong, and she would look at her four pretty friends. But it was not a matter she could come to any decision about.

On this visit, however, Mrs. Hayano sat all evening in the rocker, as motionless and unobtrusive as it was possible for her to be, and Rosie found the greater part of the evening practically anesthetic. Too, Rosie spent most of it in the girls' room, because Haru, the garrulous one, said almost as soon as the bows and other greetings were over, "Oh, you must see my new coat!"

It was a pale plaid of grey, sand, and blue, with an enormous collar, and Rosie, seeing nothing special in it, said, "Gee, how nice."

"Nice?" said Haru, indignantly. "Is that all you can say about it? It's gorgeous! And so cheap, too. Only seventeen-ninety eight, because it was a sale. The saleslady said it was twenty-five dollars regular."

"Gee," said Rosie. Natsu, who never said much and when she said anything said it shyly, fingered the coat covetously and Haru pulled it away.

"Mine," she said, putting it on. She minced in the aisle between the two large beds and smiled happily. "Let's see how your mother likes it."

She broke into the front room and the adult conversation and went to stand in front of Rosie's mother, while the rest watched from the door. Rosie's mother was properly envious. "May I inherit it when you're through with it?"

Haru, pleased, giggled and said yes, she could, but Natsu reminded gravely from the door, "You promised me, Haru."

Everyone laughed but Natsu, who shamefacedly retreated into the bedroom. Haru came in laughing, taking off the coat. "We were only kidding, Natsu," she said. "Here, you try it on now."

After Natsu buttoned herself into the coat, inspected herself solemnly in the bureau mirror, and reluctantly shed it, Rosie, Aki, and Fuyu got their turns, and Fuyu, who was eight, drowned in it while her sisters and Rosie doubled up in amusement. They all went into the front room later, because Haru's mother quaveringly called to her to fix the tea and rice cakes and open a can of sliced peaches for everybody. Rosie noticed that her mother and Mr. Hayano were talking together at the little table—they were discussing a *haiku* that Mr. Hayano was planning to send to the *Mainichi*, while her father was sitting at one end of the sofa looking through a copy of *Life*, the new picture magazine. Occasionally, her father would comment on a photograph, holding it toward Mrs. Hayano and speaking to her as he always did—loudly, as though he thought someone such as she must surely be at least a trifle deaf also.

The five girls had their refreshments at the kitchen table, and it was while Rosie was showing the sisters her trick of swallowing peach slices without chewing (she chased each slippery crescent down with a swig of tea) that her father brought his empty teacup and untouched saucer to the sink and said, "Come on, Rosie, we're going home now."

"Already?" asked Rosie.

"Work tomorrow," he said.

He sounded irritated, and Rosie, puzzled, gulped one last yellow slice and stood up to go, while the sisters began protesting, as was their wont.

"We have to get up at five-thirty," he told them, going into the front room quickly, so that they did not have their usual chance to hang onto his hands and plead for an extension of time.

Rosie, following, saw that her mother and Mr. Hayano were sipping tea and still talking together, while Mrs. Hayano concentrated, quivering, on raising the handleless Japanese cup to her lips with both her hands and lowering it back to her lap. Her father, saying nothing, went out the door, onto the bright porch, and down the steps. Her mother looked up and asked, "Where is he going?"

"Where is he going?" Rosie said. "He said we were going home now."

"Going home?" Her mother looked with embarrassment at Mr. Hayano and his absorbed wife and then forced a smile. "He must be tired," she said.

Haru was not giving up yet. "May Rosie stay overnight?" she asked, and Natsu, Aki, and Fuyu came to reinforce their sister's plea by helping her make a circle around Rosie's mother. Rosie, for once having no desire to stay, was relieved when her mother, apologizing to the perturbed Mr. and Mrs. Hayano for her father's abruptness at the same time, managed to shake her head no at the quartet, kindly but adamant, so that they broke their circle and let her go.

Rosie's father looked ahead into the windshield as the two joined him. "I'm sorry," her mother said. "You must be tired." Her father, stepping on the starter, said nothing. "You know how I get when it's *haiku*," she continued, "I forget what time it is." He only grunted.

As they rode homeward silently, Rosie, sitting between, felt a rush of hate for both—for her mother for begging, for her father for denying her mother. I wish this old Ford would crash, right now, she thought, then immediately, no, no, I wish my father would laugh, but it was too late: already the vision had passed through her mind of the green pick-up crumpled in the dark against one of the mighty eucalyptus trees they were just riding past, of the three contorted, bleeding bodies, one of them hers.

Rosie ran between two patches of tomatoes, her heart working more rambunctiously than she had ever known it to. How lucky it was that Aunt Taka and Uncle Gimpachi had come tonight, though, how very lucky. Otherwise she might not have really kept her half-promise to meet Jesus Carrasco. Jesus was going to be a senior in September at the same school she went to, and his parents were the ones helping with the tomatoes this year. She and Jesus, who hardly remembered seeing each other at Cleveland High where there were so many other people and two whole grades between them, had become great friends this summer—he always had a joke for her when he periodically drove the loaded pick-up up from the fields to the shed where she was usually sorting while her mother and father did the packing, and they laughed a great deal together over infinitesimal repartee during the afternoon break for chilled watermelon or ice cream in the shade of the shed.

What she enjoyed most was racing him to see who could finish picking a double row first. He, who could work faster, would tease her by slowing down until she thought she would surely pass him this time, then speeding up furiously to leave her several sprawling vines behind. Once he had made her screech hideously by crossing over, while her back was turned, to place atop the tomatoes in her green-stained bucket a truly monstrous, pale green worm (it had looked more like an infant snake). And it was when they had finished a contest this morning, after she had pantingly pointed a green finger at the immature tomatoes evident in the lugs at the end of his row and he had returned the accusation (with justice), that he had startlingly brought up the matter of their possibly meeting outside the range of both their parents' dubious eyes.

"What for?" she had asked.

"I've got a secret I want to tell you," he said.

"Tell me now," she demanded.

"It won't be ready till tonight," he said.

She laughed. "Tell me tomorrow then."

"It'll be gone tomorrow," he threatened.

"Well, for seven hakes, what is it?" she had asked, more than twice, and when he had suggested that the packing shed would be an appropriate place to find out, she had cautiously answered maybe. She had not been certain she was going to keep the appointment until the arrival of mother's sister and her husband. Their coming seemed a sort of signal of permission, of grace, and she had definitely made up her mind to lie and leave as she was bowing them welcome.

So as soon as everyone appeared settled back for the evening, she announced loudly that she was going to the privy outside, "I'm going to the *benjo!*" and slipped out the door. And now that she was actually on her way, her heart pumped in such an undisciplined way that she could hear it with her ears. It's because I'm running, she told herself, slowing to a walk. The shed was up ahead, one more patch away, in the middle of the fields. Its bulk, looming in the dimness, took on a sinisterness that was funny when Rosie reminded herself that it was only a wooden frame with a canvas roof and three canvas walls that made a slapping noise on breezy days.

Jesus was sitting on the narrow plank that was the sorting platform and she went around to the other side and jumped backwards to seat herself on the rim of a packing stand. "Well, tell me" she said without greeting, thinking her voice sounded reassuringly familiar.

"I saw you coming out the door," Jesus said. "I heard you running part of the way, too."

"Uh-huh," Rosie said. "Now tell me the secret."

"I was afraid you wouldn't come," he said.

Rosie delved around on the chicken-wire bottom of the stall for number two tomatoes, ripe, which she was sitting beside, and came up with a left-over that felt edible. She bit into it and began sucking out the pulp and seeds. "I'm here," she pointed out.

"Rosie, are you sorry you came?"

"Sorry? What for?" she said. "You said you were going to tell me something."

"I will, I will," Jesus said, but his voice contained disappointment, and Rosie fleetingly felt the older of the two, realizing a brand-new power which vanished without category under her recognition.

"I have to go back in a minute," she said. "My aunt and uncle are here from Wintersburg. I told them I was going to the privy."

Jesus laughed. "You funny thing," he said. "You slay me!"

"Just because you have a bathroom *inside*," Rosie said. "Come on, tell me."

Chuckling, Jesus came around to lean on the stand facing her. They still could not see each other very clearly, but Rosie noticed that Jesus became very sober again as he took the hollow tomato from her hand and dropped it back into the stall. When he took hold of her empty hand, she could find no words to protest; her vocabulary had become distressingly constricted and she thought desperately that all that remained intact now was yes and no and oh, and even these few sounds would not easily out. Thus, kissed by Jesus, Rosie fell for the first time entirely victim to a helplessness delectable beyond speech. But the terrible, beautiful sensation lasted no more than a second, and the reality of Jesus' lips and tongue and teeth and hands made her pull away with such strength that she nearly tumbled.

Rosie stopped running as she approached the lights from the windows of home. How long since she had left? She could not guess, but gasping yet, she went to the privy in back and locked herself in. Her own breathing deafened her in the dark, close space, and she sat and waited until she could hear at last the nightly calling of the frogs and crickets. Even then, all she could think to say was oh, my, and the pressure of Jesus' face against her face would not leave.

No one had missed her in the parlor, however, and Rosie walked in and through quickly, announcing that she was next going to take a bath. "Your father's in the bathhouse," her mother said, and Rosie, in her room, recalled that she had not seen him when she entered. There had been only Aunt Taka and Uncle Gimpachi with her mother at the table, drinking tea. She got her robe and straw sandals and crossed the parlor again to go outside. Her mother was telling them about the *haiku* competition in the *Mainichi* and the poem she had entered.

Rosie met her father coming out of the bathhouse. "Are you through, Father?" she asked. "I was going to ask you to scrub my back."

"Scrub your own back," he said shortly, going toward the main house.

"What have I done now?" she yelled after him. She suddenly felt like doing a lot of yelling. But he did not answer, and she went into the bathhouse. Turning on the dangling light, she removed her denims and T-shirt and threw them in the big carton for dirty clothes standing next to the washing machine. Her other things she took with her into the bath compartment to wash after her bath. After she had scooped a basin of hot water from the square wooden tub, she sat on the grey cement of the floor and soaped herself at exaggerated leisure, singing "Red Sails in the Sunset" at the top of her voice and using da-da-da where she suspected her words. Then, standing up, still singing, for she was possessed by the notion that any attempt now to analyze would result in spoilage and she believed that the larger her volume the less she would be able to hear herself think, she obtained more hot water and poured it on until she was free of lather. Only then did she allow herself to step into the steaming vat, one leg first, then the remainder of her body inch by inch until the water no longer stung and she could move around at will.

She took a long time soaking, afterwards remembering to go around outside to stoke the embers of the tin-lined fireplace beneath the tub and to throw on a few more sticks so that the water might keep its heat for her mother, and when she finally returned to the parlor, she found her mother still talking *haiku* with her aunt and uncle, the three of them on another round of tea. Her father was nowhere in sight.

At Japanese school the next day (Wednesday, it was), Rosie was grave and giddy by turns. Preoccupied at her desk in the row for students on Book Eight, she made up for it at recess by performing wild mimicry for the benefit of her friend Chizuko. She held her nose and whined a witticism or two in what she considered was the manner of Fred Allen; she assumed intoxication and a British accent to go over the climax of the Rudy Vallee recording of the pub conversation about William Ewart Gladstone; she was the child Shirley Temple piping, "On the Good Ship Lollipop"; she was the gentleman soprano of the Four Inkspots trilling, "If I Didn't Care." And she felt reasonably satisfied when Chizuko wept and gasped, "Oh, Rosie, you ought to be in the movies!"

Her father came after her at noon, bringing her sandwiches of minced ham and two nectarines to eat while she rode, so that she could pitch right into the sorting when they got home. The lugs were piling up, he said, and the ripe tomatoes in them would probably have to be taken to the cannery tomorrow if they were not ready for the produce haulers tonight. "This heat's not doing them any good. And we've got no time for a break today."

It *was* hot, probably the hottest day of the year, and Rosie's blouse stuck damply to her back even under the protection of the canvas. But she worked as efficiently as a flawless machine and kept the stalls heaped, with one part of her mind listening in to the parental murmuring about the heat and the tomatoes and with another part planning the exact words she would say to Jesus when he drove up with the first load of the afternoon. But when at last she saw that the pick-up was coming, her hands went berserk and the tomatoes started falling in the wrong stalls, and her father said, "Hey, hey! Rosie, watch what you're doing!"

"Well, I have to go to the *benjo*," she said, hiding panic.

"Go in the weeds over there," he said, only half-joking.

"Oh, Father!" she protested.

"Oh, go on home," her mother said. "We'll make out for awhile."

In the privy Rosie peered through a knothole toward the fields, watching as much as she could of Jesus. Happily she thought she saw him look in the direction of the house from time to time before he finished unloading and went back toward the patch where his mother and father worked. As she was heading for the shed, a very presentable black car purred up the dirt driveway to the house and its driver motioned to her. Was this the Hayashi home, he wanted to know. She nodded. Was she a Hayashi? Yes, she said, thinking that he was a good-looking man. He got out of the car with a huge, flat package and she saw that he warmly wore a business suit. "I have something here for your mother then," he said, in a more elegant Japanese than she was used to.

She told him where her mother was and he came along with her, patting his face with an immaculate white handkerchief and saying something about the coolness of San Francisco. To her surprised mother and father, he bowed and introduced himself as, among other things, the *haiku* editor of the *Mainichi Shimbun*, saying that since he had been coming as far as Los Angeles anyway, he had decided to bring her the first prize she had won in the recent contest.

"First prize?" her mother echoed, believing and not believing, pleased and over-whelmed. Handed the package with a bow, she bobbed her head up and down numerous times to express her utter gratitude.

"It is nothing much," he added, "but I hope it will serve as a token of our great appreciation for your contributions and our great admiration of your considerable talent."

"I am not worthy," she said, falling easily into his style. "It is I who should make some sign of my humble thanks for being permitted to contribute."

"No, no, to the contrary," he said, bowing again.

But Rosie's mother insisted, and then saying that she knew she was being unorthodox, she asked if she might open the package because her curiosity was so great. Certainly she might. In fact, he would like her reaction to it, for personally, it was one of his favorite *Hiroshiges*.

Rosie thought it was a pleasant picture, which looked to have been sketched with delicate quickness. There were pink clouds, containing some graceful calligra-phy, and a sea that was a pale blue except at the edges, containing four sampans with indications of people in them. Pines edged the water and on the far-off beach there was a cluster of thatched huts towered over by pine-dotted mountains of grey and blue. The frame was scalloped and gilt.

After Rosie's mother pronounced it without peer and somewhat prodded her father into nodding agreement, she said Mr. Kuroda must at least have a cup of tea after coming all this way, and although Mr. Kuroda did not want to impose, he soon agreed that a cup of tea would be refreshing and went along with her to the house, carrying the picture for her.

"Ha, your mother's crazy!" Rosie's father said, and Rosie laughed uneasily as she resumed judgment on the tomatoes. She had emptied six lugs when he broke into an imaginary conversation with Jesus to tell her to go and remind her mother of the tomatoes, and she went slowly.

Mr. Kuroda was in his shirtsleeves expounding some *haiku* theory as he munched a rice cake, and her mother was rapt. Abashed in the great man's presence, Rosie stood next to her mother's chair until her mother looked up inquiringly, and then she started to whisper the message, but her mother pushed her gently away and reproached, "You are not being very polite to our guest."

"Father says the tomatoes . . ." Rosie said aloud, smiling foolishly.

"Tell him I shall only be a minute," her mother said, speaking the language of Mr. Kuroda.

When Rosie carried the reply to her father, he did not seem to hear and she said again, "Mother says she'll be back in a minute."

"All right, all right," he nodded, and they worked again in silence. But suddenly, her father uttered an incredible noise, exactly like the cork of a bottle popping, and the next Rosie knew, he was stalking angrily toward the house, almost running in fact, and she chased after him crying, "Father! Father! What are you going to do?"

He stopped long enough to order her back to the shed. "Never mind!" he shouted. "Get on with the sorting!"

And from the place in the fields where she stood, frightened and vacillating, Rosie saw her father enter the house. Soon Mr. Kuroda came out alone, putting on his coat. Mr. Kuroda got into his car and backed out down the driveway onto the highway. Next her father emerged, also alone, something in his arms (it was the picture, she realized), and, going over to the bathhouse woodpile, he threw the picture on the ground and picked up the axe. Smashing the picture, glass and all (she heard the explosion faintly), he reached over for the kerosene that was used to encourage the bath fire and poured it over the wreckage. I am dreaming, Rosie said to herself, I am dreaming, but her father, having made sure that his act of cremation was irrevocable, was even then returning to the fields.

Rosie ran past him and toward the house. What had become of her mother? She burst into the parlor and found her mother at the back window watching the dying fire. They watched together until there remained only a feeble smoke under the blazing sun. Her mother was very calm.

"Do you know why I married your father?" she said without turning.

"No," said Rosie. It was the most frightening question she had ever been called upon to answer. Don't tell me now, she wanted to say, tell me tomorrow, tell me next week, don't tell me today. But she knew she would be told now, that the telling would combine with the other violence of the hot afternoon to level her life, her world to the very ground.

It was like a story out of the magazines illustrated in sepia, which she had consumed so greedily for a period until the information had somehow reached her that those wretchedly unhappy autobiographies, offered to her as the testimonials of living men and women, were largely inventions: Her mother, at nineteen, had come to America and married her father as an alternative to suicide.

At eighteen she had been in love with the first son of one of the well-to-do families in her village. The two had met whenever and wherever they could, secretly, because it would not have done for his family to see him favor her—her father had no money; he was a drunkard and a gambler besides. She had learned she was with child; an excellent match had already been arranged for her lover. Despised by her family, she had given premature birth to a stillborn son, who would be seventeen now. Her family did not turn her out, but she could no longer project herself in any direction without refreshing in them the memory of her indiscretion. She wrote to Aunt Taka, her favorite sister in America, threatening to kill herself if Aunt Taka would not send for her. Aunt Taka hastily arranged a marriage with a young man of whom she knew, but lately arrived from Japan, a young man of simple mind, it was said, but of kindly heart. The young man was never told why his unseen betrothed was so eager to hasten the day of meeting.

The story was told perfectly, with neither groping for words nor untoward passion. It was as though her mother had memorized it by heart, reciting it to herself so many times over that its nagging vileness had long since gone.

"I had a brother then?" Rosie asked, for this was what seemed to matter now; she would think about the other later, she assured herself, pushing back the illumination which threatened all that darkness that had hitherto been merely mysterious or even glamorous. "A half-brother?"

"Yes."

"I would have liked a brother," she said.

Suddenly, her mother knelt on the floor and took her by the wrists. "Rosie," she said urgently, "Promise me you will never marry!" Shocked more by the request than the revelation, Rosie stared at her mother's face. Jesus, Jesus, she called silently, not certain whether she was invoking the help of the son of the Carrascos or of God, until there returned sweetly the memory of Jesus' hand, how it had touched her and where. Still her mother waited for an answer, holding her wrists so tightly that her hands were going numb. She tried to pull free. Promise, her mother whispered fiercely, promise. Yes, yes, I promise, Rosie said. But for an instant she turned away, and her mother, hearing the familiar glib agreement, released her. Oh, you, you, you, her eyes and twisted mouth said, you fool. Rosie, covering her face, began at last to cry, and the embrace and consoling hand came much later than she expected.

1949

Maxine Hong Kingston
1940–

"When we Chinese girls listened to the adults talk-story, we learned that we failed if we grew up to be but wives or slaves. We could be heroines, swordswomen." So claims Chinese-American writer Maxine Hong Kingston, whose autobiographical book *The Woman Warrior: Memoirs of a Girlhood Among Ghosts* won the National Book Critics Circle Award for 1976. In this and other work Kingston explores the complexities of Asian-American identity, crossing genres to weave fiction, myth, cultural history, and autobiography into luminous prose. As a girl growing up in the Chinatown of Stockton, California, Kingston listened endlessly to "talk-story" from her mother, Brave Orchid, who emblazoned Chinese folk legends and family secrets on the mind of the young Maxine. To honor the family name, explains Kingston, "I would have to grow up a woman warrior."

Kingston's parents came to the United States in the 1930s from a tiny village in China, bringing with them dreams for a new life and a rich lore of Chinese tales and proverbs. The discrepancy between their fantasies of reaching "Gold Mountain," an imaginary American utopia, and the realities of racism and the immigrant experience provides the subject matter of her writing, as do the author's encounters with the stories of her heritage and the Caucasian "ghosts" among whom she lived. Kingston graduated in 1962 from the University of California at Berkeley; in that same year she married Earll Kingston, an actor. In 1967 she moved with her husband and son, Joseph, to Hawaii, where she taught at the Mid-Pacific Institute and at the University of Hawaii. She left Hawaii in the early 1990s to return to California, where she teaches at her alma mater, UC Berkeley.

Hawaiian landscape and history figure prominently in Kingston's work, since her great-grandfather, Bak Goong, was born in Hawaii and worked in the sugar cane fields there. Kingston chronicles his life in her second book, *China Men* (1980), focusing especially on his acts of resistance to white authorities in the fields: for example, he learned to cough speech when they forbade him and other workers to talk. Since "Chinese words [were] conveniently a syllable each," the author notes, Bak Goong's subversive strategy was successful. *China Men* blends childhood memory and fantasy with adult insight and compassion to portray Kingston's father, called BaBa, as a serious medical student in China, a romantic stowaway in transit between nations, and a humble but proud laundry worker in America. She also explores the miserable life of her grandfather, Ah Goong, building railroads across the U.S. West in the nineteenth century. Many of these historical and familial themes recur in Kingston's third book, *Tripmaster Monkey: His Fake Book* (1989).

In *The Woman Warrior* Kingston determines to use words as weapons to challenge racist and classist oppressors who seek to denigrate her Chinese-American identity, yet she also realizes the dangers inherent in challenging those more powerful than herself. "No Name Woman" (1976) explores the price one woman in Kingston's family pays for breaking with tradition. It also addresses the problem of breaking silence that the speaker faces in recounting the story of her aunt's secret shame. In this story Kingston powerfully articulates the anxiety many women experience as the bearers of familial silences.

⊰ No Name Woman ⊱

"You must not tell anyone," my mother said, "what I am about to tell you. In China your father had a sister who killed herself. She jumped into the family well. We say that your father has all brothers because it is as if she had never been born.

"In 1924 just a few days after our village celebrated seventeen hurry-up weddings— to make sure that every young man who went 'out on the road' would responsibly come home—your father and his brothers and your grandfather and his brothers and your aunt's new husband sailed for America, the Gold Mountain. It was your grandfather's last trip. Those lucky enough to get contracts waved good-bye from the decks. They fed and guarded the stowaways and helped them off in Cuba, New York, Bali, Hawaii. 'We'll meet in California next year,' they said. All of them sent money home.

"I remember looking at your aunt one day when she and I were dressing; I had not noticed before that she had such a protruding melon of a stomach. But I did not think, 'She's pregnant,' until she began to look like other pregnant women, her shirt pulling and the white tops of her black pants showing. She could not have been pregnant, you see, because her husband had been gone for years. No one said anything. We did not discuss it. In early summer she was ready to have the child, long after the time when it could have been possible.

"The village had also been counting. On the night the baby was to be born the villagers raided our house. Some were crying. Like a great saw, teeth strung with lights, files of people walked zigzag across our land, tearing the rice. Their lanterns doubled in the disturbed black water, which drained away through the broken bunds. As the villagers closed in, we could see that some of them, probably men and women we knew well, more white masks. The people with long hair hung it over their faces. Women with short hair made it stand up on end. Some had tied white bands around their foreheads, arms, and legs.

"At first they threw mud and rocks at the house. Then they threw eggs and began slaughtering our stock. We could hear the animals scream their deaths—the roosters, the pigs, a last great roar from the ox. Familiar wild heads flared in our night windows; the villagers encircled us. Some of the faces stopped to peer at us, their eyes rushing like searchlights. The hands flattened against the panes, framed heads, and left red prints.

"The villagers broke in the front and the back doors at the same time, even though we had not locked the doors against them. Their knives dripped with the blood of our animals. They smeared blood on the doors and walls. One woman swung a chicken, whose throat she had slit, splattering blood in red arcs about her. We stood together in the middle of our house, in the family hall with the pictures and tables of the ancestors around us, and looked straight ahead.

"At that time the house had only two wings. When the men came back, we would build two more to enclose our courtyard and a third one to begin a second courtyard. The villagers pushed through both wings, even your grandparents' rooms, to find your aunt's, which was also mine until the men returned. From this room a new wing for one of the younger families would grow. They ripped up her clothes and shoes and broke her combs, grinding them underfoot. They tore her work from the loom. They scattered the cooking fire and rolled the new weaving in it. We could hear them in the kitchen breaking our bowls and banging the pots. They overturned the great waist-high earthenware jugs; duck eggs, pickled fruits, vegetables burst out and mixed in acrid torrents. The old woman from the next field swept a broom through the air and loosed the spirits-of-the-broom over our heads. 'Pig.' 'Ghost.' 'Pig,' they sobbed and scolded while they ruined our house.

"When they left, they took sugar and oranges to bless themselves. They cut pieces from the dead animals. Some of them took bowls that were not broken and clothes that were not torn. Afterward we swept up the rice and sewed it back up into sacks. But the smells from the spilled preserves lasted. Your aunt gave birth in the pigsty that night. The next morning when I went for the water, I found her and the baby plugging up the family well.

"Don't let your father know that I told you. He denies her. Now that you have started to menstruate, what happened to her could happen to you. Don't humiliate us. You wouldn't like to be forgotten as if you had never been born. The villagers are watchful."

Whenever she had to warn us about life, my mother told stories that ran like this one, a story to grow up on. She tested our strength to establish realities. Those in the emigrant generations who could not reassert brute survival died young and far from home. Those of us in the first American generations have had to figure out how the invisible world the emigrants built around our childhoods fit in solid America.

The emigrants confused the gods by diverting their curses, misleading them with crooked streets and false names. They must try to confuse their offspring as well, who, I suppose, threaten them in similar ways—always trying to get things straight, always trying to name the unspeakable. The Chinese I know hide their names; sojourners take new names when their lives change and guard their real names with silence.

Chinese-Americans, when you try to understand what things in you are Chinese, how do you separate what is peculiar to childhood, to poverty, insanities, one family, your mother who marked your growing with stories, from what is Chinese? What is Chinese tradition and what is the movies?

If I want to learn what clothes my aunt wore, whether flashy or ordinary, I would have to begin, "Remember Father's drowned-in-the-well sister?" I cannot ask that. My mother has told me once and for all the useful parts. She will add nothing unless powered by Necessity, a riverbank that guides her life. She plants vegetable gardens rather than lawns; she carries the odd-shaped tomatoes home from the fields and eats food left for the gods.

Whenever we did frivolous things, we used up energy; we flew high kites. We children came up off the ground over the melting cones our parents brought home from work and the American movie on New Year's Day—*Oh, You Beautiful Doll* with Betty Grable one year, and *She wore a Yellow Ribbon* with John Wayne another year. After the one carnival ride each, we paid in guilt; our tired father counted his change on the dark walk home.

Adultery is extravagance. Could people who hatch their own chicks and eat the embryos and the heads for delicacies and boil the feet in vinegar for party food, leaving only the gravel, eating even the gizzard lining—could such people engender a prodigal aunt? To be a woman, to have a daughter in starvation time was a waste enough. My aunt could not have been the lone romantic who gave up everything for sex. Women in the old China did not choose. Some man had commanded her to lie with him and be his secret evil. I wonder whether he masked himself when he joined the raid on her family.

Perhaps she encountered him in the fields or on the mountain where the daughters-in-law collected fuel. Or perhaps he first noticed her in the marketplace. He was not a stranger because the village housed no strangers. She had to have dealings with him other than sex. Perhaps he worked an adjoining field, or he sold her the cloth for the dress she sewed and wore. His demand must have surprised, then terrified her. She obeyed him; she always did as she was told.

When the family found a young man in the next village to be her husband, she stood tractably beside the best rooster, his proxy, and promised before they met that she would be his forever. She was lucky that he was her age and she would be the first wife, an advantage secure now. The night she first saw him, he had sex with her. Then he left for America. She had almost forgotten what he looked like. When she tried to envision him, she only saw the black and white face in the group photograph the men had had taken before leaving.

The other man was not, after all, much different from her husband. They both gave orders: she followed. "If you tell your family, I'll beat you. I'll kill you. Be here again next week." No one talked sex, ever. And she might have separated the rapes from the rest of living if only she did not have to buy her oil from him or gather wood in the same forest. I want her fear to have lasted just as long as rape lasted so that the fear could have been contained. No drawn-out fear. But women at sex hazarded birth and hence lifetimes. The fear did not stop but permeated everywhere. She told the man, "I think I'm pregnant." He organized the raid against her.

On nights when my mother and father talked about their life back home, sometimes they mentioned an "outcast table" whose business they still seemed to be settling, their voices tight. In a commensal tradition, where food is precious, the powerful older people made wrongdoers eat alone. Instead of letting them start separate new lives like the Japanese, who could become samurais and geishas, the Chinese family, faces averted but eyes glowering sideways, hung on to the offenders and fed them leftovers. My aunt must have lived in the same house as my parents and eaten at an outcast table. My mother spoke about the raid as if she had seen it, when she and my aunt, a daughter-in-law to a different household, should not have been living together at all. Daughters-in-law lived with their husbands' parents, not their own; a synonym for marriage in Chinese is "taking a daughter-in-law." Her husband's parents could have sold her, mortgaged her, stoned her. But they had sent her back to her own mother and father, a mysterious act hinting at disgraces not told me. Perhaps they had thrown her out to deflect the avengers.

She was the only daughter; her four brothers went with her father, husband, and uncles "out on the road" and for some years became western men. When the goods were divided among the family, three of the brothers took land, and the youngest, my father, chose an education. After my grandparents gave their daughter away to her husband's family, they had dispensed all the adventure and all the property. They expected her alone to keep the traditional ways, which her brothers, now among the barbarians, could fumble without detection. The heavy, deep-rooted women were to maintain the past against the flood, safe for returning. But the rare urge west had fixed upon our family, and so my aunt crossed boundaries not delineated in space.

The work of preservation demands that the feelings playing about in one's guts not be turned into action. Just watch their passing like cherry blossoms. But perhaps my aunt, my forerunner, caught in a slow life, let dreams grow and fade and after some months or years went toward what persisted. Fear at the enormities of the forbidden kept her desires delicate, wire and bone. She looked at a man because she liked the way the hair was tucked behind his ears, or she liked the question-mark line of a long torso curving at the shoulder and straight at the hip. For warm eyes or a soft voice or a slow walk—that's all—a few hairs, a line, a brightness, a sound, a pace, she gave up family. She offered us up for a charm that vanished with tiredness, a pigtail that didn't toss when the wind died. Why, the wrong lighting could erase the dearest thing about him.

It could very well have been, however, that my aunt did not take subtle enjoyment of her friend, but, a wild woman, kept rollicking company. Imagining her free with sex doesn't fit, though. I don't know any women like that, or men either. Unless I see her life branching into mine, she gives me no ancestral help.

To sustain her being in love, she often worked at herself in the mirror, guessing at the colors and shapes that would interest him, changing them frequently in order to hit on the right combination. She wanted him to look back.

On a farm near the sea, a woman who tended her appearance reaped a reputation for eccentricity. All the married women blunt-cut their hair in flaps about their ears or pulled it back in tight buns. No nonsense. Neither style blew easily into heart-catching tangles. And at their weddings they displayed themselves in their long hair for the last time. "It brushed the backs of my knees," my mother tells me. "It was braided, and even so, it brushed the backs of my knees."

At the mirror my aunt combed individuality into her bob. A bun could have been contrived to escape into black streamers blowing in the wind or in quiet wisps about her face, but only the older women in our picture album wear buns. She brushed her hair back from her forehead, tucking the flaps behind her ears. She looped a piece of thread, knotted into a circle between her index fingers and thumbs, and ran the double strand across her forehead. When she closed her fingers as if she were making a pair of shadow geese bite, the string twisted together catching the little hairs. Then she pulled the thread away from her skin, ripping the hairs out neatly, her eyes watering from the needles of pain. Opening her fingers, she cleaned the thread, then rolled it along her hairline and the tops of her eyebrows. My mother did the same to me and my sisters and herself. I used to believe that the expression "caught by the short hairs" meant a captive held with a depilatory string. It especially hurt at the temples, but my mother said we were lucky we didn't have to have our feet bound when we were seven. Sisters used to sit on their beds and cry together, she said, as their mothers or their slaves removed the bandages for a few minutes each night and let the blood gush back into their veins. I hope that the man my aunt loved appreciated a smooth brow, that he wasn't just a tits-and-ass man.

Once my aunt found a freckle on her chin, at a spot that the almanac said predestined her for unhappiness. She dug it out with a hot needle and washed the wound with peroxide.

More attention to her looks than these pullings of hairs and pickings at spots would have caused gossip among the villagers. They owned work clothes and good clothes, and they wore good clothes for feasting the new seasons. But since a woman combing her hair hexes beginnings, my aunt rarely found an occasion to look her best. Women looked like great sea snails—the corded wood, babies, and laundry they carried were the whorls on their backs. The Chinese did not admire a bent back; goddesses and warriors stood straight. Still there must have been a marvelous freeing of beauty when a worker laid down her burden and stretched and arched.

Such commonplace loveliness, however, was not enough for my aunt. She dreamed of a lover for the fifteen days of New Year's, the time for families to exchange visits, money, and food. She plied for secret comb. And sure enough she cursed the year, the family, the village, and herself.

Even as her hair lured her imminent lover, many other men looked at her. Uncles, cousins, nephews, brothers would have looked, too, had they been home between journeys. Perhaps they had already been restraining their curiosity, and they left, fearful that their glances, like a field of nesting birds, might be startled and caught. Poverty hurt, and that was their first reason for leaving. But another, final reason for leaving the crowded house was the never-said.

She may have been unusually beloved, the precious only daughter, spoiled and mirror gazing because of the affection the family lavished on her. When her husband left, they welcomed the chance to take her back from the in-laws; she could live like the little daughter for just a while longer. There are stories that my grandfather was different from other people, "crazy ever since the little Jap bayoneted him in the head." He used to put his naked penis on the dinner table, laughing. And one day he brought home a baby girl, wrapped up inside his brown western-style greatcoat. He had traded one of his sons, probably my father, the youngest, for her. My grandmother made him trade back. When he finally got a daughter of his own, he doted on her. They must have all loved her, except perhaps my father, the only brother who never went back to China, having once been traded for a girl.

Brothers and sisters, newly men and women, had to efface their sexual color and present plain miens. Disturbing hair and eyes, a smile like no other threatened the ideal of five generations living under one roof. To focus blurs, people shouted face to face and yelled from room to room. The immigrants I know have loud voices, unmodulated to American tones even after years away from the village where they called their friendships out across the fields. I have not been able to stop my mother's screams in public libraries or over telephones. Walking erect (knees straight, toes pointed forward, not pigeon-toed, which is Chinese-feminine) and speaking in an inaudible voice, I have tried to turn myself American-feminine. Chinese communication was loud, public. Only sick people had to whisper. But at the dinner table, where the family members came nearest one another, no one could talk, not the outcasts nor any eaters. Every word that falls from the mouth is a coin lost. Silently they gave and accepted food with both hands. A preoccupied child who took his bowl with one hand got a sideways glare. A complete moment of total attention is due everyone alike. Children and lovers have no singularity here, but my aunt used a secret voice, a separate attentiveness.

She kept the man's name to herself throughout her labor and dying; she did not accuse him that he be punished with her. To save her inseminator's name she gave silent birth.

He may have been somebody in her own household, but intercourse with a man outside the family would have been no less abhorrent. All the village were kinsmen, and the titles shouted in loud country voices never let kinship be forgotten. Any man within visiting distance would have been neutralized as a lover—"brother," "younger brother," "older brother"—one hundred and fifteen relationship titles. Parents researched birth charts probably not so much to assure good fortune as to circumvent incest in a population that has but one hundred surnames. Everybody has eight million relatives. How useless then sexual mannerisms, how dangerous.

As if it came from an atavism deeper than fear, I used to add "brother" silently to boys' names. It hexed the boys, who would or would not ask me to dance, and made them less scary and as familiar and deserving of benevolence as girls.

But, of course, I hexed myself also—no dates. I should have stood up, both arms waving, and shouted out across libraries, "Hey, you! Love me back." I had no idea, though, how to make attraction selective, how to control its direction and magnitude. If I made myself American-pretty so that the five or six Chinese boys in the class fell in love with me, everyone else—the Caucasian, Negro, and Japanese boys— would too. Sisterliness, dignified and honorable, made much more sense.

Attraction eludes control so stubbornly that whole societies designed to organize relationships among people cannot keep order, not even when they bind people to one another from childhood and raise them together. Among the very poor and the wealthy, brothers married their adopted sisters, like doves. Our family allowed some romance, paying adult brides' prices and providing dowries so that their sons and daughters could marry strangers. Marriage promises to turn strangers into friendly relatives—a nation of siblings.

In the village structure, spirits shimmered among the live creatures, balanced and held in equilibrium by time and land. But one human being flaring up into violence could open up a black hole, a maelstrom that pulled in the sky. The frightened villagers, who depended on one another to maintain the real, went to my aunt to show her a personal, physical representation of the break she had made in the "roundness." Misallying couples snapped off the future, which was to be embodied in true offspring. The villagers punished her for acting as if she could have a private life, secret and apart from them.

If my aunt had betrayed the family at a time of large grain yields and peace, when many boys were born, and wings were being built on many houses, perhaps she might have escaped such severe punishment. But the men—hungry, greedy, tired of planting in dry soil, cuckolded—had had to leave the village in order to send food-money home. There were ghost plagues, bandit plagues, wars with the Japanese, floods. My Chinese brother and sister had died of an unknown sickness. Adultery, perhaps only a mistake during good times, became a crime when the village needed food.

The round moon cakes and round doorways, the round tables of graduated size that fit one roundness inside another, round windows and rice bowls—these talismen had lost their power to warn this family of the law: a family must be whole, faithfully keeping the descent line by having sons to feed the old and the dead, who in turn look after the family. The villagers came to show my aunt and her lover-in-hiding a broken house. The villagers were speeding up the circling of events because she was too shortsighted to see that her infidelity had already harmed the village, that waves of consequences would return unpredictably, sometimes in disguise, as now, to hurt her. This roundness had to be made coin-sized so that she would see its circumference: punish her at the birth of her baby. Awaken her to the inexorable. People who refused fatalism because they could invent small resources insisted on culpability. Deny accidents and wrest fault from the stars.

After the villagers left, their lanterns now scattering in various directions toward home, the family broke their silence and cursed her. "Aiaa, we're going to die. Death is coming. Death is coming. Look what you've done. You've killed us. Ghost! Dead ghost! Ghost! You've never been born." She ran out into the fields, far enough from the house so that she could no longer hear their voices, and pressed herself against the earth, her own land no more. When she felt the birth coming, she thought that she had been hurt. Her body seized together. "They've hurt me too much," she thought. "This is gall, and it will kill me." Her forehead and knees against the earth, her body convulsed and then released her onto her back. The black well of sky and stars went out and out and out forever; her body and her complexity seemed to disappear. She was one of the stars, a bright dot in blackness, without home, without a companion, in eternal cold and silence. An agoraphobia rose in her, speeding higher and higher, bigger and bigger; she would not be able to contain it; there would be no end to fear.

Flayed, unprotected against space, she felt pain return, focusing her body. This pain chilled her—a cold, steady kind of surface pain. Inside, spasmodically, the other pain, the pain of the child, heated her. For hours she lay on the ground, alternately body and space. Sometimes a vision of normal comfort obliterated reality: she saw the family in the evening gambling at the dinner table, the young people massaging their elders' backs. She saw them congratulating one another, high joy on the mornings the rice shoots came up. When these pictures burst, the stars drew yet further apart. Black space opened.

She got to her feet to fight better and remembered that old-fashioned women gave birth in their pigsties to fool the jealous, pain-dealing gods, who do not snatch piglets. Before the next spasms could stop her, she ran to the pigsty, each step a rushing out into emptiness. She climbed over the fence and knelt in the dirt. It was good to have a fence enclosing her, a tribal person alone.

Laboring, this woman who had carried her child as a foreign growth that sickened her every day, expelled it at last. She reached down to touch the hot, wet, moving mass, surely smaller than anything human, and could feel that it was human after all—fingers, toes, nails, nose. She pulled it up on to her belly, and it lay curled there, butt in the air, feet precisely tucked one under the other. She opened her loose shirt and buttoned the child inside. After resting, it squirmed and thrashed and she pushed it up to her breast. It turned its head this way and that until it found her nipple. There, it made little snuffling noises. She clenched her teeth at its preciousness, lovely as a young calf, a piglet, a little dog.

She may have gone to the pigsty as a last act of responsibility: she would protect this child as she had protected its father. It would look after her soul, leaving supplies on her grave. But how would this tiny child without family find her grave when there would be no marker for her anywhere, neither in the earth nor the family hall? No one would give her a family hall name. She had taken the child with her into the wastes. At its birth the two of them had felt the same raw pain of separation, a wound that only the family pressing tight could close. A child with no descent line would not soften her life but only trail after her, ghost-like, begging her to give it purpose. At dawn the villagers on their way to the fields would stand around the fence and look.

Full of milk, the little ghost slept. When it awoke, she hardened her breasts against the milk that crying loosens. Toward morning she picked up the baby and walked to the well.

Carrying the baby to the well shows loving. Otherwise abandon it. Turn its face into the mud. Mothers who love their children take them along. It was probably a girl; there is some hope of forgiveness for boys.

"Don't tell anyone you had an aunt. Your father does not want to hear her name. She has never been born." I have believed that sex was unspeakable and words so strong and fathers so frail that "aunt" would do my father mysterious harm. I have thought that my family, having settled among immigrants who had also been their neighbors in the ancestral land, needed to clean their name, and a wrong word would incite the kinspeople even here. But there is more to this silence: they want me to participate in her punishment. And I have.

In the twenty years since I heard this story I have not asked for details nor said my aunt's name; I do not know it. People who can comfort the dead can also chase after them to hurt them further—a reverse ancestor worship. The real punishment was not the raid swiftly inflicted by the villagers, but the family's deliberately forgetting her. Her betrayal so maddened them, they saw to it that she would suffer forever, even after death. Always hungry, always needing, she would have to beg food from other ghosts, snatch and steal it from those whose living descendants give them gifts. She would have to fight the ghosts massed at crossroads for the buns a few thoughtful citizens leave to decoy her away from village and home so that the ancestral spirits could feast unharassed. At peace, they could act like gods, not ghosts, their descent lines providing them with paper suits and dresses, spirit money, paper houses, paper automobiles, chicken, meat, and rice into eternity—essences delivered up in smoke and flames, steam and incense rising from each rice bowl. In an attempt to make the Chinese care for people outside the family, Chairman Mao encourages us now to give our paper replicas to the spirits of outstanding soldiers and workers, no matter whose ancestors they may be. My aunt remains forever hungry. Goods are not distributed evenly among the dead.

My aunt haunts me—her ghost drawn to me because now, after fifty years of neglect, I alone devote pages of paper to her, though not origamied into houses and clothes. I do not think she always means me well. I am telling on her, and she was a spite suicide, drowning herself in the drinking water. The Chinese are always very frightened of the drowned one, whose weeping ghost, wet hair hanging and skin bloated, waits silently by the water to pull down a substitute.

1976

Gloria Anzaldúa
1942–

"To survive in the Borderlands," claims U.S. poet and essayist Gloria Anzaldúa, "you must live *sin fronteras* / be a crossroads." Negotiating geographical and mental borders are acts of daily survival for Anzaldúa, a self-described Chicana/*tejana* lesbian-feminist whose writing chronicles her quest for a multiracial identity and a multilingual voice. Born on the Texas-Mexico border to working-class parents who did farm and ranch work, Anzaldúa has written an autobiographical essay, "La Prieta," describing her experience growing up as a smart, *morena* girl whose family felt "it *was* too bad I was dark like an Indian." Grateful for her parents' love and care, and conscious in her writing of not blaming them for internalized oppression, Anzaldúa nonetheless felt compelled to rebel against their sexist restrictions at an early age, to complete what she calls "the transformation of my own being." Confronted with homophobia in her Latino community and racism in her women's community, she determined to "be the black Kali. Spit in their eye and never cry. . . . Be not a rock but a razor's edge and burn with falling."

As an adult Anzaldúa has blended writing, teaching, and activism. She has taught creative writing, women's studies, and Chicano studies at a variety of institutions, including the University of Texas at Austin, San Francisco State University, Vermont College of Norwich University, and the University of California at Santa Cruz, and she has conducted writing workshops throughout the United States. In addition, she has been an activist on behalf of the migrant farm workers' movement and has served as a contributing editor to the feminist journal *Sinister Wisdom*. With CHERRÍE MORAGA, Anzaldúa edited *This Bridge Called My Back* (1981), an influential collection of writings by radical women of color, which won the Before Columbus Foundation American Book Award for 1986. In the introduction Anzaldúa and Moraga explain that this book "intends to reflect an uncompromised definition of feminism by women of color in the U.S. We named this anthology 'radical' for we were interested in the writings of women of color who want nothing short of a revolution in the hands of women. . . . Our feminist politic emerges from the roots of both our cultural oppression and heritage." Anzaldúa has also published essays in various feminist journals, including *Third Woman, Ikon, Labyris,* and *Conditions.*

"This is my home / this thin edge of barbwire," she asserts in *Borderlands/La Frontera: The New Mestiza* (1987), speaking of the Texas-Mexico border as a site of resistance and confrontation as well as the source of historical and familial wounds. This book's most distinctive feature, code-switching—its shifts from English to Spanish to "Tex-Mex" to Nahautl—is matched by its genre-crossing, a mixture of autobiography, poetry, and cultural history. "Until I am free to write bilingually and to switch codes without having always to translate," she insists, "my tongue will be illegitimate." *Borderlands* documents the vision of a woman poised between two cultures, alien to both yet aware that the space between can serve as a meeting ground for people of color and their allies as the twenty-first century dawns. Anzalduá calls for a new "consciousness of the Borderlands," a tolerance for ambiguity and contradiction that reflects the particular realities of women of color.

Other works by Anzaldúa include *Making Face, Making Soul: Hacienda Caras* (1990), a collection of creative writing and critical essays by U.S. women of color, and *Prieta Has a Friend / Preitita tiene un amigo* (1991), a bilingual children's picture book. *Making Face, Making Soul* began as a textbook for her students in feminist studies at UC Santa Cruz, a means of continuing where *This Bridge Called My Back* left off in confronting racism in the women's movement and in society at large. Anzaldúa describes this collection as both "a testimonial of survival" and a tool for learning to read in "nonwhite narrative traditions." "Speaking in Tongues: A Letter to Third World Women Writers" (1980) explores Anzaldúa's own effort to find voice as well as the difficulties of other black and brown women. Writing is for Anzaldúa both "the act of making soul, alchemy," and an essential act of survival. Learning to speak thus represents a daring and defiant political act, a transformation of cultural norms as well as individual experience.

⚞ Speaking in Tongues: A Letter to Third World Women Writers ⚟

21 mayo 80

Dear mujeres de color, companions in writing—

I sit here naked in the sun, typewriter against my knee trying to visualize you. Black woman huddles over a desk in the fifth floor of some New York tenement. Sitting on a porch in south Texas, a Chicana fanning away mosquitos and the hot air, trying to arouse the smouldering embers of writing. Indian woman walking to school or work lamenting the lack of time to weave writing into your life. Asian American, lesbian, single mother, tugged in all directions by children, lover or ex-husband, and the writing.

It is not easy writing this letter. It began as a poem, a long poem. I tried to turn it into an essay but the result was wooden, cold. I have not yet unlearned the esoteric bullshit and pseudo-intellectualizing that school brainwashed into my writing.

How to begin again. How to approximate the intimacy and immediacy I want. What form? A letter, of course.

My dear *hermanas*, the dangers we face as women writers of color are not the same as those of white women though we have many in common. We don't have as much to lose—we never had any privileges. I wanted to call the dangers "obstacles" but that would be a kind of lying. We can't *transcend* the dangers, can't rise above them. We must go through them and hope we won't have to repeat the performance.

Unlikely to be friends of people in high literary places, the beginning woman of color is invisible both in the white male mainstream world and in the white women's feminist world, though in the latter this is gradually changing. The *lesbian* of color is not only invisible, she doesn't even exist. Our speech, too, is inaudible. We speak in tongues like the outcast and the insane.

Because white eyes do not want to know us, they do not bother to learn our language, the language which reflects us, our culture, our spirit. The schools we attended or didn't attend did not give us the skills for writing nor the confidence that we were correct in using our class and ethnic languages. I, for one, became adept at, and majored in English to spite, to show up, the arrogant racist teachers who thought all Chicano children were dumb and dirty. And Spanish was not taught in grade school. And Spanish was not required in High School. And though now I write my poems in Spanish as well as English I feel the rip-off of my native tongue.

> I *lack imagination* you say
>
> *No*. I lack language.
> The language to clarify
> my resistance to the literate.
> Words are a war to me.
> They threaten my family.
>
> To gain the word
> to describe the loss
> I risk losing everything.
> I may create a monster
> the word's length and body
> swelling up colorful and thrilling
> looming over my *mother*, characterized.
> Her voice in the distance
> *unintelligible illiterate.*
> These are the monster's words.[1]
>
> Cherríe Moraga

Who gave us permission to perform the act of writing? Why does writing seem so unnatural for me? I'll do anything to postpone it—empty the trash, answer the telephone. The voice recurs in me: *Who am I, a poor Chicanita from the sticks, to think I could write?* How dare I even considered becoming a writer as I stooped over the tomato fields bending, bending under the hot sun, hands broadened and calloused, not fit to hold the quill, numbed into an animal stupor by the heat.

How hard it is for us to *think* we can choose to become writers, much less *feel* and *believe* that we can. What have we to contribute, to give? Our own expectations condition us. Does not our class, our culture as well as the white man tell us writing is not for women such as us?

The white man speaks: *Perhaps if you scrape the dark off of your face. Maybe if you bleach your bones. Stop speaking in tongues, stop writing left-handed. Don't cultivate your colored skins nor tongues of fire if you want to make it in a right-handed world.*

Man, like all the other animals, fears and is repelled by that which he does not understand, and mere difference is apt to connote something malign.[2]

I think, yes, perhaps if we go to the university. Perhaps if we become male-women or as middleclass as we can. Perhaps if we give up loving women, we will be worthy of having something to say worth saying. They convince us that we must cultivate art for art's sake. Bow down to the sacred bull, form. Put frames and metaframes around the writing. Achieve distance in order to win the coveted title "literary writer" or "professional writer." Above all do not be simple, direct, nor immediate.

Why do they fight us? Because they think we are dangerous beasts? Why *are* we dangerous beasts? Because we shake and often break the white's comfortable stereotypic images they have of us: the Black domestic, the lumbering nanny with twelve babies sucking her tits, the slant-eyed Chinese with her expert hand—"They know how to treat a man in bed," the flat-faced Chicana or Indian, passively lying on her back, being fucked by the Man *a la* La Chingada.

The Third World woman revolts: *We revoke, we erase your white male imprint. When you come knocking on our doors with your rubber stamps to brand our faces with DUMB, HYSTERICAL, PASSIVE PUTA, PERVERT, when you come with your branding irons to burn MY PROPERTY on our buttocks, we will vomit the guilt, self-denial and race-hatred you have force-fed into us right back into your mouth. We are done being cushions for your projected fears. We are tired of being your sacrificial lambs and scapegoats.*

I can write this and yet I realize that many of us women of color who have strung degrees, credentials and published books around our necks like pearls that we hang onto for dear life are in danger of contributing to the invisibility of our sister-writers. "La Vendida," the sell-out.

The danger of selling out one's own ideologies. For the Third World woman, who has, at best, one foot in the feminist literary world, the temptation is great to adopt the current feeling-fads and theory fads, the latest half truths in political thought, the half-digested new age psychological axioms that are preached by the white feminist establishment. Its followers are notorious for "adopting" women of color as their "cause" while still expecting us to adapt to *their* expectations and *their* language.

How dare we get out of our colored faces. How dare we reveal the human flesh underneath and bleed red blood like the white folks. It takes tremendous energy and courage not to acquiesce, not to capitulate to a definition of feminism that still renders most of us invisible. Even as I write this I am disturbed that I am the only Third World woman writer in this handbook.* Over and over I have found myself to be the only Third World woman at readings, workshops, and meetings.

---

* The essay was originally to have been published elsewhere but first appeared in 1981 in *This Bridge Called My Back: Writings by Radical Women of Color*, which Anzaldúa edited with Cherríe Moraga.

We cannot allow ourselves to be tokenized. We must make our own writing and that of Third World women the first priority. We cannot educate white women and take them by the hand. Most of us are willing to help but we can't do the white woman's homework for her. That's an energy drain. More times than she cares to remember, Nellie Wong, Asian American feminist writer, has been called by white women wanting a list of Asian American women who can give readings or workshops. We are in danger of being reduced to purveyors of resource lists.

Coming face to face with one's limitations. There are only so many things I can do in one day. Luisah Teish addressing a group of predominantly white feminist writers had this to say of Third World women's experience:

> If you are not caught in the maze that (we) are in, it's very difficult to explain to you the hours in the day we do not have. And the hours that we do not have are hours that are translated into survival skills and money. And when one of those hours is taken away it means an hour not that we don't have to lie back and stare at the ceiling or an hour that we don't have to talk to a friend. For me it's a loaf of bread.

> Understand.
> My family is poor.
> Poor. I can't afford
> a new ribbon. The risk
> of this one is enough
> to keep me moving
> through it, accountable.
> The repetition like my mother's
> stories retold, *each* time
> reveals more particulars
> gains more familiarity.
> You can't get me in your car so fast.[3]

Cherríe Moraga

Complacency is a far more dangerous attitude than outrage.[4]

Naomi Littlebear

Why am I compelled to write? Because the writing saves me from this complacency I fear. Because I have no choice. Because I must keep the spirit of my revolt and myself alive. Because the world I create in the writing compensates for what the real world does not give me. By writing I put order in the world, give it a handle so I can grasp it. I write because life does not appease my appetites and hunger. I write to record what others erase when I speak, to rewrite the stories others have miswritten about me, about you. To become more intimate with myself and you. To discover myself, to preserve myself, to make myself, to achieve self-autonomy. To dispel the myths that I am a mad prophet or a poor suffering soul. To convince myself that I am worthy and that what I have to say is not a pile of shit. To show that I *can* and that I *will* write, never mind their admonitions to the contrary. And I will write about the unmentionables, never mind the outraged gasp of the censor and the audience. Finally I write because I'm scared of writing but I'm more scared of not writing.

Why should I try to justify why I write? Do I need to justify being Chicana, being woman? You might as well ask me to try to justify why I'm alive.

The act of writing is the act of making soul, alchemy. It is the quest for the self, for the center of the self, which we women of color have come to think as "other"—the dark, the feminine. Didn't we start writing to reconcile this other within us? We knew we were different, set apart, exiled from what is considered "normal," white-right. And as we internalized this exile, we came to see the alien within us and too often, as a result, we split apart from ourselves and each other. Forever after we have been in search of that self, that "other" and each other. And we return, in widening spirals and never to the same childhood place where it happened, first in our families, with our mothers, with our fathers. The writing is a tool for piercing that mystery but it also shields us, gives a margin of distance, helps us survive. And those that don't survive? The waste of ourselves: so much meat thrown at the feet of madness or fate or the state.

24 mayo 80

It is dark and damp and has been raining all day. I love days like this. As I lie in bed I am able to delve inward. Perhaps today I will write from that deep core. As I grope for words and a voice to speak of writing, I stare at my brown hand clenching the pen and think of you thousands of miles away clutching your pen. You are not alone.

> Pen, I feel right at home in your ink doing a pirouette, stirring the cobwebs, leaving my signature on the window panes. Pen, how could I ever have feared you. You're quite house-broken but it's your wildness I am in love with. I'll have to get rid of you when you start being predictable, when you stop chasing dustdevils. The more you outwit me the more I love you. It's when I'm tired or have had too much caffeine or wine that you get past my defenses and you say more than what I had intended. You surprise me, shock me into knowing some part of me I'd kept secret even from myself.
>
> —Journal entry.

In the kitchen Maria and Cherríe's voices falling on these pages. I can see Cherríe going about in her terry cloth wrap, barefoot washing the dishes, shaking out the tablecloth, vacuuming. Deriving a certain pleasure watching her perform those simple tasks, I am thinking *they lied, there is no separation between life and writing*.

The danger in writing is not fusing our personal experience and world view with the social reality we live in, with our inner life, our history, our economics, and our vision. What validates us as human beings validates us as writers. What matters to us is the relationships that are important to us whether with our self or others. We must use what is important to us to get to the writing. *No topic is too trivial*. The danger is in being too universal and humanitarian and invoking the eternal to the sacrifice of the particular and the feminine and the specific historical moment.

The problem is to focus, to concentrate. The body distracts, sabotages with a hundred ruses, a cup of coffee, pencils to sharpen. The solution is to anchor the body to a cigarette or some other ritual. And who has time or energy to write after nurturing husband or lover, children, and often an outside job? The problems seem insurmountable and they are, but they cease being insurmountable once we make up our mind that whether married or childrened or working outside jobs we are going to make time for the writing.

Forget the room of one's own—write in the kitchen, lock yourself up in the bathroom. Write on the bus or the welfare line, on the job or during meals, between sleeping or waking. I write while sitting on the john. No long stretches at the type-writer unless you're wealthy or have a patron—you may not even own a typewriter.

While you wash the floor or clothes listen to the words chanting in your body. When you're depressed, angry, hurt, when compassion and love possess you. When you cannot help but write.

Distractions all—that I spring on myself when I'm so deep into the writing when I'm almost at that place, that dark cellar where some "thing" is liable to jump up and pounce on me. The ways I subvert the writing are many. The way I don't tap the well nor learn how to make the windmill turn.

Eating is my main distraction. Getting up to eat an apple danish. That I've been off sugar for three years is not a deterrent nor that I have to put on a coat, find the keys and go out into the San Francisco fog to get it. Getting up to light incense, to put a record on, to go for a walk—anything just to put off the writing.

Returning after I've stuffed myself. Writing paragraphs on pieces of paper, adding to the puzzle on the floor, to the confusion on my desk making completion far away and perfection impossible.

26 mayo 80

Dear mujeres de color, I feel heavy and tired and there is a buzz in my head—too many beers last night. But I must finish this letter. My bribe: to take myself out to pizza.

So I cut and paste and line the floor with my bits of paper. My life strewn on the floor in bits and pieces and I try to make some order out of it working against time, psyching myself up with decaffeinated coffee, trying to fill in the gaps.

Leslie, my housemate, comes in, gets on hands and knees to read my fragments on the floor and says, "It's good, Gloria." And I think: *I don't have to go back to Texas, to my family of land, mesquites, cactus, rattlesnakes and roadrunners. My family, this community of writers. How could I have lived and survived so long without it. And I remember the isolation, re-live the pain again.*

"To assess the damage is a dangerous act,"[5] writes Cherríe Moraga. To stop there is even more dangerous.

It's too easy, blaming it all on the white man or white feminists or society or on our parents. What we say and what we do ultimately comes back to us, so let us own our responsibility, place it in our own hands and carry it with dignity and strength. No one's going to do my shitwork, I pick up after myself.

It makes perfect sense to me now how I resisted the act of writing, the commitment to writing. To write is to confront one's demons, look them in the face and live to write about them. Fear acts like a magnet; it draws the demons out of the closet and into the ink in our pens.

The tiger riding our backs (writing) never lets us alone. *Why aren't you riding, writing, writing?* It asks constantly till we begin to feel we're vampires sucking the blood out of too fresh an experience; that we are sucking life's blood to feed the pen. Writing is the most daring thing I have ever done and the most dangerous. Nellie Wong calls writing "the three-eyed demon shrieking the truth."[6]

Writing is dangerous because we are afraid of what the writing reveals: the fears, the angers, the strengths of a woman under a triple or quadruple oppression. Yet in that very act lies our survival because a woman who writes has power. And a woman with power is feared.

What did it mean for a black woman to be an artist in our grandmother's time? It is a question with an answer cruel enough to stop the blood.

—*Alice Walker*[7]

I have never seen so much power in the ability to move and transform others as from that of the writing of women of color.

In the San Francisco area, where I now live, none can stir the audience with their craft and truthsaying as do Cherríe Moraga (Chicana), Genny Lim (Asian American), and Luisah Teish (Black). With women like these, the loneliness of writing and the sense of powerlessness can be dispelled. We can walk among each other talking of our writing, reading to each other. And more and more when I'm alone, though still in communion with each other, the writing possesses me and propels me to leap into a timeless, spaceless no-place where I forget myself and feel I am the universe. *This* is power.

It's not on paper that you create but in your innards, in the gut and out of living tissue—*organic writing* I call it. A poem works for me *not* when it says what I want it to say and *not* when it evokes what I want it to. It works when the subject I started out with metamorphoses alchemically into a different one, one that has been discovered, or uncovered, by the poem. It works when it surprises me, when it says something I have repressed or pretended not to know. The meaning and worth of my writing is measured by how much *I* put myself on the line and how much nakedness I achieve.

> Audre said we need to speak up. Speak loud, speak unsettling things and be dangerous and just fuck, hell, let it out and let everybody hear whether they want to or not.[8]
>
> *Kathy Kendall*

I say mujer magica, empty yourself. Shock yourself into new ways of perceiving the world, shock your readers into the same. Stop the chatter inside their heads.

Your skin must be sensitive enough for the lightest kiss and thick enough to ward off the sneers. If you are going to spit in the eye of the world, make sure your back is to the wind. Write of what most links us with life, the sensation of the body, the images seen by the eye, the expansion of the psyche in tranquility: moments of high intensity, its movement, sounds, thoughts. *Even though we go hungry we are not impoverished of experiences.*

> I think many of us have been fooled by the mass media, by society's conditioning that our lives must be lived in great explosions, by "falling in love," by being "swept off our feet," and by the sorcery of magic genies that will fulfill our every wish, our every childhood longing. Wishes, dreams, and fantasies are important parts of our creative lives. They are the steps a writer integrates into her craft. They are the spectrum of resources to reach the truth, the heart of things, the immediacy and the impact of human conflict.[9]
>
> *Nellie Wong*

Many have a way with words. They label themselves seers but they will not see. Many have the gift of tongue but nothing to say. Do not listen to them. Many who have words and tongue have no ear, they cannot listen and they will not hear.

There is no need for words to fester in our minds. They germinate in the open mouth of the barefoot child in the midst of restive crowds. They wither in ivory towers and in college classrooms.

Throw away abstraction and the academic learning, the rules, the map and compass. Feel your way without blinders. To touch more people, the personal realities and the social must be evoked—not through rhetoric but through blood and pus and sweat.

Write with your eyes like painters, with your ears like musicians, with your feet like dancers. You are the truthsayer with quill and torch. Write with your tongues of fire. Don't let the pen banish you from yourself. Don't let the ink coagulate in your pens. Don't let the censor snuff out the spark, nor the gags muffle your voice. Put your shit on the paper.

We are not reconciled to the oppressors who whet their howl on our grief. We are not reconciled.

Find the muse within you. The voice that lies buried under you, dig it up. Do not fake it, try to sell it for a handclap or your name in print.

Love,
Gloria
1980/1981

⇥ Notes ⇤

1. Cherríe Moraga's poem, "It's the Poverty" from *Living in the War Years*, an unpublished book of poems.
2. Alice Walker, ed., "What White Publishers Won't Print," *I Love Myself When I am Laughing—A Zora Neale Hurston Reader* (New York: Feminist Press, 1979) 169.
3. Moraga, "It's the Poverty."
4. Naomi Littlebear, *The Dark of the Moon* (Portland: Olive Press, 1977) 36.
5. Cherríe Moraga's essay, see "La Güera."
6. Nellie Wong, "Flows from the Dark of Monsters and Demons: Notes on Writing," *Radical Woman Pamphlet* (San Francisco, 1979).
7. Alice Walker, "In Search of Our Mothers' Gardens: The Creativity of Black Women in the South," *MS*, May 1974: 60.
8. Letter from Kathy Kendall, March 10, 1980, concerning a writer's workshop given by Audre Lorde, Adrienne Rich, and Meridel LeSeur.
9. Nellie Wong, "Flows from the Dark."

Alice Walker

1944–

An internationally renowned African-American novelist, poet, and essayist, Alice Walker was born in Eatonville, Georgia, to sharecropper parents, Willie Lee and Minnie Grant Walker. As she recounts in an essay entitled "Beauty: When the Other Dancer Is the Self," she sustained a serious eye injury at an early age when her brother shot her with a BB gun; this experience profoundly affected the way in which she views the world and identifies with the oppressed. She was later educated, on scholarship, at Spelman College and Sarah Lawrence College. Crucial to her political and literary development was her involvement in the civil rights movement of the 1960s as a cultural worker in rural Mississippi and a teacher at Jackson State University.

Walker's early novels and short story collections—*The Third Life of Grange Copeland* (1970), *In Love and Trouble* (1973), *Meridian* (1976), and *You Can't Keep a Good Woman Down* (1981)—examine the legacies of the struggle for civil rights, the vexed relationships between the sexes, and black women's efforts to speak for and about themselves. In 1983 her novel, *The Color Purple*, won the Pulitzer Prize for fiction, and in 1985 it was made into a movie by Steven Spielberg; the book recounts the compelling story of Celie, a Southern child-wife who survives incest and marital rape, in part through the ministerings of an unlikely ally and lover, Shug Avery, the mistress of Celie's abusive husband. *The Temple of My Familiar* (1989) explores the spiritual matrilineage and resilience of black women from ancient times to the present. Walker takes up the topic of female genital mutilation in her 1992 novel *Possessing the Secret of Joy* as well as in the 1993 documentary film *Warrior Marks* and its accompanying book, on which she collaborated with Pratibha Parmar. *By the Light of My Father's Smile*, a novel about familial healing, appeared in 1998. The power of women's bonding across generations and their resistance to racism and misogyny are central themes in all of Walker's fiction.

In *Search of Our Mothers' Gardens* (1983) is a collection of essays in which Walker develops the concept of "womanism," a woman-of-color alternative to feminism that emphasizes the value of black women's culture and experience as well as a commitment to the "survival and wholeness of entire people, male *and* female." In *Living by the Word* (1988) she further explores these concerns, along with issues of environmental protection, creative process, and spiritual healing. Her 1996 collection of essays, *The Same River Twice: Honoring the Difficult*, includes journal entries and her screenplay for *The Color Purple*. Walker has also published several volumes of poetry, including *Once* (1968) and *Revolutionary Petunias and Other Poems* (1973), and has been a contributing editor to *Ms.* magazine for many years. As a scholar she has been instrumental in bringing to light long-buried works by ZORA NEALE HURSTON and promoting Hurston's centrality to any African-American literary tradition. In 1997 she published an autobiographical work, *Anything We Love Can Be Saved: A Writer's Activism.*

Her essay "In Search of Our Mothers' Gardens" is widely recognized as a feminist classic for its exploration of the creative genius of ordinary/extraordinary black women and its powerful critique of VIRGINIA WOOLF'S omission of black women writers from her historical lexicon in *A Room of One's Own*. The spirits of black women have survived and soared, Walker marvels, despite seemingly insurmountable obstacles. They offer a rich legacy for their descendants, those granddaughters seeking to engender their own language and vision. "In search of my mother's garden," she concludes, "I found my own."

⊰ In Search of Our Mothers' Gardens ⊱

> I described her own nature and temperament. Told how they needed a larger life for their expression . . . . I pointed out that in lieu of proper channels, her emotions had overflowed into paths that dissipated them. I talked, beautifully I thought, about an art that would be born, an art that would open the way for women the likes of her. I asked her to hope, and build up an inner life against the coming of that day. . . . I sang, with a strange quiver in my voice, a promise song.
>
> —*Jean Toomer, "Avey," CANE[1]*

---

1. A novel by Toomer (1894–1967), a writer during the Harlem Renaissance.

The poet speaking to a prostitute who falls asleep while he's talking—

When the poet Jean Toomer walked through the South in the early twenties, he discovered a curious thing: black women whose spirituality was so intense, so deep, so *unconscious*, that they were themselves unaware of the richness they held. They stumbled blindly through their lives: creatures so abused and mutilated in body, so dimmed and confused by pain, that they considered themselves unworthy even of hope. In the selfless abstractions their bodies became to the men who used them, they became more than "sexual objects," more even than mere women: they became "Saints." Instead of being perceived as whole persons, their bodies became shrines: what was thought to be their minds became temples suitable for worship. These crazy Saints stared out at the world, wildly, like lunatics—or quietly, like suicides; and the "God" that was in their gaze was as mute as a great stone.

Who were these Saints? These crazy, loony, pitiful women?

Some of them, without a doubt, were our mothers and grandmothers.

In the still heat of the post-Reconstruction South, this is how they seemed to Jean Toomer: exquisite butterflies trapped in an evil honey, toiling away their lives in an era, a century, that did not acknowledge them, except as "the *mule* of the world." They dreamed dreams that no one knew—not even themselves, in any coherent fashion—and saw visions no one could understand. They wandered or sat about the countryside crooning lullabies to ghosts, and drawing the mother of Christ in charcoal on courthouse walls.

They forced their minds to desert their bodies and their striving spirits sought to rise, like frail whirlwinds from the hard red clay. And when those frail whirlwinds fell, in scattered particles, upon the ground, no one mourned. Instead, men lit candles to celebrate the emptiness that remained, as people do who enter a beautiful but vacant space to resurrect a God.

Our mothers and grandmothers, some of them: moving to music not yet written. And they waited.

They waited for a day when the unknown thing that was in them would be made known; but guessed, somehow in their darkness, that on the day of their revelation they would be long dead. Therefore to Toomer they walked, and even ran, in slow motion. For they were going nowhere immediate, and the future was not yet within their grasp. And men took our mothers and grandmothers, "but got no pleasure from it." So complex was their passion and their calm.

To Toomer, they lay vacant and fallow as autumn fields, with harvest time never in sight: and he saw them enter loveless marriages, without joy; and become prostitutes, without resistance; and become mothers of children, without fulfillment.

For these grandmothers and mothers of ours were not Saints, but Artists; driven to a numb and bleeding madness by the springs of creativity in them for which there was no release. They were Creators, who lived lives of spiritual waste, because they were so rich in spirituality—which is the basis of Art—that the strain of enduring their unused and unwanted talent drove them insane. Throwing away this spirituality was their pathetic attempt to lighten the soul to a weight their work-worn, sexually abused bodies could bear.

What did it mean for a black woman to be an artist in our grandmothers' time? In our great-grandmothers' day? It is a question with an answer cruel enough to stop the blood.

Did you have a genius of a great-great-grandmother who died under some ignorant and depraved white overseer's lash? Or was she required to bake biscuits for a
lazy backwater tramp, when she cried out in her soul to paint watercolors of sunsets,
or the rain falling on the green and peaceful pasturelands? Or was her body broken
and forced to bear children (who were more often than not sold away from her)—
eight, ten, fifteen, twenty children—when her one joy was the thought of modeling
heroic figures of rebellion, in stone or clay?

How was the creativity of the black woman kept alive, year after year and century after century, when for most of the years black people have been in America, it
was a punishable crime for a black person to read or write? And the freedom to paint,
to sculpt, to expand the mind with action did not exist. Consider, if you can bear to
imagine it, what might have been the result if singing, too, had been forbidden by
law. Listen to the voices of Bessie Smith, Billie Holiday, Nina Simone, Roberta
Flack, and Aretha Franklin,[2] among others, and imagine those voices muzzled for life.
Then you may begin to comprehend the lives of our "crazy," "Sainted" mothers and
grandmothers. The agony of the lives of women who might have been Poets, Novelists, Essayists, and Short-Story Writers (over a period of centuries), who died with
their real gifts stifled within them.

And, if this were the end of the story, we would have cause to cry out in my paraphrase of Okot p'Bitek's great poem:[3]

> O, my clanswomen
> Let us all cry together!
> Come,
> Let us mourn the death of our mother,
> The death of a Queen
> The ash that was produced
> By a great fire!
> O, this homestead is utterly dead
> Close the gates
> With *lacari* thorns,
> For our mother
> The creator of the Stool is lost!
> And all the young women
> Have perished in the wilderness!

But this is not the end of the story, for all the young women—our mothers and
grandmothers, *ourselves*—have not perished in the wilderness. And if we ask ourselves
why, and search for and find the answer, we will know beyond all efforts to erase it
from our minds, just exactly who, and of what, we black American women are.

One example, perhaps the most pathetic, most misunderstood one, can provide a
backdrop for our mothers' work: Phillis Wheatley, a slave in the 1700s.[4]

Virginia Woolf, in her book *A Room of One's Own*,[5] wrote that in order for a
woman to write fiction she must have two things, certainly: a room of her own (with
key and lock) and enough money to support herself.

What then are we to make of Phillis Wheatley, a slave, who owned not even herself? This sickly, frail black girl who required a servant of her own at times—her health

---

2. African-American blues singers.
3. *Song of Lawino* (1966) by the Ugandan poet Okot
p'Bitek (1931–1982).

4. Phillis Wheatley was America's first black poet.
5. British novelist and feminist whose most famous tract
on women and literature is *A Room of One's Own*.

was so precarious—and who, had she been white, would have been easily considered the intellectual superior of all the women and most of the men in the society of her day.

Virginia Woolf wrote further, speaking of course not of our Phillis, that "any woman born with a great gift in the sixteenth century [insert "eighteenth century," insert "black woman," insert "born or made a slave"] would certainly have gone crazed, shot herself, or ended her days in some lonely cottage outside the village, half witch, half wizard [insert "Saint"], feared and mocked at. For it needs little skill and psychology to be sure that a highly gifted girl who had tried to use her gift for poetry would have been so thwarted and hindered by contrary instincts [add "chains, guns, the lash, the ownership of one's body by someone else, submission to an alien religion"], that she must have lost her health and sanity to a certainty."

The key words, as they relate to Phillis, are "contrary instincts." For when we read the poetry of Phillis Wheatley—as when we read the novels of Nella Larsen or the oddly false-sounding autobiography of that freest of all black women writers, Zora Hurston[6]—evidence of "contrary instincts" is everywhere. Her loyalties were completely divided, as was, without question, her mind.

But how could this be otherwise? Captured at seven, a slave of wealthy, doting whites who instilled in her the "savagery" of the Africa they "rescued" her from . . . one wonders if she was even able to remember her homeland as she had known it, or as it really was.

Yet, because she did try to use her gift for poetry in a world that made her a slave, she was "so thwarted and hindered by . . . contrary instincts, that she . . . lost her health. . . ." In the last years of her brief life, burdened not only with the need to express her gift but also with a penniless, friendless "freedom" and several small children for whom she was forced to do strenuous work to feed, she lost her health, certainly. Suffering from malnutrition and neglect and who knows what mental agonies, Phillis Wheatley died.

So torn by "contrary instincts" was black, kidnapped, enslaved Phillis that her description of "the Goddess"—as she poetically called the Liberty she did not have—is ironically, cruelly humorous. And, in fact, has held Phillis up to ridicule for more than a century. It is usually read prior to hanging Phillis's memory as that of a fool. She wrote:

> The Goddess comes, she moves divinely fair,
> Olive and laurel binds her *golden* hair.
> Wherever shines this native of the skies,
> Unnumber'd charms and recent graces rise. [My italics]

It is obvious that Phillis, the slave, combed the "Goddess's" hair every morning; prior, perhaps, to bringing in the milk, or fixing her mistress's lunch. She took her imagery from the one thing she saw elevated above all others.

With the benefit of hindsight we ask, "How could she?"

But at last, Phillis, we understand. No more snickering when your stiff, struggling, ambivalent lines are forced on us. We know now that you were not an idiot or a traitor; only a sickly little black girl, snatched from your home and country and made a slave; a woman who still struggled to sing the song that was your gift, although in a land of barbarians who praised you for your bewildered tongue. It is not so much what you sang, as that you kept alive, in so many of our ancestors, *the notion of song.*

6. Zora Neale Hurston, African-American novelist and folklorist.

Black women are called, in the folklore that so aptly identifies one's status in society, "the *mule* of the world," because we have been handed the burdens that everyone else—*everyone* else—refused to carry. We have also been called "Matriarchs," "Super-women," and "Mean and Evil Bitches." Not to mention "Castraters" and "Sapphire's Mama." When we have pleaded for understanding, our character has been distorted; when we have asked for simple caring, we have been handed empty inspirational appellations, then stuck in the farthest corner. When we have asked for love, we have been given children. In short, even our plainer gifts, our labors of fidelity and love, have been knocked down our throats. To be an artist and a black woman, even today, lowers our status in many respects, rather than raises it: and yet, artists we will be.

Therefore we must fearlessly pull out of ourselves and look at and identify with our lives the living creativity some of our great-grandmothers were not allowed to know. I stress *some* of them because it is well known that the majority of our great-grandmothers knew, even without "knowing" it, the reality of their spirituality, even if they didn't recognize it beyond what happened in the singing at church—and they never had any intention of giving it up.

How they did it—those millions of black women who were not Phillis Wheatley, or Lucy Terry or Frances Harper or Zora Hurston or Nella Larsen or Bessie Smith; or Elizabeth Catlett, or Katherine Dunham, either[7]—brings me to the title of this essay, "In Search of Our Mothers' Gardens," which is a personal account that is yet shared, in its theme and its meaning, by all of us. I found, while thinking about the far-reaching world of the creative black woman, that often the truest answer to a question that really matters can be found very close.

In the late 1920s my mother ran away from home to marry my father. Marriage, if not running away, was expected of seventeen-year-old girls. By the time she was twenty, she had two children and was pregnant with a third. Five children later, I was born. And this is how I came to know my mother: she seemed a large, soft, loving-eyed woman who was rarely impatient in our home. Her quick, violent temper was on view only a few times a year, when she battled with the white landlord who had the misfortune to suggest to her that her children did not need to go to school.

She made all the clothes we wore, even my brothers' overalls. She made all the towels and sheets we used. She spent the summers canning vegetables and fruits. She spent the winter evenings making quilts enough to cover all our beds.

During the "working" day, she labored beside—not behind—my father in the fields. Her day began before sunup, and did not end until late at night. There was never a moment for her to sit down, undisturbed, to unravel her own private thoughts; never a time free from interruption—by work or the noisy inquiries of her many children. And yet, it is to my mother—and all our mothers who were not famous—that I went in search of the secret of what has fed that muzzled and often mutilated, but vibrant, creative spirit that the black woman has inherited, and that pops out in wild and unlikely places to this day.

But when, you will ask, did my overworked mother have time to know or care about feeding the creative spirit?

7. Lucy Terry (1730–1821) was a poet and fiction writer; FRANCES E. W. HARPER, a poet; Nella Larsen (1891–1964), a novelist of the Harlem Renaissance; Elizabeth Catlett (1915–), a sculptor; and Katherine Dunham (1910–) a dancer and choreographer.

The answer is so simple that many of us have spent years discovering it. We have constantly looked high, when we should have looked high—and low.

For example: in the Smithsonian Institution in Washington, D.C., there hangs a quilt unlike any other in the world. In fanciful, inspired, and yet simple and identifiable figures, it portrays the story of the Crucifixion. It is considered rare, beyond price. Though it follows no known pattern of quilt-making, and though it is made of bits and pieces of worthless rags, it is obviously the work of a person of powerful imagination and deep spiritual feeling. Below this quilt I saw a note that says it was made by "an anonymous Black woman in Alabama, a hundred years ago."

If we could locate this "anonymous" black woman from Alabama, she would turn out to be one of our grandmothers—an artist who left her mark in the only materials she could afford, and in the only medium her position in society allowed her to use.

As Virginia Woolf wrote further, in *A Room of One's Own*:

> Yet genius of a sort must have existed among women as it must have existed among the working class. [Change this to "slaves" and "the wives and daughters of sharecroppers."] Now and again an Emily Brontë or a Robert Burns [change this to "a Zora Hurston or a Richard Wright"][8] blazes out and proves its presence. But certainly it never got itself on to paper. When, however, one reads of a witch being ducked, of a woman possessed by devils [or "Sainthood"], of a wise woman selling herbs [our root workers], or even a very remarkable man who had a mother, then I think we are on the track of a lost novelist, a suppressed poet, of some mute and inglorious Jane Austen[9]. . . . Indeed, I would venture to guess that Anon, who wrote so many poems without signing them, was often a woman . . . .

And so our mothers and grandmothers have, more often than not anonymously, handed on the creative spark, the seed of the flower they themselves never hoped to see: or like a sealed letter they could not plainly read.

And so it is, certainly, with my own mother. Unlike "Ma" Rainey's songs, which retained their creator's name even while blasting forth from Bessie Smith's mouth, no song or poem will bear my mother's name.[10] Yet so many of the stories that I write, that we all write, are my mother's stories. Only recently did I fully realize this: that through years of listening to my mother's stories of her life, I have absorbed not only the stories themselves, but something of the manner in which she spoke, something of the urgency that involves the knowledge that her stories—like her life—must be recorded. It is probably for this reason that so much of what I have written is about characters whose counterparts in real life are so much older than I am.

But the telling of these stories, which came from my mother's lips as naturally as breathing, was not the only way my mother showed herself as an artist. For stories, too, were subject to being distracted, to dying without conclusion. Dinners must be started, and cotton must be gathered before the big rains. The artist that was and is my mother showed itself to me only after many years. This is what I finally noticed:

Like Mem, a character in *The Third Life of Grange Copeland*,[11] my mother adorned with flowers whatever shabby house we were forced to live in. And not just your typical straggly country stand of zinnias, either. She planted ambitious gardens—and still does—with over fifty different varieties of plants that bloom profusely from early

8. Emily Brontë was a British poet; Robert Burns (1759–96) a Scottish poet; Richard Wright (1908–60); an African-American novelist.
9. Jane Austen, nineteenth-century British novelist.

10. "Ma" Rainey (1886–1939) and Bessie Smith (1894?–1937) were black blues singers.
11. Walker's first novel, published in 1970.

March until late November. Before she left home for the fields, she watered her flowers, chopped up the grass, and laid out new beds. When she returned from the fields she might divide clumps of bulbs, dig a cold pit, uproot and replant roses, or prune branches from her taller bushes or trees—until night came and it was too dark to see.

Whatever she planted grew as if by magic, and her fame as a grower of flowers spread over three counties. Because of her creativity with her flowers, even my memories of poverty are seen through a screen of blooms—sunflowers, petunias, roses, dahlias, forsythia, spirea, delphiniums, verbena . . . and on and on.

And I remember people coming to my mother's yard to be given cuttings from her flowers; I hear again the praise showered on her because whatever rocky soil she landed on, she turned into a garden. A garden so brilliant with colors, so original in its design, so magnificent with life and creativity, that to this day people drive by our house in Georgia—perfect strangers and imperfect strangers—and ask to stand or walk among my mother's art.

I notice that it is only when my mother is working in her flowers that she is radiant, almost to the point of being invisible—except as Creator: hand and eye. She is involved in work her soul must have. Ordering the universe in the image of her personal conception of Beauty.

Her face, as she prepares the Art that is her gift, is a legacy of respect she leaves to me, for all that illuminates and cherishes life. She has handed down respect for the possibilities—and the will to grasp them.

For her, so hindered and intruded upon in so many ways, being an artist has still been a daily part of her life. This ability to hold on, even in very simple ways, is work black women have done for a very long time.

This poem is not enough, but it is something, for the woman who literally covered the holes in our walls with sunflowers:

> They were women then
> My mama's generation
> Husky of voice—Stout of
> Step
> With fists as well as
> Hands
> How they battered down
> Doors
> And ironed
> Starched white
> Shirts
> How they led
> Armies
> Headragged Generals
> Across mined
> Fields
> Booby-trapped
> Kitchens
> To discover books
> Desks
> A place for us
> How they knew what we

Must know
Without knowing a page
Of it
Themselves.

Guided by my heritage of a love of beauty and a respect for strength—in search of my mother's garden, I found my own.

And perhaps in Africa over two hundred years ago, there was just such a mother; perhaps she painted vivid and daring decorations in oranges and yellows and greens on the walls of her hut; perhaps she sang—in a voice like Roberta Flack's—*sweetly* over the compounds of her village; perhaps she wove the most stunning mats or told the most ingenious stories of all the village storytellers. Perhaps she was herself a poet—though only her daughter's name is signed to the poems that we know.

Perhaps Phillis Wheatley's mother was also an artist.

Perhaps in more than Phillis Wheatley's biological life is her mother's signature made clear.   *1974*

Medbh McGuckian
1950–

A prominent member of the "second generation of Ulster poets," Medbh McGuckian was born in Belfast, Northern Ireland, and educated at a Roman Catholic convent school. She later attended Queen's University in Belfast, and in 1979 she won England's National Poetry Competition. Her early poetry has been characterized as hermetic and mysterious, while her later work reveals a quest for creative and erotic identity and for a language that defies syntactical restrictions. McGuckian has received many honors for her poetry, including the Cheltenham Award, the Alice Hunt Bartlett Prize, and the Bass Ireland Award for Literature.

Her first major collection, *The Flower Master* (1982), followed two chapbooks, *Single Ladies* and *Portrait of Joanna*, both published in 1980; it offers as a poetic analogue such Japanese rituals as tea ceremonies and flower arranging. McGuckian's early poetry can be distinguished from that of her male counterparts by its indirect treatment of the Irish experience of civil war: her speakers are divided not only because of the violent struggle taking place around them but from gender turmoil as well. These poems thus evoke domestic landscapes rather than overtly political ones. *Venus and the Rain* (1984), for example, blends allusions to ancient fertility myths with modern household furnishings such as beds, tables, sofas, mirrors. McGuckian's density of language can be seen in *On Ballycastle Beach* (1987) and *Marconi's Cottage* (1991), in which Ireland plays a more central role than in earlier volumes; the latter book was shortlisted for the *Irish Times*/Aer Lingus Irish Literature Prize for Poetry. The poet has acknowledged that both *Captain Lavender* (1995) and *Shelmalier* (1998) were influenced by political poems she had recently taught and by the "Troubles" in Northern Ireland.

The poems included here are both enigmatic and lush in their imagery. In "To My Grandmother," an elegy, the speaker imagines calling her grandmother back to life. A more playful homage occurs in "From the Dressing-Room," which evokes as the poet's muse a "blue Lizard" whose job it is to serve her. "Turning the Moon into a Verb," a dreamlike love poem that examines time and loss, reveals the poet's capacity for imaginative transformation. The critic Christopher Benfrey describes McGuckian's poetry as "odd and fascinating and finally convincing"; *Collected Poems*, published in 1998 by Wake Forest University Press, reveal her status as a major international voice.

⊰ To My Grandmother ⊱

I would revive you with a swallow's nest:
For as long a time as I could hold my breath
I would feel your pulse like tangled weeds
Separate into pearls. The heart should rule
5   The summer, ringing like a sickle over
The need to make life hard. I would
Sedate your eyes with rippleseed, those
Hollow points that close as if
Your eyelids had been severed
10   To deny you sleep, imagine you a dawn.
I would push a chrysanthemum stone
Into your sleeve without your noticing
Its reaching far, its going, its returning.
When the end of summer comes, it is
15   A season by itself; when your tongue
Curls back like a sparrow's buried head,
I would fill your mouth with rice and mussels.

1982

⊰ From the Dressing-Room ⊱

Left to itself, they say, every fetus
Would turn female, staving in, nature
Siding then with the enemy that
Delicately mixes up genders. This
5   Is an absence I have passionately sought,
Brightening nevertheless my poet's attic
With my steady hands, calling him my blue
Lizard till his moans might be heard
At the far end of the garden. For I like
10   His ways, he's light on his feet and does
Not break anything, puts his entire soul
Into bringing me a glass of water.

I can take anything now, even his being
Away, for it always seems to me his
15   Writing is for me, as I walk springless
From the dressing-room in a sisterly
Length of flesh-coloured silk. Oh there
Are moments when you think you can
Give notice in a jolly, wifely tone,
20   Tossing off a very last and sunsetty
Letter of farewell, with strict injunctions
To be careful to procure his own lodgings,
That my good little room is lockable,
But shivery, I recover at the mere
25   Sight of him propping up my pillow.

1984

⊰ Turning the Moon into a Verb ⊱

A timeless winter
That wants to be now
Will go on taking shape in me.
Now everything can begin.

5   Everything can reach much
Further up; with this new
Listening, the longing at the window
For the missing season weakens.

When springtime had need of him,
10   He did not offer me the winter,
He took away each of the seasons
In its visual turn.

Dark does that to you also,
And the headlessness
15   Of a turning of light that mentions a green
A little darker than all other greens.

A secret year, a secret time,
Its flight is a written image
Of its cry, its capacity for sound
20   I call spring, the experience

When the sky becomes a womb,
And a vision of rivers slanting
Across the doubly opened page
Of the moon turns her into a verb.

25   An image I have consciously
Broken like a shoulder on your hearing,
The inconstancy within constancy
That is the price of a month.

1991

Carol Ann Duffy
1955–

Born in Glasgow, Scotland, and raised in Staffordshire, Carol Ann Duffy is best known as a critically acclaimed poet, but she has also written several plays. Since completing her studies in philosophy at the University of Liverpool in 1977, she has worked as a freelance writer in London and Manchester and has been poet in residence at various secondary schools and colleges in England and abroad. She has led more than thirty residential writing workshops for the Arvon Foundation and is a regular poetry reviewer and editor for the *Guardian* newspaper and for the poetry magazine *Ambit*.

    Duffy's first five volumes of poetry—*Standing Female Nude* (1985), *Thrown Voices* (1986), *Selling Manhattan* (1987), *The Other Country* (1990), and *Mean Times* (1993)—are populated by voices alienated by gender, culture, or class. A sixth collection, *The World's Wife* (1999), features the ironic personae of the wives of famous men from myth and history. Her plays include *Take My Husband* (1982) and *Cavern of Dreams* (1984), both of which were produced at the Liverpool Playhouse, and *Little Women, Big Boys* (1986). In 1992 Duffy edited an anthology of women's poetry intended for teenagers, *I Wouldn't Thank You for a Valentine*, whose title is taken from a poem by one of her contemporaries, Liz Lochhead. More recently she has edited a collection of poems for young people on death and loss, *We Do Not Play on Graves*, and a volume entitled *New Poets* for Anvil Press, which features nine rising British poets. Her *Selected Poems* (1994) contains meditations on time, change, and loss, as well as a humorous depiction of childhood and powerful evocations of love. In 1995 and again in 1997 her adaptations of stories by the brothers Grimm (aptly and comically entitled *Grimm Tales* and *More Grimm Tales*), were produced at the Young Vic Theatre in London. Duffy is currently completing a collection of children's poems.

Several volumes of Duffy's poetry have won major British awards, and she is widely considered one of England's finest younger poets. *Standing Female Nude* took first prize in the 1983 National Poetry Competition. She received Scottish Arts Council Book Awards for her first collection as well as for *The Other Country* and *Mean Time*; the latter volume also won the Forward Poetry Prize and the prestigious Whitbread Poetry Award. Reviewing *Mean Time* in the *London Times*, Sean O'Brien asserted that "poetry, like love, depends on a kind of recognition. So often with Duffy does the reader say 'Yes, that's it exactly,' that she could well become the representative poet of the present day."

Duffy's poems depict a wide range of women's voices, both comical and serious. The speaker in "Mrs. Aesop," for example, loses all patience with her husband's witless clichés, while "Litany," an autobiographical poem, evokes the speaker's childhood memory of tasting and regurgitating a tempting obscenity. Writing in the *Times Literary Supplement* of *The Other Country*, Ruth Padel describes Duffy's writing as "cabaret art, and her leg-flinging technique (the one-word sentences and buried rhymes, the dizzying control of line) can say practically anything." Practically anything is indeed what Carol Ann Duffy wants to say, since her goal is to break "the code I learnt at my mother's knee." Embarrassment, tension, and malice have little clout in Duffy's forthright world of words; language and love, for her, provide "moments of grace."

⊰ Standing Female Nude ⊱

Six hours like this for a few francs.
Belly nipple arse in the window light,
he drains the color from me. Further to the right,
Madame. And do try to be still.
5   I shall be represented analytically and hung
in great museums. The bourgeoisie will coo
at such an image of a river-whore. They call it Art.

Maybe. He is concerned with volume, space.
I with the next meal. You're getting thin,
10   Madame, this is not good. My breasts hang
slightly low, the studio is cold. In the tea-leaves
I can see the Queen of England gazing
on my shape. Magnificent, she murmurs,
moving on. It makes me laugh. His name

15   is Georges. They tell me he's a genius.
There are times he does not concentrate
and stiffens for my warmth.
He possesses me on canvas as he dips the brush

repeatedly into the paint. Little man,
20 you've not the money for the arts I sell.
Both poor, we make our living how we can.
I ask him *Why do you do this? Because
I have to. There's no choice. Don't talk.*
My smile confuses him. These artists
25 take themselves too seriously. At night I fill myself
with wine and dance around the bars. When it's finished
he shows me proudly, lights a cigarette. I say
Twelve francs and get my shawl. It does not look like me.

                                    1985

⊰ Litany ⊱

The soundtrack then was a litany—*candlewick
bedspread three piece suite display cabinet—*
and stiff-haired wives balanced their red smiles,
passing the catalog. *Pyrex.* A tiny ladder
5   ran up Mrs. Barr's American Tan leg, sly
like a rumor. Language embarrassed them.

The terrible marriages crackled, cellophane
round polyester shirts, and then The Lounge
would seem to bristle with eyes, hard
10 as the bright stones in engagement rings,
and sharp hands poised over biscuits as a word
was spelled out. An embarrassing word, broken

to bits, which tensed the air like an accident.
This was the code I learnt at my mother's knee, pretending
15 to read, where no one had cancer, or sex, or debts,
and certainly not leukaemia, which no one could spell.
The year a mass grave of wasps bobbed in a jam-jar;
a butterfly stammered itself in my curious hands.

A boy in the playground, I said, *told me
20 to fuck off*; and a thrilled, malicious pause
salted my tongue like an imminent storm. Then
uproar. *I'm sorry, Mrs. Barr, Mrs. Hunt, Mrs. Emery,
sorry, Mrs. Raine.* Yes, I can summon their names.
My mother's mute shame. The taste of soap.

                                    1985

⊰ Mrs. Aesop ⊱

By Christ, he could bore for Purgatory. He was small,
didn't prepossess. So he tried to impress. *Dead men,
Mrs. Aesop,* he'd say, *tell no tales.* Well, let me tell you now
that the bird in his hand shat on his sleeve,

5   never mind the two worth less in the bush. Tedious.

Going out was worst. He'd stand at our gate, look, then leap;
scour the hedgerows for a shy mouse, the fields
for a sly fox, the sky for one particular swallow
that couldn't make a summer. The jackdaw, according
10   to him,
envied the eagle. Donkeys would, on the whole, prefer
to be lions.

On one appalling evening stroll, we passed an old hare
snoozing in a ditch—he stopped and made a note—
15   and then, about a mile further on, a tortoise, somebody's pet,
creeping, slow as marriage, up the road. *Slow*
but certain, Mrs. Aesop, wins the race. Asshole.

What race? What sour grapes? What silk purse,
sow's ear, dog in a manger, what big fish? Some days,
20   I could barely keep awake as the story droned on
towards the moral of itself. *Action, Mrs. A., speaks louder*
than words. And that's another thing, the sex

was diabolical. I gave him a fable one night
about a little cock that wouldn't crow, a razor-sharp axe
25   with a heart blacker than the pot that called the kettle.
I'll cut off your tail, all right, I said, *to save my face.*
That shut him up. I laughed last, longest.

                                                                    1985

━━◆━━

Gcina Mhlophe
1959–

A prominent South African writer of poetry, plays, and fiction, Gcina Mhlophe is a distinguished actress, director, and storyteller as well. Born at Hammarsdale in the Natal
province, she was educated in boarding schools in the Eastern Cape. In the early 1980s
Mhlophe moved to the Johannesburg area to do domestic work during the day and write at
night. Several of her stories are set in Alexandra Women's Hostel, a dormitory in which
more than 2,000 migrant workers, including Mhlophe, lived during the heart of the
apartheid era. She began her career as a journalist in the mid–1980s, writing for *Learn and
Teach* magazine, and worked also as a radio announcer and as an actress in feature-length
underground films that documented the brutality of apartheid for residents in rural "homelands." In 1989 Mhlophe became the first black woman to serve as resident artistic director
at the prestigious Market Theatre in Johannesburg, where she had previously performed in
several productions.

    Mhlophe's best-known literary work is *Have You Seen Zandile?*, a play that received a
Fringefirst Award at the Edinburgh Theatre Festival in 1987 and has been performed in several U.S. cities, including Chicago and Baltimore. *Zandile* tells the story of a child sent to live

with her grandmother due to her mother's economic deprivation, and of the girl's traumatic loss of her "gogo" when her mother retrieves her without warning some years later. Written in collaboration with Thembi Mtshali and Maralin Vanrenen, two other South African performance artists, *Zendile* blends Zulu, Xhosa, and English to produce a powerful theatrical elegy. In addition, Mhlophe's short stories and poems have been published in several South African literary anthologies, including *Raising the Blinds* (1990), *Breaking the Silence* (1990), and *Sometimes When It Rains* (1988), which takes its title from one of her poems. These stories and poems explore apartheid's systematic exploitation of black women and celebrate the miracle of their survival. A multigeneric collection by Mhlophe, *Love Child* (1996), has been published in German; its subjects include indigenous girls' coming-of-age ceremonies, called by the fathers who perform them "going to the moon," and women's marriage and birthing rituals.

Mhlophe's writing is strongly influenced by oral history; in fact, she considers herself a contemporary practitioner of orature, since her work is multilingual and much of it is written to be performed. Since 1992 she has worked as artistic director for the Zanendaba Storytellers, a Johannesburg-based group that she founded and for whom she has written several performance pieces, including "My Grandmother, My Mother, Myself" and "From the Bones of Memory." "Storytelling is a way of teaching," Mhlophe has observed, "through stories we [South African women] can learn about our history." A Zulu word meaning "bring me a story or come with the news," Zanendaba seems an apt name for these women performers dedicated to carrying the living word—through mime, music, and drama—to township schools and storytelling festivals throughout South Africa. Mhlophe has also written several volumes of children's stories, including *The Snake with Seven Heads* (1989) and *Fudukazi's Magic* (1996); her stories have been set to music and recorded by Ladysmith Black Mambazo on their compact disk "Gift of the Tortoise: A Musical Journey through Southern Africa."

Mhlophe's writings document the political, economic, and creative plight of black women in South Africa. "The Toilet" (1987), which draws upon her painful experience as a domestic worker attempting to have a secret life as a writer, challenges VIRGINIA WOOLF'S thesis that a woman must have money and a room of her own if she is to write, for Mhlophe's protagonist, Mholo, has neither. Taken as a whole, Mhlophe's poems and stories offer lyrical homages to women struggling against apartheid and a scathing condemnation of its countless injustices.

⊰ The Toilet ⊱

Sometimes I wanted to give up and be a good girl who listened to her elders. Maybe I should have done something like teaching or nursing as my mother wished. People thought these professions were respectable, but I knew I wanted to do something different, though I was not sure what. I thought a lot about acting. . . . My mother said that it had been a waste of good money educating me because I did not know what to do with the knowledge I had acquired. I'd come to Johannesburg for the December holidays after writing my matric exams, and then stayed on, hoping to find something to do.

My elder sister worked in Orange Grove as a domestic worker, and I stayed with her in her back room. I didn't know anybody in Jo'burg except my sister's friends whom we went to church with. The Methodist church up Fourteenth Avenue was about the only outing we had together. I was very bored and lonely.

On weekdays I was locked in my sister's room so that the Madam wouldn't see me. She was at home most of the time: painting her nails, having tea with her friends, or lying in the sun by the swimming pool. The swimming pool was very close to the room, which is why I had to keep very quiet. My sister felt bad about locking me in there, but she had no alternative. I couldn't even play the radio, so she brought me books, old magazines, and newspapers from the white people. I just read every single thing I came across: *Fair Lady, Woman's Weekly,* anything. But then my sister thought I was reading too much.

"What kind of wife will you make if you can't even make baby clothes, or knit yourself a jersey? I suppose you will marry an educated man like yourself, who won't mind going to bed with a book and an empty stomach."

We would play cards at night when she kocked off, and listen to the radio, singing along softly with the songs we liked.

Then I got this temporary job in a clothing factory in town. I looked forward to meeting new people, and liked the idea of being out of that room for a change. The factory made clothes for ladies' boutiques.

The whole place was full of machines of all kinds. Some people were sewing, others were ironing with big heavy irons that pressed with a lot of steam. I had to cut all the loose threads that hang after a dress or a jacket is finished. As soon as a number of dresses in a certain style were finished, they would be sent to me and I had to count them, write the number down, and then start with the cutting of the threads. I was fascinated to discover that one person made only sleeves, another the collars, and so on until the last lady put all the pieces together, sewed on buttons, or whatever was necessary to finish.

Most people at the factory spoke Sotho, but they were nice to me—they tried to speak to me in Zulu or Xhosa,[1] and they gave me all kinds of advice on things I didn't know. There was this girl, Gwendolene—she thought I was very stupid—she called me a "bari" because I always sat inside the changing room with something to read when it was time to eat my lunch, instead of going outside to meet guys. She told me it was cheaper to get myself a "lunch boy"—somebody to buy me lunch. She told me it was wise not to sleep with him, because then I could dump him anytime I wanted to. I was very nervous about such things. I thought it was better to be a "bari" than to be stabbed by a city boy for his money.

The factory knocked off at four-thirty, and then I went to a park near where my sister worked. I waited there till half past six, when I could sneak into the house again without the white people seeing me. I had to leave the house before half past five in the mornings as well. That meant I had to find something to do with the time I had before I could catch the seven-thirty bus to work—about two hours. I would go to a public toilet in the park. For some reason it was never locked, so I would go in and sit on the toilet to read some magazine or other until the right time to catch the bus.

The first time I went into this toilet, I was on my way to the bus stop. Usually I went straight to the bus stop outside the OK Bazaars where it was well lit, and I could see. I would wait there, reading, or just looking at the growing number of cars and buses on their way to town. On this day it was raining quite hard, so I thought I would shelter in the toilet until the rain had passed. I knocked first to see if there was anyone inside. As there was no reply, I pushed the door open and went in. It smelled a little—a dryish kind of smell, as if the toilet was not used all that often, but it was quite clean compared to many "Non-European" toilets I knew. The floor was painted red and the walls were cream white. It did not look like it had been painted for a few years. I stood looking around, with the rain coming very hard on the zinc roof. The noise was comforting—to know I had escaped the wet—only a few of the heavy drops

---

1. Languages spoken by South Africa's indigenous people.

had got me. The plastic bag in which I carried my book and purse and neatly folded pink handkerchief was a little damp, but that was because I had used it to cover my head when I ran to the toilet. I pulled my dress down a little so that it would not get creased when I sat down. The closed lid of the toilet was going to be my seat for many mornings after that.

I was really lucky to have found that toilet because the winter was very cold. Not that it was any warmer in there, but once I'd closed the door it used to be a little less windy. Also the toilet was very small—the walls were wonderfully close to me—it felt like it was made to fit me alone. I enjoyed that kind of privacy. I did a lot of thinking while I sat on that toilet seat. I did a lot of daydreaming too—many times imagining myself in some big hall doing a really popular play with other young actors. At school, we took set books like *Buzani KuBawo* or *A Man for All Seasons* and made school plays which we toured to the other schools on weekends. I loved it very much. When I was even younger I had done little sketches taken from the Bible and on big days like Good Friday, we acted and sang happily.

I would sit there dreaming. . . .

I was getting bored with the books I was reading—the love stories all sounded the same, and besides that I just lost interest. I started asking myself why I had not written anything since I left school. At least at school I had written some poems, or stories for the school magazine, school competitions and other magazines like *Bona* and *Inkqubela*. Our English teacher was always so encouraging; I remembered the day I showed him my first poem—I was so excited I couldn't concentrate in class for the whole day. I didn't know anything about publishing then, and I didn't ask myself if my stories were good enough. I just enjoyed writing things down when I had the time. So one Friday, after I'd started being that toilet's best customer, I bought myself a notebook in which I was hoping to write something. I didn't use it for quite a while, until one evening.

My sister had taken her usual Thursday afternoon off, and she had delayed somewhere. I came back from work, then waited in the park for the right time to go back into the yard. The white people always had their supper at six-thirty and that was the time I used to steal my way in without disturbing them or being seen. My comings and goings had to be secret because they still didn't know I stayed there.

Then I realized that she hadn't come back, and I was scared to go out again, in case something went wrong this time. I decided to sit down in front of my sister's room, where I thought I wouldn't be noticed. I was reading a copy of *Drum Magazine* and hoping that she would come back soon—before the dogs sniffed me out. For the first time I realized how stupid it was of me not to have cut myself a spare key long ago. I kept on hearing noises that sounded like the gate opening. A few times I was sure I had heard her footsteps on the concrete steps leading to the servant's quarters, but it turned out to be something or someone else.

I was trying hard to concentrate on my reading again, when I heard the two dogs playing, chasing each other nearer and nearer to where I was sitting. And then, there they were in front of me, looking as surprised as I was. For a brief moment we stared at each other, then they started to bark at me. I was sure they would tear me to pieces if I moved just one finger, so I sat very still, trying not to look at them, while my heart pounded and my mouth went dry as paper.

They barked even louder when the dogs from next door joined in, glared at me through the openings in the hedge. Then the Madam's high-pitched voice rang out above the dogs' barking.

'Ireeeeeeeene!' That's my sister's English name, which we never use. I couldn't move or answer the call—the dogs were standing right in front of me, their teeth so threateningly long. When there was no reply, she came to see what was going on.

"Oh, it's you? Hello." She was smiling at me, chewing that gum which never left her mouth, instead of calling the dogs away from me. They had stopped barking, but they hadn't moved—they were still growling at me, waiting for her to tell them what to do.

"Please Madam, the dogs will bite me," I pleaded, not moving my eyes from them.

"No, they won't bite you." Then she spoke to them nicely, "Get away now—go on," and they went off. She was like a doll, her hair almost orange in color, all curls round her made-up face. Her eyelashes fluttered like a doll's. Her thin lips were bright red like her long nails, and she wore very high-heeled shoes. She was still smiling; I wondered if it didn't hurt after a while. When her friends came for a swim, I could always hear her forever laughing at something or other.

She scared me—I couldn't understand how she could smile like that but not want me to stay in her house.

"When did you come in? We didn't see you."

"I've been here for some time now—my sister isn't here. I'm waiting to talk to her."

"Oh—she's not here?" She was laughing, for no reason that I could see. "I can give her a message—you go on home—I'll tell her that you want to see her."

Once I was outside the gate, I didn't know what to do or where to go. I walked slowly, kicking my heels. The street lights were so very bright! Like big eyes staring at me. I wondered what the people who saw me thought I was doing, walking around at that time of the night. But then I didn't really care, because there wasn't much I could do about the situation right then. I was just thinking how things had to go wrong on that day particularly, because my sister and I were not on such good terms. Early that morning, when the alarm had gone for me to wake up, I did not jump to turn it off, so my sister got really angry with me. She had gone on about me always leaving it to ring for too long, as if it was set for her, and not for me. And when I went out to wash, I had left the door open a second too long, and that was enough to earn me another scolding.

Every morning I had to wake up straight away, roll my bedding and put it all under the bed where my sister was sleeping. I was not supposed to put on the light although it was still dark. I'd light a candle, and tiptoe my way out with a soap dish and a toothbrush. My clothes were on a hanger on a nail at the back of the door. I'd take the hanger and close the door as quietly as I could. Everything had to be ready set the night before. A washing basin full of cold water was also ready outside the door, put there because the sound of running water and the loud screech the taps made in the morning could wake the white people and they would wonder what my sister was doing up so early. I'd do my everything and be off the premises by five-thirty with my shoes in my bag—I only put them on once I was safely out of the gate. And that gate made such a noise too. Many time I wished I could jump over it and save myself all that sickening careful-careful business!

Thinking about all these things took my mind away from the biting cold of the night and my wet nose, until I saw my sister walking towards me.

"Mholo, what are you doing outside in the street?" she greeted me. I quickly briefed her on what had happened.

"Oh Yehovah! You can be so dumb sometimes! What were you doing inside in the first place? You know you should have waited for me so we could walk in together. Then I could say you were visiting or something. Now, you tell me, what am I supposed to say to them if they see you come in again? Hayi!"

She walked angrily towards the gate, with me hesitantly following her. When she opened the gate, she turned to me with an impatient whisper.

"And now why don't you come in, stupid?"

I mumbled my apologies, and followed her in. By some miracle no one seemed to have noticed us, and we quickly munched a snack of cold chicken and boiled potatoes and drank our tea, hardly on speaking terms. I just wanted to howl like a dog. I wished somebody would come and be my friend, and tell me that I was not useless, and that my sister did not hate me, and tell me that one day I would have a nice place to live . . . anything. It would have been really great to have someone my own age to talk to.

But also I knew that my sister was worried for me, she was scared of her employers. If they were to find out that I lived with her, they would fire her, and then we would both be walking up and down the streets. My eleven rand wages wasn't going to help us at all. I don't know how long I lay like that, unable to fall asleep, just wishing and wishing with tears running into my ears.

The next morning I woke up long before the alarm went off, but I just lay there feeling tired and depressed. If there was a way out, I would not have gone to work, but there was this other strong feeling or longing inside me. It was some kind of pain that pushed me to do everything at double speed and run to my toilet. I call it my toilet because that is exactly how I felt about it. It was very rare that I ever saw anybody else go in there in the mornings. It was like they all knew I was using it, and they had to lay off or something. When I went there, I didn't really expect to find it occupied.

I felt my spirits really lifting as I put on my shoes outside the gate. I made sure that my notebook was in my bag. In my haste I even forgot my lunchbox, but it didn't matter I was walking faster and my feet were feeling lighter all the time. Then I noticed that the door had been painted, and that a new window pane had replaced the old broken one. I smiled to myself as I reached the door. Before long I was sitting on that toilet seat, writing a poem.

Many more mornings saw me sitting there writing. Sometimes it did not need to be a poem; I wrote anything that came into my head—in the same way I would have done if I'd had a friend to talk to. I remember some days when I felt that I was hiding something from my sister. She did not know about my toilet in the park, and she was not in the least interested in my notebook.

Then one morning I wanted to write a story about what had happened at work the day before; the supervisor screaming at me for not calling her when I'd seen the people who stole two dresses at lunch time. I had found it really funny. I had to write about it and I just hoped there were enough pages left in my notebook. It all came back to me, and I was smiling when I reached for the door, but it wouldn't open—it was locked!

I think for the first time I accepted that the toilet was not mine after all. . . . Slowly I walked over to a bench nearby, watched the early spring sun come up, and wrote my story anyway.   1987

⊰ Sometimes When It Rains ⊱

Sometimes when it rains
I smile to myself
And think of times when as a child

I'd sit by myself
5   And wonder why people need clothes

Sometimes when it rains
I think of times
when I'd run into the rain
Shouting 'Nkce—nkce mlanjana
10   When will I grow?
I'll grow up tomorrow!'

Sometimes when it rains
I think of times
When I watched goats
15   running so fast from the rain
While sheep seemed to enjoy it

Sometimes when it rains
I think of times
When we had to undress
20   Carry the small bundles of uniforms and books
On our heads
And cross the river after school

Sometimes when it rains
I remember times
25   When it would rain hard for hours
And fill our drum
so we didn't have to fetch water
From the river for a day or two

Sometimes when it rains
30   Rains for many hours without break
I think of people
who have nowhere to go
No home of their own
And no food to eat
35   Only rain water to drink

Sometimes when it rains
Rains for days without break
I think of mothers
Who give birth in squatter camps
40   Under plastic shelters
At the mercy of cold angry winds

Sometimes when it rains
I think of 'illegal' job seekers
in big cities
45   Dodging police vans in the rain
Hoping for darkness to come
So they can find some wet corner to hide in

Sometimes when it rains
Rains so hard hail joins in
50   I think of life prisoners
in all the jails of the world

And wonder if they still love
To see the rainbow at the end of the rain

Sometimes when it rains
55   With hail stones biting the grass
I can't help thinking they look like teeth
Many teeth of smiling friends
Then I wish that everyone else
Had something to smile about.

1987

⊰ The Dancer ⊱

Mama,
they tell me you were a dancer
they tell me you had long
beautiful legs to carry your graceful body
5   they tell me you were a dancer

Mama,
they tell me you sang beautiful solos
they tell me you closed your eyes
always when the feeling of the song
10   was right, and lifted your face up to the sky
they tell me you were an enchanting dancer

Mama
they tell me you were always so gentle
they talk of a willow tree
15   swaying lovingly over clear running water
in early Spring when they talk of you
they tell me you were a slow dancer

Mama
they tell me you were a wedding dancer
20   they tell me you smiled and closed your eyes
your arms curving outward just a little
and your feet shuffling in the sand;
tshi tshi tshitshitshitha, tshitshi tshitshitshitha
o hee! how I wish I was there to see you
25   they tell me you were a pleasure to watch

Mama
they tell me I am a dancer too
but I don't know . . .
I don't know for sure what a wedding dancer is
30   there are no more weddings
but many, many funerals
where we sing and dance
running fast with the coffin
of a would-be bride or would-be groom
35   strange smiles have replaced our tears
our eyes are full of vengeance, Mama

Dear, dear Mama,
they tell me I am a funeral dancer.

1983–88/1990

⊰ Say No ⊱

Say No, Black Woman
Say No
When they call your jobless son
a Tsotsi[2]
5   Say No

Say No, Black Woman
Say No
When they call
Your husband at the age of 60
10   a boy
Say No

Say No, Black Woman
Say No
When they rape your daughter
15   in detention and call her
a whore
Say No

Say No, Black Woman
Say No
20   When they call your white sister
a madam
Say No

Say No, Black Woman
Say No
25   When they call your white brother
a Baas
Say No

Say No, Black woman
Say No
30   When they call a trade unionist
a terrorist
Say No

Say No, Black Woman
Say No
35   When they give you a back seat
in the liberation wagon
Say No
Yes Black Woman
a Big NO

1990

---

2. A racial slur used in apartheid South Africa.

Intertextualities

The purpose of "Intertextualities" is to help you understand the theoretical essays included in Section I—*A Room of One's Own* by Virginia Woolf and "Talking Back" by bell hooks—and to stimulate your critical thinking about all the readings in this section of the anthology. For example, the essays by Woolf and hooks might assist you in analyzing literary works by writers as diverse as Margaret Cavendish, Alice Walker, and Gcina Mhlophe. "Intertextualities" also invites you to consider the ideas of two feminist literary critics: Barbara Christian on black feminist criticism and Elaine Showalter on gynocriticism. Their critical articles provide further thoughts on issues of language, silence, and voice. Finally, the questions below offer you ideas for scholarly and creative writing about these subjects.

∽ Topics for Discussion, Journals, and Essays ∾

1. Write a dialogue between Woolf and hooks (or Woolf and Walker, or Walker and hooks) on the topic of women's creative identity, based on what you have learned from reading their essays. What are their points of contact and divergence? Consider thematic and psychological issues of breaking silence and finding voice; material issues of space, time, publishing opportunities; and aesthetic issues such as incandescence, a "woman's sentence," the "notion of song."

2. Barbara Christian offers the observation that Alice Walker, in "In Search of Our Mothers' Gardens," "turned the *idea* of Art on its head. Instead of looking high, she suggested, we should look low. On that low ground she found a multitude of artist-mothers—the women who'd transformed the material to which they'd had access into their conception of Beauty." Assume that you are a feminist critic committed to the approach of "looking low" that Christian and Walker describe. What kinds of "artist-mothers" do you find represented in hooks's "Talking Back," Walker's "In Search of Our Mothers' Gardens," Woolf's *A Room of One's Own*, and Mhlophe's "The Toilet"? What do you learn when you "hear the voiceless" that you might not learn by "looking high"?

3. If Virginia Woolf were alive in the twenty-first century to read hooks, Walker, and Mhlophe, how might she revise her thesis in *A Room of One's Own* that what women need in order to write is money and their own rooms? On what bases might she make these changes? Consider especially Walker's homage to and implicit critique of Woolf in "In Search of Our Mothers' Gardens." Which concepts from *A Room* would Woolf hold fast to and decide not to change?

4. Describe in your own words how Elaine Showalter defines "gynocriticism" in "Feminist Criticism in the Wilderness." Then, working as a gynocritic, describe the poetic language and voice in Walker's poem "Women" (incorporated into the text of "In Search of Our Mothers' Gardens"), Cavendish's "The Poetess's Hasty Resolution," and Mhlophe's "The Dancer." How do images of strength, lightness, and adversity function in each? In which lines do we find elegiac qualities, and to what end: who or what is being mourned or celebrated? To what extent can each poem's speaker be described as "gender marked"?

5. Showalter claims that gynocritics use four approaches to examine women's writing: "biological, linguistic, psychoanalytic, and cultural." The first model emphasizes women's bodies, the second women's language, the third women's psyche, and the fourth women's culture. After rereading Showalter's essay, use one of these models to write a gynocritical analysis of Mhlophe's "The Toilet" and the predicament in which the protagonist, Mholo, finds herself. Explain why you chose the model that you did. How well did it work as a tool for analyzing this story?

6. To what extent do the prose and poetry of Margaret Cavendish reveal her to be a seventeenth-century Judith Shakespeare? What historical obstacles and opportunities did

Cavendish face that were similar to those of Woolf's imaginary Judith? What might Woolf have misunderstood about Cavendish? As part of your analysis consider the passages from Woolf that discuss Cavendish and her work, along with the biographical headnote on Cavendish (*LAWL* 89).

7. In their essays Woolf, hooks, and Walker build arguments about the historical difficulties and strengths of women writers, using a combination of logical and emotional appeal. Examine the rhetorical strategies each uses—e.g., find effective examples of logical appeal, emotional appeal, digressions, interruptions, quotes from other writers, satire or irony, anger, personal anecdote, metaphor, peroration. Which of these strategies contribute most significantly to making each writer's essay a compelling feminist critique as well as an aesthetically appealing literary work?

✍ Group Writing and Performance Exercise: ✍

If your teacher asks you to lead class discussion for a day, choose someone to play the role of Virginia Woolf, who is miraculously available to others in the class for an interview. Then count off 1, 2, 3, 4 until everyone has a number; divide into four small groups by number, and sit in a circle with Woolf in the middle. The 1's are to adopt the voice of Margaret Cavendish, the 2's of Alice Walker, the 3's of Gcina Mhlophe, the 4's of bell hooks. Take a few minutes to consult with the members of each small group. What questions does the writer each group is representing want to ask Woolf? You might concentrate on questions related to engendering language, silence, and voice. Conduct the interview with the 1's asking the first question, the 2's the second, etc.

Write up your findings. What did you learn from this exercise about Woolf? About the historical circumstances of the writer whose voice you adopted? About the topic of engendering language, silence, voice? About the writings by these authors and critics that you have studied?

⊷ ⋈ ⊶

Barbara Christian
1943–

A feminist scholar and critic, Barbara Christian is best known for her groundbreaking work of African-American literary history, *Black Women Novelists: The Development of a Tradition, 1892–1976* (1980). This study, which examines the origins and evolution of a black women's literary movement, won the Before Columbus American Book Award for 1983. Christian is currently Professor of Afro-American Studies and Women's Studies at the University of California at Berkeley.

Christian was born in 1943 in St. Thomas, Virgin Islands. She received her B.A. from Marquette University in 1963, her M.A. from Columbia University in 1964, and her Ph.D. from Columbia in 1970. Divorced and the mother of one daughter, Christian has taught at UC-Berkeley since 1971 and served as chair of the Afro-American Studies Department from 1978 to 1986; she has also been president of the Women's Studies Board. Among her many honors are a 1994 MELUS Award from the Modern Language Association for her contributions to ethnic studies and African-American scholarship, a 1994 City of Berkeley Icon Award for community service, the Louise Patterson African-American Studies Award for 1992 and 1995, and the Gwendolyn Brooks Center Award for 1995.

Christian's second book, *Black Feminist Criticism: Perspectives on Black Women Writers* (1985), consists of seventeen essays on such topics as black women and motherhood, women's processes of self-discovery, and the influence of slave narratives, oral history, jazz, and blues on African-American fiction by women. She is also the author of *From the Insight Out: Afro-American Women's Literary Tradition and the State* (1987). In 1994 Christian edited and wrote an introduction to Alice Walker's popular story *Everyday Use*, and in 1997 she co-edited, with Elizabeth Abel and Helene Moglen, *Female Subjects in Black and White: Race, Psychoanalysis, Feminism*. In addition, Christian has made her mark as an editor of literary journals: *Feminist Studies* (1984–92), *Black American Literary Forum* (1985–90), and *Sage* (1987–89). In the early 1990s she edited the journal *Contentions*.

The article by Christian included here, "The Highs and Lows of Black Feminist Criticism," first appeared in *Reading Black, Reading Feminist* (1990), ed. Henry Louis Gates, Jr. In part a meditation on Alice Walker's essay "In Search of Our Mothers' Gardens," Christian's work addresses the American academy's "race to theory" (the title of another of her essays) and her decision as an African-American feminist critic to absent herself from that race. Instead, she urges readers to look "low" as well as "high" for their literary models and influences, and to interrogate the elitist assumptions that underlie such categories as "high" and "low" art.

◄ The Highs and the Lows of Black Feminist Criticism ►

In her essay, "In Search of Our Mothers' Gardens," Alice Walker asked the questions, "What is my literary tradition? Who are the black women artists who preceded me? Do I have a ground to stand on?"[1] Confronted by centuries of Afro-American women who, but for an exceptional few, lived under conditions antithetical to the creation of Art as it was then defined, how could she claim a creative legacy of foremothers, women who after all had no access to the pen, to paints, or to clay? If American cultural history was accurate, singing was the only art form in which black women participated.

But Walker turned the *idea* of Art on its head. Instead of looking high, she suggested, we should look low. On that low ground she found a multitude of artist-mothers— the women who'd transformed the material to which they'd had access into their conception of Beauty: cooking, gardening, quilting, storytelling. In retrieving that low ground, Walker not only reclaimed her foremothers, she pointed to a critical approach. For she reminded us that Art, and the thought and sense of beauty on which it is based, is the province not only of those with a room of their own, or of those in libraries, universities and literary Renaissances—that *creating* is necessary to those who work in kitchens and factories, nurture children and adorn homes, sweep streets or harvest crops, type in offices or manage them.

In the early seventies, when anyone asked me, "What do you think you're doing anyway? What is this Black Feminist Literary Critic thing you're trying to become?" I would immediately think of Alice's essay.

Like any other critic, my personal history has much to do with what I hear when I read. Perhaps because I am from the Caribbean, Alice's *high* and *low* struck chords in me. I'd grown up with a sharp division between the "high" thought, language, behavior expected in school and in church, and the "low" language that persisted at home and in the yards and the streets.

1. Alice Walker is a contemporary African-American novelist and poet.

IN SCHOOL: Proper English, Romanesque sentences, Western philosophy, jargon and exegesis; boys always before girls, lines and lines; *My Country 'Tis of Thee*, the authority of the teacher.

IN CHURCH: Unintelligible Latin and Greek, the canon, the text; the Virgin Mary and the nuclear family; priests always before nuns; Gregorian chant and tiptoeing.

AT HOME: Bad English, raunchy sayings and stories, the intoning of toasts; women in the kitchen, the parlor *and* the market; kallaloo, loud supper talk, cousins, father, aunts, god-mothers.

IN THE YARDS: Sashaying and bodies, sweat, calypso, long talk and plenty voices; women and men bantering, bad words, politics and bambooshaying.

What was real? The high, though endured, was valued. The low, though enjoyed, was denigrated even by the lowest of the low.

As I read *Jane Eyre*, I wondered what women dreamt as they gazed at men and at the sea. I knew that women as well as men gazed. My mother and aunts constantly assessed men's bodies, the sea's rhythm. But Charlotte Brontë was in print.[2] She had a language across time and space. I could not find my mother's language, far less her attitude, in any books, despite the fact that her phrasing was as complex and as subtle as Charlotte's.

Because of the 1950s (which for me was not the Eisenhower years but rather the Civil Rights movement, rhythm 'n' blues, and the works of James Baldwin), because of the 1960s (which for me was not the Free Speech Movement and the Weather-men, but rather SNCC, SEEK, the Black Muslims, Aretha and the Black Arts Move-ment), the *low* began to be valued by some of us.[3] Yet there remained the high and the low for many black women. Camouflaged by the rhetoric of the period, we were, on high ground, a monolithic Harriet Tubman or a silent Queen of Africa; on low ground, we were screaming sapphires or bourgeois bitches.[4]

But what were we saying, writing? By the early seventies, I knew some black women had written. I'd read Phillis Wheatley, Gwendolyn Brooks, and Lorraine Hansberry. I'd heard poets like Nikki Giovanni and June Jordan read. I'd known women in my childhood and adolescence who'd written stories. Yet I had never, in my years of formal schooling from kindergarten in the black Virgin Islands through a Ph.D. at white Columbia, heard even the name of *one* black woman writer. That women writers were studied, I knew. I'd had courses in which Jane Austen, George Eliot, Emily Dickinson, and Virginia Woolf appeared like fleeting phantoms.[5] I knew the university knew that black male writers existed. My professors bristled at the names of Richard Wright and James Baldwin and barely acknowledged Langston Hughes and Ralph Ellison.[6]

2. Charlotte Brontë was a British novelist; *Jane Eyre* (1847) is her most famous novel.

3. James Baldwin (1924–1987) was an African-American novelist and essayist. The Free Speech Movement flourished during the 1960s on U.S. campuses, especially at the University of California at Berkeley. The Weathermen were a revolutionary group that split off from the Students for a Democratic Society in 1969. SNCC (Student Nonviolent Coordinating Committee) was a group organized in 1960 to coordinate students' widespread civil rights protests. SEEK was a program at Hunter College in the 1960s designed to empower black youth. Black Muslims refers to members of the Nation of Islam, a black nationalist and religious group founded around 1930 by W. D. Fard. Aretha Franklin is an African-American rock and soul singer.

4. Harriet Tubman (1820–1913) was an American aboli-tionist who escaped from slavery in 1849 and thereafter helped more than 300 other slaves escape to the North on the Underground Railroad.

5. Phillis Wheatley was America's first black poet; Gwen-dolyn Brooks is a contemporary African-American poet; Lorraine Hansberry (1930–65) was a black playwright; Nikki Giovanni (1943–) and June Jordan (1936–) are African-American poets; Jane Austen and George Eliot were nineteenth-century British novelists; Emily Dickin-son was a nineteenth-century American poet; Virginia Woolf was a British novelist and essayist.

6. Richard Wright (1908–60) and Ralph Ellison (1914–1997) were African-American novelists; Langston Hughes (1902–69) was an African-American poet, nov-elist, and playwright.

But what of black women writers? No phantoms, no bristlings—not even a mention. Few of us knew they wrote; fewer of us cared. In fact, who even perceived of us, as late as the early 1970s, as writers, artists, thinkers? Why should anyone want to know what we thought or imagined? What could we tell others, far less show them, that they did not already know? After all, weren't we, as Mister taunts Celie, "black" "pore," woman, and therefore "nothing at all?"[7]

Of course we were telling stories, playing with language, speculating and specifying, reaching for wisdom, transforming the universe in our image.

Who but us could end a harrowing tale with these words to her tormentors?

Frado has passed from their memories as Joseph from the butler's but she will never cease to track them *till* beyond mortal vision. (Harriet Wilson, *Our Nig*)[8]

Who but us could use the image of a Plum Bun for the intersection of racism and sexism in this country? (Jessie Fauset, *Plum Bun*)[9]

Who but us could begin her story with this comment?

Now, women forget all those things they don't want to remember and remember everything they don't want to forget. The dream is the truth. Then they act and do things accordingly. (Zora Neale Hurston, *Their Eyes Were Watching God*)[10]

Who but us could lovingly present women poets in the kitchen? (Paule Marshall, *Poets in the Kitchen*)[11]

Who but us could tell how it was possible to clean the blood off [our] beaten men and yet receive abuse from the victim? (Toni Morrison, *The Bluest Eye*)[12]

Who but us could chant:

momma/momma/mammy/nanny/granny
woman/mistress/sista luv
(June Jordan, Trying to Get Over)[13]

But who knew that we knew? Even those of us who were telling stories or writing did not always see ourselves as artists of the word. And those of us who did know our genius were so rejected, unheard that we sometimes became crazy women crying in the wind or silenced scarecrows. Who could answer us but us? For us did need us if only to validate that which we knew, we knew. The publications of first novels, Toni Morrison's *The Bluest Eye*, Alice Walker's *The Third Life of Grange Copeland*, June Jordan's *His Own Where*, heralded the decade of the seventies.[14] While their novels were barely acknowledged in 1970, the movement of women all over the world was highlighted by American women who had some access to the Big Capital Media. Inspired, though sometimes disappointed, by movements of people of color, of blacks in the United States, of liberation struggles of "underdeveloped" nations, some American women began to seek themselves as women and to protest the truncated definition of woman in this society. In this context the

---

7. Mister and Celie are characters in Alice Walker's *The Color Purple* (1982).
8. Harriet Wilson (1828?–70?) was an African-American novelist; *Our Nig* (1859) was the first novel by an African-American to be published in the United States.
9. Jessie Redmon Fauset (1882–1961) was an African-American poet and novelist; *Plum Bun* (1929) chronicles the life of a black woman who passes for white, denying her racial heritage, but still confronts sexism in society.
10. Zora Neale Hurston was an African-American novel-

ist and ethnographer; she published *Their Eyes Were Watching God* in 1937.
11. Paule Marshall (1929–) is an African-American novelist; "Poets in the Kitchen" (1983) is one of her essays about women and creativity.
12. Toni Morrison, an African-American novelist, published *The Bluest Eye* in 1970.
13. June Jordan published this poem in 1977.
14. *The Third Life of Grange Copeland* appeared in 1970, *His Own Where* in 1971.

literature of women, the critical responses of women were published as never before during a decade when many others were asserting that *The* Movement was dead.

For those of us who came out of the sixties, the vision of women moving all over the world was not solely a claiming of our rights but also the rights of all those who had been denied their humanity. In the space created for us by our foremothers, by our sisters in the streets, the houses, the factories, the schools, we were now able to speak and to listen to each other, to hear our own language, to refine and critique it across time and space, through the written word. For me that dialogue is the kernel of what a black feminist literary critic tries to do. We listen to those of us who speak, write, read, to those who have written, to those who may write. We write to those who write, read, speak, may write, and we try to hear the voiceless. We are participants in a many-voiced palaver of thought/feeling, image/language that moves us to move—toward a world where, like Alice Walker's revolutionary petunias, all of us can bloom.[15]

We found that in order to move beyond prescribed categories we had to "rememory"—reconstruct our past. But in the literary church of the sixties, such an appeal to history was anathema. Presiding at the altar were the new critic priests, for whom the text was God, unstained by history, politics, experience, the world. Art for them was artifact. So, for example, the literature of blacks could not be literature, tainted as it was by what they called sociology. To the side of the altar were the pretenders, the political revolutionaries and new philosophers for whom creative works were primarily a pretext to expound their own ideas, their world programs. For both groups, women were neither the word nor the world, though sometimes we could be dots on some i's, muses or furies in the service of the text or the idea.

We found that we could not talk to either group unless we talked their talk, which was specialized, abstract—on high ground. So we learned their language only to find that its character had a profound effect on the questions we thought, the images we evoked, and that such thinking recalled a tradition beyond which we had to move if *we* were to be included in any authentic dialogue.

Because language is one (though not the only) way to express what one knows/feels even when one doesn't know one knows it, because storytelling *is* a dynamic form of remembering/recreating, we found that it was often in the relationship between literatures and the world that re-visioning occurred. It is often in the poem, the story, the play, rather than in Western philosophical theorizing, that feminist thought/feeling evolves, challenges and renews itself. So our Sister-bonding was presented and celebrated in novels like *Sula*, our body/spirit/erotic in works like *The Color Purple*, our revision of biography in works like *Zami*.[16] It has often been through our literatures that women have renamed critical areas of human life: mothering, sexuality, bodies, friendship, spirituality, economics, the process of literature itself. And it was to these expressions that many of us turned in order to turn to ourselves as situated in a dynamic rather than a fixed world. For many of us such a turning led us to universities where words, ideas, are, were supposed to be nurtured and valued.

And—ah, here's the rub.

As a result of the gravitation, we *have* moved to excavate the past and restore to ourselves the words of many of our foremothers who were buried in the rumble of dis-

---

15. *Revolutionary Petunias* (1973) is a volume of poetry by Walker.
16. *Sula* (1973) by Toni Morrison and *The Color Purple*

(1982) by Alice Walker are popular novels that focus on black women; *Zami* (1982) is an autobiography by the African-American poet Audre Lorde.

torted history. We have questioned the idea of great works of literature, preferences clearly determined by a powerful elite. We have asked why some forms are not considered literature—for example, the diary, the journal, the letter. We have built journals and presses through which the works of women might be published. We have developed women's studies programs. Using our stories and images, we have taught our daughters and sons about ourselves, our sisters, brothers, and lovers about our desires. And some of us have shared a palaver with our writers/readers that prompts us all to re-vision ourselves.

Yet even as we moved, the high, the low persisted, in fact moved further and further apart. For we now confronted the revelation we always knew, that there is both a She and there are many she's. And that sometimes, in our work we seemed to reduce the *both-and* to *either-or*. That revelation made itself strongly felt in the exclusion that women of color protested when Woman was defined, in the rejection that many working-class women experienced when Woman was described. The awareness that we too seek to homogenize the world of our Sisters, to fix ourselves in boxes and categories through jargon, theory, abstraction, is upon us.

Why so? Has our training led us back to the high ground that had rejected us, our education to the very language that masked our existence? So often feminist literary discussion seems riveted on defining Woman in much the same way that Western medieval scholars tried to define God. Why is it that rather than acknowledging that we are both-and, we persist in seeking the either-or. Might that be because the either-or construction, the either-or deconstruction, is so embedded in our education? Might it be because that language, whether it moves us anywhere or not, is recognized, rewarded as brilliant, intellectual, high, in contrast to the low, vulgar, ordinary language of most creative writers and readers? Is it that we too are drawn to the power that resides on the high ground?

Even as we turned to our literatures, in which language is not merely an object but is always situated in a context, in which the pleasure and emotion of language are as important as its meaning, we have gravitated toward a critical language that is riddled with abstraction and is as distanced as possible from the creative work, and from pleasure. I sometimes wonder if we critics read stories and poems, or, if as our language indicates, our reading fare is primarily that of other critics and philosophers? Do we know our own literatures? Why, for example, does it appear that white feminist critics have abandoned their contemporary novelists? Where is the palaver among them? Or are Freud, Lacan, Barthes, Foucault, Derrida inevitably more appealing?[17] Why are we so riveted on male thinkers, preferably dead or European? Why is it that in refuting essence, we become so fixed on essence? To whom are we writing when we write? Have we turned so far round that we have completed our circle? Is it that we no longer see any connections between the emotion/knowing language of women's literature, the many-voiced sounds of our own language and the re-visioning we seek?

Now when I think of Alice's *high* and *low*, I feel a new meaning. Because I am a black literary/feminist critic, I live in a sharp distinction between the high world of lit crit books, journals, and conferences, the middle world of classrooms and graduate students, and the low world of bookstores, kitchens, communities, and creative writers.

17. Sigmund Freud (1856–1939) was an Austrian neurologist and the founder of psychoanalysis; Jacques Lacan (1901–81) was a French psychoanalyst; Lacan, Roland Barthes (1915–80), Michel Foucault (1926–84), and Jacques Derrida (1930–) are French literary theorists whose philosophies have greatly influenced late twentieth-century Anglo-American literary studies.

IN THE HIGH WORLD: Discourse, theory, the canon, the body, the boys (preferably Lacan, Derrida, and Foucault) before the girls; linguistics, the authority of the critic, the exclusion of creative writings.
IN THE MIDDLE WORLD: Reading the texts, sometimes of creative writers; negotiating between advancement and appreciation; tropes, research, discourse; now I understand my mother; narrative strategies. What does it mean? The race for theory.
IN THE LOW WORLD: Stories, poems, plays. The language of the folk. Many bodies— the feeling as one with June, Alice, Toni.
I sure know what she's talking about.
I don't want to hear that.
Her words move me.
That poem changed my life.

I dream like that.
That's really disturbing.
God—that's beautiful.
Perhaps I'm not so crazy after all.
I want to write too.
Say what?

Much, of course, can be learned by all of us from all of us who speak, read, write, including those of us who look high. But as we look high, we might also look low, lest we devalue women in the world even as we define *Woman*. In ignoring their voices, we may not only truncate our movement but we may also limit our own process until our voices no longer sound like women's voices to anyone.   *1990*

⊷ ⊰◈⊱ ⊶

Elaine Showalter
1941–

ELAINE SHOWALTER established her reputation as America's foremost feminist critic with the publication of *A Literature of Their Own: British Women Novelists from Brontë to Lessing* (1977), a study that emphasizes the importance of retrieving women writers from the margins of the male literary canon. In that work and in her essay "Towards a Feminist Poetics" (1979) she coined the term "gynocriticism" to describe a critical practice concerned with "*woman as writer*—with woman as the producer of textual meaning, with the history, themes, genres and structures of literature by women." Showalter distinguished gynocriticism from "feminist critique," which she labeled "essentially political and polemical" in its Marxist overtones and problematic in its emphasis on theoretical texts by men. During the 1980s gynocriticism became one of the dominant modes of feminist criticism practiced in the United States.

Showalter was born in Boston to Paul Cottler, a self-made businessman originally from Kiev, and Violet Rottenberg Cottler. After receiving a B.A. from Bryn Mawr in 1962, she married English Showalter, a professor; they have a daughter, Vinca, and a son, Michael. Showalter went on to complete her M.A. at Brandeis in 1964 and her Ph.D. at the University of California at Davis in 1970, and from 1970 to 1983 she worked as a professor of English and women's studies at Rutgers University. Since 1984 she has been professor of English at Princeton University. Showalter was a charter member of the Modern Language Association's Commission on the Status of Women in the Profession, and in 1998 she served as president of the MLA.

Other books by Showalter include *The Female Malady: Women, Madness and English Culture 1830–1980* (1987), a landmark work of feminist cultural history; *Sexual Anarchy* (1990), which offers the concept of "endism" to theorize *fin de siècle* literature; *Sister's Choice: Tradition and Change in American Women's Writing* (1991), a study of fiction by Louisa May Alcott, KATE CHOPIN, and EDITH WHARTON, among others; and *Hystories: Hysterical Epidemics and Modern Culture* (1997), her most interdisciplinary work to date. Among her edited volumes are *Women's Liberation and Literature* (1971), the first textbook on women and literature; *The New Feminist Criticism* (1985), a major collection of essays that helped to define the field; *Speaking of Gender* (1989), a volume of essays on literature and gender studies; *Alternative Alcott* (1988), an edition of Alcott's lesser-known works; *These Modern Women* (1989), a selection of women's autobiographical writings from the 1920s; and *Where Are You Going, Where Have You Been* (1994), an edition of critical essays on Joyce Carol Oates's story by that title.

"Feminist Criticism in the Wilderness" (1981), which appeared originally in *Critical Inquiry* and was reprinted in *The New Feminist Criticism*, argues that women's writing is a "double-voiced discourse" that embodies the literary, social, and cultural legacy of "both the muted and the dominant." After critiquing feminist theoretical pluralism, Showalter suggests that female cultural analysis, an expanded form of gynocriticism, holds promise for unifying feminist theory.

⊰ Feminist Criticism in the Wilderness ⊱

PLURALISM AND THE FEMINIST CRITIQUE

Women have no wilderness in them,
They are provident instead
Content in the tight hot cell of
    their hearts
To eat dusty bread.

                        LOUISE BOGAN, "Women"[1]

In a splendidly witty dialogue of 1975, Carolyn Heilbrun and Catharine Stimpson identified two poles of feminist literary criticism.[2] The first of these modes, righteous, angry, and admonitory, they compared to the Old Testament, "looking for the sins and errors of the past." The second mode, disinterested and seeking "the grace of imagination," they compared to the New Testament. Both are necessary, they concluded, for only the Jeremiahs of ideology can lead us out of the "Egypt of female servitude" to the promised land of humanism.[3] Matthew Arnold also thought that literary critics might perish in the wilderness before they reached the promised land of disinterestedness; Heilbrun and Stimpson were neo-Arnoldian as befitted members of the Columbia and Barnard faculties.[4] But if, in the 1980s, feminist literary critics are still wandering in the wilderness, we are in good company; for, as Geoffrey Hartman tells us, *all* criticism is in the wilderness.[5] Feminist critics may be startled to find ourselves in this band of theoretical pioneers, since in the American literary tradition the wilderness has been an exclusively masculine domain. Yet between feminist ideology and the liberal ideal of disinterestedness lies the wilderness of theory, which we too must make our home.

Until very recently, feminist criticism has not had a theoretical basis; it has been an empirical orphan in the theoretical storm. In 1975, I was persuaded that no theoretical manifesto could adequately account for the varied methodologies and ideologies which called themselves feminist reading or writing.[6] By the next year, Annette Kolodny had added her observation that feminist literary criticism appeared "more like a set of interchangeable strategies than any coherent school or shared goal orientation."[7] Since then, the expressed goals have not been notably unified. Black critics protest the "massive silence" of feminist criticism about black and Third-World women writers and call for a black feminist aesthetic that would deal with both racial and sexual politics. Marxist feminists wish to focus on class along with gender as a crucial determinant of literary production.[8] Literary historians want to uncover a lost tradition. Critics trained in deconstructionist methodologies wish to "synthesize a literary criticism that is both textual and feminist."[9] Freudian and Lacanian critics want to theorize about women's relationship to language and signification.

An early obstacle to constructing a theoretical framework for feminist criticism was the unwillingness of many women to limit or bound an expressive and dynamic enterprise. The openness of feminist criticism appealed particularly to Americans who perceived the structuralist, post-structuralist, and deconstructionist debates of the 1970s as arid and falsely objective, the epitome of a pernicious masculine discourse from which many feminists wished to escape. Recalling in *A Room of One's Own* how she had been prohibited from entering the university library, the symbolic sanctuary of the male *logos,* Virginia Woolf wisely observed that while it is "unpleasant to be locked out . . . it is worse, perhaps, to be locked in." Advocates of the antitheoretical position traced their descent from Woolf and from other feminist visionaries, such as Mary Daly, Adrienne Rich, and Marguerite Duras, who had satirized the sterile narcissism of male scholarship and celebrated women's fortunate exclusion from its patriarchal methodolatry. Thus for some, feminist criticism was an act of resistance to theory, a confrontation with existing canons and judgments, what Josephine Donovan calls "a mode of negation within a fundamental dialectic." As Judith Fetterley declared in her book, *The Resisting Reader,* feminist criticism has been characterized by "a resistance to codification and a refusal to have its parameters prematurely set." I have discussed elsewhere, with considerable sympathy, the suspicion of monolithic systems and the rejection of scientism in literary study that many feminist critics have voiced. While scientific criticism struggled to purge itself of the subjective, feminist criticism reasserted the authority of experience.[10]

Yet it now appears that what looked like a theoretical impasse was actually an evolutionary phase. The ethics of awakening have been succeeded, at least in the universities, by a second stage characterized by anxiety about the isolation of feminist criticism from a critical community increasingly theoretical in its interests and indifferent to women's writing. The question of how feminist criticism should define itself with relation to the new critical theories and theorists has occasioned sharp debate in Europe and the United States. Nina Auerbach has noted the absence of dialogue and asks whether feminist criticism itself must accept responsibility:

> Feminist critics seem particularly reluctant to define themselves to the uninitiated. There is a sense in which our sisterhood has become too powerful; as a school, our belief in ourself is so potent that we decline communication with the networks of power and respectability we say we want to change.[11]

But rather than declining communication with these networks, feminist criticism has indeed spoken directly to them, in their own media: *PMLA, Diacritics, Glyph, Tel*

Quel, New Literary History, and *Critical Inquiry.*[12] For the feminist critic seeking clarification, the proliferation of communiqués may itself prove confusing.

There are two distinct modes of feminist criticism, and to conflate them (as most commentators do) is to remain permanently bemused by their theoretical potentialities. The first mode is ideological; it is concerned with the feminist as *reader,* and it offers feminist readings of texts which consider the images and stereotypes of women in literature, the omissions and misconceptions about women in criticism, and woman-as-sign in semiotic systems. This is not all feminist reading can do; it can be a liberating intellectual act, as Adrienne Rich proposes:

> A radical critique of literature, feminist in its impulse, would take the work first of all as a clue to how we live, how we have been living, how we have been led to imagine ourselves, how our language has trapped as well as liberated us, how the very act of naming has been till now a male prerogative, and how we can begin to see and name—and therefore live—afresh.[13]

This invigorating encounter with literature, which I will call *feminist reading* or the *feminist critique,* is in essence a mode of interpretation, one of many which any complex text will accommodate and permit. It is very difficult to propose theoretical coherence in an activity which by its nature is so eclectic and wide-ranging, although as a critical practice feminist reading has certainly been very influential. But in the free play of the interpretive field, the feminist critique can only compete with alternative readings, all of which have the built-in obsolescence of Buicks, cast away as newer readings take their place. As Kolodny, the most sophisticated theorist of feminist interpretation, has conceded:

> All the feminist is asserting, then, is her own equivalent right to liberate new (and perhaps different) significances from these same texts; and, at the same time, her right to choose which features of a text she takes as relevant because she is, after all, asking new and different questions of it. In the process, she claims neither definitiveness nor structural completeness for her different readings and reading systems, but only their usefulness in recognizing the particular achievements of woman-as-author and their applicability in conscientiously decoding woman-as-sign.

Rather than being discouraged by these limited objectives, Kolodny found them the happy cause of the "playful pluralism" of feminist critical theory, a pluralism which she believes to be "the only critical stance consistent with the current status of the larger women's movement."[14] Her feminist critic dances adroitly through the theoretical minefield.

Keenly aware of the political issues involved and presenting brilliant arguments, Kolodny nonetheless fails to convince me that feminist criticism must altogether abandon its hope "of establishing some basic conceptual model." If we see our critical job as interpretation and reinterpretation, we must be content with pluralism as our critical stance. But if we wish to ask questions about the process and the contexts of writing, if we genuinely wish to define ourselves to the uninitiated, we cannot rule out the prospect of theoretical consensus at this early stage.

All feminist criticism is in some sense revisionist, questioning the adequacy of accepted conceptual structures, and indeed most contemporary American criticism claims to be revisionist too. The most exciting and comprehensive case for this "revisionary imperative" is made by Sandra Gilbert: at its most ambitious, she asserts, feminist criticism "wants to decode and demystify all the disguised questions and answers that have always shadowed the connections between textuality and sexuality, genre and gender, psychosexual identity and cultural authority."[15] But in practice, the revisionary feminist critique is redressing a grievance and is built upon existing models. No one would deny that feminist criticism has affinities to other contemporary critical practices and methodologies and that the best work is also the most fully informed. Nonetheless, the feminist obsession with correcting, modifying, supplementing, revising, humanizing, or even attacking male critical theory keeps us dependent upon it and retards our progress in solving our own theoretical problems. What I mean here by "male critical theory" is a concept of creativity, literary history, or literary interpretation based entirely on male experience and put forward as universal. So long as we look to androcentric models for our most basic principles—even if we revise them by adding the feminist frame of reference—we are learning nothing new. And when the process is so one-sided, when male critics boast of their ignorance of feminist criticism, it is disheartening to find feminist critics still anxious for approval from the "white fathers" who will not listen or reply. Some feminist critics have taken upon themselves a revisionism which becomes a kind of homage; they have made Lacan the ladies' man of *Diacritics* and have forced Pierre Macherey into those dark alleys of the psyche where Engels feared to tread. According to Christiane Makward, the problem is even more serious in France than in the United States: "If neofeminist thought in France seems to have ground to a halt," she writes, "it is because it has continued to feed on the discourse of the masters."[16]

It is time for feminist criticism to decide whether between religion and revision we can claim any firm theoretical ground of our own. In calling for a feminist criticism that is genuinely women centered, independent, and intellectually coherent, I do not mean to endorse the separatist fantasies of radical feminist visionaries or to exclude from our critical practice a variety of intellectual tools. But we need to ask much more searchingly what we want to know and how we can find answers to the questions that come from *our* experience. I do not think that feminist criticism can find a usable past in the androcentric critical tradition. It has more to learn from women's studies than from English studies, more to learn from international feminist theory than from another seminar on the masters. It must find its own subject, its own system, its own theory, and its own voice. As Rich writes of Emily Dickinson in her poem "I Am in Danger—Sir—," we must choose to have the argument out at last on our own premises.

Defining the Feminine: Gynocritics and the Woman's Text

A woman's writing is always feminine; it cannot help being feminine; at its best it is most feminine; the only difficulty lies in defining what we mean by feminine.

Virginia Woolf

It is impossible to define a feminine practice of writing, and this is an impossibility that will remain, for this practice will never be theorized, enclosed, encoded—which doesn't mean that it doesn't exist.

Hélène Cixous, "The Laugh of the Medusa"

In the past decade, I believe, this process of defining the feminine has started to take place. Feminist criticism has gradually shifted its center from revisionary readings to a sustained investigation of literature by women. The second mode of feminist criticism engendered by this process is the study of women *as writers*, and its subjects are the history, styles, themes, genres, and structures of writing by women; the psychodynamics of female creativity; the trajectory of the individual or collective female career; and the evolution and laws of a female literary tradition. No English term exists for such a specialized critical discourse, and so I have invented the term "gynocritics." Unlike the feminist critique, gynocritics offers many theoretical opportunities. To see women's writing as our primary subject forces us to make the leap to a new conceptual vantage point and to redefine the nature of the theoretical problem before us. It is no longer the ideological dilemma of reconciling revisionary pluralisms but the essential question of difference. How can we constitute women as a distinct literary group? What is *the difference* of women's writing?

Patricia Meyer Spacks, I think, was the first academic critic to notice this shift from an androcentric to a gynocentric feminist criticism. In *The Female Imagination* (1975), she pointed out that few feminist theorists had concerned themselves with women's writing. Simone de Beauvoir's treatment of women writers in *The Second Sex* "always suggests an a priori tendency to take them less seriously than their masculine counterparts"; Mary Ellmann, in *Thinking about Women*, characterized women's literary success as escape from the categories of womanhood; and, according to Spacks, Kate Millett, in *Sexual Politics*, "has little interest in woman imaginative writers."[17] Spacks' wide-ranging study inaugurated a new period of feminist literary history and criticism which asked, again and again, how women's writing had been different, how womanhood itself shaped women's creative expression. In such books as Ellen Moers's *Literary Women* (1976), my *A Literature of Their Own* (1977), Nina Baym's *Woman's Fiction* (1978), Sandra Gilbert and Susan Gubar's *The Madwoman in the Attic* (1979), and Margaret Homans's *Women Writers and Poetic Identity* (1980), and in hundreds of essays and papers, women's writing asserted itself as the central project of feminist literary study.

This shift in emphasis has also taken place in European feminist criticism. To date, most commentary on French feminist critical discourse has stressed its fundamental dissimilarity from the empirical American orientation, its unfamiliar intellectual grounding in linguistics, Marxism, neo-Freudian and Lacanian psychoanalysis, and Derridean deconstruction.[18] Despite these differences, however, the new French feminisms have much in common with radical American feminist theories in terms of intellectual affiliations and rhetorical energies. The concept of *écriture féminine*, the inscription of the female body and female difference in language and text, is a significant theoretical formulation in French feminist criticism, although it describes a Utopian possibility rather than a literary practice. Hélène Cixous, one of the leading advocates of *écriture féminine*, has admitted that, with only a few exceptions, "there has not yet been any writing that inscribes femininity," and Nancy Miller explains that *écriture féminine* "privileges a textuality of the avant-garde, a literary production of the late twentieth century, and it is therefore fundamentally a hope, if not a blueprint, for the future."[19] Nonetheless, the concept of *écriture féminine* provides a way of talking about women's writing which reasserts the *value* of the feminine and identifies the theoretical project of feminist criticism as the analysis of difference. In recent years, the translations of important work by Julia Kristeva, Cixous, and Luce Irigaray and the excellent collection *New French Feminisms* have made French criticism much more accessible to American feminist scholars.[20]

English feminist criticism, which incorporates French feminist and Marxist theory but is more traditionally oriented to textual interpretation, is also moving toward a focus on women's writing.[21] The emphasis in each country falls somewhat differently:

English feminist criticism, essentially Marxist, stresses oppression; French feminist criticism, essentially psychoanalytic, stresses repression; American feminist criticism, essentially textual, stresses expression. All, however, have become gynocentric. All are struggling to find a terminology that can rescue the feminine from its stereotypical associations with inferiority.

Defining the unique difference of women's writing, as Woolf and Cixous have warned, must present a slippery and demanding task. Is difference a matter of style? Genre? Experience? Or is it produced by the reading process, as some textual critics would maintain? Spacks calls the difference of women's writing a "delicate divergency," testifying to the subtle and elusive nature of the feminine practice of writing. Yet the delicate divergency of the woman's text challenges us to respond with equal delicacy and precision to the small but crucial deviations, the cumulative weightings of experience and exclusion, that have marked the history of women's writing. Before we can chart this history, we must uncover it, patiently and scrupulously; our theories must be firmly grounded in reading and research. But we have the opportunity, through gynocritics, to learn something solid, enduring, and real about the relation of women to literary culture.

Theories of women's writing presently make use of four models of difference: biological, linguistic, psychoanalytic, and cultural. Each is an effort to define and differentiate the qualities of the woman writer and the woman's text; each model also represents a school of gynocentric feminist criticism with its own favorite texts, styles, and methods. They overlap but are roughly sequential in that each incorporates the one before. I shall try now to sort out the various terminologies and assumptions of these four models of difference and evaluate their usefulness.

WOMEN'S WRITING AND WOMAN'S BODY

More body, hence more writing.

CIXOUS, *"The Laugh of the Medusa"*

Organic or biological criticism is the most extreme statement of gender difference, of a text indelibly marked by the body: anatomy is textuality. Biological criticism is also one of the most sibylline and perplexing theoretical formulations of feminist criticism. Simply to invoke anatomy risks a return to the crude essentialism, the phallic and ovarian theories of art, that oppressed women in the past. Victorian physicians believed that women's physiological functions diverted about twenty percent of their creative energy from brain activity. Victorian anthropologists believed that the frontal lobes of the male brain were heavier and more developed than female lobes and thus that women were inferior in intelligence.

While feminist criticism rejects the attribution of literal biological inferiority, some theorists seem to have accepted the *metaphorical* implications of female biological difference in writing. In *The Madwoman in the Attic*, for example, Gilbert and Gubar structure their analysis of women's writing around metaphors of literary paternity. "In patriarchal western culture," they maintain, ". . . the text's author is a father, a progenitor, a procreator, an aesthetic patriarch whose pen is an instrument of generative power like his penis." Lacking phallic authority, they go on to suggest, women's writing is profoundly marked by the anxieties of this difference: "If the pen is a metaphorical penis, from what organ can females generate texts?"[22]

To this rhetorical question Gilbert and Gubar offer no reply; but it is a serious question of much feminist theoretical discourse. Those critics who, like myself, would protest the fundamental analogy might reply that women generate texts from the brain or that the word-processor, with its compactly coded microchips, its inputs and outputs, is a metaphorical womb. The metaphor of literary paternity, as Auerbach has pointed out in her review of *The Madwoman*, ignores "an equally timeless and, for me, even more oppressive metaphorical equation between literary creativity and childbirth."[23] Certainly metaphors of literary *maternity* predominated in the eighteenth and nineteenth centuries; the process of literary creation is analogically much more similar to gestation, labor, and delivery than it is to insemination. Describing Thackeray's plan for *Henry Esmond,* for example, Douglas Jerrold jovially remarked, "You have heard, I suppose, that Thackeray is big with twenty parts, and unless he is wrong in his time, expects the first installment at Christmas."[24] (If to write is metaphorically to give birth, from what organ can males generate texts?)

Some radical feminist critics, primarily in France but also in the United States, insist that we must read these metaphors as more than playful; that we must seriously rethink and redefine biological differentiation and its relation to women's writing. They argue that "women's writing proceeds from the body, that our sexual differentiation is also our source."[25] In *Of Woman Born*, Rich explains her belief that

> Female biology . . . has far more radical implications than we have yet come to appreciate. Patriarchal thought has limited female biology to its own narrow specifications. The feminist vision has recoiled from female biology for these reasons; it will, I believe, come to view our physicality as a resource rather than a destiny. In order to live a fully human life, we require not only *control* of our bodies . . . we must touch the unity and resonance of our physicality, the corporeal ground of our intelligence.[26]

Feminist criticism written in the biological perspective generally stresses the importance of the body as a source of imagery. Alicia Ostriker, for example, argues that contemporary American women poets use a franker, more pervasive anatomical imagery than their male counterparts and that this insistent body language refuses the spurious transcendence that comes at the price of denying the flesh. In a fascinating essay on Whitman and Dickinson, Terence Diggory shows that physical nakedness, so potent a poetic symbol of authenticity for Whitman and other male poets, had very different connotations for Dickinson and her successors, who associated nakedness with the objectified or sexually exploited female nude and who chose instead protective images of the armored self.[27]

Feminist criticism which itself tries to be biological, to write from the critic's body, has been intimate, confessional, often innovative in style and form. Rachel Blau DuPlessis's "Washing Blood," the introduction to a special issue of *Feminist Studies* on the subject of motherhood, proceeds, in short lyrical paragraphs, to describe her own experience in adopting a child, to recount her dreams and nightmares, and to meditate upon the "healing unification of body and mind based not only on the lived experiences of motherhood as a social institution . . . but also on a biological power speaking through us."[28] Such criticism makes itself defiantly vulnerable, virtually bares its throat to the knife, since our professional taboos against self-revelation are so strong. When it succeeds, however, it achieves the power and the dignity of art. Its existence is an implicit rebuke to women critics who continue to write, according to Rich, "from somewhere outside their female bodies." In comparison to this flowing confessional criticism, the tight-lipped Olympian intelligence of such texts as Elizabeth Hardwick's *Seduction and Betrayal* or Susan Sontag's *Illness as Metaphor* can seem arid and strained.

Yet in its obsessions with the "corporeal ground of our intelligence," feminist biocriticism can also become cruelly prescriptive. There is a sense in which the exhibition of bloody wounds becomes an initiation ritual quite separate and disconnected from critical insight. And as the editors of the journal *Questions féministes* point out, "it is . . . dangerous to place the body at the center of a search for female identity. . . . The themes of otherness and of the Body merge together, because the most visible difference between men and women, and the only one we know for sure to be permanent . . . is indeed the difference in body. This difference has been used as a pretext to 'justify' full power of one sex over the other" [trans. Yvonne Rochette-Ozzello, NFF 218]. The study of biological imagery in women's writing is useful and important as long as we understand that factors other than anatomy are involved in it. Ideas about the body are fundamental to understanding how women conceptualize their situation in society; but there can be no expression of the body which is unmediated by linguistic, social, and literary structures. The difference of woman's literary practice, therefore, must be sought (in Miller's words) in "the body of her writing and not the writing of her body."[29]

WOMEN'S WRITING AND WOMEN'S LANGUAGE

The women say, the language you speak poisons your glottis tongue palate lips. They say, the language you speak is made up of words that are killing you. They say, the language you speak is made up of signs that rightly speaking designate what men have appropriated.

MONIQUE WITTIG, *Les Guérillères*

Linguistic and textual theories of women's writing ask whether men and women use language differently; whether sex differences in language use can be theorized in terms of biology, socialization, or culture; whether women can create new languages of their own; and whether speaking, reading, and writing are all gender marked. American, French, and British feminist critics have all drawn attention to the philosophical, linguistic, and practical problems of women's use of language, and the debate over language is one of the most exciting areas in gynocritics. Poets and writers have led the attack on what Rich calls "the oppressor's language," a language sometimes criticized as sexist, sometimes as abstract. But the problem goes well beyond reformist efforts to purge language of its sexist aspects. As Nelly Furman explains, "It is through the medium of language that we define and categorize areas of difference and similarity, which in turn allow us to comprehend the world around us. Male-centered categorizations predominate in American English and subtly shape our understanding and perception of reality; this is why attention is increasingly directed to the inherently oppressive aspects for women of a male-constructed language system."[30] According to Carolyn Burke, the language system is at the center of French feminist theory:

The central issue in much recent women's writing in France is to find and use an appropriate female language. Language is the place to begin: a *prise de conscience* must be followed by a *prise de la parole*. . . . In this view, the very forms of the dominant mode of discourse show the mark of the dominant masculine ideology. Hence, when a woman writes or speaks herself into existence, she is forced to speak in something like a foreign tongue, a language with which she may be personally uncomfortable.[31]

Many French feminists advocate a revolutionary linguism, an oral break from the dictatorship of patriarchal speech. Annie Leclerc, in *Parole de femme*, calls on women "to invent a language that is not oppressive, a language that does not leave speechless but that loosens the tongue" [trans. Courtivron, *NFF* 179]. Chantal Chawaf, in an essay on "La chair linguistique," connects biofeminism and linguism in the view that women's language and a genuinely feminine practice of writing will articulate the body:

> In order to reconnect the book with the body and with pleasure, we must disintellectualize writing. . . . And this language, as it develops, will not degenerate and dry up, will not go back to the fleshless academicism, the stereotypical and servile discourses that we reject.
>
> . . . Feminine language must, by its very nature, work on life passionately, scientifically, poetically, politically in order to make it invulnerable. [trans. Rochette-Ozzello, *NFF* 177–78]

But scholars who want a women's language that *is* intellectual and theoretical, that works *inside* the academy, are faced with what seems like an impossible paradox, as Xavière Gauthier has lamented: "As long as women remain silent, they will be outside the historical process. But, if they begin to speak and write *as men do*, they will enter history subdued and alienated; it is a history that, logically speaking, their speech should disrupt" [trans. Marilyn A. August, *NFF* 162–63]. What we need, Mary Jacobus has proposed, is a women's writing that works within "male" discourse but works "ceaselessly to deconstruct it: to write what cannot be written," and according to Shoshana Felman, "the challenge facing the woman today is nothing less than to 'reinvent' language, . . . to speak not only against, but outside of the specular phallogocentric structure, to establish a discourse the status of which would no longer be defined by the phallacy of masculine meaning."[32]

Beyond rhetoric, what can linguistic, historical, and anthropological research tell us about the prospects for a women's language? First of all, the concept of a women's language is not original with feminist criticism; it is very ancient and appears frequently in folklore and myth. In such myths, the essence of women's language is its secrecy; what is really being described is the male fantasy of the enigmatic nature of the feminine. Herodotus, for example, reported that the Amazons were able linguists who easily mastered the languages of their male antagonists, although men could never learn the women's tongue. In *The White Goddess*, Robert Graves romantically argues that a women's language existed in a matriarchal stage of prehistory; after a great battle of the sexes, the matriarchy was overthrown and the women's language went underground, to survive in the mysterious cults of Eleusis and Corinth and the witch covens of Western Europe. Travelers and missionaries in the seventeenth and eighteenth centuries brought back accounts of "women's languages" among American Indians, Africans, and Asians (the differences in linguistic structure they reported were usually superficial). There is some ethnographic evidence that in certain cultures women have evolved a private form of communication out of their need to resist the silence imposed upon them in public life. In ecstatic religions, for example, women, more frequently than men, speak in tongues, a phenomenon attributed by anthropologists to their relative inarticulateness in formal religious discourse. But such ritualized and unintelligible female "languages" are scarcely cause for rejoicing; indeed, it was because witches were suspected of esoteric knowledge and possessed speech that they were burned.[33]

From a political perspective, there are interesting parallels between the feminist problem of a women's language and the recurring "language issue" in the general history of decolonization. After a revolution, a new state must decide which language to make official: the language that is "psychologically immediate," that allows "the kind of force that speaking one's mother tongue permits"; or the language that "is an avenue to the wider community of modern culture," a community to whose movements of thought only "foreign" languages can give access.[34] The language issue in feminist criticism has emerged, in a sense, after our revolution, and it reveals the tensions in the women's movement between those who would stay outside the academic establishments and the institutions of criticism and those who would enter and even conquer them.

The advocacy of a women's language is thus a political gesture that also carries tremendous emotional force. But despite its unifying appeal, the concept of a women's language is riddled with difficulties. Unlike Welsh, Breton, Swahili, or Amharic, that is, languages of minority or colonized groups, there is no mother tongue, no genderlect spoken by the female population in a society, which differs significantly from the dominant language. English and American linguists agree that "there is absolutely no evidence that would suggest the sexes are preprogrammed to develop structurally different linguistic systems." Furthermore, the many specific differences in male and female speech, intonation, and language use that have been identified cannot be explained in terms of "two separate sex-specific languages" but need to be considered instead in terms of styles, strategies, and contexts of linguistic performance.[35] Efforts at quantitative analysis of language in texts by men or women, such as Mary Hiatt's computerized study of contemporary fiction, *The Way Women Write* (1977), can easily be attacked for treating words apart from their meanings and purposes. At a higher level, analyses which look for "feminine style" in the repetition of stylistic devices, image patterns, and syntax in women's writing tend to confuse innate forms with the overdetermined results of literary choice. Language and style are never raw and instinctual but are always the products of innumerable factors, of genre, tradition, memory, and context.

The appropriate task for feminist criticism, I believe, is to concentrate on women's access to language, on the available lexical range from which words can be selected, on the ideological and cultural determinants of expression. The problem is not that language is insufficient to express women's consciousness but that women have been denied the full resources of language and have been forced into silence, euphemism, or circumlocution. In a series of drafts for a lecture on women's writing (drafts which she discarded or suppressed), Woolf protested against the censorship which cut off female access to language. Comparing herself to Joyce, Woolf noted the differences between their verbal territories: "Now men are shocked if a woman says what she feels (as Joyce does). Yet literature which is always pulling down blinds is not literature. All that we have ought to be expressed—mind and body—a process of incredible difficulty and danger."[36]

"All that we have ought to be expressed—mind and body." Rather than wishing to limit women's linguistic range, we must fight to open and extend it. The holes in discourse, the blanks and gaps and silences, are not the spaces where female consciousness reveals itself but the blinds of a "prison-house of language." Women's literature is still haunted by the ghosts of repressed language, and until we have exorcised those ghosts, it ought not to be in language that we base our theory of difference.

WOMEN'S WRITING AND WOMAN'S PSYCHE

Psychoanalytically oriented feminist criticism locates the difference of women's writing in the author's psyche and in the relation of gender to the creative process. It incorporates the biological and linguistic models of gender difference in a theory of the female psyche or self, shaped by the body, by the development of language, and by sex-role socialization. Here too there are many difficulties to overcome; the Freudian model requires constant revision to make it gynocentric. In one grotesque early example of Freudian reductivism, Theodor Reik suggested that women have fewer writing blocks than men because their bodies are constructed to facilitate release: "Writing, as Freud told us at the end of his life, is connected with urinating, which physiologically is easier for a woman—they have a wider bladder."[37] Generally, however, psychoanalytic criticism has focused not on the capacious bladder (could this be the organ from which females generate texts?) but on the absent phallus. Penis envy, the castration complex, and the Oedipal phase have become the Freudian coordinates defining women's relationship to language, fantasy, and culture. Currently the French psychoanalytic school dominated by Lacan has extended castration into a total metaphor for female literary and linguistic disadvantage. Lacan theorizes that the acquisition of language and the entry into its symbolic order occurs at the Oedipal phase in which the child accepts his or her gender identity. This stage requires an acceptance of the phallus as a privileged signification and a consequent female displacement, as Cora Kaplan has explained:

> The phallus as a signifier has a central, crucial position in language, for if language embodies the patriarchal law of the culture, its basic meanings refer to the recurring process by which sexual difference and subjectivity are acquired. . . . Thus the little girl's access to the Symbolic, i.e., to language and its laws, is always negative and/or mediated by introsubjective relation to a third term, for it is characterized by an identification with lack.[38]

In psychoanalytic terms, "lack" has traditionally been associated with the feminine, although Lac(k)anian critics can now make their statements linguistically. Many feminists believe that psychoanalysis could become a powerful tool for literary criticism, and recently there has been a renewed interest in Freudian theory. But feminist criticism based in Freudian or post-Freudian psychoanalysis must continually struggle with the problem of feminine disadvantage and lack. In *The Madwoman in the Attic*, Gilbert and Gubar carry out a feminist revision of Harold Bloom's Oedipal model of literary history as a conflict between fathers and sons and accept the essential psychoanalytic definition of the woman artist as displaced, disinherited, and excluded. In their view, the nature and "difference" of women's writing lies in its troubled and even tormented relationship to female identity; the woman writer experiences her own gender as "a painful obstacle or even a debilitating inadequacy." The nineteenth-century woman writer inscribed her own sickness, her madness, her anorexia, her agoraphobia, and her paralysis in her texts; and although Gilbert and Gubar are dealing specifically with the nineteenth century, the range of their allusion and quotation suggests a more general thesis:

> Thus the loneliness of the female artist, her feelings of alienation from male predecessors coupled with her need for sisterly precursors and successors, her urgent sense of her need for a female audience together with her fear of the antagonism of male readers, her culturally conditioned timidity about self-dramatization, her dread of the patriarchal authority of art, her anxiety about the impropriety of female invention—all these phenomena of

"inferiorization" mark the woman writer's struggle for artistic self-definition and differentiate her efforts at self-creation from those of her male counterpart.[39]

In "Emphasis Added," Miller takes another approach to the problem of negativity in psychoanalytic criticism. Her strategy is to expand Freud's view of female creativity and to show how criticism of women's texts has frequently been unfair because it has been based in Freudian expectations. In his essay "The Relation of the Poet to Daydreaming" (1908), Freud maintained that the unsatisfied dreams and desires of women are chiefly erotic; these are the desires that shape the plots of women's fiction. In contrast, the dominant fantasies behind men's plots are egoistic and ambitious as well as erotic. Miller shows how women's plots have been granted or denied credibility in terms of their conformity to this phallocentric model and that a gynocentric reading reveals a repressed egoistic/ambitious fantasy in women's writing as well as in men's. Women's novels which are centrally concerned with fantasies of romantic love belong to the category disdained by George Eliot and other serious women writers as "silly novels"; the smaller number of women's novels which inscribe a fantasy of power imagine a world for women outside of love, a world, however, made impossible by social boundaries.

There has also been some interesting feminist literary criticism based on alternatives to Freudian psychoanalytic theory: Annis Pratt's Jungian history of female archetypes, Barbara Rigney's Laingian study of the divided self in women's fiction, and Ann Douglas's Eriksonian analysis of inner space in nineteenth-century women's writing.[40] And for the past few years, critics have been thinking about the possibilities of a new feminist psychoanalysis that does *not* revise Freud but instead emphasizes the development and construction of gender identities.

The most dramatic and promising new work in feminist psychoanalysis looks at the pre-Oedipal phase and at the process of psychosexual differentiation. Nancy Chodorow's *The Reproduction of Mothering: Psychoanalysis and the Sociology of Gender* (1978) has had an enormous influence on women's studies. Chodorow revises traditional psychoanalytic concepts of differentiation, the process by which the child comes to perceive the self as separate and to develop ego and body boundaries. Since differentiation takes place in relation to the mother (the primary caretaker), attitudes toward the mother "emerge in the earliest differentiation of the self"; "the mother, who is a woman, becomes and remains for children of both genders the other, or object."[41] The child develops core gender identity concomitantly with differentiation, but the process is not the same for boys and girls. A boy must learn his gender identity negatively as being not-female, and this difference requires continual reinforcement. In contrast, a girl's core gender identity is positive and built upon sameness, continuity, and identification with the mother. Women's difficulties with feminine identity come after the Oedipal phase, in which male power and cultural hegemony give sex differences a transformed value. Chodorow's work suggests that shared parenting, the involvement of men as primary caretakers of children, will have a profound effect on our sense of sex difference, gender identity, and sexual preference.

But what is the significance of feminist psychoanalysis for literary criticism? One thematic carry-over has been a critical interest in the mother-daughter configuration as a source of female creativity.[42] Elizabeth Abel's bold investigation of female friendship in contemporary women's novels uses Chodorow's theory to show how not only the relationships of women characters but also the relationship of women writers to each other are determined by the psychodynamics of female bonding. Abel too confronts Bloom's paradigm of literary history, but unlike Gilbert and Gubar she sees a "triadic female pattern" in which the Oedipal relation to the male tradition is balanced by the woman writer's pre-Oedipal relation to the female tradition. "As the dynamics of female friendship differ from those of male," Abel concludes, "the dynamics of female literary influence also diverge and deserve a theory of influence attuned to female psychology and to women's dual position in literary history."[43]

Like Gilbert, Gubar, and Miller, Abel brings together women's texts from a variety of national literatures, choosing to emphasize "the constancy of certain emotional dynamics depicted in diverse cultural situations." Yet the privileging of gender implies not only the constancy but also the immutability of these dynamics. Although psychoanalytically based models of feminist criticism can now offer us remarkable and persuasive readings of individual texts and can highlight extraordinary similarities between women writing in a variety of cultural circumstances, they cannot explain historical change, ethnic difference, or the shaping force of generic and economic factors. To consider these issues, we must go beyond psychoanalysis to a more flexible and comprehensive model of women's writing which places it in the maximum context of culture.

WOMEN'S WRITING AND WOMEN'S CULTURE

I consider women's literature as a specific category, not because of biology, but because it is, in a sense, the literature of the colonized.

Christiane Rochefort, "The Privilege of Consciousness"

A theory based on a model of women's culture can provide, I believe, a more complete and satisfying way to talk about the specificity and difference of women's writing than theories based in biology, linguistics, or psychoanalysis. Indeed, a theory of culture incorporates ideas about women's body, language, and psyche but interprets them in relation to the social contexts in which they occur. The ways in which women conceptualize their bodies and their sexual and reproductive functions are intricately linked to their cultural environments. The female psyche can be studied as the product or construction of cultural forces. Language, too, comes back into the picture, as we consider the social dimensions and determinants of language use, the shaping of linguistic behavior by cultural ideals. A cultural theory acknowledges that there are important differences between women as writers: class, race, nationality, and history are literary determinants as significant as gender. Nonetheless, women's culture forms a collective experience within the cultural whole, an experience that binds women writers to each other over time and space. It is in the emphasis on the binding force of women's culture that this approach differs from Marxist theories of cultural hegemony.

Hypotheses of women's culture have been developed over the last decade primarily by anthropologists, sociologists, and social historians in order to get away from masculine systems, hierarchies, and values and to get at the primary and self-defined nature of female cultural experience. In the field of women's history, the concept of women's culture is still controversial, although there is agreement on its significance as a theoretical formulation. Gerda Lerner explains the importance of examining women's experience in its own terms:

Women have been left out of history not because of the evil conspiracies of men in general or male historians in particular, but because we have considered history only in male-centered terms. We have missed women and their activities, because we have asked questions of history which are inappropriate to women. To rectify this, and to light up areas of historical darkness we must, for a time, focus on a *woman-centered* inquiry, considering the possibility of the existence of a female culture *within* the general culture shared by men and women. History must include an account of the female experience over time and should include the development of feminist consciousness as an essential aspect of women's past. This is the primary task of women's history. The central question it raises is: What would history be like if it were seen through the eyes of women and ordered by values they define?[44]

In defining female culture, historians distinguish between the roles, activities, tastes, and behaviors prescribed and considered appropriate for women and those activities, behaviors, and functions actually generated out of women's lives. In the late-eighteenth and nineteenth centuries, the term "woman's sphere" expressed the Victorian and Jacksonian vision of separate roles for men and women, with little or no overlap and with women subordinate. Woman's sphere was defined and maintained by men, but women frequently internalized its precepts in the American "cult of true womanhood" and the English "feminine ideal." Women's culture, however, redefines women's "activities and goals from a woman-centered point of view. . . . The term implies an assertion of equality and an awareness of sisterhood, the communality of women." Women's culture refers to "the broad-based communality of values, institutions, relationships, and methods of communication" unifying nineteenth-century female experience, a culture nonetheless with significant variants by class and ethnic group [MFP 52, 54].

Some feminist historians have accepted the model of separate spheres and have seen the movement from woman's sphere to women's culture to women's-rights activism as the consecutive stages of an evolutionary political process. Others see a more complex and perpetual negotiation taking place between women's culture and the general culture. As Lerner has argued:

> It is important to understand that "woman's culture" is not and should not be seen as a subculture. It is hardly possible for the majority to live in a subculture. . . . Women live their social existence within the general culture and, whenever they are confined by patriarchal restraint or segregation into separateness (which always has subordination as its purpose), they transform this restraint into complementarity (asserting the importance of woman's function, even its "superiority") and redefine it. Thus, women live a duality—as members of the general culture and as partakers of women's culture. [MFP 52]

Lerner's views are similar to those of some cultural anthropologists. A particularly stimulating analysis of female culture has been carried out by two Oxford anthropologists, Shirley and Edwin Ardener. The Ardeners have tried to outline a model of women's culture which is not historically limited and to provide a terminology for its characteristics. Two essays by Edwin Ardener, "Belief and the Problem of Women" (1972) and "The 'Problem' Revisited" (1975), suggest that women constitute a *muted group*, the boundaries of whose culture and reality overlap, but are not wholly contained by, the *dominant (male) group*. A model of the cultural situation of women is crucial to understanding both how they are perceived by the dominant group and how they perceive themselves and others. Both historians and anthropologists emphasize the incompleteness of androcentric models of history and culture and the inadequacy of such models for the analysis of female experience. In the past, female experience which could not be accommodated by androcentric models was treated as deviant or simply ignored. Observation from an exterior point of view could never be the same as comprehension from within. Ardener's model also has many connections to and implications for current feminist literary theory, since the concepts of perception, silence, and silencing are so central to discussions of women's participation in literary culture.[45]

By the term "muted," Ardener suggests problems both of language and of power. Both muted and dominant groups generate beliefs or ordering ideas of social reality at the unconscious level, but dominant groups control the forms or structures in which consciousness can be articulated. Thus muted groups must mediate their beliefs through the allowable forms of dominant structures. Another way of putting this would be to say that all language is the language of the dominant order, and women, if they speak at all, must speak through it. How then, Ardener asks, "does the symbolic weight of that other mass of persons express itself?" In his view, women's beliefs find expression through ritual and art, expressions which can be deciphered by the ethnographer, either female or male, who is willing to make the effort to perceive beyond the screens of the dominant structure.[46]

Let us now look at Ardener's diagram of the relationship of the dominant and the muted group:

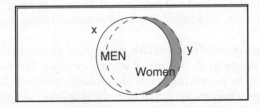

Unlike the Victorian model of complementary spheres, Ardener's groups are represented by intersecting circles. Much of muted circle Y falls within the boundaries of dominant circle X; there is also a crescent of Y which is outside the dominant boundary and therefore (in Ardener's terminology) "wild." We can think of the "wild zone" of women's culture spatially, experientially, or metaphysically. Spatially it stands for an area which is literally no-man's-land, a place forbidden to men, which corresponds to the zone in X which is off limits to women. Experientially it stands for the aspects of the female life-style which are outside of and unlike those of men; again, there is a corresponding zone of male experience alien to women. But if we think of the wild zone metaphysically, or in terms of consciousness, it has no corresponding male space since all of male consciousness is within the circle of the dominant structure and thus accessible to or structured by language. In this sense, the "wild" is always imaginary; from the male point of view, it may simply be the projection of the unconscious. In terms of cultural anthropology, women know what the male crescent is like, even if they have never seen it, because it becomes the subject of legend (like the wilderness). But men do not know what is in the wild.

For some feminist critics, the wild zone, or "female space," must be the address of a genuinely women-centered criticism, theory, and art, whose shared project is to bring into being the symbolic weight of female consciousness, to make the invisible visible, to make the silent speak. French feminist critics would like to make the wild zone the theoretical base of women's difference. In their texts, the wild zone becomes the place for the revolutionary women's language, the language of everything that is repressed, and for the revolutionary women's writing in "white ink." It is the Dark Continent in which Cixous's laughing Medusa and Wittig's *guérillères* reside. Through voluntary entry into the wild zone, other feminist critics tell us, a woman can write her way out of the "cramped confines of patriarchal space."[47] The images of this journey are now familiar in feminist quest fictions and in essays about them. The writer/heroine, often guided by another woman, travels to the "mother country" of liberated desire and female authenticity; crossing to the other side of the mirror, like Alice in Wonderland, is often a symbol of the passage.

Many forms of American radical feminism also romantically assert that women are closer to nature, to the environment, to a matriarchal principle at once biological and ecological. Mary Daly's *Gyn/Ecology* and Margaret Atwood's novel *Surfacing* are texts which create this feminist mythology. In English and American literature, women writers have often imagined Amazon Utopias, cities or countries situated in the wild zone or on its border: Elizabeth Gaskell's gentle *Cranford* is probably an Amazon Utopia; so is Charlotte Perkins Gilman's *Herland* or, to take a recent example, Joanna Russ's *While-away*. A few years ago, the feminist publishing house Daughters, Inc. tried to create a business version of the Amazon Utopia; as Lois Gould reported in the *New York Times Magazine* (2 January 1977), "They believe they are building the working models for the critical next stage of feminism: full independence from the control and influence of "male-dominated" institutions—the news media, the health, education, and legal systems, the art, theater, and literary worlds, the banks."

These fantasies of an idyllic enclave represent a phenomenon which feminist criticism must recognize in the history of women's writing. But we must also understand that there can be no writing or criticism totally outside of the dominant structure; no publication is fully independent from the economic and political pressures of the male-dominated society. The concept of a woman's text in the wild zone is a playful abstraction: in the reality to which we must address ourselves as critics, women's writing is a "double-voiced discourse" that always embodies the social, literary, and cultural heritages of both the muted and the dominant.[48] And insofar as most feminist critics are also women writing, this precarious heritage is one we share; every step that feminist criticism takes toward defining women's writing is a step toward self-understanding as well; every account of a female literary culture and a female literary tradition has parallel significance for our own place in critical history and critical tradition.

Women writing are not, then, *inside* and *outside* of the male tradition; they are inside two traditions simultaneously, "undercurrents," in Ellen Moers's metaphor, of the mainstream. To mix metaphors again, the literary estate of women, as Myra Jehlen says, "suggests . . . a more fluid imagery of interacting juxtapositions, the point of which would be to represent not so much the territory, as its defining borders. Indeed, the female territory might well be envisioned as one long border, and independence for women, not as a separate country, but as open access to the sea." As Jehlen goes on to explain, an aggressive feminist criticism must poise itself on this border and must see women's writing in its changing historical and cultural relation to that other body of texts identified by feminist criticism not simply as literature but as "men's writing."[49]

The difference of women's writing, then, can only be understood in terms of this complex and historically grounded cultural relation. An important aspect of Ardener's model is that there are muted groups other than women; a dominant structure may determine many muted structures. A black American woman poet, for example, would have her literary identity formed by the dominant (white male) tradition, by a muted women's culture, and by a muted black culture. She would be affected by both sexual and racial politics in a combination unique to her case; at the same time, as Barbara Smith points out, she shares an experience specific to her group: "Black women writers constitute an identifiable literary tradition . . . thematically, stylistically, aesthetically, and conceptually. Black women writers manifest common approaches to the act of creating literature as a direct result of the specific political, social, and economic experience they have been obliged to share."[50] Thus the first task of a gynocentric criticism must be to plot the precise cultural locus of female literary identity and to describe the forces that intersect an individual woman writer's cultural field. A gynocentric criticism would also situate women writers with respect to the variables of literary culture, such as modes of production and distribution, relations of author and audience, relations of high to popular art, and hierarchies of genre.

Insofar as our concepts of literary periodization are based on men's writing, women's writing must be forcibly assimilated to an irrelevant grid; we discuss a Renaissance which is not a renaissance for women, a Romantic period in which women played very little part, a modernism with which women conflict. At the same time, the ongoing history of women's writing has been suppressed, leaving large and mysterious gaps in accounts of the development of genre. Gynocentric criticism is already well on the way to providing us with another perspective on literary history. Margaret Anne Doody, for example, suggests that "the period between the death of Richardson and the appearance of the novels of Scott and Austen" which has "been regarded as a dead period, a dull blank" is in fact the period in which late eighteenth-century women writers were developing "the paradigm for women's fiction of the nineteenth century—something hardly less than the paradigm of the nineteenth-century novel itself."[51] There has also been a feminist rehabilitation of the female gothic, a mutation of a popular genre once believed marginal but now seen as part of the great tradition of the novel.[52] In American literature, the pioneering work of Ann Douglas, Nina Baym, and Jane Tompkins, among others, has given us a new view of the power of women's fiction to feminize nineteenth-century American culture.[53] And feminist critics have made us aware that Woolf belonged to a tradition other than modernism and that this tradition surfaces in her work precisely in those places where criticism has hitherto found obscurities, evasions, implausibilities, and imperfections.[54]

Our current theories of literary influence also need to be tested in terms of women's writing. If a man's test, as Bloom and Edward Said have maintained, is fathered, then a woman's text is not only mothered but parented; it confronts both paternal and maternal precursors and must deal with the problems and advantages of both lines of inheritance. Woolf says in A Room of One's Own that "a woman writing thinks back through her mothers." But a woman writing unavoidably thinks back through her fathers as well; only male writers can forget or mute half of their parentage. The dominant culture need not consider the muted, except to rail against "the woman's part" in itself. Thus we need more subtle and supple accounts of influence, not just to explain women's writing but also to understand how men's writing has resisted the acknowledgment of female precursors.

We must first go beyond the assumption that women writers either imitate their male predecessors or revise them and that this simple dualism is adequate to describe the influences on the woman's text. I. A. Richards once commented that the influence of G. E. Moore had had an enormous negative impact on his work: "I feel like an obverse of him. Where there's a hole in him, there's a bulge in me."[55] Too often women's place in literary tradition is translated into the crude topography of hole and bulge, with Milton, Byron, or Emerson the bulging bogeys on one side and women's literature from Aphra Behn to Adrienne Rich a pocked moon surface of revisionary lacunae on the other. One of the great advantages of the women's-culture model is that it shows how the female tradition can be a positive source of strength and solidarity as well as a negative source of powerlessness; it can generate its own experiences and symbols which are not simply the obverse of the male tradition.

How can a cultural model of women's writing help us to read a woman's text? One implication of this model is that women's fiction can be read as a double-voiced discourse, containing a "dominant" and a "muted" story, what Gilbert and Gubar call a "palimpsest." I have described it elsewhere as an object/field problem in which we must keep two alternative oscillating texts simultaneously in view: "In the purest feminist literary criticism we are . . . presented with a radical alteration of our vision, a demand that we see meaning in what has previously been empty space. The orthodox plot recedes, and another plot, hitherto submerged in the anonymity of the background, stands out in bold relief like a thumbprint." Miller too sees "another text" in women's fiction, "more or less muted from novel to novel" but "always there to be read."[56]

Another interpretative strategy for feminist criticism might be the contextual analysis that the cultural anthropologist Clifford Geertz calls "thick description." Geertz calls for descriptions that seek to understand the meaning of cultural phenomena and products by "sorting out the structures of signification . . . and determining their social ground and import."[57] A genuinely "thick" description of women's writing would insist upon gender and upon a female literary tradition among the multiple strata that make up the force of meaning in a text. No description, we must concede, could ever be thick enough to account for all the factors that go into the work of art. But we could work toward completeness, even as an unattainable ideal.

In suggesting that a cultural model of women's writing has considerable usefulness for the enterprise of feminist criticism, I don't mean to replace psychoanalysis with cultural anthropology as the answer to all our theoretical problems or to enthrone Ardener and Geertz as the new white fathers in place of Freud, Lacan, and Bloom.[58] No theory, however suggestive, can be a substitute for the close and extensive knowledge of women's texts which constitutes our essential subject. Cultural anthropology and social history can perhaps offer us a terminology and a diagram of women's cultural situation. But feminist critics must use this concept in relation to what women actually write, not in relation to a theoretical, political, metaphoric, or visionary ideal of what women ought to write.

I began by recalling that a few years ago feminist critics thought we were on a pilgrimage to the promised land in which gender would lose its power, in which all texts would be sexless and equal, like angels. But the more precisely we understand the specificity of women's writing not as a transient by-product of sexism but as a fundamental and continually determining reality, the more clearly we realize that we have misperceived our destination. We may never reach the promised land at all; for when feminist critics see our task as the study of women's writing, we realize that the land promised to us is not the serenely undifferentiated universality of texts but the tumultuous and intriguing wilderness of difference itself.   *1981*

ᴇ̧ Notes ᴇ̧

1. Louise Bogan (1897–1970) was an American poet who worked for years at the *New Yorker* magazine.

2. Carolyn Heilbrun (1926–) and Catharine Stimpson are feminist literary critics and American university professors.

3. [Carolyn G. Heilbrun and Catharine R. Stimpson, "Theories of Feminist Criticism: A Dialogue," in *Feminist Literary Criticism*, ed. Josephine Donovan (Lexington: UP of Kentucky, 1975) 64.]

4. Matthew Arnold (1822–88) was a nineteenth-century British poet and literary critic.

5. [No women critics are discussed in Geoffrey Hartman's *Criticism in the Wilderness: The Study of Literature Today* (New Haven: Yale UP, 1980), but he does describe a feminine spirit called "the Muse of Criticism": "more a governess than a Muse, the stern daughter of books no longer read under trees and in the fields" (175).]

6. [See my "Literary Criticism," Review Essay, *Signs* 1 (Winter 1975): 435–60.]

7. [Annette Kolodny, "Literary Criticism," Review Essay, *Signs* 2 (Winter 1976): 420.]

8. [On black criticism, see Barbara Smith, "Toward a Black Feminist Criticism," *The New Feminist Criticism: Essays on Women, Literature, and Theory*, ed. Elaine Showalter. New York: Pantheon Books, 1985, 168–85; and Mary Helen Washington, "New Lives and New Letters: Black Women Writers at the End of the Seventies," *College English* 43 (January 1981): 1–11. On Marxist criticism, see the Marxist-Feminist Literature Collective's "Women's Writing," *Ideology and Consciousness* 3 (Spring 1978): 27–48, a collectively written analysis of several nineteenth-century women's novels which gives equal weight to gender, class, and literary production as textual determinants.]

9. [Margaret Homans, *Women Writers and Poetic Identity: Dorothy Wordsworth, Emily Brontë, and Emily Dickinson* (Princeton: Princeton UP, 1980) 10.]

10. [Josephine Donovan, "Afterward: Critical Revision," *Feminist Literary Criticism*, 74. Judith Fetterley, *The Resisting Reader: A Feminist Approach to American Fiction* (Bloomington: Indiana UP, 1978) viii. See my "Toward a Feminist Poetics," *The New Feminist Criticism*, 125–43. *The Authority of Experience* is the title of an anthology edited by Arlyn Diamond and Lee R. Edwards (Amherst: U of Massachusetts P, 1977).]

11. [Nina Auerbach, "Feminist Criticism Reviewed," *Gender and Literary Voice*, ed. Janet Todd (New York: Holmes & Meier, 1980) 258.]

12. Journals that publish feminist and postmodern literary criticism.

13. [Adrienne Rich, "When We Dead Awaken: Writing as Re-Vision," *On Lies, Secrets, and Silence* (New York: Norton, 1979) 35.]

14. [Annette Kolodny, "Dancing through the Minefield: Some Observations on the Theory, Practice, and Politics of a Feminist Literary Criticism," *The New Feminist Criticism*. The complete theoretical case for a feminist hermeneutics is outlined in Kolodny's essays, including "Some Notes on Defining a 'Feminist Literary Criticism,'" *Critical Inquiry* 2 (Autumn 1975): 75–92; "A Map for Rereading; or, Gender and the Interpretation of Literary Texts," *The New Feminist Criticism*, 46–62; and "The Theory of Feminist Criticism," National Center for the Humanities Conference on Feminist Criticism, Research Triangle Park, NC, March 1981.]

15. [Sandra M. Gilbert, "What Do Feminist Critics Want? A Postcard from the Volcano," in *The New Feminist Criticism*, 36.]

16. [Christiane Makward, "To Be or Not to Be. . . . A Feminist Speaker," *The Future of Difference*, ed. Hester Eisenstein and Alice Jardine (Boston: G. K. Hall, 1980) 102. On Lacan,

see Jane Gallop, "The Ladies' Man," *Diacritics* 6 (Winter 1976): 28–34; on Macherey, see the Marxist-Feminist Literature Collective's "Women's Writing."]

17. [Patricia Meyer Spacks, *The Female Imagination* (New York: Knopf, 1975) 19, 32.]

18. All are schools of literary theory, based variously on the thinking of Karl Marx (1818–1833), Sigmund Freud (1856–1939), and the French philosophers Jacques Lacan (1901–81) and Jacques Derrida (1930–).

19. [Hélène Cixous, "The Laugh of the Medusa," trans. Keith and Paula Cohen, *Signs* 1 (Summer 1976): 878. Nancy K. Miller, "Emphasis Added: Plots and Plausibilities in Women's Fiction," *The New Feminist Criticism*, 339–60.]

20. [For an overview, see Domna C. Stanton, "Language and Revolution: The Franco-American Dis-Connection," in Eisenstein and Jardine, *Future of Difference*, 73–87, and Elaine Marks and Isabelle de Courtivron, eds., *New French Feminisms* (Amherst: U of Massachusetts P, 1979); all further references to *New French Feminisms*, abbreviated *NFF*, will hereafter be included with translator's name parenthetically in the text.]

21. [Two major works are the manifesto of the Marxist-Feminist Literature Collective, "Women's Writing," and the papers from the Oxford University lectures on women and literature, Mary Jacobus, ed., *Women Writing and Writing about Women* (New York: Barnes & Noble Imports, 1979).]

22. [Sandra M. Gilbert and Susan Gubar, *The Madwoman in the Attic: The Woman Writer and the Nineteenth-Century Literary Imagination* (New Haven: Yale UP, 1979) 6, 7.]

23. [Nina Auerbach, rev. of *Madwoman, Victorian Studies* 23 (Summer 1980): 506.]

24. [Douglas Jerrold, quoted in Kathleen Tillotson, *Novels of the Eighteen-Forties* (London: Oxford UP, 1961) 39 n. James Joyce imagined the creator as female and literary creation as a process of gestation; see Richard Ellmann, *James Joyce: A Biography* (London: Oxford UP, 1959) 306–8.]

25. [Carolyn G. Burke, "Report from Paris: Women's Writing and the Women's Movement," *Signs* 3 (Summer 1978): 851.]

26. [Adrienne Rich, *Of Woman Born: Motherhood as Experience and Institution* (New York: Norton, 1976) 62. Biofeminist criticism has been influential in other disciplines as well: e.g., art critics, such as Judy Chicago and Lucy Lippard, have suggested that women artists are compelled to use a uterine or vaginal iconography of centralized focus, curved lines, and tactile or sensuous forms. See Lucy Lippard, *From the Center: Feminist Essays on Women's Art* (New York: Dutton, 1976).]

27. [See Alicia Ostriker, "Body Language: Imagery of the Body in Women's Poetry," *The State of the Language*, ed. Leonard Michaels and Christopher Ricks (Berkeley: U of California P, 1980) 247–63, and Terence Diggory, "Armoured Women, Naked Men: Dickinson, Whitman, and Their Successors," *Shakespeare's Sisters: Feminist Essays on Women Poets*, ed. Sandra M. Gilbert and Susan Gubar (Bloomington: Indiana UP, 1979) 135–50.]

28. [Rachel Blau DuPlessis, "Washing Blood," *Feminist Studies* 4 (June 1978): 10. The entire issue is an important document of feminist criticism.]

29. [Nancy K. Miller, "Women's Autobiography in France: For a Dialectics of Identification," in *Women and Language in Literature and Society*, eds. Sally McConnell-Ginet, Ruth Borker, and Nelly Furman (New York: Praeger, 1980) 271.]

30. [Nelly Furman, "The Study of Women and Language: Comment on Vol. 3, No. 3," *Signs* 4 (Autumn 1978): 182.]

31. [Burke, "Report from Paris," 844.]

32. [Jacobus, "The Difference of View," in *Women's Writing and Writing about Women*, 12–13. Shoshana Felman, "Women and Madness: The Critical Phallacy," *Diacritics* 5 (Winter 1975): 10.]

33. [On women's language, see Sarah B. Pomeroy, *Goddesses, Whores, Wives, and Slaves: Women in Classical Antiquity* (New York: Schocken, 1976) 24; Sally McConnell-Ginet, "Linguistics and the Feminist Challenge," *Women and Language*, 14; and Ioan M. Lewis, *Ecstatic Religion* (1971), cited in Shirley Ardener, ed., *Perceiving Women* (New York: Halsted, 1978) 50.]

34. [Clifford Geertz, *The Interpretation of Cultures* (New York: Basic, 1973) 241–42.]

35. [McConnell-Ginet, "Linguistics and the Feminist Challenge," 13, 16.]

36. [Virginia Woolf, "Speech, Manuscript Notes," *The Pargiters: The Novel-Essay Portion of the Years 1882–1941*, ed. Mitchell A. Leaska (New York: New York Public Library, 1977) 164.]

37. [Quoted in Erika Freeman, *Insights: Conversations with Theodor Reik* (Englewood Cliffs, NJ: Prentice-Hall, 1971) 166. Reik goes on, "But what the hell, writing! The great task of a woman is to bring a child into the world."]

38. [Cora Kaplan, "Language and Gender," unpublished paper, University of Sussex, 1977, 3.]

39. [Gilbert and Gubar, *Madwoman in the Attic*, 50.]

40. [See Annis Pratt, "The New Feminist Criticisms," *Beyond Intellectual Sexism: A New Woman, a New Reality*, ed. Joan I. Roberts (New York: Longman, 1976); Barbara H. Rigney, *Madness and Sexual Politics in the Feminist Novel: Studies in Brontë, Woolf, Lessing, and Atwood* (Madison: U of Wisconsin P, 1978); and Ann Douglas, "Mrs. Sigourney and the Sensibility of the Inner Space," *New England Quarterly* 45 (June 1972): 163–81.]

41. [Nancy Chodorow, "Gender, Relation, and Difference in Psychoanalytic Perspective," in Eisenstein and Jardine, *Future of Difference*, p. 11. See also Chodorow et al., "On *The Reproduction of Mothering*: A Methodological Debate," *Signs* 6 (Spring 1981): 482–514.]

42. [See, e.g., *The Lost Tradition: Mothers and Daughters in Literature*, ed. Cathy M. Davidson and E. M. Broner (New York: Frederick Ungar, 1980); this work is more engaged with myths and images of matrilineage than with redefining female identity.]

43. [Elizabeth Abel, "(E)Merging Identities: The Dynamics of Female Friendship in Contemporary Fiction by Women," *Signs* 6 (Spring 1981): 434.]

44. [Gerda Lerner, "The Challenge of Women's History," *The Majority Finds Its Past: Placing Women in History* (New York: Oxford UP, 1979); all further references to this book, abbreviated *MFP*, will hereafter be included parenthetically in the text.]

45. [See, e.g., Tillie Olsen, *Silences* (New York: Delacorte, 1978); Sheila Rowbotham, *Woman's Consciousness, Man's World* (New York: Penguin, 1974) 31–37; and Marcia Landy, "The Silent Woman: Towards a Feminist Critique," in Diamond and Edwards, *Authority of Experience* (n. 10 above), 16–27.]

46. [Edwin Ardener, "Belief and the Problem of Women," S. Ardener, *Perceiving Women* (n. 33 above), 3.]

47. [Mari McCarty, "Possessing Female Space: 'The Tender Shoot,'" *Women's Studies* 8 (1981): 368.]

48. [Susan Lanser and Evelyn Torton Beck, "[Why] Are There No Great Women Critics? And What Difference Does It Make?" *The Prism of Sex: Essays in the Sociology of Knowledge*, ed. Beck and Julia A. Sherman (Madison: U of Wisconsin P, 1979) 86.]

49. [Myra Jehlen, "Archimedes and the Paradox of Feminist Criticism," *Signs* 6 (Fall 1981): 582.]

50. [Smith, "Black Feminist Criticism," *The New Feminist Criticism*, 168–85. See also Gloria T. Hull, "Afro-American Women Poets: A Bio-Critical Survey," in Gilbert and Gubar, *Shake-*

speare's Sisters, 165–82, and Elaine Marks, "Lesbian Intertextuality," in *Homosexualities and French Literature*, ed. Marks and George Stambolian (Ithaca, NY: Cornell UP, 1979).]

51. [Margaret Anne Doody, "George Eliot and the Eighteenth-Century Novel," *Nineteenth-Century Fiction* 35 (December 1980): 267–68.]

52. [See, e.g., Judith Wilt, *Ghosts of the Gothic: Austen, Eliot, and Lawrence* (Princeton: Princeton UP, 1980).]

53. [See Ann Douglas, *The Feminization of American Culture* (New York: Knopf, 1977); Nina Baym, *Woman's Fiction: A Guide to Novels by and about Women in America, 1820–1870* (Ithaca, NY: Cornell UP, 1978); and Jane P. Tompkins, "Sentimental Power: *Uncle Tom's Cabin* and the Politics of Literary History," *The New Feminist Criticism*, 81–104.]

54. [See, e.g., the analysis of Woolf in Sandra M. Gilbert, "Costumes of the Mind: Transvestism as Metaphor in Modern Literature," *Critical Inquiry* 7 (Winter 1980): 391–417.]

55. [I.A. Richards, quoted in John Paul Russo, "A Study in Influence: The Moore-Richards Paradigm," *Critical Inquiry* 5 (Summer 1979): 687.]

56. [Showalter, "Literary Criticism," p. 435; Miller, "Emphasis Added," *The New Feminist Criticism*, 339–60. To take one example, whereas *Jane Eyre* had always been read in relation to an implied "dominant" fictional and social mode and had thus been perceived as flawed, feminist readings foreground its muted symbolic strategies and explore its credibility and coherence in its own terms. Feminist critics revise views like those of Richard Chase, who describes Rochester as castrated, thus implying that Jane's neurosis is penis envy, and G. Armour Craig, who sees the novel as Jane's struggle for superiority, to see Jane instead as healthy within her own system, that is, a *women's* society. See Chase, "The Brontës; or, Myth Domesticated," in *Jane Eyre* (New York: Norton, 1971) 462–71; Craig, "The Unpoetic Compromise: On the Relation between Private Vision and Social Order in Nineteenth-Century English Fiction," *Self and Society*, ed. Mark Schorer (New York: 1956) 30–41; Nancy Pell, "Resistance, Rebellion, and Marriage: The Economics of *Jane Eyre*," *Nineteenth-Century Fiction* 31 (March 1977): 397–420; Helene Moglen, *Charlotte Brontë: The Self Conceived* (New York: Norton, 1977); Adrienne Rich, "*Jane Eyre*: The Temptations of a Motherless Woman," *MS*, October 1973; and Maurianne Adams, "*Jane Eyre*: Woman's Estate," in Diamond and Edwards, *Authority of Experience*, 137–59.]

57. [Geertz, *Interpretation of Cultures*, 9.]

58. Harold Bloom is the author of *The Anxiety of Influence: A Theory of Poetry* (1973) and other works of literary criticism.

SECTION II

Writing Bodies/Bodies Writing

━━◦━ ☰◈☰ ━◦━━

Write your self. Your body must be heard. Only then will the immense
resources of the unconscious spring forth.

Hélène Cixous, "The Laugh of the Medusa"

Mutuality, continuity, connection, identification, touch: this motif constitutes the imperative of intimacy in women's writing, and in this motif we
find the elements of a gynocentric erotics, metaphysics, poetics, constituting a radical challenge to some of our most cherished cultural and psychic
assumptions.

Alicia Ostriker, Stealing the Language

Many women feel ambivalent about their bodies. In significant ways women's bodies
are a source of empowerment: They create life, give birth, work out, express sensuality and sexuality. On the other hand, women may perceive their bodies as too fat, too
thin, painful during menstruation, or vulnerable to sexual abuse. Women writers
through the ages have not only written about their bodies, but have linked embodiment to female creativity and explored complex connections between women's bodies and their texts.

Contemporary French feminist theory offers creative women many reasons to
write: to disrupt and subvert patriarchal definitions of "the feminine," to reconstruct
a fluid yet forceful female identity, to locate women's subjectivity and voices centrally in the realm of the body and its pleasures. The French feminist Luce Irigaray argues
that woman's sexuality and creativity emerge through her totality of body, a huge
erotic field that brings her *jouissance*—a term that suggests both sexual satisfaction
and the pleasure of the written text. "Woman's desire most likely does not speak the
same language as man's desire," she claims (101). The practice of the woman scribe
"inscribing woman" Irigaray calls *parler femme* (or "speaking woman"), Hélène
Cixous *l'écriture féminine* (or "feminine writing"). Both women use absolute language,
direct address, in their manifestos; theirs is an urgent message—"your body must be
heard"—a seductive cry for distinctively female erotic voices (Cixous, *LAWL* 395).

Anglo-American feminist critics are especially concerned with the specificity
of women's writing about their bodies and their use of body imagery to challenge
patriarchal culture. In *Stealing the Language* Alicia Ostriker offers a lively response
to Sigmund Freud's plaintive query, "What does woman want?" Rejecting Freud's
assertions that "biology is destiny" and that a woman experiences penis envy,
Ostriker takes as her subject not woman, singular, male-defined, but *women* and
the needs of their flesh, blood, bones, and hearts. Women writing the erotic, she

suggests, want to see and be seen, some by one person of primary intensity, others by multiple lovers/others. In fact, women do not merely want such recognition and reciprocity, they insist upon it—hence Ostriker's use of the term "imperative." From mutual sight and insight comes bodily sharing or its intimate equivalent, described in terms of *need, want, look, touch, joy*. And through the power and plea-sure of these exchanges, through shared subjectivity, women's strong erotic voices emerge (164–209).

Although Irigaray, Cixous, and Ostriker offer sexuality and embodiment as sources of empowerment, their analysis of female eroticism raises the question of why writing about bodies and *as* bodies has been difficult for many women historically and why such writing continues to be controversial. The belief in a mind-body dichoto-my has characterized Western philosophy from Plato to Descartes to Nietzsche, and church fathers such as St. Augustine and St. Jerome have presented the body as the enemy of both spirituality and reason. St. Augustine railed against the "slimy desires of the flesh," and both he and Descartes provided rules for gaining control over the body and its desires. Moreover, in this conception of body and mind as inimical, women have been identified with the bodily sphere and thus devalued, while men have been posited as rational and superior beings. Aristotle, for instance, considered the sperm the active seed that gave identity to the passive ovum; he claimed that "the female is female by virtue of a certain lack of qualities" and should be viewed, therefore, as an "imperfect man." Because Western thought was founded on this fear of the corporeal, the body has been constructed as a threat to reason; it has also been presented as the "feminine," or lesser, principle in a pervasive set of binary opposites: passion/reason, sensibility/sense, other/self, immanence/transcendence, and of course female/male. Historically, the body has been seen as fundamentally passive and dan-gerous, which has led to its social devaluation and, in turn, to the devaluation and oppression of women (Grosz 3–24).

ADRIENNE RICH speaks of the body as "the geography closest in," that territory which women have a right to claim and settle on their own terms (212). However lib-erating Rich's metaphor might seem, considering women's embodiment in geographi-cal terms reminds us of how often women's bodies have been raped, plundered, and colonized. For many women writing the body, pleasure is impossible until sexual viola-tion and its aftermath have been painfully inscribed. The hurt and rage caused by rape, incest, and sexual abuse enflame many women's writings, as do issues of anorex-ia, bulimia, and other forms of bodily denial. Some women have felt compelled to conceal sexual violence even as their writing exposes it. Witness for instance HARRIET JACOBS, writing as Linda Brent, describing "incidents" in the life of a slave girl as "foulness" and "cruel wrongs" that cannot be articulated—not only because of the horror of repeated sexual harassment at the hands of her master, but because Jacobs realized full well that many whites would believe she had "asked for it." As Teresa de Lauretis notes, many African-American critics have insisted that white feminists reevaluate their discourse to reflect the lack of sexual agency experienced by poor women and women of color historically. "Sexuality is a term of power . . . and it belongs to the empowered," she concludes (de Lauretis 13). Which women writers are in a position to celebrate their desire, and which are most subject to sexual exploitation, has been historically and socially determined by race, class, nationality, sexual preference, age, and caste.

Although there are important similarities among women writers' depictions of desire, it is important to examine the salient contrasts. Differences in sexual orientation certainly affect women's attempts to write the body. As a self-described "black lesbian feminist warrior poet," AUDRE LORDE considers the erotic a long-repressed source of power in women's lives, "an assertion of the life force of women; of that creative energy empowered, the knowledge and use of which we are now reclaiming in our language, our history, our dancing, our loving, our work, our lives." Lorde refuses to locate the erotic exclusively in the realm of the sexual, preferring instead to envision it as sensual and creative: "there is, for me, no difference between writing a good poem and moving into sunlight against the body of a woman I love" (*LAWL* 539). While Ostriker claims that erotic expression offers women poets a place to shed gender, Lorde, along with many other lesbian writers, affirms and intensifies gender in her inscription of the erotic rather than erasing it. In the 1970s, lesbian writers like Mary Daly and Adrienne Rich joined VIRGINIA WOOLF in embracing androgyny, the metaphorical blending of male and female attributes, as a potent aspect of the lesbian erotic imaginary, only to reject it in the 1980s as part of the law of the fathers. Rich's critique of "compulsory heterosexuality" has influenced younger women such as JACKIE KAY and CHERRÍE MORAGA, whose writings celebrate the power and complexity of same-sex love (Rich 23–75). If Lorde is right in asserting that difference is best defined as a source of strength among women, then women of all sexual preferences and practices can learn much about sexuality and difference by reading the inscriptions of women whose sexual identities vary from their own. In the realm of desire, "an all-purpose feminist frame of reference does not exist, nor should it ever come prepackaged and ready-made" (de Lauretis 14).

Although women's writing about their bodies varies considerably, their work can be seen as inscribing desire in four general ways. For many women throughout history, to write of sexuality has been to write of loss, regret, desire unfulfilled. For others, writing the body has unleashed memories of violence and abuse, of bodies exploited. A more fortunate group of women has chosen to celebrate female sexuality in all its power and multiplicity. A daring few have attempted to represent the erotic as it has not been portrayed before—to transform desire. The sections below will explore several dimensions of these four strategies of "writing bodies/bodies writing."

DESIRE UNFULFILLED

Far and near I must
suffer the feud of my dearly loved man. . . .
I never can
find sweet rest for that heart's grief of mine.

"The Wife's Lament"

In me alone survive
The unregenerate passions of a day
When treacherous queens, with death upon the tread,
Heedless and willful, took their knights to bed.

Edna St. Vincent Millay, Fatal Interview

The study of elegies—poems about pain and grief—offers a means of exploring the ways in which cultural meanings derive from loss and its resultant mourning processes. Such meanings, of course, are profoundly gendered. Literary critics from Peter Sacks to Melissa Zeiger have treated the elegy as "heroic male narratives of renunciation" (Zeiger 6) in which women are either the objects of loss or the background to it, while male melancholia and its opportunity for male bonding are privileged elegiac subjects. If women's grief is represented at all, a melancholic male poet has often inscribed it. However, any exploration of elegy is complicated by the fact that throughout history, the role of mourner has been played by women rather than men. Early sixteenth-century consolation manuals urge men to remain stoic in the face of grief, and even Orpheus, that quintessential elegist who mourned in song the loss of his wife, Eurydice, is demasculinized because of the excesses of his grief. Some tales of Orpheus credit him with "originating" homosexuality as a means of coping with frustrated heterosexual desire. As Zeiger argues, the elegy has long been male-dominated; when women poets have written in this mode, their elegies have established a countertradition that is revisionist in nature (62–82). Although many women's elegies mourn dead or dying children or parents, the elegiac mode for women can also be linked to issues of "romantic thralldom," to use Rachel Blau DuPlessis's phrase—to their laments over frustrated desire and absent or inconstant lovers (1).

The mourning of an Anglo-Saxon woman, isolated, alone, and powerless to change her situation, lies at the heart of "The Wife's Lament," an elegy that survives as part of a tenth-century manuscript, the *Exeter Book*. It is one of two Old English elegies believed to have been composed by a woman. Despite the despair of the poem's speaker, who mourns her banished husband, her very speech challenges the boundaries of elegy by asserting that women's grief *matters*, deserves sympathy, defies gender stereotypes that expect women to remain silent or weeping as they grieve. The poet's frequent use of *min*, the possessive pronoun *mine*, reinforces her insistent, embodied connection to both her distant husband and her poetic speech. In other Old English poems a man conveys women's grief, tangentially; the *Beowulf* poet tells us, of Hildeburh, "*ides gnornoed*" ("the lady mourned"), but we do not hear her voice. When women write their bodies, Cixous proclaims, their words "must inundate, run through, go beyond the discourse," and indeed in "The Wife's Lament" unfulfilled desire overflows its shores. "I am stabbed with longing," the speaker declares with heightened emotion; "And longing smote me" (*LAWL* 417). Although the suffering in this elegy is painful to witness, as the critic Patricia Belanoff (in Damico and Olsen, 1990) has noted, its vivid representation of women's maltreatment undermines the Old English heroic ethos by focusing on the women cast aside in times of war and feud. The existence of such early women's elegies as "The Wife's Lament" and "Wulf and Eadwacer" also undermines assumptions of the elegiac tradition, in which women's voices have been construed as either missing or muted.

Some women writers of the Renaissance used the conventions of courtly love to mourn the loss of lovers. Courtly love, which culminated in the songs of Petrarch in fourteenth-century Italy and the poems of Elizabethan sonneteers in sixteenth-century England, established a literary code of lovemaking in which a male speaker idealizes his female beloved. Although each troubadour pays homage to his lady, he also asserts himself as a forceful "I," an active singer to whom others must listen. His lady, in contrast, is often designated *res*, thing. Male subjectivity and narcissism dominate the traditional courtly love poem; its focal character, finally, is not the beloved but the lover. When Renaissance women appropriate courtly conventions in their poetry, they express their grief at a lover's coldness or absence but implicitly affirm their own subjectivity and presence. One such poem is "On Monsieur's Departure" by ELIZABETH I, which offers a cathartic outpouring in a female voice, assertive and embodied, and thus subtly subverts courtly tradition. Like "The Wife's Lament," Elizabeth's poem undermines conventional elegy by voicing women's frustrations, yet it continues to represent women as victims of unfulfilled desire. A woman's version of courtly love appears as well in poems by MARY WROTH, whose sonnets were influenced by those of her uncle, Sir Philip Sidney, a renowned sonneteer. *Pamphilia to Amphilanthus,* a collection of more than 100 sonnets and songs, was the earliest sequence of love poems by a woman to be published in early modern England. As in Elizabeth's poem, Wroth's Pamphilia waits endlessly for her lover to appear, but unlike Elizabeth's speaker, she manifests bitterness at his frequent betrayals. Once again a woman presents passivity in love—"haplesse me" she often cries—as woman's lot, given the socially prescribed and rigidly patriarchal mores of the Jacobean court that constitutes her world.

Women writers of the seventeenth, eighteenth, and nineteenth centuries wrote elegies as well, although they tended not to foreground romantic thralldom so much as other kinds of loss. In colonial America the Puritan poet ANNE BRADSTREET mourned the death of her grandchildren and the burning of her house, while eighteenth-century Englishwomen lamented the death of the poets John Dryden and Elizabeth Rowe. The nineteenth-century poets LYDIA SIGOURNEY in America and FELICIA HEMANS in England wrote consolatory verse for the many mothers whose children died in infancy. Although these writers did not eroticize their elegies, they often presented graphic portraits of dying bodies and tearful mourners. In women's elegies of the nineteenth century we also find accounts of unfulfilled desire in which the woman, despite her heartbreak, claims some form of agency: that is, she articulates her own consciousness from her own authority and on her own terms. Although Petrarchan and Elizabethan sonnets of courtly love greatly influenced the Victorian poet CHRISTINA ROSSETTI, she represents both women's vulnerability in love and the force of her desire. Her *Monna Innominata,* a sonnet sequence written from the point of view of the troubadour's lady, is fraught with longing. Yet Rossetti's sonnet sequence offers moments at which the grieving speaker can proclaim her own dignity, recalling a love based not on domination but on equality. "'Love me, for I love you'—and answer me," the poet exhorts her absent beloved. "'Love me, for I love you'—so shall we stand / As happy equals in the flowering land / Of love, that knows not a dividing sea" (*LAWL* 516). Although taking refuge in memory can certainly be a danger, Rossetti claims the power of memory to be both balm and comfort.

The writings of twentieth-century poet EDNA ST. VINCENT MILLAY offer an important kind of elegiac reclamation by presenting the memory of lost love as a source of female empowerment. The sonnets of *Fatal Interview* constitute a major shift in women's presentation of romantic love; their speaker's desire is unfulfilled not because of a male lover's absence but because of the enormity of her own emotional and erotic cravings. The speaker with whom the poet aligns herself is a sexual agent; she takes men to bed rather than being taken by them. Such passion makes women vulnerable, and ultimately the sonnets in *Fatal Interview* track not enduring love but a relationship's demise. Yet even in loss the speaker affirms the power of her right to love, like lusty queens of old.

The concerns of presence, voice, and desire are central to women's elegies. Whereas modern women elegists rebel actively against male-defined concepts of romantic thralldom, however, many earlier women poets inscribe their passivity in love, as in other aspects of society. It is therefore difficult to determine the extent to which these earlier women subvert stereotypes of women waiting for their male lovers when they write their own embodied grief. Still, the fact that many women through the ages have told their stories of unfulfilled desire indicates that expressing frustration in love has never been the literary prerogative of the male writer alone.

BODIES EXPLOITED

> Oh write me a poem mother
> here, over my flesh
> get your words upon me
> as he got this child upon me
> our father lover
> thief in the night
>
> *Audre Lorde, "Chain"*

> It would have been more pleasant to me to have been silent about my own history.
> *Harriet Jacobs*, preface to *Incidents in the Life of a Slave Girl*

Throughout history women have been subjected to physical, psychological, verbal, and economic abuse at the hands of men, often those who claim to love them—husbands, lovers, fathers, uncles, brothers. For women, to speak out about sexual abuse is to risk making body and spirit doubly vulnerable, since such violence has been often sanctioned, its impact trivialized. Yet countless women have testified to their own experiences of sexual coercion and those of other women, though their testimonies have sometimes remained unpublished until years, even centuries, later. Rape, domestic violence, and incest—topics once silenced—provide subject matter today for women across races, classes, and cultures; yet women still risk censure and disbelief when they testify to abuse. Many feminists would agree with Susan Brownmiller that rather than representing "society's aberrants, or 'spoilers of purity,' men who commit rape [or other forms of sexual violence] have served in effect as frontline masculine shock troops, terrorist guerrillas in the longest sustained battle the world has ever known" (209). Writing about sexual abuse is one way that women are fighting back.

In *The Body in Pain* Elaine Scarry addresses powerfully the subject of pain's resistance to language. She cites on this matter VIRGINIA WOOLF, who claimed that "English, which can express the thoughts of Hamlet and the tragedy of Lear has no words for the shiver or the headache. . . . The merest schoolgirl when she falls in love has Shakespeare or Keats to speak her mind for her, but let a sufferer try to describe a pain in his head to a doctor and language at once runs dry." As Scarry notes, Woolf's assertion is even more true of serious and prolonged pain, which "does not simply resist language but actively destroys it, bringing about an immediate reversion to a state anterior to language, to the sounds and cries a human being makes before language is learned" (4). Both the inexpressibility of pain and a reversion to prelinguistic sounds and cries lie at the heart of women's writing about sexual abuse. Women writers attempt both to shatter language and, by naming the pain of abuse, to reconstitute language as a vehicle and sign of survival. Furthermore, much of women's writing about sexual abuse requires readers to examine not only the violations of individual girls and women but also the systemic and political implications of these acts. Both endemic and epidemic, sexual violence was for centuries denied in part *because* it lacked significant literary representation. Couragously, numerous women writers have documented sexual exploitation in sickening, searing words that cannot be ignored.

That domestic violence has a long history can be verified by considering the testimony of Lady Margaret Cuninghame, whose diary of 1608 remained unpublished until 1827, when two copies were found in Scotland, one owned by Sir Walter Scott (see Otter, 1992). Four years after her marriage, Cuninghame explains, her husband became involved with another woman, who became pregnant by him. Thereafter, "my husband conceived a great anger against me . . . and he would not come into the house I was in. . . . Being altogether destitute, I was forced to advertise my parents." Cuninghame goes on to describe "all his wonted iniquities": "he neglected his duty toward God, he kept no duty toward me, but became altogether unkind, cruel, and malicious. . . . He would not suffer any gentlewoman to remain with me . . . and cruelly, in the night, put both her and me forth of his house naked and would not suffer us to put on our clothes, but said he would strike both our backs in two with a sword." When Cuninghame gave birth to her third son, her husband refused to baptize the baby or provide for him, but after five weeks he came to her and demanded sexual access. That she refused his "filthy pleasure" attests to her strength and that of her protective parents, who managed to stop her husband's physical abuse of their daughter but could not prevent him from leaving her penniless (Otten 25–28). As Brownmiller notes, when sexual violence "operates within an emotional setting or within a dependent relationship that provides a hierarchical, authoritarian structure of its own," it all too often "weakens a victim's resistance, distorts her perspective and confounds her will" (384). The miracle of Cuninghame's narrative is that it exists at all.

In sixteenth- and seventeenth-century England, domestic violence was often tolerated, but rape was at least occasionally prosecuted, though it rarely resulted in conviction. The Statutes of Westminster, set forth by Edward I at the end of the thirteenth century, were the first legislation to authorize the prosecution of all types of rape, not just the forced deflowering of a virgin; the concept of statutory rape thus dates from this time. Nonetheless, household servants, single female dependents, unhappily married women, and widows had little protection, since their livelihood often required that they submit to unwanted sexual advances. Children were also vulnerable. As Charlotte F. Otten has noted, the *Chronicle from Aldgate* of May 12, 1587, reports that "a little girl of six and another of thirteen were murdered by rapists," and although the rapists were later identified, there exists no record of their prosecution. In the early seventeenth century, furthermore, a physician, Dr. John Lamb, was convicted of raping an eleven-year-old girl, Joan Seager, on the testimony of a neighbor, Mabel Swinnerton, who examined the frightened girl at her mother's request shortly after the rape occurred and found her genitals inflamed. Seager had been delivering a basket of medicinal herbs to the doctor's office at the time of the rape. When the king pardoned Lamb, a crowd of angry theater-goers clubbed the doctor to death (Otten 13, 18–19). Such stories from the early annals of English history are important predecessors to women's more recent writing about sexual abuse, in part because the widespread publication of these offenses helped to alert women to the realities of rape and to the role that the justice system was supposed to play in holding perpetrators accountable.

HARRIET JACOBS's *Incidents in the Life of a Slave Girl* depicts the ways in which racial and sexual abuse merged for enslaved women like Jacobs, whose master, a prominent North Carolina physician, sexually harassed her from the time she was fifteen. Foul words gave way to foul deeds, Jacobs' pseudonymous Linda Brent recounts, as her master "roved about day and night, seeking whom to devour." Angela Davis has claimed that "slavery relied as much on routine sexual abuse as it relied on the whip and the lash" (175), and certainly Jacobs's experience testifies to the truth of that observation. Jacobs consistently asserts that the violence of slavery is unspeakable: "The degradations, the wrongs, the vices, that grow out of slavery are more than I can describe. . . . [The master] came every day, and I was subjected to such insults as no pen can describe. I would not describe them if I could; they were too low, too revolting" (*LAWL* 507). This duplicitous strategy of both naming and refusing to name the terms of her abuse lies at the core of Jacobs's narrative. She conveys the sense of doubleness that pervades women's writing about the abuses of slavery, but she also sees herself as a source of power in that she is speaking for her people, generalizing from her experience to that of other women.

As Jacobs's testimonial illustrates, the sexual violation of adolescent girls and children is a particularly painful topic, and one that many women writers address. AUDRE LORDE's "Chain" takes as its point of departure a news report of two teenage girls who were placed in foster care after they had borne children by their biological father, then were removed and were returned to their father's care. A poem of both lamentation and outrage against the widespread crime of incest, "Chain" expresses the speaker's resounding grief at the repeated sexual violations of "the skeleton children / advancing against us" and in so doing indicts a whole society. "On the porch outside my door / girls are lying / like felled maples in the path of my feet," the speaker mourns; "I cannot step past them nor over them" (*LAWL* 541). Powerless to stop sexual abuse, the poet can instead bear troubled witness against it, naming the girls' unthinkable pain and rage as well as her own.

Other poems about paternal abuse document physical rather than sexual violation, as in SHARON OLDS's "That Year." This powerful poem juxtaposes the time of the speaker's first menstrual period, of "crossing over that border in the night" from girlhood to womanhood, with another pivotal transformation, her mother's shift from compliant to resistant toward her husband's abusive behavior. "That was the year my mother took us and / hid us so he could not get at us," Olds explains, "so there were no more / tyings by the wrist to the chair, / no more denial of food/ or the forcing of foods, the head held back, / down the throat at the restaurant." That year the speaker studied Auschwitz and recognized "my father's face" in the face of the guard; she recognized in "the symmetrical pile of white bodies" her own vulnerable flesh. But Olds's identification with Jews during the Holocaust does not stop with an awareness of their mutual victimization. Like many who emerged from Auschwitz, she claims a hopeful word as her mantra: "I was: / a survivor" (*LAWL* 559).

Child sexual abuse, rape, and domestic violence are painful topics that all of these writers no doubt wish would disappear from the landscape of female experience. Because such atrocities do occur, however, these women have bravely documented the violations themselves as well as the different ways they and their sisters have challenged men's misuse of power. "The secrets of slavery are concealed like those of the Inquisition," HARRIET JACOBS writes near the end of her slave narrative. "I [write] to kindle a flame of compassion in your hearts for my sisters who are still in bondage" (*LAWL* 508, 511). As Jacobs's testimony illustrates, to break silence about the exploitation of women's bodies constitutes an act of courage and reclamation.

BODIES CELEBRATED

I am she / I'm dark / in the veins / I'm intoxicant.
                                 Sandra Cisneros, "I the Woman"

Come.
Lie with me before the flame.
I will dream you a wolf
and suckle you newborn.
I will dream you a hawk
and circle this city in your
racing heart.

                                 Joy Harjo, "City of Fire"

Women writers have always celebrated their sexuality, and for this they have often been censured. "A little too loosely she writ," claimed ANNE FINCH of the predecessor she most admired, the seventeenth-century poet and playwright APHRA BEHN. Reviled by many as a woman who lived as loosely as she wrote and thus should be considered shameful, Behn scorned such criticism and became one of the most successful writers for the Restoration stage. Behn's plays are distinctive in their presentation of women as sexual agents. In *The Lucky Chance*, for example, the female characters plot ways to consummate their love as resolutely as their young male suitors do. Though popular in its own time, this play was considered too raunchy to be produced by eighteenth and nineteenth century audiences. Actually, it was only in the late 1970s, during the second wave of the women's movement, that *The Lucky Chance* found new audiences comfortable with the play's feminist treatment of adultery and female sexuality. Among the many women writers who have paid homage to Behn's originality and courage, VIRGINIA WOOLF is perhaps the most memorable. "All women together ought to let flowers fall upon the tomb of Aphra Behn," she claims in *A Room of One's Own*, "for it was she who earned them the right to speak their minds" (*LAWL* 48).

Since the time of the early Christians, remaining virgins has been a way for women to become men's equals and take away the "sins of Eve." Thus some early Englishwomen wrote not about their sexuality but about their virginity, a state of wholeness they claimed to have freely chosen. In "A Virgin Life," for example, seventeenth-century poet JANE BARKER pays homage to single womanhood as "a happy state" that frees her to pursue art more voraciously. Although she acknowledges the temptations of masculine charm and lovers' overtures, the virgin life, with its emphasis on work, friendship, and daughterly devotion, remains for her "the impress of all good." These poems offer philosophical reflections on the nature of desire, claiming women's right to withhold as well as to express it. Modern women have tended to celebrate the consummation of desire rather than its virginal alternative. Sex for these writers is often not about transcendence, nor is intimacy defined by oppressive hierarchies or traditional womanly self-sacrifice. Although she is speaking of current women poets, Alicia Ostriker's observation has broader implications: "The female desire which seems to dominate contemporary women's poetry does stress 'empathy' and 'tenderness' but is not at all 'undemanding' and is strongly opposed to polarization" (199). Such writing recounts the pleasures of sexual love and resists objectification; both the writer and her lover are subjects. There typically exist, in Ostriker's words, "an equivalence and ambivalence between the lover's body and her own" (169). Desire is mutual and contagious, that is, and who initiates the lovemaking simply doesn't matter.

Poems by two contemporary U.S. women will illustrate the way desire is celebrated by many. The first poet, SANDRA CISNEROS, offers a playful view of erotic transgression, as she discovers through poetry both her sexual and creative identities. The joy of self-naming dominates "I the Woman," in which Cisneros traces her own contours with a score of radiant images: "I'm hip / and good skin / brass / and sharp tooth / hard lip pushed / against / the air / I'm lightbeam / no stopping me." The joy of desire fulfilled appears in "Love Poem #1," as the speaker revels in pleasure after lovemaking: "then it is I want to hymn / and hallelujah /sing sweet sweet jubilee / you my religion / and I a wicked nun" (*LAWL* 577-78). JOY HARJO writes poetry that is equally celebratory. Exploring the tensions and transformations of heterosexual love, her poems blend Native American wisdom about the sacred with feminist principles. This mixture appears in "City of Fire," as the poet invites her lover to take refuge in her impassioned arms: "Come, sweet, / I am a house with many rooms. / There is no end. / Each room is a street to the next world." Such passion has tender moments—"I will dream you the wind"—and violent ones—"I take you apart raw"; but ultimately it brings healing. "We will make a river," Harjo exhorts her lover at the end, "flood this city built of passion / with fire, / with a revolutionary fire" (*LAWL* 570-71).

Contemporary women fiction writers often liberate themselves from a sense of shame, and thereby celebrate the power of their own sensuality and desire. The insouciant narrator of TONI CADE BAMBARA's "My Man Bovanne" initially asks "a nice ole gent from the block" to dance at a neighborhood gathering just because she likes dancing. "And I press up close to dance with Bovanne who is blind and I'm hummin and he hummin, chest to chest like talkin. Not jammin my breasts into the man. Wasn't bout tits. Was bout vibrations." One kind of vibrations leads to another, however, and when Hazel's grown children object to their mother's behavior, she at first is hurt that they see her as acting "like a bitch in heat." Quickly, however, she asserts her right to move her body as she pleases. When her son chastises her—"you embarrass yourself and us too dancin like that"—she retorts, "I wasn't shame"

(*LAWL* 556). Despite her children's lack of understanding, Hazel knows that she has a right to claim her sexuality at any age.

Two complicated questions about desire and difference lie at the heart of BHARATI MUKHERJEE's "A Wife's Story": What effects do the realities of diaspora and cultural dislocation have on the protagonist's transcontinental marriage? How can she conduct her erotic life in the United States? When the wife of the story, Panna Bhatt, a graduate student in Manhattan, is visited by her husband, who lives near Bombay, their gender dynamics shift as cultural assimilation and cultural dissonance intersect. At one point this conventional member of the Brahmin male elite, "who has never entered the kitchen of our Ahmadabad house," not only cooks in a microwave oven but bathes his wife's feet, using "a dish tub of steamy water to massage away the pavement heat." Although Panna Bhatt is unable fully to resolve the contradictions between U.S. and Indian cultural mores, specifically between love here and love there, what empowers her finally is the pleasure she takes in the "home" of her own body:

> In the mirror that hangs on the bathroom door, I watch my naked body turn, the breasts, the thighs glow. The body's beauty amazes. I stand here shameless, in ways he has never seen me. I am free, afloat, watching somebody else (*LAWL* 553).

For women writers celebrating their sexuality, eroticism is linked not to passivity but to power, which they redefine as self-integration, a resource within each woman that constitutes a form of knowledge. This is not to say that women's homages to desire are always solemn; they are often wildly humorous. Ostriker asserts that laughter is art's most subversive force. In claiming that "to release sexual libido is [for women] to subvert social and political order," she concurs with feminist theorists like Cixous and Irigaray, who argue that women's choice to define their own sexuality radically disrupts male authority (Ostriker 176). It thus is little wonder that these two disruptive agents, laughter and sexual power, should meet in writings that celebrate women's bodies.

DESIRE TRANSFORMED

> Our merciful Lord Christ Jesus—blessed may he be!—ravished her spirit and said to her, "Daughter, why do you weep so sorrowfully? I have come to you. . . . This is my will, daughter, that you receive my body every Sunday, and I shall flow so much grace into you that all the world shall marvel at it."
>
> *The Book of Margery Kempe*

> The body is a dwellingplace, as the Anglo-Saxons knew in naming it *banhus* (bonehouse) and *lichama* (bodyhome), and the homeliness of its nature is even livelier for a woman than for a man. . . . Through writing her body, a woman may reclaim the deed to her dwelling.
>
> *Nancy Mairs, "Reading Houses, Writing Lives"*

A few women writers through the ages have been pioneers who have written about their bodies with extraordinary vision. The fifteenth-century autobiographer

MARGERY KEMPE is one of the first women to transform the language of desire on her own terms; in this effort she joins other medieval mystics such as JULIAN OF NORWICH and Hildegard of Bingen. In *The Book of Margery Kempe* the mystic recounts both her early sexual life with her husband and her subsequent decision, after a spiritual visitation, to renounce the pleasures of the flesh. As Wendy Harding has noted, Kempe's testimony (which was dictated to male scribes) "blurs the boundaries" between the scribes' "clerical style" and "the laywoman's oral utterances," thus destabilizing ancient, hierarchical dichotomy between mind and body, male and female, the powerful and the marginalized. Rather than the mad ravings of an illiterate woman, *The Book of Margery Kempe* "can be seen as a woman's attempt to signify a mystical experience whose intensity cannot be written but must be inscribed by living flesh" (Harding 173–74). Empowered by Kempe's mystical eroticism, this text represents an early contribution to a growing body of women's literature that attempts to transform the landscape of desire.

The modernist DJUNA BARNES writes the body through an astonishing array of ancient and contemporary concerns, including lesbian desire, heterosexual ennui, and the force-feeding of suffragists. Barnes's use of bawdy comedy in *Ladies Almanack*, a celebration of lesbian sexuality, establishes her as Behn's successor, but much of her writing about women's bodily experience is painfully serious. In many works she portrays a community of outsiders and defends the sexually wounded. For example, the heroine of her play *To the Dogs*, Helena Hucksteppe, is both powerful and vulnerable because of the ways in which her female sexual identity has been socially constructed. In "How It Feels to Be Forcibly Fed" Barnes transforms her experience as a journalist covering the British women's suffrage movement into a powerful, angry account of such a force-feeding. Her narrator tells of the prison's doctor first burning her nostrils by spraying them with cocaine and disinfectant, then inserting a tube painfully into her throat. In this story Barnes condemns the British government's shameful exploitation of women's bodies for conservative political purposes.

Women who have written the body in transformational ways have often been subjected to denigration by their male peers. Reviewing work by the U.S. confessional poet ANNE SEXTON, James Dickey claimed that "It would be hard to find a writer who dwells more insistently on the pathetic and disgusting aspects of bodily experience" (qtd. in Kumin i). What Dickey deems pathetic and disgusting, however, many feminist readers find powerful and liberating. Sexton's friend and colleague Maxine Kumin explains that in focusing on women's bodies and erotic lives as subject matter, Sexton broke new ground; she "wrote openly about menstruation, abortion, masturbation, incest, adultery, and drug addiction at a time when the proprieties embraced none of these as proper topics for poetry" (Kumin ii). Such poems as "The Abortion" and "In Celebration of My Uterus" assert the power and universality of women's embodiment. "Each cell has a life," Sexton claims in honoring her uterus; "there is enough here to please a nation." Women's reproductive organs link them across class and geographical boundaries, she implies, for wombs are democratic and ubiquitous: "It is enough that the populace own these goods" (*LAWL* 533).

Among contemporary women, lesbians have been particularly involved in writing the body in transformational ways. For AUDRE LORDE, the erotic is most profoundly inscribed in the language of love, nurture, spirituality, and shared politics rather than lust. "The erotic," she asserts, "is a resource within each of us that lies in a deeply female and spiritual plane" (*LAWL* 536). Transformation occurs when black lesbians refuse to be silent about their desire, claiming their sexual orientation as part of an African-American legacy of resistance and survival, not as somehow threatening to that legacy. Thus when she published "Love Poem," a depiction of lesbian lovemaking, in *Ms.* magazine in 1971, Lorde posted it on the walls of her university office as an act of self-naming and a means of stimulating discussion of lesbianism and homophobia in her academic community. "Our erotic knowledge empowers us," Lorde declares; it "becomes a lens through which we scrutinize all aspects of our existence" (*LAWL* 538).

Some contemporary writers explore the power of the erotic even as they struggle with serious bodily limitations. The American essayist NANCY MAIRS draws upon Cixous's theory of *jouissance* to identify the female body as a space of desire once colonized by men but now reclaimed by women. Linguistic examination is central to Mairs's presentation of the erotic, as she explores the Anglo-Saxon term for the body, *banhus*, or bonehouse—a concept with particular resonance for her as a self-described "cripple," disabled by multiple sclerosis. Writing a memoir about her embodied existence, she chooses to "mention my body, certainly, quite a lot, even its secret places. Here and there I kiss, stroke, press, squeeze, even engage in sexual intercourse. Not as often, though, as I lie in bed, run across a playground, eat favorite foods, listen to the radio, tease my sister, roll in new snow. All these acts, happening to me as a body, shaping my awareness of my embodied self, form my erotic being" (*LAWL* 413). Both Lorde and Mairs present women's bodies, whether able or physically challenged, as the loci of a new erotic imaginary. These are important "bodies writing," women who seek to transform desire for their readers—of every sexual orientation.

In *The Body in the Text*, the Australian critic Anne Cranny-Francis claims that popular culture and postmodern academic theory represent female bodies in transformational ways. "'The body' is the subject of postmodernist concerns with issues of ontology (the essence of things or being in the abstract) and epistemology (theory of knowledge)," she explains. "What is the body? How are its limits defined? What space or place does it occupy? In a social context which is becoming increasingly information-based, how should the modernist conception of the body be rethought? How is this body 'known'?" (12–13). These and other questions are the subjects of inquiry across academic disciplines today. The complex space that women's bodies occupy in a postmodern age can be seen in MTV videos such as Madonna's "Material Girl," in which she presents herself erotically as the 1950s sex goddess Marilyn Monroe. Madonna's identification with this film star, notes Cranny-Francis, demonstrates the power of Monroe's sexualized image and raises interesting questions about women's bodies and contemporary representation: "After all, who is the 'star' of this video, Madonna or Monroe?" (14). In addition, the video leads viewers to consider who controls *how* women's bodies, and *which* women's bodies, are reproduced in contemporary mass media. Although whether rock stars like Madonna are transforming traditional depictions of women's sexuality or exploiting them depends upon one's perspective, one fact is clear: public representations of women's bodies are surely more prevalent and more hotly contested during this new millennium than ever before in history.

⊰ Works Cited—Section II ⊱

Note: In the introductory essay, all citations of works included in this anthology are indicated by *LAWL*, followed by the page number.

Brownmiller, Susan. *Against Our Will: Men, Women, and Rape*. New York: Simon and Schuster, 1975. A classic feminist study of rape from biblical times to the Vietnam War, this book explores how rape became a crime, how rape laws harm women and children, and why the "myth of the heroic rapist" is flawed.

Cranny-Francis, Anne. *The Body in the Text*. Melbourne, Austral.: Melbourne UP, 1995. This book analyzes literary and theoretical texts as well as film and television in examining how male and female bodies have been represented in the late twentieth century. How bodies are reconceptualized across gender, race, class, and ethnic lines and how technology is changing our views of embodiment and desire are among her topics of scrutiny.

Damico, Helen, and Alexandra Hennessey Olsen, eds. *New Readings on Women in Old English Literature*. Bloomington: U of Indiana P, 1990. This collection contains Patricia Belanoff's fine essays on "The Wife's Lament" and "Wulf and Eadwacer" and others on the representation of women in Anglo-Saxon literature.

Davis, Angela. *Women, Race and Class*. New York: Vintage, 1983. A prominent feminist political activist and scholar, Davis examines the impact of sexual abuse and racism on black women under slavery and in modern contexts and helps us better understand slave narratives by women such as Harriet Jacobs.

de Lauretis, Teresa, ed. *Feminist Studies, Critical Studies*. Bloomington: Indiana UP, 1986. This collection contains a useful introduction that discusses feminist theorizing of the body, as well as relevant essays by Jessica Benjamin, Sondra O'Neale, Cherríe Moraga, and Mary Russo.

DuPlessis, Rachel Blau. *Writing Beyond the Ending: Narrative Strategies of Twentieth-Century Women Writers*. Bloomington: Indiana UP, 1985. This study explores how women writers use gaps and ruptures, break narrative sequence, and revise myths such as romantic thralldom. Among the writers discussed are H.D., Virginia Woolf, Muriel Rukeyser, and Adrienne Rich.

Grosz, Elizabeth A. *Volatile Bodies: Toward a Corporeal Feminism*. Bloomington: Indiana UP, 1994. In this book Grosz examines how women's bodies have been socially constructed and how reevaluating women's bodily experience—menstruation, pregnancy, childbirth, menopause—can help to theorize female embodiment in new ways.

Harding, Wendy. "Body into Text: *The Book of Margery Kempe*." *Feminist Approaches to the Body in Medieval Literature*. Eds. Linda Lomperis and Sarah Stanbury. Philadelphia: U of Pennsylvania P, 1993, 168–87. This essay examines how Kempe's illiteracy freed her from patriarchal control, yet because of it she required men's aid to create her text and "enter the historical record." It also analyzes how Kempe inscribed her "living flesh," refusing to submit her body to male control.

Irigaray, Luce. "This Sex Which Is Not One." *New French Feminisms*. Eds. Elaine Marks and Isabelle de Courtivron. New York: Schocken, 1981, 99–106. This essay on the multiplicity of women's sexuality is among Irigaray's best known. The anthology as a whole contains an excellent critical and historical introduction to French feminism and includes translations of essays by Hélène Cixous, Catherine Clément, Julia Kristeva, Monique Wittig, and other French theoreticians.

Kumin, Maxine. Foreword, *The Complete Poems of Anne Sexton*. Boston: Houghton Mifflin, 1981. In this introduction to Sexton's poetry Kumin discusses her friendship with Sexton as well as the writer's themes and critical reception.

Ostriker, Alicia Suskin. *Stealing the Language: The Emergence of Women's Poetry in America.* Boston: Beacon P, 1986. This study of modern poetry contains helpful chapters on body language, embodiment, sexuality, and "the imperative of intimacy" in poems by women of different races, ages, classes.

Otten, Charlotte, ed. *English Women's Voices 1540–1700.* Miami: Florida International UP, 1992. This excellent anthology of early modern women's writings is organized in thematic sections: testifying to abuse, writing about love and marriage, taking charge of health care, etc. It offers useful historical and critical introductions to each section.

Rich, Adrienne. *Blood, Bread, and Poetry: Selected Prose, 1979–1985.* New York: Norton, 1986. This collection contains several of Rich's essays on poetry, feminism, and embodiment, including "Compulsory Heterosexuality and Lesbian Existence" and "Notes Toward a Politics of Location."

Sacks, Peter. *The English Elegy: Studies in the Genre from Spenser to Yeats.* Baltimore: Johns Hopkins UP, 1985. This examination of elegiac poetry focuses on male poets' depictions of lost love, mourning, and renunciation; Sacks reads these elegies in light of Freud's essay "Mourning and Melancholia."

Scarry, Elaine. *The Body in Pain: The Making and Unmaking of the World.* New York: Oxford UP, 1985. This brilliant interdisciplinary treatise examines the inexpressibility of physical pain, how some transform torture into testimony, and how severe bodily pain affects the imaginations of certain artists.

Zeiger, Melissa. *Beyond Consolation: Death, Sexuality, and the Changing Shapes of Elegy.* Ithaca, NY: Cornell UP, 1997. This study gives an overview of the theory of elegy and contains a valuable chapter on women's elegies and the links between grief, desire, and embodiment.

⇥ Suggestions for Further Reading ⇥

Benstock, Shari. *Women of the Left Bank: Paris, 1900–1940.* Austin: U of Texas P, 1986. This study of modernists and expatriates analyzes lesbian erotic texts by Djuna Barnes, Gertrude Stein, and Natalie Barney, among others.

Bordo, Susan. *Unbearable Weight: Feminism, Western Culture, and the Body.* Berkeley: U of California P, 1993. This book attempts to bring women's bodies from the margin to the center of philosophical discourse by examining the body as a site of pleasure, anxiety, and resistance.

Cixous, Hélène, and Catherine Clément. *The Newly Born Woman.* Trans. Betsy Wing. Minneapolis: U of Minnesota P, 1975. This work of French feminist theory considers the ways women have been pathologized as either hysterics or sorceresses and explores the multifaceted power of female sexual pleasure, or *jouissance,* as women "come to writing."

Foster, Patricia, ed. *Minding the Body: Women Writers on Body and Soul.* New York: Anchor, 1994. This anthology of women's writing about their bodies includes works by Margaret Atwood, Naomi Wulf, and Nancy Mairs, as well as a valuable introduction by Foster.

Hart, Lynda. *Between the Body and the Flesh: Theatres of Sexual Fantasy.* New York: Columbia UP, 1998. This study of lesbian literature, theater, and literary theory focuses on the sex wars among feminists, lesbian S/M, and the "queer real."

Lashgari, Dierdre, ed. *Violence, Silence, and Anger: Women's Writing as Transgression.* Charlottesville: U of Virginia P, 1995. A collection of feminist critical essays that examine women's literary texts and issues of rape, sexual abuse, and domestic violence. See especially Anne B. Dalton's essay on sexual abuse in *Incidents in the Life of a Slave Girl.*

Lochrie, Karma. "The Language of Transgression: Body, Flesh, and Word in Mystical Discourse." *Speaking Two Languages: Traditional Disciplines and Contemporary Theory in Medieval Studies*. Ed. Allen J. Frantzen. Albany, NY: SUNY Press, 1991. This examines Margery Kempe's transgressive text and its relationship to works by other medieval women mystics.

Suleiman, Susan Rubin, ed. *The Female Body in Western Culture: Contemporary Perspectives*. Cambridge: Harvard UP, 1986. This collection of feminist theoretical essays is divided into six sections: eros, death, mothers, illness, images, and difference. See especially Suleiman's introduction, "(Re)Writing the Body," and Nancy K. Miller's "Rereading as a Woman: The Body as Practice."

Thiebaux, Marcelle, ed. *The Writings of Medieval Women: An Anthology*. 2nd ed. New York: Garland, 1994. This anthology offers excellent critical and historical introductions to "The Wife's Lament," "Wulf and Eadwacer," *The Book of Margery Kempe*, and the letters of Margery Brews Paston.

◄─►◄═◊═►◄─►

Hélène Cixous

1937–

Hélène Cixous is one of France's most distinguished intellectuals and the author of more than twenty plays, novels, and works of literary theory. Her innovative writings have influenced the development of feminist theory in England and America as well as France. Cixous's project involves dismantling misogynistic works and urging women to "write yourself. Your body must be heard." In advancing *écriture feminine*, described by the scholar Isabelle de Courtivron as "the most revolutionary concept in French feminist theory," Cixous traces the contours of women's coming to voice, or "finding tongue." Furthermore, she delineates the salient characteristics of woman's embodied writing as a privileged relation to her own voice, a willingness to be emotionally wrenching, an emphasis on contextuality, and a tendency toward transgression.

Born in 1937 in Algeria to Georges Cixous, a physician, and Eva Klein, a German Jewish midwife, Cixous has described her childhood awareness of gender and ethnic oppressions as particularly intense, given her location as a Jewish girl poised between Arab and European cultures. In her essay "Coming to Writing" she remembers her beloved mother, whose beautiful and mysterious female body intrigued Hélène. Elsewhere Cixous has recalled reading male heroic texts repeatedly in her youth, works that provided few suitable role models for women. Thus she began at an early age to study saints, hysterics, and sorceresses, women whose bodies served as "the theatre for forgotten scenes." After completing her Ph.D., Cixous taught at the University of Bordeaux, the Sorbonne, and the University of Paris Nanterre. Since 1968 she has taught at University of Paris VIII (Vincennes), where she founded the Centre de Recherches en Etudes Feminines in 1974. With Catherine Clément she has co-edited "Feminin futur," a collection of feminist writings. She has served on the editorial board of the journal *Poetique* and has been a visiting professor at many universities around the world.

Among her best-known works are *The Exile of James Joyce* (1968), a critical study; *The Newly Born Woman* (1976), written with Catherine Clément and translated by Betsy Wing; *Portrait of Dora* (1976), a play about Freud's most famous patient; and *Coming to Writing and Other Essays* (1991, edited by Deborah Jenson and translated by Sarah Cornell et al.). Her novel *Dedans* won the Prix Medici in 1969 and was translated into English by Carol Barko in 1986 as *Inside*. *The Newly Born Woman* was hailed by the *New York Times Book Review* in 1986 as a "ground-breaking feminist tract"; its authors examine history, literature, and psychology to probe what culture has repressed about women: their consciousnesses, their desires. In both ideology and verbal practice Cixous's writing corresponds to the intellectual goals of "Politique and psychoanalyse," an avant-garde women's liberation group popular in France in the 1970s which argued that no feminist revolution is possible until a disruption occurs in the symbolic order—Jacques Lacan's term for the order instilled in an individual by language and overseen by a metaphoric Father. Patriarchal language must be dislocated both syntactically and linguistically, Cixous asserts.

The essay included here, "The Laugh of the Medusa," was translated into English by Paula and Keith Cohen and published in the United States in the journal *Signs* in 1976. In *New French Feminisms*, Elaine Marks and Isabelle de Courtivron describe this as an essay of French feminist theory that "seems destined, perhaps ironically, for a measure of immortality" despite "the very serious problem of reconciling language disruption, which leads to esoteric writing, and the desire to reach the masses of women." While Cixous's writing can seem at first glance bewildering, a close reading reveals a compelling exploration of female pleasure and embodiment. The empowerment that women experience through *écriture feminine* is symbolized by the revised figure of Medusa, the gorgon at the center of a horrifying patriarchal myth, a monster whose gaze turns men to stone. Cixous's reconstitutes Medusa as a source of liberation for women:

> You only have to look at the Medusa straight on to see her. And she's not deadly. She's beautiful and she's laughing.

⊰ The Laugh of the Medusa[1] ⊱

I shall speak about women's writing: about *what it will do*. Woman must write her self: must write about women and bring women to writing, from which they have been driven away as violently as from their bodies—for the same reasons, by the same law, with the same fatal goal. Woman must put herself into the text—as into the world and into history—by her own movement.

The future must no longer be determined by the past. I do not deny that the effects of the past are still with us. But I refuse to strengthen them by repeating them, to confer upon them an irremovability the equivalent of destiny, to confuse the biological and the cultural. Anticipation is imperative.

Since these reflections are taking shape in an area just on the point of being discovered, they necessarily bear the mark of our time—a time during which the new breaks away from the old, and, more precisely, the (feminine) new from the old (*la nouvelle de l'ancien*). Thus, as there are no grounds for establishing a discourse, but rather an arid millennial ground to break, what I say has at least two sides and two aims: to break up, to destroy; and to foresee the unforeseeable, to project.

I write this as a woman, toward women. When I say "woman," I'm speaking of woman in her inevitable struggle against conventional man; and of a universal woman subject who must bring women to their senses and to their meaning in history. But first it must be said that in spite of the enormity of the repression that has

---

1. [This is a revised version of "Le Rire de la Méduse," which appeared in *L'Arc* (1975), pp. 39–54.]

kept them in the "dark"—that dark which people have been trying to make them accept as their attribute—there is, at this time, no general woman, no one typical woman. What they have *in common* I will say. But what strikes me is the infinite richness of their individual constitutions: you can't talk about *a* female sexuality, uniform, homogeneous, classifiable into codes—any more than you can talk about one unconscious resembling another. Women's imaginary is inexhaustible, like music, painting, writing: their stream of phantasms is incredible.

I have been amazed more than once by a description a woman gave me of a world all her own which she had been secretly haunting since early childhood. A world of searching, the elaboration of a knowledge, on the basis of a systematic experimentation with the bodily functions, a passionate and precise interrogation of her erotogeneity. This practice, extraordinarily rich and inventive, in particular as concerns masturbation, is prolonged or accompanied by a production of forms, a veritable aesthetic activity, each stage of rapture inscribing a resonant vision, a composition, something beautiful. Beauty will no longer be forbidden.

I wished that that woman would write and proclaim this unique empire so that other women, other unacknowledged sovereigns, might exclaim: I, too, overflow; my desires have invented new desires, my body knows unheard-of songs. Time and again I, too, have felt so full of luminous torrents that I could burst—burst with forms much more beautiful than those which are put up in frames and sold for a stinking fortune. And I, too, said nothing, showed nothing; I didn't open my mouth, I didn't repaint my half of the world. I was ashamed. I was afraid, and I swallowed my shame and my fear. I said to myself: You are mad! What's the meaning of these waves, these floods, these outbursts? Where is the ebullient, infinite woman who, immersed as she was in her naiveté, kept in the dark about herself, led into self-disdain by the great arm of parental-conjugal phallocentrism, hasn't been ashamed of her strength?[2] Who, surprised and horrified by the fantastic tumult of her drives (for she was made to believe that a well-adjusted normal woman has a . . . divine composure), hasn't accused herself of being a monster? Who, feeling a funny desire stirring inside her (to sing, to write, to dare to speak, in short, to bring out something new), hasn't thought she was sick? Well, her shameful sickness is that she resists death, that she makes trouble.

And why don't you write? Write! Writing is for you, you are for you; your body is yours, take it. I know why you haven't written. (And why I didn't write before the age of twenty-seven.) Because writing is at once too high, too great for you, it's reserved for the great—that is, for "great men"; and it's "silly." Besides, you've written a little, but in secret. And it wasn't good, because it was in secret, and because you punished yourself for writing, because you didn't go all the way; or because you wrote, irresistibly, as when we would masturbate in secret, not to go further, but to attenuate the tension a bit, just enough to take the edge off. And then as soon as we come, we go and make ourselves feel guilty—so as to be forgiven; or to forget, to bury it until the next time.

Write, let no one hold you back, let nothing stop you: not man; not the imbecilic capitalist machinery, in which publishing houses are the crafty, obsequious relayers of imperatives handed down by an economy that works against us and off our backs; and not *yourself*. Smug-faced readers, managing editors, and big bosses don't like the true texts of women—female-sexed texts. That kind scares them.

2. *Phallocentrism* is a term derived from the psychoanalytic work of Ernest Jones, Jacques Lacan, and others that denotes a system of power relations which privileges the phallus as the transcendent symbol of empowerment. Some theorists view phallocentrism as synonymous with patriarchy, or male dominance in society.

I write woman: woman must write woman. And man, man. So only an oblique consideration will be found here of man; it's up to him to say where his masculinity and femininity are at: this will concern us once men have opened their eyes and seen themselves clearly.[3]

Now women return from afar, from always: from "without," from the heath where witches are kept alive; from below, from beyond "culture"; from their childhood which men have been trying desperately to make them forget, condemning it to "eternal rest." The little girls and their "ill-mannered" bodies immured, well-preserved, intact unto themselves, in the mirror. Frigidified. But are they ever seething underneath! What an effort it takes—there's no end to it—for the sex cops to bar their threatening return. Such a display of forces on both sides that the struggle has for centuries been immobilized in the trembling equilibrium of a deadlock.

Here they are, returning, arriving over and again, because the unconscious is impregnable. They have wandered around in circles, confined to the narrow room in which they've been given a deadly brainwashing. You can incarcerate them, slow them down, get away with the old Apartheid routine, but for a time only. As soon as they begin to speak, at the same time as they're taught their name, they can be taught that their territory is black: because you are Africa, you are black. Your continent is dark. Dark is dangerous. You can't see anything in the dark, you're afraid. Don't move, you might fall. Most of all, don't go into the forest. And so we have internalized this horror of the dark.

Men have committed the greatest crime against women. Insidiously, violently, they have led them to hate women, to be their own enemies, to mobilize their immense strength against themselves, to be the executants of their virile needs. They have made for women an antinarcissism! A narcissism which loves itself only to be loved for what women haven't got! They have constructed the infamous logic of antilove.

We the precocious, we the repressed of culture, our lovely mouths gagged with pollen, our wind knocked out of us, we the labyrinths, the ladders, the trampled spaces, the bevies—we are black and we are beautiful.

We're stormy, and that which is ours breaks loose from us without our fearing any debilitation. Our glances, our smiles, are spent; laughs exude from our mouths; our blood flows and we extend ourselves without ever reaching an end; we never hold back our thoughts, our signs, our writing; and we're not afraid of lacking.

What happiness for us who are omitted, brushed aside at the scene of inheritances; we inspire ourselves and we expire without running out of breath, we are everywhere!

From now on, who, if we say so, can say no to us? We've come back from always.

It is time to liberate the New Woman from the Old by coming to know her—by loving her for getting by, for getting beyond the Old without delay, by going out ahead of what the New Woman will be, as an arrow quits the bow with a movement that gathers and separates the vibrations musically, in order to be more than her self.

---

3. [Men still have everything to say about their sexuality, and everything to write. For what they have said so far, for the most part, stems from the opposition activity/passivity, from the power relation between a fantasized obligatory virility meant to invade, to colonize, and the consequential phantasm of woman as a "dark continent" to penetrate and to "pacify." (We know what "pacify" means in terms of scotomizing the other and misrecognizing the self.) Conquering her, they've made haste to depart from her borders, to get out of sight, out of body. The way man has of getting out of himself and into her whom he takes not for the other but for his own, deprives him, he knows, of his own bodily territory. One can understand how man, confusing himself with his penis and rushing in for the attack, might feel resentment and fear of being "taken" by the woman, of being lost in her, absorbed, or alone.]

I say that we must, for, with a few rare exceptions, there has not yet been any writing that inscribes femininity; exceptions so rare, in fact, that, after plowing through literature across languages, cultures, and ages,[4] one can only be startled at this vain scouting mission. It is well known that the number of women writers (while having increased very slightly from the nineteenth century on) has always been ridiculously small. This is a useless and deceptive fact unless from their species of female writers we do not first deduct the immense majority whose workmanship is in no way different from male writing, and which either obscures women or reproduces the classic representations of women (as sensitive—intuitive—dreamy, etc.)[5]

Let me insert here a parenthetical remark. I mean it when I speak of male writing. I maintain unequivocally that there is such a thing as *marked* writing; that, until now, far more extensively and repressively than is ever suspected or admitted, writing has been run by a libidinal and cultural—hence political, typically masculine—economy; that this is a locus where the repression of women has been perpetuated, over and over, more or less consciously, and in a manner that's frightening since it's often hidden or adorned with the mystifying charms of fiction; that this locus has grossly exaggerated all the signs of sexual opposition (and not sexual difference), where woman has never *her* turn to speak—this being all the more serious and unpardonable in that writing is precisely *the very possibility of change*, the space that can serve as a springboard for subversive thought, the precursory movement of a transformation of social and cultural structures.

Nearly the entire history of writing is confounded with the history of reason, of which it is at once the effect, the support, and one of the privileged alibis. It has been one with the phallocentric tradition. It is indeed that same self-admiring, self-stimulating, self-congratulatory phallocentrism.

With some exceptions, for there have been failures—and if it weren't for them, I wouldn't be writing (I-woman, escapee)—in that enormous machine that has been operating and turning out its "truth" for centuries. There have been poets who would go to any lengths to slip something by at odds with tradition—men capable of loving love and hence capable of loving others and of wanting them, of imagining the woman who would hold out against oppression and constitute herself as a superb, equal, hence "impossible" subject, untenable in a real social framework. Such a woman the poet could desire only by breaking the codes that negate her. Her appearance would necessarily bring on, if not revolution—for the bastion was supposed to be immutable—at least harrowing explosions. At times it is in the fissure caused by an earthquake, through that radical mutation of things brought on by a material upheaval when every structure is for a moment thrown off balance and an ephemeral wildness sweeps order away, that the poet slips something by, for a brief span, of woman. Thus did Kleist expend himself in his yearning for the existence of sister-lovers, maternal daughters, mother-sisters, who never hung their heads in shame.[6] Once the palace of magistrates is restored, it's time to pay: immediate bloody death to the uncontrollable elements.

---

4. [I am speaking here only of the place "reserved" for women by the Western world.]

5. [Which works, then, might be called feminine? I'll just point out some examples: one would have to give them full readings to bring out what is pervasively feminine in their significance. Which I shall do elsewhere. In France (have you noted our infinite poverty in this field?—the Anglo-Saxon countries have shown resources of distinctly greater consequence), leafing through what's come out of the twentieth century—and it's not much—the only inscriptions of femininity that I have seen were by Colette, Marguerite Duras, . . . and Jean Genêt.]

6. B. Heinrich W. von Kleist (1777–1811), a German Romantic writer whom Cixous admires, along with his contemporary E. T. A. Hoffman (1776–1822).

But only the poets—not the novelists, allies of representationalism. Because poetry involves gaining strength through the unconscious and because the unconscious, that other limitless country, is the place where the repressed manage to survive: women, or as Hoffmann would say, fairies.

She must write her self, because this is the invention of a *new insurgent* writing which, when the moment of her liberation has come, will allow her to carry out the indispensable ruptures and transformations in her history, first at two levels that cannot be separated.

a) Individually. By writing her self, woman will return to the body which has been more than confiscated from her, which has been turned into the uncanny stranger on display—the ailing or dead figure, which so often turns out to be the nasty companion, the cause and location of inhibitions. Censor the body and you censor breath and speech at the same time.

Write your self. Your body must be heard. Only then will the immense resources of the unconscious spring forth. Our naphtha will spread, throughout the world, without dollars—black or gold—nonassessed values that will change the rules of the old game.

To write. An act which will not only "realize" the decensored relation of woman to her sexuality, to her womanly being, giving her access to her native strength: it will give her back her goods, her pleasures, her organs, her immense bodily territories which have been kept under seal: it will tear her away from the superegoized structure in which she has always occupied the place reserved for the guilty (guilty of everything, guilty at every turn: for having desires, for not having any; for being frigid, for being "too hot"; for not being both at once; for being too motherly and not enough; for having children and for not having any; for nursing and for not nursing . . .)—tear her away by means of this research, this job of analysis and illuminaton, this emancipation of the marvelous text of her self that she must urgently learn to speak. A woman without a body, dumb, blind, can't possibly be a good fighter. She is reduced to being the servant of the militant male, his shadow. We must kill the false woman who is preventing the live one from breathing. Inscribe the breath of the whole woman.

b) An act that will also be marked by woman's *seizing* the occasion to *speak*, hence her shattering entry into history, which has always been based *on her suppression*. To write and thus to forge for herself the antilogos weapon. To become *at will* the taker and initiator, for her own right, in every symbolic system, in every political process.

It is time for women to start scoring their feats in written and oral language.

Every woman has known the torment of getting up to speak. Her heart racing, at times entirely lost for words, ground and language slipping away—that's how daring a feat, how great a transgression it is for a woman to speak—even just open her mouth—in public. A double distress, for even if she transgresses, her words fall almost always upon the deaf male ear, which hears in language only that which speaks in the masculine.

It is by writing, from and toward women, and by taking up the challenge of speech which has been governed by the phallus, that women will confirm women in a place other than that which is reserved in and by the symbolic, that is, in a place other than silence. Women should break out of the snare of silence. They shouldn't be conned into accepting a domain which is the margin or the harem.

Listen to a woman speak at a public gathering (if she hasn't painfully lost her wind). She doesn't "speak," she throws her trembling body forward; she lets go of herself, she flies; all of her passes into her voice, and it's with her body that she vitally supports the "logic" of her speech. Her flesh speaks true. She lays herself bare. In fact, she physically materializes what she's thinking; she signifies it with her body. In a certain way she *inscribes* what she's saying, because she doesn't deny her drives the intractable and impassioned part they have in speaking. Her speech, even when "theoretical" or political, is never simple or linear or "objectified," generalized: she draws her story into history.

There is not that scission, that division made by the common man between the logic of oral speech and the logic of the text, bound as he is by his antiquated relation—servile, calculating—to mastery. From which proceeds the niggardly lip service which engages only the tiniest part of the body, plus the mask.

In women's speech, as in their writing, that element which never stops resonating, which, once we've been permeated by it, profoundly and imperceptibly touched by it, retains the power of moving us—that element is the song: first music from the first voice of love which is alive in every woman. Why this privileged relationship with the voice? Because no woman stockpiles as many defenses for countering the drives as does a man. You don't build walls around yourself, you don't forego pleasure as "wisely" as he. Even if phallic mystification has generally contaminated good relationships, a woman is never far from "mother" (I mean outside her role functions: the "mother" as nonname and as source of goods). There is always within her at least a little of that good mother's milk. She writes in white ink.

Woman for women.—There always remains in woman that force which produces/is produced by the other—in particular, the other woman. *In* her, matrix, cradler; herself giver as her mother and child; she is her own sister-daughter. You might object, "What about she who is the hysterical offspring of a bad mother?" Everything will be changed once woman gives woman to the other woman. There is hidden and always ready in woman the source; the locus for the other. The mother, too, is a metaphor. It is necessary and sufficient that the best of herself be given to woman by another woman for her to be able to love herself and return in love the body that was "born" to her. Touch me, caress me, you the living no-name, give me my self as myself. The relation to the "mother," in terms of intense pleasure and violence, is curtailed no more than the relation to childhood (the child that she was, that she is, that she makes, remakes, undoes, there at the point where, the same, she others herself). Text: my body—shot through with streams of song; I don't mean the overbearing, clutchy "mother" but, rather, what touches you, the equivoice that affects you, fills your breast with an urge to come to language and launches your force: the rhythm that laughs you; the intimate recipient who makes all metaphors possible and desirable; body (body? bodies?), no more describable than god, the soul, or the Other; that part of you that leaves a space between yourself and urges you to inscribe in language your woman's style. In women there is always more or less of the mother who makes everything all right, who nourishes, and who stands up against separation; a force that will not be cut off but will knock the wind out of the codes. We will rethink womankind beginning with every form and every period of her body. The Americans remind us, "We are all Lesbians"; that is, don't denigrate woman, don't make of her what men have made of you.

Because the "economy" of her drives is prodigious, she cannot fail, in seizing the occasion to speak, to transform directly and indirectly *all* systems of exchange based on masculine thrift. Her libido will produce far more radical effects of political and social change than some might like to think.

Because she arrives, vibrant, over and again, we are at the beginning of a new history, or rather of a process of becoming in which several histories intersect with one another. As subject for history, woman always occurs simultaneously in several places. Woman un-thinks[7] the unifying, regulating history that homogenizes and channels forces, herding contradictions into a single battlefield. In woman, personal history blends together with the history of all women, as well as national and world history. As a militant, she is an integral part of all liberations. She must be farsighted, not limited to a blow-by-blow interaction. She foresees that her liberation will do more than modify power relations or toss the ball over to the other camp; she will bring about a mutation in human relations, in thought, in all praxis: hers is not simply a class struggle, which she carries forward into a much vaster movement. Not that in order to be a woman-in-struggle(s) you have to leave the class struggle or repudiate it; but you have to split it open, spread it out, push it forward, fill it with the fundamental struggle so as to prevent the class struggle, or any other struggle for the liberation of a class or people, from operating as a form of repression, pretext for postponing the inevitable, the staggering alteration in power relations and in the production of individualities. This alteration is already upon us—in the United States, for example, where millions of night crawlers are in the process of undermining the family and disintegrating the whole of American sociality.

The new history is coming; it's not a dream, though it does extend beyond men's imagination, and for good reason. It's going to deprive them of their conceptual orthopedics, beginning with the destruction of their enticement machine.

It is impossible to *define* a feminine practice of writing, and this is an impossibility that will remain, for this practice can never be theorized, enclosed, coded—which doesn't mean that it doesn't exist. But it will always surpass the discourse that regulates the phallocentric system; it does and will take place in areas other than those subordinated to philosophico-theoretical domination. It will be conceived of only by subjects who are breakers of automatisms, by peripheral figures that no authority can ever subjugate.

Hence the necessity to affirm the flourishes of this writing, to give form to its movement, its near and distant byways. Bear in mind to begin with (1) that sexual opposition, which has always worked for man's profit to the point of reducing writing, too, to his laws, is only a historico-cultural limit. There is, there will be more and more rapidly pervasive now, a fiction that produces irreducible effects of femininity. (2) That it is through ignorance that most readers, critics, and writers of both sexes hesitate to admit or deny outright the possibility or the pertinence of a distinction between feminine and masculine writing. It will usually be said, thus disposing of sexual difference: either that all writing, to the extent that it materializes, is feminine; or, inversely—but it comes to the same thing—that the act of writing is equivalent to masculine masturbation (and so the woman who writes cuts herself out a paper penis); or that writing is bisexual, hence neuter, which again does away with differentiation. To admit that writing is precisely working (in) the in-between, inspecting the process of the same and of the other without which nothing can live, undoing the work of death—to admit this is first to want the two, as well as both, the ensemble of the one and the other, not fixed in sequences of struggle and expulsion or some

7. "*Dé-pense,*" a neologism formed on the verb *penser*, hence "unthinks," but also "spends" (from *dépenser*) (translator's note).

other form of death but infinitely dynamized by an incessant process of exchange from one subject to another. A process of different subjects knowing one another and beginning one another anew only from the living boundaries of the other: a multiple and inexhaustible course with millions of encounters and transformations of the same into the other and into the in-between, from which woman takes her forms (and man, in his turn; but that's his other history).

In saying "bisexual, hence neuter," I am referring to the classic conception of bisexuality, which, squashed under the emblem of castration fear and along with the fantasy of a "total" being (though composed of two halves), would do away with the difference experienced as an operation incurring loss, as the mark of dreaded sectility.

To this self-effacing, merger-type bisexuality, which would conjure away castration (the writer who puts up his sign: "bisexual written here, come and see," when the odds are good that it's neither one nor the other), I oppose the *other bisexuality* on which every subject not enclosed in the false theater of phallocentric representationalism has founded his/her erotic universe. Bisexuality: that is, each one's location in self (*repérage en soi*) of the presence—variously manifest and insistent according to each person, male or female—of both sexes, nonexclusion either of the difference or of one sex, and, from this "self-permission," multiplication of the effects of the inscription of desire, over all parts of my body and the other body.

Now it happens that at present, for historico-cultural reasons, it is women who are opening up to and benefiting from this vatic bisexuality which doesn't annul differences but stirs them up, pursues them, increases their number. In a certain way, "woman is bisexual"; man—it's a secret to no one—being poised to keep glorious phallic monosexuality in view. By virtue of affirming the primacy of the phallus and of bringing it into play, phallocratic ideology has claimed more than one victim. As a woman, I've been clouded over by the great shadow of the scepter and been told: idolize it, that which you cannot brandish. But at the same time, man has been handed that grotesque and scarcely enviable destiny (just imagine) of being reduced to a single idol with clay balls. And consumed, as Freud and his followers note, by a fear of being a woman! For, if psychoanalysis was constituted from woman, to repress femininity (and not so successful a repression at that—men have made it clear), its account of masculine sexuality is now hardly refutable; as with all the "human" sciences, it reproduces the masculine view, of which it is one of the effects.

Here we encounter the inevitable man-with-rock, standing erect in his old Freudian realm, in the way that, to take the figure back to the point where linguistics is conceptualizing it "anew," Lacan preserves it in the sanctuary of the phallos (ϕ) "sheltered" from *castration's lack!* Their "symbolic" exists, it holds power—we, the sowers of disorder, know it only too well. But we are in no way obliged to deposit our lives in their banks of lack, to consider the constitution of the subject in terms of a drama manglingly restaged, to reinstate again and again the religion of the father. Because we don't want that. We don't fawn around the supreme hole. We have no womanly reason to pledge allegiance to the negative. The feminine (as the poets suspected) affirms: ". . . And yes," says Molly, carrying *Ulysses* off beyond any book and toward the new writing; "I said yes, I will Yes."

The Dark Continent is neither dark nor unexplorable.—It is still unexplored only because we've been made to believe that it was too dark to be explorable. And because they want to make us believe that what interests us is the white continent, with its monuments to Lack. And we believed. They riveted us between two horrifying myths: between the Medusa and the abyss. That would be enough to set half the world laughing, except that it's still going on. For the phallologocentric sublation[8] is with us, and it's militant, regenerating the old patterns, anchored in the dogma of castration. They haven't changed a thing: they've theorized their desire for reality! Let the priests tremble, we're going to show them our sexts!

Too bad for them if they fall apart upon discovering that women aren't men, or that the mother doesn't have one. But isn't this fear convenient for them? Wouldn't the worst be, isn't the worst, in truth, that women aren't castrated, that they have only to stop listening to the Sirens (for the Sirens were men) for history to change its meaning? You only have to look at the Medusa straight on to see her. And she's not deadly. She's beautiful and she's laughing.

Men say that there are two unrepresentable things: death and the feminine sex. That's because they need femininity to be associated with death; it's the jitters that gives them a hard-on! for themselves! They need to be afraid of us. Look at the trembling Perseuses moving backward toward us, clad in apotropes. What lovely backs! Not another minute to lose. Let's get out of here.

Let's hurry: the continent is not impenetrably dark. I've been there often. I was overjoyed one day to run into Jean Genêt. It was in *Pompes funèbres*.[9] He had come there led by his Jean. There are some men (all too few) who aren't afraid of femininity.

Almost everything is yet to be written by women about femininity: about their sexuality, that is, its infinite and mobile complexity, about their eroticization, sudden turn-ons of a certain minuscule-immense area of their bodies; not about destiny, but about the adventure of such and such a drive, about trips, crossings, trudges, abrupt and gradual awakenings, discoveries of a zone at one time timorous and soon to be forthright. A woman's body, with its thousand and one thresholds of ardor—once, by smashing yokes and censors, she lets it articulate the profusion of meanings that run through it in every direction—will make the old single-grooved mother tongue reverberate with more than one language.

We've been turned away from our bodies, shamefully taught to ignore them, to strike them with that stupid sexual modesty; we've been made victims of the old fool's game: each one will love the other sex. I'll give you your body and you'll give me mine. But who are the men who give women the body that women blindly yield to them? Why so few texts? Because so few women have as yet won back their body. Women must write through their bodies, they must invent the impregnable language that will wreck partitions, classes, and rhetorics, regulations and codes, they must submerge, cut through, get beyond the ultimate reserve-discourse, including the one that laughs at the very idea of pronouncing the word "silence," the one that, aiming for the impossible, stops short before the word "impossible" and writes it as "the end."

Such is the strength of women that, sweeping away syntax, breaking that famous thread (just a tiny little thread, they say) which acts for men as a surrogate umbilical cord, assuring them—otherwise they couldn't come—that the old lady is always right behind them, watching them make phallus, women will go right up to the impossible.

When the "repressed" of their culture and their society returns, it's an explosive, *utterly* destructive, staggering return, with a force never yet unleashed and equal to the most forbidding of suppressions. For when the Phallic period comes to an end, women will have been either annihilated or borne up to the highest and most violent

8. [Standard English term for the Hegelian *Aufhebung*, the French *la relève*.]

9. [Jean Genêt, *Pompes funèbres* (Paris, 1948), p. 185.]

incandescence. Muffled throughout their history, they have lived in dreams, in bodies (though muted), in silences, in aphonic revolts.

And with such force in their fragility; a fragility, a vulnerability, equal to their incomparable intensity. Fortunately, they haven't sublimated; they've saved their skin, their energy. They haven't worked at liquidating the impasse of lives without futures. They have furiously inhabited these sumptuous bodies: admirable hysterics who made Freud succumb to many voluptuous moments impossible to confess, bombarding his Mosaic statue with their carnal and passionate body words, haunting him with their inaudible and thundering denunciations, dazzling, more than naked underneath the seven veils of modesty. Those who, with a single word of the body, have inscribed the vertiginous immensity of a history which is sprung like an arrow from the whole history of men and from biblico-capitalist society, are the women, the supplicants of yesterday, who come as forebears of the new women, after whom no intersubjective relation will ever be the same. You, Dora, you the indomitable, the poetic body, you are the true "mistress" of the Signifier.[10] Before long your efficacity will be seen at work when your speech is no longer suppressed, its point turned in against your breast, but written out over against the other.

In body.—More so than men who are coaxed toward social success, toward sublimation, women are body. More body, hence more writing. For a long time it has been in body that women have responded to persecution, to the familial-conjugal enterprise of domestication, to the repeated attempts at castrating them. Those who have turned their tongues 10,000 times seven times before not speaking are either dead from it or more familiar with their tongues and their mouths than anyone else. Now, I-woman am going to blow up the Law: an explosion henceforth possible and ineluctable; let it be done, right now, *in* language.

Let us not be trapped by an analysis still encumbered with the old automatisms. It's not to be feared that language conceals an invincible adversary, because it's the language of men and their grammar. We mustn't leave them a single place that's any more theirs alone than we are.

If woman has always functioned "within" the discourse of man, a signifier that has always referred back to the opposite signifier which annihilates its specific energy and diminishes or stifles its very different sounds, it is time for her to dislocate this "within," to explode it, turn it around, and seize it; to make it hers, containing it, taking it in her own mouth, biting that tongue with her very own teeth to invent for herself a language to get inside of. And you'll see with what ease she will spring forth from that "within"—the "within" where once she so drowsily crouched—to overflow at the lips she will cover the foam.

Nor is the point to appropriate their instruments, their concepts, their places, or to begrudge them their position of mastery. Just because there's a risk of identification doesn't mean that we'll succumb. Let's leave it to the worriers, to masculine anxiety and its obsession with how to dominate the way things work—knowing "how it works" in order to "make it work." For us the point is not to take possession in order to internalize or manipulate, but rather to dash through and to "fly."[11]

Flying is woman's gesture—flying in language and making it fly. We have all learned the art of flying and its numerous techniques; for centuries we've been able to

---

10. Dora was a female patient of Sigmund Freud whom he considered hysterical; Cixous has published a play, *Portrait of Dora* (1976), in which she reclaims her for feminism. The "Signifier," a term taken from the linguistic theory of Ferdinand de Saussure, refers to an object of perception that may be audible as speech or visible as writing.

11. [Also, "to steal." Both meanings of the verb *voler* are played on, as the text itself explains in the following paragraph (translator's note).]

possess anything only by flying; we've lived in flight, stealing away, finding, when desired, narrow passageways, hidden crossovers. It's no accident that *voler* has a double meaning, that it plays on each of them and thus throws off the agents of sense. It's no accident: women take after birds and robbers just as robbers take after women and birds. They (*illes*)[12] go by, fly the coop, take pleasure in jumbling the order of space, in disorienting it, in changing around the furniture, dislocating things and values, breaking them all up, emptying structures, and turning propriety upside down.

What woman hasn't flown/stolen? Who hasn't felt, dreamt, performed the gesture that jams sociality? Who hasn't crumbled, held up to ridicule, the bar of separation? Who hasn't inscribed with her body the differential, punctured the system of couples and opposition? Who, by some act of transgression, hasn't overthrown successiveness, connection, the wall of circumfusion?

A feminine text cannot fail to be more than subversive. It is volcanic: as it is written it brings about an upheaval of the old property crust, carrier of masculine investments; there's no other way. There's no room for her if she's not a he. If she's a her-she, it's in order to smash everything, to shatter the framework of institutions, to blow up the law, to break up the "truth" with laughter.

For once she blazes *her* trail in the symbolic, she cannot fail to make of it the chaosmos of the "personal"—in her pronouns, her nouns, and her clique of referents. And for good reason. There will have been the long history of gynocide. This is known by the colonized peoples of yesterday, the workers, the nations, the species off whose backs the history of men has made its gold; those who have known the ignominy of persecution derive from it an obstinate future desire for grandeur; those who are locked up know better than their jailers the taste of free air. Thanks to their history, women today know (how to do and want) what men will be able to conceive of only much later. I say woman overturns the "personal," for if, by means of laws, lies, blackmail, and marriage, her right to herself has been extorted at the same time as her name, she has been able, through the very movement of mortal alienation, to see more closely the inanity of "propriety," the reductive stinginess of the masculine-conjugal subjective economy, which she doubly resists. On the one hand she has constituted herself necessarily as that "person" capable of losing a part of herself without losing her integrity. But secretly, silently, deep down inside, she grows and multiplies, for, on the other hand, she knows far more about living and about the relation between the economy of the drives and the management of the ego than any man. Unlike man, who holds so dearly to his title and his titles, his pouches of value, his cap, crown, and everything connected with his head, woman couldn't care less about the fear of decapitation (or castration), adventuring, without the masculine temerity, into anonymity, which she can merge with without annihilating herself: because she's a giver.

I shall have a great deal to say about the whole deceptive problematic of the gift. Woman is obviously not that woman Nietzsche dreamed of who gives only in order to.[13] Who could ever think of the gift as a gift-that-takes? Who else but man, precisely the one who would like to take everything?

If there is a "propriety of woman," it is paradoxically her capacity to depropriate unselfishly: body without end, without appendage, without principal "parts." If she is a whole, it's a whole composed of parts that are wholes, not simple partial objects but

---

12. [*Illes* is a fusion of the masculine pronoun *ils*, which refers back to birds and robbers, with the feminine pronoun *elles*, which refers to women (translator's note).]

13. [Reread Derrida's text, "Le Style de la femme," in *Nietzsche aujourd'hui* (Paris: Union Générale d'Editions, Coll. 10/18), where the philosopher can be seen operating an *Aufhebung* of all philosophy in its systematic reducing of woman to the place of seduction: she appears as the one who is taken for; the bait in person, all veils unfurled, the one who doesn't give but who gives only in order to (take).]

a moving, limitlessly changing ensemble, a cosmos tirelessly traversed by Eros, an immense astral space not organized around any one sun that's any more of a star than the others.

This doesn't mean that she's an undifferentiated magma, but that she doesn't lord it over her body or her desire. Though masculine sexuality gravitates around the penis, engendering that centralized body (in political anatomy) under the dictatorship of its parts, woman does not bring about the same regionalization which serves the couple head/genitals and which is inscribed only within boundaries. Her libido is cosmic, just as her unconscious is worldwide. Her writing can only keep going, without ever inscribing or discerning contours, daring to make these vertiginous crossings of the other(s) ephemeral and passionate sojourns in him, her, them, whom she inhabits long enough to look at from the point closest to their unconscious from the moment they awaken, to love them at the point closest to their drives: and then further, impregnated through and through with these brief, identificatory embraces, she goes and passes into infinity. She alone dares and wishes to know from within, where she, the outcast, has never ceased to hear the resonance of fore-language. She lets the other language speak—the language of 1,000 tongues which knows neither enclosure nor death. To life she refuses nothing. Her language does not contain, it carries; it does not hold back, it makes possible. When id is ambiguously uttered—the wonder of being several—she doesn't defend herself against these unknown women whom she's surprised at becoming, but derives pleasure from this gift of alterability. I am spacious, singing flesh, on which is grafted no one knows which I, more or less human, but alive because of transformation.

Write! and your self-seeking text will know itself better than flesh and blood, rising, insurrectionary dough kneading itself, with sonorous, perfumed ingredients, a lively combination of flying colors, leaves, and rivers plunging into the sea we feed. "Ah, there's her sea," he will say as he holds out to me a basin full of water from the little phallic mother from whom he's inseparable. But look, our seas are what we make of them, full of fish or not, opaque or transparent, red or black, high or smooth, narrow or bankless; and we are ourselves sea, sand, coral, seaweed, beaches, tides, swimmers, children, waves. . . . More or less wavily sea, earth, sky—what matter would rebuff us? We know how to speak them all.

Heterogeneous, yes. For her joyous benefit she is erogenous; she is the erotogeneity of the heterogeneous: airborne swimmer, in flight, she does not cling to herself: she is dispersible, prodigious, stunning, desirous and capable of others, of the other woman that she will be, of the other woman she isn't, of him, of you.

Woman be unafraid of any other place, of any same, or any other. My eyes, my tongue, my ears, my nose, my skin, my mouth, my body-for-(the)-other—not that I long for it in order to fill up a hole, to provide against some defect of mine, or because, as fate would have it, I'm spurred on by feminine "jealousy": not because I've been dragged into the whole chain of substitutions that brings that which is substituted back to its ultimate object. That sort of thing you would expect to come straight out of "Tom Thumb," out of the *Penisneid* whispered to us by old grandmother ogresses, servants to their father-sons. If they believe, in order to muster up some self-importance, if they really need to believe that we're dying of desire, that we are this hole fringed with desire for their penis—that's their immemorial business. Undeniably (we verify it at our own expense—but also to our amusement), it's their business to let us know they're getting a hard-on, so that we'll assure them (we the maternal mistresses of their little pocket signifier) that they still can, that it's still there—that men structure themselves only by being fitted with a feather. In the child it's not the penis that the woman desires, it's not that famous bit of skin around which every man gravitates. Pregnancy cannot be traced back, except within the historical limits of the ancients, to some form of fate, to those mechanical substitutions brought about by the unconscious of some eternal "jealous woman"; not to penis envies; and not to narcissism or to some sort of homosexuality linked to the ever-present mother! Begetting a child doesn't mean that the woman or the man must fall ineluctably into patterns or must recharge the circuit of reproduction. If there's a risk there's not an inevitable trap: may women be spared the pressure, under the guise of consciousness-raising, of a supplement of interdictions. Either you want a kid or you don't—*that's your business.* Let nobody threaten you: in satisfying your desire, let not the fear of becoming the accomplice to a sociality succeed the old-time fear of being "taken." And man, are you still going to bank on everyone's blindness and passivity, afraid lest the child make a father and, consequently, that in having a kid the woman land herself more than one bad deal by engendering all at once child—mother—father—family? No; it's up to you to break the old circuits. It will be up to man and woman to render obsolete the former relationship and all its consequences, to consider the launching of a brand-new subject, alive, with defamilialization. Let us demater-paternalize rather than deny woman, in an effort to avoid the co-optation of procreation, a thrilling era of the body. Let us defetishize. Let's get away from the dialectic which has it that the only good father is a dead one, or that the child is the death of his parents. The child is the other, but the other without violence, bypassing loss, struggle. We're fed up with the reuniting of bonds forever to be severed, with the litany of castration that's handed down and genealogized. We won't advance backward anymore; we're not going to repress something so simple as the desire for life. Oral drive, anal drive, vocal drive—all these drives are our strengths, and among them is the gestation drive—just like the desire to write: a desire to live self from within, a desire for the swollen belly, for language, for blood. We are not going to refuse, if it should happen to strike our fancy, the unsurpassed pleasures of pregnancy which have actually been always exaggerated or conjured away—or cursed—in the classic texts. For if there's one thing that's been repressed here's just the place to find it: in the taboo of the pregnant woman. This says a lot about the power she seems invested with at the time, because it has always been suspected, that, when pregnant, the woman not only doubles her market value, but—what's more important—takes on intrinsic value as a woman in her own eyes and, undeniably, acquires body and sex.

There are thousands of ways of living one's pregnancy; to have or not to have with that still invisible other a relationship of another intensity. And if you don't have that particular yearning, it doesn't mean that you're in any way lacking. Each body distributes in its own special way, without model or norm, the nonfinite and changing totality of its desires. Decide for yourself on your position in the arena of contradictions, where pleasure and reality embrace. Bring the other to life. Women know how to live detachment; giving birth is neither losing nor increasing. It's adding to life an other. Am I dreaming? Am I mis-recognizing? You, the defenders of "theory," the sacrosanct yes-men of Concept, enthroners of the phallus (but not of the penis):

Once more you'll say that all this smacks of "idealism," or what's worse, you'll splutter that I'm a "mystic."

And what about the libido? Haven't I read the "Signification of the Phallus"? And what about separation, what about that bit of self for which, to be born, you undergo an ablation—an ablation, so they say, to be forever commemorated by your desire?

Besides, isn't it evident that the penis gets around in my texts, that I give it a place and appeal? Of course I do. I want all. I want all of me with all of him. Why should I deprive myself of a part of us? I want all of us. Woman of course has a desire for a "loving desire" and not a jealous one. But not because she is gelded; not because she's deprived and needs to be filled out, like some wounded person who wants to console herself or seek vengeance: I don't want a penis to decorate my body with. But I do desire the other for the other, whole and entire, male or female; because living means wanting everything that is, everything that lives, and wanting it alive. Castration? Let others toy with it. What's a desire originating from a lack? A pretty meager desire.

The woman who still allows herself to be threatened by the big dick, who's still impressed by the commotion of the phallic stance, who still leads a loyal master to the beat of the drum: that's the woman of yesterday. They still exist, easy and numerous victims of the oldest of farces: either they're cast in the original silent version in which, as titanesses lying under the mountains they make with their quivering, they never see erected that theoretic monument to the golden phallus looming, in the old manner, over their bodies. Or, coming today out of their *infans* period and into the second, "enlightened" version of their virtuous debasement, they see themselves suddenly assaulted by the builders of the analytic empire and, as soon as they've begun to formulate the new desire, naked, nameless, so happy at making an appearance, they're taken in their bath by the new old men, and then, whoops! Luring them with flashy signifiers, the demon of interpretation—oblique, decked out in modernity—sells them the same old handcuffs, baubles, and chains. Which castration do you prefer? Whose degrading do you like better, the father's or the mother's? Oh, what pwetty eyes, you pwetty little girl. Here, buy my glasses and you'll see the Truth-Me-Myself tell you everything you should know. Put them on your nose and take a fetishist's look (you are me, the other analyst—that's what I'm telling you) at your body and the body of the other. You see? No? Wait, you'll have everything explained to you, and you'll know at last which sort of neurosis you're related to. Hold still, we're going to do your portrait, so that you can begin looking like it right away.

Yes, the naives to the first and second degree are still legion. If the New Women, arriving now, dare to create outside the theoretical, they're called in by the cops of the signifier, fingerprinted, remonstrated, and brought into the line of order that they are supposed to know; assigned by force of trickery to a precise place in the chain that's always formed for the benefit of a privileged signifier. We are pieced back to the string which leads back, if not to the Name-of-the-Father, then, for a new twist, to the place of the phallic-mother.

Beware, my friend, of the signifier that would take you back to the authority of a signified! Beware of diagnoses that would reduce your generative powers. "Common" nouns are also proper nouns that disparage your singularity by classifying it into species. Break out of the circles; don't remain within the psychoanalytic closure. Take a look around, then cut through!

And if we are legion, it's because the war of liberation has only made as yet a tiny breakthrough. But women are thronging to it. I've seen them, those who will be neither dupe nor domestic, those who will not fear the risk of being a woman: will not fear any risk, any desire, any space still unexplored in themselves, among themselves and others or anywhere else. They do not fetishize, they do not deny, they do not hate. They observe, they approach, they try to see the other woman, the child, the lover—not to strengthen their own narcissism or verify the solidity or weakness of the master, but to make love better, to invent

Other love.—In the beginning are our differences. The new love dares for the other, wants the other, makes dizzying, precipitous flights between knowledge and invention. The woman arriving over and over again does not stand still; she's every-where, she exchanges, she is the desire-that-gives. (Not enclosed in the paradox of the gift that takes nor under the illusion of unitary fusion. We're past that.) She comes in, comes-in-between herself me and you, between the other me where one is always infinitely more than one and more than me, without the fear of ever reaching a limit; she thrills in our becoming. And we'll keep on becoming! She cuts through defensive loves, motherages, and devourations: beyond selfish narcissism, in the moving, open, transitional space, she runs her risks. Beyond the struggle-to-the-death that's been removed to the bed, beyond the love-battle that claims to represent exchange, she scorns at an Eros dynamic that would be fed by hatred. Hatred: a her-itage, again, a remainder, a duping subservience to the phallus. To love, to watch-think-seek the other in the other, to despecularize, to unhoard. Does this seem difficult? It's not impossible, and this is what nourishes life—a love that has no com-merce with the apprehensive desire that provides against the lack and stultifies the strange; a love that rejoices in the exchange that multiplies. Wherever history still unfolds as the history of death, she does not tread. Opposition, hierarchizing exchange, the struggle for mastery which can end only in at least one death (one master-one slave, or two nonmasters ≠ two dead)—all that comes from a period in time governed by phallocentric values. The fact that this period extends into the pre-sent doesn't prevent woman from starting the history of life somewhere else. Else-where, she gives. She doesn't "know" what she's giving, she doesn't measure it; she gives, though, neither a counterfeit impression nor something she hasn't got. She gives more, with no assurance that she'll get back even some unexpected profit from what she puts out. She gives that there may be life, thought, transformation. This is an "economy" that can no longer be put in economic terms. Wherever she loves, all the old concepts of management are left behind. At the end of a more or less con-scious computation, she finds not her sum but her differences. I am for you what you want me to be at the moment you look at me in a way you've never seen me before: at every instant. When I write, it's everything that we don't know we can be that is written out of me, without exclusions, without stipulation, and everything we will be calls us to the unflagging, intoxicating, unappeasable search for love. In one another we will never be lacking.   *1976*

+—+ ⊨◆⊒ +—+

Nancy Mairs
1943–

NANCY MAIRS first gained literary recognition for *Plaintext* (1986), a moving collection of autobiographical essays that explores sexuali-ty, agoraphobia, and the author's struggle to cope with the physical degeneration caused by multiple sclerosis. Since that time she has continued to write and speak powerfully about eroticism, disability, motherhood, depression, and the writer's life.

Born in Long Beach, California, to John and Anne Eldredge, Mairs earned a B.A. from Wheaton College in 1964, an M.F.A. from the University of Arizona in 1975, and a Ph.D. in English (also from Arizona) in 1984. From 1966 to 1969 she worked as a technical editor at the Smithsonian Astrophysics Observatory, and from 1970 to 1972 she was an editorial assistant at Harvard Law School's International Tax Program. During the late 1970s and 1980s she taught English and women's studies at the University of Arizona before deciding to pursue writing full-time. Since 1963 she has been married to George Mairs; they live in Tucson and have three grown children.

Plaintext was followed by Remembering the Bone House (1989), a lyrical memoir that chronicles "an erotics of place and space." This volume offers Mairs's most revealing account of the homes, family members, and sexual experiences that have affected her profoundly. Carnal Acts (1990) and Ordinary Time (1992) continue her autobiographical journey, recounting both the ongoing trials of living with MS and her refusal to let the disease keep her from writing, traveling, and loving. In Voice Lessons: On Becoming a (Woman) Writer (1994) Mairs again pursues these themes but discusses as well her creative process and academic influences. She has also published two volumes of poetry: Instead It Is Winter (1977) and In All the Rooms of the Yellow House (1984), which won the Western States Arts Foundation Book Award for Poetry.

"Reading Houses, Writing Lives: The French Connection" appeared first as the introduction to Remembering the Bone House but was published in its present form in Voice Lessons. In this essay Mairs examines the body as a dwelling place, her attraction to French feminism, and her task as a feminist autobiographer. She also probes the ways in which the theoretical writings of Gaston Bachelard and HÉLÈNE CIXOUS speak to her own views of female embodiment. "As a radical feminist, pacifist, and cripple," Mairs explained in an interview in 1992, "I am most interested in theoretical bases of issues of social justice, and in particular in the power of language to privilege certain kinds of human perception and experience and to efface other kinds. In my writing I aim to speak the 'unspeakable,' in defiance of polite discourse."

◄ Reading Houses, Writing Lives: The French Connection[1] ►

On a glittering August morning in 1979 at the edge of a salt marsh in Kennebunkport, Maine, I made a psychic sick.

I had never consulted a psychic before, though as a child I had wished I could accompany my mother and grandmother and take a turn having my cards read when-

---

1. [My editor at the publishing house that commissioned my first memoir, Remembering the Bone House, cut a good bit of my original draft for the introduction, "Reading Houses, Writing Lives," on the grounds that the quoted material, with its attendant footnotes, would alienate my readers. Although her editorial judgment, identical to that of the editor of Plaintext, was probably correct—given that her task was to develop marketable books and that the people drawn to personal narratives, especially ones involving chronic illness, may well not put up with feminist reflections, replete with footnotes, about literary themes—I felt torn as "life" was thus severed from "literature."

In part, I was disgusted at the way major trade publishers nowadays, assuming that readers are boobies, tend to search out risk-free material that the boobies will go for. I'm a reader myself, and I'm no booby. I hold my readers in no lower esteem than I hold myself. I read material with footnotes all the time (though I have to admit that since finishing my doctorate I'm not awfully systematic in footnote-reading), and so do most of the people I know. By imagining a marginally literate audience and insisting that writers address that audience in the hope of producing bestsellers, preferably ones that can be transformed into made-for-television movies, publishers bring out huge quantities of safe stuff. Not necessarily bad stuff, mind you—just generic—and after the forty-leventh tale about the husband's death, or the baby's death, or the mother's death, about the descent into madness, or alcohol, or paralysis, a dutiful reviewer may positively yearn for a "bad" book—something queer, off-kilter, surprising—even if it will never sell more than a couple of thousand copies.

But everyone who loves books has these reservations about publishing as "big business." The source of my distress went deeper, I think. I perceived in my editor's rejection of my more academic writing the message that the only part of me I could interest readers in (or enough readers anyway to interest the publisher's marketing people) was the damaged part. Now, physically there isn't very much left of me. To be whittled away intellectually as well strikes me straight through with grief and fear. And defiance. I am more than a slowly crumpling heap of flesh, and I think about more than an awful failure (though I think about that more than I would wish). In fact, I think most—now, as I have nearly all my life—about literature. I could not possibly write without the texts that give texture and context to my existence. So here all the footnotes are back.]

ever they went over to Salem to a woman named Lal. Mother and Granna were two of the least spacy women I've ever known, smart and pragmatic and as ordinary in their beliefs and habits as two single matrons, one widowed and the other divorced, could be; and I can't imagine what lured them to Lal. But off they went to her, more than once in my recollection and perhaps before, returning deeply convinced of the accuracy of her predictive powers.

Whenever I asked to be taken to Lal with them, Mother and Granna told me I was too young. And then Lal stopped doing readings. She couldn't bear, they said, the accuracy of her insights when they involved disaster. So I never got my turn, and never gave my loss much thought. Then one day over lunch my friend Liz began to tell about a wonderful psychic she'd recently visited, and I felt my curiosity rekindle. "Why don't you give it a try?" my husband asked. (George never does anything weird himself, but he's very good at egging me on.) We were on vacation, with commitments, and the opportunity to take my children to Kennebunkport, where I'd spent part of my childhood summers, appealed to me. So I took the psychic's number and gave her a call that night to make an appointment.

On the scheduled morning we found the house easily, just across a little bridge on the main road into the village, and George dropped me off. He and the children would drive down to the beach and play for the hour or so I'd been told the reading would take. I felt a little nervous and shyer than usual.

The psychic, whose name I've long since forgotten, was very young and very pretty, with dark eyes and smooth, swingy dark hair set off by a delicate white summer dress. She led me through the house into a beautiful kitchen with an antique table and chairs at one end, overlooking through wide windows the silvery green marsh. We sat there, chatting a little awkwardly as I set up my tape recorder, which Liz had recommended I use so that I'd forget nothing. She took a deck of cards and began to lay them out, speaking in a light voice. I have no idea what she said, having lost the tape years ago.

Perhaps a minute or so passed before she put her hand to her forehead and complained of a headache. She tried to go back to the cards, then put her hand up again.

"There's something wrong with my eyes. My vision is so blurred I can hardly see the cards."

"I have multiple sclerosis," I told her as if to offer reassurance. "I have a scotoma, a blurry spot, in my right eye." She tried to attend to the cards again, without much luck.

"I just feel terrible," she said. "I don't know what's wrong. Maybe eating something would help." She took a reddened peach from a bowl on the sideboard behind her and bit it. She laid out a few more cards. "I'm not sure here," she said, squinting as if to focus. "I can't tell what these mean." She seemed reluctant to talk about the cards.

"Look, you don't have to go through this," I said. "I can leave."

"Oh, no," she protested without warmth.

"I'm going right now." I put the tape recorder in my bag and stood up.

"I'm so sorry," she said in a good-girl voice. "Perhaps I'm coming down with something. Listen, my in-laws live in Tucson and I'm going out to visit them this winter. Maybe I could do a reading for you then. Give me your name and address."

"Sure," I said, jotting them down. I'm not psychic, but I knew she'd rather die at this point than lay her blurred vision on me again. I made for the door.

I am a bit spacier than my mother and grandmother, but not much. Yet I felt so little doubt that my proximity was causing the psychic's distress that I was reluctant even to remain outside her house. I walked back up the road, across the bridge, and perched on the narrow railing there to pass the half-hour or so till George and the children returned for me. I sat in the startling sunshine, almost as bright as I was used to in the desert, and stared into the brown weedy water, pondering why the psychic had not been able to give me a coherent reading.

Kennebunkport had always been a powerful place for me, the most powerful in my world, in fact. My forebears had lived here, and my father lay in the small and slightly ragged cemetery a few miles up this road. Perhaps that was it. Or perhaps it was my physical condition, an incurable degenerative disease, lodging somehow in her sensitive flesh. Or perhaps she had seen something in the cards so terrible that she couldn't bear to read it to me, couldn't even bear to look at it herself. Though I didn't know it yet, I was already spiraling into a full-blown depressive episode, and by the same time a year later I would be almost lost. Now I look back and wonder if she sensed this danger. I wonder, too, whether if she had seen and warned me of it, I might have handled it better than I did.

As it was, I came away with only a fragmentary tape and a spookiness I couldn't quite communicate to George when he finally pulled up beside me and let me in. We drove on into the village, which I hardly recognized, so gentrified had it become with tourist dollars. We went up to my family's house, long since sold and converted into an apartment building. The veranda had been pulled off and the area beneath it cemented to form a barren terrace. The cavernous front hall, I saw as I peered through the glass in the door, had been constricted by flimsy blond formica paneling to a tiny square. Anne and Matthew, thirteen and ten that summer, stared at the place vacantly, not even bothering to puzzle out what magic their mother seemed to find in it. They were a bit more intrigued by the cemetery and stood respectfully enough at the foot of my father's grave. But they have all their lives had a perfectly serviceable grandfather in the person of my stepfather, and this one has no significance for them even as a ghost.

Having stopped at the shrines, we drove back into the village and walked around a little. It had all, even the Lyric movie theater, been turned into little shops selling mostly tasteful and pricey curios. The River View Restaurant was still there, but remodeled and polished and so popular that we couldn't get a table. We finally found a vacant little restaurant on the other side of the river, where we got a late lunch of fried clams before heading back down the coast. That was the end of our trip to Kennebunkport. I would not make another visit—happier, though just as brief—for thirteen years.

What I didn't know that day, or for a good while afterward, was that I'd begun to write a book. The psychic never said. Something had shifted in me, like carelessly stowed cargo, skewing my course almost imperceptibly at the first, though later I'd fetch up here in an orange desk chair in front of a word processor on a chilly November afternoon, farther afield than I could have imagined then. What moved me I'm not certain. In part, I was disturbed by the psychic's refusal, whatever its cause, to "read" my life. Something about that life now seemed, thanks to her denial, unreadable, alien, impermissible, as though I'd stepped outside for a minute and, the door blowing shut behind me, discovered that my key no longer fit the lock.

Then, too, there was the puzzle of the lost house, the lost town. A house was there, and a town, right where I had left them, but both they and I had been so transformed by the intervening years that they were, literally, not the ones I knew. The ones I knew were not there. But neither had they vanished altogether. They were perfectly present to me in both waking and sleeping dreams. They seemed to have sunk from their perch on the banks of the Mousam River into the brine of my own cells. I was the Port incarnate, all that was left of the place I meant by the Port, and the only return possible was involution.

Not long after that day on the coast of Maine, back in the desert soil I've chosen to nurture and chastise me, I bought a copybook and began to sketch some reminiscences of the houses I had grown up in as part of a preliminary study of women's autobiographical writing, but I didn't get far before other duties claimed me. Then, a year or so later, I returned to them in a workshop taught by a well-known Southwestern writer of nonfiction. His response was glum: My memoirs were not readable, he wrote on the back of the last page, "to an ordinary, bored, busy, hard-nosed, cynical, weary, cigar-smoking, whisky-drinking, fornicating old fart like—not me!—but your typical magazine or book editor. . . . Now if you were (already) a famous person this might not matter; but you're not; so it does." Well, I certainly wasn't a famous person. Not only that, but since I lacked the stature or stamina to take up football, and I was too old and funny-looking to pass a screen test, and I was more apt to hang out with the tramps at our local soup kitchen than with Beautiful People anywhere, I hadn't any chance of becoming a famous person. No fame, no life. I put the copybook with its blotchy black-and-white cardboard covers away.

I was, in some ways, a slow learner. At that time I didn't understand the kind of radical questioning that all moral life, but especially life in the academy, requires. I deferred to the values of the Fornicating Old Fart (FOF, let's call him for short) because he'd published a lot of books and I hadn't published any. In this way I remained open to his good advice—that I'd have to make my memoirs readable—but rendered it useless, since I had no permission now to write memoirs, readable or otherwise. What I didn't ask was first, whether FOF actually represented the audience I was writing for, and second, whether fame was an authentic qualification for a memoirist.

The answers to these questions unfolded for me slowly. I began to recognize that in fact nine-tenths of the literature I was familiar with had been written for FOFs— but it had also been written *by* FOFs, of which, by virtue of my gender, I could not be one. This literature forms what is known in conventional feminist parlance as the patriarchal literary canon, still firmly entrenched after centuries. So, if typical magazine or book editors were FOFs, I was going to have a tough time getting published no matter what. I could, of course, choose to write in the persona of an FOF; some women slipped by the gatekeepers of current literary taste that way. But I could also, thanks to the bravery and honesty of women writing before and beside me, choose not to. Some publishers employ editors like mine for *Remembering the Bone House* turned out to be: fresh, amused, energetic, supportive, open to quirky ideas, quick to praise. I don't think she ever smoked a cigar in her life.

As for a memoirist's fame, it's a requirement attached to the moldy definition of autobiography as the self-reporting of "the great deeds of great men." By this definition, no woman could ever compose a "life." Yet the earliest extant autobiography in English literature was dictated by a woman (illiterate, of course), fifteenth-century MARGERY KEMPE; and similar claims have been made in other literatures. And women, whose access to fame has always been severely restricted, though notoriety has been more commodious, have continued to excel at autobiographical writing— memoirs, notebooks, letters, journals—to the present. Isak Dinesen wasn't famous when she penned *Out of Africa*, though, as it turned out, *Out of Africa* made her famous. She needed to make some money, her African coffee venture having turned financially disastrous, and she was desperately homesick for a land and a life perma-nently lost to her. The strength of that yearning, which sings on every page, has touched more readers than any "great" man's memories of his "great" conquest of the Dark Continent and its peoples.

The impulse to become famous, and to make a record of that famousness, arises out of the desire to distinguish oneself, to set oneself apart from (and preferably "above") the ordinary mass of humanity. As feminist psychologists like Nancy Chodorow have made clear, when mothers provide the primary care for all infants, as they do in our cul-ture, this desire—for separation, for individuation—is more urgent from the outset in a boy. In order to establish his masculine gender identity, he must repudiate the person with whom he has identified initially and most powerfully. Girls, by contrast, whose gender identity will be the same as their mothers', "emerge with a stronger basis for experiencing another's needs and feelings as one's own . . . [and] come to experience themselves as less differentiated than boys, as more continuous with and related to the external object-world and as differently oriented to their inner object-world as well."[2]

If fame is predicated upon differentiation, and women experience differentiation in other ways than men do, then fame is likely to hold a distinctive value for them as well. I can't speak for other women. To be honest, I don't know how they feel about fame. The subject has never come up. Fame and its acquisition may be among those subjects banished from polite discourse. As for me, I recall a night when a friend prognosticated; "Nancy, one day you are going to be very rich and very famous." I laughed in reply: "Oh, I hope the 'rich' part comes true, but I don't know about fame. It seems like it would take up an awful lot of one's time." I supposed I might, like VIR-GINIA WOOLF, find it "vulgar and a nuisance"[3] (and hoped, I'm sure, for the chance to find out). That's how it's always struck me, not as an evil to be avoided (some are corrupted by fame, to be sure, but others are not), but rather as a bothersome intru-sion between oneself and the work one has chosen to do in the world. The work I have chosen demands connection, not separation: writing, weaving and mending relationships, serving people in need. Fame simply wouldn't be of use.

Thus, FOF and I have fundamentally disparate attitudes toward life (what one does day after day) and a "life" (the report one makes on the outcome of what one has done day after day). He demands that I so conduct my daily affairs as to attract public attention for my distinctions; then I will have something "worth" writing about, a "life" even an editor will look at twice, a "life," that is, which will sell. Now, I don't have any objections to selling books (remember, I liked the "rich" part), but neither have I found the prospect of selling them a motivation for writing them. What arouses me is the desire to contact others, to share my experiences with them, to stir them to recognition of the similarities that underlie their experiences and mine, to illuminate and delight in and laugh over the commonalities of human life. To this end, I *can't* be "a famous person," standing out from my audience, declaiming publicly my distinctions as a fabulously wealthy automobile company president, say, or a multiply reincarnated actress, or a venerable Speaker of the House of Represen-tatives. I want my "life," in reporting the details of my own life, to recount, at the lev-el beneath the details, the lives of others. No modesty is entailed here, simply the desire to celebrate the private rather than the public world of human habitation.

2. [Nancy Chodorow, *The Reproduction of Mothering: Psy-choanalysis and the Sociology of Gender* (Berkeley and Los Angeles: U of California P, 1978) 167.]

3. [Virginia Woolf, *A Writer's Diary* (New York: Harcourt Brace Jovanovich, 1954) 125.]

I took a long time to free myself of FOF's notion that one merits one's memoirs through acquiring fame, and to develop the divergent sense of purpose I'm describing. What returned me to my "life" wasn't a sense of this freedom and development, however. It was an accident of intellectual messiness. Because my thoughts are easily scattered, I try to read and assimilate one book at a time; but if another comes along to intrigue me, I'm apt to sneak a peek. Thus, while I was working my way through Gaston Bachelard's phenomenological study *The Poetics of Space*, a new translation I had ordered, *The Newly Born Woman*, by the French feminists Catherine Clément and HÉLÈNE CIXOUS, arrived in the mail, and I found myself shuttling back and forth between the books. Suddenly the two collided in my head, houses and female sexuality tumbling and tangling into the autobiographical project I wanted to do: a memoir of my life as a female body.

"Not only our memories, but the things we have forgotten are 'housed.' Our soul is an abode. And by remembering 'houses' and 'rooms,' we learn to 'abide' within ourselves,"[4] Bachelard writes. And "housing" for him is not an airy metaphor. He means by it the literal physical structures that have sheltered us all our lives, which "through dreams . . . copenetrate and retain the treasures of former days," so that "when memories of other places we have lived in come back to us, we travel to the land of Motionless Childhood, motionless in the way all Immemorial things are." For me, as for Bachelard, understanding the significance of habitations "is not a question of describing houses, or enumerating their picturesque features and analyzing for which reasons they are comfortable. On the contrary, we must go beyond the problems of description . . . in order to attain to the primary virtues, those that reveal an attachment that is native in some way to the primary function of inhabiting."[5] But for me the "roots of the function of inhabiting" are entwined inextricably with my gender, which shapes my relationships to both the spaces I occupy and the language in which I meditate on those spaces. Bachelard, by contrast, reveals no awareness of himself as a being engendered, in part, by the very structures, architectural and linguistic, that he contemplates.

A male French philosopher writing in the 1950s, Bachelard assumed a universality of experience that permitted him to write, without irony, "As a general thesis I believe that everything specifically human in man is *logos*."[6] To which contemporary French feminists might reply, "Ah, precisely!" For they have pointed out repeatedly the immemorial intimate connection between the phallus and the logos, both of which serve as emblems of power reserved for the masculine discursive subject.

In order to subvert such a connection, Cixous points out in her section of *The Newly Born Woman*, "now it has become rather urgent to question this solidarity between logocentrism and phallocentrism—bringing to light the fate dealt to woman, her burial—to threaten the stability of the masculine structure that passed itself off as eternal-natural, by conjuring up from femininity the reflections and hypotheses that are necessarily ruinous for the stronghold still in possession of authority."[7] At the root of the issue lies *authority*: the right of woman to author her own story, a right whose tenuousness is demonstrated in the sense of "author" as "one

4. [Gaston Bachelard, *The Poetics of Space*, trans. Marie Joles (Boston: Beacon Press, 1969) xxxiii.]
5. [Bachelard 5–6, 4.]
6. [Bachelard xix.]

7. [Hélène Cixous, "Sorties: Out and Out: Attacks/Ways Out/Forays," *The Newly Born Woman*, trans. Betsy Wing (Minneapolis: U of Minnesota P, 1986) 65.]

that fathers." Were woman to arrogate that authority to herself, "all the history," in Cixous's words, "all the stories would be there to retell differently."[8]

But the phallocentric nature of discourse makes any such project problematic because it is "the enemy," as Cixous says, "of everyone. Men's loss is different from but as serious as women's. And it is time to change. To invent the other history."[9] And what will be the burden of this new tale? Virginia Woolf knew more than half a century ago when, in "Professions for Women," she confronted the difficulty of "telling the truth about my own experiences as a body," an act prohibited her by "the extreme conventionality of the other sex."[10] Centuries of cultural repression of the knowledge of woman-as-body mean, says Cixous, that "women have almost everything to write about femininity: about their sexuality, that is to say, about the infinite and mobile complexity of their becoming erotic." Almost everything still to write, but constrained by a discourse that proscribes the feminine erotic plot. A woman's only recourse is the "theft" of language with which to "write her body"—"the act that will 'realize' the uncensored relationship of woman to her sexuality."[11]

The body is a dwelling place, as the Anglo-Saxons knew in naming it *banhus* (bonehouse) and *lichama* (bodyhome), and the homeliness of its nature is even livelier for a woman than for a man. Bachelard speaks of "inhabited space" as the "non-I that protects the I."[12] Woman may literally become that inhabited space, containing, in Cixous's words, "a thousand and one fiery hearths" of erotic desire and experiencing in childbirth "the not-me within me," thereby becoming the non-I that protects the I of the unborn child. Still, forced to function as man's Other and thus alienated from her self, "she has not been able to live in her 'own' house, her very body. . . . Women haven't had eyes for themselves. They haven't gone exploring in their house. Their sex still frightens them. Their bodies, which they haven't dared enjoy, have been colonized."[13] Through writing her body, a woman may reclaim the deed to her dwelling.

The reverberations of all these texts coalesced for me into the project of exploring my own "felicitous space," to use Bachelard's phrase, the houses where I once lived and where, time collapsing through dreams, I continue to live today. In *Remembering the Bone House* I returned to them, reentered them, in order to discover the relationships they bear to my own erotic development and thus perhaps—because I'm ever aware of my self as a cultural, not merely a personal, construct—to feminine erotic development in general.

It is difficult to redeem "eroticism" from the limitations of "genitality." The sexual pleasure of those whose view of the world dominates our language arises from a specific point in space (and time as well, for that matter)—the penis, whose set of cultural meanings has been termed the phallus—and the world so represented is divided into binary categories (you got it/you don't). Since man's pleasure is localized in his penis, he assumes that woman's is confined to some opposite location. The logical choice is her vagina, since it so neatly goes in where he goes out. But it turns out that she doesn't, as Cixous puts it, "go round and round the supreme hole"[14] as he goes round and round the paramount pole. She is not simply opposite to but absolutely different from him. Her *jouissance* can't be confined to one place (and the vagina wasn't even, it turns out, a particularly good approximation).

8. [Cixous 65.]
9. [Cixous 94.]
10. [Virginia Woolf, "Professions for Women," *Women and Writing*, ed. Michele Barrett (New York: Harcourt Brace Jovanovich, 1979) 61, 62.]
11. [Cixous, pp. 94, 97.]
12. [Bachelard 5.]
13. [Cixous 68.]
14. [Cixous 85.]

The consequences of raising to consciousness the limitlessness of feminine *jouissance* are magnificent and terrible for women both as beings in the world and as writers. (They may be equally so for men, but that's men's business. "Don't speak for me," my husband always commands. So I'm not speaking.) As I have grown older and freer of the strictures of language, I have found charms in the smallest crevices of my embodied existence. My husband doesn't understand this, I know. He cannot imagine that I might, in good health, thrill to the sun-struck petunias on the white table on our back porch or the aromatic burst of fresh basil on my tongue as to his most passionate embrace. I can't explain it to him. I can't explain it to anyone. It's just the way I am.

For these reasons, "eroticism" has a more global meaning for me than language usually permits. This semantic dissonance caused me problems with friends who asked about *Remembering the Bone House* as I was writing. "An erotics of place and space," I would tell them, waiting for the wince, the furrow, the grin. The responses varied, but plainly they all assumed that I was writing "a dirty book." Well, maybe I was. In it I mention my body, certainly, quite a lot, even its secret places. Here and there I kiss, stroke, press, squeeze, even engage in sexual intercourse. Not as often, though, as I lie in bed, run across a playground, eat favorite foods, listen to the radio, tease my sister, roll in new snow. All these acts, happening to me as a body, shaping my awareness of my embodied self, form my erotic being. It is that process I seek in all my writing to capture and comprehend: how living itself takes on an erotic tone.

For a woman saturated to the bone in Calvinist tradition, such an exploration necessitates the healing of another Western patriarchal bifurcation: body/mind or body/spirit. I grew up in the belief that my intellectual/spiritual life, reflective of my "true" self, was separate from and superior to my life as a body. My body's appearance, which preoccupied me, was dismissed as beneath my concern. Its urges were denied, or at least deferred: I was "saving" myself for marriage. In adulthood, apparently, my bodily life might begin, and I suppose it did, at least in sexual terms. After I was married, I deliberately masturbated for the first time, so I must have believed myself entitled to my body's sensations in a new way. But I got through two pregnancies and childbirths, several sexual affairs, a couple of serious suicide attempts, and the onset of a devastating degenerative disease while locked almost entirely in my head.

My body, of course, was going through all these, whether "I" was holding my "self" aloof from it or not. Fortunately, one simply cannot *be* without being a body. One simply *is* inches of supple skin and foot after foot of gut, slosh of blood, thud of heart, lick of tongue, brain humped and folded into skull. And it is as a body that one inhabits the past and it inhabits one's body, so that, as Bachelard puts it, "the house we were born in is physically inscribed in us. It is a group of organic habits. After twenty years, in spite of all the other anonymous stairways, we would recapture the reflexes of the 'first stairway,' we would not stumble on that rather high step. . . . The word habit is too worn a word to express this passionate liaison of our bodies, which do not forget, with an unforgettable house."[15] Whether or not I permitted myself to think of my self as a body at some earlier time, I cannot deny the identity today. That identity offers my only means of entering and literally making sense of my past.

Although drawn to the autobiographical task, I do not wish however to produce an autobiography bound by the narrative conventions of temporal linearity.[16] Arranging

15. [Bachelard 14–15.]
16. [For a discussion of temporal styles, see Julia Kristeva, "Women's Time," trans. Alice Jardine and Harry Blake, *The Kristeva Reader*, ed. Toril Moi (New York: Columbia UP, 1986) 187–213.]

time as a sequence of incidents aids one in establishing an alibi, say, or drawing up a list of the day's tasks. But it does not provide the means for reentering the past experientially. Its product is brittle and attenuated, a "time line," neither flexible nor massive enough to open itself to reoccupation. The past, says the philosopher Maurice Merleau-Ponty, "has its space, its paths, its nameplaces, and its monuments. Beneath the crossed but distinct orders of succession and simultaneity, beneath the train of synchronizations added onto line by line, we find a nameless network—constellations of spatial hours, of point-events." Time and space conflate: "The whole description of our landscape and the lines of our universe, and of our inner monologue, needs to be redone. Colors, sounds, and things—like Van Gogh's stars—are the focal points and radiance of being."[17]

The search for lost time, then, necessitates spatial, not merely temporal, recall. As Bachelard tells us, memory "does not record concrete duration"; rather, "we think we know ourselves in time, when all we know is a sequence of fixations in the spaces of the being's stability." Memory itself is essentially spatial: "In its countless alveoli space contains compressed time. That is what space is for."[18] We can impose a grid of time onto our memories, much as we sketch lines of latitude and longitude on a globe, a very useful device for knowing when or where we are in relation to some event or spot used as a reference point. But the memories won't yield up their freight in response. For that we have to let go of lifelines and plunge into the multiple modalities—sensory, emotional, cognitive—that have encoded the past and will release it, transformed, into the present.

To this end, I wrote a memoir—as I write most often—in the fragmented form of essays, each concentrating on a house or houses important to my growth as a woman. I sought and still seek to avoid the reassuring rigidity and muscularity I'd learned to love in the academy. To abandon the narrative structure inculcated there (exposition, complication, climax, dénouement). To refuse its critical questions (What does this mean? Why does it matter?). To embrace the past as "meaningless," as "matterless," without "worth" in an economy based on the scarcity of resources, on the fear of running out—of reasons, of memories, of precious time. To seduce the impatient reader boldly: *Here, let's take our time. We've got plenty more where it came from.* To dare to dally. These are the requisites and risks of a woman determined to experience her past—the past in which she lived as a body, which dwells in her body still—as a bower.

When we were children, we formed an enclosure of hands linked into arches and sang:

> Go in and out the window.
> Go in and out the window.
> Go in and out the window
> As you have done before.

Writing my past as a body always enacts that circle game. I invite you in because I have been schooled (not in the ivory phallus this time but in all my mothers' dim houses) in hospitality: you, my strangers, my guests. *Mi casa es su casa.*

"Writing," says Cixous, "is the passageway, the entrance, the exit, the dwelling place of the other in me."[19] Writing itself is space. It is a populated house. In the

17. [Maurice Merleau-Ponty, *Signs,* trans. Richard C. McCleary (Evanston, IL: Northwestern University P, 1964) 15.]

18. [Bachelard 8, 9.]
19. [Cixous 85–86.]

houses of my past, I often felt alone; writing about them, I am never alone. As Merleau-Ponty notes in illuminating Husserl's philosophy, "Every man [sic] reflecting upon his life does have the fundamental possibility of looking at it as a series of private states of consciousness, just as the white civilized adult does. But he can do so only if he forgets experiences which bestride this everyday and serial time, or reconstitutes them in a way which caricatures them. The fact that we die alone does not imply that we live alone."[20] I cannot be without the other. I cannot be without you.

I cannot write my self without writing you, my other. I don't believe literally that in writing my "life" I am writing yours as well. On the contrary, I feel certain I am not. You didn't get bitten on the foot by red ants when you were four, did you? You didn't sing "Lullay, Thou Little Tiny Child" in the fourth-grade Christmas pageant? Your baby bunny wasn't chewed up and swallowed, hind legs last, by your Irish setter, Pegeen? You don't eat the same thing for breakfast every morning of your life? You're not still scared of the dark? These are my details. And heaven knows I have enough trouble getting them straight without keeping track of yours as well.

In fact, this is one of the problems that dog me in autobiographical work: I can never get the details right to the satisfaction of everyone who shows up in the telling. Merleau-Ponty comments that "all action and all love are haunted by the expectation of an account which will transform them into their truth."[21] My mother's in particular. Each time I complete a project, she'd like to check it over to make sure I've told things as they "really" happened this time, having missed the mark mightily in some earlier book. Others who find themselves presented in my work no doubt wish the same. But the past, that ramshackle structure, is a fabrication. I make it up as I go along. The only promise I can state about its "reality" is that I "really" remember (reembody? flesh out anew?) the details I record; that is, I don't deliberately invent any of them.

On the whole, however, I don't seek historical accuracy either. Instead, I try, in Merleau-Ponty's words, "to give the past not a survival, which is the hypocritical form of forgetfulness, but a new life, which is the noble form of memory."[22] What my mother, for one, will have to remember is that, as Sidonie Smith puts it, "the autobiographical text becomes a narrative artifice, privileging a presence, or identity, that does not exist outside language. Given the very nature of language, embedded in the text lie alternative or deferred identities that constantly subvert any pretentions of truthfulness."[23] In these terms, I can't even tell my own truth, much less anyone else's. I can only settle the problem in the manner of Clément's sorceress: "she is true because she believes her own lies."[24]

And yet, in a deeper sense of the word, I hope that I speak truthfully about all our lives. Because I think that my "story," though intensely personal, is not at all singular. Beneath its idiosyncrasies lie vast strata of commonality, communality. It is not, at that level, an original tale. To quote Merleau-Ponty again,

> The individual drama takes place among *roles* which are already inscribed in the total institutional structure, so that from the beginning of his life the child proceeds . . . to a deciphering of meanings which from the outset generalizes his own drama into a drama of his culture. . . . Consequently, there is not a single detail of his most individual history which

20. [Merleau-Ponty 175.]
21. [Merleau-Ponty 75.]
22. [Merleau-Ponty 59.]
23. [Sidonie Smith, *A Poetics of Women's Autobiography: Marginality and the Fictions of Self-Representation* (Bloomington and Indianapolis: Indiana UP, 1987) 5.]
24. [Catherine Clément, "The Guilty One," *The Newly Born Woman*, trans. Betsy Wing (Minneapolis: U of Minnesota P, 1986) 55.]

does not contribute something to that personal significance he will manifest when . . . he finally comes to the point of reversing the relationship and . . . converting even the most secret aspects of his experience into culture. . . . These reversals, these "metamorphoses," . . . this way that cultural time and space roll up on themselves, and this perpetual overdetermination of human events which . . . makes *every other person another ourself* for us—all these things become conceivable or even visible to the philosophical attitude alone.[25]

And, I would add, they inform the autobiographical attitude, at least for the feminist autobiographer, writing out of a sense of connectedness. I don't see how anyone engaged in self-representation can fail to recognize in this self, constructed as it is in language, all the others whom the writing self shelters. The not-me dwells here in the me. We are one, and more-than-one. Our stories utter one another.

"Thus, very quickly," writes Bachelard, "at the very first word, at the first poetic overture, the reader who is 'reading a room' leaves off reading and starts to think of some place in his own past. You would like to tell everything about your room. You would like to interest the reader in yourself, whereas you have unlocked a door to daydreaming. The values of intimacy are so absorbing that the reader has ceased to read your room: he sees his own again."[26] If I do my job, the books I write vanish before your eyes. I invite you into the house of my past, and the threshold you cross leads you into your own.   *1989/1994*

+ ⋯ ⊱◆⊰ ⋯ +

The Wife's Lament
8th century?

"The Wife's Lament" is one of two surviving women's love songs from the tenth-century manuscript of English poetry and riddles called the *Exeter Book;* the poem was written before the Normans invaded England and thus records a pre-Christian woman's voice. Its fatalistic outlook is reminiscent of women's lamentations in Germanic elegies known as *frauenlieder,* in that the narrator laments the loss of her beloved and her own apparent exile in pessimistic tones. Although it is not clear whether the speaker is a queen or a noblewoman, the absence of her husband apparently leads to the loss of her independence, since an Anglo-Saxon woman's autonomy derived in large part from her husband's authority. This elegy is filled with understated longing, its tone distinguished by the Old English device of *litote,* an assertion made by disclaiming its negative: "in those days it was not worse than now." Formally, the poem includes a number of run-on lines and lengthy sentences characteristic of Old English poetry, yet it contains enough short sentences to be considered a popular rather than a classical work.

Although the poem was once assumed to have been written by a man, feminist scholars have increasingly speculated that its author might have been a woman. It is rare to find a female speaker in Old English poetry, for female grief is typically conveyed by a male narrator; only "The Wife's Lament" and "Wulf and Eadwacer" offer women's voices. Scholars who claim that the author of "The Wife's Lament" is male point to such Anglo-Saxon phrases as *fulgao secan* (to seek service) and *foehon dreogan* (to suffer a feud) as unlikely expressions to have been spoken by a woman, nor do they find the various nouns used for "lord" to be typical woman-speech. The literary scholar Patricia Belanoff argues convincingly, however, that the narrator's use of language inappropriate to women creates "polysemous" meaning, to use French theorist Julia

Kristeva's term, that it enhances the poem's power by displaying "the pulsations of the semiotic" and thus transgressing gender expectations. Belanoff links the "differentness" in the language of "The Wife's Lament" to the theory of women's writing espoused by HÉLÈNE CIXOUS, suggesting that its disjointed and fragmented syntax mirrors what Cixous calls "the unimpeded tongue that bursts partitions, classes, and rhetorics, orders and codes." The poem's extensive use of first-person pronouns, especially the pronoun *min* (mine), connect the speaker intimately to both her beloved and her own ruminations, creating a sense of bodily presence that may suggest a woman as composer. In Belanoff's words, the narrator cannot "escape the I-ness of her situation."

Furthermore, as the literary critics Helen Damico and Alexandra Hennessey Olsen suggest, the feminine endings of words such as *minre sylfre* (myself) provide evidence of the speaker as a woman who performed the poem orally. The recurring verbs *beon* (to be) and *wesan* (to be or occur) provide a sense of immediacy that would have engaged the listening audiences emotionally. Instead of encouraging listeners to aggrandize war, "The Wife's Lament" creates a bond between the female speaker and her audience, who are moved to identify with her pain and thus to respect the authority and authenticity of her expression.

⊰ The Wife's Lament ⊱

I tell this story about me, in my sorrow,
I sing the fate of my voyaging self. I may say that
whatever hardship I lived through since I grew up—
new griefs and old—in those days it was not worse than now.
5   Always I grieve in the pain of my torment.

First my lord went away from his people
over the tossing waves. I felt cold care in the dark before dawn,
wondering where my lord of the lands might be.
Then I left on a journey to seek and serve him—
10   a friendless wanderer in my terrible need.
That man's kinsmen began to plot
with secret scheming to split us both apart,
so that we two—widely asunder in the world—
lived most wretchedly. And longing smote me.

15   My lord called to me to take up my hard dwelling here.
I had few loved ones in this country,
few devoted friends. For this my mind mourns.
Then I found myself a most husbandly man,
but a man with hard luck, brooding in his heart;
20   he hid his moods, his murderous thoughts,
yet seemed blithe in his bearing. Very often we boasted that
none but death alone would drive us apart—
not anything else! All that is whorled backward, changed;
now it's as if it never had been,
25   the loving friendship the both of us had. Far and near I must
suffer the feud of my dearly loved man.

They forced me to live in a grove of the wood
under an oak tree in an earth hovel.
Old is this den of earth. I am stabbed with longing.
30   The valleys are dark, the hills rise high,

bitterly sharp is my garrison overgrown with brambles,
a joyless stronghold. Here very often what seizes me fiercely
is the want of my husband! There are friends on earth,
lovers living who lie clasped in their bed,
35 while I walk alone in the hours before daybreak
under the oak tree, throughout this earth cave
where I must remain the summerlong day,
where I can weep the sorrows
of my many hardships, because I never can
40 find sweet rest for that heart's grief of mine—
not for all of that longing laid on me in this life.

Always must the young be troubled in mood,
with thoughts harsh in their hearts, yet at the same time
seem blithe in bearing despite a care-burdened breast
45 and a swarm of sorrows. The young man must rely on himself
for all he gets of the world's joy. He must be a far-flung outlaw
in a distant country.

So my loved friend sits
under a stone cliff crusted with frost in the storm—
my lover dreary in spirit. Water flows all around him
50 in his bleak dwelling. That friend of mine suffers
great sorrow of heart. Too often he remembers
a more blissful house. Unhappy is anyone
who must longingly wait for a lover.

970–990?

Wulf and Eadwacer

8th century?

A cryptic Anglo-Saxon elegy of only nineteen lines, "Wulf and Eadwacer" has been interpreted most often as the narrative of a woman whose husband, Eadwacer, has forced her to separate from her lover, Wulf, and the child she bore him. Although this poem appears in the *Exeter Book*, a tenth-century manuscript of alliterative verse and riddles, scholars estimate that it was first performed orally centuries earlier. The Roman historian Tacitus noted the chastity and monogamy of the rugged Germanic tribes that invaded England in the fifth century and explained that adulterous women were dealt with harshly; they were stripped and their heads were shaved before being banished from their homes—perhaps the fate of the poem's speaker.

Old English scholars offer many other interpretations of "Wulf and Eadwacer"; they have viewed it as a riddle, a charm to ward off illness, a fable about actual wolves, and a mother's lament for a lost son named Wulf. Moreover, many individual words continue to be disputed, and multiple translations abound. For instance, Marcelle Thiebaux, whose translation appears here, presents line 7 as a statement—"They [the speaker's clan] will waste him [Wulf] if he crosses their path"—while other scholars pose it as a question: "Will they receive/consume/oppress him if he comes in need?" The poem's ambiguous vocabulary, abrupt shifts, frequent use of ellipses, and haunting repetitions make it enigmatic. Moreover, whether or not the elegy was written by a woman has long been disputed. Although no definitive evidence exists, many feminist scholars argue that it could have had a female author, since it shares certain characteristics—most notably, an exiled woman's voice and a strong sense of doom—with a body of ancient

Germanic elegies known as *frauenlieder*, lamentations sung and possibly composed by women. Like its counterpart, "The Wife's Lament," "Wulf and Eadwacer" demonstrates less hope of relief from suffering than do such male-voiced elegies as "The Wanderer" and "The Seafarer," which also appear in *The Exeter Book*. The rhetorical and emotional power of the female voice in "Wulf and Eadwacer" makes it an important poem to consider as part of any women's literary tradition in English, whether or not a woman actually wrote it.

Law codes, wills, and historical documents reveal that some religious and lay women had significant societal powers during the Anglo-Saxon period; they could own, inherit, and bequeath property, administer abbeys or nunneries, and manage estates in their husbands' absence or as widows. Yet most Old English literature portrays a male-centered code of war, heroism, and revenge, a world in which women were absent or, at best, marginal. Female-voiced elegies such as "Wulf and Eadwacer" thus provide a rare picture of Anglo-Saxon women's emotional landscapes, revealing what the historical records sometimes did not: that women were vulnerable to a double sexual standard that punished their transgressions more harshly than those of men and subjected them to the whims of husbands who might be vengeful or abusive.

⊰ Wulf and Eadwacer ⊱

For my clan he would be like a gift of booty—
they will waste him if he crosses their path.
With us it isn't like that.

5   Wulf is on one island, I on another—
his island is made fast, girded by fens.
Fierce men are on that island.
They will waste him if he crosses their path.
With us it isn't like that.

I yearned for Wulf in his harried wandering.
10   When the weather poured rain I sat here in tears.
When the brash fighter folded me in the branches of his arms,
I felt pleasure, yes, but I felt loathing too.

Wulf, my Wulf, to think about you
made me faint with sickness, for you seldom came.
15   It was my mood of mourning, not want of food.
Do you hear, Eadwacer? Wulf carries our forlorn
whelp to the wood.
Men can easily wrench apart what has never been wedded—
our story together.

970–990?

* ⊰◈⊱ *

Margery Kempe
1373?–1438?

Margery Kempe was a religious visionary who traveled widely and was known for her dramatic behavior. An illiterate woman, she was nonetheless well educated for her time, having hired a priest to read English and European religious and mystical texts to her. Kempe was strongly influenced by the English mystic Richard Rolle's *The Fire of Love* and by the *Revelations* of the Swedish saint Brigitta. Mistaken for a member of the Lollards, a group of church reformers who denounced vices among the clergy and were sometimes burned as heretics, Kempe was arrested several times and interrogated under suspicion of heresy—because of her unorthodox preaching, her episodes of public weeping, and her habitual wearing of white, the traditional symbol of a virginity she no longer possessed.

Details of Kempe's life can be gleaned from her book. Her father, John Burnham, served several terms as mayor of King's Lynn, a village in northeast England. She married John Kempe, a burgher, in 1393, earned a living as a brewer and a miller, and bore thirteen children, of whom, strangely, she almost never speaks. Mentally and physically ill after the birth of her first child—the point at which her narrative begins—Kempe was tormented by a sin so terrible that she found it impossible to confess. Ultimately, she claims, God restored her to sanity and health, and she resumed her worldly preoccupations until the day she experienced the "divine pull" of the Lord, at which time she eschewed sexual activity with her husband and dedicated herself to God. When she was forty years old, she visited the Bishop of Lincoln and the Archbishop of Canterbury, both of whom were perplexed by this odd and confrontational mystic. In 1413 she made a pilgrimage to the Holy Land, followed by trips to Assisi and Rome, where she recounts that God asked her to join Him in marriage. During this period she traveled without her husband, an unusually independent and even a dangerous act for a married woman. Later she journeyed throughout England and Europe, enduring many hardships.

Kempe eventually persuaded two reluctant male scribes to take down the text of her life; the manuscript that is preserved, however, is not the one she dictated but another signed by a monk named Salthouse. The role of these male scribes in transmitting Margery's *Book* raises the issue of whether mediated texts by women present their lives and voices with accuracy. Shortly after William Caxton introduced the printing press to England, brief extracts from *The Book of Margery Kempe* were published by Wynkyn de Worde (c. 1500) and Henry Pepwell (1521). Both versions omitted her many references to erotic spirituality and personal eccentricities in favor of a dialogue between an obedient Margery and an instructive God. The complete *Book*, not rediscovered until 1934 and published in its entirety until 1944, reveals an ecstatic visionary who defied the social conventions of her age: she left her husband to pursue her own calling, traveled widely and independently, affirmed her own access to divinity, and dictated a compelling account of it all to two different scribes, insisting that they bring her autobiography to fruition. *The Book of Margery Kempe* emerges as a transgressive medieval text in which the body and desire are inscribed with passion and authority.

⤙ *from* The Book of Margery Kempe ⤚

CHAPTER 21

Our Lord speaks on the merits of maidenhood, marriage, and widowhood.

AT the time that this creature[1] had revelations, Our Lord said to her: "Daughter, thou art with child."

She said to Him: "Ah! Lord, what shall I do for the keeping of my child?"

Our Lord said: "Dread thee not. I shall arrange for a keeper."

"Lord, I am not worthy to hear Thee speak, and thus to commune with my husband. Nevertheless, it is to me great pain and great dis-ease."

"Therefore it is no sin to thee, daughter, for it is rather to thee reward and merit, and thou shalt have never the less grace, for I will that thou bring Me forth more fruit."

---

1. Kempe herself, a sentient being.

Then said the creature: "Lord Jesus, this manner of living belongeth to Thy holy maidens."

"Yea, daughter, trow thou right well that I love wives also, and specially those wives who would live chaste if they might have their will, and do their business to please Me as thou dost; for, though the state of maidenhood be more perfect and more holy than the state of widowhood, and the state of widowhood more perfect than the state of wedlock, yet, daughter, I love thee as well as any maiden in the world. No man may hinder Me in loving whom I will, and as much as I will, for love, daughter, quencheth all sin. And therefore ask of Me the gifts of love. There is no gift so holy as is the gift of love, nor anything to be desired so much as love, for love may purchase what it can desire. And therefore, daughter, thou mayest no better please God than continually to think on His love."

Then this creature asked Our Lord how she should best love Him, and Our Lord said:

"Have mind of thy wickedness and think of My goodness."

She said again: "I am the most unworthy creature that ever Thou shewedest grace unto on earth."

"Ah! Daughter," said Our Lord, "fear thee nothing. I take no heed what a man hath been, but I take heed what he will be. Daughter, thou hast despised thyself; therefore thou shalt never be despised of God. Have mind, daughter, what Mary Magdalene was, Mary of Egypt, Saint Paul, and many other saints that are now in Heaven, for of unworthy, I make worthy, and of sinful, I make rightful. And so have I made thee worthy. To Me, once loved, and ever more loved by Me. There is no saint in Heaven that thou wilt speak with, but he shall come to thee. Whom God loveth, they love. When thou pleasest God, thou pleasest His Mother, and all the saints in Heaven. Daughter, I take witness of My Mother, of all the angels in Heaven, and of all the saints in Heaven, that I love thee with all My heart, and I may not forget thy love."

Our Lord said then to His Blissful Mother: "Blessed Mother, tell ye My daughter of the greatness of the love I have unto her."

Then this creature lay still, all in weeping and sobbing as if her heart would have burst for the sweetness of speech that Our Lord spoke unto her soul.

Immediately afterwards, the Queen of Mercy, God's Mother, dallied to the soul of this creature, saying:

"My dearworthy daughter, I bring thee sure tidings, as witness my sweet Son Jesus, with all the angels and all the saints in Heaven who love thee full highly. Daughter, I am thy Mother, thy Lady and thy Mistress, to teach thee in all wise how thou shalt please God best."

She taught this creature and informed her so wonderfully, that she was abashed to say it or tell it to any—the matters were so high and so holy—save only to the anchorite who was her principal confessor, for he had most knowledge of such things. And he charged this creature, by virtue of obedience, to tell him whatever she felt, and so she did.

CHAPTER 22

Our Lord praises her and promises her eternal life.

As this creature lay in contemplation for weeping, in her spirit she said to Our Lord Jesus Christ:

"Ah! Lord, maidens dance now merrily in Heaven. Shall not I do so? For, because I am no maiden, lack of maidenhood is to me now great sorrow; methinketh I would I had been slain when I was taken from the font-stone, so that I should never have displeased Thee, and then shouldst Thou, blessed Lord, have had my maidenhood without end. Ah! dear God, I have not loved Thee all the days of my life and that sore rueth me; I have run away from Thee, and Thou hast fun after me; I would fall into despair, and Thou wouldst not suffer me."

"Ah! Daughter, how often have I told thee that thy sins are forgiven thee, and that we are united (in love) together without end. Thou art to Me a singular love, daughter, and therefore I promise thee thou shalt have a singular grace in Heaven, daughter, and I promise thee that I shall come to thine end at thy dying with My Blessed Mother, and My holy angels and twelve apostles, Saint Katherine, Saint Margaret, Saint Mary Magdalene and many other saints that are in Heaven, who give great worship to Me for the grace that I give to thee, thy God, thy Lord Jesus. Thou needest dread no grievous pains in thy dying, for thou shalt have thy desire, that is to have more mind of My Passion than of thine own pain. Thou shalt not dread the devil of Hell, for he hath no power in thee. He dreadeth thee more than thou dost him. He is wroth with thee because thou tormentest him more with thy weeping than doth all the fire in Hell; thou winnest many souls from him with thy weeping. And I have promised thee that thou shouldst have no other Purgatory than the slander and speech of the world, for I have chastised thee Myself as I would, by many great dreads and torments that thou hast had with evil spirits, both asleep and awake for many years. And therefore I shall preserve thee at thine end through My mercy, so that they shall have no power over thee either in body or in soul. It is a great grace and miracle that thou hast thy bodily wits, for the vexation thou hast had with them aforetime.

"I have also, daughter, chastised thee with the dread of My Godhead, and many times have I terrified thee with great tempests of winds, so that thou thoughtst vengeance would have fallen on thee for sin. I have proved thee by many tribulations, many great griefs, and many grievous sicknesses, insomuch that thou hast been anointed for death, and all, through My grace, hast thou escaped. Therefore dread the naught, daughter, for with Mine own hands which were nailed to the Cross, I will take thy soul from thy body with great mirth and melody, with sweet smells and good odors, and offer it to My Father in Heaven, where thou shalt see Him face to face, living with Him without end.

"Daughter, thou shalt be right welcome to My Father, and My Mother, and to all My saints in Heaven, for thou hast given them drink full many times with the tears of thine eyes. All My holy saints shall rejoice at thy coming home. Thou shalt be full filled with all manner of love that thou covetest. Then shalt thou bless the time that thou wert wrought, and the Body that thee hath (dearly) bought. He shall have joy in thee and thou in Him without end.

"Daughter, I promise thee the same grace that I promised Saint Katherine, Saint Margaret, Saint Barbara, and Saint Paul, insomuch that what creature on earth unto the Day of Doom asketh thee any boon and believeth that God loveth thee, he shall have his boon or else a better thing. Therefore they that believe that God loveth thee, they shall be blessed without end. The souls in Purgatory shall rejoice in thy coming home, for they know well that God loveth thee specially. And men on earth shall rejoice in God for thee, for He shall work much grace for thee and make all the world to know that God loveth thee. Thou hast been despised for My love and therefore thou shalt be worshipped for My love.

"Daughter, when thou art in Heaven, thou shalt be able to ask what thou wilt, and I shall grant thee all thy desire. I have told thee beforetime that thou art a singular lover, and therefore thou shalt have a singular love in Heaven, a singular reward, and a singular worship. And, forasmuch as thou art a maiden in thy soul, I shall take thee by the one hand in Heaven, and My Mother by the other hand, and so shalt thou dance in Heaven with other holy maidens and virgins, for I may call thee dearly bought, and Mine own dearworthy darling. I shall say to thee, Mine own blessed spouse: 'Welcome to Me with all manner of joy and gladness, here to dwell with Me and never to depart from Me without end, but ever to dwell with Me in joy and bliss, which no eye may see, nor ear hear, nor tongue tell, nor heart think, that I have ordained for thee and all My servants who desire to love and please Me as thou dost.'"

CHAPTER 35

She is affected by the sight of children in Rome. She has a long dalliance with Our Lord.

As this creature was in the Apostles' Church in Rome on Saint Lateran's Day, the Father of Heaven said to her:

"Daughter, I am well pleased with thee, inasmuch as thou believest in all the Sacraments of Holy Church and in all faith that belongeth thereto, and especially because thou believest in the manhood of My Son, and for the great compassion thou hast for His bitter Passion."

Also the Father said to this creature: "Daughter, I will have thee wedded to My Godhead because I shall shew thee My secrets and My counsels, for thou shalt live with Me without end."

Then the creature kept silence in her soul and answered not thereto, for she was full sore afraid of the Godhead; and she had no knowledge of the dalliance of the Godhead, for all her love and all her affection were set in the manhood of Christ, and there-of she had knowledge, and she would not for anything be parted therefrom.

She had so much affection for the manhood of Christ, that when she saw women in Rome bearing children in their arms, if she could ascertain that any were men-children, she would then cry, roar, and weep as if she had seen Christ in His childhood.

And if she might have had her will, oftentimes she would have taken the children out of their mothers' arms and have kissed them in the stead of Christ.

If she saw a seemly man, she had great pain in looking at him, lest she might have seen Him Who was both God and man.

And therefore she cried many times and often when she saw a seemly man, and wept and sobbed full sore on the manhood of Christ, as she went in the streets of Rome, so that they that saw her wondered full much at her, for they knew not the cause.

Therefore it was no wonder if she was still and answered not the Father of Heaven when He told her that she should be wedded to His Godhead.

Then said the Second Person, Christ Jesus, Whose manhood she loved so much, to her:

"What sayest thou, Margery, daughter, to My Father of these words He spake to thee? Art thou well pleased that it be so?"

And then she would not answer the Second Person, but wept wondrous sore, desiring to have still Himself and in no wise to be parted from Him. Then the Second Person in the Trinity answered to His Father for her, and said:

"Father, hold her excused, for she is yet but young, and not fully learned how she should answer."

And then the Father took her by the hand, (ghostly) in her soul, before the Son and the Holy Ghost; and the Mother of Jesus and all the twelve Apostles and Saint

Katherine and Saint Margaret and many other saints and holy virgins with a great multitude of angels, saying to her soul:

"I take thee, Margery, for My wedded wife, for fairer, for fouler, for richer, for poorer, so that thou be kindly and gentle to do as I bid thee. For, daughter, there was never a child so gracious to its mother as I shall be to thee, both in weel and in woe, to help thee and comfort thee. And thereto I make thee surety."

Then the Mother of God, and all the saints that were present in her soul, prayed that they might have much joy together. And then the creature with high devotion with great plenty of tears, thanked God for His ghostly comfort, holding herself, in her own feeling, right unworthy to any such grace as she felt, for she felt many great comforts, both ghostly comforts and bodily ones. Sometimes she felt sweet smells with her nose. They were sweeter, she thought, than ever was any sweet earthly thing that she smelt before, nor could she ever tell how sweet they were, for she thought she might have lived thereby, if they had lasted.

Sometimes she heard with her bodily ears such sounds and melodies that she could not well hear what a man said to her at that time, unless he spoke the louder. These sounds and melodies had she heard nearly every day for the term of twenty-five years, when this book was written, and especially when she was in devout prayer, and also many times while she was at Rome and in England both.

She saw with her bodily eyes many white things flying all about her on every side, as thick, in a manner, as specks in a sunbeam. They were right subtle and comfortable, and the brighter the sun shone, the better might she see them. She saw them many divers times and in many divers places, both in church and in her chamber, at her meat, and at her prayers, in the fields, and in town, both going and sitting. And many times she was afraid what they might be, for she saw them as well at night in darkness, as in daylight. Then, when she was afraid of them, Our Lord said to her:

"By this token, daughter, believe that it is God Who speaketh in thee, for, wheresoever God is, Heaven is, and where God is, there be many angels, and God is in thee and thou art in Him. And therefore be not afraid, daughter, for these be tokens that there are many angels about thee, to keep both day and night so that no devil shall have power over thee, nor evil men to harm thee."

Then from that time forward, she used to say, when she saw them coming: "Benedictus qui venit in nomine Domini."[2]

Also Our Lord gave her another token which endured about sixteen years, and it increased ever more and more, and that was a flame of fire, wondrous hot and delectable, and right comfortable, not wasting but ever increasing, of love; for though the weather were never so cold, she felt the heat burning in her breast and at her heart, as verily as a man could feel the material fire if he put his hand or his finger therein.

When she first felt the fire of love burning in her breast, she was afraid thereof, and then Our Lord answered to her mind and said:

"Daughter, be not afraid, for this heat is the heat of the Holy Ghost, which shall burn away all thy sins; for the fire of love quencheth all sins. And thou shalt understand by this token that the Holy Ghost is in thee, and thou knowest well that wherever the Holy Ghost is, there is the Father, and where the Father is, there is the Son, and so thou hast fully in thy soul all the Holy Trinity. Therefore thou hast great cause to love Me right well; and yet thou shalt have greater cause than ever thou hadst to love Me, for thou shalt hear what thou hast never heard, and see what thou hast never seen, and thou shalt feel what thou hast never felt."

---

2. "Let us bless those who come in the name of the Lord" (Latin).

"For daughter, thou art as secure in the love of God, as God is God. Thy soul is more certain of the love of God, than of thine own body, for thy soul shall part from thy body, but God shall never part from thy soul, for they are united together without end. Therefore, daughter, thou hast as great cause to be merry as any lady in this world; and if thou knew, daughter, how much thou pleasest Me when thou sufferest Me wilfully to speak in thee, thou wouldst never do otherwise, for this is a holy life, and the time is right well spent. For daughter, this life pleaseth Me more than the wearing of the haburion or the haircloth, or fasting on bread and water; for, if thou saidst every day a thousand Pater Nosters, thou wouldst not please Me so well as thou dost when thou art in silence and sufferest Me to speak in thy soul."   *1436–38/1501*

Margery Brews Paston
1457?–1495

Margery Brews Paston married into the wealthy Paston family of landowners from Norfolk in England; the family's surviving letters, documents, and deeds from 1422 to 1509 chronicle the political turmoil during the thirty-year War of the Roses alongside daily life in the fifteenth century. John Paston, a third generation member of the family, was wealthy and pious enough to bequeath money to the renowned anchoress JULIAN OF NORWICH, and when his wife died she left additional funds to Julian and three other anchoresses. Their younger son, John Paston III, inherited money from his elder brother, also named John, and shortly thereafter proposed marriage to Margery Brews, whose family offered less money for their daughter than young John Paston needed—the ideology of the era treating women as property to be sold in exchange for other assets. When Margery's father, Sir Thomas Brews of Sall and Topcroft in Norfolk, initially balked at giving Paston his daughter's hand, Margery Brews wrote several valentine letters to her prospective husband, entreating him to be faithful to her despite her father's intransigence. Margery's plea was complicated by the fact that another woman, a singer with a larger dowry, was reportedly in competition with her for John's attentions.

After considerable negotiating, Margery Brews and John Paston III were married in 1477; John became a Member of Parliament for Norwich and served for a time as sheriff of Norfolk and Suffolk, and Margery bore two sons, only one of whom lived to adulthood. Although the Paston library contained works by Chaucer and Christine de Pizan as well as Arthurian legends, and Margery could and did read, she apparently dictated her letters; her valentines were penned by her father's clerk and signed in her own rough scrawl. Six of her letters remain, the two valentines below and four other epistles to her husband that discuss their children and household matters. These domestic letters, along with those by other medieval women, help readers today to "reconstruct a female peopled past" (feminist critic Nina Aeurbach's phrase) and thereby understand the Old and Middle English literary periods more fully and equitably.

⇥ Letters to her Valentine/fiancé ⇤

To my right well-beloved Valentine, John Paston, Squire, let this bill be delivered, etc.

February 1477

Most revered and worshipful and my right well-beloved Valentine, I recommend myself to you, for I most heartily desire to hear of your welfare, and I beseech

Almighty God that he will long preserve it for his own pleasure and for your heart's desire. And if you would like to hear of my own welfare, I am not in good health of body or of heart, nor shall I be till I hear from you.

> For no creature knows the pain I feel—
> Though it may cause my death, I dare it not reveal.

And my lady, my mother, has very diligently tried to persuade my father in this matter, but she is unable to get any further with him than you have already heard. And for this reason God knows I am full of sorrow. But if you love me, as I truly trust that you do, you will not leave me on account of it. Because even if you didn't have half the income that you have, I would perform the greatest tasks of any woman alive so that I would not forsake you.

> And if you command me to keep true wherever I go,
> Surely I will do all my might to love you and never another.
> And if my friends say that I do wrong,
> They shall never hinder me from doing so.
> My heart urges me forever to love you
> Truly over all earthly things,
> And even if my friends grow angry with me,
> I trust that all shall be better in the times to come.

I write no more to you at this time, but may the Holy Trinity keep you safe, and I beseech you that this bill shall not be seen by any earthly creature except yourself alone, etc. And this letter was written at Topcroft, with full heavy heart, etc.

By your own,
M.B.
1477/1872–75

To my right well-beloved cousin, John Paston, Squire, let this letter be delivered, etc.

February 1477

Right worshipful and well-beloved Valentine, in my most humble manner I recommend myself to you, etc. And heartily I thank you for the letter which you sent me by John Becurton, by which I understand and know that you plan to come to Topcroft soon, without any errand or purpose but to bring to conclusion the business between my father and you.

I would be the happiest of any creature if the matter were settled. And you say that if you come and find that the matter proves no more favorable to you now than it was before, you wouldn't put my father and my lady, my mother, to any further trouble or expense for a long time. This makes me very heavy-hearted! And if you come and the matter doesn't reach any good conclusion, I would be much more sorrowful and full of grief.

And as for me, I have done and endeavored all I could in this matter, as God knows. And I let you plainly understand that besides all this my father won't part with any more money than a hundred pounds and fifty marks, which is very far from satisfying your desire. So, if you could be content with that amount and my poor person, I would be the merriest maiden on earth. And if you think you would not be pleased with that and that you might get a richer dowry from someone else, as I have already understood you to suggest—good, true, and loving Valentine!—don't take the trouble on yourself to come here any more on this account. Let it pass, and never be spoken of again, as I may be your true lover and beadswoman during my life.

No more to you at this time, but may almighty Jesus preserve you both in body and soul, etc.

By your Valentine,
Margery Brews
1477/1872–75

Letter to her husband, John Paston

January 21, 1486

Right reverent and worshipful sir, in my most humble manner I recommend myself to you, desiring to hear of your welfare. I beseech God to preserve it, to his pleasure and to your heart's desire.

Sir, I thank you for the venison that you sent me. And your ship has sailed out of the haven as of today.

Sir, I send you by my brother William your damask waistcoat. As for your short cloak of velvet, it is not here. Ann says that you put it in your chest at London.

Sir, your children are in good health, may God be blessed.

Sir, I pray you to send me the gold that I spoke about to you, by the next man who comes to Norwich.

Sir, your mast that lay at Yarmouth is hired out to a ship from Hull for thirteen shillings and four pence. And if any damage is done to it you shall have a new mast in its place.

No more to you at this time, but may Almighty God have you in his keeping.

Written at Caister Hall the twenty-first day of January in the first year of King Harry the VII.

By your servant Margery Paston

I pray to God that no ladies continue to captivate you so you can have no leisure for your concerns.

Margery Paston
1486/1872–75

◆—══◆══—◆

Elizabeth I
1533–1603

The daughter of the ill-fated Anne Boleyn, second wife of Henry VIII, Elizabeth Tudor ascended to a vulnerable throne in 1558 and became one of the most powerful rulers in English history. Initially weakened not only by Henry's rejection of her mother but also by her low status as a woman and her designation by the Catholic church as illegitimate, Elizabeth nonetheless went on to lead England during the rise of humanism, the expansion of colonization, and the triumph of the British navy over the Spanish Armada. As a child Elizabeth suffered at the hands of her unpredictable father, who moved her from place to place along with her half-sister, Mary Tudor, and her half-brother, Edward II. Tutored by Roger Ascham and others, however, she received an outstanding humanist education and became fluent in Latin, Greek, French, and Italian. Elizabeth began to do translations while still in her teens, most notably a translation of Marguerite de Navarre's *Mirror of the Sinful Soul* (1548), and went on to translate Boethius's *Consolation of Philosophy*, which she accomplished at the age of sixty. Late in her life Elizabeth prepared some of her speeches for publication; more than a dozen of these have survived. Additional speeches that might be hers exist in manuscript or in printed editions that cannot be authenticated.

Although the legal status of women did not improve during Elizabeth's reign, in part because she was apparently uninterested in poor women's welfare, scholars differ as to whether having a forceful woman on the throne enhanced the position of women overall. Some believe that for the majority of women there was no Renaissance, while others claim that noblewomen's educational and intellectual opportunities increased. Some changes in women's education seem to have occurred before Elizabeth came to power, in part due to the influence of Henry VIII's first wife, Catherine of Aragon, active in Thomas More's humanist circle and known for her own love of learning as well as her determination to educate her daughter, the Princess Mary, who was tutored by the Spanish scholar Juan Luis Vives and received a classical education. In 1548 Nicholas Udall wrote of life at court that "it was now no news at all, to see Queens and ladies of most high estate and progeny, instead of courtly dalliance, to embrace virtuous exercise of reading and writing." The study of "God and his most holy word" was particularly sanctioned. Elizabeth's own education was partially overseen by her stepmother, Katherine Parr, to whom the young Elizabeth expressed gratitude in several letters still in existence.

Historians generally agree that one of the ways in which Queen Elizabeth kept her power was by remaining single, toying in her youth and middle years with a range of suitors and, later, ensconcing herself as the "Virgin Queen." In numerous poetic tributes during and after her lifetime, she was idealized as the goddess Diana, the mythical Cynthia, or the Faerie Queene. Elizabeth is believed to have written at least sixteen poems, although only six of those extant are definitely hers; they range in theme from grief at the departure of a beloved to a queen's proclamation of the downfall of her enemies. "On Monsieur's Departure" (1600) illustrates her mastery of the conventions of courtly love; the witty "When I Was Fair and Young" is generally attributed to Elizabeth, although some scholars consider its tone different from that of any other poem and thus find it difficult to designate. Whether ardent or self-scrutinizing, Elizabeth reminds us in these poems of the complex role Renaissance women were expected to play in matters of love, even as her life demonstrates the power of an exceptional woman to affect the course of history.

⊰ On Monsieur's Departure ⊱

I grieve and dare not show my discontent,
I love and yet am forced to seem to hate,
I do, yet dare not say I ever meant,
I seem stark mute but inwardly do prate.
5   I am and not, I freeze and yet am burned,
      Since from myself another self I turned.

My care is like my shadow in the sun,
Follows me flying, flies when I pursue it,
Stands and lies by me, doth what I have done.
10 His too familiar care doth make me rue it.

No means I find to rid him from my breast,
Till by the end of things it be supprest.

Some gentler passion slide into my mind,
For I am soft and made of melting snow;
15   Or be more cruel, love, and so be kind.
Let me or float or sink, be high or low.
        Or let me live with some more sweet content,
        Or die and so forget what love ere meant.

1600/1823

⇥ When I was Fair and Young ⇤

When I was fair and young, then favor graced me.
Of many was I sought their mistress for to be,
But I did scorn them all and answered them therefore:
Go, go, go, seek some other where, importune me no more.

5   How many weeping eyes I made to pine in woe,
How many sighing hearts I have not skill to show,
But I the prouder grew and still this spake therefore:
Go, go, go, seek some other where, importune me no more.

Then spake frair Venus' son, that brave victorious boy,[1]
10   Saying: You dainty dame, for that you be so coy,
I will so pluck your plumes as you shall say no more:
Go, go, go, seek some other where, importune me no more.

As soon as he had said, such change grew in my breast
That neither night nor day I could take any rest.
15   Wherefore I did repent that I had said before:
Go, go, go, seek some other where, importune me no more.

?/1964

Mary Wroth
1587?–1653?

A writer who served in the court of ELIZABETH I, Mary Sidney Wroth is remembered for two works: *Pamphilia to Amphilanthus* (1621), a group of eighty-three love sonnets and nineteen songs, and *The Countess of Mountgomeries Urania* (1621), an unfinished pastoral romance. Although the speakers in the sonnets bear the same names as the romance's protagonists and the two works were published in the same volume, *Urania* appears to have been intended as a separate work.

Wroth was born in 1587 into the renowned Sidney family. Her uncle, Sir Philip Sidney, the author of *Arcadia* and *Astrophel and Stella*, died the year she was born; his sister, MARY SIDNEY

---

1. Cupid, the Roman god of love.

HERBERT, Countess of Pembroke, wrote religious verse and translated works from French, Italian, and Latin; Wroth's father, Robert Sidney, second Earl of Leicester, was a poet and a servant of Queen Elizabeth; and William Herbert, Mary Sidney Herbert's son, was a poet of some renown. Raised at the family estate of Penshurst in Kent, where her father had replaced Philip Sidney as the governor of Flushing, Wroth later became Elizabeth's lady-in-waiting and went on to participate in a number of court masques, including the *Masque of Blackness* (1604), a dramatic entertainment by Ben Jonson performed for Queen Anne. That same year she married Sir Robert Wroth, the son of a wealthy landowner, with whom she was extremely unhappy; Ben Jonson once described Lady Wroth as "unworthily married on a jealous husband." A great admirer of Wroth, Jonson dedicated his play *The Alchemist* to her, referred to her as "a Sidney, tho unnamed," and claimed to have learned much from her poetry. When Robert Wroth died in 1614, he left his wife in serious debt. Their only son had been born a month before his father's death, but he too died within two years, and because English law did not allow women to inherit from either husbands or sons, Wroth's estate reverted to her uncle. For twenty years she was forced to stave off debtors, ask the crown for protection, and live with relatives. Wroth had two children after her husband's death, William and Catherine, by her first cousin, William Herbert, whom she had been forbidden to marry. The feminist scholar Germaine Greer notes that while it was unusual for noblewomen of this period to bear illegitimate children, it was even more rare for them to do so and continue to appear at court, as Wroth did, perhaps due to the influence of the Sidney family name.

With the exception of ISABELLA WHITNEY's *A Sweet Nosegay* (1573), which some scholars considered doggerel, *Pamphilia to Amphilanthus* is believed to be the first sequence of love poetry to be written by a woman in England. This fact indicates that the female sonnet sequence came rather late to England, Louise Labe and other women troubadours having written love poems in the courtly tradition more than 100 years earlier in France. Wroth was clearly influenced by the Petrarchan love sonnets of her uncle Philip Sidney and her father, as well as by her aunt Mary Sidney Herbert's psalms; yet Wroth's sonnets reflect the pessimistic mood of the Jacobean court and her own complicated relationship with William Herbert. Her romance, *Urania*, is characterized by a profound disillusionment. Because the romance offended one of Wroth's court acquaintances, who condemned it as maliciously biographical, she withdrew it from circulation almost immediately upon publication. In addition to the printed version there exists an additional manuscript of an incomplete continuation of *Urania* at the Newberry Library. Among her other extant works are manuscript copies of a pastoral entertainment, *Love's Victorie*.

In the sonnets of *Pamphilia to Amphilanthus* the melancholy of the typical Petrarchan sonnet gives way to bitterness on the part of the speaker—a tone that reflected the reality of many a Jacobean woman in court, insecure and friendless when abandoned by her husband. Certain Petrarchan conventions appear: the ritual complaint about love gone awry, the frequent use of paradox, the presentation of a variety of moods of the betrayed lover-speaker. Like other sixteenth-century English sonneteers, Wroth imitates the Petrarchan sequence loosely, achieving a unity or collectivity by grouping together ten or so sonnets on a given theme and interspersing songs between each grouping. Her sonnets tend toward direct lyrical address, whereas the songs offer cryptic dramatizations of disappointment in love. Most sonnets experiment with stanzaic and metrical patterns in a manner reminiscent of her aunt's verse; one interlocking sonnet sequence is included. The overarching themes of these poems are grief, weariness, and disdain toward love, as well as the presentation of woman's constancy as an almost spiritual ideal.

⊰ *from* Pamphilia to Amphilanthus ⊱

I

When night's black Mantle could most darkness prove,
And sleep (death's Image) did my senses hire,

From Knowledge of my self, then thoughts did move
Swifter than those, most swiftness need require:

5   In sleep, a Chariot drawn by wing'd Desire,
I saw; where sat bright *Venus* Queen of Love,
And at her feet her Son, still adding Fire
To burning hearts, which she did hold above.

But one heart flaming more than all the rest,
10   The Goddess held, and put it to my breast,
Dear Son now shut, said she, thus must we win;

He her obeyed, and martyr'd my poor heart.
I waking hop'd as dreams it would depart,
Yet since, O me, a lover I have been.

9

Be you all pleas'd, your pleasures grieve not me;
Do you delight? I envy not your joy:
Have you content? contentment with you be;
Hope you for bliss? hope still, and still enjoy.

5   Let sad misfortune, hapless me destroy,
Leave crosses to rule me, and still rule free:
While all delights their contraries employ,
To keep good back, and I but torments see.

Joys are bereav'd me, harms do only tarry,
10   Despair takes place, disdain hath got the hand:
Yet firm love holds my senses in such band;
As since despised, I with sorrow marry.

Then if with grief I now must coupled be,
Sorrow I'll wed; Despair thus governs me.

25

Like to the Indians scorched with the Sun,
The Sun which they do as their God adore:
So am I us'd by Love, for evermore
I worship him, less favors have I won.

5   Better are they who thus to blackness run,
And so can only whiteness's want deplore:
Than I who pale and white am with grief's store,
Nor can have hope, but to see hopes undone.

Besides their sacrifice receiv'd in sight,
10   Of their chose Saint, mine hid as worthless rite,
Grant me to see where I my offerings give.

Then let me wear the mark of *Cupid's* might,
In heart, as they in skin of *Phoebus's* light,[1]
Not ceasing offerings to Love while I live.

---

1. Phoebus refers to Apollo, the Greek and Roman god of music, poetry, and the sun.

Song 6

You happy blessed eyes,
  Which in that ruling place,
  Have force both to delight, and to disgrace,
Whose light allures and ties
5   All hearts to your command:
  O look on me who do at mercy stand.

'Tis you that rule my life,
  'Tis you my comforts give,
  Then let not scorn to me my ending drive:
10 Nor let the frowns of strife
  Have might to hurt those lights;
  Which while they shine they are true love's delights.

See but when Night appears
  And Sun hath lost his force,
15 How his loss doth all joy from us divorce:
And when he shines, and clears
  The Heavens from clouds of Night,
  How happy then is made our gazing sight?

But more than Sun's fair light
20 Your beams do seem to me,
  Whose sweetest looks do tie, and yet make free:
Why should you then so spite
  Poor me? as to destroy
  The only pleasure that I taste of joy.

25 Shine then, O dearest lights
  With favor and with love
  And let no cause, your cause of frowning move:
But as the soul's delights,
  So bless my then blest eyes,
30 Which unto you their true affection ties.

Then shall the Sun give place,
  As to your greater might,
  Yielding that you do show more perfect light.
Then but grant this grace,
35 Unto your Love-tide slave,
  To shine on me, who to you all faith gave.

And when you please to frown,
  Use your most killing eyes
  On them, who in untruth and falsehood lies,
40 But (Dear) on me cast down
  Sweet looks, for true desire;
  That banish do all thoughts of feigned fire.[2]

1621

2. False passion.

Aphra Behn
1640–1689

"The Life and Memoirs of Mrs. Behn, Written by One of the Fair Sex," published anonymously in 1696, asks more questions than it answers about the mysterious origins and romantic life of Aphra Behn, the playwright, poet, and novelist whom VIRGINIA WOOLF called the first Englishwoman to earn a living by her wits. ANNE FINCH, Countess of Winchilsea and an admirer of Behn, claimed that she was a barber's daughter; that barber might have been Bartholomew Johnson, whose wife, Elizabeth Denham, bore a child that was christened Eaffry in 1640. The scholar Sharon Valiant has argued that Behn was the daughter of the illegitimate daughter of MARY WROTH, author of *Pamphilia to Amphilanthus*, and thus a female literary inheritor. What is certain is that as a young woman she visited Surinam, later the setting for her novel *Oroonoko* (1688), and returned to England in 1664 as Mrs. Behn. Her husband, a Dutch merchant, is believed to have died in the 1665 plague, but Behn might well have invented him, since as a widow she could live more freely in seventeenth-century London than as a single woman.

Although Behn wrote plays as early as 1665, it was not until 1670 that *The Forced Marriage* was produced at one of the two London theaters licensed shortly after the Restoration, the Duke's Company Theatre. One reason for this delay is that Behn spent time in the Netherlands in 1665 and 1666 as a government spy, sent by Charles II to solicit information about the Dutch navy's actions from a man named William Scott, whom she had met in Surinam. When she returned home Charles ignored her findings and refused to pay her salary; shortly thereafter she was threatened with debtors' prison, where she might have spent some time between 1667 and 1670. How Behn became involved in the theater remains uncertain, although she was acquainted with Sir Thomas Killigrew, manager of the King's Company Theatre, and had once lent him an Indian feather costume from Surinam for use in a production. It is possible that either Killigrew or Lady Davenant, who ran the Duke's Company, hired Behn to write, since women playwrights were being produced and actresses were performing on the English stage for the first time during this period. Behn's earliest plays, *The Forced Marriage* and *The Amorous Prince* (1671), are tragicomedies, and *Abdelazar* (1676) is a revenge tragedy; the remaining plays are bawdy comedies that revel in complications caused by illicit desire.

Throughout her life Behn wrote about gender, sexuality, and political intrigue. *Poems Upon Several Occasions, with a Voyage to the Isle of Love* (1684) treats with comic abandon such topics as orgasm, impotence, and adultery. *Miscellany*, which she edited in 1685, contains her own verse and various poems by other women in her circle. A committed Tory who believed that a royalist court offered women more freedom than a conservative government would, Behn satirized the sexual hypocrisies of the Puritans in her work and chastised the Whigs for greed. For fifteen years she was the lover of John Hoyle, a licentious lawyer whom she described in her *Miscellany* (1685) as "A Wit uncommon, and Facetious, / A great admirer of Lucretius"—in short, an antireligious hedonist. From Hoyle, Behn probably contracted syphilis; she spent her last years ill and in poverty. Upon her death she was buried, "most scandalously but rather appropriately," in Woolf's words, in Westminster Abbey.

Of Behn's eighteen plays, *The Rover* (1677) and *The Lucky Chance* (1686) remain the best known. Based loosely on a play by Sir Thomas Killigrew entitled *Thomaso, or The Wanderer*, *The Rover* focuses on the love affairs of roaming cavaliers exiled in Italy during the Interregnum. *The Lucky Chance* (1686), arguably Behn's most feminist play, critiques unwanted marriages, especially those of young women to wealthy older men. This play is original to Behn rather than an adaptation of someone else's earlier work, and beneath the comic surface it offers a serious examination of women as property. Although this play did well at the box office, it was so roundly criticized for indecency that it was rarely revived for many years thereafter.

In the preface to *The Lucky Chance*, Behn defends her plays against accusations of licentiousness or inferiority: "Had the plays I have writ come forth under any man's name, and never known to be mine, I appeal to all unbiased judges of sense, if they had not said that person had made as many good comedies, as any one man that has writ in our age; but a devil on't, the woman damns the poet." Although she ends by describing herself as "a defenceless woman," Behn emerges as anything but weak. "I am not content to write for a third day only," she boldly tells her critics, referring to the custom of performing a mediocre play for just three days. "I value fame as much as if I had been born a hero; and if you rob me of that, I can retire from the ungrateful world, and scorn its fickle favors."

⇥ The Lucky Chance, or an Alderman's Bargain ⇤

Dramatis Personae

SIR FEEBLE FAINWOULD:	An old Alderman to be married to *Leticia*.
SIR CAUTIOUS FULBANK:	An old Banker married to *Julia*.
MR. GAYMAN:	A Spark of the Town, Lover of *Julia*.
MR. BELMOUR:	Contracted to *Leticia* disguis'd, and passes for Sir *Feeble's* Nephew.
MR. BEARJEST:	Nephew to Sir *Cautious*, a Fop.
CAPT. NOYSEY:	His Companion.
MR. BREDWELL:	Prentice to Sir *Cautious*, and Brother to *Leticia*, in love with *Diana*.
RAG:	Footman to *Gayman*.
RALPH:	Footman to Sir *Feeble*.
DICK:	Footman to Sir *Cautious*.
GINGLE:	A Musician.
LADY FULBANK:	In love with *Gayman*, honest and generous.
LETICIA:	Contracted to *Belmour*, married to Sir *Feeble*, young and virtuous.
DIANA:	Daughter to Sir *Feeble*, in love with *Bredwell*—virtuous.
PERT:	Lady *Fulbank's* Woman.
GAMMER GRIME:	Landlady to *Gayman*, a Smith's Wife in *Alsatia*.
SUSAN:	A Servant to Sir *Feeble*
PHILLIS:	*Leticia's* woman

A Parson, Fiddlers, Dancers and Singers.
Nymphs, Shepherds, A Postman, Porters

Scene

London

Prologue

Since with Old Plays you have so long been cloyed,
As with a Mistress many Years enjoy'd:

How briskly dear Variety you pursue;
Nay though for worse ye change, ye will have New.
Widows take heed, some of you in fresh Youth
Have been th' unpity'd Martyrs of this Truth.
When for a drunken Sot, that had kind hours,
And taking their own Freedoms, left you yours;
'Twas your deliberate Choice your Days to pass
With a damned, sober self-admiring Ass;
Who thinks good usage for the Sex unfit,
And slights ye out of Sparkishness and Wit.
But you can fit him—Let a worse Fool come,
If he neglect, to officiate in his room.
Vain Amorous Coxcombs everywhere are found,
Fops for all uses, but the Stage, abound.
Tho you should change them oftener than your Fashions,
There still would be enough for your Occasions:
But ours are not so easily supplied,
All that could e'er quit cost, we have already tried.
Nay, dear sometimes have bought the Frippery Stuff.
This, Widows, you—I mean the old and tough—
Will never think, be they but Fool enough.
　　Such will with any kind of Puppies play;
But we must better know for what we pay:
We must not purchase such dull Fools as they.
Should we shew each her own particular Dear,
What they admire at home, they would loath here.
Thus, though the Mall, the Ring, the Pit is full,
And every Coffee-House still swarms with Fool:
Though still by Fools all other Callings live,
Nay our own Women by fresh Cullies thrive.
Though your Intrigues which no Lampoon can cure,
Promise a long Succession to ensure,
And all your Matches Plenty do presage:
Dire is the Dearth and Famine on the Stage.
Our Store's quite wasted, and our Credit's small,
Not a Fool left to bless our selves withal.
We're forced at last to rob, (which is great pity,
Though 'tis a never-foiling Bank) the City.
　　We show you one today entirely new,
And of all Jests, none relish like the true.
Let that the value of our Play enhance,
Then it may prove indeed the *Lucky Chance*.

Act I

Scene I

The Street at Break of Day

Enter Belmour disguised in a traveling Habit.

BELMOUR: Sure 'tis the Day that gleams in yonder East,
    The Day that all but Lovers blessed by Shade
    Pay cheerful Homage to:
    Lovers! and those pursued like guilty me
    By rigid Laws, which put no Difference
    'Twixt fairly killing in my own Defense,
    And Murders bred by drunken Arguments,
    Whores, or the mean Revenges of a Coward.
    —This is Leticia's Father's House—   [Looking about.]
    And that the dear Balcony
    That has so oft been conscious of our Loves;
    From whence she's sent me down a thousand Sighs,
    A thousand Looks of Love, a thousand Vows!
    O thou dear Witness of those Charming Hours,
    How do I bless thee, how am I pleased to view thee
    After a tedious Age of six Months' Banishment
    [Enter several with Music (including Gingle).]

FIDDLER: But hark ye Mr. Gingle, is it proper to play before the Wedding?
GINGLE: Ever while you live, for many a time in playing after the first Night, the
    Bride's sleepy, the Bridegroom tired, and both so out of Humor, that perhaps they
    hate anything that puts 'em in mind they are married.   [They play and sing.]

            Rise Cloris, charming Maid arise!
                And baffle breaking Day,
            Shew the adoring World thy Eyes
                Are more surprising Gay;
            The Gods of Love are smiling round,
                And lead the Bridegroom on,
            And Hymen has the Altar crown'd,
                While all thy sighing Lovers are undone.

            To see thee pass they throng the Plain;
                The Groves with Flowers are strown,
            And every young and envying Swain
                Wishes the Hour his own.
            Rise then, and let the God of Day,
                When thou dost to the Lover yield,
            Behold more Treasure given away
                Than he in his vast Circle e're beheld.

[Enter Phillis in the Balcony, throws 'em Money.]

BELMOUR: Hah, Phillis, Leticia's Woman!
GINGLE: Fie Mrs. Phillis, do ye take us for Fiddlers that play for Hire? I came to
    compliment Mrs. Leticia on her Wedding-Morning because she is my Scholar.
PHILLIS: She sends it only to drink her Health.
GINGLE: Come Lads let's to the Tavern then—   [Exeunt (Gingle and) Music.]
BELMOUR: Hah! said he Leticia?
    Sure I shall turn to Marble at this News

I harden—and cold Damps pass through my senseless Pores
—Hah—who's here?—

[Enter Gayman wrapped in his Cloak.]

GAYMAN: 'Tis yet too early, but my Soul's impatient
And I must see Leticia—

BELMOUR: Death and the Divel—the Bridegroom—
Stay Sir, by Heaven you pass not this way—

[Goes to the Door as [Gayman] is knocking, pushes him away, and draws.]

GAYMAN: Hah! what art thou that durst forbid me Entrance?
Stand off.   *[They fight a little, and closing view each other.]*

BELMOUR: Gayman!

GAYMAN: My dearest Belmour.

BELMOUR: Oh thou false Friend, thou treacherous base Deceiver!

GAYMAN: Hah, this to me dear Harry?

BELMOUR: Whither is Honour, Truth and Friendship fled?

GAYMAN: Why there ne're was such a Virtue.
'Tis all a Poet's Dream.

BELMOUR: I thank you Sir.

GAYMAN: I am sorry for't, or that ever I did anything that could deserve it: put up
your Sword—an honest man would say how he's offended, before he rashly draws.

BELMOUR: Are not you going to be married Sir?

GAYMAN: No Sir, as long as any man in London is so, that has but a handsome
Wife Sir.

BELMOUR: Are not you in Love Sir?

GAYMAN: Most damnably—and would fain lie with the dear jilting Gypsy.

BELMOUR: Hah—who would you lie with Sir?

GAYMAN: You catechise me roundly—'tis not fair to name, but I am no Starter,
Harry; just as you left me you find me, I am for the faithless Julia still, the Old
Alderman's Wife. 'Twas high time the City should lose their Charter, when their
Wives turn honest: but pray Sir answer me a Question or two?

BELMOUR: Answer me first—what make you here this Morning?

GAYMAN: Faith to do you Service. Your Damn'd little Jade of a Mistress has learned
of her Neighbours the Art of Swearing and Lying in abundance, and is—

BELMOUR: To be married!   *[Sighing.]*

GAYMAN: Even so, God save the Mark; and she'll be a fair one for many an Arrow
besides her Husbands, though he an old Finsbury Hero this threescore Years.

BELMOUR: Who mean you?

GAYMAN: Why thy Cuckold that shall be, if thou be'st wise.

BELMOUR: Away—
Who is this Man?—thou dally'st with me.

GAYMAN: Why an old Knight, and Alderman, here o'th' City, Sir Feeble Fainwould,
a jolly old Fellow, whose Activity is all got into his Tongue, a very excellent Teas-
er; but neither Youth nor Beauty can grind his Dudgeon to an Edge.

BELMOUR: Fie what Stuff's here.

GAYMAN: Very excellent Stuff, if you have but the Grace to improve it.

BELMOUR: You banter me—but in plain English tell me
What made you here thus early,
Entering yon House with such Authority?

GAYMAN: Why your Mistress Leticia—your contracted Wife, is this Morning to be married to old Sir Feeble Fainwould, induced to't I suppose by the great Jointure he makes her, and the Improbability of your ever gaining your Pardon for your high Duel—Do I speak English now Sir?

BELMOUR: Too well, would I had never heard thee.

GAYMAN: Now I being the Confident in your Amours, the Jack-go-between —the civil Pimp, or so—you left her in charge with me at your Departure—

BELMOUR: I did so.

GAYMAN: I saw her every day—and every day she paid the Tribute of a Shower of Tears, to the dear Lord of all her Vows, Young Belmour; Till, Faith, at last, for Reasons manifold, I slacked my daily Visits.

BELMOUR: And left her to Temptation—was that well done?

GAYMAN: Now must I afflict you and myself with a long Tale of Causes why; Or be charged with want of Friendship.

BELMOUR: You will do well to clear that Point to me.

GAYMAN: I see you're peevish, and you shall be humored. —You know my Julia—Played me e'en such another Prank as your false one is going to play you, and married old Sir Cautious Fulbank here i'th' City; at which you know I stormed, and raved and swore, as thou wilt now, and to as little purpose. There was but one Way left, and that was Cuckolding him.

BELMOUR: Well that Design I left thee hot upon.

GAYMAN: And hotly have pursued it. Swore—Wept—Vowed—Wrote, upbraided, prayed and railed; then treated lavishly—and presented high—till between you and I Harry, I have presented the best part of Eight hundred a year into her Husband's hands, in Mortgage.

BELMOUR: This is the Course you'd have me steer, I thank you.

GAYMAN: No, no, Pox on't, all Women are not Jilts. Some are honest, and will give as well as take; or else there would not be so many broke i'th' City. In fine Sir, I have been in Tribulation, that is to say, Moneyless for six tedious Weeks, without either Clothes—or Equipage to appear withal; and so not only my own Love affair lay neglected—but thine too—and I am forced to pretend to my Lady, that I am i'th' Country with a Dying Uncle—from whom if he were indeed dead, I expect Two thousand a year.

BELMOUR: But what's all this to being here this Morning?

GAYMAN: Thus have I lain concealed like a winter Fly, hoping for some blessed Sunshine to warm me into Life again, and make me hover my flagging Wings; till the News of this Marriage (which fills the Town) made me crawl out this silent Hour—to upbraid the fickle Maid.

BELMOUR: Didst thou?—pursue thy kind Design. Get me to see her, and sure no Woman even possessed with a new Passion, Grown confident even to Prostitution; But when she sees the Man to whom she's sworn so very—very much, will find Remorse and Shame.

GAYMAN: For your sake though the Day be broke upon us, And I'm undone if seen—I'll venture in—   *[Throws his Cloak over (his head).]*
     [Enter Sir Feeble Fainwould—Sir Cautious Fulbank—Bearjest and Noysey. (They) pass over the Stage and go in.]

—Hah—see—the Bridegroom!
And with him my destined Cuckold, old Sir Cautious Fulbank.
—Hah—what ail'st thou Man?

BELMOUR: The Bridegroom!
Like Gorgon's Head he's turned me into Stone—

GAYMAN: Gorgon's Head—a Cuckolds Head—'twas made to graft upon—

BELMOUR: By Heaven I'll seize her even at the Altar!
And bear her thence in Triumph.

GAYMAN: Ay, and be borne to Newgate in Triumph, and be hanged in Triumph—
'twill be cold Comfort celebrating your Nuptials in the Press Yard, and be waked
next Morning like Mr. Barnardine in the Play—Will you please to Rise and be
hanged a little Sir?

BELMOUR: What wouldst thou have me do?

GAYMAN: As many an Honest Man has done before thee—Cuckold him—
Cuckold him.

BELMOUR: What—and let him marry her! She that's mine by Sacred Vow already?
By Heaven it would be Flat Adultery in her!

GAYMAN: She'll learn the Trick, and practice it the better with thee.

BELMOUR: Oh Heavens! Leticia marry him! and lie with him! Here will I stand
and see this shameful Woman,
See if she dares pass by me to this Wickedness.

GAYMAN: Hark ye, Harry—in earnest have a care of betraying yourself—and do
not venture sweet Life for a fickle Woman, who perhaps hates you.

BELMOUR: You counsel well—but yet to see her married!—
How every thought of that shocks all my Resolution—
But hang it I'll be Resolute and Saucy,
Despise a Woman who can use me ill,
And think myself above her.

GAYMAN: Why now thou art thyself—a Man again.
But see they're coming forth, now stand your ground.
[Enter Sir Feeble, Sir Cautious, Bearjest, Noysey, Leticia, sad, Diana, Phillis.]
[(They) Pass over the Stage.]

BELMOUR: 'Tis she, support me Charles, or I shall sink to Earth,
—Methought in passing by she cast a scornful Glance at me:
Such charming Pride I've seen upon her Eyes,
When our Love Quarrels armed 'em with Disdain—
—I'll after 'em, if I live she shall not scape me.

[Offers to go. Gayman holds him.]

GAYMAN: Hold, remember you're proscribed,
And die if you are taken—

BELMOUR: I've done and I will live, but he shall ne're enjoy her.
Who's yonder, Ralph, my trusty Confidant?
[Enter Ralph.]

Now though I perish I must speak to him.
—Friend, what Wedding's this?

RALPH: One that was never made in Heaven Sir,
'Tis Alderman Fainwould, and Mrs. Leticia Bredwell.
BELMOUR: Bredwell—I've heard of her—she was Mistress—
RALPH: To fine Mr. Belmour Sir—aye there was a Gentleman—But rest his Soul—
he's hanged Sir.   *[Weeps.]*
BELMOUR: How! hanged?
RALPH: Hanged Sir, hanged—at the Hague in Holland.
GAYMAN: I heard some such News, but did not credit it.
BELMOUR: For what said they was he hanged?
RALPH: Why e'en for High Treason Sir, he killed one of their Kings.
GAYMAN: Holland's a Commonwealth, and is not ruled by Kings.
RALPH: Not by one Sir, but by a great many; this was a Cheesemonger—they fell out
over a Bottle of Brandy, went to Snicker Snee—Mr. Belmour cut his Throat, and
was hanged for't, that's all Sir.
BELMOUR: And did the young Lady believe this?
RALPH: Yes,—and took on most heavily—the Doctors gave her over—and there
was the Devil to do to get her to consent to this Marriage—but her Fortune was
small, and the Hope of a Ladyship, and a Gold Chain at the Spittle Sermon did
the Business,—and so your Servant Sir.   *[Exit Ralph.]*
BELMOUR: So—here's a hopeful Account of my sweet self now.
    [Enter Postman with Letters.]

POSTMAN: Pray Sir which is Sir Feeble Fainwould's?
BELMOUR: What would you with him, Friend?
POSTMAN: I have a Letter here from the Hague for him.
BELMOUR: From the Hague! Now have I a Curiosity to see it *[Aside.]*—I am his
Servant—give it me—   *[(Postman) Gives it him and Exits.]*
Perhaps here may be the second part of my Tragedy.
I'm full of Mischief, Charles—and have a mind to see this Fellow's Secrets. For from
this hour I'll be his evil Genius, haunt him at Bed and Board, he shall not sleep nor
eat—disturb him at his Prayers, in his Embraces; and tease him into Madness.
Help me Invention, Malice, Love, and Wit.   *[Opening the Letter.]*
Ye Gods, and little Fiends instruct my Mischief.   *[Reads.]*
    *Dear Brother, according to your Desire I have sent for my Son from St. Omers, whom
    I have sent to wait on you in England, he is a very good Accountant and fit for Business,
    and much pleased he shall see that Uncle to whom he's so obliged, and which is so grate-
    fully acknowledged by—*

                                    Dear Brother, your affectionate Brother
                                                      Francis Fainwould.

—Hum—hark ye Charles, do you know who I am now?
GAYMAN: Why I hope a very honest Friend of mine, Harry Belmour.
BELMOUR: No Sir, you are mistaken in your Man.
GAYMAN: It may be so.
BELMOUR: I am d'ye see Charles, this very individual, numerical young Mr.—what ye
call um Fainwould, just come from Saint Omers into England—to my Uncle the
Alderman.
    I am, Charles, this very Man.
GAYMAN: I know you are, and will swear't upon occasion.
BELMOUR: This lucky Thought has almost calmed my mind.

And if I don't fit you my dear Uncle—
May I never lie with my Aunt.
GAYMAN: Ah Rogue—but prithee what care have you taken about your Pardon?
'twere good you should secure that.
BELMOUR: There's the Devil Charles, had I but that—but I have had a very good
Friend at work, a thousand Guineas, that seldom fails; but yet in Vain, I being the
first Transgressor since the Act against Dueling. But I impatient to see this dear
Delight of my Soul,
And hearing from none of you this six Weeks came from
Brussels in this Disguise—for the Hague I have not
Seen, though hanged there—but come—let's away
And complete me a right Saint Omers Spark, that I
May present myself as soon as they come from Church.   [*Exeunt.*]

Scene II

Sir Cautious Fulbank's House

[*Enter Lady Fulbank, Pert, and Bredwell. Bredwell gives (Lady Fulbank) a Letter.*]

LADY FULBANK [reads]: *Did my Julia know how I Languish in this cruel Separation, she
would afford me her Pity, and write oftener. If only the Expectation of two thousand a
Year kept me from you, ah! Julia how easily would I abandon that Trifle for your more
valued Sight, but that I know a Fortune will render me more agreeable to the charming
Julia, I should quit all my Interest here, to throw myself at her Feet, to make her sensible
how I am entirely her Adorer,*

Charles Gayman.

—Faith Charles you lie—you are as welcome to me now,
Now when I doubt thy Fortune is declining,
As if the Universe were thine.
PERT: That Madam is a Noble Gratitude. For if his Fortune be declining, 'tis sacri-
ficed to his Passion for your Ladyship,
'Tis all laid out on Love.
LADY FULBANK: I prize my Honor more than Life,
Yet I had rather have given him all he wished of me,
Than be guilty of his Undoing.
PERT: And I think the Sin were less.
LADY FULBANK: I must confess, such Jewels, Rings, and Presents as he made me
must needs decay his Fortune.
BREDWELL: Ay Madam, his very Coach at last was turned into a Jewel for your
Ladyship.
Then Madam what Expenses his Despairs have run him on—
As Drinking and Gaming to divert the Thought of your marrying my old Master.
LADY FULBANK: And put in Wenching too.
BREDWELL: No assure yourself Madam—
LADY FULBANK: Of that I would be better satisfied—and you too must assist me as
e're you hope I should be kind to you in gaining you Diana.   [*To Bredwell.*]

BREDWELL: Madam, I'll die to serve you.
PERT: Nor will I be behind in my Duty.

LADY FULBANK: Oh how fatal are forced Marriages!
How many Ruins one such Match pulls on—
Had I but kept my sacred Vows to Gayman
How happy had I been—how prosperous he!
Whilst now I languish in a loathed Embrace,
Pine out my Life with Age—Consumptious Coughs,
—But dost thou fear that Gayman is declining?
BREDWELL: You are my Lady, and the best of Mistresses—
Therefore I would not grieve you, for I know
You love this best—but most unhappy Man.
LADY FULBANK: You shall not grieve me—prithee on—
BREDWELL: My Master sent me yesterday to Mr. Crap his Scrivener, to send to one
Mr. Wastall, to tell him his first Mortgage was out, which is two hundred pounds a
Year—and who has since engaged five or six hundred more to my Master; but if
this first be not redeemed he'll take the Forfeit on't, as he says a Wise Man ought.
LADY FULBANK: That is to say, a Knave according to his Notion of a Wise Man.
BREDWELL: Mr. Crap being busy with a Borrowing Lord, sent me to Mr. Wastall;
whose Lodging is in a nasty Place, called Alsatia, at a Blacksmith's.
LADY FULBANK: But what's all this to Gayman?
BREDWELL: Madam, this Wastall was Mr. Gayman.
LADY FULBANK: Gayman? Saw'st thou Gayman?
BREDWELL: Madam, Mr. Gayman, yesterday.
LADY FULBANK: When came he to Town?
BREDWELL: Madam, he has not been out of it.
LADY FULBANK: Not at his Uncle's in Northamptonshire?
BREDWELL: Your Ladyship was wont to credit me.
LADY FULBANK: Forgive me—you went to a Blacksmith's—
BREDWELL: Yes Madam; and at the Door encountered the beastly thing he calls a
Landlady; who looked as if she'd been of her own Husband's making, composed of
molded Smith's Dust. I asked for Mr. Wastall, and she began to open—and did so
rail at him, that what with her Billingsgate, and her Husband's Hammers, I was
both Deaf and Dumb—at last the Hammers ceased, and she grew weary, and
called down Mr. Wastall; but he not answering—I was sent up a Ladder rather
than a pair of Stairs; at last I scaled the top, and entered the enchanted Castle;
there did I find him, spite of the Noise below, drowning his Cares in Sleep.
LADY FULBANK: Whom foundst thou, Gayman—?
BREDWELL: He Madam, whom I waked—and seeing me
Heavens what Confusion seized him! which nothing but my own
Surprise could equal. Ashamed—he would have turned away,
But when he saw by my dejected Eyes, I knew him,
He sighed, and blushed, and heard me tell my Business.
Then begged I would be secret: for he vowed, his whole Repose and Life, depend-
ed on my Silence. Nor had I told it now,
But that your Ladyship, may find some speedy means to draw him from this desperate
Condition.
LADY FULBANK: Heavens is't possible!
BREDWELL: He's driven to the last degree of Poverty—
Had you but seen his Lodgings, Madam!
LADY FULBANK: What were they?

BREDWELL: 'Tis a pretty convenient Tub Madam. He may lie along in't, there's just room for an old Joined Stool besides the Bed, which one cannot call a Cabin, about the largeness of a Pantry Bin, or a Usurer's Trunk, there had been Dornex Curtains to't in the Days of Yore; but they were now annihilated, and nothing left to save his Eyes from the Light, but my Landlady's Blue Apron, tied by the strings before the Window, in which stood a broken six penny Lookingglass, that showed as many Faces, as the Scene in Henry the Eighth, which could but just stand upright, and then the Comb-Case filled it.[1]

LADY FULBANK: What a lewd Description hast thou made of his Chamber!

BREDWELL: Then for his Equipage, 'tis banished to one small Monsieur, who (saucy with his Master's Poverty) is rather a Companion than a Footman.

LADY FULBANK: But what said he to the Forfeiture of his Land?

BREDWELL: He sighed, and cried, Why farewell dirty Acres.

It shall not trouble me, since 'twas all but for Love!

LADY FULBANK: How much redeems it?

BREDWELL: Madam, five hundred pounds.

LADY FULBANK: Enough—you shall in some Disguise convey this Money to him, as from an unknown hand: I would not have him think it comes from me, for all the World;

That Nicety and Virtue I've professed, I am resolved to keep.

PERT: If I were your Ladyship, I would make use of Sir Cautious his Cash: Pay him in his own Coin.

BREDWELL: Your Ladyship would make no Scruple of it, if you knew how this poor Gentleman has been used by my unmerciful Master.

LADY FULBANK: I have a Key already to his Countinghouse; it being lost, he had another made, and this I found and kept.

BREDWELL: Madam, this is an excellent time for't, my Master being gone to give my Sister Leticia at Church.

LADY FULBANK: 'Tis so, I'll go and commit the Theft, whilst you prepare to carry it, and then we'll to Dinner with your Sister the Bride.   *[Exeunt.]*

Scene III

The House of Sir Feeble

[Enter Sir Feeble, Leticia, Sir Cautious, Bearjest, Diana, Noysey (and Ralph). Sir Feeble sings and salutes 'em.]

SIR FEEBLE: Welcome Joan Sanderson, welcome, welcome,   *[Kiss(es) the Bride.]*
  Ods bobs,[2] and so thou art Sweetheart.   *[So the rest (Kiss Leticia).]*

BEARJEST: Methinks my Lady Bride is very Melancholy.

SIR CAUTIOUS: Ay, Ay, Women that are discreet, are always thus upon their Wedding day.

SIR FEEBLE: Always by Daylight, Sir Cautious.

  But when Bright *Phœbus* dos retire
  To *Thetis'* Bed to quench his fire,[3]

---

1. An allusion to the play *Henry VIII* (1613), believed to have been written by Shakespeare.
2. An exclamation meaning "God's body," used to avoid blasphemy.
3. Phoebus refers to the Greek and Roman god Apollo; Thetis was a Greek sea goddess.

And do the thing we need not name,
We Mortals by his influence do the same.
Then, then the Blushing Maid lays by
Her simpering, and her Modesty;
And round the Lover clasps and twines
Like Ivy, or the circling Vines.

Here Ralph, the Bottle, Rogue, of Sack ye Rascal, hadst thou been a Butler worth hanging, thou wou'dst have met us at the door with it—Ods bobs Sweetheart thy Health.

BEARJEST: Away with it, to the Bride's Haunce in Kelder.[4]

SIR FEEBLE: Gots so, go to Rogue, go to, that shall be, Knave, that shall be, by the Morrow Morning; he—ods bobs, we'll do't Sweetheart; here's to't—   *[Drinks again.]*

LETICIA: I dye but to Imagine it, would I were dead indeed.   *[Aside.]*

SIR FEEBLE: Hah—hum—how's this? Tears upon your Wedding day? Why—why— you Baggage you, ye little Thing, Fool's face—away you Rogue, you'r naughty, you'r naughty.   *[Panting, and playing, and following her.]*
Look—look—look now, buss it—buss it—and Friends, did'ums, did'ums, beat its none silly Baby—away you little Hussy, away, and pledge me—   *[She drinks a little.]*

SIR CAUTIOUS: A wise discreet Lady, I'll warrant her, my Lady would prodigally have took it off all—

SIR FEEBLE: Dear's its nown dear Fubs; buss again, buss again, away, away—ods bobs, I long for Night—look—look Sir Cautious; what an Eye's there—

SIR CAUTIOUS: Ay, so there is Brother, and a Modest Eye too.

SIR FEEBLE: Adad, I love her more and more, Ralph—call old Susan hither—*[Exit Ralph.]* Come Mr. Bearjest, put the Glass about. Ods bobs, when I was a young Fellow, I would not let the young Wenches look pale and wan—but would rouse 'em, and touse 'em, and blowze 'em, 'till I put a Color in their Cheeks, like an Apple John, affacks[5]—Nay, I can make a shift still, and Pupsey shall not be Jealous—
[Enter Susan. Sir Feeble whispers (to) her, she goes out.]

LETICIA: Indeed not I Sir. I shall be all Obedience.

SIR CAUTIOUS: A most Judicious Lady; would my Julia had a little of her Modesty, but my Lady's Wit.
[Enter Susan with a Box.]

SIR FEEBLE: Look here my little Puskin, here's fine Playthings for its n'own little Coxcomb—go—get ye gone—get ye gone and off with this Saint Martin's Trumpery, these Playhouse Glass Baubles, this Necklace, and these Pendants, and all this false Ware; ods bobs I'll have no counterfeit Gear about thee, not I. See— these are right as the Blushes on thy Cheeks and these—as true as my Heart my Girl. Go—put 'em on and be fine—   *[Gives [jewels to] her.]*

LETICIA: Believe me Sir I shall not merit this Kindness.

SIR FEEBLE: Go to—More of your Love, and less of your Ceremony—give the old Fool a hearty Buss and pay him that Way—he ye little wanton Tit, I'll steal up—and catch ye and love ye—adod I will—get ye gone—get ye gone—

---

4. Literally, *"haunch and womb,"* he means to have sexual intercourse with her.   5. In fact.

LETICIA: Heavens what a nauseous thing is an old Man turned Lover.   *[Aside.]*
                                                                    [Exeunt Leticia and Diana.]
SIR CAUTIOUS: How steal up Sir Feeble—I hope not so; I hold it most indecent
before the lawful Hour.
SIR FEEBLE: Lawful Hour! Why I hope all Hours are Lawful with a Man's own Wife.
SIR CAUTIOUS: But wise Men have Respect to Times and Seasons.
SIR FEEBLE: Wise young Men Sir Cautious, but wise old Men must nick their Incli-
nations, for it is not as 'twas wont to be, for it is not as 'twas wont to be—
                                                                    [Singing and dancing.]

[Enter Ralph.]

RALPH: Sir here's a young Gentleman without would speak with you.
SIR FEEBLE: Hum—I hope it is not that same Belmour come to forbid the Banns—
if it be, he comes too late—therefore bring me first my long Sword, and then
the Gentleman.   *[Exit Ralph.]*
BEARJEST: Pray Sir use mine it is a traveled Blade I can assure you Sir.
SIR FEEBLE: I thank you Sir—   *[Bearjest gives Sir Feeble his Sword.]*
[Enter Ralph and Belmour disguised, (Belmour) gives him a Letter, (Sir Feeble) reads.]

—How—my Nephew—*Francis Fainwould?*   *[Embraces him.]*
BELMOUR: I am glad he has told me my Christian Name.   *[Aside.]*
SIR FEEBLE: Sir Cautious know my Nephew—'tis a young Saint Omers Scholar—
but none of the Witnesses.
SIR CAUTIOUS: Marry Sir, the wiser he—for they got nothing by't.
BELMOUR: Sir I love and honor you because you are a Traveller.
SIR FEEBLE: A very proper young Fellow, and as like old Frank Fainwould as the Dev-
il to the Collier; but Francis you are come into a very lewd Town Francis for whor-
ing and plotting and roaring and drinking, but you must go to Church Francis, and
avoid ill Company, or you may make damnable Havoc in my Cash Francis—
what you can keep Merchant's Books?
BELMOUR: 'T has been my Study Sir.
SIR FEEBLE: And you will not be proud but will be commanded by me Francis?
BELMOUR: I desire not to be favored as a Kinsman Sir, but as your humblest Servant.
SIR FEEBLE: Why thou'rt an honest Fellow Francis—and thou'rt heartily welcome—
and I'll make thee Fortunate! But come Sir Cautious let you and I take a Turn
i'th'Garden, and beget a right Understanding between your Nephew Mr. Bearjest
and my Daughter Die.
SIR CAUTIOUS: Prudently thought on Sir, I'll wait on you—
                                                    [Exeunt Sir Feeble and Sir Cautious.]
BEARJEST: You are a Traveler Sir, I understand—
BELMOUR: I have seen a little part of the World Sir.
BEARJEST: So have I Sir, I thank my Stars, and have performed most of my Travels
on Foot Sir.
BELMOUR: You did not travel far then I presume Sir.
BEARJEST: No Sir, it was for my Diversion indeed; but I assure you I traveled into
Ireland afoot Sir.
BELMOUR: Sure Sir, you go by Shipping into Ireland?
BEARJEST: That's all one Sir, I was still afoot—ever walking on the Deck—
BELMOUR: Was that your farthest Travels Sir?

BEARJEST: Farthest—why that's the End of the World—and sure a Man can go no further.

BELMOUR: Sure there can be nothing worth a Man's Curiosity?

BEARJEST: No Sir? I'll assure you there are the Wonders of the World Sir; I'll hint you this one. There is a Harbor which since the Creation was never capable of receiving a Lighter, yet by another Miracle the King of France was to ride there with a vast Fleet of Ships, and to land a hundred thousand Men.

BELMOUR: This is a swinging Wonder—but are there Store of Mad Men there Sir—?

BEARJEST: That's another Rarity to see a Man run out of his Wits.

NOYSEY: Marry Sir, the wiser they I say.

BEARJEST: Pray Sir what Store of Miracles have you at St. Omers?

BELMOUR: None Sir since that of the Wonderful Salamanca Doctor, who was both here and there, at the same Instant of time.

BEARJEST: How Sir! Why that's impossible.

BELMOUR: That was the Wonder Sir, because 'twas impossible.

NOYSEY: But 'twas a greater Sir that 'twas believed.

[Enter Lady Fulbank and Pert, Sir Cautious and Sir Feeble.]

SIR FEEBLE: Enough, enough, Sir Cautious we apprehend one another, Mr. Bearjest, your Uncle here and I have struck the Bargain, the Wench is yours with three thousand Pound present, and something more after Death: Which your Uncle likes well.

BEARJEST: Does he so Sir, I'm beholding to him, then 'tis not a Pin matter whether I like or not, Sir.

SIR FEEBLE: How Sir, not like my Daughter Die?

BEARJEST: Oh Lord Sir—die or live, 'tis all one for that Sir—I'll stand to the Bargain my Uncle makes.

PERT: Will you so Sir, you'll have very good Luck if you do—   *[Aside.]*

BEARJEST: Prithee hold thy Peace, my Lady's Woman.   *[Aside.]*

LADY FULBANK: Sir I beg your Pardon for not waiting on you to Church—I knew you would be private—

[Enter Leticia fine in Jewels.]

SIR FEEBLE: You honor us too highly now Madam—
                    [Presents his Wife, who salutes (Lady Fulbank).]

LADY FULBANK: Give you Joy my dear Leticia! I find Sir you were resolved for Youth, Wit and Beauty.

SIR FEEBLE: Ay Madam to the Comfort of many a hoping Coxcomb but Lette— Rogue Lette—thou wouldst not make me free o'th'City a second time, wouldst thou entice the Rogues with the Twire and wanton Leer—the Amorous Simper that cries come kiss me—then the pretty round Lips are pouted out—he Rogue how I long to be at 'em!—well she shall never go to Church more—that she shall not.

LADY FULBANK: How Sir, not to Church, the chiefest Recreation of a City Lady?

SIR FEEBLE: That's all one Madam, that tricking and dressing and prinking and patching, is not your Devotion to Heaven, but to the young Knaves that are licked and combed—and are minding you more than the Parson—ods bobs there are more Cuckolds destined at Church than are made out of it.

SIR CAUTIOUS: Ha, ha, ha. He tickles ye i'Faith Ladies.   *[To his Lady.]*

BELMOUR: Not one chance look this Way—and yet
  I can forgive her lovely Eyes—
  Because they look not pleased with all this Ceremony;
  And yet methinks some Sympathy in Love
  Might this Way glance their Beams—I cannot hold—   *[Aside.]*
  Sir, is this fair Lady my Aunt?
SIR FEEBLE: Oh Francis! Come hither Francis.
  Lette, here's a young Rogue has a Mind to kiss thee.
                                  [Puts them together, she starts back.]
  —Nay start not, he's my own Flesh and Blood
  My Nephew—Baby—look—look how the young
  Rogues stare at one another, like will to like, I see that.
LETICIA: There's something in his Face, so like my Belmour it calls my Blushes up,
  and leaves my Heart defenseless—   *[Aside.]*
  [Enter Ralph.]

RALPH: Sir, Dinner's on the Table.
SIR FEEBLE: Come, come—let's in then—Gentlemen and Ladies—
  And share today my Pleasures and Delight
  But—
  Adds bobs they must be all mine own at Night.   *[Exeunt.]*

Act II

Scene I

Gayman's Lodging

  [Enter Gayman in a Nightcap, and an old Campaign Coat tied about him. Very melancholy.]

GAYMAN: Curse on my Birth! Curse on my faithless fortune!
  Curse on my Stars, and cursed be all—but Love!
  That dear, that charming Sin, though t'have pulled
  Innumerable Mischiefs on my Head,
  I have not, nor I cannot find Repentance for.
  No let me die despised, upbraided, poor:
  Let Fortune, Friends and all abandon me—
  But let me hold thee thou soft smiling God
  Close to my Heart while Life continues there.
  Till the last Paintings of my vital Blood
  May the last spark of Life and Fire be Love's!
  [Enter Rag.]

  —How now Rag, what's a Clock?
RAG: My Belly can inform you better than my Tongue.
GAYMAN: Why you gormandizing Vermin you, what have you done with the Three-
  pence I gave you a Fortnight ago.
RAG: Alas Sir that's all gone, long since.

GAYMAN: You gutling Rascal, you are enough to breed a Famine in a Land. I have known some industrious Footmen, that have not only gotten their own Livings, but a pretty Livelihood for their Masters too.

RAG: Ay, till they come to the Gallows Sir.

GAYMAN: Very well Sirrah, they died in an honourable Calling—but hark'y, Rag— I have Business—very earnest Business abroad this Evening, now were you a Rascal of Docity, you would invent a way—to get home my last Suit that was laid in Lavender—with the Appurtenances thereunto belonging, as Periwig, Cravat— and—so forth—

RAG: Faith Master I must deal in the black Art then, for no Human Means will do't—and now I talk of the black Art Master, try your Power once more with my Landlady—

GAYMAN: Oh! Name her not, the thought on't turns my Stomach—a Sight of her is Vomit, but he's a bold Hero that dares venture on her for a Kiss, and all beyond that sure is Hell it self—yet there's my last, last Refuge—and I must to this Wedding—I know not what—but something whispers me—this Night I shall be happy—and without Julia 'tis impossible!—

RAG: Julia; who's that, my Lady Fulbank Sir?

GAYMAN: Peace Sirrah—and call—a—no—Pox on't come back—and yet—yes— call my fullsome Landlady.   [Exit Rag.]
Sir Cautious knows me not, by Name or Person.
And I will to this Wedding, I'm sure of seeing Julia there.
And what may come of that—but here's old Nasty coming.
I smell her up—hah my dear Landlady—
    [Enter Rag and Landlady.]

Quite out of Breath—a Chair there for my Landlady—

RAG: Here's ne'er a one Sir.

LANDLADY: More of your Money and less of your Civility good Mr. Wastall.

GAYMAN: Dear Landlady—

LANDLADY: Dear me no Dears Sir, but let me have my Money—Eight Weeks' Rent last Friday. Besides Taverns, Alehouses, Chandlers, Launderesses' Scores, and ready Money out of my Purse; you know it Sir.

GAYMAN: Ay but your Husband does not; speak softly.

LANDLADY: My Husband! What do you think to fright me with my Husband—I'd have you to know I am an honest Woman and care not this—for my husband. Is this all the thanks I have for my Kindness, for patching, borrowing, and shifting for you; 'twas but last Week I pawned my best Petticoat, as I hope to wear it again it cost me six and twenty Shillings besides Making; then this Morning my new Norwich Mantua followed, and two postle Spoons, I had the whole Dozen when you came first; but they dropped, and dropped, till I had only Judas left for my Husband.

GAYMAN: Hear me good Landlady—

LANDLADY: Then I've passed my Word at the George-Tavern for forty Shillings for you, ten Shillings at my Neighbor Squabs for Ale; besides seven Shillings to Mother Suds for washing, and do you fob me off with my Husband?

GAYMAN: Here Rag—run and fetch her a Pint of Sack—there's no other way of quenching the Fire in her slaber Chops;   [(Aside to Rag) Exit Rag.]
—but my dear Landlady have a little Patience.

LANDLADY: Patience? I scorn your Words Sir—is this a place to trust in, tell me of Patience that used to have my Money before Hand; come, come pay me quickly—or old Gregory Grimes' House shall be too hot to hold you.

GAYMAN: Is't come to this, can I not be heard?

LANDLADY: No Sir, you had good Clothes when you came first, but they dwindled daily, till they dwindled to this old Campaign—with tanned colored Lining—once red—but now all Colors of the Rainbow, a Cloak to skulk in a-Nights, and a pair of Piss-burned shammy Breeches. Nay your very Badge of Manhood's gone too.

GAYMAN: How Landlady, nay then i-Faith no Wonder if you rail so.

LANDLADY: Your Silver Sword I mean—transmogrified to this two-handed Basket Hilt—this old Sir Guy of Warwick—which will sell for nothing but old Iron. In fine I'll have my Money Sir, or i-faith Alsatia shall not shelter you.

[Enter Rag.]

GAYMAN: Well Landlady—if we must part—let's drink at parting, here Landlady, here's to the Fool—that shall love you better than I have done.

[Sighing drinks.]

LANDLADY: Rot your Wine—d'[y]e think to pacify me with Wine Sir[?]

[She refusing to drink, (Gayman) holds open her Jaws; Rag throws a Glass of Wine into her Mouth.)]

—What will you force me—no—give me another Glass, I scorn to be so uncivil to be forced, my Service to you Sir—but this shan't do Sir—

[She drinks, (Gayman) embracing her sings.]

> Ah *Cloris* 'tis in vain you scold,
> Whilst your Eyes kindle such a Fire.
> Your railing cannot make me cold,
> So fast as they a Warmth inspire.

LANDLADY: Well Sir you have no Reason to complain of my Eyes nor my Tongue neither, if rightly understood.   *[Weeps.]*

GAYMAN: I know you are the best of Landladies, As such I drink your Health— *[drinks]* But to upbraid a Man in Tribulation—fie—'tis not done like a Woman of Honor, a Man that loves you too.   *[She drinks.]*

LANDLADY: I am a little hasty sometimes, but you know my good Nature.

GAYMAN: I do and therefore trust my little Wants with you. I shall be rich again— and then my dearest Landlady—

LANDLADY: Would this Wine might ne'er go through me, if I would not go as they say through Fire and Water—by Night or by Day for you.   *[She drinks.]*

GAYMAN: And as this is Wine—I do believe thee—   *[He drinks.]*

LANDLADY: Well—you have no Money in your Pocket now I'll warrant you— here—here's ten Shillings for you old Gregory knows not of.

[Opens a great greasy Purse.]

GAYMAN: I cannot in Conscience take it, good Faith I cannot—besides the next Quarrel you'll hit me in the Teeth with it.

LANDLADY: Nay pray no more of that, forget it, forget it. I own I was to blame— here—Sir you shall take it.

GAYMAN: Ay—but what should I do with Money in—these—damned Breeches? No put it up—I can't appear abroad thus—no I'll stay at home and lose my business.

LANDLADY: Why, is there no Way to redeem one of your Suits?

GAYMAN: None—none—I'll e'en lay me down and die—

LANDLADY: Die—marry Heavens forbid—I would not for the World—let me see—hum—what does it lie for?

GAYMAN: Alas! dear Landlady a Sum—a Sum.

LANDLADY: Well, say no more, I'll lay about me—

GAYMAN: By this Kiss but you shall not—Assafetida by this Light.[6]   *[Aside.]*

LANDLADY: Shall not? that's a good one i-Faith: shall you rule—or I?

GAYMAN: But should your Husband know it.

LANDLADY: Husband—marry come up, Husbands know Wives' Secrets? No sure the World's not so bad yet—where do your things lie? and for what?

GAYMAN: Five pound equips me—Rag can conduct you—but I say you shall not go—I've sworn—

LANDLADY: Meddle with your Matters—let me see, the Caudle Cup that Molly's Grandmother left her will pawn for about that Sum—I'll sneak it out—well Sir you shall have your things presently—trouble not your Head, but expect me.

[Exeunt Landlady and Rag.]

GAYMAN: Was ever Man put to such beastly Shifts? 'Sdeath, how she stunk—my Senses are most luxuriously regaled—there's my perpetual Music too—

[Knocking of Hammers on an Anvil.]

The ringing of Bells is an Ass to't.

[Enter Rag.]

RAG: Sir there's one in a Coach below would speak to you.

GAYMAN: With me—and in a Coach, who can it be?

RAG: The Devil I think, for he has a strange Countenance.

GAYMAN: The Devil, shew yourself a Rascal of Parts, Sirrah, and wait on him up with Ceremony.

RAG: Who the Devil, Sir?

GAYMAN: Ay the Devil Sir, if you mean to thrive.   *[Exit Rag.]*

—Who can this be[?]—but see he comes to inform me—withdraw—

[Enter Bredwell dressed like a Devil.]

BREDWELL: I come to bring you this—   *[Gives him a Letter.]*

GAYMAN [reads]: *Receive what Love and Fortune present you with, be grateful and be silent, or 'twill vanish like a Dream, and leave you more wretched than it found you.* Adieu —hah—   *[(Bredwell) Gives him a Bag of Money.]*

BREDWELL: Nay view it Sir, 'tis all substantial Gold.

GAYMAN: Now dare not I ask one civil Question for fear it vanish all—   *[Aside.]*

But I may ask how 'tis I ought to pay for this great Bounty.

BREDWELL: Sir all the Pay is Secrecy—

GAYMAN: And is this all that is required Sir?

BREDWELL: No you're invited to the Shades below.

GAYMAN: Hum, Shades below?—I am not prepared for such a Journey Sir.

BREDWELL: If you have Courage, Youth, or Love, you'll follow me,
    When Night's black Curtain's drawn around the World,

---

6. Assafetida refers to the fetid gum resin of various oriental plants, once used to prevent disease.

And mortal Eyes are safely locked in Sleep,   *[In feigned Heroic Tone.]*
And no bold Spy dares view when Gods caress:
Then I'll conduct thee to the Banks of Bliss.
—Durst thou not trust me?
GAYMAN: Yes sure on such substantial Security.   *[Hugs the Bag.]*
BREDWELL: Just when the Day is vanished into Night,
And only twinkling Stars inform the World,
Near to the Corner of the silent Wall
In Fields of Lincolns-Inn thy Spirit shall meet thee.
—Farewell   *[Goes out.]*
GAYMAN: Hum—I am awake sure, and this is Gold I grasp.
I could not see this Devil's cloven Foot,
Nor am I such a Coxcomb to believe,
But he was as substantial as his Gold.
Spirits, Ghosts, Hobgoblings, Furies, Fiends, and Devils
I've often heard old Wives fright Fools and Children with,
Which once arrived to common Sense they laugh at.
—No, I am for things possible and Natural,
—Some Female Devil old, and damned to Ugliness,
And past all Hopes of Courtship and Address,
    Full of another Devil called Desire,
Has seen this Face—this—Shape—this Youth
And thinks it worth her Hire. It must be so.
I must moil on in the damned dirty Road,
And sure such Pay will make the Journey easy;
And for the Price of the dull drudging Night,
All Day I'll purchase new and fresh Delight.   *[Exit.]*

Scene II

Sir Feeble's House

[Enter Leticia pursued by Phillis.]

PHILLIS: Why Madam do you leave the Garden,
    For this Retreat to Melancholy?
LETICIA: Because it suits my Fortune and my Humor.
    And even thy Presence would afflict me now.
PHILLIS: Madam, I was sent after you, my Lady Fulbank has challenged Sir Feeble at
    Bowls, and stakes a Ring of fifty Pound against his new Chariot.
LETICIA: Tell him I wish him Luck in everything
    But in his Love to me—
    Go tell him I am viewing of the Garden.   *[Exit Phillis.]*
    [Enter Belmour at a distance behind her.]

    —Blessed be this kind Retreat, this 'lone Occasion
    That lends a short Cessation to my Torments.
    And gives me leave to vent my Sighs and Tears!   *[Weeps.]*
BELMOUR: And double blessed be all the Powers of Love,
    That gives me this dear Opportunity.   *[Aside.]*

LETICIA: Where were you all ye pitying Gods of Love
    That once seemed pleased at Belmour's Flame and mine,
    And, smiling joined our Hearts, our sacred Vows
    And spread your Wings, and held your Torches high?
BELMOUR: Oh—   *[She starts, pauses.]*
LETICIA: Where were you now! When this unequal Marriage,
    Gave me from all my Joys, gave me from Belmour:
    Your Wings were flagged, your Torches bent to Earth;
    And all your little Bonnets veiled your Eyes.
    You saw not, or were deaf and pityless.
BELMOUR: Oh my Leticia!
LETICIA: Hah, 'tis there again; that very Voice was Belmour's:
    Where art thou, oh thou lovely charming Shade?
    For sure thou canst not take a Shape to fright me.
    What art thou?—speak!   *[Not looking behind her yet for Fear.]*
BELMOUR: Thy constant true Adorer.
    Who all this fatal Day has haunted thee
    To ease his tortured Soul.   *[Approaching nearer.]*
LETICIA: My Heart is well acquainted with that Voice, *[Speaking with Signs of Fear.]*
    But oh my Eyes dare not encounter thee.
BELMOUR: Is it because thou'st broken all thy Vows?
    —Take to thee Courage and behold thy Slaughters.
LETICIA: Yes, though the Sight would blast me I would view it.   *[Turns.]*
    —'tis he—'tis very Belmour? or so like—
    I cannot doubt but thou deserv'st this Welcome.   *[Embraces him.]*
BELMOUR: Oh my Leticia!
LETICIA: I'm sure I grasp not Air; thou art no Phantom.
    My Arms return not empty to my Bosom,
    But meet a solid Treasure.
BELMOUR: A Treasure thou so easily threw'st away?
    A Riddle simple Love ne're understood.
LETICIA: Alas I heard, my Belmour, thou wert dead.
BELMOUR: And was it thus you mourned my Funeral?
LETICIA: I will not justify my hated Crime.
    But Oh remember I was poor and helpless.
    And much reduced, and much imposed upon.   *[Belmour weeps.]*
BELMOUR: And Want compelled thee to this wretched Marriage—did it?
LETICIA: 'Tis not a Marriage, since my Belmour lives:
    The Consummation were Adultery.
    I was thy Wife before, wouldst thou deny me?
BELMOUR: No by those Powers that heard our mutual Vows,
    Those Vows that tie us faster than dull Priests.
LETICIA: But oh my Belmour, thy sad Circumstances
    Permit thee not to make a public Claim.
    Thou art proscribed, and die'st if thou art seen.
BELMOUR: Alas!
LETICIA: Yet I would wander with thee o're the World,
    And share thy humblest Fortune with thy Love.

BELMOUR: Is't possible Leticia thou wou'dst fly
  To foreign Shores with me?
LETICIA: Can Belmour doubt the Soul he knows so well?
BELMOUR: Perhaps in time the King may find my Innocence, and may extend his
  Mercy: Meantime I'll make Provision for our Flight.
LETICIA: But how 'twixt this and that can I defend myself from the loathed Arms of
  an impatient Dotard, that I may come a spotless Maid to thee?
BELMOUR: Thy native Modesty and my Industry
  Shall well enough secure us.
  Feign you nice Virgin-Cautions all the Day;
  Then trust at Night to my Conduct to preserve thee.
  —And wilt thou yet be mine! Oh swear anew,
  Give me again thy Faith, thy Vows, thy Soul:
  For mine's so sick with this Day's fatal Business,
  It needs a Cordial of that mighty strength;
  Swear,—Swear, so as if thou break'st——
  Thou may'st be—anything—but Damned Leticia.
LETICIA: Thus then, and hear me Heaven!   [Kneels.]
BELMOUR: And thus—I'll listen to thee   [Kneels.]
  [Enter Sir Feeble, Lady Fulbank, Sir Cautious, (Ralph).]

SIR FEEBLE: Lette, Lette, Lette, where are you little Rogue Lette.
                          [Belmour snatches her to his Bosom as if she fainted.]
  —Hah—hum—what's here—
BELMOUR: Oh Heavens, she's gone, she's gone!
SIR FEEBLE: Gone—whither is she gone?—it seems she had the Wit to take good
  Company with her—   [The Women go to her, take her up.]
BELMOUR: She's gone to Heaven Sir, for aught I know.
SIR CAUTIOUS: She was resolved to go in a young Fellow's Arms I see.
SIR FEEBLE: Go to Francis—go to.
LADY FULBANK: Stand back Sir, she recovers.
BELMOUR: Alas, I found her dead upon the Floor,
  —Should I have left her so?—if I had known your Mind—
SIR FEEBLE: Was it so—was it so?—got so, by no means Francis.
LETICIA: Pardon him Sir; For surely I had died,
  But for this timely coming.
SIR FEEBLE: Alas poor Pupsey—was it sick—look here—here's a fine thing to make
  it well again. Come buss, and it shall have it—oh how I long for Night.
  Ralph, are the Fiddlers ready?
RALPH: They are tuning in the Hall Sir.
SIR FEEBLE: That's well, they know my mind. I hate that same twang, twang, twang,
  fum, fum, fum, tweedle, tweedle, tweedle, then screw go the Pins, till a man's
  Teeth are on Edge; then snap says a small Gut, and there we are at a loss again. I
  long to be in Bed—with a hey tredodle, tredodle tredodle—with a hay tredool,
  tredodle, tredo—   [Dancing and playing on his Stick, like a Flute.]
SIR CAUTIOUS: A prudent Man would reserve himself—Good-facks I danced so on
  my Wedding Day, that when I came to Bed, to my Shame be it spoken, I fell fast
  asleep, and slept till morning.

LADY FULBANK: Where was your Wisdom then, Sir Cautious? But I know what a wise Woman ought to have done.

SIR FEEBLE: Ods bobs, that's Wormwood, that's Wormwood—I shall have my young Hussy set agog too; she'll hear there are better things in the World than she has at home, and then ods bobs, and then they'll ha't, adod they will, Sir Cautious. Ever while you live, keep a Wife ignorant, unless a Man be as brisk as his Neighbours.

SIR CAUTIOUS: A wise Man will keep 'em from bawdy Christenings then, and Gossipings.

SIR FEEBLE: Christenings, and Gossipings; why they are the very Schools that debauch our Wives, as Dancing-Schools do our Daughters.

SIR CAUTIOUS: Ay, when the overjoyed Man invites 'em all against that time twelve Month: Oh he's a dear Man, cries one—Ay marry, cries another, here's a Man indeed—my Husband—God help him—

SIR FEEBLE: Then she falls to telling of her Grievance till (half maudlin) she weeps again: Just my Condition, cries a third, so the Frolic goes round, and we poor Cuckolds are anatomized, and turned the right sides outwards; ads bobs we are Sir Cautious.

SIR CAUTIOUS: Ay, ay, this Grievance ought to be redressed Sir Feeble, the grave and sober Part o'th Nation are hereby ridiculed,—Ay, and cuckolded too, for aught I know.

LADY FULBANK: Wise men, knowing this, should not expose their Infirmities, by marrying us young Wenches; who, without Instruction, find how we are imposed upon.
 [Enter Fiddles playing, Mr. Bearjest and Diana dancing; Bredwell, Noysey etc.]

LADY FULBANK: So Cousin, I see you have found the way to Mrs. Di's Heart.

BEARJEST: Who I, my dear Lady Aunt, I never knew but one Way to a Woman's Heart, and that Road I have not yet traveled; For my Uncle, who is a wise Man, says Matrimony is a sort of a—kind of a—as it were d'ye see, of a Voyage, which every Man of Fortune is bound to make one time or other—and Madam—I am as it were—a bold Adventurer.

DIANA: And are you sure, Sir, you will venture on me?

BEARJEST: Sure?—I thank you for that—as if I could not believe my Uncle: for in this Case a young Heir has no more to do, but to come and see, settle, marry, and use you scurvily.

DIANA: How Sir, scurvily?

BEARJEST: Very scurvily, that is to say, be always fashionably drunk, despise the Tyranny of your Bed, and reign absolutely—keep a Seraglio of Women, and let my bastard Issue inherit: Be seen once a Quarter, or so, with you in the Park for Countenance, where we loll two several Ways in the gilt Coach like Janus, or a Spread-Eagle.[7]

DIANA: And do you expect I should be honest the while?

BEARJEST: Heaven forbid, not I, I have not met with that Wonder in all my Travels.

LADY FULBANK: How Sir, not an honest Woman?

BEARJEST: Except my Lady Aunt—Nay as I am a Gentleman and the first of my Family—you shall pardon me, here—Cuff me, Cuff me soundly.
 [Kneels to (Lady Fulbank).]
 [Enter Gayman richly dressed.]

---

7. Janus was a Roman god identified with doorways and gates; he was said to face two ways.

GAYMAN: This Love's a damned bewitching thing—now though I should lose my Assignation with my Devil, I cannot hold from seeing Julia tonight: hah—there, and with a Fop at her Feet—Oh Vanity of Woman!

[(Aside) Softly pulls her.]

LADY FULBANK: Oh Sir, you're welcome from Northamptonshire.

GAYMAN: Hum—surely she knows the Cheat.   *[Aside.]*

LADY FULBANK: You are so Gay, you save me Sir the Labor
   Of asking if your Uncle be alive.

GAYMAN: 'Pray Heaven she have not found my Circumstances!
   But if she have, Confidence must assist me—   *[Aside.]*
   —And Madam you're too Gay, for me to enquire
   Whether you are that Julia, which I left you?

LADY FULBANK: Oh, doubtless Sir—

GAYMAN: But why the Devil do I ask?—Yes, you are still the same; one of those hoiting Ladies, that love nothing like Fool and Fiddle; Crowds of Fops; had rather be publicly, tho dully, flattered, than privately adored; you love to pass for the Wit of the Company, by talking all and loud.

LADY FULBANK: Rail on! 'till you have made me think my Virtue at so low Ebb, it should submit to you.

GAYMAN: What—I'm not discreet enough,
   I'll babble all in my next high Debauch,
   Boast of your Favors, and describe your Charms
   To every wishing Fool?

LADY FULBANK: Or make most filthy Verses of me—
   Under the name of Cloris—you Philander,
   Who in lewd Rhymes confess the dear Appointment;
   What Hour, and where, how silent was the Night,
   How full of Love your Eyes, and Wishing, mine.
   Faith no; if you can afford me a Lease of your Love,
   'Till the Old Gentleman my Husband depart this wicked World,
   I'm for the Bargain.

SIR CAUTIOUS: Hum—what's here, a young Spark at my Wife?

[Goes about 'em.]

GAYMAN: Unreasonable Julia, is that all,
   My Love, my Sufferings, and my Vows must hope?
   Set me an Age——say when you will be kind,
   And I will languish out in starving Wish.
   But thus to gape for Legacies of Love,
   'Till Youth be past Enjoyment,
   The Devil I will as soon—farewell—   *[Offers to go.]*

LADY FULBANK: Stay, I conjure you stay—

GAYMAN: And lose my Assignation with my Devil.   *[Aside.]*

SIR CAUTIOUS: 'Tis so, Ay, Ay, 'tis so—and Wise men will perceive it; 'tis here—here in my Forehead, it more than Buds; it sprouts, it flourishes.

SIR FEEBLE: So, that young Gentleman has nettled him, stung him to th' quick: I hope he'll chain her up—the Gad Bee's in his conundrum—in Charity I'll relieve him *[Aside]*—come my Lady Fulbank, the Night grows old upon our hands, to dancing, to jiggeting—Come shall I lead your Ladyship?

LADY FULBANK: No Sir, you see I am better provided—   *[Takes Gayman's hand.]*

SIR CAUTIOUS: Ay, no doubt on't, a Pox on him for a young handsome Dog.

[They dance all.]

SIR FEEBLE: Very well, very well, now the Posset, and then—ods bobs, and then—

DIANA: And then we'll have t'other Dance.

SIR FEEBLE: Away Girls, away, and steal the Bride to Bed; they have a deal to do upon their Wedding nights; and what with the tedious Ceremonies of dressing and undressing, the smutty Lectures of the Women, by way of Instruction, and the little Stratagems of the young Wenches—ods bobs, a man's cozened half his Night: Come Gentlemen, one Bottle and then—we'll toss the Stocken.

[Exeunt all but Lady Fulbank (and) Bredwell, who are talking, and Gayman.]

LADY FULBANK: But dost thou think he'll come?

BREDWELL: I do believe so Madam—

LADY FULBANK: Be sure you contrive it so, he may not know whither, or to whom he comes.

BREDWELL: I warrant you Madam for our Parts. *[Exit Bredwell, Gayman stealing out.]*

LADY FULBANK: How now, what departing?

GAYMAN: You are going to the Bride-Chamber.

LADY FULBANK: No matter, you shall stay—

GAYMAN: I hate to have you in a Crowd.

LADY FULBANK: Can you deny me—will you not give me one Lone hour i'th' Garden?

GAYMAN: Where we shall only tantalize each other with dull Kissing, and part with the same appetite we met—no Madam, besides I have Business—

LADY FULBANK: Some Assignation—is it so indeed?

GAYMAN: Away; you cannot think me such a Traitor; 'tis most important Business.

LADY FULBANK: Oh 'tis too late for Business—let tomorrow serve.

GAYMAN: By no means—the Gentleman is to go out of Town.

LADY FULBANK: Rise the earlier then——

GAYMAN: —But Madam, the Gentleman lies dangerously—sick—and should he die—

LADY FULBANK: 'Tis not a dying Uncle, I hope Sir?

GAYMAN: Hum—

LADY FULBANK: The Gentleman a-dying, and to go out of Town tomorrow!

GAYMAN: Ay—a—he goes—in a Litter—'tis his Fancy Madam—Change of Air may recover him.

LADY FULBANK: So may your change of Mistress do me Sir—farewell.

[Goes out.]

GAYMAN: Stay Julia—Devil be damned—for you shall tempt no more,
I'll love and be undone—but she is gone—
And if I stay the most that I shall gain
Is but a reconciling Look, or Kiss.
No my kind Goblin—

I'll keep my Word with thee, as the least Evil,
A tantalizing Woman's worse than Devil.

[Exit.]

Act III

Scene I

Sir Feeble's House

The Second Song before the Entry

No more Lucinda, ah! expose no more
   To the admiring World those conqu'ring Charms:
In vain all day unhappy men adore,
   What the kind Night gives to my longing Arms.
Their vain Attempts can ne'er successful prove,
Whilst I so well maintain the Fort of Love.

Yet to the World with so bewitching Arts,
   Your dazling Beauty you around display,
And triumph in the Spoils of broken hearts,
   That sink beneath your feet, and crowd your way:
Ah! suffer now your Cruelty to cease,
And to a fruitless War prefer a Peace.

[Enter Ralph with Light, Sir Feeble, and Belmour sad.]

SIR FEEBLE: So, so; they're gone—Come Francis, you shall have the Honor of Undressing me for the Encounter, but 'twill be a Sweet one, Francis.

BELMOUR: Hell take him, how he teases me?   *[Aside.]*

                                      [Undressing [Sir Feeble] all the while.]

SIR FEEBLE: But is the young Rogue laid Francis—is she stolen to Bed? What Tricks the young Baggages have to whet a man's Appetite?

BELMOUR: Ay Sir—Pox on him—he will raise my Anger up to Madness, and I shall kill him, to prevent his going to Bed to her.   *[Aside.]*

SIR FEEBLE: A piece of those Bandstrings—the more Haste the less Speed.

BELMOUR: Be it so in all things, I beseech thee Venus?   *[Aside.]*

SIR FEEBLE: Thy Aid a little Francis—oh—oh—thou chok'st me. 'Sbobs, what dost mean?—   *[(Belmour) Pinches (Sir Feeble) by the Throat.]*

BELMOUR: You had so hampered 'em Sir—the Devil's very mischievous in me.

                                      [Aside.]

SIR FEEBLE: Come, come quick, good Francis, adod I'm as yare as a Hawk at the young Wanton—nimbly good Francis, untruss, untruss—

BELMOUR: Cramps seize ye—what shall I do—the near Approach distracts me!

                                      [Aside.]

SIR FEEBLE: So, so, my Breeches, good Francis. But well Francis, how dost think I got the young Jade my Wife?

BELMOUR: With five hundred pounds a year Jointure Sir.

SIR FEEBLE: No, that would not do, the Baggage was damnably in love with a young Fellow, they call Belmour, a handsome young Rascal he was they say, that's truth on't, and a pretty Estate, but happening to kill a Man, he was forced to fly.

BELMOUR: That was great pity Sir.

SIR FEEBLE: Pity, hang him Rogue, 'sbobs, and all the young Fellows in the Town deserve it; we can never keep our Wives and Daughters honest for rampant young Dogs; and an old Fellow cannot put in amongst 'em, under being undone, with Presenting, and the Devil and all. But what dost think I did, being damnably in Love—I feigned a Letter as from the Hague, wherein was a Relation of this same Belmour's being hanged.

BELMOUR: Is't possible Sir? could you devise such News?

SIR FEEBLE: Possible man? I did it, I did it; she swoonded at the News, shut herself up a whole Month in her Chamber; but I presented high; she sighed and wept, and swore she'd never marry. Still I presented, she hated, loathed, spit upon me, still adod I presented! till I presented myself effectually in Church to her; for she at last wisely considered her Vows were cancelled since Belmour was hanged.

BELMOUR: Faith Sir, this was very cruel to take away his Fame, and then his Mistress.

SIR FEEBLE: Cruel, thou'rt an Ass, we are but even with the brisk Rogues, for they take away our Fame, Cuckold us, and take away our Wives. So, so, my Cap Francis.

BELMOUR: And do you think this Marriage lawful Sir?

SIR FEEBLE: Lawful; it shall be when I've had Livery and Seisin[8] of her Body—and that shall be presently Rogue—quick—besides this, Belmour dares as well be hanged as come into England.

BELMOUR: If he gets his Pardon Sir—

SIR FEEBLE: Pardon, no, no, I have took care for that, for I have you must know got his Pardon already.

BELMOUR: How Sir, got his Pardon, that's some amend for robbing him of his Wife.

SIR FEEBLE: Hold honest Francis; what dost think 'twas in Kindness to him? No you Fool, I got his Pardon myself, that nobody else should have it, so that if he gets any Body to speak to his Majesty for it, his Majesty cries he has granted it; but for want of my Appearance, he's defunct, trussed up, hanged Francis.

BELMOUR: This is the most excellent Revenge I ever heard of.

SIR FEEBLE: Ay, I learnt it of a great Politician of our Times.

BELMOUR: But have you got his Pardon?—

SIR FEEBLE: I've don't, I've don't; Pox on him, it cost me five hundred pounds tho! here 'tis, my Solicitor brought it me this Evening.   [Gives it him.]

BELMOUR: This was a lucky Hit—and if it scape me, let me be hanged by a Trick indeed.   [Aside.]

SIR FEEBLE: So, put it into my Cabinet—safe Francis, safe.

BELMOUR: Safe I'll warrant you Sir.

SIR FEEBLE: My Gown, quick, quick—t'other Sleeve, man—so now my Nightcap; well I'll in, throw open my Gown to fright away the Women, and jump into her Arms.   [Exit Sir Feeble.]

BELMOUR: He's gone, quickly Oh Love inspire me!
    [Enter a Footman.]

FOOTMAN: Sir, my Master Sir Cautious Fulbank left his Watch on the little Parlor-Table to Night, and bid me call for't.

BELMOUR: Hah—the Bridegroom has it Sir, who is just gone to Bed, it shall be sent him in the Morning.

FOOTMAN: 'Tis very well Sir—your Servant—   [Exit Footman.]

8. Possession.

BELMOUR: Let me see—here is the Watch, I took it up to keep for him—but his sending has inspired me with a sudden Stratagem, that will do better than Force, to secure the poor trembling Leticia—who I am sure is dying with her Fears.   [Exit Belmour.]

Scene II

Changes, to the Bedchamber; Leticia in an Undressing,
by (Diana and) the Women at the Table

   [Enter to them Sir Feeble Fainwould.]

SIR FEEBLE: What's here? what's here? the prating Women still. Ods bobs, what not in Bed yet? for shame of Love Leticia.
LETICIA: For shame of Modesty Sir; you would not have me go to Bed before all this Company.
SIR FEEBLE: What the Women? why they must see you laid, 'tis the Fashion.
LETICIA: What with a Man? I would not for the World.
   Oh Belmour, where art thou, with all thy promised Aid?   [Aside.]
DIANA: Nay Madam, we should see you laid indeed.
LETICIA: First in my Grave Diana.   [Aside to Diana.]
SIR FEEBLE: Ods bobs, here's a Compact amongst the Women—High Treason against the Bridegroom—therefore Ladies withdraw, or adod I'll lock you all in.
                    [Throws open his Gown, they run all away, he locks the Door.]
So, so, now we're alone Leticia—off with this foolish Modesty, and Nightgown, and slide into my Arms,   [She runs from him.]
Hey my little Puskin—what fly me my Coy Daphne?
                                              [He pursues her. Knocking.]
Hah—who's that knocks—who's there?—
BELMOUR: 'Tis I Sir, 'tis I, open the Door presently.
SIR FEEBLE: Why, what's the matter, is the House o-fire?
BELMOUR [within]: Worse Sir, worse—
   [(Sir Feeble) opens the Door, Belmour enters with the Watch in his hand.]

LETICIA: 'Tis Belmour's Voice!   [Aside.]
BELMOUR: Oh Sir, do you know this Watch?
SIR FEEBLE: This Watch?
BELMOUR: Ay Sir, this Watch.
SIR FEEBLE: This Watch—why prithee, why dost tell me of a Watch, 'tis Sir Cautious Fulbank's Watch, what then, what a Pox dost trouble me with Watches?
                                        [Offers to put him out, he returns.]
BELMOUR: 'Tis indeed his Watch Sir, and by this Token he has sent for you, to come immediately to his House Sir.
SIR FEEBLE: What a Devil art Mad Francis, or is his Worship Mad, or does he think me Mad?—go prithee tell him I'll come to him to Morrow.
                                              [Goes to put him out.]
BELMOUR: Tomorrow Sir, why all our Throats may be cut before tomorrow.
SIR FEEBLE: What sayst thou, Throats cut?

BELMOUR: Why, the City's up in Arms Sir, and all the Aldermen are met at Guild-Hall; some damnable Plot Sir.

SIR FEEBLE: Hah—Plot—the Aldermen met at Guild-Hall?—hum—why let 'em meet, I'll not lose this Night to save the Nation.

LETICIA: Would you to bed Sir, when the weighty Affairs of State require your Presence?

SIR FEEBLE: —Hum—met at Guild-Hall?—my Clothes, my Gown again Francis, I'll out—out, what upon my Wedding night? no—I'll in.

[Putting on his Gown pausing, pulls it off again.]

LETICIA: For shame Sir, shall the Reverend Council of the City debate without you?

SIR FEEBLE: Ay, that's true, that's true, come truss again Francis, truss again—yet now I think on't Francis, prithee run thee to the Hall, and tell 'em 'tis my Wedding Night, d'ye see Francis; and let somebody give my Voice for—

BELMOUR: What Sir?

SIR FEEBLE: Adod I cannot tell; up in Arms say you, why, let 'em fight Dog, fight Bear; mun, I'll to Bed—go—

LETICIA: And shall his Majesty's Service and his Safety lie unregarded for a slight Woman Sir?

SIR FEEBLE: Hum, his Majesty!—come, haste Francis, I'll away, and call Ralph, and the Footmen, and bid 'em Arm; each man shoulder his Musket, and advance his Pike—and bring my Artillery Implements quick—and let's away: Pupsey, 'bye Pupsey, I'll bring it a fine thing yet before Morning, it may be—let's away; I shall grow fond, and forget the Business of the Nation—come follow me Francis—

[Exit Sir Feeble; Belmour runs to Leticia.]

BELMOUR: Now my Leticia, if thou e'r didst love!

If ever thou design'st to make me blessed—

Without delay fly this Adulterous Bed!

SIR FEEBLE [within]: Why Francis—where are you Knave?

BELMOUR: I must be gone, lest he suspect us—I'll lose him, and return to thee immediately—get thyself ready—

LETICIA: I will not fail my Love.   [Exit Belmour.]

—Old man forgive me—thou the Aggressor art,
Who rudely forced the Hand without the Heart.
She cannot from the Paths of Honor rove,
Whose Guide's Religion, and whose End is Love.   [Exit.]

Scene III

Changes to a washhouse, or outhouse

[Enter with Dark-lantern Bredwell disguised like a Devil, leading Gayman.]

BREDWELL: Stay here, till I give notice of your coming.

[Exit Bredwell, leaves his Dark-lantern.]

GAYMAN: Kind Light, a little of your Aid—now must I be peeping though my Curiosity should lose me all—hah—Zouns, what's here—a Hovel or a Hogsty? hum, see the Wickedness of Man, that I should find no time to Swear in, but just when I'm in the Devil's Clutches.

[Enter Pert, as an old Woman with a Staff.]

PERT: Good even to you, fair Sir.

GAYMAN: Ha—defend me! if this be she, I must rival the Devil, that's certain.

PERT: Come young Gentleman, dare not you venture?

GAYMAN: He must be as hot as Vesuvius, that does—I shall never earn my Morning's Present.

PERT: What do you fear a longing Woman Sir?

GAYMAN: The Devil I do—this is a damned Preparation to Love.

PERT: Why stand you gazing Sir, a Woman's Passion is like the Tide, it stays for no man when the Hour is come—

GAYMAN: I'm sorry I have took it at the Turning.
I'm sure mine's ebbing out as fast.

PERT: Will you not speak Sir—will you not on?

GAYMAN: I would fain ask—a civil Question or two first.

PERT: You know, too much Curiosity lost Paradise.

GAYMAN: Why there's it now.

PERT: Fortune and Love invite you if you dare follow me.

GAYMAN: This is the first thing in Petticoats that ever dared me in vain. Were I but sure she were but Human now—for sundry Considerations she might down—but I will on—   [Aside.]

                              [She goes, he follows; both go out.]

Scene IV

A Chamber in the Apartment of Lady Fulbank

[Enter Pert followed by Gayman in the dark.]

                              [Soft Music plays, she leaves him.]

GAYMAN: —Hah, Music—and Excellent!

Song

> Oh! Love, that stronger art than Wine,
> Pleasing Delusion, Witchery divine,
> Want to be prized above all Wealth,
> Disease that has more Joys than Health.
> Though we blaspheme thee in our Pain,
> And of thy Tyranny complain,
> We all are bettered by thy Reign.
>
> What Reason never can bestow
> We to this useful Passion owe.
> Love wakes the Dull from sluggish Ease,
> And learns a Clown the Art to please.
> Humbles the Vain, kindles the Cold,
> Makes Misers free, and Cowards bold.
> 'Tis he reforms the Sot from Drink,
> And teaches airy Fops to think.
>
> When full brute Appetite is fed,
> And choked the Glutton lies, and dead:
> Thou new Spirits does dispense,
> And fines the gross Delights of Sense.

Virtues unconquerable Aid,
That against Nature can persuade:
And makes a roving Mind retire
Within the Bounds of just Desire.
Cheerer of Age, Youth's kind unrest,
And half the Heaven of the Blessed.

GAYMAN: Ah Julia, Julia! if this soft Preparation
　Were but to bring me to thy dear Embraces;
　What different Motions would surround my Soul,
　From what perplex it now.
　　[(Enter Pert as Old Woman;) Enter Nymphs and Shepherds, and dance.]

　　　　　　　　[Then two dance alone. All go out but Pert and a Shepherd.]
—If these be Devils, they are obliging ones.
I did not care if I ventured on that last Female Fiend.
　　[Shepherd sings.]

Cease your Wonder, cease your Guess,
Whence arrives your Happiness.
Cease your Wonder, cease your Pain.
Human Fancy is in vain.

Chorus.　　　'Tis enough you once shall find,
Fortune may to Worth be kind;
　　　　　　　　　　[(Shepherd) Gives (Gayman) Gold.]
And Love can leave off being blind.

[Pert sings.]

You, before you enter here—
On this sacred Ring must swear.
　　　　　　　[Puts it on his Finger, holds his Hand.]
By the Figure which is round,
Your Passion constant and profound.
By the Adamantine Stone,
To be fixed to one alone.
By the Luster which is true,
Ne'er to break your sacred Vow.
Lastly by the Gold that's tried
For Love all Dangers to abide.
　　　[They all dance about (Gayman), while those same two sing.]

SHEPHERD:　　Once about him let us move,
　　　　　　　To confirm him true to Love.
PERT:　　　　Twice with mystic turning Feet,
　　　　　　　Make him silent and discreet.
SHEPHERD:　　Thrice about him let us tread,
　　　　　　　To keep him ever young in Bed.
　　　　　　　　[Gives (Gayman) another part (of the Gold).]

SHEPHERD: Forget Aminta's proud Disdain.
                 Taste here, and sigh no more in vain.
                 The Joy of Love without the Pain.
PERT: That God repents his former Slights,
                 And Fortune thus your Faith requites.
BOTH: Forget Aminta's proud Disdain;
                 Then taste, and sigh no more in vain,
                 The Joy of Love without the Pain.
                 The Joy of Love without the Pain.
[Exeunt all Dancers. (Gayman) Looks on himself and feels about him.]

GAYMAN: What the Devil can all this mean? If there be a Woman in the Case—Sure I have not lived so bad a Life, to gain the dull Reputation of so modest a Coxcomb, but that a Female might down with me, without all this Ceremony. Is it care of her Honor?—that cannot be—this Age affords none so nice: nor Fiend, nor Goddess can she be, for these I saw were mortal! No—'tis a Woman—I am positive. Not young nor handsome, for then Vanity had made her Glory to 'ave been seen. No— since 'tis resolved a Woman—she must be old and ugly, and will not balk my Fancy with her Sight. But baits me more with this essential Beauty.

          Well—be she young or old, Woman or Devil.
          She pays, and I'll endeavour to be civil.

                                      [Exit.]

Scene V

In the same House

[The flat Scene of the Hall. After a knocking, Enter Bredwell in his masking Habit, with his Vizard in one Hand and a Light in t'other in haste.]

BREDWELL: Hah, knocking so late at our Gate—   *[Opens the Door.]*
    [Enter Sir Feeble drest and arm'd Cap-a-pee with a broad waist Belt stuck round with Pistols, a Helmet, Scarf, Buffcoat and half Pike.]

SIR FEEBLE: How now, how now, what's the matter here?
BREDWELL: Matter, what is my Lady's innocent Intrigue found out? *[aside]*—Heavens Sir what makes you here in this warlike Equipage?
SIR FEEBLE: What makes you in this showing Equipage Sir?
BREDWELL: I have been dancing among some of my Friends.
SIR FEEBLE: And I thought to have been fighting with some of my Friends. Where's Sir Cautious? Where's Sir Cautious?
BREDWELL: Sir Cautious—Sir, in Bed.
SIR FEEBLE: Call him, call him—quickly good Edward.
BREDWELL: Sure my Lady's Frolic is betrayed and he comes to make Mischief. However I'll go and secure Mr. Gayman.   *[Exit Bredwell.]*
    [Enter Sir Cautious and Dick with Light.]

DICK: Pray Sir go to Bed, here's no Thieves; all's still and well.

SIR CAUTIOUS: This last Night's Misfortune of mine Dick, has kept me waking and methought all Night I heard a kind of a silent Noise. I am still afraid of Thieves, mercy upon me to lose five hundred Guineas at one clap Dick— Hah—bless me! What's yonder! Blow the great Horn Dick—Thieves—Murder, Murder.

SIR FEEBLE: Why what a Pox are you mad? 'Tis I, 'tis I Man.

SIR CAUTIOUS: I, who am I? Speak—declare—pronounce.

SIR FEEBLE: Your Friend old Feeble Fainwould.

SIR CAUTIOUS: How, Sir Feeble! At this late Hour, and on his Wedding Night— why what's the matter Sir—is it Peace or War with you?

SIR FEEBLE: A Mistake—a Mistake—proceed to the Business good Brother, for time you know is precious.

SIR CAUTIOUS: Some strange Catastrophe has happened between him and his Wife tonight, that makes him disturb me thus—   [Aside.]
come sit good Brother, and to the Business as you say—
  [They sit one at one end of the Table, the other at the other, Dick sets down the Light and goes out—both sit gaping and staring and expecting when either should speak.]

SIR FEEBLE: As soon as you please Sir. Lord how wildly he stares! He's much disturbed in's Mind *[aside]*—well Sir let us be brief—

SIR CAUTIOUS: As brief as you please Sir,—well Brother—   [Pausing still.]

SIR FEEBLE: So Sir.

SIR CAUTIOUS: How strangely he stares and gapes—some deep Concern!
                                                      [Aside.]

SIR FEEBLE: Hum—hum—

SIR CAUTIOUS: I listen to you, advance—

SIR FEEBLE: Sir?

SIR CAUTIOUS: A very distracted Countenance—pray Heaven he be not mad, and a young Wife is able to make any old Fellow mad, that's the Truth on't.   [Aside.]

SIR FEEBLE: Sure 'tis something of his Lady—he's so loath to bring it out *[aside]*—I am sorry you are thus disturbed Sir.

SIR CAUTIOUS: No disturbance to serve a Friend—

SIR FEEBLE: I think I am your Friend indeed Sir Cautious, or I would not have been here upon my Wedding Night.

SIR CAUTIOUS: His Wedding Night—there lies his Grief poor Heart! Perhaps she has cuckolded him already—   [Aside.]
  —Well come Brother—many such things are done—

SIR FEEBLE: Done—hum—come out with it Brother—what troubles you tonight?

SIR CAUTIOUS: Troubles me—why, knows he I am robbed?   [Aside.]

SIR FEEBLE: I may perhaps restore you to the Rest you've lost.

SIR CAUTIOUS: The Rest, why have I lost more since? Why know you then who did it? Oh how I'll be revenged upon the Rascal!

SIR FEEBLE: 'Tis—Jealousy, the old Worm that bites—   [Aside.]
  Who is it you suspect?

SIR CAUTIOUS: Alas I know not whom to suspect, I would I did; but if you could discover him—I would so swing him.—

SIR FEEBLE: I know him—what do you take me for a Pimp Sir? I know him—there's your Watch again Sir, I'm your Friend, but no Pimp Sir—
                                                      [Rises in Rage.]

SIR CAUTIOUS: My Watch, I thank you Sir—but why Pimp Sir?

SIR FEEBLE: Oh a very thriving Calling Sir—and I have a young Wife to practice with. I know your Rogues.

SIR CAUTIOUS: A young Wife—'tis so, his Gentlewoman has been at Hot-Cockles without her Husband, and he's Horn mad upon't. I suspected her being so close in with his Nephew—in a Fit with a pox—   [Aside.]

Come come Sir Feeble 'tis many an honest Man's Fortune.

SIR FEEBLE: I grant it Sir—but to the Business Sir I came for.

SIR CAUTIOUS: With all my Soul—

> [They sit gaping and expecting when either should speak.]
> [Enter Bredwell and Gayman at the Door. Bredwell sees them and puts Gayman back again.]

BREDWELL: Hah—Sir Feeble—and Sir Cautious there—what shall I do? For this Way we must pass, and to carry him back would discover my Lady to him, betray all and spoil the Jest—retire Sir; your Life depends upon your being unseen.

> [(Bredwell and Gayman) go out.]

SIR FEEBLE: Well Sir,—do you not know that I am married Sir? And this my Wedding Night?

SIR CAUTIOUS: Very good Sir.

SIR FEEBLE: And that I long to be in Bed!

SIR CAUTIOUS: Very well Sir—

SIR FEEBLE: Very good Sir, and very well Sir—why then what the Devil do I make here Sir?   [(Sir Feeble) Rises in a Rage.]

SIR CAUTIOUS: Patience Brother—and forward—

SIR FEEBLE: Forward—lend me your Hand good Brother—let's feel your Pulse—how has this Night gone with you?

SIR CAUTIOUS: Ha, ha, ha—this is the oddest conundrum—sure he's mad—and yet now I think on't, I have not slept tonight, nor shall I ever sleep again till I have found the Villain that robbed me.   [(Aside) (Sir Cautious) Weeps.]

SIR FEEBLE: So—now he weeps—far gone—this laughing and weeping is a very bad Sign! [aside] Come let me lead you to your Bed.

SIR CAUTIOUS: Mad—stark Mad [aside]—no—now I'm up 'tis no Matter—pray ease your troubled Mind—I am your Friend—out with it—what was it acted? Or but designed?

SIR FEEBLE: How Sir?

SIR CAUTIOUS: Be not ashamed—I'm under the same Premunire[9] I doubt, little better than a—but let that pass—

SIR FEEBLE: Have you any Proof?

SIR CAUTIOUS: Proof of what, good Sir?

SIR FEEBLE: Of what, why that you're a Cuckold—Sir a Cuckold if you'll ha't.

SIR CAUTIOUS: Cuckold Sir—do ye know what ye say?

SIR FEEBLE: What I say?

SIR CAUTIOUS: Ay, what you say, can you make this out?

SIR FEEBLE: I make it out—

SIR CAUTIOUS: Ay Sir—if you say it and cannot make it out—you're a—

SIR FEEBLE: What am I Sir? What am I?

---

9. Forewarning; presentiment.

SIR CAUTIOUS: A Cuckold as well as myself Sir, and I'll sue you for Scandalum
Magnatum, I shall recover swinging Damages with a City Jury.

SIR FEEBLE: I know of no such thing Sir.

SIR CAUTIOUS: No Sir?

SIR FEEBLE: No Sir.

SIR CAUTIOUS: Then what would you be at Sir?

SIR FEEBLE: I be at Sir—what would you be at Sir?

SIR CAUTIOUS: Ha, ha, ha—why this is the strangest thing—to see an old Fellow, a
Magistrate of the City, the first Night he's married forsake his Bride and Bed, and
come armed Cap-a-pee, like Gargantua, to disturb another old Fellow and banter
him with a Tale of a Tub; and all to becuckold him here *[aside]*—in plain English
what's your Business?

SIR FEEBLE: Why what the Devil's your Business and you go to that?

SIR CAUTIOUS: My Business with whom?

SIR FEEBLE: With me Sir, with me, what a Pox de ye think I do here?

SIR CAUTIOUS: 'Tis that I would be glad to know Sir.
     [Enter Dick.]

SIR FEEBLE: Here Dick, remember I've brought back your Master's Watch, next time
he sends for me o'er Night I'll come to him in the Morning.   *[Exit Dick.]*

SIR CAUTIOUS: Ha, ha, ha—I send for you? Go home and sleep Sir—ad an' ye keep
your Wife waking to so little purpose you'll go near to be haunted with a Vision of
Horns.

SIR FEEBLE: Roguery—Knavery to keep me from my Wife—Look ye this was the
Message I received—   *[Tells him seemingly.]*
     *[Enter Bredwell to the Door—in a white Sheet like a Ghost speaking to Gayman who
stands within.]*

BREDWELL: Now Sir we are two to two, for this Way you must pass or be taken in
the Ladies' Lodgings—I'll first adventure out to make you pass the safer. And that
he may not, if possible, see Sir Cautious, whom I shall fright into a Trance I am
sure.   *[Aside.]*
And Sir Feeble the Devil's in't if he know him.

GAYMAN *[within]*: A brave kind Fellow this—
     [Enter Bredwell stalking on as a Ghost by (Sir Feeble and Sir Cautious).]

SIR CAUTIOUS: Oh—undone—undone—help help—I'm dead, I'm dead— *[Falls
down on his Face, Sir Feeble stares—and stands still.]*

BREDWELL: As I could wish—   *[Aside—turns (to Gayman).]*
—Come on thou ghastly thing and follow me—
     [Enter Gayman like a Ghost with a Torch.]

SIR CAUTIOUS: Oh Lord, oh Lord—

GAYMAN: Hah—old Sir Feeble Fainwould—why where the Devil am I?—'Tis he—
and be it where it will I'll fright the old Dotard for cozening my Friend of his Mistress—   *[Stalks on.]*

SIR FEEBLE: Oh Guard me—guard me—all ye powers!   *[Trembling.]*

GAYMAN: Thou call'st in vain fond Wretch—for I am Belmour,

Whom first thou rob'st of Fame and Life
And then what dearer was—his Wife—
     [Goes out shaking his Torch at him.]

SIR CAUTIOUS: Oh Lord—oh Lord!
[Enter Lady Fulbank in an Undress, and Pert undressed.]

LADY FULBANK: Heavens what Noise is this?—So he's got safe out I see *[aside]*—
hah what thing art thou?   *[Sees Sir Feeble armed.]*
SIR FEEBLE: Stay Madam stay—'tis I, 'tis I, a poor trembling Mortal—
LADY FULBANK: Sir Feeble Fainwould?—rise—are you both mad?—
SIR CAUTIOUS: No no—Madam we have seen the Devil.
SIR FEEBLE: Ay and he was as tall as the Monument.
SIR CAUTIOUS: With Eyes like a Beacon—and a Mouth—Heaven bless us like
London Bridge at a full Tide.
SIR FEEBLE: Ay, and roared as loud—
LADY FULBANK: Idle Fancies, what makes you from your Bed? And you Sir from
your Bride?
[Enter Dick with Sack.]

SIR FEEBLE: Oh! that's the Business of another Day, a Mistake only Madam.
LADY FULBANK: Away, I'm asham'd to see wise Men so weak, the Phantoms of the
Night, or your own Shadows, the Whimsys of the Brain for want of Rest, or per-
haps Bredwell your Man—who being wiser than his Master played you this Trick
to fright you both to Bed.
SIR FEEBLE: Hum—adod and that may be, for the young Knave when he let me in
tonight, was dressed up for some Waggery—
SIR CAUTIOUS: Ha, ha, ha, 'twas even so sure enough Brother—
SIR FEEBLE: Ads bobs but they frightened me at first basely—but I'll home to
Pupsey, there may be Roguery, as well as here—Madam I ask your Pardon, I see
we're all mistaken.
LADY FULBANK: Ay, Sir Feeble; go home to your Wife.   *[Exeunt severally.]*

Scene VI

The Street

[Enter Belmour at the Door, and enter to him from the House Phillis.]

PHILLIS: Oh are you come Sir? I'll call my Lady down.
BELMOUR: Oh haste, the Minutes fly—leave all behind.   *[Exit Phillis]*
And bring Leticia only to my Arms.   *[A Noise of People.]*
—Hah—what Noise is that? 'Tis coming this Way—I tremble with my Fears—
hah—Death and the Devil—'Tis he—
[Enter Sir Feeble and his Men armed, (Sir Feeble) goes to the Door, knocks.]

Ay 'tis he—and I'm undone—what shall I do to kill him now? besides the Sin
would put me past all Hopes of pardoning.
SIR FEEBLE: A damned Rogue to deceive me thus—
BELMOUR: Hah—see by Heaven Leticia! Oh we are ruined!
SIR FEEBLE: Hum—what's here two Women?—   *[Stands a little off.]*
[Enter Leticia and Phillis softly undressed with a Box.]

LETICIA: Where are you my best Wishes? Lord of my Vows—and Charmer of my
Soul? Where are you?

BELMOUR: Oh Heavens!—   *[Draws his Sword half Way.]*

SIR FEEBLE: Hum, who's here? My Gentlewoman—she's monstrous kind of the sudden. But whom is't meant to?   *[Aside.]*

LETICIA: Give me your Hand my Love, my Life, my all—Alas! where are you?

[Aside.]

SIR FEEBLE: Hum—no, no, this is not to me—I am jilted, cozened, Cuckolded, and so forth—   *[Groping (Leticia) takes hold of Sir Feeble.]*

LETICIA: Oh are you here, indeed you frighted me with your Silence—here take these Jewels and let us haste away.

SIR FEEBLE: Hum—are you thereabouts Mistress, was I sent away with a Sham-Plot for this?—She cannot mean it to me.   *[Aside.]*

LETICIA: Will you not speak—will you not answer me?—do you repent already?— before Enjoyment are you cold and false?

SIR FEEBLE: Hum—before Enjoyment—that must be me? *[aside]* Before Enjoyment—Ay ay 'tis I—I see a little.   *[Merrily.]*
Prolonging a Woman's Joy, sets an Edge upon her Appetite.

LETICIA: What means my Dear? Shall we not haste away?

SIR FEEBLE: Haste away? there 'tis again—*[aside]* no—'tis not me she means, what at your Tricks and Intrigues already?—yes yes I am destined a Cuckold—

[Aside.]

LETICIA: Say, am I not your Wife; can you deny me?

SIR FEEBLE: Wife! adod 'tis I she means—'tis I she means—   *[aside] Merrily*

LETICIA: Oh, Belmour, Belmour!   *[Sir Feeble starts back from her Hands.]*

SIR FEEBLE: Hum—what's that—Belmour?

LETICIA: Hah! Sir Feeble!—he would not, Sir, have used me thus unkindly.

SIR FEEBLE: Oh—I'm glad 'tis no worse—Belmour quoth a; I thought the Ghost was come again.   *[Aside.]*

PHILLIS: Why did you not speak, Sir, all this while?—my Lady weeps with your Unkindness.

SIR FEEBLE: I did but hold my peace to hear how prettily she prattled Love: But fags you are nought to think of a young Fellow—ads bobs you are now.

LETICIA: I only said—he would not have been so unkind to me.

SIR FEEBLE: But what makes ye out at this Hour, and with these Jewels?

PHILLIS: Alas Sir, we thought the City was in Arms, and packed up our things to secure 'em, if there had been a Necessity for Flight. For had they come to Plundering once, they would have begun with the rich Alderman's Wives, you know Sir.

SIR FEEBLE: Ads bobs and so they would—but there was no Arms—nor Mutiny— where's Francis?

BELMOUR: Here Sir.

SIR FEEBLE: Here Sir—why what a Story you made of a Meeting in the Hall and— Arms and—a—the Devil of anything was stirring, but a couple of old Fools, that sat gaping and waiting for one another's Business—

BELMOUR: Such a Message was brought me Sir.

SIR FEEBLE: Brought, thou'rt an Ass Francis—but no more—come, come, let's to Bed.—

LETICIA: To Bed Sir? what by Daylight—for that's hasting on—I would not for the World—the Night would hide my Blushes—but the Day—would let me see my self in your Embraces.

SIR FEEBLE: Embraces, in a Fiddlestick, why are we not married?

LETICIA: 'Tis true Sir, and Time will make me more familiar with you, but yet my virgin Modesty forbids it. I'll to Diana's Chamber, the Night will come again.

SIR FEEBLE: For once you shall prevail; and this Damned Jaunt has pretty well mortified me: —a Pox of your Mutiny Francis—Come I'll conduct thee to Diana, and lock thee in, that I may have thee safe Rogue.

> We'll give young Wenches leave to whine and blush,
> And fly those Blessings which—ads bobs they wish.
>
> *[Exeunt.]*

Act IV

Scene I

Sir Feeble's House

[Enter Lady Fulbank, Gayman fine, gently pulling her back by the Hand; and Ralph meets 'em.]

LADY FULBANK: How now Ralph—Let your Lady know I am come to wait on her.
                                                                    [Exit Ralph.]

GAYMAN: Oh why this needless Visit?—
    Your Husband's safe, at least till Evening safe.
    Why will you not go back?
    And give me one soft Hour, though to torment me.

LADY FULBANK: You are at Leisure now I thank you Sir.
    Last Night when I was all Love's Rhetoric pleaded,
    And Heaven knows what last Night might have produced,
    You were engaged! False Man, I do believe it,
    And I am satisfied you love me not.   *[Walks away in scorn.]*

GAYMAN: Not love you!
    Why do I waste my Youth in vain Pursuit,
    Neglecting Interest, and despising Power?
    Unheeding, and despising other Beauties.
    Why at your Feet is all my Fortune laid,
    And why does all my Fate depend on you?

LADY FULBANK: I'll not consider why you play the Fool,
    Present me Rings and Bracelets; Why pursue me;
    Why watch whole Nights before my senseless Door,
    And take such Pains to show yourself a Coxcomb?—

GAYMAN: Oh! why all this?
    By all the Powers above! by this dear Hand,
    And by this Ring, which on this Hand I place,
    On which I've sworn Fidelity to Love;
    I never had a Wish or soft Desire
    To any other Woman,
    Since Julia swayed the Empire of my Soul!

LADY FULBANK: Hah, my own Ring I gave him last Night.   *[Aside.]*
    —Your Jewel Sir, is rich,
    Why do you part with things of so much value
    So easily, and so frequently?

GAYMAN: To strengthen the weak Arguments of Love.

LADY FULBANK: And leave yourself undone?

GAYMAN: Impossible, if I am blessed with Julia.

LADY FULBANK: Love's a thin Diet, nor will keep out Cold,
>   You cannot satisfy your Dunning Tailor,
>   To cry—I am in love!
>   Though possible you may your Seamstress.

GAYMAN: Does aught about me speak such Poverty?

LADY FULBANK: I am sorry that it does not, since to maintain this Gallantry, 'tis said you use base means, below a Gentleman.

GAYMAN: Who dares but to imagine it's a Rascal, a Slave, below a Beating—what means my Julia?

LADY FULBANK: No more dissembling, I know your Land is gone—I know each Circumstance of all your wants, therefore—as e'er you hope that I should love you ever, tell me—where 'twas you got this Jewel Sir.

GAYMAN: Hah—I hope 'tis no stolen Goods;   [Aside.]
>   Why on the sudden all this nice Examining?

LADY FULBANK: You trifle with me, and I'll plead no more.

GAYMAN: Stay—why—I bought it Madam—

LADY FULBANK: Where had you Money Sir? you see I am no Stranger to your Poverty.

GAYMAN: This is strange—perhaps it is a Secret.

LADY FULBANK: So is my love, which shall be kept from you.   [Offers to go.]

GAYMAN: Stay Julia—your Will shall be obeyed!—   [Sighing.]
>   Though I had rather die, than be obedient,
>   Because I know you'll hate me, when 'tis told.

LADY FULBANK: By all my Vows, let it be what it will,
>   It ne'er shall alter me from loving you.

GAYMAN: I have—of late—been tempted—
>   With Presents, Jewels, and large Sums of Gold.

LADY FULBANK: Tempted! by whom?

GAYMAN: The Devil, for aught I know.

LADY FULBANK: Defend me Heaven! the Devil?
>   I hope you have not made a Contract with him?

GAYMAN: No, though in the shape of Woman it appeared.

LADY FULBANK: Where met you with it?

GAYMAN: By Magic Art I was conducted—I know not how,
>   To an enchanted Palace in the Clouds,
>   Where I was so attended—
>   Young Dancing—singing Fiends innumerable!

LADY FULBANK: Imagination all.

GAYMAN: But for the Amorous Devil, the old Proserpine.

LADY FULBANK: Ay she—what said she?—

GAYMAN: Not a Word! Heaven be praised, she was a silent Devil—but she was laid in a Pavilion, all formed of gilded Clouds, which hung by Geometry, whither I was conveyed, after much Ceremony, and laid in Bed with her; where with much ado, and trembling with my Fears—I forced my Arms about her.

LADY FULBANK: And sure that undeceived him—   [Aside.]

GAYMAN: But such a Carcass 'twas—deliver me—so rivelled, lean, and rough—a Canvas Bag of wooden Ladles were a better Bedfellow.

LADY FULBANK: Now though I know that nothing is more distant than I from such a Monster—yet this angers me.   *[Aside.]*

Death could you love me and submit to this?

GAYMAN: 'Twas that first drew me in—
The tempting Hope of means to conquer you,
Would put me upon any dangerous Enterprise:
Were I the Lord of all the Universe,
I am so lost in Love,
For one dear Night to clasp you in my Arms,
I'd lavish all that World—then die with Joy.

LADY FULBANK: 'S'life after all to seem deformed, old, ugly—   *[Aside.]*
                                                                                    [Walking in a fret.]

GAYMAN: I knew you would be angry when you heard it.
                                                                [He pursues her in a submissive posture.]
  [Enter Sir Cautious, Bearjest, Noysey and Bredwell.]

SIR CAUTIOUS: —How, what's here?—my Lady with the Spark that courted her last Night—hum—with her again so soon—well this Impudence and Importunity undoes more City Wives than all their unmerciful Finery.

GAYMAN: But Madam—

LADY FULBANK: Oh here's my Husband—you'd best tell him your Story *(Angry)*— what makes him here so soon?—   *[Aside.]*

SIR CAUTIOUS: Me his Story—I hope he will not tell me he's a mind to Cuckold me!

GAYMAN: A Devil on him, what shall I say to him?   *[Aside.]*

LADY FULBANK: What—so Excellent at Intrigues, and so Dull at an Excuse?
                                                                                     [Aside.]

GAYMAN: Yes Madam, I shall tell him—
  [Enter Belmour.]

LADY FULBANK: —Is my Lady at leisure for a Visit Sir?

BELMOUR: Always to receive your Ladyship.   *[(Lady Fulbank) goes out.]*

SIR CAUTIOUS: With me Sir, would you speak?

GAYMAN: With you Sir, if your Name be Fulbank?

SIR CAUTIOUS: Plain Fulbank, methinks you might have had a Sir reverence under your Girdle Sir, I am Honoured with another Title Sir—
                                                                          [Goes talking to the rest.]

GAYMAN: With many Sir, that very well become you—
                                                                            [Pulls him a little aside.]

I've something to deliver to your Ear.

SIR CAUTIOUS: So, I'll be hanged if he do not tell me, I'm a Cuckold now. I see it in his Eyes; *[aside]* my Ear Sir, I'd have you to know I scorn any man's Secrets Sir—for aught I know you may whisper Treason to me Sir. Pox on him, how handsome he is, I hate the sight of the young Stallion.   *[Aside.]*

GAYMAN: I would not be uncivil Sir, before all this Company.

SIR CAUTIOUS: Uncivil—Ay, Ay, 'tis so, he cannot be content to Cuckold me, but he must tell me so too.   *[Aside.]*

GAYMAN: But since you'll have it Sir—you are—a Rascal—a most notorious Villain Sir, d'ye hear—

SIR CAUTIOUS: Yes, yes, I do—hear—and am glad 'tis no worse.   *[Laughing.]*

GAYMAN: Griping as Hell—and as insatiable—worse than a Brokering Jew, not all the twelve Tribes harbors such a damned Extortioner.

SIR CAUTIOUS: Pray under favor Sir—who are you?   *[Pulling off his Hat.]*

GAYMAN: One whom thou hast undone—

SIR CAUTIOUS: Hum—I'm glad of that however.   *[Aside smiling.]*

GAYMAN: Racking me up to starving Want and Misery,
Then took Advantages to ruin me.

SIR CAUTIOUS: So, and he'd revenge it on my Wife—   *[Aside smiling.]*

GAYMAN: Do you not know one Wastall Sir?
[Enter Ralph with Wine, sets it on a Table.]

SIR CAUTIOUS: Wastall—ha, ha, ha—if you are any Friend to that poor Fellow— you may return and tell him Sir—d'ye hear—that the Mortgage of two hundred pound a Year is this Day out, and I'll not bate him an Hour Sir—ha, ha, ha—what do you think to hector civil Magistrates?

GAYMAN: Very well Sir, and is this your Conscience?

SIR CAUTIOUS: Conscience—what do you tell me of Conscience? Why what a Noise's here—as if the undoing a young Heir were such a Wonder; ods so I've undone a hundred without half this ado.

GAYMAN: I do believe thee—and am come to tell you—I'll be none of that Number— for this Minute I'll go and redeem it—and free my Self from the Hell of your Indentures.

SIR CAUTIOUS: How redeem it, sure the Devil must help him then! *[aside]*—Stay Sir,—stay—Lord Sir what need you put yourself to that trouble, your Land is in safe Hands Sir, come come sit down—and let us take a Glass of Wine together Sir—

BELMOUR *[to Gayman]*: Sir my Service to you.   *[Drinks to him.]*

GAYMAN: Your Servant Sir. Would I could come to speak to Belmour which I dare not do in Public, lest I betray him. I long to be resolved where 'twas Sir Feeble was last Night—if it were he—by which I might find out my invisible Mistress.
[Aside.]

NOYSEY: Noble Mr. Wastall—   *[Salutes (Gayman); so does Bearjest.]*

BELMOUR: Will you please to sit Sir?

GAYMAN: I have a little Business Sir—but anon I'll wait on you—your Servant Gentlemen—I'll to Crap the Scrivener's.   *[(Aside) Goes out.]*

SIR CAUTIOUS: Do you know this Wastall Sir?—   *[To Noysey.]*

NOYSEY: Know him Sir? Ay too well—

BEARJEST: The World's well amended with him Captain, since I lost my Money to him and you at the George in White Friars.

NOYSEY: Ay poor Fellow—he's sometimes up and sometimes down, as the Dice favor him—

BEARJEST: Faith and that's pity; but how come he so fine o'th'sudden: 'twas but last Week he borrowed eighteen pence of me on his Waist Belt to pay his Dinner in an Ordinary.

BELMOUR: Were you so cruel Sir to take it?

NOYSEY: We are not all one Man's Children; faith Sir, we are here today and gone tomorrow—

SIR CAUTIOUS: I say 'twas done like a wise Man Sir—but under Favor Gentlemen this Wastall is a Rascal—

NOYSEY: A very Rascal Sir, and a most dangerous Fellow—he cullies in your Pren-tices and Cashiers to play—which ruins so many o'th'young Fry i'th'City—

SIR CAUTIOUS: Hum—does he so—do hear that Edward?

NOYSEY: Then he keeps a private Press and prints your Amsterdam and Leyden Libels.

SIR CAUTIOUS: Ay and makes 'em too I'll warrant him; a dangerous Fellow—

NOYSEY: Sometimes he begs for a lame Soldier with a wooden Leg.

BEARJEST: Sometimes as a blind Man sells Switches in Newmarket Road.

NOYSEY: At other times he runs the Country like a Gypsy—tells Fortunes and robs Hedges, when he's out of Linen.

SIR CAUTIOUS: Tells Fortunes too—nay I thought he dealt with the Devil—well Gentlemen you are all wide o'this Matter—for to tell you the Truth—he deals with the Devil Gentlemen—otherwise he could never have redeemed his Land.   [Aside.]

BELMOUR: How Sir, the Devil?

SIR CAUTIOUS: I say the Devil. Heaven bless every wise Man from the Devil.

BEARJEST: The Devil, sha! there's no such Animal in Nature, I rather think he pads.

NOYSEY: Oh Sir he has not Courage for that—but he's an admirable Fellow at your Lock.

SIR CAUTIOUS: Lock! My Study Lock was picked—I begin to suspect him—

BEARJEST: I saw him once open a Lock with the Bone of a Breast of Mutton, and break an Iron Bar asunder with the Eye of a needle.

SIR CAUTIOUS: Prodigious—well I say the Devil still.
    [Enter Sir Feeble.]

SIR FEEBLE: Who's this talks of the Devil—a Pox of the Devil I say, this last Night's Devil has so haunted me—

SIR CAUTIOUS: Why have you seen it since Brother?

SIR FEEBLE: In Imagination Sir.

BELMOUR: How Sir a Devil?

SIR FEEBLE: Ay, or a Ghost.

BELMOUR: Where good Sir?

BEARJEST: Ay where? I'd travel a hundred Mile to see a Ghost—

BELMOUR: Sure Sir 'twas Fancy?

SIR FEEBLE: If 'twere a Fancy, 'twas a strong one, and Ghosts and Fancies are all one, if they can deceive. I tell you—if ever I thought in my Life—I thought I saw a Ghost—Ay and a damnable impudent Ghost too; he said he was a—a Fellow here—they call Belmour.

BELMOUR: How Sir!

BEARJEST: Well I would give the World to see the Devil, provided he were a civil affable Devil, such an one as Wastall's Acquaintance is—

SIR CAUTIOUS: He can show him too soon, it may be. I'm sure as civil as he is, he helps him to steal my Gold I doubt [aside]—and to be sure—Gentlemen you say he's a Gamester—I desire when he comes anon, that you would propose to sport a Die or so—and we'll fall to play for a Teaster, or the like—and if he sets any Money—I shall go near to know my own Gold, by some remarkable Pieces amongst it; and if he have it, I'll hang him, and then all his six hundred a Year will be my own which I have in Mortgage.

BEARJEST: Let the Captain and I alone to top upon him—meantime Sir I have brought my Music—to entertain my Mistress with a Song.

SIR FEEBLE: Take your own Methods Sir—they are at Leisure—while we go drink their Healths within. Adod I long for Night, we are not half in kelter, this damned Ghost will not be out of my Head yet.   *[Exeunt all but Belmour.]*

BELMOUR: Hah—a Ghost! What can he mean? A Ghost, and Belmour's.—
Sure my good Angel, or my Genius,
In pity of my Love, and of Leticia—
But see Leticia comes, but still attended—
   [Enter Leticia, Lady Fulbank, Diana.]

—Remember—oh remember to be true!
                              [Aside to (Leticia) passing by, [Belmour] goes out.]
LADY FULBANK: I was sick to know with what Christian Patience you bore the Martyrdom of this Night.

LETICIA: As those condemned bear the last Hour of Life.
A short Reprieve I had—and by a kind Mistake.
Diana only was my Bedfellow—   *[Weeps.]*

DIANA: I wish for your Repose you ne'er had seen my Father.   *[Weeps.]*

LETICIA: And so do I, I fear he has undone me—

DIANA: And me, in breaking of his Word with Bredwell—

LADY FULBANK: —So—as Trincolo says would you were both hanged for me, for putting me in mind of my Husband. For I have e'en no better Luck than either of you—
—Let our two Fates warn your approaching one: *[To Diana.]*
I love young Bredwell and must plead for him.

DIANA: I know this Virtue Justifies my Choice.
But Pride and Modesty forbids I should unloved pursue him.

LETICIA: Wrong not my Brother so who dies for you—

DIANA: Could he so easily see me given away
Without a Sigh at parting?
For all the Day a Calm was in his Eyes,
And unconcerned he looked and talked to me.
In dancing never pressed my willing Hand,
Nor with a scornful Glance reproached my Falsehood.

LETICIA: Believe me that Dissembling was his Masterpiece.

DIANA: Why should he fear, did not my Father promise him?

LETICIA: Ay that was in his wooing time to me.
But now 'tis all forgotten—   *[Music at the Door.]*
   [After which enter Bearjest and Bredwell.]

LADY FULBANK: How now Cousin! Is this high piece of Gallantry from you?

BEARJEST: Ay Madam, I have not traveled for nothing—

LADY FULBANK: I find my Cousin is resolved to conquer, he assails with all his Artillery of Charms; we'll leave him to his Success Madam—
                              [Exeunt Leticia and Lady Fulbank.]
BEARJEST: Oh Lord Madam you oblige me—look Ned you had a mind to have a full View of my Mistress, Sir, and—here she is   *[Bredwell stands gazing.]*
Go—salute her—look how he stands now, what a sneaking thing is a Fellow who has never traveled and seen the World! *[aside]*—Madam—this is a very honest Friend of mine, for all he looks so simply.

DIANA: Come he speaks for you, Sir.   *[To Bredwell.]*

BEARJEST: He Madam, though he be but a Banker's Prentice Madam, he's as pretty a Fellow of his Inches as any i'th'City—he has made Love in Dancing Schools, and to Ladies of Quality in the middle Gallery, and shall joke ye—and repartee with any Foreman within the Walls—*[to Bredwell]* prithee to her—and commend me, I'll give thee a new Point Cravat.

DIANA: He looks as if he could not speak to me.

BEARJEST: Not speak to you?—yes Gad Madam and do anything to you too.

DIANA: Are you his Advocate Sir?   *[In Scorn.]*

BEARJEST: For Want of a Better—

                           [(Bearjest) Stands behind (Bredwell) pushing him on.]

BREDWELL: An Advocate for Love I am,

And bring you such a Message from a Heart—

BEARJEST: Meaning mine dear Madam.

BREDWELL: That when you hear it, you will pity it.

BEARJEST: Or the Devil's in her—   *[Aside.]*

DIANA: Sir I have many Reasons to believe

It is my Fortune you pursue, not Person?

BEARJEST: There's something in that I must confess.   *[Behind (Bredwell).]*

But say what you will Ned—

BREDWELL: May all the Mischiefs of despairing Love

Fall on me if it be.

BEARJEST: That's well enough—

BREDWELL: No, were you born an humble Village Maid,

That fed a Flock, upon the neighboring Plain;

With all that shining Virtue in your Soul,

By Heaven I would adore you—love you—wed you.

Though the gay World were lost by such a Nuptial.   *[Bearjest looks on him.]*

—this—I would do were I my Friend the Squire.   *[Recollecting.]*

BEARJEST: Ay if you were me—you might do what you pleased; but I'm of another Mind.   *[Aside.]*

DIANA: Should I consent, my Father is a Man whom Interest sways not Honor, and whatsoever Promises he'as made you, he means to break 'em all, and I am destined to another.

BEARJEST: How another?—his Name, his Name Madam—here's Ned and I fear ne'er a single Man i'th'Nation. What is he?—what is he?—

DIANA: A Fop, a Fool, a beaten Ass—a Blockhead.

BEARJEST: What a damned Shame's this, that Women should be sacrificed to Fools, and Fops must run away with Heiresses—whilst we Men of Wit and Parts—dress and dance, and cock, and travel, for nothing but to be tame Keepers.

DIANA: But I by Heaven will never be that Victim.

But where my Soul is vowed 'tis fix't for ever.

BREDWELL: Are you resolved, are you confirmed in this?

Oh my Diana speak it o'er again *[Runs to her and embraces her.]*

Bless me and make me happier than a Monarch.

BEARJEST: Hold, hold dear Ned—that's my part I take it.

BREDWELL: Your Pardon Sir, I had forgot myself.

—But time is short—what's to be done in this?

BEARJEST: Done, I'll enter the House with Fire and Sword d'ye'see, not that I care this—but I'll not be fobbed off—what do they take me for a Fool—an Ass?

BREDWELL: Madam, dare you run the Risk of your Father's Displeasure, and run away with the Man you love?

DIANA: With all my Soul—

BEARJEST: That's hearty—and we'll do't—Ned and I here—and I love an Amour with an Adventure in't like Amadis de Gaul[10] —harky Ned—get a Coach and fix ready to Night when 'tis dark at the back Gate—

BREDWELL: And I'll get a Parson ready in my Lodging, to which I have a Key through the Garden by which we may pass unseen.

BEARJEST: Good—Mum here's Company—

[Enter Gayman with his Hat with Money in't, Sir Cautious in a Rage—Sir Feeble, Lady Fulbank, Leticia, Captain Noysey, Belmour.]

SIR CAUTIOUS: A hundred Pound lost already! Oh Coxcomb, old Coxcomb, and a wise Coxcomb—to turn Prodigal at my Years, whe, I was bewitched!

SIR FEEBLE: Sho, 'twas a Frolic Sir, I have lost a hundred pound as well as you. My Lady has lost, and your Lady has lost, and the rest—what old Cows will kick sometimes, what's a hundred Pound?

SIR CAUTIOUS: A hundred Pound, why 'tis a Sum Sir—a Sum—why what the Devil did I do with a Box and Dice?—

LADY FULBANK: Why you made a shift to lose Sir? And where's the harm of that? We have lost, and he has won, anon it may be your Fortune.

SIR CAUTIOUS: Ay, but he could never do it fairly, that's certain. Three hundred Pound! why how came you to win so unmercifully Sir?

GAYMAN: Oh the Devil will not lose a Gamester of me—you see Sir.

SIR CAUTIOUS: The Devil!—mark that Gentlemen—

BEARJEST: The Rogue has damned Luck sure, he has got a Fly—

SIR CAUTIOUS: And can you have the Conscience to carry away all our Money Sir?

GAYMAN: Most assuredly, unless you have the Courage to retrieve it. I'll set it at a Throw, or any Way, what say you Gentlemen?

SIR FEEBLE: Ods bobs you young Fellows are too hard for us every Way, and I am engaged at an old Game with a new Gamester here—who will require all an old Man's Stock.

LADY FULBANK: Come Cousin will you venture a Guinea—Come Mr. Bredwell—

GAYMAN: Well if nobody dare venture on me I'll send away my Cash—

[They all go to play at the Table but Sir Cautious, Sir Feeble and Gayman.]

SIR CAUTIOUS: Hum—must it all go?—a rare Sum, if a Man were but sure the Devil would but stand Neuter now—   *[Aside.]*

—Sir I wish I had anything but ready Money to stake—three hundred Pound—a fine Sum!

GAYMAN: You have Moveables Sir, Goods—Commodities—

SIR CAUTIOUS: That's all one Sir; that's Money's worth Sir; but if I had anything that were worth nothing—

GAYMAN: You would venture it,—I thank you Sir, I would your Lady were worth nothing—

SIR CAUTIOUS: Why so Sir?

GAYMAN: Then I would set all this against that Nothing.

10. An allusion to the Frenchman's reputed proficiency in matters of love.

SIR CAUTIOUS: What set it against my Wife?

GAYMAN: Wife Sir, Ay your Wife—

SIR CAUTIOUS: Hum, my Wife against three hundred pounds? What All my Wife Sir?

GAYMAN: All your Wife? Why Sir, some part of her would serve my turn.

SIR CAUTIOUS: Hum—my Wife—why, if I should lose, he could not have the Impudence to take her—   [Aside.]

GAYMAN: Well, I find you are not for the Bargain, and so I put up—

SIR CAUTIOUS: Hold Sir—why so hasty—my Wife? no—put up your Money Sir— what lose my Wife, for three hundred pounds!

GAYMAN: Lose her Sir—why she shall be never the worse for my wearing Sir—the old covetous Rogue is considering on't I think [aside]—what say you to a Night? I'll set it to a Night—there's none need know it Sir.

SIR CAUTIOUS: Hum—a Night!—three hundred pounds for a Night! why what a lavish Whoremaster's this: we take Money to marry our Wives, but very seldom part with 'em, and by the Bargain get Money [aside]—for a Night say you?—gad if I should take the Rogue at his word, 'twould be a pure Jest.   [Aside.]

SIR FEEBLE: You are not Mad Brother?

SIR CAUTIOUS: No, but I'm wise—and that's as good; let me consider—

SIR FEEBLE: What whether you shall be a Cuckold or not?

SIR CAUTIOUS: Or lose three hundred pounds—consider that; a Cuckold—why, 'tis a Word—an empty Sound—'tis Breath—'tis Air—'tis nothing—but three hundred pounds—Lord, what will not three hundred pounds do! You may chance to be a Cuckold for nothing Sir—

SIR FEEBLE: It may be so—but she shall do't discreetly then.

SIR CAUTIOUS: Under favor, you're an Ass Brother, this is the discreetest way of doing it, I take it.

SIR FEEBLE: But would a wise man expose his Wife?

SIR CAUTIOUS: Why, Cato was a wiser man than I, and he lent his Wife to a young Fellow they call'd Hortensius, as Story says; and can a wise man have a better Precedent than Cato?[11]

SIR FEEBLE: I say Cato was an Ass Sir, for obliging any young Rogue of 'em all.

SIR CAUTIOUS: But I am of Cato's Mind; well, a single Night you say.

GAYMAN: A single Night—to have—to hold—possess—and so forth at discretion.

SIR CAUTIOUS: A Night—I shall have her safe and sound i'th' Morning.

SIR FEEBLE: Safe no doubt on't—but how sound?—   [Aside.]

GAYMAN: And for Nonperformance, you shall pay me Three hundred pounds, I'll forfeit as much if I tell—

SIR CAUTIOUS: Tell?—why make your Three hundred pounds six hundred, and let it be put into the Gazette if you will man—but is't a Bargain?—

GAYMAN: Done—Sir Feeble shall be witness—and there stands my Hat.

   [Puts down his Hat of Money, and each of 'em take a Box and Dice, and kneel on the Stage, the rest come about 'em.]

SIR CAUTIOUS: —He that comes first to One and thirty wins—
                                              [They throw and count.]

LADY FULBANK: What are you playing for?

---

11. Marcus Porcius Cato (95–46 BCE) was a Roman statesman.

SIR FEEBLE: Nothing, nothing—but a Trial of Skill between an Old man and a Young—and your Ladyship is to be Judge.

LADY FULBANK: I shall be partial Sir.

SIR CAUTIOUS: Six and five's eleven—

[Throws—and pulls the Hat towards him.]

GAYMAN: Cater Tray—Pox of the Dice—

SIR CAUTIOUS: Two fives—one and twenty—

[(Sir Cautious) Sets up, pulls the Hat nearer.]

GAYMAN: Now Luck—*[throws]* Doubles of sixes—nineteen.

SIR CAUTIOUS: Five and four—thirty—   *[Draws the Hat to him.]*

SIR FEEBLE: Now if he wins it, I'll swear he has a Fly indeed—'tis impossible without Doubles of sixes—

GAYMAN: Now Fortune smile—and for the future frown.   *[Throws.]*

SIR CAUTIOUS: —Hum—two sixes—   *[Rises and looks dolefully round.]*

LADY FULBANK: How now? what's the Matter you look so like an Ass, what have you lost?

SIR CAUTIOUS: A Bauble—a Bauble—'tis not for what I've lost—but because I have not won—

SIR FEEBLE: You look very simple Sir—what think you of Cato now?

SIR CAUTIOUS: A wise man may have his Failings—

LADY FULBANK: What has my Husband lost?

SIR CAUTIOUS: Only a small parcel of Ware that lay dead upon my hands, Sweetheart.

GAYMAN: But I shall improve 'em, Madam, I'll warrant you.

LADY FULBANK: Well, since 'tis no worse, bring in your fine Dancer Cousin, you say you brought to entertain your Mistress with.   *[Bearjest goes out.]*

GAYMAN: Sir, You'll take care to see me paid to Night?

SIR CAUTIOUS: Well Sir—but my Lady you must know Sir, has the common Frailties of her Sex, and will refuse what she even longs for, if persuaded to't by me.

GAYMAN: 'Tis not in my Bargain to solicit her Sir, you are to procure her—or three hundred pounds Sir; choose you whether.

SIR CAUTIOUS: Procure her? with all my Soul Sir; alas, you mistake my honest Meaning, I scorn to be so unjust as not to see you abed together; and then agree as well as you can, I have done my part—in order to this Sir—get you but yourself conveyed in a Chest to my House, with a Direction upon't for me, and for the rest—

GAYMAN: I understand you—

SIR FEEBLE: Ralph get Supper ready.

[Enter Bearjest with Dancers. All go out but Sir Cautious.]

SIR CAUTIOUS: Well, I must break my Mind, if possible, to my Lady—but if she should be refractory now—and make me pay Three hundred pounds—why sure she won't have so little Grace—Three hundred pounds saved, is Three hundred pounds got—by our account—Could All—

> Who of this City-Privilege are free,
> Hope to be paid for Cuckoldom like me;
> Th' unthriving Merchant, whom gray Hair adorns,
> Before all Ventures would ensure his Horns;
> For thus, while He but lets spare Rooms to hire,
> His Wife's cracked Credit keeps his own entire.

[Exit.]

Act V

Scene I

Sir Cautious his House

[Enter Belmour alone, sad.]

BELMOUR: The Night is come, Oh my Leticia!
   The longing Bridegroom hastens to his Bed;
   Whilst she with all the Languishment of Love,
   And sad Despair, casts her fair Eyes on me,
   Which silently implore, I would deliver her.
   But how? Ay, there's the Question—hah—   *[Pausing.]*
   I'll get myself hid in her Bed-Chamber—
   And something I will do—may save us yet—
   If all my Arts should fail—I'll have recourse   *[Draws a Dagger.]*
   To this—and bear Leticia off by Force.
   —But see she comes—
   *[Enter Lady Fulbank, Sir Cautious, Sir Feeble, Leticia, Bearjest, Noysey, Gayman.
Exit Belmour.]*

SIR FEEBLE: Lights there Ralph,
   And my Lady's Coach there—   *[Bearjest goes to Gayman.]*
BEARJEST: Well Sir, remember you have promised to grant me my diabolical Request,
   in shewing me the Devil—
GAYMAN: I will not fail you Sir.
   [Enter Ralph with the Light.]

LADY FULBANK: Madam, your Servant; I hope you'll see no more Ghosts, Sir Feeble.
SIR FEEBLE: No more of that, I beseech you Madam: Prithee Sir Cautious take away
   your Wife—Madam your Servant—
                [All (except Leticia) go out after (Ralph with) the Light.]
   —Come Lette, Lette; hasten Rogue, hasten to thy Chamber, away, here be the
   young Wenches coming—   *[Puts her out, he goes out.]*
   [Enter Diana, puts on her Hood and Scarf.]

DIANA: So—they are gone to Bed; and now for Bredwell—the Coach waits, and I'll
   take this opportunity.
   Father farewell—if you dislike my course,
   Blame the old rigid Customs of your Force.   *[Goes out.]*

Scene II

A Bed-Chamber

[Enter Sir Feeble, Leticia and Phillis.]

LETICIA: Ah Phillis! I am fainting with my Fears,   *[Aside to Phillis.]*
   Hast thou no comfort for me?   *[(Sir Feeble) undresses to his Gown.]*

SIR FEEBLE: Why what art doing there—fiddle faddling—adod you young Wenches are so loath to come to—but when your hand's in, you have no mercy upon us poor Husbands.

LETICIA: Why do you talk so Sir?

SIR FEEBLE: Was it an angered; at the Fool's Prattle; tum-a me, tum a-me, I'll undress it, effags I will—Roguy.

LETICIA: You are so wanton Sir, you make me blush—
I will not go to Bed, unless you'll Promise me—

SIR FEEBLE: No bargaining my little Hussy—what you'll tye my hands behind me, will you?   [She goes to the Table.]

LETICIA: —What shall I do?—assist me gentle Maid,
Thy Eyes methinks puts on a little hope!   [Aside to Phillis.]

PHILLIS: Take Courage Madam—you guess right—be confident.   [Aside.]

SIR FEEBLE: No whispering Gentlewoman—and putting Tricks into her Head, that shall not cheat me of another Night—

   [As (Leticia) is at the Toilet (Sir Feeble) looks over her shoulder, and sees her Face in the Glass.]

Look on that silly little round Chity-face—Look on those smiling roguish loving Eyes there—look—look how they laugh, twire and tempt—he, rogue—I'll buss 'em there, and here and everywhere—Ods bobs—away, this is fooling and spoiling of a man's Stomach, with a Bit here, and a Bit there—to Bed—to Bed—

LETICIA: Go you first, Sir, I will but stay to say my Prayers, which are that Heaven would deliver me.   [Aside.]

SIR FEEBLE: Say thy Prayers?—what art thou mad, Prayers upon thy Wedding night? a short Thanksgiving or so—but Prayers quoth a—'Sbobs you'll have time enough for that—I doubt—

LETICIA: I am ashamed to undress before you Sir, go to Bed—

SIR FEEBLE: What was it ashamed to shew its little white Foots, and its little round Bubbies—well I'll go, I'll go—I cannot think on't, no I cannot—

   [(Sir Feeble) Going towards the Bed, Belmour comes forth from between the Curtains, his Coat off, his Shirt bloody, a Dagger in his hand, and his Disguise off.]

BELMOUR: Stand—

SIR FEEBLE: Hah—

LETICIA [and] PHILLIS [squeak]: —Oh Heavens—

[LETICIA]: Why, is it Belmour?   [Aside to Phillis.]

BELMOUR: Go not to Bed, I guard this Sacred Place,
And the Adulterer dies that enters here.

SIR FEEBLE: Oh—why do I shake—sure I'm a Man? what art thou?

BELMOUR: I am the wronged, the lost, and murdered Belmour.

SIR FEEBLE: Oh Lord! it is the same I saw last Night [aside]—oh!—hold thy dread Vengeance—pity me, and hear me—oh! a Parson—a Parson—what shall I do—oh! where shall I hide myself?

BELMOUR: I'th' utmost Borders of the Earth I'll find thee—
Seas shall not hide thee, nor vast Mountains guard thee.
Even in the depth of Hell, I'll find thee out,
And lash thy filthy and Adulterous Soul—

SIR FEEBLE: Oh! I am dead, I'm dead, will not Repentance save me?—'twas that young Eye that tempted me to sin; oh!—

BELMOUR: See fair Seducer, what thou'st made me do,   [To Leticia.]
Look on this bleeding Wound, it reached my Heart,
To pluck thy dear tormenting Image thence,
When News arrived that thou hadst broke thy Vow.

SIR FEEBLE: Oh Lord! oh!—I'm glad he's dead though.

LETICIA: Oh hide that fatal Wound, my tender Heart faints with a Sight so horrid!
                                        [Seems to weep.]

SIR FEEBLE: So she'll clear herself and leave me in the Devil's Clutches.

BELMOUR: You've both offended Heaven, and must repent or die.

SIR FEEBLE: Ah—I do confess I was an old Fool—bewitched with Beauty, besotted with Love, and do repent most heartily.

BELMOUR: No, you had rather yet go on in Sin:
Thou wou'dst live on, and be a baffled Cuckold.

SIR FEEBLE: Oh, not for the World Sir: I am convinced and mortified.

BELMOUR: Maintain her fine, undo thy Peace to please her, and still be Cuckol'd on—believe her—trust her, and be Cuckold still.

SIR FEEBLE: I see my Folly—and my Age's Dotage—and find the Devil was in me— yet spare my Age—ah! spare me to repent.

BELMOUR: If thou repent'st, renounce her, fly her sight;—
Shun her bewitching Charms, as thou wouldst Hell;
Those dark eternal Mansions of the dead—
Whither I must descend.

SIR FEEBLE: Oh—would he were gone!—   [Aside.]

BELMOUR: Fly—be gone—depart, vanish forever from her to some more safe and innocent Apartment.

SIR FEEBLE: Oh that's very hard!—
        [He goes back trembling, Belmour follows in with his Dagger up; both go out.]

LETICIA: Blessed be this kind Release, and yet methinks it grieves me to consider how the poor Old man is frighted.
        [Belmour reenters, puts on his Coat.]

BELMOUR: He's gone, and locked himself into his Chamber—
And now my dear Leticia let us fly—

                Despair till now, did my wild Heart invade,
                But pitying Love has the rough Storm allayed.   [Exeunt.]

                            Scene III

                        Sir Cautious his Garden

[Enter two Porters and Rag bearing Gayman in a Chest. Set it down; (Gayman) comes forth with a dark-Lantern.]

GAYMAN: Set down the Chest behind yon Hedge of Roses—and then put on those Shapes I have appointed you—and be sure you well-favouredly bang both Bearjest and Noysey; since they have a Mind to see the Devil.

RAG: Oh Sir leave 'em to us for that, and if we do not play the Devil with 'em, we deserve they should beat us. But Sir we are in Sir Cautious his Garden, will not he sue us for a Trespass?

GAYMAN: I'll bear you out; be ready at my Call.   *[Exeunt (Rag and Porters).]*

—Let me see—I have got no ready Stuff to banter with—but no Matter, any Gibberish will serve the Fools—'tis now about the Hour of ten—but Twelve is my appointed lucky Minute, when all the Blessings that my Soul could wish Shall be resigned to me.

[Enter Bredwell.]

—Hah who's there, Bredwell?

BREDWELL: Oh are you come Sir—and can you be so kind to a poor Youth, to favor his Designs and bless his Days?

GAYMAN: Yes, I am ready here with all my Devils, both to secure you your Mistress, and to cudgel your Captain and Squire, for abusing me behind my Back so basely.

BREDWELL: 'Twas most unmanly Sir, and they deserve it—I wonder that they come not?

GAYMAN: How durst you trust her with him?

BREDWELL: Because 'tis dangerous to steal a City Heiress, and let the Theft be his— so the dear Maid be mine—Hark—sure they come—

[Enter Bearjest; runs against Bredwell.]

—Who's there, Mr. Bearjest?

BEARJEST: Who's that, Ned?—Well I have brought my Mistress—hast thou got a Parson ready—and a License?

BREDWELL: Ay, ay—but where's the Lady?

BEARJEST: In the Coach, with the Captain at the Gate. I came before to see if the Coast be clear.

BREDWELL: Ay Sir—but what shall we do?—here's Mr. Gayman come on purpose to shew you the Devil, as you desired.

BEARJEST: Shoh! a Pox of the Devil Man—I can't intend to speak with him now.

GAYMAN: How Sir? d'ye think my Devil of so little Quality to suffer an Affront unrevenged?

BEARJEST: Sir I cry this Devilship's Pardon; I did not know his Quality—I protest Sir I love and honor him, but I am not just going to be married Sir, and when that Ceremony's past, I'm ready to go to the Devil as soon as you please.

GAYMAN: I have told him your Desire of seeing him, and should you baffle him?

BEARJEST: Who I Sir? Pray let his Worship know, I shall be proud of the Honor of his Acquaintance; but Sir my Mistress and the Parson waits in Ned's Chamber.

GAYMAN: If all the World wait Sir, the Prince of Hell will stay for no Man.

BREDWELL: Oh Sir rather than the Prince of the Infernals shall be affronted, I'll conduct the Lady up, and entertain her till you come Sir.

BEARJEST: Nay I have a great Mind to kiss his—Paw Sir, but I could wish you'd shew him me by Daylight Sir.

GAYMAN: The Prince of Darkness does ahbor the Light. But Sir I will for once allow your Friend the Captain to keep you Company.

[Enter Noysey and Diana.]

BEARJEST: I'm much obliged to you Sir, oh Captain—   *[(Bearjest) Talks to (Noysey)]*

BREDWELL: —Haste Dear; the Parson waits,
 To finish what the Powers designed above.
DIANA: Sure nothing is so bold as Maids in Love!   *[They go out.]*
NOYSEY: Pshoh! he conjure—he can fly as soon.
GAYMAN: Gentlemen you must be sure to confine yourselves to this Circle, and
 have a Care you neither swear, nor pray.
BEARJEST: Pray, Sir? I dare say neither of us were ever that Way gifted.
                                                              [A horrid Noise.]

GAYMAN: Cease your Horror, cease your Haste.
                And calmly as I saw you last,
                Appear! Appear!
                By thy Pearls and Diamond Rocks,
                By thy heavy Money Box.

                By thy shining Petticoat,
                That hid thy cloven Feet from Note.
                By the Veil that hid thy Face,
                Which else had frightened human Race.
                Appear, that I Love may see   *[Soft Music ceases.]*
                Appear kind Fiends, appear to me!

 A Pox of these Rascals why come they not?   *[Aside.]*
 *[Four enter from the four Corners of the Stage to Music that plays, they dance, and in
the Dance, dance round (Bearjest and Noysey), and kick, pinch, and beat 'em.]*

BEARJEST: Oh enough, enough! Good Sir lay 'em and I'll pay the Music—
GAYMAN: I wonder at it—these Spirits are in their Nature kind, and peaceable—and
 you have basely injured somebody—and then they will be satisfied—
BEARJEST: Oh good Sir take your Cerberuses off—I do confess the Captain here and
 I have violated your Fame.
NOYSEY: Abused you—and traduced you,—and thus we beg your Pardon—
GAYMAN: Abused me? 'Tis more than I know Gentlemen.
BEARJEST: But it seems your Friend the Devil does.
GAYMAN: By this time Bredwell's married.
 Great Pantamogan hold for I am satisfied   *[Exeunt Devils.]*
 And thus undo my Charm—
                         [Takes away the Circle, (Bearjest and Noysey) run out.]
 —so—the Fools are gone, and now to Julia's Arms.   *[Going.]*
                                                           [Exit.]

Scene IV

Lady Fulbank's Anti-chamber

[(Lady Fulbank) discovered undressed at her Glass. Sir Cautious undressed.]

LADY FULBANK: But why tonight? indeed you're wonderous kind methinks.
SIR CAUTIOUS: Why I don't know—a Wedding is a sort of an Alarm to Love; it
 calls up every Man's Courage.

LADY FULBANK: Ay but will it come when 'tis called?

SIR CAUTIOUS: I doubt you'll find it to my Grief—   [Aside.]

—But I think 'tis all one to thee, thou car'st not for my Compliment; no, thou'dst rather have a young Fellow.

LADY FULBANK: I am not used to flatter much; if forty Years were taken from your Age, 'twould render you something more agreeable to my Bed, I must confess.

SIR CAUTIOUS: Ay, ay, no doubt on't.

LADY FULBANK: Yet you may take my Word without an Oath, were you as old as Time, and I were young and gay as April Flowers,

Which all are fond to gather;

My Beauties all should wither in the Shade,

E'er I'd be worn in a dishonest Bosom.

SIR CAUTIOUS: Ay but you're wondrous free methinks—sometimes, which gives shrewd Suspicions.

LADY FULBANK: What, because I cannot simper—look demure, and justify my Honor when none questions it.

—Cry fie, and out upon the naughty Women,

Because they please themselves—and so would I.

SIR CAUTIOUS: How, would, what cuckold me?

LADY FULBANK: Yes, if it pleased me better than Virtue Sir.

But I'll not change my Freedom and my Humor,

To purchase the dull Fame of being Honest.

SIR CAUTIOUS: Ay but the World, the World—

LADY FULBANK: I value not the Censures of the Crowd.

SIR CAUTIOUS: But I am old.

LADY FULBANK: That's your Fault Sir, not mine.

SIR CAUTIOUS: But being so, if I should be good-natured and give thee leave to love discreetly?—

LADY FULBANK: I'd do't without your leave Sir.

SIR CAUTIOUS: Do't—what—cuckold me?

LADY FULBANK: No, love discreetly Sir, love as I ought, love Honestly.

SIR CAUTIOUS: What in Love with anybody, but your own Husband?

LADY FULBANK: Yes.

SIR CAUTIOUS: Yes quoth a—is that your loving as you ought?—

LADY FULBANK: We cannot help our Inclinations Sir,

No more than Time, or Light from coming on—

But I can keep my Virtue Sir entire.

SIR CAUTIOUS: What I'll warrant this is your first Love Gayman?

LADY FULBANK: I'll not deny that Truth, though even to you.

SIR CAUTIOUS: Why in Consideration of my Age and your Youth, I'd bear a Conscience—provided you do things wisely.

LADY FULBANK: Do what thing Sir?

SIR CAUTIOUS: You know what I mean—

LADY FULBANK: Hah—I hope you would not be a Cuckold Sir?

SIR CAUTIOUS: Why—truly in a civil Way—or so.—

LADY FULBANK: There is but one Way Sir to make me hate you;

And that would be tame Suffering.

SIR CAUTIOUS: Nay and she be thereabouts, there's no discovering—   [Aside.]

LADY FULBANK: But leave this fond Discourse—and if you must—Let us to Bed—

SIR CAUTIOUS: Ay, ay—I did but try your Virtue, mun—dost think I was in earnest?
[Enter Servant.]

SERVANT: Sir here's a Chest directed to your Worship.
SIR CAUTIOUS: Hum—'tis Wastall—now does my Heart fail me [aside]—a Chest say you?—to me?—so late—I'll warrant it comes from Sir Nicholas Smuggle—some prohibited Goods that he has stolen the Custom of, and cheated his Majesty—well he's an honest Man, bring it in—   [Exit Servant.]
LADY FULBANK: What into my Apartment Sir, a nasty Chest!
SIR CAUTIOUS: By all Means—for if the Searchers come—they'll never be so uncivil to ransack thy Lodgings—and we are bound in Christian Charity to do for one another—Some rich Commodities I am sure—and some fine Knick-knack will fall to thy share I'll warrant thee—Pox on him for a young Rogue, how punctual he is!—   [Aside.]
[Enter (Servant) with the Chest.]

—Go my Dear, go to Bed—I'll send Sir Nicholas a Receipt for the Chest, and be with thee presently—   [Exeunt severally.]
[Gayman peeps out of the Chest, and looks round him wondering.]

GAYMAN: Hah, where am I? By Heaven my last Night's Vision—'Tis that enchanted Room and yonder the Alcove! Sure 'twas indeed some Witch, who knowing of my Infidelity—has by Enchantment brought me hither—'tis so—I am betrayed—   [Pauses.]
Hah! or was it Julia? That last Night gave me that lone Opportunity—but hark I hear some coming—   [Shuts himself in.]
[Enter Sir Cautious.]

SIR CAUTIOUS: Lifting up the Chest Lid. So you are come I see—
        [Goes and locks the Door.]
GAYMAN: Hah—he here, nay then I was deceived, and it was Julia that last Night gave me the dear Assignation.   [Aside.]
        [Sir Cautious peeps into the Bedchamber.]
LADY FULBANK [Within]: Come Sir Cautious—I shall fall asleep and then you'll waken me—
SIR CAUTIOUS: Ay my Dear I'm coming [to Lady Fulbank]—she's in Bed—I'll go put out the Candle, and then—
GAYMAN: Ay I'll warrant you for my Part—
SIR CAUTIOUS: Ay—but you may overact your Part and spoil all—but Sir I hope you'll use a Christian Conscience in this Business.
GAYMAN: Oh doubt not Sir, but I shall do you Reason.
SIR CAUTIOUS: Ah Sir, but—
GAYMAN: Good Sir no more Cautions, you unlike a fair Gamester will rook me out of half my Night—I am impatient—
SIR CAUTIOUS: Good Lord are you so hasty; if I please you shan't go at all.
GAYMAN: With all my Soul Sir, pay me three hundred Pound Sir—
SIR CAUTIOUS: Lord Sir you mistake my candid Meaning still. I am content to be a Cuckold Sir—but I would have things done decently, d'ye mind me?
GAYMAN: As decently as a Cuckold can be made Sir.
—But no more Disputes I pray Sir.

SIR CAUTIOUS: I'm gone—I'm gone—but harky Sir—you'll rise before Day?
                                                        [Going out, returns.]
GAYMAN: Yet again—
SIR CAUTIOUS: I vanish Sir—but harky—you'll not speak a Word? But let her
    think 'tis I?
GAYMAN: Be gone I say Sir—   *[(Sir Cautious) runs out.]*
    I am convinced last Night I was with Julia.
    Oh Sot—insensible and dull—
    [Enter softly Sir Cautious.]

SIR CAUTIOUS: So—the Candle's out—give me your Hand.
                                                        [Leads (Gayman) softly in.]

Scene V

Changes to a Bedchamber

[Lady Fulbank supposed in Bed. Enter Sir Cautious and Gayman by Dark.]

SIR CAUTIOUS: Where are you my Dear?   *[Leads him to the Bed.]*
LADY FULBANK: Where should I be—in Bed, what, are you by Dark?
SIR CAUTIOUS: Ay the Candle went out by Chance.
    *[Gayman signs to him to be gone, (Sir Cautious) makes grimaces as loath to go, and
Exeunt.]*

Scene VI

Draws over and represents another Room in the same House

[Enter Parson, Diana, and Pert dressed in Diana's Clothes.]

DIANA: I'll swear Mrs. Pert you look very prettily in my Clothes; and since you Sir
    have convinced me that this innocent Deceit is not unlawful, I am glad to be the
    instrument of advancing Mrs. Pert to a Husband, she already has so just a Claim to.
PARSON: Since she has so firm a Contract, I pronounce it a lawful Marriage—but
    hark they are coming sure—
DIANA: Pull your Hoods down—and keep your Face from the Light.
                                                        [Diana runs out.]
    [Enter Bearjest and Noysey disordered.]

BEARJEST: Madam I beg your Pardon—I met with a most devillish Adventure,—your
    Pardon too Mr. Doctor, for making you wait—but the Business is this Sir,—I have
    a great Mind to lie with this young Gentlewoman tonight, but she swears if I do,
    the Parson of the Parish shall know it—
PARSON: If I do Sir, I shall keep Counsel.
BEARJEST: And that's civil Sir,—come lead the Way,
    With such a Guide, the Devil's in't, if we can go astray.   *[Exeunt.]*

Scene VII

Changes to the Antichamber

[Enter Sir Cautious.]

SIR CAUTIOUS: Now cannot I sleep! But am as restless as a Merchant in stormy
Weather, that has ventured all his Wealth in one Bottom.—Woman is a leaky
Vessel—if she should like the Young Rogue now, and they should come to a
right Understanding—why then am I a—Wital—that's all, and shall be put in
Print at Snowhill with my Effigies o'th'top like the Sign of Cuckolds Haven—
hum—they're damnable silent—pray Heaven he have not murdered her, and
robbed her—hum—hark, what's that?—a Noise—he has broke his Covenant
with me, and shall forfeit the Money—how loud they are? Ay, ay, the Plot's
discovered, what shall I do—Why the Devil is not in her sure to be refractory
now and peevish, if she be I must pay my Money yet—and that would be a
damned thing—sure they're coming out—I'll retire and harken how 'tis with
them   *[Retires.]*
*[Enter Lady Fulbank undressed—Gayman half undressed upon his Knees, following
her, holding her Gown.]*

LADY FULBANK: Oh! You unkind—what have you made me do?
  Unhand me false Deceiver—let me loose—
SIR CAUTIOUS: Made her do?—so, so—'tis done—I'm glad of that—
                                                              [Aside, peeping.]
GAYMAN: Can you be angry Julia!
  Because I only seized my Right of Love.
LADY FULBANK: And must my Honor be the Price of it?
  Could nothing but my Fame reward your Passion?
  —What make me a base Prostitute, a foul Adulteress?
  Oh—be gone, be gone—dear Robber of my Quiet.   *[Weeping.]*
SIR CAUTIOUS: Oh fearful!—
GAYMAN: Oh! Calm your Rage and hear me; if you are so,
  You are an innocent Adulteress.
  It was the feeble Husband you enjoyed
  In cold Imagination, and no more,
  Shyly you turned away—faintly resigned.
SIR CAUTIOUS: Hum—did she so—?   *[Aside.]*
GAYMAN: Till my Excess of Love—betrayed the Cheat.
SIR CAUTIOUS: Ay, ay that was my Fear—   *[Aside.]*
LADY FULBANK: Away—be gone—I'll never see you more—
GAYMAN: You may as well forbid the Sun to shine.
  Not see you more!—Heavens! I before adored you
  But now I rave! And with my impatient Love,
  A thousand mad, and wild Desires are Burning!
  I have discovered now new Worlds of Charms.
  And can no longer tamely love and suffer.
SIR CAUTIOUS: So—I have brought an old House upon my Head.
  Entailed Cuckoldom upon my self.   *[Aside.]*

LADY FULBANK: I'll hear no more—Sir Cautious—where's my Husband? Why have you left my Honor thus unguarded?

SIR CAUTIOUS: Ay, ay, she's well enough pleased I fear for all that.

GAYMAN: Base as he is, 'twas he exposed this Treasure.
  Like silly Indians bartered thee for Trifles.

SIR CAUTIOUS: Oh treacherous Villain!   [Aside.]

LADY FULBANK: Hah—my Husband do this?

GAYMAN: He, by Love, he was the kind Procurer,
  Contrived the Means, and brought me to thy Bed.

LADY FULBANK: My Husband? My wise Husband!
  What Fondness in my Conduct had he seen,
  To take so shameful and so base Revenge.

GAYMAN: None—'twas filthy Avarice seduced him to't.

LADY FULBANK: If he could be so barbarous to expose me,
  Could you who lov'd me—be so cruel too!

GAYMAN: What—to possess thee when the Bliss was offered,
  Possess thee too without a Crime to thee.
  Charge not my Soul with so remiss a Flame,
  So dull a Sense of Virtue to refuse it.

LADY FULBANK: I am convinced the Fault was all my Husband's—
  And here I vow—by all things Just and sacred,
  To separate forever from this Bed.   [Kneels.]

SIR CAUTIOUS: Oh I am not able to endure it—   [Aside.]
  Hold—oh hold my dear—   [He kneels as (Lady Fulbank) rises.]

LADY FULBANK: Stand off—I do ahbor thee—

SIR CAUTIOUS: With all my Soul—but do not make rash Vows.
  They break my very Heart—regard my Reputation!

LADY FULBANK: Which you have had such Care of Sir already—
  Rise, 'tis in vain you kneel.

SIR CAUTIOUS: No—I'll never rise again—Alas! Madam I was merely drawn in, I only thought to sport a Die or so—I had only an innocent Design to have discovered whether this Gentleman had stolen my Gold—that so I might have hanged him—

GAYMAN: A very Innocent Design indeed.

SIR CAUTIOUS: Ay Sir, that's all, as I'm an honest man—

LADY FULBANK: I've sworn, nor are the Stars more fixed than I.
  [Enter Servant.]

SERVANT: How! my Lady and his Worship up?
  —Madam, a Gentleman, and a Lady below in a Coach knocked me up, and say they must speak with your Ladyship.

LADY FULBANK: This is strange!—bring 'em up—   [Exit Servant.]
  Who can it be at this odd time of neither Night nor Day?
  [Enter Leticia, Belmour and Phillis.]

LETICIA: Madam, your Virtue, Charity and Friendship to me, has made me trespass on you for my Life's Security, and beg you will protect me—and my Husband—
                                                          [Points at Belmour.]

SIR CAUTIOUS: So—here's another sad Catastrophe!

LADY FULBANK: Hah—does Belmour live, is't possible?
  Believe me Sir, you ever had my Wishes:
  And shall not fail of my Protection now.
BELMOUR: I humbly thank your Ladyship.
GAYMAN: I'm glad thou hast her Harry—but doubt thou durst not own her; nay
  dar'st not own thyself.
BELMOUR: Yes Friend, I have my Pardon—
  But hark, I think we are pursued already—
  But now I fear no force   [A noise of somebody coming in.]
LADY FULBANK: However step into my Bedchamber.
                                    [Exeunt Leticia, Gayman, and Phillis.]
  [Enter Sir Feeble in an Antic manner.]

SIR FEEBLE: Hell shall not hold thee—nor vast Mountains cover thee, but I will find
  thee out—and lash thy filthy and Adulterous Carcass.
                          [Coming up in a menacing manner to Sir Cautious.]
SIR CAUTIOUS: How—lash my filthy Carcass?—I defy thee Satan—
SIR FEEBLE: 'Twas thus he said.
SIR CAUTIOUS: Let whoso will say it, he lies in's Throat.
SIR FEEBLE: —How! the Ghostly—hush—have a care—for 'twas the Ghost of Bel-
  mour—oh! hide that bleeding Wound, it chills my Soul!—
                                            [Runs to the Lady Fulbank.]
LADY FULBANK: What bleeding Wound?—Heavens are you frantic Sir?
SIR FEEBLE: No—but for want of rest—I shall 'ere Morning.   [Weeps.]
  She's gone—she's gone—she's gone—   [He weeps.]
SIR CAUTIOUS: Ay, Ay, she's gone, she's gone indeed.   [Sir Cautious weeps.]
SIR FEEBLE: —But let her go—so I may never see that dreadful Vision—harky Sir—
  a Word in your Ear—have a care of marrying a young Wife.
SIR CAUTIOUS: Ay, but I have married one already.   [Weeping.]
SIR FEEBLE: Hast thou? Divorce her—fly her, quick—depart—be gone, she'll Cuck-
  old thee—and still she'll Cuckold thee—
SIR CAUTIOUS: Ay Brother, but whose fault was that?—
  Why, are not you married?
SIR FEEBLE: Mum—no Words on't, unless you'll have the Ghost about your Ears;
  Part with your Wife I say, or else the Devil will part ye.
LADY FULBANK: Pray go to Bed Sir?
SIR CAUTIOUS: Yes, for I shall sleep now, I shall lie alone;   [Weeps.]
  Ah Fool, old dull besotted Fool—to think she'd love me—'twas by base means I
  gained her—cozened an honest Gentleman—of Fame and Life—
LADY FULBANK: You did so Sir, but 'tis not past Redress—you may make that hon-
  est Gentleman amends.
SIR FEEBLE: Oh would I could, so I gave half my Estate—
LADY FULBANK: —That Penitence attones with him and Heaven.—Come forth
  Leticia, and your injured Ghost.
  [Enter Leticia, Belmour, and Phillis.]

SIR FEEBLE: —Hah Ghost—another Sight would make me mad indeed.
BELMOUR: Behold me Sir, I have no Terror now.
SIR FEEBLE: Hah—who's that, Francis?—my Nephew Francis?

BELMOUR: Belmour—or Francis—choose you which you like, and I am either.

SIR FEEBLE: Hah, Belmour! and no Ghost?

BELMOUR: Belmour—and not your Nephew Sir.

SIR FEEBLE: But art alive? Ods bobs I'm glad on't Sirrah,
    —But are you real Belmour?

BELMOUR: As sure as I'm no Ghost.

GAYMAN: We all can Witness for him Sir.

SIR FEEBLE: Where be the Minstrels, we'll have a Dance—adod we will—ah—art
    thou there thou cozening little Chits-face?—a Vengeance on thee—thou madest
    me an old Doting loving Coxcomb—but I forgive thee—and give thee all thy
    Jewels, and you your Pardon Sir, so you'll give me mine; for I find you young
    Knaves will be too hard for us.

BELMOUR: You are so generous Sir, that 'tis almost with grief I receive the Blessing
    of Leticia.

SIR FEEBLE: No, no, thou deserv'st her, she would have made an old fond Blockhead of
    me—and one way or other you would have had her—ods bobs you would—
    [Enter Bearjest, Diana, Pert, Bredwell, and Noysey.]

BEARJEST: Justice Sir, Justice—I have been cheated—abused—Assassinated and
    Ravished!

SIR CAUTIOUS: How, my Nephew ravished!—

PERT: No Sir, I am his Wife.

SIR CAUTIOUS: Hum—my Heir marry a Chambermaid!

BEARJEST: Sir, you must know I stole away Mrs. Di, and brought her to Ned's
    Chamber here—to marry her.

SIR FEEBLE: My Daughter Di stolen—

BEARJEST: But I being to go to the Devil a little Sir; whip—what does he, but mar-
    ries her himself Sir; and fobbed me off here with my Lady's cast Petticoat—

NOYSEY: Sir, she's a Gentlewoman, and my Sister Sir.

PERT: Madam, 'twas a pious Fraud, if it were one, for I was contracted to him
    before—see here it is—   [Gives (a paper to) 'em.]

ALL: A plain Case, a plain Case.

SIR FEEBLE: Hark y'Sir, have you had the Impudence to marry my Daugher Sir?
                                [To Bredwell, who with Diana kneels.]

BREDWELL: Yes Sir, and humbly ask your Pardon, and your Blessing—

SIR FEEBLE: You will ha't, whether I will or not—rise—you are still too hard for us,
    Come Sir forgive your Nephew—

SIR CAUTIOUS: Well Sir, I will—but all this while you little think the Tribulation I
    am in, my Lady has forsworn my Bed.

SIR FEEBLE: Indeed Sir, the wiser she.

SIR CAUTIOUS: For only performing my Promise to this Gentleman.

SIR FEEBLE: Ay, you showed her the Difference Sir, you're a wise man. Come dry
    your Eyes—and rest yourself contented, we are a couple of old Coxcombs: d'ye
    hear Sir, Coxcombs.

SIR CAUTIOUS: I grant it Sir, and if I die Sir—I bequeath my Lady to you—with my
    whole Estate—my Nephew has too much already for a Fool.   [To Gayman.]

GAYMAN: I thank you Sir—do you consent my Julia?

LADY FULBANK: No Sir—you do not like me—a canvas Bag of wooden Ladles were
    a better Bedfellow.

GAYMAN: Cruel Tormentor! oh I could kill my self with Shame and Anger!

LADY FULBANK: Come hither Bredwell—witness for my Honour—that I had no Design upon his Person, but that of trying of his Constancy.

BREDWELL: Believe me Sir, 'tis true—I feigned a danger near—just as you got to Bed—and I was the kind Devil Sir, that brought the Gold to you.

BEARJEST: And you were one of the Devils that beat me, and the Captain here Sir?

GAYMAN: No truly Sir, those were some I hired—to beat you for abusing me today—

NOYSEY: To make you 'mends Sir, I bring you the certain News of the Death of Sir Thomas Gayman your Uncle, who has left you Two Thousand pounds a year.—

GAYMAN: I thank you Sir—I heard the news before.

SIR CAUTIOUS: How's this; Mr Gayman, my Lady's first Lover? I find Sir Feeble we were a Couple of old Fools indeed, to think at our Age to cozen two lusty young Fellows of their Mistresses; 'tis no wonder that both the Men and the Women have been too hard for us, we are not fit Matches for either, that's the truth on't.

> That Warrior needs must to his Rival yield,
> Who comes with blunted Weapons to the Field.

[Exeunt.]

Epilogue

Written by a Person of Quality

Long have we turned the Point of our just Rage
On the half Wits, and Critics of the Age.
Oft has the soft, Insipid Sonneteer
In *Nice* and *Flutter*, seen his Fop-face here.
Well was the Ignorant Lampooning Pack
Of shatterhead Rhymers whipped on *Craffey's* back;
But such a trouble Weed is Poetaster,
The lower 'tis cut down, it grows the faster.
Tho Satyr then had such a plenteous Crop,
An Aftermath of *Coxcombs* is come up,
Who not content false Poetry to renew,
By sottish Censures would condemn the true.
Let writing like a *Gentleman*—fine appear,
But must you needs judge too *en Cavalier*?
These whiffling Critics, 'tis our Authoress fears,
And humbly begs a Trial by her Peers:
Or let a Poll of Fools her Fate pronounce,
There's no great harm in a good quiet Dunce.
But shield her, Heaven! from the left-handed Blow
Of Airy Blockheads, who pretend to know.
On downright Dullness let her rather split,
Than be Fop-mangled under color of Wit.
   Hear me ye Scribbling Beaus,—
Why will you in shyer Rhyme, without one stroke
Of Poetry, Lady's just Disdain provoke,
And address Songs, to whom you never spoke.

In doleful Hymns for dying Felons fit,
Why do you tax their Eyes, and blame their Wit?
Unjustly of the Innocent you complain,
'Tis Bulkers give, and Tubs must cure your Pain.
Why in Lampoons will you yourselves revile?
'Tis true, none else will think it worth their while:
But thus you're hid! oh, 'tis a Politic Fetch:
So some have hanged themselves, to ease *Jack Ketch*.
Justly your Friends and Mistresses you blame,
For being so they well deserve the Shame,
'Tis the worst Scandal to have born that Name.
At Poetry of late, and such whose Skill
Excels your own, you dart a feeble Quill;
Well may you rail at what you Ape so ill.
With virtuous Women, and all Men of Worth,
You're in a state of Mortal War by Birth.
Nature in all her Atom Fights ne'er knew
Two things so opposite as Them and You.
On such your Muse her utmost Fury spends,
They're slandered worse than any but your Friends.
More Years may teach you better, the meanwhile,
If you can't mend your Morals, mend your Style.

1686

Jane Barker
1652–1727

A Catholic convert from a Royalist family, Jane Barker published poems and narratives on such diverse topics as women's devotion to learning, friendships between women, a virgin's disappointment in love, and religious belief in the face of death. She was born in Northamptonshire to Thomas Barker, once a Royalist soldier and then in service to a rural squire, and his wife, Anne Connock. When the family relocated to Lincolnshire in 1662, Barker's brother Edward, who attended Oxford, tutored her in Latin and medicine. It seems likely that she lived for several years as a young adult in London with her mother. Much of Barker's poetry was published between 1688 and 1713 when she lived in France, having converted to Catholicism during James II's reign and followed him into exile after the Revolution of 1688. Upon returning to London she began to earn her living as a writer of fiction. Like her character Galesia, Barker never married, claiming to prefer the pleasures of literature and education to those of marriage. She was fully aware, however, of the costs of this choice for a woman of the times, including social marginalization and economic dependency.

Poetical Recreations: Consisting of Original Songs, Poems, Odes, Etc., written by Barker with others, appeared in 1688. Her fiction includes a long narrative, *Love's Intrigues: or The History of the Amours of Bosvil and Galesia* (1713); a group of short stories, *Exilus: or The Banished Roman* (1715); and most notably, *A Patch-Work Screen for the Ladies* (1723), a series of embedded narratives interspersed with poems. This work was followed by a sequel, *The Lining for the*

Patch-Work Screen (1726). A precursor to such contemporary writers as ALICE WALKER and ADRIENNE RICH in using the quilt as a metaphor for women's multifaceted writing, Barker recommends patch-work "to my Female Readers, as well in their Discourse as in their Needle-Work." She also wrote a lengthy autobiography in dialogues that reveals the strength of her Catholicism and her loyalty to the Stuart monarchy during her twenty-five year exile from her homeland to avoid religious persecution.

The poet Barker most admired was KATHERINE PHILIPS, "the matchless Orinda," and several of Barker's narratives pay homage to this female predecessor. In *The Lining of the Patch-Work Screen* she claims to have encountered Philips in a dream-vision. Her poem "A Virgin Life" is similar in tone and theme to Philips' "The Virgin"; both works praise the opportunities for art, kindness, wit, and learning offered by the single life, and neither seems unduly perturbed by the prevalent stereotype of the elderly virgin as a frustrated "Old Maid." For Barker, a virgin's life is not "all Wretchedness" or "foul Deformity" but "the Impress of all Good," a means of pursuing learning and unselfish service to others.

⊰ A Virgin Life ⊱

Since, O good Heavens! you have bestow'd on me
So great a Kindness for *Virginity*,
Suffer me not to fall into the Powers
Of Man's almost Omnipotent Amours.
5   But let me in this happy State remain,
And in chaste Verse my chaster Thoughts explain;
Fearless of *Twenty-five*, and all its Rage,
When Time with Beauty lasting Wars engage.
When once *that Clock has struck*, all Hearts retire,
10   Like *Elves* from *Daybreak*, or like *Beasts* from *Fire*,
'Tis Beauty's *Passing-Bell*; no more are slain;
But dying Lovers all revive again.
Then every Day some new Contempt we find,
As if the Scorn and Lumber of Mankind.
15   These frightful Prospects, oft our Sex betray;
Which to avoid, some fling themselves away;
Like harmless *Kids*, who when pursu'd by *Men*,
For Safety, run into a *Lion's Den*.
Ah! *happy State!* how strange it is to see,
20   What mad Conceptions some have had of *Thee!*
As if thy Being was all Wretchedness,
Or foul Deformity, in vilest Dress:
Whereas thy Beauty's pure Celestial,
Thy Thoughts Divine, thy Words Angelical:
25   And such ought all thy Votaries to be,
Or else they're so but for Necessity.
A *Virgin* bears the Impress of all Good,
Under that Name, all Vertue's understood.
So equal all her Looks, her Mien, her Dress,
30   That nought but Modesty is in Excess;
Tho Business of her Life to this extends,
To serve her God, her Neighbour and her Friends.

1723

Delarivier Manley
1663–1724

In 1785 the author of a literary study entitled *The Progress of Romance*, Clara Reeve, described Delarivier Manley as a writer who "hoarded up all the public and private scandal within her reach, and poured it forth, in a work too well known in the last age, though almost forgotten in the present." The scandalous work to which Reeve refers is *The New Atalantis* (1709–11), a lurid account of sexual intrigue based on indiscretions performed by "Several Persons of Quality, of both Sexes." In this and other narratives Manley satirized her political adversaries and adapted the stock plot device of the virtuous damsel in distress, in which a young woman is ruined by an unscrupulous older man. Although she wrote six plays, several travelogues, political tracts, and occasional poems, Manley is remembered today primarily as a scandal-monger. Yet her fiction contributed significantly to the development of the British novel.

She was born Mary Delarivier Manley in Jersey, the third child of the royalist lieutenant-governor of that district of England, Sir Roger Manley, and his wife, who died when her daughter was an infant; Manley and her sisters were subsequently cared for by a governess. In 1680 her family moved to Suffolk, where she became infatuated with a young actor and military officer, James Carlisle, and perhaps was sent away for a time to live with another family. Although she had hoped to become a Maid of Honour to Mary of Modena, joining the ranks of ANNE FINCH and ANNE KILLIGREW, King James II was deposed before this plan could be carried out. When Manley's father died in 1677, he left her 200 pounds and part of his estate, but he put his bequest in the hands of his nephew. John Manley subsequently lured his fifteen-year-old cousin into a bigamous marriage, eventually abandoning her and their son, John, in 1691 to return to his legal wife; he took his ward's fortune with him. The son's fate remains unknown, but Manley lived for a time thereafter with Barbara Villiers, the Duchess of Cleveland, who had once been Charles II's mistress.

By 1696 Manley had moved to London, where she led a volatile and independent life and earned her living as a writer. Two of her plays were performed that same year: *The Lost Lover*, produced at the Drury Lane Theatre, and *The Royal Mischief*, produced at Lincoln's Inn. The first play failed miserably, in part because she had written it in only seven days; still, Manley considered "my Treatment much severer than I deserved. I am satisfied the bare Name of being a Woman's Play damned it beyond its own want of merit." The second play, a tragedy whose opening prologue urged critics not to condemn this work as they had its predecessor, appealed to women in the audience to support her as a playwright rather than condemning her as lewd. In 1696 Manley also published her first travelogue, *Letters from Mrs. Manley*, a narrative of riding by coach from London to Exeter. During this time she reputedly had several lovers, including two theater managers, and was associated with other women playwrights such as Catherine Trotter and Mary Pix, both of whom later became her enemies. In 1700 she edited *The Nine Muses*, a group of elegies on the death of John Dryden, and in 1707 another of her plays was performed, *Almyna, or the Arabian Vow*. Manley went on to establish *The Female Tatler*, a pro-Tory journal, and to succeed Jonathan Swift as editor of *The Examiner* in 1711; she was his first choice for that prominent position.

Manley's best-known works, however, were her "scandal novels," the first of which, *The Secret History of Queen Zarah and the Zarazians*, appeared in 1705; it launched a satiric attack on Queen Anne's favorite lady-in-waiting, Sarah, Duchess of Marlborough, and was followed by a sequel, *The Lady's Pacquet of Letters* (1707). But it was *Secret Memoirs and Manners of Several Persons of Quality, of Both Sexes, From the New Atalantis* that made her reputation first plummet, then soar. Condemned especially for presenting a sordid account of the divorce proceedings of the poet SARAH FYGE and her husband, whose part Manley took, she was arrested for slander. The case was dropped after four months for lack of evidence; meanwhile, her treatise became hugely successful and went into several editions. Undaunted by those who criticized her, Manley published an autobiographical novel, *The Adventures of Rivella* (1714), which credited her success as a writer to her own wit and exposed her former friend, Catherine Trotter, as the mistress of John Tilly, warden of the Fleet, with whom Manley herself had earlier been involved. Several of Manley's poems appeared in *New Miscellany of Original Poems* (1720), edited by Anthony Hammond, and that same year she published her last novel, *The Power of Love*. Manley died in 1724 at the home of her lover John Barber, an illiterate Tory alderman and printer who later became Lord Mayor of London.

The part of *The New Atalantis* reprinted here describes a debauched duke's seduction of his naïve ward. Plotting "the manner how to corrupt her," he determines to "show her the World; Balls, Assemblies, Opera's, Comedies, Cards, and Visits." None of this is necessary, however, for the duke instead encourages her to read "the most Amorous" books from his private library. Watching her "snowy Bosom" heave as she guiltily reads about sexual pleasure, "he prest her Lips with his." Although Manley conveys here something of her own experience with her cousin, her account is based on an actual seduction by the Earl of Portland of the daughter of a friend who had been entrusted to his care. History does not record whether the Earl sued Manley for libel.

from The New Atalantis

[The Duke's Seduction of his Ward]

. . . That fatal Night the Duke felt hostile Fires in his Breast, Love was entered with all his dreadful Artillery; he took possession in a moment of the Avenues that lead to the Heart! neither did the resistance he found there serve for any thing but to make his Conquest more illustrious. The Duke try'd every corner of his uneasie Bed! whether shut or open, Charlot was still before his Eyes! his Lips and Face retain'd the dear Impression of her Kisses! the Idea of her innocent and charming Touches, wander'd o'er his Mind! he wish'd again to be so bless'd but then, with a deep and dreadful Sigh, he remembered who she was, the Daughter of his Friend! of a Friend who had at his Death left the charge of her Education to him! his Treaty with the Princess Dowager, wou'd not admit him to think of marrying of her, Ambition came in to rescue him (in that particular) from the Arms of Love. To possess her without, was a villanous detestable Thought! but not to possess her at all, was loss of Life! was Death inevitable! Not able to gain one wink of Sleep, he arose with the first Dawn, and posted back to Angela. He hop'd the hurry of Business, and the Pleasures of the Court, wou'd stifle so guilty a Passion; he was too well perswaded of his Distemper, the Symptoms were right, the Malignity was upon him! he was regularly posses'd! Love, in all its forms, had took in that formidable Heart of his! he began to be jealous of his Son, whom he had always design'd for Charlot's Husband; he cou'd not bear the thoughts that he shou'd be belov'd by her, tho' all beautiful, as the lovely Youth was. She had never had any tender Inclinations for him, nothing that exceeded the warmth of a Sister's love! whether it were that he were designed for, or that the Precepts of Education had warn'd her from too precipitate a liking: She was bred up with him, accustom'd to his Charms, they made no impression upon her Heart! neither was the Youth more sensible. The Duke cou'd distress neither of 'em by his love of that side, but this he was not so happy to know. He wrote up for the young Lord to come to Court, and gave immediate orders for forming his Equipage, that he might be sent to Travel: Mean time Charlot was never from his Thoughts. Who knows not the violence of beginning Love! especially a Love that we hold opposite to our Interest and Duty? 'Tis an unreasonable excess of Desire, which enters swiftly, but departs slowly. The love of Beauty, is the loss of Reason. Neither is it to be suppress'd by Wisdom, because it is not to be comprehended with Reason. And the Emperor Aurelius;[1] Love is a cruel Impression of that wonderful Passion, which to define is impossible, because no Words reach to the strong Nature of it, and only they know which inwardly feel it.

The Duke vainly strugled in the Snare; he wou'd live, without seeing Charlot, but then he must live in Pain, in inexplicable Torture! he applies the relief of Business, the Pleasures of Woman! Charlot's Kisses were still upon his Lips, and made all others insipid to him. In short, he try'd so much to divert his Thoughts from her, that it but more perfectly confirm'd him of the vanity and the unsuccessfulness of the attempt: He could neither eat or sleep! love and restlessness rais'd Vapours in him to that degree, he was no longer Master of his Business! Wearied with all things, hurry'd by a secret Principle of Self-Love, and Self-Preservation, the Law of Nature! he orders his Coach to carry him down once more to his Villa, there to see his Dear! this dangerous Charlot! that little innocent Sweetness! that imbitter'd his Happiness. She lov'd him tenderly, as a Benefactor, a Father, or something more; that she had been us'd to love without that severe mixture of Fear that mingles in the love we bear to Parents: She ran to meet him as he alighted; her young Face, over-spread with blushing Joys! his transport exceeded hers! he took her in his Arms with eagerness! he exchang'd all his Pains for Pleasures! there was the Cure of his past Anguish! her Kisses were the Balm to his wounded Mind! he wonder'd at the immediate alteration! she caress'd and courted him; shew'd him all things that cou'd divert or entertain. He knew not what to resolve upon; he cou'd not prudently marry her, and how to attempt to corrupt her! those excellent Principles that had been early infused into her, were all against him; but yet he must love her! he found he cou'd not live without her! he open'd a Machiavel, and read there a Maxim, That none but great Souls can be compleatly Wicked.[2] He took it for a kind of Oracle to him: He wou'd be loath to tell himself, his Soul was not great enough for any attempt. He clos'd the Book, took some turns about the Gallery to digest what he had read, and from thence concluded, that neither Religion, Honour, Gratitude nor Friendship, were ties sufficient to deprive us of an essential Good! Charlot was necessary to his very Being! all his Pleasures faded without her! and, which was worse, he was in torture! in actual pain as well as want of pleasure! therefore Charlot he would have; he had struggled more than sufficient, Virtue ought to be satisfied with the terrible Conflict he had suffered! but Love was become Master, and 'twas time for her to abscond. After he had settled his Thoughts, he grew more calm and quiet; nothing shou'd now disturb him, but the manner how to corrupt her. He was resolv'd to change her whole Form of Living to bring her to Court, to show her the World; Balls, Assemblies, Opera's, Comedies, Cards, and Visits, every thing that might enervate the Mind, and fit it for the soft play and impression of Love. One thing he a little scrupled, lest in making her susceptible of that Passion, it shou'd be for another, and not for him; he did not doubt, but upon her first appearance at Court she wou'd have many Admirers; Lovers have this opinion peculiar to themselves, they believe that others see with their Eyes: He knew that were she less agreeable, the gloss of Novelty was enough to recommend

---

1. Marcus Aurelius, a Stoic philosopher, was Roman emperor from 161 to 180 CE.
2. An allusion to Niccolò Machiavelli (1469–1527), an Italian political philosopher and author of *The Prince* (1513).

her; but the remedy he found for this, was, to caress and please her above all others; to shew such a particular regard for her, that shou'd frighten any new pretender. Few are willing to cross a first Minister, especially in such a tender Point, where all Mankind are tenacious of their Pretensions.

He had observ'd, that Charlot had been, but with disgust, deny'd the gay Part of reading: 'Tis natural for young People to chuse the diverting, before the instructive; he sent for her into the Gallery, where was a noble Library in all Languages, a Collection of the most valuable Authors, was a mixture of the most Amorous. He told her, that now her Understanding was increas'd, with her Statue, he resolv'd to make her Mistress of her own Conduct; and as the first thing that he intended to oblige her in, that Governante who had hitherto had the care of her Actions, should be dismiss'd; because he had observ'd the severity of her Temper had sometimes been displeasing to her; that she shou'd henceforward have none above her, that she shou'd need to stand in awe of; and to confirm to her that good opinion he seem'd to have, he presented her with the Key of that Gallery, to improve her Mind, and seek her Diversion, amongst those Authors he had formerly forbid her the use of. Charlot made him a very low Curtsie, and, with a blushing Grace, return'd him Thanks for the two favours he bestow'd upon her. She assur'd him, that no Action of hers shou'd make him repent the distinction; that her whole endeavour should be to walk in that Path he made familiar to her; and that Virtue shou'd ever be her only Guide. Tho' this was not what the Duke wanted, 'twas nothing but what he expected: He observ'd formerly, that she was a great lover of Poetry, especially when 'twas forbid her; he took down an *Ovid*,[3] and opening it just at the love of Myrra for her Father, conscious red overspread his Face; he gave it her to read, she obey'd him with a visible delight; nothing is more pleasing to young Girls, than in being first consider'd as Women. Charlot saw the Duke entertain'd her with an Air of Consideration more than usual, passionate and respectful; this taught her to refuge in the native Pride and Cunning of the Sex, she assum'd an Air more haughty. The leaving a Girl just beginning to believe herself capable of attaining that Empire over Mankind, which they are all born and taught by Instinct to expect. She took the Book, and plac'd herself by the Duke, his Eyes, Feasted themselves upon her Face, thence wander'd over her snowy Bosom, and saw the young swelling Breasts just beginning to distinguish themselves, and which were gently heav'd at the Impression Myrra's Sufferings made upon her Heart, by this dangerous reading, he pretended to shew her, that there were Pleasures her Sex were born for, and which she might consequently long to taste! Curiosity is an early and dangerous Enemy to Virtue, the young Charlot, who had by a noble Incli[nation] of Gratitude a strong propension of Affection for the Duke, whom she call'd and esteem'd her Papa, being a Girl of wonderful reflection, and consequently Application, wrought her Imagination up to such a lively height at the Fathers Anger after the possession of his Daughter, which she judg'd highly unkind and unnatural, that she drop'd her Book, Tears fill'd her Eyes, Sobs rose to oppress her, and she pull'd out her Handkerchief to cover the Disorder. The Duke, who was Master of all Mankind, could trace 'em in all the Meanders of Dissimulation and Cunning, was not at a loss how to interpret the Agitation of a Girl who knew no Hipocrisy, all was Artless, the beautiful product of Innocence and Nature; he drew her gently to him, drunk her Tears with his Kisses, suck'd her Sighs and gave her by that dangerous Commerce (her Soul before prepar'd to softness) new and unfelt

---

3. An allusion to the *Metamorphoses*, by Ovid (43 BCE–17 CE), a poetic treatment of several mythological tales.

Desires; her Virtue was becalm'd, or rather unapprehensive of him for an Invader; he prest her Lips with his, the nimble beatings of his Heart, apparently seen and felt thro' his open Breast! the glowings! the tremblings of his Limbs! the glorious Sparkles from his guilty Eyes! his shortness of Breath, and eminent Disorder, were things all new to her, that had never seen, heard, or read before of those powerful Operations, struck from the Fire of the two meeting Sex; nor had she leisure to examine his disorders, possess'd by greater of her own! greater! because that Modesty opposing Nature, forc'd a struggle of Dissimulation. But the Duke's pursuing Kisses overcame the very Thoughts of any thing, but that new and lazy Poison stealing to her Heart, and spreading swiftly and imperceptibly thro' all her Veins, she clos'd her Eyes with languishing Delight! deliver'd up the possession of her Lips and Breath to the amorous Invader; return'd his eager grasps, and, in a word, gave her whole Person into his Arms, in meltings full of delight! The Duke by that lovely Extasie, carry'd beyond himself, sunk over the expiring Fair, in Raptures too powerful for description! calling her his admirable Charlot! his charming Angel! his adorable Goddess! but all was so far modest, that he attempted not beyond her Lips and Breast, but cry'd that she shou'd never be anothers. The Empire of his Soul was hers; enchanted by inexplicable, irresistable Magick! she had Power beyond the Gods themselves! Charlot return'd from that amiable Disorder, was a new charm'd at the Duke's Words; Words that set her so far above what was mortal, the Woman assum'd in her, and she wou'd have no notice taken of the Transports she had shown. He saw and favour'd her modesty, secure of that fatal Sting he had fix'd within her Breast, that Taste of delight, which powerful Love and Nature wou'd call upon her to repeat. He own'd he lov'd her; that he never cou'd love any other; that 'twas impossible for him to live a day, an hour, without seeing her; that in her absence he had felt more than ever had been felt by Mortal; he begg'd her to have pity on him, to return his Love, or else he shou'd be the most lost, undone thing alive. Charlot, amaz'd and charm'd, felt all those dangerous perturbations of Nature that arise from an amorous Constitution, with Pride and Pleasure, she saw herself necessary to the happiness of one, that she had hitherto esteemed so much about her, ignorant of the Power of Love, that Leveller of Mankind; that blender of Distinction and Hearts. Her soft Answer was, That she was indeed reciprocally Charm'd, she knew not how; all he had said and done was wonderful and pleasing to her; and if he wou'd still more please her (if there were a more) it shou'd be never to be parted from her. The Duke had one of those violent Passions, where, to heighten it, resistance was not at all necessary; it had already reach'd the ultimate, it cou'd not be more ardent; yet was he loth to rush upon the possession of the Fair, lest the too early pretension might disgust her: He wou'd steal himself into her Soul, he wou'd make himself necessary to her quiet, as she was to his.

1709–10

⊱────⊰

Eliza Haywood
1693?–1756

Satirized by Jonathan Swift as the amorous "nymph Corinna," Eliza Haywood was an eighteenth-century English poet, novelist, playwright, translator, journalist, and editor known for her controversial portrayals of female sexual desire. Born to a London shopkeeper, Haywood married a clergyman, Valentine Haywood, in her late teens but somehow by 1714 had become an actress in Dublin; by 1721 she and her husband were separated, and she was earning her living as a performer and a writer in London. During her forty-year career Haywood wrote more than sixty works, many of them sensational novels that were enormously popular with a new female readership. *Love in Excess, or the Fatal Inquiry* (1719–20), her first novel and a best-seller, established her reputation as a prominent literary figure; *Letters from a Lady of Quality to a Chevalier* (1720), which chronicles a noblewoman's amorous adventures, was published in installments. *Fantomima: Or, Love in a Maze* (1724) features an unnamed heroine whose attendance at the theater becomes a means of exploring her sexual identity via masquerade. Haywood also wrote several novels of political intrigue, including *Memoirs of a Certain Island . . . Adjacent to Utopia* (1724), *The Court of Caramania* (1727), and *Eovaai* (1736).

Haywood's sometimes lurid portrayals of women's sexuality earned her the ridicule of many famous men of her time, including the satirist Alexander Pope, who criticized her for licentiousness and commercialism in his *Dunciad,* and the novelist Henry Fielding, who dubbed her "Mrs. Novel" because of her fiction's often implausible plots and her impressive, and impressionable, audience. But Haywood was capable of responding in kind. In *The Female Dunciad* (1729) she attacked both Pope and Swift for misogyny, and in 1741 she reacted to Samuel Richardson's successful novel of female virtue rewarded, *Pamela,* by writing an irreverent sequel, *Anti-Pamela, or Feign'd Innocence.* As the 1740s continued, however, Haywood responded to the decorum of the age by creating more orthodox fiction; she even composed a novel quite similar in theme and tone to *Pamela,* entitled *The Virtuous Villager: Or, Virgin's Victory* (1742), with apparently no satirical aim.

In 1744 she initiated a women's magazine, *The Female Spectator,* which she edited until 1746. In its pages she continued to produce stories of passion and intrigue, but her transgressive heroines increasingly saw the error their ways–and should they not, Haywood as editor would deliver the moral message. Late in her life she was briefly imprisoned for authoring a controversial political pamphlet, *A Letter from H——G—, Esq.* (1750), but after the 1740s she was associated more with feminine decorum than with sexual or political scandal. As a later analyst of the period, Clara Reeve, suggested in *The Progress of Romance,* Haywood is one of the few early women writers to have had "the singular good fortune to recover a lost reputation."

⊰ *from* The Female Spectator ⊱

Vol. 1, No. 1, April 1744

CHAPTER 1

The Editor introduces herself . . . and her 'Associates'

It is very much, by the Choice we make of Subjects for our Entertainment that the refin'd Taste distinguishes itself from the vulgar and more gross: Reading is universally allowed to be one of the most improving, as well as agreeable Amusements; but then to render it so, one should, among the Number of Books which are perpetually issuing from the Press, endeavor to single out such as promise to be most conducive to those Ends. In order to be as little deceiv'd as possible, I, for my own part, love to get as well acquainted as I can with an Author, before I run the risque of losing my Time in perusing his Work; and as I doubt not but most People are of this way of thinking, I shall, in imitation of my learned Brother of ever precious Memory, give some Account of what I am, and those concerned with me in this Undertaking; and likewise of the chief Intent of the Lucubrations hereafter communicated, that the Reader, on casting his Eye over the four or five first Pages, may judge how far the Book may or may not be qualified to entertain him, and either accept, or throw it aside as he thinks proper. And here I promise, that in the Pictures I shall give of myself and Associates, I will draw no flattering Lines, assume no Perfection that we are not in reality possessed of, nor attempt to shadow over any Defect with an artificial Gloss.

As a Proof of my Sincerity, I shall, in the first place, assure him, that for my own Part I never was a Beauty, and am now very far from being young, (a Confession he will find few of my Sex ready to make). I shall also acknowledge that I have run through as many Scenes of Vanity and Folly as the greatest Coquet of them all. Dress, Equipage, and Flattery, were the Idols of my Heart. I should have thought that Day lost which did not present me with some new Opportunity of showing myself. My Life, for some Years, was a continued Round of what I then called Pleasure, and my whole Time engrossed by a Hurry of promiscuous Diversions. But whatever Inconveniences such a manner of Conduct has brought upon myself, I have this Consolation, to think that the Public may reap some Benefit from it. The Company I kept was not, indeed, always so well chosen as it ought to have been, for the sake of my own Interest or Reputation; but then it was general, and by Consequence furnished me, not only with the Knowledge of many Occurrences, which otherwise I had been ignorant of, but also enabled me, when the too great Vivacity of my Nature became tempered with Reflection, to see into the secret Springs which gave rise to the Actions I had either heard, or been Witness of—to judge of the various Passions of the human Mind, and distinguish those imperceptible Degrees by which they become Masters of the Heart, and attain the Dominion over Reason. A thousand odd Adventures, which at the Time they happened made slight Impression on me, and seemed to dwell no longer on my Mind than the Wonder they occasioned, now rise fresh to my Remembrance, with this Advantage, that the Mystery I then, for want of Attention, imagined they contained, is entirely vanished, and I find it easy to account for the Cause by the Consequence.

With this Experience, added to a Genius tolerably extensive, and an Education more liberal than is ordinarily allowed to Persons of my Sex, I flatter'd myself that it might be in my Power to be in some measure both useful and entertaining to the Public; and this Thought was so soothing to those Remains of Vanity, not yet wholly extinguished in me, that I resolved to pursue it, and immediately began to consider by what Method I should be most likely to succeed. To confine myself to any one Subject, I knew could please but one kind of Taste, and my Ambition was to be as universally read as possible. From my Observations of human Nature, I found that Curiosity had, more or less, a Share in every Breast; and my Business, therefore, was to hit this reigning Humor in such a Manner, as that the Gratification it should receive from being made acquainted with other People's Affairs, should at the same Time teach every one to regulate their own.

Having agreed within myself on this important Point, I commenc'd Author, by setting down many Things which, being pleasing to myself, I imagin'd would be so to others; but on examining them the next Day, I found an infinite Deficiency both in Matter and Stile, and that there was an absolute Necessity for me to call in to my Assistance such of my Acquaintance as were qualified for that Purpose. The *first* that occurred to me, I shall distinguish by the Name of *Mira*, a Lady descended from a Family to which Wit seems hereditary, married to a Gentleman every way worthy of so excellent a Wife, and with whom she lives in so perfect a Harmony, that having nothing to ruffle the Composure of her Soul, or disturb those sparkling Ideas she received from Nature and Education, left me no Room to doubt if what she favor'd me with would be acceptable to the Public. The *next* is a Widow of Quality, who not having buried her Vivacity in the Tomb of her Lord, continues to make one in all the modish Diversions of the Times, so far, I mean, as she finds them consistent with Innocence and Honor; and as she is far from having the least Austerity in her Behavior, nor is rigid to the Failings she is wholly free from herself, those of her Acquaintance, who had been less circumspect, scruple not to make her the Confidante of Secrets they conceal from all the World beside. The *third* is the Daughter of a wealthy Merchant, charming as an Angel, but endued with so many Accomplishments, that to those who know her truly, her Beauty is the least distinguished Part of her. This fine young Creature I shall call *Euphrosine*,[1] since she has all the Cheerfulness and Sweetness ascribed to that Goddess.

These three approved my Design, assur'd me of all the Help they could afford, and soon gave a Proof of it in bringing their several Essays; but as the Reader, provided the Entertainment be agreeable, will not be interested from which Quarter it comes, whatever Productions I shall be favor'd with from these Ladies, or any others I may hereafter correspond with, will be exhibited under the general Title of *The Female Spectator*, and how many Contributors soever there may happen to be to the Work, they are to be considered only as several Members of one Body, of which I am the Mouth.

It is also highly proper I should acquaint the Town, that to secure an eternal Fund of Intelligence, Spies are placed not only in all the Places of Resort in and about this great Metropolis, but at Bath, Tunbridge, and the Spaw, and Means found out to extend my Speculations even as far as France, Rome, Germany, and other foreign Parts, so that nothing curious or worthy of Remark can escape me; and this I look upon to be a more effectual Way of penetrating into the Mysteries of the Alcove, the Cabinet, or Field, than if I had the Power of Invisibility, or could with a Wish transport myself wherever I pleased, since with the Aid of those supernatural Gifts, I could still be in no more than one Place at a Time; whereas now, by tumbling over a few Papers from my Emissaries, I have all the Secrets of Europe, at least such of them as are proper for my Purpose, laid open at one View.

I would, by no means, however, have what I say be construed into a Design of gratifying a vicious Propensity of propagating Scandal: Whoever sits down to read me with this View, will find themselves mistaken; for tho' I shall bring real Facts on the Stage, I shall conceal the Actors Names under such as will be conformable to their Characters; my Intention being only to expose the Vice, not the Person. Nor shall I confine myself to modern Transactions—Whenever I find any Example among the Anti-ents which may serve to illustrate the Topic I shall happen to be upon, I shall make no scruple to insert it. An Instance of shining Virtue in any Age, can never be too often proposed as a Pattern, nor the Fatality of Misconduct too much impress'd on the Minds of our Youth of both Sexes; and as the sole Aim of the following Pages is to reform the Faulty, and give an innocent Amusement to those who are not so, all possible Care will be taken to avoid every thing that might serve as Food for the Venom of Malice and Ill-nature. Whoever, therefore, shall pretend to fix on any particular Person the Blame of Actions they may happen to find recorded here, or make what they call a Key to these Lucubrations, must expect to see themselves treated in the next Publication with all the Severity so unfair a Proceeding merits.

And now having said as much as I think needful of this Undertaking, I shall, without being either too greatly confident, or too anxious for the Success, submit it to the Public Censure.

---

1. One of the three Graces from Greek mythology.

CHAPTER 7

The Reclamation of Dorimon

Dorimon and Alithea were married almost too young to know the Duties of the State they enter'd into; yet both being extremely good-natur'd, a mutual Desire of obliging each other appear'd in all their Words and Actions; and tho' this Complaisance was not owing to those tender Emotions which attract the Heart with a resistless Force, and bear the Name of Love, yet were the Effects so much the same as not to be distinguish'd.

The first Year of their Marriage made them the happy Parents of an Heir to a plentiful Estate. The Kindred on both Sides seem'd to vye with each other, which should give the greatest Testimonies of their Satisfaction. All their Friends congratulated this Addition to their Felicity; and for a Time, the most perfect Joy and Tranquility reigned, not only in their own Family, but in all those who had any Relation to them.

Alithea after she became a Mother began to feel, by Degrees, a greater Warmth of Affection for him that made her so; and having no Reason to doubt an equal Regard from him thought herself as happy as Woman could be, and that there were Joys in Love greater than before she had any Notion of.

Quite otherwise was it with Dorimon; the Time was now indeed arrived, which taught him what it was to love. The Hopes, the Fears, the Anxieties, the Impatiences, all the unnumber'd Cares which are attributed to that Passion, now took Possession of his Heart. He pin'd, he languish'd, but alas, not for his Wife. He had unhappily seen a young Lady at the Opera, who had Charms for him, which he had never found in the whole Sex before. As he happen'd to sit in the same Box with her, he had an Opportunity of speaking to her, which tho' only on ordinary Subjects, every Answer she made, to what he said, seem'd to him to discover a Profusion of Wit, and gave him the most longing Desire to be acquainted with her.

Fortune, favourable to his Wishes, presented her to him the next Day in the Park, accompany'd with a Lady and a Gentleman, the latter of whom he had a slight Knowledge of; he only bow'd to them the first Turn, but gather'd Courage to join Company with them on the second; and perceiving that it was to the other Lady that the Gentleman seem'd most attach'd, he was at the greater Liberty to say a thousand gallant Things to her, who was the Object of his new Flame.

Melissa, for so I shall call her, was vain, gay, and in every respect one of those modish Ladies, of which a former *Spectator* has given a Description: she receiv'd the Compliments he made her in a Manner, that made him see his Conversation was not disagreeable to her; and some mention happening to be made of a Masquerade that Night, she told him, as if by Chance, that she was to be there, and that her fair Companion and herself were going to bespeak Habits at a Warehouse she mention'd, as soon as they left the Park.

The Hint was not lost upon him, and thinking that it would seem too presuming to ask leave to wait on her at her House, the first Time of being in her Company, he resolved to make it his Business to find out, if possible, what Habit she made choice of, to go to the Masquerade, where the Freedom of the Place might give him a better Opportunity of testifying the Desire he had of improving an Acquaintance with her.

Accordingly, after their quitting him at the Park-Gate, he followed at a Distance the two Chairs that waited for them, and placing himself near enough to the Habit-Shop, to see whoever went in or out, found his Adorable had not deceiv'd him in what she said. The Ladies having dispatch'd what they came about, went again into their Chairs. They were no sooner gone than he went into the Shop, and on a pretence of ordering a *Domine* for himself, fell into Discourse with the Woman behind the Counter, whom he easily prevail'd on to let him know, not only what Habits the Ladies who had just left her had bespoke, but also of what Condition and Character they were. She inform'd him that Melissa had a large Fortune, and her Parents being dead was under the Care of Guardians, whom, notwithstanding, she did not live with, but had Lodgings to herself near Grosvenor Square. That she kept a great deal of Company, was what the World call'd a Coquet, but had hitherto preserv'd her Reputation. That the Lady who was with her was the Daughter of a Country Gentleman somewhat related to her, how nearly she could not tell, but heard she was on the point of Marriage with a Person of Rank.

Dorimon was transported at this Intelligence, as it seem'd to promise him an easy Access to her Acquaintance, and the Privilege of visiting her; which, probably, in these early Days of his Passion was all he aim'd at. Or if he thought on any thing further, the Difficulties in accomplishing his Desire seem'd less formidable than they would have done, had she been of a more reserv'd Temper, were already married, or under the Direction of Parents.

Never did Time appear so tedious as that before the Hour of going to the Masquerade. His Impatience brought him there the very first, and by that means he had the Opportunity of observing every one as they came in. Melissa, he was told, would be in the Habit of a Nun; and tho' there were several drest in that manner, yet he distinguish'd her from the others by her Tallness the Moment she appear'd.

He accosted her with the usual Phrases of—*Do you know me?*—and—*I know you!*—but was not long before he made her sensible of his more particular Attachment; and told her, that having lost his Heart that Morning in the Park, it now directed him how to discover the lovely Thief, tho' disguised, and amidst so numerous an Assembly.

This, and some other Expressions of the same nature, convincing her that he was the Gentleman who had made her so many Compliments in the Morning, immediately flatter'd her Vanity with a new Conquest; and as she found him a Man of Wit, and doubted not of his being a Person of Condition by his Appearance, resolv'd to omit nothing that might secure him. Accordingly, as all true Coquets do at first, she affected to listen with a pleas'd Attention to the Assurances he gave her of his Passion, and frequently let fall some Words, as if they escaped her inadvertently, that might make him think she would not be ungrateful if he persisted in giving her Testimonies of a constant Flame. Ladies of her Character have always this Maxim at heart,

> Kindness has resistless Charms,
> All Things else but faintly warms:
> It gilds the Lover's servile Chain,
> And makes the Slave grow pleas'd and vain.[2]

But the Misfortune is, that such a Behaviour for the most part proves fatal to themselves in the End. They toy so long with the Darts of Love, that their own Bosoms are frequently pierced when they little think of it; and the deluding She, who has made Numbers languish, becomes a Prey perhaps to one who least merits or regards the Victory he gains.

Dorimon, however, was transported to find the Offer he had made of his Heart so well received, and made so good Use of the Opportunity she gave him of entertaining

---

2. These lines are taken, not quite accurately, from "Give Me Leave to Rail at You" by John Wilmot, second Earl of Rochester (1647–1680), a poet known for his licentiousness.

her the whole Time of the Masquerade, that he obtained her Permission to attend her home, and as it was then too late for them to continue their Conversation, to visit her the next Day in the Afternoon.

This quite established an Acquaintance between them; he went every Day to see her; she admitted him when all other Company were denied; he had always the Preference of waiting on her to the Park, the Opera, the Play, and, in fine, wherever she went; and when some of her more prudent Friends took notice of their being so frequently together, and had heard that he was a married Man, she only laughed at their Remonstrances, and replied, that as she had no farther Concern with him than merely to gallant her about to public Places, she had no Business to enquire into his private Circumstances;—that if he were married, his *Wife* only had to do with it; and as for her own Part, she thought him a very pretty Fellow, and quite fit for the Use she had made of him; adding, that if she were Mistress of his Heart, it was indifferent to her who had his *Hand*.

Melissa, 'tis probable, had indeed no other View in entertaining Dorimon, and receiving his Addresses, than the same she had in treating with a like Behaviour Numbers before him, merely for the sake of hearing herself praised, and giving Pain, as she imagined, to others of her Admirers, who were less frequently admitted.

But how dangerous a Thing it is to have too great an Intimacy with a Person of a different Sex, many of a greater Share of Discretion than Melissa have experienced.— This unwary Lady, in meditating new Arts, the more to captivate her Lover, became ensnared herself; in fine, she liked, she loved as much as any Woman of that airy and volatile Disposition can be said to love. What she felt for him, however, had all the Effects which the most serious Passion in one of a different Temper could have produced, and Dorimon had as ample a Gratification of his Desires, as his most sanguine Hopes could have presented him an Idea of.

Alithea all this while lost Ground in his Affection; she every Day seemed less fair, and whatever she said or did had in it a kind of Aukwardness, which before he was far from discovering in her; every thing was now displeasing in her; if endearing, her Fondness was childish and silly; and if she was more reserved, sullen and ill-natured. One Moment he was out of Humour if she spoke, the next offended at her Silence. He was continually seeking some Pretence to find Fault with the most justifiable Conduct that ever was, and even vexed that he had nothing in reality to condemn. Unhappy, but certain Consequence of a new Attachment, which not content with the Injury it does, also adds to it Ill-Humour, and a Wish of some Occasion to hate the Object we no longer love.

The poor Lady could not but observe this Alteration in his Behaviour; but as she was far from guessing the real Motive, imputed it to some unlucky Turn in his Affairs, tho' of what Nature she could not imagine, he having a large Fortune settled on him at their Marriage, beside the Reversion of what his Father should die possessed of, and was in the Power of nobody to deprive him of.

On the first notice she took of his Discontent, she asked him, as became a tender and affectionate Wife, if any thing had happen'd either from her Family or his own to give him Subject of Complaint? But he answering with Peevishness, she desisted from any further Enquiry, judging, as he did not think proper to trust her with the Secret, it would but add to his Disquiets to testify a Desire of knowing it.

For more than a whole Year did she combat his Ill-Humour with Sweetness, Gentleness, and the most obliging Behaviour, and tho' she began to think herself lost to his Affection, bore even that afflicting Reflection with the most submissive Patience, still flattering herself that, if it were even so, he would one Day consider she deserved not her ill Fortune.

Jealousy was, however, a Passion she was wholly unacquainted with. Many very beautiful Ladies often visited at her House, and she had never seen the least Propensity in him to Gallantry with any of them; he rather behaved to them with a greater Reserve than was consistent with the good Breeding and Complaisance which might have been expected from a Man of his Years. So that she imagined rather a Disgust to the whole Sex was growing on him, than any particular Attachment to one.

Thus did her Innocence and unsuspecting Nature deceive her, till one Day a Female Friend, more busy than wise, open'd her Eyes to the true Reason of her Husband's Coldness.

This Lady, by means of a Servant Maid she had lately entertained, and who had lived with Melissa long enough to know the whole Secret of her Amour with Dorimon, and was dismissed on some Dislike, was made acquainted with all that passed between that guilty Pair. She learned from this unfaithful Creature, that Melissa had been made a Mother by Dorimon, and that the Child was disposed of to a Person, who, for a Present of fifty Guineas, had taken the sole Charge of it, so as it should never appear to the Disgrace of the unnatural Parents. Not the most minute Circumstance relating to the Affair but was betrayed by this Wretch, partly in Revenge for her having been discarded by her former Lady, and partly to gain Favour with the present, who, she easily perecived, loved to hear News of this kind.

Alithea would fain have treated this Account as fabulous, and have perswaded her Friend to regard it only as a Piece of Malice in the Reporter; but the other was positive in her Assertion, and told her, that it was utterly impossible for such a Creature to dress up a Fiction with so many Particulars, and such a Shew of Truth; *besides*, added she, *if there were nothing in it, we might easily disprove all she has said, by going to the Woman who has the Care of the Child, and whose Name and Place of Abode she has told me.*

Compelled at last to believe her Misfortune but too certain, a-while she gave a loose to Tears, and to Complainings, but her good Sense, as well as good Nature, soon got the better of this Burst of Passion; and when her Friend asked her in what Manner she would proceed in order to do herself Justice? *What can I do,* reply'd this charming Wife, *but endeavour to render myself more obliging, more pleasant, more engaging if possible than my Rival, and make Dorimon see, he can find nothing in Melissa that is wanting in me.*

O Heaven! cried the Lady, *can you forgive such an Injury?* Yes, resumed Alithea, stifling her Sighs as much as she was able, *Love is an involuntary Passion. And will you not upbraid him with his Ingratitude, and expose Melissa?* said she. *Neither the One, nor the other,* answered Alithea coldly; *either of these Methods would indeed render me unworthy of a Return of his Affection; and I conjure and beseech you,* added she, *by all the Friendship I flatter myself you have for me, that you will never make the least Mention of this Affair to any one in the World.*

This Moderation was astonishing to the Person who was Witness of it; however, she promised to be entirely silent, since it was requested with so much Earnestness. But how little she was capable of keeping her Word, most of her Acquaintance could testify, to whom not only the Fault of Dorimon, but the Manner in which his Wife received the Account of it, was not three Days a Secret.   *1744*

⊶ ⸙⸙ ⊷

Harriet Jacobs
1813?–1897

Born and raised a slave, Harriet Jacobs is famous today for her harrowing autobiographical account of sexual and racist exploitation at the hands of her master, a problem she acknowledges as both individual and systemic. *Incidents in the Life of a Slave Girl, Written by Herself* (1861) chronicles the physical, psychological, and verbal abuse encountered by the pseudonymous Linda Brent, whose owner, Dr. William Flint, "tried his utmost to corrupt the pure principles my grandmother had instilled." The actual Flint was Dr. James Norcom, a prominent physician in Edenton, North Carolina, who began sexually harassing Jacobs when she was fifteen. After years of avoiding his advances, Jacobs went into hiding in an attic in the South; eventually she escaped to the North and in 1842 became involved in New York's antislavery movement as well as in efforts to promote women's rights. She wrote her slave narrative between 1853 and 1858, composing at night after caring for the small children of her employer, the writer Nathaniel Parker Willis, during the day. Initially she published parts of her narrative anonymously in newspapers. The 1861 publication of *Incidents* was sponsored by the white abolitionists Amy Post and Lydia Marie Child; Child edited the book and wrote an introduction confirming that its language and ideas were Jacobs's own. According to biographer Jean Fagan Yellin, Jacobs worked for the Philadelphia Quakers from 1863 to 1864 distributing clothes to Civil War refugees, organizing medical care, and teaching. After the Civil War she assisted newly freed black citizens in Savannah on behalf of the New York Quakers.

Admitting that her "descriptions fall short of the facts," the speaker of Jacobs's slave narrative, Linda Brent, declares that only her ardent desire to bring an end to slavery has led her to speak at all. Certainly Jacobs knew that many white men and women viewed black women as sexually promiscuous; to present the details of her master's advances could well reinforce this pernicious stereotype, even in sympathetic readers of the time. Adopting a pseudonym afforded Jacobs some measure of protection from reprisal, as did her choice to present a metaphorical rather than a literal account of her repeated harassment. The primary metaphor that Jacobs chooses to represent this abuse is physical, linguistic, and metonymic: a demon whispers in her ear "stinging, scathing words; words that scathed ear and brain like fire." This metaphor of the violated ear appears in Brent's initial description of her master's advances: "My master began to whisper foul words in my ear. Young as I was, I could not remain ignorant of their import. I tried to treat them with indifference or contempt." The scholar Hortense Spillers has argued that Jacobs' emphasis on her ears and face in her veiled accounts might represent an unconscious form of psychosexual repression; however, Yellin asserts that Jacobs prevented her master from raping her, although she did experience sexual trauma.

Another sensitive element of Jacobs's autobiography for her white readers in 1861 was its presentation of her affair with a white slave-owner, Mr. Sands (Samuel T. Sawyer). The narrator states clearly that she undertook this relationship to protect herself from her master and assert her sexual agency. If she had to risk becoming pregnant by a white man, she could at least choose which white man. "I knew what I did," Brent proclaims, "and I did it with deliberate calculation." She goes on to write of bearing two children by Sands, but ironically, this liaison further angered her master rather than convincing him to abandon his persecution. To readers who might blame her for becoming sexually involved with Sands, Jacobs offers this emotional appeal: "You never knew what it is to be a slave; to be entirely unprotected by law or custom. . . . You never exhausted your ingenuity in avoiding the snares and eluding the power of a hated tyrant."

Although twelve percent of extant slave narratives were written by women, none are as well known as the narratives by men such as Olaudah Equiano or Frederick Douglass, whose portrayals of the struggle from slavery to freedom have long been viewed as representative of the genre. Yet women's slave narratives can be seen as equally representative in their depiction of slavery's horrors. Jacobs's inspiring narrative portrays women as active agents rather than victims, documenting not only Linda Brent's suffering but also her resistance to slavery and sexual exploitation.

◄ *from* Incidents in the Life of a Slave Girl ►

THE TRIALS OF GIRLHOOD

During the first years of my service in Dr. Flint's family, I was accustomed to share some indulgences with the children of my mistress. Though this seemed to me no more than right, I was grateful for it, and tried to merit the kindness by the faithful discharge of my duties. But I now entered on my fifteenth year—a sad epoch in the life of a slave girl. My master began to whisper foul words in my ear. Young as I was, I could not remain ignorant of their import. I tried to treat them with indifference or contempt. The master's age, my extreme youth, and the fear that his conduct would be reported to my grandmother, made him bear this treatment for many months. He was a crafty man, and resorted to many means to accomplish his purposes. Sometimes he had stormy, terrific ways, that made his victims tremble; sometimes he assumed a gentleness that he thought must surely subdue. Of the two, I preferred his stormy moods, although they left me trembling. He tried his utmost to corrupt the pure principles my grandmother had instilled. He peopled my young mind with unclean images, such as only a vile monster could think of. I turned from him in disgust and hatred. But he was my master. I was compelled to live under the same roof with him—where I saw a man forty years my senior daily violating the most sacred commandments of nature. *He told me I was his property; that I must be subject to his will in all things.* My soul revolted against the mean tyranny. But where could I turn for protection? No matter whether the slave girl be as black as ebony or as fair as her mistress. In either case, there is no shadow of law to protect her from insult, from violence, or even from death; all these are inflicted by fiends who bear the shape of men. The mistress, who ought to protect the helpless victim, has no other feelings towards her but those of jealousy and rage. The degradation, the wrongs, the vices, that grow out of slavery, are more than I can describe. They are greater than you would willingly believe. Surely, if you credited one half the truths that are told you concerning the helpless millions suffering in this cruel bondage, you at the north would not help to tighten the yoke. You surely would refuse to do for the master, on your own soil, the mean and cruel work which trained bloodhounds and the lowest class of whites do for him at the south.

Every where the years bring to all enough of sin and sorrow; but in slavery the very dawn of life is darkened by these shadows. Even the little child, who is accustomed to wait on her mistress and her children, will learn, before she is twelve years old, why it is that her mistress hates such and such a one among the slaves. Perhaps the child's own mother is among those hated ones. She listens to violent outbreaks of jealous passion, and cannot help understanding what is the cause. She will become prematurely knowing in evil things. Soon she will learn to tremble when she hears her master's footfall. She will be compelled to realize that she is no longer a child. If God has bestowed beauty upon her, it will prove her greatest curse. That which commands admiration in the white woman only hastens the degradation of the female slave. I know that some are too much brutalized by slavery to feel the humiliation of their position; but many slaves feel it most acutely, and shrink from the memory of it. I cannot tell how much I suffered in the presence of these wrongs, nor how I am still pained by the retrospect. My master met me at every turn, reminding me that I belonged to him, and swearing by heaven and earth that he would compel me to submit to him. If I went out for a breath of fresh air, after a day of unwearied toil, his footsteps dogged me. If I knelt by my mother's grave, his dark shadow fell on me even there. The light heart which nature had given me became heavy with sad forebodings. The other slaves in my master's house noticed the change. Many of them pitied me; but none dared to ask the cause. They had not need to inquire. They knew too well the guilty practices under that roof; and they were aware that to speak of them was an offense that never went unpunished.

I longed for someone to confide in. I would have given the world to have laid my head on my grandmother's faithful bosom, and told her all my troubles. But Dr. Flint swore he would kill me, if I was not as silent as the grave. Then, although my grandmother was all in all to me, I feared her as well as loved her. I had been accustomed to look up to her with a respect bordering upon awe. I was very young, and felt shamefaced about telling her such impure things, especially as I knew her to be very strict on such subjects. Moreover, she was a woman of high spirit. She was usually very quiet in her demeanor; but if her indignation was once roused, it was not very easily quelled. I had been told that she once chased a white gentleman with a loaded pistol, because he insulted one of her daughters. I dreaded the consequences of a violent outbreak; and both pride and fear kept me silent. But though I did not confide in my grandmother, and even evaded her vigilant watchfulness and inquiry, her presence in the neighborhood was some protection to me. Though she had been a slave, Dr. Flint was afraid of her. He dreaded her scorching rebukes. Moreover, she was known and patronized by many people; and he did not wish to have his villainy made public. It was lucky for me that I did not live on a distant plantation, but in a town not so large that the inhabitants were ignorant of each other's affairs. Bad as are the laws and customs in a slaveholding community, the doctor, as a professional man, deemed it prudent to keep up some outward show of decency.

O, what days and nights of fear and sorrow that man caused me! Reader, it is not to awaken sympathy for myself that I am telling you truthfully what I suffered in slavery. I do it to kindle a flame of compassion in your hearts for my sisters who are still in bondage, suffering as I once suffered.

I once saw two beautiful children playing together. One was a fair white child; the other was her slave, and also her sister. When I saw them embracing each other, and heard their joyous laughter, I turned sadly away from the lovely sight. I foresaw the inevitable blight that would fall on the little slave's heart. I knew how soon her laughter would be changed to sighs. The fair child grew up to be a still fairer woman. From childhood to womanhood her pathway was blooming with flowers, and overarched by a sunny day. Scarcely one day of her life had been clouded when the sun rose on her happy bridal morning.

How had those years dealt with her slave sister, the little playmate of her childhood? She, also, was very beautiful; but the flowers and sunshine of love were not for her. She drank the cup of sin, and shame, and misery, whereof her persecuted race are compelled to drink.

In view of these things, why are ye silent, ye free men and women of the north? Why do your tongues falter in maintenance of the right? Would that I had more ability! But my heart is so full, and my pen is so weak! There are noble men and women who plead for us, striving to help those who cannot help themselves. God bless them!

God give them strength and courage to go on! God bless those, every where, who are laboring to advance the cause of humanity!

THE JEALOUS MISTRESS

I would ten thousand times rather that my children should be the half-starved paupers of Ireland than to be the most pampered among the slaves of America. I would rather drudge out my life on a cotton plantation, to live till the grave opened to give me rest, than to live with an unprincipled master and a jealous mistress. The felon's home in a penitentiary is preferable. He may repent, and turn from the error of his ways, and so find peace; but it is not so with a favorite slave. She is not allowed to have any pride of character. It is deemed a crime in her to wish to be virtuous.

Mrs. Flint possessed the key to her husband's character before I was born. She might have used this knowledge to counsel and to screen the young and innocent among her slaves; but for them she had no sympathy. They were the objects of her constant suspicion and malevolence. She watched her husband with unceasing vigilance; but he was well practised in means to evade it. What he could not find opportunity to say in words he manifested in signs. He invented more than were ever thought of in a deaf and dumb asylum. I let them pass, as if I did not understand what he meant; and many were the curses and threats bestowed on me for my stupidity. One day he caught me teaching myself to write. He frowned, as if he was not well pleased; but I suppose he came to the conclusion that such an accomplishment might help to advance his favorite scheme. Before long, notes were often slipped into my hand. I would return them, saying, "I can't read them sir." "Can't you?" he replied; "then I must read them to you." He always finished the reading by asking, "Do you understand?" Sometimes he would complain of the heat of the tea room, and order his supper to be placed on a small table in the piazza. He would seat himself there with a well-satisfied smile, and tell me to stand by and brush away the flies. He would eat very slowly, pausing between the mouthfuls. These intervals were employed in describing the happiness I was so foolishly throwing away, and in threatening me with the penalty that finally awaited my stubborn disobedience. He boasted much of the forbearance he had exercised towards me, and reminded me that there was a limit to his patience. When I succeeded in avoiding opportunities for him to talk to me at home, I was ordered to come to his office, to do some errand. When there, I was obliged to stand and listen to such language as he saw fit to address to me. Sometimes I so openly expressed my contempt for him that he would become violently enraged, and I wondered why he did not strike me. Circumstanced as he was, he probably thought it was better policy to be forbearing. But the state of things grew worse and worse daily. In desperation I told him that I must and would apply to grandmother for protection. He threatened me with death, and worse than death, if I made any complaint to her. Strange to say, I did not despair, I was naturally of a buoyant disposition, and always I had a hope of somehow getting out of his clutches. Like many a poor simple, slave before me, I trusted that some threads of joy would yet be woven into my dark destiny.

I had entered my sixteenth year, and every day it became more apparent that my presence was intolerable to Mrs. Flint. Angry words frequently passed between her and her husband. He had never punished me himself, and he would not allow any body else to punish me. In that respect, she was never satisfied; but, in her angry moods, no terms were too vile for her to bestow upon me. Yet I, whom she detested so bitterly, had far more pity for her than he had, whose duty it was to make her life happy. I never wronged her, or wished to wrong her; and one word of kindness from her would have brought me to her feet.

After repeated quarrels between the doctor and his wife, he announced his intention to take his youngest daughter, then four years old, to sleep in his apartment. It was necessary that a servant should sleep in the same room, to be on hand if the child stirred. I was selected for that office, and informed for what purpose that arrangement had been made. By managing to keep within sight of people, as much as possible, during the day time, I had hitherto succeeded in eluding my master, though a razor was often held to my throat to force me to change this line of policy. At night I slept by the side of my great aunt, where I felt safe. He was too prudent to come into her room. She was an old woman, and had been in the family many years. Moreover, as a married man, and a professional man, he deemed it necessary to save appearances in some degree. But he resolved to remove the obstacle in the way of his scheme; and he thought he had planned it so that he should evade suspicion. He was well aware how much I prized my refuge by the side of my old aunt, and he determined to dispossess me of it. The first night the doctor had the little child in his room alone. The next morning, I was ordered to take my station as nurse the following night. A kind Providence interposed in my favor. During the day Mrs. Flint heard of this new arrangement, and a storm followed. I rejoiced to hear it rage.

After a while my mistress sent for me to come to her room. Her first question was, "Did you know you were to sleep in the doctor's room?"

"Yes, ma'am."

"Who told you?"

"My master."

"Will you answer truly all the questions I ask?"

"Yes, ma'am."

"Tell me, then, as you hope to be forgiven, are you innocent of what I have accused you?"

"I am."

She handed me a Bible, and said, "Lay your hand on your heart, kiss this holy book, and swear before God that you tell me the truth."

I took the oath she required, and I did it with a clear conscience.

"You have taken God's holy word to testify your innocence," said she. "If you have deceived me, beware! Now take this stool, sit down, look me directly in the face, and tell me all that has passed between your master and you."

I did as she ordered. As I went on with my account her color changed frequently, she wept, and sometimes groaned. She spoke in tones so sad, that I was touched by her grief. The tears came to my eyes; but I was soon convinced that her emotions arose from anger and wounded pride. She felt that her marriage-vows were desecrated, her dignity insulted; but she had no compassion for the poor victim of her husband's perfidy. She pitied herself as a martyr; but she was incapable of feeling for the condition of shame and misery in which her unfortunate, helpless slave was placed.

Yet perhaps she had some touch of feeling for me; for when the conference was ended, she spoke kindly, and promised to protect me. I should have been much comforted by this assurance if I could have had confidence in it; but my experiences in slavery had filled me with distrust. She was not a very refined woman, and had not much control over her passions. I was an object of jealousy, and, consequently, of her hatred: and I knew I could not expect kindness or confidence from her under the circumstances in which I was placed. I could not blame her. Slaveholders' wives feel as other women would under similar circumstances. The fire of her temper kindled from small sparks, and now the flame became so intense that the doctor was obliged to give up his intended arrangement.

I knew I had ignited the torch, and I expected to suffer for it afterwards; but I felt too thankful to my mistress for the timely aid she rendered me to care much about that. She now took me to sleep in a room adjoining her own. There I was an object of her especial care, though not of her especial comfort, for she spent many a sleepless night to watch over me. Sometimes I woke up, and found her bending over me. At other times she whispered in my ear, as though it was her husband who was speaking to me, and listened to hear what I would answer. If she startled me, on such occasions, she would glide stealthily away; and the next morning she would tell me I had been talking in my sleep, and ask who I was talking to. At last, I began to be fearful for my life. It had been often threatened; and you can imagine, better than I can describe, what an unpleasant sensation it must produce to wake up in the dead of night and find a jealous woman bending over you. Terrible as this experience was, I had fears that it would give place to one more terrible.

My mistress grew weary of her vigils; they did not prove satisfactory. She changed her tactics. She now tried the trick of accusing my master of crime, in my presence, and gave my name as the author of the accusation. To my utter astonishment, he replied, "I don't believe it: but if she did acknowledge it, you tortured her into exposing me." Tortured into exposing him! Truly, Satan had no difficulty in distinguishing the color of his soul! I understood his object in making this false representation. It was to show me that I gained nothing by seeking the protection of my mistress; that the power was still all in his own hands. I pitied Mrs. Flint. She was a second wife, many years the junior of her husband; and the hoary-headed miscreant was enough to try the patience of a wiser and better woman. She was completely foiled, and knew not how to proceed. She would gladly have had me flogged for my supposed false oath; but, as I have already stated, the doctor never allowed any one to whip me. The old sinner was politic. The application of the lash might had led to remarks that would have exposed him in the eyes of his children and grandchildren. How often did I rejoice that I lived in a town where all the inhabitants knew each other! If I had been on a remote plantation, or lost among the multitude of a crowded city, I should not be a living woman at this day.

The secrets of slavery are concealed like those of the Inquisition. My master was, to my knowledge, the father of eleven slaves. But did the mothers dare to tell who was the father of their children? Did the other slaves dare to allude to it, except in whispers among themselves? No, indeed! They knew too well the terrible consequences.

My grandmother could not avoid seeing things which excited her suspicions. She was uneasy about me, and tried various ways to buy me: but the neverchanging answer was always repeated: "Linda does not belong to *me*. She is my daughter's property, and I have no legal right to sell her." The conscientious man! He was too scrupulous to *sell* me; but he had no scruples whatever about committing a much greater wrong against the helpless young girl placed under his guardianship, as his daughter's property. Sometimes my persecutor would ask me whether I would like to be sold. I told him I would rather be sold to any body than to lead such a life as I did. On such occasions he would assume the air of a very injured individual, and reproach me for my ingratitude. "Did I not take you into the house, and make you the companion of my own children?" he would say. "Have I ever treated you like a negro? I have never allowed you to be punished, not even to please your mistress. And this is the recompense I get, you ungrateful girl!" I answered that he had reasons of his own for screening me from punishment, and that the course he pursued made my mistress hate me and persecute me. If I wept, he would say, "Poor child! Don't cry! don't cry! I will make peace for you with your mistress. Only let me arrange matters in my own way. Poor, foolish girl! you don't know what is for your own good. I would cherish you. I would make a lady of you. Now go, and think of all I have promised you."

I did think of it.

Reader, I draw no imaginary pictures of southern homes. I am telling you the plain truth. Yet when victims make their escape from this wild beast of Slavery, northerners consent to act the part of bloodhounds, and hunt the poor fugitive back into his den, "full of dead men's bones, and all uncleanness." Nay, more, they are not only willing, but proud, to give their daughters in marriage to slaveholders. The poor girls have romantic notions of a sunny clime, and of the flowering vines that all the year round shade a happy home. To what disappointments are they destined! The young wife soon learns that the husband in whose hands she has placed her happiness pays no regard to his marriage vows. Children of every shade of complexion play with her own fair babes, and too well she knows that they are born unto him of his own household. Jealousy and hatred enter the flowery home, and it is ravaged of its loveliness.

Southern women often marry a man knowing that he is the father of many little slaves. They do not trouble themselves about it. They regard such children as property, as marketable as the pigs on the plantation; and it is seldom that they do not make them aware of this by passing them into the slavetrader's hands as soon as possible, and thus getting them out of their sight. I am glad to say there are some honorable exceptions.

I have myself known two southern wives who exhorted their husbands to free those slaves towards whom they stood in a "parental relation;" and their request was granted. These husbands blushed before the superior nobleness of their wives' natures. Though they had only counselled them to do that which it was their duty to do, it commanded their respect, and rendered their conduct more exemplary. Concealment was at an end, and confidence took the place of distrust.

Though this bad institution deadens the moral sense, even in white women, to a fearful extent, it is not altogether extinct. I have heard southern ladies say of Mr. Such a one, "He not only thinks it no disgrace to be the father of those little niggers, but he is not ashamed to call himself their master. I declare, such things ought not to be tolerated in any decent society!"   *1861*

+·+ ⩑⧫⩒ +·+

Christina Rossetti
1830–1894

Known prior to the 1970s as a devotional poet, Christina Rossetti had been rediscovered by feminist critics as a major nineteenth-century writer who reveals much about the sexual repression and expression of her gender and era. Her subversive narrative poem, *Goblin Market* (1862), tells the tantalizing tale of two young sisters, one of whom eats forbidden fruit and must be redeemed by the other. Her Petrarchan sonnet sequence, *Monna Innominata* (1881), explores from a woman's perspective the idealization of the male beloved and the disappointments of love. Variously described as a religious zealot, a secular nun, an ardent heterosexual lover, a

repressed lesbian, or a female Gothicist, Rossetti offers a compelling glimpse into the erotic imaginary of the Victorian period.

Born into a creative Italian immigrant family, Rossetti was the youngest of four children and the most rebellious growing up. She learned politics from her father, Gabriele Rossetti, an exiled radical politician from Naples; religious zeal from her mother, Frances Polidori; and literary art from and with her brothers—William Michael, a critic, and Dante Gabriel, a painter and a poet. As a young woman she read extensively and engaged in intellectual dialogues with her brothers, her older sister Maria, and an array of Italian expatriates who visited their home. After briefly attempting a career as a governess, she left her position to devote herself to writing. In 1847 her grandfather, Gaetano Polidori, a teacher of Italian, published her first poems in his own printing press. Several later poems appeared under a pseudonym in *Germ*, a periodical published by the Pre-Raphaelite Brotherhood, a group of aspiring male artists to which her brothers belonged. The Pre-Raphaelite Movement emphasized the aesthetic ideals of clarity, simplicity, and close detail, ideals embraced by Rossetti; she was also influenced by Elizabethan sonnets and by George Herbert's religious verse. At one time she was engaged to James Collinson, a Pre-Raphaelite, but broke her engagement when he became a Roman Catholic. A striking woman, Rossetti often modeled for Dante Gabriel and his associates. According to her brother William, she fell in love during the 1860s with Charles Bagot Cayley, whose proposal of marriage she nonetheless rejected. At forty-one she was diagnosed as having Bright's disease. Although never a total recluse, she spent much of the rest of her life writing, studying, and volunteering as an aide at the St. Mary Magdalene Home for Fallen Women in London.

After her *Verses* appeared when she was only seventeen, Rossetti waited many years before publishing *Goblin Market* (1862), *The Prince's Progress, and Other Poems* (1866), and *A Pageant, and Other Poems* (1881). *Annus Domini* (1874) is her best-known volume of religious prose, while her fiction includes *Commonplace and Other Short Stories* (1870) and *Maude* (1897, published posthumously). Three later works blend prose and poetry: *Called to be Saint* (1881), *Time Flies* (1885), and *The Face of the Deep* (1892). *The Complete Poems of Christina Rossetti*, edited in three volumes in 1980 by R. W. Crump, is considered the definitive edition of her poetry.

Although the poems of *Monna Innominata* honor Dante's idealization of Beatrice and Petrarch's love of Laura, Rossetti also pays homage to the ladies of earlier troubadours, those unnamed women often sung by men but rarely given their own voice. She considers in these sonnets the possibilities "had such a lady spoken for herself." Rossetti's most prominent theme is renunciation. Melancholic and alone, her speaker alternately mourns the loss of her beloved and blesses him in his absence.

⊰ Monna Innominata ⊱

A Sonnet of Sonnets

Beatrice, immortalized by "altissimo poeta . . . cotanto amante"; Laura, celebrated by a great tho' an inferior bard—[1]have alike paid the exceptional penalty of exceptional honour, and have come down to us resplendent with charms, but (at least, to my apprehension) scant of attractiveness.

These heroines of world-wide fame were preceded by a bevy of unnamed ladies "donne innominate" sung by a school of less conspicuous poets; and in that land and that period which gave simultaneous birth to Catholics, to Albigenses, and to

---

1. Beatrice is an idealized female character in the Italian poet Dante's *Divine Comedy* (1314 ff.); Laura is the object of male desire in the courtly love poetry of Petrarch (1304–74).

Troubadours,[2] one can imagine many a lady as sharing her lover's poetic aptitude, while the barrier between them might be one held sacred by both, yet not such as to render mutual love incompatible with mutual honour.

Had such a lady spoken for herself, the portrait left us might have appeared more tender, if less dignified, than any drawn even by a devoted friend. Or had the Great Poetess of our own day and nation only been unhappy instead of happy, her circumstances would have invited her to bequeath to us, in lieu of the "Portuguese Sonnets,"[3] an inimitable "donna innominata" drawn not from fancy but from feeling, and worthy to occupy a niche beside Beatrice and Laura.

1

Come back to me, who wait and watch for you:—
   Or come not yet, for it is over then,
   And long it is before you come again.
So far between my pleasures are and few.
5 While, when you come not, what I do I do
   Thinking, "Now when he comes," my sweetest "when:"
   For one man is my world of all the men
This wide world holds; O love, my world is you.
Howbeit, to meet you grows almost a pang
10   Because the pang of parting comes so soon;
   My hope hangs waning, waxing, like a moon
    Between the heavenly days on which we meet:
Ah me, but where are now the songs I sang
   When life was sweet because you called them sweet?

2

I wish I could remember, that first day,
   First hour, first moment of your meeting me,
   If bright or dim the season, it might be
Summer or Winter for aught I can say;
5 So unrecorded did it slip away,
   So blind was I to see and to foresee,
   So dull to mark the budding of my tree
That would not blossom yet for many a May.
If only I could recollect it, such
10   A day of days! I let it come and go
   As traceless as a thaw of bygone snow;
It seemed to mean so little, meant so much:
If only now I could recall that touch,
   First touch of hand in hand—Did one but know!

3

I dream of you to wake: would that I might
   Dream of you and not wake but slumber on;

---

2. Albigenses were members of a sect of Cathars that flourished in Southern France in the twelfth and thirteenth centuries; Troubadours were lyric poets and musicians who wrote courtly poems during the same period.

3. A tribute to the British poet Elizabeth Barrett Browning (1806–61), author of *Sonnets from the Portuguese* (1850).

Nor find with dreams the dear companion gone,
As summer ended Summer birds take flight.
In happy dreams I hold you full in sight,
    I blush again who waking look so wan;
    Brighter than sunniest day that ever shone,
In happy dreams your smile makes day of night.
Thus only in a dream we are at one,
        Thus only in a dream we give and take
            The faith that maketh rich who take or give;
        If thus to sleep is sweeter than to wake,
            To die were surely sweeter than to live,
Tho' there be nothing new beneath the sun.

4

I loved you first: but afterwards your love
    Outsoaring mine, sang such a loftier song
As drowned the friendly cooings of my dove.
    Which owes the other most? my love was long,
    And yours one moment seemed to wax more strong;
I loved and guessed at you, you construed me
And loved me for what might or might not be—
    Nay, weights and measures do us both a wrong.
For verily love knows not "mine" or "thine;"
    With separate "I" and "thou" free love has done,
        For one is both and both are one in love;
Rich love knows nought of "thine that is not mine:"
        Both have the strength and both the length thereof,
        Both of us, of the love which makes us one.

5

O my heart's heart and you who are to me
    More than myself, God be with you,
    Keep you in strong obedience leal and true
To Him whose noble service setteth free,
Give you all good we see or can foresee,
    Make your joys many and your sorrows few,
    Bless you in what you bear and what you do,
Yea, perfect you as He would have you be.
So much for you: but what for me, dear friend?
    To love you without stint and all I can
Today, tomorrow, world without an end;
    To love you much and yet to love you more,
    As Jordan at his flood sweeps either shore;
Since woman is the helpmeet made for man.

6

Trust me, I have not earned your dear rebuke,
    I love, as you would have me, God the most;
    Would lose not Him, but you, must one be lost,

Nor with Lot's wife cast back a faithless look
5   Unready to forego what I forsook:
       This say I, having counted up the cost,
       This, tho' I be the feeblest of God's host,
The sorriest sheep Christ shepherds with His crook.
Yet while I love my God the most, I deem
10   That I can never love you overmuch:
           I love Him more, so let me love you too;
       Yea, as I apprehend it, love is such
I cannot love you if I love not Him,
       I cannot love Him if I love not you.

7

"Love me, for I love you"— and answer me,
       "Love me, for I love you"—so shall we stand
       As happy equals in the flowering land
Of love, that knows not a dividing sea.
5   Love builds the house on rock and not on sand,
       Love laughs what while the winds rave desperately;
And who hath found love's citadel unmanned?
       And who hath held in bonds love's liberty?
My heart's a coward tho' my words are brave—
10   We meet so seldom, yet we surely part
       So often; there's a problem for your art!
           Still I find comfort in his Book, who saith,
Tho' jealously be cruel as the grave,
       And death be strong, yet love is strong as death.

8

"I, if I perish, perish"—Esther spake:
       And bride of life or death she made her fair
       In all the lustre of her perfumed hair
And smiles that kindle longing but to slake.
5   She put on pomp of loveliness, to take
       Her husband thro' his eyes at unaware;
       She spread abroad her beauty for a snare,
Harmless as doves and subtle as a snake.
She trapped him with one mesh of silken hair,
10   She vanquished him by wisdom of her wit,
           And built her people's house that it should stand:—
       If I might take my life so in my hand,
And for my love to Love put up my prayer,
       And for love's sake by Love be granted it!

9

Thinking of you, and all that was, and all
       That might have been and now can never be,
       I feel your honoured excellence, and see

Myself unworthy of the happier call:
For woe is me who walk so apt to fall,
    So apt to shrink afraid, so apt to flee,
    Apt to lie down and die (ah, woe is me!)
Faithless and hopeless turning to the wall.
And yet not hopeless quite nor faithless quite,
Because not loveless; love may toil all night,
    But take at morning; wrestle till the break
        Of day, but then wield power with God and man:—
        So take I heart of grace as best I can,
    Ready to spend and be spent for your sake.

10

Time flies, hope flags, life plies a wearied wing;
    Death following hard on life gains ground apace;
    Faith runs with each and rears an eager face,
Outruns the rest, makes light of everything,
Spurns earth, and still finds breath to pray and sing;
    While love ahead of all uplifts his praise.
    Still asks for grace and still gives thanks for grace,
Content with all day brings and night will bring.
Life wanes; and when love folds his wings above
    Tired hope, and less we feel his conscious pulse,
        Let us go fall asleep, dear friend, in peace:
        A little while, and age and sorrow cease;
    A little while, and life reborn annuls
Loss and decay and death, and all is love.

11

Many in aftertimes will say of you
    "He loved her"—while of me what will they say?
    Not that I loved you more than just in play,
For fashion's sake as idle women do.
Even let them prate; who know not what we knew
    Of love and parting in exceeding pain,
    Of parting hopeless here to meet again,
Hopeless on earth, and heaven is out of view.
But by my heart of love laid bare to you,
    My love that you can make not void nor vain,
Love that foregoes you but to claim anew
        Beyond this passage of the gate of death,
    I charge you at the Judgment make it plain
        My love of you was life and not a breath.

12

If there be any one can take my place
    And make you happy whom I grieve to grieve,
    Think not that I can grudge it, but believe

I do commend you to that nobler grace,
5 That readier wit than mine, that sweeter face;
      Yea, since your riches make me rich, conceive
      I too am crowned, while bridal crowns I weave,
And thread the bridal dance with jocund pace.
For if I did not love you, it might be
10   That I should grudge you some one dear delight;
         But since the heart is yours that was mine own,
      Your pleasure is my pleasure, right my right,
Your honourable freedom makes me free,
         And you companioned I am not alone.

13

If I could trust mine own self with your fate,
      Shall I not rather trust it in God's hand?
      Without Whose Will one lily doth not stand,
Nor sparrow fall at his appointed date;
5   Who numbereth the unnumerable sand,
Who weighs the wind and water with a weight,
To Whom the world is neither small nor great,
      Whose knowledge foreknew every plan we planned.
Searching my heart for all that touches you,
10   I find there are only love and love's goodwill
Helpless to help and impotent to do,
         Of understanding dull, of sight most dim;
         And therefore I commend you back to Him
Whose love your love's capacity can fill.

14

Youth gone, and beauty gone if ever there
      Dwelt beauty in so poor a face as this:
      Youth gone and beatify, what remains of bliss?
I will not bind fresh roses in my hair,
5 To shame a cheek at best but little fair.—
      Leave youth his roses, who can bear a thorn,—
I will not seek for blossoms anywhere,
      Except such common flowers as blow with corn.
Youth gone and beauty gone, what doth remain?
10   The longing of a heart pent up forlorn,
         A silent heart whose silence loves and longs;
         The silence of a heart which sang its songs
      While youth and beauty made a summer morn,
Silence of love that cannot sing again.

                                                      1881

Djuna Barnes
1892–1982

A New Yorker who spent twenty years as an expatriate artist in Paris, Djuna Barnes wrote novels, short stories, plays, poems, and journalistic essays; she published some of her early works under the pseudonym Lydia Steptoe. Her best-known novel, *Nightwood* (1936), focuses on the eroticism and alienation of Robin Vote, a sexually ambiguous woman living in Paris in the 1920s. Barnes is also increasingly well regarded as a journalist whose sketches captured the tumultuous era of "new womanhood" and suffrage. Taken as a whole, Barnes's oeuvre explores female sexuality, both heterosexual and lesbian, the politics of gender, and the ambivalence of exile. Her writing is remarkable for its stylistic experimentation, which helped to define a modernist aesthetic; its sensitive portrayal of "outsider" figures; and its critique of abuses of power in European history and cultural politics.

Barnes was born into a wealthy family in Cornwall-on-Hudson, New York, and educated at home by two influential figures in her life: her paternal grandmother, Zadel Barnes, a journalist and feminist who once led a literary salon at Grosvenor Square, London; and her father, Wald Barnes, an author, a painter, and a musician. Despite their economic privilege, the Barnes family was troubled by infidelity, incest, and violence. Djuna's home life was unconventional: she lived with her mother and siblings under the same roof with her father's mistress and ten of her children, some of whom were adults. Indeed, Barnes would revisit the sexual traumas of her childhood in several later stories and plays. As a teenager she began to write and illustrate poetry, and she went on to study art at the Pratt Institute and the Art Students League, both in New York City. Writing soon replaced art as her primary interest, however, and she began her career as a journalist, eventually working for most of New York's largest newspapers. One of her assignments was to cover the activities of British suffragists, who were undertaking hunger strikes in prison and sometimes dying from infections that resulted from forced feedings. In 1920 Barnes went to Europe to interview James Joyce and Alfred Steiglitz for *McCall's* magazine. She quickly became an important figure in the expatriate community in Paris, socializing with Joyce, T. S. Eliot, and GERTRUDE STEIN; she also had a public and turbulent affair with a sculptor and artist, Thelma Wood. During the next two decades Barnes forged close ties with the lesbian artistic community led by Natalie Barney, whose salons became a Parisian institution. In 1941 Barnes returned to New York and lived in virtual seclusion in Greenwich Village until her death.

The Book of Repulsive Women (1915), her first published work, included wry poetic observations and drawings of various women in the Village. From 1919 to 1920 three of her one-act plays, including *To the Dogs*, were performed at the Provincetown Playhouse, and *The Dove* was produced at Smith College. Her second publication, *A Book* (1923), collected her stories, plays, poems, and drawings to date. In 1928 her best-selling novel *Ryder* was published, and she self-published *Ladies Almanack*, a "slight satiric wigging" that recounted the life and loves of Dame Evangeline Musset, a lesbian expatriate modeled after Natalie Barney. *Nightwood*, published in England in 1936 after being rejected in America, paid elegiac tribute to her Paris community of the 1920s. Barnes' blank-verse play, *The Antiphon* (1958), was performed at the Royal Theater of Stockholm in 1961; its controversial subject matter was the impact of sexual abuse on a troubled family. Like much of Barnes's writing, this play was described as visually exciting but enigmatic. A novel, *Spillway*, and *The Selected Works of Djuna Barnes* appeared in

1962, followed by *Vagaries Malicieux* (1974), *Creatures in an Alphabet* (1982), and *Smoke and Other Early Stories* (1982). Barnes published her epitaph, a poem entitled "Quarry," in *the New Yorker* in 1969, more than ten years prior to her death. *Interviews with Djuna Barnes* appeared posthumously in 1985, and *Poe's Mother: Selected Drawings* by Barnes in 1993. *Nightwood: The Original Version and Related Drafts,* edited by Cheryl Plumb, was published in 1996.

The scholar Shari Benstock has claimed that the primary subject matter of Barnes's writing is an "examination of internalized sexual difference," whether that difference manifests itself in heterosexual or homosexual desire. Certainly Helene Hucksteppe in *To the Dogs* struggles to define herself against enforced heterosexuality, while her would-be seducer, Gheid Storm, seeks confirmation of his own identity through her. Moreover, Barnes was acutely aware that psychologists of the era perceived lesbianism as a profoundly narcissistic "inversion" from "normal" sexuality; thus she set out to create a female-centered discourse, influenced by both Rabelais and Joyce, that could subversively transport lesbian "undercurrents" from margin to center. Archaic language, neologisms, and sexual puns dominate the unorthodox calendar of *Ladies Almanack,* whose overall effect is that of an elaborate masquerade, a carnival of women who revel in desire.

⊰ *from* Ladies Almanack ⊱

Now this be a Tale of as fine a Wench as ever wet Bed, she who was called Evangeline Musset and who was in her Heart one Grand Red Cross for the Pursuance, the Relief and the Distraction, of such Girls as in their Hinder Parts, and their Fore Parts, and in whatsoever Parts did suffer them most, lament Cruelly, be it Itch of Palm, or Quarters most horribly burning, which do oft occur in the Spring of the Year, or at those Times when they do sit upon warm and cozy Material, such as Fur, or thick and Oriental Rugs, (whose very Design it seems, procures for them such a Languishing of the Haunch and Reins as is insupportable) or who sit upon warm Stoves, whence it is known that one such flew up with an "Ah my God! What a World it is for a Girl indeed, be she ever so well abridged and cool of Mind and preserved of Intention, the Instincts are, nevertheless, brought to such a yelping Pitch and so undo her, that she runs hither and thither seeking some Simple or Unguent which shall allay her Pain ! And why is it no Philosopher of whatever Sort, has discovered, amid the nice Herbage of his Garden, one that will content that Part, but that from the day that we were indifferent Matter, to this wherein we are Imperial Personages of the divine human Race, no thing so solaces it as other Parts as inflamed, or with the Consolation every Woman has at her Finger Tips, or at the very Hang of her Tongue?"

For such then was Evangeline Musset created, a Dame of lofty Lineage, who, in the early eighties, had discarded her family Tandem, in which her Mother and Father found Pleasure enough, for the distorted Amusement of riding all smack-of-astride, like any Yeoman going to gather in his Crops; and with much jolting and galloping, was made, hour by hour, less womanly, "Though never," said she, "has the Greek Mystery occurred to me, which is known as the Dashing out of the Testicles, and all that goes with it!" Which is said to have happened to a Byzantine Baggage of the Trojan Period, more to her Surprise than her Pleasure. Yet it is an agreeable Circumstance that the Ages thought fit to hand down this Miracle, for Hope springs eternal in the human Breast.

It has been noted by some and several, that Women have in them the Pip of Romanticism so well grown and fat of Sensibility, that they, upon reaching an uncertain Age, discard Duster, Offspring and Spouse, and a little after are seen leaning, all of a limp, on a Pillar of Bathos.

Evangeline Musset was not one of these, for she had been developed in the Womb of her most gentle Mother to be a Boy, when therefore, she came forth an Inch or so less than this, she paid no Heed to the Error, but donning a Vest of a superb Blister and Tooling, a Belcher for tippet and a pair of hip-boots with a scarlet channel (for it was a most wet wading) she took her Whip in hand, calling her Pups about her, and so set out upon the Road of Destiny, until such time as they should grow to be Hounds of a Blood, and Pointers with a certainty in the Butt of their Tails; waiting patiently beneath Cypresses for this Purpose, and under the Boughs of the aloe tree, composing, as she did so, Madrigals to all sweet and ramping things.

Her Father, be it known, spent many a windy Eve pacing his Library in the most normal of Night-Shirts, trying to think of ways to bring his erring Child back into that Religion and Activity which has ever been thought sufficient for a Woman; for already, when Evangeline appeared at Tea to the Duchess Clitoressa of Natescourt, women in the way (the Bourgeoise be it noted, on an errand to some nice Church of the Catholic Order, with their Babes at Breast, and Husbands at Arm) would snatch their Skirts from Contamination, putting such wincing Terror into their Dears with their quick and trembling Plucking, that it had been observed, in due time, by all Society, and Evangeline was in order of becoming one of those who is spoken to out of Generosity, which her Father could see, would by no Road, lead her to the Altar.

He had Words with her enough, saying: "Daughter, daughter, I perceive in you most fatherly Sentiments. What am I to do?" And she answered him High enough, "Thou, good Governor, wast expecting a Son when you lay atop of your Choosing, why then be so mortal wounded when you perceive that you have your Wish? Am I not doing after your very Desire, and is it not the more commendable, seeing that I do it without the Tools for the Trade, and yet nothing complain?"

In the days of which I write she had come to be a witty and learned Fifty, and though most short of Stature and nothing handsome, was so much in Demand, and so side famed for her Genius at bringing up by Hand, and so noted and esteemed for her Slips of the Tongue that it finally brought her into the Hall of Fame, where she stood by a Statue of Venus as calm as you please, or leaned upon a lacrymal Urn with a small Sponge for such as Wept in her own Time and stood in Need of it.

⁂

Thus begins this Almanack, which all Ladies
should carry about with them, as the Priest his
Breviary, as the Cook his Recipes,
as the Doctor his Physic, as
the Bride her Fears,
and as the Lion
his Roar! . . .

FEBRUARY *hath 29 days*

THIS be a Love Letter for a Present, and when she is Catched, what shall I do with her? God knows! For 'tis safe to say I do	**SAINTS DAYS** THESE are the Days on which Dame Musset was sainted, and for these things.

not, and what we know not, is our only proof of Him!

My Love she is an Old Girl, out of Fashion, Bugles at the Bosom, and theredown a much Thumbed Mystery and a Maze. She doth jangle with last Year's attentions, she is melted with Death's Fire! Then what shall I for her that hath never been accomplished? It is a very Parcel of Perplexities! Shall one stumble on a Nuance that twenty Centuries have not pounced upon, yea worried and made a Kill of? Hath not her Hair of old been braided with the Stars? Her shin half-circled by the Moon. Hath she not been turned all ways that the Sands of her Desire know all Runnings? Who can make a New Path where there be no Wilderness? In the Salt Earth lie Parcels of lost Perfection—surely I shall not loosen her Straps a New Way, Love hath been too long a Time! Will she unpack her Panels for such a Stale Receipt, pour our her Treasures for a coin worn thin? Yet to renounce her were a thing as old; and saying "Go!" but shuts the Door that hath banged a million Years!

Oh Zeus! Oh Diane! Oh Hellebore! Oh Absalom![1] Oh Piscary Right! What shall I do with it! *To have been the First*, that alone would have gifted me! As it is, shall I not pour ashes upon my Head, gird me in Sackcloth, covering my Nothing and Despair

January
When new whelped, she was found to have missed by an Inch.

February
When but five, she lamented Mid-prayers, that the girls in the Bible were both Earth-hushed and Jew-touched forever and ever.

March
When nine she learned how the Knee termed Housemaid's is come by, when the Slavy was bedridden at the turn of the scullery and needed a kneeling-to.

April
When fast on fifteen she hushed a Near-Bride with the left Flounce of her Ruffle that her Father in sleeping might not know of the oh!

May
When sweet twenty-one prayed upon her past Bearing she went to the Cockpit and crowed with the best. And at the Full of the Moon in Gaiters and Gloves mooed with the Herd, her Heels with their Hoofs, and in the wet Dingle hooted for hoot with the Quail on the Spinney, calling for Brides Wing and a Feather to flock with.

June
When well thirty, she, like all Men before her, made a Harlot a good Woman by making her Mistress.

July
When forty she bayed up a Tree whose Leaves had no Turning and whose Name was Florella.

August
When fifty odd and a day she came upon the Wind that is labelled the second.

Septembre
When sixty some, she came to no Good as well as another.

October
When Sixty was no longer a Lodger of hers, she bought a Pair

---

1. Zeus was the king of the gods in Greek mythology; Dian(a) was the Roman goddess of the hunt. Hellebore refers to a genus of herbs in the buttercup family having showy petals and medicinal powers; Absalom was the third and favorite son of King David of Israel, who, according to the Old Testament, led a rebellion against his father.

under a Mountain of Cinders, and thus become a Monument to No-Ability for her sake?

Verily, I shall place me before her Door, and when she cometh forth I shall think she has left her Feet inward upon the Sill and when she enters in, I shall dream her Hands be yet outward upon the Door—for therein
is no way for me,
and Fancy is
my only
Craft.

✳

of extra far-off, and ultra near-to Opera Glasses, and carried them always in a Sac by her Side.

November
When eighty-eight she said, "It's a Hook Girl, not a Button, you should know your Dress better."

December
When just before her last Breath she ordered a Pasty and let a Friend eat it, renouncing the World and its Pitfalls like all Saints before her, when
she had no longer
Room for them.
Prosit!

1928

⊰ To the Dogs ⊱

PERSONS: Helena Hucksteppe
               Gheid Storm—*Her neighbor*
TIME: *Late Afternoon.*
PLACE: *In the mountains of Cornwall-on-Hudson—the* Hucksteppe *house.*
SCENE: *The inner room of the* Hucksteppe *cottage.*

To the left, in the back wall, a large window overlooks a garden. Right center, a door leads off into a bedroom, and from the bedroom one may see the woods of the mountain. The door is slightly open, showing a glimpse of a tall mirror and the polished pole of a bed.

In the right wall there is a fireplace.

A dog lies across the threshold, asleep, head on paws.

About this room there is perhaps just a little too much of a certain kind of frail beauty of object. Crystal glasses, scent bottles, bowls of an almost too perfect design, furniture that is too antiquely beautiful.

Helena Hucksteppe, a woman of about thirty-five, stands almost back view to the audience, one arm lying along the mantel. She is rather under medium in height. Her hair, which is dark and curling, is done carefully about a small fine head. She is dressed in a dark, long gown, a gown almost too faithful to the singular sadness of her body.

At about the same moment as the curtain's rising, Gheid Storm vaults the window-sill. He is a man of few years, a well-to-do man of property, brought up very carefully by upright women, the son of a conscientious physician, the kind of man who commutes with an almost religious fervor, and who keeps his wife and his lawns in the best possible trim, without any particular personal pleasure.

Gheid is tall, but much too honourable to be jaunty, he is decidedly masculine. He walks deliberately, getting all the use possible out of his boot-leather, his belt-strap and hat-bands.

His face is one of those which, for fear of misuse, has not been used at all.

Helena Hucksteppe does not appear to be in the least astonished at his mode of entrance.

GHEID STORM: As you never let me in at the door, I thought of the window. [Helena *remains silent.*] I hope I did not startle you. [*Pause.*] Women are better calm, that is, some kinds of calm—

HELENA: Yes?

GHEID: [*noticing the dog, which has not stirred*] You've got funny dogs, they don't even bark. [*Pause.*] I expected you'd set them on me; however, perhaps that will come later—

HELENA: Perhaps.

STORM: Are you always going to treat me like this? For days I've watched you walking with your dogs of an evening—that little black bull-pup, and then those three setters—you've fine ways with you Helena Hucksteppe, though there are many tales of how you came by them—

HELENA: Yes?

STORM: Yes. [*Pause.*] You know, you surprise me.

HELENA: Why? Because I do not set my dogs on you?

STORM: Something like that.

HELENA: I respect my dogs.

STORM: What does that mean?

HELENA: Had I a daughter, would I set her on every man?

STORM: [*trying to laugh*] That's meant for an insult, isn't it? Well, I like the little insulting women—

HELENA: You are a man of taste.

STORM: I respect you.

HELENA: What kind of a feeling is that?

STORM: A gentleman's—

HELENA: I see.

STORM: People say of you: "She has a great many ways—"

HELENA: Yes?

STORM: [*sitting on the edge of the table*] "But none of them simple."

HELENA: Do they?

STORM: [*without attempting to hide his admiration*] I've watched your back: "There goes a fine woman, a fine silent woman; she wears long skirts, but she knows how to move her feet without kicking up a dust—a woman who can do that, drives a man mad." In town there's a story that you come through once every Spring, driving a different man ahead of you with a riding whip; another has it, that you come in the night—

HELENA: In other words, the starved women of the town are beginning to eat.

STORM: [*pause*] Well [*laughs*] I like you.

HELENA: I do not enjoy the spectacle of men ascending.

STORM: What are you trying to say?

HELENA: I'm saying it.

STORM: [*after an awkward pause*] Do—you wish me to—go away?

HELENA: You will go.

STORM: Why won't you let me talk to you?

HELENA: Any man may accomplish anything he's capable of.

STORM: Do you know how I feel about you?

HELENA: Perfectly.

STORM: I have heard many things about you—your past——I believe none of them——

HELENA: Quite right, why should you mix trades?

STORM: What do you mean by that?

HELENA: Why confuse incapability with accomplishment—

STORM: It's strange to see a woman like you turning to the merely bitter—

HELENA: I began beyond bitterness.

STORM: Why do you treat me this way?

HELENA: How would you have me treat you?

STORM: There was one night when you seemed to know, have you forgotten? A storm was coming up, the clouds were rolling overhead—and you, you yourself started it. You kissed me.

HELENA: You say it was about to storm?

STORM: Yes.

HELENA: It even looked like rain?

STORM: Yes.

HELENA: [quickly in a different voice] It was a dark night, and I ended it.

STORM: What have I done?

HELENA: You have neglected to make any beginning in the world—can I help that?

STORM: I offer you a clean heart.

HELENA: Things which have known only one state, do not interest me.

STORM: Helena!

HELENA: Gheid Storm.

STORM: I have a son; I don't know why I should tell you about him, perhaps because I want to prove that I have lived, and perhaps not. My son is a child, I am a man of few years and my son is like what I was at his age. He is thin, I was thin; he is quiet, I was quiet; he has delicate flesh, and I had also—well, then his mother died—

HELENA: The saddle comes down from the horse.

STORM: Well, she died—

HELENA: And that's over.

STORM: Well, there it is, I have a son—

HELENA: And that's not over. Do you resent that?

STORM: I don't know, perhaps. Sometimes I say to myself when I'm sitting by the fire alone—You should have something to think of while sitting here—"

HELENA: In other words, you're living for the sake of your fire.

STORM: [to himself] Some day I shall be glad I knew you.

HELENA: You go rather fast.

STORM: Yes, I shall have you to think of.

HELENA: When the fire is hot, you'll be glad to think of me?

STORM: Yes, all of us like to have a few things to tell our children, and I have always shown all that's in my heart to my son.

HELENA: How horrible!

STORM: [startled] Why?

HELENA: Would you show everything that made your heart?

STORM: I believe in frankness—

HELENA: [with something like anger] Well, some day your son will blow his head off, to be rid of frankness, before his skin is tough.

STORM: You are not making anything easier.

HELENA: I've never been callous enough to make things easier.

STORM: You're a queer woman—

HELENA: Yes, that does describe me.

STORM: *[taking his leg off the table]* Do you really want to know why I came? Because I need you—

HELENA: I'm not interested in corruption for the many.

STORM: *[starting as if he had been struck]* By God!

HELENA: Nor in misplaced satisfactions—

STORM: By God, what a woman!

HELENA: Nor do I participate in liberations—

STORM: *[in a low voice]* I could hate you!

HELENA: I limit no man, feel what you can.

STORM: *[taking a step toward her, the dog lifts its head]* If it were not for those damned dogs of yours—I'd—I'd—

HELENA: Aristocracy of movement never made a dog bite—

STORM: That's a—strange thing to say—just at this moment.

HELENA: Not for me.

STORM: *[sulky]* Well, anyway, a cat may look at a King—

HELENA: Oh no, a cat may only look at what it sees.

STORM: Helena Hucksteppe.

HELENA: Yes.

STORM: I'm—attracted—to you.

HELENA: A magnet does not attract shavings.

STORM: *[with positive conviction]* I *could* hate you.

HELENA: I choose my enemies.

STORM: *[without warning, seizing her]* By God, at least I can kiss you! *[He kisses her full on the mouth—she makes no resistance.]*

HELENA: *[in a calm voice]* And this, I suppose, is what you call the "great moment of human contact."

STORM: *[dropping his arms—turning pale]* What are you trying to do to me?

HELENA: I'm doing it.

STORM: *[to himself]* Yet it was you that I wanted—

HELENA: Mongrels may not dig up buried treasure.

STORM: *[in a sudden rage]* You can bury your past as deep as you like, but carrion will out!

HELENA: *[softly]* And this is love.

STORM: *[his head in his arms]* Oh, God, God!

HELENA: And you who like the taste of new things, come to me?

STORM: *[in a lost voice]* Shall I have no joy?

HELENA: Joy? Oh, yes, of a kind.

STORM: And you—are angry with me?

HELENA: In the study of science, is the scientist angry when the fly possesses no amusing phenomena?

STORM: I wanted—to know—you—

HELENA: I am conscious of your failure.

STORM: I wanted something—some sign—

HELENA: Must I, who have spent my whole life in being myself, go out of my way to change some look in you?

STORM: That's why you are so terrible, you have spent all your life on yourself.

HELENA: Yes, men do resent that in women.

STORM: Yes, I suppose so. *[Pause.]* I should have liked to talk of—myself—

HELENA: You see I could not listen.

STORM: You are—intolerant.

HELENA: No—occupied——

STORM: You are probably—playing a game.

HELENA: *[with a gracious smile]* You will get some personal good out of it, won't you?

STORM: I'm uncomfortable—

HELENA: Uncomfortable!

STORM: *[beginning to be really uncomfortable]* Who *are* you?

HELENA: I am a woman, Gheid Storm, who is *not* in need.

STORM: You're horrible!

HELENA: Yes, that too.

STORM: But somewhere you're vulnerable.

HELENA: Perhaps.

STORM: Only I don't quite know the spot.

HELENA: Spot?

STORM: Something, somewhere, hidden——

HELENA: Hidden! *[She laughs.] All* of me is vulnerable.

STORM: *[setting his teeth]* You tempt me.

HELENA: *[wearily]* It's not that kind.

STORM: I've lain awake thinking of you—many nights.

HELENA: That is too bad.

STORM: What is too bad?

HELENA: That you have had—fancies.

STORM: Why?

HELENA: Theft of much, makes much to return—

STORM: The world allows a man his own thoughts.

HELENA: Oh, no—

STORM: At least my thoughts are my own.

HELENA: Not one, so far.

STORM: What does that mean?

HELENA: You'll know when you try to think them again.

STORM: You mean I'm not making headway—well, you're right, I'm not—

HELENA: Now tell me what brought you through the window.

STORM: *[relieved]* I'm glad you ask that, it's the first human thing that's happened this afternoon.

HELENA: You have forgotten our great moment of human contact.

STORM: *[nervously]* Well—

HELENA: You were about to tell me what brought you?

STORM: I don't know—something no one speaks of—some great ease in your back—the look of a great lover—

HELENA: So—you scented a great lover—

STORM: I am a man—and I love—

HELENA: What have you done for love, Gheid Storm?

STORM: I've—never gone to the dogs—

HELENA: So?

STORM: I've always respected women.

HELENA: In other words: taken the coals out of the fire with the poker—continue—

STORM: That's all.

HELENA: And you dared to come to me! *[Her entire manner has changed.]*

STORM: No matter what you've been—done—I love you.

HELENA: Do not come so near. Only those who have helped to make such death as mine may go a little way toward the ardours of that decay.

STORM: What have I done?

HELENA: You have dared to bring to a woman, who has known love, the whinny of a pauper.

STORM: What am I?

HELENA: [softly, to herself] How sensitively the handles cling to the vase, how delicate is the flesh between the fingers.

STORM: I—I don't know you.

HELENA: [dropping her hands to her sides] Come here, Gheid Storm—[Gheid approaches slowly, like a sleep walker.] Put your hand on me. [He does so as if in a dream.] So! [She looks first at his hand, then into his face, making it quite plain that he does not even know how to touch a woman.] Yet you would be my lover, knowing not one touch that is mine, nor one word that is mine. My house is for men who have done their stumbling.

STORM: [in an inaudible voice] I am going now—

HELENA: I cannot touch new things, nor see beginnings.

STORM: Helena! Helena!

HELENA: Do not call my name. There are too many names that must be called before mine.

STORM: Shall I die, and never have known you?

HELENA: Death, for you, will begin where my cradle started rocking—

STORM: Shall I have no love like yours?

HELENA: When I am an old woman, thinking of other things, you will, perhaps, be kissing a woman like me—

STORM: [moving blindly toward the door] Now I am going.

HELENA: [in a quiet, level voice] The fall is almost here.

STORM: Yes, it's almost here.

HELENA: The leaves on the mountain road are turning yellow.

STORM: Yes, the leaves are turning.

HELENA: It's late, your son will be waiting dinner for you.

STORM: Don't take everything away.

HELENA: You will not even recall having seen me.

STORM: Can memory be taken too?

HELENA: Only that memory that goes past recollection may be kept.

STORM: [at the door] Good night——

HELENA: [smiling] There is the window.

STORM: I could not lift my legs now.

HELENA: That's a memory you may keep.

STORM: Good night.

HELENA: Good-bye, Gheid Storm, and as you go down the hill, will you lock the gate, a dog thief passed in the night, taking my terrier with him.

STORM: The one with the brown spots?

HELENA: Yes.

STORM: That was a fine dog.

HELENA: Yes, she was a fine dog—restless.

STORM: They say any dog will follow any man who carries aniseed.

HELENA: Well, soon I return to the city.

STORM: You look tired.

HELENA: Yes, I am tired.

[Gheid exits. Helena takes her old position, her back almost square to the audience.]

Curtain   1919–20/1923

━━ ✦ ━━

Edna St. Vincent Millay
1892–1950

Edna St. Vincent Millay published twelve volumes of poetry in her lifetime and wrote numerous plays, in some of which she starred. Enormously popular during the 1920s and 1930s, she earned a reputation as a bohemian artist in Greenwich Village, broadcast poetry readings on weekly radio programs to thousands of Americans, and read her poems with dramatic flair around the world. In 1924 she won the Pulitzer Prize for *The Harp-Weaver and Other Poems*. Millay's lyric poems take as their subject romantic love and female empowerment; she was a somewhat scandalous advocate of women's sexual emancipation. As her humorous contemporary, the writer Dorothy Parker, once noted, Millay's public revelations of her sexual exploits started something of a trend: "We all wandered in after Miss Millay. We were all being dashing and gallant, declaring that we weren't virgins, whether we were or not."

Millay was born in Rockland, Maine, to Henry Millay, a secondary teacher and principal, and his wife Cora, a writer and musician. Her parents divorced when she was twelve, and Millay and her two sisters were raised by their mother, who became a practical nurse in order to earn a living. "Vincent," as she was called from infancy, became an actress as a schoolgirl and recited her first long poem, "La Joie de Vivre," at her high school graduation. In 1912 her poem "Renascence" won a prize in a poetry contest and was published in *The Lyric Year*. After graduating from Vassar College in 1917, Millay went to live in New York City, where she wrote plays and poems and published magazine articles under the pseudonym Nancy Boyd. Her first collection of poetry, *Renascence and Other Poems*, appeared in 1917 and was an instant success. She acted for a time at the Provincetown Playhouse and directed two of her own plays there, *Aria de Capo* (1920) and *The Princess Marries the Page* (1932). In 1932 Millay left for Europe on an assignment for *Vanity Fair* magazine; there she lived and wrote until her marriage in 1923 to a Dutch importer, Eugen Boissevain, the widower of the American feminist Inez Mulholland. After a trip around the world, the couple settled in the United States in a country estate named Steepletop in the Berkshire Mountains. The 1920s and 1930s brought Millay great fame; her ballads, sonnets, and lyric poems were beloved by many, and she was considered a master of traditional formal and metrical structures, a "lyric genius," as one contemporary put it. Throughout her life she supported feminist causes and was a committed pacifist. In the late 1930s she sustained a back injury that plagued her middle years, and in 1944, upset by the horrors of World War II, she suffered a nervous breakdown. Although she recovered to write again, her health was never fully restored, and she died at the age of fifty-eight in 1950, a year after her husband's death.

A Few Figs from Thistle (1920), Millay's most popular early collection of poetry, helped to establish her as an emotionally intense poet who wrote of passion and rebellion from a female perspective. In 1921 she published a third volume of poems, *Second April*, as well as a play, *Two Slatterns and a King*. Among her best collections of sonnets are *Sonnets from an Ungrafted Tree* (1923), which depict the struggle of an unhappily married woman at her husband's deathbed, and *Fatal Interview* (1931), which traces the contours of a doomed love affair. In 1927 she published *The King's Henchman*, a play based on an opera by Deems Taylor, and thereafter she translated Baudelaire's *Flowers of Evil*. Later works include *Invocation to the Muses* (1941), *The Murder of Lidice* (1942), *Poem and Prayer for an Invading Army* (1944), and *Mine the Harvest* (1954). Her *Collected Poems* was published posthumously in 1952.

By the 1940s Millay's poetry had fallen out of favor with modernist innovators and New Critics, who disparaged her work as simplistic and sentimental. The feminist critic Suzanne Clark has analyzed the gendered reasons why Millay's "sentimental modernism" offended these writers and critics, even though such practitioners of "aesthetic modernism" as James Joyce could also be faulted for sentimentality, but were not. Even women writers such as VIRGINIA

Woolf, Djuna Barnes, Edith Sitwell, and Louise Bogan criticized Millay and other "female songbirds" (Bogan's term), though they too wrote at times for the "women's market" to whom sentimental writing was most appealing. Such indictments reveal much about the defensiveness that female modernists felt it necessary to employ to distinguish themselves as "serious" writers from "popular" ones like Millay. For all her success with sentimental readers, however, Millay participated in establishing what Elaine Hedges has termed an "antidomestic tradition" of women's writing, one that depicts women as strong figures with sexual agency, not as passive members of the domestic sphere.

⊰ *from* Fatal Interview ⊱

XXVI

Women have loved before as I love now;
At least, in lively chronicles of the past—
Of Irish waters by a Cornish prow
Or Trojan waters by a Spartan mast
5   Much to their cost invaded—here and there,
Hunting the amorous line, skimming the rest,
I find some woman bearing as I bear
Love like a burning city in the breast.
I think however that of all alive
10   I only in such utter, ancient way
Do suffer love; in me alone survive
The unregenerate passions of a day
When treacherous queens, with death upon the tread,
Heedless and wilful, took their knights to bed.

XXVIII

When we are old and these rejoicing veins
Are frosty channels to a muted stream,
And out of all our burning there remains
No feeblest spark to fire us, even in dream,
5   This be our solace: that it was not said
When we were young and warm and in our prime,
Upon our couch we lay as lie the dead,
Sleeping away the unreturning time.
O sweet, O heavy-lidded, O my love,
10   When morning strikes her spear upon the land,
And we must rise and arm us and reprove
The insolent daylight with a steady hand,
Be not discountenanced if the knowing know
We rose from rapture but an hour ago.

XXX

Love is not all; it is not meat nor drink
Nor slumber nor a roof against the rain,
Not yet a floating spar to men that sink
And rise and sink and rise and sink again;

5   Love can not fill the thickened lung with breath,
    Nor clean the blood, nor set the fractured bone;
    Yet many a man is making friends with death
    Even as I speak, for lack of love alone.
    It well may be that in a difficult hour,
10 Pinned down by pain and moaning for release,
    Or nagged by want past resolution's power,
    I might be driven to sell your love for peace,
    Or trade the memory of this night for food.
    It well may be. I do not think I would.

XLVII

    Well, I have lost you; and I lost you fairly;
    In my own way, and with my full consent.
    Say what you will, kings in a tumbrel rarely
    Went to their deaths more proud than this one went.
5   Some nights of apprehension and hot weeping
    I will confess; but that's permitted me;
    Day dried my eyes; I was not one for keeping
    Rubbed in a cage a wing that would be free.
    If I had loved you less or played you slyly
10 I might have held you for a summer more,
    But at the cost of words I value highly,
    And no such summer as the one before.
    Should I outlive this anguish—and men do—
    I shall have only good to say of you.

                                          1931

Anne Sexton
1928–1974

Born in Newton, Massachusetts, to wealthy parents, Ralph and Mary Gray Harvey, Anne Sexton experienced an unhappy childhood wracked by sexual and emotional abuse. Her primary source of love and support, her great-aunt Nana, was placed in a mental institution when Anne was a teenager and thus cut off from her niece. After briefly training as a model and attending Garland Junior College, Sexton eloped at the age of nineteen with Alfred "Kayo" Sexton, a wool salesman; the couple had two daughters, the elder of whom, Linda Gray Sexton, has written extensively about her mother. Anne Sexton began to write poems in 1956 after her first suicide attempt; in 1957 she enrolled in a poetry workshop taught by John Holmes at the Boston Center for Adult Education, where she became friends with another woman poet studying there, Maxine Kumin. She went on to take classes from Robert Lowell at Boston University, where her classmate was SYLVIA PLATH. Although Sexton viewed poetry as a means of exploring an anguished psyche, her poems do not focus exclusively on her death wish, as some critics have contended. Her early collections—*To Bedlam and Part Way Back* (1960), *All My Pretty Ones* (1962), and *Live or Die* (1966)—present a wide range of themes, including familial dysfunction, female sexuality, the complexities of motherhood, and the erotics of suicide. In 1967 Sexton won the Pulitzer prize for *Live or Die*.

Like much of her work, *Love Songs* (1969) represents an important effort by a woman to write the body, in particular to probe the connection between art and embodiment. *Transformations* (1972) parodies familiar fairy tales from a feminist perspective, humorously decoding their misogyny and sexist stereotypes. Other volumes of poetry include *The Book of Folly* (1972) and *The Death Notebooks* (1974), titles that seem eerily prescient, for after a long struggle with depression and drug and alcohol addiction, Sexton committed suicide in 1974. Three books of poetry were published posthumously in 1975 and 1976: *The Awful Rowing Toward God*, *The Wizard's Tears*, and *45 Mercy Street*. In 1977 *Anne Sexton: A Self-Portrait in Letters* appeared, and in the early 1990s her daughter excited controversy by making taped manuscripts of her mother's therapy sessions available to her biographer, Diane Wood Middlebrook. Sexton's *Collected Poems* were published in 1981.

With Lowell and Plath, Sexton is often called a "confessional poet," one who reveals intimate details of her sexual, emotional, and relational life in order to highlight larger metaphysical questions. At their best, her poems are technically sophisticated and disciplined in their use of metrics and diction. She wrote frankly about adultery, menstruation, abortion, and orgasm before many other women did so, and to many readers today her poetry remains compelling in its forthright examination of female experience. Poetry should be "a shock to the senses," the poet once claimed. "It should also hurt." For Sexton, "the imagination and the unconscious are one and the same."

⊰ The Abortion ⊱

Somebody who should have been born
is gone.

Just as the earth puckered its mouth,
each bud puffing out from its knot,
5   I changed my shoes, and then drove south.

Up past the Blue Mountains, where
Pennsylvania humps on endlessly,
wearing, like a crayoned cat, its green hair,

its roads sunken in like a gray washboard;
10   where, in truth, the ground cracks evilly,
a dark socket from which the coal has poured,

Somebody who should have been born
is gone.

the grass as bristly and stout as chives,
15   and me wondering when the ground would break,
and me wondering how anything fragile survives;

up in Pennsylvania, I met a little man,
not Rumpelstiltskin, at all, at all . . .
he took the fullness that love began.

20   Returning north, even the sky grew thin
like a high window looking nowhere.
The road was as flat as a sheet of tin.

Somebody who should have been born
is gone.

25   Yes, woman, such logic will lead
      to loss without death. Or say what you meant,
      you coward . . . this baby that I bleed.

                                           1962

⊰ In Celebration of My Uterus ⊱

      Everyone in me is a bird.
      I am beating all my wings.
      They wanted to cut you out
      but they will not.
5   They said you were immeasurably empty
      but you are not.
      They said you were sick unto dying
      but they were wrong.
      You are singing like a school girl.
10   You are not torn.

      Sweet weight,
      in celebration of the woman I am
      and of the soul of the woman I am
      and the central creature and its delight
15   I sing for you. I dare to live.
      Hello, spirit. Hello, cup.
      Fasten, cover. Cover that does contain.
      Hello to the soil of the fields.
      Welcome, roots.

20   Each cell has a life.
      There is enough here to please a nation.
      It is enough that the populace own these goods.
      Any person, any commonwealth would say of it,
      "It is good this year that we may plant again
25   and think forward to a harvest.
      A blight had been forecast and has been cast out."
      Many women are singing together of this:
      one is in a shoe factory cursing the machine,
      one is at the aquarium tending a seal,
30   one is dull at the wheel of her Ford,
      one is at the toll gate collecting,
      one is tying the cord of a calf in Arizona,
      one is straddling a cello in Russia,
      one is shifting pots on the stove in Egypt,
35   one is painting her bedroom walls moon color,
      one is dying but remembering a breakfast,
      one is stretching on her mat in Thailand,
      one is wiping the ass of her child,
      one is staring out the window of a train
40   in the middle of Wyoming and one is
      anywhere and some are everywhere and all
      seem to be singing, although some can not
      sing a note.

Sweet weight,
45   in celebration of the woman I am
let me carry a ten-foot scarf,
let me drum for the nineteen-year-olds,
let me carry bowls for the offering
(if that is my part).
50   Let me study the cardiovascular tissue,
let me examine the angular distance of meteors,
let me suck on the stems of flowers
(if that is my part).
Let me make certain tribal figures
55   (if that is my part).
For this thing the body needs
let me sing
for the supper,
for the kissing,
60   for the correct
yes.

1969

⚔ For My Lover, Returning to His Wife ⚔

She is all there.
She was melted carefully down for you
and cast up from your childhood,
cast up from your one hundred favorite aggies.

5   She has always been there, my darling.
She is, in fact, exquisite.
Fireworks in the dull middle of February
and as real as a cast-iron pot.

Let's face it, I have been momentary.
10   A luxury. A bright red sloop in the harbor.
My hair rising like smoke from the car window.
Littleneck clams out of season.
She is more than that. She is your have to have,
has grown you your practical your tropical growth.
15   This is not an experiment. She is all harmony.
She sees to oars and oarlocks for the dinghy,

has placed wild flowers at the window at breakfast,
sat by the potter's wheel at midday,
set forth three children under the moon,
20   three cherubs drawn by Michelangelo,

done this with her legs spread out
in the terrible months in the chapel.
If you glance up, the children are there
like delicate balloons resting on the ceiling.

25 She has also carried each one down the hall
 after supper, their heads privately bent,
 two legs protesting, person to person,
 her face flushed with a song and their little sleep.

 I give you back your heart.
30 I give you permission—

 for the fuse inside her, throbbing
 angrily in the dirt, for the bitch in her
 and the burying of her wound—
 for the burying of her small red wound alive—

35 for the pale flickering flare under her ribs,
 for the drunken sailor who waits in her left pulse,
 for the mother's knee, for the stockings,
 for the garter belt, for the call—

 the curious call
40 when you will burrow in arms and breasts
 and tug at the orange ribbon in her hair
 and answer the call, the curious call.

 She is so naked and singular.
 She is the sum of yourself and your dream.
45 Climb her like a monument, step after step.
 She is solid.

 As for me, I am a watercolor.
 I wash off.

1969

Audre Lorde
1934–1992

"To whom do I owe the symbols of my survival?" Audre Lorde asks
at the beginning of her autobiographical book *Zami*, "to whom do I
owe the woman I have become?" Her answer pays tribute to the
women who have inspired her as lovers, sisters, mothers, goddesses,
and muses who "lead me home"—home to what she calls "the jour-
neywoman pieces of myself."

 Lorde was born in New York to Grenadian immigrant parents
and was educated at Catholic elementary schools, Hunter High
School, Hunter College, and Columbia University. As a child she
was legally blind, a disability that caused her teachers initially to
mistake her for willful and disobedient. In *Zami* Lorde chronicles her educational saga, with its
blend of supportive teachers, both African American and white, and dismissive white teachers
confusing to the talented child who as yet "had no words for racism." As a young adult she
lived in Mexico for a time, worked as a clerk at the New York Public Library, taught in Tuga-
loo, Mississippi, during the civil rights movement, studied and wrote poetry. She was married

for seven years and had a son, Jonathan, and a daughter, Beth. Subsequently Lorde taught English at John Jay College of Criminal Justice and at Hunter College of the City University of New York. She received many honors during her lifetime, including the Manhattan Borough President's Award for Excellence in the Arts and the Walt Whitman Citation of Merit, and in 1991 she was named the New York State Poet. During the last few years of her life Lorde lived in St. Crois, Virgin Islands, with her partner, the writer Gloria Joseph. She died in November 1992, after an extended struggle with breast cancer.

Lorde's early poetry reveals the themes that she employs throughout her work. Anger at racism and racial violence, the "transformation of silence into language and action," the effort to connect across differences, the complexities of lesbian desire provide the subject matter for *The First Cities* (1968), *Cables to Rage* (1970), *From a Land Where Other People Live* (1973), *New York Head Shop and Museum* (1975), *Coal* (1976), and *The Black Unicorn* (1978). To publish six volumes of poetry in ten years is a prodigious feat, and Lorde's early work received considerable critical acclaim; *From a Land Where Other People Live* was nominated for the 1974 National Book Award, and in 1982 W. W. Norton published a collection of Lorde's poems to date, *Chosen Poems: Old and New*. The poems in *Our Dead Behind Us* (1986) are more international in focus, reflecting her travels to Grenada and East Germany and her work as an antiapartheid activist. Lorde's poetry of the 1990s continues these emphases but also charts the effects of cancer on her body and spirit. "Death is a fractured border through the center of my days," she writes in *The Marvelous Arithmetics of Distance*, published posthumously in 1993. Shortly before her death, Lorde revised *Chosen Poems* and added new selections, publishing the work as *Undersong*.

Lorde's prose writings have brought her a wide audience. *The Cancer Journals* (1980) critiques traditional medical practice and documents her refusal to choose either breast prostheses or reconstructive surgery. *Zami: A New Spelling of My Name* (1982), which Lorde characterizes as "biomythography," combines autobiography and African and West Indian mythology to depict matrilineage. In *Sister Outsider* (1984) and *A Burst of Light* (1988) she analyzes poetry as a form of resistance, embodiment, and eroticism. Indeed, the quest to claim her identity as a "black lesbian feminist warrior poet" forms the core of Lorde's prose as well as poetry. By inscribing lesbian desire, the erotic as power, and her experience with breast cancer, Lorde became known as one of America's foremost feminist theorists of sexuality and the body.

⊰ Uses of the Erotic: The Erotic as Power ⊱

There are many kinds of power, used and unused, acknowledged or otherwise. The erotic is a resource within each of us that lies in a deeply female and spiritual plane, firmly rooted in the power of our unexpressed or unrecognized feeling. In order to perpetuate itself, every oppression must corrupt or distort those various sources of power within the culture of the oppressed that can provide energy for change. For women, this has meant a suppression of the erotic as a considered source of power and information within our lives.

We have been taught to suspect this resource, vilified, abused, and devalued within western society. On the one hand, the superficially erotic has been encouraged as a sign of female inferiority; on the other hand, women have been made to suffer and to feel both contemptible and suspect by virtue of its existence.

It is a short step from there to the false belief that only by the suppression of the erotic within our lives and consciousness can women be truly strong. But that strength is illusory, for it is fashioned within the contest of male models of power.

As women, we have come to distrust that power which rises from our deepest and nonrational knowledge. We have been warned against it all our lives by the male world, which values this depth of feeling enough to keep women around in order to exercise it in the service of men, but which fears this same depth too much to examine the possibilities of it within themselves. So women are maintained at a distant/inferior position to be psychically milked, much the same way ants maintain colonies of aphids to provide a life-giving substance for their masters.

But the erotic offers a well of replenishing and provocative force to the woman who does not fear its revelation, nor succumb to the belief that sensation is enough.

The erotic has often been misnamed by men and used against women. It has been made into the confused, the trivial, the psychotic, the plasticized sensation. For this reason, we have often turned away from the exploration and consideration of the erotic as a source of power and information, confusing it with its opposite, the pornographic. But pornography is a direct denial of the power of the erotic, for it represents the suppression of true feeling. Pornography emphasizes sensation without feeling.

The erotic is a measure between the beginnings of our sense of self and the chaos of our strongest feelings. It is an internal sense of satisfaction to which, once we have experienced it, we know we can aspire. For having experienced the fullness of this depth of feeling and recognizing its power, in honor and self-respect we can require no less of ourselves.

It is never easy to demand the most from ourselves, from our lives, from our work. To encourage excellence is to go beyond the encouraged mediocrity of our society is to encourage excellence. But giving in to the fear of feeling and working to capacity is a luxury only the unintentional can afford, and the unintentional are those who do not wish to guide their own destinies.

This internal requirement toward excellence which we learn from the erotic must not be misconstrued as demanding the impossible from ourselves nor from others. Such a demand incapacitates everyone in the process. For the erotic is not a question only of what we do; it is a question of how acutely and fully we can feel in the doing. Once we know the extent to which we are capable of feeling that sense of satisfaction and completion, we can then observe which of our various life endeavors bring us closest to that fullness.

The aim of each thing which we do is to make our lives and the lives of our children richer and more possible. Within the celebration of the erotic in all our endeavors, my work becomes a conscious decision—a longed-for bed which I enter gratefully and from which I rise up empowered.

Of course, women so empowered are dangerous. So we are taught to separate the erotic demand from most vital areas of our lives other than sex. And the lack of concern for the erotic root and satisfactions of our work is felt in our disaffection from so much of what we do. For instance, how often do we truly love our work even at its most difficult?

The principal horror of any system which defines the good in terms of profit rather than in terms of human need, or which defines human need to the exclusion of the psychic and emotional components of that need—the principal horror of such a system is that it robs our work of its erotic value, its erotic power and life appeal and fulfillment. Such a system reduces work to a travesty of necessities, a duty by which we earn bread or oblivion for ourselves and those we love. But this is tantamount to blinding a painter and then telling her to improve her work, and to enjoy the act of painting. It is not only next to impossible, it is also profoundly cruel.

As women, we need to examine the ways in which our world can be truly different. I am speaking here of the necessity for reassessing the quality of all aspects of our lives and of our work, and of how we move toward and through them.

The very word *erotic* comes from the Greek word *eros*, the personification of love in all its aspects—born of Chaos, and personifying creative power and harmony. When I speak of the erotic, then, I speak of it as an assertion of the lifeforce of women; of that creative energy empowered, the knowledge and use of which we are now reclaiming in our language, our history, our dancing, our loving, our work, our lives.

There are frequent attempts to equate pornography and eroticism, two diametrically opposed uses of the sexual. Because of these attempts, it has become fashionable to separate the spiritual (psychic and emotional) from the political, to see them as contradictory or antithetical. "What do you mean, a poetic revolutionary, a meditating gunrunner?" In the same way, we have attempted to separate the spiritual and the erotic, thereby reducing the spiritual to a world of flattened affect, a world of the ascetic who aspires to feel nothing. But nothing is farther from the truth. For the ascetic position is one of the highest fear, the gravest immobility. The severe abstinence of the ascetic becomes the ruling obsession. And it is one not of self-discipline but of self-abnegation.

The dichotomy between the spiritual and the political is also false, resulting from an incomplete attention to our erotic knowledge. For the bridge which connects them is formed by the erotic—the sensual—those physical, emotional, and psychic expressions of what is deepest and strongest and richest within each of us, being shared: the passions of love, in its deepest meanings.

Beyond the superficial, the considered phrase, "It feels right to me," acknowledges the strength of the erotic into a true knowledge, for what that means is the first and most powerful guiding light toward any understanding. And understanding is a handmaiden which can only wait upon, or clarify, that knowledge, deeply born. The erotic is the nurturer or nursemaid of all our deepest knowledge.

The erotic functions for me in several ways, and the first is in providing the power which comes from sharing deeply any pursuit with another person. The sharing of joy, whether physical, emotional, psychic, or intellectual, forms a bridge between the sharers which can be the basis for understanding much of what is not shared between them, and lessens the threat of their difference.

Another important way in which the erotic connection functions is the open and fearless underlining of my capacity for joy. In the way my body stretches to music and opens into response, hearkening to its deepest rhythms, so every level upon which I sense also opens to the erotically satisfying experience, whether it is dancing, building a bookcase, writing a poem, examining an idea.

That self-connection shared is a measure of the joy which I know myself to be capable of feeling, a reminder of my capacity for feeling. And that deep and irreplaceable knowledge of my capacity for joy comes to demand from all of my life that it be lived within the knowledge that such satisfaction is possible, and does not have to be called *marriage*, nor *god*, nor *an afterlife*.

This is one reason why the erotic is so feared, and so often relegated to the bedroom alone, when it is recognized at all. For once we begin to feel deeply all the aspects of our lives, we begin to demand from ourselves and from our life-pursuits that they feel in accordance with that joy which we know ourselves to be capable of. Our erotic knowledge empowers us, becomes a lens through which we scrutinize all aspects of our existence, forcing us to evaluate those aspects honestly in terms of their relative meaning within our lives. And this is a grave responsibility, projected from within each of us, not to settle for the convenient, the shoddy, the conventionally expected, nor the merely safe.

During World War II, we bought sealed plastic packets of white, uncolored margarine, with a tiny, intense pellet of yellow coloring perched like a topaz just inside the clear skin of the bag. We would leave the margarine out for a while to soften, and then we would pinch the little pellet to break it inside the bag, releasing the rich yellowness into the soft pale mass of margarine. Then taking it carefully between our fingers, we would knead it gently back and forth, over and over, until the color had spread throughout the whole pound bag of margarine, thoroughly coloring it.

I find the erotic such a kernel within myself. When released from its intense and constrained pellet, it flows through and colors my life with a kind of energy that heightens and sensitizes and strengthens all my experience.

We have been raised to fear the yes within ourselves, our deepest cravings. But, once recognized, those which do not enhance our future lose their power and can be altered. The fear of our desires keeps them suspect and indiscriminately powerful, for to suppress any truth is to give it strength beyond endurance. The fear that we cannot grow beyond whatever distortions we may find within ourselves keeps us docile and loyal and obedient, externally defined, and leads us to accept many facets of our oppression as women.

When we live outside ourselves, and by that I mean on external directives only rather than from our internal knowledge and needs, when we live away from those erotic guides from within ourselves, then our lives are limited by external and alien forms, and we conform to the needs of a structure that is not based on human need, let alone an individual's. But when we begin to live from within outward, in touch with the power of the erotic within ourselves, and allowing that power to inform and illuminate our actions upon the world around us, then we begin to be responsible to ourselves in the deepest sense. For as we begin to recognize our deepest feelings, we begin to give up, of necessity, being satisfied with suffering and self-negation, and with the numbness which so often seems like their only alternative in our society. Our acts against oppression become integral with self, motivated and empowered from within.

In touch with the erotic, I become less willing to accept powerlessness, or those other supplied states of being which are not native to me, such as resignation, despair, self-effacement, depression, self-denial.

And yes, there is a hierarchy. There is a difference between painting a back fence and writing a poem, but only one of quantity. And there is, for me, no difference between writing a good poem and moving into sunlight against the body of a woman I love.

This brings me to the last consideration of the erotic. To share the power of each other's feelings is different from using another's feelings as we would use a kleenex. When we look the other way from our experience, erotic or otherwise, we use rather than share the feelings of those others who participate in the experience with us. And use without consent of the used is abuse.

In order to be utilized, our erotic feelings must be recognized. The need for sharing deep feeling is a human need. But within the european-american tradition, this need is satisfied by certain proscribed erotic comings-together. These occasions are almost always characterized by a simultaneous looking away, a pretense of calling them something else, whether a religion, a fit, mob violence, or even playing doctor.

And this misnaming of the need and the deed gives rise to that distortion which results in pornography and obscenity—the abuse of feeling.

When we look away from the importance of the erotic in the development and sustenance of our power, or when we look away from ourselves as we satisfy our erotic needs in concert with others, we use each other as objects of satisfaction rather than share our joy in the satisfying, rather than make connection with our similarities and our differences. To refuse to be conscious of what we are feeling at any time, however comfortable that might seen, is to deny a large part of the experience, and to allow ourselves to be reduced to the pornographic, the abused, and the absurd.

The erotic cannot be felt secondhand. As a Black lesbian feminist, I have a particular feeling, knowledge, and understanding for those sisters with whom I have danced hard, played, or even fought. This deep participation has often been the forerunner for joint concerted actions not possible before.

But this erotic charge is not easily shared by women who continue to operate under an exclusively european-american male tradition. I know it was not available to me when I was trying to adapt my consciousness to this mode of living and sensation.

Only now, I find more and more women-identified women brave enough to risk sharing the erotic's electrical charge without having to look away, and without distorting the enormously powerful and creative nature of that exchange. Recognizing the power of the erotic within our lives can give us the energy to pursue genuine change within our world, rather than merely settling for a shift of characters in the same weary drama.

For not only do we touch our most profoundly creative source, but we do that which is female and self-affirming in the face of a racist, patriarchal, and anti-erotic society.   *1980/1984*

⊰ Love Poem ⊱

Speak earth and bless me
with what is richest
make sky flow honey out of my hips
rigid as mountains
5   spread over a valley
carved out by the mouth of rain.

And I knew when I entered her   I was
high wind in her forest's hollow
fingers whispering sound
10   honey flowed   from the split cup
impaled on a lance of tongues
on the tips of her breasts   on her navel
and my breath   howling into her entrances
through lungs of pain.

15   Greedy as herring-gulls
or a child
I swing out   over the earth
over and over   again.

1971

⇥ Chain ⇥

News item: Two girls, fifteen and sixteen, were sent to foster homes, because they had borne children by their natural father. Later, they petitioned the New York courts to be returned to their parents, who, the girls said, loved them. And the courts did so.

I

Faces surround me that have no smell or color no time
only strange laughing testaments
vomiting promise like love
but look at the skeleton children
5   advancing against us
beneath their faces there is no sunlight
no darkness
no heart remains
no legends
10   to bring them back as women
into their bodies at dawn.

Look at the skeleton children
advancing against us
we will find womanhood
15   in their eyes
as they cry
which of you bore me
will love me
will claim my blindness as yours
20   and which of you marches to battle
from between my legs?

II

On the porch outside my door
girls are lying
like felled maples in the path of my feet
25   I cannot step past them nor over them
their slim bodies roll like smooth tree trunks
repeating themselves over and over
until my porch is covered with the bodies
of young girls.
30   Some have a child in their arms.
To what death shall I look for comfort?
Which mirror to break or mourn?

Two girls repeat themselves in my doorway
their eyes are not stone
35   Their flesh is not wood nor steel
but I cannot touch them.
Shall I warn them of night
or offer them bread
or a song?
40   They are sisters. Their father has known

them over and over. The twins they carry
are his. Whose death shall we mourn
in the forest
unburied?
45   Winter has come and the children are dying.

One begs me to hold her between my breasts
Oh write me a poem mother
here, over my flesh
get your words upon me
50   as he got his child upon me
our father lover
thief in the night
do not be so angry with us. We told him
your bed was wider
55   but he said if we did it then
we would be his
good children if we did it
then he would love us
oh make us a poem mother
60   that will tell us his name
in your language
is he father or lover
we will leave your word
for our children
65   engraved on a whip or a golden scissors
to tell them the lies
of their birth.

Another says mother
I am holding your place.
70   Do you know me better than I knew him
or myself?
Am I his daughter or his girlfriend
am I your child or your rival
you wish to be gone from his bed?
75   Here is your granddaughter mother
give us your blessing before I sleep
what other secrets
do you have to tell me
how do I learn to love her
80   as you have loved me?

                                              1978

⊰ Restoration: A Memorial—9/18/91 ⊱

Berlin again   after chemotherapy
I reach behind me once more
for days to come
sweeping around the edges of authenticity

5 two years after Hugo blew one life away
Death like a burnt star
perched on the rim of my teacup
flaming the honey drips from my spoon
sunlight flouncing off the gargoyles opposite.

10 Somewhere it is Tuesday
in the ordinary world
ravishment fades
into compelling tasks
our bodies learn to perform
15 quite a bit of the house is left
our bedroom spared
except for the ankle-deep water
and terrible stench.

Would I exchange this safety of exile
20 for the muddy hand-drawn water
wash buckets stashed
where our front porch had been
half-rotten vegetables
and the antique grey settling over your face
25 that October?

I want you laughing again
After the stinking rugs are dragged away
the crystal chandelier dug
from the dining-room floor
30 refrigerator righted
broken cupboards stacked outside
to dry for our dinner fire.

A few trees still stand
in a brand-new landscape
35 but the sea road is impassable.
Your red shirt
hung out on a bush to dry
is the only flower for weeks.
No escape. No return.
40 No other life
half so sane.

In this alien and temporary haven
my poisoned fingers
slowly return to normal
45 I read your letter dreaming
the perspective of a bluefish
or a fugitive parrot
watch the chemicals leaving my nails
as my skin takes back its weaknesses.
50 Learning to laugh again.

1991/1993

——— ⊱✦⊰ ———

Bharati Mukherjee
1938–

Bharati Mukherjee was born in Calcutta to Sudhir Lal and Bina Banerjee Mukherjee, prominent Bengali Brahmins; she attended the Loreto Convent School and received a B.A. with honors from the University of Calcutta and an M.A. from the University of Baroda before emigrating to the United States in 1961 for further study. In 1969 she received her Ph.D. from the University of Iowa; since then, she has taught creative writing at Skidmore College, Columbia University, the City University of New York, and the University of Iowa. For a time she lived with her husband, the novelist Clark Blaise, and their two children in Canada, where she taught at McGill University. She now teaches at the University of California at Berkeley.

Her first novel, *The Tiger's Daughter* (1972), examines the dislocating effects of Westernization on a Brahmin woman who, upon returning to India, has difficulty reconciling herself to the poverty and the hierarchies of caste that she took for granted before. *Wife* (1975) presents an Indian woman's conflict when she rejects the passivity of the traditional wife in an arranged marriage. Also a study of dislocation, this novel examines the alienation that overwhelms its angry protagonist upon immigrating to New York. *Darkness* (1985), Mukherjee's first collection of short stories and her bleakest, focuses on the racism encountered by Southern Asian immigrants living in Canada. *The Middleman and Other Stories* (1988), which won a National Book Critics Circle Award, explores in a lighter vein what Mukherjee has called the "broken identities" of immigrants, expatriates, and assorted "others" living in cultures different from their own. *Jasmine* (1989), a novel, is based on the story by that title from *The Middleman*; in it a young Indian girl emigrates to America, where she has a series of terrible experiences but manages nonetheless to survive and flourish. *The Holder of the World* (1993) purports to be a travel narrative of Hannah Easton, born in the American colonies in 1670, who accompanies her trader-husband to India, only to take a Hindu raj as her lover. *Leave It To Me* (1997) reinvents the classical myth of Electra as an Asian-American woman searches for her inheritance from parents who abandoned her as a child.

Mukherjee has also published nonfiction. With her Canadian-born husband she wrote *Days and Nights in Calcutta* (1977), a journal that chronicles the delights and disappointments of their first visit to India together. "While changing citizenship is easy," she writes, "swapping cultures is not." Mukherjee and Blaise also collaborated on *The Sorrow and the Terror: The Haunting Legacy of the Air India Tragedy* (1987), which analyzes the international and human impact of the 1985 crash of a plane carrying 329 passengers from Toronto to Bombay, apparently the result of a terrorist bomb. In 1991 she published a study entitled *Political Culture and Leadership in India*, and she has contributed articles to numerous international periodicals.

"Mine is a clear-eyed but definite love of America," Mukherjee once explained in an interview with *Publishers Weekly*. "I'm aware of the brutality, the violences here, but in the long run my characters are survivors; they've been helped, as I have, by good people of conviction. Like Jasmine, I feel there are people born to be Americans. By American I mean an intensity of spirit and a quality of desire." In "A Wife's Story" part of Panna Bhatt's dilemma hinges on such issues of identity and desire, since what she wants as an Indian woman living in New York differs from the needs of her traditional husband. Of the many realizations that ensue, none is more grounding than Panna's recognition of her body as a source of power and truth.

⊰ A Wife's Story ⊱

Imre says forget it, but I'm going to write David Mamet. So Patels are hard to sell real estate to.[1] You buy them a beer, whisper Glengarry Glen Ross, and they smell swamp instead of sun and surf. They work hard, eat cheap, live ten to a room, stash their savings under futons in Queens, and before you know it they own half of Hoboken. You say, where's the sweet gullibility that made this nation great?

Polish jokes, Patel jokes: that's not why I want to write Mamet.

Seen their women?

Everybody laughs. Imre laughs. The dozing fat man with the Barnes & Noble sack between his legs, the woman next to him, the usher, everybody. The theater isn't so dark that they can't see me. In my red silk sari I'm conspicuous. Plump, gold paisleys sparkle on my chest.

The actor is just warming up. *Seen their women?* He plays a salesman, he's had a bad day and now he's in a Chinese restaurant trying to loosen up. His face is pink. His wool-blend slacks are creased at the crotch. We bought our tickets at half-price, we're sitting on the front row, but at the edge, and we see things we shouldn't be seeing. At least I do, or think I do. Spittle, actors goosing each other, little winks, streaks of makeup.

Maybe they're improvising dialogue too. Maybe Mamet's provided them with insult kits, Thursdays for Chinese, Wednesdays for Hispanics, today for Indians. Maybe they get together before curtain time, see an Indian woman settling in the front row off to the side, and say to each other, "Hey, forget Friday. Let's get *her* today. See if she cries. See if she walks out." Maybe, like the salesmen they play, they have a little bet on.

Maybe I shouldn't feel betrayed.

Their women, he goes again. *They look like they've just been fucked by a dead cat.*

The fat man hoots so hard he nudges my elbow off our shared armrest.

"Imre. I'm going home." But Imre's hunched so far forward he doesn't hear. English isn't his best language. A refugee from Budapest, he has to listen hard. "I didn't pay eighteen dollars to be insulted."

I don't hate Mamet. It's the tyranny of the American dream that scares me. First, you don't exist. Then you've invisible. Then you're funny. Then you're disgusting. Insult, my American friends will tell me, is a kind of acceptance. No instant dignity here. A play like this, back home, would cause riots. Communal, racist, and antisocial. The actors wouldn't make it off stage. This play, and all these awful feelings, would be safely locked up.

I long, at times, for clear-cut answers. Offer me instant dignity today, and I'll take it.

"What?" Imre moves toward me without taking his eyes off the actor. "Come again?"

Tears come. I want to stand, scream, make an awful scene. I long for ugly, nasty rage.

The actor is ranting, flinging spittle. *Give me a chance. I'm not finished, I can get back on the board. I tell that asshole, give me a real lead. And what does that asshole give me? Patels. Nothing but Patels.*

This time Imre works an arm around my shoulders. "Panna, what is Patel? Why are you taking it all so personally?"

---

1. David Mamet (1947–) is an American dramatist and the author of the Pulitzer Prize–winning play *Glengarry Glen Ross* (1983). Patel is a common Indian name like Smith or Jones in America; Mamet is using this name ironically to stand for all Indian immigrants to the U.S.

I shrink from his touch, but I don't walk out. Expensive girls' schools in Lausanne and Bombay have trained me to behave well. My manners are exquisite, my feelings are delicate, my gestures refined, my moods undetectable. They have seen me through riots, uprootings, separation, my son's death.

"I'm not taking it personally."

The fat man looks at us. The woman looks too, and shushes.

I stare back at the two of them. Then I stare, mean and cool, at the man's elbow. Under the bright blue polyester Hawaiian shirt sleeve, the elbow looks soft and runny. "Excuse me," I say. My voice has the effortless meanness of well-bred displaced Third World women, though my rhetoric has been learned elsewhere. "You're exploiting my space."

Startled, the man snatches his arm away from me. He cradles it against his breast. By the time he's ready with comebacks, I've turned my back on him. I've probably ruined the first act for him. I know I've ruined it for Imre.

It's not my fault; it's the *situation*. Old colonies wear down. Patels—the new pioneers—have to be suspicious. Idi Amin's lesson is permanent. AT&T wires move good advice from continent to continent. Keep all assets liquid. Get into 7–11s, get out of condos and motels. I know how both sides feel, that's the trouble. The Patel sniffing out scams, the sad salesmen on the stage: postcolonialism has made me their referee. It's hate I long for; simple, brutish, partisan hate.

After the show Imre and I make our way toward Broadway. Sometimes he holds my hand; it doesn't mean anything more than that crazies and drunks are crouched in doorways. Imre's been here over two years, but he's stayed very old-world, very courtly, openly protective of women. I met him in a seminar on special ed. last semester. His wife is a nurse somewhere in the Hungarian countryside. There are two sons, and miles of petitions for their emigration. My husband manages a mill two hundred miles north of Bombay. There are no children.

"You make things tough on yourself," Imre says. He assumed Patel was a Jewish name or maybe Hispanic; everything makes equal sense to him. He found the play tasteless, he worried about the effect of vulgar language on my sensitive ears. "You have to let go a bit." And as though to show me how to let go, he breaks away from me, bounds ahead with his head ducked tight, then dances on amazingly jerky legs. He's a Magyar, he often tells me, and deep down, he's an Asian too. I catch glimpses of it, knife-blade Attila cheekbones, despite the blondish hair. In his faded jeans and leather jacket, he's a rock video star. I watch MTV for hours in the apartment when Charity's working the evening shift at Macy's. I listen to WPLJ on Charity's earphones. Why should I be ashamed? Television in India is so uplifting.

Imre stops as suddenly as he'd started. People walk around us. The summer sidewalk is full of theatergoers in seersucker suits; Imre's year-round jacket is out of place. European. Cops in twos and threes huddle, lightly tap their thighs with night sticks and smile at me with benevolence. I want to wink at them, get us all in trouble, tell them the crazy dancing man is from the Warsaw Pact. I'm too shy to break into dance on Broadway. So I hug Imre instead.

The hug takes him by surprise. He wants me to let go, but he doesn't really expect me to let go. He staggers, though I weigh no more than 104 pounds, and with him, I pitch forward slightly. Then he catches me, and we walk arm in arm to the bus stop. My husband would never dance or hug a woman on Broadway. Nor would my brothers. They aren't stuffy people, but they went to Anglican boarding schools and they have a well-developed sense of what's silly.

"Imre." I squeeze his big, rough hand. "I'm sorry I ruined the evening for you."

"You did nothing of the kind." He sounds tired. "Let's not wait for the bus. Let's splurge and take a cab instead."

Imre always has unexpected funds. The Network, he calls it, Class of '56.

In the back of the cab, without even trying, I feel light, almost free. Memories of Indian destitutes mix with the hordes of New York street people, and they float free, like astronauts, inside my head. I've made it. I'm making something of my life. I've left home, my husband, to get a Ph.D. in special ed. I have a multiple-entry visa and a small scholarship for two years. After that, we'll see. My mother was beaten by her mother-in-law, my grandmother, when she'd registered for French lessons at the Alliance Française. My grandmother, the eldest daughter of a rich zamindar, was illiterate.

Imre and the cabdriver talk away in Russian. I keep my eyes closed. That way I can feel the floaters better. I'll write Mamet tonight. I feel strong, reckless. Maybe I'll write Steven Spielberg too;[2] tell him that Indians don't eat monkey brains.

We've made it. Patels must have made it. Mamet, Spielberg: they're not condescending to us. Maybe they're a little bit afraid.

Charity Chin, my roommate, is sitting on the floor drinking Chablis out of a plastic wineglass. She is five foot six, three inches taller than me, but weighs a kilo and half less than I do. She is a "hands" model. Orientals are supposed to have a monopoly on the hands-modelling business, she says. She had her eyes fixed eight or nine months ago and out of gratitude sleeps with her plastic surgeon every third Wednesday.

"Oh, good," Charity says. "I'm glad you're back early. I need to talk."

She's been writing checks. MCI, Con Ed, Bonwit Teller. Envelopes, already stamped and sealed, form a pyramid between her shapely, knee-socked legs. The checkbook's cover is brown plastic, grained to look like cowhide. Each time Charity flips back the cover, white geese fly over sky-colored checks. She makes good money, but she's extravagant. The difference adds up to this shared, rent-controlled Chelsea one-bedroom.

"All right. Talk."

When I first moved in, she was seeing an analyst. Now she sees a nutritionist.

"Eric called. From Oregon."

"What did he want?"

"He wants me to pay half the rent on his loft for last spring. He asked me to move back, remember? He *begged* me.

Eric is Charity's estranged husband.

"What does your nutritionist say?" Eric now wears a red jumpsuit and tills the soil in Rajneeshpuram.[3]

"You think Phil's a creep too, don't you? What else can he be when creeps are all I attract?"

Phil is a flutist with thinning hair. He's very touchy on the subject of *flautists* versus *flutists*. He's touchy on every subject, from music to books to foods to clothes. He teaches in a small college upstate, and Charity bought a used blue Datsun ("Nissan," Phil insists) last month so she could spend weekends with him. She returns every Sunday night, exhausted and exasperated. Phil and I don't have much to say to each other—he's the only musician I know; the men in my family are lawyers, engineers, or in business—but I like him. Around me, he loosens up. When he visits, he bakes us loaves of pumpernickel bread. He waxes our kitchen floor. Like many men in this

---

2. Steven Spielberg is a contemporary American film-maker.

3. A Hindu-influenced religious commune located in eastern Oregon during the 1980s.

country, he seems to me a displaced child, or even a woman, looking for something that passed him by, or for something that he can never have. If he thinks I'm not looking, he sneaks his hands under Charity's sweater, but there isn't too much there. Here, she's a model with high ambitions. In India, she'd be a flat-chested old maid.

I'm shy in front of the lovers. A darkness comes over me when I see them horsing around.

"It isn't the money," Charity says. Oh? I think. "He says he still loves me. Then he turns around and asks me for five hundred."

What's so strange about that, I want to ask. She still loves Eric, and Eric, red jumpsuit and all, is smart enough to know it. Love is a commodity, hoarded like any other. Mamet knows. But I say, "I'm not the person to be asking about love." Charity knows that mine was a traditional Hindu marriage. My parents, with the help of a marriage broker, who was my mother's cousin, picked out a groom. All I had to do was get to know his taste in food.

It'll be a long evening, I'm afraid. Charity likes to confess. I unpleat my silk sari—it no longer looks too showy—wrap it in muslin cloth and put it away in a dresser drawer. Saris are hard to have laundered in Manhattan, thought there's a good man in Jackson Heights. My next step will be to brew us a pot of chrysanthemum tea. It's a very special kind from the mainland. Charity's uncle gave it to us. I like him. He's a humpbacked, awkward, terrified man. He runs a gift store on Mott Street, and though he doesn't speak much English, he seems to have done well. Once upon a time he worked for the railways in Chengdu, Szechwan Province, and during the Wuchang Uprising, he was shot at.[4] When I'm down, when I'm lonely for my husband, when I think of our son, or when I need to be held, I think of Charity's uncle. If I hadn't left home, I'd never have heard of the Wuchang Uprising. I've broadened my horizons.

Very late that night my husband calls me from Ahmadabad, a town of textile mills north of Bombay. My husband is a vice president at Lakshmi Cotton Mills. Lakshmi is the goddess of wealth, but LCM (Priv.), Ltd., is doing poorly. Lockouts, strikes, rock-throwings. My husband lives on digitalis, which he calls the food for our *yoga* of discontent.

"We had a bad mishap at the mill today." Then he says nothing for seconds.

The operator comes on. "Do you have the right party, sir? We're trying to reach Mrs. Butt."

"Bhatt," I insist. "B for Bombay, H for Haryana, A for Ahmadabad, double T for Tamil Nadu." It's a litany. "This is she."

"One of our lorries was firebombed today. Resulting in three deaths. The driver, old Karamchand, and his two children."

I know how my husband's eyes looked this minute, how the eye rims sag and the yellow corneas shine and bulge with pain. He is not an emotional man—the Ahmadabad Institute of Management has trained him to cut losses, to look on the bright side of economic catastrophes—but tonight he's feeling low. I try to remember a driver named Karamchand, but can't. That part of my life is over, the way *trucks* have replaced *lorries* in my vocabulary, the way Charity Chin and her lurid love life have replaced inherited notions of marital duty. Tomorrow he'll come out of it. Soon he'll be eating again. He'll sleep like a baby. He's been trained to believe in turnovers. Every morning he rubs his scalp with cantharidine oil so his hair will grow back again.

4. The Wuchang Uprising of October 10, 1911, was a mutiny that broke out among Chinese troops unhappy with the infant emperor who ostensibly ruled China; this uprising is widely recognized as the formal beginning of the Chinese revolution.

"It could be your car next." Affection, love. Who can tell the difference in a traditional marriage in which a wife still doesn't call her husband by his first name?

"No. They know I'm a flunky, just like them. Well paid, maybe. No need for undue anxiety, please."

Then his voice breaks. He says he needs me, he misses me, he wants me to come to him damp from my evening shower, smelling of sandalwood soap, my braid decorated with jasmines.

"I need you too."

"Not to worry, please," he says. "I am coming in a fortnight's time. I have already made arrangements."

Outside my window, fire trucks whine, up Eighth Avenue. I wonder if he can hear them, what he thinks of a life like mine, led amid disorder.

"I am thinking it'll be like a honeymoon. More or less."

When I was in college, waiting to be married, I imagined honeymoons were only for the more fashionable girls, the girls who came from slightly racy families, smoked Sobranies in the dorm lavatories and put up posters of Kabir Bedi, who was supposed to have made it as a big star in the West. My husband wants us to go to Niagara. I'm not to worry about foreign exchange. He's arranged for extra dollars through the Gujarati Network, with a cousin in San Jose. And he's bought four hundred more on the black market. "Tell me you need me. Panna, please tell me again."

I change out of the cotton pants and shirt I've been wearing all day and put on a sari to meet my husband at JFK. I don't forget the jewelry; the marriage necklace of *mangalsutra*, gold drop earrings, heavy gold bangles. I don't wear them every day. In this borough of vice and greed, who knows when, or whom, desire will overwhelm.

My husband spots me in the crowd and waves. He has lost weight, and changed his glasses. The arm, uplifted in a cheery wave, is bony, frail, almost opalescent.

In the Carey Coach, we hold hands. He strokes my fingers one by one. "How come you aren't wearing my mother's ring?"

"Because muggers know about Indian women," I say. They know with us it's 24-karat. His mother's ring is showy, in ghastly taste anywhere but in India: a blood-red Burma ruby set in a gold frame of floral sprays. My mother-in-law got her guru to bless the ring before I left for the States.

He looks disconcerted. He's used to a different role. He's the knowing, suspicious one in the family. He seems to be sulking, and finally he comes out with it. "You've said nothing about my new glasses." I compliment him on the glasses, how chic and Western-executive they make him look. But I can't help the other things, necessities until he learns the ropes. I handle the money, buy the tickets. I don't know if this makes me unhappy.

Charity drives her Nissan upstate, so for two weeks we are to have the apartment to ourselves. This is more privacy than we ever had in India. No parents, no servants, to keep us modest. We play at housekeeping. Imre has lent us a hibachi, and I grill saffron chicken breasts. My husband marvels at the size of the Perdue hens. "They're big like peacocks, no? These Americans, they're really something!" He tries out pizzas, burgers, McNuggets. He chews. He explores. He judges. He loves it all, fears nothing, feels at home in the summer odors, the clutter of Manhattan streets. Since he thinks that the American palate is bland, he carries a bottle of red peppers in his pocket. I wheel a shopping cart down the aisles of the neighborhood Grand Union, and he follows, swiftly, greedily. He picks up hair rinses and high-protein diet powders. There's so much I already take for granted.

One night, Imre stops by. He wants us to go with him to a movie. In his work shirt and red leather tie, he looks arty or strung out. It's only been a week, but I feel as though I am really seeing him for the first time. The yellow hair worn very short at the sides, the wide, narrow lips. He's a good-looking man, but self-conscious, almost arrogant. He's picked the movie we should see. He always tells me what to see, what to read. He buys the *Voice*. He's a natural avant-gardist. For tonight he's chosen *Numéro Deux*.

"Is it a musical?" my husband asks. The Radio City Music Hall is on his list of sights to see. He's read up on the history of the Rockettes. He doesn't catch Imre's sympathetic wink.

Guilt, shame, loyalty. I long to be ungracious, not ingratiate myself with both men.

That night my husband calculates in rupees the money we've wasted on Godard.[5] "That refugee fellow, Nagy, must have a screw loose in his head. I paid very steep price for dollars on the black market."

Some afternoons we go shopping. Back home we hated shopping, but now it is a lovers' project. My husband's shopping list startles me. I feel I am just getting to know him. Maybe, like Imre, freed from the dignities of old-world culture, he too could get drunk and squirt Cheez Whiz on a guest. I watch him dart into stores in his gleaming leather shoes. Jockey shorts on sale in outdoor bins in Broadway entrance him. White tube socks with different bands of color delight him. He looks for microcassettes, for anything small and electronic and smuggleable. He needs a garment bag. He calls it a "wardrobe," and I have to translate.

"All of New York is having sales, no?"

My heart speeds watching him this happy. It's the third week in August, almost the end of summer, and the city smells ripe, it cannot bear more heat, more money, more energy.

"This is so smashing! The prices are so excellent!" Recklessly, my prudent husband signs away traveller's checks. How he intends to smuggle it all back, I don't dare ask. With a microwave, he calculates, we could get rid of our cook.

This has to be love, I think. Charity, Eric, Phil: they may be experts on sex. My husband doesn't chase me around the sofa, but he pushes me down on Charity's battered cushions, and the man who has never entered the kitchen in our Ahmadabad house now comes toward me with a dish tub of steamy water to massage away the pavement heat.

Ten days into his vacation my husband checks out brochures for sightseeing trips. Shortline, Grayline, Crossroads: his new vinyl briefcase is full of schedules and pamphlets. While I make pancakes out of a mix, he comparison-shops. Tour number one costs $10.95 and will give us the World Trade Center, Chinatown, and the United Nations. Tour number three would take us both uptown *and* downtown for $14.95, but my husband is absolutely sure he doesn't want to see Harlem. We settle for tour number four: Downtown and the Dame. It's offered by a new tour company with a small, dirty office at Eighth and Forty-eighth.

The sidewalk outside the office is colorful with tourists. My husband sends me in to buy the tickets because he has come to feel Americans don't understand his accent.

5. Jean-Luc Godard is a contemporary French filmmaker.

The dark man, Lebanese probably, behind the counter comes on too friendly. "Come on, doll, make my day!" He won't say which tour is his. "Number four? Honey, no! Look, you've wrecked me! Say you'll change your mind." He takes two twenties and gives back change. He holds the tickets, forcing me to pull. He leans closer. "I'm off after lunch."

My husband must have been watching me from the sidewalk. "What was the chap saying?" he demands. "I told you not to wear pants. He thinks you are Puerto Rican. He thinks he can treat you with disrespect."

The bus is crowded and we have to sit across the aisle from each other. The tour guide begins his patter on Forty-sixth. He looks like an actor, his hair bleached and blow-dried. Up close he must look middle-aged, but from where I sit his skin is smooth and his cheeks faintly red.

"Welcome to the Big Apple, folks." The guide uses a microphone. "Big Apple. That's what we native Manhattan degenerates call our city. Today we have guests from fifteen foreign countries and six states from this U.S. of A. That makes the Tourist Bureau real happy. And let me assure you that while we may be the richest city in the richest country in the world, it's okay to tip your charming and talented attendant." He laughs. Then he swings his hip out into the aisle and sings a song.

"And it's mighty fancy on old Delancey Street, you know . . . ."

My husband looks irritable. The guide is, as expected, a good singer. "The bloody man should be giving us histories of buildings we are passing, no?" I pat his hand, the mood passes. He cranes his neck. Our window seats have both gone to Japanese. It's the tour of his life. Next to this, the quick business trips to Manchester and Glasgow pale.

"And tell me what street compares to Mott Street, in July . . . ."

The guide wants applause. He manages a derisive laugh from the Americans up front. He's working the aisles now. "I coulda been somebody, right? I coulda been a star!" Two or three of us smile, those of us who recognize the parody. He catches my smile. The sun on his harsh, bleached hair. "Right, your highness? Look, we gotta maharani with us! Couldn't I have been a star?"

"Right!" I say, my voice coming out in a squeal. I've been trained to adapt; what else can I say?

We drive through traffic past landmark office buildings and churches. The guide flips his hands. "Art deco," he keeps saying. I hear him confide to one of the Americans: "Beats me. I went to a cheap guide's school." My husband wants to know more about this Art Deco, but the guide sings another song.

"We made a foolish choice," my husband grumbles. "We are sitting in the bus only. We're not going into famous buildings." He scrutinizes the pamphlets in his jacket pocket. I think, at least it's air-conditioned in here. I could sit here in the cool shadows of the city forever.

Only five of us appear to have opted for the "Downtown and the Dame" tour. The others will ride back uptown past the United Nations after we've been dropped off at the pier for the ferry to the Statue of Liberty.

An elderly European pulls a camera out of his wife's designer tote bag. He takes pictures of the boats in the harbor, the Japanese in kimonos eating popcorn, scavenging pigeons, me. Then, pushing his wife ahead of him, he climbs back on the bus and waves to us. For a second I feel terribly lost. I wish we were on the bus going back to the apartment. I know I'll not be able to describe any of this to Charity, or to Imre. I'm too proud to admit I went on a guided tour.

The view of the city from the Circle Line ferry is seductive, unreal. The skyline wavers out of reach, but never quite vanishes. The summer sun pushes through fluffy clouds and dapples the glass of office towers. My husband looks thrilled, even more than he had on the shopping trips down Broadway. Tourists and dreamers, we have spent our life's savings to see this skyline, this statue.

"Quick, take a picture of me!" my husband yells as he moves toward a gap of railings. A Japanese matron has given up her position in order to change film. "Before the Twin Towers disappear!"

I focus, wait for a large Oriental family to walk out of my range. My husband holds his pose tight against the railing. He wants to look relaxed, an international businessman at home in all the financial markets.

A bearded man slides across the bench towards me. "Like this," he says and helps me get my husband in focus. "You want me to take the photo for you?" His name, he says, is Goran. He is Goran from Yugoslavia, as though that were enough for tracking him down. Imre from Hungary, Panna from India. He pulls the old Leica out of my hand, signaling the Orientals to beat it, and clicks away. "I'm a photographer," he says. He could have been a camera thief. That's what my husband would have assumed. Somehow, I trusted. "Get you a beer?" he asks.

"I don't. Drink, I mean. Thank you very much." I say those last words very loud, for everyone's benefit. The odd bottles of Soave with Imre don't count.

"Too bad." Goran gives back the camera.

"Take one more!" my husband shouts from the railing. "Just to be sure!"

The island itself disappoints. The Lady has brutal scaffolding holding her in. The museum is closed. The snack bar is dirty and expensive. My husband reads out the prices to me. He orders two french fries and two Cokes. We sit at picnic tables and wait for the ferry to take us back.

"What was that hippie chap saying?"

As if I could say. A day-care center has brought its kids, at least forty of them, to the island for the day. The kids, all wearing name tags, run around us. I can't help noticing how many are Indian. Even a Patel, probably a Bhatt if I looked hard enough. They toss hamburger bits at pigeons. They kick styrofoam cups. The pigeons are slow, greedy, persistent. I have to shoo one off the table top. I don't think my husband thinks about our son.

"What hippie?"

"The one on the boat. With the beard and the hair."

My husband doesn't look at me. He shakes out his paper napkin and tries to protect his french fries from pigeon feathers.

"Oh, him. He said he was from Dubrovnik." It isn't true, but I don't want trouble.

"What did he say about Dubrovnik?"

I know enough about Dubrovnik to get by. Imre's told me about it. And about Mostar and Zagreb. In Mostar white Muslims sing the call to prayer. I would like to see that before I die: white Muslims. Whole peoples have moved before me; they've adapted. The night Imre told me about Mostar was also the night I saw my first snow in Manhattan. We'd walked down to Chelsea from Columbia. We'd walked and talked and I hadn't felt tired at all.

"You're too innocent," my husband says. He reaches for my hand. "Panna," he cries with pain in his voice, and I am brought back from perfect, floating memories of snow, "I've come to take you back. I have seen how men watch you."

"What?"

"Come back, now. I have tickets. We have all the things we will ever need. I can't live without you."

A little girl with wiry braids kicks a bottle cap at his shoes. The pigeons wheel and scuttle around us. My husband covers his fries with spread-out fingers. "No kicking," he tells the girl. Her name, Beulah, is printed in green ink on a heart-shaped name tag. He forces a smile, and Beulah smiles back. Then she starts to flap her arms. She flaps, she hops. The pigeons go crazy for fries and scraps.

"Special ed. course is two years," I remind him." I can't go back."

My husband picks up our trays and throws them into the garbage before I can stop him. He's carried disposability a little too far. "We've been taken," he says, moving toward the dock, though the ferry will not arrive for another twenty minutes. "The ferry costs only two dollars round-trip per person. We should have chosen tour number one for $10.95 instead of tour number four for $14.95."

With my Lebanese friend, I think. "But this way we don't have to worry about cabs. The bus will pick us up at the pier and take us back to midtown. Then we can walk home."

"New York is full of cheats and whatnot. Just like Bombay." He is not accusing me of infidelity. I feel dread all the same.

That night, after we've gone to bed, the phone rings. My husband listens, then hands the phone to me. "What is this woman saying?" He turns on the pink Macy's lamp by the bed. "I am not understanding these Negro people's accents."

The operator repeats the message. It's a cable from one of the directors of Lakshmi Cotton Mills. "Massive violent labor confrontation anticipated. Stop. Return posthaste. Stop. Cable flight details. Signed Kantilal Shah."

"It's not your factory," I say. "You're supposed to be on vacation."

"So, you are worrying about me? Yes? You reject my heartfelt wishes but you worry about me?" He pulls me close, slips the straps of my nightdress off my shoulder. "Wait a minute."

I wait, unclothed, for my husband to come back to me. The water is running in the bathroom. In the ten days he has been here he has learned American rites: deodorants, fragrances. Tomorrow morning he'll call Air India; tomorrow evening he'll be on his way back to Bombay. Tonight I should make up to him for my years away, the gutted trucks, the degree I'll never use in India. I want to pretend with him that nothing has changed.

In the mirror that hangs on the bathroom door, I watch my naked body turn, the breasts, the thighs glow. The body's beauty amazes. I stand there shameless, in ways he has never seen me. I am free, afloat, watching somebody else.   *1988*

Toni Cade Bambara
1939–1996

"It's a tremendous responsibility—responsiblity and honor—to be a writer, an artist, a cultural worker . . . whatever you want to call this vocation," explained Toni Cade Bambara in a 1981 interview with Claudia Tate, published in *Black Women Writers at Work*. "One's got to see what the factory worker sees, what the prisoner sees, what the welfare children see, what the scholar sees, got to see what the ruling-class mythmakers see as well, in order to tell the truth and not get trapped. Got to see more and dare more." Constructing truthful representations of African-American identity is important to the fiction of Bambara, whose stories affirm black women and present conflict and caring among neighbors and between generations.

Born in New York City and raised in Harlem and Bedford-Stuyvesant, she acknowledged "my mama" as the primary influence on her writing, remembering as a child how often she would daydream with pen and paper in the kitchen while her mother, Helen Cade, mopped around her. Bambara treasured her mother's stories of the Harlem Renaissance, stories that taught her about Countee Cullen, Langston Hughes, and other black writers and jazz musicians to whom her mother used to listen. For Bambara as a young writer, New York was "bebop heaven"; her own work has been influenced by music and performance. Toni Cade assumed the name Bambara to honor her female heritage after finding that surname signed in a sketch-book in her great-grandmother's trunk. After graduating from Queens College in 1959 and completing an M.A. from the City University of New York in 1964, Bambara worked at many different jobs, including welfare investigator, community organizer, youth counselor, freelance writer, and teacher. She taught in the black studies programs at Rutgers University and Duke University and in women's studies at Emory and Atlanta Universities; she also served as a writer-in-residence at Spelman College. Ill for many years, she published little after 1980, and in 1996 she died of cancer.

Bambara edited one of the first anthologies of poetry, fiction, and essays by African-American women, *The Black Woman* (1970); a second anthology, *Tales and Stories for Black Folks*, followed in 1971. She published two volumes of her own stories, *Gorilla, My Love* (1972) and *The Sea Birds Are Still Alive* (1977). A committed feminist activist, Bambara challenged negative stereotypes of black girls and women in her work. Many stories focus on intimate relationships, for Bambara insisted that nurturing the self and loving others were important pre-requisites to any kind of social transformation. Her novel *The Salt Eaters* (1980), her best-known work, began as a journal entry; it chronicles the lives of black people in a small town, some of whom are ordinary "folks on the block" and others of whom are concerned with the larger world struggle. Bambara described it as a philosophical novel that addressed the most pressing social issues of our time, for "we are a people at the crossroads."

Taken from *Gorilla, My Love*, the short story reprinted here, "My Man Bovanne," is wide-ly recognized as a classic of the genre. The scholar Eleanor Traylor considers Miss Hazel the "central consciousness" in Bambara's oeuvre, and the author herself has acknowledged her affinity with this rebellious character. All writing is ultimately autobiographical, she explained to Tate, even when it seems not to be: "Whomever we may conjure up or remember or imag-ine to get a story down, we're telling our own tale just as surely as a client on the analyst's couch, just as surely as a pilgrim on the way to Canterbury."

⤳ My Man Bovanne ⤳

Blind people got a hummin jones if you notice. Which is understandable completely once you been around one and notice what no eyes will force you into to see people, and you get past the first time, which seems to come out of nowhere, and it's like you in church again with fat-chest ladies and old gents gruntin a hum low in the throat to whatever the preacher be saying. Shakey Bee bottom lip all swole up with Sweet Peach and me explainin how come the sweet-potato bread was a dollar-quarter this time stead of dollar regular and he say uh hunh he understand, then he break into this *thizzin* kind of hum which is quiet, but fiercesome just the same, if you ain't ready for it. Which I wasn't. But I got used to it and the onliest time I had to say somethin bout it was when he was playin checkers on the stoop one time and he commenst to hummin quite churchy seem to me. So I says, "Look here Shakey Bee, I can't beat you and Jesus too." He stop.

So that's how come I asked My Man Bovanne to dance. He ain't my man mind you, just a nice ole gent from the block that we all know cause he fixes things and the kids like him. Or used to fore Black Power got hold their minds and mess em around till they can't be civil to ole folks. So we at this benefit for my niece's cousin who's runnin for somethin with this Black party somethin or other behind her. And I press up close to dance with Bovanne who blind and I'm hummin and he hummin, chest to chest like talkin. Not jammin my breasts into the man. Wasn't bout tits. Was bout vibrations. And he dug it and asked me what color dress I had on and how my hair was fixed and how I was doin without a man, not nosy but nice-like, and who was at this affair and was the canapés dainty-stingy or healthy enough to get hold of proper. Comfy and cheery is what I'm tryin to get across. Touch talkin like the heel of the hand on the tambourine or on a drum.

But right away Joe Lee come up on us and frown for dancin so close to the man. My own son who knows what kind of warm I am about; and don't grown men call me long distance and in the middle of the night for a little Mama comfort? But he frown. Which ain't right since Bovanne can't see and defend himself. Just a nice old man who fixes toasters and busted irons and bicycles and things and changes the lock on my door when my men friends get messy. Nice man. Which is not why they invited him. Grass roots you see. Me and Sister Taylor and the woman who does heads at Mamies and the man from the barber shop, we all there on account of we grass roots. And I ain't never been souther than Brooklyn Battery and no more country than the window box on my fire escape. And just yesterday my kids tellin me to take them countrified rags off my head and be cool. And now can't get Black enough to suit em. So everybody passin saying My Man Bovanne. Big deal, keep steppin and don't even stop a minute to get the man a drink or one of them cute sandwiches or tell him what's goin on. And him standin there with a smile ready case someone do speak he want to be ready. So that's how come I pull him on the dance floor and we dance squeezin past the tables and chairs and all them coats and people standin round up in each other face talkin bout this and that but got no use for this blind man who mostly fixed skates and skooters for all these folks when they was just kids. So I'm pressed up close and we touch talkin with the hum. And here come my daughter cuttin her eye at me like she do when she tell me about my "apoliti-cal" self like I got hoof and mouf disease and there ain't no hope at all. And I don't pay her no mind and just look up in Bovanne shadow face and tell him his stomach like a drum and he laugh. Laugh read loud. And here come my youngest, Task, with a tap on my elbow like he the third grade monitor and I'm cuttin up on the line to assembly.

"I was just talkin on the drums," I explained when they hauled me into the kitchen. I figured drums was my best defense. They can get ready for drums what with all this heritage business. And Bovanne stomach just like that drum Task give me when he come back from Africa. You just touch it and it hum, thizzm, thizzm. So I stuck to the drum story. "Just drummin that's all."

"Mama, what are you talkin about?"

"She had too much to drink," say Elo to Task cause she don't hardly say nuthin to me direct no more since that ugly argument about my wigs.

"Look here Mama," say Task, the gentle one. "We just tryin to pull your coat. You were makin a spectacle of yourself out there dancing like that."

"Dancin like what?"

Task run a hand over his left ear like his father for the world and his father before that.

"Like a bitch in heat," say Elo.

"Well, uhh, I was goin to say like one of them sex-starved ladies gettin on in years and not too discriminating. Know what I mean?"

I don't answer cause I'll cry. Terrible thing when your own children talk to you like that. Pullin me out the party and hustlin me into some stranger's kitchen in the back of a bar just like the damn police. And ain't like I'm old old. I can still wear me some sleeveless dresses without the meat hangin off my arm. And I keep up with some thangs through my kids. Who ain't kids no more. To hear them tell it. So I don't say nuthin.

"Dancin with that tom," says Elo to Joe Lee, who leanin on the folks' freezer. "His feet can smell a cracker a mile away and go into their shuffle number post haste. And them eyes. He could be a little considerate and put on some shades. Who wants to look into them blown-out fuses that—"

"Is this what they call the generation gap?" I say.

"Generation gap," spits Elo, like I suggested castor oil and fricasse possum in the milk-shakes or somethin. "That's a white concept for a white phenomenon. There's no generation gap among Black people. We are a col—"

"Yeh, well never mind," says Joe Lee. "The point is Mama . . . well, it's pride. You embarrass yourself and us too dancin like that."

"I wasn't shame." Then nobody say nuthin. Them standin there in they pretty clothes with drinks in they hands and gangin up on me, and me in the third-degree chair and nary a olive to my name. Felt just like the police got hold of me.

"First of all," Task say, holdin up his hand and tickin off the offenses, "the dress. Now that dress is too short, Mama, and too low-cut for a woman your age. And Tamu's going to make a speech tonight to kick off the campaign and will be introducin you and expecting you to organize the council of elders—"

"Me? Didn nobody ask me nuthin. You mean Nisi? She change her name?"

"Well, Norton was supposed to tell you about it. Nisi wants to introduce you and then encourage the older folks to form a Council of the Elders to act as an advisory—"

"And you going to be standing there with your boobs out and that wig on your head and that hem up to your ass. And people'll say, 'Ain't that the horny bitch that was grindin with the blind dude?'"

"Elo, be cool a minute," say Task, gettin to the next finger. "And then there's the drinkin. Mama, you know you can't drink cause next thing you know you be laughin loud and carryin on," and he grab another finger for loudness. "And then there's the dancin. You been tatooed on the man for four records straight and slow draggin even on the fast numbers. How you think that look for a woman your age?"

"What's my age?"

"What?"

"I'm axin you all a simple question. You keep talkin bout what's proper for a woman my age. How old am I anyhow?" And Joe Lee slams his eyes shut and squinches up his face to figure. And Task run a hand over his ear and stare into his glass like the ice cubes goin calculate for him. And Elo just starin at the top of my head like she goin rip the wig off any minute now.

"Is your hair braided up under that thing? If so, why don't you take it off? You always did do a neat cornroll."

"Uh huh," cause I'm thinkin how she couldn't undo her hair fast enough talking bout cornroll so countrified. None of which was the subject. "How old, I say?"

"Sixtee-one or —"

"You a damn lie Joe Lee Peoples."

"And that's another thing," say Task on the fingers.

"You know what you all can kiss," I say, gettin up and brushin the wrinkles out my lap.

"Oh, Mama," Elo say, puttin a hand on my shoulder like she hasn't done since she left home and the hand landin light and not sure it supposed to be there. Which hurt me to my heart. Cause this was the child in our happiness fore Mr. Peoples die. And I carried that child strapped to my chest till she was nearly two. We was close is what I'm tryin to tell you. Cause it was more me in the child than the others. And even after Task it was the girlchild I covered in the night and wept over for no reason at all less it was she was a chub-chub like me and not very pretty, but a warm child. And how did things get to this, and she can't put a sure hand on me and say Mama we love you and care about you and you entitled to enjoy yourself cause you a good woman?

"And then there's Reverend Trent," say Task, glancin from left to right like they hatchin a plot and just now lettin me in on it. "You were suppose to be talking with him tonight, Mama, about giving us his basement for campaign headquarters and—"

"Didn nobody tell me nuthin. If grass roots mean you kept in the dark I can't use it. I really can't. And Reven Trent a fool anyway the way he tore into the widow man up there on Edgecomb cause he wouldn't take in three of them foster children and the woman not even comfy in the ground yet and the man's mind messed up and—"

"Look here," say Task. "What we need is a family conference so we can get all this stuff cleared up and laid out on the table. In the meantime I think we better get back into the other room and tend to business. And in the meantime, Mama, see if you can't get to Reverend Trent and—"

"You want me to belly rub with the Reven, that it?"

"Oh damn," Elo say and go through the swingin door.

"We'll talk about all this at dinner. How's tomorrow night, Joe Lee?" While Joe Lee being self-important I'm wonderin who's doin the cookin and how come no body ax me if I'm free and do I get a corsage and things like that. Then Joe nod that it's O.K. and he go through the swingin door and just a little hubbub come through from the other room. Then Task smile his smile, lookin just like his daddy and he leave. And it just me in this stranger's kitchen, which was a mess I wouldn't never let my kitchen look like. Poison you just to look at the pots. Then the door swing the other way and it's My Man Bovanne standin there sayin Miss Hazel but lookin at the deep fry and then at the steam table, and most surprised when I come up on him from the other direction and take him on out of there. Pass the folks pushin up towards the stage where Nisi and some other people settin and ready to talk, and folks gettin to the last of the sandwiches and the booze fore they settle down in one spot and listen serious. And I'm thinkin bout tellin Bovanne what a lovely long dress Nisi got on and the earrings and her hair piled up in a cone and the people bout to hear how we all gettin screwed and gotta form our own party and everybody there listenin and lookin. But instead I just haul the man on out of there, and Joe Lee and his wife look at me like I'm terrible, but they ain't said boo to the man yet. Cause he blind and old and don't nobody there need him since they grown up and don't need they skates fixed no more.

"Where we goin, Miss Hazel?" Him knowin all the time.

"First we gonna buy you some dark sunglasses. Then you comin with me to the supermarket so I can pick up tomorrow's dinner, which is going to be grand thing proper and you invited. Then we goin to my house."

"That be fine. I surely would like to rest my feet." Bein cute, but you got to let men play out they little show, blind or not. So he chat on bout how tired he is and how he appreciate me takin him in hand this way. And I'm thinkin I'll have him change the lock on my door first thing. Then I'll give the man a nice warm bath with jasmine leaves in the water and a little Epsom salt on the sponge to do his back. And then a good rub-down with rose water and olive oil. Then a cup of lemon tea with a taste in it. And a lit-tle talcum, some of that fancy stuff Nisi mother sent over last Christmas. And then a massage, a good face massage round the forehead which is the worryin part. Cause you gots to take care of the older folks. And let them know they still needed to run the mimeo machine and keep the spark plugs clean and fix the mailboxes for folks who might help us get the breakfast program goin, and the school for the little kids and the campaign and all. Cause old folks is the nation. That what Nisi was sayin and I mean to do my part.

"I imagine you are a very pretty woman, Miss Hazel."

"I surely am," I say just like the hussy my daughter always say I was.

1960

⊹ ⹁≎⹁ ⊹

Sharon Olds
1942–

In "Sex Without Love" contemporary American poet Sharon Olds wonders "How do they do it?" How, that is, do lovers move their sweaty bodies together, take that ecstatic risk unless their union is undergirded by love? One of Olds's most moving tributes to what AUDRE LORDE has called "the erotic as power," this poem reveals the passion and compassion that Olds brings to all her poems, whose topics include incest, child abuse, rape, sexual desire, and maternal love.

Born in San Francisco and educated at Stanford University, Olds has been celebrated as one of America's most forthright poets at chronicling familial and erotic relationships. Since graduat-ing from Columbia University, where she earned a Ph.D. in 1972, she has taught at several uni-versities, most recently at New York University, where she teaches creative writing. She also helps run the NYU Writing Workshop at New York's Goldwater Hospital, where she works with physi-cally challenged patients. Her first volume of poetry, Satan Says (1980), won the San Francisco Poetry Prize; her second, The Dead and the Living (1984), received both the Lamont Prize and the National Book Critics Circle Award. Other volumes include The Gold Cell (1987) and The Father (1992). The Matter of This World: New and Selected Poems appeared in 1987, and The Sign of Sat-urn: Poems 1980–1987 was published in 1991. In 1993 Olds was honored with a Lila Wallace Reader's Digest Writing Award. In The Wellspring (1995) she traces female embodiment from the prenatal world to adulthood, celebrating adolescent sexual awakening, childbirth, and marital and sexual love in bold, musical language.

The poems included here reveal Olds's commitment to writing the body. In "The Lan-guage of the Brag" Olds asserts her American woman's voice as fully equal, if not superior, to the voices of her male predecessors. Having withstood the pain of childbirth, "my inner sex / stabbed again and again with a terrible pain like a knife," the poet is triumphant. "That Year" and "The Girl," in contrast, are graphic poems in which Olds reveals outrage at sexual vio-lence yet chronicles the power of survival.

⊰ That Year ⊱

The year of the mask of blood, my father
hammering on the glass door to get in

was the year they found her body in the hills,
in a shallow grave, naked, white as
5   mushroom, partially decomposed,
raped, murdered, the girl from my class.

That was the year my mother took us and
hid us so he could not get at us
when she told him to leave; so there were no more
10   tyings by the wrist to the chair,
no more denial of food
or the forcing of foods, the head held back,
down the throat at the restaurant,
the shame of vomited buttermilk
15   down the sweater with its shame of new breasts.

That was the year
I started to bleed
crossing over that border in the night,

and in Social Studies, we came at last
20   to Auschwitz, I recognized it
like my father's face, the face of the guard
turning away—or worse yet
turning toward me.

The symmetrical piles of white bodies,
the round white breast-shapes of the heaps,
the smell of the smoke, the dogs the wires the
rope the hunger. It had happened to others.
There was a word for us. I was: a Jew.

It had happened to six million.
And there was another word that was not
for the six million, but was a word for me
and for many others. I was:
a survivor

1980

⊰ The Language of the Brag ⊱

I have wanted excellence in the knife-throw,
I have wanted to use my exceptionally strong and accurate arms
and my straight posture and quick electric muscles
to achieve something at the center of a crowd,
5   the blade piercing the bark deep,
the haft slowly and heavily vibrating like the cock.

I have wanted some epic use for my excellent body,
some heroism, some American achievement
beyond the ordinary for my extraordinary self,
10   magnetic and tensile, I have stood by the sandlot
and watched the boys play.

I have wanted courage, I have thought about fire
and the crossing of waterfalls, I have dragged around

my belly big with cowardice and safety,
15   my stool black with iron pills,
my huge breasts oozing mucus,
my legs swelling, my hands swelling,
my face swelling and darkening, my hair
falling out, my inner sex
20   stabbed again and again with terrible pain like a knife.
I have lain down.

I have lain down and sweated and shaken
and passed blood and feces and water and
slowly alone in the center of a circle I have
25   passed the new person out
and they have lifted the new person free of the act
and wiped the new person free of that
language of blood like praise all over the body.

I have done what you wanted to do, Walt Whitman,
30   Allen Ginsberg,[1] I have done this thing,
I and the other women this exceptional
act with the exceptional heroic body,
this giving birth, this glistening verb,
and I am putting my proud American boast
35   right here with the others.

1980

⊰ The Girl ⊱

They chased her and her friend through the woods
and caught them in a small clearing, broken
random bracken, a couple of old mattresses,
the dry ochre of foam rubber,
5   as if the place had been prepared.
The thin one with black hair
started raping her best friend,
and the blond one stood above her,
thrust his thumbs back inside her jaws, she was 12,
10   stuck his penis in her mouth and throat
faster and faster and faster.
Then the black-haired one stood up—
they lay like pulled-up roots at his feet,

---

1. Walt Whitman (1819–92) and Allen Ginsberg (1926–98) were American poets who wrote about the male body and democracy.

two naked 12-year-old girls, he said
15   *Now you're going to know what it's like*
To be shot 5 times and slaughtered like a pig,
and they switched mattresses,
the blond was raping and stabbing her friend,
the black-haired one sticking inside her
20   in one place and then another,
the point of his gun pressed deep into her waist,
she felt a little click in her spine and a
sting like 7-Up in her head and then he
pulled the tree-branch across her throat
25   and everything went dark,
the gym went dark, and her mother's kitchen,
even the globes of light on the rounded
lips of her mother's nesting bowls went dark.

When she woke up she was lying on the cold
30   iron-smelling earth, she was under the mattress,
pulled up over her like a
blanket at night,
she saw the body of her best friend
and she began to run,
35   she came to the edge of the woods and she stepped
out from the trees, like a wound debriding,
and walked across the field to the tracks
and said to the railway brakeman *Please, sir. Please, sir.*

At the trial she had to say everything—
40   her big sister taught her the words—
she had to sit in the room with them and
point to them. Now she goes to parties
but does not smoke, she is a cheerleader,
she throws her body up in the air
45   and kicks her legs and comes home and does the dishes
and her homework, she has to work hard in math,
the night over the roof of her bed
filled with white planets. Every night she
prays for the soul of her best friend and
50   then thanks God for life. She knows
what all of us want never to know
and she does a cartwheel, the splits, she shakes the
shredded pom-poms in her fists.

1993

⊰ Sex Without Love ⊱

How do they do it, the ones who make love
without love? Beautiful as dancers,
gliding over each other like ice-skaters
over the ice, fingers hooked
5   inside each other's bodies, faces

red as steak, wine, wet as the
children at birth whose mothers are going to
give them away. How do they come to the
come to the   come to the   God   come to the
10   still waters, and not love
the one who came there with them, light
rising slowly as steam off their joined
skin? These are the true religious,
the purists, the pros, the ones who will not
15   accept a false Messiah, love the
priest instead of the God. They do not
mistake the lover for their own pleasure,
they are like great runners: they know they are alone
with the road surface, the cold, the wind,
20   the fit of their shoes, their over-all cardiovascular health—just factors, like the partner
in the bed, and not the truth, which is the
single body alone in the universe
against its own best time.

1992

———— ❧ ————

Slavenka Drakulić
1949–

A Croatian novelist, journalist, and feminist, Slavenka Drakulić writes about women's lives under Communism, the power of eroticism, and the tragedy of war and ethnic cleansing in Eastern Europe. She was born in Rijeka, Yugoslavia (now Croatia), to Ivan and Antonija Susanj; her father was an army colonel, her mother a government employee. After earning her B.A. in world literature in 1976, Drakulić worked as a journalist in Zagreb. She was married to Slobodan Drakulić and has a daughter, Rujana; her present husband, Richard Swartz, is also a journalist. In 1987 Drakulić participated in the International Writers' Workshop at the University of Iowa, and in 1990 she received a Fulbright Award.

Her novels were written in Croatian but have been translated into English. *Holograms of Fear* (1992) tells the story of a woman who travels from Eastern Europe to the United States for a kidney transplant and reflects upon the contrasts between the two cultures and upon the fear of death. *Marble Skin* (1994) explores the intensity of mother-daughter relationships, as a sculptor creates an erotic work that she entitles "My Mother's Body"; seeing it drives her mother to despair. A third novel, *A Woman Who Ate Her Lover* (1998) explores the perils of sexual love; a fourth, *S: A Novel about the Balkans* (1999), is set during the Bosnian war of 1992. Drakulić has also published three collections of essays. *The Deadly Sins of Feminism* appeared in Yugoslavia in 1984 and has not yet been translated into English; its subjects include prostitution, sex education, and the misrepresentation of women in the media. *How We Survived Communism and Even Laughed* (1992) chronicles the exhausting daily routines of Eastern European women who worked outside the home yet had primary responsibility for cleaning, cooking, and childcare despite the availability of state-run day care facilities that were often inadequate.

Drakulić wrote the essays that comprise *Balkan Express: Fragments from the Other Side of War* (1993) because she felt compelled to document the bloodshed in her native land, once one of the most progressive and international countries of Eastern Europe. In this collection she describes the terrors of war and ethnic hatred as well as her own flight from Zagreb to Slo[...] and later to Paris, as enemy forces invaded. Drakulić examines the reasons behind the dram[...] rise of nationalistic fervor in the former Yugoslavia in a 1991 essay in the *Nation*. Her boo[...] have been translated into twelve languages, and she has won several literary awards, including the Independent Foreign Fiction Award in 1992 for *Holograms of Fear* and a prize from the Institute of Human Sciences in Vienna in 1994. She is at work on a BBC documentary on the political situation in post-Communist countries and is writing a book about the struggle for identity experienced by people of her generation who were born under Communist rule.

"Make-up and Other Crucial Questions," first published in *How We Survived Communism and Even Laughed*, explores the lives of women in Eastern Bloc countries prior to 1989 who lacked such basic necessities as bread and sanitary napkins, let alone such "luxuries" as cosmetics or tampons. Part memoir and part social commentary, this essay probes with compassion the obsession of many women for whom the lingerie and beauty products advertised in the international edition of *Vogue* magazine, available to other women but not to them, became symbolic of their longing for political freedom. "The images that cross the borders of magazines, movies, or videos," Drakulić concludes, "are therefore more dangerous than any secret weapon, because they make one desire that 'other-ness' badly enough to risk one's life by trying to escape. Many did."

⊰ Make-up and Other Crucial Questions ⊱

When I close my eyes, I can still see her, resting on our kitchen sofa on Saturday afternoons. It's spring, she lies there in semi-darkness, and in the dim light coming through canvas shades on the window, I see her face, covered with fresh cucumber slices, like a strange white mask. She does it every Saturday—after twenty minutes she will get up, remove the rings, and wash her face with cold water. Then she will put on Dream Complex cream, the only cream available in the early 1950s. When I touch her skin, it will be fresh and tender under my fingers.

Before that, she would wash our hair, hers and mine. Her hair is very long and brown; she washes it with Camillaflor powdered shampoo. It's the only brand that exists and features a brunette or blonde on the paper package. She rinses her hair in water with vinegar so as to leave it soft and silky. My thin, blonde hair has to be rinsed with the juice of half a lemon—its smell follows me the whole afternoon. And while she lies there, with a cucumber mask—or a mask made of egg whites, or a yogurt mask if it is winter, or a camomile wrap to remove puffiness under the eyes after a bad night's sleep or quarreling with my father—I imagine that one day I will be doing the same, and I can't wait for this day to come.

Afterwards, I know she will manicure her nails and apply make-up. That is, she will put on one of the two shades of lipstick that she bought in a pharmacy and outline her eyes with a kohl pencil—these are all the cosmetics there are. She will be happy if she still has some powder left, packed in a small plastic bag, the one that her mother was able to provide for her. Finally, she will put a few drops of *eau de Cologne* behind her ears and on her ankles, a yellowish water made up by the pharmacist himself. In her blue satin evening dress that she sewed herself, she will go dancing with my father at the Army Officer's Club. Year and years later, I will remember every detail of how beautiful she was at that moment, a magician who created beauty out of nothing. She ignored reality, the fact that there was no choice, fighting it with the old beauty recipes that she had learned from the mother and grandmother. After all, one could always make a peeling mask out of cornflour, use olive oil for sun-tanning or as a dry hair treatment, or give a deep brown tone to the hair with strong black tea.

563

nist states at that time—and until they ceased to exist—had
n producing make-up, tasks like rebuilding countries devas-
rialization and electrification. Lenin's popular slogan was
viet rule equals communism. In the five-year central plans
ere was no place for such trivia as cosmetics. Anyway, aes-
superficial, "bourgeois" invention. Besides, women were
law, why would they need to please men by using all these beauty
and tricks? However, even if hungry, women still wanted to be beautiful, and
they didn't see a direct connection between beauty and state-proclaimed equality; or,
rather, they did see one, because they had to work like men, proving that they were
equal even physically. They worked on construction sites, on highways, in mines, in
fields and in factories—the communist ideal was a robust woman who didn't look
much different from a man. A nicely dressed woman was subject to suspicion, sometimes even investigation. Members of the Communist Party, for years after the war in
Yugoslavia, had to ask for official permission if they wanted to marry a woman whose
doubtful appearance would unmistakably indicate her "bourgeois" origins.

But aesthetics turned out to be a complex question that couldn't be answered by a
simple state decree. By abolishing one kind of so called "bourgeois" aesthetic, not with a
plan (except in China, where this kind of formal "equality" was carried to the extreme in
prescribed uniforms), but more as the natural result of ideology, the state created another aesthetic, a totalitarian one. Without a choice of cosmetics and clothes, with bad food
and hard work and no spare time, it wasn't at all hard to create the special kind of uniformity that comes out of an equal distribution of poverty and the neglect of people's
real needs. There was no chance for individualism—for women or men.

Once when I was in Warsaw, a friend told me about a spate of red-haired women;
suddenly it seemed that half of the women in the city had red hair, a phenomenon
that couldn't pass unnoticed. It might have been a fashion caprice. More likely, it had
to do with the failure of the chemical industry to produce or deliver other kinds of dye.
Imagine those women confronted by the fact that there is no other color in the store
where they buy their dye and knowing that if there isn't any in one store, it's generally useless to search others. There is only the one shade of red. (I've seen it; it's a bur-
gundy-red that gives hair a peculiarly artificial look, like a wig.) They have no
choice—they either appear untidy, with bleached ends and unbleached roots sticking
out, or they dye their hair whatever color they can find. So they dye it, hoping that
other women won't come to this same conclusion. They don't exactly choose.

Standing in front of a drugstore on Václavské Náme'stí in Prague last winter, I
felt as if I were perhaps thirteen years old and my mother had sent me to buy something for her—soap, perhaps, shampoo. The window of that drugstore was a time
machine for me: instantly, I was transported into years of scarcity long past, years of
the aesthetics of poverty. Even though I'm not an American, it seemed there was
absolutely nothing to buy. In front of that shop window I understood just how ironic
the advice in today's Cosmopolitan or any other women's magazine in the West is,
advice about so-called "natural" cosmetics, like olive and almond oil, lemon, egg,
lavender, camomile, cucumbers, or yogurt. I still can recall my mother's yearning to
buy a "real" cream in a tiny glass jar with a golden cap and a fancy French name,
something she would have paid dearly for on the black market.

If Western women return to the old recipes, they do so by choice; it is one of many
possibilities. Not so for Czech or Bulgarian or Polish women. I can see them arriving in
Yugoslavia after days and nights in a train or car. They go to the market, put a plastic

sheet on the street at the very edge of the market (afraid that the police migh[t] any moment) and sell the things they've brought. Among them are professional b[lack] market vendors, women who make a fortune by buying foreign currency and then sel[l]-ing it back home for five or six times as much. But I also saw a young Polish woman, a student maybe, selling a yellow rubber Teddy bear, deodorant, and a green nylon blouse (the kind you can find only in a communist country or a second-hand vintage clothing store in Greenwich Village). I couldn't help thinking that she was selling her own things. Buy why would anybody in the world travel 1500 miles just to sell a plastic toy? And what if she sells it, what is it that she wants to buy with the money? Perhaps a hair dye that is not red . . . However, she is young, and there is hope that her life will be dif-ferent. For my mother and women of her generation, it is already too late. If only they had had cosmetics, it might have changed their lives. On the other hand, it might not. But shouldn't they have had the right to find that out for themselves?

Once, when we used to play a childish adolescent guessing game, we would try to guess which of the women on the beach in Split were Polish and which Czech. It was easy to tell by their old-fashioned bathing suits, by their make-up, hairdo, and yes—the color of their hair. Somehow, everything in their appearance was wrong. Today I realize that women in Poland like green and blue eye shadow about as much as they like artificial red hair—but they wear it. There is nothing else to wear. It is the same with the spike-heeled white boots that seemed to be so popular in Prague last winter. It is the same with pullovers, coats, shoes: everyone is wearing the same thing, not because they want to, but because there is nothing else to buy. This is how the state creates fashion—by a lack of products and a lack of choice.

To avoid uniformity, you have to work very hard: you have to bribe a salesgirl, wait in line for some imported product, buy bluejeans on the black market and pay your whole month's salary for them; you have to hoard cloth and sew it, imitating the pic-tures in glamorous foreign magazines. What makes these enormous efforts touching is the way women wear it all, so you can tell they went to the trouble. Nothing is casual about them. They are over-dressed, they put on too much make-up, they match colors and textures badly, revealing their provincial attempt to imitate Western fashion. But where could they learn anything about a self-image, a style? In the party-controlled magazines for women, where they are instructed to be good workers and party mem-bers first, then mothers, housewives, and sex objects next—never themselves? To be yourself, to cultivate individualism, to perceive yourself as an individual in a mass society is dangerous. You might become living proof that the system is failing. Make-up and fashion are crucial because they are political. In Francine du Plessis Gray's book *Soviet Women*, the women say that they dress up not for men, but to cheer them-selves up in a grim everyday life or to prove their status to other women. In fact, they are doing it to show difference; there are not many other ways to differentiate oneself. Even the beginnings of consumerism in the 1960s didn't help much; there were still no choices, no variety. In fact, in spite of the new propaganda, real consumerism was impossible—except as an idea—because there was little to consume. Trying to be beautiful was always difficult; it involved an extra effort, devotion perhaps. But most women didn't have time or imagination enough even to try.

Living under such conditions and holding *Vogue* magazine in your hands is a very particular experience—it's almost like holding a pebble from Mars or a piece of a meteor that accidentally fell into your yard. "I hate it," says Agnes, an editor at a sci-entific journal in Budapest, pointing to *Vogue*. "It makes me feel so miserable I could almost cry. Just look at this paper—glossy, shiny, like silk. You can't find anything

ce you've seen it, it immediately sets not only new standards,
metimes I think that the real Iron Curtain is made of silky,
hen dressed in wonderful clothes, of pictures from women's
dvertising, a Western woman only browses through such
n with boredom. She has seen so much of it, has been
single day of her life, on TV, in magazines, on huge bill-
the movies. For us, the pictures in a magazine like *Vogue* were much more
important: we studied their every detail with the interest of those who had no other
source of information about the outside world. We tried to decode them, to read their
message. And because we were inexperienced enough to read them literally, the message that we absorbed was that the other world was a paradise. Our reading was
wrong and naive; nevertheless, it stayed in the back of our minds as a powerful force,
an inner motivation, a dormant desire for change, an opportunity to awaken. The
producers of these advertisements, Vance Packard's "hidden persuaders,"[1] should
sleep peacefully because here, in communist countries, their dream is coming true:
people still believe them, women especially. What do we care about the manipulation inherent in the fashion and cosmetic industries? To tell us they are making a
profit by exploiting our needs is like warning a Bangladeshi about cholesterol. I guess
that the average Western woman—if such a creature exists at all—still feels a slight
mixture of envy, frustration, jealousy, and desire while watching this world of images.
This is its aim anyway; this is how a consumer society works. But tomorrow she can at
least go buy what she saw. Or she can dream about it, but in a way different from us,
because the ideology of her country tells her that, one day, by hard work or by pure
chance, she can be rich. Here, you can't. Here, the images make you hate the reality
you live in, because not only can you not buy any of the things pictured (even if you
had enough money, which you don't), but the paper itself, the quality of print, is
unreachable. The images that cross the borders in magazines, movies, or videos are
therefore more dangerous than any secret weapon, because they make one desire that
"other-ness" badly enough to risk one's life by trying to escape. Many did.

In our house there was an old closet where my mother would stockpile cloth,
yards and yards of anything she could get hold of—flannel, cotton, pique, silk, tweed,
cashmere, wool, lace, elastic bands, even buttons. Sometimes she would let us play
with this cache, but it was her "boutique." She would copy a blouse or a skirt from
pattern sheets from *Svijet* (*World*), the only magazine for women, and sew it on
Grandma's Singer sewing machine. Every woman in my childhood knew how to sew,
and my mother insisted that I learn too. By the age of five I knitted my first shawl
and embroidered a duck with ducklings that she still keeps. Later on, she let me use a
sewing machine under her supervision, and by the age of fifteen I was making my
own dresses, not because it was a woman's duty, but because it was the only way to be
dressed nicely. When, for the first time, she went to Italy to visit a relative there, she
came back dressed in a white organdy blouse, a black pleated skirt, and high-heeled
black patent leather shoes. She brought back a mohair pullover, a raincoat made of a
thin, rustling plastic (it was called *suskavac* and everybody wanted to have one, since
it was a sign of prestige), an evening dress made of tulle, covered with sequins that
glittered in the night. What fascinated me most was her new pink silk nightgown and
matching silk overjacket with lace lapels. So light, almost sheer, hanging down to

---

1. Vance Packard published *The Hidden Persuaders*, a book about strategies of concealment and persuasion used by the
U.S. advertising industry, in 1957.

her ankles, with two tiny straps that would leave her shoulders bare, it was the negligée I'd ever seen. I used to tell her that she ought to wear it to the theater, n bed. Mother's nightgown was for me the very essence of femininity. This was the fir time, in 1959, that I'd seen that "otherness" with my own eyes.

My mother brought something special for me too; three dozen sanitary napkins of terrycloth and a belt. The napkins had buttonholes at each end to fasten them to the belt, so they wouldn't slip. She would hand-wash them, then hang them on a clothesline in the bathroom to dry overnight. More than thirty years later, in Sofia, my friend Katarina saw my package of tampons in her bathroom and asked if I could leave it for her. I am going on to Zagreb and she needs them when she has a performance in the theater. "We don't have sanitary napkins and sometimes not even cotton batting. I have to hoard it when I find it, or borrow it," she said. For a moment, I didn't know whether I should laugh or cry. I sprinkled Eastern Europe with tampons on my travels: I had already left one package of tampons and some napkins, ironically called "New Freedom", in Warsaw (plus Bayer aspirin and antibiotics), another package in Prague (plus Anaïs perfume), and now here in Sofia . . . After all these years, communism has not been able to produce a simple sanitary napkin, a bare necessity for women. So much of its economy and its so-called emancipation, too.

Rumiana is a Bulgarian movie director and a member of the international organization of women in the film industry known as KIWI. In Bulgaria, KIWI operates like a kind of feminist organization, helping women in different ways, for example, by taking care of the children of women prisoners, helping out girls in reform schools and orphanages, and so on. Rumiana told me that she is "in charge" of a reform school near Sofia. Every time she goes for a visit, girls there ask her to bring cotton batting. So she goes to a cotton factory, loads up her car, and then visits them. "They are so grateful," says Rumiana, "even when it is something that they have a right to." Today, when I think that my mother's silk nightdress doesn't necessarily have much to do with femininity, I still ask myself, what is the minimum you must have so you don't feel humiliated as a woman? It makes me understand a complaint I heard repeatedly from women in Warsaw, Budapest, Prague, Sofia, East Berlin: "Look at us—we don't even look like women. There are no deodorants, perfumes, sometimes even no soap or toothpaste. There is no fine underwear, no pantyhose, no nice lingerie. Worst of all, there are no sanitary napkins. What can one say except that it is humiliating?"

Walking the streets of Eastern European cities, one can easily see that the women there look tired and older than they really are. They are poorly dressed, overweight, and flabby. Only the very young are slim and beautiful, with the healthy look and grace that go with youth. For me, they are the most beautiful in the world because I know what is behind the serious, worried faces, the unattended hair, the unmanicured nails; behind a pale pink lipstick that doesn't exactly go with the color of their eyes, or hair, or dress; behind the bad teeth, the crumpled coats, the smell of their sweat in a streetcar. Their beauty should not be compared with the beauty that comes from the "otherness." Their image, fashion, and make-up should be judged by some different criteria, with knowledge of the context, and, therefore, with appreciation. They deserve more respect than they get, simply because just being a woman— not to mention a beauty—is a constant battle against the way the whole system works. When in May last year an acquaintance of mine, a Frenchwoman, visited Romania (while there was still street fighting in Bucharest) she told me this about Romanian women: "Oh they're so badly dressed, they don't have any style at all!"

Beauty is in the eye of the beholder.   *1991*

Joy Harjo
1951–

…uberant Native American poets writ-
… States today; her poems spiral and soar. A mem-
… of the Muscogee (Creek) tribe, Harjo claims that her Indian heritage "provides the underlying psychic structure" of her poetry and offers a wealth of living memory—"a delta in the skin," which implies both tribal, continental awareness and a global human consciousness. Because Harjo's father was Creek and her mother part French, part Cherokee, the history of the Trail of Tears was an important part of her childhood knowledge. Although she was raised in Tulsa, Oklahoma, and has been praised as an urban poet who creates evocative cityscapes, Harjo also uses a "land-based language" that echoes Native teachings valuing the earth as a sentient being, "as something alive with personality, breathing. Alive with names, alive with events, nonlinear." Her work is concerned with issues of social justice, the power of poetry, and the transformational potential of love.

When Harjo graduated in the late 1960s from the Institute of American Indian Arts, an experimental boarding school in Santa Fe, she planned to become a painter, influenced by her great-aunt Lois Harjo Ball, an artist of some renown whose "connection to the dream world" Harjo recalls. During her years as a student at the University of New Mexico, however, she switched to creative writing, receiving her B.A. in poetry in 1976 and in 1978, an M.F.A. from the University of Iowa, where she studied with the Native American novelist Leslie Marmon Silko. Harjo's first chapbook, *The Last Song* (1975), was published while she was a creative writing student and a budding saxophonist; it reflects her belief that both poetry and music can lead to mystical discovery. Her first full-length volume, *What Moon Drove Me To This?* (1979), evokes the moon as an archetypal feminine guide and a source of tribal insight; this book and much of Harjo's subsequent work is informed by a feminism that values all people as spiritual selves.

Harjo is best known for four books of poetry: *She Had Some Horses* (1983), *In Mad Love and War* (1990), *The Woman Who Fell from the Sky* (1994), and *A Map to the Next World* (2000). The first of these relies on the tradition of the prayer-chant, a Native talking-cure for illness and despair. This technique reveals a strong link between poetry and prayer, underscoring the importance of breaking silence and naming the sacred to Indian people's survival. *She Had Some Horses* won the American Book Award from the Before Columbus Foundation and the Delmore Schwartz Memorial Poetry Award. *In Mad Love and War* explores multiple landscapes: this earthly world and the spirit world of relatives and ancestors; physical violence enacted at Wounded Knee; the power of language and memory as tools of resistance. This book earned the William Carlos Williams Award from the Poetry Society of America. *The Woman Who Fell from the Sky* experiments with narrative and rhythm in prose-poems, luminous sagas that bear elegiac witness to the turmoil of the twentieth century. These poems and those of *A Map to the Next World* shine in what ADRIENNE RICH has called their "world-remaking language: precise, unsentimental, miraculous."

Harjo has also written a text to accompany astronomer Stephen Strom's striking collection of photographs of the Southwestern landscape, *Secrets from the Center of the World* (1989), and she has edited *Reinventing the Enemy's Language* (1999), an anthology of Native American women's writing. She is the author of several filmstrips, including *Origin of Apache Clown Dance* (1985). Although her filmmaker's eye is partly responsible for her vivid poetic language, she credits music as being even more influential, since her typical poem begins with a sound instead of an image. Poetry and music are linked in Harjo's life through her role as a saxophone player in the band Poetic Justice, which performs her poems at powwows, universities, and concert halls.

Many of Harjo's poems explore the healing power of sensuality, sexuality, and love. "Come, sweet, / I am a house with many rooms," she declares in "City of Fire." "There is no end." In her poetry Joy Harjo writes the body's sacred grace with revolutionary fire.

⇥ Fire ⇤

```
        a woman can't survive
        by her own breath
                        alone
        she must know
5       the voices of mountains
        she must recognize
        the foreverness of blue sky
        she must flow
        with the elusive
10      bodies
        of night wind women
        who will take her into
        her own self

        look at me
15      i am not a separate woman
        i am a continuance
        of blue sky
        i am the throat
        of the sandia mountains
20      a night wind woman
        who burns
        with every breath
        she takes
```

                                        1979

⇥ Deer Ghost ⇤

1

```
        I hear a deer outside; her glass voice of the invisible
        calls my heart to stand up and weep in this fragile city.
        The season changed once more, as if my childhood
        was forced from me, stolen during the dream of the lion
5       fleeing the old-style houses my people used to make of mud
        and straw to mother the source of burning. The skeleton
        of stars encircling this misty world stares through the roof;
        there is no hiding any more, and mystery is a skin that will never
        quite fit. This is a night ghosts wander, and in this place
10      they are as nameless as the nightmare the muscles in my
        left hand remember.
```

2

I have failed once more and let the fire go out. I misunderstood
and left my world on your musk angel wings. Your fire scorched
my lips, but it was sweet, a bitter poetry. I can taste you
15   now as I squat on the earth floor of this home I abandoned
for you. On this street named for a warrior people, a street
named after bravery, I am lighting the fire that crawls from my spine
to the gods with a coal from my sister's flame. This is what names
me in the ways of my people, who have called me back.
20   The deer knows what it is doing wandering the streets of this
city; it has never forgotten the songs.

3

I don't care what you say. The deer is no imaginary tale
I have created to fill this house because you left me.
There is more to this world than I have ever let on
25   to you, or anyone.

1990

⇥ City of Fire ⇤

Here is a city built of passion
where live many houses
with never falling night
in many rooms.
5   Through this entrance cold
is no longer a thief,
and in this place your heart
will never be a murderer.
Come, sweet,
10   I am a house with many rooms.
There is no end.
Each room is a sweet to the next world.
Where live other cities beneath
incendiary skies. And you have made
15   a fire in every room.
Come.
Lie with me before the flame.
I will dream you a wolf
and suckle you newborn.
20   I will dream you a hawk
and circle this city in your
racing heart.
I will dream you the wind,
taste salt air on my lips until
25   I take you apart raw.
Come here.

We will make a river,
flood this city built of passion
with fire,
30   with a revolutionary fire.

1990

᭜ Heartshed ᭝

You dream a heated chase.
Your heart pumps time through you
                into lakes of fire
and I can't sleep at night
5   because you have found me.

You keep coming back, the one who knows
the sound they call
              "in the beginning."
It doesn't mean going backward.
10   Our bones are built of spirals.
The sun
        circling.
                Ravens hang the walls
calling memory.
15   You could call it a war; it has been before.

I have killed you many times in jealousy,
beat you while you dreamed in the arms
of another lover.
                You shot me down in a war
20   that was only our own,
                my brother, my sister.
The names could be all that truly changes,
                not love.

I walk into another room inside
25   your skin house.
I open your legs with my tongue.
The war is not over but inside you
               the night is hot
and my fingers walk their way up your spine.
30   Your spirit rattles in your bones and yes
let's dance this all again
             another beginning.
Memory is triggered
            by polished stones spit up
35   from the center of the earth,
by ashy rock that crumbles in your hand.
Some are unborn children, others old ones
          who chose to learn patience, to know currents.

You dream a solid red cliff. The sun rises again
40   over the eastern horizon. Saturn spins
in her rings.
                    The names change.
                              Ravens call.
Lean up against me full with the words that have
45   kept you silent. Lean with the silence
                                        that imagines you.
I forgive you, forgive myself
from the beginning
                    this heartshed.

                                                            1990

Dionne Brand
1953–

A feminist writer of poetry, fiction, and prose, Dionne Brand was born in Trinidad but has lived in Toronto for nearly thirty years. She earned her B.A. in English and philosophy from the University of Toronto and an M.A. in philosophy of education from the Ontario Institute for Studies in Education. Brand's activist efforts include participation in the Black Education Project and the Immigrant Women's Center in Toronto. During 1983, she worked as an information and communication officer at the Agency for Rural Transformation in Grenada. A filmmaker as well as an activist, Brand served as associate director and writer of the National Film Board of Canada's Studio D documentaries *Older, Stronger, Wiser* and *Sisters in the Struggle*. She received a Canada Arts Grant in 1980 and Canada's prestigious Governor's General Award in 1998.

Brand has published six books of poetry whose vibrant language captures threads of her own complex history as a woman of color and an immigrant: *'Fore Day Morning* (1978), *Earth Magic* (1980), *Primitive Offensive* (1982), *Winter Epigrams and Epigrams to Ernesto Cardenal in Defense of Claudia* (1983), *Chronicles of the Hostile Sun* (1984), and *No Language Is Neutral* (1990). The luminous prose poems that comprise the latter work reveal her outrage at racism and sexism as well as her hope that art—her art—can effect social change. "What I say in any language is told in faultless knowledge of skin, in drunkenness and weeping, told as a woman without matches and tinder, not in words and in words and in words learned by heart, told in secret and not in secret, and listen, does not burn out of waste and is plenty and pitiless and loves." Her poetry has appeared in many journals in Canada and the United States and is included in *Piece of My Heart: A Lesbian of Colour Anthology* (1991), edited by Makeda Silver. Brand has also edited two books of feminist prose. *Rivers Have Sources, Trees Have Roots: Speaking of Racism* (with Krisantha Sri Bhaggiyadatta, 1986), seeks to educate readers about racism as experienced by the black, Native American, and Asian women interviewed. *No Burden to Carry: Narratives of Black Working Women in Ontario, 1920–1950s* (with Lois DeShield, 1991) likewise employs interviews as well as biographical sketches to probe the history of black Canadian women's lives as workers. Her first novel, *No Place But Here*, was published in 1998.

San Souci and Other Stories (1989), whose title comes from an imaginary West Indian island whose people are "as rough as the grass," explores female sexuality, the effects of the black diaspora, and the quest for social justice. As Rhonda Cobham notes in *The Women's Review of Books*, this collection traces the journey Brand herself followed, from coming of age in Trinidad to moving to Canada as a college student and returning to the Caribbean for a time, in search of her spiritual and political roots. The story included here, "Madame Alaird's Breasts," captures the erotic fantasies of adolescent schoolgirls in a language at once luminous and hilarious: "Madame Alaird's breasts were like pillows, deep purple ones, just like Madame Alaird's full lips as she expressed the personal pronouns, 'Je-u, Tu-ooo, Ell-lle, No-o-us. Mes enfants, encore . . .'" Brand's eloquent narrator is upstaged, however, by the giggling young protagonists, whose gossipy exchanges capture the exuberant rhythms of Trinidadian speech and the timeless longings of girlhood.

⊰ Madame Alaird's Breasts ⊱

Madame Alaird was our French mistress. "*Bonjour, mes enfants*," she would say on entering the classroom, then walk heavily toward her desk. Madame Alaird walked heavily because of her bosom which was massive about her thin waist. As she walked her breasts tipped her entire body forward. She was not tall, neither was she short, but her bosom made her look quite impressive and imposing and, when she entered our form room, her voice resonated through her breasts, deep and rich and Black, "*Bonjour, mes enfants*."

We, Form 3A, sing-songed back, "Bonjour, Ma-dame A-lai-air-d," smirking, as we watched her tipping heavily to her desk.

We loved Madame Alaird's breasts. All through the conjugation of verbs—*aller, acheter, appeller,* and *écouter*—we watched her breasts as she rested them on the top of her desk, the bodice of her dress holding them snugly, her deep breathing on the *eu* sounds making them descend into their warm cave and rise to take air. We imitated her voice but our *eu*'s sounded like shrill flutes, sharpened by the excitement of Madame Alaird's breasts.

We discussed Madame Alaird's breasts on the way home every Tuesday and Thursday, because French was every Tuesday and Thursday at 10:00 a.m. They weren't like Miss Henry's breasts. We would never notice Miss Henry's breasts anyway because we hated needlework and sewing. Miss Henry was our needlework and sewing mistress.

Madame Alaird wasn't fat. She wasn't thin either, but her breasts were huge and round and firm. Every Tuesday and Thursday, we looked forward to having Madame Alaird's breasts to gawk at, all of French period. Madame Alaird wore gold-rimmed bifocals which meant that she could not see very well, even though she peered over her bifocals pointedly in the direction of snickers or other rude noises during her teaching. But this was merely form; we doubted whether she could see us.

Madame Alaird's breasts were like pillows, deep purple ones, just like Madame Alaird's full lips as she expressed the personal pronouns, "*Je-u, Tu-ooo, Ell-lle, No-o-us. Mes enfants, encore . . .*"

"*No-o-us, Vo-uus, Ell-lles*," which we deliberately mispronounced to have Madame Alaird say them over. Madame Alaird's breasts gave us imagination beyond our years of possibilities, of burgundy velvet rooms with big-legged women and rum and calypso music. Next to Madame Alaird's breasts, we loved Madame Alaird's lips. They made water spring to our mouths just like when the skin bursts eating a purple fat mammy sipote fruit.

Every Tuesday and Thursday after school, bookbags and feet dragging, we'd discuss Madame Alaird's breasts.

"But you see Madame Alaird breasts!"

"Girl, you ever see how she just rest them on the table!"

"I wonder how they feel?"

"You think I go have breasts like Madame Alaird?"

Giggles.

"But Madame Alaird have more breasts than anybody I know."

"She must be does be tired carrying them, eh!"

Giggles, doubled over in laughter, near the pharmacy. Then past the boys' college,

"And you don't see how they sticking out in front like that and when she walk is like she falling over! Oui! Bon jieu!"

"But Madame Alaird ain't playing she have breast, oui!"

"And girl she know French, eh?"

"Madame Alaird must be could feed the whole world with them breasts, yes!"

Giggles reaching into belly laughs near Carib Street and in chorus, "*BONJOUR, MES ENFANTS*" rounding our lips on the *bonjour*, like Madame Alaird's kiss.

Madame Alaird was almost naked as far as we were concerned. It did not matter that she was always fully clothed. She was almost puritan in her style. Usually she wore brogues and ordinary clothing. Madame was not a snazzy dresser, but on speech day and other special occasions, she put on tan heels, stockings seamed up the back, a close-fitting beige dress with perhaps a little lace at the bosom, and her gold-rimmed bifocals hung from their gold string around her neck, resting on her breasts. Madame Alaird was beautiful. The bifocals didn't mean that Madame Alaird was old. She wasn't young either. She was what we called a full woman.

We heard that Madame Alaird had children. Heard, as adolescents hear, through self-composition. We got few glimpses of Madame Alaird's life, which is why we made up most of it. Once, we saw her husband come to pick her up after school. He drove an old sedate-looking dark green Hillman, and he was slim and short and quiet-looking with gold-rimmed peepers, like Madame Alaird's.

"But woii! Madame Alaird husband skinny, eh?!"

"It must be something when Madame Alaird sit down on him!"

That Tuesday or Thursday Madame Alaird's husband added fuel to the fire of Madame Alaird's breasts.

"He must be does have a nice time in Madame Alaird breast, oui."

"Madame Alaird must be feel sorry for him, that is why."

Madame Alaird went through a gloomy period where often the hem of her skirt hung and she wore a dark green dress with the collar frayed. We were very concerned because the period lasted a very long time and we knew that the other teachers and the head mistress were looking at her suspiciously. Among them, Madame Alaird stood out. They were not as pretty as she, though she wasn't *pretty*, for she was not a small woman, but she was as rosy as they were dry. In this time, she was absent-minded in class and didn't look at us, but looked at her desk and took us up sternly in our conjugations. Her breasts, hidden in dark green knit, were disappointing.

We were protective of Madame Alaird. In the wooden and musty paper smell of our thirteen-year-old lives, in the stifling, uniformed, Presbyterian hush of our days, in the bone and stick of our youngness, Madame Alaird was a vision, a promise of the dark-red fleshiness of real life.

"Madame Alaird looking like she catching trouble, eh?"

"But why she looking so bad?"

"It must be she husband, oui!"

"Madame Alaird don't need he."

"Is true! Madame Alaird could feed a country! How she could need he?"

"So he have Madame Alaird catching hell, or what?"

"Cheuupss! You don't see he could use a beating!"

"But Madame Alaird could beat he up easy, easy, you know!"

"You ain't see how the head teacher watching she?"

"Hmmm!"

And so it went for months until, unaccountably, her mood changed. Unaccountably, because we were not privy to Madame Alaird's life and could see only glimpses, outward and filtered, of what might be happening in it. But our stories seemed to make sense. And we saw her breasts. The only real secret that we knew about her life. Anyway, Madame Alaird was back to herself and we lapped our tongues over her breasts once again, on Tuesdays and Thursdays.

"Girl! Alaird looking good again, eh."

"She must be send that old husband packing."

"She must be get a new 'thing'."

"You ain't see how she dress up nice, nice, woi!"

We were jealous of Madame Alaird's husband and vexed with him for no reason at all. We even watched him cut-eyed when he came to pick her up from school.

"She must be find a new 'thing'! Oui foo!"

"Madame Alaird ain't playing she nice, non!"

So the talk about Madame Alaird's breasts went, for months and months, until we were so glad to see Madame Alaird's breasts again that we cooked up a treat to please her. The vogue that month was rubber spiders and snakes which we used to sneak up on each other and send down the boney backs of our still breastless bodices.

Our renewed obsession with Madame Alaird's breasts, our passion for their snug bounciness, their warm purpleness, their juicy fruitedness, had us giggling and whispering every time she walked down the hall and into Form 3A, our class. Madame Alaird's breasts drove us to extremes. She was delighted with our conjugations, rapturous about out attentiveness. Her *Bonjour, mes enfants* were more fleshy and sonorous, her *eu*'s and *ou*'s more voluptuous and dark-honeyed. We glowed at her and rivalled each other to be her favourite.

The plan was cooked up to place a rubber snake on Madame Alaird's chair, so that when she sat down she would jump up in fright. We had the idea that Madame Alaird would laugh at this trick and it would put us on even more familiar terms with her. So, that Tuesday, we put the plan in motion and stood in excited silence as Madame Alaird entered and tipped heavily toward her chair, a deeper, more sensuous than ever *Bonjour, mes enfants*, pushing out her full, purple lips. All of us burst out, shaking with laughter as Madame Alaird sat, jumped up, uttered a muffled yell, all at the same time. Then standing, looking severely at us—we, doubled over in uncontrollable laughter—she resounded, in English.

"When you are all ready to apologise, I shall be in the office. I shall not enter this class again until you do!" and strode out of the door.

After the apology, made in our forty-voiced, flutey girls' chorus, after our class mistress ordered it, Madame Alaird returned and was distant. This did not stop our irreverence about Madame Alaird's breasts. We ignored the pangs of conscience (those of us who had any) about upsetting her and rolled out laughing, for days after. Lustful and unrepentant.

"You ain't see how Madame Alaird jump up!"

"Woi! Madame Alaird breasts just fly up in the air and bounce back down."

"Oui fooo! Bon Jieu! Was like she had wings!"

"Madame Alaird ain't playing she have breasts, non!"
"Bon Jieu oiii!"
In her classes, we lowered our eyes to the burgundy velvet rooms of her beautiful
breasts, like penitents.   *1989*

＊＋ ⊠◇⊠ ＋＊

Sandra Cisneros
1955–

Called by the *Boston Globe* "the impassioned bard of the Mexican border," Latina poet and fiction writer Sandra Cisneros gives vibrant voice to young girls coming of age as well as older
women claiming their own sexual pleasure. Cisnero's spare, playful style and refreshing honesty have won her praise from many contemporary women writers, including GWENDOLYN
BROOKS, who identifies her as "one of the most brilliant of today's young writers"; Barbara
Kingsolver, who claims that Cisneros "has not made a single compromise in her language"; and
CHERRÍE MORAGA, who calls her "bold and insistent," a writer who "puts her mark on those
traveled places on the map and in the heart."

Born in Chicago to parents of Mexican-American descent, Elvira Cordero Anguiano and
Alfredo Cisneros Del Moral, Cisneros graduated from Loyola University in 1976. Two years
later she received her Master's degree in creative writing from the University of Iowa. Her first
volume of poetry, *Bad Boys* (1980), appeared as part of the Chicano Chapbook Series published by Mango Press. My *Wicked, Wicked Ways*, a second collection of poetry initially published by Third Woman Press in 1987, was reissued by Random House in 1992; *Loose Women*
appeared in 1994.

Cisneros is also known for her fiction. In *The House on Mango Street* (1984) she adopts
the compelling voice of a young girl named Esperanza, who explores her ethnic and gender
identities in luminous prose vignettes. In *Woman Hollering Creek and Other Stories* (1991), set
in San Antonio, where Cisneros now lives, she presents a stunning array of characters who celebrate the power of girlhood friendships, overcome disappointment in love, and survive
domestic violence. This book won both the Lannan Foundation Award for Fiction and the
PEN Center West Award for the Best Fiction in 1991. In both her poems and her fiction,
Cisneros celebrates women's desire and and resistance in a language that is eloquent, lyrical,
and vigorous.

⊰ I the Woman ⊱

<blockquote>
I
am she
of your stories
the notorious
5   one
leg wrapped
around
the door
bare heart
10   sticking
like a burr
</blockquote>

the fault
the back street
the weakness
15   that's me

I'm
the Thursday
night
the poor
20   excuse
I am she
I'm dark
in the veins
I'm
25   intoxicant
I'm hip
and good skin
brass
and sharp tooth
30   hard lip pushed
against
the air
I'm lightbeam
no stopping me

35   I am
your temporary
thing
your own
mad
40   dancing
I am
a live
wildness
left
45   behind
one earring
in the car
a finger-
print
50   on skin
the black smoke
in your
clothes
and in
55   your
mouth

1992

⊰ Love Poem #1 ⊱

a red flag
woman I am
all copper
chemical
5 and you an ax
and a bruised
thumb

unlikely
pas de deux
10 but just let
us wax
it's nitro
egypt
snake
15 museum
zoo

we are
connoisseurs
and commandos
20 we are rowdy
as a drum
not shy like Narcissus
nor pale as plum

then it is I want to hymn
25 and hallelujah
sing sweet sweet jubilee
you my religion
and I a wicked nun

1992

+→ ⊰◊⊱ ←+

Jackie Kay
1961–

"Writing is very important to me because it helps me to define what I want to change and why," claims Jackie Kay, a black poet, playwright, and fiction writer from Scotland. Born in Edinburgh and raised in Glasgow by adoptive white parents, Helen and John Kay, she now lives in Manchester with her son, Matthew, and works as a freelance writer. Her poems have appeared in the feminist journals *Artrage, Conditions, Spare Rib,* and *Feminist Review,* and her work is included in *A Dangerous Knowing: Four Black Women Poets* (1983), which takes as its topic the violence of and resistance to racism. She has published two collections of poems, both of which won critical acclaim. *The Adoption Papers* (1991) addresses the issue of adoption from the perspectives of the birth mother, the adoptive mother, and the daughter; this volume won a Scottish Arts Council Book Award, and a dramatization of its poems was broadcast on BBC Radio 3's *Drama Now* series in 1990. In *Other Lovers* (1993) Kay explores her identity as a black lesbian in Britain and exhibits a wide range of poetic strategies and voices.

Kay writes fiction as well as poetry and is involved in theater, television, film, and editing. Her short stories have been published in *Everyday Matters 2* (1984) and *Stepping Out* (1986). In 1986 her first play, *Chiaroscuro*, was performed by the Theatre of Black Women; it is included in a collection entitles *Lesbian Plays* (1987), edited by Jill Davis. *Twice Over*, her second play, was produced by Gay Sweatshop in 1988. Kay received the Signal Poetry Award in 1992 for her collection of children's poems, *Two's Company*. Her poetry documentary, *Twice Through the Heart*, was presented as part of the British Broadcasting System's *Words on Film* television series in 1992. With Shabnam Grewel, Liliane Landor, Gail Lewis, and Pratibha Parmar, she edited *Charting the Journey: Writings by Black and Third World Women*, published in 1988 by Sheba Press. The anthology makes an effort to portray the diversity of black womanhood in Britain and to develop a collective and harmonious black women's politics. Kay's first novel, *Trumpet* (1998), recounts the life of a female jazz trumpeteer who passed as male.

Reviewing Kay's poetry for *The Scotsman*, Elizabeth Burns claims that her poems can be loud with pain or can seem to whisper. This variety is evident in the quietly dreamy tone of "Close Shave," a poem that documents the love affair of two working-class men in a Scottish mining town, and in the noisily resistant voice of "Other Lovers," a poem that chronicles the end of a lesbian relationship. Whether angry or plaintive, the poems of Jackie Kay have contributed significantly to a growing body of literature by women of color in Britain today.

⊰ Close Shave ⊱

The only time I forget is down the pit
right down in the belly of it,
my lamp shining like a third eye,
my breath short and fast like my wife's
5   when she's knitting. Snip snap.
I've tried to tell her as many times
as I've been down this mine. I can't
bring myself to, she'd tell our girls
most probably. It doesn't bear thinking.

10   Last night he shaved me again.
Close. Such an act of trust.
And he cut my hair; the scissors snip
snipped all night as I lay beside Ella
(Good job she's not that interested)
15   I like watching him sweep it up.
He holds the brush like a dancing partner,
short steps, fox trot: 4/4 time.
I knew from the first time, he did too

Our eyes met when he came
20   to the bit above my lip. 6 years ago.
We've only slept the night together twice:
once when my wife's sister died,
once when the brother-in-law committed suicide.
She left our daughters behind that time.
25   My nerves made me come too quick
but I liked sleeping in his smooth arms
till dawn. He was gone

Before they woke, giggling round breakfast.
He says nobody else can cut my curls.
30   I laughed loud for the first time since
God knows when. You're too vain man.
We kissed, I like his beard on my skin,
how can you be a barber with a beard
I said to him; it's my daughters that worry me.
35   Course I can never tell the boys down the pit.
When I'm down here I work fast so it hurts.

1991

⊰ Other Lovers ⊱

1 WHAT WAS IT YOU SAID AGAIN THERE BY THE RIVER

And later, when the young danced to an old song,
the moon split in two, the stars smashed,
what was it again?

By the river, by the procession of trees,
5   the shadow marching across your face,
how deep do you feel?

I hold the light between us. Kiss you
hard in the dark. Ahead of us, the bright blue eyes of sheep.
Are there words for this? Words that sink to the bottom

10   of the river where ducks flap their sudden wings,
startle silence; believe me, believe me.
We walk this night, shining our bright eye ahead.
Do you love me, love me, do you.

2 THE DAY YOU CHANGE

The lace curtains go up.
15   She starts saying *you always say;*
you realize you always do.
On the living wall, strange shapes spread
like those on hospital sheets.

She closes the curtain round herself;
20   you hold your hand against the side of your cheek.
Tonight, you eat an instant meal
(no long spaghetti, no candles.)
Conversation limited

to *pass the pepper*. In the bedroom
25   the cover is stretched taut,
pulled back and forth in a battle,
till the small hours leaves one of you cold.
How long is a night like this?

3 WHEN YOU MOVE OUT

You mark each box with a thick black pen.
30   You will always be neat, no matter what's said.
And fair. You do not pack what is not yours.
Even the joint presents: the Chinese vase,
the white dinner plates, the samovar,
you leave to her. You won't miss things.

35   At night you will lie on a different side.
Listen to another station to send you to sleep.
You will never play Nina Simone, again.
Other things won't be possible. Restaurants,
parks, cinemas, pubs. Avoid them. They are dangerous.
40   Never go near another garden. There's no point,

growing peonies to blossom without you. Delphiniums.
Take up something else. *It doesn't matter what.*

4 SWIM

So, at the end of a perfect rainbow
you have upped and left, and I
45   have taken to swimming a hundred
lengths of breast-stroke per day.
This is the way of love.
Even swimming, I am obsessed
with the way your feet arc
50   when stroked, your legs,
the long length of them,
how I could have you all worked
up in seconds. My fingers
doing the butterfly, you saying,
55   *Don't stop Don't stop Don't stop .*

5 SHE NEVER THOUGHT SHE COULD WITH ANYONE ELSE

And now, here she is, whispering urgently into another ear.
Holding someone else tight. After the sixth month,
she returns the *I love you*, she's heard since day one.
In your island she lies in the sun like a traitor.
60   But you are always standing on her shoulders.
She starts to do things the way you did them.
She stacks dishes in order of size.
She begins to like your favorite cheese.
In restaurants she chooses the wine you chose.
65   She finds herself getting irritated
at the way her new lover makes a bed.
She misses smooth corners, no creases.
She scrubs the bath twice a day, and at night,
sees the wrong lover mouthing her name.

6 WORSE THAN THAT

70   One day you find you are your other lover.
      You use exactly the same expressions,
      like a child uses its mother's.
      You disapprove of the same things. Refuse
      to laugh at certain jokes. Uncertain
75   of yourself now, you start to imitate an absence.
      You don't know what to think of the News.
      Your world lack gravity. Her presence.
      You drop yourself from a height. Don't fall.
      You are scared to go from A to B
80   —she was the map-reader.
      You're scared of new things to eat.
      You poke at them on your plate, depressed.
      Long for your favorite meal, a simple life;

      until you learn to cook on your own
85   and it's good (though you say it yourself).
      Out and about, you are so confident
      you're taking short cuts, back alleys,
      winding your way past yourself,
      up a narrow cobbled close into the big High Street.
90   You stand, looking down, the air bursting
      through your raincoat like a big balloon.
      You manage to fathom one of those machines. *Easy.*
      Catch your slick tenners, *No bother,*
      and saunter off, whistling to yourself.

95   You have actually done it.
      You would never have believed it.
      You have a whole new life.

                                                    1993

Intertextualities

This case study of comparative texts draws upon two theoretical essays from Section II, "Writing Bodies/Bodies Writing": "The Laugh of the Medusa" by HÉLÈNE CIXOUS and "Reading Houses, Writing Lives: The French Connection" by NANCY MAIRS. These essays can help you analyze literary works by three representative writers from Section II: APHRA BEHN, DJUNA BARNES, and AUDRE LORDE. Also part of this set of interrelated readings are two essays of feminist literary criticism on Behn and Barnes found at the end of this section—critical pieces by CATHERINE GALLAGHER and SHARI BENSTOCK that might stimulate your critical thinking about women writers' treatment of sexuality and desire. Finally, the questions below offer ideas for scholarly and creative writing about these "intertextual" subjects.

☙ Topics for Discussion, Journals, and Essays ❧

1. In "The Laugh of the Medusa" Hélène Cixous claims that "by writing her self, woman will return to the body which has been more than confiscated from her, which has been turned

into the uncanny stranger on display." How does Helena Hucksteppe in Barnes's *To the Dogs* reclaim her confiscated body and refuse to be "the uncanny stranger on display" for Gheid Storm? How does Julia in Behn's *The Lucky Chance* do so? In what ways might drama as genre allow women a vital space in which to reclaim their bodies?

2. In "Reading Houses, Writing Lives" Nancy Mairs discusses the dualism in Western thought that can cause women to see their bodies as alien: "I grew up in the belief that my intellectual/spiritual life, reflective of my 'true' self, was separate from and superior to my life as a body." Mairs further suggests that women try to heal this "Western patriarchal bifurcation: body/mind or body/spirit." Discuss the strategies that Mairs, Cixous, Barnes, and/or Lorde use to undermine dualistic thinking about the body. What alternative views of female embodiment does each writer offer?

3. In what ways do Behn's *The Lucky Chance* and Lorde's "Uses of the Erotic: The Erotic as Power" challenge the "somatophobia," or fear of the body, that according to many feminists has characterized Western philosophy and literature since the ancient Greeks? How might Behn's play inscribe traces of somatophobia even as it critiques it? In answering this question, consider Gallagher's argument that Behn inscribes the woman playwright as a "new-fangled whore" and her writing as "sexual property."

4. Consider this quotation from Shari Benstock's "The Lesbian Other" about Barnes's *Ladies Almanack*:

   Woman's body—which has been the vehicle by which man satiates his lust—is returned to woman's control. Discovering its pleasures, the ladies of the *Almanack* celebrate women's sexuality, writing the lesbian body. The *Almanack* also discovers the pleasures of woman's speech, finds a language in which to express woman's desire for herself—a language that encompasses both heterosexual and lesbian women, that can accommodate the difference *within* womanhood.

   By what narrative strategies do Barnes (in *Ladies Almanack*) and Lorde (in "Uses of the Erotic: The Erotic as Power") "express woman's desire" in "a language that encompasses both heterosexual and lesbian women"?

5. In her essay Benstock asserts that in *Ladies Almanack* Barnes is "exploiting the female bawdy" though a frank and funny emphasis on women's sexuality. How do frankness and humor about female desire function thematically in *Ladies Almanack* and *The Lucky Chance*? Consider also ways in which "The Laugh of the Medusa" exploits (and thereby theorizes) the female bawdy/body.

6. In "Uses of the Erotic: The Erotic as Power" Audre Lorde defines the erotic as "an assertion of the lifeforce of women; that creative energy empowered, the knowledge and use of which we are now reclaiming in our language, our history, our dancing, our loving, our work, our lives." Analyze the connections that Lorde's essay and poems and Cixous's "The Laugh of the Medusa" delineate between women's erotic lifeforce and their creative energy, citing relevant examples from the texts.

7. Aphra Behn's critique of marriage in *The Lucky Chance* is clearly humorous, but might it also have a serious edge? Consider passages that reveal Behn not only as a comic genius but also as a social critic of the ideology of women as property and "occasions for the exchange of property." Is Gallagher right in asserting that this Restoration play, "the imminent danger of becoming an unwilling piece of someone else's property is at once asserted and denied?" Explain your reasoning.

◆ Group Writing and Performance Exercise ◆

After forming small groups, choose your favorite line or brief excerpt from Cixous's "The Laugh of the Medusa" and write a paragraph about why it is important to your understanding of women's creativity and embodiment. Then all group members can read their paragraphs aloud, commenting (and receiving comments) on what they have written. Finally, each group should work together to compose a "Cixous chorale," a short performance piece in which each group member reads aloud a dramatized version of the Cixous quote and then responds to it. If possible, work into the performance quotes from Mairs, Behn, Barnes, or Lorde as well. Responses may be serious, meditative, playful, ironic, or humorous. Here is an example of what one student wrote for her performance piece:

> "Write your self. Your body must be heard. Only then will the immense resources of the unconscious spring forth." If I hear my body by inscribing it, as Cixous urges, what will I hear? Will I sound shrill or strong, fearful or fierce? Will my unconscious erupt in anger, or will I claim an inner peace? Once I hear my body's voice, I can listen more intently to the world's body, hear the embodied voices of women around the globe, reflect across our sexual and cultural differences. Only by hearing other women can I understand my own body's sounds and connect with what Lorde calls "erotic knowledge"—the "lens through which we scrutinize all aspects of our existence."

⊷ ⁍◆⁌ ⊶

Catherine Gallagher
1945–

As a literary scholar Catherine Gallagher writes about a variety of periods and topics, from APHRA BEHN's Restoration drama to GEORGE ELIOT's nineteenth-century novels to contemporary Marxist theory. She was born in Denver, the daughter of John Martin and Mary Catherine (Hulton) Sullivan, and received her B.A. in 1972, her M.A. in 1974, and her Ph.D. in 1979, all from the University of California at Berkeley. Other than a brief stint as an assistant professor of English at the University of Denver (1979–80), Gallagher has spent her teaching career as an English professor as UC-Berkeley. She married Martin Jay in 1974 and they have two children, Margaret and Rebecca.

Gallagher's books of criticism include *The Making of the Modern Body* (1987), *The Industrial Reformation of English Fiction: Social Discourses and Narrative Form 1832–1867* (1988), and *Nobody's Story: The Vanishing Acts of Women Writers in the Marketplace 1670–1820* (1994). She has published on gender and the rise of the novel in *MLQ: A Journal of Literary History*, on the politics of the female subject in seventeenth-century England in *Genders*, and on "politics, the profession, and the critic" in *Diacritics*. Her article on Behn's *Oroonoko* was published in *Aphra Behn Studies* (1996), edited by Janet Todd, and essays on George Eliot have appeared in the journal *Nineteenth Century Fiction* and in *Sex, Politics, and Science in the Nineteenth-Century Novel*, edited by Ruth B. Yeazell. Gallagher has published on contemporary literary theory and the politics of culture in *Social Text* and *Representations* and on novelists Charles Dickens and Elizabeth Gaskell in *Academic Quarterly*. Since 1983 she has edited the journal *Representations*. Among Gallagher's honors are a Guggenheim Fellowship in 1989 and a National Endowment for the Humanities Fellowship in 1990.

The article reprinted here, "Who Was That Masked Woman? The Prostitute and the Playwright in the Comedies of Aphra Behn," first appeared in *Women's Studies* in 1988. In it Gallagher examines the literary and cultural context in which Behn both challenged and defiantly reconceptualized the idea of the woman dramatist as a "new-fangled whore" whose writing constitutes her "sexual property."

⊰ Who Was That Masked Woman? The Prostitute and the Playwright in the Comedies of Aphra Behn ⊱

Everyone knows that Aphra Behn, England's first professional female author, was a colossal and enduring embarrassment to the generations of women who followed her into the literary marketplace. An ancestress whose name had to be lived down rather than lived up to, Aphra Behn seemed, in Virginia Woolf's metaphor, to obstruct the very passageway to the profession of letters she had herself opened. Woolf explains in *A Room of One's Own,* "Now that Aphra Behn had done it, girls could go to their parents and say, You need not give me an allowance; I can make money by my pen. Of course the answer for many years to come was, Yes, by living the life of Aphra Behn! Death would be better! and the door was slammed faster than ever."[1]

It is impossible in this brief essay to examine all the facets of the scandal of Aphra Behn; her life and works were alike characterized by certain irregular sexual arrangements. But it is not these that I want to discuss, for they seem merely inciden-tal, the sorts of things women writers would easily dissociate themselves from if they led pure lives and wrote high-minded books. The scandal I would like to discuss is, however, with varying degree of appropriateness, applicable to all female authors, regardless of the conduct of their lives or the content of their works. It is a scandal that Aphra Behn seems quite purposely to have constructed out of the overlapping discourses of commercial, sexual, and linguistic exchange. Conscious of her historical role, she introduced to the world of English letters the professional woman writer as a new-fangled whore.

This persona has many functions in Behn's works: it titillates, scandalizes, arous-es pity, and indicates the vicissitudes of authorship and identity in general. The author-whore persona also makes of female authorship per se a dark comedy that explores the bond between the liberty the stage offered women and their confine-ment behind both literal and metaphorical vizard masks. This is the comedy played out, for example, in the prologue to her first play, *The Forced Marriage,* where she announces her epoch-making appearance in the ranks of the playwrights. She pre-sents her attainment, however, not as a daring achievement of self-expression, but as a new proof of the necessary obscurity of the "public" woman.

The prologue presents Aphra Behn's playwrighting as an extension of her erotic play. In it, a male actor pretends to have escaped temporarily the control of the intriguing female playwright; he comes on stage to warn the gallants in the audience of their danger. This was a variation on the Restoration convention of betraying the playwright in the Prologue with an added sexual dimension: the comic antagonism between playwright and audience becomes a battle in the war between the sexes. Playwrighting, warns the actor, is a new weapon in woman's amorous arsenal. She will no longer wound only through the eyes, through her beauty, but will also use wit to gain a more permanent ascendency. Here, woman's playwrighting is wholly assim-ilated to the poetic conventions of amorous battle that normally informed lyric poetry.

---

1. [*A Room of One's Own* (London, 1929), 67. Woolf here no doubt exaggerates the deterrent effects of Behn's scandal. We know that hundreds of women made some sort of living as writers in the late seventeenth and early eighteenth cen-turies. Indeed, there was no consensus that Behn was infamous until the second half of the eighteenth century. Neverthe-less, in an age that loved scandal, she seems willingly to have obliged her audience's taste.]

If the male poet had long depicted the conquering women as necessarily chaste, debarring (and consequently debarred from) the act of sex itself, then his own poetry of lyric complaint and pleas for kindness could only be understood as attempts to overthrow the conqueror. Poetry in this lyric tradition is a weapon in a struggle that takes as its most fundamental ground-rule a woman's inability to have a truly *sexual* conquest: for the doing of the deed would be the undoing of the power.

Aphra Behn's first Prologue stretches this lyric tradition to incorporate theater. However, the woman's poetry cannot have the same *end* as the man's. Indeed, according to the Prologue, ends, in the sense of terminations, are precisely what a woman's wit is directed against:

> Women those charming victors, in whose eyes
> Lie all their arts, and their artilleries,
> Not being contented with the wounds they made,
> Would by new stratagems our lives invade.
> Beauty alone goes now at too cheap rates
> And therefore they, like wise and politic states,
> Court a new power that may the old supply,
> To *keep* as well as gain the victory:
> They'll join the force of wit to beauty now,
> And so *maintain* the right they have in you.[2]

Writing is certainly on a continuum here with sex, but instead of leading to the act in which the woman's conquest is overturned, playwriting is supposed to extend the woman's erotic power beyond the moment of sexual encounter. The prologue, then, situates the drama inside the conventions of male lyric love poetry but then reverses the chronological relationship between sex and writing; the male poet writes before the sexual encounter, the woman between encounters. She thereby actually creates the possibility of a woman's version of sexual conquest. She will not be immediately conquered and discarded because she will maintain her right through her writing. The woman's play of wit is the opposite of foreplay; it is a kind of afterplay specifically designed to prolong pleasure, resuscitate desire and keep a woman who has given herself sexually from being traded in for another woman. If the woman is successful in her poetic exchange, the actor warns the gallants, then they will no longer have the freedom of briskly exchanging mistresses: "You'll never know the bliss of change; this art Retrieves (when beauty fades) the wandring heart."

Aphra Behn, then, inaugurated her career by taking up and feminizing the role of the seductive lyric poet. The drama the audience is about to see is framed by the larger comedy of erotic exchange between a woman writer and a male audience. That is, this prologue does what so many Restoration prologues do, makes of the play a drama within a drama, one series of conventional interactions inside another. But the very elaborateness of this staging of conventions makes the love battle itself (the thing supposedly revealed) seem a strategic pose in a somewhat different drama. After all, what kind of woman would stage her sexual desire as her primary motivation? The answer is a woman who might be suspected not to have any: a woman for whom professions of amorousness and theatrical authenticity are the same thing: a prostitute. Finally, just in case anyone the audience might have missed this analogy, a dramatic interruption occurs, and the prologue stages a debate about the motiva-

2. ["Prologue," *The Forced Marriage or the Jealous Bridegroom* (London, 1671), n.p.]

tion behind all this talk of strategy. The actor calls attention to the prostitutes in the audience, who were generally identified by their masks, and characterizes them as agents of the playwright, jokingly using their masks to expose them as spics in the amorous war:

> The poetess too, they say, has spies abroad.
> Which have dispers'd themselves in every road.
> I' th' upper box, pit, galleries, every face
> You find disguis'd in a black velvet case.
> My life on't: is her spy on purpose sent,
> To hold you in a wanton compliment;
> That so you may not censure what she's writ,
> Which done they face you down 'twas full of wit.

At this point, an actress comes on stage to refute the suggestion that the poetess's spies and supporters are prostitutes. She returns, then, to the conceits linking money and warfare and thus explicitly enacts the denial of prostitution that was all along implicit in the trope of amorous combat. Unlike the troop of prostitutes, she claims.

> Ours scorns the petty spoils, and do prefer
> The glory not the interest of war.
> But yet our forces shall obliging prove,
> Imposing naught but constancy in love:
> That's all our aim, and when we have it too,
> We'll sacrifice it all to pleasure you.

What the last two lines make abundantly clear, in ironically justifying female promiscuity by the pleasure it gives to men, is that the prologue has given us the spectacle of a prostitute comically denying mercenary motivations. The poetess like the prostitute is she who "stands out," as the etymology of the word "prostitute" implies, but it is also she who is masked. Indeed, as the prologue emphasizes, the prostitute is she who stands out by virtue of her mask. The dramatic masking of the prostitute and the stagey masking of the playwright's interest in money are exactly parallel cases of theatrical unmasking in which what is revealed is the parallel itself: the playwright is a whore.

This conclusion, however, is more complex than it might at first seem, for the very playfulness of the representation implies a hidden "real" woman who must remain unavailable. The prologue gives two explanations for female authorship, and they are the usual excuses for prostitution: it alludes to and disclaims the motive of money; it claims the motive of love, but in a way that makes the claim seem merely strategic. The author-whore, then, is one who comically stages her lack of self-expression and consequently implies that her true identity is the sold self's seller. She thus indicates an unseeable selfhood through the flamboyant alienation of her language.

Hence Aphra Behn managed to create the effect of an inaccessible authenticity out of the very image of prostitution. In doing so, she capitalized on a commonplace slur that probably kept many less ingenious women out of the literary marketplace. "Whore's the like reproachful name, as poetess—the luckless twins of shame,"[3] wrote Robert Gould in 1691. The equation of poetess and "punk" (in the slang of the day) was inescapable in the Restoration. A woman writer could either deny it in the content

---

3. [This quotation is from Robert Gould's *Satirical Epistle to the Female Author of a Poem called "Sylvia's Revenge"* (London, 1691). The poem acknowledges that the lines are a paraphrase from Rochester's "Letters from Artemisia in the Town to Chloe in the Country." The sentiment is presented as a commonplace.]

and form of her publications, as did Catherine Trotter, or she could embrace it, as did Aphra Behn. But she could not entirely avoid it. For the belief that "Punk and Poesie agree so pat, / You cannot well be *this*, and not be *that*"[4] was held independently of particular cases. It rested on the evidence neither of how a woman lived nor of what she wrote. It was, rather, an a priori judgement applied to all cases of female publication. As one of Aphra Behn's biographers, Angeline Goreau, has astutely pointed out, the seventeenth-century ear heard the word "public" in "publication" very distinctly, and hence a woman's publication automatically implied a public woman.[5] The woman who shared the contents of her mind instead of reserving them for one man was literally, not metaphorically, trading in her *sexual* property. If she were married, she was selling what did not belong to her, because in *mind and body* she should have given herself to her husband. In the seventeenth century, "publication," Goreau tells us, also meant sale due to bankruptcy, and the publication of the contents of a woman's mind was tantamount to the publication of her husband's property. In 1613, Lady Carey published (anonymously, of course) these lines on marital property rights, publication and female integrity:

> Then she usurps upon anther's right,
> That seeks to be by public language graced;
> And tho' her thoughts reflect with purest light
> Her mind, if not peculiar, is not chaste.
> For in a wife it is no worse to find
> A common body, than a common mind.[6]

Publication, adultery, and trading in one's husband's property were all thought of as the same thing as long as female identity, selfhold, remained an indivisible unity. As Lady Carey explained, the idea of a public mind in a private body threatened to fragment female identity, to destroy its integrated wholeness:

> When to their husbands they themselves do bind,
> Do they not wholly give themselves away?
> Or give they but their body, not their mind,
> Reserving that, tho' best, for other's prey?
> No, sure, their thoughts no more can be their own
> And therefore to none but one be known.[7]

The unique, unreserved giving of the woman's self to her husband is the act that keeps her whole. Only in this singular and total alienation does the woman maintain her complete self-identity.

We have already seen that it is precisely this ideal of a totalized woman, preserved because *wholly* given away, that Aphra Behn sacrifices to create a different idea of identity, one complexly dependent on the necessity of multiple exchanges.

---

4. [Ibid.]

5. [This discussion is heavily indebted to Angeline Goreau's *Reconstructing Aphra. A Social Biography of Aphra Behn* (Oxford, 1980), especially pp. 144–162. Goreau has gathered much of the evidence on which I draw; however, we reach very different conclusions on the basis of the evidence. Goreau writes that Behn "savagely resented" the charge of immodesty and makes no references to the playwright's own sly use of the author-whore metaphor.

For a discussion of Behn's self-presentation that recognizes her use of this trope, see Maureen Duffy, *The Passionate Shepherdess: Aphra Behn 1640–89* (London, 1977), especially pp. 94–104.]

6. [Lady Elizabeth Carey [1585–1639], *The Tragedy of Mariam, the Fair Queen of Jewry* (London, 1613) act 3, unpaginated. Quoted in Goreau, 151.]

7. [Ibid.]

She who is able to repeat the action of self-alienation an unlimited number of times is she who is constantly there to regenerate, possess, and sell a series of provisional, constructed identities. Self-possession, then, and self-alienation are just two sides of the same coin: the alienation verifies the possession. In contrast, the wife who gives herself once and completely disposes simultaneously of self-possession and self-alienation. She has no more property in which to trade and is thus rendered whole by her action. She *is* her whole, unviolated womanhood because she has given up possessing herself; she can be herself because she has given up *having* herself. Further, as Lady Carey's lines make clear, if a woman's writing is an authentic extension of herself, then she cannot have alienable property in that without violating her wholeness.

Far from denying these assumptions, Aphra Behn's comedy is based on them. Like her contemporaries, she presented her writing as part of her sexual property, not just because it was bawdy, but because it was hers. As a woman, all of her properties were at least the potential property of another; she could either reserve them and give herself whole in marriage, or she could barter them piecemeal, accepting self-division to achieve self-ownership and forfeiting the possibility of marriage. In this sense, Aphra Behn's implied identity fits into the most advanced seventeenth-century theories about selfhood: it closely resembles the possessive individualism of Locke and Hobbes, in which property in one's self both entails and is entailed by the parcelling out and serial alienation of one's self. For property by definition, in this theory, is that which is alienable. Aphra Behn's, however, is a gender specific version of possessive individualism, one constructed in opposition to the very real alternative of staying whole by renouncing self possession, an alternative that had no legal reality for men in the seventeenth century. Because the husband's right of property was in the whole of the wife, the prior alienation of any part of her had to be seen as a violation of either actual or potential marital propriety. That is, a woman who, like Aphra Behn, embraced possessive individualism, even if she were single and never bartered her sexual favors, could only do so with a consciousness that she thus contradicted the notion of female identity on which legitimate sexual property relations rested.

Publication, then, quite apart from the contents of what was published, ipso facto implied the divided, doubled, and ultimately unavailable person whose female prototype was the prostitute. By flaunting her self-sale, Aphra Behn embraced the title of whore; by writing bawdy comedies, which she then partly disclaimed, she capitalized on her supposed handicap. Finally, she even uses this persona to make herself seem the prototypical writer, and in this effort she certainly seems to have had the cooperation of her male colleagues and competitors. Thus, in the following poem, William Wycherley wittily acknowledges that the sexual innuendos about Aphra Behn rebound back on the wits who make them. The occasion of the poem was a rumor that the poetess had gonorrhea. Wycherley emphasizes how much more public is the "Sappho of the Age" than any normal prostitute, how much her fame grows as she looses her fame, and how much cheaper is the rate of the author-whore than her sister punk. But he also stresses how much more power the poetess has, since in the world of wit as opposed to the world of sexual exchange, use increases desire, and the author-whore accumulates men instead of being exchanged among them:

> More Fame you now (since talk'd of more) acquire,
> And as more Public, are more Mens Desire;
> Nay, you the more, that you are Clap'd to, now,
> Have more to like you, less to censure you:

> Now Men enjoy your Parts for Half a Crown,
> Which, for a Hundred Pound, they scarce had done,
> Before your Parts were, to the Public known.[8]

Appropriately, Wycherley ends by imagining the whole London theatrical world as a sweating-house for venereal disease:

> Thus, as your Beauty did, your Wit does now,
> The Women's envy, Men's Diversion grow;
> Who, to be clap'd, or Clap you, round you sit,
> And, tho' they Sweat for it, will crowd your Pit;
> Since lately you Lay-in, (but as they say,)
> Because, you had been Clap'd another Way;
> But, if 'tis true, that you have need to Sweat,
> Get, (if you can) at your New Play, a Seat.

If Aphra Behn's sexual and poetic parts are the same, then the wits are contaminated by her sexual distemper. Aphra Behn and her fellow wits infect one another: the theater is her body, their wits are their penises, the play is a case of gonorrhea, and the cure is the same as the disease.

Given the general Restoration delight in the equation of mental, sexual, and theatrical "parts," and its frequent likening of writing to prostitution and playwrights to bawds, one might argue that if Aphra Behn had not existed, the male playwrights would have had to invent her in order to increase the witty pointedness of their cynical self-representations. For example, in Dryden's prologue to Behn's *The Widow Ranter*, the great playwright chides the self-proclaimed wits for contesting the originality of one another's productions and squabbling over literary property. Drawing on the metaphor of literary paternity, he concludes:

> But when you see these Pictures, let none dare
> To own beyond a Limb or single share;
> For where the Punk is common, he's a Sot,
> Who needs will father what the Parish got.[9]

These lines gain half their mordancy from their reference to Aphra Behn, the poetess-punk, whose off-spring cannot seem fully her own, but whose right to them cannot be challenged with any propriety. By literalizing and embracing the playwright-prostitute metaphor, therefore, Aphra Behn was distinguished from other authors, but only as their prototypical representative. She becomes a symbolic figure of authorship for the Restoration, the writer and the strumpet muse combined. Even those who wished to keep the relationship between women and authorship strictly metaphorical were fond of the image: "What a pox have the women to do with the muses?" asks a character in a play attributed to Charles Gildon. "I grant you the poets call the nine muses by the names of women, but why so? . . . because in that sex they're much fitter for prostitution"[10] It is not hard to see how much authorial notoriety could be gained by audaciously literalizing such a metaphor.

Aphra Behn, therefore, created a persona that skillfully intertwined the age's available discourses concerning women, property, selfhood, and authorship. She

8. [William Wycherley, *Miscellany Poems*, vol. 3, *The Complete Works of William Wycherley* (London, 1924), pp. 155–156.]
9. [John Dryden, "Prologue," *The Widow Ranter or The History of Bacon in Virginia* (London, 1690). n.p. The Prologue was, in fact, first spoken to Shadwell's comedy, *The*

True Widow, in 1678, yet another reminder that the author-whore metaphor was ready-made for Behn's appropriation.]
10. [Quoted at the opening of Fidelis Morgan, *The Female Wits. Women Playwrights of The London State 1660–1720* (London, 1981), n.p.]

found advantageous openings where other women found repulsive insults; she turned self-division into identity.

The authorial effect I'm trying to describe here should not be confused with the plays' disapproving attitudes toward turning women into items of exchange. *The Lucky Chance*, which I am now going to discuss, all too readily yields a facile, right-minded thematic analysis centering on women and property exchange. It has three plots that can easily be seen as variations on this theme: Diana is being forced into a loveless marriage with a fop because of her father's family ambition. Her preference for the young Bredwell is ignored in the exchange. Diana's father, Sir Feeble Fainwood, is also purchasing himself a young bride, Leticia, whom he has tricked into believing that her betrothed lover, who had been banished for fighting a duel, is dead. Julia, having already sold herself to another rich old merchant, Sir Cautious Fulbank, is being wooed to adultery by her former lover, Gayman. That all three women are both property and occasions for the exchange of property is quite clear. Diana is part of a financial arrangement between the families of the two old men, and the intended bridegroom, Bearjest, sees her merely as the embodiment of a great fortune; Leticia is also bought by "a great jointure," and though we know, interestingly, nothing of Julia's motives, we are told that she had played such a "prank" as Leticia.[11] It is very easy, then, to make the point that the treatment of women as property is the problem that the play's comic action will set out to solve. Whether she marries for property, as in the cases of Leticia and Julia or she is married as *property* (that is, given, like Diana, as the condition of a dowry), the woman's identity *as* a form of property and item of exchange seems obviously to be the play's point of departure, and the urge to break that identification seems, on a casual reading, to license the play's impropriety. One could even redeem the fact that, in the end, the women are all *given* by the old men to their lovers by pointing out that this is, after all, a comedy and hence a form that requires female desire to flow through established channels.

Such a superficial thematic analysis of *The Lucky Chance* fits in well with that image of Aphra Behn some of her most recent biographers promote: an advocate of "free love" in every sense of the phrase and a heroic defender of the right of women to speak their own desires. However, such as interpretation does not bear the weight of the play's structure or remain steady in the face of its ellipses, nor can it sustain the pressure of the play's images. For the moments of crisis in the play are not those in which a woman becomes property but those in which a woman is burdened with a selfhood that can be neither represented (a self without properties) nor exchanged. They are the moments when the veiled woman confronts the impossibility of being represented and hence of being desired and hence of being, finally, perhaps, gratified.

Before turning to those moments, I'd like to discuss some larger organizational features of the play that complicate its treatment of the theme of women and exchange. First, then, to the emphatic way in which the plots are disconnected in their most fundamental logic. The plots of Diana and Leticia rely on the idea that there is an irreversible moment of matrimonial exchange after which the woman is "given" and cannot be given again. Thus the action is directed toward thwarting and replacing the planned marriage ceremony, in the case of Diana, and avoiding the consummation of the marriage bed in the case of Leticia. Julia, however, has crossed both these thresholds and is still somehow free to dispose of herself. The logic on which her plot is based seems to deny that there are critical or irremediable events in

11. [*The Lucky Chance or An Alderman's Bargain* (performed first in 1686) in *The Female Wits*, 76. All further quotations are from this edition of the play, and page numbers are given in the body of the essay.]

female destiny. Hence in the scene directly following Leticia's intact deliverance from Sir Feeble Fainwood's bed and Diana's elopement with Bredwell, we find Julia resignedly urging her aged husband to get the sex over with and to stop meddling with the affairs of her heart: "But let us leave this fond discourse, and, if you must, let us to bed" (p. 135). Julia proves her self-possession precisely by her indifference to the crises structuring Diana's and Leticia's experiences.

On the one hand, Julia's plot could be seen to undercut the achievement of resolution in the other plots by implying that there was never anything to resolve: the obstacles were not real, the crises were not crises, the definitive moment never did and never could arrive. Julia's would be the pervasive atmosphere of comedy that keeps the anxieties of the more "serious" love plot from truly being registered. But on the other hand, we could argue that the crisis plots drain the adultery plot not only of moral credibility but also of dramatic interest, for there would seem to be simply nothing at stake in Julia's plot. Indeed, Julia's plot in itself seems bent on making this point, turning as it so often does on attempts to achieve things that have already been achieved or gambling for stakes that have already been won. These two responses, however, tend to cancel one another, and we cannot conclude that either plot logic renders the other nugatory. The Lucky Chance achieves its effects, rather, by alternately presenting the problem and its seeming nonexistence. The imminent danger of becoming an unwilling piece of someone else's property is at once asserted and denied.

The alternating assertion/denial emphasizes the discontinuity between the two "resolutions" of the woman's sexual identity that I discussed earlier: one in which the giving of the self intact is tantamount to survival; the other in which an identity is maintained in a series of exchanges. This very discontinuity, then, as I've already pointed out, is part of an overarching discursive pattern. The proof of self-ownership is self-sale; hence, Julia has no exculpating story of deceit or coercion to explain her marriage to Fulbank. But the complete import of what she does, both of what she sacrifices and what she gains, can only be understood against the background of a one-time exchange that involves and maintains the whole self.

The disjunction between the plot exigencies Leticia is subjected to and those that hold and create Julia, (our inability to perceive these plots within a single comic perspective) reveals the oppositional relationship between the two seventeenth-century versions of the female as property. Built into this very disjunction, therefore, is a complicated presentation of the seeming inescapability for women of the condition of property. In the play, the exchange of women as property appears inevitable, and the action revolves around the terms of exchange. The crisis plots, of which Leticia's is the most important, posit wholeness as the pre-condition of exchange and as the result of its successful completion. The unitary principle dominates the logic of this plot and also, as we are about to see, the language of its actors and its representational rules. Julia's plot, on the other hand, assumes not only the fracturing and multiplication of the self as a condition and result of exchange, but also the creation of a second order of reality: a reality of representations through which the characters simultaneously alienate and protect their identities.

This split in representational procedures can be detected in the first scene, where it is associated with the characters of the leading men. In the play's opening speech, Bellmour enters complaining that the law has stolen his identity, has made him a creature of disguise and the night. His various complaints in the scene cluster around a central fear of de-differentiation, of the failure properly to distinguish essential differences. Thus it is the "rigid laws, which put no difference / 'Twixt fairly killing in my own defence, / And murders bred by drunken arguments, / Whores, or the mean revenges of a coward" that have forced his disguise, his alienation from his own identity. That is, the denial of the true, identity insuring, difference (that between duelers and murderers) necessitates false differences, disguises and theatrical representations that get more elaborate as the plot progresses. The comedy is this series of disguises and spectacles, but its end is to render them unnecessary by the reunion of Bellmour with his proper identity and his proper wife.

The very terms of Bellmour's self-alienation, moreover, are identitarian in their assumption that like must be represented by like. Bellmour has taken a life in a duel, and for that he is deprived of the life he thought he would lead. He has destroyed a body with his sword, and for that a body that belongs to him, Leticia's, will be taken from him also through puncturing. Even the comic details of Bellmour's reported death are consonant with this mode of representation:

> Ralph: Hanged, Sir, hanged at The Hague in Holland.
> Bellmour: For what, said they, was he hanged?
> Ralph: Why, e'en for high treason, Sir, he killed one of their kings.
> Gayman: Holland's a commonwealth, and is not ruled by kings.
> Ralph: Not by one, Sir, but by many. This was a cheesemonger, they fell out over a bottle of brandy, went to snicker snee, Mr. Bellmour cut his throat, and was hanged for't, that's all, Sir. (p. 81)

The *reductio ad absurdum* of like representing like is the commonwealth in which everyone is a king. It is within this comically literalist system of representation that Bellmour is imagined to have had his neck broken for slitting the throat of a cheesemonger. It is no wonder that the climax of Bellmour's performance is a simulation of the exchange of like for like. As Sir Feeble Fainwood approaches the bed on which he intends to deflower Leticia, asking her, "What, was it ashamed to show its little white foots, and its little round bubbies?," Bellmour comes out from between the curtains, naked to the waist. And, all the better to ward off that which he represents, he has Leticia's projected wound painted on his own chest and a dagger ready to make another such wound on Sir Feeble. The whole representational economy of this plot, therefore, has an underlying unitary basis in the notion that things must be paid for in kind. Even Leticia's self-sale seems not to be for money but for the jewelry to which she is often likened.

Like Bellmour, Gayman also enters the first scene in hiding, "wrapped in his cloak," but the functional differences between the two kinds of self-concealment are soon manifested. The end of Gayman's disguises is not the retrieval of his property, but the appropriation of what he thinks is the property of others: "Are you not to be married, Sir," asks Bellmour. "No Sir," returns Gayman, "not as long as any man in London is so, that has but a handsome wife, Sir" (p. 77). His attempts are not to establish essential differences, but rather to accelerate the process of de-differentiation. "The bridegroom!" exclaims Bellmour on first seeing Sir Feeble. "Like Gorgon's head he's turned me into stone." "Gorgon's head," retorts Gayman, "a cuckold's head, 'twas made to graft upon" (p. 79). The dizzying swiftness with which Gayman extends Bellmour's metaphor speaks the former's desire to destroy the paired stability of exchanges. Looking at the bridegroom's head, Bellmour sees an image of destructive female sexuality, the Gorgon. Thus, the bridegroom represents the all-too-available sexuality of Leticia. Gayman's way of disarming this insight is to deck it with horns, to introduce the third term, taking advantage of Leticia's availability to cuckold Sir Feeble. But for Bellmour this is no solution at all, since it only further collapses the distinction between lover and husband, merging him with Sir Feeble at the moment he alienates his sexual property: "What, and let him marry her! She that's mine by sacred vow already! by heaven it would be flat adultery in her!" (p. 80). "She'll learn the trick," replies Gayman, "and practise it the better with thee." The destruction of the "true" distinctions between husband and lover, cuckold and adulterer, proprietor and thief is the state for which Gayman longs.

Bellmour's comedy, then, moves toward the re-establishment of true difference through the creation of false differences; Gayman's comedy moves toward the erasure of true differences through the creation of false and abstract samenesses. Gayman is in disguise because he cannot bear to let Julia know that he is different from his former self. He wishes to appear before her always the same, to hide the new fact of his poverty. He tries to get money from his landlady so that he can get his clothes out of hock and therefore disguise himself as himself in order to go on wooing Julia. On the same principle of the effacement of difference, Gayman later tries to pass himself off as Julia's husband when he, unbeknownst to her, takes the old man's place in bed.

Moreover, just as the false differences of Bellmour's comedy conformed to a unitary like-for-like economy of representation, the false samenesses of Gayman's plotting are governed by an economy of representation through difference. The most obvious example of this is the use of money. Money in this plot often represents bodies or their sexual use, and what is generally emphasized in these exchanges are the differences between the body and money. For example, in the scenes of Gayman's two prostitutions (the first with his landlady and the second with his unknown admirer), the difference between the women's bodies and the precious metals they can be made to yield is the point of the comedy. The landlady is herself metamorphosed into iron for the sake of this contrast: she is an iron lady who emerges from her husband's blacksmith's shop. She is then stroked into metals of increasing value as she yields 'postle spoons and caudle cups that then exchange for gold. However, Gayman's expletives never allow us to forget that this sexual alchemy is being practiced on an unsublimatable body that constantly sickens the feigning lover with its stink. Even more telling is the continuation of this scene in which Gayman receives a bag of gold as advance payment for an assignation with an anonymous woman. Here the desirability of the gold (associated with its very anonymity) immediately implies the undesirability of the woman who sends it: "Some female devil, old and damned to ugliness, / And past all hopes of courtship and address, / Full of another devil called desire, / Has seen this face, this shape, this youth, / And thinks it's worth her hire. It must be so" (p. 94). Of course, as this passage emphasizes, in both cases the women's money stands for Gayman's sexual worthiness, but as such it again marks a difference, the difference in the desirability of the bodies to be exchanged. Hence the unlike substance, gold, marks the inequality of the like biological substances.

The freedom and the perils, especially the perils for women, that this comedy of representation through difference introduces into erotic life are explored in the conflict between Julia and Gayman. And this conflict returns to us the issue of authorial representation. Julia, like many of Aphra Behn's heroines, confronts a familiar predicament: she wishes to have the pleasure of sexual intercourse with her lover without the pain of the loss of honor. Honor seems to mean something wholly external in the play; it is not a matter of conscience since secret actions are outside its realm. Rather, to lose honor is to give away control over one's public representations. Hence, in the adultery plot, as opposed to the crisis plot, women's bodies are not the true stakes; representations of bodies, especially in money and language, are the focal points of conflict.

Gayman's complaint against Julia, for example, is that she prefers the public admiration of the crowd, which she gains through witty language ("talking all and loud" p. 99) to the private "adoration" of a lover, which is apparently speechless. Julia's retort, however, indicates that it is Gayman who will betray the private to public representation for the sake of his own reputation. It is Gayman who will "describe her charms," "Or make most filthy verses of me / Under the name of Cloris, you Philander, / Who, in lewd rhymes, confess the dear appointment, / What hour, and where, how silent was the night, / How full of love your eyes, and wishing mine." (We have just, by the way, heard Gayman sing a verse about Cloris's wishing eyes to his landlady.)

To escape being turned into someone else's language, losing the ability to control her own public presentation, Julia subjects herself to a much more radical severance of implied true self from self-representation than Gayman could have imagined. At once to gratify her sexual desire and preserve her honor, she arranges to have Gayman's own money (in some ways a sign of his desire for her) misrepresented to him as payment for sexual intercourse with an unknown woman. That is, Julia makes the anonymous advance earlier discussed.

Julia, then, is hiding behind the anonymity of the gold, relying on its nature as a universal equivalent for desire, universal and anonymous precisely because it doesn't resemble what it stands for and can thus stand for anything. But in this episode, she becomes a prisoner of the very anonymity of the representation. For, as we've already seen, Gayman takes it as a sign of the difference between the woman' desirability and his own. Apparently, moreover, this representation of her undesirability overwhelms the private experience itself, so that when the couple finally couples, Gayman does not actually experience Julia, but rather feels another version of his landlady. As he later reluctantly describes the sightless, wordless encounter to Julia (whom he does not suspect of having been the woman), "She was laid in a pavilion all formed of gilded clouds which hung by geometry, whither I was conveyed after much ceremony, and laid in a bed with her, where, with much ado and trembling with my fears, I forced my arms about her." "And sure," interjects Julia aside to the audience, "that undeceived him." "But," continues Gayman, "such a carcass 'twas, deliver me, so shrivelled, lean and rough, a canvas bag of wooden ladles were a better bedfellow." "Now, though, I know that nothing is more distant than I from such a monster, yet this angers me," confides Julia to the audience. "'Slife, after all to seem deformed, old, ugly." The interview ends with Gayman's final misunderstanding, "I knew you would be angry when you heard it" (p. 118).

The extraordinary thing about this interchange is that it does no matter whether or not Gayman is telling the truth about his sexual experience. The gold may have so overwhelmed his senses as to make Julia feel like its opposite: a bag of wooden ladles rather than precious coins; and, indeed, the continuity of images between this description and Gayman's earlier reactions to women who give him money tends to confirm his sincerity. The bag of ladles reminds us of the landlady, who was also a bag, but one containing somewhat more valuable table utensils: 'postle spoons and caudle cups. However, Gayman may be misrepresenting his experience to prevent Julia's jealousy. Either way, Julia was missing from that experience. Whether he did not desire her at all or desired her as someone else is immaterial; what Julia experiences as she sees herself through this doubled representation of money and language is the impossibility of keeping herself to herself and truly being gratified as at once a subject and object of desire.

By participating in this economy of difference, in which her representations are not recognizably hers, then, Julia's problem becomes her state of unexchangeability. The drive for self-possession removes her "true" self from the realms of desire and gratification.

Because she has not given herself away, she finds that her lover has not been able to take her. Surprisingly, however, the play goes on to overcome this difficulty not by taking refuge in like-for-like exchanges, but by remaining in the economy of difference until Julia seems able to adjust the claims of self-possession and gratification.

The adjustment becomes possible only after Julia has been explicitly converted into a commodity worth three hundred pounds. The process leading up to this conversion merits our scrutiny. Gayman and Sir Cautious are gambling: Gayman has won 300 pounds and is willing to stake it against something of Sir Cautious's.

> Sir Cautious: I wish I had anything but ready money to stake: three hundred pound, a fine sum!
> Gayman: You have moveables Sir, goods, commodities.
> Sir Cautious: That's all one, Sir. That's money's worth. Sir, but if I had anything that were worth nothing.
> Gayman: You would venture it. I thank you, sir. I would your lady were worth nothing.
> Sir Cautious: Why so, Sir?
> Gayman: Then I would set all 'gainst that nothing.

Sir Cautious begins this dialogue with a comical identification of everything with its universal equivalent, money. Everything he owns is convertible into money; hence, he believes that money is the real essence of everything that isn't money. Hence, everything is *really* the same thing—money. For Sir Cautious the economy of difference collapses everything into sameness. The only thing that is truly different, then, must be "nothing," a common slang word for the female genitals. One's wife is this nothing because in the normal course of things she is not a commodity. As Sir Cautious remarks, "Why, what a lavish whoremaker's this? We take money to marry our wives but very seldom part with 'em, and by the bargain get money" (p. 126). Her normal nonexchangeability for money is what makes a wife different from a prostitute; it is also what makes her the perfect nothing to set against three hundred pounds. We could say, then, that Julia is here made into a commodity only because she isn't one: she becomes the principle of universal difference and as such, paradoxically, becomes the exchangeable for the universal equivalent.

The scene provides a structural parallel for the scene of Gayman's prostitution, in which, as we have seen, money also marks difference. But the sequels of the two scenes are strikingly dissimilar. Gayman is once again back in Julia's bed, but his rather than her identity is supposedly masked. Whereas in the first encounter, Gayman went to bed with what he thought was an old woman, in the second, Julia goes to bed with what she thinks is her old husband. But the difference between these two scenes in the dark as they are later recounted stems from the relative inalienability of male sexual identity. Even in the dark, we are led to believe, the difference of men is sensible: Gayman says, "It was the feeble husband you enjoyed / In cold imagination, and no more. / Shyly you turned away, faintly resigned. . . . Till excess of love betrayed the cheat" (p. 139). Gayman's body, even unseen, is not interchangeable with Sir Cautious's. Unlike Julia's, Gayman's body will undo the misrepresentation; no mere idea can eradicate this palpable difference and sign of identity, the tumescent penis itself. Hence, when Gayman takes Sir Cautious's place in bed, he does not really risk what Julia suffered earlier: "after all to seem deformed, old, ugly." Gayman's self will always obtrude into the sphere of representation, another version of the ladle, but one that projects from the body instead of being barely discernible within it.

This inalienable masculine identity, although it seems at first Gayman's advantage, is quickly appropriated by Julia, who uses it to secure at once her own good reputation and complete liberty of action. Once again we are given a scene in which the speaker's sincerity if questionable. When Gayman's erection reveals his identity, Julia appears to be outraged at the attempted deception: "What, make me a base prostitute, a foul adult'ress? Oh, be gone, dear robber of my quiet" (p. 139). We can only see this tirade as more deceit on Julia's part, since we know she tricked the same man into bed the night before. But since her deceit was not discovered and his was, she is able to feign outrage and demand a separation from her husband. The implication is, although, once again, this cannot be represented, that Julia has found a way to secure her liberty and her "honor" by maintaining her misrepresentations.

It is, then, precisely through her nullity, her nothingness, that Julia achieves a new level of self-possession along with the promise of continual sexual exchange. But this, of course, is an inference we make from what we suspect Julia of hiding: her pleasure in Gayman's body, her delight that she now has an excuse for separating from her husband, her intention to go on seeking covert pleasure. All of this is on the other side of what we see and hear.

It is this shady effect, I want to conclude, that Aphra Behn is in the business of selling. And it is by virtue of this commodity that she becomes such a problematic figure for later women writers. For they had to overcome not only her life, her bawdiness and the author-whore metaphor she celebrated, but also her playful challenges to the very possibility of female self-representation.   *1988*

Shari Benstock
1944–

Shari Benstock is a U.S. literary critic best known for *Women of the Left Bank: Paris 1900–1940* (1986), a landmark exploration of literature by female expatriates from Natalie Barney to DJUNA BARNES to GERTRUDE STEIN. Benstock was born in San Diego to Dan and Myrl Barth Gabrielson and received her B.A. from Drake University in 1967, her M.A. from Drake in 1970, and her Ph.D. from Kent State University in 1975. In 1973 she married Bernard Benstock, an English professor; she has a son, Eric Shivvers, by a prior marriage. During the late 1970s Benstock worked in administrative posts at the University of Illinois at Urbana; from 1983 to 1986 she taught English and women's studies at the University of Tulsa, where she edited the journal *Tulsa Studies in Women's Literature*. Since 1987 she has been professor of English at the University of Miami.

Two of Benstock's publications examine the literature of James Joyce: *Who's He When He's at Home: A James Joyce Directory* (1980), coedited with Bernard Benstock, and *Coping with Joyce: Essays from the Copenhagen Symposium* (1988), coedited with Morris Beja. She has edited several collections of feminist critical essays, including *Feminist Issues in Literary Scholarship* (1987), *The Private Self: Theory and Practice of Women's Autobiography* (1988), and *Textualizing the Feminine: On the Limits of Genre* (1991). In 1994 she published a biography of Edith Wharton, *No Gifts from Chance*, and edited Wharton's *The House of Mirth*. Benstock also coedited *On Fashion* (1994) with Suzanne Ferris.

Among Benstock's many awards are a fellowship from the American Association of University Women for study in France (1981–82), a Rockefeller Foundation fellowship for study in Bellagio, Italy (1990), a Donald C. Gallup fellowship from Yale University (1991), and a National Endowment for the Humanities Grant (1993–94). Since 1987 she has edited the series Reading Women Writing for Cornell University Press, and she serves on the editorial boards of the *Journal of Modern Literature* and the *James Joyce Quarterly*.

The selection included here, "The Lesbian Other," is taken from *Women of the Left Bank;* it focuses on the comic grotesque and parodic writings of Djuna Barnes and her literary circle in Paris in the 1920s and 30s. The ways in which lesbians are "othered" in heterosexual societies, and the transgressive possibilities lesbian writers imagined for themselves as expatriate "others" in Paris, provide the focus of Benstock's subversive study.

﹛ The Lesbian Other ﹜

In the same year that *Ryder* became a bestseller in America, a slim chapbook entitled *Ladies Almanack* was published in Paris under the imprint of McAlmon's Contact Editions.[1] Published in 1,050 copies, *Ladies Almanack* contained twenty-two pen and ink drawings by [Djuna] Barnes, who hand-colored the first fifty numbered copies of the edition. It is interesting to note that McAlmon[2] underwrote the project with part of the alimony he received from Bryher's family,[3] so that Bryher—who was among the Paris lesbians who read the almanack—indirectly had a part in the printing of it. The almanack addressed itself to the particular readership of "ladies," underwriting a class association with lesbianism. If *Ryder* situated itself in the space of sexual difference, this volume, "written by a lady of fashion," made man its avowed enemy and glorified love between women. In important respects, this almanack served to counter Proust's version of Lesbos in *Sodome et Gomorrhe;*[4] indeed, it was probably written as a corrective to the Proustian version (Wickes, *Amazon of Letters*, 179).[5] Using "a lady of fashion" to address other "ladies," the language that invokes these privileged women in their art of loving conspires with the language of psychoanalysis, deconstructive practice, and feminist critical theory: "Neap-tide to the Proustian chronicle, gleanings from the shore of Mytilene, glimpses of its novitiates, its rising 'saints' and 'priestesses,' and thereon to such aptitude and insouciance that they took to gaming and to swapping that 'other' of the mystery, the anomaly that calls the hidden name. That, affronted, eats its shadow" (n.p.).[6] This commentary points toward the mystery that is woman—the mystery that the male tries to penetrate, that confounds his efforts at explication, that irritates his daily life. The "other" eerily forecasts Lacan's rereading of the Freudian Other—the mystery of the unconscious that directs our conscious lives but eludes our knowledge and our explanations.[7] The

---

1. *Ryder* (1928) was a novel and *Ladies Almanack* (1928) a satiric day book by Djuna Barnes.
2. Robert McAlmon was an American expatriate novelist and the husband of Winifred Ellerman (Bryher).
3. Bryher (Winifred Ellerman), 1894–1983, was a wealthy historical novelist, McAlmon's wife, and companion to the poet H.D.
4. Marcel Proust (1871–1922) published his seven-part novel *A la recherche du temps perdu* (*Remembrance of Things Past*) between 1913 and 1927; *Sodome et Gomorrhe* (*Sodom and Gomorrah*) was the title of the fourth part.
5. George Wickes's study of Natalie Burney and her circle, *The Amazon of Letters*, appeared in 1977.
6. [As Susan Sniader Lanser suggests, *Ladies Almanack* also responds to (and rewrites) Hall's *The Well of Loneliness*, published in the same year. By demonstrating les-

bianism to be "normative," Barnes's text undercuts the homophobia and paranoia inherent in Hall's text: "*The Well of Loneliness* is a passionate plea and cry of rage; audacious in the clarity with which it portrays lesbian existence, it cannot afford to dare in structure, language, or tone. It is only in privacy that *Ladies Almanack* was able to exist in 1928." There is only one heterosexual female character in *Ladies Almanack*, Patience Scalpel (based on Mina Loy), herself eventually tempted to lesbian experience. Even Dame Musset does not escape the mark of the heterosexual scalpel (the name "patience" suggests the inevitable nature of this mark): she admits to having been "deflowered by the Hand of a Surgeon" at age ten (*Ladies Almanack*, 24).]
7. Jacques Lacan (1901–81) was a French psychoanalyst.

"other" is the object of desire, the beloved, the woman of man's dreams. Wendell Ryder's efforts to possess this elusive object of desire lead him to polygamy, make woman "a perfect prostrate tapestry of fecundity," and force him to "gaming and to swapping that 'other' of the mystery" (*Ryder*, 50). The *Ladies Almanack* provides an alternative to this tale of heterosexual aggression, offering a lesbian creation myth in the birth of "the first Woman born with a Difference" (*Ladies Almanack*, 26). That "difference" is marked by the return of woman's sexual self, the part of her forced to "eat its shadow" in the savage ritual of the heterosexual world. In the patriarchal world, woman is denied her own desire as she becomes the object of man's lust. Carolyn Allen argues that the "difference" here is lesbian sexuality: "in their love of the same sex, they . . . admire their nonconformity, their sexual difference from the rest of the world" ("Writing toward *Nightwood*").[8] *Ladies Almanack*, several stories from the *Spillway* collection, *Nightwood*, and *The Antiphon* explore the nature of female sexuality.[9] In particular, these works examine the difference *within* sexual difference, within gender. Under the patriarchal law, not only are the male and female decreed different from each other ("the little Difference which shall be alien always," *Ladies Almanack*, 57), but each is discovered to inhabit the other. Barnes's examination of internalized sexual difference, common both to the texts that addressed a heterosexual audience and to those written for other women, becomes the primary subject matter of her writing.

In mapping the inversions and subversions of sexual difference under the law that would enforce heterosexuality, Barnes's work anticipates (and simultaneously puts into question) the Lacanian notion that heterosexuality unwrites the very law of difference it would seem to put into place. That is, heterosexuality in Western culture is really a form of what has previously been defined as homosexuality: as a search for an image of the self, a search for the twin, a search for confirmation of one's identity through the double, a reinforcement of *sameness* under the guise of *difference*.[10] Barnes's work also puts into play the prevalent scientific theories of homosexuality of her own day: that the homosexual crime constituted an "inversion" of sexual roles, an attraction of one's own sex, to a "twin." Homosexuality was seen as narcissistic, a need constantly to gaze upon the self: "woman tears her Shift for a Likeness in a Shift, and a Mystery that is lost to the proportion of Mystery" (*Ladies Almanack*, 57). As Katherine Anne Porter's comments on [Gertrude] Stein suggest, homosexuality could be viewed as a condition born of immense egotism.[11] Barnes examines all of these stereotyped notions of sexuality, both heterosexual and homosexual, with special concern for the underlying equation of "invert" and "inversion." *Nightwood* demonstrates the entire range of inversions brought about by sexual orientation toward one's own sex. This text purposely— some have said perversely—insists on conflating notions of sexual practice and

---

8. Carolyn Allen's essay "Writing toward *Nightwood*" appeared in 1986 in *Silence and Power*, edited by Mary Lynn Broe.
9. *Spillway* (1962), *Nightwood*, and *The Antiphon* (1958) are all works by Barnes.
10. [Jane Gallop discusses Jacques Lacan's reading of "difference" and "sameness" in *The Daughter's Seduction*, chs. 2–4. See also the introduction by Juliet Mitchell and Jacqueline Rose to *Jacques Lacan and the Ecole Freudienne*, 1–57. Adopting Lacan's language, Susan Sniader Lanser comments that for Dame Musset in *Ladies Almanack* "the psychotragedy of femininity, the Phallic Lack, becomes

nothing short of the signifier of superiority" ("Speaking in Tongues," in Broe, *Silence and Power*). That Dame Musset's tongue is still flicking on her funeral pyre suggests to Lanser the ways in which "the Tongue—the Word—outlives the flesh. Female sexuality and female word coalesce to form the Last Signifier, displacing the Phallus in its pre-eminence."]
11. Katherine Anne Porter (1890?–1980) was an American short story writer and novelist; Gertrude Stein (1874–1946) was an American modernist writer of fiction and poetry.

role reversal.[12] If *Nightwood* has been read as an analysis of lesbianism that damns its practices and *Ladies Almanack* is a satire of lesbian communities, it is perhaps because Barnes is so successful in inverting expected values, in putting the author at an odd angle to the literary work so that her own attitudes are simultaneously concealed and revealed by it.

The shadow presence of the other appears frequently in *Nightwood*. Guido, Robin and Felix's mentally deficient son, is called "the shadow" of his father's anxiety, one who "eats a sleep that is not our sleep" (120); he is a child who, like his mother, is described as "estranged" (108, 121). Nora sees in Robin her "other self" and thinks that in walking beside Robin she is "beside herself," seeing her own image in her lover. Robin Vote carries the past about her like a former but undiscarded self; she is described as "gracious and yet fading, like an old statue in a garden" (41). In the final scene of "Night Watch" Nora looks down on the garden in the moments before dawn, searching for Robin. Seeing a "double shadow" falling from a garden statue, she does not at first see "the body of another woman swim up into the statue's obscurity," held in Robin's embrace. Moments later, Nora meets the "double regard" of the woman's eyes and shuts her eyes against the double vision, hoping that "they will not hold together" (64). Nora discovers that she can possess Robin, have her undivided loyalty, only when Robin is "dead drunk." At other times Robin's divided identity makes her a presence "in her own nightmare": "I tried to come between and save her, but I was like a shadow in her dream that could never reach her in time . . . she was like a new shadow walking perilously close to the outer curtain" (145). This double image of woman that "holds together" a fractured female identity and sexuality is first explored in the homocentric world of *Ladies Almanack*, where woman's lesbian lover represents her "second self" and together the two discover the joys of woman's sexuality. In *Nightwood* that second (sexual) self is suppressed by society, forced to live in the secret nightwood of the unconscious, where it threatens to rob woman of her sanity. *Ladies Almanack* expresses the joy of woman's double presence and examines the richness and diversity of her character. *Nightwood* makes woman's double a "negative presence." Unable to understand this presence, woman tries to control it—as Nora tries to control Robin—and when she discovers it cannot be appropriated, she flees from it into alcoholism or insanity.

THE ALMANACK

Ladies Almanack was one of several underground "lesbian" documents of the Paris expatriate community. In histories of the period it is mentioned in passing as a satire on Natalie Barney's company of women, the Académie des Femmes, which met regularly in the garden at 20, rue Jacob, to read women's writing. In his life of Natalie Barney, George Wickes recounts that in January 1928 Barney wrote Richard Aldington to inquire whether he might be interested in publishing this little book: "All ladies fit to figure in such an almanack should of course be eager to have a copy, and all gentlemen disapproving of them. Then the public might, with a little judicious treatment,

---

12. [C. A. Tripp writes: "Only in popular thinking are homosexuality and inversion synonymous. For several decades biologists and experimental psychologists have recognized that these are distinctly different phenomena, though they may or may not occur together. Homosexuality refers to any sexual activity between members of the same sex. Inversion, on the other hand, implies nothing about the sex of the partner; it refers to a reversal of the commonly expected gender-role of the individual" (*The Homosexual Matrix*, 22).]

include those lingering on the border of such islands and those eager to be ferried across" (*Amazon of Letters*, 180). Even Barney's lighthearted tone cannot disguise her perceptive reading of the *Almanack*. It is Dame Evangeline Musset, the heroine of the *Almanack* based on Natalie Barney, whose lifelong commitment is to rescue women from the perils of heterosexuality. The community Dame Musset creates is one in which women are not estranged from themselves—from their identity and sexuality—falsely mirroring the images created for them by the men who desire them, but a community in which women have value in and of themselves—because they *are* women, not merely because they behave as men have determined they should. The community of women celebrated by the *Almanack* is one where women revel in the pleasures of their newfound freedom. As Susan Sniader Lanser has suggested, "the *Almanack* creates a lesbian-feminist culture mythology and even suggests a radical critique of patriarchy by recognizing the personal/sexual as political. As it rewrites scripture, documents lesbian rituals, muses about women's condition, and tells the mock-heroic story of its patron saint, Dame Musset, *Ladies Almanack* offers both a mockery of patriarchal values and institutions and a vision of women turning to women in pleasure and joy" ("Speaking in Tongues," 41). A document by a woman for women, *Ladies Almanack* was one of the best-known pieces of "coterie" literature of the period. Apparently not taken seriously by its author, who referred to it both as a "piece of fluff" and as a "slight satiric wigging," it has not been taken seriously by commentators. (One might argue that such disclaimers by Barnes should not be taken at face value, that the comic cloak may hide a more serious subject.) But if this work is comic satire—as its author claims—it is certainly *not* a satire at the expense of lesbianism or of such groups as Natalie Barney established. Rather, it deplores the treatment of women in the heterosexual world, suggesting the same reasons for woman's "estrangement" from herself that *Nightwood* further explores. In telling the story of Dame Musset, the *Almanack* overturns patriarchal mythologies and creates a counterculture for women; it makes love between women a radically subversive act ("Speaking in Tongues," 40–41). If, as Louis Kannenstine observed about *Ryder*, "the man of *virtu* became the homosexual O'Conner . . . , in *Ladies Almanack*, *virtu* becomes a Sapphic trait, the property of women alone" (Kannenstine, *Art of Djuna Barnes*, 50).

The frontispiece drawing shows Dame Evangeline Musset (whose name suggests her evangelistic intentions) walking on what is described as "exceeding thin ice," a long pole extended to prevent the surrounding women, who are pictured in various stages of drowning, from "sinking for the third time." Dame Musset is called "a wonder woman," whose efforts are on behalf of that "which it has pleased God more and more to call frail woman." The *Almanack* itself is not only a tribute to Dame Musset—whose life is recounted through the twelve months and who is elevated to sainthood at its close—but a collection of poems, stories, and rituals designed to provide psychic support as woman endures the hardships of life among men. Woman is given a calendar that celebrates her accomplishments and places her works in an historical context. She is provided goddesses to protect her, a zodiac whose signs describe her, and a lullaby to soothe her. Her calendar is an intimate description of her "distempers"—the signs of her "fallen" condition; it also lists her "tides and moons," her "spring fevers, love philters and winter feasts." The chapbook provides a woman's history, rewrites woman in patriarchal culture and myth, explains the workings of her body and the directions of her sexuality, and—most importantly—analyzes the reasons for her frequent unhappiness, the difficulties of her situation, and accounts for man's simultaneous hatred and love of her. *Ladies Almanack* helps woman understand her longing for the lost Eden of her existence, when woman was praised and venerated rather than belittled and despised; she learns that it was her strength, her "impudence," her beauty and knowledge that affronted man, in punishment for which "the Earth sucked down her generations, Body for Body" (62).

Woman's body—which has been made the vehicle by which man satiates his lust—is returned to woman's control. Discovering its pleasures, the ladies of the *Almanack* celebrate woman's sexuality, writing the lesbian body. The almanack also discovers the pleasure of woman's speech, finds a language in which to express woman's desire for herself—a language that encompasses both heterosexual and lesbian women, that can accommodate the difference *within* womanhood. As Susan Sniader Lanser has discovered, this woman's language speaks in "tongues." The tongue is glorified as a subtle sexual instrument (Dame Musset's tongue continues "flicking" through the ashes of her funeral pyre), an "antidote to the ethos of phallic supremacy and clitoral insufficiency of a newly Freudian age" ("Speaking in Tongues," 44). Woman is taught how to please herself, is encouraged to find "the Consolation every Woman has at her Finger Tips, or at the very Hang of her Tongue" as even Duchess Clitoressa becomes a character in the story (*Ladies Almanack*, 7). The signs of the zodiac correspond to a part of woman's body, each addressed in an attitude of sexual desire: "the longing leg," "the twining thigh," the "seeking arm," "the hungry heart." Woman's womb becomes "the spinning Centre of a spinning World" (*Ladies Almanack*, 52).

But even as woman is taught to love herself, to reject the image man has given her and love the one she herself creates, to seek a spiritual and physical soulmate in another woman, she learns that her unconquerable shame and despair is the result of patriarchal education. Entering "through the masculine Door," women have been taught that a strong, independent woman was not a woman at all, but a version of man. In the annals of history such a woman was thought to "have had a Testes of sorts, however writed and awander; that indeed she was called forth a Man, and when answering, by some Mischance, or monstrous Fury of Fate, stumbled over a Womb, and was damned then and forever to drag it about, like a Prisoner his Ball and Chain, whether she would or no" (*Ladies Almanack*, 53). The comic and antique language of this description cannot belie the seriousness of the accusation embedded here. Barnes is expressing a familiar argument—made by men and women alike— that proud, independent, intelligent, strong women are often accused of not being women at all: they are rather men in "drag." This was Katherine Anne Porter's argument against all the women of Natalie Barney's salon; it was also evident in Colette's comments on the sadism of the *Amazones*, "these mannish women [who] were able to break in and subjugate a horse, and when age and hard times deprived them of the whip and the hunting crop, they lost their final sceptre" (*The Pure and the Impure*, 72).[13] When woman frees herself of the image of femininity by which man has constrained her, sheds the clothes he has fashioned for her, she exchanges his image of her for her image of him: she remakes herself in his image. No other possibility is available for woman under the law of the patriarchy because the law can only "admit [woman] to sense through the masculine door" (*Ladies Almanack*, 53). Such "inversion"—of behavior, of dress—is an effect of the patriarchal law. In trying to discover her own true self, she only discovers man's image of her. The *Almanack*, therefore, charts a double course: to illustrate the effects of man's effort to define woman and to provide

13. Sidonie Gabrielle Colette (1873–1954) was a French author of plays, novels, short stories, and film scripts; she published *The Pure and the Impure*, a memoir.

a series of *different* images for woman. The almanack subverts the masculine image of woman by putting another in its place, one that reflects woman's diversity.

The price woman pays for displacing the patriarchal law, however, is a painful one, as the September entry, "Her Tides and Moons," illustrates. The *Almanack* suggests the complex condition of woman in the world, the illustration portraying woman as a mermaid stranded on land: "she is a fish of earth" (55). Woman is displaced in both time and place, as this entry in the calendar makes explicit: "The very Condition of Woman is so subject to Hazard, so complex, and so grievous, that to place her at one Moment is but to displace her at the next" (55). Man's jealousy of his wife does not reflect his high regard for her, but rather his fear that she will betray him with another's child, make a mockery of his masculinity, place the cuckold horns on his head. And worse awaits the woman who turns to another woman for sexual satisfaction: "see how vain is Man's suffering, change it how you will, for though that Prick is nowhere in the Flesh of Sister for Sister, they cry as loud" (57). Unable to comprehend sexuality in terms other than the phallic, man rages at his loss of woman, weeps for his wounded pride. But woman, when she remains the rib in man's side, submissive to his heterosexual law and defined by his desire, weeps "for Loneliness estranged— the unthinking returning of themselves to themselves" (58). Woman seeks the consolation of her sisters, desires the community of women, but is ashamed in betraying the master who would confine her, afraid to leave the world of patriarchal convention. The patriarchal scheme has not succeeded in reducing woman to nothing, in making her a "non-person" within the legal definition. Rather, she has been divided against herself, man has made her a fish out of water, a creature who cannot walk on land, who has been taught how to hate herself. The bizarre forms—neither man nor woman—that haunt Barnes's short stories (particularly those collected in *Spillway*) and form the company of grotesques that populate *Nightwood* are less Barnes's inventions than the creations of a world in which woman is a weaker, degraded version of man—"unmanned." Woman's gifts are wasted; she becomes waste: "She fouls everything she touches with the Droppings natural to her lost Condition!" (49). When her strength and independence have been returned to her in the company of women, she is a threat to man, who defines her as the "phallic woman."

The *Book of Repulsive Women*[14] and *Ladies Almanack* exploit what has often been termed by male critics "the bawdy." This is specifically female "bawdy" that admits no males, but nonetheless may have initially awakened a prurient male interest in the frank (and funny) emphasis on woman's sexuality. These works provide contrasting views of woman's body: the first its repulsive form, seen through the eyes of women who see themselves as a man would see them; the second the eroticized form woman sees when she has recaptured her sexuality from the patriarchal culture that appropriated it. The divided loyalty to the female body is an effect of woman's position in Western society: she quickly learns that man's desire for her body is the measure of its worth. Once that body "sags, stretches, becomes distorted" (*Ladies Almanack*, 56), it is cast aside by man. If that body is not desired by man or if its virtue is retained in chastity, woman weeps for the body's uselessness or subdues its carnal longings. As the woman ages, her body can only serve as a reminder of her lost worth—and the momentary nature of that worth, as Susan Sniader Lanser comments: "The 'September' section is the most overt in this recognition; the narrator

---

14. A book containing "eight rhythms poems and five drawings" by Barnes (1915).

complains that woman's 'very Condition' is 'so subject to Hazard, so complex, and so grievous' . . . that by middle age her body has been distorted and her mind 'corrupt with the Cash of a pick-thank existence'. . . . She suggests that although a woman may spend 'half her duration' 'upon her Back' . . . it will never be her preference" ("Speaking in Tongues," 43). Woman's body becomes in middle age the measure of her worthlessness, and as such, she despises it to the same degree as does the male who has abandoned it. Woman learns the bitter lesson that not only can the body be discarded, but it existed only to serve man's pleasure—never woman's own pleasure. It is noteworthy that Dame Musset, most unusual of women in never submitting to man's definition of her or in serving his sexual desire, recounts that she was deflow-ered "by the Hand of a Surgeon" when she was a child of ten (24), exclaiming that "I, even I, came to it as other Women." The notion that woman could teach herself the pleasures that her own body could afford her, could value her body beyond—indeed, apart from—the interest that man would have in it is one of the many lessons of *Ladies Almanack*. It is a lesson that Djuna Barnes herself desired to learn, but perhaps could not; it is a lesson that Natalie Barney seemed always to know—even into her old age.

1986

◄ Works Cited ►

Allen, Carolyn. "Writing toward *Nightwood*." *Silence and Power*, ed. Mary Lynn Broe. Carbon-dale, Ill.: Southern Illinois UP, 1986.

Barnes, Djuna. *Ladies Almanack*. New York: Harper and Row, 1972.

Gallop, Jane. *The Daughter's Seduction*. Ithaca: Cornell UP, 1982.

Kannenstine, Louis F. *The Art of Djuna Barnes*. New York: New York UP, 1977.

Lanser, Susan Sniader. "Speaking in Tongues." *Silence and Power*, ed. Mary Lynn Broe. Car-bondale, Ill.: Southern Illinois UP, 1986.

Mitchell, Juliet and Jacqueline Rose, eds. *Jacques Lacan and the Ecole Freudienne*. London: Macmillan, 1982.

Tripp, C.A. *The Homosexual Matrix*. New York: McGraw-Hill, 1975.

Wickes, George. *Amazon of Letters*. London: Allen, 1977.

SECTION III

Rethinking the Maternal

Through our mothers, the culture gave us mixed messages. Which was it to be—strong or submissive, rebellious or conforming?

Gloria Anzaldúa, Borderlands/La Frontera

Motherhood occurs in specific historical situations framed by interlocking structures of race, class, and gender, where the sons and daughters of white mothers have "every opportunity and protection," and the "colored" daughters and sons of racial ethnic mothers "know not their fate."

Patricia Hill Collins, "Shifting the Center: Race, Class and Feminist Theorizing About Motherhood"

Women writers throughout history have written with anger, ambivalence, and affirmation about motherhood, perhaps the most complex of any female experience. Many writers have questioned whether mothers are powerful or powerless in their roles as the primary caregivers of children and whether daughters should respect, revise, or challenge maternal authority. In her treatise on motherhood, *Of Woman Born*, ADRIENNE RICH distinguishes between two definitions: motherhood as experience, which encompasses the potentially powerful relationship of any woman to her reproductive capacities and her children; and motherhood as institution, which in a patriarchal society tries to keep women and children under male control. The institution of motherhood is underwritten by a series of unexamined assumptions: that motherhood is woman's destiny, her sacred calling; that mothers lack further identities and are so selfless as not to need any; that mothers feel only tenderness for their children, never resentment or rage. Motherhood is not preordained for women, Rich argues; it has a history, an ideology; it is "more fundamental than tribalism or nationalism." The experience of motherhood, varied according to race and class and geographic location, acknowledges that maternity is one part of the life process for many (not all) women rather than an identity for all time; it bears witness to guilt and anger at one's children as well as interest in their learning, joy at their growth. As women rethink the maternal in both institutional and experiential terms, Rich claims, its landscape shifts; "the words are being spoken, are being written down; the taboos are being broken, the masks of motherhood are cracking through" (24–25).

In "Writing and Motherhood" SUSAN RUBIN SULEIMAN combines autobiography, psychoanalysis, and feminist literary criticism to examine the relationship between creativity and procreativity. As a writer and a mother, Suleiman has a vested interest in her topic and demonstrates that many other women do as well. Citing theorists Juliet Mitchell and Nancy Chodorow, she argues that women's desire to find fulfillment in motherhood has been historically strong in part because women have few other sources of power in a society that devalues them. Although women have traditionally been expected (and perhaps have expected themselves) to devote their energy exclusively to their children, Suleiman notes that many mothers have spoken out about the conflict between maternal work and the desire for self-realization. Some of these mothers are creative writers, authors of fiction, poetry, and autobiography—women writing not *on* the body of the mother but *as* the body of the mother (*LAWL* 622-25).

PATRICIA HILL COLLINS provides a sociological approach in her essay "Shifting the Center," arguing that feminist theories of motherhood should foreground racial and class issues whenever they consider maternity and the mother-child bond. For women of color, she asserts, "the subjective experience of mothering / motherhood is inextricably linked to the sociocultural concern of racial ethnic communities—one does not exist without the other." To illustrate her claim, Collins discusses literary texts about mothering by Native American, African-American, Asian-American, and Hispanic women, reexamining from their perspectives certain feminist theories that posit rigid distinctions between raising a family and work outside the home, between the individual and the collective. Collins invents the term "motherwork" to describe "work for the day to come" on behalf of one's own children, the children of one's racial group, or the children of the world. When practiced with commitment and integrity, motherwork insures the physical survival of threatened children, refuses their assimilation by the dominant culture, and fosters a "meaningful racial identity in children within a society that denigrates people of color." Only by examining mothering from multiple perspectives can feminist theory "recontextualize motherhood" (*LAWL* 651).

At the same time, many feminist theoreticians offer cautionary words about efforts to rethink the maternal. In writing about mothers and daughters Marianne Hirsch notes, "I am aware of the dangers of idealizing and mystifying a certain biological female experience and of reviving an identification between femininity and maternity which certainly has not served the interests of women" (163). Writing from the perspective of peace studies, Linda Rennie Forcey echoes Hirsch's concern about "essentializing" women as kinder, gentler, and fundamentally different from men, and thereby assuming that mothers are "naturally" nurturing and thus will challenge male violence in the public sphere. Yet Forcey is sympathetic to the view of mothers as especially peace-loving—after all, she wonders, "who among us would want to imply that there could ever be too much caring in this violent world?" Who would disagree that many women act as peacemakers in their homes, or that the *feeling* of maternal difference can be used to raise human consciousness? Mothering, for Forcey, can best be defined as "a socially constructed set of activities and relationships involved in nurturing and caring for people," whether those people are biological children, stepchildren, other adults, the elderly, or the infirm. To write thoughtfully about motherhood, women must "acknowledge the tension between needing to act as women who value mothering/caring labor, and needing an identity not overdetermined by our gender" (355–75).

The texts collected here explore the insights that women from the fourteenth century to the present have offered about motherhood, motherwork, and the mother-child connection. Some women have written from their perspectives as mothers, instructing their sons and daughters and expressing care or conflict toward them.

Others have assumed the daughter's voice, whether loving or resentful, conciliatory or rebellious. Still others have recontextualized motherhood across race, class, and other lines of difference, portraying the injustices that many mothers face and thereby attempting to speak the unspeakable. These perspectives on maternity reveal that, in philosopher Sara Ruddick's words, "mothers are not any more or less wonderful than other people—they are not especially sensible or foolish, noble or ignoble, courageous or cowardly. . . . What they share is not virtuous characteristics but rather an identification and a discourse about the strengths required by their ongoing commitments to protect, nurture, and train" (25).

WRITING AS A MOTHER

You, too, will love
her thighs. The fat
sweatiness of them,
the toe-curling odor.

Kate Daniels, "Love Pig"

Is there such a thing as the writing mother's fantasy? . . . What happens to the mother's discourse when it chooses not direct expression but the indirections of fiction?

Susan Rubin Suleiman, "Writing and Motherhood"

Throughout literary history writing mothers have worked in genres that allow them to express their roles as educators, as conveyors of social mores as well as other kinds of wisdom; these genres include advice manuals, polemics, didactic poetry, and letters. Other women less concerned with adapting genres to their motherwork have written instead to celebrate their children or express what they cannot, or dare not, say: that they find a tension between their mothering and their art that is sometimes unbearable. As Suleiman notes, feminist approaches to women's literature have typically privileged the daughter's voice over the mother's. Yet "as long as our emphasis . . . continues to be on the-mother-as-she-is-written rather than on the-mother-as-she-writes, we shall continue in our ignorance" (*LAWL* 625). A chronological look at several texts from this anthology will reveal the range of discursive strategies that mothers have used to write their voices.

The medieval writer JULIANA BERNERS employs a discourse of education and instruction to address young aristocratic men in "The Book of Hunting," a fifteenth-century verse manual that "shows gentle persons how to hunt all sorts of beasts, whether they are beasts of venery or the chase." Berners frequently asserts her maternal and pedagogical authority: "Of the beasts of venery you will find; / Attend to your mistress, and she'll teach you the kinds." Addressing her reader as "my dear child" or "my son," she orders him repeatedly in the imperative mode: "learn this all"; "do so, while you have strength"; "these beasts all / You shall them call." Moreover, she refers often to herself, though by status rather than by name: "Say, child, wherever you go / It was your dame who taught you so" (*LAWL* 659–60). Clearly Berners insists on being an authoritative, maternal voice for the young men she instructs.

eventeenth-century advice books, DOROTHY LEIGH's *The Mother's Blessing*
ETH CLINTON's *The Countess of Lincoln's Nursery*, demonstrate the cultural
authority invested in a mother's right to write about maternity at a time when
women were forbidden to address politics or sexuality in the public sphere. An
extended letter to her sons written in part because Leigh feared she would fail to see
them reach adulthood, *The Mother's Blessing* offers instruction in spiritual obedience,
filial behavior, and egalitarian marriage. Published posthumously in 1616, this conduct manual became the best-selling book of its era; it was reissued often throughout
the century and praised by men and women alike. Authorized by a similar type of
maternal power, ELIZABETH CLINTON composed *The Countess of Lincoln's Nursery* as a
gentle polemic to urge wealthy Englishwomen to nurse their children. Because she
opposed the practice of wet-nursing, which was prevalent among members of her
class, the Countess drew upon her own experience as the mother of sixteen children,
none of whom she nursed, to express the error of her ways. Moreover, she refers to
Biblical passages, physicians' testimonies, and the confessions of other mothers in
building her meticulous argument. From Berners to the Countess of Lincoln, early
women writers offered their maternal knowledge as a form of cultural intervention.

Maternal instruction comes to the surface more playfully in ANNE BRADSTREET's
poem "The Author to Her Book," in which she likens her literary product to a wayward child. Ambivalence is evident in the speaker's final exhortation to her child-
book, as she dresses it in "homespun cloth" and sends it out to seek its fortune. She
sends the "child" forth with many caveats—the need to avoid criticism, a protective
gesture; the need to travel into unknown rather than familiar territory; and, most significantly, the need to disclaim paternal in favor of maternal authority. In releasing
her "ill-formed offspring" to the world, this seventeenth-century mother authorizes
herself to write (*LAWL* 669).

Women have also instructed their children by letter. Known as "the female traveler," the eighteenth-century English writer Lady MARY WORTLEY MONTAGU sent
almost 900 letters during the years she lived on the European continent, many of
them to her favorite daughter, Lady Mary Bute. Like the manuals of Barnes and
Leigh, much of Montagu's maternal instruction is directive. Yet because she is writing to a daughter rather than a son, she cannot assume that the course of action she
advocates will be easy to follow. Montagu is particularly interesting in insuring that
her eldest granddaughter be educated in Greek and Latin as well as needlework.
Learning (if a girl has a real taste for it) will make her contented, she claims. No
entertainment is as cheap as reading, nor any pleasure as lasting. "If your Daughters
are inclined to Love reading, do not check their Inclination by hindering them of the
diverting part of it" (*LAWL* 674). Here a white, upper-class mother subversively
instructs her daughter as to how to insure her granddaughter's literacy. Ironically,
Montagu both describes and enacts the role of "author in the closet," since her
maternal discourse is a private act—a letter to her daughter—but with public implications: endorsing classical education for girls, a privilege rarely granted even to England's female elite. Illustrating what Suleiman calls "the-mother-as-she-writes,"
Montagu claims both maternal and social agency, not only for herself but for her
daughter and granddaughter.

If mothers have been responsible for birthing and educating their young, they
have at times had to bury them as well. Writing as part of a nineteenth-century

American culture of mourning, which offered public testament via eulogies and monuments to the dead's continued existence, LYDIA SIGOURNEY mourned the loss of children in her poems. In "Dream of the Dead" the "sweet singer of Hartford," as this sentimental lyricist was called, depicts encounters in heaven with a dead mother, "full of fresh life and in that beauty clad / Which charmed my earliest love," and with a joyful infant, smiling as if it were still alive. Her dreams console the speaker, much as Sigourney's poems comforted parents who had suffered loss. In "The Last Words of the Dying" the poet transforms one of life's most painful moments into a mystical experience as she portrays a dying woman who spells out "mother" in sign language. The lamenting speaker wonders whether death brings a vision of the woman's long-deceased mother or causes her regret at leaving her sons, "those three fair boys" with whom her soul would linger (*LAWL* 684–87). In addition to Sigourney, such nine-teenth-century women as Helen Hunt Jackson, Elizabeth Oakes-Smith, and EMILY DICKINSON depict in their poetry dying women who seek connection with their living offspring, or living women who commune beyond the grave with their dead children.

A different kind of maternal elegy can be seen in twentieth-century Australian poet JUDITH WRIGHT's poignant "Stillborn." A chronicle of those whose "double loss" so often goes unnoticed, women whose infants are born dead, this poem confronts the "pain of that dark birth" alongside the guilt of living mothers who feel that they, not their children, should have died. Indeed, Wright gives voice to an almost preternatural grief, as these women "weep for love / of one who drew no breath" and lie in bed at night "giving the breast to death." In another poem she joins the ranks of modern women poets who share with their grown daughters their hopes for them since infancy. "Letter" acknowledges maternal frustration, as the speaker confirms her inability to protect her child from pain. "I promised you unborn / something better than that," she tells her daughter, rejecting lies that veil the truth of a relentless world. Although she knows she should repent having "promised what's not given," the mother refuses such repentance (*LAWL* 804-06). Instead, she expresses faith in her daughter's ability to find her own life path.

"What transformations does the [writing mother's] fantasy undergo in the process of its fictionalization?" wonders Suleiman in "Writing and Motherhood" (*LAWL* 634). ROSELLEN BROWN's "Good Housekeeping" reveals motherhood as a source of conflict to the woman whose mind, by necessity or choice, is not entirely focused on her children; it also inscribes a fantasy of maternal guilt. Suleiman rightly calls this story "portrait of the artist as mother; or, the momentary triumph of aggression over tenderness"; surely Brown is giving voice to that most illicit of maternal dreams, putting her own artistic needs over her child's well-being (*LAWL* 635). In *Of Woman Born* Rich discusses the "exquisite suffering" caused by her conflict between child-rearing and creativity. "It is the suffering of ambivalence: the murderous alternation between bitter resentment and raw-edged nerves, and blissful gratification and tenderness" (21). For Brown's fictional mother as for Rich, creativity and maternity refuse any comfortable coexistence.

Hirsch has stressed the importance of examining the mother as subject, "constituted in a particular relation to social reality, to sexuality, to work and historical experience, to subjectivity" (163–64). Contemporary feminist poets often address motherhood in precisely this manner. In "Poem for My Sons" MINNIE BRUCE PRATT, a lesbian mother who lost custody of her children to their father because of her sexual orientation, claims her maternal subjectivity alongside the right to write. For years she worked solely at maternity, trying to nurse her firstborn son; in those years, creativity and motherhood seemed antithetical. Only by living openly as a lesbian, "voluptuous, a lover," could the speaker become "capable of poetry" (*LAWL* 853). In this poem Pratt supports Hirsch's assertion that maternal subjects are constituted in relation to history, sexuality, and social reality. Only after claiming her own hard-won sexual identity can this mother speak openly to her sons, offering them both guidance and blessing. Another reality of the mother as subject is the desire to mourn when her adult children move away from home, leaving behind an "empty nest." How to keep her near-grown daughter close yet to let her go provides the subject for *Mother Love*, a sequence of maternal elegies by RITA DOVE. Assuming the voice of Demeter, the mythical Greek mother of Persephone, Dove confronts her yearning to capture a daughter carried off to life without her—not to the Underworld, to be sure, where Hades dragged Persephone, but to college, autonomy, and adulthood. Although Dove's speaker realizes that in time she will "forget this empty brimming" that engulfs her when her only child departs, she longs for Demeter's power to upset the balance of the seasons until her daughter comes safely home again (*LAWL* 861). Both the power of the mother-child bond and the anguish of maternal loss pervade these poems.

KATE DANIELS, a U.S. poet who has chronicled motherhood in three compelling volumes of verse, has explored courageously the effort to blend motherwork and writing. In *Four Testimonies: Poems* (1998) the speaker reveals maternal joy at her children's flesh, guilt over her absence for hours each day, and determination to write *and* mother well no matter what. "Love Pig" celebrates her newborn daughter's fat, sweaty thighs and "toe-curling odors" even as she offers to lend her infant, in friendship, to another woman so she too can "burrow / down deep in her sweet / and her sourness." "In My Office at Bennington" probes the conflict Daniels's speaker experiences when, immersed in thought, she hears "the voices of my children / returning from a meal." Her dual need—to write the poem that at last "seems possible again" and to answer her children's cries—leaves her divided: "I'm paper torn in half, / the poem that didn't work." Yet in "Prayer for My Children" she claims fervently to "regret nothing," for what she has lived has led her to "this room," to "three who love me / exactly as I am" (*LAWL* 872–74). For Daniels, no pleasure of the text can surpass the joy of mothering.

Judging from these textual examples, Suleiman seems correct in her assumption "that mothers' fantasies exist, that they are formulatable, and that they can (can, not must) provide the impetus for fictional elaboration" (*LAWL* 634). Maternal narratives include anger as well as tenderness, ambivalence as well as reconciliation. Studying the variety of discourses used by writing mothers through the ages can help readers define what Hirsch has termed "the shapes of maternal subjectivity" (163). Although maternal narratives reveal love and concern for sons as well as daughters, their connections to daughters often seem particularly intense. The power of bodily identification and a shared gender oppression might explain this intensity, as might the societal prevalence of a Freudian paradigm that posits mothers and daughters as rivals for a father's affections. By confronting these complexities from the mother's as well as the daughter's perspective, readers can "envision a feminist family romance of mothers *and* daughters, both subjects, speaking to each other and living in familial and communal contexts which enable the subjectivity of each member" (Hirsch 163).

WRITING AS A DAUGHTER

The cathexis between mother and daughter—essential, distorted, misused—
is the great unwritten story. Probably there is nothing in human nature more
resonant with charges than the flow of energy between two biologically alike
bodies, one of which has lain in amniotic bliss inside the other, one of which
has labored to give birth to the other. The materials are here for the deepest
mutuality and the most painful estrangement.

Adrienne Rich, Of Woman Born

Off, off, eely tentacle!
There is nothing between us.

Sylvia Plath, "Medusa"

In claiming the mother-daughter bond as "the great unwritten story," ADRIENNE
RICH calls upon women writers and readers to join her in exploring this powerful
connection—both its nurturing dimensions ("the deepest mutuality") and its harmful aspects ("the most painful estrangement") (226). A daughter in the Middle Ages
or the Renaissance was often married off against her will—in VIRGINIA WOOLF's
words, "locked up, beaten, and flung about the room . . . the slave of any boy whose
parents forced a ring upon her finger"; mothers either could not or would not stop
this practice. In literature, daughters who survive and flourish have often been presented as motherless, from Snow White and Cinderella to Jane Eyre and Emma
Woodhouse. Yet by the nineteenth century there existed in America what the feminist historian Carroll Smith-Rosenberg has called a "female world of love and ritual"
at whose heart lay "an intimate mother-daughter relationship" in which "mothers
and other older women carefully trained daughters in the arts of housewifery and
motherhood," while adolescent girls "helped in childbirth, nursing, and weaning"
(1–2). Surely the mother-daughter bond has long been a dual-sided one, as Plath's
angry homage to her grasping mother-as-Medusa attests. "Off, off, eely tentacle! /
There is nothing between us" seems at first glance a bitter invective, a denial of any
connection between the child and her parent. "There is nothing between us," however, has another meaning: nothing separates us, we two are one, mother-as-daughter-
as-mother.

Hirsch has argued that feminism has largely been a "daughterly" discourse
uncomfortable with the maternal, and she offers four reasons for that discomfort.
First, motherhood continues to be considered "a patriarchal construction," the mother linked to "continued bondage to men and patriarchy" (165). This view of mothers
by their feminist daughters can be seen in Rich's discussion of "matrophobia," or fear
of becoming one's mother: "Matrophobia can be seen as a womanly splitting of the
self, in the desire to become purged once and for all of our mothers' bondage, to
become individuated and free. The mother stands for the victim in ourselves, the
unfree woman, the martyr. Our personalities seem dangerously to blur and overlap
with our mothers'; and, in a desperate attempt to know where mother ends and
daughter begins, we perform radical surgery" (235). Second, feminism relates uneasily to motherhood, Hirsch claims, due to "a discomfort with the vulnerability and lack
of control that are attributed to, and certainly are elements of, maternity." Because

feminists value choice and autonomy, many see the traditional image of a mother bearing her daughter as less desirable than that of a daughter giving birth to herself. A third reason for some feminists' suspicion of the maternal, Hirsch continues, lies in their fear of essentializing the body, a fear of equating biology with destiny, of defining women by their procreative capacities. Finally, she concludes, many feminists find the maternal discomfiting because they are deeply ambivalent toward power, authority, and anger—traits that children, and many adult daughters, associate with their mothers. Hirsch cites a study by psychologists Nancy Chodorow and Susan Contratto as persuasively demonstrating that feminist writing "is permeated with fears of maternal power and with anger at maternal powerlessness" (165–66).

The daughter's fantasy is not always one of "painful estrangement," however; some women write as the daughters of loving mothers whose power they appreciate and rely upon. Known for developing the image of Christ as mother in her spiritual texts, JULIAN OF NORWICH was a medieval mystic and the first known Englishwoman to write a book. Maternity, sensuality, and spirituality are connected in Julian's writings. "Our Mother Christ" is "Our Mother of mercy in taking our sensuality," which must be "suffered for the salvation of mankind," she writes. "In our Mother Christ we profit, and in mercy he reforms and restores us, and by the power of his Passion, his death and his Resurrection, he unites us to our substance" (LAWL 655–56). By extolling the centrality of God's motherhood, and by grounding that motherhood in the specificity of female embodiment, Julian challenges medieval dichotomies that posit spirit as male and flesh as female. In this way she authorizes her own spiritual insight as a woman mystic and as a writer. Union with the symbolic mother for Julian is not a matrophobic fear but a divine privilege.

The early nineteenth-century poet MARY TIGHE pays homage to her biological mother in terms almost as ecstatic as those JULIAN OF NORWICH uses to praise Jesus as Mother, but the reward for her maternal affiliation lies not in access to divinity but in access to creativity. For Tighe, the mother's "tender smile" and "willing ear" forever "bless'd thy child"; to her mother the speaker both owes and dedicates her poetic gift: "to thee belong / The graces which adorn my first wild song." As her mother "charm'd [her] infant breast" with "eloquence of tenderness express'd," so the poet-daughter wishes to charm her mother with this sonnet dedicated to her. "Oh! ever may its accents sweet rejoice / The soul which loves to own whate'er it has is thine!"

Most women writers neither demonize nor deify their maternal figures. Instead, they attempt to untangle what Jane Lazarre has called the "mother knot," unraveling the intricate strands that provide tenuous links between generations of women. MARGARET ATWOOD's "Giving Birth" is complicated by the narrator's ambiguity as to whether the childbirth story she is telling is her mother's or the daughter's fantasy of her own experience of birthing. Precise yet evasive, the coy protagonist explains that this story about giving birth is not her story, though she too is a mother, but someone else's; she is writing it while her own daughter naps, momentarily safe from the perils of infancy. "Giving Birth" emerges as a compelling allegory of the narrator's fierce desire to know, or if not, to recreate the intimate story of her origins. If indeed the mother-daughter connection is "the great unwritten story," Atwood agrees with Rich that it need no longer remain unwritten. When a daughter is safely born, "solid, substantial, packed together like an apple," in Atwood's words, her mother too often disappears, figuratively subsumed into the child's demanding presence (*LAWL* 836). It becomes, then, the writing daughter's task to bring her mother back to life.

In her autobiographical poems and essays, Latina poet CHERRIÉ MORAGA honors her relationship with her mother but also examines its troubled contours. Defining herself in "La Güera" as "the very well-educated daughter of a woman who, by the standards of this country, would be considered largely illiterate," she describes her mother's marriage and menial labor and her own childhood memories of working in the fields, of secretly signing her mother's checks in the grocery so the clerks wouldn't know she couldn't write. Moraga's most distinguishing physical characteristic, being "la güera," or fair-skinned, furthers her assimilation into white culture but also dislocates her, until she decides in adulthood to probe her Mexican heritage (*LAWL* 864). At the same time she explores her lesbian identity, finding there another unexpected bond with her mother through the oppressions both women suffer. Moraga analyzes what feminist theoreticians have termed the "simultaneity of oppressions," the realization that racism, sexism, classism, and homophobia are interwoven. Furthermore, she recognizes her own "identity politics"—that her lesbian flesh and her brown skin are linked, and that her race, class, and sexual identities intersect with those of her mother, even where there are differences. Like another feminist writer of maternal narratives, ALICE WALKER, Moraga goes "in search of our mothers' gardens" and finds her own (*LAWL* 324).

RECONTEXTUALIZING MOTHERHOOD

Motherhood . . . today remains, after the Virgin, without a discourse.

Julia Kristeva, "Stabat Mater"

'What is a mother? What is maternal?' It is a question that situates itself at the breaking point between various feminist positions: between presence and absence, speech and silence, essentialism and constructivism, materialism and psychoanalysis. Is motherhood 'experience' or 'institution'? Is it biological or cultural? Is the mother present or absent, single or divided, in collusion with patriarchy or at odds with it, conformist or subversive? Can an analysis of motherhood point out liberation or does it inevitably ensconce feminists in constraining cultural stereotypes?

Marianne Hirsch, The Mother/Daughter Plot

Julia Kristeva's provocative statement urges readers to consider how Christian discourse idealizing the maternal has captured the imagination of Western women as well as men across the ages, yet why this ancient representation fails to provide an enduring discourse for many women today. Kristeva's "Stabat Mater" concludes that Christianity has offered women a complex form of power embodied in Mary: a virgin birth in which men had no role, a royal designation as the Queen of Heaven, a valorizing of women's breasts as the source of nurture for the infant Jesus, a fulfillment of the fantasy of eternal life through the Assumption, and a singularity that puts her above all other women. This mother's supreme role, however, is to worship her son as divine, hence insuring that the male-dominant social and symbolic order be maintained. In Kristeva's view this maternal myth has positive resonance, yet it censors many important parts of women's experience: the act of childbirth and the mother's relationship to her body; the connection of women to their own mothers and to their daughters; the relationship of women to the men or other women with whom they share child-rearing. Until women can write and read about all aspects of maternity instead of privileging the mother-son dynamic, Kristeva concludes, the inner discourse of a mother will remain a mystery.

As useful and compelling as Marianne Hirsch's questions about the meaning of "mother" and "maternal" are, her "either-or" positioning of motherhood propels readers toward a familiar quagmire, the trap of binary thinking about a subject too complex to be so categorized. What if motherhood encompasses presence, absence, *and* a fluidity of movement, positions that shift and flow throughout a lifetime? What if maternal discourses (for as Hirsch acknowledges, there is more than one discourse) inscribe not only speech and silence but also moans, blubbering, sighs, wails? What if issues frequently presented in texts about motherhood—maternal sacrifice, creativity and procreativity, mother-daughter estrangement—were considered as topics that women write not for or against but in ways that blur the boundaries? What if the categories of good and bad mothering were expanded to include such options as "good enough" and "empowering" mothering, and perhaps maternal abstention?

The work of several nineteenth- and twentieth-century writers reveals diverse approaches to the theme of maternal sacrifice and estrangement. Writing from very different circumstances, FELICIA HEMANS, KATE CHOPIN, TILLIE OLSEN, and BETH BRANT complicate the question of what a mother should be willing to give up for the sake of her children. In their texts maternal sacrifice is linked to social, political, and spiritual realities; in each work, the protagonist struggles to speak the unspeakable. Hemans' "The Hebrew Mother" is at first glance a sentimental Christian rendition of a Jewish mother's dedication of her son to God. A nineteenth-century British "songbird" widely admired for her melancholia and religious zeal, Hemans goes beyond sentimentality in her canny presentations of maternal subjectivity. Midway through, this poem shifts from an omniscient narrator, who sets the scene, to the troubled internal monologue of the mother, eager to please God but also concerned about her child and herself. The Hebrew mother's conflict lies not simply between duty and desire but probes the heart of the mother-child symbiosis: To what extent, Hemans asks implicitly, does a mother need her son—as companion, husband surrogate (no father is mentioned here), source of aesthetic joy—as much as a son needs his mother? A sacrificial mother, according to conventional assumptions, would focus on God's will and mourn only the child's pain at parting, but Hemans's mother offers a muted account of her son's sorrow, concentrating instead upon her own. The Hebrew mother speaks the unspeakable by admitting unbearable anguish at the prospect of sacrificing her son. Furthermore, hovering just below the speaker's placid surface lurks a dangerous subtext: *What if* I refuse to leave him; *what if* the pain is too severe; *why* must I keep this promise; *why* does a loving God demand maternal sacrifice? The poem's tension lies in the space between accommodation and resistance. For contemporary readers, it also lies in the problem of a Christian poet speaking for a Jewish mother, given that "the Jew" in the nineteenth century and earlier served as a site of conflict, spurious interest, and romantic desire. In choosing a Jewish woman as her speaker, Hemans risks exoticizing her as the "other." This poem can be read in interesting ways alongside writing by Heman's contemporary GRACE AGUILAR, a Jew who celebrated the strength of Hebrew mothers and asserted their equality with fathers in both the religious and the domestic spheres.

Edna Pontellier, KATE CHOPIN's protagonist in her 1899 novella *The Awakening*, is caught between accommodating her culture's assumptions about motherhood and resisting those assumptions, unable, finally, to negotiate a social, spiritual, or political middle ground. Early on in the novel, as Edna vacations at Grand Isle with other wealthy Creole families, the narrator claims that she is "not a mother woman." Her children's independence is born of Edna's own. In striking contrast is her friend Adele Ratignolle, more typical of "mother women" who "idolized their children, worshipped their husbands, and deemed it a holy privilege to efface themselves as individuals and grow wings as ministering angels." While languishing on the beach, the two women have a "rather heated argument" over the issue of maternal sacrifice. "I would give up the essential; I would give my money, I would give my life to my children," declares Edna, "but I wouldn't give myself." Adele's orthodox response cites Biblical authority: "a woman who would give her life for her children could do no more than that. Your Bible tells you so." Although the terms of the debate appear sharply defined, Chopin presents Edna's stance as vague but potent. "I can't make it more clear," she tells Adele; "it's only something which I am beginning to comprehend, which is revealing itself to me" (*LAWL* 701, 729). The racial and class privilege that Edna shares with Adele does not shelter her from maternal ambivalence.

In TILLIE OLSEN's novella "Tell Me A Riddle," the protagonist, a dying woman named Eva, is caught between accommodating her culture's assumptions about her role as grandmother and resisting those assumptions. Early in the novella, as Eva becomes increasingly silent and introspective, the narrator conveys the old woman's desire for emotional separation and the ambivalent reaction it produces:

> Now they put a baby in her lap. Do not ask me, she would have liked to beg. Enough the worn face of Vivi, the remembered grandchildren. I cannot, cannot . . .
>   *Cannot what?* Unnatural grandmother, not able to make herself embrace a baby (*LAWL* 788).

Eva loves her children and grandchildren, the narrator suggests, but can no longer bear to suffer over lives that she cannot help. Instead, she reflects upon a century of anguish, the socialist vision she has cherished, her desire to go home to die. Although neither her husband, David, nor her children can initially comprehend her needs, one granddaughter does so. With Jeannie's help and David's growing understanding, Eva seeks "a reconciled peace."

BETH BRANT's "A Long Story" juxtaposes two narratives of involuntary maternal sacrifice. The first is spoken by a Native American mother in 1890 whose son and daughter have been seized from her home and enrolled in a government-sponsored boarding school. The eerily similar second narrative is spoken in 1978 by a lesbian mother, also Native American, who has lost her daughter in a custody battle. As Collins claims, an aspect of mothering that many women of color face is "the pervasive efforts by the dominant group to control the children's minds." Due to a "legacy of conquest," Indian mothers living on reservations in the late nineteenth and early twentieth centuries were expected to sacrifice their children to the majority culture "for their own good," sanctioning their removal not only from their families but from their language and culture. In Brant's story the 1890 mother has been manipulated by government agents into signing documents that she cannot read, thus "allowing" her children to be taken away to boarding school. Imagining for weeks the voices of her missing children, she finds them more real than the letters she receives, "written in their hateful language," from "two strangers with the names Martha and Daniel." This mother's only recourse is to howl until even her husband and brother consider her crazy. By speaking what cannot be spoken, through her body and her narrative, she exposes the corrupt officials for the cowards that they are. As Collins points out, "by forbidding children to speak their native languages, and in other ways encouraging children to assimilate into Anglo culture, external agencies challenge the power of mothers to raise their children as they see fit" (*LAWL* 646). Angry fathers and homophobic courts also "challenge the power of mothers to raise their children as they see fit," as the second of Brant's interwoven narratives reveals. The 1978 story is complicated by the fact that the child's father might well be Native American himself; his ethnic identity is never specified, though he is linked implicitly to heterosexist and patriarchal forces. Brant demonstrates that a Native American lesbian mother is triply disenfranchised in a society that denigrates Indians, condemns lesbians as unfit to parent, and privileges fathers over mothers in the majority of custody cases that are not settled out of court. The dilemmas faced by the Native American mothers in Brant's story give credence to Collins' assertion that "placing racial ethnic women's motherwork in the center of analysis recontextualizes motherhood" (*LAWL* 651).

Considering maternal texts by African-American poet GWENDOLYN BROOKS and the South African fiction writer BESSIE HEAD will provide a means of further elaborating Collins's theory that racial ethnic women make race and class issues visible in their presentations of mothers' lives. In many of her best poems Brooks seeks, in critic Betsy Erkkila's words, "to retrieve the voice and place of black motherhood" in a white-dominated literary canon and a culture that devalue blackness, womanhood, and maternity. She does this through what Erkkila calls "a progressive unmasking and expansion of the voice and figure of the mother" (197). Unlike her white contemporaries such as Rich and Plath, who found writing and motherhood to be at odds, Brooks has argued that her poetry has been enhanced by her experiences as a mother, in part because motherhood in black communities has typically been not a private activity but a basis for social action and communal status. At the same time she has not hesitated to explore the sometimes brutal realities that racism and poverty have inflicted on African-American mothers. One of her most powerful dramatic monologues, "the mother," addresses the controversial subject of abortion, which for many black women raises not only issues of reproductive rights, or "choice" versus "life," but also issues of cultural genocide, since every black child has special meaning in a culture under siege. "Believe me, I loved you all," the poem ends. "Believe me, I knew you, though faintly, and I loved, I loved you / All" (*LAWL* 808). Brooks's use of repetition creates a sense of urgency in this final pronouncement; the mother, who in fact is not a mother in the usual sense of the word, feels compelled to reassure her "dim dears" that they are loved. Brooks's poem reinforces Collins's assertion that in racial ethnic women's presentations of motherhood, race and class issues demand consideration.

The misuse of class and maternal privilege rather than racism *per se* provides the theme of BESSIE HEAD's story "The Village Saint." Although Head offers sympathetic portraits of Botswanan women in many stories, portraying their suffering at the hands of men, she is ruthless in her portrayals of racial hierarchies and snobbery, in part because as a racially mixed woman she was herself an outcast in apartheid South Africa, her birthplace, and a lifelong refugee in her adopted country, Botswana. Because so many of the African mothers whose oral histories she recorded over a ten-year period could barely feed and clothe their children, Head is especially appalled by those mothers who fail to use their economic privilege for the good of families and community. She thus presents Mma Mompati in "The Village Saint" as a power-hungry figure. In Head's Afrocentric view of motherhood, children should honor their mothers but mothers should likewise honor their children and their communities.

"What is my responsibility to my roots—both white and brown, Spanish-speaking and English?" Moraga wonders near the end of "La Güera." "I am a woman with a foot in both worlds, and I refuse the split." Imagining a holistic feminist vision for the future, she speculates that this vision will emerge "out of what is dark and female," a description that recalls the "blood color of [her] mother" (*LAWL* 869). Collins, too, claims that feminism will be enhanced if motherhood is recontextualized in a way that "embraces difference as an essential part of commonality" (*LAWL* 652). Hirsch agrees that diverse maternal perspectives are vital to understanding women's literature and lives:

> A reconceptualization of power, authority, and anger can emerge only if feminism can both practice and theorize a maternal discourse, based in maternal experience and capable of combining power and powerlessness, authority and invisibility, strength and vulnerability, anger and love. Only thus can the maternal cease to polarize feminists; only thus can it be politicized from within feminist discourse (167).

For women writing today, and for many of us as readers, the stakes seem high indeed as we rethink the maternal.

⊰ Works Cited—Section III ⊱

Note: In the introductory essay, all citations of works included in this anthology are indicated by *LAWL*, followed by the page number.

Anzaldúa, Gloria. *Borderlands: La Frontera: The New Mestiza*. San Francisco: Spinsters/aunt lute, 1987. This collection of poems and essays discusses Latina women's efforts to break silence and the psychological, social, and material difficulties of being a lesbian mestiza writing on the borderlands between cultures.

Erkkila, Betsy. *The Wicked Sisters: Women Poets, Literary History and Discord*. Oxford: Oxford UP, 1993. This work of feminist criticism rethinks women's literary history, particularly recent representations that tend to "romanticize, maternalize, essentialize, and eternalize women writers and the relationships among them." It contains an excellent chapter that considers black motherhood in Gwendolyn Brooks's poetry.

Forcey, Linda Rennie. "Feminist Perspectives on Mothering and Peace." *Mothering: Ideology, Experience, and Agency*. Ed. Evelyn Nakano Glenn, Grace Chang, and Linda Rennie Forcey. New York: Routledge, 1994. 355–75. This provocative essay takes an interdisciplinary approach to the links that feminist theorists have made between mothering and peacemaking. She also considers "the feminist challenge for peace studies" at the end of the century.

Hirsch, Marianne. *The Mother/Daughter Plot: Narrative, Psychoanalysis, Feminism.* Bloomington: Indiana UP, 1989. This major feminist theoretical study of mothers and daughters considers realism and maternal silence, modernism and the maternal, and postmodern plots with maternal subjects. Among the many writers it examines are Austen, the Brontës, Chopin, Eliot, Woolf, Rich, Atwood, Morrison, and Walker. It also enters into dialogue across differences with other theorists, including Nancy Chodorow, Susan Rubin Suleiman, Julia Kristeva, Barbara Johnson, and Sara Ruddick.

Kristeva, Julia. "Stabat Mater." *The Kristeva Reader.* Ed. Toril Moi. New York: Columbia UP, 1986. 160–86. This article by a renowned French feminist theoretician demonstrates how traditional Christian discourse idealizes the Virgin Mary and offers as an alternate an experimental inner discourse that links motherhood and feminine artistic creation.

Lazarre, Jane. *The Mother Knot.* New York: Dell, 1977. This autobiography of a writer who becomes a mother explores the difficulties of learning to write in her son's presence rather than alone. Lazarre wrestles with fear of creative stasis, resentment at the stifling elements of motherhood, and passionate love for her child.

Rich, Adrienne. *Of Woman Born: Motherhood as Experience and Institution.* New York: Norton, 1976. This study of mothers' power and powerlessness under patriarchy, widely considered a major text of feminist theory, distinguishes between the experience of motherhood, comprised of both ambivalence and affirmation, and the institution of motherhood, defined primarily by men. Rich examines medical history, myth, women's literature, and her own life as a writer and a mother to analyze how motherhood can be transformed.

Rosenberg, Carroll Smith. "The Female World of Love and Ritual: Relations Between Women in Nineteenth-Century America." *Signs* 1.1 (1973): 1–29. This essay by a prominent feminist historian examines historical documents and material culture, finding "an intimate mother-daughter relationship" at the center of life for women in the nineteenth-century United States. In this context daughters accepted their mothers' world and sought support and comradeship from them and other women.

Ruddick, Sara. *Maternal Thinking: Toward a Politics of Peace.* New York: Ballantine, 1989. This important book by a philosopher and peace studies scholar asserts that the preservative love, nonviolent fostering of growth, and lucid knowledge that most mothers bring to child-raising could be the foundation of a feminist peace politics. Although many women have supported wars, maternal thinking as a "feminist standpoint" offers a viable alternative to militarism.

⊰ Suggestions for Further Reading ⊱

Allen, Paula Gunn. *The Sacred Hoop: Recovering the Feminine in American Indian Traditions.* Boston: Beacon, 1986. This book features essays on American Indian women's literature, including representations of motherhood, studies of gynocratic societies, and portrayals of the sacred, by one of America's foremost Native American literary critics. Included is Allen's essay "Who Is Your Mother? Red Roots of White Feminism."

Chodorow, Nancy. *The Reproduction of Mothering: Psychoanalysis and the Sociology of Gender.* Berkeley: U of California P, 1978. This important study posits that neither biological or social constructionist theories of why women mother are sufficient. Instead, "women are prepared psychologically for mothering through the developmental situation in which they grew up, and in which women have mothered them." Only when men also mother will the feminine psyche change, Chodorow argues.

Collin, Patricia Hill. *Black Feminist Thought: Knowledge, Consciousness, and the Politics of Empowerment.* Boston: Unwin Hyman, 1990. This study of black feminist epistemologies by a prominent African-American sociologist and feminist theoretician contains three important chapters for any consideration of black motherhood: "Work, Family, and Black Women's Oppression"; "Mammies, Matriarchs, and Other Controlling Images"; and "Black Women and Motherhood."

Daly, Brenda O. and Maureen T. Reddy, eds. *Narrating Mothers: Theorizing Maternal Subjectivities.* Knoxville: U of Tennessee P, 1991. This collection of feminist critical essays on women's writing about motherhood focuses primarily on fiction and autobiography by modern writers. Its three sections are entitled "Mothers Redefining Authority," "Mothers Mapping Boundaries," and "Mothers Transforming Practices."

Debold, Elizabeth, Marie Wilson, and Idelisse Malave. *Mother Daughter Revolution: From Betrayal to Power.* New York: Addison Wesley, 1993. This book argues that mothers are crucial to their young daughters' development of self-esteem. Powerful relationships between mothers and daughters, which require "courageous mothering," can help to prevent girls from developing eating disorders, abusing their sexuality, and losing academic confidence.

Friedman, Susan Stanford. "Creativity and the Childbirth Metaphor: Gender Difference In Literary Discourse." *Speaking of Gender.* Ed. Elaine Showalter. New York: Routledge, 1989: 73–100. This article examines ways in which women poets and novelists from different historical periods have used childbirth as a metaphor for female creativity.

Garner, Shirley Nelson, Claire Kahane, and Madelon Sprengnether, eds. *The (M)other Tongue: Essays in Feminist Psychoanalytic Interpretation.* Ithaca: Cornell UP, 1985. This collection of sixteen essays offers feminist and psychoanalytic perspectives on literary texts, including Susan Rubin Suleiman's essay "Writing and Motherhood." Its three sections are entitled "Feminists on Freud," "Rereading Patriarchal Texts," and "Women Rewriting Woman."

hooks, bell. *Feminist Theory: From Margin to Center.* Boston: South End, 1985. This important collection by a prominent black feminist thinker includes several essays that bear on the topic of motherhood, including "Rethinking the Nature of Work" and "Revolutionary Parenting."

Johnson, Barbara. "Apostrophe, Animation, and Abortion." *Diacritics* 16.1 (Spring 1986): 29–43. This frequently cited article by a prominent postmodern theorist examines the traditional use of the poetic figure of apostrophe to animate men's poems and juxtaposes it with revisionist uses of apostrophe in women's poems about abortion, including works by Gwendolyn Brooks, Anne Sexton, Adrienne Rich, and Lucille Clifton.

Jones, Vivien, ed. *Women in the Eighteenth Century: Constructions of Femininity.* New York: Routledge, 1990. This anthology contains excerpts from conduct manuals for women, medical literature (including information on midwifery, breast feeding, and childbirth), and essays on the education of daughters in the "Age of Reason."

Kaplan, E. Ann. *Motherhood and Representation: The Mother in Popular Culture and Melodrama.* New York: Routledge, 1992. This book examines motherhood as a social discourse in nineteenth- and twentieth-century culture and analyzes how mothers are represented in women's popular literature, film, and melodrama.

Lonsdale, Roger, ed. *Eighteenth Century Women Poets.* Oxford: Oxford UP, 1990. This anthology contains a number of poems to mothers and children and about motherhood by such poets as Mary Wortley Montagu, Mary Barber, Elizabeth Boyd, Maria Cowper, Charlotte Smith, and Joanna Baillie, as well as an excellent introduction to the context in which these poets wrote.

Morrison, Toni. *Beloved*. New York: Alfred A. Knopf, 1987. Morrison's Pulitzer prize-winning novel presents the maternal dilemma of Sethe, who has killed her infant daughter rather than see her taken into slavery. It examines "the return of the repressed" in the form of Beloved, the ghostly daughter who materializes, as well as the mother-daughter bond between Sethe and her other daughter, Denver. Morrison uses the term "rememory" to describe the process by which the recesses of the slave mother's consciousness are probed.

Reddy, Maureen T., Martha Roth, and Amy Sheldon. *Mother Journeys: Feminists Write About Mothering*. Minneapolis: spinsters ink, 1994. This anthology contains poems and stories as well as essays that address feminist mothering, the mother-child erotic bond, fear of childbirth, and abortion as a "motherhood issue."

Riley, Denise. *War in the Nursery: Theories of the Child and Mother*. London: Virago, 1983. Riley tries to conceptualize women without falling into the trap of either biologism or cultural construction, arguing instead that it is important to theorize women's lives without essentializing gender. Central needs of women with children include affordable child care and redistribution of labor.

Thiebaux, Marcelle, ed. *The Writings of Medieval Women: An Anthology*. 2nd ed. New York and London: Garland, 1994. This book offers excellent critical and historical introductions to writings by Julian of Norwich and Juliana Berners, each of whom wrote narratives addressing the topic of motherhood. Thiebaux analyzes Berners's maternal instruction booklets and Julian's rhapsodies on the motherhood of God.

━━ ❧ ━━

Susan Rubin Suleiman
1939–

"Will we ever be forced to write the book and deny the child . . . or love the child and postpone/renounce the book?" wonders SUSAN RUBIN SULEIMAN in "Writing and Motherhood." "It is time to let mothers have their word." Professor of Romance languages and comparative literatures at Harvard University and the mother of two grown sons, Suleiman has written extensively on motherhood, feminism, and psychoanalytic theory. In her view, "some of the most exciting, most vibrant new work in literary studies is the work of feminist critics. One does not have to write exclusively about women in order to do feminist criticism. What matters are the questions one asks, not the particular writers or works one is dealing with. And the exciting thing is that many of the questions that seem most interesting today could not even have been formulated, much less explored, twenty years ago."

Suleiman was born in Budapest, Hungary, and came with her parents to the United States in 1950. In 1960 she earned a B.A. from Barnard College, then studied at the University of Paris for a year before entering Harvard University, from which she received her Ph.D. in 1969. She is the author of *Authoritarian Fictions: The Ideological Novel as Literary Genre* (1983) and the editor, with Inge Crossman, of *The Reader in the Text: Essays on Audience and Interpretation* (1980), a collection of critical works about audience reception theory. With the aid of a Rockefeller Foundation Humanities Fellowship, which gave her time away from teaching and support for child care, she edited *The Female Body in Western Culture* (1986), an anthology of interdisciplinary essays on female embodiment and somatophobia, or fear of the body. This book includes her introductory article, "(Re)Writing the Body: The Politics and Poetics of Female Eroticism," along with essays by such feminist scholars as Catharine Stimpson, Julia Kristeva, and Nancy K. Miller. In 1990 Suleiman published *Subversive Intent: Gender, Politics, and the Avant-Garde.* Her 1996 memoir, *Risking Who One Is,* tells the story of her return to Hungary after many years away to explore her Jewish and maternal roots. Suleiman has contributed essays to *The (M)other Tongue: Essays in Feminist Psychoanalytic Interpretation* (1985), ed. Shirley Garner et al., and *The Poetics of Gender* (1986), ed. Nancy K. Miller. In addition, she has published more than thirty articles on modern French literature and literary theory, as well as several translations of literary works from the French. Suleiman has served on the editorial boards of *French Review* and *Style* and has been a member of the advisory board of *Camera Obscura: A Journal of Feminism and Film Theory.*

"Writing and Motherhood," which appears in *The (M)other Tongue,* takes issue with the conventional assumption of psychoanalytic theory that "mothers don't write, they are written." After considering problems with psychoanalysis and motherhood, she examines the guilt, anger, and alienation that characterize some maternal fictions as well as the joy many women feel at integrating writing and maternity. Suleiman considers, too, the ways radical French feminist theorists fetishize the maternal female body. In the area of writing and motherhood, she concludes, "there remains a great deal of space to explore—in fiction and in life."

⊰ Writing and Motherhood ⊱

With the approach of the climacterium, new motherhood is impossible, and the frustrated activity is directed toward other goals. Simply expressed, this attitude is: "If I cannot have any more children, I must look for something else."

Helene Duetsch

... que savons-nous du discours que (se) fait une mère?

Julia Kristeva

My epigraphs define the space I shall explore in this essay. At one end, the confident assertion of a psychoanalyst who not only knows what mothers want and feel, but does not hesitate for more than an instant ("simply expressed"—a pause) in formulating the very words that mothers speak to themselves. At the other end, a simple yet insidious question. Does the question demolish the psychoanalyst's certitudes? That is not the point. My purpose here is not to discredit psychoanalysis but, in the literal sense of the term, to put it in its place. It is a question not of distributing praise or blame but of seeing more clearly, of "knowing where it's at."

First, however, where am I at? Why did I choose to write about writing and motherhood? Is it a valid subject, is there really a connection there? Or am I indulging in a purely private pleasure, tracking a private mania, exorcising private ghosts? I am the mother of two children, boys, aged nine and two (or so they were in 1979, when these words were first written). I have written learned books and essays about fiction and the theory of literature. My first impulse, when faced with a problem or a text, is to analyze it, understand it.

I am not the first to write about writing and motherhood, their conjunction or disjunction; I need not seek justifications for doing so. But necessarily, for better or for worse, I shall write about them in my own way.

MOTHERS/WRITING: THE PSYCHOANALYTIC PROJECTION

The traditional psychoanalytic view of motherhood is indissociable from the more general theory of normal female development and female sexuality. According to Freud and his orthodox followers, the little girl's problem is to effect a satisfactory transition from the preoedipal phase of "masculine" (i.e., clitoral) eroticism to the properly feminine, vaginal eroticism that will prepare her for her role as a mother. In the process of this transition, the little girl must reject her own mother in favor of the father, whose child she longs to bear. She must reconcile herself to the "fact" of her castration, and must give up the active-sadistic impulses of the preoedipal phase in favor of the passive-masochistic gratifications appropriate to her female role. In the words of Karl Abraham, "The normal adult woman becomes reconciled to her own sexual role. . . . She desires passive gratification and longs for a child."[1] According to Helene Deutsch, the sine qua non of normal motherhood is "the masochistic-feminine willingness to sacrifice"—a sacrifice made easy by the impulse of maternal love, whose "chief characteristic is tenderness. All the aggression and sexual sensuality in the woman's personality are suppressed and diverted by the central emotional expression of motherliness."[2] The mother's sacrifice is also made easy by the fact that through the child, especially if it is a male child, she compensates for the one great lack in her life, the lack of a penis.

Feminine masochism, feminine passivity, feminine castration, feminine penis envy—every one of these notions has been challenged, both by contemporary feminists and by such earlier revisionists as Karen Horney and Clara Thompson. Significantly, however, their arguments have not borne on the *fact* of feminine masochism, passivity, or penis envy in our society, but rather on their innateness versus their culturally conditioned character. More recently, such feminists as Juliet Mitchell and Elizabeth Janeway have salvaged Freud's insights by relativizing them: whereas for Freud the course of female development was a physiologically determined process and therefore inevitable (despite his well-known demurrals, his famous statements about not knowing what women are and what they want), for Mitchell and Janeway, as for Horney and Thompson before them, the fact of feminine masochism or penis envy reflects the devalued position of women in patriarchal society. The facts are there, it is their explanation that must be corrected and their inevitability that must be challenged. As Juliet Mitchell has written: "Freud's psychoanalytic theories are about sexism; that he himself propagated certain sexist views and that his work has been the bulwark of the ideological oppression of women are doubtless of great importance. But we can understand its significance only if we first realize that it was precisely the psychological formations produced within patriarchal societies that he was revealing and analyzing."[3]

By and large I agree with this view, which also informs (by and large) Nancy Chodorow's important book *The Reproduction of Mothering*. As Chodorow shows, neither a biological-anthropological nor a behavioral role-socialization model is adequate to account for the permanence of women's mothering function: "Women's capacities for mothering and abilities to get gratification from it are strongly internalized and psychologically enforced, and are built developmentally into the feminine

1. [Quoted in Joel Kovel, "The Castration Complex Reconsidered," *Women and Analysis*, ed. Jean Strouse (New York: Viking, 1974) 136.]
2. [Helene Deutsch, *The Psychology of Women*, Vol. II (1945; rpt. New York: Bantam, 1973) 411–12, 20.]
3. [Juliet Mitchell, "On Freud and the Distinction between the Sexes." *Women and Analysis*, ed. Strouse 32.]

psychic structure. Women are prepared psychologically for mothering through the developmental situation in which they grow up, and in which women have mothered them."[4] This being the case, Chodorow argues that only a radical change in modes of parenting, so that fathers and men also "mother," can effect a change in the feminine psyche. If such a change should ever occur on a large enough scale to make a difference, the conjunction of writing and motherhood, like most other conjunctions involving motherhood, will become an altogether different subject. In the meantime, I shall argue that that particular conjunction is (1) a problem, (2) a woman's problem, and (3) a problem that must be considered as much in psychological as in sociological terms, if not more so.

Let me return, however, to the psychoanalytical view of motherhood as it exists in the traditional literature. The good and even good-enough (Winnicott) mother is characterized according to this literature, not only by tenderness and the "masochistic-feminine willingness to sacrifice" but above all by her exclusive and total involvement with her child. Chodorow quotes the psychoanalyst Alice Balint as representative in this respect. Balint states: "The ideal mother has no interests of her own. . . . For all of us it remains self-evident that the interests of mother and child are identical, and it is the generally acknowledged measure of the goodness or badness of the mother how far she really feels this identity of interests." Chodorow comments: "This statement does not mean that mothers have no interests apart from their children—we all know that this kind of overinvestment is 'bad' for children. But social commentators, legislators, and most clinicians expect women's interests to enhance their mothering and expect women to want only interests that do so." Good mothering, in other words, "requires both a constant delicate assessment of infantile needs and wants and an extreme selflessness. Analysts do not consider their prescription difficult for most 'normal' mothers to fulfill."[5]

Melanie Klein speaks with great sympathy and understanding about the murderous impulses that every child feels toward its beloved mother; she does not speak about the murderous impulses that a mother may feel toward her beloved child.[6] According to Helene Deutsch, the one permanent tragedy of motherhood is that children grow up: "Every phase of the child's development ends with intensified tendencies to liberate himself. The mother—every mother—tries to keep him attached to herself and opposes the actions that tend to dissolve the tie."[7] The notion that another tragedy of motherhood may lie in the conflict between the mother's desire for self-realization—a self-realization that has nothing to do with her being a mother— and the child's need for her selflessness seems never to have entered the psychoanalyst's mind.[8] Even Karen Horney, herself a mother and a writer, could devote a paper

---

4. [Nancy Chodorow, *The Reproduction of Mothering: Psychoanalysis and the Sociology of Gender* (Berkelely: University of California Press, 1978) 39.]

5. [Chodorow 77, 82, 84–85.]

6. [See in particular Klein's 1937 essay, "Love, Guilt, and Reparation," reprinted in *Love, Guilt, and Reparation and Other Works, 1921–1945* (New York: Doubleday, 1977) 306–43.]

7. [Deutsch 331.]

8. [It will certainly be noticed that almost all of the analysts I have been quoting are women. Their statements show either a remarkable alienation from their own experience (surely they did not become analysts and writers by adapting without problems to the "passive-masochistic gratifications" of femininity) or else a remarkable degree of self-hate (their own development was "abnormal," since they chose the route of the masculinity complex in their own lives). What seems astonishing is that Helene Deutsch recently declared herself to be a longstanding feminist, whose greatest hope for her women patients was that they would "have a passionate interest in something other than the possible man and children in [their lives]." That is a curious statement to come from the most orthodoxly Freudian theorist of "normal" femininity. As Marcia Cavell rightly points out, the statement suggests at the very least a deep split between Deutsch the therapist and Deutsch the theorist. (See Cavell, "Since 1924: Toward a New Psychology of Women," *Women and Analysis*, ed. Strouse 167.)]

to the subject of "maternal conflicts" whose entire emphasis was on the harm a mother could do to her son if her own relations to her parents were not properly worked out.[9] It is as if, for psychoanalysis, the only self worth worrying about in the mother-child relationship were that of the child. How this exclusive focus affects the mother is something we are only beginning to become aware of, as mothers begin to speak for themselves. "Most of the literature of infant care and psychology has assumed that the process toward individuation is essentially the *child's* drama, played out against and with a parent or parents who are, for better or for worse, givens. Nothing could have prepared me for the realization that I was a mother, one of those givens, when I knew I was still in a state of uncreation myself."[10] That is Adrienne Rich's testimony; the feelings it describes are not unique to her.

Mother's don't write, they are written. Simply expressed (to quote Helene Deutsch), this is the underlying assumption of most psychoanalytic theories about writing and about artistic creation in general. According to Freud, the poet is a superior daydreamer, endowed with the gift of transforming his personal fantasies into aesthetically pleasing creations. The fantasies themselves, however, are always derived from the poet's childhood self: "a piece of creative writing, like a daydream, is a continuation of, and a substitute for, what was once the play of childhood."[11] D.W. Winnicott enlarged this view with his theory of transitional objects, which function essentially as substitutes for the mother. According to Winnicott, transitional objects exist in an intermediate area between the purely subjective world of the child and the external reality of the "not-me"—more exactly, in the "potential space between the baby and the mother."[12] Artistic creation, indeed all cultural experience, belongs to the realm of transitional phenomena. Successful creation, like all creative living, depends on the trust and self-confidence first developed in the child's earliest relationship to his mother.

In Melanie Klein's theory of artistic creation, the mother—or rather, the mother's body—functions as a "beautiful land" to be explored. The creative writer, like the explorer, the scientist, the artist in general, is impelled by the "desire to rediscover the mother of the early days, whom [he] has lost actually or in [his] feelings."[13] The work of art itself stands for the mother's body, destroyed repeatedly in fantasy but restored or "repaired" in the act of creation.

The fact that for Klein, as for Freud, the poet is always a "he" is worth remarking, but it is not the point I wish to stress here. For me it is more significant that psychoanalytic theory invariably places the artist, man or woman, in the position of the child. Just as motherhood is ultimately the child's drama, so is artistic creation. In both cases the mother is the essential but silent Other, the mirror in whom the child searches for his own reflection, the body he seeks to appropriate, the thing he loses or destroys again and again, and seeks to recreate. A writer, says Roland Barthes, is "someone who plays with the body of his [her?—the French is conveniently ambiguous on this point, but Barthes's own meaning seems clear enough] mother."[14]

This is an extremely suggestive idea, one that is capable of renewing our understanding of a host of writers, such as Proust, Poe, Stendhal, Woolf (see *To the Light-*

9. [Karen Horney, "Maternal Conflicts," in *Feminine Psychology* (New York: Norton, 1973) 175–81.]
10. [Adrienne Rich, *Of Woman Born: Motherhood as Experience and Institution* (New York: Bantam, 1977) 17.]
11. [Sigmund Freud, "Creative Writers and Day-Dreaming" (1908), *Standard Edition*, IX 152.]

12. [See D.W. Winnicott, *Playing and Reality* (New York: Basic Books, 1971) 107 and *passim.*]
13. [Klein 334.]
14. [Roland Barthes, *Le Plaisir du texte* (Paris, 1973) 60. All translations from the French are my own.]

house), Robbe-Grillet (as I have tried to show elsewhere),[15] and many others. And yet . . . what about the writer who *is* "the body of the mother"? Is this a foolish question, since mothers too have mothers? Does the mother who writes write exclusively as her own mother's child?

Perhaps. Yet I contend that we know too little about what and how and why mothers write to answer the question one way or the other. We may even know too little to have asked the right questions. As Tillie Olsen has pointed out, mothers who have been "full-time" writers have been rare until our own century, and the great women writers have been, with very few exceptions, childless during all or most of their writing lives.[16] Kristeva is right, we know very little about the inner discourse of a mother; and as long as our own emphasis, encouraged by psychoanalytic theory and by the looming presence of (mostly male) mother-fixated writers, continues to be on the-mother-as-she-is-written rather than on the-mother-as-she-writes, we shall continue in our ignorance.

There are consistent reasons for psychoanalysis' failure to see mothers writing (*as* mothers). First of all, psychoanalysis is nothing if not a theory of childhood. We should not be surprised if it locates artistic creativity, as it does every other aspect of adult personality, in the child the adult once was, and often continues to be. A second and more specific reason lies, as I suggested earlier, in the psychoanalytic theory of normal female development: Mothers don't create works of art because all of their creative, aggressive drives find an outlet in the production of children. As Helene Deutsch puts it: "The urge to intellectual and artistic creation and productivity of motherhood spring from common sources, and *it seems very natural that one should be capable of replacing the other.*" As long as her motherly capacities are put to use, a mother does not need to write: "A motherly woman can give up her other interests in favor of the reproductive function, and she returns to the former when she feels the biologic restriction approaching." This might be called the menopausal theory of artistic creation (although when one reads Deutsch's description of the woman at menopause, one wonders what sort of creation she could possibly undertake: "With the lapse of the reproductive service, her beauty vanishes, and usually the warm, vital flow of feminine emotional life as well"—the grave is not far off, it would seem), itself a subcategory of the more general "either/or" theory that can be summed up as follows: writing or motherhood, work or child, never the two at the same time.[17]

The either/or theory is, of course, older than psychoanalysis. As Elaine Showalter has documented, it was already invoked by the early Victorians. Victorian critics were on the whole more kind to women writers who were mothers than to their childless sisters, but with the clear understanding that "mothers must not dream of activity beyond the domestic sphere until their families are grown."[18] This line of argument, adopted even by such writers as Mrs. Gaskell, who was the mother of four children (she published her first novel at age 38), was based on the moral obligations of the good wife and mother. "What most women rejected as unacceptable and unchristian," writes Showalter, "was the use of literary vocation to avoid the responsibilities of home life."[19] It took psychoanalysis to transform moral obligation into a

15. [Susan Suleiman, "Reading Robbe-Grillet: Sadism and Text in *Project pour une révolution à New York*," *Romantic Review*, 68 (January 1977) 43–62.]

16. [Tillie Olsen, *Silences* (New York: Doubleday, 1979) 16, 31.]

17. [Deutsch 479, 481.]

18. [Elaine Showalter, "Women Writers and the Double Standard," *Woman in Sexist Society*, ed. Vivian Gornick and Barbara Moran (New York: Basic Books, 1971) 333.]

19. [Elaine Showalter, *A Literature of Their Own: British Women Novelists from Brontë to Lessing* (Princeton: Princeton University Press, 1977) 65.]

psychological "law," equating the creative impulse with the procreative one and decreeing that she who has a child feels no need to write books.

By means of this "law," psychoanalytic theory not only offered an elegant explanation for and justification of the mother's silence (making any mother who did not wish to wait until menopause to write books feel "abnormal") but provided an equally elegant explanation for why some childless women (and men) did write books: books were obviously substitutes for children. Once the "law" was properly internalized by women (in a way it could not possibly be by men, since men cannot *choose* to bear children), its capacities for generating guilt and anguish were infinite: Corresponding to the writing mother's sense of "abnormality" was the childless woman writer's sense of "unnaturalness." Not for nothing did Virginia Woolf, who knew her Freud, "fear that writing was an act that unsexed her, made her an unnatural woman."[20] Whereas the male writer, in comparing his books to tenderly loved children (a common metaphor, at least until the recent emphasis on writing as a autoerotic activity), could see his metaphorical maternity as something *added* to his male qualities, the childless woman whose books "replaced" real children too often thought (was made to feel) that she had less, not more.

Here again, psychoanalysis cannot be held entirely responsible, since the derogation of childless and/or unmarried women writers was already common in the days of Austen and the Brontës. My point, however, is that psychoanalysis lent scientific prestige to a widespread cultural prejudice, reinforcing it and elevating it to the status of a "natural" law.

It is in this context that the protest against the "motherhood myth" perpetrated by psychoanalysis and against the fact of motherhood itself, which has characterized one branch of contemporary feminist writing and criticism, must be understood. We should also understand, however, that this protest is itself in a sense a victim of the either/or theory. The only difference is that the values attributed to book and child have been reversed. Thus Nina Auerbach, in an article significantly titled "Artists and Mothers: A False Alliance," declares that "far from endowing Austen with secondhand motherhood, her identity as an artist represented an escape from confinement into a child-free world with space for mind and spirit, time for change, and privacy for growth." Auerbach celebrates Austen and Eliot *because* they "both turned away from motherhood and embraced a creativity they defined as more spacious, more adult, more inclusive."[21]

Is there no alternative to the either/or? Will we ever be forced to write the book and deny the child (not the child we were but the child we have, or might have) or love the child and postpone/renounce the book? Or is Kristeva right in insisting that "while a certain feminism takes its pouting and its isolation for protest and perhaps even for dissidence, genuine feminine innovation . . . will not be possible until we have elucidated motherhood, feminine creation, and the relationship between them"?[22]

It is time to let mothers have their word.

WRITING AND MOTHERHOOD: AS MOTHERS SEE IT

The picture is not all rosy.

> Try telling a child that Mamma is working, when the child can see with its own eyes that she is just sitting there writing. . . . I dare not have music on when I am sitting in the basement,

20. [Phyllis Rose, as paraphrased in Showalter, *Literature of Their Own* 270.]
21. [Nina Auerback, "Artists and Mothers: A False Alliance." *Women and Literature,* 6 (Spring 1978) 9, 14.]
22. [Julia Kristeva, "Un Nouveau Type d'intellectuel: Le dissident." *Tel Quel,* no. 74 (Winter 1977) 6–7.]

writing, lest upstairs they think I am just sitting there loafing. I feel that to be respected I must produce pancakes and homebaked bread and have neat, tidy rooms. [Liv Ullman][23]

Since I had begun writing, I had sought time alone. That very self I had once sought to flee, . . . that dangerous, frightening self was precisely what I had learned to treasure, what I had begun to understand.

In order to tame [the dangerous self], I had to write, regularly and consistently, and in order to write I had to be alone.

Now suddenly I was always with Benjamin. [Jane Lazarre][24]

For me, poetry was where I lived as no one's mother, where I existed as myself. [Adrienne Rich][25]

I just started pecking away at this story set during the American Revolution. It wasn't anything I could get completely absorbed in. I had three boys at home, and there were always dishes to put in the dishwasher. [Kathleen Woodiwiss][26]

Children need one *now*. The very fact that these are real needs, that one feels them as one's own (love, not duty); that there is no one else responsible for these needs, gives them primacy. . . . Work interrupted, deferred, relinquished, makes blockage—at best, lesser accomplishment. [Tillie Olsen][27]

Every time I thought something would do, in the old days I'd race to the writing pad . . . and really be excited. Now I kept thinking: "Oh no, I don't think that's very good." Then one morning I woke up and I thought: "It's gone . . . and I don't want it to come back." [Susan Hill][28]

Guilt, desperation, splitting of the self, alienated role playing ("My writing is not serious, don't be offended by it, just look at my three children"), resignation to lesser accomplishment, renunciation of the writing self—these are some of the realities, some of the possible choices that writing mothers live with.

Kathleen Woodiwiss is a rich woman, the author of historical romances for the "housewife market." Her last book has sold more than two million copies. She calls herself "an ordinary housewife": "I enjoy cooking and cleaning, my family and home. Right now my husband is remodeling one of the bathrooms."[29] She represents what some would call the perfect accommodation between writing and motherwifehood. Perhaps she has no serious talent or ambition; perhaps she has never allowed herself to ask whether she does.

Susan Hill was a highly respected "younger" British novelist—for the cultivated reader, not the best-seller type. In her late thirties she married, and she became pregnant soon after. She was working on a novel at the time, but never finished it. She no longer writes fiction.

Between these two extremes, each of which is in its own way a renunciation of the writing self, are manifold ways of coping—some we know about because they have been written, others we can only guess at. We need to have more information—more interviews, more diaries, more memoirs, essays, reminiscences by writing mothers. I am sure I have missed many as it is, but exhaustiveness is not what I am aiming for. I wish merely to glimpse the possibilities, the principal recurrent themes in what some contemporary

23. [Liv Ullman, *Changing* (New York: Bantam, 1978) 36, 37.]

24. [Jane Lazarre, *The Mother Knot* (New York: Dell, 1977) 55–56.]

25. [Rich 12.]

26. [Kathleen E. Woodiwiss, interviewed by Judy Klemen-

srud, *New York Times Book Review*, November 4, 1979: 52.]

27. [Olsen 19.]

28. [Susan Hill, "On Ceasing to Be a Novelist" (interview with Robert Robinson), *The Listener*, February 2, 1978: 154.]

29. [Woodiwiss, interviewed by Klemesrud.]

writing mothers have said discursively (poetry and fiction are a later question) about, or out of, their own experience of the relationship between writing and motherhood.

What are the major themes? I see them clustered into two large groups: opposition and integration, motherhood as obstacle or source of conflict and motherhood as a link, a source of connection to work and world. The oppositional themes—guilt vs. love, mother's creative self vs. child needs, isolation vs. commitment—are the ones I emphasized in the above quotations. The daily conflict and self-doubt, the waste of creative energies these oppositions engender cannot be overestimated. What is involved here, furthermore, is not simply an institutional or social problem; alternate nurturers will not necessarily relieve it (although they may eventually help) because the conflicts are *inside* the mother, they are part of her most fundamental experience. One can always argue, as Rich and others have done, that the internal conflicts are the result of institutional forces, the result of women's isolation, women's victimization by the motherhood myth in patriarchal society. But while this argument can help us understand *why* the conflicts are internal, it does not eliminate them. *At the present time*, any mother of young children (and I don't mean only infants, but children of school age and beyond) who wants to do serious creative work—with all that such work implies of the will to self-assertion, self-absorption, solitary grappling—must be prepared for the worst kind of struggle which is the struggle against herself. Here I am reminded of Karen Horney's description of a certain type of neurotic disturbance in work—the disturbance she sees as typical of the "self-effacing type":

> Without being aware of it, he is up against two kinds of chronic handicaps: his self-minimizing and his inefficiency in tackling the subject matter. His self-minimizing largely results . . . from his need to keep himself down in order not to trespass against the taboo on anything "presumptuous." *It is a subtle undermining, berating, doubting*, which saps the energies without his being aware of what he is doing to himself. . . . As a result he works with the oppressive feeling of impotence and insignificance. . . . His efficiency in tackling the subject matter is caused mainly by taboos on all that implies assertion, aggression, mastery. . . . His difficulty is not in being unproductive. Good original ideas may emerge, but he is inhibited in taking hold of them, tackling them, grappling with them, wrestling with them, checking them, shaping them, organizing them. We are not usually aware of these mental operations as being assertive, aggressive moves, although the language indicates it; and we may realize this fact only when they are inhibited by a pervasive check on aggression.[30]

Mothers, or women, are of course not the only ones to whom Horney's description applies.[31] She herself obviously had both men and women in mind. But I would suggest that in the case of the writing mother, the subtle undermining, the oppressive feeling of impotence and insignificance, the pervasive check on aggression that Horney talks about are intimately linked to a sense of guilt about her child. Jean-Paul Sartre once said in an interview, when asked about the value of literature and of his own novels in particular: "En face d'un enfant qui meurt, La Nausée ne fait pas le poids" (freely translated: "When weighed against a dying child, La Nausée doesn't count").[32] If this

---

30. [Karen Horney, "Neurotic Disturbances in Work," *Neurosis and Human Growth: The Struggle toward Self-Realization* (New York: Norton, 1970) 319–20 (my emphasis).]

31. [I am struck, however, by how closely Horney's description corresponds to Simone de Beauvoir's explanation for the lack of audaciousness in women writers:

> To please is her first care; and often she fears she will be displeasing as a woman from the mere fact that she writes. . . . The writer of originality, unless dead, is always shocking, scandalous; novelty disturbs and repels. Woman is still astonished and flattered at being admitted to the world of thought, of art—a masculine world. She is on her best behavior; *she is afraid to disarrange, to investigate, to explode*; she feels she should seek pardon for literary pretensions through her modesty and good taste. She stakes on the reliable values of conformity. . . . [*The Second Sex*, trans. and ed. H.M. Parshley (New York: Bantam, 1961) 666; my emphasis]]

32. [Quoted by Jean Ricardou in Simone de Beauvoir et al., *Que peut la littérature?* (Paris: Union Générale, 1965) 59.]

statement reflects the well-known guilt of the bourgeois writer with left-wing sympathies (Sartre being a specialist on *that* question), what are we to say about the guilt of a mother who might weigh her books not against a stranger's dying child but merely against her own child who is crying?

One way to appease the crying child (and my contention is that whether or not the child actually cries while the mother writes, s/he always cries in the mother's nightmares) is to tender her/him the book as a propitiatory offering. Phyllis Chesler's *With Child*, a diary of her first pregnancy and childbirth at the age of 37, is dedicated to her son: "To my son Ariel, this handmade gift to welcome you." (I am a good mother, I make my own presents.) Liv Ullman's autobiography, from which I quoted above, is dedicated to her daughter, Linn, with a frontispiece photograph of mother and child forehead to forehead. The back cover is a close-up photo of Liv, somber, alone. The last pages are a letter to Linn—a series of self-reproaches by the mother, culminating in the astonishing question: "Do you understand that I really have no valid reason not to run out to you and live your life?" This from one of the most serious actresses of our time, who is also a genuine writer.

Another way to propitiate the crying child is not to write the book, or to write it less well than one could. "Almost no mothers—as almost no part-time, part-self persons—have created enduring literature . . . so far." That was Tillie Olsen writing, in 1972.[33]

So much for the dark side. There is also a lighter one.

> Through you, Ariel, I'm enlarged, connected to something larger than myself. Like falling in love, like ideological conversion, the connection makes me *feel* my existence. [Phyllis Chesler][34]

> And yet, somehow, something, call it Nature or that affirming fatalism of the human creature, makes me aware of the inevitable as already part of me, not to be contended against so much as brought to bear as an additional weapon against drift, stagnation and spiritual death. [Adrienne Rich][35]

> A mother can be any sort of person, great or ordinary, given to moderation or intensity, inclined toward amazonian aggression or receptivity. But whatever type you are, being a mother forces you to accept your limitations. And when you accept your limitations as a mother, you begin to accept your limitations in other areas of life as well. The daily grinding friction of motherhood will give you the chance, at least, of relinquishing some of your egotism. You will finally cease to be a child. [Jane Lazarre][36]

> . . . through the coming of the child and the beginning of a love, perhaps the only genuine feminine love for another . . . one has the chance to accede to that relationship so difficult for a woman, the relationship to the Other: to the symbolic and the ethical. If pregnancy is a threshold between nature and culture, motherhood is a bridge between the singular and the ethical. . . . [Julia Kristeva][37]

> What does it mean to love, for a woman? The same thing as to write. . . . WORD/FLESH. From one to the other, eternally, fragmented visions, metaphors of the invisible. [Julia Kristeva][38]

Integration, connection, reaching out; a defense against drift and spiritual death, a way of outgrowing the solipsism of childhood, a way to relate, a way to write—this

33. [Olsen 19.]
34. [Phyllis Chesler, *With Child: A Diary of Motherhood* (New York: Crowell, 1979) 246.]
35. [Rich 9.]
36. [Lazarre 216.]
37. [Kristeva 6.]

38. [Julia Kristeva, "Héréthique de l'amour," *Tel Quel*, no. 74 (Winter 1977) 31. Reprinted as "Stabat Mater" in Kristeva, *Histoires d'amour* (Paris: Denoël, 1983). English translation appears in *The Female Body in Western Culture: Semiotic Perspectives*, ed. Susan Rubin Suleiman (Cambridge: Harvard UP, 1986).]

too is motherhood as seen by mothers, often by the very same mothers who at other times feel torn apart by the conflicting pulls of work and child. Jane Lazarre, at the end of *The Mother Knot*, invents a debate between "the mother" and "the dark lady," the one urging Jane to have a second child, the other arguing against it. The dark lady says: "I am not speaking about mere details and practical responsibilities. It is the effect of those continuous demands on the spirit to which I commend your attention." The mother counters: "Don't you want the feeling of a baby moving inside you again?" But it turns out that the dark lady is the mother in disguise, the mother the dark lady. And Jane is both of them, they are inside her head.

Have we simply arrived here at the point where Adrienne Rich began? "My children cause me the most exquisite suffering of which I have any experience. It is the suffering of ambivalence: the murderous alternation between bitter resentment and raw-edged nerves, and blissful gratification and tenderness."[39] Yes and no. For Rich, as she expresses it in this diary entry, ambivalence is an *alternation* between resentment and tenderness, negation of the child and reaching out for the child—as if these two impulses were unconnected to each other, locked in an insurmountable opposition, corresponding perhaps to the opposition between the mother's need to affirm herself as writer and the child's need (or her belief in the child's need) for her selflessness. There is something of this struggle in Lazarre's parable, but the parable also suggests a possibility of reconciliation rather than conflict between warring elements. If the mother is the dark lady and the dark lady the mother, then the energies and aspirations of the one are also those of the other. The mother's tenderness and the dark lady's urge for self-expression may support, not hinder, each other.

This is precisely what is implied by Chesler, by Rich in another diary entry (the one I quoted above), and especially by Kristeva, who goes beyond implication to explicit statement: "Far from being in contradiction with creativity (as the existentialist myth still tries to make us believe), motherhood can—in itself and if the economic constraints are not too burdensome—favor a certain feminine creation. To the extent that it lifts the fixations, makes passion circulate between life and death, self and other, culture and nature . . ."[40] Kristeva is prudent, she makes no absolute claims (motherhood *can* favor creation, it doesn't necessarily do so); she is aware of the material obstacles (how will mother write if there is no one else to care for baby, or if she must work at other jobs to support baby?—Tillie Olsen's questions). Yet in an important turn of French feminist theory, which we also see appearing in a less abstract version in current American feminist thinking, Kristeva rejects the either/or dilemma and suggests that motherhood and feminine creation go hand in hand.

Kristeva's argument, as stated in two essays in the Winter 1977 issue of *Tel Quel*, is a very complex one and would deserve a long analysis unto itself. This is not the appropriate place for that, but I wish to pause at least briefly in order to take a closer look.

Kristeva's argument can be summed up approximately as follows: the order of the symbolic, which is the order of language, of culture, of the law, of the Name-of-the-Father (to use Lacan's terminology), is especially difficult for women to accede to, whether for historical or other reasons. Motherhood, which establishes a *natural* link (the child) between woman and the social world, provides a privileged means of entry into the order of culture and of language. This privilege belongs to the mother (if I read Kristeva correctly here) not only in contrast to women who are not mothers but also in contrast to men, whose relationship to the symbolic order is itself prob-

39. [Rich 1.]   40. [Kristeva 6.]

lematical, characterized by discontinuity, separation, absence. The symbolic, whether for men or for women, functions as the realm of the (unattainable) Other, the realm of the arbitrary signs rather than of things; it is by definition the realm of frustrated relations, of impossible loves. The love of God, that ultimate sign of the Other, is of the order of the impossible. Bur for a mother, according to Kristeva, the Other is not (only) an arbitrary sign, a necessary absence: it is the child, whose presence and whose bodily link to her are inescapable givens, material facts. If to love (her child) is, for a woman, the same thing as to write, we have in that conjunction a modern, secular equivalent of the word made flesh.

This straightforward summary is in a sense a betrayal, however, for the most interesting thing about Kristeva's argument is its quasibyzantine indirection. The first of the two essays, placed as an introduction to the special issue of the journal devoted to "*recherches féminines*," is not ostensibly about motherhood at all, or even about women, but about the possibilities of intellectuals and of intellectual dissidence in Western Culture. The remarks about motherhood and its relation to feminine creation form part of a section on the possibly dissident role of women in relation to patriarchal law. Since the more elemental law of the reproduction of the species is essentially in women's hands, Kristeva wonders whether mothers are not, in fact, at the very opposite pole of dissidence—whether by maintaining the species they do not also maintain and guarantee the existing social order. She does not answer this question directly, but my sense is that, if pressed, her answer would be: "Yes and no." The mother's body, being a place of fragmentation, cleavage, elemental pulsations that exist *before* language and meaning, is necessarily a place of exile, a place of dis-order and extreme singularity in relation to the collective order of culture. At the same time, the mother's body is the link between nature and culture, and as such must play a conserving role.

What interests me, however, is another question that Kristeva poses: "After the Virgin (Mary), what do we know about the inner discourse of a mother?" The question is both provocative and bizarre, its bizarreness residing in the opening words. Do we know more about the Virgin's inner discourse than about any other mother's? At best we know the discourse that has been attributed to her, that has in fact *created* her—it is the discourse of Christianity, of the *Fathers* of the Church.

Kristeva is aware of this. Her second and much longer essay ("Héréthique de l'amour") is devoted precisely to the question of how the myth of the Virgin Mother was gradually elaborated by Christian discourse, and how it has functioned in the imagination of the West. Above all, she seeks to answer this question: What is it about the Christian representation of ideal motherhood, as embodied in the Virgin, that was satisfactory to women for hundreds of years, and why is that representation no longer satisfactory today? Her tentative conclusion is that in the image of the Virgin Mother, Christianity provided what for a long time was a satisfactory compromise solution to female paranoia: a denial of the male's role in procreation (virgin birth), a fulfillment of the female desire for power (Mary as Queen of Heaven), a sublimation of the woman's murderous or devouring desires through the valorization of her breast (the infant Jesus suckling) and of her own pain (the *Mater dolorosa*), a fulfilling of the fantasy of deathlessness or eternal life (the Assumption), and above all a denial of other women, including the woman's own mother (Mary was "alone of all her sex")—all of this being granted upon one condition: that the ultimate supremacy and divinity of the male be maintained in the person of the Son, before whom the Mother kneels and to whom she is subservient.

According to Kristeva, the compromise solution represented by the Virgin Mother provided a model that women could, however indirectly, identify with, and at the same time allowed those in charge of the social and symbolic order to maintain their control. (It may be worth noting that the Christian representation of the Virgin Mother has some affinities with, but is much more powerful than, the representation of ideal motherhood in psychoanalytic discourse: In both cases the mother is elevated precisely to the extent that she prostrates herself before her son; for Freud, the mother's greatest satisfaction is to see her favorite son attain glory, which then reflects back on her.) For today's women, however, Kristeva argues, the myth of Mary has lost its positive powers: It leaves too many things unsaid, censors too many aspects of female experience, chief among them the experience of childbirth and of the mother's body in general, the relationship of women to their mothers (and to their daughters), and the relationship of women to men (not to male children, but to adult men). As far as all of these relationships are concerned, motherhood provides a central point from which to ask the questions and to make a first step toward answering them.

As if to demonstrate this very thing, Kristeva intersperses her analytical, discursive text with lyrical, discontinuous fragments of an "other" text—this "other" text being the inner discourse of a mother, Kristeva herself. Since the lyrical fragments are surrounded, enveloped by the discursive text, it is tempting to see the two as "mother" and "child", with the lyrical fragments representing the child. (This idea was suggested to me by Carolyn Burke). But paradoxically, in the "child-text" it is a *mother* who writes of her experiences: childbirth, playing with her infant, watching over the child sick for the first time, feeling separated from and at the same time united with the child, memories of her own mother (the "other woman"), her relationship to language, to the Law. The lyrical fragments are thus in counterpoint, both stylistically and on the level of content, to the discursive text, as the mother's *inner* discourse is in counterpoint to the discourse given to her, constructed about her, by Christianity, the dominant order of Western culture.

These essays by Kristeva seem to me to be especially important for three reasons: She seeks to analyze and show the limitations of Western culture's traditional discourse about motherhood; she offers a theory, however incomplete and tentative, about the relation between motherhood and feminine creation; finally, she *writes* her own maternal text as an example of what such creation might be. This ambitious undertaking is part of the much broader context of contemporary French feminist theory, which over the past several years has been trying both to elaborate a theory of and to exemplify the specificity of *l'écriture féminine*. Luce Irigaray and Hélène Cixous (who is a mother) have insisted on the essentially subversive, dis-orderly nature of women's writing in patriarchal culture, without attempting to differentiate between the feminine and the maternal. This may be because—at least for Cixous— the very fact of being a woman means that one is "never far from the 'mother,'" that is, from a force of reparation and nourishment that is fundamentally "other" in relation to the desiccated rationalism of male discourse.[41]

Chantal Chawaf, on the other hand, much more radically that Kristeva, has tied the practice of feminine writing to the biological fact of motherhood. Chawaf is the mother of two children and the author of several books written in a lyrical autobiographical mode. The central experience around which all her writing turns is the

---

41. [See Cixous's essay "Sorties," in Catherine Clément and Hélène Cixous, *La Jeune Née* (Paris: Union Générale, 1975) esp. 169–80.]

physical and emotional experience of motherhood and maternal love, which she endows with the quasi-cosmic significance. One of her recent books, *Maternité*, is a series of sensuous prose poems celebrating the love between a mother who is on the verge of emotional breakdown and her two children, whom she perceives as her only link to communication and light, in opposition to solitude and eternal darkness. Chawaf has stated in interviews and in commentaries on her work that for her motherhood is the only access to literary creation. In *Maternité* she speaks of a "new syntax with fatty nouns, infinitive thighs," a language so physical that it would be a nourishment and "would make every sentence the close relative of the skin and of the mucous membranes. . . ."[42]

The work of the French radical feminists represents without a doubt the most ambitious attempt so far to theorize the relationship between writing and femininity, and more or less directly between writing and motherhood. Personally, my one reservation about their work—which is clearly a work in progress, and therefore too early to make definitive pronouncements about—concerns its exclusionary aspects. To recognize that women, mothers, have been excluded from the order of patriarchal discourse, and to insist on the positive difference of maternal and feminine writing in relation to male writing, can only be beneficial at this time. But it would be a pity if the male gesture of exclusion and repression of the female "other" were to be matched by a similar gesture in reverse. I do not mean by that only the obvious exclusion of men, for some French feminists (Hélène Cixous among them) are willing to admit that certain male poets have attained a "feminine" status in their writing. Rather, I mean the exclusion of a certain *kind* of writing and discourse arbitrarily defined as "male," repressive, logical, the discourse of power, or what have you. Such a gesture necessarily places "feminine" writing in a minority position, willfully ex-centric in relation to power. I am not wholly convinced that that is the best position for women to be in.

I also have reservations about what might be called that fetishization of the female body in relation to writing. It may be true that femininity and its quintessential embodiment, motherhood, can provide a privileged mode of access to language and the mother tongue. What would worry me would be the codification, on the basis of this insight, of women's writing and writing style. In recent French feminist theory and practice, one sees tendencies toward just such codification, both on the level of themes and on the level of style: the centrality of the woman's body and blood, her closeness to Nature, her attunement to the quality of *voice* rather than to "dry" meaning; elemental rhythms, writing as flow (of menstrual blood, of mother's milk, of uterine fluid), "liquid" syntax, lyricism at all costs, receptivity, union, nonaggression. . . . We are reaching the point where a new genre is being created, and that may be all to the good. But to see in this genre the one and only genuine mode of feminine writing would, I think, be a mistake.[43]

WRITING AND MOTHERHOOD: THE MOTHER'S FICTIONS

After that ascent into theory, I want to return to more concrete ground. Mothers write, and they write fiction as well as personal statements. Tillie Olsen remarked

42. [Chantal Chawaf, *Maternité* (Paris, 1979) 20.]
43. [The debate over *l'écriture féminine*, whose implications, have properly been seen as political rather than merely stylistic, has been long and sometimes acrimonious among French feminists. The issues are clearly defined in the dialogue that concludes Cixous's and Clément's *Jeune Née*, as well as in Clément's essay "Enslaved Enclave" and Cixous's "Laugh of the Medusa," in *New French Feminisms*, ed. Elaine Marks and Isabelle de Courtivron (New York: Schocken, 1981). Like Clément, but from a different perspective, Kristeva has criticized the concept of *l'écriture féminine*; see in particular "A partir de *Polylogue*," *Revue des sciences humaines*, no. 168 (December 1977) 495–501.]

about contemporary (British and American) novelists who are mothers that "not many have directly used the material open to them out of motherhood as a central source of their work."[44] An interesting question is implied here. What fascinates me, however, is a more specific question: whether, and how, the conjunction of writing and motherhood is refracted in the fictions—as opposed to the more direct statements where the mother says "I"—of mothers who write. Here psychoanalysis may be of help, if only by analogy. Using as a starting point Freud's contention that the work of fiction is a distantiated, formally "disguised" version of the writer's fantasy, we can ask: Is there such a thing as the writing mother's fantasy? And if so, what transformations does the fantasy undergo in the process of its fictionalization? To put it somewhat differently, what happens to the mother's discourse when it chooses not direct expression but the indirections of fiction?

Having asked the question, I am not quite sure just how to go about answering it. But no matter. I shall assume that mothers' fantasies exist, that they are formulatable, and that they can (can, not must) provide the impetus for fictional elaboration. I shall further assume that they are to be found, if anywhere, in the fictions of women writers who are mothers. To demonstrate the literary-critical, if not scientific, usefulness of these assumptions, I shall propose readings of two works by a single writer. The writer is the American poet and novelist Rosellen Brown. The works are a three-page short story titled "Good Housekeeping" and a novel titled *The Autobiography of My Mother*.[45]

"Good Housekeeping"—the title is double-edged. A mother puts her baby down for a nap, first photographing his behind from close up. She is a photographer, working now after an interval long enough for all the chemicals in her darkroom to have dried up. But she is a professional, already imagining how she will hang the pictures in her next show ("utterly random, on flat matte. No implicit order, no heavy ironies"), and she works fast. After the baby's rear come the sludge-covered coffeepot, the inside of the toilet bowl, the mountain of laundry seen from the inside looking out, a bunch of peeled vegetables strewn among the peels, the rumpled bedsheets, her own vagina (seen only by the viewfinder of the camera), a handful of condoms found in a box and randomly arranged, the dirty window, fresh soil in which seedlings of vegetables are buried, a drawerful of household odds and ends, cigarette paper and the marijuana hidden in a spice jar, the inside of a pencil sharpener, a stretch of ugly wallpaper left uncovered, the welcome mat caked with mud. She rejects a row of lined-up cans and an omelet made for the occasion as inappropriate—"too much like *Good Housekeeping*"—and also a pile of bird feathers left by the cat: their function is not clear without the cat, and besides, "are murdered birds a part of every household?"

Then the baby wakes, screaming. With the shades up it is so light "you could see the baby's uvula quivering like an icicle about to drop." When he sees the camera, the baby stops crying, fascinated. "Eyes like cameras. His mother looked back at herself in them, a black box in her lap with a queer star of light in its middle." The baby smiles, reaching for his mother (or for the camera?) through the slats of the crib. The mother's next action (and the story's final paragraph):

44. [Olsen 32.]
45. ["Good Housekeeping" first appeared in *American Review*, no. 18 (1973), and was reprinted in *Bitches and Sad Ladies: An Anthology of Fiction by and about Women*, ed. Pat Rotter (New York: Dell, 1976) 68–70. *The Autobiography of My Mother* was published in 1976 (New York: Doubleday). Rosellen Brown is the mother of two young daughters.]

She put her head in her hands. Then she reached in and, focusing as well as she could with one hand, the baby slapping at her through the bars, wheezing with laughter, she found one cool bare thigh, the rosy tightness of it, and pinched it with three fingers, kept pinching hard, till she got that angry uvula again, and a good bit of very wet tongue. Through the magnifier it was spiny as some plant, some sponge, maybe, under the sea.

I find this an extraordinarily powerful story, even after several readings. In trying to account for its power (its powerful effect on me), I invariably return to the last paragraph: the mother looking at her child not directly but through the camera, transforming him into an object; feeling his thighs not as flesh, her flesh, but professionally as a "rosy tightness"; then pinching until the cry comes, and with it the thing she wants to capture, the quivering uvula—the clinicalness of it, and at the same time its possibility for endless metaphorization: icicle, spiny plant, sponge under the sea. The rosy thigh, sentimental and cloying, would be at best good for *Good Housekeeping*; the angry uvula, like the other exemplary objects ("part of every household") that preceded it, will hang in random order on flat matte. It is not propaganda (Let us all be good housekeepers and have rosy babies) but art.

Art? And what about the crying child? The power of the story, for me, lies in the fantasy that I read in (or perhaps into) it: "With every word I write, with every metaphor, with every act of genuine creation, I hurt my child."

Surely I am overreacting? Perhaps not. To me this is not only a story about the inner world of motherhood *as it is felt*, not as it is mythologized in women's magazines (think of the mess and the jumble, the receptacles of every kind, the insides so carefully observed, the hidden things growing); it is also a story about the *representation* of motherhood by a mother, "seeing herself from a great distance, doing an assignment on herself doing an assignment"; and it is a story about the specular relation between mother-as-artist and her child: seeing herself reflected, *as artist* (holding the camera), in his eyes, she reacts by pinning him down, turning him into an image, a metaphor, a text. Portrait of the artist as mother; or, the momentary triumph of aggression over tenderness.

I say momentary triumph, because the anguish and guilt that inevitably attend the real-life mother's fantasy of writing as aggression against her child are absent. The story ends at the precise moment when the artist affirms herself against both the child and her own maternal feelings, before guilt (or madness—for if she were to go on hurting the child, we would have to call her mad) has a chance to appear. The result, both in the fiction and in the effect its language produces, is a sense of freedom, of formal control, which blocks any possibility of sentimentalization or self-pity. This becomes clearer if one compares Brown's story to, say, Alta's long poem, *Momma*, which recounts a similar experience—the poet-mother chasing her child out of the room so that she can write about her, negating her physical presence in order to capture her as a name, a text. In *Momma* the tone is one of anguish, since the mother *feels* the child's pain and expresses, retrospectively, her own sense of guilt and self-reproach in the poem. By opting for a simultaneous rather than a retrospective point of view, Brown's story refuses, I think quite consciously, the relief—but also the sentimentalization—that comes from self-reproach. We do not know how the mother in the story felt about her action afterward; when she focuses her camera on the crying child (but significantly she does not *see* the child, she sees only the "angry uvula"), we know only the cool concentration with which she snaps the picture. The language of the story "doubles" her own activity by means of the concluding metaphors.

Katherine Anne Porter once said about her own work that at the moment of writing "a calculated coldness is the best mood."[46] It is the dialectic between calculated coldness and intensity of feeling—a dialectic that characterizes the mother's problematic position between work and child—which is thematized in Brown's short story and which, present in the very language of the story, gives it its particular power.

Brown's novel *The Autobiography of My Mother* is a more extended and more complex treatment of the same theme. The novel consists of the alternating narratives of a mother and a daughter, herself the mother of a very young girl child. The mother is a woman in her seventies, still actively involved in her work as a civil liberties lawyer, a public figure. The daughter is an ex-flower child of the late sixties, an escapee of various communes and the California scene, who does nothing. She and her baby daughter return to New York, to her mother's Upper West Side apartment, after a ten-year absence.

Through the mother's narrative we learn about her own disturbed and loveless childhood, her conscious repression of passion and tenderness in favor of extreme self-control and rational action; we also learn of her solitude, her emotional sterility, her inability to make contact with people on any but the most abstract level. Through the daughter's narrative we learn about her feeling of abandonment, her pathological sense of failure and worthlessness, her inability to relate to others except on the most debased sexual level, and her deep hatred of as well as emotional dependence on her mother. During a televised mother-daughter talk show, she refuses to utter a single word. Her revenge on her mother, who is never at a loss for words, takes the form of total passivity and silence.

Between these two women, too much hurt and misunderstanding have accumulated to make any renewal possible. There is the granddaughter, however; stubborn and strong-willed like her grandmother, vulnerable like her mother, she appears to hold out the possibility of a reconciliation of sorts, or at least of a new start. She even manages to awaken her grandmother's seemingly nonexistent maternal feelings.

But it doesn't work out that way. The grandmother plans to take the child away form her mother by legal force. At a picnic where she intends to announce her intentions, she and the child walk down to a waterfall, while the child's mother watches from above. The old woman is not holding on to the child, the child is suddenly no longer there. She has been swept away, drowned. Earlier, the grandmother had stated: "In life there are no accidents."

What is one to make of this very disturbing book? I begin with the title: of which mother is this the autobiography? And who is its author? Gertrude Stein, I recall, wrote *The Autobiography of Alice B. Toklas*. The grandmother's name in this novel is Gerda Stein, and at one point, in an extended allusion to Shakespeare, she refers to herself as Gertrude. She also mentions that her decision to be a lawyer came after her first desire, which was to be a writer. Is the fictional Gertrude a stand-in for the real one? Possibly. But it is Rosellen Brown who is the signed author of this "autobiography," just as Gertrude Stein was of the other one. Structurally, it is Rosellen Brown that is the stand-in for Gertrude Stein—authors both. Yet if one takes the title seriously, then one must consider (the fictional) Gerda/Gertrude Stein to be Rosellen Brown's mother. Rosellen is thus both daughter to a Gertrude and a Gertrude herself, both the author and the author's daughter. The two narratives in the novel perhaps

46. [Katherine Anne Porter, "Notes on Writing," in *The Creative Process*, ed. Brewster Ghiselin (1952; rpt. New American Library, n. d.) 199.]

reflect this split, as does the fact that in the fiction, mother and daughter manage about equally to attract (and occasionally to repel) our sympathy.

But the question that plagues me is this: Why does the granddaughter, the beautiful and innocent child, have to die? And who is it that kills her?

I will propose a reckless interpretation. The child dies as a punishment to the "unnatural" mother—not her own mother, but her mother's mother, Gerda Stein. It is a self-inflicted punishment, for Gerda loves the child and "in life there are no accidents." It is also a punishment inflicted on Gerda by her daughter, whose own life has been a slow suicide and a permanent reproach to her mother. By not intervening in time, she allows her own daughter to perish as the ultimate reproach (thereby proving herself an "unnatural" mother too).[47] And she finally gets what she wants: For the first time ever, she sees her mother cry.

But of course it is neither Gerda nor her daughter that kills the child; it is the one who is both of them, Rosellen Brown. I read the ending of this novel as a gesture of self-punishment by the writing mother, and the novel itself as a dark companion piece to "Good Housekeeping." Here the aggressive impulse of the mother as artist is turned in on herself. Gerda is a writer *manquée*, and a failed mother as well. In her relationship to her daughter, she embodies the writing mother's most nightmarish fantasy: "I had not known we were to share but one life between us, so that the fuller mine is, the more empty hers."

Brown is the only contemporary novelist I know of who has explored, in fully rendered fictional forms, the violence and guilt as well as the violent energy that attend the artistic creations of mothers. Compared to Brown on this particular subject, I find Margaret Drabble, who has been called "the novelist of maternity,"[48] surprisingly simple. In Drabble's novels, the mothers who write or pursue a creative career (the older, famous novelist in *Jerusalem the Golden*, the thesis-writing heroine of *The Millstone*, the poet protagonist of *The Waterfall*, the archaeologist heroine of *The Realms of Gold*) all have an unproblematic, quasi-idealized relationship to their children. In *Jerusalem the Golden*, where the novelist's children are already grown, we see her mothering a stranger's baby. In *The Millstone*, the heroine writes better after her child is born. In *The Waterfall*, the narrator-heroine speaks of her feelings of ambivalence during pregnancy, but these feelings miraculously evaporate once the child arrives; her problems with writing are tied up not with her children but with her husband and her lover. As for the heroine of *The Realms of Gold*, she has no problems at all, once her love life is straightened out. Indeed, if the complexity of exploration is any criterion to judge by, Drabble seems to me to be more the novelist of adult love than anything else. Her heroines are almost without exception mothers, but their motherhood is relevant above all to their relations—whether fulfilling or frustrating—with men. The question that I think underlies Drabble's novels is this: Can a creative woman with children have a satisfying, permanent relationship with a man? This question is fascinating in its own right, but it is *another* question.

As far as writing and motherhood goes, Drabble perhaps gives us the wish-fulfillment fantasies that correspond, in reverse, to the nightmare fantasies of Brown. In between, there remains a great deal of space to explore—in fiction and in life.   *1985*

---

47. [There is an interesting contrast between this scene and one of the culminating scenes in Margaret Drabble's novel *The Garrick Year* (1964), where the heroine sees her young daughter fall into a river and immediately jumps in to save her. In Drabble's fiction, as I suggest below, the mother-child bond is never problematic.]

48. [Showalter 305.]

—•— ☰◊☰ —•—

Patricia Hill Collins
1948–

A prominent sociologist and feminist theoretician, PATRICIA HILL COLLINS is professor of African-American studies and sociology at the University of Cincinnati. She is married and the mother of a grown daughter. Collins's best-known scholarly work, *Black Feminist Thought: Knowledge, Consciousness, and the Politics of Empowerment* (1990), theorizes a "black feminist epistemology" that illuminates the writing of such African-American intellectuals as BELL HOOKS, AUDRE LORDE, and ALICE WALKER. This epistemology, drawn from feminist and Afrocentric standpoints, emphasizes the need for personal accountability, concrete experience as a source of wisdom, dialogue as a tool for exploring differences, and an ethic of empathy. *Black Feminist Thought* won the C. Wright Mills Award in 1991. With Margaret Andersen, Collins has edited *Race, Class, and Gender* (1993), an anthology widely used as a text for university courses in women's studies and sociological theory. Her book *Fighting Words: Black Women and the Search for Justice* appeared in 1998.

Collins has contributed important essays to two collections on motherhood: *Double Stitch: Black Women Write about Mothers and Daughters* (1991), ed. Patricia Bell-Scott et al., and *Mothering: Ideology, Experience, and Agency* (1994), ed. Evelyn Nakano Glenn et al. In her essay from the first volume, "The Meaning of Motherhood in Black Culture and Black Mother-Daughter Relationships," Collins delineates "a distinctly Afrocentric ideology of motherhood" and traces its effects on the dynamic between African-American mothers and their daughters. In contrast to Eurocentric models of black motherhood, which include the racist and idealized "mammy" and the domineering matriarch, Afrocentric models present mothers as economic providers and nurturers of children, as figures of enormous social value, and as members of cooperative maternal groups, since child care is seen as a collective responsibility.

The second essay, "Shifting the Center: Race, Class, and Feminist Theorizing About Motherhood," argues that feminist theorists routinely downplay the importance of race and class in their analyses of motherhood. Rather than concentrating on male supremacy and the destructiveness of the traditional nuclear family, as many white feminists do, women of color who write about motherhood consider how, in Collins' words, "gender inequality has long worked in tandem with racial domination and economic exploitation." To test her theory's efficacy, Collins examines literary works by Native American, African-American, Asian-American, and Hispanic writers who address race and class issues in their presentations of motherhood. "Survival, power and identity shape motherhood for all women," she concludes. "But these themes remain muted when the mothering experiences of women of color are marginalized in feminist theorizing."

⇥ Shifting the Center: Race, Class, and Feminist Theorizing About Motherhood ⇤

> I dread to see my children grow, I know not their fate. Where the white boy has every opportunity and protection, mine will have few opportunities and no protection. It does not matter how good or wise my children may be, they are colored.
>
> *an anonymous African-American mother in 1904,*
> *reported in Lerner, 1972 p. 158.*

For Native American, African-American, Hispanic, and Asian-American women, motherhood cannot be analyzed in isolation from its context. Motherhood occurs in specific historical situations framed by interlocking structures of race, class, and gender, where the sons and daughters of white mothers have "every opportunity and protection," and the "colored" daughters and sons of racial ethnic mothers "know not their fate." Racial domination and economic exploitation profoundly shape the mothering context, not only for racial ethnic women in the United States, but for all women.[1]

Despite the significance of race and class, feminist theorizing routinely minimizes their importance. In this sense, feminist theorizing about motherhood has not been immune to the decontextualization of Western social thought overall.[2] While many dimensions of motherhood's context are ignored, the exclusion of race and/or class from feminist theorizing generally (Spelman 1988), and from feminist theorizing about motherhood specifically, merit special attention.[3]

Much feminist theorizing about motherhood assumes that male domination in the political economy and the household is the driving force in family life, and that understanding the struggle for individual autonomy in the face of such domination is central to understanding motherhood (Eisenstein 1983).[4] Several guiding principles frame such analyses. First, such theories posit a dichotomous split between the public sphere of economic and political discourse and the private sphere of family and household responsibilities. This juxtaposition of a public, political economy to a private, noneconomic and apolitical, domestic household allows work and family to be seen as separate institutions. Second, reserving the public sphere for men as a "male" domain leaves the private domestic sphere as a "female" domain. Gender roles become tied to the dichotomous constructions of these two basic societal institutions—men work and women take care of families. Third, the public/private dichotomy separating the family/household from the paid labor market shapes sex-segregated gender roles within the private sphere of the

1. [In this essay, I use the terms "racial ethnic women" and "women of color" interchangeably. Grounded in the experiences of groups who have been the targets of racism, the term "racial ethnic" implies more solidarity with men involved in struggles against racism. In contrast, the term "women of color" emerges from a feminist background where racial ethnic women committed to feminist struggle aimed to distinguish their history and issues from those of middle-class, white women. Neither term captures the complexity of African-American, Native American, Asian-American and Hispanic women's experiences.]

2. [Positivist social science exemplifies this type of decontextualization. In order to create scientific descriptions of reality, positivist researchers aim to produce ostensibly objective generalizations. But because researchers have widely differing values, experiences, and emotions, genuine science is thought to be unattainable unless all human characteristics except rationality are eliminated from the research process. By following strict methodological rules, scientists aim to distance themselves from the values, vested interests, and emotions generated by their class, race, sex, or unique situation. By decontextualizing themselves, they allegedly become detached observers and manipulators of nature. Moreover, this researcher decontextualization is paralleled by comparable efforts to remove the objects of study from their contexts (Jaggar 1983).]

3. [Dominant theories are characterized by this decontextualization. Boyd's (1989) helpful survey of literature on the mother-daughter relationship reveals that while much

work has been done on motherhood generally, and on the mother-daughter relationship, very little of it tests feminist theories of motherhood. Boyd lists two prevailing theories, psychoanalytic theory and social learning theory, that she claims form the bulk of feminist theorizing. Both of these approaches minimize the importance of race and class in the context of motherhood. Boyd ignores Marxist-feminist theorizing about motherhood, mainly because very little of this work is concerned with the mother-daughter relationship. But Marxist-feminist analyses of motherhood provide another example of how decontextualization frames feminist theories of motherhood. See, for example, Ann Ferguson's Blood at the Root: Motherhood, Sexuality, and Male Dominance (1989), an ambitious attempt to develop a universal theory of motherhood that is linked to the social construction of sexuality and male dominance. Ferguson's work stems from a feminist tradition that explores the relationship between motherhood and sexuality by either bemoaning their putative incompatibility or romanticizing maternal sexuality.]

4. [Psychoanalytic feminist theorizing about motherhood, such as Nancy Chodorow's groundbreaking work, The Reproduction of Mothering (1978), exemplifies how decontextualization of race and/or class can weaken what is otherwise strong feminist theorizing. Although I realize that other feminist approaches to motherhood exist, see Eisenstein's (1983) summary for example, I have chosen to stress psychoanalytic feminist theory because the work of Chodorow and others has been highly influential in framing the predominant themes in feminist discourse.]

family. The archetypal white, middle-class nuclear family divides family life into two oppositional spheres—the "male" sphere of economic providing and the "female" sphere of affective nurturing, mainly mothering. This normative family household ideally consists of a working father who earns enough to allow his spouse and dependent children to withdraw from the paid labor force. Due in large part to their superior earning power, men as workers and fathers exert power over women in the labor market and in families. Finally, the struggle for individual autonomy in the face of a controlling, oppressive, "public" society, or the father as patriarch, comprises the main human enterprise.[5] Successful adult males achieve this autonomy. Women, children, and less successful males, namely those who are working-class or from racial ethnic groups, are seen as dependent persons, as less autonomous, and therefore as fitting objects for elite male domination. Within the nuclear family, this struggle for autonomy takes the form of increasing opposition to the mother, the individual responsible for socializing children by these guiding principles (Chodorow 1978; Flax 1978).

Placing the experiences of women of color in the center of feminist theorizing about motherhood demonstrates how emphasizing the issue of father as patriarch in a decontextualized nuclear family distorts the experiences of women in alternative family structures with quite different political economies. While male domination certainly has been an important theme for racial ethnic women in the United States, gender inequality has long worked in tandem with racial domination and economic exploitation. Since work and family have rarely functioned as dichotomous spheres for women of color, examining racial ethnic women's experiences reveals how these two spheres actually are interwoven (Glenn 1985; Dill 1988; Collins 1990).

For women of color, the subjective experience of mothering/motherhood is inextricably linked to the sociocultural concern of racial ethnic communities—one does not exist without the other. Whether because of the labor exploitation of African-American women under slavery and its ensuing tenant farm system, the political conquest of Native American women during European acquisition of land, or exclusionary immigration policies applied to Asian-Americans and Hispanics, women of color have performed motherwork that challenges social constructions of work and family as separate spheres, of male and female gender roles as similarly dichotomized, and of the search for autonomy as the guiding human quest. "Women's reproductive labor—that is, feeding, clothing, and psychologically supporting the male wage earner and nurturing and socializing the next generation—is seen as work on behalf of the family as a whole, rather than as work benefiting men in particular," observes Asian-American sociologist Evelyn Nakano Glenn (1986, 192). The locus of conflict lies outside the household, as women and their families engage in collective effort to create and maintain family life in the face of forces that undermine family integrity. But this "reproductive labor" or "motherwork" goes beyond ensuring the survival of one's own biological children or those of one's family. This type of motherwork recognizes that individual survival, empowerment, and identity require group survival, empowerment, and identity.

In describing her relationship with her "Grandmother," Marilou Awiakta, a Native American poet and feminist theorist, captures the essence of motherwork.

---

5. [The thesis of the atomized individual that underlies Western psychology is rooted in a much larger Western construct concerning the relation of the individual to the community (Hartsock 1983). Theories of motherhood based on the assumption of the atomized human proceed to use this definition of individual as the unit of analysis, and then construct theory from this base. From this grow assumptions based on the premise that the major process to examine is one between freely choosing rational individuals engaging in bargains (Hartsock 1983).]

> Putting my arms around the Grandmother, I lay my head on her shoulder. Through touch we exchange sorrow, despair that anything really changes.

Awiakta senses the power of the Grandmother and of the motherwork that mothers and grandmothers do.

> But from the presence of her arms I also feel the stern, beautiful power that flows from all the Grandmothers, as it flows from our mountains themselves. It says, "Dry your tears. Get up. Do for yourselves or do without. Work for the day to come." (1988, 127)

Awiakta's passage places women and motherwork squarely in the center of what are typically seen as disjunctures, the place between human and nature, between private and public, between oppression and liberation. I use the term "motherwork" to soften the existing dichotomies in feminist theorizing about motherhood that posit rigid distinctions between private and public, family and work, the individual and the collective, identity as individual autonomy and identity growing from the collective self-determination of one's group. Racial ethnic women's mothering and work experiences occur at the boundaries demarking these dualities. "Work for the day to come" is motherwork, whether it is on behalf of one's own biological children, or for the children of one's own racial ethnic community, or to preserve the earth for those children who are yet unborn. The space that this motherwork occupies promises to shift our thinking about motherhood itself.

SHIFTING THE CENTER: WOMEN OF COLOR AND MOTHERWORK

What themes might emerge if issues of race and class generally, and understanding of racial ethnic women's motherwork specifically, became central to feminist theorizing about motherhood? Centering feminist theorizing on the concerns of white, middle-class women leads to two problematic assumptions. The first is that a relative degree of economic security exists for mothers and their children. The second is that all women enjoy the racial privilege that allows them to see themselves primarily as individuals in search of personal autonomy, instead of members of racial ethnic groups struggling for power. It is these assumptions that allow feminist theorists to concentrate on themes such as the connections among mothering, aggression, and death, the effects of maternal isolation on mother-child relationships within nuclear family households, maternal sexuality, relationships among family members, all-powerful mothers as conduits for gender oppression, and the possibilities of an idealized motherhood freed from patriarchy (Chodorow and Contratto 1982; Eisenstein 1983).

While these issues merit investigation, centering feminist theorizing about motherhood in the ideas and experiences of African-American, Native American, Hispanic, and Asian-American women might yield markedly different themes (Andersen 1988; Brown 1989). This stance is to be distinguished from one that merely adds racial ethnic women's experiences to preexisting feminist theories, without considering how these experiences challenge those theories (Spelman 1988). Involving much more than simply the consulting of existing social science sources, the placing of ideas and experiences of women of color in the center of analysis requires invoking a different epistemology. We must distinguish between what has been said about subordinated groups in the dominant discourse, and what such groups might say about themselves if given the opportunity. Personal narratives, autobiographical statements, poetry, fiction, and other personalized statements have all been used by women of color to express self-defined standpoints on mothering and motherhood.

Such knowledge reflects the authentic standpoint of subordinated groups. Therefore, placing these sources in the center and supplementing them with statistics, historical material, and other knowledge produced to justify the interests of ruling elites should create new themes and angles of vision (Smith 1990).[6]

Specifying the contours of racial ethnic women's motherwork promises to point the way toward richer feminist theorizing about motherhood. Themes of survival, power, and identity form the bedrock and reveal how racial ethnic women in the United States encounter and fashion motherwork. That is to understand the importance of working for the physical survival of children and community, the dialectical nature of power and powerlessness in structuring mothering patterns, and the significance of self-definition in constructing individual and collective racial identity is to grasp the three core themes characterizing the experiences of Native American, African-American, Hispanic, and Asian-American women. It is also to suggest how feminist theorizing about motherhood might be shifted if different voices became central in feminist discourse.

MOTHERWORK AND PHYSICAL SURVIVAL

When we are not physically starving we have the luxury to realize psychic and emotional starvation. (Cherríe Moraga 1979, 29)

Physical survival is assumed for children who are white and middle-class. The choice to thus examine their psychic and emotional well-being and that of their mothers appears rational. The children of women of color, many of whom are "physically starving," have no such choices however. Racial ethnic children's lives have long been held in low regard: African-American children face an infant mortality rate twice that for white infants; and approximately one-third of Hispanic children and one-half of African-American children who survive infancy live in poverty. In addition racial ethnic children often live in harsh urban environments where drugs, crime, industrial pollutants, and violence threaten their survival. Children in rural environments often fare no better. Winona LaDuke, for example, reports that Native Americans on reservations often must use contaminated water. And on the Pine Ridge Sioux Reservation in 1979, thirty-eight percent of all pregnancies resulted in miscarriages before the fifth month, or in excessive hemorrhaging. Approximately sixty-five percent of all children born suffered breathing problems caused by underdeveloped lungs and jaundice (1988, 63).

Struggles to foster the survival of Native American, Hispanic, Asian-American, and African-American families and communities by ensuring the survival of children comprise a fundamental dimension of racial ethnic women's motherwork. African-American women's fiction contains numerous stories of mothers fighting for the

---

6. [The narrative tradition in the writings of women of color addresses this effort to recover the history of mothers. Works from African-American women's autobiographical tradition, such as Ann Moody's *Coming of Age in Mississippi*, Maya Angelou's *I Know Why the Caged Bird Sings*, Linda Brent's *Incidents in the Life of a Slave Girl*, and Marita Golden's *The Heart of a Woman* contain the authentic voices of Black women centered on experiences of motherhood. Works from African-American women's fiction include Sarah Wright's *This Child's Gonna Live*, Alice Walker's *Meridian*, and Toni Morrison's *Sula* and *Beloved*. Asian-American women's fiction, such as Amy Tan's *The Joy Luck Club* and Maxine [Hong] Kingston's *Woman Warrior*, and autobiographies such as Jean Wakatsuki Houston's *Farewell to Manzanar* offer a parallel source of authentic voice. Connie Young Yu (1989) entitles her article on the history of Asian-American women "The World of Our Grandmothers," and proceeds to recreate Asian-American history with her grandmother as a central figure. Cherríe Moraga (1979) writes a letter to her mother as a way of coming to terms with the contradictions in her racial identity as a Chicana. In *Borderlands/La Frontera*, Gloria Anzaldúa (1987) weaves autobiography, poetry and philosophy together in her exploration of women and mothering.]

physical survival both of their own biological children and of those of the larger Black community.[7] "Don't care how much death it is in the land, I got to make preparations for my baby to live!" proclaims Mariah Upshur, the African-American heroine of Sarah Wright's 1986 novel *This Child's Gonna Live* (143). Like Mariah Upshur, the harsh climates which confront racial ethnic children require that their mothers "make preparations for their babies to live" as the central feature of their motherwork.

Yet, like all deep cultural themes, the theme of motherwork for physical survival contains contradictory elements. On the one hand, racial ethnic women's motherwork for individual and community survival has been essential. Without women's motherwork, communities would not survive, and by definition, women of color themselves would not survive. On the other hand, this work often extracts a high cost for large numbers of women. There is loss of individual autonomy and there is submersion of individual growth for the benefit of the group. While this dimension of motherwork remains essential, the question of women doing more than their fair share of such work for individual and community development merits open debate.

The histories of family-based labor have been shaped by racial ethnic women's motherwork for survival and the types of mothering relationships that ensued. African-American, Asian-American, Native American and Hispanic women have all worked and contributed to family economic well-being (Glenn 1985; Dill 1988). Much of their experiences with motherwork, in fact, stem from the work they performed as children. The commodification of children of color, starting with the enslavement of African children who were legally "owned" as property, to the subsequent treatment of children as units of labor in agricultural work, family businesses, and industry, has been a major theme shaping motherhood for women of color. Beginning in slavery and continuing into the post–World War II period, Black children were put to work at young ages in the fields of Southern agriculture. Sara Brooks began full-time work in the fields at the age of eleven, and remembers, "we never was lazy cause we used to really work. We used to work like men. Oh, fight sometime, fuss sometime, but worked on" (Collins 1990, 54).

Black and Hispanic children in contemporary migrant farm families make similar contributions to their family's economy. "I musta been almost eight when I started following the crops," remembers Jessie de la Cruz, a Mexican-American mother with six grown children. "Every winter, up north. I was on the end of the row of prunes, taking care of my younger brother and sister. They would help me fill up the cans and put 'em in a box while the rest of the family was picking the whole row" (de la Cruz 1980, 168). Asian-American children spend long hours working in family businesses, child labor practices that have earned Asian Americans the dubious distinction of "model minorities." More recently, the family-based labor of undocumented racial ethnic immigrants, often mother-child units doing piecework for the garment industry, recalls the sweatshop conditions confronting turn-of-the-century European immigrants.

A certain degree of maternal isolation from members of the dominant group characterizes the preceding mother-child units. For women of color working along with their children, such isolation is more appropriately seen as reflecting a placement in racially and class stratified labor systems than as a result of a patriarchal system. The unit may be isolated, but the work performed by the mother-child unit

---

7. [Notable examples include Lutie Johnson's unsuccessful attempt to rescue her son from the harmful effects of an urban environment in Ann Petry's *The Street*; and Meridian's work on behalf of the children of a small Southern town after she chooses to relinquish her own child, in Alice Walker's *Meridian*.]

closely ties the mothering experiences to wider political and economic issues. Children, too, learn to see their work and that of their mothers not as isolated from wider society, but as essential to their family's survival. Moreover, in the case of family agricultural labor or family businesses, women and children work alongside men, often performing the same work. If isolation occurs, the family, not the mother-child unit, is the focus of such isolation.

Children working in close proximity to their mothers receive distinctive types of mothering. Asian-American children working in urban family businesses, for example, report long days filled almost exclusively with work and school. In contrast, the sons and daughters of African-American sharecroppers and migrant farm children of all backgrounds have less access to educational opportunities. "I think the longest time I went to school was two months in one place," remembers Jessie de la Cruz. "I attended, I think, about forty-five schools. When my parents or my brothers didn't find work, we wouldn't attend school because we weren't sure of staying there. So I missed a lot of school" (de la Cruz 1980, 167–8). It was only in the 1950s in fact, that Southern school districts stopped the practice of closing segregated Black schools during certain times of the year so that Black children could work.

Work that separated women of color from their children also framed the mothering relationship. Until the 1960s, large numbers of African-American, Hispanic, and Asian-American women worked in domestic service. Even though women worked long hours to ensure their children's physical survival, that same work ironically denied mothers access to their children. Different institutional arrangements emerged in these mothers' respective communities, to resolve the tension between maternal separation due to employment and the needs of dependent children. The extended family structure in African-American communities endured as a flexible institution that mitigated some of the effects of maternal separation. Grandmothers are highly revered in Black communities, often because grandmothers function as primary caretakers of their daughters' and daughter-in-laws' children (Collins 1990). In contrast, exclusionary immigration policies that mitigated against intergenerational family units in the United States led Chinese-American and Japanese-American families to make other arrangements (Dill 1988).

Some mothers are clearly defeated by the demands for incessant labor they must perform to ensure their children's survival. The magnitude of their motherwork overwhelms them. But others, even while appearing to be defeated, manage to pass on the meaning of motherwork for survival to their children. African-American feminist June Jordan remembers her perceptions of her mother's work:

> As a child, I noticed the sadness of my mother as she sat alone in the kitchen at night. . . . Her woman's work never won permanent victories of any kind. It never enlarged the universe of her imagination or her power to influence what happened beyond the front door of our house. Her woman's work never tickled her to laugh or shout or dance. (Jordan 1985, 105)

But Jordan also sees her mother's work as being essential to individual and community survival.

> She did raise me to respect her way of offering love and to believe that hard work is often the irreducible factor for survival, not something to avoid. Her woman's work produced a reliable home base where I could pursue the privileges of books and music. Her woman's work invented the potential for a completely new kind of work for us, the next generation of Black women: huge, rewarding hard work demanded by the huge, different ambitions that her perfect confidence in us engendered. (Jordan 1985, 105)

MOTHERWORK AND POWER

Jessie de la Cruz, a Mexican-American migrant farm worker, experienced firsthand the struggle for empowerment facing racial ethnic women whose daily motherwork centers on issues of survival.

> How can I write down how I felt when I was a little child and my grandmother used to cry with us 'cause she didn't have enough food to give us? Because my brother was going bare-footed and he was cryin' because he wasn't used to going without shoes? How can I de-scribe that? I can't describe when my little girl died because I didn't have money for a doctor. And never had any teaching on caring for sick babies. Living out in labor camps. How can I describe that? (Jessie de la Cruz 1980, 177)

A dialectical relationship exists between efforts of racial orders to mold the insti-tution of motherhood to serve the interests of elites, in this case, racial elites, and efforts on the part of subordinated groups to retain power over motherhood so that it serves the legitimate needs of their communities (Collins 1990). African-American, Asian-American, Hispanic, and Native American women have long been preoccu-pied with patterns of maternal power and powerlessness because their mothering experiences have been profoundly affected by this dialectical process. But instead of emphasizing maternal power in dealing with father as patriarch (Chodorow 1978; Rich 1986), or with male dominance in general (Ferguson 1989), women of color are concerned with their power and powerlessness within an array of social institutions that frame their lives.

Racial ethnic women's struggles for maternal empowerment have revolved around three main themes. First is the struggle for control over their own bodies in order to preserve choice over whether to become mothers at all. The ambiguous pol-itics of caring for unplanned children has long shaped African-American women's motherwork. For example, the widespread institutionalized rape of Black women by white men, both during slavery and in the segregated South, created countless bira-cial children who had to be absorbed into African-American families and communi-ties (Davis 1981). The range of skin colors and hair textures in contemporary African-American communities bears mute testament to the powerlessness of African-American women in controlling this dimension of motherhood.

For many women of color, choosing to become a mother challenges institutional policies that encourage white, middle-class women to reproduce, and discourage and even penalize low-income racial ethnic women from doing so (Davis 1981). Rita Silk-Nauni, an incarcerated Native American woman, writes of the difficulties she encountered in trying to have additional children. She loved her son so much that she only left him to go to work. "I tried having more after him and couldn't," she laments.

> "I went to a specialist and he thought I had been fixed when I had my son. He said I would have to have surgery in order to give birth again. The surgery was so expensive but I thought I could make a way even if I had to work 24 hours a day. Now that I'm here, I know I'll never have that chance." (Brant 1988, 94)

Like Silk-Nauni, Puerto Rican and African-American women have long had to struggle with issues of sterilization abuse (Davis 1981). More recent efforts to manip-ulate the fertility of women dependent on public assistance speaks to the continued salience of this issue.

A second dimension of racial ethnic women's struggles for maternal empower-ment concerns the process of keeping the children that are wanted, whether they were planned for or not. For mothers like Jessie de la Cruz whose "little girl died" because she "didn't have money for a doctor," maternal separation from one's children becomes a much more salient issue than maternal isolation with one's children within an allegedly private nuclear family. Physical and/or psychological separation of mothers and children, designed to disempower individuals, forms the basis of a systematic effort to disempower racial ethnic communities.

For both Native American and African-American mothers, situations of conquest introduced this dimension of the struggle for maternal empowerment. In her fictional account of a Native American mother's loss of her children in 1890, Brant explores the pain of maternal separation.

> It has been two days since they came and took the children away. My body is greatly chilled. All our blankets have been used to bring me warmth. The women keep the fire blazing. The men sit. They talk among themselves. We are frightened by this sudden child-stealing. We signed papers, the agent said. This gave them rights to take our babies. It is good for them, the agent said. It will make them civilized. (1988, 101)

A legacy of conquest has meant that Native American mothers on "reservations" confront intrusive government institutions such as the Bureau of Indian Affairs in deciding the fate of their children. For example, the long-standing policy of removing Native American children from their homes and housing them in reservation boarding schools can be seen as efforts to disempower Native American mothers. For African-American women, slavery was a situation where owners controlled numerous dimensions of their children's lives. Black children could be sold at will, whipped, or even killed, all without any recourse by their mothers. In such a situation, getting to keep one's children and raise them accordingly fosters empowerment.

A third dimension of racial ethnic women's struggles for empowerment concerns the pervasive efforts by the dominant group to control the children's minds. In her short story, "A Long Memory," [sic][8] Beth Brant juxtaposes the loss felt by a Native American mother in 1890 whose son and daughter had been forcibly removed by white officials, to the loss that she felt in 1978 upon losing her daughter in a custody hearing. "Why do they want our babies?" queries the turn-of-the-century mother. "They want our power. They take our children to remove the inside of them. Our power" (Brant 1988, 105). This mother recognizes that the future of the Native American way of life lies in retaining the power to define that worldview through the education of children. By forbidding children to speak their native languages, and in other ways encouraging children to assimilate into Anglo culture, external agencies challenge the power of mothers to raise their children as they see fit.

Schools controlled by the dominant group comprise one important location where this dimension of the struggle for maternal empowerment occurs. In contrast to white, middle-class children, whose educational experiences affirm their mothers' middle-class values, culture, and authority, the educational experiences of African-American, Hispanic, Asian-American and Native American children typically denigrate their mothers' perspective. For example, the struggles over bilingual education in Hispanic communities are about much more than retaining Spanish as a second language. Speaking the language of one's childhood is a way of retaining the entire culture and honoring the mother teaching that culture (Morago 1979; Anzaldúa 1987).

8. The actual title of Brant's work is "A Long Story."

Jenny Yamoto describes the stress of continuing to negotiate with schools regarding her Black-Japanese sons.

> I've noticed that depending on which parent, Black mom or Asian dad, goes to school open house, my oldest son's behavior is interpreted as disruptive and irreverent, or assertive and clever. . . . I resent their behavior being defined and even expected on the basis of racial biases their teachers may struggle with or hold. . . . I don't have the time or energy to constantly change and challenge their teacher's and friends' misperceptions. I only go after them when the children really seem to be seriously threatened. (Yamoto 1988, 24)

In confronting each of these three dimensions of their struggles for empowerment, racial ethnic women are not powerless in the face of racial and class oppression. Being grounded in a strong, dynamic, indigenous culture can be central in these women's social constructions of motherhood. Depending on their access to traditional culture, they invoke alternative sources of power.[9]

"Equality per se, may have a different meaning for Indian women and Indian people," suggests Kate Shanley. "That difference begins with personal and tribal sovereignty—the right to be legally recognized as people empowered to determine their own destinies" (1988, 214). Personal sovereignty involves the struggle to promote the survival of a social structure whose organizational principles represent notions of family and motherhood different from those of the mainstream. "The nuclear family has little relevance to Indian women," observes Shanley. "In fact, in many ways, mainstream feminists now are striving to redefine family and community in a way that Indian women have long known" (214).

African-American mothers can draw upon an Afrocentric tradition where motherhood of varying types, whether bloodmother, othermother, or community othermother, can be invoked as a symbol of power. Many Black women receive respect and recognition within their local communities for innovative and practical approaches not only to mothering their own "blood" children, but also to being othermothers to the children in their extended family networks, and those in the community overall. Black women's involvement in fostering Black community development forms the basis of this community-based power. In local African-American communities, community othermothers can become identified as powerful figures through their work in furthering the community's well-being (Collins 1990).

Despite policies of dominant institutions that place racial ethnic mothers in positions where they appear less powerful to their children, mothers and children empower themselves by understanding each other's position and relying on each other's strengths. In many cases, children, especially daughters, bond with their mothers instead of railing against them as symbols of patriarchal power. Cherríe Moraga describes the impact that her mother had on her. Because she was repeatedly removed from school in order to work, by prevailing standards Moraga's mother would be considered largely illiterate. But she was also a fine storyteller, and found ways to empower herself within dominant institutions. "I would go with my mother to fill job applications for her, or write checks for her at the supermarket," Moraga recounts.

---

9. [Noticeably absent from feminist theories of motherhood is a comprehensive theory of power and explanation of how power relations shape theories. Firmly rooted in an exchange-based marketplace, with its accompanying assumptions of rational economic decision making and white, male control of the marketplace, this model of community stresses the rights of individuals, including feminist theorists, to make decisions in their own self-interests, regardless of the impact on larger society. Composed of a collection of unequal individuals who compete for greater shares of money as the medium of exchange, this model of community legitimates relations of domination either by denying they exist or by treating them as inevitable but unimportant (Hartsock 1983).]

We would have the scenario all worked out ahead of time. My mother would sign the check before we'd get to the store. Then, as we'd approach the checkstand, she would say—within earshot of the cashier—"oh, honey, you go 'head and make out the check,'" as if she couldn't be bothered with such an insignificant detail. (1979, 28)

Like Cherríe Moraga and her mother, racial ethnic women's motherwork involves collaborating to empower mothers and children within structures that oppress.

Motherwork and Identity

Please help me find out who I am. My mother was Indian, but we were taken from her and put in foster homes. They were white and didn't want to tell us about our mother. I have a name and maybe a place of birth. Do you think you can help me? (Brant 1988, 9)

Like this excerpt from a letter to the editor, the theme of lost racial ethnic identity and the struggle to maintain a sense of self and community pervade many of the stories, poetry and narratives in Beth Brant's volume, A Gathering of Spirit. Carol Lee Sanchez offers another view of the impact of the loss of self. "Radicals look at reservation Indians and get very upset about their poverty conditions," observes Sanchez.

But poverty to us is not the same thing as poverty is to you. Our poverty is that we can't be who we are. We can't hunt or fish or grow our food because our basic resources and the right to use them in traditional ways are denied us. (Brant 1988, 165)

Racial ethnic women's motherwork reflects the tensions inherent in trying to foster a meaningful racial identity in children within a society that denigrates people of color. The racial privilege enjoyed by white, middle-class women makes unnecessary this complicated dimension of the mothering tradition of women of color. While white children can be prepared to fight racial oppression, their survival does not depend on gaining these skills. Their racial identity is validated by their schools, the media, and other social institutions. White children are socialized into their rightful place in systems of racial privilege. Racial ethnic women have no such guarantees for their children; their children must first be taught to survive in systems that oppress them. Moreover, this survival must not come at the expense of self-esteem. Thus, a dialectical relationship exists between systems of racial oppression designed to strip subordinated groups of a sense of personal identity and a sense of collective people-hood, and the cultures of resistance extant in various racial ethnic groups that resist the oppression. For women of color, motherwork for identity occurs at this critical juncture (Collins 1990).

"Through our mothers, the culture gave us mixed messages," observes Mexican-American poet Gloria Anzaldúa. "Which was it to be—strong or submissive, rebellious or conforming?" (1987, 18). Thus women of color's motherwork requires reconciling contradictory needs concerning identity. Preparing children to cope with and survive within systems of racial oppression is extremely difficult because the pressures for children of racial ethnic groups to assimilate are pervasive. In order to compel women of color to participate in their children's assimilation, dominant institutions promulgate ideologies that belittle people of color. Negative controlling images infuse the worlds of male and female children of color (Tajima 1989; Collins 1990; Green 1990). Native American girls are encouraged to see themselves as "Pocahontases" or "squaws"; Asian-American girls as "geisha girls" or "Suzy Wongs"; Hispanic girls as "Madonnas" or "hot-blooded whores"; and African-American girls as "mammies", "matriarchs" and "prostitutes." Girls of all groups are told that their lives cannot be complete without a male partner, and that their educational and career aspirations must always be subordinated to their family obligations.

This push toward assimilation is part of a larger effort to socialize racial ethnic children into their proper, subordinate places in systems of racial and class oppression. Since children of color can never be white, however, assimilation by becoming white is impossible despite the pressures. Thus, a second dimension of the mothering tradition involves equipping children with skills to confront this contradiction and to challenge systems of racial oppression. Girls who become women believing that they are only capable of being maids and prostitutes cannot contribute to racial ethnic women's motherwork.

Mothers make varying choices in negotiating the complicated relationship of preparing children to fit into, yet resist, systems of racial domination. Some mothers remain powerless in the face of external forces that foster their children's assimilation and subsequent alienation from their families and communities. Through fiction, Native American author Beth Brant again explores the grief felt by a mother whose children had been taken away to live among whites. A letter arrives giving news of her missing children.

> This letter is from two strangers named Martha and Daniel. They say they are learning civilized ways. Daniel works in the fields, growing food for the school. Martha is being taught to sew aprons. She will be going to live with the schoolmaster's wife. She will be a live-in girl. What is a live-in girl? I shake my head. The words sound the same to me. I am afraid of Martha and Daniel. These strangers who know my name. (Brant 1988, 102–103)

Other mothers become unwitting conduits of the dominant ideology. Gloria Anzaldúa (1987, 16) asks:

> How many time have I heard mothers and mothers-in-law tell their sons to beat their wives for not obeying them, for being *hociconas* (big mouths), for being *callajeras* (going to visit and gossip with neighbors), for expecting their husbands to help with the rearing of children and the housework, for wanting to be something other than housewives?

Some mothers encourage their children to fit in, for reasons of survival. "My mother, nursed in the folds of a town that once christened its black babies Lee, after Robert E., and Jackson, after Stonewall, raised me on a dangerous generation's old belief," remembers African-American author Marita Golden.

> Because of my dark brown complexion, she warned me against my wearing browns or yellow and reds . . . and every summer I was admonished not to play in the sun "cause you gonna have to get a light husband anyway, for the sake of your children." (Golden 1983, 24)

To Cherríe Moraga's mother,

> On a basic economic level, being Chicana meant being "less." It was through my mother's desire to protect her children from poverty and illiteracy that we became "anglocized"; the more effectively we could pass in the white world, the better guaranteed our future. (1979, 28)

Despite their mothers' good intentions, the costs to children taught to submit to racist and sexist ideologies can be high. Raven, a Native American woman, looks back on her childhood:

> I've been raised in white man's world and was forbade more or less to converse with Indian people. As my mother wanted me to be educated and live a good life, free from poverty. I lived a life of loneliness. Today I am desperate to know my people. (Brant 1988, 221)

To avoid poverty, Raven's mother did what she thought best, but ultimately, Raven experienced the poverty of not being able to be who she was.

Still other mothers transmit sophisticated skills to their children, enabling them to appear to be submissive while at the same time to be able to challenge inequality. Willi Coleman's mother used a Saturday-night hair-combing ritual to impart a Black women's standpoint to her daughters:

> Except for special occasions mama came home from work early on Saturdays. She spent six days a week mopping, waxing, and dusting other women's houses and keeping out of reach of other women's husbands. Saturday nights were reserved for "taking care of them girls'" hair and the telling of stories. Some of which included a recitation of what she had endured and how she had triumphed over "folks that were lower than dirt" and "no-good snakes in the grass." She combed, patted, twisted, and talked, saying things which would have embarrassed or shamed her at other times. (Coleman 1987, 34)

Historian Elsa Barkley Brown captures this delicate balance that racial ethnic mothers negotiate. Brown points out that her mother's behavior demonstrated the "need to teach me to live my life one way and, at the same time, to provide all the tools I would need to live it quite differently" (1989, 929).

For women of color, the struggle to maintain an independent racial identity has taken many forms: All reveal varying solutions to the dialectical relationship between institutions that would deny their children their humanity and institutions that would affirm their children's right to exist as self-defined people. Like Willi Coleman's mother, African-American women draw upon a long-standing Afrocentric feminist worldview, emphasizing the importance of self-definition, self-reliance, and the necessity of demanding respect from others (Terborg-Penn 1986; Collins 1990).

Racial ethnic cultures, themselves, do not always help to support women's self-definition. Poet and essayist Gloria Anzaldúa, for example, challenges many of the ideas in Hispanic cultures concerning women. "Though I'll defend my race and culture when they are attacked by non-*mexicanos*, . . . I abhor some of my culture's ways, how it cripples its women, *como burras*, our strengths used against us" (1987, 21). Anzaldúa offers a trenchant analysis of the ways in which the Spanish conquest of Native Americans fragmented women's identity and produced three symbolic "mothers." *La Virgin de Guadalupe*, perhaps the single most potent religious, political and cultural image of the Chicano people, represents the virgin mother who cares for and nurtures an oppressed people. *La Chingada* (*Malinche*) represents the raped mother, all but abandoned. A combination of the other two, *La Llorona* symbolizes the mother who seeks her lost children. "Ambiguity surrounds the symbols of these three 'Our Mothers,'" claims Anzaldúa.

> In part, the true identity of all three has been subverted—*Guadalupe*, to make us docile and enduring, *la Chingada*, to make us ashamed of our Indian side, and *la Llorana* to make us a long-suffering people. (1987, 31)

For Anzaldúa, the Spanish conquest, which brought racism and economic subordination to Indian people, and created a new mixed-race Hispanic people, simultaneously devalued women:

> No, I do not buy all the myths of the tribe into which I was born. I can understand why the more tinged with Anglo blood, the more adamantly my colored and colorless sisters glorify their colored culture's values—to offset the extreme devaluation of it by the white culture. It's a legitimate reaction. But I will not glorify those aspects of my culture which have injured me and which have injured me in the name of protecting me. (Anzaldúa 1987, 22)

Hispanic mothers face the complicated task of shepherding their children through the racism extant in dominant society, and the reactions to that racism framing cultural beliefs internal to Hispanic communities.

Many Asian-American mothers stress conformity and fitting in as a way to challenge the system. "Our parents are painted as hard workers who were socially uncomfortable and had difficulty expressing even the smallest opinion," observes Japanese-American Kesaya Noda, in her autobiographical essay "Growing Up Asian in America" (1989, 246). Noda questioned this seeming capitulation on the part of her parents: "'Why did you go into those camps,' I raged at my parents, frightened by my own inner silence and timidity. 'Why didn't you do anything to resist?'" But Noda later discovers a compelling explanation as to why Asian-Americans are so often portrayed as conformist:

> I had not been able to imagine before what it must have felt like to be an American—to know absolutely that one is an American—and yet to have almost everyone else deny it. Not only deny it, but challenge that identity with machine guns and troops of white American soldiers. In those circumstances it was difficult to say, "I'm a Japanese-American." "American" had to do. (1989, 247)

Native American women can draw upon a tradition of motherhood and woman's power inherent in Native American cultures (Allen 1986; Awiakta 1988). In such philosophies, "water, land, and life are basic to the natural order," claims Winona LaDuke.

> All else has been created by the use and misuse of technology. It is only natural that in our respective struggles for survival, the native peoples are waging a way to protect the land, the water, and life, while the consumer culture strives to protect its technological lifeblood. (1988, 65)

Marilou Awiakta offers a powerful summary of the symbolic meaning of motherhood in Native American cultures. "I feel the Grandmother's power. She sings of harmony, not dominance," offers Awiakta. "And her song rises from a culture that repeats the wise balance of nature: the gender capable of bearing life is not separated from the power to sustain it" (1988, 126). A culture that sees the connectedness between the earth and human survival, and sees motherhood as symbolic of the earth itself, holds motherhood as an institution in high regard.

CONCLUDING REMARKS

Survival, power and identity shape motherhood for all women. But these themes remain muted when the mothering experiences of women of color are marginalized in feminist theorizing. Feminist theorizing about motherhood reflects a lack of attention to the connection between ideas and the contexts in which they emerge. While such decontextualization aims to generate universal "theories" of human behavior, in actuality, it routinely distorts, and omits huge categories of human experience.

Placing racial ethnic women's motherwork in the center of analysis recontextualizes motherhood. While the significance of race and class in shaping the context in which motherhood occurs remains virtually invisible when white, middle-class women's mothering experiences assume prominence, the effects of race and class on motherhood stand out in stark relief when women of color are accorded theoretical primacy. Highlighting racial ethnic mothers' struggles concerning their children's right to exist focuses attention on the importance of survival. Exploring the dialectical nature of racial ethnic women's empowerment in structures of racial domination and economic exploitation demonstrates the need to broaden the definition of maternal power. Emphasizing how the quest for self-definition is mediated by membership in different racial and social class groups reveals how the issues of identity are crucial to all motherwork.

Existing feminist theories of motherhood have emerged in specific intellectual and political contexts. By assuming that social theory will be applicable regardless of social context, feminist scholars fail to realize that they themselves are rooted in specific locations, and that the specific contexts in which they are located provide the thought-models of how they interpret the world. While subsequent theories appear to be universal and objective, they actually are partial perspectives reflecting the white, middle-class context in which their creators live. Large segments of experience, specifically those of women who are not white and middle-class, have been excluded (Spelman 1988).

Feminist theories of motherhood are thus valid as partial perspectives, but cannot be seen as *theories* of motherhood generalizable to all women. The resulting patterns of partiality inherent in existing theories, such as, for example, the emphasis placed on all-powerful mothers as conduits for gender oppression, reflect feminist theorists' positions in structures of power. These theorists are themselves participants in a system of privilege that rewards them for not seeing race and class privilege as being important.

Theorizing about motherhood will not be helped by supplanting one group's theory with that of another; for example, by claiming that women of color's experiences are more valid than those of white, middle-class women. Varying placement in systems of privilege, whether race, class, sexuality, or age, generates divergent experiences with motherhood; therefore, examination of motherhood and mother-as-subject from multiple perspectives should uncover rich textures of difference. Shifting the center to accommodate this diversity promises to recontextualize motherhood and point us toward feminist theorizing that embraces difference as an essential part of commonality.   1994

⊰ Works Cited ⊱

Allen, Paula Gunn. *The Sacred Hoop: Recovering the Feminine in American Indian Traditions.* Boston: Beacon, 1986.

Andersen, Margaret. "Moving Our Minds: Studying Women of Color and Reconstructing Sociology." *Teaching Sociology* 16.2 (1988): 123–132.

Anzaldúa, Gloria. *Borderlands/La Frontera: The New Mestiza.* San Francisco: Spinsters, 1987.

Awiakta, Marilou. "Amazons in Appalachia." *A Gathering of Spirit.* Ed. Beth Brant. Ithaca, NY: Firebrand (1988): 125–130.

Boyd, Carol J. "Mothers and Daughters: A Discussion of Theory and Research." *Journal of Marriage and the Family* 51(1989): 291–301.

Brant, Beth, ed. *A Gathering of Spirit: A Collection by North American Indian Women.* Ithaca, NY: Firebrand, 1988.

Brown, Elsa Barkley. "African-American Women's Quilting: A Framework for Conceptualizing and Teaching African-American Women's History." *Signs* 14.4 (1989): 921–929.

Chodorow, Nancy. *The Reproduction of Mothering.* Berkeley, CA: U of California P, 1978.

——, and Susan Contratto. "The Fantasy of the Perfect Mother." *Rethinking the Family: Some Feminist Questions.* Eds. Barrie Thorne and Marilyn Yalom. New York: Longman (1982) 54–75.

Coleman, Willi. "Closets and Keepsakes." *Sage: A Scholarly Journal on Black Women* 4.2 (1987): 34–35.

Collins, Patricia Hill. *Black Feminist Thought: Knowledge, Consciousness and the Politics of Empowerment*. New York: Unwin Hyman/Routledge, 1990.

de la Cruz, Jessie. "Interview." *American Dreams: Lost and Found*. Ed. Studs Terkel. New York: Ballantine, 1980.

Davis, Angela Y. *Women, Race, and Class*. New York: Random House, 1981.

Dill, Bonnie Thornton. "Our Mothers' Grief: Racial Ethnic Women and the Maintenance of Families." *Journal of Family History* 13.4 (1988): 415–431.

Eisenstein, Hester. *Contemporary Feminist Thought*. Boston: G.K. Hall, 1983.

Ferguson, Ann. *Blood at the Root: Motherhood, Sexuality, and Male Dominance*. New York: Unwin Hyman/Routledge, 1989.

Flax, Jane. "The Conflict between Nurturance and Autonomy in Mother-Daughter Relationships and within Feminism." *Feminist Studies* 4.2 (1978): 171–189.

Glenn, Evelyn Nakano. "Racial Ethnic Women's Labor: The Intersection of Race, Gender and Class Oppression." *Review of Radical Political Economics* 17.3 (1985): 86–108.

——. *Issei, Nisei, War Bride: Three Generations of Japanese American Women in Domestic Service*. Philadelphia: Temple UP, 1986.

Green, Rayna. "The Pocahontas Perplex: The Image of Indian Women in American Culture." *Unequal Sisters*. Eds. Ellen Carol DuBois and Vicki Ruiz. New York: Routledge (1990). 15–21.

Hartsock, Nancy. *Money, Sex and Power*. Boston: Northeastern UP, 1983.

Jordan, June. *On Call*. Boston: South End, 1985.

LaDuke, Winona. "They always come back." *A Gathering of Spirit*. Ed. Beth Brant. Ithaca, NY: Firebrand (1988). 62–67.

Lerner, Gerda. *Black Women in White America*. New York: Pantheon, 1972.

Moraga, Cherríe. "La Guera." *This Bridge Called My Back: Writings by Radical Women of Color*. Eds. Cherríe Moraga and Gloria Anzaldúa. Watertown, MA: Persephone Press (1979). 27–34.

Noda, Kesaya E. "Growing Up Asian in America." *Making Waves: An Anthology of Writings by and About Asian American Women*. Eds. Asian Women United of California. Boston: Beacon (1989). 243–50.

Rich, Adrienne. *Of Woman Born: Motherhood as Institution and Experience*. 1976. New York: Norton, 1986.

Shanley, Kate. "Thoughts on Indian Feminism." *A Gathering of Spirit*. Ed. Beth Brant. Ithaca, NY: Firebrand (1988). 213–215.

Smith, Dorothy E. *The Conceptual Practices of Power: A Feminist Sociology of Knowledge*. Boston: Northeastern UP, 1990.

Spelman, Elizabeth V. *Inessential Woman: Problems of Exclusion in Feminist Thought*. Boston: Beacon, 1988.

Tajima, Renee E. "Lotus Blossoms Don't Bleed: Images of Asian Women." *Making Waves: An Anthology of Writings by and About Asian American Women*. Eds. Asian Women United of California. Boston: Beacon (1989). 308–317.

Terborg-Penn, Rosalyn. "Black Women in Resistance: A Cross-Cultural Perspective." *In Resistance: Studies in African, Caribbean, and Afro-American History*. Ed. Gary Y. Okhiro. Amherst: U of Massachusetts P (1986). 188–209.

Wright, Sarah. *This Child's Gonna Live*. Old Westbury, NY: Feminist Press, 1986.

Yamoto, Jenny. "Mixed Bloods, Half Breeds, Mongrels, Hybrids . . ." *Changing Our Power: An Introduction to Women's Studies*. Eds. Jo Whitehorse Cochran, Donna Langston, and Carolyn Woodward. Dubuque, IA: Kendall/Hunt (1988). 22–24.

Yu, Connie Young. "The World of Our Grandmothers." *Making Waves: An Anthology of Writings by and About Asian American Women*. Eds. Asian Women United of California. Boston: Beacon (1989). 33–41.

‒‣ ⚌◆⚌ ‣‒

Julian of Norwich
1343?–1416

Julian of Norwich, a medieval mystic, was born around 1343 and may have been educated by eleven Benedictine nuns who lived at the convent of Carrow in East Anglia. She was probably a contemplative nun from an early age. In 1373, while ill, she experienced a series of sixteen spiritual revelations, or "showings," that lasted throughout the night and occurred in the presence of her mother and several friends, who believed she was dying. Julian went on to become an anchoress, or recluse, and to live in a cell adjoining the Church of St. Julian in Norwich, where she led a life of meditation and study. *The Book of Showings* (sometimes called *Revelations of Divine Love*) records her visions; it survives in a short version probably written within the decade after Julian's visionary experience and a long text completed around 1393, which offers her insights after a lifetime of reflection on her showings. Despite her claim to be "unlettered"—an ambiguous word which might mean that she was illiterate, that she could read but not write, or that she was not literate in Latin—her texts reveal rhetorical brilliance and theological sophistication. Beloved for her piety and wisdom, Julian acquired a reputation as a spiritual advisor; in her *Book*, the religious visionary MARGERY KEMPE records her visit with Julian, then about seventy-one. The records of monetary gifts to St. Julian's Church indicate that Julian of Norwich lived until at least 1416.

Both church and state leaders encouraged participation in the anchorite movement in England from 1200 to 1600, and thousands of women and men elected to lead this ascetic life, attaching themselves to churches and residing in tiny cells called anchorholds. Their daily routine included penance, meditation, and Biblical readings, and many who entered became secluded from the world forever. The *Ancrene Riwle* (sometimes called the *Ancrene Wisse*), a guidebook for anchoresses written around 1200, provides the most detailed portrait of this reclusive existence; it admonishes them to avoid displaying themselves in windows, conversing with men, or maintaining any animals other than cats. Unlike many, Julian's anchorhold was located amidst a thriving city whose resources offered her great opportunity for study. Her allusions to the scriptures and many religious treatises indicate that she was unusually well-educated.

Julian's work has undergone significant reconsideration in recent years by feminist and religious scholars. Her emphasis on the motherhood of God and her support of women's spiritual powers have endeared her to feminists, while theologians have been drawn to her visionary mysticism. A number of modern writers have also been influenced by her *Showings*, including T.S. Eliot, whose "Little Gidding" section of *Four Quartets* paraphrases Julian, and Iris Murdoch, whose novel *Nuns and Soldiers* contains a modern-day character based on Julian. In addition, scholarly books on Julian's life and teachings by Denise N. Baker, Jennifer Heimmel, Grace M. Jantzen, and Joan Nuth appeared during the 1980s and 1990s.

Although Julian was not the first writer to consider the motherhood of God, her treatment of this theme is more elaborate than that of any predecessor. Heimmel has noted that Julian presents Christ's motherhood as "a complete and connected cycle of life"; her narrative foregrounds the fetus's development in the womb, the mother's labor and delivery, nursing the infant, teaching the older child, and loving the adult child until its own demise, when it is reborn in God's womb. Women in the Middle Ages were defined by their bodies; hence Julian's portrayal of Christ's maternal embodiment would have been in keeping with cultural norms of femininity. Indeed, as Elizabeth Robertson has demonstrated, medieval texts often depict women as cold, wet, incomplete, and thus searching constantly for heat, release of moisture, and sexual union with men. In many mystical treatises by women, the emphasis is on blood, tears, and spiritual-erotic union with Christ. The body thus becomes a powerful site of women's spiritual expression, a fact that helps to explain why Julian presents Christ's maternal bodily functions—pregnancy, labor, lactation—in such vivid detail.

⊰ *from* Showings ⊱

THE FIFTY-EIGHTH CHAPTER

God the blessed Trinity, who is everlasting being, just as he is eternal from without beginning, just so was it in his eternal purpose to create human nature, which fair nature was first prepared for his own Son, the second person; and when he wished, by full agreement of the whole Trinity he created us all once. And in our creating he joined and united us to himself, and through this union we are kept as pure and as noble as we were created. By the power of that same precious union we love our Creator and delight in him, praise him and thank him and endlessly rejoice in him. And this is the work which is constantly performed in every soul which will be saved, and this is the godly will mentioned before.

And so in our making, God almighty is our loving Father, and God all wisdom is our loving Mother, with the love and the goodness of the Holy Spirit, which is all one God, one Lord. And in the joining and the union he is our very true spouse and we his beloved wife and his fair maiden, with which wife he was never displeased; for he says: I love you and you love me, and our love will never divide in two.

I contemplated the work of all the blessed Trinity, in which contemplation I saw and understood these three properties: the property of fatherhood, and the property of the motherhood, and the property of the lordship in one God. In our almighty Father we have our protection and our bliss, as regards our natural substance, which is ours by our creation from without beginning; and in the second person, in knowledge and wisdom we have our perfection, as regards our sensuality, our restoration and our salvation, for he is our Mother, brother and saviour; and in our good Lord the Holy Spirit we have our reward and our gift for our living and our labor, endlessly surpassing all that we desire in his marvelous courtesy, out of his great plentiful grace. For all our life consists of three: In the first we have our being, and in the second we have our increasing, and in the third we have our fulfillment. The first is nature, the second is mercy, the third is grace.

As to the first, I saw and understood that the high might of the Trinity is our Father, and the deep wisdom of the Trinity is our Mother, and the great love of the Trinity is our Lord; and all these we have in nature and in our substantial creation. And furthermore I saw that the second person, who is our Mother, substantially the same beloved person, has now become our mother sensually, because we are double by God's creating, that is to say substantial and sensual. Our substance is the higher part, which we have in our Father, God almighty; and the second person of the Trinity is our Mother in nature in our substantial creation, in whom we are founded and rooted, and he is our Mother of mercy in taking our sensuality. And so our Mother is working on us in various ways, in whom our parts are kept undivided; for in our Mother Christ we profit and increase, and in mercy he reforms and restores us, and by the power of his Passion, his death and his Resurrection he unites us to our substance. So our Mother works in mercy on all his beloved children who are docile and obedient to him, and grace works with mercy, and especially in two properties, as it was shown, which working belongs to the third person, the Holy Spirit. He works, rewarding and giving. Rewarding is a gift for our confidence which the Lord makes to those who have labored; and giving is a courteous act which he does freely, by grace, fulfilling and surpassing all that creatures deserve.

Thus in our Father, God almighty, we have our being, and in our Mother of mercy we have our reforming and our restoring, in whom our parts are united and all made perfect man, and through the rewards and the gifts of grace of the Holy Spirit we are fulfilled. And our substance is in our Father, God almighty, and our substance is in our Mother, God all wisdom, and our substance is in our Lord God, the Holy Spirit, all goodness, for our substance is whole in each person of the Trinity, who is one God. And our sensuality is only in the second person, Christ Jesus, in whom is the Father and the Holy Spirit; and in him and by him we are powerfully taken out of hell and out of the wretchedness on earth, and gloriously brought up into heaven, and blessedly united to our substance, increased in riches and nobility by all the power of Christ and by the grace and operation of the Holy Spirit.

THE FIFTY-NINTH CHAPTER

And we have all this bliss by mercy and grace, and this kind of bliss we never could have had and known, unless that property of goodness which is in God had been opposed, through which we have this bliss. For wickedness has been suffered to rise in opposition to that goodness; and the goodness of mercy and grace opposed that wickedness, and turned everything to goodness and honor for all who will be saved. For this is that property in God which opposes good to evil. So Jesus Christ, who opposes good to evil, is our true Mother. We have our being from him, where the foundation of motherhood begins, with all the sweet protection of love which endlessly follows.

As truly as God is our Father, so truly is God our Mother, and he revealed that in everything, and especially in these sweet words where he says: I am he; that is to say: I am he, the power and goodness of fatherhood; I am he, the wisdom and the lovingness of motherhood; I am he, the light and the grace which is all blessed love; I am he, the Trinity; I am he, the unity; I am he, the great supreme goodness of every kind of thing; I am he who makes you to love; I am he who makes you to long; I am he, the endless fulfilling of all true desires. For where the soul is highest, noblest, most honorable, still it is lowest, meekest and mildest.

And from this foundation in substance we have all the powers of our sensuality by the gift of nature, and by the help and the furthering of mercy and grace, without which we cannot profit. Our great Father, almighty God, who is being, knows us and loved us before time began. Out of this knowledge, in his most wonderful deep love, by the prescient eternal counsel of all the blessed Trinity, he wanted the second person to became our Mother, our brother and our saviour. From this it follows that as truly as God is our Father, so truly is God our Mother. Our Father wills, our Mother works, our good Lord the Holy Spirit confirms. And therefore it is our part to love our God in whom we have our being, reverently thanking and praising him for our creation, mightily praying to our Mother for mercy and pity, and to our Lord the Holy Spirit for help and grace. For in these three is all our life: nature, mercy and grace, of which we have mildness, patience and pity, and hatred of sin and wickedness; for the virtues must of themselves hate sin and wickedness.

And so Jesus is our true Mother in nature by our first creation, and he is our true Mother in grace by his taking our created nature, All the lovely works and all the sweet loving offices of beloved motherhood are appropriated to the second person, for in him we have this godly will, whole and safe forever, both in nature and in grace, from his own goodness proper to him.

I understand three ways of contemplating motherhood in God. The first is the foundation of our nature's creation; the second is his taking of our nature, where the motherhood of grace begins; the third is the motherhood at work. And in that, by the same grace, everything is penetrated, in length and in breadth, in height and in depth without end; and it is all one love.

The Sixtieth Chapter

But now I should say a little more about this penetration, as I understood our Lord to mean: How we are brought back by the motherhood of mercy and grace into our natural place, in which we were created by the motherhood of love, a mother's love which never leaves us.

Our Mother in nature, our Mother in grace, because he wanted altogether to become our Mother in all things, made the foundation of his work most humbly and most mildly in the maiden's womb. And he revealed that in the first revelation, when he brought that meek maiden before the eye of my understanding in the simple stature which she had when she conceived; that is to say that our great God, the supreme wisdom of all things, arrayed and prepared himself in this humble place, all ready in our poor flesh, himself to do the service and the office of motherhood in everything. The mother's service is nearest, readiest and surest: nearest because it is most natural, readiest because it is most loving, and surest because it is truest. No one ever might or could perform this office fully, except only him. We know that all our mothers bear us for pain and for death. O, what is that? But our true Mother Jesus, he alone bears us for joy and for endless life, blessed may he be. So he carries us within him in love and travail, until the full time when he wanted to suffer the sharpest thorns and cruel pains that ever were or will be, and at the last he died. And when he had finished, and had borne us so for bliss, still all this could not satisfy his wonderful love. And he revealed this in these great surpassing words of love: If I could suffer more, I would suffer more. He could not die any more, but he did not want to cease working; therefore he must needs nourish us, for the precious love of motherhood has made him our debtor.

The mother can give her child to suck of her milk, but our precious Mother Jesus can feed us with himself, and does, most courteously and most tenderly, with the blessed sacrament, which is the precious food of true life; and with all the sweet sacraments he sustains us most mercifully and graciously, and so he meant in these blessed words, where he said: I am he whom Holy Church preaches and teaches to you. That is to say: All the health and the life of the sacraments, all the power and the grace of my word, all the goodness which is ordained in Holy Church for you, I am he.

The mother can lay her child tenderly to her breast, but our tender Mother Jesus can lead us easily into his blessed breast through his sweet open side, and show us there a part of the godhead and of the joys of heaven, with inner certainty of endless bliss. And that he revealed in the tenth revelation, giving us the same understanding in these sweet words which he says: See, how I love you, looking into his blessed side, rejoicing.

This fair lovely word "mother" is so sweet and so kind in itself that it cannot truly be said of anyone or to anyone except of him and to him who is the true Mother of life and of all things. To the property of motherhood belong nature, love, wisdom and knowledge, and this is God. For though it may be so that our bodily bringing to birth is only little, humble and simple in comparison with our spiritual bringing to birth, still it is he who does it in the creatures by whom it is done. The kind, loving mother who knows and sees the need of her child guards it very tenderly, as the nature and condition of motherhood will have. And always as the child grows in age and in stature, she acts differently, but she does not change her love. And when it is even older, she allows it to be chastised to destroy its faults, so as to make the child receive virtues and grace. This work, with everything which is lovely and good, our Lord performs in those by whom it is done. So he is our Mother in nature by the operation of grace in the lower part, for love of the higher part. And he wants us to know it, for he wants to have all our love attached to him; and in this I saw that every debt which we owe by God's command to fatherhood and motherhood is fulfilled in truly loving God, which blessed love Christ works in us. And this was revealed in everything, and especially in the great bounteous words when he says: I am he whom you love.   *1393?*

Juliana Berners
ca. 1486

Also known as Julians Barnes, JULIANA BERNERS wrote a popular treatise, *The Book of Hunting* (also called *The Book of St. Albans*, 1486), as an instruction manual for young people of the landed gentry with increasing amounts of leisure time. Possibly the daughter of Sir James Berners, a courtier of Richard II, or perhaps the prioress of Sopwell Abbey near St. Albans, this countrywoman offered her guide in practical verse. An important influence on Berners's writing was William Twiti's fourteenth-century treatise *Craft of Venery*. While Berners's book is unusual because it was written by a woman, it is otherwise a conventional hunting manual in its linking of the seasons of the chase to holy feast days; its allusion to Tristram, a renowned hunter as well as the lover of Isolde in Arthurian legend; and its ritualized depiction of the ceremonial annunciation of the capture, accompanied by the sound of the horn. Although later versions of Berners's treatise added sections on fishing, hawking, and heraldry, her authorship has been established only on the hunting portion of the text.

Marcelle Thiebaux points out that while many medieval handbooks on hunting offer allegorical interpretations of beasts of the chase, associating the stag with Christ and the boar with Satan, Berners rejects such fancy in favor of a practical recitation of terminology and instruction. In this respect her book resembles fifteenth-century advice manuals that discuss chess, animal husbandry, weapons, and military strategy more than other hunting manuals. Moreover, Berners's use of maternal authority has caused some scholarly speculation that *The Book of St. Albans* might have been written as an advice book for her own sons or grandsons.

⤙ *from* The Book of Hunting ⤚

PROLOGUE

Just as these books about hawking are written to explain the terms of pleasure that concern gentlemen who delight in falconry, so, similarly, this book shows gentle persons how to hunt all sorts of beasts, whether they are beasts of venery or the chase, or "rascal." And it also explains all the terms used of the hounds, besides the animals we mentioned. And there is certainly a great variety of these terms, as this book will show.

1. BEASTS OF VENERY

Wherever you ride through wood or dell,
My dear child, take heed to what Tristram can tell
Of the beasts of venery you will find;
Attend to your mistress, and she'll teach you the kinds.
There are four kinds of beasts of venery:
The first is the hart, the second the hare,
    The boar is another
    And the wolf—there is no more.

2. BEASTS OF THE CHASE

And when you come to a plain or some place
I'll tell you which are the beasts of the chase:
One is the buck, another the doe,
The fox and the martron and the wild roe.
And you shall, my dear child, other beasts call—
Wherever you find them—"*rascals*" all.
    In wood or in dell
    Or in forest, as I tell.

3. THE AGE OF A HART

To speak of the hart—if you would hear—
Call him a calf in his first year,
The second year a "broket" you shall him call,
The third year a "spayad." Learn this all!
The fourth year, a "stag" call him always,
The fifth year, "a great stag," your mistress says,
    In the sixth year, "a hart" he's named.
    Do so, my child, while you have strength.

4. THE DIFFERENT HEADS OF THE HART

He's not a hart until his sixth year,
And if you'd like to speak further about this same deer
And of the horns he carries on his head—
A hart of the "first head" cannot be judged.
    In this we see
    Such diversity:

From his sixth year on, at the very least
You can judge the "perch" of this same beast.
When his antlers freely grow
"Royal" and "Surroyal," I call them so.
With two points on top, when you recognize them,
You may call him a "forked hart of ten."
And when there are three points on top of the same,
A "trochid hart of twelve" is his name.
When there are four points on the top of his head
He's termed "a summit hart of fourteen."
And beyond that, whatever happens,
However many his points—"summit" still is the term.

5. A HERD, A BEVY, A SOUNDER, A ROUT

My child, "herds" mean gatherings of hart and hind
And buck and doe, wherever they're found.
A "bevy" means roes, whatever place they're in,
And a "sounder" is for wild swine.
A "rout" is for wolves, where they may run.
That's what you call them, whatever the sum.
These beasts all
You shall them call.

                                                                    1486

—◄ ⚔ ►—

Dorothy Leigh
?–1616

The conduct book written by DOROTHY LEIGH for her children and other parents expresses its purpose in its lengthy title: "The Mother's Blessing, or The Godly Counsel of a gentlewoman not long since deceased, left behind for her children, containing many good exhortations and godly admonitions, profitable for all parents to leave as a legacy to their children, but especially for those who, by reason of their young years, stand most in need of instruction." Published after Leigh's death in 1616, *The Mother's Blessing* was one of the most popular advice manuals of its era; it was reissued nineteen times between 1616 and 1640 and was unusual in that the author did not apologize for writing for a public audience—an act that challenged prescribed notions of womanly propriety. The book consists of four sections: "Counsel to My Children"; an allegorical introductory poem about the industry of bees; two dedications, one political and one personal; and a lengthy guide to filial and spiritual conduct.

All that is known of Leigh's life comes from the book itself. Her first dedication reveals the identity of a patron, Princess Elizabeth, the eldest daughter of King James and Queen Anne of Denmark and a strong Protestant whose religious views Leigh apparently shared. As Randall Martin points out, by appealing to Elizabeth for protection Leigh implicitly acknowledges that her moderate Puritan views depart from those espoused by King James, who desired peaceful relations with Rome and was therefore cautious in promoting Protestant policies abroad. Leigh's second dedication denotes her status as a widow with three young sons; in it she explains her purpose in writing the manual and asserts her late husband's wishes that their children be educated to "follow God's counsel." In the conduct book's first chapters she addresses the boys directly, urging them to "labour for the spiritual food of the soul" and to consider entering the ministry. Leigh also implores other parents to teach their children to read so that they might better "serve God, their King and country." Subsequent chapters examine child-rearing practices and marriage in surprisingly modern ways. One chapter advances the then-radical view that servants should be made literate, for their own sake and for the well-being of the households that employed them.

In her treatise Leigh establishes motherhood as the authority that sanctions her right to public instruction. As Wendy Wall has noted, Renaissance women who wrote maternal conduct books offered their children spiritual legacies in part because they could not bequeath money or land. *The Mother's Blessing* thus testifies not only to the role of maternal nurture but also to the insistence of early women writers that wisdom was theirs to share. Although these women lacked legal control over their children, through writing they could assume "proprietorship in another realm" and thereby have an impact on their children's well-being.

ᴴ *from* The Mother's Blessing, or The Godly Counsel of a Gentlewoman, Not Long Since Deceased, Left Behind Her for Her Children ᴱ

THE OCCASION OF WRITING THIS BOOK WAS THE CONSIDERATON OF THE CARE OF PARENTS FOR THEIR CHILDREN

My children, when I did truly weigh, rightly consider, and perfectly see the great care, labor, travail, and continual study which parents take to enrich their children—some wearing their bodies with labor, some breaking their sleeps with care, some sparing from their own bellies, and many hazarding their souls, some by bribery, some by simony, others by perjury, and a multitude by usury, some stealing on the sea, others begging by land portions from every poor man, not caring if the whole commonwealth be impoverished so their children be enriched (for themselves they can be content with meat, drink and cloth, so that their children by their means may be made rich, always abusing this portion of the scripture: "he that provideth not for his own family, is worse than an infidel"), ever seeking for the temporal things of this world and forgetting those things which be eternal—when I considered these things, I say I thought it good (being not desirous to enrich you with transitory goods) to exhort and desire you to follow the counsel of Christ: "First seek the kingdom of God and his righteousness, and then all these things shall be administered unto you."

THE FIRST CAUSE OF WRITING IS A MOTHERLY AFFECTION

But lest you should marvel, my children, why I do not , according to the usual custom of women, exhort you by word and admonitions rather than by writing (a thing so unusual among us, and especially in such time when there be so many godly books in the world that they mould in some men's studies while their masters are marred because they will not meditate upon them, as many men's garments moth-eat in their chests while their Christian brethren quake with cold in the street for want of covering), know therefore that it was the motherly affection that I bare unto you all which made me now (as it often hath done heretofore) forget myself in regard of you. Neither care I what you or any shall think of me if among many words I may write but one sentence which may make you labor for the spiritual food of the soul, which must be gathered every day out of the word, as the children of Israel gathered manna in the wilderness. By the which you may see it is a labor. But what labor? A pleasant labor, a profitable labor, a labor without the which the soul cannot live. For as the children of Israel must needs starve except they gathered every day in the wilderness and fed of it, so must your souls, except you gather the spiritual manna out of the word every day and feed of it continually. . . . Whereas if you desire any food for your souls that is not in the written word of God, your souls die with it even in your hearts and mouths. Even as they that desired other food, died with it in their mouths, were it never so dainty, so shall you, and there is no recovery for you.

CHILDREN TO BE TAUGHT BETIMES AND BROUGHT UP GENTLY

I am further also to entreat you that all your children may be taught to read, beginning at four years old or before. And let them learn till ten, in which time they are not able to do any good in the commonwealth but to learn how to serve God, their king and country, by reading. And I desire, entreat, and earnestly beseech you and every one of you that you will have your children brought up with much gentleness and patience. What disposition so ever they be of, gentleness will soonest bring them to virtue. For forwardness and curstness doth harden the heart of a child and maketh him weary of virtue. Among the forward thou shalt learn forwardness. Let them therefore be gently used and always kept from idleness, and bring them up in the schools of learning, if you be able and they fit for it. If they will not be scholars, yet I hope they will be able by God's grace to read the Bible, the law of God, and to be brought to some good vocation or calling of life. Solomon saith, "Teach a child in his youth the trade of his life, and he will not forget it or depart from it when he is old."

CHOICE OF WIVES

Now for your wives the Lord direct you, for I cannot tell you what is best to be done. Our Lord saith, "First seek the kingdom of God and his righteousness, and all things else shall be ministered unto you." First you must seek a godly wife, that she may be a help to you in godliness; for God said, "It is not good for man to be alone, let him have a helper meet for him." And she cannot be meet for him except she be truly godly; for God counteth that the man is alone still if his wife be not godly. . . .

"Be not unequally yoked" saith the Holy Ghost. It is indeed very unequal for the godly and ungodly to be united together, that their hearts must be both as one, which can never be joined in the fear of God and faith of Christ. Love not the ungodly. Marry with none except you love her, and be not changeable in your love. Let nothing, after you have made your choice, remove your love from her; for it is an ungodly and very foolish thing of a man to mislike his own choice, especially since God hath given a man much choice among the godly; and it was a great cause that moved God to command his [followers] to marry with the godly, that there might be a continual agreement between them.

IT IS GREAT FOLLY FOR A MAN TO MISLIKE HIS OWN CHOICE

Methinks I never saw a man show a more senseless simplicity than in misliking his own choice, when God hath given a man almost a world of women to choose him a wife in. If a man hath not wit enough to choose him one whom he can love to the end, yet methinks he should have discretion to cover his own folly. But if he want discretion, methinks he should have policy, which never fails a man to dissemble his own simplicity in this case. If he want wit, discretion, and policy, he is unfit to marry any woman. Do not a woman that wrong as to take her from her friends that love her and after a while to begin to hate her. If she have no friends, yet thou knowest not but that she may have a husband that may love her. If thou canst not love her to the end, leave her to him that can. Methinks my son could not offend me in any thing, if he served God, except he chose a wife that he could not love to the end. I need not say if he served God, for if he served God he would obey God, and then he would choose a godly wife and live lovingly and godly with her, and not do as some man who taketh a woman to make her a companion and fellow, and after he hath her, he makes her a servant and drudge. If she be thy wife, she is always too good to be thy servant, and worthy to be thy fellow. If thou wilt have a good wife, thou must go before her in all goodness and show her a pattern of all good virtues by thy godly and discreet life, and especially in patience, according to the counsel of the Holy Ghost: 'Bear with the woman, as with the weaker vessel.' Here God showeth that it is her imperfection that honoreth thee, and that it is thy perfection that maketh thee to bear with her. Follow the counsel of God, therefore, and bear with her. God willed a man to leave father and mother for his wife. This showeth what an excellent love God did appoint to be between man and wife. In truth I cannot by any means set down the excellency of that love. But this I assure you, that if you get wives that be godly, and you love them, you shall not need to forsake me. Whereas if you have wives that you love not, I am sure I will forsake you. Do not yourselves that wrong as to marry a woman you cannot love. Show not so much childishness in your sex as to say you loved her once, and now your mind is changed. If thou canst not love her for the goodness that is in her, yet let the grace that is in thyself move thee to do it. And so I leave thee to the Lord, whom I pray to guide both thee and her with his grace, and grant that you may choose godlily, and live happily, and die comfortably through faith in Jesus Christ.

HOW TO DEAL WITH SERVANTS

Yet one thing I am to desire you to do at my request and for my sake; and though it be some trouble to you to perform it, yet I assure myself you will do it. If God shall at any time give you or any of you a servant or servants, you shall ask them if they can read. If they cannot you shall, at my request, teach them or cause them to be taught till they can read the ten commandments of almighty God. And then you shall persuade them to practice by themselves and to spend all their idle time in reading that so they may come the better to know the will of God written in his word. Remember, your servants are God's servants as well as yours. If they be not, say as David said: "There shall not an ungodly person dwell in my house; he that loveth or maketh lies shall depart out of my sight."

It is not for you by any means to keep any ungodly, profane, or wicked person in your house, for they bring a curse upon the place wherein they are and not a blessing, neither will they be taught any goodness. But you must keep those that be tractable and willing to serve God, that he may bless you and your household. For God doth not delight in that master that will suffer his servant to blaspheme his name or to misspend his sabbaths. For God commanded the master that he should see his servants to keep holy the sabbath day; and if he keep that day holy, he will learn to spend all the other days in the week well, in following the duties of his calling. I pray you keep the servants of God, and then remember they are your brethren. Use them well, and be as ready to do them good as to have their service. Be not chiding for every trifle, for that will hinder good living, and nothing enrich you. Be careful that they be godly, for "godliness hath the promise of this present life and of the life to come; godliness is great in riches if a man be contented with that he hath. For we brought nothing with us into this world, neither shall we carry anything out of the world; if we have food and raiment, let us therewith be contented."   *1616*

Elizabeth Clinton, the Countess of Lincoln
1574?–1632

One of the earliest women to endorse publicly the importance of breast-feeding was a Renaissance countess, ELIZABETH CLINTON. An impassioned plea for women to nurse their own children, *The Countess of Lincoln's Nursery* (1622) was directed to an upper-class audience who typically entrusted the breast-feeding of their infants to servants, or "wet-nurses," who had recently given birth themselves. Blending polemic and autobiography, Clinton acknowledges in this advice manual that she did not breast-feed her own children and now regrets it. Moreover, she cites as exemplary nursing mothers an array of Biblical women who obeyed this "ordinance of God," among them Eve, Sarah, Hannah, and Mary. Her presentation of the nursing Virgin is especially vivid in its bodily imagery: "as her womb bare our blessed saviour, so her paps gave him suck."

Clinton's treatise develops an argument based on physicians' authority, social propriety, and moral imperative. Most doctors recommend breast-feeding as physically and mentally healthier for babies, she insists. Although Clinton acknowledges that noblemen sometimes disapprove of their wives' nursing—the practice was widely viewed as inappropriate in public and sexually unattractive—she encourages women to explain to their husbands that it strengthens the bond between mother and child. In promoting child welfare she applauds the humanistic values endorsed by the prominent Dutch educator Desiderus Erasmus, whose 1523 essay "The New Mother" also advocated breast-feeding for ethical reasons. As the scholar Randall Martin notes, however, Clinton goes further than Erasmus in claiming that wet-nursing exploited working-class women by keeping them from devoting full attention to their own infants. In addition, it forced them to bond physically with children to whom they had no emotional connection and toward whom they might feel resentment.

In his preface to *The Countess of Lincoln's Nursery* Dr. Lodge praises Clinton for her high social standing, the uniqueness of her approach to her topic, and her brevity of words. In fact, the treatise is rather lengthy and Clinton's argument a complex one, based not only on authoritative Biblical and medical sources but also on her own wealth of experience as the mother of eighteen. She would have nursed her children, Clinton insists, but she was "overruled by another's authority"—perhaps a reference to the will of her husband, who had died two years earlier, thus freeing her to write her treatise. The book was dedicated to her daughter-in-law, whose decision to breast-feed pleased her greatly.

Clinton's treatise is well-organized, rhetorically skillful, and consistently pious; she uses both God's words and "His Works" as her proof. Children are "God's gift," she intones, and nursing a God-given duty as well as a privilege and a pleasure. Maternal duty and a sense of fairness combine in this early woman writer's unorthodox approach to the politics of motherhood.

⊰ *from* The Countess of Lincoln's Nursery ⊱

Because it hath pleased God to bless me with many children, and so caused me to observe many things falling out to mothers and to their children, I thought it good to open my mind concerning a special matter belonging to all childbearing women seriously to consider of, and to manifest my mind the better, even to write of this matter so far as God shall please to direct me. In sum, the matter I mean is the duty of nursing due by mothers to their own children.

In setting down whereof, I will first show that every woman ought to nurse her own child, and secondly, I will endeavour to answer such objections as are used to be cast out against this duty to disgrace the same.

The first point is easily performed. For it is the express ordinance of God that mothers should nurse their own children, and being his ordinance, they are bound to it in conscience. This should stop the mouths of all repliers. For God is most wise and therefore must needs know what is fittest and best for us to do. And to prevent all foolish fears or shifts, we are given to understand that he is also all sufficient, and therefore infinitely able to bless his own ordinance and to afford us means in ourselves (as continual experience confirmeth) toward the observance thereof.

If this (as it ought) be granted, then how venturous are those women that dare venture to do otherwise and so to refuse, and by refusing to despise, that order which the most wise and almighty God hath appointed, and instead thereof to choose their own pleasures? Oh what peace can there be to these women's consciences, unless through the darkness of their understanding they judge it no disobedience?

And then they will drive me to prove that this nursing and nourishing of their own children in their own bosoms is God's ordinance. They are very willful or very ignorant if they make a question of it. For it is proved sufficiently to be their duty, both by God's word and also by his works.

By his word it is proved first by examples, namely the example of Eve. For who suckled her sons Cain, Abel, Seth, etc. but herself? Which she did not only of mere necessity because yet no other woman was created, but especially because she was their mother and so saw it was her duty, and because she had a true natural affection which moved her to do it gladly. Next the example of Sarah the wife of Abraham. For she both gave her son Isaac suck, as doing the duty commanded of God, and also took great comfort and delight therein as in a duty well-pleasing to herself, whence she spake of it as of an action worthy to be named in her holy rejoicing. Now if Sarah, so great a princess, did nurse her own child, why should any of us neglect to do the like, except (which God forbid) we think scorn to follow her, whose daughters it is our glory to be, and which we be only upon this condition, that we imitate her well-doing? Let us look therefore to her worthy pattern, noting withal that she put herself to this work when she was very old, and so might the better have excused herself than we younger women can, being also more able to hire and keep a nurse than any of us. . . .

But now to another worthy example, namely that excellent woman Hannah who, having after much affliction of mind obtained a son of God whom she vowed unto God, she did not put him to another to nurse, but nursed him her own self until she had weaned him and carried him to be consecrate unto the Lord, as well knowing that this duty of giving her child suck was so acceptable to God, as for the cause thereof, she did not sin in staying with it at home from the yearly sacrifice. But now women, especially of any place and of little grace, do not hold this duty acceptable to God because it is unacceptable to themselves, as if they would have the Lord to like and dislike according to their vain lusts.

To proceed, take notice of one example more, that is of the blessed Virgin. As her womb bore our blessed saviour, so her paps gave him suck. Now whom shall deny their own mother's suckling of their own children to be their duty, since every godly matron hath walked in these steps before them: Eve the mother of all the living, Sarah the mother of all the faithful, Hannah so graciously heard of God, Mary blessed among women and called blessed of all ages? And who can say but that the rest of holy women mentioned in the holy scriptures did the like, since no doubt that speech of that noble dame, saying "Who would have said to Abraham that Sarah should have given children suck?", was taken from the ordinary custom of mothers in those less corrupted times?

And so much for proof of this office and duty to be God's ordinance by his own word according to the argument of examples. I hope I shall likewise prove it by the same word from plain precepts. First from that precept which willeth the younger women to marry and to bear children; that is, not only to bear them in the womb and to bring them forth, but also to bear them on their knee, in their arms, and at their breasts. For this bearing a little before is called nourishing and bringing up. And to enforce it the better upon women's consciences, it is numbered as the first of the good works for which godly women should be well reported of. And well it may be the first; because if holy ministers or other Christians do hear of a good woman to be brought to bed and her child to be living, their first question usually is whether she herself give it suck, yea or no. If the answer be she doth, then they commend her. If the answer be she doth not, then they are sorry for her.

And thus I come to a second precept. I pray you, who that judges aright doth not hold the suckling of her own child the part of a true mother, of an honest mother, of a just mother, of a sincere mother, of a mother worthy of love, of a mother deserving good report, of a virtuous mother, of a mother winning praise for it? All this is assented to by any of good understanding. Therefore this is also a precept. As for other duties, so for this of mothers to their children, which saith "Whatsoever things are true, whatsoever things are honest, whatsoever things are just, whatsoever things are pure, whatsoever things be worthy of love, whatsoever things be of good report, if there be any virtue, if there be any praise, think on these things, these things do, and the God of peace shall be with you." . . .

And so I come to the last part of my promise, which is to answer objections made by divers against this duty of mothers to their children.

First it is objected that Rebekah had a nurse and that therefore her mother did not give her suck of her own breasts, and so good women in the first ages did not hold them to this office of nursing their own children. To this I answer that if her mother had milk and health and yet did put this duty from her to another, it was her fault, and so proveth nothing against me. But it is manifest that she that Rebekah calleth her nurse was called so either for that she most tended her while her mother suckled her, or for that she weaned her, or for that, during her nonage and childhood, she did minister to her continually such good things as delighted and nourished her up. For to any one of these the name of a nurse is fitly given, whence a good wife is called her husband's nurse. And that Rebekah's nurse was only such a one appeareth, because afterward she is not named a nurse but a maid, saying, "Then Rebekah rose, and her maids" . . .

Secondly it is objected that it is troublesome, that it is noisome to one's clothes, that it makes one look old, etc. All such reasons are uncomely and unchristian to be objected, and therefore unworthy to be answered. They argue unmotherly affection, idleness, desire to have liberty to gad from home, pride, foolish fineness, lust, wantonness, and the like evils. Ask Sarah, Hannah, the blessed Virgin, and any modest loving mother what trouble they accounted it to give their little ones suck? Behold most nursing mothers and they be as clean and sweet in their clothes, and carry their age, and hold their beauty, as well as those that suckle not. And most likely are they so to do because, keeping God's ordinance, they are sure of God's blessing. And it hath been observed in some women that they grew more beautiful and better favored by very nursing their own children.

But there are some women that object from fear, saying that they are so weak and so tender that they are afraid to venture to give their children suck lest they endanger their health thereby. Of these I demand why then they did venture to marry and so to bear children? And if they say they could not choose and that they thought not that marriage would impair their health, I answer that for the same reasons they should set themselves to nurse their own children because they should not choose but do what God would have them do. And they should believe that this work will be for their health also, seeing it is ordinary with the Lord to give good stomach, health, and strength to almost all mothers that take this pain with their children.

One answer more to all the objections that use to be made against giving children suck is this: that now the hardness to effect this matter is much removed by a late example of a tender young lady; and you may all be encouraged to follow after in that wherein she hath gone before you and so made the way more easy and more hopeful by that which she findeth possible and comfortable by God's blessing, and no offense to her lord nor herself. She might have had as many doubts and lets as any of you, but she was willing to try how God would enable her; and he hath given her good success, as I hope he will do to others that are willing to trust in God for his help.

Now if any reading these few lines return against me that it may be I myself have given my own children suck and therefore am bolder and more busy to meddle in urging this point, to the end to insult over and to make them to be blamed that have not done it, I answer that, whether I have or have not performed this my bounden duty, I will not deny to tell my own practice. I know and acknowledge that I should have done it, and having not done it, it was not for want of will in myself, but partly I was overruled by another's authority, and partly deceived by some's ill counsel, and partly I had not so well considered of my duty in this motherly office as since I did, when it was too late for me to put it in execution. Wherefore, being pricked in heart for my undutifulness, this way I study to redeem my peace: first by repentance towards God, humbly and often craving his pardon for this my offense; secondly by studying how to show double love to my children, to make them amends for neglect of this part of love to them when they should have hung on my breasts and have been nourished in mine own bosom; thirdly by doing my endeavour to prevent many Christian mothers from sinning in the same kind against our most loving and gracious God. . . .

Do you submit yourselves to the pain and trouble of this ordinance of God? Trust not other women, whom wages hire to do it, better than yourselves, whom God and nature ties to do it. I have found by grievous experience such dissembling in nurses, pretending sufficiency of milk when indeed they had too much scarcity, pretending willingness, towardness, wakefulness, when indeed they have been most wilful, most forward, and most slothful, as I fear the death of one or two of my little babes came by the default of their nurses. Of all those which I had for eighteen children, I had but two which were thoroughly willing and careful. Divers have had their children miscarry in the nurse's hands; and are such mothers (if it were by the nurse's carelessness) guiltless? I know not how they should, since they will shut them out of the arms of nature and leave them to the will of a stranger, yea, to one that will seem to estrange herself from her own child to give suck to the nurse-child. This she may fain to do upon a covetous composition, but she frets at it in her mind if she have any natural affection.

Therefore be no longer at the trouble and at the care to hire others to do your own work. Be not so unnatural to thrust away your own children. Be not so hardy as to venture a tender babe to a less tender heart. Be not accessory to that disorder of causing a poorer woman to banish her own infant for the entertaining of a richer woman's child, as it were, bidding her unlove her own to love yours. . . .

Think always that, having the child at your breast and having it in your arms, you have God's blessing there. For children are God's blessings. Think again how your babe crying for your breast, sucking heartily the milk out of it and growing by it, is the Lord's own instruction, every hour and every day that you are suckling it, instructing you to show that you are his newborn babes by your earnest desire after his word and the sincere doctrine thereof; and by your daily growing in grace and goodness thereby, so shall you reap pleasure and profit. Again, you may consider that when your child is at your breast, it is a fit occasion to move your heart to pray for a blessing upon that work and to give thanks for your child, and for ability and freedom unto that which many a mother would have done and could not, who have tried and ventured their health and taken much pains and yet have not obtained their desire. But they that are fitted every way for this commendable act have certainly great cause to be thankful. And I much desire that God may have glory and praise for every good work, and you much comfort that do seek to honor God in all things. Amen.   *1622*

Anne Bradstreet
1612–1672

"To sing of wars, of captains, and of kings, / Of cities founded, commonwealths begun / For my mean pen are too superior things," claims ANNE BRADSTREET, stereotypically feminine in her modesty about her verse. Addressing political, social, and domestic issues in her poems, Bradstreet might have remained a private poet had not her brother-in-law, John Woodbridge, taken a collection of her verse to England, where he published it in 1650 as *The Tenth Muse Lately Sprung up in America*—without her permission, though possibly with her knowledge. Certainly her Puritan community would have considered it inappropriate for a woman to publish her own work, and in his preface Woodbridge assures prospective readers that Bradstreet's poetry "is the fruit of some few hours, curtailed from sleep and other refreshments."

Bradstreet was born in Northampton, England, to Thomas Dudley, a steward at the mansion of the Earl of Lincolnshire, and his wife, Dorothy Yorke. As a child she was tutored by her father in Greek, Latin, Hebrew, and English literature, thus receiving an unusually fine education for a girl of her times. In 1630 she came to America with her parents and her new husband, Simon Bradstreet, a Cambridge graduate; devout Puritans, her father and husband felt it was their "divine destiny" to found the Massachusetts Bay Colony. Bradstreet later acknowledged that she did not initially share their Puritan zeal: "I came into this country, where I found a new world and new manners, at which my heart rose. But after I was convinced it was the way of God, I submitted to it and joined the church at Boston." Certainly conditions at Salem were appalling: housing was makeshift, food minimal, illness rampant. Eventually, however, the Puritans made New England into a home, and Bradstreet supported her husband during his years as governor of the colony. Their marriage was by all accounts happy, as her poems to Simon reveal: "If ever two were one, then surely we, / If ever man were lov'd by wife, then thee."

Although much of her poetry is conventional in its Puritan beliefs, some of it admits religious doubt. The many hardships that they encountered in the "New World," including frequent deaths from fevers and terrible winters, caused Bradstreet and her family great "affliction" and may have contributed to her skepticism. *Contemplations*, a long poem that depicts the soul's struggle between worldly and spiritual values, anticipates nineteenth-century Romanticism in its lyrical introspection. Other philosophical works include "The Four Elements" and "Of the Four Humors in Man's Constitution," in which she laments a world in which the elements—earth, air, fire, and water—are at war with the humors—blood, choler, phlegm, and melancholy. Moreover, Bradstreet's assertions on behalf of women constitute a surprising form of rebellion, given that she witnessed the expulsion from Massachusetts Bay of Ann Hutchinson, who defied Puritan edict by holding religious meetings in her home. For this Hutchinson was tried and exiled, since women were not allowed public spiritual expression. In fact, both Thomas Dudley and Simon Bradstreet sat on the board of magistrates that convicted Hutchinson. Nonetheless, in her "Prologue" to *The Tenth Muse*, Bradstreet offers a spirited defense of women's right to write and a condemnation of men who undermine it. Her protofeminist views can also be seen in her homage to Queen Elizabeth, in which she recalls the happy time when this strong woman ruled England.

A dedicated mother, Bradstreet wrote many poems for and about her eight children. *Meditations Divine and Moral*, written for her son Simon, explores her religious doubts and beliefs in terse aphorisms. "The Author to Her Book" links motherhood and creativity, with the anxious poet addressing the literary progeny whom she must launch into the world despite her reservations. Other poems reveal a mother's fear before the birth of her child and the tender care with which she regards her "brood of chicks" well into their adulthood.

⇥ The Author to Her Book ⇤

Thou ill-formed offspring of my feeble brain,
Who after birth did'st by my side remain,
Till snatched from thence by friends, less wise than true
Who thee abroad, exposed to public view;
5   Made thee in rags, halting to th' press to trudge,
Where errors were not lessened (all may judge)
At thy return my blushing was not small,
My rambling brat (in print) should mother call,
I cast thee by as one unfit for light,
10   Thy visage was so irksome in my sight;
Yet being mine own, at length affection would
Thy blemishes amend, if so I could:
I wash'd thy face, but more defects I saw,
And rubbing off a spot, still made a flaw.
15   I stretched thy joints to make thee even feet,
Yet still thou run'st more hobbling than is meet;
In better dress to trim thee was my mind,
But nought save homespun cloth, i'th' house I find.
In this array, 'mongst vulgars mayst thou roam
20   In critics' hands, beware thou dost not come;
And take thy way where yet thou art not known,
If for thy father asked, say, thou hadst none:

And for thy mother, she alas is poor,
Which caused her thus to send thee out of door.

1678

⊰ Before the Birth of One of Her Children ⊱

All things within this fading world hath end,
Adversity doth still our joys attend;
No ties so strong, no friends so dear and sweet,
But with death's parting blow is sure to meet.
5   The sentence past is most irrevocable,
A common thing, yet oh inevitable;
How soon, my dear, death may my steps attend,
How soon't may be thy lot to lose thy friend,
We both are ignorant, yet love bids me
10   These farewell lines to recommend to thee,
That when that knot's untied that made us one,
I may seem thine, who in effect am none.
And if I see not half my days that's due,
What nature would, God grant to yours and you;
15   The many faults that well you know I have,
Let be interred in my oblivious grave;
If any worth or virtue were in me,
Let that live freshly in thy memory
And when thou feel'st no grief, as I no harms,
20   Yet love thy dead, who long lay in thine arms:
And when thy loss shall be repaid with gains
Look to my little babes my dear remains.
And if thou love thy self, or loved'st me
These O protect from step dame's injury.
25   And if chance to thine eyes shall bring this verse,
With some sad sighs honor my absent hearse;
And kiss this paper for thy love's dear sake,
Who with salt tears this last farewell did take.

1678

⊰ In Reference to her Children, 23 June, 1656 ⊱

I had eight birds hatched in one nest,
Four Cocks there were, and Hens the rest,
I nursed them up with pain and care,
Nor cost, nor labor did I spare,
5   Till at the last they felt their wing,
Mounted the Trees, and learned to sing;
Chief of the Brood then took his flight,
To Regions far, and left me quite:
My mournful chirps I after send,
10   Till he return , or I do end,

Leave not thy nest, thy Dam and Sire,
Fly back and sing amidst this Choir.
My second bird did take her flight,
And with her mate flew out of sight;
15   *Southward* they both their course did bend,
And Seasons twain they there did spend:
Till after blown by *Southern* gales,
They *Norward* steered with filled sails.
A prettier bird was nowhere seen,
20   Along the Beach among the treen.
I have a third of color white,
On whom I placed no small delight;
Coupled with mate loving and true,
Hath also bid her Dam adieu:
25   And where *Aurora* first appears,
She now hath perched, to spend her years;
One to the Academy flew
To chat among that learned crew:
Ambition moves still in his breast
30   That he might chant above the rest,
Striving for more than to do well,
That nightingales he might excel.
My fifth, whose down is yet scarce gone
Is 'mongst the shrubs and bushes flown,
35   And as his wings increase in strength,
On higher boughs he'll perch at length.
My other three, still with me nest,
Until they're grown, then as the rest,
Or here or there, they'll take their flight,
40   As is ordained, so shall they light.
If birds could weep, then would my tears
Let others know what are my fears
Lest this my brood some harm should catch,
And be surprised for want of watch,
45   Whilst pecking corn, and void of care
They fall un'wares in fowler's snare:
Or whilst on trees they sit and sing,
Some untoward boy at them do fling:
Or whilst allured with bell and glass,
50   The net be spread, and caught, alas.
Or least by lime-twigs they be foiled,
Or by some greedy hawks be spoiled.
O would my young, ye saw my breast,
And knew what thoughts there sadly rest,
55   Great was my pain when I you bred,
Great was my care, when I you fed,
Long did I keep you soft and warm,
And with my wings kept off all harm,
My cares are more, and fears than ever,
60   My throbs such now, as 'fore were never:

Alas my birds, you wisdom want,
Of perils you are ignorant,
Oft times in grass, on trees, in flight,
Sore accidents on you may light.
65   O to your safety have an eye,
So happy may you live and die:
Meanwhile my days in tunes I'll spend,
Till my weak lays with me shall end.
In shady woods I'll sit and sing,
70   And things that past, to mind I'll bring.
Once young and pleasant, as are you,
But former toys (no joys) adieu.
My age I will not once lament,
But sing, my time so near is spent.
75   And from the top bough take my flight,
Into a country beyond sight,
Where old ones, instantly grow young,
And there with Seraphims set song:
No seasons cold, nor storms they see;
80   But spring lasts to eternity,
When each of you shall in your nest
Among your young ones take your rest,
In chirping language, oft them tell,
You had a dam that loved you well,
85   That did what could be done for young,
And nursed you up till you were strong,
And 'fore she once would let you fly,
She shew'd you joy and misery;
Taught what was good, and what was ill,
90   What would save life, and what would kill?
Thus gone, amongst you I may live,
And dead, yet speak, and counsel give:
Farewell my birds, farewell adieu,
I happy am, if well with you.

1678

＋◄ Ⱟ◆Ⱟ ►＋

Lady Mary Wortley Montagu
1689–1762

"Keep my letters," LADY MARY WORLEY MONTAGU instructed her daughter, Lady Mary Bute, just prior to her death. "They will be as good as Madame de Sevigne's forty years hence." This reference to France's distinguished letter writer reveals Montagu's literary ambitions, despite the fact that few of her poems, essays, and letters were published in her lifetime. What did appear was published anonymously, since as an aristocrat she viewed commercial publication with ambivalence.

Montagu was born into a wealthy Whig family, the granddaughter of the diarist John Evelyn; her father was Evelyn Pierrepont, Earl of Kingston, her mother Lady Mary Fielding. Although she received little formal education, she taught herself Latin and, according to family accounts, never forgot anything she read. Lady Mary wrote poems as a child and compiled her first book, *Poems*,

Songs, Etc., in 1703 at age fourteen. In her late teens she was briefly tutored by Bishop Gilbert Burnet, to whom she expressed gratitude for "condescending to direct the studies of a girl." After a lengthy and tumultuous courtship she eloped in 1712 with Sir Edward Wortley Montagu, the brother of a close friend; her father disapproved of the marriage largely because he had chosen for his daughter a different suitor Although Montagu's marriage proved unhappy, it brought her the opportunity to travel to Turkey when her husband was named ambassador. *Embassy to Constantinople*, a collection of letters recounting her adventures there—she often roamed the streets dressed as a man—was published a year after her death. Although Montagu aspired to be a dramatist, her adaptation of Marivaux's *Le jeu de l'amour et du hasard*, which she entitled *Simplicity*, was never published or produced. Among her finest essays are the nine that she wrote for a journal she originated, *The Nonsense of Common Sense*, which attacked a prominent political newspaper opposed to the ministry of Sir Robert Walpole. She wrote a humorous piece on women's rights for the *Spectator*, and one unpublished essay advocates romantic love between husband and wife. In addition, she composed several influential essays advocating innoculation against smallpox, a practice that she had witnessed in Turkey and successfully introduced in England. Montagu moved to Italy in 1736 to pursue a relationship with a younger man, Francesco Algarotti; although this failed, she remained in Europe until her husband's death in 1761.

Throughout her life Lady Mary kept a journal; her daughter inherited and ultimately burned it, as her mother had requested. One probable reason for her wish to destroy her diary was the vehemence with which Montagu attacked her enemies. Literary rivalries were rampant in the eighteenth century, and hers were especially bitter. Although she had initially been friendly with the poet Alexander Pope, Montagu claimed that the two began to feud because the misshapen Pope tried to woo her and she laughed at him. Whatever the cause, she satirized Pope brutally in "Imitation of the Second Book of Horace," a poem on which she collaborated with Lord Hervey. Pope was equally vengeful, portraying her as the unkempt Sappho in *Epistle II: To a Lady*. In his *Life of Pope*, Dr. Samuel Johnson, the eighteenth-century wit, recounted that at one dinner party "the table was infested with Lady Mary Wortley"; she and Pope argued so vehemently that eventually "the one or the other quitted the house." Montagu also feuded with Horace Walpole, who represents her in his writing as a ridiculous figure. Yet Lady Mary seems to have been undaunted by such misogyny. She was a friend and supporter of many women writers, including MARY ASTELL, who shared her view that women could be as accomplished as men. Montagu also had male allies: Through her husband she became friendly with Joseph Addison and Richard Steele, publishers of the *Spectator*, and she was close to her cousin Henry Fielding and an admirer of his picaresque novel *Tom Jones*.

Montagu wrote nearly nine hundred letters during her lifetime, many of which were collected in *Letters and Works* (1837), published by her nephew, Lord Wharncliffe. Among the most engaging are those written to her daughter while Montagu was living in Italy and France. A number of letters recount her social life abroad and recall memories of London, while others express concern over her daughter's well-being and the education of her grandchildren. That Lady Bute heeded her mother's instruction to educate her daughter is evident in the writings of Lady Louisa Stuart, who in 1837 composed a biography of her grandmother's life. *Anecdotes of Lady M.W. Montagu* enhanced Montagu's literary reputation in the nineteenth century and bore witness to the close affiliation of grandmother, daughter, and granddaughter.

⊰ To Lady Bute ⊱

My Dear Child,

I am extremely concern'd to hear you complain of ill Health at a Time of Life when you ought to be in the Flower of your strength. I hope I need not recommend to you the care of it. The tenderness you have for your children is sufficient to enforce you to the utmost regard for the preservation of a Life so necessary to their well being. I do not doubt your Prudence in their Education, neither can I say anything particular relating to it at this Distance, different Tempers requiring different management. In General, never attempt to govern them (as most people do) by Deceit; if they find themselves cheated (even in Trifles) it will so far lessen the Authority of their Instructor as to make them neglect all their future admonitions. And (if possible) breed them free from Prejudices; those contracted in the Nursery often influence the whole Life after, of which I have seen many Melancholy Examples.

I shall say no more of this Subject, nor would have said this little if you had not asked my advice. 'Tis much easier to give Rules than to practice them. I am sensible my own Natural Temper is too Indulgent. I think it the least dangerous Error, yet still it is an Error. I can only say with Truth that I do not know in my whole Life having ever endeavored to impose on you or give a false color to anything that I represented to you. If your Daughters are inclined to Love reading, do not check their Inclination by hindering them of the diverting part of it. It is as necessary for the Amusement of Women as the Reputation of Men; but teach them not to expect or desire any Applause from it. Let their Brothers shine, and let them content themselves with making their Lives easier by it, which I experimentally know is more effectually done by Study than any other way. Ignorance is as much the Fountain of Vice as Idleness, and indeed generally produces it. People that do not read or work for a Livelihood have many hours they know not how to employ, especially Women, who commonly fall into Vapors or something worse. I am afraid you'll think this Letter very tedious. Forgive it as coming from your most affectionate mother,

M.W.

My Compliments to Lord Bute and Blessing to my Grandchildren.   *1750*

⊰ To Lady Bute ⊱

My Dear Child,

I gave you some general Thoughts on the Education of your children in my last Letter, but fearing you should think I neglected your request by answering it with too much conciseness, I am resolved to add to it what little I know on that Subject, and which may perhaps be useful to you in a concern with which you seem so nearly affected.

People commonly educate their children as they build their Houses, according to some plan they think beautiful, without considering whether it is suited to the purposes for which they are designed. Allmost all Girls of Quality are educated as if they were to be great Ladies, which is often as little to be expected as an immoderate Heat of the Sun in the North of Scotland. You should teach yours to confine their Desires to probabilities, to be as useful as is possible to themselves, and to think privacy (as it is) the happiest state of Life.

I do not doubt your giving them all the instructions necessary to form them to a Virtuous Life, but 'tis a fatal mistake to do this without proper restrictions. Vices are often hid under the name of Virtues, and the practice of them follow'd by the worst of Consequences. Sincerity, Friendship, Piety, Disinterestedness, and Generosity are all great Virtues, but pursued without Discretion become criminal. I have seen Ladies indulge their own ill Humor by being very rude and impertinent, and think they deserved approbation by saying, I love to speak Truth. One of your acquaintance made a Ball the next day after her Mother died, to show she was sincere. I believe your own reflection will furnish you with but too many Examples of the ill Effects of the rest of the Sentiments I have mentioned, when too warmly embraced. They are generally recommended to young People without limits or distinction, and this prejudice hurries them into great misfortunes while they are applauding themselves in the noble practise (as they fancy) of very eminent Virtues.

I cannot help adding (out [of] my real affection to you) I wish you would moderate that fondness you have for your children. I do not mean you should abate any part of your Care, or not do your Duty to them in its utmost extent, but I would have you early prepare yourself for Disappointments, which are heavy in proportion to their being surprising. It is hardly possible in such a number that none should be unhappy. Prepare yourself against a misfortune of that kind. I confess there is hardly any more difficult to support, yet it is certain Imagination has a great share in the pain of it, and it is more in our power (than it is commonly believed) to soften whatever ills are founded or augmented by Fancy. Strictly speaking, there is but one real evil; I mean acute pain. All other Complaints are so considerably diminished by Time that it is plain the Grief is owing to our Passion, since the sensation of it vanishes when that is over.

There is another mistake I forgot to mention usual in mothers. If any of their Daughters are Beauties, they take great pains to persuade them that they are ugly, or at least that they think so, which the Young Woman never fails to believe springs from Envy, and is (perhaps) not much in the wrong. I would, if possible, give them a just notion of their Figure, and show them how far it is valuable. Every advantage has its Price, and may be either over or undervalued. It is the common Doctrine of (what are called) Good Books to inspire a contempt of Beauty, Riches, Greatness etc., which has done as much mischief amongst the young of our Sex as an overeager desire of them. They should look on these things as Blessings where they are bestowed, though not necessaries that it is impossible to be happy without. I am persuaded the ruin of Lady F[rances] M[eadows] was in great measure owing to the Notions given her by the sillily good people that had the care of her. 'Tis true her Circumstances and your Daughters' are very different. They should be taught to be content with privacy, and yet not neglect good Fortune if it should be offered them.

I am afraid I have tired you with my Instructions. I do not give them as believing my Age has furnished me with Superior Wisdom, but in compliance with your desire, and being fond of every opportunity that gives a proof of the tenderness with which I am ever Your affectionate Mother,

M. Wortley.

I should be glad you sent me the 3rd Vol. of Architecture, and with it any other entertaining Books. I have seen the D[uches]s of M[arlborough]'s, but should be glad of the Apology for a Late Resignation. As to the Ale, 'tis now so late in the year it is impossible it should come good.

You do not mention your Father. My last Letter from him told me he intended soon for England. I am afraid several of mine to him have miscarryed, though directed as he ordered.

I have asked you so often the price of raw silk that I am weary of repeating it. However, I once more beg you would send me that Information.   *1750*

Mary Barber
1690–1757

Almost nothing is known of MARY BARBER prior to her marriage to Jonathan Barber, a wool-draper in Dublin, around 1710; the couple had four sons, and she began writing poetry "chiefly to form the Minds of my Children." Although she once claimed that "a Woman steps out of her Province, whenever she presumes to write for the Press," during the 1720s she published at least two poems: "A Tale Being an Addition to Mr. Gay's Fables," a petition to the queen to grant the playwright John Gay a pension; and "The Widow's Address," a request for assistance for a poverty-stricken army officer's widow. The latter work came to the attention of the Irish satirist Jonathan Swift, who became her friend and patron. A frequent visitor at his home, the Deanery, Barber was called Sapphira there, and she often presented her poems to Swift for correction. Although in her *Memoirs* the poet Laetitia Pilkerton, also a member of Swift's circle, called Barber's poems "dull . . . indigested Materials," Swift considered her the finest woman poet among his acquaintances.

When Barber went to England in 1730, Swift wrote letters of introduction to his friends and urged them to buy copies of her forthcoming book. To the English poet and wit Alexander Pope, the scholar Roger Lonsdale claims, Swift once reported that Barber was "poetically given, & for a woman, had a sort of genius that way." Barber irritated Pope, however, when she asked him to revise her poems, a request that the irascible Pope found impudent. When Barber encountered financial difficulties, Swift allowed her to keep the profits from copies she sold of his *Polite Conversation*; she, in turn, helped him by smuggling several of his banned writings into England, a crime for which she was once jailed. Barber returned to Ireland in 1732, planning to move her family to London, but ill health and her husband's death prevented her from relocating until 1734.

Barber's *Poems on Several Occasions* was published by Samuel Richardson in 1734 and reissued in 1735 and 1736; it included her own poems as well as works by Elizabeth Rowe and Constantia Grierson. One of her favorite topics was motherhood; in fact, her literary contemporaries sometimes called her "Mother Barber." In 1735, asserts Lonsdale, Anne Donnellan told Swift that Barber's poems were "generally greatly liked," although " a few severe critics . . . say they are not poetic." Apparently Barber wrote little poetry after 1734, and by 1740, ill with gout and rheumatism, she had settled once more in Dublin near her son Constantine, a physician. A number of her works were included in *Poems by Eminent Ladies*, a popular anthology published in 1755, but her writing was largely forgotten by 1800, only to be rediscovered in the late twentieth century.

☙ Written for My Son, and Spoken by Him at His First Putting on Breeches ☞

WHAT is it our mammas bewitches,
To plague us little boys with breeches?
To tyrant Custom we must yield
Whilst vanquished Reason flies the field.
Our legs must suffer by ligation,
To keep the blood from circulation;
And then our feet, though young and tender,
We to the shoemaker surrender,

Who often makes our shoes so straight
10   Our growing feet they cramp and fret;
Whilst, with contrivance most profound,
Across our insteps we are bound;
Which is the cause, I make no doubt,
Why thousands suffer in the gout.
15   Our wiser ancestors wore brogues,
Before the surgeons bribed these rogues,
With narrow toes, and heels like pegs,
To help to make us break our legs.

Then, ere we know to use our fists,
20   Our mothers closely bind our wrists;
And never think our clothes are neat,
Till they're so tight we cannot eat.
And, to increase our other pains,
The hat-band helps to cramp our brains.
25   The cravat finishes the work,
Like bowstring sent from the Grand Turk.

Thus dress, that should prolong our date,
Is made to hasten on our fate.
30   Fair privilege of nobler natures,
To be more plagued than other creatures!
The wild inhabitants of air
Are clothed by heaven with wondrous care:
The beauteous, well-compacted feathers
35   Are coats of mail against all weathers;
Enamelled, to delight the eye,
Gay as the bow that decks the sky.
The beasts are clothed with beauteous skins;
The fishes armed with scales and fins,
40   Whose lustre lends the sailor light,
When all the stars are hid in night.

O were our dress contrived like these,
For use, for ornament and ease!
Man only seems to sorrow born,
45   Naked, defenseless and forlorn.

Yet we have Reason, to supply
What nature did to man deny:
Weak viceroy! Who thy power will own,
50   When Custom has usurped thy throne?
In vain did I appeal to thee,
Ere I would wear his livery;
Who, in defiance to thy rules,
Delights to make us act like fools.
55   O'er human race the tyrant reigns,
And binds them in eternal chains.
We yield to his despotic sway,
The only monarch all obey.

⊰ The Conclusion of a Letter to the Rev. Mr C— ⊱

'Tis time to conclude, for I make it a rule
To leave off all writing, when Con. comes from school.
He dislikes what I've written, and says I had better
To send what he calls a poetical letter.

5   To this I replied, 'You are out of your wits;
A letter in verse would put him in fits;
He thinks it a crime in a woman to read—
Then what would he say should your counsel succeed?
"I pity poor Barber, his wife's so romantic:
10   A letter in rhyme!—Why the woman is frantic!
This reading the poets has quite turned her head;
On my life, she should have a dark room and straw bed.
I often heard say that St. Patrick took care
No poisonous creature should live in this air:
15   He only regarded the body, I find,
But Plato considered who poisoned the mind.[1]
Would they'd follow his precepts, who sit at the helm,
And drive poetasters from out of the realm!

       "'Her husband has surely a terrible life;
20   There's nothing I dread like a verse-writing wife:
Defend me, ye powers, from that fatal curse,
Which must heighten the plagues of *for better or worse*!

       "'May I have a wife that will dust her own floor,
And not the fine minx recommended by More.[2]
25   (That he was a dotard is granted, I hope,
Who died for asserting the rights of the Pope.)
If ever I marry, I'll choose me a spouse,
That shall *serve* and *obey*, as she's bound by her vows;
That shall, when I'm dressing, attend like a valet;
30   Then go to the kitchen, and study my palate.
She has wisdom enough, that keeps out of the dirt,
And can make a good pudding, and cut out a shirt.
What good's in a dame that will pore on a book?
No—give me the wife that shall save me a cook.'"

35   Thus far I had written—then turned to my son,
To give him advice, ere my letter was done.
'My son, should you marry, look out for a wife
That's fitted to lighten the labors of life.
Be sure, wed a woman you thoroughly know,
40   And shun, above all things, a *housewifely shrew*,
That would fly to your study, with fire in her looks,
And ask what you got by your poring on books,
Think dressing of dinner the height of all science,
And to peace and good humor bid open defiance.

1. St. Patrick was a 5th century apostole and the patron saint of Ireland; Plato (c. 428–348 BCE) was a Greek philosopher.
2. An allusion to Sir Thomas More (1478–1535), an English Renaissance statesman and author whom Barber's speaker dismisses because he preferred to die a Catholic rather than to swear allegiance to the Church of England.

45   'Avoid the fine lady, whose beauty's her care;
   Who sets a high price on her shape, and her air;
   Who in dress, and in visits, employs the whole day,
   And longs for the evening, to sit down to play.

   'Choose a woman of wisdom, as well as good breeding,
50   With a turn, or at least no aversion, to reading:
   In the care of her person, exact and refined;
   Yet still, let her principal care be her mind:
   Who can, when her family cares give her leisure,
   Without the dear cards, pass an evening with pleasure,
55   In forming her children to virtue and knowledge,
   Nor trust, for that care, to a school, or a college:
   By learning made humble, not thence taking airs
   To despise or neglect her domestic affairs:
   Nor think her less fitted for doing her duty,
60   By knowing its reasons, its use, and its beauty.

   'When you gain her affection, take care to preserve it,
   Lest others persuade her you do not deserve it.
   Still study to heighten the joys of her life;
   Nor treat her the worse for her being your wife.
65   If in judgement she errs, set her right, without pride:
   'Tis the province of insolent fools to deride.
   A husband's first praise is a Friend and Protector:
   Then change not these titles for Tyrant and Hector.
   Let your person be neat, unaffectedly clean,
70   Though alone with your wife the whole day you remain.
   Choose books, for her study, to fashion her mind,
   To emulate those who excelled of her kind.
   Be religion the principal care of your life,
   As you hope to be blessed in your children and wife;
75   So you, in your marriage, shall gain its true end,
   And find, in your wife, a Companion and Friend.'

                1734

Charlotte Smith
1749–1806

Best known as a poet and a sentimental novelist, CHARLOTTE SMITH also advocated women's educational rights and protested conventional ideologies that condemned women as "insignificant triflers" if they lacked education and "affecting masculine knowledge" if they sought it. She was born Charlotte Turner to a landed gentleman and his wife; her mother died when Charlotte was three. After receiving an excellent education, she left home at fifteen to marry Benjamin Smith, motivated in part by her father's plan to remarry. Although her husband hailed from a wealthy merchant family, he wasted his inheritance, much to the chagrin of his capable wife. Finally the couple were sent to debtors' prison, where Charlotte was forced to assume responsibility for supporting their ten children. From prison Smith published a successful volume of poetry, *Elegiac Sonnets* (1784), but once released she began to write more lucrative sentimental novels. After twenty years of marriage, she separated legally from her husband, claiming desertion, and from 1788 until 1793 lived with her children in Brighton. During this period Smith published a novel a year and enjoyed significant acclaim; nonetheless, her financial difficulties persisted, despite assistance from patrons such as William Hayley and William Cowper. In an effort to meet deadlines and pay her bills, Smith was often forced to finish a novel after its earlier chapters were already in print—a necessity that robbed some works of their structural integrity.

Enormously popular with the new reading audience of middle-class women, sentimental fiction emphasized female "sensibilities," including the desire for compatibility and love in marriage, and took issue with the prevailing view that women should be content in unhappy relationships. Such novels appealed to women because they took their emotional lives seriously and because fictional heroines often had freedoms that actual women lacked; in many cases the heroines were orphans with no family obligations. Smith's protagonists are autonomous and intelligent. Her first novel, *Emmeline* (1784), features an unrealistic but intriguing heroine who engages in brilliant conversation with wealthy aristocrats despite her youth and lack of connections. She also attracts three worthy and three unworthy suitors—an amazing plenitude, given that most women without fortunes were unlikely to attract anyone. The protagonist of *Celestina* (1791), is described as having "an active mind . . . perpetually in search of new ideas." *The Old Manor House* (1793), like many of Smith's novels, portrays a profligate man, Philip Someric, who squanders an inheritance he is supposed to divide among his siblings, thus forcing his sisters into unfortunate marriages. Smith reveals a feminist impulse in her treatment of abusive men: Celestina rejects two suitors who try to bully her into marrying them, while Leonora in *Letters of a Solitary Wanderer* (1800) remains "personally indifferent" to her adulterous husband, objecting to his affairs on financial rather than emotional grounds. Smith's exemplary heroes are gentle, responsible men like Celestina's Willoughby, "the best and most affectionate of husbands."

A number of Smith's novels were criticized for treating too generously women's sexual indiscretions—adultery, prostitution, and pregnancy outside of wedlock. Even Mary Wollstonecraft, in a 1788 review of *Emmeline* in the *Analytic Review*, disparaged Smith for allowing an adulteress, after much suffering, to marry her lover. Other reviewers objected that Smith's later novels were too political, especially those that treated sympathetically the American and French Revolutions. *Desmond* (1792) was widely condemned because its author criticized Edmund Burke's treatise against the French Revolution as the work of an English despot. Certain male critics complained that Smith's women expressed political opinions at all. Smith herself is hard on apolitical women; when Lady Ellesmere in *The Banished Man* (1794) cannot understand current events, the author presents her ignorance as an intellectual failing. In the preface Smith acknowledges her desire to subvert the sentimental novel, claiming that she would someday do what "has never yet been hazarded—to make a novel without love in it."

In addition to *Elegiac Sonnets*, Smith published two lengthy and ambitious poems, *The Emigrants* (1793) and *Beachy Head* (1807), which address themes of exile and conflicts among nations. William Wordsworth admired her poetry, and contemporaries compared her sonnets to those of John Milton. Given her difficult life, it is not surprising that Smith's poems are melancholy. "It was unaffected sorrows drew them forth," she once admitted. "I wrote mournfully because I was unhappy." Whether she writes from the perspective of a mother, as in "Verses Intended to Have Been Prefixed . . . " or a child, as in "The Glow-Worm," Smith confronts the pain of daily life for those who are vulnerable or oppressed.

⇥ The Glow-Worm ⇤

When on some balmy-breathing night of Spring
The happy child, to whom the world is new,

Pursues the evening moth, of mealy wing,
   Or from the heath-bell beats the sparkling dew;
5 He sees before his inexperienced eyes
   The brilliant Glow-worm, like a meteor, shine
On the turf-bank:—amazed, and pleased, he cries.
   "Star of the dewy grass.—I make thee mine!"—
Then, ere he sleep, collects "the moisten'd" flower,
10   And bids soft leaves his glittering prize enfold
And dreams that Fairy-lamps illume his bower:
   Yet with the morning shudders to behold
His lucid treasure, rayless as the dust.
—So turn the world's bright joys to cold and blank disgust.

1784

⚜ Verses Intended to Have Been Prefixed to the Novel of Emmeline, but then Suppressed[1] ⚜

O'erwhelm'd with sorrow, and sustaining long
"The proud man's contumely, th' oppressor's wrong,"
Languid despondency, and vain regret,
Must my exhausted spirit struggle yet?
5 Yes!—Robb'd myself of all that fortune gave,
Even of all hope—but shelter in the grave,
Still shall the plaintive lyre essay its powers
To dress the cave of Care with Fancy's flowers,
Maternal Love the fiend Despair withstand,
10 Still animate the heart and guide the hand.
—May you, dear objects of my anxious care,
Escape the evils I was born to bear!
Round my devoted head while tempests roll,
Yet there, where I have treasured up my soul,
15 May the soft rays of dawning hope impart
Reviving Patience to my fainting heart;—
And when its sharp solicitudes shall cease,
May I be conscious in the realms of peace
That every tear which swells my children's eyes,
20 From sorrows past, not present ills arise.
Then, with some friend who loves to share your pain,
For 'tis my boast that *some* such friends remain,
By filial grief, and fond remembrance pressed,
You'll seek the spot where all my sorrows rest;
25 Recall my hapless days in sad review,
The long calamities I bore for you,
And—with an happier fate—resolve to prove
How well you merited—your mother's love.

1784

---

1. Smith published *Emmeline* in 1784.

Mary Tighe
1772–1810

Mary Blachford was born in Dublin to strict Methodist parents, and in 1793 she married her cousin, Henry Tighe. From 1801 to 1803 MARY TIGHE composed *Psyche, or the Legend of Love*, a series of Spenserian sonnets addressing female creativity and eroticizing the natural world. This volume appeared in limited edition in 1805 and went through three editions, the last of which contained several new poems written before her death from tuberculosis in 1810. A second collection, *Mary, a Series of Reflections During Twenty Years*, was published posthumously in 1811 and solidified Tighe's reputation as a significant female Romanticist. She also wrote an autobiographical novel, *Selena*, which remains unpublished; the diary containing this manuscript was destroyed after her death, although a cousin copied portions of it. John Keats admired *Psyche* for its erotic content and its use of Spenserian form, and Felicia Hemans's "Grave of a Poetess" and Thomas More's "I Saw Thy Form in Youthful Prime" are elegies that reveal Tighe's influence on her contemporaries. Her unpublished manuscripts can be found in the National Library of Ireland; the only North American copy of *Mary, a Series of Reflections* is located at Harvard University.

As Andrew Ashfield has noted, early nineteenth-century collections of British poetry completely excluded women from the canon, despite the prominence of many women during the period in which these collections were compiled, 1773–1810. By the 1830s, however, women again gained modest attention, not for their contributions to Romanticism but for their "specifically feminine characteristics." Ashfield explains that women poets of this period fell into two categories: "dissenting radicals or sympathizers" and those who "embraced the notion of the 'poetess.'" Tighe fit the second category, but finally it mattered little which type of poet she was, for women of both descriptions were denied admittance to the literary canon—hence her lack of critical recognition today. In Ashfield's words, "it is a complicated law of literary history that the characterization of women's literature—be it as perversely masculine, 'unsex'd', or sweetly feminine—ensures that it can never be canonical and survive as a persistent object of attention."

Many nineteenth-century women wrote poems to their mothers or daughters, since such relationships were sanctified in what Carroll Smith Rosenberg has called "the female world of love and ritual." In "Sonnet Addressed to My Mother" Tighe pays tribute to her mother as a primary source of poetic creativity. Like women poets from KATHERINE PHILIPS to EMILY BRONTË to MAY SARTON, Tighe implores a maternal muse to grant her glorious language to speak her thoughts in poetry.

✠ Sonnet Addressed to My Mother ✠

OH, thou! whose tender smile most partially
   Hath ever bless'd thy child: to thee belong
   The graces which adorn my first wild song,
If aught of grace it knows: nor thou deny
5 Thine ever prompt attention to supply.
   But let me lead thy willing ear along,
   Where virtuous love still bids the strain prolong
His innocent applause; since from thine eye
   The beams of love first charm'd my infant breast,
10 And from thy lip Affection's soothing voice
   That eloquence of tenderness express'd,

Which still my grateful heart confess'd divine:
Oh! ever may its accents sweet rejoice
The soul which loves to own whate'er it has is thine!

1801–03/1805

+—+ ⊱✦⊰ +—+

Lydia Sigourney
1791–1865

Known during her lifetime as "the sweet singer of Hartford," LYDIA SIGOURNEY was one of nineteenth-century America's most popular poets. Her primary subjects were motherhood and death, subjects closely linked in an era in which both infant and maternal mortality rates were high. "Death of an Infant," her most widely anthologized poem, was originally attributed to the British poet Felicia Hemans, whose themes were similar to Sigourney's, but in her preface to the sixth edition of *Select Poems* (1845) Sigourney vigorously asserts her own authorship of this elegy.

She was born in Norwich, Connecticut, to Zerviah Wentworth and Ezekiel Huntley, who worked as a gardener for Mrs. Daniel Lathrop, a wealthy widow in whose home the Huntley family lived. As a child Lydia Huntley became Mrs. Lathrop's companion, reading aloud to her from the works of devotional writers and borrowing books from her library. Through Mrs. Lathrop she was introduced to Daniel Wadsworth, a prosperous Hartford businessman who later became her patron. After attending several female seminaries, which she found tedious because of their emphasis on embroidery and drawing, she decided at twenty to open her own school for young women with a friend, Nancy Maria Hyde. This school was short-lived, and in 1814 Huntley opened another school, supported monetarily by Wadsworth, which the daughters of Hartford's most prominent families attended. In 1815 she published *Moral Pieces in Prose and Verse*, which launched her writing career. When she left teaching in 1819 to marry Charles Sigourney, a wealthy merchant, however, she learned that he expected her to give up writing, an "improper" occupation for a married woman. For more than a decade Sigourney negotiated this issue with her husband, abandoning at least one book but publishing some poems anonymously in newspapers and magazines. During this time she also had five children, three of whom died at birth. By the early 1830s, in need of additional income to support an upper-class way of life, Sigourney's husband relented, and she published *Letters to Young Ladies* (1833) under the name of Lydia Huntley, although her identity was rapidly discovered. From that point on she became a prolific and successful author, contributing to such periodicals as *Lady's Book*, *Graham's Magazine*, and the *Southern Literary Messenger*, edited by Edgar Allan Poe.

Gordon Haight, Sigourney's biographer, claims that she was widely known as a female Horatio Alger, the poor girl who married a rich merchant, lived in a fabulous mansion, became a famous writer, and was received by "the crowned heads of Europe." Indeed, as Judith Fetterley has noted, Sigourney was "an intensely public figure" who "made the career of poet to some degree an extension of the service role conventionally assigned to women"; she corresponded each year with more than 2000 admirers, mostly women, and at their request wrote poems in honor of occasions in their lives. Given her popularity in pre–Civil War America, it is surprising that few modern American literary scholars took notice of Sigourney until the 1990s. Fetterley explains that few anthologies before this time included Sigourney's poems or stories, in part because even some feminist scholars dismissed her as a "songbird" rather than the serious professional writer that she was. However, critics such as Karen Kilcup, Elizabeth Petrino, and Fetterley herself have reevaluated Sigourney's significant contributions to nineteenth-century poetry, women's discourse on maternity, and the history of the elegy in the United States.

⊰ Death of an Infant ⊱

Death found strange beauty on that polished brow
And dashed it out.—
                  There was a tint of rose
On cheek and lip.—He touched the veins with ice,
5   And the rose faded.—
                  Forth from those blue eyes
There spake a wishful tenderness, a doubt
Whether to grieve or sleep, which innocence
Alone may wear.—With ruthless haste he bound
10   The silken fringes of those curtaining lids
Forever.—
                There had been a murmuring sound,
With which the babe would claim its mother's ear,
Charming her even to tears.—The Spoiler set
15   His seal of silence.—
                But there beamed a smile
So fixed, so holy, from that cherub brow,
Death gazed—and left it there.—
                        He dared not steal
20   *The signet-ring of Heaven.*

1834

⊰ The Last Word of the Dying ⊱

A Christian friend, in the last moments of life, when it was supposed all communication with mortals had ceased—spelled, with her fingers, in the dialect of the deaf and dumb, the word—"Mother."

         'Tis o'er!—'Tis o'er!
         That lip of gentle tone
         Doth speak to man no more;
     It hath given the parting kiss
5   To him with whom was learned to prove
         The climax of terrestial bliss,
           Deep, and confiding love;
         It hath sighed its last bequest
           On the weeping sister's breast,
10   Its work is done.

         The soul doth wait for thee,
         Redeemer!—strong to save
         Thy ransomed from the grave,
           It waiteth to be free.
15   Still, on the darkened eye
     It lingereth, wishful to convey
   One message more, to frail mortality,
           Then soar away.

         There is no breath to speak,
20   No life-blood in the cheek,

Listening Love doth strive in vain
    Those pearls of thought to gain,
        Which on its upward track
Thus from Heaven's threshold bright, the spirit throweth back.
25   But with remembered skill
        The *hand* interprets still,
    Though speech with broken lyre is faithless to the will,
Those poor, pale fingers weave with majestic art,
One last, lone thrilling word to echo through the heart.

30   *"Mother."*
      Oh! yet a moment stay,
    Friend!—Friend!—what would'st thou say?
What strong emotion with that word doth twine!
   She, whose soft hand did dry thine infant tear,
35   Hovereth she now, with love divine
        Thy dying pillow near?
      And is the import of thy sign
        That she is here?
Faithful to thine extremest need
40   Descends she from her blissful sphere,
    With the soft welcome of an angel's reed
Thy passage through the shadowy vale to cheer?

      Or doth affection's root
45   So to earth's soil adhere—
      That thou, in fond pursuit,
    Still turn'st to idols dear?
Drawest thou the curtain from a cherished scene
    Once more with yearning to survey
50   The little student over his book serene,
     The glad one at his play,
   The blooming babe so lately on thy breast
      Cradled to rest—
     Those three fair boys,
55 Lingers thy soul with them, even from heaven's perfect joys?
Say—wouldst thou teach us thus, how strong a mother's tie?
    That when all others fade away,
    Stricken down in moldering clay,
Springs up with agonizing hold, on vast eternity?
60   Fain would we hear thee tell,
      But ah!—the closing eye,
    The fluttering, moaning sigh,
Speak forth the disembodied friend's farewell,
We toil to break the seal, with fruitless pain,
65 Time's fellowship is riven:—earth's question is in vain.

     Yet we shall know
Thy mystery—thou who unexplained hast fled
    Where secret things are read,
70   We after thee shall go
    In the same path of woe
     Down to the dead.

Oh Christ!—whose changeless trust
Went with her to the dust,
75   Whose spirit free,
Did shield her from the victor's power,
Suffer us not, in Death's dread hour
          To fall from Thee.

1834

⊰ Dream of the Dead ⊱

Sleep brought the dead to me. Their brows were kind,
And their tones tender, and, as erst they blent
Their sympathies with each familiar scene.
It was my earthliness that robed them still
5   In their material vestments, for they seemed
Not yet to have put their glorious garments on.
Methought, 'twere better thus to dwell with them,
Than with the living.

                    'Twas a chosen friend,
10   Beloved in school-days' happiness, who came,
And put her arm through mine, and meekly walked,
As she was wont, where'er I willed to lead,
To shady grove or river's sounding shore,
Or dizzy cliff, to gaze enthralled below
15   On widespread landscape and diminished throng.
     One, too, was there, o'er whose departing steps
Night's cloud hung heavy ere she found the tomb;
One, to whose ear no infant lip, save mine,
E'er breathed the name of mother.

20   In her hour
Of conflict with the spoiler, that fond word
Fell with my tears upon her brow in vain—
She heard not, heeded not. But now she flew,
Upon the wing of dreams, to my embrace,
25   Full of fresh life, and in that beauty clad
Which charmed my earliest love. Speak, silent shade!
Speak to thy child! But with capricious haste
Sleep turned the tablet, and another came,
A stranger-matron, sicklied o'er and pale,
30   And mournful for my vanished guide I sought.
     Then, many a group, in earnest converse flocked,
Upon whose lips I knew the burial-clay
Lay deep, for I had heard its hollow sound,
In hoarse reverberation, "*dust to dust!*"
35   They put a fair, young infant in my arms,
And that was of the dead, Yet still it seemed
Like other infants. First with fear it shrank,

And then in changeful gladness smiled, and spread
Its little hands in sportive laughter forth.
40 So I awoke, and then those gentle forms
Of faithful friendship and maternal love
Did flit away, and life, with all its cares,
Stood forth in strong reality.

                      Sweet dream!
45 And solemn, let me bear thee in my soul
Throughout the livelong day, to subjugate
My earthborn hope. I bow me at your names,
Sinless and passionless and pallid train!
The seal of truth is on your breasts, ye dead!
50 Ye may not swerve, nor from your vows recede,
Nor of your faith make shipwreck. Scarce a point
Divides you from us, though we fondly look
Through a long vista of imagined years,
And in the dimness of far distance, seek
55 *To hide that tomb, whose crumbling verge we tread.*

                                               1834

Felicia Hemans
1793–1835

Born in Liverpool to George Browne, a merchant, and his wife, Felicity Wagner, FELICIA HEMANS was educated at home and encouraged by both parents to write poems at an early age. The Brownes arranged for two volumes of their daughter's poetry, *Poems* and *England and Spain*, to be published when she was only fifteen. In 1812 she married Captain Alfred Hemans; that same year *The Domestic Affections*, her first mature collection, was published. Hemans bore five children in six years before her husband abandoned her; thereafter she supported her children by writing. While married she wrote historical narrative verse, including *The Restoration of the Works of Art in Italy* (1816), *Modern Greece* (1817), *The Sceptic* (1820), and *Dartmoor* (1821). By 1825, however, she had become renowned as a lyric poet whose romantic verses exuded charm and grace.

    The Forest Sanctuary (1825) forged Hemans's reputation as a sentimental lyricist; subsequent volumes—*Lays of Many Lands* (1825), *Records of Woman* (1828), and *Songs of the Affections* (1831)—won her significant audiences in America as well as England. Readers were taken with her sweetness of temperament, religious orthodoxy, and homage to nature, all traits considered the purview of the ideal "poetess." Hemans also wrote two plays, *The Siege of Valencia* and *The Vespers of Palermo*, both in 1823, and she published poems and essays frequently in *Blackwoods*, the *New Monthly Magazine,* and other popular periodicals. These works were collected posthumously by David Moir in a volume entitled *Poetical Remains* (1836). By midnineteenth century the canon of Romantic poets had been largely established, and Hemans, denigrated as a poet both female and sentimental, was not included in it. However, as Andrew Ashfield has observed, when *The Lansdowne Poets*, a major collection of English verse, appeared in 1874, it contained one poem each by Coleridge and Shelley, two by Wordsworth, three by Keats, five by Byron, and thirteen by Hemans. This bit of literary history reveals the vicissitudes of canon formation that persist into our own time, especially as regards the inclusion of women writers. In the late twentieth century Hemans has received scholarly reconsideration for her relationship to the canonized male Romantic poets and her contributions as a poet who explores such diverse topics as nationalism, identity, and maternal sacrifice.

⊰ Casabianca ⊱

THE boy stood on the burning deck
　　Whence all but he had fled;
The flame that lit the battle's wreck
　　Shone round him o'er the dead.

5　Yet beautiful and bright he stood,
　　As born to rule the storm;
A creature of heroic blood,
　　A proud, though childlike form.

The flames roll'd on—he would not go
10　　Without his Father's word;
That Father, faint in death below,
　　His voice no longer heard.

He call'd aloud:—'Say, Father, say
　　If yet my task is done?'
15　He knew not that the chieftain lay
　　Unconscious of his son.

'Speak, Father!' once again he cried,
　　'If I may yet be gone!'
And but the booming shots replied,
20　　And fast the flames roll'd on.

Upon his brow he felt their breath,
　　And in his waving hair,
And look'd from that lone post of death
　　In still, yet brave despair.

25　And shouted but once more aloud,
　　'My Father! must I stay?'
While o'er him fast, through sail and shroud,
　　The wreathing fires made way.

They wrapped the ship in splendour wild,
30　　They caught the flag on high,
And stream'd above the gallant child,
　　Like banners in the sky.

There came a burst of thunder sound—
　　The boy—oh! where was he?
35　Ask of the winds that far around
　　With fragments strew'd the sea!—

With mast, and helm, and pennon fair,
　　That well had borne their part—
But the noblest thing which perish'd there
40　　Was that young faithful heart!

　　　　　　　　　　　　　　　　　　　　　　　　　　1835

⇥ The Hebrew Mother ⇤

The rose was in rich bloom on Sharon's plain,
When a young mother, with her firstborn, thence
Went up to Zion; for the boy was vow'd
Unto the Temple service:—by the hand
5   She led him, and her silent soul, the while,
Oft as the dewy laughter of his eye
Met her sweet serious glance, rejoiced to think
That aught so pure, so beautiful, was hers,
To bring before her God. So pass'd they on
10   O'er Judah's hills; and wheresoe'er the leaves
Of the broad sycamore made sounds at noon,
Like lulling raindrops, or the olive boughs,
With their cool dimness, cross'd the sultry blue
Of Syria's heaven, she paused, that he might rest:
15   Yet from her own meek eyelids chased the sleep
That weigh'd their dark fringe down, to sit and watch
The crimson deepening o'er his cheek's repose,
As at a red flower's heart. And where a fount
Lay, like a twilight star, 'midst palmy shades,
20   Making its bank green gems along the wild,
There, too, she linger'd, from the diamond wave
Drawing bright water for his rosy lips,
And softly parting clusters of jet curls
To bathe his brow. At last the fane was reach'd,
25   The earth's one sanctuary—and rapture hush'd
Her bosom, as before her, through the day,
It rose, a mountain of white marble, steep'd
In light like floating gold. But when that hour
Waned to the farewell moment, when the boy
30   Lifted, through rainbow-gleaming tears, his eye
Beseechingly to hers, and half in fear
Turn'd from the white-robed priest, and round her arm
Clung even as joy clings—the deep spring-tide
Of nature then swell'd high, and o'er her child
35   Bending, her soul broke forth, in mingled sounds
Of weeping and sad song.—'Alas!' she cried,—

'Alas! my boy, thy gentle grasp is on me;
The bright tears quiver in thy pleading eyes;
     And now fond thoughts arise,
40   And silver cords again to earth have won me;
And like a vine thou claspest my full heart—
     How shall I hence depart?

'How the lone paths retrace where thou wert playing
So late, along the mountains, at my side?
     And I, in joyous pride,
45   By every place of flowers my course delaying,
Wove, e'en as pearls, the lilies round thy hair,
     Beholding thee so fair!

'And, oh! the home whence thy bright smile hath parted,
50   Will it not seem as if the sunny day
         Turn'd from its door away?
While through its chambers wandering, weary-hearted,
I languish for thy voice, which past me still
         Went like a singing rill?

55   'Under the palm-trees thou no more shalt meet me,
When from the fount at evening I return,
         With the full water-urn;
Nor will thy sleep's low dovelike breathings greet me,
As 'midst the silence of the stars I wake,
         And watch for thy dear sake.

60   'And thou, will slumber's dewy cloud fall round thee,
Without thy mother's hand to smooth thy bed?
         Wilt thou not vainly spread
Thine arms, when darkness as a veil hath wound thee,
To fold my neck, and lift up, in thy fear,
65   A cry which none shall hear?

'What have I said, my child!—Will *He* not hear thee,
Who the young ravens heareth from their nest?
         Shall He not guard thy rest,
And, in the hush of holy midnight hear thee,
70   Breathe o'er thy soul, and fill its dreams with joy
         Thou shalt sleep soft, my boy.

'I give thee to thy God—the God that gave thee,
A wellspring of deep gladness to my heart!
         And, precious as thou art,
75   And pure as dew of Hermon, He shall have thee,
My own, my beautiful, my undefiled!
         And thou shalt be His child.

'Therefore, farewell!—I go, my soul may fail me,
As the hart panteth for the water brooks,
80   Yearning for thy sweet looks.
But thou, my firstborn, droop not, nor bewail me;
Thou in the Shadow of the Rock shalt dwell,
         The Rock of Strength.—Farewell!'

1835

———— ⊫◊⊨ ————

Grace Aguilar
1816–1847

Described during her lifetime as the "moral governess of the Hebrew family," GRACE AGUILAR
was the most highly regarded Jewish woman writer in Victorian England. Born in Hackney to
Sephardic (Spanish Jewish) parents, Sarah Días-Fernandez and Emmanuel Aguilar, she hailed

from a family of writers and activists: her maternal great-grandfather composed religious tracts, her father served as lay leader of London's Spanish-Portuguese community, and her mother provided the religious instruction and oral histories that Aguilar wove into many of her stories. Although she published poetry, sermons, travel journals, and a treatise on the science of conch shells, Aguilar remains best known for her novels and her prose studies of Jewish culture. Both Jews and Christians viewed Aguilar as a representative Anglo-Jewish writer, and her works were widely reprinted both during her life and after her death. Aguilar never married; she died at thirty-one of measles and consumption while visiting her brother in Frankfurt, Germany. Her epitaph, taken from Proverbs 31, extols a life of art, faith, and activism: "Give her of the fruit of her hands; and let her own works praise her from the gates."

Aguilar's early writing included two novellas, "The Friends, A Domestic Tale" (1834) and "Adah, A Simple Story" (1838); she addressed the latter to a Christian friend whom she wished to educate about Judaism. Aguilar won critical praise for her poem "The Magic Wreath" (1835) and went on to publish numerous poems in Jewish periodicals such as *Hebrew Review* and *Jewish Chronicle* and in non-Jewish ones such as *Keepsake* and *Chambers' Miscellany*. In 1838 she translated a polemic by Orobio de Castro, *Israel Defended*. *Records of Israel* (1844) blended historical romance with Jewish lore in a series of short, didactic tales. Beginning with *Home Influence; A Tale for Mothers and Daughters* (1847), all of Aguilar's novels were published posthumously, shepherded into print by her mother after her daughter's sudden death. *The Vale of Cedars; or, The Martyr* (1850), a romance that chronicles the experiences of Jews who fled the Spanish Inquisition, circulated widely in England and abroad; by 1949, the year of its last printing, it had been reprinted twenty-nine times. *Days of Bruce* (1852), a romance influenced by the works of Sir Walter Scott, was her most popular novel with the general public; Jewish and Christian women readers favored *Women's Friendship* (1850) and *The Mother's Recompense* (1851). Aguilar's novels can be described as sentimental in that they emphasize the value of sympathetic hearts and copious feeling. A compilation of her short stories, *Home Scenes and Heart Studies*, appeared in 1852.

Aguilar's prose study, *The Spirit of Judaism* (1842), offers a controversial critique of institutional religion. In it she reflects on the nature and purpose of Jewish religious rituals, and she urges mothers to instill in their sons and daughters a strong Jewish identity and to educate boys and girls equally in the faith. *Women of Israel* (1844) and *The Jewish Faith* (1846) consider the roles of women in Jewish tradition and practice. In 1847 Aguilar published in *Chambers' Miscellany* the first history of English Jews by a Jewish writer. As the scholar Michael Galchinsky notes, Aguilar's writing reflects the internal contradictions that contributed to Jewish marginalization in early Victorian culture: While she criticizes Christians for believing that all English citizens should convert to Christianity, she downplays Jewish difference and depicts Judaism primarily in the private rather than the public domain—a moderate position that may have accounted for the wide appeal of her prose.

Less moderate, however, was her assertion that in God's eyes, a woman is "a perfect equal with man." Aguilar's advocacy of equality for Jewish women and men is most evident in *Women of Israel*, from which the excerpt below is taken. This interpretation of Biblical and Talmudic heroines proceeds historically from "Wives of the Patriarchs" to "Women in the Present." Moreover, it refutes the charge that Moses viewed Hebrew women as lowly and insists that God hears women's prayers as well as men's, that the mothers of Israel are as important as the fathers. Although Aguilar supports the Victorian ideology of women's "separate sphere," she allows Jewish women more power in the home than Christian women of the era had, in part because she privileges women's role as guardian and translator of Jewish oral tradition—a task that women had undertaken since the Inquisition, when synagogues were closed and religious instruction became centered in the home. Both *Women of Israel* and *The Spirit of Judaism* received mention as groundbreaking books in an award that Aguilar won in 1847 from 300 middle-class Anglo-Jewish women, who praised her work for proving "that no female character can be more worthy than the Hebrew mother."

⇥ *from* The Exodus—Laws for the Mothers of Israel ⇤

We have seen quoted in a Jewish periodical, "that it was for the sake of the righteous women the Lord delivered our ancestors from Egypt." Scriptural authority for this assertion we certainly cannot find, as it is expressly said, "the Lord remembered the promises which he had made to Abraham, Isaac, and Jacob." We only quote it as a proof that the ancient fathers from whom we believe it taken, could not have had the low idea of women with which they are charged, to have put such an opinion forth, even in suggestion; but must have imagined the righteousness of women of no little importance towards the well-doing of the state. That so, in fact, it is, we have direct scriptural authority to believe; as not only a review of the law will make manifest, but the consequences of the sins of the women in a more distant period. Were not woman an equally responsible agent in the sight of God—were He not in His infinite mercy tenderly careful of her innocence, her honor, her well-doing, her protection by man—no law for her in particular need have been issued, nor such especial care taken to cleanse her from impurity and guilt, to free her from false charges and an unjust husband, to permit and sanctify her singular vow, and give her every incentive for a chaste, virtuous, and modest life. This need not have been—would not have been—if the Eternal had not, in His compassionating love, regarded His frailer, weaker children with even more tenderness than He looked on man, and resolved on fixing her station and her privileges, and so bringing her forward as an object at once of tenderness and respect—of cherishing, as a wife and daughter—of the deepest veneration, as a mother—the especial object of national as well as individual love and protection, as widowed and fatherless—and of the kindest, most fatherly care and gentleness, as the maid-servant. . . .

Woman is not gifted with a silvery voice and an ear for harmony, to devote to the pleasure of man alone. Let her devote them sometimes to the praises of the Lord, and bid the psalm of thanksgiving filling the sanctuary of the Lord be answered from her lips; and the sweet sanctuary of home, at morning and evening prayer, behold her leading infant lips to tune their first song in thanksgiving to their Father and their God.

As a general view of the beautiful laws constituting the Mosaic religion does not enter into the plan of this work, we shall throw together those portions on which, as they regard woman, we shall somewhat lengthily treat, without any reference to their probable dates. We know that all the laws forming our religion were given between their departure from Egypt and arrival in the promised land, and are contained principally in chapters 19, 20, 21, 22, 23, and 29 of Exodus—in the whole book of Leviticus—in chapters 5, 6, 8, 9, 15, 16, 17, 27, 28, 29, 30, 35, and 36 of Numbers—and in the whole book of Deuteronomy. From these we select and examine all that can give weight to, and throw light upon, the six divisions of our present subject.

As the first and most beautiful relationship in which woman is undeniably necessary to man—the object of his first affections, to whom he owes all of cherishing, happiness, and health, from infancy to boyhood, and often from boyhood to youth; and who, in consequence, must be entwined with every fond remembrance of childhood, the recollection of which is often the only soother, the only light, in the darker heart of man—it is but just that we should examine, first, how the holy relationship of a MOTHER in Israel is guarded and noticed by our law.

The very first command relative to the duties of man towards man, marks out the position of children with regard to their parents, male and *female*, the representatives of God on earth. It was not enough that such position should be left to the natural impulses of gratitude and affection—not enough that the love and reverence of a child to his parent should be left to his own heart, although in the cases of both Isaac and Jacob such had been so distinctly manifested. No; the same tremendous voice which bade the very earth quake, and the fast rooted mountain reel—which spoke in the midst of thunders and lightnings, "Thou shalt have no other gods but me,"—also said, "Honor thy father and thy MOTHER," and added unto its obedience a promise of reward, the only command to which recompense is annexed, that its obedience might indeed be an obedience of love. And lest there should be some natures so stubborn and obtuse that the fear of punishment only could affect, we read in the repetition, and, as it were, enlargement on the ten commandments, "And he that smiteth his father or his MOTHER shall surely be put to death, and he that curseth or revileth his father or his MOTHER shall surely be put to death" (Exodus xxi. 15–17). "Ye shall *fear* every man his MOTHER and his father, and keep my sabbaths; I am the Lord" (Levit. xix. 3). "For every one that curseth his father or his MOTHER, shall surely be put to death. He that cursed his father or his MOTHER, his blood shall be upon him." And again, in Deuteronomy v. 16, we have the repetition of the fifth commandment, the reward attending its obedience still more vividly enforced: "Honor thy father and thy MOTHER, as the Lord thy God hath commanded thee, that thy days may be prolonged, and that it may go well with thee in the land which the Lord thy God giveth thee."

With laws like these, bearing on every one of them the stamp of divine truth, of a sacred solemnity which could come from God alone, how can anyone believe in, much less assert, the Jewish degradation of woman, or call that Judaism which upholds it!

How could these solemn and often reiterated commands be obeyed, if the son of Israel beheld his mother merely the ignorant bond-slave of his father? How could he honor her? What could have such influence upon his moments of passion as to restrain him, when so tempted, from smiting, reviling, or cursing her? How could he *fear* her, when he beheld her trembling before his father, not as her husband, but as her master? But such he saw not. Weaker in frame, from her position and her duties; less mighty in mental powers, yet possessing every attribute to make home blessed, and her children holy followers of God, virtuous and patriotic citizens of their land; shrined in his heart with every memory of his infancy—such was the Hebrew mother to her son. Were the laws obeyed, there could be no neglectful or sinning mother. Not even suspicion could attack her. The law guarded her even from her own relatives, if they falsely wronged her, compelled her, even under the fear of death, to be chaste, holy, virtuous, and faithful in every duty of domestic and public life; and, therefore, it was a labor of love for her children to obey their God in honoring her, and a crime worthy of death, if indeed there could be found any sufficiently hardened and rebellious as to disobey. . . .

We here find at length a practical commentary or example, as it were, of the briefer laws on the same subject, given previously. To modern ears, and present notions of false refinement, such commands seem unnaturally harsh and terrible. In those times, they must have been needed, or they would not have been given. And beautifully, even in their harshness, do they demonstrate the reverential duty of Israelitish children to their parents. Still more powerfully do they illustrate the perfect equality of father and mother in respect to their children. It was not only that disobedience to the latter was equally punishable as to the former, but that the voice of the MOTHER was also to condemn her son, or he could not be proved guilty; a peculiarly just law in a nation where more than one wife was allowed. Without it, how often might the more favored work upon the husband to believe false tales of the off-spring of her rival! How often might innocence have been condemned, injustice and cruelty permitted, in a man's own household! Evils effectually prevented by the father's witness being unavailable without that of the accused's own mother—one, we must feel, not at all likely to come forward against her own child, unless his crimes had been so heinous as to prevent the possibility of her shielding him any longer. We have no recorded instance of such a fearful evil in Israel; but the severe law given in case of such, should never be forgotten by us, marking, as it does, the wrath and jus-tice of the Lord against all those of His chosen people who could forget, neglect, or wilfully abuse, in any one point, their duty to their early parents.

Although mothers are not individually commanded to instruct their children in the knowledge of God and His Law, they are certainly joined with the fathers in the performance of that sacred duty. Every statute, every ordinance, given by the Lord to Moses, was always introduced by the command, "Speak ye to the *Children of Israel;*" "Say ye to the children of Israel;" or, "Hear, O Israel;" words including the *whole* con-gregation, male and FEMALE. Had *man* only been included, Moses would have addressed them as sons, or as fathers of tribes, as we find Aaron and his sons, and the priests or Levites, in some few instances particularly specified. That woman is inti-mately joined with man in the religious instruction of her children, is also proved by the fact that the *mothers* of the kings of Israel and Judah are always mentioned by name, as if to them, yet more than to their fathers, they owed their early impressions of good or evil which their after lives displayed. . . .

Will, then, the Hebrew mother rest content with the station assigned her by the ignorant and the prejudiced, and not strain every nerve, rouse every energy, to make the command of the Eternal for her children to honor and fear her, easy, and joyous to obey?

She has done, and she does this! Not a slur, not a stigma, not a shadow can be flung upon the conduct of Hebrew mothers to their offspring. Neglect, injustice, par-tiality, want of affection, harshness, coldness flung by fashion between mother and child, that littleness and jealousy which would keep back youthful loveliness for a longer individual reign—such things may be known—may be common—among oth-er nations, but to the Hebrew they are utterly unknown. It is easy to assert that the woman of Israel is degraded and a slave; but did such false accusers visit a domestic circle—did they but see a Hebrew mother and her children—they would find it diffi-cult to *prove* it. Then let every son of Israel receive such religious training from his mother, in addition, or rather closely twined, to the moral and intellectual education she has so long given, that he may be ready, from his very boyhood, indignantly to repudiate the charge, and prove, by his whole conduct—alike in public career, as well as his domestic reverence and love—that his mother is as free in the sight of man, as responsible in the sight of God, and as much the possessor of an immortal spirit as his father and himself.

To the Mosaic religion, then, and to no other, does not only Israel, but every other nation by whom the Bible is acknowledged divine, owe the elevation, the dig-nity, the holiness of woman as a MOTHER, a position marked out by God Himself, and proclaimed and held sacred, not only by the awful threat of punishment, but by the solemn promise of divine reward. How sacred then to every son and daughter of Israel must be their duty to their parents! Disobedience, neglect, scorn, are no longer capital offences according to the justice of man; but, oh! let us not for one moment forget, that the same God who commanded that such they should be, is watching over Israel still, will demand from every child if His command has been obeyed—from every parent if they have done their duty, and taught their children from earliest years, that *disobedience to them is disobedience to their God, and in His eyes, and in His law, a capital offense.* Were this truth more constantly, more impressively enforced, the reciprocal duties of parent and child would be more easily and more happily fulfilled; and the heartburnings, the anguish, occasioned to parents by neglect and unkindness, and the rebellion and constant struggles of their offspring to fling off an authority which has never been exerted in infancy, and so must gall in youth, alike be at an end, and Israel's homes, as well as Israel's law, proclaim the guiding spirit and loving mercy of the Lord.   *1844*

Kate Chopin
1851–1904

"I would give up my life for my children; but I wouldn't give myself," claims Edna Pontellier, the protagonist of KATE CHOPIN's *The Awakening*, a novella that explores the complex intersection of maternity, sexuality, and selfhood. Chopin was born Katherine O'Flaherty in St. Louis, Missouri, to an Irish merchant father, Thomas O'Flaherty, and a mother of French descent, Eliza Faris. After her father was killed in a train wreck when she was four, Chopin was raised by her mother, grandmother, and great-grandmother, all widows; she attended the St. Louis Academy of the Sacred Heart and graduated in 1868. In 1870 she met and married Oscar Chopin, a banker, and after a honeymoon in Europe moved with him to New Orleans, where she was introduced to the Creole society that would later provide the subject matter for her fiction. Having observed his father's harsh treatment of his mother, Oscar Chopin supported his wife's desire for freedom and extensive amounts of solitude, and the marriage was apparently happy. During the next ten years she gave birth to six children and cared for them full-time while her husband worked as a cotton merchant; when his business failed in 1880, the family moved to the village of Cloutierville in Nachitoches Parish, Louisiana, where Oscar managed plantations and owned a general store. The colorful people and landscapes of this Acadian, or Cajun, area also populate Chopin's stories. Shortly after her husband's death in 1882 of swamp fever, Chopin returned to St. Louis to be with her mother, who died in 1885. Two years later, to support her family and entertain herself, Chopin began to write at the urging of her friend and physician, Dr. Frederick Kolbenheyer.

The primary sylistic influence on Chopin's fiction was the French writer Guy de Maupassant, who rejected the artificial plot devices that characterized nineteenth-century American fiction in favor of an introspective realism. Her development of strong female protagonists was influenced by the American regional writers Mary E. Wilkins Freeman and Sarah Orne Jewett. From early in her career editors exhorted Chopin to moderate her women characters, an admonition she appears rarely to have heeded; even her early fiction contains independent-spirited women. Her first novel, *At Fault* (1890), presents the forbidden topic of divorce in a sympathetic manner. *Bayou Folk* (1894) and *A Night in Acadie* (1897) address issues of sexuality, love, race, and class. "Desiree's Baby," one of her most highly acclaimed stories, features an orphaned woman married to a plantation owner who treats his slaves cruelly. The birth of a son who first delights but then troubles Desiree, her uneasy identification with the slaves, and her husband's ultimate rejection offer a melodramatic but powerful perspective on white Southern racism and women's treatment as men's possessions.

The Awakening (1899), called by Willa Cather a "Creole *Bovary*" after Gustave Flaubert's French classic, has been heralded since the 1970s as a major work of American fiction. In its exploration of women as sexual objects, symbolic property, and oppressed mothers it was clearly ahead of its time. The story of Edna Pontellier's attempts to gain autonomy despite the social strictures placed on her was condemned by contemporary critics, who chastised Chopin for entering "the overworked field of sex fiction." The *New Orleans Times-Democrat* denigrated Edna for being "insufficiently maternal," since she put sexual gratification above the welfare of her children. At first undaunted, Chopin issued a mock apology for the novel, claiming that "I never dreamed of Mrs. Pontellier making such a mess of things," but as friends deserted her and her literary reputation languished, Chopin was forced to take the controversy her novel had initiated more seriously; she did not publish again. The Awakening was a novel forgotten to all but a few until its rediscovery by the Norwegian scholar Per Seyersted, who published a biography of Chopin in 1969, and its subsequent embrace by feminist critics in the 1970s.

⊰ The Awakening ⊱

I

A green and yellow parrot, which hung in a cage outside the door, kept repeating over and over:

"*Allez vous-en! Allez vous-en! Sapristi!*[1] That's all right!"

He could speak a little Spanish, and also a language which nobody understood, unless it was the mockingbird that hung on the other side of the door, whistling his fluty notes out upon the breeze with maddening persistence.

Mr. Pontellier, unable to read his newspaper with any degree of comfort, arose with an expression and an exclamation of disgust. He walked down the gallery and across the narrow "bridges" which connected the Lebrun cottages one with the other. He had been seated before the door of the main house. The parrot and the mockingbird were the property of Madame Lebrun, and they had the right to make all the noise they wished. Mr. Pontellier had the privilege of quitting their society when they ceased to be entertaining.

He stopped before the door of his own cottage, which was the fourth one from the main building and next to the last. Seating himself in a wicker rocker which was there, he once more applied himself to the task of reading the newspaper. The day was Sunday; the paper was a day old. The Sunday papers had not yet reached Grand Isle. He was already acquainted with the market reports, and he glanced restlessly over the editorials and bits of news which he had not had time to read before quitting New Orleans the day before.

Mr. Pontellier wore eyeglasses. He was a man of forty, of medium height and rather slender build; he stooped a little. His hair was brown and straight, parted on one side. His beard was neatly and closely trimmed.

Once in a while he withdrew his glance from the newspaper and looked about him. There was more noise than ever over at the house. The main building was called "the house," to distinguish it from the cottages. The chattering and whistling

1. "Go away! Go away! For God's sake!"

birds were still at it. Two young girls, the Farival twins, were playing a duet from "Zampa" upon the piano. Madame Lebrun was bustling in and out, giving orders in a high key to a yardboy whenever she got inside the house, and directions in an equally high voice to a dining-room servant whenever she got outside. She was a fresh, pretty woman, clad always in white with elbow sleeves. Her starched skirts crinkled as she came and went. Farther down, before one of the cottages, a lady in black was walking demurely up and down, telling her beads. A good many persons of the *pension* had gone over to the *Chênière Caminada* in Beaudelet's lugger to hear mass. Some young people were out under the water-oaks playing croquet. Mr. Pontellier's two children were there—sturdy little fellows of four and five. A quadroon nurse followed them about with a faraway, meditative air.

Mr. Pontellier finally lit a cigar and began to smoke, letting the paper drag idly from his hand. He fixed his gaze upon a white sunshade that was advancing at snail's pace from the beach. He could see it plainly between the gaunt trunks of the water-oaks and across the stretch of yellow chamomile. The Gulf looked far away, melting hazily into the blue of the horizon. The sunshade continued to approach slowly. Beneath its pink-lined shelter were his wife, Mrs. Pontellier, and young Robert Lebrun. When they reached the cottage, the two seated themselves with some appearance of fatigue upon the upper step of the porch, facing each other, each leaning against a supporting post.

"What folly! to bathe at such an hour in such heat!" exclaimed Mr. Pontellier. He himself had taken a plunge at daylight. That was why the morning seemed long to him.

"You are burnt beyond recognition," he added, looking at his wife as one looks at a valuable piece of personal property which has suffered some damage. She held up her hands, strong, shapely hands, and surveyed them critically, drawing up her lawn sleeves above the wrists. Looking at them reminded her of her rings, which she had given to her husband before leaving for the beach. She silently reached out to him, and he, understanding, took the rings from his vest pocket and dropped them into her open palm. She slipped them upon her fingers; then clasping her knees, she looked across at Robert and began to laugh. The rings sparkled upon her fingers. He sent back an answering smile.

"What is it?" asked Pontellier, looking lazily and amused from one to the other. It was some utter nonsense; some adventure out there in the water, and they both tried to relate it at once. It did not seem half so amusing when told. They realized this, and so did Mr. Pontellier. He yawned and stretched himself. Then he got up, saying he had half a mind to go over to Klein's hotel and play a game of billiards.

"Come go along, Lebrun," he proposed to Robert. But Robert admitted quite frankly that he preferred to stay where he was and talk to Mrs. Pontellier.

"Well, send him about his business when he bores you, Edna," instructed her husband as he prepared to leave.

"Here, take the umbrella," she exclaimed, holding it out to him. He accepted the sunshade, and lifting it over his head descended the steps and walked away.

"Coming back to dinner?" his wife called after him. He halted a moment and shrugged his shoulders. He felt in his vest pocket; there was a ten-dollar bill there. He did not know; perhaps he would return for the early dinner and perhaps he would not. It all depended upon the company which he found over at Klein's and the size of "the game." He did not say this, but she understood it, and laughed, nodding goodbye to him.

Both children wanted to follow their father when they saw him starting out. He kissed them and promised to bring them back bonbons and peanuts.

II

Mrs. Pontellier's eyes were quick and bright; they were a yellowish brown, about the color of her hair. She had a way of turning them swiftly upon an object and holding them there as if lost in some inward maze of contemplation or thought.

Her eyebrows were a shade darker than her hair. They were thick and almost horizontal, emphasizing the depth of her eyes. She was rather handsome than beautiful. Her face was captivating by reason of a certain frankness of expression and a contradictory subtle play of features. Her manner was engaging.

Robert rolled a cigarette. He smoked cigarettes because he could not afford cigars, he said. He had a cigar in his pocket which Mr. Pontellier had presented him with, and he was saving it for his after-dinner smoke.

This seemed quite proper and natural on his part. In coloring he was not unlike his companion. A clean-shaved face made the resemblance more pronounced than it would otherwise have been. There rested no shadow of care upon his open countenance. His eyes gathered in and reflected the light and languor of the summer day.

Mrs. Pontellier reached over for a palm-leaf fan that lay on the porch and began to fan herself, while Robert sent between his lips light puffs from his cigarette. They chatted incessantly: about the things around them; their amusing adventure out in the water—it had again assumed its entertaining aspect; about the wind, the trees, the people who had gone to the *Chênière*; about the children playing croquet under the oaks, and the Farival twins, who were now performing the overture to "The Poet and the Peasant." Robert talked a good deal about himself. He was very young, and did not know any better. Mrs. Pontellier talked a little about herself for the same reason. Each was interested in what the other said. Robert spoke of his intention to go to Mexico in the autumn, where fortune awaited him. He was always intending to go to Mexico, but some way never got there. Meanwhile he held on to his modest position in a mercantile house in New Orleans, where an equal familiarity with English, French and Spanish gave him no small value as a clerk and correspondent.

He was spending his summer vacation, as he always did, with his mother at Grand Isle. In former times, before Robert could remember, "the house" had been a summer luxury of the Lebruns. Now, flanked by its dozen or more cottages, which were always filled with exclusive visitors from the "*Quartier Français*," it enabled Madame Lebrun to maintain the easy and comfortable existence which appeared to be her birthright.

Mrs. Pontellier talked about her father's Mississippi plantation and her girlhood home in the old Kentucky bluegrass country. She was an American woman, with a small infusion of French which seemed to have been lost in dilution. She read a letter from her sister, who was away in the East, and who had engaged herself to be married. Robert was interested, and wanted to know what manner of girls the sisters were, what the father was like, and how long the mother had been dead.

When Mrs. Pontellier folded the letter it was time for her to dress for the early dinner.

"I see Léonce isn't coming back," she said, with a glance in the direction whence her husband had disappeared. Robert supposed he was not, as there were a good many New Orleans club men over at Klein's.

When Mrs. Pontellier left him to enter her room, the young man descended the steps and strolled over toward the croquet players, where, during the half-hour before dinner, he amused himself with the little Pontellier children, who were very fond of him.

III

It was eleven o'clock that night when Mr. Pontellier returned from Klein's hotel. He was in an excellent humor, in high spirits, and very talkative. His entrance awoke his wife, who was in bed and fast asleep when he came in. He talked to her while he undressed, telling her anecdotes and bits of news and gossip that he had gathered during the day. From his trousers pockets he took a fistful of crumpled bank notes and a good deal of silver coin, which he piled on the bureau indiscriminately with keys, knife, handkerchief, and whatever else happened to be in his pockets. She was overcome with sleep, and answered him with little half utterances.

He thought it very discouraging that his wife, who was the sole object of his existence, evinced so little interest in things which concerned him, and valued so little his conversation.

Mr. Pontellier had forgotten the bonbons and peanuts for the boys. Notwithstanding he loved them very much, and went into the adjoining room where they slept to take a look at them and make sure that they were resting comfortably. The result of his investigation was far from satisfactory. He turned and shifted the youngsters about in bed. One of them began to kick and talk about a basket full of crabs.

Mr. Pontellier returned to his wife with the information that Raoul had a high fever and needed looking after. Then he lit a cigar and went and sat near the open door to smoke it.

Mrs. Pontellier was quite sure Raoul had no fever. He had gone to bed perfectly well, she said, and nothing had ailed him all day. Mr. Pontellier was too well acquainted with fever symptoms to be mistaken. He assured her the child was consuming at that moment in the next room.

He reproached his wife with her inattention, her habitual neglect of the children. If it was not a mother's place to look after children, whose on earth was it? He himself had his hands full with his brokerage business. He could not be in two places at once; making a living for his family on the street, and staying at home to see that no harm befell them. He talked in a monotonous, insistent way.

Mrs. Pontellier sprang out of bed and went into the next room. She soon came back and sat on the edge of the bed, leaning her head down on the pillow. She said nothing, and refused to answer her husband when he questioned her. When his cigar was smoked out he went to bed, and in half a minute he was fast asleep.

Mrs. Pontellier was by that time thoroughly awake. She began to cry a little, and wiped her eyes on the sleeve of her *peignoir*. Blowing out the candle, which her husband had left burning, she slipped her bare feet into a pair of satin mules at the foot of the bed and went out on the porch, where she sat down in the wicker chair and began to rock gently to and fro.

It was then past midnight. The cottages were all dark. A single faint light gleamed out from the hallway of the house. There was no sound abroad except the hooting of an old owl in the top of a water-oak, and the everlasting voice of the sea, that was not uplifted at that soft hour. It broke like a mournful lullaby upon the night.

The tears came so fast to Mrs. Pontellier's eyes that the damp sleeve of her *peignoir* no longer served to dry them. She was holding the back of her chair with one hand; her loose sleeve had slipped almost to the shoulder of her uplifted arm. Turning, she thrust her face, streaming and wet, into the bend of her arm, and she went on crying there, not caring any longer to dry her face, her eyes, her arms. She could not have told why she was crying. Such experiences as the foregoing were not uncommon in her married life. They seemed never before to have weighed much against the abundance of her husband's kindness and a uniform devotion which had come to be tacit and self-understood.

An indescribable oppression, which seemed to generate in some unfamiliar part of her consciousness, filled her whole being with a vague anguish. It was like a shadow, like a mist passing across her soul's summer day. It was strange and unfamiliar; it was a mood. She did not sit there inwardly upbraiding her husband, lamenting at Fate, which had directed her footsteps to the path which they had taken. She was just having a good cry all to herself. The mosquitoes made merry over her, biting her firm, round arms and nipping at her bare insteps.

The little stinging, buzzing imps succeeded in dispelling a mood which might have held her there in the darkness half a night longer.

The following morning Mr. Pontellier was up in good time to take the rockaway which was to convey him to the steamer at the wharf. He was returning to the city to his business, and they would not see him again at the Island till the coming Saturday. He had regained his composure, which seemed to have been somewhat impaired the night before. He was eager to be gone, as he looked forward to a lively week in Carondelet Street.

Mr. Pontellier gave his wife half of the money which he had brought away from Klein's hotel the evening before. She liked money as well as most women, and accepted it with no little satisfaction.

"It will buy a handsome wedding present for Sister Janet!" she exclaimed, smoothing out the bills as she counted them one by one.

"Oh! we'll treat Sister Janet better than that, my dear," he laughed, as he prepared to kiss her goodbye.

The boys were tumbling about, clinging to his legs, imploring that numerous things be brought back to them. Mr. Pontellier was a great favorite, and ladies, men, children, even nurses, were always on hand to say goodbye to him. His wife stood smiling and waving, the boys shouting, as he disappeared in the old rockaway down the sandy road.

A few days later a box arrived for Mrs. Pontellier from New Orleans. It was from her husband. It was filled with *friandises*,[2] with luscious and toothsome bits— the finest of fruits, *patés,* a rare bottle or two, delicious syrups, and bonbons in abundance.

Mrs. Pontellier was always very generous with the contents of such a box; she was quite used to receiving them when away from home. The *patés* and fruit were brought to the diningroom; the bonbons were passed around. And the ladies, selecting with dainty and discriminating fingers and a little greedily, all declared that Mr. Pontellier was the best husband in the world. Mrs. Pontellier was forced to admit that she knew of none better.

IV

It would have been a difficult matter for Mr. Pontellier to define to his own satisfaction or anyone else's wherein his wife failed in her duty toward their children. It was something which he felt rather than perceived, and he never voiced the feeling without subsequent regret and ample atonement.

---

2. *Friandises* are delicacies

If one of the little Pontellier boys took a tumble whilst at play, he was not apt to rush crying to his mother's arms for comfort; he would more likely pick himself up, wipe the water out of his eyes and the sand out of his mouth, and go on playing. Tots as they were, they pulled together and stood their ground in childish battles with doubled fists and uplifted voices, which usually prevailed against the other mother-tots. The quadroon nurse was looked upon as a huge encumbrance, only good to button up waists and panties and to brush and part hair; since it seemed to be a law of society that hair must be parted and brushed.

In short, Mrs. Pontellier was not a mother-woman. The mother-women seemed to prevail that summer at Grand Isle. It was easy to know them, fluttering about with extended, protecting wings when any harm, real or imaginary, threatened their precious brood. They were women who idolized their children, worshiped their husbands, and esteemed it a holy privilege to efface themselves as individuals and grow wings as ministering angels.

Many of them were delicious in the role; one of them was the embodiment of every womanly grace and charm. If her husband did not adore her, he was a brute, deserving of death by slow torture. Her name was Adèle Ratignolle. There are no words to describe her save the old ones that have served so often to picture the bygone heroine of romance and the fair lady of our dreams. There was nothing subtle or hidden about her charms; her beauty was all there, flaming and apparent: the spun-gold hair that comb nor confining pin could restrain; the blue eyes that were like nothing but sapphires; two lips that pouted, that were so red one could only think of cherries or some other delicious crimson fruit in looking at them. She was growing a little stout, but it did not seem to detract an iota from the grace of every step, pose, gesture. One would not have wanted her white neck a mite less full or her beautiful arms more slender. Never were hands more exquisite than hers, and it was a joy to look at them when she threaded her needle or adjusted her gold thimble to her taper[ed] middle finger as she sewed away on the little night-drawers or fashioned a bodice or a bib.

Madame Ratignolle was very fond of Mrs. Pontellier, and often she took her sewing and went over to sit with her in the afternoons. She was sitting there the afternoon of the day the box arrived from New Orleans. She had possession of the rocker, and she was busily engaged in sewing upon a diminutive pair of night-drawers.

She had brought the pattern of the drawers for Mrs. Pontellier to cut out—a marvel of construction, fashioned to enclose a baby's body so effectually that only two small eyes might look out from the garment, like an Eskimo's. They were designed for winter wear, when treacherous drafts came down chimneys and insidious currents of deadly cold found their way through keyholes.

Mrs. Pontellier's mind was quite at rest concerning the present material needs of her children, and she could not see the use of anticipating and making winter night garments the subject of her summer meditations. But she did not want to appear unamiable and uninterested, so she had brought forth newspapers, which she spread upon the floor of the gallery, and under Madame Ratignolle's directions she had cut a pattern of the impervious garment.

Robert was there, seated as he had been the Sunday before, and Mrs. Pontellier also occupied her former position on the upper step, leaning listlessly against the post. Beside her was a box of bonbons, which she held out at intervals to Madame Ratignolle.

That lady seemed at a loss to make a selection, but finally settled upon a stick of nougat, wondering if it were not too rich; whether it could possibly hurt her.

Madame Ratignolle had been married seven years. About every two years she had a baby. At that time she had three babies, and was beginning to think of a fourth one. She was always talking about her "condition." Her "condition" was in no way apparent, and no one would have known a thing about it but for her persistence in making it the subject of conversation.

Robert started to reassure her, asserting that he had known a lady who had subsisted upon nougat during the entire—but seeing the color mount into Mrs. Pontellier's face he checked himself and changed the subject.

Mrs. Pontellier, though she had married a Creole, was not thoroughly at home in the society of Creoles; never before had she been thrown so intimately among them. There were only Creoles that summer at Lebrun's. They all knew each other, and felt like one large family, among whom existed the most amicable relations. A characteristic which distinguished them and which impressed Mrs. Pontellier most forcibly was their entire absence of prudery. Their freedom of expression was at first incomprehensible to her, though she had no difficulty in reconciling it with a lofty chastity which in the Creole woman seems to be inborn and unmistakable.

Never would Edna Pontellier forget the shock with which she heard Madame Ratignolle relating to old Monsieur Farival the harrowing story of one of her *accouchements*,[3] withholding no intimate detail. She was growing accustomed to like shocks, but she could not keep the mounting color back from her cheeks. Oftener than once her coming had interrupted the droll story with which Robert was entertaining some amused group of married women.

A book had gone the rounds of the *pension*. When it came her turn to read it, she did so with profound astonishment. She felt moved to read the book in secret and solitude, though none of the others had done so—to hide it from view at the sound of approaching footsteps. It was openly criticised and freely discussed at table. Mrs. Pontellier gave over being astonished, and concluded that wonders would never cease.

V

They formed a congenial group sitting there that summer afternoon—Madame Ratignolle sewing away, often stopping to relate a story or incident with much expressive gesture of her perfect hands; Robert and Mrs. Pontellier sitting idle, exchanging occasional words, glances or smiles which indicated a certain advanced stage of intimacy and camaraderie.

He had lived in her shadow during the past month. No one thought anything of it. Many had predicted that Robert would devote himself to Mrs. Pontellier when he arrived. Since the age of fifteen, which was eleven years before, Robert each summer at Grand Isle had constituted himself the devoted attendant of some fair dame or damsel. Sometimes it was a young girl, again a widow; but as often as not it was some interesting married woman.

For two consecutive seasons he lived in the sunlight of Mademoiselle Duvigné's presence. But she died between summers; then Robert posed as an inconsolable, prostrating himself at the feet of Madame Ratignolle for whatever crumbs of sympathy and comfort she might be pleased to vouchsafe.

Mrs. Pontellier liked to sit and gaze at her fair companion as she might look upon a faultless Madonna.

3. Childbirths.

"Could anyone fathom the cruelty beneath that fair exterior?" murmured Robert. "She knew that I adored her once, and she let me adore her. It was 'Robert, come; go; stand up; sit down; do this; do that; see if the baby sleeps; my thimble, please, that I left God knows where. Come and read Daudet to me while I sew.'"

"Par example! I never had to ask. You were always there under my feet, like a troublesome cat."

"You mean like an adoring dog. And just as soon as Ratignolle appeared on the scene, then it *was* like a dog. '*Passez! Adieu! Allez vous-en!*'"

"Perhaps I feared to make Alphonse jealous," she interjoined, with excessive naïveté. That made them all laugh. The right hand jealous of the left! The heart jealous of the soul! But for that matter, the Creole husband is never jealous; with him the gangrene passion is one which has become dwarfed by disuse.

Meanwhile Robert, addressing Mrs. Pontellier, continued to tell of his one-time hopeless passion for Madame Ratignolle; of sleepless nights, of consuming flames till the very sea sizzled when he took his daily plunge. While the lady at the needle kept up a little running, contemptuous comment:

"*Blagueur—farceur—gros bête va!*"[4]

He never assumed this serio-comic tone when alone with Mrs. Pontellier. She never knew precisely what to make of it; at that moment it was impossible for her to guess how much of it was jest and what proportion was earnest. It was understood that he had often spoken words of love to Madame Ratignolle, without any thought of being taken seriously. Mrs. Pontellier was glad he had not assumed a similar role toward herself. It would have been unacceptable and annoying.

Mrs. Pontellier had brought her sketching materials, which she sometimes dabbled with in an unprofessional way. She liked the dabbling. She felt in it satisfaction of a kind which no other employment afforded her.

She had long wished to try herself on Madame Ratignolle. Never had that lady seemed a more tempting subject than at that moment, seated there like some sensuous Madonna, with the gleam of the fading day enriching her splendid color.

Robert crossed over and seated himself upon the step below Mrs. Pontellier, that he might watch her work. She handled her brushes with a certain ease and freedom which came, not from long and close acquaintance with them, but from a natural aptitude. Robert followed her work with close attention, giving forth little ejaculatory expressions of appreciation in French, which he addressed to Madame Ratignolle.

"*Mais ce n'est pas mal! Elle s'y connait, elle a de la force, oui.*"[5]

During his oblivious attention he once quietly rested his head against Mrs. Pontellier's arm. As gently she repulsed him. Once again he repeated the offense. She could not but believe it to be thoughtlessness on his part; yet that was no reason she should submit to it. She did not remonstrate, except again to repulse him quietly but firmly. He offered no apology.

The picture completed bore no resemblance to Madame Ratignolle. She was greatly disappointed to find that it did not look like her. But it was a fair enough piece of work, and in many respects satisfying.

Mrs. Pontellier evidently did not think so. After surveying the sketch critically she drew a broad smudge of paint across its surface, and crumpled the paper between her hands.

4. "Jester-joker-you're so silly!"   5. "But it isn't bad. She has aptitude, yes?"

The youngsters came tumbling up the steps, the quadroon following at the respectful distance which they required her to observe. Mrs. Pontellier made them carry her paints and things into the house. She sought to detain them for a little talk and some pleasantry. But they were greatly in earnest. They had only come to investigate the contents of the bonbon box. They accepted without murmuring what she chose to give them, each holding out two chubby hands scooplike, in the vain hope that they might be filled; and then away they went.

The sun was low in the west, and the breeze soft and languorous that came up from the south, charged with the seductive odor of the sea. Children, freshly befurbeloved, were gathering for their games under the oaks. Their voices were high and penetrating.

Madame Ratignolle folded her sewing, placing thimble, scissors and thread all neatly together in the roll, which she pinned securely. She complained of faintness. Mrs. Pontellier flew for the cologne water and a fan. She bathed Madame Ratignolle's face with cologne, while Robert plied the fan with unnecessary vigor.

The spell was soon over, and Mrs. Pontellier could not help wondering if there were not a little imagination responsible for its origin, for the rose tint had never faded from her friend's face.

She stood watching the fair woman walk down the long line of galleries with the grace and majesty which queens are sometimes supposed to possess. Her little ones ran to meet her. Two of them clung about her white skirts, the third she took from its nurse and with a thousand endearments bore it along in her own fond, encircling arms. Though, as everybody well knew, the doctor had forbidden her to lift so much as a pin!

"Are you going bathing?" asked Robert of Mrs. Pontellier. It was not so much a question as a reminder.

"Oh, no," she answered, with a tone of indecision. "I'm tired; I think not." Her glance wandered from his face away toward the Gulf, whose sonorous murmur reached her like a loving but imperative entreaty.

"Oh, come!" he insisted. "You mustn't miss your bath. Come on. The water must be delicious; it will not hurt you. Come."

He reached up for her big, rough straw hat that hung on a peg outside the door, and put it on her head. They descended the steps, and walked away together toward the beach. The sun was low in the west and the breeze was soft and warm.

VI

Edna Pontellier could not have told why, wishing to go to the beach with Robert, she should in the first place have declined, and in the second place have followed in obedience to one of the two contradictory impulses which impelled her.

A certain light was beginning to dawn dimly within her—the light which, showing the way, forbids it.

At the early period it served but to bewilder her. It moved her to dreams, to thoughtfulness, to the shadowy anguish which had overcome her the midnight when she had abandoned herself to tears.

In short, Mrs. Pontellier was beginning to realize her position in the universe as a human being, and to recognize her relations as an individual to the world within and about her. This may seem like a ponderous weight of wisdom to descend upon the soul of a young woman of twenty-eight—perhaps more wisdom than the Holy Ghost is usually pleased to vouchsafe to any woman.

But the beginning of things, of a world especially, is necessarily vague, tangled, chaotic, and exceedingly disturbing. How few of us ever emerge from such beginning! How many souls perish in its tumult!

The voice of the sea is seductive; never ceasing, whispering, clamoring, murmuring, inviting the soul to wander for a spell in abysses of solitude; to lose itself in mazes of inward contemplation.

The voice of the sea speaks to the soul. The touch of the sea is sensuous, enfolding the body in its soft, close embrace.

VII

Mrs. Pontellier was not a woman given to confidences, a characteristic hitherto contrary to her nature. Even as a child she had lived her own small life all within herself. At a very early period she had apprehended instinctively the dual life—that outward existence which conforms, the inward life which questions.

That summer at Grand Isle she began to loosen a little the mantle of reserve that had always enveloped her. There may have been—there must have been—influences, both subtle and apparent, working in their several ways to induce her to do this; but the most obvious was the influence of Adèle Ratignolle. The excessive physical charm of the Creole had first attracted her, for Edna had a sensuous susceptibility to beauty. Then the candor of the woman's whole existence, which every one might read, and which formed so striking a contrast to her own habitual reserve—this might have furnished a link. Who can tell what metals the gods use in forging the subtle bond which we call sympathy, which we might as well call love.

The two women went away one morning to the beach together, arm in arm, under the huge white sunshade. Edna had prevailed upon Madame Ratignolle to leave the children behind, though she could not induce her to relinquish a diminutive roll of needlework, which Adèle begged to be allowed to slip into the depths of her pocket. In some unaccountable way they had escaped from Robert.

The walk to the beach was no inconsiderable one, consisting as it did of a long, sandy path, upon which a sporadic and tangled growth that bordered it on either side made frequent and unexpected inroads. There were acres of yellow chamomile reaching out on either hand. Further away still, vegetable gardens abounded, with frequent small plantations of orange or lemon trees intervening. The dark green clusters glistened from afar in the sun.

The women were both of goodly height, Madame Ratignolle possessing the more feminine and matronly figure. The charm of Edna Pontellier's physique stole insensibly upon you. The lines of her body were long, clean and symmetrical; it was a body which occasionally fell into splendid poses; there was no suggestion of the trim, stereotyped fashionplate about it. A casual and indiscriminating observer, in passing, might not cast a second glance upon the figure. But with more feeling and discernment he would have recognized the noble beauty of its modeling, and the graceful severity of poise and movement, which made Edna Pontellier different from the crowd.

She wore a cool muslin that morning—white, with a waving vertical line of brown running through it; also a white linen collar and the big straw hat which she had taken from the peg outside the door. The hat rested any way on her yellow-brown hair, that waved a little, was heavy, and clung close to her head.

Madame Ratignolle, more careful of her complexion, had twined a gauze veil about her head. She wore dogskin gloves, with gauntlets that protected her wrists.

She was dressed in pure white, with a fluffiness of ruffles that became her. The draperies and fluttering things which she wore suited her rich, luxuriant beauty as a greater severity of line could not have done.

There were a number of bathhouses along the beach, of rough but solid construction, built with small, protecting galleries facing the water. Each house consisted of two compartments, and each family at Lebrun's possessed a compartment for itself, fitted out with all the essential paraphernalia of the bath and whatever other conveniences the owners might desire. The two women had no intention of bathing; they had just strolled down to the beach for a walk and to be alone and near the water. The Pontellier and Ratignolle compartments adjoined one another under the same roof.

Mrs. Pontellier had brought down her key through force of habit. Unlocking the door of her bathroom she went inside, and soon emerged, bringing a rug, which she spread upon the floor of the gallery, and two huge hair pillows covered with crash, which she placed against the front of the building.

The two seated themselves there in the shade of the porch, side by side, with their backs against the pillows and their feet extended. Madame Ratignolle removed her veil, wiped her face with a rather delicate handkerchief, and fanned herself with the fan which she always carried suspended somewhere about her person by a long, narrow ribbon. Edna removed her collar and opened her dress at the throat. She took the fan from Madame Ratignolle and began to fan both herself and her companion. It was very warm, and for a while they did nothing but exchange remarks about the heat, the sun, the glare. But there was a breeze blowing, a choppy, stiff wind that whipped the water into froth. It fluttered the skirts of the two women and kept them for a while engaged in adjusting, readjusting, tucking in, securing hairpins and hatpins. A few persons were sporting some distance away in the water. The beach was very still of human sound at that hour. The lady in black was reading her morning devotions on the porch of a neighboring bathhouse. Two young lovers were exchanging their hearts' yearnings beneath the children's tent, which they had found unoccupied.

Edna Pontellier, casting her eyes about, had finally kept them at rest upon the sea. The day was clear and carried the gaze out as far as the blue sky went; there were a few white clouds suspended idly over the horizon. A lateen sail was visible in the direction of Cat Island, and others to the south seemed almost motionless in the far distance.

"Of whom—of what are you thinking?" asked Adèle of her companion, whose countenance she had been watching with a little amused attention, arrested by the absorbed expression which seemed to have seized and fixed every feature into a statuesque repose.

"Nothing," returned Mrs. Pontellier, with a start, adding at once: "How stupid! But it seems to me it is the reply we make instinctively to such a question. Let me see," she went on, throwing back her head and narrowing her fine eyes till they shone like two vivid points of light. "Let me see. I was really not conscious of thinking of anything; but perhaps I can retrace my thoughts."

"Oh! never mind!" laughed Madame Ratignolle. "I am not quite so exacting. I will let you off this time. It is really too hot to think, especially to think about thinking."

"But for the fun of it," persisted Edna. "First of all, the sight of the water stretching so far away, those motionless sails against the blue sky, made a delicious picture that I just wanted to sit and look at. The hot wind beating in my face made me think—without any connection that I can trace—of a summer day in Kentucky, of a meadow that seemed as big as the ocean to the very little girl walking through the grass, which was higher than her waist. She threw out her arms as if swimming when she walked, beating the tall grass as one strikes out in the water. Oh, I see the connection now!"

"Where were you going that day in Kentucky, walking through the grass?"

"I don't remember now. I was just walking diagonally across a big field. My sunbonnet obstructed the view. I could see only the stretch of green before me, and I felt as if I must walk on forever, without coming to the end of it. I don't remember whether I was frightened or pleased. I must have been entertained."

"Likely as not it was Sunday," she laughed; "and I was running away from prayers, from the Presbyterian service, read in a spirit of gloom by my father that chills me yet to think of."

"And have you been running away from prayers ever since, *ma chère?*" asked Madame Ratignolle, amused.

"No! oh, no!" Edna hastened to say. "I was a little unthinking child in those days, just following a misleading impulse without question. On the contrary, during one period of my life religion took a firm hold upon me; after I was twelve and until—until—why, I suppose until now, though I never thought much about it—just driven along by habit. But do you know," she broke off, turning her quick eyes upon Madame Ratignolle and leaning forward a little so as to bring her face quite close to that of her companion, "sometimes I feel this summer as if I were walking through the green meadow again; idly, aimlessly, unthinking and unguided."

Madame Ratignolle laid her hand over that of Mrs. Pontellier, which was near her. Seeing that the hand was not withdrawn, she clasped it firmly and warmly. She even stroked it a little, fondly, with the other hand, murmuring in an undertone, *"Pauvre chérie."*

The action was at first a little confusing to Edna, but she soon lent herself readily to the Creole's gentle caress. She was not accustomed to an outward and spoken expression of affection, either in herself or in others. She and her younger sister, Janet, had quarreled a good deal through force of unfortunate habit. Her older sister, Margaret, was matronly and dignified, probably from having assumed matronly and housewifely responsibilities too early in life, their mother having died when they were quite young. Margaret was not effusive; she was practical. Edna had had an occasional girlfriend, but whether accidentally or not, they seemed to have been all of one type—the self-contained. She never realized that the reserve of her own character had much, perhaps everything, to do with this. Her most intimate friend at school had been one of rather exceptional intellectual gifts, who wrote fine-sounding essays, which Edna admired and strove to imitate; and with her she talked and glowed over the English classics, and sometimes held religious and political controversies.

Edna often wondered at one propensity which sometimes had inwardly disturbed her without causing any outward show or manifestation on her part. At a very early age—perhaps it was when she traversed the ocean of waving grass—she remembered that she had been passionately enamored of a dignified and sad-eyed cavalry officer who visited her father in Kentucky. She could not leave his presence when he was there, nor remove her eyes from his face, which was something like Napoleon's, with a lock of black hair falling across the forehead. But the cavalry officer melted imperceptibly out of her existence.

At another time her affections were deeply engaged by a young gentleman who visited a lady on a neighboring plantation. It was after they went to Mississippi to live. The young man was engaged to be married to the young lady, and they sometimes called upon Margaret, driving over of afternoons in a buggy. Edna was a little miss, just merging into her teens; and the realization that she herself was nothing, nothing, nothing to the engaged young man was a bitter affliction to her. But he, too, went the way of dreams.

She was a grown young woman when she was overtaken by what she supposed to be the climax of her fate. It was when the face and figure of a great tragedian began to haunt her imagination and stir her senses. The persistence of the infatuation lent it an aspect of genuineness. The hopelessness of it colored it with the lofty tones of a great passion.

The picture of the tragedian stood enframed upon her desk. Any one may possess the portrait of a tragedian without exciting suspicion or comment. (This was a sinister reflection which she cherished.) In the presence of others she expressed admiration for his exalted gifts, as she handed the photograph around and dwelt upon the fidelity of the likeness. When alone she sometimes picked it up and kissed the cold glass passionately.

Her marriage to Léonce Pontellier was purely an accident, in this respect resembling many other marriages which masquerade as the decrees of Fate. It was in the midst of her secret great passion that she met him. He fell in love, as men are in the habit of doing, and pressed his suit with an earnestness and an ardor which left nothing to be desired. He pleased her; his absolute devotion flattered her. She fancied there was a sympathy of thought and taste between them, in which fancy she was mistaken. Add to this the violent opposition of her father and her sister Margaret to her marriage with a Catholic, and we need seek no further for the motives which led her to accept Monsieur Pontellier for her husband.

The acme of bliss, which would have been a marriage with the tragedian, was not for her in this world. As the devoted wife of a man who worshiped her, she felt she would take her place with a certain dignity in the world of reality, closing the portals forever behind her upon the realm of romance and dreams.

But it was not long before the tragedian had gone to join the cavalry officer and the engaged young man and a few others; and Edna found herself face to face with the realities. She grew fond of her husband, realizing with some unaccountable satisfaction that no trace of passion or excessive and fictitious warmth colored her affection, thereby threatening its dissolution.

She was fond of her children in an uneven, impulsive way. She would sometimes gather them passionately to her heart; she would sometimes forget them. The year before they had spent part of the summer with their grandmother Pontellier in Iberville. Feeling secure regarding their happiness and welfare, she did not miss them except with an occasional intense longing. Their absence was a sort of relief, though she did not admit this, even to herself. It seemed to free her of a responsibility which she had blindly assumed and for which Fate had not fitted her.

Edna did not reveal so much as all this to Madame Ratignolle that summer day when they sat with faces turned to the sea. But a good part of it escaped her. She had put her head down on Madame Ratignolle's shoulder. She was flushed and felt intoxicated with the sound of her own voice and the unaccustomed taste of candor. It muddled her like wine, or like a first breath of freedom.

There was the sound of approaching voices. It was Robert, surrounded by a troop of children, searching for them. The two little Pontelliers were with him, and he carried Madame Ratignolle's little girl in his arms. There were other children beside, and two nursemaids followed, looking disagreeable and resigned.

The women at once rose and began to shake out their draperies and relax their muscles. Mrs. Pontellier threw the cushions and rug into the bathhouse. The children all scampered off to the awning, and they stood there in a line, gazing upon the intruding lovers, still exchanging their vows and sighs. The lovers got up, with only a silent protest, and walked slowly away somewhere else.

The children possessed themselves of the tent, and Mrs. Pontellier went over to join them.

Madame Ratignolle begged Robert to accompany her to the house; she complained of cramp in her limbs and stiffness of the joints. She leaned draggingly upon his arm as they walked.

VIII

"Do me a favor, Robert," spoke the pretty woman at his side, almost as soon as she and Robert had started on their slow, homeward way. She looked up in his face, leaning on his arm beneath the encircling shadow of the umbrella which he had lifted.

"Granted; as many as you like," he returned, glancing down into her eyes that were full of thoughtfulness and some speculation.

"I only ask for one; let Mrs. Pontellier alone."

"*Tiens!*" he exclaimed, with a sudden, boyish laugh. "*Voilà que Madame Ratignolle est jalouse!*"[6]

"Nonsense! I'm in earnest; I mean what I say. Let Mrs. Pontellier alone."

"Why?" he asked; himself growing serious at his companion's solicitation.

"She is not one of us; she is not like us. She might make the unfortunate blunder of taking you seriously."

His face flushed with annoyance, and taking off his soft hat he began to beat it impatiently against his leg as he walked. "Why shouldn't she take me seriously?" he demanded sharply. "Am I a comedian, a clown, a jack-in-the-box? Why shouldn't she? You Creoles! I have no patience with you! Am I always to be regarded as a feature of an amusing programme? I hope Mrs. Pontellier does take me seriously. I hope she has discernment enough to find in me something besides the *blagueur*.[7] If I thought there was any doubt—"

"Oh, enough, Robert!" she broke into his heated outburst. "You are not thinking of what you are saying. You speak with about as little reflection as we might expect from one of those children down there playing in the sand. If your attentions to any married women here were ever offered with any intention of being convincing, you would not be the gentleman we all know you to be, and you would be unfit to associate with the wives and daughters of the people who trust you."

Madame Ratignolle had spoken what she believed to be the law and the gospel. The young man shrugged his shoulders impatiently.

"Oh! well! That isn't it," slamming his hat down vehemently upon his head. "You ought to feel that such things are not flattering to say to a fellow."

"Should our whole intercourse consist of an exchange of compliments? *Ma foi!*"[8]

"It isn't pleasant to have a woman tell you—" he went on, unheedingly, but breaking off suddenly: "Now if I were like Arobin—you remember Alcée Arobin and that story of the consul's wife at Biloxi?" And he related the story of Alcée Arobin

6. "Ah, ha! Madame Ratignolle must be jealous!"   8. "Indeed!"
7. Joker.

and the consul's wife; and another about the tenor of the French Opera, who received letters which should never have been written; and still other stories, grave and gay, till Mrs. Pontellier and her possible propensity for taking young men seriously was apparently forgotten.

Madame Ratignolle, when they had regained her cottage, went in to take the hour's rest which she considered helpful. Before leaving her, Robert begged her pardon for the impatience—he called it rudeness—with which he had received her well-meant caution.

"You made one mistake, Adèle," he said, with a light smile; "there is no earthly possibility of Mrs. Pontellier ever taking me seriously. You should have warned me against taking myself seriously. Your advice might then have carried some weight and given me subject for some reflection. *Au revoir*.[9] But you look tired," he added, solicitously. "Would you like a cup of bouillon? Shall I stir you a toddy? Let me mix you a toddy with a drop of Angostura."

She acceded to the suggestion of bouillon, which was grateful and acceptable. He went himself to the kitchen, which was a building apart from the cottages and lying to the rear of the house. And he himself brought her the golden-brown bouillon, in a dainty Sèvres cup, with a flaky cracker or two on the saucer.

She thrust a bare, white arm from the curtain which shielded her open door, and received the cup from his hands. She told him he was a *bon garçon*,[10] and she meant it. Robert thanked her and turned away toward "the house."

The lovers were just entering the grounds of the *pension*. They were leaning toward each other as the water-oaks bent from the sea. There was not a particle of earth beneath their feet. Their heads might have been turned upside down, so absolutely did they tread upon blue ether. The lady in black, creeping behind them, looked a trifle paler and more jaded than usual. There was no sign of Mrs. Pontellier and the children. Robert scanned the distance for any such apparition. They would doubtless remain away till the dinner hour. The young man ascended to his mother's room. It was situated at the top of the house, made up of odd angles and a queer, sloping ceiling. Two broad dormer windows looked out toward the Gulf, and as far across it as a man's eye might reach. The furnishings of the room were light, cool, and practical.

Madame Lebrun was busily engaged at the sewing machine. A little black girl sat on the floor, and with her hands worked the treadle of the machine. The Creole woman does not take any chances which may be avoided of imperiling her health.

Robert went over and seated himself on the broad sill of one of the dormer windows. He took a book from his pocket and began energetically to read it, judging by the precision and frequency with which he turned the leaves. The sewing machine made a resounding clatter in the room; it was of a ponderous, bygone make. In the lulls, Robert and his mother exchanged bits of desultory conversation.

"Where is Mrs. Pontellier?"

"Down at the beach with the children."

"I promised to lend her the Goncourt. Don't forget to take it down when you go; it's there on the bookshelf over the small table." Clatter, clatter, clatter, bang! for the next five or eight minutes.

"Where is Victor going with the rockaway?"

"The rockaway? Victor?"

9. "Farewell."   10. Good fellow.

"Yes; down there in front. He seems to be getting ready to drive away somewhere."

"Call him." Clatter, clatter!

Robert uttered a shrill, piercing whistle which might have been heard back at the wharf.

"He won't look up."

Madame Lebrun flew to the window. She called "Victor!" She waved a handkerchief and called again. The young fellow below got into the vehicle and started the horse off at a gallop.

Madame Lebrun went back to the machine, crimson with annoyance. Victor was the younger son and brother—a *tête montée*,[11] with a temper which invited violence and a will which no ax could break.

"Whenever you say the word I'm ready to thrash any amount of reason into him that he's able to hold."

"If your father had only lived!" Clatter, clatter, clatter, clatter, bang! It was a fixed belief with Madame Lebrun that the conduct of the universe and all things pertaining thereto would have been manifestly of a more intelligent and higher order had not Monsieur Lebrun been removed to other spheres during the early years of their married life.

"What do you hear from Montel?" Montel was a middle-aged gentleman whose vain ambition and desire for the past twenty years had been to fill the void which Monsieur Lebrun's taking off had left in the Lebrun household. Clatter, clatter, bang, clatter!

"I have a letter somewhere," looking in the machine drawer and finding the letter in the bottom of the workbasket. "He says to tell you he will be in Vera Cruz the beginning of next month"—clatter, clatter!—"and if you still have the intention of joining him"—bang! clatter, clatter, bang!

"Why didn't you tell me so before, mother? You know I wanted—" Clatter, clatter, clatter!

"Do you see Mrs. Pontellier starting back with the children? She will be in late to luncheon again. She never starts to get ready for luncheon till the last minute." Clatter, clatter! "Where are you going?"

"Where did you say the Goncourt was?"

IX

Every light in the hall was ablaze; every lamp turned as high as it could be without smoking the chimney or threatening explosion. The lamps were fixed at intervals against the wall, encircling the whole room. Someone had gathered orange and lemon branches, and with these fashioned graceful festoons between. The dark green of the branches stood out and glistened against the white muslin curtains which draped the windows, and which puffed, floated, and flapped at the capricious will of a stiff breeze that swept up from the Gulf.

It was Saturday night a few weeks after the intimate conversation held between Robert and Madame Ratignolle on their way from the beach. An unusual number of husbands, fathers, and friends had come down to stay over Sunday; and they were being suitably entertained by their families, with the material help of Madame Lebrun. The dining tables had all been removed to one end of the hall, and the

11. Hothead.

chairs ranged about in rows and in clusters. Each little family group had had its say and exchanged its domestic gossip earlier in the evening. There was now an apparent disposition to relax; to widen the circle of confidences and give a more general tone to the conversation.

Many of the children had been permitted to sit up beyond their usual bedtime. A small band of them were lying on their stomachs on the floor looking at the colored sheets of the comic papers which Mr. Pontellier had brought down. The little Pontellier boys were permitting them to do so, and making their authority felt.

Music, dancing, and a recitation or two were the entertainments furnished, or rather, offered. But there was nothing systematic about the program, no appearance of prearrangement nor even premeditation.

At an early hour in the evening the Farival twins were prevailed upon to play the piano. They were girls of fourteen, always clad in the Virgin's colors, blue and white, having been dedicated to the Blessed Virgin at their baptism. They played a duet from "Zampa," and at the earnest solicitation of every one present followed it with the overture to "The Poet and the Peasant."

"*Allez vous-en! Sapristi!*" shrieked the parrot outside the door. He was the only being present who possessed sufficient candor to admit that he was not listening to these gracious performances for the first time that summer. Old Monsieur Farival, grandfather of the twins, grew indignant over the interruption and insisted upon having the bird removed and consigned to regions of darkness. Victor Lebrun objected; and his decrees were as immutable as those of Fate. The parrot fortunately offered no further interruption to the entertainment, the whole venom of his nature apparently having been cherished up and hurled against the twins in that one impetuous outburst.

Later a young brother and sister gave recitations, which every one present had heard many times at winter evening entertainments in the city.

A little girl performed a skirt dance in the center of the floor. The mother played her accompaniments and at the same time watched her daughter with greedy admiration and nervous apprehension. She need have had no apprehension. The child was mistress of the situation. She had been properly dressed for the occasion in black tulle and black silk tights. Her little neck and arms were bare, and her hair, artificially crimped, stood out like fluffy black plumes over her head. Her poses were full of grace, and her little black-shod toes twinkled as they shot out and upward with a rapidity and suddenness which were bewildering.

But there was no reason why everyone should not dance. Madame Ratignolle could not, so it was she who gaily consented to play for the others. She played very well, keeping excellent waltz time and infusing an expression into the strains which was indeed inspiring. She was keeping up her music on account of the children, she said; because she and her husband both considered it a means of brightening the home and making it attractive.

Almost everyone danced but the twins, who could not be induced to separate during the brief period when one or the other should be whirling around the room in the arms of a man. They might have danced together, but they did not think of it.

The children were sent to bed. Some went submissively; others with shrieks and protests as they were dragged away. They had been permitted to sit up till after the ice cream, which naturally marked the limit of human indulgence.

The ice cream was passed around with cake—gold and silver cake arranged on platters in alternate slices; it had been made and frozen during the afternoon back of the kitchen by two black women, under the supervision of Victor. It was pronounced a great success—excellent if it had only contained a little less vanilla or a little more sugar, if it had been frozen a degree harder, and if the salt might have been kept out of portions of it. Victor was proud of his achievement, and went about recommending it and urging every one to partake of it to excess.

After Mrs. Pontellier had danced twice with her husband, once with Robert, and once with Monsieur Ratignolle, who was thin and tall and swayed like a reed in the wind when he danced, she went out on the gallery and seated herself on the low windowsill, where she commanded a view of all that went on in the hall and could look out toward the Gulf. There was a soft effulgence in the east. The moon was coming up, and its mystic shimmer was casting a million lights across the distant, restless water.

"Would you like to hear Mademoiselle Reisz play?" asked Robert, coming out on the porch where she was. Of course Edna would like to hear Mademoiselle Reisz play; but she feared it would be useless to entreat her.

"I'll ask her," he said. "I'll tell her that you want to hear her. She likes you. She will come." He turned and hurried away to one of the far cottages, where Mademoiselle Reisz was shuffling away. She was dragging a chair in and out of her room, and at intervals objecting to the crying of a baby, which a nurse in the adjoining cottage was endeavoring to put to sleep. She was a disagreeable little woman, no longer young, who had quarreled with almost everyone, owing to a temper which was self-assertive and a disposition to trample upon the rights of others. Robert prevailed upon her without any too great difficulty.

She entered the hall with him during a lull in the dance. She made an awkward, imperious little bow as she went in. She was a homely woman, with a small wizened face and body and eyes that glowed. She had absolutely no taste in dress, and wore a batch of rusty black lace with a bunch of artificial violets pinned to the side of her hair.

"Ask Mrs. Pontellier what she would like to hear me play," she requested of Robert. She sat perfectly still before the piano, not touching the keys, while Robert carried her message to Edna at the window. A general air of surprise and genuine satisfaction fell upon everyone as they saw the pianist enter. There was a settling down, and a prevailing air of expectancy everywhere. Edna was a trifle embarrassed at being thus singled out for the imperious little woman's favor. She would not dare to choose, and begged that Mademoiselle Reisz would please herself in her selections.

Edna was what she herself called very fond of music. Musical strains, well rendered, had a way of evoking pictures in her mind. She sometimes liked to sit in the room of mornings when Madame Ratignolle played or practiced. One piece which that lady played Edna had entitled "Solitude." It was a short, plaintive, minor strain. The name of the piece was something else, but she called it "Solitude." When she heard it there came before her imagination the figure of a man standing beside a desolate rock on the seashore. He was naked. His attitude was one of hopeless resignation as he looked toward a distant bird winging its flight away from him.

Another piece called to her mind a dainty young woman clad in an Empire gown, taking mincing dancing steps as she came down a long avenue between tall hedges. Again, another reminded her of children at play, and still another of nothing on earth but a demure lady stroking a cat.

The very first chords which Mademoiselle Reisz struck upon the piano sent a keen tremor down Mrs. Pontellier's spinal column. It was not the first time she had heard an artist at the piano. Perhaps it was the first time she was ready, perhaps the first time her being was tempered to take an impress of the abiding truth.

She waited for the material pictures which she thought would gather and blaze before her imagination. She waited in vain. She saw no pictures of solitude, of hope, of longing, or of despair. But the very passions themselves were aroused within her soul, swaying it, lashing it, as the waves daily beat upon her splendid body. She trembled, she was choking, and the tears blinded her.

Mademoiselle had finished. She arose, and bowing her stiff, lofty bow, she went away, stopping for neither thanks nor applause. As she passed along the gallery she patted Edna upon the shoulder.

"Well, how did you like my music?" she asked. The young woman was unable to answer; she pressed the hand of the pianist convulsively. Mademoiselle Reisz perceived her agitation and even her tears. She patted her again upon the shoulder as she said:

"You are the only one worth playing for. Those others? Bah!" and she went shuffling and sidling on down the gallery toward her room.

But she was mistaken about "those others." Her playing had aroused a fever of enthusiasm. "What passion!" "What an artist!" "I have always said no one could play Chopin like Mademoiselle Reisz!" "That last prelude! Bon Dieu! It shakes a man!"

It was growing late, and there was a general disposition to disband. But someone, perhaps it was Robert, thought of a bath at that mystic hour and under that mystic moon.

X

At all events Robert proposed it, and there was not a dissenting voice. There was not one but was ready to follow when he led the way. He did not lead the way, however, he directed the way; and he himself loitered behind with the lovers, who had betrayed a disposition to linger and hold themselves apart. He walked between them, whether with malicious or mischievous intent was not wholly clear, even to himself.

The Pontelliers and Ratignolles walked ahead; the women leaning upon the arms of their husbands. Edna could hear Robert's voice behind them, and could sometimes hear what he said. She wondered why he did not join them. It was unlike him not to. Of late he had sometimes held away from her for an entire day, redoubling his devotion upon the next and the next, as though to make up for hours that had been lost. She missed him the days when some pretext served to take him away from her, just as one misses the sun on a cloudy day without having thought much about the sun when it was shining.

The people walked in little groups toward the beach. They talked and laughed; some of them sang. There was a band playing down at Klein's hotel, and the strains reached them faintly, tempered by the distance. There were strange, rare odors abroad—a tangle of the sea smell and of weeds and damp, new-plowed earth, mingled with the heavy perfume of a field of white blossoms somewhere near. But the night sat lightly upon the sea and the land. There was no weight of darkness; there were no shadows. The white light of the moon had fallen upon the world like the mystery and the softness of sleep.

Most of them walked into the water as though into a native element. The sea was quiet now, and swelled lazily in broad billows that melted into one another and did not break except upon the beach in little foamy crests that coiled back like slow, white serpents.

Edna had attempted all summer to learn to swim. She had received instructions from both the men and women; in some instances from the children. Robert had pur-

sued a system of lessons almost daily; and he was nearly at the point of discouragement in realizing the futility of his efforts. A certain ungovernable dread hung about
her when in the water, unless there was a hand near by that might reach out and
reassure her.

But that night she was like the little tottering, stumbling, clutching child, who
of a sudden realizes its powers, and walks for the first time alone, boldly and with
overconfidence. She could have shouted for joy. She did shout for joy, as with a
sweeping stroke or two she lifted her body to the surface of the water.

A feeling of exultation overtook her, as if some power of significant import had
been given her to control the working of her body and her soul. She grew daring and
reckless, overestimating her strength. She wanted to swim far out, where no woman
had swum before.

Her unlooked-for achievement was the subject of wonder, applause, and admiration. Each one congratulated himself that his special teachings had accomplished
this desired end.

"How easy it is!" she thought. "It is nothing," she said aloud; "why did I not discover before that it was nothing. Think of the time I have lost splashing about like a
baby!" She would not join the groups in their sports and bouts, but intoxicated with
her newly conquered power, she swam out alone.

She turned her face seaward to gather in an impression of space and solitude,
which the vast expanse of water, meeting and melting with the moonlit sky, conveyed to her excited fancy. As she swam she seemed to be reaching out for the unlimited in which to lose herself.

Once she turned and looked toward the shore, toward the people she had left
there. She had not gone any great distance—that is, what would have been a great
distance for an experienced swimmer. But to her unaccustomed vision the stretch of
water behind her assumed the aspect of a barrier which her unaided strength would
never be able to overcome.

A quick vision of death smote her soul, and for a second of time appalled and
enfeebled her senses. But by an effort she rallied her staggering faculties and managed
to regain the land.

She made no mention of her encounter with death and her flash of terror, except
to say to her husband, "I thought I should have perished out there alone."

"You were not so very far, my dear; I was watching you," he told her.

Edna went at once to the bathhouse, and she had put on her dry clothes and was
ready to return home before the others had left the water. She started to walk away
alone. They all called to her and shouted to her. She waved a dissenting hand, and
went on, paying no further heed to their renewed cries which sought to detain her.

"Sometimes I am tempted to think that Mrs. Pontellier is capricious," said
Madame Lebrun, who was amusing herself immensely and feared that Edna's abrupt
departure might put an end to the pleasure.

"I know she is," assented Mr. Pontellier; "sometimes, not often."

Edna had not traversed a quarter of the distance on her way home before she was
overtaken by Robert.

"Did you think I was afraid?" she asked him, without a shade of annoyance.

"No; I knew you weren't afraid."

"Then why did you come? Why didn't you stay out there with the others?"

"I never thought of it."

"Thought of what?"

"Of anything. What difference does it make?"

"I'm very tired," she uttered, complainingly.

"I know you are."

"You don't know anything about it. Why should you know? I never was so exhausted in my life. But it isn't unpleasant. A thousand emotions have swept through me tonight. I don't comprehend half of them. Don't mind what I'm saying; I am just thinking aloud. I wonder if I shall ever be stirred again as Mademoiselle Reisz's playing moved me tonight. I wonder if any night on earth will ever again be like this one. It is like a night in a dream. The people about me are like some uncanny, half-human beings. There must be spirits abroad tonight."

"There are," whispered Robert. "Didn't you know this was the twenty-eighth of August?"

"The twenty-eighth of August?"

"Yes. On the twenty-eighth of August, at the hour of midnight, and if the moon is shining—the moon must be shining—a spirit that has haunted these shores for ages rises up from the Gulf. With its own penetrating vision the spirit seeks someone mortal worthy to hold him company, worthy of being exalted for a few hours into realms of the semi-celestials. His search has always hitherto been fruitless, and he has sunk back, disheartened, into the sea. But tonight he found Mrs. Pontellier. Perhaps he will never wholly release her from the spell. Perhaps she will never again suffer a poor, unworthy earthling to walk in the shadow of her divine presence."

"Don't banter me," she said, wounded at what appeared to be his flippancy. He did not mind the entreaty, but the tone with its delicate note of pathos was like a reproach. He could not explain; he could not tell her that he had penetrated her mood and understood. He said nothing except to offer her his arm, for, by her own admission, she was exhausted. She had been walking alone with her arms hanging limp, letting her white skirts trail along the dewy path. She took his arm, but she did not lean upon it. She let her hand lie listlessly, as though her thoughts were elsewhere—somewhere in advance of her body, and she was striving to overtake them.

Robert assisted her into the hammock which swung from the post before her door out to the trunk of a tree.

"Will you stay out here and wait for Mr. Pontellier?" he asked.

"I'll stay out here. Goodnight."

"Shall I get you a pillow?"

"There's one here," she said, feeling about, for they were in the shadow.

"It must be soiled; the children have been tumbling it about."

"No matter." And having discovered the pillow, she adjusted it beneath her head. She extended herself in the hammock with a deep breath of relief. She was not a supercilious or an over-dainty woman. She was not much given to reclining in the hammock, and when she did so it was with no catlike suggestion of voluptuous ease, but with a beneficent repose which seemed to invade her whole body.

"Shall I stay with you till Mr. Pontellier comes?" asked Robert, seating himself on the outer edge of one of the steps and taking hold of the hammock rope which was fastened to the post.

"If you wish. Don't swing the hammock. Will you get my white shawl which I left on the windowsill over at the house?"

"Are you chilly?"

"No; but I shall be presently."

"Presently?" he laughed. "Do you know what time it is? How long are you going to stay out here?"

"I don't know. Will you get the shawl?"

"Of course I will," he said, rising. He went over to the house, walking along the grass. She watched his figure pass in and out of the strips of moonlight. It was past midnight. It was very quiet.

When he returned with the shawl she took it and kept it in her hand. She did not put it around her.

"Did you say I should stay till Mr. Pontellier came back?"

"I said you might if you wished to."

He seated himself again and rolled a cigarette, which he smoked in silence. Neither did Mrs. Pontellier speak. No multitude of words could have been more significant than those moments of silence, or more pregnant with the first-felt throbbings of desire.

When the voices of the bathers were heard approaching, Robert said goodnight. She did not answer him. He thought she was asleep. Again she watched his figure pass in and out of the strips of moonlight as he walked away.

XI

"What are you doing out here, Edna? I thought I should find you in bed," said her husband, when he discovered her lying there. He had walked up with Madame Lebrun and left her at the house. His wife did not reply.

"Are you asleep?" he asked, bending down close to look at her.

"No." Her eyes gleamed bright and intense, with no sleepy shadows, as they looked into his.

"Do you know it is past one o'clock? Come on," and he mounted the steps and went into their room.

"Edna!" called Mr. Pontellier from within, after a few moments had gone by.

"Don't wait for me," she answered. He thrust his head through the door.

"You will take cold out there," he said, irritably. "What folly is this? Why don't you come in?"

"It isn't cold; I have my shawl."

"The mosquitoes will devour you."

"There are no mosquitoes."

She heard him moving about the room; every sound indicating impatience and irritation. Another time she would have gone in at his request. She would, through habit, have yielded to his desire; not with any sense of submission or obedience to his compelling wishes, but unthinkingly, as we walk, move, sit, stand, go through the daily treadmill of the life which has been portioned out to us.

"Edna, dear, are you not coming in soon?" he asked again, this time fondly, with a note of entreaty.

"No; I am going to stay out here."

"This is more than folly," he blurted out. "I can't permit you to stay out there all night. You must come in the house instantly."

With a writhing motion she settled herself more securely in the hammock. She perceived that her will had blazed up, stubborn and resistant. She could not at that moment have done other than denied and resisted. She wondered if her husband had ever spoken to her like that before, and if she had submitted to his command. Of course she had; she remembered that she had. But she could not realize why or how she should have yielded, feeling as she then did.

"Léonce, go to bed," she said. "I mean to stay out here. I don't wish to go in, and I don't intend to. Don't speak to me like that again; I shall not answer you."

Mr. Pontellier had prepared for bed, but he slipped on an extra garment. He opened a bottle of wine, of which he kept a small and select supply in a buffet of his own. He drank a glass of the wine and went out on the gallery and offered a glass to his wife. She did not wish any. He drew up the rocker, hoisted his slippered feet on the rail, and proceeded to smoke a cigar. He smoked two cigars; then he went inside and drank another glass of wine. Mrs. Pontellier again declined to accept a glass when it was offered to her. Mr. Pontellier once more seated himself with elevated feet, and after a reasonable interval of time smoked some more cigars.

Edna began to feel like one who awakens gradually out of a dream, a delicious, grotesque, impossible dream, to feel again the realities pressing into her soul. The physical need for sleep began to overtake her; the exuberance which had sustained and exalted her spirit left her helpless and yielding to the conditions which crowded her in.

The stillest hour of the night had come, the hour before dawn, when the world seems to hold its breath. The moon hung low, and had turned from silver to copper in the sleeping sky. The old owl no longer hooted, and the water-oaks had ceased to moan as they bent their heads.

Edna arose, cramped from lying so long and still in the hammock. She tottered up the steps, clutching feebly at the post before passing into the house.

"Are you coming in, Léonce?" she asked, turning her face toward her husband.

"Yes, dear," he answered, with a glance following a misty puff of smoke. "Just as soon as I have finished my cigar."

XII

She slept but a few hours. They were troubled and feverish hours, disturbed with dreams that were intangible, that eluded her, leaving only an impression upon her half-awakened senses of something unattainable. She was up and dressed in the cool of the early morning. The air was invigorating and steadied somewhat her faculties. However, she was not seeking refreshment or help from any source, either external or from within. She was blindly following whatever impulse moved her, as if she had placed herself in alien hands for direction, and freed her soul of responsibility.

Most of the people at this early hour were still in bed and asleep. A few, who intended to go over to the Chênière for mass, were moving about. The lovers, who had laid their plans the night before, were already strolling toward the wharf. The lady in black, with her Sunday prayer book, velvet and gold-clasped, and her Sunday silver beads, was following them at no great distance. Old Monsieur Farival was up, and was more than half inclined to do anything that suggested itself. He put on his big straw hat, and taking his umbrella from the stand in the hall, followed the lady in black, never overtaking her.

The little negro girl who worked Madame Lebrun's sewing machine was sweeping the galleries with long, absentminded strokes of the broom. Edna sent her up into the house to awaken Robert.

"Tell him I am going to the Chênière. The boat is ready; tell him to hurry."

He had soon joined her. She had never sent for him before. She had never asked for him. She had never seemed to want him before. She did not appear conscious that she had done anything unusual in commanding his presence. He was apparently equally unconscious of anything extraordinary in the situation. But his face was suffused with a quiet glow when he met her.

They went together back to the kitchen to drink coffee. There was no time to wait for any nicety of service. They stood outside the window and the cook passed them their coffee and a roll, which they drank and ate from the windowsill. Edna said it tasted good. She had not thought of coffee nor of anything. He told her he had often noticed that she lacked forethought.

"Wasn't it enough to think of going to the *Chênière* and waking you up?" she laughed. "Do I have to think of everything?—as Léonce says when he's in a bad humor. I don't blame him; he'd never be in a bad humor if it weren't for me." They took a shortcut across the sands. At a distance they could see the curious procession moving toward the wharf—the lovers, shoulder to shoulder, creeping; the lady in black, gaining steadily upon them; old Monsieur Farival, losing ground inch by inch, and a young barefooted Spanish girl, with a red kerchief on her head and a basket on her arm, bringing up the rear.

Robert knew the girl, and he talked to her a little in the boat. No one present understood what they said. Her name was Mariequita. She had a round, sly, piquant face and pretty black eyes. Her hands were small, and she kept them folded over the handle of her basket. Her feet were broad and coarse. She did not strive to hide them. Edna looked at her feet, and noticed the sand and slime between her brown toes.

Beaudelet grumbled because Mariequita was there, taking up so much room. In reality he was annoyed at having old Monsieur Farival, who considered himself the better sailor of the two. But he would not quarrel with so old a man as Monsieur Farival, so he quarreled with Mariequita. The girl was deprecatory at one moment, appealing to Robert. She was saucy the next, moving her head up and down, making "eyes" at Robert and making "mouths" at Beaudelet.

The lovers were all alone. They saw nothing, they heard nothing. The lady in black was counting her beads for the third time. Old Monsieur Farival talked incessantly of what he knew about handling a boat, and of what Beaudelet did not know on the same subject.

Edna liked it all. She looked Mariequita up and down, from her ugly brown toes to her pretty black eyes, and back again.

"Why does she look at me like that?" inquired the girl of Robert.

"Maybe she thinks you are pretty. Shall I ask her?"

"No. Is she your sweetheart?"

"She's a married lady, and has two children."

"Oh! well! Francisco ran away with Sylvano's wife, who had four children. They took all his money and one of the children and stole his boat."

"Shut up!"

"Does she understand?"

"Oh, hush!"

"Are those two married over there—leaning on each other?"

"Of course not," laughed Robert.

"Of course not," echoed Mariequita, with a serious, confirmatory bob of the head.

The sun was high up and beginning to bite. The swift breeze seemed to Edna to bury the sting of it into the pores of her face and hands. Robert held his umbrella over her.

As they went cutting sidewise through the water, the sails bellied taut, with the wind filling and overflowing them. Old Monsieur Farival laughed sardonically at something as he looked at the sails, and Beaudelet swore at the old man under his breath.

Sailing across the bay to the *Chênière Caminada,* Edna felt as if she were being borne away from some anchorage which had held her fast, whose chains had been loosening—had snapped the night before when the mystic spirit was abroad, leaving her free to drift whithersoever she chose to set her sails. Robert spoke to her incessantly; he no longer noticed Mariequita. The girl had shrimps in her bamboo basket. They were covered with Spanish moss. She beat the moss down impatiently, and muttered to herself sullenly.

"Let us go to Grande Terre tomorrow?" said Robert in a low voice.

"What shall we do there?"

"Climb up the hill to the old fort and look at the little wriggling gold snakes, and watch the lizards sun themselves."

She gazed away toward Grande Terre and thought she would like to be alone there with Robert, in the sun, listening to the ocean's roar and watching the slimy lizards writhe in and out among the ruins of the old fort.

"And the next day or the next we can sail to the Bayou Brulow," he went on.

"What shall we do there?"

"Anything—cast bait for fish."

"No; we'll go back to Grande Terre. Let the fish alone."

"We'll go wherever you like," he said. "I'll have Tonie come over and help me patch and trim my boat. We shall not need Beaudelet nor any one. Are you afraid of the pirogue?"

"Oh, no."

"Then I'll take you some night in the pirogue when the moon shines. Maybe your Gulf spirit will whisper to you in which of these islands the treasures are hidden—direct you to the very spot, perhaps."

"And in a day we should be rich!" she laughed. "I'd give it all to you, the pirate gold and every bit of treasure we could dig up. I think you would know how to spend it. Pirate gold isn't a thing to be hoarded or utilized. It is something to squander and throw to the four winds, for the fun of seeing the golden specks fly."

"We'd share it, and scatter it together," he said. His face flushed.

They all went together up to the quaint little Gothic church of Our Lady of Lourdes, gleaming all brown and yellow with paint in the sun's glare.

Only Beaudelet remained behind, tinkering at his boat, and Mariequita walked away with her basket of shrimps, casting a look of childish ill humor and reproach at Robert from the corner of her eye.

XIII

A feeling of oppression and drowsiness overcame Edna during the service. Her head began to ache, and the lights on the altar swayed before her eyes. Another time she might have made an effort to regain her composure; but her one thought was to quit the stifling atmosphere of the church and reach the open air. She arose, climbing over Robert's feet with a muttered apology. Old Monsieur Farival, flurried, curious, stood up, but upon seeing that Robert had followed Mrs. Pontellier, he sank back into his seat. He whispered an anxious inquiry of the lady in black, who did not notice him or reply, but kept her eyes fastened upon the pages of her velvet prayer book.

"I felt giddy and almost overcome," Edna said, lifting her hands instinctively to her head and pushing her straw hat up from her forehead. "I couldn't have stayed through the service." They were outside in the shadow of the church. Robert was full of solicitude.

"It was folly to have thought of going in the first place, let alone staying. Come over to Madame Antoine's; you can rest there." He took her arm and led her away, looking anxiously and continuously down into her face.

How still it was, with only the voice of the sea whispering through the reeds that grew in the saltwater pools! The long line of little gray, weatherbeaten houses nestled peacefully among the orange trees. It must always have been God's day on that low, drowsy island, Edna thought. They stopped, leaning over a jagged fence made of seadrift, to ask for water. A youth, a mild-faced Acadian,[12] was drawing water from the cistern, which was nothing more than a rusty buoy, with an opening on one side, sunk in the ground. The water which the youth handed to them in a tin pail was not cold to taste, but it was cool to her heated face, and it greatly revived and refreshed her.

Madame Antoine's cot was at the far end of the village. She welcomed them with all the native hospitality, as she would have opened her door to let the sunlight in. She was fat, and walked heavily and clumsily across the floor. She could speak no English, but when Robert made her understand that the lady who accompanied him was ill and desired to rest, she was all eagerness to make Edna feel at home and to dispose of her comfortably.

The whole place was immaculately clean, and the big, four-posted bed, snow-white, invited one to repose. It stood in a small side room which looked out across a narrow grass plot toward the shed, where there was a disabled boat lying keel upward.

Madame Antoine had not gone to mass. Her son Tonie had, but she supposed he would soon be back, and she invited Robert to be seated and wait for him. But he went and sat outside the door and smoked. Madame Antoine busied herself in the large front room preparing dinner. She was boiling mullets over a few red coals in the huge fireplace.

Edna, left alone in the little side room, loosened her clothes, removing the greater part of them. She bathed her face, her neck and arms in the basin that stood between the windows. She took off her shoes and stockings and stretched herself in the very center of the high, white bed. How luxurious it felt to rest thus in a strange, quaint bed, with its sweet country odor of laurel lingering about the sheets and mattress! She stretched her strong limbs that ached a little. She ran her fingers through her loosened hair for a while. She looked at her round arms as she held them straight up and rubbed them one after the other, observing closely, as if it were something she saw for the first time, the fine, firm quality and texture of her flesh. She clasped her hands easily above her head, and it was thus she fell asleep.

She slept lightly at first, half awake and drowsily attentive to the things about her. She could hear Madame Antoine's heavy, scraping tread as she walked back and forth on the sanded floor. Some chickens were clucking outside the windows, scratching for bits of gravel in the grass. Later she half heard the voices of Robert and Tonie talking under the shed. She did not stir. Even her eyelids rested numb and heavily over her sleepy eyes. The voices went on—Tonie's slow, Acadian drawl, Robert's quick, soft, smooth French. She understood French imperfectly unless directly addressed, and the voices were only part of the other drowsy, muffled sounds lulling her senses.

When Edna awoke it was with the conviction that she had slept long and soundly. The voices were hushed under the shed. Madame Antoine's step was no longer to be heard in the adjoining room. Even the chickens had gone elsewhere to scratch

12. Cajun, a descendant of French Canadians who left what is now Nova Scotia in 1755, under pressure from the British, and settled in Louisiana.

and cluck. The mosquito bar was drawn over her; the old woman had come in while she slept and let down the bar. Edna arose quietly from the bed, and looking between the curtains of the window, she saw by the slanting rays of the sun that the afternoon was far advanced. Robert was out there under the shed, reclining in the shade against the sloping keel of the overturned boat. He was reading from a book. Tonie was no longer with him. She wondered what had become of the rest of the party. She peeped out at him two or three times as she stood washing herself in the little basin between the windows.

Madame Antoine had laid some coarse, clean towels upon a chair, and had placed a box of *poudre de riz*[13] within easy reach. Edna dabbed the powder upon her nose and cheeks as she looked at herself closely in the little distorted mirror which hung on the wall above the basin. Her eyes were bright and wide awake and her face glowed.

When she had completed her toilet she walked into the adjoining room. She was very hungry. No one was there. But there was a cloth spread upon the table that stood against the wall, and a cover was laid for one, with a crusty brown loaf and a bottle of wine beside the plate. Edna bit a piece from the brown loaf, tearing it with her strong, white teeth. She poured some of the wine into the glass and drank it down. Then she went softly out of doors, and plucking an orange from the low-hanging bough of a tree, threw it at Robert, who did not know she was awake and up.

An illumination broke over his whole face when he saw her and joined her under the orange tree.

"How many years have I slept?" she inquired. "The whole island seems changed. A new race of beings must have sprung up, leaving only you and me as past relics. How many ages ago did Madame Antoine and Tonie die? and when did our people from Grand Isle disappear from the earth?"

He familiarly adjusted a ruffle upon her shoulder.

"You have slept precisely one hundred years. I was left here to guard your slumbers; and for one hundred years I have been out under the shed reading a book. The only evil I couldn't prevent was to keep a broiled fowl from drying up."

"If it has turned to stone, still will I eat it," said Edna, moving with him into the house. "But really, what has become of Monsieur Farival and the others?"

"Gone hours ago. When they found that you were sleeping they thought it best not to awake you. Anyway, I wouldn't have let them. What was I here for?"

"I wonder if Léonce will be uneasy!" she speculated, as she seated herself at table.

"Of course not; he knows you are with me," Robert replied, as he busied himself among sundry pans and covered dishes which had been left standing on the hearth.

"Where are Madame Antoine and her son?" asked Edna.

"Gone to Vespers, and to visit some friends, I believe. I am to take you back in Tonie's boat whenever you are ready to go."

He stirred the smoldering ashes till the broiled fowl began to sizzle afresh. He served her with no mean repast, dripping the coffee anew and sharing it with her. Madame Antoine had cooked little else than the mullets, but while Edna slept Robert had foraged the island. He was childishly gratified to discover her appetite, and to see the relish with which she ate the food which he had procured for her.

"Shall we go right away?" she asked, after draining her glass and brushing together the crumbs of the crusty loaf.

13. Face powder.

"The sun isn't as low as it will be in two hours," he answered.

"The sun will be gone in two hours."

"Well, let it go; who cares!"

They waited a good while under the orange trees, till Madame Antoine came back, panting, waddling, with a thousand apologies to explain her absence. Tonie did not dare to return. He was shy, and would not willingly face any woman except his mother.

It was very pleasant to stay there under the orange trees, while the sun dipped lower and lower, turning the western sky to flaming copper and gold. The shadows lengthened and crept out like stealthy, grotesque monsters across the grass.

Edna and Robert both sat upon the ground—that is, he lay upon the ground beside her, occasionally picking at the hem of her muslin gown.

Madame Antoine seated her fat body, broad and squat, upon a bench beside the door. She had been talking all the afternoon, and had wound herself up to the story-telling pitch.

And what stories she told them! But twice in her life she had left the *Chênière Caminada,* and then for the briefest span. All her years she had squatted and waddled there upon the island, gathering legends of the Baratarians and the sea. The night came on, with the moon to lighten it. Edna could hear the whispering voices of dead men and the click of muffled gold.

When she and Robert stepped into Tonie's boat, with the red lateen sail, misty spirit forms were prowling in the shadows and among the reeds, and upon the water were phantom ships, speeding to cover.

XIV

The youngest boy, Etienne, had been very naughty, Madame Ratignolle said, as she delivered him into the hands of his mother. He had been unwilling to go to bed and had made a scene; whereupon she had taken charge of him and pacified him as well as she could. Raoul had been in bed and asleep for two hours.

The youngster was in his long white nightgown, that kept tripping him up as Madame Ratignolle led him along by the hand. With the other chubby fist he rubbed his eyes, which were heavy with sleep and ill humor. Edna took him in her arms, and seating herself in the rocker, began to coddle and caress him, calling him all manner of tender names, soothing him to sleep.

It was not more than nine o'clock. No one had yet gone to bed but the children.

Léonce had been very uneasy at first, Madame Ratignolle said, and had wanted to start at once for the *Chênière.* But Monsieur Farival had assured him that his wife was only overcome with sleep and fatigue, that Tonie would bring her safely back later in the day; and he had thus been dissuaded from crossing the bay. He had gone over to Klein's, looking up some cotton broker whom he wished to see in regard to securities, exchanges, stocks, bonds, or something of the sort, Madame Ratignolle did not remember what. He said he would not remain away late. She herself was suffering from heat and oppression, she said. She carried a bottle of salts and a large fan. She would not consent to remain with Edna, for Monsieur Ratignolle was alone, and he detested above all things to be left alone.

When Etienne had fallen asleep Edna bore him into the back room, and Robert went and lifted the mosquito bar that she might lay the child comfortably in his bed. The quadroon had vanished. When they emerged from the cottage Robert bade Edna good-night.

"Do you know we have been together the whole livelong day, Robert—since early this morning?" she said at parting.

"All but the hundred years when you were sleeping. Good-night."

He pressed her hand and went away in the direction of the beach. He did not join any of the others, but walked alone toward the Gulf.

Edna stayed outside, awaiting her husband's return. She had no desire to sleep or to retire; nor did she feel like going over to sit with the Ratignolles, or to join Madame Lebrun and a group whose animated voices reached her as they sat in conversation before the house. She let her mind wander back over her stay at Grand Isle; and she tried to discover wherein this summer had been different from any and every other summer of her life. She could only realize that she herself—her present self— was in some way different from the other self. That she was seeing with different eyes and making the acquaintance of new conditions in herself that colored and changed her environment, she did not yet suspect.

She wondered why Robert had gone away and left her. It did not occur to her to think he might have grown tired of being with her the livelong day. She was not tired, and she felt that he was not. She regretted that he had gone. It was so much more natural to have him stay when he was not absolutely required to leave her.

As Edna waited for her husband she sang low a little song that Robert had sung as they crossed the bay. It began with "Ah! *Si tu savais*," and every verse ended with "*si tu savais*."[14]

Robert's voice was not pretentious. It was musical and true. The voice, the notes, the whole refrain haunted her memory.

XV

When Edna entered the dining-room one evening a little late, as was her habit, an unusually animated conversation seemed to be going on. Several persons were talking at once, and Victor's voice was predominating, even over that of his mother. Edna had returned late from her bath, had dressed in some haste, and her face was flushed. Her head, set off by her dainty white gown, suggested a rich, rare blossom. She took her seat at table between old Monsieur Farival and Madame Ratignolle.

As she seated herself and was about to begin to eat her soup, which had been served when she entered the room, several persons informed her simultaneously that Robert was going to Mexico. She laid her spoon down and looked about her bewildered. He had been with her, reading to her all the morning, and had never even mentioned such a place as Mexico. She had not seen him during the afternoon; she had heard someone say he was at the house, upstairs with his mother. This she had thought nothing of, though she was surprised when he did not join her later in the afternoon, when she went down to the beach.

She looked across at him, where he sat beside Madame Lebrun, who presided. Edna's face was a blank picture of bewilderment, which she never thought of disguising. He lifted his eyebrows with the pretext of a smile as he returned her glance. He looked embarrassed and uneasy.

"When is he going?" she asked of everybody in general, as if Robert were not there to answer for himself.

14. "If you knew."

"Tonight!" "This very evening!" "Did you ever!" "What possesses him!" were some of the replies she gathered, uttered simultaneously in French and English.

"Impossible!" she exclaimed. "How can a person start off from Grand Isle to Mexico at a moment's notice, as if he were going over to Klein's or to the wharf or down to the beach?"

"I said all along I was going to Mexico; I've been saying so for years!" cried Robert, in an excited and irritable tone, with the air of a man defending himself against a swarm of stinging insects.

Madame Lebrun knocked on the table with her knife handle.

"Please let Robert explain why he is going, and why he is going tonight," she called out. "Really, this table is getting to be more and more like Bedlam every day, with everybody talking at once. Sometimes—I hope God will forgive me—but positively, sometimes I wish Victor would lose the power of speech."

Victor laughed sardonically as he thanked his mother for her holy wish, of which he failed to see the benefit to anybody, except that it might afford her a more ample opportunity and license to talk herself.

Monsieur Farival thought that Victor should have been taken out in mid-ocean in his earliest youth and drowned. Victor thought there would be more logic in thus disposing of old people with an established claim for making themselves universally obnoxious. Madame Lebrun grew a trifle hysterical; Robert called his brother some sharp, hard names.

"There's nothing much to explain, mother," he said; though he explained, nevertheless—looking chiefly at Edna—that he could only meet the gentleman whom he intended to join at Vera Cruz by taking such and such a steamer, which left New Orleans on such a day; that Beaudelet was going out with his lugger-load of vegetables that night, which gave him an opportunity of reaching the city and making his vessel in time.

"But when did you make up your mind to all this?" demanded Monsieur Farival.

"This afternoon," returned Robert, with a shade of annoyance.

"At what time this afternoon?" persisted the old gentleman, with nagging determination, as if he were cross-questioning a criminal in a court of justice.

"At four o'clock this afternoon, Monsieur Farival," Robert replied, in a high voice and with a lofty air, which reminded Edna of some gentleman on the stage.

She had forced herself to eat most of her soup, and now she was picking the flaky bits of a *court bouillon*[15] with her fork.

The lovers were profiting by the general conversation on Mexico to speak in whispers of matters which they rightly considered were interesting to no one but themselves. The lady in black had once received a pair of prayer beads of curious workmanship from Mexico, with very special indulgence attached to them, but she had never been able to ascertain whether the indulgence extended outside the Mexican border. Father Fochel of the Cathedral had attempted to explain it; but he had not done so to her satisfaction. And she begged that Robert would interest himself, and discover, if possible, whether she was entitled to the indulgence accompanying the remarkably curious Mexican prayer beads.

Madame Ratignolle hoped that Robert would exercise extreme caution in dealing with the Mexicans, who, she considered, were a treacherous people, unscrupulous and

15. Poached fish.

revengeful. She trusted she did them no injustice in thus condemning them as a race. She had known personally but one Mexican, who made and sold excellent tamales, and whom she would have trusted implicitly, so softspoken was he. One day he was arrested for stabbing his wife. She never knew whether he had been hanged or not.

Victor had grown hilarious, and was attempting to tell an anecdote about a Mexican girl who served chocolate one winter in a restaurant in Dauphine Street. No one would listen to him but old Monsieur Farival, who went into convulsions over the droll story.

Edna wondered if they had all gone mad, to be talking and clamoring at that rate. She herself could think of nothing to say about Mexico or the Mexicans.

"At what time do you leave?" she asked Robert.

"At ten," he told her. "Beaudelet wants to wait for the moon."

"Are you all ready to go?"

"Quite ready. I shall only take a handbag, and shall pack my trunk in the city."

He turned to answer some question put to him by his mother, and Edna, having finished her black coffee, left the table.

She went directly to her room. The little cottage was close and stuffy after leaving the outer air. But she did not mind; there appeared to be a hundred different things demanding her attention indoors. She began to set the toilet stand to rights, grumbling at the negligence of the quadroon, who was in the adjoining room putting the children to bed. She gathered together stray garments that were hanging on the backs of chairs, and put each where it belonged in closet or bureau drawer. She changed her gown for a more comfortable and commodious wrapper. She rearranged her hair, combing and brushing it with unusual energy. Then she went in and assisted the quadroon in getting the boys to bed.

They were very playful and inclined to talk—to do anything but lie quiet and go to sleep. Edna sent the quadroon away to her supper and told her she need not return. Then she sat and told the children a story. Instead of soothing it excited them, and added to their wakefulness. She left them in heated argument, speculating about the conclusion of the tale which their mother promised to finish the following night.

The little black girl came in to say that Madame Lebrun would like to have Mrs. Pontellier go and sit with them over at the house till Mr. Robert went away. Edna returned answer that she had already undressed, that she did not feel quite well, but perhaps she would go over to the house later. She started to dress again, and got as far advanced as to remove her *peignoir*. But changing her mind once more she resumed the *peignoir*, and went outside and sat down before her door. She was overheated and irritable, and fanned herself energetically for a while. Madame Ratignolle came down to discover what was the matter.

"All that noise and confusion at the table must have upset me," replied Edna, "and moreover, I hate shocks and surprises. The idea of Robert starting off in such a ridiculously sudden and dramatic way! As if it were a matter of life and death! Never saying a word about it all morning when he was with me."

"Yes," agreed Madame Ratignolle. "I think it was showing us all—you especially—very little consideration. It wouldn't have surprised me in any of the others; those Lebruns are all given to heroics. But I must say I should never have expected such a thing from Robert. Are you not coming down? Come on, dear; it doesn't look friendly."

"No," said Edna, a little sullenly. "I can't go to the trouble of dressing again; I don't feel like it."

"You needn't dress; you look all right; fasten a belt around your waist. Just look at me!"

"No," persisted Edna; "but you go on. Madame Lebrun might be offended if we both stayed away."

Madame Ratignolle kissed Edna goodnight, and went away, being in truth rather desirous of joining in the general and animated conversation which was still in progress concerning Mexico and the Mexicans.

Somewhat later Robert came up, carrying his handbag.

"Aren't you feeling well?" he asked.

"Oh, well enough. Are you going right away?"

He lit a match and looked at his watch. "In twenty minutes," he said. The sudden and brief flare of the match emphasized the darkness for a while. He sat down upon a stool which the children had left out on the porch.

"Get a chair," said Edna.

"This will do," he replied. He put on his soft hat and nervously took it off again, and wiping his face with his handkerchief, complained of the heat.

"Take the fan," said Edna, offering it to him.

"Oh, no! Thank you. It does no good; you have to stop fanning sometime, and feel all the more uncomfortable afterward."

"That's one of the ridiculous things which men always say. I have never known one to speak otherwise of fanning. How long will you be gone?"

"Forever, perhaps. I don't know. It depends upon a good many things."

"Well, in case it shouldn't be forever, how long will it be?"

"I don't know."

"This seems to me perfectly preposterous and uncalled for. I don't like it. I don't understand your motive for silence and mystery, never saying a word to me about it this morning." He remained silent, not offering to defend himself. He only said, after a moment:

"Don't part from me in an ill humor. I never knew you to be out of patience with me before."

"I don't want to part in any ill humor," she said. "But can't you understand? I've grown used to seeing you, to having you with me all the time, and your action seems unfriendly, even unkind. You don't even offer an excuse for it. Why, I was planning to be together, thinking of how pleasant it would be to see you in the city next winter."

"So was I," he blurted. "Perhaps that's the—" He stood up suddenly and held out his hand. "Good-by, my dear Mrs. Pontellier; goodbye. You won't—I hope you won't completely forget me." She clung to his hand, striving to detain him.

"Write to me when you get there, won't you, Robert?" she entreated.

"I will, thank you. Goodbye."

How unlike Robert! The merest acquaintance would have said something more emphatic than "I will, thank you; goodbye," to such a request.

He had evidently already taken leave of the people over at the house, for he descended the steps and went to join Beaudelet, who was out there with an oar across his shoulder waiting for Robert. They walked away in the darkness. She could only hear Beaudelet's voice; Robert had apparently not even spoken a word of greeting to his companion.

Edna bit her handkerchief convulsively, striving to hold back and to hide, even from herself as she would have hidden from another, the emotion which was troubling—tearing—her. Her eyes were brimming with tears.

For the first time she recognized anew the symptoms of infatuation which she had felt incipiently as a child, as a girl in her earliest teens, and later as a young woman. The recognition did not lessen the reality, the poignancy of the revelation by any suggestion or promise of instability. The past was nothing to her; offered no lesson which she was willing to heed. The future was a mystery which she never attempted to penetrate. The present alone was significant; was hers, to torture her as it was doing then with the biting conviction that she had lost that which she had held, that she had been denied that which her impassioned, newly awakened being demanded.

XVI

"Do you miss your friend greatly?" asked Mademoiselle Reisz one morning as she came creeping up behind Edna, who had just left her cottage on her way to the beach. She spent much of her time in the water since she had acquired finally the art of swimming. As their stay at Grand Isle drew near its close, she felt that she could not give too much time to a diversion which afforded her the only real pleasurable moments that she knew. When Mademoiselle Reisz came and touched her upon the shoulder and spoke to her, the woman seemed to echo the thought which was ever in Edna's mind; or, better, the feeling which constantly possessed her.

Robert's going had some way taken the brightness, the color, the meaning out of everything. The conditions of her life were in no way changed, but her whole existence was dulled, like a faded garment which seems to be no longer worth wearing. She sought him everywhere—in others whom she induced to talk about him. She went up in the mornings to Madame Lebrun's room, braving the clatter of the old sewing machine. She sat there and chatted at intervals as Robert had done. She gazed around the room at the pictures and photographs hanging upon the wall, and discovered in some corner an old family album, which she examined with the keenest interest, appealing to Madame Lebrun for enlightenment concerning the many figures and faces which she discovered between its pages.

There was a picture of Madame Lebrun with Robert as a baby, seated in her lap, a round-faced infant with a fist in his mouth. The eyes alone in the baby suggested the man. And that was he also in kilts, at the age of five, wearing long curls and holding a whip in his hand. It made Edna laugh, and she laughed, too, at the portrait in his first long trousers; while another interested her, taken when he left for college, looking thin, long-faced, with eyes full of fire, ambition and great intentions. But there was no recent picture, none which suggested the Robert who had gone away five days ago, leaving a void and wilderness behind him.

"Oh, Robert stopped having his pictures taken when he had to pay for them himself! He found wiser use for his money, he says," explained Madame Lebrun. She had a letter from him, written before he left New Orleans. Edna wished to see the letter, and Madame Lebrun told her to look for it either on the table or the dresser, or perhaps it was on the mantelpiece.

The letter was on the bookshelf. It possessed the greatest interest and attraction for Edna; the envelope, its size and shape, the postmark, the handwriting. She examined every detail of the outside before opening it. There were only a few lines, setting forth that he would leave the city that afternoon, that he had packed his trunk in good shape, that he was well, and sent her his love and begged to be affectionately remembered to all. There was no special message to Edna except a postscript saying that if Mrs. Pontellier desired to finish the book which he had been reading to her, his mother would find it in his room, among other books there on the table. Edna experienced a pang of jealousy because he had written to his mother rather than to her.

Every one seemed to take for granted that she missed him. Even her husband, when he came down the Saturday following Robert's departure, expressed regret that he had gone.

"How do you get on without him, Edna?" he asked.

"It's very dull without him," she admitted. Mr. Pontellier had seen Robert in the city, and Edna asked him a dozen questions or more. Where had they met? On Carondelet Street, in the morning. They had gone "in" and had a drink and a cigar together. What had they talked about? Chiefly about his prospects in Mexico, which Mr. Pontellier thought were promising. How did he look? How did he seem—grave, or gay, or how? Quite cheerful, and wholly taken up with the idea of his trip, which Mr. Pontellier found altogether natural in a young fellow about to seek fortune and adventure in a strange, queer country.

Edna tapped her foot impatiently, and wondered why the children persisted in playing in the sun when they might be under the trees. She went down and led them out of the sun, scolding the quadroon for not being more attentive.

It did not strike her as in the least grotesque that she should be making of Robert the object of conversation and leading her husband to speak of him. The sentiment which she entertained for Robert in no way resembled that which she felt for her husband, or had ever felt, or ever expected to feel. She had all her life long been accustomed to harbor thoughts and emotions which never voiced themselves. They had never taken the form of struggles. They belonged to her and were her own, and she entertained the conviction that she had a right to them and that they concerned no one but herself. Edna had once told Madame Ratignolle that she would never sacrifice herself for her children, or for anyone. Then had followed a rather heated argument; the two women did not appear to understand each other or to be talking the same language. Edna tried to appease her friend, to explain.

"I would give up the unessential; I would give my money, I would give my life for my children; but I wouldn't give myself. I can't make it more clear; it's only something which I am beginning to comprehend, which is revealing itself to me."

"I don't know what you would call the essential, or what you mean by the unessential," said Madame Ratignolle, cheerfully; "but a woman who would give her life for her children could do no more than that—your Bible tells you so. I'm sure I couldn't do more than that."

"Oh, yes you could!" laughed Edna.

She was not surprised at Mademoiselle Reisz's question the morning that lady, following her to the beach, tapped her on the shoulder and asked if she did not greatly miss her young friend.

"Oh, good morning, Mademoiselle; is it you? Why, of course I miss Robert. Are you going down to bathe?"

"Why should I go down to bathe at the very end of the season when I haven't been in the surf all summer," replied the woman, disagreeably.

"I beg your pardon," offered Edna, in some embarrassment, for she should have remembered that Mademoiselle Reisz's avoidance of the water had furnished a theme for much pleasantry. Some among them thought it was on account of her false hair, or the dread of getting the violets wet, while others attributed it to the natural aversion for water sometimes believed to accompany the artistic temperament. Mademoiselle offered Edna some chocolates in a paper bag, which she took from her pocket, by way of showing that she bore no ill feeling. She habitually ate chocolates for their sustaining quality; they contained much nutriment in small compass, she said. They saved her from starvation, as Madame Lebrun's table was utterly impossible; and no one save so impertinent a woman as Madame Lebrun could think of offering such food to people and requiring them to pay for it.

"She must feel very lonely without her son," said Edna, desiring to change the subject. "Her favorite son, too. It must have been quite hard to let him go."

Mademoiselle laughed maliciously.

"Her favorite son! Oh, dear! Who could have been imposing such a tale upon you? Aline Lebrun lives for Victor, and for Victor alone. She has spoiled him into the worthless creature he is. She worships him and the ground he walks on. Robert is very well in a way, to give up all the money he can earn to the family, and keep the barest pittance for himself. Favorite son, indeed! I miss the poor fellow myself, my dear. I liked to see him and to hear him about the place—the only Lebrun who is worth a pinch of salt. He comes to see me often in the city. I like to play to him. That Victor! hanging would be too good for him. It's a wonder Robert hasn't beaten him to death long ago."

"I thought he had great patience with his brother," offered Edna, glad to be talking about Robert, no matter what was said.

"Oh! he thrashed him well enough a year or two ago," said Mademoiselle. "It was about a Spanish girl, whom Victor considered that he had some sort of claim upon. He met Robert one day talking to the girl, or walking with her, or bathing with her, or carrying her basket—I don't remember what—and he became so insulting and abusive that Robert gave him a thrashing on the spot that has kept him comparatively in order for a good while. It's about time he was getting another."

"Was her name Mariequita?" asked Edna.

"Mariequita—yes, that was it; Mariequita. I had forgotten. Oh, she's a sly one, and a bad one, that Mariequita!"

Edna looked down at Mademoiselle Reisz and wondered how she could have listened to her venom so long. For some reason she felt depressed, almost unhappy. She had not intended to go into the water; but she donned her bathing suit, and left Mademoiselle alone, seated under the shade of the children's tent. The water was growing cooler as the season advanced. Edna plunged and swam about with an abandon that thrilled and invigorated her. She remained a long time in the water, half hoping that Mademoiselle Reisz would not wait for her.

But Mademoiselle waited. She was very amiable during the walk back, and raved much over Edna's appearance in her bathing suit. She talked about music. She hoped that Edna would go to see her in the city, and wrote her address with the stub of a pencil on a piece of card which she found in her pocket.

"When do you leave?" asked Edna.

"Next Monday; and you?"

"The following week," answered Edna, adding, "It has been a pleasant summer, hasn't it, Mademoiselle?"

"Well," agreed Mademoiselle Reisz, with a shrug, "rather pleasant, if it hadn't been for the mosquitoes and the Farival twins."

XVII

The Pontelliers possessed a very charming home on Esplanade Street in New Orleans. It was a large, double cottage, with a broad front veranda, whose round, fluted columns supported the sloping roof. The house was painted a dazzling white; the outside shutters, or jalousies, were green. In the yard, which was kept scrupulously neat, were flowers and plants of every description which flourishes in South Louisiana. Within doors the appointments were perfect after the conventional type. The softest carpets and rugs covered the floors; rich and tasteful draperies hung at doors and windows. There were paintings, selected with judgment and discrimination, upon the walls. The cut glass, the silver, the heavy damask which daily appeared upon the table were the envy of many women whose husbands were less generous than Mr. Pontellier.

Mr. Pontellier was very fond of walking about his house examining its various appointments and details, to see that nothing was amiss. He greatly valued his possessions, chiefly because they were his, and derived genuine pleasure from contemplating a painting, a statuette, a rare lace curtain—no matter what—after he had bought it and placed it among his household gods.

On Tuesday afternoons—Tuesday being Mrs. Pontellier's reception day—there was a constant stream of callers—women who came in carriages or in the street cars, or walked when the air was soft and distance permitted. A light-colored mulatto boy, in dress coat and bearing a diminutive silver tray for the reception of cards, admitted them. A maid, in white fluted cap, offered the callers liqueur, coffee, or chocolate, as they might desire. Mrs. Pontellier, attired in a handsome reception gown, remained in the drawing room the entire afternoon receiving her visitors. Men sometimes called in the evening with their wives.

This had been the program which Mrs. Pontellier had religiously followed since her marriage, six years before. Certain evenings during the week she and her husband attended the opera or sometimes the play.

Mr. Pontellier left his home in the mornings between nine and ten o'clock, and rarely returned before half-past six or seven in the evening—dinner being served at half-past seven.

He and his wife seated themselves at table one Tuesday evening, a few weeks after their return from Grand Isle. They were alone together. The boys were being put to bed; the patter of their bare, escaping feet could be heard occasionally, as well as the pursuing voice of the quadroon, lifted in mild protest and entreaty. Mrs. Pontellier did not wear her usual Tuesday reception gown; she was in ordinary house dress. Mr. Pontellier, who was observant about such things, noticed it, as he served the soup and handed it to the boy in waiting.

"Tired out, Edna? Whom did you have? Many callers?" he asked. He tasted his soup and began to season it with pepper, salt, vinegar, mustard—everything within reach.

"There were a good many," replied Edna, who was eating her soup with evident satisfaction. "I found their cards when I got home; I was out."

"Out!" exclaimed her husband, with something like genuine consternation in his voice as he laid down the vinegar cruet and looked at her through his glasses. "Why, what could have taken you out on Tuesday? What did you have to do?"

"Nothing. I simply felt like going out, and I went out."

"Well, I hope you left some suitable excuse," said her husband, somewhat appeased, as he added a dash of cayenne pepper to the soup.

"No, I left no excuse. I told Joe to say I was out, that was all."

"Why, my dear, I should think you'd understand by this time that people don't do such things; we've got to observe *les convenances*[16] if we ever expect to get on and

16. Social niceties.

keep up with the procession. If you felt that you had to leave home this afternoon, you should have left some suitable explanation for your absence.

"This soup is really impossible; it's strange that woman hasn't learned yet to make a decent soup. Any free-lunch stand in town serves a better one. Was Mrs. Belthrop here?"

"Bring the tray with the cards, Joe. I don't remember who was here."

The boy retired and returned after a moment, bringing the tiny silver tray, which was covered with ladies' visiting cards. He handed it to Mrs. Pontellier.

"Give it to Mr. Pontellier," she said.

Joe offered the tray to Mr. Pontellier, and removed the soup.

Mr. Pontellier scanned the names of his wife's callers, reading some of them aloud, with comments as he read.

"'The Misses Delasidas.' I worked a big deal in futures for their father this morning; nice girls; it's time they were getting married. 'Mrs. Belthrop.' I tell you what it is, Edna; you can't afford to snub Mrs. Belthrop. Why, Belthrop could buy and sell us ten times over. His business is worth a good, round sum to me. You'd better write her a note. 'Mrs. James Highcamp.' Hugh! the less you have to do with Mrs. Highcamp, the better. 'Madame Laforcé.' Came all the way from Carrolton, too, poor old soul. 'Miss Wiggs,' 'Mrs. Eleanor Boltons.'" He pushed the cards aside.

"Mercy!" exclaimed Edna, who had been fuming. "Why are you taking the thing so seriously and making such a fuss over it?"

"I'm not making any fuss over it. But it's just such seeming trifles that we've got to take seriously; such things count."

The fish was scorched. Mr. Pontellier would not touch it. Edna said she did not mind a little scorched taste. The roast was in some way not to his fancy, and he did not like the manner in which the vegetables were served.

"It seems to me," he said, "we spend money enough in this house to procure at least one meal a day which a man could eat and retain his self-respect."

"You used to think the cook was a treasure," returned Edna, indifferently.

"Perhaps she was when she first came; but cooks are only human. They need looking after, like any other class of persons that you employ. Suppose I didn't look after the clerks in my office, just let them run things their own way; they'd soon make a nice mess of me and my business."

"Where are you going?" asked Edna, seeing that her husband arose from table without having eaten a morsel except a taste of the highly seasoned soup.

"I'm going to get my dinner at the club. Good night." He went into the hall, took his hat and stick from the stand, and left the house.

She was somewhat familiar with such scenes. They had often made her very unhappy. On a few previous occasions she had been completely deprived of any desire to finish her dinner. Sometimes she had gone into the kitchen to administer a tardy rebuke to the cook. Once she went to her room and studied the cookbook during an entire evening, finally writing out a menu for the week, which left her harassed with a feeling that, after all, she had accomplished no good that was worth the name.

But that evening Edna finished her dinner alone, with forced deliberation. Her face was flushed and her eyes flamed with some inward fire that lighted them. After finishing her dinner she went to her room, having instructed the boy to tell any other callers that she was indisposed.

It was a large, beautiful room, rich and picturesque in the soft, dim light which the maid had turned low. She went and stood at an open window and looked out upon the deep tangle of the garden below. All the mystery and witchery of the night seemed to have gathered there amid the perfumes and the dusky and tortuous outlines of flowers and foliage. She was seeking herself and finding herself in just such sweet half-darkness which met her moods. But the voices were not soothing that came to her from the darkness and the sky above and the stars. They jeered and sounded mournful notes without promise, devoid even of hope. She turned back into the room and began to walk to and fro down its whole length, without stopping, without resting. She carried in her hands a thin handkerchief, which she tore into ribbons, rolled into a ball, and flung from her. Once she stopped, and taking off her wedding ring, flung it upon the carpet. When she saw it lying there, she stamped her heel upon it, striving to crush it. But her small boot heel did not make an indenture, not a mark upon the little glittering circlet.

In a sweeping passion she seized a glass vase from the table and flung it upon the tiles of the hearth. She wanted to destroy something. The crash and clatter were what she wanted to hear.

A maid, alarmed at the din of breaking glass, entered the room to discover what was the matter.

"A vase fell upon the hearth," said Edna. "Never mind; leave it till morning."

"Oh! you might get some of the glass in your feet, ma'am," insisted the young woman, picking up bits of the broken vase that were scattered upon the carpet. "And here's your ring, ma'am, under the chair."

Edna held out her hand, and taking the ring, slipped it upon her finger.

XVIII

The following morning Mr. Pontellier, upon leaving for his office, asked Edna if she would not meet him in town in order to look at some new fixtures for the library.

"I hardly think we need new fixtures, Léonce. Don't let us get anything new; you are too extravagant. I don't believe you ever think of saving or putting by."

"The way to become rich is to make money, my dear Edna, not to save it," he said. He regretted that she did not feel inclined to go with him and select new fixtures. He kissed her goodbye, and told her she was not looking well and must take care of herself. She was unusually pale and very quiet.

She stood on the front veranda as he quitted the house, and absently picked a few sprays of jessamine that grew upon a trellis near by. She inhaled the odor of the blossoms and thrust them into the bosom of her white morning gown. The boys were dragging along the banquette a small "express wagon," which they had filled with blocks and sticks. The quadroon was following them with little quick steps, having assumed a fictitious animation and alacrity for the occasion. A fruit vendor was crying his wares in the street.

Edna looked straight before her with a self-absorbed expression upon her face. She felt no interest in anything about her. The street, the children, the fruit vendor, the flowers growing there under her eyes, were all part and parcel of an alien world which had suddenly become antagonistic.

She went back into the house. She had thought of speaking to the cook concerning her blunders of the previous night; but Mr. Pontellier had saved her that disagreeable mission, for which she was so poorly fitted. Mr. Pontellier's arguments were usually convincing with those whom he employed. He left home feeling quite sure that he and Edna would sit down that evening, and possibly a few subsequent evenings, to a dinner deserving of the name.

Edna spent an hour or two in looking over some of her old sketches. She could see their shortcomings and defects, which were glaring in her eyes. She tried to work a little, but found she was not in the humor. Finally she gathered together a few of the sketches—those which she considered the least discreditable; and she carried them with her when, a little later, she dressed and left the house. She looked handsome and distinguished in her street gown. The tan of the seashore had left her face, and her forehead was smooth, white, and polished beneath her heavy, yellow-brown hair. There were a few freckles on her face, and a small, dark mole near the under lip and one on the temple, half-hidden in her hair.

As Edna walked along the street she was thinking of Robert. She was still under the spell of her infatuation. She had tried to forget him, realizing the inutility of remembering. But the thought of him was like an obsession, ever pressing itself upon her. It was not that she dwelt upon details of their acquaintance, or recalled in any special or peculiar way his personality; it was his being, his existence, which dominated her thought, fading sometimes as if it would melt into the mist of the forgotten, reviving again with an intensity which filled her with an incomprehensible longing.

Edna was on her way to Madame Ratignolle's. Their intimacy, begun at Grand Isle, had not declined, and they had seen each other with some frequency since their return to the city. The Ratignolles lived at no great distance from Edna's home, on the corner of a side street, where Monsieur Ratignolle owned and conducted a drugstore which enjoyed a steady and prosperous trade. His father had been in the business before him, and Monsieur Ratignolle stood well in the community and bore an enviable reputation for integrity and clear-headedness. His family lived in commodious apartments over the store, having an entrance on the side within the *porte cochère*.[17] There was something which Edna thought very French, very foreign, about their whole manner of living. In the large and pleasant salon which extended across the width of the house, the Ratignolles entertained their friends once a fortnight with a *soirée musicale*, sometimes diversified by cardplaying. There was a friend who played upon the cello. One brought his flute and another his violin, while there were some who sang and a number who performed upon the piano with various degrees of taste and agility. The Ratignolles' *soirées musicales* were widely known, and it was considered a privilege to be invited to them.

Edna found her friend engaged in assorting the clothes which had returned that morning from the laundry. She at once abandoned her occupation upon seeing Edna, who had been ushered without ceremony into her presence.

"'Cité can do it as well as I; it is really her business," she explained to Edna, who apologized for interrupting her. And she summoned a young black woman, whom she instructed, in French, to be very careful in checking off the list which she handed her. She told her to notice particularly if a fine linen handkerchief of Monsieur Ratignolle's, which was missing last week, had been returned; and to be sure to set to one side such pieces as required mending and darning.

Then placing an arm around Edna's waist, she led her to the front of the house, to the salon, where it was cool and sweet with the odor of great roses that stood upon the hearth in jars.

Madame Ratignolle looked more beautiful than ever there at home, in a negligée which left her arms almost wholly bare and exposed the rich, melting curves of her white throat.

"Perhaps I shall be able to paint your picture some day," said Edna with a smile when they were seated. She produced the roll of sketches and started to unfold them.

17. Carriage entrance.

"I believe I ought to work again. I feel as if I wanted to be doing something. What do you think of them? Do you think it worth while to take it up again and study some more? I might study for a while with Laidpore."

She knew that Madame Ratignolle's opinion in such a matter would be next to valueless, that she herself had not alone decided, but determined; but she sought the words of praise and encouragement that would help her to put heart into her venture.

"Your talent is immense, dear!"

"Nonsense!" protested Edna, well pleased.

"Immense, I tell you," persisted Madame Ratignolle, surveying the sketches one by one, at close range, then holding them at arm's length, narrowing her eyes, and dropping her head on one side. "Surely, this Bavarian peasant is worthy of framing; and this basket of apples! never have I seen anything more lifelike. One might almost be tempted to reach out a hand and take one."

Edna could not control a feeling which bordered upon complacency at her friend's praise, even realizing, as she did, its true worth. She retained a few of the sketches, and gave all the rest to Madame Ratignolle, who appreciated the gift far beyond its value and proudly exhibited the pictures to her husband when he came up from the store a little later for his midday dinner.

Mr. Ratignolle was one of those men who are called the salt of the earth. His cheerfulness was unbounded, and it was matched by his goodness of heart, his broad charity, and common sense. He and his wife spoke English with an accent which was only discernible through its un-English emphasis and a certain carefulness and deliberation. Edna's husband spoke English with no accent whatever. The Ratignolles understood each other perfectly. If ever the fusion of two human beings into one has been accomplished on this sphere it was surely in their union.

As Edna seated herself at table with them she thought, "Better a dinner of herbs," though it did not take her long to discover that it was no dinner of herbs, but a delicious repast, simple, choice, and in every way satisfying.

Monsieur Ratignolle was delighted to see her, though he found her looking not so well as at Grand Isle, and he advised a tonic. He talked a good deal on various topics, a little politics, some city news and neighborhood gossip. He spoke with an animation and earnestness that gave an exaggerated importance to every syllable he uttered. His wife was keenly interested in everything he said, laying down her fork the better to listen, chiming in, taking the words out of his mouth.

Edna felt depressed rather than soothed after leaving them. The little glimpse of domestic harmony which had been offered her, gave her no regret, no longing. It was not a condition of life which fitted her, and she could see in it but an appalling and hopeless ennui. She was moved by a kind of commiseration for Madame Ratignolle—a pity for that colorless existence which never uplifted its possessor beyond the region of blind contentment, in which no moment of anguish ever visited her soul, in which she would never have the taste of life's delirium. Edna vaguely wondered what she meant by "life's delirium." It had crossed her thought like some unsought, extraneous impression.

XIX

Edna could not help but think that it was very foolish, very childish, to have stamped upon her wedding ring and smashed the crystal vase upon the tiles. She was visited by no more outbursts, moving her to such futile expedients. She began to do as she liked and to feel as she liked. She completely abandoned her Tuesdays at home, and did not return the visits of those who had called upon her. She made no ineffectual efforts to conduct her household *en bonne ménagère*,[18] going and coming as it suited her fancy, and, so far as she was able, lending herself to any passing caprice.

Mr. Pontellier had been a rather courteous husband so long as he met a certain tacit submissiveness in his wife. But her new and unexpected line of conduct completely bewildered him. It shocked him. Then her absolute disregard for her duties as a wife angered him. When Mr. Pontellier became rude, Edna grew insolent. She had resolved never to take another step backward.

"It seems to me the utmost folly for a woman at the head of a household, and the mother of children, to spend in an atelier days which would be better employed contriving for the comfort of her family."

"I feel like painting," answered Edna. "Perhaps I shan't always feel like it."

"Then in God's name paint! but don't let the family go to the devil. There's Madame Ratignolle; because she keeps up her music, she doesn't let everything else go to chaos. And she's more of a musician than you are a painter."

"She isn't a musician, and I'm not a painter. It isn't on account of painting that I let things go."

"On account of what, then?"

"Oh! I don't know. Let me alone; you bother me."

It sometimes entered Mr. Pontellier's mind to wonder if his wife were not growing a little unbalanced mentally. He could see plainly that she was not herself. That is, he could not see that she was becoming herself and daily casting aside that fictitious self which we assume like a garment with which to appear before the world.

Her husband let her alone as she requested, and went away to his office. Edna went up to her atelier—a bright room in the top of the house. She was working with great energy and interest, without accomplishing anything, however, which satisfied her even in the smallest degree. For a time she had the whole household enrolled in the service of art. The boys posed for her. They thought it amusing at first, but the occupation soon lost its attractiveness when they discovered that it was not a game arranged especially for their entertainment. The quadroon sat for hours before Edna's palette, patient as a savage, while the housemaid took charge of the children, and the drawing-room went undusted. But the housemaid, too, served her term as model when Edna perceived that the young woman's back and shoulders were molded on classic lines, and that her hair, loosened from its confining cap, became an inspiration. While Edna worked she sometimes sang low the little air, "Ah! si tu savais!"

It moved her with recollections. She could hear again the ripple of the water, the flapping sail. She could see the glint of the moon upon the bay, and could feel the soft, gusty beating of the hot south wind. A subtle current of desire passed through her body, weakening her hold upon the brushes and making her eyes burn.

There were days when she was very happy without knowing why. She was happy to be alive and breathing, when her whole being seemed to be one with the sunlight, the color, the odors, the luxuriant warmth of some perfect Southern day. She liked then to wander alone into strange and unfamiliar places. She discovered many a sunny, sleepy corner, fashioned to dream in. And she found it good to dream and to be alone and unmolested.

There were days when she was unhappy, she did not know why—when it did not seem worth while to be glad or sorry, to be alive or dead; when life appeared to her

18. As a good housewife.

like a grotesque pandemonium and humanity like worms struggling blindly toward inevitable annihilation. She could not work on such a day, nor weave fancies to stir her pulses and warm her blood.

XX

It was during such a mood that Edna hunted up Mademoiselle Reisz. She had not forgotten the rather disagreeable impression left upon her by their last interview; but she nevertheless felt a desire to see her—above all, to listen while she played upon the piano. Quite early in the afternoon she started upon her quest for the pianist. Unfortunately, she had mislaid or lost Mademoiselle Reisz's card, and looking up her address in the city directory, she found that the woman lived on Bienville Street, some distance away. The directory which fell into her hands was a year or more old, however, and upon reaching the number indicated, Edna discovered that the house was occupied by a respectable family of mulattoes who had *chambres garnies*[19] to let. They had been living there for six months, and knew absolutely nothing of a Mademoiselle Reisz. In fact, they knew nothing of any of their neighbors; their lodgers were all people of the highest distinction, they assured Edna. She did not linger to discuss class distinctions with Madame Pouponne, but hastened to a neighboring grocery store, feeling sure that Mademoiselle would have left her address with the proprietor.

He knew Mademoiselle Reisz a good deal better than he wanted to know her, he informed his questioner. In truth he did not want to know her at all, or anything concerning her—the most disagreeable and unpopular woman who ever lived in Bienville Street. He thanked heaven she had left the neighborhood, and was equally thankful that he did not know where she had gone.

Edna's desire to see Mademoiselle Reisz had increased tenfold since these unlooked-for obstacles had arisen to thwart it. She was wondering who could give her the information she sought, when it suddenly occurred to her that Madame Lebrun would be the one most likely to do so. She knew it was useless to ask Madame Ratignolle, who was on the most distant terms with the musician, and preferred to know nothing concerning her. She had once been almost as emphatic in expressing herself upon the subject as the corner grocer.

Edna knew that Madame Lebrun had returned to the city, for it was the middle of November. And she also knew where the Lebruns lived, on Chartres Street.

Their home from the outside looked like a prison, with iron bars before the door and lower windows. The iron bars were a relic of the old *régime*, and no one had ever thought of dislodging them. At the side was a high fence enclosing the garden. A gate or door opening upon the street was locked. Edna rang the bell at this side garden gate, and stood upon the banquette, waiting to be admitted.

It was Victor who opened the gate for her. A black woman, wiping her hands upon her apron, was close at his heels. Before she saw them Edna could hear them in altercation, the woman—plainly an anomaly—claiming the right to be allowed to perform her duties, one of which was to answer the bell.

Victor was surprised and delighted to see Mrs. Pontellier, and he made no attempt to conceal either his astonishment or his delight. He was a dark-browned, good-looking youngster of nineteen, greatly resembling his mother, but with ten

19. Furnished rooms.

times her impetuosity. He instructed the black woman to go at once and inform Madame Lebrun that Mrs. Pontellier desired to see her. The woman grumbled a refusal to do part of her duty when she had not been permitted to do it all, and started back to her interrupted task of weeding the garden. Whereupon Victor administered a rebuke in the form of a volley of abuse, which, owing to its rapidity and incoherence, was all but incomprehensible to Edna. Whatever it was, the rebuke was convincing, for the woman dropped her hoe and went mumbling into the house.

Edna did not wish to enter. It was very pleasant there on the side porch, where there were chairs, a wicker lounge, and a small table. She seated herself, for she was tired from her long tramp; and she began to rock gently and smooth out the folds of her silk parasol. Victor drew up his chair beside her. He at once explained that the black woman's offensive conduct was all due to imperfect training, as he was not there to take her in hand. He had only come up from the island the morning before, and expected to return next day. He stayed all winter at the island; he lived there, and kept the place in order and got things ready for the summer visitors.

But a man needed occasional relaxation, he informed Mrs. Pontellier, and every now and again he drummed up a pretext to bring him to the city. My! but he had had a time of it the evening before! He wouldn't want his mother to know, and he began to talk in a whisper. He was scintillant with recollections. Of course, he couldn't think of telling Mrs. Pontellier all about it, she being a woman and not comprehending such things. But it all began with a girl peeping and smiling at him through the shutters as he passed by. Oh! but she was a beauty! Certainly he smiled back, and went up and talked to her. Mrs. Pontellier did not know him if she supposed he was one to let an opportunity like that escape him. Despite herself, the youngster amused her. She must have betrayed in her look some degree of interest or entertainment. The boy grew more daring, and Mrs. Pontellier might have found herself, in a little while, listening to a highly colored story but for the timely appearance of Madame Lebrun.

That lady was still clad in white, according to her custom of the summer. Her eyes beamed an effusive welcome. Would not Mrs. Pontellier go inside? Would she partake of some refreshment? Why had she not been there before? How was that dear Mr. Pontellier and how were those sweet children? Had Mrs. Pontellier ever known such a warm November?

Victor went and reclined on the wicker lounge behind his mother's chair, where he commanded a view of Edna's face. He had taken her parasol from her hands while he spoke to her, and he now lifted it and twirled it above him as he lay on his back. When Madame Lebrun complained that it was so dull coming back to the city; that she saw so few people now; that even Victor, when he came up from the island for a day or two, had so much to occupy him and engage his time; then it was that the youth went into contortions on the lounge and winked mischievously at Edna. She somehow felt like a confederate in crime, and tried to look severe and disapproving.

There had been but two letters from Robert, with little in them, they told her. Victor said it was really not worthwhile to go inside for the letters, when his mother entreated him to go in search of them. He remembered the contents, which in truth he rattled off very glibly when put to the test.

One letter was written from Vera Cruz and the other from the City of Mexico. He had met Montel, who was doing everything toward his advancement. So far, the financial situation was no improvement over the one he had left in New Orleans, but of course the prospects were vastly better. He wrote of the City of Mexico, the buildings, the people and their habits, the conditions of life which he found there. He sent his love to the family. He inclosed a check to his mother, and hoped she would affectionately remember him to all his friends. That was about the substance of the two letters. Edna felt that if there had been a message for her, she would have received it. The despondent frame of mind in which she had left home began again to overtake her, and she remembered that she wished to find Mademoiselle Reisz.

Madame Lebrun knew where Mademoiselle Reisz lived. She gave Edna the address, regretting that she would not consent to stay and spend the remainder of the afternoon, and pay a visit to Mademoiselle Reisz some other day. The afternoon was already well advanced.

Victor escorted her out upon the banquette, lifted her parasol, and held it over her while he walked to the car with her. He entreated her to bear in mind that the disclosures of the afternoon were strictly confidential. She laughed and bantered him a little, remembering too late that she should have been dignified and reserved.

"How handsome Mrs. Pontellier looked!" said Madame Lebrun to her son.

"Ravishing!" he admitted. "The city atmosphere has improved her. Some way she doesn't seem like the same woman."

XXI

Some people contended that the reason Mademoiselle Reisz always chose apartments up under the roof was to discourage the approach of beggars, peddlers and callers. There were plenty of windows in her little front room. They were for the most part dingy, but as they were nearly always open it did not make so much difference. They often admitted into the room a good deal of smoke and soot; but at the same time all the light and air that there was came through them. From her windows could be seen the crescent of the river, the masts of ships and the big chimneys of the Mississippi steamers. A magnificent piano crowded the apartment. In the next room she slept, and in the third and last she harbored a gasoline stove on which she cooked her meals when disinclined to descend to the neighboring restaurant. It was there also that she ate, keeping her belongings in a rare old buffet, dingy and battered from a hundred years of use.

When Edna knocked at Mademoiselle Reisz's front room door and entered, she discovered that person standing beside the window, engaged in mending or patching an old prunella gaiter. The little musician laughed all over when she saw Edna. Her laugh consisted of a contortion of the face and all the muscles of the body. She seemed strikingly homely, standing there in the afternoon light. She still wore the shabby lace and the artificial bunch of violets on the side of her head.

"So you remembered me at last," said Mademoiselle. "I had said to myself, 'Ah, bah! she will never come.'"

"Did you want me to come?" asked Edna with a smile.

"I had not thought much about it," answered Mademoiselle. The two had seated themselves on a little bumpy sofa which stood against the wall. "I am glad, however, that you came. I have the water boiling back there, and was just about to make some coffee. You will drink a cup with me. And how is *la belle dame?* Always handsome! always healthy! always contented!" She took Edna's hand between her strong wiry fingers, holding it loosely without warmth, and executing a sort of double theme upon the back and palm.

"Yes," she went on; "I sometimes thought: 'She will never come. She promised as those women in society always do, without meaning it. She will not come.' For I really don't believe you like me, Mrs. Pontellier."

"I don't know whether I like you or not," replied Edna, gazing down at the little woman with a quizzical look.

The candor of Mrs. Pontellier's admission greatly pleased Mademoiselle Reisz. She expressed her gratification by repairing forthwith to the region of the gasoline stove and rewarding her guest with the promised cup of coffee. The coffee and the biscuit accompanying it proved very acceptable to Edna, who had declined refreshment at Madame Lebrun's and was now beginning to feel hungry. Mademoiselle set the tray which she brought in upon a small table near at hand, and seated herself once again on the lumpy sofa.

"I have had a letter from your friend," she remarked, as she poured a little cream into Edna's cup and handed it to her.

"My friend?"

"Yes, your friend Robert. He wrote to me from the City of Mexico."

"Wrote to *you?*" repeated Edna in amazement, stirring her coffee absently.

"Yes, to me. Why not? Don't stir all the warmth out of your coffee; drink it. Though the letter might as well have been sent to you; it was nothing but Mrs. Pontellier from beginning to end."

"Let me see it," requested the young woman, entreatingly.

"No; a letter concerns no one but the person who writes it and the one to whom it is written."

"Haven't you just said it concerned me from beginning to end?"

"It was written about you, not to you. 'Have you seen Mrs. Pontellier? How is she looking?' he asks. 'As Mrs. Pontellier says,' or 'as Mrs. Pontellier once said.' 'If Mrs. Pontellier should call upon you, play for her that Impromptu of Chopin's, my favorite. I heard it here a day or two ago, but not as you play it. I should like to know how it affects her,' and so on, as if he supposed we were constantly in each other's society."

"Let me see the letter."

"Oh, no."

"Have you answered it?"

"No."

"Let me see the letter."

"No, and again, no."

"Then play the Impromptu for me."

"It is growing late; what time do you have to be home?"

"Time doesn't concern me. Your question seems a little rude. Play the Impromptu."

"But you have told me nothing of yourself. What are you doing?"

"Painting!" laughed Edna. "I am becoming an artist. Think of it!"

"Ah! an artist! You have pretensions, Madame."

"Why pretensions? Do you think I could not become an artist?"

"I do not know you well enough to say. I do not know your talent or your temperament. To be an artist includes much; one must possess many gifts—absolute gifts—which have not been acquired by one's own effort. And, moreover, to succeed, the artist must possess the courageous soul."

"What do you mean by the courageous soul?"

"Courageous, *ma foi!*[20] The brave soul. The soul that dares and defies."

20. Indeed!

"Show me the letter and play for me the Impromptu. You see that I have persistence. Does that quality count for anything in art?"

"It counts with a foolish old woman whom you have captivated," replied Mademoiselle, with her wriggling laugh.

The letter was right there at hand in the drawer of the little table upon which Edna had just placed her coffee cup. Mademoiselle opened the drawer and drew forth the letter, the topmost one. She placed it in Edna's hands, and without further comment arose and went to the piano.

Mademoiselle played a soft interlude. It was an improvisation. She sat low at the instrument, and the lines of her body settled into ungraceful curves and angles that gave it an appearance of deformity. Gradually and imperceptibly the interlude melted into the soft opening minor chords of the Chopin Impromptu.

Edna did not know when the Impromptu began or ended. She sat in the sofa corner reading Robert's letter by the fading light. Mademoiselle had glided from the Chopin into the quivering love notes of Isolde's song, and back again to the Impromptu with its soulful and poignant longing.

The shadows deepened in the little room. The music grew strange and fantastic—turbulent, insistent, plaintive and soft with entreaty. The shadows grew deeper. The music filled the room. It floated out upon the night, over the housetops, the crescent of the river, losing itself in the silence of the upper air.

Edna was sobbing, just as she had wept one midnight at Grand Isle when strange, new voices awoke in her. She arose in some agitation to take her departure. "May I come again, Mademoiselle?" she asked at the threshold.

"Come whenever you feel like it. Be careful; the stairs and landings are dark; don't stumble."

Mademoiselle reëntered and lit a candle. Robert's letter was on the floor. She stooped and picked it up. It was crumpled and damp with tears. Mademoiselle smoothed the letter out, restored it to the envelope, and replaced it in the table drawer.

XXII

One morning on his way into town Mr. Pontellier stopped at the house of his old friend and family physician, Doctor Mandelet. The Doctor was a semi-retired physician, resting, as the saying is, upon his laurels. He bore a reputation for wisdom rather than skill—leaving the active practice of medicine to his assistants and younger contemporaries—and was much sought for in matters of consultation. A few families, united to him by bonds of friendship, he still attended when they required the services of a physician. The Pontelliers were among these.

Mr. Pontellier found the doctor reading at the open window of his study. His house stood rather far back from the street, in the center of a delightful garden, so that it was quiet and peaceful at the old gentleman's study window. He was a great reader. He stared up disapprovingly over his eyeglasses as Mr. Pontellier entered, wondering who had the temerity to disturb him at that hour of the morning.

"Ah! Pontellier! Not sick, I hope. Come and have a seat. What news do you bring this morning?" He was quite portly, with a profusion of gray hair, and small blue eyes which age had robbed of much of their brightness but none of their penetration.

"Oh! I'm never sick, Doctor. You know that I come of tough fiber—of that old Creole race of Pontelliers that dry up and finally blow away. I came to consult—no, not precisely to consult—to talk to you about Edna. I don't know what ails her."

"Madame Pontellier not well?" marveled the Doctor. "Why, I saw her—I think it was a week ago—walking along Canal Street, the picture of health, it seemed to me."

"Yes, yes; she seems quite well," said Mr. Pontellier, leaning forward and whirling his stick between his two hands; "but she doesn't act well. She's odd, she's not like herself. I can't make her out, and I thought perhaps you'd help me."

"How does she act?" inquired the doctor.

"Well, it isn't easy to explain," said Mr. Pontellier, throwing himself back in his chair. "She lets the housekeeping go to the dickens."

"Well, well; women are not all alike, my dear Pontellier. We've got to consider—"

"I know that; I told you I couldn't explain. Her whole attitude—toward me and everybody and everything—has changed. You know I have a quick temper, but I don't want to quarrel or be rude to a woman, especially my wife; yet I'm driven to it, and feel like ten thousand devils after I've made a fool of myself. She's making it devilishly uncomfortable for me," he went on nervously. "She's got some sort of notion in her head concerning the eternal rights of women; and—you understand—we meet in the morning at the breakfast table."

The old gentleman lifted his shaggy eyebrows, protruded his thick nether lip, and tapped the arms of his chair with his cushioned fingertips.

"What have you been doing to her, Pontellier?"

"Doing! *Parbleu!*"[21]

"Has she," asked the Doctor, with a smile, "has she been associating of late with a circle of pseudo-intellectual women—superspiritual superior beings? My wife has been telling me about them."

"That's the trouble," broke in Mr. Pontellier, "she hasn't been associating with any one. She has abandoned her Tuesdays at home, has thrown over all her acquaintances, and goes tramping about by herself, moping in the streetcars, getting in after dark. I tell you she's peculiar. I don't like it; I feel a little worried over it."

This was a new aspect for the Doctor. "Nothing hereditary?" he asked, seriously. "Nothing peculiar about her family antecedents, is there?"

"Oh, no, indeed! She comes of sound old Presbyterian Kentucky stock. The old gentleman, her father, I have heard, used to atone for his weekday sins with his Sunday devotions. I know for a fact, that his race horses literally ran away with the prettiest bit of Kentucky farming land I ever laid eyes upon. Margaret—you know Margaret—she has all the Presbyterianism undiluted. And the youngest is something of a vixen. By the way, she gets married in a couple of weeks from now."

"Send your wife up to the wedding," exclaimed the Doctor, foreseeing a happy solution. "Let her stay among her own people for a while; it will do her good."

"That's what I want her to do. She won't go to the marriage. She says a wedding is one of the most lamentable spectacles on earth. Nice thing for a woman to say to her husband!" exclaimed Mr. Pontellier, fuming anew at the recollection.

"Pontellier," said the Doctor, after a moment's reflection, "let your wife alone for a while. Don't bother her, and don't let her bother you. Woman, my dear friend, is a very peculiar and delicate organism—a sensitive and highly organized woman, such as I know Mrs. Pontellier to be, is especially peculiar. It would require an inspired psychologist to deal successfully with them. And when ordinary fellows like you and me attempt to cope with their idiosyncrasies the result is bungling. Most women are moody and whimsical. This is some passing whim of your wife, due to some cause or

---

21. Of course!

causes which you and I needn't try to fathom. But it will pass happily over, especially if you let her alone. Send her around to see me."

"Oh! I couldn't do that; there'd be no reason for it," objected Mr. Pontellier.

"Then I'll go around and see her," said the Doctor. "I'll drop in to dinner some evening *en bon ami*."[22]

"Do! by all means," urged Mr. Pontellier. "What evening will you come? Say Thursday. Will you come Thursday?" he asked, rising to take his leave.

"Very well; Thursday. My wife may possibly have some engagement for me Thursday. In case she has, I shall let you know. Otherwise, you may expect me."

Mr. Pontellier turned before leaving to say:

"I am going to New York on business very soon. I have a big scheme on hand, and want to be on the field proper to pull the ropes and handle the ribbons. We'll let you in on the inside if you say so, Doctor," he laughed.

"No, I thank you, my dear sir," returned the Doctor. "I leave such ventures to you younger men with the fever of life still in your blood."

"What I wanted to say," continued Mr. Pontellier, with his hand on the knob; "I may have to be absent a good while. Would you advise me to take Edna along?"

"By all means, if she wishes to go. If not, leave her here. Don't contradict her. The mood will pass, I assure you. It may take a month, two, three months—possibly longer, but it will pass; have patience."

"Well, good-by, *à jeudi*,"[23] said Mr. Pontellier, as he let himself out.

The Doctor would have liked during the course of conversation to ask, "Is there any man in the case?" but he knew his Creole too well to make such a blunder as that.

He did not resume his book immediately, but sat for a while meditatively looking out into the garden.

XXIII

Edna's father was in the city, and had been with them several days. She was not very warmly or deeply attached to him, but they had certain tastes in common, and when together they were companionable. His coming was in the nature of a welcome disturbance; it seemed to furnish a new direction for her emotions.

He had come to purchase a wedding gift for his daughter, Janet, and an outfit for himself in which he might make a creditable appearance at her marriage. Mr. Pontellier had selected the bridal gift, as everyone immediately connected with him always deferred to his taste in such matters. And his suggestions on the question of dress—which too often assumes the nature of a problem—were of inestimable value to his father-in-law. But for the past few days the old gentleman had been upon Edna's hands, and in his society she was becoming acquainted with a new set of sensations. He had been a colonel in the Confederate army, and still maintained, with the title, the military bearing which had always accompanied it. His hair and mustache were white and silky, emphasizing the rugged bronze of his face. He was tall and thin, and wore his coats padded, which gave a fictitious breadth and depth to his shoulders and chest. Edna and her father looked very distinguished together, and excited a good deal of notice during their perambulations. Upon his arrival she began by introducing him to her atelier and making a sketch of him. He took the whole matter very seriously. If her talent had been tenfold greater than it was, it

22. As a good friend.   23. Till Thursday.

would not have surprised him, convinced as he was that he had bequeathed to all of his daughters the germs of a masterful capability, which only depended upon their own efforts to be directed toward successful achievement.

Before her pencil he sat rigid and unflinching, as he had faced the cannon's mouth in days gone by. He resented the intrusion of the children, who gaped with wondering eyes at him, sitting so stiff up there in their mother's bright atelier. When they drew near he motioned them away with an expressive action of the foot, loath to disturb the fixed lines of his countenance, his arms, or his rigid shoulders.

Edna, anxious to entertain him, invited Mademoiselle Reisz to meet him, having promised him a treat in her piano playing; but Mademoiselle declined the invitation. So together they attended a *soirée musicale* at the Ratignolles'. Monsieur and Madame Ratignolle made much of the colonel, installing him as the guest of honor and engaging him at once to dine with them the following Sunday, or any day which he might select. Madame coquetted with him in the most captivating and naïve manner, with eyes, gestures, and a profusion of compliments, till the colonel's old head felt thirty years younger on his padded shoulders. Edna marveled, not comprehending. She herself was almost devoid of coquetry.

There were one or two men whom she observed at the *soirée musicale*; but she would never have felt moved to any kittenish display to attract their notice—to any feline or feminine wiles to express herself toward them. Their personality attracted her in an agreeable way. Her fancy selected them, and she was glad when a lull in the music gave them an opportunity to meet her and talk with her. Often on the street the glance of strange eyes had lingered in her memory, and sometimes had disturbed her.

Mr. Pontellier did not attend these *soirées musicales*. He considered them *bourgeois*, and found more diversion at the club. To Madame Ratignolle he said the music dispensed at her *soirées* was too "heavy," too far beyond his untrained comprehension. His excuse flattered her. But she disapproved of Mr. Pontellier's club, and she was frank enough to tell Edna so.

"It's a pity Mr. Pontellier doesn't stay home more in the evenings. I think you would be more—well, if you don't mind my saying it—more united, if he did."

"Oh! dear no!" said Edna, with a blank look in her eyes. "What should I do if he stayed home? We wouldn't have anything to say to each other."

She had not much of anything to say to her father, for that matter; but he did not antagonize her. She discovered that he interested her, though she realized that he might not interest her long; and for the first time in her life she felt as if she were thoroughly acquainted with him. He kept her busy serving him and ministering to his wants. It amused her to do so. She would not permit a servant or one of the children to do anything for him which she might do herself. Her husband noticed, and thought it was the expression of a deep filial attachment which he had never suspected.

The colonel drank numerous "toddies" during the course of the day, which left him, however, imperturbed. He was an expert at concocting strong drinks. He had even invented some, to which he had given fantastic names, and for whose manufacture he required diverse ingredients that it devolved upon Edna to procure for him.

When Doctor Mandelet dined with the Pontelliers on Thursday he could discern in Mrs. Pontellier no trace of that morbid condition which her husband had reported to him. She was excited and in a manner radiant. She and her father had been to the race course, and their thoughts when they seated themselves at table were still occupied with the events of the afternoon, and their talk was still of the track. The doctor had not kept pace with turf affairs. He had certain recollections of racing in what he called "the good old times" when the Lecompte stables flourished, and he drew upon this fund of memories so that he might not be left out and seem wholly devoid of the modern spirit. But he failed to impose upon the colonel, and was even far from impressing him with this trumped-up knowledge of bygone days. Edna had staked her father on his last venture, with the most gratifying results to both of them. Besides, they had met some very charming people, according to the colonel's impressions. Mrs. Mortimer Merriman and Mrs. James Highcamp, who were there with Alcée Arobin, had joined them and had enlivened the hours in a fashion that warmed him to think of.

Mr. Pontellier himself had no particular leaning toward horseracing, and was even rather inclined to discourage it as a pastime, especially when he considered the fate of that bluegrass farm in Kentucky. He endeavored, in a general way, to express a particular disapproval, and only succeeded in arousing the ire and opposition of his father-in-law. A pretty dispute followed, in which Edna warmly espoused her father's cause and the Doctor remained neutral.

He observed his hostess attentively from under his shaggy brows, and noted a subtle change which had transformed her from the listless woman he had known into a being who, for the moment, seemed palpitant with the forces of life. Her speech was warm and energetic. There was no repression in her glance or gesture. She reminded him of some beautiful, sleek animal waking up in the sun.

The dinner was excellent. The claret was warm and the champagne was cold, and under their beneficent influence the threatened unpleasantness melted and vanished with the fumes of the wine.

Mr. Pontellier warmed up and grew reminiscent. He told some amusing plantation experiences, recollections of old Iberville and his youth, when he hunted possum in company with some friendly darky; thrashed the pecan trees, shot the grosbec, and roamed the woods and fields in mischievous idleness.

The colonel, with little sense of humor and of the fitness of things, related a somber episode of those dark and bitter days, in which he had acted a conspicuous part and always formed a central figure. Nor was the doctor happier in his selection, when he told the old, ever new and curious story of the waning of a woman's love, seeking strange, new channels, only to return to its legitimate source after days of fierce unrest. It was one of the many little human documents which had been unfolded to him during his long career as a physician. The story did not seem especially to impress Edna. She had one of her own to tell, of a woman who paddled away with her lover one night in a pirogue and never came back. They were lost amid the Baratarian Islands, and no one ever heard of them or found trace of them from that day to this. It was a pure invention. She said that Madame Antoine had related it to her. That, also, was an invention. Perhaps it was a dream she had had. But every glowing word seemed real to those who listened. They could feel the hot breath of the Southern night; they could hear the long sweep of the pirogue through the glistening moonlit water, the beating of birds' wings, rising startled from among the reeds in the salt-water pools; they could see the faces of the lovers, pale, close together, rapt in oblivious forgetfulness, drifting into the unknown.

The champagne was cold, and its subtle fumes played fantastic tricks with Edna's memory that night.

Outside, away from the glow of the fire and the soft lamplight, the night was chill and murky. The doctor doubled his old-fashioned cloak across his breast as he strode home through the darkness. He knew his fellow creatures better than most men; knew that inner life which so seldom unfolds itself to unanointed eyes. He was sorry he had accepted Pontellier's invitation. He was growing old, and beginning to need rest and an imperturbed spirit. He did not want the secrets of other lives thrust upon him.

"I hope it isn't Arobin," he muttered to himself as he walked. "I hope to heaven it isn't Alcée Arobin."

XXIV

Edna and her father had a warm, and almost violent dispute upon the subject of her refusal to attend her sister's wedding. Mr. Pontellier declined to interfere, to interpose either his influence or his authority. He was following Doctor Mandelet's advice, and letting her do as she liked. The Colonel reproached his daughter for her lack of filial kindness and respect, her want of sisterly affection and womanly consideration. His arguments were labored and unconvincing. He doubted if Janet would accept any excuse—forgetting that Edna had offered none. He doubted if Janet would ever speak to her again, and he was sure Margaret would not.

Edna was glad to be rid of her father when he finally took himself off with his wedding garments and his bridal gifts, with his padded shoulders, his Bible reading, his "toddies" and ponderous oaths.

Mr. Pontellier followed him closely. He meant to stop at the wedding on his way to New York and endeavor by every means which money and love could devise to atone somewhat for Edna's incomprehensible action.

"You are too lenient, too lenient by far, Léonce," asserted the colonel. "Authority, coercion are what is needed. Put your foot down good and hard; the only way to manage a wife. Take my word for it."

The colonel was perhaps unaware that he had coerced his own wife into her grave. Mr. Pontellier had a vague suspicion of it which he thought it needless to mention at that late day.

Edna was not so consciously gratified at her husband's leaving home as she had been over the departure of her father. As the day approached when he was to leave her for a comparatively long stay, she grew melting and affectionate, remembering his many acts of consideration and his repeated expressions of an ardent attachment. She was solicitous about his health and his welfare. She bustled around, looking after his clothing, thinking about heavy underwear, quite as Madame Ratignolle would have done under similar circumstances. She cried when he went away, calling him her dear, good friend, and she was quite certain she would grow lonely before very long and go to join him in New York.

But after all, a radiant peace settled upon her when she at last found herself alone. Even the children were gone. Old Madame Pontellier had come herself and carried them off to Iberville with their quadroon. The old madame did not venture to say she was afraid they would be neglected during Léonce's absence; she hardly ventured to think so. She was hungry for them—even a little fierce in her attachment. She did not want them to be wholly "children of the pavement," she always said when begging to have them for a space. She wished them to know the country, with its streams, its fields, its woods, its freedom, so delicious to the young. She wished them to taste something of the life their father had lived and known and loved when he, too, was a little child.

When Edna was at last alone, she breathed a big, genuine sigh of relief. A feeling that was unfamiliar but very delicious came over her. She walked all through the house, from one room to another, as if inspecting it for the first time. She tried the various chairs and lounges, as if she had never sat and reclined upon them before. And she perambulated around the outside of the house, investigating, looking to see if windows and shutters were secure and in order. The flowers were like new acquaintances; she approached them in a familiar spirit, and made herself at home among them. The garden walks were damp, and Edna called to the maid to bring out her rubber sandals. And there she stayed, and stooped, digging around the plants, trimming, picking dead, dry leaves. The children's little dog came out, interfering, getting in her way. She scolded him, laughed at him, played with him. The garden smelled so good and looked so pretty in the afternoon sunlight. Edna plucked all the bright flowers she could find, and went into the house with them, she and the little dog.

Even the kitchen assumed a sudden interesting character which she had never before perceived. She went in to give directions to the cook, to say that the butcher would have to bring much less meat, that they would require only half their usual quantity of bread, of milk and groceries. She told the cook that she herself would be greatly occupied during Mr. Pontellier's absence, and she begged her to take all thought and responsibility of the larder upon her own shoulders.

That night Edna dined alone. The candelabra, with a few candles in the center of the table, gave all the light she needed. Outside the circle of light in which she sat, the large dining-room looked solemn and shadowy. The cook, placed upon her mettle, served a delicious repast—a luscious tenderloin broiled *à point*. The wine tasted good; the *marron glacé*[24] seemed to be just what she wanted. It was so pleasant, too, to dine in a comfortable *peignoir*.

She thought a little sentimentally about Léonce and the children, and wondered what they were doing. As she gave a dainty scrap or two to the doggie, she talked intimately to him about Etienne and Raoul. He was beside himself with astonishment and delight over these companionable advances, and showed his appreciation by his little quick, snappy barks and a lively agitation.

Then Edna sat in the library after dinner and read Emerson until she grew sleepy. She realized that she had neglected her reading, and determined to start anew upon a course of improving studies, now that her time was completely her own to do with as she liked.

After a refreshing bath, Edna went to bed. And as she snuggled comfortably beneath the eiderdown a sense of restfulness invaded her, such as she had not known before.

XXV

When the weather was dark and cloudy Edna could not work. She needed the sun to mellow and temper her mood to the sticking point. She had reached a stage when she seemed to be no longer feeling her way, working, when in the humor, with sureness and ease. And being devoid of ambition, and striving not toward accomplishment, she drew satisfaction from the work in itself.

On rainy or melancholy days Edna went out and sought the society of the friends she had made at Grand Isle. Or else she stayed indoors and nursed a mood with which she was becoming too familiar for her own comfort and peace of mind. It was not despair; but it seemed to her as if life were passing by, leaving its promise broken and unfulfilled. Yet there were other days when she listened, was led on and deceived by fresh promises which her youth held out to her.

24. Glazed chestnuts.

She went again to the races, and again. Alcée Arobin and Mrs. Highcamp called for her one bright afternoon in Arobin's drag. Mrs. Highcamp was a worldly but unaffected, intelligent, slim, tall blonde woman in the forties, with an indifferent manner and blue eyes that stared. She had a daughter who served her as a pretext for cultivating the society of young men of fashion. Alcée Arobin was one of them. He was a familiar figure at the race course, the opera, the fashionable clubs. There was a perpetual smile in his eyes, which seldom failed to awaken a corresponding cheerfulness in anyone who looked into them and listened to his good-humored voice. His manner was quiet, and at times a little insolent. He possessed a good figure, a pleasing face, not overburdened with depth of thought or feeling; and his dress was that of the conventional man of fashion.

He admired Edna extravagantly, after meeting her at the races with her father. He had met her before on other occasions, but she had seemed to him unapproachable until that day. It was at his instigation that Mrs. Highcamp called to ask her to go with them to the Jockey Club to witness the turf event of the season.

There were possibly a few track men out there who knew the racehorse as well as Edna, but there was certainly none who knew it better. She sat between her two companions as one having authority to speak. She laughed at Arobin's pretensions, and deplored Mrs. Highcamp's ignorance. The racehorse was a friend and intimate associate of her childhood. The atmosphere of the stables and the breath of the bluegrass paddock revived in her memory and lingered in her nostrils. She did not perceive that she was talking like her father as the sleek geldings ambled in review before them. She played for very high stakes, and fortune favored her. The fever of the game flamed in her cheeks and eyes, and it got into her blood and into her brain like an intoxicant. People turned their heads to look at her, and more than one lent an attentive ear to her utterances, hoping thereby to secure the elusive but ever-desired "tip." Arobin caught the contagion of excitement which drew him to Edna like a magnet. Mrs. Highcamp remained, as usual, unmoved, with her indifferent stare and uplifted eyebrows.

Edna stayed and dined with Mrs. Highcamp upon being urged to do so. Arobin also remained and sent away his drag.

The dinner was quiet and uninteresting, save for the cheerful efforts of Arobin to enliven things. Mrs. Highcamp deplored the absence of her daughter from the races, and tried to convey to her what she had missed by going to the "Dante reading" instead of joining them. The girl held a geranium leaf up to her nose and said nothing, but looked knowing and noncommittal. Mr. Highcamp was a plain, bald-headed man, who only talked under compulsion. He was unresponsive. Mrs. Highcamp was full of delicate courtesy and consideration toward her husband. She addressed most of her conversation to him at table. They sat in the library after dinner and read the evening papers together under the droplight; while the younger people went into the drawing room near by and talked.

Miss Highcamp played some selections from Grieg upon the piano. She seemed to have apprehended all of the composer's coldness and none of his poetry. While Edna listened she could not help wondering if she had lost her taste for music.

When the time came for her to go home, Mr. Highcamp grunted a lame offer to escort her, looking down at his slippered feet with tactless concern. It was Arobin who took her home. The car ride was long, and it was late when they reached Esplanade Street. Arobin asked permission to enter for a second to light his cigarette—his match safe was empty. He filled his match safe, but did not light his cigarette until he left her, after she had expressed her willingness to go to the races with him again.

Edna was neither tired nor sleepy. She was hungry again, for the Highcamp dinner, though of excellent quality, had lacked abundance. She rummaged in the larder and brought forth a slice of Gruyère and some crackers. She opened a bottle of beer which she found in the icebox. Edna felt extremely restless and excited. She vacantly hummed a fantastic tune as she poked at the wood embers on the hearth and munched a cracker.

She wanted something to happen—something, anything; she did not know what. She regretted that she had not made Arobin stay a half-hour to talk over the horses with her. She counted the money she had won. But there was nothing else to do, so she went to bed, and tossed there for hours in a sort of monotonous agitation.

In the middle of the night she remembered that she had forgotten to write her regular letter to her husband; and she decided to do so next day and tell him about her afternoon at the Jockey Club. She lay wide awake composing a letter which was nothing like the one which she wrote next day. When the maid awoke her in the morning Edna was dreaming of Mr. Highcamp playing the piano at the entrance of a music store on Canal Street, while his wife was saying to Alcée Arobin, as they boarded an Esplanade Street car:

"What a pity that so much talent has been neglected! but I must go."

When, a few days later, Alcée Arobin again called for Edna in his drag, Mrs. Highcamp was not with him. He said they would pick her up. But as that lady had not been apprised of his intention of picking her up, she was not at home. The daughter was just leaving the house to attend the meeting of a branch Folk Lore Society, and regretted that she could not accompany them. Arobin appeared nonplused, and asked Edna if there were any one else she cared to ask.

She did not deem it worth while to go in search of any of the fashionable acquaintances from whom she had withdrawn herself. She thought of Madame Ratignolle, but knew that her fair friend did not leave the house, except to take a languid walk around the block with her husband after nightfall. Mademoiselle Reisz would have laughed at such a request from Edna. Madame Lebrun might have enjoyed the outing, but for some reason Edna did not want her. So they went alone, she and Arobin.

The afternoon was intensely interesting to her. The excitement came back upon her like a remittent fever. Her talk grew familiar and confidential. It was no labor to become intimate with Arobin. His manner invited easy confidence. The preliminary stage of becoming acquainted was one which he always endeavored to ignore when a pretty and engaging woman was concerned.

He stayed and dined with Edna. He stayed and sat beside the wood fire. They laughed and talked; and before it was time to go he was telling her how different life might have been if he had known her years before. With ingenuous frankness he spoke of what a wicked, ill-disciplined boy he had been, and impulsively drew up his cuff to exhibit upon his wrist the scar from a saber cut which he had received in a duel outside of Paris when he was nineteen. She touched his hand as she scanned the red cicatrice on the inside of his white wrist. A quick impulse that was somewhat spasmodic impelled her fingers to close in a sort of clutch upon his hand. He felt the pressure of her pointed nails in the flesh of his palm.

She arose hastily and walked toward the mantel.

"The sight of a wound or scar always agitates and sickens me," she said. "I shouldn't have looked at it."

"I beg your pardon," he entreated, following her; "it never occurred to me that it might be repulsive."

He stood close to her, and the effrontery in his eyes repelled the old, vanishing self in her, yet drew all her awakening sensuousness. He saw enough in her face to impel him to take her hand and hold it while he said his lingering goodnight.

"Will you go to the races again?" he asked.

"No," she said. "I've had enough of the races. I don't want to lose all the money I've won, and I've got to work when the weather is bright, instead of—"

"Yes; work; to be sure. You promised to show me your work. What morning may I come up to your atelier? Tomorrow?"

"No!"

"Day after?"

"No, no."

"Oh, please don't refuse me! I know something of such things. I might help you with a stray suggestion or two."

"No. Goodnight. Why don't you go after you have said goodnight? I don't like you," she went on in a high, excited pitch, attempting to draw away her hand. She felt that her words lacked dignity and sincerity, and she knew that he felt it.

"I'm sorry you don't like me. I'm sorry I offended you. How have I offended you? What have I done? Can't you forgive me?" And he bent and pressed his lips upon her hand as if he wished never more to withdraw them.

"Mr. Arobin," she complained, "I'm greatly upset by the excitement of the afternoon; I'm not myself. My manner must have misled you in some way. I wish you to go, please." She spoke in a monotonous, dull tone. He took his hat from the table, and stood with eyes turned from her, looking into the dying fire. For a moment or two he kept an impressive silence.

"Your manner has not misled me, Mrs. Pontellier," he said finally. "My own emotions have done that. I couldn't help it. When I'm near you, how could I help it? Don't think anything of it, don't bother, please. You see, I go when you command me. If you wish me to stay away, I shall do so. If you let me come back, I—oh! you will let me come back?"

He cast one appealing glance at her, to which she made no response. Alcée Arobin's manner was so genuine that it often deceived even himself.

Edna did not care or think whether it were genuine or not. When she was alone she looked mechanically at the back of her hand which he had kissed so warmly. Then she leaned her head down on the mantelpiece. She felt somewhat like a woman who in a moment of passion is betrayed into an act of infidelity, and realizes the significance of the act without being wholly awakened from its glamor. The thought was passing vaguely through her mind, "What would he think?"

She did not mean her husband; she was thinking of Robert Lebrun. Her husband seemed to her now like a person whom she had married without love as an excuse.

She lit a candle and went up to her room. Alcée Arobin was absolutely nothing to her. Yet his presence, his manners, the warmth of his glances, and above all the touch of his lips upon her hand had acted like a narcotic upon her.

She slept a languorous sleep, interwoven with vanishing dreams.

XXVI

Alcée Arobin wrote Edna an elaborate note of apology, palpitant with sincerity. It embarrassed her; for in a cooler, quieter moment it appeared to her absurd that she should have taken his action so seriously, so dramatically. She felt sure that the significance of the whole occurrence had lain in her own self-consciousness. If she ignored his note it would give undue importance to a trivial affair. If she replied to it in a serious spirit it would still leave in his mind the impression that she had in a susceptible moment yielded to his influence. After all, it was no great matter to have one's hand kissed. She was provoked at his having written the apology. She answered in as light and bantering a spirit as she fancied it deserved, and said she would be glad to have him look in upon her at work whenever he felt the inclination and his business gave him the opportunity.

He responded at once by presenting himself at her home with all his disarming naïveté. And then there was scarcely a day which followed that she did not see him or was not reminded of him. He was prolific in pretexts. His attitude became one of good-humored subservience and tacit adoration. He was ready at all times to submit to her moods, which were as often kind as they were cold. She grew accustomed to him. They became intimate and friendly by imperceptible degrees, and then by leaps. He sometimes talked in a way that astonished her at first and brought the crimson into her face; in a way that pleased her at last, appealing to the animalism that stirred impatiently within her.

There was nothing which so quieted the turmoil of Edna's senses as a visit to Mademoiselle Reisz. It was then, in the presence of that personality which was offensive to her, that the woman, by her divine art, seemed to reach Edna's spirit and set it free.

It was misty, with heavy, lowering atmosphere, one afternoon, when Edna climbed the stairs to the pianist's apartments under the roof. Her clothes were dripping with moisture. She felt chilled and pinched as she entered the room. Mademoiselle was poking at a rusty stove that smoked a little and warmed the room indifferently. She was endeavoring to heat a pot of chocolate on the stove. The room looked cheerless and dingy to Edna as she entered. A bust of Beethoven, covered with a hood of dust, scowled at her from the mantelpiece.

"Ah! here comes the sunlight!" exclaimed Mademoiselle, rising from her knees before the stove. "Now it will be warm and bright enough; I can let the fire alone."

She closed the stove door with a bang, and approaching, assisted in removing Edna's dripping mackintosh.

"You are cold; you look miserable. The chocolate will soon be hot. But would you rather have a taste of brandy? I have scarcely touched the bottle which you brought me for my cold." A piece of red flannel was wrapped around Mademoiselle's throat; a stiff neck compelled her to hold her head on one side.

"I will take some brandy," said Edna, shivering as she removed her gloves and overshoes. She drank the liquor from the glass as a man would have done. Then flinging herself upon the uncomfortable sofa she said, "Mademoiselle, I am going to move away from my house on Esplanade Street."

"Ah!" ejaculated the musician, neither surprised nor especially interested. Nothing ever seemed to astonish her very much. She was endeavoring to adjust the bunch of violets which had become loose from its fastening in her hair. Edna drew her down upon the sofa, and taking a pin from her own hair, secured the shabby artificial flowers in their accustomed place.

"Aren't you astonished?"

"Passably. Where are you going? to New York? to Iberville? to your father in Mississippi? where?"

"Just two steps away," laughed Edna, "in a little four-room house around the corner. It looks so cozy, so inviting and restful, whenever I pass by; and it's for rent. I'm tired looking after that big house. It never seemed like mine, anyway—like home. It's too much trouble. I have to keep too many servants. I am tired bothering with them."

"That is not your true reason, *ma belle*. There is no use in telling me lies. I don't know your reason, but you have not told me the truth." Edna did not protest or endeavor to justify herself.

"The house, the money that provides for it, are not mine. Isn't that enough reason?"

"They are your husband's," returned Mademoiselle, with a shrug and a malicious elevation of the eyebrows.

"Oh! I see there is no deceiving you. Then let me tell you: It is a caprice. I have a little money of my own from my mother's estate, which my father sends me by driblets. I won a large sum this winter on the races, and I am beginning to sell my sketches. Laidpore is more and more pleased with my work; he says it grows in force and individuality. I cannot judge of that myself, but I feel that I have gained in ease and confidence. However, as I said, I have sold a good many through Laidpore. I can live in the tiny house for little or nothing, with one servant. Old Celestine, who works occasionally for me, says she will come stay with me and do my work. I know I shall like it, like the feeling of freedom and independence."

"What does your husband say?"

"I have not told him yet. I only thought of it this morning. He will think I am demented, no doubt. Perhaps you think so."

Mademoiselle shook her head slowly. "Your reason is not yet clear to me," she said.

Neither was it quite clear to Edna herself; but it unfolded itself as she sat for a while in silence. Instinct had prompted her to put away her husband's bounty in casting off her allegiance. She did not know how it would be when he returned. There would have to be an understanding, an explanation. Conditions would some way adjust themselves, she felt; but whatever came, she had resolved never again to belong to another than herself.

"I shall give a grand dinner before I leave the old house!" Edna exclaimed. "You will have to come to it, Mademoiselle. I will give you everything that you like to eat and to drink. We shall sing and laugh and be merry for once." And she uttered a sigh that came from the very depths of her being.

If Mademoiselle happened to have received a letter from Robert during the interval of Edna's visits, she would give her the letter unsolicited. And she would seat herself at the piano and play as her humor prompted her while the young woman read the letter.

The little stove was roaring; it was red-hot, and the chocolate in the tin sizzled and sputtered. Edna went forward and opened the stove door, and Mademoiselle, rising, took a letter from under the bust of Beethoven and handed it to Edna.

"Another! so soon!" she exclaimed, her eyes filled with delight. "Tell me, Mademoiselle, does he know that I see his letters?"

"Never in the world! He would be angry and would never write to me again if he thought so. Does he write to you? Never a line. Does he send you a message? Never a word. It is because he loves you, poor fool, and is trying to forget you, since you are not free to listen to him or to belong to him."

"Why do you show me his letters, then?"

"Haven't you begged for them? Can I refuse you anything? Oh! you cannot deceive me," and Mademoiselle approached her beloved instrument and began to play. Edna did not at once read the letter. She sat holding it in her hand, while the music penetrated her whole being like an effulgence, warming and brightening the dark places of her soul. It prepared her for joy and exultation.

"Oh!" she exclaimed, letting the letter fall to the floor. "Why did you not tell me?" She went and grasped Mademoiselle's hands up from the keys. "Oh! unkind! malicious! Why did you not tell me?"

"That he was coming back? No great news, *ma foi*. I wonder he did not come long ago."

"But when, when?" cried Edna, impatiently. "He does not say when."

"He says 'very soon.' You know as much about it as I do; it is all in the letter."

"But why? Why is he coming? Oh, if I thought—" and she snatched the letter from the floor and turned the pages this way and that way, looking for the reason, which was left untold.

"If I were young and in love with a man," said Mademoiselle, turning on the stool and pressing her wiry hands between her knees as she looked down at Edna, who sat on the floor holding the letter, "it seems to me he would have to be some *grand esprit*; a man with lofty aims and ability to reach them; one who stood high enough to attract the notice of his fellow men. It seems to me if I were young and in love I should never deem a man of ordinary caliber worthy of my devotion."

"Now it is you who are telling lies and seeking to deceive me, Mademoiselle; or else you have never been in love, and know nothing about it. Why," went on Edna, clasping her knees and looking up into Mademoiselle's twisted face, "do you suppose a woman knows why she loves? Does she select? Does she say to herself: 'Go to! Here is a distinguished statesman with presidential possibilities; I shall proceed to fall in love with him.' Or, 'I shall set my heart upon this musician, whose fame is on every tongue?' Or, 'This financier, who controls the world's money markets?'"

"You are purposely misunderstanding me, *ma reine*.[25] Are you in love with Robert?"

"Yes," said Edna. It was the first time she had admitted it, and a glow overspread her face, blotching it with red spots.

"Why?" asked her companion. "Why do you love him when you ought not to?"

Edna, with a motion or two, dragged herself on her knees before Mademoiselle Reisz, who took the glowing face between her two hands.

"Why? Because his hair is brown and grows away from his temples; because he opens and shuts his eyes, and his nose is a little out of drawing; because he has two lips and a square chin, and a little finger which he can't straighten from having played baseball too energetically in his youth. Because—"

"Because you do, in short," laughed Mademoiselle. "What will you do when he comes back?" she asked.

"Do? Nothing, except feel glad and happy to be alive."

She was already glad and happy to be alive at the mere thought of his return. The murky, lowering sky, which had depressed her a few hours before, seemed bracing and invigorating as she splashed through the streets on her way home.

She stopped at a confectioner's and ordered a huge box of bonbons for the children in Iberville. She slipped a card in the box, on which she scribbled a tender message and sent an abundance of kisses.

Before dinner in the evening Edna wrote a charming letter to her husband, telling him of her intention to move for a while into the little house around the

25. My queen.

block, and to give a farewell dinner before leaving, regretting that he was not there to share it, to help her out with the menu and assist her in entertaining the guests. Her letter was brilliant and brimming with cheerfulness.

XXVII

"What is the matter with you?" asked Arobin that evening. "I never found you in such a happy mood." Edna was tired by that time, and was reclining on the lounge before the fire.

"Don't you know the weather prophet has told us we shall see the sun pretty soon?"

"Well, that ought to be reason enough," he acquiesced. "You wouldn't give me another if I sat here all night imploring you." He sat close to her on a low tabouret, and as he spoke his fingers lightly touched the hair that fell a little over her forehead. She liked the touch of his fingers through her hair, and closed her eyes sensitively.

"One of these days," she said, "I'm going to pull myself together for a while and think—try to determine what character of a woman I am; for, candidly, I don't know. By all the codes which I am acquainted with, I am a devilishly wicked specimen of the sex. But some way I can't convince myself that I am. I must think about it."

"Don't. What's the use? Why should you bother thinking about it when I can tell you what manner of woman you are." His fingers strayed occasionally down to her warm, smooth cheeks and firm chin, which was growing a little full and double.

"Oh, yes! You will tell me that I am adorable; everything that is captivating. Spare yourself the effort."

"No; I shan't tell you anything of the sort, though I shouldn't be lying if I did."

"Do you know Mademoiselle Reisz?" she asked irrelevantly.

"The pianist? I know her by sight. I've heard her play."

"She says queer things sometimes in a bantering way that you don't notice at the time and you find yourself thinking about afterward."

"For instance?"

"Well, for instance, when I left her today, she put her arms around me and felt my shoulder blades, to see if my wings were strong, she said. 'The bird that would soar above the level plain of tradition and prejudice must have strong wings. It is a sad spectacle to see the weaklings bruised, exhausted, fluttering back to earth.'"

"Whither would you soar?"

"I'm not thinking of any extraordinary flights. I only half comprehend her."

"I've heard she's partially demented," said Arobin.

"She seems to me wonderfully sane," Edna replied.

"I'm told she's extremely disagreeable and unpleasant. Why have you introduced her at a moment when I desired to talk of you?"

"Oh! talk of me if you like," cried Edna, clasping her hands beneath her head; "but let me think of something else while you do."

"I'm jealous of your thoughts tonight. They're making you a little kinder than usual; but some way I feel as if they were wandering, as if they were not here with me." She only looked at him and smiled. His eyes were very near. He leaned upon the lounge with an arm extended across her, while the other hand still rested upon her hair. They continued silently to look into each other's eyes. When he leaned forward and kissed her, she clasped his head, holding his lips to hers.

It was the first kiss of her life to which her nature had really responded. It was a flaming torch that kindled desire.

XXVIII

Edna cried a little that night after Arobin left her. It was only one phase of the multitudinous emotions which had assailed her. There was with her an overwhelming feeling of irresponsibility. There was the shock of the unexpected and the unaccustomed. There was her husband's reproach looking at her from the external things around her which he had provided for her external existence. There was Robert's reproach making itself felt by a quicker, fiercer, more overpowering love, which had awakened within her toward him. Above all, there was understanding. She felt as if a mist had been lifted from her eyes, enabling her to look upon and comprehend the significance of life, that monster made up of beauty and brutality. But among the conflicting sensations which assailed her, there was neither shame nor remorse. There was a dull pang of regret because it was not the kiss of love which had inflamed her, because it was not love which had held this cup of life to her lips.

XXIX

Without even waiting for an answer from her husband regarding his opinion or wishes in the matter, Edna hastened her preparations for quitting her home on Esplanade Street and moving into the little house around the block. A feverish anxiety attended her every action in that direction. There was no moment of deliberation, no interval of repose between the thought and its fulfillment. Early upon the morning following those hours passed in Arobin's society, Edna set about securing her new abode and hurrying her arrangements for occupying it. Within the precincts of her home she felt like one who has entered and lingered within the portals of some forbidden temple in which a thousand muffled voices bade her begone.

Whatever was her own in the house, everything which she had acquired aside from her husband's bounty, she caused to be transported to the other house, supplying simple and meager deficiencies from her own resources.

Arobin found her with rolled sleeves, working in company with the housemaid when he looked in during the afternoon. She was splendid and robust, and had never appeared handsomer than in the old blue gown, with a red silk handkerchief knotted at random around her head to protect her hair from the dust. She was mounted upon a high stepladder, unhooking a picture from the wall when he entered. He had found the front door open, and had followed his ring by walking in unceremoniously.

"Come down!" he said. "Do you want to kill yourself?" She greeted him with affected carelessness, and appeared absorbed in her occupation.

If he had expected to find her languishing, reproachful, or indulging in sentimental tears, he must have been greatly surprised.

He was no doubt prepared for any emergency, ready for any one of the foregoing attitudes, just as he bent himself easily and naturally to the situation which confronted him.

"Please come down," he insisted, holding the ladder and looking up at her.

"No," she answered; "Ellen is afraid to mount the ladder. Joe is working over at the 'pigeon house'—that's the name Ellen gives it, because it's so small and looks like a pigeon house—and some one has to do this."

Arobin pulled off his coat, and expressed himself ready and willing to tempt fate in her place. Ellen brought him one of her dustcaps, and went into contortions of mirth, which she found it impossible to control, when she saw him put it on before the mirror as grotesquely as he could. Edna herself could not refrain from smiling when she fastened it at his request. So it was he who in turn mounted the ladder, unhooking pictures and curtains, and dislodging ornaments as Edna directed. When he had finished he took off his dustcap and went out to wash his hands.

Edna was sitting on the tabouret, idly brushing the tips of a feather duster along the carpet when he came in again.

"Is there anything more you will let me do?" he asked.

"That is all," she answered. "Ellen can manage the rest." She kept the young woman occupied in the drawing room, unwilling to be left alone with Arobin.

"What about the dinner?" he asked; "the grand event, the *coup d'état?*"

"It will be day after tomorrow. Why do you call it the *'coup d'état?'* Oh! it will be very fine; all my best of everything—crystal, silver and gold, Sèvres, flowers, music, and champagne to swim in. I'll let Léonce pay the bills. I wonder what he'll say when he sees the bills."

"And you ask me why I call it a *coup d'état?*" Arobin had put on his coat, and he stood before her and asked if his cravat was plumb. She told him it was, looking no higher than the tip of his collar.

"When do you go to the 'pigeon house?'—with all due acknowledgment to Ellen."

"Day after tomorrow, after the dinner. I shall sleep there."

"Ellen, will you very kindly get me a glass of water?" asked Arobin. "The dust in the curtains, if you will pardon me for hinting such a thing, has parched my throat to a crisp."

"While Ellen gets the water," said Edna, rising, "I will say goodbye and let you go. I must get rid of this grime, and I have a million things to do and think of."

"When shall I see you?" asked Arobin, seeking to detain her, the maid having left the room.

"At the dinner, of course. You are invited."

"Not before?—not tonight or tomorrow morning or tomorrow noon or night? or the day after morning or noon? Can't you see yourself, without my telling you, what an eternity it is?"

He had followed her into the hall and to the foot of the stairway, looking up at her as she mounted with her face half turned to him.

"Not an instant sooner," she said. But she laughed and looked at him with eyes that at once gave him courage to wait and made it torture to wait.

XXX

Though Edna had spoken of the dinner as a very grand affair, it was in truth a very small affair and very select, in so much as the guests invited were few and were selected with discrimination. She had counted upon an even dozen seating themselves at her round mahogany board, forgetting for the moment that Madame Ratignolle was to the last degree *souffrante*[26] and unpresentable, and not foreseeing that Madame Lebrun would send a thousand regrets at the last moment. So there were only ten, after all, which made a cozy, comfortable number.

There were Mr. and Mrs. Merriman, a pretty, vivacious little woman in the thirties; her husband, a jovial fellow, something of a shallow-pate, who laughed a good deal at other people's witticisms, and had thereby made himself extremely popular. Mrs. High-camp had accompanied them. Of course, there was Alcée Arobin; and Mademoiselle

26. Unwell.

Reisz had consented to come. Edna had sent her a fresh bunch of violets with black lace trimmings for her hair. Monsieur Ratignolle brought himself and his wife's excuses. Victor Lebrun, who happened to be in the city, bent upon relaxation, had accepted with alacrity. There was a Miss Mayblunt, no longer in her teens, who looked at the world through lorgnettes and with the keenest interest. It was thought and said that she was intellectual; it was suspected of her that she wrote under a *nom de guerre*.[27] She had come with a gentleman by the name of Gouvernail, connected with one of the daily papers, of whom nothing special could be said, except that he was observant and seemed quiet and inoffensive. Edna herself made the tenth, and at half-past eight they seated themselves at table, Arobin and Monsieur Ratignolle on either side of their hostess.

Mrs. Highcamp sat between Arobin and Victor Lebrun. Then came Mrs. Merriman, Mr. Gouvernail, Miss Mayblunt, Mr. Merriman, and Mademoiselle Reisz next to Monsieur Ratignolle.

There was something extremely gorgeous about the appearance of the table, an effect of splendor conveyed by a cover of pale yellow satin under strips of lacework. There were wax candles in massive brass candelabra, burning softly under yellow silk shades; full, fragrant roses, yellow and red, abounded. There were silver and gold, as she had said there would be, and crystal which glittered like the gems which the women wore.

The ordinary stiff dining chairs had been discarded for the occasion and replaced by the most commodious and luxurious which could be collected throughout the house. Mademoiselle Reisz, being exceedingly diminutive, was elevated upon cushions, as small children are sometimes hoisted at table upon bulky volumes.

"Something new, Edna?" exclaimed Miss Mayblunt, with lorgnette directed toward a magnificent cluster of diamonds that sparkled, that almost sputtered, in Edna's hair, just over the center of her forehead.

"Quite new; 'brand' new, in fact; a present from my husband. It arrived this morning from New York. I may as well admit that this is my birthday, and that I am twenty-nine. In good time I expect you to drink my health. Meanwhile, I shall ask you to begin with this cocktail, composed—would you say 'composed?'" with an appeal to Miss Mayblunt—"composed by my father in honor of Sister Janet's wedding."

Before each guest stood a tiny glass that looked and sparkled like a garnet gem.

"Then, all things considered," spoke Arobin, "it might not be amiss to start out by drinking the colonel's health in the cocktail which he composed, on the birthday of the most charming of women—the daughter whom he invented."

Mr. Merriman's laugh at this sally was such a genuine outburst and so contagious that it started the dinner with an agreeable swing that never slackened.

Miss Mayblunt begged to be allowed to keep her cocktail untouched before her, just to look at. The color was marvelous! She could compare it to nothing she had ever seen, and the garnet lights which it emitted were unspeakably rare. She pronounced the colonel an artist, and stuck to it.

Monsieur Ratignolle was prepared to take things seriously: the *mets*, the *entremets*,[28] the service, the decorations, even the people. He looked up from his pompono and inquired of Arobin if he were related to the gentleman of that name who formed one of the firm of Laitner and Arobin, lawyers. The young man admitted that Laitner was a warm personal friend, who permitted Arobin's name to decorate the firm's letterheads and to appear upon a shingle that graced Perdido Street.

---

27. Fictitious name.   28. Dishes; side dishes.

"There are so many inquisitive people and institutions abounding," said Arobin, "that one is really forced as a matter of convenience these days to assume the virtue of an occupation if he has it not."

Monsieur Ratignolle stared a little, and turned to ask Mademoiselle Reisz if she considered the symphony concerts up to the standard which had been set the previous winter. Mademoiselle Reisz answered Monsieur Ratignolle in French, which Edna thought a little rude, under the circumstances, but characteristic. Mademoiselle had only disagreeable things to say of the symphony concerts, and insulting remarks to make of all the musicians of New Orleans, singly and collectively. All her interest seemed to be centered upon the delicacies placed before her.

Mr. Merriman said that Mr. Arobin's remark about inquisitive people reminded him of a man from Waco the other day at the St. Charles Hotel—but as Mr. Merriman's stories were always lame and lacking point, his wife seldom permitted him to complete them. She interrupted him to ask if he remembered the name of the author whose book she had bought the week before to send to a friend in Geneva. She was talking "books" with Mr. Gouvernail and trying to draw from him his opinion upon current literary topics. Her husband told the story of the Waco man privately to Miss Mayblunt, who pretended to be greatly amused and to think it extremely clever.

Mrs. Highcamp hung with languid but unaffected interest upon the warm and impetuous volubility of her lefthand neighbor, Victor Lebrun. Her attention was never for a moment withdrawn from him after seating herself at table; and when he turned to Mrs. Merriman, who was prettier and more vivacious than Mrs. Highcamp, she waited with easy indifference for an opportunity to reclaim his attention. There was the occasional sound of music, of mandolins, sufficiently removed to be an agreeable accompaniment rather than an interruption to the conversation. Outside the soft, monotonous splash of a fountain could be heard; the sound penetrated into the room with the heavy odor of jessamine that came through the open windows.

The golden shimmer of Edna's satin gown spread in rich folds on either side of her. There was a soft fall of lace encircling her shoulders. It was the color of her skin, without the glow, the myriad living tints that one may sometimes discover in vibrant flesh. There was something in her attitude, in her whole appearance when she leaned her head against the high-backed chair and spread her arms, which suggested the regal woman, the one who rules, who looks on, who stands alone.

But as she sat there amid her guests, she felt the old ennui overtaking her; the hopelessness which so often assailed her, which came upon her like an obsession, like something extraneous, independent of volition. It was something which announced itself; a chill breath that seemed to issue from some vast cavern wherein discords wailed. There came over her the acute longing which always summoned into her spiritual vision the presence of the beloved one, overpowering her at once with a sense of the unattainable.

The moments glided on, while a feeling of good fellowship passed around the circle like a mystic cord, holding and binding these people together with jest and laughter. Monsieur Ratignolle was the first to break the pleasant charm. At ten o'clock he excused himself. Madame Ratignolle was waiting for him at home. She was *bien souffrante,* and she was filled with vague dread, which only her husband's presence could allay.

Mademoiselle Reisz arose with Monsieur Ratignolle, who offered to escort her to the car. She had eaten well; she had tasted the good, rich wines, and they must have turned her head, for she bowed pleasantly to all as she withdrew from table. She kissed Edna upon the shoulder, and whispered: *"Bonne nuit, ma reine; soyez sage."*[29] She had been a little bewildered upon rising, or rather, descending from her cushions, and Monsieur Ratignolle gallantly took her arm and led her away.

Mrs. Highcamp was weaving a garland of roses, yellow and red. When she had finished the garland, she laid it lightly upon Victor's black curls. He was reclining far back in the luxurious chair, holding a glass of champagne to the light.

As if a magician's wand had touched him, the garland of roses transformed him into a vision of Oriental beauty. His cheeks were the color of crushed grapes, and his dusky eyes glowed with a languishing fire.

"Sapristi!" exclaimed Arobin.

But Mrs. Highcamp had one more touch to add to the picture. She took from the back of her chair a white silken scarf, with which she had covered her shoulders in the early part of the evening. She draped it across the boy in graceful folds, and in a way to conceal his black, conventional evening dress. He did not seem to mind what she did to him, only smiled, showing a faint gleam of white teeth, while he continued to gaze with narrowing eyes at the light through his glass of champagne.

"Oh! to be able to paint in color rather than in words!" exclaimed Miss Mayblunt, losing herself in a rhapsodic dream as she looked at him.

"'There was a graven image of Desire
Painted with red blood on a ground of gold.'"

murmured Gouvernail, under his breath.

The effect of the wine upon Victor was to change his accustomed volubility into silence. He seemed to have abandoned himself to a reverie, and to be seeing pleasing visions in the amber bead.

"Sing," entreated Mrs. Highcamp. "Won't you sing to us?"

"Let him alone," said Arobin.

"He's posing," offered Mr. Merriman; "let him have it out."

"I believe he's paralyzed," laughed Mrs. Merriman. And leaning over the youth's chair, she took the glass from his hand and held it to his lips. He sipped the wine slowly, and when he had drained the glass she laid it upon the table and wiped his lips with her little filmy handkerchief.

"Yes, I'll sing for you," he said, turning in his chair toward Mrs. Highcamp. He clasped his hands behind his head, and looking up at the ceiling began to hum a little, trying his voice like a musician tuning an instrument. Then, looking at Edna, he began to sing:

"Ah! si tu savais!"

"Stop!" she cried, "don't sing that. I don't want you to sing it," and she laid her glass so impetuously and blindly upon the table as to shatter it against a caraffe. The wine spilled over Arobin's legs and some of it trickled down upon Mrs. Highcamp's black gauze gown. Victor had lost all idea of courtesy, or else he thought his hostess was not in earnest, for he laughed and went on:

"Ah! si tu savais

29. Good-night, my queen; be wise.

Ce que tes yeux me disent"—[30]

"Oh! you mustn't! you mustn't," exclaimed Edna, and pushing back her chair she got up, and going behind him placed her hand over his mouth. He kissed the soft palm that pressed upon his lips.

"No, no, I won't, Mrs. Pontellier. I didn't know you meant it," looking up at her with caressing eyes. The touch of his lips was like a pleasing sting to her hand. She lifted the garland of roses from his head and flung it across the room.

"Come, Victor; you've posed long enough. Give Mrs. Highcamp her scarf."

Mrs. Highcamp undraped the scarf from about him with her own hands. Miss Mayblunt and Mr. Gouvernail suddenly conceived the notion that it was time to say good night. And Mr. and Mrs. Merriman wondered how it could be so late.

Before parting from Victor, Mrs. Highcamp invited him to call upon her daughter, who she knew would be charmed to meet him and talk French and sing French songs with him. Victor expressed his desire and intention to call upon Miss Highcamp at the first opportunity which presented itself. He asked if Arobin were going his way. Arobin was not.

The mandolin players had long since stolen away. A profound stillness had fallen upon the broad, beautiful street. The voices of Edna's disbanding guests jarred like a discordant note upon the quiet harmony of the night.

XXXI

"Well?" questioned Arobin, who had remained with Edna after the others had departed.

"Well," she reiterated, and stood up, stretching her arms, and feeling the need to relax her muscles after having been so long seated.

"What next?" he asked.

"The servants are all gone. They left when the musicians did. I have dismissed them. The house has to be closed and locked, and I shall trot around to the pigeon house, and shall send Celestine over in the morning to straighten things up."

He looked around, and began to turn out some of the lights.

"What about upstairs?" he inquired.

"I think it is all right; but there may be a window or two unlatched. We had better look; you might take a candle and see. And bring me my wrap and hat on the foot of the bed in the middle room."

He went up with the light, and Edna began closing doors and windows. She hated to shut in the smoke and the fumes of the wine. Arobin found her cape and hat, which he brought down and helped her to put on.

When everything was secured and the lights put out, they left through the front door, Arobin locking it and taking the key, which he carried for Edna. He helped her down the steps.

"Will you have a spray of jessamine?" he asked, breaking off a few blossoms as he passed.

"No; I don't want anything."

She seemed disheartened, and had nothing to say. She took his arm, which he offered her, holding up the weight of her satin train with the other hand. She looked

---

30. "Ah! if you knew / What your eyes are telling me."

down, noticing the black line of his leg moving in and out so close to her against the yellow shimmer of her gown. There was the whistle of a railway train somewhere in the distance, and the midnight bells were ringing. They met no one in their short walk.

The "pigeon house" stood behind a locked gate, and a shallow *parterre*[31] that had been somewhat neglected. There was a small front porch, upon which a long window and the front door opened. The door opened directly into the parlor; there was no side entry. Back in the yard was a room for servants, in which old Celestine had been ensconced.

Edna had left a lamp burning low upon the table. She had succeeded in making the room look habitable and homelike. There were some books on the table and a lounge near at hand. On the floor was a fresh matting, covered with a rug or two; and on the walls hung a few tasteful pictures. But the room was filled with flowers. These were a surprise to her. Arobin had sent them, and had had Celestine distribute them during Edna's absence. Her bedroom was adjoining, and across a small passage were the dining-room and kitchen.

Edna seated herself with every appearance of discomfort.

"Are you tired?" he asked.

"Yes, and chilled, and miserable. I feel as if I had been wound up to a certain pitch—too tight—and something inside of me had snapped." She rested her head against the table upon her bare arm.

"You want to rest," he said, "and to be quiet. I'll go; I'll leave you and let you rest."

"Yes," she replied.

He stood up beside her and smoothed her hair with his soft, magnetic hand. His touch conveyed to her a certain physical comfort. She could have fallen quietly asleep there if he had continued to pass his hand over her hair. He brushed the hair upward from the nape of her neck.

"I hope you will feel better and happier in the morning," he said. "You have tried to do too much in the past few days. The dinner was the last straw; you might have dispensed with it."

"Yes," she admitted; "it was stupid."

"No, it was delightful; but it has worn you out." His hand had strayed to her beautiful shoulders, and he could feel the response of her flesh to his touch. He seated himself beside her and kissed her lightly upon the shoulder.

"I thought you were going away," she said, in an uneven voice.

"I am, after I have said goodnight."

"Goodnight," she murmured.

He did not answer, except to continue to caress her. He did not say goodnight until she had become supple to his gentle, seductive entreaties.

XXXII

When Mr. Pontellier learned of his wife's intention to abandon her home and take up her residence elsewhere, he immediately wrote her a letter of unqualified disapproval and remonstrance. She had given reasons which he was unwilling to acknowledge as adequate. He hoped she had not acted upon her rash impulse; and he begged her to consider first, foremost, and above all else, what people would say. He was not

31. Flowerbed.

dreaming of scandal when he uttered this warning; that was a thing which would never have entered into his mind to consider in connection with his wife's name or his own. He was simply thinking of his financial integrity. It might get noised about that the Pontelliers had met with reverses, and were forced to conduct their *ménage* on a humbler scale than heretofore. It might do incalculable mischief to his business prospects.

But remembering Edna's whimsical turn of mind of late, and foreseeing that she had immediately acted upon her impetuous determination, he grasped the situation with his usual promptness and handled it with his well-known business tact and cleverness.

The same mail which brought to Edna his letter of disapproval carried instructions—the most minute instructions—to a well-known architect concerning the remodeling of his home, changes which he had long contemplated, and which he desired carried forward during his temporary absence.

Expert and reliable packers and movers were engaged to convey the furniture, carpets, pictures—everything movable, in short—to places of security. And in an incredibly short time the Pontellier house was turned over to the artisans. There was to be an addition—a small snuggery; there was to be frescoing, and hardwood flooring was to be put into such rooms as had not yet been subjected to this improvement.

Furthermore, in one of the daily papers appeared a brief notice to the effect that Mr. and Mrs. Pontellier were contemplating a summer sojourn abroad, and that their handsome residence on Esplanade Street was undergoing sumptuous alterations, and would not be ready for occupancy until their return. Mr. Pontellier had saved appearances!

Edna admired the skill of his maneuver, and avoided any occasion to balk his intentions. When the situation as set forth by Mr. Pontellier was accepted and taken for granted, she was apparently satisfied that it should be so.

The pigeon house pleased her. It at once assumed the intimate character of a home, while she herself invested it with a charm which it reflected like a warm glow. There was with her a feeling of having descended in the social scale, with a corresponding sense of having risen in the spiritual. Every step which she took toward relieving herself from obligations added to her strength and expansion as an individual. She began to look with her own eyes; to see and to apprehend the deeper undercurrents of life. No longer was she content to "feed upon opinion" when her own soul had invited her.

After a little while, a few days, in fact, Edna went up and spent a week with her children in Iberville. They were delicious February days, with all the summer's promise hovering in the air.

How glad she was to see the children! She wept for very pleasure when she felt their little arms clasping her; their hard, ruddy cheeks pressed against her own glowing cheeks. She looked into their faces with hungry eyes that could not be satisfied with looking. And what stories they had to tell their mother! About the pigs, the cows, the mules! About riding to the mill behind Gluglu; fishing back in the lake with their Uncle Jasper; picking pecans with Lidie's little black brood, and hauling chips in their express wagon. It was a thousand times more fun to haul real chips for old lame Susie's real fire than to drag painted blocks along the banquette on Esplanade Street!

She went with them herself to see the pigs and the cows, to look at the darkies laying the cane, to thrash the pecan trees, and catch fish in the back lake. She lived with them a whole week long, giving them all of herself, and gathering and filling herself with their young existence. They listened, breathless, when she told them the house in Esplanade Street was crowded with workmen, hammering, nailing, sawing, and filling the place with clatter. They wanted to know where their bed was; what had been done with their rocking horse; and where did Joe sleep, and where had Ellen gone, and the cook? But, above all, they were fired with a desire to see the little house around the block. Was there any place to play? Were there any boys next door? Raoul, with pessimistic foreboding, was convinced that there were only girls next door. Where would they sleep, and where would papa sleep? She told them the fairies would fix it all right.

The old Madame was charmed with Edna's visit, and showered all manner of delicate attentions upon her. She was delighted to know that the Esplanade Street house was in a dismantled condition. It gave her the promise and pretext to keep the children indefinitely.

It was with a wrench and a pang that Edna left her children. She carried away with her the sound of their voices and the touch of their cheeks. All along the journey homeward their presence lingered with her like the memory of a delicious song. But by the time she had regained the city the song no longer echoed in her soul. She was again alone.

XXXIII

It happened sometimes when Edna went to see Mademoiselle Reisz that the little musician was absent, giving a lesson or making some small necessary household purchase. The key was always left in a secret hiding place in the entry, which Edna knew. If Mademoiselle happened to be away, Edna would usually enter and wait for her return.

When she knocked at Mademoiselle Reisz's door one afternoon there was no response; so unlocking the door, as usual, she entered and found the apartment deserted, as she had expected. Her day had been quite filled up, and it was for a rest, for a refuge, and to talk about Robert, that she sought out her friend.

She had worked at her canvas—a young Italian character study—all the morning, completing the work without the model; but there had been many interruptions, some incident to her modest housekeeping, and others of a social nature.

Madame Ratignolle had dragged herself over, avoiding the too public thoroughfares, she said. She complained that Edna had neglected her much of late. Besides, she was consumed with curiosity to see the little house and the manner in which it was conducted. She wanted to hear all about the dinner party; Monsieur Ratignolle had left so early. What had happened after he left? The champagne and grapes which Edna sent over were too delicious. She had so little appetite; they had refreshed and toned her stomach. Where on earth was she going to put Mr. Pontellier in that little house, and the boys? And then she made Edna promise to go to her when her hour of trial overtook her.

"At any time—any time of the day or night, dear," Edna assured her.

Before leaving Madame Ratignolle said:

"In some way you seem to me like a child, Edna. You seem to act without a certain amount of reflection which is necessary in this life. That is the reason I want to say you mustn't mind if I advise you to be a little careful while you are living here alone. Why don't you have some one come and stay with you? Wouldn't Mademoiselle Reisz come?"

"No; she wouldn't wish to come, and I shouldn't want her always with me."

"Well, the reason—you know how evil-minded the world is—some one was talking of Alcée Arobin visiting you. Of course, it wouldn't matter if Mr. Arobin had not such a dreadful reputation. Monsieur Ratignolle was telling me that his attentions alone are considered enough to ruin a woman's name."

"Does he boast of his successes?" asked Edna, indifferently, squinting at her picture.

"No, I think not. I believe he is a decent fellow as far as that goes. But his character is so well known among the men. I shan't be able to come back and see you; it was very, very imprudent today."

"Mind the step!" cried Edna.

"Don't neglect me," entreated Madame Ratignolle; "and don't mind what I said about Arobin, or having someone to stay with you."

"Of course not," Edna laughed. "You may say anything you like to me." They kissed each other goodbye. Madame Ratignolle had not far to go, and Edna stood on the porch a while watching her walk down the street.

Then in the afternoon Mrs. Merriman and Mrs. Highcamp had made their "party call." Edna felt that they might have dispensed with the formality. They had also come to invite her to play *vingt-et-un*[32] one evening at Mrs. Merriman's. She was asked to go early, to dinner, and Mr. Merriman or Mr. Arobin would take her home. Edna accepted in a half-hearted way. She sometimes felt very tired of Mrs. Highcamp and Mrs. Merriman.

Late in the afternoon she sought refuge with Mademoiselle Reisz, and stayed there alone, waiting for her, feeling a kind of repose invade her with the very atmosphere of the shabby, unpretentious little room.

Edna sat at the window, which looked out over the housetops and across the river. The window frame was filled with pots of flowers, and she sat and picked the dry leaves from a rose geranium. The day was warm, and the breeze which blew from the river was very pleasant. She removed her hat and laid it on the piano. She went on picking the leaves and digging around the plants with her hat pin. Once she thought she heard Mademoiselle Reisz approaching. But it was a young black girl, who came in, bringing a small bundle of laundry, which she deposited in the adjoining room, and went away.

Edna seated herself at the piano, and softly picked out with one hand the bars of a piece of music which lay open before her. A half-hour went by. There was the occasional sound of people going and coming in the lower hall. She was growing interested in her occupation of picking out the aria, when there was a second rap at the door. She vaguely wondered what these people did when they found Mademoiselle's door locked.

"Come in," she called, turning her face toward the door. And this time it was Robert Lebrun who presented himself. She attempted to rise; she could not have done so without betraying the agitation which mastered her at sight of him, so she fell back upon the stool, only exclaiming, "Why, Robert!"

He came and clasped her hand, seemingly without knowing what he was saying or doing.

"Mrs. Pontellier! How do you happen—oh! how well you look! Is Mademoiselle Reisz not here? I never expected to see you."

---

32. The card game known as "twenty-one."

"When did you come back?" asked Edna in an unsteady voice, wiping her face with her handkerchief. She seemed ill at ease on the piano stool, and he begged her to take the chair by the window. She did so, mechanically, while he seated himself on the stool.

"I returned day before yesterday," he answered, while he leaned his arm on the keys, bringing forth a crash of discordant sound.

"Day before yesterday!" she repeated, aloud; and went on thinking to herself, "day before yesterday," in a sort of an uncomprehending way. She had pictured him seeing her at the very first hour, and he had lived under the same sky since day before yesterday; while only by accident had he stumbled upon her. Mademoiselle must have lied when she said, "Poor fool, he loves you."

"Day before yesterday," she repeated, breaking off a spray of Mademoiselle's geranium; "then if you had not met me here today you wouldn't—when—that is, didn't you mean to come and see me?"

"Of course, I should have gone to see you. There have been so many things—" he turned the leaves of Mademoiselle's music nervously. "I started in at once yesterday with the old firm. After all there is as much chance for me here as there was there—that is, I might find it profitable some day. The Mexicans were not very congenial."

So he had come back because the Mexicans were not congenial; because business was as profitable here as there; because of any reason, and not because he cared to be near her. She remembered the day she sat on the floor, turning the pages of his letter, seeking the reason which was left untold.

She had not noticed how he looked—only feeling his presence; but she turned deliberately and observed him. After all, he had been absent but a few months, and was not changed. His hair—the color of hers—waved back from his temples in the same way as before. His skin was not more burned than it had been at Grand Isle. She found in his eyes, when he looked at her for one silent moment, the same tender caress, with an added warmth and entreaty which had not been there before—the same glance which had penetrated to the sleeping places of her soul and awakened them.

A hundred times Edna had pictured Robert's return, and imagined their first meeting. It was usually at her home, whither he had sought her out at once. She always fancied him expressing or betraying in some way his love for her. And here, the reality was that they sat ten feet apart, she at the window, crushing geranium leaves in her hand and smelling them, he twirling around on the piano stool, saying:

"I was very much surprised to hear of Mr. Pontellier's absence; it's a wonder Mademoiselle Reisz did not tell me; and your moving—mother told me yesterday. I should think you would have gone to New York with him, or to Iberville with the children, rather than be bothered here with housekeeping. And you are going abroad, too, I hear. We shan't have you at Grand Isle next summer; it won't seem— do you see much of Mademoiselle Reisz? She often spoke of you in the few letters she wrote."

"Do you remember that you promised to write to me when you went away?" A flush overspread his whole face.

"I couldn't believe that my letters would be of any interest to you."

"That is an excuse; it isn't the truth." Edna reached for her hat on the piano. She adjusted it, sticking the hat pin through the heavy coil of hair with some deliberation.

"Are you not going to wait for Mademoiselle Reisz?" asked Robert.

"No; I have found when she is absent this long, she is liable not to come back till late." She drew on her gloves, and Robert picked up his hat.

"Won't you wait for her?" asked Edna.

"Not if you think she will not be back till late," adding, as if suddenly aware of some discourtesy in his speech, "and I should miss the pleasure of walking home with you." Edna locked the door and put the key back in its hiding place.

They went together, picking their way across muddy streets and sidewalks encumbered with the cheap display of small tradesmen. Part of the distance they rode in the car, and after disembarking, passed the Pontellier mansion, which looked broken and half torn asunder. Robert had never known the house, and looked at it with interest.

"I never knew you in your home," he remarked.

"I am glad you did not."

"Why?" She did not answer. They went on around the corner, and it seemed as if her dreams were coming true after all, when he followed her into the little house.

"You must stay and dine with me, Robert. You see I am all alone, and it is so long since I have seen you. There is so much I want to ask you."

She took off her hat and gloves. He stood irresolute, making some excuse about his mother who expected him; he even muttered something about an engagement. She struck a match and lit the lamp on the table; it was growing dusk. When he saw her face in the lamplight, looking pained, with all the soft lines gone out of it, he threw his hat aside and seated himself.

"Oh! you know I want to stay if you will let me!" he exclaimed. All the softness came back. She laughed, and went and put her hand on his shoulder.

"This is the first moment you have seemed like the old Robert. I'll go tell Celestine." She hurried away to tell Celestine to set an extra place. She even sent her off in search of some added delicacy which she had not thought of for herself. And she recommended great care in dripping the coffee and having the omelet done to a proper turn.

When she reentered, Robert was turning over magazines, sketches, and things that lay upon the table in great disorder. He picked up a photograph, and exclaimed:

"Alcée Arobin! What on earth is his picture doing here?"

"I tried to make a sketch of his head one day," answered Edna, "and he thought the photograph might help me. It was at the other house. I thought it had been left there. I must have packed it up with my drawing materials."

"I should think you would give it back to him if you have finished with it."

"Oh! I have a great many such photographs. I never think of returning them. They don't amount to anything." Robert kept on looking at the picture.

"It seems to me—do you think his head worth drawing? Is he a friend of Mr. Pontellier's? You never said you knew him."

"He isn't a friend of Mr. Pontellier's; he's a friend of mine. I always knew him—that is, it is only of late that I know him pretty well. But I'd rather talk about you, and know what you have been seeing and doing and feeling out there in Mexico." Robert threw aside the picture.

"I've been seeing the waves and the white beach of Grand Isle; the quiet, grassy street of the *Chênière*; the old fort at Grande Terre. I've been working like a machine, and feeling like a lost soul. There was nothing interesting."

She leaned her head upon her hand to shade her eyes from the light.

"And what have you been seeing and doing and feeling all these days?" he asked.

"I've been seeing the waves and the white beach of Grand Isle; the quiet, grassy street of the *Chênière Caminada;* the old sunny fort at Grande Terre. I've been working with a little more comprehension than a machine and still feeling like a lost soul. There was nothing interesting."

"Mrs. Pontellier, you are cruel," he said, with feeling, closing his eyes and resting his head back in his chair. They remained in silence till old Celestine announced dinner.

XXXIV

The dining room was very small. Edna's round mahogany would have almost filled it. As it was there was but a step or two from the little table to the kitchen, to the mantel, the small buffet, and the side door that opened out on the narrow brick-paved yard.

A certain degree of ceremony settled upon them with the announcement of dinner. There was no return to personalities. Robert related incidents of his sojourn in Mexico, and Edna talked of events likely to interest him, which had occurred during his absence. The dinner was of ordinary quality, except for the few delicacies which she had sent out to purchase. Old Celestine, with a bandana *tignon*[33] twisted about her head, hobbled in and out, taking a personal interest in everything; and she lingered occasionally to talk patois with Robert, whom she had known as a boy.

He went out to a neighboring cigar stand to purchase cigarette papers, and when he came back he found that Celestine had served the black coffee in the parlor.

"Perhaps I shouldn't have come back," he said. "When you are tired of me, tell me to go."

"You never tire me. You must have forgotten the hours and hours at Grand Isle in which we grew accustomed to each other and used to being together."

"I have forgotten nothing at Grand Isle," he said, not looking at her, but rolling a cigarette. His tobacco pouch, which he laid upon the table, was a fantastic embroidered silk affair, evidently the handiwork of a woman.

"You used to carry your tobacco in a rubber pouch," said Edna, picking up the pouch and examining the needlework.

"Yes; it was lost."

"Where did you buy this one? In Mexico?"

"It was given to me by a Vera Cruz girl; they are very generous," he replied, striking a match and lighting his cigarette.

"They are very handsome, I suppose, those Mexican women; very picturesque, with their black eyes and their lace scarfs."

"Some are; others are hideous. Just as you find women everywhere."

"What was she like—the one who gave you the pouch? You must have known her very well."

"She was very ordinary. She wasn't of the slightest importance. I knew her well enough."

"Did you visit at her house? Was it interesting? I should like to know and hear about the people you met, and the impressions they made on you."

"There are some people who leave impressions not so lasting as the imprint of an oar upon the water."

33. Knot of hair.

"Was she such a one?"

"It would be ungenerous for me to admit that she was of that order and kind." He thrust the pouch back in his pocket, as if to put away the subject with the trifle which had brought it up.

Arobin dropped in with a message from Mrs. Merriman, to say that the card party was postponed on account of the illness of one of her children.

"How do you do, Arobin?" said Robert, rising from the obscurity.

"Oh! Lebrun. To be sure! I heard yesterday you were back. How did they treat you down in Mexique?"

"Fairly well."

"But not well enough to keep you there. Stunning girls, though, in Mexico. I thought I should never get away from Vera Cruz when I was down there a couple of years ago."

"Did they embroider slippers and tobacco pouches and hatbands and things for you?" asked Edna.

"Oh! my! no! I didn't get so deep in their regard. I fear they made more impression on me than I made on them."

"You were less fortunate than Robert, then."

"I am always less fortunate than Robert. Has he been imparting tender confidences?"

"I've been imposing myself long enough," said Robert, rising, and shaking hands with Edna. "Please convey my regards to Mr. Pontellier when you write."

He shook hands with Arobin and went away.

"Fine fellow, that Lebrun," said Arobin when Robert had gone. "I never heard you speak of him."

"I knew him last summer at Grand Isle," she replied. "Here is that photograph of yours. Don't you want it?"

"What do I want with it? Throw it away." She threw it back on the table.

"I'm not going to Mrs. Merriman's," she said. "If you see her, tell her so. But perhaps I had better write. I think I shall write now, and say that I am sorry her child is sick, and tell her not to count on me."

"It would be a good scheme," acquiesced Arobin. "I don't blame you; stupid lot!"

Edna opened the blotter, and having procured paper and pen, began to write the note. Arobin lit a cigar and read the evening paper, which he had in his pocket.

"What is the date?" she asked. He told her.

"Will you mail this for me when you go out?"

"Certainly." He read to her little bits out of the newspaper, while she straightened things on the table.

"What do you want to do?" he asked, throwing aside the paper. "Do you want to go out for a walk or a drive or anything? It would be a fine night to drive."

"No; I don't want to do anything but just be quiet. You go away and amuse yourself. Don't stay."

"I'll go away if I must; but I shan't amuse myself. You know that I only live when I am near you."

He stood up to bid her goodnight.

"Is that one of the things you always say to women?"

"I have said it before, but I don't think I ever came so near meaning it," he answered with a smile. There were no warm lights in her eyes; only a dreamy, absent look.

"Good night. I adore you. Sleep well," he said, and he kissed her hand and went away.

She stayed alone in a kind of reverie—a sort of stupor. Step by step she lived over every instant of the time she had been with Robert after he had entered Mademoiselle Reisz's door. She recalled his words, his looks. How few and meager they had been for her hungry heart! A vision—a transcendently seductive vision of a Mexican girl arose before her. She writhed with a jealous pang. She wondered when he would come back. He had not said he would come back. She had been with him, had heard his voice and touched his hand. But some way he had seemed nearer to her off there in Mexico.

XXXV

The morning was full of sunlight and hope. Edna could see before her no denial—only the promise of excessive joy. She lay in bed awake, with bright eyes full of speculation. "He loves you, poor fool." If she could but get that conviction firmly fixed in her mind, what mattered about the rest? She felt she had been childish and unwise the night before in giving herself over to despondency. She recapitulated the motives which no doubt explained Robert's reserve. They were not insurmountable; they would not hold if he really loved her; they could not hold against her own passion, which he must come to realize in time. She pictured him going to his business that morning. She even saw how he was dressed; how he walked down one street, and turned the corner of another; saw him bending over his desk, talking to people who entered the office, going to his lunch, and perhaps watching for her on the street. He would come to her in the afternoon or evening, sit and roll his cigarette, talk a little, and go away as he had done the night before. But how delicious it would be to have him there with her! She would have no regrets, nor seek to penetrate his reserve if he still chose to wear it.

Edna ate her breakfast only half dressed. The maid brought her a delicious printed scrawl from Raoul, expressing his love, asking her to send him some bonbons, and telling her they had found that morning ten tiny white pigs all lying in a row beside Lidie's big white pig.

A letter also came from her husband, saying he hoped to be back early in March, and then they would get ready for that journey abroad which he had promised her so long, which he felt now fully able to afford; he felt able to travel as people should, without any thought of small economies—thanks to his recent speculations in Wall Street.

Much to her surprise she received a note from Arobin, written at midnight from the club. It was to say good morning to her, to hope she had slept well, to assure her of his devotion, which he trusted she in some faintest manner returned.

All these letters were pleasing to her. She answered the children in a cheerful frame of mind, promising them bonbons, and congratulating them upon their happy find of the little pigs.

She answered her husband with friendly evasiveness—not with any fixed design to mislead him, only because all sense of reality had gone out of her life; she had abandoned herself to Fate, and awaited the consequences with indifference.

To Arobin's note she made no reply. She put it under Celestine's stove lid.

Edna worked several hours with much spirit. She saw no one but a picture dealer, who asked her if it were true that she was going abroad to study in Paris.

She said possibly she might, and he negotiated with her for some Parisian studies to reach him in time for the holiday trade in December.

Robert did not come that day. She was keenly disappointed. He did not come the following day, nor the next. Each morning she awoke with hope, and each night she was a prey to despondency. She was tempted to seek him out. But far from yielding to the impulse, she avoided any occasion which might throw her in his way. She did not go to Mademoiselle Reisz's nor pass by Madame Lebrun's, as she might have done if he had still been in Mexico.

When Arobin, one night, urged her to drive with him, she went—out to the lake, on the Shell Road. His horses were full of mettle, and even a little unmanageable. She liked the rapid gait at which they spun along, and the quick, sharp sound of the horses' hoofs on the hard road. They did not stop anywhere to eat or to drink. Arobin was not needlessly imprudent. But they ate and they drank when they regained Edna's little dining room—which was comparatively early in the evening.

It was late when he left her. It was getting to be more than a passing whim with Arobin to see her and be with her. He had detected the latent sensuality, which unfolded under his delicate sense of her nature's requirements like a torpid, torrid, sensitive blossom.

There was no despondency when she fell asleep that night; nor was there hope when she awoke in the morning.

XXXVI

There was a garden out in the suburbs; a small, leafy corner, with a few green tables under the orange trees. An old cat slept all day on the stone step in the sun, and an old *mulatresse*[34] slept her idle hours away in her chair at the open window, till someone happened to knock on one of the green tables. She had milk and cream cheese to sell, and bread and butter. There was no one who could make such excellent coffee or fry a chicken so golden brown as she.

The place was too modest to attract the attention of people of fashion, and so quiet as to have escaped the notice of those in search of pleasure and dissipation. Edna had discovered it accidentally one day when the high-board gate stood ajar. She caught sight of a little green table, blotched with the checkered sunlight that filtered through the quivering leaves overhead. Within she had found the slumbering *mulatresse,* the drowsy cat, and a glass of milk which reminded her of the milk she had tasted in Iberville.

She often stopped there during her perambulations; sometimes taking a book with her, and sitting an hour or two under the trees when she found the place deserted. Once or twice she took a quiet dinner there alone, having instructed Celestine beforehand to prepare no dinner at home. It was the last place in the city where she would have expected to meet anyone she knew.

Still she was not astonished when, as she was partaking of a modest dinner late in the afternoon, looking into an open book, stroking the cat, which had made friends with her—she was not greatly astonished to see Robert come in at the tall garden gate.

"I am destined to see you only by accident," she said, shoving the cat off the chair beside her. He was surprised, ill at ease, almost embarrassed at meeting her thus so unexpectedly.

---

34. A woman who is part mulatto, or racially mixed.

"Do you come here often?" he asked.

"I almost live here," she said.

"I used to drop in very often for a cup of Catiche's good coffee. This is the first time since I came back."

"She'll bring you a plate, and you will share my dinner. There's always enough for two—even three." Edna had intended to be indifferent and as reserved as he when she met him; she had reached the determination by a laborious train of reasoning, incident to one of her despondent moods. But her resolve melted when she saw him before her, seated there beside her in the little garden, as if a designing Providence had led him into her path.

"Why have you kept away from me, Robert?" she asked, closing the book that lay open upon the table.

"Why are you so personal, Mrs. Pontellier? Why do you force me to idiotic subterfuges?" he exclaimed with sudden warmth. "I suppose there's no use telling you I've been very busy, or that I've been sick, or that I've been to see you and not found you at home. Please let me off with any one of these excuses."

"You are the embodiment of selfishness," she said. "You save yourself something—I don't know what—but there is some selfish motive, and in sparing yourself you never consider for a moment what I think, or how I feel your neglect and indifference. I suppose this is what you would call unwomanly; but I have got into a habit of expressing myself. It doesn't matter to me, and you may think me unwomanly if you like."

"No; I only think you cruel, as I said the other day. Maybe not intentionally cruel; but you seem to be forcing me into disclosures which can result in nothing; as if you would have me bare a wound for the pleasure of looking at it, without the intention or power of healing it."

"I'm spoiling your dinner, Robert; never mind what I say. You haven't eaten a morsel."

"I only came in for a cup of coffee." His sensitive face was all disfigured with excitement.

"Isn't this a delightful place?" she remarked. "I am so glad it has never actually been discovered. It is so quiet, so sweet, here. Do you notice there is scarcely a sound to be heard? It's so out of the way; and a good walk from the car. However, I don't mind walking. I always feel so sorry for women who don't like to walk; they miss so much—so many rare little glimpses of life; and we women learn so little of life on the whole.

"Catiche's coffee is always hot. I don't know how she manages it, here in the open air. Celestine's coffee gets cold bringing it from the kitchen to the dining-room. Three lumps! How can you drink it so sweet? Take some of the cress with your chop; it's so biting and crisp. Then there's the advantage of being able to smoke with your coffee out here. Now, in the city—aren't you going to smoke?"

"After a while," he said, laying a cigar on the table.

"Who gave it to you?" she laughed.

"I bought it. I suppose I'm getting reckless; I bought a whole box." She was determined not to be personal again and make him uncomfortable.

The cat made friends with him, and climbed into his lap when he smoked his cigar. He stroked her silky fur, and talked a little about her. He looked at Edna's book, which he had read; and he told her the end, to save her the trouble of wading through it, he said.

Again he accompanied her back to her home; and it was after dusk when they reached the little "pigeon house." She did not ask him to remain, which he was grateful for, as it permitted him to stay without the discomfort of blundering through an excuse which he had no intention of considering. He helped her to light the lamp; then she went into her room to take off her hat and to bathe her face and hands.

When she came back Robert was not examining the pictures and magazines as before; he sat off in the shadow, leaning his head back on the chair as if in a reverie. Edna lingered a moment beside the table, arranging the books there. Then she went across the room to where he sat. She bent over the arm of his chair and called his name.

"Robert," she said, "are you asleep?"

"No," he answered, looking up at her.

She leaned over and kissed him—a soft, cool, delicate kiss, whose voluptuous sting penetrated his whole being—then she moved away from him. He followed, and took her in his arms, just holding her close to him. She put her hand up to his face and pressed his cheek against her own. The action was full of love and tenderness. He sought her lips again. Then he drew her down upon the sofa beside him and held her hand in both of his.

"Now you know," he said, "now you know what I have been fighting against since last summer at Grand Isle; what drove me away and drove me back again."

"Why have you been fighting against it?" she asked. Her face glowed with soft lights.

"Why? Because you were not free; you were Léonce Pontellier's wife. I couldn't help loving you if you were ten times his wife; but so long as I went away from you and kept away I could help telling you so." She put her free hand up to his shoulder, and then against his cheek, rubbing it softly. He kissed her again. His face was warm and flushed.

"There in Mexico I was thinking of you all the time, and longing for you."

"But not writing to me," she interrupted.

"Something put into my head that you cared for me; and I lost my senses. I forgot everything but a wild dream of your some way becoming my wife."

"Your wife!"

"Religion, loyalty, everything would give way if only you cared."

"Then you must have forgotten that I was Léonce Pontellier's wife."

"Oh! I was demented, dreaming of wild, impossible things, recalling men who had set their wives free, we have heard of such things."

"Yes, we have heard of such things."

"I came back full of vague, mad intentions. And when I got here—"

"When you got here you never came near me!" She was still caressing his cheek.

"I realized what a cur I was to dream of such a thing, even if you had been willing."

She took his face between her hands and looked into it as if she would never withdraw her eyes more. She kissed him on the forehead, the eyes, the cheeks, and the lips.

"You have been a very, very foolish boy, wasting your time dreaming of impossible things when you speak of Mr. Pontellier setting me free! I am no longer one of Mr. Pontellier's possessions to dispose of or not. I give myself where I choose. If he were to say, 'Here, Robert, take her and be happy; she is yours,' I should laugh at you both."

His face grew a little white. "What do you mean?" he asked.

There was a knock at the door. Old Celestine came in to say that Madame Ratignolle's servant had come around the back way with a message that Madame had been taken sick and begged Mrs. Pontellier to go to her immediately.

"Yes, yes," said Edna, rising; "I promised. Tell her yes—to wait for me. I'll go back with her."

"Let me walk over with you," offered Robert.

"No," she said; "I will go with the servant." She went into her room to put on her hat, and when she came in again she sat once more upon the sofa beside him. He had not stirred. She put her arms about his neck.

"Goodbye, my sweet Robert. Tell me goodbye." He kissed her with a degree of passion which had not before entered into his caress, and strained her to him.

"I love you," she whispered, "only you; no one but you. It was you who awoke me last summer out of a lifelong, stupid dream. Oh! you have made me so unhappy with your indifference. Oh! I have suffered, suffered! Now you are here we shall love each other, my Robert. We shall be everything to each other. Nothing else in the world is of any consequence. I must go to my friend; but you will wait for me? No matter how late; you will wait for me, Robert?"

"Don't go; don't go! Oh! Edna, stay with me," he pleaded. "Why should you go? Stay with me, stay with me."

"I shall come back as soon as I can; I shall find you here." She buried her face in his neck, and said goodbye again. Her seductive voice, together with his great love for her, had enthralled his senses, had deprived him of every impulse but the longing to hold her and keep her.

XXXVII

Edna looked in at the drugstore. Monsieur Ratignolle was putting up a mixture himself, very carefully, dropping a red liquid into a tiny glass. He was grateful to Edna for having come; her presence would be a comfort to his wife. Madame Ratignolle's sister, who had always been with her at such trying times, had not been able to come up from the plantation, and Adèle had been inconsolable until Mrs. Pontellier so kindly promised to come to her. The nurse had been with them at night for the past week, as she lived a great distance away. And Dr. Mandelet had been coming and going all the afternoon. They were then looking for him any moment.

Edna hastened upstairs by a private stairway that led from the rear of the store to the apartments above. The children were all sleeping in a back room. Madame Ratignolle was in the salon, whither she had strayed in her suffering impatience. She sat on the sofa, clad in an ample white *peignoir*, holding a handkerchief tight in her hand with a nervous clutch. Her face was drawn and pinched, her sweet blue eyes haggard and unnatural. All her beautiful hair had been drawn back and plaited. It lay in a long braid on the sofa pillow, coiled like a golden serpent. The nurse, a comfortable looking *Griffe*[35] woman in white apron and cap, was urging her to return to her bedroom.

"There is no use, there is no use," she said at once to Edna. "We must get rid of Mandelet; he is getting too old and careless. He said he would be here at half-past seven; now it must be eight. See what time it is, Joséphine."

---

35. The child of a mulatto and a black person.

The woman was possessed of a cheerful nature, and refused to take any situation too seriously, especially a situation with which she was so familiar. She urged Madame to have courage and patience. But Madame only set her teeth hard into her under lip, and Edna saw the sweat gather in beads on her white forehead. After a moment or two she uttered a profound sigh and wiped her face with the handkerchief rolled in a ball. She appeared exhausted. The nurse gave her a fresh handkerchief, sprinkled with cologne water.

"This is too much!" she cried. "Mandelet ought to be killed! Where is Alphonse? Is it possible I am to be abandoned like this—neglected by every one?"

"Neglected, indeed!" exclaimed the nurse. Wasn't she there? And here was Mrs. Pontellier leaving, no doubt, a pleasant evening at home to devote to her? And wasn't Monsieur Ratignolle coming that very instant through the hall? And Joséphine was quite sure she had heard Doctor Mandelet's coupé. Yes, there it was, down at the door.

Adèle consented to go back to her room. She sat on the edge of a little low couch next to her bed.

Doctor Mandelet paid no attention to Madame Ratignolle's upbraidings. He was accustomed to them at such times, and was too well convinced of her loyalty to doubt it.

He was glad to see Edna, and wanted her to go with him into the salon and entertain him. But Madame Ratignolle would not consent that Edna should leave her for an instant. Between agonizing moments, she chatted a little, and said it took her mind off her sufferings.

Edna began to feel uneasy. She was seized with a vague dread. Her own like experiences seemed far away, unreal, and only half remembered. She recalled faintly an ecstasy of pain, the heavy odor of chloroform, a stupor which had deadened sensation, and an awakening to find a little new life to which she had given being, added to the great unnumbered multitude of souls that come and go.

She began to wish she had not come; her presence was not necessary. She might have invented a pretext for staying away; she might even invent a pretext now for going. But Edna did not go. With an inward agony, with a flaming, outspoken revolt against the ways of Nature, she witnessed the scene of torture.

She was still stunned and speechless with emotion when later she leaned over her friend to kiss her and softly say goodbye. Adèle, pressing her cheek, whispered in an exhausted voice: "Think of the children, Edna. Oh think of the children! Remember them!"

XXXVIII

Edna still felt dazed when she got outside in the open air. The Doctor's coupé had returned for him and stood before the *porte cochère*. She did not wish to enter the coupé, and told Doctor Mandelet she would walk; she was not afraid, and would go alone. He directed his carriage to meet him at Mrs. Pontellier's, and he started to walk home with her.

Up—away up, over the narrow street between the tall houses, the stars were blazing. The air was mild and caressing, but cool with the breath of spring and the night. They walked slowly, the doctor with a heavy, measured tread and his hands behind him; Edna, in an absentminded way, as she had walked one night at Grand Isle, as if her thoughts had gone ahead of her and she was striving to overtake them.

"You shouldn't have been there, Mrs. Pontellier," he said. "That was no place for you. Adèle is full of whims at such times. There were a dozen women she might have had with her, unimpressionable women. I felt that it was cruel, cruel. You shouldn't have gone."

"Oh, well!" she answered, indifferently. "I don't know that it matters after all. One has to think of the children some time or other; the sooner the better."

"When is Léonce coming back?"

"Quite soon. Some time in March."

"And you are going abroad?"

"Perhaps—no, I am not going. I'm not going to be forced into doing things. I don't want to go abroad. I want to be let alone. Nobody has any right—except the children, perhaps—and even then, it seems to me—or it did seem—" She felt that her speech was voicing the incoherency of her thoughts, and stopped abruptly.

"The trouble is," sighed the doctor, grasping her meaning intuitively, "that youth is given up to illusions. It seems to be a provision of Nature; a decoy to secure mothers for the race. And Nature takes no account of moral consequences, of arbitrary conditions which we create, and which we feel obliged to maintain at any cost."

"Yes," she said. "The years that are gone seem like dreams—if one might go on sleeping and dreaming—but to wake up and find—oh! well! perhaps it is better to wake up after all, even to suffer, rather than to remain a dupe to illusions all one's life."

"It seems to me, my dear child," said the doctor at parting, holding her hand, "you seem to me to be in trouble. I am not going to ask for your confidence. I will only say that if ever you feel moved to give it to me, perhaps I might help you. I know I would understand, and I tell you there are not many who would—not many, my dear."

"Some way I don't feel moved to speak of things that trouble me. Don't think I am ungrateful or that I don't appreciate your sympathy. There are periods of despondency and suffering which take possession of me. But I don't want anything but my own way. That is wanting a good deal, of course, when you have to trample upon the lives, the hearts, the prejudices of others—but no matter—still, I shouldn't want to trample upon the little lives. Oh! I don't know what I'm saying, Doctor. Good night. Don't blame me for anything."

"Yes, I will blame you if you don't come and see me soon. We will talk of things you never have dreamt of talking about before. It will do us both good. I don't want you to blame yourself, whatever comes. Good night, my child."

She let herself in at the gate, but instead of entering she sat upon the step of the porch. The night was quiet and soothing. All the tearing emotion of the last few hours seemed to fall away from her like a somber, uncomfortable garment, which she had but to loosen to be rid of. She went back to that hour before Adèle had sent for her; and her senses kindled afresh in thinking of Robert's words, the pressure of his arms, and the feeling of his lips upon her own. She could picture at that moment no greater bliss on earth than possession of the beloved one. His expression of love had already given him to her in part. When she thought that he was there at hand, waiting for her, she grew numb with the intoxication of expectancy. It was so late; he would be asleep perhaps. She would awaken him with a kiss. She hoped he would be asleep that she might arouse him with her caresses.

Still, she remembered Adèle's voice whispering, "Think of the children; think of them." She meant to think of them; that determination had driven into her soul like a death wound—but not tonight. Tomorrow would be time to think of everything.

Robert was not waiting for her in the little parlor. He was nowhere at hand. The house was empty. But he had scrawled on a piece of paper that lay in the lamplight: "I love you. Goodbye—because I love you."

Edna grew faint when she read the words. She went and sat on the sofa. Then she stretched herself out there, never uttering a sound. She did not sleep. She did not go to bed. The lamp sputtered and went out. She was still awake in the morning, when Celestine unlocked the kitchen door and came in to light the fire.

XXXIX

Victor, with hammer and nails and scraps of scantling, was patching a corner of one of the galleries. Mariequita sat near by, dangling her legs, watching him work, and handing him nails from the toolbox. The sun was beating down upon them. The girl had covered her head with her apron folded into a square pad. They had been talking for an hour or more. She was never tired of hearing Victor describe the dinner at Mrs. Pontellier's. He exaggerated every detail, making it appear a veritable Lucullean feast. The flowers were in tubs, he said. The champagne was quaffed from huge golden goblets. Venus rising from the foam could have presented no more entrancing a spectacle than Mrs. Pontellier, blazing with beauty and diamonds at the head of the board, while the other women were all of them youthful houris, possessed of incomparable charms.

She got it into her head that Victor was in love with Mrs. Pontellier, and he gave her evasive answers, framed so as to confirm her belief. She grew sullen and cried a little, threatening to go off and leave him to his fine ladies. There were a dozen men crazy about her at the *Chênière;* and since it was the fashion to be in love with married people, why, she could run away any time she liked to New Orleans with Célina's husband.

Célina's husband was a fool, a coward, and a pig, and to prove it to her, Victor intended to hammer his head into a jelly the next time he encountered him. This assurance was very consoling to Mariequita. She dried her eyes, and grew cheerful at the prospect.

They were still talking of the dinner and the allurements of city life when Mrs. Pontellier herself slipped around the corner of the house. The two youngsters stayed dumb with amazement before what they considered to be an apparition. But it was really she in flesh and blood, looking tired and a little travel-stained.

"I walked up from the wharf," she said, "and heard the hammering. I supposed it was you, mending the porch. It's a good thing. I was always tripping over those loose planks last summer. How dreary and deserted everything looks!"

It took Victor some little time to comprehend that she had come in Beaudelet's lugger, that she had come alone, and for no purpose but to rest.

"There's nothing fixed up yet, you see. I'll give you my room; it's the only place."

"Any corner will do," she assured him.

"And if you can stand Philomel's cooking," he went on, "though I might try to get her mother while you are here. Do you think she would come?" turning to Mariequita.

Mariequita thought that perhaps Philomel's mother might come for a few days, and money enough.

Beholding Mrs. Pontellier make her appearance, the girl had at once suspected a lovers' rendezvous. But Victor's astonishment was so genuine, and Mrs. Pontellier's indifference so apparent, that the disturbing notion did not lodge long in her brain. She contemplated with the greatest interest this woman who gave the most sumptuous dinners in America, and who had all the men in New Orleans at her feet.

"What time will you have dinner?" asked Edna. "I'm very hungry; but don't get anything extra."

"I'll have it ready in little or no time," he said, bustling and packing away his tools. "You may go to my room to brush up and rest yourself. Mariequita will show you."

"Thank you," said Edna. "But, do you know, I have a notion to go down to the beach and take a good wash and even a little swim, before dinner?"

"The water is too cold!" they both exclaimed. "Don't think of it."

"Well, I might go down and try—dip my toes in. Why, it seems to me the sun is hot enough to have warmed the very depths of the ocean. Could you get me a couple of towels? I'd better go right away, so as to be back in time. It would be a little too chilly if I waited till this afternoon."

Mariequita ran over to Victor's room, and returned with some towels, which she gave to Edna.

"I hope you have fish for dinner," said Edna, as she started to walk away; "but don't do anything extra if you haven't."

"Run and find Philomel's mother," Victor instructed the girl. "I'll go to the kitchen and see what I can do. By gimminy! Women have no consideration! She might have sent me word."

Edna walked on down to the beach rather mechanically, not noticing anything special except that the sun was hot. She was not dwelling upon any particular train of thought. She had done all the thinking which was necessary after Robert went away, when she lay awake upon the sofa till morning.

She had said over and over to herself: "Today it is Arobin; tomorrow it will be some one else. It makes no difference to me, it doesn't matter about Léonce Pontellier—but Raoul and Etienne!" She understood now clearly what she had meant long ago when she said to Adèle Ratignolle that she would give up the unessential, but she would never sacrifice herself for her children.

Despondency had come upon her there in the wakeful night, and had never lifted. There was no one thing in the world that she desired. There was no human being whom she wanted near her except Robert; and she even realized that the day would come when he, too, and the thought of him would melt out of her existence, leaving her alone. The children appeared before her like antagonists who had overcome her; who had overpowered and sought to drag her into the soul's slavery for the rest of her days. But she knew a way to elude them. She was not thinking of these things when she walked down to the beach.

The water of the Gulf stretched out before her, gleaming with the million lights of the sun. The voice of the sea is seductive, never ceasing, whispering, clamoring, murmuring, inviting the soul to wander in abysses of solitude. All along the white beach, up and down, there was no living thing in sight. A bird with a broken wing was beating the air above, reeling, fluttering, circling disabled down, down to the water.

Edna had found her old bathing suit still hanging, faded, upon its accustomed peg.

She put it on, leaving her clothing in the bathhouse. But when she was there beside the sea, absolutely alone, she cast the unpleasant, pricking garments from her, and for the first time in her life she stood naked in the open air, at the mercy of the sun, the breeze that beat upon her, and the waves that invited her.

How strange and awful it seemed to stand naked under the sky! how delicious! She felt like some newborn creature, opening its eyes in a familiar world that it had never known.

The foamy wavelets curled up to her white feet, and coiled like serpents about her ankles. She walked out. The water was chill, but she walked on. The water was deep, but she lifted her white body and reached out with a long, sweeping stroke. The touch of the sea is sensuous, enfolding the body in its soft, close embrace.

She went on and on. She remembered the night she swam far out, and recalled the terror that seized her at the fear of being unable to regain the shore. She did not look back now, but went on and on, thinking of the bluegrass meadow that she had traversed when a little child, believing that it had no beginning and no end.

Her arms and legs were growing tired.

She thought of Léonce and the children. They were a part of her life. But they need not have thought that they could possess her, body and soul. How Mademoiselle Reisz would have laughed, perhaps sneered, if she knew! "And you call yourself an artist! What pretensions, Madame! The artist must possess the courageous soul that dares and defies."

Exhaustion was pressing upon and overpowering her.

"Goodbye—because I love you." He did not know; he did not understand. He would never understand. Perhaps Doctor Mandelet would have understood if she had seen him—but it was too late; the shore was far behind her, and her strength was gone.

She looked into the distance, and the old terror flamed up for an instant, then sank again. Edna heard her father's voice and her sister Margaret's. She heard the barking of an old dog that was chained to the sycamore tree. The spurs of the cavalry officer clanged as he walked across the porch. There was the hum of bees, and the musky odor of pinks filled the air.   1899

Tillie Olsen
1913–

A U.S. writer of fiction and essays, TILLIE OLSEN was born in Omaha, Nebraska, to Samuel and Ida Beber Lerner, working-class Jews who had emigrated from Russia. Samuel Lerner became the secretary of the Nebraska Socialist Party, and Olsen and her five siblings were raised with a keen knowledge of labor, immigrant, and human rights issues. During the Depression, Olsen was forced to drop out of high school after the eleventh grade to earn her living. After years of working as a secretary and a manual laborer in California, she became a trade union organizer in Kansas and Minnesota in 1931, joining first the Young People's Socialist League and then the Young Communist League (YCL). In 1933 she moved to San Francisco and began a relationship with Jack Olsen, also a YCL activist, whom she married in 1943; she is the mother of four daughters. During the 1950s Olsen studied creative writing at San Francisco State University and Stanford University, and in 1956 she published her first short story, "Help Her to Believe," which she later entitled "I Stand Here Ironing." Like many works to come, this story focuses on the working-class experience and the power of the mother-daughter bond. Other stories include "Hey Sailor, What Ship?" (1957); "Baptism" (1957), later entitled "O Yes"; and "Requa I" (1970), which was reprinted in *Best American Short Stories of 1971*. Olsen has taught literature and creative writing at many colleges and universities, including Amherst College, Stanford University, the University of Massachusetts, the Massachusetts Institute of Technology, Kenyon College, and the University of California at Los Angeles. In 1983 she was awarded a senior fellowship from the National Endowment for the Humanities, and in 1994 she received the Rea Award for her contributions to the short story as an art form.

Olsen began her only novel, *Yonnondio: From the Thirties* (1974), before she was married, but the difficulties of working full-time and raising four children caused her to leave it unfinished for forty years. The novel chronicles the ways in which the lives of two women, Maizie Holbrook and her mother, are thwarted by poverty, recession, and sexism. The *New York Times Book Review* called *Yonnondio* "a remarkable book": "It is a terrible losing battle, the battle to get out from under that the poor almost never win, and Tillie Olsen portrays it with relentless compassion and with a stark, impressionistic vividness."

Olsen's landmark critical study, *Silences* (1973), examines the letters, diaries, and testimonies of many writers, women in particular, about the circumstances that have obstructed or diminished their creative output. As a writer who did not publish until she was in her forties, and who was once described as "the least prolific" of "major living American writers," Olsen is concerned with the problems women face in carving out creative identities while trying to meet the demands of work and family. Thus she theorizes the issues with which her fiction grapples, concluding that women's voices have been unnecessarily silenced, that "we who write are survivors, 'only's.'" *Silences* also includes the entire text of Rebecca Harding Davis's *Life in the Iron Mills* (1851), which Olsen is responsible for rescuing from obscurity.

Her interest in motherhood as a literary topic is evident in *Mother to Daughter/Daughter to Mother: Mothers on Mothering* (1984), a literary calendar that she edited, and in her collaboration with her daughter, Julie Olsen-Edwards, and Estelle Jussim on a series of photographs with written commentaries, *Mothers and Daughters: That Special Quality—An Exploration in Photographs* (1987). This subject is also a central theme of "Tell Me A Riddle" (1960), which won the O. Henry Prize for the best American short story in 1961. Its elderly protagonist, Eva, who is dying, refuses to play the traditional role of grandmother, preferring to reflect back on her tumultuous youth in silence and solitude; her husband, David, wishes to be with family and cannot comprehend his wife's desire. Only Eva's granddaughter Jeannie can understand her grandmother's ties to an immigrant past and a radical system of belief. Dedicated to Olsen's mother and father and to two women activists of her parents' generation, the story explores the compelling bonds of family, the passion for social justice, and the mysteries of death. The footnotes are those of Deborah Rosenfelt, who edited a recent critical edition of "Tell Me A Riddle."

ᢀ Tell Me a Riddle ᢀ

"These Things Shall Be"[1]

I

For forty-seven years they had been married. How deep back the stubborn, gnarled roots of the quarrel reached, no one could say—but only now, when tending to the needs of the others no longer shackled them together, the roots swelled up visible,

---

1. [Poem by John Addington Symonds, sung in the British labor and socialist movements, and in progressive social and religious movements in the United States.]

split the earth between them, and the tearing shook even to the children, long since grown.

Why now, why now? wailed Hannah.

As if when we grew up weren't enough, said Paul.

Poor Ma. Poor Dad. It hurts so for both of them, said Vivi. They never had very much; at least in old age they should be happy.

Knock their heads together, insisted Sammy; tell 'em: you're too old for this kind of thing; no reason not to get along now.

Lennie wrote to Clara: They've lived over so much together; what could possibly tear them apart?

Something tangible enough.

Arthritic hands, and such work as he got, occasional. Poverty all his life, and there was little breath left for running. He could not, could not turn away from this desire: to have the troubling of responsibility, the fretting with money, over and done with; to be free, to be *care*free where success was not measured by accumulation, and there was use for the vitality still in him.

There was a way. They could sell the house, and with the money join his lodge's Haven, cooperative for the aged. Happy communal life, and was he not already an official; had he not helped organize it, raise funds, served as a trustee?

But she—would not consider it.

"What do we need all this for?" he would ask loudly, for her hearing aid was turned down and the vacuum was shrilling. "Five rooms" (pushing the sofa so she could get into the corner) "furniture" (smoothing down the rug) "floors and surfaces to make work. Tell me, why do we need it?" And he was glad he could ask in a scream.

"Because I'm use't."

"Because you're use't. This is a reason, Mrs. Word Miser? Used to can get unused!"

"Enough unused I have to get used to already. . . . Not enough words?" turning off the vacuum a moment to hear herself answer. "Because soon enough we'll need only a little closet, no windows, no furniture, nothing to make work, but for worms. Because now I want room. . . . Screech and blow like you're doing, you'll need that closet even sooner. . . . Ha, again!" for the vacuum bag wailed, puffed half up, hung stubbornly limp. "This time fix it so it stays; quick before the phone rings and you get too important-busy."

But while he struggled with the motor, it seethed in him. Why fix it? Why have to bother? And if it can't be fixed, have to wring the mind with how to pay the repair? At the Haven they come in with their own machines to clean your room or your cottage; you fish, or play cards, or make jokes in the sun, not with knotty fingers fight to mend vacuums.

Over the dishes, coaxingly: "For once in your life, to be free, to have everything done for you, like a queen."

"I never liked queens."

"No dishes, no garbage, no towel to sop, no worry what to buy, what to eat."

"And what else would I do with my empty hands? Better to eat at my own table when I want, and to cook and eat how I want."

"In the cottages they buy what you ask, and cook it how you like. *You* are the one who always used to say: better mankind born without mouths and stomachs than to always worry for money to buy, to shop, to fix, to cook, to wash, to clean."

"How cleverly you hid that you heard. I said it then because eighteen hours a day I ran. And you never scraped a carrot or knew a dish towel sops. Now—for you and me—who cares? A herring out of a jar is enough. But when *I* want, and nobody to bother." And she turned off her ear button, so she would not have to hear.

But as *he* had no peace, juggling and rejuggling the money to figure: how will I pay for this now?; prying out the storm windows (there they take care of this); jolting in the streetcar on errands (there I would not have to ride to take care of this or that); fending the patronizing relatives just back from Florida (at the Haven it matters what one is, not what one can afford), he gave *her* no peace.

"Look! In their bulletin. A reading circle. Twice a week it meets."

"Haumm," her answer of not listening.

"A reading circle, Chekhov they read that you like, and Peretz.[2]" Cultured people at the Haven that you would enjoy."

"Enjoy!" She tasted the word. "Now, when it pleases you, you find a reading circle for me. And forty years ago when the children were morsels and there was a Circle, did you stay home with them once so I could go? Even once? You trained me well. I do not need others to enjoy. Others!" Her voice trembled. "Because *you* want to be there with others. Already it makes me sick to think of you always around others. Clown, grimacer, floormat, yesman, entertainer, whatever they want of you."

And now it was he who turned the television loud so he need not hear.

Old scar tissue ruptured and the wounds festered anew. Chekhov indeed. She thought without softness of that young wife, who in the deep night hours while she nursed the current baby, and perhaps held another in her lap, would try to stay awake for the only time there was to read. She would feel again the weather of the outside on his cheek when, coming late from a meeting, he would find her so, and stimulated and ardent, sniffing her skin, coax: "I'll put the baby to bed, and you—put the book away, don't read, don't read."

That had the been the most beguiling of all the "don't read, put your book away" her life had been. Chekhov indeed!

"Money?" She shrugged him off. "Could we get poorer than once we were? And in America, who starves?"

But as still he pressed.

"Let me alone about money. Was there ever enough? Seven little ones—for every penny I had to ask—and sometimes, remember, there was nothing. But always *I* had to manage. Now *you* manage. Rub your nose in it good."

But from those years she had had to manage, old humiliations and terrors rose up, lived again, and forced her to relive them. The children's needings; that grocer's face or his merchant's wife she had had to beg credit from when credit was a disgrace; the scenery of the long blocks walked around when she could not pay; school coming, and the desperate going over the old to see what could yet be remade; the soups of meat bones begged "for-the-dog" one winter. . . .

Enough. Now they had no children. Let *him* wrack his head for how they would live. She would not exchange her solitude for anything. *Never again to be forced to move to the rhythms of others.*

For in this solitude she had won to a reconciled peace.

Tranquillity from having the empty house no longer an enemy, for it stayed clean—not as in the days when it was her family, the life in it, that had seemed the

---

2. [Isaac Loeb Peretz, turn-of-the-century Russian writer of fiction in Yiddish.]

enemy: tracking, smudging, littering, dirtying, engaging her in endless defeating battle—and on whom her endless defeat had been spewed.

The few old books, memorized from rereading; the pictures to ponder (the magnifying glass superimposed on her heavy eyeglasses). Or if she wishes, when he is gone, the phonograph, that if she turns up very loud and strains, she can hear: the ordered sounds and the struggling.

Out in the garden, growing things to nurture. Birds can be kept out of the pear tree, and when the pears are heavy and ripe, the old fury of work, for all must be canned, nothing wasted.

And her once social duty (for she will not go to luncheons or meetings) the boxes of old clothes left with her, as with a life-practiced eye for finding what is still wearable within the worn (again the magnifying glass superimposed on the heavy glasses) she scans and sorts—this for rag or rummage, that for mending and cleaning, and this for sending away.

Being able at last to live within, and not move to the rhythms of others, as life had forced her to: denying; removing; isolating; taking the children one by one; then deafening, half-blinding—and at last, presenting her solitude.

And in it she had won to a reconciled peace.

Now he was violating it with his constant campaigning: *Sell the house and move to the Haven.* (You sit, you sit—there too you could sit like a stone.) He was making of her a battleground where old grievances tore. (Turn on your ear button—I am talking.) And stubbornly she resisted—so that from wheedling, reasoning, manipulation, it was bitterness he now started with.

And it came to where every happening lashed up a quarrel.

"I will sell the house anyway," he flung at her one night. "I am putting it up for sale. There will be a way to make you sign."

The television blared, as always it did on the evenings he stayed home, and as always it reached her only as noise. She did not know if the tumult was in her or outside. Snap! she turned the sound off. "Shadows," she whispered to him, pointing to the screen, "look, it is only shadows." And in a scream: "Did you say that you will sell the house? Look at me, not at that. I am no shadow. You cannot sell without me."

"Leave on the television. I am watching."

"Like Paulie, like Jenny, a four-year-old. Staring at shadows. *You cannot sell the house.*"

"I will. We are going to the Haven. There you would not hear the television when you do not want it. I could sit in the social room and watch. You could lock yourself up to smell your unpleasantness in a room by yourself—for who would want to come near you?"

"No, no selling." A whisper now.

"The television is shadows. Mrs. Enlightened! Mrs. Cultured! A world comes into your house—and it is shadows. People you would never meet in a thousand lifetimes. Wonders. When you were four years old, yes, like Paulie, like Jenny, did you know of Indian dances, alligators, how they use bamboo in Malaya? No, you scratched in your dirt with the chickens and thought Olshana[3] was the world. Yes, Mrs. Unpleasant, I will sell the house, for there better can we be rid of each other than here."

---

3. [Olsen's invented name for a typical village of tsarist Russia.]

She did not know if the tumult was outside, or in her. Always a ravening inside, a pull to the bed, to lie down, to succumb.

"Have you thought maybe Ma should let a doctor have a look at her?" asked their son Paul after Sunday dinner, regarding his mother crumpled on the couch, instead of, as was her custom, busying herself in Nancy's kitchen.

"Why not the president too?"

"Seriously, Dad. This is the third Sunday she's lain down like that after dinner. Is she that way at home?"

"A regular love affair with the bed. Every time I start to talk to her."

Good protective reaction, observed Nancy to herself. The workings of hos-til-ity.

"Nancy could take her. I just don't like how she looks. Let's have Nancy arrange an appointment."

"You think she'll go?" regarding his wife gloomily. "All right, we have to have doctor bills, we have to have doctor bills." Loudly: "Something hurts you?"

She startled, looking at his lips. He repeated: "Mrs. Take It Easy, something hurts?"

"Nothing. . . . Only you."

"A woman of honey. That's why you're lying down."

"Soon I'll get up to do the dishes, Nancy."

"Leave them, Mother, I like it better this way."

"Mrs. Take It Easy, Paul says you should start ballet. You should go to see a doctor and ask: how soon can you start ballet?"

"A doctor?" she begged. "Ballet?"

"We were talking, Ma," explained Paul, "you don't seem any too well. It would be a good idea for you to see a doctor for a checkup."

"I get up now to do the kitchen. Doctors are bills and foolishness, my son. I need no doctors."

"At the Haven," he could not resist pointing out, "a doctor is *not* bills. He lives beside you. You start to sneeze, he is there before you open up a Kleenex. You can be sick there for free, all you want."

"Diarrhea of the mouth, is there a doctor to make you dumb?"

"Ma. Promise me you'll go. Nancy will arrange it."

"It's all a piece when you think of it," said Nancy, "the way she attacks my kitchen, scrubbing under every cup hook, doing the inside of the oven so I can't enjoy Sunday dinner, knowing that half-blind or not, she's going to find every speck of dirt. . . . "

"Don't, Nancy, I've told you—it's the only way she knows to be useful. What did the *doctor* say?"

"A real fatherly lecture. Sixty-nine is young these days. Go out, enjoy life, find interests. Get a new hearing aid, this one is antiquated. Old age is sickness only if one makes it so. Geriatrics, Inc."

"So there was nothing physical."

"Of course there was. How can you live to yourself like she does without there being? Evidence of a kidney disorder, and her blood count is low. He gave her a diet, and she's to come back for follow-up and lab work. . . . But he was clear enough: Number One prescription—start living like a human being. . . . When I think of your dad, who could really play the invalid with that arthritis of his, as active as a teenager, and twice as much fun. . . . "

"You didn't tell me the doctor says your sickness is in you, how you live." He pushed his advantage. "Life and enjoyments you need better than medicine. And this diet, how can you keep it? To weigh each morsel and scrape away each bit of fat, to make this soup, that pudding. There, at the Haven, they have a dietitian, they would do it for you."

She is silent.

"You would feel better there, I know it." he says gently. "There there is life and enjoyments all around."

"What is the matter, Mr. Importantbusy, you have no card game or meeting you can go to?"—turning her face to the pillow.

For a while he cut his meetings and going out, fussed over her diet, tried to wheedle her into leaving the house, brought in visitors:

"I should come to a fashion tea. I should sit and look at pretty babies in clothes I cannot buy. This is pleasure?"

"Always you are better than everyone else. The doctor said you should go out. Mrs. Brem comes to you with goodness and you turn her away."

"Because *you* asked her to, she asked me."

"They won't come back. People you need, the doctor said. Your own cousins I asked; they were willing to come and make peace as if nothing had happened. . . . "

"No more crushers of people, pushers, hypocrites, around me. No more in *my* house. You go to them if you like."

"Kind he is to visit. And you, like ice."

"A babbler. All my life around babblers. Enough!"

"She's even worse, Dad? Then let her stew a while," advised Nancy. "You can't let it destroy you; it's a psychological thing, maybe too far gone for any of us to help."

So he let her stew. More and more she lay silent in bed, and sometimes did not even get up to make the meals. No longer was the tongue-lashing inevitable if he left the coffee cup where it did not belong, or forgot to take out the garbage or mislaid the broom. The birds grew bold that summer and for once pocked the pears, undisturbed.

A bellyful of bitterness and every day the same quarrel in a new way and a different old grievance the quarrel forced her to enter and relive. And the new torment: I am not really sick, the doctor said it, then why do I feel so sick?

One night she asked him: "You have a meeting tonight? Do not go. Stay . . . with me."

He had planned to watch "This Is Your Life," but half sick himself from the heavy heat, and sickening therefore the more after the brooks and woods of the Haven, with satisfaction he grated:

"Hah, Mrs. Live Alone and Like It wants company all of a sudden. It doesn't seem so good the time of solitary when she was a girl exile in Siberia. 'Do not go. Stay with me.' A new song for Mrs. Free As A Bird. Yes, I am going out, and while I am gone chew this aloneness good, and think how you keep us both from where if you want people, you do not need to be alone."

"Go, go. All your life you have gone without me."

After him she sobbed curses he had not heard in years, old-country curses from their childhood: Grow, oh shall you grow like an onion, with your head in the ground. Like the hide of a drum shall you be, beaten in life, beaten in death. Oh shall you be like a chandelier, to hang, and to burn. . . .

She was not in their bed when he came back. She lay on the cot on the sun porch. All week she did not speak or come near him; nor did he try to make peace or care for her.

He slept badly, so used to her next to him. After all the years, old harmonies and dependencies deep in their bodies; she curled to him, or he coiled to her, each warmed, warming, turning as the other turned, the nights a long embrace.

It was not the empty bed or the storm that woke him, but a faint singing. *She* was singing. Shaking off the drops of rain, the lightning riving her lifted face, he saw her so; the cot covers on the floor.

"This is a private concert?" he asked. "Come in, you are wet."

"I can breathe now," she answered; "my lungs are rich." Though indeed the sound was hardly a breath.

"Come in, come in." Loosing the bamboo shades. "Look how wet you are." Half helping, half carrying her, still faint-breathing her song.

A Russian love song of fifty years ago.

He had found a buyer, but before he told her, he called together those children who were close enough to come. Paul, of course, Sammy from New Jersey, Hannah from Connecticut, Vivi from Ohio.

With a kindling of energy for her beloved visitors, she arrayed the house, cooked and baked. She was not prepared for the solemn after-dinner conclave, they too probing in and tearing. Her frightened eyes watched from mouth to mouth as each spoke.

His stories were eloquent and funny of her refusal to go back to the doctor; of the scorned invitations: of her stubborn silence or the bile "like a Niagara"; of her contrariness: "If I clean it's no good how I cleaned; if I don't clean, I'm still a master who thinks he has a slave."

(Vinegar he poured on me all his life; I am well marinated; how can I be honey now?)

Deftly he marched in the rightness for moving to the Haven; their money from social security free for visiting the children, not sucked into daily needs and into the house; the activities in the Haven for him; but mostly the Haven for *her;* her health, her need of care, distraction, amusement, friends who shared her interests.

"This does offer an outlet for Dad," said Paul; "he's always been an active person. And economic peace of mind isn't to be sneezed at, either. I could use a little of that myself."

But when they asked: "And you, Ma, how do you feel about it?" could only whisper: "For him it is good. It is not for me. I can no longer live between people."

"You lived all your life *for* people," Vivi cried.

"Not with." Suffering doubly for the unhappiness on her children's faces.

"You have to find some compromise," Sammy insisted. "Maybe sell the house and buy a trailer. After forty-seven years there's surely some way you can find to live in peace."

"There is no help, my children. Different things we need."

"Then live alone!" He could control himself no longer. "I have a buyer for the house. Half the money for you, half for me. Either alone or with me to the Haven. You think I can live any longer as we are doing now?"

"Ma doesn't have to make a decision this minute, however you feel, Dad," Paul said quickly, "and you wouldn't want her to. Let's let it lay a few months, and then talk some more."

"I think I can work it out to take Mother home with me for a while," Hannah said. "You both look terrible, but especially you, Mother. I'm going to ask Phil to have a look at you."

"Sure," cracked Sammy. "What's the use of a doctor husband if you can't get free service out of him once in a while for your family? And absence might make the heart . . . you know."

"There was something after all," Paul told Nancy in a colorless voice. "That was Hannah's Phil calling. Her gall bladder. . . . Surgery."

"Her *gall* bladder. If that isn't classic. 'Bitter as gall'—talk of psychosom———"

He stepped closer, put his hand over her mouth, and said in the same colorless, plodding voice. "We have to get Dad. They operated at once. The cancer was everywhere, surrounding the liver, everywhere. They did what they could . . . at best she has a year. Dad . . . we have to tell him."

II

Honest in his weakness when they told him, and that she was not to know. "I'm not an actor. She'll know right away by how I am. Oh that poor woman. I am old too, it will break me into pieces. Oh that poor woman. She will spit on me; 'So my sickness was how I live.' Oh Paulie, how she will be, that poor woman. Only she should not suffer. . . . I can't stand sickness, Paulie. I can't go with you."

But went. And play-acted.

"A grand opening and you did not even wait for me. . . . A good thing Hannah took you with her."

"Fashion teas I needed. They cut out what tore in me; just in my throat something hurts yet. . . . Look! so many flowers, like a funeral. Vivi called, did Hannah tell you? And Lennie from San Francisco, and Clara; and Sammy is coming." Her gnome's face pressed happily into the flowers.

> It is impossible to predict these cases, but once over the immediate effects of the operation, she should have several months of comparative well-being.
>
> *The money, where will come the money?*
>
> Travel with her, Dad. Don't take her home to the old associations. The other children will want to see her.
>
> *The money, where will I wring the money?*
>
> Whatever happens, she is not to know. No, you can't ask her to sign papers to sell the house; nothing to upset her. Borrow instead, then after. . . .
>
> *I had wanted to leave you each a few dollars to make life easier, as other fathers do. There will be nothing left now. (Failure! you and your "business is exploitation." Why didn't you make it when it could be made?—Is that what you're thinking of me, Sammy?)*
>
> Sure she's unreasonable, Dad—but you have to stay with her; if there's to be any happiness in what's left of her life, it depends on you.
>
> *Prop me up, children, think of me, too. Shuffled, chained with her, bitter woman. No Haven, and the little money going. . . . How happy she looks, poor creature.*

The look of excitement. The straining to hear everything (the new hearing aid turned full). Why are you so happy, dying woman?

How the petals are, fold on fold, and the gladioli color. The autumn air.

Stranger grandsons, tall above the little gnome grandmother, the little spry grandfather. Paul in a frenzy of picture-taking before going.

She, wandering the great house. Feeling the books; laughing at the maple shoemaker's bench of a hundred years ago used as a table. The ear turned to music.

"Let us go home. See how good I walk now." "One step from the hospital," he answers, "and she wants to fly. Wait till Doctor Phil says."

"Look—the birds too are flying home. Very good Phil is and will not show it, but he is sick of sickness by the time he comes home."

"Mrs. Telepathy, to read minds," he answers; "read mine what it says: when the trunks of medicines become a suitcase, then we will go."

The grandboys, they do not know what to say to us. . . . Hannah, she runs around here, there, when is there time for herself?

Let us go home. Let us go home.

Musing; gentleness—*but for the incidents of the rabbi in the hospital, and of the candles of benediction.*

Of the rabbi in the hospital:

> Now tell me what happened, Mother.
>
> From the sleep I awoke, Hannah's Phil, and he stands there like a devil in a dream and calls me by name. I cannot hear. I think he prays. Go away, please, I tell him, I am not a believer. Still he stands, while my heart knocks with fright.
>
> You scared *him*, Mother. He thought you were delirious.
>
> Who sent him? Why did he come to *me*?
>
> It is a custom. The men of God come to visit those of their religion they might help. The hospital makes up the list for them—race, religion,—and you are on the Jewish list.
>
> Not for rabbis. At once go and make them change. Tell them to write: Race, human; Religion, none.

And of the candles of benediction:

> Look how you have upset yourself, Mrs. Excited Over Nothing. Pleasant memories you should leave.
>
> Go in, go back to Hannah and the lights. Two weeks I saw candles and said nothing. But she asked me.
>
> So what was so terrible? She forgets you never did, she asks you to light the Friday candles and say the benediction like Phil's mother when she visits. If the candles give her pleasure, why shouldn't she have the pleasure?
>
> Not for pleasure she does it. For emptiness. Because his family does. Because all around her do.
>
> That is not a good reason too? But you did not hear her. For heritage, she told you. For the boys, from the past they should have tradition.
>
> Superstition! From our ancestors, savages, afraid of the dark, of themselves: mumbo words and magic lights to scare away ghosts.
>
> She told you: How it started does not take away the goodness. For centuries, peace in the house it means.
>
> Swindler! does she look back on the dark centuries? Candles bought instead of bread and stuck into a potato for a candlestick? Religion that stifled and said: In Paradise, woman, you will be the footstool of your husband, and in life—poor chosen Jew—ground under, despised, trembling in cellars. And cremated. And cremated.[4]
>
> This is religion's fault? You think you are still an orator of the 1905 revolution?[5] Where are the pills for quieting? Which are they?
>
> Heritage. How have we come from our savage past, how no longer to be savages—this to teach. To look back and learn what humanizes—this to teach. To smash all ghettos

---

4. [Alludes to Yiddish folk saying, the basis of Peretz's story, "A Good Marriage," and to the cremations in Nazi concentration camps.]

5. [Broad uprising against the regime of Tsar Nicholas II that temporarily initiated a series of democratizing concessions.]

that divide us—not to go back, not to go back—this to teach. Learned books in the house, will humankind live or die, and she gives to her boys—superstition.

Hannah that is so good to you. Take your pill, Mrs. Excited For Nothing, swallow. Heritage! But when did I have time to teach? Of Hannah I asked only hands to help. Swallow.

Otherwise—musing; gentleness.

Not to travel. To go home.

The children want to see you. We have to show them you are as thorny a flower as ever.

Not to travel.

Vivi wants you should see her new baby. She sent the tickets—airplane tickets—a Mrs. Roosevelt she wants to make of you. To Vivi's we have to go.

A new baby. How many warm, seductive babies. She holds him stiffly, *away* from her, so that he wails. And a long shudder begins, and the sweat beads on her forehead.

"Hush, shush," croons the grandfather, lifting him back. "You should forgive your grandmamma, little prince, she has never held a baby before, only seen them in glass cases. Hush, shush."

"You're tired, Ma," says Vivi. "The travel and the noisy dinner. I'll take you to lie down."

(*A long travel from, to, what the feel of a baby evokes.*)

In the airplane, cunningly designed to encase from motion (no wind, no feel of flight), she had sat severely and still, her face turned to the sky through which they cleaved and left no scar.

So this was how it looked, the determining, the crucial sky, and this was how man moved through it, remote above the dwindled earth, the concealed human life. Vulnerable life, that could scar.

There was a steerage ship of memory that shook across a great, circular sea; clustered, ill human beings; and through the thick-stained air, tiny fretting waters in a window round like the airplane's—sun round, moon round. (The round thatched roofs of Olshana.) Eye round—like the smaller window that framed distance the solitary year of exile when only her eyes could travel, and no voice spoke. And the polar winds hurled themselves across snows trackless and endless and white—like the clouds which had closed together below and hidden the earth.

Now they put a baby in her lap. Do not ask me, she would have liked to beg. Enough the worn face of Vivi, the remembered grandchildren. I cannot, cannot. . . .

Cannot what? Unnatural grandmother, not able to make herself embrace a baby.

She lay there in the bed of the two little girls, her new hearing aid turned full, listening to the sound of the children going to sleep, the baby's fretful crying and hushing, the clatter of dishes being washed and put away. They thought she slept. Still she rode on.

It was not that she had not loved her babies, her children. The love—the passion of tending—had risen with the need like a torrent; and like a torrent drowned and immolated all else. But when the need was done—oh the power that was lost in the painful damming back and drying up of what still surged, but had nowhere to go. Only the thin pulsing left that could not quiet, suffering over lives one felt, but could no longer hold nor help.

On that torrent she had borne them to their own lives, and the riverbed was desert long years now. Not there would she dwell, a memoried wraith. Surely that was not all, surely there was more. Still the springs, the springs were in her seeking. Somewhere an older power that beat for life. Somewhere coherence, transport, meaning. If they would but leave her in the air now stilled of clamor, in the reconciled solitude, to journey on.

And they put a baby in her lap. Immediacy to embrace, and the breath of *that* past: warm flesh like this that had claims and nuzzled away all else and with lovely mouths devoured; hot-living like an animal—intensely and now; the turning maze; the long drunkenness; the drowning into needing and being needed. Severely she looked back—and the shudder seized her again, and the sweat. Not that way. Not there, not now could she, not yet. . . .

And all that visit, she could not touch the baby.

"Daddy, is it the . . . sickness she's like that?" asked Vivi. "I was so glad to be having the baby—for her. I told Tim, it'll give her more happiness than anything, being around a baby again. And she hasn't played with him once."

He was not listening, "Aahh little seed of life, little charmer," he crooned, "Hollywood should see you. A heart of ice you would melt. Kick, kick. The future you'll have for a ball. In 2050 still kick. Kick for your grandaddy then."

Attentive with the older children; sat through their performances (command performance; we command you to be the audience); helped Ann sort autumn leaves to find the best for a school program; listened gravely to Richard tell about his rock collection, while her lips mutely formed the words to remember: *igneous, sedimentary, metamorphic;* looked for missing socks, books, and bus tickets; watched the children whoop after their grandfather who knew how to tickle, chuck, lift, toss, do tricks, tell secrets, make jokes, match riddle for riddle. (Tell me a riddle, Grammy. I know no riddles, child.) Scrubbed sills and woodwork and furniture in every room; folded the laundry; straightened drawers; emptied the heaped baskets waiting for ironing (while he or Vivi or Tim nagged: You're supposed to rest here, you've been sick) but to none tended or gave food—and could not touch the baby.

After a week she said: "Let us go home. Today call about the tickets."

"You have important business, Mrs. Inahurry? The President waits to consult with you?" He shouted, for the fear of the future raced in him. "The clothes are still warm from the suitcase, your children cannot show enough how glad they are to see you, and you want home. There is plenty of time for home. We cannot be with the children at home."

"Blind to around you as always: the little ones sleep four in a room because we take their bed. We are two more people in a house with a new baby, and no help."

"Vivi is happy so. The children should have their grandparents a while, she told to me. I should have my mommy and daddy. . . ."

"Babbler and blind. Do you look at her so tired? How she starts to talk and she cries? I am not strong enough yet to help. Let us go home."

(To reconciled solitude.)

For it seemed to her the crowded noisy house was listening to her, listening for her. She could feel it like a great ear pressed under her heart. And everything knocked: quick constant raps: let me in, let me in.

How was is that soft reaching tendrils also became blows that knocked?

C'mon Grandma, I want to show you. . . .

Tell me a riddle, Grandma. (*I know no riddles.*)

Look Grammy, he's so dumb he can't even find his hands. (Dody and the baby on a blanket over the fermenting autumn mould.)

I made them—for you. (Ann) (Flat paper dolls with aprons that lifted on scalloped skirts that lifted on flowered pants; hair of yarn and great ringed questioning eyes.)

Watch me, Grandma. (Richard snaking up the tree, hanging exultant, free, with one hand at the top. Below Dody hunching over in pretend-cooking.)

(*Climb too, Dody, climb and look.*)

Be my nap bed, Grammy. (The "No!" too late.)

Morty's abandoned heaviness, while his fingers ladder up and down her hearing-aid cord to his drowsy chant, eentsiebeentsiepider. (*Children trust.*)

It's to start off your own rock collection, Grandma.

That's a trilobite fossil, 200 million years old (millions of years on a boy's mouth) and that one's obsidian, black glass.

Knocked and knocked.

Mother, I *told* you the teacher said we had to bring it back all filled out this morning. Didn't you even ask Daddy? Then tell *me* which plan and I'll check it: evacuate or stay in the city or wait for you to come and take me away, (Seeing the look of straining to hear.) It's for Disaster, Grandma. (*Children trust.*)

Vivi in the maze of the long, the lovely drunkenness. The old old noises: baby sounds; screaming of a mother flayed to exasperation; children quarreling; children playing; singing; laughter.

And Vivi's tears and memories, spilling so fast, half the words not understood.

She had started remembering out loud deliberately, so her mother would know the past was cherished, still lived in her.

Nursing the baby: My friends marvel, and I tell them, oh it's easy to be such a cow. I remember how beautiful my mother seemed nursing my brother, and the milk just flows. . . . Was that Davy? It must have been Davy. . . .

Lowering a hem: How did you ever . . . when I think how you made everything we wore . . . Tim, just think, seven kids and Mommy sewed everything . . . do I remember you sang while you sewed? That white dress with the red apples on the skirt you fixed over for me, was it Hannah's or Clara's before it was mine?

Washing sweaters: Ma, I'll never forget, one of those days so nice you washed clothes outside: one of the first spring days it must have been. The bubbles just danced while you scrubbed, and we chased after, and you stopped to show us how to blow our own bubbles with green onion stalks . . . you always. . . .

"Strong onion, to still make you cry after so many years," her father said, to turn the tears into laughter.

While Richard bent over his homework: Where is it now, do we still have it, the Book of the Martyrs? It always seemed so, well—exalted, when you'd put it on the round table and we'd all look at it together; there was even a halo from the lamp. The lamp with the beaded fringe you could move up and down; they're in style again, pulley lamps like that, but without the fringe. You know the book I'm talking about, Daddy, the book of Martyrs, the first picture was a bust of Spartacus . . . Socrates? I wish there was something like that for the children, Mommy, to give them what you. . . . (And the tears splashed again.)

(What I intended and did not? Stop it, daughter, stop it, leave that time. And he, the hypocrite, sitting there with tears in his eyes—it was nothing to you then, nothing.)

. . . The time you came to school and I almost died of shame because of your accent and because I knew you knew I was ashamed; how could I? . . . Sammy's harmonica and you danced to it once, yes you did, you and Davy squealing in your arms. . . . That time you bundled us up and walked us down to the railway station to stay the night 'cause it was heated and we didn't have any coal, that winter of the strike, you didn't think I remembered that, did you, Mommy? . . . How you'd call us out to see the sunsets. . . .

Day after day, the spilling memories. Worse now, questions, too. Even the grandchildren: Grandma, in the olden days, when you were little. . . .

It was the afternoons that saved.

While they thought she napped, she would leave the mosaic on the wall (of children's drawings, maps, calendars, pictures, Ann's cardboard dolls with their great ringed questioning eyes) and hunch in the girls' closet on the low shelf where the shoes stood, and the girls' dresses covered.

For that while she would painfully sheathe against the listening house, the tendrils and noises that knocked, and Vivi's spilling memories. Sometimes it helped to braid and unbraid the sashes that dangled, or to trace the pattern on the hoop slips.

Today she had jacks and children under jet trails to forget. Last night, Ann and Dody silhouetted in the window against a sunset of flaming manmade clouds of jet trail, their jack ball accenting the peaceful noise of dinner being made. Had she told them, yes she had told them of how they played jacks in her village though there was no ball, no jacks. Six stones, round and flat, toss them out, the seventh on the back of the hand, toss, catch and swoop up as many as possible, toss again. . . .

Of stones (repeating Richard) there are three kinds: earth's fire jetting; rock of layered centuries; crucibled new out of the old (*igneous, sedimentary, metamorphic*). But there was that other—frozen to black glass, never to transform or hold the fossil memory . . . (let not my seed fall on stone). There was an ancient man who fought to heights a great rock that crashed back down eternally[6]—eternal labor, freedom, labor . . . (stone will perish, but the word remain). And you, David, who with a stone slew, screaming: Lord, take my heart of stone and give me flesh.[7]

Who was screaming? Why was she back in the common room of the prison, the sun motes dancing in the shafts of light, and the informer being brought in, a prisoner now, like themselves. And Lisa leaping, yes, Lisa, the gentle and tender, biting at the betrayer's jugular. Screaming and screaming.

No, it is the children screaming. Another of Paul and Sammy's terrible fights?

In Vivi's house. Severely: You are in Vivi's house.

Blows, screams, a call: "Grandma!" For her? Oh please not for her. Hide, hunch behind the dresses deeper. But a trembling little body hurls itself beside her—surprised, smothered laughter, arms surround her neck, tears rub dry on her cheek, and words too soft to understand whisper into her ear (Is this where you hide too, Grammy? It's my secret place, we have a secret now).

And the sweat beads, and the long shudder seizes.

6. [Alludes to the myth of Sisyphus, who was punished eternally in Tartarus for reporting the whereabouts of Zeus, king of the gods, to the father of the maiden Zeus had seized.]

7. [Alludes to the biblical story of David's triumph over the giant Philistine, Goliath; Samuel 1:17. The quotation, which Olsen heard in a black church, paraphrases Ezekiel 11:19: "I shall remove the heart of stone from their bodies and give them a heart of flesh."]

It seemed the great ear pressed inside now, and the knocking. "We have to go home," she told him, "I grow ill here."

"It's your own fault, Mrs. Bodybusy, you do not rest, you do too much." He raged, but the fear was in his eyes. "It was a serious operation, they told you to take care. . . . All right, we will go to where you can rest."

But where? Not home to death, not yet. He had thought to Lennie's, to Clara's; beautiful visits with each of the children. She would have to rest first, be stronger. If they could but go to Florida—it glittered before him, the never-realized promise of Florida. California: of course. (The money, the money, dwindling!) Los Angeles first for sun and rest, then Lennie's in San Francisco.

He told her the next day. "You saw what Nancy wrote: snow and wind back home, a terrible winter. And look at you—all bones and a swollen belly. I called Phil: he said: 'A prescription, Los Angeles sun and rest.'"

She watched the words on his lips. "You have sold the house," she cried, "that is why we do not go home. That is why you talk no more of the Haven, why there is money for travel. After the children you will drag me to the Haven."

"The Haven! Who thinks of the Haven any more? Tell her, Vivi, tell Mrs. Suspicious: a prescription, sun and rest, to make you healthy. . . . And how could I sell the house without *you*?"

At the place of farewells and greetings, of winds of coming and winds of going, they say their good-byes.

They look back at her with the eyes of others before them: Richard with her own blue blaze; Ann with the nordic eyes of Tim; Morty's dreaming brown of a great-grandmother he will never know; Dody with the laughing eyes of him who had been her springtide love (who stands beside her now); Vivi's, all tears.

The baby's eyes are closed in sleep.

Goodbye, my children.

III

It is to the back of the great city he brought her, to the dwelling places of the cast-off old. Bounded by two lines of amusement piers to the north and to the south, and between a long straight paving rimmed with black benches facing the sand—sands so wide the ocean is only a far fluting.

In the brief vacation season, some of the boarded stores fronting the sands open, and families, young people and children, may be seen. A little tasselled tram shuttles between the piers, and the lights of roller coasters prink and tweak over those who come to have sensation made in them.

The rest of the year it is abandoned to the old, all else boarded up and still; seemingly empty, except the occasional days and hours when the sun, like a tide, sucks them out of the low rooming houses, casts them onto the benches and sandy rim of the walk—and sweeps them into decaying enclosures once again.

A few newer apartments glint among the low bleached squares. It is in one of these Lennie's Jeannie has arranged their rooms. "Only a few miles north and south people pay hundreds of dollars a month for just this gorgeous air, Grandaddy, just this ocean closeness."

She had been ill on the plane, lay ill for days in the unfamiliar room. Several times the doctor came by—left medicine she would not take. Several times Jeannie drove in the twenty miles from work, still in her Visiting Nurse uniform, the lightness and brightness of her like a healing.

"Who can believe it is winter?" he asked one morning. "Beautiful is outside like an ad. Come, Mrs. Invalid, come to taste it. You are well enough to sit in here, you are well enough to sit outside. The doctor said it too."

But the benches were encrusted with people, and the sands at the sidewalk's edge. Besides, she had seen the far ruffle of the sea: "there take me," and though she leaned against him, it was she who led.

Plodding and plodding, sitting often to rest, he grumbling. Patting the sand so warm. Once she scooped up a handful, cradling it close to her better eye; peered, and flung it back. And as they came almost to the brink and she could see the glistening wet, she sat down, pulled off her shoes and stockings, left him and began to run. "You'll catch cold," he screamed, but the sand in his shoes weighed him down—he who had always been the agile one—and already the white spray creamed her feet.

He pulled her back, took a handkerchief to wipe off the wet and the sand. "Oh no," she said, "the sun will dry," seized the square and smoothed it flat, dropped on it a mound of sand, knotted the kerchief corners and tied it to a bag—"to look at with the strong glass" (for the first time in years explaining an action of hers)—and lay down with the little bag against her cheek, looking toward the shore that nurtured life as it first crawled toward consciousness the millions of years ago.

He took her one Sunday in the evil-smelling bus, past flat miles of blister houses, to the home of relatives. Oh what is this? she cried as the light began to smoke and the houses to dim and recede. Smog, he said, everyone knows but you. . . . Outside he kept his arms about her, but she walked with hands pushing the heavy air as if to open it, whispered: Who has done this? sat down suddenly to vomit at the curb and for a long while refused to rise.

One's age as seen on the altered face of those known in youth. Is this they he has come to visit? This Max and Rose, smooth and pleasant, introducing them to polite children, disinterested grandchildren, "the whole family, once a month on Sundays. And why not? We have the room, the help, the food."

Talk of cars, of houses, of success: this son that, that daughter this. And *your* children? Hastily skimped over, the intermarriages, the obscure work—"my doctor son-in-law, Phil"—all he has to offer. She silent in a corner. (Car-sick like a baby, he explains.) Years since he has taken her to visit anyone but the children, and old apprehensions prickle: "No incidents," he silently begs, "no incidents." He itched to tell them. "A very sick woman," significantly, indicating her with his eyes, "a very sick woman." Their restricted faces did not react. "Have you thought maybe she'd do better at Palm Springs?" Rose asked. "Or at least a nicer section of the beach, nicer people, a pool." Not to have to say "money" he said instead: "would she have sand to look at through a magnifying glass?" and went on, detail after detail, the old habit betraying of parading the queerness of her for laughter.

After dinner—the other into the living room in men- or women-clusters, or into the den to watch TV—the four of them alone. She sat close to him, and did not speak. Jokes, stories, people they had known, beginning of reminiscence, Russia fifty-sixty years ago. Strange words across the Duncan Phyfe table: *hunger; secret meetings; human rights; spies; betrayals; prison; escape*—interrupted by one of the grandchildren: "Commercial's on; any Coke left? Gee, you're missing a real hairraiser." And then a granddaughter (Max proudly: "look at her, an American queen") drove them home on her way back to U. C. L. A. No incident—except that there had been no incidents.

The first few mornings she had taken with her the magnifying glass, but he would sit only on the benches, so she rested at the foot, where slatted bench shadows fell, and unless she turned her hearing aid down, other voices invaded.

Now on the days when the sun shone and she felt well enough, he took her on the tram to where the benches ranged in oblongs, some with tables for checkers or cards. Again the blanket on the sand in the striped shadows, but she no longer brought the magnifying glass. He played cards, and she lay in the sun and looked towards the waters; or they walked—two blocks down to the scaling hotel, two blocks back—past chili-hamburger stands, open-doored bars, Next-to-New and perpetual rummage sale stores.

Once, out of the aimless walkers, slow and shuffling like themselves, someone ran unevenly towards them, embraced, kissed, wept: "Dear friends, old friends." A friend of *hers*, not his: Mrs. Mays who had lived next door to them in Denver when the children were small.

Thirty years are compressed into a dozen sentences; and the present, not even in three. All is told: the children scattered; the husband dead; she lives in a room two blocks up from the sing hall—and points to the domed auditorium jutting before the pier. The leg? phlebitis; the heavy breathing? that, one does not ask. She, too, comes to the benches each day to sit. And tomorrow, tomorrow, are they going to the community sing? Of course he would have heard of it, everybody goes—the big goings they wait for all week. They have never been? She will come to them for dinner tomorrow and they will all go together.

So it is that she sits in the wind of the singing, among the thousand various faces of age.

She had turned off her hearing aid at once they came into the auditorium—as she would have wished to turn off sight.

One by one they streamed by and imprinted on her—and though the savage zest of their singing came voicelessly soft and distant, the faces still roared—the faces densened the air—chorded into

children-chants, mother-croons, singing of the chained love serenades, Beethoven storms, mad Lucia's scream drunken joy-songs, keens for the dead, work-singing

> *while from floor to balcony to dome a bare-footed sore-covered little girl threaded the sound-thronged tumult, danced her ecstasy of grimace to flutes that scratched at a cross-roads village wedding*

Yes, faces became sound, and the sound became faces; and faces and sound became weight—pushed, pressed

"Air"—her hands claw his.

"Whenever I enjoy myself. . . ." Then he saw the gray sweat on her face. "Here. Up. Help me, Mrs. Mays," and they support her out to where she can gulp the air in sob after sob.

"A doctor, we should get for her a doctor."

"Tch, it's nothing," says Ellen Mays, "I get it all the time. You've missed the tram; come to my place. Fix your hearing aid, honey . . . close . . . tea. My view. See, she *wants* to come. Steady now, that's how." Adding mysteriously: "Remember your advice, easy to keep your head above water, empty things float. Float."

The singing a fading march for them, tall woman with a swollen leg, weaving little man, and the swollen thinness they help between.

The stench in the hall: mildew? decay? "We sit and rest then climb. My gorgeous view. We help each other and here we are."

The stench along into the slab of room. A washstand for a sink, a box with oilcloth tacked around for a cupboard, a three-burner gas plate. Artificial flowers, colorless with dust. Everywhere pictures foaming: wedding, baby, party, vacation, graduation, family pictures. From the narrow couch under a slit of window, sure enough the view: lurching rooftops and a scallop of ocean heaving, preening , twitching under the moon.

"While the water heats. Excuse me . . . down the hall." Ellen Mays has gone.

"You'll live?" he asks mechanically, sat down to feel his fright; tried to pull her alongside.

She pushed him away. "For air," she said; stood clinging to the dresser. Then, in a terrible voice:

After a lifetime of room. Of many rooms.

Shhh.

You remember how she lived. Eight children.
And now one room like a coffin.

She pays rent!

Shrinking the life of her   into one room   like a coffin   Rooms and rooms like this   I lie on the quilt and hear them talk.

Please, Mrs. Orator-without-Breath.

Once you went for coffee   I walked   I saw   A Balzac   a Chekhov to write it Rummage   Alone   On scraps

Better old here than in the old country!

On scraps   Yet they sang like   like   Wondrous! *Humankind   one has to believe* So strong   for what? To rot   not grow?

Your poor lungs beg you. They sob between each word.

Singing   Unused   the life in them. She   in this poor room   with her   pictures   Max   You   The children   Everywhere unused the life   And who has meaning?   Century after century   still all in us   not   to grow?

Coffins, rummage, plants: sick woman. Oh lay down. We will get for you the doctor.

"And when will it end. Oh, *the end*." *That* nightmare thought, and this time she writhed, crumpled against him, seized his hand (for a moment again the weight the soft distant roaring of humanity) and on the strangled-for breath, begged: "Man . . . we'll destroy ourselves?"

And looking for answer—in the helpless pity and fear for her (for *her*) that distorted his face—she understood the last months, and knew that she was dying.

IV

"Let us go home," she said after several days.

"You are training for a cross-country run? That is why you do not even walk across the room? Here, like a prescription Phil said, till you are stronger from the operation. You want to break doctor's orders?"

She saw the fiction was necessary to him, was silent; then: "At home I will get better. If the doctor here says?"

"And winter? And the visits to Lennie and to Clara? All right," for he saw the tears in her eyes, "I will write Phil, and talk to the doctor."

Days passed. He reported nothing. Jeannie came and took her out for air, past the boarded concessions, and hooded and tented amusement rides, to the end of the pier. They watched the spent waves feeding the new, the gulls in the clouded sky; even up where they sat, the wind-blown sand stung.

She did not ask to go down the crooked steps to the sea.

Back in her bed, while he was gone to the store, she said: "Jeannie, this doctor, he is not one I can ask questions. Ask him for me, can I go home?"

Jeannie looked at her, said quickly: "Of course, poor Granny. You want your own things around you, don't you? I'll call him tonight. . . . Look, I've something to show you," and from her purse unwrapped a large cookie, intricately shaped like a little girl. "Look at the curls—can you hear me well, Granny?—and the darling eyelashes. I just came from a house where they were baking them."

"The dimples, there in the knees," she marveled, holding it to the better light, turning, studying, "like art. Each singly they cut, or a mold?"

"Singly," said Jeannie, "and if it is a child only the mother can make them. Oh Granny, it's the likeness of a real little girl who died yesterday—Rosita. She was three years old. *Pan del Muerto*, the Bread of the Dead. It was the custom in the part of Mexico they came from."

Still she turned and inspected. "Look, the hollow in the throat, the little cross necklace. . . . I think for the mother it is a good thing to be busy with such bread. You know the family?"

Jeannie nodded. "On my rounds. I nursed . . . Oh Granny, it is like a party; they play songs she liked to dance to. The coffin is lined with pink velvet and she wears a white dress. There are candles. . . ."

"In the house?" Surprised, "They keep her in the house?"

"Yes , said Jeannie, "and it *is* against the health law. The father said it will be sad to bury her in this country; in Oaxaca they have a feast night with candles each year; everyone picnics on the graves of those they loved until dawn."

"Yes, Jeannie, the living must comfort themselves." And closed her eyes. "You want to sleep, Granny?"

"Yes, tired from the pleasure of you. I may keep the Rosita? There stand it, on the dresser, where I can see; something of my own around me."

In the kitchenette, helping her grandfather unpack the groceries, Jeannie said in her light voice:

"I'm resigning my job, Grandaddy."

"Ah, the lucky young man. Which one is he?"

"Too late. You're spoken for." She made a pyramid of cans, unstacked, and built again.

"Something is wrong with the job?"

"With me. I can't be"—she searched for the word—"What they call professional enough. I let myself feel things. And tomorrow I have to report a family. . . ." The cans clicked again. "It's not that, either. I just don't know what I want to do, maybe go back to school, maybe go to art school. I thought if you went to San Francisco I'd come along and talk it over with Momma and Daddy. But I don't see how you can go. She wants to go home. She asked me to ask the doctor."

The doctor told her himself. "Next week you may travel, when you are a little stronger." But next week there was the fever of an infection, and by the time that was over, she could not leave the bed—a rented hospital bed that stood beside the double bed he slept in alone now.

Outwardly the days repeated themselves. Every other afternoon and evening he went out to his newfound cronies, to talk and play cards. Twice a week, Mrs. Mays came. And the rest of the time, Jeannie was there.

By the sickbed stood Jeannie's FM radio. Often into the room the shapes of music came. She would lie curled on her side, her knees drawn up, intense in listening (Jeannie sketched her so, coiled, convoluted like an ear), then thresh her hand out and abruptly snap the radio mute—still to lie in her attitude of listening, concealing tears.

Once Jeannie brought in a young Marine to visit, a friend from high-school days she had found wandering near the empty pier. Because Jeannie asked him to, gravely, without self-consciousness, he sat himself crosslegged on the floor and performed for them a dance of his native Samoa.

Long after they left, a tiny thrumming sound could be heard where, in her bed, she strove to repeat the beckon, flight, surrender of his hands, the fluttering footbeats, and his low plaintive calls.

Hannah and Phil sent flowers. To deepen her pleasure, he placed one in her hair. "Like a girl," he said, and brought the hand mirror so she could see. She looked at the pulsing red flower, the yellow skull face; a desolate, excited laugh shuddered from her, and she pushed the mirror away—but let the flower burn.

The week Lennie and Helen came, the fever returned. With it the excited laugh, and incessant words. She, who in her life had spoken but seldom and then only when necessary (never having learned the easy, social uses of words), now in dying, spoke incessantly.

In a half-whisper: "Like Lisa she is, your Jeannie. Have I told you of Lisa who taught me to read? Of the highborn she was, but noble in herself. I was sixteen; they beat me; my father beat me so I would not go to her. It was forbidden, she was a Tolstoyan.[8] At night, past dogs that howled, terrible dogs, my son, in the snows of winter to the road, I to ride in her carriage like a lady, to books. To her, life was holy, knowledge was holy, and she taught me to read. They hung her. Everything that happens one must try to understand why. She killed one who betrayed many. Because of betrayal, betrayed all she lived and believed. In one minute she killed, before my eyes (there is so much blood in a human being, my son), in prison with me. All that happens, one must try to understand.

"The name?" Her lips would work. "The name that was their pole star; the doors of the death houses fixed to open on it; I read of it my year of penal servitude. Thuban!" very excited, "Thuban, in ancient Egypt the pole star. Can you see, look out to see it, Jeannie, if it swings around *our* pole star that seems to *us* not to move.

"Yes, Jeannie, at your age my mother and grandmother had already buried children . . . yes, Jeannie, it is more than oceans between Olshana and you . . . yes, Jeannie, they danced, and for all the bodies they had they might as well be chickens, and indeed, they scratched and flapped their arms and hopped.

8. [Follower of the novelist Tolstoy, who opposed the private ownership of property and supported the dignity of peasant life.]

"And Andrei Yefimitch, who for twenty years had never known of it and never wanted to know, said as if he wanted to cry: but why my dear friend this malicious laughter?" Telling to herself half-memorized phrases from her few books. "Pain I answer with tears and cries, baseness and indignation, meanness with repulsion . . . for life may be hated or wearied of, but never despised."[9]

Delirious: "Tell me, my neighbor, Mrs. Mays, the pictures never lived, but what of the flowers? Tell them who ask: no rabbis, no ministers, no priests, no speeches, no ceremonies: ah, false—let the living comfort themselves. Tell Sammy's boy, he who flies, tell him to go to Stuttgart and see where Davy has no grave. And what? . . . And what? where millions have no graves—save air."

In delirium or not, wanting the radio on; not seeming to listen, the words still jetting, wanting the music on. Once silencing it abruptly as of old, she began to cry, unconcealed tears this time. "You have pain, Granny?" Jeannie asked.

"The music," she said, "still it is there and we do not hear; knocks, and our poor human ears too weak. What else, what else we do not hear?"

Once she knocked his hand aside as he gave her a pill, swept the bottles from her bedside table: "No pills, let me feel what I feel," and laughed as on his hands and knees he groped to pick them up.

Nighttimes her hand reached across the bed to hold his.

A constant retching began. Her breath was too faint for sustained speech now, but still the lips moved:

> *When no longer necessary   to injure others*[10]
> *Pick   pick pick   Blind chicken*
> *As a human being   reponsibility*[11]

"David!" imperious, "Basin!" and she would vomit, rinse her mouth, the wasted throat working to swallow, and begin the chant again.

She will be better off in the hospital now, the doctor said.

He sent the telegrams to the children, was packing her suitcase, when her hoarse voice startled. She had roused, was pulling herself to sitting.

"Where now?" she asked. "Where now do you drag me?"

"You do not even have to have a baby to go this time," he soothed, looking for the brush to pack. "Remember, after Davy you told me—worthy to have a baby for the pleasure of the ten-day rest in the hospital?"

"Where now? Not home yet?" Her voice mourned. "Where *is* my home?"

He rose to ease her back. "The doctor, the hospital," he started to explain, but deftly, like a snake, she had slithered out of bed and stood swaying, propped behind the night table.

"Coward," she hissed, "runner."

"You stand," he said senselessly.

"To take me there and run. Afraid of a little vomit."

He reached her as she fell. She struggled against him, half slipped from his arms, pulled herself up again.

9. [Both passages come from Chekhov, "Ward No. 6."]
10. [From Chekhov's "Rothschild's Fiddle."]
11. [From letter by Ida Lerner, Olsen's mother: "As a human being who carries responsibility for action, I think as a duty to the community we must try to understand each other."]

"Weakling," she taunted, "to leave me there and run. Betrayer. All your life you have run."

He sobbed, telling Jeannie. "A Marilyn Monroe to run for her virtue. Fifty-nine pounds she weighs, the doctor said, and she beats at me like a Dempsey. Betrayer, she cries, and I running like a dog when she calls; day and night, running to her, her vomit, the bedpan . . . ."

"She needs you, Grandaddy," said Jeannie. "Isn't that what they call love? I'll see if she sleeps, and if she does, poor worn-out darling, we'll have a party, you and I: I brought us rum babas."

They did not move her. By her bed now stood the tall hooked pillar that held the solutions—blood and dextrose—to feed her veins. Jeannie moved down the hall to take over the sickroom, her face so radiant, her grandfather asked her once: "You are in love?" (Shameful the joy, the pure overwhelming joy from being with her grandmother; the peach, the serenity that breathed.) "My darling escape," she answered incoherently, "my darling Granny"—as if that explained.

Now one by one the children came, those that were able. Hannah, Paul, Sammy. Too late to ask: and what did you learn with your living, Mother, and what do we need to know?

Clara, the eldest, clenched:

> Pay me back, Mother, pay me back for all you took from me. Those others you crowded into your heart. The hands I needed to be for you, the heaviness, the responsibility.
>
> Is this she? Noises the dying make, the crablike hands crawling over the covers. The ethereal singing.
>
> She hears that music, that singing from childhood; forgotten sound—not heard since, since. . . . And the hardness breaks like a cry: Where did we lose each other, first mother, singing mother?
>
> Annulled: the quarrels, the gibing, the harshness between; the fall into silence and the withdrawal.
>
> I do not know you, Mother, Mother, I never knew you.

Lennie, suffering not alone for her who was dying, but for that in her which never lived (for that which in him might never come to live). From him too, unspoken words: good-bye Mother who taught me to mother myself.

Not Vivi, who must stay with her children; not Davy, but he is already here, having to die again with her this time, for the living take their dead with them when they die.

Light she grew, like a bird, and, like a bird, sound bubbled in her throat while the body fluttered in agony. Night and day, asleep or awake (though indeed there was no difference now) the songs and the phrases leaping.

And he, who had once dreaded a long dying (from fear of himself, from horror of the dwindling money) now desired her quick death profoundly, for her sake. He no longer went out, except when Jeannie forced him; no longer laughed, except when, in the bright kitchenette, Jeannie coaxed his laughter (and she, who seemed to hear nothing else, would laugh too, conspiratorial wisps of laughter).

Light, like a bird, the fluttering body, the little claw hands, the beaked shadow on her face; and the throat, bubbling, straining.

He tried not to listen, as he tried not to look on the face in which only the forehead remained familiar, but trapped with her the long nights in the little room, the sounds worked themselves into his consciousness, with their punctuation of death swallows, whimpers, gurgling.

> *Even in reality* (swallow) *life's lack of it*
> *Slaveships   deathtrains   clubs   eeenough*
> *The bell   summon what enables*
> *78,000 in one minute* (whisper of a scream) *78,000 human beings   we'll destroy ourselves?*[12]

"Aah, Mrs. Miserable," he said, as if she could hear, "all your life working, and now in bed you lie, servants to tend, you do not even need to call to be tended, and still you work. Such hard work it is to die? Such hard work?"

The body threshed, her hand clung in his. A melody, ghost-thin, hovered on her lips, and like a guilty ghost, the vision of her bent in listening to it, silencing the record instantly he was near. Now, heedless of his presence, she floated the melody on and on.

"Hid it from me," he complained, "how many times you listened to remember it so?" And tried to think when she had first played it, or first begun to silence her few records when he came near—but could reconstruct nothing. There was only this room with its tall hooked pillar and its swarm of sounds.

> *No man one   except through others*
> *Strong   with the not yet   in the now*
> *Dogma dead   war dear   one country*

"It helps, Mrs. Philosopher, words from books? It helps?" And it seemed to him that for seventy years she had hidden a tape recorder, infinitely microscopic, within her, that it had coiled infinite mile on mile, trapping every song, every melody, every word read, heard, and spoken—and that maliciously she was playing back only what said nothing of him, of the children, or their intimate life together.

"Left us indeed, Mrs. Babbler," he reproached, "you who called others babbler and cunningly saved your words. A lifetime you tended and loved, and now not a word of us, for us. Left us indeed? Left me."

And he took out his solitaire deck, shuffled the cards loudly, slapped them down.

> *Lift high   banner of reason* (tatter of an orator's voice)
> *justice   freedom   light*
> *Humankind   life worthy   capacities*
> *Seeks* (blur of shudder) *belong   human being*

"Words, words," he accused, "and what human beings did *you* seek around you, Mrs. Live Alone, and what humankind think worthy?"

Though even as he spoke, he remembered she had not always been isolated, had not always wanted to be alone (as he knew there had been a voice before this gossamer one; before the hoarse voice that broke from silence to lash, make incidents, shame him—a girl's voice of eloquence that spoke their holiest dreams). But again he could reconstruct, image, nothing of what had been before, or when, or how, it had changed.

---

12. [The italicized passage contains references to the ships that transported slaves from Africa to America, to the trains that took millions of Jews and other Nazi victims to the concentration camps, and to the dropping of the atomic bomb on Hiroshima.]

Ace, queen, jack, The pillar shadow fell, so, in two tracks; in the mirror depths glistened a moonlike blob, the empty solution bottle. And it worked in him: *of reason and justice and freedom . . . Dogma dead:* he remembered the full quotation, laughed bitterly. "Hah, good you do not know what you say; good Victor Hugo died and did not see it, his twentieth century."

Deuce, ten, five. Dauntlessly she began a song of their youth of belief:

> *These things shall be, a loftier race*
> *than e'er the world hath known shall rise*
> *with flame of freedom in their souls*
> *and light of knowledge in their eyes*

King, four, jack "In the twentieth century, hah!"

> *They shall be gentle, brave and strong*
> *to spill no drop of blood, but dare*
> *all . . .*
> *on earth and fire and sea and air*

"To spill no drop of blood, hah! So, cadaver, and you too, cadaver Hugo, 'in the twentieth century ignorance will be dead, dogma will be dead, war will be dead, and for all mankind one country—of fulfillment?' Hah!"

> *And every life* (long strangling cough) *shall be a song13*

The cards fell from his fingers. Without warning, the bereavement and betrayal he had sheltered—compounded through the years—hidden even from himself—revealed itself,
> uncoiled,
> released,
> *sprung*
and with it the monstrous shapes of what had actually happened in the century.

A ravening hunger or thirst seized him. He groped into the kitchenette, switched on all three lights, piled a tray—"You have finished your night snack, Mrs. Cadaver, now I will have mine." And he was shocked at the tears that splashed on the tray.

"Salt tears. For free. I forgot to shake on salt?"

Whispered: "Lost, how much I lost."

Escaped to the grandchildren whose childhoods were childish, who had never hungered, who lived unravaged by disease in warm houses of many rooms, had all the school for which they cared, could walk on any street, stood a head taller than their grandparents, towered above—beautiful skins, straight backs, clear straightforward eyes. "Yes, you in Olshana," he said to the town of sixty years ago, "they would seem nobility to you."

And was this not the dream then, come true in ways undreamed? he asked.

And are there no other children in the world? he answered, as if in her harsh voice.

And the flame of freedom, the light of knowledge?

And the drop, to spill no drop of blood?

And he thought that at six Jeannie would get up and it would be his turn to go to her room and sleep, that he could press the buzzer and she would come now; that in the afternoon Ellen Mays was coming, and this time they would play cards and he could marvel at how rouge can stand half an inch on the cheek; that in the evening

---

13. [The italicized passages are all fragments from Hugo's "These Things Shall Be." The last verse is: "New arts shall bloom of loftier mould, / And mightier music thrill the skies, / And every life shall be a song / When all the earth is paradise."]

the doctor would come, and he could beg him to be merciful, to stop the feeding solution, to let her die.

To let her die, and with her their youth of belief out of which her bright, betrayed words foamed; stained words, that on her working lips came stainless.

Hours yet before Jeannie's turn. He could press the buzzer and wake her to come now; he could take a pill, and with it sleep; he could pour more brandy into his milk glass, though what he had poured was not yet touched.

Instead he went back, checked her pulse, gently tended with his knotty fingers as Jeannie had taught.

She was whimpering; her hand crawled across the covers for his. Compassionately he enfolded it, and with his free hand gathered up the cards again. Still was there thirst or hunger ravening in him.

That world of their youth—dark, ignorant, terrible with hate and disease—how was it that living in it, in the midst of corruption, filth, treachery, degradation, they had not mistrusted man nor themselves; had believed so beautifully, so . . . falsely?

"Aaah, children," he said out loud, "how we believed, how we belonged." And he yearned to package for each of the children, the grandchildren, for everyone, *that joyous certainty, that sense of mattering, of moving and being moved, of being one and indivisible with the great of the past, with all that freed, ennobled.* Package it, stand on corners, in front of stadiums and on crowded beaches, knock on doors, give it as a fabled gift.

"And why not in cereal boxes, in soap packages?" he mocked himself. "Aah. You have taken my senses, cadaver."

Words foamed, died unsounded. Her body writhed; she made kissing motions with her mouth. (Her lips moving as she read, pouring over the Book of Martyrs, the magnifiying glass superimposed over the heavy eyeglasses.) *Still she believed?* "Eva!" he whispered. "Still you believed? You lived by it? These Things Shall Be?"

"One pound soup meat," she answered distinctly, "one soup bone."

"My ears heard you. Ellen Mays was witness: 'Humankind . . . one has to believe.'" Imploringly: "Eva!"

"Bread, day-old." She was mumbling. "Please, in a wooden box . . . for kindling. The thread, hah, the thread breaks. Cheap thread"—and a gurgling, enormously loud, began in her throat.

"I ask for stone; she gives me bread—day–old." He pulled his hand away, shouted: "Who wanted questions? Everything you have to wake?" Then dully, "Ah, let me help you turn, poor creature."

Words jumbled, cleared. In a voice of crowded terror:

"Paul, Sammy, don't fight.

"Hannah, have I ten hands?

"How can I give it, Clara, how can I give it if I don't have?"

"You lie," he said sturdily, "there was joy too." Bitterly: "Ah how cheap you speak of us at the last."

As if to rebuke him, as if her voice had no relationship with her flaring body, she sang clearly, beautifully, a school song the children had taught her when they were little; begged:

"Not look   my hair   where they cut. . . ."

(The crown of braids shorn.)[14] And instantly he left the mute old woman poring over the Book of the Martyrs; went past the mother treading at the sewing machine,

---

14. [Reference to the Orthodox Jewish custom of cutting off the bride's hair and replacing it with a wig, and to the cutting off of prisoners' hair in Siberia.]

singing with the children; past the girl in her wrinkled prison dress, hiding her hair with scarred hands, lifting to him her awkward, shamed, imploring eyes of love; and took her in his arms, dear, personal, fleshed, in all the heavy passion he had loved to rouse from her.

"Eva!"

Her little claw hand beat the covers. How much, how much can a man stand? He took up the cards, put them down, circled the beds, walked to the dresser, opened, shut drawers, brushed his hair, moved his hand bit by bit over the mirror to see what of the reflection he could blot out with each move, and felt that at any moment he would die of what was unendurable. Went to press the buzzer to wake Jeannie, looked down, saw on Jeannie's sketch pad the hospital bed, with *her*; the double bed alongside, with him; the tall pillar feeding into her veins, and their hands, his and hers, clasped, feeding each other. And as if he had been instructed he went to his bed, lay down, holding the sketch (as if it could shield against the monstrous shapes of loss, of betrayal, of death) and with his free hand took hers back into his.

So Jeannie found them in the morning.

That last day the agony was perpetual. Time after time it lifted her almost off the bed, so they had to fight to hold her down. He could not endure and left the room; wept as if there never would be tears enough.

Jeannie came to comfort him. In her light voice she said: Grandaddy, Grandaddy don't cry. She is not there, she promised me. On the last day, she said she would go back to when she first heard music, a little girl on the road of the village where she was born. She promised me. It is a wedding and they dance, while the flutes so joyous and vibrant tremble in the air. Leave her there. Grandaddy, it is all right. She promised me. Come back, come back and help her poor body to die.

> For my mother, my father,
> and
> Two of that generation
> Seevya and Genya[15]
> Infinite, dauntless, incorruptible
> Death deepens the wonder   *1956-60/1960*

⊶ ⧓ ⊷

Judith Wright

1915–

One of Australia's most prominent poets as well as a writer of nonfiction, JUDITH WRIGHT was born in Armidale, New South Wales, on her family's sheep and cattle ranch. She was educated first by governesses, then at the New England Girls' School and the University of Sydney. Shortly after graduation she married J.P. McKinney and had a daughter; she worked as a secretary before pursuing graduate studies and becoming a professor of English at the University of Queensland. Wright is a political activist who has advocated land rights for aborigines and an environmentalist who helped to found the Wildlife Preservation Society of Queensland.

---

15. [Seevya Dinkin and Genya Gorelick, two activist immigrant women of Olsen's parents' generation. Genya Gorelick *was* an orator in the 1905 Revolution.]

Wright's poems address relationships between the sexes, the natural beauty of Australia ("my blood's country"), and environmental concerns. Her first volume of poetry, *The Moving Image*, was published in 1946 to critical acclaim. Among her thirteen subsequent collections are *Woman to Man* (1949), *The Two Fires* (1955), *The Other Half* (1966), *Fourth Quarter* (1976), and *Phantom Dwelling* (1986). *The Double Tree: Selected Poems 1942–1976*, published in America in 1977, introduced Wright's work to a U.S. audience. *Collected Poems: 1942–1970* appeared in 1971; a sequel, *Collected Poems: 1942–1985* appeared in 1994. Her subsequent books of poetry include *A Human Pattern* (1990) and *Through Broken Glass* (1992). The recipient of many honors, Wright won the Grace Leven Prize in 1949 and 1972, the Robert Frost Memorial Award in 1976, and the ASAN World Prize for Poetry in 1984.

Wright is equally renowned in Australia for her editorial work and her prose. In 1956 she edited *A Book of Australian Verse* for Oxford University Press. As a writer of nonfiction, she has published a family history, *Generation of Men* (1959); a critical biography, *Charles Harpur* (1963); a work of literary criticism, *Preoccupations in Australian Poetry* (1965); and two works on aboriginal justice, *The Cry for the Dead* (1981) and *We Call for a Treaty* (1985). She has also written short stories, including children's stories, and many essays on conservation issues.

"You inherit my own faults of character," declares Wright in "Eve To Her Daughters"; "you are submissive, follow Adam / even beyond existence." Although she treats patriarchal myth humorously in this poetic variant on the book of Genesis, Wright frequently addressed motherhood in serious, even elegiac tones. "Stillborn" portrays the agony women feel when their child is born dead, a grief that defies all rationality. "Letter" features a mother attempting to write an "honest" epistle to her daughter, "too much wanted" and now almost grown. Both poems convey with candor and poignancy the emotional perils of maternity.

⊰ Stillborn ⊱

Those who have once admitted
within their pulse and blood
the chill of that most loving
that most despairing child
5   known what is never told—
the arctic anti-god,
the secret of the cold.

Those who have once expected
the pains of that dark birth
10   which takes but without giving
and ends in double loss—
they still reach hands across
to grave from flowering earth,
to shroud from living dress.

15   Alive, they should be dead
who cheated their own death,
and I have heard them cry
when all else was lying still
"O that I stand above

20 while you lie down beneath!"
Such women weep for love
of one who drew no breath
and in the night they lie
giving the breast to death.

1971

⊰ Letter ⊱

How write an honest letter
to you, my dearest?
We know each other well—
not well enough.

5   You, the dark baby hung
in a nurse's arms,
seen through a mist—your eyes
still vague, a stranger's eyes;

hung in a hospital world
10 of drugs and fevers.
You, too much wanted,
reared in betraying love.

Yes, love is dangerous.
The innocent beginner
15 can take for crystal-true
that rainbow surface;

surprise, surprise—
paddling the slime-dark bottom
the bull-rout's sting and spine
20 stuns your soft foot.

Why try to give
what never can be given—
safety, a green world?
It's mined, the trip-wire's waiting.

25 Perhaps we should have trained you
in using weapons,
bequeathed you a straight eye,
a sure-shot trigger-finger,

or that most commonplace
30 of self-defenses,
an eye to Number One,
shop-lifting skills,

a fibrous heart, a head
sharp with arithmetic
35 to figure out the chances?
You'd not have that on.

What then? Drop-out, dry-rot?
Wipe all the questions
into an easy haze,
40   a fix for everything?

Or split the mind apart—
an old solution—
shouting to mental-nurses
your coded secrets?

45   I promised you unborn
something better than that—
the chance of love; clarity,
charity, caritas—dearest,

don't throw it in. Keep searching.
50   Dance even among these
poisoned swords; frightened only
of not being what you are—

of not expecting love
or hoping truth;
55   of sitting in lost corners
ill-willing time.

I promised what's not given,
and should repent of that,
but do not. You are you,
60   finding your own way;

nothing to do with me,
though all I care for.
I blow a kiss on paper.
I send your letter.

1971

✦

Gwendolyn Brooks
1917–

In the autobiography of her early years, *Report from Part One* (1972), U.S. poet GWENDOLYN BROOKS humorously describes her youthful realization of her literary calling: "Other girls *Had Boy Friends. I 'Wrote.'*" Born in Topeka, Kansas, to the descendant of an escaped slave, Brooks was raised in Chicago, the site and subject of much of her writing. As a schoolchild she experienced both racism from white students and interracial prejudice because of her dark skin. Viewing language as a source of empowerment, Brooks began writing poems at age seven and published her first poetry at thirteen. After graduating from Wilson Junior College in 1936, she married

Henry Blakely and became the mother of two sons. In the early 1940s Brooks participated in a poetry-writing workshop at the South Side Community Art Center led by Inez Cunningham, a wealthy white patron of the arts. Although she studied and learned from the white male modernist poets, Brooks's strongest literary influence was Langston Hughes, whom she has called "helmsman, hatchet, headlight."

In 1950 Brooks became the first African American to win the Pulitzer Prize, for *Annie Allen* (1949), a volume that employs traditional poetic forms—the sonnet, the ballad, the elegy—and revises their racial and gender associations. She went on to write a successful novel, *Maud Martha* (1953), whose youthful protagonist shares Brooks's experience of being the darkest girl in her class; the author has admitted that the book is somewhat autobiographical, though "nuanced": "There's fact-meat in the soup, among the chunks of fancy." In the late 1960s, affected by the civil rights and Black Power movements, Brooks began teaching poetry writing to gang members and other inner-city young people, a project that resulted in *Jump Bad,* an anthology of poems by BADDDD black youth "written *as* blacks, *about* blacks, *to* blacks." During this time she shifted her publishing commitment from a mainstream, white-owned press in New York, Harper and Row, to a radical black-owned press in Detroit, Broadside Press. For both her literature and her community activism Brooks has received many awards during the past thirty years; she has served as Illinois Poet Laureate, and in 1994 she won the National Book Foundation Medal of Distinguished Contribution to American Letters.

Brooks's poetry combines formal English with black idioms to depict what she has termed "life distilled." In *A Street in Bronzeville* (1945) she reveals the daily struggles of black Americans living in an urban ghetto: paying rent, "feeding a wife, satisfying a man," as she declares in the book's title poem. This collection presents a memorable array of female protagonists, including chocolate Mabbie, who loses her young love to a "lemon-hued lynx," and Sadie and Maud, two sisters who experience opposite fates—one sexually shamed, the other a spinster. *Annie Allen* traces the childhood, girlhood, and womanhood of the romantic Annie, as she shifts from adolescent self-admiration to unrealistic expectations and, finally, betrayal in love. The poems in *The Bean Eaters* (1960) are more overtly political than their predecessors: "The Lovers of the Poor" scathingly denounces white women's self-serving altruism, while "The Ballad of Rudolph Reed" depicts a black man forced to meet violence with violence when his white neighbors attack his home.

After 1967 Brooks's poetry underwent a dramatic shift, inspired by her introduction to several Black Power advocates, also poets, at the second Fisk University Writers Conference. Brooks has described this moment as pivotal in her transformation from "Negro" to "Black." Yet she rarely uses militant slogans or incendiary polemics, as do many of her counterparts, preferring instead clear language with some "hip" talk and a poetics of affirmation and love. Her goal has been "to write poems that will somehow successfully 'call'. . . all black people: black people in taverns, black people in alleys, black people in gutters, schools, offices, factories, prisons, the consulate." In *In the Mecca* (1968), a long poetic sequence remarkable for its formal range and its intensity of subject matter, the kidnapping and murder of a young black girl, offers solidarity as a source of communal healing. *Riot* (1969) opens with an epigraph from Dr. Martin Luther King, Jr., "a riot is the language of the unheard." Brooks identifies with urban rioters in the wake of the King assassination even as she realizes the futility of violence. Other volumes of poetry include *Beckonings* (1975), *Winnie* (1988), and *Primer for Blacks* (1991).

Betsy Erkkila has claimed that Brooks is seeking "to retrieve the voice and place of black motherhood"; certainly her poetry addresses such issues as abortion, racist and domestic violence, and the difficulties of raising children in poverty. In "the mother," for example, Brooks revises the poetic figure of the apostrophe by addressing the unborn, whose aborted lives are inextricably fused with their mother's. In this poem and others about motherhood, Brooks blends technical virtuosity and compassionate insight to illuminate the lives of women.

⊰ the mother ⊱

Abortions will not let you forget.
You remember the children you got that you did not get,
The damp small pulps with a little or with no hair,
The singers and workers that never handled the air.
5 You will never neglect or beat
Them, or silence or buy with a sweet.
You will never wind up the sucking-thumb
Or scuttle off ghosts that come.
You will never leave them, controlling your luscious sigh,
10 Return for a snack of them, with gobbling mother-eye.

I have heard in the voices of the wind the voices of my dim
  killed children.
I have contracted. I have eased
My dim dears at the breasts they could never suck.
15 I have said, Sweets, if I sinned, if I seized
Your luck
And your lives from your unfinished reach,
If I stole your births and your names,
Your straight baby tears and your games,
20 Your stilted or lovely loves, your tumults, your marriages,
  aches, and your deaths,
If I poisoned the beginnings of your breaths,
Believe that even in my deliberateness I was not deliberate.
Though why should I whine,
25 Whine that the crime was other than mine?—
Since anyhow you are dead.
Or rather, or instead,
You were never made.
But that too, I am afraid,
30 Is faulty: oh, what shall I say, how is the truth to be said?
You were born, you had body, you died.
It is just that you never giggled or planned or cried.

Believe me, I loved you all.
35 Believe me, I knew you, though faintly, and I loved, I loved you
All.

1945

⊰ A Bronzeville Mother Loiters in Mississippi. Meanwhile,

a Mississippi Mother Burns Bacon ⊱

From the first it had been like a
Ballad. It had the beat inevitable. It had the blood.
A wildness cut up, and tied in little bunches,
Like a four-line stanzas of the ballads she had never quite
5 Understood—the ballads they had set her to, in school.

Herself: the milk-white maid, the "maid mild"
Of the ballad. Pursued
By the Dark Villain. Rescued by the Fine Prince.
The Happiness-Ever-After.
10   That was worth anything.
It was good to be a "maid mild."
That made the breath go fast.

Her bacon burned. She
Hastened to hide it in the step-on can, and
15   Drew more strips from the meat case. The eggs and sour-milk
      biscuits
Did well. She set out a jar
Of her new quince preserve.

. . . But there was a something about the matter of the Dark Villain.
He should have been older, perhaps.
20   The hacking down of a villain was more fun to think about
When his menace possessed undisputed breadth, undisputed
      height,
And a harsh kind of vice.
And best of all, when his history was cluttered
With the bones of many eaten knights and princesses.

25   The fun was disturbed, then all but nullified
When the Dark Villain was a blackish child
Of fourteen, with eyes still too young to be dirty,
And a mouth too young to have lost every reminder
Of its infant softness.

30   That boy must have been surprised! For
These were grown-ups. Grown-ups were supposed to be
      wise.
And the Fine Prince—and that other—so tall, so broad, so
Grown! Perhaps that boy had never guessed
That the trouble with grown-ups was that under the magnifi-
      cent shell of adulthood, just under,
35   Waited the baby full of tantrums.
It occurred to her that there may have been something
Ridiculous in the picture of the Fine Prince
Rushing (right with the breadth and height and
Mature solidness whose lack, in the Dark Villain, was
      impressing her,
40   Confronting her more and more as this first day after the
      trial
And acquittal wore on) rushing
With his heavy companion to hack down (unhorsed)
That little foe.
So much had happened, she could not remember now what
      that foe had done
45   Against her, or if anything had been done.
The one thing in the world that she did know and knew
With terrifying clarity was that her composition

Had disintegrated. That, although the pattern prevailed,
Then breaks were everywhere. That she could think
50   Of no thread capable of the necessary
Sew-work.

She made the babies sit in their places at the table.
Then before calling Him, she hurried
To the mirror with her comb and lipstick. It was necessary
55   To be more beautiful than ever.
The beautiful wife.
For sometimes she fancied he looked at her as though
Measuring her. As if he considered, Had she been worth It?
Had *she* been worth the blood, the cramped cries, the little
stuttering bravado,
60   The gradual dulling of those Negro eyes,
The sudden overwhelming *little-boyness* in that barn?
Whatever she might feel or half-feel, the lipstick necessity
was something apart. He must never conclude
That she had not been worth It.

65   He sat down, the Fine Prince, and
Began buttering a biscuit. He looked at his hands.
He twisted in his chair, he scratched his nose.
He glanced again, almost secretly, at his hands.
More papers were in from the North, he mumbled. More
meddling headlines.
70   With their pepper-words, "bestiality," and "barbarism," and
"Shocking."
The half-sneers he had mastered for the trial worked across
His sweet and pretty face.

What he's like to do, he explained, was kill them all.
75   The time lost. The unwanted fame.
Still, it had been fun to show those intruders
A thing or two. To show that snappy-eyed mother,
That sassy, Northern, brown-black—

Nothing could stop Mississippi.
80   He knew that. Big Fella
Knew that.
And, what was so good, Mississippi knew that.
Nothing and nothing could stop Mississippi.
They could send in their petitions, and scar
85   Their newspapers with bleeding headlines. Their governors
Could appeal to Washington . . .

"What I want," the older baby said, "is 'lasses on my jam."
Whereupon the younger baby
Picked up the molasses pitcher and threw
90   The molasses in his brother's face. Instantly
The Fine Prince leaned across the table and slapped
The small and smiling criminal.
She did not speak. When the Hand

Came down and away, and she could look at her child,
95   At her baby-child,
She could think only of blood.
Surely her baby's cheek
Had disappeared, and in its place, surely,
Hung a heaviness, a lengthening red, a red that had no end.
100   She shook her head. It was not true, of course.
It was not true at all. The
Child's face was as always, the
Color of the paste in her paste-jar.

She left the table, to the tune of the children's lamentations,
        which were shriller
105   Than ever. She
Looked out of a window. She said not a word. *That*
Was one of the new Somethings—
The fear,
Tying her as with iron.

110   Suddenly she felt his hands upon her. He had followed her
To the window. The children were whimpering now.
Such bits of tots. And she, their mother,
Could not protect them. She looked at her shoulders, still
Gripped in the claim of his hands. She tried, but could not
        resist the idea
115   That a red ooze was seeping, spreading darkly, thickly,
        slowly,
Over her white shoulders, her own shoulders,
And over all of Earth and Mars.

He whispered something to her, did the Fine Prince, something
About love, something about love and night and intention.
120   She heard no hoof-beat of the horse and saw no flash of
        the shining steel.

He pulled her face around to meet
His, and there it was, close close,
For the first time in all those days and nights.
His mouth, wet and red,
125   So very, very, very red,
Closed over hers.

Then a sickness heaved within her. The courtroom Coca-Cola,
The courtroom beer and hate and sweat and drone,
Pushed like a wall against her. She wanted to bear it.
130   But his mouth would not go away and neither would the
Decapitated exclamation points in that Other Woman's eyes.

She did not scream.
She stood there.
But a hatred for him burst into glorious flower,
135   And its perfume enclasped them—big,
Bigger than all magnolias.

The last bleak news of the ballad.
The rest of the rugged music.
The last quatrain.

                                                        1960

◄ The Last Quatrain of the Ballad of Emmett Till[1] ►

                    after the murder,
                    after the burial

Emmett's mother is a pretty-faced thing;
                    the tint of pulled taffy.
5   She sits in a red room,
                    drinking black coffee.
She kisses her killed boy.
                    And she is sorry.
Chaos in windy grays
10   through a red prairie.

                                                        1960

Sylvia Plath
1932–1963

"I am a genius of a writer; I have it in me. I am writing the best poems of my life: they will make my name," wrote SYLVIA PLATH to her mother in 1962. A poet whose work combines psychological daring and technical virtuosity, Plath explores the complex inter-connections between women's creativity and anger. Since her sui-cide in February, 1963, fierce debates over her place in both the U.S. and feminist poetic canons have ensued; controversies have also abounded among scholars and biographers over the role her estranged husband, the late Ted Hughes, and his sister played as Plath's literary executors. Although she has sometimes been stereo-typed as "hysterical," Plath has increasingly received serious critical attention for her brilliant, acerbic poetry.

    A precocious child, Plath was encouraged to keep a journal at an early age by her mother, Aurelia Shober Plath, who became a teacher of secretarial skills after the death of her hus-band, Otto, an entomologist, when Sylvia was thirteen. Her early success as a writer came with publication of several poems in *Seventeen* magazine and her selection as winner of *Mademoiselle* magazine's college fiction contest, an experience Plath satirizes in her autobiographical novel *The Bell Jar* (1963). Also documented in this work of fiction is the author's suicide attempt and

---

1. Emmett Till was a fourteen-year-old black boy from Chicago who was murdered by white men in Mississippi in 1955 for allegedly whistling at a white woman.

subsequent hospitalization, which resulted in electric shock therapy. Despite her bout with mental illness, Plath graduated with honors from Smith College in 1955 and received a Fulbright fellowship to Cambridge University, where she met the British poet Ted Hughes, whom she married in 1956. Plath received her M.A. from Cambridge the next year, and the couple lived for a time in West Yorkshire before moving to the United States, where Plath had accepted a job teaching at her alma mater, Smith College; during this time Hughes taught at the University of Massachusetts. Shortly thereafter they decided to leave teaching and attempt to earn their living as writers, moving first to Cape Cod and then to Boston, where Plath worked part-time as a medical secretary and attended, with ANNE SEXTON, a poetry writing course taught by Robert Lowell.

After a brief stint at Yaddo, a writer's colony in upstate New York, Plath and Hughes returned to England and settled initially in London for the birth of their daughter, Frieda, in 1960 and then in Devon, where they supported each other's writing careers. Their marital content was short-lived, however, and in October of 1962, nine months after their son, Nicholas, was born, Plath and Hughes separated. Many of Plath's confessional poems trace the psychic contours of the dissolution of her marriage and her sense of betrayal at Hughes's abandonment. On February 11, 1963, after moving to a London flat in which W.B. Yeats, one of Plath's idols, had once resided, she took her own life, leaving bottles of milk beside the cribs of her sleeping infants.

Plath's poems reveal the depths of her struggle to carve out a poetic identity. On the one hand, she claimed as her goal "to be a woman famous among women," to become "a woman poet all the world will gape at." On the other, she insisted that "being born a woman is my awful tragedy." Although this paradox is charted to some extent in the poems of *The Colossus* (1962), in which she explores the complexities of familial and sexual relations, it is in *Ariel*, published posthumously in 1965, that her contradictory emotions about female subjectivity emerge most fully. Plath chose both the title and an initial selection and arrangement of the poems in this volume prior to her death, noting that the book would begin with "love" and end with "spring." As her editor, however, Hughes reconfigured the manuscript, omitting some of "the more personally aggressive poems from 1962" and adding others. Three other volumes of Plath's poetry were edited by Hughes and published after her death: *Crossing the Water* (1971), which contains most of the poems written between those of *The Colossus* and *Ariel*; *Winter Trees* (1971), which includes eighteen uncollected poems of the late period and her verse play for radio, *Three Women*; and *The Collected Poems of Sylvia Plath* (1981), which won the Pulitzer Prize for Poetry. *The Collected Poems* brings together all 224 of Plath's poems as well as fifty examples of juvenilia. Plath's *oeuvre* consists also of a collection of short stories, *Johnny Panic and the Bible of Dreams* (1978); a volume of letters written to and edited by her mother, *Letters Home* (1975); and *The Journals of Sylvia Plath* (1983), selected and edited by Hughes and Frances McCullough.

Writing especially of *Ariel*, critic Marilyn Yalom discusses the "existential dimensions" of Plath's poems, most notably her death anxiety and her obsession with motherhood; indeed, death and maternity are linked for Plath and are thus a source of profound ambivalence. Two of her best known poems, "The Disquieting Muses" and "Medusa," castigate a grasping maternal figure from whom the venomous speaker wishes either protection or separation. While it is tempting to see these poems as autobiographical, they should be read alongside Plath's letters to her mother, which present the voice of a loving, dutiful daughter. Plath's poems about her own children reveal substantially less ambivalence, even occasional joy, as seen in "Child" and "Nick and the Candlestick." In contrast, "Childless Woman" and "Edge" present bleak portraits of a woman attempting to define herself apart from her role as mother.

⊰ The Disquieting Muses ⊱

Mother, mother, what illbred aunt
Or what disfigured and unsightly
Cousin did you so unwisely keep
Unasked to my christening, that she
5 Sent these ladies in her stead
With heads like darning-eggs to nod
And nod and nod at foot and head
And at the left side of my crib?

Mother, who made to order stories
10 Of Mixie Blackshort the heroic bear,
Mother, whose witches always, always
Got baked into gingerbread, I wonder
Whether you saw them, whether you said
Words to rid me of those three ladies
15 Nodding by night around my bed,
Mouthless, eyeless, with stitched bald head.

In the hurricane, when father's twelve
Study windows bellied in
Like bubbles about to break, you fed
20 My brother and me cookies and Ovaltine
And helped the two of us to choir:
"Thor is angry: boom boom boom!
Thor is angry: we don't care!"
But those ladies broke the panes.

25 When on tiptoe the schoolgirls danced,
Blinking flashlights like fireflies
And singing the glowworm song, I could
Not lift a foot in the twinkle-dress
But, heavy-footed, stood aside
30 In the shadow cast by my dismal-headed
Godmothers, and you cried and cried:
And the shadow stretched, the lights went out.

Mother, you sent me to piano lessons
And praised my arabesques and trills
35 Although each teacher found my touch
Oddly wooden in spite of scales
And the hours of practicing, my ear
Tone-deaf and yes, unteachable.
I learned, I learned, I learned elsewhere,
40 From muses unhired by you, dear mother.

I woke one day to see you, mother,
Floating above me in bluest air
On a green balloon bright with a million
Flowers and bluebirds that never were
45 Never, never, found anywhere.
But the little planet bobbed away
Like a soap-bubble as you called: Come here!
And I faced my traveling companions.

50 Day now, night now, at head, side, feet,
    They stand their vigil in gowns of stone,
    Faces blank as the day I was born,
    Their shadows long in the setting sun
    That never brightens or goes down.
    And this is the kingdom you bore me to,
55 Mother, mother. But no frown of mine
    Will betray the company I keep.

                                        1957/1960

❧ Medusa ☙

    Off that landspit of stony mouth-plugs,
    Eyes rolled by white sticks,
    Ears cupping the sea's incoherences,
    You house your unnerving head—God-ball,
5   Lens of mercies,

    Your stooges
    Plying their wild cells in my keel's shadow,
    Pushing by like hearts,
    Red stigmata at the very center,
10 Riding the rip tide to the nearest point of departure,

    Dragging their Jesus hair.
    Did I escape, I wonder?
    My mind winds to you
    Old barnacled umbilicus, Atlantic cable,
15 Keeping itself, it seems, in a state of miraculous repair.

    In any case, you are always there,
    Tremulous breath at the end of my line,
    Curve of water upleaping
    To my water rod, dazzling and grateful,
20 Touching and sucking.

    I didn't call you.
    I didn't call you at all.
    Nevertheless, nevertheless
    You steamed to me over the sea,
25 Fat and red, a placenta

    Paralyzing the kicking lovers.
    Cobra light
    Squeezing the breath from the blood bells
    Of the fuchsia. I could draw no breath,
30 Dead and moneyless,

    Overexposed, like an X-ray.
    Who do you think you are?
    A Communion wafer? Blubbery Mary?
    I shall take no bite of your body,
35 Bottle in which I live,

Ghastly Vatican.
I am sick to death of hot salt.
Green as eunuchs, your wishes
Hiss at my sins.
40   Off, off, eely tentacle!

There is nothing between us.

1962/1965

⊰ Nick and the Candlestick ⊱

I am a miner. The light burns blue.
Waxy stalactites
Drip and thicken, tears

The earthen womb
5   Exudes from its dead boredom.
Black bat airs

Wrap me, raggy shawls,
Cold homicides.
They weld to me like plums.

10   Old cave of calcium
Icicles, old echoer.
Even the newts are white,

Those holy Joes.
And the fish, the fish——
15   Christ! they are panes of ice,

A vice of knives,
A piranha
Religion, drinking

20   Its first communion out of my live toes.
The candle
Gulps and recovers its small altitude,

Its yellows hearten.
O love, how did you get here?
25   O embryo

Remembering, even in sleep,
Your crossed position.
The blood blooms clean

30   In you, ruby.
The pain
You wake to is not yours.

Love, love,
I have hung our cave with roses,
35   With soft rugs——

The last of Victoriana.
Let the stars
Plummet to their dark address,

40   Let the mercuric
Atoms that cripple drip
Into the terrible well,

You are the one
Solid the spaces lean on, envious.
45   You are the baby in the barn.

1962/1965

⇥ Childless Woman ⇤

The womb
Rattles its pod, the moon
Discharges itself from the tree with nowhere to go.

My landscape is a hand with no lines,
5   The roads bunched to a knot,
The knot myself,

Myself the rose you achieve—
This body,
This ivory

10   Ungodly as a child's shriek.
Spiderlike, I spin mirrors,
Loyal to my image,

Uttering nothing but blood—
Taste it, dark red!
15   And my forest

My funeral,
And this hill and this
Gleaming with the mouths of corpses.

1962/1965

⇥ Edge ⇤

The woman is perfected.
Her dead

Body wears the smile of accomplishment,
The illusion of a Greek necessity

5   Flows in the scrolls of her toga,
Her bare

Feet seem to be saying:
We have come so far, it is over.

Each dead child coiled, a white serpent,
10   One at each little

Pitcher of milk, now empty.
She had folded

Them back into her body as petals
Of a rose close when the garden

15   Stiffens and odors bleed
From the sweet, deep throats of the night flower.

The moon has nothing to be sad about,
Staring from her hood of bone.

She is used to this sort of thing.
20   Her blacks crackle and drag.

1963/1965

＋—◄◆►—＋

Lucille Clifton
1936–

In "daughters" LUCILLE CLIFTON honors her African and African-American foremothers in the sort of lyrical tribute that characterizes much of her poetry: "i am / lucille, which stands for light, / daughter of thelma, daughter / of georgia, daughter of / dazzling you." A visionary voice in U.S. poetry, Clifton also writes works of children's literature that celebrate black heritage and reveal the complexity of familial bonds.

Thelma Lucille Clifton was born in Depew, New York; her parents, Samuel Louis and Thelma Moore Sayles, were day laborers. She attended Howard University from 1953 to 1955 and Fredonia State Teachers College in 1955. From 1958 until his death in 1984 she was married to Fred James Clifton, an educator, writer, and artist; she bore six children in seven years. Clifton worked briefly for the U.S. Office of Education (1969–71) but has spent most of her career as a teacher of creative writing: at Coppin State College, Columbia University, George Washington University, and, most recently, the University of California at Santa Cruz. She has received awards from the National Endowment for the Arts, and from 1979 to 1982 she served as Maryland's poet laureate. Clifton's family memoir, *Generations*, appeared in 1976. In addition, she has published more than a dozen books for children, including *Everett Anderson's Goodbye*, which won the Coretta Scott King Award for 1984.

"I am a Black woman and I write from that experience," claims Clifton. "I do not feel inhibited or bound by what I am." This credo is evident in her nine collections of poetry: *Good Times* (1969), *Good News about the Earth* (1972), *An Ordinary Woman* (1974), *Two-Headed Woman* (1980), *Good Women* (1987), *Next* (1987), *Quilting* (1991), *The Book of Light* (1993), and *The Terrible Stories* (1996). Many poems from these volumes focus on the genealogy begun by Clifton's great-great-grandmother, who was sold into slavery from her home in Dahomey, West Africa, in 1830. Clifton's language is spare, elliptical, and rhythmic; her poems often hover between elegy and celebration. The poems included here pay homage to the mother-daughter connection and reveal as well the poet's fascination with the imaginary lives of Biblical women.

⊰ june 20 ⊱

i will be born in one week
to a frowned forehead of a woman
and a man whose fingers will itch
to enter me. she will crochet
5   a dress for me of silver
and he will carry me in it.
they will do for each other
all that they can
but it will not be enough.
10   none of us know that we will not
smile again for years,
that she will not live long.
in one week i will emerge face first
into their temporary joy.

1993

⊰ daughters ⊱

woman who shines at the head
of my grandmother's bed,
brilliant woman, i like to think
you whispered into her ear
5   instructions. i like to think
you are the oddness in us,
you are the arrow
that pierced our plain skin
and made us fancy women;
10   my wild witch gran, my magic mama,
and even these gaudy girls.
i like to think you gave us
extraordinary power and to
protect us, you became the name
15   we were cautioned to forget.
it is enough,
you must have murmured,
to remember that i was
and that you are. woman, i am
20   lucille, which stands for light,
daughter of thelma, daughter
of georgia, daughter of
dazzling you.

1993

⊰ sarah's promise ⊱

who understands better than i
the hunger in old bones

for a son? so here we are,
abraham with his faith
5   and i my fury. jehovah,
i march into the thicket
of your need and promise you
the children of young women,
yours for a thousand years.
10   their faith will send them to you,
docile as abraham. now,
speak to my husband.
spare me my one good boy.

1993

⊰ naomi watches as ruth sleeps ⊱

she clings to me
like a shadow
when all that i wish
is to sit alone
5   longing for my husband,
my sons.
she has promised
to follow me,
to become me
10   if i allow it.
i am leading her
to boaz country.
he will find her beautiful
and place her among
15   his concubines.
jehovah willing
i can grieve in peace.

1993

Bessie Head
1937–86

"I write because I have authority from life to do so," declares Bessie
Head, one of Southern Africa's finest writers of fiction. "I write best
if I can hear the thunder behind my ears." As the herald of rain, a
welcome respite from the droughts that plague her adopted homeland, Botswana, thunder serves also as a metaphor for change in
Head's fiction. In five novels, three collections of short stories, and
several autobiographical works, she draws upon African oral history
and her own experiences as an outsider to present the complex lives
of African women burdened by racism and male domination.

Head was born in an asylum in Pietermaritzburg, South
Africa, to a white mother, Bessie Birch Emery; her mother's family disowned and institu-

tionalized her for becoming sexually involved with a black man—at that time a crime in apartheid South Africa—and for bearing a racially mixed child. Raised in Cape Town by "colored" foster parents and, later, in an orphanage, Head had no contact with her family of origin and was for years unaware of the circumstances of her birth. By the writer's own account she was a quiet, hardworking child who functioned as a near-servant for her foster mother, Nellie Heathcote, to whom she remained close into adulthood. When her foster family's economic circumstances changed, Head was sent as a teen to live at an Anglican mission boarding school. At first unhappy there, she eventually found a mentor in the school's headmistress, Margaret Cadmore, who encouraged her artistic pursuits. At eighteen Head began teaching at Clairwood Colored School, where she became aware of the injustices of apartheid for South African blacks, injustices from which she had been largely sheltered as a racially mixed child living in an institution. She became briefly interested in Hinduism, having rejected Christianity as oppressive, but soon became disenchanted with both her new religion and her teaching position. In the early 1960s Head worked as a journalist in Cape Town and Johannesburg, writing an advice column for teenagers in a local newspaper; during this time she became involved with a wide circle of writers and political activists who shared her pan-Africanist views. For a brief period she published her own newsletter, *The Citizen*, which pointed out the absurdities of the apartheid system. In 1961 she married Harold Head, also a struggling journalist; their son, Howard, was born in 1962. Although plagued with the first of a series of mental breakdowns, Head began to write fiction in the 1960s, including her posthumously published novella, *The Cardinals* (1993), whose protagonist is "a beautiful soul that was raised on a dung heap."

Increasingly uncomfortable with South Africa's stringent racial hierarchies, Head emigrated with her son to Botswana in 1964 and lived most of her life in a mud hut. She found pleasure in what she called "a sense of wovenness, a wholeness in life here," and the "shattered little bits" of her life "began to come together." Life for refugees in Serowe was difficult, however; Head was miserably poor and was initially shunned by the villagers, who found her odd. Still, she wrote by candlelight at night and eventually won the trust of her townspeople. Set in Botswana, her first novel, *When Rain Clouds Gather* (1967), both criticizes the villagers for their pettiness and idealizes their rural way of life. The novel examines the way that changes in traditional family structures and means of food production have affected the lives of ordinary people, especially women. *Maru* (1971), Head's second novel, chronicles the experiences of a brilliant teacher in a Botswanan village who experiences discimination because she is Masarwa, a local term for the nomadic "bushmen," or San, people. *A Question of Power* (1973), described by Head as "almost autobiographical," examines spiritual oppression and mental breakdown.

Well received in England and the United States as well as Africa, these novels launched Head's literary reputation. In 1977 she participated in the International Writing Program at the University of Iowa and traveled to Jackson State University in Mississippi at the invitation of the African-American novelist Margaret Walker. Shortly thereafter ALICE WALKER, a devoted fan, had Head's story "Witchcraft" published in Ms magazine. During the late 1970s Head collected the oral histories that resulted in *Serowe: Village of the Rain Wind* (1981), stories about the ordinary people of her village. *A Bewitched Crossroad* (1984) recounts the saga of an African clan leader, Sebina, and his resistance to colonialism. Head's autobiographical essays and sketches were compiled after her death in *A Woman Alone* (1990); also published posthumously were a collection of stories, *Tales of Tenderness and Power* (1989), and an edition of her letters, *A Gesture of Belonging* (1991). Her unpublished writings are housed at the Khama III Memorial Museum in Serowe.

Arguably Head's finest work, *The Collector of Treasures* (1977) focuses on the lives of village women in Botswana, who have conflicts with their philandering husbands and disobedient sons. Accused by an unsympathetic reviewer of putting forth "a woman's as well as a black's case," Head replied tartly, "I didn't think up a sex war. It was the truth. The men are just like that and the women suffer." Head could also be hard on women in her writing, however, as "The Village Saint" illustrates. In Mma-Mompati she creates one of her most memorable and controversial maternal figures.

⊰ The Village Saint ⊱

People were never fooled by façades. They would look quietly and humorously behind the façade at the real person—cheat, liar, pompous condescending sham, and so on—and nod their heads in a certain way until destiny caught up with the decrepit one. The village could be rocked from end to end by scandal; the society itself seemed to cater for massive public humiliations of some of its unfortunate citizens and during those times all one's fanciful, heretical, or venal tendencies would be thoroughly exposed. Despite this acute insight into human nature, the whole village was aghast the day it lost its patron saint, Mma-Mompati. She had had a long reign of twenty-six years, and a fool-proof façade.

Oh, the story was a long one. It was so long and so austere and holy that it was written into the very stones and earth of village life. And so habitual had her own pose of saintliness become to her that on the day her graven image shattered into a thousand fragments, she salvaged some of the pieces and was still seen at the head of the funeral parade or praying for the sick in hospital.

Mma-Mompati and her husband, Rra-Mompati, belonged to the elite of the village. At the time of their marriage, Rra-Mompati held an important position in tribal affairs. It was so important that he lived in a large, white-washed, colonial-style house with many large rooms. A wide porch, enclosed with mosquito netting, surrounded the whole house. It was to this house that the elders of the tribe retired to discuss top-secret affairs and it was in this house that Mma-Mompati first made her début as the great lady of the town.

Their only son, Mompati, was born a year after marriage into this state of affairs—he was born into the Bamangwato tribe, which, as most people know, was famous or notorious for a history of unexpected explosions and intrigues. The child was welcomed tenderly by his father and named Mompati—my little traveling companion. All three members of the family were spectacular in their own ways, but people tended to forget the former names of the parents—they were simply known as Father of Mompati or Mother of Mompati. The child, Mompati, hardly fulfilled the forecast of his name. Indeed, he traveled side by side with his father for sixteen years, he traveled side by side with his mother for another ten years but when he eventually emerged as a personality in his own right, he became known rather as the warmhearted, loud-voiced firm defender of all kinds of causes—marriage, morals, child care, religion, and the rights of the poor.

Mompati started his career early in that great white-washed colonial house. Whenever an explosion occurred, and there were many at one stage, the elders of the tribe did not wish the people to know of their secret deliberations and this left the people in an agony of suspense and tension. Some people, under cover of dark, would try to creep onto the wide porch of the house and hold their ears near the window to try and catch only *one* word of the hush-hush talks. A little patrolman soon appeared on stocky, stubby legs with a set, earnest expression who took turn after turn on duty around the porch to keep all eavesdroppers at bay. Seeing Mompati, the eavesdroppers would back away, laughing and shaking their heads in frustration.

"It was no good," they would report to the people. "The little policeman was on duty."

And so life went on in that great house. The tribal intrigues and explosions came; the intrigues and explosions became irrelevant. The great lady of the town, Mma-Mompati, was seen everywhere. She had the close, guarded eyes of one who knows too much and isn't telling. She presided over teas and luncheons in her home, just like any English lady, with polished etiquette and the professional smile of the highborn who don't really give a damn about people or anything. And as though to offset all the intrigues and underworld deals that went on in her home behind closed doors, Mma-Mompati assiduously cultivated her "other image" of the holy woman. No villager could die without being buried by Mma-Mompati: she attended the funerals of rich and poor. No one could fall ill without receiving the prayers of Mma-Mompati. Two days a week she set aside for visits to the hospital and in the afternoon, during visiting hours, she made the rounds of the hospital ward, Bible in hand. She would stop at each bed and enquire solicitously:

"And what may ail you, my daughter? And what may ail you, my son?"

At which, of course, the grateful ailing one would break out with a long list of woes. She had a professional smile and a professional frown of concern for everything, just like the priests. But topping it all was the fluidity and ease with which she could pray.

"Oh," she would say, stricken with sorrow. "I shall pray for you," and bending her head in deep concentration she would pray and pray to either God or Jesus for the suffering of the world. Needless to say these gestures were deeply appreciated.

Then one day, without any warning, Rra-Mompati brought his world crashing down around his ears. He just preferred another woman and walked out of the security and prestige of his job and home to live with her. It was one of those scandals that rocked the village from end to end and for a time Rra-Mompati shuffled around shame-faced at his appalling deed. He averted his face so as not to catch the angry looks of the villagers which clearly said: "Now Rra-Mompati, how could you leave a good woman like Mma-Mompati? She is matchless in her perfection. There is no other woman like her."

On this tide of indignation Mma-Mompati swept sedately into the divorce court. The whole village memorized her great court oration because she repeated it so often thereafter. It was to God, the Church, the Bible, the Sick, the Poor, the Suffering, the Honor of an Honorable Woman, the Blessings of Holy Matrimony and so on. The court was very impressed by this noble, wronged woman. They ordered that Rra-Mompati, who was rich, settle her handsomely for life, with many cattle. Life in the village became very difficult for Rra-Mompati. People muttered curses at the very sight of him, and as for his newfound lady-love, she dared not show her face. He was also advised by the elders that a man of his low morals could not be in charge of the affairs of the tribe and he ought to look for another job. Rra-Mompati failed to defend himself, except in odd ways. After a long silence he told a sympathetic friend that he was sick of the nonsense of the village and would retire permanently to his cattlepost and live henceforth the life of a cattleman. He was highly indignant, in an illogical way, at people, for turning against him.

Rra-Mompati was very indignant with his son, Mompati, for turning against him in support of his mother and he clung to these two indignations with a strange stubbornness. Soon after the father had disappeared from the village, he was pursued by Mompati in a heartbreaking attempt at reconciliation. Mompati returned to the village with a shocking story. On approaching his father's cattlepost, he said, his father had walked out of his hut and pointed his hunting gun at him. Then he'd shouted: "Get away from here! You can support that woman if you like!"

Oh, the Devil had taken Rra-Mompati's soul for good, people said. He would surely burn eternally in hellfire. Soon after this Mompati became very ill. He lay down for months. He had a terrible weakness and pain all over his body. He developed a fear of any chill or draft. It would end his life and he enveloped himself with warm clothing and blankets in an effort to save his life. Not once did he relate his nervous breakdown to the actions of his father but when he recovered a little he told people very earnestly that he was suffering from "poor blood." He kept this ailment as a kind of chronic condition and winter and summer he wrapped himself up warmly against the elements. In summer, the sweltering desert heat of the village reached temperatures of a hundred degrees in the shade. Mompati was wrapped up in two jerseys and an overcoat on such days. One day a perspiring villager remarked on the heat and looked meaningfully at Mompati's jerseys and coat. Mompati shivered and said: "I have to protect myself. I must take care of my poor blood."

Mma-Mompati settled in a little Mother Hubbard house with her son. It was neatly fenced. A water tap appeared in the yard, and vegetables and flower gardens tended by servants sprang up all round the pretty little house. Mompati found a job as a manager of the village store and together they resumed the broken thread of their lives. Mompati was seventeen then and astonishingly like his mother in appearance and behavior. Mma-Mompati kept to her round of funerals, hospital visits, and church-going and her son built up a public acclaim all his own. Like his mother, he cared about everyone and it was due to this that he managed one of the strangest stores on earth. It was always crowded with people but it often ran completely out of goods. Above the clamor of voices, every now and then rose the deep, booming bass of Mompati, either in a hearty laugh or in stern and forcefully delivered advice to those in conflict or pain. He sat in a corner with piles of accounts and bookwork but he could be easily distracted from his work. Every now and then he would look up cheerfully at the approach of a friend but that cheerful smile could, in a split second, turn to a worried frown. He would have one finger on his accounting—it would remain firmly pressed there—and a half an hour might pass in earnest discussion of the friend's latest problem. Suddenly, the bass voice would boom through the shop:

"I say, my friend, if you spare the rod, you spoil the child."

Shoppers never knew the whole story. It did not matter. It mattered that some living being cared intensely and vividly and gloriously about his fellow men. A slight hush would descend on the shop as the bass swelled out and people would smile to themselves. It swelled out about God who was important and behind all things; it swelled out about the morals of the land which were disintegrating and later, when he married, it swelled out about the virtues of family life. He threw his whole heart into peoples' affairs and then, at the end of the day took all his bookwork and accounting home, sitting up until late at night to make up for the hours lost in conversation during the day. Sometimes shoppers humorously queried:

"Mompati, why is it that there is no flour or soap in this shop? I've hunted for these goods for a whole week here and I cannot find them."

And Mompati would reply: "That's just what I was praying to God about this morning: 'Oh God,' I said 'I've forgotten to order the flour and soap again. I beg of you to help me, God, because my memory is so poor.' My prayer has been answered my friend, and I expect the flour and soap to be here next week . . ."

This went on for ten years. Both mother and son lived a busy life and people imagined they were two peas in a pod, they seemed so alike in their interests and behavior. Then Mompati fell in love with Mary Pule, a thin, wilting, willowy dreamy girl with a plaintive, tremulous voice. She had a façade too that concealed a tenacious will. She was so anxious to secure Mompati permanently as a husband that she played a hard game. All during the time he courted her, and it took months, she led him this way and that, with a charming smile. Oh, maybe she loved him. Maybe she did not. She wasn't sure. Mompati was intense about everything, so he was intensely in love. He shared his depressions and elations with his mother. The girl was invited to teas and showered with flattery and teasing until, in her own time, she accepted his proposal. It had nothing to do with either Mompati or his mother. It was her own plan.

A small flat was built in the yard in preparation for Mompati's future married life, and all proceeded well up to a certain point—the month after the marriage. Then Mma-Mompati began to undo herself. Throughout the ten years she had lived with her son, she had played a little game. Mompati used to bring his pay packet home intact but she wanted him to buy her just a teeny-weeny something—a pair of stockings, a bottle of scent, a little handkerchief or a new dress. It just pleased her, she said, that her son cared about his mother. So she always extracted a teeny bit for her share and handed him the rest. She soon informed her daughter-in-law of this procedure and like all powerful personalities, she secretly despised the weak, wilting, plaintive little wretch her son had married. She needed to dominate and shove the wretch around. So at the end of that month, she overstepped the mark. She opened the pay packet as usual and suddenly needed an enormous amount of things all at once—a pair of shoes, a new dress, and a necklace. What she handed over to her son could barely keep him and his wife in food for a week. She could not follow them into the privacy of their home, but unconsciously her vampire teeth were bared for battle. She noted that her daughter-in-law often looked gloomy and depressed in the ensuing days; her son was cold and reserved. She attacked the daughter-in-law with brittle smiles:

"Well, what's wrong with you, my child? Can't you greet an old person in a cheerful way?"

"There's nothing wrong, mother," the girl replied, with a painful smile.

At the end of the next month, Mompati walked straight to his own flat and handed his pay packet intact to his wife, ate a good supper, and fell into a sound sleep after many nights of worry and anguish. The following morning he left for work without even a glance at his mother's home. Then the storm burst. The pose of God and Jesus was blown to the winds and the demented vampire behind it was too terrible to behold. She descended on her daughter-in-law like a fury.

"You have done this to my son!" she snarled. "You have turned him against me! His duty is to respect me and honor me and you cannot take it away from me! You see that water tap? You shall not draw any more water from it while you are in this yard! Go and draw water at the village tap in future!"

And so the whole village became involved in the spectacle. They stopped and blinked their eyes as they saw the newlywed Mary carrying a water bucket a mile away from her own home to the village water taps.

"Mary," they asked curiously, "why is it you have to draw water here like everyone else when your mother-in-law has a water tap in her yard?"

Mary talked freely and at great length—a long weepy story of misery and torture. And people said: "Well, we can't believe that a good woman like Mma-Mompati could be so harsh to her own child," and they shook their heads in amazement at this thunderbolt. That was the end of Mma-Mompati. No one ever believed in her again or her God or Jesus Christ but she still buried the dead and prayed for the sick.

Her son, Mompati, set up home in a far-off part of the village. He never discussed the abrupt break with his mother to whom he had once been so overwhelmingly devoted, but one day his voice suddenly boomed out through the store in reply to some request by a friend:

"I'm sorry," he said. "I never do anything without first consulting my wife . . ."

1977

—◄ ═◈═ ►—

Margaret Atwood
1939–

"When you begin to write you're in love with the language, with the act of writing, with yourself partly; but as you go on, the writing—if you follow it—will take you places you never intended to go and show you things you would never otherwise have seen," claimed Canadian writer MARGARET ATWOOD in 1982. "I began as a profoundly apolitical writer, but then I began to do what all novelists and some poets do: I began to describe the world around me." The prolific author of nine novels, five collections of short stories, twelve volumes of poetry, and two works of nonfiction, Atwood explores cultural colonization, technology and the environment, sexuality and alienation, and women's daily lives. Her writing, called by one reviewer "sheer wizardry," has been variously described as tough, satiric, savage, compassionate, and haunting.

Born in Ottawa, Atwood was raised in northern Ontario and Quebec, where her father, an entomologist, did field work. In 1961 she graduated from the University of Toronto and went on to obtain an M.A. from Radcliffe College and study Victorian literature at Harvard University; in 1973 she earned her D Litt. from Trent University and in 1974 an L.L.D. from Queen's University. An early chapbook of poems, *Double Persephone,* was published the year she graduated from college; her first major volume of poetry, *The Circle Game* (1966) won Canada's Prestigious Governor General's Award. *Procedures for Underground* (1970) explores the vast field of the unconscious, which Atwood believes to have a life more vivid than its conscious counterpart's. *True Stories: Poems* (1981), whose title questions the reliability of human perception, bears witness to both political repression and the luminosity of love. Other poetry from the 1970s and 1980s includes *The Animals in That Country, The Journals of Susanna Moodie, Power Politics, You Are Happy, Two-Headed Poems,* and *Interlunar.* Atwood's *Selected Poems* were published in two volumes in 1987. *Morning in the Burned House* (1995) contains a series of powerful elegies to her dying father.

Critically acclaimed also as a writer of fiction, Atwood explores women's "refusal to be a victim" in *Surfacing (1972)* and the secrets and cruelties of childhood in *Cat's Eye* (1988). In *Bodily Harm* a freelance journalist whose life has been disrupted by a partial mastectomy, the break-up of a relationship, and the break-in of her house travels to the Caribbean in search of solitude but finds instead danger; this book is part political thriller, part spiritual odyssey. *The Handmaid's Tale,* which was made into a popular Hollywood movie, envisions the future as a totalitarian society run by religious extremists. Other novels include *The Edible Woman* (1969), *Lady Oracle* (1976), *Life Before Man* (1979), and *The Robber Bride* (1993). In two collections of short stories, *Dancing Girls* (1982) and *Bluebeard's Egg* (1986), Atwood probes women's interior landscapes and miscommunication between the sexes in crisp, sardonic language. *Good Bones* (1992) employs fantasy and fairy tales to consider the effects of sexism and feminism on women's emotional lives. Atwood's 1996 novel, *Alias Grace,* considers the complex character of a nineteenth-century domestic worker accused of murdering her employer.

One of Atwood's goals as a scholar has been to bring international attention to Canadian literature. This she has achieved by writing a highly praised book of criticism, *Survival: A Thematic Guide to Canadian Literature* (1972) and by compiling the *Oxford Book of Canadian Verse* (1982). An important work of nonfiction, *Second Words: Selected Critical Prose* (1982), contains fifty essays written over twenty years, including reviews of such women writers as SYLVIA PLATH, ANNE SEXTON, ADRIENNE RICH, NADINE GORDIMER, and TILLIE OLSEN; it also features several essays on Canadian writing and an account of Atwood's reaction to the early women's movement. She writes frequently for the *New York Times* and the *Chicago Sun-Times,* and her work has been translated into sixteen languages. Among her many honors are Great Britain's Sunday *Times* Award for Literary Excellence and France's Chevalier dans l'Ordre des Arts et des Lettres.

In *Second Words* Atwood contrasts the goal of political movements, which should be "to improve the quality of people's lives on all levels, spiritual and imaginative as well as material," with that of writing, which "tends to concentrate more on life, not as it ought to be, but as it is, as the writer feels it, experiences it." For Atwood, "writers are eye-witnesses, I-witnesses." The frank, sardonic account of a woman's experience of childbirth provides eyewitness in "Giving Birth," a story describing a ritual whose violence and enormity the author refuses to downplay. "But who gives it? And to whom is it given?" the narrator wonders, wryly interrogating the language used to simplify life's most intimate act of creation.

⊰ Giving Birth ⊱

But who gives it? And to whom is it given? Certainly it doesn't feel like giving, which implies a flow, a gentle handing over, no coercion. But there is scant gentleness here; it's too strenuous, the belly like a knotted fist, squeezing, the heavy trudge of the heart, every muscle in the body tight and moving, as in a slow-motion shot of a high-jump, the faceless body sailing up, turning, hanging for a moment in the air, and then—back to real time again—the plunge, the rush down, the result. Maybe the phrase was made by someone viewing the result only: in this case, the rows of babies to whom birth has occurred, lying like neat packages in their expertly wrapped blankets, pink or blue, with their labels Scotch Taped to their clear plastic cots, behind the plate-glass window.

No one ever says *giving death,* although they are in some ways the same, events, not things. And *delivering,* that act the doctor is generally believed to perform: who delivers what? Is it the mother who is delivered, like a prisoner being released? Surely not; nor is the child delivered to the mother like a letter through a slot. How can you be both the sender and the receiver at once? Was someone in bondage, is someone made free? Thus language, muttering in its archaic tongues of something, yet one more thing, that needs to be renamed.

It won't be by me, though. These are the only words I have, I'm stuck, with them, stuck in them. (That image of the tar sands, old tableau in the Royal Ontario Museum, second floor north, how persistent it is. Will I break free, or will I be sucked down, fossilized, a saber-toothed tiger or lumbering brontosaurus who ventured out too far? Words ripple at my feet, black, sluggish, lethal. Let me try once more, before the sun gets me, before I starve or drown, while I can. It's only a tableau after all, it's only a metaphor. See, I can speak, I am not trapped, and you on your part can understand. So we will go ahead as if there were no problem about language.)

This story about giving birth is not about me. In order to convince you of that I should tell you what I did this morning, before I sat down at this desk—a door on top of two filing cabinets, radio to the left, calendar to the right, these devices by which I place myself in time. I got up at twenty-to-seven, and, halfway down the stairs, met my daughter, who was ascending, autonomously she thought, actually in the arms of her father. We greeted each other with hugs and smiles; we then played with the alarm clock and the hot water bottle, a ritual we go through only on the days her father has to leave the house early to drive into the city. This ritual exists to give me the illusion that I am sleeping in. When she finally decided it was time for me to get up, she began pulling my hair. I got dressed while she explored the bathroom scales and the mysterious white altar of the toilet. I took her downstairs and we had the usual struggle over her clothes. Already she is wearing miniature jeans, miniature T-shirts. After this she fed herself: orange, banana, muffin, porridge.

We then went out to the sun porch, where we recognized anew, and by their names, the dog, the cats and the birds, blue jays and goldfinches at this time of year, which is winter. She puts her fingers on my lips as I pronounce these words; she hasn't yet learned the secret of making them. I am waiting for her first word: Surely it will be miraculous, something that has never yet been said. But if so, perhaps she's already said it and I, in my entrapment, my addiction to the usual, have not heard it.

In her playpen I discovered the first alarming thing of the day. It was a small naked woman, made of that soft plastic from which jiggly spiders and lizards and the other things people hang in their car windows are also made. She was given to my daughter by a friend, a woman who does props for movies, she was supposed to have been a prop but she wasn't used. The baby loved her and would crawl around the floor holding her in her mouth like a dog carrying a bone, with the head sticking out one side and the feet out the other. She seemed chewy and harmless, but the other day I noticed that the baby had managed to make a tear in the body with her new teeth. I put the woman into the cardboard box I use for toy storage.

But this morning she was back in the playpen and the feet were gone. The baby must have eaten them, and I worried about whether or not the plastic would dissolve in her stomach, whether it was toxic. Sooner or later, in the contents of her diaper, which I examine with the usual amount of maternal brooding, I knew I would find two small pink plastic feet. I removed the doll and later, while she was still singing to the dog outside the window, dropped it into the garbage. I am not up to finding tiny female arms, breasts, a head, in my daughter's disposable diapers, partially covered by undigested carrots and the husks of raisins, like the relics of some gruesome and demented murder.

Now she's having her nap and I am writing this story. From what I have said, you can see that my life (despite these occasional surprises, reminders of another world) is calm and orderly, suffused with that warm, reddish light, those well-placed blue high-lights and reflecting surfaces (mirrors, plates, oblong window-panes) you think of as belonging to Dutch genre paintings; and like them it is realistic in detail and slightly sentimental. Or at least it has an aura of sentiment. (Already I'm having moments of muted grief over those of my daughter's baby clothes which are too small for her to wear any more. I will be a keeper of hair, I will store things in trunks, I will weep over

Also about language.

photos.) But above all it's solid, everything here has solidity. No more of those washes of light, those shifts, nebulous effects of cloud, Turner sunsets, vague fears, the impalpables Jeanie used to concern herself with.

I call this woman Jeanie after the song. I can't remember any more of the song, only the title. The point (for in language there are always these "points," these reflections; this is what makes it so rich and sticky, this is why so many have disappeared beneath its dark and shining surface, why you should never try to see your own reflection in it; you will lean over too far, a strand of your hair will fall in and come out gold, and, thinking it is gold all the way down, you yourself will follow, sliding into those outstretched arms, towards the mouth you think is opening to pronounce your name but instead, just before your ears fill with pure sound, will form a word you have never heard before. . . .)

The point, for me, is in the hair. My own hair is not light brown, but Jeanie's was. This is one difference between us. The other point is the dreaming; for Jeanie isn't real in the same way that I am real. But by now, and I mean your time, both of us will have the same degree of reality, we will be equal: wraiths, echoes, reverberations in your own brain. At the moment though Jeanie is to me as I will someday be to you. So she is real enough.

Jeanie is on her way to the hospital, to give birth, to be delivered. She is not quibbling over these terms. She's sitting in the back seat of the car, with her eyes closed and her coat spread over her like a blanket. She is doing her breathing exercises and timing her contractions with a stopwatch. She has been up since two-thirty in the morning, when she took a bath and ate some lime Jell-O, and it's now almost ten. She has learned to count, during the slow breathing, in numbers (from one to ten while breathing in, from ten to one while breathing out) which she can actually see while she is silently pronouncing them. Each number is a different color and, if she's concentrating very hard, a different typeface. They range from plain roman to ornamented circus numbers, red with gold filigree and dots. This is a refinement not mentioned in any of the numerous books she's read on the subject. Jeanie is a devotee of handbooks. She has at least two shelves of books that cover everything from building kitchen cabinets to auto repairs to smoking your own hams. She doesn't do many of these things, but she does some of them, and in her suitcase, along with a washcloth, a package of lemon Life Savers, a pair of glasses, a hot water bottle, some talcum powder and a paper bag, is the book that suggested she take along all of these things.

(By this time you may be thinking that I've invented Jeanie in order to distance myself from these experiences. Nothing could be further from the truth. I am, in fact, trying to bring myself closer to something that time has already made distant. As for Jeanie, my intention is simple: I am bringing her back to life.)

There are two other people in the car with Jeanie. One is a man, whom I will call A., for convenience. A. is driving. When Jeanie opens her eyes, at the end of every contraction, she can see the back of his slightly balding head and his reassuring shoulders. A. drives well and not too quickly. From time to time he asks her how she is, and she tells him how long the contractions are lasting and how long there is between them. When they stop for gas he buys them each a Styrofoam container of coffee. For months he has helped her with the breathing exercises, pressing on her knee as recommended by the book, and he will be present at the delivery. (Perhaps it's to him that the birth will be given, in the same sense that one gives a performance.) Together they have toured the hospital maternity ward, in company with a small group of other pairs like them: one thin solicitous person, one slow bulbous person. They have been shown the rooms, shared and private, the sitz-baths, the delivery room itself, which gave the impression of being white. The nurse was light-brown, with limber hips and elbows; she laughed a lot as she answered questions.

"First they'll give you an enema. You know what it is? They take a tube of water and put it up your behind. Now, the gentlemen must put on this—and these, over your shoes. And these hats, this one for those with long hair, this for those with short hair."

"What about those with no hair?" says A.

The nurse looks up at his head and laughs. "Oh, you still have some," she says. "If you have a question, do not be afraid to ask."

They have also seen the film made by the hospital, a full-color film of a woman giving birth to, can it be a baby? "Not all babies will be this large at birth," the Australian nurse who introduces the movie says. Still, the audience, half of which is pregnant, doesn't look very relaxed when the lights go on. ("If you don't like the visuals," a friend of Jeanie's has told her, "you can always close your eyes.") It isn't the blood so much as the brownish-red disinfectant that bothers her. "I've decided to call this whole thing off," she says to A., smiling to show it's a joke. He gives her a hug and says, "Everything's going to be fine."

And she knows it is. Everything will be fine. But there is another woman in the car. She's sitting in the front seat, and she hasn't turned or acknowledged Jeanie in any way. She, like Jeanie, is going to the hospital. She too is pregnant. She is not going to the hospital to give birth, however, because the words, the words, are too alien to her experience, the experience she is about to have, to be used about it at all. She's wearing a cloth coat with checks in maroon and brown, and she has a kerchief tied over her hair. Jeanie has seen her before, but she knows little about her except that she is a woman who did not wish to become pregnant, who did not choose to divide herself like this, who did not choose any of these ordeals, these initiations. It would be no use telling her that everything is going to be fine. The word in English for unwanted intercourse is rape. But there is no word in the language for what is about to happen to this woman.

Jeanie has seen this woman from time to time throughout her pregnancy, always in the same coat, always with the same kerchief. Naturally, being pregnant herself has made her more aware of other pregnant women, and she has watched them, examined them covertly, every time she has seen one. But not every other pregnant woman is this woman. She did not, for instance, attend Jeanie's prenatal classes at the hospital, where the women were all young, younger than Jeanie.

"How many will be breast-feeding?" asks the Australian nurse with the hefty shoulders.

All hands but one shoot up. A modern group, the new generation, and the one lone bottle-feeder, who might have (who knows?) something wrong with her breasts, is ashamed of herself. The others look politely away from her. What they want most to discuss, it seems, are the differences between one kind of disposable diaper and another. Sometimes they lie on mats and squeeze each other's hands, simulating contractions and counting breaths. It's all very hopeful. The Australian nurse tells them not to get in and out of the bathtub by themselves. At the end of an hour they are each given a glass of apple juice.

There is only one woman in the class who has already given birth. She's there, she says, to make sure they give her a shot this time. They delayed it last time and she went through hell. The others look at her with mild disapproval. *They* are not clamoring for shots, they do not intend to go through hell. Hell comes from the wrong attitude, they feel. The books talk about discomfort.

"It's not discomfort, it's pain, baby," the woman says.

The others smile uneasily and the conversation slides back to disposable diapers.

Vitaminized, conscientious, well-read Jeanie, who has managed to avoid morning sickness, varicose veins, stretch marks, toxemia and depression, who has had no aberrations of appetite, no blurrings of vision—why is she followed, then, by this other? At first it was only a glimpse now and then, at the infants' clothing section in Simpson's Basement, in the supermarket lineup, on street corners as she herself slid by in A.'s car: the haggard face the bloated torso, the kerchief holding back the too-sparse hair. In any case, it was Jeanie who saw her, not the other way around. If she knew she was following Jeanie she gave no sign.

As Jeanie has come closer and closer to this day, the unknown day on which she will give birth, as time has thickened around her so that it has become something she must propel herself through, a kind of slush, wet earth underfoot, she has seen the woman more and more often, though always from a distance. Depending on the light, she has appeared by turns as a young girl of perhaps twenty to an older woman of forty or forty-five, but there was never any doubt in Jeanie's mind that it was the same woman. In fact it did not occur to her that the woman was not real in the usual sense (and perhaps she was, originally, on the first or second sighting, as the voice that causes an echo is real), until A. stopped for a red light during this drive to the hospital and the woman, who had been standing on the corner with a brown paper bag in her arms, simply opened the front door of the car and got in. A. didn't react, and Jeanie knows better than to say anything to him. She is aware that the woman is not really there: Jeanie is not crazy. She could even make the woman disappear by opening her eyes wider, by staring, but it is only the shape that would go away, not the feeling. Jeanie isn't exactly afraid of this woman. She is afraid for her.

When they reach the hospital, the woman gets out of the car and is through the door by the time A. has come around to help Jeanie out of the back seat. In the lobby she is nowhere to be seen. Jeanie goes through Admission in the usual way, unshadowed.

There has been an epidemic of babies during the night and the maternity ward is overcrowded. Jeanie waits for her room behind a dividing screen. Nearby someone is screaming, screaming and mumbling between screams in what sounds like a foreign language. Portuguese, Jeanie thinks. She tells herself that for them it is different, you're supposed to scream, you're regarded as queer if you don't scream, it's a required part of giving birth. Nevertheless she knows that the woman screaming is the other woman and she is screaming from pain. Jeanie listens to the other voice, also a woman's, comforting, reassuring: her mother? A nurse?

A. arrives and they sit uneasily, listening to the screams. Finally Jeanie is sent for and she goes for her prep. Prep school, she thinks. She takes off her clothes—when will she see them again?—and puts on the hospital gown. She is examined, labeled around the wrist and given an enema. She tells the nurse she can't take Demerol because she's allergic to it, and the nurse writes this down. Jeanie doesn't know whether this is true or not but she doesn't want Demerol, she has read the books. She intends to put up a struggle over her pubic hair—surely she will lose her strength if it is all shaved off—but it turns out the nurse doesn't have very strong feelings about it.

She is told her contractions are not far enough along to be taken seriously, she can even have lunch. She puts on her dressing gown and rejoins A., in the freshly vacated room, eats some tomato soup and a veal cutlet, and decides to take a nap while A. goes out for supplies.

Jeanie wakes up when A. comes back. He has brought a paper, some detective novels for Jeanie and a bottle of Scotch for himself. A. reads the paper and drinks Scotch, and Jeanie reads *Poirot's Early Cases*. There is no connection between Poirot and her labor, which is now intensifying, unless it is the egg-shape of Poirot's head and the vegetable marrows he is known to cultivate with strands of wet wool (placentae? umbilical cords?). She is glad the stories are short; she is walking around the room now, between contractions. Lunch was definitely a mistake.

"I think I have back labor," she says to A. They get out the handbook and look up the instructions for this. It's useful that everything has a name. Jeanie kneels on the bed and rests her forehead on her arms while A. rubs her back. A. pours himself another Scotch, in the hospital glass. The nurse, in pink, comes, looks, asks about the timing, and goes away again. Jeanie is beginning to sweat. She can only manage half a page or so of Poirot before she has to clamber back up on the bed again and begin breathing and running through the colored numbers.

When the nurse comes back, she has a wheelchair. It's time to go down to the labor room, she says. Jeanie feels stupid sitting in the wheelchair. She tells herself about peasant women having babies in the fields, Indian women having them on portages with hardly a second thought. She feels effete. But the hospital wants her to ride, and considering the fact that the nurse is tiny, perhaps it's just as well. What if Jeanie were to collapse, after all? After all her courageous talk. An image of the tiny pink nurse, antlike, trundling large Jeanie through the corridors, rolling her along like a heavy beach ball.

As they go by the check-in desk a woman is wheeled past on a table, covered by a sheet. Her eyes are closed and there's a bottle feeding into her arm through a tube. Something is wrong. Jeanie looks back—she thinks it was the other woman—but the sheeted table is hidden now behind the counter.

In the dim labor room Jeanie takes off her dressing gown and is helped up onto the bed by the nurse. A. brings her suitcase, which is not a suitcase actually but a small flight bag, the significance of this has not been lost on Jeanie, and in fact she now has some of the apprehensive feelings she associates with planes, including the fear of a crash. She takes out her Life Savers, her glasses, her washcloth and the other things she thinks she will need. She removes her contact lenses and places them in their case, reminding A. that they must not be lost. Now she is purblind.

There is something else in her bag that she doesn't remove. It's a talisman, given to her several years ago as a souvenir by a traveling friend of hers. It's a round oblong of opaque blue glass, with four yellow-and-white eye shapes on it. In Turkey, her friend has told her, they hang them on mules to protect against the Evil Eye. Jeanie knows this talisman probably won't work for her, she is not Turkish and she isn't a mule, but it makes her feel safer to have it in the room with her. She had planned to hold it in her hand during the most difficult part of labor but somehow there is no longer any time for carrying out plans like this.

An old woman, a fat old woman dressed all in green, comes into the room and sits beside Jeanie. She says to A., who is sitting on the other side of Jeanie, "That is a good watch. They don't make watches like that any more." She is referring to his gold pocket watch, one of his few extravagances, which is on the night table. Then

[margin annotations: "the other woman" and "blue glass"]

cruelties

she places her hand on Jeanie's belly to feel the contraction. "This is good," she says, her accent is Swedish or German. "This, I call a contraction. Before, it was nothing." Jeanie can no longer remember having seen her before. "Good. Good."

"When will I have it?" Jeanie asks, when she can talk, when she is no longer counting.

The old woman laughs. Surely that laugh, those tribal hands, have presided over a thousand beds, a thousand kitchen tables . . . "A long time yet," she says. "Eight, ten hours."

"But I've been *doing* this for twelve hours already," Jeanie says.

"Not hard labor," the woman says. "Not good, like this."

Jeanie settles into herself for the long wait. At the moment she can't remember why she wanted to have a baby in the first place. The decision was made by someone else, whose motives are now unclear. She remembers the way women who had babies used to smile at one another, mysteriously, as if there was something they knew that she didn't, the way they would casually exclude her from their frame of reference. What was the knowledge, the mystery, or was having a baby really no more inexplicable than having a car accident or an orgasm? (But these too were indescribable, events of the body, all of them; why should the mind distress itself trying to find a language for them?) She has sworn she will never do that to any woman without children, engage in those passwords and exclusions. She's old enough, she's been put through enough years of it to find it tiresome and cruel.

eath birth

But—and this is the part of Jeanie that goes with the talisman hidden in her bag, not with the part that longs to build kitchen cabinets and smoke hams—she is, secretly, hoping for a mystery. Something more than this, something else, a vision. After all she is risking her life, though it's not too likely she will die. Still, some women do. Internal bleeding, shock, heart failure, a mistake on the part of someone, a nurse, a doctor. She deserves a vision, she deserves to be allowed to bring something back with her from this dark place into which she is now rapidly descending.

She thinks momentarily about the other woman. Her motives, too, are unclear. Why doesn't she want to have a baby? Has she been raped, does she have ten other children, is she starving? Why hasn't she had an abortion? Jeanie doesn't know, and in fact it no longer matters why. *Uncross your fingers*, Jeanie thinks to her. Her face, distorted with pain and terror, floats briefly behind Jeanie's eyes before it too drifts away.

Jeanie tries to reach down to the baby, as she has many times before, sending waves of love, color, music, down through her arteries to it, but she finds she can no longer do this. She can no longer feel the baby as a baby, its arms and legs poking, kicking, turning. It has collected itself together, it's a hard sphere, it does not have time right now to listen to her. She's grateful for this because she isn't sure anyway how good the message would be. She no longer has control of the numbers either, she can no longer see them, although she continues mechanically to count. She realizes she has practiced for the wrong thing, A. squeezing her knee was nothing, she should have practiced for this, whatever it is.

"Slow down," A. says. She's on her side now, he's holding her hand. "Slow it right down."

"I can't. I can't do it, I can't do this."

"Yes, you can."

"Will I sound like that?"

"Like what?" A. says. Perhaps he can't hear it: It's the other woman, in the room next door or the room next door to that. She's screaming and crying, screaming and crying. While she cries she is saying, over and over, "It hurts. It hurts."

"No, you won't," he says. So there is someone, after all.

A doctor comes in, not her own doctor. They want her to turn over on her back.

"I can't," she says. "I don't like it that way." Sounds have receded, she has trouble hearing them. She turns over and the doctor gropes with her rubber-gloved hand. Something wet and hot flows over her thighs.

"It was just ready to break," the doctor says. "All I had to do was touch it. Four centimeters," she says to A.

"Only *four*?" Jeanie says. She feels cheated; they must be wrong. The doctor says her own doctor will be called in time. Jeanie is outraged at them. They have not understood, but it's too late to say this and she slips back into the dark place, which is not hell, which is more like being inside, trying to get out. *Out*, she says or thinks. Then she is floating, the numbers are gone, if anyone told her to get up, go out of the room, stand on her head, she would do it. From minute to minute she comes up again, grabs for air.

"You're hyperventilating," A. says. "Slow it down." He is rubbing her back now, hard, and she takes his hand and shoves it viciously further down, to the right place, which is not the right place as soon as his hand is there. She remembers a story she read once, about the Nazis tying the legs of Jewish women together during labor. She never really understood before how that could kill you.

A nurse appears with a needle. "I don't want it," Jeanie says.

"Don't be hard on yourself," the nurse says. "You don't have to go through pain like that." What pain? Jeanie thinks. When there is no pain she feels nothing, when there is pain, she feels nothing because there is no *she*. This, finally, is the disappearance of language. *You don't remember afterwards*, she has been told by almost everyone.

Jeanie comes out of a contraction, gropes for control. "Will it hurt the baby?" she says.

"It's a mild analgesic," the doctor says. "We wouldn't allow anything that would hurt the baby." Jeanie doesn't believe this. Nevertheless she is jabbed, and the doctor is right, it is very mild, because it doesn't seem to do a thing for Jeanie, though A. later tells her she has slept briefly between contractions.

Suddenly she sits bolt upright. She is wide awake and lucid. "You have to ring that bell right now," she says. "This baby is being born."

A. clearly doesn't believe her. "I can feel it, I can feel the head," she says. A. pushes the button for the call bell. A nurse appears and checks, and now everything is happening too soon, nobody is ready. They set off down the hall, the nurse wheeling. Jeanie feels fine. She watches the corridors, the edges of everything shadowy because she doesn't have her glasses on. She hopes A. will remember to bring them. They pass another doctor.

"Need me?" she asks.

"Oh no," the nurse answers breezily. "Natural childbirth."

Jeanie realizes that this woman must have been the anesthetist. "What?" she says, but it's too late now, they are in the room itself, all those glossy surfaces, tubular strange apparatus like a science-fiction movie, and the nurse is telling her to get onto the delivery table. No one else is in the room.

"You must be crazy," Jeanie says.

"Don't push," the nurse says.

"What do you mean?" Jeanie says. This is absurd. Why should she wait, why should the baby wait for them because they're late?

"Breathe through your mouth," the nurse says. "Pant," and Jeanie finally remembers how. When the contraction is over she uses the nurse's arm as a lever and hauls herself across onto the table.

From somewhere her own doctor materializes, in her doctor suit already, looking even more like Mary Poppins than usual, and Jeanie says, "Bet you weren't expecting to see me so soon!" The baby is being born when Jeanie said it would, though just three days ago the doctor said it would be at least another week, and this makes Jeanie feel jubilant and smug. Not that she knew, she'd believed the doctor.

She's being covered with a green tablecloth, they are taking far too long, she feels like pushing the baby out now, before they are ready. A. is there by her head, swathed in robes, hats, masks. He has forgotten her glasses. "Push now," the doctor says. Jeanie grips with her hands, grits her teeth, face, her whole body together, a snarl, a fierce smile, the baby is enormous, a stone, a boulder, her bones unlock, and, once, twice, the third time, she opens like a birdcage turning slowly inside out.

A pause; a wet kitten slithers between her legs. "Why don't you look?" says the doctor, but Jeanie still has her eyes closed. No glasses, she couldn't have seen a thing anyway. "Why don't you look?" the doctor says again.

Jeanie opens her eyes. She can see the baby, who has been wheeled up beside her and is fading already from the alarming birth purple. A good baby, she thinks, meaning it as the old woman did: *a good watch*, well-made, substantial. The baby isn't crying; she squints in the new light. Birth isn't something that has been given to her, nor has she taken it. It was just something that has happened so they could greet each other like this. The nurse is stringing beads for her name. When the baby is bundled and tucked beside Jeanie, she goes to sleep.

As for the vision, there wasn't one. Jeanie is conscious of no special knowledge; already she's forgetting what it was like. She's tired and very cold; she is shaking, and asks for another blanket. A. comes back to the room with her; her clothes are still there. Everything is quiet, the other woman is no longer screaming. Something has happened to her, Jeanie knows. Is she dead? Is the baby dead? Perhaps she is one of those casualties (and how can Jeanie herself be sure, yet, that she will not be among them) who will go into postpartum depression and never come out. "You see, there was nothing to be afraid of," A. says before he leaves, but he was wrong.

The next morning Jeanie wakes up when it's light. She's been warned about getting out of bed the first time without the help of a nurse, but she decides to do it anyway (peasant in the field! Indian on the portage!). She's still running adrenaline, she's also weaker than she thought, but she wants very much to look out the window. She feels she's been inside too long, she wants to see the sun come up. Being awake this early always makes her feel a little unreal, a little insubstantial, as if she's partly transparent, partly dead.

(It was to me, after all, that the birth was given, Jeanie gave it, I am the result. What would she make of me? Would she be pleased?)

The window is two panes with a venetian blind sandwiched between them; it turns by a knob at the side. Jeanie has never seen a window like this before. She closes and opens the blind several times. Then she leaves it open and looks out.

All she can see from the window is a building. It's an old stone building, heavy and Victorian, with a copper roof oxidized to green. It's solid, hard, darkened by soot, dour, leaden. But as she looks at this building, so old and seemingly immutable, she sees that it's made of water. Water, and some tenuous jellylike substance. Light flows through it from behind (the sun is coming up), the building is so thin, so fragile, that it quivers in the slight dawn wind. Jeanie sees that if the building is this way (a touch could destroy it, a ripple of the earth, why has no one noticed, guarded it against accidents?) then the rest of the world must be like this too, the entire earth, the rocks, people, trees, everything needs to be protected, cared for, tended. The enormity of this task defeats her; she will never be up to it, and what will happen then?

Jeanie hears footsteps in the hall outside her door. She thinks it must be the other woman, in her brown-and-maroon-checked coat, carrying her paper bag, leaving the hospital now that her job is done. She has seen Jeanie safely through, she must go now to hunt through the streets of the city for her next case. But the door opens, it's a nurse, who is just in time to catch Jeanie as she sinks to the floor, holding on to the edge of the air-conditioning unit. The nurse scolds her for getting up too soon.

After that the baby is carried in, solid, substantial, packed together like an apple, Jeanie examines her, she is complete, and in the days that follow Jeanie herself becomes drifted over with new words, her hair slowly darkens, she ceases to be what she was and is replaced, gradually, by someone else.   1982

⊷ ⚎ ⊶

Rosellen Brown
1939–

ROSELLEN BROWN'S novels "deal with the deeper, darker sides of family life," claims reviewer Judith Pierce Rosenberg. "Her work is not autobiographical per se, but her experience as a mother and her reflections on that experience clearly influence her fiction." Brown is the author of five novels; a collection of short stories, *Street Games* (1974); and two books of poetry, *Some Deaths in the Delta* (1970) and *Cora Fry* (1977). Born in Philadelphia, she graduated from Barnard College in 1960 and received her M.A. from Brandeis University in 1962. Brown lives in Texas with her husband, Marvin Hoffman, and their two daughters, and teaches creative writing at the University of Houston. In 1984 *Ms* magazine named her "Woman of the Year," and in 1988 she won an award from the American Academy and Institute of Arts and Letters for Literature.

In *The Autobiography of My Mother* (1976) the narration alternates between an aging mother, who is a civil liberties lawyer, and her hippie daughter, herself the mother of an infant daughter. Despite their efforts at repression, these women feel guilt and anger toward each other—violent emotions that cause them to struggle over the child they both love. *Tender Mercies* (1978) traces the marital disintegration that occurs when a happily married man accidentally runs over his wife in a power boat, leaving her a bitter paraplegic. *Civil Wars* chronicles the troubled life of the only white couple remaining in their deteriorating neighborhood in Jackson, Mississippi, where they moved during the civil rights movement of the 1960s. For reviewer Lynne Sharon Schwartz, this novel "dares to be about ideals and the perils awaiting those committed to them." *Civil Wars* won the Janet Kafka Award for the best novel of 1984. *Before and After* (1992) explores the tragedy of a stereotypical New England family—two happy parents, two intelligent teens—who must confront the realization that one of them has committed a heinous murder. Both *Before and After* and *Tender Mercies* have been made into successful Hollywood motion pictures. In 1993 Middlebury College Press published *A Rosellen Brown Reader: Selected Poetry and Prose*, which brings together her nonfictional writing. Her novel *Half a Heart* (2000) recounts the saga of a white mother's reunion with her biracial daughter and the complex emotions that ensue. Brown has also published stories in the *Atlantic Monthly*, the *Hudson Review*, and numerous literary anthologies.

That mothers do not write *as mothers* has long been an assumption of both psychoanalysis and literary studies, yet Rosellen Brown demonstrates in her fiction that mothers *do* write, and not always as loving, generous spirits. "Good Housekeeping," a title of several ironies, features a photographer caught between her profession and maternity. SUSAN RUBIN SULEIMAN has described "Good Housekeeping" as "a story about the inner world of motherhood *as it is felt*, not as it is mythologized in women's magazines." As such it invites readers to reconsider the "naturalness" of the mother-child bond.

⇥ Good Housekeeping ⇥

SHE PUT the lens of the camera up so close to the baby's rear that she suddenly thought, what if he craps on the damn thing? But she got the shot, diapered him again, lowered the shade, and closed the door. Turned the coffeepot so a wan light barely struck off the half shine under the accumulated sludge on its side. Held it over the toilet bowl, tilted so the camera wouldn't reflect in the ring of water. In the laundry mountain looking out. Carrots, parsnips, onions—then she stopped, put the camera down, shaved them all, and flung them into the long pile of their own curled skins. That was beautiful, the fingers of vegetable, the fat translucent globes of the onions like polished stones, absolute geometric definition picked out of the random garbage heap, focus on the foreground.

She was working very fast, the way the idea had come to her, before the tide of possibility receded. She laid the camera in the rumpled bedclothes so that the sheets formed great warm humps and valleys, the plaid of the blanket coasting off out of sight on one side. There was a faint impression where one of them had lain—it was more or less on his side—like grass that hasn't risen after someone's nap in the sun. Like photographing a ghost. She pulled her underpants off, sat on the bed, put her legs up the way she did in the doctor's stirrups, laid the camera on the bed—well, she couldn't see into the damn viewfinder but it seemed to be aimed—ah, it was the shutter that came, that sound of passionless satisfaction, its cool little click sucking in the core of her, reaming out the dark with its damp sweat like the seeds of some melon. So long it had been her face, she might as well have its puckered features in good light, for posterity. Some faces gape more meanly, anyway. This was so very objective, it would transcend lewdness, anger, the memory of passion. The lens like a doctor saw only fact. She found an unused box of condoms lying half covered by socks. She opened the box, arranged a few randomly, only their rolled edges peeking out, surely recognizable. Then, like a teenager nosing in her parents' drawers, she put them neatly back again and buried the box where she had found it.

And the dirty window, its shadowy design as regular as a litho. The soil in the pots waiting for the seedlings to show, that made a lovely stipple where they had been watered, light on a grainy dark, pearly vermiculite on peat. There was something so neat and purposeful about the shelf of pots. Magnified the soil reminded her of little girls she'd known who wore white blouses with Peter Pan collars and sat with a certain obedient stillness no matter what raged around them; for years and years sat that way. Her pepper seedlings, her tomatoes, under there, primly incubating in the still, protected dark.

The food didn't work, neither the lined-up cans nor the omelet she made just for the occasion, heaping it up into ridges—too much like *Good Housekeeping*. Oh, yes, the drawer in the kitchen table that held a little of everything—keys, bills, warrantees on all things electric, seed catalogues, a display so wanton she smiled. Cigarette papers—the grass to go with them was in her spice bottles marked FENUGREEK (though it looked more like basil or tarragon, finely ground. Wait till some visitor in her kitchen tried to cook with it. . . .). Straight into the bore of the pencil sharpener, a terrifying snout at 10X. Wallpaper they couldn't hide: symmetrical and graceless, cabbage roses with stars between. The welcome mat, its disordered grass lying all tamped down, caked perfectly with half-moons of mud, as though a horse had wiped his feet.

There was a little pile of feathers she had found in the bathroom—the cat had killed another bird and, proud, left this gift of fine, unmutilated evidence. They were mottled on one side, a combed gray on the other, their barbs unevenly separated as though by movement. No, that wouldn't be understood; some objects implied their function, or at the least, how they got where they were, but the feathers needed the cat and even then . . . are murdered birds a part of every household?

She was thinking of the way the show would be hung. Utterly random, on flat matte. No implicit order, no heavy ironies. In spite of the fact that the chemicals in her darkroom had probably spoiled by now from disuse multiplied by time, no bitterness. In fact there was such beauty in these banalities up close that she felt humbled. Like a lecture from her husband the evidence piled up, orderly, inside the shutter, that she was wrong again. That she was right and wrong. She walked on the balls of her feet, spying into all her likely and unlikely corners, elated.

When the baby woke, screaming and swallowing down huge hunks of air and screaming again, she took the camera coolly into the little hall room, seeing herself from a great distance, doing an assignment on herself doing an assignment. She pulled the shade all the way to the top and then knelt in front of the crib bars. So much light you could see the baby's uvula quivering like an icicle about to drop. . . . When the baby saw the camera he closed his mouth and reached out, eyes wide. Eyes like cameras. His mother looked back at herself in them, a black box in her lap with a queer star of light in its middle.

"No!" She stood up, stamping. "No, goddammit. What are you *doing?*"

The baby smiled hopefully and reached through the slats.

She put her head in her hands. Then she reached in and, focusing as well as she could with one hand, the baby slapping at her through the bars, wheezing with laughter, she found one cool bare thigh, the rosy tightness of it, and pinched it with three fingers, kept pinching hard, till she got that angry uvula again, and a good bit of very wet tongue. Through the magnifier it was spiny as some plant, some sponge, maybe, under the sea.   *1973*

✦✦✦

Beth Brant
1941–

A Bay of Quinte Mohawk from the Theyindenaga reserve in Deseronto, Ontario, BETH BRANT, or *Degonwadonti*, belongs to the Turtle Clan, as have all her female ancestors. She was born in Detroit, Michigan, at the home of her paternal grandparents on what her mother described as "the hottest day of the year"—May 6, 1941—and she lived with her grandparents until she was twelve. At seventeen, pregnant, she left high school to get married; after giving birth to three daughters she divorced her abusive husband. To support herself and her children Brant worked at a variety of jobs, including salesclerk, waitress, cleaner, and sweeper. At forty she began a writing career after having a mystical experience: While she was driving through the Mohawk Valley, a bald eagle appeared before her car, perched on a nearby tree, and urged her to write.

In 1983 Brant edited a double issue of the feminist journal *Sinister Wisdom* on literature and art by Native American women; this collection was published in 1984 as an anthology, *A Gathering of Spirit*. This anthology sold five thousand copies in less than a year and went into a second edition; since its reissue the book has been widely taught in Native American and women's studies courses at universities in the United States and Canada. Brant is cofounder of Turtle Grandmother, a library and clearinghouse for information about Native American women, and has served as a contributing editor for *Ikon: Journal of Creativity and Change* and for *Sinister Wisdom*. Her writing has been published in lesbian, feminist, and Native American journals; it appears as well in *Mother to Daughter, Daughter to Mother*, an anthology edited by TILLIE OLSEN, and in *Living the Spirit*, an anthology of gay American Indian writing. Brant's collection of stories and poems, *Mohawk Trails*, was published in 1985 by Firebrand Books.

"It has been two days since they came and took the children away," begins "A Long Story." "We are frightened by this sudden child-stealing." The theft to which Brant's narrator refers is the removal of thousands of Native American children from their homes since 1890 to place them in government-sponsored, white-run Indian boarding schools. What white leaders saw as an effort to assimilate these children through education was experienced by Native Americans mothers as a dual atrocity: Not only were they robbed of their children, their lifeline, but their children were robbed of their culture—given non-Indian names, taught "civilized ways," made strangers. Like many contemporary Indian women, including Leslie Marmon Silko and Carol Lee Sanchez, Beth Brant has written powerful fiction documenting this form of cultural genocide.

⊰ A Long Story ⊱

PART ONE: LOSS

dedicated to my Great-Grandmothers
Eliza Powless and Catherine Brant

About 40 Indian children took the train at this depot for the Philadelphia Indian School last Friday. They were accompanied by the government agent, and seemed a bright look-ing lot.

From *The Northern Observer*
Massena, NY, July 20, 1892

I am only beginning to understand what it means for a mother to lose a child.
Anna Demeter, Legal Kidnapping

1890. . . .

It has been two days since they came and took the children away. My body is greatly chilled. All our blankets have been used to bring me warmth. The women keep the fire blazing. The men sit. They talk among themselves. We are frightened by this sudden child-stealing. We signed papers, the agent said. This gave them rights to take our babies. It is good for them, the agent said. It will make them civilized, the agent said. I do not know civilized. I hold myself tight in fear of flying apart into the air. The others try to feed me. Can they feed a dead woman? I have stopped talking. When my mouth opens, only air escapes. I have used up my sound screaming their names . . . She Sees Deer! Walking Fox! My eyes stare at the room, the walls of scrubbed wood, the floor of dirt. I know there are People here, but I cannot see them. I see a darkness, like the lake at New Moon, black, unmoving. In the center, a pic-ture of my son and daughter being lifted onto the train. My daughter wearing the dark blue, heavy dress. All of the girls dressed alike. Her hair covered by a strange basket tied under her chin. Never have I seen such eyes! They burn into my head even now. My son. His hair cut. Dressed as the white men, his arms and legs covered by cloth that made him sweat. His face, wet with tears. So many children crying, screaming. The sun on our bodies, our heads. The train screeching like a crow, sounding like laughter. Smoke and dirt pumping out of the insides of the train. So many People. So many children. The women, standing as if in prayer, our hands lifted, reaching. The dust sifting down on our palms. Our palms making motions at the sky. Our fingers closing like the claws of the bear. I see this now. The hair of my son is held in my hands. I rub the strands, the heavy braids coming alive as the fire flares and casts a bright light on the black hair. They slip from my fingers and lie coiled and tangled on the ground. I see this. My husband picks up the braids, wraps them in a cloth; takes the pieces of our son away. He walks outside, the eyes of the People on him. I see this. He will find a bottle and drink with the men. Some of the women will join them. They will end the night by singing or crying. It is all the same. I see this. No sounds of children playing games and laughing. Even the dogs have ceased their noises. They lay outside each doorway, waiting. I hear this. The voices of children. They cry. They pray. They call me. . . . Nisten ha. I hear this. Nisten ha.

1978. . . .

I am awakened by the dream. In the dream, my daughter is dead. Her father is return-ing her body to me in pieces. He keeps her heart. I thought I screamed . . . Patricia! I sit up in bed, swallowing air as if for nourishment. The dream remains in the air. I rise to go to her room. Ellen tries to lead me back to bed, but I have to see once again. I open her door . . . she is gone. The room empty, lonely. They said it was in her best interests. How can it be? She is only six, a baby who needs her mothers. She loves us. This is not happening. I will not believe this. Oh god, I think I have died. Night after night, Ellen holds me as I shake. Our sobs stifling the air in our room. We lie in our bed and try to give comfort. My mind can't think beyond last week when she left. I would have killed him if I'd had the chance. He took her hand and pulled her to the car. The look in his eyes of triumph. It was a contest to him. I know he will teach her to hate us. He will! I see her dear face. Her face looking out the back window of his car. Her mouth forming the word over and over . . . Mommy Mama. Her dark braids tied with red yarn. Her front teeth missing. Her overalls with the yellow flower on the pocket, embroidered by Ellen's hands. So lovingly she sewed the yellow wool. Patricia waiting quietly until she was finished. Ellen promising to teach her the designs . . . chain stitch, french knot, split stitch. How Patricia told everyone that Ellen made the flower just for her. So proud of her overalls. I open the closet door. Almost everything is gone. A few little things hang there limp, abandoned. I pull a blue dress from a hanger and take it back to my room. Ellen tries to take it away from me, but I hold on, the soft, blue cotton smelling like her. How is it possible to feel such pain and live? Ellen?! She croons my name . . . Mary . . . Mary . . . I love you. She sings me to sleep.

1890. . . .

The agent was here to deliver a letter. I screamed at him and sent curses his way. I threw dirt in his face as he mounted his horse. He thinks I'm a crazy woman and warns me. . ."You better settle down, Annie." What can they do to me? I am a crazy woman. This letter hurts my hand. It is written in their hateful language. It is evil, but there is a message for me. I start the walk up the road to my brother. He works for the whites and understands their meanings. I think about my brother as I pull my shawl closer to my body. It is cold now. Soon there will be snow. The corn has been dried and hangs from our cabin, waiting to be used. The corn never changes. My brother is changed. He says that *I* have changed and bring shame to our clan. He says I should accept the fate. But I do not believe in the fate of child-stealing. There is evil here. There is much wrong in our village. He says I am a crazy woman because I howl at the sky every night. He is a fool! I am calling my children. He says the People are becoming afraid of me because I talk to the air, and laugh like the loon overhead. But I am talking to the children. They need to hear the sound of me. I laugh to cheer them. They cry for us. This paper in my hands has the stink of the agent. It burns my hands. I hurry to my brother. He has taken the sign of the wolf from over the doorway. He pretends to be like those who hate us. He gets more and more like the child-stealers. His eyes move away from mine. He takes the letter from me and begins the reading of it. I am confused. This letter is from two strangers with the names Martha and Daniel. They say they are learning civilized ways. Daniel works in the fields, growing food for the school. Martha cooks and is being taught to sew aprons. She will be going to live with the schoolmaster's wife. She will be a live-in girl. What is live-in girl? I shake my head. The words sound the same to me. I am afraid of Martha and Daniel. These strangers who know my name. My hands and arms are becoming numb. I tear the letters from my brother's fingers. He stares at me, his eyes traitors in his face. He calls after me . . ."Annie . . . Annie." That is not my name! I run back to the road. That is not my name! There is no Martha. There is no Daniel. This is witch work. The paper burns and burns. At my cabin, I quickly dig a hole in the field. The earth is hard and cold, but I dig with my nails. I dig, my hands feeling weaker. I tear the paper and bury the scraps. As the earth drifts and settles, the names Martha and Daniel are covered. I look to the sky and find nothing but endless blue. My eyes are blinded by the color. I begin the howling.

1978. . . .

When I get home from work, there is a letter from Patricia. I make coffee and wait for Ellen, pacing the rooms of our apartment. My back is sore from the line, bending over and down, screwing the handles on the doors of the flashy cars moving by at an incredible pace. My work protects me from questions. The guys making jokes at my expense. Some of them touching my shoulder lightly and briefly, as a sign of understanding. The few women, eyes averted or smiling at me in sympathy. No one talks. There is no time to talk. There is no room to talk, the noise taking up all space and breath. I carry the letter with me as I move from room to room. Finally I sit at the kitchen table, turning the paper around in my hands. Patricia's printing is large and uneven. The stamp has been glued on halfheartedly and is coming loose. Each time a letter arrives, I dread it, even as I long to hear from my child. I hear Ellen's key in the door. She walks into the kitchen, bringing the smell of the hospital with her. She comes toward me, her face set in new lines, her uniform crumpled and stained, her brown hair pulled back in an imitation of a french twist. She knows there is a letter. I kiss her and bring mugs of coffee to the table. We look into each other's eyes. She reaches for my hand, bringing it to her lips. Her hazel eyes are steady in her round face. I open the letter. Dear Mommy. I am fine. Daddy got me a new bike. My big teeth are coming in. We are going to see Grandma for my birthday. Daddy got me new shoes. She doesn't ask about Ellen. I imagine her father standing over her, watching the words painstakingly being printed. Coaxing her. Coaching her. The letter becomes ugly. I frantically tear it in bits and scatter them out the window. The wind scoops the pieces into a tight fist before strewing them in the street. A car drives over the paper, shredding it to mud and garbage. Ellen makes a garbled sound. "I'll leave. If it will make it better, I'll leave." I quickly hold her as the dusk swirls around the room and engulfs us. "Don't leave. Don't leave." I feel her sturdy back shiver against my hands. She begins to kiss my throat and her arms tighten as we move closer. "Ah Mary, I love you so much." As the tears threaten our eyes, the taste of salt is on our lips and tongues. We stare into ourselves, touching our place of pain; reaching past the fear, the guilt, the anger, the loneliness. We go to our room. It is beautiful again. I am seeing it as if with new eyes. The sun is barely there. The colors of cream, brown, green mixing with the wood floor. The rug with its design of wild birds. The black ash basket glowing on the dresser, holding a bouquet of dried flowers, bought at a vendor's stand. I remember the old woman, laughing and speaking rapidly in Polish as she wrapped the blossoms in newspaper. Making a present of her work. Ellen undresses me as I cry. My desire for her breaking through the heartbreak we share. She pulls the covers back, smoothing the white sheets, her hands repeating the gestures done every day at work. She guides me onto the cool material. I watch her remove the uniform of work. An aide to nurses. A healer in spirit. She comes to me full in flesh. My hands are taken with the curves and soft roundness of her. She covers me with the beating of her heart. The rhythm steadies me. Heat is centering me. I am grounded by the peace between us. I smile at her face gleaming above me, round like a moon, her long hair loose and touching my breasts. I take her breast in my hand, bring it to my mouth; suck her as a woman, in desire . . . in faith. Our bodies join. Our hair braids together on the pillow. Brown, black, silver; catching the last face of the sun. We kiss, touch, move to our place of power. Her mouth, moving over my body, stopping at curves and swells of skin, kissing, removing pain. Closer, close, together, woven, my legs are heat, the center of my soul is speaking to her, I am sliding into her, her mouth is medicine, her heart is the earth, we are dancing with flying arms, I shout, I sing, I weep salty liquid, sweet and warm, it coats her throat, this is my life. I love you Ellen, I love you Mary, I love, we love.

1891. . . .

The moon is full. The air is cold. This cold strikes at my flesh as I remove my clothes and set them on fire in the withered corn field. I cut my hair, the knife sawing through the heavy mass. I bring the sharp blade to my arms, legs, and breasts. The blood trickles like small red rivers down my body. I feel nothing. I throw the tangled webs of my hair into the flames. The smell, like a burning animal, fills my nostrils. As the fire stretches to touch the stars, the People come out to watch me . . . the crazy woman. The ice in the air touches me. They caught me as I tried to board the train and search for my babies. The white men tell my husband to watch me. I am dangerous. I laugh and laugh. My husband is only good for tipping bottles and swallowing anger. He looks at me, opening his mouth, and making no sound. His eyes are dead. He wanders from the cabin and looks out at the corn. He whispers our names. He calls after the children. He is a dead man. But I am not! Where have they taken the children? I ask the question of each one who travels the road past our house. The women come and we talk. We ask and ask. They say there is nothing we can do. The white man is a ghost. He slips in and out where we cannot see. Even in our dreams he comes to take away our questions. He works magic that has resisted our medicine. This magic has made us weak. What is the secret about them? Why do they want our babies? They sent the Blackrobes many years ago to teach us new magic. It was evil! They lied and tricked us. They spoke of gods who would forgive us if we became like them. This god is ugly!! He killed our masks. He killed our men. He sends the women screaming at the moon in terror. They want our power. They take our children to remove the inside of them. Our power. It is what makes us Hau de no sau nee. They steal our food, our sacred rattle, the stories, our names. What is left? I am a crazy woman. I look in the fire that consumes my hair and I see their faces. My daughter. My son. They are still crying for me, though the sound grows fainter. The wind picks up their keening and brings it to me. The sound has bored into my brain. I begin howling. At night, I dare not sleep. I fear the dreams. It is too terrible, the things that happen there. In my dream there is wind and blood moving as a stream. Red, dark blood in my dreams. Rushing for our village, the blood moves faster and faster. There are screams of wounded People. Animals are dead, thrown in the blood stream. There is nothing left. Only the air, echoing nothing. Only the earth, soaking up blood, spreading it in the Four Directions, becoming a thing there is no name for. I stand in the field, watching the fire, the People watching me. We are waiting, but the answer is not clear yet. A crazy woman. That is what they call me.

1979. . . .

After taking a morning off work to see my lawyer, I come home, not caring if I call in. Not caring, for once, at the loss in pay. Not caring. My lawyer says there is nothing more we can do. I must wait. As if we have done anything else. He has custody and calls the shots. We must wait and see how long it takes for him to get tired of being mommy and daddy. So . . . I wait. I open the door to Patricia's room. Ellen keeps it dusted and cleaned, in case she will be allowed to visit us. The yellow and bright blue walls are a mockery. I walk to the windows, begin to systematically tear down the curtains. I slowly start to rip the cloth apart. I enjoy hearing the sounds of destruction. Faster and faster, I tear the material into long strips. What won't come apart with my hands, I pull at with my teeth. Looking for more to destroy, I gather the sheets and bedspread in my arms and wildly shred them to pieces. Grunting and sweating, I am pushed by rage and the searing wound in my soul. Like a wolf, caught in a trap, gnawing at her own leg to set herself free, I begin to beat my breasts to deaden the pain inside. A noise gathers in my throat and finds the way out. I begin a scream that turns to howling, then turns to hoarse choking. I want to take my fists, my strong fists, my brown fists, and smash the world until it bleeds. Bleeds! And all the judges in their flapping robes, and the fathers who look for revenge, are ground, ground into dust and disappear with the wind. The word . . . lesbian. Lesbian. The word that makes them panic, makes them afraid, makes them destroy children. The word that dares them. Lesbian. *I am one.* Even for Patricia, even for her, I will not cease to be! As I kneel amidst the colorful scraps, Raggedy Anns smiling up at me, my chest gives a sigh. My heart slows to its normal speech. I feel the blood pumping outward to my veins, carrying nourishment and life. I strip the room naked. I close the door.   1984

+ ┈ ⊠⬧⊠ ┈ +

Ama Ata Aidoo
1942–

"I come from a long line of fighters," AMA ATA AIDOO told Adeola James in an interview published in 1990. "I have always been interested in the destiny of our people. I am one of those writers whose writings cannot move too far from their political involvement." This playwright, novelist, and author of short stories and children's literature was born Christina Ama Ata Aidoo in Abeadzi Kyiakor in central Ghana. Her paternal grandfather was tortured to death in a colonial prison for insubordination; her parents supported the liberal policies of Kwame Nkrumah, prime minister after Ghana became the first African country to gain independence from colonial rule in 1957. One of Nkrumah's beliefs was that the education of women educated the nation. Aidoo thus attended Wesley Girls High School in Cape Coast, where an English teacher encouraged her writing and gave her a typewriter as a gift. She went on to earn a B.A. with honors from the University of Ghana in 1964 and to enroll in the creative writing program at Stanford University in California. She taught writing at the University of Dar es Salaam in Tanzania in 1968–69 and at the University of Ghana, Cape Coast, from 1972 to 1982. During that time she also directed several national organizations, including the Ghana Broadcast Corporation and the Arts Council of Ghana, and in 1982 she served for a year as Ghana's Minister of Education—in the belief, as she explained to James, that "education is the key to everything." Since 1983 Aidoo has lived in Harare, Zimbabwe, where she has worked in the Ministry of Education and devoted herself to writing. In addition, she has been a visiting professor at the University of Richmond, Oberlin College, and Brandeis University in the United States.

Aidoo's writing reflects her view that West African literature can contribute to social change by helping people find their own voices and negotiate among ancient traditions, the legacy of colonialism, and the complexities of modernization. She writes frequently about Africans in the world diaspora and about the burdens and strengths of Ghanaian women. Aidoo began her literary career as a playwright after working in the early 1960s with Efua Sutherland, the founder of Ghana's first experimental theater, the Drama Studio. Her first play, *Dilemma of a Ghost* (1965), was produced at the Open Air Theater in Legon, Ghana, in 1964; it explores the conflicts of an African-American woman who marries a Ghanaian man and moves to Ghana in search of her African heritage. Aidoo's second play, *Anowa* (1970), emerged from a song she heard her mother singing about a woman of free spirit; this work was produced in England in 1991. Her collection of poetry, *Someone Talking to Sometime* (1985), was published in Zimbabwe and dedicated to her daughter, Kinna.

Storytelling, for Aidoo, is a social art in that it reflects her audience's cultural values and involves readers actively in a process of moral reflection. Her collection of stories, *No Sweetness Here* (1970), draws heavily on the African oral tradition in its technique, including the use of dramatic dialogue, direct address of the reader, and reliance on the "dilemma tale" popular in Ghana's Akan region, a narrative approach that presents various alternatives to a problem for readers to ponder. This volume's title story won a prize from the journal *Black Orpheus* and brought Aidoo international recognition. In 1995 this collection was reprinted by The Feminist Press, with a critical afterword by Ketu H. Katrak. Aidoo's first novel, *Our Sister Killjoy: or, Reflections from a Black-Eyed Squint* (1976), examines African expatriatism with a critical eye, exposing both the racism that Africans experience in Europe and the complacency of certain Africans who prefer living abroad to improving conditions at home. Her second novel, *Changes: A Love Story*, was published in London by the Women's Press in 1991.

Aidoo has contributed significantly to discussions of feminism to Africa. Her essay "To Be a Woman," published in Robin Morgan's *Sisterhood Is Global* (1985), can be read as a feminist manifesto. In "The African Woman Today," published in *Dissent* (1992), Aidoo asserts that "every woman and every man should be a feminist—especially if they believe that Africans should take charge of our land, its wealth, our lives, and the burden of our own development." This interweaving of feminist and postcolonial themes appears in the stories of *No Sweetness Here*, which focus on rural women's adjustments to urbanization, the complexities of Ghanaian family life, and women's experience of sexuality and motherhood. "A Gift from Somewhere," reprinted below, treats with irony and compassion the dilemma of a Ghanaian woman who has lost her first three babies to disease and now has a fourth child at risk. In this hopeful tale Aidoo chronicles the realities of domestic violence, the power of Muslim religious beliefs, and the joy a rural mother takes in her children when she manages somehow to keep them alive and safe.

⇥ A Gift from Somewhere ⇤

The Mallam had been to the village once. A long time ago. A long time ago, he had come to do these parts with Ahmadu. That had been his first time. He did not remember what had actually happened except that Ahmadu had died one night during the trip. Allah,[1] the things that can happen to us in our exile and wanderings!

Now the village was quiet. But these people. How can they leave their villages so empty every day like this? Any time you come to a village in these parts in the afternoon, you only find the too young, the too old, the maimed and the dying, or else goats and chickens, never men and women. They don't have any cause for alarm. There is no fighting here, no marauding.

He entered several compounds which were completely deserted. Then he came to this one and saw the woman. Pointing to her stomach, he said, "Mami Fanti, there is something there." The woman started shivering. He was embarrassed.

Something told him that there was nothing wrong with the woman herself. Perhaps there was a baby? Oh Allah, one always has to make such violent guesses. He looked round for a stool. When he saw one lying by the wall, he ran to pick it up. He returned with it to where the woman was sitting, placed it right opposite her, and sat down.

Then he said, "Mami, by Allah, by his holy prophet Mohamet, let your heart rest quiet in your breast. This little one, this child, he will live . . ."

And she lifted her head which until then was so bent her chin touched her breasts, and raised her eyes to the face of the Mallam for the first time, and asked "Papa Kramo, is that true?"

---

1. Allah is the Islamic term for God.

"Ah Mami Fanti," the Mallam rejoined. "Mm . . . mm," shaking awhile the fore-finger of his right hand. This movement accompanied simultaneously as it was by his turbaned head and face, made him look very knowing indeed.

"Mm . . . mm, and why must you yourself be asking me if it is true? Have I myself lied to you before, eh Mami Fanti?"

"Hmmmm. . . ." sighed she of the anxious heart. "It is just that I cannot find it possible to believe that he will live. That is why I asked you that."

His eyes glittered with the pleasure of his first victory and her heart did a little somersault.

"Mami Fanti, I myself, me, I am telling you. The little one, he will live. Now today he may not look good, perhaps not today. Perhaps even after eight days he will not be good but I tell you, Mami, one moon, he will be good . . . good . . . good," and he drew up his arms, bent them, contracted his shoulders and shook up the upper part of his body to indicate how well and strong he thought the child would be. It was a beautiful sight and for an instant a smile passed over her face. But the smile was not able to stay. It was chased away by the anxiety that seemed to have come to occupy her face forever.

"Papa Kramo, if you say that, I believe you. But you will give me something to protect him from the witches?"

"Mami Fanti, you yourself you are in too much hurry, and why? Have I got up to go?"

She shook her head and said "No" with a voice that quaked with fear.

"Aha . . . so you yourself you must be patient. I myself will do everything . . . everything. . . . Allah is present and Mohamet his holy prophet is here too. I will do everything for you. You hear?"

She breathed deeply and loudly in reply.

"Now bring to me the child." She stood up, and unwound the other cloth with which she had so far covered up her bruised soul and tied it around her waist. She turned in her step and knocked over the stool. The clanging noise did not attract her attention in the least. Slowly, she walked towards the door. The Mallam's eyes fol-lowed her while his left hand groped through the folds of his boubou in search of his last piece of cola. Then he remembered that his sack was still on his shoulder. He removed it, placed it on the floor and now with both his hands free, he fished out the cola. He popped it into his mouth and his tongue received the bitter piece of fruit with the eagerness of a lover.

The stillness of the afternoon was yet to be broken. In the hearth, a piece of coal yielded its tiny ash to the naughty breeze, blinked with its last spark and folded itself up in death. Above, a lonely cloud passed over the Mallam's turban, on its way to join camp in the south. And as if the Mallam had felt the motion of the cloud, he looked up and scanned the sky.

Perhaps it shall rain tonight? I must hurry up with this woman so that I can reach the next village before nightfall.

"Papa Kramo-e-e–!"

This single cry pierced through the dark interior of the room in which the child was lying, hit the aluminum utensils in the outer room, gathered itself together, cut through the silence of that noon, and echoed in the several corners of the village. The Mallam sprang up. "What is it, Mami Fanti?" And the two collided at the door to her rooms. But neither of them saw how she managed to throw the baby on him and how he came to himself sufficiently to catch it. But the world is a wonderful place and such things happen in it daily. The Mallam caught the baby before it fell.

"Look, look, Papa Kramo, look! Look and see if this baby is not dead. See if this baby too is not dead. Just look–o–o Papa Kramo, look!" And she started running up and down, jumping, wringing her hands and undoing the threads in her hair. Was she immediately mad? Perhaps. The only way to tell that a possessed woman of this kind is not completely out of her senses is that she does not uncloth herself to nakedness. The Mallam was bewildered.

"Mami Fanti, *hei*, Mami Fanti," he called unheeded. Then he looked down at the child in his arms.

Allah, tch, tch, tch. Now, O holy Allah. Now only you can rescue me from this trouble, since my steps found this house guided by the Prophet, but Allah, this baby is dead.

And he looked down again at it to confirm his suspicion.

Allah, the child is breathing but what kind of breath is this? I must hurry up and leave. Ah . . . what a bad day this is. But I will surely not want the baby to grow still in my arms! At all . . . for that will be bad luck, big bad luck. . . . And now where is its mother? This is not good. I am so hungry now. I thought at least I was going to earn some four pennies so I could eat. I do not like to go without food when it is not Ramaddan. No look—And I can almost count its ribs! One, two, three, four, five. . . . And Ah . . . llah, it is pale. I could swear this is a Fulani child only its face does not show that it is. If this is the pallor of sickness . . . O Mohamet! Now I must think up something quickly to comfort the mother with.

"*Hei* Mami Fanti, Mami Fanti!"

"Papaa!"

"Come."

She danced in from the doorway still wringing her hands and sucking in the air through her mouth like one who had swallowed a mouthful of scalding-hot porridge.

"It is dead, is it not?" she asked with the courtesy of the insane.

"Mami, sit down."

She sat.

"Mami, what is it yourself you are doing? Yourself you make plenty noise. It is not good. Eh, what is it for yourself you do that?"

Not knowing how to answer the questions, she kept quiet. "Yourself, look well." She craned her neck as though she were looking for an object in a distance. She saw his breath flutter.

"Yourself you see he is not dead?"

"Yes," she replied without conviction. It was too faint a breath to build any hopes on, but she did not say this to the Mallam.

"Now listen Mami," he said, and he proceeded to spit on the child: once on his forehead and then on his navel. Then he spat into his right palm and with this spittle started massaging the child very hard on his joints, the neck, shoulder blades, ankles and wrists. You could see he was straining himself very hard. You would have thought the child's skin would peel off any time. And the woman could not bear to look on.

If the child had any life in him, surely, he could have yelled at least once more? She sank her chin deeper into her breast.

"Now Mami, I myself say, you yourself, you must listen."

"Papa, I am listening."

"Mami, I myself say, this child will live. Now himself he is too small. Yourself you must not eat meat. You must not eat fish from the sea, Friday, Sunday. You hear?" She nodded in reply. "He himself, if he is about ten years," and he counted ten by flicking the five fingers of his left hand twice over, "if he is about ten, tell him he must not eat meat and fish from the sea, Friday, Sunday. If he himself he does not eat, you Mami Fanti, you can eat. You hear?"

She nodded again.

"Now, the child he will live, yourself you must stop weeping. If you do that it is not good. Now you have the blue dye for washing?"

"Yes," she murmured.

"And a piece of white cloth?"

"Yes, but it is not big. Just about a yard and a quarter."

"That does not matter. Yourself, find those things for me and I will do something and your child he shall be good."

She did not say anything.

"Did you yourself hear me, Mami Fanti?"

"Yes."

"Now take the child, put him in the room. Come back, go and find all the things."

She took the thing which might once have been a human child but now was certainly looking like something else and went back with it to the room.

And she was thinking.

Who does the Mallam think he is deceiving? This is the third child to die. The others never looked half this sick. No! In fact the last one was fat. . . . I had been playing with it. After the evening meal I had laid him down on the mat to go and take a quick bath. Nothing strange in that. When I returned to the house later, I powdered myself and finished up the last bits of my toilet. . . . When I eventually went in to pick up my baby, he was dead.

. . . O my Lord, my Mighty God, who does the Mallam think he is deceiving?

And he was thinking.

Ah . . . llah just look, I cannot remain here. It will be bad of me to ask the woman for so much as a penny when I know this child will die. Ah . . . llah, look, the day has come a long way and I have still not eaten.

He rose up, picked up his bag from the ground and with a quietness and swiftness of which only a nomad is capable, he vanished from the house. When the woman had laid the child down, she returned to the courtyard.

"Papa Kramo, Papa Kramo," she called. A goat who had been lying nearby chewing the cud got up and went out quietly too.

"Kramo, Kramo," only her own voice echoed in her brain. She sat down again on the stool. If she was surprised at all, it was only at the neatness of his escape. So he too had seen death.

Should any of my friends hear me moaning, they will say I am behaving like one who has not lost a baby before, like a fresh bride who sees her first baby dying. Now all I must do is to try and prepare myself for another pregnancy, for it seems this is the reason why I was created . . . to be pregnant for nine of the twelve months of every year. . . . Or is there a way out of it at all? And where does this road lie? I shall have to get used to it. . . . It is the pattern set for my life. For the moment, I must be quiet until the mothers come back in the evening to bury him.

Then rewrapping the other cloth around her shoulders, she put her chin in her breast and she sat, as though the Mallam had never been there.

But do you know, this child did not die. It is wonderful but this child did not die. Mmm. . . . This strange world always has something to surprise us with . . . Kweku

Nyamekye. Somehow, he did not die. To his day name Kweku, I have added Nyamekye. Kweku Nyamekye. For, was he not a gift from God through the Mallam of the Bound Mouth? And he, the Mallam of the Bound Mouth, had not taken from me a penny, not a single penny that ever bore a hole. And the way he had vanished! Or it was perhaps the god who yielded me to my mother who came to my aid at last? As he had promised her he would? I remember Maame telling me that when I was only a baby, the god of Mbemu from whom I came, had promised never to desert me and that he would come to me once in my life when I needed him most. And was it not him who had come in the person of the Mallam? . . . But was it not strange, the way he disappeared without asking for a penny? He had not even waited for me to buy the things he had prescribed. He was going to make a charm. It is good that he did not, for how can a scholar go through life wearing something like that? Looking at the others of the Bound Mouth, sometimes you can spot familiar faces, but my Mallam has never been here again.

Nyamekye, hmm, and after him I have not lost any more children. Let me touch wood. In this world, it is true, there is always something somewhere, covered with leaves. Nyamekye lived. I thought his breathing would have stopped, by the time the old women returned in the evening. But it did not. Towards nightfall his color changed completely. He did not feel so hot. His breathing improved and from then, he grew stronger every day. But if ever I come upon the Mallam, I will just fall down before him, wipe his tired feet with a silk kente, and then spread it before him and ask him to walk on it. If I do not do that then no one should call me Abena Gyaawa again.

When he started recovering, I took up the taboo as the Mallam had instructed. He is now going to be eleven years old I think. Eleven years, and I have never, since I took it up, missed observing it any Friday or Sunday. Not once. Sometimes I wonder why he chose these two days and not others. If my eyes had not been scattered about me that afternoon, I would have asked him to explain the reason behind this choice to me. And now I shall never know.

Yes, eleven years. But it has been difficult. Oh, it is true I do not think that I am one of these women with a sweet tooth for fish and meats. But if you say that you are going to eat soup, then it is soup you are going to eat. Perhaps no meat or fish may actually hit your teeth but how can you say any broth has soul when it does not contain anything at all? It is true that like everyone else, I liked kontomire. But like everyone else too, I ate it only when my throat ached for it or when I was on the farm. But since I took up the taboo, I have had to eat it at least twice two days of the week, Sunday and Friday. I have come to hate its deep-green look. My only relief came with the season of snails and mushrooms. But everyone knows that these days they are getting rarer because it does not rain as often as it used to. Then after about five years of this strict observance, someone who knew about these things advised me. He said that since the Mallam had mentioned the sea, at least I could eat freshwater fish or prawns and crabs. I did not like the idea of eating fish at all. Who can tell which minnow has paid a visit to the ocean? So I began eating freshwater prawns and crabs—but of course, only when I could get them. Normally, you do not get these things unless you have a grown-up son who would go trapping in the river for you.

But I do not mind these difficulties. If the Mallam came back to tell me that I must stop eating fish and meat altogether so that Nyamekye and the others would live, I would do it. I would. After all, he had told me that I could explain the taboo to Nyamekye when he was old enough to understand, so he could take it up himself. But I have not done it and I do not think I shall ever do it. How can a schoolboy, and who knows, one day he may become a real scholar, how can he go through life drag-ging this type of taboo along with him? I have never heard any scholar doing it, and my son is not going to be first to do it. No. I myself will go on observing it until I die. For, how could I have gone on living with my two empty hands?—I swear by every-thing, I do not understand people who complain that I am spoiling them, especially him. And anyway, is it any business of theirs? Even if I daily anointed them with shea-butter and placed them in the sun, whom would I hurt? Who else should be concerned apart from me?

But the person whose misunderstanding hurts me is their father. I do not know what to do. Something tells me it's his people and his wives who prevent him from having good thoughts about me and mine. I was his first wife and if you knew how at the outset of our lives, death haunted us, hmmm. Neither of us had a head to think in. And if things were what they should be, should he be behaving in this way? In fact, I swear by everything, he hates Nyamekye. Or how could what happened last week have happened?

It was a Friday and they had not gone to school. It was a holiday for them. I do not know what this one was for but it was one of those days they do not go. When the time came for us to leave for the farm, I showed him where food was and asked him to look after himself and his younger brother and sisters. Well my tongue was still moving when his father came in with his face shut down, the way it is when he is angry. He came up to us and asked "*Hei*, Nyamekye, are you not following your mother to the farm?" Oh, I was hurt. Is this the way to talk to a ten-year-old child? If he had been any other father, he would have said, "Nyamekye, since you are not going to school today, pick up your knife and come with me to the farm."

Would that not have been beautiful?

"Nyamekye, are you not following your mother to the farm?" As if I am the boy's only parent. But he is stuck with this habit, especially where I and my little ones are concerned.

"Gyaawa, your child is crying. . . . Gyaawa, your child is going to fall off the ter-race if you do not pay more attention to him. . . . Gyaawa, your child this, and your child that!"

Anyway, that morning I was hurt and when I opened up my mouth, all the words which came to my lips were, "I thought this boy was going to be a scholar and not a farm-goer. What was the use in sending him to school if I knew he was going to fol-low me to the farm?"

This had made him more angry. "I did not know that if you go to school, your skin must not touch a leaf!"

I did not say anything. What had I to say? We went to the farm leaving Nyamekye with the children. I returned home earlier than his father did. Nyamekye was not in the house. I asked his brother and sisters if they knew where he had gone. But they had not seen him since they finished eating earlier in the afternoon. When he had not come home by five o'clock, I started getting worried. Then his father too returned from the farm. He learned immediately that he was missing. He clouded up. After he had had his bath, he went to sit in his chair, dark as a rainy sky. Then he got up to go by the chicken coop. I did not know that he was going to fetch a cane. Just as he was sitting in the chair again, Nyamekye appeared.

"*Hei*, Kweku Nyamekye, come here."

Nyamekye was holding the little bucket and I knew where he had been to. He moved slowly up to his father.

"Papa, I went to the river to visit my trap, because today is Friday."

"Have I asked you for anything? And your traps! Is that what you go to school to learn?"

And then he pulled out the cane and fell on the child. The bucket dropped and a few little prawns fell out. Something tells me it was the sight of those prawns which finished his father. He poured those blows on him as though he were made of wood. I had made up my mind never to interfere in any manner he chose to punish the children, for after all, they are his too. But this time I thought he was going too far. I rushed out to rescue Nyamekye and then it came, wham! The sharpest blow I have ever received in my life caught me on the inside of my arm. Blood gushed out. When he saw what had happened, he was ashamed. He went away into his room. That evening he did not eat the fufu I served him.

Slowly, I picked up the bucket and the prawns. Nyamekye followed me to my room where I wept.

The scar healed quickly but the scar is of the type which rises so anyone can see it. Nyamekye's father's attitude has changed towards us. He is worse. He is angry all the time. He is angry with shame.

But I do not even care. I have my little ones. And I am sure someone is wishing she were me. I have Nyamekye. And for this, I do not even know whom to thank.

Do I thank you, O Mallam of the Bound Mouth?

Or you, Nana Mbemu, since I think you came in the person of the Mallam?

Or Mighty Jehovah-after-whom-there-is-none-other, to you alone should I give my thanks?

But why should I let this worry me? I thank you all. Oh, I thank you all. And you, our ancestral spirits, if you are looking after me, then look after the Mallam too. Remember him at meals, for he is a kinsman.

And as for this scar, I am glad it is not on Nyamekye. Any time I see it I only recall one afternoon when I sat with my chin in my breast before a Mallam came in, and after a Mallam went out.   *1970*

Minnie Bruce Pratt
1944–

"I know that in order to keep hoping, and living, and writing, I need work from other women that is rooted in the messy complexity of our daily lives, work in which we upset the predictable ending," claims MINNIE BRUCE PRATT. "I need all the voices of the women who have been destined for despisal, anonymity, or death, but who, defiant, have survived, and lived to tell their triumph." Born into a white, middle-class family in Selma, Alabama, Pratt grew up in a racially segregated community that she describes in her autobiographical essay, "Identity: Blood Skin Heart," as "the narrow circle I was raised in." Educated at the University of Alabama, she married in the late 1960s, had two sons, and moved with her family in 1974 to eastern North Carolina, where she taught English at a traditionally black college, Fayetteville State. Increasingly dissatisfied with her life as a military wife, she entered graduate school at the University of North Carolina, where she became involved with the women's liberation movement. In the late 1970s, having realized she was lesbian, Pratt left her marriage. During this time she joined the women's editorial collective that edited *Feminary*, a lesbian-feminist magazine. In the 1980s Pratt began publishing poetry and essays and became involved in antiracist work. She has taught creative writing and women's studies at the University of Maryland and at George Washington University and is now a full-time writer and activist living in Jersey City, New Jersey.

Pratt's poetry reflects many dimensions of her lesbian experience. Her first volume, *We Say We Love Each Other* (1985), pays gentle homage to her lover. *Crime Against Nature* (1989) chronicles her loss of custody of her two young sons because under North Carolina's sodomy statutes she was deemed unfit to be a mother. This volume was chosen as the Lamont Poetry Selection for 1989 by the Academy of American Poets and won the 1991 American Library Association Gay/Lesbian Book Award. Acclaimed also as an essayist, Pratt coauthored *Yours in Struggle* (1984) with Elly Bulkin and Barbara Smith, a study of anti-Semitism and racism. In *Rebellion: Essays 1980–91* Pratt confronts the "layers of deceit" that she inherited as a white Southern child and describes her civil disobedience in Washington, D.C. One essay from this volume, "Poetry in Time of War," juxtaposes Pratt's demonstrations against the Persian Gulf War of 1991 with her challenge to Senator Jesse Helms's attempts to censor her writing as "homoerotic" and therefore obscene. With AUDRE LORDE and Chrystos, two lesbian writers who, like Pratt, had won grants from the National Endowment for the Arts, she mounted a successful protest against Helms's definition of what constitutes art. In 1995 Pratt published *S/HE*, a series of vignettes that explore, in her words, "the infinities, the fluidities of sex and gender."

The poem reprinted here is taken from *Crime Against Nature*. In "Poem for My Sons" Pratt addresses her grown children directly, claiming as equally powerful her multiple identities as poet, "transgressor," and mother.

⊰ Poem for My Sons ⊱

When you were born, all the poets I knew
were men, dads eloquent on their sleeping
babes and the future: Coleridge at midnight,
Yeats' prayer that his daughter lack opinions,
5   his son be high and mighty, think and act.[1]
You've read the new father's loud eloquence,
fiery sparks written in a silent house
breathing with the mother's exhausted sleep.

When you were born, my first, what I thought was
10   milk: my breasts sore, engorged, but not enough
when you woke.   With you, my youngest, I did not
think: my head unraised for three days, mind-dead
from waist-down anesthetic labor, saddle
block, no walking either.

15   Your father was then
the poet I'd ceased to be when I got married.
It's taken me years to write this to you.

---

1. Samuel Taylor Coleridge (1772–1834) was an English Romantic poet; his poem "Frost at Midnight" (1798) pays tribute to "my cradled infant," his son Hartley. William Butler Yeats (1865–1939) was an Irish poet whose poem "A Prayer for My Daughter" (1919) expresses his hopes for her life.

I had to make a future, willful, voluble,
lascivious, a thinker, a long walker,
20 unstruck transgressor, furious, shouting,
voluptuous, a lover, a smeller of blood,
milk, a woman mean as she can be some nights,
existence I could pray to, capable of
poetry.

25   Now here we are.   You are men,
and I am not the woman who rocked you
in the sweet reek of penicillin, sour milk,
the girl who could not imagine herself
or a future more than a warm walled room,
30 had no words but the pap of the expected,
and so, those nights, could not wish for you.

But now I have spoken, my self, I can ask
for you: that you'll know evil when you smell it;
that you'll know good and do it, and see how both
35 run loose through your lives; that then you'll remember
you come from dirt and history; that you'll choose
memory, not anesthesia; that you'll have work
you love, hindering no one, a path crossing
at boundary markers where you question power;
that your loves will match you thought for thought
40 in the long heat of blood and fact of bone.

Words not so romantic nor so grandly tossed
as if I'd summoned the universe to be
at your disposal.
        I can only pray:

45 That you'll never ask for the weather, earth,
angels, women, or other lives to obey you;

that you'll remember me, who crossed, recrossed
you,
        as as woman making slowly toward
50 an unknown place where you could be with me,
like a woman on foot, in a long stepping out.

                                        1989

—·— ≡◊≡ ·—

Keri Hulme
1947–

"My imagination—theater of the head—is wholly visual," claimed New Zealand writer KERI
HULME in a 1987 interview with Jean W. Ross; "I dream in color. I illustrate with words." A
novelist and poet, Hulme is one the most famous writers of Maori descent. She was born in
Christchurch to John W. Hulme, a carpenter, and Mere Miller, a credit manager; her mother's
ancestors belonged to the Southern tribe of Kai Tahu, the first Maori group to have contact

with European settlers in the early nineteenth century. Hulme attended the University of Canterbury from 1967 to 1968 and has worked at diverse jobs, including fishing, cooking, painting, and directing television programs. She served as writer in residence at Otago University in Dunedin in 1978 and at the University of Canterbury in 1985. A member of the New Zealand Literary Fund Advisory Committee, Hulme lives and writes full-time in the remote Westland village of Okarito, population fourteen.

All of Hulme's fiction addresses issues of gender, race, cultural identity, and environmental awareness. Her highly acclaimed first novel, *The Bone People* (1984), was initially published by Spiral Collective #5, a feminist publishing cooperative, and was published the next year in America by Louisiana State University Press. It went on to win the Booker Prize, the New Zealand Book Award for Fiction, and the Pegasus Award for Maori Literature from Mobil Oil Corporation. Like Hulme, the book's central character, Kerewin Holmes, lives in self-imposed solitude in a seaside town, fishes for a living, and is one-eighth Maori; the novel focuses upon her relationship with a violent factory worker and his adopted son, as well as her efforts to confront her Maori heritage. Writing in the *New York Times*, critic Claudia Tate praised this novel's "unforgettably rich and pungent" language, its "conjuror's spell." Occasionally in her writing Hulme switches from English to vibrant words of Maori, which she has described as "a very positional and metaphoric language." Her second novel, *Lost Possessions*, appeared in 1985 but did not receive the critical attention that greeted *The Bone People*. Hulme has also published two volumes of poetry—*The Silence Between: Moeraki Conversations* (1982) and *Strands* (1988)—as well as a work of prose, *Homeplaces: Three Coasts of the South Islands of New Zealand* (1989).

Te Kaihau/The Windeater (1986), Hulme's collection of short stories, conveys her love for the country that Maori call Aotearoa, or shining light. These stories offer profound insights into Maori culture and into the spiritual and psychic conflicts of her dislocated characters. In their emphasis on family and ancestral relationships, many stories depart from a Maori saying that Hulme is fond of quoting: "We carry our ghosts on our shoulders: we are never alone." These ghosts that the unnamed protagonist in "One Whale, Singing" carries, as she drifts on a boat with her scientist husband, remain mysterious indeed. Clearly she identifies strongly with the humpback whale she watches, perhaps because she responds to its "strange and beautiful energy," perhaps because both it and she are pregnant. Like Edna Pontellier in *The Awakening*, this woman feels ambivalent toward motherhood and finds the voice of the sea seductive.

⊰ One Whale, Singing ⊱

The ship drifted on the summer night sea.

"It is a pity," she thought, "that one must come on deck to see the stars. Perhaps a boat of glass, to see the sea streaming past, to watch the nightly splendor of stars . . ." Something small jumped from the water, away to the left. A flash of phosphorescence after the sound, and then all was quiet and starlit again.

They had passed through krillswarms all day. Large areas of the sea were reddish-brown, as though an enormous creature had wallowed ahead of the boat, streaming blood.

"Whale-feed," she had said, laughing and hugging herself at the thought of seeing whales again. "Lobster-krill," he had corrected, pedantically.

The crustaceans had swum in their frightened jerking shoals, mile upon mile of them, harried by fish that were in turn pursued and torn by larger fish.

She thought, it was probably a fish after krill that had leaped then. She sighed, stroking her belly. It was the lesser of the two evils to go below now, so he didn't have an opportunity to come on deck and suggest it was better for the coming baby's health, and hers, of course, that she came down. The cramped cabin held no attraction: all that was there was boneless talk, and one couldn't see stars, or really hear the waters moving.

Far below, deep under the keel of the ship, a humpback whale sported and fed. Occasionally, she yodeled to herself, a long undulating call of content. When she found a series of sounds that pleased, she repeated them, wove them into a band of harmonious pulses.

Periodically she reared to the surface, blew, and slid smoothly back under the sea in a wheel-like motion. Because she was pregnant, and at the tailend of the southward migration, she had no reason now to leap and display on the surface.

She was not feeding seriously; the krill was there, and she swam amongst them, forcing water through her lips with her large tongue, stranding food amongst the baleen. When her mouth was full, she swallowed. It was leisurely, lazy eating. Time enough for recovering her full weight when she reached the cold seas, and she could gorge on a ton and a half of plankton daily.

Along this coast, there was life and noise in plenty. Shallow grunting from a herd of fish, gingerly feeding on the fringes of the krill shoal. The krill themselves, a thin hiss and crackle through the water. The interminable background clicking of shrimps. At times, a wayward band of sound like bass organ-notes sang through the chatter, and to this the whale listened attentively, and sometimes replied.

The krill thinned: she tested, tasted the water. Dolphins had passed recently. She heard their brief commenting chatter, but did not spend time on it. The school swept round ahead of her, and vanished into the vibrant dark.

He had the annoying habit of reading what he'd written out loud. "We can conclusively demonstrate that to man alone belong true intelligence and self-knowledge."

He coughs.

Taps his pen against his lips. He has soft, wet lips, and the sound is a fleshy slop! slop!

She thinks:

Man indeed! How arrogant! How ignorant! Woman would be as correct, but I'll settle for humanity. And it strikes me that the quality humanity stands in need of most is true intelligence and self-knowledge.

"For instance, Man alone as a species, makes significant artifacts, and transmits knowledge in permanent and durable form."

He grunts happily.

"In this lecture, I propose to . . ."

But how do they know? she asks herself. About the passing on of knowledge among other species? They may do it in ways beyond our capacity to understand . . . that we are the only ones to make artifacts I'll grant you, but that's because us needy little adapts have such pathetic bodies, and no especial ecological niche. So hooks and hoes, and steel things that gouge and slay, we produce in plenty. And build a wasteland of drear ungainly hovels to shelter our vulnerable hides.

She remembers her glass boat, and sighs. The things one could create if one made technology servant to a humble and creative imagination . . . He's booming on, getting into full lectureroom style and stride.

". . . thus we will show that no other species, lacking as they do artifacts, an organized society, or even semblances of culture . . ."

What would a whale do with an artifact, who is so perfectly adapted to the sea? Their conception of culture, of civilization, must be so alien that we'd never recognize it, even if we were to stumble on its traces daily.

She snorts.
He looks at her, eyes unglazing, and smiles.
"Criticism, my dear? Or you like that bit?"
"I was just thinking . . ."

Thinking, as for us passing on our knowledge, hah! We rarely learn from the past or the present, and what we pass on for future humanity is a mere jumble of momentarily true facts, and odd snippets of surprised self-discoveries. That's not knowledge . . .

She folds her hands over her belly. You in there, you won't learn much. What I can teach you is limited by what we are. Splotch goes the pen against his lips.

"You had better heat up that fortified drink, dear. We can't have either of you wasting from lack of proper nourishment."

Unspoken haw haw haw.

Don't refer to it as a person! It is a canker in me, a parasite. It is nothing to me. I feel it squirm and kick, and sicken at the movement.

He says he's worried by her pale face. "You shouldn't have gone up on deck so late. You could have slipped, or something, and climbing tires you now, you know."

She doesn't argue any longer. The arguments follow well-worn tracks and go in circles.

"Yes," she answers.

but I should wither without that release, that solitude, that keep away from you.

She stirs the powder into the milk and begins to mix it rhythmically.

I wonder what a whale thinks of its calf? So large a creature, so proven peaceful a beast, must be motherly, protective, a shielding benevolence against all wildness. It would be a sweet and milky love, magnified and sustained by the encompassing purity of water . . .

A swarm of insectlike creatures, sparkling like a galaxy, each a pulsing lightform in blue and silver and gold. The whale sang for them, a ripple of delicate notes, spaced in a timeless curve. It stole through the lightswarm, and the luminescence increased brilliantly.

Deep within her, the other spark of light also grew. It was the third calf she had borne; it delighted her still, that the swift airy copulation should spring so opportunely to this new life. She feeds it love and music, and her body's bounty. Already it responds to her crooning tenderness, and the dark pictures she sends it. It absorbs both, as part of the life to come, as it nests securely in the waters within.

She remembers the nautilids in the warm oceans to the north, snapping at one another in a cannibalistic frenzy.

She remembers the oil-bedraggled albatross, resting with patient finality on the water-top, waiting for death.

She remembers her flight, not long past, from killer whales, and the terrible end of the other female who had companied her south, tongue eaten from her mouth, flukes and genitals ripped, bleeding to a slow fought-against end.

And all the memories are part of the growing calf.

More krill appeared. She opened her mouth, and glided through the shoal. Sudden darkness for the krill. The whale hummed meanwhile.

He folded his papers contentedly.

"Sam was going on about his blasted dolphins the other night dear."

"Yes?"

He laughed deprecatingly. "But it wouldn't interest you. All dull scientific chatter, eh?"

"What was he saying about, umm, his dolphins?"

"O, insisted that his latest series of tests demonstrated their high intelligence. No, that's misquoting him, potentially high intelligence. Of course, I brought him down to earth smartly. Results are as you make them, I said. Nobody has proved that the animals have intelligence to a degree above that of a dog. But it made me think of the rot that's setting in lately. Inspiration for this lecture indeed."

"Lilley?" she asked, still thinking of the dolphins, "Lilley demonstrated evidence of dolphinese."

"Lilley? That mystical crackpot? Can you imagine anyone ever duplicating his work? Hah! Nobody has, of course. It was all in the man's mind."

"Dolphins and whales are still largely unknown entities," she murmured, more to herself than to him.

"Nonsense, my sweet. They've been thoroughly studied and dissected for the last century and more." She shuddered. "Rather dumb animals, all told, and probably of bovine origin. Look at the incredibly stupid way they persist in migrating straight into the hands of whalers, year after year. If they were smart, they'd have organized an attacking force and protected themselves!"

He chuckled at the thought, and lit his pipe.

"It would be nice to communicate with another species," she said, more softly still.

"That's the trouble with you poets," he said fondly. "Dream marvels are to be found from every half-baked piece of pseudoscience that drifts around. That's not seeing the world as it is. We scientists rely on reliably ascertained facts for a true picture of the world."

She sat silently by the pot on the galley stove.

An echo from the world around, a deep throbbing from miles away. It was both message and invitation to contribute. She mused on it for minutes, absorbing, storing, correlating, winding her song meanwhile experimentally through its interstices—then dropped her voice to the lowest frequencies. She sent the message along first, and then added another strength to the cold wave that traveled after the message. An ocean away, someone would collect the cold wave, and store it, while it coiled and built to uncontrollable strength. Then, just enough would be released to generate a superwave, a gigantic wall of water on the surface of the sea. It was a new thing the sea-people were experimenting with. A protection. In case.

She began to swim further out from the coast. The water flowed like warm silk over her flanks, an occasional interjectory current swept her, cold and bracing, a touch from the sea to the south. It became quieter, a calm freed from the fights of crabs and the bickerings of small fish. There was less noise too, from the strange turgid craft that buzzed and clattered across the ocean-ceiling, dropping down wastes that stank and sickened.

A great ocean-going shark prudently shifted course and flicked away to the side of her. It measured twenty feet from shovel-nose to crescentic tailfin, but she was twice as long and would grow a little yet. Her broad deep body was still well-fleshed and strong, in spite of the vicissitudes of the northward breeding trek: there were barnacles encrusting her fins and lips and head, but she was unhampered by other parasites. She blew a raspberry at the fleeing shark and beat her flukes against the ocean's pull in an ecstasy of strength.

"This lecture," he says, sipping his drink, "this lecture should cause quite a stir. They'll probably label it conservative, or even reactionary, but of course it isn't. It merely urges us to keep our feet on the ground, not go hunting off down worthless blind sidetrails. To consolidate data we already have, not, for example, to speculate about so-called ESP phenomena. There is far too much mysticism and airy-fairy folderol in science these days. I don't wholly agree with the Victorians' attitude, that science could explain all, and very shortly would, but it's high time we got things back to a solid factual basis."

"The Russians," she says, after a long moment of noncommittal silence, "the Russians have discovered a form of photography that shows all living things to be sources of a strange and beautiful energy. Lights flare from finger tips. Leaves coruscate. All is living effulgence."

He chuckles again.

"I can always tell when you're waxing poetic." Then he taps out the bowl of his pipe against the side of the bunk, and leans forward in a fatherly way.

"My dear, if they have, and that's a big if, what difference could that possibly make. Another form of energy? So what?"

"Not just another form of energy," she says somberly. "It makes for a whole new view of the world. If all things are repositories of related energy, then humanity is not alone . . ."

"Why this of solitariness, of being alone. Communication with other species, man is not alone, for God's sake! One would think you're becoming tired of us all!"

He's joking.

She is getting very tired. She speaks tiredly.

"It would mean that the things you think you are demonstrating in your paper . . ."

"Lecture."

"Work . . . those things are totally irrelevant. That we may be on the bottom of the pile, not the top. It may be that other creatures are aware of their place and purpose in the world, have no need to delve and paw a meaning out. Justify themselves. That they accept all that happens, the beautiful, the terrible, the sickening, as part of the dance, as the joy or pain of the joke. Other species may somehow be equipped to know fully and consciously what truth is, whereas we humans must struggle, must struggle blindly to the end."

He frowns, a concerned benevolent frown.

"Listen dear, has this trip been too much? Are you feeling at the end of your tether, tell us truly? I know the boat is old, and not much of a sailer, but it's the best I could do for the weekend. And I thought it would be a nice break for us, to get away from the university and home. Has there been too much work involved? The boat's got an engine after all . . . would you like me to start it and head back for the coast?"

She is shaking her head numbly.

He stands up and swallows what is left of his drink in one gulp.

"It won't take a minute to start the engine, and then I'll set that pilot thing, and we'll be back in sight of land before the morning. You'll feel happier then."

She grips the small table.

Don't scream, she tells herself, don't scream.

Diatoms of phantom light, stray single brilliances. A high burst of dolphin sonics. The school was returning. A muted rasp from shoalfish hurrying past. A thing that curled and coiled in a drifting aureole of green light.

She slows, buoyant in the water.

Green light: It brings up the memories that are bone deep in her, written in her very cells. Green light of land.

She had once gone within yards of shore, without stranding. Curiosity had impelled her up a long narrow bay. She had edged carefully along, until her long flippers touched the rocky bottom. Sculling with her tail, she had slid forward a little further, and then lifted her head out of the water. The light was bent, the sounds that came to her were thin and distorted, but she could see colors known only from dreams and hear a music that was both alien and familiar.

(Christlookitthat!)

(Fuckinghellgetoutahereitscomingin)

The sound waves pooped and spattered through the air, and things scrambled away, as she moved herself back smoothly into deeper water.

A strange visit, but it enabled her to put images of her own to the calling dream.

Follow the line to the hard and aching airswept land, lie upon solidity never before known until strained ribs collapse from weight of body never before felt. And then, the second beginning of joy . . .

She dreams a moment, recalling other ends, other beginnings. And because of the web that streamed between all members of her kind, she was ready for the softly insistent pulsation that wound itself into her dreaming. Mourning for a male of the species, up in the cold southern seas where the greenbellied krill swarm in unending abundance. Where the killing ships of the harpooners lurk. A barb sliced through the air in an arc and embedded itself in the lungs, so the whale blew red in his threshing agony. Another that sunk into his flesh by the heart. Long minutes later, his slow exhalation of death. Then the gathering of light from all parts of the drifting corpse. It condensed, vanished . . . streamers of sound from the dolphins who shoot past her, somersaulting in their strange joy.

The long siren call urges her south. She begins to surge upward to the sweet night air.

She says, "I must go on deck for a minute."

They had finished the quarrel, but still had not come together. He grunts, fondles his notes a last time, and rolls over in his sleeping bag, drawing the neck of it tightly close.

She says wistfully,
"Goodnight then," and climbs the stairs heavily up to the hatchway.
"You're slightly offskew," she says to the Southern Cross, and feels the repressed tears begin to flow down her cheeks. The stars blur.

Have I changed so much?
Or is it this interminable deadening pregnancy?
But his stolid, sullen, stupidity!
He won't see, he won't see, he won't see anything.

She walks to the bow, and settles herself down, uncomfortably aware of her protuberant belly, and begins to croon a song of comfort to herself.

And at that moment the humpback hit the ship, smashing through her old and weakened hull, collapsing the cabin, rending timbers. A mighty chaos . . .

Somehow she found herself in the water, crying for him, swimming in a circle as though among the small debris she might find a floating sleeping bag. The stern of the ship is sinking, poised a moment dark against the stars, and then it slides silently under.

She strikes out for a shape in the water, the life raft? the dinghy?

And the shape moves.

The humpback, full of her dreams and her song, had beat blindly upward, and was shocked by the unexpected fouling. She lies, waiting on the water-top.

The woman stays where she is, motionless except for her paddling hands. She has no fear of the whale, but thinks, "It may not know I am here, may hit me accidentally as it goes down."

She can see the whale more clearly now, an immense zeppelin shape, bigger by far than their flimsy craft had been, but it lies there, very still . . .

She hopes it hasn't been hurt by the impact, and chokes on the hope.

There is a long moaning call then, that reverberates through her. She is physically swept, shaken by an intensity of feeling, as though the whale has sensed her being and predicament, and has offered it all it can, a sorrowing compassion.

Again the whale makes the moaning noise, and the women calls, as loudly as she can, "Thank you, thank you" knowing that it is meaningless, and probably unheard. Tears stream down her face once more.

The whale sounded so gently she didn't realize it was going at all.

"I am now alone in the dark," she thinks, and the salt water laps round her mouth. "How strange, if this is to be the summation of my life."

In her womb the child kicked. Buoyed by the sea, she feels the movement as something gentle and familiar, dear to her for the first time.

But she begins to laugh.

The sea is warm and confiding, and it is a long long way to shore.   *1987*

Rita Dove
1952–

"When I am asked: 'What made you want to be a writer?'" claims RITA DOVE, the U.S. Poet Laureate from 1993 to 1995, "my answer has always been: 'Books.' First and foremost, now, then, and always, I have been passionate about books. From the time I began to read, as a child, I loved their heft in my hand and the warm spot caused by their intimate weight in my lap." Born in Akron, Ohio, Dove was the eldest daughter in a middle-class family of four children; her father worked as a chemist for the Goodyear Tire Company, her mother as a housekeeper. Dove shared her love of books with her older brother, a science fiction buff. Her first novel, written during elementary school, was called *Chaos* and featured robots overtaking the earth. She has credited a high school English teacher for taking her to a poetry reading by John Ciardi and thus inspiring her to become a writer. Described as "a devoted and subtle storyteller [whose] gifts are evoking, and sometimes exalting, the everyday moments we live by but may neglect or forget," Dove is Commonwealth Professor of English at the University of Virginia in Charlottesville, where she lives with her husband, Fred Viebahn. She is the mother of a daughter, Aviva.

Selected Poems (1993) contains three of Dove's previously published volumes: *The Yellow House on the Corner* (1980), which addresses the horrors of slavery and the joy of freedom; *Museum* (1983), which probes the intersections of public and familial space; and *Thomas and Beulah* (1986), a sequence about the poet's grandparents, which won the 1987 Pulitzer Prize. In *Grace Notes* (1989) Dove pays lyrical homage to her mother and her daughter. Helen Vendler has praised the economy of Dove's poetry, for she "has planed away unnecessary matter: pure shapes, her poems exhibit the thrift that Yeats called the sign of a perfected manner." At the same time, writes a reviewer for the *Chicago Tribune*, Dove's poems "draw real characters holding jobs, raising families, drinking beer, playing music, and eating catfish dripping with hot sauce." Dove has also published a collection of short stories, *Fifth Sunday* (1985); a novel, *Through the Ivory Gate* (1992); and a verse play, *The Darker Face of the Earth* (1994).

Dove's 1995 volume of poetry, *Mother Love*, draws upon the Greek myth of Demeter, ancient goddess of fertility, whose daughter, Kore, or Persephone, is abducted by Hades, King of the Underworld. Overwhelmed by loss, Demeter fails to nurture the earth, which lies in winter until her daughter is restored to her. In these poems Dove explores the power of the mother-daughter bond and the dilemma of a modern mother who finds it difficult to accept her daughter's growth into womanhood.

ᢋ Demeter Mourning[1] ᢔ

Nothing can console me. You may bring silk
to make skin sigh, dispense yellow roses
in the manner of ripened dignitaries.
You can tell me repeatedly
5   I am unbearable (and I know this):
still, nothing turns the gold to corn,
nothing is sweet to the tooth crushing in.

I'll not ask for the impossible;
one learns to walk by walking.
10   In time I'll forget this empty brimming,
I may laugh again at
a bird, perhaps, chucking the nest—
but it will not be happiness,
for I have known that.

1995

1. The Greek goddess of agriculture who lost her daughter, Koré, to Hades, god of the underworld. The crops and the land suffered neglect due to Demeter's grief, which lasted until her daughter was restored to her for six months each year.

⊰ Demeter, Waiting ⊱

No. Who can bear it. Only someone
who hates herself, who believes
to pull a hand back from a daughter's cheek
is to put love into her pocket—
5   like one of those ashen Christian
philosophers, or a war-bound soldier.

She is gone again and I will not bear
it, I will drag my grief through a winter
of my own making and refuse
10   any meadow that recycles itself into
hope. Shit on the cicadas, dry meteor
flash, finicky butterflies! I will wail and thrash
until the whole goddamned golden panorama freezes
over. Then I will sit down to wait for her. Yes.

1995

⊰ Mother Love ⊱

Who can forget the attitude of mothering?
    Toss me a baby and without bothering
to blink I'll catch her, sling him on a hip.
    Any woman knows the remedy for grief
5   is being needed: duty bugles and we'll
      climb out of exhaustion every time,
bare the nipple or tuck in the sheet,
      heat milk and hum at bedside until
they can dress themselves and rise, primed
10   for Love or Glory—those one-way mirrors
girls peer into as their fledgling heroes slip
      through, storming the smoky battlefield.

So when this kind woman approached at the urging
    of her bouquet of daughters,
15   (one for each of the world's corners,
      one for each of the winds to scatter!)
and offered up her only male child for nursing
    (a smattering of flesh, noisy and ordinary),
I put aside the lavish trousseau of the mourner
20   for the daintier comfort of pity:
I decided to save him. Each night
    I laid him on the smoldering embers,
sealing his juices in slowly so he might
    be cured to perfection. Oh, I know it
25   looked damning: at the hearth a muttering crone
    bent over a baby sizzling on a spit
as neat as a Virginia ham. Poor human—
    to scream like that, to make me remember.

1995

⊷ ⊷ ≡⊹≡ ⊶ ⊶

Cherríe Moraga
1952–

A Chicana editor, poet, playwright, and essayist, CHERRÍE MORAGA was born in Whittier, California, and raised in Los Angeles by working-class parents; her father was white and her mother Mexican-American. The first in her family to attend college, Moraga worked as a waitress and a teacher before completing her M.A. at San Francisco State University in 1980. She came to prominence as the editor (with Gloria Anzaldúa) of *This Bridge Called My Back* (1981), an anthology of stories, poems, and essays by radical U.S. women of color—feminists protesting racism in the mainstream women's movement and offering their own visions. Used as a text in many women's studies and Chicano studies courses, this book won the 1986 Before Columbus Foundation American Book Award. Moraga has also edited *Cuentos* (1983), a collection of Latina women's narratives.

Loving in the War Years (1983), Moraga's best-known volume of poetry, reconceptualizes gender, sexuality, race, and art. Like much of her work, this book engages in "code-switching," freely crossing back and forth between Spanish and English. *The Last Generation* (1993) combines prose and poetry, and mythic as well as historical analysis, to consider the role of lesbian artists' efforts to transform U.S. society at the millennium. As a dramatist Moraga has received awards from the Fund for New American Plays and the National Endowment for the Arts Playwrights Fellowship. *Giving Up the Ghost: Teatro in Two Acts* (1986) explores sexuality, desire, and incest. *Heroes and Saints* (1994) portrays the crisis of a community of Chicano farmworkers whose children are dying from exposure to pesticides. *Shadow of a Man* (1992), published in *Shattering the Myth: Plays by Hispanic Women*, addresses women's ambivalence toward the men in their lives—fathers, husbands, priests.

"My mother. On some very basic level, the woman cannot be shaken from the ground on which she walks," claims Moraga in her introduction to *This Bridge Called My Back*. "Once at a very critical point in my work on this book, when everything I loved—the people, the writing, the city—all began to cave in on me, feeling such utter despair and self-doubt, I received in the mail a card from my mother. A holy card of St. Anthony de Padua, her patron saint, her 'special' saint, wrapped in a plastic cover. She wrote in it: 'Dear Cherríe, I am sending you this prayer of St. Anthony. Pray to God to help you with this book.'" Affirmed in her work by her mother's faith, Moraga was soon able to continue her labor. In numerous essays and poems Moraga explores the love and ambivalence that characterize the mother-daughter bond.

⊰ La Güera ⊱

> It requires something more than personal experience to gain a philosophy or point of view from any specific event. It is the quality of our response to the event and our capacity to enter into the lives of others that help us to make their lives and experiences our own.
>
> *Emma Goldman[1]*

I am the very well-educated daughter of a woman who, by the standards in this country, would be considered largely illiterate. My mother was born in Santa Paula,

---

1. [Alix Kates Shulman, "Was My Life Worth Living?" *Red Emma Speaks* (New York: Random House, 1972) 388.] Emma Goldman (1869–1940) was a U.S. socialist, feminist, and anarchist.

Southern California, at a time when much of the central valley there was still farm land. Nearly thirty-five years later, in 1948, she was the only daughter of six to marry an Anglo, my father.

I remember all of my mother's stories, probably much better than she realizes. She is a fine story-teller, recalling every event of her life with the vividness of the present, noting each detail right down to the cut and color of her dress. I remember stories of her being pulled out of school at the ages of five, seven, nine, and eleven to work in the fields, along with her brothers and sisters; stories of her father drinking away whatever small profit she was able to make for the family; of her going the long way home to avoid meeting him on the street, staggering toward the same destination. I remember stories of my mother lying about her age in order to get a job as a hat-check girl at Agua Caliente Racetrack in Tijuana. At fourteen, she was the main support of the family. I can still see her walking home alone at 3 a.m., only to turn all of her salary and tips over to her mother, who was pregnant again.

The stories continue through the war years and on: walnut-cracking factories, the Voit Rubber factory, and then the computer boom. I remember my mother doing piecework for the electronics plant in our neighborhood. In the late evening, she would sit in front of the TV set, wrapping copper wires into the backs of circuit boards, talking about "keeping up with the younger girls." By that time, she was already in her mid-fifties.

Meanwhile, I was college-prep in school. After classes, I would go with my mother to fill out job applications for her, or write checks for her at the supermarket. We would have the scenario all worked out ahead of time. My mother would sign the check before we'd get to the store. Then, as we'd approach the checkstand, she would say—within earshot of the cashier—"oh honey, you go 'head and make out the check," as if she couldn't be bothered with such an insignificant detail. No one asked any questions.

I was educated, and wore it with a keen sense of pride and satisfaction, my head propped up with the knowledge, from my mother, that my life would be easier than hers. I was educated; but more than this, I was "la güera": fair-skinned. Born with the features of my Chicana mother, but the skin of my Anglo father, I had it made.

No one ever quite told me this (that light was right), but I knew that being light was something valued in my family (who were all Chicano, with the exception of my father). In fact, everything about my upbringing (at least what occurred on a conscious level) attempted to bleach me of what color I did have. Although my mother was fluent in it, I was never taught much Spanish at home. I picked up what I did learn from school and from overheard snatches of conversation among my relatives and mother. She often called other lower-income Mexicans "braceros," or "wetbacks," referring to herself and her family as "a different class of people." And yet, the real story was that my family, too, had been poor (some still are) and farmworkers. My mother can remember this in her blood as if it were yesterday. But this is something she would like to forget (and rightfully), for to her, on a basic economic level, being Chicana meant being "less." It was through my mother's desire to protect her children from poverty and illiteracy that we became "anglocized"; the more effectively we could pass in the white world, the better guaranteed our future.

From all of this, I experience, daily, a huge disparity between what I was born into and what I was to grow up to become. Because, (as Goldman suggests) these stories my mother told me crept under my "güera" skin. I had no choice but to enter into the life of my mother. *I had no choice.* I took her life into my heart, but managed to keep a lid on it as long as I feigned being the happy, upwardly mobile heterosexual.

When I finally lifted the lid to my lesbianism, a profound connection with my mother reawakened in me. It wasn't until I acknowledged and confronted my own lesbianism in the flesh, that my heartfelt identification with and empathy for my mother's oppression—due to being poor, uneducated, and Chicana—was realized. My lesbianism is the avenue through which I have learned the most about silence and oppression, and it continues to be the most tactile reminder to me that we are not free human beings.

You see, one follows the other. I had known for years that I was a lesbian, had felt it in my bones, had ached with the knowledge, gone crazed with the knowledge, wallowed in the silence of it. Silence *is* like starvation. Don't be fooled. It's nothing short of that, and felt most sharply when one has had a full belly most of her life. When we are not physically starving, we have the luxury to realize psychic and emotional starvation. It is from this starvation that other starvations can be recognized— if one is willing to take the risk of making the connection—if one is willing to be responsible to the result of the connection. For me, the connection is an inevitable one.

What I am saying is that the joys of looking like a white girl ain't so great since I realized I could be beaten on the street for being a dyke. If my sister's being beaten because she's Black, it's pretty much the same principle. We're both getting beaten any way you look at it. The connection is blatant; and in the case of my own family, the difference in the privileges attached to looking white instead of brown are merely a generation apart.

In this country, lesbianism is a poverty—as is being brown, as is being a woman, as is being just plain poor. The danger lies in ranking the oppressions. *The danger lies in failing to acknowledge the specificity of the oppression.* The danger lies in attempting to deal with oppression purely from a theoretical base. Without an emotional, heartfelt grappling with the source of our own oppression, without naming the enemy within ourselves and outside of us, no authentic, nonhierarchical connection among oppressed groups can take place.

When the going gets rough, will we abandon our so-called comrades in a flurry of racist/heterosexist/what-have-you panic? To whose camp, then, should the lesbian of color retreat? Her very presence violates the ranking and abstraction of oppression. Do we merely live hand to mouth? Do we merely struggle with the "ism" that's sitting on top of our own heads?

The answer is: Yes, I think first we do; and we must do so thoroughly and deeply. But to fail to move out from there will only isolate us in our own oppression—will only insulate, rather than radicalize us.

To illustrate: a gay male friend of mine once confided to me that he continued to feel that, on some level, I didn't trust him because he was male; that he felt, really, if it ever came down to a "battle of the sexes," I might kill him. I admitted that I might very well. He wanted to understand the source of my distrust. I responded, "You're not a woman. Be a woman for a day. Imagine being a woman." He confessed that the thought terrified him because, to him, being a woman meant being raped by men. He *had* felt raped by men; he wanted to forget what that meant. What grew from that discussion was the realization that in order for him to create an authentic alliance with me, he must deal with the primary source of his own sense of oppression. He must, first, emotionally come to terms with what it feels like to be a victim. If he—or anyone—were to truly do this, it would be impossible to discount the oppression of others, except by again forgetting how we have been hurt.

And yet, oppressed groups are forgetting all the time. There are instances of this in the rising Black middle class, and certainly an obvious trend of such "unconsciousness" among white gay men. Because to remember may mean giving up whatever privileges we have managed to squeeze out of this society by virtue of our gender, race, class, or sexuality.

Within the women's movement, the connections among women of different backgrounds and sexual orientations have been fragile, at best. I think this phenomenon is indicative of our failure to seriously address ourselves to some very frightening questions: How have I internalized my own oppression? How have I oppressed? Instead, we have let rhetoric do the job of poetry. Even the word "oppression" has lost its power. We need a new language, better words that can more closely describe women's fear of and resistance to one another; words that will not always come out sounding like dogma.

What prompted me in the first place to work on an anthology by radical women of color was a deep sense that I had a valuable insight to contribute, by virtue of my birthright and background. And yet, I don't really understand firsthand what it feels like being shitted on for being brown. I understand much more about the joys of it—being Chicana and having family are synonymous for me. What I know about loving, singing, crying, telling stories, speaking with my heart and hands, even having a sense of my own soul comes from the love of my mother, aunts, cousins. . . .

But at the age of twenty-seven, it is frightening to acknowledge that I have internalized a racism and classism, where the object of oppression is not only someone outside of my skin, but the someone inside my skin. In fact, to a large degree, the real battle with such oppression, for all of us, begins under the skin. I have had to confront the fact that much of what I value about being Chicana, about my family, has been subverted by Anglo culture and my own cooperation with it. This realization did not occur to me overnight. For example, it wasn't until long after my graduation from the private college I'd attended in Los Angeles, that I realized the major reason for my total alienation from and fear of my classmates was rooted in class and culture. CLICK.

Three years after graduation, in an apple orchard in Sonoma, a friend of mine (who comes from an Italian Irish working-class family) says to me, "Cherríe, no wonder you felt like such a nut in school. Most of the people there were white and rich." It was true. All along I had felt the difference, but not until I had put the words "class" and "color" to the experience, did my feelings make any sense. For years, I had berated myself for not being as "free" as my classmates. I completely bought that they simply had more guts than I did—to rebel against their parents and run around the country hitch-hiking, reading books and studying "art." They had enough privilege to be atheists, for chrissake. There was no one around filling in the disparity for me between their parents, who were Hollywood filmmakers, and my parents, who wouldn't know the name of a filmmaker if their lives depended on it (and precisely because their lives didn't depend on it, they couldn't be bothered). But I knew nothing about "privilege" then. White was right. Period. I could pass. If I got educated enough, there would never be any telling.

Three years after that, another CLICK. In a letter to Barbara Smith[2], I wrote:

I went to a concert where Ntosake Shange[3] was reading. There, everything exploded for me. She was speaking a language that I knew—in the deepest parts of me—existed, and that I had ignored in my own feminist studies and even in my own writing. What Ntosake caught in me is the realization that in my development as a poet, I have, in many ways, denied the voice of my brown mother—the brown in me. I have acclimated to the sound of a white language which, as my father represents it, does not speak to the emotions in my poems—emotions which stem from the love of my mother.

The reading was agitating. Made me uncomfortable. Threw me into a week-long terror of how deeply I was affected. I felt that I had to start all over again. That I turned only to the perceptions of white middle-class women to speak for me and all women. I am shocked by my own ignorance.

Sitting in that auditorium chair was the first time I had realized to the core of me that for years I had disowned the language I knew best—ignored the words and rhythms that were the closest to me. The sounds of my mother and aunts gossiping— half in English, half in Spanish—while drinking cerveza in the kitchen. And the hands—I had cut off the hands in my poems. But not in conversation; still the hands could not be kept down. Still they insisted on moving.

The reading had forced me to remember that I knew things from my roots. But to remember puts me up against what I don't know. Shange's reading agitated me because she spoke with power about a world that is both alien and common to me: "the capacity to enter into the lives of others." But you can't just take the goods and run. I knew that then, sitting in the Oakland auditorium (as I know in my poetry), that the only thing worth writing about is what seems to be unknown and, therefore, fearful.

The "unknown" is often depicted in racist literature as the "darkness" within a person. Similarly, sexist writers will refer to fear in the form of the vagina, calling it "the orifice of death." In contrast, it is a pleasure to read works such as Maxine Hong Kingston's *Woman Warrior*,[4] where fear and alienation are described as "the white ghosts." And yet, the bulk of literature in this country reinforces the myth that what is dark and female is evil. Consequently, each of us—whether dark, female, or both— has in some way *internalized* this oppressive imagery. What the oppressor often succeeds in doing is simply *externalizing* his fears, projecting them into the bodies of women, Asians, gays, disabled folks, whoever seems most "other."

> call me
> roach and presumptuous
> nightmare on your white pillow
> your itch to destroy
> the indestructible
> part of yourself
>
> *Audre Lorde*[5]

But it is not really difference the oppressor fears so much as similarity. He fears he will discover in himself the same aches, the same longings as those of the people

---

2. An African-American literary critic, born 1946.
3. Ntosake [sic] Shange (born 1948) is an African-American poet, playwright, and novelist.
4. MAXINE HONG KINGSTON (born 1940) is a Chinese-American writer who published *The Woman Warrior* in 1976.

5. [From "The Brown Menace or Poem to the Survival of Roaches," *The New York Head Shop and Museum* (Detroit: Broadside, 1974) 48.]

he has shitted on. He fears the immobilization threatened by his own incipient guilt. He fears he will have to change his life once he has seen himself in the bodies of the people he has called different. He fears the hatred, anger, and vengeance of those he has hurt.

This is the oppressor's nightmare, but it is not exclusive to him. We women have a similar nightmare, for each of us in some way has been both oppressed and the oppressor. We are afraid to look at how we have failed each other. We are afraid to see how we have taken the values of our oppressor into our hearts and turned them against ourselves and one another. We are afraid to admit how deeply "the man's" words have been ingrained in us.

To assess the damage is a dangerous act. I think of how, even as a feminist lesbian, I have so wanted to ignore my own homophobia, my own hatred of myself for being queer. I have not wanted to admit that my deepest personal sense of myself has not quite "caught up" with my "woman-identified" politics. I have been afraid to criticize lesbian writers who choose to "skip over" these issues in the name of feminism. In 1979, we talk of "old gay" and "butch and femme" roles as if they were ancient history. We toss them aside as merely patriarchal notions. And yet, the truth of the matter is that I have sometimes taken society's fear and hatred of lesbians to bed with me. I have sometimes hated my lover for loving me. I have sometimes felt "not woman enough" for her. I have sometimes felt "not man enough." For a lesbian trying to survive in heterosexist society, there is no easy way around these emotions. Similarly, in a white-dominated world, there is little getting around racism and our own internalization of it. It's always there, embodied in some one we least expect to rub up against.

When we do rub up against this person, *there* then is the challenge. *There* then is the opportunity to look at the nightmare within us. But we usually shrink from such a challenge.

Time and time again, I have observed that the usual response among white women's groups when the "racism issue" comes up is to deny the difference. I have heard comments like, "Well, we're open to *all* women; why don't they (women of color) come? You can only do so much . . ." But there is seldom any analysis of how the very nature and structure of the group itself may be founded on racist or classist assumptions. More importantly, so often the women seem to feel no loss, no lack, no absence when women of color are not involved; therefore, there is little desire to change the situation. This has hurt me deeply. I have come to believe that the only reason women of a privileged class will dare to look at *how* it is that *they* oppress, is when they've come to know the meaning of their own oppression. And understand that the oppression of others hurts them personally.

The other side of the story is that women of color and working-class women often shrink from challenging white middle-class women. It is much easier to rank oppressions and set up a hierarchy, rather than take responsibility for changing our own lives. We have failed to demand that white women, particularly those who claim to be speaking for all women, be accountable for their racism.

The dialogue has simply not gone deep enough.

I have many times questioned my right to even work on an anthology which is to be written "exclusively by Third World women." I have had to look critically at my claim to color, at a time when, among white feminist ranks, it is a "politically correct" (and sometimes peripherally advantageous) assertion to make. I must acknowledge the fact that, physically, I have had a *choice* about making that claim, in contrast to women who have not had such a choice, and have been abused for their color. I must reckon with the fact that for most of my life, by virtue of the very fact that I am white-looking, I identified with and aspired toward white values, and that I rode the wave of that Southern Californian privilege as far as conscience would let me.

Well, now I feel both bleached and beached. I feel angry about this—the years when I refused to recognize privilege, both when it worked against me, and when I worked it, ignorantly, at the expense of others. These are not settled issues. That is why this work feels so risky to me. It continues to be discovery. It has brought me into contact with women who invariably know a hell of a lot more than I do about racism, as experienced in the flesh, as revealed in the flesh of their writing.

I think: what is my responsibility to my roots—both white and brown, Spanish-speaking and English? I am a woman with a foot in both worlds; and I refuse the split. I feel the necessity for dialogue. Sometimes I feel it urgently.

But one voice is not enough, nor two, although this is where dialogue begins. It is essential that radical feminists confront their fear of and resistance to each other, because without this, there *will* be no bread on the table. Simply, we will not survive. If we could make this connection in our heart of hearts, that if we are serious about a revolution—better—if we seriously believe there should be joy in our lives (real joy, not just "good times"), then we need one another. We women need each other. Because my/your solitary, self-asserting "go-for-the-throat-of-fear" power is not enough. The real power, as you and I well know, is collective. I can't afford to be afraid of you, nor you of me. If it takes head-on collisions, let's do it: This polite timidity is killing us.

As Lorde suggests in the passage I cited earlier, it is in looking to the nightmare that the dream is found. There, the survivor emerges to insist on a future, a vision, yes, born out of what is dark and female. The feminist movement must be a movement of such survivors, a movement with a future.   *1979/1981*

⊰ For the Color of My Mother ⊱

I am a white girl gone brown to the color of my mother
speaking for her through the unnamed part of the mouth
the wide-arched muzzle of brown women

    at two
5   my upper lip split open
    clear to the tip of my nose
    it spilled forth a cry that would not yield
    that travelled down six floors of hospital
    where doctors wound me into white bandages
10   only the screaming mouth exposed

    the gash sewn back into a snarl
    would last for years

I am a white girl gone brown to the blood color of my mother
speaking for her

15   at five, her mouth
      pressed into a seam
      a fine blue child's line drawn across her face
      her mouth, pressed into mouthing english
      mouthing yes yes yes
20   mouthing stoop lift carry
      (sweating wet sighs into the field
      her red bandana comes loose from under the huge brimmed hat
      moving across her upper lip)

      at fourteen, her mouth
25   painted, the ends drawn up
      the mole in the corner colored in darker larger mouthing yes
      she praying no no no
      lips pursed and moving

      at forty-five, her mouth
30   bleeding into her stomach
      the hole gaping growing redder
      deepening with my father's pallor
      finally stitched shut from hip to breastbone
      an inverted V
35   *Vera*
      Elvira

      I am a white girl gone brown to the blood color of my mother
      speaking for her

      as it should be
40   dark women come to me
                    sitting in circles
      I pass through their hands
      the head of my mother
      painted in clay colors

45   touching each carved feature
                    swollen eyes and mouth
      they understand the explosion the splitting
      open   contained within the fixed expression

      they cradle her silence
50   nodding to me

                                        1981

Kate Daniels
1953–

In "Prayer to the Muse of Ordinary life" KATE DANIELS implores this source of inspiration to "prove you do exist: / a poem in a small, soiled / nightie, a lyric / in the sandbox voices / raised in woe." A contemporary U.S. poet and scholar, Daniels was born in Richmond and studied English literature at the University of Virginia, where she earned her B.A. and M.A. degrees;

she completed her M.F.A. at Columbia University in 1980. Daniels edited *Of Solitude and Silence: Writings on Robert Bly* (1982), and during the 1980s she served as editor of the journal *Poetry East*. In 1992 she edited *Out of Silence*, a selection of poems by MURIEL RUKEYSER, and she is currently completing a literary biography of Rukeyser. Daniels has taught literature and creative writing at the University of Massachusetts at Amherst, Louisiana State University, Wake Forest University, Bennington College, and Vanderbilt University. In addition, she has conducted writing workshops for physicians and patients at the Duke University Medical Center and the Vanderbilt Medical Center. Daniels has received grants from the National Endowment for the Arts and the Pennsylvania Council of the Arts, and in 1986 she was a fellow at the Mary Ingraham Bunting Institute. She lives in Nashville, Tennessee, with her husband, Geoffrey Macdonald, and their three children.

As the poet Maxine Kumin has noted, "Daniels gives dignity and authority to the cradle and the hearthstone as subject matter. She is at her best with details of the homely moments when disparate lives overlap or connect." Her first book of poetry, *The White Wave*, won the Agnes Lynch Starrett Poetry Prize and was published in the University of Pittsburgh Poetry Series in 1984. In this collection Daniels writes about family members, friends, and lovers—"bodies of kin," she calls them—as well as more overtly social and political topics. Her second book, *The Niobe Poems* (1988), rewrites the myth of Niobe, once the happiest and proudest of mothers, whose fourteen children were killed by the goddess Leto. The distraught Niobe sought refuge in the wilderness, where she was turned into a rock from which flowed an everlasting stream of tears. The Niobe of Daniels's poems has lost her young son in a swimming accident not even the gods can comprehend, much less the frantic mortals implicated in the tragedy.

The poems included here are taken from Daniels's third collection of poetry, *Four Testimonies* (1998). In language ranging from the terse to the luminous, they explore a woman's decision to bear children, the tension between writing and motherhood, and the joys of mothering "three who love me / exactly as I am, precisely / at the center of my ill-built being."

⊰ Genesis I: 28 ⊱

In the dank clarity of the Green Line tunnel,
we hatched our plan—to grow a creature
from those nights of love, those afternoons
of thick scents, those liquid mornings, odor
5   of coffee mingling with musk. Actually, he wanted
six, he said, standing there in the chill, a train
thundering up like an epiphany the two of us
verified together.

I knew then it was over, irrevocably
10   over, my previous life, alone and unloved, could see
how it would finally play itself out, starring him
and our creatures, the chaotic kitchen, the rumpled
beds, my wrinkled shirttails smeared with egg.
Helplessly, I tilted toward him and those sweet
15   images, to his mouth and his smell, toward my life
and my future, the nights we would recline, locked
and rocking in groaning love, the months my belly
would expand with our efforts, the bloody bringing forth
of two of him and one of me.

20   I stood for one last moment alone,
inside a cloud of grace, a pure and empty
gift of space where history released its grip.
Its bulging bag of bad memories burst open
in the doors of a train and was carried off

25   to a distant city I swore never to revisit.
And then I turned to his lips and his tongue,
to our hands in our gloves unbuckling each other,
calculating how quickly we could travel
back home. To anyone watching, it must have

30   looked like lust—two lovers emboldened
by the anonymity residing in a subway stop.
What kind of being could possibly see

a new world was being made, a universe
created? Who could have known how called

35   we were to what we were doing? How godlike
it was, how delicious, how holy?

1998

⫷ Love Pig ⫸

You, too, will love
her thighs. The fat
sweatiness of them,
the toe-curling odor.

5   The bracelets, the biscuits
of baby-flesh washed
in urine and milk.
The neck is next best.
Fat, too, bejeweled with dried

10   spit, old food, gray
gyres of tears and sweat.
If you like, I will let you
borrow her for awhile
and you can burrow

15   down deep in her sweet
and her sourness, her soft
and her softer. Belly up
to the buffet of her body, and grow
corpulent like us, guzzling

20   sweet draughts of baby breath,
gobbling mouthfuls of sticky,
tender cheek, gorging ourselves
on our own baby girl.

1998

⫷ In My Office at Bennington ⫸

Mornings, I sit by the open window
in the red barn, reading poems

and quietly thinking. Coffee idles
in a cracked blue mug, and bees burst
5   in and out of the unscreened window.
At last, a poem seems possible
again—brain knitting a scarf
of thought, purling it into words.
Metaphors emerge after long seclusion—
10   *a green crocus, crusted with dirt, thrusts*
through the rotten fabric of an ailing lawn
late in February. The season is almost
over, or it's not, in fact, begun.

But then I hear the voices of my children
15   returning from a meal, hiking up the hill
from camp. Or the plastic wheels of Janey's
carriage clattering in gravel.
The cheerful firstborn's off-key whistle,
airy through the gap in new front teeth

20   and I'm paper torn in half,

the poem that didn't work,
the wrong words, sour sounds,
ruptured rhythms, the confusion
as to what was meant, what I actually
25   desired besides those three small faces
raised to my open window, calling
my name over and over, *Mama?*

                                                            1998

⊰ After Reading Reznikoff ⊱

When I think of those mothers giving up
their children at the gates of the camps,
or choosing one over the other, or accompanying
their youngsters to the showers of gas,
5   when I think of that wrenching, that
wailing, the force of those feelings,
the terrible potency, the fear breaking
their bodies in sweat and hives,
the vomiting and shitting, the mindless
10   lunging for their infants and toddlers,
their sons and their daughters, when I think of
that universe of last images, the eyes, the unspeakable
eyes of mothers comprehending, the backs
of the children waddling away, being led
15   away, being pulled away, recalcitrant curls,
fallen hems, toys dropped on the gravel paths,
the little waves, the dipped heads, the incessant
weeping, when I think of the bleeding wombs
of dying mothers, pleading mothers, the bellies
20   of mothers with unborn babies, the breasts bursting

with unsucked milk, when I think of the various
ways the weather must have been—the cold
crunch of snow, the flowery delight of early spring
—when I think of the camps and the deaths of the Jews,
25   the millions of Jews, I think of the mothers,
the bodies of mothers, their bodies bearing
their children to death, I think of the noise
of transport trains, the terror of trains,
the engines cooling into inert steel,
30   the clatter and steam, the scenes enacted
in the railroad yards, and the trains remind me
to think of the men, at last I remember
those armies of men, their greatcoats and weapons,
no children inhabiting their rational bodies, the mystery
35   of murder, the bodies of the women so alive
with emotion, the bodies of the men so dead
to it all, I think not of God, desperately I try
to not think of God, my good, great God, neither
woman nor man, circling above in heartbroken panic,
40   the beating of wings, the cacophonous
suffering, the pungent cloud rising
of dark, dark feeling that silenced even Him.

                                                    1998

⇥ Prayer for My Children ⇤

I regret nothing.
My cruelties, my betrayals
of others I once thought
I loved. All the unlived
5   years, the unwritten
poems, the wasted nights
spent weeping and drinking.

No, I regret nothing
because what I've lived
10   has led me here, to this room
with its marvelous riches,
its simple wealth—
these three heads shining
beneath the Japanese lamp, laboring
15   over crayons and paper.
These three who love me
exactly as I am, precisely
at the center of my ill-built being.
Who rear up eagerly when I enter,
20   and fall down weeping when I leave.
Whose eyes are my eyes.
Hair, my hair.
Whose bodies I cover
with kisses and blankets.

25   Whose first meal was my own body.
      Whose last, please God, I will not live
      to serve, or share.

                                                    1998

·—· ⚏✦⚏ ·—·

Intertextualities

This case study draws upon the theoretical essays from Section III, "Rethinking the Maternal": "Writing and Motherhood" by SUSAN RUBIN SULEIMAN and "Shifting the Center: Race, Class, and Feminist Theorizing about Motherhood" by PATRICIA HILL COLLINS. These essays are used as a means of interrogating literary works by three representative writers from Section III, KATE CHOPIN, BESSIE HEAD, and BETH BRANT. Also part of this case study are a critical essay on Chopin's *The Awakening* by MARGIT STANGE and an essay on the mother's role in Native American cultures and literature by PAULA GUNN ALLEN, as well as questions related to their perspectives on the writers under consideration.

ᔌ Topics for Discussion, Journals, and Essays ᔍ

1. In "Writing and Motherhood" Susan Rubin Suleiman suggests that the major themes in women's writing about motherhood are "clustered into two large groups: opposition and integration, motherhood as obstacle or source of conflict and motherhood as link, as source of connection to work and world." Into which group do you think Chopin's novella, *The Awakening*, Head's "The Village Saint," and Brant's "A Long Story" fall? That is, to what extent do these writers view motherhood as a source of conflict, a source of connection, or both? Explain your reasoning, using examples and quotations from the texts.

2. Suleiman says in "Writing and Motherhood" that Rosellen Brown is one of the few U.S. novelists who has explored "the violence and guilt as well as the violent energy that attend the artistic creations of mothers," but one might argue that Kate Chopin addressed these issues more than seventy years earlier than Brown began writing. Using Suleiman's article as a guide, consider in what ways Chopin represents violence and guilt as part of Edna's awakening as a sexual being, an artist, and a mother in *The Awakening*.

3. Patricia Hill Collins claims in "Shifting the Center" that in Afrocentric traditions, "motherhood of varying types, whether bloodmother, othermother, or community othermother, can be invoked as a symbol of power." Paula Gunn Allen argues similarly in "Who Is Your Mother?" that in "gynocratic" Native American cultures, your mother is "not only the woman whose womb formed and released you" but "an entire generation of women." What roles do bloodmothers and othermothers fulfill in Beth Brant's "A Long Story," and who or what threatens their actions on behalf of racial-ethnic children? In Bessie Head's "The Village Saint," what differences and connections do you see between Mma-Mompati's function as a bloodmother and her role as a community othermother?

4. In discussing the nineteenth-century feminist advocacy of voluntary motherhood as a form of women's autonomy, critic Margit Stange suggests that "to put voluntary motherhood practiced without birth control devices at the center of self-ownership is to make motherhood central to a woman's life and identity." In what ways does motherhood enhance, inhibit, or define self-ownership for the protagonists in Chopin's *The Awakening* and Brant's "A Long Story"? Again, use quotations and textual references to explain your response.

5. Although Chopin describes Edna Pontellier as "not a mother woman," Stange suggests that she nonetheless is "inescapably a mother." Explain what you see as Stange's reasoning, and

consider whether the same could be said of Head's Mma-Mompati, who appears for years to be an ideal mother and community othermother but ultimately is "not a mother woman." In what ways do Edna and Mma-Mompati "fail" at mothering, and in what ways might the restrictions and expectations placed on mothers in their respective societies be said to "fail" them as women?

6. In "Who Is Your Mother?" Paula Gunn Allen claims that in Native American societies, the identity of your mother "is the key to your own identity": "naming your own mother (or her equivalent) enables people to place you precisely within the universal web of your life, in each of its dimensions: cultural, spiritual, personal, and historical." Consider Beth Brant's "A Long Story" in light of Allen's claim. Why do the two Native American mothers in this story fear that robbed of their mothers, their children will lose their identities? What cultural, spiritual, personal, and historical values does each mother want to impart to her children?

7. For Native Americans, writes Allen, memory "implies continuance rather than nostalgia"; if women fail to remember their mothers and grandmothers, they lose history and vitality. How can Allen's argument be connected to Collins's claim that racial-ethnic women's motherwork insures the survival and cultural awareness of their children? Discuss the role of motherwork and memory as tools of cultural survival in Brant's "A Long Story," using the claims of Allen and Collins as part of your reasoning.

⬿ Creative Writing Exercise ⬾

Write a letter from mother to daughter or son in the voice of either Edna Pontellier, Mma-Mompati, the 1890 Native American mother in Brant's story, or Brant's lesbian mother. Explain what kind of mother you consider yourself to be, what legacy you wish to pass along to your child (or children), and what you would like them to remember about you or learn from your life experiences. Make sure the voice of your speaker is consistent with that of the maternal subject portrayed in the relevant work of fiction.

⬿ Oral History Project ⬾

A. Using Suleiman's essay as a guide, formulate a series of questions about the conflicts and connections between mothering and creativity, and interview a mother who is an aspiring writer or artist about her perspectives on the matter.

B. Using Collins's essay as a guide, formulate a series of questions about the particular trials and joys that attend mothering and motherwork for women of color; then interview a mother or othermother from your own or a different racial-ethnic group about her perspectives on the matter.

C. As an alternative, interview your own mother, grandmother, or othermother, asking whether and how she managed to combine motherwork and creativity in her life.

D. After completing project A, B, or C, transcribe the interview, write up a feminist analysis of your findings (using insights and quotations from Suleiman and Collins), and share them with the class.

⼁⽷⼁

Margit Stange

1949–

MARGIT STANGE, an affiliated scholar with Stanford University's Institute for Research on Women and Gender, is the author of *Personal Property: Wives, White Slaves, and the Market in Women* (1998). This study of early twentieth-century literary and sociological texts investigates how women have been viewed as commodities, or objects of exchange, and how women writers have resisted commodification. Among the women whose writing she considers are KATE CHOPIN, EDITH WHARTON, CHARLOTTE PERKINS GILMAN, and Jane Addams. A feminist critic whose interests are interdisciplinary, Stange analyzes history and popular culture as well as literature in her scholarly work.

Stange was born in Bennington, Vermont, and was educated at the University of Minnesota, where she earned a B.A. in history in 1973, and at the University of California at Berkeley, where she earned a Ph.D in English literature in 1989. She has taught English at the University of California, Davis, and has been a visiting scholar of woman and gender at UC-Berkeley. Her articles on Chopin's *The Awakening* and MARY SHELLEY's *Frankenstein* have appeared in such journals as *Genders* and *Women's Studies,* and her essay on fetal alcohol syndrome and Native American selfhood was published in *Body Politics: Disease, Desire, and the Family* (1994), edited by Michael Ryan and Avery Gordon. Currently she is writing a book about nineteenth-century U.S. women public speakers and the culture of oratory.

"Personal Property: Exchange Value and the Female Self in *The Awakening*" was published in *The Awakening: A Critical Edition* (1993), edited by Nancy K. Walker, as an example of new historicism, a theoretical approach that emphasizes political and social context as central to any informed reading of literature. In this article Stange examines Chopin's novel in light of the late nineteenth-century concepts of "self-ownership," the right of a woman to refuse marital sex, and "voluntary motherhood," her right to choose whether or when to become pregnant. Drawing upon Thorstein Veblen's analysis of "conspicuous consumption" in *The Theory of the Leisure Class* (1899) and the suffragist Susan B. Anthony's theory of "self-sovereignty," Stange analyzes Edna Pontellier's struggle to refuse maternal sacrifice and thereby own herself.

⇥ Personal Property: Exchange Value and
the Female Self in *The Awakening* ⇤

In the beginning of *The Awakening,* New Orleans stockbroker Léonce Pontellier, staying with his wife, Edna, at an exclusive Creole family resort, surveys Edna as she walks up from the beach in the company of her summer flirtation, Robert Lebrun. "'You are burnt beyond recognition' [Léonce says], looking at his wife as one looks at a valuable piece of personal property which has suffered some damage" (21). Léonce's comment is the reader's introduction to Edna, whose search for self is the novel's subject. To take Léonce's hyperbole—"you are burnt beyond recognition"—as literally as Léonce takes his role as Edna's "owner" is to be introduced to an Edna who exists as a recognizable individual in reference to her status as valuable property. This status appears to determine Edna's perception of herself: in response to Léonce's anxiety, Edna makes her first self-examination in this novel about a heroine who is "beginning to realize her position in the universe as a human being, and to recognize her relations as an individual to the world within and about her" (31–32). Edna, having been told "you are burnt beyond recognition,"

> held up her hands, strong, shapely hands, and surveyed them critically, drawing up her lawn sleeves above the wrists. Looking at them reminded her of her rings, which she had given to her husband before leaving for the beach. She silently reached out to him and he, understanding, took the rings from his vest pocket and dropped them into her open palm. She slipped them upon her fingers. (21)

In the context of the property system in which Edna exists as a sign of value, Edna's body is detachable and alienable from her own viewpoint: the hands and wrists are part of the body yet can be objectified, held out and examined as if they belonged to someone else—as indeed, in some sense that Léonce insists upon very literally, they do belong to someone else. Edna's perception of her own body is structured by the detachability of the hand and arm as signs of Léonce's ownership of her. Her hands also suggest the possibility of being an owner herself when they make the proprietary gesture of reaching out for the rings that Léonce obediently drops into the palm (this gesture of Edna's contrasts with a bride's conventional passive reception of the ring). The hands are the organs of appropriation; Elizabeth Cady Stanton, in a speech on female rights given in 1892, argued that "to deny [to woman] the rights of property is like cutting off the hands."[1] In having Edna put on the rings herself (a gesture Edna will again perform at a moment when she decisively turns away from her domestic role), Chopin suggests that the chief item of property owned by the proprietary Edna is Edna herself. Thus the opening scene foreshadows the turning point of the plot at which Edna, deciding to leave Léonce's house, resolves "never again to belong to another than herself" (100).

"Self-ownership," in the second half of the nineteenth century, signified a wife's right to refuse marital sex—a right feminists were demanding as the key to female autonomy. First popularized by Lucinda Chandler in the 1840s and widely promoted by the feminists who followed her, the practice of self-ownership, as Chandler saw it, would mean that the woman "has control over her own person, independent of the desires of her husband" (2). "By the 1970s," writes historian William Leach, "self-ownership . . . had become the stock in trade of feminist thinking on birth control" (92) for it "meant that woman, not man, would decide when, where, and how the sexual act would be performed. It also meant that woman, not man, would determine when children would be conceived and how many" (89). "Voluntary motherhood"—woman's "right to choose when to be pregnant" (Gordon 109)—was usually evoked as the ground of self-ownership: "she should have pleasure or not allow access unless she wanted a child," explains advice writer Henry C. Wright (252). According to social historian Linda Gordon, by the mid–1870s, advocacy of voluntary motherhood was shared by "the whole feminist community" (109). Writing in 1881, reformer Dido Lewis demonstrates the central place of self–ownership/voluntary motherhood in the campaign for female autonomy when she evokes together the rights "of wife to be her own person, and her sacred right to deny her husband if need be; and to decide how often and when she should become a mother" (18).

While the feminist community promoted voluntary motherhood, it unanimously opposed the use of birth control devices. This opposition, which contradicts the advocacy of choice and control for women, was shared by suffragists, moral reformers, and free love advocates alike. Various kinds of contraceptive technology were accessible to middle-class women. However, as historian Gordon notes, nineteenth-century birth control practice was determined by ideology rather than the availability of technology.

---

1. ["The Solitude of Self" (qtd. in DuBois 249). In this speech Stanton gave in 1892 on the occasion of her resignation from the presidency of the suffrage movement, Stanton argued for full civil rights for woman on the grounds of her aloneness and existential "self-sovereignty." In its argument and rhetoric, this speech of Stanton's is strikingly similar to Chopin's presentations of female selfhood (*The Awakening*'s original title was *A Solitary Soul*). Like the self Chopin's heroine discovers, Stanton's self is an absolute, possessive self whose metaphorical situation is that of a lone individual "on a solitary island" or "launched on the sea of life." In Stanton and in Chopin, female subjectivity and women's rights are grounded in absolute selfhood. For an account of early English feminists' commitment to absolute selfhood, see Catherine Gallagher, "Embracing the Absolute: The Politics of the Female Subject in Seventeenth-century England," *Genders* 1 (Spring 1988): 24–39.]

In the prevailing ideology of even the most radical feminist reformers, motherhood was an inextricable part of female sexuality. Why did feminists, whose goal was to win for women the civil and proprietary rights that would make them equal to men, choose to deny women the freedom to have sex without pregnancy? As Gordon points out, the linkage of self-ownership with reproduction certainly reflects the reality of many women's lives, which were dominated by multiple births and the attendant realities of risk, disease, and pain. Some of the resistance to birth control technology, Gordon suggests, was motivated by material conditions: Birth control devices, by separating sex from reproduction, appeared to threaten the family structure that provided most middle-class women their only social standing and economic security. But even among those reformers who were not concerned with upholding the family (free love advocates and nonmarrying career women, for example), there was a strong resistance to contraception—a resistance that amounts to a refusal to separate motherhood from female sexuality.

To put voluntary motherhood practiced without birth control devices at the center of self-ownership is to make motherhood central to a woman's life and identity. The capacity to bear children is the sexual function that most dramatically distinguishes the sexual lives—and the day-to-day lives—of women from those of men. The ban on contraceptive technology enforces a lived distinction between male and female sexuality: without effective contraception, sex for a woman always means sex as a woman because it means a potential pregnancy. The opposition to contraceptive technology (as well as the idealization of motherhood of which it is a part) reflects a commitment to the sexualization of female identity. Through the practice of self-ownership, this differentiated sexuality with motherhood at its core becomes the possession that a woman makes available or withholds in order to demonstrate self-ownership. To ask why the feminist reformers opposed contraceptive technology is, then, to ask how motherhood functions in the construction of the self-owning female self. In making motherhood a central possession of the self, the feminists were defining that self as sexual and as female. The possession of this sexualized self through self-ownership amounts to the exercise of a right to alienate (confirmed by a right to withhold). This selfhood, then, consists of the alienation of female sexuality in a market. Charlotte Perkins Gilman, in her 1899 critique of this sexual market, attacked it as a market in which, "he is . . . the demand . . . she is the supply" (86). The feminists' opposition to birth control technology reflects a commitment to this market: underlying their constructions of female selfhood is the ideology of woman's sexual value in exchange.

Chopin's dramatization of female self-ownership demonstrates the central importance of the ideology of woman's value in exchange to contemporary notions of female selfhood. If, as Stanton declares in the speech on female selfhood quoted above, "in discussing the rights of woman, we are to consider, first, what belongs to her as an individual" (247), what Edna Pontellier considers as her property is, first, her body. Her body is both what she owns and what she owns with. She begins to discover a self by uncovering her hands and "surveying them critically" with her eyes, thus making an appropriative visual assessment of herself as a proprietary being. Her hands and eyes will serve her in her "venture" into her "work" of sketching and painting(75). Thus her hands, by remaining attached (and not cut off like those of the woman who is denied the rights of property), serve her visual appropriation of the world and provide the first object of this appropriation: her own body.

Edna's hands appear in two states: naked and sunburned, and ringed. In the first state, they are conventionally "unrecognizable" as signs of her status as Léonce's wife. Sunburned hands, by indicating the performance of outdoor labor, would nullify

Edna's "value" as a sign of Léonce's wealth. In the terminology of Thorstein Veblen's turn-of-the-century analysis of the ownership system, Edna is an item of "conspicuous consumption" that brings "reputability" (a degree of status) to Léonce. Such status-bearing wealth must be surplus wealth: useful articles do not serve to advertise the owner's luxurious freedom from need. Edna must, then, appear to be surplus—she must appear to perform no useful labor.[2] The rings—showy, luxurious, useless items of conspicuous consumption par excellence—restore her status as surplus. Yet this status is also constituted by the sight of her hands without the rings: the significance of the sunburned hands quickly collapses into the significance of the ringed hands when the sunburned, naked hands "remind" both Léonce and Edna of the ringed, value-bearing hands. And Edna's sunburn is directly constitutive of her "value," for it results from her conspicuous, vicarious consumption of leisure on Léonce's behalf (what Veblen calls "vicarious leisure"): She has been enjoying a holiday at the respectable, luxurious resort frequented by Léonce's Creole circle.

Thus Edna's hands appear in their naked and exposed state as a reminder of Léonce's property interests while they also, in this state, suggest an identity and proprietary interest of her own. The appropriative survey of the female body as a sign of male ownership continues to engage Edna: Her visual fascination fastens on the hands and body of her friend Adèle Ratignolle, whose "excessive physical charm" at first attracts Edna (32). Edna "like[s] to sit and gaze at her fair companion" (29). She watches Adèle at her domestic labors—"Never were hands more exquisite than [Adèle's], and it was joy to look at them when she threaded her needle or adjusted her gold thimble . . . as she sewed away on the little night-drawers" (27). Here, the hands are the organs of labor—but again, gender determines possessive status. Adèle's hands are perfectly white because she always wears dogskin gloves with gauntlets. The femininity of the laboring hands, their luxuriously aesthetic and spectacular quality, conspicuously signifies that the value of Adèle's labor does not stem from production for use: Edna "[can]not see the use" of Adèle's labor (27). Adèle's laboring hands signify her consecration to her "role" within the family, and they are marked with the gold of a thimble as Edna's are marked with the gold of a ring.

In their white, "exquisite" beauty, Adèle's hands are stably—organically—signs of her status of wealth. When Adèle jokes "with excessive naïveté" about the fear of making her husband jealous, "that made them all laugh. The right hand jealous of the left! . . . But for that matter, the Creole husband is never jealous; with him the gangrene passion is one which has become dwarfed by disuse" (29). (This ownership is not reciprocal: the question of jealousy pertains only to the husband; the wife's jealous, proprietary interest in her husband is not evoked.) Adèle's entire presence is a reminder of the property system in which woman is a form of surplus wealth whose value exists in relation to exchange. A woman of "excessive physical charm," Adèle

2. [Veblen argues that under the private property system, all personal property is a version of that original property whose "usefulness" was to serve as a trophy marking the personal "prepotence" of the trophy's barbaric owner (23, 29). The first trophy to emerge from the economic "margin worth fighting for" is woman: The original form of ownership is the ownership of women by men. In Veblens's famous characterization of the contemporary bourgeois domestic ownership system, the wife advertises her status as surplus in her role as the chief item of household property as she earns "reputability" for her husband through vicarious consumption and vicarious leisure (65–67). Veblen suggests that, because the meaning of property—and thus the identity of its owner—is produced by the perceptions and positions of others, male selfhood is always mediated by property. Chopin, like Veblen, pokes fun at the figure of the male owner who experiences himself and the world as mediated by the arbitrary conventions and relations of ownership. In the opening pages of *The Awakening*, Léonce rather ridiculously governs himself according to his notions of property rights, granting, for example, the caged birds the right to sing because they are owned by Madame Lebrun, and himself the right to retreat to "his own cottage" (19).]

is luxuriously draped in "pure white, with a fluffiness of ruffles that became her. The draperies and fluttering things which she wore suited her rich, luxuriant beauty" (33). Her body is as rich, white, and ornamental as her clothes; she appears "more beautiful than ever" in a negligee that leaves her arms "almost wholly bare" and "expose[s] the rich, melting curves of her white throat" (75).

In her rich and elaborate yet revealing clothing, Adèle is excessively covered while her body, already a sign of wealth, makes such coverings redundant. Adèle appears as a concretized *femme couverte*. Under the Napoleonic Code which was still in force in Louisiana in the 1890s, wives were legally identical with their husbands; being in *couverture*, they had no separate legal or proprietary identity and could not own property in their own right. Adèle's beauty is her conspicuousness as a form of wealth: her looks are describable by "no words . . . save the old ones that have served so often to picture the bygone heroine of romance." These words—"gold," "sapphires," "cherries or some other delicious crimson fruit"—construct femininity as tangible property. The value of the woman is emphatically defined as social wealth that exists as an effect of the public circulation of the tropes—"the old [words] that have served so often"—that identify her as beautiful. Her beauty is the product and representation of its own circulation. Adèle's "excessive physical charm" is a kind of currency that makes her the "embodiment of every womanly grace and charm" (26).

It is in public display that Adèle's beauty manifests itself. The sight of woman as social wealth is the starting point of Edna's self-seeking. "Mrs. Pontellier liked to sit and gaze at her fair companion as she might look upon a faultless Madonna" (29). An amateur artist, Edna finds such "joy" in looking at Adèle that she wants to "try herself on Madame Ratignolle" (30). Adèle, "seated there like some sensuous Madonna, with the gleam of the fading day enriching her splendid color" (30), appears to Edna as a particularly "tempting subject" of a sketch. This sketch becomes the second sight that Edna "survey[s] critically" (the first being her hands); finding that it "[bears] no resemblance to Madame Ratignolle" (and despite the fact that it is "a fair enough piece of work, and in many respects satisfying"), Edna enforces her proprietary rights in regard to the sketch as she smudges it and "crumple[s] the paper between her hands" (30). Edna is inspired to make another try when she visits Adèle at home in New Orleans and finds her again at her ornamental domestic labor (Adèle is unnecessarily sorting her husband's laundry). "Madame Ratignolle looked more beautiful than ever there at home. . . . 'Perhaps I shall be able to paint your picture some day,' said Edna. . . . 'I believe I ought to work again'" (75). The sight of Adèle at home inspires Edna to do the work that will help her get out of the home. Later she will leave Léonce and support herself on the income from her art and from a legacy of her mother's.

In her insistence on owning her own property and supporting herself, Edna is a model of the legal opposite of the *femme couverte*—she is the *femme seule*. Thus Chopin connects her to the Married Women's Property Acts, property law reforms instituted in the latter part of the century that gave married women varying rights of ownership. Edna comes from "old Presbyterian Kentucky stock" (86). Kentucky belonged to the block of states with the most advanced separation of property in marriage. In fact, Kentucky had the most advanced Married Women's Property Act in the nation, granting married women not only the right to own separate property and make contracts, but the right to keep their earnings.

Thus Chopin connects Edna to the feminist drive for women's property rights. Elizabeth Cady Stanton, in her speech on female selfhood quoted above, makes possessive individualism the first consideration among women's rights: "In discussing the right of woman, we are to consider, first, what belongs to her as an individual." Chopin suggests that what a woman owns in owning herself is her sexual exchange value. The *femme couverte*, in being both property and the inspiration to own, allows Edna to be *femme seule*. The self she owns can be owned—is property—because it is recognizable as social wealth. Adèle, who concretizes the status of the woman and mother as domestic property, makes visible to Edna the female exchange value that constitutes a self to own. Thus Edna's possessive selfhood looks "back" to the chattel form of marriage, valorizing (in a literal sense) the woman as property. In Adèle, the "bygone heroine," Edna finds the capital which she invests to produce her market selfhood.

The way that Edna owns herself by owning her value in exchange is a form of voluntary motherhood: "Edna had once told Madame Ratignolle that she would never sacrifice herself for her children, or for anyone. Then had followed a rather heated argument." In this argument Edna "explains" to Adèle, "I would give my life for my children; but I wouldn't give myself." Adèle's answer is "a woman who would give her life for her children could do no more than that. . . . I'm sure I couldn't do more than that." Withholding nothing, Adèle cannot conceive of giving more than she already gives. Edna cannot at first identify what it is she has chosen to withhold: "I wouldn't give myself. I can't make it more clear; it's only something which . . . is revealing itself to me" (67).

The self at first exists in the presumption of the right to withhold oneself as a mother. But Edna, like the feminist advocates of self-ownership, soon determines that voluntary motherhood means withholding herself sexually. After her first successful swim (during which she experiences a moment of self-support and the absolute solitariness of death), she stays on the porch, refusing Léonce's repeated orders and entreaties to come inside to bed (49–50). Later Edna stops sleeping with her husband altogether, so that Léonce complains to the family doctor, "she's making it devilishly uncomfortable for me. . . . She's got some sort of notion in her head concerning the eternal rights of women; and—you understand—we meet in the morning at the breakfast table" (85). It is by withholding herself sexually, then, that Edna exercises the "eternal rights of women" in insisting that she has a self and that she owns that self.

The freedom to withhold oneself has its complement in the freedom to give oneself. No longer sleeping with—or even living with—her husband, Edna declares herself free to have sex with whomever she chooses. She tells Robert, "I am no longer one of Mr. Pontellier's possessions to dispose of or not. I give myself where I choose" (129). Edna supposes that her self-giving is chosen because she has presumed the choice of not giving—she has made her motherhood voluntary. Adèle, in contrast, is the mother who never withholds and thus cannot choose but to give. Will and intention seem to be with Edna, whereas Adèle exercises no will (and has no self). Yet Adèle's giving is not an involuntary and therefore selfless reflex, but a consciously and intentionally developed identity. Adèle is Grand Isle's greatest exponent of the "rôle" of "mother-woman," a role that is produced through deliberate public staging (26). First presented to Edna as a beautiful vision of the "Madonna," Adèle produces her maternity through public discourse. Her children are "thoughts" brought out in speech: Adèle "thinks" (out loud) of "a fourth one" and, after giving birth to it, implores Edna, in a phrase that Edna will not be able to get out of her mind, to "think of the children . . . oh think of . . . them" (132).

"Madame Ratignolle had been married seven years. About every two years she had a baby. At that time she . . . was beginning to thing of a fourth one. She was always talking about her 'condition.' Her 'condition' was in no way apparent, and no one would have known a thing about it but for her persistence in making it the subject of conversation" (27). Adèle produces her "role" of "mother-woman" by thinking and provoking thought, but it is impossible to determine whether Adèle thinks about getting pregnant—whether, that is, she practices self-ownership and voluntary motherhood by withholding herself from sex. The two-year intervals between her pregnancies might result from chance, or they might represent intentional spacing that keeps Adèle in or nearly in the "condition" that provides her identity. This ambiguity characterizes the "condition" of motherhood that Adèle is "always" producing for herself. Motherhood is a "role" and therefore consciously produced and paraded. Yet the intention and will that are used to stage the role conflict with its content, for the role of mother demands selflessness: the mother-women of Grand Isle "efface themselves as individuals" (26). Motherhood is never voluntary or involuntary. If motherhood is a social role that Adèle intentionally inhabits, it is also a condition that she can never actually choose, since intending to become pregnant cannot make her so. Thus, motherhood has a kind of built-in selflessness that is dramatically expressed in the scene when Adèle, who is usually in control of her presence, becomes pathetically hysterical and paranoic during labor and childbirth. Here, Adèle's intentional embrace of motherhood gets its force from the unwilled nature of the "torture" that it attempts to appropriate. Hardly able to speak after her ordeal in childbirth, Adèle whispers in an "exhausted" voice, "think of the children, Edna" (132).

Adèle's histrionics insist that nothing less than the self is at stake in the speculative risk-taking that is motherhood (which includes the abstention from motherhood). The intention to become a mother is the kind of "weak" intention that Walter Benn Michaels connects with "acts that take place in the market, such as speculating in commodities" (237). Michaels places weak intention at the center of a market selfhood whose "self-possession" and "self-interest" are grounded in "the possibility of intention and action coming apart" (244, 241). Chopin's dramatization of the logic of voluntary motherhood—like Michaels's own example of Edith Wharton's self-speculating heroine Lily Bart (*The House of Mirth*)—emphasizes that self-speculation is gendered. For women, it is sexual; that is to say that sexuality is the content of the female self in the market. Contrary to Michaels's claim, Lily Bart is indeed "a victim of patriarchal capitalism" in a way that the male entrepreneurs in the novel are not (240), for the woman cannot choose whether to speculate or what to speculate in: By being a woman she is already sexually at risk. The "voluntariness" of female self-speculation is an effect of the commodity system which constructs female value along the polarities of accessibility and rarity. Lily Bart speculates in the marriage market by withholding sexual accessibility from that market—a risky behavior that results in her death (complete with hallucinated motherhood). "Voluntary motherhood" represents the inevitable risks of female self-speculation as the risk of pregnancy—which, in the nineteenth century, was the risk of life—and points to the enforced nature of female self-speculation by identifying all women as mothers.

Adèle and Edna embody the two poles of motherhood: Adèle is the "mother-woman" and Edna is "not a mother-woman." The axis of motherhood gives Edna her original sense of identity. What makes her "not a mother-woman" is her refusal to "give" herself for her children. Unlike Adèle, Edna does not embrace the role. Her motherhood seems arbitrary, externally imposed and unwilled, "a responsibility which she had blindly assumed." She is "fond of her children in an uneven, impulsive way. She [will] sometimes gather them passionately to her heart; she [will] sometimes forget them" (37). Her "half remembered" experience of childbirth is an "ecstasy" and a "stupor" (131). Edna's refusal to give herself as a mother, rather than making her the controller and proprietor of her life, entails the passivity of thoughtlessness. In refusing to be a mother-woman she absents herself from the motherhood that is thus all the more arbitrarily thrust upon her.

Indeed, Edna is inescapably a mother. Motherhood is what Edna withholds and thus she, too, is essentially a "mother-woman." Adèle's presence is a provocation and reminder of the self-constituting function of motherhood. Adèle's selflessness is an inducement to Edna to identify a self to give. For Edna, who "becom[es] herself" by "daily casting aside that fictitious self which we assume like a garment with which to appear before the world" (77), the friendship with Adèle is "the most obvious . . . influence" in the loosening of Edna's "mantle of reserve" (32). The Creole community recognizes no private sphere. Adèle's sexual and reproductive value is already located in the sphere of public exchange (or, the public is already like the private: the Creoles are like "one large family" [28]). In this Creole openness, Edna is inspired to resituate her sexual exchange value in an economy of public circulation.

"The candor of [Adèle's] whole existence, which everyone might read," is part of a Creole lack of prudery that allows for the open circulation of stories about sex and childbirth. With "profound astonishment" Edna reads "in secret and solitude" a book that "had gone the rounds" and was openly discussed at table.

> Never would Edna Pontellier forget the shock with which she heard Madame Ratignolle relating to old Monsieur Farival the harrowing story of one of her *accouchements,* withholding no intimate detail. She was growing accustomed to like shocks, but she could not keep the mounting color back from her cheeks. (28)

The candor of Adèle's motherhood provokes blushes that simultaneously constitute Edna's reserve and "give her away" to the public. Her body, whether sunburned or blushing, is red from an exposure that privatizes and valorizes that body as her domestic, private attributes—sexuality, modesty, reproduction—are manifested as social value.

Adèle has nothing to hide because her body underneath her clothes is manifestly social wealth. Her bareness is as ornamentally "beautiful" as her ornamented, clothed self. The reserved, private, domestic self of Adèle reveals itself to Edna as the valuable product of circulation, and this revelation prompts Edna to explore her own possessive privacy. She becomes aware of having "thoughts and emotions which never voiced themselves. . . . They belonged to her and were her own" (67). Her erotic longings belong in this category. "Edna often wondered at one propensity which sometimes had inwardly disturbed her without causing any outward show or manifestation on her part" (36). This is a propensity to become silently infatuated with various men. These "silent" possessions of the self are owned in a way most clearly illustrated in the story of Edna's greatest infatuation, whose object was a "great tragedian."

> The picture of the tragedian stood enframed upon her desk. Anyone may possess the portrait of a tragedian without exciting suspicion or comment. (This was a sinister reflection

which she cherished.) In the presence of others she expressed admiration for his exalted gifts, as she handed the photograph around and dwelt upon the fidelity of the likeness. When alone she sometimes picked it up and kissed the cold glass passionately. (36)

Edna's comment upon the fidelity of the likeness recapitulates the book's opening, in which Léonce's anxiety about Edna's lapse from recognizability, and his restoration of her recognizability via the wedding rings, consists of a discourse that constantly remembers and reinscribes her as a sign of him in his proprietary office. Her "fidelity" in this marital, possessive sense is her recognizability as such a sign. Edna's photograph is to Edna as Edna is to Léonce. It represents her possessive identity, her selfhood as an owner (thus there is a mirrorlike quality in the "cold glass" which shows her herself kissing herself). The photograph embodies and reflects Edna's erotic desire for the tragedian. It objectifies her sexuality in an image that is handed around, praised for its "fidelity," and kissed in private.

Like Adèle, the photograph concretizes erotic value that is both publicly produced and privately owned. The erotic availability and desirability of the actor whose photograph "anyone might possess" is a product of reproduction and circulation, as Edna's own kisses are incited by and followed by the circulation of the object. The mode of owning it is "handing it around" while she praises the "fidelity" of the likeness. That is, she assumes an individual possessive relationship to the photograph only in the context of its possession by any number of other owners, whose possession produces the "sinister reflection" of her own possessive, cherishing privacy. But Edna's position as an owner is not that of Adèle's husband—or of her own. Edna gives up possession in order to have this possessive relationship. In praising the "fidelity of the likeness" she does not praise its likeness to her but emphasizes that the photograph represents and thus "belongs to" its original—a man whose inaccessibility makes her infatuation "hopeless." Edna can see her photograph as property only by seeing it as male property—just as her own hands, in their function as signs of Léonce's ownership of her, appear detachable and therefore ownable. Yet the absence of Edna in what the photograph represents allows her to imagine a possessive self that is somehow hidden and concealed—and therefore her own. Alone with her photograph, she imagines it circulating. Circulating it, she is able to imagine being secretly alone with it. In her ownership of the photograph, Edna establishes her possessive relationship to her sexuality.

"I am no longer one of Mr. Pontellier's possessions to dispose of or not. I give myself where I choose," says Edna to Robert (129). She has withheld herself from her husband in order to give herself. Instead of being property "to dispose of or not," she intends to be property that is necessarily disposed of. The forms of value in which Edna exchanges herself are the duties and functions of the woman and wife—female sexual service, motherhood, and the performance of wifely domestic/social amenities. Edna reprivatizes and reserves this value by giving up her social and domestic duties as the lady of the house, by moving out of the impressive family home into a private domestic space, the "pigeon house," and by withholding sex from her husband. This reserved self is what she gives away at her "grand dinner," when she launches her sexual exchange value into wider circulation.

> Whatever came, she had resolved never again to belong to another than herself. "I shall give a grand dinner before I leave the old house!" Edna exclaimed. (100)

At the dinner, the "glittering circlet" of Edna's wedding ring (72) is now her crown.

> "Something new, Edna?" exclaimed Miss Mayblunt, with lorgnette directed toward a magnificent cluster of diamonds that sparkled, that almost sputtered, in Edna's hair. . . .
>
> ". . . A present from my husband. . . . I may as well admit that this in my birthday. . . . In good time I expect you to drink my health. Meanwhile, I shall ask you to begin with this cocktail, composed . . . by my father in honor of Sister Janet's wedding." (108)

Her wedding rings had "sparkled," but the tiara (a conventional adornment of the "young matron") "sputters." This dinner marks the exploding of the intramarriage market, in which she repeatedly sells herself to the same man, into the public market, in which she circulates as the owner of her own sexual exchange value. In its very conception, the dinner collapses the private and public: "though Edna had spoken of the dinner as a very grand affair, it was in truth a very small affair and very select" (107). The absent beloved, Robert, is represented by Victor, his flirtatious younger brother. Flanking Edna are representatives of two modes of the market in sex value: Arobin, the gambler and playboy, represents adulterous and extramarital serial liaisons, while Monsieur Ratignolle enjoys the quasi-organic bond of Creole marriage.

The wealth of the Pontellier household is conspicuously displayed and offered to the guests. On the other table "there were silver and gold . . . and crystal which glittered like the gems which the women wore" (107). The women, like the accoutrements, are presented as forms of wealth, and Edna is the queen among them. In her diamond crown, she both embodies and reigns over Léonce's riches. This dinner at which, like all women under exogamy, she leaves "the old house" is a version of the woman-giving potlatch, the marriage feast at which the father gives away the virgin daughter. The cocktail "composed" by the father for the daughter Janet's wedding is explicitly compared by Edna's lover Arobin to the gift of Edna herself: "it might not be amiss to start out by drinking the Colonel's health in the cocktail which he composed, on the birthday of the most charming of women—the daughter whom he invented" (108). Edna is thus the gift not just of Léonce, who makes her into a form of wealth by marking her as value, but of her father, too: that is, she is a bride. As a bride, she is an invention—manmade, brought into the world for, by, and on the occasion of the staging of ownership in the conspicuous consumption of a wedding/potlatch.

An "invention," Edna is thoroughly representational. As a sign of value she is hailed as a sign of her father's wealth of inventiveness in making signs/wealth. The dinner dramatizes the richness of her market-determined transformations: ceremonial drink, invention, queen, luxurious gift. To say that it is her "birthday" is to say that her self is born through exchange and consists of these multiple signs which circulate in the market. What Edna wears marks her as value:

> The golden shimmer of Edna's satin gown spread in rich folds on either side of her. There was a soft fall of lace encircling her shoulders. It was the color of her skin, without the glow, the myriad living tints that one may sometimes discover in vibrant flesh. There was something in her attitude, in her whole appearance . . . which suggested the regal woman, the one who rules, who looks on, who stands alone. (109)

The gold of her dress makes reference to the value in which she is robed. The lace "encircling" her shoulders refers to the skin which at the novel's opening effects Edna's transformation into "surplus." It is as if the lace is an extra skin—a conspicuously surplus skin—which in its decorative insubstantiality mirrors the meaning of Edna's skin. But the lace is not a true mirror. It points out the superior capacity of the "real" skin to change, to have "myriad tints" which allow it to be continually dissolved and recreated as a sign of value.

Edna as a sign of value is the referent of all the surrounding signs of value. She sits at the head of the table in her crown like "the regal woman, the one who rules, . . . who stands alone," as if she were the principle (and principal) of value that reigns over all its manifestations—the gold, silver, crystal, gems, and delicacies. Now Edna is like Adèle, the regal woman who has the "grace and majesty which queens are . . . supposed to possess" (31). And like Adèle, who is tortured and "exhausted" by childbirth, Edna experiences the complement of regal power in the exhausted passivity that overcomes her after the dinner, when the celebration of private wealth moves into the realization of value throughout the ceremonial enactment of breakage and loss.

Edna leaves the Pontellier house with Arobin, who pauses outside the door of the "old house" to break off a spray of jessamine, enacting this defloration. He offers it to Edna: "No; I don't want anything," she answers. Emptied, she says she feels as if "something inside of [her] had snapped." This metaphorical defloration empties Edna of the erotic desire whose ownership constitutes her selfhood. Edna's shoulders are bare of the encircling lace and Arobin caresses them. Edna is passive, but Arobin feels the "response of her flesh," which, in its consecration to value, embodies the sexuality that is created in circulation. Now, after Edna's ceremonial "self-giving," this eroticism no longer constitutes a sensation that Edna can appropriate as her own desire (112–13).

The loss of the self in maternal bloodshedding is enacted at the end of the dinner when the ceremony changes from a potlatch to a sacred, sacrificial rite. The desirous Mrs. Highcamp crowns Victor with a garland of yellow and red roses, effecting his magical transformation into a bacchanalian "vision of Oriental beauty." One of the transfixed guests mutters Swinburne under his breath: "There was a graven image of Desire / Painted with red blood on a ground of gold." This "graven image," like Edna's photograph, reflects her desire. Victor publicly sings the secret song that expresses the production of Edna's "private" desire as a suspicious reflection of circulation, *si tu savais ce que tes yeux me disent* ("if you knew what your eyes are saying to me") (110–11). She reacts with such consternation that she breaks her wineglass, and the contents—either red or gold, like the roses and the graven image—flow over Arobin and Mrs. Highcamp. Arobin has consecrated the evening's drinks as analogues of Edna, who has invited the guests to "drink her health"—that is, drink *her*—on her "birthday." In involuntarily shattering the glass, which, like the "cold glass" covering the photo, contains a possessive reflection of her value, Edna shatters the "mantle of reserve," symbolically releasing the maternal blood that constitutes her value.

The maternal quality of her self-giving—its involuntary and selfless aspects—overwhelms Edna again some time after the potlatch when, just as she is about to "give" herself to Robert, Edna is called away to witness Adèle enduring the agonies of childbirth. The sight of Adèle's "torture" overwhelms Edna (as does Adèle's exhausted plea to "think of the children"), leaving her "stunned and speechless" (132). When she returns to her little house, Robert is gone forever. Deprived of the chance to "give" herself to her desire, she spends the night thinking of her children. Later, she walks to the beach from which she will swim to her death "not thinking of these things" (136). Withholding herself from motherhood, insisting on her right to refuse to "sacrifice" herself for her children, Edna owns herself. In the logic of self-ownership and voluntary motherhood, motherhood is itself the ground on which woman claims ownership of her sexual value. Edna seizes the most extreme prerogatives of this self-ownership, withholding herself from motherhood by withholding herself from life and thus giving herself in a maternal dissolution.

Edna's death in the ocean dramatizes the self-ownership rhetoric of Elizabeth Cady Stanton. Stanton argues that "self-sovereignty" is the existential birthright of both women and men, for every human being "launched on the sea of life" is unique and "alone" (248). But women's self-sovereignty specifically denotes sexual self-determination. And Stanton insists that women—that is, mothers—earn a special presumptive self-sovereignty, for "alone [woman] goes to the gates of death to give life to every man that is born into the world; no one can share her fears, no one can mitigate her pangs; and if her sorrow is greater than she can bear, alone she passes beyond the gates into the vast unknown" (251). At the moment of extreme maternal giving, the moment when motherhood takes her life, the woman owns her self by withholding herself from motherhood.

Note: I would like to thank Catherine Gallagher and Walter Benn Michaels for their help with this essay at several stages of its composition. I am also grateful to David Lloyd, Tricia Moran, Lora Romero, and Lynn Wardley, who read this essay in draft and made helpful suggestions.   1993

⊰ Works Cited ⊱

Chandler, Lucinda. "Motherhood." *Woodhull and Claflin's Weekly*, 13 May 1871: 1–2.

Gilman, Charlotte Perkins. *Women and Economics: The Economic Factor between Men and Women as a Factor in Social Evolution.* Ed. Carl Degler. New York: Harper, 1966.

Gordon, Linda. "Voluntary Motherhood: The Beginnings of the Birth Control Movement." *Women's Body, Woman's Right: Birth Control in America.* New York: Penguin, 1974.

Lewis, Dido. *Chastity, or Our Secret Sins.* New York: Canfield, 1881.

Michaels, Walter Benn. *The Gold Standard and the Logic of Naturalism: American Literature at the Turn of the Century.* Berkeley: U of California P, 1987.

Stanton, Elizabeth Cady. "The Solitude of Self." *Elizabeth Cady Standton, Susan B. Anthony: Correspondence, Writings, Speeches.* Ed. Ellen Carol DuBois. New York: Schocken, 1981.

Veblen, Thorstein. *The Theory of the Leisure Class: An Economic Study in the Evolution of Institutions.* New York: Macmillan, 1899.

Wright, Henry C. *Marriage and Parentage.* Boston: Marsh, 1853.

⊰◈⊱

Paula Gunn Allen
1939–

A Native American writer of poetry, fiction, and essays, PAULA GUNN ALLEN was born on the Cubero land grant in New Mexico to parents of Laguna-Sioux-Lebanese-Jewish origins. Since then she has embraced fully what the theorist TRINH T. MINH-HA calls her "hyphenated identities and hybrid realities." Allen married in her teens, had children, and eventually attended college and graduate school at the University of New Mexico, where she completed her Ph.D. in American Studies. Her sister, Carol Lee Sanchez, is also a writer of renown. Allen has taught liter-ature at San Francisco State University, the University of New Mexico, and Fort Lewis College; she currently teaches Native American studies at the University of California at Berkeley.

Although she writes in multiple genres, Allen is best known as a poet; her work reflects her activism in the antiwar, feminist, and Native American rights movements. A poem, she explains, "begins as a mood that gets more and more focused, becoming a sense, a rhythm, then a scatter of words. I don't write poetry for content, but to articulate a sense, an 'intu-ition.'" Among her volumes of poetry are *The Blind Lion* (1975), *A Cannon between My Knees* (1981), *Shadow Country* (1982), and *Skin and Bones: Poems 1979–87* (1988). Much of Allen's poetry seeks to create mythic space, questing for natural harmony among humans, land, ani-mals, and spirit. Several poems address her experience as a lesbian and draw parallels between the marginalizations that occur due to ethnicity and sexual orientation. Her poems have appeared in such anthologies as *Lesbian Poetry* (1978), *A Gathering of Spirit* (1984), and *Living the Spirit* (1988). A different impulse drives Allen's fiction and criticism. "I write fiction out of interest in how people interact, how my social selves interact, how the planet and the human beings and the other beings interact." Her novel, *The Woman Who Owned the Shadows* (1983), traces the spiritual journey of Ephanie Ataencio, who suffers a mental breakdown when aban-doned by her husband but ultimately finds peace by accepting the legacy of women from her past and by reconciling native traditions with her mixed ancestry. Allen has edited an anthol-ogy of Native American women's stories, *Spider Woman's Granddaughters* (1986), that contains both contemporary narratives and traditional "told-to-people" stories. In 1991 she edited *Grandmothers of the Light: A Medicine Woman's Sourcebook*, tales of goddesses from Native American cultures; and in 1998 she published *Off the Reservation: Boundary Busting, Border Crossing, Loose Canons*.

Allen's contributions as a literary critic have also been significant. In 1983 she edited one of the first collections of critical essays on literature by Native Americans, *Studies in American Indian Literature*. In *The Sacred Hoop: Recovering the Feminine in American Indian Traditions* (1986) she explores the centrality of women to native myth and culture and analyzes literary works by such writers as JOY HARJO and Leslie Marmon Silko. This study, which began as Allen's dissertation, was written in response to a male professor who claimed that there was no such thing as Native American literature, only folklore. It was also born of her conviction that in its emphasis on gender equality and the spiritual power of women, American Indian culture serves as a precursor to the modern women's movement, an argument she makes in her essay "Who Is Your Mother? Red Roots of White Feminism."

◄ Who Is Your Mother? Red Roots of White Feminism ►

At Laguna Pueblo in New Mexico, "Who is your mother?" is an important question. At Laguna, one of several of the ancient Keres gynocratic societies of the region, your mother's identity is the key to your own identity. Among the Keres, every individual has a place within the universe—human and nonhuman—and that place is defined by clan membership. In turn, clan membership is dependent on matrilineal descent. Of course, your mother is not only that woman whose womb formed and released you—the term refers in every individual case to an entire generation of women whose psychic, and consequently physical, "shape" made the psychic existence of the following generation possible. But naming your own mother (or her equivalent) enables people to place you precisely within the universal web of your life, in each of its dimensions: cultural, spiritual, personal, and historical.

Among the Keres, "context" and "matrix" are equivalent terms, and both refer to approximately the same thing as knowing your derivation and place. Failure to know your mother, that is, your position and its attendant traditions, history, and place in the scheme of things, is failure to remember your significance, your reality, your right relationship to earth and society. It is the same as being lost—isolated, abandoned, self-estranged, and alienated from your own life. This importance of tradition in the life of every member of the community is not confined to Keres Indians; all American Indian Nations place great value on traditionalism.

The Native American sense of the importance of continuity with one's cultural origins runs counter to contemporary American ideas: In many instances, the immigrants to America have been eager to cast off cultural ties, often seeing their antecedents as backward, restrictive, even shameful. Rejection of tradition constitutes one of the major features of American life, an attitude that reaches far back into American colonial history and that now is validated by virtually every cultural institution in the country. Feminist practice, at least in the cultural artifacts the community values most, follows this cultural trend as well.

The American idea that the best and the brightest should willingly reject and repudiate their origins leads to an allied idea—that history, like everything in the past, is of little value and should be forgotten as quickly as possible. This all too often causes us to reinvent the wheel continually. We find ourselves discovering our collective pasts over and over, having to retake ground already covered by women in the preceding decades and centuries. The Native American view, which highly values maintenance of traditional customs, values, and perspectives, might result in slower societal change and in quite a bit less social upheaval, but it has the advantage of providing a solid sense of identity and lowered levels of psychological and interpersonal conflict.

Contemporary Indian communities value individual members who are deeply connected to the traditional ways of their people, even after centuries of concerted and brutal effort of the part of the American government, the churches, and the corporate system to break the connections between individuals and their tribal world. In fact, in the view of the traditionals, rejection of one's culture—one's traditions, language, people—is the result of colonial oppression and is hardly to be applauded. They believe that the roots of oppression are to be found in the loss of tradition and memory because that loss is always accompanied by a loss of a positive sense of self. In short, Indians think it is important to remember, while Americans believe it is important to forget.

The traditional Indians' view can have a significant impact if it is expanded to mean that the sources of social, political, and philosophical thought in the Americas not only should be recognized and honored by Native Americans but should be embraced by American society. If American society judiciously modeled the traditions of the various Native Nations, the place of women in society would become central, the distribution of goods and power would be egalitarian, the elderly would be respected, honored, and protected as a primary social and cultural resource, the ideals of physical beauty would be considerably enlarged (to include "fat," strong-featured women, gray-haired, and wrinkled individuals, and others who in contemporary American culture are viewed as "ugly"). Additionally, the destruction of the biota, the life sphere, and the natural resources of the planet would be curtailed, and the spiritual nature of human and nonhuman life would become a primary organizing principle of human society. And if the traditional tribal systems that are emulated included pacifist ones, war would cease to be a major method of human problem solving.

RE-MEMBERING CONNECTIONS AND HISTORIES

The belief that rejection of tradition and of history is a useful response to life is reflected in America's amazing loss of memory concerning its origins in the matrix and context of Native America. America does not seem to remember that it derived its wealth, its values, its food, much of its medicine, and a large part of its "dream" from Native America . It is ignorant of the genesis of its culture in this Native American land, and that ignorance helps to perpetuate the longstanding European and Middle Eastern monotheistic, hierarchical, patriarchal cultures' oppression of women, gays, and lesbians, people of color, working class, unemployed people, and the elderly. Hardly anyone in America speculates that the constitutional system of government might be as much a product of American Indian ideas and practices as of colonial American and Anglo-European revolutionary fervor.

Even though Indians are officially and informally ignored as intellectual movers and shapers in the United States, Britian, and Europe, they are peoples with ancient tenure on this soil. During the ages when tribal societies existed in the Americas largely untouched by patriarchal oppression, they developed elaborate systems of thought that included science, philosophy, and government based on a belief in the central importance of female energies, autonomy of individuals, cooperation, human dignity, human freedom, and egalitarian distribution of status, goods, and services. Respect for others, reverence for life, and, as a byproduct, pacifism as a way of life; importance of kinship ties in the customary order of social interaction; a sense of the sacredness and mystery of existence; balance and harmony in relationships both sacred and secular were all features of life among the tribal confederacies and nations. And in those that lived by the largest number of these principles, gynarchy was the norm rather than the exception. Those systems are as yet unmatched in any contemporary industrial, agrarian, or postindustrial society on earth.

There are many female gods recognized and honored by the tribes and Nations. Femaleness was highly valued, both respected and feared, and all social institutions reflected this attitude. Even modern sayings, such as the Cheyenne statement that a people is not conquered until the hearts of the women are on the ground, express the Indians' understanding that without the power of woman the people will not live, but with it, they will endure and prosper.

Indians did not confine this belief in the central importance of female energy to matters of worship. Among many of the tribes (perhaps as many as 70 percent of them in North America alone), this belief was reflected in all of their social institutions. The Iroquois Constitution or White Roots of Peace, also called the Great Law of the Iroquois, codified the Matrons' decision-making and economic power:

> The lineal descent of the people of the Five Fires [the Iroquois Nations] shall run in the female line. Women shall be considered the progenitors of the Nation. They shall own the land and the soil. Men and women shall follow the status of their mothers. (Article 44)
>
> The women heirs of the chieftainship titles of the League shall be called Oiner or Otinner [Noble] for all time to come. (Article 45)

If a disobedient chief persists in his disobedience after three warnings [by his female relatives, by his male relatives, and by one of his fellow council members, in that order], the matter shall go to the council of War Chiefs. The Chiefs shall then take away the title of the erring chief *by order of the women in whom the title is vested*. When the chief is deposed, the women shall notify the chiefs of the League . . . and the chiefs of the League shall sanction the act. The women will then select another of their sons as a candidate and the chiefs shall elect him. (Article 19) (Emphasis mine)[1]

The Matrons held so much policy-making power traditionally that once, when their position was threatened they demanded its return, and consequently the power of women was fundamental in shaping the Iroquois Confederation sometime in the sixteenth or early seventeenth century. It was women

who fought what may have been the first successful feminist rebellion in the New World. The year was 1600, or thereabouts, when these tribal feminists decided that they had had enough of unregulated warfare by their men. Lysistratas among the Indian women proclaimed a boycott on lovemaking and childbearing. Until the men conceded to them the power to decide upon war and peace, there would be no more warriors. Since the men believed that the women alone knew the secret of childbirth, the rebellion was instantly successful.

In the Constitution of Deganawidah the founder of the Iroquois Confederation of Nations had said: "He caused the body of our mother, the woman, to be of great worth and honor. He purposed that she shall be endowed and entrusted with the birth and upbringing of men, and that she shall have the care of all that is planted by which life is sustained and supported and the power to breathe is fortified: *and moreover that the warriors shall be her assistants.*"

The footnote of history was curiously supplied when Susan B. Anthony began her "Votes for Women" movement two and a half centuries later. Unknowingly the feminists chose to hold their founding convention of latter-day suffragettes in the town of Seneca [Falls], New York. The site was just a stone's throw from the old council house where the Iroquois women had plotted their feminist rebellion. (Emphasis mine)[2]

Beliefs, attitudes, and laws such as these became part of the vision of American feminists and of other human liberation movements around the world. Yet feminists too often believe that no one has ever experienced the kind of society that empowered women and made that empowerment the basis of its rules of civilization. The price the feminist community must pay because it is not aware of the recent presence of gynarchical societies on this continent is unnecessary confusion, division, and much lost time.

THE ROOT OF OPPRESSION IS LOSS OF MEMORY

An odd thing occurs in the minds of Americans when Indian civilization is mentioned: little or nothing. As I write this, I am aware of how far removed my version of the roots of American feminism must seem to those steeped in either mainstream or radical versions of feminism's history. I am keenly aware of the lack of image Americans have about our continent's recent past. I am intensely conscious of popular

1. [The White Roots of Peace, cited in *The Third Woman: Minority Women Writers of the United States*, ed. Dexter Fisher (Boston: Houghton Mifflin, 1980) 577. Cf. Thomas Sanders and William Peek, eds., *Literature of the American Indian* (New York: Glencoe Press, 1973) 208–239. Sanders and Peek refer to the document as "The Law of the Great Peace."]
2. [Stan Steiner, *The New Indians* (New York: Dell, 1968) 219–220.]

notions of Indian women as beasts of burden, squaws, traitors, or, at best, vanished denizens of a long-lost wilderness. How odd, then, must my contention seem that the gynocratic tribes of the American continent provided the basis for all the dreams of liberation that characterize the modern world.

We as feminists must be aware of our history on this continent. We need to recognize that the same forces that devastated the gynarchies of Britain and the Continent also devastated the ancient African civilizations, and we must know that those same materialistic, antispiritual forces are presently engaged in wiping out the same gynarchical values, along with the peoples who adhere to them, in Latin America. I am convinced that those wars were and continue to be about the imposition of patriarchal civilization over the holistic, pacifist, and spirit-based gynarchies they supplant. To that end the wars of imperial conquest have not been solely or even mostly waged over the land and its resources, but they have been fought within the bodies, minds, and hearts of the people of the earth for dominion over them. I think this is the reason traditionals say we must remember our origins, our cultures, our histories, our mothers and grandmothers, for without that memory, which implies continuance rather than nostalgia, we are doomed to engulfment by a paradigm that is fundamentally inimical to the vitality, autonomy, and self-empowerment essential for satisfying, high-quality life.

The vision that impels feminists to action was the vision of the Grandmothers' society, the society that was captured in the words of the sixteenth-century explorer Peter Martyr nearly five hundred years ago. It is the same vision repeated over and over by radical thinkers of Europe and America, from François Villon to John Locke, from William Shakespeare to Thomas Jefferson, from Karl Marx to Friedrich Engels, from Benito Juarez to Martin Luther King, from Elizabeth Cady Stanton to Judy Grahn, from Harriet Tubman to Audre Lorde, from Emma Goldman to Bella Abzug, from Malinalli to Cherríe Moraga, and from Iyatiku to me. That vision as Martyr told it is of a country where there are "no soldiers, no gendarmes or police, no nobles, kings, regents, prefects, or judges, no prisons, no lawsuits . . . All are equal and free," or so Friedrich Engels recounts Martyr's words.[3]

Columbus wrote:

> Nor have I been able to learn whether they [the inhabitants of the islands he visited on his first journey to the New World] held personal property, for it seemed to me that whatever one had, they all took shares of . . . They are so ingenuous and free with all they have, that no one would believe it who has not seen it; of anything that they possess, if it be asked of them, they never say no; on the contrary, they invited you to share it and show as much love as if their hearts went with it.[4]

At least that's how the Native Caribbean people acted when the whites first came among them; American Indians are the despair of social workers, bosses, and missionaries even now because of their deeply ingrained tendency to spend all they have, mostly on others. In any case, as the historian William Brandon notes,

> the Indian *seemed* free, to European eyes, gloriously free, to the European soul shaped by centuries of toil and tyranny, and this impression operated profoundly on the process of history and the development of America. Something in the peculiar character of the

---

3. [William Brandon, *The Last Americans: The Indian in American Culture* (New York: McGraw-Hill, 1974) 294.]

4. [Brandon, *Last Americans* 6.]

Indian world gave an impression of classlessness, of propertylessness, and that in turn led to an impression, as H.H. Bancroft put it, of "humanity unrestrained . . . in the exercise of liberty absolute."[5]

A FEMINIST HEROINE

Early in the women's suffrage movement, Eva Emery Dye, an Oregon suffragette, went looking for a heroine to embody her vision of feminism. She wanted a historical figure whose life would symbolize the strengthened power of women. She found Sacagawea (or Sacajawea) buried in the journals of Lewis and Clark. The Shoshoni teenager had traveled with the Lewis and Clark expedition, carrying her infant son, and on a small number of occasions acted as translator.[6]

Dye declared that Sacagawea, whose name is thought to mean Bird Woman, had been the guide to the historic expedition, and through Dye's work Sacagawea became enshrined in American memory as a moving force and friend of the whites, leading them in the settlement of western North America.[7]

But Native American roots of white feminism reach back beyond Sacagawea. The earliest white women on this continent were all acquainted with tribal women. They were neighbors to a number of tribes and often shared food, information, child care, and health care. Of course little is made of these encounters in official histories of colonial America, the period from the Revolution to the Civil War, or on the ever-moving frontier. Nor, to my knowledge, has either the significance or incidence of intermarriage between Indian and white or between Indian an Black been explored. By and large, the study of Indian-white relations has been focused on government and treaty relations, warfare, missionization, and education. It has been almost entirely documented in terms of formal white Christian patriarchal impacts and assaults on Native Americans, though they are not often characterized as assaults but as "civilizing the savages." Particularly in organs of popular culture and miseducation, the focus has been on what whites imagine to be degradation of Indian women ("squaws"), their equally imagined love of white government and white conquest ("princesses"), and the horrifyingly misleading, fanciful tales of "bloodthirsty, backward primitives" assaulting white Christian settlers who were looking for life, liberty, and happiness in their chosen land.

5. [Brandon, *Last Americans* 7–8. The entire chapter "American Indians and American History" (pp. 1–23) is pertinent to the discussion.]
6. [Ella E. Clark and Margot Evans, *Sacagawea of the Lewis and Clark Expedition* (Berkeley: University of California Press, 1979) 93–98. Clark details the fascinating, infuriating, and very funny scholarly escapade of how our suffragist] foremothers created a feminist hero from the scant references to the teenage Shoshoni wife of the expedition's official translator, Pierre Charbonneau.]
7. [The implications of this maneuver did not go unnoticed by either whites or Indians, for the statue of the idealized Shoshoni woman, the Native American matron Sacagawea, suggests that American tenure on American land, indeed, the right to be on this land, is given to whites by her. While that implication is not overt, it certainly is suggested in the image of her that the sculptor chose: a tall, heavy woman, standing erect, nobly pointing the way westward with upraised hand. The impression is furthered by the habit of media and scholars of referring to her as "the guide." Largely because of the popularization of the circumstances of Sacagawea's par-

ticipation in the famed Lewis and Clark expedition, Indian people have viewed her as a traitor to her people, likening her to Malinalli (La Malinche, who acted as interpreter for Cortés and bore him a son) and Pocahontas, that unhappy girl who married John Rolfe (not John Smith) and died in England after bearing him a son. Actually none of these women engaged in traitorous behavior. Sacagawea led a long life, was called Porivo (Chief Woman) by the Comanches, among whom she lived for more than twenty years, and in her old age engaged her considerable skill at speaking and manipulating white bureaucracy to help in assuring her Shoshoni people decent reservation holdings.

A full discussion is impossible here but an examination of American childrearing practices, societal attitudes toward women and exhibited by women (when compared to the same in Old World cultures) as well as the goodstuffs, medicinal materials, countercultural and alternative cultural systems, and the deeply Indian values these reflect, should demonstrate the truth about informal acculturation and crosscultural connections in the Americas.]

But, regardless of official versions of relations between Indians and whites or other segments of the American population, the fact remains that great numbers of apparently "white" or "Black" Americans carry notable degrees of Indian blood. With that blood has come the culture of the Indian, informing the lifestyles, attitudes, and values of their descendants. Somewhere along the line—and often quite recently—an Indian woman was giving birth to and raising the children of a family both officially and informally designated as white or Black—not Indian. In view of this, it should be evident that one of the major enterprises of Indian women in America has been the transfer of Indian values and culture to as large and influential a segment of American immigrant populations as possible. Their success in this endeavor is amply demonstrated in the Indian values and social styles that increasingly characterize American life. Among these must be included "permissive" childrearing practices, for as noted in an earlier chapter ("When Women Throw Down Bundles"), imprisoning, torturing, caning, strapping, starving, or verbally abusing children was considered outrageous behavior. Native Americans did not believe that physical or psychological abuse of children would result in their edification. They did not believe that children are born in sin, are congenitally predisposed to evil, or that a good parent who wishes the child to gain salvation, achieve success, or earn the respect of her or his fellows can be helped to those ends by physical or emotional torture.

The early Americans saw the strongly protective attitude of the Indian people as a mark of their "savagery"—as they saw the Indian's habit of bathing frequently, their sexual openness, their liking for scant clothing, their raucous laughter at most things, their suspicion and derision of authoritarian structures, their quick pride, their genuine courtesy, their willingness to share what they had with others less fortunate than they, their egalitarianism, their ability to act as if various lifestyles were a normal part of living, and their granting that women were of equal, or in individual cases, of greater value than men.

Yet the very qualities that marked Indian life in the sixteenth century have, over the centuries since contact between the two worlds occurred, come to mark much of contemporary American life. And those qualities, which I believe have passed into white culture from Indian culture, are the very ones that fundamentalists, immigrants from Europe, the Middle East, and Asia often find the most reprehensible. Third- and fourth-generation Americans indulge in growing nudity, informality in social relations, egalitarianism, and the rearing of women who value autonomy, strength, freedom, and personal dignity—and who are often derided by European, Asian, and middle Eastern men for those qualities. Contemporary Americans value leisure almost as much as tribal people do. They find themselves increasingly unable to accept child abuse as a reasonable way to nurture. They bathe more than any other industrial people on earth—much to the scorn of their white cousins across the Atlantic—and they sometimes enjoy a good laugh even at their own expense (though they still have a less developed sense of the ridiculous than one might wish).

Contemporary Americans find themselves more and more likely to adopt a "live and let live" attitude in matters of personal, sexual and social styles. Two-thirds of their diet and a large share of their medications and medical treatments mirror or are directly derived from Native American sources. Indianization is not a simple concept, to be sure, and it is one that Americans often find themselves resisting; but it is a process that has taken place, regardless of American resistance to recognizing the source of many if not most of Americans' vaunted freedoms in our personal, family, social, and political arenas.

This is not to say that Americans have become Indian in every attitude, value, or social institution. Unfortunately, Americans have a way to go in learning how to live in the world in ways that improve the quality of life for each individual while doing minimal damage to the biota, but they have adapted certain basic qualities of perception and certain attitudes that are moving them in that direction.

AN INDIAN-FOCUSED VERSION OF AMERICAN HISTORY

American colonial ideas of self-government came as much from the colonists' observations of tribal governments as from their Protestant or Greco-Roman heritage. Neither Greece nor Rome had the kind of pluralistic democracy as that concept has been understood in the United States since Andrew Jackson, but the tribes, particularly the gynarchical tribal confederacies, did. It is true that the *oligarchic* form of government that colonial Americans established was originally based on Greco-Roman systems in a number of important ways, such as its restriction of citizenship to propertied white males over twenty-one years of age, but it was never a form that Americans as a whole have been entirely comfortable with. Politics and government in the United States during the Federalist period also reflected the English common law system as it had evolved under patriarchal feudalism and monarchy—hence the United States' retention of slavery and restriction of citizenship to propertied white males.

The Federalists did make one notable change in the feudal system from which their political system derived on its Anglo side. They rejected blooded aristocracy and monarchy. This idea came from the Protestant Revolt to be sure, but it was at least reinforced by colonial America's proximity to American Indian nonfeudal confederacies and their concourse with those confederacies over the two hundred years of the colonial era. It was this proximity and concourse that enabled the revolutionary theorists to "dream up" a system in which all local polities would contribute to and be protected by a central governing body responsible for implementing policies that bore on the common interest of all. If should also be noted that the Reformation followed Columbus's contact with the Americas and that his and Martyr's reports concerning Native Americans' free and easy egalitarianism were in circulation by the time the Reformation took hold.

The Iroquois federal system, like that of several in the vicinity of the American colonies, is remarkably similar to the organization of the federal system of the United states. It was made up of local, "state," and federal bodies composed of executive, legislative, and judicial branches. The Council of Matrons was the executive: It instituted and determined general policy. The village, tribal (several villages), and Confederate councils determined and implemented policies when they did not conflict with the broader Council's decisions or with theological precepts that ultimately determined policy at all levels. The judicial was composed of the men's councils and the Matron's council, who sat together to make decisions. Because the matrons were the ceremonial center of the system, they were also the prime policymakers.

Obviously, there are major differences between the structure of the contemporary American government and that of the Iroquois. Two of those differences were and are crucial to the process of just government. The Iroquois system is spirit-based, while that of the United States is secular, and the Iroquois Clan Matrons formed the executive. The female executive function was directly tied to the ritual nature of the Iroquois politic, for the executive was lodged in the hands of the Matrons of particular clans across village, tribe, and national lines. The executive office was hereditary, and only sons of eligible clans could serve, at the behest of the Matrons of their clans, on the councils at the three levels. Certain daughters inherited the office of Clan Matron through their clan affiliations. No one could impeach or disempower a Matron, though her violation of certain laws could result in her ineligibility for the Matron's council. For example, a woman who married *and took her husband's name* could not hold the title Matron.

American ideas of social justice came into sharp focus through the commentaries of Iroquois observers who traveled in France in the colonial period. These observers expressed horror at the great gap between the lifestyles of the wealthy and the poor, remarking to the French philosopher Montaigne, who would heavily influence the radical communities of Europe, England, and America, that "they had noticed that in Europe there seemed to be two moities, consisting of the rich 'full gorged' with wealth, and the poor, starving 'and bare with need and poverty.' The Indian tourists not only marveled at the division, but marveled that the poor endured 'such an injustice, and that they took not the others by the throat, or set fire on their house.'"[8] It must be noted that the urban poor eventually did just that in the French Revolution. The writings of Montaigne and of those he influenced provided the theoretical framework and the vision that propelled the struggle for liberty, justice, and equality on the Continent and later throughout the British empire.

The feminist idea of power as it ideally accrues to women stems from tribal sources. The central importance of the clan Matrons in the formulation and determination of domestic and foreign policy as well as in their primary role in the ritual and ceremonial life of their respective Nations was the single most important attribute of the Iroquois, as of the Cherokee and Muskogee, who traditionally inhabited the southern Atlantic region. The latter peoples were removed to what is now Oklahoma during the Jackson administration, but prior to the American Revolution they had regular and frequent communication with and impact on both the British colonizers and later the American people, including the African peoples brought here as slaves.

Ethnographer Lewis Henry Morgan wrote an account of Iroquoian matriarchal culture, published in 1877,[9] that heavily influenced Marx and the development of communism, particularly lending it the idea of the liberation of women from patriarchal dominance. The early socialists in Europe, especially in Russia, saw women's liberation as a central aspect of the socialist revolution. Indeed, the basic ideas of socialism, the egalitarian distribution of goods and power, the peaceful ordering of society, and the right of every member of society to participate in the work and benefits of that society, are ideas that pervade American Indian political thought and action. And it is through various channels—the informal but deeply effective Indianization of Europeans, and christianizing Africans, the social and political theory of the confederacies feuding and then intertwining with European dreams of liberty and justice, and, more recently, the work of Morgan and the writings of Marx and Engels—that the age-old gynarchical systems of egalitarian government found their way into contemporary feminist theory.

When Eva Emery Dye discovered Sacagawea and honored her as the guiding spirit of American womanhood, she may have been wrong in bare historical fact, but she was quite accurate in terms of deeper truth. The statues that have been erected depicting Sacagawea as a Matron in her prime signify an understanding in the American mind, however unconscious, that the source of just government, of right ordering of

---

8. [Brandon, *Last Americans* 6.]
9. [Lewis Henry Morgan, *Ancient Society or Researches in*

the Lines of Human Progress from Savagery Through Barbarism to Civilization (New York, 1877).]

social relationships, the dream of "liberty and justice for all" can be gained only by following the Indian Matrons' guidance. For, as Dr. Anna Howard Shaw said of Sacagawea at the National American Woman's Suffrage Association in 1905:

> Forerunner of civilization, great leader of men, patient and motherly woman, we bow our hearts to do you honor! . . . May we the daughters of an alien race . . . learn the lessons of calm endurance, of patient persistence and unfaltering courage exemplified in your life, in our efforts to lead men through the Pass of justice, which goes over the mountains of prejudice and conservatism to the broad land of the perfect freedom of a true republic; one in which men and women together shall in perfect equality solve the problems of a nation that knows no caste, no race, no sex in opportunity, in responsibility or in justice! May 'the eternal womanly' ever lead us on![10]   *1986*

10. [Clark and Evans, *Sacagawea* 96.]

SECTION IV

Identity and Difference

—•— ⊱◊⊰ —•—

The self-discovery of female identity seems to acknowledge the real presence and recognition of another consciousness, and the disclosure of the
female self is linked to the identification of some 'other.'

Mary Mason, "The Other Voice: Autobiographies of Women Writers"

Identity . . . supposes that a clear dividing line can be made between I and
not-I, he and she: between depth and surface, or vertical and horizontal
identity; between us here and them over there. . . . Difference . . . is that
which undermines the very idea of identity.

*Trinh T. Minh-ha, "Not You/Like You: Postcolonial Women and the
Interlocking Questions of Identity and Difference"*

Through the ages women writers have asked a series of philosophical questions:
"Who am I?"; "What does it mean to be a *woman* writing?"; and "How am I different
from those around me?" *Identity* and *difference* represent key terms of discussion in
contemporary feminist theory, terms with important implications for the study of
autobiography, poetry, and narratives by women. Claiming a female writing identity
involves an awareness that any woman's sense of self is fluid, constantly changing,
influenced by her culture, class, race, historical circumstances, and relation to an
"other"—whether that "other" be another woman or a man; black, white, native,
person of color, British, American, African, colonial, postcolonial. Whether occupying a center or speaking from the margins, women who write about identity assure
themselves and other women that they do matter in a world that often deems them
objects rather than subjects.

A theoretical concept closely linked to identity is difference, which AUDRE
LORDE defines as "a fund of necessary polarities between which [women's] creativity
can spark like a dialectic" (111). As Lorde suggests, much of Western history has
urged humans to view difference in dichotomous terms: dominant/subordinate,
good/bad, superior/inferior. Instead of acquiescing to this hierarchical indoctrination,
she argues, women must learn to relate as equals across differences, to use difference
creatively in analyzing literature of various time periods and cultures, and to challenge
oppressive social structures. Finally, identity and difference emerge not as competitive
concepts but as interlocking questions: Who am I, who are you, how am I "not
you/like you," and how have we represented ourselves, together and apart, as women?

The links between identity and politics have been explored by the Combahee
River Collective, a group of African-American lesbians who wrote a collaborative
essay on this topic in 1977. Arguing for an emerging "identity politics" based on the

belief that, as black women, they must concentrate on their own liberation, the Collective criticized the modern women's and civil rights movements for neglecting the voices and needs of African-American women. Expanding the feminist concept that "the personal is political," the Collective linked racial, sexual, heterosexual, and class privilege as overlapping forms of oppression, which they intended to use their identity to challenge. Philosopher Linda Alcoff has expanded on the Collective's definition of identity politics, noting that identity can be "taken (and defined) as a political point of departure, as a motivation for action, and as a delineation of one's own politics" (431–32). For Alcoff, identity politics constitutes not a search for or reliance on some fixed notion of selfhood (e.g., black womanhood) but represents instead a reason and force for social change. Identity politics has also been discussed by Diana Fuss, who defines it at first narrowly, as the tendency to base one's writing or activism on self-definition (as female, black, Jewish, lesbian, etc.), but goes on to acknowledge its analytic usefulness. For feminist theorists and readers of women's literature, the task might be to dissect identity but not to disavow it. Identity thus construed has multiple, destabilizing meanings. When women view identity politics contextually, they can use it strategically to analyze various constructions of "selves" in relation to "others."

Several feminist theorists, however, have critiqued identity as a problematic concept and have explored as an alternative the idea of difference. Claiming an identity can be a triple bind for women writers of color, argues TRINH T. MINH-HA; although they may prefer to be "neither black/red/yellow nor woman but poet or writer," women of color today cannot afford to identify confidently with the profession of writing without linking it to their "color-woman condition." Which identity should take priority, Trinh asks, "Writer of color? Woman writer? Or woman of color? . . . Where does she place her loyalties?" Such polarizing levels of consciousness are troubling to her as a Vietnamese feminist living and working in the United States, and she offers difference as an alternative construct, "a tool of creativity to question multiple forms of repression and dominance" (*LAWL* 930). If identity is a potentially oppressive construct, difference may be seen as a concept that refuses to endorse hierarchies, thereby undermining oppositional thought.

For readers of women's literature, confronting identity and difference means acknowledging the interdependency of early modern women writers and women writing today; of white women who decry Native Americans as "savage" and Native American women who ask whether the "savagery" might lie on the other side; of writers from the "first world" and those from the "third world." As Trinh cautions, however, interdependency must not "be reduced to a mere question of mutual enslavement"; it suggests instead the need for "creating a ground that belongs to no one, not even to the creator. Otherness becomes empowerment, critical difference when it is not given but recreated" (*LAWL* 932). Difference can be a source of shared strength if women acknowledge, probe, and celebrate it in their writing and their lives.

The term "life writing" includes women's journals, letters, essays, and polemics, as well as poetic representations of identity and difference. Examining life writing allows readers a sense of how women have portrayed their complex, multiple selves, both autonomously and in relation to others. As Germaine Brée asks in her introduction to *Life/Lines*, "in the passage from life to writing, what strategies have women who 'writ [their] own lives' adopted, when confronting their world, to free themselves from the images of role personae and desire encoded in the language?" (Brodzki and Schenck ix). Certainly women writers have always considered the disparities and similarities between the sexes, and these considerations are fundamental to an understanding of both identity and difference. Women writers have paid homage to men as inspirers and cocreators, conceived of themselves as equal (or superior) to men, and challenged traditional assumptions about men as active and women as passive, about biology as destiny. Men are not the only oppressors, however; women have sometimes colluded in the political privilege of calling certain peoples "other." Thus it is necessary to investigate the ways in which women writers have stereotyped women who are different from themselves, as well as the ways in which women who have been so "othered" have responded.

FORGING WOMEN'S IDENTITIES: LIFE WRITING

> To the uncritical eye, autobiography presents as untroubled a reflection of identity as the surface of a mirror can provide. . . . The female autobiographer takes as a given that selfhood is mediated; her invisibility results from her lack of a tradition, her marginality in male-dominated culture, her fragmentation—social and political as well as psychic.

> Bella Brodzki and Celeste Schenck, Life/Lines

> Dare you see a Soul at the White Heat?

> Emily Dickinson, Poem 365

From St. Augustine to Jean-Jacques Rousseau to Henry Adams, male writers of autobiography have claimed to be universal, representative, the mirrors of their eras; they have assumed an essential, inviolable self from which to speak. Such a self is profoundly gendered, however, for as Susan Stanford Friedman has noted, the emphasis on individualism that has underwritten assumptions about autobiography is "a reflection of privilege, one that excludes from the canons of autobiography those writers who have been denied by history the illusion of individualism"—among them, women of most races, classes, nationalities, and time periods (34–40).

Women autobiographers have typically lacked the sense of authority to speak as an individual who commands attention or as a transcendent being. Instead, women often write autobiographies that explore the self in relation to another or others. In Friedman's words, "the self constructed in women's autobiographical writing is often based in, but not limited to, a group consciousness" (40–41). Compared to works by men, SHARI BENSTOCK notes, women's autobiographies frequently display either a tangential self or no self at all: "the self that would reside at the center of the text is decentered—and often is absent altogether" (20). Nonetheless, as Estelle Jelinek has proven in her groundbreaking study Women's Autobiography, a countertradition of women's autobiographical writing does exist, from MARGERY KEMPE to DOROTHY WORDSWORTH to MICHELLE CLIFF. Such personal narratives take different forms and are often fragmented, interrupted, characterized by "irregularity rather than orderliness" (Jelinek 17). Indeed, women's life writing breaks traditional generic boundaries and is often multigeneric. Like other forms of women's work, their life writing reflects the multiple demands and divided selves that shape the lives of those who would be sometimes daughters, mothers, sisters, wives, lovers, friends, breadwinners—as well as writers.

Dorothy Wordsworth's *Grasmere Journal* reveals the difficulty one nineteenth-century woman faced in claiming an autonomous autobiographical identity. Begun in 1800 to "give William Pleasure by it when he comes home again," the journal portrays the author's tendency toward self-denigration, toward "putting herself down," as the critic James Holt McGavran has described it (230). Still, the sister of the Romantic poet William Wordsworth wrote consistently, "putting herself down" on paper in the other sense of that idiom, keeping journals regularly for many years. Margaret Homans has noted Wordsworth's tendency to avoid using "I" in the journals and McGavran has discussed her discomfort with introspection, yet many passages do offer forthright, lyrical accounts of the speaker's moods (Homans 41–44). If indeed her pen does "stammer," as VIRGINIA WOOLF suggests in a 1929 essay on Wordsworth, her self-consciousness rarely extends to her luminous, witty descriptions of the natural world. For Woolf there is a necessary link between Wordsworth's self-effacement and the transcendent voice in which she speaks of nature. "If she let 'I' and its rights and its wrongs and its passions and its suffering get between her and the object, she would be . . . soaring into reveries and rhapsodies and forgetting to find the exact phrase for the ripple of moonlight upon the lake," declares Woolf. "It was like 'herrings in the water'—she could not have said that if she had been thinking about herself. . . . But if one subdued oneself, and resigned one's private agitations, then, as if in reward, Nature would bestow an exquisite satisfaction" (*Collected Essays* 3: 200, 203). By subduing the self, that is, Dorothy Wordsworth can attain the incandescence that Woolf advocates in *A Room of One's Own*.

In her memoirs and essays the Southern writer EUDORA WELTY tends to downplay what Friedman has called "the cultural category WOMAN" and concentrate instead on the particular blend of good parenting, curiosity about people, and fascination with language that led her to become a writer (38). Although long admired for her fiction, Welty reached new audiences with the publication of *One Writer's Beginnings*, which made the *New York Times* bestseller list for forty-six weeks in 1983–84. A series of lectures given at Harvard University, this memoir contains three sections: "Listening," "Learning to See," and "Finding a Voice." As these titles suggest, *One Writer's Beginnings*, though richly autobiographical, focuses primarily on the mysteries of the creative process and thus illuminates Welty's fictional voice as well as her autobiographical one. Writing in the realist tradition, she acknowledges links between her characters and herself. "Characters take on life sometimes by luck," she explains, "but I suspect it is when you can write most entirely out of yourself, inside the skin, heart, mind and soul of a person who is not yourself, that a character becomes in his own right another human being on the page" (100). As an other who is not the self but is of the self, the realistic character becomes, in Trinh's words, both "not me" and "like me." The narrator in Welty's "Why I Live at the P.O.," for example, and the stories she and similar characters tell, pay homage to the power of the writer's memory. "Writing fiction has developed in me an abiding respect for the unknown in a human lifetime," asserts Welty, "and a sense of where to look for the threads, how to follow, how to connect, find in the thick of the tangle what clear line persists. The strands are all there: To the memory nothing is ever really lost" (90).

As Celeste Schenck has argued, women's poetry often emerges from the same impulse toward "sketching a self in time and over time" as autobiography does:

Often the female poetic corpus, like many but by no means all women's autobiographies, serves simultaneously as a historical record of women's absence from literary culture and as evidence of one woman's presence to herself within contiguous modes of life writing, an often programmatically fragmentary, yet nonetheless inclusive record of self-inscription (Brodzki and Schenck 290–91).

Among pre-twentieth-century women, KATHERINE PHILIPS and EMILY DICKINSON stand out as poets who wrote of both "self-division and sturdy identity" in their poems. Known as the "matchless Orinda," Philips was one of the two most influential women poets of the seventeenth century, the other being APHRA BEHN; much of what Philips inscribed was her own life experience as a woman who valued both privacy and her connections to other women. Critics have long debated whether she willingly became a public writer. In 1651 and 1653 poems by Philips were published in books composed primarily by men, and in 1663 her translation of Pierre Corneille's *Pompey* was staged in Dublin; in 1664, however, when a bowdlerized collection of her poetry appeared in London, she insisted that it be withdrawn from publication. Moreover, although Philips often paid tribute to "friendship's mysteries," she viewed a writer's happiness as coming from within:

> At length this secret I have learned;
> Who will be happy, must be unconcerned,
> Must all their Comfort in their Bosom wear,
> And seek their treasure and their power there.

This assertion of autonomy and her many poems about women's affiliations reveal that "Orinda" finds delight not only in the self alone but also in the relational self.

Emily Dickinson's poetic *oeuvre* also exemplifies what Schenck has called "self/life/writing." Although Dickinson insisted to her literary correspondent, Thomas Wentworth Higginson, that "when I state myself, as the Representative of the Verse—it does not mean—me—but a supposed Person," she claimed a subjectivity more powerful and diverse than that of any other poet of her era, male or female. Nancy Walker has argued that "even now, feminist analysis is just beginning to reveal the extent to which Dickinson's poetry may constitute a record of her thoughts, an 'autobiography' of a poet for whom the private though all-encompassing life of the intellect was far richer than the public life of the social encounter" (273). Whether or not one reads her poems as autobiographical, that Dickinson meant them to be published after her death seems likely, given her careful arrangement of them into fascicles, or small bundles. Yet her public identification as a poet was ambivalent at best. "Publication—is the Auction / Of the Mind of Man—"she claims in poem 709.

> Poverty—be justifying
> For so foul a thing
>
> Possibly—but We—would rather
> From Our Garret go
> White—Unto the White Creator—
> Than invest—Our Snow—(*LAWL* 971)

Virginal and closeted, the speaker both claims an authoritative self, the royal "We," and declaims any impulse to display that self through art, to "invest—Our Snow."

The twentieth-century U.S. poet MARIANNE MOORE also may have been initially ambivalent toward publishing. Her first volume, *Poems* (1921), appeared in England without Moore's knowledge under the auspices of her friends, the poet H.D. (Hilda Doolittle) and her companion, Bryher (Winifred Ellerman). Because Moore was particularly interested in observing natural phenomena, her poems are not known for revealing the poet's own identity, nor can the majority be described as autobiographical. Yet one of Moore's finest poems, "Like a Bulwark," pays homage to her mother, Mary Warner Moore, the poet's muse and confidant for more than fifty years. Another poem, "The Paper Nautilus," reveals her ambivalent relationship with a younger poet, Elizabeth Bishop, whom she sometimes wished to control. In this poem the nautilus is a conceit for the spawning of art, and the poem serves as a tribute to motherhood as well. Cautious and gentle, the paper nautilus protects but does not crush the "cradled freight" she bears insider her body, for the fate of the mother and her young are intertwined. As Betsy Erkkila suggests, this poem reveals Moore's self-in-relation, as well as her desire to replace a traditionally male ethos of domination with a maternal ethos of nurturance. At the same time, it "appears to be an attempt by Moore to come to terms with her relationship with Bishop at a time when both women were attempting to break out of the potential constraints of the mother/daughter bond" (123). Bishop had given Moore the paper nautilus that inspired the poem, a gift she considered the "most successful" of many that she had bestowed upon her exacting tutor. Having come into her own as a poet, Bishop appreciated Moore's instruction but wished to distance herself from it. Read autobiographically, "The Paper Nautilus" represents Moore's poetic acquiescence to Bishop's unspoken desire for creative freedom.

For some women writers and theorists, the conflict lies less in how to express their identity as a woman in relation to other women than in how to negotiate their membership in a marginalized racial group. "To write as a complete Caribbean woman, or man for that matter, demands of us retracing the African part of ourselves," writes MICHELLE CLIFF, a contemporary essayist and novelist from Jamaica who is racially mixed. Cliff's theoretical narratives probe her multifaceted identity as a light-skinned Jamaican woman who could pass for white but chooses instead to embrace her darkness; they explain her difficulty in asserting her subjectivity. Initially she was able to "approach myself as a subject" only in writing that was "nonlinear, almost shorthand," notes "written in snatches on a nine-to-five job." In "If I Could Write This in Fire, I Would Write This in Fire" she determines instead to "try and locate the vanishing point: where the lines of perspective converge and disappear. Lines of color and class. Lines of history and social context. Lines of denial and rejection" (*LAWL* 920). As Elizabeth Fox-Genovese notes of black women's autobiographical prose, it is not enough to say simply that such writers suffer from the double oppression of gender and race, for each author's identity emerges from "the historical experience of being black and female in a specific society at a specific moment and over succeeding generations" (65). Cliff's experience is distinctive to the politics and culture of her island birthplace, a place she has identified as "halfway between England and Africa," as well as to her own class and color privilege and her resistance to identifying as white. It is also connected to her identity as a lesbian. As a writer who acknowledges and unsettles "otherness," Cliff reveals her status as both outsider and insider in her essays.

As these examples from women's literary history reveal, most life writing by women does not evoke some mysterious "female essence"; instead it reflects the writer's particular familial and historical circumstances, giving voice to a self-in-flux. Identifying women's positions can thus provide a basis on which to argue for their literary merit and their canonical (or political) centrality. Nowhere have women identified their location within a network of relations as vividly as in their different forms of life writing.

INSCRIBING SEXUAL DIFFERENCE: WOMEN, MEN, AND GENDER

> Sexuality and textuality both depend on difference. Deconstructive criticism has made us attend to notions of textual difference, but the complexities of sexual difference, more pervasively engrained in our culture, have largely been confined to the edges of critical debate.
>
> > *Elizabeth Abel, Writing and Sexual Difference*

> Let them be sea-captains if you will . . . every path laid open to woman as freely as to man.
>
> > *Margaret Fuller, Woman in the Nineteenth Century*

The practice known as feminist criticism began as the study of how gender informs writing and how views of sexual difference engender and structure literary works. Among the first critics to challenge the prevailing assumption that creativity was an exclusively masculine enterprise were Sandra M. Gilbert and Susan Gubar, who in *The Madwoman in the Attic* (1979) began their analysis with quotes from male writers claiming literature as a masculine prerogative. As Gilbert and Gubar suggest, these male biases against women's creativity could not help but affect women writers' perceptions of themselves:

> For all literary artists, of course, self-definition necessarily precedes self-assertion: the creative 'I AM' cannot be uttered if the 'I' knows not what it is. But for the female artist the essential process of self-definition is complicated by all those patriarchal definitions that intervene between herself and herself (17).

How, then, have women through the ages struggled to distinguish themselves from their male counterparts, thereby inscribing and challenging sexual difference? Is Abel correct in asserting that such inscriptions result in "literary differences of genre, structure, voice, and plot"? (2). And when women have collaborated with men or written from within male traditions, how have those collaborations diminished and empowered them?

One way to answer these questions is to examine works by women who have relied on a sustaining male presence or tradition yet striven to distinguish themselves as literary creators. Two such writers, MARY SIDNEY HERBERT and DOROTHY WORDSWORTH, demonstrate a brother-sister dynamic of influence (Homans 40–45). Herbert worked with her illustrious brother, Sir Philip Sidney, on a verse translation of the Biblical psalms, two-thirds of which she completed on her own after his untimely death in 1586. Certainly the thorny issue of male-female literary collaborations arises in any analysis of what have come to be called "the Sidney psalms." During the Reformation the Biblical psalms were important in both private and public worship, but until Philip Sidney and Mary Sidney Herbert began their translation, no adequate versification of them existed. Most scholars today agree that the first forty-three psalms were translated before Sidney's death and that Herbert translated psalms 44 through 150 on her own, editing several of the earlier poems as well. Nor is it contested that Herbert undertook this enterprise as a labor of love; she was devoted to her brother and devastated by his death. "Where shall I unfold my inward pain, / That my enriven heart may find relief?" she asks in "The Doleful Lay of Clorinda," a pastoral elegy written when Philip died. Clearly Herbert wished to honor her brother's memory through her own literary efforts.

Like Sidney, however, Herbert was ambitious; she shared her brother's desire to encourage Protestant activism and to further the spirit and technique of English poetry, both aims that translating the psalms would further. Moreover, Sidney's death gave her the freedom to write, for although it was frowned upon for an upper-class Renaissance woman to initiate a major public work, she could translate religious works as a tribute to her beloved brother and still observe decorum. Indeed, she presented her translation as an extended conversation with her late brother, and as such it was well received (Lamb 115–18). Yet despite accolades for the psalms from the sixteenth century to the present, Mary Sidney Herbert's reputation continues to suffer from misguided critical assumptions about sexual difference. Although she was credited as coauthor of the psalms as they circulated in manuscript during her lifetime, when they were first published in 1823 Philip Sidney was honored as primary author—a fact perhaps not surprising, given the nineteenth-century emphasis on male creative genius. But even some recent editions credit Philip Sidney with primary authorship of the first forty-three psalms, despite much evidence to the contrary. As Abel notes, women writers across time "inevitably engage a literary history and system of conventions shaped primarily by men," and Mary Sidney Herbert provides a case in point. To feminist critics falls the task of elucidating "the acts of revision, appropriation, and subversion that constitute [her] female text" (Abel 2). Herbert not only revised the psalms she and her brother had translated together, she also assigned to what could be called "the Herbert psalms" her own original and subversive signature.

The complexities of brother-sister literary coproduction can also be seen in the relationship of the diarist DOROTHY WORDSWORTH to her poet brother, William. While his sister tended house in Alfoxden and Grasmere for William, she enabled his poetic efforts and enabled him with images from her journals, which she composed for his enjoyment. To be sure, William deeply appreciated his sister, and Dorothy read his work with pleasure and encouraged him to use her descriptions of the natural world in his poetry. Yet none of Dorothy Wordsworth's writing was published in her lifetime, despite the fact that several literary men of distinction, including Wordsworth and Samuel Taylor Coleridge, recognized her creative talent. Like Mary Sidney Herbert before her, Wordsworth might well have found it difficult to make her way as a writer independently of her brother's influence, had she been temperamentally so inclined. Although her journals depict her thralldom to William, they also reveal what McGavran calls her "repressed perceptions of herself, her literary ability, and her great sacrifice" (232).

Other women writing before 1900 worked within religious or philosophical paradigms that privilege the male, either through tradition or through the influence of contemporary adherents. The seventeenth-century poet AEMELIA LANYER wrote both from within and against the whole of Biblical scholarship, arguing in *Salve Deus Rex Judaeorum* (1611) that Adam, more than Eve, was responsible for the fall of humankind. Here Lanyer refuses to be accountable to any other vision but her own. To be sure, as Janel Mueller has noted, like many writers of her era Lanyer sees masculinity and femininity as "essential, innate features of the two sexes" and assumes that God created humans invariably marked by sexual difference. But "even though her notion of culture is Christian world history and her understanding of embeddedness finds two sexes locked in a domination-subordination relationship," she resolves to transform gender relations by claiming men and women as equals (210–11). In *Salve Deus Rex Judaeorum* Lanyer declares, for example, that Eve's fault was too much love, while Adam's was not enough strength. Thus men and women together had a hand in the human fall from grace, but if either sex is to be blamed, by rights it should be men. As Mueller notes, in this poem of religious reclamation Lanyer "vindicates femininity to male critics and the misogynists of both sexes," portraying women's spiritual power in ways that have "extreme revisionary implications for men's control of society, art, and the worldly destiny of women" (227).

In a decidedly secular vein, MARGARET FULLER worked within the nineteenth-century New England group known as the Transcendentalists, who emphasized intuition as the highest truth and encouraged readers to assert their independence from religious and other authorities. Yet Fuller claims a strong identity in her writing and distinguishes herself from other Transcendentalists. Although Ralph Waldo Emerson, Bronson Alcott, Theodore Parker, and George Ripley challenge conventional opinion in their emphasis on intuition, Fuller, the lone woman in the group, is the only Transcendentalist who argues that women can be rational and men emotional, that there is in fact "no wholly masculine man, no purely feminine woman." Fuller herself defies the logic of sexual difference, asserting in *Woman in the Nineteenth Century* that "What woman needs is not as a woman to act or rule, but as a nature to grow, as an intellect to discern, as soul to live freely and unimpeded, to unfold such powers as were given her when we left our common home" (*LAWL* 958). All that remains, she concludes, is for women to have the same opportunities for intellectual development as men. In her artful refutation of the differences that nineteenth-century readers assumed existed between women and men, Fuller relies upon what Elaine Showalter has called a "double-voiced discourse," one that explores the social, literary, and cultural heritages of both "the muted and the dominant" (*LAWL* 370). Woman need not rule, but she must be allowed to think independently.

As Brodzki and Schenck assert, writers, readers, and critics must remain open to the fluidities of women's identities:

> So complex and wide-ranging has become our apprehension of the feminine presence and action in the world, past and present, that we are no longer prone to think in absolutes. At the outset it was, no doubt, essential in our Western world to speak in terms of pure "gender"— her/story, his/story—but as became clear, doing so boxed Western women into the basic habits of thought of a culture in which they did not entirely share. It closed the way— difficult to be sure—to their recognition and elaboration of a language absent from the

normative male language yet operative within the social group through which women could speak their difference and sameness as individuals within shifting cultural configurations (x).

Rather than thinking in "pure gender," women have taken diverse routes on the journey toward their place as active literary subjects. "Her/story, his/story" has given way to our/their/many stories.

EXPLORING RACISM AND ETHNOCENTRISM: BEYOND "US" AND "THEM"

> Where should the dividing line between outsider and insider stop? How should it be defined? By skin color, by language, by geography, by nation or by political affinity? What about those . . . with hyphenated identities and hybrid realities?
>
> Trinh T. Minh-ha, "Not You/Like You: Post-Colonial Women and the Interlocking Questions of Identity and Difference"

> I was of the African people, but not exclusively. My mother was a Carib woman, and when [people] looked at me, this is what they saw.
>
> Jamaica Kincaid, "Xuela"

In the quotation above, Trinh questions the conventional dichotomy between self and other and implicitly affirms the possibility of more hybrid forms of subjectivity, forms that acknowledge the value of intercultural connections and differences. Difference has often been a source of fear and hatred for women; it has been something denied or barely tolerated. As AUDRE LORDE has declared, however, respect for others demands that each woman must *"reach down into that deep place of knowledge inside herself and touch that terror and loathing of any difference that lives there. See whose face it wears.* Then the personal as the political can begin to illuminate all our choices" (113). To explore how women writers have inscribed difference, it is instructive to look at the writings of women who address issues of identity, racism, and ethnocentrism in their works.

Born in Africa and sold into slavery in the late eighteenth century, PHILLIS WHEATLEY came to poetry during her youth in America and went on to affirm an autonomous black identity even as she expressed gratitude to white patrons. As Erlene Stetson notes, critics long ignored "the mastery, skill, perceptiveness, and black female consciousness" revealed in Wheatley's poems, which she writes in conventional forms and pious language that often mask subversive strategies (4). In "On Being Brought from Africa to America," for example, she uses balanced couplets to challenge racism as hierarchical and pernicious:

Some view our sable race with scornful eye,
"Their Color is a diabolic dye."
Remember, Christians, Negros, black as Cain,
May be refined, and join th' angelic train (*LAWL* 950).

Refusing otherness, Wheatley calls Christian readers to conscience by insisting that African identity is compatible with salvation and that religious alliances can be formed across racial differences—a radical notion for America during the Revolutionary War.

The contemporary novelist JAMAICA KINCAID was born in Antigua to racially mixed parents but has lived and written in the United States since her teenage years. In much of her autobiographical fiction, and especially in *The Autobiography of My Mother* (1995), Kincaid writes about race, sex, identity, and difference, probing her maternal legacy through the lens of her colonial heritage as a West Indian. In "Xuela," a story on which her novel is based, Kincaid's protagonist identifies as dark but is criticized for looking carib by her unsympathetic African teacher and the students at her "black" school, who resent the light skin that brings her privilege. When her teacher calls the silent pupil "evil" and "possessed," Xuela knows that the instructor is insulting her mixed racial identity, not merely her demeanor (*LAWL* 1049). Confused by multiple identities and hybrid realities, Xuela withdraws into her own fantasy world of self-imposed but culturally induced exile.

A mixture of insider and outsider status, sameness and difference, can be seen in the writing of BUCHI EMECHETA, a Nigerian writer who in 1962 decided to live outside her homeland. Emecheta relocated to the seat of colonial power, London, where she could escape an abusive marriage and claim the right to write. Like that of many other writers living abroad, by force or by choice, Emecheta's diasporic consciousness evinces both painful dimensions and strengthening ones. On the one hand she is aware of a perpetual state of transition that contributes to her multiple identities and a sense of dislocation. On the other hand, a diasporic consciousness can be used to claim ideological or creative space located outside of oppressive discourses. In her fictional autobiography *Second-Class Citizen*, Emecheta probes both the negative and positive aspects of her chosen exile. Upon arriving in England, she realized that her color was a problem, and that was something she had never thought of before. As the fictional Adah's husband Francis explains when she objects to their home, "We are all blacks, all coloreds, and the only houses we can get are horrors like these." (*LAWL* 1040). Yet as a writer in Great Britain she learns to value privacy, something that would have been unavailable to her as a Nigerian living communally. The ugliness of racial and socioeconomic prejudice notwithstanding, living in the diaspora gave Emecheta the "room of one's own" she needs to write.

As a white woman writer chronicling South Africa under and beyond apartheid, INGRID DE KOK is committed to recording her country's multiple identities and to affirming what the African National Congress calls "nonracialism": the belief in humanity's oneness and equality even as cultural differences are respected. Like Emecheta, de Kok lived outside her country for some years and used her exile to scrutinize the concept of diaspora. In her poems she probes the consciousness of voluntary exiles as well as indigenous people forced to be transient. For de Kok, writing is a way to reexamine the dominant historical record for its flaws and omissions, "investigating the relationships between stories and history, staging the drama of individual and collective experiences and perspectives, examining discontinuities and lacunae" (5). In South Africa prior to 1994, of course, the historical record was distorted by apartheid. In a gesture toward reconciliation, de Kok offers her poem "Small Passing," which urges solidarity between black mothers whose children have been killed in the struggle against apartheid and middle-class white women whose babies have been stillborn. Even as she explores the possibility of shared maternal grief, however, the poet acknowledges the problems inherent in forging alliances across differences, given her country's racist history.

The ways in which issues of identity, race, and ethnocentrism converge can be seen in works by three women from different eras who write of or as Native Americans: a white colonial settler who chronicled her capture by the Indians, a turn-of-the-century Sioux writer who worked for native rights even as she assimilated into the dominant culture, and a contemporary Native American feminist who has challenged white supremacy and promoted indigenous values as healing grace. The first of these, MARY ROWLANDSON, published the first narrative by a colonial American woman of her experience as an Indian captive. *The Sovereignty and Goodness of God, Together with the Faithfulness of His Promises Displayed; Being a Narrative of the Captivity and Restoration of Mrs. Mary Rowlandson* (1682) combines autobiography, religious zeal, and the suspense of an adventure story to explore issues of identity and difference. As the poet Susan Howe has noted in an article on Rowlandson, this captivity narrative is "an avatar of the only literary-mythological form indigenous to North America"; as such it serves as "both a microcosm of colonial imperialist history, and a prophecy of our contemporary repudiation of alterity, anonymity, darkness" (313). Indeed, Rowlandson's narrative does serve as a microcosm of colonial attitudes toward civility and savagery. A Puritan, the author believed that her capture was God's will: "the Lord hereby would make us the more to acknowledge his hand, and to see that our help is always in him." She believed as well that the Indians indulged in gratuitous violence and were "murderous wretches . . . gaping before us with their guns, spears, and hatchets to devour us" (*LAWL* 944–45). This devouring "other" became more familiar to Rowlandson during her nearly three months of travel, but though the Indians apparently did her no overt harm during the journey, she never accorded them humanity.

Certainly Rowlandson suffered from what we would today call post-traumatic stress syndrome, having been taken from the structure of frontier life as she knew it and plunged into what must have seemed a living nightmare. As Howe suggests, she "wraps herself in separateness for warmth," and her ethnocentrism might be understandable, given her historical context and experience (321). In the values of Rowlandson's culture whites are the chosen race, Indians the heathen who have rejected their divinely ordained mission. On the whole Rowlandson subscribes to these hierarchies, but occasionally she interrupts her retrospective narrative to defend her captors, in one instance listing criticisms of colonial policies toward them. Momentarily, that is, she inadvertently tries to "unsettle otherness." Always she returns, however, to God's imperatives and the need for the "savages" to be redeemed or punished.

Rowlandson's narrative provides a fascinating contrast to the writing of ZITKALA-SÄ, a pan-Indian activist who wrote during the late nineteenth and early twentieth centuries. She left the Yankton reservation in South Dakota where she was born to be educated in the "white" world of Earlham College in Indiana, working thereafter as a teacher, writer, and social reformer. Although many of her essays written for white audiences were conciliatory, she often wrote to rouse Native Americans to claim their rights. She also collected traditional Native tales, which she translated from various languages. In her preface to *Old Indian Legends* she presents her goal for the collection with characteristic irony: "I have tried to transplant the native spirit of these tales—root and all—into the English language, since America in the last few centuries has acquired a second tongue" (vi). As the twentieth century dawned, Zitkala-Sä implied that indigenous people and European settlers *all* had the right to their languages and to identify as Americans—albeit as Americans with "hyphenated identities and hybrid realities" (*LAWL* 932).

Hybridity is also a topic of concern for the contemporary American Indian poet and novelist PAULA GUNN ALLEN. "I write for and to two audiences: native people and non-natives," she explains. "The first, I write for. I work to say what is in native consciousness. Not all of it, by any means, but those fragments that I focus on, that are my province. The second I write to. I write to educate, to clarify, to open up a world that has been left out of their consciousness" (23). Indeed, Allen challenges the conventional patriotic representation of the United States as a "land of liberty" in which all citizens have recourse to justice, claiming instead a country whose history has been distorted by a refusal to acknowledge the complexities of difference, to interrogate its own historical savagery. Her poem "Molly Brant, Iroquois Matron, Speaks" could function as a response to Rowlandson's captivity narrative, in which the "heathen squaw" identifies herself as a powerful clan leader. Just as Rowlandson laments the "doleful sight" of "our house on fire over our heads," so Allen's Molly Brant unhappily recalls "our Lodges burned, / our fields salted, / our Ancient fires extinguished" (*LAWL* 1028). Speaking on the eve of the American Revolution, Molly Brant reminds colonists of their own status as colonizers and prophesies a bloody future unless all people agree to honor difference.

"Hegemony works at leveling out differences and standardizing contexts and expectations in the smallest details of our everyday lives," declares Trinh. "Uncovering this leveling of differences is, therefore, resisting that very notion of difference which defined in the master's terms often resorts to the simplicity of essences" (*LAWL* 930). What Trinh advocates is a feminist reconsideration of the claims of identity and difference. Rejecting identity as a fixed essence and difference as an assertion of hierarchies—"the apartheid type of difference"—Trinh theorizes identity as a refusal to accept the dividing line between "I and not-I" and difference as a replacement for conflict, a means of conceiving otherness as empowerment. As Alcoff notes, the challenge today for readers and writers of women's literature is to "[formulate] a new theory within the process of reinterpreting our position, and reconstructing our political identity, as women and feminists in relation to the world and to one other" (436). Only then can we begin to understand women's multiple identities *and* their differences.

⊰ Works Cited—Section IV ⊱

Note: In the introductory essay, all citations of works included in this anthology are indicated by *LAWL,* followed by the page number.

Abel, Elizabeth, ed. *Writing and Sexual Difference*. Chicago: U of Chicago P, 1982. These feminist critical essays examine ways in which sexual difference has been inscribed by women writers. See especially Abel's introduction Susan Gubar on female creativity, and Judith Kegan Gardiner on women's writing and female identity.

Alcoff, Linda. "Cultural Feminism versus Poststructuralism: The Identity Crisis in Feminist Theory." *Signs* 1988 (13.3). 405–36. This essay examines two major strands of feminist theory: cultural feminism, which claims for feminists "the exclusive right to describe and evaluate woman," and poststructuralist feminism, which advocates deconstructing the category "woman" altogether. Alcoff examines the risks of each approach and offers instead "a theory of the gendered subject that does not slide into essentialism."

Allen, Paula Gunn. Interview with *The Women's Review of Books*, 6 (July 1989). 23. In this interview Allen discusses what it means to her to write in a "woman's voice," who she considers her audience, and how Native American myth and history have influenced her identity. This special issue contains interviews with ten other women writers as well.

Benstock, Shari, ed. *The Private Self: Theory and Practice of Women's Autobiographical Writings*. Chapel Hill: U of North Carolina P, 1988. This collection of essays explores women's autobiographical selves, autobiographies by black women, and female rhetorics. Benstock's introduction gives a useful overview of feminist autobiographical theory.

Brodzki, Bella and Celeste Schenck, eds. *Life/Lines: Theorizing Women's Autobiography*. Ithaca, NY: Cornell UP, 1988. These essays examine how women's autobiographies have differed from men's and from each other's through the ages. It includes a forward by Germaine Breé. In addition to works cited here, see especially Biddy Martin on "lesbian identity and autobiographical differences" and Celeste Schenck on women's poetry and autobiography.

Combahee River Collective. "A Black Feminist Statement," in *This Bridge Called My Back: Writings by Radical Women of Color*. Ed. Cherríe Moraga and Gloria Anzaldúa. New York: Kitchen Table Women of Color Press, 1983. This manifesto articulates an "identity politics" for black women, analyzes how "the major systems of oppression are interlocking" for them as lesbians and African Americans, and suggests several revolutionary goals.

de Kok, Ingrid, ed. "South African Literature in Transition." *World Literature Today*, 70: 1 (Winter 1996). This special issue of an international journal focuses on postapartheid literature and cultural identity; it contains an insightful introduction by de Kok and fiction and essays by NADINE GORDIMER and ZOË WICOMB, among others.

Erkkila, Betsy. *The Wicked Sisters: Women Poets, Literary History, and Discord*. Oxford: Oxford UP, 1992. This analysis of women poets and female influence examines Dickinson's poetic subjectivity as well as the troubled literary and personal affiliation between MARIANNE MOORE and Elizabeth Bishop.

Fox-Genovese, Elizabeth. "My Statue, My Self: Autobiographical Writings of Afro-American Women." *The Private Self*. 63–89. In this essay Fox-Genovese, a historian, argues that black women's autobiographies constitute a collective commentary on the condition of African-American women in the United States. She claims further that an emphasis on collective identity and on the links between race and gender distinguishes their work from white women's autobiographies, which tend to present their authors as individuals and to view gender as the key to self-knowledge.

Friedman, Susan Stanford. "Women's Autobiographical Selves: Theory and Practice." *The Private Self*. 34–62. Friedman considers the sense of collective as well as individual identity that many autobiographies by women feature, and she examines writing by MAXINE HONG KINGSTON, AUDRE LORDE, and H.D. from a "psychopolitical perspective."

Fuss, Diana. *Essentially Speaking: Feminism, Nature and Difference*. New York: Routledge, 1989. In this theoretical work Fuss considers the debates over woman as pure essence and woman as social construct, clarifying the issues at stake for feminist critics. Among the issues with which she grapples are identity politics as a point of departure for women and the influence of race, ethnicity, and sexual orientation on women's identity and experience.

Gilbert, Sandra M. and Susan Gubar. *The Madwoman in the Attic: The Woman Writer and the Nineteenth-Century Literary Imagination*. New Haven: Yale UP, 1979. This pioneer work of feminist criticism addresses women's creativity and sexual difference, women's "anxiety of authorship," and the possibility of a feminist poetics; it includes excellent chapters on several major figures included in this anthology, among them JANE AUSTEN and EMILY DICKINSON.

Homans, Margaret. *Women Writers and Poetic Identity*. Princeton: Princeton UP, 1980. This study of DOROTHY WORDSWORTH, EMILY DICKINSON, and EMILY BRONTË focuses on how their consciousness of being women affected their poetic imagination and identities.

Howe, Susan. "The Captivity and Restoration of Mrs. Mary Rowlandson." *Disembodied Poetics*, ed. Anne Waldman and Andrew Schelling. Albuquerque: U of New Mexico P, 1988. 313–63. In this experimental montage—part U.S. literary history, part feminist criticism— Howe examines Rowlandson's captivity narrative as a quintessential American and feminine autobiography.

Jelinek, Estelle, ed. *Women's Autobiography: Essays in Criticism*. Bloomington: Indiana UP, 1980. One of the first collections of feminist critical essays to address this genre, it attempts to distinguish women's autobiographical voices from men's and to trace the contours of a women's autobiographical tradition. See especially Jelinek's introduction and essays by Cynthia S. Pomerleau and Patricia Meyers Spacks.

Lamb, Mary Ellen. *Gender and Authorship in the Sidney Circle*. Madison: U of Wisconsin P, 1990. This book analyzes the ways in which writing and reading were gendered occupations in early modern England. It focuses especially on women writers from the famous Sidney family, most notably MARY SIDNEY HERBERT and MARY WROTH, who wrote with authority despite cultural barriers.

Lorde, Audre. *Sister Outsider: Essays and Speeches*. Trumansburg, NY: The Crossing Press, 1984. A number of Lorde's essays in this collection address issues of black women's identity and women's need to honor difference. See especially "The Master's Tools Will Never Dismantle the Master's House" and "Age, Race, Class, Sex: Women Redefining Difference."

Mason, Mary. "The Other Voice: Autobiographies of Women Writers." *Life/Lines*. 19–45. This essay provides a critical and theoretical overview of women's autobiographical writing and argues that "the disclosure of the female self is linked to the identification of some 'other.'"

McGavran, James Holt Jr. "Dorothy Wordsworth's Journals: Putting Herself Down." *The Private Self*. 230–53. McGavran argues that Wordsworth's "repressed perceptions of herself, her literary ability, and her great sacrifice *do* appear, most often indirectly, in her early journals." He analyzes as well her identification with the landscape of the Lake District and her empathy with rural women she meets.

Mueller, Janel. "The Feminist Poetics of Aemilia Lanyer's *Salve Deus Rex Judaeorum*." *Feminist Measures: Soundings in Poetry and Theory*. Ed. Lynn Keller and Cristanne Miller. Ann Arbor: U of Michigan P, 1994. 208–236. Mueller explores ways in which Lanyer links the feminine and the divine in her poem, and argues as well for the importance of her feminist theology and linguistic theory.

Sä, Zitkala-. *Old Indian Legends*. Lincoln: U of Nebraska P, 1985. In her preface to this collection of Native American legends, first published in 1901, Zitkala-Sä refers to the pleasure these tales brought to the "black-haired aborigine" by the night fire.

Stetson, Erlene, ed. *Black Sister: Poetry by Black American Women, 1746–1980*. Bloomington: Indiana UP, 1981. This anthology offers a fine collection of poems by PHILLIS WHEATLEY, FRANCES ELLEN WATKINS HARPER, ALICE DUNBAR-NELSON, JUNE JORDAN, AUDRE LORDE, MAYA ANGELOU, and others, as well as valuable critical introductions to each poet.

Walker, Nancy. "'Wider Than the Sky': Public Presence and Private Self in Dickinson, James, and Woolf." *The Private Self*. 230–53. In linking EMILY DICKINSON, a poet, VIRGINIA WOOLF, a novelist, and Alice James, a diarist, Walker claims that each "feels some ultimate public eye upon her as she writes" and thus uses her diaries or letters to express herself to the outside world.

Welty, Eudora. *One Writer's Beginnings*. Cambridge: Harvard UP, 1984. Welty's autobiographical account of how she became a writer contains three sections: "Listening," "Learning to See," and "Finding a Voice."

Woolf, Virginia. *Collected Essays*. 4 vols. New York: Harcourt, 1967. This useful edition brings together all of Woolf's published essays and thus provides insight into her identity as a prose writer and reviewer.

⊰ Suggestions for Further Reading ⊱

Braxton, Joanne. *Black Women Writing Autobiography: A Tradition Within a Tradition*. Philadelphia: Temple UP, 1989. Braxton's critical study focuses on how black women have found their autobiographical voices, "emerging from obscurity" and "claiming the Afra-American self." Among the writers she discusses are HARRIET JACOBS, ZORA NEALE HURSTON, and MAYA ANGELOU.

Davies, Carole Boyce. *Black Women, Writing and Identity: Migrations of the Subject*. New York: Routledge, 1994. This study examines black women's "renegotiation of identities," deconstructions of African women's subjectivities, women's postcolonial textualities, and issues of gender, heritage, and identity in Afro-Caribbean women's autobiographical and fictional writings.

Featherston, Elena, ed. *Skin Deep: Women Writing About Color, Culture, and Identity*. Freedom, CA: The Crossing Press, 1994. This anthology features essays, poems, and stories by women that explore the effects of skin color and ethnicity on their writing and self-actualization. Among the topics addressed are the hybrid identity of multiracial women, connecting across differences of race and culture, and art as a means of healing the wounds of oppression.

Friedman, Susan Stanford. *Mappings: Feminism and the Cultural Geographies of Encounter*. Princeton: Princeton UP, 1998. This collection of essays examines the ways in which feminist thinking about identity, difference, multiculturalism, and globalism has developed during the 1980s and 1990s. Friedman argues for a "locational feminism" in which gender is seen as interacting "with other constituents of identity."

Keeble, N.H., ed. *The Cultural Identity of Seventeenth-Century Woman*. New York: Routledge, 1994. This reader contains extracts from various early modern sources that consider how "the cultural notion of 'woman' was then constructed." Many readings inscribe a misogynist ideology but others advocate women's autonomy and egalitarian relations between the sexes. The book sheds light on the cultural contexts in which such women as MARY SIDNEY HERBERT, AEMILIA LANYER, and KATHERINE PHILIPS wrote.

Lionnet, Francoise. *Postcolonial Representations: Women, Literature, Identity*. Ithaca, NY: Cornell UP, 1995. This book examines postcolonial women writers' forms of self-representation and addresses issues of language, history, multiple subjectivities, and inscriptions of exile. Among the writers foregrounded are MICHELLE CLIFF and BESSIE HEAD.

Neuman, Shirley. "Autobiography: From a Different Poetics to a Poetics of Differences." *Essays on Life Writing: From Genre to Critical Practice*. Ed. Marlene Kadar. Toronto: U of Toronto P, 1992. 213–30. This article analyzes the different poetics of the genre of autobiography, considers women's self-depictions as complex, multiple, layered literary subjects, and calls for a "poetics of differences."

Nussbaum, Felicity. *The Autobiographical Subject: Gender and Ideology in Eighteenth-Century England*. Baltimore: The Johns Hopkins UP, 1989. This study contains excellent chapters on women's spiritual autobiographies, "scandalous memoirs," and diaries from the eighteenth century.

Smith, Sidonie and Julia Watson, eds. *De/Colonizing the Subject: The Politics of Gender in Women's Autobiography*. U of Minn. P, 1992. This collection of essays on autobiography as a genre considers the "politics of discourse" in women's autobiographical practices globally. For discussions of identity and difference, see especially essays by Julia Watson, Sidonie Smith, Carole Davies, John Beverley, and Caren Kaplan.

Thompson, Becky and Sangeeta Tyagi, eds. *Names We Call Home: Autobiography on Racial Identity*. New York: Routledge, 1996. This anthology features essays by women seeking to "claim racial identities that are not based on conquest or defacement." Topics include writing one's identity as an immigrant woman in the United States, the names women of varied racial identities have used to define themselves, and how women have negotiated race and gender amid multiple identifications.

Trinh T. Minh-ha. *When the Moon Waxes Red: Representation, Gender and Cultural Politics*. New York: Routledge, 1991. In these essays on postcolonialism, feminism, and representation, Trinh considers issues of multiple identities, spectatorship, "unwriting/inmost writing" and "questions of images and politics" in literature and film, including her own documentaries.

Williamson, Marilyn L. *Raising Their Voices: British Women Writers, 1650–1750*. Detroit: Wayne State UP, 1990. This study focuses on APHRA BEHN and KATHERINE PHILIPS as major influences on other women writers of their era, including MARY ASTELL, ANNE KILLIGREW, JANE BARKER, ANNE FINCH, SARAH FYGE, ELIZA HAYWOOD, and DELARIVIER MANLEY.

Woodward, Kathryn, ed. *Identity and Difference: Culture, Media, and Identity*. London: Sage, 1997. This anthology provides a fine collection of readings on identity and difference that have been used in courses in cultural studies at several British universities.

Michelle Cliff
1946–

A writer of fiction, autobiography, and poetry, MICHELLE CLIFF was born in Kingston, Jamaica, a place she calls "halfway between Africa and England," to a middle-class family that identified as "red," a term that "signified a degree of whiteness." This racially mixed heritage provides the primary subject matter for her writing. Although she lived in a Jamaican immigrant community in New York between the ages of three and ten, Cliff's earliest memories recall the landscape of her country of origin. She left Jamaica at eighteen to study in London, where she earned an M.Phil. in Italian Renaissance studies from the Warburg Institute. This experience,

she claims, "was responsible for giving me an intellectual belief in myself that I had not had before, while at the same time distancing me from who I am, almost rendering me speechless about who I am." Determined to claim her multiethnic identity, Cliff began writing at age thirty as a means of finding wholeness "while working within fragmentation." Her affiliation with the women's movement in the 1970s led her to edit the lesbian-feminist journal *Sinister Wisdom* with ADRIENNE RICH from 1981 to 1983. Cliff is the Allan K. Smith Professor of English Language and Literature at Trinity College in Hartford, Connecticut, where she teaches creative writing and women's studies. She conducts writing workshops across the United States and lives part-time in Santa Cruz, California.

Her writing is a mix of genres, styles, and tones that reflects her wish to break free of hegomonic language. In an essay entitled "Journey into Speech" she notes that "one of the effects of assimilation, indoctrination, passing into the anglocentrism of British West Indian culture is that you believe absolutely in the hegemony of the King's English and in the form in which it is meant to be expressed. Or else your writing is not literature; it is folklore, and folklore can never be art." To escape this double bind, Cliff endorses "speaking in the *patois* forbidden us . . . mixing in the forms taught us by the oppressor, undermining his language and coopting his style." Cliff's fiction reflects such an effort. In *Abeng* (1984) an adolescent Jamaican girl, Clare Savage, confronts the power that light skin and economic privilege bring in her relationship with Zoe, whose family is "black" and poor. Yet in her love for Zoe, Clare finds the potential for healing. *No Telephone to Heaven* (1987), a sequel to *Abeng,* depicts an older Clare who studies abroad but ultimately returns to Jamaica, joins a black guerrilla movement, and attacks a U.S. film crew to challenge its colonial consciousness. *Free Enterprise* (1993) explores the life of Mary Ellen Pleasant, who funded and helped to organize John Brown's raid at Harper's Ferry. Cliff has also published a collection of short stories that is readable as a novel, *Bodies of Water* (1990).

A number of Cliff's essays explore her identity as a Jamaican woman. *Claiming an Identity They Taught Me to Despise* (1980) affirms the long-denigrated African aspect of the author's heritage, a reclamation both racial and gendered. Cliff has described this work as "halfway between poetry and prose," but after writing it she became concerned that readers moved by its lyricism would read it apolitically. Thus her subsequent essays combine the polemic and the lyric more overtly. In "Notes on Speechlessness," published in *Sinister Wisdom* #5, she discusses her identification with Victor, the wild boy of Aveyron, who was "civilized" into English but never came to speech. "Journey into Speech" depicts her struggle to "find what has been lost to me from the darker side, what may be hidden, to be dredged from memory and dream." "Object into Subject: Some Thoughts on the Work of Black Women Artists" examines the ways in which black women are working to end their own objectification.

The essay reprinted here, "If I Could Write This in Fire, I Woul
first published in *The Land of Look Behind* (1985). In it Cliff expose
hierarchy of "colorism," which rarely allows light and dark people
her childhood memories, Cliff recalls the barriers of racial differenc
of British colonialism. Both lyrical and confrontational, this essa·
in her words, "to depict personal fragmentation and describe politicա. .
peculiar lens of the colonized."

⊰ If I Could Write This in Fire, I Would Write This in Fire ⊱

I

We were standing under the waterfall at the top of Orange River. Our chests were just beginning to mound—slight hills on either side. In the center of each were our nipples, which were losing their sideways look and rounding into perceptible buttons of dark flesh. Too fast it seemed. We touched each other, then, quickly and almost simultaneously, raised our arms to examine the hairs growing underneath. Another sign. Mine was wispy and light-brown. My friend Zoe had dark hair curled up tight. In each little patch the riverwater caught the sun so we glistened.

The waterfall had come about when my uncles dammed up the river to bring power to the sugar mill. Usually, when I say "sugar mill" to anyone not familiar with the Jamaican countryside or for that matter my family, I can tell their minds cast an image of tall smokestacks, enormous copper cauldrons, a man in a broad-brimmed hat with a whip, and several dozens of slaves—that is, if they have any idea of how large sugar mills once operated. It's a grandiose expression—like plantation, verandah, outbuilding. (Try substituting farm, porch, outside toilet.) To some people it even sounds romantic.

Our sugar mill was little more than a round-roofed shed, which contained a wheel and wood fire. We paid an old man to run it, tend the fire, and then either bartered or gave the sugar away, after my grandmother had taken what she needed. Our cane-field was about two acres of flat land next to the river. My grandmother had six acres in all—one donkey, a mule, two cows, some chickens, a few pigs, and stray dogs and cats who had taken up residence in the yard.

Her house had four rooms, no electricity, no running water. The kitchen was a shed in the back with a small pot-bellied stove. Across from the stove was a mahogany counter, which had a white enamel basin set into it. The only light source was a window, a small space covered partly by a wooden shutter. We washed our faces and hands in enamel bowls with cold water carried in kerosene tins from the river and poured from enamel pitchers. Our chamber pots were enamel also, and in the morning we carefully placed them on the steps at the side of the house where my grandmother collected them and disposed of their contents. The outhouse was about thirty yards from the back door—a "closet" as we called it—infested with lizards capable of changing color. When the door was shut it was totally dark, and the lizards made their presence known by the noise of their scurrying through the torn newspaper, or the soft shudder when they dropped from the walls. I remember most clearly the stench of the toilet, which seemed to hang in the air in that climate.

because every little piece of reality exists in relation to another little piece, our situation was not that simple. It was to our yard that people came with news first. It was in my grandmother's parlor that the Disciples of Christ held their meetings.

Zoe lived with her mother and sister on borrowed ground in a place called Breezy Hill. She and I saw each other almost every day on our school vacations over a period of three years. Each morning early—as I sat on the cement porch with my coffee cut with condensed milk—she appeared: in her straw hat, school tunic faded from blue to gray, white blouse, sneakers hanging around her neck. We had coffee together, and a piece of hard-dough bread with butter and cheese, waited a bit and headed for the river. At first we were shy with each other. We did not start from the same place.

There was land. My grandparents' farm. And there was color.

(My family was called *red*. A term which signified a degree of whiteness. "We's just a flock of red people," a cousin of mine said once.) In the hierarchy of shades I was considered among the lightest. The countrywomen who visited my grandmother commented on my "tall" hair—meaning long. Wavy, not curly.

I had spent the years from three to ten in New York and spoke—at first—like an American. I wore American clothes: shorts, slacks, bathing suit. Because of my American past I was looked upon as the creator of games. Cowboys and Indians. Cops and Robbers. Peter Pan.

(While the primary colonial identification for Jamaicans was English, American colonialism was a strong force in my childhood—and of course continues today. We were sent American movies and American music. American aluminum companies had already discovered bauxite on the island and were shipping the ore to their mainland. United Fruit bought our bananas. White Americans came to Montego Bay, Ocho Rios, and Kingston for their vacations and their cruise ships docked in Port Antonio and other places. In some ways America was seen as a better place than England by many Jamaicans. The farm laborers sent to work in American agribusiness came home with dollars and gifts and new clothes; there were few who mentioned American racism. Many of the middle class who emigrated to Brooklyn or Staten Island or Manhattan were able to pass into the white American world—saving their blackness for other Jamaicans or for trips home; in some cases, forgetting it altogether. Those middle-class Jamaicans who could not pass for white managed differently—not unlike the Bajans in Paule Marshall's *Brown Girl, Brownstones*[1]—saving, working, investing, buying property. Completely separate in most cases from Black Americans.)

I was someone who had experience with the place that sent us triple features of B-grade westerns and gangster movies. And I had tall hair and light skin. And I was the granddaughter of my grandmother. So I had power. I was the cowboy, Zoe was my sidekick, the boys we knew were Indians. I was the detective, Zoe was my "girl," the boys were the robbers. I was Peter Pan, Zoe was Wendy Darling, the boys were the lost boys. And the terrain around the river—jungled and dark green—was Tombstone, or Chicago, or Never-Never Land.

1. African-American writer Paule Marshall (born 1929) published her novel *Brown Girl, Brownstones* in 1959.

This place and my friendship with Zoe never touched my life in Kingston. We did not correspond with each other when I left my grandmother's home.

I never visited Zoe's home the entire time I knew her. It was a given: never suggested, never raised.

Zoe went to a state school held in a country church in Red Hills. It had been my mother's school. I went to a private all-girls school where I was taught by white Englishwomen and pale Jamaicans. In her school the students were caned as punishment. In mine the harshest punishment I remember was being sent to sit under the *lignum vitae* to "commune with nature." Some of the girls were out-and-out white (English and American), the rest of us were colored—only a few were dark. Our uniforms were blood-red gabardine, heavy and hot. Classes were held in buildings meant to recreate England: damp with stone floors, facing onto a cloister, or quad as they called it. We began each day with the headmistress leading us in English hymns. The entire school stood for an hour in the zinc-roofed gymnasium.

Occasionally a girl fainted, or threw up. Once, a girl had a grand mal seizure. To any such disturbance the response was always "keep singing." While she flailed on the stone floor, I wondered what the mistresses would do. We sang "Faith of Our Fathers," and watched our classmate as her eyes rolled back in her head. I thought of people swallowing their tongues. This student was dark—here on a scholarship—and the only woman who came forward to help her was the gamesmistress, the only dark teacher. She kneeled beside the girl and slid the white web belt from her tennis shorts, clamping it between the girl's teeth. When the seizure was over, she carried the girl to a tumbling mat in a corner of the gym and covered her so she wouldn't get chilled.

Were the other women unable to touch this girl because of her darkness? I think that now. Her darkness and her scholarship. She lived on Windward Road with her grandmother; her mother was a maid. But darkness is usually enough for women like those to hold back. Then, we usually excused that kind of behavior by saying they were "ladies." (We were constantly being told we should be ladies also. One teacher went so far as to tell us many people thought Jamaicans lived in trees and we had to show these people they were mistaken.) In short, we felt insufficient to judge the behavior of these women. The English ones (who had the corner on power in the school) had come all this way to teach us. Shouldn't we treat them as the missionaries they were certain they were? The creole Jamaicans had a different role: they were passing on to those of us who were light-skinned the creole heritage of collaboration, assimilation, loyalty to our betters. We were expected to be willing subjects in this outpost of civilization.

The girl left school that day and never returned.

After prayers we filed into our classrooms. After classes we had games: tennis, field hockey, rounders (what the English call baseball), netball (what the English call basketball). For games we were divided into "houses"—groups named for Joan of Arc,

Edith Cavell, Florence Nightingale, Jane Austen.[2] Four white heroines. Two martyrs. One saint. Two nurses. (None of us knew then that there were Black women with Nightingale at Scutari.) One novelist. Three involved in whitemen's wars. Two dead in whitemen's wars. *Pride and Prejudice.*

Those of us in Cavell wore red badges and recited her last words before a firing squad in W. W. I: "Patriotism is not enough. I must have no hatred or bitterness toward anyone."

Sorry to say I grew up to have exactly that.

Looking back: To try and see when the background changed places with the fore-ground. To try and locate the vanishing point: where the lines of perspective con-verge and disappear. Lines of color and class. Lines of history and social context. Lines of denial and rejection. When did *we* (the light-skinned middle-class Jamaicans) take over for *them* as oppressors? I need to see when and how this hap-pened. When what should have been reality was overtaken by what was surely unre-ality. When the house nigger became master.

"What's the matter with you? You think you're white or something?"
"Child, what you want to know 'bout Garvey[3] for? The man was nothing but a damn fool."
"They not our kind of people."

Why did we wear wide-brimmed hats and try to get into Oxford? Why did we not return?

Great Expectations:[4] a novel about origins and denial. About the futility and tragedy of that denial. About attempting assimilation. We learned this novel from a light-skinned Jamaican woman—she concentrated on what she called the "love affair" between Pip and Estella.

Looking back: Through the last page of *Sula.*[5] "And the loss pressed down on her chest and came up into her throat. 'We was girls together,' she said as though explaining something." It was Zoe, and Zoe alone, I thought of. She snapped into my mind and I remembered no one else. Through the greens and blues of the riverbank. The flame of red hibiscus in front of my grandmother's house. The cracked grave of a former landowner. The fruit of the ackee which poisons those who don't know how to prepare it.

"What is to become of us?"

2. Joan of Arc (1412?–1431), the Maid of Orleans, was a French national heroine and a female warrior who was burned at the stake after being convicted of heresy. Edith Cavell (1865–1915) founded a Belgian medical institute that became a Red Cross hospital in 1914, she helped English, French, and Belgian soldiers escape during World War I. Florence Nightingale (1820–1910) was a British nurse during the Crimean War and a writer. JANE

AUSTEN (1775–1817) was a British novelist and the author of *Pride and Predjudice* (1813).
3. Marcus Garvey (1887–1940) was a Jamaican black-nationalist leader.
4. A novel by the English writer Charles Dickens (1812–1870).
5. A novel by the African-American writer TONI MORRISON (born 1931).

We borrowed a baby from a woman and used her as our dolly. Dressed and undressed her. Dipped her in the riverwater. Fed her with the milk her mother had left with us: and giggled because we knew where the milk had come from.

A *letter:* "I am desperate. I need to get away. I beg you one fifty-dollar."

I send the money because this is what she asks for. I visit her on a trip back home. Her front teeth are gone. Her husband beats her and she suffers blackouts. I sit on her chair. She is given birth control pills which aggravate her "condition." We boil up sorrel and ginger. She is being taught by Peace Corps volunteers to embroider linen mats with little lambs on them and gives me one as a keepsake. We cool off the sorrel with a block of ice brought from the shop nearby. The shopkeeper immediately recognizes me as my grand-mother's granddaughter and refuses to sell me cigarettes. (I am twenty-seven.) We sit in the doorway of her house, pushing back the colored plastic strands which form a curtain, and talk about Babylon and Dred. About Manley and what he's doing for Jamaica.[6] About how hard it is. We walk along the railway tracks—no longer used—to Crooked River and the post office. Her little daughter walks beside us and we recite a poem for her: "Mornin' buddy / Me no buddy fe wunna / Who den, den I saw?" and on and on.

I can come and go. And I leave. To complete my education in London.

II

Their goddam kings and their goddam queens. Grandmotherly Victoria spreading herself thin across the globe. Elizabeth II on our TV screens. We stop what we are doing. We quiet down. We pay our respects.

1981: In Massachusetts I get up at 5 a.m. to watch the royal wedding. I tell myself maybe the IRA will intervene. It's got to be better than starving themselves to death. Better to be a kamikaze in St. Paul's Cathedral than a hostage in Ulster. And last week Black and white people smashed storefronts all over the United Kingdom. But I really don't believe we'll see royal blood on TV. I watch because they once ruled us. In the back of the cathedral a Maori woman[7] sings an aria from Handel, and I notice that she is surrounded by the colored subjects.

To those of us in the commonwealth the royal family was the perfect symbol of hege-mony. To those of us who were dark in the dark nations, the prime minister, the par-liament barely existed. We believed in royalty—we were convinced in this belief. Maybe it played on some ancestral memories of West Africa—where other kings and queens had been. Altars and castles and magic.

The faces of our new rulers were everywhere in my childhood. Calendars, newsreels, magazines. Their presences were often among us. Attending test matches between the West Indians and South Africans. They were our landlords. Not always absentee. And no matter what Black leader we might elect—were we to choose indepen-dence—we would be losing something almost holy in our impudence.

---

6. Robert Manley was the president of Jamaica.   7. A woman of New Zealand's indigenous people.

WE ARE HERE BECAUSE YOU WERE THERE
BLACK PEOPLE AGAINST STATE BRUTALITY
BLACK WOMEN WILL NOT BE INTIMIDATED
WELCOME TO BRITAIN . . . WELCOME TO SECOND-CLASS CITIZENSHIP
(slogans of the Black movement in Britain)

Indian women cleaning the toilets in Heathrow airport. This is the first thing I notice. Dark women in saris trudging buckets back and forth as other dark women in saris—some covered by loosefitting winter coats—form a line to have their passports stamped.

The triangle trade: molasses/rum/slaves. Robinson Crusoe was on a slave-trading journey. Robert Browning was a mulatto.[8] Holding pens. Jamaica was a seasoning station. Split tongues. Sliced ears. Whipped bodies. The constant pretense of civility against rape. Still. Iron collars. Tinplate masks. The latter a precaution: to stop the slaves from eating the sugar cane.

A pregnant woman is to be whipped—they dig a hole to accommodate her belly and place her face down on the ground. Many of us became light-skinned very fast. Traced ourselves through bastard lines to reach the duke of Devonshire. The earl of Cornwall. The lord of this and the lord of that. Our mothers' rapes were the thing unspoken.

You say: But Britain freed her slaves in 1833. Yes.

Tea plantations in India and Ceylon. Mines in Africa. The Cape-to-Cairo Railroad. Rhodes scholars. Suez Crisis. The whiteman's bloody burden. Boer War.[9] Bantustans. Sitting in a theatre in London in the seventies. A play called *West of Suez*. A lousy play about British colonials. The finale comes when several well-known white actors are machine-gunned by several lesser-known Black actors. (As Nina Simone[10] says: "This is a show tune but the show hasn't been written for it yet.")

The red empire of geography classes. "The sun never sets on the British empire and you can't trust it in the dark." Or with the dark peoples. "Because of the Industrial Revolution European countries went in search of markets and raw materials." Another geography (or was it a history) lesson.

Their bloody kings and their bloody queens. Their bloody peers. Their bloody generals. Admirals. Explorers. Livingstone. Hillary. Kitchener.[11] All the bwanas. And all their beaters, porters, sherpas. Who found the source of the Nile. Victoria Falls. The tops of mountains. Their so-called discoveries reek of untruth. How many dark people died so they could misname the physical features in their blasted gazetteer. A statistic we shall never know. Dr. Livingstone, I presume you are here to rape our land and enslave our people.

8. *Robinson Crusoe* (1719) was a novel by Daniel Defoe (1660–1731); Robert Browning (1812–1889) was a British poet.
9. The Boer War was fought in South Africa from 1899 to 1902 between Great Britain and two Afrikaner republics, the South African Republic (Transvaal) and the Orange Free State, over which white colonial group would control the country.
10. Nina Simone is an African-American blues singer.
11. David Livingstone (1813–1873) was a Scottish missionary and an explorer in Africa; Sir Edmund Hillary (born 1919) is a New Zealand mountain climber and explorer; Horatio H. Kitchener (1850–1916) was a British field marshal during World War I.

There are statues of these dead white men all over London.

An interesting fact: The swearword "bloody" is a contraction of "by my lady"—a reference to the Virgin Mary. They do tend to use their ladies. Name ages for them. Places for them. Use them as screens, inspirations, symbols. And many of the ladies comply. While the national martyr Edith Cavell was being executed by the Germans in 1915 in Belgium (called "poor little Belgium" by the allies in the war), the Belgians were engaged in the exploitation of the land and peoples of the Congo.

And will we ever know how many dark peoples were "imported" to fight in white-men's wars. Probably not. Just as we will never know how many hearts were cut from African people so that the Christian doctor might be a success—i.e., extend a white-man's life. Our Sister Killjoy[12] observes this from her black-eyed squint.

Dr. Schweitzer—humanitarian, authority on Bach, winner of the Nobel Peace Prize—on the people of Africa: "The Negro is a child, and with children nothing can be done without the use of authority. We must, therefore, so arrange the circumstances of our daily life that my authority can find expression. With regard to Negroes, then, I have coined the formula: 'I am your brother, it is true, but your elder brother.'" (*On the Edge of the Primeval Forest*, 1961)[13]

They like to pretend we didn't fight back. We did: with obeah, poison, revolution. It simply was not enough.

"Colonies . . . these places where 'niggers' are cheap and the earth is rich." (W.E.B. DuBois, "The Souls of White Folk")[14]

A cousin is visiting me from Cal Tech where he is getting a degree in engineering. I am learning about the Italian Renaissance. My cousin is recognizably Black and speaks with an accent. I am not and I do not—unless I am back home, where the "twang" comes upon me. We sit for some time in a bar in his hotel and are not served. A light-skinned Jamaican comes over to our table. He is an older man—a professor at the University of London. "Don't bother with it, you hear. They don't serve us in this bar." A run-of-the-mill incident for all recognizably Black people in this city. But for me it is not.

Henry's eyes fill up, but he refuses to believe our informant. "No, man, the girl is just busy." (The girl is a fifty-year-old white woman, who may just be following orders. But I do not mention this. I have chosen sides.) All I can manage to say is, "Jesus Christ, I hate the fucking English." Henry looks at me. (In the family I am known as the "lady cousin." It has to do with how I look. And the fact that I am twenty-seven and unmarried—and for all they know, unattached. They do not know that I am really the lesbian cousin.) Our informant says—gently, but with a distinct tone of disappointment—"My dear, is that what you're studying at the university?"

You see—the whole business is very complicated.

---

12. A character in the novel by the same title, published by the Ghanaian writer AMA ATA AIDOO in 1981.
13. Dr. Albert Schweitzer (1875–1965) was a French missionary, musician, physician, and Nobel laureate.
14. W.E.B. DuBois (1868–1963) was an African-American writer and educator.

Henry and I leave without drinks and go to meet some of his white colleagues at a restaurant I know near Covent Garden Opera House. The restaurant caters to the-ater types and so I hope there won't be a repeat of the bar scene—at least they know how to pretend. Besides, I tell myself, the owners are Italian *and* gay; they *must* be halfway decent. Henry and his colleagues work for an American company which is paying their way through Cal Tech. They mine bauxite from the hills in the middle of the island and send it to the United States. A turnaround occurs at dinner: Henry joins the whitemen in a sustained mockery of the waiters: their accents and the way they walk. He whispers to me: "Why you want to bring us to a battyman's den, lady?" (*Battyman* = *faggot* in Jamaican.) I keep quiet.

We put the whitemen in a taxi and Henry walks me to the underground station. He asks me to sleep with him. (It wouldn't be incest. His mother was a maid in the house of an uncle and Henry has not seen her since his birth. He was taken into the family. She was let go.) I say that I can't. I plead exams. I can't say that I don't want to. Because I remember what happened in the bar. But I can't say that I'm a lesbian either—even though I want to believe his alliance with the whitemen at dinner was forced: not really him. He doesn't buy my excuse. "Come on, lady, let's do it. What's the matter, you 'fraid?" I pretend I am back home and start patois to show him some-how I am not afraid, not English, not white. I tell him he's a married man and he tells me he's a ram goat. I take the train to where I am staying and try to forget the whole thing. But I don't. I remember our different skins and our different experiences with-in them. And I have a hard time realizing that I am angry with Henry. That to him—no use in pretending—a queer is a queer.

1981: I hear on the radio that Bob Marley[15] is dead and I drive over the Mohawk Trail listening to a program of his music and I cry and cry and cry. Someone says: "It wasn't the ganja that killed him, it was poverty and working in a steel foundry when he was young."

I flash back to my childhood and a young man who worked for an aunt I lived with once. He taught me to smoke ganja behind the house. And to peel an orange with the tip of a machete without cutting through the skin—"Love" it was called: a neck-lace of orange rind the result. I think about him because I heard he had become a Rastaman. And then I think about Rastas.

We are sitting on the porch of an uncle's house in Kingston—the family and I—and a Rastaman comes to the gate. We have guns but they are locked behind a false clos-et. We have dogs but they are tied up. We are Jamaicans and know that Rastas mean no harm. We let him in and he sits on the side of the porch and shows us his brooms and brushes. We buy some to take back to New York. "Peace, missis."

There were many Rastas in my childhood. Walking the roadside with their goods. Sit-ting outside their shacks in the mountains. The outsides painted bright—sometimes with words. Gathering at Palisadoes Airport to greet the Conquering Lion of Judah.

---

15. Bob Marley was a Jamaican reggae singer and a Rastafarian.

They were considered figures of fun by most middle-class Jamaicans. Harmless—like Marcus Garvey.

Later: white American hippies trying to create the effect of dred in their straight white hair. The ganja joint held between their straight white teeth. "Man, the grass is good." Hanging out by the Sheraton pool. Light-skinned Jamaicans also dred-locked, also assuming the ganja. Both groups moving to the music but not the words. Harmless. "Peace, brother."

III

My grandmother: "Let us thank God for a fruitful place."
My grandfather: "Let us rescue the perishing world."

This evening on the road in western Massachusetts there are pockets of fog. Then clear spaces. Across from a pond a dog staggers in front of my headlights. I look clos-er and see that his mouth is foaming. He stumbles to the side of the road—I go to call the police.

I drive back to the house, radio playing "difficult" piano pieces. And I think about how I need to say all this. This is who I am. I am not what you allow me to be. What-ever you decide me to be. In a bookstore in London I show the woman at the counter my book and she stares at me for a minute, then says: "You're a Jamaican." "Yes." "You're not at all like our Jamaicans."

Encountering the void is nothing more nor less than understanding invisibility. Of being fogbound.

Then: It was never a question of passing. It was a question of hiding. Behind Black and white perceptions of who we were—who they thought we were. Tropics. Plantations. Calypso. Cricket. We were the people with the musical voices and the coronation mugs on our parlor tables. I would be whatever figure these foreign imaginations cared for me to be. It would be so simple to let others fill in for me. So easy to startle them with a flash of anger when their visions got out of hand—but never to sustain the anger for myself.
It could become a life lived within myself. A life cut off. I know who I am but you will never know who I am. I may in fact lose touch with who I am.

I hid from my real sources. But my real sources were also hidden from me.

Now: It is not a question of relinquishing privilege. It is a question of grasping more of myself. I have found that in the real sources are concealed my survival. My speech. My voice. To be colonized is to be rendered insensitive. To have those parts necessary to sustain life numbed. And this is in some cases—in my case—perceived as privilege. The test of a colonized person is to walk through a shantytown in Kingston and not bat an eye. This I cannot do. Because part of me lives there—and as I grasp more of this part I realize what needs to be done with the rest of my life.

Sometimes I used to think we were like the Marranos—the Sephardic Jews forced to pretend they were Christians. The name was given to them by the Christians, and meant "pigs." But once out of Spain and Portugal, they became Jews openly again. Some settled in Jamaica. They knew who the enemy was and acted for their own survival. But they remained Jews always.

We also knew who the enemy was—I remember jokes about the English. Saying they stank. Saying they were stingy. That they drank too much and couldn't hold their liquor. That they had bad teeth. Were dirty and dishonest. Were limey bastards. And horse-faced bitches. We said the men only wanted to sleep with Jamaican women. And that the women made pigs of themselves with Jamaican men.

But of course this was seen by us—the light-skinned middle class—with a double vision. We learned to cherish that part of us that was them—and to deny the part that was not. Believing in some cases that the latter part had ceased to exist.

None of this is as simple as it may sound. We were colorists and we aspired to oppressor status. (Of course, almost any aspiration instilled by Western civilization is to oppressor status: success, for example.) Color was the symbol of our potential: color taking in hair "quality," skin tone, freckles, nose-width, eyes. We did not see that color symbolism was a method of keeping us apart: in the society, in the family, between friends. Those of us who were light-skinned, straight-haired, etc., were given to believe that we could actually attain whiteness—or at least those qualities of the colonizer which made him superior. We were convinced of white supremacy. If we failed, we were not really responsible for our failures: We had all the advantages—but it was that one persistent drop of blood, that single rogue gene that made us unable to conceptualize abstract ideas, made us love darkness rather than despise it, which was to be blamed for our failure. Our dark part had taken over: an inherited imbalance in which the doom of the creole was sealed.

I am trying to write this as clearly as possible, but as I write I realize that what I say may sound fabulous, or even mythic. It is. It is insane.

Under this system of colorism—the system which prevailed in my childhood in Jamaica, and which has carried over to the present—rarely will dark and light people comingle. Rarely will they achieve between themselves an intimacy informed with identity. (I should say here that I am using the categories light and dark both literally and symbolically. There are dark Jamaicans who have achieved lightness and the "advantages" which go with it by their successful pursuit of oppressor status.)

Under this system light and dark people will meet in those ways in which the light-skinned person imitates the oppressor. But imitation goes only so far: The light-skinned person becomes an oppressor in fact. He/she will have a dark chauffeur, a dark nanny, a dark maid, and a dark gardener. These employees will be paid badly. Because of the slave past, because of their dark skin, the servants of the middle class have been used according to the traditions of the slavocracy. They are not seen as workers for their own sake, but for the sake of the family who has employed them. It was not until Michael Manley became prime minister that a minimum wage for houseworkers was enacted—and the indignation of the middle class was profound.

During Manley's leadership the middle class began to abandon the island in droves. Toronto. Miami. New York. Leaving their houses and businesses behind and sewing cash into the tops of suitcases. Today—with a new regime—they are returning: "Come back to the way things used to be" the tourist advertisement on American TV says. "Make it Jamaica again. Make it your own."

But let me return to the situation of houseservants as I remember it: They will be paid badly, but they will be "given" room and board. However, the key to the larder will be kept by the mistress in her dresser drawer. They will spend Christmas with the family of their employers and be given a length of English wool for trousers or a few yards of cotton for dresses. They will see their children on their days off: their extended family will care for the children the rest of the time. When the employers visit their relations in the country, the servants may be asked along—oftentimes the servants of the middle class come from the same part of the countryside their employers have come from. But they will be expected to work while they are there. Back in town, there are parts of the house they are not allowed to move freely around; other parts they are not allowed to enter. When the family watches the TV the servant is allowed to watch also, but only while standing in a doorway. The servant may have a radio in his/her room, also a dresser and a cot. Perhaps a mirror. There will usually be one ceiling light. And one small square louvered window.

A true story: One middle-class Jamaican woman ordered a Persian rug from Harrod's in London. The day it arrived so did her new maid. She was going downtown to have her hair touched up, and told the maid to vacuum the rug. She told the maid she would find the vacuum cleaner in the same shed as the power mower. And when she returned she found that the fine nap of her new rug had been removed.

The reaction of the mistress was to tell her friends that the "girl" was backward. She did not fire her until she found that the maid had scrubbed the Teflon from her new set of pots, saying she thought they were coated with "nastiness."

The houseworker/mistress relationship in which one Black woman is the oppressor of another Black woman is a cornerstone of the experience of many Jamaican women.

I remember another true story: In a middle-class family's home one Christmas, a relation was visiting from New York. This woman had brought gifts for everybody, including the housemaid. The maid had been released from a mental institution recently, where they had "treated" her for depression. This visiting light-skinned woman had brought the dark woman a bright red rayon blouse and presented it to her in the garden one afternoon, while the family was having tea. The maid thanked her softly, and the other woman moved toward her as if to embrace her. Then she stopped, her face suddenly covered with tears, and ran into the house, saying, "My God, I can't, I can't."

We are women who come from a place almost incredible in its beauty. It is a beauty which can mask a great deal and which has been used in that way. But that the beauty is there is a fact. I remember what I thought the freedom of my childhood, in which the fruitful place was something I took for granted. Just as I took for granted Zoe's appearance every morning on my school vacations—in the sense that I knew she would be there. That she would always be the one to visit me. The perishing world of my grandfather's graces at the table, if I ever seriously thought about it, was somewhere else.

Our souls were affected by the beauty of Jamaica, as much as they were affected by our fears of darkness.

There is no ending to this piece of writing. There is no way to end it. As I read back over it, I see that we/they/I may become confused in the mind of the reader: but these pronouns have always coexisted in my mind. The Rastas talk of the "I and I"— a pronoun in which they combine themselves with Jah. Jah is a contraction of Jahweh and Jehova, but to me always sounds like the beginning of Jamaica. I and Jamaica is who I am. No matter how far I travel—how deep the ambivalence I feel about ever returning. And Jamaica is a place in which we/they/I connect and disconnect—change place.

1985

⊷— ⊠◈⊠ —⊶

Trinh T. Minh-ha
1952–

"What I understand of the struggle of women of color . . . is that our voices and silences across difference are so many attempts at articulating this always-emerging-already-distorted place that remains so difficult, on the one hand, for the first world even to recognize, and on the other, for our own communities to accept to venture into," writes Vietnamese theorist TRINH T. MINH-HA. In much of her theoretical writing Trinh rejects the concept of self-enclosed identity in favor of a multicultural notion of difference. A filmmaker, musician, and writer, Trinh teaches cinema at San Francisco State University. Among her prize-winning films, which fuse documentary and fictional techniques,  are *Reassemblage* (1982), *Naked Spaces: Living Is Round* (1985), and *Surname Viet Given Name Nam* (1989), which takes its title from a "recent socialist tradition" in which, when an interested man asks a woman if she is married, she responds, "Yes, his surname is Viet and his given name is Nam." In this "apparently benign reply the nation-gender relationship immediately raises questions," observes Trinh. In a 1990 interview with Judith Mayne, she explains that her films make use of "negative space," the "space that makes both composition and framing possible, that characterizes the way an image breathes"; thus she eschews the "object-oriented camera" in favor of one that obscures far less. A fourth film, *Shoot for the Contents*, was released in 1991.

Trinh Minh-ha has published three works of postcolonial and/or feminist theory, the best known of which is *Woman, Native, Other: Writing Postcoloniality and Feminism* (1989). This book examines what the author calls "postcolonial processes of displacement—cultural hybridization and decentered realities, fragmented selves and multiple identities, marginal voices and languages of rupture." *Woman, Native, Other* is comprised of four sections: "Commitment from the Mirror-Writing Box," which explores the multiple and contingent identities of women writers of color; "The Language of Nativism," a critique of the premises of traditional anthropology; "Difference: A Special Third World Women's Issue," which examines the "infinite layers" of what Trinh terms "i am not i can be you and me"; and "Grandma's Story," an analysis of the power of the Great Mother, oral tradition, and storytelling in Asian and African cultures. As Trinh explains in her interview with Mayne, because *Woman, Native, Other* "resists every easy category," the book was rejected by thirty-three presses over ten years before being accepted for publication. "The kind of problems it repeatedly encountered had precisely to do with marketable categories and disciplinary regulations; in other words, with conformist borders. Not only was the focus on postcolonial positionings and on women of color as a subject and as subjects of little interest to publishers then, but what bothered them most was the writing itself."

Trinh has described her writing as "the mixing of different modes . . . ; the mutual challenge of theoretical and poetical, discursive and nondiscursive languages." Her first theoretical work, *Un art sans oeuvre (An Art Without Masterpiece,* 1981), illustrates this mixing; one chapter links writings by the French theorist Jacques Derrida and the playwright Antonin Artaud to those of Zen Buddhist healers such as Krishnamurti. *When the Moon Waxes Red: Representation, Gender and Culture* (1991) consists of essays on myths of Chinese moon goddesses, the marginality of women of color in the art world, problems with the category "documentary," and the denial of gender in a society that reproduces "male-centered spectacle." Her articles have appeared in *French Review, French Forum, Sub-stance,* and *Camera Obscura,* and her films have been shown internationally. With Jean-Paul Bourdier she wrote *African Spaces: Designs for Living in Upper Volta* (1985). Her book of poetry, *En minuscules,* appeared in 1987 in France.

Trinh Minh-ha's writing style is strategically enigmatic. Reviewing *When the Moon Waxes Red* and *Woman, Native, Other* for *American Literary History* in 1993, Linda Alcoff claims that "by maintaining a stylistic complexity and incessantly problematizing all claims to dominance, Trinh's writing instantiates a form of guerrilla theory, powerful in its very elusiveness." Most of Trinh's works of "guerrilla theory" address issues of identity and difference. "The repressed complexities of the politics of identity have been exposed fully" by women of color, she claims. "'Identity' has now become more a point of departure than an end point in the struggle. So although we understand the necessity of acknowledging this notion of identity in politicizing the personal, we also don't want to be limited to it." Hence difference, "the necessity of speaking from a hybrid place."

The article included here, "Not You/Like You: Postcolonial Women and the Interlocking Questions of Identity and Difference," was published in *Making Face, Making Soul* (1990), edited by Gloria Anzaldúa. To investigate identity, Trinh notes, is to consider the power dynamics of the self/other relationship. Long defined as "an essential, authentic core that remains hidden to one's consciousness," identity is almost invariably conceived within a context of domination. If identity connotes sameness, then difference "remains within the boundary of that which distinguishes one identity from another." Yet notions of difference need not be defined by the majority culture, Trinh insists. As feminists we need a critical practice that considers both identity and difference.

⊰ Not You/Like You: Postcolonial Women and the Interlocking Questions of Identity and Difference ⊱

To raise the question of identity is to reopen again the discussion on the self/other relationship in its enactment of power relations. Identity as understood in the context of a certain ideology of dominance has long been a notion that relies on the concept of an essential, authentic core that remains hidden to one's consciousness and that requires the elimination of all that is considered foreign or not true to the self, that is to say, not-I, other. In such a concept the other is almost unavoidably either opposed to the self or submitted to the self's dominance. It is always condemned to remain its shadow while attempting at being its equal. Identity, thus understood, supposes that a clear dividing line can be made between I and not-I, he and she: between depth and surface, or vertical and horizontal identity; between us here and them over there. The further one moves from the core the less likely one is thought to be capable of fulfilling one's role as the real self, the real Black, Indian or Asian, the real woman. The search for an identity is, therefore, usually a search for that lost, pure, true, real, genuine, original, authentic self, often situated within a process of elimination of all that is considered other, superfluous, fake, corrupted or Westernized.

If identity refers to the whole pattern of sameness within a being, the style of a continuing me that permeated all the changes undergone, then difference remains within the boundary of that which distinguishes one identity from another. This means that at heart X must be X, Y must be Y and X cannot be Y. Those running around yelling X is not X and X can be Y usually land in a hospital, a rehabilitation center, a concentration camp or a reservation. All deviations from the dominant stream of thought, that is to say, the belief in a permanent essence of woman and in an invariant but fragile identity whose loss is considered to be a specifically human danger, can easily fit into the categories of the mentally ill or the mentally underdeveloped.

It is probably difficult for a normal, probing mind to recognize that to seek is to lose, for seeking presupposes a separation between the seeker and the sought, the continuing me and the changes it undergoes. Can identity, indeed, be viewed other than as a byproduct of a manhandling of life, one that, in fact, refers no more to a consistent pattern of sameness than to an inconsequential process of otherness? How am I to lose, maintain or gain a female identity when it is impossible for me to take up a position outside this identity from which I presumably reach in and feel for it? Difference in such a context is that which undermines the very idea of identity, differing to infinity the layers of totality that form I.

Hegemony works at leveling out differences and at standardizing contexts and expectations in the smallest details of our daily lives. Uncovering this leveling of differences is, therefore, resisting that very notion of difference which defined in the master's terms often resorts to the simplicity of essences. Divide and conquer has for centuries been his creed, his formula for success. But a different terrain of consciousness has been explored for some time now, a terrain in which clearcut divisions and dualistic oppositions such as science versus subjectivity, masculine versus feminine, may serve as departure points for analytical purpose but are no longer satisfactory if not entirely untenable to the critical mind.

I have often been asked about what some viewers call the lack of conflicts in my films. Psychological conflict is often equated with substance and depth. Conflicts in Western contexts often serve to define identities. My suggestion to the "lack" is: let difference replace conflict. Difference as understood in many feminist and non-Western contexts, difference as foreground in my film work is not opposed to sameness, nor synonymous with separateness. Difference, in other words, does not necessarily give rise to separatism. There are differences as well as similarities within the concept of difference. One can further say that difference is not what makes conflicts. It is beyond and alongside conflict. This is where confusion often arises and where the challenge can be issued. Many of us still hold on to the concept of difference not as a tool of creativity to question multiple forms of repression and dominance, but as a tool of segregation, to exert power on the basis of racial and sexual essences. The apartheid type of difference.

Let me point to a few examples of practices of such a notion of difference. There are quite a few, but I'll just select three and perhaps we can discuss those. First of all, I would take the example of the veil as reality and metaphor. If the act of unveiling has a liberating potential, so does the act of veiling. It all depends on the context in which such an act is carried out, or more precisely, on how and where women see dominance. Difference should neither be defined by the dominant sex nor the dominant culture. So that when women decide to lift the veil one can say that they do so in defiance of their men's oppressive right to their bodies. But when they decide to keep or put on the veil they once took off they might do so to reappropriate their space or to claim a new difference in defiance of genderless, hegemonic, centered standardization.

Second, the use of silence. Within the context of women's speech silence has many faces. Like the veiling of women just mentioned, silence can only be subversive when it frees itself from the male-defined context of absence, lack and fear as feminine territories. On the one hand, we face the danger of inscribing femininity as absence, as lack and as blank in rejecting the importance of the act of enunciation. On the other hand, we understand the necessity to place women on the side of negativity and to work in undertones, for example, in our attempts at undermining patriarchal systems of values. Silence is so commonly set in opposition with speech. Silence as a will not to say or a will to unsay and as a language of its own has barely been explored.

Third, the question of subjectivity. The domain of subjectivity understood as sentimental, personal and individual horizon as opposed to objective, universal, societal, limitless horizon is often attributed to both women, the other of man, and natives, the Other of the West. It is often assumed, for example, that women's enemy is the intellect, that their apprehension of life can only wind and unwind around a cooking pot, a baby's diaper or matters of the heart. Similarly, for centuries and centuries we have been told that primitive mentality belongs to the order of the emotional and the affective, and that it is incapable of elaborating concepts. Primitive man feels and participates. He does not really think or reason. He has no knowledge, "no clear idea or even no idea at all of matter and soul," as Lévi-Bruhl puts it.[1] Today this persistent rationale has taken on multiple faces, and its residues still linger on, easily recognizable despite the refined rhetoric of those who perpetuate it.

Worth mentioning again here is the question of outsider and insider in ethnographic practices. An insider's view. The magic word that bears within itself a seal of approval. What can be more authentically other than an otherness by the other, herself? Yet, every piece of cake given by the master comes with a double-edged blade. The Afrikaners[2] are prompt in saying, "you can take a Black man from the bush, but you can't take the bush from the Black man." The place of the native is always well-delimited. "Correct" cultural filmmaking, for example, usually implies that Africans show Africa; Asians, Asia; and Euro-Americans, the world. Otherness has its laws and interdictions. Since you can't take the bush from the Black man, it is the bush that is consistently given back to him, and as things often turn out it is also this very bush that the Black man shall make his exclusive territory. And he may do so with the full awareness that barren land is hardly a gift. For in the unfolding of power inequalities, changes frequently require that the rules be reappropriated so that the master be beaten at his own game. The conceited giver likes to give with the understanding that he is in a position to take back whenever he feels like it and whenever the accepter dares or happens to trespass on his preserves. The latter, however, sees no gift. Can you imagine such a thing as a gift that takes? So the latter only sees debts that, once given back, should remain his property—although land owning is a concept that has long been foreign to him and that he refused to assimilate.

Through audiences' responses and expectations of their works, nonwhite filmmakers are often informed and reminded of the territorial boundaries in which they are to remain. An insider can speak with authority about her own culture, and she's referred to as the source of authority in this matter—not as a filmmaker necessarily, but as an insider, merely. This automatic and arbitrary endowment of an insider with legitimized knowledge about her cultural heritage and environment only exerts its power when it's

---

1. Lucien Lévi-Bruhl (1857–1939) was a French philosophical writer.
2. The descendents of Dutch colonials in South Africa and the people widely identified as the architects of apartheid, South Africa's virulent system of racial hierarchies, which was in effect from 1948 to 1994.

a question of validating power. It is a paradoxical twist of the colonial mind. What the outsider expects from the insider is, in fact, a projection of an all-knowing subject that this outsider usually attributes to himself and to his own kind. In this unacknowledged self/other relation, however, the other would always remain the shadow of the self. Hence not really, not quite all-knowing. That a white person makes a film on the Goba of the Zambezi, for example, or on the Tasaday of the Philippine rainforest, seems hardly surprising to anyone, but that a Third World member makes a film on other Third World peoples never fails to appear questionable to many. The question concerning the choice of subject matter immediately arises, sometimes out of curiosity, most often out of hostility. The marriage is not consumable, for the pair is no longer outside/inside, that is to say, objective versus subjective, but something between inside/inside—objective in what is already claimed as objective. So, no real conflict.

Interdependency cannot be reduced to a mere question of mutual enslavement. It also consists in creating a ground that belongs to no one, not even to the creator. Otherness becomes empowerment, critical difference when it is not given but recreated. Furthermore, where should the dividing line between outsider and insider stop? How should it be defined? By skin color, by language, by geography, by nation or by political affinity? What about those, for example, with hyphenated identities and hybrid realities? And here it is worth noting, for example, a journalist's report in a recent *Time* issue which is entitled, "The Crazy Game of Musical Chairs." In this brief report attention is drawn to the fact that people in South Africa who are classified by race and placed into one of the nine racial categories that determine where they can live and work, can have their classification changed if they can prove they were put in a wrong group. Thus, in an announcement of racial reclassifications by the Home Affairs Ministers[3] one learns that 9 whites became colored, 506 coloreds became white, 2 whites became Malay, 14 Malay became white, 40 coloreds became Black, 666 Blacks became colored and the list goes on. However, says the minister, no Blacks apply to become whites. And no whites became Black.

The moment the insider steps out from the inside she's no longer a mere insider. She necessarily looks in from the outside while also looking out from the inside. Not quite the same, not quite the other, she stands in that undetermined threshold place where she constantly drifts in and out. Undercutting the inside/outside opposition, her intervention is necessarily that of both not quite an insider and not quite an outsider. She is, in other words, this inappropriate other or same who moves about with always at least two gestures: that of affirming 'I am like you' while persisting in her difference and that of reminding 'I am different' while unsettling every definition of otherness arrived at.

This is not to say that the historical I can be obscured and ignored and that differentiation cannot be made, but that I is not unitary, culture has never been monolithic and is always more or less in relation to a judging subject. Differences do not only exist between outsider and insider—two entities. They are also at work within the outsider herself, or the insider herself—a single entity. She who knows she cannot speak of them without speaking of herself, of history without involving her story, also knows that she cannot make a gesture without activating the to and fro movement of life.

The subjectivity at work in the context of this inappropriate other can hardly be submitted to the old subjectivity/objectivity paradigm. Acute political subject awareness cannot be reduced to a question of self-criticism toward self-improvement, nor of self-praise toward greater self-confidence. Such differentiation is useful, for a grasp

---

3. Government officials in South Africa who implemented the arbitrary racial categories of the apartheid system.

of subjectivity as, let's say, the science of the subject or merely as related to the subject, makes the fear of self-absorption look absurd. Awareness of the limits in which one works need not lead to any form of indulgence in personal partiality, nor to the narrow conclusion that it is impossible to understand anything about other peoples, since the difference is one of essence. By refusing to naturalize the I, subjectivity uncovers the myth of essential core, of spontaneity and depth as inner vision. Subjectivity, therefore, does not merely consist of talking about oneself, be this talking indulgent or critical. In short, what is at stake is a practice of subjectivity that is still unaware of its own constituted nature, hence, the difficulty to exceed the simplistic pair of subjectivity and objectivity; a practice of subjectivity that is unaware of its continuous role in the production of meaning, as if things can make sense by themselves, so that the interpreter's function consists of only choosing among the many existing readings, unaware of representation as representation, that is to say, the cultural, sexual, political interreality of the filmmaker as subject, the reality of the subject film and the reality of the cinematic apparatus. And finally unaware of the inappropriate other within every I.   *1987/1990*

<hr />

Mary Sidney Herbert
1561–1621

Described by an Elizabethan contemporary as "in Poesie the mirror of our Age," MARY SIDNEY HERBERT, Countess of Pembroke, was a highly acclaimed poet, translator, literary patron, and the sister of Sir Philip Sidney, the renowned Renaissance sonneteer. The poet Thomas Nashe, recognizing both Herbert's connection to her brother and her own talents, claimed that the "fair sister of Phoebus" outshone even "the Lesbian Sappho with her lyric Harp." Mary Sidney was raised at Ludlow and Penshurst, the family estates. Unlike her brother, who was formally educated, she studied English composition and literature at home as well as Latin, Greek, French, Italian, and Hebrew. In 1575 she became a lady-in-waiting in the court of Elizabeth I, joining her mother in that capacity; shortly thereafter her parents arranged for her to marry the middle-aged Henry Herbert, Earl of Pembroke, a patron of the arts. From 1577 until 1601 Mary Sidney Herbert lived at her husband's home, Wilton House, and served as host to such prominent English writers as Edmund Spenser and John Donne. At Wilton her three children were born, and there she presided over a literary salon without rival. Philip Sidney wrote his *Arcadia* at Wilton, and after his untimely death in 1586 his sister edited his works for publication: The *Arcadia* appeared in 1593, *Defense of Poesie* in 1595, and a corrected version of *Astrophel and Stella* in 1598.

Although women in Elizabethan England were strongly discouraged from public literary activity, her brother's death gave Herbert an opportunity to challenge that norm by completing their collaborative work. During Sidney's last years he and his sister had translated forty-three psalms into verse form; when he died, Herbert translated the remainder on her own. The *Sidney Psalms*, as they came to be called, were renowned for their technical virtuosity; completed in 1599, they were well known in the seventeenth century but not published until 1823, when they were attributed solely to Sidney. Not until the mid–1960s did literary scholars recognize Herbert's enormous contribution to the psalms' translation. Herbert translated the Italian sonneteer Petrarch's *Trionfo della Morte* (1950), and many scholars considered her reproductions of the poet's *terza rima* a prodigious accomplishment. In addition, she translated Robert Garnier's *The Tragedie of Antonie* and Philippe de Mornay's *Discours de la Vie et de la Mort*, both printed in 1592. As a poet, Herbert wrote "A Pastoral Dialogue between

Two Shepherds," which appeared in 1601 in Davison's *Poetical Rhapsody;* it was apparently composed in anticipation of a visit to Wilton by Queen Elizabeth that never occurred. This charming poem features two shepherds, Thenot and Piers, ardently praising Astrea, a literary name for the Virgin Queen. Herbert wrote "The Doleful Lay of Clorinda" shortly after her brother's death; it was published in 1595 in Spenser's *Colin Clout Comes Home Again.*

Mary Sidney Herbert died of smallpox in 1621 and was buried in Salisbury Cathedral, where a plaque bears an epitaph once ascribed to Ben Jonson but now thought to be the homage of William Browne. Called "the subject of all verse," Herbert is honored not for her own identity as a poet but as "Sydney's sister, Pembroke's mother." Browne does offer tribute, however, to her goodness and her erudition: "Death, ere thou hast slain another, / Fair, & learned, & good as she, / Time shall throw a dart at thee."

⊰ The Doleful Lay of Clorinda ⊱

Ay me, to whom shall I my case complain?
That may compassion my impatient grief?
Or where shall I unfold my inward pain,
That my enriven heart may find relief?
5   Shall I unto the heavenly powers it show?
Or unto earthly men that dwell below?

To heavens? ah they alas the authors were,
And workers of my unremedied woe:
For they foresee what to us happens here,
10   And they foresaw, yet suffered this be so.
From them comes good, from them comes also ill
That which they made, who can them warn to spill.

To men? ah, they alas like wretched be,
And subject to the heaven's ordinance:
15   Bound to abide what ever they decree,
Their best redress, is their best sufferance.
How then can they like wretched comfort me,
The which no less, need comforted to be?

Then to myself will I my sorrow mourn,
20   Since none alive like sorrowful remains:
And to myself my plaints shall back return,
To pay their usury with doubled pains.
The woods, the hills, the rivers shall resound
The mournful accent of my sorrow's ground.

25   Woods, hills and rivers, now are desolate,
Since he [1] is gone the which them all did grace:
And all the fields do wail their widow state,
Since death their fairest flower did late deface.
The fairest flower in field that ever grew,
30   Was *Astrophel:*   that was, we all may rue.

1. An allusion to her brother, the poet Philip Sidney (1554–1586), whom she also calls Astrophel after the speaker in his 1591 sonnet sequence *Astrophel and Stella.*

What cruel hand of curséd foe unknown,
Hath cropped the stalk which bore so fair a flower?
Untimely cropped, before it well were grown,
And clean defaced in untimely hour.
35   Great loss to all that ever him did see,
      Great loss to all, but greatest loss to me.

Break now your garlands, O ye shepherds' lasses,
Since the fair flower, which them adorned, is gone:
The flower, which them adorned, is gone to ashes,
40 Never again let lass put garland on:
      Instead of garland, wear sad Cypress now,
      And bitter Elder, broken from the bough.

Never sing the love-lays which he made,
Whoever made such lays of love as he?
45 Never read the riddles, which he said
Unto yourselves, to make you merry glee.
      Your merry glee is now laid all abed,
      Your merry maker now alas is dead.

Death, the devourer of all world's delight,
50 Hath robbed you and reft from me my joy:
Both you and me, and all the world he quit
Hath robbed of joyance, and left sad annoy.
      Joy of the world, and shepherds' pride was he,
      Shepherds' hope never like again to see.

55 Oh death that hast us of such riches reft,
Tell us at least, what hast thou with it done?
What is become of him whose flower here left
Is but the shadow of his likeness gone.
      Scarce like the shadow of that which he was,
60   Nought like, but that he like a shade did pass.

But that immortal spirit, which was decked
With all the dowries of celestial grace:
By sovereign choice from the heavenly choirs select,
And lineally derived from Angels' race,
65   O what is now of it become aread,
      Ay me, can so divine a thing be dead?

Ah no: it is not dead, nor can it die,
But lives for aye, in blissful Paradise:
Where like a newborn babe it soft doth lie,
70 In bed of lilies wrapped in tender wise.
      And compassed all about with roses sweet,
      And dainty violets from head to feet.

There thousand birds all of celestial brood,
To him do sweetly carol day and night:
75 And with strange notes, of him well understood,
Lull him asleep in Angel-like delight:
      Whilst in sweet dream to him presented be
      Immortal beauties, which no eye may see.

But he them sees and takes exceeding pleasure
80   Of their divine aspects, appearing plain,
And kindling love in him above all measure,
Sweet love still joyous, never feeling pain.
    For what so goodly form he there doth see,
    He may enjoy from jealous rancor free.

85   There liveth he in everlasting bliss,
Sweet spirit never fearing more to die:
Nor dreading harm from any foes of his,
Nor fearing savage beasts more cruelty.
    Whilst we here wretches wail his private lack,
90   And with vain vows do often call him back.

But live thou there still happy, happy spirit,
And give us leave thee here thus to lament:
Not thee that dost thy heaven's joy inherit,
But our own selves that here in dole are drent.
95   Thus do we weep and wail, and wear our eyes,
    Mourning in others, our own miseries.

1586–87/1595

Aemilia Lanyer
1569–1645

One of England's earliest professional women poets, AEMILIA LANYER is remembered for two works: *Salve Deus Rex Judaeorum* (1611), a verse depiction of the life of Christ, presented from a woman's point of view; and "The Description of Cooke-ham" (1611), a nostalgic poem about an English manor house that was appended to *Salve Deus Rex Judaeorum*. The latter is believed to be the first volume of poetry written by a woman in English. The poet was born Aemilia Bassano, the daughter of a Jewish court musician who hailed from Venice, Baptista Bassano, and his common-law wife, Margaret Johnson, who was English. Her father's death when she was seven left Lanyer in poor economic circumstances but with continuing access to court circles. Lady Susan, the Countess Dowager of Kent was an early patron and probable employer of Lanyer; her library might have provided the poet with a classical education while she was in service to the countess. After her mother died when Lanyer was eighteen, she became the mistress of Henry Carey, Lord Hunsdon, Queen Elizabeth's Lord Chamberlain. Her marriage in 1592 to Alfonso Lanyer, also a court musician, was probably one of convenience, since she was pregnant with Lord Hunsdon's child at the time, a boy she named Henry. In 1598 Lanyer had a daughter, Odillya, who died when she was nine months old. Although the Lanyers spent some years in near poverty, in 1604 King James granted Alfonso a patent that relieved the family's financial stress. Nonetheless, Aemilia Lanyer may well have begun writing as a means of attracting patrons.

    Sometime before 1609 Lanyer apparently spent time at Cooke-ham with Margaret Clifford, Countess of Cumberland; she dedicates her poem to both the countess and her daughter, who provided its occasion in February of 1609 by marrying the Earl of Dorset. "The Description of Cooke-ham" uses an English country house to represent nostalgia and loss. What scholars failed until recently to realize, as the critic Susanne Woods has noted, is that the publication of "Cooke-ham" predates that of the poem long thought to be the earliest of this genre, Ben Jonson's "To Penshurst" (1616); it is thus the first English country-house poem. After her husband's death in 1613, again in need of money, Lanyer founded a school in the wealthy London township of St. Giles in the Field but was forced to close it shortly thereafter due to legal disputes with her landlord. She spent her last years living with the family of her son, a court musician like his father and grandfather; when Henry Lanyer died at forty, she helped to care for her grandchildren.

As Woods notes, 1611 was the publication date of the King James Bible, John Donne's *Anatomy of the World*, three of Shakespeare's plays, and Chapman's translation of Homer; theology and literature clearly were seen as the purview of men. Thus it is astonishing that Lanyer would publish that same year a book dedicated only to women, one that assumes without self-consciousness an educated female readership. To be sure, since Protestantism granted any individual the right to communicate with God, it was becoming increasingly acceptable for women to publish religious treatises. Nonetheless, no other woman of the early modern period claimed as much religious authority as Lanyer does in *Salve Deus Rex Judaeorum*, nor does anyone offer a comparable feminist revision of religious doctrine. Along with a compassionate portrait of a feminized Christ, Lanyer's poem contains sympathetic portrayals of Eve's sin in the Garden of Eden and the Virgin Mary's sorrow; much of it is spoken in the voice of Pilate's wife, who disapproves of her husband's actions. One section, "Eve's Apology in Defense of Women," depicts Eve as ignorant of the serpent's wiles, a woman whose "harmless Heart" intended no wrong. Adam, in contrast, "cannot be excused, / Her fault though great, yet he was most to blame."

◄ *from* Salve Deus Rex Judaeorum ►

Now Pontius Pilate is to judge the cause[1]
Of faultless Jesus, who before him stands,
Who neither hath offended prince, nor laws,
Although he now be brought in woeful bands.
"O noble governor, make thou yet a pause,   5
Do not in innocent blood imbrue[2] thy hands;
    But hear the words of thy most worthy wife,[3]
    Who sends to thee, to beg her Savior's life.

Let barb'rous cruelty far depart from thee,
And in true Justice take afflictions part;   10
Open thine eyes, that thou the truth may'st see,
Do not the thing that goes against thy heart,
Condemn not him that must thy Savior be;
But view his holy Life, his good desert.
    Let not us Women glory in Men's fall,   15
    Who had power given to overrule us all.

Eve's Apology.

Till now your indiscretion sets us free,
And makes our former fault[4] much less appear;
Our Mother *Eve*, who tasted of the Tree,
Giving to *Adam* what she held most dear,   20
Was simply good, and had no power to see;
The aftercoming harm did not appear:
    The subtle Serpent that our Sex betrayed,
    Before our fall so sure a plot had laid.

1. The case against Christ.
2. Stain.
3. In the New Testament book of Matthew, Pontius Pilate's wife reportedly has a dream warning her to urge her husband not to harm Jesus; she heeds this admonition by writing her husband a letter.
4. That of Eve, whom the serpent tempted in the Garden of Eden.

25 That undiscerning Ignorance perceived
No guile, or craft that was by him intended;
For had she known, of what we were bereaved,[5]
To his request she had not condescended.
But she (poor soul) by cunning was deceived,
30 No hurt therein her harmless Heart intended:
For she alledged God's word, which he denies,
That they should die, but even as Gods, be wise.

But surely *Adam* cannot be excused,
Her fault though great, yet he was most to blame;
35 What Weakness offered, Strength might have refused,
Being Lord of all, the greater was his shame:
Although the Serpent's craft had her abused,
God's holy word ought all his actions frame,[6]
For he was Lord and King of all the earth,
40 Before poor *Eve* had either life or breath,

Who being framed by God's eternal hand,
The perfect'st man that ever breathed on earth;
And from God's mouth received that strict command,
The breach whereof he knew was present death:
45 Yea having power to rule both Sea and Land,
Yet with one Apple won to lose that breath
Which God had breathéd in his beauteous face,
Bringing us all in danger and disgrace.

And then to lay the fault on Patience's back,
50 That we (poor women) must endure it all;
We know right well he did discretion lack,
Being not persuaded thereunto at all;[7]
If *Eve* did err, it was for knowledge sake,
The fruit being fair persuaded him to fall:
55 No subtle Serpent's falsehood did betray him,
If he would eat it, who had power to stay him?

Not *Eve*, whose fault was only too much love,
Which made her give this present to her Dear,
That what she tasted, he likewise might prove,
60 Whereby his knowledge might become more clear;
He never sought her weakeness to reprove,
With those sharp words, which he of God did hear:
Yet Men will boast of Knowledge, which he took
From *Eve's* fair hand, as from a learned Book.

65 If any Evil did in her remain,
Being made of him, he was the ground of all;
If one of many Worlds[8] could lay a stain
Upon our Sex, and work so great a fall
To wretched Man, by Satan's subtle train,

---

5. Of what we humans would lose—i.e., eternal life.   7. That is, Adam ate of the fruit on his own accord.
6. Determine.   8. One woman out of the many in the world.

70   What will so foul a fault amongst you all?[9]
      Her weakness did the Serpent's words obey;
      But you in Malice God's dear Son betray,

Whom, if unjustly you condemn to die,
Her sin was small, to what you do commit;
75   All mortal sins that do for vengeance cry,
Are not to be comparéd unto it:
If many worlds would altogether try,
By all their sins the wrath of God to get,
      This sin of yours, surmounts them all as far
80   As doth the Sun, another little star.[10]

Then let us have our Liberty again,
And challenge to yourselves no Sovereignty;
You came not in the world without our pain,
Make that a bar[11] against your cruelty;
85   Your fault being greater, why should you disdain
Our being your equals, free from tyranny?
      If one weak woman simply did offend,
      This sin of yours, hath no excuse, nor end.

To which (poor souls) we never gave consent,
90   Witness thy wife (O *Pilate*) speaks for all;
Who did but dream, and yet a message sent,
That thou should'st have nothing to do at all
With that just man;[12] which, if thy heart relent,
Why wilt thou be a reprobate with *Saul*[13]
95   To seek the death of him that is so good,
      For thy soul's health to shed his dearest blood?"

1611

Katherine Philips
1632–1664

The "matchless Orinda," KATHERINE PHILIPS, was born in London to Presbyterian parents named Fowler. Her father, a well-to-do merchant, sent her at age eight to a private school in Hackney, where she met Mary Aubrey, later the "Rosania" of her poems. After her husband died in 1639, Philips's mother married a wealthy Welsh baron, and Katherine joined the newlyweds at their castle in Pembrokeshire. In 1648 she married James Philips, a Welshman thirty-eight years her senior, in what was apparently an arranged match, and for twenty-one years she lived with him in Cardigan, Wales. Although the two did not share political views—she had Royalist sympathies and he supported Oliver Cromwell during the Interregnum—the marriage appears to have been compatible. In 1651 Philips formed a "Society of Friendship," a literary salon whose members adopted classical names from pastoral literature; this society allowed her to circulate her manuscripts among friends and brought her a new *nom de plume*, "Orinda." That same year Henry

---

9. How will so foul a fault affect all members of your sex?
10. The sun was thought at the time to be larger than the stars.
11. Barrier.

12. That is, with Christ.
13. Saul was the King of Israel who tried to kill David, his former friend, out of jealousy.

Vaughan became aware of Philips's poetry and praised it publicly; she also met the woman who would become "Lucasia" in her work, Anne Owen. Philips bore two children: Hector, who died shortly after birth; and Katherine, who survived to bear sixteen children and lose fifteen of them. In 1660 Philips's husband narrowly escaped prosecution for his allegiance to Cromwell and lost the estates he had been granted; only an intervention by his wife's friend Sir Charles Cotterell, the Master of Ceremonies at the court of Charles II, saved James Philips from economic ruin.

The author of 116 extant poems, Katherine Philips also translated five verse dramas and wrote two plays. Her first poems, published in 1651 and appended to those of Henry Vaughan and Thomas Cartwright, gained immediate attention. In 1663 her translation of Pierre Corneille's *Pompey* was staged in London, the first play by a woman to be produced there professionally. An unauthorized edition of her verse, *Poems by the Incomparable, Mrs. K.P.,* appeared in 1664 but was immediately removed from circulation at her request. That same year, at the height of her career, Philips contracted smallpox and died before completing her translation of Horace. After her death Cotterell published an edition of her poems and edited *Letters from Orinda to Poliarchus* (1705).

Many of Philips's poems extol the virtues of love between women. Both "To the Excellent Mrs. A.O. upon her Receiving the Name of Lucasia, and Adoption into our Society" and "Friendship's Mysteries, to my Dearest Lucasia" were written in 1651 to honor Anne Owen. Despite her valorizing of women's relationships, Philips recognized the limits that society imposed upon them; she once commented, in a letter to Cotterell, that "we may generally conclude the Marriage of a Friend to be the Funeral of a Friendship, for then all former Endearments run naturally into the Gulf to that new and strict Relationship, and there, like Rivers in the Sea, they lose themselves forever." A loss of friendship provides the theme of "On Rosania's Apostasy, and Lucasia's Friendship," which mourns Mary Aubrey's move to London with her husband, while "Lucasia, Rosania, and Orinda Parting at a Fountain" portrays three friends' sadness upon parting. Philips's affirmation of the bonds between women and her lyrical grace inspired the next generation of women poets, including ANNE FINCH, ANNE KILLIGREW, SARAH FYGE, and JANE BARKER. As Marilyn Williamson notes, Philips's generosity and simplicity won her what no other woman of her era achieved: "a central place in mainstream discourse."

⤝ To the Excellent Mrs. A.O.[1] upon her Receiving the Name of Lucasia, and Adoption into our Society ⤜

We are complete: and faith hath now
No greater blessing to bestow:
Nay, the dull World must now confess
    We have all worth, all happiness.
5   Annalls of State are trifles to our fame,
Now 'tis made sacred by Lucasia's name.

    But as though through a burning glass
    The sun more vigorous doth pass,
    It still with general freedom shines;
10   For that contracts, but not confines:
So though by this her beams are fixed here,
Yet she diffuses glories everywhere.

    Her mind is so entirely bright,
    The splendor would but wound our sight,

---

1. Anne Owen, Viscountess of Dungannon.

15 And must to some disguise submit,
Or we could never worship it.
And we by this relation are allowed
Luster enough to be Lucasia's cloud.

Nations will own us now to be
20 A Temple of divinity;
And Pilgrims shall ten ages hence
Approach our Tombs with reverence.
May then that time, which did such bliss convey,
Be kept with us perpetual Holy day!

                                        1651/1667

◄ Friendship's Mysteries, to my Dearest Lucasia ►

1

Come, my Lucasia, since we see
That miracles men's faith do move
By wonder and by Prodigy.
To the dull, angry world let's prove
5 There's a religion in our Love.

2

For though we were designed t'agree,
That fate no liberty destroys,
But our election[2] is as free
As Angels, who with greedy choice
10 Are yet determined to their Joys.

3

Our hearts are doubled by their loss,
Here mixture is addition grown;
We both diffuse, and both engross,
And we, whose minds are so much one,
15 Never, yet ever, are alone.

4

We court our own captivity,
Then Thrones more great and innocent:
'Twere banishment to be set free,
Since we wear fetters whose intent
20 Not bondage is, but Ornament.

5

Divided Joys are tedious found,
And griefs united easier grow:
We are ourselves but by rebound,[3]
And all our titles shuffled so,
25 Both Princes, and both subjects too.

2. Our choice, with a possible allusion to the concept of   3. Reflection.
divine election.

6

Our hearts are mutual victims laid,
　　While they (such power in friendship lies)
Are Altars, Priests, and offerings made,
　　And each heart which thus kindly dies,
30　　　Grows deathless by the sacrifice.

1655/1667

On Rosania's Apostasy,[4] and Lucasia's Friendship

Great soul of Friendship, whither art thou fled?
Where dost thou now choose to repose thy head?
Or art thou nothing but voice, air and name,
Found out to put Souls in pursuit of fame?
5　Thy flames being thought Immortal, we may doubt
Whether they e're did burn, that see them out.

Go, wearied Soul, find out thy wonted rest
In the safe Harbour of Orinda's breast;
There all unknown Adventures thou has found
10　In thy late transmigrations, expound;
That so Rosania's darkness may be known
To be her want of Luster, not thy own.

Then to the Great Lucasia have recourse,
　There gather up new excellence and force,
15　Till by a free unbiased clear Commerce,
Endearments which no Tongue can e're rehearse,
Lucasia and Orinda shall thee give
Eternity, and make even Friendship live.

Hail, Great Lucasia, thou shalt doubly shine:
20　What was Rosania's own is now twice thine;
Thou saw'st Rosania's Chariot and her flight,
And so the double portion is thy right:
Though 'twas Rosania's Spirit, be content,
Since 'twas at first from thy Orinda sent.

1652/1667

⚘ Lucasia, Rosania, and Orinda Parting at a Fountain ⚘

1

Here, here are our enjoyments done,
　　And since the Love and grief we wear
　　Forbids us either word or tear,
And Art wants here expression,
5　See Nature furnish us with one.

2

The kind and mournful Nymph which here
　　Inhabits in her humble Cells,
　　No longer her own Sorrow tells,

---

4. Abandonment or renunciation by Mary Aubrey, or "Rosania," who has moved to London with her husband.

Nor for it now concerned appears,
10   But for our parting sheds these tears.

3

Unless she may afflicted be,
    Least we should doubt her Innocence;
    Since she hath lost her best pretense
Unto a matchless purity;
15   Our Love being clearer far than she.

4

Cold as the streams which from her flow,
    Or (if her privater recess
    A greater coldness can express)
Then cold as those dark beds of snow
20   Our hearts are at this parting blow.

5

But Time, that has both wings and feet,
    Our suffering Minutes being Spent,
    Will visit us with new content;
And sure, if kindness be so sweet,
25   'Tis harder to forget then meet.

6

Then though the sad Adieu we say,
    Yet as the wine we hither bring,
    Revives, and then exalts the Spring;
So let our hopes to meet allay
30   The fears and Sorrows of this day.

1663/1667

—◄►—

Mary Rowlandson
1636?–1710

"I had often before this said, that if the Indians should come, I should choose rather to be killed by them than taken alive but when it came to the trial my mind changed," claimed MARY ROWLANDSON, the author of the first colonial American narrative of Indian captivity. One of eleven children of John White, a prosperous English landowner, and his wife, Joane, she came with her family to America in 1638 and moved to Lancaster, Massachusetts, in 1653. Three years later she married Joseph Rowlandson, a Harvard graduate who served as the Puritan minister in Lancaster; the couple had four children, one of whom died shortly after birth. In 1675, after years of relative peace between Native Americans and English colonizers, discord developed when a Wampanoag chief named Metacomet realized that settlers were seizing his people's lands and depleting vital food supplies. In the ironic words of Susan Howe, "while helping the original inhabitants of Earth's millennial fourth corner to become Christians, members of the moral and profit-seeking Elect helped themselves to land." Hence

Metacomet formed an alliance with other tribes that spoke the Algonquin language, and his forces began attacking the frontier villages. On February 10 they burned Lancaster, whose fifty inhabitants were either killed or captured; Rowlandson and her youngest child, both wounded in the fray, were among the latter. Her husband was away in Boston asking the government for troops to guard the village, which had been attacked once previously, and her two older children were taken from her by the Algonquins; her sister, brother-in-law, and nephew were killed during the battle.

For eleven weeks Rowlandson traveled with the Indians on what she called "removals," witnessing the death of her six-year-old daughter and assuming that her own demise was imminent. She was ransomed by influential friends, however, near the end of her third month of captivity. Shortly thereafter she began writing her narrative, *The Sovereignty and Goodness of God, Together with the Faithfulness of His Promises Displayed, Being a Narrative of the Captivity and Restoration of Mrs. Mary Rowlandson*, which was published six years later, in 1682; it went through three editions immediately and was reprinted often during the nineteenth century. Rowlandson's narrative was so popular with Puritan readers that it gave rise to countless similar sagas and initiated a new genre of frontier literature. Although little is known of her life after her husband's death in 1678, the scholar David Greene has used genealogical records to document that in 1679 she married Captain Samuel Talcott, a wealthy farmer. If this account is correct, then she died not in 1678, as scholars previously supposed, but in 1710.

The introduction to Rowlandson's captivity narrative describes the horror of the burning village and her determination to survive, while subsequent chapters recount each day's journey with the Indians away from her known world. As Katharine Rogers points out, "the narrative of Indian captivity was a sensational form of the standard Puritan spiritual autobiography. Inner temptations and illnesses such as ANNE BRADSTREET's are replaced by external trials imposed by unbelieving Indians (seen as agents of Satan); with God's grace, the soul withstands its testing and is finally saved; redemption by ransom implies spiritual redemption as well." The demonization of difference and the celebration of her own spiritual redemption go hand in hand in Rowlandson's powerful narrative.

⇥ *from* The Sovereignty and Goodness of God, Together with the Faithfulness of His Promises Displayed, Being a Narrative of the Captivity and Restoration of Mrs. Mary Rowlandson ⇤

ON the 10th of February, 1675, came the Indians with great numbers upon Lancaster: their first coming was about sun-rising; hearing the noise of some guns, we looked out; several houses were burning, and the smoke ascending to heaven. There were five persons taken in one house, the father and mother, and a sucking child they knocked on the head, the other two they took and carried away alive. There were two others, who being out of their garrison upon occasion, were set upon; one was knocked on the head, the other escaped: Another there was who running along was shot and wounded, and fell down; he begged of them his life, promising them money (as they told me) but they would not hearken to him, but knocked him on the head, stripped him naked, and split open his bowels. Another seeing many of the Indians about his barn, ventured and went out, but was quickly shot down. There were three others belonging to the same garrison who were killed; the Indians getting up upon the roof of the barn, had advantage to shoot down upon them over their fortification. Thus these murderous wretches went on burning and destroying all before them.

At length they came and beset our house, and quickly it was the dolefulest day that ever mine eyes saw. The house stood upon the edge of a hill; some of the Indians got behind the hill, others into the barn, and others behind anything that would shelter them; from all which places they shot against the house, so that the bullets seemed to fly like hail, and quickly they wounded one man among us, then another, and then a third. About two hours (according to my observation in that amazing time) they had been about the house before they prevailed to fire it (which they did with flax and hemp, which they brought out of the barn, and there being no defense about the house, only two flankers at two opposite corners, and one of them not finished), they fired it once, and one ventured out and quenched it, but they quickly fired it again, and that took. Now is the dreadful hour come, that I have often heard of (in time of the war, as it was the case of others) but now mine eyes see it. Some in our house were fighting for their lives, others wallowing in blood, the house on fire over our heads, and the bloody heathen ready to knock us on the head if we stirred out. Now might we hear mothers and children crying out for themselves and one another, "Lord, what shall we do!" Then I took my children (and one of my sisters hers) to go forth and leave the house: but as soon as we came to the door, and appeared, the Indians shot so thick, that the bullets rattled against the house, as if one had taken a handful of stones and threw them, so that we were forced to give back. We had six stout dogs belonging to our garrison, but none of them would stir, though at another time, if an Indian had come to the door, they were ready to fly upon him and tear him down. The Lord hereby would make us the more to acknowledge his hand, and to see that our help is always in him. But out we must go, the fire increasing, and coming along behind us roaring, and the Indians gaping before us with their guns, spears, and hatchets to devour us. No sooner were we out of the house but my brother-in-law (being before wounded in defending the house, in or near the throat) fell down dead; whereat the Indians scornfully shouted and hallooed, and were presently upon him, stripping off his clothes. The bullets flying thick, one went through my side, and the same (as would seem) through the bowels and hand of my poor child in my arms. One of my elder sister's children (named William) had then his leg broke, which the Indians perceiving, they knocked him on the head. Thus were we butchered by those merciless heathens, standing amazed, with the blood running down to our heels. My eldest sister being yet in the house, and seeing those woeful sights, the infidels hauling mothers one way and children another, and some wallowing in their blood; and her eldest son telling her that her son William was dead, and myself was wounded, she said, and "Lord let me die with them:" which was no sooner said but she was struck with a bullet, and fell down dead over the threshold. I hope she is reaping the fruit of her good labors, being faithful to the service of God in her place. In her younger years she lay under much trouble upon spiritual accounts, till it pleased God to make that precious scripture take hold of her heart, 2 Cor. 12. 9. *And he said unto me, My grace is sufficient for thee*. More than twenty years after, I have heard her tell how sweet and comfortable that place was to her. But to return: The Indians laid hold of us, pulling me one way, and the children another, and said, "Come, go along with us." I told them they would kill me: they answered, "If I were willing to go along with them, they would not hurt me."

Oh! the doleful sight that now was to behold at this house! Come behold the works of the Lord, what desolations he has made in the earth. Of thirty-seven persons who were in this one house, none escaped either present death, or a bitter captivity, save only one, who might say as in Job 1, 15. *And I only am escaped alone to tell the news*. There were twelve killed, some shot, some stabbed with their spears, some knocked down with their hatchets. When we are in prosperity, oh the little that we think of such dreadful sights, to see our dear friends and relations lie bleeding out their hearts' blood upon the ground. There was one who was chopped in the head with a hatchet, and stripped naked, and yet was crawling up and down. It was a solemn sight to see so many christians lying in their blood, some here and some there, like a company of sheep torn by wolves. All of them stripped naked by a company of hell-hounds, roaring, singing, ranting and insulting, as if they would have torn our hearts out: yet the Lord by his almighty power, preserved a number of us from death; for there were twenty-four of us taken alive and carried captive.

I had often before this said that if the Indians should come, I should choose rather to be killed by them, than taken alive: but when it came to the trial, my mind changed; their glittering weapons so daunted my spirit, that I chose rather to go along with those (as I may say) ravenous bears, than that moment to end my days. And that I may the better declare what happened to me during that grievous captivity, I shall particularly speak of the several Removes we had up and down the wilderness.

THE FIRST REMOVE

NOW away we must go with those barbarous creatures, with our bodies wounded and bleeding and our hearts no less than our bodies. About a mile we went that night, up upon a hill within sight of the town, where we intended to lodge. There was hard by a vacant house (deserted by the English before, for fear of the Indians), I asked them whether I might not lodge in the house that night? to which they answered, What, will you love English-men still? This was the dolefulest night that ever my eyes saw. Oh the roaring, and singing, and dancing, and yelling of those black creatures in the night, which made the place a lively resemblance of hell: And miserable was the waste that was there made, of horses, cattle, sheep, swine, calves, lambs, roasting pigs and fowls (which they had plundered in the town) some roasting, some lying and burning, and some boiling, to feed our merciless enemies: who were joyful enough, though we were disconsolate. To add to the dolefulness of the former day, and the dismalness of the present night, my thoughts ran upon my losses and sad bereaved condition. All was gone, my husband gone (at least separated from me, he being in the Bay: and to add to my grief, the Indians told me they would kill him as he came homeward), my children gone, my relations and friends gone, our house and home, and all our comforts within door and without, all was gone (except my life) and I knew not but the next moment that might go too.

There remained nothing to me but one poor wounded babe, and it seemed at present worse than death, that it was in such a pitiful condition, bespeaking compassion, and I had no refreshing for it, nor suitable things to revive it. Little do many think, what is the savageness and brutishness of this barbarous enemy, those even that seem to profess more than others among them, when the English have fallen into their hands.

Those seven that were killed at Lancaster the summer before upon a sabbath day, and the one that was afterward killed upon a weekday, were slain and mangled in barbarous manner, by one-eyed John, and Marlborough's praying Indians, which Capt. Mosely brought to Boston, as the Indians told me. . . .

THE EIGHTEENTH REMOVE

WE took up our packs, and along we went. But a wearisome day I had of it. As we went along, I saw an Englishman stripped naked, and lying dead upon the ground, but knew not who he was. Then we came to another Indian town, where we stayed all night. In this town there were four English children captives, and one of them my own sister's. I went to see how she did, and she was well, considering her captive condition. I would have tarried that night with her, but they that owned her would not suffer. Then I went to another wigwam, where they were boiling corn and beans, which was a lovely sight to see, but I could not get a taste thereof. Then I went into another wigwam, where there were two of the English children: The Squaw was boiling horses' feet, she cut me off a little piece, and gave one of the English children a piece also. Being very hungry, I had quickly eat up mine; but the child could not bite it, it was so tough and sinewy, but lay sucking, gnawing and slabbering of it in the mouth and hand, then I took it of the child, and eat it myself, and savory it was to my taste. That I may say as Job, *Chap. 6. 7. The things that my soul refuseth to touch, are as my sorrowful meat.* Thus the Lord made that pleasant and refreshing, which another time would have been an abomination. Then I went home to my mistress's wigwam, and they told me I disgraced my master with begging, and if I did so any more, they would knock me on the head: I told them they had as good do that, as starve me to death. . . .   *1676–78/1682*

⊷⊷ ⧫ ⊶⊷

Hannah More
1745–1833

An English author of poems, plays, and social commentary, HANNAH MORE was the daughter of a schoolmaster, Jacob More, and his wife, Mary Grace; her father headed the Free School of Fishponds, Stapleton, near Bristol. From him More learned Latin, for which she showed an early proficiency; she later studied, then taught at a successful school in Bristol that her older sisters ran. A broken engagement made her financially secure, since her fiancé, Edward Turner, was legally bound to pay her an annual annuity of two hundred pounds when he ended their relationship. More's Bristol contacts ensured her entry into the literary world of London when she moved there in 1773, armed with a letter of introduction to the actor and playwright David Garrick, who became a close friend. Through Garrick and his wife, with whom More briefly lived, she met the famous writer Samuel Johnson, who once referred to her as "the most powerful versifatrix in the English language"; the painter Joshua Reynolds, whom she admired; and the group of writing women known as the "Bluestockings," whose work she praised.

More went on to enjoy a successful theatrical career. Her first play, *The Search after Happiness* (1773), written when she was eighteen, was heralded by both Garrick and the critic John Langhorne. Her tragedy *The Inflexible Captive* (1774) was produced in Bristol to great acclaim, while *Percy* (1777) was staged at Covent Garden, its prologue and epilogue written by Garrick. The actor managed More's professional life for several years, nicknaming her "Madam Nine" after the ninth muse and helping to revise her works. In 1779 *The Fatal Falsehood* was staged in London but was less well received than her prior plays had been. That same year Garrick died, effectively ending More's career in theater. She later came to regret this part of her life, convinced that to write for the theater as a woman had been imprudent.

When her work in theater ended, More became a successful writer of prose. In 1776 she published modern versions of two legendary tales, *Sir Eldred of the Bower* and *The Bleeding Rock*, which were praised by Langhorne and revised by Dr. Johnson for reissue in 1778. Her didactic writings brought her considerable fame, especially two works about education for women: *Education on Various Subjects, Principally Designed for Young Ladies* (1777) and *Strictures on the Modern System of Female Education* (1799). *Flavio: A Tale for Fine Gentlemen and Fine Ladies* (1786) won praise from Samuel Johnson; its companion work, *The Bas Bleu*, celebrated the writings of the Bluestockings. More critiqued the British aristocracy in *Thoughts on the Importance of Manners of the Great to General Society* (1788), and that same year she published *Slavery, A Poem* in protest against the immorality of that institution. Concerned by the revolutionary fervor that emerged in England on the heels of the French Revolution, she wrote *Village Politics, by "Will Chip"* (1792) in support of social hegemony. *Cheap Repository Tracts* (1795–98), a successful commercial pamphlet venture, urged the poor to work hard, remain in their proper place, learn to read for practical reasons, but accept their poverty with grace. More was known to the Romantic poets, who disliked her political conservatism; despite their differences, she praised Wordsworth's *Lyrical Ballads* when it appeared in 1798. In her later years More lived outside of London in a cottage called Bailey Wood, where many prominent literary figures visited; she died in 1833, a rich woman who bequeathed thirty thousand pounds to charities. *The Works of Hannah More* was published posthumously in two volumes in 1835 and remained popular throughout the nineteenth century.

More did not sympathize with the feminist beliefs of Catherine Macauley, MARY WOLLSTONECRAFT, and MARY HAYS, her contemporaries; indeed, she once wrote that any woman who did not adhere to conventional moral standards should be banned from polite company. In *Strictures on the Modern System of Female Education* she suggested that women caused their own discrimination: "a judicious, unrelaxing but steady and gentle curb on [women's] tempers and passions can alone insure their peace and establish their principles." She was similarly conservative on religious matters, as can be seen in *Practical Piety, or the Influence of the Religion of the Heart on the Conduct of the Life*, in which she advocates submission to the authority of the church fathers. More was liberal in certain respects, however, as *Slavery, A Poem* attests: "Perish th' illiberal thought which would debase / The native genius of the sable race!" Although More dignifies slaves as human beings, she refers as well to their "savage root" and "pagan soul," implicitly endorsing the views of racial otherness that were dominant in her era. On the other hand, she also addresses slaveholders as savages. The passage from "The Black Slave Trade" included here portrays white masters as tyrants and black slaves, especially women and children, as their unhappy victims.

⊰ *from* The Black Slave Trade ⊱

... Whene'er to Afric's shores I turn my eyes,
Horrors of deepest, deadliest guilt arise;
I see, by more than Fancy's mirror shewn,
The burning village, and the blazing town:
5   See the dire victim torn from social life,
See the scared infant, hear the shrieking wife!
She, wretch forlorn! is dragged by hostile hands,
To distant tyrants sold, in distant lands!
Transmitted miseries, and successive chains,
10   The sole sad heritage her child obtains!
E'en this last wretched boon their foes deny,
To weep together, or together die.
By felon hands, by one relentless stroke,
See the fond vital links of Nature broke!

15   The fibers twisting round a parent's heart,
       Torn from their grasp, and bleeding as they part.
          Hold, murderers, hold! nor aggravate distress;
       Respect the passions you yourselves possess;
       Even you, of ruffian heart, and ruthless hand,
20   Love your own offspring, love your native land:
       Even you, with fond impatient feelings burn,
       Though free as air, though certain of return.
       Then, if to you, who voluntary roam,
       So dear the memory of your distant home,
25   O think how absence the loved scene endears
       To him, whose food is groans, whose drink is tears;
       Think on the wretch whose aggravated pains
       To exile misery adds, to misery chains.
       If warm *your* heart, to British feelings true,
30   As dear his land to him as yours to you;
       And Liberty, in you a hallowed flame,
       Burns, unextinguished, in his breast the same.
       Then leave him holy Freedom's cheering smile,
       The heaven-taught fondness for the parent soil;
35   Revere affections mingled with our frame,
       In every nature, every clime the same;
       In all, these feelings equal sway maintain;
       In all, the love of HOME and FREEDOM reign:
       And Tempe's vale, and parched Angola's sand,
40   One equal fondness of their sons command.
       Th' unconquered Savage laughs at pain and toil,
       Basking in Freedom's beams which gild his native soil.
          Does thirst of empire, does desire of fame,
       (For these are specious crimes) our rage inflame?
45   No: sordid lust of gold their fate controls,
       The basest appetite of basest souls;
       Gold, better gained by what their ripening sky,
       Their fertile fields, their arts, and mines supply.
          What wrongs, what injuries does Oppression plead,
50   To smooth the crime and sanctify the deed? . . .

                                              1816

Phillis Wheatley
1753?–1784

PHILLIS WHEATLEY was the first African-American poet to publish in the colonies that became the United States. Born in Senegal, she was brought by slave ship in 1761 to the colonies, where a prominent Boston merchant, John Wheatley, bought her as a house servant for his wife, Suzannah. Impressed by the precocious child, the Wheatleys offered her a classical education. At ten Phillis Wheatley translated Ovid from the Latin and by her teens was writing poems, some of which were published in magazines and newspapers. In 1773 the Wheatleys sent her to England in the company of their son, in hopes of improving her poor health as well as finding a publisher for her book of poems, a project that had failed in Boston. With the aid of an English patron, the Countess of Huntington, to whom the book is dedicated, *Poems on Various Subjects, Religious and Moral* was published in 1773. Wheatley toured England to promote it, and the collection was widely read in the colonies as well, although an American edition did not appear until 1786. After her return from England John Wheatley freed her, shamed into doing so by his antislavery English friends, but freedom did not bring Wheatley prosperity. She married a free black man, John Peters, a merchant, and had three children, all of whom died in infancy; for years the family lived in poverty. Although Wheatley attempted to publish a second volume of poetry, she was unable to find an interested press. Her later poems are no longer extant, since her husband could not locate them after her death in 1784.

Most of Wheatley's poems employ such neoclassical strategies as epithets, personification, and invocations to the muse. Because of her reliance on these traditional devices, she was long considered a derivative poet, an imitator of the school of Alexander Pope. Although some African-American scholars have disparaged Wheatley for appearing to endorse a white Christian world view, others have argued that her poetry has a strong Afrocentric and feminist subtext. Many poems lament the death of mothers and children, an aspect of women's daily reality that clearly moved the poet. Although her feelings of indebtedness to white patrons are evident in poems she dedicated to famous men, her sense of African identity is likewise strong. Given her life as a slave, it seems little wonder that Wheatley reveals what ALICE WALKER has called "contrary instincts." Her multiple identities are evident in "On Being Brought from Africa to America," in which she asserts "'Twas mercy brought me from my pagan land," yet chides white Christians for their racism and hypocrisy. In contrast, one of the few poems she dedicated to a living person, the African-American artist Sapio Moorhead, also a slave, is one of her least ambivalent works. Wheatley's writing has influenced such contemporary women poets as Nikki Giovanni, whose poem "Hands" honors Wheatley; Alice Walker, who defends her foremother in "In Search of Our Mothers' Gardens"; and JUNE JORDAN, who pays homage to her in "The Difficult Miracle of Black Poetry in America or Something Like a Sonnet for Phillis Wheatley." The miracle, concludes Jordan, is that Wheatley wrote at all. "It was not natural. And she was the first."

⊰ On Being Brought from Africa to America ⊱

'TWAS mercy brought me from my pagan land,
Taught my benighted soul to understand
That there's a God, that there's a Savior too:
Once I redemption neither sought nor knew.
5   Some view our sable race with scornful eye,
"Their color is a diabolic dye."
Remember, Christians, Negros, black as Cain,
May be refined, and join th' angelic train.

1773

⊰ To S. M., a Young African Painter,[1] on Seeing his Works ⊱

To show the lab'ring bosom's deep intent,
And thought in living characters to paint,
When first thy pencil did those beauties give,
And breathing figures learnt from thee to live,
5   How did those prospects give my soul delight,
A new creation rushing on my sight?

1. Sapio (or Scipio) Moorhead of Boston.

Still, wond'rous youth! each noble path pursue,
On deathless glories fix thine ardent view:
Still may the painter's and the poet's fire
10   To aid thy pencil, and thy verse conspire!
And may the charms of each seraphic theme
Conduct thy footsteps to immortal fame!
High to the blissful wonders of the skies
Elate thy soul, and raise thy wishful eyes.
15   Thrice happy, when exalted to survey
That splendid city, crowned with endless day,
Whose twice six gates on radiant hinges ring:
Celestial Salem² blooms in endless spring.

Calm and serene thy moments glide along,
And may the muse inspire each future song!
20   Still, with the sweets of contemplation blessed,
May peace with balmy wings your soul invest!
But when these shades of time are chased away,
And darkness ends in everlasting day,
On what seraphic pinions shall we move,
25   And view the landscapes in the realms above?
There shall thy tongue in heav'nly murmurs flow,
And there my muse with heav'nly transport glow:
No more to tell of Damon's tender sighs,
Or rising radiance of Aurora's eyes,³
30   For nobler themes demand a nobler strain,
And purer language on th' ethereal plain.
Cease, gentle muse! the solemn gloom of night
Now seals the fair creation from my sight.

1773

⊰ To the Right Honorable William, Earl of DARTMOUTH, His Majesty's Principal Secretary of State for North America,⁴ &c. ⊱

HAIL, happy day, when, smiling like the morn,
Fair Freedom rose New England to adorn:
The northern clime beneath her genial ray,
Dartmouth, congratulates thy blissful sway:
5   Elate with hope her race no longer mourns,
Each soul expands, each grateful bosom burns,
While in thine hand with pleasure we behold
The silken reins, and Freedom's charms unfold.
Long lost to realms beneath the northern skies
10   She shines supreme, while hated faction dies:
Soon as appear'd the Goddess⁵ long desired,
Sick at the view, she languished and expired;

---

2. Jerusalem.
3. Damon and Aurora (the dawn) are earthly lovers, not fit for heaven.

4. In 1772 he replaced Lord Hillborough as the secretary who oversaw the American colonies.
5. Freedom.

Thus from the splendors of the morning light
The owl in sadness seeks the caves of night.

15   No more, America, in mournful strain
Of wrongs, and grievance unredressed complain,
No longer shall thou dread the iron chain,
Which wanton Tyranny with lawless hand
Had made, and with it meant t' enslave the land.

20   Should you, my lord, while you peruse my song,
Wonder from whence my love of Freedom sprung,
Whence flow these wishes for the common good,
By feeling hearts alone best understood,
I, young in life, by seeming cruel fate
25   Was snatch'd from Afric's fancied happy seat:
What pangs excruciating must molest,
What sorrows labor in my parents' breast?
Steeled was that soul and by no misery moved
That from a father seized his babe beloved:
30   Such, such my case. And can I then but pray
Others may never feel tyrannic sway?

      For favors past, great Sir, our thanks are due,
And thee we ask thy favors to renew,
Since in thy power, as in thy will before,
To sooth the griefs, which thou didst once deplore.
35   May heavenly grace the sacred sanction give
To all thy works, and thou forever live
Not only on the wings of fleeting Fame,
Though praise immortal crowns the patriot's name,
But to conduct to heaven's refulgent fane,
40   May fiery coursers sweep th' ethereal plain,
And bear thee upwards to that blessed abode,
Where, like the prophet,[6] thou shalt find thy God.

1773

—•—≡◆≡—•—

Dorothy Wordsworth
1771–1855

DOROTHY WORDSWORTH wrote vivid nature journals and travelogues, all of which remained unpublished in her lifetime. The sister of the Romantic poet William Wordsworth and the only girl of five children, she lost her parents when young and was raised by various relatives, who let her see her brothers only occasionally. She began writing when William inherited money and invited her to share a house with him in 1795; her journals continued when they moved in 1798 to Alfoxden and when they later bought Dove Cottage in Grasmere. Her depiction of the natural world influenced the poetry of both her brother and his friend Samuel Taylor Coleridge, a frequent visitor to Dove Cottage; and she in turn supported their work: Wordsworth claimed in "The Prelude" that through troubled times his sister "preserved me

6. The prophet Elijah was transported to heaven in a chariot of fire; see II Kings 2.

still a Poet." She collaborated with Wordsworth on *Guide to the Lakes*, composing the chapter entitled "Excursion on the Banks of Ullswater."

Dorothy Wordsworth's journals capture poignant details of daily life and the manners of the rural people she encountered on her walks. She began writing *The Grasmere Journal* in May, 1800, to "give William Pleasure;" she discontinued it in January, 1803, upon her brother's wedding to Mary Hutchinson. By all accounts the marriage distressed her, although she continued to share a home with her brother and his wife for many years. Subsequent journal entries reveal her devotion to William, whose writing time she protected; they also record her concern with the villagers' well-being and depict the changing face of nature. Her travelogues include *Recollections Made of a Tour in Scotland* (1803), *Excursion Up Scawfield Pike* (1818), and *Journal of a Tour of the Continent* (1820). Although Wordsworth kept journals sporadically until 1848, she wrote little after 1835, having fallen mentally and physically ill with hardening of the arteries in the brain. She spent her last twenty years as an invalid nursed by her brother and his family.

The Grasmere Journal is not only an homage to the English Lake District; it is also a record of its author's assumptions about sexual difference. Dorothy kept William's house, cooked his meals, mended his clothes, and read his poems, all the while writing constantly herself yet insisting that "I should detest the idea of setting myself up as an author." Her reward came in her brother's success as England's poet laureate and in his gratitude for her support. Although Coleridge praised Dorothy Wordsworth for "her eye watchful in minutest observation of nature—and her taste a perfect electrometer," she was not taken seriously as a writer until the twentieth century, when critics such as VIRGINIA WOOLF began to recognize her genius.

↤ *from* The Grasmere Journal ↦

May 14 1800 [Wednesday]. Wm & John[1] set off into Yorkshire after dinner at 1/2 past 2 o'clock—cold pork in their pockets. I left them at the turning of the Low-wood bay under the trees. My heart was so full that I could hardly speak to W when I gave him a farewell kiss. I sat a long time upon a stone at the margin of the lake, & after a flood of tears my heart was easier. The lake looked to me I knew not why dull and melancholy, the weltering on the shores seemed a heavy sound. I walked as long as I could amongst the stones of the shore. The wood rich in flowers. A beautiful yellow, palish yellow flower, that looked thick round & double, & smelt very sweet—I supposed it was a ranunculus—Crowfoot, the grassy-leaved Rabbit-toothed white flower, strawberries, Geranium—scentless violet, anemones two kinds, orchises, primroses. The heckberry very beautiful, the crab coming out as a low shrub. Met a blind man driving a very large beautiful Bull & a cow—he walked with two sticks. Came home by Clappersgate. The valley very green, many sweet views up to Rydale head when I could juggle away the fine houses, but they disturbed me even more than when I have been happier—one beautiful view of the Bridge, without Sir Michael's.[2] Sat down very often, tho' it was cold. I resolved to write a journal of the time till W & J return, & I set about keeping my resolve because I will not quarrel with myself, & because I shall give Wm Pleasure by it when he comes home again. At Rydale a woman of the village, stout & well-dressed, begged a halfpenny—she had never she said done it before—but these hard times!—Arrived at home with a bad headache, set some slips of privet.[3] The evening cold, had a fire—my face now flame-colored. It is nine o'clock, I shall soon go to bed. A young woman begged at the door—she had come from Manchester on Sunday morn with two

1. Her brothers, William and John Wordsworth.   3. Cuttings from a shrub.
2. The estate of Sir Michael le Fleming, RydaleHall.

shillings & a slip of paper which she supposed a Bank note—it was a cheat. She had buried her husband & three children within a year & a half—All in one grave—burying very dear—paupers all put in one place—20 shillings paid for as much ground as will bury a man—a gravestone to be put over it or the right will be lost—eleven shillings and sixpence each time the ground is opened. Oh! that I had a letter from William!

May 15 Thursday. A coldish dull morning—hoed the first row of peas, weeded &c &c—sat hard to mending till evening. The rain which had threatened all day came on just when I was going to walk—

Friday morning [16th]. Warm & mild after a fine night of rain. Transplanted radishes after breakfast. Walked to Mr. Gells with the Books—gathered mosses & plants. The woods extremely beautiful with all autumnal variety & softness—I carried a basket for mosses, & gathered some wild plants—Oh! that we had a book of botany—all flowers now are gay & deliciously sweet. The primrose still preeminent among the later flowers of the spring. Foxgloves very tall—with their heads budding. I went forward round the lake at the foot of Loughrigg fell—I was much amused with the business of a pair of stone chats. Their restless voices as they skimmed along the water following each other their shadows under them, & their returning back to the stones on the shore, chirping with the same unwearied voice. Could not cross the water so I went round by the stepping stones. The morning clear but cloudy, that is the hills were not overhung by mists. After dinner Aggy weeded onions & carrots—I helped for a little—wrote to Mary Hutchinson[4]—washed my head—worked. After tea went to Ambleside—a pleasant cool but not cold evening. Rydale was very beautiful with spear-shaped streaks of polished steel. No letters!—only one newspaper. I returned by Clappersgate. Grasmere was very solemn in the last glimpse of twilight it calls home the heart to quietness. I had been very melancholy in my walk back. I had many of my saddest thoughts & I could not keep the tears within me. But when I came to Grasmere I felt that it did me good. I finished my letter to MH.—ate hasty pudding, & went to bed. As I was going out in the morning I met a half crazy old man. He shewed me a pincushion, & begged a pin, afterwards a halfpenny. He began in a kind of indistinct voice in this manner "Matthew Jobson's lost a cow. Tom Nichol has two good horses strained—Jim Jones's cow's broken her horn, &c &c— —" He went into Aggy's & persuaded her to give him some whey & let him boil some porridge. She declares he ate two quarts.

Saturday [17th]. Incessant rain from morning till night. T. Ashburner brought us coals. Worked hard & Read *Midsummer Night's Dream, Ballads*—sauntered a little in the garden. The Skobby sat quietly in its nest rocked by the winds & beaten by the rain.

Sunday [18th]. Went to church, slight showers, a cold air. The mountains from this window look much greener & I think the valley is more green than ever. The corn begins to shew itself. The ashes are still bare. Went part of the way home with Miss Simpson . . . —A little girl from Coniston came to beg. She had lain out all night— her stepmother had turn'd her out of doors. Her father could not stay at home, "She flights so." Walked to Ambleside in the evening round the lake. The prospect exceed-ing beautiful from Loughrigg fell. It was so green, that no eye could be weary of reposing upon it. The most beautiful situation for a house in the field next to Mr. Benson's. It threatened rain all evening but was mild & pleasant. I was overtaken by 2 Cumber-land people on the other side of Rydale who complimented me upon my walking. They were going to sell cloth, & odd things which they make themselves in Hawk-shead & the neighborhood. The post was not arrived so I walked through the town,

4. The woman William Wordsworth would marry in 1802.

past Mrs. Taylor's, & met him. Letters from Coleridge[5] & Cottle—John Fisher over-took me on the other side of Rydale—he talked much about the alteration in the times, & observed that in a short time there would be only two ranks of people, the very rich & the very poor, for those who have small estates says he are forced to sell, & all the land goes into one hand. Did not reach home till 10 o'clock. . . .

Tuesday 2nd September. In the morning they all went to Stickel Tarn. A very fine, warm sunny beautiful morning. I baked a pie & c for dinner—little Sally was with me. The fair day. Miss Simpson & Mr. came down to tea—we walked to the fair. There seem'd very few people & very few stalls yet I believe there were many cakes & much beer sold. My Brothers came home to dinner at 6 o'clock. We drank Tea immediately after by Candlelight. It was a lovely moonlight night. We talked much about a house on Helvellyn. The moonlight shone only upon the village it did not eclipse the village lights & the sound of dancing & merriment came along the still air—I walked with Coleridge & Wm up the Lane & by the Church, I then lingered with Coleridge in the garden. John & Wm were both gone to bed & all the lights out.

Wednesday 3rd September. Coleridge Wm & John went from home to go upon Helvellyn with Mr Simpson. They set out after breakfast. I accompanied them up near the Blacksmith's. A fine coolish morning. I ironed till 1/2 past three—now very hot. I then went to a funeral at John Dawson's. About 10 men & 4 women. Bread cheese & ale—they talked sensibly & cheerfully about common things. The dead person 56 years of age buried by the parish—the coffin was neatly lettered & painted black & covered with a decent cloth. They set the corpse down at the door & while we stood within the threshold the men with their hats off sang with decent & solemn countenances a verse of a funeral psalm. The corpse was then borne down the hill & they sang till they had got past the Town-end. I was affected to tears while we stood in the house, the coffin lying before me. There were no near kindred, no children. When we got out of the dark house the sun was shining & the prospect looked so divinely beautiful as I never saw it. It seemed more sacred than I had ever seen it, & yet more allied to human life. The green fields, neighbors of the churchyard, were green as possible & with the brightness of the sunshine looked quite Gay. I thought she was going to a quiet spot & I could not help weeping very much. When we came to the bridge they began to sing again & stopped during 4 lines before they entered the churchyard. The priest met us—he did not look as a man ought to do on such an occasion—I had seen him half drunk the day before in a pot-house. Before we came with the corpse one of the company observed he wondered what sort of cue "our Parson would be in." NB it was the day after the Fair. I had not finished ironing till 7 o'clock. The wind was now high & I did not walk—writing my journal now at 8 o clock. Wm & John came home at 10 o clock.   *1800/1971*

Margaret Fuller
1810–1850

A key figure in the literary movement known as Transcendentalism, MARGARET FULLER was the most famous woman of letters in the United States during the nineteenth century. She was born in Cambridgeport, Massachusetts, the oldest of nine children of Timothy and Margaret Crane Fuller. Her father, a prominent lawyer and four-term congressman, took charge of his

---

5. Samuel Taylor Coleridge (1772–1834), an English Romantic poet and friend of the Wordsworths.

daughter's classical education while her mother, a former teacher, introduced her to the arts. By age six the precocious Fuller had learned Latin, and by nine she was reading Greek and Roman classics as well as English and French literature. At fourteen she was sent to Miss Prescott's Young Ladies' Seminary in Groton, a painful experience that she recounts in her "Autobiographical Sketch," written when she was thirty. A dedicated student, Fuller disliked the "finishing school" approach of her headmistress, who believed in teaching girls the social niceties. Although she spent her days in misery, Fuller later admitted that her year at the seminary "had a powerful effect on my character." In 1825 she rejoined her family in Cambridge, pursuing her education independently and adding two influential women, "the brilliant [Germaine] de Stael" and "the useful [MARIA] EDGEWORTH" to her studies. With her friend James Freeman Clarke she learned German; together they read Goethe, whom Fuller admired, and eventually she translated *Torquato Tasso,* his work on artistic development. She also began to write essays, the first of which, "In Defense of Brutus," was published in 1834 in the *Boston Daily Advertiser and Patriot;* three subsequent essays appeared in the *Western Messenger.*

When her father died in 1835, Fuller assumed the management of household affairs and the education of her siblings. To earn income for the family, she began teaching at Bronson Alcott's Temple School in Boston, where she endorsed the Socratic method of pedagogy and the then-experimental concept of coeducation. Because Alcott's radical views of education were exciting public controversy his school's enrollment diminished, and Fuller resigned her position after seven months to teach at the Greene Street School for women in Providence, Rhode Island, where her commitment to women's education was strengthened. Although she excelled at teaching, Fuller soon left to pursue a literary career, having realized that she was "fulfilling all my duties . . . except to myself." She published a translation of *Eckermann's Conversations with Goethe* in 1839 and began to host a series of "conversations" on the "woman question" for educated women and men of Boston; these popular seminars were held twice annually for five years and enrolled up to thirty-five participants per session. In addition, she renewed her friendship with Ralph Waldo Emerson, the leading proponent of Transcendentalism, whose philosophy of self-reliance she embraced. Although she found Emerson cold, Fuller appreciated his intellect, and she joined a literary circle that included Emerson, Alcott, William Ellery Channing, and Henry David Thoreau.

From 1840 until 1842 Fuller served as editor of *The Dial,* a prominent journal whose aim was intellectual reformation. Among her articles for *The Dial* were "The Great Lawsuit: Man *versus* Men. Woman *versus* Women," which argues for women's full participation in social and political life; and "Bettine Brentano and Her Friend Günderode," a meditation on women's friendships. Fuller's feminist leanings are also evident in *Summer on the Lakes* (1844), which examines the gender dynamics she observed while traveling in the West. That same year Fuller became literary editor of the *New York Daily Tribune,* for which she wrote more than two hundred columns on literature, women's rights, slavery, poverty, prison reform, and treatment of the mentally ill. *Papers on Literature and Art* (1846) collected her previously published essays. In 1846 Fuller became European correspondent for the *Tribune* and covered the Italian Revolution, which she supported. While in Rome she met an Italian nobleman, Giovanni Ossoli, with whom she had a son, Angelo, born in 1848. When the Roman Republic fell in 1850, the family left Italy to return to the United States but died together in a shipwreck near Fire Island, New York. Several of Fuller's works were published posthumously: *Memoirs of Margaret Fuller Ossoli* (1852), edited by Emerson, Channing, and Clarke; *At Home and Abroad* (1856); and *Life Without and Life Within* (1859).

Woman in the Nineteenth Century (1845), an expansion of "The Great Lawsuit," aroused immediate controversy; reviewers either lauded Fuller's "noble," "thoughtful" sentiments or damned her as "no longer a woman." In a period in which marriage and motherhood were considered women's only proper occupations, she insisted on their intellectual and professional autonomy. In the selection included below, Fuller's views are presented by her mouthpiece, Miranda, whose superior education mirrors the writer's own. Described by Mary Kelley as "manifesto, celebration, meditation, and declamation," *Woman in the Nineteenth Century* argues that assumptions about sexual difference notwithstanding, women's equality is not only desirable, it is inevitable.

⌐ *from* Woman in the Nineteenth Century ⌐

"Frailty, thy name is Woman."
"The Earth waits for her Queen."[1]

The connection between these quotations may not be obvious, but it is strict. Yet would any contradict us, if we made them applicable to the other side, and began also

Frailty, thy name is MAN.
The Earth waits for its King?

Yet man, if not yet fully installed in his powers, has given much earnest of his claims. Frail he is indeed, how frail! how impure! Yet often has the vein of gold displayed itself amid the baser ores, and Man has appeared before us in princely promise worthy of his future.

If, oftentimes, we see the prodigal son feeding on the husks in the fair field no more his own, anon, we raise the eyelids, heavy from bitter tears, to behold in him the radiant apparition of genius and love, demanding not less than the all of goodness, power and beauty. We see that in him the largest claim finds a due foundation. That claim is for no partial sway, no exclusive possession. He cannot be satisfied with any one gift of life, any one department of knowledge or telescopic peep at the heavens. He feels himself called to understand and aid nature, that she may, through his intelligence, be raised and interpreted; to be a student of, and servant to, the universe-spirit; and king of his planet, that as an angelic minister, he may bring it into conscious harmony with the law of that spirit. . . .

As to men's representing women fairly at present, while we hear from men who owe to their wives not only all that is comfortable or graceful, but all that is wise in the arrangement of their lives, the frequent remark, "You cannot reason with a woman," when from those of delicacy, nobleness, and poetic culture, the contemptuous phrase "women and children," and that in no light sally of the hour, but in works intended to give a permanent statement of the best experiences, when not one man, in the million, shall I say? no, not in the hundred million, can rise above the belief that woman was made *for man*, when such traits as these are daily forced upon the attention, can we feel that man will always do justice to the interests of woman? Can we think that he takes a sufficiently discerning and religious view of her office and destiny, *ever* to do her justice, except when prompted by sentiment, accidentally or transiently, that is, for the sentiment will vary according to the relations in which he is placed. The lover, the poet, the artist, are likely to view her nobly. The father and the philosopher have some chance of liberality; the man of the world, the legislator for expediency, none.

Under these circumstances, without attaching importance, in themselves, to the changes demanded by the champions of woman, we hail them as signs of the times. We would have every arbitrary barrier thrown down. We would have every path laid open to woman as freely as to man. Were this done and a slight temporary fermentation allowed to subside, we should see crystallizations more pure and of more various beauty. We believe the divine energy would pervade nature to a degree unknown in the history of former ages, and that no discordant collision, but a ravishing harmony of the spheres would ensue.

---

1. The first quotation is taken from William Shakespeare's *Hamlet* I. ii. 146; the source of the second quotation has never been identified.

Yet, then and only then, will mankind be ripe for this, when inward and outward freedom for woman as much as for man shall be acknowledged as a right, not yielded as a concession. As the friend of the negro assumes that one man cannot by right, hold another in bondage, so should the friend of woman assume that man cannot, by right, lay even well-meant restrictions on woman. If the negro be a soul, if the woman be a soul, appareled in flesh, to one Master only are they accountable. There is but one law for souls. and if there is to be an interpreter of it, he must come not as man, or son of man, but as son of God.

Were thought and feeling once so far elevated that man should esteem himself the brother and friend, but nowise the lord and tutor of woman, were he really bound with her in equal worship, arrangements as to function and employment would be of no consequence. What woman needs is not as a woman to act or rule, but as a nature to grow, as an intellect to discern, as soul to live freely and unimpeded, to unfold such powers as were given her when we left our common home. If fewer talents were given her, yet if allowed the free and full employment of these, so that she may render back to the giver his own with usury she will not complain; nay I dare to say she will bless and rejoice in her earthly birthplace, her earthly lot. Let us consider what obstructions impede this good era, and what signs give reason to hope that it draws near.

I was talking on this subject with Miranda,[2] a woman, who, if any in the world could, might speak without heat and bitterness of the position of her sex. Her father was a man who cherished no sentimental reverence for woman, but a firm belief in the equality of the sexes. She was his eldest child, and came to him at an age when he needed a companion. From the time she could speak and go alone, he addressed her not as a plaything, but as a living mind. Among the few verses he ever wrote was a copy addressed to this child, when the first locks were cut from her head, and the reverence expressed on this occasion for that cherished head, he never belied. It was to him the temple of immortal intellect. He respected his child, however, too much to be an indulgent parent. He called on her for clear judgment, for courage, for honor and fidelity; in short, for such virtues as he knew. In so far as he possessed the keys to the wonders of this universe, he allowed free use of them to her, and by the incentive of a high expectation, he forbade, as far as possible, that she should let the privilege lie idle.

Thus this child was early led to feel herself a child of the spirit. She took her place easily, not only in the world of organized being, but in the world of mind. A dignified sense of self-dependence was given as all her portion, and she found it a sure anchor. Herself securely anchored, her relations with others were established with equal security. She was fortunate in a total absence of those charms which might have drawn to her bewildering flatteries, and in a strong electric nature, which repelled those who did not belong to her, and attracted those who did. With men and women her relations were noble, affectionate without passion, intellectual without coldness. The world was free to her, and she lived freely in it. Outward adversity came, and inward conflict, but that faith and self-respect had early been awakened which must always lead at last, to an outward serenity and an inward peace.

Of Miranda I had always thought as an example, that the restraints upon the sex were insuperable only to those who think them so, or who noisily strive to break them. She had taken a course of her own, and no man stood in her way. Many of her

---

2. Miranda is the name of the learned daughter of Prospero in William Shakespeare's *The Tempest*; her experiences are similar to Fuller's.

acts had been unusual, but excited no uproar. Few helped, but none checked her, and the many men, who knew her mind and her life, showed to her confidence, as to a brother, gentleness as to a sister. And not only refined, but very coarse men approved and aided one in whom they saw resolution and clearness of design. Her mind was often the leading one, always effective.

When I talked with her upon these matters, and had said very much what I have written, she smilingly replied: "and yet we must admit that I have been fortunate, and this should not be. My good father's early trust gave the first bias, and the rest followed of course. It is true that I have had less outward aid, in after years, than most women, but that is of little consequence. Religion was early awakened in my soul, a sense that what the soul is capable to ask it must attain, and that, though I might be aided and instructed by others, I must depend on myself as the only constant friend. This self-dependence, which was honored in me, is deprecated as a fault in most women. They are taught to learn their rule from without, not to unfold it from within.

"This is the fault of man, who is still vain, and wishes to be more important to woman than, by right, he should be."

"Men have not shown this disposition toward you," I said.

"No! because the position I early was enabled to take was one of self-reliance. And were all women as sure of their wants as I was, the result would be the same. But they are so overloaded with precepts by guardians, who think that nothing is so much to be dreaded for a woman as originality of thought or character, that their minds are impeded by doubts till they lose their chance of fair free proportions. The difficulty is to get them to the point from which they shall naturally develop self-respect, and learn self-help.

"Once I thought that men would help to forward this state of things more than I do now. I saw so many of them wretched in the connections they had formed in weakness and vanity. They seemed so glad to esteem women whenever they could.

"'The soft arms of affection,' said one of the most discerning spirits, 'will not suffice for me, unless on them I see the steel bracelets of strength.'

"But early I perceived that men never, in any extreme of despair, wished to be women. On the contrary they were ever ready to taunt one another at any sign of weakness with,

'Art thou not like the women, who'—

"The passage ends various ways, according to the occasion and rhetoric of the speaker. When they admired any woman they were inclined to speak of her as 'above her sex.' Silently I observed this, and feared it argued a rooted skepticism, which for ages had been fastening on the heart, and which only an age of miracles could eradicate. Ever I have been treated with great sincerity; and I look upon it as a signal instance of this, that an intimate friend of the other sex said, in a fervent moment, that I 'deserved in some star to be a man.' He was much surprised when I disclosed my view of my position and hopes, when I declared my faith that the feminine side, the side of love, of beauty, of holiness, was now to have its full chance, and that, if either were better, it was better now to be a woman, for even the slightest achievement of good was furthering an especial work of our time. He smiled incredulous. 'She makes the best she can of it,' thought he. 'Let Jews believe the pride of Jewry, but I am of the better sort, and know better.'

"Another used as highest praise, in speaking of a character in literature, the words 'a manly woman.'

"So in the noble passage of Ben Jonson:[3]

> 'I meant the day-star should not brighter ride,
>   Nor shed like influence from its lucent seat:
> I meant she should be courteous, facile, sweet,
>   Free from that solemn vice of greatness, pride;
> I meant each softest virtue there should meet,
>   Fit in that softer bosom to abide.
> Only a learned and a *manly* soul,
>   I purposed her, that should with even powers,
> The rock, the spindle, and the shears control
>   Of destiny, and spin her own free hours.'"

"Methinks," said I, "you are too fastidious in objecting to this. Jonson in using the word 'manly' only meant to heighten the picture of this, the true, the intelligent fate, with one of the deeper colors."

"And yet," said she, "so invariable is the use of this word where a heroic quality is to be described, and I feel so sure that persistence and courage are the most womanly no less than the most manly qualities, that I would exchange these words for others of a larger sense at the risk of marring the fine tissue of the verse. Read, 'a heavenward and instructed soul,' and I should be satisfied. Let it not be said, wherever there is energy or creative genius, 'She has a masculine mind.'"

This by no means argues a willing want of generosity toward woman. Man is as generous toward her, as he knows how to be.

Wherever she has herself arisen in national or private history, and nobly shone forth in any form of excellence, men have received her, not only willingly, but with triumph. Their encomiums indeed, are always, in some sense, mortifying; they show too much surprise. Can this be you? he cries to the transfigured Cinderella; well I should never have thought it, but I am very glad. We will tell every one that you have "*surpassed your sex.*"

In everyday life the feelings of the many are stained with vanity. Each wishes to be lord in a little world, to be superior at least over one; and he does not feel strong enough to retain a lifelong ascendancy over a strong nature. Only a Theseus could conquer before he wed the Amazonian Queen. Hercules wished rather to rest with Dejanira, and received the poisoned robe, as a fit guerdon.[4] The tale should be interpreted to all those who seek repose with the weak.

But not only is man vain and fond of power, but the same want of development, which thus affects him morally, prevents his intellectually discerning the destiny of woman. The boy wants no woman, but only a girl to play ball with him, and mark his pocket handkerchief.

Thus, in Schiller's Dignity of Woman,[5] beautiful as the poem is, there is no "grave and perfect man," but only a great boy to be softened and restrained by the influence of girls. Poets, the elder brothers of their race, have usually seen farther; but what can you expect of everyday men, if Schiller was not more prophetic as to what women must be? Even with Richter,[6] one foremost thought about a wife was that she

3. Ben Jonson (1572–1637) was an English poet and dramatist; the poem is "On Lucy, Countess of Bedford," one of his epigraphs.
4. King Theseus, legendary Athenian ruler, kidnapped the Amazonian queen Antiope; Hercules's jealous wife, according to legend, sent him a tunic that she thought

contained a love potion but which instead poisoned his flesh.
5. Johann Christoph Friedrich von Schiller (1759–1805) was a German poet and dramatist.
6. Jean Paul Friedrich Richter (1763–1825) was a German writer.

would "cook him something good." But as this is a delicate subject, and we are in constant danger of being accused of slighting what are called "the functions," let me say in behalf of Miranda and myself, that we have high respect for those who cook something good, who create and preserve fair order in houses, and prepare therein the shining raiment for worthy inmates, worthy guests. Only these "functions" must not be a drudgery, or enforced necessity, but a part of life. Let Ulysses drive the beeves home while Penelope there piles up the fragrant loaves; they are both well employed if these be done in thought and love, willingly. But Penelope is no more meant for a baker or weaver solely, than Ulysses for a cattleherd.

The sexes should not only correspond to and appreciate, but prophesy to one another. In individual instances this happens. Two persons love in one another the future good which they aid one another to unfold. This is imperfectly or rarely done in the general life. Man has gone but little way; now he is waiting to see whether woman can keep step with him, but instead of calling out, like a good brother, "you can do it, if you only think so," or impersonally; "any one can do what he tries to do;" he often discourages with schoolboy brag: "Girls can't do that; girls can't play ball." But let anyone defy their taunts, break through and be brave and secure, they rend the air with shouts.

This fluctuation was obvious in a narrative I have lately seen, the story of the life of Countess Emily Plater, the heroine of the last revolution in Poland.[7] The dignity, the purity, the concentrated resolve, the calm, deep enthusiasm, which yet could, when occasion called, sparkle up a holy, an indignant fire, make of this young maiden the figure I want for my frontispiece. Her portrait is to be seen in the book, a gentle shadow of her soul. Short was the career—like the maid of Orleans,[8] she only did enough to verify her credentials, and then passed from a scene on which she was, probably, a premature apparition.

When the young girl joined the army where the report of her exploits had preceded her, she was received in a manner that marks the usual state of feeling. Some of the officers were disappointed at her quiet manners; that she had not the air and tone of a stage heroine. They thought she could not have acted heroically unless in buskins; had no idea that such deeds only showed the habit of her mind. Others talked of the delicacy of her sex, advised her to withdraw from perils and dangers, and had no comprehension of the feelings within her breast that made this impossible. The gentle irony of her reply to these self-constituted tutors (not one of whom showed himself her equal in conduct or reason) is as good as her indignant reproof at a later period to the general, whose perfidy ruined all.

But though, to the mass of these men, she was an embarrassment and a puzzle, the nobler sort viewed her with a tender enthusiasm worthy of her. "Her name," said her biographer, "is known throughout Europe. I paint her character that she may be as widely loved."

With pride, he shows her freedom from all personal affections; that, though tender and gentle in an uncommon degree, there was no room for a private love in her consecrated life. She inspired those who knew her with a simple energy of feeling like her own. We have seen, they felt, a woman worthy the name, capable of all sweet affections, capable of stern virtue.

It is a fact worthy of remark, that all these revolutions in favor of liberty have produced female champions that share the same traits, but Emily alone has found a

---

7. Emily Plater (1806–31) was a Polish nationalist who resisted Russian occupation.

8. A name for Joan of Arc (1412–1431), a saint, martyr, and French national heroine.

biographer. Only a near friend could have performed for her this task, for the flower was reared in feminine seclusion, and the few and simple traits of her history before her appearance in the field could only have been known to the domestic circle. Her biographer has gathered them up with a brotherly devotion.

No! man is not willingly ungenerous. He wants faith and love, because he is not yet himself an elevated being. He cries, with sneering skepticism, Give us a sign. But if the sign appears, his eyes glisten, and he offers not merely approval, but homage.

The severe nation[9] which taught that the happiness of the race was forfeited through the fault of a woman, and showed its thought of what sort of regard man owed her, by making him accuse her on the first question to his God; who gave her to the patriarch as a handmaid, and by the Mosaical law, bound her to allegiance like a self; even they greeted, with solemn rapture, all great and holy women as heroines, prophetesses, judges in Israel; and if they made Eve listen to the serpent, gave Mary as a bride to the Holy Spirit. In other nations it has been the same down to our day. To the woman who could conquer, a triumph was awarded. And not only those whose strength was recommended to the heart by association with goodness and beauty, but those who were bad, if they were steadfast and strong, had their claims allowed. In any age a Semiramis, an Elizabeth of England, a Catharine of Russia, makes her place good, whether in a large or small circle. How has a little wit, a little genius, been celebrated in a woman! What an intellectual triumph was that of the lonely Aspasia, and how heartily acknowledged! She, indeed, met a Pericles. But what annalist, the rudest of men, the most plebeian of husbands, will spare from his page one of the few anecdotes of Roman women—Sappho! Eloisa![10] The names are of threadbare celebrity. Indeed they were not more suitably met in their own time than the Countess Colonel Plater on her first joining the army. They had much to mourn, and their great impulses did not find due scope. But with time enough, space enough, their kindred appear on the scene. Across the ages, forms lean, trying to touch the hem of their retreating robes. The youth here by my side cannot be weary of the fragments from the life of Sappho. He will not believe they are not addressed to himself, or that he to whom they were addressed could be ungrateful. A recluse of high powers devotes himself to understand and explain the thought of Eloisa; he asserts her vast superiority in soul and genius to her master; he curses the fate that cast his lot in another age than hers. He could have understood her: he would have been to her a friend, such as Abelard never could. And this one woman he could have loved and reverenced, and she, alas! lay cold in her grave hundreds of years ago. His sorrow is truly pathetic. These responses that come too late to give joy are as tragic as anything we know, and yet the tears of later ages glitter as they fall on Tasso's prison bars.[11] And we know how elevating to the captive is the security that somewhere an intelligence must answer to this.

The man habitually most narrow towards women will be flushed, as by the worst assault on Christianity, if you say it has made no improvement in her condition. Indeed, those most opposed to new acts in her favor, are jealous of the reputation of those which have been done.

9. The Jewish people.
10. Semiramis was an Assyrian queen who lived in the 9th century B.C.E.; Elizabeth I ruled England from 1558 to 1603; Catherine the Great (1729–96) ruled Russia from 1762 to 1796; Aspasia (c. 470–410 B.C.E.) was a woman intellectual in classical Greece who presided over a circle of statesmen, including Pericles (495–429 B.C.E.);

Sappho was a Greek poet from Lesbos who lived in the 7th century B.C.E.; and Eloisa is another name for Heloise (c. 1098–1164), a French abbess renowned for her letters to her teacher, Peter Abelard (1079–1142).
11. Torquato Tasso (1544–95) was an Italian epic poet imprisoned for offending his patron, and the subject of a work by Goethe that Fuller translated.

We will not speak of the enthusiasm excited by actresses, improvisatrici, female singers, for here mingles the charm of beauty and grace; but female authors, even learned women, if not insufferably ugly and slovenly, from the Italian professor's daughter, who taught behind the curtain, down to Mrs. Carter and Madame Dacier,[12] are sure of an admiring audience, and what is far better, chance to use what they have learned, and to learn more, if they can once get a platform on which to stand.

But how to get this platform, or how to make it of reasonably easy access is the difficulty. Plants of great vigor will almost always struggle into blossom, despite impediments. But there should be encouragement, and a free genial atmosphere for those of more timid sort, fair play for each in its own kind. Some are like the little, delicate flowers which love to hide in the dripping mosses, by the sides of mountain torrents, or in the shade of tall trees. But others require an open field, a rich and loosened soil, or they never show their proper hues.

It may be said that man does not have his fair play either; his energies are repressed and distorted by the interposition of artificial obstacles. Aye, but he himself has put them there; they have grown out of his own imperfections. If there *is* a misfortune in woman's lot, it is in obstacles being interposed by men, which do *not* mark her state; and, if they express her past ignorance, do not her present needs. As every man is of woman born, she has slow but sure means of redress, yet the sooner a general justness of thought makes smooth the path, the better.

Man is of woman born, and her face bends over him in infancy with an expression he can never quite forget. Eminent men have delighted to pay tribute to this image, and it is a hackneyed observation, that most men of genius boast some remarkable development in the mother. The rudest tar brushes off a tear with his coat sleeve at the hallowed name. The other day, I met a decrepit old man of seventy, on a journey, who challenged the stage company to guess where he was going. They guessed aright, "To see your mother." "Yes," said he, "she is ninety-two, but has good eyesight still, they say. I have not seen her these forty years, and I thought I could not die in peace without." I should have liked his picture painted as a companion piece to that of a boisterous little boy, whom I saw attempt to declaim at a school exhibition—

> "O that those lips had language. Life has passed
> With me but roughly since I heard thee last."

He got but very little way before sudden tears shamed him from the stage.

Some gleams of the same expression which shone down upon his infancy, angelically pure and benign, visit man again with hopes of pure love, of a holy marriage. Or, if not before, in the eyes of the mother of his child they again are seen, and dim fancies pass before his mind, that woman may not have been born for him alone, but have come from heaven, a commissioned soul, a messenger of truth and love; that she can only make for him a home in which he may lawfully repose, in so far as she is

> "True to the kindred points of Heaven and home."

In gleams, in dim fancies, this thought visits the mind of common men. It is soon obscured by the mists of sensuality, the dust of routine, and he thinks it was only some meteor, or ignis fatuus that shone. But, as a Rosicrucian lamp,[13] it burns unwearied,

---

12. Anna Leferre Dacier (1647–1720) was a French scholar and translator of classical literature; Elizabeth Carter (1717–1806) was an English poet and translator.
13. An ignis fatuus is a phosphorescent light that hovers over swampy land at night; a Rosicrucian lamp is a reference to an international fraternity of religious mystics founded in the fifteenth century and active during Fuller's time.

though condemned to the solitude of tombs; and to its permanent life, as to every truth, each age has in some form borne witness. For the truths, which visit the minds of careless men only in fitful gleams, shine with radiant clearness into those of the poet, the priest, and the artist.

Whatever may have been the domestic manners of the ancients, the idea of woman was nobly manifested in their mythologies and poems, where she appears as Sita in the Ramayana, a form of tender purity, as the Egyptian Isis, of divine wisdom never yet surpassed. In Egypt, too, the Sphynx, walking the earth with lion tread, looked out upon its marvels in the calm, inscrutable beauty of a virgin's face, and the Greek could only add wings to the great emblem. In Greece, Ceres, and Proserpine, significantly termed "the great goddesses," were seen seated, side by side. They need-ed not to rise for any worshipper or any change; they were prepared for all things, as those initiated to their mysteries knew. More obvious is the meaning of these three forms, the Diana, Minerva, and Vesta. Unlike in the expression of their beauty, but alike in this—that each was self-sufficing. Other forms were only accessories and illustrations, none the complement to one like these. Another might, indeed, be the companion, and the Apollo and Diana set off one another's beauty. Of the Vesta, it is to be observed, that not only deep-eyed, deep-discerning Greece, but ruder Rome, who represents the only form of good man (the always busy warrior), that could be indifferent to woman, confided the permanence of its glory to a tutelary goddess, and her wisest legislator spoke of meditation as a nymph.

Perhaps in Rome the neglect of woman was a reaction on the manners of Etruria, where the priestess Queen, warrior Queen, would seem to have been so usual a character.

An instance of the noble Roman marriage, where the stern and calm nobleness of the nation was common to both, we see in the historic page through the little that is told us of Brutus and Portia. Shakespeare has seized on the relation in its native linea-ments, harmonizing the particular with the universal; and, while it is conjugal love, and no other, making it unlike the same relation, as seen in Cymbeline, or Othello, even as one star differeth from another in glory.

> "By that great vow
> Which did incorporate and make us one,
> Unfold to me, yourself, your half,
> Why you are heavy.   * * *
>   Dwell I but in the suburbs
> Of your good pleasure? If it be no more,
> Portia is Brutus' harlot, not his wife."

Mark the sad majesty of his tone in answer. Who would not have lent a life-long credence to that voice of honor?

> "You are my true and honorable wife,
> As dear to me as are the ruddy drops
> That visit this sad heart."

It is the same voice that tells the moral of his life in the last words—

> "Countrymen,
> My heart doth joy, that yet in all my life,
> I found no man but he was true to me."

It was not wonderful that it should be so.

Shakespeare, however, was not content to let Portia rest her plea for confidence on the essential nature of the marriage bond;

> "I grant I am a woman; but withal,
> A woman that lord Brutus took to wife.
> I grant that I am a woman; with withal,
> A woman well reputed—Cato's daughter.
> Think you I am *no stronger than my sex,*
> Being so fathered and so husbanded?"

And afterwards in the very scene where Brutus is suffering under that "insupportable and touching loss," the death of his wife, Cassius pleads—

> "Have you not love enough to bear with me,
> When that rash humor which my mother gave me
> Makes me forgetful?
> *Brutus.*—Yes, Cassius; and henceforth,
> When you are over-earnest with your Brutus,
> He'll think your mother chides and leave you so."[14]

As indeed it was a frequent belief among the ancients, as with our Indians, that the *body* was inherited from the mother, the *soul* from the father. As in that noble passage of Ovid, already quoted, where Jupiter, as his divine synod are looking down on the funeral pyre of Hercules, thus triumphs—

> Nic nisi *maternâ* Vulcanum parte potentem.
> Sentiet. Aeternum est, à me quod traxit, et expers
> At que immune necis, nullaque domabile flamma
> Idque ego defunctum terrâ coelestibus oris
> Accipiam, cunctisque meum laetabile factum
> Dis fore confido.
> "The part alone of gross *maternal* frame
> Fire shall devour, while that from me he drew
> Shall live immortal and its force renew;
> That, when he's dead, I'll raise to realms above;
> Let all the powers the righteous act approve."[15]

It is indeed a god speaking of his union with an earthly woman, but it expresses the common Roman thought as to marriage, the same which permitted a man to lend his wife to a friend, as if she were a chattel.

> "She dwelt but in the suburbs of his good pleasure."

Yet the same city as I have said leaned on the worship of Vesta, the Preserver, and in later times was devoted to that of Isis. In Sparta, thought, in this respect as in all others, was expressed in the characters of real life, and the women of Sparta were as much Spartans as the men. The citoyen, citoyenne of France was here actualized. Was not the calm equality they enjoyed as honorable as the devotion of chivalry? They intelligently shared the ideal life of their nation.

---

14. These passages are taken from William Shakespeare's *Julius Caesar.*

15. See *The Metamorphoses* by Ovid (43 B.C.E.–18 C.E.), a Roman poet.

Like the men they felt

> "Honor gone, all's gone,
> Better never have been born."

They were the true friends of men. The Spartan, surely, would not think that he received only his body from his mother. The sage, had he lived in that community, could not have thought the souls of "vain and foppish men will be degraded after death, to the forms of women, and, if they do not there make great efforts to retrieve themselves, will become birds."

(By the way it is very expressive of the hard intellectuality of the merely *mannish* mind, to speak thus of birds, chosen always by the *feminine* poet as the symbols of his fairest thoughts.)

We are told of the Greek nations in general, that woman occupied there an infinitely lower place than man. It is difficult to believe this when we see such range and dignity of thought on the subject in the mythologies, and find the poets producing such ideals as Cassandra, Iphiginia, Antigone, Macaria,[16] where Sibylline priestesses told the oracle of the highest god, and he could not be content to reign with a court of fewer than nine muses. Even victory wore a female form.

But whatever were the facts of daily life, I cannot complain of the age and nation, which represents its thought by such a symbol as I see before me at this moment. It is a zodiac of the busts of gods and goddesses, arranged in pairs. The circle breathes the music of a heavenly order. Male and female heads are distinct in expression, but equal in beauty, strength and calmness. Each male head is that of a brother and a king—each female of a sister and a queen. Could the thought, thus expressed, be lived out, there would be nothing more to be desired. There would be unison in variety, congeniality in difference.   *1845*

Emily Dickinson
1830–1886

"If I read a book, and it makes my whole body so cold no fire can ever warm me, I know *that* is poetry. If I feel physically as if the top of my head were taken off, I know *that* is poetry. These are the only ways I know it. Is there any other way?" In this statement EMILY DICKINSON described her visceral poetics to a valued correspondent, Thomas Wentworth Higginson, and wondered if he shared her sense of wonder. Born in Amherst, Massachusetts, Dickinson spent most of her life in the home of her parents, Edward Dickinson, a highly respected lawyer and U.S. congressman, and Emily Norcross Dickinson, "the Gentlest Mother." The Dickinsons were
a genteel family who treasured books and appreciated art, and although Dickinson and her sister, Lavinia, had considerable domestic responsibility, there was also time to read, reflect, and write. Dickinson was educated at Amherst Academy and Mt. Holyoke Female Seminary

16. These strong women appear in *The Odyssey*, by the epic poet Homer (fl. 850? B.C.E.), and in plays by Aeschylus (525–456 B.C.E.) and Sophocles (496?–406 B.C.E.), classical Greek tragedians.

and by all accounts enjoyed school. As a young woman she was active socially but showed no interest in marriage; "God keep me from what they call *households*," she wrote in an 1850 letter. During this period she enjoyed a close relationship with her brother, Austin, and was especially intimate with his wife, Susan Gilbert. In her youth Dickinson rejected orthodox Christianity, although she remained fascinated by images of immortality, heaven, hell, and eternity. After 1855 she rarely left home except for extended stays in Boston, where she received eye care during 1864 and 1865. Yet throughout her life she maintained a lively interest in local and national events and a voluminous correspondence with friends. As ADRIENNE RICH has observed, Dickinson "chose her seclusion, knowing she was exceptional and knowing what she needed."

What this extraordinary poet did *not* need was to expose her poems to the world. During her lifetime she published only eleven of her 1,775 poems, most of them in local newspapers; one poem, "Success is counted sweetest," appeared in an anthology entitled *A Masque of Poets* (1878), edited by her friend Helen Hunt Jackson. More than anyone else Jackson recognized Dickinson's genius: "you are a great poet—and it is wrong to the day you live in, that you will not sing aloud." Higginson, in contrast, the man most often credited with having been her mentor, found the poet's gait "spasmodic" and called her "partially cracked." When asked of her poetic influences, Dickinson named Shakespeare, who "told her knowledge"; ELIZABETH BARRETT BROWNING, by whom she was "enchanted"; Robert Browning, whose dramatic monologues she treasured; and John Keats, whose sense of being "half in love with easeful Death" she sometimes shared. Whitman, she said she had been told, was "disgraceful"; Emerson was inspiring in his nonconformity. Furthermore, Dickinson appreciated her women contemporaries, including the "female songbird" LYDIA SIGOURNEY, from whose verse she nonetheless wished to distinguish her own.

Finally, however, Dickinson was indebted to no one but herself. As a poet of unprecedented imaginative boldness, she adapted the simple rhythms of traditional hymns to suit her purposes, experimenting with prosody, grammar, syntax, punctuation, and capital letters; she employed either off rhyme or no rhyme in much of her verse. She left behind poems in manuscript copies, large numbers of which were neatly bound and meticulously revised. Thomas H. Johnson, who compiled a three-volume variorum edition of Dickinson's poetry in 1955, claims as the poet's most compelling quality her "tragic vision," and indeed her work reveals acute emotional intensity. Particularly difficult was the period from 1861 to 1863, when Dickinson acknowledged that "I had a terror since September—I could tell to none—and I sing as the Boy does by the Burying Ground—because I am afraid." Although many critics have interpreted this "terror" as disappointment in love, more convincing is the viewpoint of Elizabeth Phillips, who argues that the poet was afraid of going blind.

Dickinson composed almost a poem a day in 1862, the year in which she first wrote to Higginson to ask if her poems "breathed" and in which several Amherst friends died in the Civil War. Yet despite her emphasis on pain, dread, despair, and death, Dickinson's vision is by no means exclusively tragic. She can be sardonic about such subjects as marriage ("Title divine—is mine! / The Wife—without the Sign!") and class pretension ("What Soft—Cherubic Creatures— / These Gentlewomen are—"). Moreover, as Phillips notes, she often speaks in personae, adopting the voice of a dying child, a wry daydreamer, a literary character—Jane Eyre, Rochester, Maggie Tulliver, Desdemona. The Dickinson of her poetry is independent in spirit, determined to select "Her Own Society," and relentless in her spiritual quest, enraptured by "Awe" and assured of "Triumph." While it is true that she wrote three ambiguous letters in 1858 and 1861 to an unidentified "master," perhaps a man she loved, it is also true that late in life she had an ardent suitor, Judge Otis Lord, to whom she was devoted but whose proposal of marriage she rejected. "My business is Circumference," she declared, claiming a room of her own. The poems reprinted here depict psychic extremity, explore creative identity, or affirm the poet's autonomy. In several of them, including "Publication—is the Auction / Of the Mind of Man—," she vehemently refuses any public presentation of her art. At home in her poetry, Dickinson seeks no other venue.

Poem 258

There's a certain Slant of light,
Winter Afternoons–
That oppresses, like the Heft
Of Cathedral Tunes–

5 Heavenly Hurt, it gives us–
We can find no scar,
But internal difference,
Where the Meanings, are–

None may teach it–Any–
10 'Tis the Seal Despair–
An imperial affliction
Sent us of the Air–

When it comes, the Landscape listens–
Shadows–hold their breath–
15 When it goes, 'tis like the Distance
On the look of Death–

1861/1890

Poem 280

I felt a Funeral, in my Brain,
And Mourners to and fro
Kept treading–treading–till it seemed
That Sense was breaking through–

5 And when they all were seated,
A Service, like a Drum–
Kept beating–beating–till I thought
My Mind was going numb–

And then I heard them lift a Box
10 And creak across my Soul
With those same Boots of Lead, again,
Then Space–began to toll,

As all the Heavens were a Bell,
And Being, but an Ear,
15 And I, and Silence, some strange Race
Wrecked, solitary, here–

And then a Plank in Reason, broke,
And I dropped down, and down–

And hit a World, at every plunge,
20   And Finished knowing–then–

1861/1896

⊰ Poem 303 ⊱

The Soul selects her own Society–
Then–shuts the Door–
to her divine Majority–
Present no more–

5   Unmoved–she notes the Chariots–pausing–
At her low Gate–
Unmoved–an Emperor be kneeling
Upon her Mat–

I've known her–from an ample nation–
10   Choose One–
Then–close the Valves of her attention–
Like Stone–

1862/1890

⊰ Poem 341 ⊱

After great pain, a formal feeling comes–
The Nerves sit ceremonious, like Tombs–
The stiff Heart questions was it He, that bore,
And Yesterday, or Centuries before?

5   The Feet, mechanical, go round–
Of Ground, or Air, or Ought–
A Wooden way
Regardless grown,
A Quartz contentment, like a stone–

10   This is the Hour of Lead–
Remembered, if outlived,
As Freezing persons, recollect the Snow–
First–Chill–then Stupor–then the letting go–

1862/1929

⊰ Poem 365 ⊱

Dare you see a Soul *at the White Heat?*
Then crouch within the door–
Red–is the Fire's common tint–
But when the vivid Ore
5   Has vanquished Flame's conditions,
It quivers from the Forge

Without a color, but the light
Of unanointed Blaze.
Least Village has its Blacksmith
10   Whose Anvil's even ring
Stands symbol for the finer Forge
That soundless tugs–within–
Refining these impatient Ores
With Hammer, and with Blaze
15   Until the Designated Light
Repudiate the Forge–

1862/1891

⊰ Poem 508 ⊱

I'm ceded–I've stopped being Theirs–
The name They dropped upon my face
With water, in the country church
Is finished using, now,
5   And They can put it with my Dolls,
My childhood, and the string of spools,
I've finished threading–too–

Baptized, before, without the choice,
But this time, consciously, of Grace–
10   Unto supremest name–
Called to my Full–The Crescent dropped–
Existence's whole Arc, filled up,
With one small Diadem.

My second Rank–too small the first–
15   Crowned–Crowing–on my Father's breast–
A half unconscious Queen–
But this time–Adequate–Erect,
With Will to choose, or to reject,
And I choose, just a Crown–

1862/1890

⊰ Poem 512 ⊱

The Soul has Bandaged moments–
When too appalled to stir–
She feels some ghastly Fright come up
And stop to look at her–

5   Salute her–with long fingers–
Caress her freezing hair–
Sip, Goblin, from the very lips
The Lover–hovered–o'er–
Unworthy, that a thought so mean
10   Accost a Theme–so–fair–

The soul has moments of Escape–
When bursting all the doors–
She dances like a Bomb, abroad,
And swings upon the Hours,

15 As do the Bee–delirious borne–
Long Dungeoned from his Rose–
Touch Liberty–then know no more,
But Noon, and Paradise–

The Soul's retaken moments–
20 When, Felon led along,
With shackles on the plumed feet,
And staples, in the Song,

The Horror welcomes her, again,
These, are not brayed of Tongue–

1862/1945

⊰ Poem 709 ⊱

Publication–is the Auction
Of the Mind of Man–
Poverty–be justifying
For so foul a thing

5 Possibly–but We–would rather
From Our Garret go
White–Unto the White Creator–
Than invest–Our Snow–

Thought belong to Him who gave it–
10 Then–to Him Who bear
Its Corporeal illustration–Sell
The Royal Air–

In the Parcel–Be the Merchant
Of the Heavenly Grace–
15 But reduce no Human Spirit
To Disgrace of Price–

1863/1929

⊰ Poem 754 ⊱

My Life had stood–a Loaded Gun–
In Corners–till a Day
The Owner passed–identified–
And carried Me away–

5 And now We roam in Sovereign Woods–
And now We hunt the Doe–
And every time I speak for Him–
The Mountains straight reply–

And do I smile, such cordial light
10   Upon the Valley glow–
It is as a Vesuvian face
Had let its pleasure through–

And when at Night–Our good Day done–
I guard My Master's Head–
15   'Tis better than the Eider-Duck's[1]
Deep Pillow–to have shared–

To foe of His–I'm deadly foe–
None stir the second time–
On whom I lay a Yellow Eye–
20   Or an emphatic Thumb–

Though I than He–may longer live
He longer must–than I–
For I have but the power to kill,
Without–the power to die–

1863/1929

⊰ Poem 1072 ⊱

Title divine–is mine!
The Wife–without the Sign!
Acute Degree–conferred on me–
Empress of Calvary!
5   Royal–all but the Crown!
Betrothed–without the swoon
God sends us Women–
When you–hold–Garnet to Garnet–
Gold–to Gold–
10   Born–Bridalled–Shrouded–
In a Day–
Tri Victory
"My Husband"–women say–
Stroking the Melody–
15   Is *this*–the way?

1862/1924

Alice Dunbar-Nelson
1875–1935

Like many women who participated in the Harlem Renaissance—the flowering of African-American literature and culture that occurred in the 1920s—ALICE DUNBAR-NELSON is not as well remembered as her husband, the poet Paul Laurence Dunbar, and his most famous associ-

---

1. The duck from which eiderdown comes.

ates: Langston Hughes, Countee Cullen, and James Weldon Johnson. Yet throughout the decade a small group of women gathered regularly to share their writing at the home of Georgia Douglas Johnson, who provided the Washington locale for the Harlem Renaissance; among these women were Anne Spencer, Angelina Weld Grimké, Clarissa Scott Delaney, and Alice Dunbar-Nelson. A committed political activist, Dunbar-Nelson also wrote poems and stories, taught secondary school, and worked as a journalist.

She was born Alice Ruth Moore in New Orleans, Louisiana, to a sailor and a seamstress who had once been a slave, yet she belonged to her city's black elite, in part because of her light skin color. "Complexion did, in a manner of speaking, determine one's social status," she wrote in one of her diaries. After high school she attended a two-year teachers' training program at what is now Dillard University, and in 1895 her collection of twelve poems and seventeen sketches, *Violets and Other Tales*, was published privately. When one of the poems from that volume appeared in *Monthly Review*, a Boston literary periodical, it attracted the attention of Paul Laurence Dunbar, then at the height of his career; the two writers began a correspondence, and in 1898 they married. The marriage was not happy, although it did provide Dunbar-Nelson with the space and time to write; her second collection of stories, *The Goodness of St. Rocque*, appeared in 1899. In 1902 the couple separated, four years before Dunbar's death from tuberculosis, and Dunbar-Nelson moved to Wilmington, Delaware, where for eighteen years she served as head of the English department at Howard High School. She also gave frequent public speeches on behalf of civil rights and women's suffrage. In 1916 she married Robert John Nelson, the publisher of a civil rights newspaper, the *Washington Advocate*, and began to write regular columns on race relations for the *Washington Eagle*. Dunbar-Nelson was fired from her teaching position in 1920 for violating her school's ban on political activity, and in 1921 she became the first black woman on the state Republican Committee of Delaware, at one point unsuccessfully petitioning President Warren G. Harding to free sixty-one African-American soldiers being held in prison for allegedly leading a race riot. She switched her affiliation to the Democratic Party in 1922 because of its strong stand against lynching, and she continued to work tirelessly for political candidates who supported the causes she espoused. Among these was world peace; from 1928 to 1931 Dunbar-Nelson served as executive secretary of the American Interracial Peace Committee, an organization sponsored by the American Friends Service Committee.

Dunbar-Nelson edited two anthologies of African-American literature: *Masterpieces of Negro Eloquence* (1914) and *The Dunbar Speaker and Entertainer* (1920). Throughout the 1920s and 1930s she kept diaries that recorded her literary and political activities as well as her intimacies with women; however, as the scholar Mary Helen Washington has noted, the diarist's revelations regarding her love for women were guarded. Unpublished in her lifetime, *Give Us Each Day: The Diary of Alice Dunbar-Nelson* (1984), edited by Gloria T. Hull, sheds light on this writer's life and work. Hull has also edited, in two volumes, *The Works of Alice Dunbar-Nelson* (1988), a collection that fills an important gap in women's literary history.

The poems included here reveal Dunbar-Nelson's probing examination of gender and class differences, both of which she addresses more often in her poetry than issues of race. "I Sit and Sew," written during World War I, reveals the speaker's frustration at "the panoply of war, the martial tread of men," while "The Proletariat Speaks" juxtaposes a working-class speaker's desire for "beautiful things" with the grim realities of her life.

⊰ I Sit and Sew ⊱

I sit and sew—a useless task it seems,
My hands grown tired, my head weighed down with dreams—

The panoply of war, the martial tread of men,
Grim-faced, stern-eyed, gazing beyond the ken
5   Of lesser souls, whose eyes have not seen Death,
Nor learned to hold their lives but as a breath—
But—I must sit and sew.

I sit and sew—my heart aches with desire—
That pageant terrible, that fiercely pouring fire
10   On wasted fields, and writhing grotesque things
Once men. My soul in pity flings
Appealing cries, yearning only to go
There in that holocaust of hell, those fields of woe—
But—I must sit and sew.

15   The little useless seam, the idle patch;
Why dream I here beneath my homely thatch,
When there they lie in sodden mud and rain,
Pitifully calling me, the quick ones and the slain?
You need me, Christ! It is no roseate dream
20   That beckons me—this pretty futile seam,
It stifles me—God, must I sit and sew?

1920

⊰ The Proletariat Speaks ⊱

I love beautiful things:
Great trees, bending green winged branches to a velvet lawn,
Fountains sparkling in white marble basins,
Cool fragrance of lilacs and roses and honeysuckle.
5   Or exotic blooms, filling the air with heart-contracting odors;
Spacious rooms, cool and gracious with statues and books,
Carven seats and tapestries, and old masters
Whose patina shows the wealth of centuries.

And so I work
10   In a dusty office, whose griméd windows
Look out in an alley of unbelievable squalor,
Where mangy cats, in their degradation, spurn
Swarming bits of meat and bread;
Where odors, vile and breath taking, rise in fetid waves
15   Filling my nostrils, scorching my humid, bitter cheeks.

I love beautiful things:
Carven tables laid with lily-hued linen
And fragile china and sparkling iridescent glass;
Pale silver, etched with heraldies,
20   Where tender bits of regal dainties tempt,
And soft-stepped service anticipates the unspoken wish.

And so I eat
In the food-laden air of a greasy kitchen,

At an oil-clothed table:
25   Plate piled high with food that turns my head away,
Lest a squeamish stomach reject too soon
The lumpy gobs it never needed.
Or in a smoky cafeteria, balancing a slippery tray
To a table crowded with elbows
30   Which lately the bus boy wiped with a grimy rag.

I love beautiful things:
Soft linen sheets and silken coverlet,
Sweet coolth of chamber opened wide to fragrant breeze;
Rose shaded lamps and golden atomizers,
35   Spraying Parisian fragrance over my relaxed limbs,
Fresh from a white marble bath, and sweet cool spray.

And so I sleep
In a hot hall-room whose half opened window,
Unscreened, refuses to budge another inch;
40   Admits no air, only insects, and hot choking gasps,
That make me writhe, nun-like, in sack-cloth sheets and lumps of straw.
And then I rise
To fight my way to a dubious tub,
Whose tiny, tepid stream threatens to make me late;
45   And hurrying out, dab my unrefreshed face
With bits of toiletry from the ten cent store.

1929

Zitkala-Sä (Gertrude Simmons Bonnin)
1876–1938

A Sioux Indian born on the Yankton reservation in South Dakota, ZITKALA-SÄ chose her Lakota name, "Red Bird," following a quarrel with her sister-in-law, who accused Zitkala-Sä of having dishonored her family by leaving the reservation to seek higher education. Although she remained dedicated to the Pan-Indian movement throughout her life as a writer and an activist, the accusation and her response to it reveal much about this Indian woman's struggle to balance identity and difference.

The daughter of a Lakota mother, Tate I Yonin Win (Reaches for the Wind), and a white father named Felker, Zitkala-Sä was given the surname of her mother's second hus-band, Simmons, and called Gertrude during the eight years that she lived at Yankton. Although she described her childhood on the reservation as idyllic in "Impressions of an Indian Childhood," published in the *Atlantic Monthly* in 1900, she praised her mother's decision to send her to White's Manual Labor Institute, a Quaker school for Indian chil-dren in Wabash, Indiana, where Gertrude remained from the ages of eight to eleven. The four years after she returned to the reservation were conflicted, for the girl had absorbed nonnative ways and was ambivalent toward her mother's traditional home. At fifteen she left to study at the Santee Normal Training School in Nebraska for a year; she then returned to White's to complete her education. During her two years at Earlham College, from 1895 to 1897, Zitkala-Sä became an accomplished violinist as well as an acclaimed orator; she studied briefly at the New England Conservatory of Music and won second prize in a statewide oratory contest. Upon leaving Earlham, she accepted a teaching post at the Carlisle Indian School and began her career as a writer.

Zitkala-Sä's earliest publications were autobiographical sketches and poems that appeared in various Indian magazines. Later essays appeared in the *Atlantic Monthly,* including "The School Days of an Indian Girl" and "An Indian Teacher Among Indians," pieces fraught with tension between her anger at the government's maltreatment of Indians and her desire to promote crosscultural understanding. Zitkala-Sä published two short stories in *Harper's Magazine* in 1901, "The True Path" and "The Soft-Hearted Sioux," but it was the publication that same year of *Old Indian Legends* that ensured her literary reputation. During visits to her mother on the Yankton reservation, she spent hours gathering different versions of the *ohunkankans,* or fictional tales, that she had loved during childhood, driven by a mission "to do justice to the abandoned material around me." In writing these tales she drew upon a strong Sioux oral tradition. She published a second collection of tribal tales, *American Indian Stories,* in 1921.

Zitkala-Sä married Raymond T. Bonnin, also a Sioux, in 1921 and shifted her focus from writing to activism. For the next fourteen years the couple lived on the Uintah and Ouray reservation in Utah, where she gave birth to a son, Raymond, whose Indian name was Ohiya, "The Winner." In Utah she worked with Indian women, organizing literacy and lunch programs, sewing classes, and a children's band. In 1913 Zitkala-Sä collaborated with the composer William Hanson on "Sun Dance," an American Indian opera performed first for Indians in Utah and, years later, by the New York Light Opera Guild as part of its 1937 season. When she was elected secretary of the Society of the American Indian (SAI), an organization with which she had had connections since its founding in 1911, Zitkala-Sä and her family moved to Washington, DC, where she became a spokesperson for the Pan-Indian movement. SAI took as its mission helping Indians to challenge legal inequities, and she lectured and campaigned on behalf of fair settlement of land disputes, the hiring of more Indians in the Bureau of Indian Affairs (BIA), and the need for Indian citizenship. For two years she edited SAI's publication, *American Indian Magazine,* and thereby gained a wider audience for her political views. While editing *AIM* she published several of her own polemical poems, including "The Red Man's America," a revision of the national anthem from the Native American perspective. When SAI dissolved in 1920, Zitkala-Sä began working with the General Federation of Women's Clubs. She argued successfully for the implementation of an Indian Welfare Committee and lobbied President Hoover to appoint Indian activists to the BIA. Her political career reached its zenith with the founding of the National Council of American Indians in 1926; she served as its president until her death in 1938. Begun to ensure the "personal and property rights" of Indians, the Council also acted as an information service for Indian citizens.

In her preface to *Old Indian Legends,* Zitkala-Sä presents her goal for the collection with characteristic irony: "I have tried to transplant the native spirit of these tales—root and all—into the English language, since America in the last few centuries has acquired a second tongue." She goes on to claim as her audience all the children of the United States, for these stories "belong quite as much to the blue-eyed little patriot as to the black-haired aborigine." The story reprinted here, "The Tree-Bound," is typical of the collection in its presentation of the trickster Iktomi, the snare weaver, a figure both clever and foolish. In *Old Indian Legends,* Zitkala-Sä blends humor and dramatic appeal to tell with eloquence the stories of her Indian childhood.

ᴥ The Tree-Bound ᴥ

It was a clear summer day. The blue, blue sky dropped low over the edge of the green level land. A large yellow sun hung directly overhead.

The singing of birds filled the summer space between earth and sky with sweet music. Again and again sang a yellow-breasted birdie—"Koda Ni Dakota!" He insisted upon it. "Koda Ni Dakota!" which was "Friend, you're a Dakota! Friend, you're a Dakota!" Perchance the birdie meant the avenger with the magic arrow, for there across the plain he strode. He was handsome in his paint and feathers, proud with his great buckskin quiver on his back and a long bow in his hand. Afar to an eastern camp of cone-shaped teepees he was going. There over the Indian village hovered a large red eagle threatening the safety of the people. Every morning rose this terrible red bird out of a high chalk bluff and spreading out his gigantic wings soared slowly over the round camp ground. Then it was that the people, terror-stricken, ran screaming into their lodges. Covering their heads with their blankets, they sat trembling with fear. No one dared to venture out till the red eagle had disappeared beyond the west, where meet the blue and green.

In vain tried the chieftain of the tribe to find among his warriors a powerful marksman who could send a death arrow to the man-hungry bird. At last to urge his men to their utmost skill he bade his crier proclaim a new reward.

Of the chieftain's two beautiful daughters he would have his choice who brought the dreaded red eagle with an arrow in its breast.

Upon hearing these words, the men of the village, both young and old, both heroes and cowards, trimmed new arrows for the contest. At gray dawn there stood indistinct under the shadow of the bluff many human figures; silent as ghosts and wrapped in robes girdled tight about their waists, they waited with chosen bow and arrow.

Some cunning old warriors stayed not with the group. They crouched low upon the open ground. But all eyes alike were fixed upon the top of the high bluff. Breathless they watched for the soaring of the red eagle.

From within the dwellings many eyes peeped through the small holes in the front lapels of the teepee. With shaking knees and hard-set teeth, the women peered out upon the Dakota men prowling about with bows and arrows.

At length when the morning sun also peeped over the eastern horizon at the armed Dakotas, the red eagle walked out upon the edge of the cliff. Pluming his gorgeous feathers, he ruffled his neck and flapped his strong wings together. Then he dived into the air. Slowly he winged his way over the round camp ground; over the men with their strong bows and arrows! In an instant the long bows were bent. Strong straight arrows with red feathered tips sped upward to the blue sky. Ah! slowly moved those indifferent wings, untouched by the poison-beaked arrows. Off to the west beyond the reach of arrow, beyond the reach of eye, the red eagle flew away.

A sudden clamor of high-pitched voices broke the deadly stillness of the dawn. The women talked excitedly about the invulnerable red of the eagle's feathers, while the would-be heroes sulked within their wigwams. "Hĕ-hĕ-hĕ!" groaned the chieftain.

On the evening of the same day sat a group of hunters around a bright burning fire. They were talking of a strange young man whom they spied while out upon a hunt for deer beyond the bluffs. They saw the stranger taking aim. Following the point of his arrow with their eyes, they beheld a herd of buffalo. The arrow sprang from the bow! It darted into the skull of the foremost buffalo. But unlike other arrows it pierced through the head of the creature and spinning in the air lit into the next buffalo head. One by one the buffalo fell upon the sweet grass they were grazing. With straight quivering limbs they lay on their sides. The young man stood calmly by, counting on his fingers the buffalo as they dropped dead to the ground. When the last one fell, he ran thither and picking up his magic arrow wiped it carefully on the soft grass. He slipped it into his long fringed quiver.

"He is going to make a feast for some hungry tribe of men or beasts!" cried the hunters among themselves as they hastened away.

They were afraid of the stranger with the sacred arrow. When the hunter's tale of the stranger's arrow reached the ears of the chieftain, his face brightened with a smile. He sent forth fleet horsemen, to learn of him his birth, his name, and his deeds.

"If he is the avenger with the magic arrow, sprung up from the earth out of a clot of buffalo blood, bid him come hither. Let him kill the red eagle with his magic arrow. Let him win for himself one of my beautiful daughters," he had said to his messengers, for the old story of the badger's man-son was known all over the level lands.

After four days and nights the braves returned. "He is coming," they said. "We have seen him. He is straight and tall; handsome in face, with large black eyes. He paints his round cheeks with bright red, and wears the penciled lines of red over his temples like our men of honored rank. He carries on his back a long fringed quiver in which he keeps his magic arrow. His bow is long and strong. He is coming now to kill the big red eagle." All around the camp ground from mouth to ear passed those words of the returned messengers.

Now it chanced that immortal Iktomi, fully recovered from the brown burnt spots, overheard the people talking. At once he was filled with a new desire. "If only I had the magic arrow, I would kill the red eagle and win the chieftain's daughter for a wife," said he in his heart.

Back to his lonely wigwam he hastened. Beneath the tree in front of his teepee he sat upon the ground with chin between his drawn-up knees. His keen eyes scanned the wide plain. He was watching for the avenger.

"'He is coming!' said the people," muttered old Iktomi. All of a sudden he raised an open palm to his brow and peered afar into the west. The summer sun hung bright in the middle of a cloudless sky. There across the green prairie was a man walking bareheaded toward the east.

"Ha! ha! 'tis he! the man with the magic arrow!" laughed Iktomi. And when the bird with the yellow breast sang loud again—"Koda Ni Dakota! Friend, you're a Dakota!" Iktomi put his hand over his mouth as he threw his head far backward, laughing at both the bird and man.

"He is your friend, but his arrow will kill one of your kind! He is a Dakota, but soon he'll grow into the bark on this tree! Ha! ha! ha!" he laughed again.

The young avenger walked with swaying strides nearer and nearer toward the lonely wigwam and tree. Iktomi heard the swish! swish! of the stranger's feet through the tall grass. He was passing now beyond the tree, when Iktomi, springing to his feet, called out: "How, how, my friend! I see you are dressed in handsome deerskins and have red paint on your cheeks. You are going to some feast or dance, may I ask?" Seeing the young man only smiled Iktomi went on: "I have not had a mouthful of food this day. Have pity on me, young brave, and shoot yonder bird for me!" With these words Iktomi pointed toward the tree-top, where sat a bird on the highest branch. The young avenger, always ready to help those in distress, sent an arrow upward and the bird fell. In the next branch it was caught between the forked prongs.

"My friend, climb the tree and get the bird. I cannot climb so high. I would get dizzy and fall," pleaded Iktomi. The avenger began to scale the tree, when Iktomi cried to him: "My friend, your beaded buckskins may be torn by the branches. Leave them safe upon the grass till you are down again."

"You are right," replied the young man, quickly slipping off his long fringed quiver. Together with his dangling pouches and tinkling ornaments, he placed it on the ground. Now he climbed the tree unhindered. Soon from the top he took the bird. "My friend, toss to me your arrow that I may have the honor of wiping it clean on soft deerskin!" exclaimed Iktomi.

"How!" said the brave, and threw the bird and arrow to the ground.

At once Iktomi seized the arrow. Rubbing it first on the grass and then on a piece of deerskin, he muttered indistinct words all the while. The young man, stepping downward from limb to limb, hearing the low muttering said: "Iktomi, I cannot hear what you say!"

"Oh, my friend, I was only talking of your big heart."

Again stooping over the arrow Iktomi continued his repetition of charm words. "Grow fast, grow fast to the bark of the tree," he whispered. Still the young man moved slowly downward. Suddenly dropping the arrow and standing erect, Iktomi said aloud: "Grow fast to the bark of the tree!" Before the brave could leap from the tree he became tight-grown to the bark.

"Ah! ha!" laughed the bad Iktomi. "I have the magic arrow! I have the beaded buckskins of the great avenger!" Hooting and dancing beneath the tree, he said: "I shall kill the red eagle; I shall wed the chieftain's beautiful daughter!"

"Oh, Iktomi, set me free!" begged the tree-bound Dakota brave. But Iktomi's ears were like the fungus on a tree. He did not hear with them.

Wearing the handsome buckskins and carrying proudly the magic arrow in his right hand, he started off eastward. Imitating the swaying strides of the avenger, he walked away with a face turned slightly skyward.

"Oh, set me free! I am glued to the tree like its own bark! Cut me loose!" moaned the prisoner.

A young woman, carrying on her strong back a bundle of tightly bound willow sticks, passed near by the lonely teepee. She heard the wailing man's voice. She paused to listen to the sad words. Looking around she saw nowhere a human creature. "It may be a spirit," thought she.

"Oh! cut me loose! set me free! Iktomi has played me false! He has made me bark of his tree!" cried the voice again.

The young woman dropped her pack of firewood to the ground. With her stone ax she hurried to the tree. There before her astonished eyes clung a young brave close to the tree.

Too shy for words, yet too kind-hearted to leave the stranger tree-bound, she cut loose the whole bark. Like an open jacket she drew it to the ground. With it came the young man also. Free once more, he started away. Looking backward, a few paces from the young woman, he waved his hand, upward and downward, before her face. This was a sign of gratitude used when words failed to interpret strong emotion.

When the bewildered woman reached her dwelling, she mounted a pony and rode swiftly across the rolling land. To the camp ground in the east, to the chieftain troubled by the red eagle, she carried her story.   1901

Susan Glaspell
1882–1948

One of the United States' first experimental dramatists, SUSAN GLASPELL combined expressionistic techniques with realism in more than a dozen plays produced between 1915 and 1930. As a feminist with socialist sympathies, she brought powerful women characters to the American stage and satirized small-town morality as well as class and gender biases. Moreover, Glaspell published ten novels about life in the Midwest and more than forty short stories during her prolific career.

She was born in 1882 in Davenport, Iowa, to Elmer S. Glaspell, a feed dealer, and Alice Keating Glaspell, an Irish immigrant; her family prospered in this farming community, which would later provide the setting for many of Glaspell's works. After graduating from Drake University in 1899, she worked for two years as a journalist for the Des Moines *Daily News*, then returned to Davenport to write full-time. In 1903 she did graduate work in English at the University of Chicago, but most of the decade she spent establishing herself as a writer. Her first novel, *The Glory of the Conquered* (1909), was a conventional love story; *The Visioning* (1911) explored themes of suicide, poverty, and suffrage. In 1911 Glaspell moved to New York, and in 1912 her first collection of stories, *Lifted Masks,* was published.

Glaspell's life changed significantly in 1913, when she married George Cram Cook, a writer and a socialist who also hailed from Davenport, and moved to Cape Cod in Massachusetts. There the couple founded the Provincetown Players, a theater company conceived as an alternative to the conventionality and commercialism of Broadway. While Cook served as fundraiser and manager, Glaspell wrote, directed, and performed in *Suppressed Desires* (1915), a satirical treatment of sex and psychoanalysis that she coauthored with Cook; and *Trifles* (1916), a subtle portrait of domestic violence and sexual difference in a rural community. The theater at Provincetown succeeded, eventually attracting such playwrights as Eugene O'Neill, EDNA ST. VINCENT MILLAY, and DJUNA BARNES; and in 1916 Cook moved the Players to Greenwich Village for the winter and established the Playwright's Theater as part of what would later become known as "the little theater movement."

In New York Glaspell heard Emma Goldman lecture on feminism and Henrietta Rodman on sexual freedom, and in this bohemian atmosphere her writing flourished. In 1917 the Players produced *The People,* Glaspell's account of a socialist newspaper's struggle to survive; and 1918 saw the production of *Women's Honor,* her satirical look at women and sacrifice. Her first full-length play, *Bernice* (1919), featured debates about the meaning and nature of the title character's mysterious death. Although the 1920 publication of *Plays* enhanced Glaspell's reputation as a significant dramatist, her prominence increased with the 1921 production of *The Verge,* a treatment of the "new woman" that created controversy among New York's theater critics and audiences. *Chains of Dew* (1922) was the last of her plays to be produced at Provincetown, for Glaspell and Cook, ironically disillusioned with their company's commercial success, left America for Greece in 1922. After Cook's death there in 1924, Glaspell returned to New York and went on to write *The Comic Artist* (1928), produced in London and coauthored with her second husband, Norman Matson; and *Alison's House* (1930), produced by New York's Civic Repertory Theater. The latter work, based loosely on the poetry and secluded life of EMILY DICKINSON, won the 1931 Pulitzer Prize for Drama. From 1928 until her death in 1948 Glaspell lived in Provincetown but wrote regional novels set in the Midwest of her girlhood. Among her best-known works are *Brook Evans* (1928), *Ambrose Holt and Family* (1931), *The Morning Is Near Us* (1940), *Norma Ashe* (1942), and *Judd Rankin's Daughter* (1945).

Included here is *Trifles,* which turns upon the question of whether farm woman Minnie Wright, in jail and accused of murdering her husband, actually committed the crime. Loyalties among women and the difference between men's and women's domestic realities constitute the themes of this suspenseful drama.

⊰ Trifles ⊱

Characters

GEORGE HENDERSON, County Attorney
HENRY PETERS, Sheriff
LEWIS HALE, A Neighboring Farmer
MRS. PETERS
MRS. HALE

SCENE: *The kitchen in the now abandoned farmhouse of* JOHN WRIGHT, *a gloomy kitchen, and left without having been put in order—unwashed pans under the sink, a loaf of bread outside the bread-box, a dish-towel on the table—other signs of incompleted work. At the rear the outer door opens and the* SHERIFF *comes in followed by the* COUNTY ATTORNEY *and* HALE. *The* SHERIFF *and* HALE *are men in middle life, the* COUNTY ATTORNEY *is a young man; all are much bundled up and go at once to the stove. They are followed by the two women—the* SHERIFF'S *wife first; she is a slight wiry woman, a thin nervous face.* MRS. HALE *is larger and would ordinarily be called more comfortable looking, but she is disturbed now and looks fearfully about as she enters. The women have come in slowly, and stand close together near the door.*

COUNTY ATTORNEY: [*Rubbing his hands.*] This feels good. Come up to the fire, ladies.
MRS. PETERS: [*After taking a step forward.*] I'm not—cold.
SHERIFF: [*Unbuttoning his overcoat and stepping away from the stove as if to mark the beginning of official business.*] Now, Mr. Hale, before we move things about, you explain to Mr. Henderson just what you saw when you came here yesterday morning.
COUNTY ATTORNEY: By the way, has anything been moved? Are things just as you left them yesterday?
SHERIFF: [*Looking about.*] It's just the same. When it dropped below zero last night I thought I'd better send Frank out this morning to make a fire for us—no use getting pneumonia with a big case on, but I told him not to touch anything except the stove—and you know Frank.
COUNTY ATTORNEY: Somebody should have been left here yesterday.
SHERIFF: Oh—yesterday. When I had to send Frank to Morris Center for that man who went crazy—I want you to know I had my hands full yesterday. I knew you could get back from Omaha by today and as long as I went over everything here myself—
COUNTY ATTORNEY: Well, Mr. Hale, tell just what happened when you came here yesterday morning.
HALE: Harry and I had started to town with a load of potatoes. We came along the road from my place and as I got here I said, "I'm going to see if I can't get John Wright to go in with me on a party telephone." I spoke to Wright about it once before and he put me off, saying folks talked too much anyway, and all he asked was peace and quiet—I guess you know about how much he talked himself; but I thought maybe if I went to the house and talked about it before his

wife, though I said to Harry that I didn't know as what his wife wanted made much difference to John—

COUNTY ATTORNEY: Let's talk about that later, Mr. Hale. I do want to talk about that, but tell now just what happened when you got to the house.

HALE: I didn't hear or see anything; I knocked at the door, and still it was all quiet inside. I knew they must be up, it was past eight o'clock. So I knocked again, and I thought I heard somebody say, "Come in." I wasn't sure, I'm not sure yet, but I opened the door—this door [*indicating the door by which the two women are still standing*] and there in that rocker—[*pointing to it*] sat Mrs. Wright.

[*They all look at the rocker.*]

COUNTY ATTORNEY: What—was she doing?

HALE: She was rockin' back and forth. She had her apron in her hand and was kind of—pleating it.

COUNTY ATTORNEY: And how did she—look?

HALE: Well, she looked queer.

COUNTY ATTORNEY: How do you mean—queer?

HALE: Well, as if she didn't know what she was going to do next. And kind of done up.

COUNTY ATTORNEY: How did she seem to feel about your coming?

HALE: Why, I don't think she minded—one way or other. She didn't pay much attention. I said, "How do, Mrs. Wright, it's cold, ain't it?" And she said, "Is it?"—and went on kind of pleating at her apron. Well, I was surprised; she didn't ask me to come up to the stove, or to set down, but just sat there, not even looking at me, so I said, "I want to see John." And then she—laughed. I guess you would call it a laugh. I thought of Harry and the team outside, so I said a little sharp: "Can't I see John?" "No," she says, kind o' dull like. "Ain't he home?" says I. "Yes," says she, "he's home." "Then why can't I see him?" I asked her, out of patience. "'Cause he's dead," says she. "*Dead?*" says I. She just nodded her head, not getting a bit excited, but rockin' back and forth. "Why—where is he?" says I, not knowing what to say. She just pointed upstairs—like that [*himself pointing to the room above*]. I got up, with the idea of going up there. I walked from there to here—then I says, "Why, what did he die of?" "He died of a rope round his neck," says she, and just went on pleatin' at her apron. Well, I went out and called Harry. I thought I might—need help. We went upstairs and there he was lyin'—

COUNTY ATTORNEY: I think I'd rather have you go into that upstairs, where you can point it all out. Just go on now with the rest of the story.

HALE: Well, my first thought was to get that rope off. It looked . . . [*Stops, his face twitches*] . . . but Harry, he went up to him, and he said, "No, he's dead all right, and we'd better not touch anything." So we went back downstairs. She was still sitting that same way. "Has anybody been notified?" I asked. "No," says she, unconcerned. "Who did this, Mrs. Wright?" said Harry. He said it business-like—and she stopped pleatin' of her apron. "I don't know," she says. "You don't *know?*" says Harry. "No," says she. "Weren't you sleepin' in the bed with him?" says Harry. "Yes," says she, "but I was on the inside." "Somebody slipped a rope round his neck and strangled him and you didn't wake up?" says Harry. "I didn't wake up," she said after him. We must'a looked as if we didn't see how that could be, for after a minute she said, "I sleep sound." Harry was going to ask her more questions but I said maybe we ought to let her tell her story first to the coroner,

or the sheriff, so Harry went fast as he could to Rivers' place, where there's a telephone.

COUNTY ATTORNEY: And what did Mrs. Wright do when she knew that you had
gone for the coroner?

HALE: She moved from that chair to this one over here [*Pointing to a small chair in the
corner*] and just sat there with her hands held together and looking down. I got a
feeling that I ought to make some conversation, so I said I had come in to see if
John wanted to put in a telephone, and at that she started to laugh, and then she
stopped and looked at me—scared. [*The* COUNTY ATTORNEY, *who has had his notebook out, makes a note.*] I dunno, maybe it wasn't scared. I wouldn't like to say it
was. Soon Harry got back, and then Dr. Lloyd came, and you, Mr. Peters, and so I
guess that's all I know that you don't.

COUNTY ATTORNEY: [*Looking around.*] I guess we'll go upstairs first—and then out
to the barn and around there. [*To the* SHERIFF.] You're convinced that there was
nothing important here—nothing that would point to any motive.

SHERIFF: Nothing here but kitchen things.

[*The* COUNTY ATTORNEY, *after again looking around the kitchen, opens the door of a
cupboard closet. He gets up on a chair and looks on a shelf. Pulls his hand away, sticky.*]

COUNTY ATTORNEY: Here's a nice mess.

[*The women draw nearer.*]

MRS. PETERS: [*To the other woman.*] Oh, her fruit; it did freeze. [*To the* LAWYER.] She
worried about that when it turned so cold. She said the fire'd go out and her jars
would break.

SHERIFF: Well, can you beat the women! Held for murder and worryin' about her
preserves.

COUNTY ATTORNEY: I guess before we're through she may have something more
serious than preserves to worry about.

HALE: Well, women are used to worrying over trifles.

[*The two women move a little closer together.*]

COUNTY ATTORNEY: [*With the gallantry of a young politician.*] And yet, for all their
worries, what would we do without the ladies? [*The women do not unbend. He goes
to the sink, takes a dipperful of water from the pail and pouring it into a basin, washes his
hands. Starts to wipe them on the roller-towel, turns it for a cleaner place.*] Dirty towels! [*Kicks his foot against the pans under the sink.*] Not much of a housekeeper,
would you say, ladies?

MRS. HALE: [*Stiffly.*] There's a great deal of work to be done on a farm.

COUNTY ATTORNEY: To be sure. And yet [*With a little bow to her*] I know there are
some Dickson county farmhouses which do not have such roller towels.

[*He gives it a pull to expose its full length again.*]

MRS. HALE: Those towels get dirty awful quick. Men's hands aren't always as clean
as they might be.

COUNTY ATTORNEY: Ah, loyal to your sex, I see. But you and Mrs. Wright were
neighbors. I suppose you were friends, too.

MRS. HALE: [*Shaking her head.*] I've not seen much of her of late years. I've not been
in this house—it's more than a year.

COUNTY ATTORNEY: And why was that? You didn't like her?

MRS. HALE: I liked her all well enough. Farmers' wives have their hands full, Mr. Henderson. And then—

COUNTY ATTORNEY: Yes—?

MRS. HALE: [*Looking about.*] It never seemed a very cheerful place.

COUNTY ATTORNEY: No—it's not cheerful. I shouldn't say she had the home-making instinct.

MRS. HALE: Well, I don't know as Wright had, either.

COUNTY ATTORNEY: You mean that they didn't get on very well?

MRS. HALE: No, I don't mean anything. But I don't think a place'd be any cheer-fuller for John Wright's being in it.

COUNTY ATTORNEY: I'd like to talk more of that a little later. I want to get the lay of things upstairs now.

[*He goes to the left, where three steps lead to a stair door.*]

SHERIFF: I suppose anything Mrs. Peters does'll be all right. She was to take in some clothes for her, you know, and a few little things. We left in such a hurry yesterday.

COUNTY ATTORNEY: Yes, but I would like to see what you take, Mrs. Peters, and keep an eye out for anything that might be of use to us.

MRS. PETERS: Yes, Mr. Henderson.

[*The women listen to the men's steps on the stairs, then look about the kitchen.*]

MRS. HALE: I'd hate to have men coming into my kitchen, snooping around and criticizing.

[*She arranges the pans under sink which the* LAWYER *had shoved out of place.*]

MRS. PETERS: Of course it's no more than their duty.

MRS. HALE: Duty's all right, but I guess that deputy sheriff that came out to make the fire might have got a little of this on. [*Gives the roller towel a pull.*] Wish I'd thought of that sooner. Seems mean to talk about her for not having things slicked up when she had to come away in such a hurry.

MRS. PETERS: [*Who has gone to a small table in the left rear corner of the room, and lifted one end of a towel that covers a pan.*] She had bread set.

[*Stands still.*]

MRS. HALE: [*Eyes fixed on a loaf of bread beside the bread-box, which is on a low shelf at the other side of the room. Moves slowly toward it.*] She was going to put this in there. [*Picks up loaf, then abruptly drops it. In a manner of returning to familiar things.*] It's a shame about her fruit. I wonder if it's all gone. [*Gets up on the chair and looks.*] I think there's some here that's all right, Mrs. Peters. Yes—here; [*Holding it toward the window*] this is cherries, too. [*Looking again.*] I declare I believe that's the only one. [*Gets down, bottle in her hand. Goes to the sink and wipes it off on the outside.*] She'll feel awful bad after all her hard work in the hot weather. I remember the afternoon I put up my cherries last summer.

[*She puts the bottle on the big kitchen table, center of the room. With a sigh, is about to sit down in the rocking-chair. Before she is seated realizes what chair it is; with a slow look at it, steps back. The chair which she has touched rocks back and forth.*]

MRS. PETERS: Well, I must get those things from the front room closet. [*She goes to the door at the right, but after looking into the other room, steps back.*] You coming with me, Mrs. Hale? You could help me carry them.

[*They go in the other room; reappear,* MRS. PETERS *carrying a dress and skirt,* MRS. HALE *following with a pair of shoes.*]

MRS. PETERS: My, it's cold in there.
[*She puts the clothes on the big table, and hurries to the stove.*]

MRS. HALE: [*Examining the skirt.*] Wright was close. I think maybe that's why she kept so much to herself. She didn't even belong to the Ladies Aid. I suppose she felt she couldn't do her part, and then you don't enjoy things when you feel shabby. She used to wear pretty clothes and be lively, when she was Minnie Foster, one of the town girls singing in the choir. But that—oh, that was thirty years ago. This all you was to take in?

MRS. PETERS: She said she wanted an apron. Funny thing to want, for there isn't much to get you dirty in jail, goodness knows. But I suppose just to make her feel more natural. She said they was in the top drawer in this cupboard. Yes, here. And then her little shawl that always hung behind the door. [*Opens stair door and looks.*] Yes, here it is.
[*Quickly shuts door leading upstairs.*]

MRS. HALE: [*Abruptly moving toward her.*] Mrs. Peters?

MRS. PETERS: Yes, Mrs. Hale?

MRS. HALE: Do you think she did it?

MRS. PETERS: [*In a frightened voice.*] Oh, I don't know.

MRS. HALE: Well, I don't think she did. Asking for an apron and her little shawl. Worrying about her fruit.

MRS. PETERS: [*Starts to speak, glances up, where footsteps are heard in the room above. In a low voice.*] Mr. Peters says it looks bad for her. Mr. Henderson is awful sarcastic in a speech and he'll make fun of her sayin' she didn't wake up.

MRS. HALE: Well, I guess John Wright didn't wake when they was slipping that rope under his neck.

MRS. PETERS: No, it's strange. It must have been done awful crafty and still. They say it was such a—funny way to kill a man, rigging it all up like that.

MRS. HALE: That's just what Mr. Hale said. There was a gun in the house. He says that's what he can't understand.

MRS. PETERS: Mr. Henderson said coming out that what was needed for the case was a motive; something to show anger, or—sudden feeling.

MRS. HALE: [*Who is standing by the table.*] Well, I don't see any signs of anger around here. [*She puts her hand on the dish towel which lies on the table, stands looking down at table, one half of which is clean, the other half messy.*] It's wiped to here. [*Makes a move as if to finish work, then turns and looks at loaf of bread outside the breadbox. Drops towel. In that voice of coming back to familiar things.*] Wonder how they are finding things upstairs. I hope she had it a little more red-up up there. You know, it seems kind of *sneaking.* Locking her up in town and then coming out here and trying to get her own house to turn against her!

MRS. PETERS: But Mrs. Hale, the law is the law.

MRS. HALE: I s'pose 'tis. [*Unbuttoning her coat.*] Better loosen up your things, Mrs. Peters. You won't feel them when you go out.

[MRS. PETERS *takes off her fur tippet, goes to hang it on hook at back of room, stands looking at the under part of the small corner table.*]

MRS. PETERS: She was piecing a quilt.
[*She brings the large sewing basket and they look at the bright pieces.*]

MRS. HALE: It's log cabin pattern. Pretty, isn't it? I wonder if she was goin' to quilt it or just knot it?
[*Footsteps have been heard coming down the stairs. The* SHERIFF *enters followed by* HALE *and the* COUNTY ATTORNEY.]

SHERIFF: They wonder if she was going to quilt it or just knot it!
[*The men laugh, the women look abashed.*]

COUNTY ATTORNEY: [*Rubbing his hands over the stove.*] Frank's fire didn't do much up there, did it? Well, let's go out to the barn and get that cleared up.
[*The men go outside.*]

MRS. HALE: [*Resentfully.*] I don't know as there's anything so strange, our takin' up our time with little things while we're waiting for them to get the evidence. [*She sits down at the big table smoothing out a block with decision.*] I don't see as it's anything to laugh about.
MRS. PETERS: [*Apologetically.*] Of course they've got awful important things on their minds.
[*Pulls up a chair and joins* MRS. HALE *at the table.*]

MRS. HALE: [*Examining another block.*] Mrs. Peters, look at this one. Here, this is the one she was working on, and look at the sewing! All the rest of it has been so nice and even. And look at this! It's all over the place! Why, it looks as if she didn't know what she was about!
[*After she has said this they look at each other, then start to glance back at the door. After an instant* MRS. HALE *has pulled at a knot and ripped the sewing.*]

MRS. PETERS: Oh, what are you doing, Mrs. Hale?
MRS. HALE: [*Mildly.*] Just pulling out a stitch or two that's not sewed very good. [*Threading a needle.*] Bad sewing always made me fidgety.
MRS. PETERS: [*Nervously.*] I don't think we ought to touch things.
MRS. HALE: I'll just finish up this end. [*Suddenly stopping and leaning forward.*] Mrs. Peters?
MRS. PETERS: Yes, Mrs. Hale?
MRS. HALE: What do you suppose she was so nervous about?
MRS. PETERS: Oh—I don't know. I don't know as she was nervous. I sometimes sew awful queer when I'm just tired. [MRS. HALE *starts to say something, looks at* MRS. PETERS, *then goes on sewing.*] Well I must get these things wrapped up. They may be through sooner than we think. [*Putting apron and other things together.*] I wonder where I can find a piece of paper, and string.
MRS. HALE: In that cupboard, maybe.
MRS. PETERS: [*Looking in cupboard.*] Why, here's a birdcage. [*Holds it up.*] Did she have a bird, Mrs. Hale?
MRS. HALE: Why, I don't know whether she did or not—I've not been here for so long. There was a man around last year selling canaries cheap, but I don't know as she took one; maybe she did. She used to sing real pretty herself.

[Handwritten annotations in top margin: "John Wright — John was 'right'"]

MRS. PETERS: [*Glancing around.*] Seems funny to think of a bird here. But she must have had one, or why would she have a cage? I wonder what happened to it.

MRS. HALE: I s'pose maybe the cat got it.

MRS. PETERS: No, she didn't have a cat. She's got that feeling some people have about cats—being afraid of them. My cat got in her room and she was real upset and asked me to take it out.

MRS. HALE: My sister Bessie was like that. Queer, ain't it?

MRS. PETERS: [*Examining the cage.*] Why, look at this door. It's broke. One hinge is pulled apart.

MRS. HALE: [*Looking too.*] Looks as if someone must have been rough with it.

MRS. PETERS: Why, yes.

[*She brings the cage forward and puts it on the table.*]

MRS. HALE: I wish if they're going to find any evidence they'd be about it. I don't like this place.

MRS. PETERS: But I'm awful glad you came with me, Mrs. Hale. It would be lonesome for me sitting here alone.

MRS. HALE: It would, wouldn't it? [*Dropping her sewing.*] But I tell you what I do wish, Mrs. Peters. I wish I had come over sometimes when *she* was here. I—[*Looking around the room*]—wish I had.

MRS. PETERS: But of course you were awful busy, Mrs. Hale—your house and your children.

MRS. HALE: I could've come. I stayed away because it weren't cheerful—and that's why I ought to have come. I—I've never liked this place. Maybe because it's down in a hollow and you don't see the road. I dunno what it is, but it's a lonesome place and always was. I wish I had come over to see Minnie Foster sometimes. I can see now—
[*Shakes her head.*]

MRS. PETERS: Well, you mustn't reproach yourself, Mrs. Hale. Somehow we just don't see how it is with other folks until—something comes up.

MRS. HALE: Not having children makes less work—but it makes a quiet house, and Wright out to work all day, and no company when he did come in. Did you know John Wright, Mrs. Peters?

MRS. PETERS: Not to know him; I've seen him in town. They say he was a good man.

MRS. HALE: Yes—good; he didn't drink, and kept his word as well as most, I guess, and paid his debts. But he was a hard man, Mrs. Peters. Just to pass the time of day with him—[*Shivers.*] Like a raw wind that gets to the bone. [*Pauses, her eye falling on the cage.*] I should think she would 'a wanted a bird. But what do you suppose went with it?

MRS. PETERS: I don't know, unless it got sick and died.

[*She reaches over and swings the broken door, swings it again. Both women watch it.*] *[Handwritten: "what happened to the bird."]*

MRS. HALE: You weren't raised round here, were you? [MRS. PETERS *shakes her head.*] You didn't know—her?

MRS. PETERS: Not till they brought her yesterday.

MRS. HALE: She—come to think of it, she was kind of like a bird herself—real sweet and pretty, but kind of timid and—fluttery. How—she—did—change. [*Silence; then as if struck by a happy thought and relieved to get back to everyday things.*] Tell you what, Mrs. Peters, why don't you take the quilt in with you? It might take up her mind.

MRS. PETERS: Why, I think that's a real nice idea, Mrs. Hale. There couldn't possibly be any objection to it, could there? Now, just what would I take? I wonder if her patches are in here—and her things.
[*They look in the sewing basket.*]

MRS. HALE: Here's some red. I expect this has got sewing things in it. [*Brings out a fancy box.*] What a pretty box. Looks like something somebody would give you. Maybe her scissors are in here. [*Opens box. Suddenly puts her hand to her nose.*] Why—[MRS. PETERS *bends nearer, then turns her face away.*] There's something wrapped up in this piece of silk.
MRS. PETERS: Why, this isn't her scissors.
MRS. HALE: [*Lifting the silk.*] Oh Mrs. Peters—it's—
[MRS. PETERS *bends closer.*]

MRS. PETERS: It's the bird.
MRS. HALE: [*Jumping up.*] But, Mrs. Peters—look at it! Its neck! Look at its neck! It's all—other side to.
MRS. PETERS: Somebody—wrung—its—neck.
[*Their eyes meet. A look of growing comprehension, of horror. Steps are heard outside.* MRS. HALE *slips box under quilt pieces, and sinks into her chair. Enter* SHERIFF *and* COUNTY ATTORNEY. MRS. PETERS *rises.*]

COUNTY ATTORNEY: [*As one turning from serious things to little pleasantries.*] Well, ladies, have you decided whether she was going to quilt it or knot it?
MRS. PETERS: We think she was going to—knot it.
COUNTY ATTORNEY: Well, that's interesting, I'm sure. [*Seeing the birdcage.*] Has the bird flown?
MRS. HALE: [*Putting more quilt pieces over the box.*] We think the—cat got it.
COUNTY ATTORNEY: [*Preoccupied.*] Is there a cat?
[MRS. HALE *glances in a quick covert way at* MRS. PETERS.]

MRS. PETERS: Well, not *now.* They're superstitious, you know. They leave.
COUNTY ATTORNEY: [*To* SHERIFF PETERS, *continuing an interrupted conversation.*] No sign at all of anyone having come from the outside. Their own rope. Now let's go up again and go over it piece by piece. [*They start upstairs.*] It would have to have been someone who knew just the—
[MRS. PETERS *sits down. The two women sit there not looking at one another, but as if peering into something and at the same time holding back. When they talk now it is in the manner of feeling their way over strange ground, as if afraid of what they are saying, but as if they cannot help saying it.*]

MRS. HALE: She liked the bird. She was going to bury it in that pretty box.
MRS. PETERS: [*In a whisper.*] When I was a girl—my kitten—there was a boy took a hatchet, and before my eyes—and before I could get there—[*Covers her face an instant.*] If they hadn't held me back I would have—[*Catches herself, looks upstairs where steps are heard, falters weakly*]—hurt him.
MRS. HALE: [*With a slow look around her.*] I wonder how it would seem never to have had any children around. [*Pause.*] No, Wright wouldn't like the bird—a thing that sang. She used to sing. He killed that, too.
MRS. PETERS: [*Moving uneasily.*] We don't know who killed the bird.

MRS. HALE: I knew John Wright.

MRS. PETERS: It was an awful thing was done in this house that night, Mrs. Hale. Killing a man while he slept, slipping a rope around his neck that choked the life out of him.

MRS. HALE: His neck. Choked the life out of him.

[*Her hand goes out and rests on the birdcage.*]

dead children

MRS. PETERS: [*With rising voice.*] We don't know who killed him. We don't *know*.

MRS. HALE: [*Her own feeling not interrupted.*] If there'd been years and years of nothing, then a bird to sing to you, it would be awful—still, after the bird was still.

MRS. PETERS: [*Something within her speaking.*] I know what stillness is. When we homesteaded in Dakota, and my first baby died—after he was two years old, and me with no other then—

MRS. HALE: [*Moving.*] How soon do you suppose they'll be through, looking for the evidence?

MRS. PETERS: I know what stillness is. [*Pulling herself back.*] The law has got to punish crime, Mrs. Hale.

MRS. HALE: [*Not as if answering that.*] I wish you'd seen Minnie Foster when she wore a white dress with blue ribbons and stood up there in the choir and sang. [*A look around the room.*] Oh, I *wish* I'd come over here once in a while! That was a crime! That was a crime! Who's going to punish that?

MRS. PETERS: [*Looking upstairs.*] We mustn't—take on.

MRS. HALE: I might have known she needed help! I know how things can be—for women. I tell you, it's queer, Mrs. Peters. We live close together and we live far apart. We all go through the same things—it's all just a different kind of the same thing. [*Brushes her eyes, noticing the bottle of fruit, reaches out for it.*] If I was you I wouldn't tell her her fruit was gone. Tell her it *ain't*. Tell her it's all right. Take this in to prove it to her. She—she may never know whether it was broke or not.

MRS. PETERS: [*Takes the bottle, looks about for something to wrap it in; takes petticoat from the clothes brought from the other room, very nervously begins winding this around the bottle. In a false voice.*] My, it's a good thing the men couldn't hear us. Wouldn't they just laugh! Getting all stirred up over a little thing like a—dead canary. As if that could have anything to do with—with—wouldn't they *laugh!*

[*The men are heard coming downstairs.*]

MRS. HALE: [*Under her breath.*] Maybe they would—maybe they wouldn't.

COUNTY ATTORNEY: No, Peters, it's all perfectly clear except a reason for doing it. But you know juries when it comes to women. If there was some definite thing. Something to show—something to make a story about—a thing that would connect up with this strange way of doing it—

[*The women's eyes meet for an instant. Enter* HALE *from outer door.*]

HALE: Well, I've got the team around. Pretty cold out there.

COUNTY ATTORNEY: I'm going to stay here a while by myself. [*To the* SHERIFF.] You can send Frank out for me, can't you? I want to go over everything. I'm not satisfied that we can't do better.

SHERIFF: Do you want to see what Mrs. Peters is going to take in?

[*The* LAWYER *goes to the table, picks up the apron, laughs.*]

COUNTY ATTORNEY: Oh, I guess they're not very dangerous things the ladies have picked out. [*Moves a few things about, disturbing the quilt pieces which cover the box. Steps back.*] No, Mrs. Peters doesn't need supervising. For that matter, a sheriff's wife is married to the law. Ever think of it that way, Mrs. Peters?

MRS. PETERS: Not—just that way.

SHERIFF: [*Chuckling.*] Married to the law. [*Moves toward the other room.*] I just want you to come in here a minute, George. We ought to take a look at these windows.

COUNTY ATTORNEY: [*Scoffingly.*] Oh, windows!

SHERIFF: We'll be right out, Mr. Hale.

[HALE *goes outside. The* SHERIFF *follows the* COUNTY ATTORNEY *into the other room. Then* MRS. HALE *rises, hands tight together, looking intensely at* MRS. PETERS, *whose eyes make a slow turn, finally meeting* MRS. HALE'S. *A moment* MRS. HALE *holds her, then her own eyes point the way to where the box is concealed. Suddenly* MRS. PETERS *throws back quilt pieces and tries to put the box in the bag she is wearing. It is too big. She opens box, starts to take bird out, cannot touch it, goes to pieces, stands there helpless. Sound of a knob turning in the other room.* MRS. HALE *snatches the box and puts it in the pocket of her big coat. Enter* COUNTY ATTORNEY *and* SHERIFF.]

COUNTY ATTORNEY: [*Facetiously.*] Well, Henry, at least we found out that she was not going to quilt it. She was going to—what is it you call it, ladies?

MRS. HALE: [*Her hand against her pocket.*] We call it—knot it, Mr. Henderson.

(CURTAIN)   1916/1920

Marianne Moore

1887–1972

A poet, translator, and critic, MARIANNE MOORE was born in Kirkwood, Missouri, and grew up in Carlisle, Pennsylvania; her mother, Mary Warner Moore, cared for Marianne and her brother after their father was hospitalized for mental illness. In 1909 Moore graduated with a degree in biology and histology from Bryn Mawr College, where she met the poet H.D. After graduation Moore taught commercial law, typing, and shorthand at the Carlisle Indian School, then moved to New York with her mother; there she worked as a librarian and joined a circle of writers and artists. In 1915 H.D.,  along with her friend Bryher, recommended Moore's early poems for publication in a prominent British literary journal, *The Egoist*; her first collection, *Poems* (1921), was also published in England—without the poet's knowledge—at the behest of Bryher and H.D. From 1925 until 1929 Moore served as editor of *The Dial*, an American literary journal, and championed the work of such controversial modernists as T.S. Eliot, Ezra Pound, Hart Crane, William Carlos Williams, and Wallace Stevens.

Among Moore's enthusiasms was major league baseball; she pitched the first ball for opening day in Yankee Stadium in 1968 and in one poem compared baseball and writing. Another passion was esoteric birds and animals; Moore frequented zoos and circuses, collected glass miniatures, and wrote about such oddities as jerboas, porcupines, and pangolins. Plant and sea life, Oriental art, maps, and antique clocks captured her imagination and appeared as subjects of poems. Also unusual was Moore's favorite style of dress: a tricornered hat and flowing black cape, which her friend, the poet Elizabeth Bishop, satirizes memorably in "An Invitation to Miss Marianne Moore." Moore herself once claimed that "my writing is, if not like a cabinet of fossils, a kind of collection of flies in amber." Clearly her sense of humor was as distinctive as her verse.

With the publication of *Observations* (1924), her first collection to appear in the United States, Moore gained a reputation as a quintessential modernist whose work was characterized by linguistic virtuosity and precision, an innovative use of syllabic metrics, and radical experiments with verse forms. In a typical Moore poem the stanza is shaped typographically and rhymes lightly; except for subtle variations to effect emphasis, stanzas contain the same number of syllables and identical line lengths. Her range of themes includes not only the behavior of animals, through which she explores the nature of aesthetics and the imagination, but also the meaning of democracy, the complexities of marriage, the mysteries of grace and redemption, and the role of poetry in a changing world. *Selected Poems* (1935) was introduced by T.S. Eliot and brought Moore a wider audience. Her *Collected Poems* (1951) won the Pulitzer Prize and the National Book Award in 1952 and the Bollingen Prize in 1953. Later volumes of poetry include *Like a Bulwark* (1956), *O to Be a Dragon* (1959), *Idiosyncrasy and Technique* (1959), and *Tell Me, Tell Me* (1966). *The Complete Poems of Marianne Moore* (1981) contains the author's final revisions.

Moore's skills as a literary essayist and reviewer are evident in *Predilections* (1955) and *Poetry and Criticism* (1965); writings from these volumes and other prose are collected in *The Complete Prose of Marianne Moore*, edited by Patricia Willis (1986). Moore also translated the fables of the French writer La Fontaine and wrote a dramatic version of MARIA EDGEWORTH's 1812 novel, *The Absentee*, which Moore subtitled *A Comedy in Four Acts*. Among her many awards are the National Institute of Arts and Letters Gold Medal for Poetry, the Poetry Society of America's Gold Medal for Distinguished Achievement, and the United States' foremost literary honor, the National Medal for Literature.

The critic Yvor Winters once observed that Moore's poetry represents "the transference of the metaphysical into physical terms." The power of the visible, she believed, was invisible; and "art," she wrote in "Why I Buy Pictures," must "acknowledge the spiritual forces that made it." Of her own writing, Moore has said that "words cluster like chromosomes, determining the procedure." Moore's concern with the intricacies of the creative process is evident in "The Paper Nautilus," which has been read as a poem about the relationship between motherhood and artistic creativity. "The Fish," a meditation on the passing of time, depicts the sea as at once beautiful and treacherous. Like many of Moore's best poems—including "The Mind is an Enchanting Thing"—it is arranged mathematically, by syllable count. "In Distrust of Merits" illustrates Moore's voice during wartime, while "Like a Bulwark" pays homage to the poet's late mother. All of these poems invite readers to engage in both aesthetic and moral reflection.

⊰ The Fish ⊱

wade
through black jade.
    Of the crow-blue mussel-shells, one keeps
    adjusting the ash-heaps;
5   opening and shutting itself like

an
injured fan.
    The barnacles which encrust the side
    of the wave, cannot hide
10   there for the submerged shafts of the

sun,
split like spun
   glass, move themselves with spotlight swiftness
   into the crevices—
15   in and out, illuminating

the
turquoise sea
   of bodies. The water drives a wedge
   of iron through the iron edge
20   of the cliff; whereupon the stars,

pink
rice-grains, ink-
   bespattered jelly-fish, crabs like green
   lilies, and submarine
25   toadstools, slide each on the other.

All
external
   marks of abuse are present on this
   defiant edifice—
30   all the physical features of

ac-
cident—lack
   of cornice, dynamite grooves, burns, and
   hatchet strokes, these things stand
35   out on it; the chasm-side is

dead.
Repeated
   evidence has proved that it can live
   on what can not revive
40   its youth. The sea grows old in it.

1935

⤙ The Paper Nautilus[1] ⤚

   For authorities whose hopes
are shaped by mercenaries?
   Writers entrapped by
   teatime fame and by
5 commuters' comforts? Not for these
   the paper nautilus
   constructs her thin glass shell.

   Giving her perishable
souvenir of hope, a dull
10   white outside and smooth-

1. The female nautilus, a fish similar to an octopus, carries her eggs in a fragile shell that she holds along the water's surface with her tentacles.

edged inner surface
    glossy as the sea, the watchful
        maker of it guards it
        day and night; she scarcely

15   eats until the eggs are hatched.
    Buried eight-fold in her eight
        arms, for she is in
        a sense a devil-
    fish, her glass ram's horn-cradled freight
20   is hid but is not crushed;
        as Hercules, bitten

        by a crab loyal to the hydra,[2]
    was hindered to succeed,
        the intensively
25   watched eggs coming from
    the shell free it when they are freed,—
        leaving its wasp-nest flaws
        of white on white, and close-

        laid Ionic chiton-folds[3]
30 like the lines in the mane of
        a Parthenon horse,[4]
        round which the arms had
    wound themselves as if they knew love
        is the only fortress
35   strong enough to trust to.

1941

⊰ The Mind Is an Enchanting Thing ⊱

    is an enchanted thing
        like the glaze on a
    katydid-wing
            subdivided by sun
5   till the nettings are legion.
    Like Gieseking playing Scarlatti;[5]

    like the apteryx-awl[6]
        as a beak, or the
    kiwi's rain-shawl
10   of haired feathers, the mind
                feeling its way as though blind,
    walks along with its eyes on the ground.

2. An allusion to one of the twelve labors of Hercules, a mythical Greek hero renowned for his strength. According to legend he fought the many-headed hydra and simultaneously killed a crab that bit him.
3. The folds of an ancient Greek tunic.
4. A horse depicted in the frieze at the Parthenon in Athens.

5. Walter Wilhelm Gieseking (1895–1956) was a German pianist; Giuseppe Domenico Scarlatti (1685–1757) was an Italian composer.
6. A flightless bird from New Zealand with stout legs, a long bill (or awl), and grayish-brown plumage; more commonly called a *kiwi*.

It has memory's ear
    that can hear without
15 having to hear.
        Like the gyroscope's fall,
        truly unequivocal
because trued by regnant certainty,

it is a power of
20   strong enchantment. It
is like the dove-
        neck animated by
        sun; it is memory's eye;
it's conscientious inconsistency.

25 It tears off the veil; tears
    the temptation, the
mist the heart wears,
        from its eyes—if the heart
        has a face; it takes apart
30 dejection. It's fire in the dove-neck's

iridescence; in the
    inconsistencies
of Scarlatti.
        Unconfusion submits
35   its confusion to proof; it's
not a Herod's oath[7] that cannot change.

1944

⇥ In Distrust of Merits ⇤

Strengthened to live, strengthened to die for
    medals and positioned victories?
They're fighting, fighting, fighting the blind
    man who thinks he sees,—
5 who cannot see that the enslaver is
enslaved; the hater, harmed. O shining O
    firm star, O tumultuous
        ocean lashed till small things go
    as they will, the mountainous
10   wave makes us who look, know

depth. Lost at sea before they fought! O
    star of David, star of Bethlehem,
O black imperial lion
    of the Lord—emblem
15 of a risen world—be joined at last, be
joined. There is hate's crown beneath which all is
    death; there's love's without which none

---

7. Herod Antipas (21 B.C.E–39 C.E.) was the Roman ruler of Galilee during the time of Christ. He swore to his niece, Salome, that she could have anything in his kingdom because of her beautiful dancing, and she demanded the head of John the Baptist on a platter. Although Herod was hesitant to meet her demand, he did so because he had sworn an oath.

is king; the blessed deeds bless
the halo. As contagion
20   of sickness makes sickness,

contagion of trust can make trust. They're
fighting in deserts and caves, one by
one, in battalions and squadrons;
they're fighting that I
25 may yet recover from the disease, My
Self; some have it lightly; some will die. "Man's
wolf to man" and we devour
ourselves. The enemy could not
have made a greater breach in our
30   defenses. One pilot-

ing a blind man can escape him, but
Job disheartened by false comfort knew
that nothing can be so defeating
as a blind man who
35 can see. O alive who are dead, who are
proud not to see, O small dust of the earth
that walks so arrogantly,
trust begets power and faith is
an affectionate thing. We
40   vow, we make this promise

to the fighting—it's a promise—"We'll
never hate black, white, red, yellow, Jew,
Gentile, Untouchable." We are
not competent to
45 make our vows. With set jaw they are fighting,
fighting, fighting,—some we love whom we know,
some we love but know not—that
hearts may feel and not be numb.
It cures me; or am I what
50   I can't believe in? Some

in snow, some on crags, some in quicksands,
little by little, much by much, they
are fighting fighting fighting that where
there was death there may
55 be life. "When a man is prey to anger,
he is moved by outside things; when he holds
his ground in patience patience
patience, that is action or
beauty," the soldier's defense
60   and hardest armor for

the fight. The world's an orphans' home. Shall
we never have peace without sorrow?
without pleas of the dying for
help that won't come? O
65 quiet form upon the dust, I cannot
look and yet I must. If these great patient

dyings—all these agonies
and wound bearings and bloodshed—
can teach us how to live, these
70   dyings were not wasted.

Hate-hardened heart, O heart of iron,
iron is iron till it is rust.
There never was a war that was
not inward; I must
75   fight till I have conquered in myself what
causes war, but I would not believe it.
I inwardly did nothing.
O Iscariot-like[8] crime!
Beauty is everlasting
80   and dust is for a time.

1944

⇥ Like a Bulwark ⇤

Affirmed. Pent by power that holds it fast—
a paradox. Pent. Hard pressed,
you take the blame and are inviolate.
Abased at last?
5   Not the tempest-tossed.
Compressed; firmed by the thrust of the blast
till compact, like a bulwark against fate;
lead-saluted,
saluted by lead?
10   As though flying Old Glory[9] full mast.

1956

Katherine Mansfield
1888–1923

In "A Terribly Sensitive Mind," a 1927 review of KATHERINE MANSFIELD's journals, VIRGINIA WOOLF described her as a "born writer" whose mind stood "alone with itself; a mind which has so little thought of an audience that it will make use of a shorthand of its own now and then, or, as the mind in its loneliness tends to do, divide into two and talk to itself." Yet as a modernist writer of short fiction, Mansfield overcame any obstacles such self-absorption might imply. "Everything she feels and hears and sees," concluded Woolf, "is not fragmentary and separate; it belongs together as writing."

Born Kathleen Beauchamp in New Zealand, where she attended school as a child, Mansfield studied music at Queens College in London for four years before returning to Wellington to live. Bored with life as the daughter of a middle-class businessman, she emigrated to England in 1906

---

8. An allusion to Judas Iscariot, who betrayed Jesus Christ   9. The flag of the United States.
by denying that he knew him.

and made an unfortunate marriage to George Bowden, whom she had just met. She also reunited with a friend from her days at Queens College, Ida Baker, who became a lifelong companion; Baker changed her name to L.M. (Leslie Moore) at the same time Kathleen Beauchamp took the name of Katherine Mansfield. After becoming pregnant by a lover, Mansfield left London for Germany, where she lost her baby through miscarriage. There she wrote a series of sketches later published as *In a German Pension* (1911), stories about sexual relationships that the critic Bonnie Kime Scott considers "among her most openly feminist works." In 1910 Mansfield returned to England and wrote stories for a leading socialist periodical, *New Age;* in 1912 she became involved with aspiring literary critic John Middleton Murry, whom she married in 1918, when her divorce from Bowden became final. For the next few years she composed stories for journals edited by Murry, including *Rhythm* and the *Blue Review.* The collection many critics consider her finest, *Bliss and Other Stories* (1920), recalls her New Zealand childhood with a beloved brother who was killed in World War I. Other collections include *Je Ne Parle Pas Francais* (1918), *The Garden Party and Other Stories* (1922), *The Dove's Nest and Other Stories* (1923), *Something Childish* (1924), and *The Aloe* (1930). Mansfield is also known for her incisive but unsympathetic reviews of her women contemporaries, including Virginia Woolf, Dorothy Richardson, and May Sinclair. During the last years of her life, ill with tuberculosis, she traveled in Switzerland and France, where she pursued spiritualism and health cures. After Mansfield's death Murry edited her *Journals* (1927) and *Letters* (1928).

Katherine Mansfield was a master of the short story, the perfect form for her powerful evocation of atmosphere and quiet precision of detail. Her impressionistic technique has been compared to that of the Russian writer Anton Chekhov, whose work she admired; her experiments with stream-of-consciousness and multiple points of view link her to important modernist authors such as James Joyce and Woolf, with whom Mansfield often discussed writing. Woolf, in fact, considered Mansfield a competitor as well as an ally in fictional experimentation; she admitted in her diaries that Mansfield had produced "the only writing I have ever been jealous of." Mansfield, in turn, once described Woolf wryly as "Austen up-to-date." Mansfield's stories often satirize upper-class foibles, and they rely on a delicate emotional balance for their coherence rather than on a traditional beginning, middle, and end. This delicacy was trivialized by T.S. Eliot, who claimed that she "handled perfectly the *minimum* material—it is what I believe would be called feminine."

The story included here, "The Doll's House," hearkens back to the author's New Zealand girlhood, recalling the social boundaries and class distinctions on which certain members of her community insisted. When the prosperous Burnell children receive a wonderful doll house as a gift from a family friend, they each explore its magic in different ways. The cruelty of wealthy adults, the vulnerabilities of children, and the power of the imagination to transcend differences are themes central to this carefully crafted story.

ᗧ The Doll's House ᗤ

WHEN dear old Mrs. Hay went back to town after staying with the Burnells she sent the children a doll's house. It was so big that the carter and Pat carried it into the courtyard, and there it stayed, propped up on two wooden boxes beside the feed-room door. No harm could come to it; it was summer. And perhaps the smell of paint would have gone off by the time it had to be taken in. For, really, the smell of paint coming from that doll's house ("Sweet of old Mrs. Hay, of course; most sweet and generous!")—but the smell of paint was quite enough to make anyone seriously ill, in Aunt Beryl's opinion. Even before the sacking was taken off. And when it was . . .

There stood the doll's house, a dark, oily, spinach green, picked out with bright yellow. Its two solid little chimneys, glued on to the roof, were painted red and white, and the door, gleaming with yellow varnish, was like a little slab of toffee. Four windows, real windows, were divided into panes by a broad streak of green. There was actually a tiny porch, too, painted yellow, with big lumps of congealed paint hanging along the edge.

But perfect, perfect little house! Who could possibly mind the smell. It was part of the joy, part of the newness.

"Open it quickly, someone!"

The hook at the side was stuck fast. Pat prised it open with his penknife, and the whole house front swung back, and—there you were, gazing at one and the same moment into the drawing-room and dining-room, the kitchen and two bedrooms. That is the way for a house to open! Why don't all houses open like that? How much more exciting than peering through the slit of a door into a mean little hall with a hat stand and two umbrellas! That is—isn't it?—what you long to know about a house when you put your hand on the knocker. Perhaps it is the way God opens houses at the dead of night when He is taking a quiet turn with an angel. . . .

"Oh-oh!" The Burnell children sounded as though they were in despair. It was too marvelous; it was too much for them. They had never seen anything like it in their lives. All the rooms were papered. There were pictures on the walls, painted on the paper, with gold frames complete. Red carpet covered all the floors except the kitchen; red plush chairs in the drawing room, green in the dining room; tables, beds with real bedclothes, a cradle, a stove, a dresser with tiny plates and one big jug. But what Kezia liked more than anything, what she liked frightfully, was the lamp. It stood in the middle of the dining-room table, an exquisite little amber lamp with a white globe. It was even filled all ready for lighting, though, of course, you couldn't light it. But there was something inside that looked like oil and moved when you shook it.

The father and mother dolls, who sprawled very stiff as though they had fainted in the drawing-room, and their two little children asleep upstairs, were really too big for the doll's house. They didn't look as though they belonged. But the lamp was perfect. It seemed to smile at Kezia, to say, "I live here." The lamp was real.

The Burnell children could hardly walk to school fast enough the next morning. They burned to tell everybody, to describe, to—well—to boast about their doll's house before the schoolbell rang.

"I'm to tell," said Isabel, "because I'm the eldest. And you two can join in after. But I'm to tell first."

There was nothing to answer. Isabel was bossy, but she was always right, and Lottie and Kezia knew too well the powers that went with being eldest. They brushed through the thick buttercups at the road edge and said nothing.

"And I'm to choose who's to come and see it first. Mother said I might."

For it had been arranged that while the doll's house stood in the courtyard they might ask the girls at school, two at a time, to come and look. Not to stay to tea, of course, or to come traipsing through the house. But just to stand quietly in the courtyard while Isabel pointed out the beauties, and Lottie and Kezia looked pleased. . . .

But hurry as they might, by the time they had reached the tarred palings of the boys' playground the bell had begun to jangle. They only just had time to whip off their hats and fall into line before the roll was called. Never mind. Isabel tried to make up for it by looking very important and mysterious and by whispering behind her hand to the girls near her, "Got something to tell you at playtime."

Playtime came and Isabel was surrounded. The girls of her class nearly fought to put their arms round her, to walk away with her, to beam flatteringly, to be her special friend. She held quite a court under the huge pine trees at the side of the playground. Nudging, giggling together, the little girls pressed up close. And the only two who stayed outside the ring were the two who were always outside, the little Kelveys. They knew better than to come anywhere near the Burnells.

For the fact was, the school the Burnell children went to was not at all the kind of place their parents would have chosen if there had been any choice. But there was none. It was the only school for miles. And the consequence was all the children of the neighborhood, the Judge's little girls, the doctor's daughters, the storekeeper's children, the milkman's, were forced to mix together. Not to speak of there being an equal number of rude, rough little boys as well. But the line had to be drawn somewhere. It was drawn at the Kelveys. Many of the children, including the Burnells, were not allowed even to speak to them. They walked past the Kelveys with their heads in the air, and as they set the fashion in all matters of behavior, the Kelveys were shunned by everybody. Even the teacher had a special voice for them, and a special smile for the other children when Lil Kelvey came up to her desk with a bunch of dreadfully common-looking flowers.

They were the daughters of a spry, hardworking little washerwoman, who went about from house to house by the day. This was awful enough. But where was Mr. Kelvey? Nobody knew for certain. But everybody said he was in prison. So they were the daughters of a washerwoman and a jailbird. Very nice company for other people's children! And they looked it. Why Mrs. Kelvey made them so conspicuous was hard to understand. The truth was they were dressed in "bits" given to her by the people for whom she worked. Lil, for instance, who was a stout, plain child, with big freckles, came to school in a dress made from a green art-serge tablecloth of the Burnells', with red plush sleeves from the Logans' curtains. Her hat, perched on top of her high forehead, was a grown-up woman's hat, once the property of Miss Lecky, the postmistress. It was turned up at the back and trimmed with a large scarlet quill. What a little guy she looked! It was impossible not to laugh. And her little sister, our Else, wore a long white dress, rather like a nightgown, and a pair of little boy's boots. But whatever our Else wore she would have looked strange. She was a tiny wishbone of a child, with cropped hair and enormous solemn eyes—a little white owl. Nobody had ever seen her smile; she scarcely ever spoke. She went through life holding on to Lil, with a piece of Lil's skirt screwed up in her hand. Where Lil went, our Else followed. In the playground, on the road going to and from school, there was Lil marching in front and our Else holding on behind. Only when she wanted anything, or when she was out of breath, our Else gave Lil a tug, a twitch, and Lil stopped and turned round. The Kelveys never failed to understand each other.

Now they hovered at the edge; you couldn't stop them listening. When the little girls turned round and sneered, Lil, as usual, gave her silly, shamefaced smile, but our Else only looked.

And Isabel's voice, so very proud, went on telling. The carpet made a great sensation, but so did the beds with the real bedclothes, and the stove with an oven door.

When she finished Kezia broke in. "You've forgotten the lamp, Isabel."

"Oh yes," said Isabel, "and there's a teeny little lamp, all made of yellow glass, with a white globe that stands on the dining-room table. You couldn't tell it from a real one."

"The lamp's best of all," cried Kezia. She thought Isabel wasn't making half enough of the little lamp. But nobody paid any attention. Isabel was choosing the two who were to come back with them that afternoon and see it. She chose Emmie Cole and

Lena Logan. But when the others knew they were all to have a chance, they couldn't be nice enough to Isabel. One by one they put their arms round Isabel's waist and walked her off. They had something to whisper to her, a secret. "Isabel's *my* friend."

Only the little Kelveys moved away forgotten; there was nothing more for them to hear.

Days passed, and as more children saw the doll's house, the fame of it spread. It became the one subject, the rage. The one question was, "Have you seen the Burnells' doll's house? Oh, ain't it lovely!" "Haven't you seen it? Oh, I say!"

Even the dinner hour was given up to talking about it. The little girls sat under the pines eating their thick mutton sandwiches and big slabs of johnny cake spread with butter. While always, as near as they could get, sat the Kelveys, our Else holding on to Lil, listening too, while they chewed their jam sandwiches out of a newspaper soaked with large red blobs.

"Mother," said Kezia, "can't I ask the Kelveys just once?"

"Certainly not, Kezia."

"But why not?"

"Run away, Kezia; you know quite well why not."

At last everybody had seen it except them. On that day the subject rather flagged. It was the dinner hour. The children stood together under the pine trees, and suddenly, as they looked at the Kelveys eating out of their paper, always by themselves, always listening, they wanted to be horrid to them. Emmie Cole started the whisper.

"Lil Kelvey's going to be a servant when she grows up."

"O-oh, how awful!" said Isabel Burnell, and she made eyes at Emmie.

Emmie swallowed in a very meaning way and nodded to Isabel as she'd seen her mother do on those occasions.

"It's true—it's true—it's true," she said.

Then Lena Logan's little eyes snapped. "Shall I ask her?" she whispered.

"Bet you don't," said Jessie May.

"Pooh, I'm not frightened," said Lena. Suddenly she gave a little squeal and danced in front of the other girls. "Watch! Watch me! Watch me now!" said Lena. And sliding, gliding, dragging one foot, giggling behind her hand, Lena went over to the Kelveys.

Lil looked up from her dinner. She wrapped the rest quickly away. Our Else stopped chewing. What was coming now?

"Is it true you're going to be a servant when you grow up, Lil Kelvey?" shrilled Lena.

Dead silence. But instead of answering, Lil only gave her silly, shamefaced smile. She didn't seem to mind the question at all. What a sell for Lena! The girls began to titter.

Lena couldn't stand that. She put her hands on her hips; she shot forward. "Yah, yer father's in prison!" she hissed spitefully.

This was such a marvelous thing to have said that the little girls rushed away in a body, deeply, deeply excited, wild with joy. Someone found a long rope, and they began skipping. And never did they skip so high, run in and out so fast, or do such daring things as on that morning.

In the afternoon Pat called for the Burnell children with the buggy and they drove home. There were visitors. Isabel and Lottie, who liked visitors, went upstairs to change their pinafores. But Kezia thieved out at the back. Nobody was about; she began to swing on the big white gates of the courtyard. Presently, looking along the road, she saw two little dots. They grew bigger, they were coming towards her. Now she could see that one was in front and one close behind. Now she could see that they were the Kelveys. Kezia stopped swinging. She slipped off the gate as if she was going to run away. Then she hesitated. The Kelveys came nearer, and beside them walked their shadows, very long, stretching right across the road with their heads in the buttercups. Kezia clambered back on the gate; she had made up her mind; she swung out.

"Hullo," she said to the passing Kelveys.

They were so astounded that they stopped. Lil gave her silly smile. Our Else stared.

"You can come and see our doll's house if you want to," said Kezia, and she dragged one toe on the ground. But at that Lil turned red and shook her head quickly.

"Why not?" asked Kezia.

Lil gasped, then she said, "Your ma told our ma you wasn't to speak to us."

"Oh, well," said Kezia. She didn't know what to reply. "It doesn't matter. You can come and see our doll's house all the same. Come on. Nobody's looking."

But Lil shook her head still harder.

"Don't you want to?" asked Kezia.

Suddenly there was a twitch, a tug at Lil's skirt. She turned round. Our Else was looking at her with big, imploring eyes; she was frowning; she wanted to go. For a moment Lil looked at our Else very doubtfully. But then our Else twitched her skirt again. She started forward. Kezia led the way. Like two little stray cats they followed across the courtyard to where the doll's house stood.

"There it is," said Kezia.

There was a pause. Lil breathed loudly, almost snorted; our Else was still as stone.

"I'll open it for you," said Kezia kindly. She undid the hook and they looked inside.

"There's the drawing-room and the dining-room, and that's the—"

"Kezia!"

Oh, what a start they gave!

"Kezia!"

It was Aunt Beryl's voice. They turned round. At the back door stood Aunt Beryl, staring as if she couldn't believe what she saw.

"How dare you ask the little Kelveys into the courtyard!" said her cold, furious voice. "You know as well as I do, you're not allowed to talk to them. Run away, children, run away at once. And don't come back again," said Aunt Beryl. And she stepped into the yard and shooed them out as if they were chickens.

"Off you go immediately!" she called, cold and proud.

They did not need telling twice. Burning with shame, shrinking together, Lil huddling along like her mother, our Else dazed, somehow they crossed the big courtyard and squeezed through the white gate.

"Wicked, disobedient little girl!" said Aunt Beryl bitterly to Kezia, and she slammed the doll's house to.

The afternoon had been awful. A letter had come from Willie Brent, a terrifying, threatening letter, saying if she did not meet him that evening in Pulman's Bush, he'd come to the front door and ask the reason why! But now that she had frightened those little rats of Kelveys and given Kezia a good scolding, her heart felt lighter. That ghastly pressure was gone. She went back to the house humming.

When the Kelveys were well out of sight of Burnells', they sat down to rest on a big red drainpipe by the side of the road. Lil's cheeks were still burning; she took off the hat with the quill and held it on her knee. Dreamily they looked over the hay paddocks, past the creek, to the group of wattles where Logan's cows stood waiting to be milked. What were their thoughts?

Presently our Else nudged up close to her sister. But now she had forgotten the cross lady. She put out a finger and stroked her sister's quill; she smiled her rare smile.

"I seen the little lamp," she said softly.

Then both were silent once more.   *1921/1923*

Eudora Welty
1909–

"I am a writer who came of a sheltered life," writes EUDORA WELTY in her memoir, *One Writer's Beginning* (1983). "A sheltered life can be a daring life as well. For all serious daring starts from within." This U.S. writer of fiction was born in Jackson, Mississippi, to Christian Webb Welty, an insurance agent, and Chestina Andrews Welty, a teacher. The oldest of three children, Welty was encouraged in her love of language by her parents, who sang to each other and told endless stories: "I live in gratitude to my parents for initiating me—and as early as I begged for it, without keeping me waiting—into knowledge of the word." After completing secondary school in Jackson, Welty attended the Mississippi State College for Women for two years but transferred to the University of Wisconsin, from which she graduated in 1929; she then obtained a graduate degree from Columbia University in business, although her early ambition had been to become a painter. Upon returning to Mississippi in 1931, she worked a series of jobs as a society editor for a newspaper, a radio writer, and a junior publicity agent for the Works Progress Administration. The latter position allowed her to "see my home state at close hand" and gather material for the stories she was beginning to write.

Welty's first story, "Death of a Traveling Salesman," was published in 1936 in *Manuscript*; six subsequent stories came to the attention of Robert Penn Warren and Cleanth Brooks, who accepted them for publication in the *Southern Review*. There Katherine Ann Porter first admired the fiction she would later introduce in Welty's first collection, *A Curtain of Green and Other Stories* (1941). This volume was followed by *The Robber Bridegroom* (1942), *The Wide Net* (1943), *The Leaning Tower* (1944), and *Golden Apples* (1949). The latter collection, a series of loosely connected stories featuring related characters, Welty called "an experience in a writer's own discovery of affinities." Later volumes of short stories include *The Bride of the Innisfallen* (1955), *The Shoe Bird* (1964), *Thirteen Stories* (1965), and *Losing Battles* (1970). *The Collected Stories of Eudora Welty* appeared in 1980 to critical acclaim.

Welty has also published several novels, including *Delta Wedding* (1946), *The Ponder Heart* (1954), and *The Optimist's Daughter* (1972). Her essays and early book reviews were collected in *The Eye of the Story* (1978); recent reviews appeared in *A Writer's Eye* (1995). *One Time, One Place: Mississippi in the Depression: A Snapshot Album*, a series of photographs of rural Mississippians that Welty took while working for the WPA, was published in 1996; the accompanying text provides a vivid commentary on Southern life during the 1930s. Welty has held professorships at Smith and Bryn Mawr Colleges and has received numerous honors and awards, including the Pulitzer Prize for *The Optimist's Daughter*, the National Medal of Honor, and the Presidential Medal of Freedom. In 1996 she was inducted into the French Legion of Honor.

"Why I Live at the P.O." first appeared in 1941 in *A Curtain of Green*. Welty has described this story as "a monologue that takes possession of the speaker"; indeed, as the postmistress justifies her own behavior, "how much more gets told besides!" What Welty calls her "real subject, human relationships," lies at the heart of this hilarious tale.

⊰ Why I Live at the P.O. ⊱

I was getting along fine with Mama, Papa-Daddy and Uncle Rondo until my sister Stella-Rondo just separated from her husband and came back home again. Mr. Whitaker! Of course I went with Mr. Whitaker first, when he first appeared here in China Grove, taking "Pose Your-self" photos, and Stella-Rondo broke us up. Told him I was one-sided. Bigger on one side than the other, which is a deliberate, calculated falsehood: I'm the same. Stella-Rondo is exactly twelve months to the day younger than I am and for that reason she's spoiled.

She's always had anything in the world she wanted and then she'd throw it away. Papa-Daddy gave her this gorgeous Add-a-Pearl necklace when she was eight years old and she threw it away playing baseball when she was nine, with only two pearls.

So as soon as she got married and moved away from home the first thing she did was separate! From Mr. Whitaker! This photographer with the popeyes she said she trusted. Came home from one of those towns up in Illinois and to our complete surprise brought this child of two.

Mama said she like to made her drop dead for a second. "Here you had this marvelous blonde child and never so much as wrote your mother a word about it," says Mama. "I'm thoroughly ashamed of you." But of course she wasn't.

Stella-Rondo just calmly takes off this *hat*, I wish you could see it. She says, "Why, Mama, Shirley-T.'s adopted, I can prove it."

"How?" says Mama, but all I says was, "H'm!" There I was over the hot stove, trying to stretch two chickens over five people and a completely unexpected child into the bargain, without one moment's notice.

"What do you mean—'H'm!'?" says Stella-Rondo, and Mama says, "I heard that, Sister."

I said that oh, I didn't mean a thing, only that whoever Shirley-T. was, she was the spit-image of Papa-Daddy if he'd cut off his beard, which of course he'd never do in the world. Papa-Daddy's Mama's papa and sulks.

Stella-Rondo got furious! She said, "Sister, I don't need to tell you you got a lot of nerve and always did have and I'll thank you to make no future reference to my adopted child whatsoever."

"Very well," I said. "Very well, very well. Of course I noticed at once she looks like Mr. Whitaker's side too. That frown. She looks like a cross between Mr. Whitaker and Papa-Daddy."

"Well, all I can say is she isn't."

"She looks exactly like Shirley Temple to me," says Mama, but Shirley-T. just ran away from her.

So the first thing Stella-Rondo did at the table was turn Papa-Daddy against me.

"Papa-Daddy," she says. He was trying to cut up his meat. "Papa-Daddy!" I was taken completely by surprise. Papa-Daddy is about a million years old and's got this long-long beard. "Papa-Daddy, Sister says she fails to understand why you don't cut off your beard."

So Papa-Daddy l-a-y-s down his knife and fork! He's real rich. Mama says he is, he says he isn't. So he says, "Have I heard correctly? You don't understand why I don't cut off my beard?"

"Why," I says, "Papa-Daddy, of course I understand, I did not say any such of a thing, the idea!"

He says, "Hussy!"

I says, "Papa-Daddy, you know I wouldn't any more want you to cut off your beard than the man in the moon. It was the farthest thing from my mind! Stella-Rondo sat there and made that up while she was eating breast of chicken."

But he says, "So the postmistress fails to understand why I don't cut off my beard. Which job I got you through my influence with the government. 'Bird's nest'—is that what you call it?"

Not that it isn't the next to smallest P.O. in the entire state of Mississippi.

I says, "Oh, Papa-Daddy," I says, "I didn't say any such of a thing, I never dreamed it was a bird's nest, I have always been grateful though this is the next to smallest P.O. in the state of Mississippi, and I do not enjoy being referred to as a hussy by my own grandfather."

But Stella-Rondo says, "Yes, you did say it too. Anybody in the world could of heard you, that had ears."

"Stop right there," says Mama, looking at *me*.

So I pulled my napkin straight back through the napkin ring and left the table.

As soon as I was out of the room Mama says, "Call her back, or she'll starve to death," but Papa-Daddy says, "This is the beard I started growing on the Coast when I was fifteen years old." He would of gone on till nightfall if Shirley-T. hadn't lost the Milky Way she ate in Cairo.

So Papa-Daddy says, "I am going out and lie in the hammock, and you can all sit here and remember my words: I'll never cut off my beard as long as I live, even one inch, and I don't appreciate it in you at all." Passed right by me in the hall and went straight out and got in the hammock.

It would be a holiday. It wasn't five minutes before Uncle Rondo suddenly appeared in the hall in one of Stella-Rondo's flesh-colored kimonos, all cut on the bias, like something Mr. Whitaker probably thought was gorgeous.

"Uncle Rondo!" I says. "I didn't know who that was! Where are you going?"

"Sister," he says, "get out of my way, I'm poisoned."

"If you're poisoned stay away from Papa-Daddy," I says. "Keep out of the hammock. Papa-Daddy will certainly beat you on the head if you come within forty miles of him. He thinks I deliberately said he ought to cut off his beard after he got me the P.O., and I've told him and told him and told him, and he acts like he just don't hear me. Papa-Daddy must of gone stone deaf."

"He picked a fine day to do it then," says Uncle Rondo, and before you could say "Jack Robinson" flew out in the yard.

What he'd really done, he'd drunk another bottle of that prescription. He does it every single Fourth of July as sure as shooting, and it's horribly expensive. Then he falls over in the hammock and snores. So he insisted on zigzagging right on out to the hammock, looking like a half-wit.

Papa-Daddy woke up with this horrible yell and right there without moving an inch he tried to turn Uncle Rondo against me. I heard every word he said. Oh, he told Uncle Rondo I didn't learn to read till I was eight years old and he didn't see how in the world I ever got the mail put up at the P.O., much less read it all, and he said if Uncle Rondo could only fathom the lengths he had gone to get me that job! And he said on the other hand he thought Stella-Rondo had a brilliant mind and deserved credit for getting out of town. All the time he was just lying there swinging as pretty as you please and looping out his beard, and poor Uncle Rondo was *pleading* with him to slow down the hammock, it was making him as dizzy as a witch to watch it. But that's what Papa-Daddy likes about a hammock. So Uncle Rondo was too dizzy to get turned against me for the time being. He's Mama's only brother and is a good case of a one-track mind. Ask anybody. A certified pharmacist.

Just then I heard Stella-Rondo raising the upstairs window. While she was married she got this peculiar idea that it's cooler with the windows shut and locked. So she has to raise the window before she can make a soul hear her outdoors.

So she raises the window and says, "*Oh!*" You would have thought she was mortally wounded.

Uncle Rondo and Papa-Daddy didn't even look up, but kept right on with what they were doing. I had to laugh.

I flew up the stairs and threw the door open! I says, "What in the wide world's the matter, Stella-Rondo? You mortally wounded?"

"No," she says, "I am not mortally wounded but I wish you would do me the favor of looking out that window there and telling me what you see."

So I shade my eyes and look out the window.

"I see the front yard," I says.

"Don't you see any human beings?" she says.

"I see Uncle Rondo trying to run Papa-Daddy out of the hammock," I says. "Nothing more. Naturally, it's so suffocating-hot in the house, with all the windows shut and locked, everybody who cares to stay in their right mind will have to go out and get in the hammock before the Fourth of July is over."

"Don't you notice anything different about Uncle Rondo?" asks Stella-Rondo.

"Why, no, except he's got on some terrible-looking flesh-colored contraption I wouldn't be found dead in, is all I can see," I says.

"Never mind, you won't be found dead in it, because it happens to be part of my trousseau, and Mr. Whitaker took several dozen photographs of me in it," says Stella-Rondo. "What on earth could Uncle Rondo *mean* by wearing part of my trousseau out in the broad open daylight without saying so much as 'Kiss my foot,' *knowing* I only got home this morning after my separation and hung my negligee up on the bathroom door, just as nervous as I could be?"

"I'm sure I don't know, and what do you expect me to do about it?" I says. "Jump out the window?"

"No, I expect nothing of the kind. I simply declare that Uncle Rondo looks like a fool in it, that's all," she says. "It makes me sick to my stomach."

"Well, he looks as good as he can," I says. "As good as anybody in reason could." I stood up for Uncle Rondo, please remember. And I said to Stella-Rondo, "I think I would do well not to criticize so freely if I were you and came home with a two-year-old child I had never said a word about, and no explanation whatever about my separation."

"I asked you the instant I entered this house not to refer one more time to my adopted child, and you gave me your word of honor you would not," was all Stella-Rondo would say, and started pulling out every one of her eyebrows with some cheap Kress tweezers.

So I merely slammed the door behind me and went down and made some green-tomato pickle. Somebody had to do it. Of course Mama had turned both the Negroes loose; she always said no earthly power could hold one anyway on the Fourth of July, so she wouldn't even try. It turned out that Jaypan fell in the lake and came within a very narrow limit of drowning.

So Mama trots in. Lifts up the lid and says, "H'm! not very good for your Uncle Rondo in his precarious condition, I must say. Or poor little adopted Shirley-T. Shame on you!"

That made me tired. I says, "Well, Stella-Rondo had better thank her lucky stars it was her instead of me came trotting in with that very peculiar-looking child. Now if it had been me that trotted in from Illinois and brought a peculiar-looking child of two, I shudder to think of the reception I'd of got, much less controlled the diet of an entire family."

"But you must remember, Sister, that you were never married to Mr. Whitaker in the first place and didn't go up to Illinois to live," says Mama, shaking a spoon in my face. "If you had I would of been just as overjoyed to see you and your little adopted girl as I was to see Stella-Rondo, when you wound up with your separation and came on back home."

"You would not," I says.

"Don't contradict me, I would," says Mama.

But I said she couldn't convince me though she talked till she was blue in the face. Then I said, "Besides, you know as well as I do that that child is not adopted."

"She most certainly is adopted," says Mama, stiff as a poker.

I says, "Why, Mama, Stella-Rondo had her just as sure as anything in this world, and just too stuck up to admit it."

"Why, Sister," said Mama. "Here I thought we were going to have a pleasant Fourth of July, and you start right out not believing a word your own baby sister tells you!"

"Just like Cousin Annie Flo. Went to her grave denying the facts of life," I remind Mama.

"I told you if you ever mentioned Annie Flo's name I'd slap your face," says Mama, and slaps my face.

"All right, you wait and see," I says.

"I," says Mama, "I prefer to take my children's word for anything when it's humanly possible." You ought to see Mama, she weighs two hundred pounds and has real tiny feet.

Just then something perfectly horrible occurred to me.

"Mama," I says, "can that child talk?" I simply had to whisper! "Mama, I wonder if that child can be—you know—in any way? Do you realize," I says, "that she hasn't spoken one single, solitary word to a human being up to this minute? This is the way she looks," I says, and I looked like this.

Well, Mama and I just stood there and stared at each other. It was horrible!

"I remember well that Joe Whitaker frequently drank like a fish," says Mama. "I believed to my soul he drank *chemicals*." And without another word she marches to the foot of the stairs and calls Stella-Rondo.

"Stella-Rondo? O-o-o-o-o! Stella-Rondo!"

"What?" says Stella-Rondo from upstairs. Not even the grace to get up off the bed.

"Can that child of yours talk?" asks Mama.

Stella-Rondo says, "Can she what?"

"Talk! Talk!" says Mama. "Burdyburdyburdyburdy!"

So Stella-Rondo yells back, "Who says she can't talk?"

"Sister says so," says Mama.

"You didn't have to tell me, I know whose word of honor don't mean a thing in this house," says Stella-Rondo.

And in a minute the loudest Yankee voice I ever heard in my life yells out, "OE'm Pop-OE the Sailor-r-r-r Ma-a-an!" and then somebody jumps up and down in the upstairs hall. In another second the house would of fallen down.

"Not only talks, she can tap-dance!" calls Stella-Rondo. "Which is more than some people I won't name can do."

"Why, the little precious darling thing!" Mama says, so surprised. "Just as smart as she can be!" Starts talking baby talk right there. Then she turns on me. "Sister, you ought to be thoroughly ashamed! Run upstairs this instant and apologize to Stella-Rondo and Shirley-T."

"Apologize for what?" I says. "I merely wondered if the child was normal, that's all. Now that she's proved she is, why, I have nothing further to say."

But Mama just turned on her heel and flew out, furious. She ran right upstairs and hugged the baby. She believed it was adopted. Stella-Rondo hadn't done a thing but turn her against me from upstairs while I stood there helpless over the hot stove. So that made Mama, Papa-Daddy and the baby all on Stella-Rondo's side.

Next, Uncle Rondo.

I must say that Uncle Rondo has been marvelous to me at various times in the past and I was completely unprepared to be made to jump out of my skin, the way it turned out. Once Stella-Rondo did something perfectly horrible to him—broke a chain letter from Flanders Field—and he took the radio back he had given her and gave it to me. Stella-Rondo was furious! For six months we all had to call her Stella instead of Stella-Rondo, or she wouldn't answer. I always though Uncle Rondo had all the brains of the entire family. Another time he sent me to Mammoth Cave, with all expenses paid.

But this would be the day he was drinking that prescription, the Fourth of July.

So at supper Stella-Rondo speaks up and says she thinks Uncle Rondo ought to try to eat a little something. So finally Uncle Rondo said he would try a little cold biscuits and ketchup, but that was all. So *she* brought it to him.

"Do you think it wise to disport with ketchup in Stella-Rondo's flesh-colored kimono?" I says. Trying to be considerate! If Stella-Rondo couldn't watch out for her trousseau, somebody had to.

"Any objections?" asks Uncle Rondo, just about to pour out all the ketchup.

"Don't mind what she says, Uncle Rondo," says Stella-Rondo. "Sister has been devoting this solid afternoon to sneering out my bedroom window at the way you look."

"What's that?" says Uncle Rondo. Uncle Rondo has got the most terrible temper in the world. Anything is liable to make him tear the house down if it comes at the wrong time.

So Stella-Rondo says, "Sister says, 'Uncle Rondo certainly does look like a fool in that pink kimono!'"

Do you remember who it was really said that?

Uncle Rondo spills out all the ketchup and jumps out of his chair and tears off the kimono and throws it down on the dirty floor and puts his foot on it. It had to be sent all the way to Jackson to the cleaners and repleated.

"So that's your opinion of your Uncle Rondo, is it?" he says. "I look like a fool, do I? Well, that's the last straw. A whole day in this house with nothing to do, and then to hear you come out with a remark like that behind my back!"

"I didn't say any such of a thing, Uncle Rondo," I says, "and I'm not saying who did, either. Why, I think you look all right. Just try to take care of yourself and not talk and eat at the same time," I says. "I think you better go lie down."

"Lie down my foot," says Uncle Rondo. I ought to of known by that he was fixing to do something perfectly horrible.

So he didn't do anything that night in the precarious state he was in—just played Casino with Mama and Stella-Rondo and Shirley-T. and gave Shirley-T. a nickel with a head on both sides. It tickled her nearly to death, and she called him "Papa." But at 6:30 a.m. the next morning, he threw a whole five-cent package of some unsold one-inch firecrackers from the store as hard as he could into my bedroom and they every one went off. Not one bad one in the string. Anybody else, there'd be one that wouldn't go off.

Well, I'm just terribly susceptible to noise of any kind, the doctor has always told me I was the most sensitive person he had ever seen in his whole life, and I was simply prostrated. I couldn't eat! People tell me they heard it as far as the cemetery, and old Aunt Jep Patterson, that had been holding her own so good, thought it was Judgment Day and she was going to meet her whole family. It's usually so quiet here.

And I'll tell you it didn't take me any longer than a minute to make up my mind what to do. There I was with the whole entire house on Stella-Rondo's side and turned against me. If I have anything at all I have pride.

So I just decided I'd go straight down to the P.O. There's plenty of room there in the back, I says to myself.

Well! I made no bones about letting the family catch on to what I was up to. I didn't try to conceal it.

The first thing they knew, I marched in where they were all playing Old Maid and pulled the electric oscillating fan out by the plug, and everything got real hot. Next I snatched the pillow I'd done the needle-point on right off the davenport from behind Papa-Daddy. He went "Ugh!" I beat Stella-Rondo up the stairs and finally found my charm bracelet in her bureau drawer under a picture of Nelson Eddy.

"So that's the way the land lies," says Uncle Rondo. There he was, piecing on the ham. "Well, Sister, I'll be glad to donate my army cot if you got any place to set it up, providing you'll leave right this minute and let me get some peace." Uncle Rondo was in France.

"Thank you kindly for the cot and 'peace' is hardly the word I would select if I had to resort to firecrackers at 6:30 a.m. in a young girl's bedroom," I says back to him. "And as to where I intend to go, you seem to forget my position as postmistress of China Grove, Mississippi," I says. "I've always got the P.O."

Well, that made them all sit up and take notice.

I went out front and started digging up some four-o'clocks to plant around the P.O.

"Ah-ah-ah!" says Mama, raising the window. "Those happen to be my four-o'clocks. Everything planted in that star is mine. I've never known you to make anything grow in your life."

"Very well," I says. "But I take the fern. Even you, Mama, can't stand there and deny that I'm the one watered that fern. And I happen to know where I can send in a box top and get a packet of one thousand mixed seeds, no two the same kind, free."

"Oh, where?" Mama wants to know.

But I says, "Too late. You 'tend to your house, and I'll 'tend to mine. You hear things like that all the time if you know how to listen to the radio. Perfectly marvelous offers. Get anything you want free."

So I hope to tell you I marched in and got that radio, and they could of all bit a nail in two, especially Stella-Rondo, that it used to belong to, and she well knew she couldn't get it back, I'd sue for it like a shot. And I very politely took the sewing-machine motor I helped pay the most on to give Mama for Christmas back in 1929, and a good big calendar, with the first-aid remedies on it. The thermometer and the Hawaiian ukulele certainly were rightfully mine, and I stood on the step-ladder and got all my watermelon-rind preserves and every fruit and vegetable I'd put up, every jar. Then I began to pull the tacks out of the bluebird wall vases on the archway to the dining room.

"Who told you you could have those, Miss Priss?" says Mama, fanning as hard as she could.

"I bought 'em and I'll keep track of 'em," I says. "I'll tack 'em up one on each side the post-office window, and you can see 'em when you come to ask me for your mail, if you're so dead to see 'em."

"Not I! I'll never darken the door to that post office again if I live to be a hundred," Mama says. "Ungrateful child! After all the money we spent on you at the Normal."

"Me either," says Stella-Rondo. "You can just let my mail lie there and rot, for all I care. I'll never come and relieve you of a single, solitary piece."

"I should worry," I says. "And who you think's going to sit down and write you all those big fat letters and postcards, by the way? Mr. Whitaker? Just because he was the only man ever dropped down in China Grove and you got him—unfairly—is he going to sit down and write you a lengthy correspondence after you come home giving no rhyme nor reason whatsoever for your separation and no explanation for the presence of that child? I may not have your brilliant mind, but I fail to see it."

So Mama says, "Sister, I've told you a thousand times that Stella-Rondo simply got homesick, and this child is far too big to be hers," and she says, "Now, why don't you all just sit down and play Casino?"

Then Shirley-T. sticks out her tongue at me in this perfectly horrible way. She has no more manners than the man in the moon. I told her she was going to cross her eyes like that some day and they'd stick.

"It's too late to stop me now," I says. "You should have tried that yesterday. I'm going to the P.O. and the only way you can possibly see me is to visit me there."

So Papa-Daddy says, "You'll never catch me setting foot in that post office, even if I should take a notion into my head to write a letter some place." He says, "I won't have you reachin' out of that little old window with a pair of shears and cuttin' off any beard of mine. I'm too smart for you!"

"We all are," says Stella-Rondo.

But I said, "If you're so smart, where's Mr. Whitaker?"

So then Uncle Rondo says, "I'll thank you from now on to stop reading all the orders I get on postcards and telling everybody in China Grove what you think is the matter with them," but I says, "I draw my own conclusions and will continue in the future to draw them." I says, "If people want to write their inmost secrets on penny postcards, there's nothing in the wide world you can do about it, Uncle Rondo."

"And if you think we'll ever write another postcard you're sadly mistaken," says Mama.

"Cutting off your nose to spite your face then," I says. "But if you're all determined to have no more to do with the U.S. mail, think of this: What will Stella-Rondo do now, if she wants to tell Mr. Whitaker to come after her?"

"Wah!" says Stella-Rondo. I knew she'd cry. She had a conniption fit right there in the kitchen.

"It will be interesting to see how long she holds out," I says. "And now—I am leaving."

"Good-bye," says Uncle Rondo.

"Oh, I declare," says Mama, "to think that a family of mine should quarrel on the Fourth of July, or the day after, over Stella-Rondo leaving old Mr. Whitaker and having the sweetest little adopted child! It looks like we'd all be glad!"

"Wah!" says Stella-Rondo, and has a fresh conniption fit.

"*He* left *her*—you mark my words," I says. "That's Mr. Whitaker. I know Mr. Whitaker. After all, I knew him first. I said from the beginning he'd up and leave her. I foretold every single thing that's happened."

"Where did he go?" asks Mama.

"Probably to the North Pole, if he knows what's good for him," I says.

But Stella-Rondo just bawled and wouldn't say another word. She flew to her room and slammed the door.

"Now look what you've gone and done, Sister," says Mama. "You go apologize."

"I haven't got time, I'm leaving," I says.

"Well, what are you waiting around for?" asks Uncle Rondo.

So I just picked up the kitchen clock and marched off, without saying "Kiss my foot" or anything, and never did tell Stella-Rondo good-bye.

There was a girl going along on a little wagon right in front.

"Girl," I says, "come help me haul these things down the hill, I'm going to live in the post office."

Took her nine trips in her express wagon. Uncle Rondo came out on the porch and threw her a nickel.

And that's the last I've laid eyes on any of my family or my family laid eyes on me for five solid days and nights. Stella-Rondo may be telling the most horrible tales in the world about Mr. Whitaker, but I haven't heard them. As I tell everybody, I draw my own conclusions.

But oh, I like it here. It's ideal, as I've been saying. You see, I've got everything cater-cornered, the way I like it. Hear the radio? All the war news. Radio, sewing machine, book ends, ironing board and that great big piano lamp—peace, that's what I like. Butter-bean vines planted all along the front where the strings are.

Of course, there's not much mail. My family are naturally the main people in China Grove, and if they prefer to vanish from the face of the earth, for all the mail they get or the mail they write, why, I'm not going to open my mouth. Some of the folks here in town are taking up for me and some turned against me. I know which is which. There are always people who will quit buying stamps just to get on the right side of Papa-Daddy.

But here I am, and here I'll stay. I want the world to know I'm happy.

And if Stella-Rondo should come to me this minute, on bended knees, and *attempt* to explain the incidents of her life with Mr. Whitaker, I'd simply put my fingers in both my ears and refuse to listen.   *1941*

Doris Lessing
1919–

DORIS LESSING is renowned for both her feminist novels, *The Golden Notebook* (1962) and *The Summer Before the Dark* (1973), and her science fiction, especially *Canopus in Argus: Archives* (1979–82). Although she is generally considered a British writer, Lessing grew up in imperial England's colonies. She was born Doris Taylor to British parents living in Kermanshah, Persia (now Iran), where her father worked as a bank manager. When Lessing was five years old, her family moved to a three thousand-acre farm in Rhodesia (now Zimbabwe). Lessing's father embraced life as a homesteader, preferring, as his daughter once said, to fail on the liberating frontier than to flourish in the confines of England; her mother, on the other hand, was a reluctant exile who yearned nostalgically for home. Although Lessing loved life on the veld, her mother's misery made her childhood unhappy, and after attending a Catholic girls' secondary school she left the farm for Salisbury, Rhodesia's capital. Over a twenty-year period she worked as a secretary, was married and divorced twice, raised three children, and became active in Salisbury's intellectual and political circles. Critical of the racism that characterized British colonialism, she embraced leftist causes and even-tually joined the Communist Party. Although she resigned in 1950, disillusioned with Commu-nism's failure to bring about lasting social change, her socialism is evident in much of her fiction.

In 1949 Lessing moved to London to pursue a career as a writer. Eventually she came to love this "nightmare city," but for years she felt marginalized in both African and European cul-tures and experienced a sense of dislocation that has affected her literary work. As Judith Kegan Gardiner has noted, "being a colonial-in-exile . . . puts into play an oscillation whereby no place is home"; thus "there remains always a missing point of origin" in Lessing's texts, "a fruit-ful unsettledness." Such unsettledness is evident in the sexual and psychological disorientation of the female protagonists in her realist fiction as well as in the cosmic diaspora of the androgy-nous characters in her fantastic fiction. Her first novel, *The Grass Is Singing* (1950), addresses the tensions of African society under colonialism. *Children of Violence*, a series of five novels published between 1952 and 1969, foregrounds a woman's struggle for sexual expression and creative identity; two of these novels, *Martha Quest* (1952) and *The Four-Gated City* (1969), blend feminism, social critique, and mysticism. These themes also appear in *The Golden Note-book* (1962), whose protagonist, Anna Wulf, suffers from insecurities regarding her artistic tal-ent as well as romantic thralldom to a troubled man. *The Summer Before the Dark* (1973) chronicles a woman's effort to awaken sexually and spiritually, with mixed results. Lessing's conflicted portrayal of women's autonomy has led many critics to agree with Claire Sprague that there is "a long-term ambiguousness about feminism in Lessing's work."

In the 1970s Lessing turned her attention to science fiction and dystopian literature. This shift of interest began in 1972 with *Briefing for a Descent into Hell*, which circumvents linear time and is dystopian in tone and theme. *Memoirs of a Survivor* (1979), another dystopia, explores the threat of chaos when governments cease to function because of bureaucracies, elitism, and disregard for the environment. In *Shikasta* (1979) Lessing com-bines satire, fantasy, and realism to portray events on earth as determined by benevolent, malevolent, or ineffectual aliens who frequent this planet in disguise. *The Marriages of Zones Three, Four, and Five* (1981) presents the saga of Queen Al-Ith, who rejects the val-ues of her husband's militaristic kingdom. *Mara and Dann: An Adventure* (1999) explores enduring love between sister and brother as they struggle to survive in a barren and violent futuristic landscape.

Lessing has also continued to write novels in the realist tradition. *The Diaries of Jane Somers* (1984) considers women's roles as the nurturers of young and old; *The Good Terrorist* (1985) exam-ines a woman's complicity in political and moral intrigue; and *The Fifth Child* (1986) explores a tra-ditional family's disintegration when a severely troubled son disturbs the peace. Moreover, Lessing is an acclaimed writer of short stories and prose. Among her collections of short fiction are *A Man and Two Women* (1963), which focuses on relationships between the sexes; *African Stories* (1964), which interrogates racism from a white colonist's perspective; and *Collected Stories*, which appeared in 1979. She has published memoirs of growing up in southern Africa, includ-ing *Going Home* (1968). *A Small Personal Voice* (1975) contains many of her essays, reviews, and interviews.

Although Lessing has revealed her millennial vision in works since the 1950s, her sense of humanity's capacity for self-destruction seems particularly trenchant in the story included here. "An Old Woman and Her Cat" depicts a homeless woman's alienation from family and society. This story's apocalyptic dimensions can be seen in its opening lines: "Her name was Hetty, and she was born with the twentieth century. She was seventy when she died of cold and malnutrition." "An Old Woman and Her Cat" offers both a social commentary on homelessness and a finely tuned portrait of one woman who falls between the proverbial cracks.

⊰ An Old Woman and Her Cat ⊱

Her name was Hetty, and she was born with the twentieth century. She was seventy when she died of cold and malnutrition. She had been alone for a long time, since her husband had died of pneumonia in a bad winter soon after the Second World War. He had not been more than middle-aged. Her four children were now middle-aged, with grown children. Of these descendants one daughter sent her Christmas cards, but otherwise she did not exist for them. For they were all respectable people, with homes and good jobs and cars. And Hetty was not respectable. She had always been a bit strange, these people said, when mentioning her at all.

When Fred Pennefather, her husband, was alive and the children just growing up, they all lived much too close and uncomfortable in a Council flat in that part of London which is like an estuary, with tides of people flooding in and out: They were not half a mile from the great stations of Euston, St. Pancras, and King's Cross. The blocks of flats were pioneers in that area, standing up grim, gray, hideous, among many acres of little houses and gardens, all soon to be demolished so that they could be replaced by more tall gray blocks. The Pennefathers were good tenants, paying their rent, keeping out of debt; he was a building worker, "steady," and proud of it. There was no evidence then of Hetty's future dislocation from the normal, unless it was that she very often slipped down for an hour or so to the platforms where the locomotives drew in and ground out again. She liked the smell of it all, she said. She liked to see people moving about, "coming and going from all those foreign places." She meant Scotland, Ireland, the North of England. These visits into the din, the smoke, the massed swirling people were for her a drug, like other people's drinking or gambling. Her husband teased her, calling her a gypsy. She was in fact part gypsy, for her mother had been one, but had chosen to leave her people and marry a man who lived in a house. Fred Pennefather liked his wife for being different from the run of the women he knew, and had married her because of it, but her children were fearful that her gypsy blood might show itself in worse ways than haunting railway stations. She was a tall woman with a lot of glossy black hair, a skin that tanned easily, and dark strong eyes. She wore bright colors, and enjoyed quick tempers and sudden reconciliations. In her prime she attracted attention, was proud and handsome. All this made it inevitable that the people in those streets should refer to her as "that gypsy woman." When she heard them, she shouted back that she was none the worse for that.

After her husband died and the children married and left, the Council moved her to a small flat in the same building. She got a job selling food in a local store, but found it boring. There seem to be traditional occupations for middle-aged women living alone, the busy and responsible part of their lives being over. Drink. Gambling. Looking for another husband. A wistful affair or two. That's about it. Hetty went through a period of, as it were, testing out all these, like hobbies, but tired of them. While still

earning her small wage as a saleswoman, she began a trade in buying and selling secondhand clothes. She did not have a shop of her own, but bought clothes from householders, and sold these to stalls and the secondhand shops. She adored doing this. It
was a passion. She gave up her respectable job and forgot all about her love of trains
and travelers. Her room was always full of bright bits of cloth, a dress that had a pattern
she fancied and did not want to sell, strips of beading, old furs, embroidery, lace. There
were street traders among the people in the flats, but there was something in the way
Hetty went about it that lost her friends. Neighbors of twenty or thirty years' standing
said she had gone queer, and wished to know her no longer. But she did not mind. She
was enjoying herself too much, particularly the moving about the streets with her old
perambulator, in which she crammed what she was buying or selling. She liked the gossiping, the bargaining, the wheedling from householders. It was this last which,—and
she knew this quite well, of course—the neighbors objected to. It was the thin edge of
the wedge. It was begging. Decent people did not beg. She was no longer decent.

Lonely in her tiny flat, she was there as little as possible, always preferring the lively
streets. But she had after all to spend some time in her room, and one day she saw a kitten
lost and trembling in a dirty corner, and brought it home to the block of flats. She was on
the fifth floor. While the kitten was growing into a large strong tom, he ranged about that
conglomeration of staircases and lifts and many dozens of flats, as if the building were a
town. Pets were not actively persecuted by the authorities, only forbidden and then tolerated. Hetty's life from the coming of the cat became more sociable, for the beast was
always making friends with somebody in the cliff that was the block of flats across the
court, or not coming home for nights at a time, so that she had to go and look for him and
knock on doors and ask, or returning home kicked and limping, or bleeding after a fight
with his kind. She made scenes with the kickers, or the owners of the enemy cats,
exchanged cat lore with cat lovers, was always having to bandage and nurse her poor Tibby. The cat was soon a scarred warrior with fleas, a torn ear, and a ragged look to him. He
was a multicolored cat and his eyes were small and yellow. He was a long way down the
scale from the delicately coloured, elegantly shaped pedigree cats. But he was independent, and often caught himself pigeons when he could no longer stand the tinned cat
food, or the bread and packet gravy Hetty fed him, and he purred and nestled when she
grabbed him to her bosom at those times she suffered loneliness. This happened less and
less. Once she had realized that her children were hoping that she would leave them
alone because the old rag trader was an embarrassment to them, she accepted it, and a bitterness that always had wild humor in it only welled up at times like Christmas. She sang
or chanted to the cat: "You nasty old beast, filthy old cat, nobody wants you, do they Tibby, no, you're just an alley tom, just an old stealing cat, hey Tibs, Tibs, Tibs."

The building teemed with cats. There were even a couple of dogs. They all
fought up and down the gray cement corridors. There were sometimes dog and cat
messes which someone had to clear up, but which might be left for days and weeks as
part of neighborly wars and feuds. There were many complaints. Finally an official
came from the Council to say that the ruling about keeping animals was going to be
enforced. Hetty, like the others, would have to have her cat destroyed. This crisis
coincided with a time of bad luck for her. She had had flu; had not been able to earn
money, had found it hard to get out for her pension, had run into debt. She owed a
lot of back rent, too. A television set she had hired and was not paying for attracted
the visits of a television representative. The neighbors were gossiping that Hetty had
"gone savage." This was because the cat had brought up the stairs and along the passageways a pigeon he had caught, shedding feathers and blood all the way; a woman

coming in to complain found Hetty plucking the pigeon to stew it, as she had done with others, sharing the meal with Tibby.

"You're filthy," she would say to him, setting the stew down to cool in his dish. "Filthy old thing. Eating that dirty old pigeon. What do you think you are, a wild cat? Decent cats don't eat dirty birds. Only those old gypsies eat wild birds."

One night she begged help from a neighbor who had a car, and put into the car herself the television set, the cat, bundles of clothes, and the pram. She was driven across London to a room in a street that was a slum because it was waiting to be done up. The neighbor made a second trip to bring her bed and her mattress, which were tied to the roof of the car, a chest of drawers, an old trunk, saucepans. It was in this way that she left the street in which she had lived for thirty years, nearly half her life.

She set up house again in one room. She was frightened to go near "them" to reestablish pension rights and her identity, because of the arrears of rent she had left behind, and because of the stolen television set. She started trading again, and the little room was soon spread, like her last, with a rainbow of colors and textures and lace and sequins. She cooked on a single gas ring and washed in the sink. There was no hot water unless it was boiled in saucepans. There were several old ladies and a family of five children in the house, which was condemned.

She was in the ground floor back, with a window which opened onto a derelict garden, and her cat was happy in a hunting ground that was a mile around this house where his mistress was so splendidly living. A canal ran close by, and in the dirty city water were islands which a cat could reach by leaping from moored boat to boat. On the islands were rats and birds. There were pavements full of fat London pigeons. The cat was a fine hunter. He soon had his place in the hierarchies of the local cat population and did not have to fight much to keep it. He was a strong male cat, and fathered many litters of kittens.

In that place Hetty and he lived five happy years. She was trading well, for there were rich people close by to shed what the poor needed to buy cheaply. She was not lonely, for she made quarrelling but satisfying friendship with a woman on the top floor, a widow like herself who did not see her children either. Hetty was sharp with the five children, complaining about their noise and mess, but she slipped them bits of money and sweets after telling their mother that "she was a fool to put herself out for them, because they wouldn't appreciate it." She was living well, even without her pension. She sold the television set and gave herself and her friend upstairs some day trips to the coast, and bought a small radio. She never read books or magazines. The truth was that she could not write or read, or only so badly it was no pleasure to her. Her cat was all reward and no cost, for he fed himself, and continued to bring in pigeons for her to cook and eat, for which in return he claimed milk.

"Greedy Tibby, you greedy *thing*, don't think I don't know, oh yes I do, you'll get sick eating those old pigeons, I do keep telling you that, don't I?"

At last the street was being done up. No longer a uniform, long, disgraceful slum, houses were being bought by the middle-class people. While this meant more good warm clothes for trading—or begging, for she still could not resist the attraction of getting something for nothing by the use of her plaintive inventive tongue, her still-flashing handsome eyes—Hetty knew, like her neighbors, that soon this house with its cargo of poor people would be bought for improvement.

In the week Hetty was seventy years old came the notice that was the end of this little community. They had four weeks to find somewhere else to live.

Usually, the shortage of housing being what it is in London—and everywhere else in the world, of course—these people would have had to scatter, fending for themselves. But the fate of this particular street was attracting attention, because a municipal election was pending. Homelessness among the poor was finding a focus in this street which was a perfect symbol of the whole area, and indeed the whole city, half of it being fine converted tasteful houses, full of people who spent a lot of money, and half being dying houses tenanted by people like Hetty.

As a result of speeches by councilors and churchmen, local authorities found themselves unable to ignore the victims of this redevelopment. The people in the house Hetty was in were visited by a team consisting of an unemployment officer, a social worker, and a rehousing officer. Hetty, a strong gaunt old woman wearing a scarlet wool suit she had found among her cast-offs that week, a black knitted teacosy on her head, and black buttoned Edwardian boots too big for her, so that she had to shuffle, invited them into her room. But although all were well used to the extremes of poverty, none wished to enter the place, but stood in the doorway and made her this offer: that she should be aided to get her pension—why had she not claimed it long ago?—and that she, together with the four other old ladies in the house, should move to a Home run by the Council out in the northern suburbs. All these women were used to, and enjoyed, lively London, and while they had no alternative but to agree, they fell into a saddened and sullen state. Hetty agreed too. The last two winters had set her bones aching badly, and a cough was never far away. And while perhaps she was more of an urban soul even than the others, since she had walked up and down so many streets with her old perambulator loaded with rags and laces, and since she knew so intimately London's texture and taste, she minded least of all the idea of a new home "among green fields." There were, in fact, no fields near the promised Home, but for some reason all the old ladies had chosen to bring out this old song of a phrase, as if it belonged to their situation, that of old women not far off death. "It will be nice to be near green fields again," they said to each other over cups of tea.

The housing officer came to make final arrangements. Hetty Pennefather was to move with the others in two weeks' time. The young man, sitting on the very edge of the only chair in the crammed room, because it was greasy and he suspected it had fleas or worse in it, breathed as lightly as he could because of the appalling stink: there was a lavatory in the house, but it had been out of order for three days, and it was just the other side of a thin wall. The whole house smelled.

The young man, who knew only too well the extent of the misery due to lack of housing, who knew how many old people abandoned by their children did not get the offer to spend their days being looked after by the authorities, could not help feeling that this wreck of a human being could count herself lucky to get a place in this "Home," even if it was—and he knew and deplored the fact—an institution in which the old were treated like naughty and dimwitted children until they had the good fortune to die.

But just as he was telling Hetty that a van would be coming to take her effects and those of the other four old ladies, and that she need not take anything more with her than her clothes "and perhaps a few photographs," he saw that what he had thought was a heap of multicolored rags get up and put its ragged gingery-black paws on the old woman's skirt. Which today was a cretonne curtain covered with pink and red roses that Hetty had pinned around her because she liked the pattern.

"You can't take that cat with you," he said automatically. It was something he had to say often, and knowing what misery the statement caused, he usually softened it down. But he had been taken by surprise.

Tibby now looked like a mass of old wool that has been matting together in dust and rain. One eye was permanently half-closed, because a muscle had been ripped in a fight. One ear was vestigial. And down a flank was a hairless slope with a thick scar on it. A cat-hating man had treated Tibby as he treated all cats, to a pellet from his airgun. The resulting wound had taken two years to heal. And Tibby smelled.

No worse, however, than his mistress, who sat stiffly still, bright-eyed with suspicion, hostile, watching the well-brushed tidy young man from the Council.

"How old is that beast?"

"Ten years, no, only eight years, he's a young cat about five years old," said Hetty, desperate.

"It looks as if you'd do him a favor to put him out of his misery," said the young man.

When the official left, Hetty had agreed to everything. She was the only one of the old women with a cat. The others had budgerigars or nothing. Budgies were allowed in the Home.

She made her plans, confided in the others, and when the van came for them and their clothes and photographs and budgies, she was not there, and they told lies for her. "Oh we don't know where she can have gone, dear," the old women repeated again and again to the indifferent van driver. "She was here last night, but she did say something about going to her daughter in Manchester." And off they went to die in the Home.

Hetty knew that when houses have been emptied for redevelopment they may stay empty for months, even years. She intended to go on living in this one until the builders moved in.

It was a warm autumn. For the first time in her life she lived like her gypsy forebears, and did not go to bed in a room in a house like respectable people. She spent several nights, with Tibby, sitting crouched in a doorway of an empty house two doors from her own. She knew exactly when the police would come around, and where to hide herself in the bushes of the overgrown shrubby garden.

As she had expected, nothing happened in the house, and she moved back in. She smashed a back windowpane so that Tibby could move in and out without her having to unlock the front door for him, and without leaving a window suspiciously open. She moved to the top back room and left it every morning early, to spend the day in the streets with her pram and her rags. At night she kept a candle glimmering low down on the floor. The lavatory was still out of order, so she used a pail on the first floor, instead, and secretly emptied it at night into the canal, which in the day was full of pleasure boats and people fishing.

Tibby brought her several pigeons during that time.

"Oh you are a clever puss, Tibby, Tibby! Oh you're clever, you are. You know how things are, don't you, you know how to get around and about."

The weather turned very cold; Christmas came and went. Hetty's cough came back, and she spent most of her time under piles of blankets and old clothes, dozing. At night she watched the shadows of the candle flame on floor and ceiling—the windowframes fitted badly, and there was a draught. Twice tramps spent the night in the bottom of the house and she heard them being moved on by the police. She had to go down to make sure the police had not blocked up the broken window the cat used, but they had not. A blackbird had flown in and had battered itself to death trying to get out. She plucked it, and roasted it over a fire made with bits of floorboard in a baking pan; the gas of course had been cut off. She had never eaten very much, and was not frightened that some dry bread and a bit of cheese was all that she had eaten during her sojourn under the heap of clothes. She was cold, but did not think about that much. Outside there was slushy brown snow everywhere. She went back to her nest thinking that soon the cold spell would be over and she could get back to her trading. Tibby sometimes got into the pile with her, and she clutched the warmth of him to her. "Oh you clever cat, you clever old thing, looking after yourself, aren't you? That's right my ducky, that's right my lovely."

And then, just as she was moving about again, with snow gone off the ground for a time but winter only just begun, in January, she saw a builder's van draw up outside, a couple of men unloading their gear. They did not come into the house: they were to start work next day. By then Hetty, her cat, her pram piled with clothes and her two blankets, were gone. She also took a box of matches, a candle, an old saucepan and a fork and spoon, a tin opener, a candle and a rat-trap. She had a horror of rats.

About two miles away, among the homes and gardens of amiable Hampstead, where live so many of the rich, the intelligent and the famous, stood three empty, very large houses. She had seen them on an occasion, a couple of years before, when she had taken a bus. This was a rare thing for her, because of the remarks and curious looks provoked by her mad clothes, and by her being able to appear at the same time such a tough battling old thing and a naughty child. For the older she got, this disreputable tramp, the more there strengthened in her a quality of fierce, demanding childishness. It was all too much of a mixture; she was uncomfortable to have near.

She was afraid that "they" might have rebuilt the houses, but there they still stood, too tumbledown and dangerous to be of much use to tramps, let alone the armies of London's homeless. There was no glass left anywhere. The flooring at ground level was mostly gone, leaving small platforms and juts of planking over basements full of water. The ceilings were crumbling. The roofs were going. The houses were like bombed buildings.

But on the cold dark of a late afternoon she pulled the pram up the broken stairs and moved cautiously around the frail boards of a second-floor room that had a great hole in it right down to the bottom of the house. Looking into it was like looking into a well. She held a candle to examine the state of the walls, here more or less whole, and saw that rain and wind blowing in from a window would leave one corner dry. Here she made her home. A sycamore tree screened the gaping window from the main road twenty yards away. Tibby, who was cramped after making the journey under the clothes piled in the pram, bounded down and out and vanished into neglected undergrowth to catch his supper. He returned fed and pleased, and seemed happy to stay clutched in her hard thin old arms. She had come to watch for his return after hunting trips, because the warm purring bundle of bones and fur did seem to allay, for a while, the permanent ache of cold in her bones.

Next day she sold her Edwardian boots for a few shillings—they were fashionable again—and bought a loaf and some bacon scraps. In a corner of the ruins well away from the one she had made her own, she pulled up some floorboards, built a fire, and toasted bread and the bacon scraps. Tibby had brought in a pigeon, and she roasted that, but not very efficiently. She was afraid of the fire catching and the whole mass going up in flames; she was afraid too of the smoke showing and attracting the police. She had to keep damping down the fire, and so the bird was bloody and unappetizing, and in the end Tibby got most of it. She felt confused, and discouraged, but thought it was because of the long stretch of winter still ahead of her before spring could come. In fact, she was ill. She made a couple of attempts to trade and earn money to feed herself before she acknowledged she was ill. She knew she was not yet dangerously ill, for she had been that in her life, and would have been able to recognize the cold listless indifference of a real last-ditch illness. But all her bones ached, and her head ached, and she coughed more than she ever had. Yet she still did not think of herself as suffering particularly from the cold, even in that sleety January weather. She had never, in all her life, lived in a properly heated place, had never known a really warm home, not even when she lived in the Council flats. Those flats had electric fires, and the family had never used them, for the sake of economy, except in very bad spells of cold. They piled clothes onto themselves, or went to bed early. But she did know that to keep herself from dying now she could not treat the cold with her usual indifference. She knew she must eat. In the comparatively dry corner of the windy room, away from the gaping window through which snow and sleet were drifting, she made another nest—her last. She had found a piece of plastic sheeting in the rubble, and she laid that down first, so that the damp would not strike up. Then she spread her two blankets over that. Over them were heaped the mass of old clothes. She wished she had another piece of plastic to put on top, but she used sheets of newspaper instead. She heaved herself into the middle of this, with a loaf of bread near to her hand. She dozed, and waited, and nibbled bits of bread, and watched the snow drifting softly in. Tibby sat close to the old blue face that poked out of the pile and put up a paw to touch it. He miaowed and was restless, and then went out into the frosty morning and brought in a pigeon. This the cat put, still struggling and fluttering a little, close to the old woman. But she was afraid to get out of the pile in which the heat was being made and kept with such difficulty. She really could not climb out long enough to pull up more splinters of plank from the floors, to make a fire, to pluck the pigeon, to roast it. She put out a cold hand to stroke the cat.

"Tibby, you old thing, you brought it for me then, did you? You did, did you? Come here, come in here. . . ." But he did not want to get in with her. He miaowed again, pushed the bird closer to her. It was now limp and dead.

"You have it then. You eat it. I'm not hungry, thank you Tibby."

But the carcass did not interest him. He had eaten a pigeon before bringing this one up to Hetty. He fed himself well. In spite of his matted fur, and his scars and his half-closed yellow eye, he was a strong healthy cat.

At about four the next morning there were steps and voices downstairs. Hetty shot out of the pile and crouched behind a fallen heap of plaster and beams, now covered with snow, at the end of the room near the window. She could see through the hole in the floorboards down to the first floor, which had collapsed entirely, and through it to the ground floor. She saw a man in a thick overcoat and muffler and leather gloves holding a strong torch to illuminate a thin bundle of clothes lying on the floor. She saw that this bundle was a sleeping man or woman. She was indignant—*her* home was being trespassed upon. And she was afraid because she had not been aware of this other tenant of the ruin. Had he, or she, heard her talking to the cat? And where was the cat? If he wasn't careful he would be caught, and that would be the end of him. The man with a torch went off and came back with a second man. In the thick dark far below Hetty was a small cave of strong light, which was the torchlight. In this space of light two men bent to lift the bundle, carried it out across the dangertraps of fallen and rotting boards that made gangplanks over the water-filled basements. One man was holding the torch in the hand that supported the dead person's feet, and the light jogged and lurched over trees and grasses; the corpse was being taken through the shrubberies to a car.

There are men in London who, between the hours of two and five in the morning—when the real citizens are asleep, who should not be disturbed by such unpleasantness as the corpses of the poor—make the rounds of all the empty, rotting houses they know about, to collect the dead, and to warn the living that they ought not to be there at all, inviting them to one of the official Homes or lodgings for the homeless.

Hetty was too frightened to get back into her warm heap. She sat with the blankets pulled around her, and looked through gaps in the fabric of the house, making out shapes and boundaries and holes and puddles and mounds of rubble, as her eyes, like her cat's, became accustomed to the dark.

She heard scuffling sounds and knew they were rats. She had meant to set the trap, but the thought of her friend Tibby, who might catch his paw, had stopped her. She sat up until the morning light came in gray and cold, after nine. Now she did know herself to be very ill and in danger, for she had lost all the warmth she had huddled into her bones under the rags. She shivered violently. She was shaking herself apart with shivering. In between spasms she drooped limp and exhausted. Through the ceiling above her—but it was not a ceiling, only a cobweb of slats and planks—she could see into a dark cave which had been a garret, and through the roof above that, the gray sky, teeming with incipient rain. The cat came back from where he had been hiding, and sat crouched on her knees, keeping her stomach warm, while she thought out her position. These were her last clear thoughts. She told herself that she would not last out until spring unless she allowed "them" to find her, and take her to hospital. After that, she would be taken to a Home.

But what would happen to Tibby, her poor cat? She rubbed the old beast's scruffy head with the ball of her thumb and muttered: "Tibby, Tibby, they won't get you, no, you'll be all right, yes, I'll look after you."

Towards midday, the sun oozed yellow through miles of greasy gray cloud, and she staggered down the rotting stairs, to the shops. Even in those London streets, where the extraordinary has become usual, people turned to stare at a tall gaunt woman, with a white face that had flaming red patches on it, and blue compressed lips, and restless black eyes. She wore a tightly buttoned man's overcoat, torn brown woollen mittens, and an old fur hood. She pushed a pram loaded with old dresses and scraps of embroidery and torn jerseys and shoes, all stirred into a tight tangle, and she kept pushing this pram up against people as they stood in queues, or gossiped, or stared into windows, and she muttered: "Give me your old clothes darling, give me your old pretties, give Hetty something, poor Hetty's hungry." A woman gave her a handful of small change, and Hetty bought a roll filled with tomato and lettuce. She did not dare go into a cafe, for even in her confused state she knew she would offend, and would probably be asked to leave. But she begged a cup of tea at a street stall, and when the hot sweet liquid flooded through her she felt she might survive the winter. She bought a carton of milk and pushed the pram back through the slushy snowy street to the ruins.

Tibby was not there. She urinated down through the gap in the boards, muttering, "A nuisance, that old tea," and wrapped herself in a blanket and waited for the dark to come.

Tibby came in later. He had blood on his foreleg. She had heard scuffling and she knew that he had fought a rat, or several, and had been bitten. She poured the milk into the tilted saucepan and Tibby drank it all.

She spent the night with the animal held against her chilly bosom. They did not sleep, but dozed off and on. Tibby would normally be hunting, the night was his time, but he had stayed with the old woman now for three nights.

Early next morning they again heard the corpse removers among the rubble on the ground floor, and saw the beams of the torch moving on wet walls and collapsed beams. For a moment the torchlight was almost straight on Hetty, but no one came up: who could believe that a person could be desperate enough to climb those dangerous stairs, to trust those crumbling splintery floors, and in the middle of winter?

Hetty had now stopped thinking of herself as ill, of the degrees of her illness, of her danger—of the impossibility of her surviving. She had canceled out in her mind the presence of winter and its lethal weather, and it was as if spring were nearly here. She knew that if it had been spring when she had had to leave the other house, she and the cat could have lived here for months and months, quite safely and comfortably. Because it seemed to her an impossible and even a silly thing that her life, or, rather, her death, could depend on something so arbitrary as builders starting work on a house in January rather than in April, she could not believe it; the fact would not stay in her mind. The day before she had been quite clearheaded. But today her thoughts were cloudy, and she talked and laughed aloud. Once she scrambled up and rummaged in her rags for an old Christmas card she had got four years before from her good daughter.

In a hard harsh angry grumbling voice she said to her four children that she needed a room of her own now that she was getting on. "I've been a good mother to you," she shouted to them before invisible witnesses—former neighbors, welfare workers, a doctor. "I never let you want for anything, never! When you were little you always had the best of everything! You can ask anybody; go on, ask them, then!"

She was restless and made such a noise that Tibby left her and bounded on to the pram and crouched watching her. He was limping, and his foreleg was rusty with blood. The rat had bitten deep. When the daylight came, he left Hetty in a kind of sleep, and went down into the garden where he saw a pigeon feeding on the edge of the pavement. The cat pounced on the bird, dragged it into the bushes, and ate it all, without taking it up to his mistress. After he had finished eating, he stayed hidden, watching the passing people. He stared at them intently with his blazing yellow eye, as if he were thinking, or planning. He did not go into the old ruin and up the crumbling wet stairs until late—it was as if he knew it was not worth going at all.

He found Hetty, apparently asleep, wrapped loosely in a blanket, propped sitting in a corner. Her head had fallen on her chest, and her quantities of white hair had escaped from a scarlet woollen cap, and concealed a face that was flushed a deceptive pink—the flush of coma from cold. She was not yet dead, but she died that night. The rats came up the walls and along the planks and the cat fled down and away from them, limping still, into the bushes.

Hetty was not found for a couple of weeks. The weather changed to warm, and the man whose job it was to look for corpses was led up the dangerous stairs by the smell. There was something left of her, but not much.

As for the cat, he lingered for two or three days in the thick shrubberies, watching the passing people and beyond them, the thundering traffic of the main road. Once a couple stopped to talk on the pavement, and the cat, seeing two pairs of legs, moved out and rubbed himself against one of the legs. A hand came down and he was stroked and patted for a little. Then the people went away.

The cat saw he would not find another home, and he moved off, nosing and feeling his way from one garden to another, through empty houses, finally into an old churchyard. This graveyard already had a couple of stray cats in it, and he joined them. It was the beginning of a community of stray cats going wild. They killed birds, and the field mice that lived among the grasses, and they drank from puddles. Before winter had ended the cats had had a hard time of it from thirst, during the two long spells when the ground froze and there was snow and no puddles and the birds were hard to catch because the cats were so easy to see against the clean white. But on the whole they managed quite well. One of the cats was female, and soon there were a swarm of wild cats, as wild as if they did not live in the middle of a city surrounded by streets and houses. This was just one of half a dozen communities of wild cats living in that square mile of London.

Then an official came to trap the cats and take them away. Some of them escaped, hiding till it was safe to come back again. But Tibby was caught. He was not only getting old and stiff—he still limped from the rat's bite—but he was friendly, and did not run away from the man, who had only to pick him up in his arms.

"You're an old soldier, aren't you?" said the man. "A real tough one, a real old tramp."

It is possible that the cat even thought that he might be finding another human friend and a home.

But it was not so. The haul of wild cats that week numbered hundreds, and while if Tibby had been younger a home might have been found for him, since he was amiable, and wished to be liked by the human race, he was really too old, and smelly and battered. So they gave him an injection and, as we say, "put him to sleep."   *1963*

Oodgeroo of the tribe Noonuccal
1920–1993

Australia's best-known Aboriginal poet, OODGEROO OF THE TRIBE NOONUCCAL (formerly known as Kath Walker), participated actively in the movement to win basic human rights for her country's indigenous people. With the publication of *We Are Going* (1964) she became the first Aborigine to publish a volume of poetry. Oodgeroo once described that collection as "pure propaganda—to make people sit up and take notice." Indeed, the book did command critical attention, not only in Australia, where it sold out before it could be launched, but also in the United States, where it went through sixteen editions in the first six months of publication, due in part to its implicit links with African-American literature and history. Oodgeroo has claimed inspiration from black American writers such as Richard Wright, James Baldwin, and Amiri Baraka. Her poetry is all the more remarkable in that she received merely an elementary education before beginning domestic work at age thirteen. Only in 1967, after a lengthy civil rights movement of which she was a leader, did Aboriginal people gain the right to vote and receive higher education; and only then did indigenous Australians begin to publish a significant body of writing in English. Oodgeroo's is thus a pivotal voice in a nascent Aboriginal literature.

After *We Are Going* she wrote two other volumes of poetry, *The Dawn Is at Hand* (1966) and *My People* (1970), which record Aboriginal legends and struggles with a candid lyricism. In 1972 she published a book of prose, *Stradbroke Dreamtime*, which includes tales for children, autobiographical material, and her own versions of Aboriginal legends. Oodgeroo's illustrated volume of children's stories, *Father Sky, Mother Earth* (1982), retells an Aboriginal creation myth. Her 1985 publication, *Quandamooka: The Art of Kath Walker*, contains commentary on a series of her own illustrations. Oodgeroo lectured at the University of the South Pacific and won numerous awards for her writing and activism, including the Mary Gilmore Medal in 1970 and the Jessie Litchfield Award in 1975. In the mid–1980s she renamed herself Oodgeroo of the tribe Noonuccal after an elderly female storyteller from one of her own legends, a woman named for the paperbark tree on which she wrote her tales.

Oodgeroo's poems use irony, humor, and understatement to challenge racism and chronicle Aboriginal dispossession. "No more boomerang / No more spear; / Now all civilized— / Color bar and beer," reads one satiric verse. Such works as "Assimilation—No!," "Integration—Yes!," and "Aboriginal Charter of Rights" assert explicitly political claims of power and justice for Aborigines.

In "We Are Going," included here, she mourns the loss of Aboriginal culture, with its sacred bora rings and its lively *corroboree* (ritual ceremonies). But she likewise asserts the triumph of Aboriginal resistance and survival: "We are the lightning-bolt over Gaphembah Hill / Quick and terrible."

⊰ We Are Going ⊱

For Grannie Coolwell

They came in to the little town
A semi-naked band subdued and silent,
All that remained of their tribe.
They came here to the place of their old bora ground
5   Where now the many white men hurry about like ants.
Notice of estate agent reads: 'Rubbish May Be Tipped Here'.
Now it half covers the traces of the old bora ring.
They sit and are confused, they cannot say their thoughts:
'We are as strangers here now, but the white tribe are the strangers.
10 We belong here, we are of the old ways.
We are the corroboree and the bora ground,[1]
We are the old sacred ceremonies, the laws of the elders.
We are the wonder tales of Dream Time, the tribal legends told.
We are the past, the hunts and the laughing games, the wandering
       camp fires.
15 We are the lightning-bolt over Gaphembah Hill
Quick and terrible,
And the Thunderer after him, that loud fellow.
We are the quiet daybreak paling the dark lagoon.
We are the shadow-ghosts creeping back as the camp fires burn low.
20 We are nature and the past, all the old ways
Gone now and scattered.
The scrubs are gone, the hunting and the laughter.
The eagle is gone, the emu and the kangaroo are gone from this place.
The bora ring is gone.
25 The corroboree is gone.
And we are going.'

1964

＋━━ ⊠✧⊠ ━━＋

Anita Desai
1937–

"Writing is hell, but not writing is definitely worse," claims ANITA DESAI, an Indian writer of novels and short stories. She was born in Mussoorie, India, to D.N. and Toni (Nime) Mazumdar; her father was a businessman, and her mother hailed originally from Germany. After receiving her BA with honors from Delhi University in 1957, she married Ashvin Desai, an

1. The corroboree is an Australian aboriginal dance festival held at night to celebrate tribal victories or other occasions; the bora ring and bora ground refer to sacred space for aborigines.

executive; the couple has four children. Desai lived in India until 1986, when she became the Helen Cam Visiting Fellow at Girton College of the University of Cambridge. In 1987 she moved to the United States, where she served as Elizabeth Drew Professor of English at Smith College and as Purington Professor of English at Mt. Holyoke College. She now teaches at the Massachusetts Institute of Technology. Among her many awards are the Literary Lion Award from the New York Public Library (1993) and the Neil Gunn Fellowship from the Scottish Arts Council (1994).

Desai has written nine novels critically acclaimed for their eloquent language, vivid imagery, and sharp powers of observation. Among her best known are *Cry, the Peacock* (1963), *Voices in the City* (1965), *Bye-Bye Blackbird* (1968), and *Where Shall We Go This Summer?* (1975). *Fire on the Mountain* (1977) won the Royal Society of Literature's Winifred Holtby Prize and India's National Academy of Letters Award; *Clear Light of Day* (1980), *In Custody* (1993), and *Fasting, Feasting* (1999) were was nominated for the Booker Prize. Her novels typically portray the protagonists' struggles to cope with social and cultural transformations in postcolonial India, particularly changing relationships within families and women's quests for autonomy. Issues of exile also appear in her fiction, most notably in *Baumgartner's Bombay* (1989), which chronicles the life of a German Jewish refugee who flees Nazi Germany for India, where he lacks community and experiences a new kind of marginalization. Desai's interest in the tension between insider and outsider status may reflect the complexity of her own position as a woman of Bengali-German ancestry; writing in the *New York Times*, A.G. Mojtabai asserts that "insiders rarely notice this much; outsiders cannot have this ease of reference." *Journey to Ithaca* (1995) probes a different type of cultural dislocation, as a European couple comes to India, the husband in search of spiritual enlightenment, the wife seeking adventure. Desai has also published three prize-winning works of children's fiction, and her stories have appeared in such journals as *Quest, Indian Literature*, and *Harper's Bazaar*. In 1993 she wrote an introduction to Lady MARY WORTLEY MONTAGU's *Turkish Embassy Letters*. Two of Desai's novels have been adapted for film: *The Village by the Sea* (1982), and *In Custody* (1993).

Desai's collection of short fiction, *Games at Twilight and Other Stories* (1978), is remarkable for its compelling characters, wryly presented: the lonely child Ravi in the title story, "silenced by a terrible sense of his insignificance"; the neurotic scholar Suno, whose "brains began to jam up" whenever he took an exam; the U.S. tourist Pat, whose "first day in Bombay wilted her." "Surface Textures," the story reprinted here, dissects the crumbling marriage of Sheila and her delusional husband, Harish. Whether Harish is a lunatic or a saint, and how Sheila can feed her children in a country that offers single mothers few options, are issues at the heart of this quietly ironic tale.

⊰ Surface Textures ⊱

It was all her own fault, she later knew—but how could she have helped it? When she stood, puckering her lips, before the fruit barrow in the market and, after sullen consideration, at last plucked a rather small but nicely ripened melon out of a heap on display, her only thought had been Is it worth a *rupee* and fifty *paise*? The lichees looked more poetic, in large clusters like some prickly grapes of a charming rose colour, their long stalks and stiff gray leaves tied in a bunch above them—but were expensive. Mangoes were what the children were eagerly waiting for—the boys, she knew, were raiding the mango trees in the school compound daily and their stomachaches were a result, she told them, of the unripe mangoes they ate and for which they carried paper packets of salt to school in their pockets instead of handkerchiefs—but, leave alone the expense, the ones the fruiterer held up to her enticingly were bound to be sharp and sour for all their parakeet shades of rose and saffron; it was still too early for mangoes. So she put the melon in her string bag, rather angrily—paid the man his one *rupee* and fifty *paise* which altered his expression from one of promise and enticement to that of disappointment and contempt, and trailed off towards the vegetable barrow.

That, she later saw, was the beginning of it all, for if the melon seemed puny to her and boring to the children, from the start her husband regarded it with eyes that seemed newly opened. One would have thought he had never seen a melon before. All through the meal his eyes remained fixed on the plate in the center of the table with its big button of a yellow melon. He left most of his rice and pulses on his plate, to her indignation. While she scolded, he reached out to touch the melon that so captivated him. With one finger he stroked the coarse grain of its rind, rough with the upraised criss-cross of pale veins. Then he ran his fingers up and down the green streaks that divided it into even quarters as by green silk threads, so tenderly. She was clearing away the plates and did not notice till she came back from the kitchen.

"Aren't you going to cut it for us?" she asked, pushing the knife across to him.

He gave her a reproachful look as he picked up the knife and went about dividing the melon into quarter-moon portions with sighs that showed how it pained him.

"Come on, come on," she said, roughly, "the boys have to get back to school."

He handed them their portions and watched them scoop out the icy orange flesh with a fearful expression on his face—as though he were observing cannibals at a feast. She had not the time to pay any attention to it then but later described it as horror. And he did not eat his own slice. When the boys rushed away, he bowed his head over his plate and regarded it.

"Are you going to fall asleep?" she cried, a little frightened.

"Oh no," he said, in that low mumble that always exasperated her—it seemed a sign to her of evasiveness and pusillanimity, this mumble—"Oh no, no." Yet he did not object when she seized the plate and carried it off to the kitchen, merely picked up the knife that was left behind and, picking a flat melon seed off its edge where it had remained stuck, he held it between two fingers, fondling it delicately. Continuing to do this, he left the house.

The melon might have been the apple of knowledge for Harish—so deadly its poison that he did not even need to bite into it to imbibe it: That long, devoted look had been enough. As he walked back to his office which issued ration cards to the population of their town, he looked about him vaguely but with hunger, his eyes resting not on the things on which people's eyes normally rest—signboards, the traffic, the number of an approaching bus—but on such things, normally considered nondescript and unimportant, as the paving stones on which their feet momentarily pressed, the length of wire in a railing at the side of the road, a pattern of grime on the windowpane of a disused printing press . . . Amongst such things his eyes roved and hunted and, when he was seated at his desk in the office, his eyes continued to slide about—that was Sheila's phrase later: "slide about"—in a musing, calculating way, over the surface of the crowded desk, about the corners of the room, even across the ceiling. He seemed unable to focus them on a file or a card long enough to put to them his signature—they lay unsigned and the people in the queue outside went for another day without rice and sugar and kerosene for their lamps and Janta cookers. Harish searched—slid about, hunted, gazed—and at last found sufficiently interesting a thick book of rules that lay beneath a stack of files. Then his hand reached out—not to pull the book to him or open it, but to run the ball of his thumb across the edge of the pages. In their large number and irregular cut, so closely laid out like some crisp palimpsest, his eyes seemed to find something of riveting interest and his thumb of tactile wonder. All afternoon he massaged the cut edges of the book's seven hundred odd pages—tenderly, wonderingly. All afternoon his eyes gazed upon them with strange devotion. At five o'clock, punctually, the office shut and the queue disintegrated into vociferous grumbles and threats as people went home instead of to the ration shops, empty-handed instead of loaded with those necessary but, to Harish, so dull comestibles.

Although government service is as hard to depart from as to enter—so many letters to be written, forms to be filled, files to be circulated, petitions to be made that it hardly seems worthwhile—Harish was, after some time, dismissed—time he happily spent judging the difference between white blotting paper and pink (pink is flatter, denser, white spongier) and the texture of blotting paper stained with ink and that which is fresh, that which has been put to melt in a saucer of cold tea and that which has been doused in a pot of ink. Harish was dismissed.

The first few days Sheila stormed and screamed like some shrill, wet hurricane about the house. "How am I to go to market and buy vegetables for dinner? I don't even have enough for that. What am I to feed the boys tonight? No more milk for them. The washerwoman is asking for her bill to be paid. Do you hear? Do you *hear*? And we shall have to leave this flat. Where shall we go?" He listened—or didn't—sitting on a cushion before her mirror, fingering the small silver box in which she kept the red *kum-kum* that daily cut a gash from one end of her scalp to the other after her toilet. It was of dark, almost blackened silver, with a whole forest embossed on it—banana groves, elephants, peacocks and jackals. He rubbed his thumb over its cold, raised surface.

After that, she wept. She lay on her bed in a bath of tears and perspiration, and it was only because of the kindness of their neighbors that they did not starve to death the very first week, for even those who most disliked and distrusted Harish—"Always said he looks like a hungry hyena," said Mr. Bhatia who lived below their flat, "not human at all, but like a hungry, hunchbacked hyena hunting along the road"—felt for the distraught wife and the hungry children (who did not really mind as long as there were sour green mangoes to steal and devour) and looked to them. Such delicacies as Harish's family had never known before arrived in stainless steel and brass dishes, with delicate unobtrusiveness. For a while wife and children gorged on sweetmeats made with fresh buffalo milk, on pulses cooked according to grandmother's recipes, on stuffed bread and the first pomegranates of the season. But, although delicious, these offerings came in small quantities and irregularly and soon they were really starving.

"I suppose you want me to take the boys home to my parents," said Sheila bitterly, getting up from the bed. "Any other man would regard that as the worst disgrace of all—but not you. What is my shame to you? I will have to hang my head and crawl home and beg my father to look after us since you won't," and that was what she did. He was sorry, very sorry to see her pack the little silver *kum-kum* box in her black trunk and carry it away.

Soon after, officials of the Ministry of Works, Housing and Land Development came and turned Harish out, cleaned and painted the flat and let in the new tenants who could hardly believe their luck—they had been told so often they couldn't expect a flat in that locality for at least another two years.

The neighbors lost sight of Harish. Once some children reported they had seen him lying under the *pipal* tree at the corner of their school compound, staring fixedly at the red gashes cut into the papery bark and, later, a boy who commuted to school on a suburban train claimed to have seen him on the railway platform, sitting against a railing like some tattered beggar, staring across the crisscross of shining rails. But next day, when the boy got off the train, he did not see Harish again.

Harish had gone hunting. His slow, silent walk gave him the appearance of sliding rather than walking over the surface of the roads and fields, rather like a snail except that his movement was not as smooth as a snail's but stumbling as if he had only recently become one and was still unused to the pace. Not only his eyes and his hands but even his bare feet seemed to be feeling the earth carefully, in search of an interesting surface. Once he found it, he would pause, his whole body would gently collapse across it and hours—perhaps days—would be devoted to its investigation and worship. Outside the town the land was rocky and bare and this was Harish's especial paradise, each rock having a surface of such exquisite roughness, of such perfection in shape and design, as to keep him occupied and ecstatic for weeks together. Then the river beyond the rock quarries drew him away and there he discovered the joy of fingering silk-smooth stalks and reeds, stems and leaves.

Shepherd children, seeing him stumble about the reeds, plunging thigh-deep into the water in order to pull out a water lily with its cool, sinuous stem, fled screaming, not certain whether this was a man or a hairy water snake. Their mothers came, some with stones and some with canes at the ready, but when they saw Harish, his skin parched to a violet shade, sitting on the bank and gazing at the transparent stem of the lotus, they fell back, crying, "Wah!" gathered closer together, advanced, dropped their canes and stones, held their children still by their hair and shoulders, and came to bow to him. Then they hurried back to the village, chattering. They had never had a Swami to themselves, in these arid parts. Nor had they seen a Swami who looked holier, more inhuman than Harish with his matted hair, his blue, starved skin and single-focused eyes. So, in the evening, one brought him a brass vessel of milk, another a little rice. They pushed their children before them and made them drop flowers at his feet. When Harish stooped and felt among the offerings for something his fingers could respond to, they were pleased, they felt accepted. "Swami-ji," they whispered, "speak."

Harish did not speak and his silence made him still holier, safer. So they worshipped him, fed and watched over him, interpreting his moves in their own fashion, and Harish, in turn, watched over their offerings and worshipped.   *1978*

Paula Gunn Allen
1939–

A Native American writer of poetry, fiction, and essays, PAULA GUNN ALLEN was born on the Cubero land grant in New Mexico to parents of Laguna-Sioux-Lebanese-Jewish origins. Since then she has embraced fully what the theorist TRINH T. MINH-HA calls her "hyphenated identities and hybrid realities." Allen married in her teens, had children, and eventually attended college and graduate school at the University of New Mexico, where she completed her Ph.D. in American studies. Her sister, Carol Lee Sanchez, is also a writer of renown. Allen has taught literature at

San Francisco State University, the University of New Mexico, and Fort Lewis College; she currently teaches Native American studies at the University of California Berkeley.

Although she writes in multiple genres, Allen is best known as a poet; her work reflects her activism in the antiwar, feminist, and Native American rights movements. A poem, she explains, "begins as a mood that gets more and more focused, becoming a sense, a rhythm, then a scatter of words. I don't write poetry for content, but to articulate a sense, an 'intuition.'" Among her volumes of poetry are *The Blind Lion* (1975), *A Cannon Between My Knees* (1981), *Shadow Country* (1982), and *Skins and Bones: Poems 1979–87* (1988). Much of Allen's poetry seeks to create mythic space, questing for natural harmony among humans, land, animals, and spirit. Several poems address her experience as a lesbian and draw parallels between the marginalizations that occur due to ethnicity and sexual orientation. Her poems have appeared in such anthologies as *Lesbian Poetry* (1978), *A Gathering of Spirit* (1984), and *Living the Spirit* (1988).

A different impulse drives Allen's fiction and criticism. "I write fiction out of interest in how people interact; how my social selves interact, how the planet and the human beings and other beings interact." Her novel, *The Woman Who Owned the Shadows* (1983), traces the spiritual journey of Ephanie Ataencio, who suffers a mental breakdown when abandoned by her husband but ultimately finds peace by accepting native traditions. Allen has edited an anthology of Native American women's stories, *Spider Woman's Granddaughters* (1986), which contains both contemporary narratives and traditional "told-to-people" stories. Her contributions as a literary critic have also been significant. In 1983 she edited one of the first collections of critical essays on literature by Native Americans, *Studies in American Indian Literature*. In *The Sacred Hoop: Recovering the Feminine in American Indian Traditions* (1986) she explores the centrality of women to native myth and culture and analyzes literary works by such writers as JOY HARJO and Leslie Marmon Silko. This study, which began as Allen's dissertation, was written in response to a male professor who claimed that there was no such thing as Native American literature, only folklore. It was also born of her conviction that in its emphasis on gender equality and the spiritual power of women, American Indian culture serves as a precursor to the modern women's movement, an argument she makes in her essay "Who Is Your Mother? Red Roots of White Feminism." In 1991 Allen edited *Grandmothers of the Light: A Medicine Woman's Sourcebook*, tales of goddesses from Native American cultures; and in 1998 she published *Off the Reservation: Boundary Busting, Border Crossing, Loose Canons*.

Although many of Allen's poems are meditative in tone, some are angry and polemical. This contrast can be seen in the two works included here, "Taku Skansken" and "Molly Brant, Iroquois Matron, Speaks." The first poem considers the nature of history and divinity; its experimental form, word coinages, and verbal pyrotechnics reflect the English language's inadequacy to express Native American metaphysics. The second poem, a long dramatic monologue, is spoken by an Iroquois woman denigrated by white culture as a "heathen squaw." In these poems as in many, Allen writes as "an act of faith, an act of discovery."

⊰ Molly Brant, Iroquois Matron, Speaks ⊱

> I was, Sir, born of Indian parents, and lived while a child among those whom you are pleased to call savages; I was afterwards sent to live among the white people, and educated at one of your schools; and after every exertion to divest myself of prejudice, I am obliged to give my opinion in favor of my own people. . . . In the government you call civilized, the happiness of the people is constantly sacrificed to the splendor of empire. . . .
>
> *Joseph Brant*

We knew it was the end
long after it had ended,

my brother Joseph and I.
We were so simple then,
taking a holiday to see the war,
the one they would later call
the Revolution.
The shot sent 'round the world
was fired from the Iroquois gun; we
could not foresee its round
would lodge itself
in our breast. The fury we unleashed
in pursuit of the Great Peace
washed the Mothers away,
our Lodges burned,
our fields salted,
our Ancient fires extinguished—
no, not put out, fanned,
the flames spread far
beyond our anticipation
out of control.
We had not counted on their hate;
we had not recognized
the depth of their contempt.
How could we know I would be
no longer honored matron
but heathen squaw—
in their eyes, my beloved daughters
half-breed dirt. Along with our earth
they salted our hearts
so nothing would grow
for too long a time.
We had been arrogant
and unwise: engaged in spreading
the White Roots of Peace, we
all but forgot the little ones
dear to our Mothers
and their ancestry,
the tender fortunes
of squash, corn and beans.

Then, overnight, was I
fleeing for my life
across the new borders, my brother hunted
like a common criminal
to be tried for sedition
for his part
among the British. They
lost out just as we'd planned
a century before. But
we had forgotten the Elder's Plan.
So it was we could not know
a Council Fire would be out,
the League unable to meet

in the bitter winter that fell
55 upon us like the soldiers
and the missionaries,
the carrion birds that flew
upon the winds of Revolution
to feed upon our scarred and frozen flesh.
60 We had not counted on fate—
so far from the Roots of our being
had we flown,
carried on the wings of an Algonquin priest
we fell into the eyrie
65 of a carrion host.
Perhaps it is the Immortals alone who know
what turns the Revolution must entail,
what dreams to send to lead us on,
far beyond the borders of our Dreams.
70 The turning of centuries goes on,
revolving along some obscure path
no human woman's ever seen.

That's how it is with revolutions.
Wheels turn. So do planets.
75 Stars turn. So do galaxies.
Mortals see only this lifetime
or that. How could we know,
bound to the borders we called home,
the Revolution we conspired for
80 would turn us under
like last year's crop?

I speak now because I know
the Revolution has not let up.
Others like my brother and like me
85 conspire with other dreams,
argue whether or not
to blow earth up, or poison it mortally
or settle for alteration. They
believe, like we, that the sacred fire
90 is theirs to control, but may be
this Revolution is the plan of gods,
of beings Matrons and priests alike
cannot know.

Still, let them obliterate it, I say.
95 What do I care? What have I to lose,
having lost all I loved so long ago?
Aliens, aliens everywhere,
and so few of the People
left to dream. All that is left
100 is not so precious after all—
great cities, piling drifting clouds
of burning death, waters that last drew breath
decades, perhaps centuries ago,

105 four-leggeds, wingeds, reptiles all
drowned in bloodred rivers of an alien dream
of progress. Progress is what
they call it. I call it cemetery,
charnel house, soul sickness,
artificial mockery
110 of what we called life.

I, Matron of the Longhouse, say:
If their death is in the fire's wind,
let it wash our Mother clean.
If Revolution is to take another turn,
115 who's to say
which side will turn up next?
Maybe when the last great blast goes up
you will hear me screaming with glee,
wildly drunk at last on vindication,
120 trilling ecstatically my longed-for revenge

in the searing unearthly wind.

1988

⊰ Taku Skansken[1] ⊱

that history is an event
that life is
that I am event
ually going to do something
5 the metaphor for god.
eventuality.
activity.

what happens *to be*
what happens *to me*
10 god. history. action
the Lakota word for it is:
whatmovesmoves.
they don't call god "what moves something."
not "prime mover."
15 "first mover" "who moves everything or nothing."
"action." "lights." "movement."
not "where" or "what" or "how" but
event.   GOD
is what happens, is:
20 movesmoves.

riding a mare.
eventuality.
out of the corral into morning
taking her saddled and bridled

1. What moves moves (Lakota).

25   air thick with breath movesmoves
      horsebreath, mybreath, earthbreath
      skybreathing air. ing.
      breathesbreathes movesmoves
      in the cold. winterspringfall.
30   corral. ing. horse and breath.
      air. through the gate moveswe.
      lift we the wooden crossbar *niya*
      movesmoves unlocks movesbreathes
      lifebreath of winter soul
35   swings wide sweet corral gate
      happens to be frozenstiff in place
      happens to be cold. so I and mare
      wear clothes thatmove in event
      of frozen. shaggydressers for the air that
      breathes breathe we: flows: movesmoves:
40   god its cold.
      no other place but movemove
      horse me gate hinge air bright frost lungs burst
      swing gate far morning winter air rides
      movesmovingmoves Lakotas say: god.
45   what we do.

                                                    1988

Angela Carter
1940–1992

Lust, decadence, perversity, and female sexuality provide the subject matter for much of ANGELA CARTER's "neogothic" fiction. The gothic tradition of ghosts and horror, she once claimed, "ignores the value systems of institutions; it deals entirely with the profane. Its great themes are incest and cannibalism." Adapting the gothic for the modern age is an easy matter according to Carter, for "we live in gothic times." This highly acclaimed British novelist and short story writer was born Angela Stalker in Eastbourne, Sussex; her family moved to Yorkshire when she was three. With characteristic wit she once described her father as having descended from witches, her mother from tradeunionists. After graduating from Bristol University in 1965, she settled in London, worked as a journalist, and began to write fiction. From 1970 until 1972 she lived in Japan, an experience that informed several early stories. Although she briefly held visiting professorships at Sheffield University in England and Brown University in the United States, Carter preferred full-time writing to academia. Her friend, the novelist Salman Rushdie, described her as "the most scatologically irreligious, merrily godless of women" and "the most individual, independent, and idiosyncratic of writers." Carter died from lung cancer in 1992. She is survived by her husband, Mark, and a son, Alexander.

Many of Carter's novels examine women's erotic lives from a Freudian perspective, using dreams, myths, fairy tales, and sexual fantasies. Her first novel, *Shadow Dance* (1966), uses a highly symbolic language to interrogate sexuality. *The Magic Toyshop* (1967), which won Britain's John Llewellyn Rhys Prize, employs magic realism to trace the coming-of-age of the precocious Melanie, "pregnant with herself."

The Infernal Desire Machines of Doctor Hoffman (1972) reveals Carter's fascination with pornography and explores how fantasy can lead to sexual aggression. Androgyny and transsexualism are the subjects of *The Passion of New Eve* (1977), which challenges conventional assumptions about gender. A picaresque eroticism informs *Nights at the Circus* (1984), whose heroine is a winged woman named Fevvers, a decadent carnival performer; this novel received the James Tait Black Memorial Prize for Fiction. Other novels by Carter include *Several Perceptions* (1968), *Heroes and Villains* (1969), and *Love* (1971). Her last book, *Wise Children* (1991), has been described as "the music-hall knees-up" variety of comic fiction.

Carter is equally well known for her short stories. "I started to write short pieces when I was living in a room too small to write a novel in," she explained in 1974. "So the size of my room modified what I did inside it and it was the same with the pieces themselves. The limited trajectory of the short narrative concentrates its meaning." Her first collection, *Fireworks* (1974), contains several stories about the ceremonial pomp and hidden eroticism she found fascinating in Japan; in other stories she constructs vivid worlds through fable. *The Bloody Chamber* (1979), which includes the story "Wolf Alice," revises classic fairy tales in ways that foreground their voyeuristic and seductive aspects. In *Black Venus* (1985) and *American Ghosts and Old World Wonders* (1993) Carter turns from fantasy to the "hyperrealism" of portraiture, presenting Charles Baudelaire's black mistress, Edgar Allan Poe's secret infamy, and Lizzie Borden's axe murder. *Burning Your Boats: The Collected Angela Carter Stories* was published in 1995 to critical acclaim.

Carter also wrote essays, cultural criticism, and screenplays. *The Sadeian Woman: An Exercise in Cultural History* (1979) examines work by the Marquis de Sade and makes problematic the distinction between pornography and eroticism. Many of her essays about art and sexuality were collected in *Nothing Sacred* (1982). With Neil Jordan she created the screenplay for a movie version of *The Company of Wolves* (1984). Carter translated *The Fairy Tales of Charles Perrault* (1979) and wrote a radio drama, *Come unto These Yellow Sands*, which was produced in 1985. That same year she edited an anthology of "subversive stories" by women, *Wayward Girls and Wicked Women*.

Rushdie has described Carter's stories as having "smoky, opium-eater's cadences interrupted by harsh or comic discords, that moonstone-and-rhinestone mix of opulence and flim-flam." Many stories are set in European villages whose remoteness evokes howling wolves, bloody vampires, and other beasts of prey. As "Wolf Alice" reveals, Carter likes to make the stock female victim of the horror tale as savage and amoral as the beast itself. This tale exemplifies Carter's ability, in Rushdie's words, to "open an old story for us, like an egg, and find the new story, the now-story we want to hear, within."

⊰ Wolf Alice ⊱

Could this ragged girl with brindled legs have spoken as we do, she would have called herself a wolf, but she cannot speak, although she howls because she is lonely—yet "howl" is not the right word for it, since she is young enough to make the noise that pups do, bubbling, delicious, like that of a panful of fat on the fire. Sometimes the sharp ears of her foster kindred hear her across the irreparable gulf of absence; they answer her from faraway pine forest and the bald mountain rim. Their counterpoint crosses and crisscrosses the night sky; they are trying to talk to her but they cannot do so because she does not understand their language even if she knows how to use it, for she is not a wolf herself, although suckled by wolves.

Her panting tongue hangs out; her red lips are thick and fresh. Her legs are long, lean and muscular. Her elbows, hands and knees are thickly callused because she always runs on all fours. She never walks; she trots or gallops. Her pace is not our pace.

Two-legs looks, four-legs sniffs. Her long nose is always aquiver, sifting every scent it meets. With this useful tool, she lengthily investigates everything she glimpses. She can net so much more of the world than we can through the fine, hairy, sensitive filters of her nostrils that her poor eyesight does not trouble her. Her nose is sharper by night than our eyes are by day, so it is the night she prefers, when the cool reflected light of the moon does not make her eyes smart and draws out the various fragrances from the woodland where she wanders when she can. But the wolves keep well away from the peasants' shotguns now, and she will no longer find them there.

Wide shoulders, long arms, and she sleeps succinctly curled into a ball as if she were cradling her spine in her tail. Nothing about her is human except that she is *not* a wolf; it is as if the fur she thought she wore had melted into her skin and become part of it, although it does not exist. Like the wild beasts, she lives without a future. She inhabits only the present tense, a fugue of the continuous, a world of sensual immediacy as without hope as it is without despair.

When they found her in the wolf's den beside the bullet-riddled corpse of her foster mother, she was no more than a little brown scrap so snarled in her own brown hair they did not, at first, think she was a child but a cub; she snapped at her would-be saviors with her spiky canines until they tied her up by force. She spent her first days amongst us crouched stock-still, staring at the whitewashed wall of her cell in the convent to which they took her. The nuns poured water over her, poked her with sticks to rouse her. Then she might snatch bread from their hands and race with it into a corner to mumble it with her back towards them; it was a great day among the novices when she learned to sit up on her hind legs and beg for a crust.

They found that if she was treated with a little kindness, she was not intractable. She learned to recognize her own dish; then, to drink from a cup. They found that she could quite easily be taught a few, simple tricks, but she did not feel the cold and it took a long time to wheedle a shift over her head to cover up her bold nakedness. Yet she always seemed wild, impatient of restraint, capricious in temper; when the Mother Superior tried to teach her to give thanks for her recovery from the wolves, she arched her back, pawed the floor, retreated to a far corner of the chapel, crouched, trembled, urinated, defecated—reverted entirely, it would seem, to her natural state. Therefore, without a qualm, this nine days' wonder and continuing embarrassment of a child was delivered over to the bereft and unsanctified household of the Duke.

Deposited at the castle, she huffed and snuffed and smelled only a reek of meat, not the least whiff of sulfur, nor of familiarity. She settled down on her hunkers with that dog's sigh that is only the expulsion of breath and does not mean either relief or resignation.

The Duke is sere as old paper; his dry skin rustles against the bedsheets as he throws them back to thrust out his thin legs scabbed with old scars where thorns scored his pelt. He lives in a gloomy mansion, all alone but for this child who has as little in common with the rest of us as he does. His bedroom is painted terra cotta, rusted with a wash of pain, like the interior of an Iberian butcher's shop, but for himself, nothing can hurt him since he ceased to cast an image in the mirror.

He sleeps in an antlered bed of dull black wrought iron until the moon, the governess of transformations and overseer of somnambulists, pokes an imperative finger through the narrow window and strikes his face; then his eyes start open.

At night, those huge, inconsolable, rapacious eyes of his are eaten up by swollen, gleaming pupils. His eyes see only appetite. These eyes open to devour the world in which he sees, nowhere, a reflection of himself; he passed through the mirror and now, henceforward, lives as if upon the other side of things.

Spilt, glistering milk of moonlight on the frost-crisped grass; on such a night, in moony, metamorphic weather, they say you might easily find him, if you had been foolish enough to venture out late, scuttling along by the churchyard wall with half a juicy torso slung across his back. The white light scours the fields and scours them again until everything gleams and he will leave pawprints in the hoarfrost when he runs howling round the graves at night in his lupine fiestas.

By the red early hour of midwinter sunset, all the doors are barred for miles. The cows low fretfully in the byre when he goes by, the whimpering dogs sink their noses in their paws. He carries on his frail shoulders a weird burden of fear; he is cast in the role of the corpse eater, the body snatcher who invades the last privacies of the dead. He is white as leprosy, with scrabbling fingernails, and nothing deters him. If you stuff a corpse with garlic, why, he only slavers at the treat: cadavre provençale. He will use the holy cross as a scratching post and crouch above the font to thirstily lap up holy water.

She sleeps in the soft, warm ashes of the hearth; beds are traps, she will not stay in one. She can perform the few, small tasks to which the nuns trained her; she sweeps up the hairs, vertebrae and phalanges that litter his room into a dustpan, she makes up his bed at sunset, when he leaves it and the gray beasts outside howl, as if they know his transformation is their parody. Unkind to their prey, to their own they are tender; had the Duke been a wolf, they would have angrily expelled him from the pack; he would have had to lollop along miles behind them, creeping in submission on his belly up to the kill only after they had eaten and were sleeping, to gnaw the well-chewed bones and chew the hide. Yet, suckled as she was by wolves on the high uplands where her mother bore and left her, only his kitchen maid, who is not wolf or woman, knows no better than to do his chores for him.

She grew up with wild beasts. If you could transport her, in her filth, rags and feral disorder, to the Eden of our first beginnings where Eve and grunting Adam squat on a daisy bank, picking the lice from one another's pelts, then she might prove to be the wise child who leads them all and her silence and her howling a language as authentic as any language of nature. In a world of talking beasts and flowers, she would be the bud of flesh in the kind lion's mouth; But how can the bitten apple flesh out its scar again?

Mutilation is her lot; though, now and then, she will emit an involuntary rustle of sound, as if the unused chords in her throat were a wind harp that moved with the random impulses of the air, her whisper more obscure than the voices of the dumb.

Familiar desecrations in the village graveyard. The coffin had been ripped open with the abandon with which a child unwraps a gift on Christmas morning, and of its contents, not a trace could be found but for a rag of the bridal veil in which the corpse had been wrapped, that was caught, fluttering, in the brambles at the churchyard gate so they knew which way he had taken it, towards his gloomy castle.

In the lapse of time, the trance of being of that exiled place, this girl grew amongst things she could neither name nor perceive. How did she think, how did she feel, this perennial stranger with her furred thoughts and her primal sentience that existed in a flux of shifting impressions; there are no words to describe the way she negotiated the abyss between her dreams, those wakings strange as her sleepings. The wolves had tended her because they knew she was an imperfect wolf; we secluded her in animal privacy out of fear of her imperfection because it showed us what we might have been, and so time passed, although she scarcely knew it. Then she began to bleed.

Her first blood bewildered her. She did not know what it meant and the first stirrings of surmise that ever she felt were directed towards its possible cause. The moon had been shining into the kitchen when she woke to feel the trickle between her thighs, and it seemed to her that a wolf who, perhaps, was fond of her, as wolves were, and who lived, perhaps, in the moon? must have nibbled her cunt while she was sleeping, had subjected her to a series of affectionate nips too gentle to wake her yet sharp enough to break the skin. The shape of this theory was blurred yet, out of it, there took root a kind of wild reasoning, as it might have from a seed dropped in her brain off the foot of a flying bird.

The flow continued for a few days, which seemed to her an endless time. She had, as yet, no direct notion of past, or of future, or of duration, only of a dimensionless, immediate moment. At night, she prowled the empty house looking for rags to sop the blood up; she had learned a little elementary hygiene in the convent, enough to know how to bury her excrement and cleanse herself of her natural juices; although the nuns had not the means to inform her how it should be, it was not fastidiousness but shame that made her do so.

She found towels, sheets and pillowcases in closets that had not been opened since the Duke came shrieking into the world with all his teeth, to bite his mother's nipple off and weep. She found once-worn ball dresses in cobwebbed wardrobes and, heaped in the corners of his bloody chamber, shrouds, night-dresses and burial clothes that had wrapped items on the Duke's menus. She tore strips of the most absorbent fabrics to clumsily diaper herself. In the course of these prowlings, she bumped against the mirror over whose surface the Duke passed like a wind on ice.

First, she tried to nuzzle her reflection; then, nosing it industriously, she soon realized it gave out no smell. She bruised her muzzle on the cold glass and broke her claws trying to tussle with this stranger. She saw, with irritation, then amusement, how it mimicked every gesture of hers when she raised her fore-paw to scratch herself or dragged her bum along the dusty carpet to rid herself of a slight discomfort in her hindquarters. She rubbed her head against her reflected face, to show that she felt friendly towards it, and felt a cool, solid, immovable surface between herself and she—some kind, possibly, of invisible cage? In spite of this barrier, she was lonely enough to ask this creature to try to play with her, baring her teeth and grinning; at once she received a reciprocal invitation. She rejoiced; she began to whirl round on herself, yapping exultantly, but when she retreated from the mirror, she halted in the midst of her ecstasy, puzzled, to see how her new friend grew less in size.

The moonlight spilled into the Duke's motionless bedroom from behind a cloud and she saw how pale this wolf, not wolf who played with her was. The moon and mirrors have this much in common: You cannot see behind them. Moonlit and white, Wolf Alice looked at herself in the mirror and wondered whether there she saw the beast who came to bite her in the night. Then her sensitive ears pricked at the sound of a step in the hall; trotting at once back to her kitchen, she encountered the Duke with the leg of a man over his shoulder. Her toenails clicked against the stairs as she padded incuriously past, she, the serene, inviolable one in her absolute and verminous innocence.

Soon the flow ceased. She forgot it. The moon vanished: but, little by little, reappeared. When it again visited her kitchen at full strength, Wolf Alice was surprised into bleeding again and so it went on, with a punctuality that transformed her vague grip on time. She learned to expect these bleedings, to prepare her rags against them, and afterwards, neatly to bury the dirtied things. Sequence asserted itself with custom and then she understood the circumambulatory principle of the clock perfectly, even if all clocks were banished from the den where she and the Duke inhabited their separate solitudes, so that you might say she discovered the very action of time by means of this returning cycle.

When she curled up among the cinders, the color, texture and warmth of them brought her foster mother's belly out of the past and printed it on her flesh: her first conscious memory, painful as the first time the nuns combed her hair. She howled a little, in a firmer, deepening trajectory, to obtain the inscrutable consolation of the wolves' response, for now the world around her was assuming form. She perceived an essential difference between herself and her surroundings that you might say she could not put her *finger* on—only, the trees and grass of the meadows outside no longer seemed the emanation of her questing nose and erect ears, and yet sufficient to itself, but a kind of backdrop for her, that waited for her arrivals to give it meaning. She saw herself upon it and her eyes, with their somber clarity, took on a veiled, introspective look.

She would spend hours examining the new skin that had been born, it seemed to her, of her bleeding. She would lick her soft upholstery with her long tongue and groom her hair with her fingernails. She examined her new breasts with curiosity; the white growths reminded her of nothing so much as the night-sprung puffballs she had found, sometimes, on evening rambles in the woods, a natural if disconcerting apparition, but then, to her astonishment, she found a little diadem of fresh hairs tufting between her thighs. She showed it to her mirror littermate, who reassured her by showing her she shared it.

The damned Duke haunts the graveyard; he believes himself to be both less and more than a man, as if his obscene difference were a sign of grace. During the day, he sleeps. His mirror faithfully reflects his bed, but never the meager shape within the disordered covers.

Sometimes, on those white nights when she was left alone in the house, she dragged out his grandmother's ball dresses and rolled on suave velvet and abrasive lace because to do so delighted her adolescent skin. Her intimate in the mirror wound the old clothes round herself, wrinkling its nose in delight at the ancient yet still potent scents of musk and civet that woke up in the sleeves and bodices. This habitual, at last boring, fidelity to her every movement finally woke her up to the regretful possibility that her companion was, in fact, no more than a particularly ingenious variety of the shadow she cast on the sunlit grass. Had not she and the rest of the litter tussled and romped with their shadows long ago? She poked her agile nose around the back of the mirror; she found only dust, a spider stuck in his web, a heap of rags. A little moisture leaked from the corners of her eyes, yet her relation with the mirror was now far more intimate since she knew she saw herself within it.

She pawed and tumbled the dress the Duke had tucked away behind the mirror for a while. The dust was soon shaken out of it; she experimentally inserted her front legs in the sleeves. Although the dress was torn and crumpled, it was so white and of such a sinuous texture that she thought, before she put it on, she must thoroughly wash off her coat of ashes in the water from the pump in the yard, which she knew how to manipulate with her cunning forepaw. In the mirror, she saw how this white dress made her shine.

Although she could not run so fast on two legs in petticoats, she trotted out in her new dress to investigate the odorous October hedgerows, like a debutante from the castle, delighted with herself but still, now and then, singing to the wolves with a kind of wistful triumph, because now she knew how to wear clothes and so had put on the visible sign of her difference from them.

Her footprints on damp earth are beautiful and menacing as those Man Friday left.[1]

The young husband of the dead bride spent a long time planning his revenge. He filled the church with an arsenal of bells, books and candles; a battery of silver bullets; they brought a ten-gallon tub of holy water in a wagon from the city, where it had been blessed by the Archbishop himself, to drown the Duke, if the bullets bounced off him. They gathered in the church to chant a litany and wait for the one who would visit with the first deaths of winter.

She goes out at night more often now. The landscape assembles itself about her; she informs it with her presence. She is its significance.

It seemed to her the congregation in the church was ineffectually attempting to imitate the wolves' chorus. She lent them the assistance of her own, educated voice for a while, rocking contemplatively on her haunches by the graveyard gate; then her nostrils twitched to catch the rank stench of the dead that told her her cohabitor was at hand; raising her head, who did her new, keen eyes spy but the lord of cobweb castle intent on performing his cannibal rituals?

And if her nostrils flare suspiciously at the choking reek of incense and his do not, that is because she is far more sentient than he. She will, therefore, run, run! when she hears the crack of bullets, because they killed her foster mother: so, with the selfsame lilting lope, drenched with holy water, will he run, too, until the young widower fires the silver bullet that bites his shoulder and drags off half his fictive pelt, so that he must rise up like any common forked biped and limp distressfully on as best he may.

When they saw the white bride leap out of the tombstones and scamper off towards the castle with the werewolf stumbling after, the peasants thought the Duke's dearest victim had come back to take matters into her own hands. They ran screaming from the presence of a ghostly vengeance on him.

Poor, wounded thing . . . locked half and half between such strange states, an aborted transformation, an incomplete mystery, now he lies writhing on his black bed in the room like a Mycenaean tomb,[2] howls like a wolf with his foot in a trap or a woman in labor, and bleeds.

First, she was fearful when she heard the sound of pain, in case it hurt her, as it had done before. She prowled round the bed, growling, snuffing at his wound, that does not smell like her wound. Then, she was pitiful as her gaunt gray mother; she leapt upon his bed to lick, without hesitation, without disgust, with a quick, tender gravity, the blood and dirt from his cheeks and forehead.

The lucidity of the moonlight lit the mirror propped against the red wall; the rational glass, the master of the visible, impartially recorded the crooning girl.

As she continued her ministrations, this glass, with infinite slowness, yielded to the reflexive strength of its own material construction. Little by little, there appeared within it, like the image on photographic paper that emerges, first, a formless web of tracery, the prey caught in its own fishing net, then in firmer yet still shadowed outline until at last as vivid as real life itself, as if brought into being by her soft, moist, gentle tongue, finally, the face of the Duke.   *1978*

---

1. An allusion to Daniel Defoe's *Robinson Crusoe* (1719).   2. Mycenae is an ancient Greek city.

—•—☰◈☲—•—

Buchi Emecheta
1944–

A Nigerian author of nine novels and an autobiography, BUCHI EMECHETA was born Florence Onye Buchi in a village near Lagos to parents from the town of Ibuza. Despite the traditional Nigerian bias against education for girls, she attended a Methodist high school and aspired to be a writer. In 1962 she moved to London to join her husband, Sylvester Onwordi, to whom she had been betrothed at the age of eleven; there she worked in a public library, raised the two children she had brought with her from Nigeria, and bore three others. When her husband burned the manuscript of her first novel, declaring that she would never be a writer because she was black and a woman, she left him even though divorce was not sanctioned in the Ibo culture. Emecheta earned a degree in sociology from the University of London and turned again to fiction in the early 1970s. Except for a brief stint of teaching at the University of Calabar, she has continued to live and write in London, where she has established her own publishing company, Ogugwu Afor, named for an Ibo goddess. Emecheta's novels reveal the difficulties of girls' and women's lives due to the oppressive aspects of African traditions; they also examine the psychic split that can result when women's allegiance to their culture and their desire for self-determination clash. *Head Above Water*, her autobiography, was published in 1986.

Emecheta has identified her first two novels as slightly fictionalized accounts of her own experiences. *In the Ditch* (1972) describes the painful childhood of Adah Obi, who confronts her family's sexism and satisfies her desire to be educated. *Second-Class Citizen* (1974) chronicles Adah's move to England, where she encounters both racial prejudice and domestic violence. Both *The Bride Price* (1976), a rewriting of the novel Emecheta's husband burned, and *The Slave Girl* (1977) consider women's changing roles in Nigeria from the early colonial period to World War II. The first novel scrutinizes the custom of paying dowry, the second, marriage's oppressive potential. *The Joys of Motherhood* (1979) explores the ways that assumptions about motherhood punish Nnu Ego, a married Nigerian woman who fails to conceive a child. This novel won England's Jock Campbell Award for Fiction. Subsequent novels address issues of feminism, sexual violence, militarism, and cultural dislocation. *Destination Biafra* (1982) recounts the Nigerian Civil War from the perspective of Debbi Ogedemgbe, an Oxford graduate who joins the Nigerian army and is twice raped in the line of duty. *The Rape of Shavi* (1983), a futuristic tale, explores the disaster that occurs when a group of Europeans fleeing nuclear holocaust come to a remote African village. *Double Yoke* (1983) examines the sexual harassment with which women often contend when pursuing higher education. *Gwendolyn* (1989) portrays the alienation experienced by a Caribbean girl whose family moves to England as part of the African diaspora.

In a 1995 interview with Dolly McPherson, Emecheta discussed her attempt to "bridge a gap between these two cultures—the Nigerian and the British." This struggle with hybrid identities can be seen in the chapter from *Second-Class Citizen* included here, as Emecheta's dislocated protagonist confronts the pernicious effects of racism as well as the destructive elements of sexual exploitation.

⊰ A Cold Welcome ⊱

There was a sudden burst of excitement on the deck of the ship. Adah could hear it from where she was sitting in her cabin, changing Vicky's napkin. For a moment she stopped what she was doing, straining her ears to make out what the excitement was about, but she could hear nothing coherent. There were voices jabbering loudly, somebody laughed hysterically, and there were sounds of someone running as if chased by demons.

What could it be? wondered Adah, as she hurried through the diaper routine. Perhaps it was a fire, or an accident, or could it be that they were drowning? She knew they would be in Liverpool in a day or two, but what was the rushing for? She was unable to bear the suspense any longer so she quickly slipped a dress on and ran out onto the deck.

She had forgotten that they had passed the Bay of Biscay, she had forgotten that they were now in Europe and that it was March. The cold wind that blew on her face as she emerged on the deck was as heavy and hurtful as a blow from a boxer. She ran back, with her arms folded across her chest, to get more clothes. Then she ran to the ship's nurse. The nurse had a fat face, small eyes and a fat body. She was all smiles when she saw Adah and her eyes were lost in creases.

"Have you seen it?" she burbled. "Have you seen Liverpool? It's too early and a bit dark, but we are in Liverpool. We've arrived in England!"

Adah opened her eyes wide and closed them again, still shivering. So they had arrived. She had arrived in the United Kingdom. *Pa, I'm in the United Kingdom*, her heart sang to her dead father.

The nurse stared at her for a second, then dashed past her, anxious to spread the good news.

Adah put on the woollies which she bought at Las Palmas. Then she ran out on to the deck.

England gave Adah a cold welcome. The welcome was particularly cold because only a few days previously they had been enjoying bright and cheerful welcomes from ports like Takoradi, Freetown and Las Palmas. If Adah had been Jesus, she would have passed England by. Liverpool was gray, smoky and looked uninhabited by humans. It reminded Adah of the loco-yard where they told her Pa had once worked as a molder. In fact the architectural designs were the same. But if, as people said, there was plenty of money in England, why then did the natives give their visitors this poor cold welcome? Well, it was too late to moan, it was too late to change her mind. She could not have changed it even if she had wanted to. Her children must have an English education and, for that reason, she was prepared to bear the coldest welcome, even if it came from the land of her dreams. She was a little bit disappointed, but she told herself not to worry. If people like Lawyer Nweze and others could survive it, so could she.

The Francis that came to meet them was a new Francis. There was something very, very different about him. Adah was stunned when he kissed her in public, with everybody looking. Oh, my God, she thought; if her mother-in-law could see them, she would go and make sacrifices to Oboshi for forgiveness. Francis was delighted with Vicky.

"Just my image, I can now die in peace!"

"What do you mean, die in peace?" Adah challenged.

Francis laughed. "In England, people make jokes of everything, even things as serious as death. People still laugh about them."

"Yes?" Adah was beginning to be scared. She looked round her wildly.

There were hundreds of people rushing around clutching their luggage, and pulling their children, but it was not as noisy as it would have been had they been in Lagos. The whites she saw did not look like people who could make jokes about things like death. They looked remote, happy in an aloof way, but determined to keep their distance.

"These people don't look as if they know how to joke. You're lying, Francis. You're making it all up. English people don't joke about death."

"This separation of ours has made you bold. You've never in your life told me that I was lying before," Francis accused.

Adah was quietened by the sharpness in his voice. The sharpness seemed to say to her: "It is allowed for African males to come and get civilized in England. But that privilege has not been extended to females yet." She would have liked to protest about it from the very beginning, but what was the point of their quarreling on the very first day of their meeting after such a long separation? It was a sad indication, though, of what was coming, but she prayed that the two of them would be strong enough to accept civilization into their relationship. Because if they did not, their coming would have been a very big mistake.

After the tedious check by the immigration officers, they shivered themselves into the train. It sped on and on for hours. For the first time Adah saw real snow. It all looked so beautiful after the grayness of Liverpool. It was as if there were beautiful white clouds on the ground. She saw the factory where Ovaltine was made. Somehow that factory, standing there isolated, clean and red against the snowy background, lightened her spirit. She was in England at last. She was beginning to feel like Dick Whittington!

Francis had told her in his letter that he had accommodation for them in London. He did not warn Adah what it was like. The shock of it all nearly drove her crazy.

The house was gray with green windows. She could not tell where the house began and where it ended, because it was joined to other houses in the street. She had never seen houses like that before, joined together like that. In Lagos houses were usually completely detached with the yards on both sides, the compound at the back and verandahs in front. These ones had none of those things. They were long solid blocks, with doors opening into the street. The windows were arranged in straight rows along the streets. On looking round, Adah noticed that one could tell which windows belonged to which door by the color the frames were painted. Most of the houses seemed to have the same curtains for their windows.

"They all look like churches, you know; monasteries," Adah remarked.

"They build their houses like that here because land is not as plentiful as it is in Lagos. I am sure that builders of the future will start building our houses like that when Nigeria is fully industrialized. At the moment we can afford to waste land in building spacious verandahs and back yards."

"We may never be as bad as this. Jammed against each other."

Francis did not make any comment. There was no need. He opened the door into what looked to Adah like a tunnel. But it was a hall; a hall with flowered walls! It was narrow and it seemed at first as if there were no windows. Adah clutched at Titi, and she in turn held her mother in fear. They climbed stairs upon stairs until they seemed to be approaching the roof of the house. Then Francis opened one door and showed them into a room, or a half-room. It was very small, with a single bed at one end and a new settee which Francis had bought with the money Adah sent him to buy her a top coat with. The space between the settee and the bed was just enough for a formica-topped table, the type she had had in the kitchen in Lagos.

"Are we going to live here?" she managed to ask.

"Well, I know you will not like it, but this is the best I can do. You see, accommodation is very short in London, especially for black people with children. Everybody is coming to London. The West Indians, the Pakistanis and even the Indians, so that African students are usually grouped together with them. We are all blacks, all coloreds, and the only houses we can get are horrors like these."

Well, what could she say? She simply stared. She said nothing even when she learned that the toilet was outside, four flights of stairs down, in the yard; nor when she learned that there was no bath and no kitchen. She swallowed it all, just like a nasty pill.

In the evening, the other tenants returned from the factories where they worked. They all came to welcome her. Then, to her horror, she saw that she had to share the house with such Nigerians who called her madam at home; some of them were of the same educational background as her paid servants. She knew she had had a terrible childhood, but still, in Nigeria, class distinctions were beginning to be established. *Oh Francis,* she wailed inwardly, *how could you have done this to us. After all we have friends who, though they may be living in slums like this, still live apart from this type of people.*

"You could have tried, Francis. Look at your friend, Mr. Eke—when he knew that his wife was coming with their daughter, he made sure he moved away from this lot," she said aloud.

"Sorry, but I was too busy. It's not bad, you can keep to yourself, you don't have to mix with them. You have your children to look after, you don't have to see them!"

"You make it all sound so easy—'I don't have to see them'. You forget I have young children, and they will bring me into contact with the neighbors. You should have thought of that before. Have you no shame at all or have you lost your sense of shame in this Godforsaken country? Oh, I wish I had not come. I wish I had been warned. I wish . . ."

"Why don't you stop wishing and face reality? It is too late now. We just have to make the best of the situation. I shouldn't start moaning, if I were you."

"Don't talk to me. I don't want to hear. You could have got better accommodation if you had really tried. But you didn't try hard enough," Adah yelled.

Francis's temper snapped. He lifted his hand as if to slap her, but thought better of it. There would be plenty of time for that, if Adah was going to start telling him what to do. This scared Adah a little. He would not have dreamt of hitting her at home because his mother and father would not have allowed it. To them, Adah was like the goose that laid the golden eggs. It seemed that in England, Francis didn't care whether she laid the golden egg or not. He was free at last from his parents, he was free to do what he liked, and not even hundreds of Adahs were going to curtail that new freedom. The ugly glare he gave Adah made that clear.

The he spat out in anger: "You must know, my dear young *lady,* that in Lagos you may be a million publicity officers for the Americans; you may be earning a million pounds a day; you may have hundreds of servants: you may be living like an elite, but the day you land in England, you are a second-class citizen. So you can't discriminate against your own people, because we are all second-class."

He stopped to see the effect of his warning. He was happy to see that it had made an impression. Adah sat crumpled on the edge of the new settee, just like the dying Ayesha in Rider Haggard's *She.*

Francis went on, enjoying the rhythm of his voice. That man should have been an actor, Adah thought.

He laughed. A joyless sort of laugh, dry and empty. "I remember at one of your Old Girls' Association meetings where that white lady . . . yes, I remember, she was from Oxford, wasn't she?—I remember her telling you all that young women with your background should never in all your lives talk to bus conductors. Well, my darling, in England the middle-class black is the one that is lucky enough to get the post of bus conductor. So you'd better start respecting them."

At first Adah thought Francis hated her. This was his first opportunity of showing her what he was really like. Had she made a mistake in rushing into this marriage? But she had needed a home. And the immigration authorities were making it very difficult for single girls to come to England. You were allowed only as long as you were coming to join a husband who was already there. It was very bad, sad in fact. But even if she had nothing to thank Francis for, she could still thank him for making it possible for her to come to England, for giving her her own children, because she had never really had anything of her own before.

They made it up that night, forgetting, in their intense disappointment and loneliness which was fast descending upon them like a gloomy cloud, that they were not supposed to have more children for some time. Adah did remember in the confusion that her nickname at home was "Touch Not." But how could she protest to a man who was past reasoning? The whole process was an attack, as savage as that of any animal.

At the end of it all, Francis gasped and said, "Tomorrow you are going to see a doctor. I want them to see to this frigidity. I am not going to have it."

When, days later, Adah discovered what frigidity meant, she realized that Francis had become sophisticated in many things. She kept all this to herself, though. There was no point in arguing with Francis; he was as remote as the English people Adah had seen at Liverpool. And the house where they now lived was a place in which one could not have a good family ding-dong in peace.

What worried her most was the description "second-class." Francis had become so conditioned by this phrase that he was not only living up to it but enjoying it, too. He kept pressing Adah to get a job in a shirt factory. Adah refused. Working in a factory was the last thing she would do. After all, she had several "O" and "A" levels and she had part of the British Library Association Professional Certificate, to say nothing of the experience. Why should she go and work with her neighbors who were just learning to join their letters together instead of printing them? Some of them could not even speak any English even though it was becoming a colloquial language for most Ibos. To cap it all, these people were Yorubas, the type of illiterate Yoruba who would take joy in belittling anything Ibo. But Francis mixed with them very well, and they were pushing him to force her to take the type of job considered suitable for housewives, especially black housewives.

This was all too much for Adah, and she recoiled into her shell, telling it all, as the Protestant hymn book says, "to God in prayers."

But, as usual, God had a funny way of answering people's prayers. An envelope arrived one morning telling her that she had been accepted as a senior library assistant at North Finchley Library subject to certain conditions. She was so happy about this that she ran into the backyard where she hung out the babies' nappies and started to whirl round and round in a kind of Ibo dance. She was forced to stop suddenly because she was dizzy. She was unwell. She was, in fact, feeling sick.

Then she remembered that first night. Oh, God help her, what was she going to do? Tell Francis in his present mood? He would kill her. He had started accusing her of all sorts of things. He had told her that he married her in the first place because she could work harder than most girls of her age and because she was orphaned very early in life. But since she had arrived in England, she had grown too proud to work.

The news of the new job would have cheered him up, but not if it was coupled with the knowledge that another child was on the way when Titi was barely two and Vicky nine months old; not when the two children were not yet out of nappies? Oh, God, what was she going to do? Francis would say she had invented the pregnancy to avoid work. Had he not taken her to see a female gynecologist the very next day because, as he said, no marriage succeeds without a good sex life? As far as he was concerned, marriage was sex and lots of it, nothing more. The doctor was very sympathetic towards Adah and guessed that she was frightened of another child. She was sent home equipped with all sorts of gadgets to prevent a baby that was already sitting there prettily. Oh, yes, Bubu was determined to come into the world, and nobody was able to stop him even though he chose a very unorthodox way of doing so, nine months later. Meanwhile his mother went through hell.

Adah felt very ill, but kept it quiet. Francis was dissatisfied and started shopping around outside for willing women. Adah was quite happy about this; she even encouraged him. At least she would have some peaceful nights.

As she expected, Francis blamed her for the baby, and was sure she would lose the job because there was to be a medical examination. Adah was scared about this, but she was determined to get that job.

She put on her best skirt and blouse, the set she had bought from St. Michael's in Lagos. She had not been able to buy any clothes since she arrived in England as all the money she had brought with her went on food. Francis would not work as he was studying and he said this would interfere with his progress. Well, she put on this outfit, feeling great. She had not really dressed up for a very long time. Apart from making her feel good, the skirt and blouse covered the gentle bulge that was already forming. Being the third child, it showed early.

She stopped panicking when she saw that the doctor was a man, and an old man at that. There was a woman sitting by him, though, a scribe or something, for she held a pen and paper and sat on a chair, as stiff as dry twigs. Adah ignored the latter and set to work on the old doctor. She beamed at him, charmed him and even wanted to flirt with him. In short, the doctor got carried away and forgot to look at Adah's belly button, even though she was stripped to the waist.

She got the job. Only God Almighty knew what happened to the poor doctor, especially as it was clear from the first month that she was pregnant and she inquired about maternity leave. Adah was sorry for him, but what could she have done? If she had not got that job her marriage would have broken up, and that would have been very difficult because she did not yet know her way about. The fact that she was still laying the golden eggs stopped Francis from walking out on her. As before, her pay bound him to her but the difference was that she now knew it.

She had had to travel all the way from Lagos to London to find that out, and to discover another very weak point: she cared for Francis, she wanted him to make good, she hated to disappoint him. So, sorry though she was for making a fool of an old doctor, this was just one of those cases where honesty would not have been the best policy.   *1974*

Jamaica Kincaid
1949–

A fiction writer raised on the Caribbean island of Antigua, JAMAICA KINCAID was born Elaine Potter Richardson to racially mixed parents and was educated at colonial schools. At sixteen she left Antigua to study in the United States, eventually pursuing a career as a freelance journalist. After publishing a number of articles for *Ingenue* magazine, she became a regular contributor to the *New Yorker*, where she worked for over a decade as a staff writer. Many of her stories were first published in that magazine, including seven from her first collection, *At the Bottom of the River* (1983). In addition to fiction, she has published a memoir of growing up in Antigua, *A Small Place* (1988). As the critic Carole Boyce Davies notes, Kincaid's "is never an

uncritical, unproblematized acceptance of Caribbean identity"; indeed, she rejects the colonization and political corruption there, but with the eye of both an insider and an exile. Although Kincaid sets much of her fiction in Antigua, she lives in Vermont with her husband, Allen Shawn, and their two children.

Known for its musical prose, Kincaid's fiction typically features a young female protagonist involved in a process of self-discovery. *At the Bottom of the River* contains ten prize-winning stories that recount the pains and pleasures of childhood in the Caribbean and probe the bittersweet nature of family love. *Annie John* (1985), a novella, chronicles a young girl's coming of age in Antigua, focusing especially on her complex relationship with her mother. *Lucy* (1990) portrays the sexual awakening of an insouciant *au pair* from the West Indies who comes to the United States to work for the "perfect" upper-class family. *The Autobiography of My Mother* (1996) tells the story of Xuela Claudette Richardson, the daughter of a Carib mother who dies in childbirth and a father who is half Scots, half African. *My Brother* (1997) recounts the death from AIDS of the author's brother in Antigua.

Excerpted from *The Autobiography of My Mother*, "Xuela" was published in the *New Yorker* in 1994. It presents the intimate musings of a motherless girl who struggles to understand her maternal legacy and claim her emotional and sexual autonomy. As she learns to negotiate racial, linguistic, and familial identities, Xuela begins to decode her mysterious world and construct a fluid female subjectivity.

⇥ Xuela ⇤

My mother died at the moment I was born, and so for my whole life there was nothing standing between myself and eternity; at my back was always a bleak, black wind. I could not have known at the beginning of my life that this would be so; I only came to know this in the middle of my life, just at the time when I was no longer young and realized that I had less of some of the things I used to have in abundance and more of some of the things I had scarcely had at all. And this realization of loss and gain made me look backward and forward: at my beginning was this woman whose face I had never seen, but at my end was nothing, no one between me and the black room of the world. I came to feel that for my whole life I had been standing on a precipice, that my loss had made me vulnerable, hard, and helpless; on knowing this I became overwhelmed with sadness and shame and pity for myself.

When my mother died, leaving me a small child vulnerable to all the world, my father took me and placed me in the care of the same woman he paid to wash his clothes. It is possible that he emphasized to her the difference between the two bundles: one was his child, not his only child in the world but the only child he had with the only woman he had married so far; the other was his soiled clothes. He would have handled one more gently than the other, he would have given more careful instructions for the care of one over the other, he would have expected better care for one than the other, but which one I do not know, because he was a very vain man, his appearance was very important to him. That I was a burden to him, I know; that his soiled clothes were a burden to him, I know; that he did not know how to take care of me by himself, or how to clean his own clothes himself, I know.

He had lived in a very small house with my mother. He was poor, but it was not because he was good; he had not done enough bad things yet to get rich. This house was on a hill and he had walked down the hill balancing in one hand his child, in the other his clothes, and he had given them, bundle and child, to a woman. She was not a relative of his or of my mother's; her name was Eunice Paul, and she had six children already, the last one was still a baby. That was why she still had some milk in her breast to give me, but in my mouth it tasted sour and I would not drink it. She lived in a house that was far from other houses, and from it there was a broad view of the sea and the mountains, and when I was irritable and unable to console myself, she would prop me up on pieces of old cloth and place me in the shade of a tree, and at the sight of that sea and those mountains, so unpitying, I would exhaust myself in tears.

Ma Eunice was not unkind: She treated me just the way she treated her own children—but this is not to say she was kind to her own children. In a place like this, brutality is the only real inheritance and cruelty is sometimes the only thing freely given. I did not like her, and I missed the face I had never seen; I looked over my shoulder to see if someone was coming, as if I were expecting someone to come, and Ma Eunice would ask me what I was looking for, at first as a joke, but when, after a time, I did not stop doing it, she thought it meant I could see spirits. I could not see spirits at all, I was just looking for that face, the face I would never see, even if I lived forever.

I never grew to love this woman my father left me with, this woman who was not unkind to me but who could not be kind because she did not know how—and perhaps I could not love her because I, too, did not know how. She fed me food forced through a sieve when I would not drink her milk and did not yet have teeth; when I grew teeth, the first thing I did was to sink them into her hand as she fed me. A small sound escaped her mouth then, more from surprise than from pain, and she knew this for what it was—my first act of ingratitude—and it put her on her guard against me for the rest of the time we knew each other.

Until I was four I did not speak. This did not cause anyone to lose a minute of happiness; there was no one who would have worried about it in any case. I knew I could speak, but I did not want to. I saw my father every fortnight, when he came to get his clean clothes. I never thought of him as coming to visit me; I thought of him as coming to pick up his clean clothes. When he came, I was brought to him and he would ask me how I was, but it was a formality; he would never touch me or look into my eyes. What was there to see in my eyes? Eunice washed, ironed, and folded his clothes; they were wrapped up like a gift in two pieces of clean nankeen cloth and placed on a table, the only table in the house, waiting for him to come and pick them up. His visits were quite regular, and so when he did not appear as he usually did, I noticed it. I said, "Where is my father?"

I said it in English—not French patois or English patois, but plain English—and that should have been the surprise: not that I spoke, but that I spoke English, a language I had never heard anyone speak. Ma Eunice and her children spoke the language of Dominica, which is French patois, and my father when he spoke to me spoke that language also, not because he disrespected me, but because he thought I understood nothing else. But no one noticed; they only marveled at the fact that I had finally spoken and inquired about the absence of my father. That the first words I said were in the language of a people I would never like or love is not now a mystery to me; everything in my life, good or bad, to which I am inextricably bound is a source of pain.

I was then four years old and saw the world as a series of soft lines joined together, a sketch in charcoal; and so when my father would come and take his clothes away I saw only that he suddenly appeared on the small path that led from the main road to the door of the house in which I lived and then, after completing his mission, disappeared as he turned onto the road where it met the path. I did not know what lay beyond the path, I did not know if after he passed from my sight he remained my father or dissolved into something altogether different and I would never see him again in the form of my father. I would have accepted this. I would have come to believe that this is the way of the world. I did not talk and I would not talk.

One day, without meaning to, I broke a plate, the only plate of its kind that Eunice had ever owned, a plate made of bone china, and the words "I am sorry" would not pass my lips. The sadness she expressed over this loss fascinated me; it was so thick with grief, so overwhelming, so deep, as if the death of a loved one had occurred. She grabbed the thick pouch that was her stomach, she pulled at her hair, she pounded her bossom; large tears rolled out of her eyes and down her cheeks, and they came in such profusion that if a new source of water had sprung up from them, as in a myth or a fairy tale, my small self would not have been surprised. I had been warned repeatedly by her not to touch this plate, for she had seen me look at it with an obsessive curiosity. I would look at it and wonder about the picture painted on its surface, a picture of a wide-open field filled with grass and flowers in the most tender shades of yellow, pink, blue, and green; the sky had a sun in it that shone but did not burn bright; the clouds were thin and scattered about like a decoration, not thick and banked up, not harbingers of doom. This picture was nothing but a field full of grass and flowers on a sunny day, but it had an atmosphere of secret abundance, happiness, and tranquility; underneath it was written in gold letters the one word HEAVEN. Of course it was not a picture of heaven at all; it was a picture of the English countryside idealized, but I did not know that, I did not know that such a thing as the English countryside existed. And neither did Eunice; she thought that this picture was a picture of heaven, offering as it did a secret promise of a life without worry or care or want.

When I broke the china plate on which this picture was painted and caused Ma Eunice to cry so, I did not immediately feel sorry, I did not feel sorry shortly after, I felt sorry only long afterward, and by then it was too late to tell her so, she had died; perhaps she went to heaven and it fulfilled the promise on that plate. When I broke the plate and would not say that I was sorry, she cursed my dead mother, she cursed my father, she cursed me. The words she used were without meaning; I understood them but they did not hurt me, for I did not love her. And she did not love me. She made me kneel down on her stone heap, which as it should be was situated in a spot that got direct sun all day long, with my hands raised high above my head and with a large stone in each hand. She meant to keep me in this position until I said the words "I am sorry," but I would not say them, I could not say them. It was beyond my own will; those words could not pass my lips. I stayed like that until she exhausted herself cursing me and all whom I came from.

Why should this punishment have made a lasting impression on me, redolent as it was in every way of the relationship between captor and captive, master and slave, with its motif of the big and the small, the powerful and the powerless, the strong and the weak, and against a background of earth, sea, and sky, and Eunice standing over me, metamorphosing into a succession of things furious and not human with each syllable that passed her lips—with her dress of a thin, badly woven cotton, the bodice of a color and pattern contrary to the skirt, her hair, uncombed, unwashed for many months, wrapped in a piece of old cloth that had been unwashed for longer than her hair? The dress again—it had once been new and clean, and dirt had made it old, but dirt had made it new again by giving it shadings it did not have before, and dirt would finally cause it to disintegrate altogether, though she was not a dirty woman, she washed her feet every night.

The day was clear, it was not the rainy time, some men were on the sea casting nets for fish, but they would not catch too many because it was a clear day; and three of her children were eating bread and they rolled up the inside of the bread into small pebble-like shapes and threw them at me as I knelt there, and laughed at me; and the sky was without a cloud and there was not a breeze; a fly flew back and forth across my face, sometimes landing on a corner of my mouth; an overripe breadfruit fell off its tree, and that sound was like a fist meeting the soft, fleshy part of a body. All this, all this I can remember—why should it have made a lasting impression on me?

As I was kneeling there I saw three land turtles crawling in and out of the small space under the house, and I fell in love with them, I wanted to have them near me, I wanted to speak only to them each day for the rest of my life. Long after my ordeal was over—resolved in a way that did not please Ma Eunice, for I did not say I was sorry—I took all three turtles and placed them in an enclosed area where they could not come and go as they pleased and so were completely dependent on me for their existence. I would bring to them the leaves of vegetables and water in small seashells. I thought them beautiful, their shells dark gray with faint yellow circles, their long necks, their unjudging eyes, the slow deliberateness of their crawl. But they would withdraw into their shells when I did not want them to, and when I called them, they would not come out. To teach them a lesson, I took some mud from the riverbed and covered up the small hole from which each neck would emerge, and I allowed it to dry up. I covered over the place where they lived with stones, and for many days afterward I forgot about them. When they came into my mind again, I went to take a look at them in the place where I had left them. They were by then all dead.

It was my father's wish that I be sent to school. It was an unusual request; girls did not attend school, none of Ma Eunice's girl children attended school. I shall never know what made him do such a thing. I can only imagine that he desired such a thing for me without giving it too much thought, because in the end what could an education do for someone like me? I can only say what I did not have; I can only measure it against what I did have and find misery in the difference. And yet, and yet . . . it was for this reason that I came to see for the first time what lay beyond the path that led away from my house. And I can so well remember the feel of the cloth of my skirt and blouse—coarse because it was new—a green skirt and beige blouse, a uniform, its colors and style mimicking the colors and style of a school somewhere else, somewhere far away; and I had on a pair of brown thick cloth shoes and brown cotton socks which my father had gotten for me, I did not know where. And to mention that I did not know where these things came from, to say that I wondered about them, is really to say that this was the first time I had worn such things as shoes and socks, and they caused my feet to ache and swell and the skin to blister and break, but I was made to wear them until my feet got used to them, and my feet—all of me— did. That morning was a morning like any other, so ordinary it was profound: it was sunny in some places and not in others, and the two (sunny, cloudy) occupied different parts of the sky quite comfortably; there was the green of the leaves, the red burst of the flowers from the flamboyant trees, the sickly yellow fruit of the cashew, the smell of lime, the smell of almonds, the coffee on my breath, Eunice's skirt blowing in my face, and the stirring up of the smells that came from between her legs, which I shall never forget, and whenever I smell myself I am reminded of her. The river was low, so I did not hear the sound of the water rushing over stones; the breeze was soft, so the leaves did not rustle in the trees.

I had these sensations of seeing, smelling, and hearing on my journey down the path on the way to my school. When I reached the road and placed my newly shod feet on it, this was the first time I had done so. I was aware of this. It was a road of small stones and tightly packed dirt, and each step I took was awkward; the ground shifted, my feet slipped backward. The road stretched out ahead of me and vanished around a bend; we kept walking toward this bend and then we came to the bend and the bend gave way to more of the same road and then another bend. We came to my school before the end of the last bend. It was a small building with one door and four windows; it had a wooden floor; there was a small reptile crawling along a beam in the roof; there were three long desks lined up one behind the other; there was a large wooden table and a chair facing the three long desks; on the wall behind the wooden table and chair was a map; at the top of the map were the words "THE BRITISH EMPIRE." These were the first words I learned to read.

In that room always there were ony boys; I did not sit in a schoolroom with oth-er girls until I was older. I was not afraid in that new situation: I did not know how to be that then and do not know how to be that now. I was not afraid, because my mother had already died and that is the only thing a child is really afraid of; when I was born, my mother was dead, and I had already lived all those years with Eunice, a woman who was not my mother and who could not love me, and without my father, never knowing when I would see him again, so I was not afraid for myself in this situ-ation. (And if it is not really true that I was not afraid then, it was not the ony time that I did not admit to myself my own vulnerability.)

If I speak now of those first days with clarity and insight, it is not an invention, it should not surprise; at the time, each thing as it took place stood out in my mind with a sharpness that I now take for granted; it did not then have a meaning, it did not have a context, I did not yet know the history of events, I did not know their antecedents. My teacher was a woman who had been trained by Methodist mission-aries; she was of the African people, that I could see, and she found in this a source of humiliation and self-loathing, and she wore despair like an article of clothing, like a mantle, or a staff on which she leaned constantly, a birthright which she would pass on to us. She did not love us; we did not love her; we did not love one another, not then, not ever. There were seven boys and myself. The boys, too, were all of the African people. My teacher and these boys looked at me and looked at me: I had thick eyebrows; my hair was coarse, thick, and wavy; my eyes were set far apart from each other and they had the shape of almonds; my lips were wide and narrow in an unexpected way. I was of the African people, but not exclusively. My mother was a Carib woman, and when they looked at me this is what they saw: The Carib people had been defeated and then exterminated, thrown away like the weeds in a garden; the African people had been defeated but had survived. When they looked at me, they saw only the Carib people. They were wrong but I did not tell them so.

I started to speak quite openly then—to myself frequently, to others only when it was absolutely necessary. We spoke English in school—proper English, not patois—and among ourselves we spoke French patois, a language that was not considered proper at all, a language that a person from France could not speak and could only with difficulty understand. I spoke to myself because I grew to like the sound of my own voice. It had a sweetness to me, it made my loneliness less, for I was lonely and wished to see people in whose faces I could recognize something of myself. Because who was I? My mother was dead; I had not seen my father for a long time.

I learned to read and write very quickly. My memory, my ability to retain information, to retrieve the tiniest detail, to recall who said what and when, was regarded as unusual, so unusual that my teacher, who was trained to think only of good and evil and whose judgment of such things was always mistaken, said I was evil, I was possessed—and to establish that there could be no doubt of this, she pointed again to the fact that my mother was of the Carib people.

My world then—silent, soft, and vegetable-like in its vulnerability, subject to the powerful whims of others, diurnal, beginning with the pale opening of light on the horizon each morning and ending with the sudden onset of dark at the beginning of each night—was both a mystery to me and the source of much pleasure: I loved the face of a gray sky, porous, grainy, wet, following me to school for mornings on end, sending down on me soft arrows of water; the face of that same sky when it was a hard, unsheltering blue, a backdrop for a cruel sun; the harsh heat that eventually became a part of me, like my blood; the overbearing trees (the stems of some of them the size of small trunks) that grew without restraint, as if beauty were only size, and I could tell them all apart by closing my eyes and listening to the sound the leaves made when they rubbed together; and I loved that moment when the white flowers from the cedar tree started to fall to the ground with a silence that I could hear, their petals at first still fresh, a soft kiss of pink and white, then a day later, crushed, wilted, and brown, a nuisance to the eye; and the river that had become a small lagoon when one day on its own it changed course, on whose bank I would sit and watch families of birds, and frogs laying their eggs, and the sky turning from black to blue and blue to black, and rain falling on the sea beyond the lagoon but not on the mountain that was beyond the sea. It was while sitting in this place that I first began to dream about my mother; I had fallen asleep on the stones that covered the ground around me, my small body sinking into this surface as if it were feathers. I saw my mother come down a ladder. She wore a long white gown, the hem of it falling just above her heels, and that was all of her that was exposed, just her heels; she came down and down, but no more of her was ever revealed. Only her heels, and the hem of her gown. At first I longed to see more, and then I became satisfied just to see her heels coming down toward me. When I awoke, I was not the same child I had been before I fell asleep. I longed to see my father and to be in his presence constantly.

On a day that began in no special way that I can remember, I was taught the principles involved in writing an ordinary letter. A letter has six parts: the address of the sender, the date, the address of the recipient, the salutation or greeting, the body of the letter, the closing of the letter. It was well known that a person in the position that I was expected to occupy—the position of a woman and a poor one—would have no need whatsoever to write a letter, but the sense of satisfaction it gave everyone connected with teaching me this, writing a letter, must have been immense. I was beaten and harsh words were said to me when I made a mistake. The exercise of copying the letters of someone whose complaints or perceptions or joys were of no interest to me did not make me angry then—I was too young to understand that vanity could be a weapon as dangerous as any knife; it only made me want to write my own letters, letters in which I would express my feelings about my own life as it appeared to me at seven years old. I started to write to my father. I wrote, "My dear Papa," in a lovely, decorative penmanship, a penmanship born of beatings and harsh words. I would say to him that I was mistreated by Eunice in word and deed and that I missed him and loved him very much. I wrote the same thing over and over again. It was without detail. It was nothing but the plaintive cry of a small wounded animal: "My dear Papa, you are the only person I have left in the world, no one loves me, only you can, I am beaten with words, I am beaten with sticks, I am beaten with stones, I love you more than anything, only you can save me." These words were not meant for my father at all but for the person of whom I could see only her heels. Night after night I saw her heels, only her heels coming down to meet me, coming down to meet me forever.

I wrote these letters without any intention of sending them to my father; I did not know how to do that, to send them. I folded them up in such a way that if they were torn apart they would make eight small squares. There was no mysterious significance to this; I did it only to make them fit more discreetly under a large stone just outside the gate to my school. Each day, as I left, I would place a letter I had written to my father under it. I had written these letters in secret, during the small amount of time allotted to us as recess, or during the time when I had completed my work and had gone unnoticed. Pretending to be deeply involved in what I was supposed to be doing, I would write a letter to my father.

This small cry for help did not bring me instant relief. I recognized my own misery, but that it could be alleviated—that my life could change, that my circumstances could change—did not occur to me.

My letters did not remain a secret. A boy named Roman had seen me putting them in their secret place, and behind my back, he removed them. He had no empathy, no pity; any instinct to protect the weak had been destroyed in him. He took my letters to our teacher. In my letters to my father I had said, "Everyone hates me, only you love me," but I had not truly meant these letters to be sent to my father, and they were not really addressed to my father; if I had been asked then if I really felt that everyone hated me, that only my father loved me, I would not have known how to answer. But my teacher's reaction to my letters, those small scribblings, was a tonic to me. She believed the "everybody" I referred to was herself, and only herself. She said my words were a lie, libelous, that she was ashamed of me, that she was not afraid of me. My teacher said all this to me in front of the other pupils at my school. They thought I was humiliated and they felt joy seeing me brought so low. I did not feel humiliated at all. I felt something. I could see her teeth were crooked and yellow, and I wondered how they had got that way. Large half-moons of perspiration stained the underarms of her dress, and I wondered if when I became a woman I, too, would perspire so profusely and how it would smell. Behind her shoulder on the wall was a large female spider carrying its sac of eggs, and I wanted to reach out and crush it with the bare palm of my hand, because I wondered if it was the same kind of spider or a relative of the spider that had sucked saliva from the corner of my mouth the night before as I lay sleeping, leaving three small, painful bites. There was a drizzle of rain outside, I could hear the sound of it on the galvanized roof.

She sent my letters to my father, to show me that she had a clear conscience. She said that I had mistaken her scoldings, which were administered out of love for me, as an expression of hatred, and that this showed I was guilty of the sin of pride. And she said that she hoped I would learn to tell the difference between the two: love and hate. To this day, I have tried to tell the difference between the two, and I cannot, because often they wear so much the same face. When she said this, I did look in her face to see if I could tell whether it was true that she loved me and to see if her words, which so often seemed to be a series of harsh blows, were really an expression of love. Her face to me then did not appear loving, but perhaps I was mistaken—perhaps I was too young to judge, too young to know.

I did not immediately recognize what had happened, what I had done: However unconsciously, however without direction, I had, through the use of some words, changed my situation; I had perhaps even saved my life. To speak of my own situation, to myself or to others, is something I would always do thereafter. It is in this way that I came to be so extremely conscious of myself, so interested in my own needs, so interested in fulfilling them, aware of my grievances, aware of my pleasures. From this unfocused, childish expression of pain, my life was changed and I took note of it.

My father came to fetch me wearing the uniform of a jailer. To him this had no meaning, it was without significance. He was returning to Roseau from the village of St. Joseph, where he had been carrying out his duties as a policeman. I was not told that he would arrive on that day; I had not expected him. I returned from school and saw him standing at the final bend in the road that led to the house in which I lived. I was surprised to see him, but I would admit this only to myself; I did not let anyone know. The reason I had missed my father so—the reason he no longer came to the house in which I lived, bringing his dirty clothes and taking away clean ones—was that he had married again. I had been told about this, but it was a mystery to me what it might mean; it was not unlike the first time I had been told that the world was round; I thought, What can it mean, why should it be? My father had married again. He took my hand, he said something, he spoke in English, his mouth began to curl around the words he spoke, and it made him appear benign, attractive, even kind. I understood what he said: He had a home for me now, a good home; I would love his wife, my new mother; he loved me as much as he loved himself, perhaps even more, because I reminded him of someone whom he knew with certainty he had loved even more than he had loved himself. I would love my new home; I would love the sky above and the earth below.

The word "love" was spoken with such frequency that it became a clue to my seven-year-old heart and my seven-year-old mind that this thing did not exist. My father's eyes grew small and then they grew big; he believed what he said, and that was a good thing, because I did not. But I would not have wanted to stop this progression, this new thing, this going away from here; and I did not believe him, but I did not have any reason to, no real reason. I was not yet cynical and thought that behind everything I heard lay another story altogether, the real story.

I thanked Eunice for taking care of me. I did not mean it, I could not mean it, I did not know how to mean it, but I would mean it now. I did not say goodbye; in the world that I lived in then and the world that I live in now, good-byes do not exist, it is a small world. All my belongings were in a muslin knapsack and he placed them in a bag that was on the donkey he had been riding. He placed me on the donkey and sat behind me. And this was how we looked as my back was turned on the small house in which I spent the first seven years of my life: an already important man and his small daughter on the back of a donkey at the end of the day, an ordinary day, a day that had no meaning if you were less than a smudge on a page covered with print. I could hear my father's breath; it was not the breath of my life. The back of my head touched his chest from time to time, I could hear the sound of his heart beating through his shirt, the uniform that, when people saw him wearing it coming toward them, made them afraid, for his presence when wearing these clothes was almost always not a good thing. In my life then his presence was a good thing, it was too bad that he had not thought of changing his clothes; it was too bad that I had noticed he had not done so, it was too bad that such a thing would matter to me.

This new experience of really leaving the past behind, of going from one place to the other and knowing that whatever had been would remain just so, was something I immediately accepted as a gift, as a right of nature. This most simple of movements, the turning of your back, is among the most difficult to make, but once it has been made you cannot imagine it was at all hard to accomplish. I had not been able to do it by myself, but I could see that I had set in motion events that would make it possible. If I were ever to find myself sitting in that schoolroom again, or sitting in Eunice's yard again, sleeping in her bed, eating with her children, none of it would have the same power it once had over me—the power to make me feel helpless and ashamed at my own helplessness.

I could not see the look on my father's face as he rode, I did not know what he was thinking, I did not know him well enough to guess. He set off down the road in the opposite direction from the schoolhouse. The stretch of road was new to me, and yet it had a familiarity that made me sad. Around each bend was the familiar dark green of the trees that grew with a ferociousness that no hand had yet attempted to restrain, a green so unrelenting that it attained great beauty and great ugliness and yet great humility all at once; it was itself: Nothing could be added to it; nothing could be taken away from it. Each precipice along the road was steep and dangerous, and a fall down one of them would have resulted in death or a lasting injury. And each climb up was followed by a slope down, at the bottom of which was the same choke of flowering plants, each with a purpose not yet known to me. And each curve that ran left would soon give way to a curve that ran right.

The day then began to have the colors of an ending, the colors of a funeral, gray, mauve, black; my sadness inside became manifest to me. I was a part of a procession of sadness, which was moving away from my old life, a life I had lived for only seven years. I did not become overwhelmed, though. The dark of night came on with its usual suddenness, without warning. Again I did not become overwhelmed. My father placed an arm around me, as if to ward off something—a danger I could not see in the cool air, an evil spirit, a fall. His clasp was at first gentle; then it grew till it had the strength of an iron band, but even then I did not become overwhelmed.

We entered the village in the dark. There were no lights anywhere, no dog barked, we did not pass anyone. We entered the house in which my father lived, there was a light coming from a beautiful glass lamp, something I had never seen before; the light was fueled by a clear liquid that I could see through the base of the lamp, which was embossed with the heads of animals unfamiliar to me. The lamp was on a shelf, and the shelf was made of mahogany, its brackets ended in the shape of two tightly closed paws. The room was crowded, with a chair on which two people could sit at once, two other chairs on which only one person could sit, and a small, low table draped with a piece of white linen. The walls of the house and the partition that separated this room from the rest of the house were covered with paper, and the paper was decorated with small pink roses. I had never seen anything like this before, except once, while looking through a book at my school—but the picture I had seen then was a drawing illustrating a story about the domestic goings-on of a small mammal who lived in a field with his family. In their burrow, the walls had been covered with similar paper. I had understood that story about the small mammal to be a pretense, something to amuse a child, but this was my very real father's house, a house with a bright lamp in a room, and a room that seemed to exist only for an occasional purpose.

At that moment I realized that there were so many things I did not know, not including the very big thing I did not know—my mother. I did not know my father; I did not know where he was from or whom or what he liked; I did not know the land whose surface I had just come through on an animal's back; I did not know who I was or why I was standing there in that room of the occasional purpose with the lamp. A great sea of what I did not know opened up before me, and its powerful treacherous currents pulsed over my head repeatedly until I was sure I was dead.

I had only fainted. I opened my eyes soon after to see the face of my father's wife not too far above mine. She had the face of evil. I had no other face to compare it with; I knew only that hers was the face of evil as far as I could tell. She did not like me. I could see that. She did not love me. I could see that. I could not see the rest of her right away—only her face. She was of the African people and the people from France. It was nighttime and she was in her own house, so her hair was exposed; it was smooth and yet tightly curled, and she wore it parted in the middle and plaited in two braids that were pinned up in the back. Her lips were shaped like those of people from a cold climate: thin and ungenerous. Her eyes were black, not with beauty but with deceit. Her nose was long and sharp, like an arrow; her cheekbones were also sharp. She did not like me. She did not love me. I could see it in her face. My spirit rose to meet this challenge. No love: I could live in a place like this. I knew this atmosphere all too well. Love would have defeated me. Love would always defeat me. In an atmosphere of no love I could live well; in this atmosphere of no love I could make a life for myself. She held a cup to my mouth, one of her hands brushed against my face, and it felt cold; she was feeding me a tea, something to revive me, but it tasted bitter, like a bad potion. My small tongue allowed no more than a drop of it to come into my mouth, but the bitter taste of it warmed my young heart. I sat up. Our eyes did not meet and lock; I was too young to throw out such a challenge, I could then act only on instinct.

I was led down a short hallway to a room. It was to be my own room; my father lived in a house in which there were enough rooms for me to occupy my own. This small event immediately became central to my life: I adjusted to this evidence of privacy without question. My room was lit by a small lamp, the size of my now large, aged fist, and I could see my bed: small, of wood, a white sheet on its copra-filled mattress, a square, flat pillow. I had a wash-stand on which stood a basin and an urn that had water in it. I did not see a towel. (I did not then know how to wash myself properly, in any case, and the lesson I eventually got came with many words of abuse.) There was not a picture on the wall. The walls were not covered with paper; the bare wood, pine, was not painted. It was the plainest of plain rooms, but it had in it more luxury than I had ever imagined, it offered me something I did not even know I needed: it offered me solitude. All of my little being, physical and spiritual, could find peace here, in this little place of my own where I could sit and take stock.

I sat down on the bed. My heart was breaking; I wanted to cry, I felt so alone. I felt in danger, I felt threatened; I felt as each minute passed that someone wished me dead. My father's wife came to say good night, and she turned out the lamp. She spoke to me then in French patois; in his presence she had spoken to me in English. She would do this to me through all the time we knew each other, but that first time, in the sanctuary of my room, at seven years old, I recognized this to be an attempt on her part to make an illegitimate of me, to associate me with the made-up language of people regarded as not real—the shadow people, the forever humiliated, the forever low. She then went to the part of the house where she and my father slept; it was far enough away that I could hear the sound of her footsteps fade; still, I could hear their voices as they spoke, the sounds swirling upward to the empty space beneath the ceiling. They had a conversation; I could not make out the words; the emotions seemed neutral, neither hot nor cold. There was some silence; there were short gasps and sighs; there were the sounds of people sleeping, breath escaping through the mouth.

I lay down to sleep and to dream of my mother—for I knew I would do that, I knew I would make myself do that, I needed to do that. She came down the ladder again and again, over and over, just her heels and the hem of her white dress visible; down, down, over and over. I watched her all night in my dream. I did not see her face. I was not disappointed. I would have loved to see her face, but I didn't long for it anymore. She sang a song, but it had not words; it was not a lullaby, it was not sentimental, not meant to calm me when my soul roiled at the harshness of life; it was only a song, but the sound of her voice was like a small treasure found in an abandoned chest, a treasure that inspires not astonishment but contentment and eternal pleasure.

All night I slept, and in my sleep saw her feet come down the ladder, step after step, never seeing her face, hearing her voice sing that song, sometimes humming, sometimes through an open mouth. To this day she will appear in my dreams from time to time but never again to sing or utter a sound of any kind—only as before, coming down a ladder, her heels visible and the white hem of her garment above them.

I came to my father's house in the blanket of voluptuous blackness that was the night; a morning naturally followed. I awoke in the false paradise into which I was born, the false paradise in which I will die, the same landscape that I had always known, each aspect of it beyond reproach, at once beautiful, ugly, humble, and proud; full of life, full of death, able to sustain the one, inevitably to claim the other.

My father's wife showed me how to wash myself. It was not done with kindness. My human form and odor were an opportunity to heap scorn on me. I responded in a fashion by now characteristic of me: Whatever I was told to hate I loved and loved the most. I loved the smell of the thin dirt behind my ears, the smell of my unwashed mouth, the smell that came from between my legs, the smell in the pit of my arm, the smell of my unwashed feet. Whatever about me caused offense, whatever was native to me, whatever I could not help and was not a moral failing—those things about me I loved with the fervor of the devoted. Her hands as they touched me were cold and caused me pain. We would never love each other. In her was a despair rooted in a desire long thwarted: She had not yet been able to bear my father a child. She was afraid of me; she was afraid that because of me my father would think of my mother more often than he thought of her. On that first morning she gave me some food and it was old, moldy, as if she had saved it specially for me in order to make me sick. I did not eat what she gave me after that; I learned then how to prepare my own food and made this a trait by which others would know me: I was a girl who prepared her own food.

Parts of my life, incidents in my life then, seem, when I remember them now, as if they were happening in a very small, dark place, a place the size of a dollhouse, and the dollhouse is at the bottom of a big hole, and I am way up at the top of the hole, peering down into this little house, trying to make out exactly what it is that happened down there. And sometimes when I look down at this scene, certain things are not in the same place they were in the last time I looked: Different things are in the shadows at different times, different things are in the light.

My father's wife wished me dead, at first in a way that would have allowed her to make a lavish display of sorrow over my death: an accident, God's desire. And then when no accident occurred and God did not seem to care one way or the other whether I lived or died, she tried to accomplish this herself. She made me a present of a necklace fashioned from dried berries and polished wood and stone and shells from the sea. It was most beautiful, too beautiful for a child, but a child, a real child, would have been dazzled by it, would have been seduced by it, would have immediately placed it around her neck. I was not a real child. I thanked and thanked her. I thanked her again. I did not take it into my small room. I did not want to hold on to it for very long. I had made a small place in the everlastingly thick grove of trees at the back of the house. She did not know of it yet; when eventually she discovered it, she sent something that I could not see to live there and it drove me away. It was in this secret place that I left the necklace until I could decide what to do with it. She would look at my neck and notice that I was not wearing it, but she never mentioned it again. Not once. She never urged me to wear it at all. She had a dog that she took to ground with her; this dog was a gift from my father, it was to protect her from real human harm, a harm that could be seen, it was meant to make her feel a kind of safety. One day I placed the necklace around the dog's neck, hiding it in the hair there; within twenty-four hours he went mad and died. If she found the necklace around his neck she never mentioned it to me. She became pregnant then and bore the first of her two children, and this took her close attention away from me; but she did not stop wishing me dead.

The school I attended was five miles away in the next village, and I walked to it with some other children, most of them boys. We had to cross a river, but in the dry season that meant stepping on the stones in the riverbed. When it rained and the water had risen very high, we would remove our clothes and tie them in a bundle, placing them on our heads, and cross the river naked. One day when the river was very high and we were crossing naked, we saw a woman in the part of the river where the mouth met the sea. It was deep there and we could not tell if she was sitting or standing, but we knew she was naked. She was a beautiful woman, more beautiful than any woman we had ever seen, beautiful in a way that made sense to us, not a European way: she was dark brown in skin, her hair was black and shiny and twisted into small coils all around her head. Her face was like a moon, a soft, brown, glistening moon. She opened her mouth and a strange yet sweet sound came out. It was mesmerizing; we stood and stared at her. She was surrounded by fruit, mangoes—it was the season for them—and they were all ripe, and those shades of red, pink, and yellow were tantalizing and mouth-watering. She beckoned to us to come to her. Someone said it was not a woman at all, that we should not go, that we should run away. We could not move away. And then this boy, whose face I can remember because it was the male mask of heedlessness and boastfulness that I have come to know, started forward and forward, and he laughed as he went forward. When he seemed to get to the place where she was, she moved farther away, yet she was always in the same place; he swam toward her and the fruit, and each time he was almost near, she became farther away. He swam in this way until he began to sink from exhaustion; we could see only the top of his head, we could see only his hands; then we could see nothing at all, only a set of expanding circles where he used to be, as if a pebble had been thrown there. And then the woman with her fruit vanished, too, as if she had not been there, as if the whole thing had never happened.

The boy disappeared; he was never seen again, not dead even, and when the water got low in that place, we would go and look, but he wasn't there. It was if it had never happened, and the way we talked about it was as if we had imagined it, because we never spoke about it out loud, we only accepted that it had happened, and it came to exist only in our minds, an act of faith, like the Virgin Birth for some people, or other such miracles; and it had the same power of belief and disbelief, only unlike the Virgin Birth we had seen this ourselves. I saw it happen. I saw a boy in whose company I would walk to school swim out naked to meet a woman who was also naked and surrounded by ripe fruit and disappear in the muddy waters where the river met the sea. He disappeared there and was never seen again. That woman was not a woman; she was something that took the shape of a woman. It was almost as if the reality of this terror was so overwhelming that it became a myth, as if it had happened a very long time ago and to other people, not us. I know of friends who witnessed this event with me and, forgetting that I was present, would tell it to me in a certain way, daring me to believe them; but it is only because they do not themselves believe what they are saying; they no longer believe what they saw with their own eyes, or in their own reality. This is no longer without an explanation to me. Everything about us is held in doubt and we the defeated define all that is unreal, all that is not human, all that is without love, all that is without mercy. Our experience cannot be interpreted by us; we do not know the truth of it. Our God was not the correct one, our understanding of heaven and hell was not a respectable one. Belief in that apparition of a naked woman with outstretched arms beckoning a small boy to his death was the belief of the illegitimate, the poor, the low. I believed in that apparition then and I believe in it now.

Who was my father? Not just who was he to me, his child—but who was he? He was a policeman, but not an ordinary policeman; he inspired more than the expected amount of fear for someone in his position. He made appointments to see people, men, at his house, the place where he lived with his family—this entity of which I was now a sort of member—and he would make these people wait for hours; at times he never showed up at all. They waited for him, sometimes sitting on a stone that was just inside the gate of the yard, sometimes pacing back and forth from inside the yard to outside the yard, causing the gate to creak, and this always made his wife cross, and she would complain to these people, speaking rudely to them, the rudeness way out of proportion to the annoyance of the creaky gate. They waited for him without complaint, falling asleep standing up, falling asleep as they sat on the ground, flies drinking from the saliva that leaked out of the corners of their open mouths. They waited, and when he did not show up they left and returned the next day, hoping to see him; sometimes they did, sometimes they did not. He suffered no consequences for his behavior; he just treated people in this way. He did not care, or so I thought at first— but of course he did care; it was well thought out, this way he had of causing suffering; he was a part of a whole way of life on the island which perpetuated pain.

At the time I came to live with him, he had just mastered the mask that he wore as a face for the remainder of his life: the skin taut, the eyes small and drawn back as though deep inside his head, so that it wasn't possible to get a clue to him from them, the lips parted in a smile. He seemed trustworthy. His clothes were always well ironed, clean, spotless. He did not like people to know him very well; he tried never to eat food in the presence of strangers, or in the presence of people who were afraid of him.

Who was he? I ask myself this all the time, to this day. Who was he? He was a tall man; his hair was red; his eyes were gray. His wife, the woman he married after my mother died while giving birth to me, was the only daughter of a thief, a man who grew bananas and coffee and cocoa on his own land (these crops were sold to someone else, a European man who exported them). She came to my father with no money, but her father made possible many connections for him. They bought other people's land together, they divided the profits in a way satisfactory to them both, they never quarreled, but they did not seem to be close friends; my father did not have that, a close friend. When he met the daughter of his sometime partner in crime

I do not know. It might have been a night full of stars, or a night with no light at all from above, or a day with the sun big in the sky or so bleak it felt sad to be alive. I do not know and I do not want to find out. Her voice had a harsh, heated quality to it; if there is a language that would make her voice sound musical and so invite desire, I do not yet know of it.

My father must have loved me then, but he never told me so. I never heard him say those words to anyone. He wanted me to keep going to school, he made sure of this, but I do not know why. He wanted me to go to school beyond the time that most girls were in school. I went to school past the age of thirteen. No one told me what I should do with myself after I was finished with school. It was a great sacrifice that I should go to school, because as his wife often pointed out, I would have been more useful at home. He gave me books to read. He gave me a life of John Wesley, and as I read it I wondered what the life of a man so full of spiritual tumult and piety had to do with me. My father had become a Methodist, he attended church every Sunday; he taught Sunday school. The more he robbed, the more money he had, the more he went to church; it is not an unheard-of linking. And the richer he became, the more fixed the mask of his face grew, so that now I no longer remember what he really looked like when I first knew him long ago, before I came to live with him. And so my mother and father then were a mystery to me: one through death, the other through the maze of living; one I had never seen, the other I saw constantly.

The world I came to know was full of danger and treachery, but I did not become afraid, I did not become cautious. I was not indifferent to the danger my father's wife posed to me, and I was not indifferent to the danger she thought my presence posed to her. So in my father's house, which was her home, I tried to cloak myself in an atmosphere of apology. I did not in fact feel sorry for anything at all, I had not done anything, either deliberately or by accident, that warranted my begging for forgiveness, but my gait was a weapon—a way of deflecting her attention from me, of persuading her to think of me as someone who was pitiable, an ignorant child. I did not like her, I did not wish her dead, I only wanted her to leave me alone. I was very careful how far I carried this attitude of piousness, because I did not wish to draw the sympathy of anyone else, especially not my father, for I calculated she might become jealous of that. I had a version of this piety that I took with me to school. To my teachers I seemed quiet and studious; I was modest, which is to say, I did not seem to them to have any interest in the world of my body or anyone else's body. This wearying demand was only one of many demands made on me simply because I was female. From the moment I stepped out of my bed in the early morning to the time I covered myself up again in the dark of night, I negotiated many treacherous acts of deception, but it was clear to me who I really was.

I lay in my bed at night, and turned my ear to the sounds that were inside and outside the house, identifying each noise, separating the real from the unreal: whether the screeches that crisscrossed the night, leaving the blackness to fall to earth like so many ribbons, were the screeches of bats or someone who had taken the shape of a bat; whether the sound of wings beating in that space so empty of light was a bird or someone who had taken the shape of a bird. The sound of the gate being opened was my father coming home long after the stillness of sleep had overtaken most of his household, his footsteps stealthy but sure, coming into the yard, up the steps; his hand opening the door to his house, closing the door behind him, turning the bar that made the door secure, walking to another part of the house; he never ate meals when he returned home late at night. The sound of the sea then, at night, could be heard so clearly, sometimes as a soft swish, a lapping of waves against the shore of black stones, sometimes with the anger of water boiling in a cauldron resting unsteadily on a large fire. And sometimes when the night was completely still and completely black, I could hear, outside, the long sigh of someone on the way to eternity; and this, of all things, would disturb the troubled peace of all that was real: the dogs asleep under houses, the chickens in the trees, the trees themselves moving about, not in a way that suggested an uprooting, just moving about, as if they wished they could run away. And if I listened again I could hear the sound of those who crawled on their bellies, the ones who carried poisonous lances, and those who carried a deadly poison in their saliva; I could hear the ones who were hunting, the ones who were hunted, the pitiful cry of the small ones who were about to be devoured, followed by the temporary satisfaction of the ones doing the devouring: all this I heard night after night, again and again. And it ended only after my hands had traveled up and down all over my own body in a loving caress, finally coming to the soft, moist spot between my legs, and a gasp of pleasure had escaped my lips which I would allow no one to hear.   *1994*

— ⋙◆⋘ —

Ingrid de Kok
1951–

"Home is where the heart is: / a tin can tied to a stray dog. / The only truth is home truth: / preserves on the winter shelf." So writes South African poet INGRID DE KOK, whose poems frequently reveal the distorted sense of "truth" under which her country labored during the apartheid era. Born and raised in Stilfontein, a small mining town near Johannesburg, de Kok was educated at the University of the Witwatersrand and the University of Cape Town. For years she lived in Canada, where she studied at Queen's University. Residing now in Cape Town with her husband and child, she works for the department of adult education and extramural studies at the University of Cape Town. Active in politics, she conducted a workshop on gender issues in 1995 for the women members of the newly elected South African parliament. In 1996 she directed an international writers' conference on poetry of witness at the University of Cape Town.

Familiar Ground (1988), de Kok's first collection of poetry, reflects her sense of responsibility as a white South African who lived in voluntary exile during the worst years of political upheaval in her nation's history. One reviewer described this volume as "deeply political" in its probing of "the human suffering caused by apartheid and its repercussions." While her elegiac verse recounts both memory and loss, other poems explore, with irony and wit, the pleasures of heterosexual love and the speaker's connections with other women. Transfer (1998), de Kok's second volume, addresses the poet's changing role in the new South Africa. The author sees continuity between this book and her first, however, in that both examine how childhood acts reflect on later political choices, and both contain a deep, inchoate rage that she struggles to tamp down as well as to voice. Especially compelling to de Kok is the testimony of children injured by apartheid and its legacy, some of whose stories were broadcast on radio and television during the late 1990s as South Africa's Truth and Reconciliation Commission gathered data on crimes against humanity. de Kok also edited (with Karen Press) Spring Is Rebellious: Arguments About Cultural Freedom (1990), a collection of essays written in response to a paper by African National Congress attorney Albie Sachs in which he argues that South African art should no longer be "a weapon of struggle." In addition, she edited a 1996 issue of *World Literature Today* that focuses on "South African Literature in Transition." Poems by de Kok have appeared in South African literary anthologies and international journals and have been translated into French, Spanish, Italian, and Japanese.

In "Standing in the Doorway: A Preface," de Kok claims that when a "literary project revisits history, it does so not to produce an authorized account, not to resolve history. Its charge is private, not public. Its bid is to unwrite, retell, and reorganize the nature of the record." This statement is an apt description of her poetry, which challenges the "nature of the record" regarding life in apartheid and postapartheid South Africa. Growing up white in the racist 1950s provides the subject of "Our Sharpeville," which probes the speaker's troubled family history against the political backdrop of the 1960 Sharpeville massacre, when sixty-nine unarmed black demonstrators were gunned down by government forces. "Small Passing" presents the difficulties of forming alliances between black and white women, while "Transfer" chronicles the ambiguous landscape to which political exiles returned at century's end. For de Kok, South Africa remains a country that is fractured and dissonant, even as many citizens work together across differences to ensure a democratic future.

⊰ Our Sharpeville[1] ⊱

I was playing hopscotch on the slate
when miners roared past in lorries,
their arms raised, signals at a crossing,
their chanting foreign and familiar,
5   like the call and answer of road gangs
across the veld, building hot arteries
from the heart of the Transvaal[2] mine.

I ran to the gate to watch them pass.
And it seemed like a great caravan
10   moving across the desert to an oasis
I remembered from my Sunday school book:
olive trees, a deep jade pool,
men resting in clusters after a long journey,
the danger of the mission still around them,
15   and night falling, its silver stars just like the ones
you got for remembering your Bible texts.

Then my grandmother called from behind the front door,
her voice a stiff broom over the steps:
"Come inside; they do things to little girls."

20   For it was noon, and there was no jade pool.
Instead, a pool of blood that already had a living name
and grew like a shadow as the day lengthened.
The dead, buried in voices that reached even my gate,

---

1. A black township in the Gauteng province of South Africa and the site in 1960 of a massive demonstration against the racist laws of apartheid, a protest led by the Pan-Africanist Congress. When some of the twenty thousand African demonstrators stoned police, the police opened fire with machine guns, killing sixty-nine Africans, including forty-eight women and children.
2. The South African province in which Johannesburg is located.

the chanting men on the ambushed trucks,
25   these were not heroes in my town,
but maulers of children,
doing things that had to remain nameless.
And our Sharpeville was this fearful thing
that might tempt us across the wellswept streets.

30   If I had turned I would have seen
brocade curtains drawn tightly across sheer net ones,
known there were eyes behind both,
heard the dogs pacing in the locked yard next door.
But, walking backwards, all I felt was shame,
35   at being a girl, at having been found at the gate,
at having heard my grandmother lie
and at my fear her lie might be true.
Walking backwards, called back,
I returned to the closed rooms, home.

1988

⇥ Small Passing ⇤

For a woman whose baby died stillborn, and who was told by a man to stop mourning,
"because the trials and horrors suffered daily by black women in this country are more significant than the loss of one white child."

1

In this country you may not
suffer the death of your stillborn,
remember the last push into shadow and silence,
the useless wires and cords on your stomach,
5   the nurse's face, the walls, the afterbirth in a basin.
Do not touch your breasts
still full of purpose.
Do not circle the house,
pack, unpack the small clothes.
10   Do not lie awake at night hearing
the doctor say "It was just as well"
and "You can have another."
In this country you may not
mourn small passings.

15   See: the newspaper boy in the rain
will sleep tonight in a doorway.
The woman in the busline
may next month be on a train
to a place not her own.
20   The baby in the backyard now
will be sent to a tired aunt,
grow chubby, then lean,
return a stranger.

Mandela's[3] daughter tried to find her father
25   through the glass. She thought they'd let her touch him.

And this woman's hands are so heavy when she dusts
the photographs of other children
they fall to the floor and break.
Clumsy woman, she moves so slowly
30   as if in a funeral rite.

On the pavements the nannies meet.
These are legal gatherings.
They talk about everything, about home,
while the children play among them,
35   their skins like litmus, their bonnets clean.

2

Small wrist in the grave.
Baby no one carried live
between houses, among trees.
Child shot running,
40   stones in his pocket,
boy's swollen stomach
full of hungry air.
Girls carrying babies
not much smaller than themselves.
45   Erosion. Soil washed down to the sea.

3

I think these mothers dream
headstones of the unborn.
Their mourning rises like a wall
no vine will cling to.
50   They will not tell you your suffering is white.
They will not say it is just as well.
They will not compete for the ashes of infants.
I think they may say to you:
Come with us to the place of mothers.
55   We will stroke your flat empty belly,
let you weep with us in the dark,
and arm you with one of our babies
to carry home on your back.

1988

ᶔ Transfer ᶕ

All the family dogs are dead.
A borrowed one, its displaced hip
at an angle to its purebred head,

3. Nelson Mandela (born 1918), South Africa's President from 1994 to 1999, was imprisoned as a political dissident for more than twenty years on Robben Island during the apartheid regime.

bays at a siren's emergency climb
5   whining from the motorway.
Seven strangers now have keys
to the padlock on the gate,
where, instead of lights, a mimosa tree
burns its golden blurred bee-fur
10   to lead you to the door.

"So many leaves, so many trees"
says the gardener who weekly
salvages an ordered edge;
raking round the rusted rotary hoe
15   left standing where my uncle last
cranked it hard to clear a space
between the trees, peach orchard,
nectarine and plum, to prove
that he at least could move
20   the future's rankness to another place.

Forty years ago the house was built
to hold private unhappiness intact,
safe against mobile molecular growths
of city, developers and blacks.
25   Now rhubarb spurs grow wild and sour;
the mulberries, the ducks and bantams gone.
In the fishpond's sage-green soup,
its fraying goldfish decompose the sun,
wax-white lilies float upon the rot.
30   And leaves in random piles are burning.

Townhouses circle the inheritance.
The fire station and franchised inn
keep neighborhood watch over its fate.
The municipality leers over the gate,
35   complains of dispossession and neglect,
dark tenants and the broken fence.
But all the highveld birds are here,
weighing their metronomic blossoms
upon the branches in the winter air.
40   And the exiles are returning.

1996

✦ ⊰◆⊱ ✦

Intertextualities

This case study draws upon the theoretical essays from Section IV, "Identity and Difference": "If I Could Write This in Fire, I Would Write This in Fire" by MICHELLE CLIFF and "Not You/Like You: Postcolonial Women and the Interlocking Questions of Identity and Difference" by TRINH T. MINH-HA. You might find it helpful to refer to these essays as you examine works by three representative writers from Part IV: PHILLIS WHEATLEY, EMILY DICKINSON, and INGRID DE KOK. Also part of this case study are two essays by literary critics—JUNE JORDAN on

Wheatley and JOANNE FEIT DIEHL on Dickinson—that can help you sharpen your critical think-ing skills. Finally, the questions below suggest topics for creative and scholarly writing about women's literature, identity, and difference.

⤚ Topics for Discussion, Journals, and Essays ⤙

1. Analyze in your own words how Trinh defines both *identity* and *difference*. In what ways do Cliff, Wheatley, and Dickinson construct their own literary identities in their writing? Find and briefly discuss a passage from each writer that offers an example of such construction. Which of these writers' works (if any) articulate a connection between identity and differ-ence, in your view? Explain your reasoning.

2. To what extent might Wheatley's, Dickinson's, and de Kok's poems be considered as auto-biographical "life writing"? Reflect in your response upon Celeste Schenck's view that poems emerge from the same desire to "sketch a self in time or over time" that autobiogra-phy does, Jordan's suggestion that Wheatley's middle name ought to be "Miracle," and Diehl's argument that Dickinson constructs "shifting personae of identity."

3. "Identity . . . supposes that a clear dividing line can be made between I and not-I," claims Trinh T. Minh-ha. "Difference . . . is that which undermines the very idea of identity, dif-fering to infinity the layers of totality that forms I." Using these definitions as part of your thinking, analyze the ways that identity as a dividing line "between I and not-I" is both constructed and undermined in Wheatley's "On Being Brought from Africa to America," Dickinson's "My Life Had Stood—a Loaded Gun," de Kok's "Our Sharpeville," and Cliff's description of being in London with her cousin Henry. Consider Jordan's interpretation of Wheatley's poem and Diehl's discussion of Dickinson's "transgendered poetic ego" in your response.

4. Why does Cliff entitle her essay "If I Could Write This in Fire, I Would Write This in Fire"? How does fire function metaphorically and rhetorically in this title and essay? Discuss the similar or different ways in which Dickinson's "Dare You See a Soul *at the White Heat?*" uses fire as an extended metaphor. Is Wheatley's use of fire imagery in "To S.M., a Young African Painter" like or unlike Cliff's and Dickinson's use of it? Explain your response, referring to the critical essays by Jordan and Diehl as needed.

5. In "Not You/Like You" Trinh Minh-ha speaks of the "voices and silences across differ-ence" in which women, especially women of color, attempt to "articulate [an] always-emerging-already-distorted place." To what sort of voices, silences, and emerging but distorted place does Trinh refer? Think here not only of place in its most literal sense—Africa, Jamaica—but of place as a psychic and creative landscape. Discuss the poetic and rhetorical strategies that Trinh, Wheatley, de Kok, and Cliff use to articulate such a place in their writing.

6. "Claiming an Identity They Taught Me to Despise" is the title of a book by Cliff, but it could perhaps apply to Wheatley and Dickinson as writers, too. What aspects of their iden-tity was each of these three writers taught to hate, and by what or whom in their environ-ment? To what extent did each writer shift from denial to affirmation in her writing? As textual examples, please consider Wheatley's "On Being Brought from Africa to America"; Dickinson's "I'm ceded—I've Stopped being Theirs—"; and Cliff's depiction of her rela-tionship with Zoë and her experience at the British colonial school.

⤚ Creative Writing Exercise ⤙

Writing Home

Choose two women in your family (one can be yourself if you like) and compose a narrative of identity and difference in which each woman "writes home"—that is, describes a place or situa-tion in her life that she has left, probes her emotions regarding that place and her leavetaking, and considers how she has changed as a result of leaving this landscape for another. "Who am I (is she) here that I (she) was not when I (she) was there?" You might want to reread Trinh's discussion of identity as fluid, contingent, and multiple. You may write your narrative in interview format, as a play for two voices, as a narrative poem, or in any other form that you wish.

⊷ ⊱⊰ ⊶

June Jordan
1936–

An African-American poet, essayist, playwright, and children's writer, JUNE JORDAN chronicles what she calls "black survivor-consciousness"; she is committed in her work to "telling the truth as I know it." Jordan is best known for her political poetry and essays, which explore African-American history, culture, and experience. In this writing she documents the terrible effects of racism and economic exploitation on people of color, in the United States and around the world.

She was born in Harlem to Granville Ivanhoe and Mildred Fisher Jordan and would later write about the life and death of her father, a postal clerk, and the 1966 suicide of her mother. Raised in the Bedford-Stuyvesant area of New York City, she enrolled at Barnard College from 1953 to 1955 and again in 1956–57 but dropped out because, she later claimed, no one ever introduced her to a single black writer. Her marriage to Michael Meyer in 1955 ended in divorce in 1963; she has one son, Christopher David Meyer. A civil rights activist, Jordan served as assistant producer of "The Cool World," a 1964 film about the police murder of a young black boy in New York City that led to the 1964 Harlem Riots. From 1967 to 1969 she directed New York City's SEEK program for inner-city students. After the 1969 publication of her first book of poetry, *Who Look at Me?*, Jordan began to teach creative writing, first at Sarah Lawrence College (1969–74) and then at City College of the City University of New York (1975–76). During the 1980s she was a professor of English at the State University of New York at Stonybrook; she is now a professor of African-American studies at the University of California at Berkeley. A longtime member of PEN (the International Association of Poets, Playwrights, Editors, Essayists, and Novelists), Jordan also serves on the boards of the American Writers Congress, the Center for Constitutional Rights, and the Nicaraguan Culture Alliance.

Jordan's poetic voice is perhaps best described as combative, yet faith and optimism are prevalent in her vision. People of color, she claims, "are not powerless. We are indispensable despite all atrocities of state and corporate power to the contrary." Her many volumes of poetry include *Some Changes* (1971), *New Days: Poems of Exile and Return* (1973), *Things That I Do in the Dark* (1977), *Passion* (1980), *Living Room: New Poems 1980–84*, and *Naming Our Destiny: New and Selected Poems* (1989). As an essayist Jordan addresses a wide range of topics that link personal life and political struggle, including the welfare of children, racism in the media, revolution in Nicaragua and Haiti, and the Israeli bombings of Lebanon. Among her collections of essays are *Civil Wars* (1981), *On Call: New Political Essays 1981–85* (1985), *Moving Towards Home: Political Essays* (1989), *Technical Difficulties* (1994), and *Affirmative Acts: Political Essays* (1998).

Jordan has also written plays, most notably *In the Spirit of Sojourner Truth*, produced at New York's Public Theater in 1979, and *From the Arrow that Flies by Day*, produced at New York City's Shakespeare Festival in 1981. An author of children's literature, she was nominated for a National Book Award for *His Own Where* (1971) and edited, with Terri Bush, a reader entitled *The Voice of the Children* (1971), selected by the *New York Times* as one of the year's outstanding books for young adults. Other works for young people include *Dry Victories* (1972), *Fannie Lou Hamer* (1972), *New Room, New Life* (1975), and *Kimako's Story* (1981).

The essay reprinted here, from *On Call*, pays lyrical homage to Jordan's eighteenth-century foremother and America's first black poet, PHILLIS WHEATLEY. It meditates as well on slavery and its atrocities, the complexities of white literary patronage, and the price and perils of survival. Wheatley's life and art are nothing short of miraculous, Jordan concludes, and for this the poet deserves "something like a sonnet."

⊰ The Difficult Miracle of Black Poetry in America or Something Like a Sonnet for Phillis Wheatley ⊱

It was not natural. And she was the first. Come from a country of many tongues tortured by rupture, by theft, by travel like mismatched clothing packed down into the cargo hold of evil ships sailing, irreversible, into slavery. Come to a country to be docile and dumb, to be big and breeding, easily, to be turkey/horse/cow, to be cook/carpenter/plow, to be 5'6" 140 lbs., in good condition and answering to the name of Tom or Mary: to be bed bait: to be legally spread legs for rape by the master/the master's son/the master's overseer/the master's visiting nephew: to be nothing human nothing family nothing from nowhere nothing that screams nothing that weeps nothing that dreams nothing that keeps anything/anyone deep in your heart: to live forcibly illiterate, forcibly itinerant: to live eyes lowered head bowed: to be worked without rest, to be worked without pay, to be worked without thanks, to be worked day up to nightfall: to be three-fifths of a human being at best: to be this valuable/this hated thing among strangers who purchased your life and then cursed it unceasingly: to be a slave: to be a slave. Come to this country a slave and how should you sing? After the flogging the lynch rope the general terror and weariness what should you know of a lyrical life? How could you, belonging to no one, but property to those despising the smiles of your soul, how could you dare to create yourself: a poet?

A poet can read. A poet can write.

A poet is African in Africa, or Irish in Ireland, or French on the left bank of Paris, or white in Wisconsin. A poet writes in her own language. A poet writes of her own people, her own history, her own vision, her own room, her own house where she sits at her own table quietly placing one word after another word until she builds a line and a movement and an image and a meaning that somersaults all of these into the singing, the absolutely individual voice of the poet: at liberty. A poet is somebody free. A poet is someone at home.

How should there be black poets in America?

It was not natural. And she was the first. It was 1761—so far back before the revolution that produced these United States, so far back before the concept of freedom disturbed the insolent crimes of this continent—in 1761, when seven-year-old Phillis stood, as she must, when she stood nearly naked, as small as a seven-year-old, by herself, standing on land at last, at last after the long, annihilating horrors of the Middle Passage. Phillis, standing on the auctioneer's rude platform: Phillis For Sale.

Was it a nice day?:

Does it matter? Should she muse on the sky or remember the sea? Until Phillis had been somebody's child. Now she was about to become somebody'

Suzannah and John Wheatley finished their breakfast and ordered th' brought 'round. They would ride to the auction. This would be an impor'

They planned to buy yet another human being to help with the hap' comfortable life in Boston. You don't buy a human being, you don't purchase a slave, without thinking ahead. So they had planned this excursion. They were dressed for the occasion, and excited, probably. And experienced, certainly. The Wheatleys already owned several slaves. They had done this before; the transaction would not startle or confound or embarrass or appall either one of them.

Was it a nice day?

When the Wheatleys arrived at the auction they greeted their neighbors, they enjoyed this business of mingling with other townsfolk politely shifting about the plat-form, politely adjusting positions for gain of a better view of the bodies for sale. The Wheatleys were good people. They were kind people. They were openminded and thoughtful. They looked at the bodies for sale. They looked and they looked. This one could be useful for that. That one might be useful for this. But then they looked at that child, the black child standing nearly naked, by herself. Seven or eight years old, at the most, and frail. Now that was a different proposal! Not a strong body, not a grown set of shoulders, not a promising wide set of hips, but a little body, a delicate body, a young, surely terrified face! John Wheatley agreed to the whim of his wife, Suzannah. He put in his bid. He put down his cash. He called out the numbers. He competed successfully. He had a good time. He got what he wanted. He purchased yet another slave. He bought that black girl standing on the platform, nearly naked. He gave this new slave to his wife and Suzannah Wheatley was delighted. She and her husband went home. They rode there by carriage. They took that new slave with them. An old slave commanded the horses that pulled the carriage that carried the Wheatleys home, along with the new slave, that little girl they named Phillis.

Why did they give her that name?

Was it a nice day?

Does it matter?

It was not natural. And she was the first: Phillis Miracle: Phillis Miracle Wheatley: the first black human being to be published in America. She was the second female to be published in America.

And the miracle begins in Africa. It was there that a bitterly anonymous man and a woman conjoined to create this genius, this lost child of such prodigious apti-tude and such beguiling attributes that she very soon interposed the reality of her particular, dear life between the Wheatleys' notions about slaves and the predictable outcome of such usual blasphemies against black human beings.

Seven-year-old Phillis changed the slaveholding Wheatleys. She altered their minds. She entered their hearts. She made them see her and when they truly saw her, Phillis, darkly amazing them with the sweetness of her spirit and the alacrity of her forbidden, strange intelligence, they, in their own way, loved her as a prodigy, as a girl mysterious but godly.

Sixteen months after her entry into the Wheatley household Phillis was talking the language of her owners. Phillis was fluently reading the Scriptures. At eight and a half years of age, this black child, or "Africa's Muse," as she would later describe her-self, was fully literate in the language of this slaveholding land. She was competent and eagerly asking for more: more books, more and more information. And Suzannah Wheatley loved this child of her whimsical good luck. It pleased her to teach and to train and to tutor this black girl, this black darling of God. And so Phillis delved into kitchen studies commensurate, finally, to a classical education available to young white men at Harvard.

She was nine years old.

What did she read? What did she memorize? What did the Wheatleys give to this African child? Of course, it was white, all of it: white. It was English, most of it, from England. It was written, all of it, by white men taking their pleasure, their walks, their pipes, their pens and their paper, rather seriously, while somebody else cleaned the house, washed the clothes, cooked the food, watched the children: probably not slaves, but possibly a servant, or, commonly, a wife. It was written, this white man's literature of England, while somebody else did the other things that have to be done. And that was the literature absorbed by the slave, Phillis Wheatley. That was the writing, the thoughts, the nostalgia, the lust, the conceits, the ambitions, the mannerisms, the games, the illusions, the discoveries, the filth and the flowers that filled up the mind of the African child.

At fourteen, Phillis published her first poem, "To the University of Cambridge": not a brief limerick or desultory teenager's verse, but thirty-two lines of blank verse telling those fellows what for and whereas, according to their own strict Christian codes of behavior. It is in that poem that Phillis describes the miracle of her own black poetry in America:

> While an intrinsic ardor bids me write
> the muse doth promise to assist my pen

She says that her poetry results from "an intrinsic ardor," not to dismiss the extraordinary kindness of the Wheatleys, and not to diminish the wealth of white men's literature with which she found herself quite saturated, but it was none of these extrinsic factors that compelled the labors of her poetry. It was she who created herself a poet, notwithstanding and despite everything around her.

Two years later, Phillis Wheatley, at the age of sixteen, had composed three additional, noteworthy poems. This is one of them, "On Being Brought from Africa to America":

> Twas mercy brought me from my Pagan land,
> Taught my benighted soul to understand
> That there's a God, that there's a Savior too:
> Once I redemption neither sought nor knew
> Some view our sable race with scornful eye,
> "Their color is a diabolic die."
> Remember, *Christians*, Negroes, black as Cain,
> May be refined, and join the angelic train.

Where did Phillis get these ideas?

It's simple enough to track the nonsense about herself "benighted": *benighted* means surrounded and preyed upon by darkness. That clearly reverses what had happened to that African child, surrounded by and captured by the greed of white men. Nor should we find puzzling her depiction of Africa as "Pagan" versus somewhere "refined." Even her bizarre interpretation of slavery's theft of black life as a merciful rescue should not bewilder anyone. These are regular kinds of iniquitous nonsense found in white literature, the literature that Phillis Wheatley assimilated, with no choice in the matter.

But here, in this surprising poem, this first black poet presents us with something wholly her own, something entirely new. It is her matter of fact assertion that, "Once I redemption neither sought nor knew," as in: once I existed beyond and without these terms under consideration. *Once I existed on other than your terms.* And, she says, *but* since we are talking your talk about good and evil/redemption and damnation, let me tell you something you had better understand. I am black as Cain and I may very well be an angel of the Lord. Take care not to offend the Lord!

Where did that thought come to Phillis Wheatley?

Was it a nice day?

Does it matter?

Following her "intrinsic ardor," and attuned to the core of her own person, this girl, the first black poet in America, had dared to redefine herself from house slave to, possibly, an angel of the Almighty.

She was making herself at home.

And, depending whether you estimated that nearly naked black girl on the auction block to be seven or eight years old, in 1761, by the time she was eighteen or nineteen, she had published her first book of poetry, *Poems on Various Subjects Religious and Moral*. It was published in London, in 1773, and the American edition appeared, years later, in 1786. Here are some examples from the poems of Phillis Wheatley:

From "On the Death of Rev. Dr. Sewell":

> Come let us all behold with wishful eyes
> The saint ascending to his native skies.

From "On the Death of the Rev. Mr. George Whitefield":

> Take him, ye Africans, he longs for you,
> *Impartial Savior* is his title due,
> Washed in the fountain of redeeming blood,
> You shall be sons and kings, and priest to God.

Here is an especially graceful and musical couplet, penned by the first black poet in America:

> But, see the softly stealing tears apace,
> Pursue each other down the mourner's face;

This is an especially awful, virtually absurd set of lines by Ms. Wheatley:

> "Go Thebons! great nations will obey
> And pious tribute to her altars pay:
> With rights divine, the goddess be implored,
> Nor be her sacred offspring nor adored."
> Thus Manto spoke. The Thebon maids obey,
> And pious tribute to the goddess pay.

Awful, yes. Virtually absurd; well, yes, except, consider what it took for that young African to undertake such personal abstraction and mythologies a million million miles remote from her own ancestry, and her own darkly formulating face! Consider what might meet her laborings, as poet, should she, instead, invent a vernacular precise to Senegal, precise to slavery, and, therefore, accurate to the secret wishings of her lost and secret heart?

If she, this genius teenager, should, instead of writing verse to comfort a white man upon the death of his wife, or a white woman upon the death of her husband, or verse commemorating weirdly fabled white characters bereft of children diabolically dispersed; if she, instead, composed poetry to speak her pain, to say her grief, to find her parents, or to stir her people into insurrection, what would we now know about God's darling girl, that Phillis?

Who would publish that poetry, then?

But Phillis Miracle, she managed, nonetheless, to write, sometimes, towards the personal truth of her experience.

For example, we find in a monumental poem entitled "Thoughts on the Works of Providence," these five provocative lines, confirming every suspicion that most of the published Phillis Wheatley represents a meager portion of her concerns and inclinations:

> As reason's powers by day our God disclose,
> So we may trace him in the night's repose.
> Say what is sleep? and dreams how passing strange!
> When action ceases, and ideas range
> Licentious and unbounded o'er the plains.

And, concluding this long work, there are these lines:

> Infinite *love* whene'er we turn our eyes
> Appears: this ev'ry creature's wants supplies,
> This most is heard in Nature's constant voice,
> This makes the morn, and this the eve rejoice,
> This bids the fost'ring rains and dews descend
> To nourish all, to serve one gen'ral end,
> The good of man: Yet man ungrateful pays
> But little homage, and but little praise.

Now and again and again these surviving works of the genius Phillis Wheatley veer incisive and unmistakable, completely away from the verse of good girl Phillis ever compassionate upon the death of someone else's beloved, pious Phillis modestly enraptured by the glorious trials of virtue on the road to Christ, arcane Phillis intent upon an "Ode to Neptune," or patriotic Phillis penning an encomium to General George Washington ("Thee, first in peace and honor"). Then do we find that "Ethiop," as she once called herself, that "Africa's muse," knowledgeable, but succinct, on "dreams how passing strange! / When action ceases, and ideas range / Licentious and unbounded o'er the plains."

Phillis Licentious Wheatley?

Phillis Miracle Wheatley in contemplation of love and want of love?

Was it a nice day?

It was not natural. And she was the first.

Repeatedly singing for liberty, singing against the tyrannical, repeatedly avid in her trusting support of the American Revolution (how could men want freedom enough to die for it but then want slavery enough to die for that?), repeatedly lifting witness to the righteous and the kindly factors of her days, this was no ordinary teenaged poet, male or female, black or white. Indeed, the insistently concrete content of her tribute to the revolutionaries who would forge America, an independent nation state, indeed the specific daily substance of her poetry establishes Phillis Wheatley as the first decidedly American poet on this continent, black or white, male or female.

Nor did she only love the ones who purchased her, a slave, those ones who loved her, yes, but with astonishment. Her lifelong friend was a young black woman, Obour Tanner, who lived in Newport, Rhode Island, and one of her few poems dedicated to a living person, neither morbid nor ethereal, was written to the young black visual artist Sapio Moorhead, himself a slave. It is he who crafted the portrait of Phillis that serves as her frontispiece profile in her book of poems. Here are the opening lines from her poem, "To S.M., A Young African Painter, On Seeing His Works."

> To show the lab'ring bosom's deep intent,
> And thought in living characters to paint.
> When first thy pencil did those beauties give,
> And breathing figures learnt from thee to live,
> How did those prospects give my soul delight,
> A new creation rushing on my sight?
> Still, wondrous youth! each noble path pursue,
> On deathless glories fix thine ardent view:
> Still may the painter's and the poet's fire
> To aid thy pencil, and thy verse conspire!
> And many the charms of each seraphic theme
> Conduct thy footsteps to immortal fame!

Remember that the poet so generously addressing the "wondrous youth" is certainly no older than eighteen, herself! And this, years before the American Revolution, and how many many years before the 1960s! This is the first black poet of America addressing her Brother Artist not as so-and-so's boy, but as "Scipio Moorhead, A Young African Painter."

Where did Phillis Miracle acquire this consciousness?

Was it a nice day?

It was not natural. And she was the first.

But did she—we may persevere, critical from the ease of the 1980s—did she love, did she need, freedom?

In the poem (typically titled at such length and in such deferential rectitude as to discourage most readers from scanning what follows), in the poem titled "To the Right Honorable William, Earl of Dartmouth, His Majesty's Principal Secretary of State for North America, etc.," Phillis Miracle has written these irresistible, authentic, felt lines:

> No more America in mournful strain
> Of wrongs, and grievance unredressed complain,
> No longer shalt Thou dread the iron chain,
> Which wanton tyranny with lawless head
> Had made, and with it meant t' enslave the land.
> Should you, my Lord, while you peruse my song,
> Wonder from whence my love of Freedom sprung,
> Whence flow these wishes for the common good,
> By feeling hearts alone best understood,
> I, young in life, by seeming cruel fate
> Was snatched from Afric's fancied happy seat.
> What pangs excruciating must molest
> What sorrows labour in my parent's breast?
> Steeled was that soul and by no misery moved
> That from a father seized his babe beloved
> Such, such my case. And can I then but pray
> Others may never feel tyrannic sway?

So did the darling girl of God compose her thoughts, prior to 1772.

And then.

And then her poetry, these poems, were published in London.

And then, during her twenty-first year, Suzannah Wheatley, the white woman slaveholder who had been changed into the white mother, the white mentor, the white protector of Phillis, died.

Without that white indulgence, that white love, without that white sponsorship, what happened to the young African daughter, the young African poet?

No one knows for sure.

With the death of Mrs. Wheatley, Phillis came of age, a black slave in America.

Where did she live?

How did she eat?

No one knows for sure.

But four years later she met and married a black man, John Peters. Mr. Peters apparently thought well of himself, and of his people. He comported himself with dignity, studied law, argued for the liberation of black people, and earned the every-day dislike of white folks. His wife bore him three children; all of them died.

His wife continued to be Phillis Miracle.

His wife continued to obey the "intrinsic ardor" of her calling and she never ceased the practice of her poetry. She hoped, in fact, to publish a second volume of her verse.

This would be the poetry of Phillis the lover of John, Phillis the woman, Phillis the wife of a black man pragmatically premature in his defiant self-respect, Phillis giving birth to three children, Phillis, the mother, who must bury the three children she delivered into American life.

None of these poems was ever published.

This would have been the poetry of someone who had chosen herself, free, and brave to be free in a land of slavery.

When she was thirty-one years old, in 1784, Phillis Wheatley, the first black poet in America, she died.

Her husband, John Peters, advertised and begged that the manuscript of her poems she had given to someone, please be returned. But no one returned them.

And I believe we would not have seen them, anyway. I believe no one would have published the poetry of black Phillis Wheatley, that grown woman who stayed with her chosen black man. I believe that the death of Suzannah Wheatley, coincident with the African poet's twenty-first birthday, signalled, decisively, the end of her status as a child, as a dependent. From there we would hear from an independent black woman poet in America.

Can you imagine that, in 1775?

Can you imagine that, today?

America has long been tolerant of black children, compared to its reception of independent black men and black women.

She died in 1784.

Was it a nice day?

It was not natural. And she was the first.

Last week, as the final judge for this year's Loft McKnight Awards in creative writing, awards distributed in Minneapolis, Minnesota, I read through sixteen manuscripts of rather fine poetry.

These are the terms, the lexical items, that I encountered there:

Rock, moon, star, roses, chimney, Prague, elms, lilac, railroad tracks, lake, lilies, snow geese, crow, mountain, arrow feathers, ear of corn, marsh, sandstone, rabbit-bush, gulley, pumpkins, eagle, tundra, dwarf willow, dipper-bird, brown creek, lizards, sycamores, glacier, canteen, skate eggs, birch, spruce, pumphandle

Is anything about that listing odd? I didn't suppose so. These are the terms, the lexical items accurate to the specific white Minnesota daily life of those white poets.

And so I did not reject these poems, I did not despise them saying, "How is this possible? Sixteen different manuscripts of poetry written in 1985 and not one of them uses the terms of my own black life! Not one of them writes about the police murder of Eleanor Bumpurs or the Bernard Goetz shooting of four black boys or apartheid in South Africa, or unemployment, or famine in Ethiopia, or rape, or fire escapes, or cruise missiles in the New York harbor, or Medicare, or alleyways, or napalm, or $4.00 an hour, and no time off for lunch."

I did not and I would not presume to impose my urgencies upon white poets writing in America. But the miracle of black poetry in America, the *difficult* miracle of black poetry in America, is that we have been rejected and we are frequently dismissed as "political" or "topical" or "sloganeering" and "crude" and "insignificant" because, like Phillis Wheatley, we have persisted for freedom. We will write against South Africa and we will seldom pen a poem about wild geese flying over Prague, or grizzlies at the rain barrel under the dwarf willow trees. We will write, published or not, however we may, like Phillis Wheatley, of the terror and the hungering and the quandaries of our African lives on this North American soil. And as long as we study white literature, as long as we assimilate the English language and its implicit English values, as long as we allude and defer to gods we "neither sought nor knew," as long as we, black poets in America, remain the children of slavery, as long as we do not come of age and attempt, then to speak the truth of our difficult maturity in an alien place, alien place, then we will be beloved, and sheltered, and published,

But not otherwise. And yet we persist.

And it was not natural. And she was the first.

This is the difficult miracle of black poetry in America: that we persist, published or not, and loved or unloved: we persist.

And this is: "Something Like A Sonnet for Phillis Miracle Wheatley":

Girl from the realm of birds florid and fleet
flying full feather in far or near weather
Who fell to a dollar lust coffled like meat
Captured by avarice and hate spit together
Trembling asthmatic alone on the slave block
built by a savagery travelling by carriage
viewed like a species of flaw in the livestock
A child without safety of mother or marriage

Chosen by whimsy but born to surprise
They taught you to read but you learned how to write
Begging the universe into your eyes:
They dressed you in light but you dreamed
with the night.
From Africa singing of justice and grace,
Your early verse sweetens the fame of our Race.

And because we black people in North America persist in an irony profound, black poetry persists in this way:

> Like the trees of winter and
> like the snow which has no power
> makes very little sound
> but comes and collects itself
> edible light on the black trees
> The tall black trees of winter
> lifting up a poetry of snow
> so that we may be astounded
> by the poems of Black
> trees inside a cold environment

1985

━•━ ≡◊≡ ━•━

Joanne Feit Diehl
1947–

JOANNE FEIT DIEHL is best known for two books on nineteenth- and twentieth-century women's poetry: *Emily Dickinson and the Romantic Imagination* (1981) and *Women Poets and the American Sublime* (1990). She was born in 1947 to Hadassah A. and Charles Feit. After receiving her Ph.D. from Yale University, Diehl taught briefly at the University of Texas; since 1981 she has been a professor of English at the University of California at Davis. She is married to Carl Diehl and has a daughter.

Diehl has published articles on Dickinson's poetry in such journals as *Women's Studies, ELH,* and *Texas Studies in Language and Literature,* as well as in the collection *Feminist Critics Read Emily Dickinson* (1983), edited by Suzanne Juhasz. Her work on the modern U.S. poet Elizabeth Bishop appeared in *Coming to Light* (1985), a volume of articles on women's poetry edited by Diane Wood Middlebrook and Marilyn Yalom. Diehl has published on ADRIENNE RICH's poetry in *Feminist Studies* and on Nathaniel Hawthorne's fiction in *New Literary History.* Her well-known essay on women poets and their muses appeared in 1981 in the feminist journal *Signs.*

"Selfish Desires: Dickinson's Poetic Ego and the Rites of Subjectivity," first published in *The Emily Dickinson Journal* in 1996, examines Dickinson's forging of a strong subjective voice. Focusing on a number of the poet's lesser-known works, Diehl argues that Dickinson presents "a desiring subject, a self that may elude as well as submit to a specific gender identity, a subject that constitutes itself as transgendered, responsive to libidinous longings yet escaping the confines of gender."

⊰ Selfish Desires: Dickinson's Poetic Ego and the Rites of Subjectivity ⊱

The self that emerges from Dickinson's poems is singular yet multifarious, "columnar" yet labile, personified yet "costumeless." Observing the construction of this self allows us to see the underlying identifications Dickinson makes between her subjectivity and gender; an examination of the shifting personae of identity entitles us to speculate regarding Dickinson's experiential and interpretive understanding of self-states and her fashioning from these a poetic ego. How Dickinson constructs that poetic ego and that construction's relation to desire will be my subject here. My initial assertion is that in whatever forms the self appears, it is significantly associated with a scene of contestation, a scene that dramatizes the struggle with dependence, faces the challenge of submission, and wins through to the hard-won position of transcendence or release. Such contestatory moments occur both on an inter-and intrapsychic level. The self may ward off external adversaries or it may split into discordant or harmonious parts most commonly identified as the "soul," the "body," and "consciousness." Indeed, these aspects of the self may individually comprise a desiring subject, a self that may elude as well as submit to a specific gender identity, a subject that constitutes itself as transgendered, responsive to libidinous longings yet escaping the confines of gender. Before we can broach the issue of a transgendered poetic ego, a subjectivity that evades the specificity of gender yet constitutes a desiring subject, we need to attend to the kinds of individuated selves Dickinson presents; we need to attest to the various guises the poetic ego assumes as it emerges from the poems.

Sandra Gilbert and Susan Gubar have argued that Dickinson's assumption of various personae was "essential to her poetic self-achievement;" they go on to elucidate the numerous manifestations of her poetic self. Tellingly, they note that Dickinson's "impersonating 'a woman—white' . . . gave her exactly the 'Amplitude' and 'Awe' she knew she needed in order to write great poetry. . . ." (Gilbert and Gubar, *The Madwoman in the Attic*, 586). They discuss Dickinson's role as "defiant childwoman" (595) as well as the other images Dickinson invokes to articulate her split self. What I choose to emphasize are the psychodynamics which inform these avatars of Dickinsonian selfhood. Particularly, I am interested in the psychosexual implications of the assumption of these distinct roles and the impact of these transmutations on a theory of the self. Dickinson escapes the conflictual position she assumes in her evocations of the male-female relationship, which, as Gilbert and Gubar have observed, constitutes a "father / daughter, master / scholar / slave" paradigm, by relinquishing the individuating attributes of gender (587). Such relinquishment is attained by two alternative strategies: a splitting of the self into autonomous entities or a decorporealizing of subjective presence.

By dissecting the self, by representing aspects of existence as themselves singular entities, Dickinson converts those entities into personae who refigure power relationships within and beyond the self. Preeminent among these aspects of the self is, of course, consciousness, which is the self-defining subject that stands in for all others. As Dickinson writes, "Captivity is Consciousness— / So's Liberty" (384). Elsewhere Dickinson notes its inviolability: "How adequate unto itself / It's properties shall be / Itself unto itself and none / Shall make discovery" (822). Indeed, for Dickinson, "Consciousness—is Noon" (1056). Yet such cerebral autonomy may be challenged when the self is bound by an Other in an experience of identification and commitment that threatens the self's free will:

> Bind me—I still can sing—
> Banish—my mandolin
> Strikes true within—
>
> Slay—and my Soul shall rise
> Chanting to Paradise—
> Still thine.

(1005)

Here the ego is at the service of the other; to whom the bound and banished self, with renewed, possibly masochistic fervor, declares her allegiance. Yet this devotion is, in other poems, not so much a question of dependence as it is one of mutuality. In "I make His Crescent fill or lack—" (909), such mutuality presents the self as a presence that has a power equal to the masculine Other:

> I make His Crescent fill or lack—
> His Nature is at Full
> Or Quarter—as I signify—
> His Tides—do I control—
>
> He holds superior in the Sky
> Or gropes, at my Command
> Behind inferior Clouds—or round
> A Mist's slow Colonnade—
>
> But since We hold a Mutual Disc—
> And front a Mutual Day—
> Which is the Despot, neither knows—
> Nor Whose—the Tyranny—

Such reciprocity creates a "Mutual Disc," wherein potential violence and exclusive sovereignty are eradicated. Indeed, throughout Dickinson's poems, representations of equality and dependence both play their part; and, thus, each may be understood as constituting an historical moment in the formation of a changing identity that assumes a variety of positions reflecting shifts in self-other boundaries and fluctuations in ego strength.

At times this self in her solitude is so expansive she fills the entire horizon, as in "Behind Me—dips Eternity—" (721). At other times, the self assumes a diminutive persona, "a speck upon a ball" (378). Both the moments of expansion and those of diminution attest to the fluctuation of boundaries and are related to labile aspects of the self. Filling up the entire world, however, is not simply an ego syntonic event; for this consolidation of power threatens to burst beyond control; the image of a "Bomb, abroad" signifies the threat of a power that potentially cannot be contained by the self (512). But the bomb, at other moments, may prove a balm to soothe the self and the self's pain. What creates the possibilities of both representations of the self and allows these contradictory images to coexist throughout the poems is the creation of an ego that possesses a remarkable capacity for change, a self that is discontinuous, one that refuses to be limited to a specific size or a specific gender.

Along with such wildly divergent representations of the ego, the body *qua* body undergoes a process of depersonalization with similarly uncanny results. At times, consciousness is represented as so remote from the body that one can only infer that one exists through studied observation. In "It Was Not Death, For I Stood Up," (510), evidence is gathered as if the self examined were distinct from the speaking subject, who, nevertheless, addresses that bodily ego as "I." Here, as elsewhere in Dickinson, sensation must be witnessed to acquire proof of one's existence. Such ontological uncertainty produces a tortuous route to self-knowledge as it testifies to the degree of dissociation that may occur within the self.

> It was not Death, for I stood up,
> And all the Dead, lie down—

It was not Night, for all the Bells
Put out their Tongues, for Noon.

It was not Frost, for on my Flesh
I felt Siroccos—crawl—
Nor Fire—for just my Marble feet
Could keep a Chancel, cool—

And yet, it tasted, like them all,
The Figure I have seen
Set orderly, for Burial,
Reminded me, of mine—

As if my life were shaven,
And fitted to a frame,
And could not breathe without a key,
And 'twas like Midnight, some—

When everything that ticked—has stopped—
And Space stares all around—
Or Grisly frosts—first Autumn morns,
Repeal the Beating Ground—

But, most like Chaos—Stopless—cool—
Without a Chance, or Spar—
Or even a Report of Land—
To justify—Despair.

(510)

Knowledge of the self is brought to consciousness but only at one remove. The poem performs the act of knowing through a process of negative definition that signals a lack of immediate self-state recognition. The awful stasis here described is a temporal as well as a physical phenomenon that creates an interpretive scenario in which consciousness itself is problematized, making the acquisition of self-awareness synonymous with the process of reading the poem. Thus, the poem functions as a means of working through to cognitive as well as subjective understanding. In what follows, that sense of working through is commensurate with a survey of both abstractions and physical materiality that constitutes an attempt to identify the self in a moment of crisis:

I felt my life with both my hands
To see if it was there—
I held my spirit to the Glass,
To prove it possibler—

I turned my Being round and round
And paused at every pound
To ask the Owner's name—
For doubt that I should know the Sound—

I judged my features—jarred my hair—
I pushed my dimples by, and waited—
If they—twinkled back—
conviction might, of me—

> I told myself, "Take Courage, Friend—
> That—was a former time—
> But we might learn to like the Heaven,
> As well as our Old Home!"

(351)

This poem underscores the distanced objectivity with which the cognitive self may assess the experiential subject. Although the speaker's features are noted, the very necessity for such deliberate scrutiny bespeaks the depersonalization that has already occurred. Addressing us from an imagined afterlife, the self experiences physicality as severed from consciousness; the marks of gender, hair and dimples, are observed only at secondhand.

In order to achieve an aura of invincibility, to acquire transcendent power, Dickinson invents a self that sloughs off gender, that eschews a sexualized identity to assume what I have called a transgendered position. When the ego is completely severed from the body, it may acquire the attributes of invulnerability; by divesting itself of the corporeal, the self comes into full possession of its autonomy. Dickinson praises an identity so monumental, stoic, and assured:

> On a Columnar Self—
> How ample to rely
> In Tumult—or Extremity—
> How good the Certainty
>
> That Lever cannot pry—
> And Wedge cannot divide
> Conviction—That Granitic Base—
> Though None be on our Side—
>
> Suffice Us—for a Crowd—
> Ourself—and Rectitude—
> And that Assembly—not far off
> From furthest Spirit—God—

(789)

Although the wound of dissociation is healed, although lever cannot pry and wedge cannot divide this columnar self, the price for such conviction is isolation and disengenderment. When the soul is "admitted to itself—," the state achieved constitutes a "polar privacy" (1695) which is only the most extreme manifestation of the desire for autonomy that is a dominant force in Dickinson's poems. Elsewhere, however, there is a commensurate yearning for merger, a longing for erotic fulfillment. The "Battle fought between the Soul / And No Man—" (594) remains internal, but the poetic ego does not remain immune to the lure of desire. How can the poet reconcile this passionate, transgendered striving for autonomy with an eroticized, desiring subject?

In her assumption of positions that reflect and evade the ascriptions of gender, Dickinson configures alternative approaches to desire. By complicating the issue of agency, Dickinson paradoxically intensifies the role of eros in her work; for, when the poetic ego undergoes shifts in identity, the lineaments of desire, its ebb and flow, become the crux in determining the character of the self and assessing its capacities. Identity, for example, may be acquired through the advent of an Other (see "I heard, as if I had no Ear / Until a Vital Word / Came all the way from Life to me / And then I knew I heard" [1039]) or the self may reaffirm its autonomy through rejection of external presence (see "Art thou the thing I wanted?" [1282]). Desire may be transformed into disavowal, and self-fulfillment predicated upon abstention. In poem 1282, exclusivity serves as a means to distinguish the self as power accrues to the individual who exercises her right to choose. Similarly, in "The Soul selects her own Society—," (303) the authority to reject consolidates power within the self.

In Dickinson's poems, autonomy and mutuality may be understood as vying for preeminence, as constituting the two interrelational positions between which the poetic ego veers. Fluid ego boundaries create a permeable conception of identity, and Dickinson responds to this permeability either by embracing the eroticized Other or by sealing off the threatened self. When relationality is the choice, Dickinson constructs a poetics that privileges the self through interactions with the Other. When autonomy becomes the goal, Dickinson constructs a self that appears rejecting, isolate, and alone. From within these alternatives, a poetic ego emerges that constitutes a world defined by its projected power. Consciousness, at once proliferating and expansive, inhabits a sphere predicated upon its capacity for rejection and desire. Finally, refusing to be restricted by traditional notions of the dependent, female self, Dickinson creates a multifarious persona that, taken in its entirety, incorporates wildly divergent possibilities. Whether evoking a dissociative state, a split self, or an imperial, autonomous subject, Dickinson forges an identity that transcends the categories of gender. Through repeated literary encounters, what we might call the rites of subjectivity, Dickinson defines a poetic ego that is drawn to the possibilities of merger yet attests to the triumph of individuation. Engaged in the psychosexual drama of ego differentiation and the rigors of poetic self-assertion, the Dickinsonian subject assumes an eroticized yet, frequently, transgendered character. Reading Dickinson, we bear witness to the emergence of this impassioned ego as it strives to articulate a trajectory of desire that is unequivocally its own.

1996

SECTION V

Resistance and Transformation

Resistance literature calls attention to itself, and to literature in general, as a political and politicized activity. The literature of resistance sees itself further as immediately and directly involved in a struggle against ascendant or dominant forms of ideological and cultural production.

Barbara Harlow, Resistance Literature

How do we share equitably the world's wealth and concomitant power among the races and between the sexes?

Chikwenye Okonjo Ogunyemi, "Womanism"

Women have always resisted tyranny, both individually and collectively. They have challenged misogyny, sexual abuse, and rape; slavery, apartheid, and other racist systems; poverty, exploitation, and harassment. They have resisted on behalf of their children, their husbands and fathers, other women, their homes and countries, themselves. Moreover, they have said NO in writing as well as speech and action. Women's ways of voicing this NO are manifested in an international literature of resistance and transformation—a literature to which women from the Renaissance to the present have contributed. Refusing both elitism and the guise of objectivity, resistance texts opt instead for inclusiveness and impassioned engagement. They are works of witness and confrontation. Writers of resistance literature view nonviolent struggle and literary reclamation as equally important areas of cultural terrain; they challenge notions of art as detached, objective, "universal." Whether cleverly subversive or overtly polemical, resistance writing addresses the historical context from which it emerges and chronicles the writer's perspective on injustice.

It is important that the term "resistance" be defined as an active quest for fairness, not merely as a reactive phenomenon created in response to power and its abuses. At its richest, resistance literature offers various models of racial, gender, or class empowerment, and it engages in acts of aesthetic intervention in the service of one or more of these models. Moreover, resistance literature typically blends politics, theory, and practice. Different genres often have different focuses: as Harlow notes, poetry may preserve and redefine cultural images for particular historical moments, while narratives may analyze the past in order to reinterpret the present and envision alternative futures (82). Resistance is an especially important concept in feminist theory articulated by women of color, many of whom recognize, because of their positions on the margins of institutional structures, that radical systemic transformation is necessary to remove social inequities. Chicana theoretician Chela Sandoval asserts that women of color are "survivors in a dynamic which places them as the final 'other' in a complex of power moves"; their goal in challenging the system extends beyond self-interest toward a commitment to an alternative world view that nurtures everyone (64). In *Black Feminist Thought* PATRICIA HILL COLLINS delineates several traits that characterize a "black women's epistemology": an emphasis on personal accountability, the belief that concrete experience is a source of wisdom and knowledge, a commitment to dialogue as a tool for exploring differences, and an ethic of empathy (221–38). This blend of caring and confrontation can be seen in the writing produced by feminists of color worldwide. Many First and Third World women writers share the realization that their linguistic, literary, and cultural traditions have been dismantled by racism, sexism, militarism, or colonialism; they likewise share s strong commitment to radical reclamation and change.

Because misogynists, colonizers, and other oppressors try to rob the people they oppress of their control of language, many women writers use linguistic forms of resistance, from name calling to protest songs to code switching. For the seventeenth-century polemicist RACHEL SPEGHT, enraged at Joseph Swetnam's misogynist pamphlet about women's infamy, linguistic resistance occurred in the title of her tract *A Muzzle for Melastomus*; here Speght portrayed her adversary as a "blackmouth," or slanderer, in need of muzzling. For South African women protesting apartheid's racist laws in the 1950s, linguistic resistance emerged as a militant slogan shouted at police and government officials attempting to break up their demonstrations:

> You have touched a woman
> You have struck a rock.
> You have dislodged a boulder.
> You will be crushed.

Women's linguistic resistance can often be seen in contemporary South African women's narratives. ZOË WICOMB's young protagonist in "Bowl like Hole," for example, recognizes the tone of racist superiority in the voice of her father's white visitor and resists it in the only way she can: by spying from beneath the kitchen table and resolving not to pronounce "bowl" in "correct" English, as her mother does. Likewise ELLEN KUZWAYO's women of Sobokeng, though powerless to stop their homes from being raided by police, respond with quiet dignity and refuse to give out information, withholding language to "survive the ordeal" (*LAWL* 1114). For Latina women, philosopher Maria Lugones claims, linguistic resistance may occur as code-switching, writing alternatively in Spanish and English without translation. This form of rebellion reveals the writer's multiple identities and challenges readers who privilege English: "to play in this way is then an act of resistance as well as an act of self-affirmation." (46).

Although resistance literature by women varies according to time period and cultural context, it generally is political in the broadest sense of the term: it questions how individuals, societies, and human relations should be governed. Many resistance texts offer angry challenges of dominant ways of constructing societies, poignant laments for the mistreated, and fierce calls for social change. Some resistance literature foregrounds what Harlow called "the catastrophic disruption of Third World people's cultural and literary traditions," thereby reclaiming history, honoring oral traditions, and rewriting cultures from the perspective of the marginalized (*Resistance Literature* 33). Often resistance texts reveal the writer's awareness of the larger cultural context from which she writes. They may allude to a variety of struggles for self-determination or bear witness to the horrors of racism, sexism, and other forms of dehumanization; in so doing, they reappropriate the terms of human knowledge. Finally, women's literature of resistance is often visionary: neither utopian nor dystopian, but forward looking, imaginative, committed to a future of peace and justice.

The sections below offer further insight into the themes and strategies of resistance literature by women. "Challenging Patriarchy and Racial Oppression" examines ways in which women writers from the seventeenth through the nineteenth centuries have resisted racism and sexism through anger, humor, lyricism, and reason. "Giving Testimony, Bearing Witness" considers powerful testimonials to World War II, the Holocaust, and Hiroshima by several twentieth-century women poets. "Developing a Politics of Location" explores how U.S. poet ADRIENNE RICH's concept of *location* helps us understand modern women writers who have interrogated racial and cultural privilege. And "Raising These Questions in the World" considers the idea that in women writers' dialogues across class, race, and national differences lies the hope of feminist transformation.

CHALLENGING PATRIARCHY AND RACIAL OPPRESSION

Is one half of the human species, like the poor African slaves, to be subject to prejudices that brutalize them, when principles would be a surer guard, only to sweeten the cup of man? Is not this indirectly to deny woman reason? For a gift is mockery, if it be unfit for use.

Mary Wollstonecraft, A Vindication of the Rights of Woman

Look at me! Look at my arm! I have ploughed and planted, and gathered into barns, and no man could head me! And ain't I a woman? I could work as much and eat as much as a man—when I could get it—and bear the lash as well! And ain't I a woman? I have borne thirteen children, and seen them most all sold off to slavery, and when I cried out with my mother's grief, none but Jesus heard me! And ain't I a woman?

Sojourner Truth, "Ain't I a Woman?"

In the early eighteenth century, views of a woman's place were articulated by such prominent patriarchs as the journalist Richard Steele, who claimed that "All she has to do in this World, is contained within the Duties of a Daughter, a Sister, a Wife, and a Mother" (quoted in Rogers 124). Although Steele's journal *Spectator* tried to instill bourgeois values in its readers, it also promoted the changing view of marriage that characterized the century, as an ideology that marriage should forge economic alliances between families gave way to a view of husband and wife as intimate life companions. With this social change came a new interest in women's rights that is reflected in the literature of the period. While even liberal thinkers typically believed that woman was man's subordinate, many did support an upper-class woman's right to choose her husband and be educated so that she might be a better helpmate, although few working-class women benefited from this shift. Between 1690 and 1800 radical thinkers like SARAH FYGE and the three feminist Mary's—Astell, Wollstonecraft, and Hays—would assert that woman was equal to man in intellect and reason, not created merely to serve.

Interestingly, however, such challenges to patriarchy occurred primarily in the last decades of the seventeenth and eighteenth centuries, during eras of political and social revolution in England, France, and the American colonies. In England between 1700 and 1790, most women based their appeals for betterment on notions of sentimentality that fit the century's glorification of tenderness and delicacy in females. Advocates of women's rights, especially in marriage, had little legal protection or precedence, since husband and wife were considered one person under the law and only men could make contracts, control property, govern children, or determine inheritance. Divorce was virtually impossible, adultery was condemned only in women, and nothing short of life-threatening physical abuse would allow a woman freedom from her husband.

Educated by a clergyman uncle, MARY ASTELL moved to London in 1686 at the age of twenty and became a writer, supported financially and otherwise by wealthy women friends such as Lady MARY WORTLEY MONTAGU and Elizabeth Hastings. Because her scholarly treatises on church and state upheld the status quo, she earned the respect of prominent clergy and civic leaders who, although not pleased with her feminist tracts, nonetheless did not denounce them. A Serious Proposal to the Ladies (1694) and Some Reflections upon Marriage (1700) were popular enough for several editions to be published. As one of England's first feminists, Astell devalued sex and romance, articulated the difficulties many women experienced in marriage, and proposed that women be allowed to retire to female monasteries as a form of marriage resistance. Because she considered celibacy a valid option, she offered few suggestions as to how to improve women's situation in marriage. Though many read her treatise, no one acted on her idea of establishing women's separate communities. Earlier Astell had predicted her proposal's fate when she claimed she would rather find her project condemned as "foolish" and "impertinent" than to find it received with some approbation, and yet "nobody endeavoring to put it in practice" (LAWL 1127). Despite her project's failure, Astell argued fiercely that women needed education to improve their intellects rather than their utility.

Although not as systematic in her feminist resistance as Astell, SARAH FYGE began challenging misogyny at age fourteen, when she wrote and published anonymously The Female Advocate (1686) in response to Robert Gould's misogynist treatise Love Given O'er or, a Satyr against the Pride, Lust, and Inconstancy, Etc. of Woman (1682). Forced by her father into a loveless marriage, Fyge became a widow in her mid-twenties, wrote about her infatuation with a friend of her late husband (called "Alexis" in her poems), and married a second husband whom she later sued for divorce on the grounds of cruelty, unleashing a sordid public debate over the merits of her case. Through it all Fyge wrote both traditional verse, including odes honoring John Dryden upon his death, and unconventionally feminist poems like "The Liberty," in which she refuses to be "one of those obsequious Fools, / That square their lives, by Custom's scanty Rules." The "dull fulsome Rules" that govern women's behavior Fyge finds especially offensive: "My Sex forbids, I should my Silence break, / I lose my Jest, cause Women must not speak" (LAWL 1130-31). Yet speak she does, and with "bolder Sallies" than most women writers of her time.

Resisting patriarchal strictures was also the aim of MARY WOLLSTONECRAFT, who wrote A Vindication of the Rights of Men (1790) as a critique of Edmund Burke's Reflections on the Revolution in France and shortly thereafter composed A Vindication of the Rights of Woman (1792), a pioneer text of the early women's rights movement. In her treatise Wollstonecraft drew upon Astell's argument that women should develop themselves as strong, rational beings rather than be sexual objects governed by men.

Yet Wollstonecraft went further, denouncing as "poetical story" John Milton's account in *Paradise Lost* of woman as having been created for and from man. She also advocated that men become "content with rational fellowship instead of slavish obedience" from women (*LAWL* 1139).

A close friend of Wollstonecraft and her husband, William Godwin, MARY HAYS followed the feminist rationalist tradition in *Appeal to the Men of Great Britain in Behalf of Women* (1798), which argued that women, like men, should have the right to education and ambition without being condemned. Men "do not upon the whole like [women] the better, or at least they do not treat them better—which is the only true test of love—for their forced humility and submission," insisted Hays. More sentimental than Wollstonecraft in emphasizing woman's duty to husband, father, and children, Hays considered women "not formed for warlike enterprises" and expressed objections to their "taking any active part in popular assemblies." Still, Hays advocated women's rights throughout her life, believing fiercely that anything other than free thinking and free speaking is "at variance with nature, with reason, and with common sense" (*LAWL* 1144).

While Astell, Fyge, Wollstonecraft, and Hays challenged patriarchal restrictions of women, none of them analyzed in any depth the links between sexism and racism. Wollstonecraft did pity "the poor African slaves" and offered an analogy between their brutal treatment and that meted out to women by abusive men, but it was not until the late 1790s that certain white feminists became abolitionists, and even then some used stereotypical notions of women's "natural" humanity to justify their positions. Two white British women, HARRIET MARTINEAU and ELIZABETH BARRETT BROWNING, both esteemed public figures in the nineteenth century, were especially effective opponents of slavery; and both linked race and gender in their writings. In *Society in America* (1837) Martineau condemned the disparity between democratic principle and reality in the pre–Civil War United States, through which she traveled for two years. Noting parallels between the maltreatment even of free "people of color," as she called black Americans, and of women, she recognized that citizenship was unfairly denied to both groups. Martineau quoted the U.S. elder statesman Thomas Jefferson, who excluded from the business of state "women, who to prevent depravation of morals, and ambiguity of issue, could mix not promiscuously in the public meetings of men," and slaves, "from whom the unfortunate state of things with us takes away the rights of will and property." That Jefferson gives neither women nor slaves rights of will or property is simply unjust, she countered; the excuses Jefferson offers—"the unfortunate state of things," the danger of "promiscuous" meetings—she labeled ridiculous, "not worth another word"(*LAWL* 1151).

One of Victorian England's most renowned women writers and a fervent abolitionist, Elizabeth Barrett Browning published "The Runaway Slave at Pilgrim's Point" in 1848 in an annual antislavery journal, *The Liberty Bell*, as part of a fundraising effort by the Boston National Anti-Slavery Bazaar. A "ferocious" (Barrett Browning's word) denunciation of racism and sexism, this poem drew upon an incident from Jamaican slave history that she had been told as a child by her cousin; in fact, her hatred of slavery stemmed in part from the fact that her family had owned plantations and slaves in Jamaica prior to the Emancipation Act of 1833. Because she feared that the U.S. North might accept slavery to placate the South, Barrett Browning set her poem on the shores of liberty, near Boston Harbor, and had her slavewoman recount her saga to the white "pilgrim fathers." As ANN PARRY has suggested, this poem "prophesies a society on the brink of revolution" and offers both "a radical critique of racist discourse" and a fierce inversion of "the existing racist and gender structure" (*LAWL* 1307-08).

No nineteenth-century white woman writing against racism and sexism could match the eloquence of SOJOURNER TRUTH, a former slave who traveled for forty years across the United States, preaching and lecturing against slavery and in favor of women's rights. Blending logical and emotional appeal, Truth took on religious as well as political ideologies in such feminist speeches as "Ain't I A Woman?". In 1867 Truth courageously opposed the Fourteenth Amendment to the U.S. Constitution, which awarded suffrage to black men but to neither black nor white women. In "Keeping the Things Going While Things Are Stirring" she argued that if black men gain their rights at the expense of women, "the colored men will be masters over the women, and it will be just as bad as it was before" (*LAWL* 1146). White supremacy and patriarchy go hand in hand, she realized, and must be challenged simultaneously. This was FRANCES ELLEN WATKINS HARPER's realization as well. Born in 1825 to free black parents, Harper was educated in a school her uncle opened for former slaves, and many of her best poems dealt with the power education has to improve black women's lives. Her expressed poetic goal was "to make songs for the people . . . for the old and the young"; her poems sang of anguish as well as rebellion. For Harper as for the African-American statesman Frederick Douglass, the ultimate act of self-determination for black citizens in the 1870s was learning to read. She thus invents Aunt Chloe, a character who, when she is "rising sixty," begins to use literacy as a tool of resistance (*LAWL* 1168).

Resistance writing of the eighteenth and nineteenth centuries reveals that to challenge misogyny and racism effectively, women must use whatever literary strategy is most productive, given their historical, social, and artistic contexts. Often such literature raises, and tries to answer, a question asked by Nigerian scholar Chikwenye Okonjo Ogunyemi: how can women, the poor, and people of color worldwide gain fair access to the world's resources? (63–64). It also asks, implicitly or explicitly, how political art can contribute to social change.

GIVING TESTIMONY, BEARING WITNESS

The process of the testimony indeed sheds new light, both on the psychoanalytical relation between speech and survival, and on the historical processes of the Holocaust itself, whose uniquely devastating aspect can be interpreted as a radical historical *crisis of witnessing*, and as the unprecedented, inconceivable, historical occurrence of "an event without a witness"—an event eliminating its own witness.

Shoshana Felman and Dori Laub, Testimony

To be a Jew in the twentieth century
Is to be offered a gift. If you refuse,
Wishing to be invisible, you choose
Death of spirit, the stone insanity.

Accepting, take full life. Full agonies:
Your evening deep in labyrinthine blood
Of those who resist, fail, and resist; and God
Reduced to a hostage among hostages.

Muriel Rukeyser, "Letter to the Front"

In settings from the courthouses of U.S. villages to the International War Crimes Tribunals in eastern Europe, victims of individual crimes and government atrocities came forward in the 1990s as never before, giving testimony that they hoped would bring perpetrators of violence to justice. Indeed, the act of bearing witness was a major cultural phenomenon of the twentieth century, as Shoshana Felman and Dori Laub reveal in *Testimony*. For Felman and Laub, the century's landmark event was the Holocaust, a trauma "which is essentially *not over*, a history whose repercussions are not simply omnipresent (whether consciously or not) in all our cultural activities, but whose traumatic consequences are still actively *evolving*." Literature, they claim, can teach us much about testimony as both subject and medium of transmission. If testimony, the rhetoric of witnessing, is in fact "the literary—or discursive—mode par excellence of our times," if "our era can precisely be defined as the age of testimony," what is the effect of such witness on contemporary cultural representation? (1–5).

To engage in a literary act of witness requires the writer to examine the circumstances of a shock or wound and move on, a process that may result in temporary muteness, acute anxiety, or verbal overkill. In addition, it asks that a writer consider the connection between violence and language—what Felman describes as "the passage of the language through the violence and the passage of the violence through the language" (19); or what Teresa deLauretis terms "the rhetoric of violence and the violence of rhetoric" (32). Is to write about horror at once to remove some of that horror's reality through the act of making art? Such fear has motivated the German critic Theodor Adorno to claim that "after Auschwitz, it is no longer possible to write poems" (quoted in Felman and Laub 33); it has caused the U.S. poet CAROLYN FORCHÉ to question whether metaphor can be ethically employed in the service of witness against atrocity; it has led the Chilean poet Pablo Neruda to write poignantly, "the blood of the children flowed into the streets like . . . like . . . the blood of the children" (quoted in Forché, "El Salvador" 7). Perhaps, as Felman claims, literature about and after the Holocaust must write "against *itself*"—or, in Forché's words, "against forgetting."

Of the many modern writers who have testified against forgetting, four of the poets included in this section of this anthology have been among the most vital. H.D. (HILDA DOOLITTLE) considers the impact of World War II on a woman writer struggling to find voice amidst the bombs that rained down on London during the blitz. A feminist pacifist, this poet determines not only to chronicle the destruction but also somehow to find a path toward gender harmony and "spiritual realism." MURIEL RUKEYSER, a Jewish socialist whose poems offer stringent critiques of materialism and injustice, assesses the role of "a Jew in the twentieth century" as fraught with contradictions. It brings an unparalleled opportunity for witnessing a moral crisis, but to disclaim it may cause psychic or literal death; to claim it, an agony of mind and spirit. IRENA KLEPFISZ, a child survivor of the Holocaust who came with her mother to America shortly after the war, pays equal homage in her poem "Bashert" to those who survived the atrocities and those who did not. An accident of fate more often than an act of selfishness, selflessness, or will, both victim and survivor status are arbitrary, Klepfisz implies; both victims and survivors must thus be honored and mourned. Carolyn Forché, in *The Angel of History*, enters into dialogue with two women who came through the war as both victims and survivors: a Jewish woman living in France, Ellie, whom the poet meets in a Paris hospital forty years after the trauma; and a Japanese *hibakusha*, one of many women who lived through the bombing of Hiroshima and, maimed but articulate, bears witness to her experience. All four poets undertake the profoundly troubling and the profoundly freeing act of testimony. Indeed, considered collectively, their texts offer contemporary readers a vision of transfiguring illumination.

Trilogy, H.D.'s brilliant poetic triptych, has been compared to T.S. Eliot's *Four Quartets* and Ezra Pound's *Pisan Cantos* as a major modernist poem to emerge from a civilian's experience of war. The German air raids over London in 1943–44, or "incidents," as the newspapers called them, brought first anguish, then creative renewal to H.D.; "inspiration stalks us / through gloom," she writes near the beginning of Book One, *The Walls Do Not Fall* (*LAWL* 1202). As a civilian exposed daily to the trauma of war, H.D. claims, "one seems to shed a skin or husk; in fact, the whole race has got to slough off, out of it—the past I mean—and this 'new creation' is already on us." The opportunity for witness is unprecedented; the crisis of witnessing enormous. "We do not know if we live to tell the tale," H.D. wrote her friend Norman Holmes Pearson in August, 1943, "but we shall cling to our standards—to this, I mean, OUR PROFESSION" (H.D. v–vi). As *The Walls Do Not Fall* ends, the poet is uncertain but hopeful that the war will conclude and that she and other writers, "companions of the flame," will survive to bear witness to it. For H.D. the miracle of walls that refuse to fall despite the pressure of repeated bombings reveals the possibility of spiritual, cultural, and gender transformation.

Much of Muriel Rukeyser's poetry bears witness to the fierce conjunction of womanhood, pacifism, and Judaism, three crucial aspects of her identity. In "Bubble of Air" she makes this intersection explicit, naming herself "Woman, American, Jew." Exhorted by "the angel of the century" in a dream, the speaker realizes that her task is to "resist the evil of [her] age." She goes on to imagine "three guardsmen watching over" her who will assist in this calling: "life, freedom, and memory" (*LAWL* 1207). With their help she must testify to the effects of World War II's atrocities on Jews and on Americans living far from Europe. In "Letter to the Front" Rukeyser, like H.D., attributes special insight to poets and to women who interpret such events. As a Jewish woman poet and a pacifist, moreover, Rukeyser finds her creative gift and the responsibility she bears to be a torment. Yet with pain come glimmers of hope that justice will prevail. Surely, "Letter to the Front" enacts "the passage of the language through the violence and the passage of the violence through the language."

That the process of testimony illumines the relationship between speech and survival can be seen in Irena Klepfisz's long poem about Holocaust and memory, "Bashert," which in Yiddish means "predestined." This poem grapples with the conundrum discussed in depth by Felman and Laub: does the accident of history pursue the witness, or does the witness pursue the accident? If the former is the case, then "the compulsive character of testimony is brought into relief," as the poet-witness is compelled and bound by what is "both incomprehensible and unforgettable" (22–24). If the latter is true, the witness pursues the accident because it in some way offers unexpected liberation. Both compulsion and liberation undergird this poem's testimony. Adrienne Rich has called "Bashert" "one of the great 'borderland' poems—poems which emerge from the consciousness of being of no one geography, time zone or culture; of moving inwardly as well as outwardly between continents, land-masses, eras of history." As a poem of witness to a terrible historical moment, it touches something universal, "a consciousness that tries to claim all its legacies: courage, endurance, vision, fierceness of human will, and also the underside of oppression, the distortions that quarantine and violent deracination inflict on the heart." The poem's subject is the *shoah*, its aftermath, its survival—which is to say, the landscape of the human psyche and spirit. Rich praises the poem for "its verse and prose rhythms, its insistence on memory without idealization, its refusal to let go" (*What Is Found There* 139). Like Rukeyser, Klepfisz will not forget.

In *The Country Between Us* Carolyn Forché documents the U.S.-sponsored civil war that wracked the tiny Central American country of El Salvador from 1979 to 1991. Posing as a journalist there during the early days of the war, Forché encountered death squads and mutilated *compesinos* (peasants), wealthy colonels without conscience and starving children without hope. Despite her impulse not to write of this experience—she feared aestheticizing the suffering of others, creative voyeurism—the poems insisted on coming, and she determined to record them. These poems call readers to conscience, asking us to stop behaving "exactly like netted fish" and to face squarely the atrocities countries commit in the name of their citizens— to become "ourselves or nothing" (*LAWL* 1285). History is refracted through memory and conscience in poetry of witness, and Forché's poems convey this historical testimony.

Poetry of witness exhibits a powerful capacity to transform pain even as it marks it. The voices of poets who give language to atrocity—voices like those of H.D., Rukeyser, Klepfisz, and Forché—refuse to let atrocity or language go. In broken, wounded words, they remember the past, speak the present, and haunt the future.

DEVELOPING A POLITICS OF LOCATION

How does the white Western feminist define theory? It is something made only by white women and only by women acknowledged as writers? How does the white Western feminist define "an idea"? How do we actively work to build a white Western feminist consciousness that is not simply centered on itself, that resists white circumscribing?

Adrienne Rich, "Notes toward a Politics of Location"

Only when we utilize the notion of location to destabilize unexamined or stereotypical images that are vestiges of colonial discourse and other manifestations of modernity's structural inequalities can we recognize and work through the complex relationships between women in different parts of the world.

Caren Kaplan, "The Politics of Location as Transnational Feminist Critical Practice"

The term "politics of location" first appeared in a 1984 essay by poet and theorist Adrienne Rich, who offers a forthright assessment of herself as a white feminist and a U.S. citizen engaged in "a struggle to keep moving, a struggle for accountability." In this essay Rich invites readers to reflect upon the multiple locations, or literal and psychic sites, in which they reside: their bodies, the "geography closest in"; their houses, modest or fancy, with or without family ties; their towns, cities, or suburbs; their countries of origin; the world all humans share (*LAWL* 1096). To consider the sociopolitical implications of these locations, readers must scrutinize the meaning of race and sex to the bodies in which they live, of any ethnic or religious as well as national identity they embrace, and of the policies of justice or domination that their country's government enacts—toward its own citizens or toward other countries. Only if women and men honor the locations and historical realities of diverse people, Rich argues, can they ethically combat racism, sexism, and other injustice. As Caren Kaplan explains, "the key to Rich's politics of location lies in her recognition that as marginal as white, Western women appear to be in relation to the real movers and shakers in this world—white men—there are others made marginal by white, Western women themselves. Rich desires 'us' to take responsibility for these marginalizations, to acknowledge 'our' part in this process in order to change these unequal dynamics" (140).

As Rich claims, white Western feminists must learn of other "great movements for self-determination and justice," and surely the resistance to apartheid by South African blacks and their white allies is one of the most powerful movements of the twentieth century (*LAWL* 1106). This resistance is the subject of ELLEN KUZWAYO's testimonial, *Call Me Woman*. Published in 1985 during the "state of emergency," when the apartheid government had virtually declared war on its rebellious black citizens, this book celebrates the power of one woman, in solidarity with many, to participate in social change. Kuzwayo's account of this struggle reveals her strength as a social worker and an activist called the "mother of Soweto" for her empowerment of black women there. She experiences a five-month prison detention at the age of sixty-three and survives to tell of it—with clarity of moral vision, compassion for others still imprisoned, and an unswerving commitment to the truth regardless of its cost. Her final chapter, "Nkosi Sikelel'i Afrika," pays tribute to the central role black women have played throughout the century as resisters of apartheid. Writing from London in 1984, watching on television as the South African police raid the black township of Sebokeng, a site of massive student protests, Kuzwayo expresses confidence that the antiapartheid movement will prevail. Despite the government's show of force, women will continue in the vanguard of the struggle. In Rich's words from "Movement," these women did not "join a movement"; they stepped into that "deep current" that guides lives "bent toward freedom"—lives committed to resistance, solidarity, transformation (*LAWL* 1110). For Kuzwayo and the black women whose struggle she chronicles, a "politics of location" is no abstraction; it is instead the wellspring of their lives—as Africans, as women, as residents of a black township, poor in a wealthy country. "The black women in South Africa have shown outstanding tenacity against great odds," Kuzwayo concludes. "We shall never give in to defeat. Today we remain determined, like the women of our community of previous generations, who have left us a living example of strength and integrity" (*LAWL* 1116). Feminist theory remains woefully incomplete without the testimonies of South African women like Kuzwayo, whose struggle against racism inspires all women to grasp their life's direction.

Progressive white women in South Africa have also contributed to the antiapartheid movement as writers and activists, and foremost among these is the Nobel Prize-winning author of fiction NADINE GORDIMER. Commending Kuzwayo, Gordimer writes in her foreword to *Call Me Woman* that "this book is true testimony from a wonderful woman. For myself, she is one of those people who give me faith in the new and different South Africa they will create" (quoted in Kuzwayo xii). That such a new South Africa is being created as the twenty-first century dawns—with Nelson Mandela, a former political prisoner, and Thabo Mbeki, his successor, as the first black presidents and Ellen Kuzwayo as a member of Parliament—gives Gordimer's words from 1985 particular resonance. Much of her fiction grapples with the responsibilities of liberal white citizens in racist South Africa; in her essays and interviews she struggles similarly with the role of the white writer in challenging apartheid. "The white artist may perhaps take [her] place in an indigenous culture of the future," writes Gordimer, "by claiming that place in the implicit nature of the artist as an agent of change" (quoted in Kuzwayo xii). As an agent of change Gordimer has resisted what Rich calls "white circumscribing" by scrutinizing her own politics of location as a white woman writer in South Africa (*LAWL* 1100).

This effort toward accountability has caused Gordimer to be wary of feminism, a movement which, in the South African context, she has viewed as white, bourgeois, and politically naive. In a 1992 interview with Karen Lazar she indicates that feminism for her cannot be separated from the larger issue of human rights, and although she believes that black women in South Africa have been oppressed because of gender as well as race, she is not convinced that most white women there have suffered from gender oppression (Hunter and Mackenzie 27). During the apartheid era Gordimer rarely wrote from the perspective of black women, and her white protagonists typically explored their sexuality, familial dynamics, and racial complicity rather than sexism *per se*. In her story, "Amnesty," however, from her 1991 collection *Jump*, she writes in the voice of a young black woman waiting in the countryside for her lover, a former revolutionary, to come home. When he does return, he has little time for his lover and behaves toward her in sexist ways. In this story Gordimer questions the value that amnesty for political prisoners has had for women in remote villages, whose lives have changed little despite major social transformation in their country. For the revolution against apartheid to be fully realized, she implies, *all* South Africans must have a physically and psychically affirming place to call home.

RAISING THESE QUESTIONS IN THE WORLD

> The absolute necessity to raise these questions in the world: where, when, and under what conditions have women acted and been acted on, as women?
>
> Adrienne Rich, *"Notes toward a Politics of Location"*

Rich addresses in many essays the question of what feminist movement should be in the twenty-first century. "A movement for change lives in feelings, actions, and words," she declares in "Notes toward a Politics of Location." "Whatever circumscribes or mutilates our feelings makes it more difficult to act, keeps our actions reactive, repetitive." Among these sources of circumscription, or limitation, Rich lists abstract thinking, "narrow tribal loyalties," self-righteousness, arrogance, fears, and denials—all of which affect each one of us every day, despite our best efforts. What, then, allows us to release ourselves from such limits? How do we shift from a static vision, one in which we see ourselves at the center, to a dynamic vision of community and solidarity? "Let us get back to earth," Rich implores, "not as paradigm for 'women,' but as a place of location" (*LAWL* 1098). Living with integrity on earth will take all our strength, patience, labor, and desire; only with these resources can freedom be imagined, let alone attained.

Many different forms of feminism will enhance the twenty-first century, concludes ZOË WICOMB in her essay "To Hear the Variety of Discourses," if all of them consider "race and class as interlocking factors" across cultures. Only then can "an aligned feminist criticism" emerge that addresses the lives and writings of *all* women (42). As both Wicomb and Rich suggest, a multicultural approach to women's literature will of necessity ask, in Rich's words, "where, when, and under what conditions have women acted and been acted on, as women?" (*LAWL* 1097) Some of this multicultural literature will foreground the lives of working-class women, as do the stories of the U.S. writers REBECCA HARDING DAVIS and ANZIA YEZIERSKA. In *Life in the Iron-Mills* Davis depicts the physical and spiritual deprivation of West Virginia mill workers she had known since childhood. Deb, a young woman misshapen from working in a cotton mill, suffers from both class and gender marginalization. Yezierska's protagonist in "Soap and Water" is a laundry worker who, like Davis's Deb, is frustrated by her marginal status. Unlike Deb, however, she has some hope of social mobility by virtue of having won a scholarship to a teacher's college. She suffers from class bias, however, at the hands of a professor who threatens to withhold her diploma because of her unkempt appearance. "Soap and water are cheap. Any one can be clean," insists the unfeeling dean, who neither knows nor cares that her student works long hours before and after classes with no time to wash herself, only wealthy people's clothes. Davis's Deb has no recourse but active rebellion, but Yezierska's heroine fights with words, unleashing "the suppressed wrath of all the unwashed of the earth" (*LAWL* 1193).

What Wicomb describes as a "stealthy negotiation of race and gender" (43) that occurs in much writing by African and African-American women can be seen in TONI MORRISON'S story "Recitatif." In "To Hear the Variety of Discourses" Wicomb praises Morrison's 1987 novel *Beloved* for "elegantly articulating a black feminism which is a far cry from the crude womanism of empowering men or asserting imaginary wholeness;" instead, Morrison's black feminist text offers a "discourse of desire" (39). The same can be said of "Recitatif," although the problem of conflicting desires in this text occurs between two women of different races, bound by their childhood wounds, rather than between a black woman and a black man, as in *Beloved*. By leaving certain questions about the women's lives unanswered, Morrison invites readers to fill the gaps with racial and gendered desires of their own. A feminist criticism of the sort Wicomb envisions might usefully examine the ambiguities and contradictions in Morrison's representation of black and white women's subjectivities.

A multicultural approach to women's literature will also explore national origin as a source of identity for women writers. Certainly interrogating their country's history is a concern shared by Rich in the United States, Kuzwayo and Wicomb in South Africa, and EAVAN BOLAND in Ireland. "I came to know history as a woman and a poet when I apparently left the site of it," writes Boland, commenting on her early poems, many of which were written when she was an isolated young mother and a temporary exile studying abroad. "I came to know my country when I went to live at its margin. I grew to understand the Irish poetic tradition only when I went into exile with it" (i). As these paradoxes reveal, Boland takes seriously Rich's claim that recognizing one's own politics of location begins invariably with self-knowledge, and only thereafter with cultural interrogation. For many women, coming to know their body enhances the knowledge of other terrain. As Boland explains, her poems are "about Ireland, about the body, about growing older in both and using each as a text for the other"(ii). Like Rich, she describes complex connections between nationality and embodiment, conditions of the state and conditions of the flesh.

In "Dwelling in Decencies" Lillian S. Robinson argues that "to be effective, feminist criticism cannot be simply bourgeois criticism in drag. It must be ideological and moral criticism; it must be revolutionary" (889). Certainly a revolutionary feminist criticism demands a body of revolutionary literature worthy of its full consideration. That such a body of literature has been written by women across cultures and time periods is evident from the works included in "Resistance and Transformation." From Astell to Boland, from Truth to Kuzwayo, women have written political art that matters and transformed political matters into art.

⚔ Works Cited—Section V ⚕

Note: In the introductory essay, all citations of works included in this anthology are indicated by *LAWL*, followed by the page number.

Boland, Eavan. *Outside History: Selected Poems, 1980–1990*. New York: Norton, 1990. This collection of one of Ireland's most distinguished poets contains five previously published volumes of poetry and an introduction that links her writing to her country's tumultuous political history.

Collins, Patricia Hill. *Black Feminist Thought: Knowledge, Consciousness, and the Politics of Empowerment*. Boston: Unwin Hyman, 1990. This book examines characteristics of a "black women's epistemology" drawn from feminist, womanist, and Afrocentric standpoints: an emphasis on personal accountability, concrete experience as a source of knowledge, dialogue as a tool for exploring differences, and an ethic of empathy.

de Lauretis, Teresa. *Technologies of Gender: Essays on Theory, Film, and Fiction*. Bloomington: U of Indiana P, 1987. This book contains several strong theoretical essays on gender and representation, but see especially chapter 2, "The Violence of Rhetoric."

Felman, Shoshana and Dori Laub, M.D. *Testimony: Crises of Witnessing in Literature, Psychoanalysis, and History*. New York and London: Routledge, 1992. This collaborative study, written by a literary critic and a psychoanalyst, considers the complex meanings of Holocaust literature and oral testimony; it also examines the effect that witnessing atrocities, whether firsthand or vicariously, has on readers and in the classroom.

Forché, Carolyn. Introduction to *Against Forgetting: Twentieth Century Poetry of Witness*. New York: Norton, 1993. 29–47. Forché has collected and analyzed a wide range of poetry dealing with war, torture, imprisonment, and physical and psychic extremity—poetry that testifies "against forgetting." Her introduction examines the theoretical and ethical issues that such poems raise.

———. "El Salvador: An Aide Memoir." *American Poetry Review*, July–Aug. 1981: 1–8. This testimony recounts Forché's experience as a journalist in El Salvador during the war there and offers her views on poetry of witness.

Harlow, Barbara. *Resistance Literature*. New York: Metheun, 1987. This study traces the contours of contemporary resistance literature as an "arena of struggle." Harlow theorizes that such writing is political and politicized and that it challenges dominant forms of cultural and ideological production.

H.D. *Trilogy*. New York: New Directions, 1973. This volume includes all three of the poet's "epic" poems from World War II, as well as a useful introduction in which her friend and editor, Norman Holmes Pearson, quotes from H.D.'s letters.

Hunter, Eva and Craig Mackenzie, eds. *Between the Lines II*. Grahamstown, South Africa: National English Literary Museum, 1993. A collection of excellent interviews with four of South Africa's most prominent women writers, including Zoë Wicomb (interviewed by Eva Hunter) and Nadine Gordimer (interviewed by Karen Lazar and by Robert Dorsman and Gitte Postel).

Kaplan, Caren. "The Politics of Location as Transnational Feminist Critical Practice." *Scattered Hegemonies: Postmodernity and Transnational Feminist Practices*. Eds. Inderpal Grewal and Caren Kaplan. Minneapolis: U of Minnesota P, 1994. 137–51. This essay thoughtfully considers the implications of Rich's concept of a politics of location for postcolonial and postmodern criticism and urges feminists to examine their politics of location cross-culturally in the production and reception of theory.

Kuzwayo, Ellen. *Call Me Woman*. San Francisco: Spinsters Ink, 1985. This autobiographical account of the life and resistance of Kuzwayo—a black South African social worker, activist, African National Congress member, and member of Parliament—offers an inspiring challenge to apartheid. It includes a preface by Nadine Gordimer and a foreword by Bessie Head.

Lugones, Maria. "*Hablando cara a cara*/ Speaking Face to Face: An Exploration of Ethnocentric Racism." *Making Face, Making Soul: haciendo caras: Creative and Critical Perspectives by Women of Color*. Ed. Gloria Anzaldúa. San Francisco: aunt lute, 1990. 46–54. This essay proposes creative ways in which white women can think seriously about their complicity in a racist state and discuss their own racism and ethnocentrism with women of color in a spirit of friendship and collective struggle.

Ogunyemi, Chikwenye Okonjo. "Womanism: The Dynamics of the Contemporary Black Female Novel in English." *Signs* 11:1 (1985): 63–80. This widely cited essay argues that womanism better describes the world view of African women writers who focus on gender issues than does feminism. Wicomb takes issue with Ogunyemi on this point in "To Hear the Variety of Discourses."

Rich, Adrienne. *Blood, Bread, and Poetry: Selected Prose, 1979–1985*. New York: Norton, 1986. This collection contains many essays in which Rich discusses feminist critical practice across cultures, including the title essay and "Notes toward a Politics of Location"; these essays also shed light on her poetry and poetic sensibility.

———. *What Is Found There: Notebooks on Poetry and Politics*. New York: Norton, 1993. These impressionistic essays consider how and under what circumstances poetry, politics, and the examined life intersect. The collection contains a fine introduction to Irena Klepfisz's political poetry and explores Rich's own texts, contexts, and influences.

Robinson, Lillian S. "Dwelling in Decencies: Radical Criticism and the Feminist Perspective." *College English* 32:8 (May 1971): 879–89. This landmark essay of early feminist criticism challenges critics to go beyond "bourgeois feminism" to an approach that links the production and study of literature to social change.

Rogers, Katharine M. *Feminism in Eighteenth Century England*. Urbana: U of Illinois P, 1982. This study examines feminist literature and polemical tracts by such early feminists as Mary Astell, Mary Wollstonecraft, and Mary Hays; it also sheds light on the historical context and literary climate in which these women wrote.

Sandoval, Chela. "Feminism and Racism: A Report on the 1981 National Women's Studies Association Conference." *Making Face, Making Soul*. 55–71. Although this essay is in part an evaluation of a particular organization and historical moment, it offers considerable insight into the problem of racism in the women's movement and the response to this problem by U.S. women of color.

Wicomb, Zoë. "To Hear the Variety of Discourses." *Current Writing: Text and Reception in Southern Africa* 2 (1990): 37–44. This essay by a South African feminist theorist and activist calls for "an aligned feminist criticism" that considers race and class as well as gender in analyzing women's resistance literature across cultures.

⊰ Suggestions for Further Reading ⊱

COSAW Women's Collective, eds. *Like a House on Fire: Contemporary Women's Writing, Art and Photography from South Africa*. Johannesburg: COSAW Publishing, 1994. This anthology of women's writing from postapartheid South Africa addresses gender as well as political struggle as an issue of revolutionary importance; women of all racial-ethnic groups are represented.

DeShazer, Mary K. *A Poetics of Resistance: Women Writing in El Salvador, South Africa, and the United States*. Ann Arbor: U of Michigan P, 1994. This study examines contemporary women's poetry that is political, ideological, and gendered and draws comparisons among poets from three countries. Women's combat poetry and solidarity poetry by women who have been engaged in struggles for political and social justice are a primary focus.

———. "'The End of a Century': Feminist Millennial Vision in Adrienne Rich's *Dark Fields of the Republic*." *NWSA Journal* (Fall 1996): 36–62. Rich's 1995 volume of poetry is the subject of this essay, which examines "Inscriptions" and other poems in light of Rich's feminist theory and perspective on the United States at century's end.

Delamotte, Eugenia C. et al., eds. *Women Imagine Change: A Global Anthology of Women's Resistance*. New York and London: Routledge, 1997. This collection of women's resistance writing covers twenty-six centuries, from 600 B.C. to the present, and is geographically diverse. Its last two sections, "Identifying Sources of Resistance" and "Vision and Transformation," are especially valuable.

Forché, Carolyn. "The Province of Radical Solitude." *The Writer on Her Work, II*. Ed. Janet Sternberg. New York: Norton, 1991. In this essay on poetry of witness and creative process, Forché pays homage to her Slovak grandmother, considers what it means to write poetry after the Holocaust, and describes the dilemma of the poet-witness who writes out of extremity.

Harlow, Barbara. *Barred: Women, Writing, and Political Detention*. Hanover and London: Wesleyan UP, 1992. This book examines the writing of women political prisoners and dissidents in El Salvador, South Africa, Northern Ireland, the West Bank and Gaza, and elsewhere in the world and discusses why this work matters to U.S. feminist theory.

Helle, Anita Plath. "Elegy as History: Three Women Poets 'By the Century's Deathbed.'" *South Atlantic Review* 61:2 (Spring 1996): 51–68. This essay examines how elegy functions at the end of the twentieth century and offers cogent analyses of Rich's *Dark Fields of the Republic* and Forché's *The Angel of History* as works of witness and mourning.

Mohanty, Chandra Talpede et al, eds. *Third World Women and the Politics of Feminism*. Bloomington: Indiana UP, 1991. This collection of essays examines resistance literature and feminist theory as applicable to the writings of women of the "Third World" and explains and interrogates that term. "Writing often becomes the context through which new political identities are forged," writes Mohanty in the introduction. "It becomes a space for struggle and contestation about reality itself."

Adrienne Rich
1929–

"Poetry is not resting on the given, but a questing toward what might otherwise be," claims ADRIENNE RICH, one of the United States' best contemporary poets. Rich has published sixteen volumes of poetry and four books of prose; her work has been translated into eight languages, and she is the recipient of numerous literary awards, including the Ruth Lilly Prize for Poetry, the Lenore Marshall/*Nation* Prize for Poetry, two Guggenheim Fellowships, and the MacArthur Fellowship for lifetime achievement. In 1997 she refused to accept the prestigious National Medal for the Arts, asserting that "democracy in this country has been in decline" and that "art means nothing if it simply decorates the dinner table of power which holds it hostage."

Born in Baltimore, Maryland, Rich was educated at home until fourth grade; her father, a professor of medicine, and her mother, a classical pianist, encouraged her literary pursuits. She graduated from Radcliffe College in 1951 and two years later married Alfred Conrad, an economist with whom she had three sons; the family lived in Cambridge, Massachusetts, for the next thirteen years. These were years of personal and political growth for Rich, who struggled to combine writing and raising children in a stifling environment; the marriage ended in 1969. Her work during the late 1960s as a teacher in the SEEK and Open Admissions Programs of the City College of New York reflected her commitment to the civil rights, antiwar, and women's movements. A sense of urgency has characterized Rich's poetry from its beginnings, although it has undergone significant stylistic and thematic shifts. Her first volume, *A Change of World*, was selected by W.H. Auden for the 1951 Yale Younger Poets Award. While Auden described her verse condescendingly as "neatly and modestly dressed," he also praised her technical virtuosity. *The Diamond Cutters* (1955) likewise featured elegant poems that were tightly controlled. In her essay "'When We Dead Awaken': Writing as Re-Vision," Rich likens her early formalist strategy to the use of asbestos gloves, since emphasizing form allowed her to present "objectively" content otherwise too difficult to handle. In the 1960s her work became more technically experimental and began to encompass feminist themes: "I was able to write, for the first time, directly about experiencing myself as a woman." This change is evident in *Snapshots of a Daughter-in-Law* (1963), whose title poem "was an extraordinary relief to write." A scrapbook comprised of ten related "snapshots," this poem chronicles the efforts of a daughter-in-law—a woman defined by her relationship to her family—to forge an autonomous identity. Themes of self-definition, sexuality, intimacy, and pacifism also appear in *The Will to Change* (1971) and *Diving into the Wreck* (1973). The latter volume won the National Book Award, which Rich rejected for herself but accepted with two other nominees, ALICE WALKER and AUDRE LORDE, on behalf of women everywhere. *The Dream of a Common Language* (1978) celebrates lesbian love and redefines separation, relation, and poetry. Subsequent volumes—*A Wild Patience Has Taken Me This Far* (1981), *Sources* (1983), *The Fact of a Doorframe* (1984), and *Your Native Land, Your Life* (1986)—explore women's forgotten contributions to history, the meaning of Judaism in the poet's life, and the intersections of race, class, and gender.

Poetry, for Rich, is a means of reconceptualizing language and "reconstituting the world," for poetry serves as a "criticism of language." The cultural and aesthetic implications of this criticism can be seen in Rich's poems of the 1990s, which traverse new political ground. "This is no place you ever knew me," she claims in *An Atlas of the Difficult World* (1991); "these are not the roads / you knew me by." Written during and just after the Persian Gulf War, these poems probe the heart of a national conscience. "A patriot is one who wrestles for the soul of her country / as she wrestles for her own being," Rich asserts, as she asks three crucial questions about America and Americans: "Where are we moored? What are the bindings? What behooves us?" Rich investigates further what it means to be a U.S. poet in *Dark Fields of the Republic* (1995). Although her title reveals a barren national landscape, her poems offer compassionate knowledge, beauty worth grasping, fierce connections with comrades: "Surely the love of life is never-ending, / the failure of nerve, a charred fuse? / I want more from you than I ever knew to ask." In *Midnight Salvage: Poems 1995–1998* (1999) she continues to grapple with themes of national and personal identity.

Rich is also a distinguished writer of feminist theory. *Of Woman Born* (1976) distinguishes between the institution of motherhood and women's experience of maternity, which she views as a potential source of empowerment. *On Lies, Secrets, and Silence* (1979) includes "When We Dead Awaken" as well as critical studies of *Jane Eyre* and EMILY DICKINSON's poems. *Blood, Bread, and Poetry* (1986) reflects Rich's "struggle for accountability" and her view of poetry as a global political force. *What Is Found There: Notebooks on Poetry and Politics* (1993) contains impressionistic essays that "lay claim to poetry" as a source of sensual and historical vitality.

The poems included here are "Diving into the Wreck" and four parts of the sequence "Inscriptions," taken from *Dark Fields of the Republic*. "Diving into the Wreck" challenges patriarchal world views and offers an androgynous vision, while the poems from "Inscriptions" explore the poet's relationship to "this tenuous, still unbirthed democracy, my country." "Inscriptions" seems revolutionary in Rich's sense of the word:

> A revolutionary poem will not tell you who or when to kill, what and when to burn, or even how to theorize. It reminds you (for you have known, somehow, all along, maybe lost track) where and when and how you are living and might live—it is a wick of desire.

Revolution, desire, and living are also themes of "Notes toward a Politics of Location," originally published in *Blood, Bread, and Poetry*. In this compelling essay Rich considers how to forge a lasting connection between writing and resistance, and why such a connection matters.

⊰ Notes toward a Politics of Location ⊱

I am to speak these words in Europe, but I have been searching for them in the United States of America. A few years ago I would have spoken of the common oppression of women, the gathering movement of women around the globe, the hidden history of women's resistance and bonding, the failure of all previous politics to recognize the universal shadow of patriarchy, the belief that women now, in a time of rising consciousness and global emergency, may join across all national and cultural boundaries to create a society free of domination, in which "sexuality, politics, . . . work, . . . intimacy . . . thinking itself will be transformed."[1]

I would have spoken these words as a feminist who "happened" to be a white United States citizen, conscious of my government's proven capacity for violence and arrogance of power, but as self-separated from that government, quoting without second thought Virginia Woolf's statement in *Three Guineas* that "as a woman I have no country. As a woman I want no country. As a woman my country is the whole world."[2]

1. [Talk given at the first Summer School of Critical Semiotics, Conference on Women, Feminist Identity and Society in the 1980s, Utrecht, Holland, June 1, 1984. Different versions of this talk were given at Cornell University for the Women's Studies Research Seminar, and as the Burgess Lecture, Pacific Oaks College, Pasadena, California.] [Adrienne Rich, *Of Woman Born: Motherhood as Experience and Institution*. New York: Norton, 1976. 286.]

2. Virginia Woolf, a British novelist and feminist, published her essay *Three Guineas* in 1938.

This is not what I come here to say in 1984. I come here with notes but without absolute conclusions. This is not a sign of loss of faith or hope. These notes are the marks of a struggle to keep moving, a struggle for accountability.

Beginning to write, then getting up. Stopped by the movements of a huge early bumble-bee which has somehow gotten inside this house and is reeling, bumping, stunning itself against windowpanes and sills. I open the front door and speak to it, trying to attract it outside. It is looking for what it needs, just as I am, and, like me, it has gotten trapped in a place where it cannot fulfill its own life. I could open the jar of honey on the kitchen counter, and perhaps it would take honey from that jar; but its life process, its work, its mode of being cannot be fulfilled inside this house.

And I, too, have been bumping my way against glassy panes, falling half-stunned, gathering myself up and crawling, then again taking off, searching.

I don't hear the bumblebee any more, and I leave the front door. I sit down and pick up a secondhand, faintly annotated student copy of Marx's *The German Ideology*,[3] which "happens" to be lying on the table.

I will speak these words in Europe, but I am having to search for them in the United States of North America. When I was ten or eleven, early in World War II, a girl-friend and I used to write each other letters which we addressed like this:

Adrienne Rich
14 Edgevale Road
Baltimore, Maryland
The United States of America
The Continent of North America
The Western Hemisphere
The Earth
The Solar System
The Universe

You could see your own house as a tiny fleck on an ever-widening landscape, or as the center of it all from which the circles expanded into the infinite unknown.

It is that question of feeling at the center that gnaws at me now. At the center of what?

As a woman I have a country; as a woman I cannot divest myself of that country merely by condemning its government or by saying three times "As a woman my country is the whole world." Tribal loyalties aside, and even if nation-states are now just pretexts used by multinational conglomerates to serve their interests, I need to understand how a place on the map is also a place in history within which as a woman, a Jew, a lesbian, a feminist I am created and trying to create.

Begin, though, not with a continent or a country or a house, but with the geography closest in—the body. Here at least I know I exist, that living human individual whom the young Marx called "the first premise of all human history."[4] But it was not as a Marxist that I turned to this place, back from philosophy and literature and science and theology in which I had looked for myself in vain. It was as a radical feminist.

3. Karl Marx (1818–1883) was a German socialist and political philosopher; he published *The German Ideology* in 1845.

4. [Karl Marx and Frederick Engels, *The German Ideology*, ed. C.J. Arthur (New York: International Publishers, 1970) 42.]

The politics of pregnability and motherhood. The politics of orgasm. The politics of rape and incest, or abortion, birth control, forcible sterilization. Of prostitution and marital sex. Of what had been named sexual liberation. Of prescriptive heterosexuality. Of lesbian existence.

And Marxist feminists were often pioneers in this work. But for many women I knew, the need to begin with the female body—our own—was understood not as applying a Marxist principle *to* women, but as locating the grounds from which to speak with authority *as* women. Not to transcend this body, but to reclaim it. To reconnect our thinking and speaking with the body of this particular living human individual, a woman. Begin, we said, with the material, with matter, mma, madre, mutter, moeder, modder, etc., etc.

Begin with the material. Pick up again the long struggle against lofty and privileged abstraction. Perhaps this is the one core of the revolutionary process, whether it calls itself Marxist or Third World or feminist or all three. Long before the nineteenth century, the empirical witch of the European Middle Ages, trusting her senses, practicing her tried remedies against the antimaterial, antisensuous, antiempirical dogmas of the Church. Dying for that, by the millions. "A female-led peasant rebellion"?—in any event, a rebellion against the idolatry of pure ideas, the belief that ideas have a life of their own and float along and above the heads of ordinary people—women, the poor, the uninitiated.[5]

Abstractions severed from the doings of living people, fed back to people as slogans.

Theory—the seeing of patterns, showing the forest as well as the trees—theory can be a dew that rises from the earth and collects in the rain cloud and returns to earth over and over. But if it doesn't smell of the earth, it isn't good for the earth.

I wrote a sentence just now and x'd it out. In it I said that women have always understood the struggle against free-floating abstraction even when they were intimidated by abstract ideas. I don't want to write that kind of sentence now, the sentence that begins "Women have always. . . ." We started by rejecting the sentences that began "Women have always had an instinct for mothering" or "Women have always and everywhere been in subjugation to men." If we have learned anything in these years of late twentieth-century feminism, it's that that "always" blots out what we really need to know: When, where, and under what conditions has the statement been true?

The absolute necessity to raise these questions in the world: where, when, and under what conditions have women acted and been acted on, as women? Wherever people are struggling against subjection, the specific subjection of women, through our location in a female body, from now on has to be addressed. The necessity to go on speaking of it, refusing to let the discussion go on as before, speaking where silence has been advised and enforced, not just about our subjection, but about our active presence and practice as women. We believed (I go on believing) that the liberation of women is a wedge driven into all other radical thought, can open out the structures of resistance, unbind the imagination, connect what's been dangerously disconnected. Let us pay attention now, we said, to women: let men and women make a conscious act of attention when women

---

5. [Barbara Ehrenreich and Deirdre English, *Witches, Midwives, and Nurses: A History of Women Healers* (Old Westbury, NY: Feminist Press, 1973).]

speak; let us insist on kinds of process which allow more women to speak; let us get back to earth—not as paradigm for "women," but as place of location.

Perhaps we need a moratorium on saying "the body." For it's also possible to abstract "the" body. When I write "the body," I see nothing in particular. To write "my body" plunges me into lived experience, particularity: I see scars, disfigurements, discolorations, damages, losses, as well as what pleases me. Bones well nourished from the placenta; the teeth of a middle-class person seen by the dentist twice a year from childhood. White skin, marked and scarred by three pregnancies, an elected sterilization, progressive arthritis, four joint operations, calcium deposits, no rapes, no abortions, long hours at a typewriter—my own, not in a typing pool—and so forth. To say "the body" lifts me away from what has given me a primary perspective. To say "my body" reduces the temptation to grandiose assertions.

This body. White, female; or female, white. The first obvious, lifelong facts. But I was born in the white section of a hospital which separated black and white women in labor and black and white babies in the nursery, just as it separated black and white bodies in its morgue. I was defined as white before I was defined as female.

The politics of location. Even to begin with my body I have to say that from the outset that body had more than one identity. When I was carried out of the hospital into the world, I was viewed and treated as female, but also viewed and treated as white—by both black and white people. I was located by color and sex as surely as a black child was located by color and sex—though the implications of white identity were mystified by the presumption that white people are the center of the universe.

To locate myself in my body means more than understanding what it has meant to me to have a vulva and clitoris and uterus and breasts. It means recognizing this white skin, the places it has taken me, the places it has not let me go.

The body I was born into was not only female and white, but Jewish—enough for geographic location to have played, in those years, a determining part. I was a *Mischling,* four years old when the Third Reich began. Had it been not Baltimore, but Prague or Lódz or Amsterdam, the ten-year-old letter writer might have had no address. Had I survived Prague, Amsterdam, or Lódz and the railway stations for which they were deportation points, I would be some body else. My center, perhaps, the Middle East or Latin America, my language itself another language. Or I might be in no body at all.

But I am a North American Jew, born and raised three thousand miles from the war in Europe.

Trying as women to see from the center. "A politics," I wrote once, "of asking women's questions."[6] We are not "the woman question" asked by somebody else; we are the women who ask the questions.

Trying to see so much, aware of so much to be seen, brought into the light, changed. Breaking down again and again the false male universal. Piling piece by piece of concrete experience side by side, comparing, beginning to discern patterns. Anger, frustration with Marxist or Leftist dismissals of these questions, this struggle. Easy now to call this disillusionment facile, but the anger was deep, the frustration real, both in personal relationships and political organizations. I wrote in 1975:

6. [Adrienne Rich, *On Lies, Secrets, and Silence: Selected Prose 1966–1978* (New York: Norton, 1979) 17.]

Much of what is narrowly termed "politics" seems to rest on a longing for certainty even at the cost of honesty, for an analysis which, once given, need not be reexamined. Such is the deadendedness—for women—of Marxism in our times.[7]

And it has felt like a dead end whenever politics has been externalized, cut off from the ongoing lives of women or of men, rarefied into an elite jargon, an enclave, defined by little sects who feed off each others' errors.

But even as we shrugged away Marx along with the academic Marxists and the sectarian Left, some of us, calling ourselves radical feminists, never meant anything less by women's liberation than the creation of a society without domination; we never meant less than the making new all of relationships. The problem was that we did not know whom we meant when we said "we."

> The power men everywhere wield over women, power which has become a model for every other form of exploitation and illegitimate control.[8]

I wrote these words in 1978 at the end of an essay called "Compulsory Heterosexuality and Lesbian Existence." Patriarchy as the "model" for other forms of domination—this idea was not original with me. It has been put forward insistently by white Western feminists, and in 1972 I had quoted from Lévi-Strauss: *I would go so far as to say that even before slavery or class domination existed, men built an approach to women that would serve one day to introduce differences among us all.*[9]

Living for fifty-some years, having watched even minor bits of history unfold, I am less quick than I once was to search for single "causes" or origins in dealings among human beings. But suppose that we could trace back and establish that patriarchy has been everywhere the model. To what choices of action does that lead us in the present? Patriarchy exists nowhere in a pure state; we are the latest to set foot in a tangle of oppressions grown up and around each other for centuries. This isn't the old children's game where you choose one strand of color in the web and follow it back to find your prize, ignoring the others as mere distractions. The prize is life itself, and most women in the world must fight for their lives on many fronts at once.

> We . . . often find it difficult to separate race from class from sex oppression because in our lives they are most often experienced simultaneously. We know that there is such a thing as racial-sexual oppression which is neither solely racial nor solely sexual. . . . We need to articulate the real class situation of persons who are not merely raceless, sexless workers but for whom racial and sexual oppression are significant determinants in their working/economic lives.

This is from the 1977 Combahee River Collective statement, a major document of the U.S. women's movement, which gives a clear and uncompromising black-feminist naming to the experience of simultaneity of oppressions.[10]

---

7. [Rich, *On Lies, Secrets and Silence* 193.] A. R., 1986: For a vigorous indictment of dead-ended Marxism and a call to "revolution in permanence," see Raya Dunayevskaya, *Women's Liberation and the Dialectics of Revolution* (Atlantic Highlands, NJ: Humanities Press, 1985).
8. [Adrienne Rich, "Compulsory Heterosexuality and Lesbian Existence," *Blood, Bread, and Poetry: Selected Prose 1979–1985* (New York: Norton, 1986) 68.]
9. [Rich, *On Lies, Secrets, and Silence* 84.]
10. [Barbara Smith, ed., *Home Girls: A Black Feminist Anthology* (New York: Kitchen Table/Women of Color Press, 1983). 272–283. See also Audre Lorde, *Sister Outsider: Essays and Speeches* (Trumansburg, NY: Crossing Press, 1984). See Hilda Bernstein, *For Their Triumphs and for Their Tears: Women in Apartheid South Africa* (London: International Defence and Aid Fund, 1978), for a description of simultaneity of African women's oppressions under apartheid. For a biographical and personal account, see Ellen Kuzwayo, *Call Me Woman* (San Francisco: Spinsters/aunt lute, 1985).]

Even in the struggle against free-floating abstraction, we have abstracted. Marxists and radical feminists have both done this. Why not admit it, get it said, so we can get on to the work to be done, back down to earth again? The faceless, sexless, raceless proletariat. The faceless, raceless, classless category of "all women." Both creations of white Western self-centeredness.

To come to terms with the circumscribing nature of (our) whiteness.[11] Marginalized though we have been as women, as white and Western makers of theory, we also marginalize others because our lived experience is thoughtlessly white, because even our "women's cultures" are rooted in some Western tradition. Recognizing our location, having to name the ground we're coming from, the conditions we have taken for granted—there is a confusion between our claims to the white and Western eye and the woman-seeing eye,[12] fear of losing the centrality of the one even as we claim the other.

How does the white Western feminist define theory? Is it something made only by white women and only by women acknowledged as writers? How does the white Western feminist define "an idea"? How do we actively work to build a white Western feminist consciousness that is not simply centered on itself, that resists white circumscribing?

It was in the writings but also the actions and speeches and sermons of black United States citizens that I began to experience the meaning of my whiteness as a point of location for which I needed to take responsibility. It was in reading poems by contemporary Cuban women that I began to experience the meaning of North America as a location which had also shaped my ways of seeing and my ideas of who and what was important, a location for which I was also responsible. I traveled then to Nicaragua, where, in a tiny impoverished country, in a four-year-old society dedicated to eradicating poverty, under the hills of the Nicaragua-Honduras border, I could physically feel the weight of the United States of North America, its military forces, its vast appropriations of money, its mass media, at my back; I could feel what it means, dissident or not, to be part of that raised boot of power, the cold shadow we cast everywhere to the south.

I come from a country stuck fast for forty years in the deep-freeze of history. Any United States citizen alive today has been saturated with Cold War rhetoric, the horrors of communism, the betrayals of socialism, the warning that any collective restructuring of society spells the end of personal freedom. And, yes, there have been horrors and betrayals deserving open opposition. But we are not invited to consider the butcheries of Stalinism, the terrors of Russian counterrevolution alongside the butcheries of white supremacism and Manifest Destiny. We are not urged to help create a more human society here in response to the ones we are taught to hate and dread. Discourse itself is frozen at this level. Tonight as I turned a switch searching for "the news," that shinily animated silicone mask was on television again, telling the citizens of my country we are menaced by communism from El Salvador, that

11. [Gloria I. Joseph, "The Incompatible Ménage à Trois: Marxism, Feminism and Racism," in *Women and Revolution*, ed. Lydia Sargent (Boston: South End Press, 1981).]

12. [See Marilyn Frye, *The Politics of Reality* (Trumansburg, NY: Crossing Press, 1983) 171.]

communism—Soviet variety, obviously—is on the move in Central America, that freedom is imperiled, that the suffering peasants of Latin America must be stopped, just as Hitler had to be stopped.

The discourse has never really changed; it is wearingly abstract. (Lillian Smith, white antiracist writer and activist, spoke of the "deadly sameness" of abstraction.)[13] It allows no differences among places, times, cultures, conditions, movements. Words that should possess a depth and breadth of allusions—words like *socialism, communism, democracy, collectivism*—are stripped of their historical roots, the many faces of the struggles for social justice and independence reduced to an ambition to dominate the world.

Is there a connection between this state of mind—the Cold War mentality, the attribution of all our problems to an external enemy—and a form of feminism so focused on male evil and female victimization that it, too, allows for no differences among women, men, places, times, cultures, conditions, classes, movements? Living in the climate of an enormous either/or, we absorb some of it unless we actively take heed.

In the United States large numbers of people have been cut off from their own process and movement. We have been hearing for forty years that we are the guardians of freedom, while "behind the Iron Curtain" all is duplicity and manipulation, if not sheer terror. Yet the legacy of fear lingering after the witch hunts of the fifties hangs on like the aftersmell of a burning. The sense of obliquity, mystery, paranoia surrounding the American Communist party after the Krushchev Report of 1956: the party lost 30,000 members within weeks, and a few who remained were talking about it. To be a Jew, a homosexual, any kind of marginal person was to be liable for suspicion of being "Communist." A blanketing snow had begun to drift over the radical history of the United States.

And, though parts of the North American feminist movement actually sprang from the black movements of the sixties and the student left, feminists have suffered not only from the burying and distortion of women's experience, but from the overall burying and distortion of the great movements for social change.[14]

The first American woman astronaut is interviewed by the liberal-feminist editor of a mass-circulation women's magazine. She is a splendid creature, healthy, young, thick dark head of hair, scientific degrees from an elite university, an athletic self-confidence. She is also white. She speaks of the future of space, the potential uses of space colonies by private industry, especially for producing materials which can be advantageously processed under conditions of weightlessness. Pharmaceuticals, for example. By extension one thinks of chemicals. Neither of these two spirited women speak of the alliances between the military and the "private" sector of the North American economy. Nor do they speak of Depo-Provera, Valium, Librium, napalm, dioxin. *When big companies decide that it's now to their advantage to put a lot of their money into production of materials in space . . . we'll really get the funding we need,* says the astronaut. No mention of who "we" are and what "we" need funding for; no questions about the

13. [Lillian Smith, "Autobiography as a Dialogue between King and Corpse," in *The Winner Names the Age*, ed. Michelle Cliff (New York: Norton, 1978) 189.]
14. [See Elly Bulkin, "Hard Ground: Jewish Identity, Racism, and Anti-Semitism," in E. Bulkin, M.B. Pratt, and B. Smith, *Yours in Struggle: Three Feminist Perspectives on Anti-Semitism and Racism* (Brooklyn, NY: Long Haul, 1984; distributed by Firebrand Books, 141 The Commons, Ithaca, NY, 14850).]

poisoning and impoverishment of women here on earth or of the earth itself. Women, too, may leave the earth behind.[15]

The astronaut is young, feels her own power, works hard for her exhilaration. She has swung out over the earth and come back, one more time passed all the tests. It's not that I expect her to come back to earth as Cassandra.[16] But this experience of hers has nothing as yet to do with the liberation of women. A female proletariat—uneducated, ill nourished, unorganized, and largely from the Third World—will create the profits which will stimulate the "big companies" to invest in space.

On a split screen in my brain I see two versions of her story: the backward gaze through streaming weightlessness to the familiar globe, pale blue and green and white, the strict and sober presence of it, the true intuition of relativity battering the heart;

and the swiftly calculated move to a farther suburb, the male technocrats and the women they have picked and tested, leaving the familiar globe behind: the toxic rivers, the cancerous wells, the strangled valleys, the closed-down urban hospitals, the shattered schools, the atomic desert blooming, the lilac suckers run wild, the blue grape hyacinths spreading, the ailanthus and kudzu doing their final desperate part—the beauty that won't travel, that can't be stolen away.

A movement for change lives in feelings, actions, and words. Whatever circumscribes or mutilates our feelings makes it more difficult to act, keeps our actions reactive, repetitive: abstract thinking, narrow tribal loyalties, every kind of self-righteousness, the arrogance of believing ourselves at the center. It's hard to look back on the limits of my understanding a year, five years ago—how did I look without seeing, hear without listening? It can be difficult to be generous to earlier selves, and keeping faith with the continuity of our journeys is especially hard in the United States, where identities and loyalties have been shed and replaced without a tremor, all in the name of becoming "American." Yet how, except through ourselves, do we discover what moves other people to change? Our old fears and denials—what helps us let go of them? What makes us decide we have to re-educate ourselves, even those of us with "good" educations? A politicized life ought to sharpen both the senses and the memory.

The difficulty of saying I—a phrase from the East German novelist Christa Wolf.[17] But once having said it, as we realize the necessity to go further, isn't there a difficulty of saying "we"? You cannot speak for me. I cannot speak for us. Two thoughts: there is no liberation that only knows how to say "I"; there is no collective movement that speaks for each of us all the way through.

And so even ordinary pronouns become a political problem.[18]

- 64 cruise missiles in Greenham Common and Molesworth.
- 112 at Comiso.
- 96 Pershing II missiles in West Germany.
- 96 for Belgium and the Netherlands.

15. [Ms. (January 1984): 86.]
16. A legendary Greek woman who was endowed with the gift of prophecy. She predicted disasters but was destined never to be believed.
17. [Christa Wolf, The Quest for Christa T, trans. Christo-
pher Middleton (New York: Farrar, Straus & Giroux, 1970), 174.]
18. [See Bernice Reagon, "Turning the Century," in Barbara Smith 356–368; Bulkin 103, 190–193.]

That is the projection for the next few years.[19]

- Thousands of women, in Europe and the United States, saying *no* to this and to the militarization of the world.

An approach which traces militarism back to patriarchy and patriarchy back to the fundamental quality of maleness can be demoralizing and even paralyzing. . . . Perhaps it is possible to be less fixed on the discovery of "original causes." It might be more useful to ask, How do these values and behaviors get repeated generation after generation?[20]

The valorization of manliness and masculinity. The armed forces as the extreme embodiment of the patriarchal family. The archaic idea of women as a "home front" even as the missiles are deployed in the backyards of Wyoming and Mutlangen. The growing urgency that an anti-nuclear, anti-militarist movement must be a feminist movement, must be a socialist movement, must be an antiracist, antiimperialist movement. That it's not enough to fear for the people we know, our own kind, ourselves. Nor it is empowering to give ourselves up to abstract terrors of pure annihilation. The antinuclear, antimilitary movement cannot sweep away the missiles as a movement to save white civilization in the West.

The movement for change is a changing movement, changing itself, demasculinizing itself, de-Westernizing itself, becoming a critical mass that is saying in so many different voices, languages, gestures, actions: *It must change; we ourselves can change it.*

We who are not the same. We who are many and do not want to be the same.

Trying to watch myself in the process of writing this, I keep coming back to something Sheila Rowbotham, the British socialist feminist, wrote in *Beyond the Fragments*:

A movement helps you to overcome some of the oppressive distancing of theory and this has been a . . . continuing creative endeavour of women's liberation. But some paths are not mapped and our footholds vanish. . . . I see what I'm writing as part of a wider claiming which is beginning. I am part of the difficulty myself. The difficulty is not out there.[21]

My difficulties, too, are not out there—except in the social conditions that make all this necessary. I do not any longer *believe*—my feelings do not allow me to believe—that the white eye sees from the center. Yet I often find myself thinking as if I still believed that were true. Or, rather, my thinking stands still. I feel in a state of arrest, as if my brain and heart were refusing to speak to each other. My brain, a woman's brain, has exulted in breaking the taboo against women thinking, has taken off on the wind, saying, *I am the woman who asks the questions*. My heart has been learning in a much more humble and laborious way, learning that feelings are useless without facts, that all privilege is ignorant at the core.

The United States has never been a white country, though it has long served what white men defined as their interests. The Mediterranean was never white. England, northern Europe, if ever absolutely white, are so no longer. In a Leftist bookstore in Manchester, England, a Third World poster: *WE ARE HERE BECAUSE YOU WERE THERE*. In Europe there have always been the Jews, the original ghetto

---

19. [Information as of May 1984, thanks to the War Resisters League.]

20. [Cynthia Enloe, *Does Khaki Become You? The Militarization of Women's Lives* (London: Pluto Press, 1983), ch. 8.]

21. [Sheila Rowbotham, Lynne Segal, and Hilary Wainwright, *Beyond the Fragments: Feminism and the Making of Socialism* (Boston: Alyson, 1981), 55–56.]

dwellers, identified as a racial type, suffering under pass laws and special entry taxes, enforced relocations, massacres: the scapegoats, the aliens, never seen as truly European but as part of that darker world that must be controlled, eventually exterminated. Today the cities of Europe have new scapegoats as well: the diaspora from the old colonial empires. Is anti-Semitism the model for racism, or racism for anti-Semitism? Once more, where does the question lead us? Don't we have to start here, where we are, forty years after the Holocaust, in the churn of Middle Eastern violence, in the midst of decisive ferment in South Africa—not in some debate over origins and precedents, but in the recognition of simultaneous oppressions?

I've been thinking a lot about the obsession with origins. It seems a way of stopping time in its tracks. The sacred Neolithic triangles, the Minoan vases with staring eyes and breasts, the female figurines of Anatolia—weren't they concrete evidence of a kind, like Sappho's fragments,[22] for earlier woman-affirming cultures, cultures that enjoyed centuries of peace? But haven't they also served as arresting images, which kept us attached and immobilized? Human activity didn't stop in Crete or Çatal Hüyük. We can't build a society free from domination by fixing our sights backward on some long-ago tribe or city.

The continuing spiritual power of an image lives in the interplay between what it reminds us of—what it *brings to mind*—and our own continuing actions in the present. When the labrys becomes a badge for a cult of Minoan goddesses, when the wearer of the labrys has ceased to ask herself what she is doing on this earth, where her love of women is taking her, the labrys, too, becomes abstraction—lifted away from the heat and friction of human activity. The Jewish star on my neck must serve me both for reminder and as a goad to continuing and changing responsibility.

When I learn that in 1913, mass women's marches were held in South Africa which caused the rescinding of entry permit laws; that in 1956, 20,000 women assembled in Pretoria to protest pass laws for women,[23] that resistance to these laws was carried out in remote country villages and punished by shootings, beatings, and burnings; that in 1959, 2,000 women demonstrated in Durban against laws which provided beerhalls for African men and criminalized women's traditional home brewing; that at one and the same time, African women have played a major role alongside men in resisting apartheid, I have to ask myself why it took me so long to learn these chapters of women's history, why the leadership and strategies of African women have been so unrecognized as theory in action by white Western feminist thought. (And in a book by two men, entitled *South African Politics* and published in 1982, there is one entry under "Women" [franchise] and no reference anywhere to women's political leadership and mass actions.)[24]

When I read that a major strand in the conflicts of the past decade in Lebanon has been political organizing by women of women, across class and tribal and religious lines, women working and teaching together within refugee camps and armed

---

22. Sappho (610?–580 B.C.E.) was an ancient poet from Lesbos whose only extant verse exists in fragments.
23. In 1956 the South African, apartheid government attempted to require black women to carry pass books that would identify them and serve to restrict their movement to certain locations. Black men were already required to carry these books.
24. [*Women Under Apartheid* (London: International

Defence and Aid Fund for Southern Africa in cooperation with the United Nations Centre Against Apartheid, 1981) 87–99; Leonard Thompson and Andrew Prior, *South African Politics* (New Haven, Conn.: Yale University Press, 1982). An article in *Sechaba* (published by the African National Congress) refers to "the rich tradition of organization and mobilization by women" in the Black South African struggle ([October 1984]: 9).]

communities, and of the violent undermining of their efforts through the civil war and the Israeli invasion, I am forced to think.[25] Iman Khalife, the young teacher who tried to organize a silent peace march on the Christian-Moslem border of Beirut—a protest which was quelled by the threat of a massacre of the participants—Iman Khalife and women like her do not come out of nowhere. But we Western feminists, living under other kinds of conditions, are not encouraged to know this background.

And I turn to Etel Adnan's brief, extraordinary novel *Sitt Marie Rose,* about a middle-class Christian Lebanese woman tortured for joining the Palestinian Resistance, and read:

> She was also subject to another great delusion believing that women are protected from repression, and that the leaders considered political fights to be strictly between males. In fact, with women's greater access to certain powers, they began to watch them more closely, and perhaps with even greater hostility. Every feminine act, even charitable and seemingly unpolitical ones, were regarded as a rebellion in this world where women had always played servile roles. Marie Rose inspired scorn and hate long before the fateful day of her arrest.[26]

Across the curve of the earth, there are women getting up before dawn, in the blackness before the point of light, in the twilight before sunrise; there are women rising earlier than men and children to break the ice, to start the stove, to put up the pap, the coffee, the rice, to iron the pants, to braid the hair, to pull the day's water up from the well, to boil water for tea, to wash the children for school, to pull the vegetables and start the walk to market, to run to catch the bus for work that is paid. I don't know when most women sleep. In big cities at dawn women are traveling home after cleaning offices all night, or waxing the halls of hospitals, or sitting up with the old and sick and frightened at the hour when death is supposed to do its work.

In Peru: "Women invest hours in cleaning tiny stones and chaff out of beans, wheat, and rice; they shell peas and clean fish and grind spices in small mortars. They buy bones or tripe at the fish market and cook cheap, nutritious soups. They repair clothes until they will not sustain another patch. They . . . search . . . out the cheapest school uniforms, payable in the greatest number of installments. They trade old magazines for plastic washbasins and buy secondhand toys and shoes. They walk long distances to find a spool of thread at a slightly lower price."[27]

This is the working day that has never changed, the unpaid female labor which means the survival of the poor.

In minimal light I see her, over and over, her inner clock pushing her out of bed with her heavy and maybe painful limbs, her breath breathing life into her stove, her house, her family, taking the last cold swatch of night on her body, meeting the sudden leap of the rising sun.

In my white North American world they have tried to tell me that this woman—politicized by intersecting forces—doesn't think and reflect on her life. That her ideas are not real ideas like those of Karl Marx and Simone de Beauvoir.[28] That her calculations, her spiritual philosophy, her gifts for law and ethics, her daily emergency political

25. [Helen Wheatley, "Palestinian Women in Lebanon: Targets of Repression," *TWANAS, Third World Student Newspaper,* University of California, Santa Cruz (March 1984).]

26. [Etel Adnan, *Sitt Marie Rose,* trans. Georgina Kleege (Sausalito, CA: Post Apollo Press, 1982), 101.]

27. [Blanca Figuera and Jeanine Anderson, "Women in Peru," *International Reports: Women and Society* (1981).

See also Ximena Bunster and Elsa M. Chaney, *Sellers and Servants: Working Women in Lima, Peru* (New York: Praeger, 1985), and Madhu Kishwar and Ruth Vanita, *In Search of Answers: Indian Women's Voices from "Manushi"* (London: Zed, 1984) 56–57.]

28. Simone de Beauvoir (1908–1986) was a French existentialist philosopher, writer, and feminist.

decisions are merely instinctual or conditioned reactions. That only certain kinds of people can make theory; that the white-educated mind is capable of formulating everything; that white middle-class feminism can know for "all women"; that only when a white mind formulates is the formulation to be taken seriously.

In the United States, white-centered theory has not yet adequately engaged with the texts—written, printed, and widely available—which have been for a decade or more formulating the political theory of black American feminism: the Combahee River Collective statement, the essays and speeches of Gloria I. Joseph, Audre Lorde, Bernice Reagon, Michele Russell, Barbara Smith, June Jordan, to name a few of the most obvious.[29] White feminists have read and taught from the anthology *This Bridge Called My Back: Writings by Radical Women of Color,* yet often have stopped at perceiving it simply as an angry attack on the white women's movement. So white feelings remain at the center. And, yes, I need to move outward from the base and center of my feelings, but with a corrective sense that my feelings are not *the* center of feminism.[30]

And if we read Audre Lorde or Gloria Joseph or Barbara Smith, do we understand that the intellectual roots of this feminist theory are not white liberalism or white Euro-American feminism, but the analyses of Afro-American experience articulated by Sojourner Truth, W.E.B. Du Bois, Ida B. Wells-Barnett, C.L.R. James, Malcolm X, Lorraine Hansberry, Fannie Lou Hamer, among others?[31] That black feminism cannot be marginalized and circumscribed as simply a response to white feminist racism or an augmentation of white feminism; that it is an organic development of the black movements and philosophies of the past, their practice and their printed writings? (And that, increasingly, black American feminism is actively in dialogue with other movements of women of color within and beyond the United States?)

To shrink from or dismiss that challenge can only isolate white feminism from the other great movements for self-determination and justice within and against which women define ourselves.

Once again: Who is *we?*

This is the end of these notes, but it is not an ending.   1984

⊰ Diving into the Wreck ⊱

First having read the book of myths,
and loaded the camera,
and checked the edge of the knife-blade,
I put on
5   the body-armor of black rubber
the absurd flippers
the grave and awkward mask.
I am having to do this

29. Gloria I. Joseph is an African-American feminist critic; Audre Lorde (1934–1992) was an African-American poet; Bernice Johnson Reagon (born 1942) is an African-American writer and the originator of the feminist gospel choir Sweet Honey in the Rock; Michele Russell and Barbara Smith (born 1946) are African-American feminist critics; June Jordan (born 1936) is an African-American poet. 30. [Gloria Anzaldúa and Cherríe Moraga, eds., *This Bridge Called My Back: Writings by Radical Women of Color* (Watertown, MA: Persephone, 1981; distributed by Kitchen Table/Women of Color Press, Albany, New York).]

31. Sojourner Truth (1797?–1883) was a black orator and abolitionist; W.E.B. DuBois (1868–1963) was an African-American educator and writer; Ida B. Wells-Barnett (1862–1931) was an African-American journalist and anti-lynching activist; C.L.R. James (1901–1989) was a socialist revolutionary from Trinidad; Malcolm X (1922–1965) was a civil rights activist and leader of the Black Muslims; Lorraine Hansberry (1930–1965) was an African-American playwright; Fannie Lou Hamer (1917–1977) was a civil rights activist.

not like Cousteau with his
10   assiduous team
aboard the sun-flooded schooner
but here alone.

There is a ladder.
The ladder is always there
15   hanging innocently
close to the side of the schooner.
We know what it is for,
we who have used it.
Otherwise
20   it is a piece of maritime floss
some sundry equipment.

I go down.
Rung after rung and still
the oxygen immerses me
25   the blue light
the clear atoms
of our human air.
I go down.
My flippers cripple me,
30   I crawl like an insect down the ladder
and there is no one
to tell me when the ocean
will begin.

First the air is blue and then
35   it is bluer and then green and then
black I am blacking out and yet
my mask is powerful
it pumps my blood with power
the sea is another story
40   the sea is not a question of power
I have to learn alone
to turn my body without force
in the deep element.

And now: it is easy to forget
45   what I came for
among so many who have always
lived here
swaying their crenellated fans
between the reefs
50   and besides
you breathe differently down here.

I came to explore the wreck.
The words are purposes.
The words are maps.
55   I came to see the damage that was done
and the treasures that prevail.
I stroke the beam of my lamp

slowly along the flank
of something more permanent
60   than fish or weed

the thing I came for:
the wreck and not the story of the wreck
the thing itself and not the myth
the drowned face always staring
65   toward the sun
the evidence of damage
worn by salt and sway into this threadbare beauty
the ribs of the disaster
curving their assertion
70   among the tentative haunters.

This is the place.
And I am here, the mermaid whose dark hair
streams black, the merman in his armored body
We circle silently
75   about the wreck
we dive into the hold.
I am she: I am he

whose drowned face sleeps with open eyes
whose breasts still bear the stress
80   whose silver, copper, vermeil cargo lies
obscurely inside barrels
half-wedged and left to rot
we are the half-destroyed instruments
that once held to a course
85   the water-eaten log
the fouled compass

We are, I am, you are
by cowardice or courage
the one who find our way
90   back to this scene
carrying a knife, a camera
a book of myths
in which
our names do not appear.   *1972/1973*

⊰ *from* Inscriptions ⊱

ONE: COMRADE

Little as I knew you I know you: little as you knew me you
          know me
—that's the light we stand under when we meet.
I've looked into flecked jaws
5   walked injured beaches footslick in oil

watching licked birds stumble in flight
while you drawn through the pupil of your eye
across your own oceans in visionary pain and in relief
headlong and by choice took on the work of charting
10   your city's wounds ancient and fertile
listening for voices within and against.
My testimony: yours: Trying to keep faith
not with each other exactly yet it's the one known and unknown
who stands for, imagines the other   with whom faith could
15   be kept.

In city your mind burns wanes waxes with hope
(no stranger to bleakness you: worms have toothed at
          your truths
but you were honest regarding that).
20   You conspired to compile the illegal discography
of songs forbidden to sing or to be heard.
If there were ethical flowers one would surely be yours
and I'd hand it to you headlong across landmines
across city's whyless sleeplight I'd hand it
25   purposefully, with love, and a hand trying to keep beauty afloat
on the bacterial waters.

When a voice learns to sing it can be heard as dangerous
when a voice learns to listen it can be heard as desperate.
The self unlocked to many selves.
30   A mirror handed to one who just released
from the locked ward from solitary from preventive detention
sees in her thicket of hair her lost eyebrows
whole populations.
One who discharged from war stares in the looking-glass of home
35   at what he finds there, sees in the undischarged tumult of his
          own eye
how thickskinned peace is, and those who claimed to promote it.

TWO: MOVEMENT

Old backswitching road bent toward the ocean's light
Talking of angles of vision   movements   a black or a red tulip
          opening
Times of walking across a street   thinking
not *I have joined a movement* but   *I am stepping in this deep current*
5   *Part of my life washing behind me   terror I couldn't swim with*
part of my life waiting for me   a part I had no words for
I need to live each day through   have them and know them all
though I can see from here where I'll be standing at the end.

—∙— ⇝✦⇜ —∙—

When does a life bend toward freedom?   grasp its direction?
10   How do you know you're not circling in pale dreams, nostalgia,
          stagnation

but entering that deep current   malachite, colorado
requiring all your strength wherever found
your patience and your labor
15   desire pitted against desire's inversion
all your mind's fortitude?
Maybe through a teacher: someone with facts with numbers
             with poetry
who wrote on the board: IN EVERY GENERATION ACTION FREES
20   OUR DREAMS.
Maybe a student: one mind unfurling like a redblack peony
quenched into percentile, dropout, stubbed-out bud
—Your journals Patricia: Douglas your poems: but the repeti-
             tive blows
25   on spines whose hopes you were, on yours:
to see that quenching and decide.

—And now she turns her face brightly on the new morning in
             the new classroom
new in her beauty her skin lashes her lively body:
30   *Race, class . . . all that . . . but isn't all that just history?*
Aren't people bored with it all?

She could be
myself at nineteen   but free of reverence for past ideas
ignorant of hopes piled on her   She's a mermaid
35   momentarily precipitated from a solution
which could stop her heart   She could swim or sink
like a beautiful crystal.

THREE: ORIGINS

Turning points.   We all like to hear about those.   Points
             on a graph.
Sudden conversions.   Historical swings.   Some kind of
             dramatic structure.
5   But a life doesn't unfold that way   it moves
in loops   by switchbacks loosely strung
around the swelling of one hillside toward another
one island toward another
A child's knowing   a child's forgetting   remain childish
10   till you meet them   mirrored and echoing   somewhere else
Don't ask me when I learned love
Don't ask me when I learned fear
Ask about the size of rooms   how many lived in them
             what else the rooms contained
15   what whispers of the histories of skin

Should I simplify my life for you?
The Confederate Women of Maryland
on their dried-blood granite pedestal incised
             IN DIFFICULTY AND IN DANGER . . .
20   "BRAVE AT HOME:"

—words a child could spell out
standing in wetgreen grass stuck full of yellow leaves
monumental women bandaging wounded men
Joan of Arc in a book   a peasant in armor
25   Mussolini   Amelia Earhart   the President on the radio[32]
        —what's taught, what's overheard

FOUR: HISTORY

Should I simplify my life for you?
Don't ask how I began to love men.
Don't ask how I began to love women.
Remember the forties songs, the slowdance numbers
5   the small sex-filled gas-rationed Chevrolet?
Remember walking in the snow and who was gay?
Cigarette smoke of the movies, silver-and-gray
profiles, dreaming the dreams of he-and-she
breathing the dissolution of the wisping silver plume?
10   Dreaming that dream we leaned applying lipstick
by the gravestone's mirror when we found ourselves
playing in the cemetery.   In Current Events she said
the war in Europe is over, the Allies
and she wore no lipstick have won the war
15   and we raced screaming out of Sixth Period.

Dreaming that dream
we had to maze our ways through a wood
where lips were knives breasts razors and I hid
in the cage of mind scribbling
20   *this map stops where it all begins*
into a red-and-black notebook.
Remember after the war when peace came down
as plenty for some and they said we were saved
in an eternal present and we knew the world could end?
25   —remember after the war when peace rained down
on the winds from Hiroshima Nagasaki Utah Nevada?[33]
and the socialist queer Christian teacher jumps from the
                hotel window?[34]
and L. G. saying *I want to sleep with you but not for sex*
30   and the red-and-black enamelled coffee-pot dripped slow through
                the dark grounds
        —appetite terror power tenderness
the long kiss in the stairwell the switch thrown
on two Jewish Communists married to each other[35]

---

32. Joan of Arc (1412–1431) was a Christian martyr and a French national hero; Benito Mussolini (1883–1945) was a Fascist and Italy's premier from 1923 to 1943; Amelia Earhart (1897–1937) was a U.S. aviator. "The President" refers to Franklin Delano Roosevelt (1882–1945), the thirty-second president of the United States.
33. Hiroshima and Nagasaki were Japanese cities bombed by the Allies during World War II; Utah and Nevada deserts provided nuclear testing sites.
34. A reference to F.O. Matthiessen (1902–1950), a Harvard professor who committed suicide in 1956 during the McCarthy era.
35. A reference to Julius (1918–1953) and Ethel (1915–1953) Rosenberg, who were executed in the U.S. in 1953 as alleged Russian spies.

35   the definitive crunch of glass at the end of the wedding?
        (*When shall we learn, what should be clear as day,*
        We cannot choose what we are free to love?)   *1993–94/1995*

❈

Ellen Kuzwayo
1914–

Called "the mother of Soweto" for her social work in South Africa's largest black township, ELLEN KUZWAYO is best known for her autobiography *Call Me Woman* (1985), which links her life to the struggle of her people. She has also published a collection of short stories, *Sit Down and Listen* (1990), contemporary narratives informed by African oral tradition. In all her writing Kuzwayo has spoken out against racism and sexism, which she views as related forms of oppression.

Born in Thaba Patchoa in the Orange Free State, Kuzwayo hails from a rural family once wealthy in stock and land, a family enlightened to the equality of the sexes; her grandparents worked side by side as partners on their farm. After her family was forcibly removed from their land, Kuzwayo lived in urban townships and attended black schools. She was married to an abusive husband from whom she eventually fled, seeking refuge with her mother-in-law and temporarily losing custody of her younger son. After serving a brief stint as "a disgruntled schoolteacher," she turned to social work. Between 1964 and 1976 she worked with Tsonga women in rural areas outside of Johannesburg, helping them adjust to resettlement by the apartheid government, which "made people squatters in the country of their birth"; she also helped the women produce food, improve sanitation, and combat their children's chronic dysentery. One of her greatest accomplishments was the founding of the Zomani Sisters' Council, an informal, cooperative credit union for black women, who produce goods collectively, pool money, and share debts.

In her sixties Kuzwayo returned to school to complete a graduate degree in social work at the University of the Witswatersrand. In 1977, at sixty-three, she was detained without trial and imprisoned under the so-called Terrorism Act, an experience that enhanced her feelings of solidarity with the young activists who instigated the Soweto uprisings of 1976. By this time progressive South Africans, both white and black, had become aware of her unswerving commitment to justice, and in 1979 the *Johannesburg Star*, a mainstream newspaper, named her Woman of the Year. During the 1980s Kuzwayo served as president of the Black Consumer Union of South Africa and as chairperson of the Maggie Magaba Trust, a philanthropic organization. Two documentary films have been made about her life, both directed by Betty Wolpert: *Awake from Mourning*, which presents Kuzwayo's views of social change; and *Tsiamelo: A Place of Goodness*, which explores her family's dislocation during the early years of apartheid. Since the first free elections took place in 1994, Kuzwayo has served as a member of the South African Parliament representing the African National Congress.

The last chapter of *Call Me Woman*, "Nkosi Sikelel'i Afrika," reviews the history of black South African women's resistance in Kuzwayo's lifetime. Women have long protested against apartheid, defied tradition by migrating to cities in search of their husbands, entered occupations not formally open to them, and challenged illiteracy. *Call Me Woman* reflects Kuzwayo's own philosophy of resistance and transformation. "We've just got to go on—even if we feel hopeless," she told an interviewer in the 1980s, the bleakest decade of the apartheid era. "We are people in this country, we are South Africans by birth and nobody can deny us this."

⊰ Nkosi Sikelel' i Afrika ⊱
(God Bless Africa)

Today, 22 October 1984, I am once more in London, completing this final chapter[1] and watching on television 7,000 police and military in a dawn raid surround and seal off the township of Sebokeng. Sebokeng has a population of 180,000 and has been the scene of massive student protest in the past few months, during which many young lives have been taken. The police and military are marching through the streets in full battledress, in platoons, with rifles at the ready. Hundreds of military lorries filled with more soldiers surround the township. 18,000 homes are being searched for "terrorists and agitators." It is as though a state of war has been declared against the entire black population. A massive demonstration of the mighty armed strength of the regime, against a defenceless, unarmed people. A show to create terror! The *Guardian* described this action as "the indiscriminate lashing out of an enraged, blinded cyclops." And the London *Times* commented "It would have been suicide for any of the people to resist at this time."

But does this mean an end to struggle? Looking back over the history of my people's resistance through this century, I know it cannot be. Here are but a few of the campaigns black women have been through:

> The 1913 Orange Free State Women's Anti-Pass Campaign, against the proposed extension of the pass system to women. They staved off the carrying of passes by women for more than 40 years. All the women who ran that campaign have died nameless and faceless.
>
> The 1956 Anti-Pass Campaign[2] culminating in a silent demonstration by 50,000 women from all over the country at the Union Building, Pretoria. They were contemptuously ignored by the government.
>
> The Defiance of Unjust Laws Campaign of 1952, in which women participated and served prison sentences, side by side with their men.
>
> The 1960 Sharpeville Massacre,[3] where once more women were killed and wounded with the menfolk.
>
> The 1976 uprising[4] in which young girls participated equally with young boys; and through which thousands of mothers suffered the disappearance, detention and death of their children, some of them as young as twelve years old.

The physical activities of a people can be temporarily contained, but the spirit behind that movement lives on forever. That alone, if nothing else, should be an inspiration for the black women. If we needed to be convinced again, two days after the massive display of military force by the authorities in October 1984, the children of Sebokeng again went into the streets to protest.

British television revealed the faces of the women of Sebokeng while their homes were being searched by the police, and the dignified, composed way they moved from room to room at the order of the armed officials on that fateful 23 October 1984. They shed no tears, showed no panic. They survived the ordeal.

---

1. This is the last chapter in her autobiography, *Call Me Woman*.
2. A campaign in which women protested the apartheid government's attempt to require black women to carry pass books that would identify them and serve to restrict their movement to certain locations. Black men were already required to carry these books.
3. A massacre that occurred when South African govern- ment troops opened fire on black union protestors who were demonstrating at first peacefully and then by throwing rocks. Sixty-nine protesters were killed, forty-eight of them women and children.
4. An uprising led by students in the township of Soweto who were protesting their inadequate education under apartheid.

When I look back over the history of women in South Africa as I have told it in this book and over the changes that have taken place in my own lifetime, I find myself amazed all over again, first by the extraordinary disabilities under which the women of my country have had to struggle, and then by the spirit with which so many of the challenges have been overcome.

These are the same women who over the past century have been compelled to remain home in the rural areas, penniless, faced with severe droughts, to mind the young and elderly, to till the land and raise flocks, as well as administer the neighbourhood and larger communities.

Gradually some of these very women decided to defy tradition and dare the cities, going first in search of their husbands, fathers, brothers, and sons, then becoming trapped in the urban economy. They were forced to accept domestic work and menial earnings.

Today women from rural areas come to the cities as migrant laborers like the men, on permits granted by their relevant "homeland governments." These women have to have their "homeland" passports or reference (identity) books endorsed monthly by government officials. You can see them in long queues at the beginning of every month at the segregated women's influx control office. These women are forced by poverty to leave the rural areas, and today they take jobs as road diggers or newspaper vendors as well as domestic servants.

New generations of black women have also brought about unprecedented transformation in the old loathed stereotype of the domestic servant. During the 1960s a kind of "trade union" called the Domestic Workers Employer Program (DWEP) was established. Leah Tutu (her husband, Bishop Tutu, won the Nobel Peace Prize in 1984. Leah deserves a good share of it) is director of this movement. In this program, run mostly from church halls in Johannesburg, Durban, Capetown and elsewhere, domestic workers are being trained in new skills such as fine sewing, cookery, literacy, money handling, car driving, first aid and other skills. The women of this movement are also fighting for living wages, paid annual leave, pension schemes, all of which have been denied to them in the past by their white employers.

Indeed, the determination and fortitude of black women pushes them to try their hand at everything. Now that the era of the computer is with us black women have joined such of the training programs as are open to them and became competent in handling keyboards and punch card machines.

So began a slow but steadfast growth in the number of black women cashiers in the large department stores in the city centres of South Africa. Today most of these stores employ predominantly black women. Whilst these women have arrived there on their own steam and thanks to their unquestioned efficiency, it is equally true that they save these white establishments thousands of rands, as their wages are far below those of their white counterparts.

Many black women are also tellers in different banks in the country, particularly those established in Soweto and other black townships in industrialized South Africa, and in the so-called "homelands." Building societies also employ a few black women, as tellers and in other skilled jobs.

A good number of black women are prominent in large industrial and commercial firms in cities and towns, at secretarial level, as personal secretaries, typists and receptionists. These numbers are not growing fast, as there are no properly run schools for such training.

Today as I look around me, I see that black women have broken into a whole range of new occupations; that they expect a great deal in their lives, such that young women of fifty years ago never dreamed of; and welcome their ambition as a very exciting, and overdue development.

But this dynamic process among black women, revolutionary as it is, brings with it its own complications. New achievements in employment for women brings women a new kind of equality with their menfolk, at work, at home and in the community. This situation has become a threat to some men.

The changing role of the urban black woman as she makes an increasing contribution towards the family income, even brings in more money than the husband, has added to the problems of family relationships. This factor hits at the root of the traditional acceptance of the man as the head of the family, and is made more complex by the cultural dimensions in the black community where the man has always been accorded a special authority as father and master, with his word the last in family decisions. Women are now taking a very firm stand against such behavior in their husbands, who often still expect their wives to accept in silence some of their most unacceptable practices. The men may completely refuse to listen to and reason with the women, even in matters very crucial to the existence of family life.

When such feelings of threat surface they can have serious effects between spouses. These may be so serious that the marriage survives only within a very unhealthy climate, for the spouses and their children alike, while in others it may even end in divorce courts. The divorce rates in Soweto and other similar black urban townships have risen in recent years (though there are many reasons for this, besides male resistance to the liberation of women!).

So in addition to the growing number of single women with children who for one reason or another have never been married, we also have growing numbers of divorced women in our community. They have at last won the right to own their homes in recent years: a major victory for black women.

Taking into consideration that the rate of illiteracy of the whole population is very high and that for generations black girls have had extra problems in entering schools the rate of illiteracy among women must therefore be higher than that among men. This fact makes the educational achievements of those women who have managed to excel all the more admirable. But it also underlines the need for more education, even at primary school level, for girls. This is a responsibility black women have made their own. For more than forty years our women have worked collectively, through small and large organizations, to improve educational and social facilities, for deprived urban communities in particular. Many of these organizations have already been mentioned in this book. But there are many others.

Orlando Mothers' Welfare Association, established in the early thirties, was the brain child of Mabel Ngakane, who was concerned about the growth of truancy and juvenile delinquency in the young Orlando of those years, the first township of Soweto. Among the issues she raised with the Non-European Affairs Department was the lack of recreational facilities—playgrounds and community centres—and the dearth of toilets in the center city for black women. It is striking that fifty years later there is very little improvement!

I remember too, how at the close of 1940s and the beginning of the 1950s black women in Soweto formed groups known as "Service Committees" to raise funds and equipment to build neighborhood creches to serve as day care centers for the children of working mothers. There are now about forty to fifty of these. These are far too few to meet the demands of the population of two million people, but the government of South Africa has never valued black children, and never offered any assistance for building more of these.

These organizations and several others mentioned earlier in this book sent representatives to an historic meeting held in Johannesburg on 17 March 1984. It was attended by about 250 women representing at least 50,000 members of various organizations, and unanimously resolved to established a "Black Consumer Union." The delegates referred to the great economic buying power of the millions of black people in South Africa who make up 75 percent of the population.

The black women in South Africa have shown outstanding tenacity against great odds. We shall never give in to defeat. Today we remain determined, like the women of our community of previous generations, who have left us a living example of strength and integrity.

Even now, at the age of seventy years, I tremble for what the future has in store for my grandchildren and those of their age group if things continue in the state in which they are at present. I am all the more determined to join the struggle, and fight with all the means I have at my disposal for change in my country so that the coming generations can enjoy a better life in their ancestor's country.

The commitment of the women of my community is my commitment—to stand side by side with our menfolk and our children in this long struggle to liberate ourselves and to bring about our *peace* and *justice* for all in a country we love so deeply.

The old Setswana proverb has come alive with a fresh meaning for me at this point:

> *Mmangoana o tshwara thipa ka fa bogaleng*

It means:

> "The child's mother grabs the sharp end of the knife."

Nkosi Sikelel' i Afrika
God Bless Africa.
1985

Rachel Speght
1597?–1630?

"Many propositions have you framed which (as you think) make much against women," wrote English polemicist RACHEL SPEGHT in 1617 to her adversary, Joseph Swetnam, "but if one would make a logical assumption, the conclusion would be flat against your own sex." Speght was one of only a few Englishwomen who participated publicly in the Jacobean pamphlet wars on the nature and status of women. These debates resembled in tone their medieval predecessors, which the French called the *querelles des femmes*. In 1615 Swetnam, a fencing instructor, published his scathing and somewhat confusing invective, *Arraignment of Lewd, Idle, Forward, and Unconstant Women*, under the pseudonym "Thomas Tell-Troth"; in it he posed as a cynical traveler struck by the many instances of women's depravity that he had witnessed or overheard. In her spirited response, *A Muzzle for Melastomus, The Cynical Baiter of, and Foul-mouthed Barker Against Eve's Sex*, Speght grounded her argument in scripture, invoking Biblical authority to vindicate women of the charges leveled against them. Indeed, she insisted that women were God's handiwork and Eve was Adam's equal.

Speght's date of birth remains uncertain because the Great Fire of 1666 in London destroyed most birth records in the city's churches. However, she appears to have been born around 1597, since she claimed in her preface to *A Muzzle for Melastomus* to have "not yet seen twenty years"; at the time of her marriage in 1621 she was 24. Her father, James Speght, a Calvinist minister, served as rector for two different London churches, St. Mary Magdalene and St. Clement. A writer whose pamphlets and sermons were published between 1613 and 1615, Speght probably supported his daughter's writing career, for it would have been difficult for her to publish without his permission. Little information exists regarding Speght's life after her marriage to William Procter, an Oxford graduate, but birth registrations for two Procter children, Rachel and William, suggest that she became a mother in 1626.

Speght's second publication, *Mortalities Memorandum* (1621), a long poem reflecting upon the meaning of death, was accompanied by *A Dream*, an allegorical dream vision. *Mortalities Memorandum* paid homage to the author's mother, who died shortly before it was published, and to her godmother, Mary Moundford. Although nothing is known of Speght's mother, her godmother was the wife of a prominent London physician, Thomas Moundford, a patron of King James's learned cousin Arbella Stuart. It is possible that Speght's belief in education for women was influenced by the Moundfords; clearly she herself had received a classical education, tutored either by her father or at one of the rare schools in existence for "young gentlewomen." However, as the scholar Barbara Lewalski points out, Speght reveals in the preface to *A Muzzle for Melastomus* that some "obviously gendered circumstance" caused the termination of her studies earlier than she would have liked.

In her preface to *Mortalities Memorandum* Speght acknowledges that not only did many readers of *A Muzzle for Melastomus* criticize her work, but many assumed that her father must have written it, a charge she vehemently denies. She recognizes, however, that censure is "inevitable to a public act," especially for a woman, and insists that her resistance to the scurrilous Swetnam—a "blackmouth," or slanderer—was justified. Again she condemns his tract as a "mingle-mangle invective against women" and labels its author a blasphemer against God's creation, "a fit scribe for the devil." In challenging Swetnam's misogyny, notes Lewalski, Speght became "the first English-woman to identify herself, by name, as a polemicist and critic of contemporary gender ideology."

◄ *from* A Muzzle for Melastomus, the Cynical Baiter of, and Foul-Mouthed Barker Against Eve's Sex, or an Apologetical Answer to That Irreligious and Illiterate Pamphlet Made by Joseph Swetnam and by Him Entitled "The Arraignment of Women" ►

The Epistle dedicatory to all virtuous ladies honorable or worshipful, and to all other of Eve's sex fearing God and loving their just reputation, grace and peace through Christ, to eternal glory.

It was the simile of that wise and learned Lactantius[1] that if fire, though but with a small spark kindled, be not at the first quenched, it may work great mischief and damage. So likewise may the scandals and defamations of the malevolent in time prove pernicious if they be not nipped in the head at their first appearance. The consideration of this, right honorable and worshipful ladies, hath incited me (though young, and the unworthiest of thousands) to encounter with a furious enemy to our sex, lest if his unjust imputations should continue without answer, he might insult and account himself a victor, and by such a conceit deal as historiographers report the viper to do (who in the winter time doth vomit forth her poison and in the spring

---

1. An early Christian writer of the third and fourth centuries.

time sucketh the same up again, which becometh twice as deadly as the former). And this our pestiferous enemy, by thinking to provide a more deadly poison for women than already he hath foamed forth, may evaporate by an addition unto his former illiterate pamphlet entitled *The Arraignment of Women* a more contagious obtrectation[2] than he hath already done, and indeed hath threatened to do.

Secondly, if it should have had free passage without any answer at all (seeing that *tacere* is *quasi consentire*)[3], the vulgar ignorant might have believed his diabolical infamies to be infallible truths not to be infringed, whereas now they may plainly perceive them to be but the scum of heathenish brains, or a building raised without a foundation (at least from sacred scripture), which the wind of God's truth must needs cast down to the ground.

A third reason why I have adventured to fling this stone at vaunting Goliath is to comfort the minds of all Eve's sex, both rich and poor, learned and unlearned, with this antidote, that if the fear of God reside in their hearts, maugre[4] all adversaries, they are highly esteemed and accounted of in the eyes of their gracious redeemer, so that they need not fear the darts of envy or obtrectators; for shame and disgrace, saith Aristotle, is the end of them that shoot such poisoned shafts. Worthy therefore of imitation is that example of Seneca[5], who when he was told that a certain man did exclaim and rail against him, made this mild answer: "Some dogs bark more upon custom than cursedness, and some speak evil of others not that the defamed deserve it, but because through custom and corruption of their hearts they cannot speak well of any." This I allege as a paradigmatical pattern for all women, noble and ignoble, to follow, that they be not inflamed with choler against this our enraged adversary, but patiently consider of him according to the portraiture which he hath drawn of himself (his writings being the very emblem of a monster).

This my brief apology, right honorable and worshipful, did I enterprise not as thinking myself more fit than others to undertake such a task, but as one who, not perceiving any of our sex to enter the lists of encountering with this our grand enemy among men (I being out of all fear, because armed with the truth—which though often blamed, yet can never be shamed—and the word of God's spirit, together with the example of virtue's pupils for a buckler), did no whit dread to combat with our said malevolent adversary. And if in so doing I shall be censured by the judicious to have the victory, and shall have given content unto the wronged, I have both hit the mark whereat I aimed and obtained that prize which I desired. But if Zoilus[6] shall adjudge me presumptuous in dedicating this my chirograph[7] unto personages of so high rank, both because of my insufficiency in literature and tenderness in years, I thus apologise for myself, that seeing the Baiter of women hath opened his mouth against noble as well is ignoble, against the rich as well as the poor, therefore meet it is that they should be joint spectators of this encounter. And withal, in regard to my imperfection both in learning and age, I need so much the more to impetrate patronage from some of power to shield me from the biting wrongs of Momus,[8] who oftentimes setteth a rankling tooth into the sides of truth. Wherefore I, being of Decius[9] his mind (who deemed himself safe under the shield of Ceasar), have presumed to

---

2. Slander.
3. Latin: "to remain silent is the same as to consent."
4. Despite.
5. Aristotle (384–322 B.C.E.) was a Greek philosopher and rhetorician; Seneca (4 B.C.E.–65 C.E.) was a stoic philosopher and poet.

6. A fourth-century B.C.E. Sophist and critic.
7. A penned work.
8. Greek god of satire.
9. A Roman senator who accompanied the statesman Julius Caesar (100–44 B.C.E.) to the senate on the day of his assassination.

shelter myself under the wings of you honourable personages against the persecuting heat of this fiery and furious dragon, desiring that you would be pleased not to look so much *ad opus*, as *ad animum*.[10] And so, not doubting of the favorable acceptance and censure of all virtuously affected, I rest

Your honors' and worships'
Humbly at commandment,
Rachel Speght.

THE PREFACE

Not unto the veriest idiot that ever set pen to paper, but to the cynical
baiter of women, or metamorphosed misogynist, Joseph Swetnam.

From standing water, which soon putrefies, can no good fish be expected, for it produceth no creatures but those that are venomous or noisome, as snakes, adders, and such like. Semblably, no better stream can we look should issue from your idle corrupt brain than that whereto the rough of your fury (to use your own words) hath moved you to open the sluice. In which excrement of your roving cogitations you have used such irregularities touching concordance, and observed so disordered a method, as I doubt not to tell you that a very accidence-scholar would have quite put you down in both. You appear herein not unlike that painter who, seriously endeavouring to portray Cupid's bow, forgot the string; for you, being greedy to botch up your mingle-mangle invective against women, have not therein observed in many places so much as grammar sense. But the emptiest barrel makes the loudest sound, and so we will account of you.

Many propositions have you framed which (as you think) make much against women; but if one would make a logical assumption, the conclusion would be flat against your own sex. Your dealing wants so much discretion that I doubt whether to bestow so good a name as the dunce upon you. But minority bids me keep within my bounds, and therefore I only say unto you that your corrupt heart and railing tongue hath made you a fit scribe for the devil.

In that you have termed your virulent foam "The Bear-baiting of Women," you have plainly displayed your own disposition to be cynical, in that there appears no other dog or bull to bait them but yourself. Good had it been for you to have put on that muzzle which St. James would have all Christians to wear: "Speak not evil one of another."[11] And then had you not seemed so like the serpent Porphyrus[12] as now you do (which, though full of deadly poison yet being toothless, hurteth none so much as himself). For you having gone beyond the limits not of humanity alone but of Christianity, have done greater harm unto your own soul than unto women, as may plainly appear. First, in dishonoring of God by palpable blasphemy, wresting and perverting every place of scripture that you have alleged, which by the testimony of St. Peter is to the destruction of them that so do. Secondly, it appears by your disparaging of, and opprobrious speeches against, that excellent work of God's hands, which in his great love he perfected for the comfort of man. Thirdly and lastly, by this your hodge-podge of heathenish sentences, similes, and examples, you have set forth yourself in your right colors

---

10. Latin: "to the work as to the motivation."
11. See James 4.6–11 in the Bible.

12. A deadly snake indigenous to India.

unto the view of the world, and I doubt not but the judicious will account of you according to your demerit. As for the vulgar sort, which have no more learning than you have showed in your book, it is likely they will applaud you for your pains.

As for your "bugbear" or advice unto women, that whatsoever they do think of your work they should conceal it, lest in finding fault they bewray their galled backs to the world (in which you allude to the proverb, "Rub a galled horse and he will kick"), unto it I answer by way of apology that, though every galled horse being touched doth kick, yet every one that kicks is not galled; so that you might as well have said that because burnt folks dread the fire, therefore none fear fire but those that are burnt, as made that illiterate conclusion which you have absurdly inferred.

In your title-leaf you arraign none but lewd, idle, forward, and unconstant women, but in the sequel (through defect of memory as it seemeth), forgetting that you had made a distinction of good from bad, condemning all in general, you advise men to beware of and not to match with any of these six sorts of women; *viz.* good and bad, fair and foul, rich and poor. But this doctrine of devils St. Paul, foreseeing would be broached in the latter times, gives warning of.

There also you promise a commendation of wise, virtuous, and honest women, whenas in the subsequent, the worst words and filthiest epithets that you can devise you bestow on them in general, excepting no sort of women. Herein may you be likened unto a man which upon the door of a scurvy house sets this superscription, "Here is a very fair house to be let," whereas the door being opened, it is no better than a dog-hole and dark dungeon.

Further, if your own words be true that you wrote with your hand but not with your heart, then are you an hypocrite in print. But it is rather to be thought that your pen was the bewrayer of the abundance of your mind, and that this was but a little mortar to daub up against the wall which you intended to break down.

The revenge of your railing work we leave to him who hath appropriated vengeance unto himself, whose pen-man hath included railers in the catalogue of them that shall not inherit God's kingdom, and yourself unto the mercy of that just judge who is able to save and to destroy.

Your undeserved friend,

Rachel Speght.

A MUZZLE FOR MELASTOMUS

Proverbs 18.22: He that findeth a wife findeth a good thing, and receiveth favor of the Lord.

If lawful it be to compare the potter with his clay, or the architect with the edifice, then may I in some sort resemble that love of God towards man in creating woman unto the affectionate care of Abraham for his son Isaac, who, that he might not take to wife one of the daughters of the Canaanites, did provide him one of his own kindred.[13]

Almighty God, who is rich in mercy, having made all things of nothing and created man in his own image (that is, as the apostle expounds it, "In wisdom, right-

---

13. See Genesis 24.4 in the Bible for the story of Isaac and his wife, Rebecca.

eousness, and true holiness,"[14] making him lord over all), to avoid that solitary condition that he was then in, having none to commerce or converse withal but dumb creatures, it seemed good unto the Lord that as of every creature he had made male and female, and man only being alone without mate, so likewise to form an helpmeet for him. Adam for this cause being cast into a heavy sleep, God, extracting a rib from his side, thereof made or built woman, showing thereby that man was an unperfect building afore woman was made, and, bringing her unto Adam, united and married them together.

Thus the resplendent love of God toward man appeared, in taking care to provide him an helper before he saw his own want, and in providing him such an helper as should be meet for him. Sovereignty had he over all creatures, and they were all serviceable unto him; but yet afore woman was formed there was not a meet help found for Adam. Man's worthiness not meriting this great favor at God's hands, but his mercy only moving him thereunto, I may use those words which the Jews uttered when they saw Christ weep for Lazarus: "Behold how he loved him."[15] Behold, and that with good regard, God's love, yea his great love which from the beginning he hath borne unto man; which as it appears in all things, so, next his love in Christ Jesus, apparently in this: that for man's sake, that he might not be an unit when all other creatures were for procreation dual, he created woman to be a solace unto him, to participate of his sorrows, partake of his pleasures, and as a good yoke-fellow bear part of his burden. Of the excellency of this structure (I mean of women), whose foundation and original of creation was God's love, do I intend to dilate.

> Of woman's excellency, with the causes of her creation, and of the sympathy which ought to be in man and wife each toward other.

The work of creation being finished, this approbation thereof was given by God himself, that "All was very good."[16] If all, then woman, who, excepting man, is the most excellent creature under the canopy of heaven. But if it be objected by any:

First, that woman, though created good, yet by giving ear to Satan's temptations, brought death and misery upon all her posterity.

Secondly, that "Adam was not deceived, but that the woman was deceived and was in the transgression."[17]

Thirdly, that St. Paul saith, "It were good for a man not to touch a woman."[18]

Fourthly and lastly, that of Solomon, who seems to speak against all of our sex: "I have found one man of a thousand, but a woman among them all have I not found" (whereof in its due place).[19]

To the first of these objections I answer that Satan first assailed the woman because where the hedge is lowest, most easy it is to get over, and she being the weaker vessel was with more facility to be seduced (like as a crystal glass sooner receives a crack than a strong stone pot). Yet we shall find the offense of Adam and Eve almost to parallel; for as an ambitious desire of being made like unto God was the motive which caused her to eat, so likewise was it his, as may plainly appear by that *ironia:* "Behold, man is become as one of us."[20] Not that he was so

---

14. A reference to St. Paul; see Ephesians 4.24.
15. See John 11.36.
16. See Genesis 1.31.
17. See 1 Timothy 2.14.
18. See 1 Corinthians 7.1.
19. See Ecclesiastes 7.28.
20. See Genesis 3.22.

indeed, but hereby his desire to attain a greater perfection than God had given him was reproved. Woman sinned, it is true, by her infidelity in not believing the word of God but giving credit to Satan's fair promises that "she should not die,"[21] but so did the man too. And if Adam had not approved of that deed which Eve had done, and been willing to tread the steps which she had gone, he, being her head, would have reproved her and have made the commandment a bit to restrain him from breaking his maker's injunction. For if a man burn his hand in the fire, the bellows that blowed the fire are not to be blamed, but himself rather for not being careful to avoid the danger. Yet if the bellows had not blowed, the fire had not burnt; no more is woman simply to be condemned for man's transgression. For by the free will, which before his fall he enjoyed, he might have avoided and been free from being burnt or singed with that fire which was kindled by Satan and blown by Eve. It therefore served not his turn a whit afterwards to say: "The woman which thou gavest me gave me of the tree, and I did eat."[22] For a penalty was inflicted upon him as well as on the woman, the punishment of her transgression being particular to her own sex and to none but the female kind; but for the sin of man the whole earth was cursed. And he, being better able than the woman to have resisted temptation because the stronger vessel, was first called to account, to show that to whom much is given, of them much is required: and that he who was the sovereign of all creatures visible should have yielded greatest obedience to God. . . .

To the second objection I answer that the Apostle doth not hereby exempt man from sin, but only giveth to understand that the woman was the primary transgressor and not the man; but that man was not at all deceived was far from his meaning, for he afterward expressly saith, that as "in Adam all die, so in Christ shall all be made alive."[23]

For the third objection . . . the Apostle makes it not a positive prohibition, but speaks it only because of the Corinthians' present necessity, who were then persecuted by the enemies of the church; for which cause and no other he saith, "Art thou loosed from a wife? Seek not a wife" (meaning whilst the time of these perturbations should continue in their heat),

> but if thou art bound, seek not to be loosed; if thou marriest thou sinnest not, only increasest thy care. For the married careth for the things of this world, and I wish that you were without care, that ye might cleave fast unto the Lord without separation. For the time remaineth that they which have wives be as though they had none; for the persecutors shall deprive you of them, either by imprisonment, banishment, or death.[24]

So that manifest it is that the Apostle doth not hereby forbid marriage but only adviseth the Corinthians to forbear a while till God in mercy should curb the fury of their adversaries. For, as Eusebius[25] writeth, Paul was afterward married himself, the which is very probable, being that interrogatively he saith.

> Have we not power to lead about a wife being a sister, as well as the rest of the Apostles, and as the brethren of the Lord, and Cephas?

---

21. See Genesis 3.4.
22. See Genesis 3.12.
23. See 1 Corinthians 15.22.
24. See 1 Corinthians 7.27–31.

25. Eusebius (260–340) was an early church historian; Speght uses his *Ecclesiastical History* to reinterpret St. Paul's views of women (see 1 Corinthians 9.5).

The fourth and last objection is that of Solomon. . . . For answer of which, if we look into the story of his life we shall find therein a commentary upon this enigmatical sentence included; for it is there said that Solomon had seven hundred wives and three hundred concubines, which number connexed make one thousand. These women, turning his heart away from being perfect with the Lord his God, sufficient cause had he to say that among the thousand women found he not one upright. He saith not that among a thousand women never any man found one worthy of commendation, but speaks in the first person singularly, "I have not found," meaning in his own experience. For this assertion is to be holden a part of the confessing of his former follies and no otherwise, his repentance being the intended drift of Ecclesiastes. . . .[26]

Woman was made . . . to be a companion and helper for man; and if she must be an helper, and but an helper, then are those husbands to be blamed which lay the whole burden of domestical affairs and maintenance on the shoulders of their wives. For as yoke-fellows they are to sustain part of each other's cares, griefs, and calamities. But as if two oxen be put in one yoke, the one being bigger than the other, the greater bears most weight; so the husband being the stronger vessel is to bear a greater burden than his wife. And therefore the Lord said to Adam, "In the sweat of thy face shalt thou eat thy bread, till thou return to the dust."[27] And St. Paul saith that "he that provideth not for his household is worse than an infidel."[28] Nature hath taught senseless creatures to help one another, as the male pigeon, when his hen is weary with sitting on her eggs and comes off from them, supplies her place, that in her absence they may receive no harm, until such time as she is fully refreshed. Of small birds the cock always helps his hen to build her nest, and while she sits upon her eggs he flies abroad to get meat for her, who cannot then provide any for herself. The crowing cockerel helps his hen to defend her chickens from peril, and will endanger himself to save her and them from harm. Seeing then that these unreasonable creatures by the instinct of nature bear such affection each to other that without any grudge they willingly, according to their kind, help one another, I may reason *a minore ad maius*[29] that much more should man and woman, which are reasonable creatures, be helpers each to other in all things lawful, they having the law of God to guide them, his word to be a lantern unto their feet and a light unto their paths, by which they are excited to a far more mutual participation of each other's burden than other creatures. So that neither the wife may say to her husband nor the husband unto his wife, "I have no need of thee,"[30] no more than the members of the body may so say each to other, between whom there is such a sympathy, that if one member suffer, all suffer with it. Therefore, though God bade Abraham forsake his country and kindred, yet he bade him not forsake his wife, who, being "flesh of his flesh, and bone of his bone"[31] was to be co-partner with him of whatsoever did betide him, whether joy or sorrow. Wherefore Solomon saith, "Woe to him that is alone";[32] for when thoughts of discomfort, troubles of this world, and fears of dangers do possess him, he wants a companion to lift him up from the pit of perplexity into which he is fallen; for a good wife, saith Plautus,[33] is the wealth of the mind and the welfare of

---

26. She argues that the book of Ecclesiastes focuses on male repentance for sexual promiscuity, not female imperfection.
27. See Genesis 3.19.
28. See 1 Timothy 5.8.

29. Latin: "from smaller to greater."
30. See 1 Corinthians 12.21.
31. See Genesis 21.12.
32. See Ecclesiastes 4.10.
33. Plautus (254–184 B.C.E.) was a Roman dramatist.

the heart, and therefore a meet associate for her husband; and "woman," saith
Paul, "is the glory of the man". . . .[34]   *1617*

⊷⊶ ⛧◈⛧ ⊷⊶

Mary Astell
1666–1731

A British polemicist, poet, and social theorist, MARY ASTELL was born in Newcastle-upon-
Tyne to Anglican and Tory parents; her father, Peter Astell, was a coal merchant and her
mother, Mary Errington, hailed from a wealthy family with financial interests in the coal
mines. She was educated at home by her uncle, Ralph Astell, a clergyman who taught his
niece philosophy, logic, and mathematics. In 1688 Astell moved to London, where she
wrote poetry dedicated to William Sancroft, the Archbishop of Canterbury, who assisted
her financially during her early years as a writer. She later would receive economic support
from Lady MARY WORTLEY MONTAGU, whose intellectual acumen and travel narratives
Astell admired and whose friendship she valued. In 1693 Astell began a correspondence
with John Norris, a Cambridge Platonist whose *Practical Discourses on Divine Subjects*
(1691–93) interested her; their correspondence was published in 1695 as *Letters Concerning
the Love of God*. Although her first original work, *A Serious Proposal to the Ladies* (1697),
was presented anonymously, Astell's authorial identity was widely known. In this polemic
she advocates the establishment of religious and educational institutions for Protestant
gentlewomen, utopian "seminaries" in which both learning and spirituality would reign.
Women could reside for as long as they liked in these seminaries, pursuing "a stock of solid
and useful Knowledge."

Astell's ideas in *A Serious Proposal to the Ladies* influenced several of her male contemporaries, particularly Daniel Defoe, who incorporated her thinking into his *Essay on Projects*
(1697), and Richard Steele, who, according to Germaine Greer, included over one hundred
pages of Astell's work in his book *The Ladies Library* (1714) without proper attribution. In
1697 Astell published a sequel to *A Serious Proposal,* a philosophical tract urging women to
undertake strenuous abstract thinking as a means of exercising their minds. She took up the
subject of marriage in her tract of 1700, *Some Reflections upon Marriage, Occasioned by the
Duke and Duchess of Magazine's Case.* In it she examines the misery and powerlessness experienced by women married to tyrannical men and characterizes the Duke as "an absolute Lord
and Master, whose follies all [his wife's] prudence cannot hide, and whose Commands she
cannot but despise." Unsurprisingly, Astell herself never married, and her denunciation of
marriage solidified her reputation as a resolute defender of women's autonomy. Despite her
liberal attitudes toward women, Astell was conservative politically, a lifelong supporter of
Tory causes and an opponent of Whig tolerance. Her later publications include *Moderation
Truly Stated* (1704), a philosophical interrogation of political extremism; *A Fair Way with the
Dissenters* (1704), an argument against the Whigs' belief in religious dissent; *An Impartial
Enquiry into the Causes of Rebellion and Civil War in this Kingdom* (1704), a defense of Charles
I; and *Bartlemy Fair or an Enquiry after Wit* (1709). In 1709 she and several associates estab-
lished a charity school for girls in Chelsea, affirming once more her progressive attitudes
toward women's education.

In *A Serious Proposal to the Ladies* Astell argues that friendship between women is among
life's most meaningful endeavors. Whereas marriage often reinforces the inequality of men

---

34. See 1 Corinthians 11.7.

and women, friendship occurs between two same-sex equals; thus it models virtue and piety. In the educational community of women whose establishment she supports, "we shall have the opportunity of contracting the purest and noblest Friendship; a Blessing, the purchase of which were richly worth all the World besides!"

⇥ *from* A Serious Proposal to the Ladies ⇤

LADIES,

Since the Profitable Adventures that have gone abroad in the World have met with so great Encouragement, tho' the highest advantage they can propose, is an uncertain Lot for such matters as Opinion, not real worth, gives a value to; things which if obtained are as flitting and fickle as that Chance which is to dispose of them; I therefore persuade my self, you will not be less kind to a Proposition that comes attended with more certain and substantial Gain; whose only design is to improve your Charms and heighten your Value, by suffering you no longer to be cheap and contemptible. Its aim is to fix that Beauty, to make it lasting and permanent, which Nature with all the helps of Art cannot secure, and to place it out of the reach of Sickness and Old Age. . . . Would have you all be wits, or what is better, Wise. Raise you above the Vulgar by something more truly illustrious, than a sounding Title or a great Estate. Would excite in you a generous Emulation to excel in the best things, and not in such Trifles as every mean person who has but Money enough may purchase as well as you. Not suffer you to take up with the low thought of distinguishing your selves by any thing that is not truly valuable, and procure you such Ornaments as all the Treasures of the Indies are not able to purchase. Would help you to surpass the Men as much in Virtue and Ingenuity, as you do in Beauty; that you may not only be as lovely, but as wise as Angels. Exalt and Establish your Fame, more than the best wrought Poems and loudest Panegyrics, by ennobling your Minds with such Graces as really deserve it. And instead of the Fustian Compliments and Fulsome Flatteries of your Admirers, obtain for you the Plaudit of Good Men and Angels, and the approbation of Him who cannot err. In a word, render you the Glory and Blessing of the present Age, and the Admiration and Pattern of the next.

And sure, I shall not need many words to persuade you to close with this *Proposal*. . . . Since you can't be so unkind to yourselves, as to refuse your *real* Interest, I only entreat you to be so wise as to examine wherein it consists; for nothing is of worse consequence than to be deceived in a matter of so great concern. 'Tis as little beneath your Grandeur as your Prudence, to examine curiously what is in this case offered you, and to take care that cheating Hucksters don't impose upon you with deceitful Ware. This is a Matter infinitely more worthy your Debates, than what Colors are most agreeable, or what's the Dress becomes you best. Your Glass will not do you half so much service as a serious reflection on your own Minds, which will discover Irregularities more worthy your Correction, and keep you from being either too much elated or depressed by the representations of the other. 'Twill not be near so advantageous to consult with your Dancing-Master as with your own Thoughts, how you may with greatest exactness tread in the Paths of Virtue, which has certainly the most attractive *Air*, and Wisdom the most graceful and becoming *Mien*: Let these attend you and your Carriage will be always well composed, and every thing you do will carry its Charm with it. No solicitude in the adornation of yourselves is discommended, provided you employ your care about that which is really your *self*; and do not neglect that particle of Divinity within you, which must survive, and may (if you please) be happy and perfect, when it's unsuitable and much inferior Companion is moldering into Dust. Neither will any pleasure be denied you, who are only desired not to catch at the Shadow and let the Substance go. You may be as ambitious as you please, so you aspire to the best things; and contend with your Neighbors as much as you can, that they may not outdo you in any commendable Quality. Let it never be said, That they to whom preeminence is so very agreeable, can be tamely content that others should surpass them in *this*, and precede them in a *better* World! Remember, I pray you, the famous Women of former Ages, the *Orinda's*[1] of late, and the more Modern Heroines, and blush to think how much is now, and will hereafter be said of them, when you yourselves (as great a Figure as you make) must be buried in silence and forgetfulness! Shall your Emulation fail *there only* where 'tis commendable? Why are you so preposterously humble, as not to contend for one of the highest Mansions in the Court of Heaven? . . . How can you be content to be in the World like Tulips in a Garden, to make a fine *show* and be good for nothing; have all your Glories set in the Grave, or perhaps much sooner! What your own sentiments are I know not, but I can't without pity and resentment reflect, that those Glorious Temples on which your kind Creator has bestowed such exquisite workmanship, should enshrine no better than *Egyptian* Deities; be like a garnished Sepulchre, which for all its glittering, has nothing within but emptiness or putrefaction! What a pity it is, that whilst your Beauty casts a luster all around you, your Souls which are infinitely more bright and radiant, . . . should be suffered to overrun with Weeds, lie fallow and neglected, unadorned with any Grace! . . . For shame let's abandon that Old, and therefore one would think, unfashionable employment of pursuing Butterflies and Trifles! No longer drudge on in the dull beaten road of Vanity and Folly, which so many have gone before us, but dare to break the enchanted Circle that custom has placed us in, and scorn the vulgar way of imitating all the Impertinencies of our Neighbors. Let us learn to pride ourselves in something more excellent than the invention of a Fashion; and not entertain such a degrading thought of our own *worth*, as to imagine that our Souls were given us only for the service of our Bodies, and that the best improvement we can make of these, is to attract the Eyes of Men. We value *them* too much, and our *selves* too little, if we place any part of our desert in their Opinion; and don't think our selves capable of Nobler Things than the pitiful Conquest of some worthless heart. She who has opportunities of making an interest in Heaven, of obtaining the love and admiration of GOD and Angels, is too prodigal of her Time, and injurious to her Charms, to throw them away on vain insignificant men. She need not make her self so cheap, as to descend to court their Applauses; for at the greater distance she keeps, and the more she is above them, the more effectually she secures their esteem and wonder. Be so generous then, Ladies, as to do nothing unworthy of you; so true to your Interest, as not to lessen your Empire and depreciate your Charms. Let not your Thoughts be wholly busied in observing what respect is paid you, but a part of them at least, in studying to deserve it. And after all, remember that Goodness is the truest Greatness; to be wise for yourselves the greatest Wit; and *that* Beauty the most desirable which will endure to Eternity.

Pardon me the seeming rudeness of this Proposal, which goes upon a supposition that there's something amiss in you, which it is intended to amend. My design is not to expose, but to rectify your Failures. To be exempt from mistake, is a privilege few

---

1. Orinda was the classical pseudonym used by the British poet Katherine Philips (1632–1664).

can pretend to, the greatest is to be past Conviction and too obstinate to reform. Even the *Men*, as exact as they would seem, and as much as they divert themselves with our Miscarriages, are very often guilty of greater faults, and such, as considering the advantages they enjoy, are much more inexcusable. But I will not pretend to correct their Errors, who either are, or at least *think* themselves too wise to receive Instruction from a Woman's Pen. My earnest desire is, That you Ladies, would be as perfect and happy as 'tis possible to be in this imperfect state, ... I would have you live up to the dignity of your Nature, and express your thankfulness to GOD for the benefits you enjoy by a due improvement of them: As I know very many of you do, who countenance that Piety which the men decry, and are the brightest Patterns of Religion that the Age affords; 'tis my grief that all the rest of our Sex do not imitate such Illustrious Examples, ... The Men perhaps will cry out that I teach you false Doctrine, for because by their seductions some amongst us are become very mean and contemptible, they would fain persuade the rest to be as despicable and forlorn as they. We're indeed obliged to them for their management, in endeavoring to make us so, who use all the artifice they can to spoil, and deny us the means of improvement. So that instead of inquiring why all Women are not wise and good, we have reason to wonder that there are any so. Were the Men as much neglected, and as little care taken to cultivate and improve them, perhaps they would be so far from surpassing those whom they now despise, that they themselves would sink into the greatest stupidity and brutality. The preposterous returns that the most of them make, to all the care and pains that is bestowed on them, renders this no uncharitable, nor improbable Conjecture. One would therefore almost think, that the wise disposer of all things, foreseeing how unjustly Women are denied opportunities of improvement from *without* has therefore by way of compensation endowed them with greater propensions to Virtue and a natural goodness of Temper within, which if duly managed, would raise them to the most eminent pitch of heroic Virtue. Hither, Ladies, I desire you would aspire, 'tis a noble and becoming Ambition, and to remove such Obstacles as lie in your way is the design of this Paper. We will therefore enquire what it is that stops your flight, that keeps you groveling here below, like *Domitian* catching Flies when you should be busied in obtaining Empires.

Altho' it has been said by Men of more Wit than Wisdom, and perhaps of more malice than either, that Women are naturally incapable of acting Prudently, or that they are necessarily determined to folly, I must by no means grant it; that Hypothesis would render my endeavors impertinent, for then it would be in vain to advise the one, or endeavor the Reformation of the other. Besides, there are Examples in all Ages, which sufficiently confute the Ignorance and Malice of this Assertion.

The Incapacity, if there be any, is acquired not natural; and none of their Follies are so necessary, but that they might avoid them if they pleased themselves. Some disadvantages indeed they labor under, and what these are we shall see by and by and endeavor to surmount; but Women need not take up with mean things, since (if they are not wanting to themselves) they are capable of the best. Neither God nor Nature have excluded them from being Ornaments to their Families and useful in their Generation; there is therefore no reason they should be content to be Ciphers in the World, useless at the best, and in a little time a burden and nuisance to all about them. And 'tis very great pity that they who are so apt to overrate themselves in smaller Matters, should, where it most concerns them to know and stand upon their Value, be so insensible of their own worth. The Cause therefore of the defects we labor under is, if not wholly, yet at least in the first place, to be ascribed to the mistakes of our Education, which like an Error in the first Concoction, spreads its ill Influence through all our Lives. [. . .]

Now as to the Proposal, it is to erect a *Monastery,* or if you will (to avoid giving offense to the scrupulous and injudicious, by names which tho' innocent in themselves, have been abused by superstitious Practices,) we will call it a *Religious Retirement,* and such as shall have a double aspect, being not only a Retreat from the World for those who desire that advantage, but likewise, an Institution and previous discipline, to fit us to do the greatest good in it; such an Institution as this (if I do not mightily deceive myself) would be the most probable method to amend the present and improve the future Age. For here those who are convinced of the emptiness of earthly Enjoyments, who are sick of the vanity of the world and its impertinencies, may find more substantial and satisfying entertainments, and need not be confined to what they justly loath. Those who are desirous to know and fortify their weak side, first do good to themselves, that hereafter they may be capable of doing more good to others; or for their greater security are willing to avoid *temptation,* may get out of that danger which a continual stay in view of the Enemy, and the familiarity and unwearied application of the Temptation may expose them to; and gain an opportunity to look into themselves to be acquainted at home and no longer the greatest strangers to their own hearts. Such as are willing in a more peculiar and undisturbed manner, to attend the great business they came into the world about, the service of GOD and improvement of their own Minds, may find a convenient and blissful recess from the noise and hurry of the World. . . .

You are therefore Ladies, invited into a place, where you shall suffer no other confinement, but to be kept out of the road of sin: You shall not be deprived of your grandeur, but only exchange the vain Pomps and Pageantry of the world, empty Titles and Forms of State, for the true and solid Greatness of being able to despise them. You will only quit the Chat of insignificant people for an ingenious Conversation; the froth of flashy Wit for real Wisdom; idle tales for instructive discourses. The deceitful Flatteries of those who under pretence of loving and admiring you, really served their *own* base ends for the seasonable Reproofs and wholsom Counsels of your hearty wellwishers and affectionate Friends, which will procure you those perfections your feigned lovers pretended you had, and kept you from obtaining. . . . Happy Retreat! which will be the introducing you into such a *Paradise* as your Mother *Eve* forfeited, where you shall feast on Pleasures, that do not like those of the World, disappoint your expectations, pall your Appetites, and by the disgust they give you put you on the fruitless search after new Delights, which when obtained are as empty as the former; but such as will make you *truly* happy *now*, and prepare you to be *perfectly* so hereafter. Here are no Serpents to deceive you, whilst you entertain yourselves in these delicious Gardens. No Provocations will be given in this Amicable Society, but to Love and to good Works, which will afford such an entertaining employment, that you'll have as little inclination as leisure to pursue those Follies, which in the time of your ignorance passed with you under the name of love, altho' there is not in nature two more different things, than *true Love* and that *brutish Passion* which pretends to ape it. Here will be no Rivaling but for the of Love of GOD, no Ambition but to procure his Favor, to which nothing will more effectually recommend you, than a great and dear affection to each other. Envy that Canker, will not here disturb your Breasts; for how can she repine at another's welfare, who reckons it the greatest part of her own? No Covetousness will gain admittance in this blessed abode, but to amass huge Treasures of good Works, and to procure one of the brightest Crowns of Glory.

You will not be solicitous to increase your Fortunes, but to enlarge your Minds, esteeming no Grandeur like being conformable to the meek and humble JESUS. So that you only withdraw from the noise and trouble, the folly and temptation of the world, that you may more peaceably enjoy yourselves, and all the innocent Pleasures it is able to afford you, and particularly that which is worth all the rest, a Noble Virtuous and Disinterested Friendship. . . . In fine, the place to which you are invited is a Type and Antepast of Heaven, where your Employment will be as there, to magnify GOD, to love one another, and to communicate that useful *knowledge*, which by the due improvement of your time in Study and Contemplation you will obtain, and which when obtained, will afford you a much sweeter and more durable delight, than all those pitiful diversions, those revellings and amusements, which now through your ignorance of better, appear the only grateful and relishing Entertainments.

But because we were not made for ourselves, nor can by any means so effectually glorify GOD and do good to our own Souls, as by doing Offices of Charity and Beneficence to others: . . . . your Retreat shall be so managed as not to exclude the good Works of an *Active*, from the pleasure and serenity of a *Contemplative* Life, but by a due mixture of both retain all the advantages and avoid the inconveniences that attend either. It shall not so cut you off from the world as to hinder you from bettering and improving it, but rather qualify you to do it the greatest Good, and be a Seminary to stock the Kingdom with pious and prudent Ladies, whose good Example it is to be hoped, will so influence the rest of their Sex, that Women may no longer pass for those little useless and impertinent Animals, which the ill conduct of too many has caused 'em to be mistaken for.   *1694*

—•—➤⧦✦⧧◄—•—

Sarah Fyge
1670–1723

Best known for her response to a misogynist treatise by Robert Gould, *Love Given O'er* (1683), SARAH FYGE claimed to have composed her spirited rebuttal in fourteen days at the youthful age of fourteen. In *The Female Advocate, or an Answer to a late Satyr against the Pride, Lust and Inconstancy, Etc. of Woman* (1686), "written by a lady in vindication of her sex," Fyge challenges the traditional interpretation of Genesis that blames Eve, and by extension all women, for the fall of humankind. Published anonymously with a preface signed "S.F.," *The Female Advocate* appeared as one of a series of replies to Gould's treatise, both serious and satirical, and received enough acclaim to be reissued in an expanded version in 1687.

Fyge was born in London to Mary Beacham and Thomas Fyge, a physician and city councilman who did not approve of his daughter's writing. Shortly after the second edition of *The Female Advocate* was published, Fyge sent his daughter to an isolated village, Shenley in Buckingham, to live with relatives whom she scarcely knew. Fyge refused to let her father's maltreatment go unmentioned; in a poem addressed to Lady Cambell she depicts her banishment as directly related to her art: "But ah! My Poetry, did fatal prove, / And robbed me of a tender Father's Love." Around 1687 Fyge was married, apparently against her will, to an attorney, Edward Field, who died in the mid-1690s. A wealthy, childless widow who might have chosen to remain single, Fyge instead married an older second cousin, Thomas Egerton, a clergyman with whom she lived unhappily. According to Germaine Greer, Fyge sued Egerton for divorce in 1703 on the grounds of cruelty and Egerton countersued, claiming adultery, in an attempt to win from Fyge and her father the estate she had inherited from Field. This spectacular set of divorce proceedings was recounted in grim and sometimes humorous detail by Fyge's literary rival DELARIVIER MANLEY, who in *The New Atalantis* (1704) portrayed Fyge pelting her husband with a hot apple pie. Despite such colorful publicity, the divorce was never finalized. Greer claims that Fyge was infatuated for much of her life with Field's former clerk, Henry Pierce, who appears in her poetry as Alexis.

Fyge's poems are collected in *Poems on Several Occasions, Together with a Pastoral* (1703), which was reissued in 1706. Three of her elegies on the death of John Dryden appeared in *The Nine Muses* (1700), a collection of verse edited by Manley. In "The Liberty," reprinted below, Fyge refuses to be silent because women are supposed to be, nor will she limit her work to "transcribing old Receipts of Cookery / . . . Good Cures for Agues, and a cancered Breast." Instead, "My daring Pen, will bolder Sallies make." Her resistance to the strictures placed on writing women made Fyge's life painful, as Greer notes. Indeed, the inscription on her tombstone "depicts Fyge as a victim of Fate, an image she often elaborated in her poetry":

> In vain I strove to be with quiet blessed;
> Various sorrows wrecked my destined breast,
> And I could only in the grave find rest.

❧ The Liberty ❧

Shall I be one of those obsequious Fools,
That square their lives, by Custom's scanty Rules;
Condemned forever, to the puny Curse,
Of Precepts taught, at Boarding-school, or Nurse,
5   That all the business of my Life must be,
Foolish, dull Trifling, Formality.
Confined to a strict Magic complaisance,
And round a Circle, of nice visits Dance,
Nor for my Life beyond the Chalk advance:[1]
10   The Devil Censure, stands to guard the same,
One step awry, he tears my ventrous[2] Fame.
So when my Friends, in a facetious Vein,
With Mirth and Wit, a while can entertain;
Tho' ne'er so pleasant, yet I must not stay,
15   If a commanding Clock, bids me away:
But with a sudden start, as in a Fright,
I must be gone indeed, 'tis after Eight.
Sure these restraints, with such regret we bear,
That dreaded Censure, can't be more severe,
20   Which has no Terror, if we did not fear;
But let the Bug-bear, timorous Infants fright,
I'll not be scared, from Innocent delight:
Whatever is not vicious, I dare do,
I'll never to the Idol Custom bow,
25   Unless it suits with my own Humor too.
Some boast their Fetters, of Formality,

---

1. According to Germaine Greer in *Kissing the Rod*, Fyge refers here to conjuring and necromance, in which a person is confined within a chalk circle in order to see apparitions outside it.
2. Adventurous.

Fancy they ornamental Bracelets be,
I'm sure their Gyves,[3] and Manacles to me.
To their dull fulsome Rules, I'd not be tied,
30   For all the Flattery that exalts their Pride:
My Sex forbids, I should my Silence break,
I lose my Jest, cause Women must not speak.
Mysteries must not be, with my search Profaned,
My Closet not with Books, but Sweet-meats crammed
35   A little *China*, to advance the show,
My *Prayer Book*, and seven *Champions*,[4] or so.
My pen if ever used employed must be,
In lofty Themes of useful Houswifery,
Transcribing old Receipts[5] of Cookery:
40   And what is necessary 'mongst the rest,
Good Cures for Agues, and a cancered Breast,
But I can't here, write my *Probatum est*.[6]
My daring Pen, will bolder Sallies make,
And like myself, an unchecked freedom take;
45   Not chained to the nice Order of my Sex,
And with restraints my wishing Soul perplex:
I'll blush at Sin, and not what some call Shame,
Secure my Virtue, slight precarious Fame.
This Courage speaks me, Brave, 'tis surely worse,
50   To keep those Rules, which privately we Curse:
And I'll appeal, to all the formal Saints,[7]
With what reluctance they endure restraints.   *1703*

Mary Wollstonecraft
1759–1797

"How much more respectable is the woman who earns her own bread by fulfilling any duty, than the most accomplished beauty!" claims MARY WOLLSTONECRAFT in *A Vindication of the Rights of Woman* (1792). Written during the French Revolution over a period of six weeks, this feminist treatise captures the revolutionary fervor of the times and offers an impassioned exposé of social and sexual injustice. As the daughter of a failed English gentleman farmer, Edward John Wollstonecraft, and a mother who showed preferential treatment to her eldest son, Wollstonecraft learned firsthand about injustice in a family torn by sexism, domestic violence, economic insecurities, and alcohol abuse. Educated sporadically at home, she left her family at the age of nineteen to work in Bath as the companion of an elderly widow, only to return several years later to nurse her mother through a long illness. Upon her mother's death Wollstonecraft sought refuge with the indigent family of her friend Fanny Blood, her primary source of comfort during her childhood. With her sister Everina and Fanny, she established a school for girls at Newington Green near London, an effort supported by the reformer Richard

---

3. Shackles.
4. An allusion to *The Seven Champions of Christendom* (c. 1597), a decorous romance.
5. Recipes.

6. A phrase indicating that a medicine has been tested and approved.
7. Those women who remain compliant.

Price. When Fanny, already ill with tuberculosis, moved to Portugal to marry her longtime suitor and became pregnant there, Wollstonecraft left England to assist with the delivery. Fanny's death in childbirth caused her friend a deep depression from which she spent years trying to recover. Returning to London to find that her financially distressed school had to be closed only deepened Wollstonecraft's malaise.

To meet the debts her school had incurred, Wollstonecraft wrote *Thoughts on the Education of Daughters* (1787), a series of conventional essays based on her experience as a teacher and an administrator. After working briefly in Ireland as a governess, she returned to London and became an editor and a translator of French and German texts; she also wrote essays for a radical publication, *Analytical Review*. In 1788 she published *Mary, A Fiction*, a sentimental novel, partly autobiographical, which implicitly challenges Jean-Jacques Rousseau's influential view of the inherent inequality of the sexes. That same year she wrote a children's book, *Original Stories from Real Life*. An immediate success; the collection was translated into German, and its second edition was illustrated by the poet and engraver William Blake. With funds earned from these books and from *The Female Reader* (1789), a volume of children's literature, Wollstonecraft made enough income to support her impoverished family and that of Fanny Blood.

Having come to espouse revolutionary beliefs, Wollstonecraft took issue with the statesman Edmund Burke's analysis in his 1790 treatise *Reflections on the Revolution in France;* the terms of her disagreement are set forth in *A Vindication of the Rights of Men* (1790). Hers was not the only critical response to Burke but was among the most fervent. Still, it was Wollstonecraft's 1792 sequel, *A Vindication of the Rights of Woman*, that brought her fame. Influenced by Catharine Macauley's *Letters on Education* (1790), *A Vindication* argues that women should be educated to use their reason and thereby prove themselves equal to men. Moreover, Wollstonecraft asserts that only major social reform can liberate women, reform that the rising British middle class must lead. She planned but never wrote a second volume on discriminatory laws related to women.

In 1793–94 Wollstonecraft lived in France, observing the upheaval and composing *A History and Moral View of the Origin and Progress of the French Revolution* (1794). During that time she fell in love with an American entrepreneur, Gilbert Imlay, with whom she had a daughter, Fanny. Having followed Imlay to London, feeling despondent over losing his affections, she attempted suicide but was prevented by Imlay from succeeding. Eager to be rid of Wollstonecraft and their child, he hired her to travel on business to Scandinavia. Wollstonecraft's account of traveling abroad with only her infant and a nurse was published in 1796 as *Letters from Scandinavia*. Upon returning to London she began a novel, *Maria, or the Wrongs of Woman*, a portrait of the lives of women governed by men who regard them as property; it was published posthumously, unfinished, in 1798. Wollstonecraft also began a relationship with the philosopher William Godwin, whom she married in 1797, shortly before her untimely death; she died of complications from childbirth after bearing another daughter, Mary, who grew up to become the writer MARY SHELLEY. To pay homage to his late wife, Godwin published a memoir of Wollstonecraft that praised her political writings and recounted her affair with Imlay. The unintended result was that Wollstonecraft earned a reputation as a licentious woman unworthy of note by proper Victorians; her writings thus fell into obscurity until their revival in the twentieth century.

Chapter nine of *A Vindication of the Rights of Woman* claims that only when society becomes more egalitarian will morality "gain ground." Women's first duty "is to themselves as rational creatures"; the second is to motherhood; the third, to good citizenship. If men would only desire "rational fellowship instead of slavish obedience," she concludes, "they would find us more observant daughters, more affectionate sisters, more faithful wives, more reasonable mothers—in a word, better citizens."

⊰ *from* A Vindication of the Rights of Woman ⊱

Chapter IX

Of the pernicious effects which arise from the unnatural distinctions established in society

From the respect paid to property flow, as from a poisoned fountain, most of the evils and vices which render this world such a dreary scene to the contemplative mind. For it is in the most polished society that noisome reptiles and venomous serpents lurk under the rank herbage; and there is voluptuousness pampered by the still sultry air, which relaxes every good disposition before it ripens into virtue.

One class presses on another; for all are aiming to procure respect on account of their property: and property, once gained, will procure the respect due only to talents and virtue. Men neglect the duties incumbent on man, yet are treated like demigods; religion is also separated from morality by a ceremonial veil, yet men wonder that the world is almost literally speaking, a den of sharpers or oppressors.

There is a homely proverb, which speaks a shrewd truth, that whoever the devil finds idle he will employ. And what but habitual idleness can hereditary wealth and titles produce? For man is so constituted that he can only attain a proper use of his faculties by exercising them, and will not exercise them unless necessity, of some kind, first set the wheels in motion. Virtue likewise can only be acquired by the discharge of relative duties; but the importance of these sacred duties will scarcely be felt by the being who is cajoled out of his humanity by the flattery of sycophants. There must be more equality established in society, or morality will never gain ground, and this virtuous equality will not rest firmly even when founded on a rock, if one half of mankind [be] chained to its bottom by fate, for they will be continually undermining it through ignorance or pride.

It is vain to expect virtue from women till they are, in some degree, independent of men; nay, it is vain to expect that strength of natural affection, which would make them good wives and mothers. Whilst they are absolutely dependent on their husbands they will be cunning, mean, and selfish, and the men who can be gratified by the fawning fondness of spaniel-like affection, have not much delicacy, for love is not to be bought, in any sense of the words, its silken wings are instantly shrivelled up when any thing beside a return in kind is sought. Yet whilst wealth enervates men; and women live, as it were, by their personal charms, how can we expect them to discharge those ennobling duties which equally require exertion and self-denial. Hereditary property sophisticates the mind, and the unfortunate victims to it, if I may so express myself, swathed from their birth, seldom exert the locomotive faculty of body or mind; and, thus viewing everything through one medium, and that a false one, they are unable to discern in what true merit and happiness consist. False, indeed, must be the light when the drapery of situation hides the man, and makes him stalk in masquerade, dragging from one scene of dissipation to another the nerveless limbs that hang with stupid listlessness, and rolling round the vacant eye which plainly tells us that there is no mind at home.

I mean, therefore, to infer that the society is not properly organized which does not compel men and women to discharge their respective duties, by making it the only way to acquire that countenance from their fellow creatures, which every human being wishes some way to attain. The respect, consequently, which is paid to wealth and mere personal charms, is a true northeast blast, that blights the tender blossoms of affection and virtue. Nature has wisely attached affections to duties, to sweeten toil, and to give that vigour to the exertions of reason which only the heart can give. But, the affection which is put on merely because it is the appropriated insignia of a certain character, when its duties are not fulfilled, is one of the empty compliments which vice and folly are obliged to pay to virtue and the real nature of things.

To illustrate my opinion, I need only observe, that when a woman is admired for her beauty, and suffers herself to be so far intoxicated by the admiration she receives, as to neglect to discharge the indispensable duty of a mother, she sins against herself by neglecting to cultivate an affection that would equally tend to make her useful and happy. True happiness, I mean all the contentment, and virtuous satisfaction, that can be snatched in this imperfect state, must arise from well regulated affections; and an affection includes a duty. Men are not aware of the misery they cause, and the vicious weakness they cherish, by only inciting women to render themselves pleasing; they do not consider that they thus make natural and artificial duties clash, by sacrificing the comfort and respectability of a woman's life to voluptuous notions of beauty, when in nature they all harmonize.

Cold would be the heart of a husband, were he not rendered unnatural by early debauchery, who did not feel more delight at seeing his child suckled by its mother, than the most artful wanton tricks could ever raise; yet this natural way of cementing the matrimonial tie, and twisting esteem with fonder recollections, wealth leads women to spurn.[1] To preserve their beauty, and wear the flowery crown of the day, [which] gives them a kind of right to reign for a short time over the sex, they neglect to stamp impressions on their husbands' hearts, that would be remembered with more tenderness when the snow on the head began to chill the bosom, than even their virgin charms. The maternal solicitude of a reasonable affectionate woman is very interesting, and the chastened dignity with which a mother returns the caresses that she and her child receive from a father who has been fulfilling the serious duties of his station, is not only a respectable, but a beautiful sight. So singular, indeed, are my feelings, and I have endeavored not to catch factitious ones, that after having been fatigued with the sight of insipid grandeur and the slavish ceremonies that with cumberous pomp supplied the place of domestic affections, I have turned to some other scene to relieve my eye by resting it on the refreshing green everywhere scattered by nature. I have then viewed with pleasure a woman nursing her children, and discharging the duties of her station with, perhaps, merely a servant maid to take off her hands the servile part of the household business. I have seen her prepare herself and her children, with only the luxury of cleanliness, to receive her husband, who returning weary home in the evening found smiling babes and a clean hearth. My heart has loitered in the midst of the group, and has even throbbed with sympathetic emotion, when the scraping of the well-known foot has raised a pleasing tumult.

Whilst my benevolence has been gratified by contemplating this artless picture, I have thought that a couple of this description, equally necessary and independent of each other, because each fulfilled the respective duties of their station, possessed all that life could give—raised sufficiently above abject poverty not to be obliged to weigh the consequence of every farthing they spend, and having sufficient to prevent their attending to a frigid system of economy, which narrows both heart and mind. I declare, so vulgar are my conceptions, that I know not what is wanted to render this the happiest as well as the most respectable situation in the world, but a taste for literature, to throw a little variety and interest into social converse, and some superfluous

1. She refers here to the practice of wet nursing employed by many upper-class women in England at this time.

money to give to the needy and to buy books. For it is not pleasant when the heart is opened by compassion and the head active in arranging plans of usefulness, to have a prim urchin continually twitching back the elbow to prevent the hand from drawing out an almost empty purse, whispering at the same time some prudential maxim about the priority of justice.

Destructive, however, as riches and inherited honors are to the human character, women are more debased and cramped, if possible, by them, than men, because men may still, in some degree, unfold their faculties by becoming soldiers and statesmen.

As soldiers, I grant, they can now only gather, for the most part, vain glorious laurels, whilst they adjust to a hair the European balance, taking especial care that no bleak northern nook or sound incline the beam. But the days of true heroism are over, when a citizen fought for his country like a Fabricius or a Washington, and then returned to his farm to let his virtuous fervor run in a more placid, but not a less salutary, stream.[2] No, our British heroes are oftener sent from the gaming table than from the plow; and their passions have been rather inflamed by hanging with dumb suspense on the turn of a die, than sublimated by panting after the adventurous march of virtue in the historic page.

The statesman, it is true, might with more propriety quit the Faro Bank, or card table, to guide the helm, for he has still but to shuffle and trick. The whole system of British politics, if system it may courteously be called, consisting in multiplying dependents and contriving taxes which grind the poor to pamper the rich; thus a war, or any wild goose chase, is, as the vulgar use the phrase, a lucky turnup of patronage for the minister, whose chief merit is the art of keeping himself in place. It is not necessary then that he should have bowels for the poor, so he can secure for his family the odd trick. Or should some show of respect, for what is termed with ignorant ostentation an Englishman's birthright, be expedient to bubble the gruff mastiff that he has to lead by the nose, he can make an empty show, very safely, by giving his single voice, and suffering his light squadron to file off to the other side. And when a question of humanity is agitated he may dip a sop in the milk of human kindness, to silence Cerberus,[3] and talk of the interest which his heart takes in an attempt to make the earth no longer cry for vengeance as it sucks in its children's blood, though his cold hand may at the very moment rivet their chains, by sanctioning the abominable traffic.[4] A minister is no longer a minister, than while he can carry a point, which he is determined to carry—yet it is not necessary that a minister should feel like a man, when a bold push might shake his seat.

But, to have done with these episodical observations, let me return to the more specious slavery which chains the very soul of woman, keeping her forever under the bondage of ignorance.

The preposterous distinctions of rank, which render civilization a curse, by dividing the world between voluptuous tyrants, and cunning envious dependents, corrupt, almost equally, every class of people, because respectability is not attached to the discharge of the relative duties of life, but to the station, and when the duties are not fulfilled the affections cannot gain sufficient strength to fortify the virtue of which they are the natural reward. Still there are some loopholes out of which a man

2. Fabricius was a Roman soldier who died in poverty; George Washington (1732–99), a Revolutionary soldier and the first U.S. president, returned to his family home, Mount Vernon, in 1796 after his retirement.

3. The three-headed dog that guarded the gate to Hades in Greek mythology.
4. The slave traffic.

may creep, and dare to think and act for himself; but for a woman it is an herculean task, because she has difficulties peculiar to her sex to overcome, which require almost superhuman powers.

A truly benevolent legislator always endeavors to make it the interest of each individual to be virtuous; and thus private virtue becoming the cement of public happiness, an orderly whole is consolidated by the tendency of all the parts towards a common center. But, the private or public virtue of woman is very problematical; for Rousseau,[5] and a numerous list of male writers, insist that she should all her life be subjected to a severe restraint, that of propriety. Why subject her to propriety—blind propriety, if she be capable of acting from a nobler spring, if she be an heir of immortality? Is sugar always to be produced by vital blood? Is one half of the human species, like the poor African slaves, to be subject to prejudices that brutalize them, when principles would be a surer guard, only to sweeten the cup of man? Is not this indirectly to deny woman reason? for a gift is a mockery, if it be unfit for use.

Women are, in common with men, rendered weak and luxurious by the relaxing pleasures which wealth procures; but added to this they are made slaves to their persons, and must render them alluring that man may lend them his reason to guide their tottering steps aright. Or should they be ambitious, they must govern their tyrants by sinister tricks, for without rights there cannot be any incumbent duties. The laws respecting woman, which I mean to discuss in a future part, make an absurd unit of a man and his wife; and then, by the easy transition of only considering him as responsible, she is reduced to a mere cipher.

The being who discharges the duties of its station is independent; and, speaking of women at large, their first duty is to themselves as rational creatures, and the next, in point of importance, as citizens, is that, which includes so many, of a mother. The rank in life which dispenses with their fulfilling this duty, necessarily degrades them by making them mere dolls. Or, should they turn to something more important than merely fitting drapery upon a smooth block, their minds are only occupied by some soft platonic attachment; or, the actual management of an intrigue may keep their thoughts in motion; for when they neglect domestic duties, they have it not in their power to take the field and march and countermarch like soldiers, or wrangle in the senate to keep their faculties from rusting.

I know that, as a proof of the inferiority of the sex, Rousseau has exultingly exclaimed, How can they leave the nursery for the camp![6]—And the camp has by some moralists been termed the school of the most heroic virtues; though, I think, it would puzzle a keen casuist to prove the reasonableness of the greater number of wars that have dubbed heroes. I do not mean to consider this question critically; because, having frequently viewed these freaks of ambition as the first natural mode of civilization, when the ground must be torn up, and the woods cleared by fire and sword, I do not choose to call them pests; but surely the present system of war has little connection with virtue of any denomination, being rather the school of *finesse* and effeminacy, than of fortitude.

Yet, if defensive war, the only justifiable war, in the present advanced state of society, where virtue can show its face and ripen amidst the rigors which purify the air on the mountain's top, were alone to be adopted as just and glorious, the true

---

5. Jean-Jacques Rousseau (1712–78) was a French writer and philosopher with whose conservative views of women Wollstonecraft takes issue.

6. In *Emile* IV, v, Rousseau asks, "Can a woman be one day a nurse, and the next a soldier?"

heroism of antiquity might again animate female bosoms. But fair and softly, gentle reader, male or female, do not alarm thyself, for though I have compared the character of a modern soldier with that of a civilized woman, I am not going to advise them to turn their distaff into a musket, though I sincerely wish to see the bayonet converted into a pruning-hook. I only recreated an imagination, fatigued by contemplating the vices and follies which all proceed from a feculent stream of wealth that has muddied the pure rills of natural affection, by supposing that society will some time or other be so constituted, that man must necessarily fulfill the duties of a citizen, or be despised, and that while he was employed in any of the departments of civil life, his wife, also an active citizen, should be equally intent to manage her family, educate her children, and assist her neighbors.

But, to render her really virtuous and useful, she must not, if she discharge her civil duties, want, individually, the protection of civil laws; she must not be dependent on her husband's bounty for her subsistence during his life, or support after his death—for how can a being be generous who has nothing of its own? or virtuous, who is not free? The wife, in the present state of things, who is faithful to her husband, and neither suckles nor educates her children, scarcely deserves the name of a wife, and has no right to that of a citizen. But take away natural rights, and [duties become null].

Women [then must be considered as only the wanton solace of men, when they become] so weak in mind and body, that they cannot exert themselves, unless to pursue some frothy pleasure, or to invent some frivolous fashion. What can be a more melancholy sight to a thinking mind, than to look into the numerous carriages that drive helter-skelter about this metropolis in a morning full of pale-faced creatures who are flying from themselves. I have often wished, with Dr. Johnson,[7] to place some of them in a little shop with half a dozen children looking up to their languid countenances for support. I am much mistaken, if some latent vigor would not soon give health and spirit to their eyes, and some lines drawn by the exercise of reason on the blank cheeks, which before were only undulated by dimples, might restore lost dignity to the character, or rather enable it to attain the true dignity of its nature. Virtue is not to be acquired even by speculation, much less by the negative supineness that wealth naturally generates.

Besides, when poverty is more disgraceful than even vice, is not morality cut to the quick? Still to avoid misconstruction, though I consider that women in the common walks of life are called to fulfill the duties of wives and mothers, by religion and reason, I cannot help lamenting that women of a superior cast have not a road open by which they can pursue more extensive plans of usefulness and independence. I may excite laughter, by dropping an hint, which I mean to pursue, some future time, for I really think that women ought to have representatives, instead of being arbitrarily governed without having any direct share allowed them in the deliberations of government.

But, as the whole system of representation is now, in this country, only a convenient handle for despotism, they need not complain, for they are as well represented as a numerous class of hard working mechanics, who pay for the support of royalty when they can scarcely stop their children's mouths with bread. How are they represented whose very sweat supports the splendid stud of an heir apparent, or varnishes the chariot of some female favorite who looks down on shame? Taxes on the very necessaries of life, enable an endless tribe of idle princes and princesses to pass with stupid pomp before a gaping crowd, who almost worship the very parade which costs

7. Samuel Johnson (1709–84) was an English author and lexicographer.

them so dear. This is mere gothic grandeur, something like the barbarous useless parade of having sentinels on horseback at Whitehall, which I could never view without a mixture of contempt and indignation.[8]

How strangely must the mind be sophisticated when this sort of state impresses it! But, till these monuments of folly are levelled by virtue, similar follies will leaven the whole mass. For the same character, in some degree, will prevail in the aggregate of society: and the refinements of luxury, or the vicious repinings of envious poverty, will equally banish virtue from society, considered as the characteristic of that society, or only allow it to appear as one of the stripes of the harlequin coat, worn by the civilized man.

In the superior ranks of life, every duty is done by deputies, as if duties could ever be waved, and the vain pleasures which consequent idleness forces the rich to pursue, appear so enticing to the next rank, that the numerous scramblers for wealth sacrifice every thing to tread on their heels. The most sacred trusts are then considered as sinecures, because they were procured by interest, and only sought to enable a man to keep *good company*. Women, in particular, all want to be ladies. Which is simply to have nothing to do, but listlessly to go they scarcely care where, for they cannot tell what.

But what have women to do in society? I may be asked, but to loiter with easy grace; surely you would not condemn them all to suckle fools and chronicle small beer! No. Women might certainly study the art of healing, and be physicians as well as nurses. And midwifery, decency seems to allot to them, though I am afraid the word midwife, in our dictionaries, will soon give place to *accoucheur*,[9] and one proof of the former delicacy of the sex be effaced from the language.

They might, also, study politics, and settle their benevolence on the broadest basis; for the reading of history will scarcely be more useful than the perusal of romances, if read as mere biography; if the character of the times, the political improvements, arts, etc. be not observed. In short, if it be not considered as the history of man; and not of particular men, who filled a niche in the temple of fame, and dropped into the black rolling stream of time, that silently sweeps all before it, into the shapeless void called eternity. For shape, can it be called, "that shape hath none?"

Business of various kinds, they might likewise pursue, if they were educated in a more orderly manner, which might save many from common and legal prostitution. Women would not then marry for a support, as men accept of places under government, and neglect the implied duties; nor would an attempt to earn their own subsistence, a most laudable one! sink them almost to the level of those poor abandoned creatures who live by prostitution. For are not milliners and mantua-makers[10] reckoned the next class? The few employments open to women, so far from being liberal, are menial; and when a superior education enables them to take charge of the education of children as governesses, they are not treated like the tutors of sons, though even clerical tutors are not always treated in a manner calculated to render them respectable in the eyes of their pupils, to say nothing of the private comfort of the individual. But as women educated like gentlewomen, are never designed for the humiliating situation which necessity sometimes forces them to fill; these situations are considered in the light of a degradation; and they know little of the human heart, who need to be told, that nothing so painfully sharpens sensibility as such a fall in life.

---

8. She refers here to the guards on horseback who protect the government offices housed at Whitehall in London.

9. A male obstetrician.

10. Dressmakers.

Some of these women might be restrained from marrying by a proper spirit or delicacy, and others may not have had it in their power to escape in this pitiful way from servitude; is not that government then very defective, and very unmindful of the happiness of one half of its members, that does not provide for honest, independent women, by encouraging them to fill respectable stations? But in order to render their private virtue a public benefit, they must have a civil existence in the state, married or single; else we shall continually see some worthy woman, whose sensibility has been rendered painfully acute by undeserved contempt, droop like "the lily broken down by a plowshare."[11]

It is a melancholy truth; yet such is the blessed effect of civilization! the most respectable women are the most oppressed; and, unless they have understandings far superior to the common run of understandings, taking in both sexes, they must, from being treated like contemptible beings, become contemptible. How many women thus waste life away the prey of discontent, who might have practiced as physicians, regulated a farm, managed a shop, and stood erect, supported by their own industry, instead of hanging their heads surcharged with the dew of sensibility, that consumes the beauty to which it at first gave lustre; nay, I doubt whether pity and love are so near akin as poets feign, for I have seldom seen much compassion excited by the helplessness of females, unless they were fair; then, perhaps, pity was the soft hand-maid of love, or the harbinger of lust.

How much more respectable is the woman who earns her own bread by fulfilling any duty, than the most accomplished beauty!—beauty did I say?—so sensible am I of the beauty of moral loveliness, or the harmonious propriety that attunes the passions of a well-regulated mind, that I blush at making the comparison; yet I sigh to think how few women aim at attaining this respectability by withdrawing from the giddy whirl of pleasure, or the indolent calm that stupifies the good sort of women it sucks in.

Proud of their weakness, however, they must always be protected, guarded from care, and all the rough toils that dignify the mind. If this be the fiat of fate, if they will make themselves insignificant and contemptible, sweetly to waste "life away," let them not expect to be valued when their beauty fades, for it is the fate of the fairest flowers to be admired and pulled to pieces by the careless hand that plucked them. In how many ways do I wish, from the purest benevolence, to impress this truth on my sex; yet I fear that they will not listen to a truth that dear-bought experience has brought home to many an agitated bosom, nor willingly resign the privileges of rank and sex for the privileges of humanity, to which those have no claim who do not discharge its duties.

Those writers are particularly useful, in my opinion, who make man feel for man, independent of the station he fills, or the drapery of factitious sentiments. I then would fain convince reasonable men of the importance of some of my remarks; and prevail on them to weigh dispassionately the whole tenor of my observations. I appeal to their understandings; and, as a fellow-creature, claim, in the name of my sex, some interest in their hearts. I entreat them to assist to emancipate their companion, to make her a *helpmeet* for them!

Would men but generously snap our chains, and be content with rational fellowship instead of slavish obedience, they would find us more observant daughters, more

11. A quotation from *The Adventures of Telemachus* (1699) by Francois Fénelon (1651–1715), a French author and prelate.

affectionate sisters, more faithful wives, more reasonable mothers—in a word, better citizens. We should then love them with true affection, because we should learn to respect ourselves; and the peace of mind of a worthy man would not be interrupted by the idle vanity of his wife, nor the babes sent to nestle in a strange bosom, having never found a home in their mother's.   *1792*

✦

Mary Hays
1760–1843

"Of all the systems—if indeed a bundle of contradictions and absurdities may be called a system— which human nature in its moments of intoxication has produced; that which men have con- trived with a view to forming the minds, and regulating the conduct of women, is perhaps the most completely absurd." So begins MARY HAYS's uncompromising treatise of 1798, *Appeal to the Men of Great Britain in Behalf of Women*. Despite her provocative words, Hays intended to disarm men by evoking their reason rather than their passions on the inflammatory issue of women's rights. Arguing that women's weakness is not innate but has resulted from inferior education, Hays claims that educating women would promote compatibility rather than estrangement between married couples.

This feminist thinker was born to a large family of religious and political dissenters in Southwark, near London. Educated at home, she fell in love at sixteen with a fellow dissenter who was also her teacher, John Eccles; the two lovers corresponded for three years until their parents granted them permission to marry. Eccles died of a fever shortly before their wedding; in her diary Hays describes his death as that "fatal day, which blasted all the fond hopes of my youth." Although she published her first story in 1786, Hays did not begin to write in earnest until the 1790s, after beginning to correspond with William Godwin and other prominent radicals. In 1792 she became a friend of MARY WOLLSTONECRAFT, whose views of women's emancipation she shared; her writing of this decade promoted sexual, intellectual, and eco- nomic independence for women. Such views appealed to many, but by century's end conserv- ative men were fighting back. In his 1798 poem *The Unsexed Females*, the Reverend Richard Polwhele satirized Hays and other women writers as rebels against "Nature's law"; that same year she appeared as the self-righteous Lady Gertrude Sinclair in Charles Floyd's novel *Edmund Oliver*. Perhaps dismayed by such attacks, Hays never wrote as radically after 1800 as she had before.

In her long career Hays published poetry, fiction, essays, and letters. Her first prose trea- tise, *Cursory Remarks on an Enquiry into the Expediency and Propriety of Public or Social Worship* (1791), criticizes the Church of England. *Letters and Essays* (1793) addresses issues of gender equality and pleads for a "reformation of manners" so that women might be more useful in society. Throughout the 1790s she published essays on women's education, sexual difference, and political reform for *Monthly Magazine* and, like Mary Wollstonecraft, wrote for the *Analytical Review*. By the time that *Appeal to the Men of Great Britain* was published, Hays had earned a reputation as a feminist polemicist second only to Wollstonecraft.

Her fiction also challenged sexual mores and stereotypes. *The Memoirs of Emma Courtney* (1796), at once a philosophical novel and a fictional autobiography, is based on Hays's attrac- tion to a Cambridge reformer, William Frend, who corresponded with her about intellectual issues but did not return her affections. *The Victim of Prejudice* (1799) advocates egalitarian rela- tionships between women and men and among social classes. A gothic novel in which rape, courtrooms, and prison figure prominently, it dramatizes the links between gender and class oppression. Some critics consider *The Victim of Prejudice* a rewriting of Samuel Richardson's

Clarissa, but while the protagonists of both works recount rape and its aftermath, Hays's novel is more realistic: Her heroine, Mary, endures not only the insults of friends, servants, and prospective employers after she is sexually violated, but poverty and near-starvation as well. Unlike Richardson, Hays argues that there is "too-great stress laid on the reputation for chastity in women."

By the publication of *Female Biography* (1803), Hays's five-volume study of the accomplishments of famous women, antifeminist pressure was strong enough to prevent her from including a portrait of Mary Wollstonecraft. This was in part due to negative response to William Godwin's frank portrayal of Wollstonecraft's sexual liaisons in his 1799 memoir, which led critics of "scribbling women" to associate them all with licentiousness. In 1806 Hays collaborated with CHARLOTTE SMITH on *The History of England*; she subsequently published both a life of Smith and a volume entitled *Historical Dialogues for Young Persons* (1808). *Memoirs of Queens, Illustrious and Celebrated* (1821) chronicles the lives of royalty and recalls the egalitarian zeal of the 1790s. In her introduction Hays claims that during that decade women rebelled against overprotection: "Every manly mind shrank from the idea of driving, by protracted and endless persecutions, a desolate impoverished female from her family, her rank, from society and from the world. *Woman* considered it as a common cause of the tyranny and despotism of men."

Appeal to the Men of Great Britain in Behalf of Women appeared anonymously in 1798 but has since been attributed to Hays; it launches an argument for women's equality similar to Wollstonecraft's in *A Vindication of the Rights of Woman* but with greater emphasis on the Christian duties of both sexes. As Eleanor Ty has observed, "Hays's radicalism involved what feminists today would call the politics of the personal," since the solutions she offers to the problem of women's inequality are practical as well as philosophical.

from Appeal to the Men of Great Britain in Behalf of Women

> Implicit faith, all hail! Imperial Man Exacts submission.
>
> *Yearsley*[1]

WHAT MEN WOULD HAVE WOMEN TO BE

Of all the systems—if indeed a bundle of contradictions and absurdities may be called a system—which human nature in its moments of intoxication has produced; that which men have contrived with a view to forming the minds, and regulating the conduct of women, is perhaps the most completely absurd. And, though the consequences are often very serious to both sexes, yet if one could for a moment forget these, and consider it only as a system, it would rather be found a subject of mirth and ridicule than serious anger.

What a chaos!—What a mixture of strength and weakness—of greatness and littleness—of sense and folly—of exquisite feeling and total insensibility—have they jumbled together in their imaginations—and then given to their pretty darling the name of woman! How unlike the father of gods and men, the gay, the gallant Jupiter, who on producing wisdom the fruit of his brains, presented it to admiring worlds under the character of a female.[2]

1. Ann Yearsley (1752–1806) was a British working-class poet, novelist, and dramatist.
2. An allusion to the Greek myth in which Athene, god-dess of wisdom, sprang fully formed from the head of Zeus, the chief god in the pantheon, whose Roman name was Jupiter.

But in the composition of Man's woman, wisdom must not be spoken of, nay nor even hinted at, yet strange to tell! there it must be in full force, and come forth upon all convenient occasions. This is a mystery which, as we are not allowed to be amongst the initiated, we may admire at an awful distance, but can never comprehend.

Again how great in some parts of their conduct, and how insignificant upon the whole, would men have women to be! For one example—when their love, their pride, their delicacy; in short, when all the finest feelings of humanity are insulted and put to the rack, what is the line of conduct, then expected from them?

I need not explain that the situation I here allude to is—when a woman finds that the husband of her choice, the object of her most sincere and constant love, abandons himself to other attachments; and not only this, but when—the natural consequences of these—estrangement of affection and estrangement of confidence follow, which are infinitely cutting to a woman of sensibility and soul; what I say is the line of conduct then expected from a creature declared to be—weak by nature, and who is rendered still weaker by education?

Now here is one of those absurdities of which I accuse men in their system of contradictions. They expect that this poor weak creature, setting aside in a moment, love, jealousy, and pride, the most powerful and universal passions interwoven in the human heart, and which even men, clothed in wisdom and fortitude, find so difficult to conquer, that they seldom attempt it—that she shall notwithstanding lay all these aside as easily as she would her gown and petticoat, and plunge at once into the cold bath of prudence, of which though the wife only is to receive the shock, and make daily use of, yet if she does so, it has the virtue of keeping both husband and wife in a most agreeable temperament. Prudence being one of those rare medicines which affect by sympathy, and this being likewise one of those cases, where the husbands have no objections to the wives acting as principals, nor to their receiving all the honors and emoluments of office; even if death should crown their martyrdom, as has been sometimes known to happen.

Dear, generous creatures!

This reminds me of a singular circumstance which I heard the other day, of a poor man who had the misfortune to have a cataract on each eye. The one was cut, or extracted, or what you please to call it, and suffered as one may suppose the most extreme anguish. The other immediately wore off, or, I really don't know well how to express myself, dispersed, nobody knows how, except by the power of sympathy; but certainly without any operation being performed upon it. Now this last eye—this not guiltless though unsuffering luminary, is what learned physicians call the *male* eye; and this operation when followed by such consequences, in honor of those consequences they have been pleased to distinguish by a most expressive name, which I have however entirely forgot; but under it they mean in future to class, all those cases, where one part only suffers, and the other receives all the benefit. For, I had almost forgot to mention, that the poor eye on which the experiment was made, soon "Closed in endless night."

But to return to our subject; the situations before alluded to, though perhaps the most trying for human nature in general, and to minds of sensibility in particular, are not the only ones prepared for women upon which to exercise their patience and temper. For, there are no vices to which a man addicts himself, no follies he can take it into his head to commit, but his wife and his nearest female relations are expected to connive at, are expected to look upon, if not with admiration, at least with respectful silence, and at awful distance. Any other conduct is looked upon, as a breach of that fanciful system of arbitrary authority, which men have so assiduously erected in their own favor; and any other conduct is accordingly resisted, with the most acrimonious severity.

A man, for example, is addicted to the destructive vice of drinking. His wife sees with terror and anguish the approach of this pernicious habit, and by anticipation beholds the evils to be dreaded to his individual health, happiness, and consequence; and the probable misery to his family. Yet with this melancholy prospect before her eyes, it is reckoned an unpardonable degree of harshness and imprudence, if she by any means whatever endeavour to check in the bud, this baleful practice; and she is in this case accused at all hands of driving him to pursue in worse places, that which he cannot enjoy in peace at home. And, when this disease gains ground, and ends in an established habit, she is treated as a fool for attempting a cure for what is incurable.

Thus there is no stage of this disorder, or any other to which man is morally liable, when it is accounted necessary or proper for women to interfere; or if they do so, men suppose themselves fully justified to plunge deeper and deeper into those vices, which create most misery to their wives, in order to punish their presumption. And thus it is that the designs of Providence seem to be counteracted, by the pride and obstinacy of man. For, the design of Providence seems evidently to be—that the sexes should restrain, discourage, and prevent vice in each other; as much as they should encourage, promote, and reward virtue.

Again, women are often connected with men, whose shameful extravagance leave little for their families to hope for, but poverty, and the consequent neglect of a hard-hearted world. In this case perhaps, in the little sphere in which she is permitted to move, a wife may likewise be permitted to economize; but the fruits of her economy are still at the mercy of an imperious master, who thinks himself entitled to spend upon his unlawful pleasures, what might have procured her, innocent enjoyment, and rational delight. And, I am sorry to add, that the men in general are but too apt in these cases, as well as upon most other occasions, to take the part of their own sex; and to consider nothing as blameable in them to such a degree, as to justify opposition from the women connected with them.

Again, women of liberal sentiments and expanded hearts—and surely there are such, in consequence of good, or in spite of bad education—who would willingly employ fortune in acts of benevolence and schemes of beneficence; are connected with men, sordid in principle, rapacious in acquiring riches, and contemptibly mean in restraining them from returning again into society, through their proper channels. Woman here again is the sport, of the vices and infirmities of her tyrant: and however formed by nature to virtue and benevolence—however trained by education—here she finds all this against her. Here she finds that her time and endeavors would have been much more happily employed, in strengthening the opposite habits of selfishness, and uncharitableness. Since, the highest pitch of virtue, to which a woman can possibly aspire on the present system of things; is to please her husband, in whatever line of conduct pleasing him consists. And, to this great end, this one thing needful, men are impolitic enough to advance, and to expect, that everything else should be sacrificed. Reason, religion—or at least many of the most important maxims of religion—private judgment, prejudices; all these, and much more than these must be swallowed up in the gulp of authority; which requiring everything as a right, disdains to return anything but as a concession.

I wish not however to be misunderstood, if even but for a moment; for though this is not the place to enlarge upon the subject, it must be acknowledged, that to please a reasonable and worthy husband—let me repeat my own words—in whatever pleasing him consists, is one of the most heartfelt, and purest pleasures, which a woman such as she ought to be, can possibly enjoy. But for women to be obliged to humor the follies, the caprice, the vices of men of a very different stamp, and to be obliged to consider this as their duty; is perhaps as unfortunate a system of politics in morals, as ever was introduced for degrading the human species.

I could here enumerate numberless instances, of WHAT MEN WOULD HAVE WOMEN TO BE, under circumstances the most trying and the most humiliating; but as I neither wish to tire out the reader nor myself with what may be well imagined without repetition, I shall only say; that though they are allowed, and even expected, to assume upon proper occasions, and when it happens to indulge the passions, or fall in with the humors of men, all that firmness of character, and greatness of mind commonly esteemed masculine; yet this is in so direct opposition, and so totally inconsistent with that universal weakness, which men first endeavor to affix upon women for their own convenience, and then for their own defense affect to admire; that really it requires more than female imbecility and credulity to suppose that such extremes can unite with any degree of harmony, in such imperfect beings as we all of us, men and women, must acknowledge ourselves to be. And therefore, except a woman has some schemes of her own to accomplish by this sort of management—which necessity is most galling to an ingenuous mind; or except she is herself a mere nothing—in which case her merit is next to nothing; these violent extremes—these violent exertions of the mind—are by no means natural or voluntary ones; but are on the contrary at variance with nature, with reason, and with common sense.

Indeed by preparatory tortures any mode of conduct, however unnatural, may be forced upon individuals.

Even inferior animals are taught not only to dance, but to dance to appearance in time, and with alacrity, when their tyrant pipes. Bears and Turkeys for example. But we ought not to forget, that to produce these wonderful exertions; the first have had their eyes put out, to render them more docile to the cruel caprice of man; and that nothing less than hot iron applied to the feet of the latter, had furnished that singular spectacle, with which many had the barbarity to be amused.[1]

So alas! women often go through scenes with apparent cheerfulness, that did the most indifferent spectators, but consider what such appearances must have previously cost them, they would execrate the mean and sordid system; and join in endeavoring to expel from society those errors in theory, which produce such consequences in practice. For, from exertions made under such circumstances—against nature—against reason—and against common sense—can good be expected? Can such mend the understanding, or purify the heart? No, never! On the contrary they debase the one, and they corrupt the other. But it is a melancholy truth, that the whole system raised and supported by the men, tends to, nay I must be honest enough to say hangs upon, degrading the understandings, and corrupting the hearts of women; and yet! they are unreasonable enough to expect, discrimination in the one, and purity in the other. . . .   *1798*

---

1. Hays refers here to the sports of bearbaiting and cockfighting.

Sojourner Truth

1797?–1883

> That man over there says that women need to be helped into carriages, and lifted over ditches, and to have the best place everywhere. Nobody ever helps me into carriages, or over mud puddles, or gives me any best place! And ain't I a woman?

SOJOURNER TRUTH's 1851 speech distinguishes her experience as a slave from that of privileged white women, protected by the nineteenth-century ideology of the "cult of true womanhood." This evangelist, abolitionist, and women's rights activist claims equality as her birthright, grounded in the strength of women forced to work the land of others. Born into slavery in Hurley, New York, Isabella Bomefree sought emancipation at age thirty with the help of a white family whose surname, Van Wagenen, she adopted. Having seen two of her four children sold from their home into slavery, she fled in part to prevent the sale of the other two. For a time she did domestic work in New York City, where she joined forces with Elijah Pierson, an evangelical minister attempting to convert prostitutes, and later with Robert Matthew, the leader of an interracial religious community called Zion Hill, where she lived briefly. In 1843, after a visionary experience, she renamed herself Sojourner Truth and began what would be a forty-year career of preaching and lecturing across the United States.

Because Truth was illiterate, most of what was known about her during her lifetime was culled from journalists' reports of her speeches. A gifted orator, Truth used rhetorical flourishes, Biblical and historical allusions, and logical argument in her lectures and mesmerized crowds with her tall, commanding presence and keen intelligence. "I can't read," she once proclaimed, "but I can read people." During the 1840s and 1850s she combined religious fervor with abolitionist aims, becoming connected with George W. Benson, William Lloyd Garrison, and other antislavery advocates and touring the Midwest with copies of her autobiography in tow. *The Narrative of Sojourner Truth* (1850) recounts in detail Truth's life as recorded and transcribed by the white abolitionist Olive Gilbert. Harriet Beecher Stowe's article "Sojourner Truth: The Libyan Sibyl," published in 1863 in the *Atlantic Monthly,* also enhanced her fame. A little-known fact about Truth's life, as reported by Gloria I. Joseph, is that she was responsible for Congress's banning of segregated streetcars in Washington, D.C., in the early 1860s, nearly 100 years before Rosa Parks began the Montgomery, Alabama, bus boycotts that sparked the contemporary civil rights movement. Calling out in her booming voice, "I WANT TO RIDE," Truth commandeered the car she desired and once successfully sued a conductor who tried to eject her from his "whites only" coach, causing him to lose his job.

Truth's speeches reveal her intellect, wit, and determination that justice should prevail. "Ain't I a Woman?" (sometimes called "Ar'n't I a Woman?") was presented at an 1851 women's rights convention in Akron, Ohio, and has become a classic text of the modern feminist movement; it claims that none of us are free until all of us are free. Since the most familiar version of the speech was recorded twelve years later by the white feminist Frances Gage, however, readers today cannot know precisely what Truth actually said. Her 1867 speech "Keeping the Thing Going While Things Are Stirring" was given when the Fourteenth Amendment to the U.S. Constitution was proposed, insuring black men's right to vote but failing to mention women. Although many male and female abolitionists, black and white, argued that the amendment should pass, for the black man's hour had come, Truth supports freedom for people of all races and both genders, for slavery must be "root and branch destroyed." Her speeches were published by Elizabeth Cady Stanton in *The History of Woman Suffrage* (1881–86) and have been modernized by Miriam Schneir in *Feminism: The Essential Historical Writings* (1972). A 1996 biography by NELL IRVIN PAINTER provides insight into Truth's courageous life and voice.

⊰ Ain't I a Woman? ⊱

Well, children, where there is so much racket there must be something out of kilter. I think that 'twixt the negroes of the South and the women at the North, all talking about rights, the white men will be in a fix pretty soon. But what's all this here talking about?

That man over there says that women need to be helped into carriages, and lifted over ditches, and to have the best place everywhere. Nobody ever helps me into carriages, or over mud puddles, or gives me any best place! And ain't I a woman? Look at me! Look at my arm! I have plowed and planted, and gathered into barns, and no man could head me! And ain't I a woman? I could work as much and eat as much as a man—when I could get it—and bear the lash as well! And ain't I a woman? I have borne thirteen children, and seen them most all sold off to slavery, and when I cried out with my mother's grief, none but Jesus heard me! And ain't I a woman?

Then they talk about this thing in the head; what's this they call it? [Intellect, someone whispers.] That's it, honey. What's that got to do with women's rights or negro's rights? If my cup won't hold but a pint, and yours holds a quart, wouldn't you be mean not to let me have my little half-measure full?

Then that little man in black there, he says women can't have as much rights as men, 'cause Christ wasn't a woman! Where did your Christ come from? Where did your Christ come from? From God and a woman! Man had nothing to do with Him.

If the first woman God ever made was strong enough to turn the world upside down all alone, these women together ought to be able to turn it back, and get it right side up again! And now they is asking to do it, the men better let them.

Obliged to you for hearing me, and now old Sojourner ain't got nothing more to say.   *1851/1881–86*

⊰ Keeping the Thing Going While Things Are Stirring ⊱

My friends, I am rejoiced that you are glad, but I don't know how you will feel when I get through. I come from another field—the country of the slave. They have got their liberty—so much good luck to have slavery partly destroyed; not entirely. I want it root and branch destroyed. Then we will all be free indeed. I feel that if I have to answer for the deeds done in my body just as much as a man, I have a right to have just as much as a man. There is a great stir about colored men getting their rights, but not a word about the colored women; and if colored men get their rights, and not colored women theirs, you see the colored men will be masters over the women, and it will be just as bad as it was before. So I am for keeping the thing going while things are stirring; because if we wait till it is still, it will take a great while to get it going again. White women are a great deal smarter, and know more than colored women, while colored women do not know scarcely anything. They go out washing, which is about as high as a colored woman gets, and their men go about idle, strutting up and down;

and when the women come home, they ask for their money and take it all, and then scold because there is no food. I want you to consider on that, chil'n. I call you chil'n; you are somebody's chil'n, and I am old enough to be mother of all that is here. I want women to have their rights. In the courts women have no right, no voice; nobody speaks for them. I wish woman to have her voice there among the pettifoggers. If it is not a fit place for women, it is unfit for men to be there.

I am above eighty years old; it is about time for me to be going. I have been forty years a slave and forty years free, and would be here forty years more to have equal rights for all. I suppose I am kept here because something remains for me to do; I suppose I am yet to help to break the chain. I have done a great deal of work; as much as a man, but did not get so much pay. I used to work in the field and bind grain, keeping up with the cradler; but men doing no more, got twice as much pay; so with the German women. They work in the field and do as much work, but do not get the pay. We do as much, we eat as much, we want as much. I suppose I am about the only colored woman that goes about to speak for the rights of the colored women. I want to keep the thing stirring, now that the ice is cracked. What we want is a little money. You men know that you get as much again as women when you write, or for what you do. When we get our rights we shall not have to come to you for money, for then we shall have money enough in our own pockets; and may be you will ask us for money. But help us now until we get it. It is a good consolation to know that when we have got this battle once fought we shall not be coming to you any more. You have been having our rights so long, that you think, like a slaveholder, that you own us. I know that it is hard for one who has held the reins for so long to give up; it cuts like a knife. It will feel all the better when it closes up again. I have been in Washington about three years, seeing about these colored people. Now colored men have the right to vote. There ought to be equal rights now more than ever, since colored people have got their freedom. I am going to talk several times while I am here; so now I will do a little singing. I have not heard any singing since I came here.   *1867/1881–86*

+━ ⊫◊⊨ ━+

Harriet Martineau
1802–1876

One of Victorian England's foremost women of letters, HARRIET MARTINEAU published theoretical treatises on a wide range of subjects, including the abolition of slavery, women's rights, household arrangements, public education, prison reform, political economy, religion, illness, and deafness. Martineau adopted a utilitarian philosophy influenced by the positivism and rationality espoused by John Stuart Mill and Jeremy Bentham. In the obituary that she wrote for herself, which appeared in the *Daily News* on June 29, 1876, she claimed that her "original power was nothing more than was due to earnestness and intellectual clearness. . . . In short, she could popularize, while she could neither discover nor invent." As Deirdre David argues, however, Martineau was a formidable intellectual in her own right, not merely one who popularized others' ideas.

Martineau was born in Norwich, the sixth of eight children of Huguenot parents, Thomas and Elizabeth Rankin Martineau. A sickly child, she was tutored at home in French, Latin, rhetoric, and mathematics by her older siblings until the age of eleven, when she attended a Unitarian school run by Isaac Perry. After two years there she studied again with private tutors until, at sixteen, she began to lose her hearing; she was then sent to live with an aunt in Bristol, where she was exposed to the tenets of utilitarianism. Her first published essays addressed feminist topics: "Female Writers on Practical Divinity" (1822) and "On Female Education" (1823) both appeared in a dissident journal, the *Monthly Repository*. She also published works influenced by her Unitarian faith, including *Devotional Exercises for the Use of Young Persons* (1823) and *Addresses with Prayers* (1826). Her tales for working-class readers, *The Turn-Out* and *The Rioters* (1827), were so successful that in the early 1830s she published a series of fictional works advocating social reform, *Illustrations of Political Economy*, which also received critical acclaim. For the rest of her life Martineau, a single deaf woman, would earn her living as a writer.

Among her best-known works are *Society in America* (1837) and *A Retrospect of Western Travel* (1838), social critiques based on her two-year journey to the United States, where she became a fervent spokesperson for the rights of women and people of color. A compelling cultural analysis, *Society in America* was as influential in its time as Alexis de Tocqueville's *Democracy in America* (1835–40) had been. Although bedridden from 1839 to 1844, Martineau produced *Deerbrook* (1839), a novel about two orphaned sisters and their governess in a small English village; *The Hour and the Man* (1841), a historical novel about a black Haitian revolutionary; and *The Playfellows* (1841), a collection of children's stories. Critics compared Martineau's writing to JANE AUSTEN's, and CHARLOTTE BRONTË later claimed *Deerbrook* as an important influence. After recovering from her mysterious illness, Martineau published an autobiographical account, *Life in the Sick Room* (1844), and a study of the hypnotic treatment she felt had cured her, *Letters on Mesmerism* (1845). Her major historical work, *The History of England During the Thirty Years' Peace 1816–1846* (1849–50), recorded not only political and military but social and economic history as well. In 1853 Martineau published *The Positive Philosophy of Comte*, and in 1855 she began writing her *Autobiography*, which appeared in 1877.

The essays included here, "Citizenship of People of Color" and "Political Nonexistence of Women," are taken from volume one of *Society in America*. As Martineau traveled around the United States from 1834 to 1836, she determined to "compare the existing state of society in America with the principles on which it is professedly founded." Unhappy with what she saw, she criticizes the hypocrisy of both Southern slave holders and New Englanders who believe "their" blacks are fairly treated. In "Political Nonexistence of Women" she claims that the lack of women's rights constitutes a major flaw in the maintenance of democratic values. Women should be treated as full citizens, Martineau argues, if they are expected to obey a country's laws, for "governments can derive their just powers only from the consent of the governed."

⇥ *from* Society in America ⇤

CITIZENSHIP OF PEOPLE OF COLOR

BEFORE I entered New England, while I was ascending the Mississippi, I was told by a Boston gentleman that the people of color in the New England States were perfectly well-treated; that the children were educated in schools provided for them; and that their fathers freely exercised the franchise. This gentleman certainly believed he was telling me the truth. That he, a busy citizen of Boston, should know no better, is now as striking an exemplification of the state of the case to me as a correct representation of the facts would have been. There are two causes for his mistake. He was not aware that the schools for the colored children in New England are, unless they escape by their insignificance, shut up, or pulled down, or the schoolhouse wheeled away upon rollers over the frontier of a pious State, which will not endure that its colored citizens should be educated. He was not aware of a gentleman of color, and his family, being locked out of their own hired pew in a church, because their white brethren will not worship by their side. But I will not proceed with an enumeration of injuries, too familiar to Americans to excite any feeling but that of weariness; and too disgusting to all others to be endured. The other cause of this gentleman's mistake was, that he did not, from long custom, feel some things to be injuries, which he would call anything but good treatment, if he had to bear them himself. Would he think it good treatment to be forbidden to eat with fellow citizens; to be assigned to a particular gallery in his church; to be excluded from college, from municipal office, from professions, from scientific and literary associations? If he felt himself excluded from every department of society, but its humiliations and its drudgery, would he declare himself to be "perfectly well-treated in Boston?" Not a word more of statement is needed.

The colored race are citizens. They stand, as such, in the law, and in the acknowledgment of everyone who knows the law. They are citizens, yet their houses and schools are pulled down, and they can obtain no remedy at law. They are thrust out of offices, and excluded from the most honorable employments, and stripped of all the best benefits of society by fellow citizens who, once a year, solemnly lay their hands on their hearts, and declare that all men are born free and equal, and that rulers derive their just powers from the consent of the governed.

This system of injury is not wearing out. Lafayette,[1] on his last visit to the United States, expressed his astonishment at the increase of the prejudice against color. He remembered, he said, how the black soldiers used to mess with the whites in the revolutionary war.[2] It should ever be remembered that America is the country of the best friends the colored race has ever had. The more truth there is in the assertions of the oppressors of the blacks, the more heroism there is in their friends. The greater the excuse for the pharisees of the community, the more divine is the equity of the redeemers of the colored race. If it be granted that the colored race are naturally inferior, naturally depraved, disgusting, cursed—it must be granted that it is a heavenly charity which descends among them to give such solace as it can to their incomprehensible existence. As long as the excuses of the one party go to enhance the merit of the other, the society is not to be despaired of, even with this poisonous anomaly at its heart.

Happily, however, the colored race is not cursed by God, as it is by some factions of his children. The less clear-sighted of them are pardonable for so believing. Circumstances, for which no living man is answerable, have generated an erroneous conviction in the feeble mind of man, which sees not beyond the actual and immediate. No remedy could ever have been applied, unless stronger minds than ordinary had been brought into the case. But it so happens, wherever there is an anomaly, giant minds rise up to overthrow it: minds gigantic, not in understanding, but in faith. While the mass of common men and women are despising, and disliking, and fearing, and keeping down the colored race, blinking the fact that they are citizens, the few of Nature's aristocracy are putting forth a strong hand to lift up this degraded race out of oppression, and their country from the reproach of it. If they were but one or two, trembling and toiling in solitary energy, the world afar would be confident of their success. But they number hundreds and thousands; and if ever they feel a passing doubt of their progress, it is only because they are pressed upon by the meaner multitude. Over the sea, no one doubts of their victory. It is as certain as that the risen sun will reach the meridian. Already have people of color crossed the thresholds of many whites, as

---

1. Marquis de Lafayette (1757–1834) was a French general and statesman who aided the American revolutionaries during the War of Independence.

2. "Mess with" here means to eat together in a mess hall.

guests, not as drudges or beggars. Already are they admitted to worship, and to exercise charity, among the whites.

The world has heard and seen enough of the reproach incurred by America, on account of her colored population. It is now time to look for the fairer side. Already is the world beyond the sea beginning to think of America, less as the country of the double-faced pretender to the name of Liberty, than as the home of the single-hearted, clear-eyed Presence which, under the name of Abolitionism, is majestically passing through the land which is soon to be her throne.   *1837*

POLITICAL NONEXISTENCE OF WOMEN

ONE of the fundamental principles announced in the Declaration of Independence is, that governments derive their just powers from the consent of the governed. How can the political condition of women be reconciled with this?

Governments in the United States have power to tax women who hold property; to divorce them from their husbands; to fine, imprison, and execute them for certain offences. Whence do these governments derive their powers? They are not "just," as they are not derived from the consent of the women thus governed.

Governments in the United States have power to enslave certain women; and also to punish other women for inhuman treatment of such slaves. Neither of these powers are "just;" not being derived from the consent of the governed.

Governments decree to women in some States half their husbands' property; in others one-third. In some, a woman, on her marriage, is made to yield all her property to her husband; in others, to retain a portion, or the whole, in her own hands. Whence do governments derive the unjust power of thus disposing of property without the consent of the governed?

The democratic principle condemns all this as wrong; and requires the equal political representation of all rational beings. Children, idiots, and criminals, during the season of sequestration, are the only fair exceptions.

The case is so plain that I might close it here; but it is interesting to inquire how so obvious a decision has been so evaded as to leave to women no political rights whatever. The question has been asked, from time to time, in more countries than one, how obedience to the laws can be required of women, when no woman has, either actually or virtually, given any assent to any law. No plausible answer has, as far as I can discover, been offered; for the good reason, that no plausible answer can be devised. The most principled democratic writers on government have on this subject sunk into fallacies, as disgraceful as any advocate of despotism has adduced. In fact, they have thus sunk from being, for the moment, advocates of despotism. Jefferson in America, and James Mill at home,[3] subside, for the occasion, to the level of the author of the Emperor of Russia's Catechism for the young Poles.

Jefferson says,[4]

Were our State a pure democracy, in which all the inhabitants should meet together to transact all their business, there would yet be excluded from their deliberations,

1. Infants, until arrived at years of discretion;

2. Women, who, to prevent depravation of morals, and ambiguity of issue, could not mix promiscuously in the public meetings of men;

3. Thomas Jefferson (1743–1826) was the third president of the United States; James Mill (1773–1836) was a Scottish philosopher, historian, and economist.

4. [Correspondence vol. iv 295.]

3. Slaves, from whom the unfortunate state of things with us takes away the rights of will and of property.

If the slave disqualification, here assigned, were shifted up under the head of Women, their case would be nearer the truth than as it now stands. Woman's lack of will and of property, is more like the true cause of her exclusion from the representation, than that which is actually set down against her. As if there could be no means of conducting public affairs but by promiscuous meetings! As if there would be more danger in promiscuous meetings for political business than in such meetings for worship, for oratory, for music, for dramatic entertainments—for any of the thousand transactions of civilized life! The plea is not worth another word.

Mill says, with regard to representation, in his Essay on Government, "One thing is pretty clear; that all those individuals, whose interests are involved in those of other individuals, may be struck off without inconvenience. . . . In this light, women may be regarded, the interest of almost all of whom is involved, either in that of their fathers or in that of their husbands."

The true democratic principle is, that no person's interests can be, or can be ascertained to be, identical with those of any other person. This allows the exclusion of none but incapables.

The interests of women who have fathers and husbands can never be identical with theirs, while there is a necessity for laws to protect women against their husbands and fathers. This statement is not worth another word.

Some who desire that there should be an equality of property between men and women, oppose representation, on the ground that political duties would be incompatible with the other duties which women have to discharge. The reply to this is, that women are the best judges here. God has given time and power for the discharge of all duties; and, if he had not, it would be for women to decide which they would take, and which they would leave. But their guardians follow the ancient fashion of deciding what is best for their wards. The Emperor of Russia discovers when a coat of arms and title do not agree with a subject prince. The King of France early perceives that the air of Paris does not agree with a free-thinking foreigner. The English Tories feel the hardship that it would be to impose the franchise on every artisan, busy as he is in getting his bread. The Georgian planter perceives the hardship that freedom would be to his slaves. And the best friends of half the human race peremptorily decide for them as to their rights, their duties, their feelings, their powers. In all these cases, the persons thus cared for feel that the abstract decision rests with themselves; that, though they may be compelled to submit, they need not acquiesce.

I cannot enter upon the commonest order of pleas of all—those which relate to the virtual influence of woman; her swaying the judgment and will of man through the heart; and so forth. One might as well try to dissect the morning mist. I knew a gentleman in America who told me how much rather he had be a woman than the man he is—a professional man, a father, a citizen. He would give up all this for a woman's influence. I thought he was mated too soon. He should have married a lady, also of my acquaintance, who would not at all object to being a slave, if ever the blacks should have the upper hand; "it is so right that the one race should be subservient to the other!" Or rather—I thought it a pity that the one could not be a woman, and the other a slave; so that an injured individual of each class might be exalted into their places, to fulfill and enjoy the duties and privileges which they despise, and, in despising, disgrace.

That woman has power to represent her own interests, no one can deny till she has been tried. The modes need not be discussed here: they must vary with circumstances.

The fearful and absurd images which are perpetually called up to perplex the question—images of women on woolsacks in England, and under canopies in America, have nothing to do with the matter.[5] The principle being once established, the methods will follow, easily, naturally, and under a remarkable transmutation of the ludicrous into the sublime. The kings of Europe would have laughed mightily, two centuries ago, at the idea of a commoner, without robes, crown, or sceptre, stepping into the throne of a strong nation. Yet who dared to laugh when Washington's superroyal voice greeted the New World from the presidential chair, and the Old World stood still to catch the echo?[6]

The principle of the equal rights of both halves of the human race is all we have to do with here. It is the true democratic principle which can never be seriously controverted, and only for a short time evaded. Governments can derive their just powers only from the consent of the governed.   *1837*

Elizabeth Barrett Browning
1806–1861

The most highly regarded woman writer in Victorian England, ELIZ-ABETH BARRETT BROWNING was praised by her peers as "the Shakespeare of her sex." She was the oldest of eleven children of wealthy parents, Edward and Mary Moulton Barrett, and grew up on the family estate in Herefordshire. Tutored at home in Greek and classical philosophy, she began writing poems at thirteen and published two volumes of juvenilia: *The Battle of Marathon* (1820), an epic poem that her proud father copied privately for friends; and *An Essay on Mind* (1826), a long, philosophical poem that she composed at six-
teen. A nervous disorder, diagnosed when she was a teen, was exacerbated by the death of her mother in 1828. During the 1830s Elizabeth Barrett acquired a significant literary reputation as a translator of Aeschylus's *Prometheus Bound* (1833) and as a poet in her own right; *The Seraphim, and Other Poems* appeared in 1838 to much acclaim. After the death of her favorite brother in 1838, however, she was confined as an invalid in London with her beloved but tyrannical father. Still, she continued to write and in 1842 published an analysis of Greek Christian poetry in the *Athenaeum*. A two-volume U.S. edition of her poetry appeared in 1844 with an introduction by Edgar Allan Poe.

In 1845 Elizabeth Barrett began corresponding with Robert Browning, a younger poet who wrote to express his admiration for her work. Eventually the couple eloped and settled in Florence, Italy, where they lived for the remainder of her life. At forty-three, Barrett Browning gave birth to a son, Robert Weidemann Barrett Browning, affectionately called Pen, whom she describes as "my own young Florentine" with "brave blue English eyes." In 1850 she was seriously considered for poet laureate, an honor that went to Alfred, Lord Tennyson. *Poems* (1850) features forty-four love sonnets that purport to be translations

---

5. She alludes here to the possibility of a woman as head of state in England or the United States and suggests that women deserve political power despite the controversies that such empowerment might evoke. "Woolsack" refers to the official seat of the Lord Chancellor in England's House of Lords.
6. George Washington (1732–99), the first U.S. president, was not of royal blood, yet he wielded enormous political power.

from the Portuguese but are really an homage to Robert Browning (who called her "my little Portuguese"). Barrett Browning's health improved by living abroad, and she published prolifically throughout the 1850s. *Casa Guidi Windows* (1851) supports Italian nationalism, a subject also central to her 1860 collection, *Poems Before Congress*—a volume which so offended one reviewer that he claimed she was stricken with a "fit of insanity," for "to bless and not to curse is woman's function." Acutely conscious of the woman writer's plight, Barrett Browning addresses this topic in *Aurora Leigh* (1856). A verse-novel that recounts the literary and romantic struggles of a woman poet, this feminist work became an unlikely bestseller. She continued to espouse liberal causes until her death in 1861; *Last Poems* (1862) was compiled by her husband.

Elizabeth Barrett Browning experimented with a wide range of poetic forms, including sonnets, allegories, epics, and political odes. Many of her best poems express concern over the major social issues of her day: the exploitation of child workers, the immorality of slavery, racial and sexual oppression. In "The Runaway Slave at Pilgrim's Point" an escaped slave speaks from Plymouth Rock, where victims of religious persecution landed in the early 1600s in search of religious liberty. In "A Curse for a Nation" the speaker lambastes the United States for endorsing slavery and selling its national soul. Although many modern readers know only Barrett Browning's love poetry, these other works define her clearly as a poet of resistance.

⊰ The Runaway Slave at Pilgrim's Point[1] ⊱

I

I stand on the mark beside the shore
   Of the first white pilgrim's bended knee,
Where exile turned to ancestor,[2]
   And God was thanked for liberty.
5   I have run through the night, my skin is as dark,
I bend my knee down on this mark:
   I look on the sky and the sea.

II

O pilgrim-souls, I speak to you!
   I see you come proud and slow
10 From the land of the spirits pale as dew
   And round me and round me ye go.
O pilgrims, I have gasped and run
All night long from the whips of one
   Who in your names works sin and woe!

III

15 And thus I thought that I would come
   And kneel here where ye knelt before,
And feel your souls around me hum
   In undertone to the ocean's roar;

---

1. The point at which the Pilgrims landed their ships upon arriving in the New World, a spot near Plymouth Rock, Massachusetts.

2. Where those exiled from one nation became the founders of another.

And lift my black face, my black hand,
20   Here, in your names, to curse this land
        Ye blessed in freedom's, evermore.

IV

I am black, I am black,
        And yet God made me, they say:
But if He did so, smiling back
25   He must have cast his work away
Under the feet of his white creatures,
With a look of scorn, that the dusky features
        Might be trodden again to clay.

V

And yet He has made dark things
30   To be glad and merry as light:
There's a little dark bird sits and sings,
        There's a dark stream ripples out of sight,
And the dark frogs chant in the safe morass,
And the sweetest stars are made to pass
35   O'er the face of the darkest night.

VI

But *we* who are dark, we are dark!
        Ah God, we have no stars!
About our souls in care and cark[3]
        Our blackness shuts like prison-bars:
40   The poor souls crouch so far behind
That never a comfort can they find
        By reaching through the prison-bars.

VII

Indeed we live beneath the sky,
        That great smooth Hand of God stretched out
45   On all his children fatherly,
        To save them from the dread and doubt
Which would be if, from this low place,
All opened straight up to his face
        Into the grand eternity.

VIII

50   And still God's sunshine and his frost,
        They make us hot, they make us cold,
As if we were not black and lost;
        And the beasts and birds, in wood and fold,
Do fear and take us for very men:

3. Distress.

55   Could the whippoorwill or the cat of the glen
          Look into my eyes and be bold?

                          IX

      I am black, I am black!
          But, once, I laughed in girlish glee,   *woman's voice*
      For one of my color stood in the track
60   Where the drivers drove, and looked at me,
      And tender and full was the look he gave—
      Could a slave look *so* at another slave?—
          I look at the sky and the sea.

                          X

      And from that hour our spirits grew
65   As free as if unsold, unbought:
      Oh, strong enough, since we were two,
          To conquer the world, we thought.
      The drivers drove us day by day;
      We did not mind, we went one way,
70   And no better a freedom sought.

                          XI

      In the sunny ground between the canes,
          He said "I love you" as he passed;
      When the shingle-roof rang sharp with the rains,
          I heard how he vowed it fast:
75   While others shook he smiled in the hut,
      As he carved me a bowl of the cocoa-nut
          Through the roar of the hurricanes.

                          XII

      I sang his name instead of a song,
          Over and over I sang his name,
80   Upward and downward I drew it along
          My various notes—the same, the same!
      I sang it low, that the slave-girls near
      Might never guess, from aught they could hear,
          It was only a name—a name.

                          XIII

85   I look on the sky and the sea.
          We were two to love and two to pray:
      Yes, two, O God, who cried to Thee,
          Though nothing didst Thou say!
      Coldly Thou sat'st behind the sun:
90   And now I cry who am but one,
          Thou wilt not speak today.

XIV

We were black, we were black,
  We had no claim to love and bliss,
What marvel if each went to wrack?
    They wrung my cold hands out of his,
They dragged him—where? I crawled to touch
His blood's mark in the dust . . . not much,
    Ye pilgrim-souls, though plain as *this!*[4]

XV

Wrong, followed by a deeper wrong!
    Mere grief's too good for such as I:
So the white men brought the shame ere long
  To strangle the sob of my agony.
They would not leave me for my dull
Wet eyes!—it was too merciful
    To let me weep pure tears and die.

XVI

I am black, I am black!
  I wore a child upon my breast,
An amulet that hung too slack,
  And, in my unrest, could not rest:
Thus we went moaning, child and mother,
One to another, one to another,
    Until all ended for the best.

XVII

For hark! I will tell you low, low,
  I am black, you see—
And the babe who lay on my bosom so,
  Was far too white, too white for me;
As white as the ladies who scorned to pray
Beside me at church but yesterday,
    Though my tears had washed a place for my knee.

XVIII

My own, own child! I could not bear
  To look in his face, it was so white;
I covered him up with a kerchief there,
  I covered his face in close and tight:
And he moaned and struggled, as well might be,
For the white child wanted his liberty—
    Ha, ha! he wanted the master-right.

XIX

He moaned and beat with his head and feet,

95

100

105

110

115

120

125

---

4. This "pilgrim point" at which the speaker stands.

His little feet that never grew;
He struck them out, as it was meet.
130   Against my heart to break it through:
I might have sung and made him mild,
But I dared not sing to the white-faced child
      The only song I knew.

XX

I pulled the kerchief very close:
135   He could not see the sun, I swear,
More, then, alive, than now he does
      From between the roots of the mango . . . where?
I know where. Close! A child and mother
Do wrong to look at one another
140   When one is black and one is fair.

XXI

Why, in that single glance I had
      Of my child's face, . . . I tell you all,
I saw a look that made me mad!
      The master's look, that used to fall
145 On my soul like his lash . . . or worse!
And so, to save it from my curse,
      I twisted it round in my shawl.

XXII

And he moaned and trembled from foot to head,
      He shivered from head to foot;
150 Till after a time, he lay instead
      Too suddenly still and mute.
I felt, beside, a stiffening cold:
I dared to lift up just a fold,
      As in lifting a leaf of the mango-fruit.

XXIII

155 But my fruit . . . ha, ha!—there, had been
      (I laugh to think on 't at this hour!)
Your fine white angels (who have seen
      Nearest the secret of God's power)
And plucked my fruit to make them wine,
160 And sucked the soul of that child of mine
      As the hummingbird sucks the soul of the flower.

XXIV

Ha, ha, the trick of the angels white!
      They freed the white child's spirit so.
I said not a word, but day and night
165   I carried the body to and fro,
And it lay on my heart like a stone, as chill.

—The sun may shine out as much as he will:
   I am cold, though it happened a month ago.

XXV

From the white man's house, and the black man's hut,
170   I carried the little body on;
The forest's arms did round us shut,
   And silence through the trees did run:
They asked no question as I went,
They stood too high for astonishment,
175   They could see God sit on his throne.

XXVI

My little body, kerchiefed fast,
   I bore it on through the forest, on;
And when I felt it was tired at last,
   I scooped a hole beneath the moon:
180 Through the forest-tops the angels far,
With a white sharp finger from every star,
   Did point and mock at what was done.

XXVII

Yet when it was all done aright—
   Earth, 'twixt me and my baby, strewed—
185 All, changed to black earth—nothing white—
   A dark child in the dark!—ensued
Some comfort, and my heart grew young;
I sate down smiling there and sung
   The song I learnt in my maidenhood.

Liberation

XXVIII

190 And thus we two were reconciled,
   The white child and black mother, thus;
For as I sang it soft and wild,
   The same song, more melodious,
Rose from the grave whereon I sate:
195 It was the dead child singing that,
   To join the souls of both of us.

XXIX

I look on the sea and the sky.
   Where the pilgrims' ships first anchored lay
The free sun rideth gloriously,
200   But the pilgrim-ghosts have slid away
Through the earliest streaks of the morn:
My face is black, but it glares with a scorn
   Which they dare not meet by day.

confidence

XXX

Ha!—in their stead, their hunter sons!

205   Ha, ha! they are on me—they hunt in a ring!
Keep off! I brave you all at once,
    I throw off your eyes like snakes that sting!
You have killed the black eagle at nest, I think:
Did you ever stand still in your triumph, and shrink
210   From the stroke of her wounded wing?

XXXI

(Man, drop that stone you dared to lift!—)
    I wish you who stand there five abreast,
Each, for his own wife's joy and gift,
    A little corpse as safely at rest
215 As mine in the mangoes! Yes, but *she*
May keep live babies on her knee,
    And sing the song she likes the best.

XXXII

I am not mad: I am black.
    I see you staring in my face—
220 I know you staring, shrinking back,
    Ye are born of the Washington-race,[5]
And this land is the free America,
And this mark on my wrist—(I prove what I say)
    Ropes tied me up here to the flogging-place.

XXXIII

225 You think I shrieked then? Not a sound
    I hung, as a gourd hangs in the sun;
I only cursed them all around
    As softly as I might have done
My very own child: from these sands
230 Up to the mountains, lift your hands,
    O slaves, and end what I begun!

XXXIV

Whips, curses; these must answer those!
    For in this UNION you have set
Two kinds of men in adverse rows,
235   Each loathing each; and all forget
The seven wounds in Christ's body fair,
While HE sees gaping everywhere
    Our countless wounds that pay no debt.

---

5. The race of George Washington (1732–99), the first president of the United States. Ironically, Washington himself owned slaves.

XXXV

Our wounds are different. Your white men
240   Are, after all, not gods indeed,
Nor able to make Christs again
    Do good with bleeding. We who bleed
(Stand off!) we help not in our loss!
We are too heavy for our cross,
245   And fall and crush you and your seed.

XXXVI

I fall, I swoon! I look at the sky.
    The clouds are breaking on my brain;
I am floated along, as if I should die
    Of liberty's exquisite pain.
250 In the name of the white child waiting for me
In the death-dark where we may kiss and agree,
White men, I leave you all curse-free
    In my broken heart's disdain!

                                                    1847/1850

⊰ A Curse for a Nation[6] ⊱

PROLOGUE

I heard an angel speak last night,
        And he said "Write!
Write a Nation's curse for me,
And send it over the Western Sea."

5   I faltered, taking up the word:
            "Not so, my lord!
    If curses must be, choose another
    To send thy curse against my brother.

"For I am bound by gratitude,
10   By love and blood,
    To brothers of mine across the sea,
    Who stretch out kindly hands to me."

"Therefore," the voice said, "shalt thou write
            My curse tonight.
15   From the summits of love a curse is driven,
    As lightning is from the tops of heaven."

"Not so," I answered. "Evermore
            My heart is sore
    For my own land's sins: for little feet
20   Of children bleeding along the street:

"For parked-up honors[7] that gainsay

---

6. The United States, which, unlike England, was continuing the practice of slavery in 1860, when this poem was
written.
7. Honors collected in one place.

        The right of way:
For almsgiving through a door that is
Not open enough for two friends to kiss:

25   "For love of freedom which abates
                Beyond the Straits:[8]
For patriot virtue starved to vice on
Self-praise, self-interest, and suspicion:

        "For an oligarchic parliament,
30   And bribes well-meant.
What curse to another land assign.
When heavy-souled for the sins of mine?"

        "Therefore," the voice said, "shalt thou write
                My curse tonight.
35   Because thou hast strength to see and hate
A foul thing done *within* thy gate."

        "Not so," I answered once again.
                "To curse, choose men.
For I, a woman, have only known
40   How the heart melts and the tears run down."

        "Therefore," the voice said, "shalt thou write
                My curse tonight.
Some women weep and curse, I say
(And no one marvels), night and day.

45   "And thou shalt take their part tonight,
                Weep and write.
A curse from the depths of womanhood
Is very salt, and bitter, and good."

        So thus I wrote, and mourned indeed,
50   What all may read.
And thus, as was enjoined on me,
I sent it over the Western Sea.

THE CURSE

I

Because ye have broken your own chain
           With the strain
Of brave men climbing a Nation's height,
Yet thence bear down with brand and thong
5   On souls of others—for this wrong
           This is the curse.   Write.

Because yourselves are standing straight
           In the state
Of Freedom's foremost acolyte,

---

8. The Strait of Gibralter separated Europe from Africa.

10   Yet keep calm footing all the time
      On writhing bond-slaves—for this crime
            This is the curse.   Write.

      Because ye prosper in God's name,
            With a claim
15   To honor in the old world's sight,
      Yet do the fiend's work perfectly
      In strangling martyrs—for this lie
            This is the curse.   Write.

                        II

      Ye shall watch while kings conspire
20   Round the people's smoldering fire,
            And, warm for your part,
      Shall never dare—O shame!
      To utter the thought into flame
            Which burns at your heart.
25   This is the curse. Write.

      Ye shall watch while nations strive
      With the bloodhounds, die or survive,
            Drop faint from their jaws,
      Or throttle them backward to death;
30   And only under your breath
            Shall favor the cause.
                  This is the curse. Write.

      Ye shall watch while strong men draw
      The nets of feudal law
35   To strangle the weak;
      And, counting the sin for a sin,
      Your soul shall be sadder within
            Than the word ye shall speak.
                  This is the curse. Write.

40   When good men are praying erect
      That Christ may avenge his elect
            And deliver the earth,
      The prayer in your ears, said low,
      Shall sound like the tramp of a foe
45   That's driving you forth.
                  This is the curse. Write.

      When wise men give you their praise,
      They shall pause in the heat of the phrase,
            As if carried too far.
50   When ye boast your own charters kept true,
      Ye shall blush; for the thing which ye do
            Derides what ye are.
                  This is the curse. Write.

      When fools cast taunts at your gate,

55   Your scorn ye shall somewhat abate
            As ye look o'er the wall;
        For your conscience, tradition, and name
        Explode with a deadlier blame
            Than the worst of them all.
60   This is the curse. Write.

        Go. wherever ill deeds shall be done,
        Go. plant your flag in the sun
            Beside the ill-doers!
        And recoil from clenching the curse
65   Of God's witnessing Universe
            With a curse of yours.
                THIS is the curse. Write.

                                        1860

❧ ⟪◊⟫ ☙

Frances Ellen Watkins Harper
1825–1911

Best known for her novel *Iola Leroy, or Shadows Uplifted* (1892), FRANCES E.W. HARPER was also a distinguished poet whose work combines Victorian restraint, Christian piety, and political subject matter from slavery to suffrage to temperance. In many poems Harper portrays powerful black "sheroes" (MAYA ANGELOU's term) from history, Biblical literature, and myth—for example, the proud and noble Vashti, the queen banished by the Old Testament king who later chose Esther as his concubine. Harper's writing emphasizes Christian humanism, yet she frequently challenges the passivity expected of women and people of color. Concerned with her own salvation and that of her neighbors, black and white, Harper both empathizes with sufferers and calls them to resistance.

Harper was born in Baltimore, Maryland, to free black parents but was orphaned at age three; she lived thereafter with her clergyman uncle, William Watkins, and attended the school he ran for former slaves. She earned her living first as a nurse and seamstress, then as a teacher, and later as a lecturer for various antislavery societies. In 1860 she married Fenton Harper and temporarily ceased lecturing, only to return four years later after his death to speak in favor of temperance, black education, and women as the moral centers of the home. Although conservative in her views of women as men's ethical guardians, Harper resolutely challenged white women's racism and called for solidarity among women against the institution of slavery. After settling in Philadelphia with her daughter in 1876, Harper served as director of the American Association for the Education of Colored Youth and as vice president of the National Association of Colored Women. The motto of many nineteenth-century black women's organizations, "lift as we climb," lay at the heart of her work.

Harper's earliest collection of poetry, *Forest Leaves* (1845), is no longer extant. Her second collection, *Poems on Miscellaneous Subjects* (1854), was hugely successful; twenty editions of it were published in as many years. "The Two Offers," which Harper sold to *Anglo-African Magazine* in 1859, is believed to be the first story published by an African American. *Moses: A Story of the Nile* (1869), which reveals her attachment to revisionist Biblical themes, portrays a bold, rebellious woman, Princess Charmian, as the savior of Moses from the death her father decreed. *Sketches of Southern Life* (1872) recounts among other tales the saga of the Biblical

Deborah, both a rebel and a deliverer of her people. *Iola Leroy* combines historical romance and realism to depict the Reconstruction era in the Southern United States; it was long considered the first novel published by an African-American woman until the rediscovery of Harriet Wilson's *Our Nig,* which was published thirty years earlier. As Barbara Christian has noted, Harper's idealized portrayal of Iola attempts to counteract racist stereotypes of black women: "since positive female qualities were all attributed to the white lady," Harper "based [her] counterimage on her ideal qualities, more than on those of any real black women." In *Idylls of the Bible* (1901), however, Harper satirizes Alfred, Lord Tennyson's *Idylls of the King* for its sentimental portrayals of white women's purity.

As a poet Harper wrote odes, lyrics, eulogies, ballads, and political protests. Most of her poems contain the regular rhyme scheme and rhythm patterns, narrative flourishes, folk influences, and didacticism of the traditional ballad. Harper's most powerful poetry uses emotional appeal to critique slavery, particularly the hypocrisy of white Christians who supported this heinous institution. She reserves her strongest anger for white women, whose silence on this issue is an act of complicity. Harper believed that black and white women shared a common oppression based on gender. Arguing in 1859 that suffrage would not solve the problems of racism and sexism if it meant joining forces with corrupt white men, she asserted that "it is no honor to shake hands politically with men who whip women and steal babies." The women whom Harper most honors, finally, are black women like Aunt Chloe of "Learning to Read," who defies the racist stereotypes of "Yankee teachers" to embrace at sixty, in her own dialect, both literacy and independence.

⇥ The Slave Mother ⇤

Heard you that shriek? It rose
　　So wildly on the air,
It seemed as if a burdened heart
　　Was breaking in despair.

5　Saw you those hands so sadly clasped—
　　The bowed and feeble hand—
The shuddering of that fragile form—
　　That look of grief and dread?

Saw you the sad, imploring eye?
10　　Its every glance was pain,
As if a storm of agony
　　Were sweeping through the brain.

She is a mother, pale with fear,
　　Her boys clings to her side,
15　And in her kirtle vainly tries
　　His trembling form to hide.

He is not hers, although she bore
　　For him a mother's pains;
He is not hers, although her blood
20　　Is coursing through his veins!

He is not hers, for cruel hands
　　May rudely tear apart
The only wreath of household love
　　That binds her breaking heart.

25 His love has been a joyous light
    That o'er her pathway smiled,
A fountain gushing ever new,
    Amid life's desert wild.

His lightest word has been a tone
30   Of music round her heart,
Their lives a streamlet blent in one—
    Oh, Father! must they part?

They tear him from her circling arms.
    Her last and fond embrace.
35 Oh! never more may her sad eyes
    Gaze on his mournful face.

No marvel, then, these bitter shrieks
    Disturb the listening air;
She is a mother, and her heart
40   Is breaking in despair.

1854

⊰ Free Labor ⊱

I wear an easy garment,
    O'er it no toiling slave
Wept tears of hopeless anguish,
    In his passage to the grave.

5 And from its ample folds
    Shall rise no cry to God,
Upon its warp and woof shall be
    No stain of tears and blood.

Oh, lightly shall it press my form,
10   Unladen with a sigh,
I shall not 'mid its rustling hear,
    Some sad despairing cry.

This fabric is too light to bear
    The weight of bondsmen's tears,
15 I shall not in its texture trace
    The agony of years.

Too light to bear a smothered sigh,
    From some lorn woman's heart,
Whose only wreath of household love
20   Is rudely torn apart.

Then lightly shall it press my form,
    Unburdened by a sigh;
And from its seams and folds shall rise,
    No voice to pierce the sky,

25   And witness at the throne of God,
           In language deep and strong,
       That I have nerved Oppression's hand,
           For deeds of guilt and wrong.

                                                   1874

⇥ An Appeal to My Country Women ⇤

       You can sigh o'er the sad-eyed Armenian
           Who weeps in her desolate home.
       You can mourn o'er the exile of Russia
           From kindred and friends doomed to roam.

5   You can pity the men who have woven
           From passion and appetite chains
       To coil with a terrible tension
           Around their heartstrings and brains.

       You can sorrow o'er little children
10   Disinherited from their birth,
       The wee waifs and toddlers neglected,
           Robbed of sunshine, music and mirth.

       For beasts you have gentle compassion;
           Your mercy and pity they share.
15   For the wretched, outcast and fallen
           You have tenderness, love and care.

       But hark! from our Southland are floating
           Sobs of anguish, murmurs of pain,
       And women heart-stricken are weeping
20   Over their tortured and their slain.

       On their brows the sun has left traces;
           Shrink not from their sorrow in scorn.
       When they entered the threshold of being
           The children of a King were born.

25   Each comes as a guest to the table
           The hands of our God has outspread,
       To fountains that ever leap upward,
           To share in the soil we all tread.

       When we plead for the wrecked and fallen,
30   The exile from far-distant shores,
       Remember that men are still wasting
           Life's crimson around our own doors.

       Have ye not, oh, my favored sisters,
           Just a plea, a prayer or a tear,
35   For mothers who dwell 'neath the shadows
           Of agony, hatred and fear?

Men may tread down the poor and lowly,
    May crush them in anger and hate,
But surely the mills of God's justice
40   Will grind out the grist of their fate.

Oh, people sin-laden and guilty,
    So lusty and proud in your prime,
The sharp sickles of God's retribution
    Will gather your harvest of crime.

45   Weep not, oh my well-sheltered sisters,
    Weep not for the Negro alone,
But weep for your sons who must gather
    The crops which their fathers have sown.

Go read on the tombstones of nations
50   Of chieftains who masterful trod,
The sentence which time has engraven,
    That they had forgotten their God.

'Tis the judgment of God that men reap
    The tares which in madness they sow,
55   Sorrow follows the footsteps of crime,
    And Sin is the consort of Woe.

1894

⊰ Learning to Read ⊱

Very soon the Yankee teachers
    Came down and set up school;
But, oh! how the Rebs did hate it—
    It was agin' their rule.

5   Our masters always tried to hide
    Book learning from our eyes;
Knowledge didn't agree with slavery—
    'Twould make us all too wise.

But some of us would try to steal
10   A little from the book,
And put the words together,
    And learn by hook or crook.

I remember Uncle Caldwell,
    Who took pot liquor fat
15   And greased the pages of his book,
    And hid it in his hat

And had his master ever seen
    The leaves upon his head,
He'd have thought them greasy papers,
20   But nothing to be read.

And there was Mr. Turner's Ben,
  Who heard the children spell,
And picked the words right up by heart,
  And learned to read 'em well.

25 Well, the Northern folks kept sending
  The Yankee teachers down;
And they stood right up and helped us,
  Though Rebs did sneer and frown.

And, I longed to read my Bible,
30   For precious words it said;
But when I begun to learn it,
  Folks just shook their heads,

And said there is no use trying,
  Oh! Chloe, you're too late;
35 But as I was rising sixty,
  I had no time to wait.

So I got a pair of glasses,
  And straight to work I went,
And never stopped till I could read
40   The hymns and Testament.

Then I got a little cabin
  A place to call my own—
And I felt as independent
  As the queen upon her throne.

1872

Rebecca Harding Davis
1831–1910

Early in *Life in the Iron-Mills* (1861) the narrator exclaims mysteriously, "there is a secret down here, in this nightmare fog, that has lain dumb for centuries: I want to make it a real thing to you." She further hints that from the fog a kind of hope emerges—the hope that through the telling of their tale, the "thwarted, wasted lives" and "mighty hungers" of the unheard working poor will be made manifest. Silence must be broken, REBECCA HARDING DAVIS believed, so that the privileged reader would know the abuses of industrialization.

    Davis was born in Washington County, Pennsylvania, into an upper-middle-class family; her father, Richard W. Harding, was a successful businessman, while her mother, Rachel Wilson Harding, raised and tutored five children, of whom Rebecca was the eldest. At the age of fourteen she was sent from Wheeling, where her family had moved when she was five, back to Pennsylvania to live with an aunt and attend finishing school. There she read voraciously; there, too, she met Francis Le Moyne, a renowned physician, abolitionist, and social reformer who helped her see what she would later call "a gulf of pain and wrong . . . the underlife of America." Upon her return to Wheeling, Davis became a reclusive writer secretly observing the negative effects of mill life on the workers around her. Although she sent *Life in the Iron-Mills* to the *Atlantic Monthly* without expecting it to be published, it was accepted at once by the editor, James T. Fields, who paid her the then-huge sum of fifty dollars for the story and offered her a one hundred dollar advance for the right to publish any writing she might have in progress. *Life in the Iron-Mills* was an overnight success, disturbing readers unfamiliar with the "dark satanic mills" and the "living death" that mill work caused. Davis then sent her first novel, *Margret Howth: A Story of Today*, to Fields at the *Atlantic Monthly* only to have it rejected because, in his words, "it assembles the gloom too depressingly." Fields agreed to read a revised version, however, and during 1861–62 *Margret Howth* was published serially in his magazine.

That same year L. Clarke Davis invited Rebecca Harding to write a mystery novel for *Peterson's* magazine, to which he was a regular contributor; she accepted this assignment and went on to write numerous stories for this popular publication. Later that year she visited James Fields and his wife, Annie, at their home in Boston, where she met such luminaries as Oliver Wendell Holmes, Ralph Waldo Emerson, Louisa May Alcott, and Nathaniel Hawthorne—an experience she would record many years later in *Bits of Gossip* (1904). On her way home from Boston she visited Davis, who had begun to court her through the mail, and in 1863 she married this writer and abolitionist, moving with him to Philadelphia to live in a crowded home with his sister and her children. The couple had a daughter, Nora, and two sons, Richard Harding and Charles Belmont Davis. To increase the household income Davis wrote what she described as mediocre fiction for *Peterson's*. Eventually she became a contributing editor for the *New York Tribune* and again began to address social problems in her novels and essays.

Waiting for the Verdict (1867) examines how the United States might redress the ills of slavery; another novel, *John Andross* (1874), explores government corruption. Davis's essay "Put Out of Her Way" (1871), which criticizes laws that favor institutionalizing the insane, helped to change a Pennsylvania law defining lunacy. "Earthen Pitchers" (1873–74), a story serialized in *Scribner's*, features two professional women artists and reveals a surprising disillusionment with marriage, which Davis at times idealized. Although none of these works brought her the praise she had won with *Life in the Iron-Mills*, her first collection of short stories, *Silhouettes of American Life* (1892), renewed critical interest in her work.

Life in the Iron-Mills, or *The Korl Woman*, was, in the words of TILLIE OLSEN, "a forgotten American classic" until its reprinting in 1972 by the Feminist Press. Davis's powerful characters—Hugh Wolfe, a consumptive millhand who is also an artist; Deborah, a young girl afflicted from years of working the cotton looms—reveal the painful existence of those who must labor incessantly to feed themselves and their families. As Olsen asserts in her introduction to the 1972 edition, "No one in literature has opposed the prevalent 'American right to rise . . . A man may make himself anything he chooses' with Rebecca Harding's living question: 'What are rights without means?'"

⊰ Life in the Iron-Mills ⊱

"Is this the end?
O Life, as futile, then, as frail!
What hope of answer or redress?"[1]

A cloudy day: do you know what that is in a town of ironworks? The sky sank down before dawn, muddy, flat, immovable. The air is thick, clammy with the breath of crowded human beings. It stifles me. I open the window, and, looking out, can

1. A quotation from "In Memoriam A.H.H." (1833), an elegy by the English poet Alfred, Lord Tennyson (1809–1892).

scarcely see through the rain the grocer's shop opposite, where a crowd of drunken Irishmen are puffing Lynchburg tobacco in their pipes. I can detect the scent through all the foul smells ranging loose in the air.

The idiosyncrasy of this town is smoke. It rolls sullenly in slow folds from the great chimneys of the iron foundries, and settles down in black, slimy pools on the muddy streets. Smoke on the wharves, smoke on the dingy boats, on the yellow river—clinging in a coating of greasy soot to the housefront, the two faded poplars, the faces of the passerby. The long train of mules, dragging masses of pin-iron through the narrow street, have a foul vapor hanging to their reeking sides. Here, inside, is a little broken figure of an angel pointing upward from the mantel shelf; but even its wings are covered with smoke, clotted and black. Smoke everywhere! A dirty canary chirps desolately in a cage beside me. Its dream of green fields and sunshine is a very old dream—almost worn out, I think.

From the back window I can see a narrow brickyard sloping down to the riverside, strewed with rain-butts and tubs. The river, dull and tawny-colored, (*la bella rivière!*) drags itself sluggishly along, tired of the heavy weight of boats and coal barges. What wonder? When I was a child, I used to fancy a look of weary, dumb appeal upon the face of the negro-like river slavishly bearing its burden day after day. Something of the same idle notion comes to me today, when from the street window I look on the slow stream of human life creeping past, night and morning, to the great mills. Masses of men, with dull, besotted faces bent to the ground, sharpened here and there by pain or cunning; skin and muscle and flesh begrimed with smoke and ashes; stooping all night over boiling cauldrons of metal, laired by day in dens of drunkenness and infamy; breathing from infancy to death an air saturated with fog and grease and soot, vileness for soul and body. What do you make of a case like that, amateur psychologist? You call it an altogether serious thing to be alive: to these men it is a drunken jest, a joke—horrible to angels perhaps, to them common-place enough. My fancy about the river was an idle one: It is no type of such a life. What if it be stagnant and slimy here? It knows that beyond there waits for it odorous sunlight— quaint old gardens, dusky with soft, green foliage of apple trees, and flushing crimson with roses—air, and fields, and mountains. The future of the Welsh puddler passing just now is not so pleasant. To be stowed away, after his grimy work is done, in a hole in the muddy graveyard, and after that—*not* air, nor green fields, nor curious roses.

Can you see how foggy the day is? As I stand here, idly tapping the windowpane, and looking out through the rain at the dirty back yard and the coal boats below, fragments of an old story float up before me—a story of this old house into which I happened to come today. You may think it a tiresome story enough, as foggy as the day, sharpened by no sudden flashes of pain or pleasure.—I know: only the outline of a dull life, that long since, with thousands of dull lives like its own, was vainly lived and lost: thousands of them—massed, vile, slimy lives, like those of the torpid lizards in yonder stagnant water-butt.—Lost? There is a curious point for you to settle, my friend, who study psychology in a lazy, *dilettante* way. Stop a moment. I am going to be honest. This is what I want you to do. I want you to hide your disgust, take no heed to your clean clothes, and come right down with me—here, into the thickest of the fog and mud and foul effluvia. I want you to hear this story. There is a secret down here, in this nightmare fog, that has lain dumb for centuries: I want to make it a real thing to you. You, Egoist, or Pantheist, or Arminian,[2] busy in making straight paths for your feet on the hills, do not see it clearly—this terrible question which men here have gone mad and

2. Followers of Dutch theologian James Arminius (1560–1609), who challenged the Calvinist belief in predestination.

died trying to answer. I dare not put this secret into words. I told you it was dumb. These men, going by with drunken faces and brains full of unawakened power, do not ask it of Society or of God. Their lives ask it; their deaths ask it. There is no reply. I will tell you plainly that I have a great hope; and I bring it to you to be tested. It is this: that this terrible dumb question is its own reply; that it is not the sentence of death we think it, but, from the very extremity of its darkness, the most solemn prophecy which the world has known of the Hope to come. I dare make my meaning no clearer, but will only tell my story. It will, perhaps, seem to you as foul and dark as this thick vapor about us, and as pregnant with death; but if your eyes are free as mine are to look deeper, no perfume-tinted dawn will be so fair with promise of the day that shall surely come.

My story is very simple—only what I remember of the life of one of these men—a furnace-tender in one of Kirby & John's rolling-mills—Hugh Wolfe. You know the mills? They took the great order for the Lower Virginia railroads there last winter; run usually with about a thousand men. I cannot tell why I choose the half-forgotten story of this Wolfe more than that of myriads of these furnacehands. Perhaps because there is a secret underlying sympathy between that story and this day with its impure fog and thwarted sunshine—or perhaps simply for the reason that this house is the one where the Wolfes lived. There were the father and son—both hands, as I said, in one of Kirby & John's mills for making railroad iron—and Deborah, their cousin, a picker in some of the cotton mills. The house was rented then to half a dozen families. The Wolfes had two of the cellar rooms. The old man, like many of the puddlers and feeders of the mills, was Welsh—had spent half of his life in the Cornish tin mines. You may pick the Welsh emigrants, Cornish miners, out of the throng passing the windows, any day. They are a trifle more filthy; their muscles are not so brawny; they stoop more. When they are drunk, they neither yell, nor shout, nor stagger, but skulk along like beaten hounds. A pure, unmixed blood, I fancy: shows itself in the slight angular bodies and sharply cut facial lines. It is nearly thirty years since the Wolfes lived here. Their lives were like those of their class: incessant labor, sleeping in kennel-like rooms, eating rank pork and molasses, drinking—God and the distillers only know what; with an occasional night in jail, to atone for some drunken excess. Is that all of their lives?—of the portion given to them and these their duplicates swarming the streets today?—nothing beneath?—all? So many a political reformer will tell you,—and many a private reformer, too, who has gone among them with a heart tender with Christ's charity, and come out outraged, hardened.

One rainy night, about eleven o'clock, a crowd of half-clothed women stopped outside of the cellar-door. They were going home from the cotton mill.

"Good night, Deb," said one, a mulatto, steadying herself against the gas post. She needed the post to steady her. So did more than one of them.

"Dah 's a ball to Miss Potts' tonight. Ye 'd best come."

"Inteet, Deb, if hur 'll come, hur 'll hef fun," said a shrill Welsh voice in the crowd.

Two or three dirty hands were thrust out to catch the gown of the woman, who was groping for the latch of the door.

"No."

"No? Where 's Kit Small, then?"

"Begorra! on the spools. Alleys behint, though we helped her, we dud. An wid ye! Let Deb alone! It 's ondacent frettin' a quite body. Be the powers, an' we 'll have a night of it! there 'll be lashin's o' drink,—the Vargent be blessed and praised for 't!"

They went on, the mulatto inclining for a moment to show fight, and drag the woman Wolfe off with them; but, being pacified, she staggered away.

Deborah groped her way into the cellar, and, after considerable stumbling, kindled a match, and lighted a tallow dip, that sent a yellow glimmer over the room. It was low, damp—the earthen floor covered with a green, slimy moss—a fetid air smothering the breath. Old Wolfe lay asleep on a heap of straw, wrapped in a torn horse blanket. He was a pale, meek little man, with a white face and red rabbit-eyes. The woman Deborah was like him; only her face was even more ghastly, her lips bluer, her eyes more watery. She wore a faded cotton gown and a slouching bonnet. When she walked, one could see that she was deformed, almost a hunchback. She trod softly, so as not to waken him, and went through into the room beyond. There she found by the half-extinguished fire an iron saucepan filled with cold boiled potatoes, which she put upon a broken chair with a pint cup of ale. Placing the old candlestick beside this dainty repast, she untied her bonnet, which hung limp and wet over her face, and prepared to eat her supper. It was the first food that had touched her lips since morning. There was enough of it, however: there is not always. She was hungry—one could see that easily enough—and not drunk, as most of her companions would have been found at this hour. She did not drink, this woman—her face told that, too—nothing stronger than ale. Perhaps the weak, flaccid wretch had some stimulant in her pale life to keep her up—some love or hope, it might be, or urgent need. When that stimulant was gone, she would take to whiskey. Man cannot live by work alone. While she was skinning the potatoes, and munching them, a noise behind her made her stop.

"Janey!" she called, lifting the candle and peering into the darkness. "Janey, are you there?"

A heap of ragged coats was heaved up, and the face of a young girl emerged, staring sleepily at the woman.

"Deborah," she said, at last, "I'm here the night."

"Yes, child. Hur 's welcome," she said, quietly eating on.

The girl's face was haggard and sickly; her eyes were heavy with sleep and hunger: real Milesian eyes they were, dark, delicate blue, glooming out from black shadows with a pitiful fright.

"I was alone," she said, timidly.

"Where 's the father?" asked Deborah, holding out a potato, which the girl greedily seized.

"He 's beyant—wid Haley—in the stone house." (Did you ever hear the word *jail* from an Irish mouth?) "I came here. Hugh told me never to stay me-lone."

"Hugh?"

"Yes."

A vexed frown crossed her face. The girl saw it, and added quickly—

"I have not seen Hugh the day, Deb. The old man says his watch lasts till the mornin'."

The woman sprang up, and hastily began to arrange some bread and flitch in a tin pail, and to pour her own measure of ale into a bottle. Tying on her bonnet, she blew out the candle.

"Lay ye down, Janey dear," she said, gently, covering her with the old rags. "Hur can eat the potatoes, if hur 's hungry."

"Where are ye goin', Deb? The rain 's sharp."

"To the mill, with Hugh's supper."

"Let him bide till th' morn. Sit ye down."

"No, no,"—sharply pushing her off. "The boy 'll starve."

She hurried from the cellar, while the child wearily coiled herself up for sleep. The rain was falling heavily, as the woman, pail in hand, emerged from the mouth of the alley, and turned down the narrow street, that stretched out, long and black, miles before her. Here and there a flicker of gas lighted an uncertain space of muddy foot-walk and gutter; the long rows of houses, except an occasional lager-bier shop, were closed; now and then she met a band of millhands skulking to or from their work.

Not many even of the inhabitants of a manufacturing town know the vast machinery of system by which the bodies of workmen are governed, that goes on unceasingly from year to year. The hands of each mill are divided into watches that relieve each other as regularly as the sentinels of an army. By night and day the work goes on, the unsleeping engines groan and shriek, the fiery pools of metal boil and surge. Only for a day in the week, in half-courtesy to public censure, the fires are partially veiled; but as soon as the clock strikes midnight, the great furnaces break forth with renewed fury, the clamor begins with fresh, breathless vigor, the engines sob and shriek like "gods in pain."

As Deborah hurried down through the heavy rain, the noise of these thousand engines sounded through the sleep and shadow of the city like far-off thunder. The mill to which she was going lay on the river, a mile below the city limits. It was far, and she was weak, aching from standing twelve hours at the spools. Yet it was her almost nightly walk to take this man his supper, though at every square she sat down to rest, and she knew she should receive small word of thanks.

Perhaps, if she had possessed an artist's eye, the picturesque oddity of the scene might have made her step stagger less, and the path seem shorter; but to her the mills were only "summat deilish to look at by night."

The road leading to the mills had been quarried from the solid rock, which rose abrupt and bare on one side of the cinder-covered road, while the river, sluggish and black, crept past on the other. The mills for rolling iron are simply immense tent-like roofs, covering acres of ground, open on every side. Beneath these roofs Deborah looked in on a city of fires, that burned hot and fiercely in the night. Fire in every horrible form: pits of flame waving in the wind; liquid metal flames writhing in tortu-ous streams through the sand; wide cauldrons filled with boiling fire, over which bent ghastly wretches stirring the strange brewing; and through all, crowds of half-clad men, looking like revengeful ghosts in the red light, hurried, throwing masses of glit-tering fire. It was like a street in Hell. Even Deborah muttered, as she crept through, "'T looks like t' Devil's place!" It did—in more ways than one.

She found the man she was looking for, at last, heaping coal on a furnace. He had not time to eat his supper; so she went behind the furnace, and waited. Only a few men were with him, and they noticed her only by a "Hyur comes t' hunchback, Wolfe."

Deborah was stupid with sleep; her back pained her sharply; and her teeth chat-tered with cold, with the rain that soaked her clothes and dripped from her at every step. She stood, however, patiently holding the pail, and waiting.

"Hout, woman! ye look like a drowned cat. Come near to the fire," said one of the men, approaching to scrape away the ashes.

She shook her head. Wolfe had forgotten her. He turned, hearing the man, and came closer.

"I did no' think; gi' me my supper, woman."

She watched him eat with a painful eagerness. With a woman's quick instinct, she saw that he was not hungry—was eating to please her. Her pale, watery eyes began to gather a strange light.

"Is 't good, Hugh? T' ale was a bit sour, I feared."

"No, good enough." He hesitated a moment. "Ye 're tired, poor lass! Bide here till I go. Lay down there on that heap of ash, and go to sleep."

He threw her an old coat for a pillow, and turned to his work. The heap was the refuse of the burnt iron, and was not a hard bed; the half-smothered warmth, too, penetrated her limbs, dulling their pain and cold shiver.

Miserable enough she looked, lying there on the ashes like a limp, dirty rag—yet not an unfitting figure to crown the scene of hopeless discomfort and veiled crime: more fitting, if one looked deeper into the heart of things—at her thwarted woman's form, her colorless life, her waking stupor that smothered pain and hunger—even more fit to be a type of her class. Deeper yet if one could look, was there nothing worth reading in this wet, faded thing, half-covered with ashes? no story of a soul filled with groping passionate love, heroic unselfishness, fierce jealousy? of years of weary trying to please the one human being whom she loved, to gain one look of real heart-kindness from him? If anything like this were hidden beneath the pale, bleared eyes, and dull, washed-out-looking face, no one had ever taken the trouble to read its faint signs: not the half-clothed furnace-tender, Wolfe, certainly. Yet he was kind to her: it was his nature to be kind, even to the very rats that swarmed in the cellar: kind to her in just the same way. She knew that. And it might be that very knowledge had given to her face its apathy and vacancy more than her low, torpid life. One sees that dead, vacant look steal sometimes over the rarest, finest of women's faces—in the very midst, it may be, of their warmest summer's day; and then one can guess at the secret of intolerable solitude that lies hid beneath the delicate laces and brilliant smile. There was no warmth, no brilliancy, no summer for this woman; so the stupor and vacancy had time to gnaw into her face perpetually. She was young, too, though no one guessed it; so the gnawing was the fiercer.

She lay quiet in the dark corner, listening, through the monotonous din and uncertain glare of the works, to the dull plash of the rain in the far distance, shrinking back whenever the man Wolfe happened to look towards her. She knew, in spite of all his kindness, that there was that in her face and form which made him loathe the sight of her. She felt by instinct, although she could not comprehend it, the finer nature of the man, which made him among his fellow workmen something unique, set apart. She knew, that, down under all the vileness and coarseness of his life, there was a groping passion for whatever was beautiful and pure—that his soul sickened with disgust at her deformity, even when his words were kindest. Through this dull consciousness, which never left her, came, like a sting, the recollection of the dark blue eyes and lithe figure of the little Irish girl she had left in the cellar. The recollection struck through even her stupid intellect with a vivid glow of beauty and of grace. Little Janey, timid, helpless, clinging to Hugh as her only friend: that was the sharp thought, the bitter thought, that drove into the glazed eyes a fierce light of pain. You laugh at it? Are pain and jealousy less savage realities down here in this place I am taking you to than in your own house or your own heart—your heart, which they clutch at sometimes? The note is the same, I fancy, be the octave high or low.

If you could go into this mill where Deborah lay, and drag out from the hearts of these men the terrible tragedy of their lives, taking it as a symptom of the disease of their class, no ghost Horror would terrify you more. A reality of soul-starvation, of living death, that meets you every day under the besotted faces on the street—I can paint nothing of this, only give you the outside outlines of a night, a crisis in the life of one man: whatever muddy depth of soul-history lies beneath you can read according to the eyes God has given you.

Wolfe, while Deborah watched him as a spaniel its master, bent over the furnace with his iron pole, unconscious of her scrutiny, only stopping to receive orders. Physically, Nature had promised the man but little. He had already lost the strength and instinct vigor of a man, his muscles were thin, his nerves weak, his face (a meek, woman's face) haggard, yellow with consumption. In the mill he was known as one of the girl-men: "Molly Wolfe" was his *sobriquet*. He was never seen in the cockpit, did not own a terrier, drank but seldom; when he did, desperately. He fought sometimes, but was always thrashed, pummeled to a jelly. The man was game enough, when his blood was up: but he was no favorite in the mill; he had the taint of school-learning on him—not to a dangerous extent, only a quarter or so in the free school in fact, but enough to ruin him as a good hand in a fight.

For other reasons, too, he was not popular. Not one of themselves, they felt that, though outwardly as filthy and ash-covered; silent, with foreign thoughts and longings breaking out through his quietness in innumerable curious ways: this one, for instance. In the neighboring furnace buildings lay great heaps of the refuse from the ore after the pig metal is run. *Korl* we call it here: a light, porous substance, of a delicate, waxen, flesh-colored tinge. Out of the blocks of this korl, Wolfe, in his off hours from the furnace, had a habit of chipping and molding figures—hideous, fantastic enough, but sometimes strangely beautiful: even the mill-men saw that, while they jeered at him. It was a curious fancy in the man, almost a passion. The few hours for rest he spent hewing and hacking with his blunt knife, never speaking, until his watch came again—working at one figure for months, and, when it was finished, breaking it to pieces perhaps, in a fit of disappointment. A morbid, gloomy man, untaught, unled, left to feed his soul in grossness and crime, and hard, grinding labor. I want you to come down and look at this Wolfe, standing there among the lowest of his kind, and see him just as he is, that you may judge him justly when you hear the story of this night. I want you to look back, as he does every day, at his birth in vice, his starved infancy; to remember the heavy years he has groped through as boy and man—the slow, heavy years of constant, hot work. So long ago he began, that he thinks sometimes he has worked there for ages. There is no hope that it will ever end. Think that God put into this man's soul a fierce thirst for beauty—to know it, to create it; to *be*—something, he knows not what—other than he is. There are moments when a passing cloud, the sun glinting on the purple thistles, a kindly smile, a child's face, will rouse him to a passion of pain—when his nature starts up with a mad cry of rage against God, man, whoever it is that has forced this vile, slimy life upon him. With all this groping, this mad desire, a great blind intellect stumbling through wrong, a loving poet's heart, the man was by habit only a coarse, vulgar laborer, familiar with sights and words you would blush to name. Be just: when I tell you about this night, see him as he is. Be just—not like man's law, which seizes on one isolated fact, but like God's judging angel, whose clear, sad eye saw all the countless cankering days of this man's life, all the countless nights, when, sick with starving, his soul fainted in him, before it judged him for this night, the saddest of all.

I called this night the crisis of his life. If it was, it stole on him unawares. These great turning-days of life cast no shadow before, slip by unconsciously. Only a trifle, a little turn of the rudder, and the ship goes to heaven or hell.

Wolfe, while Deborah watched him, dug into the furnace of melting iron with his pole, dully thinking only how many rails the lump would yield. It was late—nearly Sunday morning; another hour, and the heavy work would be done—only the furnaces to replenish and cover for the next day. The workmen were growing more noisy, shouting, as they had to do, to be heard over the deep clamor of the mills. Suddenly they grew less boisterous—at the far end, entirely silent. Something unusual had happened. After a moment, the silence came nearer; the men stopped their jeers and drunken choruses. Deborah, stupidly lifting up her head, saw the cause of the quiet. A group of five or six men were slowly approaching, stopping to examine each furnace as they came. Visitors often came to see the mills after night: except by growing less noisy, the men took no notice of them. The furnace where Wolfe worked was near the bounds of the works; they halted there hot and tired: a walk over one of these great foundries is no trifling task. The woman, drawing out of sight, turned over to sleep. Wolfe, seeing them stop, suddenly roused from his indifferent stupor, and watched them keenly. He knew some of them: the overseer, Clarke—a son of Kirby, one of the mill owners—and a Doctor May, one of the town physicians. The other two were strangers. Wolfe came closer. He seized eagerly every chance that brought him into contact with this mysterious class that shone down on him perpetually with the glamor of another order of being. What made the difference between them? That was the mystery of his life. He had a vague notion that perhaps tonight he could find it out. One of the strangers sat down on a pile of bricks, and beckoned young Kirby to his side.

"This *is* hot, with a vengeance. A match, please?"—lighting his cigar. "But the walk is worth the trouble. If it were not that you must have heard it so often, Kirby, I would tell you that your works look like Dante's Inferno."

Kirby laughed.

"Yes. Yonder is Farinata[3] himself in the burning tomb—" pointing to some figure in the shimmering shadows.

"Judging from some of the faces of your men," said the other, "they bid fair to try the reality of Dante's vision, some day."

Young Kirby looked curiously around, as if seeing the faces of his hands for the first time.

"They're bad enough, that 's true. A desperate set, I fancy. Eh, Clarke?"

The overseer did not hear him. He was talking of net profits just then—giving, in fact, a schedule of the annual business of the firm to a sharp peering little Yankee, who jotted down notes on a paper laid on the crown of his hat: a reporter for one of the city papers, getting up a series of reviews of the leading manufactories. The other gentlemen had accompanied them merely for amusement. They were silent until the notes were finished, drying their feet at the furnaces, and sheltering their faces from the intolerable heat. At last the overseer concluded with—

"I believe that is a pretty fair estimate, Captain."

"Here, some of you men!" said Kirby, "bring up those boards. We may as well sit down, gentlemen, until the rain is over. It cannot last much longer at this rate."

"Pig metal," mumbled the reporter, "um!—coal facilities—um!—hands employed, twelve hundred—bitumen—um!—all right, I believe, Mr. Clarke—sinking fund— what did you say was your sinking fund?"

"Twelve hundred hands?" said the stranger, the young man who had first spoken. "Do you control their votes, Kirby?"

"Control? No." The young man smiled complacently. "But my father brought seven hundred votes to the polls for his candidate last November. No force work, you understand—only a speech or two, a hint to form themselves into a society, and a bit of red and blue bunting to make them a flag. The Invincible Roughs—I believe that is their name. I forget the motto: 'Our country's hope,' I think."

There was a laugh. The young man talking to Kirby sat with an amused light in his cool gray eye, surveying critically the half-clothed figures of the puddlers, and the slow swing of their brawny muscles. He was a stranger in the city, spending a couple of months in the borders of a slave state, to study the institutions of the South—a brother-in-law of

3. A thirteenth-century Florentine revolutionary leader whom the Italian poet Dante Aleghieri (1265–1321) portrayed as a heretic. Dante's *Inferno* depicted his vision of hell.

Kirby's—Mitchell. He was an amateur gymnast, hence his anatomical eye; a patron, in a *blasé* way, of the prize ring; a man who sucked the essence out of a science or philosophy in an indifferent, gentlemanly way; who took Kant, Novalis, Humboldt,[4] for what they were worth in his own scales; accepting all, despising nothing, in heaven, earth, or hell, but one-idea'd men; with a temper yielding and brilliant as summer water, until his Self was touched, when it was ice, though brilliant still. Such men are not rare in the States.

As he knocked the ashes from his cigar, Wolfe caught with a quick pleasure the contour of the white hand, the blood-glow of a red ring he wore. His voice, too, and that of Kirby's, touched him like music—low, even, with chording cadences. About this man Mitchell hung the impalpable atmosphere belonging to the thoroughbred gentleman. Wolfe, scraping away the ashes beside him, was conscious of it, did obeisance to it with his artist sense, unconscious that he did so.

The rain did not cease. Clarke and the reporter left the mills; the others, comfortably seated near the furnace, lingered, smoking and talking in a desultory way. Greek would not have been more unintelligible to the furnace tenders, whose presence they soon forgot entirely. Kirby drew out a newspaper from his pocket and read aloud some article, which they discussed eagerly. At every sentence, Wolfe listened more and more like a dumb, hopeless animal, with a duller, more stolid look creeping over his face, glancing now and then at Mitchell, marking acutely every smallest sign of refinement, then back to himself, seeing as in a mirror his filthy body, his more stained soul.

Never! He had no words for such a thought, but he knew now, in all the sharpness of the bitter certainty, that between them there was a great gulf never to be passed. Never!

The bell of the mills rang for midnight. Sunday morning had dawned. Whatever hidden message lay in the tolling bells floated past these men unknown. Yet it was there. Veiled in the solemn music ushering the risen Savior was a keynote to solve the darkest secrets of a world gone wrong—even this social riddle which the brain of the grimy puddler grappled with madly tonight.

The men began to withdraw the metal from the cauldrons. The mills were deserted on Sundays, except by the hands who fed the fires, and those who had no lodgings and slept usually on the ash heaps. The three strangers sat still during the next hour, watching the men cover the furnaces, laughing now and then at some jest of Kirby's.

"Do you know," said Mitchell, "I like this view of the works better than when the glare was fiercest? These heavy shadows and the amphitheatre of smothered fires are ghostly, unreal. One could fancy these red smoldering lights to be the half-shut eyes of wild beasts, and the spectral figures their victims in the den."

Kirby laughed. "You are fanciful. Come, let us get out of the den. The spectral figures, as you call them, are a little too real for me to fancy a close proximity in the darkness—unarmed, too."

The others rose, buttoning their overcoats, and lighting cigars.

"Raining, still," said Doctor May, "and hard. Where did we leave the coach, Mitchell?"

"At the other side of the works. Kirby, what 's that?"

Mitchell started back, half-frightened, as, suddenly turning a corner, the white figure of a woman faced him in the darkness—a woman, white, of giant proportions, crouching on the ground, her arms flung out in some wild gesture of warning.

"Stop! Make that fire burn there!" cried Kirby, stopping short.

---

4. Immanuel Kant (1724–1804) was a German philosopher; Novalis was the pseudonym of Friedrich Leopold Freiherr von Hardenberg (1722–1801), a German Romantic poet; Wilhelm von Humboldt (1767–1835) was a Prussian statesman and humanist.

The flame burst out, flashing the gaunt figure into bold relief.

Mitchell drew a long breath.

"I thought it was alive," he said, going up curiously.

The others followed.

"Not marble, eh?" asked Kirby, touching it.

One of the lower overseers stopped.

"Korl, Sir."

"Who did it?"

"Can't say. Some of the hands; chipped it out in off hours."

"Chipped to some purpose, I should say. What a flesh-tint the stuff has! Do you see, Mitchell?"

"I see."

He had stepped aside where the light fell boldest on the figure, looking at it in silence. There was not one line of beauty or grace in it: a nude woman's form, muscular, grown coarse with labor, the powerful limbs instinct with some one poignant longing. One idea: there it was in the tense, rigid muscles, the clutching hands, the wild, eager face, like that of a starving wolf's. Kirby and Doctor May walked around it, critical, curious. Mitchell stood aloof, silent. The figure touched him strangely.

"Not badly done," said Doctor May. "Where did the fellow learn that sweep of the muscles in the arm and hand? Look at them! They are groping—do you see?—clutching: the peculiar action of a man dying of thirst."

"They have ample facilities for studying anatomy," sneered Kirby, glancing at the half-naked figures.

"Look," continued the Doctor, "at this bony wrist, and the strained sinews of the instep! A working woman—the very type of her class."

"God forbid!" muttered Mitchell.

"Why?" demanded May. "What does the fellow intend by the figure? I cannot catch the meaning."

"Ask him," said the other, dryly. "There he stands—" pointing to Wolfe, who stood with a group of men, leaning on his ash-rake.

The doctor beckoned him with the affable smile which kind-hearted men put on, when talking to these people.

"Mr. Mitchell has picked you out as the man who did this—I'm sure I don't know why. But what did you mean by it?"

"She be hungry."

Wolfe's eyes answered Mitchell, not the Doctor.

"Oh-h! But what a mistake you have made, my fine fellow! You have given no sign of starvation to the body. It is strong—terribly strong. It has the mad, half-despairing gesture of drowning."

Wolfe stammered, glanced appealingly at Mitchell, who saw the soul of the thing, he knew. But the cool, probing eyes were turned on himself now—mocking, cruel, relentless.

"Not hungry for meat," the furnace tender said at last.

"What then? Whiskey?" jeered Kirby, with a coarse laugh.

Wolfe was silent a moment, thinking.

"I dunno," he said, with a bewildered look. "It mebbe. Summat to make her live, I think—like you. Whiskey ull do it, in a way."

The young man laughed again. Mitchell flashed a look of disgust somewhere—not at Wolfe.

"May," he broke out impatiently, "are you blind? Look at that woman's face! It asks questions of God, and says, 'I have a right to know.' Good God, how hungry it is!"

They looked a moment; then May turned to the mill owner:

"Have you many such hands as this? What are you going to do with them? Keep them at puddling iron?"

Kirby shrugged his shoulders. Mitchell's look had irritated him.

"*Ce n'est pas mon affaire.* I have no fancy for nursing infant geniuses. I suppose there are some stray gleams of mind and soul among these wretches. The Lord will take care of his own; or else they can work out their own salvation. I have heard you call our American system a ladder which any man can scale. Do you doubt it? Or perhaps you want to banish all social ladders, and put us all on a flat table-land—eh, May?"

The doctor looked vexed, puzzled. Some terrible problem lay hid in this woman's face, and troubled these men. Kirby waited for an answer, and, receiving none, went on, warming with his subject.

"I tell you, there 's something wrong that no talk of '*Liberté*' or '*Égalité*' will do away. If I had the making of men, these men who do the lowest part of the world's work should be machines—nothing more—hands. It would be kindness. God help them! What are taste, reason, to creatures who must live such lives as that?" He pointed to Deborah, sleeping on the ash heap. "So many nerves to sting them to pain. What if God had put your brain, with all its agony of touch, into your fingers, and bid you work and strike with that?"

"You think you could govern the world better?" laughed the doctor.

"I do not think at all."

"That is true philosophy. Drift with the stream, because you cannot dive deep enough to find bottom, eh?"

"Exactly," rejoined Kirby. "I do not think. I wash my hands of all social problems— slavery, caste, white or black. My duty to my operatives has a narrow limit—the pay hour on Saturday night. Outside of that, if they cut korl, or cut each other's throats, (the more popular amusement of the two), I am not responsible."

The doctor sighed—a good honest sigh, from the depths of his stomach.

"God help us! Who is responsible?"

"Not I, I tell you," said Kirby, testily. "What has the man who pays them money to do with their souls' concerns, more than the grocer or butcher who takes it?"

"And yet," said Mitchell's cynical voice, "look at her! How hungry she is!"

Kirby tapped his boot with his cane. No one spoke. Only the dumb face of the rough image looking into their faces with the awful question, "What shall we do to be saved?" Only Wolfe's face, with its heavy weight of brain, its weak, uncertain mouth, its desperate eyes, out of which looked the soul of his class—only Wolfe's face turned towards Kirby's. Mitchell laughed—a cool, musical laugh.

"Money has spoken!" he said, seating himself lightly on a stone with the air of an amused spectator at a play. "Are you answered?"—turning to Wolfe his clear, magnetic face.

Bright and deep and cold as arctic air, the soul of the man lay tranquil beneath. He looked at the furnace tender as he had looked at a rare mosaic in the morning; only the man was the more amusing study of the two.

"Are you answered? Why, May, look at him! '*De profundis clamavi.*'[5] Or, to quote in English, 'Hungry and thirsty, his soul faints in him.' And so Money sends back its

5. I have cried out of the deep [unto thee, O Lord] – Psalm 130:1.

answer into the depths through you, Kirby! Very clear the answer, too! I think I remember reading the same words somewhere—washing your hands in eau de cologne, and saying, 'I am innocent of the blood of this man. See ye to it!'"[6]

Kirby flushed angrily.

"You quote Scripture freely."

"Do I not quote correctly? I think I remember another line, which may amend my meaning: 'Inasmuch as ye did it unto one of the least of these, ye did it unto me.' Deist? Bless you, man, I was raised on the milk of the Word. Now, Doctor, the pocket of the world having uttered its voice, what has the heart to say? You are a philanthropist, in a small way—*n'est ce pas?* Here, boy, this gentleman can show you how to cut korl better—or your destiny. Go on, May!"

"I think a mocking devil possesses you tonight," rejoined the doctor, seriously.

He went to Wolfe and put his hand kindly on his arm. Something of a vague idea possessed the doctor's brain that much good was to be done here by a friendly word or two: a latent genius to be warmed into life by a waited-for sunbeam. Here it was: he had brought it. So he went on complacently:

"Do you know, boy, you have it in you to be a great sculptor, a great man?—do you understand?" (talking down to the capacity of his hearer: it is a way people have with children, and men like Wolfe)—"to live a better, stronger life than I, or Mr. Kirby here? A man may make himself anything he chooses. God has given you stronger powers than many men—me, for instance."

May stopped, heated, glowing with his own magnanimity. And it was magnanimous. The puddler had drunk in every word, looking through the doctor's flurry, and generous heat, and self-approval, into his will, with those slow, absorbing eyes of his.

"Make yourself what you will. It is your right."

"I know," quietly. "Will you help me?"

Mitchell laughed again. The Doctor turned now, in a passion,—

"You know, Mitchell, I have not the means. You know, if I had, it is in my heart to take this boy and educate him for"—

"The glory of God, and the glory of John May."

May did not speak for a moment; then, controlled, he said—

"Why should one be raised, when myriads are left?—I have not the money, boy," to Wolfe, shortly.

"Money?" He said it over slowly, as one repeats the guessed answer to a riddle, doubtfully. "That is it? Money?"

"Yes, money—that is it," said Mitchell, rising, and drawing his furred coat about him. "You've found the cure for all the world's diseases. Come, May, find your good humor, and come home. This damp wind chills my very bones. Come and preach your Saint-Simonian doctrines[7] tomorrow to Kirby's hands. Let them have a clear idea of the rights of the soul, and I'll venture next week they'll strike for higher wages. That will be the end of it."

"Will you send the coach driver to this side of the mills?" asked Kirby, turning to Wolfe.

He spoke kindly: It was his habit to do so. Deborah, seeing the puddler go, crept after him. The three men waited outside. Doctor May walked up and down, chafed. Suddenly he stopped.

---

6. These words of Pontius Pilate, the Roman judge who allowed Christ to be crucified, reveal an unwillingness to accept responsibility (see Matthew 27:24).

7. Beliefs of Claude-Henri de Rouvroy de Saint-Simon (1760–1825), a French philosopher who founded a socialist and utopian sect.

"Go back, Mitchell! You say the pocket and the heart of the world speak without meaning to these people. What has its head to say? Taste, culture, refinement? Go!"

Mitchell was leaning against a brick wall. He turned his head indolently, and looked into the mills. There hung about the place a thick, unclean odor. The slightest motion of his hand marked that he perceived it, and his insufferable disgust. That was all. May said nothing, only quickened his angry tramp.

"Besides," added Mitchell, giving a corollary to his answer, "it would be of no use. I am not one of them."

"You do not mean—" said May, facing him.

"Yes, I mean just that. Reform is born of need, not pity. No vital movement of the people's has worked down, for good or evil; fermented, instead, carried up the heaving, cloggy mass. Think back through history, and you will know it. What will this lowest deep—thieves, Magdalens, negroes—do with the light filtered through ponderous Church creeds, Baconian theories, Goethe schemes? Some day, out of their bitter need will be thrown up their own light-bringer—their Jean Paul, their Cromwell, their Messiah."[8]

"Bah!" was the doctor's inward criticism. However, in practice, he adopted the theory; for, when, night and morning, afterwards, he prayed that power might be given these degraded souls to rise, he glowed at heart, recognizing an accomplished duty.

Wolfe and the woman had stood in the shadow of the works as the coach drove off. The doctor had held out his hand in a frank, generous way, telling him to "take care of himself, and to remember it was his right to rise." Mitchell had simply touched his hat, as to an equal, with a quiet look of thorough recognition. Kirby had thrown Deborah some money, which she found, and clutched eagerly enough. They were gone now, all of them. The man sat down on the cinder road, looking up into the murky sky.

"'T be late, Hugh. Wunnot hur come?"

He shook his head doggedly, and the woman crouched out of his sight against the wall. Do you remember rare moments when a sudden light flashed over yourself, your world, God? when you stood on a mountain peak, seeing your life as it might have been, as it is? one quick instant, when custom lost its force and everyday usage? when your friend, wife, brother, stood in a new light? your soul was bared, and the grave—a foretaste of the nakedness of the Judgment Day? So it came before him, his life, that night. The slow tides of pain he had borne gathered themselves up and surged against his soul. His squalid daily life, the brutal coarseness eating into his brain, as the ashes into his skin: before, these things had been a dull aching into his consciousness; tonight, they were reality. He griped the filthy red shirt that clung, stiff with soot, about him, and tore it savagely from his arm. The flesh beneath was muddy with grease and ashes—and the heart beneath that! And the soul? God knows.

Then flashed before his vivid poetic sense the man who had left him—the pure face, the delicate, sinewy limbs, in harmony with all he knew of beauty or truth. In his cloudy fancy he had pictured a Something like this. He had found it in this Mitchell, even when he idly scoffed at his pain: a Man all-knowing, all-seeing, crowned by Nature, reigning—the keen glance of his eye falling like a sceptre on other men. And yet his instinct taught him that he too—He! He looked at himself with sudden loathing, sick, wrung his hands with a cry, and then was silent. With all the phantoms of his heated, ignorant fancy, Wolfe had not been vague in his

---

8. Francis Bacon (1561–1626) was an English philosopher; Johann Wolfgang von Goethe (1749–1832) was a poet and philosopher; Jean Paul Richter (1763–1825) was a German novelist; Oliver Cromwell (1599–1658) led a revolt against the British monarchy.

ambitions. They were practical, slowly built up before him out of his knowledge of what he could do. Through years he had day by day made this hope a real thing to himself—a clear, projected figure of himself, as he might become.

Able to speak, to know what was best, to raise these men and women working at his side up with him: sometimes he forgot this defined hope in the frantic anguish to escape—only to escape—out of the wet, the pain, the ashes, somewhere, anywhere—only for one moment of free air on a hillside, to lie down and let his sick soul throb itself out in the sunshine. But tonight he panted for life. The savage strength of his nature was roused; his cry was fierce to God for justice.

"Look at me!" he said to Deborah, with a low, bitter laugh, striking his puny chest savagely. "What am I worth, Deb? Is it my fault that I am no better? My fault? My fault?"

He stopped, stung with a sudden remorse, seeing her hunchback shape writhing with sobs. For Deborah was crying thankless tears, according to the fashion of women.

"God forgi' me, woman! Things go harder wi' you nor me. It 's a worse share."

He got up and helped her to rise; and they went doggedly down the muddy street, side by side.

"It 's all wrong," he muttered, slowly," all wrong! I dunnot understan'. But it'll end some day."

"Come home, Hugh!" she said, coaxingly; for he had stopped, looking around bewildered.

"Home—and back to the mill!" He went on saying this over to himself, as if he would mutter down every pain in this dull despair.

She followed him through the fog, her blue lips chattering with cold. They reached the cellar at last. Old Wolfe had been drinking since she went out, and had crept nearer the door. The girl Janey slept heavily in the corner. He went up to her, touching softly the worn white arm with his fingers. Some bitterer thought stung him, as he stood there. He wiped the drops from his forehead, and went into the room beyond, livid, trembling. A hope, trifling, perhaps, but very dear, had died just then out of the poor puddler's life, as he looked at the sleeping, innocent girl—some plan for the future, in which she had borne a part. He gave it up that moment, then and forever. Only a trifle, perhaps, to us: his face grew a shade paler—that was all. But, somehow, the man's soul, as God and the angels looked down on it, never was the same afterwards.

Deborah followed him into the inner room. She carried a candle, which she placed on the floor, closing the door after her. She had seen the look on his face, as he turned away: her own grew deadly. Yet, as she came up to him, her eyes glowed. He was seated on an old chest, quiet, holding his face in his hands.

"Hugh!" she said, softly.

He did not speak.

"Hugh, did hur hear what the man said—him with the clear voice? Did hur hear? Money, money—that it wud do all?"

He pushed her away—gently, but he was worn out; her rasping tone fretted him.

"Hugh!"

The candle flared a pale yellow light over the cobwebbed brick walls, and the woman standing there. He looked at her. She was young, in deadly earnest; her faded eyes, and wet, ragged figure caught from their frantic eagerness a power akin to beauty.

"Hugh, it is true! Money ull do it! Oh, Hugh, boy, listen till me! He said it true! It is money!"

"I know. Go back! I do not want you here."

"Hugh, it is t' last time. I 'll never worrit hur again."

There were tears in her voice now, but she choked them back.

"Hear till me only tonight! If one of t' witch people wud come, them we heard of t' home, and gif hur all hur wants, what then? Say, Hugh!"

"What do you mean?"

"I mean money."

Her whisper shrilled through his brain.

"If one of t' witch dwarfs wud come from t' lane moors tonight, and gif hur money, to go out—*out*, I say—out, lad, where t' sun shines, and t' heath grows, and t' ladies walk in silken gownds, and God stays all t' time—where t' man lives that talked to us tonight—Hugh knows—Hugh could walk there like a king!"

He thought the woman mad, tried to check her, but she went on, fierce in her eager haste.

"If *I* were t' witch dwarf, if I had t' money, wud hur thank me? Wud hur take me out o' this place wid hur and Janey? I wud not come into the gran' house hur wud build, to vex hur wid t' hunch—only at night, when t' shadows were dark, stand far off to see hur."

Mad? Yes! Are many of us mad in this way?

"Poor Deb! poor Deb!" he said, soothingly.

"It is here," she said, suddenly jerking into his hand a small roll. "I took it! I did it! Me, me!—not hur! I shall be hanged, I shall be burnt in hell, if anybody knows I took it! Out of his pocket, as he leaned against t' bricks. Hur knows?"

She thrust it into his hand, and then, her errand done, began to gather chips together to make a fire, choking down hysteric sobs.

"Has it come to this?"

That was all he said. The Welsh Wolfe blood was honest. The roll was a small green pocketbook containing one or two gold pieces, and a check for an incredible amount, as it seemed to the poor puddler. He laid it down, hiding his face again in his hands.

"Hugh, don't be angry wud me! It 's only poor Deb—hur knows?"

He took the long skinny fingers kindly in his.

"Angry? God help me, no! Let me sleep. I am tired."

He threw himself heavily down on the wooden bench, stunned with pain and weariness. She brought some old rags to cover him.

It was late on Sunday evening before he awoke. I tell God's truth, when I say he had then no thought of keeping this money. Deborah had hid it in his pocket. He found it there. She watched him eagerly, as he took it out.

"I must gif it to him," he said, reading her face.

"Hur knows," she said with a bitter sigh of disappointment. "But it is hur right to keep it."

His right! The word struck him. Doctor May had used the same. He washed himself, and went out to find this man Mitchell. His right! Why did this chance word cling to him so obstinately? Do you hear the fierce devils whisper in his ear, as he went slowly down the darkening street?

The evening came on, slow and calm. He seated himself at the end of an alley leading into one of the larger streets. His brain was clear tonight, keen, intent, mastering. It would not start back, cowardly, from any hellish temptation, but meet it face to face. Therefore the great temptation of his life came to him veiled by no sophistry, but bold, defiant, owning its own vile name, trusting to one bold blow for victory.

He did not deceive himself. Theft! That was it. At first the word sickened him; then he grappled with it. Sitting there on a broken cartwheel, the fading day, the noisy groups, the church bells' tolling passed before him like a panorama, while the sharp struggle went on within. This money! He took it out, and looked at it. If he gave it back, what then? He was going to be cool about it.

People going by to church saw only a sickly mill boy watching them quietly at the alley's mouth. They did not know that he was mad, or they would not have gone by so quietly: mad with hunger; stretching out his hands to the world, that had given so much to them, for leave to live the life God meant him to live. His soul within him was smothering to death; he wanted so much, thought so much, and *knew*— nothing. There was nothing of which he was certain, except the mill and things there. Of God and heaven he had heard so little, that they were to him what fairy-land is to a child: something real, but not here; very far off. His brain, greedy, dwarfed, full of thwarted energy and unused powers, questioned these men and women going by, coldly, bitterly, that night. Was it not his right to live as they—a pure life, a good, true-hearted life, full of beauty and kind words? He only wanted to know how to use the strength within him. His heart warmed, as he thought of it. He suffered himself to think of it longer. If he took the money?

Then he saw himself as he might be, strong, helpful, kindly. The night crept on, as this one image slowly evolved itself from the crown of other thoughts and stood triumphant. He looked at it. As he might be! What wonder, if it blinded him to delirium—the madness that underlies all revolution, all progress, and all fall?

You laugh at the shallow temptation? You see the error underlying its argument so clearly—that to him a true life was one of full development rather than self-restraint? that he was deaf to the higher tone in a cry of voluntary suffering for truth's sake than in the fullest flow of spontaneous harmony? I do not plead his cause. I only want to show you the mote in my brother's eye: then you can see clear-ly to take it out.

The money—there it lay on his knee, a little blotted slip of paper, nothing in itself; used to raise him out of the pit; something straight from God's hand. A thief! Well, what was it to be a thief? He met the question at last, face to face, wiping the clammy drops of sweat from his forehead. God made this money—the fresh air, too— for his children's use. He never made the difference between poor and rich. The Something who looked down on him that moment through the cool gray sky had a kindly face, he knew—loved his children alike. Oh, he knew that!

There were times when the soft floods of color in the crimson and purple flames, or the clear depth of amber in the water below the bridge, had somehow given him a glimpse of another world than this—of an infinite depth of beauty and of quiet somewhere—somewhere—a depth of quiet and rest and love. Looking up now, it became strangely real. The sun had sunk quite below the hills, but his last rays struck upward, touching the zenith. The fog had risen, and the town and river were steeped in its thick, gray damp; but overhead, the sun-touched smoke clouds opened like a cleft ocean—shifting, rolling seas of crimson mist, waves of billowy sil-ver veined with blood-scarlet, inner depths unfathomable of glancing light. Wolfe's artist eye grew drunk with color. The gates of that other world! Fading, flashing before him now! What, in that world of Beauty, Content, and Right, were the petty laws, the mine and thine, of mill owners and millhands?

A consciousness of power stirred within him. He stood up. A man—he thought, stretching out his hands—free to work, to live, to love! Free! His right! He folded the scrap of paper in his hand. As his nervous fingers took it in, limp and blotted, so his soul took in the mean temptation, lapped it in fancied rights, in dreams of improved existences, drifting and endless as the cloud-seas of color. Clutching it, as if the tight-ness of his hold would strengthen his sense of possession, he went aimlessly down the street. It was his watch at the mill. He need not go, need never go again, thank God!—shaking off the thought with unspeakable loathing.

Shall I go over the history of the hours of that night? how the man wandered from one to another of his old haunts, with a half-consciousness of bidding them farewell—lanes and alleys and backyards where the millhands lodged—noting, with a new eagerness, the filth and drunkenness, the pigpens, the ash heaps covered with potato skins, the bloated, pimpled women at the doors—with a new disgust, a new sense of sudden triumph, and, under all, a new, vague dread, unknown before, smothered down, kept under, but still there? It left him but once during the night, when, for the second time in his life, he entered a church. It was a somber gothic pile, where the stained light lost itself in far-retreating arches; built to meet the requirements and sympathies of a far other class than Wolfe's. Yet it touched, moved him uncontrollably. The distances, the shadows, the still, marble figures, the mass of silent kneeling worshippers, the mysterious music, thrilled, lifted his soul with a wonderful pain. Wolfe forgot himself, forgot the new life he was going to live, the mean terror gnawing underneath. The voice of the speaker strengthened the charm; it was clear, feeling, full, strong. An old man, who had lived much, suffered much; whose brain was keenly alive, dominant; whose heart was summer-warm with charity. He taught it tonight. He held up Humanity in its grand total; showed the great world-cancer to his people. Who could show it better? He was a Christian reformer; he had studied the age thoroughly; his outlook at man had been free, worldwide, over all time. His faith stood sublime upon the Rock of Ages; his fiery zeal guided vast schemes by which the gospel was to be preached to all nations. How did he preach it tonight? In burning, light-laden words he painted the incarnate Life, Love, the universal Man: words that became reality in the lives of these people—that lived again in beautiful words and actions, trifling, but heroic. Sin, as he defined it, was a real foe to them; their trials, temptations, were his. His words passed far over the furnace tender's grasp, toned to suit another class of culture; they sounded in his ears a very pleasant song in an unknown tongue. He meant to cure this world-cancer with a steady eye that had never glared with hunger, and a hand that neither poverty nor strychnine whiskey had taught to shake. In this morbid, distorted heart of the Welsh puddler he had failed.

Wolfe rose at last, and turned from the church down the street. He looked up; the night had come on foggy, damp; the golden mists had vanished, and the sky lay dull and ash-colored. He wandered again aimlessly down the street, idly wondering what had become of the cloud-sea of crimson and scarlet. The trial day of this man's life was over, and he had lost the victory. What followed was mere drifting circumstance—a quicker walking over the path—that was all. Do you want to hear the end of it? You wish me to make a tragic story out of it? Why, in the police reports of the morning paper you can find a dozen such tragedies: hints of shipwrecks unlike any that ever befell on the high seas; hints that here a power was lost to heaven—that there a soul went down where no tide can ebb or flow. Commonplace enough the hints are—jocose sometimes, done up in rhyme.

Doctor May, a month after the night I have told you of, was reading to his wife at breakfast from this fourth column of the morning paper: an unusual thing—these police reports not being, in general, choice reading for ladies; but it was only one item he read.

"Oh, my dear! You remember that man I told you of, that we saw at Kirby's mill?—that was arrested for robbing Mitchell? Here he is; just listen:—'Circuit Court. Judge Day. Hugh Wolfe, operative in Kirby & John's Loudon Mills. Charge, grand larceny. Sentence, nineteen years hard labor in penitentiary.' Scoundrel! Serves him right! After all our kindness that night! Picking Mitchell's pocket at the very time!"

His wife said something about the ingratitude of that kind of people, and then they began to talk of something else.

Nineteen years! How easy that was to read! What a simple word for Judge Day to utter! Nineteen years! Half a lifetime!

Hugh Wolfe sat on the window ledge of his cell, looking out. His ankles were ironed. Not usual in such cases; but he had made two desperate efforts to escape. "Well," as Haley, the jailer, said, "small blame to him! Nineteen years' imprisonment was not a pleasant thing to look forward to." Haley was very good-natured about it, though Wolfe had fought him savagely.

"When he was first caught," the jailer said afterwards, in telling the story, "before the trial, the fellow was cut down at once—laid there on that pallet like a dead man, with his hands over his eyes. Never saw a man so cut down in my life. Time of the trial, too, came the queerest dodge of any customer I ever had. Would choose no lawyer. Judge gave him one, of course. Gibson it was. He tried to prove the fellow crazy; but it wouldn't go. Thing was plain as daylight: money found on him. 'T was a hard sentence—all the law allows; but it was for 'xample's sake. These millhands are gettin' onbearable. When the sentence was read, he just looked up, and said the money was his by rights, and that all the world had gone wrong. That night, after the trial, a gentleman came to see him here, name of Mitchell—him as he stole from. Talked to him for an hour. Thought he came for curiosity, like. After he was gone, thought Wolfe was remarkable quiet, and went into his cell. Found him very low; bed all bloody. Doctor said he had been bleeding at the lungs. He was as weak as a cat; yet, if ye'll b'lieve me, he tried to get a-past me and get out. I just carried him like a baby, and threw him on the pallet. Three days after, he tried it again: that time reached the wall. Lord help you! he fought like a tiger—giv' some terrible blows. Fightin' for life, you see; for he can't live long, shut up in the stone crib down yonder. Got a death-cough now. 'T took two of us to bring him down that day; so I just put the irons on his feet. There he sits, in there. Goin' tomorrow, with a batch more of 'em. That woman, hunchback, tried with him—you remember?—she's only got three years. 'Complice. But *she's* a woman, you know. He's been quiet ever since I put on irons: giv' up, I suppose. Looks white, sick-lookin'. It acts different on 'em, bein' sentenced. Most of 'em gets reckless, devilish-like. Some prays awful, and sings them vile songs of the mills, all in a breath. That woman, now, she's desper't'. Been beggin' to see Hugh, as she calls him, for three days. I'm a-goin' to let her in. She don't go with him. Here she is in this next cell. I'm a-goin' now to let her in."

He let her in. Wolfe did not see her. She crept into a corner of the cell, and stood watching him. He was scratching the iron bars of the window with a piece of tin which he had picked up, with an idle, uncertain, vacant stare, just as a child or idiot would do.

"Tryin' to get out, old boy?" laughed Haley. "Them irons will need a crowbar beside your tin, before you can open 'em."

Wolfe laughed, too, in a senseless way.

"I think I'll get out," he said.

"I believe his brain's touched," said Haley, when he came out.

The puddler scraped away with the tin for half an hour. Still Deborah did not speak. At last she ventured nearer, and touched his arm.

"Blood?" she said, looking at some spots on his coat with a shudder.

He looked up at her. "Why, Deb!" he said, smiling—such a bright, boyish smile, that it went to poor Deborah's heart directly, and she sobbed and cried out loud.

"Oh, Hugh, lad! Hugh! dunnot look at me, when it wur my fault! To think I brought hur to it! And I loved hur so! Oh, lad, I dud!"

The confession, even in this wretch, came with the woman's blush through the sharp cry.

He did not seem to hear her—scraping away diligently at the bars with the bit of tin.

Was he going mad? She peered closely into his face. Something she saw there made her draw suddenly back—something which Haley had not seen, that lay beneath the pinched, vacant look it had caught since the trial, or the curious gray shadow that rested on it. The gray shadow—yes, she knew what that meant. She had often seen it creeping over women's faces for months, who died at last of slow hunger or consumption. That meant death, distant, lingering: but this——Whatever it was the woman saw, or thought she saw, used as she was to crime and misery, seemed to make her sick with a new horror. Forgetting her fear of him, she caught his shoulders, and looked keenly, steadily, into his eyes.

"Hugh!" she cried, in a desperate whisper—"oh, boy, not that! for God's sake, not *that!*"

The vacant laugh went off his face, and he answered her in a muttered word or two that drove her away. Yet the words were kindly enough. Sitting there on his pallet, she cried silently a hopeless sort of tears, but did not speak again. The man looked up furtively at her now and then. Whatever his own trouble was, her distress vexed him with a momentary sting.

It was market day. The narrow window of the jail looked down directly on the carts and wagons drawn up in a long line, where they had unloaded. He could see, too, and hear distinctly the clink of money as it changed hands, the busy crowd of whites and blacks shoving, pushing one another, and the chaffering and swearing at the stalls. Somehow, the sound, more than anything else had done, wakened him up—made the whole real to him. He was done with the world and the business of it. He let the tin fall, and looked out; pressing his face close to the rusty bars. How they crowded and pushed! And he—he should never walk that pavement again! There came Neff Sanders, one of the feeders at the mill, with a basket on his arm. Sure enough, Neff was married the other week. He whistled, hoping he would look up; but he did not. He wondered if Neff remembered he was there—if any of the boys thought of him up there, and thought that he never was to go down that old cinder road again. Never again! He had not quite understood it before; but now he did. Not for days or years, but never!—that was it.

How clear the light fell on that stall in front of the market! and how like a picture it was, the dark-green heaps of corn, and the crimson beets, and golden melons! There was another with game: how the light flickered on that pheasant's breast, with the purplish blood dripping over the brown feathers! He could see the red shining of the drops, it was so near. In one minute he could be down there. It was just a step. So easy, as it seemed, so natural to go! Yet it could never be—not in all the thousands of years to come—that he should put his foot on that street again! He thought of himself with a sorrowful pity, as of someone else. There was a dog down in the market, walking after his master with such a stately, grave look!—only a dog, yet he could go backwards and forwards just as he pleased: he had good luck! Why, the very vilest cur, yelping there in the gutter, had not lived his life, had been free to act out whatever thought God had put into his brain; while he—No, he would not think of that! He tried to put the thought away, and to listen to a dispute between a countryman and a woman about some meat; but it would come back. He, what had he done to bear this?

Then came the sudden picture of what might have been, and now. He knew what it was to be in the penitentiary—how it went with men there. He knew how in these long years he should slowly die, but not until soul and body had become corrupt and rotten—how, when he came out, if he lived to come, even the lowest of the mill-hands would jeer him—how his hands would be weak, and his brain senseless and stupid. He believed he was almost that now. He put his hand to his head, with a puzzled, weary look. It ached, his head, with thinking. He tried to quiet himself. It was only right, perhaps; he had done wrong. But was there right or wrong for such as he? What was right? And who had ever taught him? He thrust the whole matter away. A dark, cold quiet crept through his brain. It was all wrong; but let it be! It was nothing to him more than the others. Let it be!

The door grated, as Haley opened it.

"Come, my woman! Must lock up for t' night. Come, stir yerself!"

She went up and took Hugh's hand.

"Good night, Deb," he said, carelessly.

She had not hoped he would say more; but the tired pain on her mouth just then was bitterer than death. She took his passive hand and kissed it.

"Hur 'll never see Deb again!" she ventured, her lips growing colder and more bloodless.

What did she say that for? Did he not know it? Yet he would not be impatient with poor old Deb. She had trouble of her own, as well as he.

"No, never again," he said, trying to be cheerful.

She stood just a moment, looking at him. Do you laugh at her, standing there, with her hunchback, her rags, her bleared, withered face, and the great despised love tugging at her heart?

"Come, you!" called Haley, impatiently.

She did not move.

"Hugh!" she whispered.

It was to be her last word. What was it?

"Hugh, boy, not THAT!"

He did not answer. She wrung her hands, trying to be silent, looking in his face in an agony of entreaty. He smiled again, kindly.

"It is best, Deb. I cannot bear to be hurted any more."

"Hur knows," she said, humbly.

"Tell my father goodbye; and—and kiss little Janey."

She nodded, saying nothing, looked in his face again, and went out of the door. As she went, she staggered.

"Drinkin' today?" broke out Haley, pushing her before him. "Where the Devil did you get it? Here, in with ye!" and he shoved her into her cell, next to Wolfe's, and shut the door.

Along the wall of her cell there was a crack low down by the floor, through which she could see the light from Wolfe's. She had discovered it days before. She hurried in now, and, kneeling down by it, listened, hoping to hear some sound. Nothing but the rasping of the tin on the bars. He was at his old amusement again. Something in the noise jarred on her ear, for she shivered as she heard it. Hugh rasped away at the bars. A dull old bit of tin, not fit to cut korl with.

He looked out of the window again. People were leaving the market now. A tall mulatto girl, following her mistress, her basket on her head, crossed the street just below, and looked up. She was laughing; but, when she caught sight of the haggard face peering out through the bars, suddenly grew grave, and hurried by. A free, firm step, a clear-cut olive face, with a scarlet turban tied on one side, dark, shining eyes, and on the head the basket poised, filled with fruit and flowers, under which the scarlet turban and bright eyes looked out half-shadowed. The picture caught his eye. It was good to see a face like that. He would try tomorrow, and cut one like it. *Tomorrow!* He threw down the tin, trembling, and covered his face with his hands. When he looked up again, the daylight was gone.

Deborah, crouching near by on the other side of the wall, heard no noise. He sat on the side of the low pallet, thinking. Whatever was the mystery which the woman had seen on his face, it came out now slowly, in the dark there, and became fixed—a something never seen on his face before. The evening was darkening fast. The market had been over for an hour; the rumbling of the carts over the pavement grew more infrequent: he listened to each, as it passed, because he thought it was to be for the last time. For the same reason, it was, I suppose, that he strained his eyes to catch a glimpse of each passerby, wondering who they were, what kind of homes they were going to, if they had children—listening eagerly to every chance word in the street, as if—(God be merciful to the man! what strange fancy was this?)—as if he never should hear human voices again.

It was quite dark at last. The street was a lonely one. The last passenger, he thought, was gone. No—there was a quick step: Joe Hill, lighting the lamps. Joe was a good old chap; never passed a fellow without some joke or other. He remembered once seeing the place where he lived with his wife. "Granny Hill" the boys called her. Bedridden she was; but so kind as Joe was to her! kept the room so clean!—and the old woman, when he was there, was laughing at "some of t' lad's foolishness." The step was far down the street; but he could see him place the ladder, run up, and light the gas. A longing seized him to be spoken to once more.

"Joe!" he called, out of the grating. "Goodbye, Joe!"

The old man stopped a moment, listening uncertainly; then hurried on. The prisoner thrust his hand out of the window, and called again, louder; but Joe was too far down the street. It was a little thing; but it hurt him—this disappointment.

"Goodbye, Joe!" he called, sorrowfully enough.

"Be quiet!" said one of the jailers, passing the door, striking on it with his club.

Oh, that was the last, was it?

There was an inexpressible bitterness on his face, as he lay down on the bed, taking the bit of tin, which he had rasped to a tolerable degree of sharpness, in his hand—to play with, it may be. He bared his arms, looking intently at their corded veins and sinews. Deborah, listening in the next cell, heard a slight clicking sound, often repeated. She shut her lips tightly, that she might not scream; the cold drops of sweat broke over her, in her dumb agony.

"Hur knows best," she muttered at last, fiercely clutching the boards where she lay.

If she could have seen Wolfe, there was nothing about him to frighten her. He lay quite still, his arms outstretched, looking at the pearly stream of moonlight coming into the window. I think in that one hour that came then he lived back over all the years that had gone before. I think that all the low, vile life, all his wrongs, all his starved hopes, came then, and stung him with a farewell poison that made him sick unto death. He made neither moan nor cry, only turned his worn face now and then to the pure light, that seemed so far off, as one that said, "How long, O Lord? how long?"

The hour was over at last. The moon, passing over her nightly path, slowly came nearer, and threw the light across his bed on his feet. He watched it steadily, as it crept up, inch by inch, slowly. It seemed to him to carry with it a great silence. He had been so hot and tired there always in the mills! The years had been so fierce and cruel! There was coming now quiet and coolness and sleep. His tense limbs relaxed, and settled in a calm languor. The blood ran fainter and slow from his heart. He did not think now with a savage anger of what might be and was not; he was conscious only of deep stillness creeping over him. At first he saw a sea of faces: the mill men—women he had known, drunken and bloated—Janeys timid and pitiful—poor old Debs: then they floated together like a mist, and faded away, leaving only the clear, pearly moonlight.

Whether, as the pure light crept up the stretched-out figure, it brought with it calm and peace, who shall say? His dumb soul was alone with God in judgment. A Voice may have spoken for it from far-off Calvary, "Father, forgive them, for they know not what they do!" Who dare say? Fainter and fainter the heart rose and fell, slower and slower the moon floated from behind a cloud, until, when at last its full tide of white splendor swept over the cell, it seemed to wrap and fold into a deeper stillness the dead figure that never should move again. Silence deeper than the Night! Nothing that moved, save the black, nauseous stream of blood dripping slowly from the pallet to the floor!

There was outcry and crowd enough in the cell the next day. The coroner and his jury, the local editors, Kirby himself, and boys with their hands thrust knowingly into their pockets and heads on one side, jammed into the corners. Coming and going all day. Only one woman. She came late, and outstayed them all. A Quaker, or Friend, as they call themselves. I think this woman was known by that name in heaven. A homely body, coarsely dressed in gray and white. Deborah (for Haley had let her in) took notice of her. She watched them all—sitting on the end of the pallet, holding his head in her arms—with the ferocity of a watchdog, if any of them touched the body. There was no meekness, no sorrow, in her face; the stuff out of which murderers are made, instead. All the time Haley and the woman were laying straight the limbs and cleaning the cell, Deborah sat still, keenly watching the Quaker's face. Of all the crowd there that day, this woman alone had not spoken to her—only once or twice had put some cordial to her lips. After they all were gone, the woman, in the same still, gentle way, brought a vase of wood leaves and berries, and placed it by the pallet, then opened the narrow window. The fresh air blew in, and swept the woody fragrance over the dead face. Deborah looked up with a quick wonder.

"Did hur know my boy wud like it? Dud hur know Hugh?"

"I know Hugh now."

The white fingers passed in a slow, pitiful way over the dead, worn face. There was a heavy shadow in the quiet eyes.

"Did hur know where they 'll bury Hugh?" said Deborah in a shrill tone, catching her arm.

This had been the question hanging on her lips all day.

"In t' town yard? Under t' mud and ash? T' lad 'll smother, woman! He wur born on t' lane moor, where t' air is frick and strong. Take hur out, for God's sake, take hur out where t' air blows!"

The Quaker hesitated, but only for a moment. She put her strong arm around Deborah and led her to the window.

"Thee sees the hills, friend, over the river? Thee sees how the light lies warm there, and the winds of God blow all the day? I live there—where the blue smoke is, by the trees. Look at me." She turned Deborah's face to her own, clear and earnest. "Thee will believe me? I will take Hugh and bury him there tomorrow."

Deborah did not doubt her. As the evening wore on, she leaned against the iron bars, looking at the hills that rose far off, through the thick sodden clouds, like a bright, unattainable calm. As she looked, a shadow of their solemn repose fell on her face: its fierce discontent faded into a pitiful, humble quiet. Slow, solemn tears gathered in her eyes: the poor weak eyes turned so hopelessly to the place where Hugh was to rest, the grave heights looking higher and brighter and more solemn than ever before. The Quaker watched her keenly. She came to her at last, and touched her arm.

"When thee comes back," she said, in a low, sorrowful tone, like one who speaks from a strong heart deeply moved with remorse or pity, "thee shall begin thy life again—there on the hills. I came too late; but not for thee—by God's help, it may be."

Not too late. Three years after, the Quaker began her work. I end my story here. At evening-time it was light. There is no need to tire you with the long years of sunshine, and fresh air, and slow, patient Christ-love, needed to make healthy and hopeful this impure body and soul. There is a homely pine house, on one of these hills, whose windows overlook broad, wooded slopes and clover-crimsoned meadows—niched into the very place where the light is warmest, the air freest. It is the Friends' meeting house. Once a week they sit there, in their grave, earnest way, waiting for the Spirit of Love to speak, opening their simple hearts to receive His words. There is a woman, old, deformed, who takes a humble place among them: waiting like them: in her gray dress, her worn face, pure and meek, turned now and then to the sky. A woman much loved by these silent, restful people; more silent than they, more humble, more loving. Waiting: with her eyes turned to hills higher and purer than these on which she lives—dim and far off now, but to be reached some day. There may be in her heart some latent hope to meet there the love denied her here—that she shall find him whom she lost, and that then she will not be all unworthy. Who blames her? Something is lost in the passage of every soul from one eternity to the other—something pure and beautiful, which might have been and was not: a hope, a talent, a love, over which the soul mourns, like Esau deprived of his birthright.[9] What blame to the meek Quaker, if she took her lost hope to make the hills of heaven more fair?

Nothing remains to tell that the poor Welsh puddler once lived, but this figure of the mill woman cut in korl. I have it here in a corner of my library. I keep it hid behind a curtain—it is such a rough, ungainly thing. Yet there are about it touches, grand sweeps of outline, that show a master's hand. Sometimes—tonight, for instance—the curtain is accidentally drawn back, and I see a bare arm stretched out imploringly in the darkness, and an eager, wolfish face watching mine: a wan, woeful face, through which the spirit of the dead korl-cutter looks out, with its thwarted life, its mighty hunger, its unfinished work. Its pale, vague lips seem to tremble with a terrible question. "Is this the End?" they say—"nothing beyond?—no more?" Why, you tell me you have seen that look in the eyes of dumb brutes—horses dying under the lash. I know.

The deep of the night is passing while I write. The gaslight wakens from the shadows here and there the objects which lie scattered through the room: only faintly, though; for they belong to the open sunlight. As I glance at them, they each recall some task or pleasure of the coming day. A half-molded child's head; Aphrodite;[10] a bough of forest leaves; music; work; homely fragments, in which lie the secrets of all eternal truth and beauty. Prophetic all! Only this dumb, woeful face seems to belong to and end with the night. I turn to look at it. Has the power of its desperate need commanded the darkness away? While the room is yet steeped in heavy shadow, a cool, gray light suddenly touches its head like a blessing hand, and its groping arm points through the broken cloud to the far East, where, in the flickering, nebulous crimson, God has set the promise of the Dawn.   *1861*

9. Esau sold his birthright to his brother, Jacob (Genesis   10. Greek goddess of love.
25:31).

+—+ ⊨◊⊒ +—+

Anzia Yezierska
1881?–1970

"My body was worn to the bone from overwork, my footsteps dragged with exhaustion, but my eyes still sought the sky, praying, ceaselessly praying, the dumb, inarticulate prayer of the lost immigrant: 'America! Ach, America! Where is America?'" So wrote ANZIA YEZIERSKA in "Soap and Water" (1920), documenting the exhaustion and disillusionment of immigrant women and attempting in her work both to ask and answer questions regarding the United States' lost promise of full democracy. Born in Plinsk on the Russian-Polish border, Yezierska was one of ten children of poor but devout Jewish parents, Bernard and Pearl Yezierska, who lived at one time in a mud hut; her father was a Talmudic scholar. When she was an adolescent her family joined countless other eastern European Jews in emigrating to New York City's Lower East Side, where she worked in a nonregulated clothing factory, or sweatshop, by day and attended school at night. In 1900 she won a scholarship to Columbia College's domestic science teacher training program; although she found the environment hostile, she managed to obtain a degree and began to teach. She became friends in 1905 with the feminist Henrietta Rodman, who encouraged her writing; around this time she stopped calling herself Hattie Mayer, the name she had been given at Ellis Island when she emigrated, and took back her given name, Anzia Yezierska. She was married twice, to a lawyer, Jacob Gordon, and a teacher, Arnold Levitas, both times briefly; in 1915 she left her second husband and their young daughter, Louise, to pursue her writing but continued to see Louise on a weekly basis. In 1917 Yezierska began attending the classes of the educator and philosopher John Dewey at Columbia University; each inspired the other's writing, and they were briefly involved romantically.

Much of Yezierska's fiction portrays the tensions between a vibrant Jewish culture enriched by the Yiddish language, on the one hand, and the indignities of working-class women's lives in a crowded, dirty urban ghetto on the other. In 1919 she published her first short story, "The Fat of the Land," which won the Edmund J. O'Brien Prize and brought her modest critical attention; it portrayed the humiliation experienced by New York's poor at the hands of insensitive charitable organizations. She sold the movie rights to her first collection of short fiction, *Hungry Hearts* (1920), to Hollywood mogul Samuel Goldwyn for the then huge some of $10,000; the movie was released in 1922. In her autobiographical novel *Bread Givers* (1925) an immigrant protagonist resolves to thwart poverty and ignorance through education, even if it means alienation from her orthodox relatives and her patriarchal father. Refusing to marry a well-off suitor and become "another piece of property," the protagonist instead chooses autonomy and self-determination. Yezierska wrote prolifically throughout the 1920s, publishing a novel, *Salome of the Tenements* (1922) and another volume of stories, *Children of Loneliness*, (1923); *Arrogant Beggar* appeared in 1927. During the 1930s she worked with the WPA Writers' Project, and in 1932 she published *All I Could Never Be*, a popular work of fiction based on her relationship with Dewey. During the 1940s, however, Yezierska had trouble finding a publisher, and her works fell into obscurity. Although she wrote her autobiography, *Red Ribbon on a White Horse*, in 1950, it was not discovered until the late 1960s, shortly before her death.

Yezierska knew that for a Jew, a woman, and an immigrant, refusing muteness was an act of survival. "As one of the dumb, voiceless ones I speak," she writes in "America and Me"; "one of the millions of immigrants beating, beating out their hearts at your gates for a breath of understanding." As Andrew Ettin has noted in *Speaking Silences*, Yezierska addresses all immigrants who feel their talents have been wasted, their dreams deferred: "her seeming humility in sharing alleged voicelessness 'as one . . . of the millions' actually gives her the privilege to speak on behalf of them." "Soap and Water," the story reprinted here, inscribes both the resistance and the transformation that for Yezierska lie at the heart of immigrant experience.

⊰ Soap and Water ⊱

What I so greatly feared, happened! Miss Whiteside, the dean of our college, withheld my diploma. When I came to her office, and asked her why she did not pass me, she said that she could not recommend me as a teacher because of my personal appearance.

She told me that my skin looked oily, my hair unkempt, and my fingernails sadly neglected. She told me that I was utterly unmindful of the little niceties of the well-groomed lady. She pointed out that my collar did not set evenly, my belt was awry, and there was a lack of freshness in my dress. And she ended with: "Soap and water are cheap. Anyone can be clean."

In those four years while I was under her supervision, I was always timid and diffident. I shrank and trembled when I had to come near her. When I had to say something to her, I mumbled and stuttered, and grew red and white in the face with fear.

Every time I had to come to the dean's office for a private conference, I prepared for the ordeal of her cold scrutiny, as a patient prepares for a surgical operation. I watched her gimlet eyes searching for a stray pin, for a spot on my dress, for my unpolished shoes, for my uncared-for fingernails, as one strapped on the operating table watches the surgeon approaching with his tray of sterilized knives.

She never looked into my eyes. She never perceived that I had a soul. She did not see how I longed for beauty and cleanliness. How I strained and struggled to lift myself from the dead toil and exhaustion that weighed me down. She could see nothing in people like me, except the dirt and the stains on the outside.

But this last time when she threatened to withhold my diploma, because of my appearance, this last time when she reminded me that "Soap and water are cheap. Anyone can be clean," this last time, something burst within me.

I felt the suppressed wrath of all the unwashed of the earth break loose within me. My eyes blazed fire. I didn't care for myself, nor the dean, nor the whole laundered world. I had suffered the cruelty of their cleanliness and the tyranny of their culture to the breaking point. I was too frenzied to know what I said or did. But I saw clean, immaculate, spotless Miss Whiteside shrivel and tremble and cower before me, as I had shriveled and trembled and cowered before her for so many years.

Why did she give me my diploma? Was it pity? Or can it be that in my outburst of fury, at the climax of indignities that I had suffered, the barriers broke, and she saw into the world below from where I came?

Miss Whiteside had no particular reason for hounding and persecuting me. Personally, she didn't give a hang if I was clean or dirty. She was merely one of the agents of clean society, delegated to judge who is fit and who is unfit to teach.

While they condemned me as unfit to be a teacher, because of my appearance, I was slaving to keep them clean. I was slaving in a laundry from five to eight in the morning, before going to college, and from six to eleven at night, after coming from college. Eight hours of work a day, outside my studies. Where was the time and the strength for the "little niceties of the well-groomed lady"?

At the time when they rose and took their morning bath, and put on their fresh-laundered linen that somebody had made ready for them, when they were being served with their breakfast, I had already toiled for three hours in a laundry.

When college hours were over, they went for a walk in the fresh air. They had time to rest, and bathe again, and put on fresh clothes for dinner. But I, after college hours, had only time to bolt a soggy meal, and rush back to the grind of the laundry till eleven at night.

At the hour when they came from the theater or musical, I came from the laundry. But I was so bathed in the sweat of exhaustion that I could not think of a bath of soap and water. I had only strength to drag myself home, and fall down on the bed and sleep. Even if I had had the desire and the energy to take a bath, there were no such things as bathtubs in the house where I lived.

Often as I stood at my board at the laundry, I thought of Miss Whiteside, and her clean world, clothed in the snowy shirtwaists I had ironed. I was thinking—I, soaking in the foul vapors of the steaming laundry, I, with my dirty, tired hands, I am ironing the clean, immaculate shirtwaists of clean, immaculate society. I, the unclean one, am actually fashioning the pedestal of their cleanliness, from which they reach down, hoping to lift me to the height that I have created for them.

I look back at my sweatshop childhood. One day, when I was about sixteen, someone gave me Rosenfeld's poem, "The Machine," to read. Like a spark thrown among oily rags, it set my whole being aflame with longing for self-expression. But I was dumb. I had nothing but blind, aching feeling. For days I went about with agonies of feeling, yet utterly at sea how to fathom and voice those feelings—birth throes of infinite worlds, and yet dumb.

Suddenly, there came upon me this inspiration. I can go to college! There I shall learn to express myself, to voice my thoughts. But I was not prepared to go to college. The girl in the cigar factory, in the next block, had gone first to a preparatory school. Why shouldn't I find a way, too?

Going to college seemed as impossible for me, at that time, as for an ignorant Russian shop girl to attempt to write poetry in English. But I was sixteen then, and the impossible was a magnet to draw the dreams that had no outlet. Besides, the actual was so barren, so narrow, so strangling, that the dream of the unattainable was the only air in which the soul could survive.

The ideal of going to college was like the birth of a new religion in my soul. It put new fire in my eyes, and new strength in my tired arms and fingers.

For six years I worked daytimes and went at night to a preparatory school. For six years I went about nursing the illusion that college was a place where I should find self-expression, and vague, pent-up feelings could live as thoughts and grow as ideas.

At last I came to college. I rushed for it with the outstretched arms of youth's aching hunger to give and take of life's deepest and highest, and I came against the solid wall of the well-fed, well-dressed world—the frigid whitewashed wall of cleanliness.

Until I came to college I had been unconscious of my clothes. Suddenly I felt people looking at me at arm's length, as if I were crooked or crippled, as if I had come to a place where I didn't belong, and would never be taken in.

How I pinched, and scraped, and starved myself, to save enough to come to college! Every cent of the tuition fee I paid was drops of sweat and blood from underpaid laundry work. And what did I get for it? A crushed spirit, a broken heart, a stinging sense of poverty that I never felt before.

The courses of study I had to swallow to get my diploma were utterly barren of interest to me. I didn't come to college to get dull learning from dead books. I didn't come for that dry, inanimate stuff that can be hammered out in lectures. I came because I longed for the larger life, for the stimulus of intellectual associations. I came because my whole being clamored for more vision, more light. But everywhere I went I saw big fences put up against me, with the brutal signs: "No trespassing. Get off the grass."

I experienced at college the same feeling of years ago when I came to this country, when after months of shut-in-ness, in dark tenements and stifling sweatshops, I had come to Central Park for the first time. Like a bird just out from a cage, I stretched out my arms, and then flung myself in ecstatic abandon on the grass. Just as I began to breathe in the fresh-smelling earth, and lift up my eyes to the sky, a big, fat policeman with a club in his hand seized me, with: "Can't you read the sign? Get off the grass!" Miss Whiteside, the dean of the college, the representative of the clean, the educated world, for all her external refinement, was to me like that big, brutal policeman, with the club in his hand, that drove me off the grass.

The death blows to all aspiration began when I graduated from college and tried to get a start at the work for which I had struggled so hard to fit myself. I soon found other agents of clean society, who had the power of giving or withholding the positions I sought, judging me as Miss Whiteside judged me. One glance at my shabby clothes, the desperate anguish that glazed and dulled my eyes and I felt myself condemned by them before I opened my lips to speak.

Starvation forced me to accept the lowest-paid substitute position. And because my wages were so low and so unsteady, I could never get the money for the clothes to make an appearance to secure a position with better pay. I was tricked and foiled. I was considered unfit to get decent pay for my work because of my appearance, and it was to the advantage of those who used me that my appearance should damn me, so as to get me to work for the low wages I was forced to accept. It seemed to me the whole vicious circle of society's injustices was thrust like a noose around my neck to strangle me.

The insults and injuries I had suffered at college had so eaten into my flesh that I could not bear to get near it. I shuddered with horror whenever I had to pass the place blocks away. The hate which I felt for Miss Whiteside spread like poison inside my soul, into hate for all clean society. The whole clean world was massed against me. Whenever I met a well-dressed person, I felt the secret stab of a hidden enemy.

I was so obsessed and consumed with my grievances that I could not get away from myself and think things out in the light. I was in the grip of that blinding, destructive, terrible thing—righteous indignation. I could not rest. I wanted the whole world to know that the college was against democracy in education, that clothes form the basis of class distinctions, that after graduation the opportunities for the best positions are passed out to those who are best-dressed, and the students too poor to put up a front are pigeonholed and marked unfit and abandoned to the mercy of the wind.

A wild desire raged in the corner of my brain. I knew that the dean gave dinners to the faculty at regular intervals. I longed to burst in at one of those feasts, in the midst of their grand speech-making, and tear down the fine clothes from these well-groomed ladies and gentlemen, and trample them under my feet, and scream like a lunatic: "Soap and water are cheap! Soap and water are cheap! Look at me! See how cheap it is!"

There seemed but three avenues of escape to the torments of my wasted life, madness, suicide, or a heart-to-heart confession to some one who understood. I had not energy enough for suicide. Besides, in my darkest moments of despair, hope clamored loudest. Oh, I longed so to live, to dream my way up on the heights, above the unreal realities that ground me and dragged me down to earth.

Inside the ruin of my thwarted life, the *unlived* visionary immigrant hungered and thirsted for America. I had come a refugee from the Russian pogroms, aflame with dreams of America. I did not find America in the sweatshops, much less in the schools and colleges. But for hundreds of years the persecuted races all over the world were nurtured on hopes of America. When a little baby in my mother's arms, before I was old enough to speak, I saw all around me weary faces light up with thrilling tales of the far-off "golden country." And so, though my faith in this so-called America was shattered, yet underneath, in the sap and roots of my soul, burned the deathless faith that America is, must be, somehow, somewhere. In the midst of my bitterest hates and rebellions, visions of America rose over me, like songs of freedom of an oppressed people.

My body was worn to the bone from overwork, my footsteps dragged with exhaustion, but my eyes still sought the sky, praying, ceaselessly praying, the dumb, inarticulate prayer of the lost immigrant: "America! Ach, America! Where is America?"

It seemed to me if I could only find some human being to whom I could unburden my heart, I would have new strength to begin again my insatiable search for America.

But to whom could I speak? The people in the laundry? They never understood me. They had a grudge against me because I left them when I tried to work myself up. Could I speak to the college people? What did these icebergs of convention know about the vital things of the heart?

And yet, I remembered, in the freshman year, in one of the courses in chemistry, there was an instructor, a woman, who drew me strangely. I felt she was the only real teacher among all the teachers and professors I met. I didn't care for the chemistry, but I liked to look at her. She gave me life, air, the unconscious emanation of her beautiful spirit. I had not spoken a word to her, outside the experiments in chemistry, but I knew her more than the people around her who were of her own class. I felt in the throb of her voice, in the subtle shading around the corner of her eyes, the color and texture of her dreams.

Often in the midst of our work in chemistry I felt like crying out to her: "Oh, please be my friend. I'm so lonely." But something choked me. I couldn't speak. The very intensity of my longing for her friendship made me run away from her in confusion the minute she approached me. I was so conscious of my shabbiness that I was afraid maybe she was only trying to be kind. I couldn't bear kindness. I wanted from her love, understanding, or nothing.

About ten years after I left college, as I walked the streets bowed and beaten with the shame of having to go around begging for work, I met Miss Van Ness. She not only recognized me, but stopped to ask how I was, and what I was doing.

I had begun to think that my only comrades in this world were the homeless and abandoned cats and dogs of the street, whom everybody gives another kick, as they slam the door on them. And here was one from the clean world human enough to be friendly. Here was one of the well-dressed, with a look in her eyes and a sound in her voice that was like healing oil over the bruises of my soul. The mere touch of that woman's hand in mine so overwhelmed me, that I burst out crying in the street.

The next morning I came to Miss Van Ness at her office. In those ten years she had risen to a professorship. But I was not in the least intimidated by her high office. I felt as natural in her presence as if she were my own sister. I heard myself telling her the whole story of my life, but I felt that even if I had not said a word she would have understood all I had to say as if I had spoken. It was all so unutterable, to find one from the other side of the world who was so simply and naturally that miraculous thing—a friend. Just as contact with Miss Whiteside had tied and bound all my thinking processes, so Miss Van Ness unbound and freed me and suffused me with light.

I felt the joy of one breathing on the mountaintops for the first time. I looked down at the world below. I was changed and the world was changed. My past was the forgotten night. Sunrise was all around me.

I went out from Miss Van Ness's office, singing a song of new life: "America! I found America."   *1920*

━┥━◆━┝━

H.D. (Hilda Doolittle)
1886–1961

"Why must I write?" wonders the U.S. poet H.D. in *Hermetic Definition* (1972); who or what inspires such persistent and controversial poetry? H.D. identifies her source of inspiration as a potent female muse, a goddess who unveils, unbinds, and subsequently commands the elderly poet to "write, write or die." The relentless "She" of the poem is Isis, most protean of Egyptian deities, but Isis is one of many names for H.D.'s muse. In her early poems the inspiring forces appear as women from Greek mythology—Artemis, Athene, Aphrodite—transformed from secondary figures in a patriarchal drama to powerful wellsprings of female creative identity. In *Trilogy* (1944–46), H.D.'s tripartite epic of World War II, the muse is "Our Lady," who appears not with the traditional holy child, the Savior of Christian legend, but with a blank book, "the unwritten volume of the new." In *Helen in Egypt* (1961) the questing Helen seeks affirmation from Thetis, the maternal sea goddess, a fertile source of the woman poet's art. Throughout her varied career—as poet, fiction writer, and critic of modernist movements—H.D. was fascinated with the goddess as a metaphor for female creativity.

H.D. documented her life in works of fiction that are thinly veiled autobiography. *The Gift* (1969) describes the author's childhood in a Moravian community in Bethlehem, Pennsylvania, and explores the tensions the child Hilda felt between her "father's science" (he was an astronomer at the University of Pennsylvania) and her "mother's art" (she was a painter and a musician). After two years at Bryn Mawr College, where she met MARIANNE MOORE and William Carlos Williams, H.D. moved in 1911 to London and was engaged for a time to Ezra Pound. Her novel *HERmione* (1981) presents the conflict she experienced between the influence of Pound and her desire for creative and sexual autonomy. It was Pound who, in the tea room of the British Museum in 1913, christened the poet H.D., a *nom de plume* she thereafter adopted, and who sent her Imagist poems to Harriet Monroe of *Poetry* magazine. H.D. married the British poet Richard Aldington in 1913, although she lived with him for only a brief time; their breakup during World War I is the subject of her novella *Bid Me to Live* (1939), which was not published until 1960.

Bryher (Winifred Ellerman), an historical novelist and heiress, entered H.D.'s life in 1919, when the poet was estranged from Aldington, pregnant by musician Cecil Gray, and ill with pneumonia. A fan of H.D.'s verse, Bryher nursed her back to health, adopted her daughter, Perdita, and became the poet's lover and lifelong friend. During the 1920s H.D. and Bryher traveled in Greece and Egypt, gathering material for H.D.'s writing, and in the late 1920s Bryher introduced her companion to the newly developing art form of cinema. Both women became involved in filmmaking, and in 1930 H.D. starred with Paul Robeson in *Borderline*, an avant-garde film that explores issues of race, class, and sexuality. In the 1930s she studied a variety of spiritual and psychological practices: Moravian mysticism, Kabbalism, gnosticism, astrology, the tarot, and psychoanalysis. In *Tribute to Freud* (1956) H.D. chronicles her 1933 analysis with Sigmund Freud, whom she admires but also criticizes for his misogyny. Although she published a translation of Euripides' *Ion* in 1937, H.D. wrote little from 1935 to 1942. During the early 1940s she lived with Bryher and Perdita in London, where they survived the

bombings of World War II and H.D. enjoyed a creative resurgence. But in 1946 she was hospitalized for depression in Kusnacht, Switzerland, where she lived for much of the remainder of
her life. In 1956 H.D. celebrated her seventieth birthday by visiting the United States for the
first time in thirty-five years, and in 1960 she received a medal from the American Academy of
Arts and Letters, the first woman to be so honored.

H.D.'s poetry can be divided into Imagist and epic phases. Poems in her early volumes—*Sea Garden* (1916), *Hymen* (1921), *Heliodora* (1924) and *Collected Poems* (1925)—
are characterized by linguistic compression, dramatic juxtaposition of images, and frequent
allusions to Greek mythology. The new aesthetic of Imagism appealed to the reclusive H.D.
because it provided a means of poetic camouflage and indirection. H.D.'s poems became
more experimental in *Hippolytus Temporizes* (1928) and *Red Roses for Bronze* (1931). During
this period she also began to reclaim maligned women from classical and Near Eastern
mythology. *Trilogy* explores the role of matriarchal goddesses and the sacred word in healing
the destruction caused by World War II, while *Helen in Egypt* undertakes both a personal
and a universal quest, as the poet reclaims Helen of Troy and chastises the "iron ring of the
patriarchy."

Included here are "Eurydice," in which H.D. challenges the arrogance of Orpheus and
charts Hades as female territory, and "Oread," the most famous of her Imagist verses. Also
included are the first four poems from Part I of *Trilogy*, *The Walls Do Not Fall*. Written in
1942 and published first as a separate volume in 1944, this long poem rejects misogyny, war,
and militant Christianity in favor of "the secret of Isis." H.D.'s vision of divinity combines
ancient and modern, male, and female; in her poetic theory words can transform reality, naming and thus effecting spiritual truths. Linguistic anagrams can venerate Isis and reconstruct a
female-centered, pacifist world view, and writers must initiate such an effort. Despite the
chaos that surrounds her, the poet finds in language, feminism, and "spiritual realism" the
possibility of redemption.

⊰ Eurydice ⊱

I

So you have swept me back,
I who could have walked with the live souls
above the earth,
I who could have slept among the live flowers
5   at last;

so for your arrogance
and your ruthlessness
I am swept back
where dead lichens drip
10   dead cinders upon moss of ash;

so for your arrogance
I am broken at last,
I who had lived unconscious,
who was almost forgot;

15   if you had let me wait
I had grown from listlessness
into peace,

if you had let me rest with the dead,
I had forgot you
20   and the past.

II

Here only flame upon flame
and black among the red sparks,
streaks of black and light
grown colorless;

25   why did you turn back,
that hell should be reinhabited
of myself thus
swept into nothingness?

why did you turn?
30   why did you glance back?
why did you hesitate for that moment?
why did you bend your face
caught with the flame of the upper earth,
above my face?

35   what was it that crossed my face
with the light from yours
and your glance?
what was it you saw in my face?
the light of your own face,
40   the fire of your own presence?

What had my face to offer
but reflex of the earth,
hyacinth color
caught from the raw fissure in the rock
45   where the light struck,
and the color of azure crocuses
and the bright surface of gold crocuses
and of the wind-flower,
swift in its veins as lightning
50   and as white.

III

Saffron from the fringe of the earth,
wild saffron that has bent
over the sharp edge of earth,
all the flowers that cut through the earth,
55   all, all the flowers are lost;

everything is lost,
everything is crossed with black,
black upon black
and worse than black,
60   this colorless light.

IV

Fringe upon fringe
of blue crocuses,
crocuses, walled against blue of themselves,
blue of that upper earth,
65   blue of the depth upon depth of flowers,
lost;

flowers,
if I could have taken once my breath of them,
enough of them,
70   more than earth,
even than of the upper earth,
had passed with me
beneath the earth;

if I could have caught up from the earth,
75   the whole of the flowers of the earth,
if once I could have breathed into myself
the very golden crocuses
and the red,
and the very golden hearts of the first saffron,
80   the whole of the golden mass,
the whole of the great fragrance,
I could have dared the loss.

V

So for your arrogance
and your ruthlessness
85   I have lost the earth
and the flowers of the earth,
and the live souls above the earth,
and you who passed across the light
and reached
90   ruthless;

you who have your own light,
who are to yourself a presence,
who need no presence;

yet for all your arrogance
95   and your glance,
I tell you this:

such loss is no loss,
such terror, such coils and strands and pitfalls
of blackness,
100   such terror
is no loss;

hell is no worse than your earth
above the earth,
hell is no worse,
105   no, nor your flowers

nor your veins of light
nor your presence,
a loss;

my hell is no worse than yours
110 though you pass among the flowers and speak
with the spirits above earth.

VI

Against the black
I have more fervor
than you in all the splendor of that place,
115 against the blackness
and the stark grey
I have more light;

and the flowers,
if I should tell you,
120 you would turn from your own fit paths
toward hell,
turn again and glance back
and I would sink into a place
even more terrible than this.

VII

125 At least I have the flowers of myself,
and my thoughts, no god
can take that;
I have the fervor of myself for a presence
and my own spirit for light;

130 and my spirit with its loss
knows this;
though small against the black,
small against the formless rocks,
hell must break before I am lost;

135 before I am lost,
hell must open like a red rose
for the dead to pass.

1917

⊰ Oread ⊱

Whirl up, sea—
whirl your pointed pines,
splash your great pines
on our rocks,
5 hurl your green over us,
cover us with your pools of fir.

1917

⊰ *from* The Walls Do Not Fall ⊱

1

An incident here and there,
and rails gone (for guns)
from your (and my) old town square:

mist and mist-gray, no color,
5   still the Luxor bee, chick and hare
pursue unalterable purpose

in green, rose-red, lapis;
they continue to prophesy
from the stone papyrus:

10   there, as here, ruin opens
the tomb, the temple; enter,
there as here, there are no doors:

the shrine lies open to the sky,
the rain falls, here, there
15   sand drifts; eternity endures:

ruin everywhere, yet as the fallen roof
leaves the sealed room
open to the air,

so, through our desolation,
20   thoughts stir, inspiration stalks us
through gloom:

unaware, Spirit announces the Presence;
shivering overtakes us,
as of old, Samuel:[1]

25   trembling at a known street-corner,
we know not nor are known;
the Pythian[2] pronounces—we pass on

to another cellar, to another sliced wall
where poor utensils show
30   like rare objects in a museum;

Pompeii[3] has nothing to teach us,
we know crack of volcanic fissure,
slow flow of terrible lava,

pressure on heart, lungs, the brain
35   about to burst its brittle case
(what the skull can endure!):

---

1. The Old Testament prophet.
2. Pytho is an ancient name for Delphi in Greece, where
the legendary oracle of Apollo was located.

3. Ancient Italian city destroyed in 79 C.E. by the eruption of Mount Vesuvius.

over us, Apocryphal fire,
under us, the earth sway, dip of a floor,
slope of a pavement

40   where men roll, drunk
with a new bewilderment,
sorcery, bedevilment:

the bone-frame was made for
no such shock knit within terror,
45   yet the skeleton stood up to it:

the flesh? it was melted away,
the heart burnt out, dead ember,
tendons, muscles shattered, outer husk dismembered,

yet the frame held:
50   we passed the flame: we wonder
what saved us? what for?

2

Evil was active in the land,
Good was impoverished and sad;

Ill promised adventure,
55   Good was smug and fat;

Dev-ill was after us,
tricked up like Jehovah;

Good was the tasteless pod,
stripped from the manna-beans, pulse, lentils:

60   they were angry when we were so hungry
for the nourishment, God;

they snatched off our amulets,
charms are not, they said, grace;

but gods always face two-ways,
65   so let us search the old highways

for the true-rune, the right-spell,
recover old values;

nor listen if they shout out,
your beauty, Isis, Aset or Astarte,[4]

70   is a harlot; you are retrogressive,
zealot, hankering after old flesh-pots;

your heart, moreover,
is a dead canker,

---

4. Isis and Aset were ancient Egyptian nature goddesses; Astarte was a Phoenician goddess of fertility and sexual love.

they continue, and
75   your rhythm is the devil's hymn,

your stylus is dipped in corrosive sublimate,
how can you scratch out

indelible ink of the palimpsest
of past misadventure?

3

80   Let us, however, recover the Sceptre,
the rod of power:

it is crowned with the lily-head
or the lily-bud:

it is Caduceus;[5] among the dying
85   it bears healing:

or evoking the dead,
it brings life to the living.

4

There is a spell, for instance,
in every sea-shell:

90   continuous, the sea-thrust
is powerless against coral,

bone, stone, marble
hewn from within by that craftsman,

the shell-fish:
95   oyster, clam, mollusk

is master-mason planning
the stone marvel:

yet that flabby, amorphous hermit
within, like the planet

100   senses the finite,
it limits its orbit

of being, its house,
temple, fane, shrine:

it unlocks the portals
105   at stated intervals:

prompted by hunger,
it opens to the tide-flow:

---

5. The symbolic staff of a herald, decorated with two entwined snakes and two wings at the top; also, an insignia that symbolizes a physician.

but infinity? no,
of nothing-too-much:

110   I sense my own limit,
my shell-jaws snap shut

at invasion of the limitless,
ocean-weight; infinite water

can not crack me, egg in egg-shell;
115   closed in, complete, immortal

full-circle, I know the pull
of the tide, the lull

as well as the moon;
the octopus-darkness

120   is powerless against
her cold immortality;

so I in my own way know
that the whale

can not digest me:
125   be firm in your own small, static, limited

orbit and the shark-jaws
of outer circumstance

will spit you forth:
be indigestible, hard, ungiving.

130   so that, living within,
you beget, self-out-of-self,

selfless,
that pearl-of-great-price.

1942

━━━ ❧❦❧ ━━━

Muriel Rukeyser
1913–1980

MURIEL RUKEYSER is one of the twentieth century's most powerful poets of witness. In more than twenty volumes written over fifty years, she blends poetry and social activism to protest the executions of the anarchists Sacco and Vanzetti, the exposure of silicon miners to lung disease, the atrocity of the Holocaust, segregation in the South, the Viet Nam War, and the oppression of women. As poet and editor KATE DANIELS has suggested, Rukeyser was never "a poet's poet—the exquisite practitioner of craft capable of making other poets envy her sheer technical skill." Instead, she was a democratic poet who write and cared for ordinary people. "Writing is only another way of giving," she once declared, "a courtesy, if you will, and a form of love."

Rukeyser was born into a wealthy, conservative Jewish family in New York who provided her with a privileged but not a sheltered childhood. From an early age she seemed aware of the painful aftermath of World War I as well as the familial tensions generated by her unhappily married parents. Her progressive politics emerged during her teenage years at the Ethical Cultural School in New York, where she determined to become a writer. From 1930 to 1932 she attended Vassar College, where she met Elizabeth Bishop and Mary McCarthy. Like many radical writers of the era, she joined the Communist Party, which she hoped would undermine class hierarchies worldwide. At Vassar she edited the *Student Review*, which had Communist leanings, and wrote for the *New Masses*, the official party newspaper in the United States. Her Communist sympathies led her to document the second trial of the Scottsboro boys in Alabama in 1933 and to visit silica mines in West Virginia in 1936 and write about unsafe working conditions there. During the Spanish Civil War she worked in Spain as a journalist and supported the Republican movement. By the end of the 1930s she was less committed to Communism than to an eclectic, progressive political vision that contested all forms of violence and injustice.

Her first volume of poetry, *Theory of Flight* (1935), won the prestigious Yale Younger Poets Award. It was quickly followed by two collections: *U.S. 1* (1938), which contains "The Book of the Dead," her long poem exposing the United States' failed promise, and *A Turning Wind* (1939), which mourns the rise of fascism and foreshadows war. *Beast in View* (1944) examines the atrocities of World War II from the perspective of "a Jew in the twentieth century." During the mid–1940s Rukeyser wrote *The Life of Poetry* (1949), in which she explores the "very different set of laws" by which the language of poetry operates. "One writes in order to feel," she claims. She described the period between 1947, the year her son was born, through 1958 as "the intercepted years," when raising a child as a single mother dominated her life. In this period she published two volumes of poetry, *The Green Wave* (1948) and *Elegies* (1949), and began teaching at Sarah Lawrence College, where she worked through the 1960s. During the McCarthy era she was the subject of anti-Communist investigations but, unlike many of her peers, was able to retain her teaching position because her college supported her. *Body of Waking* (1958) probes the responsibilities of motherhood, to one's own child, the world's children, and the body politic.

During the last two decades of her life Rukeyser wrote extensively and was actively involved in the feminist and antiwar movements. In the 1960s she was imprisoned for demonstrating against the Viet Nam War, and in 1975 she traveled to Hanoi as President of PEN-America, a writers' group dedicated to social justice, to protest the death sentence levied against poet Kim Chi-Ha. *The Speed of Darkness* (1968) contains her celebrated sequence "Käthe Kollwitz," both a tribute to the life and work of a German expressionist artist and an homage to women's sexuality and embodiment. *Breaking Open* (1973) offers Rukeyser's most staunchly antipatriarchal poems, including "Myth" and "Despisals." "I write from the body, a female body," she proclaimed in 1976, once referring to herself as a "a rare battered she-poet."

Rukeyser's oeuvre inscribes transformation as well as resistance, a radically hopeful vision of the possibility for change. "What would happen if one woman told the truth about her life?" she muses in "Käthe Kollwitz." "The world would split open." Indeed, Rukeyser's poetic example has opened up worlds for many younger women poets and their readers. Two pivotal feminist anthologies of poetry, *No More Masks!* and *The World Split Open*, have taken their titles from her poems; and poets from ADRIENNE RICH to SHARON OLDS consider Rukeyser a formidable and inspiring foremother. Like Kollwitz, Rukeyser resolved to "wrestle with grief with time" and "from the material make / an art harder than bronze."

⇥ Bubble of Air ⇤

The bubbles in the blood sprang free,
crying from roots, from Darwin's[1] beard.

---

1. Charles Darwin (1809–1882) was an English naturalist known today for his theories of evolution.

The angel of the century
stood on the night and would be heard;
5   turned to my dream of tears and sang:
Woman, American, and Jew,
three guardians watch over you,
three lions of heritage
resist the evil of your age:
10   life, freedom, and memory.
And all the dreams cried from the camps
and all the steel of torture rang.
The angel of the century
stood on the night and cried the great
15   notes Give Create and Fight—
while war
runs through your veins, while life
a bubble of air stands in your throat,
answer the silence of the weak:
20   Speak!

                           1944

⇥ *from* Letter to the Front ⇤

VII

To be a Jew in the twentieth century
Is to be offered a gift.   If you refuse,
Wising to be invisible, you choose
Death of the spirit, the stone insanity.
5   Accepting, take full life.   Full agonies:
Your evening deep in labyrinthine blood
Of those who resist, fail, and resist; and God
Reduced to a hostage among hostages.

The gift is torment.   Not alone the still
10   Torture, isolation; or torture of the flesh.
That may come also.   But the accepting wish,
The whole and fertile spirit as guarantee
For every human freedom, suffering to be free,
Daring to live for the impossible.

                           1944

⇥ Käthe Kollwitz[1] ⇤

I

Held between wars
my lifetime
           among wars, the big hands of the world of death

---

1. Käthe Kollwitz (1867–1945) was a German graphic artist who portrayed in her work the suffering of ordinary citizens during war, especially mothers and children. Rukeyser quotes from a number of Kollwitz's written works in this poem.

my lifetime
5   listens to yours.

The faces of the sufferers
in the street, in dailiness,
their lives showing
through their bodies
10   a look as of music
the revolutionary look
that says   I am in the world
to change the world
my lifetime
15   is to love to endure to suffer the music
to set its portrait
up as a sheet of the world
the most moving the most alive
Easter and bone
20   and Faust[2] walking among the flowers of the world
and the child alive within the living woman, music of man,
and death holding my lifetime between great hands
the hands of enduring life
that suffers the gifts and madness of full life, on earth, in our time,
25   and through my life, through my eyes, through my arms and hands
may give the face of this music in portrait waiting for
the unknown person
held in the two hands, you.

II

Woman as gates, saying :
30   "The process is after all like music,
like the development of a piece of music.
The fugues come back and
                                          again and again
interweave.
35   A theme may seem to have been put aside,
but it keeps returning—
the same thing modulated,
somewhat changed in form.
Usually richer.
40   And it is very good that this is so."

A woman pouring her opposites.
"After all there are happy things in life too.
Why do you show only the dark side?"
"I could not answer this. But I know—
45   in the beginning my impulse to know
the working life
                          had little to do with
pity or sympathy.

2. The questing hero of an epic poem by Johann Wolfgang von Goethe (1749–1832).

I simply felt
50   that the life of the workers was beautiful."

She said, "I am groping in the dark."

She said, "When the door opens, of sensuality,
the you will understand it too. The struggle begins.
Never again to be free of it,
55   often you will feel it to be your enemy.
Sometimes
you will almost suffocate,
such joy it brings."

Saying of her husband : "My wish
60   is to die after Karl.[3]
I know no person who can love as he can,
with his whole soul.
Often this love has oppressed me;
I wanted to be free.
65   But often too it has made me
so terribly happy."

She said : "We rowed over to Carrara at dawn,
climbed up to the marble quarries
and rowed back at night. The drops of water
70   fell like glittering stars
from our oars."

She said: "As a matter of fact,
I believe
            that bisexuality
75   is almost   a necessary factor
in artistic production; at any rate,
the tinge of masculinity within me
helped me
            in my work."

80   She said : "The only technique I can still manage.
It's hardly a technique at all, lithography.
In it
            only the essentials count."

A tight-lipped man in a restaurant last night saying to me :
85   "Kollwitz?   She's too black-and-white."

III

Held among wars, watching
    all of them
    all these people

3. Her husband, Karl Kollwitz, a physician.

weavers,
90   Carmagnole[4]

Looking at
all of them
death, the children
patients in waiting-rooms
95   famine
the street
the corpse with the baby
floating, on the dark river

A woman seeing
100   the violent, inexorable
movement of nakedness
and the confession of No
the confession of great weakness, war,
all streaming to one son killed, Peter;
105   even the son left living; repeated,
the father, the mother; the grandson
another Peter killed in another war;[5] firestorm;
dark, light, as two hands,
this pole and that pole as the gates.

110   What would happen if one woman told the truth about her life?
The world would split open

IV / Song: The Calling-Up

Rumor, stir of ripeness
rising within this girl
sensual blossoming
115   of meaning, its light and form.

The birth-cry summoning
out of the male, the father
from the warm woman
a mother in response.

120   The word of death
calls up the fight with stone
wrestle with grief with time
from the material make
an art harder than bronze.

V / Self-Portrait

125   Mouth looking directly at you
eyes in their inwardness looking
directly at you
half light   half darkness
woman, strong, German, young artist

---

4. Italian for revolution.
5. Kollwitz's son Peter was killed in World War I; her

grandson, also named Peter, was killed in World War II.

130 flows into
     wide sensual mouth meditating
     looking right at you
     eyes shadowed with brave hand
     looking deep at you
135 flows into
     wounded brave mouth
     grieving and hooded eyes
     alive, German, in her first War
     flows into
140 strength of the worn face
     a skein of lines
     broods, flows into
     mothers among the war graves
     bent over death
145 facing the father
     stubborn upon the field
     flows into
     the marks of her knowing—
     Nie Wieder Krieg[6]
150 repeated in the eyes
     flows into
     "Seedcorn must not be ground"[7]
     and the grooved cheek
     lips drawn fine
155 the down-drawn grief
     face of our age
     flows into
     Pieta,[8] mother and
     between her knees
160 life as her son in death
     pouring from the sky of
     one more war
     flows into
     face almost obliterated
165 hand over the mouth forever
     hand over one eye now
     the other great eye
     closed

                                        1968

⊰ Despisals ⊱

In the human cities, never again to
despise the backside of the city, the ghetto,

---

6. "No More War" in German.
7. This was the title of Kollwitz's last work, which depicts a mother attempting to shield her children from war.

8. A term used to describe artistic representations of the Virgin Mary mourning over Christ's dead body.

or build it again as we build the despised
backsides of houses.   Look at your own building.
5   You are the city.

Among our secrecies, not to despise our Jews
(that is, ourselves) or our darkness, our blacks,
or in our sexuality   wherever it takes us
and we now know we are productive
10   too productive, too reproductive
for our present invention — never to despise
the homosexual who goes building another

with touch   with touch   (not to despise any touch)
each like himself, like herself each.
15   You are this.
                              In the body's ghetto
never to go despising the asshole
nor the useful shit that is our clean clue
to what we need.   Never to despise
20   the clitoris in her least speech.

Never to despise in myself what I have been taught
to despise.   Nor to despise the other.
Not to despise the *it*.   To make this relation
with the it : to know that *I* am it.   *1973*

━ ❖ ━

Nadine Gordimer
1923–

In eleven novels and ten collections of stories written over more than forty years, NADINE
GORDIMER has exposed the patterns of racist dominance that characterized South Africa under
apartheid. Until the 1970s the political perspective of her realist fiction was liberal, but after
the publication of *The Conservationist* in 1974 her work became increasingly radical; indeed,
two of her best novels, *Burger's Daughter* (1979) and *July's People* (1981), were initially banned
in their country of origin. As a writer, Gordimer has explained, she finds "two presences within—creative self-absorption and conscionable awareness"; her quest has been to "resolve
whether these are locked in death-struggle, or are really fetuses in a twinship of fecundity." Her
fiction bears witness to one writer's ability to be a creative genius and an agent of change, and
its power has been widely recognized: in 1991 she received the Nobel Prize for Fiction.

Born in Springs, a mining town outside of Johannesburg, Gordimer was raised by Jewish
parents; her father, Isidore Gordimer, emigrated to South Africa from Latvia at the age of thirteen, while her mother, Nan, was of English descent. Influenced by her mother, she began as a
child to notice the inequities around her. Gordimer links the beginning of her moral development most directly, however, to the reading she did as a teen in the library of a wealthy family
friend. Affected particularly by Upton Sinclair's *The Jungle*, she transposed his social critique of
the terrible working conditions in Chicago's stockyards to those in the South African mines
that surrounded her home. Gordimer began writing fiction as a student in a girls' convent
school; by 1950 she had published numerous stories in regional magazines, and in 1951 *The
New Yorker* accepted one of her stories. After a brief marriage and divorce in her twenties,
Gordimer married Reinhold Cassirer, a Johannesburg businessman; the couple have two grown

children. Since the 1950s she has staunchly supported black South African writers, promoting their work for publication, offering creative writing workshops to aspiring novelists, and helping to found a nonracial writers' guild, the Congress of South African Writers. She founded South Africa's Anti-Censorship Action Group and is a member of the African National Congress.

Gordimer's first novel, *The Lying Days* (1953), is set in an East Rand mining community similar to the one in which she grew up. Like much of her early fiction, it explores repressive sexual relations and familial dynamics in a middle-class white household. This novel was followed by *A World of Strangers* (1966), *A Guest of Honor* (1970), and *The Conservationist*, which won Britain's Booker Prize for Fiction. *Burger's Daughter* and *July's People* examine white guilt and responsibility for racism, as well as the possibility of civil war as the only vehicle for change in South Africa, while *A Sport of Nature* (1987) imagines a future of independent black rule. *My Son's Story* (1990) considers the impact a father's sexual behavior has on his idealistic son. *None to Accompany Me* (1995) is set during the early 1990s in a South Africa in transition. Its white female protagonist, a human rights attorney, experiences frustration with both her family life and the slow pace of change, while its central black characters, a married couple returned at last from exile, struggle to understand gender politics in the new South Africa.

Although Gordimer's novels have received more critical attention than her stories, her work in this genre is also impressive. Most of her best early stories appear in *Selected Stories* (1975); more recent volumes include *No Place Like* (1979), *A Soldier's Embrace* (1980), and *Jump* (1991). Gordimer is also a renowned essayist whose prose addresses politics, writing, censorship, and travel. A number of her published essays have been collected in *The Essential Gesture: Writing, Politics and Places*, edited in 1988 by Stephen Clingman. Interviews with Gordimer conducted over a thirty-year period are represented in *Conversations with Nadine Gordimer* (1990).

Although Gordimer does not consider herself a feminist, her writing explores gender as well as racial and class concerns; many of her protagonists experience tensions between their personal lives and political commitments. The story included here, "Amnesty," is written in the anxious voice of a rural black village woman who for five years has waited for her lover, a revolutionary jailed on Robben Island, to come home. In "Amnesty" Gordimer implies that no revolution is complete until transformation occurs in rural as well as urban areas, in the economic as well as the political sphere, and for women as well as men.

⊰ Amnesty ⊱

When we heard he was released I ran all over the farm and through the fence to our people on the next farm to tell everybody. I only saw afterwards I'd torn my dress on the barbed wire, and there was a scratch, with blood, on my shoulder.

He went away from this place nine years ago, signed up to work in town with what they call a construction company—building glass walls up to the sky. For the first two years he came home for the weekend once a month and two weeks at Christmas; that was when he asked my father for me. And he began to pay. He and I thought that in three years he would have paid enough for us to get married. But then he started wearing that T-shirt, he told us he'd joined the union, he told us about the strike, how he was one of the men who went to talk to the bosses because some others had been laid off after the strike. He's always been good at talking, even in English—he was the best at the farm school, he used to read the newspapers the Indian wraps soap and sugar in when you buy at the store.

There was trouble at the hostel where he had a bed, and riots over paying rent in the townships and he told me—just me, not the old ones—that wherever people were fighting against the way we are treated they were doing it for all of us, on the farms as well as the towns, and the unions were with them, he was with them, making speeches, marching. The third year, we heard he was in prison. Instead of getting married. We didn't know where to find him, until he went on trial. The case was heard in a town far away. I couldn't go often to the court because by that time I had passed my Standard 8 and I was working in the farm school. Also my parents were short of money. Two of my brothers who had gone away to work in town didn't send home; I suppose they lived with girlfriends and had to buy things for them. My father and other brother work here for the Boer[1] and the pay is very small, we have two goats, a few cows we're allowed to graze, and a patch of land where my mother can grow vegetables. No cash from that.

When I saw him in the court he looked beautiful in a blue suit with a striped shirt and brown tie. All the accused—his comrades, he said—were well-dressed. The union bought the clothes so that the judge and the prosecutor would know they weren't dealing with stupid yes-baas black men who didn't know their rights. These things and everything else about the court and trial he explained to me when I was allowed to visit him in jail. Our little girl was born while the trial went on and when I brought the baby to court the first time to show him, his comrades hugged him and then hugged me across the barrier of the prisoners' dock and they had clubbed together to give me some money as a present for the baby. He chose the name for her, Inkululeko.

Then the trial was over and he got six years. He was sent to the Island. We all knew about the Island. Our leaders had been there so long. But I have never seen the sea except to color it in blue at school, and I couldn't imagine a piece of earth surrounded by it. I could only think of a cake of dung, dropped by the cattle, floating in a pool of rainwater they'd crossed, the water showing the sky like a looking-glass, blue. I was ashamed only to think that. He had told me how the glass walls showed the pavement trees and the other buildings in the street and the colors of the cars and the clouds as the crane lifted him on a platform higher and higher through the sky to work at the top of a building.

He was allowed one letter a month. It was my letter because his parents didn't know how to write. I used to go to them where they worked on another farm to ask what message they wanted to send. The mother always cried and put her hands on her head and said nothing, and the old man, who preached to us in the veld every Sunday, said tell my son we are praying, God will make everything all right for him. Once he wrote back, That's the trouble—our people on farms, they're told God will decide what's good for them so that they won't find the force to do anything to change their lives.

After two years had passed, we—his parents and I—had saved up enough money to go to Cape Town to visit him. We went by train and slept on the floor at the station and asked the way, next day, to the ferry. People were kind; they all knew that if you wanted the ferry it was because you had somebody of yours on the Island.[2]

And there it was—there was the sea. It was green and blue, climbing and falling, bursting white, all the way to the sky. A terrible wind was slapping it this way and that; it hid the Island, but people like us, also waiting for the ferry, pointed where the Island must be, far out in the sea that I never thought would be like it really was.

There were other boats, and ships as big as buildings that go to other places, all over the world, but the ferry is only for the Island, it doesn't go anywhere else in the

1. White South Africans of Dutch descent.
2. Robben Island, where President Nelson Mandela and other antiapartheid activists with the African National Congress were imprisoned during the 1960s, 1970s, and 1980s.

world, only to the Island. So everybody waiting there was waiting for the Island, there could be no mistake we were not in the right place. We had sweets and biscuits, trousers and a warm coat for him (a woman standing with us said we wouldn't be allowed to give him the clothes) and I wasn't wearing, any more, the old beret pulled down over my head that farm girls wear, I had bought relaxer cream from the man who comes round the farms selling things out of a box on his bicycle, and my hair was combed up thick under a flowered scarf that didn't cover the gold-colored rings in my ears. His mother had her blanket tied round her waist over her dress, a farm woman, but I looked just as good as any of the other girls there. When the ferry was ready to take us, we stood all pressed together and quiet like the cattle waiting to be let through a gate. One man kept looking round with his chin moving up and down, he was counting, he must have been afraid there were too many to get on and he didn't want to be left behind. We all moved up to the policeman in charge and everyone ahead of us went onto the boat. But when our turn came and he put out his hand for something, I didn't know what.

We didn't have a permit. We didn't know that before you come to Cape Town, before you come to the ferry for the Island, you have to have a police permit to visit a prisoner on the Island. I tried to ask him nicely. The wind blew the voice out of my mouth.

We were turned away. We saw the ferry rock, bumping the landing where we stood, moving, lifted and dropped by all that water, getting smaller and smaller until we didn't know if we were really seeing it or one of the birds that looked black, dipping up and down, out there.

The only good thing was one of the other people took the sweets and biscuits for him. He wrote and said he got them. But it wasn't a good letter. Of course not. He was cross with me; I should have found out, I should have known about the permit. He was right—I bought the train tickets, I asked where to go for the ferry, I should have known about the permit. I have passed Standard 8. There was an advice office to go to in town, the churches ran it, he wrote. But the farm is so far from town, we on the farms don't know about these things. It was as he said: Our ignorance is the way we are kept down, this ignorance must go.

We took the train back and we never went to the Island—never saw him in the three more years he was there. Not once. We couldn't find the money for the train. His father died and I had to help his mother from my pay. For our people the worry is always money, I wrote. When will we ever have money? Then he sent such a good letter. That's what I'm on the Island for, far away from you, I'm here so that one day our people will have the things they need, land, food, and end of ignorance. There was something else—I could just read the word 'power' the prison had blacked out. All his letters were not just for me; the prison officer read them before I could.

He was coming home after only five years!

That's what is seemed to me, when I heard—the five years were suddenly disappeared—nothing!—there was no whole year still to wait. I showed my—our—little girl his photo again. That's your daddy, he's coming, you're going to see him. She told the other children at school, I've got a daddy, just as she showed off about the kid goat she had at home.

We wanted him to come at once, and at the same time we wanted time to prepare. His mother lived with one of his uncles; now that his father was dead there was no house of his father for him to take me to as soon as we married. If there had been time, my father would have cut poles, my mother and I would have baked bricks, cut thatch, and built a house for him and me and the child.

We were not sure what day he would arrive. We only heard on my radio his name and the names of some others who were released. Then at the Indian's store I noticed the newspaper, *The Nation*, written by black people, and on the front a picture of a lot of people dancing and waving—I saw at once it was at that ferry. Some men were being carried on other men's shoulders. I couldn't see which one was him. We were waiting. The ferry had brought him from the Island but we remembered Cape Town is a long way from us. Then he did come. On a Saturday, no school, so I was working with my mother, hoeing and weeding round the pumpkins and mealies, my hair, that I meant to keep nice, tied in an old *doek*.[3] A combi[4] came over the veld and his comrades had brought him. I wanted to run away and wash but he stood there stretching his legs, calling, hey! hey! with his comrades making noise around him, and my mother started shrieking in the old style aie! aie! and my father was clapping and stamping towards him. He held his arms open to us, this big man in town clothes, polished shoes, and all the time while he hugged me I was holding my dirty hands, full of mud, away from him behind his back. His teeth hit me hard through his lips, he grabbed at my mother and she struggled to hold the child up to him. I thought we would all fall down! Then everyone was quiet. The child hid behind my mother. He picked her up but she turned her head away to her shoulder. He spoke to her gently but she wouldn't speak to him. She's nearly six years old! I told her not to be a baby. She said, That's not him.

The comrades all laughed, we laughed, she ran off and he said, She has to have time to get used to me.

He has put on weight, yes; a lot. You couldn't believe it. He used to be so thin his feet looked too big for him. I used to feel his bones but now—that night—when he lay on me he was so heavy, I didn't remember it was like that. Such a long time. It's strange to get stronger in prison; I thought he wouldn't have enough to eat and would come out weak. Everyone said, Look at him!—he's a man, now. He laughed and banged his fist on his chest, told them how the comrades exercised in their cells, he would run three miles a day, stepping up and down on one place on the floor of the small cell where he was kept. After we were together at night we used to whisper a long time but now I can feel he's thinking of some things I don't know and I can't worry him with talk. Also I don't know what to say. To ask him what it was like, five years shut away there; or to tell him something about school or about the child. What else has happened, here? Nothing. Just waiting. Sometimes in the daytime I do try to tell him what it was like for me, here at home on the farm, five years. He listens, he's interested, just like he's interested when people from the other farms come to visit and talk to him about little things that happened to them while he was away all that time on the Island. He smiles and nods, asks a couple of questions and then stands up and stretches. I see it's to show them it's enough, his mind is going back to something he was busy with before they came. And we farm people are very slow; we tell things slowly, he used to, too.

He hasn't signed on for another job. But he can't stay at home with us; we thought, after five years over there in the middle of that green and blue sea, so far, he would rest with us a little while. The combi or some car comes to fetch him and he says don't worry, I don't know what day I'll be back. At first I asked, what week, next week? He tried to explain to me: in the Movement it's not like it was in the union, where you do your

---

3. Scarf.   4. Truck.

work every day and after that you are busy with meetings; in the Movement you never know where you will have to go and what is going to come up next. And the same with money. In the Movement, it's not like a job, with regular pay—I know that, he doesn't have to tell me—it's like it was going to the Island, you do it for all our people who suffer because we haven't got money, we haven't got land—look, he said, speaking of my parents', my home, the home that has been waiting for him, with his child: Look at this place where the white man owns the ground and lets you squat in mud and tin huts here only as long as you work for him—*Baba* and your brother planting his crops and looking after his cattle, Mama cleaning his house and you in the school without even having the chance to train properly as a teacher. The farmer owns us, he says.

I've been thinking we haven't got a home because there wasn't time to build a house before he came from the Island; but we haven't got a home at all. Now I've understood that.

I'm not stupid. When the comrades come to this place in the combi to talk to him here I don't go away with my mother after we've brought them tea or (if she's made it for the weekend) beer. They like her beer, they talk about our culture and there's one of them who makes a point of putting his arm around my mother, calling her the mama of all of them, the mama of Africa. Sometimes they please her very much by telling her how they used to sing on the Island and getting her to sing an old song we all know from our grandmothers. Then they join in with their strong voices. My father doesn't like this noise traveling across the veld; he's afraid that if the Boer finds out my man is a political, from the Island, and he's holding meetings on the Boer's land, he'll tell my father to go, and take his family with him. But my brother says if the Boer asks anything just tell him it's a prayer meeting. Then the singing is over; my mother knows she must go away into the house.

I stay, and listen. He forgets I'm there when he's talking and arguing about something I can see is important, more important than anything we could ever have to say to each other when we're alone. But now and then, when one of the other comrades is speaking I see him look at me for a moment the way I will look up at one of my favorite children in school to encourage the child to understand. The men don't speak to me and I don't speak. One of the things they talk about is organizing the people on the farms—the workers, like my father and brother, and like his parents used to be. I learn what all these things are: minimum wage, limitation of working hours, the right to strike, annual leave, accident compensation, pensions, sick and even maternity leave. I am pregnant, at last I have another child inside me, but that's women's business. When they talk about the Big Man, the Old Men, I know who these are: Our leaders are also back from prison. I told him about the child coming; he said, And this one belongs to a new country, he'll build the freedom we've fought for! I know he wants to get married but there's no time for that at present. There was hardly time for him to make the child. He comes to me just like he comes here to eat a meal or put on clean clothes. Then he picks up the little girl and swings her round and there!—it's done, he's getting into the combi, he's already turning to his comrade that face of his that knows only what's inside his head, those eyes that move quickly as if he's chasing something you can't see. The little girl hasn't had time to get used to this man. But I know she'll be proud of him, one day!

How can you tell that to a child six years old. But I tell her about the Big Man and the Old Men, our leaders, so she'll know that her father was with them on the Island, this man is a great man, too.

On Saturday, no school and I plant and weed with my mother, she sings but I don't; I think. On Sunday there's no work, only prayer meetings out of the farmer's way under the trees, and beer drinks at the mud and tin huts where the farmers allow us to squat on their land. I go off on my own as I used to do when I was a child, making up games and talking to myself where no one would hear me or look for me. I sit on a warm stone in the late afternoon, high up, and the whole valley is a path between the hills, leading away from my feet. It's the Boer's farm but that's not true, it belongs to nobody. The cattle don't know that anyone says he owns it, the sheep—they are gray stones, and then they become a thick gray snake moving—don't know. Our huts and the old mulberry tree and the little brown mat of earth that my mother dug over yesterday, way down there, and way over there the clump of trees round the chimneys and the shiny thing that is the TV mast of the farmhouse—they are nothing, on the back of this earth. It could twitch them away like a dog does a fly.

I am up with the clouds. The sun behind me is changing the colors of the sky and the clouds are changing themselves, slowly, slowly. Some are pink, some are white, swelling like bubbles. Underneath is a bar of gray, not enough to make rain. It gets longer and darker, it grows a thin snout and long body and then the end of it is a tail. There's a huge gray rat moving across the sky, eating the sky.

The child remembered the photo; she said *That's not him.* I'm sitting here where I came often when he was on the Island. I came to get away from the others, to wait by myself.

I'm watching the rat, it's losing itself, its shape, eating the sky, and I'm waiting. Waiting for him to come back.

Waiting.

I'm waiting to come back home.   *1991*

⊷ ⚹ ⊶

Janet Frame
1924–

New Zealand novelist JANET FRAME documents her country's complex cultural history in her writing, as well as her own pilgrimage from mental illness to recovery. She grew up in Oamaru, New Zealand, the daughter of a poor railroad worker. In her three-volume autobiography she describes her family's financial difficulties and her own creative growth, as well as a painful childhood colored by the drowning death of two younger sisters and her brother's struggles with epilepsy. Academically talented, Frame attended Dunedin Teachers College from 1943 to 1945 but left due to stress; in 1947 she admitted herself into Seacliff Mental Hospital and for the next seven years lived there or in other sanitariums. In 1951, while still a patient, she published *The Lagoon*, a volume of short stories that won New Zealand's prestigious Herbert Church Memorial Award. After leaving the hospital she lived for a time on the land of a fellow writer, Frank Sargeson, and in 1956 she traveled to Spain and England on a State Literary Fund grant, remaining abroad for the next seven years. Since 1963 she has resided in New Zealand and worked full-time as a writer.

Frame has published eleven novels, beginning with *Owls Do Cry* (1957); she uses an experimental narrative technique to investigate how language can obfuscate truth and distort reality. Among her novels are *Faces in the Water* (1961), *The Edge of the Alphabet* (1962), *A State of Siege* (1966), *Daughter Buffalo* (1972), *Living in the Maniototo* (1979), and *The Carpathians* (1988). In addition to *The Lagoon* she has published three collections of prize-winning short stories: *The Reservoir* (1963), *Snowman, Snowman* (1963), and *You Are Now Entering the Human Heart* (1984). In 1967 she published a volume of poetry, *The Pocket Mirror*, and in 1969 a children's book, *Mona Minim and the Smell of the Sun*. Frame writes about her childhood in *To the Island* (1983) and about her mental breakdown and gradual recovery in *An Angel at My Table* (1984); this latter work was made into a 1990 film directed by Jane Campion. Frame's subsequent development as a writer and a world traveler is chronicled in the third volume of her autobiography, *The Envoy from Mirror City* (1985).

"The Chosen Image," taken from *The Reservoir*, offers an allegorical account of a male poet who determines to grow a lovely hothouse plant in his meager rooms by breathing on it constantly. The effects of this decision on the poet and his resistant muse emerge as an ironic commentary on the artistic process, the politics of gender, and the writer's quest for truth.

⊰ The Chosen Image ⊱

In late winter when the seed catalogs were thrust through the letter box, the poet, having a spare hour or two, gathered them upon his table, studied them carefully, and from the many magnificent illustrations he chose the bloom which he had decided to plant in a wooden box upon his window sill, for he did not possess a garden. That same afternoon he went to the local post office and after waiting in the queue which extended from the stationery beyond the frozen foods to the cheeses which were next to the door, the poet bought a postal order for two and threepence, put it in an envelope with the number of the packet of seed, and sent it to the seed company. Then he returned home and for three days waited impatiently for the seed to arrive. At night after he had gone to bed he would take the catalog and read it, and on the third night when he was gazing at the picture of his chosen seed which he already loved very dearly, he happened to read the small print beneath the advertisement.

"Hothouse bloom only," he read.

For a moment he was alarmed. He knew that his room would not provide much warmth for the plant, because he did not earn much money as a poet, in spite of the occasional television interviews where he was asked, What do you think of the world situation? Do you think Success comes too early in this modern age? If you had to live your life over again which one thing would you change? And in spite of the occasional poem printed in a literary journal, and the advertisement jingle which he wrote for a friend in an agency, his slight income did not allow for central heating. How would a hothouse bloom ever survive? he wondered.

"Well," he said at last to himself, "I will breathe on it. My body is warm, well stoked, blood flows from rafter to basement and even the rats have been driven inside this winter to seek shelter in me. By the way, one day when I am free of dreams and light, hawkers, carrion crows and enchantments I shall take time to sprinkle an appetizing sweet poison for the rats in my sealed cabinet. In the meantime I shall await my packet of wonderful blossom."

So he waited, sitting down to work the next morning with his mind continually straying to the thought of growing a hothouse bloom upon his window sill.

In due course the packet of seed arrived. The poet planted it, following the instructions as carefully as his individual temperament would allow. He resolved to breathe upon the soil, the seed and the resulting plant as often as he remembered or was free to do so when he took time from writing his poems to walk about the room counting the faded leaves upon the carpet or looking from the window at the man in the battered gray cap who walked from door to door asking, "Have you any old watches, old gold, bracelets, wedding rings?"

The poet was not married, although like all poets he possessed an invisible muse, a mistress and wife to him, and a wedding ring with which he pledged his devotion to the Chosen Image. Unfortunately, when he turned the wedding ring three times upon his finger it did not provide him with a poem. There had been much controversy. Some poets had said that the wedding ring should provide poems in this way.

Nor could the poet give to the man in the gray battered cap any old watches, old gold or bracelets. How could he possess such valuables? He lived in a small flat where his only treasures which were yet not his alone but were accessible to all, lay arranged in dictionaries and grammars upon his bookshelves. Strange, wasn't it, that no burglar had been know to raid the premises in order to steal suitcases of words?

As for old watches, well, the poet owned a wristwatch which he preferred to keep in his pocket or upon his table. Strapped on his wrist it reminded him of a too genial handcuff to which he had no key, for which no key had yet been made.

Did I tell you that he was a poet who could not write good poetry (there are many such) but unearthed clichés as if they were archaeological treasures arranged on a silver spade? After he had written each poem he was pleased with it, he confused the warmth and excitement which the act of writing gave him with the feelings naturally provided by a thing of beauty; therefore he thought his poem beautiful, and was most distressed and could not understand when later, from somewhere in the cave roof, the dampening idea leaked through that his poem was bad. Yet he could not stop writing just as he could not stop counting the leaves on the carpet or looking from his window at the man calling for Old Watches, Old Gold, Bracelets; or breathing warmth upon the tender leaves that had sprung from his chosen seed.

One evening when he looked at the plant he noticed a tiny bud with its petals beginning to open, and he knew that when morning came the plant would be in full blossom. So he went quickly to bed, pulling the blankets well over him in the belief that concealment means escape and acceleration of time, and soon he was fast asleep and dreaming, but the anonymous voices which inhabit all dreams said to him, "What can you call entirely your own? You cannot write a poem without using the words, often the thoughts, of others. The words of the world lie like stagnant water in the ponds for the poets masquerading as the sun to quench their thirst, spitting out the dead tadpoles and the dry sticks and stones and bones. If ever you have precious thoughts of your own which do not lie accessible to all beneath the sky, how can you safeguard them? Where are your security measures for putting thoughts under lock and key?

"But then, no thoughts belong entirely to you. You have no talent for your work. Your only talent and personal possession is breath, and yet since late winter when the seed catalogs were thrust through your letter box you have bestowed your breath upon a mere plant in order that it should give you pleasure by blossoming on your window sill. Do you think that is wise? Should you not conserve your breath, issue it according to a planned system of economy, and not waste it upon objects like flowers which perish almost as soon as they have bloomed?"

The poet heeded the voices in his dream and the next morning when he looked at the plant, although he knew that the flower was almost in blossom, he refused to breathe upon it, and all day it shivered upon the window sill, feeling for the first time the bitterness of the March winds that moaned up and down the street, and the chill touch of the tendrils of frost and fog that crept down the chimney, under the door, and through the top of the window into the poet's room. And the petals of the flower never opened, their promise was never fulfilled. By nightfall the leaves had blackened at the edges and the bud was a shriveled silken cocoon of nothing.

The saddened poet gazed at the corpse of his Chosen Image, then uprooting it from the window box and taking it outside onto the landing, he thrust the plant and flower down the chute which extended from the top floor to the basement and which carried away all the refuse of the block of flats where he lived—cataracts of detergent packets, drums, soup tins, sardine keys, torn letters, parcel wrappings, newspapers, ends of bread, eggshells, orange peel, used cotton wool. Sorrowfully the poet watched the plant join its traveling companions, finding its place almost as if it belonged there, taking up the new rhythm of its journey, jostling, struggling in the narrow chute, being trampled and crushed by overbearing jam jars, bottles, and a rusted paraffin container.

For a moment the poet regretted his action. He longed to be in his room again with the plant there on the window sill, almost in blossom, and with him breathing tenderly upon it to provide it with the warmth it needed in order to survive.

Then he shrugged, and smiled cheerfully. What was the use of feeling dejected when one had only done what was right, and refused to waste one's breath upon a negligible hothouse bloom which had been deceitful anyway as its real nature had not been known until the small print of the contract was studied?

"I will forget the whole episode," the poet said.

And he tried to forget.

He returned to his room and began to write his new poem. Now and again he glanced at the empty window box and sighed. The poem refused to be composed. The poet turned his wedding ring three times. Still the poem refused to be composed.

Well, that was nothing unusual.

He glanced once again at the empty window box and stilled his conscience by remarking to himself, "Anyway it was a hothouse bloom and would never have survived the rigors of this climate; not even if it had been allowed to blossom. It was not selfish of me to deny it my breath, to dispose of it. Rather was it an act of thoughtfulness which is rare these days."

He smoothed the paper before him, ready to imprint his poem.

Then a fit of coughing seized him, and he died.

In her silk and ivory tower the Muse turned from her window. "He was a hothouse plant, anyway. I chose him at random without reading the small print at the bottom of the contract. He would never have blossomed. In future I shall keep my breath to myself—well at least I shall not be tempted when aspiring poets thrust their souls cataloged, numbered, illustrated, through my letter box."   *1963*

Maya Angelou
1928–

One of the most distinguished writers in the contemporary United States, MAYA ANGELOU achieved instant fame with *I Know Why the Caged Bird Sings* (1970), the life story of a black girl growing up in rural Stamps, Arkansas. In this work, as in many other autobiographies and poems, Angelou celebrates the vitality of African-American life, explores how families and communities prevail despite poverty and racism, and examines with candor the self in relation to others. Angelou's work offers both an account of the artist's development and a spiritual chronicle of the African-American people, whom she calls "a tongued folk, a race of singers."

Angelou was born Marguerite Annie Johnson in St. Louis, Missouri, to Bailey and Vivian Baxter Johnson. When her parents' marriage ended, she and her brother, Bailey Jr., ages three and four, were sent by train to live with their grandmother, Mrs. Annie Henderson. Although she attended public schools, Angelou recalls most vividly her informal education; she read the Bible twice in its entirety, for she "loved its cadences," and she was introduced to Shakespeare by one of Stamps' women of humanity and intelligence, Mrs. Bertha Flowers. After moving to California at sixteen Angelou gave birth to a son, Guy Johnson, and left her mother's home to work a series of jobs, including cook, secretary, and nightclub dancer. After a brief marriage at twenty-two, she became a professional dancer and actor who traveled to Europe in the 1950s with the cast of *Porgy and Bess*. Angelou later produced, directed, and starred in *Cabaret for Freedom* with Godfrey Cambridge at New York's Village Gate and starred in Jean Genet's *The Blacks* at St. Mark's Playhouse. She traveled to Egypt with a South African freedom fighter, Vusumzi Make, with whom she lived for two years in Cairo, and during the early 1960s she spent three years with her son in Ghana. Angelou was active in the U.S. civil rights movement, serving at the request of Martin Luther King, Jr., as northern coordinator of the Southern Christian Leadership Conference.

I Know Why the Caged Bird Sings was published in 1970 to enormous critical acclaim. Through vivid dialogue and characterization, it introduces readers to a memorable array of personalities in addition to the girl Maya herself: her indomitable Momma Henderson, who teaches her granddaughter courage and dignity; her beloved brother, Bailey, with whom she seeks to decipher adult codes; the "peckerwood dentist" whose racism unleashes the young Maya's wrath. In five successive volumes Angelou has described her life journey with lyricism and wit. *Gather Together in My Name* (1974) presents a young woman seeking economic and emotional security in postwar America, constantly asking the question "what kind of self am I?" *Singin' and Swingin' and Gettin' Merry Like Christmas* (1976) profiles a more mature woman, a professional entertainer who finds traditional marriage oppressive and determines to build her career. *The Heart of a Woman* (1981) scrutinizes female identity, motherhood, and political responsibility. *All God's Children Need Traveling Shoes* (1986) chronicles Angelou's three years as an expatriate living in Ghana and presents international travel as a window to the world. *Wouldn't Take Nothin' for My Journey Now* (1993) offers insights about U.S. life and the indomitable human spirit.

Angelou has also been praised as a poet. Among her many honors was President Bill Clinton's request that she write and read a poem, "On the Pulse of Morning," for his 1993 inauguration. Her first volume of poetry, *Just Give Me a Cool Drink of Water 'Fore I Die*, appeared in 1971; it was followed by *O Pray My Wings Are Gonna Fit Me Well* (1975), *And Still I Rise* (1978), and *Shaker Why Don't You Sing?* (1983). The titles of these works reveal Angelou's love for African-American spirituals. Indeed, spirituality, art, and the examined life intersect for Angelou. "I try to live what I consider a 'poetic existence,'" she told Claudia Tate in an interview published in 1981. "That means I take responsibility for the air I breathe and the space I take up. I try to be immediate, to be totally present for all my work."

Angelou's work is varied and demanding. Over the past twenty years she has written numerous screenplays and musical scores; starred in plays and films for PBS and Hollywood, some of which she has also directed; taught students at Wake Forest University in North Carolina, where she is Reynolds Professor of American Studies; and toured the world addressing more than 300 organizations, universities, and civic groups each year—all the while continuing to write and publish. She has also served as an informal adviser to President Clinton and as an international ambassador for UNICEF. "All of my work, my life, everything I do is about survival," Angelou claimed in a conversation with the scholar Dolly McPherson, published in *Order Out of Chaos: The Autobiographical Works of Maya Angelou* (1990): "Not just bare, awful, plodding survival, but survival with grace and faith. While one may encounter many defeats, one must not be defeated."

⊰ Still I Rise ⊱

You may write me down in history
With your bitter, twisted lies,
You may trod me in the very dirt
But still, like dust, I'll rise.

5   Does my sassiness upset you?
Why are you beset with gloom?
'Cause I walk like I've got oil wells
Pumping in my living room.

Just like moons and like suns,
10   With the certainty of tides,
Just like hopes springing high,
Still I'll rise.

Did you want to see me broken?
Bowed head and lowered eyes?
15   Shoulders falling down like teardrops,
Weakened by my soulful cries.

Does my haughtiness offend you?
Don't you take it awful hard
'Cause I laugh like I've got gold mines
20   Diggin' in my own back yard.

You may shoot me with your words,
You may cut me with your eyes,
You may kill me with your hatefulness,
But still, like air, I'll rise.

25   Does my sexiness upset you?
Does it come as a surprise
That I dance like I've got diamonds
At the meeting of my thighs?

Out of the huts of history's shame
30   I rise
Up from a past that's rooted in pain
I rise
I'm a black ocean, leaping and wide,
Welling and swelling I bear in the tide.

35   Leaving behind nights of terror and fear
I rise
Into a daybreak that's wondrously clear
I rise
Bringing the gifts that my ancestors gave,
40   I am the dream and the hope of the slave.

I rise
I rise
I rise.

1978

✦⧓⧓✦

Toni Morrison
1931–

"Writing has to do with the imagination," claims U.S. novelist TONI MORRISON. "It's being willing to open a door or think the unthinkable." Indeed, the unthinkable occurs often in Morrison's fiction: Cholly Breedlove abuses his daughter in *The Bluest Eye* (1970); Sula Peace sleeps with her best friend's husband and expects to be forgiven in *Sula* (1973); Sethe in *Beloved* (1987) commits infanticide rather than send her children into slavery. Since Morrison treats these "outlaws" with compassion and empathy, readers feel compelled to do the same. Her philosophical novels examine universal themes—good, evil, beauty, ugliness, love and its absence—within the context of black communities; they also explore the effects of racism, sexism, and poverty on members of these communities. Despite its sometimes grim subject matter, Morrison's fiction is characterized by luminous prose that seems poetic in its lyrical precision and emotional resonance.

Morrison was born Chloe Anthony Wofford in Lorain, Ohio, to parents who worked several jobs at once to make ends meet. After graduating from Howard University in 1953, she pursued an M.A. at Cornell University, where she wrote a thesis on suicide in fiction by VIRGINIA WOOLF and William Faulkner. While at Howard she married Harold Morrison and had two sons; she was later divorced and moved with her children from Washington to New York, where she worked as an editor for Random House. Morrison's first novel, *The Bluest Eye* (1970), addresses such themes as women and self-esteem, hierarchies based on skin color, and the painful effects of incest. *Sula* (1973) centers on an unconventional black woman, determined to gain autonomy regardless of the cost, who becomes her community's pariah. *Song of Solomon* (1977), which won the National Book Critics Circle Award for fiction, blends folklore and memory to probe the familial legacy of its protagonist, Milkman Dead. *Tar Baby* (1981) examines the tensions that arise when Jadine, a wealthy fashion model, travels to a Caribbean island and falls in love with Son, a vagrant. *Beloved* (1987), which won the Pulitzer Prize for Fiction, traces the spiritual journey of Sethe from slavery and its aftermath toward a reconciled peace. *Jazz* (1992) exposes both the vibrancy and the underbelly of 1920s Harlem from the perspectives of three characters seeking love and redemption, while *Paradise* (1997), an American epic, explores the sexist violence that explodes in a community founded to resist racism. These seven novels confirm Morrison's status as a major figure in U.S. literature.

Morrison's work as a literary theorist and cultural critic can be seen in *Playing in the Dark: Whiteness and the Literary Imagination* (1992). This study stretches the boundaries of U.S. literature by considering the "Africanist presence" in classic texts by white writers, a presence that embodies their hidden anxieties and desire about race, identity, and democracy. She has also edited *Race-ing Justice, En-gendering Power* (1992), a collection of essays about the sexual harassment charges brought against Judge Clarence Thomas, a nominee for the Supreme Court, by law professor Anita Hill. In addition, Morrison has published several short stories and a play, *Dreaming Emmett*, about Emmett Till, a fourteen-year-old black boy from Chicago murdered in Mississippi in 1955 for allegedly whistling at a white woman. In 1993 she was awarded the Nobel Prize for Literature, the first African American to be so recognized.

Regarding her fictional method, Morrison asserted in a 1981 interview with Claudia Tate that "My writing expects, demands, participatory reading, and that I think is what literature is supposed to do. It's not just about telling a story; it's about involving the reader. The reader supplies the emotions. The reader supplies even some of the color, some of the sound. My language has to have holes and spaces so the reader can come into it." The themes and techniques of "Recitatif" illustrate Morrison's philosophy by inviting readers into its holes and spaces, as we trace the interracial friendship of Roberta and Twyla across decades, class lines, and the vicissitudes of memory.

⊨ Recitatif ⊭

My mother danced all night and Roberta's was sick. That's why we were taken to St. Bonny's. People want to put their arms around you when you tell them you were in a shelter, but it really wasn't bad. No big long room with one hundred beds like Bellevue. There were four to a room, and when Roberta and me came, there was a shortage of state kids, so we were the only ones assigned to 406 and could go from bed to bed if we wanted to. And we wanted to, too. We changed beds every night and for the whole four months we were there we never picked one out as our own permanent bed.

It didn't start out that way. The minute I walked in and the Big Bozo introduced us, I got sick to my stomach. It was one thing to be taken out of your own bed early in the morning—it was something else to be stuck in a strange place with a girl from a whole other race. And Mary, that's my mother, she was right. Every now and then she would stop dancing long enough to tell me something important and one of the things she said was that they never washed their hair and they smelled funny. Roberta sure did. Smell funny, I mean. So when the Big Bozo (nobody ever called her Mrs. Itkin, just like nobody ever said St. Bonaventure)—when she said, "Twyla, this is Roberta. Roberta, this is Twyla. Make each other welcome." I said, "My mother won't like you putting me in here."

"Good," said Bozo. "Maybe then she'll come and take you home."

How's that for mean? If Roberta had laughed I would have killed her, but she didn't. She just walked over to the window and stood with her back to us.

"Turn around," said the Bozo. "Don't be rude. Now Twyla. Roberta. When you hear a loud buzzer, that's the call for dinner. Come down to the first floor. Any fights and no movie." And then, just to make sure we knew what we would be missing, "*The Wizard of Oz.*"

Roberta must have thought I meant that my mother would be mad about my being put in the shelter. Not about rooming with her, because as soon as Bozo left she came over to me and said, "Is your mother sick too?"

"No," I said. "She just likes to dance all night."

"Oh," she nodded her head and I liked the way she understood things so fast. So for the moment it didn't matter that we looked like salt and pepper standing there and that's what the other kids called us sometimes. We were eight years old and got F's all the time. Me because I couldn't remember what I read or what the teacher said. And Roberta because she couldn't read at all and didn't even listen to the teacher. She wasn't good at anything except jacks, at which she was a killer: pow scoop pow scoop pow scoop.

We didn't like each other all that much at first, but nobody else wanted to play with us because we weren't real orphans with beautiful dead parents in the sky. We were dumped. Even the New York City Puerto Ricans and the upstate Indians ignored us. All kinds of kids were in there, black ones, white ones, even two Koreans. The food was good, though. At least I thought so. Roberta hated it and left whole pieces of things on her plate: Spam, Salisbury steak—even jello with fruit cocktail in it, and she didn't care if I ate what she wouldn't. Mary's idea of supper was popcorn and a can of Yoo-Hoo. Hot mashed potatoes and two weenies was like Thanksgiving for me.

It really wasn't bad, St. Bonny's. The big girls on the second floor pushed us around now and then. But that was all. They wore lipstick and eyebrow pencil and wobbled their knees while they watched TV. Fifteen, sixteen, even, some of them were. They were put-out girls, scared runaways most of them. Poor little girls who fought their uncles off but looked tough to us, and mean. God did they look mean. The staff tried to keep them separate from the younger children, but sometimes they caught us watching them in the orchard where they played radios and danced with each other. They'd light out after us and pull our hair or twist our arms. We were scared of them, Roberta and me, but neither of us wanted the other one to know it. So we got a good list of dirty names we could shout back when we ran from them through the orchard. I used to dream a lot and almost always the orchard was there. Two acres, four maybe, of these little apple trees. Hundreds of them. Empty and crooked like beggar women when I first came to St. Bonny's but fat with flowers when I left. I don't know why I dreamt about that orchard so much. Nothing really happened there. Nothing all that important, I mean. Just the big girls dancing and playing the radio. Roberta and me watching. Maggie fell down there once. The kitchen woman with legs like parentheses. And the big girls laughed at her. We should have helped her up, I know, but we were scared of those girls with lipstick and eyebrow pencil. Maggie couldn't talk. The kids said she had her tongue cut out, but I think she was just born that way: mute. She was old and sandy-colored and she worked in the kitchen. I don't know if she was nice or not. I just remember her legs like parentheses and how she rocked when she walked. She worked from early in the morning till two o'clock, and if she was late, if she had too much cleaning and didn't get out till two-fifteen or so, she'd cut through the orchard so she wouldn't miss her bus and have to wait another hour. She wore this really stupid little hat—a kid's hat with ear flaps—and she wasn't much taller than we were. A really awful little hat. Even for a mute, it was dumb—dressing like a kid and never saying anything at all.

"But what about if somebody tries to kill her?" I used to wonder about that. "Or what if she wants to cry? Can she cry?"

"Sure," Roberta said. "But just tears. No sounds come out."

"She can't scream?"

"Nope. Nothing."

"Can she hear?"

"I guess."

"Let's call her," I said. And we did.

"Dummy! Dummy!" She never turned her head.

"Bow legs! Bow legs!" Nothing. She just rocked on, the chin straps of her baby-boy hat swaying from side to side. I think we were wrong. I think she could hear and didn't let on. And it shames me even now to think there was somebody in there after all who heard us call her those names and couldn't tell on us.

We got along all right, Roberta and me. Changed beds every night, got F's in civics and communication skills and gym. The Bozo was disappointed in us, she said. Out of 130 of us state cases, 90 were under twelve. Almost all were real orphans with beautiful dead parents in the sky. We were the only ones dumped and the only ones with F's in three classes including gym. So we got along—what with her leaving whole pieces of things on her plate and being nice about not asking questions.

I think it was the day before Maggie fell down that we found out our mothers were coming to visit us on the same Sunday. We had been at the shelter twenty-eight days (Roberta twenty-eight and a half) and this was their first visit with us. Our mothers would come at ten o'clock in time for chapel, then lunch with us in the teachers' lounge. I thought if my dancing mother met her sick mother it might be good for her. And Roberta thought her sick mother would get a big bang out of a dancing one. We got excited about it and curled each other's hair. After breakfast we sat on the bed watching the road from the window. Roberta's socks were still wet. She washed them the night before and put them on the radiator to dry. They hadn't, but she put them on anyway because their tops were so pretty—scalloped in pink. Each of us had a purple construction-paper basket that we had made in craft class. Mine had a yellow crayon rabbit on it. Roberta's had eggs with wiggly lines of color. Inside were cellophane grass and just the jelly beans because I'd eaten the two marsh-mallow eggs they gave us. The Big Bozo came herself to get us. Smiling she told us we looked very nice and to come downstairs. We were so surprised by the smile we'd never seen before, neither of us moved.

"Don't you want to see your mommies?"

I stood up first and spilled the jelly beans all over the floor. Bozo's smile disap-peared while we scrambled to get the candy up off the floor and put it back in the grass.

She escorted us downstairs to the first floor, where the other girls were lining up to file into the chapel. A bunch of grown-ups stood to one side. Viewers mostly. The old biddies who wanted servants and the fags who wanted company looking for children they might want to adopt. Once in a while a grandmother. Almost never anybody young or anybody whose face wouldn't scare you in the night. Because if any of the real orphans had young relatives they wouldn't be real orphans. I saw Mary right away. She had on those green slacks I hated and hated even more now because didn't she know we were going to chapel? And that fur jacket with the pocket linings so ripped she had to pull to get her hands out of them. But her face was pretty—like always, and she smiled and waved like she was the little girl look-ing for her mother—not me.

I walked slowly, trying not to drop the jelly beans and hoping the paper handle would hold. I had to use my last Chiclet because by the time I finished cutting every-thing out, all the Elmer's was gone. I am left-handed and the scissors never worked for me. It didn't matter, though; I might just as well have chewed the gum. Mary dropped to her knees and grabbed me, mashing the basket, the jelly beans, and the grass into her ratty fur jacket.

"Twyla, baby. Twyla, baby!"

I could have killed her. Already I heard the big girls in the orchard the next time saying, "Twyyyyyla, baby!" But I couldn't stay mad at Mary while she was smiling and hugging me and smelling of Lady Esther dusting powder. I wanted to stay buried in her fur all day.

To tell the truth I forgot about Roberta. Mary and I got in line for the traipse into chapel and I was feeling proud because she looked so beautiful even in those ugly green slacks that made her behind stick out. A pretty mother on earth is better than a beautiful dead one in the sky even if she did leave you all alone to go dancing.

I felt a tap on my shoulder, turned, and saw Roberta smiling. I smiled back, but not too much lest somebody think this visit was the biggest thing that ever happened in my life. Then Roberta said, "Mother, I want you to meet my roommate, Twyla. And that's Twyla's mother."

I looked up it seemed for miles. She was big. Bigger than any man and on her chest was the biggest cross I'd ever seen. I swear it was six inches long each way. And in the crook of her arm was the biggest Bible ever made.

Mary, simple-minded as ever, grinned and tried to yank her hand out of the pocket with the raggedy lining—to shake hands, I guess. Roberta's mother looked down at me and then looked down at Mary too. She didn't say anything, just grabbed Roberta with her Bible-free hand and stepped out of line, walking quickly to the rear of it. Mary was still grinning because she's not too swift when it comes to what's really going on. Then this light bulb goes off in her head and she says "That bitch!" really loud and us almost in the chapel now. Organ music whining; the Bonny Angels singing sweetly. Everybody in the world turned around to look. And Mary would have kept it up—kept calling names if I hadn't squeezed her hand as hard as I could. That helped a little, but she still twitched and crossed and uncrossed her legs all through service. Even groaned a couple of times. Why did I think she would come there and act right? Slacks. No hat like the grandmothers and viewers, and groaning all the while. When we stood for hymns she kept her mouth shut. Wouldn't even look at the words on the page. She actually reached in her purse for a mirror to check her lipstick. All I could think of was that she really needed to be killed. The sermon lasted a year, and I knew the real orphans were looking smug again.

We were supposed to have lunch in the teachers' lounge, but Mary didn't bring anything, so we picked fur and cellophane grass off the mashed jelly beans and ate them. I could have killed her. I sneaked a look at Roberta. Her mother had brought chicken legs and ham sandwiches and oranges and a whole box of chocolate-covered grahams. Roberta drank milk from a thermos while her mother read the Bible to her.

Things are not right. The wrong food is always with the wrong people. Maybe that's why I got into waitress work later—to match up the right people with the right food. Roberta just let those chicken legs sit there, but she did bring a stack of grahams up to me later when the visit was over. I think she was sorry that her mother would not shake my mother's hand. And I liked that and I liked the fact that she didn't say a word about Mary groaning all the way through the service and not bringing any lunch.

Roberta left in May when the apple trees were heavy and white. On her last day we went to the orchard to watch the big girls smoke and dance by the radio. It didn't matter that they said, "Twyyyyyla, baby." We sat on the ground and breathed. Lady Esther. Apple blossoms. I still go soft when I smell one or the other. Roberta was going home. The big cross and the big Bible was coming to get her and she seemed sort of glad and sort of not. I thought I would die in that room of four beds without her and I knew Bozo had plans to move some other dumped kid in there with me. Roberta promised to write every day, which was really sweet of her because she couldn't read a lick so how could she write anybody. I would have drawn pictures and sent them to her but she never gave me her address. Little by little she faded. Her wet socks with the pink scalloped tops and her big serious-looking eyes—that's all I could catch when I tried to bring her to mind.

I was working behind the counter at the Howard Johnson's on the Thruway just before the Kingston exit. Not a bad job. Kind of a long ride from Newburgh, but okay once I got there. Mine was the second night shift—eleven to seven. Very light until a Greyhound checked in for breakfast around six-thirty. At that hour the sun was all the way clear of the hills behind the restaurant. The place looked better at night—more like shelter—but I loved it when the sun broke in, even if it did show all the cracks in the vinyl and the speckled floor looked dirty no matter what the mop boy did.

It was August and a bus crowd was just unloading. They would stand around a long while: going to the john, and looking at gifts and junk-for-sale machines, reluctant to sit down so soon. Even to eat. I was trying to fill the coffee pots and get them all situated on the electric burners when I saw her. She was sitting in a booth smoking a cigarette with two guys smothered in head and facial hair. Her own hair was so big and wild I could hardly see her face. But the eyes. I would know them anywhere. She had on a powder-blue halter and shorts outfit and earrings the size of bracelets. Talk about lipstick and eyebrow pencil. She made the big girls look like nuns. I couldn't get off the counter until seven o'clock, but I kept watching the booth in case they got up to leave before that. My replacement was on time for a change, so I counted and stacked my receipts as fast as I could and signed off. I walked over to the booth, smiling and wondering if she would remember me. Or even if she wanted to remember me. Maybe she didn't want to be reminded of St. Bonny's or to have anybody know she was ever there. I know I never talked about it to anybody.

I put my hands in my apron pockets and leaned against the back of the booth facing them.

"Roberta? Roberta Fisk?"

She looked up. "Yeah?"

"Twyla."

She squinted for a second and then said, "Wow."

"Remember me?"

"Sure. Hey. Wow."

"It's been a while," I said, and gave a smile to the two hairy guys.

"Yeah. Wow. You work here?"

"Yeah," I said. "I live in Newburgh."

"Newburgh? No kidding?" She laughed then a private laugh that included the guys but only the guys, and they laughed with her. What could I do but laugh too and wonder why I was standing there with my knees showing out from under that uniform. Without looking I could see the blue and white triangle on my head, my hair shapeless in a net, my ankles thick in white oxfords. Nothing could have been less sheer than my stockings. There was this silence that came down right after I laughed. A silence it was her turn to fill up. With introductions, maybe, to her boyfriends or an invitation to sit down and have a Coke. Instead she lit a cigarette off the one she'd just finished and said, "We're on our way to the Coast. He's got an appointment with Hendrix." She gestured casually toward the boy next to her.

"Hendrix? Fantastic," I said. "Really fantastic. What's she doing now?"

Roberta coughed on her cigarette and the two guys rolled their eyes up at the ceiling.

"Hendrix. Jimi Hendrix,[1] asshole. He's only the biggest—Oh, wow. Forget it."

I was dismissed without anyone saying goodbye, so I thought I would do it for her.

1. Jimi Hendrix (1942–1970) was a legendary African-American rock singer.

"How's your mother?" I asked. Her grin cracked her whole face. She swallowed. "Fine," she said. "How's yours?"

"Pretty as a picture," I said and turned away. The backs of my knees were damp. Howard Johnson's really was a dump in the sunlight.

James is as comfortable as a house slipper. He liked my cooking and I liked his big loud family. They have lived in Newburgh all of their lives and talk about it the way people do who have always known a home. His grandmother is a porch swing older than his father and when they talk about streets and avenues and buildings they call them names they no longer have. They still call the A & P Rico's because it stands on property once a mom and pop store owned by Mr. Rico. And they call the new community college Town Hall because it once was. My mother-in-law puts up jelly and cucumbers and buys butter wrapped in cloth from a dairy. James and his father talk about fishing and baseball and I can see them all together on the Hudson in a raggedy skiff. Half the population of Newburgh is on welfare now, but to my husband's family it was still some upstate paradise of a time long past. A time of ice houses and vegetable wagons, coal furnaces and children weeding gardens. When our son was born my mother-in-law gave me the crib blanket that had been hers.

But the town they remembered had changed. Something quick was in the air. Magnificent old houses, so ruined they had become shelter for squatters and rent risks, were bought and renovated. Smart IBM people moved out of their suburbs back into the city and put shutters up and herb gardens in their backyards. A brochure came in the mail announcing the opening of a Food Emporium. Gourmet food it said—and listed items the rich IBM crowd would want. It was located in a new mall at the edge of town and I drove out to shop there one day—just to see. It was late in June. After the tulips were gone and the Queen Elizabeth roses were open everywhere. I trailed my cart along the aisle tossing in smoked oysters and Robert's sauce and things I knew would sit in my cupboard for years. Only when I found some Klondike ice cream bars did I feel less guilty about spending James's fireman's salary so foolishly. My father-in-law ate them with the same gusto little Joseph did.

Waiting in the check-out line I heard a voice say, "Twyla!"

The classical music piped over the aisles had affected me and the woman leaning toward me was dressed to kill. Diamonds on her hand, a smart white summer dress. "I'm Mrs. Benson," I said.

"Ho. Ho. the Big Bozo," she sang.

For a split second I didn't know what she was talking about. She had a bunch of asparagus and two cartons of fancy water.

"Roberta!"

"Right."

"For heaven's sake. Roberta."

"You look great," she said.

"So do you. Where are you? Here? In Newburgh?"

"Yes. Over in Annandale."

I was opening my mouth to say more when the cashier called my attention to her empty counter.

"Meet you outside." Roberta pointed her finger and went into the express line.

I placed the groceries and kept myself from glancing around to check Roberta's progress. I remembered Howard Johnson's and looking for a chance to speak only to be greeted with a stingy "wow." But she was waiting for me and her huge hair was sleek now, smooth around a small, nicely shaped head. Shoes, dress, everything love-ly and summery and rich. I was dying to know what happened to her, how she got from Jimi Hendrix to Annandale, a neighborhood full of doctors and IBM execu-tives. Easy, I thought. Everything is so easy for them. They think they own the world.

"How long," I asked her. "How long have you been here?"

"A year. I got married to a man who lives here. And you, you're married too, right? Benson, you said."

"Yeah. James Benson."

"And is he nice?"

"Oh, is he nice?"

"Well is he?" Roberta's eyes were steady as though she really meant the question and wanted an answer.

"He's wonderful, Roberta. Wonderful."

"So you're happy."

"Very."

"That's good," she said and nodded her head. "I always hoped you'd be happy. Any kids? I know you have kids."

"One. A boy. How about you?"

"Four."

"Four?"

She laughed. "Stepkids. He's a widower."

"Oh."

"Got a minute? Let's have a coffee."

I thought about the Klondikes melting and the inconvenience of going all the way to my car and putting the bags in the trunk. Served me right for buying all that stuff I didn't need. Roberta was ahead of me.

"Put them in my car. It's right here."

And then I saw the dark blue limousine.

"You married a Chinaman?"

"No," she laughed. "He's the driver."

"Oh, my. If the Big Bozo could see you now."

We both giggled. Really giggled. Suddenly, in just a pulse beat, twenty years dis-appeared and all of it came rushing back. The big girls (whom we called gar girls—Roberta's misheard word for the evil stone faces described in a civics class) there dancing in the orchard, the ploppy mashed potatoes, the double weenies, the Spam with pineapple. We went into the coffee shop holding on to one another and I tried to think why we were glad to see each other this time and not before. Once, twelve years ago, we passed like strangers. A black girl and a white girl meeting in a Howard Johnson's on the road and having nothing to say. One in a blue and white triangle waitress hat—the other on her way to see Hendrix. Now we were behaving like sis-ters separated for much too long. Those four short months were nothing in time. Maybe it was the thing itself. Just being there, together. Two little girls who knew what nobody else in the world knew—how not to ask questions. How to believe what had to be believed. There was politeness in that reluctance and generosity as well. Is your mother sick too? No, she dances all night. Oh—and an understanding nod.

We sat in a booth by the window and fell into recollection like veterans.

"Did you ever learn to read?"

"Watch." She picked up the menu. "Special of the day. Cream of corn soup. Entrées. Two dots and a wriggly line. Quiche. Chef salad, scallops . . ."

I was laughing and applauding when the waitress came up.

"Remember the Easter baskets?"

"And how we tried to *introduce* them?"

"Your mother with that cross like two telephone poles."

"And yours with those tight slacks."

We laughed so loudly heads turned and made the laughter harder to suppress.

"What happened to the Jimi Hendrix date?"

Roberta made a blow-out sound with her lips.

"When he died I thought about you."

"Oh, you heard about him finally?"

"Finally. Come on, I was a small-town country waitress."

"And I was a small-town country dropout. God, were we wild. I still don't know how I got out of there alive."

"But you did."

"I did. I really did. Now I'm Mrs. Kenneth Norton."

"Sounds like a mouthful."

"It is."

"Servants and all?"

Roberta held up two fingers.

"Ow! What does he do?"

"Computers and stuff. What do I know?"

"I don't remember a hell of a lot from those days, but Lord, St. Bonny's is as clear as daylight. Remember Maggie? The day she fell down and those gar girls laughed at her?"

Roberta looked up from her salad and stared at me. "Maggie didn't fall," she said.

"Yes, she did. You remember."

"No, Twyla. They knocked her down. Those girls pushed her down and tore her clothes. In the orchard."

"I don't—that's not what happened."

"Sure it is. In the orchard. Remember how scared we were?"

"Wait a minute. I don't remember any of that."

"And Bozo was fired."

"You're crazy. She was there when I left. You left before me."

"I went back. You weren't there when they fired Bozo."

"What?"

"Twice. Once for a year when I was about ten, another for two months when I was fourteen. That's when I ran away."

"You ran away from St. Bonny's?"

"I had to. What do you want? Me dancing in that orchard?"

"Are you sure about Maggie?"

"Of course I'm sure. You've blocked it, Twyla. It happened. Those girls had behavior problems, you know."

"Didn't they, though. But why can't I remember the Maggie thing?"

"Believe me. It happened. And we were there."

"Who did you room with when you went back?" I asked her as if I would know her. The Maggie thing was troubling me.

"Creeps. They tickled themselves in the night."

My ears were itching and I wanted to go home suddenly. This was all very well but she couldn't just comb her hair, wash her face and pretend everything was hunky-dory. After the Howard Johnson's snub. And no apology. Nothing.

"Were you on dope or what that time at Howard Johnson's?" I tried to make my voice sound friendlier than I felt.

"Maybe, a little. I never did drugs much. Why?"

"I don't know; you acted sort of like you didn't want to know me then."

"Oh, Twyla, you know how it was in those days: black—white. You know how everything was."

But I didn't know. I thought it was just the opposite. Busloads of blacks and whites came into Howard Johnson's together. They roamed together then: students, musicians, lovers, protesters. You got to see everything at Howard Johnson's and blacks were very friendly with whites in those days. But sitting there with nothing on my plate but two hard tomato wedges wondering about the melting Klondikes it seemed childish remembering the slight. We went to her car, and with the help of the driver, got my stuff into my station wagon.

"We'll keep in touch this time," she said.

"Sure," I said. "Sure. Give me a call."

"I will," she said, and then just as I was sliding behind the wheel, she leaned into the window. "By the way. Your mother. Did she ever stop dancing?"

I shook my head. "No. Never."

Roberta nodded.

"And yours? Did she ever get well?"

She smiled a tiny sad smile. "No. She never did. Look, call me, okay?"

"Okay," I said, but I knew I wouldn't. Roberta had messed up my past somehow with that business about Maggie. I wouldn't forget a thing like that. Would I?

Strife came to us that fall. At least that's what the paper called it. Strife. Racial strife. The word made me think of a bird—a big shrieking bird out of 1,000,000,000 B.C. Flapping its wings and cawing. Its eye with no lid always bearing down on you. All day it screeched and at night it slept on the rooftops. It woke you in the morning and from the *Today* show to the eleven o'clock news it kept you an awful company. I couldn't figure it out from one day to the next. I knew I was supposed to feel something strong, but I didn't know what, and James wasn't any help. Joseph was on the list of kids to be transferred from the junior high school to another one at some far-out-of-the-way place and I thought it was a good thing until I heard it was a bad thing. I mean I didn't know. All the schools seemed dumps to me, and the fact that one was nicer looking didn't hold much weight. But the papers were full of it and then the kids began to get jumpy. In August, mind you. Schools weren't even open yet. I thought Joseph might be frightened to go over there, but he didn't seem scared so I forgot about it, until I found myself driving along Hudson Street out there by the school they were trying to integrate and saw a line of women marching. And who do you suppose was in line, big as life, holding a sign in front of her bigger than her mother's cross? MOTHERS HAVE RIGHTS TOO! it said.

I drove on, and then changed my mind. I circled the block, slowed down, and honked my horn.

Roberta looked over and when she saw me she waved. I didn't wave back, but I didn't move either. She handed her sign to another woman and came over to where I was parked.

"Hi."

"What are you doing?"

"Picketing. What's it look like?"

"What for?"

"What do you mean, 'What for?' They want to take my kids and send them out of the neighborhood. They don't want to go."

"So what if they go to another school? My boy's being bussed too, and I don't mind. Why should you?"

"It's not about us, Twyla. Me and you. It's about our kids."

"What's more *us* than that?"

"Well, it is a free country."

"Not yet, but it will be."

"What the hell does that mean? I'm not doing anything to you."

"You really think that?"

"I know it."

"I wonder what made me think you were different."

"I wonder what made me think you were different."

"Look at them," I said. "Just look. Who do they think they are? Swarming all over the place like they own it. And now they think they can decide where my child goes to school. Look at them, Roberta. They're Bozos."

Roberta turned around and looked at the women. Almost all of them were standing still now, waiting. Some were even edging toward us. Roberta looked at me out of some refrigerator behind her eyes. "No, they're not. They're just mothers."

"And what am I? Swiss cheese?"

"I used to curl your hair."

"I hated your hands in my hair."

The women were moving. Our faces looked mean to them of course and they looked as though they could not wait to throw themselves in front of a police car, or better yet, into my car and drag me away by my ankles. Now they surrounded my car and gently, gently began to rock it. I swayed back and forth like a sideways yo-yo. Automatically I reached for Roberta, like the old days in the orchard when they saw us watching them and we had to get out of there, and if one of us fell the other pulled her up and if one of us was caught the other stayed to kick and scratch, and neither would leave the other behind. My arm shot out of the car window but no receiving hand was there. Roberta was looking at me sway from side to side in the car and her face was still. My purse slid from the car seat down under the dashboard. The four policemen who had been drinking Tab in their car finally got the message and strolled over, forcing their way through the women. Quietly, firmly they spoke. "Okay, ladies. Back in line or off the streets."

Some of them went away willingly; others had to be urged away from the car doors and the hood. Roberta didn't move. She was looking steadily at me. I was fumbling to turn on the ignition, which wouldn't catch because the gearshift was still in drive. The seats of the car were a mess because the swaying had thrown my grocery coupons all over it and my purse was sprawled on the floor.

"Maybe I am different now, Twyla. But you're not. You're the same little state kid who kicked a poor old black lady when she was down on the ground. You kicked a black lady and you have the nerve to call me a bigot."

The coupons were everywhere and the guts of my purse were bunched under the dashboard. What was she saying? Black? Maggie wasn't black.

"She wasn't black," I said.

"Like hell she wasn't, and you kicked her. We both did. You kicked a black lady who couldn't even scream."

"Liar!"

"You're the liar! Why don't you just go on home and leave us alone, huh?"

She turned away and I skidded away from the curb.

The next morning I went into the garage and cut the side out of the carton our portable TV had come in. It wasn't nearly big enough, but after a while I had a decent sign: red spray-painted letters on a white background—AND SO DO CHILDREN****. I meant just to go down to the school and tack it up somewhere so those cows on the picket line across the street could see it, but when I got there, some ten or so others had already assembled—protesting the cows across the street. Police permits and everything. I got in line and we strutted in line on our side while Roberta's group strutted on theirs. That first day we were all dignified, pretending the other side didn't exist. The second day there was name calling and finger gestures. But that was about all. People changed signs from time to time, but Roberta never did and neither did I. Actually my sign didn't make sense without Roberta's. "And so do children what?" one of the women on my side asked me. Have rights, I said, as though it was obvious.

Roberta didn't acknowledge my presence in any way and I got to thinking maybe she didn't know I was there. I began to pace myself in the line, jostling people one minute and lagging behind the next, so Roberta and I could reach the end of our respective lines at the same time and there would be a moment in our turn when we would face each other. Still, I couldn't tell whether she saw me and knew my sign was for her. The next day I went early before we were scheduled to assemble. I waited until she got there before I exposed my new creation. As soon as she hoisted her MOTHERS HAVE RIGHTS TOO I began to wave my new one, which said, HOW WOULD YOU KNOW? I know she saw that one, but I had gotten addicted now. My signs got crazier each day, and the women on my side decided that I was a kook. They couldn't make heads or tails out of my brilliant screaming posters.

I brought a painted sign in queenly red with huge black letters that said, IS YOUR MOTHER WELL? Roberta took her lunch break and didn't come back for the rest of the day or any day after. Two days later I stopped going too and couldn't have been missed because nobody understood my signs anyway.

It was a nasty six weeks. Classes were suspended and Joseph didn't go to any-body's school until October. The children—everybody's children—soon got bored with that extended vacation they thought was going to be so great. They looked at TV until their eyes flattened. I spent a couple of mornings tutoring my son, as the other mothers said we should. Twice I opened a text from last year that he had never turned in. Twice he yawned in my face. Other mothers organized living room ses-sions so the kids would keep up. None of the kids could concentrate so they drifted back to *The Price Is Right* and *The Brady Bunch*. When the school finally opened there were fights once or twice and some sirens roared through the streets every once in a while. There were a lot of photographers from Albany. And just when ABC was about to send up a news crew, the kids settled down like nothing in the world had happened. Joseph hung my HOW WOULD YOU KNOW? sign in his bedroom. I don't know what became of AND SO DO CHILDREN****. I think my father-in-law cleaned some fish on it. He was always puttering around in our garage. Each of his five chil-dren lived in Newburgh and he acted as though he had five extra homes.

I couldn't help looking for Roberta when Joseph graduated from high school, but I didn't see her. It didn't trouble me much what she had said to me in the car. I mean the kicking part. I know I didn't do that, I couldn't do that. But I was puzzled by her telling me Maggie was black. When I thought about it I actually couldn't be certain. She wasn't pitch-black, I knew, or I would have remembered that. What I remember was the kiddie hat, and the semicircle legs. I tried to reassure myself about the race thing for a long time until it dawned on me that the truth was already there, and Roberta knew it. I didn't kick her; I didn't join in with the gar girls and kick that lady, but I sure did want to. We watched and never tried to help her and never called for help. Maggie was my dancing mother. Deaf, I thought, and dumb. Nobody inside. Nobody who would hear you if you cried in the night. Nobody who could tell you anything important that you could use. Rocking, dancing, swaying as she walked. And when the gar girls pushed her down, and started roughhousing, I knew she wouldn't scream, couldn't—just like me—and I was glad about that.

We decided not to have a tree, because Christmas would be at my mother-in-law's house, so why have a tree at both places? Joseph was at SUNY New Paltz and we had to economize, we said. But at the last minute, I changed my mind. Nothing could be that bad. So I rushed around town looking for a tree, something small but wide. By the time I found a place, it was snowing and very late. I dawdled like it was the most important purchase in the world and the tree man was fed up with me. Finally I chose one and had it tied onto the trunk of the car. I drove away slowly because the sand trucks were not out yet and the streets could be murder at the beginning of a snowfall. Downtown the streets were wide and rather empty except for a cluster of people coming out of the Newburgh Hotel. The one hotel in town that wasn't built out of cardboard and Plexiglas. A party, probably. The men huddled in the snow were dressed in tails and the women had on furs. Shiny things glittered from underneath their coats. It made me tired to look at them. Tired, tired, tired. On the next corner was a small diner with loops and loops of paper bells in the window. I stopped the car and went in. Just for a cup of coffee and twenty minutes of peace before I went home and tried to finish everything before Christmas Eve.

"Twyla?"

There she was. In a silvery evening gown and dark fur coat. A man and another woman were with her, the man fumbling for change to put in the cigarette machine. The woman was humming and tapping on the counter with her fingernails. They all looked a little bit drunk.

"Well. It's you."

"How are you?"

I shrugged. "Pretty good. Frazzled. Christmas and all."

"Regular?" called the woman from the counter.

"Fine," Roberta called back and then, "Wait for me in the car."

She slipped into the booth beside me. "I have to tell you something, Twyla. I made up my mind if I ever saw you again, I'd tell you."

"I'd just as soon not hear anything, Roberta. It doesn't matter now, anyway."

"No," she said. "Not about that."

"Don't be long," said the woman. She carried two regulars to go and the man peeled his cigarette pack as they left.

"It's about St. Bonny's and Maggie."

"Oh, please."

"Listen to me. I really did think she was black. I didn't make that up. I really thought so. But now I can't be sure. I just remember her as old, so old. And because she couldn't talk—well, you know, I thought she was crazy. She'd been brought up in an institution like my mother was and like I thought I would be too. And you were right. We didn't kick her. It was the gar girls. Only them. But, well, I wanted to. I really wanted them to hurt her. I said we did it, too. You and me, but that's not true. And I don't want you to carry that around. It was just that I wanted to do it so bad that day—wanting to is doing it."

Her eyes were watery from the drinks she'd had, I guess. I know it's that way with me. One glass of wine and I start bawling over the littlest thing.

"We were kids, Roberta."

"Yeah. Yeah. I know, just kids."

"Eight."

"Eight."

"And lonely."

"Scared, too."

She wiped her cheeks with the heel of her hand and smiled. "Well, that's all I wanted to say."

I nodded and couldn't think of any way to fill the silence that went from the diner past the paper bells on out into the snow. It was heavy now. I thought I'd better wait for the sand trucks before starting home.

"Thanks, Roberta."

"Sure."

"Did I tell you? My mother, she never did stop dancing."

"Yes. You told me. And mine, she never got well." Roberta lifted her hands from the tabletop and covered her face with her palms. When she took them away she really was crying. "Oh shit, Twyla. Shit, shit, shit. What the hell happened to Maggie?"   1983

＋＋ ⋈◊⋈ ＋＋

Caryl Churchill
1938–

"Women are traditionally expected not to initiate action, and plays are action, in a way that words are not. So perhaps that's one reason why comparatively few women have written plays," claimed the British dramatist CARYL CHURCHILL in a 1988 interview with Linda Fitzsimmons. A socialist-feminist playwright, Churchill is among the most prolific of these women, the author of more than forty plays, many of which have been produced in collaboration with Max Stafford Clark's Joint Stock Company or with feminist collectives such as Monstrous Regiment. Among her best-known plays are *Light Shining in Buckinghamshire* (1976), which explores a working-class millennial movement that occurred during the English civil war of the 1640s; *Cloud Nine* (1978), which examines issues of gender and sexual politics in the context of British imperialism; *Top Girls* (1982), which critiques the corporate values of women struggling to "break the glass ceiling," to the detriment of other women and themselves; and *Serious Money* (1987), which satirizes junk bonds tradesmen and other swindlers who manipulate the stock market.

Born in London, Churchill came from a family interested in politics and theater; her father was a political cartoonist and her mother a model and part-time actress. As an adolescent Churchill lived with her family in Canada, where she attended the Trafalgar School in Montreal. She began composing plays while a student at Lady Margaret Hall, Oxford, where several of her works were performed by the college company. After she married David Harter, a barrister, in 1961 and gave birth to three children, she turned to radio theater—not only because she had listened with pleasure to radio drama as a child, but because raising three children allowed her time to write only short pieces. Among her most popular radio dramas were *You've No Need to be Frightened* (1961) and *The Ants* (1962). She began to write for the stage full-time in the early 1970s, when her play *Owners* (1972) was produced at London's Royal Court Theatre, the venue since 1956 for many new and exciting British plays. Since then she has won numerous prizes, including three Obie Awards for the Broadway production of *Cloud Nine*, which had a successful two-year run in New York, and the Susan Smith Blackburn Prize for *Fen* (1983), which portrays the difficult lives of rural English women working in potato fields.

Churchill's plays blend fantastic, even surrealistic elements with realistic and sometimes satiric themes. *Top Girls*, for example, opens with a carnivalesque dinner party featuring an array of women guests from art, literature, and history: Brueghel's Dull Gret, Chaucer's Patient Griselda, the Japanese courtesan Lady Nijo, and the legendary Italian Pope Joan—all of whom share with Marlene, the newly hired manager of the Top Girls Employment Agency, the burden of having lost their children. These characters talk simultaneously, interrupt each other in midstream, and indicate through gesture and body language the chaos of their lives. Her 1997 play *Blue Heart*, also produced at the Royal Court, uses postmodern and absurdist techniques to question the dynamics by which traditional families are both constructed and destroyed.

Set in a seventeenth-century English village, *Vinegar Tom* (1976), the play included here, examines how a community's misogyny caused its members to label outspoken women as troublemakers, and how these women's social marginalization led them to be condemned and executed as witches. Churchill confronts the sexual and economic tensions that moved women to turn on one another, as well as the church-sanctioned sexism that motivated such men as Heinrich Kramer and James Sprenger to write the *Malleus Maleficarum* (*The Hammer of Witches*), a handbook on how to identify and capture witches that was widely read during the seventeenth century, the era of the last major English witchhunts. This play was written collaboratively with the actors in the Monstrous Regiment company, with whom Churchill decided to "write a play about witches but with no witches in it; a play not about evil, hysteria, and possession by the devil but about poverty, humiliation, and prejudice, and how the women accused of witchcraft saw themselves." After meeting with the company, Churchill drafted the play in three days, left it during the summer of 1976 to do other work, and expanded it in the fall to include fourteen roles for nine women actors—a financial necessity that led to creative staging, as women who played witches hanged in one scene reappeared as their persecutors in the next. *Vinegar Tom*, named for the cat accused of being a witch's familiar, was well received by British reviewers, who recognized its radical message. As a writer for the London *Tribune* asserted, this play "is set in the world of seventeenth-century witchcraft, but it speaks, through its striking images and its plethora of ironic contradictions, of and to this century's still deep-rooted antifeminism and women's oppression."

ᣥ Vinegar Tom ᣤ

Vinegar Tom was written for Monstrous Regiment and was first presented at the Humberside Theatre, Hull on October 12, 1976, directed by Pam Brighton, designed by Andrea Montag, with music composed by Helen Glavin. The cast was as follows:

JOAN	Mary McCusker	SUSAN	Sue Todd
ALICE	Gillian Hanna	GOODY	Helen Glavin
BETTY	Josefina Cupido	MARGERY	Linda Broughton
ELLEN	Chris Bowler	JACK	Ian Blower
MAN, DOCTOR, BELLRINGER, PACKER		Roger Allam	

Scene One

MAN: Am I the devil?

ALICE: What, sweet?

MAN: I'm the devil. Man in black, they say, they always say, a man in black met me in the night, took me into the thicket and made me commit uncleanness unspeakable.

ALICE: I've seen men in black that's no devils unless clergy and gentlemen are devils.

MAN: Have I not got great burning eyes then?

ALICE: Bright enough eyes.

MAN: Is my body not rough and hairy?

ALICE: I don't like a man too smooth.

MAN: Am I not ice cold?

ALICE: In a ditch in November.

MAN: Didn't I lie on you so heavy I took your breath? Didn't the enormous size of me terrify you?

ALICE: It seemed a fair size like other men's.

MAN: Didn't it hurt you? Are you saying I didn't hurt you?

ALICE: You don't need be the devil, I been hurt by men. Let me go now, you're hurting my shoulder.

MAN: What it is, you didn't see my feet.

ALICE: You never took off your shoes. Take off your shoes if your feet's cloven.

MAN: If you come with me and give me body and soul, you'll never want in this world.

ALICE: Are you saying that as a man?

MAN: Am I saying it as the devil?

ALICE: If you're saying it as a man I'll go with you. There's no one round here knows me going to marry me. There's no way I'll get money. I've a child, mind, I'll not leave the child.

MAN: Has it a father?

ALICE: No, never had.

MAN: So you think that was no sin we did?

ALICE: If it was I don't care.

MAN: Don't say that.

ALICE: You'd say worse living here. Any time I'm happy someone says it's a sin.

MAN: There's some in London says there's no sin. Each man has his own religion nearly, or none at all, and there's women speak out too. They smoke and curse in the tavern and they say flesh is no sin for they are God themselves and can't sin. The men and women lie together and say that's bliss and that's heaven and that's no sin. I believe it for there's such changes.

ALICE: I'd like to go to London and hear them.

MAN: But then I believe with Calvin[1] that few are saved and I am damned utterly. Then I think if I'm damned anyway I might as well sin to make it worthwhile. But I'm afraid to die. I'm afraid of the torture after. One of my family was burnt for a Catholic and they all changed to Protestant and one burnt for that too. I wish I was a Catholic and could confess my sins and burn them away in candles. I believe it all in turn and all at once.

1. John Calvin (1509–1564) was a French Protestant theologian and reformer.

ALICE: Would you take me to London? I've nothing to keep me here except my mother and I'd leave her.

MAN: You don't think I'm sent you by the devil? Sometimes I think the devil has me. And then I think there is no devil. And then I think the devil would make me think there was no devil.

ALICE: I'll never get away from here if you don't take me.

MAN: Will you do everything I say, like a witch with the devil her master?

ALICE: I'll do like a wife with a husband her master and that's enough for man or devil.

MAN: Will you kiss my arse like the devil makes his witches?

ALICE: I'll do what gives us pleasure. Was I good just now?

MAN: In Scotland I saw a witch burnt.

ALICE: Did you? A real witch? Was she a real one?

MAN: She was really burnt for one.

ALICE: Did the spirits fly out of her like black bats? Did the devil make the sky go dark? I've heard plenty tales of witches and I've heard some called witch, there's one in the next village some say and others say not, but she's nothing to see. Did she fly at night on a stick? Did you see her flying?

MAN: I saw her burnt.

ALICE: Tell then. What did she say?

MAN: She couldn't speak, I think. They'd been questioning her. There's wrenching the head with a cord. She came to the stake in a cart and men lifted her out, and the stake held her up when she was tied. She'd been in the boots you see that break the bones.

ALICE: And wood was put round? And a fire lit just like lighting a fire? Oh, I'd have shrieked, I cry the least thing.

MAN: She did shriek.

ALICE: I long to see that. But I might hide my face. Did you hide your face?

MAN: No, I saw it.

ALICE: Did you like seeing it then?

MAN: I may have done.

ALICE: Will you take me with you, to London, to Scotland? Nothing happens here.

MAN: Take you with me?

ALICE: Please, I'd be no trouble . . .

MAN: A whore? Take a whore with me?

ALICE: I'm not that.

MAN: What are you then? What name would you put to yourself? You're not a wife or a widow. You're not a virgin. Tell me a name for what you are.

ALICE: You're not going? Stay a bit.

MAN: I've stayed too long. I'm cold. The devil's cold. Back to my warm fire, eh?

ALICE: Stay with me!

MAN: Get away will you.

ALICE: Please.

MAN: Get away.

He pushes her and she falls.

ALICE: Go to hell then, go to the devil, you devil.

MAN: Cursing is it? I can outcurse you.

ALICE: You foul devil, you fool, bastard, damn you, you devil!

MAN: Devil take you, whore, whore, damned strumpet, succubus, witch!

ALICE: But come back. I'll not curse you. Don't you curse. We were friends just now.

MAN: You should have behaved better.

ALICE: Will I see you again?

MAN: Unless I see you first.

ALICE: But will I see you? How can I find you?

MAN: You can call on me.

ALICE: How? Where? How shall I call on you?

MAN: You know how to curse. Just call on the devil.

ALICE: Don't tease me, you're not the devil, what's your name?

MAN: Lucifer, isn't it, and Beelzebub.

ALICE: No, what's your name?

MAN: Darling was my name, and sweeting, till you called me devil.

ALICE: I'll not call you devil, come back, what's your name?

MAN: You won't need to know it. You won't be seeing me.

Scene Two

JACK: The river meadow is the one to get.

MARGERY: I thought the long field up the hill.

JACK: No, the river meadow for the cattle.

MARGERY: But Jack, for corn. Think of the long field full of wheat.

JACK: He's had a bad crop two years. That's why he can't pay the rent.

MARGERY: No, but he's got no cattle. We'd be all right.

JACK: If we took both fields.

MARGERY: Could we? Both?

JACK: The more we have the more we can afford.

MARGERY: And we'll pray God sends us sunshine.

JACK: Who's that down by the river?

MARGERY: That Alice, is it, wandering about?

JACK: I'm surprised Mother Noakes can pay her rent.

MARGERY: Just a cottage isn't much.

JACK: I've been wondering if we'll see them turned out.

MARGERY: I don't know why she's let stay. If we all lived like her it wouldn't be the fine estate it is. And Alice . . .

JACK: You can't blame Alice.

MARGERY: You can blame her. You can't be surprised. She's just what I'd expect of a girl brought up by Joan Noakes.

JACK: If we rent both fields, we'll have to hire a man to help with the harvest.

MARGERY: Hire a man?

JACK: That's not Alice.

MARGERY: It's not Miss Betty out by herself again?

JACK: I wouldn't be her father, not even to own the land.

MARGERY: That's a fine idea, hire a man.

JACK: She's coming here.

MARGERY: What we going to do?

JACK: Be respectful.

MARGERY: No but shall we take her home? She's not meant to. She's still shut up in her room, everyone says.

JACK: I won't be sorry to see her.

MARGERY: I love to see her. She was always so soft on your lap, not like ours all hard edges. I could sit all afternoon just to smell her hair. But she's not a child, now, you can have run in and out and touch her. She's in trouble at home and we shouldn't help her do wrong.

JACK: We can't stop her, can we, if she walks in?

They wait and in a moment BETTY *does comes in.*

MARGERY: Miss Betty, how nice.

BETTY: I came to see you milking the cows.

JACK: We finished milking, miss. The cows are in.

BETTY: Is it that late?

MARGERY: You want to get home before dark.

BETTY: No I don't. I want to be out in the dark. It's not late, it's dark in the daytime. I could stay out for hours if it was summer.

JACK: If you want to come and see the farm, Miss Betty, you should ask your father to bring you one morning when he's inspecting the estate.

BETTY: I'm not let go where I like.

JACK: I've business with your father.

MARGERY: We're going to take on the river meadow for the cattle.

JACK: And the long field up the hill.

BETTY: I used to play here all day. Nothing's different. Have you still got Betty's mug?

MARGERY: That's right, she had her special mug.

BETTY: I milked the red cow right into it one day. I got milk in my eye.

JACK: She died, that red cow. But we've four new cows you've not seen.

MARGERY: Died last week. There's two or three cows died in the neighborhood.

BETTY: I wish she hadn't.

JACK: That don't matter, losing one, we're going well enough.

MARGERY: And you're doing well, I hear, miss.

BETTY: What?

MARGERY: I hear you're leaving us for better things.

BETTY: No.

MARGERY: I was only saying yesterday, our little Miss Betty that was and now to be a lady with her own house and . . .

BETTY: They lock me up. I said I won't marry him so they lock me up. Don't you know that?

MARGERY: I had heard something.

BETTY: I get out the window.

MARGERY: Hadn't you better have him, Betty, and be happy? Everyone hopes so. Everyone loves a wedding.

BETTY: Margery, can I stay here tonight?

MARGERY: They'd worry for you.

BETTY: Can I? Please?

JACK: There's no bed fit for you, miss.

BETTY: On my way here I climbed a tree. I could see the whole estate. I could see the other side of the river. I wanted to jump off. And fly.

MARGERY: Shall Jack walk home with you, miss, now it's getting dark?

Scene Three

JOAN: Alice?

ALICE: No need wake up, mum.

JOAN: You'll catch cold out all night in this weather.

ALICE: Don't wake up if it's only to moan at me.

JOAN: Who were you with?

ALICE: Did he wake up?

JOAN: No, not a sound.

ALICE: He's sleeping better. Not so much bad dreams.

JOAN: Come on, child, there's some broth left.

ALICE: I couldn't eat.

JOAN: You stay out half the night, you don't even enjoy it. You stay in with the boy. You sit by the fire with no one to talk to but old Vinegar Tomcat. I'll go out.

ALICE: You go out?

JOAN: Funny, isn't it? What would I do going out?

ALICE: I'll stay in if you like.

JOAN: Where would I go? Who wants an old woman?

ALICE: You want me to stay with you more?

JOAN: An old woman wandering about in the cold.

ALICE: Do you want some broth, mum?

JOAN: Who were you with this time? Anyone I know?

ALICE: Oh mum, I'm sick of myself.

JOAN: If we'd each got a man we'd be better off.

ALICE: You weren't better off, mum. You've told me often you're glad he's dead. Think how he used to beat you.

JOAN: We'd have more to eat, that's one thing.

Nobody Sings

I met an old old woman
Who made my blood run cold.
You don't stop wanting sex, she said,
Just because you're old.
    Oh nobody sings about it,
    but it happens all the time.

I should be glad of the change of life,
But it makes me feel so strange.
If your life is being wanted
Do you want your life to change?
    Oh nobody sings about it,
    but it happens all the time.

Do you want your skin to wrinkle
And your cunt get sore and dry?
And they say it's just your hormones
If you cry and cry and cry.

Oh nobody sings about it,
but it happens all the time.

Nobody ever saw me,
She whispered in a rage.
They were blinded by my beauty, now
They're blinded by my age.
    Oh nobody sings about it,
    but it happens all the time.

Scene Four

MARGERY *is churning.*
JACK: Hurry up with that butter, woman.
MARGERY: Butter won't come.
JACK: There's other work to do.
MARGERY: Butter won't come.
JACK: You don't churn. You sit gossiping.
MARGERY: Who would I talk to?
JACK: I heard your voice now.
MARGERY: Mother Noakes.
JACK: Always hanging about.
MARGERY: Her girl's no better.
JACK: Was her girl here? No.
MARGERY: I told her be on her way. Mother Noakes.
JACK: You tell her.
MARGERY: I told her.
JACK: Get on now with the butter and don't be always gossiping.
    JACK *goes.* MARGERY *churns and sings very quietly.*

MARGERY: Come butter come, come butter come. Johnny's standing at the gate
    waiting for a butter cake. Come butter come, come butter come. Johnny's stand-
    ing at the gate waiting for a butter cake. Come butter come, come butter come.
    Johnny's standing at the gate . . .
    She stops as she realises JOAN NOAKES *has come in and is standing behind her.*

JOAN: Just passing by.
MARGERY: Again.
JOAN: I wonder could you lend me a little yeast? I've no yeast, see. I'm fresh out of
    yeast. I've no bread in the house and I thought, I thought . . . I'll do a little baking
    now and brew a little beer maybe . . . and I went to get some yeast and I've no
    yeast. Who'd have thought it? No yeast at all.
MARGERY: You'd be better without beer.
JOAN: I thought a little yeast as I was passing.
MARGERY: You get drunk. You should be ashamed.
JOAN: To bake a couple of little small loaves.
MARGERY: I've no yeast.
JOAN: A couple of little small loaves wouldn't take much yeast. A woman comfort-
    able off with a fine man and a nice field and five cows and three pigs and plenty of
    apples that makes a good cider, bless you, Margery, many's the time . . . you'd not

grudge a neighbor a little loaf? Many's the good times, eh, Margery? I've my own flour, you know, I'm not asking for flour.

MARGERY: I gave you yeast last week.

JOAN: A little small crumb of yeast and God will bless you for kindness to your poor old neighbor.

MARGERY: You're not so badly off, Joan Noakes. You're not on the parish.

JOAN: If I was I'd be fed. I should be on relief, then I'd not trouble you. There's some on relief, better off than me. I get nothing.

MARGERY: What money you get you drink.

JOAN: If you'd my troubles, Margery, you'd be glad of a drink, but as you haven't, thank God, and lend me a little yeast like a good woman.

MARGERY: I've no yeast.

JOAN: I know you, Margery.

MARGERY: What do you know?

JOAN: I know you've got yeast. My eyes are old, but I see through you. You're a cold woman and getting worse and you'll die without a friend in this parish when if you gave yeast to your good neighbors everyone would bless you . . .

MARGERY: I've no yeast.

JOAN: But you don't give and they say what a mean bitter woman and curse you.

MARGERY: There's nobody curses me. Now get out of my dairy. Dirty old woman you are, smelling of drink, come in here day after day begging, and stealing, too, I shouldn't wonder . . .

JOAN: You shouldn't say that.

MARGERY: . . . and your great ugly cat in here stealing the cream. Get out of my dairy.

JOAN: You'll be sorry you spoke to me like that. I've always been your friend, Margery, but now you'll find I'm not.

MARGERY: I've work to do. Now get out. I'm making my butter.

JOAN: Damn your butter to hell.

MARGERY: Will you get out?

JOAN: Devil take you and your man and your fields and your cows and your butter and your yeast and your beer and your bread and your cider and your cold face . . .

MARGERY: Will you go?

JOAN *goes.* MARGERY *churns.*

MARGERY: Come butter come, come butter come. Johnny's standing at the gate waiting for a butter cake. Come butter . . . It's not coming, this butter. I'm sick of it.

JACK *comes.*

JACK: What's all this? You're a lazy woman, you know that? Times are bad enough. The little black calf don't look well.

MARGERY: Butter won't come. Mother Noakes said damn the butter to hell.

JACK: Lazy slut, get on with it.

MARGERY: Come butter come. Come butter come. Come butter come. Come butter come. Come butter come. Come butter . . . Mother Noakes come begging and borrowing. She still got my big bowl I give her some eggs in that time she was poorly. She makes out I've treated her bad. I've been a good neighbor to that woman years out of mind and no return. We'll get that bowl back off her. Jack, do you hear me? Go over Mother Noakes and get my bowl. And we'll heat a horse-shoe red hot and put it in the milk to make the butter come.

Scene Five

SUSAN: Don't always talk of men.

ALICE: He knew what he was doing.

SUSAN: You'll know what he was doing in a few months.

ALICE: No, it never happens. The cunning woman put a charm inside me.

SUSAN: Take more than a charm to do me good.

ALICE: Not again? Does he know?

SUSAN: He wants it. I know the night it was. He said, "Let's hope a fine child comes of it."

ALICE: And what did you say?

SUSAN: Devil take it.

ALICE: What he say to that?

SUSAN: He don't like me swearing.

ALICE: But the baby's not a year.

SUSAN: Two weeks late, so.

ALICE: But the baby's not weaned.

SUSAN: The boy wasn't weaned when I fell for the baby.

ALICE: You could go see the cunning woman.

SUSAN: What for?

ALICE: She's a good midwife.

SUSAN: I don't want a midwife. I got my mother, anyway. I don't want to think about it. Nearly died last time. I was two days.

ALICE: Go and see the cunning woman. Just go see.

SUSAN: What for?

ALICE: She could say for certain.

SUSAN: I'm sure for certain.

ALICE: She could give you a charm.

SUSAN: They do say the pain is what's sent to a woman for her sins. I complained last time after churching, and he said I must think on Eve who brought the sin into the world that got me pregnant. I must think on how woman tempts man, and how she pays God with her pain having the baby. So if we try to get round the pain, we're going against God.

ALICE: I hate my body.

SUSAN: You mustn't say that. God sent his son . . .

ALICE: Blood every month, and no way out of that but to be sick and swell up, and no way out of that but pain. No way out of all that till we're old and that's worse. I can't bear to see my mother if she changes her clothes. If I was a man, I'd go to London and Scotland and never come back and take a girl under a bush and on my way.

SUSAN: You could go to the cunning woman.

ALICE: What for?

SUSAN: Charm.

ALICE: What for?

SUSAN: Love charm bring him back.

ALICE: I don't want him back.

SUSAN: Did he look wonderful, more than anyone here, that he's got you so low?

ALICE: It was dark, I wouldn't know him again.

SUSAN: Not so much how he looked as how he felt?

ALICE: I could do with it now, I can tell you. I could do with walking across that field again and finding him there just the same. I want a man I can have when I want, not if I'm lucky to meet some villain one night.

SUSAN: You always say you don't want to be married.

ALICE: I don't want to be married. Look at you. Who'd want to be you?

SUSAN: He doesn't beat me.

ALICE: He doesn't beat you.

SUSAN: What's wrong with me? Better than you.

ALICE: Three babies and what, two, three times miscarried and wonderful he doesn't beat you.

SUSAN: No one's going to marry you because they know you here. That's why you say you don't want to be married—because no one's going to ask you round here, because they know you.

They move apart. JACK *has been lingering in the background a while, and now comes up to* ALICE.

JACK: It's not you I've come to see.

ALICE: Never thought it was.

JACK: You should have done then.

ALICE: Why?

JACK: You know why.

ALICE: You've come to see my mum, have you?

JACK: I've business with her, yes. That's why I came.

ALICE: She's somewhere around. I'll get her.

JACK: No hurry. Wait a bit. Never seem to talk.

ALICE: Nothing to talk about.

JACK: I'm forgetting. I brought something.

He gives her two apples.

ALICE: Thank you. What then?

JACK: Am I not handsome enough, is that it?

ALICE: I don't want trouble.

JACK: No one's to know.

ALICE: If I say you're not handsome enough, will you go away?

JACK: Alice, you must. I have dreams.

ALICE: You've a wife.

JACK: I'm no good to my wife. I can't do it. Not these three months. It's only when I dream of you or like now talking to you . . .

ALICE: Mum. There's someone to see you.

JACK: Alice, have some pity . . .

ALICE: Do you hear me? Mum? She'll be out to see you.

She moves away. JOAN *comes.*

JOAN: What's the matter?

JACK: I've come for the bowl.

JOAN: Bowl? Bowl?

JACK: Bowl my wife gave you some eggs in, you ungrateful old hag.

JOAN: You're asking for the bowl? You think I wouldn't give you back your bowl? You think I'm stealing your bowl? When have I ever kept anything? Have your bowl. I'll get your bowl and much good may it do you.

JACK: Then get it, damn you, and quick or you'll feel my hand.

She goes.

ALICE: Why treat her like that?

JACK: Don't speak to me. Let me get the bowl and go.

ALICE: And don't come back.

JACK: Alice, I'd be good to you. I'm not a poor man. I could give you things for your boy . . .

ALICE: Go away to hell.

JOAN comes back.

JOAN: Here's your bowl, Jack, and the devil go with it. Get away home and I hope you've more trouble there than I have here.

JACK: I'll break your neck if you speak to me.

JOAN: You lift your hand to me, may it drop off.

ALICE: Go home away to hell, man.

JACK goes.

JOAN: Away to hell with him. Never liked the man. Never liked the wife.

ALICE: Don't think on them, mum. They're not worth your time. Go in by the fire, go on, go in and be warm.

JOAN goes. SUSAN approaches.

ALICE: Nobody likes my mother. That's what it is why nobody wants me.

SUSAN: I'm sorry for what I said, Alice.

ALICE: Going to see the cunning woman then?

SUSAN: Are you going for a love charm?

ALICE: It's something to do, isn't it? Better than waiting and waiting for something to happen. If I had a charm I could make him just appear in front of me now, I'd do anything. Will you come?

ALICE gives SUSAN apple.

SUSAN: I'll keep you company then. Just tell her my trouble. There's no harm.

Oh Doctor

> Oh, doctor, tell
> me, make me well.
> What's wrong with me
> the way I am?
> I know I'm sad.
> I may be sick.
> I may be bad.
> Please cure me quick,
> oh doctor.

Scene Six

BETTY *tied to a chair.*

BETTY: Why am I tied? Tied to be bled. Why am I bled? Because I was screaming. Why was I screaming? Because I'm bad. Why was I bad? Because I was happy. Why was I happy? Because I ran out by myself and got away from them and—Why was I screaming? Because I'm bad. Why am I bad? Because I'm tied. Why am I tied? Because I was happy. Why was I happy? Because I was screaming.

DOCTOR: Hysteria is a woman's weakness. Hysteron, Greek, the womb. Excessive blood causes an imbalance in the humors. The noxious gases that form inwardly every month rise to the brain and cause behaviour quite contrary to the patient's real feelings. After bleeding you must be purged. Tonight you shall be blistered. You will soon be well enough to be married.

Oh Doctor

Where are you taking my skin?
Where are you putting my bones?
I shut my eyes and I opened wide,
But why is my heart on the other side?
Why are you putting my brain in my cunt?
You're putting me back all back to front.

Stop looking up me with your metal eye.
Stop cutting me apart before I die.
Stop, put me back.
Stop, put me back.
Put back my body.

Who are you giving my womb?
Who are you showing my breath?
Tell me what you whisper to nurse,
Whatever I've got, you're making it worse.
I'm wide awake, but I still can't shout.
Why can't I see what you're taking out?

Stop looking up me with your metal eye.
Stop cutting me apart before I die.
Stop, put me back.
Stop, put me back.
Put back my body.

Oh, doctor, tell
me, make me well.
What's wrong with me
the way I am?
I know I'm sad
I may be sick.
I may be bad.
Please cure me quick,
oh doctor.

What's wrong with me the way I am?
What's wrong with me?

I want to see myself.
I want to see inside myself.
Give me back my head.
I'll put my heart in straight.
Let me out of bed now.
I can't wait
To see myself.
Give me back my body.
I can see myself.
Give me back my body.
I can see myself.

Scene Seven

MARGERY: Jack, Jack, come quick—Jack.

JACK: What's the matter now?

MARGERY: The calves. Have you seen the calves?

JACK: What's the woman on about?

MARGERY: The calves are shaking and they've a terrible stench, so you can't go near them and their bellies are swollen up. (JACK *goes off.*) There's no good running. There's nothing you can do for them. They'll die like the red cow. You don't love me. Damn this stinking life to hell. Calves stinking and shaking there. No good you going to see, Jack. Better stand and curse. Everything dying on us. Aah. What's that? Who's there? Get out, you beast, get out. (*She throws her shoe.*)Jack, Jack.

JACK: Hold your noise.

MARGERY: That nasty old cat of Mother Noakes. I'll kill that cat if I get it, stinking up my clean dairy, stealing my cream. Where's it gone?

JACK: Let it go.

MARGERY: What you think of those calves then? Nothing to be done is there? What can we do? Nothing. Nothing to be done. Can't do nothing. Oh. Oh.

JACK: Now what is it?

MARGERY: Jack!

JACK: What is it? Don't frighten me, woman.

MARGERY: My head, oh, my stomach. Oh, Jack, I feel ill.

   She sits on the ground.

JACK: Get up, woman. It's no time. There's things to do.

MARGERY: Nothing.

JACK: Lie there a bit then. You'll maybe feel better. I can hardly stir myself. What have I done to deserve it? Why me? Why my calves shaking? Why my wife falling down?

MARGERY: It's passing now.

JACK: Why me?

MARGERY: That was a terrible pain. I still feel it. I'm shaking, look.

JACK: Other people sin and aren't punished so much as we are.

MARGERY: We must pray to God.

JACK: We do pray to God, and he sends afflictions.

MARGERY: It must be we deserve it somehow, but I don't know how. I do my best. I do my best, Jack, God knows, don't I, Jack? God knows I do my best.

JACK: Don't other people sin? Is it just me?

MARGERY: You're not a bad man, Jack.

JACK: I must be the worst man.

MARGERY: No, dear.

JACK: Would God send all this to a good man? Would he? It's my sins those calves shaking and stinking and swelling up their bellies in there.

MARGERY: Don't talk so.

JACK: My sins stinking and swelling up.

MARGERY: Unless it's not God.

JACK: How can I bear it?

MARGERY: If it's not God.

JACK: What?

MARGERY: If it's not God sends the trouble.

JACK: The devil?

MARGERY: One of his servants. If we're bewitched, Jack, that explains all.

JACK: If we're bewitched . . .

MARGERY: Butter not coming. Calves swelling. Me struck in the head.

JACK: Then it's not my sins. Good folk get bewitched.

MARGERY: Good folk like us.

JACK: It can happen to anyone.

MARGERY: Rich folk can have spells against them.

JACK: It's good people the witches want to hurt.

MARGERY: The devil can't bear to see us so good.

JACK: You know who it is?

MARGERY: Who?

JACK: The witch. Who it is.

MARGERY: Who?

JACK: You know who.

MARGERY: She cursed the butter to hell.

JACK: She cursed me when I got the bowl.

MARGERY: She said I'd be sorry I'd spoken to her.

JACK: She wished me trouble at home.

MARGERY: Devil take your man and your cows, she said that, and your butter. She cursed the calves see and she's made them shake. She struck me on the head and in the stomach.

JACK: I'll break her neck.

MARGERY: Be careful now, what she might do.

JACK: I'm not afraid of an old witch.

MARGERY: You should be. She could kill you.

JACK: I'll kill her first.

MARGERY: Wait, Jack. Let's meet cunning with cunning. What we must do is get the spell off.

JACK: She's not going to take it off for asking. She might for a few hard knocks.

MARGERY: No, wait, Jack. We can take the spell off and never go near her. Serve her right.

JACK: What we do then? Burn something?

MARGERY: Burn an animal alive, don't we? Or bury it alive. That takes witchcraft off the rest.

JACK: Burn the black calf then shall we? We'll get some straw and wood and put it in the yard and the calf on top and set it on fire.

MARGERY: Will it walk?

JACK: Or I'll carry it.

MARGERY: It stinks terrible.

JACK: Stink of witchcraft it is. Burn it up.

MARGERY: We must pray to God to keep us safe from the devil. Praying's strong against witches.

JACK: We'll pray God help us and help ourselves too.

MARGERY: She'll see the fire and smell it and she'll know we're fighting her back, stinking old witch, can't hurt us.

Something to Burn

What can we do, there's nothing to do,
about sickness and hunger and dying.
What can we do, there's nothing to do,
nothing but cursing and crying.
    Find something to burn.
    Let it go up in smoke.
    Burn your troubles away.

Sometimes it's witches, or what will you choose?
Sometimes it's lunatics, shut them away.
It's blacks and it's women and often it's Jews.
We'd all be quite happy if they'd go away.
    Find something to burn.
    Let it go up in smoke.
    Burn your troubles away.

Scene Eight

ELLEN: Take it or leave it, my dear, it's one to me. If you want to be rid of your trouble, you'll take it. But only you know what you want.

SUSAN: It's not what I came for.

ALICE: Of course it is.

SUSAN: I wanted to know for certain.

ALICE: You know for certain.

SUSAN: I want a charm against pain.

ELLEN: I'll come as your midwife if you send for me near the time and do what I can, if that's all you want.

ALICE: She wants to be rid of it. Well, do you want it?

SUSAN: I don't want it but I don't want to be rid of it. I want to be rid of it, but not do anything to be rid of it.

ELLEN: If you won't do anything to help yourself you must stay as you are.

SUSAN: I shall pray to God.

ALICE: It's no sin. You just give yourself the drink.

SUSAN: Oh, I don't know.

ELLEN: Let her go home. She can come back. You have your charm safe, Alice? I could
do more if you could come at the young man and give him a potion I'd let you have.

ALICE: If I could come at him he wouldn't need potion.

ELLEN: And you're sure you've nothing of his?

ALICE: He gave me nothing.

ELLEN: A few hairs or a drop of blood makes all the difference. It's part of him and
the powers can work on it to call him.

ALICE: I'll pull a few hairs out next time I've a lover. Come on, Susan.

ELLEN: For your heartache I'll give you these herbs to boil up in water and drink at
night. Give you a sound sleep and think less of him.

ALICE: Don't want to think less of him.

ELLEN: You have your sleep. There'll be other men along if not that one. Clever girl
like you could think of other things.

ALICE: Like what?

ELLEN: Learn a trade.

ALICE: Nothing dangerous.

ELLEN: Where's the danger in herbs?

ALICE: Not just herbs.

ELLEN: Where's the danger in healing?

ALICE: Not just healing, is it.

ELLEN: There's powers, and you use them for healing or hurt. You use them how you
like. There's no hurt if you're healing so where's the danger? You could use them.
Not everyone can.

ALICE: Learn the herbs?

ELLEN: There's all kinds of wisdom. Bit by bit I'd teach you.

ALICE: I'd never thought.

ELLEN: There's no hurry. I don't want you unless it's what you want. You'll be coming by to leave a little something for me in a few days, since I have to live and
wouldn't charge you. You can tell me how you've got on with your young man and
what you're thinking.

ALICE: Yes, I'll be coming by. Goodnight then. What are you standing there for, Susan?

SUSAN: Maybe I'll take some potion with me. And see when I get home whether I
take it.

ELLEN: Don't be afraid if it makes you very sick. It's to do you good.

Scene Nine

BETTY: I don't know what I'm here for. I've had so much treatment already. The
doctor comes every day.

ELLEN: You know what you're here for.

BETTY: The doctor says people like you don't know anything. He thinks he's cured me
because I said I would get married to stop them locking me up. But I'll never do it.

ELLEN: Do you want a potion to make you love the man?

BETTY: I'd rather have one to make him hate me so he'd leave me alone. Or make
him die.

ELLEN: The best I can do for you is help you sleep. I won't harm him for you, so
don't ask. Get some sleep and think out what you want.

BETTY: Can I come again sometimes just to be here? I like it here.

ELLEN: Come when you like. I don't charge but you'll bring a little present.

BETTY: I'll give you anything if you can help me.

ELLEN: Come when you like.

Scene Ten

ELLEN: I'm not saying I can't do anything. But if I can't, it's because you've left it too late.

JACK: Lift your hand to me, she said, may it drop off. Then next day it went stiff.

MARGERY: We want to be certain. I've talked to others and they've things against her too. She's cursed and scolded two or three, and one's lame and the other lost her hen. And while we were talking we thought of her great cat that's always in my dairy, stinking it up and stealing the cream. Ah what's that, I said crying out, didn't I, and that was the cat, and I was struck down with a blow inside my head. That's her familiar sent her by Satan.

JACK: I've seen a rat run out of her yard into ours and I went for it with a pitchfork and the spikes were turned aside and nearly went in my own foot by her foul magic. And that rat's another of her imps.

MARGERY: But you don't like to think it of your neighbor. Time was she was neighborly enough. If you could tell us it was true, we could act against her more certain in our minds.

JACK: I shouted at her over the fence, I said I'll have you hanged you old strumpet, burnt and hanged, and she cursed me again.

MARGERY: We burnt a calf alive to save our calves but it was too late. If I knew for certain it was her I'd be easier.

ELLEN: I've a glass here, a cloudy glass. Look in the glass, so, and see if any face comes into it.

She gives them a mirror.

MARGERY: Come on, Jack, don't be afraid.

JACK: I don't like it.

MARGERY: Come on, it's good magic to find a witch.

ELLEN: Look in the glass and think on all the misfortunes you've had and see what comes.

MARGERY: Nothing yet. Do you see anything?

JACK: No.

MARGERY: Nothing still.

JACK: Don't keep talking.

MARGERY: Look.

JACK: What?

MARGERY: Did something move in the glass? My heart's beating so.

JACK: It's too dark.

MARGERY: No. Look.

JACK: I did see something.

MARGERY: It's the witch.

JACK: It's her sure enough.

MARGERY: It is, isn't it, Jack? Mother Noakes, isn't it?

JACK: It was Mother Noakes in that glass.

ELLEN: There then. You have what you came for.

MARGERY: Proves she's a witch then?

ELLEN: Not for me to say one's a witch or not a witch. I give you the glass and you
    see in it what you see in it.

JACK: Saw Mother Noakes.

MARGERY: Proves she's a witch.

ELLEN: Saw what you come to see. Is your mind easy?

Scene Eleven

JACK: Want to ask you something private. It's about my . . . (He gestures, embar-
    rassed.) It's gone. I can't do anything with it, haven't for some time. I accepted
    that. But now it's not even there, it's completely gone. There's a girl bewitched me.
    She's daughter of that witch. And I've heard how witches sometimes get a whole
    boxful and they move and stir by themselves like living creatures and the witch
    feeds them oats and hay. There was one witch told a man in my condition to climb
    a tree and he'd find a nest with several in it and take which he liked, and when he
    took the big one she said no, not that one, because that one belongs to the parish
    priest. I don't want a big one, I want my own back, and this witch has it.

ELLEN: You'd better go and ask her nicely for it.

JACK: Is that all you can say? Can't you force her to give it me?

ELLEN: It's sure to come back. You ask the girl nicely, she'll give it you back. I'll give
    you a little potion to take.

JACK: Kill her else.

Scene Twelve

JOAN: That's a foul stink. I don't know how you can stay there. Whatever is it?

MARGERY: Do you know why you've come?

JOAN: I was passing.

MARGERY: Why were you passing?

JOAN: Can't I pass by your door now? Time was it was always open for me.

MARGERY: And what's that?

JOAN: A foul stink. Whatever are you making? I thought I'd come and see you as I
    was passing. I don't want any trouble between us. I thought, come and see her,
    make it all right.

MARGERY: You come to see me because of that. That's my piss boiling. And two
    feathers of your chicken burning. It's a foul stink brings a witch. If you come when
    I do that, proves you've a spell on me. And now I'll get it off. You know how?

JOAN: Come and see you. Make it all right.

MARGERY: Blood you, that's how.

    MARGERY scratches JOAN's head.

JOAN: Damn you, get away.

MARGERY: Can't hurt me now. And if that doesn't bring the spell off I'll burn your
    thatch.

If Everybody Worked as Hard as Me

    If everybody worked as hard as me,
    if our children's shirts are white,

if their language is polite,
if nobody stays out late at night . . .
Oh, happy family.
Oh, the country's what it is because
the family's what it is because
the wife is what she is
to her man.
Oh I do all I can.
Yes, I do all I can.
I try to do what's right,
so I'll never be alone and afraid in the night.
And nobody comes knocking at my door in the night.
The horrors that are done will not be done to me.

Nobody loves a scold,
nobody loves a slut,
nobody loves you when you're old,
unless you're someone's gran.
Nobody loves you
unless you keep your mouth shut.
Nobody loves you
if you don't support your man.
Oh you can,
oh you can
have a happy family.

If everybody worked as hard as me,
sometimes you'll be bored,
you'll often be ignored,
but in your heart you'll know you are adored.
Oh, happy family.
Your dreams will all come true.
You'll make your country strong.
Oh the country's what it is because
the family's what it is because
the wife is what she is
to her man.
Oh please do all you can.
Yes, please do all you can.
Oh please don't do what's wrong,
so you'll never be alone and afraid in the night.
So nobody comes knocking at your door in the night.
So the horrors that are done will not be done to you.

Yes you can.
Yes you can.
Oh the country's what it is because
the family's what it is because
the wife is what she is
to her man.

Scene Thirteen

SUSAN: You're sure it was him? You said you wouldn't know him.

ALICE: I did when I saw him.

SUSAN: Riding? Couldn't see him close.

ALICE: Close enough to be spattered with his mud. He saw me.

SUSAN: But he didn't show he knew you.

ALICE: Pretended not to.

SUSAN: It wasn't him.

ALICE: It was him.

SUSAN: And you don't know the beautiful lady?

ALICE: I'll know her again. Scratch her eyes if I come at her.

SUSAN: What was she wearing?

ALICE: What was she wearing? How should I know? A fine rich dress made her beautiful, I suppose. Are you trying to plague me?

SUSAN: Was he in black still?

ALICE: Blue velvet jacket.

SUSAN: Blue velvet.

ALICE: Yes, damn you, I said that before. Are you stupid? (*Silence*) For God's sake, now what is it? Are you crying? Shouldn't I be crying?

SUSAN: It's not your fault, Ally. I cry all the time.

ALICE: You're still weak, that's what it is. It's the blood you lost. You should rest more.

SUSAN: I don't want him to know.

ALICE: Doesn't he know?

SUSAN: He may guess but I don't dare ask. He was out all day that day and I said I'd been ill, but not why.

ALICE: It's done anyway.

SUSAN: Can't be undone.

ALICE: You're not sorry now?

SUSAN: I don't know.

ALICE: You'd be a fool to be sorry.

SUSAN: I am sorry. I'm wicked. You're wicked.

   She cries.

ALICE: Oh, Susan, you're tired out, that's all. You're not wicked. You'd have cried more to have it. All the extra work, another baby.

SUSAN: I like babies.

ALICE: You'll have plenty more, God, you'll have plenty. What's the use of crying?

SUSAN: You were crying for that lover.

ALICE: I'm not now. I'd sooner kill him. If I could get at him. If thoughts could get at him he'd feel it.

SUSAN: I'm so tired, Ally.

ALICE: Do you think it's true thoughts can reach someone?

SUSAN: What are you thinking of?

ALICE: Like if I had something of his, I could bring him. Or harm him.

SUSAN: Don't try that.

ALICE: But I've nothing of his. I'd have to make a puppet.

SUSAN: Don't talk so. Oh, don't, Alice, when I'm so tired.

ALICE: Does it have to be like? Is it like just if you say it's like?

SUSAN: Alice!

ALICE: If I get this wet mud, it's like clay. There should be at least a spider or some ashes of bones, but mud will do. Here's a man's shape, see, that's his head and that's arms and legs.

SUSAN: I'm going home. I'm too tired to move.

ALICE: You stay here and watch. This is the man. We know who though we don't know his name. Now here's a pin, let's prick him. Where shall I prick him? Between the legs first so he can't get on with his lady.

SUSAN: Alice, stop.

ALICE: Once in the head to drive him mad. Shall I give him one in the heart? Do I want him to die yet? Or just waste till I please.

SUSAN: Alice . . .

SUSAN tries to get the mud man, it falls on the ground and breaks.

ALICE: Now look. You've broken him up. You've killed him.

SUSAN: I haven't.

ALICE: All in pieces. Think of the poor man. Come apart.

SUSAN: I didn't. Alice, I didn't. It was you.

ALICE: If it was me, I don't care.

SUSAN: Alice, what have you done? Oh Alice, Alice,

ALICE: It's not true, stupid. It's not him.

SUSAN: How do you know?

ALICE: It's a bit of mud.

SUSAN: But you said.

ALICE: That's just words.

SUSAN: But . . .

ALICE: No. I did nothing. I never do anything. Might be better if I did. (*They sit in silence.*) You're crying again. Here, don't cry.

ALICE holds SUSAN while she cries.

SUSAN: Little clay puppet like a tiny baby not big enough to live and we crumble it away.

JACK comes.

JACK: Witch.

ALICE: Are you drunk?

JACK: Give it back.

ALICE: What?

JACK: Give it back.

ALICE: What now, Jack?

JACK: Give it me back. You know. You took it from me these three months. I've not been a man since. You bewitched me. You took it off me.

ALICE: Is he mad?

SUSAN: What is it?

ALICE: Susan's ill, will you leave us alone?

JACK: Everyone comes near you is ill. Give it back, come on, give it back.

ALICE: How can I?

JACK: She said speak nicely to you. I would, Alice, if you were good to me. I never wanted this. Please, sweet good Alice, give it back.

ALICE: What? How can I?
JACK: Give it me.
  He grabs her round the neck. SUSAN *screams.*

ALICE: Damn you!
SUSAN: You'll kill her . . .
JACK: Give it me . . .
SUSAN: Let her go, she'll give it you whatever it is, you'll kill her Jack.
  JACK *lets go.*

JACK: Give it me then. Come on.
SUSAN: Wait, she can't move, leave her alone.
JACK: Give it me.
  ALICE *gets up and puts her hand between his thighs.*

ALICE: There. It's back.
JACK: It is. It is back. Thank you, Alice. I wasn't sure you were a witch till then.
  JACK *goes.*

SUSAN: What you doing Alice? Alice? Alice?
  ALICE *turns to her.*

ALICE: It's nothing. He's mad. Oh my neck, Susan. Oh, I'd laugh if it didn't hurt.
SUSAN: Don't touch me. I'll not be touched by a witch.

Scene Fifteen

BELLRINGER: Whereas if anyone has any complaint against any woman for a witch,
  let them go to the townhall and lay their complaint. For a man is in town that is a
  famous finder of witches and has had above thirty hanged in the country round
  and he will discover if they are or no. Whereas if anyone has any complaint
  against any woman for a witch, let them go . . .
MARGERY: Stopped the butter.
JACK: Killed the calves.
MARGERY: Struck me in the head.
JACK: Lamed my hand.
MARGERY: Struck me in the stomach.
JACK: Bewitched my organ.
MARGERY: When I boiled my urine she came.
JACK: Blooded her and made my hand well.
MARGERY: Burnt her thatch.
JACK: And Susan, her friend, is like possessed screaming and crying and lay two days
  without speaking.
MARGERY: Susan's baby turned blue and its limbs twisted and it died.
JACK: Boy threw stones and called them witch, and, after, he vomited pins and
  straw.
MARGERY: Big nasty cat she has in her bed and sends it to people's dairies.
JACK: A rat's her imp.
MARGERY: And the great storm last night brought a tree down in the lane, who
  made that out of a clear sky?

PACKER: I thank God that he has brought me again where I am needed. Don't be afraid any more. You have been in great danger but the devil can never overcome the faithful. For God in his mercy has called me and shown me a wonderful way of finding out witches, which is finding the place on the body of the witch made insensitive to pain by the devil. So that if you prick that place with a pin no blood comes out and the witch feels nothing at all.

PACKER and GOODY take JOAN, and GOODY holds her, while PACKER pulls up her skirts and pricks her legs. JOAN curses and screams throughout. PACKER and GOODY abuse her: a short sharp moment of great noise and confusion.

GOODY: Hold still you old witch. Devil not help you now, no good calling him. Strong for your age, that's the devil's strength in her, see. Hold still, you stinking old strumpet . . .
PACKER: Hold your noise, witch, how can we tell what we're doing? Ah, ah, there's for you devil, there's blood, and there's blood, where's your spot, we'll find you out Satan . . .
JOAN: Damn you to hell, oh Christ help me! Ah, ah, you're hurting, let go, damn you, oh sweet God, oh you devils, oh devil take you . . .
PACKER: There, there, no blood here, Goody Haskins. Here's her spot. Hardly a speck here.
GOODY: How she cries the old liar, pretending it hurts her.
PACKER: There's one for hanging, stand aside there. We've others to attend to. Next please, Goody.

GOODY takes ALICE. PACKER helps, and her skirts are thrown over her head while he pricks her. She tries not to cry out and her cries are muffled by the skirt but slight whimpers are heard.

GOODY: Why so much blood?
PACKER: The devil's cunning here.
GOODY: She's not crying much, she can't feel it.
PACKER: Have I the spot though? Which is the spot? There. There. There. No, I haven't the spot. Oh, it's tiring work. Set this one aside. Maybe there's others will speak against her and let us know more clearly what she is.

ALICE is stood aside.

PACKER: If anyone here knows anything more of this woman why she might be a witch, I charge them in God's name to speak out, or the guilt of filthy witchcraft will be on you for concealing it.
SUSAN: I know something of her.
PACKER: Don't be shy then girl, speak out.
ALICE: Susan, what you doing? Don't speak against me.
SUSAN: Don't let her at me.
ALICE: You'll have me hanged.

SUSAN starts to shriek hysterically.

GOODY: Look, she's bewitched.
MARGERY: It's Alice did it to her.
ALICE: Susan, stop.
SUSAN: Alice. Alice. Alice.

PACKER: Take the witch out and the girl may be quiet.
> GOODY *takes* ALICE *off*. SUSAN *stops*.

MARGERY: See that.

JACK: Praise God I escaped such danger.

SUSAN: She met with the devil, she told me, like a man in black she met him in the night and did uncleanness with him, and ever after she was not herself but wanted to be with the devil again. She took me to a cunning woman and they made me take a foul potion to destroy the baby in my womb and it was destroyed. And the cunning woman said she would teach Alice her wicked magic, and she'd have powers and not everyone could learn that, but Alice could because she's a witch, and the cunning woman gave her something to call the devil, and she tried to call him, and she made a puppet, and stuck pins in, and tried to make me believe that was the devil, but that was my baby girl, and next day she was sick and her face blue and limbs all twisted up and she died. And I don't want to see her.

PACKER: These cunning women are worst of all. Everyone hates witches who do harm but good witches they go to for help and come into the devil's power without knowing it. The infection will spread through the whole country if we don't stop it. Yes, all witches deserve death, and the good witch even more than the bad one. Oh God, do not let your kingdom be overrun by the devil. And you, girl, you went to this good witch, and you destroyed the child in your womb by witchcraft, which is a grievous offense. And you were there when this puppet was stuck with pins, and consented to the death of your own baby daughter?

SUSAN: No, I didn't. I didn't consent. I never wished her harm. Oh if I was angry sometimes or cursed her for crying, I never meant it. I'd take it back if I could have her back. I never meant to harm her.

PACKER: You can't take your curses back, you cursed her to death. That's two of your children you killed. And what other harm have you done? Don't look amazed, you'll speak soon enough. We'll prick you as you pricked your babies.

Scene Sixteen

> GOODY *takes* SUSAN *and* PACKER *pulls up her skirt*.

GOODY: There's no man finds more witches than Henry Packer. He can tell by their look, he says, but of course he has more ways than that. He's read all the books and he's traveled. He says the reason there's so much witchcraft in England is England is too soft with its witches, for in Europe and Scotland they are hanged and burned and if they are not penitent they are burnt alive, but in England they are only hanged. And the ways of discovering witches are not so good here, for in other countries they have thumbscrews and racks and the bootikens which is said to be the worst pain in the world, for it fits tight over the legs from ankle to knee and is driven tighter and tighter till the legs are crushed as small as might be and the blood and marrow spout out and the bones crushed and the legs made unserviceable forever. And very few continue their lies and denials then. In England we haven't got such thorough ways, our ways are slower but they get the truth in the end when a fine skillful man like Henry Packer is onto them. He's well worth the twenty shillings a time, and I get the same, which is very good of him to insist on and well worth it though some folk complain and say, "What, the price of a cow, just to have a witch hanged?" But I say to them think of the expense a witch is to you in the damage she does to property, such as a cow killed one or two pounds, a horse maybe four pounds, besides all the pigs and sheep at a few shillings a time, and chickens at sixpence all adds up. For two pounds and our expenses at the inn, you have all that saving, besides knowing you're free of the threat of sudden illness and death. Yes, it's interesting work being a searcher and nice to do good at the same time as earning a living. Better than staying home a widow. I'd end up like the old women you see, soft in the head and full of spite with their muttering and spells. I keep healthy keeping the country healthy. It's an honor to work with a great professional.

Scene Seventeen

BETTY: I'm frightened to come any more. They'll say I'm a witch.

ELLEN: Are they saying I'm a witch?

BETTY: They say because I screamed that was the devil in me. And when I ran out of the house they say where was I going if not to meet other witches. And some know I come to see you.

ELLEN: Nobody's said it yet to my face.

BETTY: But the doctor says he'll save me. He says I'm not a witch, he says I'm ill. He says I'm his patient so I can't be a witch. He says he's making me better. I hope I can be better.

ELLEN: You get married, Betty, that's safest.

BETTY: But I want to be left alone. You know I do.

ELLEN: Left alone for what? To be like me? There's no doctor going to save me from being called a witch. Your best chance of being left alone is marry a rich man, because it's part of his honor to have a wife who does nothing. He has his big house and rose garden and trout stream, he just needs a fine lady to make it complete and you can be that. You can sing and sit on the lawn and change your dresses and order the dinner. That's the best you can do. What would you rather? Marry a poor man and work all day? Or go on as you're going, go on strange? That's not safe. Plenty of girls feel like you've been feeling, just for a bit. But you're not one to go on with it.

BETTY: If it's true there's witches, maybe I've been bewitched. If the witches are stopped, maybe I'll get well.

ELLEN: You'll get well, my dear, and you'll get married, and you'll tell your children about the witches.

BETTY: What's going to happen? Will you be all right?

ELLEN: You go home now. You don't want them finding you here.

   BETTY goes.

ELLEN: I could ask to be swum. They think the water won't keep a witch in, for Christ's baptism sake, so if a woman floats she's a witch. And if she sinks they have to let her go. I could sink. Any fool can sink. It's how to sink without drowning. It's whether they get you out. No, why should I ask to be half drowned? I've done nothing. I'll explain to them what I do. It's healing, not harm. There's no devil in it. If I keep calm and explain it, they can't hurt me.

Scene Eighteen

ALICE *is sitting crosslegged, tied up, on the floor.* GOODY *is eating and yawning.*

GOODY: You'd better confess, my dear, for he'll have you watched night and day and there's nothing makes a body so wretched as not sleeping. I'm tired myself. It's for your own good, you know, to save you from the devil. If we let you stay as you are, you'd be damned eternally and better a little pain now than eternal ... (*She realizes* ALICE *is nodding to sleep and picks up a drum and bangs it loudly. Gives it several bangs to keep* ALICE *awake.* PACKER *comes in.*) She's an obstinate young witch, this one, on her second night. She tires a body out.

PACKER: Go and sleep, Goody, I'll watch her a while.

GOODY: You're a considerate man, Mr. Packer. We earn our money.

　　GOODY *goes.*

PACKER: I'm not a hard man. I like to have my confession so I'm easy in my mind I've done right.

ALICE: Where's my boy?

PACKER: Safe with good people.

ALICE: He wants me.

PACKER: He's safe from the devil, where you'll never come.

ALICE: I want him.

PACKER: Why won't you confess and make this shorter?

ALICE: It isn't true.

PACKER: Tell me your familiars. Tell me your imps' names. I won't let them plague you for telling. God will protect you if you repent.

ALICE: I haven't any. (PACKER *drums.*) I want my boy.

PACKER: Then you should have stayed home at night with him and not gone out after the devil.

ALICE: I want him.

PACKER: How could a mother be a filthy witch and put her child in danger?

ALICE: I didn't.

PACKER: Night after night, it's well known.

ALICE: But what's going to happen to him? He's only got me.

PACKER: He should have a father. Who's his father? Speak up, who's his father?

ALICE: I don't know.

PACKER: You must speak.

ALICE: I don't know.

PACKER: You must confess.

　　PACKER *drums.*

ALICE: Oh my head. Please don't. Everything's drumming.

PACKER: I'll watch. Your imps will come to see you.

ALICE: Drumming.

　　PACKER *suddenly stops.*

PACKER: Ah. Ah. What's this? A spider. A huge black one. And it ran off when it saw a godly man. Deny if you can that spider's one of your imps.

ALICE: No.

PACKER: Then why should it come? Tell me that.

ALICE: I want my boy.

PACKER: Why? Why do you keep on about the boy? Who's his father? Is the devil his father?

ALICE: No, no, no.

PACKER: I'll have the boy to see me in the morning. If he's not the devil's child he'll speak against you. (*Alice cries.*) I'll watch you. I've watched plenty of witches and hanged them all. I'll get that spider too if it comes back.

Scene Nineteen

GOODY *is shaving* SUSAN *under her arm.*

GOODY: There, that's the second arm done, and no mark yet. Devil hides his marks all kinds of places. The more secret the better he likes it. Though I knew one witch had a great pink mark on her shoulder and neck so everyone could see. And a woman last week with a big lump in her breast like another whole teat where she sucked her imps, a little black one she had and a little white one and kept them in wool in a bottle. And when I squeezed it first white stuff came out like milk and then blood, for she fed those horrid creatures on milk and blood and they sucked her secret parts in the night too. Now let's see your secret parts and see what the devil does there.

She makes SUSAN *lie down, and pulls up her skirt to shave her.* PACKER *comes in.*

PACKER: What devil's marks?

GOODY: No need to shave the other for she has three bigs in her privates almost an inch long like great teats where the devil sucks her and a bloody place on her side where she can't deny she cut a lump off herself so I wouldn't find it.

PACKER: Such a stinking old witch I won't look myself. Is there nothing here?

GOODY: She's clean yet but we'll shave her and see what shameful thing's hidden.

PACKER: Though a mark is a sure sign of a witch's guilt having no mark is no sign of innocence for the devil can take marks off.

JOAN: And the devil take you.

PACKER: You'll be with the devil soon enough.

JOAN: And I'll be glad to see him. I been a witch these ten years. Boys was always calling after me and one day I said to a boy, Boy boy you call me witch but when I did I make your arse to itch. And he ran off and I met a little gray kitling and the kitling said, "You must go with me" and I said, "Avoid Satan." And he said, "You must give me your body and soul and you'll have all happiness." And I did. And I gave him my blood every day, and that's my old cat Vinegar Tom. And he lamed John Peter's son that's a cripple this day, that was ten years ago. And I had two more imps sent me crept in my bed in the night sucked my privy parts so sore they hurt me and wouldn't leave me. And I asked them to kill Mary Johnson who crossed me and she wasted after. And everyone knows Anne that had fits and would gnash her teeth and took six strong men to hold her. That was me sent those fits to her. My little imps are like moles with four feet but no tails and a black color. And I'd send them off and they'd come back in the night and say they did what I said. Jack is lucky I didn't bewitch him to death and Margery, but she was kind to me long ago. But I killed their cows like I killed ten cows last year. And the great storm and tempest comes when I call it and strikes down trees. But now I'm in prison my powers all gone or I'd call down thunder and twist your guts.

PACKER: Is there any reason you shouldn't be hanged?

JOAN: I'm with child.

GOODY: Who'd believe that?

Scene Twenty

JOAN and ELLEN are hanged while MARGERY prays.

MARGERY: Dear God, thank you for saving us. Let us live safe now. I have scrubbed the dairy out. You have shown your power in destroying the wicked, and you show it in blessing the good. You have helped me in my struggle against the witches, help me in my daily struggle. Help me work harder and our good harvests will be to your glory. Bless Miss Betty's marriage and let her live happy. Bless Jack and keep him safe from evil and let him love me and give us the land, amen.

Scene Twenty One

JOAN and ELLEN hanging.

SUSAN: Alice, how can you look? Your poor mother. You're not even crying.

ALICE: She wasn't a witch. She wouldn't know how.

SUSAN: Alice, she was.

ALICE: The cunning woman was, I think. That's why I was frightened of her.

SUSAN: I was a witch and never knew it. I killed my babies. I never meant it. I didn't know I was so wicked. I didn't know I had that mark on me. I'm so wicked. Alice, let's pray to God we won't be damned. If we're hanged, we're saved, Alice, so we mustn't be frightened. It's done to help us. Oh God, I know now I'm loathsome and a sinner and Mr. Packer has shown me how bad I am and I repent I never knew that but now I know and please forgive me and don't make me go to hell and be burnt forever—

ALICE: I'm not a witch.

SUSAN: Alice, you know you are. God, don't hear her say that.

ALICE: I'm not a witch. But I wish I was. If I could live I'd be a witch now after what they've done. I'd make wax men and melt them on a slow fire. I'd kill their animals and blast their crops and make such storms, I'd wreck their ships all over the world. I shouldn't have been frightened of Ellen, I should have learnt. Oh if I could meet with the devil now I'd give him anything if he'd give me power. There's no way for us except by the devil. If I only did have magic, I'd make them feel it.

Lament for the Witches

Where have the witches gone?
Who are the witches now?
Here we are.

All the gentle witches spells
blast the doctors' sleeping pills.
The witches hanging in the sky

haunt the courts where lawyers lie.
Here we are.

They were gentle witches
with healing spells.
They were desperate witches
with no way out but the other side of hell.

A witch's crying in the night
switches out your children's light.
All your houses safe and warm
are struck at by the witches' storm.
Here we are.

Where have all the witches gone?
Who are the witches now?
Here we are.

They were gentle witches
with healing spells.
They were desperate witches
with no way out but the other side of hell.
Here we are.

Look in the mirror tonight.
Would they have hanged you then?
Ask how they're stopping you now.
Where have the witches gone?
Who are the witches now?
Ask how they're stopping you now.
Here we are.

Scene Twenty Two

SPRENGER: He's Kramer.
KRAMER: He's Sprenger.[2]
KRAMER & SPRENGER: Professors of Theology . . .
KRAMER: . . . delegated by letters apostolic . . .
SPRENGER: (here's a toast, nonalcoholic).
KRAMER: Inquisitors of heretical pravities . . .
SPRENGER: . . . we must fill those moral cavities . . .
KRAMER: . . . so we've written a book . . .
SPRENGER: . . . *Malleus Maleficarum* . . .
KRAMER: . . . *The Hammer of Witches*.
SPRENGER: It works like a charm . . .
KRAMER: . . . to discover witches . . .
SPRENGER: . . . and torture with no hitches.
KRAMER: Why is a greater number of witches found in the fragile feminine sex than
    in men?

---

2. Jakob Sprenger (1436?–1495) and Heinrich Kramer (1430–1505) were the authors of the *Malleus Maleficarum*, or
The Hammer of Witches (1486), a handbook used to determine whether a woman was a witch.

SPRENGER: Why is a greater number of witches found in the fragile feminine sex than in men?

KRAMER: "All wickedness is but little to the wickedness of a woman." Ecclesiastes.

SPRENGER: Here are three reasons, first because . . .

KRAMER: . . . woman is more credulous and since the aim of the devil is to corrupt faith he attacks them. Second because . . .

SPRENGER: . . . women are more impressionable. Third because . . .

KRAMER: . . . women have slippery tongues and cannot conceal from other women what by their evil art they know.

SPRENGER: Women are feebler in both body and mind so it's not surprising.

KRAMER: In intellect they seem to be of a different nature from men . . .

SPRENGER: . . . like children . . .

KRAMER: . . . yes . . .

SPRENGER: . . . but the main reason is . . .

KRAMER & SPRENGER: . . . she is more carnal than a man . . .

KRAMER: . . . as may be seen from her many carnal abominations.

SPRENGER: She was formed from a bent rib . . .

KRAMER: . . . and so is an imperfect animal.

SPRENGER: Fe mina, female, that is fe faith minus without . . .

KRAMER: . . . so cannot keep faith.

SPRENGER: A defect of intelligence.

KRAMER: A defect of inordinate passions.

SPRENGER: They brood on vengeance.

KRAMER & SPRENGER: Wherefore it is no wonder they are witches.

KRAMER: Women have weak memories . . .

SPRENGER: . . . follow their own impulses.

KRAMER: Nearly all the kingdoms of the world have been overthrown by women . . .

SPRENGER: . . . as Troy, etc.

KRAMER: She's a liar by nature . . .

SPRENGER: . . . vain . . .

KRAMER: . . . more bitter than death . . .

SPRENGER: . . . contaminating to touch . . .

KRAMER: . . . their carnal desires . . .

SPRENGER: . . . their insatiable malice . . .

KRAMER: . . . their hands are as bands for binding when they place their hands on a creature to bewitch it with the help of the devil.

SPRENGER: To conclude.

KRAMER: All witchcraft . . .

SPRENGER: . . . comes from carnal lust . . .

KRAMER: . . . which is in woman . . .

KRAMER & SPRENGER: . . . insatiable.

KRAMER: It is no wonder there are more women than men found infected with the heresy of witchcraft.

SPRENGER: And blessed be the Most High, which has so far preserved the male sex from so great a crime.

Evil Women

Evil women
Is that what you want?

Is that what you want to see?
On the movie screen
Of your own wet dream
Evil women.

If you like sex sinful, what you want is us.
You can be sucked off by a succubus.
We had this man, and afterwards he died.

Does she do what she's told or does she nag?
Are you cornered in the kitchen by a bitching hag?
Satan's lady, Satan's pride.
Satan's baby, Satan's bride,
A devil woman's not easily satisfied.

Do you ever get afraid
You don't do it right?
Does your lady demand it
Three times a night?
If we don't say you're big
Do you start to shrink?
We earn our own money
And buy our own drink.

Did you learn you were dirty boys, did you learn
Women were wicked to make you burn?
Satan's lady, Satan's pride,
Satan's baby, Satan's bride,
Witches were wicked and had to burn.

Evil women
Is that what you want?
Is that what you want to see?
In your movie dream
Do they scream and scream?
Evil women
Evil women
Women.   1976

＋⊢ ☰◆☰ ⊣＋

Irena Klepfisz
1941–

IRENA KLEPFISZ is a lesbian poet, a scholar of Yiddish language and literature, and an essayist on
the intersections of Judaism and feminism. Born in Poland, she spent her infancy as one of
500,000 Jews crowded forcibly into the Warsaw ghetto; her father, Michael Klepfisz, a Bundist
and a Nazi resister, was killed in 1943 during the Warsaw ghetto uprising. For the remainder of
World War II Klepfisz and her mother were hidden by Polish peasants. In 1949 mother and
daughter emigrated to the United States via Sweden, eventually settling in New York City in
a community of survivors. After attending both public schools and Workmen's Circle schools

as a youth, Klepfisz earned a B.A. from City College and, later, a Ph.D. in English literature from the University of Chicago. As a postdoctoral fellow at the Institute for Jewish Research, she served as translator-in-residence.

For more than twenty-five years Klepfisz has been a writer and political activist. A founder of the lesbian-feminist journal *Conditions*, she helped to institute the Jewish Women's Committee to End the Occupation of the West Bank and Gaza and worked for two years as director of New Jewish Agenda. Klepfisz has taught women's studies, Judaic studies, Yiddish, and English literature at Columbia University, the University of Illinois, Wake Forest University, and Michigan State University; she has lectured widely and conducted workshops on Yiddish women writers, Jewish secular feminism, women and peace in the Middle East, lesbian identity, homophobia, and anti-Semitism. Klepfisz defines herself as "an incorrigible secularist and socialist, the product of a Bundist upbringing." Though not a Zionist, she explains, "I do feel that I am in *goles*/exile, . . . that I've lost my home, been torn my roots—not the Bible and Israel, but *yidishkayt* and Eastern Europe."

Klepfisz's poems are collected in *A Few Words in the Mother Tongue: Poems Selected and New 1971–1990* (1990). In this volume, she explores memory and loss, the legacy of Jewish people after genocide, and what it means to be a Holocaust survivor or the child of survivors. She also writes of lesbian identity and eroticism, of working-class women in the sexist and classist United States, of Yiddish as the *mame-loshen*, or mother tongue. As ADRIENNE RICH claims in her introduction to *A Few Words in the Mother Tongue*, "because 'history stops for no one,' Klepfisz has gone on to write poetry of uncompromising complexity, clothed in apparently simple, even spare language—simple and bare as the stage of a theater in which strict economies of means release a powerful concentrate of feeling."

During the 1980s Klepfisz coedited (with Melanie Kaye/Kantrowitz) an anthology of Jewish women's writing, *The Tribe of Dina*, published by Beacon Press; and a collection of articles entitled *Jewish Women's Call for Peace*, published by Firebrand Books. Klepfisz's prose has been collected in *Dreams of an Insomniac: Jewish Feminist Essays, Speeches, and Diatribes* (1990). An article on four eastern European women activists' work and writing, "*Di mame, dos los* / The Mothers, the Language: Feminism, *Yidishkayt*, and the Politics of Memory," appeared in the Jewish-feminist journal *Bridges* in 1994. That same year she wrote a scholarly introduction to *Found Treasures: Stories by Yiddish Women*, edited by Frieda Forman et al. Klepfisz has translated a number of Yiddish women poets, including Fradel Schtok and Kadya Molodowsky.

In her poems in response to the Holocaust, Klepfisz confronts the human capacity for atrocity and inscribes both resistance and transformation. "death camp," for instance, depicts in graphic imagery the sights and sounds of burning flesh, thereby singeing the reader's consciousness and conscience. "Bashert," which means "predestined" in Yiddish, traces the impossibility and the necessity of survival. And "Etlekhe verter oyf mame-loshn / A few words in the mother tongue" explores Klepfisz's location as a writer living, in Rich's words, "not only between landscapes, but also between languages; the words of the mother-tongue are handled and savored with extreme delicacy, as a precious yet also tenuous legacy."

⊰ *from* Bashert[1] ⊱

These words are dedicated to those who died

These words are dedicated to those who died
because they had no love and felt alone in the world
because they were afraid to be alone and tried to stick it out

---

1. *Bashert* (Yiddish)—inevitable, predestined.

because they could not ask
because they were shunned
because they were sick and their bodies could not resist the
disease
because they played it safe
because they had no connections
because they had no faith
because they felt they did not belong and wanted to die

These words are dedicated to those who died
because they were loners and liked it
because they acquired friends and drew others to them
because they took risks
because they were stubborn and refused to give up
because they asked for too much

These words are dedicated to those who died
because a card was lost and a number was skipped
because a bed was denied
because a place was filled and no other place was left

These words are dedicated to those who died
because someone did not follow through
because someone was overworked and forgot
because someone left everything to God
because someone was late
because someone did not arrive at all
because someone told them to wait and they just couldn't
any longer

These words are dedicated to those who died
because death is a punishment
because death is a reward
because death is the final rest
because death is eternal rage

These words are dedicated to those who died

Bashert

These words are dedicated to those who survived

These words are dedicated to those who survived
because their second grade teacher gave them books
because they did not draw attention to themselves and got lost
in the shuffle
because they knew someone who knew someone else who could
help them and bumped into them on a corner on a Thursday
afternoon
because they played it safe
because they were lucky

These words are dedicated to those who survived
because they knew how to cut corners
because they drew attention to themselves and always got

picked
because they took risks
because they had no principles and were hard

50   These words are dedicated to those who survived
because they refused to give up and defied statistics
because they had faith and trusted in God
because they expected the worst and were always prepared
because they were angry
55   because they could ask
because they mooched off others and saved their strength
because they endured humiliation
because they turned the other cheek
because they looked the other way

60   These words are dedicated to those who survived
because life is a wilderness and they were savage
because life is an awakening and they were alert
because life is a flowering and they blossomed
because life is a struggle and they struggled
65   because life is a gift and they were free to accept it

These words are dedicated to those who survived

Bashert

                                                                1982

⊰ death camp ⊱

when they took us   to the shower   i saw
the rebitsin[2]   her sagging breasts   sparse
pubic hairs   i knew   and remembered
the old rebe[3]   and turned   my eyes away
5   i could still hear   her advice   a woman
with a husband   a scholar

when they turned   on the gas   i smelled
it   first   coming at me   pressed myself
hard to the wall   crying   rebitsin   rebitsin
10   i am here with you   and the advice you gave me
i screamed   into the wall   as the blood burst from

my lungs   cracking   her nails in women's flesh   i watched

her capsize   beneath me   my blood in her mouth   i screamed

when they dragged my body   into the oven   i burned
15   slowly at first   i could smell my own flesh   and could
hear   them grunt   with the weight of the rebitsin
and they flung   her on top   of me   and i could smell
her hair burning   against my stomach

---

2. Rabbi's wife.   3. Rabbi.

<blockquote>

20
</blockquote>

when i pressed through   the chimney
it was sunny   and clear   my smoke
was distinct   i rose quiet   left her
beneath

1975

⊰ *Etlekhe verter oyf mame-loshn/* ⊱
A few words in the mother tongue

lemoshl: for example

di kurve   the whore
a woman who acknowledges her passions

di yidene   the Jewess   the Jewish woman
5
ignorant   overbearing
let's face it: every woman is one

di yente   the gossip   the busybody
who knows what's what
and is never caught off guard

10
di lezbianke   the one with
a roommate   though we never used
the word

dos vaybl   the wife
or the little woman

*   *   *

15
in der heym   at home
where she does everything to keep
yidishkayt alive

yidishkayt   a way of being
Jewish   always arguable

20
in mark   where she buys
di kartofl un khalah
(yes, potatoes and challah)

di kartofl   the material counterpart of *yidishkayt*

25
mit tsibeles   with onions
that bring *trern tsu di oygn*
tears to her eyes   when she sees
how little it all is
veyniker un veyniker
30
less and less

di khalah   braided
vi ir hor far der khasene
like her hair before the wedding
when she was *aza sheyn meydl*
35
such a pretty girl

di lange shvartse hor
the long black hair
di lange shvartse hor

*   *   *

a froy kholmt   a woman
40   dreams ir ort oyf der velt
her place in this world
un zi hot moyre   and she is afraid
so afraid of the words

kurve
45   yidene
yente
lezbianke
vaybl

zi kholmt   she dreams
50   un zi hot moyre   and she is afraid
ir ort
di velt
di heym
der mark

55   a meydl kholmt
a kurve kholmt
a yidene kholmt
a yente kholmt
a lezbianke kholmt

60   a vaybl kholmt
di kartofl
di khalah

yidishkayt

zi kholmt
65   di hor
di lange shvartse hor

zi kholmt
zi kholmt
zi kholmt

1990

Eavan Boland
1944–

A contemporary Irish poet, EAVAN BOLAND explores links between female identity and the history, culture, and nationhood of Ireland. "I know now that I began writing in a country where the word *woman* and the word *poet* were almost magnetically opposed," wrote Boland in 1995. "One word was used to evoke collective nurture, the other to sketch out self-reflective individualism. . . . I became used to the flawed space between them. In a certain sense I found my poetic voice by shouting across that distance."

Born in Dublin, Boland was educated in London and New York and attended Trinity College, where she later served as a lecturer. She is married to the novelist Kevin Casey, and they have two daughters. For many years she strove to balance writing and mother-hood: "In a house with small children, with no time to waste, I gradually reformed my working habits. I learned that if I could not write a poem, I could make an image, and if I could not make an image, I could take out a word, savor it and store it." In addition to pub-lishing eight acclaimed volumes of poetry, she has written regular reviews for the *Irish Times* and published numerous essays on Irish literary texts and contexts. Boland has docu-mented the dilemma of women poets writing in Ireland in two prose works: *A Kind of Scar: The Woman Poet in a National Tradition* (1989) and *Object Lessons: The Life of the Woman and the Poet in Our Time* (1995). She has taught literature at University College, Dublin, at Bowdoin College in Maine, and in the International Writing Program at the University of Iowa.

Poetry "enters at the point where myth touches history," asserts Boland. Her first vol-umes, *New Territory* (1974), and *The War Horse* (1975), bear witness to her Irish "politics of location." *In Her Own Image* (1980) celebrates women's sexuality and embodiment in lush, defiant language, while *Night Feed* (1982) explores the effects of caring for children on a woman's creativity. *The Journey* (1987) brings a "painterly consciousness" to women in the shadows of Irish history. *Outside History* (1990), Boland's selected poems, takes its title from her belief that the "official" historical record is not the whole story. *In a Time of Vio-lence* probes "the meeting place between womanhood and history," as the poet recalls not only her own younger voice but also the voices of nineteenth-century women silenced by famine and war. Boland's first five volumes of poetry were collected in 1996 in *An Origin Like Water*.

Boland notes in *Object Lessons* that when she began writing in the early 1960s, male poets in Ireland were taken seriously, even honored, while women belonged to an invisible domestic world. By 1995 this was no longer true: "A woman's life—its sexuality, its ritual, its history—has become a brilliantly lit motif, influencing the agenda of culture and commerce alike," she claimed, writing as an Irish woman whose life and art must be politicized. This politicization is evident in *In a Time of Violence*. In the poems included here, Boland meditates on language, his-torical consciousness, and creative process:

> The time of violence in the title happens in the present and in the past. It happens in the soul and the event. It is that demanding state of process where things are revealed about womanhood and identity which lead on to an investigation—in the title sequence—of the poignant and dangerous mischances between expression and experience.

⇥ Inscriptions ⇤

About holiday rooms there can be
a solid feel at first. Then, as you go upstairs,
the air gets
a dry rustle of excitement

5   the way a new dress comes out of tissue paper,
up and out of it, and
the girl watching this thinks:
Where will I wear it? Who will kiss me in it?

Peter
10   was the name on the cot.
The cot was made of the carefully bought
scarcities of the nineteen-forties:
Oak. Tersely planed and varnished.
Cast-steel hinges.

15   I stood where the roof sloped into
paper roses,
in a room where a child once went to sleep,
looking at blue, painted lettering:

as he slept
20   someone had found for him
five pieces of the alphabet which said
the mauve petals of his eyelids as they closed out
the scalded hallway moonlight made of the ocean at
the end of his road.

25   Someone knew
the importance of giving him a name.

For years I have known
how important it is
not to name
30   the coffins, the murdered in them,
the deaths in alleyways and on doorsteps—

in case they rise out of their names
and I recognize

the child who slept peacefully
35   and the girl who guessed at her future in
the dress as it came out of its box,
falling free in
kick pleats of silk.

And what comfort can there be
40   in knowing that
in a distant room
his sign is safe tonight
and reposes its modest blues in darkness?

Or that outside his window
45   the name-eating elements—the salt wind, the rain—
must find
headstones to feed their hunger?

1994

⊰ Writing in a Time of Violence ⊱

In my last year in College
I set out

to write an essay on
the Art of Rhetoric. I had yet to find

5   the country already lost to me
in song and figure as I scribbled down
names for sweet euphony
and safe digression.

And when I came to the word *insinuate*
10   I saw that language could writhe and creep
and the lore of snakes
which I had learned as a child not to fear—
because the Saint had sent them out of Ireland—
came nearer.

15   *Chiasmus. Litotes. Periphrasis.* Old
indices and agents of persuasion. How
I remember them in that room where
a girl is writing at a desk with
dusk already in
20   the streets outside. I can see her. I could say to her—

we will live, we have lived
where language is concealed. Is perilous.
We will be—we have been—citizens
of its hiding place. But it is too late

25   to shut the book of satin phrases,
to refuse to enter
an evening bitter with peat smoke,
where newspaper sellers shout headlines
and friends call out their farewells in
30   a city of whispers
and interiors where

the dear vowels
Irish Ireland ours are
absorbed into Autumn air,
35   are out of earshot in the distances
we are stepping into where we never

imagine words such as *hate*
and *territory* and the like—unbanished still
as they always would be—wait
40   and are waiting under
beautiful speech. To strike.

1994

Zoë Wicomb

1948–

Zoë Wicomb, a South African writer of fiction and literary criticism, was born in the Western Cape Province in an isolated Griqua ("colored") settlement near Vredendal, outside of Cape Town. Educated in the local school and encouraged by her father, a teacher, she began at age nine to write poetry in Afrikaans, the official language of apartheid South Africa. As an adolescent she was sent to an English-speaking school in Cape Town, where she felt humiliated when her mother showed her poems to a condescending white teacher of Afrikaans; for a time she stopped writing altogether. Wicomb completed an arts degree at the University of the Western Cape, one of the few South African universities that racially mixed Africans could attend in the 1960s. In 1970 she left for England to study literature at Reading University, where she became fascinated with the fiction of BESSIE HEAD—like her, a woman classified as "colored" under apartheid and a voluntary exile from South Africa. But in England Wicomb again felt silenced. "The subtle British racism made me feel that it would be presumptuous of me to write and even to speak. . . . It took a very long time, and immense effort, to find my voice." During the 1980s she divided her time between writing and teaching English and women's studies at the University of Nottingham; she was also active in the antiapartheid movement. In 1991 Wicomb returned to South Africa to teach at the University of the Western Cape. She has been a visiting professor at the University of Strathclyde and serves on the editorial board of the *South African Review of Books*.

Wicomb's critically acclaimed volume of fiction, *You Can't Get Lost in Cape Town* (1987), chronicles the emotional and political growth of Frieda Shenton, a young South African who is racially mixed. From her rural childhood to her departure for boarding school, from her sexual awakening to her complicated homecoming, Frieda struggles to find a space from which to speak. Wicomb is ambivalent toward the critical praise she won for this collection, some of which she calls "solidarity criticism"; she considers her book "overwritten." As the critic Dorothy Driver notes, however, what Wicomb considers excessive language can be seen as discursive play. Wicomb's stories have appeared in *The Penguin Book of Southern African Stories* (1985), *Colors of a New Day* (1990), and *World Literature Today* (1996). Her novel-in-progress presents the postapartheid conflicts of former revolutionaries now dissatisfied with daily life. In this work Wicomb participates in a South African literary project that INGRID DE KOK has described as "unmaking and remaking *inheritance* . . . after a censored, exiled and broken history."

As a critic Wicomb advocates multiculturalism: "If cultural diversity is not celebrated, there seems little hope that a national literature will be able to avoid the monocultural hell to which nationalism can be prone." She is concerned with gender as well as race and class. During the transition from apartheid, she complains, political discourse has not "taken into account what women are actually saying. . . . The discourse of feminism ought to inform the national liberation struggle." Wicomb clarifies her views in "To Hear the Variety of Discourses," an essay first published in 1990 in *Current Writing: Text and Reception in Southern Africa*. If South Africa is to find a literary theory appropriate to its own situation, she argues, it must privilege a "conflictual model of society" to which various discourses respond. Neither womanism, which she considers insufficient to challenge African men's sexism, nor feminism, which too often is created by and for white women, will suffice. Instead, she calls for "an aligned feminist criticism" for the twenty-first century—a criticism that is transnational, nonracial, and multivoiced.

The story included here, "Bowl Like Hole," examines the inequities of apartheid from the perspective of a curious girl. Internationalized oppression, racism, and linguistic imperialism are key themes in this quietly ironic tale.

⊰ Bowl Like Hole ⊱

At first Mr. Weedon came like any white man in a motor car, inquiring about sheep or goats or servants.

A vehicle swerving meteor-bright across the veld signaled a break in the school day as rows of children scuttled out to hide behind the corner, their fingers plugged into their nostrils with wonder and admiration. They examined the tracks of the car or craned their necks in turn to catch a glimpse of the visitor even though all white men looked exactly the same. Others exploited the break to find circuitous routes to the bank of squat ghanna bushes where they emptied their bowels and bladders. On such occasions they did not examine each other's genitals. They peered through the scant foliage to admire the shiny vehicle from a safe distance. They brushed against the bushes, competing to see, so that the shriveled little leaf-balls twisted and showered into dust. From this vantage point they would sit, pants down, for the entire visit while the visitor conducted his business from the magnificence of his car.

At an early age I discovered the advantage of curling up motionless in moments of confusion, a position which in further education I found to be fetal. On these topsy-turvy days I crept at great risk of being spotted to the kitchen which jutted out at a near ninety degrees of mud-brick wall from the school building. Under the narrow rectangular table I lay very still. The flutter inside subsided the instant I drew my knees up and became part of the arrangement of objects, shared in the solidity of the table and the cast-iron buckets full of water lined up on it. I could depend on Mamma being too absorbed by the event to notice me. Or if she did, she would not shout while the car squinted at the kitchen door.

So under the kitchen table I invariably found myself when vehicles arrived. And at first Mr. Weedon arrived like any other white man inquiring about sheep or goats or servants.

As the time between sunrises and sunsets began to arrange itself into weeks and months and seasons, Mr. Weedon's arrivals became regular. Something to do with the tax year, at the end of March, Mamma explained. The children still ran out to whisper and admire from a distance, and I with a new knowledge of geography still crept under the kitchen table, but with the buckets of water was now swept along on the earth's elliptical journey around the sun.

Mr. Weedon spoke not one word of Afrikaans.[1] For people who were born in England the g's and r's of the language were impossible, barbaric.

"A gentleman, a true Englishman," Mamma said as she handed Father his best hat. For the Mercedes could be seen miles away, a shining disc spun in a cloud of dust. A week or so after the autumn equinox he arrived. He did not blow a horn like the uncouth Boers from the dorp. There was no horn in the back seat. Neither did he roll down a window to rest a forearm on the door. Perhaps the chrome was too hot even in autumn and he did not wish to scorch the blond hairs on his arm. With the help of the person who occupied the driver's seat, Mr. Weedon's door was opened, and despite a light skirmish between the two men, he landed squarely on both feet. The cloud of dust produced by the car and the minor struggle subsided. So Mr. Weedon puffed deeply on a thick cigar, producing a cloud of smoke. Mr. Weedon loved

---

1. The language spoken by the Dutch settlers of South Africa, some of whose ancestors were the architects of apartheid. This language is also spoken by many racially mixed citizens of South Africa's Western Cape province.

clouds. Which may explain why his eyes roved about as he spoke, often to rest pon-
derously on a fleecy cloud above.

"A true gentleman," Mamma whispered to herself from the kitchen window as
he shook hands with Father, "these Boers could learn a few things from him."

"Well and how are you, how's the wife?" The English r's slid along without the
vibration of tongue against palate. Mamma's asthma mentioned, he explained how
his wife suffered with hers. And Cape Town so damp in winter she was forced to
spend a hideous season in the Bahamas. Father tutted sympathetically. He would
hate to spend several days away from home, let alone months.

"Yes," said Mr. Weedon, braiding his lapel with delicate fingers. How frail we all
are . . . an uncertain world . . . even health cannot be bought . . . we must all march
past as Death the Leveler makes his claim, and he looked up at a floating cloud in
support of his theory of transience.

Father too held his chin slightly to the left, his goiter lifted as he scanned the sky.
Possibly to avoid the cigar smoke, for he supported the school of thought that doubted
whether God intended man to smoke; why else had he not provided him with a chimney?

Mr. Weedon dropped his cigar and rubbed his palms together, which indicated
that he was ready for the discussion held annually in the schoolroom. Father smiled,
"Certainly," and tapped the black ledger already tucked under his arm. He rushed to
open the door and another cloud of dust ensued as the man who opened doors tried
to oust him. Everyone mercifully kept their balance and the man retreated sourly to
lean against his Mercedes.

"Good heavens," whispered Mamma, "he's picking his nose." Was she talking to
me? Even in the topsy-turviness of the day I dared not say anything, ask who or
where. Only the previous day I had been viciously dragged by the hair from under the
table with threats of thrashings if ever I was found there again. It was not worth the
risk. Fortunately she went on. "I wouldn't be surprised if he were Colored,[2] from
Cape Town I suppose, a play-white . . . one can never tell with Capetonians. Or perhaps a registered Colored. Mr. Weedon being a civilized man might not mind a
brown person driving his car."

So she knew that I was there, must have known all along, for I had been careful
not to move. I turned my head towards the window and through the iron crossbars of
the table saw in her two great buttocks the opposing worlds she occupied. The humiliation of the previous day still smarted; she was not to be trusted and I pursed my lips
in disgust when she sat down, occupying her two worlds so fully.

"Oom Klaas Dirkse has been off work again. You must take him an egg and a
mug of milk, and no playing on the way."

A brief silence, then she carried on, "And I've warned you not to speak
Afrikaans to the children. They ought to understand English and it won't hurt them
to try. Your father and I managed and we all have to put up with things we don't
understand. Anyway, those Dirkse children have lice; you're not to play with them."

As if the Dirkse children would want to play with me. Kaatjie Dirkse may lower
her head and draw up her thin shoulders, but her plaited horns would stand erect and
quiver their contempt.

Oh how Mamma spoiled things. The space under the table grew into the vast
open veld so that I pressed against the wall and bored my chin into clasped knees.

---

2. Under apartheid legislation people were classified according to four racial and hierarchical categories: White, Indian,
Colored (racially mixed), and Black. Boers are white South Africans of Dutch descent.

Outside the shiny Capetonian leaned against his car; only Kaatjie Dirkse would have dared to slink past him with a single sullen glare. The murmur from the schoolroom rose and fell and I was glad, very glad, that Kaatjie's horns crawled with lice.

"Stay there, you're not to hang over the lower door and gawp," Mamma hissed unnecessarily. She heard the shuffling towards the school door and, finding her hands empty, reached for the parts of our new milk separator. These she started to assemble, tentatively clicking the parts into place, then confidently, as if her finger-tips drew strength from the magic machine. Its scarecrow arms flung resolutely apart, the assembled contraption waited for the milk that it would drive through the aluminium maze and so frighten into separation. I watched her pour the calf's milk into the bowl and turn the handle viciously to drown the sound of the men's shuffling conversation outside. Out of the left arm the startled thin bluish milk spurted, and seconds later yellow cream trickled confidently from the right.

"That's Flossie's milk. She's not had any today," I accused.

"We'll milk again tonight. There'll be more tonight," and her eyes begged as if she were addressing the cow herself, as if her life depended on the change of routine.

Father did not report back to the kitchen. He was shown to the front seat of the car in order to accompany Mr. Weedon to the gypsum mine on the edge of the settlement. Mr. Weedon's cigar smoke wrapped itself in blue bands around Father's neck. He coughed and marveled at the modesty of the man who preferred to sit alone in the back seat of his own car.

Children tumbled out from behind the schoolroom or the ghanna bushes to stare at the departing vehicle. Little ones recited the CA 3654 of the number plate and carried the transported look throughout the day. The older boys freed their nostrils and with hands plunged in their pockets suggested by a new swaggering gait that it was not so wonderful a spectacle after all. How could it be if their schoolmaster was carried away in the Mercedes? But it was, because Father was the only person for miles who knew enough English, who could interpret. And Mr. Weedon had a deep fear of appearing foolish. What if he told a joke and the men continued to look at him blankly, or if they with enameled faces said something irreverent or just something not very nice? How they would laugh later at his blank or smiling face. For Mr. Weedon understood more than he admitted, and was not above the occasional pretense.

With Father by his side Mr. Weedon said the foreign Good Afternoon to the miners, followed by a compliment on how well they looked, their naked torsos glistening with sweat, rivaling only the glory of the pink desert rose that they heaved out of the earth. Distanced by the translation, the winged words fluttered; he was moved to a poetic comparison. A maddening rhythm as the picks swung with a bulge of biceps in unison, up, cutting the air, the blades striking the sunbeams in one long stroke of lightning; then down the dark torsos fell, and a crash of thunder as the blades struck the earth, baring her bosom of rosy gypsum. Mr. Weedon, so overcome, was forced to look away, at a cloud that raced across the sky with such apparent panting that in all decency he had to avert his eyes once again.

And so midst all that making of poetry, two prosaic mounds rose on either side of the deepening pit. One of these would ultimately blend in with the landscape; fine dust cones would spin off it in the afternoons just as they spun off the hills that had always been there. There was no telling, unless one kicked ruthlessly and fixed an expert eye on the telltale tiredness of the stone, that this hill was born last year and that had always been. The other mound of gypsum was heaved by the same glistening torsos on to lorries that arrived at the end of the week. These hobbled over gravel roads to the siding at Moedverloor from where the transformed plaster of paris was carried away.

Mr. Weedon turned a lump of jagged gypsum in the sun so that its crystal peaks shimmered like a thousand stars in the dead stone.

"For my daughter," he said, "a sample of nature's bounty. She collects rocks, just loves the simple things in life. It's nature, the simple things," he said to Father, who could not decide whether to translate or not, "the simple things that bring the greatest joy. Oh Sylvia would love our Brakwater, such stark beauty," and his gaze shifted . . . "the men are doing a marvelous job" . . . as his eyes settled on a rippled chest thrown back.

"These manmade mountains and the bowls they once fitted into, beautiful and very useful for catching the rain, don't you think?"

So he had no idea that it never rained more than the surface of the earth could hold, enough to keep the dust at rest for a day or so. Father decided not to translate.

"Tell them that I'm very happy with things," and he turned, clicking his fingers at the man who opened doors. An intricate system of signals thus triggered itself off. The boot of the car flew open, a cardboard box appeared, and after a particularly united blow at the rock the men laid down their picks and waited in semaphoric obedience. Mr. Weedon smiled. Then they stepped forward holding out their hands to receive the green and white packet of Cavalla cigarettes that the smiling man dealt out. Descants of "Dankie Meneer"[3] and he flushed with pleasure for he had asked many times before not to be called Baas as the Boers insisted on being called. This time not one of the men made a mistake or even stuttered over the words. A day to be remembered, as he reviewed the sinewed arms outstretched, synchronized with simple words of thanks and the happy contingent of the kind angle of sun so that a bead of sweat could not gather at his brow and at a critical moment bounce on to the green and white Cavalla packet, or, and here he clenched his teeth, trail along the powdered arm of a miner who would look away in disgust.

"I don't smoke thank you, sir," Father seemed very tall as his rigid arm held out the box. Mr. Weedon's musings on harmony splintered to the dissonance of Father's words, so that he stared vacantly at the box of one hundred Cavallas held at him between thumb and index finger. Where in God's name was the man who opened doors?

Was the wind changing direction? Moisture seeped on to his brow and little mercurial drops rolled together until a shining bead gathered dead center then slid perpendicularly to the tip of his nose where it waited. Mr. Weedon brushed the back of his hand across the lower half of his face, rubbed the left jaw in an improvised itch and said, "Well we must be off." The box of cigarettes had somehow landed in his free arm.

The men waited, leaning on their picks, and with the purr of the engine shouted a musical Goodbye Sir in Afrikaans, words which Mr. Weedon fortunately knew the meaning of. The wheels swung, a cigar moved across the back window and a cloud of dust swallowed all. The men screwed their eyes and tried to follow the vehicle. When it finally disappeared over the ridge they took up their picks once more.

"Here he co-omes," the children crooned, as they do about all vehicles flashing in the distance. I ran to meet Father who would be dropped just above the school. From behind a bush I watched the Mercedes move on. A cloud of dust shaped itself into a festive trail following the car. A dozen brackhounds, spaced at intervals along

3. "Thank you, sir" (Afrikaans).

the road and barking theatrically, ran in the manner of a relay race alongside the vehicle until the next dog took over.

I trotted to keep up with Father's long stride, my hand locked in his. His eyes like the miners' were red-rimmed in his powdered face. He handed me a lump of gypsum which I turned about in the sun until its crystal peaks shimmered like a thousand stars in the dead stone.

"That was quick," Mamma said. Obscure words of praise that would invite him to give a full account.

"Funny," Father replied, "Mr. Weedon said that the mine was like a bowl in the earth. Bowl like hole, not bowl like howl. Do you think that's right?"

She frowned. She had been so sure. She said, "Of course, he's English, he ought to know."

Then, unexpectedly, interrupting Father as he gave details of the visit, she turned on me. "And don't you think you'll get away with it, sitting under the table like a tame Griqua."[4]

But revenge did not hold her attention. A wry smile fluttered about her lips. She muttered. "Fowl, howl, scowl and not bowl." She would check the pronunciation of every word she had taken for granted.

I knew that unlike the rest of us it would take her no time at all to say bowl like hole, smoothly, without stuttering.   1987

⊁◆⊱

Carolyn Forché
1950–

Raised in rural Michigan near Detroit, CAROLYN FORCHÉ began writing poems at age nine with her mother's encouragement. "I think I used writing as an escape," the poet has explained. "Writing and daydreaming. . . . I suspected, when I was young, that this was madness, but I couldn't give it up." Forché was educated at Michigan State University and received her M.F.A. from Bowling Green State University in 1975. The sense of urgency that she attributes to her childhood writing also characterizes her three volumes of poetry: *Gathering the Tribes*, which won the Yale Series of Younger Poets Award in 1975; *The Country Between Us*, the Lamont Poetry Selection for 1981 from the Academy of American Poets; and *The Angel of History* (1994), which received the Los Angeles Times Book Award for Poetry.

Poet Stanley Kunitz, who chose *Gathering the Tribes* for the Yale Award, has described it as a work centered on kinship in which the poet "remembers her childhood in rural Michigan, evokes her Slovak ancestors, immerses herself in the American Indian culture of the Southwest, explores the mysteries of flesh, tries to understand the bonds of family, race, and sex." During the five years between her first and second volumes she worked with Amnesty International as a journalist and a human rights activist in El Salvador, where she witnessed firsthand the starvation of countless children who lacked access to modern medicine and the disappearance and dismemberment of Salvadoran *campesinos* at the hands of paramilitary death squads attempting to quell a revolution. One result of this experience was the poetry of *The Country Between Us*. Forché has claimed that although she tried not to write poems about El Salvador, the poems refused to stop coming. "There is no such thing as nonpolitical poetry," she argues; what matters is the quality of the poet's engagement, which is reflected not only in writing but in the whole of one's life.

---

4. A name given to one group of "colored" Africans living in rural areas in the Western Cape Province.

For several years after returning from El Salvador, Forché could not write poems; instead, she traveled with her husband, Harry Mattison, a photojournalist, to countries wracked by wars past or present—Ireland, Mexico, Japan, Lebanon, South Africa—keeping notebooks and sketches. From these fragments emerged a new poetic form and voice: "the first-person free verse lyric-narrative poem of my earlier years has given way to a work which has desired its own bodying forth: broken, haunted, and in ruins, with no possibility of restoration." *The Angel of History* inscribes this change, exploring the aftermath of World War II and referring as well to the poet's experiences in El Salvador and Lebanon. The title figure was first imagined by the German critic and philosopher Walter Benjamin as a recorder of human misery who lacks the power to heal the suffering he sees; Forché depicts the angel similarly as a witness to horror who bears the weight of the century's burdens and serves as an apocalyptic muse to the weary poet. Reviewer Calvin Bedient has praised *The Angel of History* as "instantly recognizable as a great book, the most humanitarian and aesthetically 'inevitable' response to a half-century of atrocities that has yet been written in English." It offers "a new tone, at once sensitive and bleak; a new rhythm, at once prose-like and exquisite; a new line and method of sequencing, at once fluid and fragmentary."

In addition to her poetry, Forché has edited (with Martha Jane Soltow) an annotated bibliography, *Women in the Labor Movement, 1835–1925,* and *Women and War in El Salvador* (1980). She has translated Salvadoran poet Claribel Alegria's *Flores del volcan/Flowers from the Volcano* (1982) into English and has published poems and essays in such journals as *American Poetry Review, The New York Times Book Review, Atlantic Monthly,* and *Ms.* Moreover, she has edited an anthology of twentieth-century poetry of witness, *Against Forgetting* (1993), which reveals the barbarism evident across cultures. Forché describes this volume as a tribute to "144 poets who endured conditions of historical and social extremity during the twentieth century—through exile, state censorship, political persecution, house arrest, torture, imprisonment, military occupation, warfare, and assassination."

Forché has written extensively on what it means to be a poet of witness at the start of a new century. The poet cannot remove herself from situations of extremity, she declares, and proximity to the terror brings with it the risk of being wounded. Poems can no longer be easily categorized as either personal or political; metaphor may be inadequate to the task of naming the unnameable:

> The witness who writes out of extremity writes his or her wound, as if such writing were making an incision. . . . The self is fragmented and the vessel of self breaks into shards. . . . The narrative also breaks. At the site of the wound, language breaks, interrogates itself, becomes tentative, kaleidoscopic.

Such fragmented language is characterized by questions, aphorisms, quotations, bits of memory and conversation, severed lyrical passages. Forché's poems serve as newsreels from a war correspondent, testimonies to the power and resilience of the human spirit.

⊰ The Colonel ⊱

WHAT YOU HAVE HEARD is true. I was in his house. His wife carried a tray of coffee and sugar. His daughter filed her nails, his son went out for the night. There were daily papers, pet dogs, a pistol on the cushion beside him. The moon swung bare on its black cord over the house. On the television was a cop show. It was in English. Broken bottles were embedded in the walls around the house to scoop the kneecaps from a man's legs or cut his hands to lace. On the windows there were gratings like those in liquor stores. We had dinner, rack of lamb, good wine, a gold bell was on the table for calling the maid. The maid brought green mangoes, salt, a type of bread. I was asked how I enjoyed the country. There was a brief commercial

in Spanish. His wife took everything away. There was some talk then of how difficult it had become to govern. The parrot said hello on the terrace. The colonel
told it to shut up, and pushed himself from the table. My friend said to me with his
eyes: say nothing. The colonel returned with a sack used to bring groceries home.
He spilled many human ears on the table. They were like dried peach halves.
There is no other way to say this. He took one of them in his hands, shook it in
our faces, dropped it into a water glass. It came alive there. I am tired of fooling
around he said. As for the rights of anyone, tell your people they can go fuck
themselves. He swept the ears to the floor with his arm and held the last of his
wine in the air. Something for your poetry, no? he said. Some of the ears on the
floor caught this scrap of his voice. Some of the ears on the floor were pressed to
the ground.

1978/1981

⊰ Message ⊱

Your voices sprayed over the walls
dry to the touch by morning.
Your women walk among *champas*
with baskets of live hens, grenades and fruit.
5   Tonight you begin to fight
for the most hopeless of revolutions.
Pedro, you place a host on each
man's chant of *Body of Christ Amen.*
Margarita, you slip from your house
10   with plastiques wrapped in newsprint,
the dossier of your dearest friend
whose hair grew to the floor of her cell.
Leonel, you load your bare few guns
with an idea for a water pump and
15   cooperative farm.
                    You will fight
and fighting, you will die. I will live
and living cry out until my voice is gone
to its hollow of earth, where with our
20   hands and by the lives we have chosen
we will dig deep into our deaths.
I have done all that I could do.
Link hands, link arms with me
in the next of lives everafter,
25   where we will not know each other
or ourselves, where we will be a various
darkness among ideas that amounted
to nothing, among men who amounted
to nothing, with a belief that became
30   but small light
in the breadth of time where we began
among each other, where we lived
in the hour farthest from God.

1980/1981

⫷ Ourselves or Nothing ⫸

For Terrence Des Pres

After seven years and as the wine
leaves and black trunks of maples wait
beyond the window, I think of you
north, in the few lighted rooms
5   of that ruined house, a candle in each
open pane of breath, the absence of anyone,
snow in a hurry to earth, my fingernails
pressing half moons into the sill
as I watched you pouring three
10   then four fingers of Scotch over ice,
the chill in your throat like a small
blue bone, those years of your work
on the Holocaust. You had to walk
off the darkness, miles of winter
15   riverfront, windows the eyes in skulls
along the river, gratings in the streets
over jeweled human sewage, your breath
hanging about your face like tobacco.
I was with you even then, your face
20   the face of a clock as you swept
through the memoirs of men and women
who would not give up. In the short light
of Decembers, you took suppers of whole
white hens and pans of broth
25   in a city of liquor bottles and light.
Go after that which is lost
and all the mass graves of the century's dead
will open into your early waking hours:
Belsen, Dachau, Saigon, Phnom Penh
30   and the one meaning Bridge of Ravens,
Sao Paulo, Armagh, Calcutta, Salvador,
although these are not the same.
You wrote too of Theresienstadt,[1]
that word that ran screaming into
35   my girlhood, lifting its grey wool dress,
the smoke in its violent plumes and feathers,
the dark wormy heart of the human desire to die.
In Prague, Anna[2] told me, there was bread,
stubborn potatoes and fish, armies and the women
40   who lie down with them, eggs perhaps but never
meat, never meat but the dead.
In Theresienstadt she said there was only the dying.
Never bread, potatoes, fish or women.
They were all as yet girls then.

---

1. Belsen, Dachau, and Theresienstadt were concentration camps in which Jewish people were exterminated during World War II. Terrence Des Pres (d.1987) was the author of *The Survivor*, to which Forché alludes. She refers as well to the wars in Viet Nam, El Salvador, and Northern Ireland.
2. Anna was the poet's Czech grandmother.

45   *Vast numbers of men and women died,* you wrote,
        because they did not have time, the blessing
        of sheer time, to recover. Your ration of time
        was smaller then, a tin spoon of winter,
        piano notes one at a time from the roof
50   to the gutter. I am only imagining this,
        as I had not yet entered your life
        like the dark fact of a gun on your pillow,
        or Anna Akhmatova's "Requiem"[3]
        and its final *I can* when the faceless woman
55   before her asked *can you describe this?*
        I was not yet in your life when you turned
        the bullet toward the empty hole in yourself
        and whispered: finish this or die.
        But you lived and what you wrote became
60   *The Survivor,* that act of contrition for despair:
        They turned to face the worst
        straight-on, without sentiment or hope,
        simply to keep watch over life. Now,
        as you sleep face down on your papers,
65   the book pages turning of themselves
        in your invisible breath, I climb
        the stairs of that house, fragile
        with age and the dry fear of burning
        and I touch the needle to music to wake you,
70   the snow long past falling, something
        by Vivaldi or Brahms.[4]
        I have come from our cacophonous
        ordinary lives where I stood at the sink
        last summer scrubbing mud from potatoes
75   and listening to the supper fish
        in the skillet, my eyes on the narrowed
        streets of rain through the window
        as I thought of the long war
        that misted country turned to the moon's surface,
80   gray and ring-wormed with ridges of light.
        the women in their silk *ao dais* along
        the river, those flowers under fire, rolled
        at night in the desperate arms of American men.
        Once I walked your rooms with my
85   nightdress open, a cigarette from my lips
        to the darkness and back as you worked
        at times through to the morning.
        Always on my waking you were gone,
        the blue holes of your path through snow
90   to the road, your face still haggard
        in the white mirror, the pained note

---

3. Anna Akhmatova (1889–1966) was a Russian poet whose long poem "Requiem" (1963) links her personal tragedies with those of her country.

4. Antonio Vivaldi (1678–1741) and Johannes Brahms (1833–1897) were composers of classical music.

where ten times you had written
the word *recalcitrance* and once:
you will die and live

95 *under the name of someone*
who has actually died.
I think of that night in a tropic hotel,
the man who danced with a tray over his head
and offered us free because we were *socialistas,*

100 not only that, he sang, but young and pretty.
Later as I lay on a cot in the heat naked
my friend was able to reach for the guns
and load them clicking in the moonlight
with only the barest of sounds;

105 he had heard them before me moving among the palms.
We were going to die there.
I remember the moon notching its way
through the palms and the calm sense that came
for me at the end of my life. In that moment

110 the woman beside me became my sister,
her hand cupping her mouth, the blood
that would later spill from her face
if what we believed were the truth.
Her blood would crawl black and belly-down

115 onto a balcony of hands and flashlights,
cameras, flowers, propaganda.
Her name was Renée and without knowing
her you wrote: *all things human take time,*
time which the damned never have, time for life

120 *to repair at least the worst of its wounds;*
it took time to wake, time for horror
to incite revolt, time for the recovery
of lucidity and will.
In the late afternoons you returned,

125 the long teeth shining from the eaves,
a clink in the wood half-burnt
and as you touched it alive:
ici repose un déporté inconnu.[5]
In the mass graves, a woman's hand

130 caged in the ribs of her child,
a single stone in Spain beneath olives,
in Germany the silent windy fields,
in the Soviet Union where the snow
is scarred with wire, in Salvador

135 where the blood will never soak
into the ground, everywhere and always
go after that which is lost.
There is a cyclone fence between
ourselves and the slaughter and behind it

---

5. Here lies an unknown victim of the Holocaust.

140   we hover in a calm protected world like
    netted fish, exactly like netted fish.
    It is either the beginning or the end
    of the world, and the choice is ourselves
    or nothing.

1981

⇥ The Garden Shukkei-en[6] ⇤

By way of a vanished bridge we cross this river
as a cloud of lifted snow would ascend a mountain.

She has always been afraid to come here.

    It is the river she most
5   remembers, the living
    and the dead both crying for help.

A world that allowed neither tears nor lamentation.

The *matsu* trees brush her hair as she passes
beneath them, as do the shining strands of barbed wire.

10 Where this lake is, there was a lake,
    where these black pine grow, there grew black pine.

Where there is no teahouse I see a wooden teahouse
and the corpses of those who slept in it.

On the opposite bank of the Ota, a weeping willow
15 etches its memory of their faces into the water.

Where light touches the face, the character for heart is written.

She strokes a burnt trunk wrapped in straw:
I was weak and my skin hung from my fingertips like cloth

Do you think for a moment we were human beings to them?

20 She comes to the stone angel holding paper cranes.
    Not an angel, but a woman where she once had been,

who walks through the garden Shukkei-en
calling the carp to the surface by clapping her hands.

Do Americans think of us?

25 So she began as we squatted over the toilets:
    If you want, I'll tell you, but nothing I say will be enough.

We tried to dress our burns with vegetable oil.

Her hair is the white froth of rice rising up kettlesides, her mind also.
In the postwar years she thought deeply about how to live.

---

6. An ornamental garden in Hiroshima that was restored after the city was destroyed by a nuclear bomb in 1945.

30   The common greeting *dozo-yiroshku* is please take care of me.
     All *hibakusha*[7] still alive were children then.

     A cemetery seen from the air is a child's city.

     I don't like this particular red flower because
     it reminds me of a woman's brain crushed under a roof.

     Perhaps my language is too precise, and therefore difficult to understand?

     We have not, all these years, felt what you call happiness.
     But at times, with good fortune, we experience something close.
     As our life resembles life, and this garden the garden.
     And in the silence surrounding what happened to us

40   it is the bell to awaken God that we've heard ringing.

                            1994

⊰ The Testimony of Light ⊱

Our life is a fire dampened, or a fire shut up in stone.
            —*Jacob Boehme, De Incarnatione Verbi*[8]

     Outside everything visible and invisible a blazing maple.
     Daybreak: a seam at the curve of the world. The trousered legs of the
          women shimmered.
     They held their arms in front of them like ghosts.

5   The coal bones of the house clinked in a kimono of smoke.
     An attention hovered over the dream where the world had been.

     For if Hiroshima in the morning, after the bomb has fallen,
        is like a dream, one must ask whose dream it is.[9]

     Must understand how not to speak would carry it with us.
10   With bones put into rice bowls.
     While the baby crawled over its dead mother seeking milk.

     Muga-muchu:[10] without self, without center. Thrown up in the sky by a wind.

     The way back is lost, the one obsession.
     The worst is over.
15   The worst is yet to come.

                            1994

---

7. Women who were burned by nuclear fallout as children but survived the bombing of Hiroshima.
8. Jacob Boehme (1575–1624) was a German mystic.
9. Forché notes that this question is asked by Peter Schwenger in *Letter Bomb: Nuclear Holocaust and the Exploding Word* (1992).
10. A term taken from Robert Jay Lifton's *Death in Life: Survivors of Hiroshima* (1967).

⊶ ⊰◆⊱ ⊷

Louise Erdrich

1954–

What gives LOUISE ERDRICH'S fiction its "heartbreaking fierceness?" wonders the novelist Anne Tyler. "Is it her unblinking gaze—her firm refusal to overlook the less than beautiful? Is it the hammered clarity of her language, or the grace with which she slips from realistic to mythic and back again?" Whatever the source of her narrative skill, Erdrich is one of the finest contemporary Native American writers. With the publication of *Love Medicine* (1984), which won the National Book Critics Circle Award, she began a series of novels that engage Indian history and legends even as they chronicle the complexities of Native life in the twentieth century.

Erdrich was raised in Wahpeton, North Dakota, on the Turtle Mountain Reservation, where her maternal grandmother had once been tribal chief; her Chippewa mother and German-American father both taught at the Bureau of Indian Affairs boarding school there. As a child she wrote stories for her family, which they subsequently "published" in notebooks for safekeeping, and early on she aspired to become a writer. She has worked in road construction, edited the Boston Indian Council's newsletter, and taught poetry in the schools. After graduating from Dartmouth College in 1976, she earned her M.F.A. at Johns Hopkins University before returning to Dartmouth as writer-in-residence. Erdrich has five children and was married to the writer Michael Dorris from 1981 until his death in 1997.

Each of Erdrich's novels contains an intricately woven group of stories that defies chronology. In *Love Medicine* readers meet the Kashpaws, Lazarres, Nanapushes, and Lamartines, as Erdrich traces each family's history from 1934 to 1984. *The Beet Queen* presents a mother-daughter saga that further explores these families' histories. *Tracks* (1988), notes one reviewer, "has the quiet pull of [Erdrich's] other work but feels even truer and more unerring in its arc"; in this novel Erdrich "writes unflinchingly about God and love and hunger and death and vengeance—the forces that can save or devastate an entire culture." *The Bingo Palace* (1994) focuses on Lipsha Morrissey, who enlists the aid of his great-grandmother in concocting a love medicine; the dilemmas that follow raise questions of ethics, economics, and traditional Native culture. *Tales of Burning Love* (1996) presents the saga of four wives of Jack Mauser, each of whom recounts what the author calls a "strange mixture of devotion and misunderstanding," while *The Antelope Wife* (1998) features, among other characters, a man who nurses a foundling with his own breast milk.

Other works by Erdrich include *The Crown of Columbus* (1991), a novel written with Michael Dorris, two volumes of poetry, and a memoir. Named by the *San Francisco Chronicle* as an outstanding book of poetry for 1984, *Jacklight* presents Potchikoo, a Chippewa trickster interested in sex and mischief. *Baptism of Desire* (1987) features poems of redemption and grace that are populated by sinners, saints, and figures from mythology. In 1995 Erdrich published *The Blue Jay's Dance: A Birth Year*, which documents a year she spent at home with her newborn daughter.

The story included here, "Fleur," was first published in *Esquire* magazine in 1986 and later appeared as a chapter in *Tracks*. A modern allegory, it chronicles the life of a Chippewa woman who causes men to disappear or die mysteriously. "Fleur" tells the story of how she "almost destroyed the town," and how it tried to destroy her.

⊰ Fleur ⊱

The first time she drowned in the cold and glassy waters of Lake Turcot, Fleur Pillager was only a girl. Two men saw the boat tip, saw her struggle in the waves. They rowed over to the place she went down, and jumped in. When they dragged her over the gunwales, she was cold to the touch and stiff, so they slapped her face, shook her by the heels, worked her arms back and forth, and pounded her back until she coughed up lake water. She shivered all over like a dog, then took a breath. But it wasn't long afterward that those two men disappeared. The first wandered off, and the other, Jean Hat, got himself run over by a cart.

It went to show, my grandma said. It figured to her, all right. By saving Fleur Pillager, those two men had lost themselves.

The next time she fell in the lake, Fleur Pillager was twenty years old and no one touched her. She washed onshore, her skin a dull dead gray, but when George Many Women bent to look closer, he saw her chest move. Then her eyes spun open, sharp black riprock, and she looked at him. "You'll take my place," she hissed. Everybody scattered and left her there, so no one knows how she dragged herself home. Soon after that we noticed Many Women changed, grew afraid, wouldn't leave his house, and would not be forced to go near water. For his caution, he lived until the day that his sons brought him a new tin bathtub. Then the first time he used the tub he slipped, got knocked out, and breathed water while his wife stood in the other room frying breakfast.

Men stayed clear of Fleur Pillager after the second drowning. Even though she was good-looking, nobody dared to court her because it was clear that Misshepeshu, the waterman, the monster, wanted her for himself. He's a devil, that one, love-hungry with desire and maddened for the touch of young girls, the strong and daring especially, the ones like Fleur.

Our mothers warn us that we'll think he's handsome, for he appears with green eyes, copper skin, a mouth tender as a child's. But if you fall into his arms, he sprouts horns, fangs, claws, fins. His feet are joined as one and his skin, brass scales, rings to the touch. You're fascinated, cannot move. He casts a shell necklace at your feet, weeps gleaming chips that harden into mica on your breasts. He holds you under. Then he takes the body of a lion or a fat brown worm. He's made of gold. He's made of beach moss. He's a thing of dry foam, a thing of death by drowning, the death a Chippewa cannot survive.

Unless you are Fleur Pillager. We all knew she couldn't swim. After the first time, we thought she'd never go back to Lake Turcot. We thought she'd keep to herself, live quiet, stop killing men off by drowning in the lake. After the first time, we thought she'd keep the good ways. But then, after the second drowning, we knew that we were dealing with something much more serious. She was haywire, out of control. She messed with evil, laughed at the old women's advice, and dressed like a man. She got herself into some half-forgotten medicine, studied ways we shouldn't talk about. Some say she kept the finger of a child in her pocket and a powder of unborn rabbits in a leather thong around her neck. She laid the heart of an owl on her tongue so she could see at night, and went out, hunting, not even in her own body. We know for sure because the next morning, in the snow or dust, we followed the tracks of her bare feet and saw where they changed, where the claws sprang out, the pad broadened and pressed into the dirt. By night we heard her chuffing cough, the bear cough. By day her silence and the wide grin she threw to bring down our guard made us frightened. Some thought that Fleur Pillager should be driven off the reservation, but not a single person who spoke like this had the nerve. And finally, when people were just about to get together and throw her out, she left on her own and didn't come back all summer. That's what this story is about.

During that summer, when she lived a few miles south in Argus, things happened. She almost destroyed that town.

When she got down to Argus in the year of 1920, it was just a small grid of six streets on either side of the railroad depot. There were two elevators, one central, the other a few miles west. Two stores competed for the trade of the three hundred citizens, and three churches quarreled with one another for their souls. There was a frame building for Lutherans, a heavy brick one for Episcopalians, and a long narrow shingled Catholic church. This last had a tall slender steeple, twice as high as any building or tree.

No doubt, across the low, flat wheat, watching from the road as she came near Argus on foot, Fleur saw that steeple rise, a shadow thin as a needle. Maybe in that raw space it drew her the way a lone tree draws lightning. Maybe, in the end, the Catholics are to blame. For if she hadn't seen that sign of pride, that slim prayer, that marker, maybe she would have kept walking.

But Fleur Pillager turned, and the first place she went once she came into town was to the back door of the priest's residence attached to the landmark church. She didn't go there for a handout, although she got that, but to ask for work. She got that too, or the town got her. It's hard to tell which came out worse, her or the men or the town, although the upshot of it all was that Fleur lived.

The four men who worked at the butcher's had carved up about a thousand carcasses between them, maybe half of that steers and the other half pigs, sheep, and game animals like deer, elk, and bear. That's not even mentioning the chickens, which were beyond counting. Pete Kozka owned the place, and employed Lily Veddar, Tor Grunewald, and my stepfather, Dutch James, who had brought my mother down from the reservation the year before she disappointed him by dying. Dutch took me out of school to take her place. I kept house half the time and worked the other in the butcher shop, sweeping floors, putting sawdust down, running a hambone across the street to a customer's bean pot or a package of sausage to the corner. I was a good one to have around because until they needed me, I was invisible. I blended into the stained brown walls, a skinny, big-nosed girl with staring eyes. Because I could fade into a corner or squeeze beneath a shelf, I knew everything, what the men said when no one was around, and what they did to Fleur.

Kozka's Meats served farmers for a fifty-mile area, both to slaughter, for it had a stock pen and chute, and to cure the meat by smoking it or spicing it in sausage. The storage locker was a marvel, made of many thicknesses of brick, earth insulation, and Minnesota timber, lined inside with sawdust and vast blocks of ice cut from Lake Turcot, hauled down from home each winter by horse and sledge.

A ramshackle board building, part slaughterhouse, part store, was fixed to the low, thick square of the lockers. That's where Fleur worked. Kozka hired her for her strength. She could lift a haunch or carry a pole of sausages without stumbling, and she soon learned cutting from Pete's wife, a string-thin blonde who chain smoked and handled the razor-sharp knives with nerveless precision, slicing close to her stained fingers. Fleur and Fritzie Kozka worked afternoons, wrapping their cuts in paper, and Fleur hauled the packages to the lockers. The meat was left outside the heavy oak doors that were only opened at 5:00 each afternoon, before the men ate supper.

Sometimes Dutch, Tor, and Lily ate at the lockers, and when they did I stayed too, cleaned floors, restoked the fires in the front smokehouses, while the men sat around the squat cast-iron stove spearing slats of herring onto hardtack bread. They played long games of poker or cribbage on a board made from the planed end of a salt crate. They talked and I listened, although there wasn't much to hear since almost nothing ever happened in Argus. Tor was married, Dutch had lost my mother, and Lily read circulars. They mainly discussed about the auctions to come, equipment, or women.

Every so often, Pete Kozka came out front to make a whist, leaving Fritzie to smoke cigarettes and fry raised doughnuts in the back room. He sat and played a few rounds but kept his thoughts to himself. Fritzie did not tolerate him talking behind her back, and the one book he read was the New Testament. If he said something, it concerned weather or a surplus of sheep stomachs, a ham that smoked green or the markets for corn and wheat. He had a good-luck talisman, the opal-white lens of a cow's eye. Playing cards, he rubbed it between his fingers. That soft sound and the slap of cards was about the only conversation.

Fleur finally gave them a subject.

Her cheeks were wide and flat, her hands large, chapped, muscular. Fleur's shoulders were broad as beams, her hips fishlike, slippery, narrow. An old green dress clung to her waist, worn thin where she sat. Her braids were thick like the tails of animals, and swung against her when she moved, deliberately, slowly in her work, held in and half-tamed, but only half. I could tell, but the others never saw. They never looked into her sly brown eyes or noticed her teeth, strong and curved and very white. Her legs were bare, and since she padded around in beadwork moccasins they never saw that her fifth toes were missing. They never knew she'd drowned. They were blinded, they were stupid, they only saw her in the flesh.

And yet it wasn't just that she was a Chippewa, or even that she was a woman, it wasn't that she was good-looking or even that she was alone that made their brains hum. It was how she played cards.

Women didn't usually play with men, so the evening that Fleur drew a chair up to the men's table without being so much as asked, there was a shock of surprise.

"What's this," said Lily. He was fat, with a snake's cold pale eyes and precious skin, smooth and lily-white, which is how he got his name. Lily had a dog, a stumpy mean little bull of a thing with a belly drum-tight from eating pork rinds. The dog liked to play cards just like Lily, and straddled his barrel thighs through games of stud, rum poker, vingt-un. The dog snapped at Fleur's arm that first night, but cringed back, its snarl frozen, when she took her place.

"I thought," she said, her voice soft and stroking, "you might deal me in."

There was a space between the heavy bin of spiced flour and the wall where I just fit. I hunkered down there, kept my eyes open, saw her black hair swing over the chair, her feet solid on the wood floor. I couldn't see up on the table where the cards slapped down, so after they were deep in their game I raised myself up in the shadows, and crouched on a sill of wood.

I watched Fleur's hands stack and ruffle, divide the cards, spill them to each player in a blur, rake them up and shuffle again. Tor, short and scrappy, shut one eye and squinted the other at Fleur. Dutch screwed his lips around a wet cigar.

"Gotta see a man," he mumbled, getting up to go out back to the privy. The others broke, put their cards down, and Fleur sat alone in the lamplight that glowed in a sheen across the push of her breasts. I watched her closely, then she paid me a beam of notice for the first time. She turned, looked straight at me, and grinned the white wolf grin a Pillager turns on its victims, except that she wasn't after me.

"Pauline there," she said, "how much money you got?"

We'd all been paid for the week that day. Eight cents was in my pocket.

"Stake me," she said, holding out her long fingers. I put the coins in her palm and then I melted back to nothing, part of the walls and tables. It was a long time before I understood that the men would not have seen me no matter what I did, how I moved. I wasn't anything like Fleur. My dress hung loose and my back was already curved, an old woman's. Work had roughened me, reading made my eyes sore, caring for my mother before she died had hardened my face. I was not much to look at, so they never saw me.

When the men came back and sat around the table, they had drawn together. They shot each other small glances, stuck their tongues in their cheeks, burst out laughing at odd moments, to rattle Fleur. But she never minded. They played their vingt-un, staying even as Fleur slowly gained. Those pennies I had given her drew nickels and attracted dimes until there was a small pile in front of her.

Then she hooked them with five-card draw, nothing wild. She dealt, discarded, drew, and then she sighed and her cards gave a little shiver. Tor's eye gleamed, and Dutch straightened in his seat.

"I'll pay to see that hand," said Lily Veddar.

Fleur showed, and she had nothing there, nothing at all.

Tor's thin smile cracked open, and he threw his hand in too.

"Well, we know one thing," he said, leaning back in his chair, "the squaw can't bluff."

With that I lowered myself into a mound of swept sawdust and slept. I woke up during the night, but none of them had moved yet, so I couldn't either. Still later, the men must have gone out again, or Fritzie come out to break the game, because I was lifted, soothed, cradled in a woman's arms and rocked so quiet that I kept my eyes shut while Fleur rolled me into a closet of grimy ledgers, oiled paper, balls of string, and thick files that fit beneath me like a mattress.

The game went on after work the next evening. I got my eight cents back five times over, and Fleur kept the rest of the dollar she'd won for a stake. This time they didn't play so late, but they played regular, and then kept going at it night after night. They played poker now, or variations, for one week straight, and each time Fleur won exactly one dollar, no more and no less, too consistent for luck.

By this time, Lily and the other men were so lit with suspense that they got Pete to join the game with them. They concentrated, the fat dog sitting tense in Lily Veddar's lap, Tor suspicious, Dutch stroking his huge square brow, Pete steady. It wasn't that Fleur won that hooked them in so, because she lost hands too. It was rather that she never had a freak hand or even anything above a straight. She only took on her low cards, which didn't sit right. By chance, Fleur should have gotten a full or flush by now. The irritating thing was she beat with pairs and never bluffed, because she couldn't, and still she ended up each night with exactly one dollar. Lily couldn't believe, first of all, that a woman could be smart enough to play cards, but even if she was, that she would then be stupid enough to cheat for a dollar a night. By day I watched him turn the problem over, his hard white face dull, small fingers probing at his knuckles, until he finally thought he had Fleur figured out as a bit-time player, caution her game. Raising the stakes would throw her.

More than anything now, he wanted Fleur to come away with something but a dollar. Two bits less or ten more, the sum didn't matter, just so he broke her streak.

Night after night she played, won her dollar, and left to stay in a place that just Fritzie and I knew about. Fleur bathed in the slaughtering tub, then slept in the unused brick smokehouse behind the lockers, a windowless place tarred on the inside with scorched fats. When I brushed against her skin I noticed that she smelled of the walls, rich and woody, slightly burnt. Since that night she put me in the closet I was no longer afraid of her, but followed her close, stayed with her, became her moving shadow that the men never noticed, the shadow that could have saved her.

August, the month that bears fruit, closed around the shop, and Pete and Fritzie left for Minnesota to escape the heat. Night by night, running, Fleur had won thirty dollars, and only Pete's presence had kept Lily at bay. But Pete was gone now, and one payday, with the heat so bad no one could move but Fleur, the men sat and played and waited while she finished work. The cards sweat, limp in their fingers, the table was slick with grease, and even the walls were warm to the touch. The air was motionless. Fleur was in the next room boiling heads.

Her green dress, drenched, wrapped her like a transparent sheet. A skin of lake-weed. Black snarls of veining clung to her arms. Her braids were loose, half-unraveled, tied behind her neck in a thick loop. She stood in steam, turning skulls through a vat with a wooden paddle. When scraps boiled to the surface, she bent with a round tin sieve and scooped them out. She'd filled two dishpans.

"Ain't that enough now?" called Lily. "We're waiting." The stump of a dog trembled in his lap, alive with rage. It never smelled me or noticed me above Fleur's smoky skin. The air was heavy in my corner, and pressed me down. Fleur sat with them.

"Now what do you say?" Lily asked the dog. It barked. That was the signal for the real game to start.

"Let's up the ante," said Lily, who had been stalking this night all month. He had a roll of money in his pocket. Fleur had five bills in her dress. The men had each saved their full pay.

"Ante a dollar then," said Fleur, and pitched hers in. She lost, but they let her scrape along, cent by cent. And then she won some. She played unevenly, as if chance was all she had. She reeled them in. The game went on. The dog was stiff now, poised on Lily's knees, a ball of vicious muscle with its yellow eyes slit in concentration. It gave advice, seemed to sniff the lay of Fleur's cards, twitched and nudged. Fleur was up, then down, saved by a scratch. Tor dealt seven cards, three down. The pot grew, round by round, until it held all the money. Nobody folded. Then it all rode on one last card and they went silent. Fleur picked hers up and blew a long breath. The heat lowered like a bell. Her card shook, but she stayed in.

Lily smiled and took the dog's head tenderly between his palms.

"Say, Fatso," he said, crooning the words, "you reckon that girl's bluffing?"

The dog whined and Lily laughed. "Me too," he said, "let's show." He swept his bills and coins into the pot and then they turned their cards over.

Lily looked once, looked again, then he squeezed the dog up like a fist of dough and slammed it on the table.

Fleur threw her arms out and drew the money over, grinning that same wolf grin that she'd used on me, the grin that had them. She jammed the bills in her dress, scooped the coins up in waxed white paper that she tied with string.

"Let's go another round," said Lily, his voice choked with burrs. But Fleur opened her mouth and yawned, then walked out back to gather slops for the one big hog that was waiting in the stock pen to be killed.

The men sat still as rocks, their hands spread on the oiled wood table. Dutch had chewed his cigar to damp shreds, Tor's eye was dull. Lily's gaze was the only one to follow Fleur. I didn't move. I felt them gathering, saw my stepfather's veins, the ones in his forehead that stood out in anger. The dog had rolled off the table and curled in a knot below the counter, where none of the men could touch it.

Lily rose and stepped out back to the closet of ledgers where Pete kept his private stock. He brought back a bottle, uncorked and tipped it between his fingers. The lump in his throat moved, then he passed it on. They drank, quickly felt the whiskey's fire, and planned with their eyes things they couldn't say out loud.

When they left, I followed. I hid out back in the clutter of broken boards and chicken crates beside the stock pen, where they waited. Fleur could not be seen at first, and then the moon broke and showed her, slipping cautiously along the rough board chute with a bucket in her hand. Her hair fell, wild and coarse, to her waist, and her dress was a floating patch in the dark. She made a pig-calling sound, rang the tin pail lightly against the wood, froze suspiciously. But too late. In the sound of the ring Lily moved, fat and nimble, stepped right behind Fleur and put out his creamy hands. At his first touch, she whirled and doused him with the bucket of sour slops. He pushed her against the big fence and the package of coins split, went clinking and jumping, winked against the wood. Fleur rolled over once and vanished in the yard.

The moon fell behind a curtain of ragged clouds, and Lily followed into the dark muck. But he tripped, pitched over the huge flank of the pig, who lay mired to the snout, heavily snoring. I sprang out of the weeds and climbed the side of the pen, stuck like glue. I saw the sow rise to her neat, knobby knees, gain her balance, and sway, curious, as Lily stumbled forward. Fleur had backed into the angle of rough wood just beyond, and when Lily tried to jostle past, the sow tipped up on her hind legs and struck, quick and hard as a snake. She plunged her head into Lily's thick side and snatched a mouthful of his shirt. She lunged again, caught him lower, so that he grunted in pained surprise. He seemed to ponder, breathing deep. Then he launched his huge body in a swimmer's dive.

The sow screamed as his body smacked over hers. She rolled, striking out with her knife-sharp hooves, and Lily gathered himself upon her, took her foot-long face by the ears and scraped her snout and cheeks against the trestles of the pen. He hurled the sow's tight skull against an iron post, but instead of knocking her dead, he merely woke her from her dream.

She reared, shrieked, drew him with her so that they posed standing upright. They bowed jerkily to each other, as if to begin. Then his arms swung and flailed. She sank her black fangs into his shoulder, clasping him, dancing him forward and backward through the pen. Their steps picked up pace, went wild. The two dipped as one, box-stepped, tripped each other. She ran her split foot though his hair. He grabbed her kinked tail. They went down and came up, the same shape and then the same color, until the men couldn't tell one from the other in that light and Fleur was able to launch herself over the gates, swing down, hit gravel.

The men saw, yelled, and chased her at a dead run to the smokehouse. And Lily too, once the sow gave up in disgust and freed him. That is where I should have gone to Fleur, saved her, thrown myself on Dutch. But I went stiff with fear and couldn't unlatch myself from the trestles or move at all. I closed my eyes and put my head in my arms, tried to hide, so there is nothing to describe but what I couldn't block out, Fleur's hoarse breath, so loud it filled me, her cry in the old language, and my name repeated over and over among the words.

The heat was still dense the next morning when I came back to work. Fleur was gone but the men were there, slack-faced, hung over. Lily was paler and softer than ever, as if his flesh had steamed on his bones. They smoked, took pulls off a bottle. It wasn't noon yet. I worked awhile, waiting shop and sharpening steel. But I was sick, I was smothered, I was sweating so hard that my hands slipped on the knives, and I wiped my fingers clean of the greasy touch of the customers' coins. Lily opened his mouth and roared once, not in anger. There was no meaning to the sound. His boxer dog, sprawled limp beside his foot, never lifted its head. Nor did the other men.

They didn't notice when I stepped outside, hoping for a clear breath. And then I forgot them because I knew that we were all balanced, ready to tip, to fly, to be crushed as soon as the weather broke. The sky was so low that I felt the weight of it like a yoke. Clouds hung down, witch teats, a tornado's green-brown cones, and as I watched one flicked out and became a delicate probing thumb. Even as I picked up my heels and ran back inside, the wind blew suddenly, cold, and then came rain.

Inside, the men had disappeared already and the whole place was trembling as if a huge hand was pinched at the rafters, shaking it. I ran straight through, screaming for Dutch or for any of them, and then I stopped at the heavy doors of the lockers, where they had surely taken shelter. I stood there a moment. Everything went still. Then I heard a cry building in the wind, faint at first, a whistle and then a shrill scream that tore through the walls and gathered around me, spoke plain so I understood that I should move, put my arms out, and slam down the great iron bar that fit across the hasp and lock.

Outside, the wind was stronger, like a hand held against me. I struggled forward. The bushes tossed, the awnings flapped off storefronts, the rails of porches rattled. The odd cloud became a fat snout that nosed along the earth and sniffled, jabbed, picked at things, sucked them up, blew them apart, rooted around as if it was following a certain scent, then stopped behind me at the butcher shop and bored down like a drill.

I went flying, landed somewhere in a ball. When I opened my eyes and looked, stranger things were happening.

A herd of cattle flew through the air like giant birds, dropping dung, their mouths opened in stunned bellows. A candle, still lighted, blew past, and tables, napkins, garden tools, a whole school of drifting eyeglasses, jackets on hangers, hams, a checkerboard, a lampshade, and at last the sow from behind the lockers, on the run, her hooves a blur, set free, swooping, diving, screaming as everything in Argus fell apart and got turned upside down, smashed, and thoroughly wrecked.

Days passed before the town went looking for the men. They were bachelors, after all, except for Tor, whose wife had suffered a blow to the head that made her forgetful. Everyone was occupied with digging out, in high relief because even though the Catholic steeple had been torn off like a peaked cap and sent across five fields, those huddled in the cellar were unhurt. Walls had fallen, windows were demolished, but the stores were intact and so were the bankers and shop owners who had taken refuge in their safes or beneath their cash registers. It was a fair-minded disaster, no one could be said to have suffered much more than the next, at least not until Fritzie and Pete came home.

Of all the businesses in Argus, Kozka's Meats had suffered worst. The boards of the front building had been split to kindling, piled in a huge pyramid, and the shop equipment was blasted far and wide. Pete paced off the distance the iron bathtub had been flung—a hundred feet. The glass candy case went fifty, and landed without so much as a cracked pane. There were other surprises as well, for the back rooms where Fritzie and Pete lived were undisturbed. Fritzie said the dust still coated her china figures, and upon her kitchen table, in the ashtray, perched the last cigarette she'd put out in haste. She lit it up and finished it, looking through the window. From there, she could see that the old smokehouse Fleur had slept in was crushed to a reddish sand and the stockpens were completely torn apart, the rails stacked helter-skelter. Fritzie asked for Fleur. People shrugged. Then she asked about the others and, suddenly, the town understood that three men were missing.

There was a rally of help, a gathering of shovels and volunteers. We passed boards from hand to hand, stacked them, uncovered what lay beneath the pile of jagged splinters. The lockers, full of the meat that was Pete and Fritzie's investment, slowly came into sight, still intact. When enough room was made for a man to stand on the roof, there were calls, a general urge to hack through and see what lay below. But Fritzie shouted that she wouldn't allow it because the meat would spoil. And so the work continued, board by board, until at last the heavy oak doors of the freezer were revealed and people pressed to the entry. Everyone wanted to be the first, but since it was my stepfather lost, I was let go in when Pete and Fritzie wedged through into the sudden icy air.

Pete scraped a match on his boot, lit the lamp Fritzie held, and then the three of us stood still in its circle. Light glared off the skinned and hanging carcasses, the crates of wrapped sausages, the bright and cloudy blocks of lake ice, pure as winter. The cold bit into us, pleasant at first, then numbing. We must have stood there a couple of minutes before we saw the men, or more rightly, the humps of fur, the iced and shaggy hides they wore, the bearskins they had taken down and wrapped around themselves. We stepped closer and tilted the lantern beneath the flaps of fur into their faces. The dog was there, perched among them, heavy as a doorstop. The three had hunched around a barrel where the game was still laid out, and a dead lantern and an empty bottle, too. But they had thrown down their last hands and hunkered tight, clutching one another, knuckles raw from beating at the door they had also attacked with hooks. Frost stars gleamed off their eyelashes and the stubble of their beards. Their faces were set in concentration, mouths open as if to speak some careful thought, some agreement they'd come to in each other's arms.

Power travels in the bloodlines, handed out before birth. It comes down through the hands, which in the Pillagers were strong and knotted, big, spidery, and rough, with sensitive fingertips good at dealing cards. It comes through the eyes, too, belligerent, darkest brown, the eyes of those in the bear clan, impolite as they gaze directly at a person.

In my dreams, I look straight back at Fleur, at the men. I am no longer the watcher on the dark sill, the skinny girl.

The blood draws us back, as if it runs through a vein of earth. I've come home and, except for talking to my cousins, live a quiet life. Fleur lives quiet too, down on Lake Turcot with her boat. Some say she's married to the waterman, Misshepeshu, or that she's living in shame with white men or windigos, or that she's killed them all. I'm about the only one here who ever goes to visit her. Last winter, I went to help out in her cabin when she bore the child, whose green eyes and skin the color of an old penny made more talk, as no one could decide if the child was mixed blood or what, fathered in a smoke-house, or by a man with brass scales, or by the lake. The girl is bold, smiling in her sleep, as if she knows what people wonder, as if she hears the old men talk, turning the story over. It comes up different every time and has no ending, no beginning. They get the middle wrong too. They only know that they don't know anything.

1986

Intertextualities

This case study draws upon the theoretical essays from Section V, "Resistance and Transformation": "Notes toward a Politics of Location" by ADRIENNE RICH and "Nkosi Sikelel'i Afrika" by ELLEN KUZWAYO. These essays might stimulate your thinking as you consider literary works by three representative writers from Section V: ELIZABETH BARRETT BROWNING, SOJOURNER TRUTH, and CAROLYN FORCHÉ. Also part of this case study are essays of feminist historical criticism on Browning and Truth—by ANN PARRY and NELL IRVIN PAINTER—that shed light on these women's works. Finally, the questions below offer you ideas for scholarly and creative writing about women's literature of resistance and transformation.

◞ Topics for Discussion, Journals, and Essays ◝

1. In "Notes toward a Politics of Location" Rich argues that feminist theory must be multicultural and multivoiced. "How does the white Western feminist define theory?" she wonders. "Is it something made only by white women and only by women acknowledged as writers?" What solution does Rich offer to the problem of feminist theory as the province of white, educated women? Consider, for example, her self-critique and the concept of a "politics of location." How do the readings of Kuzwayo and Truth shed light on the idea of feminist theory as multicultural and multivoiced?

2. Although Barrett Browning's runaway slave and Truth, a freed slave, both lost children under desperate circumstances, the two speakers differ on the power of religion to sustain them in their grief. Standing on America's "pilgrim shores," Barrett Browning's slave implicitly refuses the rhetoric of white Christians: "God made me, they say: / But if he did so ... / He must have cast his work away." Truth, in contrast, claims (if we accept Gage's version of her "Ain't I a Woman?" speech) that "I have borne thirteen children, and seen them most all sold off to slavery, and when I cried out with my mother's grief, none but Jesus heard me!" Discuss how religious allusions function as a means of resistance and/or transformation in Barrett Browning's poem and Truth's speeches, referring to the essays by Parry and Painter in your response.

3. In "Notes toward a Politics of Location" Rich asks, "How do we actively work to build a white Western feminist consciousness that is not simply centered on itself, that resists white circumscribing?" In what ways does Rich's "struggle for accountability" manifest itself in "Inscriptions"? How does her attempt to avoid "white circumscribing" compare and contrast with that of Barrett Browning, as revealed in "The Runaway Slave at Pilgrim's Point" and in Ann Parry's explanation of why Barrett Browning composed this poem?

4. In her article, Parry asserts that Barrett Browning viewed "The Runaway Slave at Pilgrim's Point" as "ferocious" and that contemporary reviewers generally agreed, compelled by its author's "adamant belief that women in particular had the right and duty to speak out against slavery." Truth obviously shared this belief that women must challenge slavery from a gendered perspective, as her speeches and Painter's essay make clear. Which aspects of Barrett Browning's poem and Truth's orations do you consider most effective in evoking the reader's outrage against slavery? Consider in your answer the poem's ballad form, the poem's and the speeches' allusions to patriarchy, and the use of drama and melodrama by Barrett Browning and Truth. In what ways do the runaway slave and Truth as a speaker articulate what Rich calls a "politics of location"?

5. Barrett Browning, Rich, and Forché all have created poems of resistance in response to particular historical events. Barrett Browning wrote to support the U.S. abolitionist movement of 1848, Rich in response to the Cold War and its aftermath, and Forché to critique the Salvadoran government's repression of its rebellious citizens in the 1980s. Choose two of these poets and analyze what their poems resist, and *how* they resist.

❧ Group Research Assignment ❧

Members of each group should read historical accounts of at least one event to which the writers in this case study allude: e.g., a slave narrative or a journalistic account of an actual runaway slave in the 1840s in the United States (Barrett Browning), two competing accounts of one of Truth's speeches (Painter), the testimony of a survivor of the bombings of Hiroshima (Forché), newspaper accounts of the Allies' victory at the close of World War II (Rich), the testimony of a survivor of the Salvadoran civil war of the 1980s (Forché), or newspaper accounts of the antiapartheid struggle in South Africa in the 1980s (Kuzwayo). What perspective on these events does the journalistic or testimonial account offer that literary work cannot? On the other hand, what insight into the event does each literary work offer that the journalistic or testimonial account cannot? In what ways do the various genres of communicating "truths" intersect? Each group should present your findings orally and in writing to the entire class.

━━ ᴈ◆ᴇ ━━

Ann Parry
1949?–

ANN PARRY is a British literary critic who specializes in Victorian literature and culture; she teaches at Staffordshire Polytechnic in England. Her articles on Rudyard Kipling have appeared in the *Kipling Journal, Literature and History,* and *QWERTY,* a French literary journal. She has published essays on nineteenth-century history in *Victorian Periodicals Review* and on the middle-class periodical press in the *Journal of Newspaper and Periodical History.* In 1990 Parry coedited a special issue of *Text and Context: A Journal of Interdisciplinary Studies* on the "new realism" and the role of Irish literary studies in contemporary Britain.

"Sexual Exploitation and Freedom: Religion, Race, and Gender in Elizabeth Barrett Browning's 'The Runaway Slave at Pilgrim's Point'," first appeared in the journal *Studies in Browning and His Circle* in 1988. In this essay Parry provides insight into the historical circumstances and context in which Elizabeth Barrett Browning wrote her famous antislavery poem. She also offers a salient reading of the poem's impassioned challenge to racial, gender, and religious oppression.

⚔ Sexual Exploitation and Freedom: Religion, Race, and Gender in Elizabeth Barrett Browning's "The Runaway Slave at Pilgrim's Point" ⚔

Dorothy Mermin's synthesis each year in *Victorian Poetry* of publications about Elizabeth Barrett Browning is an indication of the revival of interest in this writer. Unfortunately, a significant number of critics accept and reinvigorate Robert Browning's view of his wife as essentially a Shelleyan, subjective poet, saying and showing her full self in her writings. Reference to some of the most recent writing about Elizabeth Barrett Browning clearly illustrates this point.

John Bayley, writing in the *London Review of Books* about a recently published biography of the poet and a new selection of her poetry, claimed that *Aurora Leigh* was, "a record of Elizabeth's deep, instinctual feelings." He added that, as a tale about "the Victorian Woman Problem, it is completely unconvincing, and boring, because the reader sees that the poet is bored with her own story, interested only in herself." Feminists who read this review would have had no doubt about the gender of the reader who could see that Elizabeth obviously created her own health problems, as well as being "a conscious and loving masochist in relation to her father and family."[1]

Yet, feminists too allow biography the ultimate determination of Barrett Browning's poetry. Angela Leighton's book is organized around the major family figures in Elizabeth Barrett Browning's life, by far the most important of whom was, of course, her father. He is portrayed both as the object of her desire and the force that prohibits it: the inspiration for and the obstacle to her writing.[2] Similarly, Margaret Forster's description of the poem which is the subject of this article is a disconcerting example of the limited critical insight produced by an overemphasis on the familial perspective, an overemphasis which, in some shape or form, Elizabeth Barrett Browning seems always to have been a victim. Forster comments that, while its author thought of the poem's theme as antislavery it "reads more like anti-men."[3]

If, however, "The Runaway Slave at Pilgrim's Point" is returned to its proper range of contemporary discursive practices its determinations are seen to be multiple and complex. Written for a specific occasion in the American abolitionist campaign it adopts an explicitly radical position that interrogates attitudes towards religion, race, and gender through the least lyrical of forms, the ballad. It is only when the formal means and the larger context of this poem are reinstated that a reader can acknowledge just how far-reaching and far-seeing was the statement made in it.

What we now know as "The Runaway Slave at Pilgrim's Point" was first published in 1848 in *The Liberty Bell*, the annual antislavery yearbook. The poem appeared amidst miscellaneous articles by leading reformers of the abolitionist movement. This volume was displayed at the Boston National Antisavery Bazaar, which offered for sale a multiplicity of items donated by friends of the slave in America and from abroad.[4] The success of these fairs owed most to the efforts of Maria Weston Chapman. She was the leader of those women, who, from the start, refused to accept the roles of listener and spectator which most of the men, except Garrison, expected them to take in the campaign to end slavery.[5] Elizabeth Barrett Browning was in full sympathy with these women who refused to accept a nonactive role, but she went further, emphasizing not only the necessity for involvement but the implications for a woman of failing to declare against the "peculiar institution." It would mean that:

> she had better subside into slavery and concubinage herself . . . shut herself up with the Penelopes in the 'women's apartment,' and take no rank among thinkers and speakers.[6]

If women refused to make the slave's case their own they would be reaffirming the oppression they had suffered from the earliest times; they would be abdicating their right *now* to a place in male ranks of speakers and thinkers.

1. [John Bayley, "A Question of Breathing," *London Review of Books*, vol. 10, No. 13, August 1988; 20; Margaret Forster, *Elizabeth Barrett Browning* (London: Chatto & Windus, 1988)].
2. [Angela Leighton, *Elizabeth Barrett Browning*, Key Women Writers Series (Bloomington: Indiana UP, 1986).]
3. [Forster 203.]
4. [W. M. Merrill, *Against Wind & Tide: A Biography of William Lloyd Garrison* (Boston: Harvard UP, 1963)

196–99; Betty Fladeland, *Men & Brothers: Anglo-American Anti-Slavery Cooperation* (Urbana: U of Illinois P, 1972) 281, 295, 300.]
5. [Blanche Glassman Hersh, "Am I not a Woman and a Sister: Abolitionist Beginnings of Nineteenth Century Feminism," *Antislavery Reconsidered: New Perspectives on Abolition*, ed. Lewis Perry and Michael Fellman (Baton Rouge: Louisiana State UP, 1979), pp. 258–59.]
6. [*Letters of Elizabeth Barrett Browning*, ed. Frederic Kenyon, Vol. II (London: Smith and Elder, 1987) 111.]

Historians frequently refer to the link between the antislavery campaign and the movement for women's rights, both in Britain and America. However, letters in the Boston collection show that the kind of connection made by Elizabeth Barrett Browning was by no means universally accepted by women of that time.[7] Although led by Maria Weston Chapman, a Garrisonian, who connected slavery with women's chattel status, the first and last loyalty of many female supporters was to the antislavery campaign. The activities of the Boston Female Antislavery Society were devoted for the most part to fundraising, which provided an important source of revenue for the movement. The success of the Christmas Bazaars had derived from the establishment of a network of women sympathizers all over the world. Maria Weston Chapman, having been educated partly in England, had been responsible for developing connections there on her extended visits to the country.[8] Elizabeth Barrett Browning had been approached for she wrote "The Runaway Slave" specifically "at the request of anti-slavery friends in America."[9]

To have received a contribution from her must have delighted the organizers of the Boston fair, for Barrett Browning's work had been well-received in America, and by 1844 she was held in higher esteem there than in England. James Russell Lowell had praised her, Edgar Allan Poe dedicated a volume of his own to her and her poetry had been widely reviewed.[10] However, when she sent her poem Barrett Browning was aware that it might prove unpalatable to its recipients. She told her friend H.S. Boyd that:

I am just sending off an anti-slavery poem for America, too ferocious perhaps for the Americans to publish: but they asked for a poem and shall have it.[11]

Her suspicions were correct. Although the poem was received in America in January, 1847, it was not included in the annual of that year, but held over until December, 1848.

None of the recent criticisms of "The Runaway Slave" have given any other than a general indication of what, in a contemporary context, would have been considered "ferocious." In her biography of the poet Margaret Forster dismisses the poem as "melodramatic" and "sometimes unintentionally ludicrous," and it has not found a place in her new edition of Elizabeth Barrett Browning's *Selected Poems*.[12] Gardner B. Taplin, similarly, had little to say about the poem, describing it as devoid of inspiration and "too blunt and shocking."[13] Feminist critics, such as Helen Cooper, have been enthusiastic about and receptive of the poem, speaking of its "explosive exposure of racism and sexism," but ultimately they have done little more than reassert the intensity of which Elizabeth Barrett Browning herself spoke.[14] An appreciation of the poem today must inevitably include an understanding of what accounted for the hesitancy with which it was received in 1847.

Elizabeth Barrett Browning wrote three poems on the subject of slavery and "The Runaway Slave" is the least oblique and mannered of them. In "Hiram Powers'

7. [Clare Taylor, *British & American Abolitionists: An Episode in Transatlantic Understanding* (Edinburgh UP, 1974) 4.]
8. [Taylor 9.]
9. [Kenyon, Vol. I 462.]
10. [Dorothy Hewlett, *Elizabeth Barrett Browning* (London: Cassell & Co. Ltd., 1953) 89, 124. Elizabeth Barrett Browning's popularity in America grew in spite of the ferocity of this poem. *Poems Before Congress*, 1860, was well-received in contrast to its reception in England. Theodore Tilton of *The New Yorker* offered her a hundred dollars for any poem

she might choose to send him. See Hewlett 324–5.]
11. [Kenyon, Vol. I 315.]
12. [Margaret Forster, *Selected Poems of Elizabeth Barrett Browning* (London: Chatto & Windus, 1988).]
13. [Gardner B. Taplin, *The Life of Elizabeth Barrett Browning* (London: John Murray, 1957) 194.]
14. [Helen Cooper, "Working into Light: Elizabeth Barrett Browning," in *Shakespeare's Sisters*, ed. Susan Gubar and Sandra M. Gilbert (Bloomington: Indiana UP, 1979) 80.]

Greek Slave" the institution of slavery assumes the same air of unreality and remoteness as the personifications, such as "Ideal Beauty," with which the sonnet is interspersed. "A Curse for a Nation," although written in the form of Blake's prophetic books, with an excoriating angel commanding the poet, was, nevertheless, as David DeLaura has shown, inspired by a specific incident.[15] When it was published critics were confused by the indirection of the poem, believing that it was addressed to England. Such a confusion was not possible in the case of "The Runaway Slave."

On its appearance at the Antislavery Bazaar the poem was entitled "The Runaway Slave at Hurst Point," and it is narrated on a promontory at Cape Cod that marked the spot where the Pilgrim Fathers landed.[16] However, these details of location make the poem specific not only in geographical terms, but historical ones too. In the twenty years following the American Revolution most of the Northern states ended slavery, either by bills of gradual abolition or by court jurisdiction. When the first federal census was taken in 1790 Massachusetts, the scene of the poem, reported that it had no more slaves.[17] At the height of her passion (XXXII),[18] the slave woman refers to the Declaration of Independence, which indicates that, in chronological terms, the poem refers to the period in the North between then and 1790. When, therefore, Elizabeth Barrett Browning wrote her poem, although there were still groups who opposed the abolition of slavery, the North had been free of the institution for fifty years.

This reference back in the poem to Northern slavery cannot be put down to ignorance, to her imagining that it persisted there. Elizabeth Barrett Browning's letters show that she avidly followed events across the Atlantic. In 1843 she wrote to Miss Mitford, "Yesterday, I had a heap of newspapers and magazines from America," and we find comments on such things as the Boundary Crisis and presidential addresses; and until her death she was following the war crisis daily.[19] Moreover, a great deal of thought had gone into the compiling of the poem. It had involved her in transferring an incident from Jamaican history into a context that called on the originating events of modern American history. "The Runaway Slave" was based on a story written out for Elizabeth Barrett Browning when she was a child, by her cousin Richard Barrett. Although she disliked him she had recognized "even then. . . . a subject for a poem."[20] Her assumption that a story from one slave culture could be translated in that of another, so that it became a ferocious satire on the other country's national history and character, tells us a great deal about her standpoint on slavery and about her political view of the situation in America.

Elizabeth Barrett Browning and all those in her family that she most revered abhorred slavery, even though they had plantations in Jamaica, and even though the Emancipation Act of 1833 severely damaged their financial standing.[21] It was irrelevant to her in 1846, and during the war period, how individuals or interests might be adversely affected by abolition, because "It is the difference between the death of the

15.[David DeLaura, "A Robert Browning Letter: The Occasion of Mrs. Browning's 'A Curse for a Nation'" *Victorian Poetry* 4 (1966): 210–212.]

16. [Hewlett 211.]

17. [Arthur Zilversmit, *The First Emancipation, the Abolition of Slavery in the North* (Chicago: U of Chicago P, 1967) 115.]

18. [All references to the poem are to the edition printed in Elizabeth Barrett Browning, *Aurora Leigh and Other Poems*, ed. Cora Kaplan (London: The Women's Press Ltd., 1978) 392–402.]

19. [*Elizabeth Barrett to Miss Mitford*, ed. Betty Miller

(London: John Murray, 1954) 100–01.]

20. [Kenyon, Vol. II 411, 419, 439.]

21. [Although Edward Moulton-Barrett derived his wealth from sugar plantations in Jamaica, he was all for ending slavery. See *Diary by E.B.B.: Unpublished Diary of Elizabeth Barrett Browning 1831–1832*. Philip Kelley and Ronald Hudson (Athens: Ohio UP, 1969) 282. Mr. Barrett's brother and his wife, who lived on the plantation, worked hard for the cause of abolition. See *Elizabeth Barrett Browning: Letters to Her Sister 1846–1859*, ed. Leonard Huxley (London: J. Murray, 1929) vii.]

soul and of the body. . . . a compromise of principle would be fatal." Where slavery was an institution, "the nation perishes morally," and it was her purpose in "The Runaway Slave" to show that this had been so in the Northern states and would prevail wherever slavery was maintained.[22] The existence of slavery indicated a deep corruption in national history and identity. The poem was no doubt intended to shake the self-image of white Americans generally should they read it, but it was addressed in the first instance to Northerners. By displaying Negro slavery at its very worst Elizabeth Barrett Browning can only have wished to inspire feelings of guilt in Northerners about their own history so that they would bind themselves unequivocally to the movement for abolition in the Union as a whole. Her poetic purposes and tactics in "The Runaway Slave" must be related to one of Elizabeth Barrett Browning's recurrent political concerns. It is a concern which again indicates how closely she had been following events in America.

What Barrett Browning feared in 1846, and in later years, "was that the North would compromise. . . . that they are not heroically strong on their legs on the moral question." Every aspect of the political situation was for her entirely subordinate to the moral principle at stake; it might "rain blood," but "If they compromise in the North it is a moral death."[23] Ironically, it was this perception of political problems as being of easy solution, because they were entirely subordinate to moral issues, that allowed her to maintain that she was "an abolitionist, not to the fanatical degree, because I hold that compensation should be given by the North to the South."[24] The purpose of "The Runaway Slave" in terms of its immediate context of 1846, therefore, was to impress upon its Northern audience in particular, the necessity for a moral choice that paid no heed even to the state of the Union. It was "A difficult question yes! All virtue is difficult."[25] The reestablishment of these contextual details, that were based upon an adamant belief that women in particular had the right and duty to speak out against slavery, indicates some of the reasons why the initial recipients of the poem found it indeed "ferocious."

The ferocity that derived from the setting of the poem was in no way mitigated by the images and incidents of the narrative. It turned on what abolitionists and commentators from abroad pointed to as the cruel paradox that existed in America at this time: how a country which, more than any other, boasted of its freedom and democracy was also the largest single slaveholding power in the Western hemisphere? This contradictory aspect of American society, with its declaration of libertarian principles and its great slave population, is evoked immediately and deliberately in the poem through the potent symbol of the pilgrim fathers of the seventeenth century.

The first stanza recalls the historic moment over two hundred years previously when the pilgrims stepped ashore, as they believed to their promised land, and laid the basis for a new society whose architect and builder was God. The runaway slave has sought out the very spot, the "mark," where "God was thanked for liberty" by the "first white pilgrim" (I). She kneels where "ye knelt before" (III), and before she is murdered by the "hunter sons" (XXX) of these same "pilgrim-souls" (XIV) the poem encompasses her efforts to discover an identity in relation to the white God, the white fathers, her own kind and the liberty that the land of America had promised. By these two recurrent images, that of the pilgrim and the runaway slave, the first stanzas clearly "mark" out, as the heavy emphasis on that word shows, the history of America as the terrain on

22. [Kenyon, Vol. II 417.]
23. [Kenyon, Vol. II 439, 419, 411.]

24. [Kenyon, Vol. II 111.]
25. [Kenyon, Vol. II 111.]

which all the other discourses of the poem operate. The poem recounts how "exile turned to ancestor" (I) and in this way two points in time are counterpointed and brought into deliberate collision: the place that saw the Godly inception of America, "blessed in freedom, evermore" (III) is shown also to be the place where, "Whips and curses . . . answer those" with "countless wounds that pay no debt" (XXXIV).

However, not only the imagery but the poetic form of "The Runaway Slave" contributes to the occasion of the poem. Elizabeth Barrett Browning herself had recognized this when she told Miss Mitford that her response to the request for a poem from abolitionists had been to write a poem of a particular kind, "a rather long ballad."[26] *ballad* The characteristics of the ballad form predicated certain ways in which the subject of the poem would be dealt. In a traditional ballad circumstances and action are given baldly; cause and motivation are left to the imagination. Interest is in the type and not the individual. Hence, in "The Runaway Slave" the pilgrims are only of significance in the poem in terms of their symbolic function, as the founding fathers of America. Why they were exiled from England or what might be the influence of the old country on the new, such questions are of no importance. Similarly, we are never told why the woman's lover was murdered, and throughout we know only the barest details of her predicament. In short, the historical framework of the poem is peopled with symbolic figures and the reader is presented with effects rather than their causes. In such a poetic environment moral evil is starkly delineated; the rape of the woman, because it occurs without reason or encouragement, can be seen in no other light than as sexual exploitation. The ballad form was, therefore, particularly well-adapted to Elizabeth Barrett Browning's wish to show that all political considerations paled when compared with the inverted moral order that was produced by slavery.

The history of the North during these years, traversed as it is in the poem only by the images of the pilgrims, their descendants and the black slave appears to be one of increasing meaninglessness and cruelty. The story told by the slave systematically negates all those contemporary discourses that offered transcendent possibilities. Christianity, shown throughout as the historical foundation of the American nation, is the first to be dismissed:

> God made me, they say:
> But if he did so . . . . .
> He must have cast His work away. (IV)

By the last movement of the poem "the pilgrim-ghosts have slid away" (XXIX), indicating that where slavery existed Christian values became insubstantial, disappearing gradually, retreating in shame.

Love seems to offer the slave girl an alternative spiritual dimension:

> our spirits grew
> As free as if unsold, unbought
> Oh, strong enough, since we were two,
> To conquer the world, we thought. (X)

However, as with religion this faith is degraded by the slave system, and is subject to the power of racist discourse:

> We were black, we were Black,
> We had no claim to love and bliss (XIV)

26. [Kenyon, Vol. II 111.]

The ballad, therefore, dismisses the transcendent, replacing it with a nightmarish world of actuality. The only beyond that the poem concedes is the "death-dark" (XXXVI).

America by its participation in slavery has reversed rational understanding; it has opened a world of inverted meanings. The definition of "UNION" has become:

> Two kinds of men in adverse rows,
> Each loathing each (XXXIV)

And "free America" has become "the flogging place" (XXXII).

In a balladic world such as this melodrama is appropriate, not "ludicrous." The histrionic emotion involved in the slave's imprecations to "the sea and the sky" (XXIX), the pitiful but passionate assertion that "I am not mad: I am black" (XXXII), her rallying call to her brothers and sisters:

> from these sands
> Up to the mountains, lift your hands,
> O slaves, and end what I began. (XXXIII)

These cries are not the indulgent emotionalism of a middle-class English poetess carried away by her own excess; this is to ignore their formal and political context. Rather, they are the dramatic extremity that was appropriate to a situation that Elizabeth Barrett Browning believed had exceeded rational and human bounds and needed articulation in all its enormity. The melodrama serves to polarize the ideological conflicts at stake and the final stanza shows the process to effect:

> I fall, I swoon! I look at the sky.
> The clouds are breaking on my brain;
> I am floated along, as if I should die
> Of liberty's exquisite pain
> In the name of the white child waiting for me
> In the death-dark where we may kiss and agree,
> White men I leave you all curse-free
> In my broken heart's disdain!

Here, the operatic gestures of the speaker as her killers draw closer—"I fall, I swoon"—draw attention to the fundamental opposition of black and white which, at this time, disjoints all human relationships and negates the egalitarian principles on which the country was founded and for which it had recently undergone a revolution. Through slavery freedom is denied, joy is set against pain, mother against child, death against reconciliation, escape against capture. In the context of the poem these polarizations are subversive because the contradictions they reveal cannot be accommodated in the existing present, only in the emptiness of the "death-dark." In such a world all that can be attained is a "broken heart's disdain" (XXXVI).

By the end of the poem the melodrama has opened a space in which the contradictions of American society are not only revealed but shown to be a threat to the existing order:

> . . . Your white men
> Are, after all, not gods indeed,
> . . . . WE who bleed
> (Stand off!) we help not in our loss!
> WE are too heavy for our cross,
> And fall and crush you and your seed. (XXXV)

The Christlike burden of the Negroes has become so great that it threatens to crush the white perpetrators of it. Melodrama has here created an excess which allows the reader to see beyond the confident surface of America, where "The free sun rideth gloriously," to another reality where, although

> My face is black,
> . . . it glares with a scorn
> Which they dare not meet by day.

"The Runaway Slave" prophesies a society on the brink of revolution and it was a radical critique of racist discourse.

As this racism is exposed in the poem by the slave its central purpose is to transform racial difference into moral and metaphysical difference. The Negroes were made to feel the need to be totally reconstituted by God, "that the dusky features / Might be trodden again to clay" (IV) because they were "black and lost" (VIII). As black humanity they differed from all other dark creatures that God had made.

> There's a little dark bird sits and sings,
> . . . . ,
> And the sweetest stars are made to pass
> O'er the face of the darkest night. (V)
>
> But WE who are dark, we are dark! (VI)

As another kind of being they were in a world apart from the rest of human kind:

> Our blackness shuts like prison bars:
> The poor souls crouch so far behind
> That never a comfort can they find
> By reaching through the prison-bars. (VI)

Such a racist ideology was intended to justify white superiority by suggesting the irrevocability of the Negro's difference; indeed, God had ordained that he be "Under the feet of his white creatures" (IV).

The worst effect of the racist discourse on the Negroes in the poem is that they come to see themselves in white terms—as commodities. Even when the girl falls in love it is clear that her individuality and subjectivity are anaesthetized. She is only able to respond as a generic being. When she first notices the attentions of "one of my color," she asks, "Could a slave look SO at another slave?" She is fully interpellated within the racist system so that the only freedom she sees lies in the vast anonymity of "sky and the sea" (IX), and she and her lover accept that it is out of reach:

> The drivers drove us day by day;
> We did not mind, we went one way,
> And no better a freedom sought. (X)

The way in which she tries to surmount the separation that occurs because they are slaves is to sing "his name instead of a song" (XII). A song would particularize and individuate; it would put them in relation to one another and because the social structure has forbidden this she does not know how to become a subject. This is acknowledged, implicitly, when she admits that all she could do was chant "a name—only a name" (XII). The "only" suggests that, as was often the case with the names of slaves, it was either borne by many individuals, or was that of a common object. The name was, as she indicates, another sign of her race's invisibility, because she chanted it, ". . . the slave-girls near / Might never guess, from aught they could hear" (XII) the specific person to whom it referred. In a racist society the subordinate must remain generic types, not individuals, even in love, the most individual of all human situations.

Ironically, the rape, which initially the woman experiences as the nightmare expression of white dominance that displays her as a subject space, with no power to take any part in her own destiny, eventually becomes a source of transformation, through which she herself attains mastery and radically inverts the existing racist and gender structure. Ultimately, sexual exploitation provides a passage through to the same freedom of the pilgrim fathers, symbolically achieved on the same "mark." As with the melodramatic tenor a space is opened to reveal a revolutionary future.

At first when the black slave discovers she has given birth to a white child she is traumatized

> . . . I could not bear
> To look in his face (XVIII)

because

> the babe who lay on my bosom so,
> Was far too white, too white for me. (VII)

However, "The *masters's* look" on the child's face maddens her so that she is able to shatter the normally sacred bond between mother and child. She realizes that she herself now has the same power over the white race that it has had over her lover. Just as they murdered him, she disposes of the child, and is then, as previous critics have failed to note, joyously transformed:

liberation

> I sate down smiling there and sung
> The song I learnt in my maidenhood. (XXVII)

Significantly, the name has now become a song, a meaningful pattern, not a chant. "All," is "changed to black earth," there is "—nothing white—" as the white child becomes "A dark child in the dark!" and sings the song of the Negroes (XXVII). Then, and only then, "we two were reconciled" (XXVIII). It is from this moment with the world made black and the power structure inverted that the slave throws off the racist interpellations, roundly condemning those "born of the Washington race" (XXXII), calling her fellow slaves to rebellion, and in her last moment achieving in her defiance the freedom that can be theirs, as she dies "Of Liberty's exquisite pain" (XXXVI).

The effect in "The Runaway Slave" of exposing ideological contradictions through *a black woman's voice*, that has joyously freed itself from racist interpellation and asserts *equality with the white man*, as she stands in his former place, must have been both a warning and a threat to the first readers of the poem. It is also likely to have been offensive to some Northerners, as Elizabeth Barrett Browning recognized in her own description of the poem. The admonition to remember your slaving past with shame and penitence by the representative of a country that had itself only recently shed its own complicity in slavery may have seemed ironic to some and to others insulting. In American eyes, those so recently out of glass houses may not

no mention of her father

have been the best placed to deliver lessons in good faith. Nevertheless, it is clear that by restoring "The Runaway Slave" to its original historical context the multi-leveled quality of the poem is revealed. It is resistant to unification and cannot easily be subsumed beneath a grid of feminism or biographical detail. Indeed, the participation of the poem in such a variety of discourses does much to dispel the myth of Elizabeth Barrett Browning as a writer incapable, whatever her subject, of escaping her preoccupation with her father. The fierceness and passion of this poem does not bespeak a writer only able to evince the "indignation . . . that goes with reading things, not experiencing them."[27]   *1988*

Nell Irvin Painter
1942–

A distinguished historian of U.S. and African-American history, NELL IRVIN PAINTER is best known to scholars of women's literature as the celebrated biographer of Sojourner Truth. In *Sojourner Truth: A Life, A Symbol* (1996) Painter rightly describes Truth as "one of the two most famous African-American women of the nineteenth century," the other being Harriet Tubman of Underground Railroad fame. "As an abolitionist and feminist," Painter writes of Truth, "she put her mind and body to a unique task, that of physically representing women who had been enslaved."

Painter was born in Houston, Texas, to Frank Edward and Dona McGruder Irvin. She received her B.A. from the University of California at Berkeley in 1964, her M.A. from the University of California at Los Angeles in 1967, and her Ph.D. in 1974 from Harvard University. Formerly affiliated with the W.E.B. DuBois Center at Harvard, she has taught history and women's studies at the University of Pennsylvania, the University of North Carolina at Chapel Hill, and, currently, Princeton University. Among her many honors are the Coretta Scott King Award from the American Association of University Women in 1969, a fellowship from the Radcliffe Institute in 1976–77, a National Humanities Center Fellowship in 1978–79, and grants from the Andrew W. Mellon Foundation and the National Endowment for the Humanities in the early 1990s.

In addition to her celebrated biography of Truth, Painter is the author of *Exodusters: Black Migration to Kansas after Reconstruction* (1977), which examines the relocation of Southern African Americans in the 1880s; and *The Narrative of Hosea Hudson: His Life as a Negro Communist in the South* (1979), a compilation of the oral memoirs of a union organizer. A historian of the Progressive era, Painter has also published *The Progressive Era* (1984) and *Standing at Armageddon: The United States, 1877–1919* (1987). She has contributed essays to numerous periodicals, including the *New England Quarterly* and the *Nation*.

"Ar'n't I a Woman?," a chapter from Painter's life of Truth, chronicles the feminist abolitionist's relationship with her white counterpart, Frances Dana Gage, the woman largely responsible for turning into legend Truth's 1851 speech to the Women's Rights Convention in Akron, Ohio. Painter contrasts Gage's version of Truth's oration with that of the African-American journalist Marius Robinson, also present at the convention. In addition, she explores the problem of translation that results when an illiterate black woman's eloquent words are recorded by an educated white woman who might well have had her own agenda.

27. [Bayley 20.]

⇥ "Ar'n't I a Woman?" ⇤

[Sojourner] Truth's feminist comrade Frances Dana Gage was volunteering with the freedpeople in Union-occupied South Carolina in April 1863, when "The Libyan Sibyl" appeared.[1] [Harriet Beecher] Stowe's commercialism chagrined Gage, a far less renowned writer still dedicating her talent to reform. Reading Stowe on Parris Island, Gage realized immediately that she possessed the raw materials for a more riveting and true-to-life version of Sojourner Truth. In answer to Stowe's "Frederick, *is God dead?*", Gage reached back to a different setting and invented "and ar'n't I a woman?"

On 23 April 1863, less than a month after the publication of Stowe's "Libyan Sibyl," the New York *Independent* ran Gage's long account of Truth. Its centerpiece was Truth's intervention at the women's rights convention that Gage had chaired twelve years earlier in Akron. This portrait comprises today's essence of Sojourner Truth:

> The story of "Sojourner Truth," by Mrs. H.B. Stowe, in the April number of *The Atlantic* will be read by thousands in the East and West with intense interest; and as those who knew this remarkable woman will lay down this periodical, there will be heard in home circles throughout Ohio, Michigan, Wisconsin, and Illinois many an anecdote of the weird, wonderful creature, who was at once a marvel and a mystery.
>
> Mrs. Stowe's remarks on Sojourner's opinion of Woman's Rights bring vividly to my mind a scene in Ohio, never to be forgotten by those who witnessed it. In the spring of 1851, a Woman's Rights Convention was called in Akron, Ohio, by the friends of that then wondrously unpopular cause. I attended that Convention. No one at this day can conceive of the state of feeling of the multitude that came together on that occasion.
>
> The Convention in the spring of 1850, in Salem, Ohio, reported at length in *The New York Tribune* by that staunch friend of Human rights, Oliver Johnson, followed in October of the same year by another convention at Worcester, Mass., well reported and well abused, with divers minor conventions, each amply vilified and caricatured, had set the world all agog, and the people, finding the women *in earnest*, turned out in large numbers to see and hear.
>
> The leaders of the movement, staggering under the weight of disapprobation already laid upon them, and tremblingly alive to every appearance of evil that might spring up in their midst, were many of them almost thrown into panics on the first day of the meeting, by seeing a tall, gaunt black woman in a gray dress and white turban, surmounted by an uncouth sunbonnet, march deliberately into the church, walk with the air of a queen up the aisle, and take her seat upon the pulpit steps. A buzz of disapprobation was heard all over the house, and such words as these fell upon listening ears:
>
> "An abolition affair!" "Women's Rights and niggers!" "We told you so. Go it, old darkey!"
>
> I chanced upon that occasion to wear my first laurels in public life, as president of the meeting. At my request, order was restored, and the business of the hour went on. The morning session closed; the afternoon session was held; the evening exercises came and went; old Sojourner, quiet and reticent as the "Libyan Statue," sat crouched against the wall on a corner of the pulpit stairs, her sunbonnet shading her eyes, her elbow on her knee, and her chin resting on her broad, hard palm.

---

1. [Clara Cornelia Holtzman, "Frances Dana Gage," unpublished M.A. thesis (Ohio State University, 1931) 36–39. For a view of Gage through the eyes of her friend and admirer, the pioneer Civil War nurse Clara Barton, see Stephen B. Oates, *A Woman of Valor: Clara Barton and the Civil War* (New York: Free Press, 1994) 145–148, 153, 189–197, 362.] Stowe's "The Libyan Sibyl" gave a flamboyant account of Truth's career as an activist and portrayed her relationship with fellow activist Frederick Douglass (1817?–1895) as central to her indentity.

At intermissions she was busy selling the "Life of Sojourner Truth," a narrative of her own strange and adventurous life.

Again and again timorous and trembling ones came to me and said with earnestness, "Don't let her speak, Mrs. G. It will ruin us. Every newspaper in the land will have our cause mixed with abolition and niggers, and we shall be utterly denounced." My only answer was, "We shall see when the time comes."

The second day the work waxed warm. Methodist, Baptist, Episcopal, Presbyterian, and Universalist ministers came in to hear and discuss the resolutions brought forth. One claimed superior rights and privileges for man because of superior intellect; another because of the manhood of Christ. If God had desired the equality of woman, he would have given some token of his will through the birth, life, and death of the Savior. Another gave us a theological view of the awful sin of our first mother. There were few women in those days that dared to "speak in meeting," and the august teachers of the people, with long-winded bombast, were seeming to get the better of us, while the boys in the galleries and sneerers among the pews were enjoying hugely the discomfiture, as they supposed, of the strong-minded. Some of the tender-skinned friends were growing indignant and on the point of losing dignity, and the atmosphere of the convention betokened a storm.

Slowly from her seat in the corner rose Sojourner Truth, who, till now, had hardly lifted her head. "Don't let her speak," gasped a half-dozen in my ear. She moved slowly and solemnly to the front; laid her old bonnet at her feet, and turned her great speaking eyes to me.

There was a hissing sound of disapprobation above and below. I rose and announced "Sojourner Truth," and begged the audience to keep silence for a few moments. The tumult subsided at once, and every eye was fixed on this almost Amazon form, which stood nearly six feet high, head erect, and eye piercing the upper air like one in a dream. At her first word there was a profound hush. She spoke in deep tones, which, though not loud, reached every ear in the house, and away through the throng at the doors and windows.

"Well, chillen, whar dar's so much racket dar must be som'ting out o' kilter. I tink dat, 'twixt the niggers of de South and de women at de Norf, all a-talking 'bout rights, de white men will be in a fix pretty soon. But what's all this here talking 'bout? Dat man over dar say dat woman needs to be helped into carriages, and lifted over ditches, and to have de best place eberywhar. Nobody eber helps me into carriages, or ober mud-puddles, or gives me any best place;" and, raising herself to her full height, and her voice to a pitch like rolling thunder, she asked, "And ar'n't I a woman? Look at me. Look at my arm," and she bared her right arm to the shoulder, showing its tremendous muscular power. "I have plowed and planted and gathered into barns, and no man could head me—and ar'n't I a woman? I could work as much and eat as much as a man (when I could get it), and bear de lash as well—and ar'n't I a woman? I have borne thirteen chillen, and seen 'em mos' all sold off into slavery, and when I cried out with a mother's grief, none but Jesus heard— and ar'n't I a woman? When dey talks 'bout dis ting in de head. What dis dey call it?" "Intellect," whispered someone near. "Dat's it, honey. What's dat got to do with woman's rights or niggers' rights? If my cup won't hold but a pint and yourn holds a quart, wouldn't ye be mean not to let me have my little half-measure full?" and she pointed her significant finger and sent a keen glance at the minister who had made the argument. "Den dat little man in black dar, he say woman can't have as much right as man 'cause Christ wa'n't a woman. *Whar did your Christ come from?*"

Rolling thunder could not have stilled that crowd as did those deep wonderful tones, as she stood there with outstretched arms and eye of fire. Raising her voice still louder, she repeated,

"Whar did your Christ come from? From God and a woman. Man had noting to do with him." Oh! what a rebuke she gave the little man. Turning again to another objector, she took up the defense of Mother Eve. I cannot follow her through it all. It was pointed and witty and solemn; eliciting at almost every sentence deafening applause; and she ended by asserting "that if de fust woman God ever made was strong enough to turn de world upside down all her one lone, all dese togeder," and she glanced her eye over us, "ought to be able to turn it back and git it right side up again, and now dey is asking to, de men better let 'em." (Long continuous cheering.) "'Bleeged to ye for hearin' on me, and now old Sojourner ha'n't got nothin' more to say."

Amid roars of applause she turned to her corner, leaving more than one of us with streaming eyes and hearts beating with gratitude. She had taken us up in her great strong arms and carried us safely over the slough of difficulty, turning the whole tide in our favor.

I have given but a faint sketch of her speech. I have never in my life seen anything like the magical influence that subdued the mobbish spirit of the day, and turned the jibes and sneers of an excited crowd into notes of respect and admiration. Hundreds rushed up to shake hands and congratulate the glorious old mother, and bid her "God-speed" on her mission of "testifying agin concernin' the wickedness of this here people."

Once upon a Sabbath in Michigan an abolition meeting was held. Parker Pillsbury was speaker, and expressed himself freely upon the conduct of the churches regarding slavery. While he spoke, there came up a fearful thunderstorm. A young Methodist rose and, interrupting him, said he felt alarmed; he felt as if God's judgment was about to fall upon him for daring to sit and hear such blasphemy; that it made his hair almost rise with terror. Here a voice sounding above the rain that beat upon the roof, the sweeping surge of the winds, the crashing of the limbs of trees, swaying of branches, and the rolling of thunder, spoke out: "Chile, don't be skeered; you're not goin' to be harmed. I don't speck God's ever heern tell on ye!"

It was all she said, but it was enough. I might multiply anecdotes (and some of the best cannot be told) till your pages would not contain them, and yet the fund not be exhausted. Therefore, I will close, only saying to those who think public opinion does not change, that they have only to look at the progress of ideas from the standpoint of old Sojourner Truth twelve years ago.

The despised and mobbed African, now the heroine of an article in the most popular periodical in the United States. Then Sojourner could say, "If woman wants rights, let her take 'em." Now, women do take them, and public opinion sustains them.

Sojourner Truth is not dead; but, old and feeble, she rests from her labors near Battle Creek, Michigan.

Gage's rendition of Truth far exceeds in drama Marius Robinson's straightforward report from 1851. Through framing and elaboration, she turns Truth's comments into a spectacular performance four times longer than his.

The antiblack setting, though crucial to latter-day users of Sojourner Truth the symbol, is Gage's creation. The call to the conference had specifically invited a wide range of reformers, including antislavery people, the backbone of antebellum feminism. Gage's depiction of a roomful of women unskilled in debate and timorous in their claims applied to only a few in the Akron meeting, to one person in particular: the Pittsburgh journalist Jane Swisshelm, Gage's main rival in the feminist press. Swisshelm plays several invisible roles in Gage's "Sojourner Truth."

Gage introduces Truth in motion: she strides into the church and sits on the pulpit steps. In 1851 someone did stride in to perch on the pulpit steps, but it was Jane Swisshelm, not Sojourner Truth. Swisshelm had sat there because the sanctuary was overcrowded; she had removed her bonnet—normally considered an unladylike gesture—because of the heat.[2] Gage sets Truth in Swisshelm's place, refashions Swiss-helm's bonnet into an "uncouth sunbonnet," and has Truth scandalize by not removing it. Gage informs her 1863 readers that she was presiding at a meeting for the first time in her life, a piece of information that does not contribute to her depiction of Truth but points again to Swisshelm, who had criticized Gage repeatedly for incompetence as chair. Swisshelm had complained that Gage "was a dignified, fine-looking *woman*, but she was *not* a good president. Literary abilities and fine personal appearance are not enough to make a good presiding officer."[3]

To describe Truth during the first day's deliberations, Gage borrows liberally from Stowe with more or less acknowledgment, calling Truth the "Libyan Statue" and copying the pose of Story's sculpture. Her depiction of the events of the second day differs markedly from what appeared in newspaper accounts in 1851. Instead of the confident interchange between Swisshelm, Mary Ann Johnson, Emma Coe, and other outspoken women, Gage hands the initiative to antifeminist ministers seeking to undermine women's claim to equal rights.

In Gage's scenario, Truth addresses male critics and antiblack women, not a meeting full of people who agreed with and supported her. Gage does two things with her set-up: she reiterates a familiar Christian narrative in which a lone preacher—like Sojourner Truth against the rowdies at Northampton—subdues and converts a body of unruly nonbelievers. And she plays on the irony of white women advocating women's rights while ignoring women who are black. White feminists' hostility is the bedrock of the emblematic Sojourner Truth who emerges from Gage's narrative. Their antagonism proves the power of Truth, the preacher able to convert them.

As Gage builds the scene, Truth rises from a sea of foes. Beginning quietly, in puissant tones, she commands the meeting to hush. Then she establishes an alliance between slaves and the women before her: "'twixt the niggers of de South and de women at de Norf, all a-talking 'bout rights, de white men will be in a fix pretty soon." In Robinson's 1851 report, this thought had come at the end, not the beginning.

Gage's Truth speaks in an inconsistent dialect that may have been inspired by the South Carolinians around Gage in 1863. As in "The Libyan Sibyl," the dialect serves primarily to measure the distance between Truth and her white audience.

Gage has Truth personify an argument familiar to Gage's work: to anti–women's-righters who declare women too fragile for the rights of men, Gage answers that legions of strong women are already doing men's work without getting men's pay. In 1851, Truth made this argument in a very personal way that Gage repeats in 1863: "I could work as much and eat as much as a man (when I could get it)." Speaking on woman suffrage platforms in the 1860s, Truth would often reclaim the right of equal pay for equal work, based on her own experience.

"Ar'n't I a woman?" was Gage's invention. Had Truth said it several times in 1851, as in Gage's article, Marius Robinson, who was familiar with Truth's diction, most certainly would have noted it. If he had an unusually tin ear, he might have missed it once, perhaps even twice. But not four times, as in Gage's report. This rhetorical question inserts blackness into feminism and gender into racial identity.

One of only a few black women regulars on the feminist and antislavery circuit, Truth was doing in Gage's report the very same symbolic work of her personal presence

---

2. [Swisshelm describes her own actions in the Pittsburgh *Saturday Visiter*, 28 June 1851.]
3. [Pittsburgh *Saturday Visiter*, 7 June 1851; 30 August 1851; and 11 October 1851. The quotation is in the 11 October 1851 issue.]

in these meetings: she was the pivot that linked two causes—of women (presumed to be white) and of blacks (presumed to be men)—through one black female body. One phrase sums up the meaning of the emblematic Sojourner Truth today: "ar'n't I a woman?"

Gage shines a spotlight on Truth's body: a massive, towering figure straining upward and thundering a riveting refrain, "ar'n't I a woman?" In Gage's "Sojourner Truth," that body is once again undressed and on display. With the force of Truth's use of slave auction imagery in Indiana in 1858, Gage describes Truth's disrobing a part of her body. The naked limb is a mighty right arm, the arm of a worker, the arm of a powerful woman, the body subject to the whip, and again, in counterpoint, "ar'n't I a woman?" The productive labor that Truth describes is men's fieldwork, but Gage inserts the reproductive work of women through an allusion to the tragedy of slave motherhood: the loss of one's children to the slave trade. With the grief of the mother comes one final time, "and ar'n't I a woman?"

Gage's Truth has borne and lost thirteen children. We will never know whether Truth, appropriating her own mother's tragedy, had claimed in 1851 to have lost thirteen children to the slave trade or whether Gage first puts the number thirteen into Truth's mouth in 1863. We know only that Robinson did not have Truth mention thirteen children and that Gage used that number in connection with a slave mother's pain shortly after the Akron convention.

Although she did not write about Truth by name until 1863, Gage had immediately recognized Truth's magnetism and used her as a model in an October 1851 episode of a fictional series she was publishing in Swisshelm's *Saturday Visitor* [sic.]. She described a fugitive slave whom she called Winna in "Aunt Hanna's Quilt: Or the Record of the West. 'A Tale of the Apple Cellar'":

> She was black—black as November night itself—tall, straight and muscular. Her wool was sprinkled with gray, that showed her years and sorrows, and her countenance was strikingly interesting. Her features once must have been fine, and even yet beamed with more than ordinary intelligence; her language was a mixture of the African lingo and the manner of the whites among whom she lived.

Winna lamented that all her children had been lost to the slave trade: "I'se had thirteen of 'em. They are all gone—all gone, Miss, I don't know where. . . ."[4]

The Sojourner Truth-like Winna is one of two strong characters in the story. The second is another symbolic type that fascinated Gage and many other American writers, black and white—a type Gage would highlight in her woman suffrage work after the war. Gage was enthralled by the enslavement of near-white women. In "Aunt Hanna's Quilt," the only one of Winna's children said to be of mixed race is subject to sale despite—or because of—her whiteness and beauty.[5]

In "Sojourner Truth," Gage echoes Truth's use of the Bible, but without Truth's skill. Gage recites Truth on original sin, Eve, and woman's ability to set the world right side up again, and she repeats Truth's assertion that God and a woman produced Jesus without any help from man. But Gage is not so agile as Truth in making her way around the Bible. She omits Mary, Martha, and Lazarus, and she stumbles

---

4. [Pittsburgh *Saturday Visiter*, 18 October 1851.]

5. [For example, in "The Market-Woman of San Domingo," Gage describes a mixed-race woman, formerly a slave in Baltimore, who was "tall, symmetrical, almost white, with hair glossy, and wavy, and black as (not a raven's wing) but as the diamonds of the coal mine, just brought to light and flashing the hues of the rainbow in the sun. Unlike those about her, her head was unturbaned, and her hair was gorgeous." New York *Independent*, 24 December 1863.]

when she has Truth argue for equal rights because "I have plowed and planted and gathered into barns. . . ." This evokes Matthew 6:26, in which the fowls of the air "sow not, neither do they reap, nor gather into barns. . . ." Yet the point in Matthew is that God feeds the birds even without their doing this work, a theme incompatible with what Gage presents as Truth's point: equal work demands equal pay. Truth's biblical allusions always fit her meaning, enabling her Bible-literate public to amplify that meaning, not merely take comfort in the familiarity of her language. Gage closes this section with Truth in the posture of the prophet, silencing the crowd with her "deep wonderful tones," her arms outstretched, her eyes afire.

Gage appropriates from Stowe Truth's single-handed capture and remolding of her audience. As in "The Libyan Sibyl," the white audience is mesmerized. Stowe's Truth electrifies her listeners with a single line, "Frederick, *is* God dead?" Gage's Truth holds them with a spellbinding performance: "I have never in my life seen anything like the magical influence that subdued the mobbish spirit of the day, and turned the jibes and sneers of an excited crowd into notes of respect and admiration." In Stowe's essay, Truth leaves her audience stunned; in Gage's, she moves them from hushed silence to "deafening applause." In both reports, Truth's intervention ruptures business as usual through a logic all her own that cannot be refuted by ordinary (white) people. She puts an end to discussion.

Gage presents Truth as a figure of strength, and that characterization, punctuated with the unforgettable refrain—"ar'n't I a woman?"—has captivated feminists since the late nineteenth century. Not only does Truth exhibit her muscular right arm, she figuratively rescues the timid white women and carries them to safety.[6] Gage overturns Stowe's burlesque of Truth's feminism. Stowe's Truth was impatient with feminists: they should simply take their rights. Gage exhibits Truth as an embodiment of women's power and gives Stowe's throwaway line real meaning. Women can take their rights and make a difference.

Stowe and Gage each append anecdotes to seal Truth's reputation as a natural wit. Gage's Truth demolishes the pretensions of a conventional young Christian with "I don't speck God's ever heern tell on ye!" The stringing together of such stories became a hallmark of Truth narratives, which sometimes were little more than listings of Truth's greatest lines, each abstracted from its context or larger meaning.

We cannot know exactly what Truth said at Akron in 1851, an unusually well reported appearance. We know even less of what she said most other times she spoke. She put her soul and genius into extemporaneous speech, not dictation, and lacking sound recordings or reliable transcripts, seekers after Truth are now at the mercy of what other people said that she said. Accounts of her words in 1851 differ, and today the one that historians judge the more reliable—because it was written close to the time when Truth spoke—is Marius Robinson's.

Unlike professional historians, whose eyes are fixed on accuracy, Truth's modern admirers almost universally prefer the account that Gage presented twelve years after the fact. It fits far better with what we believe Truth to have been like. But this is testimony to the role of symbol in our public life and to our need for this symbol. To

---

6. [For different readings of Gage's version of Sojourner Truth, see Jean Fagan Yellin, *Women and Sisters: The Antislavery Feminists in American Culture* (New Haven: Yale University Press, 1989) 81–87, and Erlene Stetson and Linda David, *Glorying in Tribulation: The Lifework of Sojourner Truth* (East Lansing, MI: Michigan State UP, 1994) 112–118, 125.]

Robinson's contemporaneous report in standard English, we prefer the Sojourner Truth in dialect of a skilled feminist writer.

Everything we know of Sojourner Truth comes through other people, mostly educated white women. Does this make Truth unusually remote? Consider the obstacles standing in the way of knowing anyone from the past, whether or not they wrote and preserved testaments to their existence. Every source, every document, comes from a person in a particular relationship to the subject, and every source, every document has a reason for existing. No means of knowing the past is objective, and none is transparent. The layers of interpretation between us and Sojourner Truth are simply different from those that separate us from people who document their own lives and try to supply their own meaning.[7]

After the summer of 1863, Truth began to portray herself in photographs; but photographs, too, have their own rhetoric of representation and are not a transparent window onto history.[8] In every instance, layers of interpretation separate the past from the present. Those who shape their own presentation of self—in words or in pictures—do so for their, not our own ends.

Gage crafted her "Sojourner Truth" carefully, and her sensibility was remarkably modern. Her account is still compelling. But it is by no means the real Sojourner Truth.

Painting in 1863 a positive word portrait of a powerful black woman, Gage was as usual in the vanguard. An Ohio abolitionist with roots in Massachusetts, Frances Dana Gage (1808–1884) was known throughout her life as a woman's rights woman. In the early 1860s, her writing appeared now and then alongside Stowe's in the New York *Independent*, the nation's foremost religious newspaper. But whereas Stowe was a featured writer whose Italian travelogues appeared weekly in 1859–60, Gage contributed occasional pieces that most likely were not paid.

Largely self-educated, Gage was a popular public speaker who wrote under the pen name "Aunt Fanny" for a number of feminist and agricultural newspapers in the 1850s and 1860s. She was the first woman suffragist to lecture in Iowa, and in 1856 she toured with Susan B. Anthony.[9] As a Western antislavery feminist, Gage was known for being both a sharp critic of the patriarchal family and a folksy wife and mother of eight.

In the mid–1850s, Gage corresponded with Elizabeth Cady Stanton, the leading woman suffragist, to whom she sent this self-deprecating ditty:

> The woman is tallish, but not very slender.
> Her feelings are kind; some think very tender.
> She's some common sense, but is not very witty.
> Her features are coarse and not very pretty.
> Her eyes a clear gray, her hair once was brown,
> Her forehead is narrow and graced with a frown;
> A nose rather flat and lips rather thick,
> A mouth pretty large, a tongue glib and quick,
> A voice middling so-so, a skin without pimples,
> A fairish complexion, a chin without dimples,

7. [For a thoughtful discussion on the writing of history and the use of historical sources, see Michel de Certeau, *The Writing of History*, trans. Tom Conley (New York: Columbia University Press, 1988), pp. 56–113.]
8. [See "The Rhetoric of the Image," Roland Barthes, *Image—Music—Text*, ed. and trans. Stephen Heath (New York: Farrar, Straus & Giroux, 1977) 32–51.]
9. [Elizabeth Cady Stanton, Susan B. Anthony, and

Matilda Joslyn Gage, eds., *History of Woman Suffrage*. Vol. 3 (New York, Fowler & Wells, 1883), p. 613. Gage gave a series of lectures in the summer of 1854. Philadelphia *Woman's Advocate*, 26 February 1856; undated letter [ca. 1856] from Gage to Susan B. Anthony in the Papers of Frances Dana Barker Gage, 1808–1884, the Schlesinger Library, Radcliffe College, Cambridge, MA.]

A light merry laugh and a will of her own,
And a heart as love-craving as ever was known . . .
She has eight boys and girls (Mrs. Swisshelm said ten) . . .
She tries with the world to be open and true,
To do unto others as she'd have them, too, do.[10]

As in "Sojourner Truth," Jane Swisshelm plays a role.

Gage's support of woman suffrage stemmed from her temperance convictions. She contended that "*nine-tenths* of all the manufacturers of ardent spirits, of all the drinkers of ardent spirits, and of all the criminals made by ardent spirits, are *men*," while "the greatest sufferers from all this crime, and shame, and wrong, are *women*."[11] Women needed to vote, hold office, elect representatives, and frame laws that would control the liquor traffic so ruinous to families. At the end of the nineteenth century, this same logic would make Frances Willard, the leader of the Woman's Christian Temperance Union (WCTU), into a woman suffragist, an advocate of what the WCTU called the "home protection ballot."

Gage was radical for her time. Antagonists charged she was for free love because she criticized the institution of marriage as it then existed in the United States; in virtually every state married women lacked the right to control their own wages and property and had no rights in the custody of their children. By rejecting the logic of separate spheres and natural proclivities by sex, and by insisting that women be included as people with full civil, financial, and human rights under state and federal constitutions, Gage placed herself among the extremists in American reform.

Gage contended, for instance, that women would make just as good doctors as men, that they were already doing a good deal of doctoring. Male doctors who cited women's natural unfitness for medicine were hypocrites: "We have always noticed that literary men do not like literary ladies. I suppose from the same reason that the village doctor dislikes his [women] colleagues [who carry] pill-boxes. They don't like competition—are afraid of losing ground by comparison."[12]

When Swisshelm celebrated differences between the sexes, wondering why women would "contend for the right to get upon the housetop and nail shingles," Gage had answers. A widow with children to feed would gladly nail shingles for a dollar a day, for a dollar was more than she could make through knitting or sewing. "[L]et me tell you," Gage harangued Swisshelm, that where there is one lady perched complacently on a stool doing nothing, there are "ten women in this same country of ours that roll logs, mall rails, plough, hoe corn, dig potatoes, burn brush heaps, pitch hay, &c . . . and they do it from necessity."[13]

Throughout her career, Gage focused her women's rights rhetoric on strong, working-class women. Where Swisshelm waxed sentimental about man's strength and woman's weakness, Gage extolled strong women: a woman in rags walked a canal path in Cincinnati with "half a cartload of old fence-rails set into a big sack that was strapped round her neck . . . half bent to the earth with a burden that few men could have carried"; another

10. [Frances Dana Gage to Elizabeth Cady Stanton, 4 September [1853?], in Patricia G. Holland and Ann D. Gordon, eds., *The Papers of Elizabeth Cady Stanton and Susan B. Anthony* (Wilmington, DE: Scholarly Resources, Inc., 1990); reel 7, 817.]

11. [Frances Dana Gage to Susan B. Anthony, McConnellsville, Ohio, 5 April 1852, in the Seneca Falls, NY, *Lily*, May 1852, quoted in Holland and Gordon, eds.,

The Papers of Elizabeth Cady Stanton and Susan B. Anthony, microfilm: reel 7, 199–200. Anthony read Gage's letter to the founding convention of the Woman's New York State Temperance Society in Rochester, New York.]

12. [*Proceedings of the Free Convention Held at Rutland, VT.*, June 25th, 26th, 27th, 1858 (Boston: G. B. Yerrinton & Son, 1858) 74–76; Pittsburgh *Saturday Visiter*, 10 May 1851.]

13. [Pittsburgh *Saturday Visiter*, 29 June 1850.]

woman in St. Louis walked two miles "with a child six months old—a large fat boy on her left shoulder, while on her head she is holding some thirty, forty, or fifty pounds of flour. She walks with a firm step, and carries her burden with apparent ease."[14]

When antifeminists contended that equal rights would expose women to the rough-and-tumble of economic and political strife, Gage pointed to poor women drowning in an acute struggle for existence, working as hard as men in thoroughly unpleasant circumstances, but handicapped by their lack of civil rights and equal pay.

In 1863, Gage seized on Truth as another working woman who deserved her rights as a worker. Such views were too extreme for readers of prestigious magazines. Unlike the more moderate Harriet Beecher Stowe, Gage never stepped up to the *Atlantic Monthly* or other widely read, fashionable journals. Throughout her life, she remained with the religious and feminist press. Among her eleven books of fiction, those published for temperance organizations predominate.

With the publication of the Stowe and Gage profiles during the Civil War, Sojourner Truth became a well-known symbol among liberals, as well as a particular person with her own life history. She began to appear in mainstream newspapers like the Boston *Commonwealth,* the *New York Tribune,* and the Philadelphia *Bulletin,* her access to their columns opened by the wartime influence of the antislavery community. But writers did not invent Truth entirely as they pleased. They nearly always built on Stowe and Gage, whose writing elaborated encounters that Truth initiated. Truth had approached Stowe, and in Akron in 1851 she had turned up on her own and sought permission to speak. Before either woman wrote about her, Truth presented herself to them as a dynamic, attractive person. In light of her tragic youthful experience, this creation represents an extraordinary accomplishment.

When Truth met Stowe and Gage, she had already forged a powerful persona that each writer found compelling—albeit for different reasons. This achievement did not come automatically by dint of Truth's having been enslaved—quite to the contrary, slavery was something she had actively to surmount. As a slave, Truth had been abused, like millions of her counterparts in bondage. Women who have been enslaved and beaten are far more likely to appear depressed than to project intriguing strength of character. They tend to fade from memory rather than make an indelible impression. The legacy of abuse helps explain why Truth's success on the antislavery lecture circuit was unique among women who had actually been enslaved.

Truth in public was extraordinary as an ex-slavewoman, and her vitality needs an explanation. The key lies in Truth's refashioning herself over long years of adult life and through access to uncommon sources of power. Relying on the gifts of the Holy Spirit and a remarkable network of abolitionist, feminist, and spiritualist supporters, she healed the fear and insecurity embedded in her wretched childhood.

A powerfully *re*-made character attracted Stowe and Gage. Truth was no longer a timid victim who might let herself be fondled by Sally Dumont or Ann Folger or beaten by John Dumont or the Prophet Matthias.[15] She was a forceful, indefatigable speaker for political causes that needed the strength and the body she brought to them.   *1996*

---

14. [Pittsburgh *Saturday Visiter,* 16 November 1850, and Philadelphia *Woman's Advocate,* 21 June 1856.]
15. Sally and John Dumont were Truth's abusive mistress and master for sixteen years, beginning when she was twelve years old; Ann Folger was a member of the Matthias Kingdom, a religious community in which Sojourner Truth lived as a freed slave; the Prophet Matthias was its founder.

HISTORICAL APPENDICES

Old English and Middle English Literature
449–1485

Literary scholars have traditionally designated the medieval period "from *Beowulf* to Chaucer" and defined it historically from 449, the approximate year that Anglo-Saxon tribes invaded England, to 1485, the year that Henry VII, the first of the Tudor kings, ascended to the English throne. The establishment of William Caxton's printing press in 1485 inaugurated the mass production of books and furthered the gradual transition from oral to written literature. The Norman Conquest of 1066, when invading Norsemen defeated King Harold at the Battle of Hastings, has conventionally been the dividing line between the Old English period and the Middle English period. Although these dates and descriptions reveal the male-centered nature of literary history, they provide a convenient framework for discussing medieval culture, masculine literary traditions, images of women in men's writings, and the place of women's writing in this culture.

The Anglo-Saxon invasion of England during the first half of the fifth century was part of a massive folk migration that had been taking place for centuries. The three invading tribes—the Angles, the Saxons, and the Jutes—shared a Germanic heritage and language (though with different dialects). Early Germanic society was centered on the family, headed by a chieftain who maintained his kin; eventually a number of families gathered around a king, who protected his small band of clansmen. The Roman historian Tacitus was the first to explain the *comitatus,* the close-knit group consisting of a king, or lord, and the youthful warriors, or thanes, who vowed military service in exchange for economic and legal protection. This bond became central to the heroic ideal, along with the belief that the skill, courage, and generosity of a king and his warriors constituted the greatest social good. During the sixth century, however, this war-prone culture was challenged when Pope Gregory I sent a mission to Britain determined to Christianize the nation. Led by St. Augustine, who became the first Archbishop of Canterbury (not the same Augustine who wrote *The City of God,* 413–426), the missionaries slowly converted the Germanic and Anglo-Saxon peoples and emphasized the desirability of peace rather than war between factions. In addition, the commingling of pagan and Christian themes, legends, and styles had a powerful influence on literary culture.

Old English poetry emerged from a long Germanic oral tradition and was usually recited by wandering professional bards, or *scops,* who went from court to court; eventually monks transcribed these poems and compiled them in manuscripts such as *The Exeter Book* (c. 975). Poets employed an alliterative form whose verse unit is the single line, in which three or more words begin with the same consonant sound or with any vowel. The single line was, in fact, two half lines separated by a distinct pause, which perhaps marked the place at which the *scop* played a note on his harp.

In addition to rhythm and alliteration, Anglo-Saxon poetry used such devices as the kenning, a compound of two terms that substituted for a common word (e.g., the sea as "swan's path"); the litote, an ironic negative statement or understatement (e.g., "Far different his fate / From that which befell him in former days!"); and variation, the use of repetition of thought for poetic purposes (e.g., "Widsith spoke his word-hoard unlocked"). These devices, scholars believe, also functioned as aids to the *scop's* memory. Much Anglo-Saxon poetry was heroic in nature: it told the stories of courageous warriors, battles fought, and glorious deeds accomplished, thus presenting tribal history in a manner designed to educate audiences of listeners. Other poetic forms included the elegy, a lament for someone or something dead or lost; the riddle, either tame or bawdy, designed to test the listener's canniness; and religious verse— dream visions, Old Testament narratives, and saints' lives. Much of this literature expressed an awareness of the transience of earthly goods and blended Christian ethical doctrine with an ancient sense of foreboding.

BEOWULF, THE OLD ENGLISH EPIC, AND CHRISTIAN POETRY

This fusion of pagan and Christian motifs occurs in *Beowulf* (650–750?), generally considered the greatest extant Old English poem. Composed by an anonymous poet of considerable artistry, it celebrates the exploits of the youthful hero, Beowulf, as he tracks and kills the monster Grendel and his mother, who have ravaged the court of the Danish king Hrothgar. The second part of *Beowulf*, set many years later in his native Geatland, presents him as a king who has ruled wisely for fifty years; it goes on to chronicle the destruction of the country by a terrible fire dragon and the elderly Beowulf's heroic death in battle, even as he slays the monster. Although such a summary fails to do justice to the poem's vitality and the beauty of its language, it reveals the masculine nature of heroic society. As Gillian R. Overing notes, *Beowulf* is "an overwhelmingly masculine poem; it could be seen as a chronicle of male desire, a tale of men dying. In the masculine economy of the poem, desire expresses itself as desire for the other, as a continual process of subjugation and appropriation of the other. The code of vengeance and the heroic choice demand above all a *resolution* of opposing elements, a decision must always be made. . . . One death must pay for another" (69–70). Overing further claims, however, that the poem is not without female intervention. Although women have little space from which to speak, they constitute a disruptive force in this male universe: from the silent Queen Hildeburh, whose presence indicts the warring society that would avenge her, to the outspoken Queen Wealhtheow, whose exhortations to the warriors call into question the masculine symbolic order, to the rebellious Modthryth, who embraces violence, refusing the feminine role of peace-weaver. Long studied as a poem that celebrates a male heroic code, *Beowulf* expands its parameters through the insights of feminist critics such as Overing, Jane Chance, and Helen Damico, who approach the text from the voices of those at its margins as well as those at its center.

Other Old English poems of note include works by Caedmon, Cynewulf, and one or more "Cynewulfian" poets. Introduced by the Venerable Bede in his *Ecclesiastical History of the English People* (731), Caedmon was the reputed leader of a poetic school in Northumbria that flourished during the late seventh and early eighth centuries;

according to Bede, he "did not learn the art of poetry from men, but from God." As Clare A. Lees and Gillian R. Overing have noted, however, Bede's designation of Caedmon as the "Father of English poetry" participates in a narrative of origin that is profoundly masculinist in its assumptions about gender and the production of meaning (35–38). Certainly the nine-line "Hymn" attributed to Caedmon strikingly celebrates the wonders of God, and Anglo-Saxons invested it with significant power. Other poems from the Caedmonian school include *Genesis A and B*, narrative poems that closely paraphrase their Biblical source; *Exodus*, which treats with narrative power Moses' life as a lawmaker and military leader; and *Daniel*, two versions of which recount the reign of Nebuchadnezzar, Daniel's interpretation of the king's dreams, and an angel's deliverance of three young men from the fiery vaults of hell. Unlike Caedmon, whose poetic identity is hypothetical, Cynewulf wrote his name in runic letters on the texts of four poems: *The Fates of the Apostles, The Ascension, Juliana,* and *Elene*. The two latter works, the lives of saints, shed light on the role of women as early Christian martyrs and present Juliana and Elene as participants in the Christian heroic code. Poems written in the Cynewulfian manner include *Andreas*, a saint's life culled from Greek sources; *Guthlac A and B*, the tale of a saint's resistance to devils that would destroy his faith; *Phoenix*, an elaborate allegory of natural history transmitted as the saga of a self-rejuvenating bird; and *The Dream of the Rood*, a dream-vision and one of the finest religious lyrics in English.

WOMEN'S CONTRIBUTIONS TO OLD ENGLISH LITERARY CULTURE

As far as modern scholarship can determine, Anglo-Saxon women did not compose heroic epics or saints' lives; women's literacy was rare, the purview of a few well-educated nuns and abbesses. It is possible that women composed anonymous secular elegies, however, for, as VIRGINIA WOOLF claimed in *A Room of One's Own*, "Anon" must often have been a woman. *The Wife's Lament* and *Wulf and Eadwacer*, two of many elegies collected in *The Exeter Book*, feature female speakers who mourn their exile from a male beloved. These poems contrast significantly with better known male-voiced elegies from the same manuscript collection, such as *The Wanderer* and *The Seafarer*, in that they refuse Christian consolation and assert female sexual authority.

Scholars today debate how much power Anglo-Saxon women actually were accorded and to what extent they fared better than did women after the Norman Conquest. According to Frank M. Stenton, "one of the interesting features of Anglo-Saxon history is the number of women who impressed themselves on the consciousness of the time. They appear in all periods from the legendary foreworld to the eve of the Norman Conquest, and they occur in the religious as well as the temporal sphere. . . . There is no doubt that Old English society allowed to women, not only private influence, but also the widest liberty in public affairs" (79). This assessment could help to explain the positions of authority of women like the nun Leoba, an eighth-century missionary to Germany who assisted the prominent scholar Boniface and wrote him to express her love of learning and devotion to her mentor. Recent feminist scholars have challenged the idea of a "golden age" for Anglo-Saxon women, however, by noting close links between the restricted lives of female religious and the Church's misogynist teachings and by suggesting that such a linear model obscures very real differences among women of different classes (Hollis, Lees and Overing). Whether or not Anglo-Saxon women experienced a "golden age," letters written by and to nuns and abbesses reveal much about religious life and about the influx of Christianity into England and beyond its borders. These letters are worthy of study alongside important prose documents by men, such as King Alfred's *Anglo-Saxon Chronicle* (891) and Aelfric's 120 religious maxims, the *Homilies* (1020).

MIDDLE ENGLISH CULTURE, LANGUAGE, AND LITERATURE

After the Norman Conquest, England and the English language were transformed by the initiation of feudalism and the empire-building of William the Conqueror and his successors. After William rewarded his followers with the lands of defeated English nobles, thus insuring the feudal allegiance of knights to their lords, literature no longer depended on the patronage of *scops* by tribal chiefs. In fact, for over a hundred years the vernacular English language itself seems rarely to have been used as a literary vehicle. As orality gradually gave way to literacy, what writing there was took place in monasteries by religious scribes recording texts in Latin. During this apparent hiatus, however, thousands of French words entered the English language, and various dialects of Middle English developed, the most prominent of which was East Midland, the language of medieval London and the source of modern English. As it reemerged around 1200, English popular literature assumed a variety of styles and forms: prose romances, religious and secular poetry, moral tales (allegories, fables, or exempla), mystery and morality plays, and humorous narratives. Most of this literature concerned itself with the issue of sin and redemption and with an emphasis on the vanity and treachery of this earthly home in comparison with the one to come— themes also prominent in Anglo-Saxon elegies.

Worship of God and loyalty to an earthly lord were not the only subjects to preoccupy medieval writers; admiration for a pure and distant lady who served as a source of inspiration was also prevalent in the conventions of courtly love. Initially knighthood constituted a way of building an army of fighters for a king's conflicts, but ultimately it was idealized as an exemplary form of courtly behavior known as chivalry, taken from the French word *chevalier* (horseman). Like the knight in Chaucer's *The Canterbury Tales* (1386–1400), the chivalric gentleman must manifest valor, piety, kindness, and courtesy. A literary doctrine linked to chivalry is that of courtly love, which developed in the eleventh century with the lyrics of troubadors in Provence, the southern region of France. Most of these troubadours were men who, as Gale Sigal has demonstrated, either placed their lady on a pedestal or condemned her to a metaphoric pit. However, research by Meg Bogin has revealed the presence of twenty powerful women troubadours in twelfth-century Provence who described love in less flowery language than that of their male peers, preferring instead the casual language of conversation. More of a European phenomenon than an English one, courtly love allegedly reached its peak in twelfth-century France at the court of Eleanor of Aquitaine and her daughter, the Countess Marie. In *The Art of Courtly Love* Andreas Capellanus codified the rules of the game and recounted mock courts in which Eleanor and Marie "tried" would-be lovers according to the complex guidelines of the courtly ideal. Although love was considered possible between husband and wife, the knight more often worshipped the wife of someone else, causing courtly love to be disparaged by advocates of conventional Christianity. The values of chivalry and courtly love, though modified by the end of the Middle Ages, affected writers well into the Renaissance as they extolled the virtue of the ideal courtier.

Chivalry and courtly love dominated the popular medieval genre of romance, which told of knights' bold and sometimes mysterious deeds of courage and the ladies who admired them. Medieval romance originated in twelfth-century France. Among the most accomplished French romances, as Alexandra Barratt notes, are those of Marie de France, who wrote short narrative poems, or lays, about adulterous love during the last half of the twelfth century. During the thirteenth century the romance developed further; its typical subjects included battles with dragons, trials by combat, rash promises betrayed, and encounters with fairies, magicians, or magic swords. The most beloved English romances focus on the legendary King Arthur, a figure based loosely on the saga of an actual sixth-century king described by Geoffrey of Monmouth in *History of the Kings of Britain* (1137). In this history Merlin the Magician first appears, a character central to many Arthurian romances; one of his accomplishments is to orchestrate an affair between King Uther Pendragon and a beautiful married woman called Igraine, from whose union Arthur is born. Many of Arthur's exploits are told by Geoffrey, including his conquest of Britain and invasion of Gaul, the infidelity of Queen Guinevere, and the perfidy of his advisor Mordred. Although this popular manuscript circulated initially in Latin, English translations soon appeared, most notably by the Norman poet Wace, who embellished Geoffrey's account by adding the Knights of the Round Table. The French poet Chrétien de Troyes, a courtier of Marie de Champagne, was the first to unify the Arthurian legends and to invent the key characters of Perceval and Lancelot.

These and other sources influenced Thomas Malory in his *Morte d'Arthur* (1469), a superb prose version of Arthur's career, the chivalrous and adulterous exploits of Lancelot, and the reward of Lancelot's virtuous son, Sir Galahad, the first to see the long-desired Holy Grail. Courtly love is prominent in Malory's version of the saga, although it takes a more fleshly form than in its thirteenth-century idealization by Dante. Adultery and secrecy are central parts of Arthur's court, especially the affair of Lancelot and Guinevere, and the errant knight verges on perjury at one point rather than have his lover's reputation sullied. Although Arthur hopes that romantic love will yield primacy to knightly friendship, the values of the Round Table are finally destroyed, and Guinevere renounces human vanity, withdrawing to a nunnery, that medieval haven for both devout and wayward women.

Important poetic works were also produced in the late Middle Ages during the "alliterative revival," a fourteenth-century outpouring of verse based on alliteration rather than rhyme. Two extraordinary achievements of this revival were composed by the same writer, known only as the Pearl poet: *Sir Gawain and the Green Knight*, an account of the physical and spiritual ordeal the Arthurian knight Gawain faces in confronting two adversarial situations, the beheading game and the exchange of gifts game; and *Pearl*, a dream-vision that functions as religious allegory, with the pearl representing the purity of a maiden, the dreamer the fallen human seeking the innocence lost in the Garden of Eden. A third significant poem is *Piers Plowman* (1362 ff.), an intriguing blend of social history, satire, and religious allegory by William Langland that presents the quest of its protagonist, Will, for social and spiritual reform.

Many scholars agree that Middle English literature reached its zenith in the work of Geoffrey Chaucer, author of *The Canterbury Tales*. Although Chaucer projected 120 stories, he completed only twenty-two, each of which reveals the character of a pilgrim brought together "by aventure" with other "sundry folk" on the road to Canterbury. With genial irony Chaucer conveys tales by a sensitive Knight and his romantically excessive son, a wanton Friar who chases "faire wyves" and "yonge wommen," a greedy Pardoner who passes off a pillowcase as the veil of Our Lady, and a Nun's Priest who tells of a proud rooster who must learn humility. Most interesting to readers of women's literature are the narratives spoken by female characters, most notably the Prioress's tale and the Wife of Bath's tale, for they reveal the antifeminism that pervaded the Middle Ages and affected even the generous-spirited Chaucer. The Prioress, Madame Eglantyne, is excessive in her social grace and intractable in her disobedience to the rules of the priory. She adores the small, prim dogs she keeps although forbidden to do so; she wears a brooch ambiguously inscribed with *Amor vincit omnia* (Love conquers all); and she exhibits virulent anti-Semitism despite her professed belief in tolerance. Although the narrator of the General Prologue pretends to admire her, Chaucer clearly satirizes the Prioress as a foolish woman and a religious hypocrite. The Wife of Bath's tale, in many ways the culmination of centuries of misogyny encouraged by the medieval church, presents female sexuality as a dangerous excess. The "monstrous feminism" (as one male critic put it) of an old woman who has outlasted five husbands and searches for a sixth clearly threatens the men in her company, most notably the Clerk, the Merchant, and the Franklin, who go on to debate the merits and demerits of marriage. Whether female sexual power also threatened Chaucer, who makes the Wife of Bath humorous in her excesses but seems to denigrate her as well, has been debated by readers for centuries.

WOMEN'S CONTRIBUTIONS TO MIDDLE ENGLISH LITERATURE

As this overview reveals, women provided ample subject matter for male writers during the medieval period; they were alternately praised for their virtue and scorned for their fickleness and deception. A few Middle English women documented their own lives, however, mostly in prose and letters. Books by JULIAN OF NORWICH (1343–1416) and MARGERY KEMPE (1373?–1438?), two medieval mystics, raise complex issues of female authority and embodiment and provide intriguing contrasts with mystical texts by men, most notably Walter Hilton and Richard Rolle. They also serve as useful analogues to the *Ancrene Riwle*, or *Rule for Anchoresses* (c. 1200), written presumably by a witty male author to provide instruction to young women preparing to become recluses. Although Julian probably composed her book in her own hand, Margery dictated hers to scribes, a fact that raises concerns about women's authorship and mediation.

Medieval women's themes range from expressions of religious faith to interventions in political conflicts to the education of their children. Women's writings were not, of course, part of the literary mainstream; religious readers, mostly priests and monks, favored classical texts written in Latin, whereas wealthy landowners, a growing part of the reading public, preferred Arthurian romances such as Layamon's *Brut* (1189–1207) or, later, Malory's *Morte d'Arthur* and the stories of *The Canterbury Tales*. Nonetheless, for readers of women's writing today, examining female-voiced elegies and riddles, letters to husbands and mentors, and spiritual autobiographies reveals a valuable and otherwise absent side of medieval life and art. Moreover, these works lie at the center of important debates by feminist critics of medieval literature regarding which texts are considered canonical and who has had the authority to say.

GENDER, SEXUALITY, AND AUTHORSHIP: ELEGIES AND RIDDLES IN *THE EXETER BOOK*

The Exeter Book is a tenth-century manuscript, housed in Exeter Cathedral, which includes a number of elegies spoken by men and women; nearly one hundred riddles, ten of which rely on sexually explicit *double entendres*; *Widsith*, a compendium of heroic myth and history that may be the earliest surviving poem in English; and several intricate poems presumably written by Cynewulf, a cultured eighth-century cleric, or his imitators. Although none of these early poems can be definitively attributed to women, authorship assumed less centrality in Anglo-Saxon culture—which privileged the communal and oral over the individual, written text—than it has assumed since the advent of the printing press in 1485. What is important is that many poems and riddles are *female-voiced* as well as possibly female-authored. A feminist reconsideration of these elegies and riddles provides enormous insight into portrayals of gender, sexuality, and transgressive language in Anglo-Saxon literature.

It is useful to examine the elegies that most strikingly inscribe women's voices, *The Wife's Lament* and *Wulf and Eadwacer*, in comparison with the two most famous poems in which men relay their grief, *The Wanderer* and *The Seafarer*. In all four cases exile lies at the heart of the lament, but in a masculine heroic culture in which warring tribes dominate, women's forms of exile differ significantly from those of men. As Helen T. Bennett explains, exiled men have lost the security previously found in the bond between lord and thane; they mourn their loss of security as they sail "wave-tossed" seas, as well as a lack of the male camaraderie that they previously found in the mead halls of these noblemen. Still, since as Robert Bjork points out, exile constitutes "a constant tradition in the Anglo-Saxon world," and since men are central to that society, the wanderer and the seafarer are tied even in exile to the social order (119–21). Exiled women, in contrast, appear even before banishment on the peripheries of Anglo-Saxon society, their social role identified primarily through their connection to their husbands and their place as "peace-weavers"—a role which, as Overing notes, amounts to "utter nonsignification" for women in a society based on war (85). Hence their mourning is more ambivalent than that of their male counterparts, and they typically lament their separation from a husband or lover, express their anguish at enforced dislocation, and in the case of the speaker of *Wulf and Eadwacer*, reveal mixed emotions at embracing a mate less desirable than the absent beloved. The speaker in *The Wanderer*, for example, laments his lost relationship with his master, recalling "that he embraced and / kissed his liege lord, and on his knee / lay his hands and head, as he formerly, / in bygone days, enjoyed the gift-stool." The speaker of *The Wife's Lament*, in contrast, mourns the absence of her *hlaford* (husband or lord) and the loss of their sexual relationship: "There are friends on earth, / lovers living who lie clasped in their bed / while I walk alone in the hours before daybreak, / under the oak tree."

Other noteworthy differences between men's and women's elegies include their adherence to or divergence from traditional linguistic formulae of Old English poetry, their embracing or eschewing of solace, and their treatment of time or timelessness. Both men's and women's elegies reveal certain stock characteristics of Old English alliterative poetry: the linguistic compression necessitated by the metrical requirements of a half-line as a unit of meaning, the expansion of ideas through repetition and parallel variation, and a reliance on the kenning. Yet *The Wanderer* and *The Seafarer* rely on run-on lines, long, involved sentences, and numerous dependent clauses, while the women's elegies, as both Kemp Malone and Patricia Belanoff have demonstrated, exhibit shorter sentences and a fragmented syntax more reminiscent of Old Icelandic poetry than Old English. These critics also link *The Wife's Lament* and *Wulf and Eadwacer* to the international genre of *frauenlieder*, popular rather than courtly Germanic women's songs, pieces typically enigmatic and allusive in their mourning for a lost beloved and their frank presentation of sexuality. Drawing upon Overing's research, Bennett associates the male-spoken elegies with metaphor, a tightly controlled comparison that relies on similarity, and the female-spoken elegies with metonymy, a mode of delivery based on contiguity, deferral, and resistance to decisive analysis. For instance, the wanderer attempts to order his speech and draw conclusions about his status as exile, while the lamenting woman in *Wulf and Eadwacer* expresses her desire for contiguity and mourns Wulf's *seldymes* (seldom-comings) in "wandering thoughts."

Moreover, the speakers in *The Wanderer* and *The Seafarer* find ultimate solace in God and the hope of a better world in heaven, while the speakers in *The Wife's Lament* and *Wulf and Eadwacer* refer neither to God nor to any hope of an afterlife. This difference can best be seen in the poems' endings. *The Wanderer* concludes with Christian resignation: "Well it is for him who seeks mercy, / comfort from Father in heaven, where / for us all security stands"; *The Seafarer*, similarly, urges listeners, "Let us think where we have our home, / and then think how we may come there, / and then strive that we may come to / eternal happiness, where life derives / from the love of God, joy in heaven." In turn, *Wulf and Eadwacer* ends only with remorse—"Men can easily wrench apart what has never been wedded— / our story together"—while *The Wife's Lament* offers a pessimistic warning: "Unhappy is anyone who must longingly wait for a lover." Bennett argues convincingly that women are doubly exiled in exogamous Anglo-Saxon society, forced first to leave "my people" for "his people" and then to absent themselves from their husbands. Finally, although all four poems deal with time and timelessness, the male speakers believe in an afterlife in heaven, which offers salvation from the unreliable world, while the female speakers portray time as nonlinear and cyclical; they are always already suffering, endlessly waiting.

Marilynn Desmond claims that for feminist readers of Old English elegies, considering *The Wife's Lament* and *Wulf and Eadwacer* as *frauenlieder* offers "the opportunity to short-circuit issues of historical gender and focus instead on the gender of the text" (577). Neither masculine authority nor authorship need be inherent in these anonymous, female-voiced works. There are at least three advantages of focusing on the gendered voices of these elegies rather than the disputable issue of authorship. One advantage, as Belanoff asserts, is the subsequent realization that the heroic, war-centered vision widely considered the ethos of Old English poetry exists alongside an alternate women's ethos of suffering and separation, an ethos that appealed both rhetorically and emotionally to the oral audiences of the times. A second advantage is that focusing on the gendered voices of these poems paves the way for new feminist interpretations. Both Dolores Frees and Marijane Osborn, for example, have offered alternative readings of *Wulf and Eadwacer* not as a lament by an adulterous woman, as most critics view it, but as the mourning of a mother who has lost her son—a pervasive theme in Old English poetry. A final advantage, in Desmond's words, is that once we interpret *The Wife's Lament* and *Wulf and Eadwacer* "as women's language, we do more than simply open up a space for a female voice; we also begin to envision a female literary history that might include medieval texts and culture" (590). Rather than assuming that Julian of Norwich and Margery Kempe initiated a women's literary tradition in English, we can instead begin that tradition with thousand-year-old *frauenlieder* of the Anglo-Saxon era.

A feminist examination of the bawdy riddles of *The Exeter Book* yields similarly fruitful insights into female sexuality and authority in Old English poetry. Ninety-five riddles appear in this book, ranging from four to one hundred lines. As Edith Whitehurst Williams and John W. Tanke have noted, male and female sexual experience are represented in surprising ways in the ten bawdy riddles. Specifically, the riddles reveal that women as well as men were viewed as capable of sexual pleasure and control, and they imply that no stigma adhered to women who sought out such pleasure. These conclusions seem consistent with research showing that although Christianity had made inroads into English culture by the eighth century, the antifeminism characteristic of the patristic writings by St. Paul and St. Jerome had not fully penetrated the society.

One example of a bawdy riddle in which a woman claims her right to sexual pleasure is #23. Since Victorian times, when these pun-ridden riddles from *The Exeter Book* were first solved and labeled obscene, this riddle has been answered as either "onion" (the "correct" or "moral" response) or "penis" (the "incorrect" or "immoral" response):

> I am a remarkable creature, a joy to women, useful to neighbors; I harm no citizen except my slayer alone. Lofty is my position, I stand in a bed, am shaggy somewhere beneath. Sometimes a very beautiful daughter of a freeman, a proud-minded woman, ventures to get hold of me, rushes upon me who am red, ravages my head, binds me in a fastness. She soon feels that encounter with me, she who confines me, the woman with braided locks. Her eye becomes wet.

The woman in this riddle is portrayed as joyful, willing, and assertive in her sexual desire. Furthermore, the positive connotations of the nouns and adjectives that describe her suggest that she pays no social price for her sexual pleasure.

As Williams claims, these sexually explicit riddles could have been composed by women, since "there were many double religious houses [abbeys in which men and women lived] in the Anglo-Saxon period and the behavior of their inmates often lapsed into a secularity which caused consternation among the Church fathers." For instance, one monastery at Coldringham is described by the Venerable Bede as troubling the monk Adanman because its cells had been "converted into places for eating, drinking, gossip, or other amusement." Given the difficulty the Roman church had in imposing celibacy upon its priests, "other amusement" could refer to sexual activity, about which women religious might be as knowledgeable as their male counterparts.

Whether or not any of the riddles were written by women, however, several of them feature female speakers, as in riddle #87, which Williams solves as "keyhole," or female genitalia:

My head is beaten by a hammer, wounded by a pointed instrument, rubbed by a file. Often I open wide to that which pricks against me. Then, girded with rings, I must thrust hard against the hard, pierced from the rear, press forth that joy which my lord cherishes at midnight. Sometimes, by means of my countenance, I move to and fro, backwards, the entrance of the treasure when my lord wishes to receive what is left of that which he commanded from life, which he thrust with deadly power according to his desire.

An active female receptacle rather than a male instrument, the keyhole functions as a metaphor for female sexual pleasure and draws upon conventional associations of sexual intercourse with symbolic death. Thus the female speaker inscribes her own sexual gratification as well as that of her "lord."

Tanke notes that riddle #12 is the only one that denigrates a sexually active woman, the "wonfeax wale," or dark-haired servant woman; he argues convincingly that this woman is scapegoated because of gender *and* class, as well as other factors. The ox, and the leather object it becomes after death, lies at the center of the riddle's scrutiny; the leather object has been variously interpreted as glove, jerkin (a close-fitting jacket), hat, and boot. The dark-haired woman, in turn, either works in some way with the leather while masturbating or masturbates with the object itself:

I walk with feet, slit the earth, the green fields, while I bear a spirit. If life is loosed from me, I bind fast the dark slave men, sometimes better men. Sometimes I give a bold man to drink from my bosom; sometimes a woman treads me, very proud with her feet; sometimes a dark-haired servant woman, brought from afar, silly drunken slave, moves and presses me on dark nights, wets me in water, warms me at times, fairly by the fire; the lustful one's hand sticks in my embrace, turns often, moves through me, the dark one. Say what I am called, I who, living, plunder the land and, dead, serve people.

As Tanke asserts, this riddle meditates on slavery, sexuality, and the body, and it is potentially subversive in presenting a slave woman, however "drunken" or "silly," who takes her pleasure literally into her own hands. "The *wale* here is the riddle subject's master. She is, in fact, her own master" (35). In contrast to the presentation of male servants in the riddles, who typically are applauded for transgressive behaviors, the servant woman here must be condemned by the riddle poser on the basis not only of her class but also her subordinate gender, her ethnicity as a Welshwoman (*wale* carried the double meaning of Welsh and slave), and her illicit sexual activity. Ironically, Tanke concludes, the "wonfeax wale" is so subversive in her behavior that she threatens the established Anglo-Saxon social order—indeed, she represents "a subject so enslaved to the law that she is quite capable of toppling it" (39).

The risqué riddles in *The Exeter Book* portray male and female sexuality frankly and enthusiastically. Like *The Wife's Lament* and *Wulf and Eadwacer*, these riddles participate in constructing a sexual order in which women, although marginalized, could exert subversive power.

MEDIEVAL LETTERS AND PRACTICAL DOMESTIC DOCUMENTS

Letters written between women and men from the seventh to the fifteenth centuries provide insight into the dynamic between the genders, the authority accorded to certain Anglo-Saxon and medieval women, and life in the Middle Ages more generally.

Among the most engaging set of extant letters is the Boniface correspondence, a group of 150 Latin letters dating from 670 to 770 that center on the work of the noted missionary St. Boniface, his successor, Lull, and the nuns and abbesses aligned with Boniface in the mission fields. Christine Fell considers these letters the most revealing about women's lives of any in the Anglo-Saxon period; she further suggests that they might have survived when many other letters did not because they were copied abroad, thus avoiding destruction by Viking raids, or because their literary value was recognized. Of these 150 letters, sixteen were written from men to women, two from Boniface to "all our brothers and sisters consecrated and devoted to God," nine by women to men, and one by a woman to another woman: from Aelflaed, abbess of Whitby, to Adola, abbess of Pfalzel, asking that young Englishwomen undertaking a pilgrimage to Rome be given shelter at the German abbey. As many scholars note, these letters reveal much about women's attitudes toward community and their desire to replace kinship ties with spiritual ties (Fell, Lees, and Overing, and Cherewatuk and Wiethaus).

Of the other letters composed by women, four written to Boniface from the abbess Ecgburg, one written to Boniface from the nun LEOBA, and three written from the nun Berhtgyd to her brother Baldhard are extant. A few letters from Boniface to various abbesses survive but none of his missives to Leoba, with whom—according to her biographer, the monk Rudolf of Fulda—Boniface enjoyed an especially close relationship. Leoba's extant letter to Boniface, written before she left England to serve as a missionary in Germany, expresses her devotion to the bishop along with her love of learning. It also reveals the emotional intensity that accompanied the mentor-student bond and her desire to win Boniface's approval for her intellectual endeavors, as witnessed by a poem she enclosed for him to critique. Leoba's unpretentious verses imitate the Latin poems of Aldhelm of Malmesbury, a monk well known for his poetic virtuosity, and reveal the literary interest Leoba shared with many abbesses.

Other letters in the Boniface correspondence provide us with knowledge of medieval women's lives as well. A surviving letter written to a much older Leoba by Boniface's successor, Lull, stimulates speculation regarding the nun's latter days. Described by Fell as "a magnificent piece of thinly disguised irritation," Lull's letter to Leoba makes frequent use of the rhetorical device of *occupatio,* or pointed reminder ("I do not believe that you forget, in your wisdom and energy . . ."); it also implores Leoba not to consider him forgetful or negligent (35). Fell hypothesizes that since Boniface before his death begged Leoba not to abandon her German post, and since the loneliness of many medieval women missionaries is acknowledged in their writings, Leoba might have entreated Lull to release her, or at least asked him for emotional support after Boniface's death. However, it is worth noting that Leoba's biographer does not attribute any feelings of isolation to the elderly Leoba but presents her as the much beloved center of her religious community. Several interesting letters from Lull to an abbess named Cyneburg, moreover, reveal the extensive administrative power abbesses had as legal protectors of lordless men who committed themselves to their care, as well as the guardians of young women whom they instructed in their monasteries. Finally, one letter from the abbess Ecgburg to Boniface suggests that a friendly rapport must often have existed between women and men in religious communities, since a monk adds a casual postscript greeting Boniface fondly.

Two other sets of medieval letters that reveal information about women's lives are the twelfth-century correspondence between Anselm, Archbishop of Canterbury, and MATILDA, QUEEN OF ENGLAND and the fifteenth-century Paston family letters. As Marcelle Thiebaux points out, Matilda wrote many letters to Anselm that reveal her devotion to him as well as her shrewdness in negotiating on behalf of her husband, King Henry I. Anselm's letters, in turn, express his religious and political concerns in a somewhat distant tone, indicating his awareness of the queen's mixed motivations. The hundreds of letters written by members of the Paston family from Norfolk date from 1422, when the Pastons were ordinary farmers, to nearly a century later, when they had become wealthy through clever economic and legal maneuvers. Social and domestic matters were discussed in these letters, from the lack of police protection to the behavior of wayward children; their style was straightforward in the manner of those not writing letters for posterity. Among the letters are those written by Margery Paston to the bailiff Richard Calle, whom she wished to wed; her family's agreement to allow her to marry "beneath her" constituted an important exception to the cultural norm permitting fathers to arrange their daughters' marriages, often selling them to the highest bidder. Similarly, the refreshing verse epistles written in 1477 by MARGERY BREWS to her future husband, John Paston, reveal her insistence on a love match despite the resistance of her father, who tried to negotiate a more substantial dowry than Paston was initially willing to pay. The Paston letters offer valuable insight into rural customs as well as women's language and experience.

MEN'S AND WOMEN'S RELIGIOUS PROSE OF THE LATE MIDDLE AGES

Volumes of religious prose were compiled during the medieval period, including sermons, proverbs, translations, conduct books, and mystical texts. Although the best known of these were by men—namely the anonymously authored *Ancrene Riwle* and the writings of Richard Rolle, the "hermit of Hampole" (1300–49)—many nuns, abbesses, and lay women composed works that documented their spiritual lives. A number of these women, and a few men such as Rolle, were mystics: persons whose intense communication with God caused them to experience fasting, self-flagellation, excessive tears, involuntary seizures, or stigmata. As Carolyn Walker Bynum has noted, "compared to other periods of Christian history and other world religions, medieval spirituality—especially female spirituality—was peculiarly bodily; this was so not only because medieval assumptions associated female with flesh, but also because theology and natural philosophy saw persons as in some real sense body as well as soul" (162). Comparing spiritual guidebooks and autobiographies by men and women of the Middle Ages reveals both the similarities and the differences in their treatment of embodiment, mysticism, suffering, and identification with Christ.

The goal of the *Ancrene Riwle* was to instruct young women how best to live an enclosed life; in doing so its author blends wit and practical wisdom with strict religious discipline. He soberly urges the aspiring anchoress, for example, never to break a vow, yet in the next breath he acknowledges that "if she does not vow it, she may, nevertheless, do it, and leave it off when she will." Although the author offers instruction in a good-natured manner, he also reinforces misogynistic stereotypes of women. By temperament, he suggests, women are flirtatious and seductive; they thus must strive to avoid the label of "roving-eyed anchoresses, or of having catching looks or expressions, which some, at times, alas, put on contrary to nature." He assumes that the anchoress will be subject to sexual temptations she must avoid by refusing to think of love "when she ought to attend diligently to something else." The only appropriate suitor is Christ, who is presented in chivalrous terms: "and, for His lady's love, He, like a bold knight, had his shield pierced in every part in the fight." Furthermore, the author associates women with excessive speech and exhorts them, through a barnyard analogy, not to talk too much: "The hen, when she hath laid, can do nothing but cackle. And what does she get from it? The stealthy man cometh right away, and taketh from her her eggs." As Karma Lochrie has noted, the *Ancrene Riwle* "advocates a sealing of the borders, particularly the border of speech" for women, who must "dam up [their] speech and thoughts" by meditating on Christ's suffering (126–27).

Elizabeth Robertson has traced ways in which the *Ancrene Riwle* develops a bodily imagery linking the cells, or "anchorholds," in which anchoresses or recluses lived to the womb to be prepared for the entry of Christ. The book's last three chapters— "Confession," "Penance," and "Love"—focus especially on blood, which is viewed as interchangeable with tears. Because of women's association with blood through menstruation, these images must have been particularly powerful for them, since purgation could be seen as enhancing spiritual as well as physical health. Once cleansed, the anchoress could contemplate a spiritual union with Christ through the fire of desire, a union the author presents as far more satisfying than intercourse with an earthly man could ever be. God's incendiary love, present in the text as uncontrollable wildfire, may represent a discreet reference to orgasm; in any event, both Christ and women are associated here with desire as well as love—an acceptable desire as long as it is properly focused. The representation of female spirituality in the *Ancrene Riwle*, Robertson concludes, thus differs significantly from portrayals of male spirituality, even in mystical texts that emphasize Christ's suffering humanity, since for women, "union with Christ occurs not as an allegory of the ascent of the mind to God, but as concretized erotic experience" (153).

Other striking contrasts exist between the writings of male and female mystics. As over four hundred extant manuscripts attest, Rolle was one of the most widely read writers of his time, the prolific author of more than a dozen works of poetry and prose, most notably *Meditations on the Passion* and *The Form of Living*. Although Rolle and other men such as Bernard of Clairvaux, Rupert of Deutz, and the Monk of Farne use sensuous and erotic language, both Robertson and Karma Lochrie have argued that male mystics do not linger on images of moisture or blood unless they are focusing on Christ's passion. In contrast, female mystics such as Julian of Norwich and Margery Kempe express their identification with Christ through bodily activities considered in medieval times essentially feminine: blood, tears, purgation of excessive moisture, and erotic union with the "hot" male principle. In Julian's *Showings* (1393), the dominant motif is the redemption of her body through that of a feminized Christ. Like Julian, Christ is wounded and bloody; like her, he must undergo excessive purgation for redemption's sake. Rolle's evocation of Jesus's blood in his *Meditation on the Passion* elicits more pity than identification, and he identifies more with Mary's suffering than with Jesus's. For Julian, claims Robertson, "the biological parity between blood, sweat, tears, milk, and urine meant that a woman's contemplation of Christ's blood was a contemplation of her own blood, and further that her tears were equivalent to Christ's blood. Therefore she could not only pity Christ but identify in him her own perceived bodily suffering" (149).

Like Julian of Norwich, Margery Kempe filters her mystical visions through the lens of medieval views of women's bodies. In *The Book of Margery Kempe* (1436–38) she identifies her blood with Christ's, literalizes her marriage to Him, and emphasizes his sensuality. In fact, she eroticizes God much more explicitly than does Julian:

> When she first felt the fire of love burning in her breast, she was afraid thereof, and then Our Lord answered to her mind and said:
> "Daughter, be not afraid, for this heat is the heat of the Holy Ghost, which shall burn away all thy sins; for the fire of love quencheth all sins." (*LAWL* 424).

While an erotic component is a part of certain male mystics' texts—the Monk of Farne imagines plunging himself into Christ's wounds, while Rupert of Deutz kisses Christ passionately—it is central to Kempe's autobiography.

Feminist scholars have raised interesting questions about whether medieval women's mystical texts, in Lochrie's words, "radically subvert or surreptitiously reinforce the dominant patriarchal discourse of the medieval Church" (115). As the fleshly lover of Christ, the female mystic in some ways excludes herself from conventional notions of transcendence and reifies her own position as immanence, to use Simone de Beauvoir's terms from *The Second Sex* (1949). Perhaps these early women writers speak neither through patriarchal constructions of woman nor from fully autonomous and liberating perspectives of their own, but from somewhere in the borderlands—those same borderlands the author of the *Ancrene Riwle* exhorted religious women to seal. For Carolyn Walker Bynum, medieval female mystics may well constitute the first women's movement in Western history, while for Lochrie they practice an "affirmative transgression" (137). Robertson claims similarly that Julian of Norwich and Margery Kempe ultimately can be seen as "subtle strategists" (161) who challenge male-centered assumptions about femininity and celebrate women's identification with Christ in revolutionary ways.

⊰ Works Cited ⊱

Barratt, Alexandra, ed. *Women's Writing in the Middle Ages*. London and New York: Longman, 1992.

Belanoff, Patricia A. "Women's Songs, Women's Language: *Wulf and Eadwacer* and *The Wife's Lament*." *New Readings on Women in Old English Literature*, eds. Helen Damico and Alexandra Hennessey Olsen. Bloomington: Indiana UP, 1990. 193–203.

Bennett, Helen T. "Exile and the Semiosis of Gender in Old English Elegies." *Class and Gender in Early English Literature*, eds. Britton J. Harwood and Gillian R. Overing. Bloomington: Indiana UP, 1994. 43–58.

Bjork, Robert. "*Sundor Aet Rune*: The Voluntary Exile of the Wanderer." *Neophilologus* 73 (1989): 109–21.

Bogin, Meg, ed. *The Women Troubadours*. New York: Norton, 1980.

Bynum, Carolyn Walker. "The Female Body and Religious Practice in the Later Middle Ages." *Fragments for a History of the Human Body*, Part I, ed. Michel Feher. New York: Urzone Inc., 1989. 161–219.

Chance, Jane. *Woman as Hero in Old English Literature*. Syracuse: Syracuse UP, 1986.

Cherewatuk, Karen and Ulrike Wiethaus. *Dear Sister: Medieval Women and the Epistolary Genre*. Philadelphia: U of Pennsylvania P, 1993.

Damico, Helen. *Beowulf's Wealhtheow and the Valkyrie Tradition*. Madison: U of Wisconsin P, 1984.

de Beauvoir, Simone. *The Second Sex*. Trans. H. M. Parshley, 1949; rpt. Harmondsworth: Penguin, 1972.

Desmond, Marilynn. "The Voice of Exile: Feminist Literary History and the Anonymous Anglo-Saxon Elegy," *Critical Inquiry* 16 (Spring 1990): 572–590.

Fell, Christine E. *Women in Anglo-Saxon England*. Oxford: Basil Blackwell, 1984.

———. "Some Implications of the Boniface Correspondence," *New Readings on Women in Old English Literature*, eds. Helen Damico and Alexandra Hennessey Olsen. Bloomington: Indiana UP, 1990. 29–43.

Frese, Dolores Warwick. "*Wulf and Eadwacer*: The Adulterous Woman Reconsidered." *Notre Dame English Journal* 15 (1983): 1–22.

Hollis, Stephanie. *Anglo-Saxon Women and the Church: Sharing a Common Fate*. Woodbridge, Suffolk: Boydell, 1992.

Lees, Clare A. "Engendering Religious Desire: Sex, Knowledge, and Christian Identity in Anglo-Saxon England." *The Journal of Medieval and Early Modern Studies* 27:1 (Winter 1997): 17–45.

Lees, Clare A. and Gillian R. Overing. "Birthing Bishops and Fathering Poets: Bede, Hild, and the Relations of Cultural Production." *Exemplaria* 6:1 (1995): 35–65.

Lochrie, Karma. "The Language of Transgression: Body, Flesh, and Word in Mystical Discourse." *Speaking Two Languages: Traditional Disciplines and Contemporary Theory in Medieval Studies*, ed. Allen J. Frantzen. Albany: SUNY Press, 1991.

Malone, Kemp. "Two English *Frauenlieder*." *Comparative Literature* 14 (Winter 1962): 106–17.

Osborn, Marijane. "Text and Context of *Wulf and Eadwacer*." *The Old English Elegies: New Essays in Criticism and Research*, ed. Martin Green. Rutherford: Fairleigh Dickinson UP, 1983. 123–32.

Overing, Gillian R. *Language, Sign, and Gender in Beowulf*. Carbondale: Southern Illinois UP, 1990.

Robertson, Elizabeth. "Medieval Medical Views of Women and Female Spirituality in the *Ancrene Wisse* and Julian of Norwich's *Showings*." *Feminist Approaches to the Body in Medieval Literature*, eds. Linda Lomperis and Sarah Stanbury. Philadelphia: U of Pennsylvania P, 1993. 142–67.

Sigal, Gale. *Erotic Dawn-Songs of the Middle Ages: Voicing the Lyric Lady*. Gainesville: The U of Florida P, 1994.

Stenton, Frank M. "The Historical Bearing of Place-Name Studies: The Place of Women in Anglo-Saxon Society." *New Readings on Women in Old English Literature*, eds. Damico and Olsen, 79–88.

Tanke, John W. "*Wonfeax wale*: Ideology and Figuration in the Sexual Riddles of the Exeter Book." *Class and Gender in Early English Literature*, eds. Britton J. Harwood and Gillian R. Overing. Bloomington: Indiana UP, 1994. 21–42.

Thiebaux, Marcelle, ed. *The Writings of Medieval Women: An Anthology*. 2nd ed. New York and London: Garland Publishing Co., 1994.

Williams, Edith Whitehurst. "What's So New about the Sexual Revolution? Some Comments on Anglo-Saxon Attitudes Toward Sexuality in Women Based on Four Exeter Book Riddles." *New Readings on Women in Old English Literature*, eds. Damico and Olsen. 137–45.

Renaissance and Early Seventeenth-Century Literature

1485–1660

The word "Renaissance" comes from the French verb *renaitre*, to be born again, and is associated historically with the rebirth of knowledge after a time of stasis. The period from 1485, when the first Tudor king of England, Henry VII, ascended to the throne, until 1603, when Queen Elizabeth I died, constitutes the English Renaissance, a period of intellectual flowering, nationalistic expansion, and religious reformation. The early seventeenth-century reign of James I (1603–25) and his successor Charles I (1625–49), both Stuart kings, saw increasing political and religious upheaval as well as a continuation of the literary and scholarly awakening that had begun during the preceding century. Because many literary traditions, both male and female, extend through the Tudor and early Stuart periods, it is useful to examine the sixteenth and early seventeenth centuries in tandem.

In literary studies the Renaissance was once synonymous with the flourishing of English literature by men and in particular the age of William Shakespeare (1564–1616), the author of thirty-seven brilliant plays and 154 extraordinary sonnets. During the past twenty years, however, scholars have reconceptualized early modern literature not as a series of works by great men but as texts embedded in their cultural circumstances. Moreover, feminist critics and historians have rediscovered and represented anew both women's writing and ideas about women in the sixteenth and seventeenth centuries. As Helen Wilcox has noted, many paradoxes exist regarding women, writing, and early modern history. While a number of women expressed themselves with creative vitality, they did so in a "gendered world"—"a world of genres and traditions, muses and authors, in which the woman was constructed as the inspiration rather than the creator, the subject of fascination rather than the speaking or controlling subject" (1–2). Nonetheless, the number of women who read and wrote and the quality and range of their writing far exceeded that of medieval Englishwomen. Women in England published nearly one hundred literary works between 1500 and 1600, and between 1600 and 1700 nearly three hundred women published 822 first editions of their work—figures that point toward a burgeoning of female literary production during the seventeenth century. Moreover, these figures do not include the writings of numerous women who circulated their work in manuscripts rather than risking infamy by publishing it. As Wilcox suggests, it was "not straightforward for a woman to circulate or publish her own writings in the early modern era; to do so was a bold, much criticized and frequently isolated action" (2).

In the 1970s the feminist historian Joan Kelly-Gadol asked whether Englishwomen *had* a Renaissance, given the daily realities of their lives (Bridenthal and Koonz 137). Indeed, ordinary women were greatly constrained by law and in society. Legally, women had no status at all but were merely men's wives, daughters, or widows; moreover, religious orthodoxy held that women should be silent and reflect upon the sins of Eve. Despite these painful realities, a number of "firsts" occurred for writing women during this period: "the first autobiography (male or female) in English

(MARGERY KEMPE, 1501), the first English publication of a secular text translated by a woman (Margaret Tyler, 1578), the first original play known to have been written by a woman (Elizabeth Cary, 1613)" (Wilcox 4). One can therefore argue, as does Marion Wynne-Davies, that for Englishwomen this period was a "naissance," a birth rather than a rebirth of knowledge (4). An examination of writing by early modern women will reveal the changing contours of the Renaissance and early seventeenth-century literary canons in English.

Before turning to the literature of the period, it is necessary to consider its historical and cultural context. The era from the late fifteenth to the early sixteenth century was the age of three generations of Tudor monarchs, beginning with Henry VII, who in 1485 won the crown by defeating the infamous Richard III at Bosworth Field, thus ending the thirty-year Wars of the Roses. When Henry, a member of the house of Lancaster, married Elizabeth, a member of the house of York and the niece of Richard III, feudal power was consolidated and the way was paved for the rise of a new nation-state. During the sixteenth century the English established colonies overseas, and as the country shifted from a sheep-raising to a commercial economy, Henry VII made treaties that caused the city of London to triple in size and develop as a metropolitan market. William Caxton's printing press was introduced into England in the 1480s, making printing easier and cheaper over time; as a result literacy rose from 30 to 60 percent from 1470 to 1530. Another effect of increased access to print was the rise of humanism, an emphasis on arts and letters that promoted a new aesthetic based on classical models and individual worth. An important supporter of humanistic learning was Sir Thomas More (1478–1535), who wrote, in Latin, *Utopia* (1514–16), the chronicle of an imaginary and enlightened society based on reason. Ironically, perhaps, he was executed in 1535 for refusing to take Henry VII's oath to the succession and, more decisively, his oath to the royal supremacy. Along with the Dutch scholar Desiderus Erasmus (1466?–1536), More advocated during his lifetime both the classical education of the "Christian gentleman" and the education at home of that gentleman's sisters. At this time the question of whether scholars should write literature and philosophy in Latin, the language of the church fathers as well as that of rediscovered classical texts, or in the Midland dialect that was becoming standard English was very much in question. Eventually the humanistic desire to reach audiences of men and women who did not know Latin, alongside the Protestant Reformation's goal of teaching both women and men to read the Bible for themselves, caused the English language to dominate.

Religious reform was an important issue of the era. Although More and Erasmus favored a united Christendom, conflict developed when Henry VIII divorced his first wife, Catherine of Aragon, and married Anne Boleyn, who would bear him a female heir. Because the Roman Catholic Church would not recognize his second marriage as valid, Henry made himself Supreme Head of the Church of England and renounced the primacy of the "bishop of Rome." What began as a king's stubborn rebellion fast became a revolution that led to the English monarch's establishment as head of both church and state, thus linking nationhood and religion. Ironically, despite his renegade tendencies, Henry VIII remained a Catholic champion who wrote against religious dissenters such as Martin Luther, who longed for a Christianity less dependent on the excesses of a corrupt Catholic hierarchy. After the brief reign of the boy king Edward VI (1547–53), the succession to the throne in 1553 by Mary Tudor, a devout Catholic and the daughter of Catherine of Aragon, caused many Protestants to flee the country. By this time, however, most of Henry VIII's acts in establishing the

Church of England, such as his seizure of the monasteries and his attacks on popular religion and the doctrine of purgatory, were irreversible. Hence after 1558, when Mary died and ELIZABETH I took the throne, the Reformation was resumed in England.

Elizabeth chose to define the church broadly in ways acceptable to most of her subjects, a strategy that freed her to create a strong, united, and ambitious England. Moreover, she manipulated foreign powers by refusing to marry but always holding open the possibility of marriage to other heads of state eager to seize control of England; at the same time she funded merchant adventurers in their voyages to the New World and greatly increased her country's colonial holdings. When a papal decree of 1570 excommunicated Elizabeth, she tightened the oath of allegiance and placed further restrictions on Catholics, by 1585 making priest-harboring a treasonable offense. Ironically, Elizabeth's excommunication inadvertently contributed to national solidarity, although its purpose had been to support the bid of Elizabeth's Catholic cousin, Mary Queen of Scots, to seize the throne. The defeat of the Spanish Armada in 1588 further consolidated Elizabeth's power. Ireland was also being colonized at this time, as the English supported rebellion against Church authorities there in an attempt to eradicate Catholicism. Many of these historical events were chronicled, directly or indirectly, in the nationalistic literature of the age, most notably in Edmund Spenser's *The Faerie Queen* (1590–96), an important admonitory epic that both glorified and advised Elizabeth near the end of her forty-five-year reign.

The writings of Spenser and Shakespeare were made possible in part because of the growth under Queen Elizabeth of a system of literary patronage, the financial support of courtiers seeking to please their monarch by paying tribute to and entertaining her in verse. Sir Philip Sidney, one of the most important Renaissance courtiers, developed the first major English sonnet cycle in *Astrophel and Stella* (1591), which adapted the Petrarchan sonnets first brought to England by the Earl of Surrey to a distinctly English form. Not only was the queen a patron of the arts, but so were certain noblemen and a few noblewomen with resources and energy to spare. MARY SIDNEY HERBERT, who entertained writers at her family home of Wilton, and Margaret Clifford, Countess of Cumberland, are among those who established intellectual circles that encouraged both men and women toward humanistic writing and learning. The development of two major British universities, Oxford and Cambridge, also enhanced literary production, as did the growth of London as a powerful city in which many of the world's foremost printers and book sellers were located. Between 1475 and 1640 more than 26,000 literary works and editions were published in England; authors sold books to publishers outright with no royalties, and since there were no copyright laws, bowdlerization was common. Moreover, Anglican bishops had to approve any work to be published. Both censorship laws and the exigencies of social class led to the circulation of many manuscripts by unorthodox noblemen and a number of noblewomen amongst a circle of friends. In response to Parliament's Licensing Order of 1643, which made the printing, selling, or importing of seditious or offensive books a punishable offense, John Milton wrote *Areopagitica* (1644), which he published without license or registration, although it did bear his name.

Despite many restrictions, an authentically English literature did develop during the Renaissance and early seventeenth century, a literature dominated by men but populated as well by a number of writing women. To understand the development of this literature, we will examine the rise of lyric poetry and drama, genres that few women wrote but many consumed. We will also consider types of writing in which larger numbers of women expressed themselves: religious tracts, conduct manuals, and translations of men's works. Finally, we will examine women's contributions to an important form of polemical writing of the Renaissance and seventeenth century, debates about woman's nature that were known as the *querelles des femmes*.

GENDER AND LYRIC POETRY

Numerous modes of poetic expression developed during the Renaissance: pastoral, heroic, satiric, elegiac, comic, and tragic as well as lyric. The Elizabethans, and later the Jacobeans, especially enjoyed pastoral and epic poetry; thus both Spenser and Milton built their reputations by writing pastoral verse and then turned to epics. Spenser's *The Faerie Queene* celebrated the history and legends of England and admonished its reigning monarch, while Milton's *Paradise Lost* (1667) recounted Biblical along with secular history in an effort to "justify the ways of God to man." Pastoral poetry depicted a simple, idealized world of pleasant shepherds and their nymphs, while epic poetry presented battles and their aftermath; hence the blend reflected in the opening line of Spenser's romantic epic, "Fierce wars and faithful loves shall moralize my song." Sir Philip Sidney's *Arcadia* (1578; 1590) also blended pastoral and heroic properties into a new literary mode, the prose romance, a form that would be developed further in the next generation by his niece, LADY MARY WROTH. Linked to romance by theme and form, lyric poetry took as its subjects love, nature, and the good life. In ancient Greece the term "lyric" was given to verse written to be accompanied by a musical instrument, the lyre, but in Renaissance England the term applied not only to verse set to music but also to odes, poems written to celebrate worthy people and occasions; epithalamia, or marriage tributes; and sonnets, fourteen-line poems depicting courtly love, the ritualized expression of a knight's unrequited passion for his absent, idealized lady.

By the end of the sixteenth century the sonnet had become the quintessential lyric genre. The earliest writers of sonnets in English were Sir Thomas Wyatt and the Earl of Surrey, who wrote sonnets modeled after those of the Italian poet Petrarch. Petrarchan sonnets consisted of fourteen lines of iambic pentameter verse divided into two stanzas, an eight-line octave and a six-line sestet, but Surrey invented a different form that allowed more flexibility than did the Petrarchan sonnet. The poetic experiments of Wyatt and Surrey were published in the popular anthology of 1559, *Tottel's Miscellany*. Beloved for its blend of discipline, amplitude, and musicality, the sonnet typically expressed some aspect of courtly love. The 1591 publication of Sidney's *Astrophel and Stella* launched the first English sequence of love sonnets; the most important sequence after Sidney's, that of Shakespeare, was printed in a pirated edition in 1609, though its composition is believed to date from 1595 to 1599. The first 126 poems are addressed to a male beloved, the remainder to a woman, the so-called "dark lady" of the sonnets; though long speculated, the identity of neither addressee is known, and critics disagree as to whether the poems are autobiographical or formally and thematically experimental. After 1600 the sonnet continued to be popular with the metaphysical poets—John Donne, George Herbert, Henry Vaughan— although less for amorous themes than for religious ones. John Milton used the sonnet form to express personal tribulation in "On His Blindness," as well as political dissent in "On the Late Massacre in Piedmont." For many readers even today, the sonnet remains the quintessential English poetic form.

Several Englishwomen contributed as well to the development of the sonnet. A translator of the sermons of John Calvin, ANNE LOCK, wrote what probably was the first sonnet sequence in English, published in 1560. Presenting her work as "a meditation of a penitent sinner," Lock used Surrey's model to compose a sequence of twenty-one sonnets based on Psalm 51. The five prefatory sonnets were her own and were written syntactically as one continuous utterance. Lock's musical ear was faultless, claims Michael Spiller in his recent history of the sonnet, and her expression of religious passion was unequaled (92). Among the other Renaissance noblewomen who wrote sonnets were Lady Mary Sidney Herbert and LADY MARY WROTH. Herbert, Countess of Pembroke and the sister of Philip Sidney, used the sonnet form to express her religious zeal and to complete the work of translating the Biblical psalms that she and her brother had begun together before his untimely death. As Mary Ellen Lamb points out, issues of gender and authorship were complicated for Herbert: "the Countess creates her authorship as a form of mourning. Not only is Philip the author's only meaningful audience, but he is also her poetry's real author, inspiring her after his death" (116). Elizabeth Hageman, however, attributes more originality to Herbert, arguing that she "applies the psalms to her own situation" and adds references to "such topics as marriage, pregnancy, childbirth, child rearing and gender autonomy" (193). Herbert's niece, Mary Wroth, extended the Elizabethan penchant for the love sonnet to the cynical Jacobean age. *Pamphilia to Amphilanthus* (1621), a group of eighty-three sonnets and nineteen songs, was influenced by the writings of her uncle, aunt, and father but reflected as well the grim mood of the Jacobean court and her own unhappy relationship with her cousin, William Herbert. These sonnets respond to traditional Petrarchan treatments of women as distant, cold, angelic figures by having a woman express her love and demonstrate her constancy. Women sonneteers such as Herbert and Wroth, along with male sonneteers such as Wyatt and Surrey, Sidney, Spenser, and Shakespeare, experimented with many different sonnet forms and are thus remembered for their technical virtuosity as well as their themes of devotion, love, and loss.

Other women poets of the sixteenth and early seventeenth centuries experimented not with sonnets but with different lyric forms. Queen Elizabeth composed numerous lyric poems, several of which expressed courtly conventions—for example, the contrast of paired opposites, or despair at love denied—from a woman's point of view. ISABELLA WHITNEY, the first professional woman poet in England, published 110 "philosophical flowers," as she called her verse, in a 1573 volume entitled *A Sweet Nosegay*. As Randall Martin notes, Whitney "must have needed extraordinary resources of self-motivation and confidence simply to compose and publish original verse in the absence of any contemporary role models; the only woman to do so at this time beside herself was the Queen—an exception in every sense" (279). A later secular poet, MARGARET CAVENDISH, showed remarkable courage as well in defying propriety and publishing verse. *Poems and Fancies*, published in 1653 to some acclaim, was by all accounts a daring work, especially to the growing female readership of the era. "They say it is ten times more extravagant than her dress," wrote Dorothy Osborne to her friend William Temple of Cavendish's book in 1653. "For God sake if you meet with it send it me" (Greer 164). Indeed, the most popular woman poet of the seventeenth century, KATHERINE PHILIPS, the "matchless Orinda," geared some of her work toward a female audience and celebrated friendship between women. Her verse, known for its grace and charm, generally upheld propriety rather than challenging it, as had the work of Whitney and Cavendish. Despite significant differences, these early women lyricists all fit the description Cavendish had etched on her tombstone in Westminster Abbey: they were "wise, witty, and learned ladies."

THE RISE OF AN ENGLISH DRAMATIC TRADITION

The earliest form of drama in England was the mystery plays, which began as scriptural interpretation in churches during the Middle Ages. By the middle of the fifteenth century these plays were performed as part of religious festivals in churchyards or in towns on moveable stages. In this century morality plays developed as well, allegorical narratives such as the anonymous *Everyman* (c.1500), whose protagonists enacted human foibles and apparently reinforced by example the need to follow Christian doctrine. Because of audience interest in religious drama, a secular form arose during the sixteenth century for the purpose of entertaining nobility in their estates or at court. The theater became professional at this time as well, as the actors changed from clergymen to trade guildsmen and performers who attached themselves to noblemen; only men acted, for women were not allowed on stage until the Restoration. In 1576 the first public theater (aptly called "The Theater") was established by the actor James Burbage in Shoreditch, just outside the city of London; it was eventually followed in 1599 by the Globe, where many of Shakespeare's plays were performed. Additionally, a rise in the status of actors occurred during Shakespeare's day, as can be seen in the shift from the penurious and dangerous working conditions of Shakespeare's initial company, the Lord Chamberlain's Men, to the patronage of theater by Queen Elizabeth, who established the Queen's Men in 1583 and thus challenged Puritan attacks on the theater.

The two main theatrical genres to succeed mystery and morality plays were comedies and tragedies. Nicholas Udall's *Ralph Roister Doister* (1550), an English adaptation of a Latin farce, was the first comedy produced in England; among its characters was the prototype for the braggart soldier that led to Shakespeare's figure Sir John Falstaff in *Henry IV* and *Henry V*. Shakespeare's earliest comedy, *The Comedy of Errors* (1592), was based on Plautus' *Menaechmi* but rejected the mercenary view of society promulgated by its classical source in favor of a farcical but benign treatment of confusion in love. Henceforth many of Shakespeare's best comedies—*A Midsummer Night's Dream* (1595–96), for example, and *As You Like It* (1599–1600)—used mythology, fancy, and pastoral romance to depict strong female characters as well as sexual desire and its resolution in marriage. Because of its popularity during the Renaissance, comedy as a theatrical genre developed in diverse ways. Shakespeare turned to tragicomedy in *Measure for Measure* (1600), Ben Jonson composed comedy of intrigue in *The Alchemist* (1610), and Thomas Middleton wrote "citizen comedy" in *A Chaste Maid in Cheapside* (1613), in which a merchant conducts a war of wits against a country gentleman. Shakespeare's foremost rival during his lifetime, Jonson, became known as one of the seventeenth century's finest comic playwrights. Unlike most of his rival's comedies, Jonson's masterpiece, *Volpone* (1606), a concentrated satire, revealed the cynicism that dominated the Jacobean court.

If the gaiety and extravagance of comedy lightened the hearts of Renaissance and Jacobean playgoers, surely the seriousness and intensity of tragedy troubled them. The four principles that lay at the heart of tragedy were first set forth by Aristotle in his *Poetics*: the noble protagonist must reveal an irredeemable flaw; that flaw must cause him to fall from great heights; his fall must be accompanied by a series of reversals and discoveries; and his destruction must evoke the audience's fear and pity. The first English tragedy, Sackville and Norton's *Gorboduc* (1561), was acted initially in a law school and eventually performed for Queen Elizabeth; indeed, tragedy became almost as popular as comedy in the Queen's court. *Gorboduc* was based on the violent model of the Roman dramatist Seneca, whose plays were translated into English and published in 1581; his bloody plots, intense rhetorical speeches, and frequent ghosts influenced subsequent tragedians from Thomas Kyd (*The Spanish Tragedy*, 1592) to Shakespeare, whose *Hamlet* (1601) was indebted to both Seneca and Kyd. Other Renaissance tragedies, most notably Christopher Marlowe's *Dr. Faustus* (1592) and Shakespeare's *Othello* (1604), owed their treatment of the struggle between good and evil to medieval morality plays as well as to Senecan depictions of revenge. Seventeenth-century tragedy became bleaker still with John Webster's *The White Devil* (1612), which based its plot on a sensational murder of the era, and John Ford's *'Tis Pity She's a Whore* (1633), which dealt with incestuous love. Anxiety and ambivalence lay at the core of the Renaissance and seventeenth-century tragic paradigm, as the emphasis on individual freedom of conscience promoted by humanism and the Reformation came into conflict with tightening social structures: a closed family system, prescribed gender roles, an increasingly difficult system of patronage, and a centralized government.

One Renaissance woman who contributed significantly to the rise of drama wrote "closet drama" intended only for staged readings rather than for production. Elizabeth Cary, Lady Falkland (1585–1639) composed *The Tragedy of Mariam* between 1602 and 1604; the first original play by an Englishwoman, it concerns the marital and political struggles of the Jewish Queen Mariam, who ultimately rebels against her husband, King Herod, by speaking her conscience. Although Senecan in its construction, *The Tragedy of Mariam* maintains fidelity to the unities of time and place recommended by Aristotle and explores the equivocal potential of a conventional chorus; its primary source was the *Antiquities* of Josephus. A second play, *History of the Life, Reign, and Death of Edward II* (1627), is widely accepted as Cary's; if so, it was the first political history written by a woman in England. Insisting in the preface that she would not set forth a "dull" chronicle, she determined instead to examine the moral and political lessons to be learned from her characters' experiences. Isobel Grundy has called *Edward II* a "hybrid" text—"highly literary, morally questioning, sometimes elaborately and sometimes stiffly rhetorical" (82–83). Cary might well have identified with her female protagonist, Queen Isabel, for in 1626 she converted to Catholicism and was subsequently persecuted by her Protestant husband, who seized both her children and her money. Writing with her "melancholy pen" became a source of comfort for Cary, according to her daughter, who wrote a biography of her mother while in the Catholic convent at Lille, where the manuscript remains; it was copied around 1655 and published in 1861 by Richard Simpson. Although Cary as a woman could not have participated in the public and professional life of the theater as did Shakespeare and his male contemporaries, she deserves recognition as the first female tragedian in English.

WOMEN WRITERS AND RELIGIOUS DISSENT

In his 1997 anthology of Renaissance women writers Randall Martin argues that contemporary scholars have been slow to recover hidden texts by women of the period because they lack sympathy for the religious subjects about which these women wrote. He goes on to implore readers not to collude with such silences by ignoring this important area of writing (8–11). The Protestant Reformation, after all, enhanced women's literacy and led to their greater participation in public life, since religion and politics were closely linked. In fact, this sweeping movement so greatly changed the lives of English citizens that the scholar Janel Mueller has reframed Joan Kelly-Gadol's question "did women have a Renaissance?" to wonder "did women have a Reformation?" (Mueller 15) By emphasizing a person's unmediated relationship with God, Reformation doctrine helped many women justify their wish to read and write, since, as Martin claims, "divine atonement and personal salvation [were] dependent upon individual agency" (9). Moreover, the desire to write and publish could be justified on religious terms as contributing to the spiritual well-being of self and others. For some women, publication led to self-consciousness and subjectivity, to the rethinking of traditional discourses and prescribed gender roles.

To be sure, the phenomenon of the learned lady was short-lived, in part because to express alternative knowledge was dangerous for Renaissance women. From St. Paul to St. Augustine to Tertullian, the early church fathers had prohibited women from speaking publicly on religious topics. The infamous *Malleus Maleficarum*, or *Witches' Hammer* (1486), associated European women healers and spiritual leaders with witchcraft; it was the foremost handbook of an inquisition in continental Europe that led to the martyrdom of hundreds of thousands of unconventional women, burned at the stake as witches. In Renaissance England, too, outspoken women were punished for religious and domestic insubordination, though relatively few were executed. Many fathers simply found it unnecessary to educate their daughters, and as Protestantism and its outgrowth, Puritanism, gained currency, women's education was increasingly and negatively associated with the Catholic humanism of Sir Thomas More and other early advocates. Nonetheless, as Elaine Beilin demonstrates in *Redeeming Eve* (1987), the advent of a scripture-reading culture that let women speak with authority on religious subjects did emerge in the seventeenth century, and this phenomenon led to women's enhanced awareness of themselves as literary agents.

More than half of all literature to reach print in Renaissance England was religious in nature. From William Dunbar's *Dance of the Seven Deadly Sins* (1507) to William Tyndale's translation of the New Testament (1525) to John Knox's *History of the Reformation in Scotland* (1584), men published religious arguments, scriptures, and histories better known in their time than the secular masterpieces of Sidney and Shakespeare. Although many women who wrote on religious subjects prior to 1650 did not reach publication, those who did used scriptural reinterpretation to examine both received notions of spiritual authority and the landscape of their own lives. Here we shall examine four such women, two of whom wrote religious tracts and two of whom used religious analogies and images to justify their secular writing: Anne Askew, Katherine Parr, Anne Dowriche, and AEMILIA LANYER.

The Protestant dissenter Anne Askew (1520–1546) apparently sought to escape an oppressive arranged marriage by claiming that her husband was an unbeliever, but the conservative court before which she brought her complaint refused to accept her argument. Instead, Roman Catholic authorities who wished to eradicate religious reform tried to brand her as a member of the renegade party, arresting her in 1545 and cross-examining her to determine whether she accepted the controversial doctrine of transubstantiation. Although Henry VIII had by this time broken with Rome and seized the English monasteries, Catholicism remained dominant in England. The last wife of Henry VIII, Katherine Parr, may have helped to secure Askew's acquittal, perhaps because the elderly king's ministers feared public reaction to her conviction. Askew's *First Examination* (1546) gave a searing account of the inquiries to which she was subjected, including her forced signing of a statement of faith prepared by Bishop Bonner, although one that she insisted on altering to protect her right to individual religious expression. Askew's troubles were not over, however; later in 1545 she was again brought to trial, this time for heresy, and was tortured by two of Henry's most ruthless ministers; when she refused to submit, they used St. Paul's restrictions on women's public speech in an effort to silence her. Even after Askew was condemned to death and taken to the Tower of London she was tortured on the rack, an unprecedented abuse of an English gentlewoman. *The Latter Examination,* written in prison and published posthumously in 1547, offered a detailed account of that abuse and therefore had enormous emotional appeal. Indeed, Askew inspired other religious dissenters through her terse, angry, and clever rhetoric: "Then the bishop said I should be burned. I answered that I had searched all the scriptures yet could I never find there that either Christ or his apostles put any creature to death. 'Well, well,' said I, 'God will laugh your threatenings to scorn' (Psalm 2). Then I was commanded to stand aside." After her execution Askew's *Examinations* were published by the Protestant polemicist John Bale, who proclaimed her the foremost female religious martyr of the age but downplayed both her rhetorical skills and her heroic resistance (Beilin 1996).

Few female religious writers died for their beliefs, as Anne Askew did, in part because they were protected by their associations with powerful men. Many historians believe, in fact, that the ministers who interrogated and executed Askew really wished to silence Katherine Parr (1512–1548), the aging Henry's influential queen after 1543 and a Protestant convert. Although Parr failed to assert spiritual authority in as radical a manner as Askew did, she revealed in her actions and her writing a commitment to spiritual and political renewal. Educated by the Spanish humanist Juan Luis Vives, she chose humanist tutors for Prince Edward and Princess Elizabeth, Henry's children by his prior marriages, and she convinced Henry to restore Elizabeth and her sister Mary to the line of royal succession, from which they had been excluded on the grounds of illegitimacy. In 1545, when Askew was arrested for the second time, the Queen's rooms were searched for evidence of Protestant subversion, but since nothing incriminating was found she escaped arrest. However, she was forced to submit publicly to Henry's authority and could no longer intervene on Askew's behalf. Only after Henry's death in 1547 did she publish *The Lamentation of a Sinner,* both an autobiography and a statement of faith. Janel Mueller has described it as "an unfolding of the momentous significance [Parr] discerned in her Protestant conversion," but scholars agree that although it criticized the self-righteousness of certain Catholic authorities, it had a less defiant tone than Askew's polemic (15).

Askew's *Examinations* and Parr's *Lamentation* were two of many assertions of faith published by Englishwomen prior to the civil war of 1642. In addition, numerous Renaissance women cited scriptural authority as a justification for their writing on unorthodox topics. In her preface to *The French History* (1589), a verse-chronicle of the sufferings of the Huguenots (French Protestants) by one who sympathized with their plight, Anne Dowriche quoted a famous section of Corinthians: "What is to be done then, brethren? When ye come together, according as every one of you hath a psalm, or hath doctrine, or hath a tongue, or hath revelation, or hath interpretation, let all things be done unto edifying." For the edification of other Christians, therefore, Dowriche offered her treatise in full awareness that St. Paul also forbade women to speak in public, a proscription she chose to ignore. Like many women of the times, Dowriche tried to protect herself and her writing from male censure through a pose of modesty; as Beilin notes, she hesitated to call herself a poet yet attempted "no less than to write God's truth, to regenerate poetry, and to move a wide audience with her power" (102). In its argument that English Protestants should show solidarity with their French brethren, *The French History* anticipated the strategies used later by Christopher Marlowe in his *Massacre at Paris* (1592), which drew on similar sources to advocate English support of French Protestant dissent. Dowriche's text can be seen as radical in combining secular history, religious dissent, and political intervention; at the end she daringly implored Queen Elizabeth to respond to Huguenot requests for aid and to resist any attempt to make England Catholic.

One of the most overtly feminist revisions of religious doctrine of the early modern period was written by Aemilia Lanyer (1569–1645), the daughter of a court musician who probably began writing out of economic need, as a means of attracting patrons. Despite prohibitions against women's public speech, women were accorded increasing authority to publish writing on religious matters; few, however, wrote poetry. While *Salve Deus Rex Judaeorum* (1611) focused on Christ's passion, it contained as well a commentary on Adam as a sinner worse than Eve, sympathy for the suffering of the Virgin, and a reflection on the relationship between the feminized Christian soul and the crucified Jesus. In its lyricism Lanyer's work followed in the footsteps of Anne Lock's poetic meditations on Psalm 51, which, Susanne Woods speculates, were probably known to her, and Mary Sidney Herbert's translations of the Psalms, which Lanyer certainly read, since they circulated widely in manuscript. Yet Lanyer claimed a Biblical and historical authority that these earlier women writers did not. Moreover, as Woods points out, Lanyer's volume was unique in being dedicated only to women patrons and in refusing to endorse the dominant ideology that a woman should write religious poetry only if she apologized for it (xxx–xxxv). Finally, her baroque description of Christ's blood anticipated the sensual religiosity of Richard Crashawe, the seventeeth-century Catholic metaphysical poet.

As Margaret Ezell has noted, the period from 1642 to 1660, when the English civil war took place, witnessed the claim to public voice of many female religious dissenters (132–60). Among the most vocal were Quakers such as the itinerant minister Priscilla Cotton, who defended women's preaching in *To the Priests and the People of England* (1655), and the polemicist Margaret Fell (1614–1702), who wrote pamphlets defending her faith to Oliver Cromwell in the 1650s and produced a defense of her religious writing, *Women's Speaking Justified*, in 1666. Like Lanyer, these women found in Christ's "feminine" qualities of love and mercy a means of challenging conventional sexual dichotomies and prohibitions against women's expression of spiritual equality. In the words of Randall Martin, "while social changes brought about by humanist theories and Reformation ideologies admittedly had little effect in achieving greater female participation in politics, government, and related areas, they did gradually encourage many women to develop a heightened awareness about their own nature and status, and to prompt a few into writing eloquently creative challenges to gender restrictions" (11).

WOMEN'S CONDUCT MANUALS

During the Renaissance and the early seventeenth century numerous women wrote conduct manuals that reflected their sense of responsibility for child rearing, household management, community health care, and midwifery. Yet no clear public and private spheres existed in this period: home was not yet exclusively defined for the nuclear family but rather extended to friends, servants, tenants, and distant family as well. Hence communal child rearing was dominant, and men as well as women discussed the nature of that care and gave written advice to other parents and to children. These advice books typically offered moral precepts and adages; both men's and women's counsel was didactic and stressed godly living above all. As Valerie Wayne notes, such books were "a counterpart to our modern self-help books in that they offered early modern women advice on how to improve their lives" (156). Here we shall concentrate on four female writers of conduct books, all of whom address the topic of motherhood.

Elizabeth Grymeston (1563?–1603) completed *Miscellanea, Meditations, Memoratives* shortly before her death; it was published posthumously in 1604 and was probably edited by her husband. This treatise offered an account of the "true portraiture" of her mind as well as her interest in classical literature, theology, and languages; its mix of genres raises the question of whether advice manuals offered early women an approved format for raising their voices on diverse topics. Grymeston's declared purpose was the instruction of her son Bernye, whom she addressed during an illness that she feared might prove fatal; her spiritual counsel focused on the importance of renouncing worldly goods. A number of miscellanea were added to the second edition in 1606, however, addressing such civil subjects as political leadership, murder, treason, and the qualifications required of judges—areas of inquiry normally reserved for men. Grymeston's perspective was complicated by the fact that she was Catholic, a faith whose practice was illegal in England at this time and for which her cousin Robert Southwell, a prominent priest, had been executed in 1595; hence she realized that civil, religious, and domestic matters were inseparable. Expressions of maternal love, spiritual piety, and ethical reflection dominated Grymeston's essays. Her work was popular enough to be published in four editions and thus represents a major contribution to this developing genre (Wayne 165–66, Martin 97–116, Travitsky 49–55).

The conduct manuals of DOROTHY LEIGH and Elizabeth Jocelin contained a similar emphasis to Grymeston's, that of instilling traditional moral values in their children. Like Grymeston they justified their decision to write because they anticipated their own deaths, not from illness but from childbirth, the leading cause of death among young women during this era. A sense of urgency allowed Leigh, for instance, to "forget the usual custom of woman"—to keep silent—and instead instruct not only her young children but other parents as well. Leigh's narrative strategy suggests a self-conscious positioning of herself as authority; she opened with an introductory poem, offered two dedications, one to Princess Elizabeth of Denmark, and justified her writing as supported by her husband. Interestingly, Leigh ignored the rules of primogeniture, a complex system of transferring property to the eldest male heir, and instead treated her sons as equals. Also radical for the time was her refusal to apologize for her sex; indeed, she denounced the social abuses against women in an almost angry tone. Leigh also defended literacy for women and for servants in her tract and supported the emerging ideology of the companionate marriage, a union based not wholly on female subservience but on mutual obligation and at least nominal gender reciprocity. Published in 1616, *The Mother's Blessing* determined "to broaden the scope of legitimate discussion open to a female author and to emphasize the national consequences of individual approaches to child rearing and education" (Martin 117–25, Beilin 280–85, Travitsky 55–57).

Elizabeth Jocelin's conduct book, *The Mother's Legacy to Her Unborn Child* (1624), was one of the most popular original works by a Renaissance woman; it was reissued eleven times between 1624 and 1674, translated into Dutch in 1699, and widely printed in the eighteenth and nineteenth centuries. Its popularity stemmed in part from its apologetic tone, a combination of self-deprecation and maternal solicitude, and in part from its conventional gender ideology, which advocated different strategies for raising boys and girls. Boys should be well educated, she asserted, prepared ideally for the life of an evangelizing Calvinist minister, while girls should be taught Biblical scripture, basic writing skills, and housework—"other learning a woman needs not." Jocelin presented her advice as a model of ideal conduct for one day in the life of her unborn child; she wrote it during pregnancy and did indeed die in childbirth. Her introductory epistle to her husband declared her devotion and emphasized that her comments would address the domestic sphere only. Unlike Grymeston and Leigh, Jocelin did not offer public counsel on nonmaternal topics, although an "Approbation" written by the clergyman Thomas Goad claimed a wider value for her treatise (Martin 34–41, Travitsky 60–63).

ELIZABETH CLINTON's advice manual differed from those of her contemporaries in arguing that noblewomen should breast-feed their children, an unorthodox notion for the time; she also challenged the upper-class custom of wet-nursing as an "unnatural practice" and one exploitative of working-class women. In *The Countess of Lincoln's Nursery* (1622) Clinton claimed that breast-feeding had a long and honorable history and that women and their infants would benefit emotionally and medically from this practice; in addition, she confessed her own regret at having hired a wet-nurse for her children. Although Clinton apparently convinced few women of the need for "giving the sweet milk of your own breasts to your own child," her treatise represented a distinctively feminine form of the advice manual (Martin 148–59, Travitsky 57–60).

A number of important sixteenth and seventeenth century works of prose were written or commissioned by men: Thomas More's *Utopia* (1514), a major proponent of humanistic learning; *The Book of Common Prayer*, commissioned by King Edward VI in 1549; and the King James Bible of 1611. To understand Renaissance culture and literary history fully, one must examine conduct manuals by women alongside religious texts and philosophical treatises. These manuals reveal the ways in which philosophy, parenting, and early modern women's lives intersected.

MEN, WOMEN, AND TRANSLATION

Reverence for classical literature dominated the early Renaissance, and numerous male and female scholars translated works of importance to the development of humanistic learning. Henry Howard, Earl of Surrey, translated Virgil's *Aeneid* in the

1540s; William Tyndale translated the New Testament from the Greek (1525); and George Chapman produced definitive translations of Homer's *Iliad* (1611) and *Odyssey* (1615). Sir Thomas Hoby translated Castiglione's *The Courtier* (1561), a treatise that influenced behavior at court as well as poetic conventions. Another great translation of the period was Ann Bacon's translation of John Jewell's *Apology of the Church of England* (1564). Since Renaissance society did not place the same emphasis on "originality" as do readers today—many of Shakespeare's finest plays relied heavily upon earlier sources—translation was widely considered an art rather than a craft, and scholars typically received considerable praise and some money for successful translations. Typically the goal of translation was less a precise rendering of a foreign text than its presentation in an English spirit. Translating was one of the few literary endeavors open to educated Renaissance women, since bringing the work of famous men to an elite male audience did not conflict with the established moral values associated with women: piety, chastity, and obedience. Although women found it especially congenial to write and occasionally to publish religious translations, a few made their mark with secular works.

Elizabeth I initiated her work as a translator at the age of fifteen, when she completed a translation of Marguerite de Navarre's *Mirror of the Sinful Soul* (1548). Fluent in Latin, Greek, French, and Italian, she went on to translate classical works such as Horace's *Art of Poetry*, Boethius's *Consolation of Philosophy*, Xenophon's dialogues, and Isocrates's speeches, as well as modern ones such as Petrarch's "Triumph of Eternity." For Elizabeth, translation represented a scholarly interest and a source of intellectual stimulation, and her work as a translator paid homage to the classical literature that humanism extolled. In contrast, ANNE LOCK's motivation for translation was primarily religious. In 1560 she published her French-to-English translation, *Sermons of John Calvin, Upon the Song that Ezechias Made*, to advertise the religious teachings of a man she admired. In her dedication to the Duchess of Suffolk, Lock justified her publication as a means of helping men "oppressed with poverty, tossed with worldly adversity, and tormented with pain, soreness, and sickness of body," to develop "minds armed and furnished with prepared patience" (*Sermons*, A1). Reading Calvin's sermons, she claimed, would bring hope and relief to the spiritually weary.

Another female translator was Margaret Tyler, who translated a Spanish romance by Ortuñez, *The Mirror of Princely Deeds and Knighthood*, into English in 1578. In the "Epistle to the Reader" that accompanied her translation, Tyler claimed in print women's intellectual equality with men, defending her choice of a chivalric text on the grounds that it was "a legitimate exercise of the creative imagination." To offset Protestant objections to her translation of a work suspected of being Catholic in its origins, as well as humanist objections that the text revealed excessive courtly passion, she denigrated translation as a derivative literary form, "a matter of more heed than of deep invention or exquisite learning" (Martin 15). During Tyler's lifetime women were not only prohibited from writing romances, they were forbidden as well to read them, an effort led by the otherwise liberal Juan Luis Vives, a Spanish tutor who favored women's education but felt that their exposure to European romances might lead to immorality. The prohibition on women's writing romances was not broken until 1621, when Lady Mary Wroth published *The Countess of Montgomery's Urania*. However, Tyler paved the way for Wroth in arguing successfully that women should be allowed to translate romances because they promoted chivalry. She further argued that if women's opinions could be so highly valued that men would dedicate their literary works to women, then women should not be prohibited from translating the works of men (Martin 15–24).

In 1585 Mary Sidney Herbert began collaborating with her brother on a translation of the Biblical psalms into verse form; they had completed forty-three psalms by the time of Philip Sidney's death in 1586, and Herbert translated the rest herself over the next thirteen years. The "Sidney Psalms," renowned for their technical brilliance and lyric beauty, were well known in seventeenth-century literary circles but remained unpublished until 1823. The fact that Herbert translated under her brother's auspices gave her tacit permission to continue after his death. In 1590 she published a translation of Petrarch's *Trionfo della Morte* widely praised for its *terza rima* renditions; she went on to translate *The Tragedie of Marc Antonie* by Robert Garnier and *Discours de la Vie et de la Mort* by Philippe de Mornay. By undertaking religious translation with her brother, Sidney gained access to the world of secular translation as well (Martin 311–36; see also Waller).

Several seventeenth-century women also made their marks as translators, most notably the poet Katherine Philips, whose translation of Corneille's *La Mort de Pompee* was performed in Dublin in 1663 to such great acclaim that the translation was published three weeks later. Philips had Royalist sympathies and relied heavily on the favors of men connected with Charles II's court to promote her translations, but her publisher also advertised that the translation was done by her. Indeed, by the mid-seventeenth century it had become acceptable for women to publish their translations and for those translations to be praised as works of art.

GENDER AND THE *QUERELLES DES FEMMES*

Literary debates about the nature and status of women, or "querelles des femmes," began during the Middle Ages in France and England and continued in various forms during the Renaissance and early seventeenth century. In these debates women were censured by men for insufficient piety, excessive sexuality, and improper public speech. Typically women were condemned for expressing opinions on any issue other than the religious or domestic, and sometimes for addressing these topics as well. As Katherine Henderson and Barbara McManus have demonstrated, during the fifteenth century the number of tracts about women increased dramatically in England, although all of them were initially written by men. Many men wrote both for and against women. John Lydgate, for example, alternately praised and blamed women in his *Pilgrimage of the Life of a Man* (1426–30). Moreover, the first half of the sixteenth century witnessed English translations of texts by European writers participating in debates about women, most notably Christine de Pisan, the German Cornelius Agrippa, the Dutch humanist Desiderus Erasmus, and the Spanish humanist Juan Luis Vives. These writers all supported education for women, a bold stance for the times, and the three men in particular greatly influenced English humanists. In 1540 Sir Thomas Elyot published *The Defense of Good Women*, composed as a Platonic dialogue to counter the misogynistic accusations "with praise of modest, pious, obedient" members of the female sex; among the women he lauded was Zenobia, the ancient queen of Palmyra, an important figure in his dialogue.

The sixteenth-century "pamphlet wars" that debated women's nature and roles differed from their predecessors for several reasons. The rise of the printing press resulted in an increase in the number of attacks on women and a wider distribution of these texts to eager middle-class readers. As these treatises developed, they became less courtly in nature. They also became more secular, although many still relied upon biblical sources for their proscriptions on women's activities. Interestingly, the number of defenses of women rose with the number of attacks, although more attacks were reprinted during the Renaissance than were defenses. The "woman question" appeared in all types of literature—poetry, drama, romance—not merely in pamphlets; however, polemical tracts became the most popular genre to advance these debates.

The first significant antiwoman pamphlets of the sixteenth century were *The Schoolhouse of Women*, a long and thorough attack on women, and *Mulierium Paean*, a diatribe often attributed to Edward Gosynhill; both appeared around 1541. In 1542 an anonymous response to these attacks, *The Praise of All Women*, defended women's piety in conventional ways and offered a lengthy account of the difficulties women faced in giving birth and raising children. Shortly thereafter *A Dialogue Defensive for Women Against Malicious Detractors*, attributed to Robert Vaughan, used the medieval form of an argument between birds to present its thesis. After a magpie cast aspersions on female character, a falcon defended women, ultimately winning the debate through reason and common sense. In 1558 John Knox, a Protestant dissenter, wrote a misogynist attack directed against the Catholic ruler Mary Tudor in which he argued that a female monarch offended nature, religion, and reason. *The First Blast of the Trumpet Against the Monstrous Regiment of Women* appeared, ironically, just before Elizabeth I ascended to the throne of England. Needless to say, both patriotism and expediency provoked a number of male courtiers to rise to the defense of the queen. The best known of these, John Aylmer's untitled response (1559), purported to defend women's right to rule yet asserted their inferiority to men, thus undercutting its own argument. Old debates resurfaced during this period as well. In 1560 a late response to *The Schoolhouse of Women* appeared, this one by Edward More, the grandson of Sir Thomas More, the Christian humanist beheaded by Henry VIII. *A Little and Brief Treatise Called the Defense of Women*, composed by this twenty-year-old bachelor, apologized for its author's youth and inexperience but challenged accusations of women's sexual improprieties. Despite his defense of women, More employed chivalrous terms that often relied on stereotypes; he asserted, for instance, that English women could be only virtuous because they lacked the hot blood of Roman women! Near the end of the 1560s C. Perryl wrote *The Praise and Dispraise of Women*, two poems and a dialogue in which he alternated between attacking women as monsters and praising them as angels. Together with other pamphleteers, Perryl reinforced the long-established demon-whore paradigm that would haunt literary representations of women for centuries to come (Henderson and McManus 11–14).

The formal controversy over women's status then died down for nearly twenty years, although it appeared less formally in several literary works, including John Lyly's popular prose romance *Eupheus* (1578). The year 1589 marked a new burst of writing on this topic and women writers' entry into the debates. In this year Thomas Nashe's *The Anatomy of Absurdity* appeared, challenging the "unsavory duncery" of the many works that praised women and quoting diverse misogynist views by classical authorities. Nashe's work provoked a response by Jane Anger, who was once believed to be a man writing pseudonymously but is now widely accepted as the woman who wrote the first defense of her sex in English. *Protection for Women* (1589) was a self-possessed work that not only failed to offer the traditional apologies of women who dared to write but also berated men for their unfairness. Anger's introduction, "To All Women in General," began, "Fie on the falsehood of men, whose minds go oft a-meddling and whose tongues cannot so soon be wagging but straight they fall a-railing"—an ingenious reversal of the stereotype of the gossiping woman. Declaring herself a "clamorous avenger," Anger took to task both Nashe's pamphlet and an even more egregious one known as the *Book of Surfeit*, whose author is unknown. Arguing by compilation, she gathered antiwoman allusions from the *Book of Surfeit* in order to refute them. Although Anger's contribution to the *querelles des femmes* was important, feminist scholars disagree as to whether her work was derivative or original. Some scholars have claimed that *Protection for Women* did not differ significantly from male defenses because it stigmatized women who expressed their sexuality, but Henderson and McManus argue that Anger wrote with conviction of women's "intellectual and moral worth" and that she was bold in critiquing men for failing to recognize these virtues (24–31).

In 1615 another series of debates was spawned with the publication of Joseph Swetnam's *Arraignment of Lewd, Idle, Forward, and Unconstant Women*, a tract published under the pseudonym Thomas Tell-Troth. Relying heavily on the arguments of John Lyly, Swetnam parodied advice manuals for women and posed as a worldly traveler whose duty was to list the many examples of women's depravity that he had encountered. A fierce response appeared in 1617 by RACHEL SPEGHT, who condemned Swetnam as a blackmouth, or slanderer. Diane Purkiss has argued that Swetnam wrote his tract not out of deeply held misogyny but instead to generate titillation and pleasure for male readers, whom he hoped would enter the pamphlet debates themselves to earn money and have fun at women's expense (73–78). He might also have intended to console bachelors whose marriage prospects were poor. Speght's response, however, *A Muzzle for Melastomus, The Cynical Baiter of, and Foul-Mouthed Barker Against Eve's Sex*, mounted a serious defense of women grounded in scripture and showed impressive learning for a woman of nineteen. Both Swetnam's attack on women and Speght's defense were published by the bookseller Thomas Archer, who hoped to make a profit on these debates and evidently did so. Yet Swetnam's misogynist tract was reprinted ten times between 1615 and 1637, while Speght's treatise fell quickly out of print. Although Swetnam's pamphlet provided the impetus for Speght's defense of women, her treatise revealed a larger goal: the use of religious doctrine to assert a woman's right to a public voice. This right was also asserted by Speght's successor in the Jacobean pamphlet wars, the pseudonymous Esther Sowernam (perhaps a man posing as a woman). Sowernam claimed that Speght was too young to respond adequately to Swetnam and criticized her tract as "slender." On the other hand, another essayist who challenged Swetnam, Constantia Munda (also a pseudonym and perhaps a man), praised Speght's treatise as an impressive defense of womanhood to which her own was indebted. Certainly Speght deserves praise, in Barbara Lewalski's words, as "the first Englishwoman to identify herself, by name, as a polemicist and critic of contemporary gender ideology" (xi).

Another interesting aspect of the seventeenth-century pamphlet wars about women was a debate launched by King James himself in 1620 when he spoke publicly against women who donned male clothing. In a letter to his bishops the king urged them to "inveigh vehemently" in their sermons against "the insolence of our women and their wearing of broad-brimmed hats, pointed doublets, their hair cut short or shorn, and some of their stilettes or pomaids, and such other trinkets of like moment." Just how many women were guilty of these sartorial offenses is unclear, but James's outburst provoked three immediate responses by pamphleteers whose identities are today unknown. The first of these, *The Man-Woman*, supported the king's position, arguing that women's masculine style was "unnatural." The second pamphlet, *The Womanish Man*, countered by claiming that not only did women sometimes adopt male dress but men often adopted women's; it went on to critique the clothing and habits of the fop as unseemly. *Mulled Sack*, the third treatise, attacked both masculine women and feminine men as blasphemous. These debates reveal the amount of insecurity experienced by men of the era when traditional sex roles and long-accepted dress codes began to be challenged (Henderson and McManus 17–18).

Christopher Newstead's *An Apology for Women* (1620) heralded a return to more scholarly debate about women's status, as he offered a humanistic defense of women's piety, continence, and chastity. This dignified tone prevailed until the 1639 publication of John Taylor's vituperative tracts, *A Juniper Lecture* and *Divers Crabtree Lectures*. These pamphlets portrayed women as extravagant shrews, thus shifting the terms of the debates from sexuality to domestic power and economics. Again women came to the rescue of their sex: *A Woman's Sharp Revenge* (1640), written under the pseudonyms Mary Tattlewell and Joan Hit-Him-Home, responded to Taylor point by point and attempted to refute misogynist claims about women. While some scholars argue that Tattlewell and Hit-Him-Home were actually Taylor answering himself, others claim these as independent women's voices of resistance (Henderson and McManus 18–20).

Women such as Anger, Speght, Sowernam, Munda, Tattlewell, and Hit-Him-Home are important today because they added female voices to the *querelles des femmes*, contributing both knowledge and passion to the debates. As Henderson and McManus point out, their interventions raise two key questions for readers today: were these polemicists really women, and can the positions they took be considered feminist? They argue, in response to the first question, that there is no good reason to discount these writers' claims to be women, since men would have encountered no advantage in pretending to be women. Moreover, the enlightened attitudes and impassioned defenses of the writers thought now to have been women suggest their strong stake in the outcome of the quarrel: "there is a zeal and conviction in these pamphlets that is absent from the defenses written by men, even the most eloquent of which are marked by a certain dispassionate detachment of tone" (22). These women were feminist in that they brought "moral outrage" to their writing, even where humor was evident, as in the choice of pseudonyms such as "Tattlewell" and "Hit-Him-Home." Anger began her preface by shouting "Fie on the falsehood of men!"; Speght denounced Swetnam as "an hypocrite in print"; Tattlewell called misogynist pamphleteers "lime twigs of Lust and Schoolmasters of Folly." Such women shifted the grounds of the debate from women's chastity to the injustices men could impose on women. They used wit, satire, and outrage to voice their protest against such maltreatment, and at times they supported each other in their resistance. Even when their arguments were derivative, their learning and passion were impressive; Speght, for instance, quoted not only scriptures but Stoic philosophers, Greek sophists, and numerous church fathers in her defense of "all Eve's sex, both rich and poor." Finally, these women directed their defenses not exclusively toward male readers, many of whom found them humorous, but toward a growing female readership that took them seriously—"to all virtuous ladies honorable and worshipful" whose reputations were at stake. "So may the scandals and defamations of the malevolent in time prove pernicious if they be not nipped in the head at their first appearance," insisted Speght, defending her right to write on behalf of her maligned sex.

⊰ Works Cited ⊱

Beilin, Elaine V. *Redeeming Eve: Women Writers of the English Renaissance*. Princeton: Princeton UP, 1987.

Ezell, Margaret J.M. *Writing Women's Literary History*. Baltimore: The Johns Hopkins UP, 1993.

Greer, Germaine et al, ed. *Kissing the Rod: An Anthology of Seventeenth-Century Women's Verse*. New York: Farrar Straus Giroux, 1988.

Grundy, Isobel. "Falkland's *History of . . . Edward II*," *Bodleian Library Record* 13 (1988): 82–83.

Hageman, Elizabeth H. "Women's Poetry in Early Modern England." In *Women and Literature in Britain 1500–1799*, ed. Helen Wilcox. Cambridge: Cambridge UP, 1996. 190–208.

Henderson, Katherine Usher and Barbara F. McManus. *Half Humankind: Contexts and Texts of the Controversy about Women in England, 1540–1640*. Urbana: U of Illinois P, 1985.

Kelly-Gadol, Joan. "Did Women Have a Renaissance?" *Becoming Visible: Women in European History*, eds. Renate Bridenthal and Claudia Koonz. Boston: Houghton Mifflin, 1977. 137–64.

Lamb, Mary Ellen. *Gender and Authorship in the Sidney Circle*. Madison: The U of Wisconsin P, 1990.

Lewalski, Barbara Kiefer, ed. *The Polemics and Poems of Rachel Speght*. Oxford: Oxford UP, 1996.

Lock, Anne, trans. *Sermons of John Calvin, Upon the Song that Ezechias Made . . .* London: John Day Publishers, 1650. (Copies in the British and Folger Libraries)

Martin, Randall, ed. *Women Writers in Renaissance England*. London and New York: Longman, 1997.

Mueller, Janel. "A Tudor Queen Finds Voice: Katherine Parr's *Lamentation of a Sinner*." *This Historical Renaissance*, eds. Heather Dubrow and Richard Strier. Chicago: The U of Chicago P, 1988. 15–47.

Purkiss, Diane. "Material Girls: The Seventeenth-Century Woman Debate." *Women, Texts and Histories, 1575–1760*, eds. Clare Brant and Diane Purkiss. London and New York: Routledge, 1992. 69–101.

Spiller, Michael R.G. *The Development of the Sonnet: An Introduction*. London and New York: Routledge, 1992.

Travitsky, Betty, ed. *The Paradise of Women: Writings by Englishwomen of the Renaissance*. Westport, CT: Greenwood Press, 1981.

Waller, Gary F. *Mary Sidney, Countess of Pembroke: A Critical Study of Her Writings and Literary Milieu*. Salzberg: Institut fur Anglistik und Amerikanistik, 1979.

Wayne, Valerie. "Advice for Women from Mothers and Patriarchs." In *Women and Literature in Britain 1500–1700*, ed. Helen Wilcox. Cambridge: Cambridge UP, 1996. 156–79.

Wilcox, Helen, ed. *Women and Literature in Britain 1500–1700*. Cambridge: Cambridge UP, 1996.

Woods, Susanne, ed. *The Poems of Aemilia Lanyer: Salve Deus Rex Judaeorum*. Oxford: Oxford UP, 1993.

Wynne-Davis, Marian, ed. *The Renaissance: A Guide to English Renaissance Literature: 1500–1660*. London: Bloomsbury Publishing, 1992.

Late Seventeenth and Eighteenth-Century Literature
1660–1800

The period between the restoration of King Charles II to the throne of England in 1660 and the publication of *Lyrical Ballads* by the Romantic poets William Wordsworth and Samuel Taylor Coleridge in 1798 is often called by literary scholars the "long eighteenth century." During the 1660s the English people, exhausted by twenty years of civil war and religious turmoil, experienced two other calamities: the bubonic plague of 1665, which took the lives of 70,000 citizens of London and many more in the countryside, and the Great Fire of 1666, which left two-thirds of the city's population without homes. The ascension of Charles II led to a series of political crises, but eventually the nation became an international power. In 1707 an Act of Union united England and Scotland as Great Britain; thereafter the country continued to acquire territory abroad as part of a growing empire. By the end of the eighteenth century England had lost the American colonies in the Revolutionary War of 1776 but governed Canada, India, and parts of Africa.

A brief look at English history from 1600 to 1800 will help to establish a context for the literature of the era. During the first half of the seventeenth century the English people fiercely debated issues of political and religious authority. Unlike Queen Elizabeth I (1558–1603), a flexible and shrewd monarch, James I (1603–25) and Charles I (1625–49) attempted to eradicate Puritans and other religious groups dissenting from the Church of England, impose restrictions on an increasingly divided Parliament, and assert the absolute authority of the king. Opposition to these Stuart monarchs came especially from members of the House of Commons—lawyers, merchants, and the landed gentry—who challenged the doctrine of royal absolutism. To squelch this challenge Charles I resolved to govern without Parliament and did so for the last ten years of his reign, supported by the Anglican bishops and leaders of the military. In 1642, however, civil war erupted, with the king and a Puritan-influenced Parliament as the key adversaries, and in 1649 Charles was taken prisoner, tried by a militant minority of the House of Commons, and executed as a traitor. The leader of this militant branch of Parliament, Oliver Cromwell, assumed control of the English government and established a protectorate, which he ruled until his death in 1658. Because his son and successor, Richard Cromwell, lacked his father's power, his regime weakened, and certain officials began secret negotiations with Charles II, the son of Charles I, who was exiled in France. In 1660 he returned to restore the monarchy and the Anglican Church to power and elect a new Parliament. Both church and state were profoundly affected by the Puritan revolution, which led to crucial questions about the nature of authority; government of necessity would become less hierarchical and more tolerant of dissent over the succeeding decades.

Charles II promised to govern through Parliament and did so, not wishing to suffer his father's fate. Nonetheless, during his reign two distinct political factions developed: the Tories, clergymen and landed gentry who supported the king, and the

Whigs, merchants and dissenters interested in limiting the power of the Crown and promoting religious freedom. Real anxiety gripped the nation over Charles's failure to produce a legitimate heir, leading to a series of political plots and crises in the late 1670s and early 1680s. When Charles's Catholic brother, James II, acceded to the throne in 1685, another crisis developed as the new king began to fill important government posts with members of his faith, upsetting the Anglican Parliament and causing widespread fear of a succession of Catholic monarchs. Again secret negotiations were established, this time with James's Protestant daughter, Mary, and her Dutch husband, William of Orange. In 1689 James II was forced to flee England, and William and Mary took the throne in a "Glorious," or "Bloodless," Revolution. That same year Parliament passed a Bill of Rights limiting the king's power, reaffirming the authority of Parliament, and guaranteeing individual legal rights for men; a subsequent Toleration Act insured freedom of worship for dissenters.

Still, tensions between Whigs and Tories continued during the reign of James II's younger daughter, Queen Anne (1702–14), the last of the Stuart monarchs. At this time England engaged in the War of the Spanish Succession against France and Spain, a conflict supported and brought to a victorious conclusion by wealthy Whig ministers. Anne, a High Anglican who opposed dissenters, ultimately dismissed her Whig ministers to appoint Tories to the posts. These Tory ministers were served by such literary figures as the satirist Jonathan Swift (1667–1745) and the novelist DELARIVIER MANLEY (1663?–1724). Queen Anne was a great patron of the arts, and literature and theater flourished at court until her death. At that time the Whigs returned to power with the ascension of George I, the son of Sophia, Electress of Hanover. Thus began a century-long reign of Hanoverians: George I (1714–27), George II (1727–60), and George III (1760–1820). The first two kings were more interested in spending time in Germany than in ruling England, a fact that allowed Whig ministers to gain power, most notably Sir Robert Walpole, who served as Britain's prime minister from 1721 to 1742 and virtually governed the country. George III, who wished to rule absolutely, struggled to restore the Tories to power and challenge the Whig oligarchy.

For the sake of convenience, scholars have divided the literature of the long eighteenth century into three periods: 1660–1700, sometimes called the Restoration, when the theaters reopened after twelve years of closure by the Puritans and mainstream writers began to favor clarity and simplicity; 1700–1745, when neoclassical aesthetics dominated poetry and ancient Greek and Roman concepts of style and decorum were privileged; and 1745–1798, when new literary ideas developed that led to Romanticism. Although such divisions are necessarily reductive, they are helpful to highlight the major literary trends of the long century.

The period from 1660 to 1700 produced a variety of important literary works, some recalling the Renaissance emphasis on boldness and wit, others anticipating the eighteenth-century emphasis on balance and restraint. The major epic poems of John Milton (1608–1774) appeared in the 1660s: *Paradise Lost* (1667), an effort to "justify the ways of God to Man"; and *Paradise Regained* (1671), four books that depict Christ's temptation in the wilderness. *Samson Agonistes*, a "closet" tragedy not intended for theatrical production, was also published in 1671. Although Milton's works were widely admired, the dominant figure of the Restoration period was John Dryden (1631–1700), whose rhymed heroic plays and critical essays helped to establish the standards by which writing would be governed in the neoclassical age.

Restoration theater challenged Puritan rigidities and enjoyed the support of Charles II, who established two acting companies in 1660. Many writers depended on the court for patronage, although women playwrights like APHRA BEHN (1640–89) often earned their living, as VIRGINIA WOOLF would later claim, "by their wits." The political anxiety surrounding Charles II's final years shaped the literature produced in this period. Thomas Otway's *Venice Preserv'd* (1682) is one of many plays with overt references to the turbulence surrounding Parliament, and Behn's later work is colored by a persistent uneasiness over the failure of authority to establish order. By the end of the seventeenth century mainstream literature had become increasingly skeptical of religious orthodoxy and inclined toward ancient Greek models of good sense.

The period from 1700 to 1745 produced an Age of Reason and an Age of Feeling, since both rationality and sentiment found literary favor. Each literary genre was viewed as having a distinctive language, subject, and style. An emphasis on wit resulted, defined by Dryden not as mere cleverness but as "a propriety of thoughts and words; or, in other terms, thoughts and words elegantly adopted to the subject." The literature of the period was dominated by brilliant satirists such as Swift and Alexander Pope (1688–1744), and mock heroics emerged as a major literary form. Yet alongside this satiric impulse grew an increased emphasis on exploring and arousing human emotions that coincided with the development of a working-class and middle-class reading public. One result was the rise of the novel, a new literary genre that appealed to the sentiments of men and women of these classes as well as to upper-class women. Behn is generally credited with having written the first English novel, *Oroonoko* (1689), the story of a "royal slave" and an intriguing representation of blackness. Other women began to write novels as well: DELARIVIER MANLEY (1663–1724) and ELIZA HAYWOOD (1693?–1756) published "scandal fiction" that focused on illicit sexuality, while JANE BARKER (1652–1727), Penelope Aubin (1679–1731), and Mary Davys (1674–1732) wrote more virtuous narratives. Prominent male practitioners of the new novel form were Samuel Richardson (1689–1761) and Henry Fielding (1707–54).

The period from 1745 to 1798 witnessed the development of interest in the irrational and wild, manifested in Edmund Burke's (1729–1797) influential work on the Sublime, the exploration of gothic themes by novelists such as Horace Walpole (1717–1797) and Ann Radcliffe (1764–1823), who set their tales of terror in the haunted castles of the Middle Ages, and an experimentation with literary form, as in the fragmentary novels of Henry Mackenzie (1745–1831) or the mock medieval manuscripts of Thomas Chatterton (1752–1770.) Simultaneously, literature of the period continued to emphasize classical wit and decorum, best represented by the achievements of Dr. Samuel Johnson (1709–84), England's foremost man of letters. Moreover, revolutionary fervor increased, as exemplified by MARY WOLLSTONECRAFT's *A Vindication of the Rights of Men* (1790) and its feminist successor, *A Vindication of the Rights of Woman* (1792). The renewal of lyric poetry in volumes such as Oliver Goldsmith's *The Deserted Village* (1770) and CHARLOTTE SMITH's *Elegiac Sonnets* (1784) led to a climate receptive to Romantic poetry.

Colonial literature of the late seventeenth and eighteenth centuries was dominated by Puritanism, since between 1629 and 1640 thousands of middle-class dissenters had left England for the New World in search of religious freedom. The first poet of the colonies, ANNE BRADSTREET (1612–72), published on motherhood and domestic life as well as Christian virtue. Some of her writing reveals an ambivalence toward patriarchal authority, whether religious or secular, and a "gynecocratic vision that is based on nurturance, cooperation, and relationship" (Martin 16, 38). Male Puritan writers such as Cotton Mather (1663–1728) and Jonathan Edwards (1703–58) scrutinized the nature of sin in harsh but effective sermons. Writers also turned to satire, however, as illustrated by Benjamin Franklin's response to Mather's *Essays to Do Good* (1710), the *Silence Dogood Papers* (1722). As the colonists stepped up their resistance to English rule, Puritan fervor waned and colonial literature became increasingly secular and nationalistic.

In neither England nor the colonies did women have significant legal, political, economic, or social rights. Neither nation allowed women to own or inherit property or to write their own wills; nor could they file for divorce or retain custody of their children if their husbands left them. Due to the rise of industrialization and the increasing authority of a male medical establishment, working-class women lost access to home industries—weaving, spinning, farming, and midwifery—that had once brought them income. Near the century's end some women were forced into long hours of factory work or into domestic service. However, more upper- and middle-class women acquired an education during this period than ever before, although they were admonished by moralists such as Dr. Gregory in *A Father's Legacy to His Daughters* (1774) to keep their "cultivated understanding" a "profound secret, especially from the men." Because of a rise in the belief in companionate marriage, more women were able to choose their own husbands rather than having marriages arranged by their families. However, many married woman had only "veto power" rather than full equality with their spouses. Perhaps the most extraordinary change for eighteenth-century women, however, was that many began to write, in part because they began to gain access to literacy. Earlier, in the seventeenth century, women such as KATHERINE PHILIPS had participated alongside men in coterie writing, circulating their manuscripts to a supportive circle of friends. During the eighteenth century, increasing numbers of women published their writing professionally.

The long eighteenth century witnessed a remarkable amount of social, political, and literary change. To understand better the culture of the period, it is helpful to examine five major literary developments: the link between politics, religion, and literature; the decline and development of literary forms; the professionalization of writing; the emphasis on education; and new literary depictions of sexuality, virginity, and marriage.

POLITICS, RELIGION, AND LITERARY PRODUCTION

Politics and religion were inextricably linked for men as well as women throughout the long eighteenth century. It is no accident that many of the best-known male and female writers in England were Tory—pro-Stuart, High Church Anglican—in their sentiments, as this allegiance enabled their search for elite patronage and facilitated their access to both stage and print. Due to educational, legal, and political advantages, men were more successful than women in achieving patronage and audiences for their work.

John Dryden and Aphra Behn offer an intriguing comparison as rival dramatists who were both loyal Stuart supporters. While Dryden was named poet laureate in 1668 (when he was thirty-seven), there is no evidence that Behn was successful in her many applications to royal patrons. On the contrary, King Charles II's failure to pay her expenses resulted in her brief stay in debtors' prison upon her return from spying on his behalf in Belgium in 1667. The success of Dryden's tragedy *All for Love* (1677) and the fact that he wrote prolifically and well in many different genres, from prose to comedy to ode to satire, made him the most influential man of letters of the last three decades of the seventeenth century. Although Behn's *The Rover* (1677) and *The Lucky Chance* (1686) were successful with Restoration audiences, and she too wrote in many genres—poetry, prose, fiction, translations from the French—she was judged harshly for "indecency." As she wrote in her preface to *The Lucky Chance*," a devil on't—the woman damns the poet"; women, that is, could not write freely even in a more tolerant age. Dryden was a friend of Charles and his ministers, while Behn's primary connection at court was Nell Gwynn, a comic actress and the King's favorite mistress. Furthermore, while Dryden used learned allusions to the Bible and ancient philosophy in his verse, Behn preferred pastoral images of a community free of gender bias and mercenary exchange. This contrast reflects the different education given to men and women during the Restoration, but it also suggests that although many male writers supported the king in maintaining the status quo, many women sensed in Charles II's love of the arts and delight in female companionship the potential for a social order based on egalitarian erotics rather than hierarchical politics, an order in which men and women would be partners rather than adversaries. This partnership remained an elusive hope, and although Behn was a popular and prolific playwright, she never acquired Dryden's centrality as a spokesperson for the age.

ANNE KILLIGREW (1660–85), ANNE FINCH (1661–1720), and Jane Barker provide excellent additional examples of the way Royalist politics offered women a rationale to enter the public arena of debate during this period. Indeed, the Interregnum (1649–1660) at first gave Royalist women the opportunity to speak as female protectors or "brides" (loyal subjects) of the young exiled king, Charles II. When the Restoration and Charles's licentious behavior made this pose problematic, women like Katherine Philips linked sexual and national politics more discreetly (Hobby 128–42). Such a linkage can be seen in Philips's elegy "On the Death of the Queen of Bohemia" (1664), which praised the virtue of Queen Elizabeth (sister to Charles I of England) and mourned her difficult life (Greer 200). Restrained by changing cultural mores during the brief reign of James II (1685–89), Killigrew, Barker, and other women poets developed literary cults based on James's queen, Mary of Modena. This trend can be seen in Killigrew's "To the Queen," which confesses the inadequacy of the poet's muse to sing of so noble a queen. Literary homage to Mary eventually gave way to the devotion to Queen Anne found in poems and prefaces by Finch, SARAH FYGE (1670–1723), and MARY ASTELL (1666–1731). As Carol Barash has shown, Anne's authority as a female ruler allowed Astell to question men's "natural" superiority and enabled Anne's female literary defenders "to sanction women's political and linguistic forwardness" (Grundy and Wiseman 69).

For Jonathan Swift, too, in the literary generation that followed Behn and Dryden, politics and religion were united in a lifelong passion. Like many of his women contemporaries, Swift identified Queen Anne as the defender of the High Church, and he sought political influence during her reign. In 1710 he abandoned the Whig Party because he objected to its lack of concern about the Anglican church's status in Ireland. After Anne's death and his appointment in 1713 as dean of St. Patrick's cathedral in Dublin, Swift worked as a Tory journalist who inveighed against George I and II, deriding their sympathy for dissenting Protestants. He persistently linked the Hanoverians with political corruption, dishonest stock-market schemes, and the "abolition" of Christianity. In *Gulliver's Travels* (1726), for instance, Swift makes clear his revulsion at the leadership of the Whig minister Sir Robert Walpole. In addition, Swift led Irish resistance to English oppression; under the pseudonym "M.B., Drapier" he published a series of letters that convinced his impoverished countrymen to reject 100,000 pounds of newly minted English currency that threatened more harm to the Irish economy. The effect of Swift's political involvement on his literary output may be usefully compared to that of his contemporary Mary Astell, whose politics shaped her strong reformist views. Like Swift, her social criticism was matched with a political and religious conservatism, as she also saw Queen Anne as the chief representative of her faith. Moreover, she viewed the queen as the potential sponsor of her own political goal, the amelioration of women's low social position, about which she writes passionately in *A Serious Proposal to the Ladies* (1697). Astell petitioned the queen for support of better schooling for women, a petition that failed after the queen's death in 1713, as had Swift's proposals for less tolerance of religious dissenters. Surely, the decline in Tory fortunes shaped both writers' career and influence.

Alexander Pope likewise was haunted by religion and politics: his Tory affiliation was partly dictated by the party's association with the Catholic Stuarts. Born a Catholic, Pope was disenfranchised throughout his life, yet he worked assiduously to support Tory aristocrats throughout the reigns of George I and II. Many of his mature poems—*The Dunciad* (1728), *An Essay on Man* (1732), and *Epistles to Several Persons* (1735)—reflect his denunciations of ruling Whigs for their moral, political, social, and literary corruption. All the while he tried to maintain a delicate balance between identifying himself as a "catholic" subject and a communicant in the outlawed Catholic church. "The life of a wit is a warfare on earth," he insisted, a claim based on his own experience as a Tory writer devoted to satirizing the Whigs. Pope's situation as a marginalized Catholic contrasted vividly with that of his one-time friend LADY MARY WORTLEY MONTAGU (1689–1762), who was born into privilege as the daughter of a Whig grandee and enjoyed friendships with prominent Whigs such as Joseph Addison and Sir Robert Walpole. Her essays supported Sir Robert's affiliates and his policies as strenuously as Pope's attempted to abuse them, especially those that appeared in her periodical *The Nonsense of Common Sense* (1737–38). On the other hand, Lady Mary faced difficulties as a writer because of her gender and class status that Pope did not face. Certainly her class and gender kept her from speaking publicly about political matters, and although she circulated her literary works by subscription, she refused to publish under her own name, wary of the negative attention that might accompany any ventures into print. After Pope and she quarreled over religious and personal differences, he vilified her in "Epistle: To a Lady" as "Sappho at her toilet's greasy task" an insult that her gender made difficult to return in kind. However, in "Imitation of the Second Book of Horace," Montagu and her friend Lord Hervey gave Pope a taste of his own venom, characterizing him as a toad, a porcupine, and Satan himself (Thomas 121–30).

Samuel Johnson offers another noteworthy example of a man for whom religion and politics were linked. A conservative, High-Church Anglican, Johnson made his religious and political views clear in *The Rambler* (1750–52), *The Idler* (1758–60), and other periodicals replete with moral instruction. Even the *Dictionary* (1755), as Allen Reddick has demonstrated, was flooded with instructive quotations from Johnson's favorite seventeenth-century theologians. When offered the chance to augment the series *Lives of the Poets* (1779), Johnson chose several minor writers of undoubted piety to complete the collection. Supporting the established Church meant for Johnson supporting the established monarchy, although he was often suspected of nostalgic partiality for the Stuarts. Shared political views led Johnson to form lifelong friendships with Elizabeth Carter (1717–1800), who contributed to *The Rambler*, and other "Bluestockings" such as Elizabeth Montagu (1720–1800) and HANNAH MORE (1745–1833), women so named because at their literary gatherings men wore casual, blue-worsted stockings. More's life and literary career were especially shaped by her religious views. Despite a promising beginning as a dramatist, she gave up writing for the stage as immoral and turned her considerable energies to writing religious tracts and novels while fighting poverty and illiteracy. Early poems and essays by the pious Elizabeth Singer Rowe (*Poems on Several Occasions by Philomela*, 1696) had opened the door for these later women to publish, although the Bluestockings received criticism that Rowe had escaped due to her emphasis on female propriety.

The political views of other late-eighteenth-century women writers were yet more explicit. When the American Revolution occurred (1776) and the French called for liberty, equality, and fraternity (1789), women joined men in composing political poems and essays. In America the English-born essayist Thomas Paine defended the right of the colonies to resist English rule, and Philip Freneau argued for separation from England on the grounds of an emerging national identity. As the number of English colonists grew—by 1760 there were more than a million and a half—so did the number of African slaves: each year after 1770 more than 70,000 slaves were forcibly removed from their homeland and brought by ship to the colonies. One African-American slave who was educated by her master, PHILLIS WHEATLEY (1753?–84), developed a style of writing poetry that enabled her to speak publicly from her ambiguous position as a black woman and a domestic servant. It is not surprising that she alluded heavily to Milton and Pope, since such allusions added authority to her words. During the Revolutionary War Wheatley wrote from the vantage point of one whose personal bondage paralleled the political status of the colonies. Like many Englishwomen of the era, she used national political turmoil to justify her public speech. Many of Wheatley's poems were commissioned elegies; remarkably, she found a market niche specializing in these pious occasional poems. However, she also used the American desire for liberty and the Christian doctrine of charity to plead her case for the humanity of slaves, who had the right to join the "celestial train."

In England more than in France itself the French Revolution produced calls for social and political reform, including that of women's lot. Along with Paine and William Godwin, Mary Wollstonecraft (1759–97) revealed her democratic idealism in *A Vindication of the Rights of Man* (1790), and two years she later called for women's equality in *A Vindication of the Rights of Woman*. Wollstonecraft's argument depends upon an appeal both to reason and to religious duty, urging her readers to let women "attain conscious dignity by feeling themselves only dependent on God." Along with MARY HAYS (1760–1843), whose *Letter to the Men of Great Britain on Behalf of Women* (1798) owed much to her friend's argument, Wollstonecraft exemplifies what Gary Kelly has called "revolutionary feminism," which advocates liberty for women in a revolutionary context (25–29). Indeed, the emancipatory spirit of the age made possible Wollstonecraft's interest in women's rights. However, the failure of the French Revolution diminished interest in cultural change among English progressives; the feminist impulse faded in little more than a decade, and the writing of Wollstonecraft and Hays was neglected, and often vilified, for much of the nineteenth century.

DECLINE AND DEVELOPMENT OF LITERARY FORMS

The Restoration and eighteenth century saw the rise of new literary genres and the decline of old forms. During this period a reaction occurred against the intricacy and extravagance associated with the late Renaissance, and clarity, restraint and good sense were newly valued. This preference can be seen in Dryden's emphasis on natural wit, his praise of Augustus Caesar, the first Roman emperor, and the influence of the sophisticated poetry of Virgil, Horace, and Ovid—the "ancients." The goal of good poetry was to bring sweetness and usefulness (*dulce et utile*) to the reader; moreover, poetry was considered a visual as well as a verbal art form. As dictated by Horace's *Art of Poetry*, the poet's task was to represent nature as a universal aspect of human experience. In its exterior form nature referred to the landscape, while its interior form referred to human nature, the concern explored by Pope in *An Essay on Man* and Swift in *Gulliver's Travels*. Between 1660 and 1700, the ode—a formal, ceremonial, and balanced form—became the favored type of poetry, while the lyric, a popular form during the Renaissance, became a minor mode. The heroic couplet—two lines of rhymed iambic pentameter that contained an entire moral or philosophical precept—became a major literary device, as illustrated most famously in Pope's declaration, "Know then thyself; presume not God to scan; / The proper study of mankind is man." This quotation also reveals the increasing secularization that characterized the "Age of Reason."

Drama changed as well during the Restoration and eighteenth century. With the reopening of the theatres came a resurgence in dramatic writing, most boisterously represented by the new comedies of manners. Devoted to capturing and mocking the flamboyant society that grew up around Charles's court, these comedies reached their apogee in the witty, seductive plays of Behn, William Wycherley (1640–1716), and William Congreve (1670–1729). As the century turned, however, these plays faded in popularity, partly because reformist critics viewed the stage and playwrights as immoral, partly because cultural attitudes emphasized refinement and elegance. Comedy was softened, its bawdy excesses purged, and sentimental scenes of reunited families or virtue in distress were interwoven with more traditional spoofs of country manners or witty servants. Tragedy also enjoyed a revival in the late seventeenth century. Initially written in rhyming couplets, which later gave way to blank verse, these plays took up heroic themes that centered on the conflict between love and duty and featured exotic locations and extravagent, impassioned characters. Dryden's *All for Love*, which adapted the story of Antony and Cleopatra to the unities of time and place, is the most famous example. Yet no lasting tragedy was written during the long eighteenth century, despite critical fascination with establishing the aesthetics of the form.

Satire flourished from 1700 to 1745, with Pope and Swift as its exemplary practitioners. Conservative by definition, the satirist criticizes changes that undermine the moral fabric of society. Pope, for instance, felt that civilization was threatened by Whig barbarians and ridiculed their greed and ignorance in *The Dunciad* (1728), while Swift preferred the "right reason" of Tory politics and satirized the "madness" of the Whigs. Certain women writers challenged the sexism of male satirists, most notably ANNE FINCH in "The Answer" (1717), a response to Pope's negative portrayal of women in *The Rape of the Lock* (1717); and Eliza Haywood in *The Female Dunciad* (1729), an attack on Swift's misogyny.

The most remarkable generic advance of the eighteenth century was the development of the novel. Certainly there had been prose fiction written before 1700, including Philip Sidney's *Arcadia* (1590), John Bunyan's *The Pilgrim's Progress* (1675), and Behn's *Oroonoko* (1688). But the appearance of a working- and middle-class reading audience of women and men increased demand for this evolving genre. Daniel Defoe (1660–1731), one of its earliest practitioners, expressed middle-class desires for adventure and concerns with economic issues in such popular novels as *Robinson Crusoe* (1719) and *Captain Singleton* (1720). Moreover, by portraying roguish women sympathetically in *Moll Flanders* (1722) and *Roxana* (1724), he challenged the prevailing notion that a woman's chastity mattered more than her individual rights or economic survival. Also a friend to women as well as a pioneering novelist was Samuel Richardson, who portrayed his society's social and sexual tensions in such epistolary novels as *Pamela, or Virtue Rewarded* (1740), the story of a servant girl who resists her master's advances and ultimately wins his love, and *Clarissa* (1747–48), which pits a manipulative aristocrat against an angelic woman from the middle class. Few other male authors had shown an interest in women's lives or their exploitation, and readers responded with an enthusiasm that encouraged women novelists as well as men to write for this new female audience.

Henry Fielding, Tobias Smollett (1721–71), and Lawrence Sterne (1712–68) exploited the new genre's comic potential. Fielding's parody of *Pamela*, a novel that he considered unrealistic and didactic, brought him instant fame, while *Joseph Andrews* (1742) burlesqued a male servant's prim resistance to the advances of his mistress, Lady Booby, and popularized the wandering hero of the "picaresque" novel. Fielding's most famous work, *The History of Tom Jones, A Foundling* (1749), a "comic epic in prose," chronicles an impulsive young man's coming of age. The picaresque tradition was furthered by Smollett, whose *Roderick Random* (1748) and *Humphrey Clinker* (1771) recount the grotesque and comic journeys of ribald protagonists through English cities and countryside. More experimental in style was Sterne, a sentimental humorist whose masterpiece, *The Life and Opinions of Tristram Shandy* (1760–67), presents engaging comic characters in a form that looked back to such models as Rabelais and Swift to effect a simulation of the mind's associational processes.

Many eighteenth-century women contributed to the novel's development. Among the most successful "daughters of Aphra" were Delarivier Manley and Eliza Haywood. Manley's *The New Atalantis* (1709–10) showed the victimization of an innocent young woman raped and abandoned by her older guardian. Its combination of salaciousness and didacticism made it attractive to male and female readers alike, and the novel rapidly became a bestseller. Haywood's *Love in Excess* (1719) enjoyed a popularity that Katharine M. Rogers has compared to that of *Gulliver's Travels* and *Robinson Crusoe*. It too portrayed a relationship between an older man and his ward, although the male protagonist was less diabolical than that of *The New Atalantis* (101). In her introduction to a late novel, *The Fatal Secret* (1724), Haywood acknowledged gender as a factor in her choice of intricate but stereotypical plots of love and its intrigues: "But as I am a Woman, and consequently depriv'd of those Advantages of Education which the other Sex enjoy, I cannot so far flatter my Desires, as to imagine it in my Power to soar to any Subject higher than that which

Nature is not negligent to teach us. Love is a Topick which I believe few are ignorant of. . . . a shady Grove and purling Stream are all Things that's necessary to give us an Idea of the tender Passion."

Many other women novelists were successful in the marketplace. Frances Brooke (1724–89), Frances Sheridan (1724–66), Sophia Lee (1750–1824), and CHARLOTTE SMITH (1749–1806) wrote popular novels featuring sensitive and thoughtful heroines, and Smith in particular created intelligent women with minds of their own in *Celestina* (1791) and *Marchmont* (1796). With such novels as *The Mysteries of Udolpho* (1794) and *The Italian* (1797) Ann Radcliffe revitalized the form. The most famous woman novelist of the late eighteenth century was FRANCES BURNEY, whose *Evelina* (1778), though published anonymously, made her a celebrity. Presenting both women and men as tender and considerate, Burney wrote sentimental novels that refused to downplay women's economic dependence but also emphasized what decent men could learn from their female companions. As CATHERINE GALLAGHER (1994) has argued, "Burney's relationship to the literary marketplace differed from that of . . . Aphra Behn, Delarivier Manley, and Charlotte Lennox" because Burney "was born and raised in a 'literary' milieu"; her father was an aspiring writer, and indeed "the writings of the Burneys were the business of their lives" (215–17). These authors capitalized on their femaleness and feminized literary capital.

THE PROFESSIONALIZATION OF WRITING

The period between 1660 and 1800 saw the development of writing as a profession whose earning power for women Virginia Woolf would later celebrate in *A Room of One's Own*: "Money dignifies what is frivolous if unpaid for. It might still be well to sneer at 'Bluestockings with an itch for scribbling,' but it could not be denied that they could put money in their purses. Thus, toward the end of the eighteenth century a change came about which, if I were rewriting history, I should describe more fully and think of greater importance than the Crusades or the War of the Roses. The middle-class woman began to write" (65). Although Woolf's version of eighteenth-century history has been widely accepted by feminist scholars, critics such as Margaret Ezell offer a more cautionary view of what women's entry into the literary marketplace meant. In the Renaissance and seventeenth century a woman could be a public writer without having published a word; she instead would distribute her writing to circles of friends, or coteries, or distribute by subscription, a form of patronage. Well into the eighteenth century many women published only after they became well-known writers, as in the cases of Lady Mary Wortley Montagu and MARY BARBER (Lonsdale 54–56, 118–19). Moreover, becoming professional writers did not necessarily free women to be more creative or less subject to gender subordination, Ezell argues, since for many women it meant virtual servitude to the demands of greedy publishers (36–38). The professionalization of writing aided literary men, but its effects on women were mixed.

When John Milton published *Paradise Lost* in 1667, he earned only ten pounds for it; thirty years later, when John Dryden published his translation of Virgil, he earned twelve hundred pounds in subscription fees and royalties. Dryden was among the first male writers to boast of his professionalism, but he suffered the constant insults of wealthier peers and had to seek payment from many patrons. Swift never accepted money for his writing and rarely published under his own name, proud of his amateur status. Pope, in contrast, called his writing "idle trade," thus perfectly summarizing his aspiration to independent gentility even as he amassed the first fortune earned by a professional writer. Samuel Johnson asserted that "no one but a blockhead ever writ for money": the proud boast of an assured professional. Certainly Johnson recognized the appeal of "Grub Street" to hack writers as well as to more serious ones; by midcentury he claimed that book merchants had become the new patrons of literature, replacing the king and his courtiers.

Predictably, women had a more difficult time entering the profession of writing than men did. Behn's career was far more tenuous than Dryden's, for example; by her own words she was "forced to write for bread and not ashamed to own it." Although Woolf and others have called Behn the first woman to earn her living by her pen, Germaine Greer has questioned whether Behn did earn much money from her writing. It is clear that she died poor, while Dryden was financially secure. Moreover, Behn and other "female wits"—Susanna Centlivre, Mary Pix, Catherine Trotter— contended with vicious attacks on their reputations once they entered the marketplace. As Gallagher has shown, Restoration women playwrights were considered prostitutes. Not until Astell and Rowe began writing did this judgment reverse to allow women to enter the marketplace if they wrote on appropriate topics such as religion or education. Even so, many women preferred to publish through subscription so that their writing would be purchased by known readers rather than open to the public. Writing for subscribers let women preserve a ladylike privacy; thus Dr. Johnson urged women to follow this route to publication.

The success of early women novelists caused many other women to attempt the genre. For women such as Charlotte Lennox, this career proved a form of drudgery necessary to support their families; it produced many novels but few financial rewards. For writers such as Frances Burney and Ann Radcliffe, however, early success led to substantial earnings throughout their careers. Burney received not only praise from the upper classes for *Evelina* but also their patronage; *Camilla* (1796) earned two thousand pounds in subscriptions. Radcliffe made five hundred pounds from *The Mysteries of Udolpho* and six hundred pounds from *The Italian* without even seeking subscriptions. Indeed, by the end of the century, at least half the novels composed in England were by women, although many of them fell into oblivion during the nineteenth century. Throughout the 1700s the novel was considered a lesser art form than poetry, prose, or scholarly writings, since one did not need a classical education to compose novels, and "even" women wrote them.

Eighteenth-century women published scholarly writings as well, although often anonymously and apologetically. Encouraged by Dr. Johnson, the Bluestockings wrote translations, histories, and criticism as well as imaginative literature. Elizabeth Carter's translation of Epictetus from the Greek (1758) was highly praised in the prestigious journal *Monthly Review*, whose reviewer claimed that this work illustrated a woman's use of "the more solid and noble faculties" of intellect that had once been considered the domain of men. Anna Barbauld (1743–1825) edited and wrote prefaces for more than fifty British novels, and by century's end the radical histories of Catherine Macauley (1731–91) were widely read. Late in his life Dr. Johnson noted the "amazing progress made . . . in literature by women," claiming that not long ago "a woman who could spell a common letter was regarded as all accomplished, but now they vie with the men in everything."

Improvement in women's education in the late eighteenth century led to a growing parity between intellectual women and men. In 1791 the renowned bookseller James Lackington claimed that the hundreds of women who frequented his shop "know as well what books to choose, and are as well acquainted with works of taste and genius, as any gentleman in the kingdom, notwithstanding they sneer against novel readers." In addition, some educated women participated as peers in discussions with male intellectuals: At Bluestocking parties, famous men like Johnson often acknowledged learning from women. Although the Bluestockings published little enduring literature themselves, they urged other women to become professional writers and contributed to the growing sentiment for women's education.

MEN, WOMEN, AND EDUCATION

The topic of education attracted the attention of men as well as women in the long eighteenth century. The Whig philosopher and essayist John Locke, who formulated the first "modern" psychological theories about the learning process, argued in *Essay Concerning Human Understanding* (1690) for a secular, tolerant view of human knowledge: "our business here is not to know all things, but those which concern our conduct." Although he advocated parental authority over children, he questioned the family's hierarchical structure and insisted that girls as well as boys should be educated. Daniel Defoe expressed protofeminist sentiments in *An Essay upon Projects* (1697), which owed much of its reasoning to Mary Astell. In this treatise Defoe proposed that public girls' schools comparable to boys' academies be founded and argued that women were poorly educated rather than naturally inferior to men, as was the dominant belief of the time. Like many progressive men of his era, Defoe believed that the main goal of women's education was to make them more intelligent companions and better mothers. Pope also advanced liberal views on education, and poems such as *The Essay on Man* suggested that all humans should be educated beyond self-love to love of humankind. Dr. Johnson facilitated the education of his Bluestocking friends; when Elizabeth Carter's translation of Epictetus appeared, one male reviewer argued that "if women had the benefit of liberal instructions, if they were inured to study, and accustomed to learned conversation . . . if they had the same opportunity of improvement as the men, there can be no doubt but that they would be equally capable of reaching any intellectual attainment." Although Jonathan Swift's writings on education exemplified an older Christian tradition about human culpability, he too advocated women's education and tutored female pupils, including his beloved friend Esther Johnson (the Stella of his poems) and the poet Laetitia Pilkington. Moreover, in *Gulliver's Travels* he imagined an environment in which both girls and boys were educated in state-run boarding schools. Elsewhere in the tale both male and female Houyhnhnms were taught "Strength, Speed, and Hardiness"; indeed, one Houyhnhnm master claimed that it was "monstrous in us to give Females a different kind of Education from the Males, except in Some Articles of Domestic Management." For Swift, who scorned conventional femininity, educated women should seek to develop the best qualities of men, which he defined as reason, virtue, and courage.

Joseph Addison and Richard Steele wrote essays designed to educate "the fair," and the popularity of *The Spectator* gave rise to many magazines designed for educated women, including Eliza Haywood's *The Female Spectator* (1744–46), Charlotte Lennox's *Lady's Museum* (1760–61), and *The Lady's Magazine* (1770–1850). Moreover, *The Gentleman's Magazine* (1731–1914) often featured articles arguing in favor of women's education. Despite such advocacy, many early women writers bemoaned their lack of education, while others pleaded for more opportunity. Behn, for instance, alternately used her lack of education to assert the originality of her work and to excuse herself from harsh criticism. In fact, she was apparently rather well educated for a woman of her class and probably knew more Latin than she claimed. Both Killigrew's and Finch's poems express tension between what women were expected to be taught and what they aspired to know; in "Upon the Saying that My Verses Were Made by Another" Killigrew defends her poems from the accusation that only a man could have written them, while in "The Introduction" Finch laments that women's education fits them only for "the dull manage of a servile house." An elderly and disillusioned Lady Mary Wortley Montagu instructed her daughter, Lady Bute, to train her own daughter to conceal any learning she might acquire as carefully as if it were a hump or any other deformity, lest it be used against her. For most women, Montagu explained, education would simply provide a means of passing tedious hours profitably.

As Katharine Rogers has noted, in the eighteenth century there existed a double standard regarding women's education that was accepted even by many women. Eliza Haywood, who published *The Female Spectator* for an audience of educated women, nonetheless claimed that a woman could learn all she needed to know of natural philosophy by spending her summers "reading a few easy books and go[ing] for walks"; this she could accomplish "without the least trouble or study" (28). Similarly Anna Barbauld, a teacher as well as a writer, once said that women had no need of higher education and that the classroom's competitive atmosphere was inappropriate for girls. Jane Barker had Galesia, her female protagonist in *A Patchwork Screen for the Ladies*, claim that learning was pointless for women, even though Galesia herself was fiercely intellectual and pursued her education independently. Even the feminist MARY HAYS believed that women could cultivate "every branch of knowledge" by participating in "the domestic scenes of life." Apparently many women questioned the propriety of extensive education for women.

Others insisted upon it. Mary Astell used her Tory sentiments and religious learning to plead for women's right to education in *A Serious Proposal to the Ladies*. Her reasoning, like Pope's, was that well-educated women would be better wives and mothers. As Ruth Perry explains, Astell not only advocated women's education, she founded a charitable school with two female patrons and disciples, Lady Catherine Jones and Lady Ann Coventry, under the auspices of the Society for the Propagation of Christian Knowledge (7). Early education was the responsibility of mothers, as Astell pointed out; eighteenth-century women writers took advantage of this cultural approbation to publish their opinions on children's education. Hannah More wrote *Education on Various Subjects, Principally Designed for Young Ladies* (1777), and she made a long career out of educating the lower classes in practical and Christian knowledge, most notably in *Cheap Repository Tracts* (1795–98). As *Strictures on the Modern System of Female Education* (1799) reveals, she emphasized women's education as a moral duty rather than a political right. Mary Wollstonecraft began her career with *Notes on the Education of Daughters* (1788), and certainly *A Vindication on the Rights of Woman* argued forcefully for women's educational equality. In the century's last decade Catherine Macauley (in *Letters on Education*, 1790) and Mary Robinson (in *A Letter to the Women of England, on the Injustice of Mental Subordination*, 1799) made overtly feminist arguments on behalf of women's education.

The development of the novel in the eighteenth century offered another venue for exploring the theme of women's education. While Henry Fielding chronicled Joseph Andrews' growth to maturity, his sister, Sarah Fielding, and her friend Charlotte Smith featured the maturation of both women and men in such novels as *The Adventures of David Simple* (1747) and *The Old Manor House* (1793). Sarah Fielding also published the first educational novella specifically for girls, *The Governess* (1749), which was reprinted well into the nineteenth century. Haywood, Burney, Wollstonecraft, and Hays all wrote novels detailing the progress of young women toward adulthood; their plots "feminized" the picaresque motif favored by Fielding. Yet while a Fielding or a Smollett hero misbehaved on his path to manhood but was finally rewarded, no heroine could afford to sin egregiously and reach her goal of a happy marriage. Haywood's charming heroine in *The History of Miss Betsy Thoughtless* (1751) was careless, but she never violated feminine propriety to an extent that would exile her from polite society.

Moreover, the sheer mobility of male heroes, from Tom Jones and Roderick Random to Smith's Orlando Somerive, was necessarily denied heroines of "realistic" novels. Short of having a heroine kidnapped, as Richardson did in *Clarissa*, novelists were hard pressed to invent a female *bildungsroman* with a gripping plot; women's initiation into the world was simply not as thrilling as men's, it seemed. Yet many women novelists did create heroines to whom adventures came, as in Lennox's *The Life of Harriet Stuart* (1750). A few even portrayed heroines falsely detained in asylums, as in Wollstonecraft's *Maria, or The Wrongs of Woman* (1798). Ann Radcliffe's gothic heroines wandered in haunted landscapes, while Fanny Burney's late novel *The Wanderer* (1814) featured a disguised heroine hiding from political assassins after escaping from revolutionary France. Regardless of her circumstances, each heroine in women's novels of education negotiated her way toward death or marriage, the primary options available to women at the time.

SEXUALITY, VIRGINITY, AND MARRIAGE

Sexuality, virginity, and marriage were satirized, parodied, explored dramatically, and examined rationally in eighteenth-century literature and culture. The literary mode most flagrantly celebratory of women's sexual desire was the Restoration comedy of manners, with Behn one of its most erotic practitioners. *The Lucky Chance*, for instance, pokes sympathetic fun at Leticia's efforts to avoid sex with her elderly husband and portrays the impassioned desires of a married woman, Julia, for her sexy suitor, Gayman. Male playwrights also exploited this theme. George Etherege's *She Would If She Could* (1668) explores the sexual double standard in a comic vein, while Edward Ravenscroft's *The Careless Lovers* (1673) presents an assertive young woman, Hillaria, who tells her meddlesome uncle that she will choose her own husband. William Wycherley's *The Country Wife* (1672–74) punishes male adultery by having abusive husbands stripped of their desirable wives, while William Congreve's *The Way of the World* (1700) offers a witty protagonist, Millamant, who will marry her suitor, Mirabell, only if she can maintain her independence. Despite its flippant tone the play envisions a stable marital relationship between equals.

The profligate behavior of Charles II encouraged frank treatment of sexuality, but as the seventeenth century ended, accusations by Anglican clergymen caused bawdy dramatists to fall into disfavor. Even the distinguished John Dryden came under attack in Jeremy Collier's *Short View of the Immorality and Profaneness of the English Stage* (1698). As drama became more proper, however, fiction became less so. Scandal novels by Delarivier Manley and Eliza Haywood flourished, while Fielding's *Moll Flanders* and *Roxana* (1724) portrayed the erotic lives of prostitutes, although to be sure they reformed in the course of the book. In addition, "scandalous memoirs" by Laetitia Pilkington (1712–50), Charlotte Charke (?–1760), and others inaugurated the "nonreligious confession" as a literary genre (Nussbaum 179). After 1700 chastity was widely considered the primary factor in determining a woman's virtue; adultery in women was deemed criminal behavior, though in men it was overlooked or blamed on a wife's inadequacies. Virginity was also a popular topic. No longer did Robert Herrick and Andrew Marvell, cavalier poets of the mid-1600s, urge women to give up their virginity in poems with a "carpe diem," or "seize the day" theme. Instead, Elizabeth Taylor Wythens (1659?–1708) and Jane Barker wrote compellingly of the pleasures of a virgin's life. In *Some Reflections upon Marriage* (1700) Mary Astell presented celibacy as a viable and even a desirable alternative to marriage, which would make women miserable if they found themselves wed to tyrants. Astell herself never married, fearing that marriage would severely restrict her freedom to write. In "To the Ladies" (1703) Lady Mary Chudleigh echoed Astell in advocating celibacy and imploring women to forego the "wretched state" altogether.

Other women presented marriage as negative but inevitable. In many letters Lady Mary Wortley Montagu portrayed marriage as women's only option, in contrast to men, who had "so many roads" from which to choose. Yet despite the economic imperative of marriage for women, she concluded that it was a union "surrounded by precipices, and perhaps, after all, better miss'd than found." It is most interesting to compare the disillusioned view of marriage expressed in Montagu's letters, written after her own romantic elopement failed to produce a satisfactory marriage, with the ironic view envisioned fifty years later by Fanny Burney in *Camilla,* in which the husband-to-be seems as confused about his role as does the naïve heroine. Nevertheless, Burney, too, is concerned by marriage's limitations, particularly in *Cecilia,* which is a devastating account of women's lack of options and the obstacles to finding a satisfactory union.

Yet the possibility of a new kind of marriage was an important topic for other women writers. Modern scholars debate the extent to which women's married lives altered during this period. Lawrence Stone has defined the eighteenth century as moving from a hierarchical, patriarchal model to one of "companionate marriage," while Susan Staves has questioned whether women actually made the gains in their married lives that Stone has claimed. Staves, for example, argues that married women's legal right to own and manage property actually declined throughout the era. Still, many novelists enshrined the ideal of married friendship, as Sarah Fielding's *The Adventures of David Simple* (1744) and Frances Brooke's *The History of Emily Montague* (1769) reveal. In many novels of the 1780s and 1790s, moreover, writers such as

Frances Burney and Charlotte Smith created portraits of couples who eased each other's burdens and marriages to which both partners contributed strengths. Burney's Lord Orville exhibited "sweetness, politeness, and diffidence" toward Evelina, and Orlando in Smith's *The Old Manor House* displayed both gentleness and strength toward the woman he loved. Unequal marriages were often mourned: Smith's *Elegiac Sonnets* (1784), for example, lamented the failure of a marital relationship to fulfill emotional expectations undreamed of by earlier women. And for all their despair, Wollstonecraft's novels critiqued not the institution of marriage itself but her culture's failure to foster affectionate partnerships as the norm. Even behind the facade of a tragic novel like Mary Hays's *The Memoirs of Emma Courtney* (1796), in which the heroine's unrequited love leads her to despair, madness, and death, the longing for egalitarian relationships is evident. Such longing revealed a century-long development of the concept of companionate marriage.

Marriage occupied the minds of women writers more than those of men, given that it was the "career destiny" of most women; certainly no man approached the topic with the radicalism of Milton, who wrote a series of pamphlets (1643–45) arguing that divorce should be granted on the grounds of incompatibility. Neither Dryden, Swift, nor Pope was particularly interested in the topic of marriage or divorce; marriage among the idealized Houyhnhnms in Swift's *Gulliver's Travels* was nearly devoid of emotion, a fact that suggests its lack of centrality in many male writers' lives. Some men argued against women's autonomy in matters of marriage; James Boswell (1740–95), Dr. Johnson's biographer, claimed that a young woman who married without her parents' permission "ought to suffer" because her action "disturbed the settled order of society." But the rise of companionate marriage did draw the attention of certain male writers. Daniel Defoe wrote prolifically on the subject in essays for *The Review* (1704–13) and in three manuals on family relations: *The Family Instructor* (1715), *Religious Courtship* (1722), and *Conjugal Lewdness* (1727), which despite its lurid title was about marital inequality, not sex. These writings asserted women's rights within marriage and challenged the notion of female submission. Only Astell matched Defoe's awareness of the oppression many married women suffered. Though less feminist than Defoe, Richard Steele also argued that the role of wife should be valorized: "I have very long entertained an ambition to make the word *wife* the most agreeable and delightful name in Nature. Marriage is an institution calculated for a constant Scene of as much Delight as our Being is capable of."

As more women read novels, more men extolled a happy marriage as the prime reward for hero and heroine alike. In Fielding's *Joseph Andrews* and *Tom Jones* the heroes found domestic bliss at the conclusion of their travails, as did Richardson's protagonists in *Pamela* and *Sir Charles Grandison* (1753–54). Dr. Johnson wrote essays on marriage and commented wittily on it in *Rasselas* (1759): "Marriage has many pains, but celibacy has no pleasures." Most male writers through the century agreed, as even scoundrels such as Defoe's Moll Flanders and Smollett's Roderick Random were finally allowed to rest with suitable mates. Indeed, these eighteenth-century works anticipated the marriage-focused writing of JANE AUSTEN, CHARLOTTE BRONTË, and many other women who would take the novel to further heights in the nineteenth century.

⊰ Works Cited ⊱

Ezell, Margaret. *Writing Women's Literary History*. Baltimore: The Johns Hopkins UP, 1993.

Gallagher, Catherine. *Nobody's Story: The Vanishing Acts of Women Writers in the Marketplace, 1670–1820*. Berkeley: U of California P, 1994.

————. "Who Was That Masked Woman? The Prostitute and the Playwright in the Comedies of Aphra Behn." *Women's Studies* 15 (1988): 23–42.

Greer, Germaine et al., eds. *Kissing the Rod: An Anthology of Seventeenth-Century Women's Verse*. New York: Farrar Straus Giroux, 1988.

Grundy, Isobel and Susan Wiseman, eds. *Women, Writing, History 1640–1740*. Athens: The U of Georgia P, 1992.

Hobby, Elaine. *Virtue of Necessity: English Women's Writing 1649–88*. London: Virago Press, 1988.

Kelly, Gary. *Women, Writing, and Revolution, 1790–1827*. Oxford: Clarendon Press, 1993.

Lonsdale, Roger, ed. *Eighteenth-Century Women's Poetry: An Oxford Anthology*. Oxford: Oxford UP, 1989.

Martin, Wendy. *An American Triptych: Anne Bradstreet, Emily Dickinson, Adrienne Rich*. Chapel Hill: The U of North Carolina P, 1984.

Nussbaum, Felicity. *The Autobiographical Subject: Gender and Ideology in Eighteenth-Century England*. Baltimore: The Johns Hopkins University P, 1989.

Perry, Ruth. *The Celebrated Mary Astell: An Early English Feminist*. Chicago: The U of Chicago P, 1986.

Reddick, Allen. *The Making of Johnson's Dictionary, 1746–1773*. Cambridge: Cambridge UP, 1990.

Staves, Susan. *Married Women's Separate Property in England, 1660–1833*. Cambridge: Harvard UP, 1990.

Stone, Lawrence. *Uncertain Unions: Marriage in England 1660–1753*. Oxford: Oxford UP, 1992.

Thomas, Claudia N. *Alexander Pope and His Eighteenth-Century Women Readers*. Carbondale: Southern Illinois UP, 1994.

Nineteenth-Century Literature
1800–1900

The nineteenth century spawned a variety of literary movements and genres, and a literary marketplace developed that opened its doors to women as well as men. In England, William Wordsworth and his fellow Romantics revolutionized poetry by privileging imagination over reason; the publication of *Lyrical Ballads* in 1798 articulated poetic principles that ran counter to the emphasis on decorum of eighteenth-century verse. As women turned increasingly to poetry, it was possible by 1850 for a woman, ELIZABETH BARRETT BROWNING, to be seriously considered for the British honor of poet laureate to replace Wordsworth; the award ultimately went, however, to Alfred, Lord Tennyson. England also saw the further development of a still emerging genre, the novel, with four women among its finest practitioners: JANE AUSTEN, CHARLOTTE BRONTË, EMILY BRONTË, and GEORGE ELIOT. Charles Dickens became the most popular novelist of the 1830s, combining social protest with comedy and sentimentality; in the 1840s William Makepeace Thackeray probed social mores, and in the 1850s Anthony Trollope represented the optimism of the Victorian Age. By 1870 Eliot was considered England's premier novelist, renowned for her philosophical and moral reflection.

Both England and the United States were affected by the revolutionary spirit of the last decades of the eighteenth century, and for both countries the nineteenth century was an age of industrialization and expansion. The industrial and scientific revolutions, along with increasing religious skepticism, sent these previously agrarian societies into a chaotic transition. In England, displaced workers came to the cities and found only dangerous, low-paying jobs because the new technology, while efficient, was unsafe. With laissez-faire capitalism, these numerous workers were ill paid and wretched; as a result, many of them lost confidence in providential explanations of their life conditions. During the first half of the century, for example, as workers in the industrial north protested poor wages and dangerous working conditions, writers took up their cause. Their plight was acknowledged in poetry by William Blake, who protested the "dark Satanic mills," and by Percy Bysshe Shelley, who wrote "England in 1819" and "To Sidmouth and Castlereagh" in sympathy with downtrodden workers. In addition, Elizabeth Barrett Browning's "The Cry of the Children" (1843) exposed the terrible treatment of child laborers. In fiction, Charlotte Brontë's *Shirley* (1849), Dickens's *David Copperfield* (1849) and *Hard Times* (1854), and Elizabeth Gaskell's *Mary Barton* (1848) portrayed the misery of the working classes. Friedrich Engels's *Condition of the Working Class in England in 1844* examined these problems in compelling prose that influenced political leaders like Benjamin Disraeli, who acknowledged that by midcentury England was "two nations," rich and poor.

Scientific along with technological advancement affected literature, as Charles Darwin's 1859 *The Origins of Species* set forth the theory of evolution and natural selection. The embrace of science and technology provoked a corresponding turn away from religion, and both the secularization of the culture and the commodification of its people created profound religious anxiety to which writers also responded. In the 1860s the poet Matthew Arnold pondered the loss of religious faith in poems like "Dover Beach"

(1867), while Gerard Manley Hopkins experimented privately with sprung rhythm, elliptical syntax, and alliterative diction as a means of expressing his spiritual zeal. In prose, Utilitarians like Jeremy Bentham and HARRIET MARTINEAU critiqued organized religion, joining public debates between believers and nonbelievers.

Social as well as religious issues provoked controversy. The "Woman Question," which considered whether men and women should be socially and politically equal, continued to be debated; it was stirred in part by John Stuart Mill's *The Subjection of Women* (1869), which challenged patriarchal assumptions about women's roles. Although Victoria ruled as queen from 1837 to 1901, she did little to support women's rights. However, through the efforts of women like Caroline Norton, who wrote about losing her children when her husband divorced her (in *The Natural Right of a Mother to the Custody of Her Child*, 1837), Parliament passed the Infants' Custody Act in 1839. Emily Davies and others lobbied for women to be admitted to major British universities; her efforts reached fruition in 1870, when Cambridge admitted women to Girton. By 1884 Oxford had established two colleges for women, although at neither institution could women actually earn degrees. Between 1870 and 1908 a series of Married Women's Property Acts was passed, reducing women's economic dependence on their husbands. Despite these important changes, the dominant ideology remained one of "separate spheres," as historian Barbara Welter has termed it; Tennyson described this ideology as "man for the field and woman for the hearth." Conduct books written by Sarah Ellis defined proper feminine behavior conservatively, as did Coventry Patmore's popular poem "The Angel in the House" (1854). Women who were not aristocrats or middle-class did not have the option of making the home the center of their life, of course. They worked in other people's houses as governesses or domestics; as seamstresses who took in piecework; in dark, poorly ventilated factories; or in brothels.

In America after the Revolutionary War of 1776, Northern states became increasingly industrialized while the South developed an agrarian economy. Although the United States outlawed the slave trade in 1819, it nonetheless continued, and by 1860 there were almost four million slaves in America, most brought forcibly from Africa, working in the cotton and tobacco producing states. Economic conflicts between North and South and debates regarding the morality of slavery led to the Civil War (1861–65), which cost $8 billion and 600,000 lives but ended slavery as an institution. Many prominent African Americans contributed to its demise, including orators such as SOJOURNER TRUTH, authors of slave narratives such as Frederick Douglass and HARRIET JACOBS, and poets such as FRANCES ELLEN WATKINS HARPER. White writers also spoke out against slavery, including Henry David Thoreau, Ralph Waldo Emerson, and Walt Whitman. Herman Melville called slavery "man's foulest crime," and Harriet Beecher Stowe's *Uncle Tom's Cabin* (1852) brought worldwide attention to the problem. British writers, too, protested slavery in the United States. Elizabeth Barrett Browning adopted a slave mother's point of view in her powerful poem "A Runaway Slave at Pilgrim's Point" (1848), while Martineau argued persuasively for the "citizenship of people of color" (1837). As the century progressed, British writers wrote both in favor of and against colonialism. By 1890 the British Empire encompassed one-quarter of the world's territory, and nationalistic male writers like Rudyard Kipling spoke piously of the "white man's burden" to "civilize natives," while such women of letters as Vernon Lee expressed antinationalistic sentiments.

Most nineteenth-century U.S. literature was engaged not in social protest but in attempting to forge a national identity. Fiction was dominated in the early century by the German-influenced tales of Washington Irving; his popularity was rivaled in the 1830s by that of James Fenimore Cooper, who fictionalized life on the frontier. Emerson speculated in "The Poet" as to what a truly American literature would entail, and his Transcendentalist philosophy of self-reliance became an important literary theme—one that Thoreau embraced in *Walden* and MARGARET FULLER gave a feminist spin in *Woman in the Nineteenth Century* (1845). The humorist Mark Twain became the most popular U.S. novelist of the last half of the century, while the poet Walt Whitman spoke in a uniquely American and democratic voice. Another major U.S. poet, EMILY DICKINSON, chose seclusion as a context from which to explore nature, theology, and the inner life. Since she published few poems during her lifetime, however, it was not until the twentieth century that her greatness was recognized.

The "Woman Question" was debated in Unites States as well as England. Margaret Fuller's treatise espoused women's equality just as Lucy Stone, Lucretia Mott, Elizabeth Cady Stanton, and Susan B. Anthony began what would be a seventy-year drive toward women's suffrage. Sojourner Truth spoke in the 1850s on behalf of women's and civil rights, while Frances E.W. Harper advocated liberty for both slaves and women. Other women writers espoused a feminine ideal, however: in *Little Women* (1868) Louisa May Alcott wrote that "a woman's happiest kingdom is home," while the popular sentimental poet LYDIA SIGOURNEY sang the virtues of domesticity and maternity. Still, social reforms benefiting women did take place. By 1860 the Married Women's Property Act had passed fourteen states, and by century's end it was national law. In 1837 Oberlin College became the first U.S. college to admit women; that same year Mt. Holyoke Academy was established to educate women in rhetoric, logic, philosophy, and science. In 1890 Anna Julia Cooper argued persuasively in "The Higher Education of Women" for black women's right to be educated, and by 1904 Mary McLeod Bethune had established a Normal and Industrial Institute for African-American Women that later became Bethune-Cookman College. This push for women's rights was reflected in the fiction of the century's last decades, including Harper's *Iola Leroy* (1892), which condemned sexual and racial exploitation; CHARLOTTE PERKINS GILMAN's "The Yellow Wallpaper" (1892), which protested women's postpartum treatment by male doctors; and KATE CHOPIN's *The Awakening* (1899), which challenged traditional sexual mores. The ideology of "separate spheres" would never again be as powerful.

Although nineteenth-century literature encompasses many genres, ideologies, and movements, four general areas of consideration seem especially fruitful for examining women's literature of the era in comparison with that of men: Romantic poetry and prose, the Victorian novel, sentimental and popular literature, and literature of social protest.

ROMANTICISM

The term "Romanticism" describes a broadly defined artistic movement of revolutionary fervor, radical individualism, and poetic reconfiguration. Histories of the Romantic movement in literature have traditionally foregrounded masculine contributions, with six British figures—William Wordsworth, Samuel Taylor Coleridge, William Blake, Percy Bysshe Shelley, John Keats, and George Gordon, Lord Byron—dominating the landscape. These writers share a commitment to imagination, vision, and transcendence. A postmodern understanding of Romanticism defines it as a questioning of any vision not mediated through language, while to new historicists Romanticism is an ideology linked to specific political and social events. However, as Anne K. Mellor has argued, it is reductive to view Romanticism only in terms of these six male writers, since women wrote at least half of the literature published in England and the United States between 1780 and 1830 and since, in fact, there were many Romanticisms (1988: 3–8). Women poets popular in their own time but little known today, such as Joanna Baillie and MARY TIGHE; writers who published nothing in their lifetimes, such as DOROTHY WORDSWORTH; and renowned writers such as Emily Brontë, MARY SHELLEY, and Mary Wollstonecraft can also be considered important Romantics.

The Romantic period has traditionally been thought to begin in 1798, when William Wordsworth and Samuel Taylor Coleridge published *Lyrical Ballads*, and end in 1832, when England's first Reform Bill shifted conventional economic hierarchies. However, Mellor argues that Romanticism started in 1780, and its roots could surely be found in the ferment that led to the French Revolution of 1789, with which all of the male Romantics were initially in sympathy (1993: 1–11). In his *Prelude* (1850) Wordsworth wrote retrospectively of "France standing on the top of golden hours, / And human nature seeming born again"; the "whole Earth, / The beauty wore of promise." Even after these poets became disillusioned with the Reign of Terror and its bloody aftermath—when, as Wordsworth noted, the protesters "became oppressors in their turn"—younger writers like Shelley, Byron, and the essayist William Hazlitt continued to think that revolutionary zeal, if stripped of its terrors, represented the best hope of humankind. For Hazlitt, revolution presaged "the dawn of a new era," for "a new impulse had been given to men's minds." The Romantic poets were influenced by Thomas Paine's *Rights of Man* (1791–92) and Mary Wollstonecraft's *Vindication of the Rights of Men* (1790), both of which challenged Edmund Burke's critique of the French Revolution, and especially by William Godwin's *Inquiry Concerning Political Justice* (1793), which envisioned a utopian future in which property would be equally redistributed and government would be obsolete.

As articulated in *Lyrical Ballads*, the major tenets of Romanticism represented an aesthetic as well as a political shift from the Enlightenment emphasis on rationality. Poetry was born not of the outer but of the inner world of the poet's emotions, Wordsworth and Coleridge proclaimed; it should represent the "spontaneous overflow of powerful feelings" remembered in tranquility rather than "a mirror held up to nature," as eighteenth-century poets had asserted. Both Blake and Shelley considered the poet's imaginative vision central to the making of a poem, and even in narrative or dramatic poems like Byron's *Childe Harold*, the speaker's "I" was read not as a literary persona but as the poet's own lyric voice. In his *Prelude* and elsewhere Wordsworth conceptualized the poet as bard, a "chosen son" destined to write at times of crisis. The Romantic emphasis on spontaneity was an important contrast to the previous century's attention to craft; Keats claimed that "if poetry comes not as naturally as the leaves to a tree it had better not come at all." Blake believed that good poetry emerged from "inspiration and vision," while Percy Shelley appropriated the metaphor of female procreativity in *Defense of Poetry* to describe the generative process: "a great [work] grows under the power of the artist as a child in the mother's womb."

Romantic poetry emphasized a close observation of nature, the glorification of the simple and ordinary, and an intrigue with the supernatural and magical. Wordsworth felt compelled to "look steadily at my subject," which in poems like "Lines Composed a Few Miles Above Tintern Abbey" (1798) was the changing face of nature; such examination led to consideration of human transformations as well. Coleridge's "Frost at Midnight," Shelley's "Ode to the West Wind," and Keats's "Ode to a Nightingale" pay homage to nature and its creatures, drawing human inspiration from the landscape and taking pleasure in its beauty. In *Songs of Innocence* (1789) and *Songs of Experience* (1794) Blake drew links between natural objects and the spiritual world, investing nature with metaphysical significance; in *Defense of Poetry* Shelley claimed that "poetry reproduces the common universe" but "purges from our inward sight the film of familiarity which obscures from us the wonder of one's being," thus articulating the paradoxical Romantic fascination with both the commonplace and the exotic. Wordsworth determined to "choose incidents and situations from ordinary life" as subjects for his poems, including humble people—"female vagrants, gypsies, peasants, peddlars." Coleridge, in contrast, used mysticism and superstition to explore the powers of the unknown in such poems as "The Rime of the Ancient Mariner" and "Kubla Khan"; the latter poem exhibited a fascination with orientalism that Coleridge shared with other Romantics. At times the emphasis on exoticism indicated a fear of female power, as in Keats's "La Belle Dame Sans Merci"; for Byron it was manifested as a fascination with the Satanic hero, a proudly unrepentant violator of social and sacred norms.

The Romantic poets and the principles they articulated influenced the Victorian Age, conventionally dated 1832–1900. Although Victorian writers at first celebrated and emulated Romantic principles, most eventually came to believe that duty to others should replace pleasure and private visions as motivation for writing. According to the historian Thomas Carlyle, Victorians should prefer the pleasing sound and polished texture of Keats and the musings of German idealist philosopher Goethe to the revolutionary tendencies of Wordsworth or Byron. "Close thy Byron, open thy Goethe," urged Carlyle in 1834, heralding the Victorian era's shift of emphasis. Despite Carlyle's admonition, Romantic poets were both popular and powerful in Victorian England: Robert Southey, now considered a minor Romantic, was poet laureate from 1813 to 1843; upon his death Wordsworth received the honor and served until 1850. Alfred, Lord Tennyson, whose poem "The Lady of Shalott" (1832; 1842) revealed a Romantic preoccupation with the exotic past, held the post from 1850 until his death in 1892. Moreover, the development of the personal essay, as practiced by Charles Lamb, William Hazlitt, and Leigh Hunt, and the growth of spiritual biographies such as Thomas De Quincey's *Confessions of an English Opium-Eater* (1822), Newman's *Apologia Pro Vita Sua* (1864), and Carlyle's *Sartor Resartus* (1833–34) can be traced to the Romantic primacy of the individual.

U.S. writers developed their own form of Romanticism. In particular, Transcendentalism as delineated by Ralph Waldo Emerson was a late manifestation of British and European Romantic thought. Transcendentalists emphasized intuition over reason, a philosophy of self-reliance, a resistance to customary restraint, and a mystical union with nature. In three closely related essays Emerson defined the essential preoccupations of Transcendentalism: in "Nature" (1836) he explored how humans discover their spiritual nature; in "The American Scholar" (1837) he advocated literary independence from Europe and urged men of letters to develop a self-reliant nationhood; and in his "Divinity School Address at Cambridge" (1838) he encouraged listeners to become "newborn bards of the Holy Ghost," eschewing traditional dogmas and relying on personal experience for knowledge. His view of the writer's quest for a definitive

American voice hearkens back to the theme of Romantic individualism, while his notion of the Oversoul (discussed in "Compensation," 1841) owes something to the Romantics' fascination with the mystical and the pantheistic. For Emerson and his New England coterie—Bronson Alcott, Henry David Thoreau, William Ellery Channing, and Margaret Fuller—Transcendentalism provided an alternative to the growing materialism of the United States in the 1830s and 1840s. Thus Thoreau could advocate civil disobedience on principle, refusing to pay a poll tax that he realized would be used to promulgate the institute of slavery, and Transcendentalism could offer an ethical vision to a new and growing nation and its increasingly national literature.

Romanticism affected two of nineteenth-century America's most distinctive male poets, Edgar Allan Poe and Walt Whitman. Poe's early volume, *Tamerlane and Other Poems* (1827), caused him to be seen as a U.S. imitator of Byron, but "The Raven" (1845), with its air of mystery and melancholy, brought him international fame. His emphasis on the death of a beautiful woman as the ultimate poetic subject, his tales of the supernatural, and such mysterious poems as "Ulalume" and "The Bells" relied on Romantic mysticism. In contrast, Whitman's concern in *Leaves of Grass* (1855) with finding a democratic American voice was more closely linked to Emerson's exhortations in "The Poet" and Wordsworth's emphasis on common people and the beauty in ordinary life than to Byron. To be sure, Whitman's celebration of homosexual desire and the "body electric" took the romantic impulse in a new direction, but like Wordsworth he set out to revolutionize poetry by rejecting didacticism in favor of "genuineness." Certainly a poem like "Song of Myself" displays the Romantic qualities of the lyrical "I," enchantment with nature, and democratizing zeal.

WOMEN'S CONTRIBUTIONS TO THE ROMANTIC TRADITION

What traditional histories of Romanticism have left out is the role of women in this literary movement. Several women writers were influential on Romanticism's major male figures. The poet CHARLOTTE SMITH, for example, published a successful volume, *Elegiac Sonnets* (1784), which Coleridge commended in 1796 for helping to reestablish the sonnet form in England. Wordsworth also admired Smith's work: in 1791 he visited her in Brighton, delighted by her blend of natural description and mysterious melancholy, and in 1802 he acknowledged reading over her sonnets before writing his own. Forced to support a large family when her husband was sent to debtors' prison, Smith turned to popular fiction to earn money but continued to write poetry during the nineteenth century.

Two of the best known women poets writing during the Romantic period have been largely forgotten today, the Scottish Joanna Baillie and the Irish Mary Tighe. Baillie's *Poems* (1790) described a mind alternately fearful, discontented, sorrowful, and joyful, prefiguring a Romantic sensibility. Wordsworth admired her early nineteenth-century verse dramas, and Sir Walter Scott called her "the best dramatic writer since the days of Shakespeare." Tighe's *Psyche, or the Legend of Love* (1805), a series of Shakespearean sonnets that eroticized the natural world, went through three editions and was admired by Keats for its ecstatic portrayals of nature. The contributions to Romanticism of women poets like Baillie and Tighe deserved more note than they received by Victorian critics eager to judge women's writing on what Isobel Armstrong has called "the gush of the feminine" (1995: 15).

Dorothy Wordsworth was extremely influential on her brother, William, and his circle of friends. She began writing journals when she lived with her brother in Alfoxden and continued when they moved together to the English Lake District; her *Grasmere Journal* (1800–1803) is noteworthy for its splendid and meticulous observation of the natural world. Wordsworth admired his sister's prose depictions of nature and expressed gratitude to her in the *Prelude* for "preserving me still a poet." Coleridge called her a "woman of Genius," while DeQuincey praised the "subtle fire of impassioned intellect" that "burned within her." Like many women who wrote journals and letters for familial consumption, however, Dorothy Wordsworth never considered herself "an author" and published nothing during her lifetime.

The finest women poets to be affected by Romantic sensibilities were Emily Brontë in England and Emily Dickinson in the United States. Neither poet had an audience during her lifetime—Brontë because the poems she and her sisters published in 1846 were ignored (the volume sold two copies), Dickinson because she chose to publish only eleven of her 1,775 poems. Charlotte Brontë said after her sister's death that Emily had loved nature (particularly the Yorkshire moors), solitude, and liberty—all popular themes of Romanticism—and described her poetry as "wild, melancholy, and elevating." Many of her lyric poems were part of a long narrative saga concerning Gondal, an imaginary kingdom populated by exotic knights and vindictive queens; in these poems she comfortably adopted male as well as female personae. Her highest ideal was reserved for a "God of Visions," a muse of the natural world whom she designated in one poem as "my slave, my comrade, and my king." Mellor has argued that Brontë's "personal history and ideological investments more closely approximate masculine Romanticism than feminine" (1993: 186). Like the male Romantics, Brontë found Enlightenment rationality suspect, preferring instead the energy and passion of the natural world. Both her poetry and her novel, *Wuthering Heights* (1847), may be seen as triumphs of Romanticism.

Like Emily Brontë, Emily Dickinson loved to write of nature, although in her poems it appears as luminous rather than wild. A seascape offers epiphanic vision in Poem 884, "An Everywhere of Silver"; a hummingbird leads to illumination in Poem 1463, "A Route of Evanescence." For Dickinson, closely observing the natural world led to inner vision, as in Poem 258, "There's a certain Slant of light," which explores the oppressive emotional landscape wrought by certain "Winter Afternoons." Dickinson often alluded to her interest in Wordsworth's poetry: she called him "the Stranger" in an 1886 letter to Elizabeth Holland (perhaps, as the critic Elizabeth Phillips suggests, because she had not read him for a while) and paraphrased a line from his "Elegiac Stanzas" to describe "the light that never was on sea or land" (Phillips 139). Dickinson was also intrigued as a young woman by Emerson's emphasis on self-reliance and liberation from mundane values. Although she was by no means exclusively a nature poet—Dickinson wrote also of psychic extremity, the possibilities of language, and poetic identity—natural phenomena both inspired and delighted her. Her poetic distinction, however, lies in her richly elliptical language and quiet philosophical power, which contrast with the large rhetorical flourishes of the era.

Women writers of Romantic fiction and prose exhibited concerns different from those of their male counterparts. The writing of Mary Shelley, for instance, provides a contrast to the radical social transformation that Wordsworth, Coleridge, Blake, and Percy Shelley supported, offering what Mellor has called "an alternative program grounded on the trope of the family-politic," a program guided by a mother as well as a father (1993: 65). At one point in *Frankenstein* (1818) Shelley's protagonist suggests that if man were to make "the tranquillity of his domestic affections" his first priority, wars would cease and empires never be established. Shelley shared with her mother, Mary Wollstonecraft, a belief in the equality or perhaps even the superiority of women in maintaining the well-being of the family-politic.

Margaret Fuller's link to U.S. Romanticism came in part through Emerson, whom she met in 1836 and whose Transcendental philosophy she embraced, although she modified it significantly to fit her own egalitarian beliefs. She appreciated Emerson's emphasis on intuition, yet she criticized her sometime mentor for having "faith in the Universal, but not in the Individual Man; he met men, not as a brother, but as a critic" (quoted in Kelley xviii). Fuller edited the Transcendentalist journal *The Dial* from 1840 to 1842, embracing radical individualism and publishing her own mystical contemplations, analyses of Goethe, and essays on literature and on gender relations. Like Coleridge, she felt that the creative mind was androgynous, declaring in *Woman in the Nineteenth Century* that there was "no wholly masculine man, no purely feminine woman." Praised by the scholar Mary Kelley as "manifesto, celebration, meditation, and declamation," Fuller's controversial treatise recalls the revolutionary fervor of Wollstonecraft and Wordsworth and champions autonomy for women as well as men (xxiv).

ACHIEVEMENTS IN THE VICTORIAN NOVEL

The British novel flourished in the nineteenth century. From Jane Austen's witty *Pride and Prejudice* (1813) to Charles Dickens's delightful *Pickwick Papers* (1837), from Charlotte Brontë's passionate *Jane Eyre* (1847) to George Eliot's philosophical *Middlemarch* (1872), an impressive array of men and women novelists produced masterpieces loved by their contemporaries and still enjoyed by readers today. While such prominent writers as Jane Austen and William Makepeace Thackeray were concerned with what the critic Lionel Trilling called "manners, morals, and the novel," Charles Dickens, Charlotte Brontë, and Elizabeth Gaskell expanded the genre to include social criticism. In the 1850s, after the publication of *Vanity Fair* (1848), Thackeray rivaled Dickens's ongoing popularity and prominence; in the 1860s Anthony Trollope portrayed the optimism of the Victorian Age at midcentury; and in the 1870s Eliot wrestled with problems of conscience and ethical choice. In the century's final decade Thomas Hardy challenged the Victorians' sexual codes, especially the strictures on women's sexuality, in such novels as *Tess of the D'Urbervilles* (1891) and *Jude the Obscure* (1895).

Taken as a whole, these novelists contributed to the development of the realist tradition in fiction. As Thackeray noted, "the Art of Novels *is* to represent Nature: to convey as strongly as possible the sentiment of reality." Like their predecessors Henry Fielding and Samuel Richardson, nineteenth-century novelists typically focused on the struggles of a male or female protagonist in relation to family members and neighbors. Although the settings varied from Emily Brontë's Yorkshire moors to Dickens's teeming London to Hardy's rural Wessex, realist novels provided readers with a recognizable slice of daily life. Moreover, the relationship between writer and audience shifted during midcentury as novels began to be published in serial form.

Although some later critics felt that serial publication detracted from the genre's art—Henry James would call Victorian novels "large loose baggy monsters"—novels published serially had to be told more artfully to keep readers engaged from one installment to the next, and such works as Dickens's *Bleak House* (1852) reveal meticulous rather than fragmented construction. Writers learned how readers were responding to their work while it was still in progress, a fact that empowered a growing and diverse reading audience comprised of women as well as men, newly literate factory and domestic workers as well as aristocrats.

The two most prominent male Victorian novelists, Dickens and Thackeray, represented different attitudes toward the century in which they lived. Along with many of his compatriots, Dickens criticized industrialization as more of a curse than a blessing, noting the terrible living and working conditions of the poor and that "progress" was for many an illusion. He was influenced by Engels's *The Condition of the Working Class in England*, written after Dickens spent nearly two years observing industrial life near Manchester, and by such social critics as Thomas Carlyle and William Morris, who mourned the loss of what Karl Marx described as the "feudal, patriarchal, idyllic relations" established in previous centuries between employers and workers. Perhaps the most trenchant fictional critique of industrialization was Dickens's *Hard Times* (1854), which portrayed the "ill-smelling" village of Coketown as "severely workful," a monotonous and exhausting factory town in which to live and die. The Victorian essayist John Ruskin claimed that this novel "should be studied with close and earnest care by persons interested in social questions." Dickens's skillful reportage was combined with an artful stylization that many Victorian critics considered overly theatrical; Walter Bagehot, however, praised his realism in describing London "like a special correspondent for posterity."

Rather than offer dramatic social criticism, Thackeray examined social mores, though in a more trenchant way than Dickens. *Vanity Fair* has been praised for its "magisterial omniscience" as well as its satire and cynicism, and for its compelling contribution to what F.R. Leavis termed the "great tradition" of the English novel. Thackeray was much admired by women novelists of the period; Charlotte Brontë called him a "genius" who "stands alone—alone in his sagacity, alone in his truth, alone in his feeling," and both George Eliot and her close friend, the feminist Barbara Bodichon, praised his forthright attack on discriminatory marriage and divorce laws in *The Newcomes* (1855). Like Trollope, Thackeray regarded the Victorian era and progress with cautious optimism.

THE RISE OF WOMEN NOVELISTS

Certainly British women made major contributions to the nineteenth-century novel. Indeed, as Sandra Gilbert and Susan Gubar have claimed, "beginning with APHRA BEHN and burgeoning with FRANCES BURNEY, Ann Radcliffe, MARIA EDGEWORTH, and Jane Austen, the English novel seems to have been in great part a female invention" (540). Women wrote hundreds of novels during the century. Scholars Gaye Tuchman and Nina Forten have demonstrated that until the 1870s women published more than six times as many serialized novels as men did; only in the 1880s, when the genre came to be considered "serious" literature, did men outpublish women. For many women the novel seemed an ideal genre for depicting the pleasures and problems of the drawing room, as pioneering works by Burney and Austen reveal. An early novel of manners, Burney's popular *Evelina* (1778) presented in epistolary form the struggle of the shy protagonist to avoid social ruin at the hands of the devious Madame Duval. Both *Evelina* and its more substantive successor, *Cecilia* (1782), influenced Austen, who parodied Burney's histrionic language and sentimental plot in *Northanger Abbey* (1818) but took both the title of *Pride and Prejudice* (1813) and its central theme from *Cecilia*. However, Austen's social satire and lively female protagonists were unprecedented in comic fiction. Tennyson called her a "prose Shakespeare," a comparison that Virginia Woolf would also make a century later in praising the incandescence of Shakespeare and Austen, for "the minds of both had consumed all impediments" (*LAWL* 49).

Not all nineteenth-century women novelists concentrated on the parlor or the ballroom, however. Maria Edgeworth, Charlotte Brontë, and George Eliot in particular addressed important social, ethical, and philosophical concerns of the age: equality between women and men, the human desire for meaningful work, the pursuit of liberty, aristocratic and patriarchal arrogance and irresponsibility, and the individual's duty to his or her fellow humans. Edgeworth's *Castle Rackrent* (1800) criticized the decadence of Irish landowners and their abuse of women; Brontë's *Jane Eyre* (1847) explored the economic plight of orphans and governesses and pilloried the evangelical clergy; Eliot's *Middlemarch* (1872) made problematic Dorothea Brooke's sacrifice of her own ill-defined ambitions to the service of her pedantic husband, Casaubon, and questioned the viability of a young woman's marriage to a man twice her age. As Elaine Showalter has argued, in much women's fiction "the orthodox plot recedes, and another plot, hitherto submerged in the anonymity of the background, stands out in bold relief like a thumbprint" (435).

Most women novelists of the nineteenth century struggled with the politics of authorship, since prevailing gender ideologies denied them literary authority. Burney and Austen initially published their works anonymously, while others assumed male pseudonyms: Charlotte, Emily, and Anne Brontë became Currer, Ellis, and Acton Bell, and Marian Evans published only one scholarly work before beginning to write fiction as George Eliot. Moreover, these women had difficulty negotiating with prominent and overly directive male critics and publishers as well as other writers. Richard Lovell Edgeworth, Maria's father and an Enlightenment scientist and theorist, trivialized her as "a mere writer of pretty stories and novellettes," insisting that she abandon fiction and assist him with his research. Robert Southey, then England's poet laureate, told Charlotte Brontë that "literature cannot be the business of a woman's life: and it ought not to be" (*LAWL* 239). Even George Henry Lewes, the literary critic with whom Eliot lived and a man generally supportive of women's intellectual pursuits, once opined that maternity was "the grand function of woman."

Yet these women novelists persevered, writing against the grain. Edgeworth wrote *Castle Rackrent* in secret, without her father's knowledge, and both there and in *Letters to Literary Ladies* (1795) she challenged the patriarchal assumptions that her father and his friends advanced. Brontë responded to Southey by insisting that she would continue to write: "You do not forbid me to write; you do not say that what I write is utterly destitute of merit" (*LAWL* 239). Eliot sometimes heeded Lewes's editorial advice but often defied it; in 1860, when he urged her to write a historical novel about the life of Savonarola, she insisted instead on writing "another English story." The perseverence of Edgeworth, Brontë, and Eliot paid off, for critical reception of their novels was positive. *Castle Rackrent* was praised as a brilliant treatment of Ireland's declining Ascendency class; *Jane Eyre* was reviewed as "not merely a work of great promise" but "one of absolute performance"; and the greatness of *Middlemarch* was celebrated by Emily Dickinson, among many other contemporaries: "What do I think of *Middlemarch?* What do I think of glory? . . . The mysteries of human nature surpass the 'mysteries of redemption'" (*Letters* 2: 506).

The undeniable accomplishment of nineteenth-century women novelists has a darker side, however. As Gilbert and Gubar have demonstrated, much fiction by Austen, Mary Shelley, the Brontës, and Eliot reflects their "anxiety of authorship," a fear and ambivalence toward female creativity (45). Such novels as *Sense and Sensibility* (1811), *Frankenstein* (1818), *Wuthering Heights* (1847), and *The Mill on the Floss* (1860) are "both literally and figuratively concerned with disease, as if to emphasize the effort with which health and wholeness were won from the infectious 'vapors' of despair and fragmentation" suffered by their protagonists (57). As a strategy for overcoming this anxiety, Gilbert and Gubar argue, many women writers revised male genres, "using them to record their own dreams and their own stories *in disguise*" (72–73). Thus Emily Brontë created not only an amoral Byronic hero in Heathcliff but a Byronic heroine in the passionate Catherine Earnshaw; Charlotte Brontë portrayed Jane Eyre's mad double, Bertha Mason Rochester, as an extension of herself; Shelley evoked both conflict and affinity between the noble but arrogant Victor Frankenstein and his monstrous creation. These fictional "monsters" often escaped from their actual or imagined cages. To be sure, such doubling can also be found in certain male texts of the period—in *Vanity Fair*, for example, Thackeray pits the meek and angelic Amelia Sedley against the cunning and destructive Becky Sharp—but there such oppositions reveal stereotypes about women, not ambivalence toward authorship.

"We women are always in danger of living too exclusively in the affections," wrote George Eliot to Mrs. Robert Lifton in 1870, "and though our affections are perhaps the best gift we have, we also ought to have our share of the more independent life." Feminist critics such as Ellen Moers and Elaine Showalter have remarked how ironic it is that nineteenth-century women novelists often could not imagine for their heroines the sort of independent lives that they themselves led; certainly it is true that in most of these novels the female protagonists either marry or die. However, Kathleen Blake has complicated this interpretation, noting that Charlotte Brontë and George Eliot criticized the notion of woman's "self-postponement" in favor of love rather than endorsing it. Moreover, Margaret Homans has argued that the Brontës, Eliot, Shelley, and Gaskell opted courageously to "bear the word" by writing about the relationship between women and language; indeed, they defied cultural prohibitions to "mark their treacherous, liberating moves between repression and expression" (1986: 29–32). As writers during the "heroic age" of the English novel, these women novelists insisted that heroes came in both genders and that literary conception was a female as well as a male province.

SENTIMENTAL AND DOMESTIC LITERATURE AND CULTURE

Women's literary production in the nineteenth century includes not only participation in major genres and literary movements, but also contributions to a more diffuse spectrum of popular sentimental and domestic writing. The word "sentimental" was originally applied during the eighteenth century to a certain type of novel exemplified by the adventures of sensitive heroines such as Samuel Richardson's Pamela. In the nineteenth century the definition of sentimental and domestic writing was expanded and applied to a vast literature of bestselling fiction and poetry, as well as nonfiction genres such as letters, diaries, and journals, often explicitly tied to domestic consumption and circulation. The "sentimental" became a term of style, linked to the rise of mass culture and entangled in the popular ideology of "separate spheres."

In women's writing, sentimental themes assumed that individual differences were less important than the private "language of the heart" and shared sympathy. Sentimental fiction romanticized home and hearth; it venerated motherhood and female friendships as important sources of support and, as Jane Tompkins has pointed out, "moral power." These themes and ideas lay close to the material culture and public/private divisions of nineteenth-century women's lives in the United States and Britain, as Barbara Welter emphasizes in her description of the virtues of "true womanhood"—piety, purity, domesticity, and submissiveness. Because the values and motifs of the sentimental were so closely tied to gender ideology, the growing market for sentimental writing became a stylistic and politically fraught issue in both countries.

Issues of the sentimental developed differently in different cultural contexts. In England, sentimental traditions were associated with evangelical religious and political dissent, but also with bourgeois culture and the reading habits of those who would aspire to gentility. Seduction-and-betrayal plots of sensational novels were altered to appeal to more ordinary women's situations in novels such as *Charlotte Temple* (1791) by Susanna Rowson, a novel that enjoyed great popularity in England and the United States. English versions included novels by Mary Elizabeth Braddon and Rhoda Broughton. George Eliot's 1855 condemnation of the "frothy, the prosy, the pious, and the pedantic" in "Silly Novels by Lady Novelists" set the tone for a debate that typically pitted the values of common sense, reason, realism, and emotional constraint against suspicion of the dangers of emotional excess and commodity culture.

In U.S. culture at midcentury the politics of authorship was framed by a debate between masculine versions of the novels of Nathaniel Hawthorne and James Fenimore Cooper and feminine versions of the popular domestic novel, which often had strong sentimental overtones. U.S. "literary domestics," as the popular fiction was called, flooded the market with commercial successes during the period from 1855 to 1865; works such as Susan Warner's *The Wide, Wide World* (1851) and Maria Cummins's *The Lamplighter* (1854) defined the meaning of the literary bestseller. At the same time, novelists such as Hawthorne were struggling to define a tradition of romance with symbolism and Puritan allegory as its predominant values. Hawthorne's complaint about the "d——d mob of scribbling women" and Mark Twain's satire in *The Adventures of Huckleberry Finn* of Emmeline Grangerford, the girl who could write anything "so long as it was mournful," functioned to trivialize a growing female authorship seen as a threat to founding a distinctive national literature. Melville, too, conceived of two audiences for U.S. fiction: the group of book-buying women whose tastes he tried to appease in conceiving of an audience for his incest novel, *Pierre* (1852), written to make money; and the reader (assumed to be male) interested in the drama of cosmic forces and worldly adventure such as *Moby Dick* (1851).

Yet the influence of the sentimental and domestic novel was not altogether separate from men's literary production during this period. Just as earlier sensation novels were sometimes written by men—William Brown's *The Power of Sympathy* (1789) was an early example—U.S. "classics" such as Hawthorne's *The Scarlet Letter* (1850) folded their seduction-and-betrayal themes in moral allegories. Gender studies of the nineteenth-century British and U.S. traditions note that male novelists in the realist tradition from Dickens to Twain and Henry James measured their popularity against that of "flagrantly bad bestsellers" and worried about cultural "feminization." Ironically, as Nina Baym has argued, male-authored fiction that has been taken as representative of U.S. culture as a whole also contained its melodramatic plots in which "men on the run" evaded the women who would domesticate them, engineering feats of evasion through male-bonding and self-fathering acts.

POPULAR POETRY

In England and the United States, women's poetic productions included a number of genres associated with popular verse culture: elegies on the death of a child, war elegies, patriotic verse, didactic odes, hymns and ballads, and other occasional verse. These works appeared in an array of venues from gift books to magazines to sheet music. Nearly as well known as the popular novelists, poets such as FELICIA HEMANS, Letitia Elizabeth Landon, Maria Jane Jewsbury in England and LYDIA SIGOURNEY, Alice Cary, Elizabeth Oakes Smith, Sarah Josepha Hale, Helen Hunt Jackson, and Hannah Gould in America shared a problematic relationship to the literary marketplace. Popular poets in the United States learned much from Hemans, whose patriotic elegy "Casabianca" (1826) was a schoolroom classic well into the end of the century and whose style was deemed a model of feminine diction and decorum in U.S. finishing schools. Sigourney once defined the "genius" of Hemans as "the whole sweet circle of the domestic affections—the hallowed ministries of woman at the cradle, the hearthstone, and the deathbed." Emily Dickinson, whose reading of popular poets was influenced by Emersonian Transcendentalism, was put off precisely by these "dimity convictions"; she feared the "auction of the mind" would lead to an "admiring bog." So resistant was Dickinson to the new commercialization and democratization of literature that the sentimental market represented—and so certain she may have been that her work, too, would be trivialized—that anxiety about alliance with a sisterhood of sentimental poets appears to have been one of the reasons for her reluctance to publish. CHRISTINA ROSSETTI and Elizabeth Barrett Browning, in contrast, while defining themselves as "serious" rather than sentimental poets, were nonetheless influenced by their female colleagues; both, for example, wrote elegies at the death of Landon. Dickinson, in turn, wrote an elegy at the death of Barrett Browning, a fact that suggests varied spheres of influence among nineteenth-century women poets.

Not all readers shared Dickinson's prejudices or her precise insights about the ironies of popular domestic and sentimental verse-culture. A number of male editors, including Thomas Buchanan Read, Rufus Griswold, and Evert and George Duyckinck, gathered large and relatively diverse groups of popular poets together in bestselling anthologies—not always because they admired the poetry but because they wanted to make money, and, more problematically, because they thought variety might be "broadly representative" of U.S. womanhood (Ezell 95–96). Generally, the so-called "nightingale" poets (Cheryl Walker's term) consciously identified themselves with the muselike songbirds of the British Romantic tradition, but their poetic agendas, as Walker has shown, need to be understood on their own terms. These terms include the recognition of issues of pain and insight intertwined with problems of love and domesticity, which the contradictory burdens of nineteenth-century womanhood evoked. Seen in this light, the elegies for dead children written by Lydia Sigourney and other women of the nineteenth century revealed divided and ambivalent sentiments.

LITERATURE AND SOCIAL PROTEST

Some sentimental and domestic novels and poems might indeed have been "tearful floods," as detractors typically portrayed them. But U.S. culture at midcentury also shaped a radical tradition that joined appeals to sympathy with protest writing and social criticism. David S. Reynolds has called this the literature of the "other American Renaissance." The category includes didactic writing in popular genres, antislavery and Civil War literature, immigrant narratives, and polemical rhetoric. Harriet Beecher Stowe's famed abolitionist novel, *Uncle Tom's Cabin* (1852), and REBECCA HARDING DAVIS's critique of industrialization, *Life in the Iron-Mills* (1861), exemplified what TILLIE OLSEN has called "trespass vision," crossing the ideology of separate spheres (68–69). Other writers known for sentimental and domestic fiction such as Elizabeth Stuart Phelps, Catherine Sedgwick, Caroline Kirkland, Lydia Maria Child, and Frances E.W. Harper rejected the separation of art from rhetoric, adapting sentimental fiction to social agendas or extending their repertoires to include political essays, narrative poems, and other forms of journalism and social commentary. Critics of the time had difficulty knowing whether to classify Harper, for example, as "genteel," "black liberationist," or "profeminist" for her wide-ranging concerns as a novelist, poet, and polemicist. Labeling may miss the point: a number of these women considered themselves professional writers rather than creative artists, and although they identified with "feminine" values, many simply refused to define themselves narrowly as writers. Certainly the influence of many popular women fiction writers, through the range of their audience and their flexible use of genres, was enormous. In Europe for most of the nineteenth century, Stowe's *Uncle Tom's Cabin,* not Twain's *The Adventures of Huckleberry Finn,* was seen as the "great American novel," and Harper was described by a contemporary reviewer as the "most eloquent woman" in the country.

In the 1850s and 60s much protest literature took the form of antislavery sermons, oratory, slave narratives, and polemical rhetoric, genres that revealed the influence and intertwining of oral and written culture. Abolitionists and suffragists such as the Grimké sisters, Frederick Douglass, Maria Stewart, and CHARLOTTE PERKINS GILMAN were as well known as public speakers as they were for their writing. African-American rhetoric in particular was adapted to a variety of audiences, with its goal a "stirring to action." While standard English and traditional rhetorical style and delivery were commonly used by black orators speaking to white audiences, in African-American settings these same orators frequently incorporated devices designed to solicit audience participation, such as the evangelical "call and response" technique. Antislavery literature as well as oratory demonstrated the flexibility of black women in particular in moving among different audiences. It also raised problems of literacy, race, and mediation. For example, the recorded versions of speeches by Sojourner Truth have come down to us through the mediation of white suffragists like Frances Dana Gage, and the bestselling *Narrative of Sojourner Truth* (1850), the story of her life, was transcribed and edited by the white abolitionist Olive Gilbert. Similarly, Harriet Jacobs's *Incidents in the Life of a Slave Girl, Written by Herself* (1861) was sponsored by Amy Post and Lydia Maria Child; Child edited the book and certified in her introduction that its language and ideas were Jacobs's own. Raising the issue of mediation should not detract from these texts' value: Truth's brilliant speeches linking racial and gender exploitation and Jacobs's powerful rendition of the physical and psychological abuse she suffered from her master stand as forceful antislavery testimonies. Instead, reading these works as mediated can enhance our understanding of their frequent "cross-talk," or switching of tone, cadence, and metaphor to appeal to white as well as black audiences.

After the Civil War much literature of protest focused on women's restricted lives. Mark Twain's Gilded Age, a term often applied to the last decades of the nineteenth century, was a more crass, less idealistic literary era. New laws gradually permitted women the "wider sphere of activity" that Charlotte Brontë's governess, Jane Eyre, had yearned for earlier in the century. But there were many contradictions. In the United States the Married Women's Property Act was passed in 1860 but had to be ratified slowly, from state to state. A storm of protest that followed publication of KATE CHOPIN's The Awakening (1899), the story of an adulterous woman who committed suicide rather than return to her stultifying married life, showed that legal reforms had not readily transformed deep-seated cultural beliefs about gender or overthrown regional customs. In crucial matters such as divorce law, women remained the legal property of their husbands; in Chopin's Lousiana, where local courts still operated under Napoleonic codes late in the century, laws that would have made it possible under the best of circumstances for a divorced woman to have custody of her children were not passed until 1888. "Local color" artists—as Chopin was considered when her popular tales of Creole and Bayou folk life were first published—are now recognized for having pointed to a number of the ways in which regional prejudices about women persisted. There were also racial subtexts in both Chopin's and Charlotte Perkins Gilman's work: "mulattos" often figured as complex symbols of difference in Chopin's stories, and in California, where Gilman lived when she wrote "The Yellow Wallpaper," the "yellow peril" of Asiatic immigration was as much a social issue as the developing freedoms of new womanhood.

Stylistically and philosophically, fiction such as Chopin's and Gilman's was linked to the pervasive influence of literary "naturalism," an outgrowth of realism informed by quasiscientific and Darwinian philosophies about human nature and evolution. In the work of Stephen Crane and Theodore Dreiser, naturalism introduced a new frankness of presentation about sexuality and economic oppression that emphasized the role of social determinism in the formation of character but also introduced a new "essentialism" about male and female natures that reinforced sexual stereotypes. The complex, often terrifying psychosocial dilemmas and determinisms portrayed in fin de siecle women's fiction sometimes made earlier "women's fiction" seem naïve. However, both Chopin's and Gilman's fiction drew upon some of the strategies used by earlier novelists in valuing emotional intensity and maximizing the reader's involvement with the text.

Whether subversively or overtly, nineteenth-century women writers began to challenge masculine representations that associated femininity with nature and excluded women from speaking subjectivity. To become autonomous writers, as Margaret Homans has noted, women had to "shift from agreeing to see themselves as daughters of nature and as part of the world of objects to seeing themselves as daughters of an Eve reclaimed for their [literature]" (216). From Charlotte Brontë's orphaned governess, who not only marries her chastened "master" but writes the saga of their courtship on her own terms, to Emily Dickinson's liberated Soul, who "dances like a Bomb abroad," the characters and personae of nineteenth-century women inscribe social rebellion, self-definition, and unquestionable literary authority.

⊰ Works Cited ⊱

Armstrong, Isobel. *Victorian Poetry: Poetry, Poetics and Politics.* London and New York: Routledge, 1993.

———. "The Gush of the Feminine: How Can We Read Women's Poetry of the Romantic Period?" *Romantic Women Writers: Voices and Countervoices.* Eds. Paula R. Feldman and Theresa M. Kelley. Hanover and London: UP of New England, 1995. 13–32.

Baym, Nina. *Feminism and American Literary History.* New Brunswick: Rutgers UP, 1992.

———. *American Women Writers and the Work of History, 1790–1860.* New Brunswick: Rutgers UP, 1995.

Blake, Kathleen. *Love and the Woman Question in Victorian Literature.* Totowa, NJ: Barnes and Noble Books, 1983.

Dickinson, Emily. *The Letters of Emily Dickinson.* Eds. Thomas H. Johnson and Theodora Ward. Cambridge, MA: Harvard UP, 1958.

Ezell, Margaret J. M. *Writing Women's Literary History.* Baltimore: The Johns Hopkins UP, 1993.

Gilbert, Sandra M. and Susan Gubar. *The Madwoman in the Attic: The Woman Writer and the Nineteenth-Century Literary Imagination.* New Haven: Yale UP, 1979.

Homans, Margaret. *Bearing the Word: Language and Female Experience in Nineteenth-Century Women's Writing.* Chicago: The U of Chicago P, 1986.

———. *Women Writers and Poetic Identity: Dorothy Wordsworth, Emily Brontë, and Emily Dickinson.* Princeton: Princeton UP, 1980.

Kelley, Mary, ed. *The Portable Margaret Fuller.* New York: Penguin, 1994.

Leavis, F.R. *The Great Tradition.* Garden City, NY: Doubleday, 1954.

Mellor, Anne K., ed. *Romanticism and Feminism.* Bloomington: Indiana UP, 1988.

———. *Romanticism and Gender.* New York and London: Routledge, 1993.

Moers, Ellen. *Literary Women.* Garden City, NY: Doubleday, 1976.

Olsen, Tillie. *Silences.* New York: Dell, 1972.

Phillips, Elizabeth. *Emily Dickinson: Personae and Performance.* University Park: The Pennsylvania State UP, 1988.

Reynolds, David S. *Beneath the American Renaissance: The Subversive Imagination in the Age of Emerson and Melville.* New York: Alfred E. Knopf, 1988.

Showalter, Elaine. "Review Essay," *Signs* 1: 2 (Winter 1975): 435.

Tompkins, Jane. *Sensational Designs: The Cultural Work of American Fiction, 1790–1860.* New York and Oxford: Oxford UP, 1985.

Trilling, Lionel. *The Liberal Imagination: Essays on Literature and Society.* Garden City, NY: Doubleday, 1950.

Tuchman, Gaye and Nina E. Fortin. *Edging Women Out: Victorian Novelists, Publishers, and Social Change.* New Haven: Yale UP, 1989.

Walker, Cheryl. *The Nightingale's Burden: Women Poets and American Culture Before 1900.* Bloomington: Indiana UP, 1982.

Welter, Barbara. "The Cult of True Womanhood, 1820–1860." *American Quarterly* 18 (1966): 151–74.

Modernist Literature
1900–1945

The term "modernism" has generally referred to a distinctive experimental tradition in post-Romantic literature, as early twentieth century writers shifted from the composed, meditative voice of the Romantic lyricist and the philosophical, often ponderous voice of the Victorian sage to an ironic and fragmented sensibility. Much modernist literature reflects a sense of crisis in human existence, a crisis manifested in the writers' preoccupation with the present and its lack of meaning, due in part to an increase in technology and urbanization; in the quest for a new context and new literary techniques to depict past losses and the complex reality of the here and now; and in an inward-focused, frequently disillusioned vision that conveys alienation and psychic fragmentation. Although some scholars have dated modernism from 1910, when VIRGINIA WOOLF claimed that "human character changed," for practical purposes it can be designated as beginning with Queen Victoria's death in 1901 and concluding at the end of World War II in 1945 (Woolf 1950: 94).

Modernism is usually associated with writers that the critic Wyndham Lewis called "the men of 1914": Ezra Pound, T.S. Eliot, James Joyce, and himself—writers whose work was, in the words of Bonnie Kime Scott, "experimental, audience challenging, and language focused" (1995: xxvi; 1990: 4). Lewis might have added to his list the Irish poet William Butler Yeats, widely considered one of the greatest poets of the age due to his bold, vigorous voice and his exploration of myth, mysticism, and apocalyptic thought. Modernist fiction left behind the comic realism of JANE AUSTEN and the Victorian earnestness of Charles Dickens to explore the complex workings of the human psyche, while poetry tended toward free verse innovations. Pound was a pivotal man of 1914 because of his development of Imagist tenets, which emphasized the centrality of the image to poetic representation, direct treatment of the thing, and no word except the exact one. "Make it new," he urged his fellow poets, encouraging them to find original literary techniques to represent the shifting terms of modern reality. Heeding this exhortation was Pound's sometime pupil T.S. Eliot; in *The Waste Land* he presented modern malaise in an avant-garde style that was fragmented, highly allusive, and filled with torment. *The Waste Land* and Joyce's innovative novel *Ulysses* were published in the same year, 1922, and together set the standard for an evolving experimentalism.

As Scott has argued convincingly, however, modernism has long been "unconsciously gendered masculine" in its emphasis on a "language-centered" form of experimentation, its attempts to articulate a discourse that represents the trauma of world war, its preoccupation with redefining masculinity for the modern age, and its presentation of expatriatism as reflecting a generational experience of loss (1990: 2). Alternate or neglected approaches to issues of language and formal experimentation, gender anxieties and affirmations, race and the "New Negro" of the Harlem Renaissance, war and its tolls on men and women, and the complexities of expatriate experience can be found if we consider women's modernist innovations and texts alongside men's. Certainly, too, there exist strands of interconnection in men's and women's approaches to these historical issues and movements, as well as differences among men and among women, that undercut any essentialist notion of there being a "male modernism" or a "female modernism" per se.

Finally, it is worth noting that modernism is not monolithic; radical styles do not necessarily connote radicalism in political content. Moreover, modernism refers to a cultural movement as well as a period style. The linguistic orders of modernism, that is, relate somewhat uneasily to the social orders of modernity. If defined in the broader historical context of modernity, modernism would include among its key features the redefinition of national and transnational boundaries; the struggle for freedom of artistic expression in relation to various forms of difference, especially racial and gender difference; the loss and questioning of traditional foundations of institutional and spiritual authority; and a reexamination of the relationship between art and everyday life.

INNOVATIVE USES OF LANGUAGE

Although the concept of "stream of consciousness" was initially developed by the psychologist William James, twentieth-century literary critics have applied it to the writing of James Joyce, Dorothy Richardson, and Virginia Woolf to describe fiction that blends multiple and shifting narrative perspectives, fluidity of time and space, and free association of ideas. The stream-of-consciousness novel focuses on the psychological states and mental processes of one or more characters by probing their inner consciousness. Widely viewed as a quintessentially modernist novel, Joyce's *Ulysses* is a modern epic placed on the frame of a classical text, Homer's *Odyssey*; it explores the psychic lives of three central characters—the spiritually haunted Stephen Daedalus, the wandering advertising solicitor Leopold Bloom, and Bloom's unfaithful wife, Molly—and uses a cinematic technique to provide a panoramic view of Dublin. Joyce displays his virtuosity in *Ulysses* to imply that life and time are continuous, that the wanderings of the ancient Odysseus and those of his antiheroic successor, Bloom, emerge from the same complex cycle of life. Ultimately Joyce's modernist vision challenges any notion of a stable external reality to which an inward search can be connected.

Since 1914, when his work was first touted by Pound (who heard of him through Yeats), Joyce has been considered by male writers and critics the most important modernist experimenter. Women writers also used Joyce's prose as a standard by which to judge their own. Woolf, for instance, took copious notes on *Ulysses*, admiring Joyce's attempt "to do away with the machinery—to extract the marrow" and wondering whether he was right in suggesting that "the subconscious mind dwells on indecency"; in "Modern Fiction" (1919) she praised him for being "concerned at all costs to reveal the flickerings of that innermost flame which flashes its messages through the brain," even if in this effort he had to forego probability, coherence, or other "signposts" that have traditionally aided the reader (152–53). Other women modernists—most notably Richardson, DJUNA BARNES, Mina Loy, and Rebecca West—reviewed Joyce's writing positively, praising his experimental aspects and, in the case of Barnes, lauding his lyricism and sexual boldness. No evidence suggests, however, that Joyce regarded his female contemporaries with the same degree of interest they showed in his work, a fact that explains in part why women's contributions to modernist fiction and poetry have been minimalized.

Studying women's contributions paints a richer picture of the aims and achievements of the modernist novel, for as Scott notes, female modernists offer "an unassessed vitality in form and content" (1990: 3). The artistic innovators best known for their fluid, associative representations of women's interior lives are two canonical writers, Virginia Woolf and GERTRUDE STEIN. However, as "midwives of modernism," literary figures such as May Sinclair, KATHERINE MANSFIELD, and Dorothy Richardson—writers considered "minor" in the traditional canon—also played significant roles in developing a twentieth-century aesthetic (Scott 1995: 55–83). Sinclair first used the term "stream-of-consciousness" to describe the fiction of Dorothy Richardson, thereby linking psychology and modernism. Moreover, in her thoughtful reviews of Richardson and other experimental women novelists she evinced a serious interest in representations of the human psyche that many male modernists found less compelling. In her multivolume novel *Pilgrimage* (1915–17), which predated *Ulysses* by seven years, Richardson attempted to break with the "masculine" realism in favor of an experimental "feminine" equivalent that was more fluid and less linear in style. And although marginalized because she did not write novels (a genre privileged in masculine modernism), Katherine Mansfield contributed significantly to the development of the short story as a modernist literary form. Furthermore, Mansfield's critical review of Woolf's early novel *Night and Day* (1919) as insufficiently experimental pushed Woolf, who considered her both a friend and a rival, to develop a stream-of-consciousness narrative style in *Jacob's Room* (1922), the fragmented account of a young man's tragic life and death in World War I.

Many modernist writers used gendered metaphors to assert difference. Woolf described Richardson's accomplishment, and her own stylistic goal, as creating "the psychological sentence of the feminine gender," a strategy that would allow her to "descend to the depths and investigate the crannies" of the human mind, and the minds of women in particular (1979: 191–92). Woolf modified this technique in her representations of Clarissa Dalloway and her shell-shocked "other," Septimus Warren Smith, in *Mrs. Dalloway* (1925) and of Mrs. Ramsay and Lily Briscoe in *To the Lighthouse* (1927). In *A Room of One's Own* (1929) Woolf theorized this method of writing the feminine; she praised JANE AUSTEN for creating a "woman's sentence" and articulated her own aesthetic of "incandescence" and the "androgynous mind."

Like Woolf, Gertrude Stein experimented with form as well as content. In *Three Lives* (1936), for example, she offered multiple and fluid narrative perspectives, rhythmic repetition, an emphasis on words as words, and an innovative representation of the refusal of a black woman, Melanctha, to be objectified as a racial "other." As Marianne DeKoven notes, Stein "went a great deal further than anyone else in the modernist period in reinventing literary language in a way that undoes conventional, hierarchical, patriarchal modes of signification" (Scott 1990: 480). In their place she offered a diverse range of stylistic modes, an open-ended syntax, and a rich semantic field. Michael Hoffman has called Stein's technique "abstractionism," an emphasis on language itself rather than on narrative strategies (21–23). Stein also used lesbian erotic humor and a playfully defiant satire of "patriarchal poetry" in her experimental chicanery.

Influenced by Pound, Eliot, H.D., and Stein, the modernist movement in poetry also embraced aesthetic experimentation. Between 1900 and 1917 Pound extolled the virtues of Imagism, a poetic approach that presented a particular image exactly, making it concrete and clear, not blurred or diffuse; he edited *Des Imagistes*, an anthology, in 1913 and in 1915 issued an "Imagist Manifesto" defining the image as "that which presents an intellectual and emotional complex in an instant of time." Proponents of Imagism—along with Pound, H.D., T.E. Hulme, F.S. Flint, Richard Aldington, and Amy Lowell—employed the language of common speech, created new rhythms to follow the sequence of the musical phrase, endorsed total freedom of subject matter, and claimed concentration as the essence of poetry. Eliot's poetry blended erudition and ordinary speech, employed subtle irony, juxtaposed unexpected and sometimes shocking images, and shifted topics and voices in a discontinuous manner. "The Love Song of J. Alfred Prufrock" (1915), a dramatic monologue, presented the alienation of an ineffectual, sexually inhibited man, while *The Waste Land* (1922) assumed epic proportions to chronicle the sexual malaise and spiritual desolation experienced by many after World War I. This latter poem was distinctively modern not only in its disillusionment but also in its merging of ancient and modern prophetic figures and its unrealized quest for regeneration.

Eliot considered Pound and Lewis London's finest literary men; he benefited especially from Pound's editorial support and claimed that meeting him changed his life. Pound, on the other hand, perpetuated the myth of masculine originality by writing to Harriet Monroe, editor of *Poetry* magazine, that Eliot "modernized himself *on his own*." Eliot was an influential critic as well as a poet; his landmark essay "Tradition and the Individual Talent" espoused a set of ordering categories that delineated how traditional and new aesthetics might most effectively mix. The poet should write "not merely with his own generation in his bones but with a feeling that the whole of the literature of his country has a simultaneous existence and composes a simultaneous order," he claimed. Tradition evolves because "the existing monuments form an ideal order among themselves, which is modified by the introduction of the new (the really new) work of art among them" (1920). Eliot went a step beyond Pound in emphasizing the "really new" over the "new," revealing a tendency toward hierarchy and demonstrating in the essay's language and content what the critic Harold Bloom has called the male writer's "anxiety of influence."

Although their innovations have been critically underrepresented until recently, modernist women also experimented with poetic technique. Living in London in 1913–14, H.D. worked with Pound to develop the principles of Imagism, refining a crystalline precision in such poems as "Oread," renowned for its stark imagery and slightly discordant musical rhythms. Pound considered H.D.'s poems the finest representatives of Imagist technique: hard, clear, and offering "always the *exact* word." Like Pound, however, H.D. finally found Imagism too limiting. In her later epic works, most notably *Trilogy* (1942–44) and *Helen in Egypt* (1956), she inscribed "the disintegration of traditional symbolic systems and myth-making quest for new meanings" by identifying with a female-centered divinity (Scott 1990: 85). Another poetic innovator, MARIANNE MOORE, paid close attention to metrics and syllabication, joining Stein and H.D. in a concern with the poetics of the word. Eliot praised Moore for three formal qualities: her distinctive choice of rhythm, her "peculiar and brilliant" use of American idioms, and "an almost primitive simplicity of phrase" (quoted in Scott 1990: 14). William Carlos Williams also admired Moore's experimentation because she cut "soiled words" out of the "greasy" conventional poetic line (quoted in Scott 1990: 331).

Despite certain differences of style and subject matter, various interconnections characterized men's and women's approaches to modernist experimentation and supported networks of influence. During the 1920s the British novelist, biographer, and suffragist Violet Hunt offered her London home as a literary gathering spot where older writers like Henry James, Thomas Hardy, Ford Madox Ford, H.G. Wells, and May Sinclair could meet "les jeunes," or younger writers, a category that included Eliot, H.D., Lewis, D.H. Lawrence, and Rebecca West, among others. Many of these writers read, edited, and promoted one another's work. Sinclair's feminist novel *Mary Olivier: A Life* (1919), also an experiment in stream-of-consciousness, was published in an influential literary magazine, the *Little Review*, at the same time as the middle chapters of *Ulysses*. Pound theorized Imagism and H.D. perfected its practice, while Woolf admired Joyce for his mythic scaffolding and his penetration of mind. Eliot and Woolf visited each other's homes in London, alternately intimidating and entertaining one another. Finally, male and female modernists joined forces to oppose censorship and support Radclyffe Hall in 1928 when her pioneer lesbian novel *The Well of Loneliness* went on trial for obscenity, though with some ambivalence on the part of Virginia Woolf, who disliked the novel, and men such as Eliot and Leonard Woolf, who were uncomfortable with its content. In their shared commitment to formal and/or thematic experimentation and their support of free artistic expression, women and men could band together in defense of modernism.

Psychology, Sexuality, and the "New Woman"

Modernist women also "made it new" by becoming politically active and by revising male-defined fictions of their sexuality, thereby "modernizing desire" (Felski 1). On the activist front, militant suffragists such as Emmeline and Cristabel Pankhurst in England and Alice Paul in the United States engaged in a provocative public campaign to win women the vote by any means necessary during the first two decades of the century. Their tactics included mass demonstrations and hunger strikes, which often resulted in imprisonment and forced feedings. In 1907 a U.S. writer living abroad, Elizabeth Robins, published *The Convert*, a novel that chronicled a skeptical woman's conversion to suffragism, while as a journalist from 1913 to 1915 Djuna Barnes covered many of these protests and wrote compellingly of the suffragists' plight. Although many suffragists were sexually conservative, profoundly opposed to birth control and horrified at the notion of abortion, others such as Dora Marsden and Rebecca West felt that the agenda of women's suffrage should be expanded to include reflection on marriage and sexuality. In 1911 Marsden began *Freewoman A Weekly Feminist Review*, a journal formed in reaction to the Pankhursts' exclusive emphasis on suffrage; West, in contrast, published articles that linked sexual morality and women's oppression.

On the erotic front, the work of the psychoanalyst Sigmund Freud and the sexologist Havelock Ellis early in the century provoked public discussion of human sexuality and legitimized it as a field of scientific study. Beginning with *The Interpretation of Dreams* (1900) and continuing in published works through the 1930s, Freud argued that the mind was comprised not only of its conscious personality, or "ego," but also of an irrational and desiring unconscious, the "id," and a socially acceptable, moralistic "superego." In his view the primitive, self-absorbed, "polymorphously perverse" infant (generally conceived as male) was eventually socialized into adult heterosexuality through an Oedipus complex, a rivalry between father and son for the affections of the mother. Regardless of Freud's inability, in essays like "On Femininity," to determine what women want—to theorize female sexuality as well as male—his theories of sexual repression and expression revolutionized modern psychology and lent credence to modern women's efforts to articulate a desire of their own. Ellis's *Studies in the Psychology of Sex* (1897–1910) contributed a theory of the "invert," a "mannish woman" who manifested confusion of gender identity and same-sex erotic desire. In his introduction to Hall's *The Well of Loneliness* Ellis praised the novel for its psychological and sociological value in presenting homosexuality as a way of life.

As Scott points out, an important link among H.D., Mansfield, Woolf, Stein, and Loy was their interest in language, psychoanalysis, and the unconscious, manifested in "texts that write the erotics of the female body" (1990: 13). H.D., who underwent psychoanalysis with Freud during the 1930s but considered herself his pupil rather than analysand, viewed the womb as a feminine source of creativity and eventually developed rich myths of female creative quest that she found psychologically and erotically sustaining. Although she paid homage to her mentor in *Tribute to Freud* (1944) and continued throughout her life to be intrigued by his conception of the family romance, she chose finally to embrace her own metaphors of self-healing. Loy analyzed *Ulysses* in a language of embodiment, considering both its phallic properties and the womb as a source of "sanguine introspection." Stein's "Lifting Belly" (1915–17) and Barnes's *Ladies Almanack* (1928) celebrated lesbian eroticism and offered feminist myths of origin and triumph that were informed by theories of psychoanalysis and sexology but not wedded to them. Moreover, by representing such "perversities" as sadism, masquerade, and transvestism in both playful and sober manners, Stein, Barnes, and Hall contributed to the emergence of lesbian and gay male sexuality as serious literary themes. Barnes's *Nightwood* (1937), which T.S. Eliot considered stylistically innovative and the feminist critic Jane Marcus has called "modernism's most representative text," featured not only two lesbian protagonists but also a bisexual transvestite, Dr. O'Connor, a complex character of heightened spiritual consciousness as well as profound social alienation (quoted in Scott 1990: 22).

Some modernist women, most notably EDNA ST. VINCENT MILLAY, Jean Rhys, and Djuna Barnes, wrote about heterosexual women's burgeoning sexual freedom. They were empowered to choose this subject by the challenge of social reformers working to broaden women's sexual options. In the second decade of the twentieth century, for example, birth control became a reality for women who had formerly had no choice but to link sexuality and reproduction. Led by Margaret Sanger in America and Marie Stopes in England, the birth control movement allowed women more control over their erotic and their reproductive lives. Moreover, radicals like the anarchist Emma Goldman, who lectured throughout the United States between 1890 and 1917 and published *The Traffic in Women* (1910), identified not only birth control but also free love, a critique of marriage, and prostitutes' rights as issues that women needed to address. In writing about the "new womanhood," Millay tended to celebrate it, while Rhys and Barnes wrote about it more ambivalently. Appropriating the sonnet form used by male poets through the ages to express longing for a female beloved, Millay focused instead on women's desire, depicting it as bold, brazen, and lusty (Dickie and Travisano 143–88). As Suzanne Clark has shown, many women poets of the 1920s participated in a "sentimental modernism" that did not emphasize technical experimentation but was nonetheless innovative in treating the "new woman's" sexual pleasure seriously, whether in the defiant tone of Millay or the elegiac tones of Elinor Wylie, Sara Teasdale, or Louise Bogan.

In fiction, Jean Rhys explored the social and psychic costs of sexual freedom. Her story "Vienne," for instance, presented women as sexual objects, victims of their own romantic fantasies and men's detachment; Rhys showed the underside of free love by depicting the lives of prostitutes, artists' models, and other economically vulnerable women who traded in sexuality. Moreover, her novel *Voyage in the Dark* (1934) ended with its "new woman" protagonist, Anne Morgan, nearly dying from the results of a botched abortion. Barnes also critiqued heterosexuality, presenting Helena Hucksteppe, the protagonist of her play *To the Dogs* (1923), as a nonconformist who refused to become Gheid Storm's mistress or the object of his sexual fantasy. In revising stage space to become more woman-centered—the play opens with Helena's back to the audience, her body stretched toward the room's interior and away from Storm—and in presenting Helena's cool self-possession, Barnes portrayed her protagonist as autonomous and triumphant. However, Helena's solitary alienation suggested the price a woman paid for sexual freedom in a society that embraced different standards for women and men.

Many male modernist writers were ambivalent toward women writers' emphasis on female sexuality and toward homosexual themes, an ambivalence they revealed in their responses to women's writing and in their own texts. Both Ezra Pound and Havelock Ellis discouraged H.D. from developing her fluid style of prose poem, complaining that it was too feminine. Rhys's male editor forced her to change the ending of *Voyage in the Dark* (1934), which initially concluded with Anne Morgan's interior monologue at the moment of her death from an abortion-induced infection but was revised to end with the words of the male doctor who saved her life. Although Eliot supported Barnes's writing and offered a trenchant analysis of Dr. O'Connor in *Nightwood*, he failed to mention in his review that this character's lust for men and desire to become a woman motivated his behavior. Critics today differ in their views as to whether Joyce's representation of the lusty Molly Bloom constitutes a protofeminist celebration of women's sexuality or a misogynistic portrayal of nymphomania. The same conflict in interpretation exists over Ernest Hemingway's portrait of Brett Ashley in *The Sun Also Rises* (1926), D.H. Lawrence's depiction of Constance Chatterley in *Lady Chatterley's Lover* (1928), and F. Scott Fitzgerald's portrayal of Daisy Buchanan in *The Great Gatsby* (1925). Regardless of whether one considers male modernists supportive of or threatened by women's sexual emancipation, examining the writing of women modernists alongside that of men reveals that not just language and form were "made new" but also, as Scott points out, mind, body, sexual desire, and family (1990: 12–15).

RACE, GENDER, AND THE "NEW NEGRO" OF THE HARLEM RENAISSANCE

Concerns about race as well as concerns about gender and sexuality characterize modernist literature. The term "Harlem Renaissance" refers to a period of creative awakening and intense literary and artistic output by African-American writers centered in or near Harlem, a section of New York City that, along with Greenwich Village, became an important site of U.S. intellectual life and modernist innovation during the 1920s and 30s. Originally used to describe a movement led by black male writers—Jean Toomer, James Weldon Johnson, Countee Cullen, Langston Hughes, Paul Laurence Dunbar, Claude McKay—the Harlem Renaissance has more recently designated the literary production of black women of the era as well: Georgia Douglas Johnson, Jessie Redmon Fauset, ALICE DUNBAR-NELSON, Anne Spencer, Nella Larsen, and ZORA NEALE HURSTON, among others. This period of cultural transformation began in 1921, when James Weldon Johnson edited *The Book of American Negro Poetry*, an anthology that he hoped would enlighten an uninformed public as to the literary achievements of African Americans. As the critic Barbara Johnson has noted, in his introduction Johnson used passive voice, avoided any opposition of blacks and whites, and employed syllogistic logic to argue for the greatness of "Negro" poetry and, by extension, for black people's contributions to U.S. culture (204–207). Subject to critical debate, therefore, is the question of whether the representations of blacks in the Harlem Renaissance advanced or constrained women's and men's freedom. The answer frequently depended on audiences' perceptions, and often the audiences were white.

That James Weldon Johnson's anthology was not particularly successful raises an important political concern that plagued black writers during the Harlem Renaissance, the issue of white patronage. What was considered then and is still today seen as the defining publication of this movement, the anthology entitled *The New Negro* (1925), was edited by a prominent white critic, Alain Locke. Although African-American writers at the turn of the century had taken care to maintain independence from white editorial controls—in 1900 the staff of the *Colored American Magazine* refused the aid of white philanthropists, although they later had a black patron, Colonel William H. Dupress—writers such as Hughes and Hurston were later forced for economic reasons to accept the aid, and often the interference, of white patrons. Johnson's introduction to *The Book of American Negro Poetry* was clearly geared toward a white audience; he catalogued contributions to U.S. culture with which all African-Americans would already be quite familiar—spirituals, Uncle Remus stories, ragtime music, jazz—and used emotional appeal to argue that black writers have achieved much against great odds. For example, he claimed a brief passage from Countee Cullen's poem "The Heritage" as "the two most poignant lines in American literature": "Yet I do marvel at this curious thing— / To make a poet black and bid him sing" (quoted in Johnson 205–208).

As Hazel Carby has noted, the emphasis on separating art from life that has characterized literary critical analysis of the Harlem Renaissance has downplayed the social radicalism of many of the intellectuals involved in it. For men like Asa Philip Randolph and Chandler Owens, editors of *The Messenger*, a journal designed to appeal to working-class as well as elite black readers, the "New Negro" movement was "the product of the same worldwide forces that have brought into being the great liberal and radical movements that are now seizing the reins of political, economic, and social power in all the civilized countries of the world"—socialism and communism (165). Moreover, some black critics writing about the Harlem Renaissance after its heyday criticized its representatives for gearing their writing to liberal whites. In his 1937 "Blueprint for Negro Writing" Richard Wright revealed his bitter ambivalence toward writers of the Renaissance when he suggested that they "had been confined to humble novels, poems, and plays"; they were "prim and decorous ambassadors who went a-begging to white Americans" and had been "received as though they were French poodles who do clever tricks" (37).

Gender tensions also characterized the Harlem Renaissance, tensions that had historical roots. In the 1890s, as Mary Helen Washington has pointed out, when a group of black scholars formed an organization of writers and artists designed to "improve the intellectual output of blacks" they deliberately excluded women (xviii). This exclusion took place even though women had been in the forefront of speaking and writing against lynching and in favor of improved education for black children. In a similar fashion, argues Cheryl A. Wall, Alain Locke's 1925 representation of the "New Negro" as a male figure celebrating a new racial identity, "shaking off the psychology of imitation and implied inferiority" that had been slavery's legacy, ran counter to the experience of many black women writers. The work of poets and fiction writers such as Johnson, Spencer, Fauset, and Larsen was haunted by the racial stereotypes that Locke sought to dismiss, Wall suggests. She argues, moreover, that although their writing was "less innovative in form and less race conscious in theme" than that of their male counterparts, it did "encode the experience of racism and sexism" in profound ways (5, 11–13). Johnson and Spenser wrote of women's conflict between repression and expression in such poems as "The Heart of a Woman" and "Letter to My Sister." Fauset's novels tended toward the sentimental but revealed a thorough knowledge of racial and sexual politics; *Plum Bun* (1928), for example, examined the difficulties black women experienced in marriage and their ambivalence in passing for white. Larsen also explored these painful topics in her 1929 novel *Passing*. As Susan Gubar has argued, the "passing" novels of the Harlem Renaissance, "in which African-American characters masqueraded as white so as to assimilate into mainstream culture," portrayed a "type of racechange [that] functions as *the* crucial subscript of a supremacist society" (11).

Jessie Redmon Fauset was one of the few women of the Harlem Renaissance actually to live in Harlem, perhaps another reason that women's achievements were overlooked. Alice Dunbar-Nelson, Anne Spencer, Angelina Weld Grimké, and other black women met regularly throughout the 1920s at Johnson's home in Washington, D.C., reading and supporting each other's writing, but their work never received the critical attention that the writing of men in Harlem did. To be sure, Zora Neale Hurston and Gwendolyn Bennett worked collaboratively with men, including Langston Hughes, to produce the inaugural issue of a journal of experimental writing, *Fire* (1926), but they were not seen as the Renaissance's pivotal figures. Hurston would later distinguish her approach toward retrieving a racial heritage from the approaches of W.E.B. DuBois and Langston Hughes, whom she considered "Race Champions"; she preferred instead to write "a Negro story . . . without special pleading," one that presents its characters (as in *Jonah's Gourd Vine*, 1934) "in relation to themselves and not in relation to whites as has been the rule." Hurston paid a high price for her autonomous voice, however: she and Hughes had an argument during the 1920s that led to her marginalization within the movement, and when *Their Eyes Were Watching God* was published in 1937, Richard Wright dismissed the novel as having "no theme, no message, no thought" (quoted in Scott 1990: 173–74). After *Native Son* was published in 1940, Wright became a major U.S. literary figure, while Hurston's novels went out of print. Although the Harlem Renaissance brought much black literature to prominence in the U.S. literary scene, it was clearly gender-encoded; for many black women it reinforced a sense of difference and otherness.

MEN, WOMEN, AND WAR

World War I (1914–1918) and World War II (1939–1945) were defining cultural events of the first half of the twentieth century. A technological nightmare of trenches, land mines, poisonous gases, and zeppelins, World War I resulted in massive human destruction. Postwar medical discoveries included the realization that under stress in war, men exhibited a number of the same pathological symptoms that psychologists such as Freud had begun to ascribe to female hysteria. The horror worsened as the illusion of chivalry and heroism in battle gave way for many men to the awareness of a senseless slaughter designed, in U.S. president Woodrow Wilson's words, to "make the world safe for democracy." As cultural historian Malcolm Bradbury notes, the "Great War," as it was known to its contemporaries, provided "the apocalypse that leads the way into modernism," to be reflected in literature as "violation, intrusion, wound, [a] source of psychic anxiety, generational instability, and . . . mechanistic humanity" (quoted in Gilbert and Gubar 260).

Male modernists in England and America responded to the Great War in a variety of ways. Certainly some writers were idealistic at the outbreak of the war; shortly before his death the poet Rupert Brooke declared "Now, God be thanked Who has matched us with His hour, / And caught our youth, and wakened us from sleeping." Others chose not to respond at all. W.B. Yeats, in "On Being Asked for a War Poem," urged that "A poet's mouth be silent, for in truth / We have no gift to set a statesman right." Many writers did take on this enormous topic, however, and were quickly disillusioned; they presented as speakers or characters antiheroes horrified at the circumstances in which they found themselves. In *Death of a Hero* (1929) Richard Aldington portrayed a hero who "lived among smashed bodies and human remains in an infernal cemetery"; in his war memoir *Goodbye to All That* (1929) Robert Graves recalled his terror in encountering "the slimy body of an old corpse." Ford Madox Ford's *Parade's End: Some Do Not* (1924) documented the ironic sacrifice of a Welsh miner, O'Nine Morgan, who could not leave the front because his wife was having an affair with a man who he feared might kill him.

As Sandra Gilbert and Susan Gubar have shown, the "unmanning terrors of combat" not only caused men enormous pain but led many to an irrational ambivalence toward women, who were not forced to suffer through the onslaught (260). Siegfried Sassoon's sardonic "Glory of Women" (1917) offered a mocking direct address: "You love us when we're heroes, home on leave, / Or wounded in a mentionable place." But women know nothing, he continued angrily, of "hell's last horror," of running from the enemy and "trampling the terrible corpses—blind with blood." Hemingway's male protagonist Jake Barnes in *The Sun Also Rises* (1926) was emasculated not only by his war wound but by the insatiable desire of a woman who "wants what she can't have," Brett Ashley, while Frederic Henry in *A Farewell to Arms* (1929) both appreciated Catherine Barkley's ministrations and found her tenderness overwhelming. Rudyard Kipling's 1917 short story "Mary Postgate" featured a vengeful nurse-governess, angry at the wartime death of her young pupil, who refused medical care to a dying German pilot whose plane crashed into her garden. And D.H. Lawrence's last novel, *Lady's Chatterley's Lover* (1928), lambasted the war for causing Clifford Chatterley's paralysis and his wife's erotic defection.

The end of the war brought celebration but also resentment and malaise. In *Three Soldiers* (1921) the experimental novelist John Dos Passos made World War I and the U.S. Army symbolic representatives of a repressive, mechanized society that stifled men from different class and regional backgrounds; he resumed this theme in his three-volume *USA Trilogy* (1930–36), revealing a pronounced but typical postwar disillusion. "War shut up the progressives (no more nonsense about trustbusting, controlling monopolies, the public good)," his cynical narrator explained in *The Big Money* (1936); war and its aftermath brought to power materialistic tycoons whose mantra was "*I can do what I like.*" Moreover, the country's virulent racism, witnessed by the rise of the Ku Klux Klan in the early twentieth century, did not end despite the sacrifice of countless black soldiers. As W.E.B. DuBois documented in "Essay Toward a History of the Black Man in the Great War," the war was a double hell for African Americans, since they "gained the right to fight for civilization at the cost of being 'Jim-crowed'" and insulted "by a white Negro-hating oligarchy" (quoted in Gilbert and Gubar 269).

Although only men died in the trenches and returned home wounded, women did write about the effects of the two wars on their lives at home or, in some cases, as ambulance drivers or nurses at the front. Some writers celebrated war's glories, most notably EDITH WHARTON, whose "A Son at the Front" (1917) depicted a mother's satisfaction at having her boy participate in such a heroic enterprise. Wharton apparently felt this sentiment herself, since she once wrote to congratulate a cousin whose son had enlisted on the young's soldier's embrace of this historical moment. Moreover, women undoubtedly had new freedoms as a result of the war. A popular song during the Great War, written by Nina Macdonald, proclaimed that "Girls are doing things / They've never done before." Many a woman "desired our splendid war," Woolf wrote sadly in *Three Guineas* (1938), "so profound was [her] unconscious loathing for the education of the private house that she would undertake any task, however menial . . . that enabled her to escape" (37–39). Women who drove ambulances, as Vera Brittain did, wrote of the glamour of changing men's bandages; according to both historians of the period and men's fiction, many women's sexual passion was unleashed by men in uniform, and the expression of that desire became more permissible due to the cultural extremity of war. For lesbians, as Radclyffe Hall revealed in *The Well of Loneliness*, driving an ambulance at the front was a liberating role reversal. Ambivalent toward her status as an "invert," Stephen Gordon at first felt like a "freak" when she arrived at the front, only to learn that "war and death" would bring her freedom.

Other women wrote of lives wrecked by war or expressed pacifistic sentiments. In *Testament of Youth* Brittain claimed that the war erected "a barrier of indescribable experience between men and the women whom they loved," as she knew from her own estrangement from her fiance (quoted in Gilbert and Gubar 262). H.D.'s *roman à clef*, *Bid Me To Live*, also explored the breach between a husband and wife which caused him to take a lover and her to miscarry. Katherine Mansfield's story "The Fly" (1922) bleakly portrayed a father unable to grieve for his only son; when memories intruded he focused obsessively on a fly that fell into his inkwell, ultimately torturing and killing it though "admiring the fly's courage." In "I Sit and Sew" (1920) Alice Dunbar-Nelson's speaker deplored "the panoply of war, the martial tread of men" and expressed frustration at women's helplessness to provide comfort. Fiction by English women about the suffering of noncombatants—Rose Macauley's *Noncombatants and Others* (1916), Rebecca West's *The Return of the Soldier* (1918), and Antonia White's "The House of Clouds" (1928)—questioned the gender conventions of war fiction and probed the psyches of women back home. Perhaps the most sustained criticism of war's toll came from Woolf, whose novel *Jacob's Room* paid brooding, elegiac homage to a young man's senseless loss. In *Mrs. Dalloway* the psychological trauma and suicide of a victim of shell shock, Septimus Warren Smith, figure prominently. By the 1930s, as Mussolini ruled Italy and Hitler rose to power in Germany, Woolf urged women to "refuse . . . to make munitions or nurse the wounded." Ultimately, in *Three Guineas*, she advocated that women withdraw from participation in men's efforts at war or peace, forming instead a "Society of Outsiders" and rejecting all symbols of nationalism: "As a woman I have no country. As a woman I want no country. As a woman my country is the whole world" (108–109).

As a second world war loomed on the horizon, other British women of the 1930s wrote antiwar poems and essays, among them Lilian Bowes Lyon, Naomi Mitchison, Dorothy Wellesley, and Vita Sackville-West. Compelling accounts of the actual experience of World War II also came from two women writers in the United States with pacifist leanings, H.D. and MURIEL RUKEYSER. As Adalaide Morris has argued, H.D.'s *Trilogy*, an epic poem in three parts written between 1942 and 1944 during the bombing of London, blended feminism, politics, and mysticism to consider the role of the poet in times of cultural crisis. Typing at night between the "fifty thousand incidents" of the Blitz gave H.D. new access to cultural authority and motivated her to defend poetry from the charges of those who felt it was obsolete during war. H.D. ritualized the past through dream vision and mysticism, which she used to imagine spiritual and cultural rejuvenation. *Trilogy* functioned, in Morris's words, as "at once a warning and an incitement to concerted action," warning readers "against the impulses that bring culture into crisis—our racism, misogyny, materialism, and despair" and reminding us "of the remedies we know—our capacity for concerted action, our access to mystery, our membership in a community much vaster than this one time, this small place" (133).

Like Macauley, H.D., Elizabeth Bishop, and others, Rukeyser was interested in the effects of war on noncombatants, especially women, and in the possibility of communal healing via art. "Women and poets see the truth arrive," began "Letter to the Front," her long, meditative poem on the tragedy of World War II. "Then it is acted out, / The lives are lost, and all the newsboys shout." Amidst the fanfare and human drama of war, "women and poets believe and resist forever." As a pacifist, Rukeyser bemoaned what she viewed as "the savage waste of the battlefield"; as a socialist, she realized that struggles such as the Spanish Civil War provided a necessary antidote to fascism; as a Jew, she recognized that to be silent while European Jews were slaughtered constituted a "death of the spirit." Still, the role of women and poets during wartime, as Rukeyser saw it, was to envision peace as actively as others sang of battle. "Surely it is time for the true grace of women / Emerging, in their lives' colors, from the rooms, from the harvests, / From the delicate prisons, to speak their promises," she proclaimed in "Letter to the Front." In the midst of despair, only "signs of belief, offered in time of war," would suffice (*LAWL* 1207).

GENDER AND EXPATRIATISM

In her reference to a "Society of Outsiders" Woolf evoked another important category in a gender-balanced reading of modernism. Although not herself an expatriate, Woolf's society suggested what expatriatism became for many artists, writers, and intellectuals between 1900 and 1945: a social, cultural, and linguistic challenge as well as an important fact of modern literature's historical background. For a number of major male modernists, including figures as diverse as Sherwood Anderson, James Joyce, Ernest Hemingway, F. Scott Fitzgerald, Ezra Pound, T.S. Eliot, Ford Madox Ford, e.e. cummings, and Richard Wright, as well as for such women as Djuna Barnes, Gertrude

Stein, H.D., Kay Boyle, Jessie Redmon Fauset, Nancy Cunard, Sylvia Beach, and Anaïs Nin, it was not only the Great War but the experience of living and writing abroad that framed a generational experience and anxiety around meanings of loss and adventure, exile and escape. Whether they flocked to Paris and London, as did many of the Americans, or to Paris, Mexico, Berlin, and Switzerland, as did such writers as H.D., Winifred Ellerman (Bryher), Jane Bowles, and Mina Loy; whether they lived abroad intermittently, as did William Carlos Williams, T.S. Eliot, Jessie Fauset, and Robert Frost; whether they stayed for some duration, as did Edith Wharton, Gertrude Stein, and Djuna Barnes; whether they left home because the dollar and pound were strong and European currencies weak or were independently wealthy, expatriates inevitably experienced new freedoms associated with modern convenience, travel, opportunity, and distance from confining origins. Yet their writing was also tinged with the chronic homelessness that the accelerated pace of modern life encouraged.

Another way to acknowledge the significance of expatriatism is to note that it provided the twentieth century with its first glimpses of multiculturalism and the possibility of world community. From the fabulous opening of Stravinsky's modernist musical work *The Rites of Spring* in Paris (1913), with its international cast of performers, to the dense network of allusions to modern European history and contemporary events in Eliot's *The Waste Land*, modernism was an international and crosscultural phenomenon. Its cultural and artistic movements signaled both a creative opportunity and the problem of reaching increasingly diverse and fragmented audiences. Furthermore, critics are still divided about whether artistic and social ferment associated with expatriate communities was a phenomenon that ended with the rise of fascism in Europe as World War II approached or whether the contemporary emphasis in the arts on challenging singular notions of gender and identity is, at least in part, rooted in exposure to transnational artistic influences. In any case, it is clear that national boundaries in the 1920s and 1930s were not the only "approved" space of cultural and social insurgency. Among the many contradictory meanings of modernism that the study of expatriatism among literary women and men has unlocked is that it both expanded the horizons of cultural understanding and opened up the notion of the modern to include the marginalities of race, class, and exilic subjectivity.

Memoirs, autobiographies, histories, and literary works by male modernists told conflicting stories of expatriate experience. In *Exile's Return: A Literary Odyssey of the 1920s* Malcolm Cowley, writing about the so-called "lost generation" of American writers whose Paris sojourns took place predominately during the "peak" years of artistic immigration between 1922 and 1929, highlighted generational "confraternity" and masculine rites of passage. His prototypical exile was one who, in the manner of previous generations of U.S. writers such as Nathaniel Hawthorne and Henry James, used expatriate experience to reexamine "native" materials. Neoprimitivism in the styles of William Carlos Williams's epic poetry (especially *Paterson*, 1946) or Ernest Hemingway's stories was linked to the alienation that European experience provided a number of U.S. male writers. But such narratives of loss and reestablishment of national identity were limited. For other writers, such as Eliot and Pound, the broadening of intellectual horizons and exploration of new textual topographies were an important byproduct of exposure to European intellectual and artistic influences. In *The Waste Land*, a classic expression of modern alienation, Eliot drew upon crosscultural research on fertility cults and masculine heroism in the West from Sir James Frazier's *The Golden Bough* and reflected early twentieth-century interests in the archetypal representations of the "collective unconscious" studied by the psychoanalyst Carl Jung. Pound's poetry, although troubled by anti-Semitism, also made conscious use of the studied effects of European cosmopolitanism. In *The Cantos*, a group of 116 poems written between 1916 and 1969, Pound explored the more radical possibility of the "lost" or disused fragment for unsettling modern civilization. Finally, expatriate myths and actualities formed an important historical bridge between writers, artists, and intellectuals who chose to leave home for the opportunity of adventure and insight that a new milieu might provide, and those disenfranchised figures such as the novelist Richard Wright, the dancer Josephine Baker, and other artists of color who, often with fewer choices, were part of modernity's history of expulsions and exclusions.

Women chose to live abroad for many reasons, but most often for something having to do with the pleasures and dangers of exploring what H.D. called "borderline" existence. Women writers living ex-patria in Paris in particular defined a tone of parodic excess, exuberance, and radical critiques of patriarchal institutions that many critics have compared to later twentieth-century literary and social movements. Anarchism, antifascism, bohemianism, communism, and antiracist sentiments were boldly expressed in alternative coterie settings, although the primary form of activism in avant-garde circles was literary and cultural. When a number of English-speaking writers joined dadaists and surrealist artists in the Transition Manifesto and called for a "revolution of the word" (Hart Crane and Kay Boyle, among others), they were allying themselves with unfinished traditions of French revolution and asserting that the "primary matter" of words would be their revolutionary practice. Often mythologized, the liberal social atmosphere of Paris in the 1920s and 1930s also had its terrifying underside. Barnes's *Nightwood* and Boyle's short stories indicated an awareness of the growing presence of fascism in Europe and the Jew as cultural "other." Even the more transgressive and radical experiments of expatriate writers in Paris, such as Barnes's *Ladies' Almanack*, Jean Rhys's novels of female exile, and Mina Loy's poems in *The Last Lunar Baedecker* (1923), suggested that sisterhood among expatriate literary women could be a fragile enterprise, and that some women without money or privilege paid a high price for what Loy called "chronic itinerancy" (Benstock 381–88).

Expatriate experience also gave rise to new forms of dialogue among literary men and women through coterie memoirs, collaborative books, and reviews, both supportive and antagonistic. The most famous antagonistic partnership was that of Stein and Hemingway: Hemingway lampooned Stein as didactic and overbearing in his memoir of Paris in the 1920s, *A Moveable Feast*, while Stein memorialized Hemingway as her boyish apprentice in *The Autobiography of Alice B. Toklas* (1933). The equanimity of Robert McAlmon and Kay Boyle's collaborative memoir, *Being Geniuses Together* (1968), presented a contrast, but it also reflected the decision Boyle made earlier in her career to maintain her credentials as a social activist but to be the "perfect lady" (297). In memoirs such as Williams's *A Voyage to Pagany* (1928) and John Glassco's *Memoirs of Montparnesse* (1973), Paris was portrayed as a city dominated by literary women before men arrived, and hence a source of possible "unmanning."

MODERNIST WOMEN AND MEN AS PROMULGATORS OF CULTURE

As editors, publishers, journalists, archivists, and critics, women such as Dora Marsden, Harriet Shaw Weaver, Sylvia Beach, Jane Heap, Margaret Anderson, Harriet Monroe, Nancy Cunard, and Jessie Redmon Fauset challenged canonical tastes and prejudice. Weaver, the editor of the *Egoist* (the successor to Marsden's *Freewoman*), published Joyce's *Portrait of the Artist as a Young Man* (1916) and became his lifelong patron. As proprietor of the Parisian bookstore Shakespeare and Company, Beach spent her own money to publish *Ulysses* when no one else dared and sponsored countless other writers, male and female. The editor of the *Little Review*, Anderson published both Joyce and May Sinclair; she and Heap risked imprisonment in the United States to bring out *Ulysses* there. Monroe, the editor of *Poetry*, published Eliot, H.D., and Moore, among others. As editor of a massive anthology on African and African-American art, literature, and culture, *Negro* (1934), Cunard shared modernist biases toward "authentic" negritude based on primitivist stereotypes, but her anthology represented an important landmark in the construction of what the social critic Paul Gilroy has referred to as the "Black Atlantic" connections in the global history of black-white relations. And as editor after 1919 of the *Crisis*, a black periodical with a circulation of 100,000, Fauset published Langston Hughes's "The Negro Speaks of Rivers" and was considered by him a "midwife" of the Renaissance, along with Locke and Charles S. Johnson. She also supported black women writers, publishing Nella Larsen's writing for children and singling out for praise the work of Georgia Douglas Johnson and Anne Spencer in her review of James Weldon Johnson's anthology of black verse (Scott 1995: 36–49, 232–26).

To be sure, men also edited prominent modernist journals and published women's writing as well as men's. Ford Madox Ford edited the *English Review* and, later, *transatlantic review*; John Middleton Murry edited the *Athenaeum* and, later, *Adelphi*; Pound promoted Imagist work as foreign correspondent for *Poetry* in 1912–13 and launched Vorticism as editor, with Lewis, of *Blast* in 1914–15; and Leonard Woolf, with his wife, Virginia, founded Hogarth Press, which published Eliot's *Prufrock and Other Poems* in 1919, as well as works by Mansfield and Joyce. For the first time in history, however, many women had both the financial resources and the cultural clout to influence literary publication, and they used that power in the service of the women as well as the men of modernism.

⊰ Works Cited ⊱

Benstock, Shari. *Women of the Left Bank: Paris 1900–1940*. Austin: U of Texas P, 1986.

Bloom, Harold. *The Anxiety of Influence: A Theory of Poetry*. New York: Oxford UP, 1973.

Carby, Hazel. *Reconstructing Womanhood: The Emergence of the Afro-American Woman Novelist*. Oxford and New York: Oxford UP, 1987.

Clark, Suzanne. *Sentimental Modernism: Women Writers and the Revolution of the Word*. Bloomington: Indiana UP, 1991.

Cowley, Malcolm. *Exile's Return: A Literary Odyssey of the 1920s*. New York: The Viking Press, 1951.

Dickie, Margaret and Thomas Travisano, eds. *Gendered Modernisms: American Women Poets and Their Readers*. Philadelphia: U of Pennsylvania P, 1996.

Eliot, T.S. "Tradition and the Individual Talent." In *The Sacred Wood*. New York: Harcourt Brace, 1920.

Felski, Rita. *The Gender of Modernity*. Cambridge: Harvard UP, 1995.

Gilbert, Sandra M. and Susan Gubar. *No Man's Land: The Place of the Woman Writer in the Twentieth Century*. Vol. 2, "Sexchanges." New Haven: Yale UP, 1989.

Gilroy, Paul. *The Black Atlantic: Modernity and Double Consciousness*. Cambridge: Harvard UP, 1993.

Gubar, Susan. *Racechanges: White Skin, Black Face in American Culture*. New York and Oxford: Oxford UP, 1997.

Hoffman, Michael J. *Gertrude Stein*. Boston: Twayne Publishers, 1976.

Johnson, Barbara. "Euphemism, Understatement, and the Passive Voice: A Genealogy of Afro-American Poetry. *Reading Black, Reading Feminist: A Critical Anthology*. Ed. Henry Louis Gates, Jr. New York: Penguin, 1990. 204–211.

McAlmon, Robert and Kay Boyle. *Being Geniuses Together, 1920–1930*. Garden City, NY: Doubleday, 1968.

Morris, Adelaide. "Signaling: Feminism, Politics, and Mysticism in H.D.'s War Trilogy." *Sagetrieb* 9: 3 (Winter 1990): 121–33.

Scott, Bonnie Kime, ed. *The Gender of Modernism: A Critical Anthology*. Bloomington: Indiana UP, 1990.

———. *Refiguring Modernism*. Vol. 1, "The Women of 1928." Bloomington: Indiana UP, 1995.

Wall, Cheryl. *Women of the Harlem Renaissance*. Bloomington: Indiana UP, 1995.

Washington, Mary Helen. *Invented Lives: Narratives of Black Women 1860–1960*. Garden City, NY: Doubleday, 1987.

Williams, William Carlos. *In the American Grain*. New York: New Directions, 1925.

Woolf, Virginia. "Dorothy Richardson." *Women and Writing*. Ed. Michele Barrett. New York: Harcourt Brace, 1979.

———. "Modern Fiction." *The Common Reader*. 1925; rpt. New York: Harcourt Brace, 1953.

———. "Mr. Bennett and Mrs. Brown." *The Captain's Death Bed and Other Essays*. New York and London: Harcourt Brace, 1950.

———. *Three Guineas*. 1938; rpt. New York: Harcourt Brace, 1966.

Wright, Richard. *The Richard Wright Reader*. Eds. Ellen Wright and Michel Fabre. New York: Harper and Row. 1978.

Contemporary Literature
1945–2000
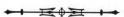

The period between the end of World War II and the end of the century is widely called the contemporary era, although to those readers born in the 1980s and raised with cell phones and notebook computers as prevalent in their homes as books, the middle decades of the twentieth century might seem remote indeed. Like their modernist predecessors, literary works of the contemporary period typically refuse metaphysical and transcendental absolutes in favor of culturally relative and transgressive visions of the world. Although poetry and fiction in the realistic tradition continue to be written and read, technically experimental writers of the past five decades have disrupted the realist link between an actual object or event and its literary representation. They have written free-verse poems exploring violence and chaos, novels with no plots or recognizable characters, plays in which "nothing happens, nobody comes, nobody goes, it's awful" (Samuel Beckett's *Waiting for Godot*). Politically oriented writers have struggled to make sense of the aftermath of World War II, the Holocaust, and the bombing of Hiroshima and Nagasaki; their work has reflected worldwide liberation movements for peace, civil rights, women's liberation, gay rights, and freedom from colonialism.

The post–World War II era has been dominated by complex political events to which many writers have responded. The Cold War between the U.S.S.R. and the United States, which began with the annexation of parts of eastern Europe by Russian forces during the 1950s, the formation of an "Iron Curtain" around this new "Soviet bloc," and anti-Communist fervor in the West, abated only with the fall of the Berlin Wall and the subsequent demise of the Soviet Union in 1989. During the 1950s and 1960s such novelists as Norman Mailer and Joseph Heller wrote novels that explored the cost of war; later, poets Adrienne Rich and May Sarton documented retrospectively their experience of living in the United States during the Cold War. In England in the 1960s socialist playwrights such as Howard Brenton, David Hare, Caryl Churchill, and Michelene Wandor developed a vibrantly political fringe theater and promoted the oppositional policies of the Labour Party, which had governed briefly in the 1950s only to fall to the Tories and not return to power until the mid–1990s.

Many writers living in the United States in the 1960s protested the Viet Nam War in their work, among them Robert Lowell, Norman Mailer, Denise Levertov, and Adrienne Rich. The late 1960s and early 1970s was a period of political turmoil, with the assassinations of John F. Kennedy, Robert Kennedy, and Martin Luther King, Jr. dominating the political scene. The Watergate scandal forced the resignation of President Richard Nixon in 1973 and contributed to widespread distrust of government. In South Africa during the 1970s and 80s a vibrant antiapartheid literature sprang up not only from university-educated, liberal white writers such as J.M. Coetzee, Nadine Gordimer, and Ingrid de Kok but also from rebellious students in Soweto. Internationally known black poets and novelists exposed the horrors of a virulent racist system, among them Njabulo S. Ndebele, Mongane Wally Serote, Bessie Head, and Ellen Kuzwayo. In the United States during the 1980s, moreover,

African-American and women poets protested their government's policies in South Africa and Central America. AUDRE LORDE, Essex Hemphill, JUNE JORDAN, MICHELLE CLIFF, and CAROLYN FORCHÉ, along with such Latin American writers as Ernesto Cardenal, Claribel Alegria, and Marta Benevides, wrote political literature decrying imperialism.

For women in the West, the second half of the twentieth century brought about many changes in lifestyle, work, and motherhood to which women writers responded. Simone de Beauvoir's *The Second Sex* (1949) developed a radical theory of women as a subordinate "sex class" that viewed gender as the foundation for unequal distribution of society's privileges and resources. Betty Friedan's *The Feminine Mystique* (1963) urged liberation for stifled middle-class housewives suffering from "the oppression that has no name." In the late 1960s and the 1970s both black and white women involved in the U.S. civil rights and antiwar movements determined that serving as men's subordinates in struggles was not sufficient; they proclaimed the need for women's liberation, which espoused full equality between the sexes, women's right to work for pay inside or outside the home, and women's abilities to be leaders, not just followers, in movements against racism, economic injustice, and militarism. This is not to say that the women's movement was devoid of racism; for example, theorists like Angela Davis (*Women, Race and Class*, 1981) have rightly challenged white feminists for advocating abortion rights without promoting a full agenda of reproductive rights, including a campaign against the unwanted sterilization procedures to which many women of color were being subjected by white physicians. Other challenges to the social status quo include the emergence of a gay and lesbian liberation movement in the 1970s after police raided a gay bar at the Stonewall in New York City, arresting hundreds of men on suspicion of same-sex love. Lesbian feminists formed such organizations as Radicalesbians (1970) and the Furies (1971), and such women as Jill Johnston, Rita Mae Brown, Adrienne Rich, and Audre Lorde began to theorize the intersection of oppression based on gender and sexual orientation. In addition, the development of women's studies programs in U.S., British, and Australian universities during the 1970s and 1980s produced a significant body of feminist theory that has profoundly influenced literary studies.

Literature of the 1990s continued to reflect the movement in literary studies toward postmodern explorations of texts and textual strategies. Postmodernism can be distinguished from modernism in that while both approaches challenge the dominant culture, postmodern theorists question the very notion of boundaries and truths. Certain writing by women who made their mark as feminist writers during the 1970s and 1980s has been influenced more recently by postmodern theories of the breakdown and ultimate inadequacy of language, for example Kathleen Fraser's *Notes Preceding Trust* (1987) and Caryl Churchill's *Blue Heart* (1997). In the last decade many writers expressed discouragement at the political cynicism and apathy of their governments and fellow citizens. Some literature written near the end of the century had a decidedly apocalyptic tone, e.g. Kathy Acker's *Empire of the Senseless* (1988), Carolyn Forché's *The Angel of History* (1994), and Adrienne Rich's *Dark Fields of the Republic* (1995). Although such works may seem pessimistic, many passages reflect the writers' continued commitment to feminist or progressive movements and the possibility of meaningful transformation toward a more just society.

Since the middle of the century U.S. and British poets have questioned received notions of what constitutes poetic discourse. In the 1960s and 1970s a women's poetry movement emerged that would evoke women's voices out of silence. Realistic fiction has continued to be powerfully represented in men's and women's novels about ethics, identity, culture, and desire, and experimental fiction and drama has gained credence, as writers from Salman Rushdie to ANGELA CARTER to Jeanette Winterson have won praise for their comically grotesque portrayals of once-sacred themes. Since the 1960s, moreover, an African-American literary renaissance has produced outstanding fiction, poetry, drama, and autobiography, including James Baldwin's urgent *The Fire Next Time* (1963), MAYA ANGELOU's luminous *I Know Why the Caged Bird Sings* (1969), and TONI MORRISON's Pulitzer-Prize-winning *Beloved* (1987). Finally, international fiction and poetry written in English has become increasingly influential during the late twentieth century. Writers from India, Africa, Australia, New Zealand, Canada, Latin America, and the West Indies have protested fundamentalism and neocolonialism and in doing so have challenged, in a vital and politically urgent manner, what has traditionally been considered "English" literature.

POETRY AT MID-CENTURY: THE MOVEMENT, THE BEATS, THE CONFESSIONALS, OTHERS

Several schools of poetic thought developed in England and the United States in the aftermath of World War II, some of them hearkening back nostalgically to prewar ideals, others rebellious and innovative. One of the best-known British schools, commonly called "the Movement," is associated with the publication of three key anthologies: *Poets of the 1950s*, edited by D.J. Enright (1955); *New Lines*, edited by Robert Conquest (1956); and *Poetry Now*, edited by G.S. Frazer (1956). Typically lucid, ironic, and self-conscious, Movement poetry challenged the romantic sensibility of prewar poets. In his introduction to *New Lines*, Conquest defined this new poetry as philosophical and empirical. Movement poetry privileged rational structure and concise language; it thus aligned itself with witty neoclassical verse rather than with Romantic excess. Among its major figures were Philip Larkin, an ironic conformist whose carefully wrought phrases and melancholic resignation in *The Less Deceived* (1955) indicate both humility and conformity; Elizabeth Jennings, a Catholic poet living in Oxford who combined mysticism and traditional verse techniques in such works as *A Way of Looking* (1955); and Donald Davie, whose cool, rational verse revealed a verbal austerity in *Brides of Reason* (1955) and other volumes. It is worth noting that with the exception of the prolific Jennings, all of the Movement poets were men, perhaps because many late modernist women resisted any impulse toward provincialism and parochial restriction of language. Davie's critical study of 1952, *Purity of Diction in English Verse*, greatly influenced other Movement poets in its emphasis on stylistic discipline and its refutation of poetic excess; indeed, Davie presciently challenged the Beat and confessional poets who would succeed him.

Across the ocean, the radical iconoclasm of the Beat generation did not draw large numbers of women adherents either, perhaps because of the rampant misogyny of certain Beat writers. Poets such as Allen Ginsberg, Lawrence Ferlinghetti, and Gregory Corso took their name from their affinity with the downtrodden, or beaten, people of society as well as from their interest in the "beatific" elements of Eastern religions, while the term "beatnik" was initially a derogatory designation intended to label the socialistically inclined Beat circle as Soviet sympathizers, or fans of Sputnik, the Soviet moon rocket. The Beats were greatly influenced by the poetry of the U.S. bard Walt Whitman, by the exotic and intricate rhythms of jazz, and by an anarchic vision. The quintessential Beat poem, Ginsberg's *Howl* (1956), brought protest poetry into the mainstream; it was daring in its celebration of same-sex desire in an era in which homosexuality was still illegal. The Beat generation included writers of fiction as well, most notably William S. Burroughs and Jack Kerouac, whose novel *On the Road* (1957) challenged the materialism and political conservatism of the 1950s. To be sure, a few women writers were affiliated with the Beats—Hettie Jones, Diane DiPrima, and Eileen Kaufman, for example—but none gained the prominence of the men. Although some critics decried the disillusionment of Beat poetry as nihilistic, it can also be viewed as ethically astute in anticipating protest poetry of the 1960s and 1970s, when writers spoke out against the military-industrial complex and the Viet Nam War.

A different poetic movement of the 1950s and 60s was noted for its liberating frankness and its impulse toward personal exploration. The autobiographical fervor of Robert Lowell's *Life Studies* (1959) sent shock waves through the poetic establishment; no longer would the "man who suffers be entirely separate from the mind that creates," as T.S. Eliot had advocated in his landmark modernist treatise of 1919, "Tradition and the Individual Talent." "Confessional" poetry, as it came to be called by the British critic A. Alvarez, explored the psyche in a state of extremity. In part a reaction to the reserve of the Movement poets, confessionalism took emotional and linguistic risks, explored pathological rather than rational states of consciousness, and reflected on the horrors of war, evil, and the individual or cultural "death drive." Perhaps the foremost confessional poet was SYLVIA PLATH; as Linda R. Williams has noted, the posthumous publication of Plath's *Ariel* (1965) was a major literary event that "aroused more interest in Britain than any other since Dylan Thomas's *Deaths and Entrances* (1946)" (254). Plath's poetic voice was influenced by that of her husband, British poet Ted Hughes, and his by hers; Plath was influenced as well by Robert Lowell, with whom she studied in Boston in the mid-1950s. Also part of Lowell's workshop was the U.S. poet ANNE SEXTON, who became well known during the 1960s as a confessional and a feminist poet. In *All My Pretty Ones* (1962) and elsewhere she wrote frankly about women's experience of madness, abortion, adultery, and sexual desire. Although most men poets were uncomfortable with such forthright discussion of female experience, several male confessionals joined Lowell in criticizing the "tranquilized Fifties" in their verse and writing frankly about emotional distress and erotic longings. Originally drawn to Auden and Yeats, John Berryman moved toward confessionalism in *The Dream Songs* (1964), while W.D. Snodgrass wrote lyrically of a husband's feelings about divorce in *Heart's Needle* (1969). As university professors, Lowell and Berryman became influential literary critics as well as poets, and their analyses, along with those of British critics such as A. Alvarez, enabled scholars to consider confessional poetry as technically and thematically experimental rather than dismiss it as self-indulgent. Or, as Plath's and Sexton's work was sometimes deemed, "hysterical"—a term that reveals the sexual double standard that developed regarding confessional poetry, since men of the school could write about their emotional lives and have their writing called art, while women who did so ran the risk of being labeled exhibitionists.

Other schools of poetry developed after World War II. The Black Mountain poets gathered in North Carolina to rail against the closed forms and "objective" poems of the early 1940s; they heralded instead open forms that would reveal more vividly the mind's spontaneity, confusions, and insights. The leader of the Black Mountain school was Charles Olson, whose manifesto "Projective Verse" (1950) claimed as the unit of poetic expression not the metrical foot but the "poet's breath" and other bodily rhythms; he urged that lines of poetry be placed anywhere on the page and that the poem represent the moment of composition rather than undergoing extensive revision (Hoover 613–20). Other Black Mountain poets were Robert Creeley, Robert Duncan, and Denise Levertov. This belief in poetry as provisional and the poem as indicative of the poet's growth influenced both the Beat poets and the confessionals.

In short, British and U.S. poetry at midcentury and beyond was exciting and eclectic. Women poets such as May Sarton in the United States and STEVIE SMITH in England, who wrote in traditional form, were influenced by older female peers such as Louise Bogan and Ruth Pitter as well as by "major" male modernists: Eliot, Stevens, and W.B. Yeats. As these poets relied on time-honored techniques and values, others anticipated the conflicts and tensions that would characterize the late 1960s and 1970s: a questioning of familial and sexual norms, a suspicion of government, and the autobiographical (and sometimes narcissistic) fervor that would come to be associated with the "me" generation.

THE WOMEN'S POETRY MOVEMENT

Although some critics would argue that there exists no women's poetry movement per se, few would disagree that an extraordinary wave of poems by women swelled during the last four decades of the twentieth century, a wave that shows little sign of abating as a new century dawns, although it has undergone varied undulations. Alicia Ostriker has dated this movement in the United States from 1960 and has listed a number of pivotal books by women poets, published during this decade, that expressed anger at patriarchal definitions of womanhood and redefined male-dominated myths and paradigms from a woman-centered perspective (7). Among these signal publications were GWENDOLYN BROOKS's The Bean Eaters (1960), Hilda Doolittle's Helen in Egypt (1961), Anne Sexton's To Bedlam and Part Way Back (1960), Sylvia Plath's Ariel (1963), Adrienne Rich's Snapshots of a Daughter-in-law (1963), Denise Levertov's O Taste and See (1964), MURIEL RUKEYSER's The Speed of Darkness (1968), Diane Wakoski's Inside the Blood Factory (1968), Mona Van Dyne's To See, To Take (1970), and Maxine Kumin's The Nightmare Factory (1970). To Ostriker's list of noteworthy U.S. publications we might add the Canadian poet MARGARET ATWOOD's The Journals of Susanna Moodie (1969), the British poet Ruth Fainlight's Cages (1966), and the British poet Libby Houston's A Stained Glass Raree Show (1967).

The women's poetry movement challenged male dominance in art, politics, and culture. In a 1980 article examining the movement's contours, Jan Clausen asserted that "feminism has made possible the recent notable development of women's poetry (what term is, by the way, adequately descriptive of this phenomenon: renaissance? flowering? earthquake? volcanic eruption?)" and that "this tremendous release of poetic energy cannot be understood without reference to the catalytic role of feminism as ideology, political movement, and cultural/material support network" (5). Clausen went on to hypothesize that in a certain sense poets were the movement, in that Rich, Lorde, and others were important feminist activists as well as theorists and that poetry had become a popular means of self-expression and consciousness raising among women who had not previously written. In addition, she noted the rise of small feminist presses that distributed women's poetry to avid readers in the 1970s, well before mainstream presses added these writers to their publication lists—such presses as the Women's Press Collective, which published Judy Grahn in 1971; Shameless Hussy, which published Pat Parker and Susan Griffin in 1972; and Violet Press, which published *We Are All Lesbians* (1973), an early anthology of lesbian poetry. Anthologies such as *Rising Tides* (1973), *No More Masks* (1973), and *The World Split Open* (1974) further enhanced the availability of women's poetry to the general public and to literature and women's studies professors. Although some members of the male poetry establishment denigrated women's poetry as "strident" or "mediocre," it flourished nonetheless, and several feminist poets are widely considered among the finest writing today—Rich and Atwood, most notably. Other women poets who have won acclaim for their compelling treatment of feminist subjects are SHARON OLDS, Olga Broumas, and RITA DOVE in the United States, Ursula Fanthorpe and CAROL ANN DUFFY in England, and EAVAN BOLAND and MEDBH MCGUCKIAN in Ireland.

The development of feminist literary criticism led to thoughtful critical analysis of the women's poetry movement. Ostriker, for example, has described the U.S. movement in terms of several recurring themes, among them the divided female self and the "quest for autonomous self-definition"; the use of "body language," including subversive references to anatomical parts and sexual acts; an "imperative of intimacy" that presents love and desire in female terms; the cathartic release of anger, violence, and polarization; and "revisionist mythmaking," the appropriation of male-dominant myths for feminist purposes (10–13). In contrast, feminist critic Jan Montefiore has deemed the women's poetry movement a British as well as a U.S. phenomenon and has explored such topics as unrecognized Romanticism in verse by women, imaginary identities in women's love poems, and poetic ambiguity and contradictions. Moreover, Montefiore has demonstrated connections between recent women's poetry and that of significant predecessors: EMILY DICKINSON, who "created a truly great and original poetry by exploiting the duplicity of language through a series of fictional masks"; CHRISTINA ROSSETTI, who defined an aesthetics of renunciation; EDNA ST. VINCENT MILLAY, who promoted romantic transcendence; and Stevie Smith, a consummate and wicked poetic teller of women's subversive tales (61). As part of their effort to come to voice, many women poets of the 1960s and 1970s reimagined muses of their own, female-centered sources and images of inspiration, rather than continuing to define themselves as the muses of male poets, husbands, or lovers. H.D.'s Helen, for instance, invoked Thetis, goddess of the sea and mother of her lover, Achilles, as a source of creative sustenance. May Sarton's speaker in "The Muse as Medusa" thanked the mythic gorgon for helping her claim her own subversive power. Sylvia Plath's "The Disquieting Muses" identified a bald-headed, unsightly trio come to punish rather than sustain her literary endeavors, while Audre Lorde drew strength from Yoruba mother-goddesses such as Yemanja, whose breasts flow like rivers. As Sandra M. Gilbert and Susan Gubar asserted, to achieve literary autonomy, the woman writer must "come to terms with . . . those mythic masks male artists have fastened over her human face both to lessen their dread of her 'inconsistency' and—by identifying her with the 'eternal types' they themselves have invented—to possess her more thoroughly" (17). One such "eternal type" is the traditional female muse, a figure central to the oldest extant myths used to explain men's relationship to their art. Women wishing to assume the role of poet rather than muse, of powerful creator, often revised male myths by invoking potent female muses (DeShazer 1–7). They thus related their creativity to complex and original mythic structures yet redefined what Rich has called "a whole new psychic geography" of female literary imagination.

The 1970s and 1980s saw the emergence of many African-American, Afro-British, Jewish, Asian-American, Chicana, and Native American women poets who celebrated their racial-ethnic traditions and chronicled their experience of womanhood, social marginalization, and political dissidence. Among the best-known African-American poets were June Jordan, Nikki Giovanni, and Sonia Sanchez, all of whom protested sexual and racial "othering." Afro-British poet Grace Nichols (*The Fat Black Woman's Poems*, 1984) and Afro-Scots poet JACKIE KAY (*A Dangerous Knowing*, 1983) affirmed their identities as women of color and challenged racist stereotyping. Prominent Jewish poets who identified explicitly as Jews, in addition to Rukeyser and Rich, included IRENA KLEPFISZ and Melanie Kaye-Kantrowitz; they recalled the horrors of the Holocaust in their poems, reclaimed Yiddish language and culture, and probed the intersections of lesbianism, feminism, and Judaism. Asian-American women such as Nellie Wong, Mitsuye Yamada, Merle Woo, and Janice Mirikatani confronted the stereotype of silence and submission associated with women from China and Japan, asserting instead powerful voices of self-definition and resistance. Chicana poets GLORIA ANZALDÚA, CHERRÍE MORAGA, and Lorna Dee Cervantes developed metaphors of mestiza consciousness and borderlands to proclaim their "resistance to the literate." And poets from PAULA GUNN ALLEN, a Laguna Sioux, to JOY HARJO, a Creek, to BETH BRANT, a Canadian Mohawk, explored Indian legends and legacies while decrying the painful ravages of cultural genocide, poverty, and alcoholism on native peoples.

Women's poetry in the 1990s became increasingly eclectic and experimental, and anthologies continued to proliferate. Furthermore, women poets are increasingly included in dual-gender anthologies, although their numbers still have not reached parity with those of men. *Postmodern American Poetry* (1994), edited by Paul Hoover, for example, includes Levertov, Howe, and Wakoski as well as lesser-known women from a variety of ethnic backgrounds, such as Jayne Cortez, Wanda Coleman, and Jessica Hagedorn. In the words of British poet Anne Stevenson, "no artist can be optimistic in days of spiritual decay, but it is possible to be honest. And joyful!" Such joy can be the individual woman poet's, "the sense of a creature constrained too long, wanting to taste earthy pleasures," as Linda France puts it, or it can be a collective joy born of struggle (13–19). In Gloria Anzaldúa's view, women poets today "have not one movement but many. Our political, literary and artistic movements are discarding the patriarchal model of the hero/leader leading the rank and file. . . . Now here, now there, *aquí y alla*, we and our *movimientos* are firmly committed to transforming all our cultures" (v).

REALIST REPRESENTATIONS IN POSTWAR FICTION

In his essay "The Postwar English Novel" (1983) Gilbert Phelps claims that fiction since 1945 has been characterized by "a turning aside from the mainstream of European literature and a tendency to retreat into parochialism and defeatism" (quoted in Williams 43). Some critics warn against such wholesale dismissal of British fiction, preferring instead to celebrate the diversity and richness of a culture that has produced realistic, experimental, and politically committed novels over the past half-century (Williams 43–44). In the United States, on the other hand, literary critics have welcomed the onset of a fictional renaissance, particularly since the Viet Nam War, and have credited the women's movement for bringing new subjects, new materials, and new visions to contemporary U.S. fiction. One way of considering contemporary fiction in the realist tradition is to examine it in three categories, each of which overlaps somewhat with the others. Moral and philosophical fiction after World War II has been influenced by Judeo-Christian values, existentialism, and movements for social justice. Satire and social comedy have offered playful or grim cultural critiques that analyze the present through the lens of the fictive past or future. And feminist fiction has articulated women's process of self-discovery while challenging patriarchal structures of oppression.

Certain postwar novelists in Britain have presented moral fables that interrogate the nature and possibilities of good and evil. William Golding's *Lord of the Flies* (1954), for example, considers what happens when humans become morally and physically desperate for survival. Catholic novelist Graham Greene's *The Heart of the Matter* (1948) and *The End of the Affair* (1951) portray the guilt and frustration of characters saved from their moral malaise by spiritual dignity, even in the face or failure and squalor. Other British novelists influenced by Roman Catholicism include Evelyn Waugh, whose *Brideshead Revisited* (1945) foregrounds a battle for ethical control between an atheist and his lover's disintegrating Catholic family; Muriel Spark, whose *The Ballad of Peckham Rye* (1960) focuses on the manipulations of the charmingly diabolical Dougal Douglas; and Anthony Burgess, whose *A Clockwork Orange* (1962) presents its protagonist's struggle between the evil pull of violence and sadism, on the one hand, and free will on the other. Philosophical novelists such as Iris Murdoch in England and Patrick White in Australia have been influenced by French existential philosophy, which argues that "existence precedes essence" (in Jean Paul Sartre's famous words), that individuals freely choose their behaviors and define themselves rather than those acts and definitions being god-ordained. Murdoch's *Under the Net* (1954) offers a tragic examination of ethical responsibility and individual freedom, while White's *The Tree of Man* (1955) and *Voss* (1957) starkly depict the human struggle against nature, with the Australian interior as a spiritual testing ground. A.S. Byatt's philosophical fiction (*The Virgin in the Garden*, 1979; *Still Life*, 1985; and *Babel Tower*, 1996) has been influenced by Murdoch and informed by a broadly humanistic set of concerns: the quest for goodness, the healing properties of love, and the process of cultural change.

In the United States, moral and philosophical writers since World War II include several novelists of the Southern gothic school. Carson McCullers's *The Member of the Wedding* (1946), EUDORA WELTY's *The Golden Apples* (1947), Flannery O'Connor's *A Good Man Is Hard to Find* (1955), and Truman Capote's *Other Voices, Other Rooms* (1948) best represent this literary style. Other philosophical novelists include Susan Sontag, who has probed the nature of generosity and greed in *The Benefactor* (1963) and brought the historical romance to new heights in *The Volcano Lover* (1992); and the prolific Joyce Carol Oates, who has explored the dark side of the human (and national) psyche in such novels as *Them* (1969) and *Black Water* (1992). William Styron's *The Confessions of Nat Turner* (1967) and *Sophie's Choice* (1979) show protagonists struggling with moral choices during historically charged moments, while TILLIE OLSEN's *Tell Me A Riddle* (1963) examines a Jewish woman's confrontation with aging and death in a lyrical and compassion way. Among the most powerful philosophical novels written in the United States since 1970 are those of Nobel Prize winner Toni Morrison, who meditates on African-American cultural identity in luminous works like *Sula* (1973), *Beloved* (1987), and *Jazz* (1992). These novels chronicle both the pain experienced by racism and the healing power of communal redemption.

Some of the most powerful ethical critiques of U.S. values since 1970 have been written by Native Americans, who have portrayed their people's genocide and mistreatment at the hands of the government as well as their love of the land and determination to survive. Leslie Marmon Silko's *Ceremony* (1977) blends the mythic and the real to explore the pain of the divided native self, while in *Mean Spirit* (1990) Linda Hogan explores with reverence the natural world, the sacredness of all forms of life, and the need to build a peaceful global community. Among the most popular and prolific of American Indian fiction writers has been LOUISE ERDRICH, whose novel *Love Medicine* won the National Book Critics Circle Award in 1984, when she was only thirty; subsequent novels—*The Beet Queen*, 1986; *Tracks*, 1988; and *The Bingo Palace*, 1994—have continued the saga of multiple generations of Nanapushes, Lazarres, and Kashpaws, all of whom faced the pressures of dislocation and psychic exile. The fiction of N. Scott Momaday and Sherman Alexie documents American Indian men's struggles to survive the ravages of economic injustice and alcoholism.

[handwritten margin note: Am. Indian]

Satire and social comedy have also been prevalent in postwar fiction of Britain and the United States. Kingsley Amis's *Lucky Jim* (1954) initiated the tradition of the academic satire in England, a subgenre to which such writers as Angus Wilson (*Anglo-Saxon Attitudes*, 1956), Malcolm Bradbury (*The History Man*, 1975), and David Lodge (*Changing Places*, 1975) have contributed. The fiction of Barbara Pym, influenced by the wry social comedy of JANE AUSTEN, takes a shrewd, ironical look at middle-class life in England in the 1970s; such works as *The Sweet Dove Died* (1978) and *An Unsuitable Attachment* (1982) focus specifically on the social contexts of women's lives. A darker satire is written by Martin Amis, who presents the violent, sordid, and misogynistic behavior of a decadent protagonist in *Dead Babies* (1975) and *Money* (1984). His work is matched for originality and satiric thrust by the writing of Fay Weldon, whose sardonic novels both endorse and parody feminist attitudes about sexuality, maternity, and sisterhood.

The most popular satiric work of U.S. fiction of the 1950s was J.D. Salinger's *The Catcher in the Rye* (1951), whose adolescent hero exposes the commercialism, phoniness, and sexual malaise of the adult society that tries to suppress him. In the 1960s Joseph Heller's *Catch–22* (1961) satirized the military-industrial complex, and Ken Kesey's *One Flew over the Cuckoo's Nest* (1962) condemned an oppressive medical establishment that labeled iconoclasts insane. Kurt Vonnegut's novels from the late 1960s and 1970s, most notably *Slaughterhouse Five* (1969), blended fantasy and social criticism to show the inanities of war and other forms of systemic oppression. Philip Roth's *Portnoy's Complaint* (1969) and John Updike's *Rabbit Run* (1960) and *Rabbit Redux* (1971) explored comically the sexual hypocrisies of the U.S. upper and middle classes. In the next decades Laurie Colwin (*Goodbye before Leaving*, 1990) and Alison Lurie (*The Truth about Lorin Jones*, 1988) presented wry portraits of sexual desire and betrayal from the privileged woman's point of view. Since the 1980s a number of

Southern women writers—among them Bobbie Ann Mason, Doris Betts, and Lee Smith—have extended the tradition of the comic grotesque begun by Welty and O'Connor to reveal working-class foibles in the American South. The disaffection and resilience of ordinary small-town Americans also contribute to the dark humor of Raymond Carver's stories.

What exactly constitutes feminist fiction has been hotly debated over the past thirty years. Many critics believe this genre originated with the publication of DORIS LESSING's *The Golden Notebook* in 1962, although this designation is complicated by the fact that Lessing has claimed that she did not consider her novel feminist. Nonetheless, the struggle of Anna Wulf, Lessing's protagonist, to become a sexually and spiritually autonomous woman artist spoke to many "free women" as few previous novels about female experience had done. Reclaiming women's previously silenced or muted voices has been a trademark of feminist fiction, as have explorations of madness or vengeful rage and the challenging of male authority and violence. If these themes are used as a guide—and they can be presented in a variety of traditional or innovative narrative forms—then such disparate British writers as Jean Rhys, Margaret Drabble, Eva Figes, Zoe Fairbairns, and ANGELA CARTER can be considered feminist. In *The Wide Sargasso Sea* (1966) Rhys gives voice to Bertha Mason Rochester, Jane Eyre's mad double in CHARLOTTE BRONTË's famous novel, and in so doing explored how racism, sexual excess, and violence combine to impose on powerful women a label of insanity. In *The Millstone* (1965) Drabble presents with compassion the efforts of a single woman, Rosamund, to raise her illegitimate infant daughter in an ethically responsible way. In *The Seven Ages* (1986) Figes recounts the conflicts and celebrations of seven generations of women who struggled against poverty and violence to bring the next generation of daughters to life. In *Stand We At Last* (1983), a novel sometimes compared with *The Seven Ages*, Fairbairns traces the lineage of a group of women from the nineteenth century to the present, documenting their increasingly feminist consciousnesses. And in *The Bloody Chamber* (1979), a collection of short stories, Angela Carter offers feminist and surreal versions of European fairy tales, with the women as likely to be the big bad wolves as the men.

Feminist fiction in the United States has many popular practitioners, including Tillie Olsen, Grace Paley, ROSELLEN BROWN, Marge Piercy, Ursula LeGuin, ALICE WALKER, Jane Smiley, and SANDRA CISNEROS. In such volumes of short stories as *Tell Me A Riddle* (1962) and *Enormous Changes at the Last Minute* (1974), Olsen and Paley "hear other people's voices," in Paley's words, especially the voices of downtrodden women trying to rise up with dignity and self-affirmation. Piercy and LeGuin have used the genre of science fiction to explore issues of gender and power. In Piercy's *Woman on the Edge of Time* (1976) a woman discovers her uncanny ability to project herself into a future in which she is no longer socially marginalized; in LeGuin's *The Left Hand of Darkness* (1969) a person named Genly Ai experiences the perils and possibilities of androgyny. Alice Walker has portrayed an African-American woman's struggle against her husband's abuse and the power of love between women in her Pulitzer Prize-winning work *The Color Purple* (1982) and has critiqued the worldwide problem of female genital mutilation in *Possessing the Secret of Joy* (1992). Jane Smiley has offered a compelling portrait of the dysfunctional family, paternal incest, and women's enforced silences in her Pulitzer Prize-winning novel *A Thousand Acres* (1991). And Sandra Cisneros has celebrated the sexual awakening of a young

Latina girl in *The House on Mango Street* (1984) and has documented women's resistance to economic and sexual domination in *Woman Hollering Creek* (1991).

"The question of what constitutes 'feminist writing' is a contentious issue, but what is certain is that novels concerned with women's experience represent a significant section of the contemporary fiction market, and make rich use of innovations in narrative technique and of a range of styles and genres" (Williams 47). Whether they chronicle women's journeys to self-knowledge, resistance to oppression, or the deconstruction of gender altogether, feminist fiction writers suggest that new types of women are emerging, sexual relationships are changing, and female autonomy and community continue to serve as topics of celebration and interrogation.

POSTMODERN NARRATIVE EXPERIMENTATION

The term "postmodernism" has been variously defined. Certainly it represents a shift from the rebellious strategies of modernism toward a focus on a series of insoluble social debates over gender, class, race, colonialism and its breakdown, and new world economies. In literary studies postmodernism is associated with a self-conscious awareness of fictionality, a challenge to traditional notions of authorship and genre, and an emphasis on intertextuality, the belief that no text can be read in isolation from other texts. Theories of cultural postmodernism consider how culture itself has become a commodity in a technological, capitalistic, and multicultural age.

In extending the modernist narrative experimentation of James Joyce, Samuel Beckett anticipated postmodernist strategies of minimalism and self-conscious parody in his novels and plays. *Waiting for Godot* (1953), *Molloy* (1956), and *The Unnameable* (1959) reveal both a fascination with words and an awareness of their limitations, as well as a compulsion to assert the texts' fictionality. Whether language is capable of referring to a nonlinguistic reality is also the question raised by many other British novelists, including Lawrence Durrell, whose "game of mirrors" in his novelistic sequence *The Alexandria Quartet* (1957–60) includes traditional first- and third-person narratives as well as journals, letters, and excerpts from a novel by one of its characters. In *The French Lieutenant's Woman* (1969) John Fowles explores narrative's possibilities as a means of structuring individual and cultural experience in a pastiche that interweaves Victorian social history with a purportedly nineteenth-century saga of love and betrayal. To call attention to the novel's fictionality, Fowles presents readers with a choice of endings, abnegating his authorial autonomy and tossing a coin to determine the order of the two conclusions. A fascination with pastiche and fantasy can also be seen in the antirealistic and feminist writing of Angela Carter, most notably in *Nights at the Circus* (1984) and *Wise Children* (1991). Two of the most popular novelists writing in Britain in the 1990s, Jeanette Winterson and Salman Rushdie, have been strongly influenced by postmodernism, although in different ways. In *The Passion* (1988) and *Written on the Body* (1992) Winterson uses fantasy and parody to reveal new possibilities for women who have been limited by restrictive socialization. Rushdie uses magic realism and self-conscious narrative multiplicity to resist imperialism in works like *The Satanic Verses* (1988), a novel whose religious irreverence so infuriated the Iranian Islamic leader the Ayatollah Khomeini that he imposed a death sentence on Rushdie, forcing the writer into hiding. A link between postmodernism and difference can also be seen in the historiographic metafiction of MAXINE HONG KINGSTON. *The Woman Warrior* (1976) blends fiction, autobiography, and biography, in a self-reflexive narrative, to construct the racial and gender subjectivity of Chinese women in America. More recently, Don Delillo has wryly challenge orthodoxies of God, man, state, and sport in such novels as *White Noise* (1985) and *Underworld* (1997).

Some late-twentieth-century dramatic narratives can also be considered postmodern, particularly the plays of British dramatists Tom Stoppard and Caryl Churchill. Influenced by the German expressionist and Marxist playwright Bertolt Brecht, whose Berliner Ensemble visited London in 1956 to rave reviews, and by other theatrical innovators such as Samuel Beckett, Stoppard combined parody, pastiche, and intertextuality in his first major play, *Rosencrantz and Guildenstern Are Dead* (1966), which played with and off of Shakespeare's *Hamlet*. Churchill's plays are both postmodern and feminist: postmodern in their use of witty doublings, cross-dressing and gender-bending of characters, feminist in their trenchant examination of sexuality and power. In *Vinegar Tom* (1976), for example, the same two actresses who play women hanged for witchcraft in one scene return as leaders of the Inquisition in the next. Churchill's 1997 play *Blue Heart* experiments with the breakdown of language altogether, as characters are reduced to primal consonant sounds in their frustrated efforts to communicate: "T b k k k k l?" "B. K."

As Linda Hutcheon notes, postmodernism challenges our dominant, liberal humanistic culture by refuting the notion of what the philosopher Jean-Francois Lyotard has called consolatory "master narratives"—art, for instance, or myth, or religion. "What this means is that the familiar humanist separation of art and life (or human imagination and order *versus* chaos and disorder) no longer holds. Postmodernist contradictory art still installs that order, but it then uses it to demystify our everyday processes of structuring chaos, of imparting or assigning meaning" (6–7). Literature can be called postmodern when it interrogates human certainties and declines to resolve contradictions; typically, it calls attention to itself as what Julia Kristeva has called "writing-as-experience-of-limits," whether those limits be linguistic, subjective, sexual, or systemic (quoted in Hutcheon 8).

THE AFRICAN-AMERICAN LITERARY TRADITION

Of the many movements for human liberation that developed during the 1950s and 1960s, the U.S. civil rights movement has been perhaps the most far-reaching. Although much important African-American literature was written during the nineteenth and early twentieth centuries, African-American writing has flourished since the 1950s. Indeed, an impressive literary tradition developed that has had a major impact on U.S. literary studies. Twentieth-century Afrrican-American literature has sometimes been divided into two categories: protest writing, illustrated by Richard Wright's *Native Son* (1940), Ann Petry's *The Street* (1946), and Chester Himes's *Lonely Crusade* (1947)—writing that expresses rage at living in a racist system—and literature of the African-American renaissance, embodied in such lyrical works as Ralph Ellison's *Invisible Man* (1952), James Baldwin's *Go Tell It on the Mountain* (1953), and Toni Morrison's *Song of Solomon* (1977). This distinction is problematic, however, in that these lyrical works implicitly, and often explicitly, present the furious ravages of racism, while protest writing sometimes presents moments of redemption and transformation.

Despite many common concerns, contemporary African-American women writers' themes and strategies differ from those of their male contemporaries in significant ways. Critic Mary Helen Washington has described an African-American women's tradition succinctly:

> Their literature is about black women; it takes the trouble to record the thoughts, words, feelings, and deeds of black women, experiences that make the realities of being black in America look very different from what men have written. There are no women in this tradition hibernating in dark holes contemplating their invisibility; there are no women dismembering the bodies or crushing the skulls of either women or men; and few, if any women in the literature of black women succeed in heroic quests without the support of other women or men in their communities. Women talk to other women in this tradition, and their friendships with other women—mothers, sisters, grandmothers, friends, lovers—are vital to their growth and well-being (xxi).

Their emphasis on women's communities and self-definition does not mean that African-American women writers are apolitical, Washington cautions; they also explore issues of social justice, from rape to lynching to workplace discrimination. Moreover, they treat sexuality differently from their male peers. Historically, rather than avoiding discussion of their own sexual lives, as authors of male slave narratives typically did, women like HARRIET JACOBS presented and examined their sexual abuse and their strategies of resistance. Contemporary women such as Toni Morrison (*The Bluest Eye*, 1970), Ntozake Shange (*For colored girls who have considered suicide/when the rainbow is enuf*, 1976), and Alice Walker (*The Color Purple*, 1982) have likewise insisted on naming their exploiters, usually white but sometimes black men. However, prominent women writers also show black women's fulfillment of their own sexual desire, following the tradition of Zora Neale Hurston's Janie Crawford in *Their Eyes Were Watching God* (1937): Sethe in *Beloved* ultimately finds sexual and emotional satisfaction in the arms of Paul D, while Celie in *The Color Purple* learns about sexual pleasure from her husband's lover, Shug Avery.

Viewed as a whole, African-American fiction since 1945 has focused on challenging racist constructions of otherness, documenting black history and culture, promoting racial empowerment and transformation, and examining universal human struggles for autonomy and self-realization. Among the most important fictional works of this period are Ellison's *Invisible Man* (1952), a novel of startling linguistic intensity and luminosity; Baldwin's *Another Country* (1962), an exploration of racism, poverty, sexism, and bisexuality; Paule Marshall's *Brown Girl, Brownstones* (1959), a portrait of a Barbadian immigrant family transplanted to New York; and Morrison's *Beloved* (1987), a retrospective account of the horrors of slavery as it affected "fifty million and more" lives. Other African-American fiction writers of note include Margaret Walker (*Jubilee*, 1966), Ernest Gaines (*The Autobiography of Miss Jane Pittman*, 1971), Ishmael Reed (*Mumbo Jumbo*, 1972), TONI CADE BAMBARA (*The Salt Eaters*, 1980), Gloria Naylor (*The Women of Brewster Place*, 1982), Charles Johnson (*Middle Passage*, 1990), and Terri McMillan (*Waiting to Exhale*, 1992).

African-American poets since 1945 have forged racial identities as well as critiqued racist practices. From her first collection, *A Street in Bronzeville* (1945) to her Pulitzer Prize-winning *Annie Allen* (1949) to *The Bean Eaters* (1960) and beyond, Gwendolyn Brooks has been a major chronicler of black identities. Other poets who rose to prominence in the turbulent 1960s were Nikki Giovanni, whose *Black Feeling,*

Black Talk (1967) and *Black Judgement* (1968) document the black struggle for civil rights, in which Giovanni was both a participant and a witness; Etheridge Knight, whose *Black Voices from Prison* (1970) documents desperation and entrapment as well as the possibility of liberation; Sterling A. Brown, whose *Collected Poems* (1980) recalls the spirit of slave poems even as it reflects modern black culture; and Maya Angelou, whose *Just Give Me a Cool Drink of Water 'fore I Die* (1971) and *And Still I Rise* (1978) evoke lyrical reminiscences of her growth as a black woman and celebrate the legacy of African-American resistance and survival. And since the 1970s a number of African-American feminist poets have risen to prominence, most notably June Jordan (*Things That I Do in the Dark: Selected Poetry,* 1977), who sees challenging racism and sexism as the African-American poet's first duty; Audre Lorde (*Chosen Poems: Old and New,* 1982), who defined herself until her untimely death in 1992 as a "black lesbian feminist warrior poet"; and LUCILLE CLIFTON (*An Ordinary Woman,* 1974), who speaks as an empowered black woman indebted to a family whose genesis lay in slavery.

African-American drama has focused on the economic and emotional struggles of black families, external and internalized violence among black people, and men's and women's quests for identity, autonomy, and community. Lorraine Hansberry's *A Raisin in the Sun* (1959), a huge hit on Broadway, portrayed both the discord of a family who failed to meet its own aspirations and the pervasive injustice of a racist system; it won the New York Drama Critics Circle Award for Best Play of 1959 and brought black drama to the attention of the general public. Adrienne Kennedy's *Funnyhouse of a Negro* (1962) dramatized the negative effects of prejudice, hatred, and rejection on an anguished black girl, using highly stylized and surrealistic theatrical techniques; this dreamscape won an Obie for 1964. Amiri Baraka's *Dutchman* (1964) likewise drew on techniques of surrealism and mythic realism to present a violent conflict between a black man and a seductive white woman on a subway train in the "underbelly of the city," which for Baraka symbolizes entombment and incarceration. Alice Childress's *Trouble in Mind* (1971) critiqued negative stereotypes of black people perpetuated by white playwrights and producers and challenged sexist treatment of black women, especially actresses; for this play she won an Obie, the first African-American woman to do so. August Wilson's *Fences* (1985) depicted the breakdown of a black family in the 1950s because of its desperate construction of emotional barriers; it won both a Tony award for Best Play of 1985 and a Pulitzer Prize for drama.

African-American autobiography has a long and eloquent history, beginning with the slave narratives of Frederick Douglass and Harriet Jacobs and continuing with the autobiographical writings of James Weldon Johnson (*The Autobiography of an Ex-Colored Man,* 1912) and Zora Neale Hurston (*Dust Tracks on a Road,* 1942). Among the most important autobiographies published since World War II are Richard Wright's *Black Boy* (1945), which documents the ordeal of growing up in the segregated South; and *The Autobiography of W.E.B. Dubois* (1968), which traces his ninety-year journey as a civil rights activist and statesman. Alex Haley's *The Autobiography of Malcolm X* (1965) was written from interviews that Haley conducted with Malcolm just before his assassination; the book chronicles his life as a black separatist and the philosophical changes his thinking underwent when he embraced the Nation of Islam. Probably the most famous of black autobiographies is Maya Angelou's *I Know Why the Caged Bird Sings* (1969), a major contribution to the history of U.S. autobiography, the literature of African-American experience, and women's writing in general. Other important examples of contemporary black autobiography include Gwendolyn Brooks's *Maud Martha* (1953) and Claude Brown's *Manchild in the Promised Land* (1965), both of which present themselves as fiction; Eldridge Cleaver's riveting *Soul on Ice* (1968), which documents this militant activist's prison experience; and Nikki Giovanni's *Gemini* (1971), subtitled "An Extended Autobiographical Statement on My First Twenty-five Years of Being a Black Poet." Of the many distinguished collections of prose essays by African-American writers, James Baldwin's *The Fire Next Time* (1963) is perhaps the most trenchant. He speaks directly to his readers on subjects ranging from the violence of segregation to black Islamic militancy to the need for social justice and racial reconciliation. Other collections of essays that have challenged racist policies and texts and probed the intersections of racism, sexism, and homophobia include June Jordan's *On Call* (1985), Audre Lorde's *Sister Outsider* (1984), and Toni Morrison's *Playing in the Dark* (1992). Black autographical and prose writings, in summary, have told the truth about slavery and black experience and celebrated the culture through the individual voice, which speaks with and of the African-American community as well as to it. They have also served as a bridge to those white communities willing to listen to stories of black struggle and triumph and examine their own complicity in racist behaviors and policies.

LITERARY INTERNATIONALIZATION: BORDER CROSSINGS

Especially since 1945, an important contribution to literature written in English has been made by writers for whom English is a first or second language bequeathed by a legacy of colonialism. Britain's relations with the rest of the world changed dramatically with the steady dismantling of the British Empire in the 1950s and 1960s, and writers from the former colonies have critiqued the legacy of colonialism and explored the parameters of cultural diversity and literary crossfertilization. One characteristic of much postcolonial literature is its hybrid quality, indicating a blend of English societal values and those of the indigenous culture. Writers of the former British Commonwealth have crossed symbolic borders by examining their societies' historical pasts and entering into debates about gender, race, and class oppression. They have also considered the role of nationalism and internationalism in their countries' movements forward.

The writing of postcolonial women has been especially vital to postwar literary internationalization. Among the best known of these writers are Kamala Das and BHARATI MUKHERJEE from India; BESSIE HEAD, Ellen Kuzwayo, and ZOË WICOMB from South Africa; Flora Nwapa and BUCHI EMECHETA from Nigeria; AMA ATA AIDOO from Ghana; OODGEROO OF THE TRIBE NOONUCCAL and KERI HULME from aboriginal cultures; and Beth Brant, a Bay of Quinte Mohawk Indian from Canada. As Chandra Mohanty suggests, these writers have reconceptualized "ideas of resistance, community, and agency in daily life," questioned their cultural construction as "native," and explored questions of politicized consciousness and identity in their work. Among the "crucial elements" that link writing, memory, and consciousness in postcolonial women's literature are "(a) the codification of covert images of resistance during non-revolutionary times; (b) the creation of communal (feminist) political consciousness through the practice of storytelling; and (c) the redefinition of the very possibilities of political consciousness and action through the act of writing" (35).

Because the histories and cultural landscapes of former British colonies differ so greatly, it is useful to consider new developments in international literature in English by region or country. In the disrupted cultures of West Africa, novelists like Chinua Achebe (*Things Fall Apart*, 1958) and Buchi Emecheta (*The Joys of Motherhood*, 1979) and playwrights like Wole Soyinka (*A Dance of the Forests*, 1960), all of whom are from Nigeria, present the writer as modern-day "griot," or storyteller/historian, and insist that the artist plays a crucial role in national reconstruction. In South Africa under apartheid (1948–1994) black male writers such as Dennis Brutus, Achmed Dangor, Mafeka Pascal Gwala, Keorapetse Kgositsile, Mazisi Kunene and black female writers such as Sankie Dolly Nkondo, Gladys Thomas, and GCINA MHLOPHE have challenged this racist system and enhanced their audience's will to struggle and survive. White South African writers such as the novelists NADINE GORDIMER and J.M. Coetzee and the playwright Athol Fugard have chronicled the injustices of apartheid, its demise and its aftermath, and the decay of the white middle classes resulting from their complicity in this system.

In India writers such as R.K. Narayan, ANITA DESAI, and Arundhati Roy have explored their society from within, while Indian expatriates such as Salman Rushdie and Bharati Mukherjee have combined traditional and Western literary characteristics to produce cultural and narrative hybrids. Narayan's novels *Waiting for the Mahatma* (1955), *The Guide* (1958), and *A Tiger for Malgudi* (1983) draw upon such disparate legacies as Hindu beliefs in reincarnation and the British influence on the Indian system of education. The novels of Desai, including *Where Shall We Go This Summer* (1975) and *Clear Light of Day* (1980), address in an impressionistic style the dilemmas of Indian women torn between traditional customs and Westernization. Roy's *The God of Small Things*, which won the Booker Prize for 1997, portrays the tragedies of gender discrimination, class and caste conflict, and family violence in contemporary India and their effects on two lost children. Rushdie's *Midnight's Children* (1981) presents an innovative collage of classical, modern, and popular traditions— Hindu, Islamic, and Western—while Mukherjee's *Darkness* (1985), a collection of stories in the realist tradition, explore the racism and cultural dislocation experienced by Indian women expatriates living in Canada.

Canadian, Australian, and New Zealand writers comprise a group designated by Linda R. Williams as "transplanted New World society," whose majority peoples are European in origin and who have had to transform Old World cultural forms to New World landscapes and social realities (132–33). The Canadian writer Margaret Atwood has explored the problems settlers had in constructing a national identity in poems from *The Animals in That Country* (1968) and has drawn parallels between Canadians and women as suffering from a victim mentality in her novel *Surfacing* (1972). Beth Brant has examined in her poems the cultural estrangement experienced by Canadian native peoples and lesbians. In Australia, the poet JUDITH WRIGHT has traced the contours of "my blood's country . . . the high lean country / full of old stories that still go walking in my sleep," while the novelist Patrick White has linked linguistic transformation to nationalistic quest. The short story writer Peter Carey, in turn, has presented a nightmarish Australian landscape in a postmodern style and context. In New Zealand JANET FRAME has explored the effects of a repressive landscape on the individual imagination in such novels as *Owls Do Cry* (1957) and *The Edge of the Alphabet* (1962). Moreover, indigenous writers such as

Colin Johnson and Oodgeroo of the tribe Noonuccal, aborigines in Australia, and Witi Ihimaera and Keri Hulme, New Zealanders of Maori descent, have forged complex self-definitions, validated ancestral customs, and critiqued those forces that would deny them social justice and cultural expression.

West Indian writers have written of both cultural disruption and transplantation. The Nobel Prize-winning poet Derek Walcott, from St. Lucia, documents his conflict as a racially mixed Caribbean man forced to "choose / Between this Africa and the English tongue I love" in such poems as "A Far Cry from Africa"; he promotes in his poetry a "creative schizophrenia" that would turn the divisions of colonialism into sources of cultural strength. Performance poets such as Linton Kwesi Johnson and Michael Smith reject English metrical forms and embrace reggae rhythms, while oral poets such as Edward Kamau Brathwaite and Louise Bennett and poet-essayists such as M. Nourbese Philip inscribe the polyphonies of Caribbean speech. The lesbian feminist writer Michelle Cliff, originally from Jamaica, labels her country "a place halfway between Africa and England" and herself as "red," a hybrid blend of Black, Indian, and English influences, in her autobiographical work *Claiming an Identity They Taught Me to Despise* (1981). JAMAICA KINCAID, originally from Antigua, renders Caribbean identity problematic through the lens of a racially mixed girl growing into womanhood in the stories that comprise *At the Bottom of the River* (1978).

Although literature written by these postcolonial writers is diverse in theme and style, all of them have responded to the cultural legacy of colonialism and have had to mediate between local or ancestral traditions and those imposed from the outside. Many of them have crossed cultural and national boundaries by advocating a multicultural vision of consciousness that would heal fragmentation and lead to psychic and social integration. Finally, these writers have created a dialogue between past legacies and present realities—between indigenous, disrupted, and transplanted peoples and their allies—that promises to continue unabated into the twenty-first century.

⊰ Works Cited ⊱

Anzaldúa, Gloria, ed. Introduction to *Making Face, Making Soul/haciendo caras: Creative and Critical Perspectives by Women of Color*. San Francisco: aunt lute, 1990.

Clausen, Jan. *A Movement of Poets: Thoughts on Poetry and Feminism*. Brooklyn: Long Haul Press, 1980.

Davis, Angela. *Women, Race, and Class*. New York: Vintage Books, 1983.

de Beauvoir, Simone. *The Second Sex*. Trans. H.M. Parshley. 1949; Harmondsworth: Penguin, 1972.

DeShazer, Mary K. *Inspiring Women: Reimagining the Muse*. New York: Pergamon Press, 1986.

France, Linda, ed. *Sixty Women Poets*. Newcastle-upon-Tyne: Bloodaxe Books, 1993.

Friedan, Betty. *The Feminine Mystique*. New York: Norton, 1963.

Hoover, Paul, ed. *Postmodern American Poetry: A Norton Anthology*. New York: Norton, 1994.

Hutcheon, Linda. *A Poetics of Postmodernism: History, Theory, Fiction*. New York and London: Routledge, 1988.

Mohanty, Chandra Talpede et al., eds. *Third World Women and the Politics of Feminism*. Bloomington: Indiana UP, 1991.

Montefiore, Jan. *Feminism and Poetry: Language, Experience, Identity in Women's Writing*. London and New York: Pandora, 1987.

Moraga, Cherríe. "La Guera." *This Bridge Called My Back: Writings by Radical Women of Color*. Eds. Cherríe Moraga and Gloria Anzaldúa. 1981; rpt. Latham, NY: Kitchen Table Women of Color Press, 1983.

Olson, Charles. "Projective Verse." *Collected Prose*. Eds. Donald Allen and Benjamin Friedlander. Berkeley: U of California P, 1997. 239–49.

Ostriker, Alicia. *Stealing the Language: The Emergence of Women's Poetry in America*. Boston: Beacon Press, 1986.

Rich, Adrienne. "'When We Dead Awaken': Writing as Re-Vision." *On Lies, Secrets, and Silence: Selected Prose 1966–1979*. New York: Norton, 1979.

Washington, Mary Helen, ed. *Invented Lives: Narratives of Black Women 1860–1960*. Garden City, NY: Doubleday, 1987.

Williams, Linda R., ed. *The Twentieth Century: From 1900 to the Present Day*. London: Bloomsbury, 1992.

Selected Bibliographies

Grace Aguilar

Works by Aguilar: See biographical headnote pp. 690-91.

Criticism: Michael Galchinsky, *The Origin of the Modern Jewish Woman Writer: Romance and Reform in Victorian England* (1996) • Galchinsky, "Modern Jewish Women's Dilemmas: Grace Aguilar's Bargains," *Literature and Theology* 11 (1997).

Ama Ata Aidoo

Works by Aidoo: See biographical headnote pp. 844-45.

Interview: Rosemary Marangoly George and Helen Scott, "'A New Tail to an Old Tale': An Interview with Ama Ata Aidoo," *Novel* 26 (1993).

Criticism: Marion Kilson, "Women and African Literature," *Journal of African Studies* 4 (1977) • Kathleen McCaffrey, "Images of the Mother in the Stories of Ama Ata Aidoo," *African Women* 23 (1979) • Chikwenye Okonjo Ogunyemi, "Womanism: The Dynamics of the Contemporary Black Female Novel in English," *Signs* 11:1 (1985) • Chimalum Nwanko, "The Feminist Impulse and Social Realism in Ama Ata Aidoo's *No Sweetness Here* and *Our Sister Killjoy*," *Nganbika: Studies of Women in African Literature*, eds. Carole Boyce Davies and Anne Adams Graves (1986) • Caroline Rooney, "Dangerous Knowledge and the Poetics of Survival: A Reading of *Our Sister Killjoy* and *A Question of Power*," in *Motherlands: Black Women's Writing from Africa, the Caribbean, and South Asia*, ed. Susheila Nasta (1992) • Ada U. Azodo and Gay Wilentz, eds., *Emerging Perspectives on Ama Ata Aidoo* (1999).

Paula Gunn Allen

Works by Allen: See biographical headnote pp. 1026-27.

Interview: "An Interview with Paula Gunn Allen," *Women's Review of Books* 6 (1989).

Criticism: Mary Tallmountain, "Paula Gunn Allen's 'The One Who Skins Cats': An Inquiry into Spiritedness," *Studies in American Indian Literatures* 5 (1993) • Vanessa Holford, "Remembering Ephanie: A Woman's Recreation of Self in Paula Gunn Allen's *The Woman Who Owned the Shadows*," *Studies in American Indian Literatures* 6 (1994) • AnaLouise Keating, *Women Reading Women Writing: Self-Invention in Paula Gunn Allen, Gloria Anzaldúa, and Audre Lorde* (1996) • Tara Prince-Hughes, "Contemporary Two-Spirit Identity in the Fiction of Paula Gunn Allen and Beth Brant," *Studies in American Indian Literatures* 10 (1998).

Maya Angelou

Works by Angelou: See biographical headnote pp. 1221-23.

Biographies: Miles Shapiro, *Maya Angelou* (1994) • Margaret Courtney-Clarke, *Maya Angelou: The Poetry of Living* (1999).

Criticism: Sidonie A. Smith, "The Song of a Caged Bird: Maya Angelou's Quest After Self-Acceptance," *Southern Humanities Review* 7 (1973) • R.B. Stepto, "The Phenomenal Woman and the Severed Daughter," *Parnassus* (1980) • Selwyn R. Cudjoe, "Maya Angelou and the Autobiographical Statement," *Black Women Writers (1950–1980)*, ed. Mari Evans (1984) • Sondra O'Neale, "Reconstruction of the Composite Self," *Black Women Writers* (1984) • Joanne M. Braxton, *Black Women Writing Autobiography: A Tradition Within a Tradition* (1989) • Dolly A. McPherson, *Order Out of Chaos: The Autobiographical Works of Maya Angelou* (1990) • Ekaterini Georgoudaki, *Race, Gender, and Class Perspectives: Works of Maya Angelou, Gwendolyn Brooks, Rita Dove, Nikki Giovanni, and Audre Lorde* (1991) • Valerie Baisnee, *Gendered Resistance: The Autobiographies of Simone deBeauvoir, Maya Angelou, Janet Frame, and Marguerite Duras* (1997) • *Maya Angelou's "I Know Why the Caged Bird Sings,"* ed. Harold Bloom (1998).

Gloria Anzaldúa

Works by Anzaldúa: See biographical headnote pp. 315-16.

Biography: Gloria Anzaldúa, "To(o) Queer the Writer—*Loca, escritora y chicana*," in *Inversions: Writing by Dykes, Queers, and Lesbians*, ed. Betsy Warland (1991).

Criticism: AnaLouise Keating, "Writing, Politics, and *Las Lesberados—Platicando—con Gloria Anzaldúa*," *Frontiers: A Journal of Women's Studies* 14 (1994) • Yvonne Yarbro-Bejarano, "Gloria

Anzaldúa's *Borderlands/La Frontera:* Cultural Studies, 'Difference,' and the Non-Unitary Subject," *Cultural Critique* 28 (1994) • Carol Thomas Neely, "Women/Utopia/Fetish: Disavowal and Satisfied Desire in Margaret Cavendish's *New Blazing World* and Gloria Anzaldúa's *Borderlands/La Frontera*," in *Heterotopia: Postmodern Utopia and the Body Politic,* ed. Tobin Siebers (1995) • Jane Hedley, "Nepantilist Poetics: Narrative and Cultural Identity in the Mixed-Language Writings of Irena Klepfisz and Gloria Anzaldúa," *Narrative* 4 (1996) • AnaLouise Keating, *Women Reading Women Writing: Self-Invention in Paula Gunn Allen, Gloria Anzaldúa, and Audre Lorde* (1996) • Diane L. Fowlkes, "Moving from Feminist Identity Politics to Coalition Politics through a Feminist Materialist Standpoint: Intersubjectivity in Gloria Anzaldúa's *Borderlands/La Frontera: The New Mestiza,*" *Hypatia* 12 (1997) • Jennifer Browdy de Hernandez, "Mothering the Self: Writing through the Lesbian Sublime in Audre Lorde's *Zami* and Gloria Anzaldúa's *Borderlands/La Frontera,*" in *Other Sisterhoods: Literary Theory and U.S. Women of Color,* ed. Sandra Kumamoto Stanley (1998).

Mary Astell

Works by Astell: See biographical headnote pp. 1224-25.

Editions: Bridget Hill, ed., *The First English Feminist: Reflections upon Marriage and Other Writings by Mary Astell* (1986) • Patricia Springborg, ed., *A Serious Proposal to the Ladies,* parts I and II (1997).

Biography: Ruth Perry, *The Celebrated Mary Astell: An Early English Feminist* (1986).

Criticism: Catherine Gallagher, "Embracing the Absolute: The Politics of the Female Subject in Seventeenth-Century England," *Genders* 1 (1988) • Christine Mason Sutherland, "Mary Astell: Reclaiming Rhetorica in the Seventeenth Century," in *Reclaiming Rhetorica: Women in the Rhetorical Tradition,* ed. Andrea Lunsford (1995) • Alessa Johns, "Mary Astell's 'Excited Needles': Theorizing Feminist Utopia in Seventeenth-Century England," *Utopian Studies* 7 (1996) • Patricia Springborg, "Mary Astell and John Locke," in *English Literature 1650–1740,* ed. Steven N. Zwicker (1998).

Margaret Atwood

Works by Atwood: See biographical headnote pp. 826-27.

Biography: Coral Ann Howells, *Margaret Atwood* (1996).

Criticism: Sherrill Grace, *Violent Duality: A Study of Margaret Atwood* (1980) • *The Art of Margaret Atwood: Essays in Criticism,* ed. Arnold E. Davidson and Cathy N. Davidson (1981) • *Margaret Atwood: Language, Text, and System,* ed. Sherrill E. Grace and Lorraine Weir (1983) • Kathryn Van Spanckeren and Jan Garden Castro, *Margaret Atwood: Vision and Form* (1988) • *Critical Essays on Margaret Atwood,* ed. Judith McCombs (1988) • Eleanora Rao, *Strategies for Identity: The Fiction of Margaret Atwood* (1993) • Sharon Rose Wilson, *Margaret Atwood's Fairy-tale Sexual Politics* (1993) • *Margaret Atwood, Writing, and Subjectivity: New Critical Essays,* ed. Colin Nicholson (1994) • Roxanne J. Fand, *The Dialogic Self: Reconstructing Subjectivity in Woolf, Lessing, and Atwood* (1999).

Jane Austen

Works by Austen: See biographical headnote pp. 112-13.

Editions: *The Works of Jane Austen,* ed. R.W. Chapman (1920) • *Jane Austen's Letters,* ed. R.W. Chapman (1979) • *Selected Letters, 1796–1817,* ed. R.W. Chapman (1985) • *Jane Austen's Manuscript Letters in Facsimile,* ed. Jo Modert (1990) • *My Dear Cassandra: The Letters of Jane Austen,* ed. Penelope Hughes-Hellet (1991) • *The Poetry of Jane Austen and the Austen Family,* ed. David Selwyn (1997).

Biographies: Mary A. Austen-Leigh, *Personal Aspects of Jane Austen* (1920) • Valerie Grosvenor-Myer, *Jane Austen: Obstinate Heart* (1997) • Claire Tomalin, *Jane Austen: A Life* (1997) • Deirdre LeFaye, *Jane Austen* (1998).

Criticism: Julia P. Brown, *Jane Austen's Novels: Social Change and Literary Form* (1979) • Susan Morgan, *In the Meantime: Character and Perception in Jane Austen's Fiction* (1980) • *Jane Austen: New Perspectives,* ed. Janet Todd (1983) • Mary Poovey, *The Proper Lady and the Woman Writer* (1984) • Laura G. Mooneyham, *Romance, Language, and Education in Jane Austen's Novels* (1986) • Claudia L. Johnson, *Jane Austen: Women, Politics, and the Novel* (1988) • Alison Sulloway, *Jane Austen and the Province of Womanhood* (1989) • Deborah Kaplan, *Jane Austen Among Women* (1992) • Maaja A. Stewart, *Domestic Realities and Imperial Fictions: Jane Austen's Novels in Eighteenth-century Contexts* (1993) • Audrey Bilger, *Laughing Feminism: Subversive Comedy in Fanny Burney, Maria Edgeworth, and Jane Austen* (1998) • *Jane Austen in Hollywood,* eds. Linda Troost and Sayer Greenfield (1998).

Toni Cade Bambara

Works by Bambara: See biographical headnote pp. 553-54.

Interview: "Toni Cade Bambara," in *Black Women Writers at Work*, ed. Claudia Tate (1983).

Criticism: Elliott Butler-Evans, *Race, Gender, and Desire: Narrative Strategies in the Fiction of Toni Cade Bambara, Toni Morrison, and Alice Walker* (1989) • Nancy Porter, "Women's Interracial Friendships and Visions of Community in *Meridian, The Salt Eaters, Civil Wars, and Dessa Rose*," in *Tradition and the Talents of Women*, ed. Florence Howe (1991).

Mary Barber

Works by Barber: See biographical headnote p. 676.

Criticism: Roger Lonsdale, ed., *Eighteenth-Century Women Poets* (1990) • A.C. Elias Jr., "Editing Minor Writers: The Case of Laetitia Pilkington and Mary Barber," in *1650–1850: Ideas, Aesthetics, and Inquiries in the Early Modern Era*, III, ed. Kevin L. Cope (1997).

Jane Barker

Works by Barker: See biographical headnote pp. 492-93.

Edition: *The Galesia Trilogy and Selected Manuscript Poems of Jane Barker*, ed. Carol Shiner Wilson (1997).

Biography: Kathryn R. King and Jeslyn Medoff, "Jane Barker and Her Life," *Eighteenth-century Life* 21 (1997).

Criticism: Kathryn R. King, "Galesia, Jane Barker, and a Coming to Authorship," in *Anxious Power: Reading, Writing, and Ambivalence in Narrative by Women*, eds. Carol J. Singley and Susan E. Sweeney (1993) • King, "The Unaccountable Wife and Other Tales of Female Desire in Jane Barker's *A Patchwork Screen for the Ladies*," *The Eighteenth Century: Theory and Interpretation* 35 (1994) • King, "Of Needles and Pens and Women's Work," *Tulsa Studies in Women's Literature* 14 (1995) • Tom Bowers, "Jacobite Difference and the Poetry of Jane Barker," *ELH* 64 (1997).

Djuna Barnes

Works by Barnes: See biographical headnote pp. 519-20.

Editions: *The Selected Works of Djuna Barnes: Smoke and Other Early Stories*, ed. Douglas

Messerli (1982) • *Interviews*, ed. Alyce Barry (1985) • *New York*, ed. Alyce Barry (1989) • *Selected Letters of Djuna Barnes* (1993).

Biographies: Andrew Field, *Djuna: The Life and Times of Djuna Barnes* (1983) • Phillip F. Herring, *Djuna: The Life and Work of Djuna Barnes* (1995).

Criticism: Susan Sniader Lanser, "Speaking in Tongues: *Ladies' Almanack* and the Language of Celebration," *Frontiers* 4 (1979) • Shari Benstock, *Women of the Left Bank* (1986) • Bonnie Kime Scott, *The Gender of Modernism* (1990) • *Silence and Power: A Reevaluation of Djuna Barnes*, ed. Mary Lynn Broe (1991) • Carolyn J. Allen, "Sexual Narrative in the Fiction of Djuna Barnes," in *Sexual Practice, Textual Theory: Lesbian Cultural Criticism*, eds. Susan J. Wolfe and Julia Penelope (1993) • Karen Kaivola, *All Contraries Confounded: The Lyric Fiction of Virginia Woolf, Djuna Barnes, and Marguerite Duras* (1993) • Frann Michael, "'I Just Loved Thelma': Djuna Barnes and the Construction of Bisexuality," *The Review of Contemporary Fiction* 13 (1993) • Tyrus Miller, *Late Modernism: Politics, Fiction, and the Arts Between the World Wars* (1999).

Aphra Behn

Works by Behn: See biographical headnote pp. 433-34.

Editions: *Five Plays*, ed. Maureen Duffy (1990) • *The Works of Aphra Behn*, 7 vols., ed. Janet Todd (1992–) • *Oroonoko, The Rover, and Other Works*, ed. Janet Todd (1992).

Biographies: Maureen Duffy, *The Passionate Shepherdess: Aphra Behn, 1640–1689* (1977) • Angeline Goreau, *Reconstructing Aphra: A Social Biography of Aphra Behn* (1980) • Janet Todd, *The Secret Life of Aphra Behn* (1997).

Criticism: Judith Kegan Gardiner, "Aphra Behn: Sexuality and Self-Respect," *Women's Studies* 7 (1980) • Fidelis Morgan, *The Female Wits* (1981) • Laura Brown, "The Romance of Empire: Oronooko and the Trade in Slaves," in *The New Eighteenth Century: Theory, Politics, English Literature*, eds. Laura Brown and Felicity Nussbaum (1987) • Susan Carlson, *Women and Comedy: Rewriting the British Theatrical Tradition* (1991) • Ros Ballaster, *Seductive Forms: Women's Amatory Fiction from 1684–1740* (1992) • *Rereading Aphra Behn: History, Theory, Criticism*, ed. Heidi Hutner (1993) • Catherine Gallagher, *Nobody's Story: The Vanishing Acts of Women Writers in the Marketplace, 1670–1820* (1994) • Robert A. Erickson, "Lady Fulbank and the Poet's Dream in Behn's *The Lucky Chance*," in *Broken Boundaries: Women and Feminism in Restoration Drama*, ed. Katherine M. Quinsey (1996) • *Shakespeare, Aphra Behn, and the Canon*, eds. W.R. Owens and Lizbeth Goodman (1996) • *Aphra Behn Studies*, ed. Janet Todd (1996) • Margaret Ferguson, "The Authorial Ciphers of Aphra Behn," in *English Literature 1650–1740*, ed. Steven N. Zwicker (1998) • *Aphra Behn*, ed. Janet Todd (1999).

Shari Benstock

Works by Benstock: see biographical head-note pp. 597-98.

Juliana Berners (Julians Barnes)

Works by Berners: See biographical headnote p. 658.

Edition: *Julians Barnes: Boke of Hunting*, ed. Gunnar Tilander (1964).

Criticism: Rachel Hands, "Juliana Berners and the *Boke of St. Albans*," *Review of English Studies* 18 (1967) • Alexandra Barrett, ed., *Women's Writing in Middle English* (1992) • Marcelle Thiebaux, ed., *The Works of Medieval Women: An Anthology*, 2nd ed. (1994).

Eavan Boland

Works by Boland: See biographical headnote pp. 1273-74.

Interview: Deborah McWilliams Conslavo, "An Interview with Eavan Boland," *Studies: An Irish Quarterly Review* 81 (1992).

Criticism: Sheila C. Conboy, "'What You Have Seen Is Beyond Speech': Female Journeys in the Poetry of Eavan Boland and Eilean Ni Chuilleanain," *Canadian Journal of Irish Studies* 16 (1990) • Patricia L. Hagen and Thomas W. Zelman, "'We Were Never on the Scene of the Crime': Eavan Boland's Repossession of History," *Twentieth-Century Literature* 37 (1991) • Patricia Boyle Haberstroh, *Women Creating Women: Contemporary Irish Women Poets* (1996) • *The Wake Forest Book of Irish Women Poets*, ed. Peggy O'Brien (1999).

Anne Bradstreet

Works by Bradstreet: See biographical head-note pp. 668-69.

Edition: *The Complete Works of Anne Bradstreet*, eds. Joseph McElrath and Allan Robb (1981).

Biographies: Elizabeth W. White, *Anne Bradstreet: The Tenth Muse* (1971) • Ann Stanford,

Anne Bradstreet: The Worldly Puritan (1977).

Criticism: Wendy Martin, "Anne Bradstreet's Poetry: A Study in Subversive Piety," in *Shakespeare's Sisters*, eds. Sandra M. Gilbert and Susan Gubar (1979) • Adrienne Rich, "Anne Bradstreet," in *On Lies, Secrets, and Silence* (1979) • Ellen B. Brandt, "Anne Bradstreet: The Erotic Component in Puritan Poetry," *Women's Studies* 7 (1980) • Eileen Margerum, "Anne Bradstreet's Public Poetry and the Tradition of Humility," *Early American Literature* 17 (1982) • Wendy Martin, *An American Triptych* (1984) • Raymond F. Dalle, *Anne Bradstreet: A Reference Guide* (1990) • Jane D. Eberwein, "Civil War and Bradstreet's 'Monarchies,'" *Early American Literature* 26 (1991) • Rosamund Rosenmeier, *Anne Bradstreet Revisited* (1991) • Amanda Porterfield, *Female Piety in Puritan New England: The Emergence of Religious Humanism* (1992) • Jeffrey A. Hammond, *Sinful Self, Saintly Self: The Puritan Experience of Poetry* (1993) • Stephanie Jed, "The Tenth Muse: Gender, Rationality, and the Making of Knowledge," in *Women, 'Race,' and Writing in Early Modern Poetry*, eds. Margo Hendricks and Patricia Parker (1994) • Carrie Galloway Blackstock, "Anne Bradstreet and Performativity: Self-Cultivation, Self-Deployment," *Early American Literature* 32 (1997).

Dionne Brand

Works by Brand: See biographical headnote pp. 572-73.

Biography: Frank Birbalsingh, "Dionne Brand: No Language Is Neutral," in *Frontiers of Caribbean Literatures in English*, ed. Birbalsingh (1996).

Criticism: Charlotte Sturgess, "Spirits and Transformation in Dionne Brand's *San Souci and Other Stories*," *ECCS* 35 (1993) • Maria Casas, "Codes as Identity: The Bilingual Representation of a Fragmented Literary Subject," *Language and Discourse* 2 (1994) • Judith L. Raiskin, *Snow on the Cane Fields: Women's Writing and Creole Subjectivity* (1996) • Kathleen J. Renk, "'Her Words Are Like Fire': The Storytelling Magic of Dionne Brand," *ARIEL* 27 (1996) • Charlotte Sturgiss, "Dionne Brand's Short Stories: Warring Forces and Narrative Poetics," *Anglophonia: French Journal of English Studies* (1997).

Beth Brant

Works by Brant: See biographical headnote pp. 838-39.

Biography: Dorothy Allison, "Beth Brant (1941–)," in *Contemporary Lesbian Writers of the United States: A Bio-Bibliographical Critical Sourcebook*, ed. Sandra Pollock et al. (1993).

Criticism: Patricia Hill Collins, "Shifting the Center: Race, Class, and Feminizing Theorizing About Motherhood," in *Mothering: Ideology, Experience, Agency*, eds. Evelyn Nakano Glenn et al. (1994) • Tara Prince-Hughes, "Contemporary Two-Spirit Identity in the Fiction of Paula Gunn Allen and Beth Brant," *Studies in American Indian Literatures* 10 (1998).

Charlotte Brontë

Works by Brontë: See biographical headnote pp. 236-37.

Editions: *The Shakespeare Head Brontë*, ed. Thomas James Wise and John Alexander Symington (1931–38) • *The Poems of Charlotte Brontë*, ed. Victor A. Neufeldt (1985) • *The Early Writings of Charlotte Brontë: The Rise of Angria*, 2 vols., ed. Christine Alexander (1991).

Biographies: Elizabeth Gaskell, *The Life of Charlotte Brontë* (1857) • Winifred Gerin, *Charlotte Brontë: The Evolution of Genius* (1967) • Helene Moglen, *Charlotte Brontë: The Self Conceived* (1976) • Lyndall Gordon, *Charlotte Brontë: A Passionate Life* (1994).

Criticism: Patricia Beer, *Reader, I Married Him* (1974) • *The Brontës: The Critical Heritage*, ed. Miriam Allot (1974) • Terry Eagleton, *Myths of Power: A Marxist Study of the Brontës* (1975) • Elaine Showalter, *A Literature of Their Own* (1977) • Barbara Hill Rigney, *Madness and Sexual Politics in the Feminist Novel* (1978) • Sandra M. Gilbert and Susan Gubar, *The Madwoman in the Attic* (1979) • Judith Lowder Newton, *Women, Power, and Subversion* (1981) • Rebecca Crump, *Charlotte and Emily Brontë: A Reference Guide* (1982) • *Critical Essays on Charlotte Brontë*, ed. Barbara Timm Gates (1990) • Carol Bock, *Charlotte Brontë and the Storyteller's Audience* (1992) • Jerome Beaty, *Misreading Jane Eyre: A Postformalist Paradigm* (1996) • Patsy Stoneman, *Brontë Transformations: The Cultural Dissemination of Jane Eyre and Wuthering Heights* (1996) • Diane Hoevler Long and Lisa Jadwin, *Charlotte Brontë* (1997) • Diane Hoevler Long, *Gothic Feminism: The Professionalization of Gender from Charlotte Smith to the Brontës* (1998).

Emily Brontë

Works by Brontë: See biographical headnote pp. 241-42.

Editions: *Selections from Poems by Ellis Bell*, ed. Charlotte Brontë (1850) • *The Complete Poems of Emily Jane Brontë*, ed. C.W. Hatfield (1941).

Biographies: Winifred Gerin, *Emily Brontë* (1971) • Edward Chitham, *A Life of Emily Brontë* (1987) • Katherine Frank, *A Chainless Soul: A Life of Emily Brontë* (1990) • Steven Vine, *Emily Brontë* (1998).

Criticism: *The Art of Emily Brontë*, ed. Anne Smith (1977) • Sandra M. Gilbert and Susan Gubar, *The Madwoman in the Attic* (1979) • Margaret Homans, *Women Writers and Poetic Identity* (1980) • Janet M. Barclay, *Emily Brontë Criticism, 1900–1980: An Annotated Checklist* (1984) • Nina Aeurbach, *Romantic Imprisonment: Women and Other Glorified Outcasts* (1985) • Margaret Homans, *Bearing the Word: Language and Female Experience in Nineteenth-century Women's Writing* (1986) • *The Brontës: Modern Critical Views*, ed. Harold Bloom (1987) • Judith Weissman, *Half Savage and Hearty and Free: Women and Rural Radicalism in the Nineteenth-century Novel* (1987) • Patricia Yaeger, *Honey-Mad Women: Emancipatory Strategies in Women's Writing* (1988) • Elise B. Michie, *Outside the Pale: Cultural Exclusion, Gender Difference, and the Victorian Woman Writer* (1993) • Virginia Jill Dix Ghnassia, *Metaphysical Rebellion in the Works of Emily Brontë: A Reinterpretation* (1994) • Joseph Bristow, ed., *Victorian Women Poets: Emily Brontë, Elizabeth Barrett Browning, Christina Rossetti* (1995) • Patsy Stoneman, *Brontë Transformations: The Cultural Dissemination of Jane Eyre and Wuthering Heights* (1996) • Edward Chitham, *The Birth of Wuthering Heights: Emily Brontë at Work* (1998) • Diane Hoevler Long, *Gothic Feminism: The Professionalization of Gender from Charlotte Smith to the Brontës* (1998).

Gwendolyn Brooks

Works by Brooks: See biographical headnote pp. 806-07.

Biography: George E. Kent, *A Life of Gwendolyn Brooks* (1990).

Criticism: *A Life Distilled: Gwendolyn Brooks, Her Poetry and Fiction*, eds. Maria K. Mootry and Gary Smith (1987) • *Say That the River Turns Twice: The Impact of Gwendolyn Brooks*, ed. Haki Madhubuti (1987) • D.W. Melham, *Gwendolyn Brooks: Poetry and the Heroic Voice* (1987) • Betsy Erkkila, *The Wicked Sisters: Women Poets, Literary History, and Discord* (1992) • Stephen Caldwell Wright, *On Gwendolyn Brooks: Reliant*

Contemplation (1995) • Philip Greasley, "Gwendolyn Brooks at Eighty: A Retrospective," *MidAmerica* 23 (1996) • Barbara Johnson, "Apostrophe, Animation, and Abortion," in *Feminisms: An Anthology of Literary Theory and Criticism*, eds. Robin R. Warhol and Diane Price Herndl (1997).

Rosellen Brown

Works by Brown: See biographical headnote pp. 836-37.

Interviews: "An Interview with Rosellen Brown," *The Missouri Review* 17 (1994) • Kay Bonetti, "Rosellen Brown," in *Conversations with American Novelists*, eds. Kay Bonetti et al. (1997).

Criticism: Susan Rubin Suleiman, "Writing and Motherhood," in *The (M)other Tongue: Essays in Feminist Psychoanalytic Interpretation*, eds. Shirley Nelson Garner et al. (1985) • Dee Seligman, "Jewish Mothers' Stories: Rosellen Brown's *The Autobiography of My Mother*," in *Mother Puzzles: Daughters and Mothers in Contemporary American Fiction*, ed. Mickey Pearlman (1989) • Nancy Porter, "Women's Interracial Friendships and Visions of Community in *Meridian*, *The Salt Eaters*, *Civil Wars*, and *Dessa Rose*," in *Tradition and the Talents of Women*, ed. Florence Howe (1991).

Elizabeth Barrett Browning

Works by Browning: See biographical headnote pp. 1152-53.

Editions: *Complete Works of Elizabeth Barrett Browning*, 6 vols., eds. Charlotte Porter and Helen Clarke (1900) • *The Letters of Robert Browning and Elizabeth Barrett Browning, 1845–46*, 2 vols., eds. Meredith Raymond and Mary Rose Sullivan (1964) • *Aurora Leigh and Other Poems*, ed. Cora Kaplan (1978) • *Selected Poems of Elizabeth Barrett Browning*, ed. Margaret Forster (1988).

Biographies: Margaret Forster, *Elizabeth Barrett Browning: A Biography* (1988) • Marjorie Stone, *Elizabeth Barrett Browning* (1995).

Criticism: Sandra M. Gilbert and Susan Gubar, *The Madwoman in the Attic* (1979) • Angela Leighton, *Elizabeth Barrett Browning* (1986) • Deirdre David, *Intellectual Women and Victorian Patriarchy: Harriet Martineau, Elizabeth Barrett Browning, George Eliot* (1987) • Helen Cooper, *Elizabeth Barrett Browning: Woman and Artist* (1988) • Dorothy Mermin, *Elizabeth Barrett Browning: The Origins of a New Poetry* (1989) • Sandra Donaldson, *Elizabeth Barrett Browning: An Annotated Bibliography of the Commentary and Criticism, 1826–1990* (1993) • Joseph Bristow, ed., *Victorian Women Poets: Emily Brontë, Elizabeth Barrett Browning, Christina Rossetti* (1995) • Linda M. Lewis, *Elizabeth Barrett Browning's Spiritual Progress: Face to Face with God* (1998).

Frances Burney

Works by Burney: See biographical headnote pp. 102-03.

Editions: Fanny Burney, *Selected Letters and Journals*, ed. Joyce Hemlow (1986) • *The Early Journals and Letters of Fanny Burney*, ed. Lars Troide (1988).

Biographies: Winifred Gerin, *The Young Fanny Burney* (1961) • Margaret Anne Doody, *Frances Burney: The Life in the Works* (1988).

Criticism: Joseph A. Grau, *Fanny Burney: An Annotated Bibliography* (1981) • Kristina Straub, *Divided Fictions: Fanny Burney and the Feminine Strategy* (1987) • Julia Epstein, *The Iron Pen: Frances Burney and the Politics of Women's Writing* (1989) • Katharine M. Rogers, *Frances Burney: The World of "Female Difficulties"* (1990) • Joanne Cutting-Gray, *Woman as "Nobody" and the Novels of Fanny Burney* (1992) • Lois L. McNeil, *Female Difficulties: Self Dependence in the Novels of Frances Burney* (1993) • Claudia L. Johnson, *Equivocal Beings: Politics, Gender, and Sentimentality in the 1790s* (1995).

Angela Carter

Works by Carter: See biographical headnote pp. 1031-32.

Edition: *Burning Your Boats: The Collected Angela Carter Stories*, ed. Salman Rushdie (1995).

Criticism: Ellen Kronin Rose, "Through the Looking Glass: When Women Tell Fairy Tales," in *The Voyage In: Fictions of Female Development*, eds. Elizabeth Abel and Marianne Hirsch (1983) • Sally Robinson, *Engendering the Subject: Gender and Self-Representation in Contemporary Women's Fiction* (1991) • *Flesh and the Mirror: Essays on the Art of Angela Carter*, ed. Lorna Sage (1994) • Yvonne Martinsson, *Eroticism, Ethics and Reading: Angela Carter in Dialogue with Roland Barthes* (1996) • *Infernal Desires of Angela Carter: Fiction, Femininity, Feminism*, eds. Joseph Bristow and Trev Lynn Broughton (1997) • Alison Lee, *Angela Carter* (1997).

Margaret Cavendish, Duchess of Newcastle

Works by Cavendish: See biographical headnote p. 89.

Biographies: Louisa Costello, *Memoirs of Eminent Englishwomen* (1844) • Kathleen Jones, *A Glorious Fame: The Life of Margaret Cavendish, Duchess of Newcastle, 1623–1673* (1988).

Criticism: Patricia A. Sullivan, "Female Writing Beside the Rhetorical Tradition," *International Journal of Women's Studies* 3 (1981) • Moira Ferguson, "A 'Wise, Wittie and Learned Lady': Margaret Lucas Cavendish," in *Women Writers of the Seventeenth Century*, ed. Katharina M. Wilson (1989) • Catherine Gallagher, "Embracing the Absolute: The Politics of the Female Subject in Seventeenth-century England," *Genders* 1 (1989) • Linda Payne, "Dramatic Dreamscape: Women's Dreams and Utopian Vision in the Works of Margaret Cavendish, Duchess of Newcastle," in *Curtain Calls: British and American Women and the Theater, 1660–1820*, ed. Mary Anne Schofield (1991) • Carol Thomas Neely, "Women/Utopia/Fetish: Disavowal and Satisfied Desire in Margaret Cavendish's *New Blazing World* and Gloria Anzaldúa's *Borderlands/ La Frontera*," in *Heterotopia: Postmodern Utopia and the Body Politic*, ed. Tobin Siebers (1995) • John Rogers, *Matter of Revolution: Science, Poetry, and Politics in the Age of Milton* (1996) • Alice Fulton, *Feeling as a Foreign Language: The Good Strangeness of Poetry* (1999).

Kate Chopin

Works by Chopin: See biographical headnote pp. 695-96.

Editions: *Complete Works of Kate Chopin*, ed. Per Seyersted (1969) • *A Kate Chopin Miscellany*, eds. Per Seyersted and Emily Toth (1979).

Biographies: Per Seyersted, *Kate Chopin: A Critical Biography* (1969) • Emily Toth, *Kate Chopin* (1994).

Criticism: Cynthia Griffin Wolff, "Thanatos and Eros: Kate Chopin's *The Awakening*," *American Quarterly* 25 (1973) • Marlene Springer, *Edith Wharton and Kate Chopin: A Reference Guide* (1976) • Jane P. Tompkins, "*The Awakening*: An Evaluation," *Feminist Studies* 3 (1976) • Priscilla Allen, "Old Critics and New: The Treatment of Chopin's *The Awakening*," in *The Authority of Experience*, eds. Arlyn Diamond and Lee R. Edwards (1977) • Sandra M. Gilbert, "The Second Coming of Aphrodite: Kate Chopin's Fantasy of Desire," *Kenyon Review* 5 (1983) • Linda Wagner Martin, "Recent Books on Kate Chopin," *Mississippi Quarterly* 42 (1989) • *Kate Chopin Reconsidered: Beyond the Bayou*, eds. Lynda S. Boren and Sara deSaussure Davis (1992) • *Critical Essays on Kate Chopin*, ed. Alice Hall Petry (1996) • Janet Beer, *Kate Chopin, Edith Wharton, Charlotte Perkins Gilman: Studies in Short Fiction* (1997).

Barbara Christian

Works by Christian: See biographical headnote pp. 346-47.

Caryl Churchill

Works by Churchill: See biographical headnote pp. 1237-38.

Editions: *Plays: 1* (1983) • *Plays: 2* (1990) • *Churchill Shorts: Short Plays* (1990).

Biography: Geraldine Cousin, *Churchill, the Playwright* (1989).

Criticism: Alisa Solomon, "Witches, Ranters, and the Middle Class: The Plays of Caryl Churchill," *Theater* 12 (1981) • Helene Keyssar, "The Dramas of Caryl Churchill: The Politics of Possibility," *Massachusetts Review* 24 (1983) • Linda Fitzsimmons, "'I Won't Turn Back for You or Anyone': Caryl Churchill's Socialist-Feminist Theatre," *Essays in Theatre* 6 (1987) • Elin Diamond, "(In)Visible Bodies in Churchill's Theater," in *Making a Spectacle: Feminist Essays on Contemporary Women's Theatre*, ed. Lynda Hart (1989) • Linda Fitzsimmons, *File on Churchill* (1989) • Austin E. Quigley, "Stereotype and Prototype: Character in the Plays of Caryl Churchill," in *Feminine Focus: The New Women Playwrights*, ed. Enoch Brater (1989) • Amelia Howe Kritzer, *The Plays of Caryl Churchill: Theatre of Empowerment* (1991) • Elaine Aston, *Caryl Churchill* (1997).

Sandra Cisneros

Works by Cisneros: See biographical headnote p. 576.

Criticism: Jacqueline Doyle, "More Room of Her Own: Sandra Cisneros's *The House on Mango Street*," *MELUS* 19 (1994) • Jean Wyatt, "On Not Being La Malinche: Border Negotiations of Gender in Sandra Cisneros's 'Never Marry a Mexican' and 'Woman Hollering Creek,'" *Tulsa Studies in Women's Literature* 14 (1995) • Maria Gonzalez, "Love and Conflict: Mexican American Women Writers as Daughters," in *Women of Color: Mother-Daughter Relationships in 20th-century Literature*, ed. Elizabeth Brown-Guillory (1996) • Susan E. Griffin, "Resistance and Reinvention in Sandra Cisneros' *Woman Hollering Creek*," in *Ethnicity and the American Short Story*, ed. Julia Brown (1997) • Laura Gutierrez Spencer, "Fairy Tales and Opera: The Fate of the Heroine in the Work of Sandra Cisneros," in *Speaking the Other Self: American Women Writers*, ed. Jeanne Campbell Reisman (1997).

Helene Cixous

Works by Cixous: See biographical headnote pp. 390-91.

Michelle Cliff

Works by Cliff: See biographical headnote pp. 916-17.

Interviews: Judith Raiskin, "The Art of History: An Interview with Michelle Cliff," *The Kenyon Review* 15 (1993) • Meryl F. Schwartz, "An Interview with Michelle Cliff," *Contemporary Literature* 34 (1993).

Criticism: Michelle Cliff, "Clare Savage as a Crossroads Character," in *Caribbean Women Writers*, ed. Selwyn R. Cudjoe (1990) • Francoise Lionnet, "Of Mangoes and Maroons: Language, History, and the Multicultural Subject of Michelle Cliff's *Abeng*," in *De/colonizing the Subject: The Politics of Gender in Women's Autobiography*, eds. Sidonie Smith and Julia Watson (1992) • Maria Helena Lima, "Revolutionary Developments: Michelle Cliff's 'No Telephone to Heaven' and Merle Collins' 'Angel,'" *Ariel* 24 (1993) • Carole Boyce Davies, *Black Women, Writing and Identity: The Migration of the Subject* (1994) • Judith L. Raiskin, *Snow on the Cane Fields: Women's Writing and Creole Subjectivity* (1996) • Suzanne Bost, "Fluidity Without Postmodernism: Michelle Cliff and the 'Tragic Mulatta' Tradition," *African American Review* 32 (1998) • *Postcolonialism and Autobiography: Michelle Cliff, David Dabydeen, Opal Palmer Adisa*, eds. Alfred Hornung and Ernstpeter Ruhe (1998).

Lucille Clifton

Works by Clifton: See biographical headnote p. 818.

Criticism: Audrey McCluskey, "Tell the Good News: A View of the Works of Lucille Clifton" in *Black Women Writers (1950–1980)*, ed. Mari Evans (1984) • Andrea Benton Rushing, "Lucille Clifton: A Changing Voice for Changing Times," in *Coming to Light: American Women Poets in the Twentieth Century*, eds. Diane Wood Middlebrook and Marilyn Yalom (1985) • Sandi

Russell, *Render Me My Song: African-American Women Writers from Slavery to the Present* (1990) • Akasha Hull, "Channeling the Ancestral Muse: Lucille Clifton and Dolores Kendrick," in *Feminist Measures: Soundings in Poetry and Theory*, eds. Lynn Keller and Cristanne Miller (1994) • Akasha Hull, "In Her Own Images: Lucille Clifton and the Bible," in *Dwelling in Possibility: Women Poets and Critics on Poetry*, eds. Yopie Prins and Maerra Shreiber (1997).

Elizabeth Clinton, the Countess of Lincoln

Works by Clinton: See biographical headnote p. 664.

Edition: *The Female Spectator*, eds. Mary R. Mahl and Helene Koon (1977).

Criticism: Christine W. Sizemore, "Early Seventeenth-Century Advice Books: The Female Viewpoint," *South Atlantic Bulletin* 41 (1976) • *The Paradise of Women*, ed. Betty Travitsky (1981) • Hilda Smith, *Reason's Disciples: Seventeenth-Century English Feminists* (1982) • *English Women's Voices*, ed. Charlotte F. Otten (1992) • Virginia Brackett, "*The Countesse of Lincolne's Nurserie* as Inspiration for Anne Bradstreet," *Notes and Queries* 240 (1995) • *Women Writers in Renaissance England*, ed. Randall Martin (1997).

Patricia Hill Collins

Works by Collins: See biographical headnote p. 638.

Kate Daniels

Works by Daniels: See biographical headnote pp. 870-71.

Criticism: Kate Daniels, "Porch Sitting and Southern Poetry," in *The Future of Southern Letters*, eds. Jefferson Humphries and John Lowe (1996).

Rebecca Harding Davis

Works by Davis: See biographical headnote pp. 1168-69.

Biographies: Jean Pfaelzer, "Legacy Profile: Rebecca Harding Davis (1831–1910)," *Legacy* 7 (1990) • Jane Atteridge Rose, *Rebecca Harding Davis* (1993).

Criticism: Jean Pfaelzer, "Rebecca Harding Davis: Domesticity, Social Order, and the Industrial Novel," *International Journal of Women's Studies* 4 (1981) • Jean Fagan Yellin, "The 'Feminization' of Rebecca Harding Davis," *American Literary History* 2 (1990) • Sharon Harris, *Rebecca Harding Davis and American*

Realism (1991) • Jane Attenridge Rose, "The Artist Manqué in the Fiction of Rebecca Harding Davis," in *Writing the Woman Artist: Essays on Poetics, Politics, and Portraiture,* ed. Suzanne Jones (1991).

Ingrid de Kok

Works by de Kok: See biographical headnote pp. 1058-59.

Criticism: Colin Gardner, "Negotiating Poetry: A New Poetry for a New South Africa," *Theoria* 77 (1991) • Mary K. DeShazer, *A Poetics of Resistance: Women Writing from El Salvador, South Africa, and the United States* (1994).

Anita Desai

Works by Desai: See biographical headnote pp. 1022-23.

Criticism: Jayshree Odin, "Gender and Identity in Anita Desai's Novels," *Journal of Commonwealth and Postcolonial Studies* 1 (1993) • Pushpa Naidu Parekh, "Redefining the Postcolonial Female Self: Women in Anita Desai's *Clear Light of Day,*" in *Between the Lines: South Asians and Post-coloniality,* eds. Deepika Bahri and Mary Vasudeva (1996) • Bishnupriya Ghosh, "Feminist Critiques of Nationalism and Communalism from Bangladesh and India: A Transnational Reading," in *Interventions: Feminist Dialogues on Third World Women's Literature and Film,* eds. Bishnupriya Ghosh and Brinda Bose (1997) • Radha Chakravarty, "Figuring the Maternal: 'Freedom' and 'Responsibility' in Anita Desai's Novels," *ARIEL* 29 (1998).

Emily Dickinson

Works by Dickinson: See biographical headnote pp. 966-68.

Editions: *The Letters of Emily Dickinson,* eds. Thomas H. Johnson and Theodora Ward (1958) • *The Complete Poems of Emily Dickinson,* ed. Thomas H. Johnson (1960) • *The Master Letters of Emily Dickinson,* ed. Ralph W. Franklin (1986) • *New Poems of Emily Dickinson,* ed. William H. Shurr et al. (1993).

Biographies: Richard B. Sewell, *The Life of Emily Dickinson* (1974) • Cynthia Griffin Wolff, *Emily Dickinson* (1986).

Bibliographies: Karen Dandurand, *Dickinson Scholarship: An Annotated Bibliography, 1965-1985* (1988) • Jeanetta Boswell, *Emily Dickinson: A Bibliography of Secondary Sources, 1890-1987* (1989) • Joseph Duchac, *The Poems of Emily Dickinson: An Annotated Guide to Commentary Published in English, 1978-1989* (1993).

Criticism: Albert J. Gelpi, *Emily Dickinson: The Mind of the Poet* (1965) • Joanne Feit Diehl, *Dickinson and the Romantic Imagination* (1981) • Barbara Clarke Mossberg, *Emily Dickinson: When a Writer Is a Daughter* (1982) • Suzanne Juhasz, *The Undiscovered Continent: Emily Dickinson and the Space of the Mind* (1983) • Vivian R. Pollok, *Dickinson: The Anxiety of Gender* (1984) • *Emily Dickinson: Modern Critical Views,* ed. Harold Bloom (1985) • Christanne Miller, *Emily Dickinson: A Poet's Grammar* (1987) • Elizabeth Phillips, *Emily Dickinson: Personae and Performance* (1988) • Paula Bennett, *Emily Dickinson: Woman Poet* (1990) • Mary Loeffelholz, *Dickinson and the Boundaries of Feminist Theory* (1990) • Judith Farr, *The Passion of Emily Dickinson* (1992) • Martha Nell Smith, *Rowing in Eden: Rereading Emily Dickinson* (1992) • Dorothy Huff Oberhaus, *Emily Dickinson's Fascicles: Method and Meaning* (1995) • James R. Guthrie, *Emily Dickinson's Vision: Illness and Identity in her Poetry* (1998) • Elizabeth Petrino, *Emily Dickinson and her Contemporaries: Women's Verse in America, 1820-1885* (1998).

Joanne Feit Diehl

Works by Diehl: See biographical headnote p. 1073.

H.D. (Hilda Doolittle)

Works by H.D.: See biographical headnote pp. 1197-98.

Biography: Barbara Guest, *Herself Defined: The Poet H.D. and Her World* (1984).

Bibliography: Michael Boughn, *H.D.: A Bibliography, 1905-1990* (1993).

Criticism: Susan Stanford Friedman, "Who Buried H.D.?" *College English* 36 (1975) • Susan Stanford Friedman, *Psyche Reborn: The Emergence of H.D.* (1981) • *H.D.: Woman and Poet,* ed. Michael King (1986) • Rachel Blau DuPlessis and Susan Stanford Friedman, *Signets: Reading H.D.* (1990) • Susan Stanford Friedman, *Penelope's Web: Gender, Modernity, and H.D.'s Fiction* (1990) • Donna K. Hollenberg, *H.D.: The Poetics of Childbirth and Creativity* (1991) • Dianne Chisholm, *H.D.'s Freudian Poetics: Psychoanalysis in Translation* (1992) • *Richard Aldington and H.D.: The Early Years in Letters,* ed. Caroline Zilboorg (1992) • Susan Edmunds, *Out of Line: History, Psychoanalysis, and Montage in H.D.'s Long Poems* (1994) •

Between History and Poetry: The Letters of H.D. and Norman Holmes Pearson, ed. Donna K. Hollenberg (1997) • Johanna Dehler, *Fragments of Desire: Sapphic Fictions in Works by H.D., Judy Grahn, and Monique Wittig* (1999).

Rita Dove

Works by Dove: See biographical headnote pp. 860-61.

Interview: Steven Schneider, "Coming Home: An Interview with Rita Dove," *The Iowa Review* 19 (1989).

Criticism: Arnold Rampersad, "The Poems of Rita Dove," *Callaloo* 9 (1986) • Ekaterini Georgoudaki, "Rita Dove: Crossing Boundaries," *Callaloo* 14 (1991) • Bonnie Costello, "Scars and Wings: Rita Dove's *Grace Notes*," *Callaloo* 14 (1991) • Patricia Wallace, "Divided Loyalties: Literal and Literary in the Poetry of Lorna Dee Cervantes, Cathy Song, and Rita Dove," *MELUS* 18 (1993) • Helen Vendler, *The Given and the Made: Strategies of Poetic Redefinition* (1995).

Slavenka Drakulić

Works by Drakulić: See biographical headnote pp. 562-63.

Criticism: Gordana P. Crnkovic, "That Other Place," *Stanford Humanities Review* 1 (1990) • Anne Cubilie, "Cosmopolitanism as Resistance: Fragmented Identities, Women's Testimonials and the War in Yugoslavia," in *Critical Ethics: Text, Theory and Responsibility*, eds. Dominic Rainsford and Tim Woods (1999).

Carol Ann Duffy

Works by Duffy: See biographical headnote pp. 333-34.

Biography: Deryn Rees-Jones, *Carol Ann Duffy* (1999).

Criticism: Jane E. Thomas, "'The Intolerable Wrestle with Words': The Poetry of Carol Ann Duffy," *Bête Noire* 6 (1988) • Ian Gregson, *Contemporary Poetry and Postmodernism: Dialogue and Estrangement* (1996).

Alice Dunbar-Nelson

Works by Dunbar-Nelson: See biographical headnote pp. 972-73.

Editions: *An Alice Dunbar-Nelson Reader*, ed. Ruby Ora Williams (1978) • *Give Us Each Day: The Diary of Alice Dunbar-Nelson*, ed. Gloria T. Hull (1985).

Biography: Jean Marie Lutes, "Alice Ruth Moore Dunbar-Nelson," in *Nineteenth-Century American Women Writers: A Bio-Bibliographical Critical Sourcebook*, eds. Denise D. Knight and Emmanuel S. Nelson (1997).

Criticism: Gloria T. Hull, "Alice Dunbar-Nelson: A Personal and Literary Perspective," in *Between Women*, ed. Carol Ascher et al. (1984) • Gloria T. Hull, *Color, Sex, and Poetry: Three Women Writers of the Harlem Renaissance* (1987) • Violet Harrington Bryan, "Race and Gender in the Early Works of Alice Dunbar-Nelson," in *Louisiana Women Writers*, eds. Dorothy H. Brown and Barbara C. Ewell (1992).

Maria Edgeworth

Works by Edgeworth: See biographical headnote pp. 105-06.

Edition: *Letters from England, 1813–1844*, ed. Christina Colvin (1971).

Biographies: Constance Clarke, *Maria Edgeworth, Her Family and Friends* (1950) • Oleta E. M. Harden, *Maria Edgeworth* (1984).

Criticism: Patricia Voss-Clesly, *Tendencies of Character Depiction in the Domestic Novels of Burney, Edgeworth, and Austen* (1979) • Mitzi Myers, "The Dilemmas of Gender as Double-Voiced Narrative; or, Maria Edgeworth Mothers the Bildungsroman," in *The Idea of the Novel in the Eighteenth Century*, ed. Robert W. Uphaus (1988) • Elizabeth Kowalski-Wallace, *Their Fathers' Daughters: Hannah More, Maria Edgeworth, and Patriarchal Complicity* (1991) • Caroline Gonda, *Reading Daughters' Fictions 1709–1834: Novels and Society from Manley to Edgeworth* (1996).

George Eliot

Works by Eliot: See biographical headnote pp. 247-48.

Editions: *The George Eliot Letters*, ed. Gordon S. Haight (1954–1978) • *A Writer's Notebook*, ed. Joseph Wiesenfarth (1981) • *Uncollected Writings*, ed. Joseph Wiesenfarth (1981) • *Collected Poems*, ed. Lucien Jenkins (1989) • *Selected Essays, Poems, and Other Writings*, eds. A.S. Byatt and Nicholas Warren (1990).

Bibliography: *An Annotated Critical Bibliography of George Eliot*, ed. George Levine with Patricia O'Hara (1988).

Biographies: Gordon S. Haight, *George Eliot* (1968) • Ina Taylor, *A Woman of Correspondence: The Life of George Eliot* (1989).

Criticism: Patricia Meyer Spacks, *The Female Imagination* (1975) • Elaine Showalter, *A Literature of Their Own* (1977) • Sandra M. Gilbert and Susan Gubar, *The Madwoman in the Attic* (1979) • Mary Ellen Doyle, *The Sympathetic Response: George Eliot's Fictional Rhetoric* (1981) • Karen S. Mann, *The Language that Makes George Eliot's Fiction* (1983) • Suzanne Graver, *George Eliot and Community* (1984) • Deirdre David, *Intellectual Women and Victorian Patriarchy: Harriet Martineau, Elizabeth Barrett Browning, George Eliot* (1987) • *The Critical Response to George Eliot*, ed. Karen L. Pangello (1994) • *The Transformation of Rage: Mourning and Creativity in George Eliot's Fiction*, ed. Peggy Fitzhugh Johnstone • *George Eliot and the Politics of National Inheritance*, ed. Bernard Semmel (1994) • Carol A. Martin, *George Eliot's Serial Fiction* (1994) • Reina Lewis, *Gendering Orientalism: Race, Femininity and Representation* (1996) • Josephine McDonagh, *George Eliot* (1997).

Elizabeth I

Works by Elizabeth I: See biographical headnote pp. 427-28.

Biographies: Thomas Heywood, *England's Elizabeth* (1631) • Wallace T. MacCaffrey, *Elizabeth I* (1993).

Criticism: Alison Plowden, *Elizabeth Regina: The Age of Triumph, 1588–1603* (1980) • Frances Teague, "Elizabeth I," in *Women Writers of the Renaissance and Reformation*, ed. Katharina M. Wilson (1987) • Susan Frye, *Elizabeth I: The Competition for Representation* (1993) • Susan Doran, *Elizabeth I and Religion, 1558–1603* (1994) • Carole Levin, *Heart and Stomach of a King: Elizabeth I and the Politics of Sex and Power* (1994) • Helen Hackett, *Virgin Mother, Maiden Queen* (1995).

Buchi Emecheta

Works by Emecheta: See biographical headnote p. 1038.

Criticism: Abioseh Michael Porter, "Second Class Citizen: The Point of Departure for Understanding Buchi Emecheta's Major Fiction," *International Fiction Review* 15 (1988) • M.J. Daymond, "Buchi Emecheta, Laughter and Silence: Changes in the Concepts 'Woman' and 'Mother,'" *Journal of Literary Studies* 4 (1988) • Eva Lennox Birch, "Autobiography: The Art of Self-definition," in *Black Women's Writing*, ed. Gina Wisker (1993) • Cynthia Ward, "What They Told Buchi Emecheta: Oral Subjectivity and the Joys of 'Otherhood,'" *PMLA* 105

(1990) • Katherine Fishburn, *Reading Buchi Emecheta: Cross-Cultural Conversations* (1995).

Louise Erdrich

Works by Erdrich: See biographical headnote pp. 1289-90.

Bibliography: Mickey Pearlman, "A Bibliography of Writings About Louise Erdrich," in *American Women Writing Fiction: Memory, Identity, Family, Space* (1989).

Interviews: *Conversations with Louise Erdrich and Michael Dorris*, eds. Allan R. Chavkin and Nancy Feyl Chavkin (1994).

Criticism: Susan Stanford Friedman, "Identity Politics, Syncretism, Catholicism, and Anishanabe Religion in Louise Erdrich's *Tracks*," *Religion and Literature* 26 (1994) • Victoria Brehm, "The Metamorphosis of an Ojibwa Manido," *American Literature* 68 (1996) • Alan Kelie, "Magic Realism and Ethnicity: The Fantastic in the Fiction of Louise Erdrich," *Native American Women in Literature and Culture*, eds. Susan Castillo and Victor M.P. DaRosa (1997) • Jeanne Rosier Smith, *Writing Tricksters: Mythic Gambols in American Ethnic Literature* (1997) • Meldan Tanrisal, "Mother and Child Relationships in the Novels of Louise Erdrich," *American Studies International* 35 (1997) • Tom Berninghausen, "'This Ain't Real Estate': Land and Culture in Louise Erdrich's Chippawa Tetralogy," in *Women, America, and Movement: Narratives of Relocation*, ed. Susan L. Robertson (1998) • *The Chippewa Landscape of Louise Erdrich*, ed. Allen R. Chavkin (1999).

Anne Finch, Countess of Winchilsea

Works by Finch: See biographical headnote pp. 96-97.

Editions: Myra Reynolds, ed., *The Poems of Anne Finch, Countess of Winchilsea* (1903) • Katharine M. Rogers, ed., *Selected Poems of Anne Finch* (1979).

Biography: Barbara McGovern, *Anne Finch and Her Poetry* (1992).

Criticism: Katharine M. Rogers, "An Augustan Woman Poet," in *Shakespeare's Sisters*, eds. Sandra M. Gilbert and Susan Gubar (1979) • Rogers *Before Their Time: Six Women Writers of the Eighteenth Century* (1979) • Ann Messenger, *His and Hers: Essays in Restoration and Eighteenth-century Literature* (1986) • Dorothy Mermin, "Women Becoming Poets: Katherine Philips, Aphra Behn, Anne Finch," *ELH* 57 (1990) • Jean

Mallinson, "Anne Finch: A Woman Poet and the Tradition," in *Gender at Work: Four Women Writers of the Eighteenth Century*, ed. Ann Messenger (1990) • Charles H. Hinnant, *The Poetry of Anne Finch: An Essay in Interpretation* (1994) • Jayne Elizabeth Lewis, "Invading the 'Transparent Laberynth': Anne Finch and the Politics of Translation," in *Dwelling in Possibility: Women Poets and Critics on Poetry*, eds. Yopie Prins and Maerra Shreiber (1997) • Ruth Salvaggio, "Anne Finch Placed and Displaced," in *Early Women Writers: 1600–1720*, ed. Anita Pacheco (1998).

Carolyn Forché

Works by Forché: See biographical headnote pp. 1282-83.

Interviews: "Jill Taft-Kaufman Talks with Carolyn Forché," *Text and Performance Quarterly* 10 (1990) • "Interview with David Montenegro," in *Points of Departure*, ed. David Montenegro (1991).

Criticism: Michael Greer, "Politicizing the Modern: Carolyn Forché in El Salvador and America," *The Centennial Review* 30 (1986) • Carole Stone, "Elegy as Political Expression in Women's Poetry: Ahkmatova, Levertov, Forché," *College Literature* 18 (1991) • Leonora Smith, "Carolyn Forché: Poet of Witness," in *Still the Frame Holds: Essays on Women Poets and Writers*, eds. Sheila Roberts and Yvonne Pacheco Tevis (1993) • Peter Balakian, "Carolyn Forché and the Poetry of Witness: Another View," *Agni* 40 (1994) • Mary K. DeShazer, *A Poetics of Resistance* (1994) • Anite Helle, "Elegy as History: Three Women Poets 'By the Century's Deathbed,'" *South Atlantic Review* 61 (1996).

Janet Frame

Works by Frame: See biographical headnote pp. 1218-19.

Bibliography: Alexander Hart and W.H. New, "Janet Frame: An Enumerative Bibliography to 1990," in *The Ring of Fire: Essays on Janet Frame*, ed. Jeanne Delbaere (1992).

Interview: Elizabeth Alley, "'An Honest Record': An Interview with Janet Frame," in *Landfall: New Zealand Arts and Letters* 45 (1991).

Criticism: Peter Simon, "Janet Frame and the Languages of Autobiography," *Australian and New Zealand Studies in Canada* 5 (1991); Diane Caney, "Janet Frame and *The Tempest*," *Journal of New Zealand Literature* 11 (1993; entire issue devoted to Frame) • Alison Lambert, "The

Memory Flower, the Gravity Star, and the Real World: Janet Frame's *The Carpathians*," in *New Zealand Literature Today*, eds. R.K. Dhawan and Walter Tonetto (1993) • Lorna M. Irvine, *Critical Spaces: Margaret Laurence and Janet Frame* (1995) • Karin Hanssen, *The Unstable Manifold: Janet Frame's Challenge to Determinism* (1996) • Susan Schwartz, "Dancing in the Asylum: The Uncanny Truth of the Madwoman in Janet Frame's Autobiographical Fiction," *ARIEL* 27 (1996) • Valerie Baisnee, *Gendered Resistance: The Autobiographies of Simone de Beauvoir, Maya Angelou, Janet Frame, and Marguerite Duras* (1997).

Margaret Fuller

Works by Fuller: See biographical headnote pp. 955-56.

Editions: *The Letters of Margaret Fuller*, 5 vols., ed. Robert N. Hudspeth (1983–88) • *The Portable Margaret Fuller*, ed. Mary Kelley (1994).

Biographies: Donna Dickenson, *Margaret Fuller: Writing a Woman's Life* (1993) • Bell Gale Chevigny, *The Woman and the Myth: Margaret Fuller's Life and Writings* (1994).

Criticism: Paula Blanchard, *Margaret Fuller, from Transcendentalism to Revolution* (1978) • Margaret Allen, *The Achievement of Margaret Fuller* (1979) • Marie Urbanski, *Margaret Fuller's "Woman in the Nineteenth Century": A Literary Study of Form and Content, of Sources and Influence* (1980) • *Woman in the Nineteenth Century and Other Writings*, ed. Bell Gale Chevigny (1994) • Theresa F. Nicolay, *Gender Roles, Literary Authority, and Three American Writers: Anne Dudley Bradstreet, Mercy Otis Warren, Margaret Fuller Ossoli* (1995).

Sarah Fyge

Works by Fyge: See biographical headnote pp. 1129-30.

Criticism: Jeslyn Medoff, "New Light on Sarah Fyge (Field, Egerton)," *Tulsa Studies in Women's Literature* 1 (1982) • *Kissing the Rod: An Anthology of 17th Century Women's Verse*, ed. Germaine Greer (1988) • Carol Barash, "'The Native Liberty . . . of the Subject': Configurations of Gender and Authority in the Works of Mary Chudleigh, Sarah Fyge Egerton, and Mary Astell," in *Women, Writing, History: 1640–1799*, eds. Isobel Grundy and Susan Wiseman (1992).

Catherine Gallagher

Works by Gallagher: See biographical headnote p. 584.

Charlotte Perkins Gilman

Works by Gilman: See biographical headnote pp. 263-64.

Editions: *The Charlotte Perkins Gilman Reader*, ed. Ann J. Lane (1980) • *Charlotte Perkins Gilman: A Nonfiction Reader*, ed. Larry Ceplair (1991).

Bibliography: Gary Scharnhorst, *Charlotte Perkins Gilman: A Bibliography* (1985).

Biography: Mary A. Hill, *Charlotte Perkins Gilman: The Making of a Radical Feminist, 1860–1896* (1980) • Ann J. Lane, *To "Herland" and Beyond: The Life and Work of Charlotte Perkins Gilman* (1990).

Criticism: Laura E. Donaldson, "The Eve of Destruction: Charlotte Perkins Gilman and the Feminist Re-creation of Paradise," *Women's Studies* 16 (1989) • *Charlotte Perkins Gilman: The Woman and Her Work*, ed. Sheryl L. Meyering (1989) • *Critical Essays on Charlotte Perkins Gilman*, ed. Joanne B. Karpinski (1992) • *The Captive Imagination: A Casebook on "The Yellow Wallpaper"*, ed. Catherine Golden (1992) • Janet Beer, *Kate Chopin, Edith Wharton, and Charlotte Perkins Gilman: Studies in Short Fiction* (1997) • *A Very Different Story: Studies in the Fiction of Charlotte Perkins Gilman*, eds. Val Gough and Jill Rudd (1998) • Thomas Peyser, *Utopia and Cosmopolis: Globalization in the Era of American Literary Realism* (1998).

Susan Glaspell

Works by Glaspell: See biographical headnote pp. 980-81.

Editions: *Plays by Susan Glaspell*, ed. C.W.E. Bigsby (1987) • *Lifted Masks and Other Works*, ed. Eric S. Rabkin (1993).

Bibliography: *Susan Glaspell: A Research and Production Sourcebook*, ed. Mary E. Papke (1993).

Biography: Arthur E. Waterman, *Susan Glaspell* (1966).

Criticism: Christine Dymkowski, "On the Edge: The Plays of Susan Glaspell," *Modern Drama* 31 (1988) • Linda Ben-Zvi, "Susan Glaspell's Contributions to Contemporary Women Playwrights," in *Feminine Focus: The New Women*

Playwrights, ed. Enoch Brater (1989) • Barbara Ozieblo, "Rebellion and Rejection: The Plays of Susan Glaspell," in *Modern American Drama: The Female Canon*, ed. June Schlueter (1990) • Veronica Makowsky, *Susan Glaspell's Century of American Women* (1993) • *Susan Glaspell: Essays on Her Theater and Fiction*, ed. Linda Ben-Zvi (1995) • Barbara Ozieblo, "Susan Glaspell," in *American Drama*, ed. Clive Bloom (1995).

Nadine Gordimer

Works by Gordimer: See biographical headnote pp. 1212-13.

Bibliography: *Nadine Gordimer: A Bibliography of Primary and Secondary Sources, 1937–1992*, ed. Dorothy Driver (1993).

Biography: *Conversations with Nadine Gordimer*, ed. Nancy Topping Bazin (1990) • Carol P. Marsh-Lockett, "Nadine Gordimer (1923–)," in *Postcolonial African Writers: A Bio-Bibliographical Critical Sourcebook*, ed. Pushpa Naidu Parekh et al. (1998).

Criticism: *Critical Essays on Nadine Gordimer*, ed. Rowland Smith (1990) • Stephen Clingman, *The Novels of Nadine Gordimer: History from the Inside* (1993) • Andrew Vogel Ettin, *Betrayals of the Body Politic: The Literary Commitments of Nadine Gordimer* (1993) • *The Later Fiction of Nadine Gordimer*, ed. Bruce Alvin King (1993) • Cherry Clayton, "White Writing and Postcolonial Politics," *ARIEL* 25 (1994) • Dominic Head, *Nadine Gordimer* (1994) • Nancy Topping Bazin, "Southern Africa and the Themes of Madness: Novels by Doris Lessing, Bessie Head, and Nadine Gordimer," in *International Women's Writing: New Landscapes of Identity*, ed. Marjanne E. Gooze (1995) • Barbara Temple-Thurston, *Nadine Gordimer Revisited* (1999).

Joy Harjo

Works by Harjo: See biographical headnote pp. 568-69.

Interviews: *Spiral of Memory: Interviews with Joy Harjo*, ed. Laura Coltelli (1996).

Criticism: Kathleen McNerney Donovan, "Dark Continent/Dark Woman: Transformation and Healing in the Work of Hélène Cixous and Joy Harjo," in *Native American Literatures*, ed. Laura Coltelli (1994) • Jeannie Ludlow, "Working (In) the In-Between: Poetry, Criticism, Interrogation, and Interruption," *Studies in American*

Indian Literatures 6 (1994) • Kristine Holmes, "'This Woman Can Cross Any Line': Feminist Trickster in the Works of Nora Naranjo-Morse and Joy Harjo," *Studies in American Indian Literature* 7 (1995) • Janet McAdams, "Castings for a (New) New World: The Poetry of Joy Harjo," in *Women Poets of the Americas: Toward a Pan-American Gathering*, eds. Jacqueline Vaught Brogan and Cordelia Chavez Candelaria (1999).

Frances E.W. Harper

Works by Harper: See biographical headnote pp. 1163-64.

Editions: *The Complete Poems of Frances E.W. Harper*, ed. Maryemma Graham (1988) • *Three Classic African-American Novels*, ed. Henry Louis Gates, Jr. (1990) • *A Brighter Coming Day: A Frances Ellen Watkins Harper Reader*, ed. Frances Smith Foster (1990) • *Minnie's Sacrifice, Sowing and Reaping, Trial and Triumph: Three Rediscovered Novels*, ed. Frances Smith Foster (1994).

Biography: Gretchen Holbrook Gerzina, "Frances E.W. Harper (1825–1911)," in *Nineteenth-Century American Women Writers: A Bio-Bibliographical Critical Sourcebook*, eds. Denise D. Knight and Emmanuel S. Nelson (1997).

Criticism: Patricia L. Hill, "Let Me Make the Songs for the People: A Study of Frances W. Harper's Poetry," *Black American Literature Forum* 15 (1981) • Elizabeth Aamons, *Conflicting Stories: American Women Writers at the Turn of the Twentieth Century* (1991) • Lauren Berlant, "The Queen of America Goes to Washington City: Harriet Jacobs, Frances Harper, Anita Hill," *American Literature* 65 (1993) • Carla L. Peterson, "'Further Liftings of the Veil,': Gender, Class, and Labor in Frances E.W. Harper's *Iola Leroy*," in *Listening to Silences: New Essays in Feminist Criticism*, eds. Elaine Hedges and Shelley Fisher Fishkin (1994) • Gabrielle P. Foreman, "'Reading Aright': White Slavery, Black Referents, and the Strategy of Histotextuality in *Iola Leroy*," *Yale Journal of Criticism* 10 (1997).

Mary Hays

Works by Hays: See biographical headnote pp. 1140-41.

Criticism: Katharine M. Rogers, "The Contribution of Mary Hays," *Prose Studies* 10 (1987) • Gary Kelly, *Women, Writing, and Revolution, 1790–1827* (1993) • Eleanor Ty, *Unsex'd Revolutionaries: Five Women Novelists of the 1790s* (1993) • Tilottama Rajan, "Autonarration and Genotext in Mary Hays' *Memoirs of Emma Courtney*," in *Romanticism, History and the Possibilities of Genre: Re-Forming Literature, 1789–1837*, eds. Tilottama Rajan and Julia M. Wright (1998).

Eliza Haywood

Works by Haywood: See biographical headnote pp. 498-99.

Editions: *The Plays of Eliza Haywood*, ed. Valerie C. Rudolph (1983) • *The Masquerade Novels of Eliza Haywood*, ed. Mary Anne Schofield (1986) • *Selections from "The Female Spectator*," ed. Gabrielle M. Firmager (1993).

Biography: Mary Anne Schofield, *Eliza Haywood* (1983).

Criticism: Mary Anne Schofield, "Exposé of the Popular Heroine: The Female Protagonists of Eliza Haywood," *Studies in Eighteenth-Century Culture* 12 (1983) • Kathryn Shevelow, "Rewriting the Moral Essay: Eliza Haywood's Female Spectator," *Reader* 13 (1985) • Ros Ballaster, *Seductive Forms: Women's Amatory Fiction from 1684–1740* (1992) • William B. Warner, "Formulating Fiction: Romancing the General Reader in Early Modern Britain," in *Cultural Institutions of the Novel*, eds. Deidre Lynch and William B. Warner (1996) • Kathryn R. King, "Spying upon the Conjurer: Haywood, Curiosity, and 'the Novel' in the 1720s," *Studies in the Novel* 30 (1998) • Karen Haywood, "Eliza Haywood and the Gender of Print," *Eighteenth Century: Theory and Interpretation* 38 (1997).

Bessie Head

Works by Head: See biographical headnote pp. 820-22.

Bibliography: *Bessie Head: A Bibliography*, ed. Craig Mackenzie (1992).

Biographies: Craig Mackenzie, *Bessie Head: An Introduction* (1989) • Virginia Uzoma Ola, *The Life and Work of Bessie Head* (1994).

Criticism: Susan Gardiner, "Bessie Head: Production Under Drought Conditions," in *Women and Writing in South Africa: A Critical Anthology*, ed. Cherry Clayton (1989) • Dorothy Driver, "Reconstructing the Past, Shaping the Future: Bessie Head and the Question of Feminism in a New South Africa," in *Black Women's Writing*, ed. Gina Wisker (1993) • Nancy Topping Bazin, "Southern Africa and the Themes of Madness: Novels by Doris Lessing, Bessie Head, and Nadine Gordimer," in *International Women's*

Writing: New Landscapes of Identity, ed. Marjanne E. Gooze (1997) • Huma Ibrahim, Bessie Head: Subversive Identities in Exile (1996) • A Gesture of Belonging, ed. Randolph Vigne (1997) • Craig Mackenzie, Bessie Head (1999).

Felicia Hemans

Works by Hemans: See biographical headnote pp. 687-88.

Criticism: Kathleen Hickok, Representations of Women: Nineteenth-Century British Women's Poetry (1984) • Norma Clarke, Ambitious Heights: Writing, Friendship, Love: The Jewsbury Sisters, Felicia Hemans, and Jane Welsh Carlyle (1990) • Tricia Lootens, "Hemans and Home: Victorianism, Feminine 'Internal Enemies,' and the Domestication of National Identity," PMLA 109 (1994) • Jerome J. McGann, "Literary History, Romanticism, and Felicia Hemans," in Re-Visioning Romanticism: British Women Writers, 1776–1837, eds. Carol Shiner Wilson and Joel Haefner (1994) • Nanora Sweet, "History, Imperialism, and the Aesthetics of the Beautiful: Hemans and the Post-Napoleonic Moment," in At the Limits of Romanticism, eds. Mary A. Favret and Nicola J. Watson (1994) • Susan J. Wolfson, "'Domestic Affections' and 'the Spear of Minerva': Felicia Hemans and the Dilemma of Gender," in Re-Visioning Romanticism (1994) • Paula R. Feldman, "The Poet and the Profits: Felicia Hemans and the Literary Marketplace," Keats Shelley Journal 46 (1997) • Karen Eubanks, "Minerva's Veil: Hemans, Critics, and the Construction of Gender," European Romantic Review 8 (1997).

Mary Sidney Herbert

Works by Herbert: See biographical headnote pp. 933-34.

Editions: The Psalms of Sir Philip Sidney and the Countess of Pembroke, ed. J.C.A. Rathbone (1963) • The Triumph of Death and Other Unpublished and Uncollected Poems, ed. G.F. Waller (1977).

Biography: Frances B. Young, Mary Sidney, Countess of Pembroke (1912).

Criticism: G. F. Waller, Mary Sidney, Countess of Pembroke, a Critical Study of Her Writings and Literary Milieu (1979) • Margaret Hannay, "'Do What Men May Sing': Mary Sidney and the Tradition of Admonitory Dedication," in Silent but for the Word: Tudor Women as Patrons, Translators, and Writers of

Religious Works, ed. Margaret Hannay (1985) • Mary Ellen Lamb, Gender and Authorship in the Sidney Circle (1990) • Mary Sidney Herbert, ed. Gary Waller (1996) • Collected Works of Mary Sidney Herbert, Countess of Pembroke, ed. Margaret Hannay (1998) • Three Tragedies by Renaissance Women, ed. Diane Purkiss (1998).

bell hooks

Works by hooks: See biographical headnote pp. 72-73.

Criticism: Marilyn Edelstein, "Resisting Postmodernism: Or, 'A Postmodern Resistance': bell hooks and the Theory Debates," Other Sisterhoods, ed. Sandra Kumamoto Stanley (1998).

Keri Hulme

Works by Hulme: See biographical headnote pp. 853-54.

Interview: "Keri Hulme," Spiritcarvers: Interviews with Eighteen Writers from New Zealand, ed. Antonella Sarti (1994).

Criticism: Giovanna Covi, "Keri Hulme's The Bone People: A Critique of Gender," in Imagination and the Creative Impulse in the New Literatures in English, eds. M.T. Bindella and G.V. Davis (1993) • Margery Fee, "Who Can Write as Other?" in The Postcolonial Studies Reader, ed. Bill Ashcroft et al. (1995) • Gay Wilentz, "Instruments of Change: Healing Cultural Dis-Ease in Keri Hulme's The Bone People," Literature and Medicine 14 (1995).

Zora Heale Hurston

Works by Hurston: See biographical headnote pp. 288-89.

Bibliography: Adele S. Newson, Zora Neale Hurston: A Reference Guide (1987).

Edition: I Love Myself When I am Laughing . . . And Then Again When I Am Looking Mean and Impressive: A Zora Neale Hurston Reader, ed. Alice Walker (1979).

Biographies: Robert E. Hemenway, Zora Neale Hurston (1977) • Janelle Yates, Zora Neale Hurston: A Storyteller's Life (1993).

Criticism: Cheryl A. Wall, "Zora Neale Hurston: Changing Her Own Words," in American Novelists Revisited: Essays in Feminist Criticism, ed. Fritz Fleischmann (1982) • Karla F. C. Holloway, The Character of the Word: The Texts of Zora Neale Hurston (1987) • New Essays on Their Eyes Were Watching God, ed. Michael

Awkward (1990) • *Zora Neale Hurston: Critical Perspectives Past and Present*, eds. Henry Louis Gates, Jr. and Anthony Appiah (1993) • Mae Gwendolyn Henderson, "Speaking in Tongues: Dialogics, Dialectics, and the Black Woman Writer's Literary Tradition," in *Aesthetics in Feminist Perspective*, eds. Hilde Hein and Carolyn Korsmeyer (1993) • *Alice Walker and Zora Neale Hurston: The Common Bond*, ed. Lillie P. Howard (1993) • Janet Carter-Sigglow, *Making Her Way with Thunder: A Reappraisal of Zora Neale Hurston's Narrative Art* (1995) • Cheryl A. Wall, *Women of the Harlem Renaissance* (1995) • Lynda M. Hill, *Social Rituals and the Verbal Art of Zora Neale Hurston* (1996) • Trudier Harris, *Power of the Porch: The Storyteller's Craft in Zora Neale Hurston, Gloria Naylor, and Randall Kenan* (1996) • Yvonne Johnson, *Voices of African-American Women: The Use of Narrative and Authorial Voice in the Works of Harriet Jacobs, Zora Neale Hurston, and Alice Walker* (1998) • Susan E. Meisenhelder, *Hitting a Straight Lick with a Crooked Stick: Race and Gender in the Work of Zora Neale Hurston* (1998).

Harriet Jacobs

Works by Jacobs: See biographical headnote pp. 506-07.

Edition: *Incidents in the Life of a Slave Girl, Written by Herself*, ed. Jean Fagan Yellin (1987).

Biography: Jean Fagan Yellin, "Harriet Jacobs' Family History," *American Literature* 66 (1994).

Criticism: Mary Helen Washington, *Invented Lives: Narratives of Black Women, 1860–1960* (1987) • Valerie Smith, *Self-Discovery and Authority in Afro-American Narrative* (1988) • Frances Smith Foster, *Written by Herself: Literary Production of African-American Women, 1746–1892* (1993) • Carla Kaplan, "Narrative Contracts and Emancipatory Readers: *Incidents in the Life of a Slave Girl*," *The Yale Journal of Criticism* 6 (1993) • *Harriet Jacobs and Incidents in the Life of a Slave Girl: New Critical Readings*, eds. Deborah M. Garfield and Rafia Zafar (1996) • Carla Kaplan, *The Erotics of Talk: Women's Writing and Feminist Paradigms* (1996) • Yvonne Johnson, *Voices of African-American Women: The Use of Narrative and Authorial Voice in the Works of Harriet Jacobs, Zora Neale Hurston, and Alice Walker* (1998).

June Jordan

Works by Jordan: See biographical headnote pp. 1064-65.

Julian of Norwich

Works by Julian: See biographical headnote pp. 654-55.

Edition: *A Book of Showings*, eds. Edmund Colledge and James Walsh (1978).

Criticism: Jennifer P. Hummel, "God Is Our Mother": *Julian of Norwich and the Medieval Image of Feminine Divinity* (1982) • Grace Jantzen, *Julian of Norwich: Mystic and Theologian* (1988) • Lynn Staley Johnson, "The Trope of the Scribe and the Question of Literary Authority in the Works of Julian of Norwich and Margery Kempe," *Speculum* 66 (1991) • Frances Beer, *Women and Mystical Experience in the Middle Ages* (1992) • Elizabeth Robertson, "Medieval Medical Views of Women and Female Spirituality in the *Ancrene Wisse* and Julian of Norwich's *Showings*," in *Feminist Approaches to the Body in Medieval Literature*, eds. Linda Lomperis and Sarah Stanbury (1993) • Denise N. Baker, *Julian of Norwich's Showings: From Vision to Book* (1994) • Sheila Upjohn, *Why Julian Now? A Voyage of Discovery* (1997) • *Julian of Norwich: A Book of Essays*, ed. Sandra J. McEntire (1998).

Jackie Kay

Works by Kay: See biographical headnote pp. 578-79.

Criticism: Ian Gregson, *Contemporary Poetry and Postmodernism: Dialogue and Estrangement* (1996).

Margery Kempe

Works by Kempe: See biographical headnote pp. 419-20.

Edition: *Margery Kempe: A Book of Essays*, ed. Sandra J. McEntire (1992).

Biography: Clarissa W. Atkinson, *Mystic and Pilgrim: The Book and the World of Margery Kempe* (1983).

Criticism: Lynn Staley Johnson, "The Trope of the Scribe and the Question of Literary Authority in the Works of Julian of Norwich and Margery Kempe," *Speculum* 66 (1991) • Karma Lochrie, *Margery Kempe and the Translations of the Flesh* (1991) • Wendy Harding, "Body into Text: *The Book of Margery Kempe*," in *Feminist Approaches to the Body in Medieval Literature*, eds. Linda Lomperis and Sarah Stanbury (1993) • Lynn Staley Johnson, *Margery Kempe's Dissenting Fictions* (1994) • Verena A. Neuberger, *Margery Kempe: A Study in Early*

English Feminism (1994) • Margaret Gallyon, Margery Kempe of Lynn and Medieval England (1995) • Santha Bhattacharji, God Is an Earthquake: The Spirituality of Margery Kempe (1997) • Rosalynn Voaden, God's Words, Women's Voices: The Discernment of Spirit in the Writings of Late-Medieval Women Visionaries (1999).

Anne Killigrew

Works by Killigrew: See biographical headnote pp. 93-94.

Criticism: Ann Messenger, His and Hers: Essays in Restoration and Eighteenth-Century Literature (1986) • Kristina Straub, "Indecent Liberties with a Poet: Audience and the Metaphor of Rape in Killigrew's 'Upon the Saying that My Verses . . .' and Pope's 'Arbuthnot,'" Tulsa Studies in Women's Literature 6 (1987) • Elaine Hobby, Virtue of Necessity: English Women's Writing, 1646–1688 (1988).

Jamaica Kincaid

Works by Kincaid: See biographical headnote pp. 1043-44.

Biographies: Selwyn R. Cudjoe, "Jamaica Kincaid and the Modernist Project: An Interview," in Caribbean Women Writers, ed. Selwyn R. Cudjoe (1990) • Diane Simmons, Jamaica Kincaid (1994).

Criticism: Gay Wilentz, "English is a Foreign Anguish: Caribbean Writers and the Disruption of the Colonial Canon," in Decolonizing Tradition: New Views of Twentieth-Century "British" Literary Canons, ed. Karen R. Lawrence (1992) • Moira Ferguson, Jamaica Kincaid: Where the Land Meets the Body (1994) • Merle Hodge, "Caribbean Writers and the Caribbean Language: A Study of Jamaica Kincaid's Annie John," in Winds of Change: The Transforming Voices of Caribbean Women Writers and Scholars, ed. Linda Strong-Leek (1998) • Diane Simmons, "Coming-of-Age in the Snare of History: Jamaica Kincaid's The Autobiography of My Mother," in The Girl: Constructions of the Girl in Contemporary Fiction by Women, ed. Ruth O. Saxton (1998).

Maxine Hong Kingston

Works by Kingston: See biographical headnote pp. 307-08.

Biographies: Shelley Fisher Fishkin, "An Interview with Maxine Hong Kingston," American Literary History 3 (1991) • Conversations with Maxine Hong Kingston, eds. Paul Skenazy and

Tera Martin (1998) • Diane Simmons, Maxine Hong Kingston (1999).

Criticism: Sidonie Smith, A Poetics of Women's Autobiography: Marginality and the Fictions of Self-Representation (1987) • Modern Chinese Women Writers: Critical Appraisals, ed. Michael S. Duke (1989) • Amy Ling, Between Worlds: Women Writers of Chinese Ancestry (1990) • King-kok Cheung, Articulate Silences: Hisaye Yamamoto, Maxine Hong Kingston, Joy Kogawa (1993) • Jeanne Rosier Smith, Writing Tricksters: Mythic Gambols in American Ethnic Literature (1997) • Critical Essays on Maxine Hong Kingston, ed. Laura E. Skandera-Trombley (1998) • Maxine Hong Kingston's The Woman Warrior: A Casebook, ed. Sau-ling Cynthia Wong (1999).

Irena Klepfisz

Works by Klepfisz: See biographical headnote pp. 1268-69.

Biography: Michelle Keventner, "Irena Klepfisz," in Contemporary Lesbian Writers of the United States: A Bio-Bibliographical Critical Sourcebook, ed. Sandra Pollock et al. (1993).

Criticism: Irena Klepfisz, "Forging a Woman's Link in Di Goldene Keyt: Some Possibilities for Jewish American Poetry," in Conversant Essays: Contemporary Poets on Poetry, ed. James McCorkle (1990) • James McCorkle, "Contemporary Poetics and History: Pinsky, Klepfisz and Rothenberg," The Kenyon Review 14 (1992) • Adrienne Rich, "'History Stops for No One,'" What Is Found There: Notebooks on Poetry and Politics (1993) • Jane Hedley, "Nepantilist Poetics: Narrative and Cultural Identity in the Mixed-Language Writings of Irena Klepfisz and Gloria Anzaldúa," Narrative 4 (1996) • Maerra Y. Shreiber, "The End of Exile: Jewish Identity and Its Diasporic Poetics," PMLA 113 (1998).

Ellen Kuzwayo

Works by Kuzwayo: See biographical headnote pp. 1112-13.

Biographies: "Interview with Ellen Kuzwayo," in Between the Lines, eds. Cherry Clayton and Craig MacKenzie (1989) • Lindsay Pentolfe Algerter, "Ellen Kuzwayo (1914–)," in Post-colonial African Writers: A Bio-Bibliographical Critical Source Book, eds. Pushpa Naidu Parekh et al. (1998).

Criticism: Arlene A. Elder, "'Who Can Take the Multitude and Lock It in a Cage?': Noemia De Sousa, Micere Mugo, Ellen Kuzwayo: Three African Women's Voices of Resistance," in Moving Beyond Boundaries, II: Black Women's

Diasporas, ed. Carole Boyce Davies (1994) • Julie Phelps Dietche, "Voyaging Toward Freedom: New Voices from South Africa," *Research in African Literatures* 26 (1995) • Carmela J. Garritano, "At an Intersection of Humanism and Postmodernism: A Feminist Reading of Ellen Kuzwayo's *Call Me Woman*," *Research in African Literatures* 28 (1997).

Aemelia Lanyer

Works by Lanyer: See biographical headnote pp. 936-37.

Edition: *The Poems of Aemilia Lanyer*, ed. Susanne Woods (1993).

Biography: Susanne Woods, *Aemilia Lanyer: A Renaissance Woman Poet* (1999).

Criticism: Barbara K. Lewalski, "Of God and Good Women: The Poems of Aemilia Lanyer," in *Silent but for the Word: Tudor Women as Patrons, Translators, and Writers of Religious Works*, ed. Margaret Hannay (1985) • Elaine V. Beilin, *Redeeming Eve: Women Writers of the English Renaissance* (1987) • Wendy Wall, "Our Bodies/Our Texts? Renaissance Women and the Trials of Authorship," in *Anxious Power: Reading, Writing, and Ambivalence in Narrative by Women*, eds. Carol J. Singley and Susan E. Sweeney (1993) • Janel Mueller, "The Feminist Poetics of Aemilia Lanyer's "Salve Deus Rex Judaeorum," in *Feminist Measures: Soundings in Poetry and Theory*, eds. Lynn Keller and Cristanne Miller (1994) • *Aemilia Lanyer: Gender, Genre, and the Canon*, ed. Marshall Grossman (1998).

Dorothy Leigh

Works by Leigh: See biographical headnote pp. 660-61.

Edition: *A Paradise of Women*, ed. Betty Travitsky (1981).

Criticism: Christine W. Sizemore, "Early Seventeenth-century Advice Books: The Female Viewpoint," *South Atlantic Bulletin* 41 (1976) • *English Women's Voices, 1540–1700*, ed. Charlotte F. Otten (1992) • *Women Writers in Renaissance England*, ed. Randall Martin (1997).

Leoba of England and Germany

Works by Leoba: See biographical headnote pp. 76-77.

Biography: *The Anglo-Saxon Missionaries in Germany*, ed. C.H. Talbot (1954).

Criticism: Christine B. Fell, "Some Implications of the Boniface Correspondence," in *New Readings on Women in Old English Literature*, eds. Helen Damico and Alexandra Hennessey Olsen (1990) • Marcelle Thiebaux, ed., *The Works of Medieval Women: An Anthology*, 2nd ed. (1994).

Doris Lessing

Works by Lessing: See biographical headnote pp. 1010-12.

Edition: *The Doris Lessing Reader* (1989).

Biographies: Lorna Sage, *Doris Lessing* (1983) • Mona Kapp, *Doris Lessing* (1984) • Margaret Moan Rowe, *Doris Lessing* (1994).

Criticism: *Doris Lessing: Critical Essays*, eds. Annis Pratt and L.S. Dembo (1974) • Roberta Rubenstein, *The Novelistic Vision of Doris Lessing* (1979) • *Notebooks, Memoirs, Archives: Reading and Rereading Doris Lessing*, ed. Jenny Taylor (1982) • Katherine Fishburn, *The Unexpected Universe of Doris Lessing: A Study in Narrative Technique* (1985) • *Critical Essays on Doris Lessing*, eds. Claire Sprague and Virginia Tiger (1990) • *In Pursuit of Doris Lessing: Nine Nations Reading*, ed. Claire Sprague (1990) • Gayle Greene, *Doris Lessing: The Poetics of Change* (1994) • *Woolf and Lessing: Breaking the Mold*, eds. Ruth Sexton and Jean Tobin (1994) • Nancy Topping Bazin, "Southern Africa and the Themes of Madness: Novels by Doris Lessing, Bessie Head, and Nadine Gordimer," in *International Women's Writing: New Landscapes of Identity*, ed. Marjanne E. Gooze (1995) • Roxanne J. Fand, *The Dialogic Self: Reconstructing Subjectivity in Woolf, Lessing, Atwood* (1999).

Anne Lock

Works by Lock: See biographical headnote pp. 81-82.

Edition: *Meditation of a Penitent Sinner: Anne Locke's Sonnet Sequence with Locke's Epistles*, ed. Kel Parsons Morin (1997).

Biography: Susan M. Felch, "'Deir Sister': The Letters of John Knox to Anne Vaughan Lok," *Renaissance and Reformation* 19 (1995).

Criticism: Patrick Collinson, *The Elizabethan Puritan Movement* (1967) • Michael R. G. Spiller, *The Development of the Sonnet* (1992) • Margaret P. Hannay, "'Strengthning the Walles of . . . Ierusalem': Anne Vaughan Lok's Dedication to the Countess of Warwick," *ANQ* 5 (1992) • Michael R. G. Spiller, "A Literary 'First': The Sonnet Sequence of Anne Lock," *Renaissance Studies* 11 (1997).

Audre Lorde

Works by Lorde: See biographical headnote pp. 535-36.

Interview: "Audre Lorde," in *Black Women Writers at Work*, ed. Claudia Tate (1983).

Criticism: R.G. Stepto, "The Phenomenal Woman and the Severed Daughter," *Parnassus* 8 (1980) • *Black Women Writers (1950–1980)*, ed. Mari Evans (1984) • Mary K. DeShazer, *Inspiring Women: Reimagining the Muse* (1986) • Gloria T. Hull, "Living on the Line: Audre Lorde and *Our Dead Behind Us*," in *Changing Our Words: Essays on Criticism, Theory, and Writing by Black Women*, ed. Cheryl Wall (1989) • Estella Lauter, "Re-Visioning Creativity: Audre Lorde's Refiguration of Eros as the Black Mother Within," in *Writing the Woman Artist: Essays on Poetics, Politics, and Portraiture*, ed. Suzanne W. Jones (1991) • Anna Wilson, "Audre Lorde and the African-American Tradition: When the Family Is Not Enough," in *New Lesbian Criticism: Literary and Cultural Readings*, ed. Sally Munt (1992) • Erin G. Carlson, "*Zami* and the Politics of Plural Identity," in *Sexual Practice, Textual Theory: Lesbian Cultural Criticism*, eds. Susan J. Wolfe and Julia Penelope (1993) • Eva Lennox Birch, *Black Women's Writing: a Quilt of Many Colors* (1994).

Nancy Mairs

Works by Mairs: See biographical headnote pp. 405-06.

Criticism: Jeanne Braham, "A Lens of Empathy," *Inscribing the Daily*, ed. Cynthia A Huff and Suzanne L. Bunkers (1996).

Delarivier Manley

Works by Manley: See biographical headnote pp. 494-95.

Edition: *The Novels of Mary Delarivier Manley, 1705–1714*, ed. P. Koster (1971).

Biography: *A Woman of No Character: An Autobiography of Mrs. Manley*, ed. Fidelis Morgan (1986).

Criticism: Constance Clark, *Three Augustan Women Playwrights* (1986) • Ros Ballaster, *Seductive Forms: Women's Amatory Fiction, 1684–1740* (1992) • Caroline Gonda, *Reading Daughters' Fictions, 1709–1834: Novels and Society from Manley to Edgeworth* (1996) • Paula McDowell, *The Women of Grub Street: Press, Politics, and Gender in the London Literary Marketplace, 1678–1730* (1998).

Katherine Mansfield

Works by Mansfield: See biographical headnote pp. 996-97.

Editions: *Letters and Journals of Katherine Mansfield*, ed. C.K. Stead (1977) • *The Collected Letters of Katherine Mansfield*, 3 vols., eds. Vincent O'Sullivan and Margaret Scott (1984).

Bibliography: *A Bibliography of Katherine Mansfield*, ed. Brownlee Jean Kirkpatrick (1989).

Biographies: Jeffrey Meyers, *Katherine Mansfield: A Biography* (1978) • Anthony Alpers, *The Life of Katherine Mansfield* (1980).

Criticism: Gillian Boddy, *Katherine Mansfield: The Woman and the Writer* (1988) • Heather Murray, *Double Lives: Women in the Stories of Katherine Mansfield* (1990) • Sydney Janet Kaplan, *Katherine Mansfield and the Origins of Modernist Fiction* (1991) • *Critical Essays on Katherine Mansfield*, ed. Rhoda B. Nathan (1993) • *Katherine Mansfield: In from the Margin*, ed. Roger Robinson (1994) • Pamela Dunbar, *Radical Mansfield: Double Discourse in Katherine Mansfield's Stories* (1997) • Angela Smith, *Katherine Mansfield and Virginia Woolf: A Public of Two* (1999).

Harriet Martineau

Works by Martineau: See biographical headnote pp. 1147-48.

Edition: *Harriet Martineau: Selected Letters*, ed. Valerie Sanders (1990).

Biography: Gillian Thomas, *Harriet Martineau* (1985).

Criticism: Valerie Pichanick, *Harriet Martineau, The Woman and Her Work, 1802–76* (1980) • Valerie Sanders, *Reason over Passion: Harriet Martineau and the Victorian Novel* (1986) • Deirdre David, *Intellectual Women and Victorian Patriarchy: Harriet Martineau, Elizabeth Barrett Browning, George Eliot* (1987) • Linda H. Peterson, "Harriet Martineau: Masculine Discourse, Female Sage," in *Victorian Sages and Cultural Discourse: Renegotiating Gender and Power*, ed. Thais E. Morgan (1990) • Elaine Freedgood, "Banishing Panic: Harriet Martineau and the Popularization of Political Economy," *Victorian Studies* 39 (1995) • Shelagh Hunter, *Harriet Martineau: The Poetics of Moralism* (1995).

Matilda, Queen of England

Works by Matilda: See biographical headnote pp. 78-79.

Criticism: Marcelle Thiebaux, ed., *The Works of Medieval Women: An Anthology*, 2nd ed. (1994).

Medbh McGuckian

Works by McGuckian: See biographical headnote p. 331.

Interview: Susan Shaw Sailer, "An Interview with Medbh McGuckian," *Michigan Quarterly Review* 32 (1993).

Criticism: Molly Bendall, "Flower Logic: The Poems of Medbh McGuckian," *The Antioch Review* 48 (1990) • Thomas Docherty, "Initiations, Tempers, Seductions: Postmodern McGuckian," in *The Chosen Ground: Essays on Contemporary Poetry of Northern Ireland*, ed. Neil Corcoran (1992) • Susan Porter, "The 'Imaginative Space' of Medbh McGuckian," in *International Women's Writing: New Landscapes of Identity*, ed. Marjanne E. Gooze (1995) • Patricia Boyle Haberstroh, *Women Creating Women: Contemporary Irish Women Poets* (1996) • Mary O'Connor, "'Rising Out': Medbh McGuckian's Destabilizing Poetics," *Eire Ireland* 30 (1996) • Guinn Batten, "'The More with Which We Are Connected': The Muse of the Minus in the Poetry of McGuckian and Kinsella," in *Gender and Sexuality in Modern Ireland*, eds. Anthony Bradley and Maryann Gialanella Valiulis (1997) • *The Wake Forest Book of Irish Women Poets*, ed. Peggy O'Brien (1999).

Gcina Mhlophe

Works by Mhlophe: See biographical headnote pp. 336-37.

Criticism: Mary K. DeShazer, *A Poetics of Resistance* (1994).

Edna St. Vincent Millay

Works by Millay: See biographical headnote pp. 529-30.

Editions: *Letters of Edna St. Vincent Millay*, ed. Allan Ross McDougal (1952) • *Collected Poems: Edna St. Vincent Millay*, ed. Norma Millay (1956) • *Selected Poems: The Centenary Edition*, ed. Colin Falck (1991).

Bibliography: Judith Nierman, *Edna St. Vincent Millay: A Reference Guide* (1977).

Biographies: Anne Cheney, *Millay in Greenwich Village* (1975) • Norman A. Brittin, *Edna St. Vincent Millay* (1982).

Criticism: Jane Stanbrough, "Edna St. Vincent Millay and the Language of Vulnerability," in *Shakespeare's Sisters*, eds. Sandra M. Gilbert and Susan Gubar (1979) • Debra Fried, "Andromeda Unbound: Gender and Genre in Millay's Sonnets," *Twentieth-Century Literature* 32 (1986) • Suzanne Clark, "The Unwarranted Discourse: Sentimental Community, Modernist Women, and the Case of Millay," *Genre* 20 (1987) • William Drake, *The First Wave: Women Poets in America, 1915–1945* (1987) • Suzanne Clark, *Sentimental Modernism: Women Writers and the Revolution of the Word* (1991) • Cheryl Walker, *Masks Outrageous and Austere: Culture, Psyche, and Persona in Modern Women Poets* (1991) • *Critical Essays on Edna St. Vincent Millay*, ed. William B. Thesing (1993) • Sandra M. Gilbert and Susan Gubar, *Letters from the Front* (1994) • *Millay at 100: A Critical Reappraisal*, ed. Diane P. Freedman (1995).

Mary Wortley Montagu

Works by Montagu: See biographical headnote pp. 672-73.

Editions: *Essays and Poems of Lady Mary Wortley Montagu*, eds. Isobel Grundy and Robert Halsband (1977) • *Turkish Embassy Letters*, ed. Malcolm Jack (1993).

Biography: Isobel Grundy, *Lady Mary Wortley Montagu* (1999).

Criticism: Jill Rubenstein, "Women's Biography as a Family Affair: Lady Louisa Stuart's 'Biographical Anecdotes' of Lady Wortley Montagu," *Prose Studies: History, Theory, Criticism* 9 (1986) • Cynthia Wall, "Editing Desire: Pope's Correspondence with (and without) Lady Mary," *Philological Quarterly* 71 (1992) • Isobel Grundy, "'Trash, Trumpery, and Idle Time': Lady Mary Wortley Montagu and Fiction," *Eighteenth-Century Fiction* 5 (1993) • Jill Campbell, "Lady Wortley Montagu and the Historical Machinery of Female Identity," in *History, Gender, and Eighteenth-Century Literature*, ed. Beth Fowkes Tobin (1994) • Cynthia Lowenthal, *Lady Mary Wortley Montagu and the Eighteenth-Century Familiar Letter* (1994).

Marianne Moore

Works by Moore: See biographical headnote pp. 990-91.

Edition: *The Complete Poems of Marianne Moore* (1967) • *The Complete Prose of Marianne Moore*, ed. Patricia C. Willis (1986).

Bibliography: *Marianne Moore: A Reference Guide*, ed. Craig S. Abbot (1978).

Biography: Charles Molesworth, *Marianne Moore: A Literary Life* (1990).

Criticism: Pamela W. Hadas, *Marianne Moore, Poet of Affection* (1977) • Bonnie Costello, *Marianne Moore: Imaginary Possessions* (1981) • Elizabeth Phillips, *Marianne Moore* (1982) • Taffy Martin, *Marianne Moore: Subversive Modernist* (1986) • Lynn Keller, *Re-Making It New: Contemporary American Poetry and the Modernist Tradition* (1987) • Patricia C. Willis, *Marianne Moore: Vision into Verse* (1987) • *Marianne Moore: The Art of a Modernist*, ed. Joseph Parisi (1990) • *Marianne Moore: Woman and Poet*, ed. Patricia C. Willis (1990) • Joanne Feit Diehl, *Elizabeth Bishop and Marianne Moore: The Psychodynamics of Creativity* (1993) • Sandra M. Gilbert and Susan Gubar, *Letters from the Front* (1994) • Cristanne Miller, *Marianne Moore: Questions of Authority* (1995) • Sabine Sielke, *Fashioning the Female Subject: The Intertextual Networking of Dickinson, Moore, and Rich* (1997) • Elizabeth W. Joyce, *Cultural Critique and Abstraction: Marianne Moore and the Avant-Garde* (1998).

Cherríe Moraga

Works by Moraga: See biographical headnote p. 863.

Biographies: Cherríe Moraga and Amber Hollibaugh, "What We're Rollin' Around in Bed With—Sexual Silences in Feminism: A Conversation Toward Ending Them," *Heresies* 12 (1981) • Skye Ward, "Cherríe Moraga," in *Contemporary Lesbian Writing of the United States: A Bio-Bibliographical Critical Sourcebook*, eds. Sandra Pollack et al. (1993).

Criticism: Lora Romero, "'When Something Goes Queer': Familiarity, Formalism, and Minority Intellectuals in the 1980s," *The Yale Journal of Criticism* 6 (1993) • Kate Adams, "Northamerican Silences: History, Identity, and Witness in the Poetry of Gloria Anzaldúa, Cherríe Moraga, and Leslie Marmon Silko," in *Listening to Silences: New Essays in Feminist Criticism*, eds. Elaine Hedges and Shelley Fisher Fishkin (1994) • Norma Alarcón, "Making *Familia* from Scratch: Split Subjectivities in the Work of Helena Maria Viramontes and Cherríe Moraga," in *Chicana Creativity and Criticism: New Frontiers in American Literature*, eds. Maria Hererra-Sobek and Helena Maria Viramontes (1996) • Julia DeFoor Jay, "(Re)Claiming the Race of the Mother: Cherríe Moraga's *Shadow of a Man*, *Giving Up the Ghost*, and *Heroes and*

Saints," in *Women of Color: Mother-Daughter Relationships in Twentieth-Century Literature*, ed. Elizabeth Guillory Brown (1996).

Hannah More

Works by More: See biographical headnote pp. 947-48.

Biography: Charles H. Ford, *Hannah More: A Critical Biography* (1996).

Criticism: Elizabeth Kowalski-Wallace, *Their Fathers' Daughters: Hannah More, Maria Edgeworth, and Patriarchal Complicity* (1991) • Patricia Demers, *The World of Hannah More* (1996).

Toni Morrison

Works by Morrison: See biographical headnote pp. 1224-25.

Bibliography: *Toni Morrison: An Annotated Bibliography*, ed. David L. Middleton (1987).

Interviews: *Conversations with Toni Morrison*, ed. Danille Taylor-Guthrie (1994).

Criticism: Karla F.C. Holloway and Stephanie A. Demetrakopoulos, *New Dimensions of Spirituality: The Novels of Toni Morrison* (1987) • *Critical Essays on Toni Morrison*, ed. Nellie Y. McKay (1988) • *Callaloo* 13 (1990; issue devoted to Morrison) • *Toni Morrison: Modern Critical Views*, ed. Harold Bloom (1990) • Trudier Harris, *Fiction and Folklore: The Novels of Toni Morrison* (1991) • Denise Heinze, *The Dilemma of "Double Consciousness": Toni Morrison's Novels* (1993) • Jan Furman, *Toni Morrison's Fiction* (1996) • *Toni Morrison: Critical and Theoretical Approaches*, ed. Nancy J. Peterson (1997) • Gurleen Grewal, *Circles of Sorrow, Lines of Struggle: The Novels of Toni Morrison* (1998) • Jill L. Matus, *Toni Morrison* (1998) • Aoi Mori, *Toni Morrison and Womanist Discourse* (1999).

Bharati Mukherjee

Works by Mukherjee: See biographical headnote pp. 544-45.

Biography: Fakrul Alam, *Bharati Mukherjee* (1996).

Criticism: Carmen Wickramagamage, "Relocation as Positive Act: The Immigrant Experience in Bharati Mukherjee's Novels," *Diaspora* 2 (1992) • *Bharati Mukherjee: Critical Perspectives*, ed. Emmanuel S. Nelson (1993) • Gail Ching Liang Low, "In a Free State: Postcolonialism and Postmodernism in Bharati Mukherjee's Fiction," *Women: A Cultural*

Review 4 (1993) • Deborah R. Geis, "'You're Exploiting My Space': Ethnicity, Spectatorship, and the Postcolonial Condition in Mukherjee's 'A Wife's Story' and Mamet's *Glengarry, Glen Ross*," in *David Mamet's Glengarry, Glen Ross: Text and Performance*, ed. Leslie Kane (1996) • Deepika Bahri, "Always Becoming: Narratives of Nation and Self in Bharati Mukherjee's *Jasmine*," in *Women, America, Movement: Narratives of Relocation*, ed. Susan L. Roberson (1998).

Sharon Olds

Works by Olds: See biographical headnote p. 558.

Criticism: Suzanne Matson, "Talking to Our Father: The Political and Mythical Appropriations of Adrienne Rich and Sharon Olds," *The American Poetry Review* 18 (1989) • Calvin Bedient, "Sentencing Eros," *Salmagundi* 97 (1993) • Alicia Ostriker, "I Am (Not) This: Erotic Discourse in Bishop, Olds, and Stevens," *The Wallace Stevens Journal* 19 (1995).

Tillie Olsen

Works by Olsen: See biographical headnote pp. 778-79

Biography: Mickie Pearlman and Abby H.P. Werlock, *Tillie Olsen* (1991).

Criticism: Deborah Rosenfelt, "From the Thirties: Tillie Olsen and the Radical Tradition," *Feminist Studies* 7 (1981) • Elaine Orr, *Tillie Olsen and a Feminist Spiritual Vision* (1987) • Mara Faulkner, *Protest and Possibility in the Writing of Tillie Olsen* (1993) • *Listening to Silences: New Essays in Feminist Criticism*, eds. Elaine Hedges and Shelley Fisher Fishkin (1994) • Nancy Huse, *The Critical Response to Tillie Olsen* (1994) • Joanne S. Frye, *Tillie Olsen: A Study of the Short Fiction* (1995) • Constance Coiner, *Better Red: The Writing and Resistance of Tillie Olsen and Meridel LeSeuer* (1995).

Oodgeroo of the tribe Noonuccal

Works by Oodgeroo: See biographical headnote pp. 1021-22.

Bibliography: Janine Little, "Oodgeroo: A Selective Checklist," *Australian Literary Studies* 16 (1994).

Criticism: Geoff Page, "The Poetry of Oodgeroo," *Island* 57 (1993) • Anne Brewster, "Oodgeroo: Orator, Poet, Storyteller," *Australian Literary Studies* 16 (1994; issue devoted to Oodgeroo).

Nell Irvin Painter

Works by Painter: See biographical headnote p. 1309.

Ann Parry

Works by Parry: See biographical headnote p. 1300.

Margery Brews Paston

Works by Paston: See biographical headnote p. 425.

Criticism: *Private Life in the Fifteenth Century: Illustrated Letters of the Paston Family*, ed. Roger Virgoe (1989) • *The Paston Family in the Fifteenth Century: The First Phase*, ed. Colin Richmond (1990) • *The Works of Medieval Women: An Anthology*, 2nd ed., ed. Marcelle Thiebaux (1994).

Katherine Philips

Works by Philips: See biographical headnote pp. 939-40.

Edition: *Collected Works of Katherine Philips, the "Matchless Orinda"*, 3 vols., eds. Patrick Thomas et al. (1990).

Biography: Elizabeth H. Hageman, "Katherine Philips: The Matchless Orinda," in *Women Writers of the Renaissance and Reformation* (1987).

Criticism: Fidelis Morgan, *The Female Wits* (1981) • Elaine Hobby, *Virtue of Necessity: English Women's Writing, 1646–1688* (1988) • Harriette Andreadis, "The Sapphic Platonics of Katherine Philips, 1632–1644," *Signs* 15 (1989) • Claudia A. Lambert, "Katherine Philips: Controlling a Life and a Reputation," *South Atlantic Review* 56 (1991) • Arlene Stiebel, "Subversive Sexuality: Masking the Erotic in Poems by Katherine Philips and Aphra Behn," *Renaissance Discourses of Desire*, eds. Claudia J. Summers and Ted Larry Pebworth (1993) • Stella P. Revard, "Katherine Philips, Aphra Behn, and the Female Pindaric," in *Representing Women in Renaissance England*, eds. Claudia J. Summers and Ted Larry Pebworth (1997) • Kathleen M. Swain, "Matching the 'Matchless Orinda' to Her Times," in *1650–1850: Ideas, Aesthetics, and Inquiries in the Early Modern Era*, III, ed. Kevin L. Cope (1997) • Celia A. Easton, "Excusing the Breach of Nature's Laws: The Discourse of Denial and Disguise in Katherine Philips' Friendship Poetry," in *Early Women Writers 1600–1720*, ed. Anita Pacheco (1998) • Elaine Hobby, "Orinda and Female Intimacy," in *Early Women Writers*

1600–1720, ed. Anita Pacheco (1998).

Sylvia Plath

Works by Plath: See biographical headnote pp. 812-13.

Editions: *The Collected Poems*, ed. Ted Hughes (1981) • *Letters Home: Correspondence, 1950–1963*, ed. Aurelia Schober Plath (1975) • *The Journals of Sylvia Plath*, eds. Ted Hughes and Frances McCullough (1982).

Bibliography: Sheryl L. Meyering, *Sylvia Plath: A Reference Guide, 1973–1988* (1990).

Biographies: Linda Wagner-Martin, *Sylvia Plath: A Biography* (1982) • Anne Stevenson, *Bitter Fame: A Life of Sylvia Plath* (1989) • Janet Malcolm, *The Silent Woman: Sylvia Plath and Ted Hughes* (1993).

Criticism: Judith Kroll, *Chapters in a Mythology: The Poetry of Sylvia Plath* (1976) • Mary Lynn Broe, *Protean Poetics: The Poetry of Sylvia Plath* (1980) • Lynda K. Bundtzen, *Plath's Incarnations: Women and the Creative Process* (1983) • *Ariel Ascending: Writings about Sylvia Plath*, ed. Paul Alexander (1985) • Pamela J. Annas, *A Disturbance of Mirrors: The Poetry of Sylvia Plath* (1988) • *Sylvia Plath: The Critical Heritage*, ed. Linda Wagner (1988) • *Sylvia Plath: Modern Critical Views*, ed. Harold Bloom (1989) • Jacqueline Rose, *The Haunting of Sylvia Plath* (1991) • Elaine Connell, *Sylvia Plath: Killing the Angel in the House* (1993) • Susan R. Van Dyne, *Revising Life: Sylvia Plath's Ariel Poems* (1993) • Sandra M. Gilbert and Susan Gubar, *Letters from the Front* (1994) • Caroline King Bernard Hill, *Sylvia Plath Revisited* (1998).

Minnie Bruce Pratt

Works by Pratt: See biographical headnote pp. 851-52.

Biographies: Elly Bulkin, Minnie Bruce Pratt, and Barbara Smith, *Yours in Struggle: Three Feminist Perspectives on Anti-Semitism and Racism* (1984) • V. Hunt, "An Interview with Minnie Bruce Pratt," *Southern Quarterly* 35 (1997).

Criticism: Adrienne Rich, "The Transgressor Mother," in *What Is Found There: Notebooks on Poetry and Politics* (1993) • Biddy Martin and Chandra Talpede Mohanty, "Feminist Politics: What's Home Got to Do with It?" in *Feminisms*, eds. Robin R. Warhol and Diane Price Herndl (1997).

Adrienne Rich

Works by Rich: See biographical headnote pp. 1094-95.

Edition: *Adrienne Rich's Poetry and Prose*, eds. Barbara Charlesworth Gelpi and Albert Gelpi (1993).

Criticism: Marilyn R. Farwell, "Adrienne Rich and an Organic Feminist Criticism," *College English* 39 (1977) • Joanne Feit Diehl, "'Cartographies of Silence': Rich's Common Language and the Woman Poet," *Feminist Studies* 6 (1980) • *Reading Adrienne Rich: Reviews and Re-Visions, 1951–81*, ed. Jane Roberta Cooper (1984) • Wendy Martin, *An American Triptych* (1984) • Mary K. DeShazer, *Inspiring Women: Reimagining the Muse* (1986) • Claire Keyes, *The Aesthetics of Power: The Poetry of Adrienne Rich* (1986) • Helen M. Dennis, "Adrienne Rich: Consciousness Raising as Poetic Method," in *Contemporary Poetry Meets Modern Theory*, eds. Antony Easthope and John O. Thompson (1991) • Alice Templeton, *The Dream and the Dialogue: Adrienne Rich's Feminist Poetics* (1994) • Krista Ratcliffe, *Anglo-American Feminist Challenges to the Rhetorical Tradition: Virginia Woolf, Mary Daly, Adrienne Rich* (1996) • Mary K. DeShazer, "'The End of a Century': Feminist Millennial Vision in Adrienne Rich's *Dark Fields of the Republic*," *NWSA Journal* (1997) • Margaret Dickie, *Stein, Bishop and Rich: Lyrics of Love, War, and Place* (1997) • Sabine Sielke, *Fashioning the Female Subject: The Intertextual Networking of Dickinson, Moore, and Rich* (1997).

Christina Rossetti

Works by Rossetti: See biographical headnote pp. 512-13.

Edition: *The Complete Poems of Christina Rossetti*, 3 vols., ed. Rebecca Crump (1979–90).

Bibliography: *Christina Rossetti: A Reference Guide* (1976).

Biographies: Georgina Battiscombe, *Christina Rossetti: A Divided Life* (1981) • Jan Marsh, *Christina Rossetti: A Writer's Life* (1995).

Criticism: Sandra M. Gilbert and Susan Gubar, *The Madwoman in the Attic* (1979) • Jerome J. McGann, "Christina Rossetti's Poems: A New Edition and Revaluation," *Victorian Studies* 23 (1980) • *Christina Rossetti: Critical Perspectives, 1862–1982*, ed. Edna Kotin Charles (1985) • Dolores Rosenblum, *Christina Rossetti: The Poetry of Endurance* (1986) • *The Achievement of Christina Rossetti*, ed. David Kent (1987) • Sharon Leder and Andrea Abbott, *The Language of Exclusion: The Poetry of Emily Dickinson and Christina Rossetti* (1987) • Katherine J. Mayberry, *Christina Rossetti and the Poetry of Discovery* (1990) • *Victorian Women Poets: Emily Brontë, Elizabeth Barrett Browning, Christina Rossetti*, ed. Joseph Bristow (1995) • Tricia A. Lootens, *Lost Saints: Silence, Gender, and Victorian Literary Canonization* (1996) • Claudia Ottlinger, *The Death-Motif in the Poetry of Emily Dickinson and Christina Rossetti* (1996) • Sharon Smulders, *Christina Rossetti Revisited* (1996) • *The Culture of Christina Rossetti: Female Poetics and Victorian Contexts*, eds. Mary Arseneau et al. (1999).

Mary Rowlandson

Works by Rowlandson: See biographical headnote pp. 943-44.

Criticism: Mitchell R. Breitweiser, *American Puritanism and the Defense of Mourning: Religion, Grief, and Ethnology in Mary White Rowlandson's Captivity Narrative* (1991) • Teresa Toulouse, "'My Own Credit': Strategies of (E)valuation in Mary Rowlandson's Captivity Narrative," *American Literature* 64 (1992) • Susan Howe, *The Birth-Mark: Unsettling the Wilderness in American Literary History* (1993) • Christopher Castiglia, *Bound and Determined: Captivity, Culture-crossing, and White Womanhood from Mary Rowlandson to Patty Hearst* (1996).

Muriel Rukeyser

Works by Rukeyser: See biographical headnote pp. 1205-06.

Editions: *Out of Silence: Selected Poems*, ed. Kate Daniels (1992) • *A Muriel Rukeyser Reader*, ed. Jan Heller Levi (1994).

Criticism: Rachel Blau DuPlessis, "The Critique of Consciousness and Myth in Levertov, Rich, and Rukeyser," in *Shakespeare's Sisters*, eds. Sandra M. Gilbert and Susan Gubar (1979) • Louise Kertesz, *The Poetic Vision of Muriel Rukeyser* (1980) • Adrienne Rich, "Beginners," *What Is Found There: Notebooks on Poetry and Politics* (1993) • Kate Daniels, "Muriel Rukeyser and Her Critics," in *Gendered Modernisms: American Women Poets and Their Readers*, eds. Margaret Dickie and Thomas Travisano (1996) • *How Shall We Tell Each Other of the Poet?: The Life and Writing of Muriel Rukeyser*, eds. Anne F. Herzog and Janet E. Kaufman (1999).

May Sarton

Works by Sarton: See biographical headnote

pp. 295-96.

Editions: *Sarton Selected: An Anthology of Novels, Journals, and Poetry*, ed. Bradford D. Daziel (1991) • *May Sarton: Among the Usual Days*, ed. Susan Sherman (1993).

Bibliography: *May Sarton*, ed. Lenora Blouin (1978).

Biographies: *Conversations with May Sarton*, ed. Earl G. Ingersoll (1991) • Margot Peters, *May Sarton* (1997).

Criticism: *May Sarton, Woman and Poet*, ed. Constance Hunting (1982) • Mary K. DeShazer, *Inspiring Women: Re-imagining the Muse* (1986) • Elizabeth Evans, *May Sarton Revisited* (1989) • Carolyn Heilbrun, *Hamlet's Mother and Other Women* (1990) • Anne Wyatt-Brown, "Another Model of the Aging Writer: Sarton's Politics of Old Age," in *Aging and Gender in Literature: Studies in Creativity*, eds. Anne Wyatt-Brown and Janice Rossen (1993) • *A Celebration for May Sarton: Essays from the National Conference "May Sarton at Eighty"*, ed. Constance Hunting (1994) • Leah E. White, "Silenced Stories: May Sarton's Journals as a Form of Discursive Resistance," in *Women's Life-Writing: Finding Voice/Building Community*, ed. Linda S. Coleman (1997).

Anne Sexton

Works by Sexton: See biographical headnote pp. 531-32.

Editions: *Selected Poems of Anne Sexton*, eds. Diane Wood Middlebrook and Diana Hume George (1988) • *No Evil Star: Selected Essays, Interviews, and Prose*, ed. Steven E. Colburn (1985).

Bibliography: *Sylvia Plath and Anne Sexton: A Reference Guide*, ed. R.P. Walsh (1974).

Biographies: Diane Wood Middlebrook, *Anne Sexton: A Biography* (1991) • Linda Gray Sexton, *Searching for Mercy Street: My Journey Back to My Mother* (1994).

Criticism: Suzanne Juhasz, "Seeking the Exit or the Home: Poetry and Salvation in the Career of Anne Sexton," in *Shakespeare's Sisters*, eds. Sandra M. Gilbert and Susan Gubar (1979) • Alicia Ostriker, "That Story: Anne Sexton and Her Transformations," *American Poetry Review* 11 (1982) • *Sexton: Selected Criticism*, ed. Diana Hume George (1988) • *Critical Essays on Anne Sexton*, ed. Linda Wagner (1989) • Diane Wood Middlebrook, "Spinning Straw into Gold," in *The Literary Biography:*

Problems and Solutions, ed. Dale Salwak (1996) • Dawn Skorczewski, "What Prison Is This? Literary Critics Cover Incest in Anne Sexton's 'Briar Rose,'" *Signs* 21 (1996).

Mary Shelley

Works by Shelley: See biographical headnote pp. 232-33.

Editions: *The Journals of Mary Shelley, 1814–1844,* eds. Paula R. Feldman and Diana Scott-Kilvert (1987) • *The Mary Shelley Reader,* eds. Betty T. Bennett and Charles E. Robinson (1990) • *Mary Shelley: Collected Tales and Stories,* ed. Charles E. Robinson (1990).

Bibliography: *Mary Shelley: An Annotated Bibliography,* ed. W.H. Lyles (1975).

Biography: Bonnie R. Neumann, *The Lonely Muse: A Critical Biography of Mary Shelley* (1979).

Criticism: Ellen Moers, *Literary Women* (1976) • Sandra M. Gilbert and Susan Gubar, *The Madwoman in the Attic* (1979) • *The Endurance of Frankenstein,* eds. George Levine and U.C. Knoepflmacher (1979) • Mary Poovey, *The Proper Lady and the Woman Writer* (1984) • Mary A. Favret, "A Woman Writes the Fiction of the Body in *Frankenstein,*" *Genders* 14 (1992) • *The Other Mary Shelley: Beyond Frankenstein,* eds. Audrey A. Fisch et al. (1993) • Bette London, "Mary Shelley, *Frankenstein,* and the Spectacle of Masculinity," *PMLA* 108 (1993) • *Iconoclastic Departures: Mary Shelley After Frankenstein,* eds. Syndy M. Conger et al. (1997) • Betty T. Bennett, *Mary Wollstonecraft Shelley: An Introduction* (1998).

Elaine Showalter

Works by Showalter: See biographical headnote pp. 352-53.

Lydia Sigourney

Works by Sigourney: See biographical headnote p. 683.

Biography: Karen L. Kilcup, "Lydia Howard Huntley Sigourney (1791–1865)," in *Nineteenth-century American Women Writers: A Bio-Bibliographical Critical Sourcebook,* eds. Denise D. Knight and Emmanuel S. Nelson (1997).

Criticism: Sandra A. Zagarell, "Expanding 'America': Lydia Sigourney's Sketch of Connecticut, Catharine Sedgwick's Hope Leslie," *Tulsa Studies in Women's Literature* 6 (1987) •

Elizabeth Petrino, "'Feet So Precious Charged': Dickinson, Sigourney, and the Child Elegy," *Tulsa Studies in Women's Literature* 13 (1994) • Nina Baym, "Reinventing Lydia Sigourney," in *Redefining the Political Novel: American Women Writers,* ed. Sharon M. Harris (1995) • Elizabeth Petrino, *Emily Dickinson and her Contemporaries: Women's Verse in America, 1820–1885* (1998).

Charlotte Smith

Works by Smith: See biographical headnote pp. 679-80.

Edition: *The Poems of Charlotte Smith,* ed. Stuart Curran (1993).

Biography: Katharine M. Rogers, *Before Their Time* (1979).

Criticism: Judith P. Stanton, "Charlotte Smith's 'Literary Business': Income, Patronage, and Indigence," *The Age of Johnson: A Scholarly Annual* 1 (1987) • Eleanor Ty, *Unsex'd Revolutionaries: Five Female Novelists of the 1790s* (1993) • Jacqueline Labbe, "Selling One's Sorrows: Charlotte Smith, Mary Robinson, and the Marketing of Poetry," *The Wordsworth Circle* 25 (1994) • Deborah Kennedy, "Thorns and Roses: The Sonnets of Charlotte Smith," *Women's Writing* 92 (1995) • Silvia Mergenthal, "Charlotte Smith and the Romantic Sonnet Revival," in *Feminist Contributions to the Literary Canon,* ed. Susanne Fendler (1997) • Diane Hoevler Long, *Gothic Feminism: The Professionalization of Gender from Charlotte Smith to the Brontës* (1998).

Stevie Smith

Works by Smith: See biographical headnote p. 292.

Edition: *Collected Poems,* ed. James MacGibbon (1976).

Bibliography: *Stevie Smith: A Bibliography,* eds. Jack Barbera et al. (1986).

Biography: Frances Spalding, *Stevie Smith* (1988).

Criticism: Mark Storey, "Why Stevie Smith Matters," *Critical Quarterly* 21 (1979) • Arthur C. Rankin, *The Poetry of Stevie Smith: "Little Girl Lost"* (1985) • *In Search of Stevie Smith,* ed. Stanford Sternlicht (1991) • Romana Huk, "Eccentric Concentrism: Traditional Poetic Forms and Refracted Discourse in Stevie Smith's Poetry," *Contemporary Literature* 43

(1993) • Sheryl Stevenson, "Stevie Smith's Voices," *Contemporary Literature* 43 (1993).

Rachel Speght

Works by Speght: See biographical headnote pp. 1116-17.

Edition/Biography: *The Polemics and Poems of Rachel Speght,* ed. Barbara Kiefer Lewalski (1996).

Criticism: Katherine Usher Henderson and Barbara F. McManus, *Half Humankind: Contexts and Texts of the Controversy about Women in England, 1540–1640* (1985) • Cis van Heertum, "A Hostile Annotation of Rachel Speght's A Muzzle for Melastomus, 1617," *English Studies* 68 (1987) • *Women Writers in Renaissance England,* ed. Randall Martin (1997) • Barbara Kiefer Lewalski, "Female Text, Male Reader Response: Contemporary Marginalia in Rachel Speght's A Mouzell for Melastomus," in *Representing Women in Renaissance England,* eds. Claudia J. Summers and Ted Larry Pebworth (1997).

Margit Stange

Works by Stange: See biographical headnote pp. 876-77.

Gertrude Stein

Works by Stein: See biographical headnote pp. 282-83.

Editions: *The Yale Edition of the Unpublished Writings of Gertrude Stein,* ed. Carl Van Vechten (1951–58) • *A Stein Reader,* ed. Ulla E. Dydo (1993).

Bibliographies: *Gertrude Stein,* ed. Maureen R. Liston (1979) • *Gertrude Stein and Alice B. Toklas: A Reference Guide,* ed. Ray L. White (1984).

Biographies: Janet Hobhouse, *Everybody Who Was Anybody* (1975).

Criticism: Carolyn F. Copeland, *Language and Time and Gertrude Stein* (1975) • Wendy Steiner, *Exact Resemblance to Exact Resemblance: The Literary Portraiture of Gertrude Stein's Experimental Writing* (1983) • Marianne deKoven, *A Different Language: Gertrude Stein's Experimental Writing* (1983) • *A Gertrude Stein Companion,* ed. Bruce Kellner (1988) • Judy Grahn, *Really Reading Gertrude Stein* (1989) • Lisa Cole Ruddick, *Reading Gertrude Stein: Body, Text, Gnosis* (1990) • Ellen E. Berry, *Curved Thought and Textual Wandering: Gertrude Stein's Postmodernism* (1992).

Susan Rubin Suleiman

Works by Suleiman: See biographical headnote pp. 620-21.

Mary Tighe

Works by Tighe: See biographical headnote p. 682.

Criticism: Greg Kucich, "Gender Crossings: Keats and Tighe," *Keats Shelley Journal* 44 (1995) • Harriet Kramer Linker, "Romanticism and Mary Tighe's Psyche: Peering at the Hem of Her Blue Stockings," *Studies in Romanticism* 35 (1996) • "Romantic Aesthetics in Mary Tighe and Letitia Landon: How Women Poets Recuperate the Gaze," *European Romanticism Review* 7 (1997).

Trinh T. Minh-ha

Works by Trinh: See biographical headnote pp. 928-29.

Sojourner Truth

Works by Truth: See biographical headnote pp. 1145-46.

Edition: Elizabeth Cady Stanton et al., *The History of Woman Suffrage,* vols. I–III (1881–86).

Biographies: Carleton Mabee, *Sojourner Truth—Slave, Prophet, Legend* (1993) • Nell Irvin Painter, *Sojourner Truth: A Life, A Symbol* (1996).

Criticism: Jean Fagan Yellin, *Women and Sisters: The Antislavery Feminists in American Culture* (1989) • Nell Irvin Painter, "Sojourner Truth in Life and Memory: Writing the Biography of an American Exotic," *Gender and History* 2 (1990) • Gloria I. Joseph, "Sojourner Truth: Archetypal Black Feminist," in *Wild Women in the Whirlwind: Afra-American Culture and the Contemporary Literary Renaissance,* eds. Joanne M. Braxton and Andree Nicola McLaughlin (1991) • Linda David and Erlene Stetson, *Glorying in Tribulation: The Lifework of Sojourner Truth* (1994) • Nell Irvin Painter, "Difference, Slavery, and Memory: Sojourner Truth in Feminist Abolitionism," in *The Abolitionist Sisterhood,* ed. Jean Fagan Yellin (1994) • Drema R. Lipscomb, "Sojourner Truth: A Practical Public Discourse," in *Reclaiming Rhetorica: Women in the Rhetorical Tradition,* ed. Andrea Lunsford (1995) • Jean M. Humez, "Reading the *Narrative of Sojourner Truth* as a Collaborative Text," *Frontiers* 16 (1996) • Joann P. Krieg, "Whitman and

Sojourner Truth," *Walt Whitman Quarterly Review* 16 (1998).

Alice Walker

Works by Walker: See biographical headnote pp. 323-24.

Bibliography: Louise H. Pratt, *Alice Walker: An Annotated Bibliography 1968–1986* (1988).

Interviews: "Alice Walker," in *Black Women Writers at Work*, ed. Claudia Tate (1983) • John O'Brien, "Interview with Alice Walker," in *Alice Walker: "Everyday Use"*, ed. Barbara T. Christian (1994).

Criticism: Trudier Harris, "Folklore in the Fiction of Alice Walker," *Black American Literature Forum* 11 (1977) • Mary Helen Washington, "An Essay on Alice Walker" in *Sturdy Black Bridges: Visions of Black Women in Literature*, ed. Roseann Bell et al. (1979) • Barbara Christian, *Black Feminist Criticism* (1986) • Lauren Berlant, "Race, Gender, and Nation in *The Color Purple*," *Critical Inquiry* 14 (1988) • Elliott Butler-Evans, *Race, Gender, and Desire: Narrative Strategies in the Fiction of Toni Cade Bambara, Toni Morrison, and Alice Walker* (1989) • bell hooks, "Writing the Subject: Reading *The Color Purple*," in *Reading Black, Reading Feminist: A Critical Anthology*, ed. Henry Louis Gates, Jr. (1990) • Donna Haisty Winchell, *Alice Walker* (1992) • *Alice Walker: Critical Perspectives Past and Present*, eds. Henry Louis Gates, Jr. and Kwame Anthony Appiah (1993) • *Alice Walker and Zora Neale Hurston: The Common Bond*, ed. Lillie P. Howard (1993) • Yvonne Johnson, *The Voices of African-American Women: The Use of Narrative and Authorial Voice in the Works of Harriet Jacobs, Zora Neale Hurston, and Alice Walker* (1998) • *Critical Essays on Alice Walker*, ed. Ikenna Dieke (2000).

Eudora Welty

Works by Welty: See biographical headnote p. 1002.

Bibliography: Noel Polk, *Eudora Welty: A Bibliography of Her Work* (1994).

Criticism: *A Still Moment: Essays on the Art of Eudora Welty*, ed. John F. Desmond (1978) • Elizabeth Evans, *Eudora Welty* (1981) • Louise Westling, *Sacred Groves and Ravaged Gardens: The Fiction of Eudora Welty, Carson McCullers, and Flannery O'Connor* (1985) • *Critical Essays on Eudora Welty*, ed. Craig Turner (1989) • *Eudora Welty*, ed. Louise Westling (1989) • Peter Schmidt, *The Heart of the Story: Eudora Welty's Short Fiction* (1991) • *The Critical*

Responses to Eudora Welty's Fiction, ed. Laurie Champion (1994) • Gail Mortimer, *Daughter of the Swan: Love and Knowledge in Eudora Welty's Fiction* (1994) • *The Late Novels of Eudora Welty*, eds. Jan N. Gretlund and Karl Heinz Westerp (1998) • Michael Kreyling, *Understanding Eudora Welty* (1999).

Edith Wharton

Works by Wharton: See biographical headnote pp. 274-75.

Editions: *The Edith Wharton Reader*, ed. Louis Auchincloss (1965) • *The Collected Short Stories of Edith Wharton*, ed. R.W.B. Lewis (1968) • *The Letters of Edith Wharton*, eds. R.W.B. Lewis and Nancy Lewis (1988).

Bibliography: Kristin O. Lauer, *Edith Wharton: An Annotated Secondary Bibliography* (1990).

Biographies: R.W.B. Lewis, *Edith Wharton: A Biography* (1975) • Cynthia Griffin Wolff, *A Feast of Words: The Triumph of Edith Wharton* (1977) • Shari Benstock, *No Gifts from Chance: A Biography of Edith Wharton* (1994).

Criticism: Elizabeth Aamons, *Edith Wharton's Argument with America* (1980) • Carol Wershaven, *The Female Intruder in the Novels of Edith Wharton* (1982) • Josephine Donovan, *After the Fall: The Demeter-Persephone Myth in Wharton, Cather, and Glasgow* (1988) • Sandra M. Gilbert and Susan Gubar, *Sexchanges* (1989) • Elaine Showalter, *Sister's Choice: Tradition and Change in American Women's Writing* (1991) • Candace Wait, *Edith Wharton's Letters from the Underworld: Fictions of Women and Writing* (1991) • Barbara A. White, *Edith Wharton: A Study of the Short Fiction* (1991) • *Edith Wharton: New Critical Essays*, eds. Alfred Bendixen and Annette Zilversmith (1992) • *The Cambridge Companion to Edith Wharton*, ed. Millicent Bell (1995) • Kathy A. Fedorko, *Gender and the Gothic in the Fiction of Edith Wharton* (1995) • Carol J. Singley, *Edith Wharton: Matters of Mind and Spirit* (1995) • Sarah Bird Wright, *Edith Wharton's Travel Literature: The Making of a Connoisseur* (1997) • *Forward Glance: New Essays on Edith Wharton*, eds. Claire Colquitt et al. (1999) • Adeline R. Tintner, *Edith Wharton in Context: Essays on Intertextuality* (1999).

Phillis Wheatley

Works by Wheatley: See biographical headnote pp. 949-50.

Edition: *The Collected Works of Phillis Wheatley*, ed. John C. Shields (1988).

Bibliography: William Henry Robinson, *Phillis Wheatley: A Bio-Bibliography* (1981).

Biography: Merle Richmond, *Phillis Wheatley* (1988).

Criticism: *Bid the Vassal Soar: Interpretive Essays on the Life and Poetry of Phillis Wheatley and George Moses*, ed. M.A. Richmond (1974) • *Critical Essays on Phillis Wheatley*, ed. William Henry Robinson (1982) • Helen Burke, "Problematizing American Dissent: The Subject of Phillis Wheatley," in *Cohesion and Dissent in America*, eds. Carol Colabretta and Joseph Alkana (1994) • Karla F.C. Holloway, "The Body Politic," in *Subjects and Citizens: Nation, Race, and Gender from Oroonoko to Anita Hill*, eds. Michael Moon and Cathy Davidson (1995) • Carla Willard, "Wheatley's Turns of Praise: Heroic Entrapment and the Paradox of Revolution," *American Literature* 67 (1995) • Paula Bennett, "Phillis Wheatley's Vocation and the Paradox of the 'Afric Muse,'" *PMLA* 113 (1998).

Isabella Whitney

Works by Whitney: See biographical headnote p. 85.

Criticism: Elaine V. Beilin, *Redeeming Eve: Women Writers of the English Renaissance* (1987) • Ann Rosalind Jones, "Nets and Bridles: Early Modern Conduct Books and Sixteenth-century Women's Lyrics," in *The Ideology of Conduct: Essays in Literature and the History of Sexuality*, eds. Nancy Armstrong and Leonard Tennenhouse (1987) • Wendy Wall, "Isabella Whitney and the Female Legacy," *English Literary History* 58 (1991) • Ilona Bell, "Women in the Lyric Dialogue of Courtship: Whitney's 'Admonition to a Yong Gentilwoman' and Donne's 'The Legacy,'" in *Representing Women in Renaissance England*, eds. Claudia J. Summers and Ted Larry Pebworth (1997) • Patricia Phillippy, "The Maid's Lawful Liberty: Service, the Household, and 'Mother B' in Isabella Whitney's *A Sweet Nosegay*," *Modern Philology* 95 (1998).

Zoë Wicomb

Works by Wicomb: See biographical headnote p. 1277.

Interview: Eva Hunter, "Interview with Zoë Wicomb," in *Between the Lines II*, eds. Eva Hunter and Craig MacKenzie (1993).

Criticism: Mary K. DeShazer, *A Poetics of Resistance* (1994) • Sue Marais, "Getting Lost in Cape Town: Spatial and Temporal Disloca-tion in the South African Short Fiction Cycle," *English in Africa* 22 (1995) • Dorothy Driver, "Transformation Through Art: Writing, Representation, and Subjectivity in Recent South African Fiction," *World Literature Today* 70 (1996) • Rob Gaylard, "Exile and Homecoming: Identity in Zoë Wicomb's 'You Can't Get Lost in Cape Town,'" *ARIEL* 27 (1996) • Zoë Wicomb, "Shame and Identity: The Case of the Colored in South Africa," in *Writing South Africa: Literature, Apartheid, and Democracy, 1970–1995*, eds. Derek Attridge and Rosemary Jolly (1998).

"The Wife's Lament"

Criticism: Susan Schibanoff, "Medieval *Frauenlieder*: Anonymous Was a Man?" *Tulsa Studies in Women's Literature* 1 (1982) • Anne L. Klinck, "The Old English Elegy as a Genre," *English Studies in Canada* 10 (1984) • Patricia A. Belanoff, "Women's Songs, Women's Language: *Wulf and Eadwacer* and *The Wife's Lament*," in *New Readings on Women in Old English Literature*, eds. Helen Damico and Alexandra Hennessey Olsen (1990) • Marilynn Desmond, "The Voice of Exile: Feminist Literary History and the Anonymous Anglo-Saxon Elegy," *Critical Inquiry* 16 (1990) • Helen T. Bennett, "Exile and the Semiosis of Gender in Old English Elegies," in *Class and Gender in Early English Literature: Intersections*, eds. Britton J. Harwood and Gillian R. Overing (1994) • Fiona Gameson and Richard Gameson, "'Wulf and Eadwacer,' 'The Wife's Lament,' and the Discovery of the Individual in Old English Verse," in *Studies in English Language and Literature: "Doubt Wisely,"* eds. M.J. Toswell and E.M. Tyler (1996).

Mary Wollstonecraft

Works by Wollstonecraft: See biographical headnote pp. 1131-32.

Editions: *The Works of Mary Wollstonecraft*, 7 vols., eds. Janet M. Todd and Marilyn Butler (1989) • *The Collected Letters*, ed. Ralph M. Wardle (1979) • *Political Writings*, ed. Janet Todd (1993).

Bibliography: Leigh Williams and Rosemarie Johnstone, "Updating Mary Wollstonecraft: A Bibliography of Criticism, 1976–1989," *Bulletin of Bibliography* 48 (1991).

Biographies: Janet M. Todd and Moira Ferguson, *Mary Wollstonecraft* (1984) • Claire Tomalin, *The Life and Death of Mary Wollstonecraft* (1992).

Criticism: Mary Poovey, *The Proper Lady and the Woman Writer* (1984) • Laurie Langbaeur, "An Early Romance: Motherhood and Women's Writing in Mary Wollstonecraft's Novels," in *Romanticism and Feminism*, ed. Anne K. Mellor (1988) • Virginia Sapiro, *A Vindication of Political Virtue: The Political Theory of Mary Wollstonecraft* (1992) • Syndy M. Conger, *Mary Wollstonecraft and the Language of Sensibility* (1994) • *Feminist Interpretations of Mary Wollstonecraft*, ed. Maria J. Falco (1996) • Jane Moore, *Mary Wollstonecraft* (1999).

Virginia Woolf

Works by Woolf: See biographical headnote pp. 14-15.

Editions: *Women and Writing*, ed. Michele Barrett (1979) • *The Essays of Virginia Woolf*, ed. Andrew McNeillie (1986–89) • *The Diary of Virginia Woolf*, ed. Anne Olivier Bell, 5 vols. (1977–1994).

Bibliographies: Brownlee Jean Kirkpatrick, *A Bibliography of Virginia Woolf* (1980) • Edward L. Bishop, *A Virginia Woolf Chronology* (1989).

Biographies: Quentin Bell, *Virginia Woolf*, 2 vols. (1972) • Phyllis Rose, *Woman of Letters: A Life of Virginia Woolf* (1978) • Louise de Salvo, *Virginia Woolf: The Impact of Childhood Sexual Abuse on Her Life and Work* (1989) • James King, *Virginia Woolf* (1995).

Criticism: Herbert Marder, *Feminism and Art: A Study of Virginia Woolf* (1968) • James Naremore, *The World Without a Self* (1973) • Winifred Holtby, *Virginia Woolf* (1978) • Maria DeBattista, *Virginia Woolf's Major Novels* (1980) • *New Feminist Essays on Virginia Woolf*, ed. Jane Marcus (1981) • *Virginia Woolf: A Feminist Slant*, ed. Jane Marcus (1983) • Susan M. Squier, *Woolf and London: The Sexual Politics of the City* (1985) • *Virginia Woolf: Modern Critical Views*, ed. Harold Bloom (1986) • Jane Marcus, *Virginia Woolf and the Languages of Patriarchy* (1987) • *Virginia Woolf and Bloomsbury: A Centenary Celebration*, ed. Jane Marcus (1987) • Makiko Minow-Pinckney, *Virginia Woolf and the Problem of the Subject* (1987) • Rachel Bowlby, *Virginia Woolf: Feminist Destinations* (1988) • Elizabeth Abel, *Virginia Woolf and the Fictions of Psychoanalysis* (1989) • Alice Fox, *Virginia Woolf and the Literature of the English Renaissance* (1990) • Sandra M. Gilbert and Susan Gubar, *Letters from the Front* (1994) • *Virginia Woolf: A Collection of Critical Essays*, ed. Margaret Homans (1993) • *New Essays on Virginia Woolf*, ed. Helen Wussow (1994) • Gillian Beer, *Virginia Woolf: The Common Ground* (1996) • *Virginia Woolf: Lesbian Readings*, eds. Eileen Barrett and Patricia Cramer (1997) • Leila Brosnan, *Reading Virginia Woolf's Essays and Journalism: Breaking the Surface of Silence* (1997) • Laura Marcus, *Virginia Woolf* (1997) • Jane Goldman, *The Feminist Aesthetics of Virginia Woolf: Modernism, Post-Impressionism, and the Politics of the Visual* (1998).

Dorothy Wordsworth

Works by Wordsworth: See biographical headnote pp. 952-53.

Editions: *The Letters of William Wordsworth and Dorothy Wordsworth*, 6 vols., eds. C.L. Shaver et al. (1967–82) • *Dorothy Wordsworth: Selections from the Journals* (1992).

Biography: Pamela Woof, *Dorothy Wordsworth, Writer* (1988).

Criticism: Margaret Homans, *Women Writers and Poetic Identity* (1980) • Susan Levin, *Dorothy Wordsworth and Romanticism* (1987) • James Holt McGavran, Jr., "Dorothy Wordsworth's Journals: Putting Herself Down," in *The Private Self: Theory and Practice of Women's Autobiographical Writings*, ed. Shari Benstock (1988) • Lucinda Cole and Richard G. Swartz, "'Why Should I Wish for Words?': Literacy, Articulation, and the Borders of Literary Culture," in *At the Limits of Romanticism: Essays in Cultural, Feminist, and Materialist Criticism*, eds. Mary A. Favret and Nicole J. Watson (1994) • Elizabeth A. Fay, *Becoming Wordsworthian: A Performative Aesthetics* (1995) • Alexis Easley, "Wandering Women: Dorothy Wordsworth's *Grasmere Journal* and the Discourse on Female Vagrancy," *Women's Writing* 3 (1996).

Judith Wright

Works by Wright: See biographical headnote pp. 803-04.

Criticism: Stephen Tatum, "Tradition of the Exile: Judith Wright's Australian 'West,'" in *Women, Women Writers, and the West*, ed. Stephen Tatum (1979) • Harry Heseltine, "Wrestling with the Angel: Judith Wright's Poetry in the 1950s," in *The Uncertain Self: Essays in Australian Literature and Criticism*, ed. Heseltine (1986) • Jennifer Strauss, "Within the Bounds of Feminine Sensibility? The Poetry of Rosemary Dobson, Gwen Harwood, and Judith Wright," in *Still the Frame Holds: Essays on Women Poets and Writers*, eds. Sheila Roberts and Yvonne Pacheo Tevis (1993) • Robert Zeller, "Judith Wright's

Nature Poetry—The Problem of Living 'Through a Web of Language,'" *Antipodes* 12 (1998).

Mary Wroth

Works by Wroth: See biographical headnote pp. 429-30.

Editions: *Pamphilia to Amphilanthus*, ed. Gary Waller (1977) • *The Poems of Lady Mary Wroth*, ed. Josephine Roberts (1983).

Biography: Gary Waller, *The Sidney Family Romance* (1993).

Criticism: May N. Paulissen, *The Love Sonnets of Lady Mary Wroth: A Critical Introduction* (1982) • Josephine Roberts, "The Biographical Problem of *Pamphilia to Amphilanthus*," *Tulsa Studies in Women's Literature* 1 (1982) • Elaine V. Beilin, *Redeeming Eve: Women Writers of the English Renaissance* (1987) • Maureen Quilligan, "Lady Mary Wroth: Female Authority and the Family Romance," in *Unfolded Tales: Essays on Renaissance Romance*, ed. George Logan and Gordon Teskey (1989) • Ann Rosalind Jones, *The Currency of Eros: Women's Love Lyric in Europe, 1540–1620* (1990) • Mary Ellen Lamb, *Gender and Authorship in the Sidney Circle* (1990) • *Reading Mary Wroth: Representing Alternatives in Early Modern England*, eds. Naomi J. Miller and Gary Waller (1991) • Barbara Kiefer Lewalski, *Writing Women in Jacobean England* (1993) • Naomi J. Miller, *Changing the Subject: Mary Wroth and Figurations of Gender in Early Modern England* (1996) • Elizabeth Hanson, "Boredom and Whoredom: Reading Renaissance Women's Sonnet Sequences," *Yale Journal of Criticism* 10 (1997) • Jeff Masten, "'Shall I turne blabb?': Circulation, Gender, and Subjectivity in Mary Wroth's Sonnets," in *Early Women Writers: 1600–1720*, ed. Anita Pacheco (1998).

"Wulf and Eadwacer"

Criticism: Susan Schibanoff, "Medieval *Frauenlieder*: Anonymous Was a Man?" *Tulsa Studies in Women's Literature* 1 (1982) • Dolores Frese, "*Wulf and Eadwacer*: The Adulterous Woman Reconsidered," *Religion and Literature* 15 (1983) • Anne L. Klinck, "The Old English Elegy as a Genre," *English Studies in Canada* 10 (1984) • Patricia A. Belanoff, "Women's Songs, Women's Language: *Wulf and Eadwacer* and *The Wife's Lament*," in *New Readings on Women in Old English Literature*, eds. Helen Damico and Alexandra Hennessey Olsen (1990) • Marilynn Desmond, "The Voice of Exile: Feminist Literary History and the Anonymous Anglo-Saxon Elegy," *Critical Inquiry* 16

(1990) • Marijane Osborn, "The Text and Context of *Wulf and Eadwacer*," in *Old English Shorter Poems: Basic Readings*, ed. Katherine O'Brien O'Keeffe (1994) • Fiona Gameson and Richard Gameson, "'Wulf and Eadwacer,' 'The Wife's Lament,' and the Discovery of the Individual in Old English Verse," in *Studies in English Language and Literature: "Doubt Wisely"*, eds. M.J. Toswell and E.M. Tyler (1996).

Hisaye Yamamoto

Works by Yamamoto: See biographical headnote pp. 289-99.

Edition: *Seventeen Syllables and Other Stories*, ed. and intro. King-kok Cheung (1988).

Criticism: Stan Yogi, "Rebels and Heroines: Subversive Narratives in the Stories of Wakako Yamauchi and Hisaye Yamamoto," in *Reading the Literatures of Asian America*, eds. Shirley Geok-lin Lim and Amy Ling (1992) • King-kok Cheung, *Articulate Silences: Hisaye Yamamoto, Maxine Hong Kingston, Joy Kogawa* (1993) • Ming L. Cheng, "The Unrepentant Fire: Tragic Limitations in Hisaye Yamamoto's 'Seventeen Syllables,'" *MELUS* 19 (1994) • King-kok Cheung, "Reading Between the Syllables: Hisaye Yamamoto's *Seventeen Syllables and Other Stories*," in *Teaching American Ethnic Literatures*, eds. John R. Maitino and David R. Peck (1996) • Naoko Sugiyama, "Issei Mothers' Silence, Nisei Daughters' Stories: The Short Fiction of Hisaye Yamamoto," *Comparative Literature Studies* 33 (1996).

Anzia Yezierska

Works by Yezierska: See biographical headnote pp. 1192-93.

Edition: *The Open Cage: An Anzia Yezierska Collection*, ed. Alice Kessler-Harris (1979).

Biographies: Carol B. Shoe, *Anzia Yezierska* (1982) • Louise Levitas Henriksen, *Anzia Yezierska: A Writer's Life* (1988).

Criticism: Laura Wexler, "Looking at Yezierska," in *Women of the Word: Jewish Women and Jewish Writing*, ed. Judith R. Baskin (1994) • Ann R. Shapiro, "The Ultimate Shaygets and the Fiction of Anzia Yezierska," *MELUS* 21 (1996) • Delia Caparoso-Konzett, "Administered Identities and Linguistic Assimilation: The Politics of Immigrant English in Anzia Yezierska's *Hungry Hearts*," *American Literature* 69 (1997) • Lisa Muir, "Lady Liberty's Colonization and Anzia Yezierska's 'Bread Givers,'" *Centennial Review* 41 (1997).

Zitkala-Sä

Works by Zitkala-Sä: See biographical head-note pp. 975-76.

Biography: *American Indian Women*, ed. Marion E. Gridley (1974).

Criticism: Dexter Fisher, "Zitkala-Sä: The Evolution of a Writer," *American Indian Quarterly* 5 (1979) • Dorothea M. Susag, "Zitkala-Sä (Gertrude Simmons Bonnin): A Powerful Literary Voice," *Studies in American Indian Literature* 5 (1993) • Martha J. Cutter, "Zitkala-Sä's Autiobiographical Writings: The Problems of a Canonical Search for Language and Identity," *MELUS* 19 (1994) • Patricia Okker, "Native American Literatures and the Canon: The Case of Zitkala-Sä," in *American Realism and the Canon*, eds. Tom Quirk and Gary Scharnhorst (1994) • Roseanne Hoefel, "Writing, Performance, Activism: Zitkala-Sä and Pauline Johnson," in *Native American Literature and Culture*, eds. Susan Castillo and Victor M. DaRosa (1997) • Margaret A. Lukens, "The American Story of Zitkala-Sä," in *In Her Own Voice: Nineteenth-Century American Women Essayists*, ed. Sherry-Lee Linkon (1997) • Ruth Spack, "Re-Visioning Sioux Women: Zitkala-Sä's Revolutionary American Indian Stories," *Legacy* 14 (1997).

Credits

Index

Abortion, The, 532

Abortions will not let you forget, 808

About holiday rooms there can be, 1274

Affirmed. pent by power that holds it fast—, 996

After great pain, a formal feeling comes— (341), 969

After Reading Reznikoff, 873

After seven years and as the wine, 1285

after the murder, 812

Aguilar, Grace, 690

Aidoo, Ama Ata, 844

Ain't I a Woman?, 1146

All the family dogs are dead, 1061

All things within this fading world hath end, 670

Allen, Paula Gunn, 888, 1026

[*Alone I Sat; the Summer Day*], 242

Amnesty, 1213

An incident here and there, 1202

And later, when the young danced to an old song, 580

And now, here she is, whispering urgently into another ear, 581

And when you come to a plain or some place, 659

Angelou, Maya, 1221

Answer, The, 101

Anzaldúa, Gloria, 315

Appeal to My Country Women, An, 1165

Appeal to the Men of Great Britain in Behalf of Women, 1141

Ardelia to Melancholy, 100

a red flag, 578

Arn't I a Woman?, 1310

Astell, Mary, 1124

A timeless winter, 333

At last, my old inveterate foe, 100

Atwood, Margaret, 826

Austen, Jane, 112

Author. . . Maketh Her Will and Testament, The, 85

Author to Her Book, The, 669

Awakening, The, 696

a woman can't survive, 569

Ay me, to whom, shall I my case complain?, 934

Bambara, Toni Cade, 553

Barber, Mary, 676

Barker, Jane, 492

Barnes, Djuna, 519

Bashert, 1269

Be you all pleas'd, your pleasures grieve not me, 431

Before the Birth of One of Her Children, 670

Behn, Aphra, 433

Benstock, Shari, 597

Berlin again after chemotherapy, 542

Berners, Juliana, 658

Black Slave Trade, The, 948

Boland, Eavan, 1273

Book of Hunting, The, 659

Book of Margery Kempe, The, 420

Bowl Like Hole, 1278

Bradstreet, Anne, 668

Brand, Dionne, 572

Brant, Beth, 838

Brontë, Charlotte, 2360

Brontë, Emily, 241

Bronzeville Mother Loiters in Missis-sippi. Meanwhile, a Mississippi Mother Burns Bacon, A, 808

Brooks, Gwendolyn, 806

Brown, Rosellen, 836

Browning, Elizabeth Barrett, 1152

Bubble of Air, 1206

Burney, Frances (Fanny), 102

But render me my wonted joys again, 83

By Christ, he could bore for Pur-gatory. He was small, 335

By way of a vanished bridge we cross this river, 1288

Carter, Angela, 1031

Casabianca, 688

Cavendish, Margaret, Duchess of Newcastle, 89

Chain, 541

Childless Woman, 817

Chopin, Kate, 695

Chosen Image, The, 1219

Christian, Barbara, 346

Churchill, Caryl, 1237

Cisneros, Sandra, 576

Citizenship of People of Color, 1148

City of Fire, 570

Cixous, Hélène, 390

Cliff, Michelle, 916

Clifton, Lucille, 818

Clinton, Elizabeth, the Coun-tess of Lincoln, 664

Close Shave, 574

Cold in the earth, and the deep snow piled above thee!, 244

Cold Welcome, A, 1038

Coleridge received the Person from Porlock, 293

Collins, Patricia Hill, 638

Colonel, The, 1283

Come back to me, who wait and watch for you:—, 514

Come, my Lucasia, since we see, 941

Comrade, 1108

Conclusion of a Letter to the Rev. Mr C—, The, 678

Condemn me not for making such a coyle, 91

Countess of Lincoln's Nursery, The, 665

Curse for a Nation, A, 1160

Dancer, The, 343

Daniels, Kate, 870

Dare you see a Soul *at the White Heat?* (365), 969

daughters, 819

Davis, Rebecca Harding, 1168

death camp, 1271

Death found strange beauty on that polished brow, 684

Death is the *Cook of Nature*: and we find, 91

Death of an Infant, 684

Deer Ghost, 569

de Kok, Ingrid, 1058

Demeter Mourning, 861

Demeter, Waiting, 862

Desai, Anita, 1022

Despisals, 1211

Diary of Frances Burney, The, 103

Dickinson, Emily, 966

Did I my lines intend for public view, 97

Diehl, Joanne Feit, 1073

Difficult Miracle of Black Poetry in America or Something Like a Sonnet for Phillis Wheatley, The, 1065

Disarmed with so genteel an air, 101

Disquieting Muses, The, 814

Diving into the Wreck, 1106

Doleful Lay of Clorinda, The, 934

Doll's House, The, 997

Doolittle, Hilda (H. D.), 1197

Dove, Rita, 860

Drakulić, Slavenka, 562

Dream of Comparison, A, 293

Dream of the Dead, 686

Duffy, Carol Ann, 333

Dunbar-Nelson, Alice, 972

Dust Tracks on a Road, 289

Edge, 817

Edgeworth, Maria, 105

Eliot, George, 247

Elizabeth I, 427
Emecheta, Buchi, 1038
Engendering Language, Silence, and Voice, 1
Erdrich, Louise, 1290
Etlekhe verter oyf mame-loshn/A few words in the mother tongue, 1272
Eurydice, 1198
Everyone in me is a bird, 533
Excuse for So Much Writ upon My Verses, An, 91
Exodus—Laws for the Mothers of Israel, The, 692

Faces surround me that have no smell or color no time, 541
Fatal Interview, 530
Female Spectator, The, 499
Feminist Criticism in the Wilderness, 353
Finch, Anne, Countess of Winchilsea, 96
Fire, 569
First having read the book of myths, 1106
First that beautiful mad exploration, 296
Fish, The, 991
Fleur, 1290
For authorities whose hopes, 992
For lo, in sin, Lord, I begotten was, 82
For my clan he would be like a gift of booty—, 419
For My Lover, Returning to His Wife, 534
For the Color of My Mother, 869
Forché, Carolyn, 1282
Frame, Janet, 1218
Free Labor, 1165
Friendship Between Ephelia and Ardelia, 101
Friendship's Mysteries, to my Dearest Lucasia, 941
From the Dressing-Room, 332
From the first it had been like a, 808
Fuller, Margaret, 955
Fyge, Sarah, 1129

Gallagher, Catherine, 584
Garden Shukkei-en, The, 1288
Genesis I: 28, 871
Gift from Somewhere, A, 845
Gilman, Charlotte Perkins, 263
Girl, The, 560
Giving Birth, 827
Glaspell, Susan, 980
Glow-Worm, The, 680
Good Housekeeping, 837
Gordimer, Nadine, 1212
Grasmere Journal, The, 953
Great soul of Friendship, whither art thou fled?, 942

Hail, happy day, when, smiling like the morn, 951
Harjo, Joy, 568
Harper, Frances Ellen Watkins, 1163
Have mercy, God, for thy great mercy's sake, 82
Hays, Mary, 1140
Haywood, Eliza, 498
Head, Bessie, 820
Heard you that shriek? It rose, 1164
Heartshed, 571
Hebrew Mother, The, 689
Held between wars, 1207
Hemans, Felicia, 687
Herbert, Mary Sidney, 933
Here, here are our enjoyments done, 942
Here is a city built of passion, 570
He's not a hart until his sixth year, 659
Highs and Lows of Black Feminist Criticism, The, 347
History, 111
hooks, bell, 72
How do they do it, the ones who make love, 561
How write an honest letter, 805
Hulme, Keri, 853
Hurston, Zora Neale, 288

I, 576
I am a miner. The light burns blue, 816
I am a white girl gone brown to the color of my mother, 869
Identity and Difference, 899
I dream of you to wake: would that I might, 514
I felt a Funeral, in my Brain (280), 968
If I could trust mine own self with your fate, 518
If I Could Write This in Fire, I Would Write This in Fire, 917
If there be any one can take my place, 517
I grieve and dare not show my discontent, 428
I had eight birds hatched in one next, 670
I have wanted excellence in the knife-throw, 559
I hear a deer outside; her glass voice of the invisible, 569
I heard an angel speak last night, 1160
"I, if I perish, perish"—Esther spake:, 516
I love beautiful things:, 974
I loved you first: but afterwards your love, 515
I'm ceded—I've stopped being Theirs— (508), 970

In Celebration of My Uterus, 533
Incidents in the Life of a Slave Girl, Written by Herself, 507
In Distrust of Merits, 994
In my last year in college, 1275
In My Office at Bennington, 872
In Reference to her Children, 23 June, 1656, 670
Inscriptions (Boland), 1274
Inscriptions (Rich), 1108
In Search of Our Mothers' Gardens, 324
In such a Night, when every louder Wind, 98
In summer's mellow midnight, 243
Intertextualities, 345, 582, 875, 1062, 1299
In the dank clarity of the Green Line tunnel, 871
In the human cities, never again to, 1211
In this country you may not, 1060
Introduction, The, 97
Introduction to Frankenstein, 233
I regret nothing, 874
is an enchanted thing, 993
I saw you once, Medusa; we were alone, 296
I Sit and Sew, 973
I sit and sew—a useless task it seems, 973
I stand on the mark beside the shore, 1153
I tell this story about me, in my sorrow, 417
I, the Woman, 576
I was playing hopscotch on the slate, 1059
I wear an easy garment, 1165
i will be born in one week, 819
I wish I could remember, that first day, 514
I whole in body and in mind, 86
I would revive you with a swallow's nest, 332

Jacobs, Harriet, 506
Jordan, June, 1064
Journey, A, 275
Journey Toward Poetry, 296
Julian of Norwich, 654
june 20, 819

Käthe Kollwitz, 1207
Kay, Jackie, 578
Keeping the Thing Going While Things Are Stirring, 1146
Kempe, Margery, 419
Killigrew, Anne, 93
Kincaid, Jamaica, 1043
Kingston, Maxine Hong, 307
Klepfisz, Irena, 1268
Kuzwayo, Ellen, 1112

Ladies Almanack, 520
La Güera, 863

Language of the Brag, The, 559
Lanyer, Aemilia, 936
Last Quatrain of the Ballad of Emmett Till, The, 812
Last Word of the Dying, The, 684
Laugh of the Medusa, The, 391
Learning to Read, 1167
Left to itself, they say, every fetus, 332
Leigh, Dorothy, 660
lemoshl: for example, 1272
Leoba of England and Germany, 76
Lesbian Other, The, 598
Lessing, Doris, 1010
Letter, 805
Letter from Robert Southey, 238
Letter to Archbishop Anselm, 79
Letter to George Henry Lewes, 240
Letter to her husband, John Paston, 427
Letter to Lord Boniface, 77
Letter to Pope Pascal, 80
Letter to Robert Southey, 239
Letter to the Front, 1207
Letters for Literary Ladies, 106
Letters to her Valentine/fiance, 425
Liberty, The, 1130
Life in the Iron-Mills, 1169
Like a Bulwark, 996
Like to a Fever's pulse my heart doth beat, 90
Like to the Indians scorched with the sun, 431
Litany, 335
Little as I knew you I know you: little as you knew me you, 1108
Lock, Anne, 81
Long Story, A, 839
Look on me, Lord: though trembling I beknow, 83
Lorde, Audre, 535
Love is not all; it is not meat nor drink, 530
"Love me, for I love you"—and answer me, 516
Love Pig, 872
Love Poem, 540
Love Poem #1, 578
Lucasia, Rosania, and Orinda parting at a Fountain, 942
Lucky Chance, or an Alderman's Bargain, The, 434

Madame Alaird's Breasts, 573
Mairs, Nancy, 405
Make-up and Other Crucial Questions, 563
Mama, 343
Manley, Delarivier, 494
Manner of Her Will, The, 86
Mansfield, Katherine, 996
Many in aftertimes will say of you, 517
Martineau, Harriet, 1147

Matilda, Queen of England, 78
McGuckian, Medbh, 331
Meditation of a Penitent Sinner, upon the 51 Psalm, A, 82
Medusa, 815
Message, 1284
Mhlophe, Gcina, 336
Millay, Edna St. Vincent, 529
Mind is an Enchanting Thing, The, 993
Molly Brant, Iroquois Matron, Speaks, 1027
Monna Innominata, 513
Montagu, Lady Mary Wortley, 672
Moore, Marianne, 990
Moraga, Cherríe, 863
More, Hannah, 947
Mornings, I sit by the open window, 872
Morrison, Toni, 1224
Mother Love, 862
Mother, mother, what illbred aunt, 814
mother, the, 808
Mother's Blessing, The, 661
Movement, 1109
Mrs. Aesop, 335
Muse as Medusa, The, 296
Muzzle for Melastomus, A, 1117
My child, "herds"mean gatherings of hart and hind, 660
My Life had stood—a Loaded Gun— (754), 971
My Man Bovanne, 554
My Muse, 292

naomi watches as ruth sleeps, 820
Nature's Cook, 91
New Atalantis, The, 495
Next Heaven my vows to thee (O Sacred Muse!), 94
Nick and the Candlestick, 816
Night Wind, The, 243
Nkosi Sikelel'i Afrika (God Bless Afrika), 1113
[*No Coward Soul is Mine*], 245
No. Who can bear it. Only someone, 862
Nocturnal Reverie, A, 98
No Name Woman, 308
Northanger Abbey, 114
Not You/Like You: Postcolonial Women and the Interlocking Questions of Identity and Difference, 929
Notes toward a Politics of Location, 1095
Nothing can console me. You may bring silk, 861
Now Pontius Pilate is to judge the cause, 937

O'erwhelm'd with sorrow, and sustaining long, 681

Of the Muse, 297
Off that landspit of stony mouthplugs, 815
Often rebuked, yet always back returning, 246
Oh, thou! whose tender smile most partially, 682
Old backswitching road bent toward the ocean's light, 1109
Old Woman and Her Cat, An, 1012
Olds, Sharon, 558
Olsen, Tillie, 778
O my heart's heart and you who are to me, 515
On a Picture Painted by Herself, 95
On Being Brought from Africa to America, 950
On Monsieur's Departure, 428
On Rosania's Apostasy and Lucasia's Friendship, 942
One day you find you are your other lover, 582
One Whale, Singing, 854
Oodgeroo of the tribe Noonuccal, 1021
Oread, 1201
Origins, 1110
Other Lovers, 580
Ourselves or Nothing, 1285
Our Sharpeville, 1059
Outside everything visible and invisible a blazing maple, 1289

Painter, Nell Irvin, 1309
Pamphilia to Amphilanthus, 430
Paper Nautilus, The, 992
Parry, Ann, 1300
Paston, Margery Brews, 425
Patriarchal Poetry, 284
Personal Property: Exchange Value and the Female Self in The Awakening, 877
Philips, Katherine, 939
Plath, Sylvia, 812
Poem for My Sons, 852
Poetess's Hasty Resolution, The, 90
Poetess's Petition, The, 90
Political Nonexistence of Women, 1150
Pratt, Minnie Bruce, 851
Prayer for My Children, 874
Proletariat Speaks, The, 974
Publication—is the Auction (709), 971

R. Alcona to J. Brenzaida, 244
Reading Houses, Writing Lives: The French Connection, 406
Reading my Verses, I liked them so well, 90
Recitatif, 1225

Resistance and Transformation, 1079
Restoration: A Memorial— 9/18/91, 542
Rethinking the Maternal, 605
Rich, Adrienne, 1094
Room of One's Own, A, 16
Rossetti, Christina, 512
Rowlandson, Mary, 943
Rukeyser, Muriel, 1205
Runaway Slave at Pilgrim's Point, The, 1153

Salve Deus Rex Judaeorum, 937
sarah's promise, 819
Sarton, May, 295
Say No, 344
Say No, Black Woman, 344
Selfish Desires: Dickinson's Poetic Ego and the Rites of Subjectivity, 1073
Serious Proposal to the Ladies, A, 1125
Seventeen Syllables, 299
Sex Without Love, 561
Sexton, Anne, 531
Sexual Exploitation and Freedom: Religion, Race, and Gender in Elizabeth Barrett Browning's "The Runaway Slave at Pilgrim's Point," 1300
Shall I be one of those obsequious Fools, 1130
She clings to me, 820
She is all there, 534
Shelley, Mary, 232
Shifting the Center: Race, Class, and Feminist Theorizing About Motherhood, 638
Should I simplify my life for you?, 1111
Showalter, Elaine, 352
Showings, 655
Show mercy, Lord, not unto me alone:, 84
Sigourney, Lydia, 683
Silly Novels by Lady Novelists, 248
Since, O good Heavens! you have bestow'd on me, 493
Six hours like this for a few francs, 334
Slave Mother, The, 1164
Sleep brought the dead to me. Their brows were kind, 686
Small Passing, 1060
Smith, Charlotte, 679
Smith, Stevie, 292
So, at the end of a perfect rainbow, 581
So you have swept me back, 1198
Soap and Water, 1193
Society in America, 1148
Somebody who should have been born, 532
Sometimes When It Rains, 341

Sonnet Addressed to My Mother, 682
Sovereignty and Goodness of God, Together with the Faithfulness of His Promises Displayed, Being a Narrative of the Captivity and Restoration of Mrs. Mary Rowlandson, The, 944
Speak earth and bless me, 540
Speaking in Tongues: A Letter to Third World Women Writers, 316
Speght, Rachel, 1116
Standing Female Nude, 334
Stange, Margit, 876
Stanzas, 246
Stein, Gertrude, 282
Still I Rise, 1223
Stillborn, 804
Strengthened to live, strengthened to die for, 994
Suleiman, Susan Rubin, 620
Surface Textures, 1023

Taku Skansken, 1030
Talking Back, 73
Tell Me A Riddle, 779
Testimony of Light, The, 1289
that history is an event, 1030
That Year, 559
The boy stood on the burning deck, 688
The bubbles in the blood sprang free, 1206
The lace curtains go up, 580
The only time I forget is down the pit, 579
The rose was in rich bloom on Sharon's plain, 689
The Soul has Bandaged moments— (512), 970
The Soul selects her own Society— (303), 969
The soundtrack then was a litany—candlewick, 335
The time is come I must depart, 85
The woman is perfected, 817
The womb, 817
The year of the mask of blood, my father, 559
There is no poetry in lies, 297
There's a certain Slant of light (258), 968
These words are dedicated to those who died, 1269
They came into the little town, 1022
They chased her and her friend through the woods, 560
Thinking of you, and all that was, and all, 516
Those who have once admitted, 804
Thou ill-formed offspring of my feeble brain, 669

Thou shalt receive the pleasing sacrifice, 84
Thoughts about the Person from Porlock, 293
Tighe, Mary, 682
Time flies, hope flags, life plies a wearied wing, 517
'Tis o'er!—'Tis o'er!, 684
'Tis time to conclude, for I make it a rule, 678
Title divine—is mine! (1072), 972
To All Writing Ladies, 92
To be a Jew in the twentieth century, 1207
Toilet, The, 337
To Imagination, 243
To Lady Bute, 673
To My Grandmother, 332
To show the lab'ring bosom's deep intent, 950
To S.M., a Young African Painter, On Seeing His Works, 950
To speak of the hart—if you would hear—, 659
To the Dogs, 523
To the Excellent Mrs. A.O. upon her Receiving the Name of Lucasia, and Adoption into Our Society, 940
To the Right Honorable William, Earl of DARTMOUTH, His Majesty's Principal Secretary of State for North America, &c, 951
Transfer, 1061
Tree-Bound, The, 976
Trifles, 981
Trinh T. Minh-ha, 928
Truth, Sojourner, 1145
Trust me, I have not earned your dear rebuke, 515
Turning points. We all like to hear about those. Points, 1110
Turning the Moon into a Verb, 333
'Twas mercy brought me from my pagan land, 950
Two ladies walked on the soft green grass, 293

Upon the Saying That My Verses Were Made by Another, 94
Uses of the Erotic: The Erotic as Power, 536

Verses Intended to Have Been Prefixed to the Novel of Emmeline, but Then Suppressed, 681
Very soon the Yankee teachers, 1167
Village Saint, The, 822
Vindication of the Rights of Woman, A, 1133

Index 1465

Vinegar Tom, 1238
Virgin Life, A, 493

wade, 991
Walker, Alice, 323
Walls Do Not Fall, The, 1202
We are complete: and faith hath
  now, 940
We are Diana's Virgin-Train, 95
We Are Going, 1022
We knew it was the end, 1027
Well, I have lost you; and I lost
  you fairly, 531
Welty, Eudora, 1002
Wharton, Edith, 274
What Friendship is, Ardelia
  show, 101
What is it our mammas bewitch-
  es, 676
WHAT YOU HAVE HEARD is
  true, 1283
Wheatley, Phillis, 949
Whene'er to Afric's shores I turn
  my eyes, 948
When I think of those mothers
  giving up, 873
When I Was Fair and Young, 429
When I was fair and young, then
  favor graced me, 429
When night's black mantle could
  most darkness prove, 430
When on some balmy-breathing
  night of spring, 680
When they took us to the shower
  i saw, 1271

When we are old and these
  rejoicing veins, 530
When weary with the long day's
  care, 243
When you were born, all the
  poets I knew, 852
Whenever you ride through
  wood or dell, 659
Whirl up, sea—, 1201
Whitney, Isabella, 85
Who can forget the attitude of
  mothering?, 862
Who Is Your Mother? Red Roots of
  White Feminism, 889
who understands better than i,
  819
Who Was That Masked Woman!
  The Prostitute and the Play-
  wright in the Comedies of
  Aphra Behn, 585
Why I Live at the P.O., 1003
Wicomb, Zoë, 1277
Wife's Lament, The, 416
Wife's Story, A, 545
With sweet hyssop besprinkle
  thou my sprite, 83
Wolf Alice, 1032
Wollstonecraft, Mary, 1131
Woman in the Nineteenth Century,
  957
woman who shines at the head,
  819
Women have loved before as I
  love now, 530
Woolf, Virginia, 14

Wordsworth, Dorothy, 952
Wright, Judith, 803
Wroth, Mary, 429
Writing and Motherhood, 621
Writing Bodies/Bodies Writing, 375
Writing in a Time of Violence,
  1275
Written for My Son, and Spoken
  by Him at His First Putting on
  Breeches, 676
Wulf and Eadwacer, 418

Xuela, 1044

Yamamoto, Hisaye, 298
Yellow Wallpaper, The, 264
Yezierska, Anzia, 1192
You can sigh o'er the sad-eyed
  Armenian, 1166
You dream a heated chase, 571
You happy blessed eyes, 432
You mark each box with a thick
  black pen, 581
You may write me down in
  history, 1223
Your voices sprayed over the
  walls, 1284
Youth gone, and beauty gone if
  ever there, 518
You, too, will love, 872

Zitkala-Ša (Gertrude Simmons
  Bonnin), 975